Washington
Information Directory
2016–2017

Washington
Information Directory
2016–2017

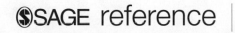

FOR INFORMATION:

CQ Press
An Imprint of SAGE Publications, Inc.
2455 Teller Road
Thousand Oaks, California 91320
E-mail: order@sagepub.com

SAGE Publications Ltd.
1 Oliver's Yard
55 City Road
London, EC1Y 1SP
United Kingdom

SAGE Publications India Pvt. Ltd.
B 1/I 1 Mohan Cooperative Industrial Area
Mathura Road, New Delhi 110 044
India

SAGE Publications Asia-Pacific Pte. Ltd.
3 Church Street
#10-04 Samsung Hub
Singapore 049483

Editor: Laura Notton
Editorial Assistant: Jordan Enobakhare
Researchers: Lisa Bhattacharji,
    Cynthia Canterbury, Megan Freiberg,
    Diane Goldenberg-Hart, Vicki Heitsch,
    Mary Hunter, Heather Kerrigan,
    Meisha Mossayebi, Theresa Munt,
    Jack Rockwood, Ronald Stouffer
Production Editor: David C. Felts
Typesetter: Hurix Systems Pvt. Ltd.
Proofreaders: Sally Jaskold, Bonnie Moore
Indexers: Hurix Systems Pvt. Ltd., Joan Shapiro
Cover Designer: Michael Dubowe
Marketing Manager: Leah Watson

Cover photos: ©istockphoto.com

Library of Congress Cataloging-in-Publication Data

The Library of Congress catalogued the first edition of this title as follows:

Washington information directory. 1975/76—
    Washington. Congressional Quarterly Inc.
    1. Washington, D.C.—Directories.
    2. Washington metropolitan area—Directories.
    3. United States—Executive departments—
        Directories. I. Congressional Quarterly Inc.
F192.3.W33   975.3'0025   75-646321

ISBN: 978-1-5063-3401-1
ISSN: 0887-8064

This book is printed on acid-free paper.

16 17 18 19 20 10 9 8 7 6 5 4 3 2 1

Contents

Reference Boxes and Organization Charts

Each chapter also features a box listing the relevant committee and subcommittee resources in Congress.

Preface

Since 1975, the *Washington Information Directory* has been the essential resource for locating information on governmental and nongovernmental organizations in the national capital region. This trusted and user-friendly directory helps researchers find the right contact at the right organization, whether their interest is consumer product and food safety, equal employment opportunities, finance and investments, housing, immigration, terrorism, or a wealth of other timely topics. The directory allows the user to locate accurate, complete, and current information quickly and easily in a way that free Internet searches cannot.

In updating the *Washington Information Directory* every year, we research each existing organization entry to provide current addresses; phone, fax, TTY, and toll-free numbers; email and Web addresses; and key officers and descriptions. Our team calls each organization and speaks with a member of its Washington office to obtain this information. In directory listings, we include contacts' direct lines whenever possible (many organizations do not publish these numbers on their Web sites in an attempt to channel all calls through an operator or answering service). When a federal department reorganizes, we assess the new divisions and directorates and reorganize the book, along with providing updated organization charts. Each year we add new government agencies and new nongovernmental organizations, which comprise national organizations and international organizations with Washington offices. Entries are arranged by topic, subtopic, and organization type. The result is an indispensable reference engine that makes finding up-to-date information easy, whether you are using the print edition or navigating the online edition.

Readers will find a comprehensive listing of the members of the 114th Congress as well as a handy "Resources in Congress" box at the beginning of each chapter listing relevant committees and subcommittees for that chapter's topic, along with their Web site and phone number. Readers may also turn to the first appendix, which offers a complete listing of each 114th Congress committee for which information is available and includes full contact information, leadership, membership, and jurisdictions.

Every edition of the *Washington Information Directory* brings something altogether new. New to the 2016–2017 edition are more than 150 federal and nongovernmental organizations, new sections covering fields of health research, victim assistance, equal employment for older adults, and general finance, and an updated and expanded listing of more than 200 House and Senate caucuses. Federal organizations new to the Washington Directory this year include a variety of offices: the Health and Human Services Department's National Vaccine Program Office, which informs the public about vaccines and immunizations as well as provides interactive community disease mapping, and the Food and Nutrition Service's National School Lunch Program, which provides nutritional low-cost or free school lunches to students in more than 100,000 schools and child care institutions, serving 224 billion lunches since the program began in 1946. Among new nongovernmental organizations are: Active Minds, which encourages education and openness about youth mental health and supports student-run chapters nationwide that provide resources and support for students seeking help with mental illness, and the Brookings Institute's Africa Growth Initiative, which seeks to improve the industrial and political health and living conditions in African nations to better enable them to compete in a dynamic global economy.

The fully updated chapters of the *Washington Information Directory* are supplemented by two appendices comprising a guide to the members and committees of the 114th Congress; a directory of government Web sites; a list of governors and other state officials; a list of foreign diplomats and embassies, U.S. ambassadors, and State Department country offices; and current information on the Freedom of Information Act and legislation and recent Supreme Court cases related to privacy. Also in the congressional delegation section, we have included Facebook and Twitter information in all members' profiles. Print readers can also search and cross-search across the edition in three ways: through the name index, the organization index, or the subject index.

CQ Press seeks to continue the *Washington Information Directory*'s reputation as an invaluable, comprehensive, and authoritative reference of its kind. We welcome feedback related to the book's quality and functionality, as well as suggestions for future editions.

Laura Notton
Editor

How to Use This Directory

The *Washington Information Directory* is designed to make your search for information quick and easy.

Each chapter covers a broad topic, and within the chapters, information is divided into more specific subject areas. This arrangement allows you to find in one place the departments and agencies of the federal government, congressional committees, and nongovernmental organizations that have the information you need.

The directory divides information sources into three main categories: (1) agencies, (2) Congress, and (3) nongovernmental organizations. There is also a small international organizations category. Each entry includes the name, address, and telephone and fax numbers of the organization; the name and title of the director or the best person to contact for information; press, hotline, and TTY numbers, and email, Internet, Twitter, and Facebook addresses whenever available; and a description of the work performed by the organization. Congressional committees and subcommittees appear in a box at the beginning of each chapter; a full entry for each committee appears in the first appendix.

HOW INFORMATION IS PRESENTED

The following examples represent the three main categories of entries and the other resources provided in the directory. The examples are drawn from the History and Preservation section in Chapter 4, Culture and Religion. (To read the mailing addresses, check the abbreviations at the end of this guide.)

Agencies

In the first category, government agencies are listed. For example, the National Park Service and its acronym appear in bold type. Next, in parentheses, is the name of its parent organization, the Interior Department. Entries may also include the name of an office within the agency, in this case the Office of Cultural Resources.

National Park Service (NPS), *(Interior Dept.),* *Cultural Resources, Partnerships, and Science,* 1849 C St. N.W., #3128, 20240-0001; (202) 208-7625. Fax, (202) 273-3237. Stephanie Toothman, Associate Director.
Web, www.nps.gov/history

Oversees preservation of federal historic sites and administration of buildings programs. Programs include the National Register of Historic Places, National Historic and National Landmark Programs, Historic American Building Survey, Historic American Engineering Record, Archeology and Antiquities Act Program, and Technical Preservation Services. Gives grant and aid assistance and tax benefit information to properties listed in the National Register of Historic Places.

Congress

Congressional committees and subcommittees relevant to each chapter are listed in a box in the beginning of each chapter. Each committee's phone number and Web site are listed here. For a complete listing of congressional committees, including their full contact information, leadership, memberships, and jurisdictions, please refer to the first appendix. Entries that appear under the "Congress" heading within each chapter are agencies under congressional authority, such as the Government Accountability Office or the Library of Congress. Each entry includes a description of the agency's activities relating to the section in which it appears.

Senate Office of Conservation and Preservation, *S416 CAP, 20510; (202) 224-4550. Leona Faust, Director, Acting*

Develops and coordinates programs related to the conservation and preservation of Senate records and materials for the secretary of the Senate.

Nongovernmental

Thousands of nongovernmental groups have headquarters or legislative offices in or near Washington. Their staffs are often excellent information sources, and these organizations frequently maintain special libraries or information centers. Here is an example of a group with an interest in the preservation of historic sites:

Civil War Trust, *1156 15th St. N.W., #900, 20005; (202) 367-1861. Fax, (202) 367-1865. James Lighthizer, President. General email, info@civilwar.org Web, www.civilwar.org and Twitter, @civilwartrust*

Membership: preservation professionals, historians, conservation activists, and citizens. Preserves endangered Civil War battlefields throughout the United States. Conducts preservation conferences and workshops. Advises local preservation groups. Monitors legislation and regulations at the federal, state, and local levels.

How the *Washington Information Directory* Works

The *Washington Information Directory* (WID) directs your search more efficiently and effectively than any other print or online search. This resource does the hard work of pinpointing the information you need. Here is an example of how to use it to find information on the preservation of historic sites and materials:

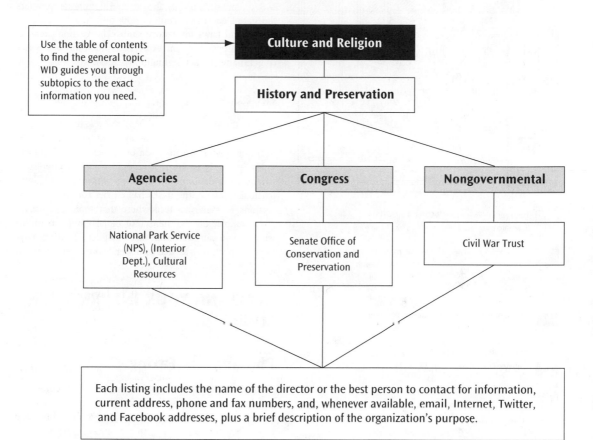

Use the table of contents to find the general topic. WID guides you through subtopics to the exact information you need.

Culture and Religion

History and Preservation

Agencies — National Park Service (NPS), (Interior Dept.), Cultural Resources

Congress — Senate Office of Conservation and Preservation

Nongovernmental — Civil War Trust

Each listing includes the name of the director or the best person to contact for information, current address, phone and fax numbers, and, whenever available, email, Internet, Twitter, and Facebook addresses, plus a brief description of the organization's purpose.

Charts and Boxes

This directory includes organization charts to make the hierarchy of federal departments and agencies easy to grasp, as well as reference boxes that provide essential agency contacts and other information. On the topic of historic sites, you can locate the National Park Service within the Interior Department (see chart on p. 293) or consult a list of sites administered by the National Park Service (see box on p. 141). The National Park Service's organization chart appears on page 582. The general organization chart for the federal government appears on page 907.

REFERENCE RESOURCES

Tables of Contents

The table of contents (p. v) lists the directory's chapters and their major subheadings. A list of reference boxes

and organization charts within the chapters is provided on page vii. Each chapter opens with a detailed table of contents, including the boxes and charts that appear in the chapter.

Congressional Information

A section on the 114th Congress, beginning on page 779, provides extensive information about members and committees:

State Delegations. Here (p. 780) you can locate senators, representatives, and delegates by state (or territory) and congressional district.

Committees. These sections list the jurisdictions and memberships of committees and subcommittees of the House (p. 785) and Senate (p. 863), as well as the joint committees of Congress (p. 861). Also included are party leaderships and partisan committees of the House (p. 803) and Senate (p. 876).

Members' Offices. For the House (p. 804) and Senate (p. 877), we provide each member's Capitol Hill office

Map of Capitol Hill

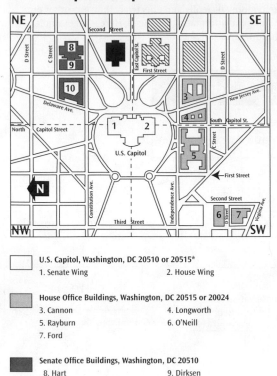

U.S. Capitol, Washington, DC 20510 or 20515*
1. Senate Wing   2. House Wing

House Office Buildings, Washington, DC 20515 or 20024
3. Cannon   4. Longworth
5. Rayburn   6. O'Neill
7. Ford

Senate Office Buildings, Washington, DC 20510
8. Hart   9. Dirksen
10. Russell

Supreme Court, Washington, DC 20543

Library of Congress, Washington, DC 20540

* Mail sent to the U.S. Capitol should bear the zip code of the chamber to which it is addressed.

Note: Dashed lines indicate the city's quadrants, which are noted in the corners of the map.

address, telephone and fax numbers, Internet address, social media (if available), key professional aide, committee assignments, and district office contact information.

House and Senate Caucuses. For congressional caucuses (p. 897), we provide a listing of the most active caucuses with contact information and staff members.

Ready Reference

A section of reference lists, beginning on page 902, provides information on the following subjects:

Government Information on the Internet. Organized by branch of government, this section (p. 904) lists Web addresses for locating information and social media on the White House, cabinet departments, Congress, and the judiciary.

State Government. The list of state officials (p. 909) provides the name, address, and telephone number for each governor, lieutenant governor, secretary of state, attorney general, and state treasurer. It includes a press

contact for the governor and, where applicable, the governor's office representative in Washington, D.C.

Diplomats. The foreign embassies section (p. 920) gives the names, official addresses, and telephone numbers of foreign diplomats in Washington; the names of ranking U.S. diplomatic officials abroad; and the phone numbers for State Department country desk offices.

Federal Laws on Information. This section presents current information on the Freedom of Information Act (p. 935) and privacy legislation (p. 939).

Indexes

Use the name index (p. 943) to look up any person listed in the directory. Use the organization index (p. 985) to find a specific organization or agency. Use the subject index (p. 1035) to locate a particular area of interest. If you need information on a specific topic but do not know a particular source, the index has entries for chapter subsections to help you find where that topic is covered. For example, on the subject of equal employment for women, you can find index entries under Equal Employment Opportunity as well as under Women.

REACHING YOUR INFORMATION SOURCE

Phoning and Faxing

Call information or toll-free numbers first. Often you can get the answer you need without searching any further. If not, an explanation of your query should put you in touch with the person who can answer your question. Rarely will you need to talk to the top administrator.

Offer to fax your query if it is difficult to explain over the phone, but make sure that the person helping you knows to expect your fax. Faxing promptly and limiting your transmission to a single page brings the best results.

Remember that publications and documents are often available from a special office (for federal agencies, see p. 95) and, increasingly, on Web sites. Ask what is the fastest way to receive the information you need.

Keep in mind the agency or organization, not the name of the director. Personnel changes are common, but for most inquiries you will want to stay within the organization you call, rather than track down a person who may have moved on to a new job.

Concerning congressional questions, first contact one of your members of Congress; representatives have staff assigned to answer questions from constituents. Contact a committee only if you have a technical question that cannot be answered elsewhere.

Writing

Address letters to the director of an office or organization—the contact person listed. Your letter will be directed to the person who can answer your question. Be prepared to follow up by phone.

Using the Internet

Most agencies and governmental organizations have sites on the Internet (for federal departments and agencies, see pp. 104, 904–908) and an email address for general inquiries. Information available from these sources is expanding and is usually free once you are online. However, this approach is not always faster or better than a phone call—Internet connections can be slow, site menus can be complex or confusing, and information can be incomplete or out of date. The office also may be able to alert you to any upcoming changes.

As with faxing, reserve email for inquiries that may be too complex for a phone call, but phone first to establish that someone is ready to help.

ADDRESSES AND AREA CODES

Listings in the directory include full contact information, including telephone area code and, when available, room or suite number and nine-digit zip code. If an office prefers a mailing address that is different from the physical location, we provide both.

Washington, D.C., Addresses

For brevity, entries for agencies, organizations, and congressional offices in the District of Columbia (area code 202) do not include the city as part of the address. Here is the beginning of a typical Washington entry:

Equal Employment Opportunity Commission (EEOC), *131 M St. N.E., 20507; (202) 663-4001.*

To complete the mailing address, add "Washington, DC" before the zip code.

Building Addresses

Departments and agencies generally have their own zip codes. Updates to our directory reflect the increasing use of street addresses by the federal government. Federal offices at the following locations are listed by building name or abbreviation:

The White House. Located at 1600 Pennsylvania Ave. N.W., 20500.

Dwight D. Eisenhower Executive Office Building. Located at 17th St. and Pennsylvania Ave. N.W., 20500.

New Executive Office Building. Located at 725 17th St. N.W., 20503.

Main State Department Building. Located at 2201 C St. N.W., 20520.

The Pentagon. Located in Arlington, Virginia, but has a Washington mailing address and different zip codes for each branch of the military.

Navy Annex. Located at Columbia Pike and Southgate Rd., Arlington, VA 20370, but most offices use a Washington mailing address.

U.S. Capitol. Abbreviated as CAP; the letters *H* and *S* before the room number indicate the House or Senate side of the building. Zip codes are 20510 for the Senate, 20515 for the House.

Senate Office Buildings. Mail for delivery to Senate office buildings does not require a street address. The zip code is 20510. Abbreviations, building names, and street locations are as follows:

SDOB	Dirksen Senate Office Bldg., Constitution Ave. between 1st and 2nd Sts. N.E.
SHOB	Hart Senate Office Bldg., 2nd St. and Constitution Ave. N.E.
SROB	Russell Senate Office Bldg., Constitution Ave. between Delaware Ave. and 1st St. N.E.

House Office Buildings. Mail for delivery to House office buildings does not require a street address. The zip code is 20515. Abbreviations, building names, and street locations are as follows:

CHOB	Cannon House Office Bldg., Independence Ave. between New Jersey Ave. and 1st St. S.E.
FHOB	Ford House Office Bldg., 2nd and D Sts. S.W.
LHOB	Longworth House Office Bldg., Independence Ave. between S. Capitol St. and New Jersey Ave. S.E.
OHOB	O'Neill House Office Bldg., 200 C St. S.W. 20024
RHOB	Rayburn House Office Bldg., Independence Ave. between S. Capitol and 1st Sts. S.W.

SAGE was founded in 1965 by Sara Miller McCune to support the dissemination of usable knowledge by publishing innovative and high-quality research and teaching content. Today, we publish over 900 journals, including those of more than 400 learned societies, more than 800 new books per year, and a growing range of library products including archives, data, case studies, reports, and video. SAGE remains majority-owned by our founder, and after Sara's lifetime will become owned by a charitable trust that secures our continued independence.

Los Angeles | London | New Delhi | Singapore | Washington DC | Melbourne

1

Agriculture, Food, and Nutrition

GENERAL POLICY AND ANALYSIS

Basic Resources

▶AGENCIES

Agricultural Dept. (USDA), *People's Garden,* 1400
Independence Ave. S.W., 20250; (202) 577-7462.
Annie Ceccarini, Program Manager.
General email, oc.news@usda.gov
Web, peoplesgarden.usda.gov/gardens/18952/usda-
national-headquarters-peoples-garden and Twitter,
@People'sGarden

Works with Agriculture Dept. agencies and offices
to promote healthy eating, sustainable agricultural and
landscaping practices, and locally produed agricultural
products through school gardens, community gardens,
urban farms, and small-scale agriculture projects.

Agricultural Marketing Service (AMS) *(Agriculture*
Dept.), 1400 Independence Ave. S.W., #3933S, MS 0201,
20250-0201; (202) 720-5115. Fax, (202) 690-1718.
Anne L. Alonzo, Administrator. Public Affairs, (202) 720-
8998.
Web, www.ams.usda.gov

Provides domestic and international marketing services to the agricultural industry. Administers marketing,
standardization, grading, inspection, and regulatory programs; maintains a market news service to inform producers of price changes; conducts agricultural marketing
research and development programs; studies agricultural
transportation issues.

Agriculture Dept. (USDA), *1400 Independence Ave. S.W.,*
#200A, 20250-0002; (202) 720-3631. Fax, (202) 720-2166.
Thomas J. Vilsack, Secretary; Krysta Harden, Deputy
Secretary. Press, (202) 720-4623. Locator, (202) 720-8732.
Web, www.usda.gov

Serves as principal adviser to the president on agricultural policy; works to increase and maintain farm income
and to develop markets abroad for U.S. agricultural
products.

Agriculture Dept. (USDA), *Advocacy and Outreach,* 1400
Independence Ave. S.W., #526-A, Whitten Bldg., 20250;
(202) 720-6350. Fax, (202) 720-7136. Carolyn Parker,
Director. Toll-free, (800) 880-4183.
General email, outreachandadvocacy@usda.gov
Web, www.outreach.usda.gov

Develops, manages, and supports programs that provide information, training, and technical assistance to
socially disadvantaged farmers and ranchers and small
and beginning farmers and ranchers. Administers the
Small Farmer Outreach, Training, and Technical Assistance Program and the USDA Farm Worker Initiative.
Provides policy guidance and feedback to the Agriculture
Dept. on all outreach-related activities and functions.

Agriculture Dept. (USDA), *Chief Economist,* 1400
Independence Ave. S.W., #112A, Whitten Bldg.,
20250-3810; (202) 720-4955. Fax, (202) 690-4915.
Robert Johansson, Chief Economist. Alternate phone, (202)
720-5955.
Web, www.usda.gov/oce

Prepares economic and statistical analyses used to plan
and evaluate short-range and intermediate-range agricultural policy. Evaluates Agriculture Dept. policy, proposals,
and legislation for their impact on the agricultural economy. Administers Agriculture Dept. economic agencies,
including the Office of Risk Assessment and Cost-
Benefit Analysis, the Office of Energy Policy and New
Uses, the Global Change Program Office, and the World
Agricultural Outlook Board.

Agriculture Dept. (USDA), *National Appeals Division,*
3101 Park Center Dr., #1100, Alexandria, VA 22302; (703)
305-1166. Fax, (703) 305-2108. Steven Silverman, Director.
TTY, (703) 305-2007.
General email, nadinfo@usda.gov
Web, www.nad.usda.gov

Conducts impartial administrative appeals hearings
and reviews of adverse program decisions for participants
of programs administered by the Farm Service Agency,
Risk Management Agency, Natural Resources Conservation Service, and Rural Development.

Animal and Plant Health Inspection Service (APHIS)
(Agriculture Dept.), **Legislative and Public Affairs,** *South*
Bldg., 1400 Independence Ave. S.W., #1147, 20250; (202)
799-7030. Abbey Fretz, Legislative Director.
*Web, www.aphis.usda.gov/aphis/banner/contactus/sa_*
aphis_contacts/ct_contact_lpa

Manages communications with Congress, industry
stakeholders, trading partners, and the media.

Bureau of Economic and Business Affairs *(State Dept.),*
Agriculture Policy, *2201 C St. N.W., #4686, 20520-0002;*
(202) 647-3090. Fax, (202) 647-1894. Eric W. Luftman,
Director, (202) 647-0133.
Web, www.state.gov/e/eb/tpp/agp

Develops agricultural trade policy; handles questions
pertaining to international negotiations on all agricultural
products covered by the World Trade Organization
(WTO) and bilateral trade agreements. Oversees the distribution of biotechnology outreach funds to promote
international acceptance of the technology.

Farm Service Agency (FSA) *(Agriculture Dept.),* 1400
Independence Ave. S.W., #3086, MS 0501, 20250-0506;
(202) 720-3467. Fax, (202) 720-9105. Val J. Dolcini,
Administrator. Press, (202) 720-7807.
Web, www.fsa.usda.gov

Oversees farm commodity programs that provide
crop loans and purchases. Administers price support programs that provide crop payments when market prices
fall below specified levels; conducts programs to help
obtain adequate farm and commercial storage and drying
equipment for farm products; directs conservation
and environmental cost sharing projects and programs
to assist farmers during natural disasters and other
emergencies.

AGRICULTURE RESOURCES IN CONGRESS

For a complete listing of congressional committees, including their full contact information, leadership, membership, and jurisdictions, please refer to the Appendix on pages 779–896.

HOUSE:

House Agriculture Committee, (202) 225-2171.
Web, agriculture.house.gov
  Subcommittee on Biotechnology, Horticulture, and Research, (202) 225-2171.
  Subcommittee on Commodity Exchanges, Energy, and Credit, (202) 225-2171.
  Subcommittee on Conservation and Forestry, (202) 225-2171.
  Subcommittee on General Farm Commodities and Risk Management, (202) 225-2171.
  Subcommittee on Livestock and Foreign Agriculture, (202) 225-2171.
  Subcommittee on Nutrition, (202) 225-2171.
House Appropriations Committee, (202) 225-2771.
Web, appropriations.house.gov
  Subcommittee on Agriculture, Rural Development, Food and Drug Administration, and Related Agencies, (202) 225-2638.
House Education and the Workforce Committee, (202) 225-4527.
Web, edworkforce.house.gov
  Subcommittee on Early Childhood, Elementary, and Secondary Education, (202) 225-4527.
House Energy and Commerce Committee, (202) 225-2927.
Web, energycommerce.house.gov
  Subcommittee on Health, (202) 225-2927.
House Foreign Affairs Committee, (202) 225-5021.
Web, foreignaffairs.house.gov

House Science, Space, and Technology Committee, (202) 225-6371.
Web, science.house.gov
  Subcommittee on Research and Technology, (202) 225-6371.
House Small Business Committee, (202) 225-5821.
Web, smallbusiness.house.gov
  Subcommittee on Agriculture, Energy, and Trade, (202) 225-5821.

SENATE:

Senate Agriculture, Nutrition, and Forestry Committee, (202) 224-2035.
Web, ag.senate.gov
  Subcommittee on Commodities, Risk Management, and Trade, (202) 224-2035.
  Subcommittee on Conservation and Forestry, (202) 224-2035.
  Subcommittee on Livestock, Marketing, and Agriculture Security, (202) 224-2035.
  Subcommittee on Nutrition, Specialty Crops, and Agricultural Research, (202) 224-2035.
  Subcommittee on Rural Development and Energy, (202) 224-2035.
Senate Appropriations Committee, (202) 224-7363.
Web, appropriations.senate.gov
  Subcommittee on Agriculture, Rural Development, Food and Drug Administration, and Related Agencies, (202) 224-8090.

▶CONGRESS

For a listing of relevant congressional committees and subcommittees, please see text box above or the Appendix.

Government Accountability Office (GAO), *Natural Resources and Environment, 441 G St. N.W., #2057, 20548 (mailing address: 441 G St. N.W., #2T23A, Washington, DC 20548); (202) 512-3841. Fax, (202) 512-8774. Mark Gaffigan, Managing Director.*
Web, www.gao.gov/careers/nre.html

Independent nonpartisan agency in the legislative branch that audits the Agriculture Dept. and analyzes and reports on its handling of agriculture issues and food safety.

▶NONGOVERNMENTAL

American Farm Bureau Federation (AFBF), *600 Maryland Ave. S.W., #1000W, 20024-2520; (202) 406-3600. Fax, (202) 406-3606. Zippy Duvall, President.*

General email, reception@fb.org
Web, www.fb.org

Federation of state farm bureaus in fifty states and Puerto Rico. Promotes agricultural research. Interests include commodity programs, domestic production, marketing, education, research, financial assistance to the farmer, foreign assistance programs, rural development, the world food shortage, and inspection and certification of food.

National Assn. of State Departments of Agriculture, *4350 N. Fairfax Dr., #910, Arlington, VA 22203; (202) 296-9680. Fax, (703) 880-0509. Barbara P. Glenn, Chief Executive Officer.*
General email, nasda@nasda.org
Web, www.nasda.org

Membership: commissioners, secretaries, and directors of agriculture from the fifty states, Puerto Rico, Guam, American Samoa, and the Virgin Islands. Serves as liaison between federal agencies and state governments to coordinate agricultural policies and laws. Provides data collection, emergency planning, and training. Seeks to protect consumers and the environment. Monitors legislation and regulations.

National Council of Agricultural Employers (NCAE), *525 9th St. N.W., #800, 20004; (202) 629-9320. Frank A. Gasperini Jr., Executive Vice President. General email, info@ncaeonline.org*

Web, www.ncaeonline.org

Membership: employers of agricultural labor. Encourages establishment and maintenance of conditions conducive to an adequate supply of domestic and foreign farm labor.

National Farmers Union, *20 F St. N.W., #300, 20001-1560; (202) 554-1600. Fax, (202) 554-1654. Roger Johnson, President. General email, info@nfu.org*

Web, www.nfu.org, Twitter, @NFUDC and Facebook, www.facebook.com/nationalfarmersunion

Advocates economic and social well-being and quality of life of family farmers, ranchers, fishermen, and consumers and their communities through education, cooperation, and legislation. Encourages sustainable production of food, fiber, feed, and fuel.

National Grange, *1616 H St. N.W., 10th Floor, 20006-4999; (202) 628-3507. Fax, (202) 347-1091. Betsy Huber, President. Toll-free, (888) 447-2643. General email, info@nationalgrange.org*

Web, www.nationalgrange.org

Membership: farmers and others involved in agricultural production and rural community service activities. Coordinates community service programs with state grange organizations.

National Sustainable Agriculture Coalition, *110 Maryland Ave. N.E., #209, 20002-5622; (202) 547-5754. Fax, (202) 547-1837. Ferd Hoefner, Policy Director; Jeremy Emmi, Managing Director. General email, info@sustainableagriculture.net*

Web, www.sustainableagriculture.net

National alliance of farm, rural, and conservation organizations. Advocates federal policies that promote environmentally sustainable agriculture, natural resources management, and rural community development. Monitors legislation and regulations.

Rural Coalition, *1029 Vermont Ave., #601, 20005; (202) 628-7160. Fax, (202) 393-1816. Lorette Picciano, Executive Director. General email, ruralco@ruralco.org*

Web, www.ruralco.org and Twitter, @RuralCo

Alliance of organizations that develop public policies benefiting rural communities. Collaborates with community-based groups on agriculture and rural development issues, including health and the environment, minority farmers, farm workers, Native Americans' rights, and rural

community development. Provides rural groups with technical assistance.

Union of Concerned Scientists, *Food and Environment Program, 1825 K St. N.W., #800, 20006-1232; (202) 223-6133. Fax, (202) 223-6162. Ricardo Salvador, Director. General email, ucs@ucsusa.org*

Web, www.ucsusa.org

Promotes a food system that encourages innovative and environmentally sustainable ways of producing high-quality, safe, and affordable food. Focuses on reducing the unnecessary use of antibiotics and strengthening federal oversight of genetically engineered products for food and agriculture and promoting climate-friendly agricultural practices. (Headquarters in Cambridge, Mass.)

Agricultural Research, Education

▶**AGENCIES**

Agricultural Research Service *(Agriculture Dept.), 1400 Independence Ave. S.W., #302A, MS 0300, 20250-0300; (202) 720-3656. Fax, (202) 720-5427. Chavonda Jacobs-Young, Administrator. Web, www.ars.usda.gov*

Conducts research on crops, livestock, poultry, soil and water conservation, agricultural engineering, and control of insects and other pests; develops new uses for farm commodities.

Agriculture Dept. (USDA), *Research, Education, and Economics, 1400 Independence Ave. S.W., #214W, MS 0110, 20250-0110; (202) 720-5923. Fax, (202) 690-2842. Catherine E. Woteki, Under Secretary, (202) 720-1542. Web, www.ree.usda.gov*

Coordinates agricultural research, extension, and teaching programs in the food and agricultural sciences, including human nutrition, home economics, consumer services, agricultural economics, environmental quality, natural and renewable resources, forestry and range management, animal and plant production and protection, aquaculture, and the processing, distribution, marketing, and utilization of food and agricultural products. Oversees the Agricultural Research Service, the National Institute of Food and Agriculture, the Economic Research Service, and the National Agricultural Statistics Service.

Agriculture Dept. (USDA), *Small and Disadvantaged Business Utilization (OSDBU), 1400 Independence Ave. S.W., #1085-S, Ag Stop 9501, 20250-9501; (202) 720-7117. Fax, (202) 720-3001. Carmen Jones, Director, Acting, (202) 720-3291. Web, www.usda.gov/osdbu*

Provides guidance and technical assistance to small businesses seeking to do business with the USDA; monitors the development and implementation of contracting policies to prevent barriers to small business participation; works with other federal agencies and public/private partners to increase the number of small businesses participating in the contracting arena.

Agriculture Department

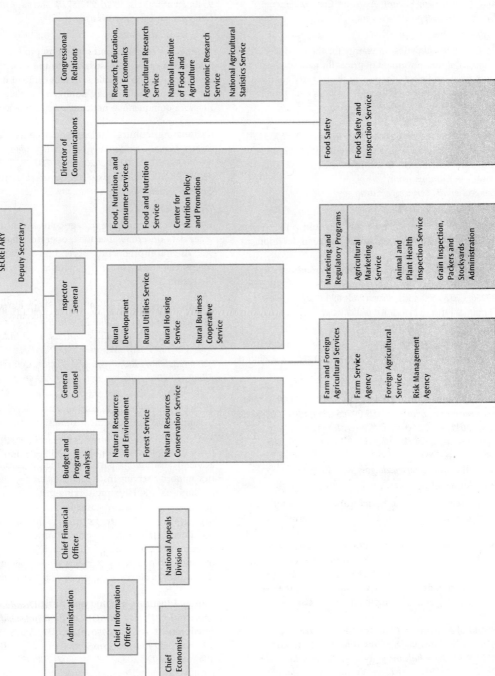

Bureau of Labor Statistics (BLS) *(Labor Dept.),* *Industrial Prices and Price Index,* 2 Massachusetts Ave. N.E., #3840, 20212-0001; (202) 691-7700. Fax, (202) 691-7753. Alaric Brown, Manager, Agriculture, Food, Tobacco, and Paper Team; Vacant, Assistant Commissioner. General email, ppi-info@bls.gov

Web, www.bls.gov/ppi

Compiles statistics on energy for the Producer Price Index; analyzes movement of prices for natural gas, petroleum, coal, and electric power in the primary commercial and industrial markets. Records changes over time in the prices domestic producers receive.

Economic Research Service *(Agriculture Dept.),* 355 E St. S.W., 20024-8221; (202) 694-5000. Fax, (202) 245-5467. Mary Bohman, Administrator; Greg Pompelli, Associate Administrator. General email, service@ers.usda.gov

Web, www.ers.usda.gov

Conducts research on economic and policy issues involving food, natural resources, and rural development.

Foreign Agricultural Service (FAS) *(Agriculture Dept.),* *Global Analysis,* 1400 Independence Ave. S.W., #4083S, 20250; (202) 720-6301. Fax, (202) 690-0727. Daniel Whitley, Deputy Administrator. Web, www.fas.usda.gov

Conducts research relevant to USDA's trade initiatives. Develops and maintains USDA's data on agricultural production, supply, and demand.

National Agricultural Library *(Agriculture Dept.),* 10301 Baltimore Ave., Beltsville, MD 20705-2351; (301) 504-5248. Fax, (301) 504-7042. Paul Wester, Libray Director. Reference desk, (301) 504-5755, 8:30 a.m.–4:30 p.m. TTY, (301) 504-6856. General email, agref@usda.gov

Web, www.nal.usda.gov

Principal source of agricultural information in the United States. Makes significant information available to researchers, educators, policymakers, and the public; coordinates with state land-grant and Agriculture Dept. field libraries; promotes international cooperation and exchange of information. Deeper interests include food production, food safety, human nutrition, animal welfare, water quality, rural development, and invasive species.

National Agricultural Library *(Agriculture Dept.),* *Alternative Farming Systems Information Center (AFSIC),* 10301 Baltimore Ave., #123, Beltsville, MD 20705-2351; (301) 504-6559. Vacant, Coordinator. Web, http://afsic.nal.usda.gov

Serves individuals and agencies seeking information on sustainability in agriculture, alternative plants and crops, farm energy options, grazing systems and alternative livestock breeds, alternative marketing and business practices, organic production, ecological pest management, and soil and water management.

National Agricultural Statistics Service *(Agriculture Dept.),* 1400 Independence Ave. S.W., #5041, MS 2001, 20250-2001; (202) 720-2707. Fax, (202) 720-9013. Joseph T. Reilly, Administrator. Information, (800) 727-9540. Print reports, (800) 999-6779. General email, nass@nass.usda.gov

Web, www.nass.usda.gov

Prepares estimates and reports on production, supply, prices, and other items relating to the U.S. agricultural economy. Reports include statistics on field crops, fruits and vegetables, cattle, hogs, poultry, and related products. Prepares quinquennial national census of agriculture.

National Agricultural Statistics Service *(Agriculture Dept.), Census and Survey,* 1400 Independence Ave. S.W., #6306, MS 2020, 20250-2020; (202) 720-4557. Fax, (202) 720-8738. Joseph T. Reilly, Administrator. General email, nass@nass.usda.gov

Web, www.nass.usda.gov

Conducts a quinquennial agricultural census that provides data on crops, livestock, operator characteristics, land use, farm production expenditures, machinery and equipment, and irrigation for counties, states, regions, and the nation.

National Institute of Food and Agriculture (NIFA) *(Agriculture Dept.),* Jaime L. Whitten Bldg., #305A, 800 9th St. S.W., 20024 (mailing address: 1400 Independence Ave. S.W., MS 2201, Washington, DC 20250-2201); (202) 720-4423. Sonny Ramaswamy, Director. Communications, (202) 720-4242. Information, (202) 720-4651. Web, www.nifa.usda.gov

Supports research, education, and extension of issues pertaining to agricultural production, nutrition, food safety, energy independence, and the sustainability of natural resources. Partners with and funds scientists at academic institutions, particularly the land-grant universities, minority-serving institutions, including black colleges and universities, Hispanic-serving institutions, and tribal colleges, as well as government, private, and nonprofit organizations to address critical issues in agriculture, including global food security and hunger, water resources, climate change, sustainable energy, childhood obesity, and food safety. Partners with agricultural extension offices in all counties, states, and territories.

National Institute of Food and Agriculture (NIFA) *(Agriculture Dept.), Institute of Bioenergy, Climate, and Environment,* 800 9th St. S.W., #3231, 20024 (mailing address: 1400 Independence Ave. S.W., MS 2210, Washington, DC 20250-2215); (202) 720-4926. Luis Tupas, Deputy Director. Web, www.nifa.usda.gov/office/institute-bioenergy-climate-and-environment

Administers programs to address national science priorities that advance energy independence and help agricultural, forest, and range production systems adapt to climate change variables. Provides grants to support the development of sustainable bioenergy production systems, agricultural production systems, and natural resource management activities that are adapted to climate variation and activities that otherwise support sustainable natural resource use.

National Institute of Food and Agriculture (NIFA) *(Agriculture Dept.),* ***Institute of Food Production and Sustainability,*** *800 9th St. S.W., #3305, 20024 (mailing address: 1400 Independence Ave. S.W., MS 2240, Washington, DC 20250-2240); (202) 401-5024. Fax, (202) 401-1782. Parag R. Chitnis, Deputy Director.* *Web, www.nifa.usda.gov/office/institute-food-production-and-sustainability*

Enhances food security through productive and sustainable agricultural systems. Includes divisions of Animal Safety, Plant Systems, Protection, Plant Systems Production, and Agriculture Systems.

National Institute of Food and Agriculture (NIFA) *(Agriculture Dept.),* ***Institute of Youth, Family, and Community,*** *800 9th St. S.W., #4343, 20024 (mailing address: 1400 Independence Ave. S.W., MS2250, Washington, DC 20250-2225); (202) 720-5305. Fax, (202) 720-3945. Muquarrab Qureshi, Deputy Director.* *Web, www.nifa.usda.gov/office/institute-youth-family-and-community*

Provides grants and programmatic training to support youth and family development; partners with county governments, the private sector, and state land-grant universities. Program areas include food and agricultural science education, particularly in minority-serving institutions; childhood nutrition; community food projects; and community service. Includes divisions of Community Education, Family and Consumer Sciences, and Youth and 4-H.

Rural Development *(Agriculture Dept.),* ***Business–Cooperative Service, Business Programs,*** *1400 Independence Ave. S.W., #5803-S, MS 3201, 20250-3201; (202) 690-4730. William Smith, Deputy Administrator. Press, (202) 690-4737.* *Web, www.rd.usda.gov/about-rd/agencies/rural-business-cooperative-service*

Conducts economic research and provides financial assistance and business planning to help farmers market their products and purchase supplies.

Rural Development *(Agriculture Dept.),* ***Business–Cooperative Service, Cooperative Programs,*** *1400 Independence Ave. S.W., #5803-S, MS 3201, 20250-3201; (202) 690-4730. Fax, (202) 690-4737. Chad Parker, Deputy Administrator.* *Web, www.rd.usda.gov/about-rd/agencies/rural-business-cooperative-service*

Conducts economic research and helps people living in rural areas obtain business services through cooperatives.

▶ **NONGOVERNMENTAL**

National 4-H Council, *7100 Connecticut Ave., Chevy Chase, MD 20815-4999; (301) 961-2800. Fax, (301)*

961-2894. Jennifer L. Sirangelo, President, (301) 961-2820. Press, (301) 961-2973. *Web, www.4-h.org, Twitter, @4H and Facebook, www.facebook.com/4-h*

4-H membership: young people across the United States engaged in hands-on learning activities in leadership, citizenship, life skills, science, healthy living, and food security. National 4-H Council is a national, private-sector partner of the 4-H Youth Development Program and its parent, the Cooperative Extension System of the Agriculture Dept. In the United States, 4-H programs are implemented by 109 land-grant universities and more than 3,000 cooperative extension offices. Outside the United States, 4-H programs operate through independent, country-led organizations in more than 50 countries.

National Council of Farmer Cooperatives (NCFC), *50 F St. N.W., #900, 20001-1530; (202) 626-8700. Fax, (202) 626-8722. Charles F. Conner, President.* *General email, info@ncfc.org* *Web, www.ncfc.org*

Membership: cooperative businesses owned and operated by farmers. Conducts educational programs and encourages research on agricultural cooperatives; provides statistics and analyzes trends; presents awards for research papers.

National Ecological Observatory Network, Inc. (NEON), *Washington Office, 1100 Jefferson Dr. S.W., #3123, MRC 705, 20560-0001; (202) 370-7891. Fax, (202) 204-0128. Brian Wee, Chief of Strategic Alliances; Gene Kelly, Chief Executive Officer, Acting. Press, (720) 746-4936.* *General email, bwee@neoninc.org* *Web, www.neoninc.org, Twitter, @NEONInc and Facebook, www.facebook.com/NEONInc*

Collects data across the United States on the impact of climate change, land use change, and invasive species on natural resources and biodiversity, with the goal of detecting and forecasting ecological change on a continental scale over multiple decades. Works with various government agencies to develop standards for environmental observations and data interoperability; expected to become fully operational by 2017. Funded by the National Science Foundation in partnership with NEON. (Visitors note: Co-located in the Smithsonian's S. Dillon Ripley Center.) (Headquarters in Boulder, Colo.)

National FFA Organization, *1410 King St., #400, Alexandria, VA 22314-2749; (703) 838-5889. Steve A. Brown, National FFA Advisor.* *Web, www.ffa.org, Twitter, @NationalFFA and Facebook, www.facebook.com/nationalffa*

Membership: local chapters of high school students enrolled in agricultural, food, and natural resources sciences education and agribusiness programs. Coordinates leadership training and other activities with local chapters across the United States. Formerly known as the Future Farmers of America. (Business Center in Indianapolis, Ind.)

Fertilizer and Pesticides

►AGENCIES

Environmental Protection Agency (EPA), *Chemical Safety and Pollution Prevention, 1200 Pennsylvania Ave. N.W., #4146, MC 7101M, 20460; (202) 564-2902. Fax, (202) 564-0801. James J. Jones, Assistant Administrator.*
Web, www2.epa.gov/aboutepa/about-office-chemical-safety-and-pollution-prevention-ocspp

Studies and makes recommendations for regulating chemical substances under the Toxic Substances Control Act. Compiles list of chemical substances subject to the act. Registers, controls, and regulates use of pesticides and toxic substances. Manages the Endocrine Disruptor Screening Program.

Environmental Protection Agency (EPA), *Chemical Safety and Pollution Prevention, Pesticide Programs, 1 Potomac Yard, 2777 Crystal Dr., Arlington, VA 22202 (mailing address: 1200 Pennsylvania Ave. N.W., MC 7501P, Washington, DC 20460); (703) 305-7090. Fax, (703) 308-4776. Jack Housenger, Director. National Pesticide Information Center, (800) 858-7378.*
General email, pesticidewebcomments@epa.gov
Web, www.epa.gov/aboutepa/about-office-chemical-safety-and-pollution-prevention-ocspp#opp and www.epa.gov/aboutepa/organization-chart-office-chemical-safety-and-pollution-prevention-ocspp

Regulates the manufacturing and use of all pesticides, including insecticides, herbicides, rodenticides, disinfectants, and sanitizers, in the United States. Establishes maximum levels for pesticide residues in food. Develops rules that govern labeling and literature accompanying pesticide products. Administers the Integrated Pest Management in Schools and the Pesticide Environmental Stewardship programs. Operates the National Pesticide Information Center (8 a.m.–12 p.m. PST).

Natural Resources Conservation Service *(Agriculture Dept.), Pest Management, 1400 Independence Ave. S.W., #5103, 20250; (202) 720-4630. Fax, (202) 720-2646. Noeller Herbert, Chief.*
General email, jason.weller@usda.gov
Web, www.nrcs.usda.gov

Formulates and recommends agency policy in coordination with the Environmental Protection Agency and other USDA agencies for the establishment of standards, procedures, and management of agronomic, forest, and horticultural use of pesticides.

►NONGOVERNMENTAL

Beyond Pesticides, *701 E St. S.E., #200, 20003; (202) 543-5450. Fax, (202) 543-4791. Jay Feldman, Executive Director.*
General email, info@beyondpesticides.org
Web, www.beyondpesticides.org and Twitter, @bpncamp

Coalition of family farmers, farm workers, consumers, home gardeners, physicians, lawyers, and others concerned about pesticide hazards and safety. Issues information to increase public awareness of environmental, public health, and economic problems caused by pesticide abuse; promotes alternatives to pesticide use, such as organic pest management program.

Croplife America, *1156 15th St. N.W., #400, 20005-1752; (202) 296-1585. Fax, (202) 463-0474. Jay J. Vroom, President.*
General email, agriesser@croplifeamerica.org
Web, www.croplifeamerica.org

Membership: pesticide manufacturers. Provides information on pesticide safety, development, and use. Monitors legislation and regulations. (Formerly the American Crop Protection Assn.)

Entomological Society of America, *3 Park Pl., #307, Annapolis, MD 21401-3722; (301) 731-4535. Fax, (301) 731-4538. David Gammel, Executive Director.*
General email, esa@entsoc.org
Web, www.entsoc.org and Twitter, @EntsocAmerica

Scientific association that promotes the science of entomology and the interests of professionals in the field, with branches throughout the United States. Advises on crop protection, food chain, and individual and urban health matters dealing with insect pests.

Fertilizer Institute, *425 3rd St. S.W., #950, 20024; (202) 962-0490. Fax, (202) 962-0577. Chris Jahn, President, (202) 515-2700.*
General email, info@tfi.org
Web, www.tfi.org and Twitter, @Fertilizer_Inst

Membership: manufacturers, dealers, and distributors of fertilizer. Provides statistical data and other information concerning the effects of fertilizer and its relationship to world food production, food supply, and the environment.

Migrant Legal Action Program, *1001 Connecticut Ave. N.W., #915, 20036-5524; (202) 775-7780. Fax, (202) 775-7784. Roger C. Rosenthal, Executive Director.*
General email, mlap@mlap.org
Web, www.mlap.org

Assists local legal services groups and private attorneys representing farm workers. Monitors legislation, regulations, and enforcement activities of the Environmental Protection Agency and the Occupational Safety and Health Administration in the area of pesticide use as it affects the health of migrant farm workers. Litigates cases concerning living and working conditions experienced by migrant farm workers. Works with local groups on implementation of Medicaid block grants.

National Agricultural Aviation Assn., *1440 Duke St., Alexandria, VA 22314; (202) 546-5722. Fax, (202) 546-5726. Andrew D. Moore, Executive Director.*
General email, information@agaviation.org
Web, www.agaviation.org

Membership: agricultural pilots; operating companies that seed, fertilize, and spray land by air; and allied industries. Monitors legislation and regulations. (Affiliated with National Agricultural Aviation Research and Education Foundation.)

National Pest Management Assn., *10460 North St., Fairfax, VA 22030; (703) 352-6762. Fax, (703) 352-3031. Robert M. Rosenberg, Corporate Executive Officer. Toll-free, (800) 678-6722.*
Web, www.npmapestworld.org

Membership: pest control operators. Monitors federal regulations that affect pesticide use; provides members with technical information. Web site has a Spanish-language link.

Horticulture and Gardening

►AGENCIES

National Arboretum *(Agriculture Dept.), Floral and Nursery Plants Research, 3501 New York Ave. N.E., #100, 20002; (202) 245-2701. Fax, (202) 245-5973. Ramon Jordan, Associate Director.*
Web, www.ars.usda.gov/main/site_main.htm?modecode= 80-20-05-05

Supports research and implementation of new technologies in florist and nursery industries. Areas of research include development of new floral, nursery, and turf plants; detection and control of pathogens in ornamental plants; ornamental plant taxonomy; improvement of nursery production systems; and curation of woody landscape plant germplasm as part of the National Plant Germplasm System.

National Arboretum *(Agriculture Dept.), Gardens Research, 3501 New York Ave. N.E., 20002; (202) 245-4533. Scott Aker, Supervisory Research Horticulturalist.*
Web, www.ars.usda.gov/main/site_main.htm?modecode= 80-20-05-10

Collects, displays, documents, evaluates, and introduces woody and herbaceous landscape ornamentals; interprets plant collections, display gardens, and Agricultural Research Service and National Arboretum research for the public through signage, exhibits, and programs; and provides educational programs for gardeners and green industry professionals.

National Arboretum *(Agriculture Dept.), 3501 New York Ave. N.E., 20002-1958; (202) 245-2726. Fax, (202) 245-4575. Richard T. Olsen, Director.*
Web, www.usna.usda.gov

Maintains public display of plants on 446 acres; provides information and makes referrals concerning cultivated plants (exclusive of field crops and fruits); conducts plant breeding and research; maintains herbarium.

Smithsonian Institution, *Botany and Horticulture Library, 10th St. and Constitution Ave. N.W., #W422, 20560-0166 (mailing address: P.O. Box 37012, MRC 154, Washington, DC 20013-7012); (202) 633-1685. Fax, (202) 786-2866. Robin Everly, Branch Librarian.*
General email, askalibrarian@si.edu
Web, www.library.si.edu/libraries/botany

Collection includes books, periodicals, and videotapes on horticulture, garden history, and landscape design. Specializes in American gardens and gardening of the late nineteenth and early twentieth centuries. Open to the public by appointment 9:00 a.m.–4:30 p.m. (Housed at the National Museum of Natural History.)

U.S. Botanic Garden, *100 Maryland Ave. S.W., 20001 (mailing address: 245 1st St. S.W., Washington, DC 20024); (202) 225-8333. Fax, (202) 225-1561. Ari Novy, Executive Director, (202) 225-6670. Horticulture hotline, (202) 226-4785. Program registration information, (202) 225-1116. Special events, (202) 226-7674. Tour line, (202) 226-2055. Press, (202) 226-4145.*
General email, usbg@aoc.gov
Web, www.usbg.gov

Collects, cultivates, and grows various plants for public display and study; identifies botanic specimens and furnishes information on proper growing methods. Conducts horticultural classes and tours.

►NONGOVERNMENTAL

American Horticultural Society, *River Farm, 7931 E. Boulevard Dr., Alexandria, VA 22308-1300; (703) 768-5700, ext. 119. Fax, (703) 768-8700. Tom Underwood, Executive Director, (703) 768-5700, ext. 123. Toll-free, (800) 777-7931.*
Web, www.ahs.org

Promotes the expansion of horticulture in the United States through educational programs for amateur and professional horticulturists. Publishes gardening magazine. Oversees historic house and farm once owned by George Washington, with gardens maintained by staff; house and grounds are rented for special occasions.

American Society for Horticultural Science (ASHS), *1018 Duke St., Alexandria, VA 22314; (703) 836-4606. Fax, (703) 836-2024. Michael W. Neff, Executive Director, ext. 106.*
General email, webmaster@ashs.org
Web, www.ashs.org and Twitter, @ASHA_Hort

Membership: educators, government workers, firms, associations, and individuals interested in horticultural science. Promotes scientific research and education in horticulture, including international exchange of information.

AmericanHort, *Government Relations, 525 9th St. N.W., #800, 20004 (mailing address: 2130 Stella Ct., Columbus OH 43215); (202) 789-2900. Fax, (202) 789-1893. David Savoia, President, Acting.*
General email, hello@AmericanHort.org
Web, www.AmericanHort.org and Twitter, @American_ Hort

Membership: wholesale growers, garden center retailers, landscape firms, and suppliers to the horticultural community. Monitors legislation and regulations on agricultural, environmental, and small business issues; conducts educational seminars on business management for members.

National Assn. of Plant Patent Owners, *525 9th St. N.W., #800, 20004; (202) 789-2900. Fax, (202) 789-1893. Craig Regelbrugge, Administrator. Web, www.americanhort.org*

Membership: owners of patents on newly propagated horticultural plants. Informs members of plant patents issued, provisions of patent laws, and changes in practice. Promotes the development, protection, production, and distribution of new varieties of horticultural plants. Works with international organizations of plant breeders on matters of common interest. (Affiliated with AmericanHort, formerly the American Nursery and Landscape Assn.)

Society of American Florists, *1601 Duke St., Alexandria, VA 22314-3406; (703) 836-8700. Fax, (703) 836-8705. Peter J. Moran, Chief Executive Officer. Toll-free, (800) 336-4743. General email, pmoran@safnow.org Web, www.safnow.org*

Membership: growers, wholesalers, and retailers in the floriculture and ornamental horticulture industries. Interests include labor, pesticides, the environment, international trade, and toxicity of plants. Mediates industry problems.

Soil and Watershed Conservation

►AGENCIES

Farm Service Agency (FSA) *(Agriculture Dept.), Conservation and Environmental Programs, 1400 Independence Ave. S.W., MS 0513, 20250-0513; (202) 720-6221. Fax, (202) 720-4619. Matthew Ponish, Director. Web, www.fsa.usda.gov*

Directs conservation and environmental projects and programs to help farmers and ranchers prevent soil erosion and contamination of natural resources.

National Agricultural Library *(Agriculture Dept.), Water Quality Information Center, 10301 Baltimore Ave., 1st Floor, Beltsville, MD 20705-2351; (301) 504-6077. Fax, (301) 504-5181. Joe Makuch, Coordinator. Web, http://wqic.nal.usda.gov*

Serves individuals and agencies seeking information on water quality and agriculture. Special subject areas include agricultural environmental management, irrigation, water availability, and water quality.

Natural Resources Conservation Service *(Agriculture Dept.), 1400 Independence Ave. S.W., #5105AS, 20250 (mailing address: P.O. Box 2890, Washington, DC 20013-2890); (202) 720-4525. Fax, (202) 720-7690. Jason Weller,*

Chief, (202) 720-7246. Chief's Office, (202) 720-7246. Public Affairs, (202) 720-5776. General email, nrcsdistributioncenter@ia.usda.gov Web, www.nrcs.usda.gov

Responsible for soil and water conservation programs, including watershed protection, flood prevention, river basin surveys, and resource conservation and development. Provides landowners, operators, state and local units of government, and community groups with technical assistance in carrying out local programs. Inventories and monitors soil, water, and related resource data and resource use trends. Provides information about soil surveys, farmlands, and other natural resources.

►NONGOVERNMENTAL

American Farmland Trust (AFT), *1150 Connecticut Ave. N.W., #600, 20036; (202) 331-7300. Fax, (202) 659-8339. Ralph Grossi, President, Acting. Toll-free, (800) 431-1499. General email, info@farmland.org Web, www.farmland.org*

Works to protect farmland, promote sound farming practices, and keep farmers on the land through local, regional, and national efforts. Works to help farmers implement practices that protect water quality. Conducts independent analyses of policies that affect farmland and advocates government policies that support farmland conservation and keep farms economically viable.

Irrigation Assn., *8280 Willow Oaks Corporate Dr., #400, Fairfax, VA 22031; (703) 536-7080. Fax, (703) 536-7019. Deborah Hamlin, Executive Director. General email, info@irrigation.org Web, www.irrigation.org*

Membership: companies and individuals involved in irrigation, drainage, and erosion control worldwide. Promotes efficient and effective water management through training, education, and certification programs. Interests include economic development and environmental enhancement.

National Assn. of Clean Water Agencies, *1816 Jefferson Pl. N.W., 20036; (202) 833-2672. Fax, (888) 267-9505. Adam Krantz, Chief Executive Officer. General email, info@nacwa.org Web, www.nacwa.org*

Represents public wastewater treatment works, public and private organizations, law firms representing public clean water agencies, and nonprofit or academic organizations. Interests include water quality and watershed management. Sponsors conferences. Monitors legislation and regulations.

National Assn. of Conservation Districts (NACD), *509 Capitol Court N.E., 20002-4937; (202) 547-6223. Fax, (202) 547-6450. Jeremy Peters, Chief Executive Officer. General email, bethany-shively@nacdet.org Web, www.nacdnet.org*

Membership: conservation districts (local subdivisions of state government). Works to promote the conservation of land, forests, and other natural resources. Interests include erosion and sediment control; water quality; forestry, water, flood plain, and range management; rural development; and urban and community conservation.

Winrock International, *2121 Crystal Dr., #500, Arlington, VA 22202; (703) 302-6500. Fax, (703) 302-6512. Rodney Ferguson, President. General email, information@winrock.org*

Web, www.winrock.org and Twitter, @WinrockIntl

Addresses international water issues through programs targeting sustainable strategies for use and conservation within communities, and watersheds. (Headquarters in Little Rock, Ark.)

COMMODITIES, FARM PRODUCE

General

▶AGENCIES

Agricultural Marketing Service (AMS) *(Agriculture Dept.), Transportation and Marketing Programs, 1400 Independence Ave. S.W., #4543, MS 0266, 20250-0264; (202) 690-1300. Fax, (202) 690-0338. Arthur Neal, Deputy Administrator, (202) 690-1300; Bruce Blanton, Director, Transportation Services Division, (202) 690-0435; Billy Cox, Director, Marketing Services Division, (202) 720-8317.*

Web, www.ams.usda.gov/about-ams/programs-offices/ transportation-marketing-program

Promotes efficient, cost-effective marketing and transportation for U.S. agricultural products; sets standards for domestic and international marketing of organic products. Provides exporters with market information, educational services, and regulatory representation.

Agricultural Research Service *(Agriculture Dept.), National Plant Germplasm System, 5601 Sunnyside Ave., #4-2212, Beltsville, MD 20705-5139; (301) 504-5541. Fax, (301) 504-6191. Peter Bretting, National Program Leader.*

Web, www.ars-grin.gov

Network of federal and state gene banks that preserve samples of all major field crops and horticultural crops. Collects, preserves, evaluates, and catalogs germplasm and distributes it for specific purposes.

Agriculture Dept. (USDA), *Marketing and Regulatory Programs, 1400 Independence Ave. S.W., #228W, MS 0109, 20250-0109; (202) 720-4256. Fax, (202) 720-5775. Edward M. Avalos, Under Secretary.*

Web, www.usda.gov/wps/portal/usda/usdahome? contentid=missionarea_MRP.xml

Administers inspection and grading services and regulatory programs for agricultural commodities through the Agricultural Marketing Service; Animal and Plant Health Inspection Service; and Grain Inspection, Packers and Stockyards Administration.

Animal and Plant Health Inspection Service (APHIS) *(Agriculture Dept.), 1400 Independence Ave. S.W., #312E, MS 3401, 20250-3401; (202) 799-7030. Fax, (202) 720-3982. Kevin A. Shea, Administrator. Press, (301) 851-4100. Veterinary Services, (301) 851-3300. Plants and Plant Products, (877) 770-5990. Customer Service, (844) 820-2234.*

Web, www.aphis.usda.gov and Twitter, @USDA_APHIS

Administers programs in cooperation with the states to prevent the spread of pests and plant diseases; certifies that U.S. exports are free of pests and disease.

Bureau of Economic and Business Affairs *(State Dept.), Agriculture Policy, 2201 C St. N.W., #4686, 20520-0002; (202) 647-3090. Fax, (202) 647-1894. Eric W. Luftman, Director, (202) 647-0133.*

Web, www.state.gov/e/eb/tpp/agp

Negotiates bilateral textile trade agreements with foreign governments concerning cotton, wool, and synthetic textile and apparel products.

Commodity Futures Trading Commission, *Three Lafayette Centre, 1155 21st St. N.W., 20581-0001; (202) 418-5000. Fax, (202) 418-5521. Timothy G. Massad, Chair. TTY, (202) 418-5514. Toll-free, (866) 366-2382. General email, questions@cftc.gov*

Web, www.cftc.gov and Twitter, @CFTC

Oversees the Commodity Exchange Act, which regulates all commodity futures and options to prevent fraudulent trade practices.

Farm Service Agency (FSA) *(Agriculture Dept.), 1400 Independence Ave. S.W., #3086, MS 0501, 20250-0506; (202) 720-3467. Fax, (202) 720-9105. Val J. Dolcini, Administrator. Press, (202) 720-7807.*

Web, www.fsa.usda.gov

Administers farm commodity programs providing crop loans and purchases; provides crop payments when market prices fall below specified levels; sets acreage allotments and marketing quotas; assists farmers in areas affected by natural disasters.

Farm Service Agency (FSA) *(Agriculture Dept.), Commodity Credit Corp., 1400 Independence Ave. S.W., MS 0599, 20250-0571; (202) 720-0402. Fax, (202) 245-4786. Sandra G. Wood, Assistant Secretary, Acting. General email, Robert.Stephenson@wdc.usda.gov*

Web, www.fsa.usda.gov/ccc

Finances commodity stabilization programs, domestic and export surplus commodity disposal, foreign assistance, storage activities, and related programs.

Foreign Agricultural Service (FAS) *(Agriculture Dept.), 1400 Independence Ave. S.W., #5071S, MS 1001, 20250-1001; (202) 720-3935. Fax, (202) 690-2159. Philip (Phil) Karsting, Administrator. Public Affairs, (202) 720-7115. TTY, (202) 720-1786.*

Web, www.fas.usda.gov and Twitter, USDAForeignAg

Promotes exports of U.S. commodities and assists with trade negotiations; coordinates activities of U.S. representatives in foreign countries who report on crop and market conditions; sponsors trade fairs in foreign countries to promote export of U.S. agricultural products; analyzes world demand and production of various commodities; administers food aid programs; monitors sales by private exporters; provides technical assistance and trade capacity building programs.

Foreign Agricultural Service (FAS) *(Agriculture Dept.),* **Trade Programs,** *1400 Independence Ave. S.W., MS 1020, 20250-1020; (202) 720-9516. Fax, (202) 401-0135. Christian Foster, Deputy Administrator. Web, www.fas.usda.gov*

Administers market development, export credit guarantees, dairy export incentive programs, and import programs for sugar, dairy, and trade adjustment assistance.

Rural Development *(Agriculture Dept.),* **Business–Cooperative Service, Business Programs,** *1400 Independence Ave. S.W., #5803-S, MS 3201, 20250-3201; (202) 690-4730. William Smith, Deputy Administrator. Press, (202) 690-4737. Web, www.rd.usda.gov/about-rd/agencies/rural-business-cooperative-service*

Conducts economic research and provides financial assistance and business planning to help farmers market their products and purchase supplies.

▶**CONGRESS**

For a listing of relevant congressional committees and subcommittees, please see page 3 or the Appendix.

▶**NONGOVERNMENTAL**

American Seed Trade Assn., *1701 Duke St., #275, Alexandria, VA 22314-2878; (703) 837-8140. Fax, (703) 837-9365. Andrew (Andy) W. LaVigne, President. Toll-free, (888) 890-7333. Web, www.amseed.org and Twitter, @AMSEED2*

Membership: producers and merchandisers of seeds. Conducts seminars on research developments in corn, sorghum, soybean, and other farm and garden seeds; promotes overseas seed market development.

Commodity Markets Council (CMC), *1300 L St. N.W., #1020, 20005-4166; (202) 842-0400. Gregg Doud, President. Web, http://commoditymkts.org and Twitter, @CommodityMkts*

Federation of commodity futures exchanges, boards of trade, and industry stakeholders, including commodity merchandisers, processors, and refiners; futures commission merchants; food and beverage manufacturers; transportation companies; and financial institutions. Combines members' expertise to formulate positions on market, policy, and contracting issues involving commodities, with an overall goal of facilitating growth in liquidity and transparency in cash and derivative markets. Monitors legislation and regulations. (Formerly the National Grain Trade Council.)

Global Cold Chain Alliance, *1500 King St., #201, Alexandria, VA 22314-2730; (703) 373-4300. Fax, (703) 373-4301. Corey Rosenbusch, President. General email, email@gcca.org Web, www.gcca.org*

Membership: owners and operators of public refrigerated warehouses. Interests include labor, transportation, taxes, environment, safety, regulatory compliance, and food distribution. Monitors legislation and regulations. (Affiliated with the International Refrigerated Transportation Assn., the International Assn. for Cold Storage Construction, and the World Food Logistics Assn.)

National Cooperative Business Assn., CLUSA International (NCBA CLUSA), *1775 Eye St. N.W., #800, 20006; (202) 638-6222. Fax, (202) 638-1374. Judy Ziewacz, President. General email, info@ncba.coop Web, www.ncba.coop, Twitter, @NCBACLUSA and Facebook, www.facebook.com/NCBACLUSA*

Alliance of cooperatives, businesses, and state cooperative associations. Provides information about starting and managing agricultural cooperatives in the United States and in developing nations. Monitors legislation and regulations.

National Council of Farmer Cooperatives (NCFC), *50 F St. N.W., #900, 20001-1530; (202) 626-8700. Fax, (202) 626-8722. Charles F. Conner, President. General email, info@ncfc.org Web, www.ncfc.org*

Membership: cooperative businesses owned and operated by farmers. Encourages research on agricultural cooperatives; provides statistics and analyzes trends. Monitors legislation and regulations on agricultural trade, transportation, energy, and tax issues.

U.S. Agricultural Export Development Council, *8233 Old Courthouse Rd., #200, Vienna, VA 22182; (703) 556-9290. Fax, (703) 790-0845. Annie Durbin, Executive Director. General email, adurbin@usaedc.org Web, www.usaedc.org*

Membership: agricultural growers and processors, commodity trade associations, farmer cooperatives, and state regional trade groups. Works with the Foreign Agricultural Service on projects to create, expand, and maintain agricultural markets abroad. Sponsors seminars and workshops.

Cotton

▶**AGENCIES**

Agricultural Marketing Service (AMS) *(Agriculture Dept.),* **Cotton and Tobacco Programs,** *1400 Independence Ave. S.W., #2641S, MS 0224, 20250-0224; (202) 720-2145. Fax, (202) 690-1718. Darryl W. Earnest, Deputy Administrator. Web, www.ams.usda.gov/about-ams/programs-offices/cotton-tobacco*

Administers cotton marketing programs; sets cotton and tobacco grading standards and conducts quality inspections based on those standards. Maintains market news service to inform producers of daily price changes.

Farm Service Agency (FSA) *(Agriculture Dept.), Fibers, Peanuts, and Tobacco Analysis, 1400 Independence Ave. S.W., #37605, MS 0515, 20250-0515; (202) 720-3392. Fax, (202) 690-2186. Scott Sanford, Director.*
Web, www.fsa.usda.gov/programs-and-services/economic-and-policy-analysis/fibers-peanuts-tobacco

Develops production adjustment and price support programs to balance supply and demand for cotton, peanuts, and tobacco.

▶ **INTERNATIONAL ORGANIZATIONS**

International Cotton Advisory Committee, *1629 K St. N.W., #702, 20006-1636; (202) 463-6660. Fax, (202) 463-6950. José Sette, Executive Director, ext. 116.*
General email, secretariat@icac.org
Web, www.icac.org

Membership: cotton producing and consuming countries. Provides information on cotton production, trade, consumption, stocks, and prices.

▶ **NONGOVERNMENTAL**

Cotton Council International, *1521 New Hampshire Ave. N.W., 20036-1203; (202) 745-7805. Fax, (202) 483-4040. Bruce Atherley, Executive Director.*
General email, cottonusa@cotton.org
Web, www.cottonusa.org and Twitter, @CottonUSA

Division of National Cotton Council of America. Promotes U.S. raw cotton and cotton-product exports.

Cotton Warehouse Assn. of America, *316 Pennsylvania Ave. S.E., #401, 20003; (202) 544-5875. Fax, (202) 544-5874. Larry Combest, Executive Vice President.*
General email, cwaa@cottonwarehouse.org
Web, www.cottonwarehouse.org

Membership: cotton compress and warehouse operators. Serves as a liaison between members and government agencies; monitors legislation and regulations.

National Cotton Council of America, *Washington Office, 1521 New Hampshire Ave. N.W., 20036-1205; (202) 745-7805. Fax, (202) 483-4040. Reece Langley, Vice President, Washington Operations.*
Web, www.cotton.org

Membership: all segments of the U.S. cotton industry. Provides statistics and information on such topics as cotton history and processing. (Headquarters in Memphis, Tenn.)

Dairy Products and Eggs

▶ **AGENCIES**

Agricultural Marketing Service (AMS) *(Agriculture Dept.), Dairy Programs, 1400 Independence Ave. S.W.,*
#2968, 20250-0225; (202) 720-4392. Fax, (202) 690-3410. Dana H. Coale, Deputy Administrator.
Web, www.ams.usda.gov/about-ams/programs-offices/dairy-program

Administers dairy product marketing and promotion programs; grades dairy products; maintains market news service on daily price changes; sets minimum price that farmers receive for milk.

Agricultural Marketing Service (AMS) *(Agriculture Dept.), Livestock, Poultry, and Seed, 1400 Independence Ave. S.W., #2092S, MS 0249, 20250-0249; (202) 720-5705. Fax, (202) 720-3499. Craig Morris, Deputy Administrator.*
Web, www.ams.usda.gov/about-ams/programs-offices/livestock-poultry-seed-program

Sets poultry and egg grading standards. Provides promotion and market news services for domestic and international markets.

Farm Service Agency (FSA) *(Agriculture Dept.), Dairy and Sweeteners Analysis, 1400 Independence Ave. S.W., #3752, MS 0516, 20250-0516; (202) 720-4146. Fax, (202) 690-1480. Barbara Fecso, Group Director.*
Web, www.fsa.usda.gov/programs-and-services/economic-and-policy-analysis/dairy-and-sweeteners-analysis

Develops production adjustment and price support programs to balance supply and demand for certain commodities, including dairy products, sugar, and honey.

▶ **NONGOVERNMENTAL**

American Butter Institute (ABI), *2101 Wilson Blvd., #400, Arlington, VA 22201-3062; (703) 243-5630. Fax, (703) 841-9328. Annja Miner, Executive Director.*
General email, AMiner@nmpf.org
Web, www.nmpf.org/abi

Membership: butter manufacturers, packagers, and distributors. Interests include dairy price supports and programs, packaging and labeling, and imports. Monitors legislation and regulations.

Humane Farm Animal Care, *P.O. Box 727, Herndon, VA 20172-0727; (703) 435-3883. Fax, (703) 435-3981. Adele Douglass, Executive Director.*
General email, info@certifiedhumane.org
Web, www.certifiedhumane.org

Seeks to improve the welfare of farm animals by providing viable, duly monitored standards for humane food production. Administers the Certified Humane Raised and Handled program for meat, poultry, eggs, and dairy products.

International Dairy Foods Assn., *1250 H St. N.W., #900, 20005-3952; (202) 737-4332. Fax, (202) 331-7820. Constance (Connie) E. Tipton, President.*
Web, www.idfa.org

Membership: processors, manufacturers, marketers, and distributors of dairy foods in the United States and abroad. Provides members with marketing, public relations, training, and management services. Monitors legislation and regulations. (Affiliated with the Milk

Industry Foundation, the National Cheese Institute, and the International Ice Cream Assn.)

National Milk Producers Federation, *2101 Wilson Blvd., #400, Arlington, VA 22201-3062; (703) 243-6111. Fax, (703) 841-9328. Jim Mulhern, Chief Executive Officer. General email, info@nmpf.org*

Web, www.nmpf.org

Membership: dairy farmer cooperatives. Provides information on development and modification of sanitary regulations, product standards, and marketing procedures for dairy products.

Fruits and Vegetables

▶**AGENCIES**

Agricultural Marketing Service (AMS) *(Agriculture Dept.), Specialty Crops Program, 1400 Independence Ave. S.W., #2077-S, MS 0235, 20250-0235; (202) 720-4722. Fax, (202) 720-0016. Charles Parrott, Deputy Administrator.*
Web, www.ams.usda.gov/about-ams/programs-offices/specialty-crops-program

Administers research, marketing, promotional, and regulatory programs for fruits, vegetables, nuts, ornamental plants, and other specialty crops; focus includes international markets. Sets grading standards for fresh and processed fruits and vegetables; conducts quality inspections; maintains market news service to inform producers of price changes.

Economic Research Service *(Agriculture Dept.), 355 E St. S.W., 20024-8221; (202) 694-5000. Fax, (202) 245-5467. Mary Bohman, Administrator; Greg Pompelli, Associate Administrator.*
General email, service@ers.usda.gov

Web, www.ers.usda.gov

Conducts market research; studies and forecasts domestic supply-and-demand trends for fruits and vegetables.

▶**NONGOVERNMENTAL**

U.S. Apple Assn., *8233 Old Courthouse Rd., #200, Vienna, VA 22182; (703) 442-8850. Fax, (703) 790-0845. James (Jim) Bair, President.*
General email, info@usapple.org

Web, www.usapple.org

Membership: U.S. commercial apple growers and processors, distributors, exporters, importers, and retailers of apples. Promotes nutrition research and marketing; provides information about apples and nutrition to educators. Monitors legislation and regulations.

United Fresh Produce Assn., *1901 Pennsylvania Ave. N.W., #1100, 20006; (202) 303-3400. Fax, (202) 303-3433. Tom Stenzel, President, (202) 303-3406.*
Web, www.unitedfresh.org

Membership: growers, shippers, wholesalers, retailers, food service operators, importers, and exporters involved

in producing and marketing fresh fruits and vegetables. Represents the industry before the government and the public sector.

Wine Institute, *Federal Relations, 601 13th St. N.W., #330 South, 20005-3866; (202) 408-0870. Fax, (202) 371-0061. Charles Jefferson, Vice President; Linda Ulrich, Vice President.*
Web, www.wineinstitute.org

Membership: California wineries and affiliated businesses. Seeks international recognition for California wines; conducts promotional campaigns in other countries. Monitors legislation and regulations. (Headquarters in San Francisco, Calif.)

Grains and Oilseeds

▶**AGENCIES**

Agricultural Marketing Service (AMS) *(Agriculture Dept.), Livestock, Poultry, and Seed, 1400 Independence Ave. S.W., #2092S, MS 0249, 20250-0249; (202) 720-5705. Fax, (202) 720-3499. Craig Morris, Deputy Administrator.*
Web, www.ams.usda.gov/about-ams/programs-offices/livestock-poultry-seed-program

Administers programs for marketing grain, including rice; maintains market news service to inform producers of grain market situation and daily price changes. Sets poultry and egg grading standards. Provides promotion and market news services for domestic and international markets.

Farm Service Agency (FSA) *(Agriculture Dept.), Feed Grains and Oilseeds Analysis, 1400 Independence Ave. S.W., #3740S, MS 0532, 20250-0532; (202) 720-2711. Fax, (202) 690-2186. Philip Sronce, Group Director.*
Web, www.fsa.usda.gov/programs-and-services/economic-and-policy-analysis/feed-grains-and-oilseeds-analysis

Develops, analyzes, and implements domestic farm policy focusing on corn, soybeans, and other feed grains and oilseeds. Develops production adjustment and price support programs to balance supply and demand for these commodities.

Farm Service Agency (FSA) *(Agriculture Dept.), Food Grains Analysis, 1400 Independence Ave. S.W., MS 0518, 20250-0532; (202) 720-2891. Fax, (202) 690-2186. Thomas F. Tice, Director.*
Web, www.fsa.usda.gov/programs-and-services/economic-and-policy-analysis/food-grains-analysis

Develops marketing loan and contract crop programs in support of food grain commodities, including wheat, rice, and pulse crops.

Grain Inspection, Packers and Stockyards Administration *(Agriculture Dept.), 1400 Independence Ave. S.W., #2055, South Bldg., MS 3601, 20250-3601; (202) 720-0219. Fax, (202) 205-9237. Larry Mitchell, Administrator. Toll-free, (800) 455-3447.*

General email, larry.mitchell@gipsa.usda.gov

Web, www.gipsa.usda.gov

Administers inspection and weighing program for grain, soybeans, rice, sunflower seeds, and other processed commodities; conducts quality inspections based on established standards.

▶ NONGOVERNMENTAL

American Feed Industry Assn. (AFIA), *2101 Wilson Blvd., #916, Arlington, VA 22201; (703) 524-0810. Fax, (703) 524-1921. Joel Newman, President.*

General email, afia@afia.org

Web, www.afia.org

Membership: more than 5,000 feed manufacturers, pharmaceutical companies, and ingredient suppliers and integrators. Conducts seminars on feed grain production, marketing, advertising, and quality control; interests include international trade.

American Soybean Assn., Washington Office, *600 Pennsylvania Ave. S.E., #320, 20003-6300; (202) 969-7040. Fax, (202) 969-7036. John Gordley, Washington Representative.*

Web, www.soygrowers.com

Membership: soybean farmers. Promotes expanded world markets and research for the benefit of soybean growers; maintains a network of state and international offices. Monitors legislation and regulations. (Headquarters in St. Louis, Mo.)

Corn Refiners Assn., *1701 Pennsylvania Ave. N.W., #950, 20006-5805; (202) 331-1634. Fax, (202) 331-2054. John Bode, Chief Executive Officer; David Knowles, Communications Director, (202) 534-3494.*

General email, comments@corn.org

Web, www.corn.org and Twitter, @CornRefiners

Promotes research on technical aspects of corn refining and product development; acts as a clearinghouse for members who award research grants to colleges and universities. Monitors legislation and regulations.

National Assn. of Wheat Growers, *415 2nd St. N.E., 20002-4993; (202) 547-7800. Fax, (202) 546-2638. Jim Palmer, Chief Executive Officer.*

General email, wheatworld@wheatworld.org

Web, www.wheatworld.org

Federation of state wheat grower associations. Monitors legislation and regulations.

National Corn Growers Assn., Public Policy, *20 F St. N.W., #600, 20001; (202) 628-7001. Fax, (202) 628-1933. Jon Doggett, Vice President, Public Policy.*

General email, corninfo@ncga.com and doggett@dc.ncga.com

Web, www.ncga.com, Twitter, @NationalCorn and Facebook, www.facebook.com/corngrowers

Represents the interests of U.S. corn farmers, including in international trade; promotes the use, marketing, and efficient production of corn; conducts research and educational activities; monitors legislation and regulations. (Headquarters in St. Louis, Mo.)

National Grain and Feed Assn., *1250 Eye St. N.W., #1003, 20005-3939; (202) 289-0873. Fax, (202) 289-5388. Randall (Randy) C. Gordon, President.*

General email, ngfa@ngfa.org

Web, www.ngfa.org and Twitter, @NGFA

Membership: firms that process, handle, and use U.S. grains and oilseeds in domestic and export markets; commodity futures brokers; and others involved with futures markets. Additional panel resolves disputes over trade and commercial regulations.

National Institute of Oilseed Products, *529 14th St. N.W., 750 National Press Bldg., 20045; (202) 591-2461. Fax, (202) 591-2445. Lauren LeMunyan, Executive Director.*

General email, niop@kellencompany.com

Web, www.niop.org

Membership: companies and individuals involved in manufacturing and trading oilseed products. Maintains standards for trading and transport of vegetable oils and oilseeds worldwide.

National Oilseed Processors Assn., *1300 L St. N.W., #1020, 20005-4168, (202) 842-0463. Fax, (202) 842-9126. Thomas A. Hammer, President.*

General email, jseibert@nopa.org

Web, www.nopa.org

Provides information on oilseed crops, products, processing, and commodity programs; interests include international trade.

North American Export Grain and Oilseed Assn. (NAEGA), *1250 Eye St. N.W., #1003, 20005-3939; (202) 682-4030. Fax, (202) 682-4033. Gary C. Martin, President.*

General email, info@naega.org

Web, www.naega.org

Membership: grain and oilseed exporting firms and others interested in the grain export industry. Provides information on grain export and contracting; sponsors foreign seminars. Monitors domestic and international legislation and regulations.

North American Millers' Assn., *600 Maryland Ave. S.W., #825W, 20024-2573; (202) 484-2200. Fax, (202) 488-7416. James A. McCarthy, President.*

General email, generalinfo@namamillers.org

Web, www.namamillers.org

Trade association representing the dry corn, wheat, oats, and rye milling industry. Seeks to inform the public, the industry, and government about issues affecting the domestic milling industry. Monitors legislation and regulations.

U.S. Grains Council, *20 F St. N.W., #600, 20001; (202) 789-0789. Fax, (202) 898-0522. Thomas Sleight, President.*

General email, grains@grains.org

Web, www.grains.org

Membership: barley, corn, and sorghum producers and exporters; and chemical, machinery, malting, and seed companies interested in feed grain exports. Promotes development of U.S. feed grain markets overseas.

U.S. Wheat Associates, *3103 10th St. North, #300, Arlington, VA 22201; (202) 463-0999. Fax, (703) 524-4399. Alan Tracy, President.*
General email, info@uswheat.org
Web, www.uswheat.org

Membership: wheat farmers. Develops export markets for the U.S. wheat industry; provides information on wheat production and marketing. Interests include trade policy, food aid, and biotechnology.

USA Rice Federation, *2101 Wilson Blvd., #610, Arlington, VA 22201; (703) 236-2300. Fax, (703) 236-2301. Betsy Ward, Chief Executive Officer. Toll-free, (800) 888-7423. General email, riceinfo@usarice.com*
Web, www.usarice.com

Membership: rice producers, millers, merchants, and related firms. Provides U.S. and foreign rice trade and industry information; assists in establishing quality standards for rice production and milling. Monitors legislation and regulations.

Sugar

▶**AGENCIES**

Economic Research Service *(Agriculture Dept.), 355 E St. S.W., 20024-8221; (202) 694-5000. Fax, (202) 245-5467. Mary Bohman, Administrator; Greg Pompelli, Associate Administrator.*
General email, service@ers.usda.gov
Web, www.ers.usda.gov

Conducts market research; studies and forecasts domestic supply-and-demand trends for sugar and other sweeteners.

Farm Service Agency (FSA) *(Agriculture Dept.), Dairy and Sweeteners Analysis, 1400 Independence Ave. S.W., #3752, MS 0516, 20250-0516; (202) 720-4146. Fax, (202) 690-1480. Barbara Fecso, Group Director.*
Web, www.fsa.usda.gov/programs-and-services/economic-and-policy-analysis/dairy-and-sweeteners-analysis

Develops production adjustment and price support programs to balance supply and demand for certain commodities, including dairy products, sugar, and honey.

▶**NONGOVERNMENTAL**

American Sugar Alliance, *2111 Wilson Blvd., #600, Arlington, VA 22201-3051; (703) 351-5055. Fax, (703) 351-6698. Vickie R. Myers, Executive Director.*
General email, info@sugaralliance.org
Web, www.sugaralliance.org

National coalition of sugarcane and sugarbeet farmers, processors, refiners, suppliers, workers, and others dedicated to preserving a strong domestic sweetener industry. Monitors legislation and regulations.

American Sugarbeet Growers Assn., *1156 15th St. N.W., #1101, 20005-1756; (202) 833-2398. Fax, (240) 235-4291. Luther Markwart, Executive Vice President.*
General email, info@americansugarbeet.org
Web, www.americansugarbeet.org

Membership: sugarbeet growers associations. Serves as liaison to U.S. government agencies, including the Agriculture Dept. and the U.S. Trade Representative; interests include international trade. Monitors legislation and regulations.

National Confectioners Assn., *1101 30th St. N.W., #200, 20007; (202) 534-1440. Fax, (202) 337-0637. John H. Downs Jr., President.*
General email, info@candyusa.com
Web, www.candyusa.com, Twitter, @CandyUSA and Facebook, www.facebook.com/NationalConfectionersAssociation

Membership: confectionery manufacturers and suppliers. Provides information on confectionery consumption and nutrition; sponsors educational programs and research on candy technology. Monitors legislation and regulations.

Sugar Assn., *1300 L St. N.W., #1001, 20005-4263; (202) 785-1122. Fax, (202) 785-5019. P. Courtney Gaine, President, Acting. Media, (202) 740-1997.*
General email, sugar@sugar.org
Web, www.sugar.org

Membership: sugar processors, growers, refiners, and planters. Provides nutritional information, public education, and research on sugar.

U.S. Beet Sugar Assn., *1156 15th St. N.W., #1019, 20005-1704; (202) 296-4820. Fax, (202) 331-2065. James W. Johnson Jr., President. Toll-free, (800) 872-0127. General email, beetsugar@aol.com*
Web, www.beetsugar.org

Membership: beet sugar processors. Monitors legislation and regulations.

Tobacco and Peanuts

▶**AGENCIES**

Agricultural Marketing Service (AMS) *(Agriculture Dept.), Cotton and Tobacco Programs, 1400 Independence Ave. S.W., #2641S, MS 0224, 20250-0224; (202) 720-2145. Fax, (202) 690-1718. Darryl W. Earnest, Deputy Administrator.*
Web, www.ams.usda.gov/about-ams/programs-offices/cotton-tobacco

Administers cotton marketing programs; sets cotton and tobacco grading standards and conducts quality inspections based on those standards. Maintains market news service to inform producers of daily price changes.

Economic Research Service *(Agriculture Dept.), 355 E St. S.W., 20024-8221; (202) 694-5000.*

Fax, (202) 245-5467. Mary Bohman, Administrator; Greg Pompelli, Associate Administrator.

General email, service@ers.usda.gov

Web, www.ers.usda.gov

Conducts market research; studies and forecasts domestic supply-and-demand trends for tobacco.

Farm Service Agency (FSA) *(Agriculture Dept.), Farm Programs, 1400 Independence Ave. S.W., MS 0510, 20250-0510; (202) 720-3175. Fax, (202) 720-4726. Brad Pfaff, Deputy Administrator. Press, (202) 720-7807. Web, www.fsa.usda.gov*

Administers and manages aid programs for farmers and ranchers, including conservation efforts, disaster relief, marketing loans, and safety-net subsidies. Operates through county offices spread throughout the continental United States, Hawaii, and several American territories.

Farm Service Agency (FSA) *(Agriculture Dept.), Fibers, Peanuts, and Tobacco Analysis, 1400 Independence Ave. S.W., #37605, MS 0515, 20250-0515; (202) 720-3392. Fax, (202) 690-2186. Scott Sanford, Director. Web, www.fsa.usda.gov/programs-and-services/economic-and-policy-analysis/fibers-peanuts-tobacco*

Develops production adjustment and price support programs to balance supply and demand for cotton, peanuts, and tobacco.

▶**NONGOVERNMENTAL**

American Peanut Council, *1500 King St., #301, Alexandria, VA 22314-2737; (703) 838-9500. Fax, (703) 838-9508. Patrick Archer, President.*

General email, info@peanutsusa.com

Web, www.peanutsusa.com and Twitter, @pnutsusa

Membership: peanut growers, shellers, brokers, and manufacturers, as well as allied domestic and international companies. Provides information on economic and nutritional value of peanuts; coordinates research; promotes U.S. peanut exports, domestic production, and market development.

Cigar Assn. of America, *1100 G St. N.W., #1050, 20005-7405; (202) 223-8204. Fax, (202) 833-0379. Craig P. Williamson, President.*

General email, cwilliamson@cigarassociation.org

Web, www.cigarassociation.org and Twitter, @CigarAssoc

Membership: growers and suppliers of cigar leaf tobacco; manufacturers, packagers, importers, and distributors of cigars; and suppliers to the cigar industry. Monitors legislation and regulations.

Tobacco Associates, Inc., *Washington Office, 8452 Holly Leaf Dr., McLean, VA 22102; (703) 821-1255. Fax, (703) 821-1511. Clyde (Kirk) N. Wayne, President.*

General email, taw@tobaccoassociatesinc.org

Web, www.tobaccoassociatesinc.org

Membership: U.S. producers of flue-cured tobacco. Promotes exports; provides information to encourage overseas market development. (Headquarters in Raleigh, N.C.)

FARM LOANS, INSURANCE, AND SUBSIDIES

General

▶**AGENCIES**

Farm Credit Administration, *1501 Farm Credit Dr., McLean, VA 22102-5090; (703) 883-4056. Fax, (703) 790-3260. Kenneth A. Spearman, Chief Executive Officer, (703) 883-4004. TTY, (703) 883-4056.*

General email, info-line@fca.gov

Web, www.fca.gov

Examines and regulates the cooperative Farm Credit System, which comprises farm credit banks, one agricultural credit bank, agricultural credit associations, and federal land credit associations. Oversees credit programs and related services for farmers, ranchers, producers and harvesters of aquatic products, farm-related service businesses, rural homeowners, agricultural and aquatic cooperatives, and rural utilities.

Farm Credit Administration, *Examination, 1501 Farm Credit Dr., McLean, VA 22102-5090; (703) 883-4160. Fax, (703) 893-2978. S. Robert Coleman, Chief Examiner, (703) 883-4246.*

General email, info-line@fca.gov

Web, www.fca.gov/about/offices/offices.html

Enforces and oversees compliance with the Farm Credit Act. Monitors cooperatively owned member banks' and associations' compliance with laws prohibiting discrimination in credit transactions.

Farm Service Agency (FSA) *(Agriculture Dept.), 1400 Independence Ave. S.W., #3086, MS 0501, 20250-0506; (202) 720-3467. Fax, (202) 720-9105. Val J. Dolcini, Administrator. Press, (202) 720-7807. Web, www.fsa.usda.gov*

Administers farm commodity programs providing crop loans and purchases; provides crop payments when market prices fall below specified levels; sets acreage allotments and marketing quotas; assists farmers in areas affected by natural disasters.

Farm Service Agency (FSA) *(Agriculture Dept.), Commodity Credit Corp., 1400 Independence Ave. S.W., MS 0599, 20250-0571; (202) 720-0402. Fax, (202) 245-4786. Sandra G. Wood, Assistant Secretary, Acting. General email, Robert.Stephenson@wdc.usda.gov*

Web, www.fsa.usda.gov/ccc

Administers and finances the commodity stabilization program through loans, purchases, and supplemental payments; sells through domestic and export markets commodities acquired by the government under this program; administers some aspects of foreign food aid through the Food for Peace program; provides storage facilities.

Farm Service Agency (FSA) *(Agriculture Dept.), Farm Loan Programs, 1400 Independence Ave. S.W., #3605S,*

MS 0520, 20250-0520; (202) 720-4671. Fax, (202) 690-3573. James F. Radintz, Deputy Administrator.
Web, www.fsa.usda.gov

Provides services and loans to beginning farmers and ranchers and administers emergency farm and ranch loan programs.

Farm Service Agency (FSA) *(Agriculture Dept.), Minority and Socially Disadvantaged Farmers Assistance, 1400 Independence Ave. S.W., MS 0503, 20250-0503; (202) 690-1700. Fax, (202) 690-4727. J. Latrice Hill, Director, Outreach. TTY, (202) 720-5132.*
General email, oasdfr@osec.usda.gov
Web, www.fsa.usda.gov

Works with minority and socially disadvantaged farmers who have concerns and questions about loan applications filed with local offices or other Farm Service Agency programs.

Farmer Mac, *1999 K St. N.W., 4th Floor, 20036; (202) 872-7700. Fax, (800) 999-1814. Timothy Buzby, President. Toll-free, (800) 879-3276.*
Web, www.farmermac.com

Private corporation chartered by Congress to provide a secondary mortgage market for farm and rural housing loans. Guarantees principal and interest repayment on securities backed by farm and rural housing loans. (Farmer Mac stands for Federal Agricultural Mortgage Corp.)

Risk Management Agency *(Agriculture Dept.), 1400 Independence Ave. S.W., #6092S, MS 0801, 20250-0801; (202) 690-2803. Fax, (202) 690-2818. Brandon C. Willis, Administrator. Media, (202) 690-0437.*
General email, rma.cco@rma.usda.gov
Web, www.rma.usda.gov

Operates and manages the Federal Crop Insurance Corp. Provides farmers with insurance against crops lost because of bad weather, insects, disease, and other natural causes.

Rural Development *(Agriculture Dept.), Civil Rights, 1400 Independence Ave. S.W., #1341, MS 0703, 20250-0703; (202) 692-0252. Fax, (202) 692-0279. Angilla Denton, Director. Toll-free, (800) 787-8821.*
General email, rd.civilrights@wdc.usda.gov
Web, www.rd.usda.gov/about-rd/offices/civil-rights

Enforces compliance with laws prohibiting discrimination in credit transactions on the basis of sex, marital status, race, color, religion, age, or disability. Ensures equal opportunity in granting Rural Economic and Community Development housing, farm ownership, and operating loans and a variety of community and business program loans.

▶**CONGRESS**

For a listing of relevant congressional committees and subcommittees, please see page 3 or the Appendix.

▶**NONGOVERNMENTAL**

Environmental Working Group, *1436 U St. N.W., #100, 20009-3987; (202) 667-6982. Fax, (202) 232-2592. Kenneth A. Cook, President.*
General email, generalinfo@ewg.org
Web, www.ewg.org and Twitter, @ewg

Research and advocacy group that studies and publishes reports on a wide range of agricultural and environmental issues, including farm subsidies and industrial pollution. Monitors legislation and regulations.

Farm Credit Council, *50 F St. N.W., #900, 20001-1530; (202) 626-8710. Fax, (202) 626-8718. Ken Auer, President, (202) 879-0843.*
General email, auer@fccouncil.com
Web, www.fccouncil.com and Twitter, @thefccouncil

Represents the Farm Credit System, a national financial cooperative that makes loans to agricultural producers, rural homebuyers, farmer cooperatives, and rural utilities. Finances the export of U.S. agricultural commodities.

FOOD AND NUTRITION

General

▶**AGENCIES**

Agricultural Marketing Service (AMS) *(Agriculture Dept.), Science and Technology, 1400 Independence Ave. S.W., #3533, 20250-0003; (202) 720-5231. Fax, (202) 720-6496. Ruihong Guo, Deputy Administrator, (202) 720-8556.*
Web, www.ams.usda.gov/science/index.htm

Provides analytical testing to AMS community programs, federal and state agencies, and the private sector food industry; participates in international food safety organizations. Tests commodities traded with specific countries and regions, including butter, honey, eggs, nuts, poultry, and meat; analyzes nutritional value of U.S. military rations.

Agricultural Research Service *(Agriculture Dept.), 1400 Independence Ave. S.W., #302A, MS 0300, 20250-0300; (202) 720-3656. Fax, (202) 720-5427. Chavonda Jacobs-Young, Administrator.*
Web, www.ars.usda.gov

Conducts studies on agricultural problems of domestic and international concern through nationwide network of research centers. Studies include research on human nutrition; livestock production and protection; crop production, protection, and processing; postharvest technology; and food distribution and market value.

Animal and Plant Health Inspection Service (APHIS) *(Agriculture Dept.), 1400 Independence Ave. S.W., #312E, MS 3401, 20250-3401; (202) 799-7030. Fax, (202) 720-3982. Kevin A. Shea, Administrator. Press, (301) 851-4100. Veterinary Services, (301) 851-3300. Plants and Plant Products, (877) 770-5990. Customer Service, (844) 820-2234.*
Web, www.aphis.usda.gov and Twitter, @USDA_APHIS

Administers animal disease control programs in cooperation with states; inspects imported animals, flowers, and plants; licenses the manufacture and marketing of veterinary biologics to ensure purity and effectiveness.

Center for Nutrition Policy and Promotion *(Agriculture Dept.), 3101 Park Center Dr., 10th Floor, Alexandria, VA 22302-1594; (703) 305-7600. Fax, (703) 305-3300. Angela Tagtow, Executive Director. Newsroom, (703) 305-7600.*
Web, www.cnpp.usda.gov

Defines and coordinates nutrition education policy, promotes food and nutrition guidance, and develops nutrition information materials for consumers, policymakers, and professionals in health, education, industry, and media.

Food and Drug Administration (FDA) *(Health and Human Services Dept.), Center for Food Safety and Applied Nutrition, 5100 Paint Branch Pkwy., HFS-009, College Park, MD 20740-3835; (240) 402-1600. Fax, (301) 436-2668. Susan T. Mayne, Director.*
General email, consumer@fda.gov

Web, www.fda.gov/AboutFDA/CentersOffices/ OfficeofFoods/CFSAN/default.htm

Develops standards of composition and quality of foods (except meat and poultry but including fish); develops safety regulations for food and color additives for foods, cosmetics, and drugs; monitors pesticide residues in foods; conducts food safety and nutrition research; develops analytical methods for measuring food additives, nutrients, pesticides, and chemical and microbiological contaminants; recommends action to Justice Dept.

Food and Drug Administration (FDA) *(Health and Human Services Dept.), Nutrition, Labeling, and Dietary Supplements, 5100 Paint Branch Pkwy., CPK-1 Bldg., #4C-095, College Park, MD 20740-3835; (240) 402-2373. Fax, (301) 436-2639. Douglas A. Balentine, Director.*
Web, www.fda.gov/Aboutfda/centersoffices/ organizationcharts/ucm385139.htm

Scientific and technical component of the Center for Food Safety and Applied Nutrition. Conducts research on nutrients; develops regulations and labeling requirements on infant formulas, medical foods, and dietary supplements, including herbs.

Food and Nutrition Service *(Agriculture Dept.), 3101 Park Center Dr., #906, Alexandria, VA 22302-1500; (703) 305-2060. Fax, (703) 305-2908. Audrey Rowe, Administrator. Information, (703) 305-2286.*
Web, www.fns.usda.gov and Twitter, @USDANutrition

Administers all Agriculture Dept. domestic food assistance, including the distribution of funds and food for school breakfast and lunch programs (preschool through secondary) to public and nonprofit private schools; the Supplemental Nutrition Assistance Program (SNAP, formerly the food stamp program); and a supplemental nutrition program for women, infants, and children (WIC).

Food and Nutrition Service *(Agriculture Dept.), Child Nutrition, 3101 Park Center Dr., #640, Alexandria, VA 22302-1500; (703) 305-2590. Fax, (703) 305-2879. Cindy Long, Deputy Administrator, (703) 305-2054. Press, (202) 720-4623.*
General email, cndinternet@fns.usda.gov

Web, www.fns.usda.gov/school-meals/child-nutrition-programs

Administers the transfer of funds to state agencies for the National School Lunch Program; the School Breakfast Program; the Special Milk Program, the Child and Adult Care Food Program, and the Summer Food Service Program. These programs help fight hunger and obesity by reimbursing organizations such as schools, child care centers, and after-school programs for providing healthy meals to children.

Food and Nutrition Service *(Agriculture Dept.), Communications and Governmental Affairs, 3101 Park Center Dr., #926, Alexandria, VA 22302; (703) 305-2281. Fax, (703) 305-2312. Bruce Alexander, Director.*
Web, www.fns.usda.gov/cga

Provides information concerning the Food and Nutrition Service and its fifteen nutrition assistance programs to the media, program participants, advocates, members of Congress, and the general public. Monitors and analyzes relevant legislation.

Food and Nutrition Service *(Agriculture Dept.), Food Distribution, 3101 Park Center Dr., #504, Alexandria, VA 22302-1500; (703) 305-2680. Fax, (703) 305-2964. Laura Castro, Director.*
General email, fdd-psl@fns.usda.gov

Web, www.fns.usda.gov/fdd

Provides food for the National School Lunch Program, the Summer Food Service Program, and the Child and Adult Care Food Program. Administers the Commodity Supplemental Food Program for low-income pregnant and breastfeeding women, new mothers, infants, children, and the elderly. Supplies food to relief organizations for distribution following disasters. Makes commodity food and cash available through the Nutrition Services Incentive Program (formerly the Nutrition Program for the Elderly). Administers the Emergency Food Assistance Program through soup kitchens and food banks and the Food Distribution Program on Indian reservations and to Indian households elsewhere.

Food and Nutrition Service *(Agriculture Dept.), National School Lunch Program, 3101 Park Center Dr., #926, Alexandria, VA 22302; (703) 305-2590. Cindy Long, Deputy Administrator. Communications, (703) 305-2281.*
Web, www.fns.usda.gov/nslp/national-school-lunch-program-nslp

Administers the federal assistance meal program operating in public and nonprofit private schools and residential child care institutions. Provides daily nutritionally balanced, low-cost or free lunches to children.

Food and Nutrition Service *(Agriculture Dept.), Policy Support, 3101 Park Center Dr., #1014, Alexandria, VA*

22302-1500; (703) 305-2017. Fax, (703) 305-2576.
Richard Lucas, Deputy Associate Administrator.
General email, oaneweb@fns.usda.gov

Web, www.fns.usda.gov/ora

Evaluates federal nutrition assistance programs; provides results to policymakers and program administrators. Funds demonstration grants for state and local nutrition assistance projects.

Food and Nutrition Service *(Agriculture Dept.), Special Supplemental Nutrition Program for Women, Infants, and Children (WIC),* 3101 Park Center Dr., #528, Alexandria, VA 22302-1594; (703) 305-2746. Fax, (703) 305-2196. Sarah Widor, Director.
Web, www.fns.usda.gov/wic

Provides health departments and agencies with federal funding for food supplements and administrative expenses to make food, nutrition education, and health services available to infants, young children, and pregnant, nursing, and postpartum women.

Food and Nutrition Service *(Agriculture Dept.), Supplemental Nutrition Assistance Program (SNAP),* 3101 Park Center Dr., #808, Alexandria, VA 22302-1500; (703) 305-2026. Fax, (703) 305-2454. Jessica Shahin, Associate Administrator, (703) 305-2022.
Web, www.fns.usda.gov/snap

Administers SNAP through state welfare agencies to provide needy persons with Electronic Benefit Transfer cards to increase food purchasing power. Provides matching funds to cover half the cost of EBT card issuance.

Food Safety and Inspection Service *(Agriculture Dept.),* 1400 Independence Ave. S.W., #331E, 20250-3700; (202) 720-7025. Fax, (202) 205-0158. Alfred Almanza, Deputy Under Secretary. Press, (202) 720-9113. Consumer inquiries, (800) 535-4555. TTY, (800) 877-8339.
Web, www.usda.gov/fsis

Inspects meat, poultry, and egg products moving in interstate commerce for use as human food to ensure that they are safe, wholesome, and accurately labeled. Provides safe handling and labeling guidelines.

Food, Nutrition, and Consumer Services *(Agriculture Dept.),* 1400 Independence Ave. S.W., #216E, 20250-0106; (202) 720-7711. Fax, (202) 690-3100.
Kevin W. Concannon, Under Secretary; Katie Wilson, Deputy Under Secretary.
Web, www.usda.gov/wps/portal/usda/usdahome?
contentid=missionarea_FNC.xml

Oversees the Food and Nutrition Service and the Center for Nutrition Policy and Promotion.

Health and Human Services Dept. (HHS), *President's Council on Fitness, Sports, and Nutrition,* 1101 Wootton Pkwy., #560, Tower Bldg., Rockville, MD 20852; (240) 276-9567. Fax, (240) 276-9860. Shellie Pfohl, Executive Director.
General email, fitness@hhs.gov

Web, www.fitness.gov, www.presidentschallenge.org and Twitter, @FitnessGov

Provides schools, state and local governments, recreation agencies, and employers with information on designing and implementing physical fitness and nutrition programs; conducts award programs for children and adults and for schools, clubs, and other institutions.

National Agricultural Library *(Agriculture Dept.), Food and Nutrition Information Center,* 10301 Baltimore Ave., #108, Beltsville, MD 20705-2351; (301) 504-5414. Fax, (301) 504-6409. Wendy Davis, Nutrition and Food Safety Program Leader.
General email, fnic@ars.usda.gov

Web, http://fnic.nal.usda.gov

Serves primarily educators, health professionals, and consumers seeking information about nutrition assistance programs and general nutrition. Serves as an online provider of science-based information about food and nutrition and links to such information. Lends books and audiovisual materials for educational purposes through interlibrary loan; maintains a database of food and nutrition software and multimedia programs; provides reference services; develops resource lists of health and nutrition publications. Library open to the public.

National Agricultural Library *(Agriculture Dept.), Food Safety Information Center,* 10301 Baltimore Ave., #304B, Beltsville, MD 20705-2351; (301) 504-5515. Fax, (301) 504-7680. Wendy Davis, Nutrition and Food Safety Program Leader.
General email, fsrio@ars.usda.gov

Web, http://fsrio.nal.usda.gov

Provides food safety information to educators, industry, researchers, and the general public. Special subject areas include pathogens and contaminants, sanitation and quality standards, food preparation and handling, and food processing and technology. The center includes the Food Safety Research Information Office, which focuses on providing information and reference services to the research community and the general public.

National Institute of Food and Agriculture (NIFA) *(Agriculture Dept.),* Jaime L. Whitten Bldg., #305A, 800 9th St. S.W., 20024 (mailing address: 1400 Independence Ave. S.W., MS 2201, Washington, DC 20250-2201); (202) 720-4423. Sonny Ramaswamy, Director. Communications, (202) 720-4242. Information, (202) 720-4651.
Web, www.nifa.usda.gov

Supports research, education, and extension of issues pertaining to agricultural production, nutrition, food safety, energy independence, and the sustainability of natural resources. Partners with and funds scientists at academic institutions, particularly the land-grant universities, minority-serving institutions, including black colleges and universities, Hispanic-serving institutions, and tribal colleges, as well as government, private, and nonprofit organizations to address critical issues in agriculture, including global food security and hunger, water resources, climate change, sustainable energy, childhood obesity, and food safety. Partners with agricultural extension offices in all counties, states, and territories.

National Institute of Food and Agriculture (NIFA) *(Agriculture Dept.), Institute of Food Safety and Nutrition,* 1400 Independence Ave. S.W., MS 2225, 20250-2225; (202) 702-5004. Fax, (202) 401-4888. *Denise Riordan Eblen, Deputy Director. Web, www.nifa.usda.gov/office/institute-food-safety-and-nutrition*

Works toward safe food supply by reducing food-borne illness. Addresses causes of microbial contamination and antimicrobial resistance; educates consumer and food safety professionals; and develops food processing technologies. Promotes programs to improve citizens' health through better nutrition, reducing childhood obesity, and improving food quality.

National Oceanic and Atmospheric Administration (NOAA) *(Commerce Dept.), Seafood Inspection Program,* 1315 East-West Hwy., Silver Spring, MD 20910; (301) 427-8300. Fax, (301) 713-1081. Steven Wilson, Deputy Director; John Henderschedt, Director, (301) 427-8314. Toll-free, (800) 422-2750. *General email, nmfs.seafood.services@noaa.gov*

Web, www.seafood.nmfs.noaa.gov

Administers voluntary inspection program for fish products and fish processing plants; certifies fish for wholesomeness, safety, and condition; grades for quality. Conducts training and workshops to help U.S. importers and foreign suppliers comply with food regulations.

► **CONGRESS**

For a listing of relevant congressional committees and sub-committees, please see page 3 or the Appendix.

► **INTERNATIONAL ORGANIZATIONS**

Codex Alimentarius Commission, *U.S. Codex Office,* 1400 Independence Ave. S.W., South Bldg., #4861, 20250-3700; (202) 205-7760. Fax, (202) 720-3157. Mary Frances Lowe, U.S. Codex Manager; Paulo Almeida, U.S. Associate Manager. Toll-free TTY, (800) 877-8339. Meat and Poultry Hotline, (888) 674-6854. *General email, uscodex@fsis.usda.gov*

Web, www.fsis.usda.gov/codex and Twitter, @USDAFoodSafety

Operates within the Food and Agricultural Organization (FAO) and the World Health Organization (WHO) to establish international food and food safety standards and to ensure fair trade practices. Convenes committees in member countries to address specific commodities and issues including labeling, additives in food and veterinary drugs, pesticide residues and other contaminants, and systems for food inspection. (Located in the USDA Food Safety and Inspection Service; international headquarters in Rome at the UN's Food and Agricultural Organization.)

Cultivating New Frontiers in Agriculture (CNFA), 1828 L St. N.W., #710, 20036; (202) 296-3920. Fax, (202) 296-3948. Sylvain Roy, President. *General email, info@cnfa.org*

Web, www.cnfa.org

International development organization that has worked in over 42 countries to provide agricultural solutions to stimulate economic growth and improve livelihoods by cultivating entrepreneurship.

International Food Information Council, 1100 Connecticut Ave. N.W., #430, 20036-4120; (202) 296-6540. Fax, (202) 296-6547. Kimberly Reed, President. *General email, info@foodinsight.org*

Web, www.foodinsight.org

Membership: food and beverage companies and manufacturers of food ingredients. Provides the media, health professionals, and consumers with science-based information about food safety, health, and nutrition. Interests include harmonization of international food safety standards.

► **NONGOVERNMENTAL**

Academy of Nutrition and Dietetics, *Washington Office,* 1120 Connecticut Ave. N.W., #460, 20036-3989; (202) 775-8277. Fax, (202) 775-8284. Jeanne Blankenship, Vice President. Toll-free, (800) 877-0877. *General email, govaffairs@eatright.org*

Media email, media@eatright.org Web, www.eatright.org

Membership: dietitians and other nutrition professionals. Promotes public health and nutrition; accredits academic programs in clinical nutrition and food service management; sets standards of professional practice. Sponsors the National Center for Nutrition and Dietetics. (Headquarters in Chicago, Ill.)

American Herbal Products Assn., 8630 Fenton St., #918, Silver Spring, MD 20910; (301) 588-1171. Fax, (301) 588-1174. Michael McGuffin, President. *General email, ahpa@ahpa.org*

Web, www.ahpa.org

Membership: U.S. companies and individuals that grow, manufacture, and distribute botanicals and herbal products, including foods, beverages, dietary supplements, and personal care products; associates in education, law, media, and medicine. Supports research; promotes quality standards, consumer access, and self-regulation in the industry. Monitors legislation and regulations.

Center for Science in the Public Interest, 1220 L St. N.W., #300, 20005; (202) 332-9110. Fax, (202) 265-4954. Michael F. Jacobson, President. *General email, cspi@cspinet.org*

Web, www.cspinet.org

Conducts research on food and nutrition. Interests include eating habits, food safety regulations, food additives, organically produced foods, and links between diet and disease. Publishes *Nutrition Action Healthletter.* Monitors U.S. and international policy.

Congressional Hunger Center, Hall of the States Bldg., 400 N. Capitol St. N.W., #G100, 20001-1592; (202) 547-7022. Fax, (202) 547-7575. Shannon Maynard, Executive Director. *Web, www.hungercenter.org and Twitter, @HungerCenter*

Food Safety Resources and Contacts

AGENCIES

Center for Food Safety and Applied Nutrition, Food and Drug Administration (FDA), (Health and Human Services Department),
Susan T. Mayne, Director, (888) 723-3366
Office of Analytics and Outreach, Jody Menikheim, Director, (240) 402-1864
Office of Food Additive Safety, Dr. Dennis M. Keefe, Director, (240) 402-1200
Office of Food Safety, Dr. Nega Beru, Director, (240) 402-1700
Office of Nutritional Products, Labeling and Dietary Supplements, Douglas A. Balentine, Director, (240) 402-2373

Food Safety and Inspection Service (FSIS), (Agriculture Department),
Alfred V. Almanza, Administrator (Acting), (202) 720-7025
Office of Data Integration and Food Protection, Terri Nintemann, Assistant Administrator, (202) 690-6486

Food Safety Information Center (FSIC), National Agricultural Library, (Agriculture Department),
Paul Webster, Director, (301) 504-5248

Office of Ground Water and Drinking Water, Environmental Protection Agency, Peter Grevatt, Director, (202) 564-8954

Seafood Inspection Program, National Oceanic and Atmospheric Administration (NOAA), (Commerce Department),
John Henderschedt, Director, (301) 427-8300

ORGANIZATIONS

Center for Food Safety,
Andrew Kimbrell, Executive Director, (202) 547-9359

Center for Science in the Public Interest,
Michael F. Jacobson, Executive Director, (202) 332-9110

Food and Water Watch,
Wenonah Hauter, Executive Director, (202) 683-2500

International Food Information Council,
Kimberly Reed, President, (202) 296-6540

HOTLINES

24-Hour Emergency Number: (866) 395-9701
www.fsis.usda.gov

FDA Center for Food Safety and Applied Nutrition, (888) SAFEFOOD;
(888) 723-3366
www.fda.gov/aboutfda/centersoffices/officeoffoods/cfsan/default.htm

Gateway to Government Food Safety Information,
www.foodsafety.gov; www.facebook.com/FoodSafety.gov

Safe Drinking Water Hotline, (800) 426-4791
http://water.epa.gov/drink

USDA Meat and Poultry Hotline,
(888) 674-6854
mphotline.fsis@usda.gov

Works to increase public awareness of hunger in the United States and abroad. Develops strategies and trains leaders to combat hunger and facilitates collaborative efforts between organizations.

Council for Responsible Nutrition (CRN), *1828 L St. N.W., #510, 20036-5114; (202) 204-7700. Fax, (202) 204-7701. Steven Mister, President.*
General email, webmaster@crnus.org

Web, www.crnusa.org and Twitter, @CRN_Supplements

Membership: manufacturers, distributors, and ingredient suppliers of dietary supplements. Provides information to members; monitors Food and Drug Administration, Federal Trade Commission, and Consumer Product Safety Commission regulations.

D.C. Central Kitchen, *425 2nd St. N.W., 20001; (202) 234-0707. Fax, (202) 986-1051. Mike Curtin, Chief Executive Officer, (202) 266-2018.*
Email, www.dccentralkitchen.org

Distributes food to D.C.-area homeless shelters, transitional homes, low-income schoolchildren, and corner store "food deserts."

Food & Water Watch, *1616 P St. N.W., #300, 20036; (202) 683-2500. Fax, (202) 683-2501. Wenonah Hauter, Executive Director.*
General email, info@fwwatch.org

Web, www.foodandwaterwatch.org and Twitter, @foodandwater

Consumer organization that advocates stricter water and food safety regulations. Organizes public awareness campaigns and lobbies Congress. Publishes studies of agricultural, food preparation, and drinking water sanitation practices. Chapters in fifteen states and international chapter in Brussels, Belgium.

Food Allergy Research and Education (FARE), *7925 Jones Branch Dr., #1100, McLean, VA 22102; (703) 691-3179. Fax, (703) 691-2713. James R. Baker Jr., Chief Executive Officer. Toll-free, (800) 929-4040.*
General email, faan@foodallergy.org

Web, www.foodallergy.org and Twitter, @FoodAllergy

Membership: dietitians, nurses, physicians, school staff, government representatives, members of the food and pharmaceutical industries, and food-allergy patients and their families. Provides information and educational resources on food allergies and allergic reactions. Offers research grants.

Food Policy Action, *1436 U St. N.W., #200, 20009; (202) 631-6362. Claire Benjamin, Executive Director, (202) 631-6362.*
General email, info@foodpolicyaction.org
Web, http://foodpolicyaction.org

Promotes policies that support healthy food options; works to reduce hunger and improve food access; publishes a congressional vote and legislation scorecard.

Food Research and Action Center (FRAC), *1200 18th St. N.W., #400, 20036; (202) 986-2200. Fax, (202) 986-2525. James D. Weill, President.*
General email, comments@frac.org
Web, www.frac.org and Twitter, @fractweets

Public interest advocacy center that works to end hunger and undernutrition in the United States. Offers organizational aid, training, and information to groups seeking to improve or expand federal food programs, including food stamp, child nutrition, and WIC (women, infants, and children) programs; conducts studies relating to hunger and poverty; coordinates network of antihunger organizations. Monitors legislation and regulations.

International Life Sciences Institute (ILSI), *North America, 1156 15th St. N.W., #200, 20005-5802; (202) 659-0074. Fax, (202) 659-3859. Eric J. Hentges, Executive Director; Sharon Weiss, Deputy Executive Director.*
General email, info@ilsi.org
Web, www.ilsi.org

Acts as liaison among scientists from international government agencies, concerned industries, research institutes, and universities regarding the safety of foods and chemical ingredients. Conducts research on caffeine, food coloring, oral health, human nutrition, and other food issues. Promotes international cooperation among scientists.

National Center for Food and Agricultural Policy, *1616 P St. N.W., 1st Floor, 20036; (202) 328-5183. Fax, (202) 328-5133. Joe Dunn, Chief Executive Officer.*
General email, info@ncfap.org
Web, www.ncfap.org

Research and educational organization concerned with domestic and international food and agricultural issues. Examines public policy concerning agriculture, food safety and quality, natural resources, and the environment.

National Research Council (NRC), *Agriculture and Natural Resources Board, Keck Center, 500 5th St. N.W., #WS632, 20001; (202) 334-3062. Fax, (202) 334-1978. Robin Schoen, Director.*
General email, banr@nas.edu
Web, http://dels.nas.edu/banr

Promotes and oversees research on the environmental impact of agriculture and food sustainability, including forestry, fisheries, wildlife, and the use of land, water, and other natural resources.

Public Citizen, *Health Research Group, 1600 20th St. N.W., 20009-1001; (202) 588-1000. Fax, (202) 588-7798. Michael Carome, Director.*
General email, hrg1@citizen.org
Web, www.citizen.org/hrg and Twitter, @CitizenHRG

Citizens' interest group that studies and reports on unsafe foods; monitors and petitions the Food and Drug Administration.

United Food and Commercial Workers International Union (UFCW), *1775 K St. N.W., 20006-1598; (202) 223-3111. Fax, (202) 728-1803. Marc Perrone, President.*
Web, www.ufcw.org and Twitter, @UFCW

Membership: approximately 1.3 million workers primarily in the retail, meatpacking, food processing, and poultry industries. Interests include health care reform, living wages, retirement security, safe working conditions, and the right to unionize. Monitors legislation and regulations.

Beverages

▶AGENCIES

Alcohol and Tobacco Tax and Trade Bureau (TTB) *(Treasury Dept.), 1310 G St. N.W., #300E, 20005; (202) 453-2250. John J. Manfreda, Administrator. Press, (202) 453-2180. TTY, (202) 882-9914.*
General email, alfd@ttb.gov
Web, www.ttb.gov

Regulates the advertising and labeling of alcohol beverages, including the size of containers; enforces federal taxation of alcohol and tobacco. Authorized to refer violations to Justice Dept. for criminal prosecution.

▶NONGOVERNMENTAL

American Beverage Assn., *1101 16th St. N.W., 20036-6396; (202) 463-6732. Fax, (202) 659-5349. Susan Neely, President. Press, (202) 463-6770.*
General email, info@ameribev.org
Web, www.ameribev.org

Membership: companies engaged in producing or distributing carbonated and noncarbonated soft drinks and bottled water. Acts as industry liaison with government and the public. (Formerly the National Soft Drink Assn.)

American Beverage Institute, *1090 Vermont Ave. N.W., #800, 20005; (202) 463-7110. Fax, (202) 463-7107. Sarah Longwell, Managing Director.*
General email, info@abionline.org
Web, www.abionline.org

Promotes responsible alcohol consumption in restaurants and bars. Opposes restrictions on alcohol use. Monitors legislation and regulations.

American Beverage Licensees (ABL), *5101 River Rd., #108, Bethesda, MD 20816-1560; (301) 656-1494. Fax, (301) 656-7539. John D. Bodnovich, Executive Director.*

General email, info@ablusa.org

Web, www.ablusa.org

Membership: state associations of on-premise and off-premise beverage alcohol licensees. Monitors legislation and regulations affecting the alcohol beverage industry.

Beer Institute, 440 1st St. N.W., #350, 20001; (202) 737-2337. Fax, (202) 737-7004. James McGreevy, President.
General email, info@beerinstitute.org

Web, www.beerinstitute.org and Twitter, @beerinstitute

Membership: domestic brewers and beer importers and suppliers to the domestic brewing industry. Monitors legislation and regulations.

Distilled Spirits Council of the United States, 1250 Eye St. N.W., #400, 20005-3998; (202) 628-3544. Fax, (202) 682-8888. Kraig Naasz, President.
Web, www.discus.org

Membership: manufacturers and marketers of distilled spirits sold in the United States. Provides consumer information on alcohol-related issues and topics. Monitors legislation and regulations.

International Bottled Water Assn. (IBWA), 1700 Diagonal Rd., #650, Alexandria, VA 22314-2864; (703) 683-5213. Fax, (703) 683-4074. Joseph K. Doss, President, (703) 647-4605. Information, 800-WATER-11. Press, (703) 647-4609.
General email, info@bottledwater.org

Web, www.bottledwater.org

Serves as a clearinghouse for industry-related consumer, regulatory, and technical information; interests include international trade. Monitors state and federal legislation and regulations.

National Alcohol Beverage Control Assn. (NABCA), 4401 Ford Ave., #700, Alexandria, VA 22302; (703) 578-4200. Fax, (703) 820-3551. James M. Sgueo, President.
Web, www.nabca.org

Membership: distilleries, importers, brokers, trade associations, and state agencies that control the purchase, distribution, and sale of alcohol beverages. Promotes responsible sale and consumption of these beverages. Serves as an information clearinghouse. Monitors legislation and regulations.

National Beer Wholesalers Assn., 1101 King St., #600, Alexandria, VA 22314-2944; (703) 683-4300. Fax, (703) 683-8965. Craig A. Purser, President. Toll-free, (800) 300-6417.
General email, info@nbwa.org

Web, www.nbwa.org

Works to enhance the independent beer wholesale industry. Advocates before government and the public; encourages responsible consumption of beer; sponsors programs and services to benefit members; monitors legislation and regulations.

Wine and Spirits Wholesalers of America (WSWA), 805 15th St. N.W., #430, 20005-2273; (202) 371-9792. Fax, (202) 789-2405. Craig Wolf, President.

General email, info@wswa.org

Web, www.wswa.org and Twitter, @wswamedia

Trade association of wholesale distributors of domestic and imported wine and distilled spirits. Provides information on drinking awareness. Represents members' interests before Congress and federal agencies.

Wine Institute, Federal Relations, 601 13th St. N.W., #330 South, 20005-3866; (202) 408-0870. Fax, (202) 371-0061. Charles Jefferson, Vice President; Linda Ulrich, Vice President.
Web, www.wineinstitute.org

Membership: California wineries and affiliated businesses. Seeks international recognition for California wines; conducts promotional campaigns in other countries. Monitors legislation and regulations. (Headquarters in San Francisco, Calif.)

Food Industries

▶NONGOVERNMENTAL

American Bakers Assn. (ABA), 601 Pennsylvania Ave., #230, 20004; (202) 789-0300. Fax, (202) 898-1164. Robb MacKie, President.
General email, info@americanbakers.org

Web, www.americanbakers.org

Membership: wholesale baking companies and their suppliers. Promotes increased consumption of baked goods; provides consumers with nutritional information; conducts conventions. Monitors legislation and regulations.

American Frozen Food Institute, 2000 Corporate Ridge Blvd., #1000, McLean, VA 22102-7862; (703) 821-0770. Fax, (703) 821-1350. Joseph Clayton, President, Acting.
General email, info@affi.com

Web, www.affi.org

Membership: frozen food packers, distributors, and suppliers. Testifies before Congress and federal agencies.

Bakery, Confectionery, Tobacco Workers, and Grain Millers International Union, 10401 Connecticut Ave., 4th Floor, Kensington, MD 20895-3940; (301) 933-8600. Fax, (301) 946-8452. David B. Durkee, President.
General email, bctgmwebmater@gmail.com

Web, www.bctgm.org and Twitter, @BCTGM

Membership: approximately 120,000 workers from the bakery, confectionery, grain miller, and tobacco industries. Helps members negotiate pay, benefits, and better working conditions; conducts training programs and workshops. Monitors legislation and regulations. (Affiliated with the AFL-CIO.)

Biscuit and Cracker Manufacturers' Assn. (B&CMA), 6325 Woodside Court, #125, Columbia, MD 21046-3215; (443) 545-1645. Fax, (410) 290-8585. Dave Van Laar, President.
Web, www.thebcma.org

Membership: companies in the cookie and cracker industry. Provides education, training, and networking services.

Food Marketing Institute (FMI), *2345 Crystal Dr., #800, Arlington, VA 22202-4813; (202) 452-8444. Fax, (202) 429-4519. Leslie G. Sarasin, President.*
General email, info@fmi.org
Web, www.fmi.org and Twitter, @FMI_ORG

Trade association of food retailers and wholesalers. Conducts programs in research, education, industry relations, and public affairs; participates in international conferences. Library open to the public by appointment.

Food Processing Suppliers Assn. (FPSA), *1451 Dolley Madison Blvd., #101, McLean, VA 22101-3850; (703) 761-2600. Fax, (703) 761-4334. David Seckman, President, (703) 663-1200.*
General email, info@fpsa.org
Web, www.fpsa.org and Twitter, @FPSAorg

Membership: equipment and ingredient manufacturers, suppliers, and servicers for the food, dairy, and beverage processing industry. Sponsors food engineering scholarships and the biannual Process Expo. (Merger of the International Assn. of Food Industry Suppliers and the Food Processing Machinery Assn.)

Grocery Manufacturers Assn. (GMA), *1350 Eye St. N.W., #300, 20005-3377; (202) 639-5900. Fax, (202) 639-5932. Pamela Bailey, President. Press, (202) 295-3957.*
General email, info@gmaonline.org
Web, www.gmaonline.org

Membership: manufacturers of food, beverage, and consumer packaged goods sold through the retail grocery trade. Interests include holistic waste management solutions, nutritional labeling, and the safety and security of the food supply. Supplies industry information to members. Monitors legislation and regulations.

International Foodservice Distributors Assn., *1410 Spring Hill Rd., #210, McLean, VA 22102; (703) 532-9400. Fax, (703) 538-4673. Mark S. Allen, President.*
General email, info@ifdaonline.org
Web, www.ifdaonline.org

Trade association of foodservice distribution companies that promotes the interests of members in government and industry affairs through research, education, and communication.

National Assn. of Convenience Stores (NACS), *1600 Duke St., 7th Floor, Alexandria, VA 22314-3421; (703) 684-3600. Fax, (703) 836-4564. Henry Armour, President. Toll-free, (800) 966-6227.*
General email, nacs@nacsonline.com
Web, www.nacsonline.com

Membership: convenience store retailers and industry suppliers. Promotes industry position on labor, tax, environment, alcohol, and food-related issues; conducts research and training programs. Monitors legislation and regulations.

National Automatic Merchandising Assn. (NAMA), *Washington Office, 1600 Wilson Blvd., #650, Arlington, VA 22209; (571) 346-1900. Fax, (703) 836-8262. Carla Balakgie, President, (312) 346-0370; Eric Dell, Senior Vice President, Government Affairs.*
Web, www.vending.org

Membership: service companies, equipment manufacturers, and product suppliers for the food and refreshment vending, coffee service, and foodservice management industries. Seeks to advance and promote the automatic merchandising and coffee service industries, provide administrative, logistical, and financial assistance to its members. (Headquarters in Chicago, Ill.)

National Council of Chain Restaurants (NCCR), *1101 New York Ave. N.W., #1200, 20005; (202) 626-8183. Fax, (202) 737-2849. Robert (Rob) Green, Executive Director. Toll-free, (800) 673-4692.*
General email, purviss@nccr.net
Web, www.nrf.com/who-we-are/retail-communities/chain-restaurants-nccr

Trade association representing chain restaurant companies. Affiliated with the National Retail Federation. Monitors legislation and regulations.

National Grocers Assn., *1005 N. Glebe Rd., #250, Arlington, VA 22201-5758; (703) 516-0700. Fax, (703) 516-0115. Peter J. Larkin, President.*
General email, feedback@nationalgrocers.org
Web, www.nationalgrocers.org

Trade association that represents independent retail and wholesale grocers. Membership also includes affiliated associations, manufacturers, and service suppliers. Provides members with educational materials through a Web site, publications, and conferences. Monitors legislation and regulations.

National Pasta Assn. (NPA), *750 National Press Bldg., 529 14th St. N.W., 20045-1806; (202) 591-2459. Fax, (202) 591-2445. Carol Freysinger, Executive Director.*
General email, info@ilovepasta.org
Web, www.ilovepasta.org

Membership: U.S. pasta manufacturers, related suppliers, and allied industry representatives. Represents the industry on public policy issues; monitors and addresses technical issues; and organizes events and seminars for the industry.

National Restaurant Assn., *2055 L St. N.W., #700, 20036; (202) 331-5900. Fax, (202) 331-2429. Dawn Sweeney, Chief Executive Officer. Toll-free, (800) 424-5156.*
Web, www.restaurant.org

Membership: restaurants, cafeterias, clubs, contract feeders, caterers, institutional food services, and other members of the food industry. Supports food service education and research. Monitors legislation and regulations.

North American Meat Institute, *1150 Connecticut Ave. N.W., 12th Floor, 20036; (202) 587-4200. Fax, (202) 587-4300. Barry Carpenter, President; Eric Mittenthal, Communications, (202) 587-4238.*

Web, www.meatami.com and Twitter, @MeatInstitute

General email, emittenthal@meatinstitute.org

Membership: national and international meat and poultry packers, suppliers, and processors. Provides statistics on meat production and exports. Funds research projects and consumer education programs. Monitors legislation and regulations. (Formed from merger of the North American Meat Assn. and American Meat Institute.)

Snack Food Assn. (SFA), *1600 Wilson Blvd., #650, Arlington, VA 22209-2510; (703) 836-4500. Fax, (703) 836-8262. Thomas Dempsey Jr., Chief Executive Officer, ext. 209. Toll-free, (800) 628-1334.*

General email, sfa@sfa.org

Web, www.sfa.org

Membership: snack food manufacturers and suppliers. Promotes industry sales; compiles statistics; conducts research and surveys; assists members with training and education; provides consumers with industry information. Monitors legislation and regulations.

Soyfoods Assn. of North America, *1050 17th St. N.W., #600, 20036-5570; (202) 659-3520. Fax, (202) 659-3522. Nancy Chapman, Executive Director.*

General email, info@soyfoods.org

Web, www.soyfoods.org

Membership: large and small soyfood companies, growers and suppliers of soybeans, nutritionists, equipment representatives, food scientists, and retailers. Promotes soybean consumption. Helps establish standards for soyfoods. Monitors legislation and regulations.

Tortilla Industry Assn., *1600 Wilson Blvd., #650, Arlington, VA 22209; (800) 944-6099. Fax, (800) 944-6177. Jim Kabbani, Executive Director, ext. 206.*

General email, jkabbaani@tortilla-info.com

Web, www.tortilla-info.com

Membership: tortilla manufacturers, industry suppliers, and distributors. Promotes tortilla consumption. Provides market research and other industry-related information to its members. Sponsors conferences, seminars, and educational events for the industry.

UNITE HERE, *Washington Office, 1775 K St. N.W., #620, 20006-1530; (202) 393-4373. Fax, (202) 223-6213. Fax, (202) 342-2929. Vacant, Political Director; D. Taylor, President.*

Web, www.unitehere.org

Membership: more than 270,000 workers in the United States and Canada who work in the hospitality, gaming, food service, manufacturing, textile, laundry, and airport industries. Assists members with contract negotiation and grievances; conducts training programs and workshops. Monitors legislation and regulations. (Headquarters in New York. Formed by the merger of the former Union of Needletrades, Textiles and Industrial Employees and the Hotel Employees and Restaurant Employees International Union.)

World Cocoa Foundation, *1411 K St. N.W., 500, 20005; (202) 737-7870. Fax, (202) 737-7832. Timothy S. McCoy, President, Acting.*

General email, wcf@worldcocoa.org

Web, www.worldcocoafoundation.org and Twitter, @WorldCocoa

Promotes a sustainable cocoa economy through economic and social development and environmental conservation in cocoa-growing communities. Helps raise funds for cocoa farmers and increases their access to modern farming practices.

Vegetarianism

▶**NONGOVERNMENTAL**

Compassion Over Killing, *6930 Carroll Ave., #910, Tacoma Park, MD 20912 (mailing address: P.O. Box 9773, Washington, DC 20016); (301) 891-2458. Fax, (301) 891-6815. Erica Meier, Executive Director.*

General email, info@cok.net

Web, www.cok.net and Twitter, @TryVeg

Animal rights organization that focuses primarily on cruelty to animals in agriculture. Promotes vegetarianism.

Farm Animal Rights Movement (FARM), *10101 Ashburton Lane, Bethesda, MD 20817-1729; (301) 530-1737. Fax, (301) 530-5683. Michael A. Weberman, Executive Director; Alex Hershaft, President. Toll-free, 888-FARM-USA.*

General email, info@farmusa.org

Web, www.farmusa.org, www.livevegan.org and Twitter, @FARMUSA

Works to end use of animals for food. Interests include animal protection, consumer health, agricultural resources, and environmental quality. Conducts national educational campaigns, including World Farm Animals Day, the Live Vegan program, and the Great American Meatout. Monitors legislation and regulations.

Great American Meatout, *10101 Ashburton Lane, Bethesda, MD 20817-1729; (800) 632-8688. Fax, (301) 530-5683. Alex Hershaft, President.*

General email, info@farmusa.org

Web, www.meatout.org

Promotes the dietary elimination of meat. Facilitates vegan-diet information tables, exhibits, cooking demonstrations, and festivals nationwide. (Affiliated with Farm Animal Rights Movement.)

Vegetarian Resource Group, *P.O. Box 1463, Baltimore, MD 21203-1463; (410) 366-8343. Fax, (410) 366-8804. Charles Stahler, Co-Director; Debra Wasserman, Co-Director.*

General email, vrg@vrg.org

Press email, press@vrg.org and Web, www.vrg.org

Works to educate the public on vegetarianism and veganism and issues of health, nutrition, ecology, ethics, and world hunger.

World Food Assistance

Agency for International Development (USAID), *Farmer-to-Farmer Program,* 1424 K St. N.W., #700, 20007; (202) 712-4086. Gary E. Alex, Program Manager.
General email, galex@usaid.gov

Web, www.usaid.gov/what-we-do/agriculture-and-food-security/supporting-agricultural-capacity-development/john-ogonowski

Promotes sustainable improvements in food security and agricultural processing, production, and marketing. Provides voluntary assistance to farmers, farm groups, and agribusinesses in developing countries. Formally the John Ogonowski and Doug Bereuter Farmer-to-Farmer Program.

Agriculture Dept. (USDA), *World Agricultural Outlook Board,* 1400 Independence Ave. S.W., #4419S, 20250-3812; (202) 720-2831. Fax, (202) 720-1805. Seth Meyer, Chair, (202) 720-6030; Susan Carter, Information Officer, (202) 720-5447.
Web, www.usda.gov/oce/commodity

Reports to the USDA chief economist. Coordinates the department's commodity forecasting program, which develops the official prognosis of supply, utilization, and prices for commodities worldwide. Works with the National Weather Service to monitor the impact of global weather on agriculture.

Bureau of Economic and Business Affairs *(State Dept.),* *Agriculture Policy,* 2201 C St. N.W., #4686, 20520-0002; (202) 647-3090. Fax, (202) 647-1894. Eric W. Luftman, Director, (202) 647-0133.
Web, www.state.gov/e/eb/tpp/agp

Makes recommendations on international food policy issues including effects of U.S. food aid on foreign policy; studies and drafts proposals on the U.S. role in Food for Peace and World Food programs.

Foreign Agricultural Service (FAS) *(Agriculture Dept.),* *Capacity Building and Development,* 1400 Independence Ave. S.W., #3008S, MS 1030, 20250-1030; (202) 720-6887. Fax, (202) 720-0069. Jocelyn Brown, Deputy Administrator.
Web, www.fas.usda.gov

Operates food aid programs, trade, science, and regulatory capacity-building projects, including training and technical assistance programs, and supports USDA's postconflict and postdisaster reconstruction efforts.

State Dept., *Global Food Security,* 2201 C St. N.W., #5323, 20520; (202) 647-4027. Nancy Stetson, Special Representative.
Web, www.state.gov/s/globalfoodsecurity/index.htm

Supports country-driven approaches to address the root causes of hunger and poverty, and helps countries transform their own agricultural sectors to grow enough food to sustainably feed their people.

Food and Agriculture Organization of the United Nations (FAO), *Liaison Office in Washington,* 2121 K St. N.W., #800B, 20037-0001; (202) 653-2400. Fax, (202) 653-5760. Ajay Markanday, Director.
General email, faolow@fao.org

Web, www.fao.org/north-america/en, www.worldfooddayusa.org and Twitter, @WorldFoodDayUSA

Offers development assistance; collects, analyzes, and disseminates information; provides policy and planning advice to governments; acts as an international forum for debate on food and agricultural issues, including animal health and production, fisheries, and forestry; encourages sustainable agricultural development and a long-term strategy for the conservation and management of natural resources. Coordinates World Food Day. (International headquarters in Rome.)

International Fund for Agricultural Development (IFAD), *North American Liaison Office,* 1775 K St. N.W., #410, 20006-1502; (202) 331-9099. Fax, (202) 331-9366. Thomas Pesek, Partnership Officer.
General email, t.pesek@ifad.org
Web, www.ifad.org

Financial institution and specialized agency of the United Nations that provides the rural poor of developing nations with cost-effective ways of overcoming hunger, poverty, and malnutrition. Advocates a community-based approach to reducing rural poverty. (International headquarters in Rome.)

TechnoServe, 1120 19th St. N.W., 8th Floor, 20036; (202) 785-4515. Fax, (202) 785-4544. Will Warshauer, President. Press, (202) 650-5713. Donor Support, (800) 999-6757.
General email, info@technoserve.org
Web, www.technoserve.org

International nonprofit that assists entrepreneurs in poor and developing countries. Provides access to technology, information, and resources that connect business owners to suppliers and industry networks to increase their revenue. Specializes in farming and agricultural enterprises.

ACDI/VOCA, 50 F St. N.W., #1000, 20001-1530; (202) 469-6000. Fax, (202) 469-6257. William Polidoro, President.
General email, webmaster@acdivoca.org
Web, www.acdivoca.org

Promotes agribusiness systems that improve production and link farmers to national, regional, and international markets. Partners with farm supply, processing, and marketing cooperatives; farm credit banks; national farmer organizations; and insurance cooperatives. Provides cooperatives with training and technical, management, and marketing assistance; supports farm credit systems, agribusiness, and government agencies in developing countries.

American Red Cross, *National Headquarters, 2025 E St. N.W., 20006-5009; (202) 303-5000. Gail J. McGovern, President. Press, (202) 303-5551. Toll-free, 800-RED-CROSS (733-2767).*
Web, www.redcross.org and Twitter, @RedCross

Humanitarian relief and health education organization chartered by Congress. Provides food and supplies to assist in major disaster and refugee situations worldwide. U.S. delegate of the international Red Cross and Red Crescent Societies in international response efforts.

Bread for the World/Bread for the World Institute,
425 3rd St. S.W., #1200, 20024; (202) 639-9400. Fax, (202) 639-9401. David Beckmann, President. Information, (800) 822-7323.
General email, bread@bread.org and institute@bread.org
Web, www.bread.org and Twitter, @bread4theworld

Christian citizens' movement that works to eradicate world hunger. Organizes and coordinates political action on issues and public policy affecting the causes of hunger.

CARE, *Washington Office, 1899 L St. N.W., #500, 20036; (202) 595-2800. Fax, (202) 296-8695. David Ray, Head of Policy and Advocacy. Toll-free, (800) 422-7385.*
General email, info@care.org
Web, www.care.org and Twitter, @CARE

Assists the developing world's poor through emergency assistance and community self-help programs that focus on sustainable development, agriculture, agroforestry, water and sanitation, health, family planning, and income generation. Community-based efforts are centered on providing resources to poor women. (U.S. headquarters in Atlanta, Ga.; international headquarters in Geneva.)

International Food Policy Research Institute (IFPRI),
2033 K St. N.W., #400, 20006-1002; (202) 862-5600. Fax, (202) 862-8129. Shenggen Fan, Director General. Library, (202) 862-5614.
General email, ifpri@cgiar.org
Web, www.ifpri.org

Research organization that analyzes the world food situation and suggests ways of making food more available in developing countries. Provides various governments with information on national and international food policy. Sponsors conferences and seminars; publishes research reports. Library open to the public by appointment.

National Center for Food and Agricultural Policy, *1616 P St. N.W., 1st Floor, 20036; (202) 328-5183. Fax, (202) 328-5133. Joe Dunn, Chief Executive Officer.*
General email, info@ncfap.org
Web, www.ncfap.org

Research and educational organization concerned with domestic and international food and agricultural issues. Examines public policy concerning agriculture, food safety and quality, natural resources, and the environment.

Oxfam America, *Policy and Campaigns, 1101 17th St. N.W. #1300, 20036-4710; (202) 496-1180. Fax, (202) 496-1190. Raymond C. Offenheiser, President; Paul O'Brien,*

Vice President for Policy and Campaigns. Information, (800) 776-9326. Press, (202) 496-1169.
General email, info@oxfamamerica.org
Web, www.oxfamamerica.org and Twitter, @OxfamAmerica

Funds disaster relief and long-term development programs internationally. Organizes grassroots support in the United States for issues affecting global poverty and hunger.

RESULTS, *1101 15th St. N.W., #1200, 20005; (202) 783-7100. Fax, (202) 466-1397. Joanne Carter, Executive Director.*
General email, results@results.org
Web, www.results.org and Twitter, @RESULTS_Tweets

Works to end hunger and poverty nationally and worldwide; encourages grassroots and legislative support of programs and proposals dealing with hunger and hunger-related issues. Monitors legislation and regulations.

Winrock International, *2121 Crystal Dr., #500, Arlington, VA 22202; (703) 302-6500. Fax, (703) 302-6512. Rodney Ferguson, President.*
General email, information@winrock.org
Web, www.winrock.org and Twitter, @WinrockIntl

Works to increase economic opportunity; sustain natural resources; protect the environment; and increase long-term productivity, equity, and responsible resource management to benefit the world's poor and disadvantaged communities. Matches innovative approaches in agriculture, natural resources management, clean energy, and leadership development with the unique needs of its partners. Links local individuals and communities with new ideas and technology. (Headquarters in Little Rock, Ark.)

Worldwatch Institute, *1400 16th St. N.W., #430, 20036; (202) 745-8092. Fax, (202) 478-2534. Ed Groark, President, Acting.*
General email, worldwatch@worldwatch.org
Web, www.worldwatch.org and Twitter, @worldwatch

Environmental think tank that studies the environmental, political, and economic links to world population growth and health trends. Interests include food and sustainable agriculture.

LIVESTOCK AND POULTRY

General

▶ **AGENCIES**

Agricultural Marketing Service (AMS) *(Agriculture Dept.), Livestock, Poultry, and Seed, 1400 Independence Ave. S.W., #2092S, MS 0249, 20250-0249; (202) 720-5705. Fax, (202) 720-3499. Craig Morris, Deputy Administrator.*
Web, www.ams.usda.gov/about-ams/programs-offices/livestock-poultry-seed-program

Administers meat marketing program; maintains market news service to inform producers of meat market situation and daily price changes; develops, establishes, and revises U.S. standards for classes and grades of livestock and meat; grades, examines, and certifies meat and meat products. Sets poultry and egg grading standards. Provides promotion and market news services for domestic and international markets.

Food and Drug Administration (FDA) *(Health and Human Services Dept.), Center for Veterinary Medicine,* *7519 Standish Pl., HFV-1, Rockville, MD 20855-0001;* *(240) 402-7002. Fax, (240) 276-9001.* *Dr. Bernadette Dunham, Director.* *General email, askcvm@fda.hhs.gov*
Web, www.fda.gov/animalveterinary

Regulates the manufacture and distribution of drugs, food additives, feed, and devices for livestock and pets. Conducts research; works to ensure animal health and the safety of food derived from animals.

Food Safety and Inspection Service *(Agriculture Dept.),* *1400 Independence Ave. S.W., #331E, 20250-3700; (202)* *720-7025. Fax, (202) 205-0158. Alfred Almanza, Deputy* *Under Secretary. Press, (202) 720-9113. Consumer* *inquiries, (800) 535-4555. TTY, (800) 877-8339.* *Web, www.usda.gov/fsis*

Inspects meat and poultry products and provides safe handling and labeling guidelines.

Grain Inspection, Packers and Stockyards Administration *(Agriculture Dept.), 1400 Independence* *Ave. S.W., #2055, South Bldg., MS 3601, 20250-3601; (202)* *720-0219. Fax, (202) 205-9237. Larry Mitchell,* *Administrator. Toll-free, (800) 455-3447.* *General email, larry.mitchell@gipsa.usda.gov*
Web, www.gipsa.usda.gov

Maintains competition in the marketing of livestock, poultry, grain, and meat by prohibiting deceptive and monopolistic marketing practices; tests market scales and conducts check weighings for accuracy.

▶CONGRESS

For a listing of relevant congressional committees and sub committees, please see page 3 or the Appendix.

▶NONGOVERNMENTAL

Animal Health Institute, *1325 G St. N.W., #700,* *20005-3104; (202) 637-2440. Fax, (202) 393-1667.* *Alexander S. Mathews, President.* *Web, www.ahi.org*

Membership: manufacturers of drugs and other products (including vaccines, pesticides, and vitamins) for pets and food-producing animals. Interests include pet health, livestock health, and disease outbreak prevention. Monitors legislation and regulations.

Farm Animal Rights Movement (FARM), *10101* *Ashburton Lane, Bethesda, MD 20817-1729; (301) 530-* *1737. Fax, (301) 530-5683. Michael A. Weberman,* *Executive Director; Alex Hershaft, President. Toll-free, 888-* *FARM-USA.*

General email, info@farmusa.org
Web, www.farmusa.org, www.livevegan.org and Twitter, *@FARMUSA*

Works to end use of animals for food. Interests include animal protection, consumer health, agricultural resources, and environmental quality. Conducts national educational campaigns, including World Farm Animals Day, the Live Vegan program, and the Great American Meatout. Monitors legislation and regulations.

Humane Farm Animal Care, *P.O. Box 727, Herndon, VA* *20172-0727; (703) 435-3883. Fax, (703) 435-3981.* *Adele Douglass, Executive Director.* *General email, info@certifiedhumane.org*
Web, www.certifiedhumane.org

Seeks to improve the welfare of farm animals by providing viable, duly monitored standards for humane food production. Administers the Certified Humane Raised and Handled program for meat, poultry, eggs, and dairy products.

National Cattlemen's Beef Assn., *Government Affairs,* *1301 Pennsylvania Ave. N.W., #300, 20004-1701; (202)* *347-0228. Fax, (202) 638-0607. Tracy Brunner, Association* *President; Colin Woodall, Vice President, Government* *Affairs.* *Web, www.beefusa.org*

Membership: individual cattlemen, state cattlemen's groups, and breed associations. Provides information on beef research, agricultural labor, beef grading, foreign trade, taxes, marketing, cattle economics, branding, animal health, and environmental management. (Headquarters in Denver, Colo.)

National Chicken Council, *1152 15th St. N.W., #430,* *20005-2622; (202) 296-2622. Fax, (202) 293-4005.* *Michael J. Brown, President.* *General email, ncc@chickenusa.org*
Web, www.nationalchickencouncil.org and Twitter, *@chickencouncil*

Trade association that represents the vertically integrated producers of 95 percent of the chickens raised and processed for meat in the United States. Monitors domestic and international legislation and regulations.

National Pork Producers Council, *122 C St. N.W., #875,* *20001; (202) 347-3600. Fax, (202) 347-5265. Ron Prestage,* *President.* *General email, pork@nppc.org*
Web, www.nppc.org

Membership: pork producers and state pork producer organizations. Interests include pork production, food safety, the environment, trade, and federal regulations. Monitors legislation and regulations. (Headquarters in Des Moines, Iowa.)

National Renderers Assn., *500 Montgomery St., #310,* *Alexandria, VA 22314; (703) 683-0155. Fax, (571) 970-* *2279. Nancy Foster, President.*

General email, renderers@nationalrenderers.com

Web, http://nationalrenderers.org

Membership: manufacturers of meat meal and tallow. Compiles industry statistics; sponsors research; conducts seminars and workshops. Monitors legislation and regulations.

National Turkey Federation, *1225 New York Ave. N.W., #400, 20005-6404; (202) 898-0100. Fax, (202) 898-0203. Joel Brandenberger, President.*

General email, info@turkeyfed.org

Web, www.eatturkey.com

Membership: turkey growers, hatcheries, breeders, and processors. Promotes turkey consumption. Monitors legislation and regulations.

North American Meat Institute, *1150 Connecticut Ave. N.W., 12th Floor, 20036; (202) 587-4200. Fax, (202) 587-4300. Barry Carpenter, President; Eric Mittenthal, Communications, (202) 587-4238.*

General email, emittenthal@meatinstitute.org

Web, www.meatami.com and Twitter, @MeatInstitute

Membership: national and international meat and poultry packers, suppliers, and processors. Provides statistics on meat production and consumption, livestock, and feed grains. Funds meat research projects and consumer education programs; sponsors conferences and correspondence courses on meat production and processing. Monitors legislation and regulations. (Formed from merger of the North American Meat Assn. and American Meat Institute.)

Shelf-Stable Food Processors Assn. (SFPA), *1150 Connecticut Ave. N.W., 12th Floor, 20036; (202) 587-4200. Fax, (202) 587-4300. Barry Carpenter, President, (202) 587-4262.*

General email, sfpa@meatinstitute.org

Web, www.meatinstitute.org

Membership: shelf-stable food manufacturers and their suppliers. Provides information on the shelf-stable industry, particularly as it pertains to meat products. (Subsidiary of the American Meat Institute.)

U.S. Hide, Skin, and Leather Assn. (USHSLA), *1150 Connecticut Ave. N.W., 12th Floor, 20036; (202) 587-4250. Fax, (202) 587-4300. Stephen Sothmann, President.*

Web, www.ushsla.org

Membership: meatpackers, brokers, dealers, processors, and exporters of hides and skins. Maintains liaison with allied trade associations and participates in programs on export statistics, hide price reporting, and freight rates; conducts seminars and consumer information programs. (Division of American Meat Institute.)

2 Business and Economics

GENERAL POLICY AND ANALYSIS

Basic Resources

▶AGENCIES

Bureau of Economic and Business Affairs *(State Dept.),* *Commercial and Business Affairs,* 2201 C St. N.W., #5820, 20520-5820; (202) 647-1625. Fax, (202) 647-3953. Vacant, Special Representative; Caryn R. McClelland, Deputy Special Representative.
General email, cbaweb@state.gov
Web, www.state.gov/e/eb/cba

Serves as primary contact in the State Dept. for U.S. businesses. Coordinates efforts to facilitate U.S. business interests abroad, ensures that U.S. business interests are given sufficient consideration in foreign policy, and provides assistance to firms with problems overseas (such as claims and trade complaints). Oversees the Global Entrepreneurship Program.

Census Bureau *(Commerce Dept.), Economic Programs,* 4600 Silver Hill Rd., #8H132, Suitland, MD 20746 (mailing address: 4600 Silver Hill Rd., #8H132 Washington, DC 20233-6000); (301) 763-8842. Fax, (301) 763-8150. William G. Bostic Jr., Associate Director.
Web, www.census.gov/econ

Compiles comprehensive statistics on the level and structure of U.S. economic activity and the characteristics of industrial and business establishments at the national, state, and local levels; collects and publishes foreign trade statistics.

Commerce Dept., 1401 Constitution Ave. N.W., 20230; (202) 482-2000. Fax, (202) 482-5168. Penny Pritzker, Secretary, Acting. Press, (202) 482-4883. Library, (202) 482-1154.
Web, www.commerce.gov and Twitter, @CommerceGov

Acts as a principal adviser to the president on federal policy affecting industry and commerce; promotes job creation, national economic growth and development, competitiveness, international trade, and technological development; provides business and government with economic statistics, research, and analysis; encourages minority business; promotes tourism. Library open to the public by appointment.

Commerce Dept., *Business Liaison,* 1401 Constitution Ave. N.W., #5062, 20230; (202) 482-1360. Fax, (202) 482-4054. Shannon Roche, Director.
General email, businessliaison@doc.gov
Web, www.commerce.gov/office-secretary/office-business-liaison

Serves as the federal government's central office for business assistance. Handles requests for information and services as well as complaints and suggestions from businesses; provides a forum for businesses to comment on federal regulations; initiates meetings on policy issues with industry groups, business organizations, trade and small business associations, and the corporate community.

Consumer Product Safety Commission (CPSC), *Economic Analysis,* 4330 East-West Hwy., Bethesda, MD 20814; (301) 504-7705. Fax, (301) 504-0109. Gregory B. Rodgers, Associate Executive Director, (301) 504-7702.
Web, www.cpsc.gov

Conducts studies to determine the impact of CPSC's regulations on consumers, the economy, industry, and production. Studies the potential environmental effects of commission actions.

Council of Economic Advisers *(Executive Office of the President),* 725 17th St. N.W., 20502; (202) 395-5084. Fax, (202) 395-5630. Jason Furman, Chair; Andrea Taverna, Chief of Staff.
Web, www.whitehouse.gov/administration/eop/cea

Advisory body consisting of three members and supporting staff of economists. Monitors and analyzes the economy and advises the president on economic developments, trends, and policies and on the economic implications of other policy initiatives. Prepares the annual *Economic Report of the President* for Congress. Assesses economic implications of international policy.

Economics and Statistics Administration *(Commerce Dept.),* 1401 Constitution Ave. N.W., #4848, 20230; (202) 482-3727. Fax, (202) 482-0432. Justin F. Antonipillai, Deputy Under Secretary.
General email, esa@doc.gov
Web, www.esa.doc.gov

Advises the secretary on economic policy matters, including consumer and capital spending, inventory status, and the short- and long-term outlook in output and unemployment. Seeks to improve economic productivity and growth. Serves as departmental liaison with the Council of Economic Advisers and other government agencies concerned with economic policy. Supervises and sets policy for the Census Bureau and the Bureau of Economic Analysis.

Federal Reserve System, *Board of Governors,* 20th St. and Constitution Ave., N.W., 20551; (202) 452-3000. Fax, (202) 452-3819. Janet L. Yellen, Chair; Stanley Fischer, Vice Chair. Information (meetings), (202) 452-3204. Public Affairs, (202) 452-2955. Congressional Liaison, (202) 452-3003. Publications, (202) 452-3245. TTY, (202) 263-4869.
General email, eric.j.kollig@frb.gov
Web, www.federalreserve.gov

Sets U.S. monetary policy. Supervises the Federal Reserve System and influences credit conditions through the buying and selling of Treasury securities in the open market by fixing the amount of reserves depository institutions must maintain and by determining discount rates.

Federal Trade Commission (FTC), 600 Pennsylvania Ave. N.W., 20580; (202) 326-2222. Edith Ramirez, Chair; David B. Robbins, Executive Director. Press, (202) 326-2180. Library, (202) 326-2395. Congressional Relations, (202) 326-2195. Identity theft hotline, (877) 438-4338.
Web, www.ftc.gov and Twitter, @FTC

Promotes policies designed to maintain strong competitive enterprise and consumer protection within the

U.S. economic system. Monitors trade practices and investigates cases involving monopoly, unfair restraints, or deceptive practices. Enforces Truth in Lending and Fair Credit Reporting acts. Library open to the public (Monday–Friday, 8:30 a.m.–5:00 p.m.).

Federal Trade Commission (FTC), *Bureau of Economics,*
600 Pennsylvania Ave. N.W., 20580; (202) 326-3420.
Fax, (202) 326-2380. Ginger Zhe Jin, Director.
Web, www.ftc.gov/about-ftc/bureaus-offices/bureau-economics

Provides economic analyses for consumer protection and antitrust investigations, cases, and rulemakings; advises the commission on the effect of government regulations on competition and consumers in various industries; develops special reports on competition, consumer protection, and regulatory issues.

National Economic Council *(Executive Office of the President),* *The White House, 20502; (202) 456-2800.*
Fax, (202) 456-2223. Jeffrey Zients, Assistant to the President for Economic Policy.
Web, www.whitehouse.gov/administration/eop/nec

Comprises cabinet members and other high-ranking executive branch officials. Coordinates domestic and international economic policymaking, provides economic policy advice to the president, ensures that policy decisions and programs are consistent with the president's economic goals, and monitors the implementation of the president's economic agenda.

National Institute of Standards and Technology (NIST) *(Commerce Dept.), Baldrige Performance Excellence Program,* *100 Bureau Dr., MS 1020, Gaithersburg, MD 20899-1020; (301) 975-2036. Fax, (301) 948-3716.*
Robert Fangmeyer, Director.
General email, baldrige@nist.gov
Web, www.nist.gov/baldrige

Public-private partnership that educates business, education, and organization leaders on industry-specific best-practices management. Offers organizational assessment tools and criteria.

National Institute of Standards and Technology (NIST) *(Commerce Dept.), Special Programs Office,* *100 Bureau Dr., MS 1000, Gaithersburg, MD 20899-1000; (301) 975-4447. Fax, (301) 975-8972. Richard R. Cavanagh, Director.*
General information, (301) 975-2756.
Web, www.nist.gov/director/spo

Fosters collaboration among government, military, academia, professional, and private organizations to respond to critical national needs through science-based standards and technology innovation, including the areas of manufacturing and physical infrastructure.

National Institute of Standards and Technology (NIST) *(Commerce Dept.), Standards Services,* *100 Bureau Dr., MS 2100, Gaithersburg, MD 20899; (301) 975-4000.*
Fax, (301) 975-4715. Nancy Evans, Director.
General email, standardsinfo@nist.gov
Web, http://gsi.nist.gov/global

Monitors and participates in industries' development of federal and global standards and standard-enforcement mechanisms. Conducts standards-related research and training and holds workshops for domestic and international audiences. Provides information on industry standards and specifications, conformity assessment, test methods, domestic and international technical regulations, codes, and recommended practices.

National Institute of Standards and Technology (NIST) *(Commerce Dept.), Weights and Measures, Laws and Metric Group,* *100 Bureau Dr., MS 2600, Gaithersburg, MD 20899-2600; (301) 975-4004. Fax, (301) 975-8091.*
Kenneth S. Butcher, Group Leader.
General email, owm@nist.gov
Web, www.nist.gov/metric

Coordinates federal metric conversion transition to ensure consistency in the interpretation and enforcement of packaging, labeling, net content, and other laws; provides the public with technical and general information about the metric system; assists state and local governments, businesses, and educators with metric conversion activities.

National Women's Business Council, *409 3rd St. S.W., 5th Floor, 20416; (202) 205-3850. Fax, (202) 205-6825.*
Amanda Brown, Executive Director.
General email, info@nwbc.gov
Web, www.nwbc.gov

Independent, congressionally mandated council established by the Women's Business Ownership Act of 1988. Reviews the status of women-owned businesses nationwide and makes policy recommendations to the president, Congress, and the Small Business Administration. Assesses the role of the federal government in aiding and promoting women-owned businesses.

Small Business Administration (SBA), *409 3rd St. S.W., 20416-7000; (202) 205-6605. Fax, (202) 205-6802.*
Maria Contreras-Sweet, Administrator; Douglas J. Kramer, Deputy Administrator. Toll-free information (Answer Desk), (800) 827-5722. Locator, (202) 205-6600. TTY, (800) 877-8339.
General email, answerdesk@sba.gov
Web, www.sba.gov

Maintains and strengthens the nation's economy by aiding, counseling, assisting, and protecting the interests of small businesses and by helping families and businesses recover from natural disasters.

Treasury Dept., *1500 Pennsylvania Ave. N.W., #3330, 20220; (202) 622-2000. Fax, (202) 622-6415. Jacob J. Lew, Secretary, (202) 622-1100; Sarah Bloom Raskin, Deputy Secretary. Information, (202) 622-5500. Library, (202) 622-0990. TTY, (877) 304-9709. Press, (202) 622-2960.*
Web, www.treasury.gov

Serves as chief financial officer of the government and adviser to the president on economic policy. Formulates and recommends domestic and international financial, economic, tax, and broad fiscal policies; manages the public debt; collects monies owed to the U.S. government;

BUSINESS AND ECONOMICS RESOURCES IN CONGRESS

For a complete listing of congressional committees, including their full contact information, leadership, membership, and jurisdictions, please refer to the Appendix on pages 779–896.

HOUSE:

House Agriculture Committee, (202) 225-2171.
Web, agriculture.house.gov
    Subcommittee on Biotechnology, Horticulture, and Research, (202) 225-2171.
House Appropriations Committee, (202) 225-2771.
Web, appropriations.house.gov
    Subcommittee on Commerce, Justice, Science, and Related Agencies, (202) 225-3351.
    Subcommittee on Financial Services and General Government, (202) 225-7245.
    Subcommittee on Transportation, HUD, and Related Agencies, (202) 225-2141.
House Budget Committee, (202) 226-7270.
Web, budget.house.gov
House Energy and Commerce Committee, (202) 225-2927.
Web, energycommerce.house.gov
    Subcommittee on Commerce, Manufacturing, and Trade, (202) 225-2927.
    Subcommittee on Energy and Power, (202) 225-2927.
    Subcommittee on Environment and the Economy, (202) 225-2927.
    Subcommittee on Health, (202) 225-2927.
House Financial Services Committee, (202) 225-7502.
Web, financialservices.house.gov
    Subcommittee on Housing and Insurance, (202) 225-7502.
House Foreign Affairs Committee, (202) 225-5021.
Web, foreignaffairs.house.gov
    Subcommittee on Terrorism, Nonproliferation, and Trade, (202) 225-5021.

House Judiciary Committee, (202) 225-3951.
Web, judiciary.house.gov
    Subcommittee on Courts, Intellectual Property, and the Internet, (202) 226-7680.
    Subcommittee on Regulatory Reform, Commercial, and Antitrust Law, (202) 226-7680.
House Oversight and Government Reform Committee, (202) 225-5074.
Web, oversight.house.gov
    Subcommittee on Transportation and Public Assets, (202) 225-5074.
House Science, Space, and Technology Committee, (202) 225-6371.
Web, science.house.gov
    Subcommittee on Research and Technology, (202) 225-6371.
House Small Business Committee, (202) 225-5821.
Web, smallbusiness.house.gov
    Subcommittee on Agriculture, Energy, and Trade, (202) 225-5821.
    Subcommittee on Contracting and Workforce, (202) 225-5821.
    Subcommittee on Economic Growth, Tax, and Capital Access, (202) 225-5821.
    Subcommittee on Health and Technology, (202) 225-5821.
    Subcommittee on Investigations, Oversight, and Regulations, (202) 225-5821.
House Ways and Means Committee, (202) 225-3625.
Web, waysandmeans.house.gov
    Subcommittee on Trade, (202) 225-6649.

---

supervises national banks and thrifts. Library open to the public by appointment.

Treasury Dept., *Economic Policy, 1500 Pennsylvania Ave. N.W., #3454, 20220; (202) 622-2200. Fax, (202) 622-2633. Karen Dynan, Assistant Secretary.*
Web, www.treasury.gov/about/organizational-structure/offices/Pages/Economic-Policy.aspx

Assists and advises the Treasury secretary in the formulation and execution of domestic and international economic policies and programs; helps prepare economic forecasts for the federal budget.

▶CONGRESS

For a listing of relevant congressional committees and subcommittees, please see pages 34–35 or the Appendix.

Government Accountability Office (GAO), *441 G St. N.W., 20548; (202) 512-5500. Fax, (202) 512-5507.*

Gene L. Dodaro, Comptroller General. Information, (202) 512-3000. Publications and Documents, (202) 512-6000. Congressional Relations, (202) 512-4400.
Web, www.gao.gov

Independent, nonpartisan agency in the legislative branch. Serves as the investigating agency for Congress; carries out legal, accounting, auditing, and claims settlement functions; makes recommendations for more effective government operations; publishes monthly lists of reports available to the public.

▶NONGOVERNMENTAL

American Business Conference, *1828 L St. N.W., #280, 20036; (202) 822-9300. Fax, (202) 467-4070. John Endean, President.*
General email, info@americanbusinessconference.org
Web, www.americanbusinessconference.org

JOINT:

Joint Committee on Taxation, (202) 225-3621.
Web, jct.gov

Joint Economic Committee, (202) 224-5171.
Web, jec.senate.gov

SENATE:

**Senate Agriculture, Nutrition, and Forestry
    Committee,** (202) 224-2035.
Web, ag.senate.gov

    **Subcommittee on Commodities, Risk
        Management, and Trade,** (202) 224-2035.

Senate Appropriations Committee, (202) 224-7363.
Web, appropriations.senate.gov

    **Subcommittee on Commerce, Justice, Science,
        and Related Agencies,** (202) 224-5202.

    **Subcommittee on Labor, Health and Human
        Services, Education, and Related Agencies,**
        (202) 224-9145.

**Senate Banking, Housing, and Urban Affairs
    Committee,** (202) 224-7391.
Web, banking.senate.gov

    Subcommittee on Economic Policy,
        (202) 224-3753.

    **Subcommittee on Financial Institutions and
        Consumer Protection,** (202) 224-2315.

    **Subcommittee on National Security and
        International Trade and Finance,**
        (202) 224-2023.

    **Subcommittee on Securities, Insurance, and
        Investment,** (202) 224-4642.

Senate Budget Committee, (202) 224-0642.
Web, budget.senate.gov

**Senate Commerce, Science, and Transportation
    Committee,** (202) 224-0411.
Web, commerce.senate.gov

    **Subcommittee on Consumer Protection, Product
        Safety, Insurance and Data Security,**
        (202) 224-0411.

Senate Finance Committee, (202) 224-4515.
Web, finance.senate.gov

    **Subcommittee on Energy, Natural Resources, and
        Infrastructure,** (202) 224-4515.

    **Subcommittee on Fiscal Responsibility and
        Economic Growth,** (202) 224-4515.

    Subcommittee on Health Care, (202) 224-4515.

    **Subcommittee on International Trade, Customs,
        and Global Competitiveness,** (202) 224-4515.

    **Subcommittee on Social Security, Pensions and
        Family Policy,** (202) 224-4515.

    Subcommittee on Taxation and IRS Oversight,
        (202) 224-4515.

**Senate Health, Education, Labor, and Pensions
    Committee,** (202) 224-5375.
Web, help.senate.gov

**Senate Homeland Security and Governmental Affairs
    Committee,** (202) 224-2627.
Web, hsgac.senate.gov

    Permanent Subcommittee on Investigations,
        (202) 224-4462.

Senate Judiciary Committee, (202) 224-7703.
Web, judiciary.senate.gov

    **Subcommittee on Antitrust, Competition Policy,
        and Consumer Rights,** (202) 224-6884.

    Subcommittee on Bankruptcy and the Courts,
        (202) 224-7703.

Membership: chief executive officers of midsize, high-growth companies. Seeks a public policy role for growth companies. Studies capital formation, tax policy, regulatory reform, and international trade.

American Chamber of Commerce Executives, *1330 Braddock Pl., #300, Alexandria, VA 22314; (703) 998-0072. Fax, (888) 577-9883. Michael Fleming, President, (703) 998-3537.*
General email, info@acce.org

Web, www.acce.org

Membership: executives of local, state, and international chambers of commerce. Conducts for members educational programs and conferences on topics of interest, including economic development, government relations, management symposiums, and membership drives. Assembles special interest committees for members.

American Council for Capital Formation (ACCF), *1001 Conneticut Ave. N.W., #620, 20036; (202) 293-5811.*

Fax, (202) 785-8165. Mark A. Bloomfield, President.
Press, (202) 420-9361.
General email, info@accf.org

Web, www.accf.org

Promotes tax, trade, and environmental policies conducive to saving, investment, and economic growth. Affiliated with the ACCF Center for Policy Research, which conducts and funds research on capital formation topics.

American Enterprise Institute (AEI), *1150 17th St. N.W., 20036; (202) 862-5800. Fax, (202) 862-7177.*
Arthur C. Brooks, President. Press, (202) 862-5829.
Web, www.aei.org

Conducts research. Sponsors events. Interests include monetary, tax, trade, financial services, regulatory policy, labor, social security issues, and retirement.

American Management Assn. International,
Washington Office, 2345 Crystal Dr., #200, Arlington, VA

Commerce Department

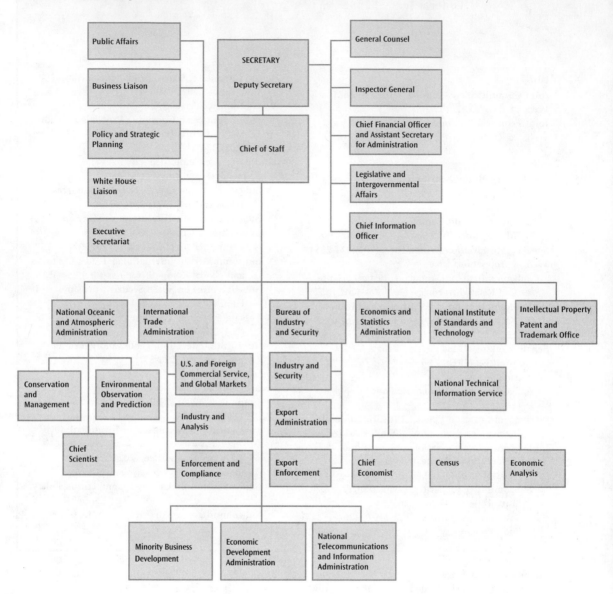

22202-4807; (571) 481-2200. Fax, (571) 481-2211. *Richard Nusbaum, Center Manager.* Toll-free, (877) 566-9441.

Web, www.amanet.org and Twitter, @AMAnet

Membership: managers and other corporate professionals. Offers training and education programs to members. (Headquarters in New York.)

American Society of Assn. Executives (ASAE), *1575 Eye St. N.W., #1100, 20005-1103; (202) 371-0940. Fax, (202) 371-8315. John H. Graham IV, President, (202) 626-2741. Press, (202) 326-9505.* Toll-free, (888) 950-2723.

General email, pr@asaecenter.org

Web, www.asaecenter.org

Membership: managers of trade associations, membership societies, and volunteer organizations. Conducts research and provides educational programs on association management, trends, and developments. Library open to the public.

Americans for Prosperity, *1310 N. Courthouse Rd., #700, Arlington, VA 22201; (703) 224-3200. Fax, (703) 224-3201. Tim Phillips, President.* Toll-free, (866) 730-0150.

General email, info@AFPhq.org

Web, www.americansforprosperity.org

Grassroots organization that seeks to educate citizens about economic policy and encourage their participation in the public policy process. Supports limited government and free markets on the local, state, and federal levels. Specific interests include Social Security, trade, and taxes. Monitors legislation and regulations.

Federal Trade Commission

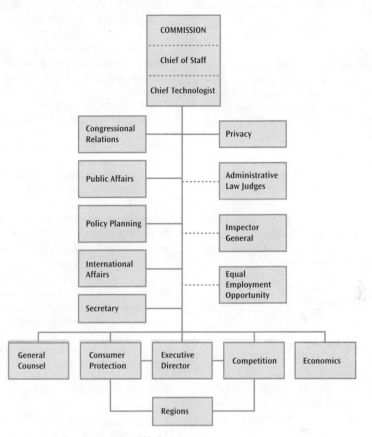

- - - - Denotes independent operation within the agency

Aspen Institute, *1 Dupont Circle N.W., #700, 20036-7133; (202) 736-5800. Fax, (202) 467-0790. Walter Isaacson, President. Press, (202) 736-3849.*
General email, info@aspeninstitute.org
Web, www.aspeninstitute.org and Twitter, @AspenInstitute

Educational and policy studies organization. Promotes consideration of the public good in a wide variety of policy areas, including business management and economic development. Working with international partners, offers educational seminars, nonpartisan policy forums, public conferences and events, and leadership development initiatives.

Atlas Network, *1201 L St. N.W., 20005; (202) 449-8449. Fax, (202) 280-1259. Alejandro A. Chafuen, President. Press, (202) 449-8441.*
General email, info@atlasnetwork.org
Web, www.atlasnetwork.org and Twitter, @AtlasNetwork

Connects free market-oriented think tanks who seek to reform global economic policy. Distributes grants to new institutes, international student groups, and select partner projects. Administers awards and training programs for free-enterprise organization leaders. Holds forums and events that focus on the advancement of a free-market economic system.

The Brookings Institution, *Climate and Energy Economics Project, 1775 Massachusetts Ave. N.W., 20036; (202) 797-6000. Warwick McKibbin, Co-Director; Pete Wilcoxen, Co-Director. Press, (202) 797-6105.*
Web, www.brookings.edu/about/projects/climate-energy-economics

Promotes economically efficient approaches to mitigating human impacts on climate change, including cap-and-trade.

The Brookings Institution, *Economic Studies, 1775 Massachusetts Ave. N.W., 20036-2188; (202) 797-6000. Fax, (202) 797-6181. Ted Gayer, Director. Press, (202) 797-6105.*
General email, escomment@brookings.edu
Web, www.brookings.edu/economics

Sponsors economic research and publishes studies on domestic and international economics, macroeconomics, worldwide economic growth and stability, public finance, industrial organization and regulation, labor economics, social policy, and the economics of human resources.

The Brookings Institution, *Metropolitan Policy Program,* *1755 Massachusetts Ave. N.W., 20036; (202) 797-6000. Fax, (202) 797-2965. Amy Liu, Director. Press, (202) 797-6105.*
General email, metro@brookings.edu

Web, www.brookings.edu/metro

Provides research and policy analysis to public, private, and nonprofit leaders to drive economic growth and prosperity. Interests include human capital and economic mobility, industrial innovation and productivity, global marketplace engagement, and infrastructure sustainability.

The Business Council, *1901 Pennsylvania Ave. N.W., #701, 20006; (202) 298-7650. Fax, (202) 785-0296. Marlene Colucci, Executive Director.*
Web, www.thebusinesscouncil.org

Membership: current and former chief executive officers of major corporations. Serves as a forum for business and government to exchange views and explore public policy as it affects U.S. business interests.

The Business Roundtable, *300 New Jersey Ave. N.W., #800, 20001; (202) 872-1260. Fax, (202) 466-3509. Gov. John Engler, President. Press, (202) 496-3269.*
General email, info@brt.org

Web, www.businessroundtable.org and Twitter, @BizRoundtable

Membership: chief executives of the nation's largest corporations. Examines issues of taxation, antitrust law, corporate governance, international trade, employment policy, and the federal budget. Monitors legislation and regulations.

Business–Higher Education Forum, *2025 M St. N.W., #800, 20036; (202) 367-1189. Fax, (202) 367-2100. Brian K. Fitzgerald, Chief Executive Officer.*
General email, info@bhef.com

Web, www.bhef.com and Twitter, @BHEF

Membership: chief executive officers of major corporations, foundations, colleges, and universities. Develops and promotes policy positions to enhance U.S. competitiveness. Interests include improving student achievement and readiness for college and work; and strengthening higher education, particularly in the fields of science, technology, engineering, and math.

Center for Economic and Policy Research (CEPR), *1611 Connecticut Ave. N.W., #400, 20009; (202) 293-5380. Fax, (202) 588-1356. Dean Baker, Co-Director; Mark Weisbrot, Co-Director.*
General email, info@cepr.net

Web, www.cepr.net and Twitter, @ceprdc

Researches economic and social issues and the impact of related public policies. Presents findings to the public with the goal of better preparing citizens to choose among various policy options. Promotes democratic debate and voter education. Areas of interest include health care, trade, financial reform, Social Security, taxes, housing, and the labor market.

Center for Study of Public Choice *(George Mason University), Carow Hall, MS 1D3, 4400 University Dr., Fairfax, VA 22030-4444; (703) 993-2330. Fax, (703) 993-2323. Alexander Tabarrok, Director.*
Web, www.gmu.edu/centers/publicchoice

Promotes research in public choice, an interdisciplinary approach to the study of the relationship between economic and political institutions. Interests include constitutional economics, public finance, federalism and local government, econometrics, and trade protection and regulation. Sponsors conferences and seminars.

Committee for Economic Development, *1530 Wilson Blvd., #400, Arlington, VA 22209; (202) 296-5860. Fax, (202) 223-0776. Steve Odland, Chief Executive Officer; Joseph J. Minarik, Senior Vice President. Toll-free, (800) 676-7353.*
General email, info@ced.org; email addresses are first.last@ced.org

Web, www.ced.org and Twitter, @CEDupdate

Nonpartisan, business-led public-policy organization that offers research and analysis. Interests include tax and health care reform, corporate governance and the role of women as administrators, education, immigration, older workers, and international trade.

Competitive Enterprise Institute, *1899 L St. N.W., 12th Floor, 20036; (202) 331-1010. Fax, (202) 331-0640. Gregory Conko, Executive Director; Kent Lassman, President. Press, (202) 331-2258.*
General email, info@cei.org

Web, www.cei.org and Twitter, @ceidotorg

Advocates free enterprise and limited government. Produces policy analyses on tax, budget, financial services, antitrust, biotechnological, and environmental issues. Monitors legislation and litigates against restrictive regulations through its Free Market Legal Program.

Corporation for Enterprise Development (CFED), *1200 G St. N.W., #400, 20005; (202) 408-9788. Fax, (202) 408-9793. Andrea Levere, President.*
General email, info@cfed.org

Web, www.cfed.org and Twitter, @cfed

Works to alleviate poverty by expanding economic opportunity and participation, bringing together community practice, public policy, and private markets in new and effective ways.

Council on Competitiveness, *900 17th St. N.W., #700, 20006; (202) 682-4292. Fax, (202) 682-5150. Deborah Wince-Smith, President; Jay Hamilton, Senior Vice President, Communications and Public Affairs.*
General email, info@compete.org

Web, www.compete.org and Twitter, @CompeteNow

Nonpartisan peer organization. Membership: chief executives from business, education, and labor. Seeks increased public awareness of issues related to economic competitiveness. Works to set a national action agenda for U.S. competitiveness in global markets.

Economic Policy Institute, *1333 H St. N.W., East Tower, #300, 20005-4707; (202) 775-8810. Fax, (202) 775-0819. Lawrence Mishel, President.*
General email, epi@epi.org
Web, www.epi.org

Research and educational organization that publishes analyses on economics, economic development, competitiveness, income distribution, industrial competitiveness, and investment. Conducts public conferences and seminars.

Essential Information, *Center for Corporate Policy, 1530 P St. N.W., 20005 (mailing address: P.O. Box 19505); (202) 387-8030. Fax, (202) 234-5176. Gary Ruskin, Director.*
General email, ruskin@corporatepolicy.org
Web, www.corporatepolicy.org

Nonpartisan public interest group that supports corporate accountability and the prevention of corporate misconduct. Educates public about and analyzes national and international corporate corruption. Requests government reports on corporate crime.

Ethics Research and Compliance Initiative, *2345 Crystal Dr., #201, Arlington, VA 22202; (703) 647-2185. Fax, (703) 647-2180. Patricia J. Harned, President. Information, (800) 777-1285.*
General email, ethics@ethics.org
Web, www.ethics.org and Twitter, @ethicsRC

Nonpartisan research organization that fosters ethical practices among individuals and institutions. Interests include research, knowledge building, education, and advocacy.

Good Jobs First, *1616 P St. N.W., #210, 20036; (202) 232-1616. Greg LeRoy, Executive Director.*
General email, info@goodjobsfirst.org
Web, www.goodjobsfirst.org

Promotes corporate and government accountability in economic development incentives; primary focus is on state and local job subsidies with emerging work on federal development programs and federal regulatory violations data. Maintains Subsidy Tracker database. Includes Good Jobs New York and the Corporate Research Project.

Greater Washington Board of Trade, *800 Connecticut Ave., #10001, 20006; (202) 857-5900. Fax, (202) 223-2648. James (Jim) C. Dinegar, President.*
General email, info@bot.org and danielflores@bot.org
Web, www.bot.org

Promotes and plans economic growth for the capital region. Supports business-government partnerships, technological training, and transportation planning; promotes international trade; works to increase economic viability of the city of Washington. Monitors legislation and regulations at local, state, and federal levels.

Institute for Credentialing Excellence, *2025 M St. N.W., #800, 20036-3309; (202) 367-1165. Fax, (202) 367-2165. Denise Roosendaal, Executive Director.*

General email, info@credentialingexcellence.org
Web, www.credentialingexcellence.org

Membership: certifying agencies and other groups that issue credentials for professions and occupations. Promotes public understanding of competency assurance certification programs. Oversees commission that establishes certification program standards. Monitors regulations.

International Business Ethics Institute, *1776 Eye St. N.W., 9th Floor, 20006; (202) 296-6938. Fax, (202) 296-5897. Lori Tansey Martens, President.*
General email, info@business-ethics.org
Web, www.business-ethics.org

Nonpartisan educational organization that promotes business ethics and corporate responsibility. Works to increase public awareness and dialogue about international business ethics issues through various educational resources and activities. Works with companies to assist them in establishing effective international ethics programs.

Mercatus Center *(George Mason University), 3434 Washington Blvd., 4th Floor, Arlington, VA 22201; (703) 993-4930. Fax, (703) 993-4935. Tyler Cowen, Director. Information, (800) 815-5711.*
General email, mercatus@mercatus.gmu.edu
Web, www.mercatus.org

Research center that studies sustained prosperity in societies and the conditions that contribute to economic success. Interests include the drivers of social, political, and economic change; international and domestic economic development; entrepreneurship and the institutions that enable it; the benefits and costs of regulatory policy; government performance and transparency; and good governance practices. Also studies the benefits of market-oriented systems using market process analysis.

National Assn. of Corporate Directors, *2001 Pennsylvania Ave. N.W., #500, 20006; (202) 775-0509. Fax, (202) 775-4857. Peter Gleason, President.*
General email, join@nacdonline.org
Web, www.nacdonline.org

Membership: executives of public, private, and nonprofit companies. Serves as a clearinghouse on corporate governance and current board practices. Sponsors seminars, peer forums, research, publications, and board development programs.

National Assn. of Manufacturers (NAM), *State Associations Group, 733 10th St. N.W., #700, 20001; (202) 637-3000. Fax, (202) 637-3182. Jay Timmons, President.*
Web, www.nam.org

Membership: employer associations at the regional, state, and local levels. Works to strengthen the U.S. competitive enterprise system. Represents views of the industry on business and economic issues; sponsors conferences and seminars.

National Assn. of State Budget Officers, *444 N. Capitol St. N.W., #642, 20001-1511; (202) 624-5382. Fax, (202) 624-7745. Stacey Mazer, Executive Director, Acting.*

General email, nasbo-direct@nasbo.org

Web, www.nasbo.org

Membership: state budget and financial officers. Publishes research reports on budget-related issues; shares best practices; provides training and technical assistance. (Affiliate of the National Governors Assn.)

National Chamber Litigation Center, *1615 H St. N.W., 20062-2000; (202) 463-5337. Fax, (202) 463-5346. Lily Fu Claffee, Executive Vice President.*
General email, litigationcenter@uschamber.com

Web, www.chamberlitigation.com

Public policy law firm of the U.S. Chamber of Commerce. Advocates businesses' positions in court on such issues as antitrust, bankruptcy, and employment, environmental, and constitutional law. Provides businesses with legal assistance and amicus support in legal proceedings before federal courts and agencies.

National Cooperative Business Assn., CLUSA International (NCBA CLUSA), *1775 Eye St. N.W., #800, 20006; (202) 638-6222. Fax, (202) 638-1374. Judy Ziewacz, President.*
General email, info@ncba.coop

Web, www.ncba.coop, Twitter, @NCBACLUSA and Facebook, www.facebook.com/NCBACLUSA

Alliance of cooperatives, businesses, and state cooperative associations. Supports development of cooperative businesses; promotes and develops trade among domestic and international cooperatives. Monitors legislation and regulations.

National Economists Club, *P.O. Box 33511, 20033-3511; (703) 493-8824. Thomas Oakley, President.*
General email, manager@national-economists.org

Web, www.thenationaleconomistsclub.shuttlepod.org

Provides venues for scholars, policymakers, business leaders, and public figures to present and defend their views on timely economic topics. Offers members employment and networking opportunities.

National Retail Federation, *1101 New York Ave. N.W., 20005; (202) 783-7971. Fax, (202) 737-2849. Matthew R. Shay, President; David French, Senior Vice President, Government Relations. Toll-free, (800) 673-4692.*
Web, www.nrf.com

Membership: international, national, and state associations of retailers and major retail corporations. Concerned with federal regulatory activities and legislation that affect retailers, including tax, employment, trade, and credit issues. Provides information on retailing through seminars, conferences, and publications.

Partnership for Public Service, *1100 New York Ave. N.W., #200E, 20005; (202) 775-9111. Fax, (202) 775-8885. Max Stier, President.*
Web, www.ourpublicservice.org

Membership: large corporations and private businesses, including financial and information technology organizations. Seeks to improve government efficiency, productivity, and management through a cooperative effort of the public and private sectors.

Private Equity Growth Capital Council (PEGCC), *799 9th St. N.W., #200, 20001; (202) 465-7700. Fax, (202) 639-0209. Vacant, President; James Maloney, Vice President, Public Affairs.*
General email, info@pegcc.org

Web, www.pegcc.org

Advocacy, communications, and research organization and resource center that develops, analyzes, and distributes information about the private equity industry and its contributions to the national and global economy.

Technology CEO Council, *1341 G St. N.W., #1100, 20005; (202) 585-0258. Fax, (202) 393-3031. Bruce Mehlman, Executive Director.*
General email, info@techceocouncil.org

Web, www.techceocouncil.org

Membership: chief executive officers from U.S. information technology companies. Monitors legislation and regulations on technology and trade issues.

U.S. Business and Industry Council (USBIC), *512 C St. N.E., 20002; (202) 266-3980. Fax, (202) 266-3981. Kevin L. Kearns, President.*
General email, usbicef@aol.com

Web, www.americaneconomicalert.org

Membership: owners of privately held manufacturing, farming, processing, and fabricating companies. Advocates energy independence, reindustrialization, and effective use of natural resources and manufacturing capacity. Interests include business tax reduction, the liability crisis, defense and other federal spending, and the trade deficit. Media network distributes op-ed pieces to newspapers and radio stations. (Affiliated with AmericanEconomic Alert.org.)

U.S. Chamber of Commerce, *1615 H St. N.W., 20062-2000; (202) 659-6000. Fax, (202) 463-5327. Thomas J. Donohue, Chief Executive Officer. Press, (202) 463-5682. Customer Service, (800) 638-6582.*
Web, www.uschamber.com

Federation of businesses; trade and professional associations; state and local chambers of commerce; and American chambers of commerce abroad. Sponsors programs on management, business confidence, small business, consumer affairs, economic policy, minority business, and tax policy. Monitors legislation and regulations.

U.S. Chamber of Commerce, *Congressional and Public Affairs, 1615 H St. N.W., 20062-2000; (202) 463-5600. Jack Howard, Senior Vice President.*
Web, www.uschamber.com

Advocates businesses' position on government and regulatory affairs. Monitors legislation and regulations on antitrust and corporate policy, product liability, and business-consumer relations.

U.S. Chamber of Commerce, *Economic Policy, 1615 H St. N.W., 20062-2000; (202) 463-5620. Fax, (202) 463-3174. Martin A. Regalia, Chief Economist. Web, www.uschamber.com/economic-policy*

Represents the business community's views on economic policy, including government spending, the federal budget, and tax issues. Forecasts the economy of the United States and other industrialized nations and projects the impact of major policy changes. Studies economic trends and analyzes their effect on the business community.

Coins and Currency

▶AGENCIES

Bureau of Engraving and Printing (BEP) *(Treasury Dept.), 14th and C Sts. S.W., 20228; (202) 874-4000. Fax, (202) 874-3177. Leonard R. Olijar, Director. Information, (877) 874-4114. Tours, (202) 874-2330. Web, www.moneyfactory.gov*

Designs, engraves, and prints Federal Reserve notes, military certificates, White House invitations, presidential portraits, and special security documents for the federal government. Provides information on history, design, and engraving of currency; offers public tours; maintains reading room where materials are brought for special research (for appointment, write to the BEP's Historical Resource Center).

Bureau of Engraving and Printing (BEP) *(Treasury Dept.), Mutilated Currency Division, 14th and C Sts. S.W., 20018 (mailing address: BEP/MCD, #344A, P.O. Box 37048, Washington, DC 20013); (202) 874 2141. Fax, (202) 874-4082. Tryst Hensell, Head, (202) 874-2131. Toll-free, (866) 575-2361. General email, mcdstatus@bep.gov Web, www.moneyfactory.gov*

Redeems U.S. currency that has been mutilated.

Bureau of the Fiscal Service *(Treasury Dept.), 401 14th St. S.W., #545, 20227; (202) 874-7000. Fax, (202) 874-6743. Sheryl Morrow, Commissioner. Public Affairs, (202) 874-6750. Savings Bonds, (800) 553-2663. Media and congressional inquiries, (202) 504-3535. Web, www.fiscal.treasury.gov, Buy and redeem securities online, www.treasurydirect.gov and Twitter, @FiscalService*

Prepares and publishes for the president, Congress, and the public monthly, quarterly, and annual statements of government financial transactions, including reports on U.S. currency and coins in circulation.

Federal Reserve System, *Board of Governors, 20th St. and Constitution Ave., N.W., 20551; (202) 452-3000. Fax, (202) 452-3819. Janet L. Yellen, Chair; Stanley Fischer, Vice Chair. Information (meetings), (202) 452-3204. Public Affairs, (202) 452-2955. Congressional Liaison, (202) 452-3003. Publications, (202) 452-3245. TTY, (202) 263-4869. General email, eric.j.kollig@frb.gov Web, www.federalreserve.gov*

Influences the availability of money as part of its responsibility for monetary policy; maintains reading room for inspection of records that are available to the public.

National Museum of American History *(Smithsonian Institution), Armed Forces History, National Numismatic Collection, 14th St. and Constitution Ave. N.W., 20013 (mailing address: P.O. Box 37012, MRC609, Washington, DC 20013-7012); (202) 633-3950. Ellen Feingold, Curator of Numismatic Collection. Web, http://americanhistory.si.edu/collections/numismatics*

Develops and maintains collections of ancient, medieval, modern, U.S., and world coins; U.S. and world currencies; tokens; medals; orders and decorations; and traditional exchange media. Conducts research and responds to public inquiries. Collection can be viewed online.

Treasury Dept., *1500 Pennsylvania Ave. N.W., #3330, 20220; (202) 622-2000. Fax, (202) 622-6415. Jacob J. Lew, Secretary, (202) 622-1100; Sarah Bloom Raskin, Deputy Secretary. Information, (202) 622-5500. Library, (202) 622-0990. TTY, (877) 304-9709. Press, (202) 622-2960. Web, www.treasury.gov*

Oversees the manufacture of U.S. coins and currency; submits to Congress final reports on the minting of coins or any changes in currency. Library open to the public by appointment.

Treasury Dept., *Treasurer of the United States, 1500 Pennsylvania Ave. N.W., #2134, 20220; (202) 622-0100. Rosie G. Rios, Treasurer. Web, www.treasury.gov/about/organizational-structure/ offices/Pages/Office-of-the-Treasurer.aspx*

Advises the secretary of the Treasury on matters relating to coinage, currency, and the production of other instruments issued by the United States. Serves as the national honorary director of the Savings Bond Program. Represents the department in public engagement efforts.

U.S. Mint *(Treasury Dept.), 801 9th St. N.W., 8th Floor, 20220; (202) 756-6468. Fax, (202) 756-6160. Rhett Jeppson, Deputy Director. Information, (202) 354-7227. Press, (202) 354-7222. Customer service, (800) 872-6468. TTY, (888) 321-6468. Web, www.usmint.gov and Twitter, @usmint*

Manufactures and distributes all domestic coins; safeguards the government's holdings of precious metals; manufactures and sells commemorative coins and medals of historic interest. Maintains a kiosk at its main building.

▶NONGOVERNMENTAL

Americans for Common Cents, *1301 K St. N.W., #600, East Tower, 20005-3364; (800) 561-7909. Fax, (202) 408-6399. Mark Weller, Executive Director. General email, info@pennies.org Web, www.pennies.org*

Educates policymakers and the public about the penny's impact on the economy. Monitors legislation and regulations to advocate keeping the one-cent coin in the U.S. monetary system.

Treasury Department

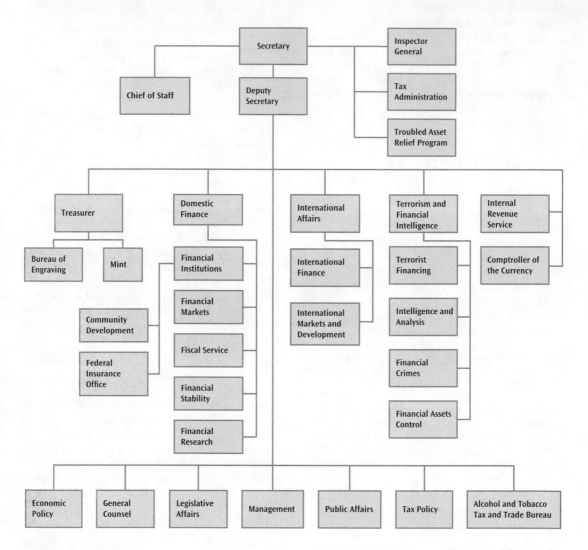

Federal Budget

▶AGENCIES

Bureau of the Fiscal Service *(Treasury Dept.),* 401 14th St. S.W., #545, 20227; (202) 874-7000. Fax, (202) 874-6743. Sheryl Morrow, Commissioner. Public Affairs, (202) 874-6750. Savings Bonds, (800) 553-2663. Media and congressional inquiries, (202) 504-3535.
Web, www.fiscal.treasury.gov, Buy and redeem securities online, www.treasurydirect.gov and Twitter, @FiscalService

Borrows to finance federal government operations by selling public debt securities, Treasury notes, and bonds; maintains all records on series EE and HH savings bonds.

Federal Financing Bank *(Treasury Dept.),* 1500 Pennsylvania Ave. N.W., 20220; (202) 622-2470. Fax, (202) 622-0707. Gary H. Burner, Chief Financial Officer. General email, ffb@do.treas.gov
Web, www.treasury.gov/ffb

Coordinates federal agency borrowing by purchasing securities issued or guaranteed by federal agencies; funds its operations by borrowing from the Treasury.

Office of Management and Budget (OMB) *(Executive Office of the President),* 725 17th St. N.W., 20503; (202) 395-3080. Fax, (202) 395-3888. Shaun Donovan, Director. Press, (202) 395-7254.
Web, www.whitehouse.gov/omb

Prepares president's annual budget; works with the Council of Economic Advisers and the Treasury Dept. to develop the federal government's fiscal program; oversees administration of the budget; reviews government regulations; coordinates administration procurement and management policy.

Treasury Dept., *Domestic Finance, Debt Management,* 1500 Pennsylvania Ave. N.W., #2417, 20220; (202) 622-1885. Fax, (202) 622-0244. Fred Pietrangeli, Director.

General email, Debt.Management@do.treas.gov

Web, www.treasury.gov/about/organizational-structure/offices/Pages/-Debt-Management.aspx

Provides financial and economic analysis on government financing and Treasury debt management. Coordinates, analyzes, and reviews government borrowing, lending, and investment activities. Determines interest rates for government borrowing and lending programs.

Treasury Dept., *Domestic Finance, Financial Market Policy,* 1500 Pennsylvania Ave. N.W., #5011, 20220; (202) 622-2000. Seth Carpenter, Assistant Secretary, Acting.
Web, www.treasury.gov/about/organizational-structure/offices/Pages/-Financial-Market-Policy.aspx

Provides analyses and policy recommendations on financial markets, government financing, and securities, tax implications, and related regulations.

Treasury Dept., *Domestic Finance, Policy and Legislative Review,* 1120 Vermont Ave. N.W., #916B, 20005; (202) 622-2450. Fax, (202) 622-0427. Paula Farrell, Director.
General email, policyandlegislativereview@do.treas.gov

Web, www.treasury.gov/about/organizational-structure/offices/Pages/-Office-of-Policy-and-Legislative-Review.aspx

Analyzes federal credit program principles and standards, legislation, and proposals related to government borrowing, lending, and investment. Furnishes actuarial and mathematical analysis required for Treasury market financing, the Federal Financing Bank, and other government agencies.

Treasury Dept., *Economic Policy,* 1500 Pennsylvania Ave. N.W., #3454, 20220; (202) 622-2200. Fax, (202) 622-2633. Karen Dynan, Assistant Secretary.
Web, www.treasury.gov/about/organizational-structure/offices/Pages/Economic-Policy.aspx

Assists and advises the Treasury secretary in the formulation and execution of domestic and international economic policies and programs; helps prepare economic forecasts for the federal budget.

►**CONGRESS**

For a listing of relevant congressional committees and subcommittees, please see pages 34–35 or the Appendix.

Congressional Budget Office, FHOB, 2nd and D Sts. S.W., 4th Floor, 20515-6925; (202) 226-2602. Fax, (202) 225-7509. Keith Hall, Director. Information, (202) 226-2600. Publications, (202) 226-2809.
Web, www.cbo.gov and Twitter, @USCBO

Nonpartisan office that provides the House and Senate with analyses needed for economic and budget decisions, and with the information and estimates required for the congressional budget process.

►**NONGOVERNMENTAL**

Committee for a Responsible Federal Budget, 1900 M St. N.W., #850, 20036; (202) 596-3597. Fax, (202) 478-0681. Maya MacGuineas, President.

General email, crfb@crfb.org

Web, www.crfb.org and Twitter, @BudgetHawks

Bipartisan nonprofit organization that educates the public about issues that have significant fiscal policy impact. Monitors legislation and regulation. (Affiliated with the New America Foundation.)

Concord Coalition, 1011 Arlington Blvd., #300, Arlington, VA 22209; (703) 894-6222. Fax, (703) 894-6231. Robert L. Bixby, Executive Director.
General email, concordcoalition@concordcoalition.org

Web, www.concordcoalition.org and Twitter, @ConcordC

Nonpartisan grassroots organization dedicated to educating the public about the causes and consequences of federal budget deficits, the long-term challenges facing America's unsustainable entitlement programs, how to build a sound foundation for economic growth, and ensuring that Social Security, Medicare, and Medicaid are secure for all generations.

Institute for Policy Studies, *Foreign Policy in Focus,* 1301 Connecticut Ave. N.W., #600, 20036; (202) 234-9382. Fax, (202) 387-7915. John Feffer, Co-Director.
General email, fpif@ips-dc.org

Web, www.fpif.org

Think tank that provides analysis of U.S. foreign policy and international affairs and recommends progressive policy alternatives. Publishes reports; organizes briefings for the public, media, and policymakers. Interests include climate change, global poverty, nuclear weapons, terrorism, and military conflict.

Statistics, Economic Projections

►**AGENCIES**

Bureau of Economic Analysis *(Commerce Dept.),* 1441 L St. N.W., #6006, 20230; (202) 606-9900. Fax, (202) 606-5311. Brian C. Moyer, Director. Press, (202) 606-2649.
General email, CustomerService@bea.gov

Web, www.bea.gov and Twitter, @BEA_NEWS

Compiles, analyzes, and publishes data on measures of aggregate U.S. economic activity, including gross domestic product; prices by type of expenditure; personal income and outlays; personal savings; corporate profits; capital stock; U.S. international transactions; and foreign investment. Provides statistics of personal income and employment by industry for regions, states, metropolitan areas, and counties. Refers specific inquiries to economic specialists in the field.

Bureau of Labor Statistics (BLS) *(Labor Dept.),* 2 Massachusetts Ave. N.E., #4040, 20212-0001; (202) 691-5200. Fax, (202) 691-7890. Erica Lynn Groshen, Commissioner, (202) 691-7800. Press, (202) 691-5902. TTY, (800) 877-8339.
General email, blsdata_staff@bls.gov

Web, www.bls.gov and Twitter, @BLS_gov

Provides statistical data on labor economics, including labor force, employment and unemployment, hours of work, wages, employee compensation, prices, living conditions, labor-management relations, productivity, technological developments, occupational safety and health, and structure and growth of the economy. Publishes reports on these statistical trends, including the *Consumer Price Index, Producer Price Index,* and *Employment and Earnings.*

Census Bureau *(Commerce Dept.), Economic Programs,* *4600 Silver Hill Rd., #8H132, Suitland, MD 20746 (mailing address: 4600 Silver Hill Rd., #8H132, Washington, DC 20233-6000); (301) 763-8842. Fax, (301) 763-8150.* *William G. Bostic Jr., Associate Director.* *Web, www.census.gov/econ*

Provides data and explains proper use of data on county business patterns, classification of industries and commodities, and business statistics. Compiles quarterly reports listing financial data for corporations in certain industrial sectors.

Census Bureau *(Commerce Dept.), Economy-Wide Statistics, 4700 Silver Hill Rd., #8K154, Suitland, MD 20746-2401 (mailing address: 4700 Silver Hill Rd., #8K154, Washington, DC 20233-6500); (301) 763-5170. Fax, (301) 735-8741. Kevin E. Deardorff, Chief.* *Web, www.census.gov/econ/economywide.html*

Provides data of five-year census programs on retail, wholesale, and service industries. Conducts periodic monthly or annual surveys for specific items within these industries.

Census Bureau *(Commerce Dept.), Manufacturing and Construction, Mining, 4600 Silver Hill Rd., Suitland, MD 20746 (mailing address: 4600 Silver Hill Rd., Washington, DC 20233); (301) 763-4750. Fax, (301) 763-8398.* *Edward Watkins, Chief.* *Web, www.census.gov/mcd*

Collects, tabulates, and publishes statistics for the mining and construction sectors of the Economic Census.

Council of Economic Advisers *(Executive Office of the President), Statistical Office, 725 17th St. N.W., 20502; (202) 395-5062. Fax, (202) 395-5630. Adrienne Pilot, Director.* *Web, www.whitehouse.gov/administration/eop/cea*

Compiles and reports aggregate economic data, including national income and expenditures, employment, wages, productivity, production and business activity, prices, money stock, credit, finance, government finance, agriculture, and international statistics.

Economic Research Service *(Agriculture Dept.), 355 E St. S.W., 20024-8221; (202) 694-5000. Fax, (202) 245-5467. Mary Bohman, Administrator; Greg Pompelli, Associate Administrator.* *General email, service@ers.usda.gov* *Web, www.ers.usda.gov*

Conducts market research; studies and forecasts domestic supply-and-demand trends for fruits and vegetables.

Federal Reserve System, *Monetary Affairs, 20th and C Sts. N.W., #B3022B, 20551; (202) 452-3327. Fax, (202) 452-2301. Thomas B. Laubach, Director.* *Web, www.federalreserve.gov/mastaff.htm*

Assists the Federal Reserve Board and the Federal Open Market Committee in the conduct of monetary policy, especially in the areas of finance, money and banking, and monetary policy design and implementation. Provides expertise on open market operations, discount window policy, and reserve markets.

Federal Reserve System, *Research and Statistics, 20th and C Sts. N.W., #B3048, 20551; (202) 452-3300. Fax, (202) 452-5296. David W. Wilcox, Director.* *Web, www.federalreserve.gov/econresdata/rsstaff.htm*

Publishes statistical data and analyses on business finance, real estate credit, consumer credit, industrial production, construction, and flow of funds.

Internal Revenue Service (IRS) *(Treasury Dept.), Statistics of Income, 1111 Constitution Ave. N.W., #K-4112, 20224 (mailing address: P.O. Box 2608, Washington, DC 20013-2608); (202) 803-9285. Fax, (202) 803-9393. Susan Boehmer, Director. Publications, (202) 874-0410.* *General email, sis@irs.gov* *Web, www.irs.ustreas.gov/uac/Tax-Stats-2*

Provides the public and the Treasury Dept. with statistical information on tax laws. Prepares statistical information for the Commerce Dept. to use in formulating the gross national product (GNP). Publishes *Statistics of Income,* a series available at cost to the public.

International Trade Administration (ITA) *(Commerce Dept.), Industry and Analysis, Trade Policy and Analysis, 1401 Constitution Ave. N.W., #21028, 20230; (202) 482-3177. Fax, (202) 482-4614. Praveen Dixit, Deputy Assistant Secretary, (202) 482-6232.* *Web, www.trade.gov/mas/ian/otpahome*

Analyzes international and domestic competitiveness of U.S. industry and component sectors. Assesses impact of regulations on competitive positions. Produces and disseminates U.S. foreign trade and related economic data. Supports U.S. international trade negotiations initiative.

National Agricultural Statistics Service *(Agriculture Dept.), 1400 Independence Ave. S.W., #5041, MS 2001, 20250-2001; (202) 720-2707. Fax, (202) 720-9013. Joseph T. Reilly, Administrator. Information, (800) 727-9540. Print reports, (800) 999-6779.* *General email, nass@nass.usda.gov* *Web, www.nass.usda.gov*

Prepares estimates and reports on production, supply, prices, and other items relating to the U.S. agricultural economy. Reports include statistics on field crops, fruits and vegetables, cattle, hogs, poultry, and related products. Prepares quinquennial national census of agriculture.

Securities and Exchange Commission (SEC), *Economic and Risk Analysis, 100 F St. N.E., 20549; (202) 551-6600. Fax, (202) 756-0505. Mark J. Flannery, Director.*

General email, DERA@sec.gov

Web, www.sec.gov/dera

Advises the SEC and its staff on economic issues as they pertain to the commission's regulatory activities. Publishes data on trading volume of the stock exchanges; compiles statistics on financial reports of brokerage firms.

U.S. International Trade Commission, *Industries, 500 E St. S.W., #504-A, 20436; (202) 205-3296. Fax, (202) 205-3161. Michael G. Anderson, Director, Acting, (202) 205-3380. Web, www.usitc.gov/research_and_analysis/office_industry.htm*

Identifies, analyzes, and develops data on economic and technical matters related to the competitive position of the United States in domestic and world markets in agriculture and forest production, chemicals, textiles, energy, electronics, transportation, services and investments, minerals, metals, and machinery.

►**CONGRESS**

Library of Congress, *Science, Technology, and Business, John Adams Bldg., 101 Independence Ave. S.E., #LA 508, 20540; (202) 707-5639. Fax, (202) 707-1925. Ron Bluestone, Chief. Business Reference Services, (202) 707-7934. Science Reference Services, (202) 707-6401. Technical reports, (202) 707 5655. Web, www.loc.gov/rr/scitech*

Offers reference service by telephone, by correspondence, and in person. Maintains a collection of more than 3 million reports on science, technology, business management, and economics.

►**NONGOVERNMENTAL**

American Statistical Assn., *732 N. Washington St., Alexandria, VA 22314-1943; (703) 684-1221. Fax, (703) 684-2037. Ronald Wasserstein, Executive Director. Toll-free, (888) 231-3473.*

General email, asainfo@amstat.org

Web, www.amstat.org

Membership: statistical practitioners in industry, government, and academia. Supports excellence in the development, application, and dissemination of statistical science through meetings, publications, membership services, education, accreditation, and advocacy.

Taxes and Tax Reform

►**AGENCIES**

Alcohol and Tobacco Tax and Trade Bureau (TTB) *(Treasury Dept.), 1310 G St. N.W., #300E, 20005; (202) 453-2250. John J. Manfreda, Administrator. Press, (202) 453 2180. TTY, (202) 882-9914.*

General email, alfd@ttb.gov

Web, www.ttb.gov

Enforces and administers revenue laws relating to firearms, explosives, alcohol, and tobacco.

Internal Revenue Service (IRS) *(Treasury Dept.), 1111 Constitution Ave. N.W., 20224 (mailing address from outside the U.S.: IRS International Accounts, Philadelphia, PA 19255-0725); (202) 622-5000. John A. Koskinen, Commissioner. Information and assistance, (800) 829-1040. Press, (202) 622-4000. TTY, (800) 829-4059. Phone from outside the U.S., (267) 941-1000. Fax from outside the U.S., (267) 941-1055. Information for businesses, (800) 829-4933. Identity theft hotline, (800) 908-4490. National Taxpayer Advocates helpline, (877) 777-4778.*

Web, www.irs.gov

Administers and enforces internal revenue laws and related statutes (except those relating to firearms, explosives, alcohol, and tobacco).

Internal Revenue Service (IRS) *(Treasury Dept.), Art Advisory Panel, 1111 Constitution Ave., #700, C:AP:SO: ART ATTN: AAS, 20004; (305) 982-5364. MariCarmen Quello, Director, Acting, (305) 982-5364. Web, www.irs.gov/Individuals/Art-Appraisal-Services*

Panel of twenty-five art professionals that assists the IRS by reviewing and evaluating taxpayers' appraisals on works of art valued at $50,000 or more involved in federal income, estate, and gift taxes.

Internal Revenue Service (IRS) *(Treasury Dept.), Passthroughs and Special Industries, Excise Tax Branch, 1111 Constitution Ave. N.W., #5314, 20224; (202) 317-3100. Stephanie Bland, Chief. Web, www.irs.gov*

Administers excise tax programs, including taxes on diesel, gasoline, and special fuels. Advises district offices, internal IRS offices, and general inquirers on tax policy, rules, and regulations.

Internal Revenue Service (IRS) *(Treasury Dept.), Taxpayer Advocate, 1111 Constitution Ave. N.W., #3031, 20224; (202) 622-6100. Fax, (202) 622-7854. Nina E. Olson, National Taxpayer Advocate. Toll-free, (877) 777-4778. TTY, (800) 829-4059. Web, www.irs.gov/uac/Taxpayer-Advocate-Service-At-a-Glance*

Helps taxpayers resolve problems with the IRS and recommends changes to prevent the problems. Represents taxpayers' interests in the formulation of policies and procedures.

Justice Dept. (DOJ), *Tax Division, 950 Pennsylvania Ave. N.W., #4141, 20530; (202) 514-2901. Fax, (202) 514-5479. Caroline D. Ciraolo, Assistant Attorney General, Acting, (202) 514-2901. Web, www.usdoj.gov/tax*

Acts as counsel for the Internal Revenue Service (IRS) in court litigation between the government and taxpayers (other than those handled by the IRS in the U.S. Tax Court).

Multistate Tax Commission, *444 N. Capitol St. N.W., #425, 20001-1538; (202) 650-0300. Gregory S. Matson, Director. General email, mtc@mtc.gov*

Web, www.mtc.gov

Membership: state governments that have enacted the Multistate Tax Compact. Promotes fair, effective, and efficient state tax systems for interstate and international commerce; works to preserve state tax sovereignty. Encourages uniform state tax laws and regulations for multistate and multinational enterprises. Maintains three regional audit offices that monitor compliance with state tax laws and encourage uniformity in taxpayer treatment. Administers program to identify businesses that do not file tax returns with states.

Treasury Dept., *Tax Policy,* 1500 Pennsylvania Ave. N.W., #3120, 20220; (202) 622-0050. Fax, (202) 622-0605. Mark J. Mazur, Assistant Secretary.
Web, www.treasury.gov/about/organizational-structure/offices/Pages/Tax-Policy.aspx

Formulates and implements domestic and international tax policies and programs; conducts analyses of proposed tax legislation and programs; participates in international tax treaty negotiations; responsible for receipts estimates for the annual budget of the United States.

Treasury Dept., *Tax Policy, International Tax Counsel,* 1500 Pennsylvania Ave. N.W., #3058, 20220; (202) 622-1782. Fax, (202) 622-2969. Robert Stack, Deputy Assistant Secretary.
Web, www.treasury.gov/about/organizational-structure/offices/Pages/Office-of-the-International-Tax-Counsel.aspx

Analyzes tax policies affecting businesses and international taxation. Negotiates tax treaties with foreign governments and participates in meetings of international organizations. Develops legislative proposals and regulations.

▶JUDICIARY

U.S. Tax Court, 400 2nd St. N.W., #134, 20217; (202) 521-0700. Michael B. Thornton, Chief Judge, (202) 521-0777.
Web, www.ustaxcourt.gov

Tries and adjudicates disputes involving income, estate, and gift taxes and personal holding company surtaxes in cases in which deficiencies have been determined by the Internal Revenue Service.

▶NONGOVERNMENTAL

American Enterprise Institute (AEI), *Economic Policy Studies,* 1150 17th St. N.W., #1100, 20036; (202) 862-5800. Fax, (202) 862-7177. Kevin Hassett, Director, (202) 862-7157.
Web, www.aei.org

Conducts research on fiscal policy and taxes. Sponsors events.

Americans for Tax Reform, 722 12th St. N.W., #400, 20005; (202) 785-0266. Fax, (202) 785-0261.
Grover G. Norquist, President.
General email, ideas@atr.org
Web, www.atr.org and Twitter, @taxreformer

Advocates reduction of federal and state taxes; encourages candidates for public office to pledge their opposition to income tax increases through a national pledge campaign.

The Brookings Institution, *Economic Studies,* 1775 Massachusetts Ave. N.W., 20036-2188; (202) 797-6000. Fax, (202) 797-6181. Ted Gayer, Director. Press, (202) 797-6105.
General email, escomment@brookings.edu
Web, www.brookings.edu/economics

Researches and analyzes U.S. tax policy; provides information to policymakers, journalists, and researchers.

Center on Budget and Policy Priorities, 820 1st St. N.E., #510, 20002; (202) 408-1080. Fax, (202) 408-1056.
Robert Greenstein, President.
General email, center@cbpp.org
Web, www.cbpp.org and Twitter, @CenterOnBudget

Research group that analyzes changes in federal and state programs, such as tax credits, Medicaid coverage, and food stamps, and their effect on low-income and moderate-income households.

Citizens Against Government Waste, 1301 Pennsylvania Ave. N.W., #1075, 20004; (202) 467-5300. Fax, (202) 467-4253. Thomas A. Schatz, President.
General email, membership@cagw.org
Web, www.cagw.org and Twitter, @GovWaste

Taxpayer watchdog group that monitors government spending to identify how waste, mismanagement, and inefficiency in government can be eliminated. Has created criteria to identify pork-barrel spending. Publishes the annual *Congressional Pig Book*, which lists the names of politicians and their pet pork-barrel projects. Monitors legislation and regulations.

Citizens for Tax Justice, 1616 P St. N.W., #200, 20036; (202) 299-1066. Fax, (202) 299-1065. Robert S. McIntyre, Executive Director.
General email, ctj@ctj.org
Web, www.ctj.org and Twitter, @taxjustice

Research and advocacy organization that works for progressive taxes at the federal, state, and local levels.

Federation of Tax Administrators, 444 N. Capitol St. N.W., #348, 20001; (202) 624-5890. Fax, (202) 624-7888.
Gale Garriott, Executive Director.
Web, www.taxadmin.org

Membership: tax agencies in the fifty states, plus New York City, Philadelphia, and the District of Columbia. Provides information upon written request on tax-related issues, including court decisions and legislation. Conducts research and sponsors workshops.

FreedomWorks, 400 N. Capitol St. N.W., #765, 20001; (202) 783-3870. Fax, (202) 942-7649. Adam Brandon, President. Toll-free, (888) 564-6273.
Web, www.freedomworks.org and Twitter, @FreedomWorks

Recruits, educates, trains, and mobilizes citizens to promote lower taxes, less government, and greater economic freedom. Maintains scorecards on members of the Senate and House based on adherence to FreedomWorks positions.

Institute on Taxation and Economic Policy, *1616 P St. N.W., #200, 20036; (202) 299-1066. Fax, (202) 299-1065. Matthew Gardner, Executive Director.*
General email, itep@itep.org

Web, www.itep.org and Twitter, @iteptweets

Research and education organization that promotes tax fairness and sustainability in federal, state, and local tax policy.

National Assn. of Manufacturers (NAM), *Tax and Domestic Economic Policy, 733 10th St. N.W., #700, 20001; (202) 637-3096. Fax, (202) 637-3182. Dorothy B. Coleman, Vice President, (202) 637-3077.*
Web, www.nam.org

Represents and advocates for manufacturers on federal tax and budget policies; acts as a spokesperson for manufacturers on fiscal issues in the media; works with the broader business community to advance pro-growth, pro-competitiveness tax policy; conducts conferences. Monitors legislation and regulations.

National Campaign for a Peace Tax Fund, *2121 Decatur Pl. N.W., 20008-1923; (202) 483-3751. Jack McHale, Executive Director. Toll-free, (888) 732-2382.*
General email, info@peacetaxfund.org

Web, www.peacetaxfund.org

Supports legislation permitting taxpayers who are conscientiously opposed to military expenditures to have the military portion of their income tax money placed in a separate, nonmilitary fund.

National Tax Assn., *725 15th St. N.W., #600, 20005-2109; (202) 737-3325. Fax, (202) 737-7308. W. Bareley Hildreth, Executive Director, (404) 413-0271.*
General email, natltax@aol.com

Web, www.ntanet.org

Membership: tax lawyers and accountants, academics, legislators, and students. Seeks to advance understanding of tax theory, practice, and policy, as well as other aspects of public finance. Holds conferences and symposiums, including the Annual Conference on Taxation. Publishes the *National Tax Journal.*

National Taxpayers Union, *Communications, 25 Massachusetts Ave. N.W., #140, Alexandria, VA 20001; (703) 683-5700. Peter Sepp, President; Nan Swift, Federal Affairs.*
General email, ntu@ntu.org

Web, www.ntu.org

Citizens' interest group that promotes tax and spending reduction at all levels of government. Supports constitutional amendments to balance the federal budget and limit taxes.

Tax Analysts, *400 S. Maple Ave., #400, Falls Church, VA 22046; (703) 533-4400. Fax, (703) 533-4444. Christopher Bergin, President. Customer Service, (800) 955-2444.*
General email, cservice@tax.org

Web, www.taxanalysts.com

Nonpartisan publisher of state, federal, and international tax news and analysis. Advocates tax reforms to develop tax systems that are fair, simple, and efficient. Provides publications to educate tax professionals and the public about tax reform.

The Tax Council, *600 13th St. N.W., #1000, 20005; (202) 822-8062. Fax, (202) 315-3413. Lynda K. Walker, Executive Director, (202) 414-1460.*
General email, general@thetaxcouncil.org

Web, www.thetaxcouncil.org

Organization of corporations concerned with tax policy and legislation. Interests include tax rate, capital formation, capital gains, foreign source income, and capital cost recovery. (Affiliated with the Tax Council Policy Institute [TCPI].)

Tax Executives Institute, *1200 G St. N.W., #300, 20005-3814; (202) 638-5601. Fax, (202) 638-5607. Eli J. Dicker, Executive Director, (202) 464-8354.*
General email, asktei@tei.org

Web, www.tei.org

Membership: accountants, lawyers, and other corporate and business employees dealing with tax issues. Sponsors seminars and conferences on federal, state, local, and international tax issues. Develops and monitors tax legislation, regulations, and administrative procedures.

Tax Foundation, *1325 G. St. N.W., #950, 20005; (202) 464-6200. Scott A. Hodge, President. Media, (202) 464-5120.*
General email, tf@taxfoundation.org

Web, www.taxfoundation.org

Membership: individuals and businesses interested in federal, state, and local fiscal matters. Conducts research and analysis and prepares reports on taxes and government expenditures. Advocates a simple, transparent, neutral, and stable tax policy.

Urban-Brookings Tax Policy Center, *Brookings Institution, 1775 Massachusetts Ave. N.W., 20036; Urban Institute, 2100 M St. N.W., 4th Floor, 20037; Fax, (202) 728-0232. Leonard Burman, Director. Brookings Institution Phone, (202) 797-6000. Urban Institute Phone, (202) 833-7200.*
Web, www.taxpolicycenter.org

Provides analysis of current and pending tax issues to policymakers, journalists, researchers, and citizens. (Joint venture of the Urban Institute and the Brookings Institution.)

CONSUMER PROTECTION

General

►AGENCIES

Civil Division *(Justice Dept.), Consumer Protection, 450 5th St. N.W., #6400, 20001; (202) 307-0066. Fax, (202) 514-8742. Michael Blume, Director.*
Web, www.justice.gov/civil/consumer-protection-branch

Consumer Product Safety Commission

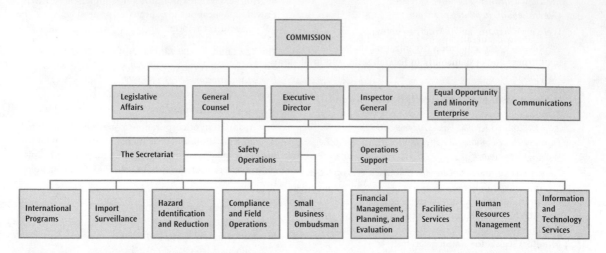

Enforces consumer protection statutes to protect health, safety, and economic security of consumers. Handles cases in the areas of pharmaceuticals and medical devices, deceptive trade practices and telemarketing fraud, food and dietary supplements, consumer product safety, odometer fraud, tobacco products, and civil defense litigation.

Comptroller of the Currency *(Treasury Dept.),* **Ombudsman,** *Constitution Center, 400 7th St. S.W., MS 10E-12, 20024; (202) 649-5530. Fax, (202) 649-5727. Larry L. Hattix, Ombudsman.* Web, www.occ.gov

Ensures that bank customers and the banks the agency supervises receive fair and expeditious resolution of their concerns.

Consumer Product Safety Commission (CPSC), *4330 East-West Hwy., #820, Bethesda, MD 20814; (301) 504-7923. Fax, (301) 504-0124. Elliott Kaye, Chair; Patricia Adkins, Executive Director, (301) 504-7907. Congressional Relations, (301) 504-7660. Product safety hotline, (800) 638-2772. TTY, (301) 595-7054. National Injury Information Clearinghouse, (301) 504-7921. Communications, (301) 504-7908. General email, info@cpsc.gov* Web, www.cpsc.gov *and Twitter, @USCPSC*

Establishes and enforces product safety standards; collects data; studies the causes and prevention of product-related injuries; identifies hazardous products, including imports, and recalls them from the marketplace.

Consumer Product Safety Commission (CPSC), **Communications,** *4330 East-West Hwy., #717, Bethesda, MD 20814-4408; (301) 504-7908. Fax, (301) 504-0862. Scott J. Wolfson, Director, (301) 504-7051. Product safety hotline, (800) 638-2772. TTY, (800) 638-8270. General email, info@cpsc.gov* Web, www.cpsc.gov

Provides information concerning consumer product safety; works with local and state governments, school systems, and private groups to develop product safety information and education programs. Toll-free hotline accepts consumer complaints on hazardous products and injuries associated with a product and offers recorded information on product recalls and CPSC safety recommendations.

Consumer Product Safety Commission (CPSC), *Small Business Ombudsman, 4330 East-West Hwy., Bethesda, MD 20814; (888) 531-9070. Will Cusey, Ombudsman, (301) 504-7833. TTY, (301) 595-7054. General email, sbo@cpsc.gov* Web, www.cpsc.gov

Provides guidance and advice to small businesses and small batch manufacturers about compliance with CPSC laws and regulations as well as technical assistance in resolving problems.

Federal Communications Commission (FCC), *Consumer and Governmental Affairs Bureau, 445 12th St. S.W., #5C758, 20554; (202) 418-1400. Fax, (202) 418-2839. Alison Kutler, Chief. TTY, (888) 835-5322. General email, cgbweb@fcc.gov* Web, www.fcc.gov/consumer-governmental-affairs

Develops and implements FCC policies, including disability access. Operates a consumer center that responds to consumer inquiries and complaints. Partners with state, local, and tribal governments in areas of emergency preparedness and implementation of new technologies.

Federal Deposit Insurance Corp. (FDIC), *Depositor and Consumer Protection, Consumer and Community Affairs, 1310 Court House Rd., #11060, Arlington, VA 22201; (877) 275-3342. Fax, (703) 254-0222. Elizabeth Ortiz, Deputy Director; Joni Cremean, Associate Director, Consumer Protection. Information, 877-ASK-FDIC. TTY, (800) 925-4618.*

General email, consumer@fdic.gov

Web, www.fdic.gov/about/contact/directory/index.
html#DDCP

Coordinates and monitors complaints filed by consumers against federally insured state banks that are not members of the Federal Reserve System; handles complaints concerning truth-in-lending and other fair credit provisions, including charges of discrimination on the basis of sex or marital status; responds to general banking inquiries; answers questions on deposit insurance coverage.

Federal Maritime Commission (FMC), *Consumer Affairs and Dispute Resolution Services,* *800 N. Capitol St. N.W., #939, 20573; (202) 523-5807. Fax, (202) 275-0059. Rebecca A. Fenneman, Director. Toll-free, (866) 448-9586. General email, complaints@fmc.gov*

Web, www.fmc.gov/bureaus_offices/consumer_affairs_
and_dispute_resolution_services.aspx

Provides ombudsman, mediation, facilitation, small claims adjudication, and arbitration services to assist shippers, carriers, marine terminal operators, and the shipping public to resolve commercial cargo shipping disputes. Provides assistance to cruise passengers to resolve disputes with cruise operators for cruises between the United States and international ports. Library open to the public (Monday through Friday, 8:00 a.m.–4:30 p.m.).

Federal Reserve System, *Consumer and Community Affairs,* *1709 New York Ave. N.W., 20006; (202) 452-2955. Fax, (202) 452-3849. Arturo Gonzalez, Chief, (202) 785-6024. Complaints, (888) 851-1920.*

Web, www.federalreserve.gov/econresdata/ccastaff.htm

Receives consumer complaints concerning truth-in-lending, fair credit billing, equal credit opportunity, electronic fund transfer, home mortgage disclosure, consumer leasing, and advertising; receives complaints about unregulated practices; refers complaints to district banks. The Federal Reserve monitors enforcement of fair lending laws with regard to state-chartered banks that are members of the Federal Reserve System.

Federal Trade Commission (FTC), *Bureau of Consumer Protection, Enforcement Division,* *400 7th Ave. S.W., CC-9423, 20024; (202) 326-2996. Fax, (202) 326-3197. James A. Kohm, Associate Director.*

Web, www.ftc.gov/about-ftc/bureaus-offices/bureau-
consumer-protection/our-divisions/division-enforcement

Enforces consumer protection, including advertising and financial practices, data security, high-tech fraud, and telemarketing and other scams. Coordinates FTC actions with criminal law enforcement agencies; litigates civil actions against those who defraud consumers; and develops, reviews, and enforces a variety of consumer protection rules.

Federal Trade Commission (FTC), *Consumer Protection,* *600 Pennsylvania Ave. N.W., #470, 20580; (202) 326-2148. Fax, (202) 326-3799. Jessica L. Rich, Director, (202) 326-2148. Complaint hotline, 877-FTC-HELP.*

Web, www.ftc.gov/about-ftc/bureaus-offices/bureau-
consumer-protection

Stops unfair, deceptive, and fraudulent business practices by collecting complaints and conducting investigations, suing companies and people that break the law, developing rules to maintain a fair marketplace, and educating consumers and businesses about their rights and responsibilities.

Federal Trade Commission (FTC), *Consumer Response Center,* *600 Pennsylvania Ave. N.W., #240, 20580; (202) 326-3075. Fax, (202) 326-2012. David Torok, Associate Director. Identity fraud report line, (877) ID-THEFT. Toll-free, (877) FTC-HELP. Do-Not-Call Registry, (888) 382-1222.*

Web, www.ftc.gov

Handles complaints about regulations dealing with unfair or deceptive business practices in advertising, credit, marketing, and service industries; educates consumers and businesses about these regulations.

Food and Drug Administration (FDA) *(Health and Human Services Dept.), External Affairs,* *10903 New Hampshire Ave., Bldg. 32, #5360, Silver Spring, MD 20993; (301) 796-4540. Fax, (301) 827-8030. Lisa Turner, Associate Commissioner. Consumer inquiries, (888) 463-6332.*

Web, www.fda.gov/AboutFDA/CentersOffices/OC/
OfficeofExternalAffairs/default.htm

Responds to inquiries on issues related to the FDA. Conducts consumer health education programs for specific groups, including women, older adults, and the educationally and economically disadvantaged. Serves as liaison with national health and consumer organizations.

General Services Administration (GSA), *USAGov,* *1800 F St. N.W., 20405; (202) 501-1794. Fax, (202) 357-0078. Sarah Crane, Director. Toll-free, (844) 872-4681.*

Web, www.publications.usa.gov and www.gobiernoUSA.gov
and www.gsa.gov/portal/category/101011

Manages the portal site to U.S. government information, www.usa.gov. Manages kids.gov, a resource that provides government information to younger Americans. Distributes free and low-cost federal publications of consumer interest via the Internet at www.publications.usa .gov, or when callers dial (888) 878-3256 for a catalog. Publishes the *Consumer Action Handbook*, a free resource that can be used online at http://consumeraction.gov or obtained when callers dial (888) 8-PUEBLO. Assists people with questions about American government agencies, programs, and services via telephone, (800) FED-INFO ([800] 333-4636), or Web site, http://answers .usa.gov. Operates a contact center to provide information in English or Spanish on all federal government agencies, programs, and services via toll-free telephone, email, and chat. Operated under contract by Sykes in Pennsylvania and Florida. Responds to inquiries about federal programs and services. Gives information about or referrals to appropriate offices. (Formerly Federal Citizen Information Center.)

National Institute of Standards and Technology (NIST) *(Commerce Dept.), Public Affairs,* *100 Bureau Dr., Stop*

1070, Gaithersburg, MD 20899-1070; (301) 975-6478. Fax, (301) 926-1630. Gail Porter, Director. TTY, (800) 877-8339.
General email, inquiries@nist.gov
Web, www.nist.gov

Responds to public and media inquiries concerning NIST.

Postal Regulatory Commission, *Public Affairs and Government Relations, 901 New York Ave. N.W., #200, 20268; (202) 789-6800. Fax, (202) 789-6891. Ann C. Fisher, Director.*
General email, prc-pagr@prc.gov
Web, www.prc.gov/offices/pagr

Supports public outreach and education and media relations; provides information for consumers and responds to their inquiries. Informal complaints regarding individual rate and service inquiries are referred to the Consumer Advocate of the Postal Service.

Securities and Exchange Commission (SEC), *Investor Education and Advocacy, 100 F St. N.E., 20549-0213; (202) 942-8088. Fax, (202) 772-9295. Lori Schock, Director, (202) 551-6500. Toll-free, (800) 732-0330.*
Web, www.sec.gov/oiea

Assists individual consumers in investing wisely and avoiding fraud. Provides a variety of services and tools, including publications on mutual funds and annuities, studies and recommendations concerning the evaluation of brokers and advisors, online calculators, and explanations about fees and expenses. Information is also available in Spanish.

Small Business Administration (SBA), *Capital Access, 409 3rd St. S.W., #8200, 20416; (202) 205-6657. Fax, (202) 205-7230. Ann Marie Mehlum, Associate Administrator. TTY, (800) 877-8339.*
Web, www.sba.gov/offices/headquarters/oca

Provides financial assistance to small business, including microloans, surety bond guarantees, investment, and international trade.

Transportation Dept. (DOT), *Aviation Consumer Protection, 1200 New Jersey Ave. S.E., 20590; (202) 366-2220. Norman Strickman, Director, (202) 366-5960. Air travelers with disabilities hotline, (800) 778-4838. TTY, (202) 366-0511.*
Web, www.dot.gov/airconsumer

Processes consumer complaints; advises the secretary on consumer issues; investigates air travel consumer rule violations; educates the public about air travel via reports and Web site.

Transportation Security Administration (TSA) *(Homeland Security Dept.), Contact Center, 601 S. 12th St., 7th Floor, Arlington, VA 20598; (866) 289-9673. Michelle Cartagena, Program Manager.*
General email, tsa-contactcenter@tsa.dhs.gov
Web, www.tsa.gov

Answers questions and collects concerns from the public regarding travel security.

Treasury Dept., *Public Affairs, 1500 Pennsylvania Ave. N.W., #3442, 20220; (202) 622-2960. Fax, (202) 622-2808. Victoria Esser, Assistant Secretary.*
Web, www.treasury.gov/about/organizational-structure/offices/Pages/Public-Affairs.aspx

Serves as the department's liaison to the media and public.

U.S. Postal Service (USPS), *Office of the Consumer Advocate, 475 L'Enfant Plaza S.W., #4100, 20260-0004; (202) 268-6308. Fax, (202) 636-5344. James A. Nemec, Vice President and Consumer Advocate, (202) 268-2681. Inquiries, (800) ASK-USPS or (800) 275-8777. TTY, (877) 889-2457.*
General email, usps_ca_response@usps.gov
Web, www.usps.com

Handles consumer complaints; oversees investigations into consumer problems; intercedes in local areas when problems are not adequately resolved; provides information on specific products and services; represents consumers' viewpoint before postal management bodies; initiates projects to improve the U.S. Postal Service.

► CONGRESS

For a listing of relevant congressional committees and subcommittees, please see pages 34–35 or the Appendix.

► NONGOVERNMENTAL

American National Standards Institute (ANSI), *1899 L St. N.W., 11th Floor, 20036; (202) 293-8020. Fax, (202) 293-9287. Joe Bhatia, President, (202) 331-3605.*
Web, www.ansi.org

Oversees norms and guidelines of many private sectors to strengthen the U.S. market position in a global economy; seeks to protect the health and saftey of consumers and the environment.

Call for Action, *11820 Parklawn Dr., #340, Rockville, MD 20852; (240) 747-0229. Fax, (240) 747-0239. Shirley Rooker, President; Eduard Bartholme, Executive Director.*
Web, www.callforaction.org

International network of consumer hotlines affiliated with local broadcast partners. Helps consumers resolve problems with businesses, government agencies, and other organizations through mediation. Provides information on privacy concerns.

Center for Auto Safety, *1825 Connecticut Ave. N.W., #330, 20009-5708; (202) 328-7700. Fax, (202) 387-0140. Clarence Ditlow, Executive Director.*
General email, accounts@autosafety.org
Web, www.autosafety.org

Public interest organization that receives written consumer complaints against auto manufacturers; monitors federal agencies responsible for regulating and enforcing auto and highway safety rules.

Consumer Financial Protection Bureau

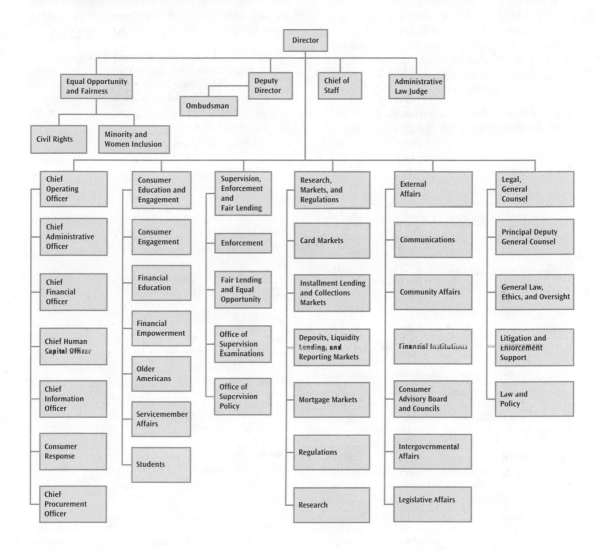

The Center for Consumer Freedom, *P.O. Box 34557, 20043; (202) 463-7112. Richard Berman, Executive Director.*
General email, info2consumerfreedom.com
Web, www.consumerfreedom.com and *Twitter, @consumerfreedom*

Membership: restaurants, food companies, and consumers. Seeks to promote personal freedom and protect consumer choices in lifestyle-related and health-related areas such as diet and exercise. Monitors legislation and regulations.

Consumer Federation of America, *1620 Eye St. N.W., #200, 20006; (202) 387-6121. Fax, (202) 265-7989. Stephen Brobeck, Executive Director. Press, (202) 737-0766. General email, cfa@consumerfed.org*
Web, www.consumerfed.org and *Twitter, @ConsumerFed*

Federation of national, regional, state, and local pro-consumer organizations. Promotes consumer interests in banking, credit, and insurance; telecommunications; housing; food, drugs, and medical care; safety; and energy and natural resources development.

Consumers Union of the United States, *Washington Office, 1101 17th St. N.W., #500, 20036; (202) 462-6262. Fax, (202) 265-9548. Martha Tellado, President; David Butler, Director, Acting, Washington Office. Web, www.consumersunion.org*

Independent, nonprofit consumer advocacy group that represents consumer interests before Congress; litigates consumer affairs cases involving government policy, corporate wrongdoing, and harmful products and services. Interests include health care, product safety, energy, government policies, privacy, and banking. Publishes *Consumer Reports* magazine. (Headquarters in Yonkers, N.Y.)

Council of Better Business Bureaus, *3033 Wilson Blvd., #600, Arlington, VA 22201-3843; (703) 276-0100. Fax, (703) 525-8277. Mary E. Power, President. Web, www.bbb.org/council and Twitter, @bbb_us*

Membership: businesses and Better Business Bureaus in the United States and Canada. Promotes ethical business practices and truth in national advertising; mediates disputes between consumers and businesses.

National Assn. of Consumer Advocates, *1215 17th St. N.W., 5th Floor, 20036; (202) 452-1989. Fax, (202) 452-0099. Ira J. Rheingold, Executive Director. General email, info@consumeradvocates.org Web, www.consumeradvocates.org*

Membership: consumer advocate attorneys. Seeks to protect the rights of consumers from fraudulent, abusive, and predatory business practices. Provides consumer law training through conferences and publications. Monitors legislation and regulations on banking, credit, and housing laws.

National Consumers League, *1701 K St. N.W., #1200, 20006; (202) 835-3323. Fax, (202) 835-0747. Sally Greenberg, Executive Director. General email, info@nclnet.org Web, www.nclnet.org, Twitter, @ncl_tweets and Facebook, www.facebook.com/nationalconsumersleague*

Advocacy group that engages in research and educational activities related to consumer and worker issues. Interests include fraud, privacy, child labor, product safety, and food and drug safety. Web resources include fakechecks.org, fraud.org, lifesmarts.org, sosrx.org, and stopchildlabor.org.

Public Justice Foundation, *1825 K St. N.W., #200, 20006; (202) 797-8600. Fax, (202) 232-7203. F. Paul Bland Jr., Executive Director, ext. 223; Arthur H. Bryant, Chair. Web, www.publicjustice.net and Twitter, @Public_Justice*

Membership: consumer activists, trial lawyers, public interest lawyers, and law professors and students. Litigates to influence corporate and government decisions about products or activities adversely affecting health or safety. Interests include toxic torts, environmental protection, civil rights and civil liberties, workers' safety, consumer protection, and the preservation of the civil justice system. (Formerly Trial Lawyers for Public Justice.)

SAFE KIDS Worldwide, *1301 Pennsylvania Ave. N.W., #1000, 20004-1707; (202) 662-0600. Fax, (202) 393-2072. Dana Points, Chair; Kate Carr, Chief Executive Officer. General email, kphillips@safekids.org Web, www.safekids.org and Twitter, @safekids*

Promotes awareness among adults that unintentional injury is the leading cause of death among children ages nineteen and under. Conducts educational programs on childhood injury prevention.

U.S. Chamber of Commerce, *Congressional and Public Affairs, 1615 H St. N.W., 20062-2000; (202) 463-5600. Jack Howard, Senior Vice President. Web, www.uschamber.com*

Monitors legislation and regulations regarding business and consumer issues, including legislation and policies affecting the Federal Trade Commission, the Consumer Product Safety Commission, and other agencies.

U.S. Public Interest Research Group (USPIRG), *218 D St. S.E., 1st Floor, 20003; (202) 546-9707. Fax, (202) 543-6489. Andre Delattre, Executive Director (in Boston), (312) 544-4436, ext. 203; Ed Mierzwinski, Consumer Program Director, ext. 314. General email, uspirg@pirg.org Web, www.uspirg.org and Twitter, @uspirg*

Conducts research and advocacy on consumer and environmental issues, including telephone rates, banking practices, insurance, campaign finance reform, product safety, and toxic and solid waste; monitors private and governmental actions affecting consumers; supports efforts to challenge consumer fraud and illegal business practices. Serves as national office for state groups.

Credit Practices

▶AGENCIES

Civil Division *(Justice Dept.),* **Consumer Protection,** *450 5th St. N.W., #6400, 20001; (202) 307-0066. Fax, (202) 514-8742. Michael Blume, Director. Web, www.justice.gov/civil/consumer-protection-branch*

Files suits to enforce the Truth-in-Lending Act and other federal statutes protecting consumers, generally upon referral by client agencies.

Comptroller of the Currency *(Treasury Dept.),* **Chief Counsel,** *Constitution Center, 400 7th St. S.W., 20506; (202) 649-5400. Fax, (202) 649-6077. Amy S. Friend, Senior Deputy Comptroller and Chief Counsel. Web, www.occ.gov*

Enforces and oversees compliance by nationally chartered banks with laws prohibiting discrimination in credit transactions on the basis of sex or marital status. Enforces regulations concerning bank advertising; may issue cease-and-desist orders.

Comptroller of the Currency *(Treasury Dept.),* **Compliance and Community Affairs,** *Constitution Center, 400 7th St. S.W., MS 7E512, 20024; (202) 649-5470. Grovetta Gardineer, Senior Deputy Comptroller. Web, www.occ.treas.gov*

Develops policy for enforcing consumer laws and regulations that affect national banks, including the Bank Secrecy (BSA/AML), Truth-in-Lending, Community Reinvestment, and Equal Credit Opportunity acts.

Comptroller of the Currency *(Treasury Dept.),* **Public Affairs,** *Constitution Center, 400 7th St. S.W., 20506; (202) 649-6870. Fax, (202) 874-5678. Paul M. Nash, Senior Deputy Comptroller; Robert M. Garsson, Deputy Comptroller, Public Affairs. Congressional Liaison, (202) 649-6440. Customer Assistance Group, (800) 613-6743.*

General email, publicaffairs3@occ.treas.gov

Web, www.occ.gov

http://helpwithmybank.gov

Advises the comptroller on banking industry relations, employee communicationns, congressional affairs, disclosure, media relations, minority affairs, and publishing.

Consumer Financial Protection Bureau (CFPB), *1275 1st St. N.E., 20002; (202) 435-7000. Fax, (855) 237-2392. Richard Cordray, Director. Toll-free, (855) 411-2372. RESPA enquiries, (855) 411-2372. TTY, (855) 729-2372.*

General email, info@consumerfinance.gov

RESPA email, cfpb_respaenquiries@consumerfinance.gov, Web, www.consumerfinance.gov and Twitter, @cfpb

An independent government agency created per the Dodd-Frank Act of 2010. Functions include implementing and enforcing federal laws pertaining to mortgages, credit cards, and other consumer financial products and services. Supervises bank and nonbank financial institutions for compliance with consumer financial protection regulations. Accepts consumer complaints about financial products and services. Administers regulations including the Truth in Lending Act (TILA), Real Estate Settlement Procedures Act (RESPA), Fair Debt Collection Practices Act (FDCPA), Electronic Fund Transfer Act (EFTA), and Equal Credit Opportunity Act (ECOA).

Federal Deposit Insurance Corp. (FDIC), *Depositor and Consumer Protection, 1776 F St. N.W., #F6074, 20429; (202) 898-7088. Fax, (202) 898-3909. Mark Pearce, Director.*

Web, www.fdic.gov/about/contact/directory/#DDCP

Examines and supervises federally insured state banks that are not members of the Federal Reserve System to ascertain their safety and soundness.

Federal Deposit Insurance Corp. (FDIC), *Depositor and Consumer Protection, Consumer and Community Affairs, 1310 Court House Rd., #11060, Arlington, VA 22201; (877) 275-3342. Fax, (703) 254-0222. Elizabeth Ortiz, Deputy Director; Joni Cremean, Associate Director, Consumer Protection. Information, 877-ASK-FDIC. TTY, (800) 925-4618.*

General email, consumer@fdic.gov

Web, www.fdic.gov/about/contact/directory/index. html#DDCP

Coordinates and monitors complaints filed by consumers against federally insured state banks that are not members of the Federal Reserve System; handles complaints concerning truth-in-lending and other fair credit provisions, including charges of discrimination on the basis of sex or marital status; responds to general banking inquiries; answers questions on deposit insurance coverage.

Federal Reserve System, *Consumer and Community Affairs, 1709 New York Ave. N.W., 20006; (202) 452-2955. Fax, (202) 452-3849. Arturo Gonzalez, Chief, (202) 785-6024. Complaints, (888) 851-1920.*

Web, www.federalreserve.gov/econresdata/ccastaff.htm

Receives consumer complaints concerning truth-in-lending, fair credit billing, equal credit opportunity, electronic fund transfer, home mortgage disclosure, consumer leasing, and advertising; receives complaints about unregulated practices; refers complaints to district banks. The Federal Reserve monitors enforcement of fair lending laws with regard to state-chartered banks that are members of the Federal Reserve System.

Federal Trade Commission (FTC), *Bureau of Consumer Protection, Financial Practices, 400 7th Ave. S.W., CC-10416, 20024; (202) 326-3224. Fax, (202) 326-3768. Malini Maithal, Associate Director, Acting.*

Web, www.ftc.gov/about-ftc/bureaus-offices/bureau-consumer-protection/our-divisions/division-financial-practices

Challenges unfair or deceptive financial practices, including those involving lending, loan servicing, debt negotiation, and debt collection. Enforces specific consumer credit statutes, including the Fair Debt Collection Practices Act, Equal Credit Opportunity Act, Truth-in-Lending Act, Credit Repair Organization Act, Home Ownership and Equity Protection Act, Electronic Fund Transfer Act, Consumer Leasing Act, Holder-In-Due-Course Rule, and Credit Practices Rule.

National Credit Union Administration (NCUA), *Consumer Protection, 1775 Duke St., Alexandria, VA 22314; (703) 518-1140. Fax, (703) 837-2460. Gail Laster, Director.*

General email, ocpmail@ncua.gov

Web, www.mycreditunion.gov/about-ncua/Pages/Office-of-Consumer-Protection.aspx and Consumer Assistance Center, www.mycreditunion.gov/consumer-assistance-center/Pages/default.aspx

Responsible for consumer financial protection compliance policy and rulemaking, fair lending examinations, and consumer financial literacy efforts. Administers the NCUA's Consumer Assistance Center for consumer inquiries and complaints.

National Credit Union Administration (NCUA), *Examination and Insurance, 1775 Duke St., Alexandria, VA 22314-3428; (703) 518-6360. Fax, (703) 518-6499. Larry D. Fazio, Director. Toll-free investment hotline, (800) 755-5999.*

General email, eimail@ncua.gov

Web, www.ncua.gov

Oversees and enforces compliance by federally chartered credit unions with the Truth-in-Lending Act, the Equal Credit Opportunity Act, and other federal statutes protecting consumers.

Small Business Administration (SBA), *Diversity, Inclusion, and Civil Rights, 409 3rd St. S.W., #6400, 20416; (202) 205-6750. Tinisha Agramonte, Associate Administrator. TTY, (800) 877-8339.*

Web, www.sba.gov/offices/headquarters/dicr

Reviews complaints based on disability against the Small Business Administration by recipients of its assistance in cases of alleged discrimination in credit transactions; monitors recipients for civil rights compliance.

▶NONGOVERNMENTAL

American Bankers Assn. (ABA), Communications, *1120 Connecticut Ave. N.W., 8th Floor, 20036; (202) 663-5315. Fax, (202) 663-7578. John Hall, Executive Vice President. Web, www.aba.com*

Provides information on a wide range of banking issues and financial management.

American Financial Services Assn. (AFSA), *919 18th St. N.W., #300, 20006-5517; (202) 296-5544. Fax, (202) 223-0321. Chris Stinebert, President. Press, (202) 466-8613. General email, info@afsamail.org*

Web, www.afsaonline.org

Trade association for the consumer credit industry. Focus includes government relations and consumer education. Monitors legislation and regulations.

National Assn. of Consumer Advocates, *1215 17th St. N.W., 5th Floor, 20036; (202) 452-1989. Fax, (202) 452-0099. Ira J. Rheingold, Executive Director. General email, info@consumeradvocates.org*

Web, www.consumeradvocates.org

Membership: consumer advocate attorneys. Seeks to protect the rights of consumers from fraudulent, abusive, and predatory business practices. Provides consumer law training through conferences and publications. Monitors legislation and regulations on banking, credit, and housing laws.

National Retail Federation, *1101 New York Ave. N.W., 20005; (202) 783-7971. Fax, (202) 737-2849. Matthew R. Shay, President; David French, Senior Vice President, Government Relations. Toll-free, (800) 673-4692. Web, www.nrf.com*

Membership: national and state associations of retailers and major retail corporations. Provides information on credit, truth-in-lending laws, and other fair credit practices.

Product Safety, Testing

▶AGENCIES

Consumer Product Safety Commission (CPSC), *4330 East-West Hwy., #820, Bethesda, MD 20814; (301) 504-7923. Fax, (301) 504-0124. Elliott Kaye, Chair; Patricia Adkins, Executive Director, (301) 504-7907. Congressional Relations, (301) 504-7660. Product safety hotline, (800) 638-2772. TTY, (301) 595-7054. National Injury Information Clearinghouse, (301) 504-7921. Communications, (301) 504-7908. General email, info@cpsc.gov*

Web, www.cpsc.gov and Twitter, @USCPSC

Establishes and enforces product safety standards; collects data; studies the causes and prevention of product-related injuries; identifies hazardous products, including imports, and recalls them from the marketplace.

Consumer Product Safety Commission (CPSC), Compliance and Field Operations, *4330 East-West Hwy., #610, Bethesda, MD 20814; (301) 504-7912. Jay Howell, Director, Acting, (301) 504-7621. Web, www.cpsc.gov*

Identifies and acts on defective consumer products; enforces industry compliance with safety standards for domestic and imported products; conducts enforcement litigation. Monitors recall of defective products and issues warnings to consumers.

Consumer Product Safety Commission (CPSC), Engineering Sciences, *5 Research Pl., Rockville, MD 28050; (301) 987-2036. Fax, (978) 367-9122. Joel R. Recht, Associate Executive Director. Web, www.cpsc.gov*

Develops and evaluates consumer product safety standards, test methods, performance criteria, design specifications, and quality standards; conducts and evaluates engineering tests. Collects scientific and technical data to determine potential hazards of consumer products.

Consumer Product Safety Commission (CPSC), Epidemiology, *4330 East-West Hwy., Bethesda, MD 20814-4408; (301) 504-7416. Fax, (301) 504-0081. Kathleen Stralka, Associate Executive Director, (301) 504-7416. Web, www.cpsc.gov*

Collects data on consumer product–related hazards and potential hazards; determines the frequency, severity, and distribution of the various types of injuries and investigates their causes; and assesses the effects of product safety standards and programs on consumer injuries. Conducts epidemiological studies and research in the fields of consumer-related injuries.

Consumer Product Safety Commission (CPSC), Hazard Identification and Reduction, *4330 East-West Hwy., #611, Bethesda, MD 20814-4408; (301) 504-7622. Fax, (301) 504-0038. George Borlase, Associate Executive Director. Web, www.cpsc.gov*

Establishes labeling and packaging regulations. Develops standards in accordance with the Poison Prevention Packaging Act, the Federal Hazardous Substances Act, the Consumer Products Safety Act, and the Consumer Products Safety Improvement Act.

Consumer Product Safety Commission (CPSC), Health Sciences, *4330 East-West Hwy., #600, Bethesda, MD 20814-4408; (301) 987-2240. Fax, (978) 967-8401. Alice Thaler, Associate Executive Director. Web, www.cpsc.gov*

Evaluates potential health effects and hazards of consumer products and their foreseeable uses and misuses, and performs exposure and risk assessments for product-related hazards.

Consumer Product Safety Commission (CPSC), Laboratory Sciences, *5 Research Pl., Rockville, MD 20850;*

Federal Deposit Insurance Corporation

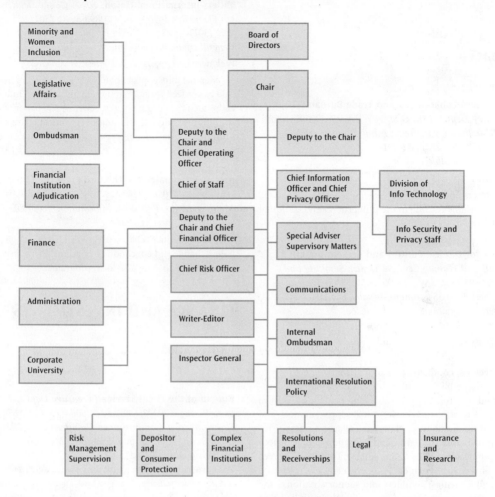

(301) 987-2037. Fax, (301) 427-1955. Andrew Stadnik,
Associate Executive Director.
Web, www.cpsc.gov

Conducts engineering analyses and testing of consumer products, supports the development of voluntary and mandatory standards, and supports the agency's compliance activities through product safety assessments.

National Injury Information Clearinghouse *(Consumer Product Safety Commission),* 4330 East-West Hwy., #820, Bethesda, MD 20814; (301) 504-7921. Fax, (301) 504-0025. Shoma Ramaswamy, Program Analyst. TTY, (301) 595-7054. To report consumer product-related accidents or injuries, (800) 638-2772.
General email, clearinghouse@cpsc.gov

Web, www.cpsc.gov/en/About-CPSC/National-Injury-Information-Clearinghouse/

Disseminates statistics and information relating to the prevention of death and injury associated with consumer products. Provides injury data from electronic data sources and distributes publications, including hazard analysis, special studies, and data summaries.

American Academy of Pediatrics, *Federal Affairs,* 601 13th St. N.W., #400N, 20005; (202) 347-8600. Fax, (202) 393-6137. Karen Remley, Executive Director. Information, (800) 336-5475.
General email, kids1st@aap.org

Web, www.aap.org

Promotes legislation and regulations concerning child health and safety. Committee on Injury and Poison Prevention drafts policy statements and publishes information on toy safety, poisons, and other issues that affect children and adolescents. (Headquarters in Elk Grove Village, Ill.)

Cosmetic Ingredient Review, 1620 L St. N.W., #1200, 20036-4702; (202) 331-0651. Fax, (202) 331-0088. Lillian Gill, Director.
General email, cirinfo@cir-safety.org

Web, www.cir-safety.org

Voluntary self-regulatory program funded by the Personal Products Council. Reviews and evaluates published and unpublished data to assess the safety of cosmetic ingredients.

Tobacco

Alcohol and Tobacco Tax and Trade Bureau (TTB) *(Treasury Dept.),* *1310 G St. N.W., #300E, 20005; (202) 453-2250. John J. Manfreda, Administrator. Press, (202) 453-2180. TTY, (202) 882-9914.*
General email, alfd@ttb.gov

Web, www.ttb.gov

Enforces and administers existing federal laws and tax code provisions relating to the production and taxation of alcohol and tobacco.

Centers for Disease Control and Prevention (CDC) *(Health and Human Services Dept.),* **Smoking and Health,** *395 E St. S.W., #9100, 20201; (202) 245-0550. Fax, (202) 245-0554. Simon McNabb, Senior Policy Adviser. Information, (800) 232-4636.*
General email, tobaccoinfo@cdc.gov

Web, www.cdc.gov/tobacco and Twitter, @CDCTobaccoFree

Develops, conducts, and supports strategic efforts to protect the public's health in the area of tobacco prevention and control. Funds, trains, and provides technical assistance to states, territories, tribal support centers, and national networks (e.g., National Tobacco Control Program); increases awareness and education about tobacco (e.g., publications, CDC's Smoking & Tobacco Use Web site, Tips from Former Smokers campaign, earned and digital media); conducts and supports national and international surveillance (e.g., National Youth Tobacco Survey, Global Tobacco Surveillance System).

Food and Drug Administration (FDA) *(Health and Human Services Dept.),* **Center for Tobacco Products,** *10903 New Hampshire Ave., Bldg. 75, Room G335, Silver Spring, MD 20993; (877) 287-1373. Mitch Zeller, Director.*
General email, askctp@fda.hhs.gov

Web, www.fda.gov/tobaccoproducts and Twitter, @FDATobacco

Regulates the manufacture, distribution, and marketing of tobacco products.

Action on Smoking and Health (ASH), *701 4th St. N.W., 20001; (202) 659-4310. Fax, (202) 289-7166. Laurent Huber, Executive Director.*
General email, info@ash.org

Web, www.ash.org

Educational and legal organization that works to protect nonsmokers from cigarette smoking; provides information about smoking hazards and nonsmokers' rights.

Bakery, Confectionery, Tobacco Workers, and Grain Millers International Union, *10401 Connecticut Ave., 4th Floor, Kensington, MD 20895-3940; (301) 933-8600. Fax, (301) 946-8452. David B. Durkee, President. General email, bctgmwebmater@gmail.com*

Web, www.bctgm.org and Twitter, @BCTGM

Membership: approximately 120,000 workers from the bakery, confectionery, grain miller, and tobacco industries. Helps members negotiate pay, benefits, and better working conditions; conducts training programs and workshops. Monitors legislation and regulations. (Affiliated with the AFL-CIO.)

National Campaign for Tobacco-Free Kids, *1400 Eye St. N.W., #1200, 20005; (202) 296-5469. Fax, (202) 296-5427. Matthew Myers, President. Information, (800) 803-7178. Web, www.tobaccofreekids.org*

Seeks to reduce tobacco use by children through public policy change and educational programs. Provides technical assistance to state and local programs.

FINANCE AND INVESTMENTS

General

Bureau of the Fiscal Service *(Treasury Dept.),* *401 14th St. S.W., #545, 20227; (202) 874-7000. Fax, (202) 874-6743. Sheryl Morrow, Commissioner. Public Affairs, (202) 874-6750. Savings Bonds, (800) 553-2663. Media and congressional inquiries, (202) 504-3535.*
Web, www.fiscal.treasury.gov, Buy and redeem securities online, www.treasurydirect.gov and Twitter, @FiscalService

Serves as the government's central financial manager, responsible for cash management and investment of government trust funds, credit administration, and debt collection. Handles central accounting for government fiscal activities; promotes sound financial management practices and increased use of automated payments, collections, accounting, and reporting systems.

Federal Deposit Insurance Corp. (FDIC), *Complex Financial Institutions, 1776 F St. N.W., #F-3080, 20429; (202) 898-3922. Fax, (202) 808-3800. Arthur J. Murton, Director.*
Web, www.fdic.gov/about/contact/directory/#OCFI

Reviews and oversees large bank holding companies and nonbank financial companies designated as systemically important by the Financial Stability Oversight Council. Implements orderly liquidations of such companies that fail.

Federal Reserve System, *Financial Stability Policy and Research, 20th and C Sts. N.W., #B2046, 20551; (202) 452-3000. Fax, (202) 263-4852. Bora Durdu, Chief, Financial and Macroeconomics Stability Studies; J. Nellie Liang, Director, (202) 452-2918.*
Web, www.federalreserve.gov/econresdata/fsprstaff.htm

Federal Reserve System

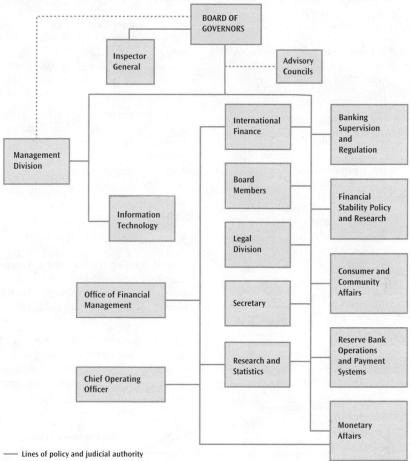

— Lines of policy and judicial authority
---- Lines of management and administrative authority

Identifies and analyzes potential threats to financial stability; monitors financial markets, institutions, and structures; and assesses and recommends policy alternatives to address these threats. Conducts long-term research in banking, finance, and macroeconomics.

►CONGRESS

For a listing of relevant congressional committees and subcommittees, please see pages 34–35 or the Appendix.

Government Accountability Office (GAO), *Financial Markets and Community Investment,* 441 G St N.W., #2440B, 20548; (202) 512-8678. Joan Holloway, Staff Assistant.
Web, www.gao.gov/careers/fmci.html

Supports congressional efforts to ensure that U.S. financial markets function smoothly and effectively, identify fraud and abuse, and promote sound, sustainable community investment by assessing the effectiveness of federal initiatives aimed at small businesses, state, and local governments, and communities.

►NONGOVERNMENTAL

Americans for Financial Reform, *1629 K St. N.W., 10th Floor, 20006; (202) 466-1885. Lisa Donner, Executive Director.*
General email, info@ourfinancialsecurity.org
Web, www.ourfinancialsecurity.org

Coalition of groups seeking to increase economic transparency and financial institution accountability. Analyzes economic public policies. Interests include protecting consumers, reducing large-bank bailouts, improving the Federal Reserve, regulating Wall Street, and limiting the influence of financial institutions on policy matters. Monitors legislation and regulations.

The Brookings Institution, *Economic Studies, 1775 Massachusetts Ave. N.W., 20036-2188; (202) 797-6000. Fax, (202) 797-6181. Ted Gayer, Director. Press, (202) 797-6105.*
General email, escomment@brookings.edu
Web, www.brookings.edu/economics

Sponsors economic research and publishes studies on domestic and international economics, macroeconomics, worldwide economic growth and stability, public finance, industrial organization and regulation, labor economics, social policy, and the economics of human resources.

Certified Financial Planner Board of Standards, *1425 K St. N.W., #800, 20005; (202) 379-2200. Fax, (202) 379-2299. Kevin R. Keller, Chief Executive Officer. Toll-free, (800) 487-1497.*
General email, mail@cfpboard.org
Web, www.cfp.net and Twitter, @CFPBoard

Grants certification to professional financial planners through education, examination, and regulation of industry standards. Publishes handbooks and newsletters to advance financial planning ethics and awareness.

Consumer Data Industry Assn., *1090 Vermont Ave. N.W., #200, 20005-4905; (202) 371-0910. Fax, (202) 371-0134. Stuart Pratt, President. Press, (202) 408-7406.*
General email, cdia@cdiaonline.org
Web, www.cdiaonline.org

Membership: credit reporting, mortgage reporting, and collection service companies. Provides information about credit rights to consumers. Monitors legislation and regulations.

Financial Executives International, *Government Affairs, 1825 K St. N.W., #510, 20006; (202) 626-7801. Fax, (973) 843-1222. Robert Kramer, Vice President, Government Affairs, (202) 626-7804.*
General email, rkramer@financialexecutives.org
Web, www.financialexecutives.org and Twitter, @FEINews

Membership: chief financial officers, treasurers, controllers, and other corporate financial managers involved in policymaking. Offers professional development opportunities through peer networking, career management services, conferences, teleconferences, and publications. Provides regulatory updates and continuing education on financial management and reporting, including Sarbanes-Oxley Act compliance. (Headquarters in Morristown, N.J.)

National Assn. of State Auditors, Comptrollers, and Treasurers, *Washington Office, 444 N. Capitol St. N.W., #234, 20001; (202) 624-5451. Fax, (202) 624-5473. Cornelia Chebinou, Washington Director.*
Web, www.nasact.org

Membership: elected and appointed state and territorial officials who deal with the financial management of state government. Provides information on financial best practices and research. Monitors legislation and regulations. (Headquarters in Lexington, Ky.)

National Disability Institute, *1667 K St. N.W., #640, 20006; (202) 296-2040. Michael Morris, Executive Director.*
General email, info@realeconomicimpact.org
Web, www.realeconomicimpact.org

Advocates public policies that address the economic interests of those with disabilities and their families.

Interests include tax education and preparation, asset development, financial education, and employment programs.

National Venture Capital Assn., *25 Massachusetts Ave. N.W., #730, 20001; (202) 864-5920. Fax, (202) 864-5930. Bobby Franklin, President; Ben Veghte, Vice President, Communications. Media, (202) 864-5923.*
General email, info@nvca.org
Web, www.nvca.org

Membership: venture capital organizations and individuals and corporate financiers. Promotes understanding of venture capital investment. Facilitates networking opportunities and provides research data on equity investment in emerging growth companies. Monitors legislation.

Banking

▶**AGENCIES**

Antitrust Division *(Justice Dept.), Networks and Technology Enforcement, 450 5th St. N.W., #7100, 20530; (202) 307-6200. Fax, (202) 616-8544. James J. Tierney, Chief.*
General email, antitrust.atr@usdoj.gov
Web, www.justice.gov/atr/about/ntes.html

Investigates and litigates certain antitrust cases involving financial institutions, including securities, commodity futures, computer hardware and software, professional associations, and high-technology component manufacturing; participates in agency proceedings and rulemaking in these areas; monitors and analyzes legislation.

Comptroller of the Currency *(Treasury Dept.), Constitution Center, 400 7th St. S.W., 20219; (202) 649-6800. Thomas J. Curry, Comptroller. Press, (202) 649-6870.*
General email, publicaffairs3@occ.treas.gov
Web, www.occ.treas.gov and Twitter, @USOCC

Charters and examines operations of national banks, federal savings associations, and U.S. operations of foreign-owned banks; establishes guidelines for bank examinations; handles mergers of national banks with regard to antitrust law. Ensures that national banks and savings associations operate in a safe and sound manner, provide fair access to financial services, treat customers fairly, and comply with applicable laws and regulations.

Comptroller of the Currency *(Treasury Dept.), Licensing, Constitution Center, 400 7th St. S.W., #3E-218, 20024; (202) 649-6260. Fax, (202) 649-5728. Stephen A. Lybarger, Deputy Comptroller.*
Web, www.occ.gov

Advises the comptroller on policy matters and programs related to bank corporate activities and is the primary decision maker on national bank corporate applications, including charters, mergers and acquisitions, conversions, and operating subsidiaries.

Comptroller of the Currency *(Treasury Dept.), Ombudsman, Constitution Center, 400 7th St. S.W., MS*

10E-12, 20024; (202) 649-5530. Fax, (202) 649-5727. *Larry L. Hattix, Ombudsman.*
Web, www.occ.gov

Ensures that bank customers and the banks the agency supervises receive fair and expeditious resolution of their concerns.

Federal Deposit Insurance Corp. (FDIC), *550 17th St. N.W., 20429; (703) 562-2222. Fax, (202) 898-3543. Martin J. Gruenberg, Chair. Press, (202) 898-6993. TTY, (800) 925-4618. Toll-free information, (877) 275-3342.*
Web, www.fdic.gov

Insures deposits in national banks and state banks. Conducts examinations of insured state banks that are not members of the Federal Reserve System.

Federal Deposit Insurance Corp. (FDIC), *Ombudsman, 3501 N. Fairfax Dr., #E-2022, Arlington, VA 22226; (703) 562-6049. Fax, (703) 562-6058. Cottrell L. Webster, Director. TTY, (800) 925-4618.*
Web, www.fdic.gov/about/contact/directory/#HQOO

An independent, neutral, and confidential source of assistance for the public. Provides answers to the public in the areas of depositor concerns, loan questions, asset information, bank closing issues, and any FDIC regulation or policy.

Federal Deposit Insurance Corp. (FDIC), *Resolutions and Receiverships, 3701 N. Fairfax Dr., #10072, Arlington, VA 22226; (202) 898-6525. Fax, (202) 898-6528. Bret Edwards, Director.*
Web, www.fdic.gov/about/contact/directory/#HQDRR

Plans, executes, and monitors the orderly and least-cost resolution of failing FDIC-insured institutions. Manages remaining liability of the federal savings and deposit insurance funds.

Federal Deposit Insurance Corp. (FDIC), *Risk Management Supervision, 550 17th St. N.W., #5036, 20429; (202) 898-6519. Fax, (202) 898-3638. Doreen R. Eberly, Director.*
Web, www.fdic.gov/about/contact/#HQDSC

Serves as the federal regulator and supervisor of insured state banks that are not members of the Federal Reserve System. Conducts regular examinations and investigations of banks under the jurisdiction of FDIC; advises bank managers on improving policies and practices. Administers the Bank Insurance Fund, which insures deposits in commercial and savings banks, and the Savings Assn. Insurance Fund, which insures deposits in savings and loan institutions.

Federal Housing Finance Agency (FHFA), *400 7th St. S.W., 20219; (202) 649-3800. Fax, (202) 649-1071. Melvin L. Watt, Director. Ombudsman, (888) 665-1474. Media, (202) 649-3700.*
General email, fhfainfo@fhfa.gov
Web, www.fhfa.gov

Regulates and works to ensure the financial soundness of Fannie Mae (Federal National Mortgage Assn.), Freddie Mac (Federal Home Loan Mortgage Corp.), and the eleven Federal Home Loan banks. FHFA was formed by a legislative merger of the Office of Federal Housing Enterprise Oversight (OFHEO), the Federal Housing Finance Board, and HUD's Government-sponsored Enterprise (GSE) mission team.

Federal Reserve System, *Banking Supervision and Regulation, 20th St. and Constitution Ave. N.W., 20551; (202) 973-6999. Michael Gibson, Director, (202) 452-2495.*
Web, www.federalreserve.gov/econresdata/bsrstaff.htm

Supervises and regulates state banks that are members of the Federal Reserve System; supervises and inspects all bank holding companies; monitors banking practices; approves bank mergers, consolidations, and other changes in bank structure.

Federal Reserve System, *Board of Governors, 20th St. and Constitution Ave., N.W., 20551; (202) 452-3000. Fax, (202) 452-3819. Janet L. Yellen, Chair; Stanley Fischer, Vice Chair. Information (meetings), (202) 452-3204. Public Affairs, (202) 452-2955. Congressional Liaison, (202) 452-3003. Publications, (202) 452-3245. TTY, (202) 263-4869. General email, eric.j.kollig@frb.gov*
Web, www.federalreserve.gov

Serves as the central bank and fiscal agent for the government. Examines Federal Reserve banks and state member banks; supervises bank holding companies. Controls wire system transfer operations and supplies currency for depository institutions.

Federal Reserve System, *Reserve Bank Operations and Payment Systems, 20th and C Sts. N.W., MS 190, 20551; (202) 452-2789. Fax, (202) 452-2746. Jeffrey C. Marquardt, Deputy Director.*
Web, www.federalreserve.gov/econresdata/rbopsstaff.htm

Oversees the Federal Reserve banks' provision of financial services to depository institutions and fiscal agency services to the Treasury Dept. and other federal agencies; provides support, such as information technology and financial cost accounting. Develops policies and regulations to foster the efficiency and integrity of U.S. payment systems; works with other central banks and international organizations to improve payment systems more broadly; and conducts research on payment issues.

National Credit Union Administration (NCUA), *1775 Duke St., Alexandria, VA 22314-3428; (703) 518-6300. Fax, (703) 518-6319. Deborah (Debbie) Matz, Chair. Information, (703) 518-6440. Media, (703) 518-6336. General email, consumerassistance@ncua.gov*
Web, www.ncua.gov, Twitter, @TheNCUA and Facebook, www.facebook.com/NCUAgov

Administers the National Credit Union Share Insurance Fund, which, with the backing of the full faith and credit of the U.S. government, operates and manages the National Credit Union, which insures the deposits of nearly 96 million account holders. Regulates all federally chartered credit unions; charters new credit unions; supervises and examines federal credit unions and insures their member accounts up to $250,000. Insures state-chartered credit unions that apply and are eligible. Manages the

Central Liquidity Facility, which supplies emergency short-term loans to members. Conducts research on economic trends and their effect on credit unions and advises the administration's board on economic and financial policy and regulations.

Office of Management and Budget (OMB) *(Executive Office of the President), Housing, Treasury, and Commerce,* 725 17th St. N.W., #9201, 20503; (202) 395-4516. Fax, (202) 395-6889. Mark Weatherly, Chief. Press, (202) 395-7254.
Web, www.whitehouse.gov/omb

Monitors the financial condition of deposit insurance funds including the Bank Insurance Fund, the Savings Assn. Insurance Fund, and the Federal Savings and Loan Insurance Corp. (FSLIC) Resolution Fund. Monitors the Securities and Exchange Commission. Has limited oversight over the Federal Housing Finance Board and the Federal Home Loan Bank System.

Securities and Exchange Commission (SEC), *Corporation Finance,* 100 F St. N.E., MS 4613, 20549; (202) 551-3100. Fax, (202) 772-9215. Keith F. Higgins, Director, (202) 551-3110.
Web, www.sec.gov/corpfin

Receives and examines disclosure statements and other information from publicly held companies, including bank holding companies.

Securities and Exchange Commission (SEC), *Economic and Risk Analysis,* 100 F St. N.E., 20549; (202) 551-6600. Fax, (202) 756-0505. Mark J. Flannery, Director.
General email, DERA@sec.gov
Web, www.sec.gov/dera

Provides the commission with economic analyses of proposed rule and policy changes and other information to guide the SEC in influencing capital markets. Evaluates the effect of policy and other factors on competition within the securities industry and among competing securities markets; compiles financial statistics on capital formation and the securities industry.

Treasury Dept., *Domestic Finance, Financial Institutions,* 1500 Pennsylvania Ave. N.W., #2326, 20220; (202) 622-2610. Fax, (202) 622-4774. Amias Gerety, Assistant Secretary, Acting.
Web, www.treasury.gov/about/organizational-structure/offices/Pages/Financial-Institutions.aspx

Advises the under secretary for domestic finance and the Treasury secretary on financial institutions, banks, and thrifts.

Treasury Dept., *Domestic Finance, Financial Institutions Policy,* 1500 Pennsylvania Ave. N.W., #1310, 20220; (202) 622-2000. Amias Gerety, Assistant Secretary, Acting.
General email, OFIP@treasury.gov
Web, www.treasury.gov/about/organizational-structure/offices/Pages/-Office-of-Financial-Institutions-Policy.aspx

Coordinates department efforts on all legislation and regulations affecting financial institutions. Develops

department policy on all matters relating to agencies responsible for supervising financial institutions and financial markets.

Treasury Dept., *Domestic Finance, Financial Stability,* 1500 Pennsylvania Ave. N.W., #2428, 20220; (202) 622-2000. Fax, (202) 622-6415. Timothy Massad, Assistant Secretary.
Web, www.treasury.gov/about/organizational-structure/offices/Pages/Financial-Stability.aspx

Seeks to normalize lending. Provides eligible financial institutions with capital assistance; administers mortgage modification programs. Manages the Troubled Asset Relief Program (TARP).

Treasury Dept., *Special Inspector General for the Troubled Asset Relief Program (SIGTARP),* 1801 L St. N.W., 20220; (202) 622-1419. Fax, (202) 622-4559. Peggy Ellen, Deputy Special Inspector General. Fraud, waste, and abuse hotline, 877-SIG-2009. Press, (202) 927-8940.
Web, www.sigtarp.gov

Conducts, supervises, and coordinates audits and investigations of the purchase, management, and sale of assets under the Troubled Asset Relief Program (TARP).

▶**CONGRESS**

For a listing of relevant congressional committees and subcommittees, please see pages 34–35 or the Appendix.

▶**NONGOVERNMENTAL**

American Bankers Assn. (ABA), 1120 Connecticut Ave. N.W., 20036; (202) 663-5000. Fax, (202) 663-7578. Rob Nichols, President. Information, 800-BANKERS.
General email, custserv@aba.com
Web, www.aba.com

Membership: commercial banks. Operates schools to train banking personnel; conducts conferences; formulates government relations policies for the banking community.

American Council of State Savings Supervisors, 1129 20th St. N.W., 9th Floor, 20036; (202) 728-5707. Thomas E. Harlow, Executive Director.
Web, www.acsss.org

Membership: supervisors and regulators of state-chartered savings associations; associate members include state-chartered savings associations and state savings banks. Trains state financial regulatory examiners. Monitors legislation and regulations affecting the state-chartered thrift industry.

American Institute of Certified Public Accountants, *Washington Office,* 1455 Pennsylvania Ave. N.W., 10th Floor, 20004-1081; (202) 737-6600. Fax, (202) 638-4512. Mark Peterson, Senior Vice President of Congressional and Public Affairs. Press, (202) 434-9266.
Web, www.aicpa.org

Establishes voluntary professional and ethical regulations for the profession; sponsors conferences and training workshops. Answers technical auditing and accounting questions. (Headquarters in Durham, N.C.)

Assn. for Financial Professionals, *4520 East-West Hwy., #750, Bethesda, MD 20814; (301) 907-2862. Fax, (301) 907-2864. James A. Kaitz, President.*
Web, www.afponline.org and Twitter, @AFPonline

Membership: more than 16,000 members from a wide range of industries throughout all stages of their careers in various aspects of treasury and financial management. Acts as a resource for continuing education, financial tools and publications, career development, certifications, research, representation to legislators and regulators, and the development of industry standards.

BAFT, *1120 Connecticut Ave. N.W., 5th Floor, 20036-3902; (202) 663-7575. Fax, (202) 663-5538. Tod R. Burwell, Chief Executive Officer.*
General email, info@baft-ifsa.com
Web, www.baft.org

Membership: international financial services providers, including U.S. and non-U.S. commercial banks, financial services companies, and suppliers with major international operations. Interests include international trade, trade finance, payments, compliance, asset servicing, and transaction banking. Monitors and acts as advocate globally on activities that affect the business of commercial and international banks and nonfinancial companies. (Formerly Bankers' Assn. for Financial Trade.)

Conference of State Bank Supervisors, *1129 20th St. N.W., 9th Floor, 20036; (202) 296-2840. Fax, (202) 296-1928. John Ryan, President, (202) 728-5724.*
Web, www.csbs.org

Membership: state officials responsible for supervision of state-chartered banking institutions. Conducts educational programs. Monitors legislation and regulations.

Consumer Bankers Assn., *1225 Eye St. N.W., #550, 20005; (202) 552-6380. Richard Hunt, President, (202) 552-6382. Media, (703) 869-1246.*
Web, www.cbanet.org and Twitter, @ConsumerBankers

Membership: federally insured financial institutions. Provides information on retail banking, including industry trends. Operates the Graduate School of Retail Bank Management to train banking personnel; conducts research and analysis on retail banking trends; sponsors conferences.

Credit Union National Assn., *Washington Office, South Bldg., 601 Pennsylvania Ave. N.W., #600, 20004-2601; (202) 638-5777. Fax, (202) 638-7734. Jim Nussle, President.*
Web, www.cuna.org

Confederation of credit unions from every state, the District of Columbia, and Puerto Rico. Represents federal and state chartered credit unions. Monitors legislation and regulations. (Headquarters in Madison, Wisc.)

Electronic Funds Transfer Assn., *4000 Legato Rd., #1100, Fairfax, VA 22033; (571) 318-5556. Fax, (571) 318-5557. Kurt Helwig, President, (571) 318-5555.*
Web, www.efta.org

Membership: financial institutions, electronic funds transfer hardware and software providers, automatic teller machine networks, and others engaged in electronic commerce. Promotes electronic payments and commerce technologies; sponsors industry analysis. Monitors legislation and regulations.

Employee Benefit Research Institute, *1100 13th St. N.W., #878, 20005; (202) 659-0670. Fax, (202) 775-6312. Harry Conaway, President.*
General email, info@ebri.org
Web, www.ebri.org

Research institute that focuses on economic security and employee benefit issues. Seeks to raise public awareness about long-term personal financial independence and encourage retirement savings. Does not lobby and does not take public policy positions.

Financial Services Roundtable, *600 13th St. N.W., #400, 20005; (202) 289-4322. Fax, (202) 628-2507. Tim Pawlenty, Chief Executive Officer; Eric Hoplin, Executive Director.*
General email, info@fsroundtable.org
Web, www.fsroundtable.org and Twitter, @FSRoundtable

Membership: one hundred integrated financial services companies. Provides banking, insurance, investment products, and services to American consumers.

Independent Community Bankers of America, *1615 L St. N.W., #900, 20036; (202) 659-8111. Fax, (202) 659-3604. Camden Fine, President. Information, (800) 422-8439.*
General email, info@icba.org
Web, www.icba.org

Membership: medium-sized and smaller community banks. Interests include farm credit, deregulation, interstate banking, deposit insurance, and financial industry standards.

Mortgage Bankers Assn., *1919 M St. N.W., 5th Floor, 20036; (202) 557-2700. Fax, (202) 408-4961. David H. Stevens, President. Information, (800) 793-6222.*
Web, www.mba.org, Twitter, @MBAMortgage and Facebook, www.facebook.com/mbamortgage

Membership: institutions involved in real estate finance. Maintains School of Mortgage Banking and sponsors educational seminars; collects statistics on the industry.

NACHA: The Electronic Payments Assn., *2550 Wasser Terrace, #400, Herndon, VA 20171; (703) 561-1100. Fax, (703) 787-0996. Janet O. Estep, President.*
General email, info@nacha.org
Web, www.nacha.org

Membership: ACH Network participants. Supports ACH Network growth by managing its development, administration, and governance. Facilitates the expansion and diversification of electronic payments, supporting Direct Deposit and Direct Payment via ACH transactions, including credit and debit transactions; recurring and one-time payments; government, consumer, and business-to-business transactions; international payments; and payments plus payment-related information. Develops operating rules and business practices through its

Securities and Exchange Commission

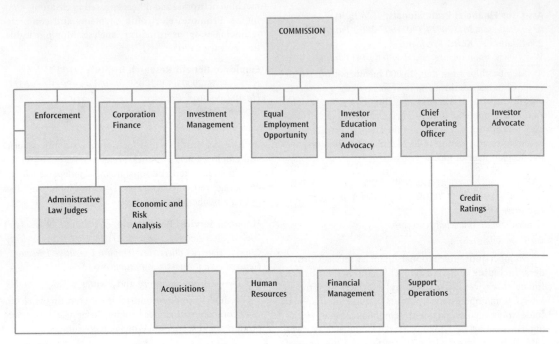

collaborative, self-regulatory model. Sponsors workshops and seminars. (Formerly the National Automated Clearing House Assn.)

National Assn. of Federal Credit Unions (NAFCU), *3138 10th St. North, Arlington, VA 22201-2149; (703) 842-2240. Fax, (703) 522-2734. B. Dan Berger, President. Web, www.nafcu.org*

Membership: federally chartered credit unions. Issues legislative and regulatory alerts for members and consumers. Sponsors briefings on current financial trends, legislation and regulations, and management techniques.

National Assn. of State Credit Union Supervisors, *1655 N. Fort Myer Dr., #650, Arlington, VA 22209-3113; (703) 528-8351. Fax, (703) 528-3248. Lucy Ito, Chief Executive Officer. General email, offices@nascus.org Web, www.nascus.org*

Membership: state credit union supervisors, state-chartered credit unions, and credit union leagues. Interests include state regulatory systems; conducts educational programs for examiners.

National Bankers Assn., *1513 P St. N.W., 20005; (202) 588-5432. Fax, (202) 588-5443. Michael A. Grant, President. Web, www.nationalbankers.org*

Membership: minority-owned and women-owned financial institutions. Monitors legislation and regulations.

National Society of Accountants, *1330 Braddock Pl., #540, Alexandria, VA 22314; (703) 549-6400. Fax, (703) 549-2984. John G. Ams, Executive Vice President, ext. 1313. Toll-free, (800) 966-6679. General email, members@nsacct.org Web, www.nsacct.org*

Seeks to improve the accounting profession and to enhance the status of individual practitioners. Sponsors seminars and correspondence courses on accounting, auditing, business law, and estate planning; monitors legislation and regulations affecting accountants and their small-business clients.

Transparency International USA, *1023 15th St. N.W., #300, 20005; (202) 589-1616. Fax, (202) 589-1512. Claudia J. Damas, President. General email, administration@transparency-usa.org Web, www.transparency-usa.org*

Seeks to curb corruption in international transactions. Promotes reform of government, business, and development assistance transactions through effective anti-corruption laws and policies. (Headquarters in Berlin, Germany.)

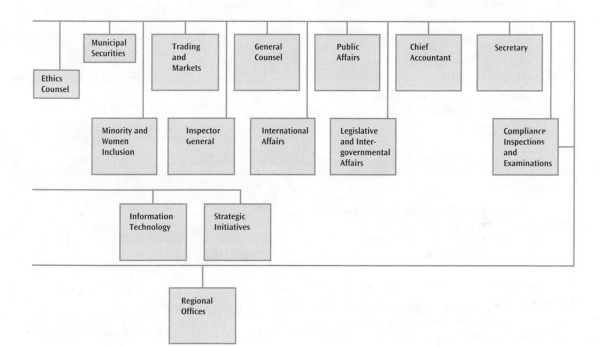

Stocks, Bonds, and Securities

▶AGENCIES

Bureau of the Fiscal Service *(Treasury Dept.),*
Legislative and Public Affairs, 401 14th St. S.W., 5th
Floor, 20227; (202) 504-3502. Fax, (202) 874-7016.
Joyce Harris, Director.
Web, www.treasurydirect.gov and www.fiscal.treasury.gov

Plans, develops, and implements communication
regarding Treasury securities.

Federal Reserve System, *Board of Governors,* 20th St.
and Constitution Ave., N.W., 20551; (202) 452-3000.
Fax, (202) 452-3819. Janet L. Yellen, Chair; Stanley Fischer,
Vice Chair. Information (meetings), (202) 452-3204. Public
Affairs, (202) 452-2955. Congressional Liaison, (202) 452-
3003. Publications, (202) 452-3245. TTY, (202) 263-4869.
General email, eric.j.kollig@frb.gov
Web, www.federalreserve.gov

Regulates amount of credit that may be extended and
maintained on certain securities in order to prevent excessive use of credit for purchase or carrying of securities.

Securities and Exchange Commission (SEC), *100 F St.*
N.E., 20549; (202) 551-5410. Fax, (202) 772-9200. Mary
Jo White, Chair, (202) 551-2100. Press, (202) 551-4120.
Investor Information and Complaints, (202) 551-6551.

Toll-free, (800) 732-0330. Legislative and
Intergovernmental Affairs, (202) 551-2010. Library, (202)
551-8090. Personnel locator, (202) 551-6000. TTY, (800)
877-8339.
Web, www.sec.gov

Requires public disclosure of financial and other information about companies whose securities are offered
for public sale, traded on exchanges, or traded over the
counter; issues and enforces regulations to prevent fraud
in securities markets and investigates securities frauds and
violations; supervises operations of stock exchanges and
activities of securities dealers, investment advisers, and
investment companies; regulates purchase and sale of
securities; participates in bankruptcy proceedings involving
publicly held companies; has some jurisdiction over municipal securities trading. Public Reference Section makes available corporation reports and statements filed with the SEC.
The information is available via the Web (www.sec.gov/
edgar.shtml). Library open to the public by appointment.

Securities and Exchange Commission (SEC), *Compliance*
Inspections and Examinations, 100 F St. N.E., 20549;
(202) 551-6200. Marc Wyatt, Director.
Web, www.sec.gov/ocie/Article/about.html

Analyzes data and conducts examinations in order to
ensure compliance with federal security laws, identify and
monitor risks, improve industry practices, and to prevent
fraud.

Securities and Exchange Commission (SEC), *Economic and Risk Analysis,* *100 F St. N.E., 20549; (202) 551-6600. Fax, (202) 756-0505. Mark J. Flannery, Director.*
General email, DERA@sec.gov

Web, www.sec.gov/dera

Provides the commission with economic analyses of proposed rule and policy changes and other information to guide the SEC in influencing capital markets. Evaluates the effect of policy and other factors on competition within the securities industry and among competing securities markets; compiles financial statistics on capital formation and the securities industry.

Securities and Exchange Commission (SEC), *Investor Advocate,* *100 F St. N.E., 20549; (202) 551-3302. Rick Fleming, Director.*
Web, www.sec.gov/investorad

Considers investors' interests in policymaking; addresses complaints from retail investors concerning the commission; studies investor behavior.

Securities and Exchange Commission (SEC), *Office of the Whistleblower,* *100 F St. N.E., MS 5628, 20549; (202) 551-4790. Fax, (703) 813-9322. Sean McKessy, Chief.*
Web, www.sec.gov/whistleblower

Receives information about possible securities law violations and provides information about the whistleblower program.

Securities and Exchange Commission (SEC), *Trading and Markets,* *100 F St. N.E., 20549; (202) 551-5777. Fax, (202) 772-9273. Stephen Luparaello, Director, (202) 551-5500.*
General email, tradingandmarkets@sec.gov

Web, www.sec.gov/tm

Oversees and regulates the operations of securities exchanges, the Financial Industry Regulatory Authority (FINRA), nationally recognized statistical rating organizations, brokers-dealers, clearing agencies, transfer agents, alternative trading systems, large traders, security-based swap dealers, security futures product exchanges, and securities information processors. Promotes the establishment of a national system for clearing and settling securities transactions. Facilitates the development of a national market system.

Treasury Dept., *Domestic Finance, Financial Market Policy,* *1500 Pennsylvania Ave. N.W., #5011, 20220; (202) 622-2000. Seth Carpenter, Assistant Secretary, Acting.*
Web, www.treasury.gov/about/organizational-structure/offices/Pages/-Financial-Market-Policy.aspx

Provides analyses and policy recommendations on financial markets, government financing, and securities, tax implications, and related regulations.

▶**NONGOVERNMENTAL**

Council of Institutional Investors, *888 17th St. N.W., #500, 20006; (202) 822-0800. Fax, (202) 822-0801. Ken Bertsch, Executive Director.*
Web, www.cii.org and Twitter, @InfoCil

Membership: pension funds and other employee benefit funds, foundations, and endowments. Studies investment issues that affect pension plan assets. Focuses on corporate governance and shareholder rights. Monitors legislation and regulations.

Financial Industry Regulatory Authority (FINRA), *1735 K St. N.W., 20006-1506; (202) 728-8000. Fax, (202) 728-8075. Richard G. Ketchum, Chief Executive Officer. Member services, (301) 590-6500. Public disclosure, (800) 289-9999.*
Web, www.finra.org and Twitter, @FINRA_News

Membership: investment brokers and dealers authorized to conduct transactions of the investment banking and securities business under federal and state laws. Serves as the self-regulatory mechanism in the over-the-counter securities market. Operates speakers bureau. (Formerly the National Assn. of Securities Dealers.)

Futures Industry Assn. (FIA), *2001 Pennsylvania Ave. N.W., #600, 20006; (202) 466-5460. Fax, (202) 296-3184. Walter L. Lukken, President.*
General email, info@fia.org

Web, www.fia.org and Twitter, @FIAAmericas

Membership: futures commission merchants, introducing brokers, exchanges, clearinghouses, and others interested in derivative markets. Serves as a forum for discussion of industry issues; engages in regulatory and legislative advocacy; provides market information and statistical data; offers educational programs; works to establish professional and ethical standards for members.

Intercontinental Exchange, *Washington Office,* *801 Pennsylvania Ave. N.W., #630, 20004-2685; (202) 347-4300. Fax, (202) 347-4372. Alex Albert, Vice President.*
Web, www.intercontinentalexchange.com

Provides information about risk management services to market participants around the world. Washington office monitors legislation and regulations. (Headquarters in Atlanta, Ga.)

Investment Company Institute, *1401 H St. N.W., #1200, 20005-2148; (202) 326-5800. Fax, (202) 326-5899. Paul Schott Stevens, President.*
General email, matthew.beck@ici.org

Web, www.ici.org

Membership: mutual funds, exchange-traded funds, and closed-end funds registered under the Investment Company Act of 1940 (including investment advisers to and underwriters of such companies) and the unit investment trust industry. Conducts research and disseminates information on issues affecting mutual funds.

Investor Protection Trust, *1020 19th St. N.W., #890, 20036; (202) 775-2112. Don M. Blandin, President.*
General email, iptinfo@investorprotection.org

Web, www.investorprotection.org

Provides noncommercial investment information to consumers to help them make informed investment decisions. Serves as an independent source of noncommercial investor education materials. Operates programs under its own auspices and uses grants to underwrite important initiatives carried out by other organizations.

Municipal Securities Rulemaking Board, *1300 Eye St. N.W., #1000, 20005; (202) 838-1500. Fax, (202) 898-1500. Lynnette Kelly, Executive Director.*
Web, www.msrb.org

Congressionally chartered self-regulatory organization for the municipal securities market. Regulates municipal securities dealers and municipal advisers and seeks to provide market transparency through the Electronic Municipal Market Access Web site. Conducts education and outreach. Subject to oversight by the Securities and Exchange Commission.

National Assn. of Bond Lawyers, *601 13th St., #800-S, 20005-3875; (202) 503-3300. Fax, (202) 637-0217. Linda H. Wyman, Chief Operating Officer.*
General email, nabl@nabl.org
Web, www.nabl.org

Membership: state and municipal finance lawyers. Educates members and others on the law relating to state and municipal bonds and other obligations. Provides advice and comment at the federal, state, and local levels on legislation, regulations, rulings, and court and administrative proceedings regarding public obligations.

National Assn. of Real Estate Investment Trusts, *1875 Eye St. N.W., #600, 20006-5413; (202) 739-9400. Fax, (202) 739-9401. Steven Wechsler, President. Toll-free, (800) 362-7348.*
Web, www.reit.com

Membership: real estate investment trusts and corporations, partnerships, and individuals interested in real estate securities and the industry. Interests include federal taxation, securities regulation, financial standards and reporting standards and ethics, and housing and education; compiles industry statistics. Monitors federal and state legislation and regulations.

National Investor Relations Institute, *225 Reinekers Lane, #560, Alexandria, VA 22314; (703) 562-7700. Fax, (703) 562-7701. James M. Cudahy, President.*
Web, www.niri.org

Membership: executives engaged in investor relations and financial communications. Provides publications, educational training sessions, and research on investor relations for members; offers conferences and workshops; maintains job placement and referral services for members.

North American Securities Administrators Assn., *750 1st St. N.E., #1140, 20002; (202) 737-0900. Fax, (202) 783-3571. Joseph Brady, Executive Director.*
Web, www.nasaa.org

Membership: state, provincial, and territorial securities administrators of the United States, Canada, and Mexico. Serves as the national representative of the state agencies responsible for investor protection. Works to prevent fraud in securities markets and provides a national forum to increase the efficiency and uniformity of state regulation of capital markets. Operates the Central Registration

Depository, a nationwide computer link for agent registration and transfers, in conjunction with the National Assn. of Securities Dealers. Monitors legislation and regulations.

Private Equity Growth Capital Council (PEGCC), *799 9th St. N.W., #200, 20001; (202) 465-7700. Fax, (202) 639-0209. Vacant, President; James Maloney, Vice President, Public Affairs.*
General email, info@pegcc.org
Web, www.pegcc.org

Advocacy, communications, and research organization and resource center that develops, analyzes, and distributes information about the private equity industry and its contributions to the national and global economy.

Public Company Accounting Oversight Board, *1666 K St. N.W., #800, 20006-2803; (202) 207-9100. Fax, (202) 862-8430. James R. Doty, Chair; Suzanne Kinzer, Chief Administrative Officer, ext. 2139. Information, (202) 591-4135.*
Web, www.pcaobus.org and Twitter, @PCAOB_News

Established by Congress to oversee the audits of public companies in order to protect the interests of investors and the public. Also oversees the audits of broker-dealers, including compliance reports filed pursuant to federal securities laws.

Securities Industry and Financial Markets Assn. (SIFMA), Washington Office, *1101 New York Ave. N.W., 8th Floor, 20005; (202) 962-7300. Fax, (202) 962-7305. Kenneth E. Bentsen Jr., Chief Executive Officer.*
General email, inquiry@sifma.org
Web, www.sifma.org and Twitter, @SIFMA

Membership: securities firms, banks, and asset managers. Focuses on enhancing the public's trust in markets. Provides educational resources for professionals and investors in the industry. Monitors legislation and regulations. (Headquarters in New York. Merger of the Securities Industry Assn. and the Bond Market Assn.)

Securities Investor Protection Corp. (SIPC), *1667 K St. N.W., #1000, 20006-1620; (202) 371-8300. Fax, (202) 223-1679. Stephen P. Harbeck, Chief Executive Officer.*
General email, asksipc@sipc.org
Web, www.sipc.org and Twitter, @sipc

Private corporation established by Congress to administer the Securities Investor Protection Act. Acts as a trustee or works with an independent, court-appointed trustee to recover funds in brokerage insolvency cases.

Small Business Investor Alliance, *1100 H St. N.W., #1200, 20005; (202) 628-5055. Brett Palmer, President.*
General email, info@sbia.org
Web, www.sbia.org

Membership: private equity, venture capital, and middle market funds that invest in small businesses. Provides training to fund managers and holds industry networking events. Monitors legislation and regulations.

US SIF: The Forum for Sustainable and Responsible Investment, *1660 L St. N.W., #306, 20036; (202) 872-5361. Fax, (202) 775-8686. Lisa Woll, Chief Executive Officer. Web, www.ussif.org*

Membership association promoting sustainable and socially responsible investing. Conducts research, events, and courses on investments considering environmental, social, and corporate governance criteria. Monitors legislation and regulations. (Formerly Social Investment Forum.)

Tangible Assets

▶**AGENCIES**

Commodity Futures Trading Commission, *Three Lafayette Centre, 1155 21st St. N.W., 20581-0001; (202) 418-5000. Fax, (202) 418-5521. Timothy G. Massad, Chair. TTY, (202) 418-5514. Toll-free, (866) 366-2382. General email, questions@cftc.gov*

Web, www.cftc.gov and Twitter, @CFTC

Enforces federal statutes relating to commodity futures and options, including gold and silver futures and options. Monitors and regulates gold and silver leverage contracts, which provide for deferred delivery of the commodity and the payment of an agreed portion of the purchase price on margin.

Defense Logistics Agency *(Defense Dept.),* **Strategic Materials,** *8725 John Jay Kingman Rd., #3229, Fort Belvoir, VA 22060-6223; (703) 767-5500. Fax, (703) 767-3316. Ronnie Favors, Administrator; Vacant, Deputy Administrator. Press, (703) 767-6479. Web, www.dla.mil/HQ/Acquisition/Strategicmaterials. aspx*

Manages the national defense stockpile of strategic and critical materials. Purchases strategic materials, including beryllium and newly developed high-tech alloys. Disposes of excess materials, including tin, silver, industrial diamond stones, tungsten, and vegetable tannin.

U.S. Geological Survey (USGS) *(Interior Dept.),* **Global Minerals Analysis,** *12201 Sunrise Valley Dr., MS 991, Reston, VA 20192-0002; (703) 648-4976. Fax, (703) 648-7737. Steven D. Textoris, Chief. Web, http://minerals.usgs.gov/minerals*

Collects, analyzes, and disseminates information on ferrous and nonferrous metals, including gold, silver, platinum group metals, iron, iron ore, steel, chromium, and nickel.

U.S. Mint *(Treasury Dept.),* *801 9th St. N.W., 8th Floor, 20220; (202) 756-6468. Fax, (202) 756-6160. Rhett Jeppson, Deputy Director. Information, (202) 354-7227. Press, (202) 354-7222. Customer Service, (800) 872-6468. TTY, (888) 321-6468. Web, www.usmint.gov and Twitter, @usmint*

Produces and distributes the national coinage so that the nation can conduct trade and commerce. Produces gold, silver, and platinum coins for sale to investors.

▶**NONGOVERNMENTAL**

Silver Institute, *1400 Eye St. N.W., #550, 20005; (202) 835-0185. Fax, (202) 835-0155. Michael DiRienzo, Executive Director. General email, info@silverinstitute.org Web, www.silverinstitute.org*

Membership: companies that mine, refine, fabricate, or manufacture silver or silver-containing products. Conducts research on new technological and industrial uses for silver. Compiles statistics on mining; coinage; and the production, distribution, and use of refined silver.

Silver Users Assn., *3930 Walnut St., Fairfax, VA 22030; (703) 383-1330. Fax, (703) 383-1332. Paul Miller, Executive Director. General email, pmiller@mwcapitol.com Web, www.silverusersassociation.org*

Membership: users of silver, including the photographic industry, silversmiths, and other manufacturers. Conducts research on the silver market; monitors government activities in silver; analyzes government statistics on silver consumption and production. Monitors legislation and regulations.

INDUSTRIAL PRODUCTION, MANUFACTURING

General

▶**AGENCIES**

Bureau of Industry and Security *(Commerce Dept.),* *14th St. and Constitution Ave. N.W., #3898, 20230; (202) 482-1455. Fax, (202) 482-2387. Eric L. Hirschhorn, Under Secretary. Press, (202) 482-2721. Export licensing information, (202) 482-4811. Web, www.bis.doc.gov and Twitter, @BISgov*

Assists in providing for an adequate supply of strategic and critical materials for defense activities and civilian needs, including military requirements, and other domestic energy supplies; develops plans for industry to meet national emergencies. Studies the effect of imports on national security and recommends actions. Manages the nation's dual-use export control laws and regulations.

Bureau of Labor Statistics (BLS) *(Labor Dept.),* **Industrial Prices and Price Index,** *2 Massachusetts Ave. N.E., #3840, 20212-0001; (202) 691-7700. Fax, (202) 691-7754. Amber Fink, Manager, Apparel, Pharmaceuticals, Printing, and Construction Materials Team; David M. Friedman, Assistant Commissioner. General email, ppi-info@bls.gov Web, www.bls.gov/ppi*

Compiles statistics on apparel, pharmaceuticals, printing, construction materials, and all U.S. products for the Producer Price Index.

Economic Development Administration *(Commerce Dept.)*, *1401 Constitution Ave. N.W., #78006, 20230; (202) 482-5081. Fax, (202) 273-4781. Jay Williams, Assistant Secretary.*
Web, www.eda.gov

Assists U.S. firms in increasing their competitiveness against foreign imports. Certifies eligibility and provides domestic firms and industries adversely affected by increased imports with technical assistance under provisions of the Trade Act of 1974. Administers eleven regional Trade Adjustment Assistance Centers that offer services to eligible U.S. firms.

International Trade Administration (ITA) *(Commerce Dept.), Industry and Analysis, 1401 Constitution Ave. N.W., #2854, 20230; (202) 482-1461. Fax, (202) 482-5697. Marcus Jadotte, Assistant Secretary; Maureen Smith, Deputy Assistant Secretary.*
Web, www.trade.gov/industry

Conducts industry trade analysis. Shapes U.S. trade policy. Participates in trade negotiations. Organizes trade capacity building programs. Evaluates the impact of domestic and international economic and regulatory policies on U.S. manufacturers and service industries.

International Trade Administration (ITA) *(Commerce Dept.), Industry and Analysis, Manufacturing, 1401 Constitution Ave. N.W., #28004, 20230; (202) 482-1872. Fax, (202) 482-0856. Scott Kennedy, Deputy Assistant Secretary, Acting.*
Web, www.trade.gov/td/manufacturing and *www.manufacturing.gov*

Conducts analyses and competitive assessments of high-tech industries, including aerospace, automotive, industrial machinery, medical devices, and the pharmaceutical industry. Develops trade policies for these industries, negotiates market access for U.S. companies, and assists in promoting exports through trade missions, shows, and fairs in major overseas markets.

National Institute of Standards and Technology (NIST) *(Commerce Dept.), Hollings Manufacturing Extension Partnership, 100 Bureau Dr., MS 4800, Gaithersburg, MD 20899-4800; (301) 975-5020. Fax, (301) 963-6556. Carroll Thomas, Director. Toll-free, (800) 637-4634. General email, mfg@nist.gov*
Web, www.nist.gov/mep

Collaborates with and advises private manufacturers in the United States on innovation strategies, process improvements, green manufacturing, and market diversification.

National Institute of Standards and Technology (NIST) *(Commerce Dept.), Weights and Measures, 100 Bureau Dr., MS 2600, Gaithersburg, MD 20899-2600; (301) 975-4004. Fax, (301) 975-8091. Carol Hockert, Chief; Barbara Turner, Public Relations. General email, owm@nist.gov*
Web, www.nist.gov/pml/wmd

Promotes uniform standards among the states for packaging and labeling products and for measuring devices, including scales and commercial measurement instruments; advises manufacturers on labeling and packaging laws and on measuring device standards. Partners with the National Conference on Weights and Measures to develop standards.

▶NONGOVERNMENTAL

American Chemistry Council, *700 2nd St. N.E., 20002; (202) 249-7000. Fax, (202) 249-6100. Calvin (Cal) M. Dooley, President.*
Web, www.americanchemistry.com

Membership: manufacturers of basic industrial chemicals. Provides members with technical research, communications services, and legal affairs counseling. Sponsors research on chemical risk assessments, biomonitoring, and nanotechnology. Interests include environmental safety and health, transportation, energy, and international trade and security. Monitors legislation and regulations.

American National Standards Institute (ANSI), *1899 L St. N.W., 11th Floor, 20036; (202) 293-8020. Fax, (202) 293-9287. Joe Bhatia, President, (202) 331-3605.*
Web, www.ansi.org

Administers and coordinates the voluntary U.S. private sector-led consensus standards and conformity assessment system. Serves as the official U.S. representative to the International Organization of Standardization (ISO) and, via the U.S. National Committee, the International Electrotechnical Commission (IEC), and is a U.S. representative to the International Accreditation Forum (IAF).

Assn. for Manufacturing Technology (AMT), *7901 Westpark Dr., McLean, VA 22102-4206; (703) 893-2900. Fax, (703) 893-1151. Douglas Woods, President. Toll-free, (800) 524-0475. General email, amt@amtonline.org*
Web, www.amtonline.org and *Twitter, @amtonline*

Supports the U.S. manufacturing industry; sponsors workshops and seminars; fosters safety and technical standards. Monitors legislation and regulations.

Can Manufacturers Institute, *1730 Rhode Island Ave. N.W., #1000, 20036; (202) 232-4677. Fax, (202) 232-5756. Robert Budway, President.*
Web, www.cancentral.com

Represents can manufacturers and suppliers; promotes the use of the can as a form of food and beverage packaging. Conducts market research. Monitors legislation and regulations.

Chlorine Institute Inc., *1300 Wilson Blvd., #525, Arlington, VA 22209; (703) 894-4140. Fax, (703) 894-4130. Frank Reiner, President. General email, info@cl2.com*
Web, www.chlorineinstitute.org

Safety, health, and environmental protection center of the chlor-alkali (chlorine, caustic soda, caustic potash, and hydrogen chloride) industry. Interests include employee health and safety, resource conservation and pollution abatement, control of chlorine emergencies, product specifications, and public and community relations. Publishes technical pamphlets and drawings.

Consumer Specialty Products Assn., *1667 K St. N.W., #300, 20006; (202) 872-8110. Fax, (202) 223-2636. Christopher Cathcart, President. General email, info@cspa.org*

Web, www.cspa.org and Twitter, @The_CSPA

Membership: manufacturers, marketers, packagers, and suppliers in the chemical specialties industry. Focus includes cleaning products and detergents, nonagricultural pesticides, disinfectants, automotive and industrial products, polishes and floor finishes, antimicrobials, air care products and candles, and aerosol products. Monitors legislation and regulations.

Envelope Manufacturers Assn., *500 Montgomery St., #550, Alexandria, VA 22314-1565; (703) 739-2200. Fax, (703) 739-2209. Maynard H. Benjamin, President. General email, mhbenjamin@envelope.org*

Web, www.envelope.org

Membership: envelope manufacturers and suppliers. Monitors legislation and regulations.

Flexible Packaging Assn., *185 Admiral Cochrane Dr., #105, Annapolis, MD 21401; (410) 694-0800. Fax, (410) 694-0900. Marla Donahue, President. General email, fpa@flexpack.org*

Web, www.flexpack.org

Membership: companies that supply or manufacture flexible packaging. Researches packaging trends and technical developments. Compiles industry statistics. Monitors legislation and regulations.

Glass Packaging Institute, *1220 N. Fillmore St., #400, Arlington, VA 22201; (703) 684-6359. Fax, (703) 546-0588. Lynn Bragg, President. General email, info@gpi.org*

Web, www.gpi.org

Membership: manufacturers of glass containers and their suppliers. Promotes industry policies to protect the environment, conserve natural resources, and reduce energy consumption; conducts research; monitors legislation affecting the industry. Interests include glass recycling.

Green Seal, *1001 Connecticut Ave. N.W., #827, 20036; (202) 872-6400. Fax, (202) 872-4324. Arthur B. Weissman, President. General email, greenseal@greenseal.org*

Web, www.greenseal.org

Grants certification to environmentally sustainable products, services, hotels, restaurants, and other companies.

Independent Lubricant Manufacturers Assn., *400 N. Columbus St., #201, Alexandria, VA 22314; (703) 684-5574. Fax, (703) 836-8503. Holly Alfano, Executive Director.*

General email, ilma@ilma.org

Web, www.ilma.org

Membership: U.S. and international companies that manufacture automotive, industrial, and metalworking lubricants; associates include suppliers and related businesses. Conducts two workshops and conferences annually; compiles statistics. Monitors legislation and regulations.

Independent Office Products and Furniture Dealers Assn., *3601 E. Joppa Rd., Baltimore, MD 21234; (410) 931-8100. Fax, (410) 931-8111. Michael Tucker, President. General email, info@iopfda.org*

Web, www.iopfda.org

Membership: independent dealers of office products and office furniture. Serves independent dealers and works with their trading partners to develop programs and opportunities that help strengthen the dealer position in the marketplace.

Industrial Designers Society of America, *555 Grove St., #200, Herndon, VA 20170; (703) 707-6000. Fax, (703) 787-8501. Daniel Martinage, Executive Director. General email, idsa@idsa.org*

Web, www.idsa.org

Membership: designers of products, equipment, instruments, furniture, transportation, packages, exhibits, information services, and related services, and educators of industrial design. Provides the Bureau of Labor Statistics with industry information. Monitors legislation and regulations.

Industrial Energy Consumers of America, *1776 K St. N.W., #720, 20006; (202) 223-1420. Paul N. Cicio, President, (202) 223-1661.*

Web, www.ieca-us.com

National trade association that represents the manufacturing industry and advocates on energy, environmental, and public policy issues. Advocates greater diversity of and lower costs for energy. Monitors legislation and regulations.

Industrial Research Institute Inc., *2300 Clarendon Blvd., #400, Arlington, VA 22201; (703) 647-2580. Fax, (703) 647-2581. Edward Bernstein, President. Web, www.iriweb.org*

Membership: companies that maintain laboratories for industrial research. Seeks to improve the process of industrial research by promoting cooperative efforts among companies and federal laboratories, between the academic and research communities, and between industry and the government. Monitors legislation and regulations concerning technology, industry, and national competitiveness.

International Sleep Products Assn., *501 Wythe St., Alexandria, VA 22314-1917; (703) 683-8371. Fax, (703) 683-4503. Ryan Trainer, President. General email, info@sleepproducts.org*

Web, www.sleepproducts.org

Membership: manufacturers of bedding and mattresses. Compiles statistics on the industry. (Affiliated with Sleep Products Safety Council and the Better Sleep Council.)

Manufacturers Alliance/MAPI, *1600 Wilson Blvd., #1100, Arlington, VA 22209; (703) 841-9000. Fax, (703) 841-9514. Steven V. Gold, President.*
Web, www.mapi.net

Membership: companies involved in advanced manufacturing industries, including electronics, telecommunications, precision instruments, computers, and the automotive and aerospace industries. Seeks to increase industrial productivity. Conducts research; organizes discussion councils. Monitors legislation and regulations.

National Assn. of Chemical Distributors (NACD), *1560 Wilson Blvd., #1100, Arlington, VA 22209; (703) 527-6223. Fax, (703) 527-7747. Eric Byer, President.*
General email, nacdpublicaffairs@nacd.com
Web, www.nacd.com

Membership: firms involved in purchasing, processing, blending, storing, transporting, and marketing of chemical products. Provides members with information on such topics as training, safe handling and transport of chemicals, liability insurance, and environmental issues. Manages the NACD Chemical Educational Foundation. Monitors legislation and regulations.

National Assn. of Manufacturers (NAM), *733 10th St. N.W., #700, 20001; (202) 637-3000. Fax, (202) 637-3182. Jay Timmons, President. Toll-free, (800) 814-8468.*
General email, manufacturing@nam.org
Web, www.nam.org

Membership: public and private manufacturing companies. Interests include manufacturing technology, economic growth, international trade, national security, taxation, corporate finance and governance, labor relations, occupational safety, workforce education, health care, energy and natural resources, transportation, and environmental quality. Monitors legislation and regulations.

National Council on Advanced Manufacturing, *2025 M St. N.W., #800, 20036; (202) 367-1178. Fax, (202) 367-2178. Robert (Rusty) Patterson, Chief Executive Officer.*
General email, wentzelf@nacfam.org
Web, www.nacfam.org

Promotes public policies supportive of advanced manufacturing and industrial modernization conducive to global economic competitiveness. Advocates greater national focus on industrial base modernization, increased investment in plants and equipment, accelerated development and deployment of advanced manufacturing technology, and reform of technical education and training.

Society of Chemical Manufacturers and Affiliates (SOCMA), *1850 M St. N.W., #700, 20036-5810; (202) 721-4100. Fax, (202) 296-8120. Lawrence (Larry) D. Sloan, President.*
General email, info@socma.com
Web, www.socma.com

Membership: companies that manufacture, distribute, and market organic chemicals; producers of chemical components; and providers of custom chemical services. Interests include international trade, environmental and occupational safety, chemical security, and health issues; conducts workshops and seminars. Promotes commercial opportunities for members. Monitors legislation and regulations.

Society of the Plastics Industry (SPI), *1425 K St. N.W., #500, 20005; (202) 974-5200. Fax, (202) 296-7005. William (Bill) R. Carteaux, President.*
General email, feedback@plasticsindustry.org
Web, www.plasticsindustry.org

Promotes the plastics industry and its processes, raw materials suppliers, and machinery manufacturers. Monitors legislation and regulations.

Clothing and Textiles

▶AGENCIES

International Trade Administration (ITA) *(Commerce Dept.), Industry and Analysis, Textiles and Apparel, 1401 Constitution Ave. N.W., #30003, 20230; (202) 482-5078. Fax, (202) 482-2331. Joshua Teitelbaum, Deputy Assistant Secretary, (202) 482-3737; Janet Heinzen, Director.*
General email, otcxa@trade.gov
Web, http://otexa.trade.gov

Participates in negotiating bilateral textile and apparel import restraint agreements; responsible for export expansion programs and reduction of nontariff barriers for textile and apparel goods; provides data on economic conditions in the domestic textile and apparel markets, including impact of imports.

▶NONGOVERNMENTAL

American Apparel and Footwear Assn. (AAFA), *740 6th St. N.W., 3rd and 4th Floors, 20001; (202) 853-9080. Fax, (202) 853-9076. Rick Helfenbein, President. Toll-free, (800) 520-2262.*
Web, www.apparelandfootwear.org

Membership: manufacturers of apparel, sewn products, footwear and their suppliers, importers, and distributors. Provides members with information on the industry, including import and export data. Interests include product flammability and trade promotion. Monitors legislation and regulations.

American Fiber Manufacturers Assn., *1530 Wilson Blvd., #700, Arlington, VA 22209; (703) 875-0432. Fax, (703) 875-0907. Paul T. O'Day, President.*
General email, feb@afma.org
Web, www.fibersource.com

Membership: U.S. manufacturers of synthetic and cellulosic fibers, filaments, and yarns. Interests include international trade, education, and environmental and technical services. Monitors legislation and regulations.

American Textile Machinery Assn., *201 Park Washington Court, Falls Church, VA 22046-4527; (703) 538-1789. Fax, (703) 241-5603. Clay D. Tyeryar, President.*
General email, info@atmanet.org
Web, www.atmanet.org

Membership: U.S.-based manufacturers of textile machinery and related parts and accessories. Interests include competitiveness and expansion of foreign markets. Monitors legislation and regulations.

Dry Cleaning and Laundry Institute, *14700 Sweitzer Lane, Laurel, MD 20707; (301) 622-1900. Fax, (240) 295-0685. Mary Scalco, Chief Executive Officer. Toll-free, (800) 638-2627.*
General email, techline@dlionline.org
Web, www.dlionline.org

Membership: dry cleaners and launderers. Conducts research and provides information on products and services. Monitors legislation and regulations.

Footwear Distributors and Retailers of America, *1319 F St. N.W., #700, 20004-1179; (202) 737-5660. Fax, (202) 645-0789. Matt Priest, President.*
General email, info@fdra.org
Web, www.fdra.org and Twitter, @FDRA

Membership: companies that operate shoe retail outlets and wholesale footwear companies with U.S. and global brands. Provides business support and government relations to members. Interests include intellectual property rights, ocean shipping rates, trade with China, and labeling regulations.

National Cotton Council of America, Washington Office, *1521 New Hampshire Ave. N.W., 20036-1205; (202) 745-7805. Fax, (202) 483-4040. Reece Langley, Vice President, Washington Operations.*
Web, www.cotton.org

Membership: all segments of the U.S. cotton industry. Formulates positions on trade policy and negotiations; seeks to improve competitiveness of U.S. exports; sponsors programs to educate the public about flammable fabrics. (Headquarters in Memphis, Tenn.)

National Council of Textile Organizations, *1701 K St. N.W., #625, 20006; (202) 822-8028. Fax, (202) 822-8029. Augustine Tantillo, President.*
Web, www.ncto.org

Membership: U.S. companies that spin, weave, knit, or finish textiles from natural fibers, and associate members from affiliated industries. Interests include domestic and world markets. Monitors legislation and regulations.

Secondary Materials and Recycled Textiles Assn. (SMART), *3465 Box Hill Corporate Center Dr., Suite H, Abingdon, MD 21009; (443) 640-1050. Fax, (443) 640-1086. Jackie King, Executive Director, ext. 105.*
General email, smartinfo@kingmgmt.org
Web, www.smartasn.org and Twitter, @SMARTTextile

Membership: organizations and individuals involved in producing, shipping, and distributing recycled textiles and other textile products. Sponsors educational programs; publishes newsletters. Monitors legislation and regulations.

UNITE HERE, Washington Office, *1775 K St. N.W., #620, 20006-1530; (202) 393-4373. Fax, (202) 223-6213. Fax, (202) 342-2929. Vacant, Political Director; D. Taylor, President.*
Web, www.unitehere.org

Membership: more than 270,000 workers in the United States and Canada who work in the hospitality, gaming, food service, manufacturing, textile, laundry, and airport industries. Assists members with contract negotiation and grievances; conducts training programs and workshops. Monitors legislation and regulations. (Headquarters in New York. Formed by the merger of the former Union of Needletrades, Textiles and Industrial Employees and the Hotel Employees and Restaurant Employees International Union.)

Electronics and Appliances

▶**NONGOVERNMENTAL**

Air-Conditioning, Heating, and Refrigeration Institute (AHRI), *2111 Wilson Blvd., #500, Arlington, VA 22201; (703) 524-8800. Fax, (703) 562-1942. Stephen R. Yurek, President.*
General email, ahri@ahrinet.org
Web, www.ahrinet.org

Membership: manufacturers of gas appliances and equipment for residential and commercial use and related industries. Advocates product improvement; provides market statistics. Monitors legislation and regulations. (Merger of the Air-Conditioning and Refrigeration Institute [ARI] and the Gas Appliance Manufacturers Assn. [GAMA].)

Assn. of Electrical Equipment and Medical Imaging Manufacturers (NEMA), *1300 N. 17th St., #900, Rosslyn, VA 22209-3801; (703) 841-3200. Fax, (703) 841-5900. Kevin Cosgriff, President. Press, (703) 841-3241.*
Web, www.nema.org and Twitter, @NEMAupdates

Membership: manufacturers of products used in the generation, transmission, distribution, control, and end-use of electricity, including manufacturers of medical diagnostic imaging equipment. Develops technical standards; collects, analyzes, and disseminates industry data. Interests include Smart Grid, high-performance building, carbon footprint, energy storage, and an intelligence portal. Monitors legislation, regulations, and international trade activities.

Consumer Technology Assn., *1919 S. Eads St., Arlington, VA 22202; (703) 907-7600. Fax, (703) 907-7675. Gary Shapiro, President. Toll-free, (866) 858-1555. Press, (703) 907-7650.*

General email, cea@ce.org

Web, www.cta.tech and Twitter, @CTATech

Membership: 2,000 U.S. consumer electronics companies. Promotes the industry; sponsors seminars and conferences; conducts research; consults with member companies. Monitors legislation and regulations. (Affiliated with Electronic Industries Alliance. Formerly Consumer Electronics Assn.)

Electronic Components Industry Association, *2214 Rock Hill Rd., #265, Herndon, VA 20170; (571) 323-0294. Fax, (571) 323-0245. John Denslinger, President.*
Web, www.ecianow.org

Membership: manufacturers, distributors, and manufacturer representatives of electronic components and semiconductor products. Provides information and data on industry trends; advocates the authorized sale of electronics components to prevent counterfeit product moving through the supply chain. Monitors legislation and regulations.

National Electrical Contractors Assn., *3 Bethesda Metro Center, #1100, Bethesda, MD 20814; (301) 657-3110. Fax, (301) 215-4500. John M. Grau, Chief Executive Officer.*
Web, www.necanet.org, Twitter, @necanet and Facebook, www.facebook.com/NECANET

Membership: electrical contractors who build and service electrical wiring and equipment, including high-voltage construction and service. Represents members in collective bargaining with union workers; sponsors research and educational programs.

Optoelectronics Industry Development Associates, *2010 Massachusetts Ave. N.W., 20036; (202) 416-1982. Fax, (202) 416-6130. Hans-Juergen Schmidtke, Chair.*
General email, industry@oida.org

Web, www.oida.org/industry

Membership: optoelectronics components and systems providers, businesses, and research institutions in North America. Activities include workshops and conferences, industry reports, and advocacy. Monitors legislation and regulations. (Affiliated with The Optical Society.)

United Electrical, Radio, and Machine Workers of America, *Washington Office, P.O. Box 10031, Alexandria, VA 22310-0031; (703) 341-9446. Chris Townsend, Director, Political Action. Information, (412) 471-8919.*
General email, uewashingtonoffice@gmail.com

Web, www.ueunion.org

Membership: manufacturing assembly workers, plastic injection molders, tool and die makers, electrical workers, sheet metal workers, truck and bus drivers, warehouse workers, custodians, clerical workers, graduate instructors, graduate researchers, scientists, librarians, social workers, and day care workers. (National headquarters in Pittsburgh, Pa.)

Steel, Metalworking, Machinery

▶NONGOVERNMENTAL

American Boiler Manufacturers Assn., *8221 Old Courthouse Rd., #380, Vienna, VA 22182; (703) 356-7172. Fax, (703) 356-4543. Scott Lynch, President; Robert Stemen, Chair.*
Web, www.abma.com

Membership: manufacturers of boiler systems and boiler-related products, including fuel-burning systems. Interests include energy and environmental issues.

American Gear Manufacturers Assn., *1001 N. Fairfax St., #500, Alexandria, VA 22314; (703) 684-0211. Fax, (703) 684-0242. Joe T. Franklin Jr., President.*
General email, agma@agma.org

Web, www.agma.org

Membership: gear manufacturers, suppliers, and industry consultants. Conducts workshops, seminars, and conferences; develops industry standards; sponsors research. Monitors legislation and regulations.

American Institute for International Steel, *701 W. Broad St., #301, Falls Church, VA 22046; (703) 245-8075. Fax, (703) 610-0215. Richard Chriss, Executive Director, ext. 301.*
General email, chriss@aiis.org

Web, www.aiis.org

Membership: importers and exporters of steel, logistics companies, and port authorities. Conducts research and provides analysis on steel market and importing and exporting. Holds annual conferences.

American Iron and Steel Institute (AISI), *Washington Office, 25 Massachusetts Ave. N.W., #800, 20001; (202) 452-7100. Fax, (202) 463-6573. Thomas Gibson, President. Press, (202) 452-7116.*
General email, steelnews@steel.org

Web, www.steel.org and Twitter, @aisisteel

Represents the iron and steel industry. Publishes statistics on iron and steel production; promotes the use of steel; conducts research. Monitors legislation and regulations. (Maintains offices in Southfield, Mich., and Pittsburgh, Pa.)

American Wire Producers Assn., *P.O. Box 151387, Alexandria, VA 22315; (703) 299-4434. Fax, (703) 299-9233. Kimberly A. Korbel, Executive Director.*
General email, info@awpa.org

Web, www.awpa.org

Membership: companies that produce carbon, alloy, and stainless steel wire and wire products in the United States, Canada, and Mexico. Interests include imports of rod, wire, and wire products. Publishes survey of the domestic wire industry. Monitors legislation and regulations.

International Assn. of Bridge, Structural, Ornamental, and Reinforcing Iron Workers, *1750 New York Ave. N.W., #400, 20006; (202) 383-4800. Fax, (202) 638-4856. Eric Dean, President.*

General email, iwmagazine@iwintl.org

Web, www.ironworkers.org

Membership: approximately 140,000 iron workers. Helps members negotiate pay, benefits, and better working conditions; conducts training programs and workshops. Monitors legislation and regulations. (Affiliated with the AFL-CIO.)

International Assn. of Machinists and Aerospace Workers, 9000 Machinists Pl., Upper Marlboro, MD 20772-2687; (301) 967-4500. Fax, (301) 967-4588. Robert Martinez, International President. Information, (301) 967-4520. TTY, (800) 201-7165.

General email, websteward@iamaw.org

Web, www.goiam.org

Membership: machinists in more than 200 industries. Helps members negotiate pay, benefits, and better working conditions; conducts training programs and workshops. Monitors legislation and regulations. (Affiliated with the AFL-CIO, the Canadian Labour Congress, the International Metalworkers Federation, the International Transport Workers' Federation, and the Railway Labor Executives Assn.)

Machinery Dealers National Assn., 315 S. Patrick St., Alexandria, VA 22314; (703) 836-9300. Fax, (703) 836-9303. Mark Robinson, Executive Vice President. Toll-free, (800) 872-7807.

General email, office@mdna.org

Web, www.mdna.org, Twitter, @MDNA_Machines and Facebook, www.facebook.com/Machinery-Dealers-National-Association-270644229632807

Membership: companies that buy and sell used capital equipment. Establishes a code of ethics for members; publishes a buyer's guide that lists members by types of machinery they sell.

Outdoor Power Equipment Institute, 341 S. Patrick St., Alexandria, VA 22314; (703) 549-7600. Fax, (703) 549-7604. Kris Kiser, President.

General email, info@opei.org

Web, www.opei.org

Membership: manufacturers of powered lawn and garden maintenance products, components and attachments, and their suppliers. Promotes safe use of outdoor power equipment; keeps statistics on the industry; fosters exchange of information. Monitors legislation and regulations.

Packaging Machinery Manufacturers Institute, 11911 Freedom Dr., #600, Reston, VA 20190; (571) 612-3200. Fax, (703) 243-8556. Charles D. Yuska, President.

General email, pmmi@pmmi.org

Web, www.pmmi.org

Membership: manufacturers of packaging, machinery, packaging-related converting machinery, components, processing materials, and containers. Provides industry information and statistics; offers educational programs to members.

Sheet Metal, Air, Rail, and Transportation Workers (SMART), 1750 New York Ave. N.W., 6th Floor, 20006; (202) 662-0880. Joseph Sellers Jr., General President. Toll-free, 800-662 0800.

General email, info@smart-union.org

Web, http://smart-union.org

Membership: U.S., Puerto Rican, and Canadian workers in the building and construction trades, manufacturing, and the railroad and shipyard industries. Assists members with contract negotiation and grievances; conducts training programs and workshops. Monitors legislation and regulations. (Affiliated with the Sheet Metal and Air Conditioning Contractors' Assn., the AFL-CIO, and the Canadian Labour Congress.)

Specialty Steel Industry of North America, 3050 K St. N.W., #400, 20007; (202) 342-8630. Fax, (202) 342-8451. Carl R. Moulton, Chair. Toll-free, (800) 982-0355.

General email, dhorquist@kelleydrye.com

Web, www.ssina.com

Membership: manufacturers of products in stainless and other specialty steels. Establishes manufacturing techniques and issues technical guides; operates a hotline for technical questions.

Steel Manufacturers Assn., 1150 Connecticut Ave. N.W., #715, 20036-3101; (202) 296-1515. Fax, (202) 296-2506. Phil Bell, President.

General email, webmail@steelnet.org

Web, www.steelnet.org

Membership: steel producers and their vendors in North America. Helps members exchange information on technical matters; provides information on the steel industry to the public and government. Monitors legislation and regulations.

United Electrical, Radio, and Machine Workers of America, *Washington Office,* P.O. Box 10031, Alexandria, VA 22310-0031; (703) 341-9446. Chris Townsend, Political Action Director. Information, (412) 471-8919.

General email, uewashingtonoffice@gmail.com

Web, www.ueunion.org

Membership: manufacturing assembly workers, plastic injection molders, tool and die makers, electrical workers, sheet metal workers, truck and bus drivers, warehouse workers, custodians, clerical workers, graduate instructors, graduate researchers, scientists, librarians, social workers, and day care workers. (National headquarters in Pittsburgh, Pa.)

United Steelworkers, 1155 M St. N.W., #500, 20036; (202) 778-4384. Fax, (202) 419-1486. Holly Hart, Legislative Director.

Web, www.usw.org

Membership: more than one million workers in the steel, paper, rubber, energy, chemical, pharmaceutical, and allied industries. Helps members negotiate pay, benefits, and better working conditions; conducts training programs and workshops. Monitors legislation and regulations. (Affiliated with the AFL-CIO; headquarters in Pittsburgh, Pa.)

INSURANCE

General

▶AGENCIES

Federal Emergency Management Agency (FEMA) *(Homeland Security Dept.), Federal Insurance and Mitigation Administration,* 1800 S. Bell St., MS 3020, Arlington, VA 22202; (202) 646-2781. Fax, (202) 646-7970. Vacant, Associate Administrator.
Web, www.fema.gov/what-mitigation/federal-insurance-mitigation-administration

Administers federal flood insurance programs, including the National Flood Insurance Program. Makes low-cost flood insurance available to eligible homeowners.

Small Business Administration (SBA), *Disaster Assistance,* 409 3rd St. S.W., #6050, 20416; (202) 205-6734. Fax, (202) 205-7728. James Rivera, Associate Administrator. Service Center, (800) 659-2955. TTY, (800) 877-8339.
Web, www.sba.gov/offices/headquarters/oda

Provides victims of physical disasters with disaster and economic injury loans for homes, businesses, and personal property. Lends funds for uncompensated losses incurred from any disaster declared by the president of the United States or the administrator of the SBA. Lends funds to individual homeowners, business concerns of all sizes, and nonprofit institutions to repair or replace damaged structures and furnishings, business machinery, equipment, and inventory. Provides economic injury loans to small businesses for losses to meet necessary operating expenses, provided the business could have paid these expenses prior to the disaster.

▶CONGRESS

For a listing of relevant congressional committees and subcommittees, please see pages 34–35 or the Appendix.

▶NONGOVERNMENTAL

American Academy of Actuaries, 1850 M St. N.W., #300, 20036; (202) 223-8196. Fax, (202) 872-1948. Tom Wildsmith, President; Mary Downs, Executive Director.
Web, www.actuary.org

Membership: professional actuaries practicing in the areas of life, health, liability, property, and casualty insurance; pensions; government insurance plans; and general consulting. Provides information on actuarial matters, including insurance and pensions; develops professional standards; advises public policymakers.

American Assn. for Justice, 777 6th St. N.W., #200, 20001; (202) 965-3500. Fax, (202) 342-5484. Linda Lipsen, Chief Executive Officer. Toll-free, (800) 424-2725.

General email, aaj@justice.org
Web, www.justice.org

Membership: attorneys, judges, law professors, and students. Interests include aspects of legal and legislative activity relating to the adversary system and trial by jury, including property and casualty insurance. (Formerly the Assn. of Trial Lawyers of America.)

American Council of Life Insurers, 101 Constitution Ave. N.W., #700, 20001-2133; (202) 624-2000. Fax, (202) 624-2319. Dirk A. Kempthorne, President.
Web, www.acli.com

Membership: life insurance companies authorized to do business in the United States. Conducts research and compiles statistics at state and federal levels. Monitors legislation and regulations.

American Insurance Assn., 2101 L St. N.W., #400, 20037; (202) 828-7100. Fax, (202) 293-1219. Leigh Ann Pusey, President.
General email, info@aiadc.org
Web, www.aiadc.org and Twitter, @AIADC

Membership: companies providing property and casualty insurance. Conducts public relations and educational activities; provides information on issues related to property and casualty insurance.

American Society of Pension Professionals and Actuaries, 4245 N. Fairfax Dr., #750, Arlington, VA 22203-1648; (703) 516-9300. Fax, (703) 516-9308. Brian H. Graff, Chief Executive Officer.
General email, asppa@asppa.org
Web, www.asppa.org

Membership: administrators, actuaries, advisers, lawyers, accountants, and other financial services professionals who provide consulting and administrative services for employee-based retirement plans. Sponsors educational conferences, webcasts, and credentialing programs for retirement professionals. Monitors legislation and regulations.

Assn. for Advanced Life Underwriting, 11921 Freedom Dr., #1100, Reston, VA 20190; 101 Constitution Ave. N.W., #703 East, 20001; (703) 641-9400. Fax, (703) 641-9885. David J. Stertzer, Chief Executive Officer, (703) 641-8114. Toll-free, (888) 275-0092.
General email, info@aalu.org
Web, www.aalu.org

Membership: specialized underwriters in the fields of estate analysis, charitable planning, business insurance, pension planning, and employee benefit plans. Monitors legislation and regulations on small-business taxes and capital formation. (Maintains an additional office in Washington, D.C.)

Council of Insurance Agents and Brokers, 701 Pennsylvania Ave. N.W., #750, 20004; (202) 783-4400. Fax, (202) 783-4410. Ken A. Crerar, President, (202) 662-4420.

General email, ciab@ciab.com

Web, www.ciab.com and Twitter, @TheCIAB

Represents commercial property and casualty insurance agencies and brokerage firms. Members offer insurance products and risk management services to business, government, and the public.

ERISA Industry Committee, 1400 L St. N.W., #350, 20005; (202) 789-1400. Fax, (202) 789-1120.
Annette Guarisco Fildes, President, (202) 627-1910.
General email, eric@eric.org

Web, www.eric.org

Membership: major U.S. employers. Advocates members' positions on employee retirement, health care coverage, and welfare benefit plans. Monitors legislation and regulations.

GAMA International, 2901 Telestar Court, #140, Falls Church, VA 22042-1205; (571) 499-4300. Fax, (571) 499-4302. Bonnie Godsman, Chief Executive Officer, (571) 661-4311. Information, (800) 345-2687.
Web, www.gamaweb.com

Membership: general agents and managers who provide life insurance and related financial products and services. Provides information, education, and training for members.

Independent Insurance Agents and Brokers of America, 127 S. Peyton St., Alexandria, VA 22314; (703) 683-4422. Fax, (703) 683-7556. Robert Rusbuldt, President. Toll-free, (800) 221-7917.
General email, info@iiaba.net

Web, www.independentagent.com

Provides educational and advisory services; researches issues pertaining to auto, home, business, life, and health insurance; offers cooperative advertising program to members. Political action committee monitors legislation and regulations.

National Assn. of Independent Life Brokerage Agencies, 11325 Random Hills Rd., #110, Fairfax, VA 22030; (703) 383-3081. Fax, (703) 383-6942. Jack Chiasson, Executive Director.
Web, www.nailba.org

Membership: owners of independent life insurance agencies. Fosters the responsible and effective distribution of life and health insurance and related financial services; provides a forum for exchange of information among members. Monitors legislation and regulations.

National Assn. of Insurance and Financial Advisors, 2901 Telestar Court, Falls Church, VA 22042-1205; (703) 770-8100. Kevin M. Mayeux, Chief Executive Officer. Toll-free, (877) 866-2432.
General email, membersupport@naifa.org

Web, www.naifa.org

Federation of state and local life underwriters, agents, and financial advisers. Provides information on life and health insurance and other financial services; sponsors education and training programs.

National Assn. of Insurance Commissioners, Government Relations, 444 N. Capitol St. N.W., #700, 20001-1509; (202) 471-3990. Andy Beal, Chief Executive Officer, Acting.
Web, www.naic.org

Membership: state insurance commissioners, directors, and supervisors. Provides members with information on legal and market conduct, and financial services; publishes research and statistics on the insurance industry. Monitors legislation and regulations. (Affiliated with the Center for Insurance Policy and Research. Headquarters in Kansas City, Mo.)

National Assn. of Professional Insurance Agents, 400 N. Washington St., Alexandria, VA 22314-2353; (703) 836-9340. Fax, (703) 836-1279. Mike Becker, Executive Vice President; Jon Gentile, Director, Federal Affairs, (703) 518-1365. Information, (800) 742-6900. Press, (703) 518-1352.
General email, web@pianet.org

Web, www.pianet.com

Membership: independent insurance agents and brokers. Provides basic and continuing education for agents through courses, seminars, and educational materials. Monitors legislation and regulations.

Nonprofit Risk Management Center, 204 S. King St., Leesburg, VA 20175; (703) 777-3504. Fax, (703) 443-1990. (202) 785-3891. Melanie L. Herman, Executive Director. phone, (202) 785-3891.
General email, info@nonprofitrisk.org

Web, www.nonprofitrisk.org

Provides information on insurance and risk management issues through conferences, consulting, online tools, and publications for nonprofit organizations.

Property Casualty Insurers Assn. of America, Washington Office, 444 N. Capitol St., #801, 20001; (202) 639-0490. Fax, (202) 639-0494. David A. Sampson, Chief Executive Officer.
Web, www.pciaa.net

Membership: companies providing property and casualty insurance. Monitors legislation and compiles statistics; interests include personal and commercial property and casualty insurance. (Headquarters in Chicago, Ill.)

Reinsurance Assn. of America, 1445 New York Ave. N.W., 7th Floor, 20005; (202) 638-3690. Fax, (202) 638-0936. Franklin W. Nutter, President.
General email, infobox@reinsurance.org

Web, www.reinsurance.org and Twitter, @TheRAA

Membership: companies writing property and casualty reinsurance. Monitors legislation and regulations.

PATENTS, COPYRIGHTS, AND TRADEMARKS

General

Bureau of Economic and Business Affairs *(State Dept.),* **International Intellectual Property Enforcement,** *2201 C St. N.W., #4931, 20520-4931; (202) 647-3251. Fax, (202) 647-1537. Jean A. Bonilla, Director.*
General email, ebtpp@state.gov
Web, www.state.gov/e/eb/tpp/ipe

Handles multilateral and bilateral policy formulation involving patents, copyrights, and trademarks, and international industrial property of U.S. nationals.

Civil Division *(Justice Dept.),* **Intellectual Property,** *1100 L St. N.W., #11116, 20005; (202) 514-7223. Fax, (202) 307-0345. John Fargo, Director.*
General email, john.fargo@usdoj.gov
Web, www.justice.gov/civil/intellectual-property-section

Represents the United States in patent, copyright, and trademark cases. Includes the defense of patent infringement suits; legal proceedings to establish government priority of invention; defense of administrative acts of the Register of Copyrights; and actions on behalf of the government involving the use of trademarks.

Patent and Trademark Office *(Commerce Dept.),*
Madison West Bldg., 600 Dulany St., #10-D44, Alexandria, VA 22314 (mailing address: P.O. Box 1450, Alexandria, VA 22313-1450); (571) 272-1000. Fax, (571) 273-8300. Michelle Lee, Under Secretary; Russell Slider, Deputy Director. Customer support, (800) 786-9199. Press, (571) 272-8400. Patent search library, (571) 272-3275. TTY, (800) 877-8339.
Web, www.uspto.gov

Grants patents, registers trademarks, and provides patent and trademark information. Library and search file of U.S. and foreign patents available for public use.

U.S. Customs and Border Protection *(Homeland Security Dept.),* **Intellectual Property Rights and Restrictions,** *1300 Pennsylvania Ave. N.W., Mint Annex, 20229; (202) 325-0020. Fax, (202) 572-8744. Michael B. Walsh, Director, (202) 863-6447.*
General email, hqiprbranch@cbp.dhs.gov
Web, www.cbp.gov

Responsible for customs recordation of registered trademarks and copyrights. Enforces rules and regulations pertaining to intellectual property rights. Coordinates enforcement of International Trade Commission exclusion orders against unfairly competing goods. Determines admissibility of restricted merchandise and cultural properties. Provides support to and coordinates with international organizations and the Office of the U.S. Trade Representative.

For a listing of relevant congressional committees and subcommittees, please see pages 34–35 or the Appendix.

Library of Congress, *Copyright Office, Licensing, James Madison Memorial Bldg., 101 Independence Ave. S.E., #LM 504, 20557; (202) 707-8150. Fax, (202) 707-0905. James Enzinna, Chief. Information, (202) 707-3000. General email, licensing@loc.gov*
Web, www.copyright.gov/licensing

Administers statutory licensing for cable television companies and satellite carriers, for making and distributing digital audio recording products, and for use of certain noncommercial broadcasting. Collects and distributes royalty payments under the copyright law. Administers Section 115 licensing for making and distributing phonorecords.

Library of Congress, *United States Copyright Office, 101 Independence Ave. S.E., #403, 20540; (202) 707-8350. Maria A. Pallante, Register of Copyrights. Information, (202) 707-3000. Forms and publications hotline, (202) 707-9100. Toll-free, (877) 476-0778.*
Web, www.copyright.gov

Administers the United States copyright laws. Provides information to the public on copyright registration procedures and requirements, and on other Copyright Office services. Registers copyright claims and maintains public records of copyright ownership. Conducts Copyright records searches on a fee basis. Provides information regarding U.S. and foreign copyright laws, but does not give legal advice on copyright matters. Principal advisor to the United States Congress on domestic and international copyright issues.

U.S. Court of Appeals for the Federal Circuit, *717 Madison Pl. N.W., 20439; (202) 275-8000. Fax, (202) 275-9678. Sharon Prost, Chief Judge; Daniel E. O'Toole, Clerk, (202) 272-8020. Help Desk, (202) 275-8036. Mediation, (202) 275-8120.*
Web, www.cafc.uscourts.gov

Reviews decisions of U.S. Patent and Trademark Office on applications and interferences regarding patents and trademarks; hears appeals on patent infringement cases from district courts.

American Intellectual Property Law Assn., *241 18th St. South, #700, Arlington, VA 22202; (703) 415-0780. Fax, (703) 415-0786. Lisa Jorgenson, Executive Director. General email, aipla@aipla.org*
Web, www.aipla.org and Twitter, @aipla

Membership: lawyers practicing in the field of patents, trademarks, and copyrights (intellectual property law). Holds continuing legal education conferences.

Assn. of American Publishers, *Government Affairs, 455 Massachusetts Ave. N.W., #700, 20001; (202) 347-3375.*

Fax, (202) 347-3690. Allan R. Adler, Vice President, Legal and Government Affairs.

General email, info@publishers.org

Web, www.publishers.org and Twitter, @AmericanPublish

Represents U.S. book and journal publishing industry priorities on policy, legislation, and regulatory issues regionally, nationally, and worldwide. Interests include intellectual property rights, worldwide copyright enforcement, digital and new technology issues, tax and trade, and First Amendment rights.

Intellectual Property Owners Assn., 1501 M St. N.W., #1150, 20005; (202) 507-4500. Fax, (202) 507-4501. Mark Lauroesch, Executive Director; Samantha Aguayo, Director, Government Relations.

General email, info@ipo.org

Web, www.ipo.org

Monitors and acts as advocate for intellectual property legislation. Conducts educational programs to protect intellectual property through patents, trademarks, copyrights, and trade secret laws.

International Anticounterfeiting Coalition, 1730 M St. N.W., #1020, 20036; (202) 223-6667. Robert Barchiesi, President.

General email, iacc@iacc.org

Web, www.iacc.org

Works to combat counterfeiting and piracy by promoting laws, regulations, and directives to render theft of intellectual property unprofitable. Oversees anticounterfeiting programs that increase patent, trademark, copyright, service mark, trade dress, and trade secret protection. Provides information and training to law enforcement officials to help identify counterfeit and pirate products.

International Intellectual Property Alliance, 1818 N St. N.W., 8th Floor, 20036; (202) 355-7900. Fax, (202) 355-7899. Michael Schlesinger, Counsel.

General email, info@iipa.com

Web, www.iipa.com

Represents U.S. copyright-based industries in efforts to improve international protection of copyrighted materials. Monitors legislation domestically and abroad; promotes enforcement reform abroad.

International Intellectual Property Institute, 1900 K St. N.W., #725, 20006; (202) 544-6610. Bruce A. Lehman, President.

General email, ahirsch@iipi.org

Web, www.iipi.org

Aims to combat patent infringement and eliminate counterfeit products being imported into the U.S. Holds conferences to educate the public on intellectual property rights. Offers training programs and intellectual property guidance for leaders in developing countries.

National Assn. of Manufacturers (NAM), *Technology Policy,* 733 10th St. N.W., #700, 20001; (202) 637-3096. Fax, (202) 637-3182. Bryan Raymond, Director, (202) 637-3072.

Web, www.nam.org

Represents manufacturers in government and the media, advocating pro-manufacturing positions on technology policy issues, including cybersecurity, telecommunication, R&D funding, and intellectual property protection; develops policy and legislation on patents, copyrights, trademarks, and trade secrets; works with the broader business community to advance pro-growth, pro-competitiveness technology policy.

National Assn. of Patent Practitioners, 1629 K St. N.W., #300, 20006; (703) 634-3423. Sarah Gabriel, Executive Director.

General email, representative@napp.org

Web, www.napp.org

Membership: patent attorneys and consultants. Connects intellectual property professionals and provides malpractice insurance benefits. Holds annual conferences on patent-related topics. Maintains a national database for registered patent practitioners.

National Assn. of Plant Patent Owners, 525 9th St. N.W., #800, 20004; (202) 789-2900. Fax, (202) 789-1893. Craig Regelbrugge, Administrator.

Web, www.americanhort.org

Membership: owners of patents on newly propagated horticultural plants. Informs members of plant patents issued, provisions of patent laws, and changes in practice. Promotes the development, protection, production, and distribution of new varieties of horticultural plants. Works with international organizations of plant breeders on matters of common interest. (Affiliated with AmericanHort, formerly the American Nursery and Landscape Assn.)

National Music Publishers' Assn., 975 F St. N.W., #375, 20004; (202) 393-6672. Fax, (202) 393-6673. David M. Israelite, President.

General email, pr@nmpa.org

Web, www.nmpa.org

Works to enforce music copyrights. Sponsors litigation against copyright violators. Monitors and interprets legislation and regulations.

National School Boards Assn., 1680 Duke St., Alexandria, VA 22314-3493; (703) 838-6722. Fax, (703) 549-7590. Thomas Gentzel, Executive Director, (703) 838-6700; Francisco Negron, General Counsel, (703) 838-6710.

General email, info@nsba.org

Web, www.nsba.org

Promotes a broad interpretation of copyright law to permit legitimate scholarly use of published and musical works, videotaped programs, and materials for computer-assisted instruction.

SoundExchange, 733 10th St. N.W., 10th Floor, 20001; (202) 640-5858. Fax, (202) 640-5859. Michael Huppe, President. Press, (202) 559-0558.

General email, info@soundexchange.com

Web, www.soundexchange.com

Artists' rights advocacy group that represents record labels and unsigned artists whose work is broadcast on national and global digital radio. Distributes royalties to musicians, performers, and music copyright owners. Monitors legislation and regulations related to digital music licensing.

U.S. Chamber of Commerce, *Congressional and Public Affairs, 1615 St. N.W., 20062-2000; (202) 463-5600. Jack Howard, Senior Vice President. Web, www.uschamber.com*

Monitors legislation and regulations on patents, copyrights, and trademarks.

SALES AND SERVICES

General

▶AGENCIES

Bureau of Labor Statistics (BLS) *(Labor Dept.), Prices and Living Conditions, 2 Massachusetts Ave. N.E., #3120, 20212-0001; (202) 691-6960. Fax, (202) 691-7080. David M. Friedman, Associate Commissioner. Information, (202) 691-7000. Web, www.bls.gov/cpi*

Collects, processes, analyzes, and disseminates data relating to prices and consumer expenditures; maintains the Consumer Price Index.

Census Bureau *(Commerce Dept.), Economy-Wide Statistics, 4700 Silver Hill Rd., #8K154, Suitland, MD 20746-2401 (mailing address: change city, state, and zip code Washington, DC 20233-6500); (301) 763-5170. Fax, (301) 735-8741. Kevin E. Deardorff, Chief. Web, www.census.gov/econ/economywide.html*

Provides data of five-year census programs on retail, wholesale, and service industries. Conducts periodic monthly or annual surveys for specific items within these industries.

▶NONGOVERNMENTAL

American Society of Appraisers (ASA), *11107 Sunset Hills Rd., #310, Reston, VA 20190; (703) 478-2228. Fax, (703) 742-8471. Jim Hirt, Chief Executive Officer, (703) 733-2112. Toll-free, (800) 272-8258. General email, asainfo@appraisers.org Web, www.appraisers.org and Twitter, @ASAappraisers*

Membership: accredited appraisers of real property, including land, houses, and commercial buildings; business valuation; machinery and technical specialties; yachts; aircraft; public utilities; personal property, including antiques, fine art, residential contents; and gems and jewelry. Affiliate members include students and professionals interested in appraising. Provides technical information; accredits appraisers; provides consumer information programs.

ASIS International, *1625 Prince St., Alexandria, VA 22314-2882; (703) 519-6200. Fax, (703) 519-6299. Peter J. O'Neil, Chief Executive Officer.*

General email, asis@asisonline.org

Web, www.asisonline.org and Twitter, @ASIS_Intl

Membership: security administrators who oversee physical and logistical security for private and public organizations, including law enforcement and the military. Develops security standards; offers educational programs and materials on general and industry-specific practices; and administers certification programs.

Convenience Distribution Assn., *11311 Sunset Hills Rd., Reston, VA 20190; (703) 208-3358. Fax, (703) 573-5738. Scott Ramminger, President. Toll-free, (800) 482-2962. General email, info@cdaweb.net Web, www.cdaweb.net*

Membership: wholesalers, manufacturers, retailers, and brokers who sell or distribute convenience products. Conducts educational programs. Monitors legislation and regulations. (Formerly American Wholesale Marketers Assn.)

Council of Better Business Bureaus, *3033 Wilson Blvd., #600, Arlington, VA 22201-3843; (703) 276-0100. Fax, (703) 525-8277. Mary E. Power, President. Web, www.bbb.org/council and Twitter, @bbb_us*

Membership: businesses and Better Business Bureaus in the United States and Canada. Promotes ethical business practices and truth in national advertising; mediates disputes between consumers and businesses.

Equipment Leasing and Finance Assn., *1825 K St. N.W., #900, 20006; (202) 238-3400. Fax, (202) 238-3401. Ralph Petta, President. General email, rscoggins@elfaonline.org Web, www.elfaonline.org and Twitter, @ELFAOnline*

Membership: independent leasing companies, banks, financial service companies, and independent brokers and suppliers to the leasing industry. Promotes the interests of the equipment leasing and finance industry; assists in the resolution of industry problems; encourages standards. Monitors legislation and regulations.

Grocery Manufacturers Assn. (GMA), *1350 Eye St. N.W., #300, 20005-3377; (202) 639-5900. Fax, (202) 639-5932. Pamela Bailey, President. Press, (202) 295-3957. General email, info@gmaonline.org Web, www.gmaonline.org*

Membership: sales and marketing agents and retail merchandisers of food and consumer products worldwide. Sponsors research, training, and educational programs for members and their trading partners. Monitors legislation and regulations.

International Cemetery, Cremation, and Funeral Assn., *107 Carpenter Dr., #100, Sterling, VA 20164; (703) 391-8400. Fax, (703) 391-8416. Robert M. Fells, Executive Director, ext. 1212. Information, (800) 645-7700. General email, hq@iccfa.com Web, www.iccfa.com*

Membership: owners and operators of cemeteries, crematories, funeral homes, mausoleums, and columbariums.

Promotes the building and proper maintenance of modern interment places; promotes high ethical standards in the industry; encourages prearrangement of funerals.

International Council of Shopping Centers, *Global Public Policy, 555 12th St. N.W., #660, 20004; (202) 626-1400. Fax, (202) 626-1418. Betsy Laird, Senior Staff Vice President; Christopher Gerlach, Director, Public Policy Research, (202) 626-1413.*
General email, gpp@icsc.org
Web, www.icsc.org

Membership: shopping center owners, developers, managers, retailers, contractors, and others in the industry worldwide. Provides information, including research data. Monitors legislation and regulations. (Headquarters in New York.)

International Franchise Assn., *1900 K St. N.W., #700, 20006; (202) 628-8000. Fax, (202) 628-0812. Robert Cresanti, President.*
Web, www.franchise.org

Membership: national and international franchisers. Sponsors seminars, workshops, trade shows, and conferences. Monitors legislation and regulations.

National Assn. of Convenience Stores (NACS), *1600 Duke St., 7th Floor, Alexandria, VA 22314-3421; (703) 684-3600. Fax, (703) 836-4564. Henry Armour, President. Toll-free, (800) 966-6227.*
General email, nacs@nacsonline.com
Web, www.nacsonline.com

Membership: convenience store retailers and industry suppliers. Promotes industry position on labor, tax, environment, alcohol, and food-related issues; conducts research and training programs. Monitors legislation and regulations.

National Assn. of Wholesaler-Distributors, *1325 G St. N.W., #1000, 20005-3100; (202) 872-0885. Fax, (202) 785-0586. Dirk Van Dongen, President.*
General email, naw@naw.org
Web, www.naw.org

Membership: wholesale distributors and trade associations, product sellers, manufacturers, and their insurers. Provides members and government policymakers with research, education, and government relations information. Promotes federal product liability tort reform. Monitors legislation and regulations.

National Retail Federation, *1101 New York Ave. N.W., 20005; (202) 783-7971. Fax, (202) 737-2849. Matthew R. Shay, President; David French, Senior Vice President, Government Relations. Toll-free, (800) 673-4692.*
Web, www.nrf.com

Membership: international, national, and state associations of retailers and major retail corporations. Concerned with federal regulatory activities and legislation that affect retailers, including tax, employment, trade, and credit issues. Provides information on retailing through seminars, conferences, and publications.

Personal Care Products Council, *1620 L St. N.W., #1200, 20036; (202) 331-1770. Fax, (202) 331-1969. Lezlee Westine, President.*
Web, www.personalcarecouncil.org; www.cosmeticsinfo.org

Membership: manufacturers and distributors of finished personal care products. Conducts product safety research and advocacy. Represents the industry at the local, state, and national levels. Interests include legal issues, international trade, legislation, and regulatory policy. (Formerly Cosmetic, Toiletry, and Fragrance Assn.)

Retail Industry Leaders Assn., *1700 N. Moore St., #2250, Arlington, VA 22209-1998; (703) 841-2300. Fax, (703) 841-1184. Sandra (Sandy) Kennedy, President.*
Web, www.rila.org and Twitter, @RILAtweets

Membership: retailers, consumer product manufacturers, and service suppliers in the United States and abroad. Interests include supply chain, trade, finance, asset protection, and workforce issues, and energy. Monitors legislation and regulations. (Formerly International Mass Retail Assn.)

Security Industry Assn., *8405 Colesville Rd., #500, Silver Spring, MD 20910; (301) 804-4700. Fax, (301) 804-4701. Donald Erickson, Chief Executive Officer, (301) 804-4747.*
General email, info@siaonline.org
Web, www.securityindustry.org and Twitter, @SIAOnline

Membership: manufacturers, service providers, and integrators of electronic security equipment. Sponsors trade shows, develops industry standards, supports educational programs and job training, and publishes statistical research. Monitors legislation and regulations.

Service Station Dealers of America and Allied Trades, *1532 Pointer Ridge Pl., Suite G, Bowie, MD 20716; (301) 390-4405. Fax, (301) 390-3161. Billy Hillmulth, Vice President, (301) 390-0900.*
General email, mgates@wmda.net
Web, www.ssda-at.com

Membership: state associations of gasoline retailers, repair facilities, car washes, and convenience stores. Interests include environmental issues, retail marketing, oil allocation, imports and exports, prices, and taxation. Monitors legislation and regulations.

Society of Consumer Affairs Professionals in Business (SOCAP International), *625 N. Washington St., #304, Alexandria, VA 22314; (703) 519-3700. Fax, (703) 549-4886. Brian Costanzo, President, (703) 910-2470.*
General email, socap@socap.org
Web, www.socap.org

Membership: managers and supervisors who are responsible for consumer affairs, customer service, market research, and sales and marketing operations. Provides information on customer service techniques, market trends, and industry statistics; sponsors seminars and conferences. Monitors legislation and regulations.

Advertising

►AGENCIES

Federal Highway Administration (FHWA)
(Transportation Dept.), Planning, Environment, and Realty, 1200 New Jersey Ave. S.E., #E76-306, 20590; (202) 366-0116. Fax, (202) 366-3713. Gloria M. Shepherd, Associate Administrator.
Web, www.fhwa.dot.gov/real_estate

Administers laws concerning outdoor advertising along interstate and federally-aided primary highways.

Federal Trade Commission (FTC), *Bureau of Consumer Protection, Advertising Practices,* 400 7th Ave. S.W., #10418, 20024; (202) 326-3090. Fax, (202) 326-3259. Mary Engle, Associate Director.
Web, www.ftc.gov/about-ftc/bureaus-offices/bureau-consumer-protection/our-divisions/division-advertising-practices

Protects consumers from deceptive and unsubstantiated advertising through law enforcement, public reports, and industry outreach. Focuses on national advertising campaigns for food, dietary supplements, and over-the-counter drugs, particularly advertising that makes claims difficult for consumers to evaluate. Monitors alcohol advertising for unfair practices; issues reports on alcohol labeling, advertising, and promotion. Issues reports on the marketing to children of violent movies, video games, and music recordings.

Food and Drug Administration (FDA) *(Health and Human Services Dept.), Prescription Drug Promotion,* 10903 New Hampshire Ave., Bldg. 51, #3203, Silver Spring, MD 20993-0002; (301) 796-1200. Fax, (301) 847-8444. Thomas W. Abrams, Director.
Web, www.fda.gov/aboutfda/centersoffices/officeofmedicalproductsandtobacco/cder/ucm090142.htm

Monitors prescription drug advertising and labeling; investigates complaints; conducts market research on health care communications and drug issues.

►NONGOVERNMENTAL

Ad Council, 1707 L St. N.W., #600, 20036; (202) 331-9153. Lisa Sherman, President.
General email, info@adcouncil.org
Web, www.adcouncil.org

Produces and distributes public service advertisements for nonprofit organizations and federal agencies.

American Advertising Federation, 1101 Vermont Ave. N.W., #500, 20005; (202) 898-0089. Fax, (202) 898-0159. James Edmund Datri, President. Toll-free, (800) 999-2231.
General email, aaf@aaf.org
Web, www.aaf.org

Membership: advertising companies (ad agencies, advertisers, media, and services), clubs, associations, and college chapters. A founder of the National Advertising Review Board, a self-regulatory body. Sponsors annual awards for outstanding advertising.

American Assn. of Advertising Agencies, *Government Relations,* 1707 L St. N.W., #600, 20036; (202) 331-7345. Fax, (202) 857-3675. Richard (Dick) O'Brien, Executive Vice President.
General email, wash@aaaadc.org
Web, www.aaaa.org

Co-sponsors the National Advertising Review Board (a self-regulatory body), the Advertising Council, and the Media/Advertising Partnership for a Drug Free America. Monitors legislation and regulations at the federal, state, and local level to protect the agency business and the advertising industry as a whole. (Headquarters in New York.)

Color Marketing Group, 1908 Mount Vernon Ave., Alexandria, VA 22301; (703) 329-8500. Fax, (703) 535-3190. Sharon Griffis, Executive Director.
General email, sgriffis@colormarketing.org
Web, www.colormarketing.org and Twitter, @ColorSells

Provides a forum for the exchange of noncompetitive information by color design professionals; seeks to create color forecast information for design and marketing. Holds meetings; sponsors special events in the United States as well as abroad.

Direct Marketing Assn., Washington Office, 1615 L St. N.W., #1100, 20036-5624; (202) 955-5030. Fax, (202) 955-0085. Thomsa Benton, Chief Executive Officer; Michael Uehlein, Communications. Press, (202) 861-2441.
General email, info@the-dma.org
Web, www.the-dma.org

Membership: businesses and nonprofit organizations using and supporting direct marketing tools. Advocates standards for marketing, focusing on relevance to consumers. Provides research, education, and networking opportunities to members. Operates a service that removes consumer names from unwanted mailing lists. Monitors legislation and regulations. (Headquarters in New York.)

International Sign Assn., 1001 N. Fairfax St., #301, Alexandria, VA 22314; (703) 836-4012. Fax, (703) 836-8353. Lori Anderson, President, ext. 116.
General email, info@signs.org
Web, www.signs.org

Membership: manufacturers and distributors of signs and other visual communications systems. Promotes the sign industry; conducts workshops and seminars; sponsors annual competition.

Outdoor Advertising Assn. of America, 1850 M St. N.W., #1040, 20036; (202) 833-5566. Fax, (202) 833-1522. Nancy Fletcher, President.
General email, info@oaaa.org
Web, www.oaaa.org

Membership: outdoor advertising companies, operators, suppliers, and affiliates. Serves as a clearinghouse for public service advertising campaigns. Monitors legislation and regulations.

Small Business Administration

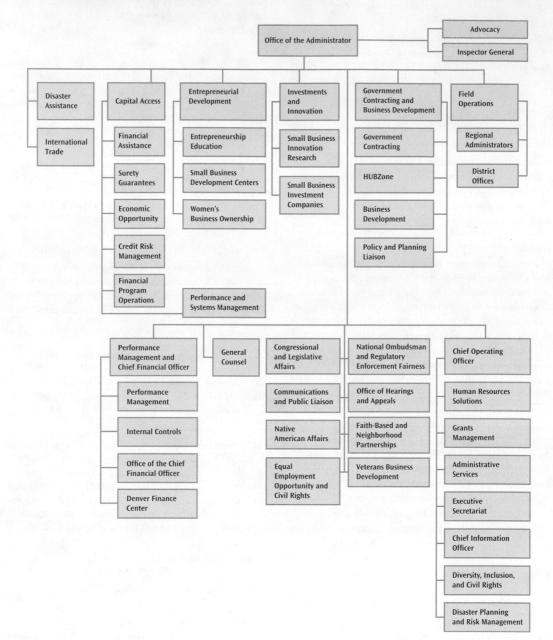

SMALL AND DISADVANTAGED BUSINESS

General

▶AGENCIES

Agency for International Development (USAID), *Small and Disadvantaged Business Utilization (OSDBU),* 301 4th St., #SA-44, 20024; (202) 567-4730. Mauricio P. Vera, Director, (202) 567-4730.
Web, www.usaid.gov/who-we-are/organization/ independent-offices/office-small-and-disadvantaged-business-utilization

Counsels small and minority-owned businesses on how to do business with USAID. Identifies opportunities for small businesses in subcontracting with the agency.

Commerce Dept., *Business Liaison,* 1401 Constitution Ave. N.W., #5062, 20230; (202) 482-1360. Fax, (202) 482-4054. Shannon Roche, Director.
General email, businessliaison@doc.gov
Web, www.commerce.gov/office-secretary/office-business-liaison

Serves as the federal government's central office for business assistance. Handles requests for information and services as well as complaints and suggestions from businesses; provides a forum for businesses to comment on federal regulations; initiates meetings on policy issues with industry groups, business organizations, trade and small business associations, and the corporate community.

Commerce Dept., *Small and Disadvantaged Business Utilization,* *1401 Constitution Ave. N.W., #6411, 20230; (202) 482-1472. LaJuene Desmukes, Director.*
General email, osdbu@doc.gov

Web, www.osec.doc.gov/osdbu

An advocacy and advisory office that works toward increasing Commerce Dept. contract awards to small, disadvantaged, women-owned, veteran-owned, and HUB-Zone small businesses.

Consumer Product Safety Commission (CPSC), *Small Business Ombudsman,* *4330 East-West Hwy., Bethesda, MD 20814; (888) 531-9070. Will Cusey, Ombudsman, (301) 504-7833. TTY, (301) 595-7054.*
General email, sbo@cpsc.gov

Web, www.cpsc.gov

Provides guidance and advice to small businesses and small batch manufacturers about compliance with CPSC laws and regulations as well as technical assistance in resolving problems.

Education Dept., *White House Initiative on Asian Americans and Pacific Islanders,* *550 12th St. S.W., 10th Floor, 20202; (202) 245-6418. Fax, (202) 245-7166. Doua Thor, Executive Director. Press, (202) 245-6353.*
General email, whitehouseaapi@ed.gov

Web, http://sites.ed.gov/whieeaa and Twitter, @whitehouseAAPI

Works to increase Asian American and Pacific Islander participation in federal business and economic development programs.

Farm Service Agency (FSA) *(Agriculture Dept.), Minority and Socially Disadvantaged Farmers Assistance,* *1400 Independence Ave. S.W., MS 0503, 20250-0503; (202) 690-1700. Fax, (202) 690-4727. J. Latrice Hill, Director, Outreach. TTY, (202) 720-5132.*
General email, oasdfr@osec.usda.gov

Web, www.fsa.usda.gov

Works with minority and socially disadvantaged farmers who have concerns and questions about loan applications filed with local offices or other Farm Service Agency programs.

Federal Emergency Management Agency (FEMA) *(Homeland Security Dept.), Federal Insurance and Mitigation Administration,* *1800 S. Bell St., MS 3020, Arlington, VA 22202; (202) 646-2781. Fax, (202) 646-7970. Vacant, Associate Administrator.*
Web, www.fema.gov/what-mitigation/federal-insurance-mitigation-administration

Administers federal crime and flood insurance programs. Makes low-cost flood and crime insurance available to eligible small businesses.

General Services Administration (GSA), *Small Business Utilization,* *1275 1st St. N.E., 20417; (202) 208-5938. Fax, (202) 501-2590. Jerome Fletcher II, Associate Administrator, (202) 969-7089.*
General email, smallbusiness@gsa.gov

Web, www.gsa.gov/osbu and Twitter, @GSAOSBU

Works to increase small business access to government contract procurement opportunities. Provides policy guidance and direction for GSA Regional Small Business Offices, which offer advice and assistance to businesses interested in government procurement.

Minority Business Development Agency *(Commerce Dept.),* *1401 Constitution Ave. N.W., #5053, 20230; (202) 482-2332. Fax, (202) 501-4698. Alejandra Castillo, Director.*
Web, www.mbda.gov

Assists minority business owners in obtaining federal loans and contract awards; produces an annual report on federal agencies' performance in procuring from minority-owned businesses. Assists minority entrepreneurs one-on-one with financial planning, marketing, management, and technical assistance. Focuses on promoting wealth in minority communities.

National Science Foundation (NSF), *Small Business Innovation Research / Small Business Technology Transfer Program,* *4201 Wilson Blvd., #590N, Arlington, VA 22230; (703) 292-8050. Fax, (703) 292-9057. Prakash Balan, Director, (703) 292-7069.*
Web, www.nsf.gov/eng/iip/sttr

Serves as liaison between the small-business community and NSF offices; awards grants and contracts. Administers the Small Business Innovation Research and Small Business Technology Transfer Programs, which fund research proposals from small science/high technology firms and startups. Interests include hard science and technology with high technical risk and potential for significant commercial or societal impact. Offers incentives for commercial development, including NSF-funded research.

National Women's Business Council, *409 3rd St. S.W., 5th Floor, 20416; (202) 205-3850. Fax, (202) 205-6825. Amanda Brown, Executive Director.*
General email, info@nwbc.gov

Web, www.nwbc.gov

Independent, congressionally mandated council established by the Women's Business Ownership Act of 1988. Reviews the status of women-owned businesses nationwide and makes policy recommendations to the president, Congress, and the Small Business Administration. Assesses the role of the federal government in aiding and promoting women-owned businesses.

Securities and Exchange Commission (SEC), *Economic and Risk Analysis,* 100 F St. N.E., 20549; (202) 551-6600. Fax, (202) 756-0505. Mark J. Flannery, Director.
General email, DERA@sec.gov

Web, www.sec.gov/dera

Provides the commission with economic analyses of proposed rule and policy changes and other information to guide the SEC in influencing capital markets. Evaluates the effect of policy and other factors on competition within the securities industry and among competing securities markets; compiles financial statistics on capital formation and the securities industry.

Small Business Administration (SBA), 409 3rd St. S.W., 20416-7000; (202) 205-6605. Fax, (202) 205-6802. *Maria Contreras-Sweet, Administrator; Douglas J. Kramer, Deputy Administrator. Toll-free information (Answer Desk), (800) 827-5722. Locator, (202) 205-6600. TTY, (800) 877-8339.*
General email, answerdesk@sba.gov

Web, www.sba.gov

Provides small businesses with financial and management assistance; offers loans to victims of floods, natural disasters, and other catastrophes; licenses, regulates, and guarantees some financing of small-business investment companies; conducts economic and statistical research on small businesses. SBA Answer Desk is an information and referral service. District or regional offices can be contacted for specific loan information.

Small Business Administration (SBA), *Advocacy,* 409 3rd St. S.W., 20416; (202) 205-6533. Fax, (202) 205-6928. *Daryl L. Post, Chief Counsel, Acting. TTY, (800) 877-8339.*
General email, advocacy@sba.gov

Web, www.sba.gov/advocacy

Acts as an advocate for small business viewpoints in regulatory and legislative proceedings. Economic Research Office analyzes the effects of government policies on small businesses and documents the contributions of small business to the economy.

Small Business Administration (SBA), *Business Development,* 409 3rd St. S.W., #8800, 20416; (202) 205-5852. Fax, (202) 205-7259. Jackquline Robinson-Burnette, Associate Administrator. TTY, (800) 877-8339.
General email, 8abd@sba.gov

Web, www.sba.gov/offices/obd

Coordinates the services provided by private industry, banks, the SBA, and other government agencies—such as business development and management and technical assistance—to increase the number of small businesses owned by socially and economically disadvantaged Americans.

Small Business Administration (SBA), *Capital Access,* 409 3rd St. S.W., #8200, 20416; (202) 205-6657. Fax, (202) 205-7230. Ann Marie Mehlum, Associate Administrator. TTY, (800) 877-8339.
Web, www.sba.gov/offices/headquarters/oca

Small and Disadvantaged Business Contacts at Federal Departments and Agencies

DEPARTMENTS

Agriculture, Carmen Jones, (202) 720-7117

Commerce, LaJuene Desmukes, (202) 482-1472

Defense, Kenyata Wesley, (571) 256-7791

  Air Force, Mark Teskey, (571) 256-8052

  Army, James Lloyd (Acting), (703) 697-2868

  Marine Corps, Dave Dawson, (703) 432-3946

  Navy, Emily Harman, (202) 685-6485

Education, Janet D. Scott, (202) 245-6300

Energy, John Hale, (202) 586-7377

Health and Human Services, Teresa Lewis, (202) 690-7300

Homeland Security, Kevin Boshears, (202) 447-0826

  Coast Guard, Carla Thomas, (202) 475-5786

Housing and Urban Development, Karen A. Newton Cole, (202) 402-5477

Interior, Vacant, (202) 208-3493

Justice, Bob Connolly, (202) 616-0521

Labor, Gladys Bailey, (202) 693-7299

State, George L. Price, (703) 875-6822

Transportation, Brandon Neal, (202) 366-1930

Treasury, Jose Arrieta, (202) 622-0530

Veterans Affairs, Tom Leney, (202) 461-4300

AGENCIES

Agency for International Development, Mauricio Vera, (202) 567-4730

Consumer Product Safety Commission, William Cusey, (301) 504-7945

Environmental Protection Agency, Kimberly Patrick, (202) 566-2075

General Services Administration, A. Jerome Fletcher, (855) 672-8472

National Aeronautics and Space Administration, Glenn Delgado, (202) 358-2088

Nuclear Regulatory Commission, Vonna Ordaz, (301) 415-7380

Small Business Administration, Maria Contreras-Sweet, (800) 827-5722

Social Security Administration, Wayne McDonald, (410) 965-7467

Provides financial assistance to small business, including microloans, surety bond guarantees, investment, and international trade.

Small Business Administration (SBA), *Credit Risk Management,* 409 3rd St. S.W., #8200, 20416; (202) 205-3049. Fax, (202) 205-6831. Linda S. Rusche, Director.

TTY, (800) 205-7230.
Web, www.sba.gov/offices/headquarters/ocrm

Conducts on-site and off-site analysis and reviews of SBA lending partners' activities; reviews the quality of the SBA loan portfolio through trend analysis and assessment of risk indicators.

Small Business Administration (SBA), *Entrepreneurial Development,* *409 3rd St. S.W., #6200, 20416; (202) 205-6239. Fax, (202) 205-6903. Tameka Montgomery, Associate Administrator. TTY, (800) 877-8339.*
Web, www.sba.gov/offices/headquarters/oed

Responsible for business development programs of the offices of the Small Business Development Centers and the offices of Business Initiatives and Women's Business Ownership.

Small Business Administration (SBA), *Entrepreneurship Education,* *409 3rd St. S.W., #6200, 20416; (202) 205-6665. Fax, (202) 205-6093. Jack Bienko, Associate Administrator. TTY, (800) 877-6903.*
Web, www.sba.gov/offices/headquarters/oee

Outreach and education arm of SBA. Provides small businesses with instruction and counseling in marketing, accounting, product analysis, production methods, research and development, and management problems. Provides in-person as well as online training and specialized services for underserved markets.

Small Business Administration (SBA), *International Trade,* *409 3rd St. S.W., #2400, 20416; (202) 205-6720. Fax, (202) 205-7272. Eileen Sánchez, Associate Administrator. TTY, (800) 877-8339.*
Web, www.sba.gov/offices/headquarters/oit

Ensures interests of small businesses are considered and reflected in trade negotiations; promotes ability of small businesses to export.

Small Business Administration (SBA), *Investment and Innovation,* *409 3rd St. S.W., #6300, 20416; (202) 205-6510. Fax, (202) 205-6959. Mark Walsh, Associate Administrator. TTY, (800) 877-8339.*
Web, www.sba.gov/offices/headquarters/ooi

Administers and runs the Small Business Investment Company, Small Business Investment Research, and Small Business Technology Transfer programs.

Small Business Administration (SBA), *Women's Business Ownership,* *409 3rd St. S.W., #6600, 20416; (202) 205-6673. Fax, (202) 205-7287. Erin Andrew, Assistant Administrator.*
Web, www.sba.gov/offices/headquarters/wbo

Acts as an advocate for current and potential women business owners throughout the federal government and in the private sector. Provides training, counseling, and mentoring through a nationwide network of women's business centers; offers information on national and local resources, including SBA small business programs.

Small Business Administration, (SBA), *Native American Affairs,* *409 3rd St. S.W., #6700, 20416; (202) 205-7364.*

Fax, (202) 205-6139. Nathan Segal, Assistant Administrator. TTY, (800) 877-8339.
Web, www.sba.gov/offices/headquarters/naa

Offers tools and resources to increase Native American involvement and opportunities in small business.

▶**CONGRESS**

For a listing of relevant congressional committees and sub-committees, please see pages 34–35 or the Appendix.

▶**NONGOVERNMENTAL**

AHHA: The Voice of Hispanic Marketing, *8280 Willow Oaks Corporate Dr., #600, Fairfax, VA 22031; (703) 745-5531. Horacio Gavilan, Executive Director, (703) 256-5069.*
General email, info@ahaa.org
Web, www.ahaa.org

Works to grow, strengthen, and protect the Hispanic marketing and advertising industry. Strives to increase Hispanics' awareness of market opportunities and enhance professionalism of the industry. (Formerly the Assn. of Hispanic Advertising Agencies.)

Capital Region Minority Supplier Development Council, *10750 Columbia Pike, #200, Silver Spring, MD 20901; (301) 593-5860. Fax, (301) 593-1364. Sharon Pinder, President; Jonice Adams, Vice President.*
General email, info@mddcmsdc.org
Web, www.crmsdc.org and Twitter, @CRMSDC

Certifies minority (Asian, African American, Hispanic, and Native American) business enterprises. Refers corporate buyers to minority suppliers and supports the development, expansion, and promotion of corporate minority supplier development programs. Offers networking opportunities and gives awards. Disseminates statistics and information. Provides consultation services, educational seminars, technical assistance, and training opportunities. (Regional council of the National Minority Supplier Development Council.)

ECDC Enterprise Development Group (EDG), *901 S. Highland St., Arlington, VA 22204; (703) 685-0441. Fax, (703) 685-4200. Kevin Kelly, Managing Director, ext. 225.*
General email, info@entdevgroup.org
Web, www.entdevgroup.org

Provides microloans to clients in the Washington metropolitan area with low-to-moderate income in order to promote new business enterprises and individual self-sufficiency. Offers business training and pre loan and post-loan technical assistance to entrepreneurs. Operates a matched savings program for low-income refugees and a car loan program for those with inadequate transportation. An independent subsidiary of the Ethiopian Community Development Council.

Institute for Liberty (IFL), *1250 Connecticut Ave. N.W., #200, 20036; (202) 261-6592. Fax, (877) 350-6147. Andrew Langer, President.*
Web, www.instituteforliberty.org

Seeks to protect small businesses. Interests include energy and tax policy, health care, property rights, and Internet freedom. Monitors policy and legislation.

National Assn. of Investment Companies, *1300 Pennsylvania Ave. N.W., #700, 20005; (202) 204-3001. Fax, (202) 204-3022. Robert L. Greene, President.*
General email, info@naicpe.com
Web, www.naicpe.com

Membership: investment companies that provide minority-owned businesses with venture capital and management guidance. Provides technical assistance; monitors legislation and regulations.

National Assn. of Negro Business and Professional Women's Clubs Inc., *1806 New Hampshire Ave. N.W., 20009; (202) 483-4206. Fax, (202) 462-7253. Robin M. Waley, Executive Director.*
General email, executivedirector@nanbpwc.org
Web, www.nanbpwc.org

Promotes and protects the interests of business and professional women, serves as advisors to young people seeking to enter business and the professions, provides scholarship support for secondary education, sponsors workshops, and works to improve the quality of life in local and global communities to foster good fellowship. Monitors legislation and regulations.

National Assn. of Women Business Owners, *601 Pennsylvania Ave. N.W., South Bldg., #900, 20004; (202) 609-9817. Fax, (202) 403-3788. Jen Earle, Chief Executive Officer. Toll-free, (800) 556-2926.*
General email, national@nawbo.org
Web, www.nawbo.org

Promotes the economic, social, and political interests of women business owners through networking, leadership and business development training, and advocacy.

National Black Chamber of Commerce, *4400 Jenifer St. N.W., #331, 20015; (202) 466-6888. Fax, (202) 466-4918. Harry C. Alford, President.*
General email, info@nationalbcc.org
Web, www.nationalbcc.org

Membership: Black-owned businesses. Educates and trains the Black community in entrepreneurship and other economic areas. Monitors legislation and regulations.

National Federation of Independent Business (NFIB), Washington Office, *1201 F St. N.W., #200, 20004-1221; (202) 314-2000. Fax, (202) 554-0496. Juanita Duggan, President; Caitlin McDevitt, Legislative Services Representative; Sarah Feagan, Legislative Services Representative. Toll-free, (800) 634-2669. Press, (202) 554-9000.*
General email, media@nfib.com
Web, www.nfib.com

Membership: independent businesses. Monitors public policy issues and legislation affecting small and independent businesses, including taxation, government regulation, labor-management relations, and liability insurance. (Headquarters in Nashville, Tenn.)

National Gay and Lesbian Chamber of Commerce, *729 15th St. N.W., 9th Floor, 20005; (202) 234-9181. Fax, (202) 234-9185. Justin G. Nelson, President.*
General email, info@nglcc.org
Web, www.nglcc.org, Twitter, @NGLCC and Facebook, www.facebook.com/NGLCC

Communicates ideas and information for and between businesses and organizations. Works with state and local chambers of commerce and business groups on various issues. Acts as an advocate on behalf of lesbian-, gay-, bisexual-, and transgender- owned businesses; professionals; students of business; and corporations.

National Small Business Assn., *1156 15th St. N.W., #1100, 20005; (202) 293-8830. Fax, (202) 872-8543. Todd McCracken, President. Toll-free, (800) 345-6728.*
General email, info@nsba.biz
Web, www.nsba.biz

Membership: manufacturing, wholesale, retail, service, exporting, and other small business firms and regional small-business organizations. Represents the interests of small business before Congress, the administration, and federal agencies. Services to members include a toll-free legislative hotline and group insurance.

SCORE Assn., *1175 Herndon Pkwy., #900, Herndon, VA 20170; (703) 487-3612. Fax, (703) 487-3066. W. Kenneth (Ken) Yancey Jr., Chief Executive Officer. Information, (800) 634-0245.*
General email, help@score.org
Web, www.score.org and Twitter, @SCOREMentors

Independent volunteer organization funded by the Small Business Administration through which retired, semiretired, and active business executives use their knowledge and experience to counsel small businesses. (Formerly Service Corps of Retired Executives Assn.)

Small Business and Entrepreneurship Council (SBE Council), *301 Maple Ave. West, Vienna, VA 22180; (703) 242-5840. Fax, (703) 242-5841. Karen Kerrigan, President.*
General email, info@sbecouncil.org
Web, www.sbecouncil.org

Membership: U.S. entrepreneurs and business owners. Seeks to protect small business and promotes entrepreneurship. Provides networking opportunities, educational resources, and market intelligence for its members. Monitors legislation and regulations.

Small Business Legislative Council, *4800 Hampden Lane, #64, Bethesda, MD 20814; (301) 652-8302. Paula Calimafde, President; Jerry Heppes, Chair.*
General email, email@sblc.org
Web, www.sblc.org

Membership: trade associations that represent small businesses in the manufacturing, retail, professional, service, and technical services and the agricultural, transportation, tourism, and construction sectors. Monitors and proposes legislation and regulations to benefit small businesses.

U.S. Chamber of Commerce, *Small Business Policy,* *1615 H St. N.W., 20062-2000; (202) 463-5498. Fax, (202) 463-3174. Giovanni Coratolo, Vice President.*
Web, www.uschambersmallbusinessnation.com

Seeks to enhance visibility of small businesses within the national chamber and the U.S. business community. Provides members with information on national small business programs and legislative issues.

U.S. Hispanic Chamber of Commerce, *1424 K St. N.W., #401, 20015; (202) 842-1212. Fax, (202) 842-3221. Javier Palomarez, President. Press, (619) 721-5148. General email, info@ushcc.com*
Web, www.ushcc.com

Membership: Hispanic Chambers of Commerce and business organizations. Monitors legislation. Provides technical assistance to Hispanic business associations and owners. Promotes public policies that enhance the economic development of its members, trade between Hispanic businesses in the United States and Latin America, and partnerships with the larger business community.

U.S. Pan Asian American Chamber of Commerce, *1329 18th St. N.W., 20036; (202) 296-5221. Fax, (202) 296-5225. Susan Au Allen, Chief Executive Officer, (202) 378-1130. Toll-free, (800) 696-7818.*
General email, info@uspaacc.com and michelle@paacc.com
Web, www.uspaacc.com

Helps Asian American-owned businesses gain access to government and corporate contracts.

U.S. Women's Chamber of Commerce, *700 12th St. N.W., #700, 20005; (888) 418-7922. Margot Dorfman, Chief Executive Officer.*
General email, notify@uswcc.org
Web, www.uswcc.org

Provides services and career opportunities to women in business, including networking, leadership training, political advocacy, access to government procurement markets, and technical expertise. Monitors legislation and regulations.

3

Communications and the Media

GENERAL POLICY AND ANALYSIS

Basic Resources

▶AGENCIES

Access Board, *1331 F St. N.W., #1000, 20004-1111; (202) 272-0080. Fax, (202) 272-0081. David M. Capozzi, Executive Director, (202) 272-0010. Toll-free technical assistance, (800) 872-2253. TTY, (202) 272-0082. Toll-free TTY, (800) 993-2822.*
General email, info@access-board.gov

Web, www.access-board.gov

Develops and maintains accessibility requirements for buildings, transit vehicles, telecommunications equipment, medical diagnostic equipment, and electronic and information technology. Provides technical assistance and training on these guidelines and standards. Enforces access standards for federally funded facilities through the Architectural Barriers Act.

Federal Communications Commission (FCC), *445 12th St. S.W., 20554; (888) 225-5322. Fax, (202) 418-2801. Tom Wheeler, Chair, (202) 418-1000. Toll-free fax, (866) 418-0232. Reference Information Center, (202) 418-0270. Media Relations, (202) 418-0503. Consumer and Government Affairs, (202) 418-1400. Legislative Affairs, (202) 418-1900. TTY, (888) 835-5322. Videophone, (844) 432-2275.*
General email, fccinfo@fcc.gov

Web, www.fcc.gov

Regulates interstate and foreign communications by radio, television, wire, cable, microwave, and satellite; consults with other government agencies and departments on national and international matters involving wire and radio telecommunications and with state regulatory commissions on telegraph and telephone matters; reviews applications for construction permits and licenses for such services. Reference Information Center open to the public (except under high-alert status orange and higher).

Federal Communications Commission (FCC), *Media Bureau, Policy Division, 445 12th St. S.W., 20554; (202) 418-1450. Fax, (202) 418-1069. Martha Heller, Chief.*
Web, www.fcc.gov/media/policy/policy-division

Conducts proceedings concerning broadcast, cable, and post-licensing Direct Broadcast Satellite issues. Facilitates competition in the multichannel video programming marketplace by resolving carriage and other complaints involving access to facilities. Administers FCC's programs for political broadcasting and equal opportunity matters. Interests include children's TV, closed captioning, digital broadcasting, leased access, low-power FM and TV, public broadcasting, and V chip.

National Telecommunications and Information Administration (NTIA) *(Commerce Dept.), 1401 Constitution Ave. N.W., #4898, 20230; (202) 482-2000.*

Fax, (202) 501-0536. Lawrence E. Strickling, Assistant Secretary; Linda Kinney, Senior Adviser, Internet Policy; Derek Khlopin, Senior Adviser, Spectrum; Jennifer Duane, Senior Adviser, Broadband & Public Safety. Press, (202) 482-7002.
Web, www.ntia.doc.gov

Develops domestic and international telecommunications policy for the executive branch; manages federal use of radio spectrum; conducts research on radiowave transmissions and other aspects of telecommunications; serves as information source for federal and state agencies on the efficient use of telecommunications resources.

▶CONGRESS

For a listing of relevant congressional committees and subcommittees, please see page 89 or the Appendix.

Library of Congress, *Copyright Office, Licensing, James Madison Memorial Bldg., 101 Independence Ave. S.E., #LM 504, 20557; (202) 707-8150. Fax, (202) 707-0905. James Enzinna, Chief. Information, (202) 707-3000.*
General email, licensing@loc.gov

Web, www.copyright.gov/licensing

Administers statutory licensing for cable television companies and satellite carriers, for making and distributing digital audio recording products, and for use of certain noncommercial broadcasting. Collects and distributes royalty payments under the copyright law. Administers Section 115 licensing for making and distributing phonorecords.

U.S. House of Representatives, *Legislative Resource Center, 135 CHOB, 20515; Fax, (202) 226-5208. Ronald (Dale) Thomas, Chief. Bill status, (202) 226-5200.*
General email, info.clerkweb@mail.house.gov

Web, http://clerk.house.gov/about/offices_lrc.aspx

Records, stores, and provides legislative status information on all bills and resolutions pending in Congress. Print publications include a biographical directory, a guide to research collections of former House members, and books on African Americans and women who have served in Congress.

▶INTERNATIONAL ORGANIZATIONS

Inter-American Telecommunication Commission (CITEL) *(Organization of American States), 1889 F St. N.W., 6th Floor, 20006; (202) 370-4713. Fax, (202) 458-6854. Oscar Léon, Executive Secretary.*
General email, citel@oas.org

Web, www.citel.oas.org

Membership: OAS member states and associate members from the telecommunications, internet, electronic, and media industries, and others. Works with the public and private sectors to facilitate the development of universal telecommunications in the Americas.

►NONGOVERNMENTAL

Accuracy in Media (AIM), *4350 East-West Hwy., #555, Bethesda, MD 20814; (202) 364-4401. Fax, (202) 364-4098. Donald K. Irvine, Chair.*
General email, info@aim.org
Web, www.aim.org

Analyzes print and electronic news media for bias, omissions, and errors in news; approaches media with complaints. Maintains a speakers bureau and a library on political and media topics.

Alliance for Telecommunications Industry Solutions (ATIS), *1200 G St. N.W., #500, 20005; (202) 628-6380. Fax, (202) 393-5453. Susan M. Miller, President, (202) 434-8828.*
General email, atispr@atis.org
Web, www.atis.org

Develops and promotes the worldwide technical and operations standards for information, entertainment, and communications technologies. Sponsors industry forums; serves as an information clearinghouse. Member of the Inter-American Telecommunication Commission (CITEL). Monitors legislation and regulations.

Center for Media and Public Affairs (CMPA), *2338 S. Queen St., Arlington, VA 22202; (202) 302-5523. S. Robert Lichter, President.*
General email, mail@cmpa.com
Web, www.cmpa.com and Twitter, @CMPAatGMU

Nonpartisan research and educational organization that studies media coverage of social and political issues and campaigns, specifically information about health risks, scientific matters, and presidential campaigns. Conducts surveys; publishes materials and reports. (Affiliated with George Mason University.)

Free Press, *Washington Office, 1025 Connecticut Ave. N.W., #1110, 20036; (202) 265-1490. Fax, (202) 265-1489. Craig Aaron, President.*
General email, info@freepress.net
Web, www.freepress.net and Twitter, @freepress

Seeks to engage the public in media policymaking. Advocates policies for more competitive and public interest-oriented media. (Headquarters in Florence, Mass.)

INCOMPAS, *1200 G St. N.W., #350, 20005; (202) 296-6650. Fax, (202) 296-7585. Chip Pickering, Chief Executive Officer.*
Web, www.incompas.org and Twitter, @INCOMPAS

Membership: Broadband, cloud, business and enterprise, fiber, international, Internet, tower and backhaul, and wireless providers. Acts as advocate for the competitive telecommunications industry before Congress, the FCC, and state regulatory agencies; sponsors trade shows, conferences, and policy summits. Monitors legislation and regulations. (Formerly COMPTEL.)

Info Comm International, *11242 Waples Mill Rd., #200, Fairfax, VA 22030; (703) 273-7200. Fax, (703) 278-8082.*

David Labuskes, Executive Director. Information, (800) 659-7469.
Web, www.infocomm.org

Membership: video and audiovisual dealers, manufacturers and producers, and individuals. Promotes the professional AV communications industry and seeks to enhance members' ability to conduct business successfully through tradeshows, education, certification, market research, and government relations. Interests include small business issues, intellectual property, sustainable buildings, e-waste, and standards. Monitors legislation and regulations. (Formerly the International Communications Industries Assn.)

Institute for Public Representation, *600 New Jersey Ave. N.W., #312, 20001; (202) 662-9535. Fax, (202) 662-9634. Hope Babcock, Co-Director; Angela Campbell, Co-Director; Michael Kirkpatrick, Co-Director.*
General email, gulcipr@law.georgetown.edu
Web, www.law.georgetown.edu/academics/academic-programs/clinical-programs/our-clinics/institute-for-public-representation.cfm
Blog, instituteforpublicrepresentation.org

Public interest law firm and clinical education program founded by Georgetown University Law Center. Attorneys act as counsel for groups and individuals unable to obtain effective legal representation in the areas of First Amendment and media law, environmental law, civil rights, and general public interest matters. Gives graduate fellows an opportunity to work on unique, large-scale projects.

Media Institute, *2300 Clarendon Blvd., #602, Arlington, VA 22201; (703) 243-5700. Fax, (703) 243-8808. Patrick D. Maines, President.*
General email, info@mediainstitute.org
Web, www.mediainstitute.org

Research foundation that conducts conferences, files court briefs and regulatory comments, and sponsors programs on communications topics. Advocates a competitive media and communications industry and free-speech rights for individuals, media, and corporate speakers.

Media Matters for America, *P.O. Box 52155, 20091; (202) 756-4100. Fax, (202) 756-4101. Bradley Beychok, President. Press, (202) 772-8195.*
Web, www.mediamatters.org

Web-based research and information center concerned with monitoring and analyzing print, broadcast, cable, radio, and Internet media for inaccurate news and commentary. Seeks to inform journalists and the general public about specific instances of misinformation and provide resources for taking action against false claims.

Media Research Center, *1900 Campus Commons Dr., #600, Reston, VA 20191; (571) 267-3500. Fax, (571) 375-0099. Toll-free, (800) 672-1423. L. Brent Bozell III, President; David Martin, Executive Vice President.*

COMMUNICATIONS AND MEDIA RESOURCES IN CONGRESS

For a complete listing of congressional committees, including their full contact information, leadership, membership, and jurisdictions, please refer to the Appendix on pages 779–896.

HOUSE:

House Administration Committee, (202) 225-8281. Web, cha.house.gov

House Appropriations Committee, (202) 225-2771. Web, appropriations.house.gov

 Subcommittee on Labor, Health and Human Services, Education, and Related Agencies, (202) 225-3508.

House Energy and Commerce Committee, (202) 225-2927. Web, energycommerce.house.gov

 Subcommittee on Communications and Technology, (202) 225-2927.

House Judiciary Committee, (202) 225-3951. Web, judiciary.house.gov

 Subcommittee on Courts, Intellectual Property, and the Internet, (202) 226-7680.

 Subcommittee on the Constitution and Civil Justice, (202) 225-2825.

House Oversight and Government Reform Committee, (202) 225-5074. Web, oversight.house.gov

 Subcommittee on Information Technology, (202) 225-5074.

House Science, Space, and Technology Committee, (202) 225-6371. Web, science.house.gov

 Subcommittee on Research and Technology, (202) 225-6371.

House Small Business Committee, (202) 225-5821. Web, smallbusiness.house.gov

 Subcommittee on Health and Technology, (202) 225-5821.

JOINT:

Joint Committee on Printing, (202) 225-2061. Web, cha.house.gov/jointcommittees/joint-committee-on-printing

Joint Committee on the Library of Congress, (202) 225-8281. Web, cha.house.gov/jointcommittees/joint-committee-library

SENATE:

Senate Agriculture, Nutrition, and Forestry Committee, (202) 224-2035. Web, ag.senate.gov

 Subcommittee on Rural Development and Energy, (202) 224-2035.

Senate Appropriations Committee, (202) 224-7363. Web, appropriations.senate.gov

 Subcommittee on Labor, Health and Human Services, Education, and Related Agencies, (202) 224-9145.

Senate Commerce, Science, and Transportation Committee, (202) 224-0411. Web, commerce.senate.gov

 Subcommittee on Communications, Technology, Innovation, and the Internet, (202) 224-9340.

Senate Foreign Relations Committee, (202) 224-4651. Web, foreign.senate.gov

 Subcommittee on East Asia, The Pacific, and International Cybersecurity Policy, (202) 224-4651.

Senate Judiciary Committee, (202) 224-7703. Web, judiciary.senate.gov

 Subcommittee on Antitrust, Competition Policy, and Consumer Rights, (202) 224-6884, (202) 224-7703.

 Subcommittee on Crime and Terrorism, (202) 224-6791.

 Subcommittee on the Constitution, (202) 224-7840.

Senate Rules and Administration Committee, (202) 224-6352. Web, rules.senate.gov

---

General email, mrc@mrc.org

Web, www.mrc.org

 Media-watch organization working for balanced and responsible news coverage of political issues. Records and analyzes network news programs; analyzes print media; maintains profiles of media executives and library of recordings.

National Captioning Institute, *3725 Concorde Pkwy., #100, Chantilly, VA 20151; Fax, (703) 917-9853. Gene Chao, Chief Executive Officer. Phone/TTY, (703) 917-7600.*

General email, mail@ncicap.org

Web, www.ncicap.org

 Captions television programs for the deaf and hard-of-hearing and produces audio descriptions for the blind on behalf of public and commercial broadcast television networks, cable networks, syndicators, program producers, government agencies, advertisers, and home video distributors. Offers subtitling and language translation services. Produces and disseminates information about the national closed-captioning service and audio description services.

Federal Communications Commission

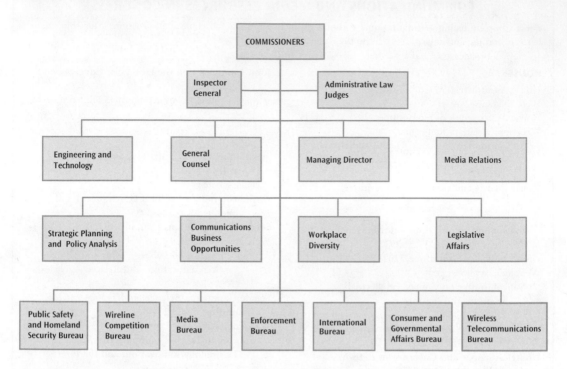

National Journalism Center, *11480 Commerce Park Dr., 600, Reston, VA 20191; Fax, (703) 318-9122. Vacant, Executive Director. Toll-free, (800) 872-1776.*
Web, www.nationaljournalismcenter.org

Sponsors a comprehensive internship program in journalism composed of a series of training seminars that enhance students' knowledge of policy reporting in the areas of economics, education, and business. (Affiliated with the Young America's Foundation.)

Pew Research Center, *U.S. Politics and Policy Project, 1615 L St. N.W., #700, 20036; (202) 419-4350. Fax, (202) 419-4399. Carroll Doherty, Director, (202) 419-4363.*
Web, http://people-press.org

Studies attitudes toward politics and public policy issues as well as the changing U.S. electorate through public opinion research. Conducts national surveys measuring public attentiveness to major news stories; charts trends in values and political and social attitudes. Makes survey results available online, free of charge.

TDI, *8630 Fenton St., #121, Silver Spring, MD 20910-3803; Claude L. Stout, Executive Director.*
Phone (voice/video), (301) 563-9112.
General email, info@TDIforaccess.org
Web, www.TDIforaccess.org

Membership: individuals, organizations, and businesses that advocate equal access to telecommunications, media, and information technologies for Americans who are deaf and hard of hearing. Interests include closed captioning for television, movies, DVDs, and online videos; emergency access (911); and TTY and Telecommunications Relays

Services. Publishes a quarterly magazine and an annual resource directory. Monitors legislation and regulations.

Telecommunications Industry Assn. (TIA), *1320 N. Courthouse Rd., #200, Arlington, VA 22201; (703) 907-7700. Fax, (703) 907-7727. James Reid, Chief Executive Officer; Danielle Coffey, Vice President, Government Affairs, (703) 907-7707.*
General email, tia@tiaonline.org
Web, www.tiaonline.org

Trade association for the information and communications technology industry, including broadband, mobile wireless, information technology, networks, cable, satellite, and unified communications. Develops standards; provides market intelligence; analyzes environmental regulations; hosts trade shows and facilitates business opportunities for members. Monitors legislation and regulations.

Cable Services

▶**AGENCIES**

Federal Communications Commission (FCC), *Media Bureau, 445 12th St. S.W., 3rd Floor, 20554; (202) 418-7200. Fax, (202) 418-2376. William T. Lake, Chief; Janice Wise, Director of Media Relations, (202) 418-8165.*
General email, mbinfo@fcc.gov
Web, www.fcc.gov/media

Makes, recommends, and enforces rules governing cable television and other video distribution services; promotes industry growth, competition, and availability to the public; ensures reasonable rates for consumers in areas that do not have competition in cable service. Responsible for the regulation of analog and digital broadcast services. Licenses, regulates, and develops audio and video services in traditional broadcasting and emerging television delivery systems, including digital television (DTV). Processes applications for licensing commercial and noncommercial radio and television broadcast equipment and facilities; handles renewals and changes of ownership; investigates public complaints.

Federal Communications Commission (FCC), *Media Bureau, Engineering Division,* *445 12th St. S.W., #4-C838, 20554; (202) 418-7000. Fax, (202) 418-1189. John Wong, Chief.*
Web, www.fcc.gov/encyclopedia/engineering-division-media-bureau

Provides technical advice for digital television (DTV) transition, latest cable technologies, and spectrum and broadband policies. Oversees the processing of routine cable applications.

▶NONGOVERNMENTAL

CTAM: Cable and Telecommunications Assn. for Marketing, *120 Waterfront St., #200, National Harbor, MD 20745; (301) 485-8900. Fax, (301) 560-4964. Vicki Lins, President, (301) 485-8920.*
General email, info@ctam.com
Web, www.ctam.com

Promotes innovation in the cable and related industries in areas of marketing, research, management, and new product development. Sponsors annual marketing and research conferences; interests include international markets.

National Cable Telecommunications Assn., *25 Massachusetts Ave. N.W., #100, 20001-1413; (202) 222-2300. Fax, (202) 222-2514. Michael K. Powell, President. Press, (202) 222-2350. Government Relations, (202) 222-2410.*
General email, info@ncta.com
Web, www.ncta.com and Twitter, @NCTAcable

Membership: companies that operate cable television systems, cable television programmers, and manufacturers and suppliers of hardware and software for the industry. Represents the industry before federal regulatory agencies, Congress, and in the courts; provides management and promotional aids and information on legal, legislative, and regulatory matters.

Enforcement, Judicial, and Legal Actions

▶AGENCIES

Antitrust Division *(Justice Dept.), Networks and Technology Enforcement, 450 5th St. N.W., #7100, 20530; (202) 307-6200. Fax, (202) 616-8544. James J. Tierney, Chief.*

General email, antitrust.atr@usdoj.gov
Web, www.justice.gov/atr/about/ntes.html

Reviews mergers in the areas of information technology, Internet-related businesses, computer hardware and software, high-technology components, manufacturing, professional associations, financial services, and the securities industry.

Antitrust Division *(Justice Dept.), Telecommunications and Media Enforcement, 450 5th St. N.W., #7000, 20530; (202) 514-5621. Fax, (202) 514-6381. Scott A. Scheele, Chief. Press, (202) 514-2007.*
Web, www.justice.gov/atr/about/tel.html

Investigates and litigates antitrust cases dealing with communications and media, including mobile wireless services, broadband Internet, satellite communications services, voice communication services, video programming distribution, and business telecommunications services. Participates in agency proceedings and rulemaking concerning communications and media; monitors and analyzes legislation.

Federal Bureau of Investigation (FBI) *(Justice Dept.), CALEA Implementation Unit, Engineering Research Facility, Bldg. 27958A, Quantico, VA 22135; (540) 361-4600. Fax, (540) 361-7082. Marybeth Paglino, Unit Chief, (540) 361-2300.*
Web, http://askcalea.fbi.gov

Administers enforcement of the Communications Assistance for Law Enforcement Act (CALEA). Sets standards for telecommunications carriers concerning the development and deployment of electronic surveillance technologies. Promotes cooperation between the telecommunications industry, government entities, and law enforcement officials to develop intercept capabilities required by law enforcement.

Federal Communications Commission (FCC), *Administrative Law Judges, 445 12th St. S.W., #1C768, 20554; (202) 418-2280. Fax, (202) 418-0195. Richard L. Sippel, Chief Judge; Mary Gosse, Administrative Officer.*
Web, www.fcc.gov/administrative-law-judges

Presides over hearings and issues initial decisions in disputes concerning FCC adjudication proceedings and applications for licensing.

Federal Communications Commission (FCC), *Enforcement Bureau, 445 12th St. S.W., 3rd Floor, #7C723, 20554; (202) 418-7450. Fax, (202) 418-2810. Travis LeBlanc, Chief. Media Relations, (202) 418-0500. Toll-free, (888) 225-5322.*
Web, www.fcc.gov/enforcement-bureau

Enforces the provisions of the Communications Act, the FCC's rules and orders, and various licensing terms and conditions. Investigates and responds to potential unlawful conduct to ensure consumer protection, robust competition, efficient and responsible use of the public airwaves, and compliance with public safety-related rules.

►NONGOVERNMENTAL

Federal Communications Bar Assn., *1020 19th St. N.W., #325, 20036-6101; (202) 293-4000. Fax, (202) 293-4317. Kerry Loughney, Executive Director.*
General email, fcba@fcba.org
Web, www.fcba.org

Membership: attorneys, nonattorneys, and law students in communications law who practice before the Federal Communications Commission, the courts, and state and local regulatory agencies. Cooperates with the FCC and other members of the bar on legal aspects of communications issues.

International and Satellite Communications

►AGENCIES

Broadcasting Board of Governors, *330 Independence Ave. S.W., #3300, 20237; (202) 203-4545. Fax, (202) 203-4585. Vacant, Executive Director. Press, (202) 203-4400. Locator, (202) 203-4000.*
General email, publicaffairs@bbg.gov
Web, www.bbg.gov and Twitter, @BBGov

Established by Congress to supervise all U.S. government nonmilitary international broadcasting, including Voice of America, Radio and TV Martí, Radio Free Europe/Radio Liberty, Radio Free Asia, and the Middle East Broadcasting Networks (MBN). Assesses the quality and effectiveness of broadcasts with regard to U.S. foreign policy objectives; reports annually to the president and to Congress.

Bureau of Economic and Business Affairs *(State Dept.),* ***International Communications and Information Policy,*** *2201 C St. N.W., #4634, EB/CIP, 20520-5820; (202) 647-5212. Fax, (202) 647-5957. Daniel A. Sepulveda, Deputy Assistant Secretary.*
General email, EB-A-CIP-ACC-DL@state.gov
Web, www.state.gov/e/eeb/cip

Coordinates U.S. government international communication and information policy. Acts as a liaison for other federal agencies and the private sector in international communications issues. Promotes advancement of information and communication technology with expanded access and improved efficiency and security; the creation of business opportunities at home and abroad in this sector; resolution of telecommunications trade issues in conjunction with the Office of the U.S. Trade Representative; and the expansion of access to this technology globally.

Federal Communications Commission (FCC), *International Bureau, 445 12th St. S.W., 6th Floor, 20554; (202) 418-0437. Fax, (202) 418-2818. Mindel De La Torre, Chief.*
General email, contact_ib@fcc.gov
Web, www.fcc.gov/international-bureau

Coordinates the FCC's international policy activities; represents the FCC in international forums. Licenses international telecommunications carriers, undersea cables, international short-wave broadcasters, and satellite facilities. Coordinates the FCC's collection and dissemination of information on communications and telecommunications policy, regulation, and market developments in other countries and the policies and regulations of international organizations.

Federal Communications Commission (FCC), *Media Bureau, Policy Division, 445 12th St. S.W., 20554; (202) 418-1450. Fax, (202) 418-1069. Martha Heller, Chief.*
Web, www.fcc.gov/media/policy/policy-division

Conducts proceedings concerning broadcast, cable, and post-licensing Direct Broadcast Satellite issues, including the Satellite Home Viewer Improvement Act.

Federal Communications Commission (FCC), *Wireline Competition Bureau, 445 12th St. S.W., #5C343, 20554; (202) 418-1500. Fax, (202) 418-2825. Matthew DelNero, Chief.*
Web, www.fcc.gov/wireline-competition

Develops and recommends FCC policies involving common carriers (wireline facilities that furnish interstate communications services for hire). Interests include deregulation, pricing policy, economic and technical aspects, numbering resources, and competition in telecommunications markets.

National Telecommunications and Information Administration (NTIA) *(Commerce Dept.), 1401 Constitution Ave. N.W., #4898, 20230; (202) 482-2000. Fax, (202) 501-0536. Lawrence E. Strickling, Assistant Secretary; Linda Kinney, Senior Adviser, Internet Policy; Derek Khlopin, Senior Adviser, Spectrum; Jennifer Duane, Senior Adviser, Broadband & Public Safety. Press, (202) 482-7002.*
Web, www.ntia.doc.gov

Represents the U.S. telecommunications sector (along with the State Dept.) in negotiating international agreements, including conferences with the International Telecommunication Union.

►INTERNATIONAL ORGANIZATIONS

Intelsat, *Washington Office, 7900 Tysons One Pl., McLean, VA 22102-5972; (703) 559-6800. Stephen Spengler, Chief Executive Officer.*
Web, www.intelsat.com

Owns and operates a global satellite communications system and complementary terrestrial network. Helps service providers, broadcasters, corporations, and governments transmit information and content internationally; provides broadband connectivity, multi-format video broadcasting, secure satellite communications, and mobility services. (Headquarters in Luxembourg.)

**Satellite Broadcasting and Communications Assn.
(SBCA),** *1100 17th St. N.W., #1150, 20036; (202) 349-3620.
Fax, (202) 318-2618. Joseph Widoff, Executive Director,
(202) 349-3656. Toll-free, (800) 541-5981.
General email, info@sbca.org*

Web, www.sbca.org and Twitter, @sbacomm

Membership: owners, operators, manufacturers, dealers, and distributors of satellite receiving stations; software
and program suppliers; and others in the satellite services
industry. Promotes use of satellite technology for broadcast
delivery of video, audio, voice, broadband, and interactive
services and as part of the national and global information
infrastructure. Monitors legislation and regulations.

Satellite Industry Association (SIA), *1200 18th St. N.W.,
#1001, 20036; (202) 503-1560. Tom Stroup, President.
General email, info@sia.org*

Web, www.sia.org

Trade association representing global satellite operators, service providers, manufacturers, launch services
providers, and ground equipment suppliers. Promotes
the benefits and uses of commercial satellite technology.
Monitors legislation and regulations, domestically and
abroad.

Radio and Television

Corporation for Public Broadcasting, *401 9th St. N.W.,
20004-2129; (202) 879-9600. Fax, (202) 879-9700.
Patricia de Stacy Harrison, Chief Executive Officer;
Anne Brachman, Vice President, Corp. and Public Affairs.
Comments, (800) 272-2190.
General email, press@cpb.org*

Web, www.cpb.org and Twitter, @CPBmedia

Private corporation chartered by Congress under the
Public Broadcasting Act of 1967 and funded by the federal
government. Helps support the operation of more than
1,400 locally owned and locally operated public television
and radio stations nationwide; provides general support
for national program production and operation, including
content for underserved communities; helps fund projects
on U.S. and international news, education, arts, culture,
history, and natural history; invests in emerging technologies, such as cable and satellite transmission, the Internet
and broadband communication networks, for use by public media.

Federal Communications Commission (FCC),
*Enforcement Bureau, 445 12th St. S.W., 3rd Floor,
#7C723, 20554; (202) 418-7450. Fax, (202) 418 2810.
Travis LeBlanc, Chief. Media Relations, (202) 418-0500.
Toll-free, (888) 225-5322.
Web, www.fcc.gov/enforcement-bureau*

Monitors the radio spectrum and inspects broadcast
stations; ensures that U.S. radio laws and FCC rules are

observed. Develops activities to inform, assist, and educate
licensees; provides presentations and information. Manages the Emergency Alert System. Operates the National
Call Center in Gettysburg, Pa.

Federal Communications Commission (FCC),
*Engineering and Technology, 445 12th St. S.W., 7th Floor,
20554; (202) 418-2470. Fax, (202) 418-1944. Julius Knapp,
Chief Engineer.
General email, oetinfo@fcc.gov*

Web, www.fcc.gov/office-engineering-technology

Advises the FCC on technical and spectrum matters
and assists in developing U.S. telecommunications policy.
Identifies and reviews developments in telecommunications and related technologies. Studies characteristics
of radio frequency spectrum. Certifies radios and other
electronic equipment to meet FCC standards.

National Endowment for the Arts (NEA), *Media Arts, 400
7th St. S.W., 20506; (202) 682-5452. Fax, (202) 682-5721.
Jax Deluca, Director, (202) 682-5742. TTY, (202) 682-5496.
Web, www.arts.gov/artistic-fields/media-arts*

Awards grants to nonprofit organizations for film,
video, and radio productions; supports arts programming
broadcast nationally on public television and radio.

National Assn. of Broadcasters (NAB), *1771 N St. N.W.,
20036; (202) 429-5300. Fax, (202) 429-5406. Gordon Smith,
President. Communications, (202) 429-5350.
General email, nab@nab.org*

Web, www.nab.org

Membership: radio and television broadcast stations
and broadcast networks holding an FCC license or construction permit; associate members include producers
of equipment and programs. Assists members in areas of
management, engineering, and research. Monitors legislation and regulations.

National Public Radio, *1111 N. Capitol St. N.E., 20002;
(202) 513-2000. Fax, (202) 513-3329. Jarl Mohn, President;
Emma Carrasco, Senior Vice President, (202) 513-2313.
Press, (202) 513-2300.
General email, ombudsman@npr.org*

Web, www.npr.org

Multimedia news organization composed of 849 member stations operated by 269 member organizations
nationwide that are locally owned and operated. Produces
and distributes news, music, and entertainment programming in all 50 states. Provides program distribution
service via satellite. Represents member stations before
Congress, the FCC, and other regulatory agencies. Supported by member station programming fees (about
40 percent of funding); corporate sponsorships; and institutional grants.

Public Broadcasting Service, *2100 Crystal Dr., Arlington,
VA 22202; (703) 739-5000. Fax, (703) 739-0775.
Paula Kerger, President, (703) 739-5015; Michael Getler,
Ombudsman, (703) 739-5290.*

General email, pbs@pbs.org

Web, www.pbs.org and Twitter, @PBS

Membership: public television stations nationwide. Selects, schedules, promotes, and distributes national programs; provides public television stations with educational, instructional, and cultural programming; also provides news and public affairs, science and nature, and children's programming. Assists members with technology development and fund-raising.

Telephone and Telegraph

For cellular telephones, see Wireless Telecommunications.

▶AGENCIES

Federal Communications Commission (FCC), *Wireline Competition Bureau,* 445 12th St. S.W., #5C343, 20554; (202) 418-1500. Fax, (202) 418-2825. Matthew DelNero, Chief.
Web, www.fcc.gov/wireline-competition

Creates and recommends policy goals, objectives, programs, and plans for the FCC on matters concerning wireline telecommunications. Objectives include promoting competition in wireline services and markets, deregulation, encouraging economically efficient investment in wireline telecommunications infrastructure, expanding the availability of wireline telecommunications services, and fostering economic growth.

General Services Administration (GSA), *Federal Relay Service (FedRelay),* 10304 Eaton Pl., Fairfax, VA 22030; (703) 306-6308. Angela Officer, Program Manager, Acting, (703) 689-5654. Customer Service, (800) 877-0996 (Voice/ TTY, ASCII, Spanish). TTY/ASCII, (800) 877-8339. VCO (Voice Carry Over), (877) 877-6280. Speech-to-Speech, (877) 877-8982. Voice, (866) 377-8642. TeleBraille, (866) 893-8340.
General email, ITCSC@gsa.gov

Web, www.gsa.gov/fedrelay

Provides telecommunications services for conducting official business with and within the federal government to individuals who are deaf, hard of hearing, or have speech disabilities. Federal Relay Service features are Voice, TTY, *HCO,* Speech-to-Speech, Spanish, Telebraille, Captioned Telephone Service (CTS), IP Relay, Video Relay Service (VRS), Internet Relay (FRSO), and Relay Conference Captioning (RCC). For those with limited English proficiency, contact fas.car@gsa.gov, as services are available in Spanish, Vietnamese, Russian, Portuguese, Polish, Haitian, Creole, and Arabic.

▶NONGOVERNMENTAL

National Assn. of Regulatory Utility Commissioners, 1101 Vermont Ave. N.W., #200, 20005-3521; (202) 898-2200. Fax, (202) 898-2213. Greg White, Executive Director.
General email, admin@naruc.org

Web, www.naruc.org

Membership: members of federal, state, municipal, and international regulatory commissions that have jurisdiction over utilities and carriers of transportation services. Interests include telecommunications.

National Assn. of State Utility Consumer Advocates (NASUCA), 8380 Colesville Rd., #101, Silver Spring, MD 20910-6267; (301) 589-6313. Fax, (301) 589-6380. David Springe, Executive Director.
General email, nasuca@nasuca.org

Web, www.nasuca.org

Membership: public advocate offices authorized by states to represent ratepayer interests before state and federal utility regulatory commissions. Supports privacy protection for telephone customers.

National Telecommunications Cooperative Assn. (NTCA), 4121 Wilson Blvd., #1000, Arlington, VA 22203-1801; (703) 351-2000. Fax, (703) 351-2001. Shirley Bloomfield, Chief Executive Officer.
General email, pubrelations@ntca.org

Web, www.ntca.org

Membership: locally owned and controlled telecommunications cooperatives and companies serving rural and small-town areas. Offers educational seminars, workshops, publications, technical assistance, and various employee benefits programs to members. Monitors legislation and regulations.

U.S. Telecom Assn. (USTA), 607 14th St. N.W., #400, 20005; (202) 326-7300. Fax, (202) 315-3603. Walter B. McCormick Jr., President.
General email, policy@ustelecom.org

Web, www.ustelecom.org

Membership: broadband telecommunication service providers and manufacturers and suppliers for these companies. Provides members with information on the industry; conducts webinars; participates in FCC regulatory proceedings.

Wireless Telecommunications

▶AGENCIES

Federal Communications Commission (FCC), *Wireless Telecommunications Bureau,* 445 12th St. S.W., #6408, 20554; (202) 418-0600. Fax, (202) 418-0787. Roger C. Sherman, Chief.
Web, www.fcc.gov/wireless-telecommunications

Regulates domestic wireless communications, including cellular telephone, paging, personal communications services, public safety, air and maritime navigation, and other commercial and private radio services. Responsible for implementing the competitive bidding authority for spectrum auctions. Assesses new uses of wireless technologies, including electronic commerce. (Gettysburg office handles all licensing: FCC Wireless Telecommunications Bureau, Spectrum Management Resources and Technologies Division, 1270 Fairfield Rd., Gettysburg, PA 17325; [717] 338-2510.)

U.S. Secret Service *(Homeland Security Dept.), Criminal Investigative Division, 950 H St. N.W., #5000, 20223; (202) 406-9330. Fax, (202) 406-5016. Stuart Tryon, Special Agent-in-Charge.*
Web, www.secretservice.gov/investigation

Plans, reviews, and coordinates criminal investigations involving reports of bank fraud, credit fraud, telecommunications and computer crimes, fraudulent securities, and electronic funds transfer fraud.

▶NONGOVERNMENTAL

CTIA—The Wireless Assn., *1400 16th St. N.W., #600, 20036; (202) 736-3200. Fax, (202) 785-0721. Meredith Baker, President.*
General email, ctiaadministration@ctia.org
Web, www.ctia.org

Membership: system operators, equipment manufacturers, engineering firms, and others engaged in the cellular telephone and mobile communications industry in domestic and world markets. Monitors legislation and regulations.

Enterprise Wireless Alliance (EWA), *2121 Cooperative Way, #225, Herndon, VA 20171; (703) 528-5115. Fax, (703) 524-1074. Mark E. Crosby, Chief Executive Officer. Toll-free, (800) 482-8282.*
General email, info@enterprisewireless.org
Web, www.ita-relay.com

Membership: enterprise wireless companies, dealers, and trade associations. Serves as an information source on radio frequencies, licensing, new products and technology, and market conditions. Monitors legislation and regulations.

National Assn. of Regulatory Utility Commissioners, *1101 Vermont Ave. N.W., #200, 20005-3521; (202) 898-2200. Fax, (202) 898-2213. Greg White, Executive Director. General email, admin@naruc.org*
Web, www.naruc.org

Membership: members of federal, state, municipal, and international regulatory commissions that have jurisdiction over utilities and carriers of transportation services. Interests include telecommunications.

PCIA: The Wireless Infrastructure Assn., *500 Montgomery St., #500, Alexandria, VA 22314; (703) 739-0300. Fax, (703) 836-1608. Jonathan Adelstein, President. Information, (800) 759-0300. Press, (703) 535-7424.*
Web, www.pcia.com and Twitter, @PCIA

Represents companies that make up the wireless telecommunications infrastructure industry. Supports wireless communications and information infrastructure.

Utilities Telecom Council (UTC), *1129 20th St. N.W., #350, 20036; (202) 872-0030. Fax, (202) 872-1331. Stephen Vick, President, Acting.*
General email, marketing@utc.org
Web, www.utc.org

Membership: companies that own, manage, or provide critical telecommunications systems in support of their core business, including energy, gas, and water utility companies, pipeline companies, and radio and international critical infrastructure organizations. Participates in FCC rulemaking proceedings. Interests include fiber security; radio spectrum for fixed and mobile wireless communication; and technological, legislative, and regulatory developments affecting telecommunications operations of energy utilities.

GOVERNMENT INFORMATION

General

▶AGENCIES

Bureau of Engraving and Printing (BEP) *(Treasury Dept.), 14th and C Sts. S.W., 20228; (202) 874-4000. Fax, (202) 874-3177. Leonard R. Olijar, Director. Information, (877) 874-4114. Tours, (202) 874-2330.*
Web, www.moneyfactory.gov

Designs, engraves, and prints Federal Reserve notes, military certificates, White House invitations, presidential portraits, and special security documents for the federal government. Provides information on history, design, and engraving of currency; offers public tours, maintains reading room where materials are brought for special research (for appointment, write to the BEP's Historical Resource Center).

Bureau of International Information Programs *(State Dept.), 1250 23rd St. N.W., #5B17, 20037; (202) 632-9942. Fax, (202) 632-9901. Macon Phillips, Coordinator. General email, Contact_IIP@state.gov*
Web, www.state.gov/r/iip and Twitter, @IIPState

Implements strategic communications programs—including Internet and print publications, traveling and electronically transmitted speaker programs, and information resource services—that reach key international audiences and support department initiatives. Explains U.S. foreign policy. Develops governmentwide technology policies that help disseminate this information.

General Services Administration (GSA), *USAGov, 1800 F St. N.W., 20405; (202) 501-1794. Fax, (202) 357-0078. Sarah Crane, Director. Toll-free, (844) 872-4681.*
Web, www.publications.usa.gov and www.gobiernoUSA .gov and www.gsa.gov/portal/category/101011

Manages the portal site to U.S. government information, www.usa.gov. Manages kids.gov, a resource that provides government information to younger Americans. Distributes free and low-cost federal publications of consumer interest via the Internet at www.publications.usa.gov, or when callers dial (888) 878-3256 for a catalog. Publishes the *Consumer Action Handbook,* a free resource that can be used online at http://consumeraction.gov or obtained when callers dial (888) 8-PUEBLO. Assists people with questions about American government agencies, programs, and services via telephone, (800) FED-INFO ([800] 333-4636), or Web site, http://answers.usa.gov. Operates a contact center

Chief Information Officers for Federal Departments and Agencies

DEPARTMENTS

Agriculture, Jonathan Alboum, (202) 720-8833

Commerce, Steve Cooper, (202) 482-4797

Defense, Terry Halvorsen, (703) 695-0348

  Air Force, Lt. Gen. William Bender, (703) 695-6829

  Army, Lt. Gen. Robert Ferrell, (703) 695-4366

  Navy, Robert W. Foster, (703) 695-1840

Education, Danny Harris, (202) 245-6252

Energy, Michael Johnson, (202) 586-0166

Health and Human Services, Frank Baitman, (202) 690-6162

Homeland Security, Luke McCormack, (202) 514-0507

Housing and Urban Development, Rafael Diaz, (202) 708-0306

Interior, Sylvia Burns, (202) 208-6194

Justice, Joseph Klimavicz, (202) 514-0507

Labor, Dawn Leas, (202) 693-4220

State, Steven C. Taylor, (202) 647-2889

Transportation, Richard McKinney, (202) 366-9201

Treasury, Sonny Bhagowalia, (202) 622-1200

Veterans Affairs, Stephen Warren (Acting), (202) 461-6910

AGENCIES

Environmental Protection Agency, Ann E. Dunkin, (202) 564-6665

Federal Communications Commission, David A. Bray, (202) 418-2020

Federal Emergency Management Agency, Adrian R. Gardner, (202) 646-3006

Federal Trade Commission, Raghav Bajjhala, (202) 326-2667

General Services Administration, David Shive, (202) 501-1000

Government Accountability Office, Howard Williams Jr., (202) 512-5589

Government Printing Office, Chuck Riddle, (202) 512-1040

National Aeronautics and Space Administration, Renee Wynn, (202) 358-1824

National Archives and Records Administration, Swarnali Haldar, (301) 837-1583

National Science Foundation, Amy Northcutt, (703) 292-8100

Nuclear Regulatory Commission, Darren Ash, (301) 415-7443

Office of Management and Budget, Tony Scott, (202) 395-3018

Office of Personnel Management, Donna Seymour, (202) 606-2150

Office of the Director of National Intelligence, Raymond Cook (Acting), (703) 733-8600

Securities and Exchange Commission, Pamela Dyson, (202) 551-8800

Small Business Administration, Keith Bluestein (Deputy), (202) 205-6708

Social Security Administration, Robert Klopp, (800) 772-1213

---

to provide information in English or Spanish on all federal government agencies, programs, and services via toll-free telephone, email, and chat. Operated under contract by Sykes in Pennsylvania and Florida. Responds to inquiries about federal programs and services. Gives information about or referrals to appropriate offices. (Formerly Federal Citizen Information Center.)

National Archives and Records Administration (NARA),
700 Pennsylvania Ave. N.W., 20408; (866) 272-6272. Fax, (301) 837-0483. David S. Ferriero, Archivist of the United States. Press and Public Affairs, (202) 357-5300. TTY, (301) 837-0482.
Web, www.archives.gov

Identifies, preserves, and makes available federal government documents of historic value; administers a network of regional storage centers and archives and operates the presidential library system. Collections include photographs, graphic materials, films, and maps; holdings include records generated by foreign governments (especially in wartime) and by international conferences, commissions, and exhibitions.

National Archives and Records Administration (NARA),
Agency Services, 8601 Adelphi Rd., #3600, College Park,

MD 20740-6001; (301) 837-3064. Fax, (301) 837-1617. Jay A. Trainer, Executive.
Web, www.archives.gov

Manages the federal record centers throughout the country. Works with the record managers to feed records into the National Archives. Oversees the National Declassification Center, the Office of Government Information Services, and the Information Security Oversight Office.

National Archives and Records Administration (NARA),
Electronic Records Division, 8601 Adelphi Rd., #5320, College Park, MD 20740-6001; (301) 837-0470. Fax, (301) 837-3681. Theodore J. Hull, Director.
General email, cer@nara.gov
Web, www.archives.gov/research/electronic-records

Preserves, maintains, and makes available electronic records of the U.S. government. Provides researchers with magnetic tape, CD, DVD, and other copies of electronic records on a cost-recovery basis. Offers direct downloads and searches of selected holdings.

National Archives and Records Administration (NARA),
Federal Register, 800 N. Capitol St. N.W., #700, 20001 (mailing address: NF, 8601 Adelphi Rd., College Park, MD

20740-6001); (202) 741-6000. Fax, (202) 741-6012.
Oliver Potts, Director. TTY, (202) 741-6086.
General email, fedreg.info@nara.gov

Web, www.archives.gov/federal_register/the-federal-register

Informs citizens of their rights and obligations by providing access to the official texts of federal laws, presidential documents, administrative regulations and notices, and descriptions of federal organizations, programs, and activities. Provides online and in-person access to documents on file before their publication. Administers the Electoral College and the constitutional amendment process. Publications available from the U.S. Government Printing Office, (301) 317-3953, http://bookstore.gpo.gov.

National Archives and Records Administration (NARA),
Modern Records Program, 8601 Adelphi Rd., #2100, College Park, MD 20740; (301) 837-3570. Fax, (301) 837-3697. Laurence Brewer, Director, (301) 837-1539.
Web, www.archives.gov

Administers programs that establish standards, guidelines, and procedures for agency records administration. Manages training programs; inspects records management practices; monitors certain records not contained in National Archives depositories.

National Archives and Records Administration (NARA),
Presidential Libraries, 8601 Adelphi Rd., #2200, College Park, MD 20740-6001; (301) 837-3250. Fax, (301) 837-3199. Susan K. Donius, Director, (301) 837-1662.
Web, www.archives.gov/presidential-libraries

Administers thirteen presidential libraries. Directs all programs relating to acquisition, preservation, and research use of materials in presidential libraries; conducts oral history projects; publishes finding aids for research sources; provides reference service, including information from and about documentary holdings. Conducts community outreach; oversees museum exhibition programming.

National Archives and Records Administration (NARA),
Reference Services, 8601 Adelphi Rd., #2400, College Park, MD 20740-6001; (301) 837-3510. Fax, (301) 837-1752.
Richard W. Peuser, Branch Chief.
Web, www.archives.gov/frc/reference-services.html

Provides reference service for unpublished civil and military federal government records. Maintains central catalog of all archival materials. Compiles comprehensive bibliographies of materials related to archival administration and records management. Permits research in American history, archival science, and records management. Maintains collections of the papers of the Continental Congress (1774–1789), U.S. State Dept. diplomatic correspondence (1789–1963), and general records of the U.S. government.

National Archives and Records Administration (NARA),
Research Services, 8601 Adelphi Rd., #3400, College Park, MD 20740-6001; (301) 837-1893. Fax, (301) 837-3633.
William A. Mayer, Executive.
Web, www.archives.gov/research

Preserves and makes available federal records at fifteen National Archives facilities across the country.

National Security Staff (NSS) *(Executive Office of the President),* **Strategic Communications and Speechwriting,** Dwight D. Eisenhower Executive Office Bldg., #302, 20500; (202) 456-9271. Fax, (202) 456-9270. Benjamin (Ben) J. Rhodes, Deputy National Security Adviser. Administrative office, (202) 456-9301.
Web, www.whitehouse.gov/administration/eop/nsc

Advises U.S. government agencies on the direction and theme of the president's message. Assists in the development and coordination of communications programs that disseminate consistent and accurate messages about the U.S. government and policies to the global audience.

National Technical Information Service (NTIS) *(Commerce Dept.),* 5301 Shawnee Rd., Alexandria, VA 22312; (703) 605-6000. Fax, (703) 605-6900. Bruce Borzino, Director, (703) 605-6400. Toll-free, (800) 553-6847. Bookstore, (703) 605-6040. TTY, (703) 487-4639. Customer support, (703) 605-6050. Toll-free customer support, (888) 584-8332.
General email, customerservice@ntis.gov

Web, www.ntis.gov

Collects and organizes technical, scientific, engineering, and business-related information generated by U.S. and foreign governments and makes it available for commercial use in the private sector. Makes available approximately 3 million works covering research and development, current events, business and management studies, translations of foreign open source reports, foreign and domestic trade, general statistics, environment and energy, health and social sciences, and hundreds of other areas. Provides computer software and computerized data files in a variety of formats, including Internet downloads. Houses the Homeland Security Information Center, a centralized source on major security concerns for health and medicine, food and agriculture, and biochemical war.

Treasury Dept., *Public Affairs,* 1500 Pennsylvania Ave. N.W., #3442, 20220; (202) 622-2960. Fax, (202) 622-2808. Victoria Esser, Assistant Secretary.
Web, www.treasury.gov/about/organizational-structure/offices/Pages/Public-Affairs.aspx

Serves as the department's liaison to the media and public.

▶ **CONGRESS**

For a listing of relevant congressional committees and subcommittees, please see page 89 or the Appendix.

Government Accountability Office (GAO), *Publications and Dissemination,* 441 G St. N.W., #1T61B, 20548; (202) 512-3992. Leo Barbour, Director.
General email, info@gao.gov

Web, www.gao.gov

Provides information to the public on federal programs, reports, and testimonies. GAO publications and information about GAO publications are available upon request in print or online.

Publications Contacts at Federal Departments and Agencies

Many publications for federal departments and agencies may be available through the Government Printing Office (GPO) and the National Technical Information Service (NTIS). For GPO and NTIS contact information, see below.

GENERAL

Government Printing Office (GPO), (202) 512-1800, Toll-free, (866) 512-1800, Fax, (202) 512-2104; www.gpo.gov

House Document Room, (202) 226-5210; http://clerk.house.gov/about/offices_lrc.aspx

Library of Congress, Orders, (202) 707-5093; www.loc.gov/loc/pub

National Technical Information Service (NTIS), (703) 605-6000 or (888) 584-8332; www.ntis.gov/help/order-methods

DEPARTMENTS

Agriculture, Information, (202) 694-5050; Orders via NTIS; www.usda.gov/newsroom

Commerce, Orders via NTIS

Defense, Orders via NTIS; www.defense.gov/pubs

Education, Orders, (877) 433-7827, TTY, (877) 576-7734, Fax, (703) 605-6794; http://www2.ed.gov/about/pubs/intro/index.html

Energy, Orders via NTIS and GPO; www1.eere.energy.gov/library or www.osti.gov/home/publications

Health and Human Services, Toll-free, (877) 696-6775; www.hhs.gov

Homeland Security, www.dhs.gov/publications-0

Housing and Urban Development, Orders, (800) 767-7468, Fax, (202) 708-2313; www.huduser.org/portal/taxonomy/term/1

Justice, Orders, (800) 851-3420; www.justice.gov/publications/publications_a.html

Labor, Statistic orders, (202) 691-5200, Employee benefits, (866) 444-3272; www.dol.gov/ebsa/publications or www.dol.gov/odep/topics/OrderPublications.htm or www.dol.gov/dol/topic/statistics/publications.htm

State, Orders via GPO; www.state.gov/r/pa/ei/rls

Transportation, Orders via NTIS; www.fhwa.dot.gov/research/publications/periodicals.cfm

Treasury, Orders via NTIS and GPO; www.treasury.gov/tigta/publications.shtml

Veterans Affairs, www.va.gov/opa/publications

AGENCIES

Census Bureau, Orders, (301) 763-4400; http://census.gov/library/publications.html

Commission on Civil Rights, Orders, (202) 376-8128; www.usccr.gov/pubs

Consumer Product Safety Commission, Orders, (301) 504-7921; www.cpsc.gov/en/Safety-Education/Safety-Guides/General-Information/Publications-Listing

Corporation for National and Community Service (AmeriCorps), Orders, (800) 942-2677; https://pubs.nationalservice.gov

Energy Information Administration, Orders, (202) 586-8800; www.eia.gov/reports

Environmental Protection Agency, Orders, (800) 490-9198; www.epa.gov/nscep

Equal Employment Opportunity Commission, Orders, (202) 663-4191, TTY, (202) 663-4494; www1.eeoc.gov/eeoc/publications

Government Publishing Office (GPO), *732 N. Capitol St. N.W., 20401; (202) 512-0000. Fax, (202) 512-2104. Davita E. Vance-Cooks, Director. Public Relations, (202) 512-1957. Congressional documents, (202) 512-1808. To order government publications, (202) 512-1800. General email, contactcenter@gpo.gov*

Web, www.gpo.gov

The federal government's official digital secure resource for producing, procuring, cataloging, indexing, authenticating, disseminating, and preserving the official information products of the U.S. government. Responsible for the production and distribution of information products and services for all three branches of the federal government, including U.S. passports for the Department of State as well as the official publications of Congress, the White House, and other federal agencies in digital and print formats. Provides for free permanent public access to federal government information through the Federal Digital System (www.fdsys.gov), partnerships with approximately 1,200 libraries nationwide participating in the Federal Depository Library Program, and a secure online bookstore.

Library of Congress, *Federal Library and Information Network (FEDLINK), John Adams Bldg., 101 Independence Ave. S.E., #LA 217, 20540; (202) 707-4800. Fax, (202) 707-4818. Meg Tulloch, Executive Director, Acting; Robin Harvey, Editor-in-Chief, (202) 707-4820. FEDLINK hotline, (202) 707-4900. General email, fliccffo@loc.gov*

Web, www.loc.gov/flicc

Promotes better utilization of federal library and information resources by seeking to provide the most cost-effective and efficient administrative mechanisms for delivering services and materials to federal libraries and information centers; serves as a forum for discussion of federal library and information policies, programs, and procedures; helps inform Congress, federal agencies, and others concerned with libraries and information centers.

Federal Communications Commission, Orders, (202) 418-7512; www.fcc.gov

Federal Election Commission, Orders, (800) 424-9530; www.fec.gov/info/publications.shtml

Federal Emergency Management Agency, Toll-free, (800) 237-3239, Fax, (240) 699-0525; www.fema.gov/publications-archive or www.ready.gov/publications

Federal Reserve System, Orders, (202) 452-3245, Fax, (202) 728-5886; www.federalreserve.gov/pubs/order.htm

Federal Trade Commission, Orders, (877) 382-4357; https://bulkorder.ftc.gov

General Services Administration, Orders, (800) 488-3111; www.gsa.gov/portal/content/101674

Government Accountability Office, Orders, (202) 512-6000, Toll-free, (866) 801-7077, TTY, (202) 512-2537; www.gao.gov/ordering.htm

International Bank for Reconstruction and Development (World Bank), Orders, (703) 661-1580, Toll-free, (800) 645-7247, Fax, (703) 661-1501; www.worldbank.org/reference

International Trade Administration, Orders via NTIS and GPO; http://trade.gov/publications

National Aeronautics and Space Administration, Orders, (202) 358-0000; www.hq.nasa.gov/office/hqlibrary/ic/ic2.htm#pubs

National Archives and Records Administration, Orders, (202) 357-5332, Toll-free, (866) 272-6272; www.archives.gov/publications

National Endowment for the Humanities, Orders, (202) 606-8435

National Park Service, Orders by mail only; www.nps.gov/aboutus/publications.htm

National Science Foundation, Orders, (703) 292-7827; www.nsf.gov/publications

National Transportation Safety Board, Information, (202) 314-6551; www.ntsb.gov/publications/Pages/default.aspx; Post-publication orders via NTIS.

Nuclear Regulatory Commission, Orders, (301) 415-4737 or (800) 397-4209, TTY, (800) 635-4512; Orders also from GPO; www.nrc.gov/reading-rm/pdr.html

Occupational Safety and Health Administration, Orders, (202) 693-1888, Fax, (202) 693-2498; www.osha.gov/pls/publications/publication.html

Office of Personnel Management, Orders via GPO; Retirement and insurance information, (202) 606-1800; http://apps.opm.gov/publications

Peace Corps, Toll-free hotline, (855) 855-1961; http://www.peacecorps.gov/about/policies/docs

Securities and Exchange Commission, Orders, (202) 551-4040; Public documents, (202) 551-8090; www.sec.gov/investor/pubs.shtml

Social Security Administration, Orders, (410) 965-2039, Fax, (410) 965-2037; www.ssa.gov/pubs

U.S. Fish and Wildlife Service, Orders, (303) 236-7639, Fax, (303) 236-0845; Orders via NTIS; www.fws.gov/external-affairs/marketing-communications/printing-and-publishing

U.S. Geological Survey, Orders, (888) 275-8747; http://store.usgs.gov

U.S. Institute of Peace, Book orders, (800) 868-8064, Fax, (703) 661-1501; http://bookstore.usip.org

---

Library of Congress, *Federal Research Division, John Adams Bldg., 101 Independence Ave. S.E., #LA 5281, 20540-4840; (202) 707-3900. Fax, (202) 707-3920. Mukta Ohri, Chief.*
General email, frds@loc.gov

Web, www.loc.gov/rr/frd

Provides research and analytical support to federal agencies and authorized federal contractors.

Library of Congress, *Serial and Government Publications, James Madison Memorial Bldg., 101 Independence Ave. S.E., #LM 133, 20540-4760; (202) 707-5690. Teri Sierra, Chief. Reference desk, (202) 707-5208. Current periodical reading room, (202) 707-5691.*
Web, www.loc.gov/rr/news

Operates Newspaper and Current Periodical Reading Room; maintains library's collection of domestic and foreign newspapers, current periodicals, comic books, and current serially issued publications of federal, state, and foreign governments; maintains a selective U.S. federal government publication depository since 1979, a United Nations document collection, and a Federal Advisory Committee (FAC) collection. Responds to written or telephone requests for information on newspapers, periodicals, or government publications, or online through Ask a Librarian. Lends some microfilm through interlibrary loans.

Senate Historical Office, *201 SHOB, 20510; (202) 224-6900. Betty K. Koed, Historian.*
General email, historian@sec.senate.gov

Web, www.senate.gov/artandhistory/history/common/generic/Senate_Historical_Office.htm

Serves as an information clearinghouse on Senate history, traditions, and members. Collects, organizes, and distributes to the public unpublished Senate documents; collects and preserves photographs and pictures related to Senate history; conducts an oral history program; advises senators and Senate committees on the disposition of their noncurrent papers and records. Produces publications on the history of the Senate.

U.S. House of Representatives, *Legislative Resource Center,* *135 CHOB, 20515; Fax, (202) 226-5208. Ronald (Dale) Thomas, Chief. Bill status, (202) 226-5200. General email, info.clerkweb@mail.house.gov*

Web, http://clerk.house.gov/about/offices_lrc.aspx

Provides legislative information, records and registration, historical information, and library services to the House and the public. Reading room contains computer terminals where collections may be viewed or printed out. Collections include House and Senate journals (1st Congress to present); *Congressional Record* and its predecessors (1st Congress to present); House reports, documents, bills, resolutions, and hearings; Senate reports and documents; U.S. statutes, treaties, the *Federal Register,* U.S. codes, and numerous other documents. (See Web site or call for a complete list of collections.)

U.S. House of Representatives, *Office of Art and Archives,* *B53 CHOB, 20515; (202) 226-1300. Fax, (202) 226-4635. Farar P. Elliott, Chief, Art and Archives. General email, art@mail.house.gov*

Archives email, archives@mail.house.gov

Office of the Historian email, history@mail.house.gov

Web, http://history.house.gov

Works with the Office of the Historian to provide access to published documents and historical records of the House. Advises members on the disposition of their records and papers; maintains information on manuscript collections of former members; maintains biographical files on former members; houses photographs and artifacts of former members. Produces publications on Congress and its members.

U.S. House of Representatives, *Office of the Historian,* *B53 CHOB, 20515; (202) 226-1300. Matthew A. Wasniewski, House Historian. General email, history@mail.house.gov*

Web, http://history.house.gov

Works with the Office of Art and Archives to provide access to published documents and historical records of the House. Conducts historical research. Advises members on the disposition of their records and papers; maintains information on manuscript collections of former members; maintains biographical files on former members. Produces publications on Congress and its members.

Freedom of Information

▶**AGENCIES**

Justice Dept. (DOJ), *Information Policy,* *1425 New York Ave. N.W., #11050, 20530; (202) 514-3642. Fax, (202) 514-1009. Melanie Ann Pustay, Director. Information, (202) 514-2000. General email, doj.oip.foia@usdoj.gov*

Web, www.justice.gov/oip

Provides federal agencies with advice and policy guidance on matters related to implementing and interpreting the Freedom of Information Act (FOIA). Processes FOIA requests on behalf of the Department's Senior Leadership Offices; adjudicates administrative appeals from Justice Department denials of public requests for access to documents; litigates selected FOIA and Privacy Act cases; conducts FOIA training for government agencies.

National Archives and Records Administration (NARA), *Information Security Oversight (ISOO),* *700 Pennsylvania Ave. N.W., #100, 20408-0001; (202) 357-5250. Fax, (202) 357-5907. William A. Cira, Director, Acting, (202) 357-5323. General email, isoo@nara.gov*

Web, www.archives.gov/isoo

Receiving guidance from the National Security Council, oversees policy on security classification/declassification on documents and programs for the federal government and industry; develops policies and procedures for sensitive unclassified information.

National Archives and Records Administration (NARA), *National Declassification Center,* *8601 Adelphi Rd., #6350, College Park, MD 20740; (301) 837-0405. Fax, (301) 837-0346. Sheryl Shenberger, Director. General email, ndc@nara.gov*

Web, www.archives.gov/declassification

Directs the review and declassification of records and security-classified materials in the National Archives in accordance with Executive Order 13526 and the Freedom of Information Act; assists other federal archival agencies in declassifying security-classified documents in their holdings.

▶**NONGOVERNMENTAL**

American Civil Liberties Union (ACLU), *Washington Legislative Office,* *915 15th St. N.W., 20005; (202) 544-1681. Fax, (202) 546-0738. Michael Macleod-Ball, Chief of Staff. Press, (202) 544-2312. General email, media@dcaclu.org*

Web, www.aclu.org/legiupdate

Advocates legislation to guarantee constitutional rights and civil liberties. Monitors agency compliance with the Privacy Act and other access statutes. Produces publications. (Headquarters in New York maintains docket of cases.)

American Society of Access Professionals, *1444 Eye St. N.W., #700, 20005; (202) 712-9054. Fax, (202) 216-9646. Claire Shanley, Executive Director. General email, asap@bostrom.com*

Web, www.accesspro.org and *Twitter, @ASAPAccessPro*

Membership: federal employees, attorneys, journalists, and others working with or interested in access-to-information laws. Seeks to improve the administration of the Freedom of Information Act, the Privacy Act, and other access statutes.

Public Affairs Contacts at Federal Departments and Agencies

DEPARTMENTS

Agriculture, Matt Paul, (202) 720-4623

Commerce, Erin Weinstein (Acting), (202) 482-4883

Defense, Peter Cook, (703) 697-5131

  Air Force, Brig. Gen. Kathleen A. Cook, (703) 697-6061

  Army, Brig. Gen. Malcolm Frost, (703) 693-4723

  Marine Corps, Brig. Gen. James Glynn, (703) 614-4309

  Navy, Rear Adm. Dawn Cuttler, (703) 697-5342

Education, Jonathan Schorr (Acting), (202) 401-6359

Energy, Aoife McCarthy, (202) 586-4940

Health and Human Services, Kevin Griffis (Acting), (202) 401-2281

Homeland Security, Clark W. Stevens, (202) 282-8010

  Coast Guard, David French, (202) 372-4630

Housing and Urban Development, Betsaida Alcantara, (202) 708-0980

Interior, Blake Androff, (202) 208-6416

Justice, Melanie Newman, (202) 514-2007

Labor, Dori Henry (Acting), (202) 693-4676

State, John Kirby, (202) 647-6575

Transportation, Jane Mellow, (202) 366-0660

Treasury, Victoria Esser, (202) 622-2960

Veterans Affairs, Gary Tallman (Acting), (202) 461-7500

AGENCIES

Agency for International Development, T. Charles Cooper, (202) 712-4320

Commission on Civil Rights, Gerfon Gomez, (202) 376-8371

Commodity Futures Trading Commission, Steven W. Adamske, (202) 418-5080

Consumer Product Safety Commission, Scott Wolfson, (301) 504-7051

Corporation for National and Community Service, Ted Miller, (202) 606-6689

Environmental Protection Agency, Liz Purchia (Acting), (202) 564-8368

Equal Employment Opportunity Commission, Kimberly Smith Brown, (202) 663-4950

Export-Import Bank, Cattrel Brown, (202) 565-3203

Farm Credit Administration, Michael A. Stokke, (703) 883-4056

Federal Communications Commission, Shannon Gilson, (202) 418-0503

Federal Deposit Insurance Corporation, Barbara Hagenbaugh, (877) 275-3342

Federal Election Commission, Eileen J. Leamon, (202) 694-1120

Federal Emergency Management Agency, Joshua Batkin, (202) 646-4600

Federal Labor Relations Authority, Sarah Whittle Spooner, (202) 218-7791

Federal Mediation and Conciliation Service, John Arnold, (202) 606-5442

Federal Reserve System, Michelle Smith, (202) 452-2955

Federal Trade Commission, Justin Cole, (202) 326-2180

General Services Administration, Brett Prather, (202) 208-0128

Government Accountability Office, Chuck Young, (202) 512-4800

Government Printing Office, Gary Somerset, (202) 512-1957

Institute of Museum and Library Services, Janelle Carter Brevard, (202) 653-4757

National Aeronautics and Space Administration, David Weaver, (202) 358-1600

National Archives and Records Administration, Miriam Kleiman, (202) 357-5300

National Capital Planning Commission, Julia Koster, (202) 482-7211

National Credit Union Administration, Todd Harper, (703) 518-6330

National Endowment for the Arts, Jessamyn Sarmiento, (202) 682-5759

National Endowment for the Humanities, Theola Debose, (202) 606-8255

National Labor Relations Board, Celine McNicholas, (202) 273-1991

National Science Foundation, Vacant, (703) 292-8070

National Transportation Safety Board, Kelly A. Nantel, (202) 314-6100

Nuclear Regulatory Commission, Eliot Brenner, (301) 415-8200

Occupational Safety and Health Review Commission, Mabeline Pope, (202) 606-5370

Office of Personnel Management, Michael J. Amato, (202) 606-2402

Office of Special Counsel, Nick Schwellenbach, (202) 254-3631

Pension Benefit Guaranty Corporation, Martha Threatt (Acting), (202) 326-4343

Securities and Exchange Commission, John Nester, (202) 551-4120

Selective Service System, Richard S. Flahaven, (703) 605-4017

Small Business Administration, Brian Weiss, (202) 205-6740

Social Security Administration, LaVenia J. LaVelle, (410) 965-8904

U.S. International Trade Commission, Peg O'Laughlin, (202) 205-1819

U.S. Postal Service, Toni DeLancey, (202) 268-6915

Center for National Security Studies, *1730 Pennsylvania Ave. N.W., 7th Floor, 20006; (202) 721-5650. Fax, (202) 530-0128. Kate A. Martin, Director.*
General email, cnss@cnss.org
Web, www.cnss.org

Human rights and civil liberties organization specializing in national security, access to government information, government secrecy, government surveillance, intelligence oversight, and detentions.

Radio Television Digital News Assn., *529 14th St. N.W., #1240, 20045; (202) 659-6510. Fax, (202) 223-4007. Mike Cavender, Executive Director, (770) 622-7011.*
Web, www.rtdna.org and Twitter, @RTDNA

Membership: electronic journalists in radio, television, and all digital media. Sponsors and promotes education and advocacy concerning First Amendment issues, freedom of information, and government secrecy issues; ethics in reporting; improving coverage; implementing technology; and other news industry issues. Radio and Television News Directors Foundation (RTNDF) is the educational arm of the association.

INTERNET AND RELATED TECHNOLOGIES

General

▶**AGENCIES**

Criminal Division *(Justice Dept.), Computer Crime and Intellectual Property Section, 1301 New York Ave. N.W., #600, 20530; (202) 514-1026. Fax, (202) 514-6113. John Lynch, Chief.*
Web, www.justice.gov/criminal-ccips

Investigates and litigates criminal cases involving computers, intellectual property, and the Internet. Administers the Computer Crime Initiative, a program designed to combat electronic penetrations, data theft, and cyberattacks on critical information systems. Provides specialized technical and legal assistance to other Justice Dept. divisions; coordinates international efforts; formulates policies and proposes legislation on computer crime and intellectual property issues.

Defense Advanced Research Projects Agency *(Defense Dept.), 675 N. Randolph St., Arlington, VA 22203-2114; (703) 696-2400. Arati Prabhakar, Director; Richard Weiss, External Relations, (571) 218-4988.*
Web, www.darpa.mil

Develops technologically advanced research ideas, assesses technical feasibility, and develops prototypes.

Federal Communications Commission (FCC), *Strategic Planning and Policy Analysis, 445 12th St. S.W., #7-C347, 20554; (202) 418-2030. Fax, (202) 418-2807. Jonathan Chambers, Chief.*
Web, www.fcc.gov/osp

Monitors developments in expansion of the global Internet and the communications industry. Reviews legal trends in intellectual property law and e-commerce issues.

General Services Administration (GSA), *Governmentwide Policy, Information, Integrity, and Access, 1800 F St. N.W., 20405; (202) 219-1279. Fax, (202) 357-0044. Dominic Keith Sale, Deputy Associate Administrator.*
Web, www.gsa.gov/portal/category/21399

Develops, coordinates, and defines ways that electronic and information technology business strategies can assist the Office of Management and Budget and other federal agencies to enhance access to and delivery of information and services to citizens.

Immigration and Customs Enforcement (ICE) *(Homeland Security Dept.), Cyber Crimes Center (C3), 500 12th St. S.W., 20536; (703) 293-8005. Fax, (703) 293-9127. Patrick J. Lechleitner, Deputy Assistant Director, (703) 877-3211. Press, (202) 732-4242.*
Web, www.ice.gov/cyber-crimes

Focuses on the investigation of international Internet crimes, such as money laundering, financing of terrorist activities, child sexual exploitation, human smuggling and trafficking, intellectual property rights violations, identity and document fraud, illegal arms trafficking, and drug trafficking.

National Science Foundation (NSF), *Computer and Information Science and Engineering Directorate, 4201 Wilson Blvd., #1105N, Arlington, VA 22230; (703) 292-8900. Fax, (703) 292-9074. James Kurose, Assistant Director.*
Web, www.nsf.gov/dir/index.jsp?org=cise

Supports investigator-initiated research in computer science and engineering. Promotes the use of advanced computing, communications, and information systems. Provides grants for research and education.

National Telecommunications and Information Administration (NTIA) *(Commerce Dept.), 1401 Constitution Ave. N.W., #4898, 20230; (202) 482-2000. Fax, (202) 501-0536. Lawrence E. Strickling, Assistant Secretary; Linda Kinney, Senior Adviser, Internet Policy; Derek Khlopin, Senior Adviser, Spectrum; Jennifer Duane, Senior Adviser, Broadband & Public Safety. Press, (202) 482-7002.*
Web, www.ntia.doc.gov

Responsible for oversight of the technical management of the Internet domain name system (DNS) and the Institute for Telecommunication Science (ITS).

Office of Management and Budget (OMB) *(Executive Office of the President), Information and Regulatory Affairs, 725 17th St. N.W., #10236, 20503; (202) 395-5897. Fax, (202) 395-6102. Harold Shelanski, Administrator. Press, (202) 395-7254.*
Web, www.whitehouse.gov/omb/inforeg_infopoltech

Oversees implementation and policy development under the Information Technology Reform Act of 1996

Freedom of Information Contacts at Federal Departments and Agencies

DEPARTMENTS

Agriculture, Alexis Graves, (202) 690-3318

Commerce, Brenda Dolan, (202) 482-3258

Defense, Jim Hogan, (866) 574-4970

  Air Force, Anh Trinh, (703) 614-8500

  Army, Steven A. Raho, (703) 428-6238

  Marine Corps, Sally Hughes, (703) 614-4008

  Navy, Robin Patterson, (202) 685-0412

Education, Gregory Smith, (202) 401-8365

Energy, Kevin T. Hagerty, (202) 586-5955

Health and Human Services, Michael Marquiz (Acting), (202) 690-7453

Homeland Security, Angela Washington, (202) 343-1743

  Coast Guard, Amanda Ackerson, (202) 475-3522

Housing and Urban Development, Vicky J. Lewis, (202) 708-3054

Interior, Cindy Cafaro, (202) 208-5342

Justice, Melanie Ann Pustay, (202) 514-3642

Labor, Thomas G. Hicks Sr., (202) 693-5427

State, Marianne Manheim, (202) 261-8484

Transportation, Judith S. Kaleta, (202) 366-4542

Treasury, Ryan Law, (202) 622-0930

Veterans Affairs, Laurie Karnay, (202) 632-7465

AGENCIES

Agency for International Development, Alecia S. Sillah, (202) 712-1371

Central Intelligence Agency, Michael Labergne, (703) 613-1287

Commission on Civil Rights, Jennifer Cron Hepler, (202) 376-8351

Commodity Futures Trading Commission, Linda Mauldin, (202) 418-5497

Consumer Product Safety Commission, Deborah Acosta, (301) 504-6821

Council on Environmental Quality, Brooke Dorner, (202) 456-6224

Environmental Protection Agency, Larry F. Gottesman, (202) 566-1667

Equal Employment Opportunity Commission, Stephanie Garner, (202) 663-4634

Export-Import Bank, Lennell Jackson, (202) 565-3290

Farm Credit Administration, Jane Virga, (703) 883-4071

Federal Communications Commission, Stephanie Kost, (202) 418-1379

Federal Deposit Insurance Corp., Cottrell L. Webster, (703) 562-6040

Federal Election Commission, Katie Higginbothom, (202) 694-1650

Federal Emergency Management Agency, Charlene Myrthil, (202) 646-3323

Federal Labor Relations Authority, Gina Grippando, (202) 218-7776

Federal Maritime Commission, Karen Gregory, (202) 523-5725

Federal Reserve, Jeanne McLaughlin, (202) 452-2407

Federal Trade Commission, Richard Gold, (202) 326-3355

General Services Administration, Audrey Corbett Brooks, (202) 205-5912

Legal Services Corp., Cheryl DuHart, (202) 295-1500

Merit Systems Protection Board, Bernard Parker, (202) 254-4475

National Aeronautics and Space Administration, Miriam Brown-Lam, (202) 358-0718

National Archives and Records Administration, Gary M. Stern, (301) 837-1750

National Credit Union Administration, Linda Dent, (703) 518-6450

National Endowment for the Humanities, Lisette Voyatzis, (202) 606-8322

National Labor Relations Board, Diane Bridge, (202) 273-3843

National Mediation Board, Angela Heverling, (202) 692-5000

National Science Foundation, Sandra Evans, (703) 292-8060

National Transportation Safety Board, Melba D. Moye, (202) 314-6540

Nuclear Regulatory Commission, Patricia Hirsch, (301) 415-0563

Office of Government Ethics, Diana J. Veilleux, (202) 482-9203

Office of Management and Budget, Lauren Wright, (202) 395-7250

Office of National Drug Control Policy, Jeffrey Teitz, (202) 395-6601

Office of Personnel Management, Trina Porter, (202) 606-1153

Office of Science and Technology Policy, Rachael Leonard, (202) 456-6125

Office of the U.S. Trade Representative, Jacqueline B. Caldwell, (202) 395-3419

Peace Corps, Denore Miller, (202) 692-1236

Pension Benefit Guaranty Corp., Michelle Y. Chase, (202) 326-4040

Securities and Exchange Commission, John Livornese, (202) 551-7900

Selective Service, Betty Lou Wingo, (703) 605-4005

Small Business Administration, Linda Digiandomenico, (202) 401-8203

Social Security Administration, Debbie Verzi, (410) 965-1727

U.S. International Trade Commission, Jacqueline N. Gross, (202) 205-1816

Federal Government Web Sites

CONGRESS

Government Accountability Office, www.gao.gov

House of Representatives, www.house.gov

Library of Congress, www.loc.gov

Senate, www.senate.gov

WHITE HOUSE

General Information, www.whitehouse.gov

DEPARTMENTS

Agriculture, www.usda.gov

Commerce, www.commerce.gov

Defense, www.defense.mil

  Air Force, www.af.mil

  Army, www.army.mil

  Marine Corps, www.marines.mil

  Navy, www.navy.mil

Education, www.ed.gov

Energy, www.energy.gov

Health and Human Services, www.hhs.gov

Homeland Security, www.dhs.gov

  Coast Guard, www.uscg.mil

Housing and Urban Development, www.hud.gov

Interior, www.doi.gov

Justice, www.justice.gov

Labor, www.dol.gov

State, www.state.gov

Transportation, www.dot.gov

Treasury, www.treasury.gov

Veterans Affairs, www.va.gov

AGENCIES

Agency of International Development, www.usaid.gov

Consumer Product Safety Commission, www.cpsc.gov

Corporation for Public Broadcasting, www.cpb.org

Drug Enforcement Administration, www.dea.gov

Environmental Protection Agency, www.epa.gov

Export-Import Bank, www.exim.gov

Federal Aviation Administration, www.faa.gov

Federal Bureau of Investigation, www.fbi.gov

Federal Communications Commission, www.fcc.gov

Federal Deposit Insurance Corporation, www.fdic.gov

Federal Election Commission, www.fec.gov

Federal Emergency Management Agency, www.fema.gov

Federal Energy Regulatory Commission, www.ferc.gov

Federal Reserve System, www.federalreserve.gov

Federal Trade Commission, www.ftc.gov

Food and Drug Administration, www.fda.gov

General Services Administration, www.gsa.gov

Government Accountability Office, www.gao.gov

Government Publishing Office, www.gpo.gov

Internal Revenue Service, www.irs.gov

National Aeronautics and Space Administration, www.nasa.gov

National Archives and Records Administration, www.archives.gov

National Institute of Standards and Technology, www.nist.gov

National Institutes of Health, www.nih.gov

National Oceanic and Atmospheric Administration, www.noaa.gov; www.climate.gov

National Park Service, www.nps.gov

National Railroad Passenger Corporation (Amtrak), www.amtrak.com

National Science Foundation, www.nsf.gov

National Technical Information Service, www.ntis.gov

National Transportation Safety Board, www.ntsb.gov

Nuclear Regulatory Commission, www.nrc.gov

Occupational Safety and Health Administration, www.osha.gov

Patent and Trademark Office, www.uspto.gov

Peace Corps, www.peacecorps.gov

Pension Benefit Guaranty Corporation, www.pbgc.gov

Securities and Exchange Commission, www.sec.gov

Small Business Administration, www.sba.gov

Smithsonian Institution, www.si.edu

Social Security Administration, www.ssa.gov

U.S. Fish and Wildlife Service, www.fws.gov

U.S. Geological Survey, www.usgs.gov

U.S. International Trade Commission, www.usitc.gov

U.S. Postal Service, www.usps.com

and the Paperwork Reduction Act of 1995; focuses on information technology management and substantive information policy, including records management, privacy, and computer security, and the Freedom of Information Act.

►CONGRESS

Government Accountability Office (GAO), *Applied Research and Methods, 441 G St. N.W., #6H19, 20548; (202) 512-2700. Fax, (202) 512-3938. Nancy Kingsbury, Managing Director.*
Web, www.gao.gov/careers/arm.html

Assesses the quality of the nation's major statistical databases and helps adapt the government's dissemination of information to a new technological environment. Conducts congressional studies that entail specialized analysis.

Government Accountability Office (GAO), *Information Technology, 441 G St. N.W., #4T21B, 20548; (202) 512-6408. Joel C. Willemssen, Managing Director.*
Web, www.gao.gov

Seeks to make the federal government more effective in its information management by improving performance and reducing costs. Assesses best practices in the public and private sectors; makes recommendations to government agencies. Interests include information security.

National Digital Information Infrastructure and Preservation Program (NDIIPP) *(Library of Congress), Office of Strategic Initiatives, 101 Independence Ave. S.E., 20540-1300; (202) 707-3300. Fax, (202) 707-0815. Vacant, Associate Librarian.*
Web, www.digitalpreservation.gov, Twitter, @ndiipp and Facebook, www.facebook.com/digitalpreservation

Oversees development of a national strategy to collect, archive, and preserve digital content, and directs the activities of the Information Technology Directorate.

►NONGOVERNMENTAL

Accredited Standards Committee (ASC X12), *8300 Greensboro Dr., #800, McLean, VA 22102; (703) 970-4480. Fax, (703) 970-4488. Gary Beatty, Chair.*
Web, www.x12.org

Promotes the development and maintenence of cross-industry Electronic Data Interchange (EDI) and Context Inspired Component Architecture (CICA) standards in electronic commerce that help organizations improve business methods, lower costs, and increase productivity. Provides administrative and technical support. Chartered by the American National Standards Institute. (Formerly Data Interchange Standards Assn.)

American Library Assn., *Office for Information Technology Policy, 1615 New Hampshire Ave. N.W., 1st Floor, 20009-2520; (202) 628-8410. Fax, (202) 628-8419. Alan Inouye, Director. Toll-free, (800) 941-8478.*

General email, oitp@alawash.org
Web, www.ala.org/offices/oitp

Provides policy research and analysis of developments in technology and telecommunications as they affect libraries and library users. Interests include information policy, law, and regulations; free expression on the Internet; equitable access to electronic information resources; and treaty negotiations of the United Nations World Intellectual Property Organization. (Headquarters in Chicago, Ill.)

Assn. for Competitive Technology (ACT), *1401 K St. N.W., #501, 20005; (202) 331-2130. Fax, (202) 331-2139. Jonathan Zuck, President.*
General email, info@actonline.org
Web, www.actonline.org and Twitter, @actonline

Membership: businesses that engage in or support the information technology industry. International education and advocacy organization for information technology companies worldwide. Interests include intellectual property, international trade, e-commerce, privacy, tax policy, antitrust, and commercial piracy issues. Focuses predominantly on the interests of small and midsized entrepreneurial technology companies. Monitors legislation and regulations.

Assn. for Information Science and Technology (ASIS&T), *8555 16th St., #850, Silver Spring, MD 20910; (301) 495-0900. Fax, (301) 495-0810. Richard Hill, Executive Director.*
General email, asist@asist.org
Web, www.asist.org

Membership: information specialists from such fields as computer science, linguistics, management, librarianship, engineering, law, medicine, chemistry, and education. Advocates research and development in basic and applied information science. Offers continuing education programs.

Assn. of Research Libraries (ARL), *21 Dupont Circle N.W., #800, 20036-1118; (202) 296-2296. Fax, (202) 872-0884. Elliott Shore, Executive Director.*
General email, webmgr@arl.org
Web, www.arl.org and Twitter, @ARLnews

Federation of 126 research and academic libraries in the United States and Canada. Interests include public access to federally funded research; federal, state, and international copyright and intellectual property laws; information technology and telecommunications policies; appropriations for selected federal and congressional agencies, national libraries, and agency programs and initiatives; scholarly communication, including publication and dissemination systems; the library's role in the transformation of research, teaching, and learning; and library performance assessment.

Center for Democracy and Technology, *1401 K St. N.W., 2nd Floor, 20005; (202) 637-9800. Fax, (202) 637-0968. Nuala O'Connor, President.*

General email, info@cdt.org

Web, www.cdt.org and Twitter, @CenDemTech

Promotes and defends privacy and civil liberties on the Internet. Interests include free expression, social networking and access to the Internet, consumer protection, health information privacy and technology, and government surveillance.

Center for Digital Democracy, *1621 Connecticut Ave. N.W., #550, 20009; (202) 986-2220. Jeffrey Chester, Executive Director, (202) 494-7100.*
General email, jeff@democraticmedia.org

Web, www.democraticmedia.org and Twitter, @DigitalDemoc

Seeks to ensure that the public interest is a fundamental part of the digital communications landscape. Conducts public education designed to protect consumer privacy and works to ensure competition in the new media industries, especially at the Federal Trade Commission and the Justice Dept. Tracks and analyzes the online advertising market, including areas affecting public health, news and information, children and adolescents, and financial industries.

Coalition for Networked Information, *21 Dupont Circle N.W., #800, 20036; (202) 296-5098. Fax, (202) 872-0884. Clifford A. Lynch, Executive Director.*
General email, info@cni.org

Web, www.cni.org and Twitter, @cni_org

Membership: higher education, publishing, network and telecommunications, information technology, and libraries and library organizations, as well as government agencies and foundations. Promotes networked information technology, scholarly communication, intellectual productivity, and education.

Common Cause, *805 15th St. N.W., #800, 20005; (202) 833-1200. Fax, (202) 659-3716. Miles Rapoport, President, (202) 736-5740. Press, (202) 736-5788.*
General email, mrapoport@commoncause.org

Web, www.commoncause.org and Twitter, @CommonCause

Nonpartisan citizens' lobby that works to promote laws and regulations safeguarding the free flow of information online. Supports strong open Internet protections; opposes media consolidation.

CompTIA, *Public Advocacy, 515 2nd St. N. E., 20002; (202) 682-9110. Fax, (202) 682-9111. Todd Thibodeaux, President; Elizabeth (Liz) Hyman, Executive Vice President, Public Advocacy. Press, (202) 682-4458.*
General email, techvoice@comptia.org

Web, www.comptia.org

Trade association for technology companies offering hardware, software, electronics, telecommunications, and information technology products and services. Offers business services and networking programs to members. Monitors legislation and regulations. (Headquarters in Downers Grove, Ill.)

Computer and Communications Industry Assn. (CCIA), *900 17th St. N.W., #1100, 20006; (202) 783-0070. Fax, (202) 783-0534. Edward J. Black, President; Heather Greenfield, Director of Communications.*
General email, hgreenfield@ccianet.org

Web, www.ccianet.org and Twitter, @ccianet

Membership: Internet service providers, software providers, and manufacturers and suppliers of computer data processing and communications-related products and services. Interests include Internet freedom, privacy and neutrality, government electronic surveillance, telecommunications policy, tax policy, federal procurement policy, communications and computer industry standards, intellectual property policies, encryption, international trade, and antitrust reform.

Cyber Security Policy and Research Institute *(George Washington University), Tompkins Hall, 725 23rd St. N.W., #106, 20052; (202) 994-5613. Lance J. Hoffman, Director.*
General email, cspri@gwu.edu

Web, www.cspri.seas.gwu.edu

Promotes education, research, and policy analysis in the areas of computer security and privacy, computer networks, electronic commerce, e-government, and the cultural aspects of cyberspace. (Affiliated with George Washington University.)

Electronic Privacy Information Center (EPIC), *1718 Connecticut Ave. N.W., #200, 20009; (202) 483-1140. Fax, (202) 483-1248. Marc Rotenberg, President.*
General email, info@epic.org

Web, www.epic.org

Public interest research center. Conducts research and conferences on domestic and international civil liberties issues, including privacy, free speech, information access, computer security, and encryption; litigates cases. Monitors legislation and regulations. Operates an online bookstore.

Entertainment Software Assn. (ESA), *575 7th St. N.W., #300, 20004; (202) 223-2400. Fax, (202) 223-2401. Michael (Mike) D. Gallagher, President.*
General email, esainfo@theesa.com

Web, www.theesa.com

Membership: publishers of interactive entertainment software. Distributes marketing statistics and information. Administers a worldwide antipiracy program. Established an independent rating system for entertainment software. Monitors legislation and regulations. Interests include First Amendment and intellectual property protection efforts.

Family Online Safety Institute, *400 7th St. N.W., #506, 20004; (202) 775-0158. Stephen (Steve) Balkam, Chief Executive Officer.*
General email, fosi@fosi.org

Web, www.fosi.org and Twitter, @FOSI

Membership: Internet safety advocates in business, government, academia, the media, and the general public. Identifies risks to children on the Internet; develops and promotes solutions to keep children safe while protecting free speech. Issues reports on online trends among young people; hosts conferences and other educational events; monitors legislation and regulations internationally. Offices in Washington, D.C., and London.

IDEAlliance, *1600 Duke St., #420, Alexandria, VA 22314; (703) 837-1070. Fax, (703) 837-1072. David J. Steinhardt, President.*
General email, registrar@idealliance.org
Web, www.idealliance.org

Membership: firms and customers in printing, publishing, and information technology. Helps set industry standards for electronic and Web commerce and conducts studies on new information technologies.

Info Comm International, *11242 Waples Mill Rd., #200, Fairfax, VA 22030; (703) 273-7200. Fax, (703) 278-8082. David Labuskes, Executive Director. Information, (800) 659-7469.*
Web, www.infocomm.org

Membership: video and audiovisual dealers, manufacturers and producers, and individuals. Promotes the professional AV communications industry and seeks to enhance members' ability to conduct business successfully through tradeshows, education, certification, market research, and government relations. Interests include small business issues, intellectual property, sustainable buildings, e-waste, and standards. Monitors legislation and regulations. (Formerly the International Communications Industries Assn.)

Information Sciences Institute, *Washington Office, 3811 Fairfax Dr., #200, Arlington, VA 22203; (703) 812-3700. Fax, (703) 812-3712. Joseph Sullivan, Associate Director, (310) 448-8206.*
Web, www.isi.edu

Conducts basic and applied research in advanced computer, communications, and information processing technologies. Works with public- and private-sector customers to develop diverse information technologies for civilian and military uses, often bridging multiple technology disciplines. Projects include advanced communications and network research; distributed databases and pattern recognition with applications in law enforcement, inspection systems, and threat detection; and computing architectures and devices. (Headquarters in Marina del Rey, Calif.; part of the University of Southern California.)

Information Technology Industry Council (ITI), *1101 K St. N.W., #610, 20005; (202) 737-8888. Fax, (202) 638-4922. Dean C. Garfield, President. Press, (202) 524-5543.*
General email, info@itic.org
Web, www.itic.org and Twitter, @ITI_TechTweets

Membership: providers of information and communications technology products and services. Acts as advocate for member companies in the areas of privacy, immigration reform, cybersecurity, intellectual property, tax reform, telecommunications, STEM education, trade, accessibility, voluntary standards, sustainability, and Internet governance.

Internet Coalition, *1615 L St. N.W., #1100, 20036; (802) 279-3534. Tammy Cota, Executive Director.*
Web, www.theinternetcoalition.com

Membership: companies involved in the online industry, including marketing agencies, consulting and research organizations, entrepreneurs, financial institutions, interactive service providers, software vendors, telecommunications companies, and service bureaus. Promotes consumer confidence and trust in the Internet and monitors the effect of public policy on the Internet and its users with a focus on privacy, taxation, intellectual property, online security, unsolicited email, and content regulation.

Internet Education Foundation, *1401 K St. N.W., #200, 20005; (202) 638-4370. Fax, (202) 637-0968. Tim Lordan, Executive Director.*
General email, tlordan@neted.org
Web, www.neted.org

Sponsors educational initiatives promoting the Internet as a valuable medium for democratic participation, communications, and commerce. Funds the Congressional Internet Caucus Advisory Committee, which works to inform Congress of important Internet-related policy issues. Monitors legislation and regulations.

Internet Engineering Task Force (IETF), *c/o Internet Society (ISOC), 1775 Wiehle Ave., #201, Reston, VA 20190-5108; (703) 439-2133. Fax, (703) 326-9881. Ray Pelletier, Administrative Director.*
General email, iad@ietf.org
Web, www.ietf.org

Membership: network designers, operators, vendors, and researchers from around the world who are concerned with the evolution, smooth operation, and continuing development of the Internet. Establishes working groups to address technical concerns. IETF is an organized activity of the Internet Society. (Headquarters in Fremont, Calif.)

Internet Society (ISOC), *1775 Wiehle Ave., #201, Reston, VA 20190-5108; (703) 439-2120. Fax, (703) 326-9881. Kathy Brown, President.*
General email, media@isoc.org
Web, www.internetsociety.org

Membership: individuals, corporations, nonprofit organizations, and government agencies. Focused on ensuring that the Internet continues to evolve as an open platform for innovation, collaboration, and economic development. Engages in a wide spectrum of Internet issues, including policy, governance, technology, and development and availability of the Internet. Conducts research and educational programs; provides information about the Internet.

National Research Council (NRC), *Computer Science and Telecommunications Board, Keck Center, 500 5th St. N.W., 20001; (202) 334-2605. Fax, (202) 334-2318. Farnam Jahanian, Chair, (412) 268-3363; Jon Eisenberg, Director, (202) 334-2605.*

General email, cstb@nas.edu

Web, http://sites.nationalacademies.org/CSTB

Advises the federal government on technical and public policy issues relating to computing and communications. Research includes computer science, cybersecurity, privacy, the Internet, and electronic voting and voter registration.

Pew Research Center, *Internet, Science, and Technology Project,* 1615 L St. N.W., #700, 20036; (202) 419-4500. Fax, (202) 419-4505. Lee Rainie, Director.

Web, www.pewinternet.org

Conducts research, surveys, and analyses to explore the impact of the Internet on families, communities, teens, education, health care, mobile technologies, and civic and political life. Makes its reports available online for public and academic use. (A project of the Pew Research Center.)

Public Knowledge, 1818 N St. N.W., #410, 20036; (202) 861-0020. Fax, (202) 861-0040. Gene Kimmelman, President, ext. 117.

General email, pk@publicknowledge.org

Web, www.publicknowledge.org and Twitter, @publicknowledge

Coalition of libraries, educators, scientists, artists, musicians, journalists, lawyers, and consumers interested in intellectual property law and technology policy as it pertains to the Internet and electronic information. Encourages openness, access, and competition in the digital age. Supports U.S. laws and policies that provide incentives to innovators as well as ensure a free flow of information and ideas to the public.

The Software Alliance (BSA), 20 F St. N.W., #800, 20001; (202) 872-5500. Fax, (202) 872-5501. Victoria Espinel, President. Toll-free, (888) 667-4722.

General email, info@bsa.org

Web, www.bsa.org and Twitter, @BSAnews

Membership: personal and business computer software publishing companies. Promotes growth of the software industry worldwide; helps develop electronic commerce. Investigates claims of software theft within corporations, financial institutions, academia, state and local governments, and nonprofit organizations. Provides legal counsel and initiates litigation on behalf of members.

Software and Information Industry Assn. (SIIA), 1090 Vermont Ave. N.W., 6th Floor, 20005; (202) 289-7442. Fax, (202) 289-7097. Kenneth (Ken) Wasch, President, (202) 789-4440.

Web, www.siia.net

Membership: software and digital content companies. Promotes the industry worldwide; conducts antipiracy program and other intellectual property initiatives; sponsors conferences, seminars, and other events. Monitors legislation and regulations.

StaySafeOnline.org/National Cyber Security Alliance, 1010 Vermont Ave. N.W., #821, 20005; (202) 570-7431. Michael Kaiser, Executive Director.

General email, info@staysafeonline.org

Web, www.staysafeonline.org

Public-private partnership that promotes computer safety and responsible online behavior. Designated by the Homeland Security Dept. to provide tools and resources to help home users, small businesses, and schools stay safe online. Online resources include tips, a self-guided cyber security test and checklist, and educational materials.

Technology CEO Council, 1341 G St. N.W., #1100, 20005; (202) 585-0258. Fax, (202) 393-3031. Bruce Mehlman, Executive Director.

General email, info@techceocouncil.org

Web, www.techceocouncil.org

Membership: chief executive officers from U.S. information technology companies. Monitors legislation and regulations on technology and trade issues. Interests include health care information technology, telecommunications, international trade, innovation, digital rights management, export and knowledge controls, and privacy.

The Telework Coalition (TelCoa), 204 East St. N.E., 20002; (202) 266-0046. Fax, (202) 465-3776. Chuck Wilsker, President.

General email, info@telcoa.org

Web, www.telcoa.org

Promotes telework and access to broadband services to increase productivity and provide employment opportunities for disabled, rural, and older workers, while reducing vehicular travel and energy use. Monitors legislation and regulations.

MEDIA PROFESSIONS AND RESOURCES

General

▶AGENCIES

Federal Communications Commission (FCC), *Communications Business Opportunities,* 445 12th St. S.W., #4A624, 20554; (202) 418-0990. Fax, (202) 418-0235. Thomas Reed, Director.

General email, ocboinfo@fcc.gov

Web, www.fcc.gov/communications-business-opportunities

Provides technical and legal guidance and assistance to the small, minority, and female business communities in the telecommunications industry. Advises the FCC chair on small, minority, and female business issues. Serves as liaison between federal agencies, state and local governments, and trade associations representing small, minority, and female enterprises concerning FCC policies, procedures, rulemaking activities, and increased ownership and employment opportunities.

Federal Communications Commission (FCC), *Media Bureau, Policy Division, Equal Employment Opportunity,* 445 12th St. S.W., #3A738, 20554; (202)

Media Contacts in Washington, D.C.

MAGAZINES

The Atlantic, 600 New Hampshire Ave. N.W., 20037;
(202) 266-6000

CQ Weekly, 77 K St. N.E., 20002-4681; (202) 650-6500

National Journal, 600 New Hampshire Ave. N.W., 20037;
(202) 739-8400

Time, 1130 Connecticut Ave. N.W., Suite 900, 20036;
(202) 861-4000

U.S. News & World Report, 1050 Thomas Jefferson St. N.W.,
4th Floor, 20007; (202) 955-2155

NEWS SERVICES

Agence France-Presse, 1500 K St. N.W., #600, 20005;
(202) 289-0700

Associated Press, 1100 13th St. N.W., #500, 20005;
(202) 641-9000

McClatchy, 700 12th St. N.W., #1000, 20005; (202) 383-6000

Reuters, 1333 H St. N.W., #510, 20005; (202) 898-8300

Scripps-Howard Newspapers, 1100 13th St. N.W., 20005;
(202) 408-1484

United Press International, 1133 19th St. N.W., #9, 20036;
(202) 898-8000

Washington Post News Services, 1150 15th St. N.W.,
4th Floor, 20071; (202) 334-6375

NEWSPAPERS

New York Times, 1627 Eye St. N.W., #700, 20006;
(202) 862-0300

USA Today, 1575 Eye St. N.W., #350, 20005

Wall Street Journal, 1025 Connecticut Ave. N.W., #800,
20036; (202) 862-9200

Washington City Paper, 1400 Eye St. N.W., #900, 20005;
(202) 332-2100

Washington Post, 1301 K St. N.W., 20071; (202) 334-6000

Washington Times, 3600 New York Ave. N.E., 20002;
(202) 636-3000

TELEVISION/RADIO NETWORKS

ABC News, 1717 DeSales St. N.W., 20036; (202) 222-7700

CBS News, 2020 M St. N.W., 20036; (202) 457-4385

CNN, 820 1st St. N.E., 20002; (202) 898-7900

C-SPAN, 400 N. Capitol St. N.W., #650, 20001; (202) 737-3220

Fox News, 400 N. Capitol St. N.W., #550, 20001;
(202) 824-6300

National Public Radio, 1111 N. Capitol St. N.E., 20002;
(202) 513-2000

NBC News, 4001 Nebraska Ave. N.W., 20016; (202) 885-4111

Public Broadcasting Service, 2100 Crystal Dr, Arlington, VA
22202; (703) 739-5000

418-1450. *Fax, (202) 418-1797. Lewis Pulley, Assistant Chief, Policy Division, (202) 418-2120.*
Web, www.fcc.gov/encyclopedia/equal_employment_opportunity_0

Responsible for the annual certification of cable television equal employment opportunity compliance. Oversees broadcast employment practices.

National Endowment for the Arts (NEA), *Media Arts, 400 7th St. S.W., 20506; (202) 682-5452. Fax, (202) 682-5721. Jax Deluca, Director, (202) 682-5742. TTY, (202) 682-5496.*
Web, www.arts.gov/artistic-fields/media-arts

Awards grants to nonprofit organizations for screen-based projects presented by film, television, video, radio, Internet, mobile technologies, video games, transmedia storytelling, and satellite; supports film and video exhibitions and workshops.

▶NONGOVERNMENTAL

Alicia Patterson Foundation, *1100 Vermont Ave. N.W., #900, 20005; (202) 393-5995. Fax, (301) 951-8512. Alice Arlen, Chair.*
General email, info@aliciapatterson.org
Web, www.aliciapatterson.org

Awards grants to professional journalists to continue projects based on their previous investigative work for *The APF Reporter,* a Web magazine published by the Foundation.

American News Women's Club, *1607 22nd St. N.W., 20008; (202) 332-6770. Fax, (202) 265-6092. Helen (Jean) Gleason White, President.*
General email, anwclub@comcast.net
Web, www.anwc.org and Twitter, @NewsWomensClub

Membership: women in communications. Promotes the advancement of women in all media. Sponsors professional receptions and lectures.

Center for Public Integrity, *910 17th St. N.W., #700, 20006; (202) 466-1300. Fax, (202) 466-1102. Peter Bale, Chief Executive Officer.*
General email, contact@icij.org
Web, www.publicintegrity.org and Twitter, @Publici

Nonpartisan organization that seeks to produce original investigative journalism on significant issues in the United States and around the world. Organizes and supports investigative journalists committed to transparent and comprehensive reporting. Interests include the environment, public health, public accountability, federal and state lobbying, war profiteering, and financial disclosure.

Communications Workers of America (CWA), *501 3rd St. N.W., 20001; (202) 434-1100. Fax, (202) 434-1279. Christopher M. Shelton, President.*
Web, www.cwa-union.org and Twitter, @CWAUnion

Membership: approximately 700,000 workers in telecommunications, journalism, publishing, cable television, electronics, and other fields. Interests include workplace

Congressional News Media Galleries

The congressional news media galleries serve as liaisons between members of Congress and their staffs and accredited newspaper, magazine, and broadcasting correspondents. The galleries provide facilities to cover activities of Congress, and gallery staff members ensure that congressional press releases reach appropriate correspondents. Independent committees of correspondents working through the press galleries are responsible for accreditation of correspondents.

House Periodical Press Gallery, H-304 CAP, Washington, DC 20515; (202) 225-2941. Robert M. Zatkowski, Director.

House Press Gallery, H-315 CAP, Washington, DC 20515; (202) 225-3945. Annie Tin, Superintendent.

House Radio and Television Gallery, H-320 CAP, Washington, DC 20515; (202) 225-5214. Olga Ramirez Kornacki, Director.

Press Photographers Gallery, S-317 CAP, Washington, DC 20510; (202) 224-6548. Jeffrey S. Kent, Director.

Senate Periodical Press Gallery, S-320 CAP, Washington, DC 20510; (202) 224-0265. Ed Pesce, Director.

Senate Press Gallery, S-316 CAP, Washington, DC 20510; (202) 224-0241. Laura Lytle, Director.

Senate Radio and Television Gallery, S-325 CAP, Washington, DC 20510; (202) 224-6421. Michael Mastrian, Director.

democracy and restoring bargaining rights. Represents members in contract negotiations and grievances; conducts training programs and workshops. Monitors legislation and regulations. (Affiliated with the AFL-CIO.)

Freedom Forum, *555 Pennsylvania Ave. N.W., 20001; (202) 292-6100. Fax, (202) 292-6148. Gene Policinski, Chief Operating Officer, (202) 292-6290. Toll-free inquiries, (888) 639-7386.*
General email, news@freedomforum.org
Web, www.freedomforum.org

Sponsors training and research that promote free press, free speech, and freedom of information. Interests include the First Amendment and newsroom diversity. Primary funder for the Newseum, an interactive museum of news.

Fund for Investigative Journalism, *529 14th St. N.W., 13th Floor, 20045; (202) 662-7564. Sandy Bergo, Executive Director.*
General email, fundfij@gmail.com
Web, www.fij.org and Twitter, @fundFIJ

Provides investigative reporters working outside the protection and backing of major news organizations with grants to cover the expenses of investigative pieces involving corruption, malfeasance, incompetence, and domestic and international societal ills.

International Center for Journalists (ICFJ), *2000 M St. N.W., #250, 20036; (202) 737-3700. Fax, (202) 737-0530. Joyce Barnathan, President.*
General email, editor@icfj.org
Web, www.icfj.org

Fosters international freedom of the press through hands-on training, workshops, seminars, online courses, fellowships, and international exchanges. Offers online mentoring and consulting; publishes media training manuals in various languages.

International Women's Media Foundation (IWMF), *1625 K St. N.W., #1275, 20006; (202) 496-1992. Fax, (202) 496-1977. Elisa Lees Munoz, Executive Director.*
General email, info@iwmf.org
Web, http://iwmf.org

Conducts reporting trips and safety training for women journalists, acts as advocate on behalf of women journalists who work under adverse conditions, and makes grants to support women journalists in their projects and endeavors worldwide.

J-Lab: The Institute for Interactive Journalism *(American University), School of Communications, 4400 Massachusetts Ave. N.W., 20016; (202) 255-2571. Fax, (202) 885-2019. Jan Schaffer, Executive Director.*
General email, jans@j-lab.org
Web, www.j-lab.org, Twitter, @jlab and Twitter, @janjlab

Develops research and discrete projects around new ideas to help journalists and citizens engage in public life. Projects include community news startups, innovations in journalism, news entrepreneurship, participatory and civic journalism, training, and publications.

Multicultural Media, Telecom, and Internet Council (MMTC), *1620 L St. N.W., #250, 20036; (202) 332-0500. Fax, (202) 332-0503. Kim Keenan, President.*
General email, info@mmtconline.org
Web, www.mmtconline.org

Membership: lawyers, engineers, broadcasters, cablecasters, telecommunicators, and scholars. Provides pro bono services to the civil rights community on communication policy matters. Represents civil rights groups before the FCC on issues concerning equal opportunity and diversity. Promotes equal opportunity and civil rights in the mass media and telecommunications industries. Operates nonprofit media brokerage and offers fellowships for lawyers and law students interested in FCC practice.

National Assn. of Black Journalists (NABJ), *1100 Knight Hall, #3100, College Park, MD 20742; (301) 405-0248. Fax, (301) 314-1714. Drew Berry, Executive Director, Acting.*
General email, sberry@nabj.org
Web, www.nabj.org

Membership: African American students and media professionals. Works to increase recognition and career advancement of minority journalists, to expand opportunities for minority students entering the field, and to promote balanced coverage of the African American community. Sponsors scholarships, internship program, and annual convention.

National Assn. of Government Communicators (NAGC), *201 Park Washington Court, Falls Church, VA 22046-4527; (703) 538-1787. Fax, (703) 241-5603. Elizabeth B. Armstrong, Executive Director. General email, info@nagconline.org*

Web, www.nagconline.org

National network of federal, state, and local government communications employees. Provides professional development through public meetings, exhibitions, workshops, and formal courses of instruction. Promotes high standards for the government communications profession and recognizes noteworthy service.

National Assn. of Hispanic Journalists (NAHJ), *1050 Connecticut Ave., 6th Floor, 20036; (202) 853-7754. Fax, (202) 662-7144. Alberto B. Mendoza, Executive Director. General email, nahj@nahj.org*

Web, www.nahj.org

Membership: professional journalists, educators, students, and others interested in encouraging and supporting the study and practice of journalism and communications by Hispanics. Promotes fair representation and treatment of Hispanics by the media. Provides professional development and computerized job referral service; compiles and updates national directory of Hispanics in the media; sponsors national high school essay contest, journalism awards, and scholarships.

National Hispanic Foundation for the Arts (NHFA), *Washington Square, 1050 Connecticut Ave. N.W., 5th Floor, #500, 20036; (202) 293-8330. Fax, (202) 772-3101. Felix Sanchez, Chair. General email, info@hispanicarts.org*

Web, www.hispanicarts.org

Strives to increase the presence of Hispanics in the media, telecommunications, entertainment industries, and performing arts, and to increase programming for the U.S. Latino community. Provides scholarships for Hispanic students to pursue graduate study in the arts.

National Lesbian and Gay Journalists Assn. (NLGJA), *2120 L St. N.W., #850, 20037; (202) 588-9888. Adam Pawlus, Executive Director. General email, info@nlgja.org*

Web, www.nlgja.org

Works within the journalism industry to foster fair and accurate coverage of lesbian, gay, bisexual, and transgender issues. Opposes workplace bias against all minorities and provides professional development for its members.

National Press Club, *529 14th St. N.W., 13th Floor, 20045; (202) 662-7500. Fax, (202) 662-7537. Thomas Burr, President. Library and Research Center, (202) 662-7523. General email, info@press.org*

Web, www.press.org

Membership: reporters, editors, writers, publishers, cartoonists, producers, librarians, and teachers of journalism at all levels. Interests include advancement of professional standards and skills, and the promotion of free expression. Provides networking opportunities and manages an online job listing site for members. Library available to members for research.

National Press Foundation (NPF), *1211 Connecticut Ave. N.W., #310, 20036; (202) 663-7280. Fax, (202) 530-2855. Sandy Johnson, President. General email, npf@nationalpress.org*

Web, www.nationalpress.org

Works to enhance the professional competence of journalists through in-career education projects. Sponsors conferences, seminars, fellowships, and awards; conducts public forums and international exchanges. Supports the National Press Club library.

The Newspaper Guild–CWA, *501 3rd St. N.W., 6th Floor, 20001-2797; (202) 434-7177. Fax, (202) 434-1472. Bernard J. Lunzer, President. General email, guild@cwa-union.org*

Web, www.newsguild.org

Membership: journalists, sales and media professionals. Advocates higher standards in journalism; equal employment opportunity in the print, broadcast, wire, and Web media industries; and advancement of members' economic interests. (Affiliated with Communications Workers of America, the AFL-CIO, CLC, and IFJ.)

Pew Research Center, *Journalism and Media Project, 1615 L St. N.W., #700, 20036; (202) 419-3650. Fax, (202) 419-3699. Amy Mitchell, Director. Press, (202) 419-3650. General email, journalism@pewresearch.org*

Web, www.journalism.org

Evaluates and studies the performance of the press, particularly content analysis using empirical research to quantify what is occurring in the press. Tracks key industry trends. Publishes a daily digest of media news and an annual report on American journalism. (Formerly Project for Excellence in Journalism.)

Society for Technical Communication (STC), *9401 Lee Hwy., #300, Fairfax, VA 22031; (703) 522-4114. Fax, (703) 522-2075. Chris Lyons, Executive Director; Molly Jin, Education Director. General email, stc@stc.org*

Web, www.stc.org

Membership: writers, publishers, educators, editors, illustrators, and others involved in technical communication. Encourages research and develops training programs; aids educational institutions in devising curricula; awards scholarships.

Statistical Assessment Service (STATS), *933 N. Kenmore St., #405, Arlington, VA 22201; (571) 319-0029. Fax, (202) 872-4014. S. Robert Lichter, President; Rebecca Goldin, Director.*

Web, www.stats.org

Research and resource organization. Interests include improving the quality of scientific and statistical information in public discourse. Acts as a resource for journalists and policymakers on scientific issues and controversies. (Affiliated with George Mason University.)

Washington Press Club Foundation, *National Press Club Bldg., 529 14th St. N.W., #1115, 20045; (202) 393-0613. Fax, (202) 662-7040. Margaret Talev, President.*
General email, wpcf@wpcf.org
Web, www.wpcf.org

Seeks to advance professionalism in journalism. Sponsors programs and events to educate students and the public on the role of a free press. Awards paid internships for minorities in D.C.–area newsrooms. Administers an oral history of women in journalism. Sponsors annual Congressional Dinner in February to welcome Congress back into session.

White House Correspondents' Assn., *600 New Hampshire Ave., N.W., #800, 20037; (202) 266-7453. Fax, (202) 266-7454. Julia Whiston, Executive Director.*
General email, whca@starpower.net
Web, www.whca.net and Twitter, @whca

Membership: reporters with permanent White House press credentials. Acts as a liaison between reporters and White House staff. Sponsors annual WHCA Journalism Awards and Scholarships fund-raising dinner.

Women in Film and Video (WIFV), *4000 Albemarle St. N.W., #305, 20016; (202) 429-9438. Fax, (202) 429-9440. Rebecca Bustamante, President.*
General email, director@wifv.org
Web, www.wifv.org and Twitter, @WIFV_DC

Membership organization dedicated to promoting equal employment opportunities and advancing career development and achievement for women working in all areas of screen-based media and related disciplines.

Women's Institute for Freedom of the Press, *1940 Calvert St. N.W., 20009-1502; (202) 656-0893. Martha Allen, Director.*
General email, mediademocracywifp@gmail.com
Web, www.wifp.org and Twitter, @WIFP

Conducts research and publishes in areas of communications and the media that are of particular interest to women. Promotes freedom of the press. Publishes a free online directory of media produced by and for women.

Accreditation in Washington

▶AGENCIES

Defense Dept. (DoD), *Public Affairs, The Pentagon, #2D961, 20301-1400; (703) 571-3343. Fax, (703) 697-3501. Peter Cook, Assistant Secretary, Acting, (703) 697-9312. Press, (703) 697-5131.*
Web, www.defense.gov/news

Selects staff of accredited Washington-based media organizations by lottery for rotating assignments with the National Media Pool. Correspondents must be familiar with U.S. military affairs, be available on short notice to deploy to the site of military operations, and adhere to pool ground rules. Issues Pentagon press passes to members of the press regularly covering the Pentagon.

Metropolitan Police Dept., *Police Public Information, 300 Indiana Ave. N.W., #5128, 20001; (202) 727-4383. Fax, (202) 727-4822. Dustin Sternbeck, Director.*
General email, mpd@dc.gov
Web, www.mpdc.dc.gov

Serves as connection between the media and the police department.

National Park Service (NPS) *(Interior Dept.),* **National Capital Region,** *1100 Ohio Dr. S.W., 20242; (202) 619-7023. Bob Vogel, Regional Director. Permits, (202) 245-4715.*
Web, www.nps.gov/ncro

Regional office that administers national parks, monuments, historic sites, and recreation areas in the Washington metropolitan area. Issues special permits required for commercial filming on public park lands. News media representatives covering public events that take place on park lands must notify the Office of Public Affairs and Tourism in advance. A White House, Capitol Hill, metropolitan police, or other policy-agency-issued press pass is required in some circumstances. Commercial filming on park lands requires a special-use permit.

State Dept., *Public Affairs, Foreign Press Centers, 529 14th St. N.W., #800, 20045; (202) 504-6300. Fax, (202) 504-6334. Orna Blum, Director, Foreign Press Centers.*
Web, http://fpc.state.gov and Twitter, @ForeignPressCtr

Provides foreign journalists with access to news sources, including wire services and daily briefings from the White House, State Dept., and Pentagon. Holds live news conferences. Foreign journalists wishing to use the center should check the Web site for information on what documents to present for admission.

State Dept., *Public Affairs, Press Relations, 2201 C St. N.W., #2109, 20520-6180; (202) 647-2492. Fax, (202) 647-0244. Elizabeth Trudeau, Director.*
General email, PAPressDuty@state.gov
Web, www.state.gov/media

Each U.S. journalist seeking a long-term building pass must apply in person with a letter from his or her editor or publisher, two application forms (available from the press office), and proof of citizenship. In addition, foreign correspondents need a letter from the embassy of the country in which their organization is based. Applicants should allow three months for security clearance. Members of the press wishing to attend an individual briefing must present a U.S. government-issued photo ID, a media-issued photo ID, or a letter from their employer and photo ID.

White House, *Press Office, White House, 1600 Pennsylvania Ave. N.W., 20502; (202) 456-2580. Fax, (202) 456-3347. Josh Earnest, Press Secretary. Comments and information, (202) 456-1111. TTY, (202) 456-6213.*

General email, press@who.eop.gov

Web, www.whitehouse.gov

Briefing Room, http://whitehouse.gov/briefing-room

White House blog, http://whitehouse.gov/blog

Journalists seeking permanent accreditation must meet four criteria. The journalist must be a designated White House correspondent and expected to cover the White House daily; must be accredited by the House and Senate press galleries; must be a resident of the Washington, D.C., area, and must be willing to undergo the required Secret Service background investigation. A journalist's editor, publisher, or employer must write to the press office requesting accreditation. Freelance journalists, cameramen, or technicians wishing temporary accreditation must send letters from at least two news organizations indicating the above criteria.

▶CONGRESS

House Periodical Press Gallery, *H304 CAP, 20515; (202) 225-2941. Robert M. Zatkowski, Director.*

General email, periodical.press@mail.house.gov

Web, http://periodical.house.gov

Open by application to periodical correspondents whose chief occupation is gathering and reporting news for periodicals not affiliated with lobbying or membership organizations. Accreditation with the House Gallery covers accreditation with the Senate Gallery.

▶JUDICIARY

Supreme Court of the United States, *1 1st St. N.E., 20543; (202) 479-3000. John G. Roberts Jr., Chief Justice; Kathleen Arberg, Public Information Officer, (202) 479-3211. TTY, (202) 479-3472. Visitor Information, (202) 479-3030.*

Web, www.supremecourtus.gov

Journalists seeking to cover the Court should be accredited by either the White House or the House or Senate press galleries, but others may apply by submitting a letter from their editors. Contact the public information office to make arrangements.

Broadcasting

▶AGENCIES

Federal Communications Commission (FCC), *Media Bureau, Policy Division, 445 12th St. S.W., 20554; (202) 418-1450. Fax, (202) 418-1069. Martha Heller, Chief.*

Web, www.fcc.gov/media/policy/policy-division

Handles complaints and inquiries concerning the equal time rule, which requires equal broadcast opportunities for all legally qualified candidates for the same office, and other political broadcast, cable, and satellite rules. Interprets and enforces related Communications Act provisions, including the requirement for sponsorship identification of all paid political broadcast, cable, and satellite announcements and the requirement for

broadcasters to furnish federal candidates with reasonable access to broadcast time for political advertising. Administers Equal Employment Opportunity (EEO) matters.

▶NONGOVERNMENTAL

Alliance for Women in Media Information, *1250 24th St. N.W., #300, 20037; (202) 750-3664. Becky Brooks, Executive Director.*

Web, www.allwomeninmedia.org

Membership: professionals in the electronic media and full-time students in accredited colleges and universities. Promotes industry cooperation and advancement of women. Maintains foundation supporting educational programs, charitable activities, public service campaigns, and scholarships.

Broadcast Education Assn. (BEA), *1771 N St. N.W., 20036-2891; (202) 602-0587. Fax, (202) 609-9940. Heather Birks, Executive Director, (202) 602-0584.*

General email, HELP@BEAweb.org

Web, www.beaweb.org and Twitter, @BEAWebTweets

Membership: universities, colleges, and faculty members offering specialized training in the radio, television, and electronic media industries. Promotes improvement of curriculum and teaching methods. Fosters working relationships among academics, students, and professionals in the industry. Interests include documentaries, international business and regulatory practices, gender issues, interactive media and emerging technologies, and electronic media law and policy. Administers scholarships in the field.

National Academy of Television Arts and Sciences (NATAS), *National Capital Chesapeake Bay Chapter Office, 12100 Sunset Hills Rd., #130, Reston, VA 20910; (703) 234-4055. Fax, (703) 435-4390. Carol Wynne, Executive Director; Dianne E. Bruno, Administrator.*

General email, capitalemmys@aol.com

Web, www.capitalemmys.tv

Membership: professionals in television and related fields and students in communications. Serves the Virginia, Maryland, and Washington, D.C., television community. Works to upgrade television programming; awards scholarships to junior, senior, or graduate students in communications. Sponsors annual Emmy Awards. (Headquarters in New York.)

National Assn. of Black Owned Broadcasters (NABOB), *1201 Connecticut Ave. N.W., #200, 20036; (202) 463-8970. Fax, (202) 429-0657. James L. Winston, President.*

General email, nabobinfo@nabob.org

Web, www.nabob.org

Membership: minority owners and employees of radio and television stations and telecommunications properties. Provides members and the public with information on the broadcast industry and the FCC. Provides members with legal and advertising research facilities. Monitors legislation and regulations.

National Assn. of Broadcast Employees and Technicians (NABET-CWA), *501 3rd St. N.W., 6th Floor,*

20001; (202) 434-1254. Fax, (202) 434-1426.
Charlie Braico, President.
General email, nabet@nabetcwa.org

Web, www.nabetcwa.org

Membership: approximately 10,000 commercial broadcast and cable television and radio personnel. Helps members negotiate pay, benefits, and better working conditions; conducts training programs and workshops. Monitors legislation and regulations. (Broadcast and Cable Television Workers Sector of the Communications Workers of America.)

National Assn. of Broadcasters (NAB), 1771 N St. N.W., 20036; (202) 429-5300. Fax, (202) 429-5406. Gordon Smith, President. Communications, (202) 429-5350.
General email, nab@nab.org

Web, www.nab.org

Membership: radio and television broadcast stations and broadcast networks holding an FCC license or construction permit; associate members include producers of equipment and programs. Assists members in areas of management, engineering, and research. Monitors legislation and regulations.

Radio Television Digital News Assn., 529 14th St. N.W., #1240, 20045; (202) 659-6510. Fax, (202) 223-4007. Mike Cavender, Executive Director, (770) 622-7011.
Web, www.rtdna.org and Twitter, @RTDNA

Membership: local and network news executives in broadcasting, cable, and other electronic media in more than thirty countries. Serves as information source for members; provides advice on legislative, political, and judicial problems of electronic journalism; conducts international exchanges.

Senate Radio-Television Gallery, S325 CAP, 20515; (202) 224-6421. Fax, (202) 224-4882. Michael Mastrian, Director.
General email, senatetvg@saa.senate.gov

Web, www.radiotv.senate

Membership: broadcast correspondents who cover Congress. Sponsors annual dinner. Officers also serve on the executive committee of the Congressional Radio-Television Galleries and determine eligibility for broadcast media credentials in Congress. Acts as a liaison between congressional offices and members of the media, and facilitates broadcast coverage of Senate activities.

Walter Kaitz Foundation, 25 Massachusetts Ave. N.W., #100, 20001; (202) 222-2490. Fax, (202) 222-2491. David M. Porter Jr., Executive Director. Press, (202) 222-2350.
General email, info@walterkaitz.org

Web, www.walterkaitz.org and Twitter, @WalterKaitz

Nonprofit that promotes women and minorities working in the cable industry. Financially supports and creates programs that provide internships to minority students, educate women on leadership, and advocate diversity in

telecommunications. Awards scholarships to professionals in the cable community.

Press Freedom

▶**NONGOVERNMENTAL**

Reporters Committee for Freedom of the Press, 1156 15th St. N.W., #1250, 20005; (202) 795-9300. Fax, (202) 795-9310. Bruce D. Brown, Executive Director, (202) 795-9301. Legal defense hotline, (800) 336-4243.
General email, info@rcfp.org

Legal defense hotline email, hotline@rcfp.org, and
Web, www.rcfp.org

Committee of reporters and editors that provides journalists and media lawyers with a 24-hour hotline for media law and freedom of information questions. Provides assistance to journalists and media lawyers in media law court cases, and to student journalists. Produces publications on newsgathering legal issues. Interests include freedom of speech abroad, primarily as it affects U.S. citizens in the press.

Reporters Without Borders (Reporters Sans Frontières), **Washington Office,** Southern Railway Bldg., 1500 K St. N.W., #600, 20005; (202) 879-9295. Delphine Halgand, Director.
General email, dcdesk@rsf.org

Web, www.rsf.org and Twitter, @RSF_RWB

Defends journalists who have been imprisoned or persecuted while conducting their work. Works to improve the safety of journalists. Advocates freedom of the press internationally through its offices in 11 countries. Sponsors annual events and awards. (Headquarters in Paris, France.)

Student Press Law Center, 1608 Rhode Island Ave. N.W., #211, 20036; (202) 785-5450. Fax, (202) 822-5045. Frank LoMonte, Executive Director.
General email, admin@splc.org

Web, www.splc.org

Collects, analyzes, and distributes information on free expression and freedom of information rights of student journalists (print, online, and broadcast) and on violations of those rights in high schools and colleges. Provides free legal advice and referrals to students and faculty advisers experiencing censorship. (Affiliated with the Reporters Committee for Freedom of the Press.)

Women's Institute for Freedom of the Press, 1940 Calvert St. N.W., 20009-1502; (202) 656-0893. Martha Allen, Director.
General email, mediademocracywifp@gmail.com

Web, www.wifp.org and Twitter, @WIFP

Conducts research and publishes in areas of communications and the media that are of particular interest to women. Promotes freedom of the press. Publishes a free online directory of media produced by and for women.

Print and Online Media

▶NONGOVERNMENTAL

American Press Institute (API), *4401 Wilson Blvd., #900, Arlington, VA 22203; (571) 366-1200. Fax, (703) 620-5814. Thomas (Tom) Rosenstiel, Executive Director, (571) 366-1035.*
General email, hello@pressinstitute.org
Web, www.americanpressinstitute.org and Twitter, @AmPress

Conducts research and training for journalists. Interests include sustaining a free press, and understanding changing audiences, new revenue models, and best practices for journalism in the digital age.

Assn. Media and Publishing, *12100 Sunset Hills Rd., #130, Reston, VA 20190; (703) 234-4063. Fax, (703) 435-4390. John T. Adam III, Executive Director.*
General email, info@associationmediaandpublishing.com
Web, www.associationmediaandpublishing.org, Twitter, @AssnMediaPub and Facebook, www.facebook.com/ AssociationMediaandPublishing

Membership: association publishers and communications professionals. Works to develop high standards for editorial and advertising content in members' publications. Compiles statistics; bestows editorial and graphics awards; monitors postal regulations. (Formerly Society of National Assn. Publications.)

Assn. of American Publishers, *Government Affairs, 455 Massachusetts Ave. N.W., #700, 20001; (202) 347-3375. Fax, (202) 347-3690. Allan R. Adler, Vice President, Legal and Government Affairs.*
General email, info@publishers.org
Web, www.publishers.org and Twitter, @AmericanPublish

Membership: U.S. publishers of books, scholarly journals, and multiplatform K–12 and higher education course materials. Represents industry priorities on policy, legislation, and regulatory issues regionally, nationally, and worldwide. Interests include intellectual property rights and copyright protection, tax and trade, new technology, educational and library funding, and First Amendment rights.

Essential Information, *1530 P St. N.W., 20005 (mailing address: P.O. Box 19405, Washington, DC); (202) 387-8030. Fax, (202) 234-5176. John Richard, Executive Director.*
General email, info@essential.org
Web, www.essential.org

Provides writers and the public with information on public policy matters; awards grants to investigative reporters; sponsors conference on investigative journalism. Interests include activities of multinational corporations in developing countries.

Graphic Communications Conference of the International Brotherhood of Teamsters (GCC/IBT), *25 Louisiana Ave. N.W., 20001; (202) 508-6660. Fax, (202) 624-8145. George Tedeschi, President.*

General email, webmessenger@gciu.org
Web, www.gciu.org

Membership: approximately 60,000 members of the print and publishing industries, including lithographers, photoengravers, and bookbinders. Assists members with contract negotiation and grievances; conducts training programs and workshops. Monitors legislation and regulations.

IDEAlliance, *1600 Duke St., #420, Alexandria, VA 22314; (703) 837-1070. Fax, (703) 837-1072. David J. Steinhardt, President.*
General email, registrar@idealliance.org
Web, www.idealliance.org

Membership: firms and customers in printing, publishing, and related industries. Assists members in production of color graphics and conducts studies on print media management methods.

Magazine Publishers of America (MPA), *Government Affairs, 1211 Connecticut Ave. N.W., #610, 20036; (202) 296-7277. Fax, (202) 296-0343. James Cregan, Executive Vice President.*
Web, www.magazine.org/advocacy

Membership: publishers of consumer magazines. Washington office represents members in all aspects of government relations in Washington and state capitals. Interests include intellectual property, the First Amendment, consumer protection, advertising, and postal, environmental, and tax policy. (Headquarters in New York.)

National Newspaper Publishers Assn. (NNPA), *1816 12th St. N.W., 2nd Floor, 20009; (202) 588-8764. Fax, (202) 588-8960. Denise Rolark Barnes, President, Washington region.*
General email, info@nnpa.org
Web, www.nnpa.org

Membership: newspapers owned by African Americans serving an African American audience. Assists in improving management and quality of the African American press through workshops and merit awards. Sponsors NNPA Media Services, a print and Web advertising-placement and press release distribution service.

Newspaper Assn. of America, *4401 Wilson Blvd., #900, Arlington, VA 22203-1867; (571) 366-1000. Fax, (571) 366-1195. David Chavern, President, (571) 366-1100; Paul Boyle, Senior Vice President, Public Policy, (571) 366-1150. Press, (571) 366-1009.*
Web, www.naa.org

Membership: daily and weekly newspapers, other papers, and online products published in the United States, Canada, other parts of the Western Hemisphere, and Europe. Conducts research and disseminates information on newspaper publishing, including labor relations, legal matters, government relations, technical problems and innovations, telecommunications, economic and statistical data, marketing, and training programs.

NPES: The Assn. for Suppliers of Printing, Publishing, and Converting Technologies, *1899 Preston White Dr., Reston, VA 20191-4367; (703) 264-7200. Fax, (703) 620-0994. Ralph J. Nappi, President.*
General email, npes@npes.org

Web, www.npes.org

Trade association representing companies that manufacture and distribute equipment, supplies, systems, software, and services for printing, publishing, and converting.

Print Communications Professionals International Inc. (PCPI), *2100 N. Potomac St., Arlington, VA 22205; (703) 534-9305. Fax, (703) 534-1858. Suzanne Morgan, President.*
General email, smorgan@pcpi.org

Web, www.pcpi.org

Membership: print buyers, communications professionals, and other purchasers of printing services. Educates members about best practices in the industry.

Printing Industries of America (PIA), *Washington Office, 1001 G St. N.W., #800, 20001; (202) 627-6924. Fax, (202) 730-7987. Lisbeth Lyons, Vice President, Government Affairs. Government Affairs, (202) 627-6925, ext. 504.*
General email, llyons@printing.org

Web, www.printing.org

Membership: printing firms and businesses that service printing industries. Represents members before Congress and regulatory agencies. Assists members with

labor relations, human resources management, and other business management issues. Sponsors graphic arts competition. Monitors legislation and regulations. (Headquarters in Warrendale, Pa.)

Specialized Information Publishers Assn. (SIPA), *1090 Vermont Ave. N.W., 6th Floor, 20005; (202) 289-7442. Fax, (202) 289-7097. Ken Wasch, President, (202) 739-4440.*
General email, sipa@sipaonline.com

Web, www.sipaonline.com

Membership: newsletter publishers, specialized information services, and vendors to that market. Serves as an information clearinghouse and provides educational resources in the field. Monitors legislation and regulations. Library open to the public. (Division of SIIA; formerly the Newsletter and Electronic Publishers Assn.)

Specialty Graphic Imaging Assn., *10015 Main St., Fairfax, VA 22031-3489; (703) 385-1335. Fax, (703) 273-0456. Ford Bowers, President. Toll-free, (888) 385-3588.*
General email, sgia@sgia.org

Web, www.sgia.org

Provides screen printers, graphic imagers, digital imagers, suppliers, manufacturers, and educators with technical guidebooks, training videos, managerial support, and guidelines for safety programs. Monitors legislation and regulations.

4

Culture and Religion

ARTS AND HUMANITIES

General

▶ **AGENCIES**

General Services Administration (GSA), *Design and Construction, Office of the Chief Architect,* 1800 F St. N.W., #3300, 20405-0001; (202) 501-1888. Fax, (202) 501-3393. Leslie Shepherd, Chief Architect, (202) 501-2289.
General email, les.shepherd@gsa.gov

Web, www.gsa.gov/portal/content/104549

Administers the Art in Architecture Program, which commissions publicly scaled works of art for government buildings and landscapes, and the Fine Arts Program, which manages the GSA's collection of fine artwork that has been commissioned for use in government buildings. Administers the historic preservation of historic federal buildings, and the Design Excellence Program, which reviews designs of federal buildings and courthouses.

John F. Kennedy Center for the Performing Arts, 2700 F St. N.W., 20566-0001; (202) 416-8000. Deborah F. Rutter, President, (202) 416-8011; David M. Rubenstein, Chair. Performance and ticket information, (202) 467-4600. Toll-free, (800) 444-1324. TTY, (202) 416-8524.
Web, www.kennedy-center.org

National cultural center created by Congress that operates independently; funded in part by federal dollars but primarily through private gifts and sales. Sponsors educational programs; presents American and international performances in theater, music, dance, and film; sponsors the John F. Kennedy Center Education Program, which produces the annual American College Theater Festival; and presents and subsidizes events for young people. The Kennedy Center stages free daily performances open to the public 365 days a year on its Millennium Stage in the Grand Foyer.

National Endowment for the Arts (NEA), 400 7th St. S.W., 20506; (202) 682-5400. Jane Chu, Chair, (202) 682-5414. Press, (202) 682-5570. TTY, (202) 682-5496.
General email, webmgr@arts.gov

Web, www.arts.gov, Twitter, @NEAarts and Facebook, www.facebook.com/NationalEndowmentfortheArts

Independent grant-making agency. Awards grants to support artistic excellence, creativity, and innovation for the benefit of individuals and communities. Works through partnerships with state arts agencies, local leaders, other federal agencies, and the philanthropic sector. Main funding categories include Art Works (replaces Access to Artistic Excellence and Learning in the Arts for Children and Youth); Challenge America Fast-Track (for art projects in underserved communities); and Our Town (for art projects that contribute to the livability of communities).

National Endowment for the Arts (NEA), *Artist Communities,* 400 7th St. S.W., 20506; (202) 682-5428. Fax, (202) 682-5669. Michael Orlove, Director. TTY, (202) 682-5496.
Web, www.arts.gov/artistic-fields/artist-communities

Awards grants and provides assistance to artist communities for projects that encourage and nurture the development of individual artists.

National Endowment for the Arts (NEA), *Presenting and Multidisciplinary Arts,* 400 7th St. S.W., 20506; (202) 682-5428. Fax, (202) 682-5669. Michael Orlove, Director. TTY, (202) 682-5496.
Web, www.arts.gov/artistic-fields/presenting-multidisciplinary-works

Awards grants to traditional presenting programs as well as artistic works and events that present multiple disciplines, combine or integrate art forms, explore boundaries between art disciplines, and seek to create new forms of expression.

National Endowment for the Humanities (NEH), 400 7th St. S.W., 20506; Fax, (202) 606-8608. William Adams, Chair, (202) 606-8310; Donna McClish, Librarian; Katja Zelljadt, Director, Challenge Grants. Information, (202) 606-8400. Toll-free, 800-NEH-1121. Library, (202) 606-8244. Public Affairs, (202) 606-8446. TTY, (202) 606-8282. Toll-free TTY, (866) 372-2930.
General email, info@neh.gov

Web, www.neh.gov and Facebook, www.facebook.com/ National-Endowment-for-the-Humanities-131252093552454

Independent federal grant-making agency. Awards grants to individuals and institutions for research, scholarship, and educational and public programs (including broadcasts, museum exhibitions, lectures, and symposia) in the humanities (defined as study of archaeology; history; jurisprudence; language; linguistics; literature; philosophy; comparative religion; ethics; history, criticism, and theory of the arts; and humanistic aspects of the social sciences). Funds preservation of books, newspapers, historical documents, and photographs. Library open by appointment only.

President's Committee on the Arts and the Humanities, 400 7th St. S.W., 20506; (202) 682-5409. Fax, (202) 682-5668. Megan Beyer, Executive Director; Margo Lion, Co-Chair; George Stevens Jr., Co-Chair.
General email, pcah@pcah.gov

Web, www.pcah.gov

Helps to incorporate the arts and humanities into White House objectives. Bridges federal agencies and the private sector. Recognizes cultural excellence, engages in research, initiates special projects, and stimulates private funding.

U.S. Commission of Fine Arts, 401 F St. N.W., #312, 20001-2728; (202) 504-2200. Fax, (202) 504-2195. Earl A. Powell III, Chair; Thomas Luebke, Secretary, tluebke@cfa.gov.
General email, cfastaff@cfa.gov

Web, www.cfa.gov and Twitter, @CFA_GOV

Advises the federal and D.C. governments on matters of art and architecture that affect the appearance of the nation's capital.

CULTURE AND RELIGION RESOURCES IN CONGRESS

For a complete listing of congressional committees, including their full contact information, leadership, membership, and jurisdictions, please refer to the Appendix on pages 779–896.

HOUSE:

House Administration Committee, (202) 225-8281.
Web, cha.house.gov

House Agriculture Committee, (202) 225-2171.
Web, agriculture.house.gov

House Appropriations Committee,
(202) 225-2771.
Web, appropriations.house.gov
  Subcommittee on Interior, Environment, and Related Agencies, (202) 225-3081.
  Subcommittee on Labor, Health and Human Services, Education, and Related Agencies, (202) 225-3508.
  Subcommittee on Legislative Branch, (202) 226-7252.

House Education and the Workforce Committee, (202) 225-4527.
Web, edworkforce.house.gov
  Subcommittee on Early Childhood, Elementary, and Secondary Education, (202) 225-4527.
  Subcommittee on Higher Education and Workforce Training, (202) 225-4527.

House Energy and Commerce Committee, (202) 225-2927.
Web, energycommerce.house.gov
  Subcommittee on Commerce, Manufacturing, and Trade, (202) 225-2927.
  Subcommittee on Communications and Technology, (202) 225-2927.

House Judiciary Committee, (202) 225-3951.
Web, judiciary.house.gov
  Subcommittee on the Constitution and Civil Justice, (202) 225-2825.

House Natural Resources Committee,
(202) 225-2761.
Web, naturalresources.house.gov
  Subcommittee on Indian, Insular, and Alaska Native Affairs, (202) 225-9725.

House Science, Space, and Technology Committee, (202) 225-6371.
Web, science.house.gov
  Subcommittee on Research and Technology, (202) 225-6371.

House Ways and Means Committee,
(202) 225-3625.
Web, waysandmeans.house.gov

JOINT:

Joint Committee on the Library of Congress,
(202) 225-8281.
Web, cha.house.gov/jointcommittees/joint-committee-library

SENATE:

Senate Agriculture, Nutrition, and Forestry Committee, (202) 224-2035.
Web, ag.senate.gov
  Subcommittee on Nutrition, Specialty Crops, and Agricultural Research, (202) 224-2035.

Senate Appropriations Committee,
(202) 224-7363.
Web, appropriations.senate.gov
  Subcommittee on Interior, Environment, and Related Agencies, (202) 228-0774.
  Subcommittee on Labor, Health and Human Services, Education, and Related Agencies, (202) 224-7363.

Senate Banking, Housing, and Urban Affairs Committee, (202) 224-7391.
Web, banking.senate.gov

Senate Commerce, Science, and Transportation Committee, (202) 224-0411.
Web, commerce.senate.gov
  Subcommittee on Science, Space and Competitiveness, (202) 224-0415.

Senate Energy and Natural Resources Committee, (202) 224-4971.
Web, energy.senate.gov
  Subcommittee on National Parks, (202) 224-4971.

Senate Finance Committee, (202) 224-4515.
Web, finance.senate.gov

Senate Health, Education, Labor, and Pensions Committee, (202) 224-5375.
Web, help.senate.gov
  Subcommittee on Children and Families, (202) 224-5375.

Senate Indian Affairs Committee, (202) 224-2251.
Web, indian.senate.gov

Senate Judiciary Committee, (202) 224-7703.
Web, judiciary.senate.gov

Senate Rules and Administration Committee, (202) 224-6352.
Web, rules.senate.gov

►CONGRESS

For a listing of relevant congressional committees and sub-committees, please see page 119 or the Appendix.

►NONGOVERNMENTAL

Americans for the Arts, *1000 Vermont Ave. N.W., 6th Floor, 20005; (202) 371-2830. Fax, (202) 371-0424. Robert L. Lynch, President.*
General email, info@artsusa.org
Web, www.americansforthearts.org

Membership: groups and individuals promoting advancement of the arts and culture in U.S. communities. Provides information on programs, activities, and administration of local arts agencies; on funding sources and guidelines; and on government policies and programs. Conducts, sponsors, and disseminates research on the social, educational, and economic benefits of arts programs. Monitors legislation and regulations.

Assn. of Performing Arts Presenters, *1211 Connecticut Ave. N.W., #200, 20036; (202) 833-2787. Fax, (202) 833-1543. Mario Garcia Durham, President. Toll-free, (888) 820-2787.*
General email, info@artspresenters.org
Web, www.apap365.org and Twitter, @APAP365

Connects performing artists to audiences and communities around the world. Facilitates the work of presenters, artist managers, and consultants through continuing education, regranting programs, and legislative advocacy.

Federation of State Humanities Councils, *1600 Wilson Blvd., #902, Arlington, VA 22209-2511; (703) 908-9700. Fax, (703) 908-9706. Esther Mackintosh, President.*
General email, info@statehumanities.org
Web, www.statehumanities.org and Twitter, @HumFed

Membership: humanities councils from U.S. states and territories. Provides members with information; forms partnerships with other organizations and with the private sector to promote the humanities. Monitors legislation and regulations.

National Assembly of State Arts Agencies, *1200 18th St. N.W., #1100, 20036; (202) 347-6352. Fax, (202) 737-0526. Pam Breaux, Chief Executive Officer. TTY, (202) 296-0567.*
General email, nasaa@nasaa-arts.org
Web, www.nasaa-arts.org

Membership: state and territorial arts agencies. Provides members with information, resources, and representation. Interests include arts programs for rural and underserved populations and the arts as a catalyst for economic development. Monitors legislation and regulations.

National Humanities Alliance, *21 Dupont Circle N.W., #800, 20036; (202) 296-4994. Fax, (202) 872-0884. Stephen Kidd, Executive Director, ext. 149.*

General email, humanities@nhalliance.org
Web, www.nhalliance.org, Twitter, @HumanitiesAll and Facebook, www.facebook.com/ NationalHumanitiesAlliance

Represents scholarly and professional humanities associations; associations of museums, libraries, and historical societies; higher education institutions; state humanities councils; and independent and university-based research centers. Promotes the interests of individuals engaged in research, writing, and teaching.

National League of American Pen Women, *1300 17th St. N.W., 20036-1973; (202) 785-1997. Fax, (202) 452-8868. Candace Long, National President.*
General email, contact@nlapw.org
Web, www.nlapw.org

Promotes the development of the creative talents of professional women in the fields of art, letters, and music composition. Conducts and promotes literary, educational, and charitable activities. Offers scholarships, workshops, and discussion groups.

Performing Arts Alliance, *1211 Connecticut Ave. N.W., #200, 20036; (202) 207-3850. Fax, (202) 833-1543. Cristine Davis, General Manager.*
General email, info@theperformingartsalliance.org
Web, www.theperformingartsalliance.org

Membership: organizations of the professional, non-profit performing arts and presenting fields. Through legislative and grassroots activities, advocates policies favorable to the performing arts and presenting fields.

Provisions Library Resource Center for Arts and Social Change *(George Mason University), Art and Design Bldg., 4400 University Dr., #L002, MS 1C3, Fairfax, VA 22030; (202) 670-7768. Donald H. Russell, Executive Director.*
General email, provisionslibrary@gmail.com
Web, http://provisionslibrary.com, http://soa.gmu.edu/ provisions

Library collection on politics and culture open to the public by appointment. Offers educational and arts programs concerning social change and social justice.

Wolf Trap Foundation for the Performing Arts, *1645 Trap Rd., Vienna, VA 22182-2064; (703) 255-1900. Fax, (703) 255-1905. Arvind Manocha, President. Press, (703) 255-4096. TTY, (703) 255-1849. Tickets, (877) 965-3872.*
General email, wolftrap@wolftrap.org
Web, www.wolftrap.org and Twitter, @wolf_trap

Established by Congress; operates as a public-private partnership between the National Park Service, which maintains the grounds, and the Wolf Trap Foundation, which sponsors performances in theater, music, and dance. Conducts educational programs for children, internships for college students, career-entry programs for young singers, and professional training for teachers and performers.

Education

▶ **AGENCIES**

Education Dept., *Innovation and Improvement, Arts in Education—Model Development and Dissemination,* 400 Maryland Ave. S.W., #4W210, 20202-5950; (202) 260-1280. Fax, (202) 205-5630. Anna Hinton, Director.
General email, artsdemo@ed.gov
Web, www2.ed.gov/programs/artsedmodel

Supports the development of innovative model programs that integrate and strengthen the arts into core elementary and middle school curricula and that strengthen arts instruction in those grades. Provides grants to local education agencies and nonprofit art organizations.

Education Dept., *Innovation and Improvement, Professional Development for Arts Educators,* 400 Maryland Ave. S.W., #4W214, 20202-5950; (202) 260-2072. Fax, (202) 205-5630. Michelle Johnson Armstrong, Program Manager, (202) 205-1729.
General email, Michelle.Armstrong@ed.gov
Web, www2.ed.gov/programs/artsedprofdev

Supports the implementation of high-quality professional development model programs in elementary and secondary education for music, dance, drama, and visual arts educators in high-poverty schools. Funds support innovative instructional methods, especially those linked to scientifically based research.

John F. Kennedy Center for the Performing Arts, *Education,* 2700 F St. N.W., 20566-0001; (202) 416-8854. Mario Rossero, Vice President. Press, (202) 416-8447. TTY, (202) 416-8728.
General email, kced@kennedy-center.org
Web, www.kennedy-center.org/education

Establishes and supports state committees to encourage arts education in schools; promotes community partnerships between performing arts centers and school systems (Partners in Education); provides teachers, artists, and school and arts administrators with professional development classes; offers in-house and touring performances for students, teachers, families, and the general public; arranges artist and company residencies in schools; sponsors the National Symphony Orchestra education program; presents lectures, demonstrations, and classes in the performing arts for the general public; offers internships in arts management; and produces annually the Kennedy Center American College Theater Festival.

John F. Kennedy Center for the Performing Arts, *National Partnerships,* 2700 F St. N.W., 20566-0001; (202) 416-8854. Barbara Shepherd, Director. Press, (202) 416-8447. TTY, (202) 416-8728.
Web, www.kennedy-center.org/education/partners

Supports community-based educational partnerships and state alliances by providing professional development, technical support, and resource development through the Ensuring the Arts for Any Given Child program, the Kennedy Center Alliance for Arts Education Network

(KCAAEN), and the Partners in Education program. These three national networks provide communities with such services as teacher professional development, policy and research formation, and arts education programming.

National Endowment for the Arts (NEA), *Arts Education,* 400 7th St. S.W., 20506; (202) 682-5707. Fax, (202) 682-5002. Ayanna N. Hudson, Director, (202) 682-5515. TTY, (202) 682-5496.
General email, artseducation@arts.gov
Web, www.arts.gov

Provides grants for curriculum-based arts education for children and youth (generally between ages 5 and 18) in schools or other community-based settings. Projects must provide participatory learning that engages students with accomplished artists and teachers, align with national or state arts education standards, and include assessments of participant learning. Also provides funding to support professional development opportunities for teachers, teaching artists, and other educators.

National Endowment for the Humanities (NEH), *Digital Humanities,* 400 7th St. S.W., 20506; (202) 606-8401. Fax, (202) 606-8411. Brett Bobley, Director.
General email, odh@neh.gov
Web, www.neh.gov/divisions/odh

Encourages and supports projects that utilize or study the impact of digital technology on research, education, preservation, access, and public programming in the humanities.

National Endowment for the Humanities (NEH), *Education Programs,* 400 7th St. S.W., 20506; (202) 606-8500. Fax, (202) 606-8394. William Craig Rice, Director.
General email, education@neh.gov
Web, www.neh.gov/divisions/education

Supports the improvement of education in the humanities. Supports classroom resources and faculty training and development.

National Endowment for the Humanities (NEH), *Research Programs,* 400 7th St. S.W., 20506; (202) 606-8200. Fax, (202) 606-8558. Jane Aikin, Director, (202) 606-8212.
General email, research@neh.gov
Web, www.neh.gov/divisions/research

Sponsors fellowship programs for humanities scholars, including summer stipend programs. Provides support to libraries, museums, and independent centers for advanced study.

National Gallery of Art, *Education,* 4th St. and Constitution Ave. N.W., 20565 (mailing address: 2000B S. Club Dr., Landover, MD 20785); (202) 842-6246. Fax, (202) 842-6935. Lynn Russell, Head. TTY, (202) 842-6176.
General email, EdResources@nga.gov
Web, www.nga.gov/education

Serves as an educational arm of the gallery by providing free programs for schools, families, and adults. Lends audiovisual educational materials free of charge to schools, colleges, community groups, libraries, and individuals. Provides answers to written and telephone inquiries about European and American art.

Smithsonian Center for Learning and Digital Access, *600 Maryland Ave. S.W., #1005W, 20024 (mailing address: P.O. Box 37012, MRC 508, Washington, DC 20013-7012); (202) 633-5330. Fax, (202) 633-5489. Stephanie Norby, Director.*
General email, learning@si.edu
Web, www.smithsonianeducation.org

Serves as the Smithsonian's central education office. Provides elementary and secondary teachers with programs, publications, audiovisual materials, regional workshops, and summer courses on using museums and primary source materials as teaching tools. Publishes books and other educational materials for teachers.

Smithsonian Institution, *Smithsonian Associates, 1100 Jefferson Dr. S.W., #3077, 20560 (mailing address: P.O. Box 23293, Washington, DC 20026-3293); (202) 633-3030. Fax, (202) 786-2034. Frederica Adelman, Director.*
General email, customerservice@smithsonianassociates.org
Web, http://smithsonianassociates.org

National cultural and educational membership organization that offers courses and lectures for adults and young people. Presents films and offers study tours on subjects related to the arts, humanities, and science; sponsors performances, studio arts workshops, and research.

▶ **NONGOVERNMENTAL**

National Art Education Assn., *901 Prince St., Alexandria, VA 22314; (703) 860-8000. Fax, (703) 860-2960. Deborah Reeve, Executive Director. Toll-free, (800) 299-8321.*
General email, info@arteducators.org
Web, www.arteducators.org

Membership: art teachers (pre-K through university), school administrators, museum staff, and manufacturers and suppliers of art materials. Issues publications on art education theory and practice, research, and current trends; provides technical assistance to art educators. Sponsors awards.

National Assn. of Schools of Art and Design, *11250 Roger Bacon Dr., #21, Reston, VA 20190-5248; (703) 437-0700. Fax, (703) 437-6312. Karen Moynahan, Executive Director.*
General email, info@arts-accredit.org
Web, http://nasad.arts-accredit.org

Specialized professional accrediting agency for postsecondary programs in art and design. Conducts and shares research and analysis on topics pertinent to art and design programs and fields of art and design. Offers professional development opportunities for executives of art and design programs.

Wolf Trap Foundation for the Performing Arts, *1645 Trap Rd., Vienna, VA 22182-2064; (703) 255-1900. Fax, (703) 255-1905. Arvind Manocha, President. Press, (703) 255-4096. TTY, (703) 255-1849. Tickets, (877) 965-3872.*

General email, wolftrap@wolftrap.org
Web, www.wolftrap.org and Twitter, @wolf_trap

Established by Congress; operates as a public-private partnership between the National Park Service, which maintains the grounds, and the Wolf Trap Foundation, which sponsors performances in theater, music, and dance. Conducts educational programs for children, internships for college students, career-entry programs for young singers, and professional training for teachers and performers.

Film, Photography, and Broadcasting

▶ **AGENCIES**

American Film Institute (AFI), *Silver Theatre and Cultural Center, 8633 Colesville Rd., Silver Spring, MD 20910-3916; (301) 495-6720. Fax, (301) 495-6777. Ray Barry, Director. Recorded information, (301) 495-6700.*
General email, silverinfo@afi.com
Web, www.afi.com/silver

Shows films of historical and artistic importance. AFI theater open to the public.

National Archives and Records Administration (NARA), *Motion Picture, Sound, and Video Branch, 8601 Adelphi Rd., #3360, College Park, MD 20740-6001; (301) 837-0526. Fax, (301) 837-3620. Daniel Rooney, Chief. TTY, (301) 837-0482.*
General email, mopix@nara.gov
Web, www.archives.gov

Selects and preserves audiovisual records produced or acquired by federal agencies; maintains collections from the private sector, including newsreels. Research room open to the public Monday–Saturday, 9:00 a.m.–5:00 p.m.

National Archives and Records Administration (NARA), *Still Picture Branch, 8601 Adelphi Rd., NWCS #5360, College Park, MD 20740-6001; (301) 837-3530. Fax, (301) 837-3621. Deborah Lelansky, Director, Acting. Reference desk, (301) 837-0561.*
General email, stillpix@nara.gov
Web, www.archives.gov/dc-metro/college-park/photographs-dc.html

Provides the public with access to and copies of still picture and poster records created or acquired by the federal government; supplies research assistance (both offsite and onsite), finding aids and guides to these materials. Records include still pictures and posters (some in digital format) from more than 200 federal agencies, from the mid-nineteenth century to the present.

National Endowment for the Arts (NEA), *Media Arts, 400 7th St. S.W., 20506; (202) 682-5452. Fax, (202) 682-5721. Jax Deluca, Director, (202) 682-5742. TTY, (202) 682-5496.*
Web, www.arts.gov/artistic-fields/media-arts

Awards grants to nonprofit organizations for screen-based projects presented by film, television, video, radio, Internet, mobile technologies, video games, transmedia storytelling, and satellite; supports film and video exhibitions and workshops.

National Endowment for the Humanities (NEH), *Public Programs,* *400 7th St. S.W., 20506; (202) 606-8269. Fax, (202) 606-8557. Karen Mittelman, Director, (202) 606-8631.*
General email, publicpgms@neh.gov
Web, www.neh.gov/divisions/public

Awards grants to libraries, museums, special projects, and media for projects that enhance public appreciation and understanding of the humanities through books and other resources in American library collections. Promotes public appreciation of the humanities through support of quality public programs of broad significance, reach, and impact. Awards grants for projects that meet NEH goals and standards, including excellence in content and format, broad public appeal, and wide access to diverse audiences.

►CONGRESS

For a listing of relevant congressional committees and subcommittees, please see page 119 or the Appendix.

Library of Congress, *Motion Picture, Broadcasting, and Recorded Sound Division,* James Madison Memorial Bldg., 101 Independence Ave. S.E., #LM 336, 20540; (202) 707-8572. Gregory Lukow, Chief. Recorded Sound Reference Center, (202) 707-7833. Fax for Recorded Sound Reference Center, (202) 707-8464. Fax for Motion Picture and Television Reading Room, (202) 707-2371.
Web, www.loc.gov/rr/mopic

Motion Picture and Broadcasting archives include an extensive range from 1894 to the present of feature films, shorts, animated cartoons, newsreels, television shows, and more. Recorded Sound archives include sound recordings from 1890 to present; tapes the library's concert series and other musical events for radio broadcast; produces recordings of music and poetry for sale to the public. American Film Institute film archives are interfiled with the division's collections. Use of collections restricted to scholars and researchers; reading room open to the public.

Library of Congress, *National Film Preservation Board,* 19053 Mount Pony Rd., Culpeper, VA 22701-7551; (202) 707-5912. Fax, (202) 707-2371. Steve Leggett, Staff Coordinator. TTY, (202) 707-6362.
Web, www.loc.gov/programs/national-film-preservation-board/about-this-program

Administers the National Film Preservation Plan. Establishes guidelines and receives nominations for the annual selection of twenty-five films of cultural, historical, or aesthetic significance; selections are entered in the National Film Registry to ensure archival preservation in their original form.

Library of Congress, *National Recording Preservation Board,* 1010 Independence Ave. S.E., 20540-5698; (202) 707-5912. Fax, (202) 707-2371. Steve Leggett, Staff Coordinator. TTY, (202) 707-6362.
Web, www.loc.gov/programs/national-recording-preservation-board/about-this-program

Administers the National Recording Preservation Plan aimed at studying the state of and advances in sound recording. Receives nominations for the annual selection of twenty-five recordings demonstrating the range and diversity of American recorded sound heritage. Makes selections to the National Recording Registry.

Library of Congress, *Prints and Photographs Division,* James Madison Memorial Bldg., 101 Independence Ave. S.E., #LM 337, 20540-4730; (202) 707-6394. Fax, (202) 707-6647. Helena Zinkham, Chief.
Web, www.loc.gov/rr/print

Maintains Library of Congress's collection of pictorial material not in book format, totaling more than 15 million items. U.S. and international collections include artists' prints; historical prints, posters, and drawings; photographs (chiefly documentary); political and social cartoons; and architectural plans, drawings, prints, and photographs. Reference service provided in the Prints and Photographs Reading Room. Reproductions of nonrestricted material available through the Library of Congress's Photoduplication Service; prints and photographs may be borrowed through the Exhibits Office for exhibits by qualified institutions. A portion of the collections and an overview of reference services are available on the World Wide Web.

►NONGOVERNMENTAL

CINE (Council on International Nontheatrical Events), *1003 K St. N.W., #208, 20001; (507) 400-2463. Jon Gann, Executive Director.*
General email, info@cine.org
Web, www.cine.org and Twitter, @cinegoldeneagle

Builds and supports a community of professional, emerging, and student film, television, and digital content creators through the CINE Golden Eagle Awards, the CINE Connects alumni network, the Marvin Hamlisch Film Scoring Contest, and related skill-building events and programming.

Motion Picture Assn. of America, *1600 Eye St. N.W., 20006; (202) 293-1966. Fax, (202) 296-7410. Christopher J. Dodd, Chief Executive Officer. Anti-piracy hotline, (800) 662-6797.*
General email, ContactUs@mpaa.org
Web, www.mpaa.org

Membership: motion picture producers and distributors. Advises state and federal governments on copyrights, censorship, cable broadcasting, and other topics; administers volunteer rating system for motion pictures; works to prevent video piracy.

Special Collections in Mass Media and Culture *(University of Maryland),* Hornbake Library, 4130 Campus Dr., College Park, MD 20742-7011; (301) 405-9160.

Fax, (301) 314-2634. Douglas McElrath, Curator, Acting, (301) 405-9210. Reference desk, (301) 405-9212. General email, bcast@umd.edu

Web, www.lib.umd.edu/special

Maintains library and archives on the history of radio and television. Houses the National Public Broadcasting Archives. Open to the public. (Formerly Library of American Broadcasting.)

Language and Literature

▶AGENCIES

Administration for Native Americans *(Health and Human Services Dept.), 330 C. St. S.W., 20201; (202) 690-7776. Fax, (202) 690-7441. Lillian A. Sparks, Commissioner. Toll-free, (877) 922-9262. General email, ana@acf.hhs.gov*

Web, www.acf.hhs.gov/programs/ana

Promotes revitalization and continuation of tribal languages.

National Endowment for the Arts (NEA), *Literature, 400 7th St. S.W., 20506; (202) 682-5707. Fax, (202) 682-5002. Amy Stolls, Director, (202) 682-5771. TTY, (202) 682-5496. General email, literature@arts.gov*

Web, www.arts.gov/artistic-fields/literature

Awards grants to published writers, poets, and translators of prose and poetry; awards grants to nonprofit presses, literary magazines, and literature organizations that publish poetry and fiction.

▶CONGRESS

For a listing of relevant congressional committees and subcommittees, please see page 119 or the Appendix.

Library of Congress, *Center for the Book, James Madison Memorial Bldg., 101 Independence Ave. S.E., #LM 650, 20540; (202) 707-5221. Fax, (202) 707-0269. John Y. Cole, Director. General email, cfbook@loc.gov*

Web, www.read.gov/cfb

Seeks to broaden public appreciation of books, reading, literacy, and libraries; sponsors lectures and conferences on the educational and cultural role of the book worldwide, including the history of books and printing, television and the printed word, and the publishing and production of books; cooperates with state centers and with other organizations. Projects and programs are privately funded except for basic administrative support from the Library of Congress.

Library of Congress, *Children's Literature Center, Thomas Jefferson Bldg., 101 Independence Ave. S.E., #LJ 129, 20540; (202) 707-5535. Fax, (202) 707-4632. Sybille A. Jagusch, Chief. General email, childref@loc.gov*

Web, www.loc.gov/rr/child

Provides reference and information services by telephone, by correspondence, and in person; maintains reference materials on all aspects of the study of children's literature. Serves children indirectly through assistance given to teachers, librarians, and others who work with youth.

Library of Congress, *Main Reading Room, Thomas Jefferson Bldg., 101 Independence Ave. S.E., #LJ 100, 20540-4660; (202) 707-3399. Fax, (202) 707-1957. Barbie Morland, Head. Web, www.loc.gov/rr/main*

Point of access to the general collection of books and bound periodicals as well as electronic resources including microform. Offers research orientations.

Library of Congress, *Poetry and Literature Center, Thomas Jefferson Bldg., 101 Independence Ave. S.E., #A102, 20540-4861; (202) 707-5394. Fax, (202) 707-9946. Robert Casper, Head; Juan Felipe Herrera, Poet Laureate. General email, poetry@loc.gov*

Web, www.loc.gov/poetry

Advises the library on public literary programs and on the acquisition of literary materials. Sponsors public poetry and fiction readings, lectures, symposia, occasional dramatic performances, and other literary events. Arranges for poets to record readings of their work for the library's tape archive. The poet laureate is appointed annually by the Librarian of Congress on the basis of literary distinction.

Library of Congress, *Young Readers Center, Thomas Jefferson Bldg., 10 1st St. S.E., #LJ G29, 20540; (202) 707-1950. Fax, (202) 707-0269. Karen Jaffe, Head. General email, yrc@loc.gov*

Web, http://read.gov/yrc

Promotes books, reading, literacy, libraries, and the scholarly study of books through affiliates and promotional programs. Places special emphasis on young readers through reading and writing contests.

▶NONGOVERNMENTAL

Alliance Française de Washington, *2142 Wyoming Ave. N.W., 20008-3906; (202) 234-7911. Fax, (202) 234-0125. Sarah Diligenti, Executive Director. General email, alliance@francedc.org*

Web, www.francedc.org

Offers courses in French language and literature; presents lectures and cultural events; maintains library of French-language publications for members; offers language programs, including on-site corporate language programs.

Center for Applied Linguistics, *4646 40th St. N.W., #200, 20016-1859; (202) 362-0700. Fax, (202) 362-3740. Terrence Wiley, President. General email, info@cal.org*

Web, www.cal.org

Research and technical assistance organization that serves as a clearinghouse on application of linguistics to practical language problems. Interests include English as a second language (ESL), teacher training and material development, language education, language proficiency test development, bilingual education, and sociolinguistics.

English First, *8001 Forbes Pl., #102, Springfield, VA 22151-2205; (703) 321-8818. Fax, (703) 321-8408. Frank McGlynn, Executive Director. Web, www.englishfirst.org*

Seeks to make English the official language of the United States. Advocates policies that make English education available to all children. Monitors legislation and regulations. Opposes multilingual education and governmental policies, including *Clinton Executive Order 13166.*

Folger Shakespeare Library, *201 E. Capitol St. S.E., 20003-1004; (202) 544-4600. Fax, (202) 544-4623. Michael Witmore, Director, (202) 675-0301. Press, (202) 675-0326. Box Office, (202) 544-7077. General email, info@folger.edu Web, www.folger.edu and Twitter, @FolgerLibrary*

Maintains major Shakespearean and Renaissance materials; awards fellowships for postdoctoral research; presents concerts, theater performances, poetry and fiction readings, exhibits, and other public events. Offers educational programs for elementary, secondary, high school, college, and graduate school students and teachers. Publishes the Folger Shakespeare editions, *Folger Magazine,* and, in association with the George Washington University, *Shakespeare Quarterly.*

The Herb Block Foundation, *1730 M St. N.W., #901, 20036; (202) 223-8801. Fax, (202) 223-8804. Marcela Brane, President; Sarah Alex, Executive Director. General email, info@herbblock.org Web, www.herbblockfoundation.org*

Maintains an archive of Herb Block's editorial cartoons through the Library of Congress.

Japan–America Society of Washington, *1819 L St. N.W., Level B2, 20036-3807; (202) 833-2210. Amb. John R. Malott, President. General email, info@jaswdc.org Web, www.jaswdc.org*

Offers lectures and films on Japan; operates a Japanese-language school and an annual nationwide language competition for high school students; partner of the National Cherry Blossom Festival. Maintains library for members.

Joint National Committee for Languages / National Council for Languages and International Studies, *4600 Waverly Ave., Garrett Park, MD 20896 (mailing address: P.O. Box 386, Garrett Park, MD 20896); (202) 580-8684. William Rivers, Executive Director. General email, info@languagepolicy.org Web, www.languagepolicy.org*

Coalition of professional organizations in teaching, translation, interpreting, testing, and research. Supports

a national policy on language study and international education. Provides forum and clearinghouse for professional language and international education associations. National Council for Languages and International Studies is the political arm.

Linguistic Society of America, *522 21st St. N.W., #120, 20006-5012; (202) 835-1714. Fax, (202) 835-1717. Alyson Reed, Executive Director. General email, lsa@lsadc.org Web, www.linguisticsociety.org*

Membership: individuals and institutions interested in the scientific analysis of language. Holds linguistic institutes every other year and an annual meeting.

Malice Domestic Ltd., *P.O. Box 8007, Gaithersburg, MD 20898-8007; (301) 730-1675. Verena Rose, Chair; Shawn Reilly Simmons, Public Relations. General email, malicedomesticPR@gmail.com Web, www.malicedomestic.org and Facebook, www.facebook.com/Malice-Domestic-137517609649969*

Membership: authors and readers of traditional mysteries. Sponsors annual Agatha Awards and an annual convention. Awards grants to unpublished writers in the genre.

National Foreign Language Center *(University of Maryland), 5245 Greenbelt Rd., Severn Bldg. 810, College Park, MD 20742 (mailing address: P.O. Box 93, Severn Bldg. 810, 5245 Greenbelt Rd., College Park, MD 20742); (301) 405-9828. Fax, (301) 405-9829. David P. Ellis, Executive Director. General email, inquiries@nflc.org Web, www.nflc.umd.edu*

Research and policy organization that develops new strategies for strengthening foreign language competence in the United States. Conducts research on national language needs and assists policymakers in identifying priorities, allocating resources, and designing programs. Interests include the role of foreign language in higher education, national competence in critical languages, ethnic language maintenance, and K–12 and postsecondary language programs.

PEN/Faulkner Foundation, *201 E. Capitol St. S.E., 20003-1094; (202) 898-9063. Fax, (202) 675-0360. Emma Snyder, Executive Director. General email, info@penfaulkner.org Web, www.penfaulkner.org*

Sponsors an annual juried award for American fiction. Brings authors to visit public schools to discuss their work. Holds readings by noted authors of American fiction.

U.S. English Inc., *2000 L St. N.W., #702, 20036; (202) 833-0100. Fax, (202) 833-0108. Mauro E. Mujica, Chair. Toll-free, (800) 787-8216. General email, info@usenglish.org Web, www.usenglish.org*

Museum Education Programs

Alexandria Archaeology, (703) 746-4399

American Alliance of Museums, Museum Assessment Program, (202) 289-1818

Arlington Arts Center, (703) 248-6800

Assn. of Science-Technology Centers, (202) 783-7200

B'nai B'rith Klutznick Museum, (202) 857-6600

C & O Canal, (301) 739-4200

Corcoran Gallery of Art, (202) 994-1700

Daughters of the American Revolution (DAR) Museum, (202) 628-1776

Decatur House, (202) 842-0917

Dumbarton Oaks, (202) 339-6401

Federal Reserve Board Fine Arts Program, (202) 452-3778

Folger Shakespeare Library, (202) 544-4600

Gadsby's Tavern Museum, (703) 746-4242

Institute of Museum and Library Services, (202) 653-4657

J.F.K. Center for the Performing Arts, (202) 467-4600

The Lyceum: Alexandria's History Museum, (703) 746-4994

Mount Vernon, (703) 780-2000

National Arboretum, (202) 245-2726

National Archives, (866) 272-6272

National Building Museum, (202) 272-2448

National Gallery of Art, (202) 737-4215

National Museum of Women in the Arts, (202) 783-5000

Navy Museum, (202) 433-6826

Octagon Museum, (202) 626-7439

Phillips Collection, (202) 387-2151

Smithsonian Institution, (202) 633-1000

  Anacostia Community Museum, (202) 633-4820

  Arthur M. Sackler Gallery, (202) 633-0457

  Center for Education and Museum Studies, (202) 633-5330

  Freer Gallery of Art, (202) 633-0457

  Hirshhorn Museum and Sculpture Garden, (202) 633-3382

  National Air and Space Museum, (202) 633-2540

  National Museum of African Art, (202) 633-4640

  National Museum of American Art, (202) 633-7970

  National Museum of American History, (202) 633-3717

  National Museum of Natural History, (202) 633-1077

  National Museum of the American Indian, (202) 633-6644

  National Portrait Gallery, (202) 633-8500

  Renwick Gallery, (202) 633-2850

Textile Museum, (202) 667-0441

Woodrow Wilson House, (202) 387-4062

Advocates English as the official language of federal and state government. Affiliate U.S. English Foundation promotes English language education for immigrants.

The Writer's Center, *4508 Walsh St., Bethesda, MD 20815; (301) 654-8664. Fax, (240) 223-0458. Joe Callahan, Executive Director.*
General email, post.master@writer.org
Web, www.writer.org and Twitter, @writerscenter

Membership: writers, editors, and interested individuals. Supports the creation, publication, presentation, and dissemination of literary texts. Sponsors workshops in writing. Presents author readings. Maintains a book gallery.

Museums

▶AGENCIES

Anacostia Community Museum *(Smithsonian Institution), 1901 Fort Pl. S.E., 20020 (mailing address: P.O. Box 37012, MRC 0777, Washington, DC 20013-7012); (202) 633-4820. Fax, (202) 287-3183. Camille Akeju, Director. Press, (202) 633-4876. Public Affairs, (202) 633-4869. Public programs, (202) 633-4844. Recorded information, (202) 633-1000. Special events, (202) 633-4867. General email, ACMinfo@si.edu*
Web, http://anacostia.si.edu and Twitter, @AnacostiaMuseum

Explores, documents, and interprets social and cultural issues that impact contemporary urban communities. Presents changing exhibits and programs.

Federal Council on the Arts and the Humanities, *400 7th St. S.W., 20506; (202) 682-5541. Fax, (202) 682-5721. Patricia Loiko, Indemnity Administrator.*
Web, http://arts.gov/artistic-fields/museums/arts-and-artifacts-indemnity-program-domestic-indemnity and
http://arts.gov/artistic-fields/museums/arts-and-artifacts-indemnity-program-international-indemnity

Membership: leaders of federal agencies sponsoring arts-related activities. Administers the Arts and Artifacts Indemnity Act, which helps museums reduce the costs of commercial insurance for traveling exhibits.

Ford's Theatre National Historic Site, *511 10th St. N.W., 20004; (202) 426-6924. Fax, (202) 426-1845. William Cheek, Site Manager. Recorded ticket information, (202) 638-2941.*
General email, NACC_FOTH_Interpretation@nps.gov
Web, www.nps.gov/foth and Facebook, www.facebook.com/fordstheatrenps

Administered by the National Park Service, which manages Ford's Theatre, Ford's Theatre Museum, and the Peterson House (house where Lincoln died). Presents interpretive talks, exhibits, and tours. Research library open by appointment. Functions as working stage for theatrical productions.

Frederick Douglass National Historic Site, *1411 W St. S.E., 20020; (202) 426-5961. Fax, (202) 426-0880. Julie A. Kutruff, District Manager; Ka'mal McClarin, Site Curator. Reservations, (877) 444-6777.*
General email, julie_kutruff@nps.gov

Web, www.nps.gov/frdo and Twitter, @FredDouglassNPS

Administered by the National Park Service. Museum of the life and work of abolitionist Frederick Douglass and his family. Offers tours of the home and special programs, such as documentary films, videos, and slide presentations; maintains visitors center and bookstore. Reservations are required for parties of more than ten. Online reservations can be made at www.recreation.gov.

Freer Gallery of Art and Arthur M. Sackler Gallery *(Smithsonian Institution), 1050 Independence Ave. S.W., 20560 (mailing address: P.O. Box 37012, MRC 707, Washington, DC 20013-7012); (202) 633-4880. Fax, (202) 357-4911. Julian Raby, Director. Press, (202) 633-0519. Public programs, (202) 633-1000 (recording). TTY, (202) 633-5285. Library, (202) 633-0477. Education Office, (202) 633-0457.*
General email, publicaffairsasia@si.edu

Web, www.asia.si.edu and Twitter, @FreerSackler

Exhibits ancient and contemporary Asian art from the Mediterranean to Japan and late nineteenth- and early twentieth-century American art from its permanent collection, including works by James McNeill Whistler. Presents films, lectures, and concerts. Library open to the public Monday through Friday, 10:00 a.m.–5:00 p.m.

Hirshhorn Museum and Sculpture Garden *(Smithsonian Institution), 7th St. and Independence Ave. S.W., 20560 (mailing address: P.O. Box 37012, HMSG, MRC 350, Washington, DC 20013-7012); (202) 633-4674. Fax, (202) 633-8796. Melissa Chiu, Director. Press, (202) 633-2807. TTY, (202) 633-8043.*
General email, hmsginquiries@si.edu

Web, www.hirshhorn.si.edu

Preserves and exhibits modern and contemporary art. Offers films, lectures, and tours of the collection.

L'Enfant Institute of Museums and Libraries, *955 L'Enfant Plaza North S.W., #4000, 20024; (202) 653-4700. Fax, (202) 653-4600. Kathryn K. Matthew, Director. Main IMLS office, (202) 653-4700. Library services, (202) 653-4700. Museum services, (202) 653-4789. fax, (202) 653-4600. Communications and Government Affairs, (202) 653-4799. TTY, (202) 653-4614.*
General email, imlsinfo@imls.gov

Web, www.imls.gov and Twitter, @US_IMLS

Independent federal agency established by Congress to assist museums and libraries in increasing and improving their services. Awards grants for the professional development of museum and library staff, conservation projects, and creation of new tools, services, practices, and alliances. Also funds research, conferences, and publications.

National Archives and Records Administration (NARA), *National Archives Museum, 700 Pennsylvania Ave. N.W.,* *#G9, 20408; (202) 357-5210. Fax, (202) 357-5926. Lisa Royce, Director. Information, (202) 357-5000. Press, (202) 357-5300.*
General email, inquire@nara.gov/museum

Web, www.archives.gov

Plans and directs activities to acquaint the public with the mission and holdings of the National Archives; conducts behind-the-scenes tours; presents hands-on workshops; develops both traditional and interactive exhibits; produces publications, including teaching packets that feature historic documents and online educational tools.

National Cryptologic Museum *(National Security Agency), 8290 Colony Seven Rd., Annapolis Junction, MD 20701 (mailing address: 9800 Savage Rd., Fort Meade, MD 20755); (301) 688-5849. Fax, (301) 688-5847. Patrick Weadon, Curator. NSA Public and Media Affairs, (301) 688-6524.*
General email, crypto_museum@nsa.gov

Web, www.nsa.gov/about/cryptologic_heritage/museum

Documents the history of the cryptologic profession.

National Endowment for the Arts (NEA), *Museums, 400 7th St. S.W., 20506; (202) 682-5452. Fax, (202) 682-5721. Wendy Clark, Director. TTY, (202) 682-5496.*
Web, www.arts.gov/artistic-fields/museums

Awards grants to museums for installing and cataloging permanent and special collections; conducts traveling exhibits; trains museum professionals; conserves and preserves museum collections; and develops arts-related educational programs.

National Gallery of Art, *4th St. and Constitution Ave. N.W., 20565 (mailing address: 2000B S. Club Dr., Landover, MD 20785); (202) 737-4215. Fax, (202) 842-2356. Earl A. Powell III, Director. Press, (202) 842-6353. TTY, (202) 842-6176. Visitor services, (202) 842-6691. Library, (202) 842-6511.*
Web, www.nga.gov, Twitter, @ngadc and Facebook, www.facebook.com/nationalgalleryofart

Created by a joint resolution of Congress, the museum is a public-private partnership that collects, preserves, and exhibits European and American paintings, sculpture, and decorative and graphic arts. Offers concerts, demonstrations, lectures, symposia, films, tours, and teacher workshops to enhance exhibitions, the permanent collection, and related topics. Lends art to museums in all fifty states and abroad through the National Lending Service. Publishes a bimonthly calendar of events.

National Museum of African Art *(Smithsonian Institution), 950 Independence Ave. S.W., 20560 (mailing address: P.O. Box 37012, MRC 708, Washington, DC 20013-7012); (202) 633-4600. Fax, (202) 357-4879. Johnnetta B. Cole, Director. Press, (202) 633-4649. General Smithsonian information, (202) 633-1000.*
General email, nmafaweb@nmafa.si.edu

Web, http://africa.si.edu

Collects, studies, and exhibits traditional and contemporary arts of Africa. Exhibits feature objects from the permanent collection and from private and public collections worldwide. Museum is open 10 a.m. to 5:30 p.m. daily except December 25. Library and photo archive open to the public by appointment.

National Museum of American History *(Smithsonian Institution), 14th St. and Constitution Ave. N.W., #4260, MRC 622, 20560-0630 (mailing address: P.O. Box 37012, Washington, DC 20013); (202) 633-3435. Fax, (202) 633-4717. John Gray, Director. Library, (202) 633-2240. Press, (202) 633-3129. TTY, (202) 633-5285. General Smithsonian information, (202) 633-1000.*
General email, info@si.edu

Web, http://americanhistory.si.edu

Collects and exhibits objects representative of American cultural history, applied arts, industry, national and military history, and science and technology. Library open to the public by appointment.

National Museum of Health and Medicine *(Defense Dept.), 2460 Linden Lane, Silver Spring, MD 20910 (mailing address: 2460 Linden Lane, Bldg. 2500, Silver Spring, MD 20910); (301) 319-3300. Fax, (301) 319-3373. Dr. Adrianne Noe, Director. Tours, (301) 319-3312.*
General email, usarmy.detrick.medcom-usamrmc.list .medical-museum@mail.mil

Web, www.medicalmuseum.mil and Twitter, @medicalmuseum

Collects and exhibits medical models, tools, and pathological specimens. Maintains exhibits on military medicine and surgery. Open to the public 10:00 a.m.–5:30 p.m., 7 days a week. Study collection available to scholars by appointment.

National Museum of the American Indian *(Smithsonian Institution), 4th St. and Independence Ave. S.W., 20560; (202) 633-6803. Fax, (202) 633-6920. Kevin Gover, Director, (202) 633-6707. Group reservations, (202) 633-6644. TTY, (202) 633-5285. TTY group reservations, (202) 633-6751. General Smithsonian information, (202) 633-1000.*
General email, NMAI-info@si.edu

Web, www.americanindian.si.edu

Collects, exhibits, preserves, and studies American Indian languages, literature, history, art, and culture. Operates ImagiNations activity center, open to the public. (Affiliated with the George Gustav Heye Center, 1 Bowling Green, New York, NY 10004 and the Cultural Resources Center, 4220 Silver Hill Rd., Suitland, MD 20746.)

National Portrait Gallery *(Smithsonian Institution), 800 F St. N.W., 20001 (mailing address: P.O. Box 37012, Victor Bldg., MRC 973, Washington, DC 20013-7012); (202) 633-8300. Fax, (202) 633-8243. Kim Sajet, Director; Brandon Fortune, Chief Curator; Bethany Bentley, Communications, (202) 633-8293. Library, (202) 633-8227. Press, (202) 633-2585. General Smithsonian information, (202) 633-1000.*
General email, npgnews@si.edu

Web, www.npg.si.edu

Exhibits paintings, photographs, sculpture, drawings, and prints of individuals who have made significant contributions to the history, development, and culture of the United States. Library open to the public.

National Postal Museum *(Smithsonian Institution), 2 Massachusetts Ave. N.E., 20002 (mailing address: P.O. Box 37012, Washington, DC 20013); (202) 633-5555. Fax, (202) 633-9393. Allen Kane, Director. Tours and education, (202) 633-5534. Press, (202) 633-5518.*
Web, http://postalmuseum.si.edu

Exhibits postal history and stamp collections; provides information on world postal and stamp history.

Naval History and Heritage Command *(Navy Dept.), Navy Art Collection, Washington Navy Yard, 822 Sicard St. S.E., Bldg. 67, 20374 (mailing address: 805 Kidder Breese St. S.E., Washington Navy Yard, DC 20374); (202) 433-3815. Gale Munro, Head.*
General email, NavyArt@navy.mil

Web, www.history.navy.mil

Holdings include more than 18,000 paintings, prints, drawings, and sculptures. Artworks depict naval ships, personnel, and action from all eras of U.S. naval history, especially the eras of World War II, the Korean War, and Desert Shield/Storm. Open to the public. Visitors without Defense Dept. or military identification must call in advance. Photo identification required.

Renwick Gallery of the Smithsonian American Art Museum *(Smithsonian Institution), 17th St. and Pennsylvania Ave. N.W., 20006 (mailing address: Renwick Gallery, MRC 510, P.O. Box 37012, Washington, DC 20013-7012); (202) 633-1000. Fax, (202) 633-8538. Robyn Kennedy, Chief. Press, (202) 633-8530. Information, (202) 633-7970.*
General email, AmericanArtRenwick@si.edu

Web, www.renwick.americanart.si.edu

Curatorial department of the Smithsonian American Art Museum. Exhibits contemporary American crafts and decorative arts.

Smithsonian American Art Museum *(Smithsonian Institution), 8th and F Sts. N.W., 20004 (mailing address: P.O. Box 37012, MRC 970, Washington, DC 20013-7012); (202) 633-7970. Fax, (202) 633-8424. Elizabeth Broun, Director. Library, (202) 633-8230. Press, (202) 633-8530.*
General email, americanartinfo@si.edu

Web, www.americanart.si.edu

Exhibits and interprets American painting, sculpture, photographs, folk art, and graphic art in the permanent collection and temporary exhibition galleries. Library open to the public. (Includes the Renwick Gallery.)

Smithsonian Institution, *1000 Jefferson Dr. S.W., 20560 (mailing address: P.O. Box 37012, SIB 153, MRC 010, Washington, DC 20013-7012); (202) 633-1000. David J. Skorton, Secretary; John Kress, Under Secretary for Science; Richard Kurin, Under Secretary for History, Art, and Culture; Albert Horvath, Under Secretary for Finance* and Administration. Information, (202) 633-1000. Library, (202) 633-1700. Press (journalists only), (202) 633-2400. General email, info@si.edu

Web, www.si.edu

Conducts research; publishes results of studies, explorations, and investigations; presents study and reference collections on science, culture, and history; presents exhibitions in the arts, American history, technology, aeronautics and space exploration, and natural history. Smithsonian Institution sites in Washington, D.C., include the Anacostia Community Museum, Archives of American Art, Arthur M. Sackler Gallery, Arts and Industries Building, Freer Gallery of Art, Hirshhorn Museum and Sculpture Garden, National Air and Space Museum, National Museum of African Art, Renwick Gallery, Smithsonian American Art Museum, National Museum of American History, National Museum of the American Indian, National Museum of Natural History, National Portrait Gallery, National Postal Museum, National Zoological Park, S. Dillon Ripley Center, and Smithsonian Institution Building. Libraries open to the public by appointment; library catalogs are available on the Web. Affiliated with more than 175 organizations in 41 states, Panama, and Puerto Rico. Autonomous organizations affiliated with the Smithsonian Institution include John F. Kennedy Center for the Performing Arts, National Gallery of Art, and Woodrow Wilson International Center for Scholars.

Smithsonian Institution, *International Relations,* 1100 Jefferson Dr. S.W., #3123, 20560 (mailing address: P.O. Box 37012, Quad MRC 705, Washington, DC 20013-7012); (202) 633-4795. Fax, (202) 786-2557. Molly Fannon, Director.

General email, global@si.edu

Web, www.smithsonianofi.com/sors-index/office-of-international-relations.oir

Fosters the development and coordinates the international aspects of Smithsonian cultural activities; facilitates basic research in history and art and encourages international collaboration among individuals and institutions.

Smithsonian Institution, *Office of Fellowships and Internships,* 470 L'Enfant Plaza S.W., #7102, 20013 (mailing address: P.O. Box 37012, MRC 902, Washington, DC 20013-7012); (202) 633-7070. Fax, (202) 633-7069. Eric Woodard, Director.

General email, siofi@si.edu

Web, www.smithsonianofi.com

Provides fellowships to students and scholars for independent research projects in association with members of the Smithsonian professional research staff. Provides central management for all Smithsonian research fellowship programs. Facilitates the Smithsonian's scholarly interactions with universities, museums, and research institutions around the world.

Smithsonian Institution, *Smithsonian Museum Support Center,* 4210 Silver Hill Rd., MRC 534, Suitland, MD 20746-2863; (301) 238-1026. Fax, (301) 238-3661. Elizabeth Dietrich, Management Officer, (301) 238-1010.

General email, libmail@si.edu

Web, www.mnh.si.edu

Museum collections management facility dedicated to collections, storage, research, and conservation. Library serves Smithsonian staff, other government agencies, and researchers. Open to the public by appointment.

Steven F. Udvar-Hazy Center *(Smithsonian Institution), National Air and Space Museum,* 14390 Air and Space Museum Pkwy., Chantilly, VA 20151; (703) 572-4118. Gen. John R. Dailey, Director. Public Affairs, (202) 633-1000. TTY, (202) 633-5285.

General email, nasm-visitorservices@si.edu

Web, www.airandspace.si.edu/visit/udvar-hazy-center

Displays and preserves a collection of historical aviation and space artifacts, including the B-29 Superfortress, Enola Gay, the Lockheed SR-71 Blackbird, the prototype of the Boeing 707, the space shuttle Discovery, and the Concord. Provides a center for research into the history, science, and technology of aviation and space flight. Open to the public daily 10:00 a.m.–5:30 p.m., except December 25.

U.S. Botanic Garden, 100 Maryland Ave. S.W., 20001 (mailing address: 245 1st St. S.W., Washington, DC 20024); (202) 225-8333. Fax, (202) 225-1561. Ari Novy, Executive Director, (202) 225-6670. Horticulture hotline, (202) 226-4785. Program registration information, (202) 225-1116. Special events, (202) 226-7674. Tour line, (202) 226-2055. Press, (202) 226-4145.

General email, usbg@aoc.gov

Web, www.usbg.gov

Educates the public on the aesthetic, cultural, economic, therapeutic, and ecological importance of plants to the well-being of humankind.

U.S. Navy Museum *(Naval Historical Center),* Bldg. 76, 805 Kidder Breese St. S.E., Washington Navy Yard, DC 20374-5060; (202) 433-4882. Fax, (202) 433-8200. Laura Hockensmith, Deputy Director, Education and Public Programs; James H. Bruns, Director of Museum; Rear Adm. Samuel Cox (USN, Ret.), Director of Naval History. Tours, (202) 433-6826. Internships, (202) 433-6901.

General email, navymuseum@navy.mil

Web, www.history.navy.mil/museum/NationalMuseums/org8-1.htm

Collects, preserves, displays, and interprets historic naval artifacts and artwork. Presents a complete overview of U.S. naval history. Open to the public. Photo identification required.

▶ CONGRESS

For a listing of relevant congressional committees and subcommittees, please see page 119 or the Appendix.

Library of Congress, *Interpretive Programs,* John Adams Bldg., 101 Independence Ave. S.E., #LA G25, 20540; (202) 707-5223. Fax, (202) 707-9063. Vacant, Interpretive Programs Officer. Information, (202) 707-4604.

Web, www.loc.gov/exhibits

Handles exhibits within the Library of Congress; establishes and coordinates traveling exhibits; handles loans of library material.

▶ NONGOVERNMENTAL

American Alliance of Museums, *2451 Crystal Dr., #1005, Arlington, VA 22202; (202) 289-1818. Fax, (202) 289-6578. Laura Lott, President.*
General email, infocenter@aam-us.org
Web, www.aam-us.org

Membership: individuals, institutions, museums, and museum professionals. Accredits museums; conducts educational programs; promotes international professional exchanges.

Art Services International, *119 Duke St., Alexandria, VA 22314; (703) 548-4554. Fax, (703) 548-3305. Lynn K. Rogerson, Director.*
General email, asi@asiexhibitions.org
Web, www.asiexhibitions.org

Develops, organizes, and circulates fine arts exhibitions throughout the world.

Dumbarton Oaks, *1703 32nd St. N.W., 20007-2961; (202) 339-6400. Fax, (202) 625-0280. Jan M. Ziolkowski, Director. Information, (202) 339-6401.*
General email, museum@doaks.org
Tours email, tours@doaks.org
Web, www.doaks.org

Exhibits Byzantine and pre-Columbian art and artifacts; conducts advanced research and maintains publication programs and library collections in Byzantine and pre-Columbian studies and garden and landscape studies. Offers guided tours of museum and gardens. Gardens open to the public Tuesday through Sunday 2:00–6:00 p.m. in summer, and 2:00–5:00 p.m. in winter (except during inclement weather and on federal holidays; fee charged March 15 through October 31); library open to qualified scholars by advance application. Administered by the trustees for Harvard University.

Fondo del Sol Visual Arts Center/Museum of Cultures and Heritages of America (MOCHA), *2112 R St. N.W., 20008; (202) 483-2777. Marc Zuver, Director.*
General email, info@fondodelsol.org
Web, www.fondodelsol.org

Multicultural artist-run bilingual museum exhibiting twentieth-century Latino and Caribbean art, pre-Columbian, Santero, and select Afro-American works. Collection includes paintings, prints, drawings, photographs, objects, and a film and video archive. Offers bilingual educational programs; internships in art, history, and language; workshop spaces; and art consultation services.

Hillwood Estate, Museum, and Gardens, *4155 Linnean Ave. N.W., 20008-3806; (202) 686-5807. Fax, (202) 966-7846. Kate Markert, Executive Director, (202) 243-3900. Press, (202) 243-3975.*
General email, info@hillwoodmuseum.org
Web, www.hillwoodmuseum.org

Former residence of Marjorie Merriweather Post. Maintains and exhibits collection of Russian imperial art, including Fabergé eggs, and eighteenth-century French decorative arts; twelve acres of formal gardens. Gardens and museum open to the public Tuesday through Sunday, 10:00 a.m.–5:00 p.m.; reservations required for large groups.

International Spy Museum, *800 F St. N.W., 20004; (202) 393-7798. Fax, (202) 393-7797. Peter Earnest, Executive Director. Toll-free, (866) 779-6873. TTY, (202) 654-0977.*
General email, info@spymuseum.org
Web, www.spymuseum.org

Dedicated to educating the public about the tradecraft, history, and contemporary role of espionage, particularly human intelligence, by examining its role in and effect on current and historical events. Offers a collection of international espionage artifacts. (Affiliated with the Malrite Company.)

Marian Koshland Science Museum *(National Academy of Sciences), 525 E St. N.W., entrance at corner of 6th and E Sts. N.W., 20001 (mailing address: 500 5th St. N.W., Washington, DC 20001); (202) 334-1201. Fax, (202) 334-1548. Patrice Legro, Director. Toll-free, (888) 567-4526. TTY, (202) 334-1306.*
General email, ksm@nas.edu
Web, www.koshland-science-museum.org, Twitter, @koshlandscience and Facebook, www.facebook.com/KoshlandScience

Encourages teenagers and adults to use science to solve problems in their communities through exhibits, public events, and educational programs. Provides information aimed at stimulating discussion and insight into how science supports decision making.

National Building Museum, *401 F St. N.W., 20001-2637; (202) 272-2448. Fax, (202) 272-2564. Chase W. Rynd, Executive Director. Press, (202) 272-2448, ext. 3109.*
Web, www.nbm.org

Celebrates achievements in building, architecture, urban planning, engineering, and historic preservation through educational programs, exhibitions, tours, lectures, workshops, and publications.

National Children's Museum. *Vacant, Executive Director.*
General email, info@ncm.museum
Press email, media@ncm.museum
Web, www.ncm.museum and Facebook, www.facebook.com/NationalChildrensMuseum

A cultural and educational institution serving children and families onsite and through national partners and programs. Exhibits and activities focus on the arts, civic engagement, the environment, global citizenship, health and well-being, and play. Affiliated with the Association of Children's Museums Reciprocal Network. (In the process of moving to Washington, D.C.)

National Geographic Museum, *1145 17th St. N.W., 20036-4688; Kathryn Keane, Vice President, Exhibitions. Exhibit information, (202) 857-7588. Tickets and tour information, (202) 857-7700.*
Web, http://events.nationalgeographic.com/national-geographic-museum

Maintains self-guided exhibits about past and current expeditions, scientific research, and other themes in history and culture. Admission is free; some special exhibitions require ticket purchase.

National Guard Memorial Museum, *1 Massachusetts Ave. N.W., 20001; (202) 789-0031. Fax, (202) 682-9358. Anne Armstrong, Deputy Director, (202) 408-5890. Toll-free, (888) 226-4287.*
General email, ngef@ngaus.org
Web, www.ngef.org/national-guard-memorial-museum, Twitter, @NGMuseum and Facebook, www.facebook.com/ NationalGuardMemorialMuseum

Features exhibit areas that explore the National Guard from colonial times through the world wars and the cold war to the modern era through timelines, photographs, artifacts, light, and sound.

National Museum of Civil War Medicine, *48 E. Patrick St., Frederick, MD 21705 (mailing address; P.O. Box 470, Frederick, MD 21705); (301) 695-1864. Fax, (301) 695-6823. David Price, Executive Director.*
General email, info@civilwarmed.org
Web, www.civilwarmed.org

Maintains artifacts and exhibits pertaining to general and wartime medicine in the 1800s, including dentistry, veterinary medicine, and medical evacuation. Presents information about individual soldiers, surgeons, medics, and nurses. Research department assists with questions about individuals injured in the Civil War.

National Museum of Women in the Arts, *1250 New York Ave. N.W., 20005-3970; (202) 783-5000. Fax, (202) 393-3234. Susan Fisher Sterling, Director; Susan Manerina, Director, Communications. Information, (800) 222-7270. Library, (202) 783-7338. Press, (202) 783-7373.*
Web, www.nmwa.org

Acquires, researches, and presents the works of women artists from the Renaissance to the present. Promotes greater representation and awareness of women in the arts. Library open for research to the public by appointment.

Newseum, *555 Pennsylvania Ave. N.W., 20001; (202) 292-6100. Jeffrey Herbst, Chief Executive Officer. Press, (202) 292-6200.*
General email, info@newseum.org
Web, www.newseum.org

World's only interactive museum of news. Collects items related to the history of news coverage; offers multimedia presentations and exhibits on the past, present, and future of news coverage; emphasizes the importance of the First Amendment to news coverage. (Affiliated with Freedom Forum.)

Octagon Museum, *1799 New York Ave. N.W., 20006-5207; (202) 626-7439. Sherry-Lea Bloodworth Botop, Executive Director.*
General email, octagonmuseum@aia.org
Web, www.theoctagon.org

Federal period historic residence open to the public for tours; served as the executive mansion during the War of 1812. Sponsors exhibits, lectures, publications, and educational programs. (Owned by the AIA Foundation [American Institute of Architects].) Guided tours available by appointment. Open for self-guided tours Thursday to Sunday from 1:00 p.m.–4:00 p.m.

Phillips Collection, *1600 21st St. N.W., 20009; (202) 387-2151. Fax, (202) 387-2436. Dorothy Kosinski, Director. Press, (202) 387-2151, ext. 220. Membership, (202) 387-3036. Shop, (202) 387-2151, ext. 239.*
General email, communications@phillipscollection.org
Web, www.phillipscollection.org

Maintains permanent collection of European and American paintings, primarily of the nineteenth through twenty-first centuries, and holds special exhibitions from the same periods. Sponsors lectures, gallery talks, and special events, including Sunday concerts (October–May). Library open to researchers and members.

Sewall-Belmont House & Museum, *144 Constitution Ave. N.E., 20002-5608; (202) 546-1210. Fax, (202) 546-3997. Page Harrington, Executive Director, ext. 20. Press, (202) 546-1210, ext. 12.*
General email, info@sewallbelmont.org
Web, www.sewallbelmont.org

Maintains archives and artifacts documenting women's equality under the law. Interests include the suffragists, the National Women's Party, and the Equal Rights Amendment campaign.

Society of the Cincinnati, *2118 Massachusetts Ave. N.W., 20008; (202) 785-2040. Fax, (202) 785-0729. Jack Duane Warren Jr., Executive Director, ext. 410. Press, ext. 445. Library appointments, ext. 426.*
General email, admin@societyofthecincinnati.org
Web, www.societyofthecincinnati.org

Collects and exhibits books, manuscripts, paintings, and other artifacts from the Revolutionary War. Maintains a library for research on the American Revolution. Preserves and operates the Anderson House as a historic landmark and museum. Collects and preserves American manuscripts and books from the 1700s. Specializes in documents and artifacts related to the American Revolution.

Textile Museum *(George Washington University), 701 21st St. N.W., 20052; (202) 994-5200. Fax, (202) 483-0994. John Wetenhall, Director.*
General email, museuminfo@gwu.edu
Web, https://museum.gwu.edu

Exhibits historic and handmade textiles and carpets with the goal of expanding appreciation of the artistic and cultural importance of the world's textiles. Exhibitions draw from loans and the permanent collection, specializing in the

Eastern Hemisphere. Offers annual Fall Symposium, Celebration of Textiles festival, and other programs. Library open to the public during restricted hours Wednesdays and Saturdays.

Tudor Place, *1644 31st St. N.W., 20007; (202) 965-0400. Fax, (202) 965-0164. Mark Hudson, Executive Director, ext. 101.*
General email, info@tudorplace.org
Web, www.tudorplace.org

Operates a historic property, home of Martha Washington's granddaughter and six generations of Custis-Peter family descendants. Seeks to educate the public about American history and culture, focusing on the capital region from the 18th century. Maintains and displays artifacts, maintains a manuscript collection, conducts guided tours, and sponsors educational programs for students and teachers.

U.S. Holocaust Memorial Museum, *100 Raoul Wallenberg Pl. S.W., 20024-2126; (202) 488-0400. Fax, (202) 488-2690. Sara J. Bloomfield, Director. Library, (202) 479-9717. Press, (202) 488-6133. TTY, (202) 488-0406. Toll-free, (866) 998-7466.*
Web, www.ushmm.org

Preserves documentation about the Holocaust and works to prevent genocide worldwide. Hosts exhibitions and Web site; conducts public programs, educational outreach, leadership training programs, and Holocaust commemorations; operates the Mandel Center for Advanced Holocaust Studies and the Genocide Prevention Task Force. Library and archives are open to the public.

Woodrow Wilson House *(National Trust for Historic Preservation), 2340 S St. N.W., 20008-4016; (202) 387-4062. Fax, (202) 483-1466. Robert A. Enholm, Executive Director; Linna Barnes, Chair.*
General email, wilsonhouse@woodrowwilsonhouse.org
Events email, sandrews@woodrowwilsonhouse.org
Web, www.woodrowwilsonhouse.org

Georgian Revival home that exhibits state gifts, furnishings, and memorabilia from President Woodrow Wilson's political and postpresidential years.

Music

▶**AGENCIES**

National Endowment for the Arts (NEA), *Music, 400 7th St. S.W., 20506; (202) 682-5438. Fax, (202) 682-5076. Ann Meier Baker, Director. TTY, (202) 682-5496.*
Web, www.arts.gov/artistic-fields/music

Awards grants to support a wide range of music, including classical, opera, contemporary, and jazz. Supports both performing ensembles and music institutions, including chamber music ensembles, opera companies, choruses, early music programs, jazz ensembles, music festivals, and symphony orchestras.

National Museum of American History *(Smithsonian Institution), Culture and the Arts, 12th St. and Constitution Ave. N.W., Room 4212, 20560-0616 (mailing address: P.O. Box 37012, MRC 616, Washington, DC 20013-7012); (202) 633-1707. Fax, (202) 786-2883. Stacey Kluck, Chair. Press, (202) 633-3129.*
General email, info@si.edu
Web, www.americanhistory.si.edu/about/departments/culture-and-the-arts

Preserves American culture and heritage through collections, research, exhibitions, publications, teaching and lectures, and broadcasts. Sponsors Jazz Appreciation Month and a chamber music program. Research areas are open by appointment.

National Symphony Orchestra *(John F. Kennedy Center for the Performing Arts), 2700 F St. N.W., 20566-0004 (mailing address: P.O. Box 101510, Arlington, VA 22210); (202) 416-8100. Fax, (202) 416-8105. Christoph Eschenbach, Music Director; Steven Reineke, Principal Pops Conductor; Rita Shapiro, Executive Director. Information and reservations, (202) 467-4600. Toll-free, (800) 444-1324. TTY, (202) 416-8524. Tours, (202) 416-8340. Tour accessibility, (202) 416-8727. Tour accessibility TTY, (202) 416-8728.*
Web, www.kennedy-center.org/nso

Year-round orchestra that presents a full range of symphonic activities: classical, pops, and educational events; national and international tours; recordings; and special events.

National Symphony Orchestra *(John F. Kennedy Center for the Performing Arts), Education Dept., 2700 F St. N.W., 20566-0004 (mailing address: P.O. Box 101510, Arlington, VA 22210); (202) 416-8835. Carole J. Wysocki, Director, (202) 416-8828. TTY, (202) 416-8728.*
General email, kced@kennedy-center.org
Web, http://education.kennedy-center.org//education/schoolguide/accessaccommodations.pdf

Commissions, produces, presents, and tours performances for students, teachers, adults, and families; offers professional development opportunities in the arts for teachers and artists; creates and implements model programs for performing arts centers and schools; develops community and national outreach programs; fosters careers of young artists and arts managers; and provides arts education resources via satellite, the Internet, in print, and in person. Publishes an accessibility brochure and an annual performance brochure.

▶**CONGRESS**

For a listing of relevant congressional committees and subcommittees, please see page 119 or the Appendix.

Library of Congress, *Motion Picture, Broadcasting, and Recorded Sound Division, James Madison Memorial Bldg., 101 Independence Ave. S.E., #LM 336, 20540; (202) 707-8572. Gregory Lukow, Chief. Recorded Sound Reference Center, (202) 707-7833. Fax for Recorded Sound*

Reference Center, (202) 707-8464. Fax for Motion Picture and Television Reading Room, (202) 707-2371.
Web, www.loc.gov/rr/mopic

Maintains library's collection of musical and vocal recordings; tapes the library's concert series and other musical events for radio broadcast; produces recordings of music and poetry for sale to the public. Collection also includes sound recordings (1890–present). Reading room open to the public Monday through Friday, 8:30 a.m. to 5:00 p.m.; listening and viewing by appointment only.

Library of Congress, *Music Division,* James Madison Memorial Bldg., 101 Independence Ave. S.E., #LM 113, 20540; (202) 707-5503. Fax, (202) 707-0621. Susan H. Vita, Chief. Concert information, (202) 707-5502. Performing Arts Reading Room, (202) 707-5507.
Web, www.loc.gov/rr/perform

Maintains and services, through the Performing Arts Reading Room, the library's collection of music manuscripts, sheet music, books, and instruments. Coordinates the library's chamber music concert series; produces radio broadcasts and, for sale to the public, recordings of concerts sponsored by the division; issues publications relating to the field of music and to division collections.

Library of Congress, *National Recording Preservation Board,* 1010 Independence Ave. S.E., 20540-5698; (202) 707-5912. Fax, (202) 707-2371. Steve Leggett, Staff Coordinator. TTY, (202) 707-6362.
Web, www.loc.gov/programs/national-recording-preservation-board/about-this-program

Administers the National Recording Preservation Plan aimed at studying the state of and advances in sound recording. Receives nominations for the annual selection of twenty-five recordings demonstrating the range and diversity of American recorded sound heritage. Makes selections to the National Recording Registry.

▶ **NONGOVERNMENTAL**

American Music Therapy Assn., 8455 Colesville Rd., #1000, Silver Spring, MD 20910; (301) 589-3300. Fax, (301) 589-5175. Andrea Farbman, Executive Director.
General email, info@musictherapy.org
Web, www.musictherapy.org and Twitter, @AMTAInc

Promotes the therapeutic use of music by approving degree programs and clinical training sites, establishing professional competencies and clinical practice standards for music therapists, and conducting research in the music therapy field.

Future of Music Coalition, 2217 14th St. N.W., 2nd Floor, 20009; (202) 822-2051. Casey Rae, Chief Executive Officer.
General email, suggestions@futureofmusic.org
Web, www.futureofmusic.org and Twitter, @future_of_music

Seeks to educate the media, policymakers, and the public on music technology issues. Identifies and promotes innovative business models that will help musicians and citizens benefit from new technologies.

League of American Orchestras, *Advocacy and Government,* 910 17th St. N.W., #800, 20006; (202) 776-0215. Fax, (202) 776-0224. Heather Noonan, Vice President for Advocacy.
Web, www.americanorchestras.org/advocacy-government.html, Twitter, @OrchLeague and Facebook, www.facebook.com/orchleague

Service and educational organization dedicated to strengthening orchestras. Provides information and analysis on subjects of interest to orchestras through reports, seminars, and other educational forums. Seeks to improve policies that increase public access to orchestral music. Monitors legislation and regulations. (Headquarters in New York.)

National Assn. for Music Education, 1806 Robert Fulton Dr., Reston, VA 20191-4348; (703) 860-4000. Fax, (703) 860-1531. Michael Butera, Executive Director.
Information, (800) 336-3768.
General email, memberservices@nafme2.org
Web, www.nafme.org

Membership: music educators (preschool through university). Holds biennial conference. Publishes books and teaching aids for music educators.

National Assn. of Schools of Music, 11250 Roger Bacon Dr., #21, Reston, VA 20190-5248; (703) 437-0700. Fax, (703) 437-6312. Karen Moynahan, Executive Director.
General email, info@arts-accredit.org
Web, http://nasm.arts-accredit.org

Specialized professional accrediting agency for postsecondary programs in music. Conducts and shares research and analysis on topics pertinent to music programs and the field of music. Offers professional development opportunities for executives of music programs.

Recording Industry Assn. of America, 1025 F St. N.W., 10th Floor, 20004; (202) 775-0101. Fax, (202) 775-7253. Cary Sherman, Chief Executive Officer.
Web, www.riaa.com and Twitter, @RIAA

Membership: creators, manufacturers, and marketers of sound recordings. Educates members about new technology in the music industry. Advocates copyright protection and opposes censorship. Works to prevent recording piracy, counterfeiting, bootlegging, and unauthorized rental and imports. Certifies gold, platinum, and multiplatinum recordings. Publishes statistics on the recording industry. Monitors legislation and regulations.

SoundExchange, 733 10th St. N.W., 10th Floor, 20001; (202) 640-5858. Fax, (202) 640-5859. Michael Huppe, President. Press, (202) 559-0558.
General email, info@soundexchange.com
Web, www.soundexchange.com

Artists' rights advocacy group that represents record labels and unsigned artists whose work is broadcast on national and global digital radio. Distributes royalties to musicians, performers, and music copyright owners. Monitors legislation and regulations related to digital music licensing.

Washington Area Music Assn., *6263 Occoquan Forest Dr., Manassas, VA 20112-3011; (703) 368-3300. Fax, (703) 393-1028. Mike Schreibman, President.*
General email, dcmusic@wamadc.com

Web, www.wamadc.com

Membership: musicians, concert promoters, lawyers, recording engineers, managers, contractors, and other music industry professionals. Sponsors workshops on industry-related topics. Represents professionals from all musical genres. Serves as a liaison between the Washington-area music community and music communities nationwide.

Theater and Dance

▶AGENCIES

Ford's Theatre National Historic Site, *511 10th St. N.W., 20004; (202) 426-6924. Fax, (202) 426-1845. William Cheek, Site Manager. Recorded ticket information, (202) 638-2941.*
General email, NACC_FOTH_Interpretation@nps.gov

Web, www.nps.gov/foth and Facebook, www.facebook.com/fordstheatrenps

Administered by the National Park Service, which manages Ford's Theatre, Ford's Theatre Museum, and the Peterson House (house where Lincoln died). Presents interpretive talks, exhibits, and tours. Research library open by appointment. Functions as working stage for theatrical productions.

National Endowment for the Arts (NEA), *Dance, 400 7th St. S.W., 20506; (202) 682-5438. Fax, (202) 682-5612. Douglas Sonntag, Director. TTY, (202) 682-5496.*
Web, www.arts.gov/artistic-fields/dance

Awards grants to dance companies and presenters for projects in all dance styles, including ballet, modern dance, jazz, folkloric, tap, hip-hop, and other contemporary forms.

National Endowment for the Arts (NEA), *Theater and Musical Theater, 400 7th St. S.W., 20506; (202) 682-5438. Fax, (202) 682-5612. Greg Reiner, Director. TTY, (202) 682-5496.*
Web, www.arts.gov/artistic-fields/theater-musical-theater

Awards grants to organizations and artists in all venues of theater, including traditional, musical, classical, new plays, works for young audiences, experimental work, community-based work, circus arts, and puppetry.

Smithsonian Institution, *Discovery Theater, 1100 Jefferson Dr. S.W., 20024 (mailing address: Discovery Theater, P.O. Box 23293, Washington, DC 20026-3293); (202) 633-8700. Fax, (202) 633-1322. Roberta Gasbarre, Director.*
General email, info@discoverytheater.org

Web, www.discoverytheater.org

Presents live theatrical performances, including storytelling, dance, music, puppetry, and plays, for young people and their families.

▶NONGOVERNMENTAL

Dance/USA, *1029 Vermont Ave. N.W., #400, 20005; (202) 833-1717. Fax, (202) 833-2686. Amy Fitterer, Executive Director.*
General email, danceusa@danceusa.org

Web, www.danceusa.org

Membership: professional dance companies, artists, artist managers, presenters, service organizations, educators, libraries, businesses, and individuals. Advances the art form by addressing the needs, concerns, and interests of the professional dance community through public communications, research and information services, professional development, advocacy, re-granting initiatives, and other projects.

National Assn. of Schools of Dance, *11250 Roger Bacon Dr., #21, Reston, VA 20190-5248; (703) 437-0700. Fax, (703) 437-6312. Karen Moynahan, Executive Director.*
General email, info@arts-accredit.org

Web, http://nasd.arts-accredit.org

Specialized professional accrediting agency for postsecondary programs in dance. Conducts and shares research and analysis on topics pertinent to dance programs and the field of dance. Offers professional development opportunities for executives of dance programs.

National Assn. of Schools of Theatre, *11250 Roger Bacon Dr., #21, Reston, VA 20190-5248; (703) 437-0700. Fax, (703) 437-6312. Karen Moynahan, Executive Director.*
General email, info@arts-accredit.org

Web, http://nast.arts-accredit.org

Specialized professional accrediting agency for postsecondary programs in theatre. Conducts and shares research and analysis on topics pertinent to theatre programs and the field of theatre. Offers professional development opportunities for executives of theatre programs.

National Conservatory of Dramatic Arts, *1556 Wisconsin Ave. N.W., 20007; (202) 333-2202. Raymond (Ray) G. Ficca, President; Nan Ficca, Vice President.*
General email, NCDAdrama@aol.com

Web, www.theconservatory.org

Offers an accredited two-year program in postsecondary professional actor training and a one-year program in advanced professional training. Emphasizes both physical and mental preparedness for acting in the professional entertainment industry.

Shakespeare Theatre Company, *Lansburgh Theatre, 450 7th St. N.W., and Sidney Harmon Hall, 610 F St. N.W., 20004 (mailing address: 516 8th St. S.E., Washington, DC 20003-2834); (202) 547-3230. Fax, (202) 547-0226. Michael Kahn, Artistic Director; Chris Jennings, Executive Director; Michael R. Klein, Chair. Toll-free, (877) 487-8849. TTY, (202) 546-9606. Box office, (202) 547-1122. Educational programs, (202) 547-5688.*
Web, www.shakespearetheatre.org

Professional resident theater that presents Shakespearean and other classical plays. Offers actor training program for youths, adults, and professional actors. Produces free outdoor summer Shakespeare plays and free Shakespeare plays for schools.

Visual Arts

▶AGENCIES

National Endowment for the Arts (NEA), *Design,* 400 7th St. S.W., 20506; (202) 682-5452. Fax, (202) 682-5721. *Jason Schupbach, Director. TTY, (202) 682-5496.*
Web, www.arts.gov/artistic-fields/design

Provides grants to nonprofit organizations to fund the role of creative design and visual arts in economic revitalization and creating sustainable communities.

National Endowment for the Arts (NEA), *Visual Arts,* 400 7th St. S.W., 20506; (202) 682-5400. Fax, (202) 682-5721. *Wendy Clark, Director. TTY, (202) 682-5496.*
Web, www.arts.gov/artistic-fields/visual-arts

Awards grants to nonprofit organizations for creative works and programs in the visual arts, including painting, sculpture, crafts, video, photography, printmaking, drawing, artists' books, and performance art

State Dept., *Art in Embassies,* 1701 N. Fort Myer Dr., #663, Arlington, VA 22209; (703) 875-4202. Fax, (703) 875-4182. *Ellen Susman, Director, (703) 875-7205.*
General email, artinembassies@state.gov
Web, http://art.state.gov

Exhibits American art in U.S. ambassadorial residences. Borrows artworks from artists, collectors, galleries, and museums.

▶CONGRESS

For a listing of relevant congressional committees and subcommittees, please see page 119 or the Appendix.

Library of Congress, *Prints and Photographs Division,* James Madison Memorial Bldg., 101 Independence Ave. S.E., #LM 337, 20540-4730; (202) 707-6394. Fax, (202) 707-6647. *Helena Zinkham, Chief.*
Web, www.loc.gov/rr/print

Maintains Library of Congress's collection of pictorial material not in book format, totaling more than 15 million items. U.S. and international collections include artists' prints; historical prints, posters, and drawings; photographs (chiefly documentary); political and social cartoons; and architectural plans, drawings, prints, and photographs. Reference service provided in the Prints and Photographs Reading Room. Reproductions of nonrestricted material available through the Library of Congress's Photoduplication Service; prints and photographs may be borrowed through the Exhibits Office for exhibits by qualified institutions. A portion of the collections and an overview of reference services are available on the Web.

▶NONGOVERNMENTAL

American Institute of Architects, 1735 New York Ave. N.W., 20006-5292; (202) 626-7300. Fax, (202) 626-7547. *Robert Ivy, Chief Executive Officer. Press, (202) 626-7467. Toll-free, (800) 242-3837. Government Advocacy, (202) 626-7507.*
General email, infocentral@aia.org
Web, www.aia.org and Twitter, @AIANational

Membership: licensed American architects, interns, architecture faculty, engineers, planners, and those in government, manufacturing, or other fields in a capacity related to architecture. Works to advance the standards of architectural education, training, and practice. Promotes the aesthetic, scientific, and practical efficiency of architecture, urban design, and planning; monitors international developments. Offers continuing and professional education programs; sponsors scholarships, internships, and awards. Houses archival collection, including documents and drawings of American architects and architecture. Library open to the public by appointment. Monitors legislation and regulations.

Foundation for Art and Preservation in Embassies (FAPE), 1725 Eye St. N.W., #300, 20006-2423; (202) 349-3724. Fax, (202) 349-3727. *Jennifer A. Duncan, Director.*
General email, info@fapeglobal.org
Web, www.fapeglobal.org

Works with the State Dept. to contribute fine art for placement in U.S. embassies worldwide.

International Arts and Artists, 9 Hillyer Court N.W., 20008; (202) 338-0680. Fax, (202) 333-0758. *David Furchgott, President.*
General email, info@artsandartists.org
Web, www.artsandartists.org

Collects multicultural art and plans art exhibits for museums. Offers affordable print and digital services to artists and organizations. Assists international artists and institutions in obtaining visas. Provides international internships and training programs. Offers an exchange program for artists to travel and complete international art-related internships. Local gallery, the Hillyer Arts Space, exhibits contemporary art.

National Assn. of Schools of Art and Design, 11250 Roger Bacon Dr., #21, Reston, VA 20190-5248; (703) 437-0700. Fax, (703) 437-6312. *Karen Moynahan, Executive Director.*
General email, info@arts-accredit.org
Web, http://nasad.arts-accredit.org

Specialized professional accrediting agency for postsecondary programs in art and design. Conducts and shares research and analysis on topics pertinent to art and design programs and fields of art and design. Offers professional development opportunities for executives of art and design programs.

HISTORY AND PRESERVATION

General

▶AGENCIES

Advisory Council on Historic Preservation, *401 F St. N.W., #308, 20001; (202) 517-0200. Fax, (202) 517-6381. John M. Fowler, Executive Director; Milford W. Donaldson, Chair. General email, achp@achp.gov*

Web, www.achp.gov

Advises the president and Congress on historic preservation; reviews and comments on federal projects and programs affecting historic, architectural, archaeological, and cultural resources.

Bureau of Educational and Cultural Affairs *(State Dept.), Cultural Heritage Center, 2200 C St. N.W., #C2O19/SA-5, 20037; (202) 632-6197. Maria Kouroupas, Director. General email, culprop@state.gov*

Web, http://eca.state.gov/cultural-heritage-center and *Twitter, @HeritageatState*

Protects and preserves ancient and historic monuments, objects, and archaeological sites. Reviews country requests for import restrictions on archaeological or ethnological artifacts and makes recommendations on them to the State Dept. Distributes information to police, customs, museums, dealers, and collectors about cultural heritage objects stolen from archaeological sites, museums, and churches.

Bureau of Land Management (BLM) *(Interior Dept.), Cultural, Paleontological Resources, and Tribal Consultation, 20 M St. S.E., #2134, 20003; (202) 912-7208. Fax, (202) 245-0015. Byron Loosle, Division Chief. General email, bloosle@blm.gov*

Web, www.blm.gov/wo/st/en/prog/more/CRM.html

Develops bureau policy on historic preservation, archaeological resource protection, consultation with Native Americans, curation of artifacts and records, heritage education, and paleontological resource management.

General Services Administration (GSA), *Urban Development/Good Neighbor Program, 1800 F St. N.W., #3341, 20405-0001; (202) 501-1856. Fax, (202) 501-3393. Frank Giblin, Program Manager. General email, frank.giblin@gsa.gov*

Web, www.gsa.gov/portal/content/104461 and *Twitter, @GSA_urbder*

Advises on locations, designs, and renovations of federal facilities in central business areas, historic districts, and local redevelopment areas where they can anchor or promote community development. Collaborates with local and national civic and other organizations. Serves as clearinghouse for good practices.

National Archives and Records Administration (NARA), *Cartographic and Architectural Unit, 8601 Adelphi Rd.,*

#3320, College Park, MD 20740-6001; (301) 837-3200. Fax, (301) 837-3622. Deborah Lelansky, Cartographic Supervisor, (301) 837-1911. General email, carto@nara.gov

Web, www.archives.gov/dc-metro/college-park/researcher-info.html#cartographic

Preserves and makes available historical records of federal agencies, including maps, charts, aerial photographs, architectural engineering drawings, patents, lighthouse plans, and ships' plans. Research room open to the public. Records are available for reproduction.

National Archives and Records Administration (NARA), *National Archives Museum, 700 Pennsylvania Ave. N.W., #G9, 20408; (202) 357-5210. Fax, (202) 357-5926. Lisa Royce, Director. Information, (202) 357-5000. Press, (202) 357-5300. General email, inquire@nara.gov/museum*

Web, www.archives.gov

Plans and directs activities to acquaint the public with the mission and holdings of the National Archives; conducts behind-the-scenes tours; presents hands-on workshops; develops both traditional and interactive exhibits; produces publications, including teaching packets that feature historic documents and online educational tools.

National Archives and Records Administration (NARA), *Preservation Programs, 8601 Adelphi Rd., #2800, College Park, MD 20740-6001; (301) 837-1785. Fax, (301) 837-3701. Doris A. Hamburg, Director. General email, preservation@nara.gov*

Web, www.archives.gov/preservation

Manages the preservation program for the 44 National Archives facilities across the country. Develops preservation policy, regulations, and planning. Responsible for conserving and reformatting archival holdings. Ensures that the storage environments are designed and maintained to prolong the life of records. Manages records during emergency preparedness and response for the agency; advises other federal agencies in event of need. Conducts research and testing for materials purchased by and used in the archives, as well as deterioration and preservation processes. Monitors and maintains the condition of the Charters of Freedom.

National Archives and Records Administration (NARA), *Research Services, 8601 Adelphi Rd., #3400, College Park, MD 20740-6001; (301) 837-1893. Fax, (301) 837-3633. William A. Mayer, Executive. Web, www.archives.gov/research*

Preserves and makes available federal records at fifteen National Archives facilities across the country.

National Endowment for the Arts (NEA), *Folk and Traditional Arts, 400 7th St. S.W., 20506; (202) 682-5428. Fax, (202) 682-5669. Clifford Murphy, Director. TTY, (202) 682-5496. Web, www.arts.gov/artistic-fields/folk-traditional-arts*

Awards grants to the folk and traditional arts that are rooted in and reflective of the cultural life of communities.

National Endowment for the Humanities (NEH), *Preservation and Access, 400 7th St. S.W., 20506; (202) 606-8570. Fax, (202) 606-8639. Nadina Gardner, Director, (202) 606-8442.*

General email, preservation@neh.gov

Web, www.neh.gov/divisions/preservation

Sponsors preservation and access projects, the stabilization and documentation of material culture collections, and the National Digital Newspaper program.

National Museum of American History *(Smithsonian Institution), Culture and the Arts, 12th St. and Constitution Ave. N.W., Room 4212, 20560-0616 (mailing address: P.O. Box 37012, MRC 616, Washington, DC 20013-7012); (202) 633-1707. Fax, (202) 786-2883. Stacey Kluck, Chair. Press, (202) 633-3129.*

General email, info@si.edu

Web, www.americanhistory.si.edu/about/departments/culture-and-the-arts

Collects and preserves artifacts related to U.S. cultural heritage; supports research, exhibits, performances, and educational programs. Areas of focus include sports, recreation, and leisure; popular culture; music and dance; theater, film, broadcast media, graphic arts, printing, and photographic history.

National Museum of American History *(Smithsonian Institution), Curatorial Affairs, 12th St. and Constitution Ave. N.W., 20560 (mailing address: P.O. Box 37012, MRC 664, Washington, DC 20013-7012); (202) 633-3497. Fax, (202) 633-4284. David K. Allison, Associate Director.*

General email, info@si.edu

Web, www.americanhistory.si.edu/about/departments/curatorial-affairs

Conducts research, develops collections, and creates exhibits on American social and public history, based on collections of folk and popular arts, ethnic and craft objects, textiles, coins, costumes and jewelry, ceramics and glass, graphic arts, musical instruments, photographs, technological innovations, appliances, and machines. Research areas are open by appointment.

National Park Service (NPS) *(Interior Dept.), 1849 C St. N.W., #3115, 20240; (202) 208-3818. Fax, (202) 208-7889. Jonathan B. Jarvis, Director. Press, (202) 208-6843.*

General email, asknps@nps.gov

Web, www.nps.gov and Twitter, @NatlParkService

Administers national parks, monuments, historic sites, and recreation areas. Oversees coordination, planning, and financing of public outdoor recreation programs at all levels of government. Conducts recreation research surveys; administers financial assistance program to states for planning and development of outdoor recreation programs. (Some lands designated as national recreation areas are not under NPS jurisdiction.)

National Park Service (NPS) *(Interior Dept.), Cultural Resources, Partnerships, and Science, 1849 C St. N.W., #3128, MIB, 20240-0001; (202) 208-7625. Fax, (202)*

273-3237. Stephanie Toothman, Associate Director.

Web, www.nps.gov/history

Oversees preservation of federal historic sites and administration of building programs. Programs include the National Register of Historic Places, National Historic and National Landmark Programs, Historic American Building Survey, Historic American Engineering Record, Archeology and Antiquities Act Program, and Technical Preservation Services. Gives grant and aid assistance and tax benefit information to properties listed in the National Register of Historic Places.

▶**CONGRESS**

For a listing of relevant congressional committees and subcommittees, please see page 119 or the Appendix.

Senate Office of Conservation and Preservation, *S416 CAP, 20510; (202) 224-4550. Leona Faust, Director, Acting, (202) 224-5730.*

Develops and coordinates programs related to the conservation and preservation of Senate records and materials for the secretary of the Senate.

▶**NONGOVERNMENTAL**

American Historical Assn., *400 A St. S.E., 20003; (202) 544-2422. Fax, (202) 544-8307. James Grossman, Executive Director.*

General email, info@historians.org

Web, www.historians.org

Membership: university academics, colleges, museums, historical organizations, libraries and archives, independent historians, students, K–12 teachers, government and business professionals, and individuals interested in history. Interests include academic freedom, professional standards, publication, teaching, professional development, networking, and advocacy. Supports public access to government information; publishes original historical research, journals, bibliographies, historical directories, and a job placement bulletin.

American Institute for Conservation of Historic and Artistic Works, *1156 15th St. N.W., #320, 20005-1714; (202) 452-9545. Fax, (202) 452-9328. Eryl P. Wentworth, Executive Director.*

General email, info@conservation-US.org

Web, www.conservation-US.org and Twitter, @conservators

Membership: professional conservators, scientists, students, administrators, cultural institutions, collection care professionals, and others. Promotes the knowledge and practice of the conservation of cultural property; supports research; and disseminates information on conservation.

American Studies Assn., *1120 19th St. N.W., #301, 20036-3614; (202) 467-4783. Fax, (202) 467-4786. John F. Stephens, Executive Director.*

General email, asastaff@theasa.net

Web, www.theasa.net

Fosters the interdisciplinary exchange of ideas about American culture and history in local and global contexts; awards annual prizes for contributions to American studies; provides curriculum resources.

Civil War Trust, *1156 15th St. N.W., #900, 20005; (202) 367-1861. Fax, (202) 367-1865. James Lighthizer, President. General email, info@civilwar.org*

Web, www.civilwar.org and Twitter, @civilwartrust

Membership: preservation professionals, historians, conservation activists, and citizens. Preserves endangered Civil War battlefields throughout the United States. Conducts preservation conferences and workshops. Advises local preservation groups. Monitors legislation and regulations at the federal, state, and local levels.

Daughters of the American Revolution, National Society, *1776 D St. N.W., 20006-5303; (202) 628-1776. Fax, (202) 879-3227. Lynn Young, President General. Web, www.dar.org*

Membership: women descended from American Revolutionary War patriots. Conducts historical, educational, and patriotic activities; maintains a genealogical library, fine arts museum, and documentary collection antedating 1830. Library open to the public.

David S. Wyman Institute for Holocaust Studies, *1200 G St. N.W., #800, 20005; (202) 434-8994. Rafael Medoff, Director. General email, info@wymaninstitute.org*

Web, www.wymaninstitute.org

Educates the public about U.S. response to Nazism and the Holocaust through scholarly research, public events and exhibits, publications, conferences, and educational programs.

Heritage Preservation, *1012 14th St. N.W., #1200, 20005-3408; (202) 233-0800. Fax, (202) 233-0807. Tom Clareson, President, Acting. General email, info@heritagepreservation.org*

Web, www.heritagepreservation.org

Membership: museums, libraries, archives, historic preservation organizations, historical societies, and conservation groups. Advocates the conservation and preservation of works of art, anthropological artifacts, documents, historic objects, architecture, and natural science specimens. Programs include Save Outdoor Sculpture, which works to inventory all U.S. outdoor sculpture; the Conservation Assessment Program, which administers grants to museums for conservation surveys of their collections; the Heritage Health Index, which documents the condition of U.S. collections; the Heritage Emergency Task Force, which helps institutions protect their collections from disasters and emergencies and Rescue Public Murals, which aids in the conservation of public murals throughout the United States.

National Conference of State Historic Preservation Officers, *444 N. Capitol St. N.W., #342, 20001-1512; (202) 624-5465. Fax, (202) 624-5419. Erik Hein, Executive Director. Web, www.ncshpo.org*

Membership: state and territorial historic preservation officers and deputy officers. Compiles statistics on programs; monitors legislation and regulations.

National Park Trust, *401 E. Jefferson St., #203, Rockville, MD 20850; (301) 279-7275. Fax, (301) 279-7211. Grace K. Lee, Executive Director. General email, npt@parktrust.org*

Web, www.parktrust.org

Protects national parks, wildlife refuges, and historic monuments. Uses funds to purchase private land within or adjacent to existing parks and land suitable for new parks; works with preservation organizations to manage acquired resources.

National Preservation Institute, *P.O. Box 1702, Alexandria, VA 22313; (703) 765-0100. Fax, (703) 768-9350. Jere Gibber, Executive Director; Elizabeth Hebron, President. General email, info@npi.org*

Web, www.npi.org

Conducts seminars in historic preservation and cultural resource management for those involved in the management, preservation, and stewardship of historic and cultural resources.

National Society of Colonial Dames of America, *2715 Que St. N.W., 20007-3071; (202) 337-2288. Fax, (202) 337-0348. Karen L. Daly, Executive Director. General email, hqassistant@dumbartonhouse.org*

Web, www.nscda.org

Membership: descendants of colonists in America before 1750. Conducts historical and educational activities; maintains Dumbarton House, a museum open to the public Tuesday–Sunday; and offers lectures and concerts.

National Society of Colonial Dames XVII Century, *1300 New Hampshire Ave. N.W., 20036-1502; (202) 293-1700. Fax, (202) 466-6099. Elizabeth Snuggs McAteer, President General. General email, cd17th@verizon.net*

Web, www.colonialdames17c.org

Membership: American women who are lineal descendants of persons who rendered civil or military service and lived in America or one of the British colonies before 1701. Preserves records and shrines; encourages historical research; awards scholarships to undergraduate and graduate students and scholarships in medicine to persons of Native American descent.

National Society of the Children of the American Revolution, *1776 D St. N.W., #224, 20006-5303; (202) 638-3153. Fax, (202) 737-3162. Joanne Zumbrun, Senior National President. General email, hq@nscar.org*

Web, www.nscar.org

Membership: descendants, age twenty-two years and under, of American soldiers and patriots of the American Revolution. Conducts historical, educational, and patriotic activities; preserves places of historical interest.

National Trust for Historic Preservation, *2600 Virginia Ave. N.W., #1000, 20037; (202) 588-6000. Fax, (202) 588-6038. Stephanie Meeks, President; Robin Scullin, Public Affairs. Toll-free, (800) 944-6847. Press, (202) 588-6141.*
General email, info@savingplaces.org

Web, www.preservationnation.org

Conducts seminars, workshops, and conferences on topics related to preservation, including neighborhood conservation, main street revitalization, rural conservation, and preservation law; offers financial assistance through loan and grant programs; provides advisory services; operates historic house sites, which are open to the public; and publishes quarterly magazine and e-newsletters.

Preservation Action, *1307 New Hampshire Ave. N.W., 3rd Floor, 20036; (202) 463-0970. Fax, (202) 463-1299. Robert Naylor, Program Manager.*
General email, mail@preservationaction.org

Web, www.preservationaction.org

Monitors legislation affecting historic preservation and neighborhood conservation. Maintains a nationwide database of activists. Promotes adequate funding for historic preservation programs and policies that support historic resource protection.

Society for American Archaeology, *1111 14th St. N.W., #800, 20005-5622; (202) 789-8200. Fax, (202) 789-0284. Tobi Brimsek, Executive Director.*
General email, headquarters@saa.org

Web, www.saa.org

Promotes greater awareness, understanding, and research of archaeology on the American continents; works to preserve and publish results of scientific data and research; serves as information clearinghouse for members.

Archives and Manuscripts

▶**AGENCIES**

National Archives and Records Administration (NARA), *700 Pennsylvania Ave. N.W., 20408; (866) 272-6272. Fax, (301) 837-0483. David S. Ferriero, Archivist of the United States. Press and public affairs, (202) 357-5300. TTY, (301) 837-0482.*
Web, www.archives.gov

Identifies, preserves, and makes available federal government documents of historic value; administers a network of regional storage centers and archives and operates the presidential library system. Collections include photographs, graphic materials, films, and maps; holdings include records generated by foreign governments (especially in wartime) and by international conferences, commissions, and exhibitions.

National Archives and Records Administration (NARA), *Center for Legislative Archives, 700 Pennsylvania Ave. N.W., #8E, 20408; (202) 357-5350. Fax, (202) 357-5911. Richard H. Hunt, Director.*
Web, www.archives.gov/legislative

Collects and maintains records of congressional committees and legislative files from 1789 to the present. Publishes inventories and guides to these records.

National Archives and Records Administration (NARA), *Electronic Records Division, 8601 Adelphi Rd., #5320, College Park, MD 20740-6001; (301) 837-0470. Fax, (301) 837-3681. Theodore J. Hull, Director.*
General email, cer@nara.gov

Web, www.archives.gov/research/electronic-records

Preserves, maintains, and makes available electronic records of the U.S. government. Provides researchers with magnetic tape, CD, DVD, and other copies of electronic records on a cost-recovery basis. Offers direct downloads and searches of selected holdings.

National Archives and Records Administration (NARA), *Presidential Libraries, 8601 Adelphi Rd., #2200, College Park, MD 20740-6001; (301) 837-3250. Fax, (301) 837-3199. Susan K. Donius, Director, (301) 837-1662.*
Web, www.archives.gov/presidential-libraries

Administers thirteen presidential libraries. Directs all programs relating to acquisition, preservation, and research use of materials in presidential libraries; conducts oral history projects; publishes finding aids for research sources; provides reference service, including information from and about documentary holdings. Conducts community outreach; oversees museum exhibition programming.

National Archives and Records Administration (NARA), *Reference Services, 8601 Adelphi Rd., #2400, College Park, MD 20740-6001; (301) 837-3510. Fax, (301) 837-1752. Richard W. Peuser, Branch Chief.*
Web, www.archives.gov/frc/reference-services.html

Provides reference service for unpublished civil and military federal government records. Maintains central catalog of all archival materials. Compiles comprehensive bibliographies of materials related to archival administration and records management. Permits research in American history, archival science, and records management. Maintains collections of the papers of the Continental Congress (1774–1789), U.S. State Dept. diplomatic correspondence (1789–1963), and general records of the U.S. government.

National Historical Publications and Records Commission *(National Archives and Records Administration), 700 Pennsylvania Ave. N.W., #114, 20408-0001; (202) 357-5010. Fax, (202) 357-5914. Kathleen Williams, Executive Director, (202) 357-5263. Toll-free, (866) 272-6272.*
General email, nhprc@nara.gov

Web, www.archives.gov/nhprc

Awards grants to nonprofit institutions, educational institutions, and local and state governments to preserve and make accessible historical records, including the papers of nationally significant Americans. Helps preserve electronic records and digitize and publish online collections.

National Museum of American History *(Smithsonian Institution), Archives Center, 14th St. and Constitution*

Ave. N.W., 20560-0601 (mailing address: P.O. Box 37012, NMAH MRC 601, Washington, DC 20013-7012); (202) 633-3270. Fax, (202) 312-1990. Robert Horton, Chair. Press, (202) 633-3129. TTY, (202) 357-1729.
General email, archivescenter@si.edu
Web, www.americanhistory.si.edu/archives

Acquires, organizes, preserves, and makes available for research the museum's archival and documentary materials relating to American history and culture. Three-dimensional objects and closely related documents are in the care of curatorial divisions. Research areas are open by appointment.

Smithsonian Institution, *Archives of American Art,*
750 9th St. N.W., #2200, 20001 (mailing address: P.O. Box 37012, Victor Bldg., #2200, MRC 937, Washington, DC 20013-7012); (202) 633-7940. Fax, (202) 633-7994. Katie Haw, Director, (202) 633-7992. Reference desk, (202) 633-7950.
Web, www.aaa.si.edu

Collects and preserves manuscript items, such as note-books, sketchbooks, letters, and journals; photos of artists and works of art; tape-recorded interviews with artists, dealers, and collectors; exhibition catalogs; directories; and biographies on the history of visual arts in the United States. Library open to scholars and researchers. Reference centers that maintain microfilm copies of a selection of the Archives' collection include New York; Boston; San Francisco; and San Marino, Calif.

▶ **CONGRESS**

For a listing of relevant congressional committees and sub-committees, please see page 119 or the Appendix.

Library of Congress, *Main Reading Room, Thomas Jefferson Bldg., 101 Independence Ave. S.E., #LJ 100, 20540-4660; (202) 707-3399. Fax, (202) 707-1957. Barbie Morland, Head.*
Web, www.loc.gov/rr/main

Point of access to the general collection of books and bound periodicals as well as electronic resources including microform. Offers research orientations.

Library of Congress, *Manuscript Division, James Madison Memorial Bldg., 101 Independence Ave. S.E., #LM 102, 20540; (202) 707-5383. Fax, (202) 707-7791. James H. Hutson, Chief. Reading room, (202) 707-5387.*
Web, www.loc.gov/rr/mss

Maintains, describes, and provides reference service on the library's manuscript collections, including the papers of U.S. presidents and other eminent Americans. Manu-script reading room primarily serves serious scholars and researchers; historians and reference librarians are available for consultation.

Library of Congress, *Microform and Electronic Resources Center, Thomas Jefferson Bldg., 101 Independence Ave. S.E., #LJ 139, 20540-4660; (202) 707-3399. Fax, (202) 707-1957. James P. Sweany, Head.*
Web, www.loc.gov/rr/microform

Has custody of and services the library's general micro-form collection. Provides work stations for searching the library's online catalog and accessing the Internet. Open to the public, hours posted on the Web site.

Library of Congress, *Preservation Directorate,*
101 Independence Ave. S.E., 20540; (202) 707-2958. Adarija Henley, Director, Acting.
General email, preserve@loc.gov
Web, www.loc.gov/preservation

Responsible for preserving book and paper materials in the library's collections.

Library of Congress, *Rare Book and Special Collections Division, Thomas Jefferson Bldg., 101 Independence Ave. S.E., #LJ 239, 20540; (202) 707-3448. Fax, (202) 707-4142. Mark G. Dimunation, Chief.*
Web, www.loc.gov/rr/rarebook

Maintains collections of incunabula (books printed before 1501) and other early printed books; early imprints of American history and literature; illustrated books; early Spanish American, Russian, and Bulgarian imprints; Con-federate states imprints; libraries of famous personalities (including Thomas Jefferson, Woodrow Wilson, and Oliver Wendell Holmes); special format collections (miniature books, broadsides, almanacs, and pre-1870 copyright records); special interest collections; and special prove-nance collections. Reference assistance is provided in the Rare Book and Special Collections Reading Room.

National Digital Information Infrastructure and Preservation Program (NDIIPP) *(Library of Congress), James Madison Memorial Bldg., 101 Independence Ave. S.E., 20540-1300; (202) 707-3300. Fax, (202) 707-0815. Vacant, Associate Librarian.*
Web, www.digitalpreservation.gov, Twitter, @ndiipp and Facebook, www.facebook.com/digitalpreservation

Oversees development of a national strategy to collect, archive, and preserve digital content, and directs the activities of the Information Technology Directorate.

Senate Historical Office, *201 SHOB, 20510; (202) 224-6900. Betty K. Koed, Historian.*
General email, historian@sec.senate.gov
Web, www.senate.gov/artandhistory/history/common/ generic/Senate_Historical_Office.htm

Serves as an information clearinghouse on Senate history, traditions, and members. Collects, organizes, and distributes to the public unpublished Senate documents; collects and preserves photographs and pictures related to Senate history; conducts an oral history program; advises senators and Senate committees on the disposition of their noncurrent papers and records. Produces publica-tions on the history of the Senate.

U.S. House of Representatives, *Office of Art and Archives, B53 CHOB, 20515; (202) 226-1300. Fax, (202) 226-4635. Farar P. Elliott, Chief, Art and Archives.*
General email, art@mail.house.gov
Archives email, archives@mail.house.gov
Office of the Historian email, history@mail.house.gov
Web, http://history.house.gov

National Park Service Sites in the Capital Region

The National Park Service administers most parks, circles, and monuments in the District of Columbia, as well as sites in nearby Maryland, Virginia, and West Virginia. For information on facilities not listed here, visit www.nps.gov/parks.html.

Go to www.recreation.gov for information on visiting and making reservations at federal recreation sites nationwide.

Antietam National Battlefield, (301) 432-5124

Arlington House, Robert E. Lee Memorial, (703) 235-1530

C & O Canal National Historical Park, (301) 739-4200

Great Falls Area (C & O Canal Maryland), (301) 767-3714

Catoctin Mountain Park, (301) 663-9330

Clara Barton National Historic Site, (301) 320-1410

Ford's Theatre National Historic Site, (202) 426-6924

Fort Washington Park (includes Piscataway Park), (301) 763-4600

Frederick Douglass National Historic Site, (202) 426-5961

George Washington Memorial Parkway (includes memorials to Theodore Roosevelt, Lyndon Johnson, and U.S. Marine Corps), (703) 289-2500

Glen Echo Park, (703) 289-2500

Great Falls Park, Virginia, (703) 757-3101

Greenbelt Park, (301) 344-3948

Harpers Ferry National Historical Park, (304) 535-6029

Manassas National Battlefield Park, (703) 754-1861

Mary McLeod Bethune Council House National Historic Site, (202) 673-2402

Monocacy National Battlefield, (301) 662-3515

National Mall (includes presidential and war memorials and Pennsylvania Avenue National Historic Site), (202) 426-6841

President's Park (White House), (202) 456-7041

Prince William Forest Park, (703) 221-7181

Rock Creek Park, (202) 895-6000

Thomas Stone National Historic Site, (301) 392-1776

Wolf Trap National Park for the Performing Arts, (703) 255-1800

Works with the Office of the Historian to provide access to published documents and historical records of the House. Advises members on the disposition of their records and papers; maintains information on manuscript collections of former members; maintains biographical files of former members; houses photographs and artifacts of former members. Produces publications on Congress and its members.

U.S. House of Representatives, *Office of the Historian,* B53 CHOB, 20515; (202) 226-1300. *Matthew A. Wasniewski, House Historian.*

General email, history@mail.house.gov

Web, http://history.house.gov

Works with the Office of Art and Archives to provide access to published documents and historical records of the House. Conducts historical research. Advises members on the disposition of their records and papers; maintains information on manuscript collections of former members; maintains biographical files on former members. Produces publications on Congress and its members.

▶NONGOVERNMENTAL

Assassination Archives and Research Center, *962 Wayne Ave., #910, Silver Spring, MD 20910; (301) 565-0249. James Lesar, President.*

General email, aarc@uarclibrary.org

Web, www.aarclibrary.org

Acquires, preserves, and disseminates information on political assassinations. Materials and information available on Web site and by request through mail. On-site access available to the public by appointment only.

Moorland-Spingarn Research Center (MSRC) *(Howard University),* 500 Howard Pl. N.W., #129, 20059; (202) 806-7239. Fax, (202) 806-6405. Clifford Muse Jr., Director, Acting. Library, (202) 806-7266.

Web, www.howard.edu/msrc

Comprehensive repository for the documentation of the history and culture of people of African descent in Africa, the Americas, and other parts of the world; collects, preserves, and makes available for research a wide range of resources chronicling the black experience.

Society of the Cincinnati, 2118 Massachusetts Ave. N.W., 20008; (202) 785-2040. Fax, (202) 785-0729. Jack Duane Warren Jr., Executive Director, ext. 410. Press, ext. 445. Library appointments, ext. 426.

General email, admin@societyofthecincinnati.org

Web, www.societyofthecincinnati.org

Collects and exhibits books, manuscripts, paintings, and other artifacts from the Revolutionary War. Maintains a library for research on the American Revolution. Preserves and operates the Anderson House as a historic landmark and museum. Collects and preserves American manuscripts and books from the 1700s. Specializes in documents and artifacts related to the American Revolution.

Genealogy

▶AGENCIES

National Archives and Records Administration (NARA), 700 Pennsylvania Ave. N.W., 20408; (866) 272-6272. Fax, (301) 837-0483. David S. Ferriero, Archivist of the United States. Press and public affairs, (202) 357-5300. TTY, (301) 837-0482.

Web, www.archives.gov

Makes available resources for genealogy research, including military, passport, immigration, census, and land records. Holds genealogy consultations at the Microfilm Research desk one Saturday every month. Genealogy lectures and workshops are available nationwide; events may be found on the National Archives calendar www .archives.gov/calendar.

National Archives and Records Administration (NARA), *Archives 1, References Services Branch,* 700 Pennsylvania Ave. N.W., #G13, 20408; (202) 357-5400. Fax, (202) 357-5934. Trevor Plante, Branch Chief; Dennis Edelin, Section Chief.
General email, archives1reference@nara.gov
Web, www.archives.gov

Assists individuals interested in researching record holdings of the National Archives, including genealogical records; issues research cards to researchers who present photo identification. Users must be at least fourteen years of age.

►CONGRESS

For a listing of relevant congressional committees and subcommittees, please see page 119 or the Appendix.

Library of Congress, *Local History and Genealogy Reference Services,* Thomas Jefferson Bldg., 101 Independence Ave. S.E., #LJ 100, 20540; (202) 707-3399. Fax, (202) 707-1957. James P. Sweany, Head.
Web, www.loc.gov/rr/genealogy

Provides reference and referral service on topics related to local history, genealogy, and heraldry throughout the United States.

►NONGOVERNMENTAL

Daughters of the American Revolution, National Society, 1776 D St. N.W., 20006-5303; (202) 628-1776. Fax, (202) 879-3227. Lynn Young, President General.
Web, www.dar.org

Membership: women descended from American Revolutionary War patriots. Maintains a genealogical library, which is open to the public.

National Genealogical Society, 3108 Columbia Pike, #300, Arlington, VA 22204-4370; (703) 525-0050. Fax, (703) 525-0052. Jordan Jones, President. Toll-free, (800) 473-0060.
General email, ngs@ngsgenealogy.org
Web, www.ngsgenealogy.org, Twitter, @ngsgenealogy and Facebook, www.facebook.com/ngsgenealogy

Encourages study of genealogy and publication of all records that are of genealogical interest. Provides online courses and an in-depth home study program; holds an annual conference.

National Museum of Civil War Medicine, 48 E. Patrick St., Frederick, MD 21705 (mailing address: P.O. Box 470, Frederick, MD 21705); (301) 695-1864. Fax, (301) 695-6823. David Price, Executive Director.
General email, info@civilwarmed.org
Web, www.civilwarmed.org

Assists individuals with questions about ancestors injured in the Civil War.

National Society Daughters of the American Colonists, 2205 Massachusetts Ave. N.W., 20008-2813; (202) 667-3076. Fax, (202) 667-0571. Phyllis Best Jones, President.
General email, cc@nsdac.org
Web, www.nsdac.org

Membership: women descended from men and women who were resident in or gave civil or military service to the colonies prior to the Revolutionary War. Maintains library of colonial and genealogical records, open to the public by appointment.

Washington D.C. Family History Center, 10000 Stoneybrook Dr., Kensington, MD 20895 (mailing address: P.O. Box 49, Kensington, MD 20895); (301) 587-0042. Linda Christensen, Director.
General email, info@wdcfhc.org
Web, www.wdcfhc.org

Maintains genealogical library for research. Collection includes international genealogical index, family group record archives, microfiche registers, and the Family Search Computer Program (www.familysearch.org). Library open to the public. (Sponsored by the Church of Jesus Christ of Latter-day Saints.)

Specific Cultures

►AGENCIES

Interior Dept. (DOI), *Indian Arts and Crafts Board,* 1849 C St. N.W., #2528-MIB, 20240-0001; (888) 278-3253. Fax, (202) 208-5196. Meridith Z. Stanton, Director.
General email, iacb@ios.doi.gov
Web, www.doi.gov/iacb

Advises Native American artisans and craft guilds; produces a source directory on arts and crafts of Native Americans (including Alaska Natives); maintains museums of native crafts in Montana, South Dakota, and Oklahoma; provides information on the Indian Arts and Crafts Act.

Smithsonian Institution, *Center for Folklife and Cultural Heritage,* 600 Maryland Ave. S.W., #2001, 20024 (mailing address: P.O. Box 37012, MRC 520, Washington, DC 20013-7012); (202) 633-6440. Fax, (202) 633-6474. Michael Atwood Mason, Director. Press, (202) 633-0644.
General email, folklife@si.edu
Web, www.folklife.si.edu

Promotes and conducts research into traditional U.S. cultures and foreign folklife traditions; produces folkways recordings, films, videos, and educational programs; presents annual Smithsonian Folklife Festival in Washington, D.C.

►CONGRESS

For a listing of relevant congressional committees and subcommittees, please see page 119 or the Appendix.

Library of Congress, *American Folklife Center,* Thomas Jefferson Bldg., 101 Independence Ave. S.E., #LJ G49, 20540; (202) 707-5510. Fax, (202) 707-2076. Elizabeth (Betsy) Peterson, Director. Reading room, (202) 707-5510.
General email, folklife@loc.gov

Web, www.loc.gov/folklife

Coordinates national, regional, state and local government, and private folklife activities; contracts with individuals and groups for research and field studies in American folklife and for exhibits and workshops; maintains the National Archive of Folk Culture (an ethnographic collection of American and international folklore, grassroots oral histories, and ethnomusicology) and the Veterans History Project (a collection of oral histories and documentary materials from veterans of World Wars I and II and the Korean, Vietnam, and Persian Gulf wars). Conducts internships at the archive; lectures; sponsors year-round concerts of traditional and ethnic music. American Folklife Center Reading Room is located in room #LJ G43.

▶**NONGOVERNMENTAL**

National Council for the Traditional Arts, 8757 Georgia Ave., #450, Silver Spring, MD 20910; (301) 565-0654. Fax, (301) 565-0472. Julia Olin, Executive Director.
General email, info@ncta-usa.org

Web, www.ncta-usa.org

Seeks to celebrate and honor arts of cultural and ethnic significance, including music, crafts, stories, and dance. Promotes artistic authenticity in festivals, national and international tours, concerts, radio and television programs, CD recordings, and films. Works with national parks and other institutions to create, plan, and present cultural events, exhibits, and other programs. Sponsors the annual National Folk Festival.

National Hispanic Foundation for the Arts (NHFA), Washington Square, 1050 Connecticut Ave. N.W., 5th Floor, #500, 20036; (202) 293-8330. Fax, (202) 772-3101. Felix Sanchez, Chair.
General email, info@hispanicarts.org

Web, www.hispanicarts.org

Strives to increase the presence of Hispanics in the media, telecommunications, entertainment industries, and performing arts, and to increase programming for the U.S. Latino community. Provides scholarships for Hispanic students to pursue graduate study in the arts.

National Italian American Foundation, 1860 19th St. N.W., 20009; (202) 387-0600. Fax, (202) 387-0800. John Viola, Chief Operating Officer, (202) 939-3115. Media, (202) 939-3106.
General email, information@niaf.org

Web, www.niaf.org

Membership: U.S. citizens of Italian ancestry. Promotes recognition of Italian American contributions to American society; funds cultural events, educational symposia, antidefamation programs, and grants and scholarships; serves as an umbrella organization for local Italian American clubs throughout the United States.

Pew Research Center, *Hispanic Trends Project,* 1615 L St. N.W., #700, 20036; (202) 419-3600. Fax, (202) 419-3608. Mark Hugo Lopez, Director. Information, (202) 419-3606. Press, (202) 419-4372.
Web, www.pewhispanic.org

Seeks to improve understanding of the U.S. Hispanic population and its impact on the nation, as well as explore Latino views on a range of social matters and public policy issues, including public opinion, identity, and trends in voting, immigration, work, and education. Conducts public opinion surveys and other studies that are made available to the public. (A project of the Pew Research Center.)

Washington Area

▶**AGENCIES**

National Capital Planning Commission, 401 9th St. N.W., North Lobby, #500, 20004; (202) 482-7200. Fax, (202) 482-7272. Marcel Acosta, Executive Director.
General email, info@ncpc.gov

Web, www.ncpc.gov

Central planning agency for the federal government in the national capital region, which includes the District of Columbia and suburban Maryland and Virginia. Reviews and approves plans for the preservation of certain historic and environmental features in the national capital region, including the annual federal capital improvement plan.

National Park Service (NPS) *(Interior Dept.),* **National Capital Region,** 1100 Ohio Dr. S.W., 20242; (202) 619-7023. Bob Vogel, Regional Director. Permits, (202) 245-4715.
Web, www.nps.gov/ncro

Provides visitors with information on Washington-area parks, monuments, and Civil War battlefields; offers press services for the media and processes special event applications and permits.

White House Visitor Center *(President's Park),* 1450 Pennsylvania Ave. N.W., 20230; 1100 Ohio Dr. S.W., 20242; (202) 208-1631. Fax, (202) 208-1643. Peter Lonsway, Park Manager; Kathy Langley, Manager, Visitor Center; John Stanwich, National Park Service White House Liaison, (202) 619-6344. TTY, (800) 877-8339.
General email, presidents_park@nps.gov

Web, www.nps.gov/whho

Administered by the National Park Service. Educates visitors about the White House through videos, exhibits, and historical artifacts. Public tours of the White House are available to those who submit requests to their member of Congress and are accepted up to six months in advance. (Ellipse Visitor Pavillon Complex located just west of the intersection of 15th and E Sts. N.W.)

▶**CONGRESS**

For a listing of relevant congressional committees and subcommittees, please see page 119 or the Appendix.

Senate Commission on Art, *S411 CAP, 20510; (202) 224-2955. Melinda K. Smith, Curator of the Senate.*
General email, curator@sec.senate.gov
Web, www.senate.gov/pagelayout/art/one_item_and_teasers/Explore_Senate_Art.htm

Accepts artwork and historical objects for display in Senate office buildings and the Senate wing of the Capitol. Maintains and exhibits Senate collections (paintings, sculptures, furniture, and manuscripts); oversees and maintains old Senate and Supreme Court chambers.

▶NONGOVERNMENTAL

Assn. for Preservation of Historic Congressional Cemetery, *1801 E St. S.E., 20003-2499; (202) 543-0539. Fax, (202) 449-8364. Paul Williams, President.*
General email, staff@congressionalcemetery.org
Web, www.congressionalcemetery.org and Twitter, @CongCemetery

Administers and maintains the Washington Parish Burial Ground (commonly known as the Congressional Cemetery). Tours available Saturdays at 11:00 a.m. in warm weather. See Web site for tour information.

Historical Society of Washington, D.C., *801 K St. N.W., 2nd Floor, 20001-3746; (202) 249-3955. John Suau, Executive Director; Anne McDonough, Library and Collections Director. Library, (202) 249-3954.*
General email, info@dchistory.org
Web, www.dchistory.org

Maintains research collections on the District of Columbia. Publishes *Washington History* magazine. Library open to the public by appointment. Permanent exhibit about the history of Washington, D.C., open Tuesday–Friday, 10:00 a.m.–4:00 p.m.

Martin Luther King Jr. Memorial Library,
Washingtoniana Division, 901 G St. N.W., #307, 20001-1443; (202) 727-1213. Kerrie Cotten Williams, Manager, Special Collections.
General email, wash.dcpl@dc.gov
Web, www.dclibrary.org/research/collections

Maintains reference collections of District of Columbia current laws and regulations, history, and culture. Collections include biographies; travel books; memoirs and diaries; family, church, government, and institutional histories; maps (1612–present); plat books; city, telephone, and real estate directories (1822–present); census schedules; newspapers (1800–present), including the Washington Star microfilm (1852–1981) and microfilm of several other historic newspapers dating back to 1800, and a collection of clippings and photographs (1940–1981); periodicals; and oral history materials on local neighborhoods, ethnic groups, and businesses.

National Mall Coalition, *9507 Overlea Dr., Rockville, MD 20850 (mailing address: P.O. Box 4709, Rockville, MD 20849); (301) 335-8490. Fax, (301) 340-3947. Judy Scott Feldman, Chair.*
General email, jfeldman@nationalmallcoalition.org
Web, www.nationalmallcoalition.org

Coalition of architects, historians, educators, and citizens promoting the protection and long-range vision planning of the National Mall in Washington, D.C.

Supreme Court Historical Society, *224 E. Capitol St. N.E., 20003; (202) 543-0400. Fax, (202) 547-7730. David T. Pride, Executive Director.*
Web, www.supremecourthistory.org

Acquires, preserves, and displays historic items associated with the Court; conducts and publishes scholarly research. Conducts lecture programs; promotes and supports educational activities about the Court.

U.S. Capitol Historical Society, *200 Maryland Ave. N.E., 20002; (202) 543-8919. Fax, (202) 544-8244. Ronald A. Sarasin, President; William C. diGiacomantonio, Chief Historian. Information, (800) 887-9318.*
General email, uschs@uschs.org
Web, www.uschs.org

Membership: members of Congress, individuals, and organizations interested in the preservation of the history and traditions of the U.S. Capitol. Conducts historical research; offers tours, lectures, workshops, and films; holds events involving members of Congress; publishes an annual historical calendar.

White House Historical Assn., *740 Jackson Pl. N.W., 20006 (mailing address: P.O. Box 27624, Washington, DC 20038-7624); (202) 737-8292. Fax, (202) 789-0440. Stewart McLaurin, President. Toll-free for purchases, (800) 555-2451.*
General email, webmaster@whha.org
Web, www.whitehousehistory.org and Twitter, @WhiteHouseHstry

Seeks to enhance the understanding and appreciation of the White House. Publishes books on the White House, its inhabitants, its artworks, its furnishings, and its history. Net proceeds from book sales, videos and DVDs, traveling exhibits, the museum shop, and gift shop go toward the purchase of historic items for the White House permanent collection.

PHILANTHROPY, PUBLIC SERVICE, AND VOLUNTEERISM

General

▶AGENCIES

AmeriCorps *(Corp. for National and Community Service), 250 E St. S.W., 20024-3208; (202) 606-5000. Fax, (202) 606-3475. Wendy M. Spencer, Chief Executive Officer. Volunteer recruiting information, (800) 942-2677. TTY, (800) 833-3722. Local TTY, (202) 606-3472.*

General email, info@cns.gov

Web, www.nationalservice.gov and *Twitter, @AmeriCorps*

Provides Americans age seventeen and older with opportunities to serve their communities on a full-time or part-time basis. Participants work in the areas of education, public safety, human needs, and the environment and earn education awards for college or vocational training.

AmeriCorps *(Corp. for National and Community Service), National Civilian Community Corps, 250 E St. S.W., 20024-3208; (202) 606-5000. Fax, (202) 606-3462. Gina Cross, Director, Acting, (202) 606-6706. Volunteer recruiting information, (800) 942-2677. TTY, (800) 833-3722. Local TTY, (202) 565-2799.*

General email, info@cns.gov

Web, www.nationalservice.gov/programs/americorps/ americorps-nccc and *Twitter, @nationalservice*

Provides a 10-month residential service and leadership program for men and women ages eighteen to twenty-four of all social, economic, and educational backgrounds. Works to restore and preserve the environment. Working in teams of 8 to 10, members provide disaster relief, fight forest fires, restore homes and habitats after natural disasters, and work in a variety of other service projects in every state.

AmeriCorps *(Corp. for National and Community Service), State and National Program, 250 E St. S.W., 20024-3208; (202) 606-5000. Bill Basl, Director, (202) 606-6790. Alternate phone, (202) 606-6790. Volunteer recruiting information, (800) 942-2677. TTY, (800) 833-3722.*

General email, questions@americorps.gov

Web, www.nationalservice.gov/programs/americorps/ americorps-state-and-national and *Twitter, @nationalservice*

AmeriCorps State administers and oversees AmeriCorps funding distributed to governor-appointed state commissions, which distribute grants to local organizations and to such national organizations as Habitat for Humanity. AmeriCorps National provides grants directly to national public and nonprofit organizations that sponsor service programs, Indian tribes, and consortia formed across two or more states, including faith-based and community organizations, higher education institutions, and public agencies.

AmeriCorps *(Corp. for National and Community Service), Volunteers in Service to America (VISTA), 250 E St. S.W., 20024-3208; (202) 606-5000. Fax, (202) 565-2789. Max Finberg, Director. Volunteer recruiting information, (800) 942-2677. TTY, (800) 833-3722.*

General email, questions@americorps.gov

Web, www.americorps.gov/programs/americorps/ americorps-vista and *Twitter, @nationalservice*

Assigns full-time volunteers to public and private nonprofit organizations for one year to alleviate poverty in local communities. Volunteers receive a living allowance, health care, and other benefits and their choice of a post-service stipend or education award.

Corporation for National and Community Service, *250 E St. N.W., 20525; (202) 606-5000. Fax, (202) 606-3460. Wendy M. Spencer, Chief Executive Officer, (202) 606-5000, ext. 6735. Press, (202) 606-6775. Volunteer recruiting information, (800) 942-2677. TTY, (800) 833-3722.*

General email, info@cns.gov

Web, www.nationalservice.gov and *Twitter, @nationalservice*

Partners people of all ages with national and community-based organizations, schools, faith-based groups, and local agencies to assist with community needs in education, the environment, public safety, homeland security, and other areas. Programs include AmeriCorps-VISTA (Volunteers in Service to America), AmeriCorps-NCCC (National Civilian Community Corps), and the Senior Corps, among others.

Federal Emergency Management Agency (FEMA) *(Homeland Security Dept.), Individual and Community Preparedness, Techworld Bldg., 800 K St. N.W., #5127, 20472-3630; (202) 786-9557. Helen Lowman, Director. Flood insurance information, (888) 379-9531. Storm shelter information, (866) 222-3580.*

General email, citizencorps@dhs.gov

Web, www.ready.gov/citizen-corps

Conducts research on individual, business, and community preparedness. Administers Citizen Corps, a national network of state, territory, tribal, and local councils that coordinate with local first responders to develop community-specific public education, outreach, training, and volunteer opportunities that address community preparedness and resiliency.

Peace Corps, *1111 20th St. N.W., 20526; (202) 692-1040. Fax, (202) 692-8400. Carrie Hessler-Radelet, Director. Information, (855) 855-1961. Press, (202) 692-2230.*

Web, www.peacecorps.gov and *Twitter, @PeaceCorps*

Promotes world peace, friendship, and mutual understanding between the United States and developing nations. Administers volunteer programs to assist developing countries in education, the environment, health (particularly HIV awareness and prevention), small business development, agriculture, and urban youth development.

Senior Corps *(Corporation for National and Community Service), Retired and Senior Volunteer Program, Foster Grandparent Program, and Senior Companion Program, 1201 New York Ave. N.W., 20525; (202) 606-5000. Erwin Tan, Director, (202) 606-3237. National service information hotline, (800) 942-2677. TTY, (800) 833-3722.*

General email, info@cns.gov

Web, www.seniorcorps.gov

Network of programs that help older Americans find service opportunities in their communities, including the Retired and Senior Volunteer Program, which encourages older citizens to use their talents and experience in community service; the Foster Grandparent Program, which gives older citizens opportunities to work with exceptional children and children with special needs; and the Senior

Companion Program, which recruits older citizens to help homebound adults, especially seniors, with special needs.

►CONGRESS

For a listing of relevant congressional committees and sub-committees, please see page 119 or the Appendix.

Government Accountability Office (GAO), *Education, Workforce, and Income Security,* 441 G St. N.W., #5928, 20548; (202) 512-7215. Barbara D. Bovbjerg, Managing Director.
Web, www.gao.gov/careers/ewis.html

Independent nonpartisan agency in the legislative branch. Audits, analyzes, and evaluates programs of the Corporation for National and Community Service; makes reports available to the public.

►NONGOVERNMENTAL

Arca Foundation, 1308 19th St. N.W., 20036; (202) 822-9193. Anna Lefer Kuhn, Executive Director.
General email, proposals@arcafoundation.org
Web, www.arcafoundation.org

Awards grants to nonprofit organizations in the areas of social equity and justice. Interests include corporate accountability, and civic participation domestically and internationally.

Assn. of Fundraising Professionals (AFP), 4300 Wilson Blvd., #300, Arlington, VA 22203-4168; (703) 684-0410. Fax, (703) 684-0540. Andrew Watt, President.
Information, (800) 666-3863.
General email, afp@afpnet.org
Web, www.afpnet.org

Membership: individuals who serve as fundraising executives for nonprofit institutions or as members of counseling firms engaged in fundraising management. Promotes ethical standards; offers workshops; provides resources for member certification; monitors legislation and regulations. AFP Foundation promotes philanthropy and volunteerism. Library open to the public by appointment.

BoardSource, 750 9th St. N.W., #650, 20001; (202) 349-2500. Fax, (202) 349-2599. Anne Wallestad, Chief Executive Officer. Toll-free, (877) 892-6273.
Web, www.boardsource.org and Twitter, @BoardSource

Works to improve the effectiveness of nonprofit organizations by strengthening their boards of directors. Operates an information clearinghouse; publishes materials on governing nonprofit organizations; assists organizations in conducting training programs, workshops, and conferences for board members and chief executives.

Capital Research Center, 1513 16th St. N.W., 20036; (202) 483-6900. Fax, (202) 483-6990. Scott Walter, President.
General email, contact@capitalresearch.org
Web, www.capitalresearch.org

Conservative think tank that researches funding sources of public interest and advocacy groups. Analyzes the impact these groups have on public policy. Publishes findings in newsletters and reports.

Caring Institute, 228 7th St. S.E., 20003; (202) 547-4273. Fax, (202) 546-4510. Kathleen Brennan, President.
General email, info@caring.org
Web, www.caring.org

Promotes selflessness and public service. Recognizes the achievements of individuals who have demonstrated a commitment to serving others. Operates the Frederick Douglass Museum and Hall of Fame for Caring Americans. Sponsors the National Caring Award and offers internships to high school and college students.

The Congressional Award, 379 FHOB, 20515 (mailing address: P.O. Box 77440, Washington, DC 20013-7440); (202) 226-0130. Fax, (202) 226-0131. Erica Wheelan Heyse, National Director. Toll-free, (888) 802-9273.
General email, information@congressionalaward.org
Web, www.congressionalaward.org and Twitter, @theaward

Nonpartisan noncompetitive program established by Congress that recognizes the achievements of young people ages thirteen and one-half to twenty-three. Participants are awarded certificates or medals for setting and achieving goals in four areas: volunteer public service, personal development, physical fitness, and expeditions and exploration.

The Corps Network, 1275 K St. N.W., #1050, 20005; (202) 737-6272. Fax, (202) 737-6277. Mary Ellen Sprenkel, President.
Web, www.corpsnetwork.org and Twitter, @TheCorpsNetwork

Membership: youth corps programs. Produces publications and workshops on starting and operating youth corps and offers technical assistance programs. Holds annual conference. Monitors legislation and regulations.

Council of Better Business Bureaus, *Wise Giving Alliance,* 3033 Wilson Blvd., #600, Arlington, VA 22201-3843; (703) 276-0100. Fax, (703) 525-8277. H. Art Taylor, President.
General email, give@council.bbb.org
Web, www.give.org

Serves as a donor information service on national charities. Evaluates charities in relation to Better Business Bureau standards for charitable solicitation, which address charity finances, solicitations, fund-raising practices, and governance. Produces quarterly guide that summarizes these findings.

Council on Foundations, 2121 Crystal Dr., #700, Arlington, VA 22202; (703) 879-0600. Vikki N. Spruill, President. Toll-free, (800) 673-9036.
General email, membership@cof.org
*Web, www.cof.org and Twitter, @COF_*

Membership: independent community, family, and public-sponsored and company-sponsored foundations; corporate giving programs; and foundations in other countries. Promotes responsible and effective philanthropy through educational programs, publications, government relations, and promulgation of a set of principles and practices for effective grant making.

Earth Share, *7735 Old Georgetown Rd., #900, Bethesda, MD 20814; (240) 333-0300. Fax, (240) 333-0301. Deb Furry, President, Acting. Information, (800) 875-3863. General email, info@earthshare.org*

Web, www.earthshare.org

Federation of environmental and conservation organizations. Works with government and private payroll contribution programs to solicit contributions to member organizations for environmental research, education, and community programs. Provides information on establishing environmental giving options in the workplace.

Evangelical Council for Financial Accountability, *440 W. Jubal Early Dr., #100, Winchester, VA 22601-6319; (540) 535-0103. Fax, (540) 535-0533. Dan Busby, President. Information, (800) 323-9473. General email, information@ecfa.org*

Web, www.ecfa.org and Twitter, @ecfa

Membership: charitable, religious, international relief, and educational nonprofit U.S.–based organizations committed to evangelical Christianity. Assists members in making appropriate public disclosure of their financial practices and accomplishments. Certifies organizations that conform to standards of financial integrity and Christian ethics.

Exponent Philanthropy, *1720 N St. N.W., 20036; (202) 580 6560. Fax, (202) 580-6579. Henry L. Berman, Chief Executive Officer. Toll-free, (888) 212-9922. General email, info@exponentphilanthropy.org*

Web, www.smallfoundations.org and Twitter, @exponentphil

Membership: donors, trustees, consultants, and employees of philanthropic foundations that have few or no staff. Offers educational programs and publications, referrals, networking opportunities, and liability insurance to members. (Formerly the Assn. of Small Foundations.)

Foundation Center, *Washington Field Office, 1627 K St. N.W., 3rd Floor, 20006-1708; (202) 331-1400. Fax, (202) 331-1739. Kim Patton, Director. General email, jzr@foundationcenter.org*

Web, www.foundationcenter.org/washington, http://grantspace.org and Twitter, @FCWashington

Publishes foundation guides and electronic databases. Serves as a clearinghouse on foundations and corporate giving, nonprofit management, fund-raising, and grants for individuals. Provides training and seminars on fundraising and grant writing. Operates libraries in Atlanta, Cleveland, New York, San Francisco, and Washington, D.C.; library catalog available on the Web site. Libraries open to the public. (Headquarters in New York.)

General Federation of Women's Clubs, *1734 N St. N.W., 20036-2990; (202) 347-3168. Fax, (202) 835-0246. Rosemary Thomas, Chief Operating Officer. Toll-free, (800) 443-4392.*

General email, gfwc@gfwc.org

Web, www.gfwc.org and Twitter, @GFWCHQ

Nondenominational, nonpartisan international organization of women volunteers. Interests include conservation, education, international and public affairs, and the arts.

Good360, *675 N. Washington St., #330, Alexandria, VA 22314; (703) 836-2121. Fax, (877) 798-3192. Shabab Gruberg, President. General email, press@good360.org*

Web, www.good360.org

Online product-donation marketplace that seeks to meet the needs of nonprofit organizations by encouraging corporations to donate newly manufactured products to domestic and international charities. Works with companies to develop in-kind programs, coordinates the distribution of gifts to nonprofit agencies, collects tax documentation from recipients, and conducts communitywide public relations activities to encourage product giving. Serves schools and health, recreational, housing, arts, and environmental groups. (Formerly Gifts in Kind International.)

Grantmakers in Health, *1100 Connecticut Ave. N.W., #1200, 20036; (202) 452-8331. Fax, (202) 452-8340. Faith Mitchell, President. General email, info@gih.org*

Web, www.gih.org and Twitter, @GIHealth

Seeks to increase the capacity of health foundations and giving programs to enhance public health. Fosters information exchange among grantmakers. Publications include a bulletin on current news in health and human services.

GuideStar, *1250 H St. N.W., #1150, 20005; (202) 637-7604. Fax, (202) 637-7619. Jacob Harold, President. Toll-free, (800) 421-8656. General email, info@guidestar.org*

Web, www.guidestar.org

Public charity that curates a database gathering and distributing information about IRS-registered nonprofit organizations. Reports on organizations' purpose, impact, finances, and legitimacy.

Habitat for Humanity International, *Government Relations and Advocacy, 1424 K St. N.W., #600, 20005-2429; (202) 628-9171. Fax, (202) 628-9169. Chris Vincent, Vice President, Advocacy and Government Relations. General email, advocacy@habitat.org*

Web, www.habitat.org

Christian ministry that seeks to eliminate poverty housing. Helps people attain housing through home construction, rehabilitation and repairs, and increased access to improved shelter through programs. Offers housing support services that enable low-income families to make improvements on their homes. Works in more than 70 countries.

Independent Sector, *1602 L St. N.W., #900, 20036; (202) 467-6100. Fax, (202) 467-6101. Candy Hill, President,*

Acting; Jeffrey Moore, Co-Chief Executive Officer, Acting;
Claire Wellington, Co-Chief Executive Officer, Acting.
General email, info@independentsector.org

Web, www.independentsector.org

Membership: corporations, foundations, and national
voluntary, charitable, and philanthropic organizations.
Advocates supportive government policies and encourages volunteering, giving, and best practice not-for-profit
nonpartisan initiatives by the private sector for public
causes.

Institute for Justice, 901 N. Glebe Rd., #900, Arlington,
VA 22203; (703) 682-9320. Fax, (703) 682-9321.
Scott Bullock, President.
General email, general@ij.org

Web, www.ij.org

Sponsors seminars to train law students, grassroots
activists, and practicing lawyers in applying advocacy
strategies in public-interest litigation. Seeks to protect
individuals from arbitrary government interference in free
speech, private property rights, parental school choice,
and economic liberty. Litigates cases.

Institute for Sustainable Communities, Washington
Office, 888 17th St. N.W., #610, 20006; (202) 777-7575.
Fax, (202) 777-7577. George Hamilton, President;
Debra Perry, Senior Program Manager, U.S.
General email, isc@iscvt.org

Web, www.iscvt.org

Public interest organization that offers mentoring and
training in advocacy skills and strategies to nonprofit and
international groups interested in such issues as civil and
human rights, public health, arms control, and environmental and consumer affairs. Aids groups in making better
use of resources, such as access to the media and coalition
building. (Headquarters in Montpelier, Vt.)

Lutheran Volunteer Corps, 1226 Vermont Ave. N.W.,
20005; (202) 387-3222. Fax, (202) 667-0037. Sam Collins,
President.
General email, op.associate@lutheranvolunteercorps.org

Web, www.lutheranvolunteercorps.org and Twitter,
@LVCorps

Administers volunteer program in selected U.S. cities;
coordinates activities with health and social service agencies, educational institutions, and environmental groups.
Places volunteers in full-time positions in direct service,
community organizing, advocacy, and public policy.

Mars Foundation, 6885 Elm St., McLean, VA 22101; (703)
821-4900. Fax, (703) 448-9678. Sue Martin, Assistant
Secretary; O. O. Otih, Secretary-Treasurer.

Awards grants in education, arts, health care concerns,
animal wildlife environment, and history.

National Committee for Responsive Philanthropy,
1331 H St. N.W., #200, 20005; (202) 387-9177. Fax, (202)
332-5084. Aaron Dorfman, Executive Director.
General email, info@ncrp.org

Web, www.ncrp.org, Twitter, @NCRP and Facebook,
www.facebook.com/NCRPcommunity

Directs philanthropic giving to benefit the socially, economically, and politically disenfranchised; acts as advocate
for groups that represent the poor, minorities, and women.
Conducts research; organizes local coalitions. Monitors
legislation and regulations.

National Conference on Citizenship (NCOC), 1100 17th
St. N.W., 12th Floor, 20036; (202) 601-7096. Sally Prouty,
Chief Executive Officer, Acting. Press, (202) 864-5518.
General email, conference@ncoc.net

Web, www.ncoc.net, Twitter, @NCoC and Facebook,
www.facebook.com/NCoC1

Congressionally chartered nonpartisan nonprofit that
supports the Civic Health Initiative. Encourages citizens
to participate in civic services. Holds annual conferences to promote public-service activities in local communities. Produces the Civic Health Index to measure civic
engagement.

Nexus Global Youth Summit, 1400 16th St. N.W., #710,
20036; (202) 780-6180. Jonah Wittcamper, Global Director.
General email, info@nexusyouthsummit.org

Web, www.nexusyouthsummit.com

Seeks to increase the philanthropic efforts of young
investors and entrepreneurs. Holds summits for philan-
thropists and social entrepreneurs to network and discuss
their current projects. Affiliated with Search for Common
Ground and The Giving Back Fund.

Philanthropy Roundtable, 1730 M St. N.W., #601, 20036;
(202) 822-8333. Fax, (202) 822-8325. Adam Meyerson,
President.
General email, main@philanthropyroundtable.org

Web, www.philanthropyroundtable.org

Membership: individual donors, foundation trustees
and staff, and corporate giving officers. Helps donors
achieve their charitable objectives by offering counsel and
peer-to-peer exchange opportunities.

Points of Light Institute, 1625 K St. N.W., #500, 20006;
(404) 979-2900. Fax, (404) 979-2901. Tracy Hoover, Chief
Executive Officer. Media, (202) 729-8282.
General email, info@pointsoflight.org

Web, www.pointsoflight.org

Promotes mobilization of people for volunteer community service aimed at solving social problems. Through
HandsOn Network regional centers, offers technical assistance, training, and information services to nonprofit
organizations, public agencies, corporations, and others
interested in volunteering. (Headquarters in Atlanta, Ga.)

United Way Worldwide, 701 N. Fairfax St., Alexandria,
VA 22314-2045; (703) 836-7112. Fax, (703) 519-0097.
Brian A. Gallagher, President.
Web, www.unitedway.org

Membership: independent United Way organizations
in 41 countries and territories, including 1,300 in the
United States. Provides staff training; fund-raising, planning, and communications assistance; resource management; and national public service advertising. Activities
support education, financial stability, and health.

Urban Institute, *Center on Nonprofits and Philanthropy,* 2100 M St. N.W., 20037; (202) 833-7200. Fax, (202) 833-6231. Shena Ashley, Director.
Web, www.urban.org/center/cnp

Conducts and disseminates research on the role and impact of nonprofit organizations and philanthropy.

Volunteers of America, 1660 Duke St., Alexandria, VA 22314; (703) 341-5000. Fax, (703) 341-7000. Michael King, President. Toll-free, (800) 899-0089.
General email, info@voa.org
Web, www.voa.org

Faith-based organization that promotes local human services and outreach programs. Facilitates individual and community involvement. Focuses on children at risk, abused and neglected children, older adults, homeless individuals, people with disabilities, and others.

W. O'Neil Foundation, 5454 Wisconsin Ave., #730, Chevy Chase, MD 20815; (301) 656-5848. Helene O'Neil Shere, President.

Awards grants primarily to Roman Catholic organizations providing programs and basic needs of the poor, such as food, clothing, shelter, and basic medical care, both nationally and internationally.

Youth Service America, 1101 15th St. N.W., #200, 20005; (202) 296-2992. Fax (202) 296 1030. Steven A. Culbertson, President.
General email, info@ysa.org
Web, www.ysa.org and Twitter, @youthservice

Advocates youth service at national, state, and local levels. Promotes opportunities for young people to be engaged in community service. Sponsors Global Youth Service Day. Hosts database of U.S. volunteer opportunities.

Washington Area

▶ NONGOVERNMENTAL

Boy Scouts of America, *National Capitol Area Council,* Marriott Scout Service Center, 9190 Rockville Pike, Bethesda, MD 20814-3897; (301) 530-9360. Fax, (301) 564-9513. Les Baron, Scout Executive, (301) 214-9101.
Web, www.NCACBSA.org and Twitter, @NCACBSA

Educational service organization for youth that supports more than 1,700 local units that provide quality youth programs, including cub scouting, boy scouting, venturing, and exploring. National Capitol Area Council covers the Washington, D.C. metro area, sixteen counties in Maryland and Virginia, and the U.S. Virgin Islands. (Headquarters in Irving, Tex.)

D.C. Preservation League, 1221 Connecticut Ave. N.W., #5A, 20036; (202) 783-5144. Fax, (202) 783-5596. Rebecca A. Miller, Executive Director.
General email, info@dcpreservation.org
Web, www.dcpreservation.org

Participates in planning and preserving buildings and sites in Washington, D.C. Programs include protection and enhancement of the city's landmarks; educational

lectures, tours, and seminars; and technical assistance to neighborhood groups. Monitors legislation and regulations.

Eugene and Agnes E. Meyer Foundation, 1250 Connecticut Ave. N.W., #800, 20036; (202) 483-8294. Fax, (202) 328-6850. Nicky Goren, President.
General email, meyer@meyerfdn.org
Web, www.meyerfoundation.org and Twitter, @MeyerFoundation

Seeks to improve the quality of life in Washington, D.C. Awards grants to nonprofit organizations in four program areas: education, health communities, economic security, and a strong nonprofit sector.

Eugene B. Casey Foundation, 800 S. Frederick Ave., #100, Gaithersburg, MD 20877; (301) 948-6500. Betty Brown Casey, Trustee.

Philanthropic organization that supports the arts, education, and social services in the metropolitan Washington area.

The Herb Block Foundation, 1730 M St. N.W., #901, 20036; (202) 223-8801. Fax, (202) 223-8804. Marcela Brane, President; Sarah Alex, Executive Director.
General email, info@herbblock.org
Web, www.herbblockfoundation.org

Awards grants to charitable and educational programs that combat discrimination and poverty, and promote citizen involvement in government. Provides scholarships to individuals seeking to attend community colleges in the Washington, D.C., area. Awards prizes for excellence in editorial cartooning to serve as as a tool for freedom and to address social issues.

International Order of the Rainbow For Girls, *Washington Assembly,* 2800 16th St. N.W., 20009; (202) 232-8155. Vicky Starr, Advisor, (301) 460-3088.
Web, www.gomarylandrainbow.org

Membership: girls ages 11 through 20. Promotes leadership training through community service and volunteerism. Includes local assemblies throughout the United States (Headquarters in McAlester, Okla.)

Junior League of Washington, 3039 M St. N.W., 20007; (202) 337-2001. Fax, (202) 342-3148. Cameron Gilreath, President.
General email, office@jlw.org
Web, www.jlw.org

Educational and charitable women's organization that promotes volunteerism and works for community improvement through leadership of trained volunteers. Interests include promoting volunteerism and developing the potential of women. Current emphasis is on literacy. (Assn. of Junior Leagues International headquarters in New York.)

Morris and Gwendolyn Cafritz Foundation, 1825 K St. N.W., #1400, 20006; (202) 223-3100. Fax, (202) 296-7567. Calvin Cafritz, Chair; Rose Ann Cleveland, Executive Director.
General email, info@cafritzfoundation.org
Web, www.cafritzfoundation.org

Awards grants to educational, arts, and social services institutions in the metropolitan Washington area.

Quota International, *1420 21st St. N.W., 20036; (202) 331-9694. Fax, (202) 331-4395. Barbara Schreiber, Executive Director.*
General email, staff@quota.org
Web, www.quota.org and
https://quotainternational.org and Twitter, @QuotaIntl

International service organization that links members in twelve countries in a worldwide network of service and friendship. Interests include deaf, hard-of-hearing, and speech-impaired individuals and disadvantaged women and children. Maintains the We Share Foundation, a charitable organization.

Washington Humane Society, *1201 New York Ave N.E., 20002; (202) 576-6664. Claudia Roll, Director, Operations. Press, (202) 375-7750. 24-hour animal cruelty and emergency hotline, (202) 723-5730.*
General email, adopt@washhumane.org
Press, matt.williams@warl.org
Web, http://support.washhumane.org

Congressionally chartered animal welfare agency and open-access animal shelter. Promotes pet adoption; offers low-cost spay and neuter services and trap-and-neuter programs.

Washington Regional Assn. of Grantmakers, *1400 16th St. N.W., #740, 20036; (202) 939-3440. Fax, (202) 939-3442. Tamara Lucas Copeland, President, (202) 939-3441.*
General email, info@washingtongrantmakers.org
Web, www.washingtongrantmakers.org and Twitter, @WRAGtweets

Network of funders that partners with agencies and nongovernmental organizations in the Washington, D.C., region. Identifies and implements new and innovative forms of philanthropy. Shares best practices. Advocates collective philanthropic community in the region and publishes issue briefs.

RECREATION AND SPORT

General

▶AGENCIES

Bureau of Land Management (BLM) *(Interior Dept.), Recreation and Visitor Services, 20 M St. S.E., 6th Floor, 20003 (mailing address: 1849 C St. N.W., MS 2134, Washington, DC 20240); (202) 912-7256. Fax, (202) 912-7362. Andy Tenney, Division Chief.*
Web, www.blm.gov/wo/st/en/prog/Recreation.html

Develops recreation opportunities on public lands.

Health and Human Services Dept. (HHS), *President's Council on Fitness, Sports, and Nutrition, 1101 Wootton Pkwy., #560, Tower Bldg., Rockville, MD 20852; (240) 276-9567. Fax, (240) 276-9860. Shellie Pfohl, Executive Director.*

Faith-Based and Neighborhood Partnerships Contacts at Federal Departments and Agencies

White House Office of Faith-Based and Neighborhood Partnerships, Melissa Rogers (202) 456-3394, www.whitehouse.gov/administration/eop/ofbnp

DEPARTMENTS

Agriculture, Norah Deluhery, (202) 720-2032; www.usda.gov/partnerships

Commerce, Josh Dickson, (202) 482-2770; www.commerce.gov/office-secretary/center-faith-based-and-neighborhood-partnerships

Education, Rev. Brenda Girton-Mitchell, (202) 401-1876; www2.ed.gov/edblogs/fbnp

Health and Human Services, Acacia Bamberg Salatti, (202) 358-3595; www.hhs.gov/partnerships

Homeland Security, David L. Myers, (202) 646-3487; www.dhs.gov/dhs-center-faith-based-neighborhood-partnerships

Housing and Urban Development, Paula Lincoln, (202) 708-2404; www.hud.gov/offices/fbci

Justice, Eugene Schneeberg, (202) 305-7462; http://ojp.gov/fbnp

Labor, Ben Seigel (Acting), (202) 693-6017; www.dol.gov/cfbnp

State, Shaun Casey, (202) 647-3137; www.state.gov/s/fbci

Veterans Affairs, Rev. E. Terri LaVelle, (202) 461-7689; www.va.gov/cfbnpartnerships

AGENCIES

Agency for International Development, J Mark. Brinkmoeller, (202) 712-5236; www.usaid.gov/partnership-opportunities/fbci

Corporation for National and Community Service, John Kelly, (202) 606-6743; www.nationalservice.gov/special-initiatives/communities/faith-based-and-other-community-initiatives-and-neighborhood

Environmental Protection Agency, Shakeba Carter-Jenkins, (202) 564-7263

Small Business Administration, DeJuana Thompson (202) 205-6677; www.sba.gov/offices/headquarters/ofbnp

---

General email, fitness@hhs.gov
Web, www.fitness.gov, www.presidentschallenge.org and Twitter, @FitnessGov

Provides schools, state and local governments, recreation agencies, and employers with information on designing and implementing physical fitness and nutrition programs; conducts award programs for children and adults and for schools, clubs, and other institutions.

National Park Service (NPS) *(Interior Dept.), 1849 C St. N.W., #3115, 20240; (202) 208-3818. Fax, (202) 208-7889. Jonathan B. Jarvis, Director. Press, (202) 208-6843.*

General email, asknps@nps.gov

Web, www.nps.gov and *Twitter, @NatlParkService*

Administers national parks, monuments, historic sites, and recreation areas. Oversees coordination, planning, and financing of public outdoor recreation programs at all levels of government. Conducts recreation research surveys; administers financial assistance program to states for planning and development of outdoor recreation programs. (Some lands designated as national recreation areas are not under NPS jurisdiction.)

► NONGOVERNMENTAL

American Canoe Assn., *503 Sophia St., #100, Fredericksburg, VA 22401; (540) 907-4460. Fax, (888) 229-3792. Wade Blackwood, Executive Director.*
General email, aca@americancanoe.org
Web, www.americancanoe.org

Membership: individuals and organizations interested in the promotion of canoeing, kayaking, and other paddle sports. Works to preserve the nation's recreational waterways. Sponsors programs in safety education, competition, recreation, public awareness, conservation, and public policy. Monitors legislation and regulations.

American Gaming Assn., *799 9th St. N.W., #700, 20001; (202) 552-2675. Fax, (202) 552-2676. Geoff Freeman, President.*
General email, info@americangaming.org
Web, www.americangaming.org

Membership: casinos, casino and gaming equipment manufacturers, and financial services companies. Compiles statistics and serves as an information clearinghouse on the gaming industry. Administers a task force to study gambling addiction, raise public awareness of the condition, and develop assistance programs for it. Monitors legislation and regulations.

American Hiking Society, *8605 2nd Ave., Silver Spring, MD 20910; (301) 565-6704. Fax, (301) 565-6714. Gregory Miller, President. Toll-free, (800) 972-8608.*
General email, info@americanhiking.org
Web, www.americanhiking.org

Membership: individuals and clubs interested in preserving America's trail system and protecting the interests of hikers and other trail users. Sponsors research on trail construction and a trail maintenance summer program. Provides information on outdoor volunteer opportunities on public lands.

American Medical Athletic Assn., *4405 East-West Hwy., #405, Bethesda, MD 20814-4535; (301) 913-9517. Fax, (301) 913-9520. David Watt, Executive Director, ext. 13. Toll-free, (800) 776-2732.*
General email, amaa@americanrunning.org
Web, www.amaasportsmed.org

Membership: sports medicine and allied health professionals. Assists members in promoting running and physical fitness to their patients and in developing their own physical fitness programs. Promotes and reports on sports medicine research and discussion. (Sister organization to American Running Assn.)

American Recreation Coalition, *1200 G St. N.W., #650, 20005; (202) 682-9530. Fax, (202) 682-9529. Derrick A. Crandall, President.*
General email, arc@funoutdoors.com
Web, www.funoutdoors.com and *Twitter, @AmerRecreation*

Membership: recreation industry associations, recreation enthusiast groups, and leading corporations in the recreation products and services sectors. Promotes health and well-being through outdoor recreation.

American Running Assn., *4405 East-West Hwy., #405, Bethesda, MD 20814-4535; (301) 913-9517. Fax, (301) 913-9520. David Watt, Executive Director. Toll-free, (800) 776-2732.*
General email, milerun@americanrunning.org
Web, www.americanrunning.org

Membership: athletes, health clubs, physicians, businesses, and individuals. Promotes proper nutrition and regular exercise. Provides members with medical advice and referrals, fitness information, and assistance in developing fitness programs. (Sister organization to American Medical Athletic Assn.)

American Sportfishing Assn., *1001 N. Fairfax St., #501, Alexandria, VA 22314; (703) 519-9691. Fax, (703) 519-1872. Michael (Mike) Nussman, President.*
General email, info@asafishing.org
Web, www.asafishing.org and *Twitter, @ASAfishing*

Works to ensure healthy and sustainable fisheries resources and to expand market growth for its members through increased participation in sportfishing. Programs include Keep America Fishing and the Fish America Foundation.

Assn. of Pool and Spa Professionals, *2111 Eisenhower Ave., #500, Alexandria, VA 22314-4698; (703) 838-0083. Fax, (703) 549-0493. Rich Gottwald, President.*
General email, MemberServices@apsp.org
Web, www.apsp.org and *Twitter, @TheAPSP*

Membership: manufacturers, dealers and retailers, service companies, builders, and distributors of pools, spas, and hot tubs. Promotes the industry; provides educational programs for industry professionals; establishes standards for construction and safety. Monitors legislation and regulations.

Boat U.S. (Boat Owners Assn. of the United States), *880 S. Pickett St., Alexandria, VA 22304-4606; (703) 461-2878. Fax, (703) 461-2847. Margaret Podlich, President.*
General email, govtaffairs@boatus.com
Web, www.boatus.com and *Twitter, @BoatUS*

Membership: owners of recreational boats. Represents boat-owner interests before the federal, state, and local governments.

Club Managers Assn. of America, *1733 King St., Alexandria, VA 22314; (703) 739-9500. Fax, (703) 739-0124. Jeffrey Morgan, Chief Executive Officer.*
General email, cmaa@cmaa.org

Web, www.cmaa.org

Membership: managers of membership clubs. Promotes the profession of club management through education and other assistance.

Disabled Sports USA, *451 Hungerford Dr., #100, Rockville, MD 20850; (301) 217-0960. Fax, (301) 217-0968. Kirk M. Bauer, Executive Director, (301) 217-9838.*
General email, info@dsusa.org

Web, www.dsusa.org and www.disabledsportsusa.org

Offers nationwide sports rehabilitation programs in more than forty summer and winter sports; promotes independence, confidence, and fitness through programs for people with permanent disabilities, including wounded service personnel; conducts workshops and competitions through community-based chapters; participates in world championships.

FishAmerica Foundation, *1001 N. Fairfax St., #501, Alexandria, VA 22314; (703) 519-9691. Fax, (703) 519-1872. Ruth Jackson, Grants Manager, (703) 519-9691, ext. 247.*
General email, fafgrants@asafishing.org

Web, www.fishamerica.org and Twitter, @fafgrants

Invests in local communities to restore habitat, improve water quality, and advance fisheries research to increase sportfish populations and sportfishing opportunities. (Affiliated with the American Sportfishing Assn.)

National Aeronautic Assn., *Reagan National Airport, Hangar 7, #202, 20001-6015; (703) 416-4888. Fax, (703) 416-4877. Jonathan Gaffney, President.*
General email, naa@naa.aero

Web, www.naa.aero

Membership: persons interested in development of general and sporting aviation, including skydiving, commercial and military aircraft, and spaceflight. Supervises sporting aviation competitions; administers awards in aviation; oversees and approves official U.S. aircraft, aeronautics, and space records. Serves as U.S. representative to the International Aeronautical Federation in Lausanne, Switzerland.

National Center for Bicycling & Walking, *Project for Public Spaces, 1612 K St. N.W., #802, 20006; (202) 223-3621. Mark Plotz, Program Manager.*
General email, info@bikewalk.org

Web, www.bikewalk.org

Promotes bicycle use; conducts research, planning, and training projects; develops safety education and public information materials; offers consulting services for long-range planning and policy analysis. Works to increase public awareness of the benefits and opportunities of bicycling and walking. (Headquarters in New York.)

National Club Assn., *1201 15th St. N.W., #450, 20005; (202) 822-9822. Fax, (202) 822-9808. Henry Wallmeyer, President.*
General email, info@nationalclub.org

Web, www.nationalclub.org and Twitter, @NatlClubAssn

Promotes the interests of private, social, and recreational clubs. Monitors legislation and regulations.

National Collegiate Athletic Assn. (NCAA), *Government Relations, 1 Dupont Circle N.W., #310, 20036-1139; (202) 293-3050. Fax, (202) 293-3075. Abe L. Frank, Director, ext. 2122.*
Web, www.ncaa.org

Membership: colleges and universities, conferences, and organizations interested in the administration of intercollegiate athletics. Certifies institutions' athletic programs; compiles records and statistics; produces publications and television programs; administers youth development programs; awards student athletes with postgraduate scholarships and degree-completion grants. (Headquarters in Indianapolis, Ind.)

National Football League Players Assn., *1133 20th St. N.W., #600, 20036; (202) 463-2200. Fax, (202) 756-9310. DeMaurice Smith, Executive Director. Toll-free, (800) 372-2000.*
Web, www.nflpa.com, Twitter, @NFLPA and Facebook, www.facebook.com/NFLPA

Membership: professional football players. Represents members in matters concerning wages, hours, and working conditions. Provides assistance to charitable and community organizations. Sponsors programs and events to promote the image of professional football and its players.

National Indian Gaming Assn. (NIGA), *224 2nd St. S.E., 20003; (202) 546-7711. Fax, (202) 546-1755. Jason Giles, Executive Director.*
General email, questions@indiangaming.org

Web, www.indiangaming.org and Facebook, www.facebook.com/NIGAIndianGaming

Membership: more than 180 Indian nations as well as other organizations, tribes, and businesses engaged in gaming enterprises. Operates as a clearinghouse for tribes, policymakers, and the public on Indian gaming issues and tribal community development.

National Recreation and Park Assn., *22377 Belmont Ridge Rd., Ashburn, VA 20148-4501; (703) 858-0784. Fax, (703) 858-0794. Barbara Tulipane, Chief Executive Officer, (703) 858-2144. Toll-free, (800) 626-6772.*
General email, customerservice@nrpa.org

Web, www.nrpa.org

Membership: park and recreation professionals and interested citizens. Promotes support and awareness of park, recreation, and leisure services; advances environmental and conservation efforts; facilitates development, expansion, and management of resources; provides technical assistance for park and recreational programs; and provides professional development to members. Monitors legislation and regulations.

Poker Players Alliance, *705 8th St. S.E., #300, 20003; (202) 552-7429. Fax, (202) 552-7423. John A. Pappas, Executive Director. Toll-free, (888) 448-4772. General email, email@theppa.org*

Web, www.theppa.org

Membership: poker players and enthusiasts. Seeks to promote the game and protect players' rights. Monitors legislation and regulations.

Road Runners Club of America, *1501 Lee Hwy., #140, Arlington, VA 22209; (703) 525-3890. Fax, (703) 525-3891. Jean Knaack, Executive Director. General email, office@rrca.org*

Web, www.rrca.org and Twitter, @RRCAnational

Develops and promotes road races and fitness programs, including the Kids Run the Nation Program and the Women's Distance Festival. Issues guidelines on road races concerning safety, legal issues, and runners with disabilities. Facilitates communication between clubs.

SnowSports Industries America, *8377-B Greensboro Dr., McLean, VA 22102-3587; (703) 556-9020. Fax, (703) 821-8276. Nick Sargent, President. General email, siamail@snowsports.org*

Web, www.snowsports.org

Membership: manufacturers and distributors of ski and other outdoor sports equipment, apparel, and accessories. Interests include international markets and reducing global warming. Monitors legislation and regulations.

Society of Health and Physical Educators (SHAPE) America, *1900 Association Dr., Reston, VA 20191-1598; (703) 476-3400. Fax, (703) 476-9527. E. Paul Roetert, Chief Executive Officer. Toll-free, (800) 213-7193. Press, (703) 476-1461. General email, info@shapeamerica.org*

Web, www.shapeamerica.org

Membership: teachers and others who work with school health, physical education, athletics, recreation, dance, and safety education programs (kindergarten through postsecondary levels). Member associations are National Assn. for Girls and Women in Sport, American Assn. for Health Education, National Dance Assn., National Assn. for Sport and Physical Education, and American Assn. for Physical Activity and Recreation.

Special Olympics International Inc., *1133 19th St. N.W., 20036-3604; (202) 628-3630. Fax, (202) 824-0354. Mary Davis, Chief Executive Officer, Acting; Timothy P. Shriver, Chair. Toll-free, (800) 700-8585. General email, info@specialolympics.org*

Web, www.specialolympics.org

Offers individuals with intellectual disabilities opportunities for year-round sports training; sponsors athletic competition for 4 million athletes worldwide in twenty-two individual and Olympic-type team sports.

StopPredatoryGambling.org, *100 Maryland Ave. N.E., #311, 20002; (202) 567-6996. Les Bernal, Executive Director, (202) 567-6996, ext. 1. Toll-free and fax, (800) 664-2680.*

General email, mail@stoppredatorygambling.org

Web, www.stoppredatorygambling.org

Seeks to end government support of exploitive forms of gambling. Compiles information on the personal, social, economic, and public health impacts of gambling and disseminates it to citizens and policymakers at the local, state, and national levels. Monitors legislation and regulations.

U.S. Eventing Assn. (USEA), *525 Old Waterford Rd. N.W., Leesburg, VA 20176-2050; (703) 779-0440. Fax, (703) 779-0550. Rob Burk, Chief Executive Officer, (703) 779-9895. General email, info@useventing.com*

Web, www.useventing.com

Membership: individuals interested in eventing, an Olympic-recognized equestrian sport featuring dressage, cross-country, and show jumping. Registers all national events to ensure that they meet the standards set by the U.S. Equestrian Federation. Sponsors three-day events for members from beginner novice to Olympic levels. Provides educational materials on competition, riding, and care of horses.

U.S. Olympic Committee, *Government Relations, 1100 H St. N.W., #600, 20005; (202) 466-3399. Fax, (202) 466-5068. Desiree Filippone, Managing Director; Karen Irish, Associate Director. General email, communications@usoc.org*

Web, www.teamusa.org

Responsible for training, entering, and underwriting U.S. teams in the Olympic, Paralympic, Pan American, and Parapan Games. Supports the bid of U.S. cities to host the Games; recognizes the national governing body of each sport in these games. Promotes international athletic competition. (Headquarters in Colorado Springs, Colo.)

U.S. Parachute Assn., *5401 Southpoint Centre Blvd., Fredericksburg, VA 22407-2612; (540) 604-9740. Fax, (540) 604-9741. Edward Scott, Executive Director, ext. 325. General email, uspa@uspa.org*

Web, www.uspa.org

Membership: individuals and organizations interested in skydiving. Develops safety procedures; maintains training programs; issues skydiving licenses and ratings; certifies skydiving instructors; sanctions national competitions; and documents record attempts. Offers liability insurance to members. Monitors legislation and regulations.

RELIGION

General

▶NONGOVERNMENTAL

American Assn. of Pastoral Counselors, *9504A Lee Hwy., Fairfax, VA 22031-2303; (703) 385-6967. Fax, (703) 352-7725. Douglas M. Ronsheim, Executive Director. General email, info@aapc.org*

Web, www.aapc.org

Membership: mental health professionals with training in both religion and the behavioral sciences. Nonsectarian organization that accredits pastoral counseling centers, certifies pastoral counselors, and approves training programs.

American Friends Service Committee (AFSC), *Public Policy,* *1822 R St. N.W., 20009-1604; (202) 483-3341. Fax, (202) 232-3197. Aura Kanegis, Director.*
General email, WashOfficeInfo@afsc.org
Web, www.advocacy/dc

Education, outreach, and advocacy office for the AFSC, an independent organization affiliated with the Religious Society of Friends (Quakers) in America. Sponsors domestic and international service, development, justice, and peace programs. Priorities include Iraq, Israel/Palestine, civil rights and liberties, and economic justice in the United States. Interests include peace education; arms control and disarmament; social and economic justice; gay and lesbian rights, racism, sexism, and civil rights; refugees and immigration policy; crisis response and relief efforts; and international development efforts, especially in Central America, the Middle East, and southern Africa. (Headquarters in Philadelphia, Pa.)

American Humanist Assn., *1777 T St. N.W., 20009-7125; (202) 238-9088. Fax, (202) 238-9003. Rebecca Hale, President. Toll-free, (800) 837-3792.*
General email, aha@americanhumanist.org
Web, www.americanhumanist.org and Twitter, @americanhumanist

Seeks to educate the public about Humanism and bring Humanists together for mutual support and action. Defends the civil liberties and constitutional freedoms of Humanists and leads both local and national Humanist organizations toward progressive societal change.

American Islamic Congress, *1718 M St. N.W., #243, 20036; (202) 595-3160. Fax, (202) 621-6005. Zainab Al-Suwaij, Executive Director.*
General email, info@aicongress.org
Web, www.aicongress.org

Independent, nonpartisan initiative of American Muslims challenging negative perceptions of Muslims by advocating interethnic and interfaith understanding. Promotes open multicultural society and civil liberties; advocates women's equality, free expression, and nonviolence. Encourages the denouncement of terrorism, extremism, and hate speech within the Muslim community. Maintains offices in Tunisia and Iraq.

American Jewish Committee, *Government and International Affairs, 1156 15th St. N.W., 20005; (202) 785-4200. Fax, (202) 785-4115. Alan Ronkin, Washington Regional Director.*
Web, www.ajc.org

Human relations agency devoted to protecting civil and religious rights for all people. Interests include church-state issues, research on energy security, Israel and the Middle East, the security and well-being of Jewish diasporic communities worldwide, immigration, social discrimination, civil and women's rights, education, and

international cooperation for peace and human rights. (Headquarters in New York.)

Americans United for Separation of Church and State, *1901 L St. N.W., #400, 20036; (202) 466-3234. Fax, (202) 466-2587. Barry W. Lynn, Executive Director.*
General email, americansunited@au.org
Web, www.au.org and Twitter, @americansunited

Citizens' interest group. Opposes federal and state aid to parochial schools; works to ensure religious neutrality in public schools; supports free religious exercise; initiates litigation; maintains speakers bureau. Monitors legislation and regulations.

Atheist Alliance of America, *1777 T St. N.W., 20009-7125; (866) 437-3842. Melissa Pugh, President.*
General email, info@atheistalliance.org
Web, www.atheistallianceamerica.org

Federation of international atheists and groups who seek to educate the public about atheism. Supports secularism in developing countries and responds to discrimination against atheists. Hosts related conventions.

Baptist Joint Committee for Religious Liberty, *200 Maryland Ave. N.E., 3rd Floor, 20002; (202) 544-4226. Fax, (202) 544-2094. J. Brent Walker, Executive Director.*
General email, bjc@bjconline.org
Web, www.bjconline.org and Twitter, @BJContheHill

Membership: Baptist conventions and conferences. Interests include religious liberty, separation of church and state, First Amendment religious issues, and government regulation of religious institutions. Files court briefs, leads educational programs, and monitors legislation.

Baptist World Alliance, *405 N. Washington St., Falls Church, VA 22046; (703) 790-8980. Fax, (703) 893-5160. Neville Callam, General Secretary.*
General email, bwa@bwanet.org
Web, www.bwanet.org and Twitter, @TheBWA

International Baptist organization. Conducts religious teaching and works to create a better understanding among nations. Organizes development efforts and disaster relief worldwide. Interests include human rights and religious liberty.

Becket Fund for Religious Liberty, *1200 New Hampshire Ave. N.W., #700, 20036; (202) 955-0095. Fax, (202) 955-0090. William Mumma, President; Kristina Arriaga de Bucholz, Executive Director. Press, (202) 349-7226.*
Web, www.becketfund.org and Twitter, @TheBecketFund

Public interest law firm that promotes freedom of expression for people of all faiths. Works to ensure that people and institutions of all faiths, domestically and abroad, are entitled to a voice in public affairs.

B'nai B'rith International, *1120 20th St. N.W., #300N, 20036; (202) 857-6600. Fax, (202) 857-2700. Daniel S. Mariaschin, Executive Vice President. Toll-free, (888) 388-4224.*
General email, info@bnaibrith.org
Web, www.bnaibrith.org and Twitter, @BnaiBrith

International Jewish organization that promotes the security and continuity of the Jewish people and the State of Israel; defends human rights; combats anti-Semitism; and promotes Jewish identity through cultural activities. Interests include strengthening family life and the education and training of youth, providing broad-based services for the benefit of senior citizens, and advocacy on behalf of Jews throughout the world.

Catholic Charities USA, *2050 Ballenger Ave., #400, Alexandria, VA 22314; (703) 549-1390. Fax, (703) 549-1656. Sister Donna Markham, President.*
General email, info@catholiccharitiesusa.org
Web, www.catholiccharitiesusa.org and Twitter, @CCharitiesUSA

Member agencies and institutions provide assistance to persons of all backgrounds; community-based services include day care, counseling, food, and housing. National office provides members with advocacy and professional support, including networking, training and consulting, program development, and financial benefits. Represents the Catholic community in times of domestic disaster.

Catholic Information Center, *1501 K St. N.W., #175, 20005; (202) 783-2062. Fax, (202) 783-6667.*
Rev. Arne Panula, Director
General email, events@cicdc.org
Web, www.cicdc.org and Twitter, @CICDC

Catholic cultural center, hosts lectures and events, offers free counseling services. Includes Catholic bookstore and chapel.

Chaplain Alliance for Religious Liberty, *P.O. Box 151353, Alexandria, VA 22315; (571) 293-2427. Fax, (910) 221-2226. Col. Ron Crews (USAR, Ret.), Executive Director; Brig. Gen. Doug Lee (USAR, Ret.), President.*
General email, info@chaplainalliance.org
Web, http://chaplainalliance.org

Membership: military chaplains and others who support orthodox Christian doctrines. Seeks to ensure that all chaplains and those they serve may exercise their religious liberties without fear of reprisal. Interests include the conflict between official protection for gays in the military and orthodox Christian teachings. Issues press releases; grants media interviews; monitors legislation and regulations.

Christian Science Committee on Publication, *Federal Office, 1001 G St., #1000 West, 20001 (mailing address: P.O. Box 15726, Washington, DC 20003); (202) 296-2190. Fax, (202) 296-2426. Gary Jones, Manager.*
General email, federal@christianscience.com
Web, www.christianscience.com/member-resources/committee-on-publications

Public service organization that provides information on the religious convictions and practices of Christian Scientists; works with Congress and regulatory agencies to ensure that the interests of Christian Science are not adversely affected by law or regulations.

Conference of Major Superiors of Men (CMSM), *8808 Cameron St., Silver Spring, MD 20910; (301) 588-4030. Fax, (301) 587-4575. John A. Pavlik, Executive Director.*
General email, postmaster@cmsm.org
Web, www.cmsm.org

National representative body for more than 17,000 men in 240 religious and apostolic communities in the United States, including foreign missionaries. Collaborates with U.S. bishops and other key groups and organizations that serve church and society.

Council on American–Islamic Relations, *453 New Jersey Ave. S.E., 20003-4034; (202) 488-8787. Fax, (202) 488-0833. Nihad Awad, National Executive Director; Ibrahim Hooper, Communications, (202) 744-7726.*
General email, info@cair.com
Web, www.cair.com and Twitter, @CAIRNational

Promotes the understanding of Islam to the American public. Seeks to empower the Muslim community in the United States and protect civil liberties through political and social activism.

Episcopal Church, *Government Relations, 110 Maryland Ave. N.E., #309, 20002; (202) 547-7300. Fax, (202) 547-4457. Alexander Baumgarten, Director. Toll-free, (800) 228-0515.*
Web, www.episcopalchurch.org/eppn and www.episcopalchurch.org/office/office-government-relations

Informs Congress, the executive branch, and governmental agencies about the actions and resolutions of the Episcopal Church. Monitors legislation and regulations. (Denominational headquarters in New York.)

Ethics and Public Policy Center, *1730 M St. N.W., #910, 20036; (202) 682-1200. Fax, (202) 408-0632. M. Edward Whelan III, President.*
General email, ethics@eppc.org
Web, www.eppc.org and Twitter, @EPPCdc

Considers implications of Judeo-Christian moral tradition for domestic and foreign policymaking.

Evangelical Lutheran Church in America, *Advocacy, 122 C St. N.W., #125, 20001; (202) 783-7507. Stacy Martin, Director. Toll-free, (800) 638-3522.*
General email, washingtonoffice@elca.org
Web, www.elca.org/advocacy and Twitter, @ELCA

Represents the church's ministries, relationships, projects, and relief efforts on behalf of underrepresented people in order to effect policy change. Monitors and responds to proposed legislation and regulations. (Headquarters in Chicago, Ill.)

Faith in Public Life, *1111 14th St. N.W., #900, 20005; (202) 499-4095. Fax, (202) 315-0469. Rev. Jennifer Butler, Chief Executive Officer.*
General email, admin@faithinpubliclife.org
Web, www.faithinpubliclife.org and Twitter, @BuildFaithType

Provides organizing and communications support to diverse faith leaders and organizations working to further justice and the common good in public policy; designs and implements coalitions and initiatives to promote faith as a force for the common good.

Friends Committee on National Legislation (FCNL), *245 2nd St. N.E., 20002-5795; (202) 547-6000. Fax, (202) 547-6019. Diane Randall, Executive Secretary. Toll-free, (800) 630-1330. Recorded information, (202) 547-4343.*
General email, fcnl@fcnl.org

Web, www.fcnl.org

Advocates economic justice, world disarmament, international cooperation, and religious rights. Advocates on behalf of Native Americans in such areas as treaty rights, self-determination, and U.S. trust responsibilities. Conducts research and educational activities through the FCNL Education Fund. Opposes the death penalty. Monitors national legislation and policy. (Affiliated with the Religious Society of Friends [Quakers].)

General Board of Church and Society of the United Methodist Church, *100 Maryland Ave. N.E., 20002; (202) 488-5600. Fax, (202) 488-5619.*
Rev. Dr. Susan Henry-Crowe, General Secretary, (202) 488-5629. Press, (202) 488-5630.
General email, gbcs@umc-gbcs.org

Web, www.umc-gbcs.org and Twitter, @GBCSUMC

One of four international general program boards of the United Methodist Church. Provides training and educational resources to member churches on social concerns. Monitors legislation and regulations. (Has offices at the Church Center for the United Nations.)

General Conference of Seventh-day Adventists, *12501 Old Columbia Pike, Silver Spring, MD 20904-6600; (301) 680-6000. Ted N. C. Wilson, President; Williams Costa Jr., Director, Communications. Press, (301) 680-6315.*
General email, info@contact.adventist.org

Web, www.adventist.org and Twitter, @adventistchurch

World headquarters of the Seventh-day Adventist Church. Interests include education, health care, humanitarian relief, and development. Supplies educational tools for the blind and the hard of hearing. Operates schools worldwide. Organizes community service-oriented youth groups.

Institute on Religion and Democracy, *1023 15th St. N.W., #601, 20005-2601; (202) 682-4131. Fax, (202) 682-4136. Mark Tooley, President.*
General email, info@theird.org

Web, www.theird.org

Interdenominational bipartisan organization that supports democratic and constitutional forms of government consistent with the values of Christianity. Serves as a resource center to promote Christian perspectives on U.S. foreign policy questions. Interests include international conflicts, religious liberties, and the promotion of democratic forms of government in the United States and worldwide.

Interfaith Alliance, *1250 24th St. N.W., #300, 20037; (202) 466-0567. Fax, (202) 466-0502. Rabbi Jack Welton Moline, President.*
General email, info@interfaithalliance.org

Web, www.interfaithalliance.org

Membership: seventy-five faith traditions, including Protestant, Catholic, Jewish, and Muslim clergy, laity, and others who favor a positive, nonpartisan role for religious faith in public life. Advocates mainstream religious values; promotes tolerance and social opportunity; opposes the use of religion to promote political extremism at national, state, and local levels. Monitors legislation and regulations.

International Religious Liberty Assn., *12501 Old Columbia Pike, Silver Spring, MD 20904-6600; (301) 680-6686. Fax, (301) 680-6695. Robert Seiple, President.*
General email, info@irla.org

Web, www.irla.org

Seeks to preserve and expand religious liberty and freedom of conscience; advocates separation of church and state; sponsors international and domestic meetings and congresses.

Islamic Society of North America (ISNA), *Office of Interfaith and Community Alliances, 110 Maryland Ave. N.E., #304, 20002; (202) 544-6565. Fax, (202) 544-6636. Sayyid M. Syeed, National Director.*
General email, info@isna.net

Web, www.isna.net

Conducts outreach to grassroots organizations and engages in joint programs with other religious organizations, including the National Council of Churches, the United States Conference of Catholic Bishops, and the Union for Reform Judaism. Seeks to promote a positive image of Islam and Muslims to national political leaders and strong relationships with U.S. congressional staff and federal government officials. Serves as an outreach resource to the American Muslim community. (Headquarters in Plainfield, Ind.)

Jesuit Conference, *Social and International Ministries, 1016 16th St. N.W., 4th Floor, 20036; (202) 462-0400. Fax, (202) 328-9212. Shaina Aber, Policy Director; Fr. William J. Kelley, S.J., Secretary.*
General email, usjc@jesuit.org

Web, www.jesuit.org

Information and advocacy organization of Jesuits and laypersons concerned with peace and social justice issues. Interests include peace and disarmament, domestic poverty, socially responsible investing, and migration and immigration.

Jewish Federations of North America, *Washington Office, 1720 Eye St. N.W., 20006; (202) 785-5900. Fax, (202) 785-4937. William Daroff, Director.*
General email, dc@JewishFederations.org

Web, www.jewishfederations.org

Acts as advocate for the 153 Jewish federations across the United States on issues of concern, including long-term care, families at risk, and naturally occurring retirement communities. Offers marketing, communications, and public relations support; coordinates a speakers bureau. (Headquarters in New York.)

Jewish Women International, *1129 20th St. N.W., #801, 20036; (202) 857-1300. Fax, (202) 857-1380. Loribeth Weinstein, Chief Executive Officer. Toll-free, (800) 343-2823.*
General email, jwi@jwi.org
Web, www.jwi.org

Membership: Jewish women, supporters, and partners in the United States and Canada. Interests include empowerment of women and girls, ending domestic and sexual violence, financial literacy and economic security, and highlighting women's leadership at multi-generational intersections.

Leadership Conference of Women Religious, *8808 Cameron St., Silver Spring, MD 20910; (301) 588-4955. Fax, (301) 587-4575. Joan Marie Steadman, Executive Director.*
Web, www.lcwr.org

Membership: Roman Catholic women who are the principal administrators of their congregations in the United States and around the world. Offers programs and support to members; conducts research; serves as an information clearinghouse.

Loyola Foundation, *10335 Democracy Lane, #202, Fairfax, VA 22030; (571) 435-9401. Fax, (571) 435-9402. A. Gregory McCarthy IV, Executive Director.*
General email, info@loyolafoundation.org
Web, www.loyolafoundation.org

Assists overseas Catholic mission activities. Awards grants to international missionaries and Catholic dioceses for vehicle and equipment purchase and construction.

Maryknoll Office for Global Concerns (*Catholic Foreign Mission Society of America*), *200 New York Ave. N.W., 20001; (202) 832-1780. Fax, (202) 832-5195. Gerry Lee, Executive Director.*
General email, ogc@maryknoll.org
Web, www.maryknollogc.org

Conducts education and advocacy for international policies that promote peace, social justice, and ecological integrity. (Headquarters in Maryknoll, N.Y.)

Mennonite Central Committee, *Washington Office, 920 Pennsylvania Ave. S.E., 20003; (202) 544-6564. Fax, (202) 544-2820. J. Ron Byler, Executive Director.*
General email, mccwash@mcc.org
Web, http://mcc.org/get-involved/advocacy/washington

Christian organization engaged in service and development projects. Monitors legislation and regulations affecting issues of interest to Mennonite and Brethren in Christ churches. Interests include human rights in developing countries, military spending, the environment, world hunger, poverty, and civil and religious liberties. (Headquarters in Akron, Pa.)

Muslim Public Affairs Council, *Washington Office, 1020 16th St. N.W., 20036; (202) 547-7701. Fax, (202) 547-7704. Salam Al-Marayati, National President; Hoda Hawa, Director.*
General email, rabiah@mpac.org
Web, www.mpac.org and Twitter, @mpac_national

Promotes the civil rights of American Muslims and the integration of Islam into American pluralism. Seeks an accurate portrayal of Islam and Muslims in the media and popular culture. (Headquarters in Los Angeles, Calif.)

National Assn. of Evangelicals, *P.O. Box 23269, 20026; (202) 479-0815. Fax, (202) 379-9955. Leith Anderson, President.*
General email, info@nae.net
Web, www.nae.net

Membership: evangelical denominations, nonprofits, churches, schools, and individuals. Works to connect and represent Christian evangelical denominations, nonprofits, churches, schools, and individuals. Interests include church and faith; family; religious liberty; economic policy; church-state relations; immigration and refugee policy; and world relief efforts. Provides networking opportunities and commissions chaplains. Monitors legislation and regulations.

National Clergy Council, *109 2nd St. N.E., 20002; (202) 546-8329. Fax, (202) 546-6864. Rev. Robert L. Schenck, President; Peggy Nienaber, Chief of Programs.*
General email, peggy@faithandaction.org
Web, www.faithandaction.org

Informal network of conservative and traditional Christian clergy and heads of religious organizations and societies. Advocates injecting religious morality into public policy debates. Monitors legislation and regulations.

National Council of Catholic Women, *200 N. Glebe Rd., #725, Arlington, VA 22203; (703) 224-0990. Fax, (703) 224-0991. Juanita Balenger, Administrator; Sheila Hopkins, President. Toll-free, (800) 506-9407.*
General email, nccw01@nccw.org
Web, www.nccw.org and Facebook, www.facebook.com/nationalcouncilofcatholicwomen

Roman Catholic women's organization. Provides education and information to Catholic women regarding social issues. Interests include women and poverty, employment, family life, abortion, care for older adults, world hunger, global water supplies, genetic engineering research, pornography, capital punishment, immigration, domestic violence, and human trafficking. Special programs include volunteer respite care, leadership training for women, mentoring of mothers, and drug and alcohol abuse education. Monitors legislation and regulations.

National Council of Churches, *110 Maryland Ave. N.E., #108, 20002-5603; (202) 544-2350. Fax, (202) 543-1297. Jim Winkler, President.*

General email, info@nationalcouncilofchurches.us

Web, www.nationalcouncilofchurches.us, Twitter, @nccusa and *Facebook, www.facebook.com/ nationalcouncilofchurches*

Membership: thirty-eight Protestant, Anglican, and Orthodox denominations. Interests include interreligious relations, racial and social equality; social welfare, economic justice, environmental justice, peace, and international issues, with a focus on peacemaking and mass incarceration issues; and church-state relations.

National Council of Jewish Women, *Washington Office,* *1707 L St. N.W., #950, 20036-4206; (202) 296-2588. Fax, (202) 331-7792. Jody Rabhan, Director, Washington Operations.*

General email, action@ncjwdc.org

Web, www.ncjw.org, Twitter, @NCJW and *Facebook, www.facebook.com/NCJWInc*

Progressive Jewish women's membership organization. Activities include education, community service, and advocacy. Interests include women's issues, reproductive, civil, and constitutional rights, child care, judicial nominations, religion-state separation, and human needs funding issues. (Headquarters in New York.)

NCSEJ: National Coalition Supporting Eurasian Jewry, *1120 20th St. N.W, #300N, 20006-3413; (202) 898-2500. Fax, (202) 898-0822. Mark B. Levin, Executive Director; Daniel Rubin, Chair.*

General email, ncsj@ncsj.org

Web, www.ncsej.org

Advocacy group promoting political and religious freedom on behalf of Jews in Russia, Ukraine, the Baltic states, and Eurasia. Works with community and government leadership in the United States and in the former Soviet Union addressing issues of anti-Semitism, community relations, and promotion of democracy, tolerance, and U.S. engagement in the region.

Operation Understanding DC, *3000 Connecticut Ave. N.W., #335, 20008; (202) 234-6832. Fax, (202) 234-6669. Aaron Jenkins, Executive Director.*

General email, info@oudc.org

Web, www.oudc.org

African American and Jewish youth education program promoting leadership and antidiscrimination.

Orthodox Union, *Advocacy Center, 820 1st St. N.E., #730, 20002; (202) 513-6484. Fax, (202) 513-6497. Nathan Diament, Executive Director.*

General email, info@ouadvocacy.org

Web, www.ou.org/public_affairs

Works to protect Orthodox Jewish interests and freedoms through dissemination of policy briefings to government officials. Encourages Jewish law and a traditional perspective on public policy issues. Coordinates grassroots activities. (Headquarters in New York.)

Pew Research Center, *Religion and Public Life Project, 1615 L St. N.W., #700, 20036; (202) 419-4550. Fax, (202)*

419-4559. Alan Cooperman, Director. Media, (202) 419-4564. General email, religion@pewresearch.org

Web, www.pewforum.org

Nonpartisan organization that seeks to explore the impact of religion on public affairs, political behavior, the law, domestic policy, and international affairs. Conducts polling and independent research; serves as a clearinghouse and forum on these issues. Delivers findings to journalists, government officials, and other interested groups. (A Pew Research Center project.)

Presbyterian Mission (U.S.A.), *Office of Public Witness, 100 Maryland Ave. N.E., #410, 20002; (202) 543-1126. Fax, (202) 543-7755. Rev. J. Herbert Nelson II, Director. Toll-free, (800) 728-7228.*

General email, ga_washington_office@pcusa.org

Web, www.presbyterianmission.org/ministries/washington

Provides information on the views of the general assembly of the Presbyterian Church on public policy issues; monitors legislation affecting issues of concern. Interests include budget priorities, foreign policy, arms control, civil rights, religious liberty, church-state relations, economic justice, environmental justice, and public policy issues affecting women. (Headquarters in Louisville, Ky.)

Progressive National Baptist Convention Inc., *601 50th St. N.E., 20019; (202) 396-0558. Fax, (202) 398-4998. Rev. James C. Perkins, President. Toll-free, (800) 876-7622.*

General email, info@pnbc.org

Web, www.pnbc.org

Baptist denomination that supports missionaries, implements education programs, and acts as advocate for civil and human rights.

Public Religion Research Institute, *2027 Massachusetts Ave. N.W., 3rd Floor, 20036; (202) 238-9424. Fax, (202) 238-9427. Robert P. Jones, Chief Executive Officer, (202) 238-9426. Press, (202) 776-7700.*

General email, info@publicreligion.org

Web, www.publicreligion.org and *Twitter, @publicreligion*

Nonpartisan nonprofit that conducts surveys and publishes research on the junction of public life and religion. Serves as a resource to help journalists and the public understand the impact of religion on American life and discussions on public policy.

Sojourners, *3333 14th St. N.W., #200, 20010; (202) 328-8842. Fax, (202) 328-8757. Rob Wilson-Black, Chief Executive Officer; Lisa Sharon Harper, Chief Church Engagement Officer. Toll-free, (800) 714-7474. Press, (202) 328-8842.*

General email, sojourners@sojo.net

Web, www.sojo.net

Membership: Catholics, Protestants, Evangelicals, and other interested Christians. Grassroots network that focuses on social injustices and the intersection of faith, politics, and culture. (Merger of Sojourners and Call to Renewal.)

U.S. Conference of Catholic Bishops (USCCB), *3211 4th St. N.E., 20017; (202) 541-3000. Fax, (202) 541-3166.*

James Rogers, Chief Communications Officer, (202) 541-3200. Toll-free, (800) 235-8722.
Web, www.usccb.org

Serves as a forum for bishops to exchange ideas, debate concerns of the church, and draft responses to religious and social issues. Provides information on doctrine and policies of the Roman Catholic Church; develops religious education and training programs; formulates policy positions on social issues, including the economy, employment, federal budget priorities, voting rights, energy, health, housing, rural affairs, international military and political matters, human rights, the arms race, global economics, and immigration and refugee policy.

Union for Reform Judaism, *Religious Action Center of Reform Judaism, 2027 Massachusetts Ave. N.W., 20036; (202) 387-2800. Fax, (202) 667-9070. Rabbi Jonah Pesner, Director.*
General email, rac@rac.org
Web, www.rac.org

Religious and educational organization that mobilizes the American Jewish community on legislative and social concerns. Interests include economic justice, civil rights, religious liberty, and international peace.

United Church of Christ, *Washington Office, 100 Maryland Ave. N.E., #330, 20002; (202) 543-1517. Fax, (202) 543-5994. Sandra (Sandy) Sorensen, Director.*
Web, www.ucc.org

Studies public policy issues and promotes church policy on these issues; organizes legislative advocacy to address church views. Interests include health care, international peace, economic justice, the environment, climate change, civil rights, and immigration. (Headquarters in Cleveland, Ohio.)

Washington Ethical Society, *7750 16th St. N.W., 20012; (202) 882-6650. Amanda Poppei, Senior Leader.*
General email, wes@ethicalsociety.org
Web, www.ethicalsociety.org

A humanistic religious community that sets standards, distributes ethical culture materials, trains leaders, awards grants, publishes statements on moral issues and public policy, and coordinates national projects such as youth programs. (Affiliated with the American Ethical Union and the Unitarian Universalist Assn.)

Women's Alliance for Theology, Ethics, and Ritual (WATER), *8121 Georgia Ave., #310, Silver Spring, MD 20910; (301) 589-2509. Fax, (301) 589-3150. Diann L. Neu, Co-Director; Mary E. Hunt, Co-Director.*
General email, water@hers.com
Web, www.waterwomensalliance.org and Twitter, @watervoices

Feminist theological organization that focuses on issues concerning women and religion. Interests include social issues; work skills for women with disabilities; human rights in Latin America; and liturgies, rituals, counseling, and research.

TRAVEL AND TOURISM

General

▶ **AGENCIES**

Bureau of Consular Affairs *(State Dept.), Passport Services, 600 19th St. N.W., #6826, 20006; (202) 647-9584. Brenda Sprague, Deputy Assistant Secretary. National passport information, (877) 487-2778.*
Web, https://travel.state.gov/content/passports/en/passports.html
National Passport Information Center, NPIC@state.gov

Creates passports and provides information and resources to citizens about how to obtain, replace, and change a U.S. passport.

Bureau of Consular Affairs *(State Dept.), Special Issuance Agency, 600 19th St. N.W., #3.200, 20006; (202) 485-8244. Christine Harold-Aluyen, Director. National passport information, (877) 487-2778.*
Web, http://travel.state.gov/content/passports/en/passports/information/where-to-apply/agencies/special-issuance-agency.html

Administers passport laws and issues passports. (Most branches of the U.S. Postal Service and most U.S. district and state courts are authorized to accept applications and payment for passports and to administer the required oath to U.S. citizens. Completed applications are sent from the post office or court to the nearest State Dept. regional passport office for processing.) Maintains a variety of records received from the Overseas Citizens Services, including consular certificates of witness to marriage and reports of birth and death. (Individuals wishing to apply for a U.S. passport may seek additional information via the phone number or Web address listed above.)

International Trade Administration (ITA) *(Commerce Dept.), Industry and Analysis, National Travel and Tourism, 1401 Constitution Ave. N.W., #1003, 20230-0001; (202) 482-0140. Fax, (202) 482-2887. Kelly Craighead, Executive Director.*
General email, ntto@trade.gov
Web, http://travel.trade.gov

Fosters international tourism trade development, including public-private partnerships; represents the United States in tourism-related meetings with foreign government officials. Assembles, analyzes, and disseminates data and statistics on travel and tourism to and from the United States.

National Park Service (NPS) *(Interior Dept.), Sustainable Tourism, 1201 Eye St. N.W., #933, 20005; (202) 354-6986. Fax, (202) 371-5179. Dean T. Reeder, Chief.*
General email, dean_reeder@nps.gov
Web, www.nps.gov/tourism

Directs and supports the National Park Service's tourism program. Acts as liaison to government departments and agencies on tourism issues. Serves as the primary contact for national and international travel and tourism industry officials and professionals.

►CONGRESS

For a listing of relevant congressional committees and subcommittees, please see page 119 or the Appendix.

►NONGOVERNMENTAL

American Hotel and Lodging Assn., *1250 Eye St. N.W., #1100, 20005-3931; (202) 289-3100. Fax, (202) 289-3199. Katherine Lugar, President; Jim Abrahamson, Chair. General email, info@ahla.com*

Web, www.ahla.com

Membership: state and city partner lodging associations. Provides operations, technical, educational, marketing, and communications services to members. Monitors legislation and regulations.

American Resort Development Assn., *1201 15th St. N.W., #400, 20005; (202) 371-6700. Fax, (202) 289-8544. Howard Nusbaum, President. Web, www.arda.org*

Membership: U.S. and international developers, builders, financiers, marketing companies, and others involved in resort, recreational, and community development. Serves as an information clearinghouse; monitors federal and state legislation affecting land, time share, and community development industries.

American Society of Travel Agents (ASTA), *675 N. Washington St., #490, Alexandria, VA 22314-2963; (703) 739-2782. Fax, (703) 739-3268. Zane Kerby, President. Toll-free, (800) 275-2782. General email, askasta@asta.org*

Web, www.asta.org and Twitter, @ASTAAgents

Membership: representatives of the travel industry. Works to safeguard the traveling public against fraud, misrepresentation, and other unethical practices. Offers training programs for travel agents. Consumer affairs department offers help for anyone with a travel complaint against a member of the association.

Center for Responsible Travel, *1333 H St. N.W., #300, East Tower, 20005; (202) 347-9203, ext. 417. Fax, (202) 775-0819. Martha Honey, Director. General email, staff@responsibletravel.org*

Web, www.responsibletravel.org and Twitter, @CRESTResTravel

Designs, monitors, evaluates, and seeks to improve ecotourism and sustainable tourism principles and practices. (Affiliated with Stanford University.)

Cruise Lines International Assn., *1201 F St. N.W., #250, 20004; (202) 759-9370. Fax, (202) 759-9344. Cindy D'Aoust, President, Acting. General email, info@cruising.org*

Web, www.cruising.org

Membership: more than sixty cruise lines as well as other cruise industry professionals. Advises domestic and international regulatory organizations on shipping policy. Works with U.S. and international agencies to promote safety, public health, security, medical facilities, environmental awareness, and passenger protection. Monitors legislation and regulations.

Destination Marketing Assn. International, *2025 M St. N.W., #500, 20036-3309; (202) 296-7888. Fax, (202) 296-7889. Charles Jeffers II, Chief Executive Officer, Acting; Jim McCaul, Communications, (202) 835-4205. General email, jmccaul@destinationmarketing.org*

Web, www.destinationmarketing.org

Membership: travel- and tourism-related businesses, convention and meeting professionals, and tour operators. Encourages business travelers and tourists to visit local historic, cultural, and recreational areas; assists in meeting preparations. Monitors legislation and regulations.

Global Business Travel Assn., *123 N. Pitt St., 1st Floor, Alexandria, VA 22314; (703) 684-0836. Fax, (703) 342-4324. Michael (Mike) McCormick, Executive Director, (703) 236-1129. General email, info@gbta.org*

Web, www.gbta.org

Membership: corporate travel managers and travel service suppliers. Promotes educational advancement of members and provides a forum for exchange of information on U.S. and international travel. Monitors legislation and regulations.

Hostelling International USA—American Youth Hostels, *8401 Colesville Rd., #600, Silver Spring, MD 20910-9663; (301) 495-1240. Fax, (240) 650-2094. Russell Hedge, Chief Executive Officer. General email, members@hiusa.org*

Web, www.hiusa.org

Seeks to improve cultural understanding through a nationwide network of hostels and travel-based programs. Provides opportunities for outdoor recreation and inexpensive educational travel and accommodations through hostelling. Member of the International Youth Hostel Federation.

International Assn. of Amusement Parks and Attractions, *1448 Duke St., Alexandria, VA 22314; (703) 836-4800. Fax, (703) 836-4801. Paul Noland, President, ext. 772. Press, (703) 299-5127. General email, iaapa@iaapa.org*

Web, www.iaapa.org

Membership: companies from around the world in the amusement parks and attractions industry. Monitors legislation and regulations.

International Ecotourism Society, *P.O. Box 96503, #34145, 20090-6503; (202) 506-5033. Fax, (202) 789-7279. Kelly Bricker, Chair. General email, info@ecotourism.org*

Web, www.ecotourism.org

Promotes tourism practices that conserve the environment and improve the situation of local peoples. Sponsors meetings and workshops for ecotourism professionals; publishes guide for travelers.

Passenger Vessel Assn., *103 Oronoco St., #200, Alexandria, VA 22314; (703) 518-5005. Fax, (703) 518-5151. John R. Groundwater, Executive Director. Toll-free, (800) 807-8360.*
General email, pvainfo@passengervessel.com

Web, www.passengervessel.com

Membership: owners, operators, and suppliers for U.S. and Canadian passenger vessels and international vessel companies. Interests include insurance, safety and security, and U.S. congressional impact upon dinner and excursion boats, car and passenger ferries, overnight cruise ships, and riverboat casinos. Monitors legislation and regulations.

U.S. Travel Assn., *1100 New York Ave. N.W., #450, 20005-3934; (202) 408-8422. Fax, (202) 408-1255. Roger Dow, President.*
General email, feedback@ustravel.org

Web, www.USTravel.org, Project Time Off, www.projecttimeoff.com and Twitter, @ustravel

Membership: travel-related companies and associations, state tourism offices, convention and visitors bureaus. Advocates increased travel to and within the United States; conducts research, provides marketing, and hosts trade shows. Monitors legislation and regulations.

UNITE HERE, *Washington Office, 1775 K St. N.W., #620, 20006-1530; (202) 393-4373. Fax, (202) 223-6213. or fax, (202) 342-2929. Vacant, Political Director; D. Taylor, President.*
Web, www.unitehere.org

Membership: more than 270,000 workers in the United States and Canada who work in the hospitality, gaming, food service, manufacturing, textile, laundry, and airport industries. Assists members with contract negotiation and grievances; conducts training programs and workshops. Monitors legislation and regulations. (Headquarters in New York. Formed by the merger of the former Union of Needletrades, Textiles and Industrial Employees and the Hotel Employees and Restaurant Employees International Union.)

5

Education

GENERAL POLICY AND ANALYSIS

Basic Resources

▶AGENCIES

Education Dept., *400 Maryland Ave. S.W., #7W301, 20202-0001; (202) 401-3000. Fax, (202) 260-7867. John B. King Jr., Secretary; James Cole Jr., General Counsel, (202) 401-6000. Federal Student Aid Information Center, (800) 433-3243. Information Resource Center, (202) 401-2000. Toll-free, (800) 872-5327. TTY, (800) 877-8339. Press, (202) 401-1576.*
Web, www.ed.gov and Twitter, @usedgov

Establishes education policy and acts as principal adviser to the president on education matters; administers and coordinates most federal assistance programs on education.

Education Dept., *Educational Technology, 400 Maryland Ave. S.W., #5W114, 20202; (202) 401-1444. Joseph South, Director, Acting.*
General email, tech@ed.gov
Web, www.tech.ed.gov and Twitter, @OfficeofEdTech

Develops national educational policy and advocates the transition from print-based to digital learning

Education Dept., *Innovation and Improvement, 400 Maryland Ave. S.W., #4W300, 20202-0001; (202) 205-4500. Fax, (202) 205-4123. Nadya Chinoy Dabby, Assistant Deputy Secretary.*
Web, www.ed.gov/edblogs/oii and Twitter, @ED_OII

Provides grants for innovative K–12 educational practices in areas such as alternative routes to teacher certification, traditional teaching of American history, financial literacy and economic education, and arts in education. Supports the establishment of charter schools, magnet schools, and other public and nonpublic education alternatives. Serves as liaison and resource to the nonpublic education community.

Education Dept., *International Affairs, 400 Maryland Ave. S.W., #6W108, 20202-0001; (202) 401-0430. Fax, (202) 401-2508. Maureen McLaughlin, Director, (202) 401-8964.*
General email, international.affairs@ed.gov
Web, www.ed.gov/international

Responsible for the overall coordination of the Education Dept.'s international presence. Works with department program offices, support units, and senior leadership as well as with external partners, including other federal agencies, state and local agencies, foreign governments, international organizations, and the private sector.

Education Dept., *Legislative and Congressional Affairs, 400 Maryland Ave. S.W., #6W315, 20202-3500; (202) 401-0020. Lloyd Horwich, Assistant Secretary, Acting.*
General email, olca@ed.gov
Web, www2.ed.gov/about/offices/list/olca

Directs and supervises all legislative activities of the Education Dept. Participates on legislation and regulation development teams within the department and provides legislative history behind the current law.

Education Dept., *School Support and Rural Programs, 400 Maryland Ave. S.W., #3W205, 20202-6400; (202) 401-0039. Fax, (202) 205-5870. Lisa Ramirez, Director, Acting.*
Web, www2.ed.gov/about/offices/list/oese/sst

Provides a coordinated strategy to focus federal resources on supporting improvements in schools; promotes development and implementation of comprehensive improvement plans that direct resources toward improved achievement for all students.

Educational Resources Information Center (ERIC) *(Education Dept.), 400 Maryland Ave. S.W., #BE101, 20202-5950; (800) 538-3742. Erin Pollard, Program Director, (202) 219-3400.*
General email, eric@ed.gov
Web, http://eric.ed.gov

Coordinates an online national information system of education literature and resources. Provides a centralized bibliographic and full-text database of journal articles and other published and unpublished materials. Available at no charge to educators worldwide. Managed by the Applied Engineering Management Corp.

▶CONGRESS

For a listing of relevant congressional committees and subcommittees, please see page 164 or the Appendix.

Government Accountability Office (GAO), *Education, Workforce, and Income Security, 441 G St. N.W., #5928, 20548; (202) 512-7215. Barbara D. Bovbjerg, Managing Director.*
Web, www.gao.gov/careers/ewis.html

Independent nonpartisan agency in the legislative branch. Audits, analyzes, and evaluates Education Dept. programs; makes reports available to the public.

▶NONGOVERNMENTAL

APPA: Leadership in Educational Facilities, *1643 Prince St., Alexandria, VA 22314-2818; (703) 684-1446. Fax, (703) 549-2772. E. Lander Medlin, Executive Vice President.*
General email, info@appa.org
Web, www.appa.org and Twitter, @APPA_facilities

Membership: professionals involved in the administration, maintenance, planning, and development of buildings and facilities used by colleges and universities, K–12 private and public schools, museums, libraries, and other educational institutions. Interests include maintenance and upkeep of housing facilities. Provides information on campus energy management programs and campus accessibility for people with disabilities. (Formerly the Assn. of Higher Education Facilities Officers.)

EDUCATION RESOURCES IN CONGRESS

For a complete listing of congressional committees, including their full contact information, leadership, membership, and jurisdictions, please refer to the Appendix on pages 779–896.

HOUSE:

House Administration Committee, (202) 225-8281. Web, cha.house.gov

House Agriculture Committee, (202) 225-2171. Web, agriculture.house.gov

  Subcommittee on Biotechnology, Horticulture, and Research, (202) 225-2171.

House Appropriations Committee, (202) 225-2771. Web, appropriations.house.gov

  Subcommittee on Interior, Environment, and Related Agencies, (202) 225-3081.

  Subcommittee on Labor, Health and Human Services, Education, and Related Agencies, (202) 225-3508.

  Subcommittee on Legislative Branch, (202) 226-7252.

House Armed Services Committee, (202) 225-4151. Web, armedservices.house.gov

  Subcommittee on Military Personnel, (202) 225-7560.

House Education and the Workforce Committee, (202) 225-4527. Web, edworkforce.house.gov

  Subcommittee on Early Childhood, Elementary, and Secondary Education, (202) 225-4527.

  Subcommittee on Higher Education and Workforce Training, (202) 225-4527.

House Natural Resources Committee, (202) 225-2761. Web, naturalresources.house.gov

House Oversight and Government Reform Committee, (202) 225-5074. Web, oversight.house.gov

  Subcommittee on Information Technology, (202) 225-5074.

House Science, Space, and Technology Committee, (202) 225-6371. Web, science.house.gov

  Subcommittee on Research and Technology, (202) 225-6371.

JOINT:

Joint Committee on the Library of Congress, (202) 225-8281.

Web, cha.house.gov/jointcommittees/joint-committee-library

SENATE:

Senate Agriculture, Nutrition, and Forestry Committee, (202) 224-2035. Web, ag.senate.gov

  Subcommittee on Nutrition, Specialty Crops, and Agricultural Research, (202) 224-2035.

Senate Appropriations Committee, (202) 224-7363. Web, appropriations.senate.gov

  Subcommittee on Interior, Environment, and Related Agencies, (202) 228-0774.

  Subcommittee on Labor, Health and Human Services, Education, and Related Agencies, (202) 224-9145.

  Subcommittee on Legislative Branch, (202) 224-7256.

Senate Armed Services Committee, (202) 224-3871. Web, armed-services.senate.gov

  Subcommittee on Personnel, (202) 224-3871.

Senate Banking, Housing, and Urban Affairs Committee, (202) 224-7391. Web, banking.senate.gov

Senate Commerce, Science, and Transportation Committee, (202) 224-0411. Web, commerce.senate.gov

  Subcommittee on Science, Space and Competitiveness, (202) 224-0415.

Senate Health, Education, Labor, and Pensions Committee, (202) 224-5375. Web, help.senate.gov

  Subcommittee on Children and Families, (202) 224-5375.

Senate Indian Affairs Committee, (202) 224-2251. Web, indian.senate.gov

Senate Rules and Administration Committee, (202) 224-6352. Web, rules.senate.gov

---

Aspen Institute, *1 Dupont Circle N.W., #700, 20036-7133; (202) 736-5800. Fax, (202) 467-0790. Walter Isaacson, President. Press, (202) 736-3849.*
General email, info@aspeninstitute.org

Web, www.aspeninstitute.org and Twitter, @AspenInstitute

   Educational and policy studies organization. Promotes consideration of the public good in a wide variety of policy areas, including education. Working with international partners, offers educational seminars, nonpartisan policy forums, public conferences and events, and leadership development initiatives.

Center for Education Reform, *1901 L St. N.W., #705, 20036; (202) 750-0016. Fax, (202) 290-2492. Jeanne Allen, President, Acting. Toll-free, (800) 521-2118.*
General email, cer@edreform.com

Web, www.edreform.com and Twitter, @edreform

Education Department

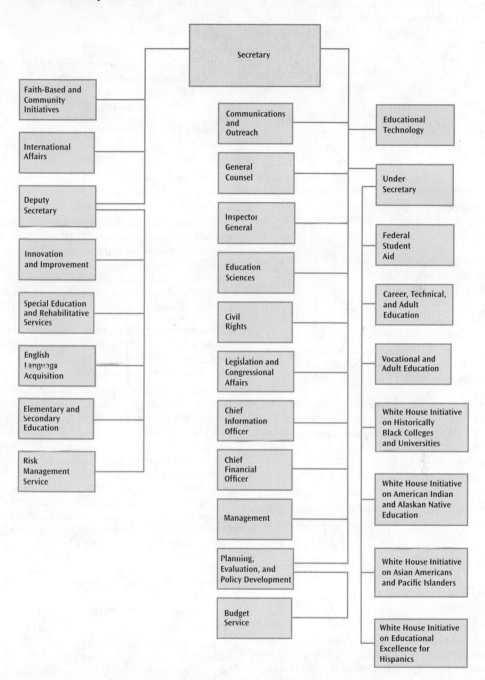

Research and informational organization that promotes education reform through grassroots advocacy. Interests include charter school laws, school choice programs, teacher qualifications, and educational standards. Web site serves as a networking forum for parents, educators, policymakers, and others interested in education reform, providing news reports and information on education seminars throughout the country.

Center for Law and Education, *7101 Holly Ave., Takoma Park, MD 20912-4225; (202) 986-3000. Fax, (202)*

986-6648. Paul Weckstein, Co-Director, (202) 986-3000, ext. 101; Kathleen Boundy, Co-Director (located in Boston). General email, cle@cleweb.org

Web, www.cleweb.org

Works to advance the right of all students, in particular those from low-income families, to a high-quality education. Focuses on assessments, testing, and tracking; rights of students with disabilities (including special education); students with limited English proficiency, including bilingual education; implementation of key parent participation provisions under Title 1; vocational education; excessive/discriminatory discipline; and the education of youth in juvenile justice facilities. (Headquarters in Boston, Mass.)

Council for Advancement and Support of Education, *1307 New York Ave. N.W., #1000, 20005-4701; (202) 328-2273. Fax, (202) 387-4973. Sue Cunningham, President.*
General email, memberservicecenter@case.org
Web, www.case.org and Twitter, @CASEAdvance

Membership: two-year and four-year colleges, universities, and independent schools. Offers professional education and training programs to members; advises members on institutional advancement issues, including fundraising, public relations programs, government relations, and management. Library open to professional members by appointment.

DECA Inc., *1908 Association Dr., Reston, VA 20191-1594; (703) 860-5000. Fax, (703) 860-4013. Paul Wardinski, Executive Director.*
General email, info@deca.org
Web, www.deca.org

Educational organization that helps high school and college students develop skills in marketing, management, and entrepreneurship. Promotes business and education partnerships.

Ethics Research and Compliance Initiative, *2345 Crystal Dr., #201, Arlington, VA 22202; (703) 647-2185. Fax, (703) 647-2180. Patricia J. Harned, President. Information, (800) 777-1285.*
General email, ethics@ethics.org
Web, www.ethics.org and Twitter, @ethicsRC

Nonpartisan research organization that fosters ethical practices among individuals and institutions. Interests include research, knowledge building, education, and advocacy.

Institute for Educational Leadership, *4301 Connecticut Ave. N.W., #100, 20008; (202) 822-8405. Fax, (202) 872-4050. Martin Blank, President.*
General email, iel@iel.org
Web, www.iel.org

Works with educators, human services personnel, government officials, and association executives to improve educational opportunities for youths; conducts research on education issues.

National Assn. of State Boards of Education, *333 John Carlyle St., #530, Alexandria, VA 22314; (703) 684-4000. Kristen Amundson, Executive Director.*
General email, boards@nasbe.org
Web, www.nasbe.org

Membership: members of state boards of education, state board attorneys, and executives to state boards. Works to strengthen state boards as the preeminent educational policymaking bodies for students and citizens.

National Center on Education and the Economy (NCEE), *2121 K St. N.W., #700, 20037; (202) 379-1800. Fax, (202) 293-1560. Marc S. Tucker, President.*
General email, info@ncee.org
Web, www.ncee.org

Provides research, analysis, advocacy, tools, and technical assistance to improve the nation's school systems and student performances. (Administers the National Institute for School Leadership.)

National Children's Museum,
Vacant, Executive Director.
General email, info@ncm.museum
Press email, media@ncm.museum
Web, www.ncm.museum and Facebook, www.facebook .com/NationalChildrensMuseum

A cultural and educational institution serving children and families onsite and through national partners and programs. Exhibits and activities focus on the arts, civic engagement, the environment, global citizenship, health and well-being, and play. Affiliated with the Association of Children's Museums Reciprocal Network. (In the process of moving to Washington, DC)

National Governors Assn. (NGA), *Center for Best Practices, Education Division, 444 N. Capitol St. N.W., #267, 20001-1512; (202) 624-7801. Richard Laine, Director.*
Web, www.nga.org/cms/center/edu

Provides information, research, policy analysis, and technical assistance to governors and their staff in the areas of early childhood, K–12, and postsecondary education. Focus areas include early education access, readiness, and quality; teacher and principal preparation, evaluation, and professional development; postsecondary education standards and assessments, including Common Core Standards, Science, Technology, Engineering, and Math (STEM), and ready assessments; competency-based learning and charter schools; higher education and career training access, success, and affordability; and finance, data, and accountability.

National Humanities Institute (NHI), *P.O. Box 1387, Bowie, MD 20718-1387; (301) 464-4277. Fax, (301) 464-4277. Michael P. Federici, President.*
General email, mail@nhinet.org
Web, www.nhinet.org

Promotes research, publishing, and teaching in the humanities. Interests include the effect of the humanities on society. Publishes *Humanitas* journal.

National Institute for School Leadership, Inc. (NISL), *2121 K St. N.W., #700, 20037; (202) 449-5060. Fax, (202) 293-1560. Jason Dougal, Chief Operating Officer.*
General email, info@ncee.org
Web, www.nisl.net

Offers research-based professional development programs designed to give principals the knowledge and skills they need to be instructional leaders and improve student achievement in their schools. (Subsidiary of National Center on Education and the Economy [NCEE].)

National Research Council (NRC), *Testing and Assessment Board, Keck Center, 500 5th St. N.W., 20001; (202) 334-2000. Patricia Morison, Director, Acting; David J. Francis, Chair.*
General email, bota@nas.edu

Web, http://sites.nationalacademies.org/dbasse/bota

Assists policymakers by providing scientific expertise about critical issues of testing and assessment in education and the workplace.

National School Public Relations Assn., *15948 Derwood Rd., Rockville, MD 20855; (301) 519-0496. Fax, (301) 519-0494. Richard D. Bagin, Executive Director.*
General email, info@nspra.org

Web, www.nspra.org

Membership: educators and individuals interested in improving communications in education. Works to improve communication between educators and the public on the needs of schools. Provides educators with information on public relations and policy developments.

Internships, Fellowships, Grants

▶ AGENCIES

Bureau of Educational and Cultural Affairs *(State Dept.), Academic Exchange Programs, 2200 C St. N.W., #4-B06/SA-5, 20520; (202) 632-3234. Mary Kirk, Director. Web, http://eca.state.gov/about-bureau-0/organizational-structure/office-academic-exchanges*

Provides opportunities for international study and research from the undergraduate through postdoctoral and professional levels. Works with the Fulbright Program, Critical Language Scholarship Program, Global Undergraduate Exchange Program, Edmund S. Muskie Graduate Fellowship Program, and Study of the United States Institutes.

Bureau of Educational and Cultural Affairs *(State Dept.), Global Educational Programs, 2200 C St. N.W., #4-CC17/SA-5, 20520; (202) 632-6345. Anthony D. Koliha, Director.*
Web, http://eca.state.gov/about-bureau-0/organizational-structure/office-global-educational-programs

Administers the Hubert H. Humphrey Fellowship Program, the Community College Initiative Program, and the Benjamin A. Gilman International Scholarship Program, and programs for the exchange and professional development of secondary school teachers and educators.

Harry S. Truman Scholarship Foundation, *712 Jackson Pl. N.W., 3rd Floor, 20006-4901; (202) 395-4831. Fax, (202) 395-6995. Andrew Rich, Executive Secretary, (202) 395-3545.*
General email, office@truman.gov

Web, www.truman.gov and Twitter, @TrumanApp

Memorial to Harry S. Truman established by Congress. Provides students preparing for careers in public service with graduate school scholarship funding. (Candidates are nominated by their respective colleges or universities while in their third year of undergraduate study.)

National Endowment for the Arts (NEA), *400 7th St. S.W., 20506; (202) 682-5400. Jane Chu, Chair, (202) 682-5414. Press, (202) 682-5570. TTY, (202) 682-5496.*
General email, webmgr@arts.gov

Web, www.arts.gov, Twitter, @NEAarts and Facebook, www.facebook.com/NationalEndowmentfortheArts

Independent grant-making agency. Awards grants to support artistic excellence, creativity, and innovation for the benefit of individuals and communities. Works through partnerships with state arts agencies, local leaders, other federal agencies, and the philanthropic sector. Main funding categories include Art Works (replaces Access to Artistic Excellence and Learning in the Arts for Children and Youth); Challenge America Fast-Track (for art projects in underserved communities); and Our Town (for art projects that contribute to the livability of communities).

National Endowment for the Humanities (NEH), *400 7th St. S.W., 20506; Fax, (202) 606-8608. William Adams, Chair, (202) 606-8310; Donna McClish, Librarian; Katja Zelljadt, Director, Challenge Grants. Information, (202) 606-8400. Toll-free, 800-NEH-1121. Library, (202) 606-8244. Public Affairs, (202) 606-8446, TTY, (202) 606-8282. Toll-free TTY, (866) 372-2930.*
General email, info@neh.gov

Web, www.neh.gov and Facebook, www.facebook.com/National-Endowment-for-the-Humanities-131252093552454

Independent federal grant making agency. Awards grants to individuals and institutions for research, scholarship, and educational and public programs (including broadcasts, museum exhibitions, lectures, and symposia) in the humanities (defined as study of archaeology; history; jurisprudence; language; linguistics; literature; philosophy; comparative religion; ethics; history, criticism, and theory of the arts; and humanistic aspects of the social sciences). Funds preservation of books, newspapers, historical documents, and photographs. Library open by appointment only.

National Endowment for the Humanities (NEH), *Education Programs, 400 7th St. S.W., 20506; (202) 606-8500. Fax, (202) 606-8394. William Craig Rice, Director.*
General email, education@neh.gov

Web, www.neh.gov/divisions/education

Offers seminars and institutes for higher education faculty, school teachers, and independent scholars. Promotes research and development.

National Institute of Food and Agriculture (NIFA) *(Agriculture Dept.), Institute of Youth, Family, and Community, 800 9th St. S.W., #4343, 20024 (mailing address: 1400 Independence Ave. S.W., MS 2250, Washington, DC 20250-2225); (202) 720-5305. Fax, (202) 720-3945. Muquarrab Qureshi, Deputy Director.*
Web, www.nifa.usda.gov/office/institute-youth-family-and-community

Provides grants and programmatic training to support youth and family development; partners with county governments, the private sector, and state land-grant universities. Program areas include food and agricultural science education, particularly in minority-serving institutions; childhood nutrition; community food projects; and community service. Includes divisions of Community Education, Family and Consumer Sciences, and Youth and 4-H.

National Science Foundation (NSF), *Graduate Education Division*, *4201 Wilson Blvd., #875S, Arlington, VA 22230; (703) 292-8630. Fax, (703) 292-9048. Dean Evasius, Division Director. TTY, (800) 281-8749. Web, www.nsf.gov/div/index.jsp?div=dge*

Supports activities to strengthen the education of research scientists and engineers; promotes career development; offers pre doctoral fellowships and traineeships for study and research.

President's Commission on White House Fellowships, *712 Jackson Pl. N.W., 20503; (202) 395-4522. Fax, (202) 395-6179. Jennifer Yeager Kaplan, Director. General email, whitehousefellows@whf.eop.gov Web, www.whitehouse.gov/about/fellows*

Nonpartisan commission that provides professionals from all sectors of national life with the opportunity to observe firsthand the processes of the federal government. Fellows work for one year as special assistants to cabinet members or to principal members of the White House staff. Qualified applicants have demonstrated superior accomplishments early in their careers and have a commitment to leadership and public service.

Smithsonian Institution, *Fellowships and Internships*, *470 L'Enfant Plaza S.W., #7102, 20013 (mailing address: P.O. Box 37012, MRC 902, Washington, DC 20013-7012); (202) 633-7070. Fax, (202) 633-7069. Eric Woodard, Director. General email, siofi@si.edu Web, www.smithsonianofi.com*

Administers internships and fellowships in residence for study and research at the Smithsonian Institution in history of science and technology, American and cultural history, history of art, anthropology, evolutionary and systematic biology, environmental sciences, astrophysics and astronomy, earth sciences, and tropical biology.

Woodrow Wilson International Center for Scholars, *1300 Pennsylvania Ave. N.W., 20004-3027; (202) 691-4000. Fax, (202) 691-4001. Jane Harman, President, (202) 691-4202; Blair A. Ruble, Vice President for Programs. Press, (202) 691-4217. General email, wwics@wilsoncenter.org Library, library.email@wilsoncenter.org Fellowship information, fellowships@wilsoncenter.org Web, www.wilsoncenter.org and Twitter, @thewilsoncenter*

Supports research in the social studies and humanities. Awards fellowships to individuals from a wide variety of backgrounds, including academia, government, the nonprofit sector, and the corporate world. Hosts public policy and senior scholars who conduct research and write in a variety of disciplines. Offers grant competitions through regional programs, including the Asia Program, the Kennan Institute, East European Studies, and the Canada Institute.

▶ NONGOVERNMENTAL

American Architectural Foundation, *750 15th St. N.W., #225, 20005; (202) 787-1001. Fax, (202) 787-1002. Ronald E. Bogle, President. General email, info@archfoundation.org Web, www.archfoundation.org*

Seeks to advance the quality of American architecture. Works to increase public awareness and understanding and to apply new technology to create more humane environments. Acts as liaison between the profession and the public. Awards grants for architecture-oriented projects. Operates the historic Octagon Museum.

American Assn. of University Women (AAUW), *1111 16th St. N.W., 20036-4873; (202) 785-7700. Fax, (202) 872-1425. Linda D. Hallman, Chief Executive Officer. Toll-free, (800) 326-2289. TTY, (202) 785-7777. General email, connect@aauw.org Web, www.aauw.org*

Awards fellowships and grants to women for various areas of study and educational pursuit. Offers fellowships to foreign women coming to the United States for one year of graduate study. Awards grants to women returning to school for postbaccalaureate education or professional development.

American Political Science Assn. (APSA), *Congressional Fellowship Program*, *1527 New Hampshire Ave. N.W., 20036-1206; (202) 483-2512. Fax, (202) 483-2657. Kara Abramson, Program Director. General email, cfp@apsanet.org Web, www.apsanet.org/cfp*

Places midcareer political scientists, journalists, faculty of medical schools (Robert Wood Johnson Fellowships, Health and Aging Policy Fellowships), and federal executives in congressional offices and committees for nine-month fellowships. Individual government agencies nominate federal executive participants.

Center for the Study of the Presidency and Congress, *601 13th St., N.W., #1050N, 20005; (202) 872-9800. Fax, (202) 872-9811. Maximillian Angerholtzer III, President. General email, ann.packo@thepresidency.org Web, www.thepresidency.org*

Provides fellowships to undergraduate and graduate students studying the U.S. presidency, the public policy-making process, the presidential relations with Congress, allies, the media, and the public.

Congressional Black Caucus Foundation, *1720 Massachusetts Ave. N.W., 20036-1903; (202) 263-2800. Fax, (202) 775-0773. A. Shuanise Washington, President.*

General email, info@cbcfinc.org

Web, www.cbcfinc.org and Twitter, @CBCFInc

Conducts public policy research on issues of concern to African Americans. Sponsors internships and scholarships, as well as fellowship programs in which professionals and academic candidates work on congressional committees and subcommittees.

Council for International Exchange of Scholars, 1400 K St. N.W., #700, 20005; (202) 686-4000. Fax, (202) 686-4029. Maria de los Angeles Crummett, Executive Director, (202) 686-4001.

General email, scholars@iie.org

Web, www.cies.org

Cooperates with the U.S. government in administering Fulbright grants for university teaching and advanced research abroad. (A division of the Institute of International Education.)

Council on Foundations, 2121 Crystal Dr., #700, Arlington, VA 22202; (703) 879-0600. Vikki N. Spruill, President. Toll-free, (800) 673-9036.

General email, membership@cof.org

Web, www.cof.org and Twitter, @COF_

Membership: independent community, family, and public-sponsored and company-sponsored foundations; corporate giving programs, and foundations in other countries. Promotes responsible and effective philanthropy through educational programs, publications, government relations, and promulgation of a set of principles and practices for effective grant making.

Education Trust, 1250 H St. N.W., #700, 20005; (202) 293-1217. Fax, (202) 293-2605. Kati Haycock, President; Loretta Singleton, Communications.

General email, lsingleton@edtrust.org

Web, www.edtrust.org

Researches and disseminates data on student achievement. Provides assistance to school districts, colleges, and other organizations to raise student achievement, especially among poor and minority students. Monitors legislation and regulations.

Foundation Center, Washington Field Office, 1627 K St. N.W., 3rd Floor, 20006-1708; (202) 331-1400. Fax, (202) 331-1739. Kim Patton, Director.

General email, jzr@foundationcenter.org

Web, www.foundationcenter.org/washington

http://grantspace.org and Twitter, @FCWashington

Publishes foundation guides and electronic databases. Serves as a clearinghouse on foundations and corporate giving, nonprofit management, fundraising, and grants for individuals. Provides training and seminars on fundraising and grant writing. Operates libraries in Atlanta, Cleveland, New York, San Francisco, and Washington, D.C.; library catalog available on the Web site. Libraries open to the public. (Headquarters in New York.)

The Fund for American Studies (TFAS), 1706 New Hampshire Ave. N.W., 20009; (202) 986-0384. Fax, (202) 986-0390. Roger R. Ream, President.

General email, info@tfas.org

Web, www.tfas.org

Sponsors internships for college students on comparative political and economic systems, business and government affairs, political journalism, philanthropy, and voluntary service; grants scholarships. Interests include political and economic freedoms.

The Herb Block Foundation, 1730 M St. N.W., #901, 20036; (202) 223-8801. Fax, (202) 223-8804. Marcela Brane, President; Sarah Alex, Executive Director.

General email, info@herbblock.org

Web, www.herbblockfoundation.org

Awards grants to charitable and educational programs that combat discrimination and poverty, and promote citizen involvement in government. Provides scholarships to individuals seeking to attend community colleges in the Washington, D.C., area. Awards prizes for excellence in editorial cartooning to serve as as a tool for freedom and to address social issues.

Institute for Responsible Citizenship, 1227 25th St. N.W., 6th Floor, 20037; (202) 660-2501. William A. Keyes, President.

Web, www.theinstitute.net

Offers grants, internships, and leadership courses for African American men scholars. Academic areas for internships include art, business, finance, philanthropy, education, government, science, law, public relations, medicine, journalism, and religion.

Institute of Current World Affairs, 1779 Massachusetts Ave. N.W., #615, 20036; (202) 364-4068. Ellen Kozak, Program Manager.

General email, icwa@icwa.org

Web, www.icwa.org

Offers two-year fellowships to support the independent study of international region-specific issues. Fellows write monthly newsletters to update the institute on their progress and findings.

Institute of International Education, National Security Education Program, 1101 Wilson Blvd., #1210, Arlington, VA 22209 (mailing address: P.O. Box 20010, Arlington, VA 22209); (571) 256-0711. Fax, (703) 696-5667. Michael Nugent, Director. Information, (800) 618-6737.

General email, nsep@nsep.gov

Web, www.nsep.gov

Administers Boren Awards and Language Flagship programs; provides scholarships, fellowships, and institutional grants to students and academics with an interest in foreign affairs and national security.

National Journalism Center, 11480 Commerce Park Dr., #600, Reston, VA 20191; Fax, (703) 318-9122. Vacant, Executive Director. Toll-free, (800) 872-1776.

Web, www.nationaljournalismcenter.org

Sponsors a comprehensive internship program in journalism composed of a series of training seminars that enhance students' knowledge of policy reporting in the areas of economics, education, and business. (Affliliated with the Young America's Foundation.)

The Next Generation Initiative, *P.O. Box 7322, Arlington, VA 22207; (202) 360-5119. Fax, (703) 532-7130. Leon Stavrou, Executive Director.*
General email, info@hellenext.org
Web, www.hellenext.org

Assists students in obtaining career internships and fellowships related to their academic field. Connects students to mentors in their profession of interest. Offers academic scholarships and provides leadership programs to encourage students to participate in public service.

The Washington Center for Internships and Academic Seminars, *1333 16th St. N.W., 20036-2205; (202) 238-7900. Fax, (202) 238-7700. Christopher Norton, President. Information, (800) 486-8921.*
General email, info@twc.edu
Web, www.twc.edu and Twitter, @TWCInternships

Arranges congressional, agency, and public service internships for college undergraduate students for credit. Sponsors classes and lectures as part of the internship program. Scholarships and stipends available. Fee for internship and housing assistance.

Washington Center for Politics and Journalism, *600 New Hampshire Ave. N.W., #4, 20037 (mailing address: P.O. Box 15603, Washington, DC 20003-0603); (202) 210-8455. Terry Michael, Executive Director.*
General email, terrymichael@wcpj.org
Web, www.wcpj.org

Offers internships in political journalism to undergraduate and graduate students and recent graduates; provides a $3,000 stipend for living expenses. The Politics & Journalism Semester provides for free sixteen-week fall and winter/spring sessions, which include full-time work in Washington news bureaus and twice-weekly seminars in campaign, governance, and interest-group politics for future political reporters.

Women's Research and Education Institute (WREI), *3808 Brighton Ct., Alexandria, VA 22305; (703) 837-1977. Susan Scanlan, President.*
General email, wrei@wrei.org
Web, www.wrei.org

Provides data and analysis of issues affecting women and their families to policymakers, the press, and the public. Its Women in the Military project acts as an advocate on policy issues affecting women in uniform through publications and conferences.

Professional Interests and Benefits

▶**NONGOVERNMENTAL**

American Assn. of Colleges for Teacher Education, *1307 New York Ave. N.W., #300, 20005-4701; (202) 293-2450. Fax, (202) 457-8095. Sharon P. Robinson,*

President, (202) 478-4505.
General email, aacte@aacte.org
Web, www.aacte.org

Membership: colleges and universities with teacher education programs. Informs members about state and federal policies affecting teacher education and about professional issues such as accreditation, certification, and assessment. Collects and analyzes information on education.

American Assn. of School Administrators, *1615 Duke St., Alexandria, VA 22314; (703) 528-0700. Fax, (703) 841-1543. Daniel Domenech, Executive Director.*
General email, info@aasa.org
Web, www.aasa.org

Membership: more than 13,000 educational leaders, including superintendents, chief executive officers, senior-level school administrators, and professors, as well as aspiring school system leaders. Seeks to support and develop effective school system leaders through publications and professional development workshops.

American Federation of School Administrators, *1101 17th St. N.W., #408, 20036-4704; (202) 986-4209. Fax, (202) 986-4211. Diann Woodard, President.*
General email, afsa@afsaadmin.org
Web, www.afsaadmin.org

Membership: approximately 20,000 school administrators, including principals, vice principals, directors, and supervisors in the United States, Puerto Rico, and U.S. Virgin Islands. Helps members negotiate pay, benefits, and better working conditions; conducts training programs and workshops. Monitors legislation and regulations. (Affiliated with the AFL-CIO.)

American Federation of Teachers (AFT), *555 New Jersey Ave. N.W., 20001-2079; (202) 879-4400. Fax, (202) 879-4556. Randi Weingarten, President.*
General email, online@aft.org
Web, www.aft.org

Membership: 1.5 million public school teachers and staff, higher education faculty and staff, state and local government employees, and nurses and health care professionals. Assists members with contract negotiation and grievances; conducts training programs and workshops. Monitors legislation and regulations. (Affiliated with the AFL-CIO.)

American Political Science Assn. (APSA), *1527 New Hampshire Ave. N.W., 20036-1206; (202) 483-2512. Fax, (202) 483-2657. Steven Rathgeb Smith, Executive Director.*
General email, apsa@apsanet.org
Web, www.apsanet.org and Twitter, @APSAtweets

Membership: political scientists, primarily college and university professors. Promotes scholarly inquiry into all aspects of political science, including international affairs and comparative government. Works to increase public understanding of politics; provides services to facilitate and enhance research, teaching, and professional development of its members. Acts as liaison with federal agencies,

Congress, and the public. Seeks to improve the status of women and minorities in the profession. Offers congressional fellowships, workshops, and awards. Provides information on political science issues.

Assn. of School Business Officials International, *11401 N. Shore Dr., Reston, VA 20190-4232; (703) 478-0405. Fax, (703) 478-0205. John Musso, Executive Director. Toll-free, (866) 682-2729.*
General email, asboreq@asbointl.org
Web, www.asbointl.org and Twitter, @ASBOUSA

Membership: administrators, directors, and others involved in school business management. Provides news and information concerning management best practices and the effective use of educational resources. Hosts conferences; sponsors research; monitors legislation and regulations.

Assn. of Teacher Educators, *11350 Random Hills Rd., #800, Fairfax, VA 22030 (mailing address: P.O. Box 793, Manassas, VA 20113); (703) 659-1708. Fax, (703) 595-4792. David A. Ritchey, Executive Director.*
General email, info@ate1.org
Web, www.ate1.org and Twitter, @AssocTeacherEd

Membership: individuals and public and private agencies involved with teacher education. Seeks to improve teacher education at all levels; conducts workshops and conferences; produces and disseminates publications.

Council of Chief State School Officers, *1 Massachusetts Ave. N.W., #700, 20001-1431; (202) 336-7000. Fax, (202) 408-8072. Chris Minnich, Executive Director. Press, (202) 336-7034.*
General email, communications@ccsso.org
Web, www.ccsso.org and Twitter, @CCSSO

Membership: the public officials who head departments of elementary and secondary education in the states, the District of Columbia, the Department of Defense Education Activity, and five U.S. extrastate jurisdictions. Provides leadership, advocacy, and technical assistance on major educational issues. Seeks member consensus on major educational issues and advocates issue positions to civic and professional organizations, federal agencies, Congress, and the public.

Federal Education Assn., *1201 16th St. N.W., #117, 20036; (202) 822-7850. Fax, (202) 822-7867. Chuck McCarter, President.*
General email, fea@feaonline.org
Web, www.feaonline.org

Membership: teachers and personnel of Defense Dept. schools for military dependents in the United States and abroad. Helps members negotiate pay, benefits, and better working conditions. Provides professional development through workshops and publications. Monitors legislation and regulations.

International Test and Evaluation Assn., *4400 Fair Lakes Court, #104, Fairfax, VA 22033-3801; (703) 631-6220. Fax, (703) 631-6221. James M. Gaidry, Executive Director, ext. 204.*

General email, info@itea.org
Web, www.itea.org

Membership: engineers, scientists, managers, and other industry, government, and academic professionals interested in testing and evaluating products and complex systems. Provides a forum for information exchange; monitors international research.

National Assn. of Biology Teachers, *11 Main St., Suite D, Warrenton, VA 20186 (mailing address: P.O. Box 3363, Warrenton, VA 20188); (703) 264-9696. Fax, (703) 435-4390. Jaclyn Reeves-Pepin, Executive Director. Information, (888) 501-6228.*
General email, office@nabt.org
Web, www.nabt.org

Membership: biology teachers and others interested in life sciences education at the elementary, secondary, and collegiate levels. Provides professional development opportunities through its publication program, summer workshops, conventions, and national award programs. Interests include teaching standards, science curriculum, and issues affecting biology and life sciences education.

National Business Education Assn., *1914 Association Dr., Reston, VA 20191-1596; (703) 860-8300. Fax, (703) 620-4483. Janet M. Treichel, Executive Director*
General email, nbea@nbea.org
Web, www.nbea.org

Membership: business education teachers and others interested in the field. Provides information on business education; offers teaching materials; sponsors conferences. Monitors legislation and regulations affecting business education.

National Council for the Social Studies (NCSS), *8555 16th St., #500, Silver Spring, MD 20910; (301) 588-1800. Fax, (301) 588-2049. Susan Griffin, Executive Director, ext. 103. Publications, (800) 683-0812.*
General email, information@ncss.org
Web, www.socialstudies.org and Twitter, @NCSSNetwork

Membership: curriculum developers, educational administrators, state supervisors, and social studies educators, including K–12 classroom teachers and university professors of history, political science, geography, economics, civics, psychology, sociology, and anthropology. Promotes the teaching of social studies; encourages research; sponsors publications; works with other organizations to advance social studies education.

National Council of Teachers of Mathematics, *1906 Association Dr., Reston, VA 20191-1502; (703) 620-9840. Fax, (703) 476-2970. Robert M. Doucette, Executive Director. Toll-free, (800) 235-7566.*
General email, nctm@nctm.org
Web, www.nctm.org, Twitter, @NCTM and Facebook, www.facebook.com/TeachersofMathematics

Membership: mathematics educators, researchers, students, and other interested persons. Works for the improvement of classroom instruction at all levels. Serves as forum and information clearinghouse on issues related to mathematics education. Offers educational materials and conferences. Monitors legislation and regulations.

National Council on Teacher Quality, *1120 G St. N.W., #800, 20005; (202) 393-0020. Fax, (202) 393-0095. Kate Walsh, President.*
Web, www.nctq.org, www.pathtoteach.org, Twitter, @NCTQ and Facebook, www.facebook.com/teacherquality

Advocacy group for teacher quality and effectiveness. Interests include state and district teacher policy reform. Reviews and reports on national teacher training programs, layoff policies, teacher contracts, and state performance. Analyzes school board policies, teacher performance evaluations, and salary schedules to aid dialogue between school officials and teachers unions.

National Education Assn. (NEA), *1201 16th St. N.W., 20036-3290; (202) 833-4000. Fax, (202) 822-7974. Lily Eskelson Garcia, President; John C. Stocks, Executive Director. Press, (202) 822-7823.*
Web, www.nea.org

Membership: more than 3.2 million educators from preschool to university graduate programs. Promotes the interest of the profession of teaching and the cause of education in the United States. Monitors legislation and regulations at state and national levels.

National Science Teachers Assn., *1840 Wilson Blvd., Arlington, VA 22201-3000; (703) 243-7100. Fax, (703) 243-7177. David L. Evans, Executive Director.*
Web, www.nsta.org

Membership: science teachers from elementary through college levels. Seeks to improve science education; provides forum for exchange of information. Monitors legislation and regulations.

NEA Foundation, *1201 16th St. N.W., #416, 20036-3207; (202) 822-7840. Fax, (202) 822-7779. Harriet Sanford, President.*
General email, NEAFoundation@nea.org
Web, www.neafoundation.org

Offers grants and programs to public educators to improve teaching techniques, increase classroom innovations, and otherwise further professional development. Grant areas include science, technology, engineering, and mathematics teaching and learning, with a current special emphasis on "green" grants. Program specialties include strategies for improving achievement rates for poor and minority students.

NRTA: AARP's Educator Community, *601 E St. N.W., 20049; (202) 434-2380. Fax, (202) 434-3439. Dara L. Dann, Vice President. Information, (888) 687-2277.*
General email, gruiz@aarp.org
Web, www.aarp.org/nrta

Membership: active and retired teachers, other school personnel (elementary through postsecondary), and those interested in education and learning over age fifty. Provides members with information on relevant national issues. Provides state associations of retired school personnel

with technical assistance. (Formerly the National Retired Teachers Assn.)

Teachers of English to Speakers of Other Languages Inc. (TESOL), *1925 Ballenger Ave., #550, Alexandria, VA 22314-6820; (703) 836-0774. Fax, (703) 836-7864. Rosa Aronson, Executive Director, ext. 505. Information, (888) 891-0041.*
General email, info@tesol.org
Web, www.tesol.org

Provides professional development programs and career services for teachers of English to speakers of other languages. Sponsors professional development programs and provides career management services.

Research

▶**AGENCIES**

Education Dept., *National Library of Education, 400 Maryland Ave. S.W., 20202-5721; (202) 205-5015. Fax, (202) 401-0547. Pamela Tripp-Melby, Director, (202) 453-6536. Information, (800) 424-1616. TTY, (800) 877-8339. Reference, (202) 205-5015.*
General email, askalibrarian@ed.gov
Web, http://ies.ed.gov/ncee/projects/nle

Federal government's main resource center for education information. Provides information, statistical, and referral services to the Education Dept. and other government agencies, the education community, and the public. Collection focuses on education research, but also includes fields such as law, public policy, economics, urban affairs, and sociology. Includes current and historical Education Dept. publications. Provides information and answers questions on education statistics and research. Library open to the public by appointment only.

Institute of Education Sciences *(Education Dept.), 400 Maryland Ave. S.W., 20202; (202) 219-1385. Fax, (202) 245-6752. Ruth Nield, Director. Library, (202) 205-4945.*
General email, contact.ies@ed.gov
Web, www.ies.ed.gov and Twitter, @IESResearch

Provides evidence on which to ground education practice and policy through the work of four centers dealing with education research, education statistics, education evaluation and regional assistance, and special education research. Funds studies on ways to improve academic achievement, conducts large-scale evaluations of federal education programs, and reports a wide array of statistics on the condition of education.

Institute of Education Sciences *(Education Dept.), National Center for Education Evaluation and Regional Assistance, 555 New Jersey Ave. N.W., #500E, 20208-5500; (202) 208-1200. Ruth Nield, Commissioner.*
Web, www.ies.ed.gov/ncee

Conducts large-scale evaluations of education programs and practices supported by federal funds; provides research-based technical assistance to educators and policymakers; and supports the synthesis and dissemination of the results of research and evaluation.

Institute of Education Sciences *(Education Dept.),* *National Center for Education Research,* 550 12th St. S.W., 20004; (202) 245-8123. Thomas W. Brock, Commissioner.
Web, www.ies.ed.gov/ncer

Supports research that addresses the nation's education needs, from early childhood to adult education.

Institute of Education Sciences *(Education Dept.),* *National Center for Education Statistics,* 550 12th St. S.W., 20202; (202) 403-5551. Fax, (202) 245-6101. Peggy G. Carr, Commissioner, Acting, (202) 245-6168.
Web, https://nces.ed.gov

Primary federal entity for collecting and analyzing data related to education. Administers the National Assessment of Educational Progress (NAEP), the "Nation's Report Card."

Institute of Education Sciences *(Education Dept.),* *National Center for Special Education Research,* 555 New Jersey Ave. N.W., #510F, 20208-5500; (202) 219-1309. Fax, (202) 219-1402. Joan McLaughlin, Commissioner.
Web, www.ies.ed.gov/ncser

Sponsors a comprehensive program of special education research designed to expand the knowledge and understanding of infants, toddlers, and children with disabilities.

▶**NONGOVERNMENTAL**

American Councils for International Education: ACTR/ ACCELS, 1828 L St. N.W., #1200, 20036; (202) 833-7522. Fax, (202) 833-7523. Dan E. Davidson, President.
General email, general@americancouncils.org
Web, www.americancouncils.org

Advances education and research worldwide through international programs focused on academic exchange, professional training, distance learning, curriculum and test development, delivery of technical assistance, research, evaluation, and institution building.

American Educational Research Assn., 1430 K St. N.W., #1200, 20005; (202) 238-3200. Fax, (202) 238-3250. Felice J. Levine, Executive Director.
General email, members@aera.net
Web, www.aera.net

Membership: educational researchers affiliated with universities and colleges, school systems, think tanks, and federal and state agencies. Publishes original research in education; sponsors publication of reference works in educational research; conducts continuing education programs; studies status of women and minorities in the education field.

American Institutes for Research, 1000 Thomas Jefferson St. N.W., 20007; (202) 403-5000. Fax, (202) 403-5001. David Myers, President. TTY, (877) 334-3499. Media, (202) 403-6043.

General email, inquiry@air.org
Web, www.air.org and Twitter, @AIR_Info

Conducts research on educational evaluation and improvement. Develops and implements assessment and testing services that improve student education as well as meet the requirements set forth by state and federally mandated programs.

The Brookings Institution, *Governance Studies,* 1755 Massachusetts Ave. N.W., 20036; (202) 797-6090. Fax, (202) 797-6144. Darrell M. West, Director, (202) 797-6481. Information, (202) 797-6000. Press, (202) 797-6105.
Web, www.brookings.edu/governance

Conducts research and provides policy recommendations on topics in education.

Council on Governmental Relations, 1200 New York Ave. N.W., #460, 20005; (202) 289-6655. Fax, (202) 289-6698. Anthony DeCrappeo, President.
Web, www.cogr.edu

Membership: research universities, institutes, and medical colleges maintaining federally supported programs. Advises members and makes recommendations to government agencies regarding policies and regulations affecting federally funded university research.

Knowledge Alliance, 20 F St. N.W., #700, 20001; (202) 507-6370. Michele McLaughlin, President.
General email, waters@knowledgeall.net
Web, www.knowledgeall.net

Membership: university-based educational research and development organizations, educational entrepreneurs, and technical assistance providers. Promotes use of scientifically based solutions for improving teaching and learning. (Formerly the National Education Knowledge Industry Assn.)

National Assn. of Independent Colleges and Universities, 1025 Connecticut Ave. N.W., #700, 20036-5405; (202) 785-8866. Fax, (202) 835-0003. David L. Warren, President.
General email, geninfo@naicu.edu
Web, www.naicu.edu

Membership: liberal arts colleges, research universities, church-related and faith-related institutions, historically black colleges and universities, women's colleges, performing and visual arts institutions, two-year colleges; graduate schools of law, medicine, engineering, business, and other professions. Tracks campus trends, conducts research, analyzes higher education issues, and helps coordinate state-level activities. Interests include federal policies that affect student aid, taxation, and government regulation. Monitors legislation and regulations.

RAND Corporation, *Washington Office,* 1200 S. Hayes St., Arlington, VA 22202-5050; (703) 413-1100. Fax, (703) 413-8111. Richard M. Moore, Director, ext. 5399; Anita Chandra, Director, Justice, Infrastructure, and Environment, ext. 5323.
Web, www.rand.org

Research organization partially funded by federal agencies. Conducts research on education policy. (Headquarters in Santa Monica, Calif.)

LIBRARIES, TECHNOLOGY, AND EDUCATIONAL MEDIA

General

▶AGENCIES

Institute of Museums and Libraries, *955 L'Enfant Plaza North S.W., #4000, 20024; Fax, (202) 653-4600. Kathryn K. Matthew, Director. Main IMLS office, (202) 653-4700. Library Services, (202) 653-4700. Museum Services, (202) 653-4789. Communications and Government Affairs, (202) 653-4799. TTY, (202) 653-4614. General email, imlsinfo@imls.gov*

Web, www.imls.gov and Twitter, @US_IMLS

Awards federal grants to support learning experiences in all types of libraries and all types of museums, including opportunities for formal and informal learning, 21st-century skills development, STEM (science, technology, engineering, and math), and early learning. Promotes access to information through electronic networks, links between libraries, and services to individuals having difficulty using a library. Provides federal grants for improved care of museum collections and increased professional development, including the training and development of library students, librarians, and museum professionals. Provides museum grants for African American history and culture, and funding for improved library services to Native American tribal communities, Native Alaskan villages, and Native Hawaiian library users.

National Archives and Records Administration (NARA), *National Archives Museum, 700 Pennsylvania Ave. N.W., #G9, 20408; (202) 357-5210. Fax, (202) 357-5926. Lisa Royce, Director. Information, (202) 357-5000. Press, (202) 357-5300. General email, inquire@nara.gov/museum*

Web, www.archives.gov

Plans and directs activities to acquaint the public with the mission and holdings of the National Archives; conducts behind-the-scenes tours; presents hands-on workshops; develops both traditional and interactive exhibits; produces publications, including teaching packets that feature historic documents and online educational tools.

National Archives and Records Administration (NARA), *Presidential Libraries, 8601 Adelphi Rd., #2200, College Park, MD 20740-6001; (301) 837-3250. Fax, (301) 837-3199. Susan K. Donius, Director, (301) 837-1662. Web, www.archives.gov/presidential-libraries*

Administers thirteen presidential libraries. Directs all programs relating to acquisition, preservation, and research use of materials in presidential libraries; conducts oral history projects; publishes finding aids for research

sources; provides reference service, including information from and about documentary holdings. Conducts community outreach; oversees museum exhibition programming.

National Endowment for the Humanities (NEH), *Digital Humanities, 400 7th St. S.W., 20506; (202) 606-8401. Fax, (202) 606-8411. Brett Bobley, Director. General email, odh@neh.gov*

Web, www.neh.gov/divisions/odh

Encourages and supports projects that utilize or study the impact of digital technology on research, education, preservation, access, and public programming in the humanities.

National Endowment for the Humanities (NEH), *Public Programs, 400 7th St. S.W., 20506; (202) 606-8269. Fax, (202) 606-8557. Karen Mittelman, Director, (202) 606-8631. General email, publicpgms@neh.gov*

Web, www.neh.gov/divisions/public

Awards grants to libraries, museums, special projects, and media for projects that enhance public appreciation and understanding of the humanities through books and other resources in American library collections. Projects include conferences, exhibitions, essays, documentaries, radio programs, and lecture series. Promotes public appreciation of the humanities through support of quality public programs of broad significance, reach, and impact. Awards grants for projects that meet NEH goals and standards, including excellence in content and format, broad public appeal, and wide access to diverse audiences.

Smithsonian Center for Learning and Digital Access, *600 Maryland Ave. S.W., #1005W, 20024 (mailing address: P.O. Box 37012, MRC 508, Washington, DC 20013-7012); (202) 633-5330. Fax, (202) 633-5489. Stephanie Norby, Director. General email, learning@si.edu*

Web, www.smithsonianeducation.org

Serves as the Smithsonian's central education office. Provides elementary and secondary teachers with programs, publications, audiovisual materials, regional workshops, and summer courses on using museums and primary source materials as teaching tools. Publishes books and other educational materials for teachers.

Smithsonian Institution, *Office of the Director, Libraries, 10th St. and Constitution Ave. N.W., National Museum of Natural History, 20560 (mailing address: P.O. Box 37012, MRC 154, Washington, DC 20013-7012); (202) 633-2240. Fax, (202) 786-2866. Nancy E. Gwinn, Director. Web, http://library.si.edu*

Unites twenty libraries into one system supported by an online catalog of the combined collections. Maintains collection of general reference, biographical, and interdisciplinary materials; serves as an information resource on institution libraries and museum studies. Open to the public by appointment.

Libraries at Federal Departments and Agencies

DEPARTMENTS

Agriculture, (301) 504-5755

Commerce, (202) 482-1154

Defense, (703) 695-1992

Education, (202) 205-5015

Energy (Main), (202) 586-2886

Energy (Law), (202) 586-4849

Health and Human Services (Law), (202) 619-0190

Homeland Security, (831) 272-2437

Housing and Urban Development, (202) 402-2680

Interior, (202) 208-5815

Justice, (202) 532-4895

Labor, (202) 693-6600

State, (202) 647-1099

Transportation, (202) 366-3282

Treasury, (202) 622-2000

Veterans Affairs, (202) 461-7573

AGENCIES

Agency for International Development, (202) 712-0579

Commission on Civil Rights, (202) 376-8110

Commodity Futures Trading Commission, (202) 418-5254

Consumer Product Safety Commission, (301) 504-7923

Drug Enforcement Administration, (202) 307-8932

Environmental Protection Agency, (202) 566-0556

Equal Employment Opportunity Commission, (202) 663-4630

Export-Import Bank, (202) 565-3980

Federal Communications Commission, (202) 418-0450

Federal Deposit Insurance Corporation, (202) 898-3631

Federal Election Commission, (202) 694-1516

Federal Labor Relations Authority, www.flra.gov/history_index

Federal Maritime Commission, (202) 523-5762

Federal Reserve Board, (202) 452-2018

Federal Trade Commission, (202) 326-2395

Government Accountability Office (Law), (202) 512-5941

International Bank for Reconstruction and Development (World Bank)/International Monetary Fund, (202) 623-7054

Merit Systems Protection Board, (202) 653-7200

National Aeronautics and Space Administration, (202) 358-0168

National Archives and Records Administration, (301) 837-3415

National Credit Union Administration (Law), (703) 518-6540

National Endowment for the Humanities, (202) 606-8244

National Institutes of Health, (301) 496-1080 or (301) 496-5611

National Labor Relations Board, (202) 273-3720

National Library of Medicine, (301) 594-5983

National Science Foundation, (703) 292-7830

Nuclear Regulatory Commission, (301) 415-6239

Occupational Safety and Health Review Commission, (202) 606-5729

Overseas Private Investment Corporation, (202) 336-8566

Peace Corps, (202) 692-1236

Postal Regulatory Commission, (202) 789-6800

Securities and Exchange Commission, (202) 551-5450

Small Business Administration Law Library, (202) 401-8203

Smithsonian Institution, (202) 633-2240

Social Security Administration, (410) 965-6107

U.S. International Trade Commission, https://www.usitc.gov/elearning/hts/library/htms/resources1.htm

Main Library, (202) 205-2630

Law, (202) 205-3287

U.S. Postal Service, (202) 268-2904

►CONGRESS

For a listing of relevant congressional committees and subcommittees, please see page 164 or the Appendix.

Library of Congress, *101 Independence Ave. S.E., 20540; (202) 707-5000. David Mao, Librarian of Congress, Acting. Public Affairs, (202) 707-2905. General reference, (202) 707-3399. Copyright information, (202) 707-3000. Visitor information, (202) 707-8000.*

Web, www.loc.gov and General reference, www.loc.gov//rr/askalib and Copyright information, www.copyright.gov, Legislative information, www.congress.gov, Twitter, @librarycongress and Facebook, www.facebook.com/libraryofcongress

The nation's library.

Library of Congress, *Center for the Book, James Madison Memorial Bldg., 101 Independence Ave. S.E., #LM 650,*

Library of Congress Divisions and Programs

African and Middle Eastern Division, (202) 707-7937

American Folklife Center, (202) 707-5510

Asian Division, (202) 707-3766

Business Enterprises, (202) 707-3156

Cataloging Distribution Service, (202) 707-6100

Center for the Book, (202) 707-5221

Children's Literature Center, (202) 707-5535

Computer Catalog Center, (202) 707-3370

Copyright Office, (202) 707-3000 or (202) 707-9100

European Division, (202) 707-4515

Federal Library and Information Center Committee, (202) 707-4800

Geography and Map Division, (202) 707-6277

Hispanic Division, (202) 707-5397

Humanities and Social Science Division, (202) 707-3399

Interlibrary Loan Division (CALM), (202) 707-5444

Interpretive Programs, (202) 707-5223

Law Library, (202) 707-5079

Law Library Reading Room, (202) 707-5080

Local History and Genealogy Reference Services, (202) 707-3399

Manuscript Division, (202) 707-5383

Mary Pickford Theater, (202) 707-5677

Microform Reading Room, (202) 707-5471

Motion Picture, Broadcasting, and Recorded Sound Division, Audio-Visual, (202) 707-5840; Moving Image, (202) 707-8572; Recorded Sound, (202) 707-7833

Music Reference, (202) 707-5507

National Library Service for the Blind and Physically Handicapped, (202) 707-5100

Poetry and Literature Center, (202) 707-5394

Preservation Directorate, (202) 707-8345

Prints and Photographs Division, (202) 707-6394

Rare Book and Special Collections Division, (202) 707-3448

Science, Technology and Business Division, (202) 707-5639

Serial and Government Publications Division, (202) 707-5690

20540; (202) 707-5221. Fax, (202) 707-0269. John Y. Cole, Director.
General email, cfbook@loc.gov
Web, www.read.gov/cfb

Seeks to broaden public appreciation of books, reading, literacy, and libraries; sponsors lectures and conferences on the educational and cultural role of the book worldwide, including the history of books and printing, television and the printed word, and the publishing and production of books; cooperates with state centers and with other organizations. Projects and programs are privately funded except for basic administrative support from the Library of Congress.

Library of Congress, *Children's Literature Center,* Thomas Jefferson Bldg., 101 Independence Ave. S.E., #LJ 129, 20540; (202) 707-5535. Fax, (202) 707-4632. Sybille A. Jagusch, Chief.
General email, childref@loc.gov
Web, www.loc.gov/rr/child

Provides reference and information services by telephone, by correspondence, and in person; maintains reference materials on all aspects of the study of children's literature. Serves children indirectly through assistance given to teachers, librarians, and others who work with youth.

Library of Congress, *Federal Library and Information Network (FEDLINK),* John Adams Bldg., 101 Independence Ave. S.E., #LA 217, 20540; (202) 707-4800. Fax, (202) 707-4818. Meg Tulloch, Executive Director,

Acting; Robin Harvey, Editor-in-Chief, (202) 707-4820. FEDLINK hotline, (202) 707-4900.
General email, fliccffo@loc.gov
Web, www.loc.gov/flicc

Promotes better utilization of federal library and information resources by seeking to provide the most cost-effective and efficient administrative mechanisms for delivering services and materials to federal libraries and information centers; serves as a forum for discussion of federal library and information policies, programs, and procedures; helps inform Congress, federal agencies, and others concerned with libraries and information centers.

Library of Congress, *Main Reading Room,* Thomas Jefferson Bldg., 101 Independence Ave. S.E., #LJ 100, 20540-4660; (202) 707-3399. Fax, (202) 707-1957. Barbie Morland, Head.
Web, www.loc.gov/rr/main

Point of access to the general collection of books and bound periodicals as well as electronic resources including microform. Offers research orientations.

▶ **NONGOVERNMENTAL**

American Library Assn., *Washington Office,* 1615 New Hampshire Ave. N.W., 1st Floor, 20009-2520; (202) 628-8410. Fax, (202) 628-8419. Emily Sheketoff, Executive Director. Information, (800) 941-8478.
General email, alawash@alawash.org
Web, www.ala.org/offices/wo

Educational organization of librarians, trustees, and educators. Washington office monitors legislation and regulations on libraries and information science. (Headquarters in Chicago, Ill.)

Assn. for Information and Image Management (AIIM), *1100 Wayne Ave., #1100, Silver Spring, MD 20910; (301) 587-8202. Fax, (301) 587-2711. John F. Mancini, President. Information, (800) 477-2446.*
General email, aiim@aiim.org
Web, www.aiim.org and Twitter, @AIIMIntl

Membership: manufacturers and users of image-based information systems. Works to advance the profession of information management; develops training standards on information management and document formats.

Assn. for Information Science and Technology (ASIS&T), *8555 16th St., #850, Silver Spring, MD 20910; (301) 495-0900. Fax, (301) 495-0810. Richard Hill, Executive Director.*
General email, asist@asist.org
Web, www.asist.org

Membership: information specialists from such fields as computer science, linguistics, management, librarianship, engineering, law, medicine, chemistry, and education. Advocates research and development in basic and applied information science. Offers continuing education programs.

Assn. of Research Libraries (ARL), *21 Dupont Circle N.W., #800, 20036-1118; (202) 296-2296. Fax, (202) 872-0884. Elliott Shore, Executive Director.*
General email, webmgr@arl.org
Web, www.arl.org and Twitter, @ARLnews

Membership: major research libraries, mainly at universities, in the United States and Canada. Interests include development of library resources in all formats, subjects, and languages; computer information systems and other bibliographic tools; management of research libraries; preservation of library materials; worldwide information policy; and publishing and scholarly communication.

The Brookings Institution, *Center for Technology Innovation, 1775 Massachusetts Ave. N.W., 20036; (202) 797-6090. Darrell M. West, Director, (202) 797-6481.*
Web, www.brookings.edu/about/centers/techinnovation

Research center promoting policymaking and public debate about technology innovation, including digital infrastructure, the mobile economy, e-governance, digital media and entertainment, cybersecurity and privacy, digital medicine, and virtual education.

Consortium for School Networking (CoSN), *1025 Vermont Ave. N.W., #1010, 20005; (202) 861-2676. Fax, (202) 393-2011. Keith R. Krueger, Chief Executive Officer. Certification hotline, (202) 524-8464. Membership hotline, (202) 558 0059. Toll-free, (866) 267-8747.*
General email, info@cosn.org
Web, www.cosn.org and Twitter, @CoSN

Membership: teachers and school officials who support educational technology for grades K–12. Grants certification to educators who are fluent in technology and promote the role of technology in teaching. Assists schools in implementing educational technologies. Holds an annual policy summit to support legislation that affects technology education.

Council on Library and Information Resources, *1707 L St. N.W., #650, 20036; (202) 939-4750. Fax, (202) 600-9628. Charles Henry, President.*
Web, www.clir.org and Twitter, @CLIRnews

Acts on behalf of the nation's libraries, archives, and universities to develop and encourage collaborative strategies for preserving the nation's intellectual heritage; seeks to strengthen its information systems and learning environments.

Digital Promise, *1001 Connecticut Ave. N.W., #830, 20036; (202) 450-3675. Karen Cator, President.*
General email, contact@digitalpromise.org
Web, www.digitalpromise.org

Assists educators, technology developers, and researchers in applying and creating educational technologies that improve student learning. Grants micro-credentials to teachers and equips schools with mobile learning technology.

Gallaudet University, Library, *800 Florida Ave. N.E., 20002-3695; (202) 651-5217. Some numbers require state relay service for voice transmission. Sarah Hamrick, Director, Library Public Services, (202) 651-5214; Michael (Mike) Olson, Director, Archives Preservation Specialist.*
General email, library.help@gallaudet.edu
Web, www.gallaudet.edu/library.html

Maintains extensive special collection on deafness, including archival materials relating to deaf cultural history and Gallaudet University.

Info Comm International, *11242 Waples Mill Rd., #200, Fairfax, VA 22030; (703) 273-7200. Fax, (703) 278-8082. David Labuskes, Executive Director. Information, (800) 659-7469.*
Web, www.infocomm.org

Membership: manufacturers, dealers, and specialists in educational communications products. Provides educators with information on federal funding for audiovisual, video, and computer equipment and materials; monitors trends in educational technology; conducts audiovisual trade shows worldwide. (Formerly the International Communications Industries Assn.)

Lubuto Library Partners, *5614 Connecticut Ave N.W., #368, 20015; (202) 558-5609. Jane Kinney Meyers, Director.*
General email, webmail@lubuto.org
Web, www.lubuto.org

Works with public and private libraries and other partners to construct an open-access library collection and accessible services for children and youth in Africa. Sponsors library programs to foster education in the arts and technology; offers services for children with disabilities.

Special Libraries Assn., *331 S. Patrick St., Alexandria, VA 22314-3501; (703) 647-4900. Fax, (703) 647-4901. Doug Newcomb, Deputy Chief Executive Officer, (703) 647-4923.*
General email, sla@sla.org
Web, www.sla.org

Membership: librarians and information managers serving institutions that use or produce information in specialized areas, including business, engineering, law, the arts and sciences, government, museums, and universities. Conducts professional development programs, research projects, and an annual conference. Monitors legislation and regulations.

POSTSECONDARY EDUCATION

General

▶AGENCIES

Bureau of Educational and Cultural Affairs *(State Dept.), Academic Exchange Programs, 2200 C St. N.W., #4-B06/SA-5, 20520; (202) 632-3234. Mary Kirk, Director. Web, http://eca.state.gov/about-bureau-0/organizational-structure/office-academic-exchanges*

Provides opportunities for international study and research from the undergraduate through postdoctoral and professional levels. Works with the Fulbright Program, Critical Language Scholarship Program, Global Undergraduate Exchange Program, Edmund S. Muskie Graduate Fellowship Program, and Study of the United States Institutes.

Education Dept., *Postsecondary Education, 1990 K St. N.W., 7th Floor, 20006; (202) 502-7750. Fax, (202) 502-7677. Ericka Miller, Assistant Secretary, Acting. TTY, (800) 437-0833.*
Web, www2.ed.gov/about/offices/list/ope/index.html and Twitter, @EDPostsecondary

Formulates federal postsecondary education policy. Administers federal assistance programs for public and private postsecondary institutions; provides financial support for faculty development, construction of facilities, and improvement of graduate, continuing, cooperative, and international education; awards grants and loans for financial assistance to eligible students.

Education Dept., *Postsecondary Education, Fund for the Improvement of Postsecondary Education, 1990 K St. N.W., 6th Floor, 20006-8544; (202) 502-7500. Fax, (202) 502-7877. Ralph Hines, Director, (202) 502-7618.*
General email, fipse@ed.gov
Web, www2.ed.gov/FIPSE

Works to improve postsecondary education by administering grant competitions.

Education Dept., *Postsecondary Education, Higher Education Programs, 1990 K St. N.W., 6th Floor, 20006;*
(202) 502-7555. James T. Minor, Deputy Assistant Secretary. Web, www2.ed.gov/about/offices/list/ope/hep.html

Administers programs to increase access to postsecondary education for low-income, first-generation students and students with disabilities. Supports higher education facilities and programs through financial support to eligible institutions, and management of programs that recruit and prepare low-income students for successful completion of college. Programs include eight TRIO programs, institutional development programs for minority-serving institutions, and the Fund for the Improvement of Postsecondary Education.

National Institutes of Health (NIH) *(Health and Human Services Dept.), Intramural Training and Education, 2 Center Dr., Bldg. 2, #2E04, MSC 0230, Bethesda, MD 20892-0240; (301) 496-2427. Fax, (301) 594-9606. Sharon Milgram, Director.*
General email, trainingwww@mail.nih.gov
Web, www.training.nih.gov

Administers programs and initiatives to recruit and develop individuals who participate in research training activities on the NIH's campuses. Maintains an interactive Web site for the various research training programs. Supports the training mission of the NIH Intramural Research Program through placement, retention, support, and tracking of trainees at all levels, as well as program delivery and evaluation. Administers the NIH Academy, the Summer Internship Program, the Undergraduate Scholarship Program, the Graduate Partnerships Program, and the Postbac and Technical Intramural Research Training Award programs.

▶CONGRESS

For a listing of relevant congressional committees and subcommittees, please see page 164 or the Appendix.

▶NONGOVERNMENTAL

Accuracy in Academia (AIA), *4350 East-West Hwy., #555, Bethesda, MD 20814; (202) 364-3085. Fax, (202) 364-4098. Malcolm A. Kline, Executive Director.*
General email, info@academia.org
Web, www.academia.org

Seeks to eliminate political bias in university education, particularly discrimination against students, faculty, or administrators on the basis of political beliefs. Publishes a monthly newsletter.

ACT Inc. (American College Testing), *Washington Office, 1 Dupont Circle N.W., #220, 20036-1170; (202) 223-2318. Fax, (202) 293-2223. Tom Lindsley, Director of Federal Advocacy. TTY, (319) 337-1701.*
Web, www.act.org

Administers ACT assessment planning and examination for colleges and universities. Provides more than one hundred assessment, research, information, and program management services in the areas of education and workforce development to elementary and secondary schools, colleges, professional associations, businesses, and government agencies. (Headquarters in Iowa City, Iowa.)

American Assn. of Colleges of Pharmacy, *1727 King St., Alexandria, VA 22314-2700; (703) 739-2330. Fax, (703) 836-8982. Lucinda L. Maine, Executive Vice President.*
General email, mail@aacp.org

Web, www.aacp.org

Represents and acts as advocate for pharmacists in the academic community. Conducts programs and activities in cooperation with other national health and higher education associations.

American Assn. of Collegiate Registrars and Admissions Officers, *1 Dupont Circle N.W., #520, 20036-1135; (202) 293-9161. Fax, (202) 872-8857. Michael Reilly, Executive Director.*
General email, info@uacrao.org

Web, www.aacrao.org

Membership: degree-granting postsecondary institutions, government agencies, higher education coordinating boards, private education organizations, and education-oriented businesses. Promotes higher education and contributes to the professional development of members working in admissions, enrollment management, financial aid, institutional research, records, and registration.

American Assn. of Community Colleges, *1 Dupont Circle N.W., #410, 20036-1176; (202) 728-0200. Fax, (202) 833-2467. Walter G. Bumphus, President.*
Web, www.aacc.nche.edu

Membership: accredited two-year community technical and junior colleges, corporate foundations, international associates, and institutional affiliates. Studies include policies for lifelong education, workforce training programs and partnerships, international curricula, enrollment trends, and cooperative programs with public schools and communities. (Affiliated with the Council for Resource Development.)

American Assn. of State Colleges and Universities, *1307 New York Ave. N.W., 5th Floor, 20005; (202) 293-7070. Fax, (202) 296-5819. Muriel Howard, President, (202) 478-4647.*
General email, info@aascu.org

Web, www.aascu.org

Membership: presidents and chancellors of state colleges and universities. Promotes equity in education and fosters information exchange among members. Interests include student financial aid, international education programs, academic affairs, teacher education, and higher education access and affordability. Monitors legislation and regulations.

American Assn. of University Professors (AAUP), *1133 19th St. N.W., #200, 20036; (202) 737-5900. Fax, (202) 737-5526. Julie Schmid, Chief Executive Officer.*
General email, aaup@aaup.org

Web, www.aaup.org

Membership: college and university faculty members. Defends faculties' and professional staffs' academic freedom and tenure; advocates collegial governance; assists in the development of policies ensuring due process. Conducts workshops and education programs. Monitors legislation and regulations.

American Conference of Academic Deans, *1818 R St. N.W., 20009; (202) 884-7419. Fax, (202) 265-9532. Laura A. Rzepka, Executive Director.*
General email, info@acad-edu.org

Web, www.acad-edu.org

Membership: academic administrators of two- and four-year accredited colleges, universities, and community colleges (private and public). Fosters information exchange among members on college curricular and administrative issues.

American Council of Trustees and Alumni, *1726 M St. N.W., #600, 20036-4525; (202) 467-6787. Fax, (202) 467-6784. Anne D. Neal, President. Toll-free, (800) 258-6648.*
General email, info@goacta.org

Web, www.goacta.org

Membership: college and university alumni and trustees interested in promoting academic freedom and excellence. Seeks to help alumni and trustees direct their financial contributions to programs that will raise educational standards at their alma maters. Promotes the role of alumni and trustees in shaping higher education policies.

American Council on Education (ACE), *1 Dupont Circle N.W., #800, 20036-1193; (202) 939-9300. Fax, (202) 833-4762. Molly Corbett Broad, President. Press, (202) 939-9328.*
General email, comments@acenet.edu

Web, www.acenet.edu

Membership: presidents of universities and other education institutions. Conducts and publishes research; maintains offices dealing with government relations, women and minorities in higher education, management of higher education institutions, adult learning and educational credentials (academic credit for nontraditional learning, especially in the armed forces), leadership development, and international education.

ASCD, *1703 N. Beauregard St., Alexandria, VA 22311-1714; (703) 578-9600. Fax, (703) 575-5400. Deb Delisle, Executive Director. Information, (800) 933-2723.*
General email, member@ascd.org

Web, www.ascd.org

Membership: approximately 140,000 professional educators internationally, including superintendents, supervisors, principals, teachers, professors of education, and school board members. Develops programs, products, and services for educators. (Formerly the Assn. for Supervision and Curriculum Development.)

Assn. of American Colleges and Universities (AACU), *1818 R St. N.W., 20009; (202) 387-3760. Fax, (202) 265-9532. Carol Geary Schneider, President.*
Web, www.aacu.org, Twitter, @aacu and Facebook, www.facebook.com/Association-of-American-Colleges-and-Universities-48308128458

Colleges and Universities in the Washington Metropolitan Area

Agriculture Dept. Graduate School, 600 Maryland Ave. S.W., 20024. Switchboard: (888) 744-4723. Interim President: Elaine Ryan, (202) 314-3300

American University, 4400 Massachusetts Ave. N.W., 20016. Switchboard: (202) 885-1000. President: Cornelius Kerwin, (202) 885-2121

Catholic University of America, 620 Michigan Ave. N.E., 20064. Switchboard: (202) 319-5000. President: John Garvey, (202) 319-5100

Corcoran School of the Arts and Design, George Washington University, 500 17th St. N.W., 20006. Switchboard: (202) 994-1700. Director: Sanjit Sethi, (202) 994-1700

Gallaudet University, 800 Florida Ave. N.E., 20002. Switchboard: (202) 651-5000 (voice and TTY). President: Roberta (Bobbi) Cordano, (202) 651-5005 (voice and TTY)

George Mason University, 4400 University Dr., Fairfax, VA 22030. Switchboard: (703) 993-1000. President: Ángel Cabrera, (703) 993-8700

George Washington University, 2121 Eye St. N.W., 20052. Switchboard: (202) 994-1000. President: Steven Knapp, (202) 994-6500

George Washington University at Mount Vernon Campus, 2100 Foxhall Rd. N.W., 20007. Switchboard: (202) 242-6670. Associate Provost: Rachelle S. Heller, (202) 242-6698

Georgetown University, 3700 O St. N.W., 20057. Switchboard: (202) 687-0100. President: John J. DeGioia, (202) 687-4134

Howard University, 2400 6th St. N.W., 20059. Switchboard: (202) 806-6100. President: Wayne A.I. Frederick, (202) 806-2500

The Institute of World Politics, 1521 16th St. N.W., 20036-1464. Switchboard: (202) 462-2101. President: John Lenczowski, (202) 462-2101 ext. 333

Marymount University, 2807 N. Glebe Rd., Arlington, VA 22207. Switchboard: (703) 522-5600. President: Matthew D. Shank, (703) 284-1598

Paul H. Nitze School of Advanced International Studies (SAIS), Johns Hopkins University, 1740 Massachusetts Ave. N.W., 20036. Switchboard: (202) 663-5600. Dean: Vali R. Nasr, (202) 663-5624

Strayer University, 2303 Dulles Station Blvd., Herndon, VA 20171. Switchboard: (888) 311-0355. President: Brian W. Jones, (888) 311-0355

Trinity Washington University, 125 Michigan Ave. N.E., 20017. Switchboard: (202) 884-9000. President: Patricia A. McGuire, (202) 884-9050

University of Maryland, College Park, MD 20742. Switchboard: (301) 405-1000. President: Wallace D. Loh, (301) 405-5803

University of the District of Columbia, 4200 Connecticut Ave. N.W., 20008. Switchboard: (202) 274-5000. President: Ronald Mason Jr., (202) 274-6016

University of Virginia (Northern Virginia Center), 7054 Haycock Rd., Falls Church, VA 22043. Switchboard: (703) 536-1100. Interim Dean: Steve Laymon, (434) 982-5206

Virginia Tech (Northern Virginia Center), 7054 Haycock Rd., Falls Church, VA 22043 Switchboard: (540) 231-6000. Director of Northern Virginia Campus: Kenneth H. Wong, (703) 538-8310

Virginia Theological Seminary, 3737 Seminary Rd., Alexandria, VA 22304. Switchboard: (703) 370-6600. Dean: The Very Rev. Ian S. Markham, (703) 461-1701

Washington Adventist University, 7600 Flower Ave., Takoma Park, MD 20912. Switchboard: (301) 891-4000. President: Weymouth Spence, (301) 891-4128

Wesley Theological Seminary, 4500 Massachussetts Ave. N.W., 20016. Switchboard: (202) 885-8600. President: Rev. Dr. David McAllister-Wilson, (202) 885-8611

Membership: two-year and four-year public and private colleges, universities, and postsecondary consortia. Works to develop effective academic programs and improve undergraduate curricula and services. Seeks to encourage, enhance, and support student achievement through liberal education for all students, regardless of academic specialization or intended career.

The Assn. of American Law Schools, *1614 20th St. N.W., 20009-1001; (202) 296-8851. Fax, (202) 296-8869. Judith Areen, Executive Director. General email, aals@aals.org*

Web, www.aals.org and Twitter, @TheAALS

Membership: law schools, subject to approval. Membership criteria include high-quality academic programs, faculty, scholarship, and students; academic freedom; diversity of people and viewpoints; and emphasis on public service. Hosts meetings and workshops; publishes a directory of law teachers. Acts as advocate on behalf of legal education; monitors legislation and judicial decisions.

Assn. of American Universities, *1200 New York Ave. N.W., #550, 20005; (202) 408-7500. Fax, (202) 408-8184. Hunter R. Rawlings III, President. Web, www.aau.edu and Twitter, @AAUniversities*

Membership: public and private universities in the United States and Canada with emphasis on graduate and professional education and research. Fosters information exchange among presidents of member institutions.

Assn. of Catholic Colleges and Universities, *1 Dupont Circle N.W., #650, 20036; (202) 457-0650. Fax, (202) 728-0977. Michael Galligan-Stierle, President. General email, accu@accunet.org Web, www.accunet.org and Twitter, @CatholicHighrEd*

Membership: regionally accredited American Catholic colleges and universities. Offers affiliated status for selected international Catholic universities. Acts as a clearinghouse for information on Catholic institutions of higher education.

Assn. of Community College Trustees (ACCT), *1101 17th St. N.W., #300, 20036; (202) 775-4667. Fax, (202) 223-1297. J. Noah Brown, President.*
General email, acctinfo@acct.org

Web, www.acct.org and Twitter, @CCTrustees

Provides members of community college governing boards with training in educational programs and services. Monitors federal education programs and acts as advocate on behalf of community colleges and their trustees.

Assn. of Governing Boards of Universities and Colleges, *1133 20th St. N.W., #300, 20036; (202) 296-8400. Fax, (202) 223-7053. Richard D. Legon, President. Toll-free, (800) 356-6317.*
Web, www.agb.org and Twitter, @AGBtweets

Membership: presidents, boards of trustees, regents, commissions, and other groups governing colleges, universities, and institutionally related foundations. Interests include the relationship between the president and board of trustees and other subjects relating to governance.

Assn. of Jesuit Colleges and Universities, *1 Dupont Circle N.W., #405, 20036-1140; (202) 862-9893. Fax, (202) 862-8523. Rev. Michael J. Sheeran, President.*
General email, dhowes@ajcunet.edu

Web, www.ajcunet.edu and Twitter, @jesuitcolleges

Membership: American Jesuit colleges and universities. Monitors government regulatory and policymaking activities affecting higher education. Publishes the AJCU Directory and a monthly newsletter. Promotes national and international cooperation among Jesuit higher education institutions.

Assn. of Private Sector Colleges and Universities (APSCU), *1101 Connecticut Ave. N.W., #900, 20036; (202) 336-6700. Fax, (202) 336-6828. Steve Gunderson, President. Toll-free, (866) 711-8574.*
General email, apscu@apscu.org

Web, www.career.org and Twitter, @apscunow

Membership: private postsecondary colleges and career schools in the United States. Works to expand the accessibility of postsecondary career education and to improve the quality of education offered by member institutions. (Formerly Career College Assn.)

Assn. of Public and Land-Grant Universities, *1307 New York Ave. N.W., #400, 20005-4722; (202) 478-6040. Fax, (202) 478-6046. M. Peter McPherson, President, (202) 478-6060.*
General email, info@aplu.org

Web, www.aplu.org and Twitter, @APLU_News

Membership: land grant colleges; state and public research universities. Serves as clearinghouse on issues of public higher education.

Business–Higher Education Forum, *2025 M St. N.W., #800, 20036; (202) 367-1189. Fax, (202) 367-2100. Brian K. Fitzgerald, Chief Executive Officer.*
General email, info@bhef.com

Web, www.bhef.com and Twitter, @BHEF

Membership: chief executive officers of major corporations, foundations, colleges, and universities. Develops and promotes policy positions to enhance U.S. competitiveness. Interests include improving student achievement and readiness for college and work; and strengthening higher education, particularly in the fields of science, technology, engineering, and math.

College Board, *Advocacy and Policy, 1919 M St. N.W., #300, 20034; (202) 741-4700. Fax, (202) 223-7035. Stephanie Sanford, Chief, Washington Office.*
General email, govrelations@collegeboard.org

Web, www.collegeboard.org and Twitter, @CollegeBoard

Membership: colleges and universities, secondary schools, school systems, and education associations. Provides direct student support programs and professional development for educators; conducts policy analysis and research; and advocates public policy positions that support educational excellence and promote student access to higher education. (Headquarters in New York.)

Consortium of Universities for Global Health, *1608 Rhode Island Ave. N.W., #211B, 20036; (202) 974-6363. Fax, (202) 833-5078. Keith Martin, Executive Director.*
General email, info@cugh.org

Web, www.cugh.org and Twitter, @CUGHnews

Assists in regulating curricula and standards for university global health programs. Coordinates academic partnerships between national universities and international educational institutions in developing countries.

Council for Christian Colleges & Universities, *321 8th St. N.E., 20002; (202) 546-8713. Fax, (202) 546-8913. Shirley V. Hoogstra, President.*
General email, council@cccu.org

Web, www.cccu.org and Twitter, @CCCUtweets

Membership: accredited four-year Christian liberal arts colleges. Offers faculty development conferences on faith and the academic disciplines. Coordinates annual gathering of college administrators. Sponsors internship/seminar programs for students at member colleges. Promotes Christian affiliated higher education. Interests include religious and educational freedom.

Council for Resource Development, *8720 Georgia Ave., #700, Silver Spring, MD 20910; (202) 822-0750. Leah Goss, President.*
General email, crd@crdnet.org

Web, www.crdnet.org and Twitter, @CRD_DC

Membership: college presidents, administrators, fundraisers, grant writers, and development officers at two-year colleges. Educates members on how to secure resources for their institution; conducts workshops and training programs. Monitors legislation and regulations. (Affiliated with the American Assn. of Community Colleges.)

Council of Graduate Schools, *1 Dupont Circle N.W., #230, 20036-1173; (202) 223-3791. Fax, (202) 331-7157. Suzanne T. Ortega, President.*
General email, general_inquiries@cgs.nche.edu

Web, www.cgsnet.org and Twitter, @CGSGradEd

Membership: private and public colleges and universities with significant involvement in graduate education, research, and scholarship. Produces publications and information about graduate education; provides a forum for member schools to exchange information and ideas.

Council of Independent Colleges, *1 Dupont Circle N.W., #320, 20036-1142; (202) 466-7230. Fax, (202) 466-7238. Richard Ekman, President.*
General email, cic@cic.nche.edu
Web, www.cic.edu

Membership: independent liberal arts colleges and universities, and higher education affiliates and organizations. Sponsors development programs for college presidents, deans, and faculty members and communications officers on topics such as leadership, financial management, academic quality, visibility, and other issues crucial to high-quality education and independent liberal arts colleges. Holds workshops and annual meetings, conducts research, and produces publications.

Council on Education for Public Health, *1010 Wayne Ave., #220, Silver Spring, MD 20910; (202) 789-1050. Fax, (202) 789-1895. Laura Rasar King, Executive Director. Web, www.ceph.org*

Accredits schools of public health and undergraduate and graduate programs in public health. Works to strengthen public health programs through research and other means.

Council on Social Work Education, *1701 Duke St., #200, Alexandria, VA 22314-3457; (703) 683-8080. Fax, (703) 683-8099. Darla Spence Coffey, President.*
General email, info@cswe.org
Web, www.cswe.org

Membership: educational and professional institutions, social welfare agencies, and private citizens. Promotes high-quality education in social work. Accredits social work programs.

Educational Testing Service (ETS), *Communications and Public Affairs, 1800 K St. N.W., #900, 20006-2202; (202) 659-0616. Fax, (202) 659-8075. Kurt Landgraf, President; Tom Ewing, Communications. TTY, (202) 659-8067.*
General email, etsinfo@ets.org
Web, www.ets.org

Administers examinations for admission to educational programs and for graduate and licensing purposes; conducts instructional programs in testing, evaluation, and research in education fields. Washington office handles government and professional relations. Fee for services. (Headquarters in Princeton, N.J.)

NASPA: Student Affairs Administrators in Higher Education, *111 K St. N.E., 10th Floor, 20002; (202) 265-7500. Fax, (202) 898-5737. Kevin Kruger, President.*
General email, office@naspa.org
Web, www.naspa.org, Twitter, @NASPAtweets and Facebook, www.facebook.com/naspaFB

Membership: student affairs administrators, deans, faculty, and graduate and undergraduate students at 2,100 campuses, representing 25 countries. Seeks to develop leadership and improve practices in student affairs administration. Initiates and supports programs and legislation to improve student affairs administration.

National Assn. for College Admission Counseling, *1050 N. Highland St., #400, Arlington, VA 22201; (703) 836-2222. Fax, (703) 243-9375. Joyce Smith, Chief Executive Officer. Information, (800) 822-6285.*
General email, info@nacacnet.org
Web, www.nacacnet.org

Membership: high school guidance counselors, independent counselors, college and university admissions officers, and financial aid officers. Promotes and funds research on admission counseling and on the transition from high school to college. Acts as advocate for student rights in college admissions. Sponsors national college fairs and continuing education for members.

National Assn. of College and University Attorneys, *1 Dupont Circle N.W., #620, 20036-1182; (202) 833-8390. Fax, (202) 296-8379. Kathleen Curry Santora, Chief Executive Officer.*
General email, nacua@nacua.org
Web, www.nacua.org

Provides information on legal developments affecting postsecondary education. Operates a clearinghouse through which in-house and external legal counselors are able to network with their counterparts on current legal problems.

National Assn. of College and University Business Officers, *1110 Vermont Ave. N.W., #800, 20005; (202) 861-2500. Fax, (202) 861-2583. John D. Walda, President. Toll-free, (800) 462-4916.*
General email, support@nacubo.org
Web, www.nacubo.org

Membership: chief business officers at higher education institutions. Provides members with information on financial management, federal regulations, and other subjects related to the business administration of universities and colleges; conducts workshops on issues such as student aid, institutional budgeting, and accounting.

National Assn. of Independent Colleges and Universities, *1025 Connecticut Ave. N.W., #700, 20036-5405; (202) 785-8866. Fax, (202) 835-0003. David L. Warren, President.*
General email, geninfo@naicu.edu
Web, www.naicu.edu

Membership: liberal arts colleges, research universities, church-related and faith-related institutions, historically black colleges and universities, women's colleges, performing and visual arts institutions, two-year colleges; graduate schools of law, medicine, engineering, business, and other professions. Tracks campus trends, conducts research, analyzes higher education issues, and helps coordinate state-level activities. Interests include federal policies that affect student aid, taxation, and government regulation. Monitors legislation and regulations.

National Council of University Research Administrators, *1015 18th St. N.W., #901, 20036; (202)*

466-3894. Fax, (202) 223-5573. Kathleen Larmett, Executive Director.

General email, info@ncura.edu

Web, www.ncura.edu, Twitter, @NCURA and Facebook, www.facebook.com/ncura1959

Membership: individuals involved in grant administration at colleges, universities, and teaching hospitals. Encourages development of effective policies and procedures in the administration of these programs.

Network of Schools of Public Policy, Affairs, and Administration (NASPAA), 1029 Vermont Ave. N.W., #1100, 20005-3517; (202) 628-8965. Fax, (202) 626-4978. Laurel McFarland, Executive Director.

General email, naspaa@naspaa.org

Web, www.naspaa.org

Membership: universities involved in education, research, and training in public management in the United States and internationally.

U.S. Student Assn., 1211 Connecticut Ave. N.W., #406, 20036; (202) 640-6570. Fax, (202) 223-4005. Alexandra Flores-Quilty, President.

General email, manager@usstudents.org

Web, www.usstudents.org

Represents postsecondary students, student government associations, and state student lobby associations. Monitors legislation and regulations. Organizes students to participate in the political process through congressional testimony, letter-writing campaigns, and lobbying visits. Represents students in various coalitions, including the Committee for Education Funding, the Student Aid Alliance, the Generational Alliance, and the Leadership Conference on Civil Rights.

Washington Higher Education Secretariat, 1 Dupont Circle N.W., #800, 20036-1110; (202) 939-9444. Fax, (202) 833-4760. Molly Corbett Broad, Chair.

General email, whs@acenet.edu

Web, www.whes.org

Membership: national higher education association chief executives representing the different sectors and functions in postsecondary institutions. Provides forum for discussion on national and local education issues. (Coordinated by the president of the American Council on Education.)

College Accreditation

Many college-based or university-based independent post-secondary education programs are accredited by member associations. See specific headings and associations within the chapter.

▶**AGENCIES**

Education Dept., *Accreditation Group,* 1990 K St. N.W., #8065, 20006-8509; (202) 219-7011. Herman Bounds Jr., Director.

General email, Herman.Bounds@ed.gov

Web, www2.ed.gov

Reviews accrediting agencies and state approval agencies that seek initial or renewed recognition by the secretary; provides the National Advisory Committee on Institutional Quality and Integrity with staff support.

▶**NONGOVERNMENTAL**

Accrediting Council for Independent Colleges and Schools (ACICS), 750 1st St. N.E., #980, 20002-4241; (202) 336-6780. Fax, (202) 842-2593. Albert C. Gray, Chief Executive Officer.

General email, info@acics.org

Web, www.acics.org

Accredits postsecondary institutions offering programs of study through the master's degree level that are designed to train and educate persons for careers or professions where business applications and concepts constitute or support the career or professional activity. Promotes educational excellence and ethical business practices in its member schools.

American Academy for Liberal Education (AALE), 1200 G St., #883, 20005; (703) 717-9719. Diane Auer Jones, President.

General email, aaleinfo@aale.org

Web, www.aale.org

Accredits colleges, universities, and charter schools whose general education program in the liberal arts meets the academy's accreditation requirements. Provides support for institutions that maintain substantial liberal arts programs and desire to raise requirements to meet AALE standards.

Council for Higher Education Accreditation, 1 Dupont Circle N.W., #510, 20036; (202) 955-6126. Fax, (202) 955-6129. Judith S. Eaton, President.

General email, chea@chea.org

Web, www.chea.org, www.cheainternational.org and Twitter, @CHEAnews

Advocates voluntary self-regulation of colleges and universities through accreditation; conducts recognition processes for accrediting organizations; coordinates research, debate, and processes that improve accreditation; mediates disputes and fosters communications among accrediting bodies and the higher education community.

Council for the Accreditation of Educator Preparation, 1140 19th St., #400, 20036; (202) 223-0077. Fax, (202) 296-6620. James (Jim) G. Cibulka, President.

General email, caep@caep.org

Web, www.ncate.org

Evaluates and accredits schools and departments of education at colleges and universities. Publishes list of accredited institutions and standards for accreditation. (Formerly National Council for Accreditation of Teacher Education.)

National Assn. of Schools of Dance, *11250 Roger Bacon Dr., #21, Reston, VA 20190-5248; (703) 437-0700. Fax, (703) 437-6312. Karen Moynahan, Executive Director. General email, info@arts-accredit.org*

Web, http://nasd.arts-accredit.org

Specialized professional accrediting agency for post-secondary programs in dance. Conducts and shares research and analysis on topics pertinent to dance programs and the field of dance. Offers professional development opportunities for executives of dance programs.

National Assn. of Schools of Music, *11250 Roger Bacon Dr., #21, Reston, VA 20190-5248; (703) 437-0700. Fax, (703) 437-6312. Karen Moynahan, Executive Director. General email, info@arts-accredit.org*

Web, http://nasm.arts-accredit.org

Specialized professional accrediting agency for post-secondary programs in music. Conducts and shares research and analysis on topics pertinent to music programs and the field of music. Offers professional development opportunities for executives of music programs.

National Assn. of Schools of Theatre, *11250 Roger Bacon Dr., #21, Reston, VA 20190-5248; (703) 437-0700. Fax, (703) 437-6312. Karen Moynahan, Executive Director. General email, info@arts-accredit.org*

Web, http://nast.arts-accredit.org

Specialized professional accrediting agency for postsecondary programs in theatre. Conducts and shares research and analysis on topics pertinent to theatre programs and the field of theatre. Offers professional development opportunities for executives of theatre programs.

Network of Schools of Public Policy, Affairs, and Administration (NASPAA), *1029 Vermont Ave. N.W., #1100, 20005-3517; (202) 628-8965. Fax, (202) 626-4978. Laurel McFarland, Executive Director. General email, naspaa@naspaa.org*

Web, www.naspaa.org

Accredits master's degree programs in public affairs, public policy, and public administration.

Financial Aid to Students

▶AGENCIES

Education Dept., *Federal Student Aid, 830 1st St. N.E., 20202; (202) 377-3000. Fax, (202) 275-5000. James Runcie, Chief Operating Officer. Student Aid Information Center, (800) 433-3243. TTY, (800) 730-8913. Web, https://studentaid.ed.gov/sa*

Administers federal loan, grant, and work-study programs for postsecondary education to eligible individuals. Administers the Pell Grant Program, the Perkins Loan Program, the Stafford Student Loan Program (Guaranteed Student Loan)/PLUS Program, the College Work-Study Program, the Supplemental Loans for Students (SLS), and the Supplemental Educational Opportunity Grant Program.

Education Dept., *Health Education Assistance Loan Program, 830 1st St. N.E., #44B, 20202; (844) 509-8957. Tawana Lewis, Supervisor. Email, heal@ed.gov*

Web, www.ifap.ed.gov/HEALInfo/HEALInfo.html

Insures loans provided by private lenders to students attending eligible health professions schools under the Public Health Service Act. New loans to student borrowers have been discontinued. Refinancing has been terminated.

▶NONGOVERNMENTAL

College Board, *Advocacy and Policy, 1919 M St. N.W., #300, 20034; (202) 741-4700. Fax, (202) 223-7035. Stephanie Sanford, Chief, Washington Office. General email, govrelations@collegeboard.org*

Web, www.collegeboard.org and Twitter, @CollegeBoard

Membership: colleges and universities, secondary schools, school systems, and education associations. Provides direct student support programs and professional development for educators; conducts policy analysis and research; and advocates public policy positions that support educational excellence and promote student access to higher education. (Headquarters in New York.)

Education Finance Council, *1850 M St. N.W., #920, 20036; (202) 955-5510. Fax, (202) 955-5530. Debra J. Chromy, President. General email, info@efc.org*

Web, www.efc.org

Membership: Nonprofit and state-based student loan secondary market organizations. Participates in the Federal Family Education Loan Program (FFELP). Works to maintain and expand student access to higher education through tax-exempt funding for loans.

National Assn. of Student Financial Aid Administrators, *1101 Connecticut Ave. N.W., #1100, 20036-4303; (202) 785-0453. Fax, (202) 785-1487. Justin Draeger, President. General email, info@nasfaa.org*

Web, www.nasfaa.org and Twitter, @nasfaa

Membership: more than 20,000 financial aid professionals at nearly 3,000 colleges, universities, and career schools. Interests include student aid legislation, regulatory analysis, and training for financial aid administrators.

National Council of Higher Education Resources, *1100 Connecticut Ave. N.W., #1200, 20036-4110; (202) 822-2106. Fax, (202) 822-2142. James (Shelly) P. Bergeron, President. General email, info@nchelp.org*

Web, www.ncher.us

Membership: agencies and organizations involved in servicing and collecting federal student loans and providing debt management, financial literacy, student loan counseling, and other college access and success services. Fosters information exchange among members.

Student Aid Alliance, *1 Dupont Circle N.W., #800, 20036-1193; (202) 939-9355. Fax, (202) 833-4762.*

Molly Corbett Broad, President, ACE; David L. Warren, President, NAICU.
Web, studentaidalliance.org

Membership: more than seventy organizations representing students, administrators, and faculty members from all sectors of higher education. Seeks to ensure adequate funding of federal aid programs. Monitors legislation and regulations. (Co-chaired by the National Assn. of Independent Colleges and Universities [NAICU] and the American Council on Education [ACE].)

PRESCHOOL, ELEMENTARY, SECONDARY EDUCATION

General

▶AGENCIES

Education Dept., *Elementary and Secondary Education,* 400 Maryland Ave. S.W., #3W315, 20202; (202) 401-0113. Fax, (202) 205-0310. Ann Whalen, Assistant Secretary, Acting.
General email, oese@ed.gov
Web, www2.ed.gov/about/offices/list/oese

Administers federal assistance programs for preschool, elementary, and secondary education (both public and private). Program divisions include Student Achievement and School Accountability (including Title I aid for disadvantaged children); Migrant Education; Impact Aid; School Support and Rural Programs; Early Learning; Safe and Healthy Students; and Academic Improvement and Teacher Quality Programs.

Education Dept., *Elementary and Secondary Education, Academic Improvement and Teacher Quality Programs,* 400 Maryland Ave. S.W., 20202; (202) 260-8228. Fax, (202) 260-8969. Sylvia Lyles, Director, (202) 260-2551.
General email, oese@ed.gov
Web, www2.ed.gov/about/offices/list/oese/aitq

Provides financial assistance to state and local educational agencies, community and faith-based organizations, and other entities to support activities to recruit and retain high-quality teaching staff and to strengthen the quality of elementary and secondary education. Divided into four program groups: the Academic Improvement Program, the High School Programs, the Teacher Quality Program, and Literacy Programs; implements programs providing support for reopening and rebuilding schools in areas impacted by natural disasters; implements the 21st Century Community Learning Centers, which provide academic enrichment opportunities during nonschool hours for students attending high-poverty and low-performing schools.

Education Dept., *Elementary and Secondary Education, Academic Improvement and Teacher Quality Programs, Reading First,* 400 Maryland Ave. S.W., #3E314, 20202-6132; (202) 260-2551. Fax, (202) 260-8969. Sylvia Lyles, Director.

Administers formula and discretionary grants that support family literacy programs that provide early childhood, adult literacy, and parenting education to low-income families (Even Start); enhance early childhood literacy instruction for children in the two years before kindergarten (Early Reading First); and support partnerships between institutions of higher education and other entities to improve the professional development of early childhood instructors (Early Childhood Educator Professional Development).

Education Dept., *Elementary and Secondary Education, Impact Aid,* 400 Maryland Ave. S.W., #3E105, 20202-6244; (202) 260-3858. Alfred Lott, Director. Toll-free fax, (866) 799-1272.
General email, impact.aid@ed.gov
Web, www2.ed.gov/about/offices/list/oese/impactaid

Provides funds for elementary and secondary educational activities to school districts in federally impacted areas (where federal activities such as military bases enlarge staff and reduce taxable property).

Education Dept., *Elementary and Secondary Education, Safe and Healthy Students,* 400 Maryland Ave. S.W., #3E328, 20202-6135; (202) 453-6777. Fax, (202) 453-6742. David Esquith, Director.
General email, osdfs.safeschl@ed.gov
Web, www2.ed.gov/about/offices/list/oese/oshs

Develops policy for the department's drug and violence prevention initiatives for students in elementary and secondary schools and institutions of higher education. Provides financial assistance for drug and violence prevention activities. Coordinates education efforts in drug and violence prevention with those of other federal departments and agencies.

Education Dept., *English Language Acquisition, Language Enhancement and Academic Achievement for Limited English Proficient Students,* 400 Maryland Ave. S.W., #5E106, 20202-6510; (202) 401-4300. Fax, (202) 205-1229. Libia Gil, Assistant Deputy Secretary. NCELA helpline, (866) 347-6864.
Web, www2.ed.gov/about/offices/list/oela

Provides grants for the professional development of teachers of English learners and administers the Native American/Alaska-Native Children in School Program and National Professional Development Discretionary Grant Programs.

Health and Human Services Dept. (HHS), *Head Start,* 330 C St. S.W., 8th Floor, 20201; (202) 205-8573. Blanca Enriquez, Director.
Web, www.acf.hhs.gov/programs/ohs

Awards grants to nonprofit and for-profit organizations and local governments for operating community Head Start programs (comprehensive development programs for children, ages three to five, of low-income families); manages a limited number of parent and child centers for families with children up to age five. Conducts research and manages demonstration programs, including those under the Comprehensive Child Care Development

Act of 1988; administers the Child Development Associate scholarship program, which trains individuals for careers in child development, often as Head Start teachers.

Health and Human Services Dept. (HHS), *President's Council on Fitness, Sports, and Nutrition,* *1101 Wootton Pkwy., #560, Tower Bldg., Rockville, MD 20852; (240) 276-9567. Fax, (240) 276-9860. Shellie Pfohl, Executive Director.*
General email, fitness@hhs.gov
Web, www.fitness.gov, www.presidentschallenge.org and Twitter, @FitnessGov

Provides schools, state and local governments, recreation agencies, and employers with information on designing and implementing physical fitness and nutrition programs; conducts award programs for children and adults and for schools, clubs, and other institutions.

National Agricultural Library *(Agriculture Dept.),* *Food and Nutrition Information Center,* *10301 Baltimore Ave., #108, Beltsville, MD 20705-2351; (301) 504-5414. Fax, (301) 504-6409. Wendy Davis, Nutrition and Food Safety Program Leader.*
General email, fnic@ars.usda.gov
Web, http://fnic.nal.usda.gov

Serves as a resource center for school and child nutrition program personnel who need information on food service management and nutrition education. Library open to the public.

National Assessment Governing Board, *800 N. Capitol St. N.W., #825, 20002-4233; (202) 357-6938. Fax, (202) 357-6945. Bill Bushaw, Executive Director. Toll-free, (877) 977-6938.*
General email, nagb@ed.gov
Web, www.nagb.org

Independent board of local, state, and federal officials, educators, and others appointed by the secretary of education and funded under the National Assessment of Educational Progress (NAEP) program. Sets policy for NAEP, a series of tests measuring achievements of U.S. students since 1969.

United States Presidential Scholars Program *(Education Dept.),* *400 Maryland Ave. S.W., #5E228, 20202-8173; (202) 401-0961. Fax, (202) 260-7465. Simone M. Olson, Executive Director.*
General email, Presidential.Scholars@ed.gov
Web, www2.ed.gov/programs/psp

Honorary recognition program that selects high school seniors of outstanding achievement in academics, community service, artistic ability, and leadership to receive the Presidential Scholars Award. Scholars travel to Washington during national recognition week to receive the award.

▶**CONGRESS**

For a listing of relevant congressional committees and subcommittees, please see page 164 or the Appendix.

▶**NONGOVERNMENTAL**

Achieve, Inc., *1400 16th St. N.W., #510, 20036; (202) 419-1540. Fax, (202) 828-0911. Michael Cohen, President.*
Web, www.achieve.org

Bipartisan organization that seeks to raise academic standards, improve performance assessments, and strengthen personal accountability among young people. Encourages high school graduates to pursue postsecondary education and rewarding careers. Monitors legislation and regulations.

Afterschool Alliance, *1616 H St. N.W., #820, 20006; (202) 347-2030. Fax, (202) 347-2092. Jodi Grant, Executive Director.*
General email, info@afterschoolalliance.org
Web, www.afterschoolalliance.org

Advocacy group that campaigns for afterschool programs. Partners include Congressional and local government leaders. Trains selected Afterschool Ambassadors to educate policymakers about afterschool programs. Publishes reports supporting afterschool daycare.

Alliance for Excellent Education, *1201 Connecticut Ave. N.W., #901, 20036; (202) 828-0828. Fax, (202) 828-0821. Bob Wise, President.*
Web, www.all4ed.org

Policy and advocacy organization that promotes secondary education reform, with a focus on the most at-risk students. Works to increase public awareness through conferences, reports, and press releases. Monitors legislation and regulations.

American Coal Foundation, *101 Constitution Ave. N.W., #500 East, 20001-2133; (202) 463-9785. Fax, (202) 463-9786. Alma Paty, Executive Director.*
General email, info@teachcoal.org
Web, www.teachcoal.org

Provides coal-related educational materials designed for elementary school teachers and students. Web site provides free coal sample kits. Supported by coal producers and manufacturers of mining equipment and supplies.

ASCD, *1703 N. Beauregard St., Alexandria, VA 22311-1714; (703) 578-9600. Fax, (703) 575-5400. Deb Delisle, Executive Director. Information, (800) 933-2723.*
General email, member@ascd.org
Web, www.ascd.org

Membership: approximately 140,000 professional educators internationally, including superintendents, supervisors, principals, teachers, professors of education, and school board members. Develops programs, products, and services for educators. (Formerly the Assn. for Supervision and Curriculum Development.)

Assn. for Childhood Education International, *1200 18th St. N.W., #700, 20036; (202) 372-9986. Fax, (202) 372-9989. Diane Whitehead, Executive Director. Information, (800) 423-3563.*
General email, headquarters@acei.org
Web, www.acei.org and Twitter, @acei.org

Membership: educators, parents, and professionals who work with children (infancy to adolescence). Works to promote the rights, education, and well-being of children worldwide. Holds annual conference.

Center for Inspired Teaching, *1436 U St. N.W., #400, 20009; (202) 462-1956. Fax, (202) 462-1905.*
Aleta Margolis, Executive Director.
General email, info@inspiredteaching.org
Web, www.inspiredteaching.org and Twitter, @InspireTeach

Promotes teaching skills that make the most of children's innate desire to learn. Provides professional development through course, mentoring, new teacher certification and residency programs, school partnerships, and a demonstration charter school.

Center on Education Policy, *2129 G St. N.W., 1st Floor, 20052; (202) 994-9050. Fax, (202) 994-8859.*
Maria Voles Ferguson, Executive Director.
General email, cep-dc@cep-dc.org
Web, www.cep-dc.org and Twitter, @CEPDC

Acts as advocate for public education. Interests include the federal role in education and the status and effects of state high school exit examinations. Provides expert advice upon request. Works with many other education, business, state, and civic organizations. Monitors local, state, and federal legislation and regulations.

Character Education Partnership, *1634 Eye St. N.W., #550, 20006; (202) 296-7743. Fax, (202) 296-7779.*
Becky Sipos, President, ext. 20.
General email, information@character.org
Web, www.character.org and Twitter, @CharacterDotOrg

Promotes the integration of character development in schools and education. Trains education professionals to support character development and social-emotional learning skills, and decrease student behavioral problems. Sponsors an annual forum and publication on effective character education practices.

Council for Professional Recognition, *2460 16th St. N.W., 20009-3547; (202) 265-9090. Fax, (202) 265-9161.*
Valora Washington, Chief Executive Officer.
Toll-free, (800) 424-4310.
CDA Candidates email, cdafeedback@cda.org
Web, www.cdacouncil.org and Twitter, @cdacouncil

Promotes high standards for early childhood teachers. Awards credentials to family day care, preschool, home visitor, and infant-toddler caregivers. Administers the Child Development Associate National Credentialing Program, designed to assess and credential early childhood education professionals.

Council of Chief State School Officers, *1 Massachusetts Ave. N.W., #700, 20001-1431; (202) 336-7000. Fax, (202) 408-8072. Chris Minnich, Executive Director. Press, (202) 336-7034.*
General email, communications@ccsso.org
Web, www.ccsso.org and Twitter, @CCSSO

Membership: the public officials who head departments of elementary and secondary education in the states, the District of Columbia, the Department of Defense Education Activity, and five U.S. extrastate jurisdictions. Provides leadership, advocacy, and technical assistance on major educational issues. Seeks member consensus on major educational issues and advocates issue positions to civic and professional organizations, federal agencies, Congress, and the public.

Council of the Great City Schools, *1301 Pennsylvania Ave. N.W., #702, 20004-1758; (202) 393-2427. Fax, (202) 393-2400. Mike Casserly, Executive Director.*
Web, www.cgcs.org and Twitter, @GreatCitySchls

Membership: superintendents and school board members of large urban school districts. Provides research, legislative, and support services for members; interests include elementary and secondary education and school finance.

Editorial Projects in Education, Inc., *6935 Arlington Rd., #100, Bethesda, MD 20814-5233; (301) 280-3100.*
Fax, (301) 280-3200. Virginia Edwards, President.
Toll-free, (800) 346-1834.
General email, gined@epe.org
Web, www.edweek.org

Promotes awareness of important issues in K–12 education among professionals and the public. Publishes books and special reports on topics of interest to educators.

National Assn. for College Admission Counseling, *1050 N. Highland St., #400, Arlington, VA 22201; (703) 836-2222. Fax, (703) 243-9375. Joyce Smith, Chief Executive Officer. Information, (800) 822-6285.*
General email, info@nacacnet.org
Web, www.nacacnet.org

Membership: high school guidance counselors, independent counselors, college and university admissions officers, and financial aid officers. Promotes and funds research on admission counseling and on the transition from high school to college. Acts as advocate for student rights in college admissions. Sponsors national college fairs and continuing education for members.

National Assn. for the Education of Young Children, *1313 L St. N.W., #500, 20005; (202) 232-8777. Fax, (202) 328-1846. Rhian Allvin, Executive Director.*
Information, (800) 424-2460.
General email, naeyc@naeyc.org
Web, www.naeyc.org

Membership: early childhood teachers, administrators, college faculty, and directors of early childhood programs at the state and local levels. Works to improve the education of and the quality of services to children from birth through age eight. Sponsors professional development opportunities for early childhood educators. Offers an accreditation program and conducts two conferences annually; issues publications.

National Assn. of Elementary School Principals, *1615 Duke St., Alexandria, VA 22314; (703) 684-3345.*

Fax, (703) 549-5568. Gail Connelly, Executive Director. Toll-free, (800) 386-2377.

General email, naesp@naesp.org

Web, www.naesp.org

Membership: elementary school and middle school principals. Conducts workshops for members on federal and state policies and programs and on professional development. Offers assistance in contract negotiations.

National Assn. of Secondary School Principals, *1904 Association Dr., Reston, VA 20191-1537; (703) 860-0200. Fax, (703) 476-5432. JoAnn Bartoletti, Executive Director.*

Web, www.nassp.org

Membership: principals and assistant principals of middle schools and senior high schools, both public and private, and college-level teachers of secondary education. Conducts training programs for members; serves as clearinghouse for information on secondary school administration. Student activities office provides student councils, student activity advisers, and national and junior honor societies with information on national associations.

National Head Start Assn., *1651 Prince St., Alexandria, VA 22314; (703) 739-0875. Fax, (703) 739-0878. Yasmina S. Vinci, Executive Director. Toll-free, (866) 677-8724.*

Web, www.nhsa.org

Membership: organizations that represent Head Start children, families, and staff. Recommends strategies on issues affecting Head Start programs; provides training and professional development opportunities. Monitors legislation and regulations.

National PTA, *1250 N. Pitt St., Alexandria, VA 22314; (703) 518-1200. Fax, (703) 836-0942. Nathan R. Monell, Executive Director; Elizabeth Rorick, Government Affairs and Communications. Toll-free, (800) 307-4782.*

General email, info@pta.org

Web, www.pta.org

Membership: parent-teacher associations at the preschool, elementary, and secondary levels. Washington office represents members' interests on education, funding for education, parent involvement, child protection and safety, comprehensive health care for children, AIDS, the environment, children's television and educational technology, child care, and nutrition.

National School Boards Assn., *1680 Duke St., Alexandria, VA 22314-3493; (703) 838-6722. Fax, (703) 549-7590. Thomas Gentzel, Executive Director, (703) 838-6700; Francisco Negron, General Counsel, (703) 838-6710.*

General email, info@nsba.org

Web, www.nsba.org

Federation of state school board associations. Interests include funding of public education, local governance, and quality of education programs. Sponsors seminars, an annual conference, and an information center. Publishes a monthly journal and various newsletters. Monitors legislation and regulations. Library open to the public by appointment.

Reading Is Fundamental, *1730 Rhode Island Ave. N.W., #1100, 20036; (202) 536-3400. Fax, (202) 536-3518. Carol H. Rasco, President. Information, 877-RIF-READ. Press, (202) 536-3458.*

General email, contactus@rif.org

Web, www.rif.org and Twitter, @RIFWEB

Conducts programs and workshops to motivate young people to read. Provides young people in low-income neighborhoods with free books and parents with services to encourage reading at home.

School Nutrition Assn., *120 Waterfront St., #300, National Harbor, MD 20745; (301) 686-3100. Fax, (301) 686-3115. Patricia Montague, Chief Executive Officer. Information, (800) 877-8822.*

General email, servicecenter@schoolnutrition.org

Web, www.schoolnutrition.org and Twitter, @SchoolLunch

Membership: state and national food service workers and supervisors, school cafeteria managers, nutrition educators, industry members, and others interested in school food programs and child nutrition. Offers credentialing and sponsors National School Lunch Week and National School Breakfast Week. (Formerly the American School Food Service Assn.)

Teach for America, *Washington Office, 1805 7th St. N.W., 6th Floor, 20001; (202) 552-2400. Fax, (202) 371-9272. Adele Fabrikant, Executive Director. Information, (800) 832-1230.*

General email, admissions@teachforamerica.org

Web, https://dc.teachforamerica.org

A national teacher corps of recent college graduates who teach in underfunded urban and rural public schools. Promotes outstanding teaching methodologies and educational equity. Monitors legislation and regulations. (Headquarters in New York.)

Thomas B. Fordham Institute, *National Office, 1016 16th St. N.W., 8th Floor, 20036; (202) 223-5452. Fax, (202) 223-9226. Michael J. Petrilli, President.*

General email, thegadfly@edexcellence.net

Web, www.edexcellence.net

Advocates education reform to improve the quality of children's school systems. Researches and analyzes education policy issues. Brings scholars to the Capitol to brainstorm solutions to national education issues with education policy experts. Distributes an online course that educates the public about fundamental education policies that affect young students. Publishes the newsletter *The Education Gadfly Weekly.*

Private, Parochial, and Home Schooling

▶ **AGENCIES**

Education Dept., *Non-Public Education, 400 Maryland Ave. S.W., #4W339, 20202-5940; (202) 401-1365. Fax, (202) 401-1368. Maureen Dowling, Director, (202) 260-7820.*

General email, onpe@ed.gov

Web, www2.ed.gov/about/offices/list/oii/nonpublic

Acts as ombudsman for interests of teachers and students in nonpublic schools (elementary and secondary levels); reports to the secretary of education on matters relating to nonpublic education.

▶NONGOVERNMENTAL

Americans United for Separation of Church and State, *1901 L St. N.W., #400, 20036; (202) 466-3234. Fax, (202) 466-2587. Barry W. Lynn, Executive Director.*
General email, americansunited@au.org

Web, www.au.org and Twitter, @americansunited

Citizens' interest group. Opposes federal and state aid to parochial schools; works to ensure religious neutrality in public schools; supports free religious exercise; initiates litigation; maintains speakers bureau. Monitors legislation and regulations.

Council for American Private Education, *13017 Wisteria Dr., #457, Germantown, MD 20874; (301) 916-8460. Fax, (301) 916-8485. Joe McTighe, Executive Director.*
General email, cape@capenet.org

Web, www.capenet.org

Coalition of national private school associations serving private elementary and secondary schools. Acts as a liaison between private education and government, other educational organizations, the media, and the public. Seeks greater access to private schools for all families. Monitors legislation and regulations.

Home School Legal Defense Assn., *1 Patrick Henry Circle, Purcellville, VA 20132 (mailing address: P.O. Box 3000, Purcellville, VA 20134-9000); (540) 338-5600. Fax, (540) 338-2733. J. Michael Smith, President.*
General email, info@hslda.org

Web, www.hslda.org

Membership: families who practice home schooling. Provides members with legal consultation and defense. Initiates civil rights litigation on behalf of members. Monitors legislation and regulations.

National Assn. of Independent Schools, *Government Relations, 1129 20th St. N.W., #800, 20036; (202) 973-9700. Fax, (888) 316-3862. Donna Orem, President, Acting. Press, (202) 973-9717.*
General email, info@nais.org

Web, www.nais.org

Membership: independent elementary and secondary schools in the United States and abroad. Provides statistical and educational information to members. Monitors legislation and regulations.

National Catholic Educational Assn., *1005 N. Glebe Rd., #525, Arlington, VA 22201; (571) 257-0010. Fax, (703) 243-0025. Brother Thomas W. Burnford, President, Acting. Toll-free, (800) 711-6232.*

General email, ncea@ncea.org

Web, www.ncea.org

Membership: Catholic schools (preschool through college and seminary) and school administrators. Provides consultation services to members for administration, curriculum, continuing education, religious education, campus ministry, boards of education, and union and personnel negotiations; conducts workshops and conferences; supports federal aid for private education. (Affiliated with the Assn. of Catholic Colleges and Universities.)

National PTA, *1250 N. Pitt St., Alexandria, VA 22314; (703) 518-1200. Fax, (703) 836-0942. Nathan R. Monell, Executive Director; Elizabeth Rorick, Government Affairs and Communications. Toll-free, (800) 307-4782.*
General email, info@pta.org

Web, www.pta.org

Membership: parent-teacher associations at the preschool, elementary, and secondary levels. Coordinates the National Coalition for Public Education, which opposes tuition tax credits and vouchers for private education.

U.S. Conference of Catholic Bishops (USCCB), *Secretariat of Catholic Education, 3211 4th St. N.E., 20017-1194; (202) 541-3132. Fax, (202) 541-3390. Sr. John Mary Fleming, Executive Director.*
Web, www.usccb.org/beliefs-and-teachings/how-we-teach/catholic-education

Represents Catholic bishops in the United States in public policy educational issues.

SPECIAL GROUPS IN EDUCATION

Gifted and Talented

▶NONGOVERNMENTAL

Council for Exceptional Children (CEC), *2900 Crystal Dr., #1000, Arlington, VA 22202-3557; (703) 620-3660. Fax, (703) 264-9494. Alexander T. Graham, Executive Director. Toll-free, (888) 232-7733. TTY, (866) 915-5000.*
General email, service@cec.sped.org

Web, www.cec.sped.org and Twitter, @CECMembership

Membership association that acts as advocate on behalf of children with disabilities and gifts and talents as well as special educators. Sets professional standards for the field; publishes books, journals, newsletters, and other resources; and offers professional development for teachers and administrators, including an annual convention. Sponsors the Yes I Can! Awards for children with disabilities who excel. Monitors legislation and regulations.

National Assn. for Gifted Children, *1331 H St. N.W., #1001, 20005; (202) 785-4268. Fax, (202) 785-4248. Rene Islas, Executive Director.*
General email, nagc@nagc.org

Web, www.nagc.org

Membership: teachers, administrators, state coordinators, and parents. Acts as advocate for increased federal support for intellectually and creatively gifted children in public and private schools. Produces publications and conducts training for educators and parents.

Learning and Physically Disabled

▶**AGENCIES**

Education Dept., *Special Education and Rehabilitative Services,* 550 12th St. S.W., 5th Floor, 20202-7100 (mailing address: 400 Maryland Ave. S.W., Washington, DC 20202-7000); (202) 245-7468. Fax, (202) 245-7638. Main phone is voice and TTY accessible. Michael Yudin, Assistant Secretary.
Web, www2.ed.gov/about/offices/list/osers

Administers federal assistance programs for the education and rehabilitation of people with disabilities through the Office of Special Education Programs and the Rehabilitation Services Administration; maintains a national information clearinghouse for people with disabilities. Provides information on federal legislation and programs and national organizations concerning individuals with disabilities.

Education Dept., *Special Education and Rehabilitative Services, Special Education Programs,* 550 12th St. S.W., 5th Floor, 20202-3600; (202) 245-7459. Fax, (202) 245-7323. Ruth Ryder, Director, Acting.
Web, www2.ed.gov/about/offices/list/osers/osep

Responsible for special education programs and services designed to meet the needs and develop the full potential of children from infancy through age 21. Programs include support for training of teachers and other professional personnel; grants for research; financial aid to help states initiate and improve their resources; and media services and captioned films for hearing-impaired persons.

Institute of Education Sciences *(Education Dept.),* **National Center for Special Education Research,** 555 New Jersey Ave. N.W., #510F, 20208-5500; (202) 219-1309. Fax, (202) 219-1402. Joan McLaughlin, Commissioner.
Web, www.ies.ed.gov/ncser

Sponsors a comprehensive program of special education research designed to expand the knowledge and understanding of infants, toddlers, and children with disabilities.

John F. Kennedy Center for the Performing Arts, *VSA and Accessibility,* 2700 F St. N.W., 20566 (mailing address: P.O. Box 101510, Arlington, VA 22210); (202) 416-8898. Fax, (202) 416-4840. Betty Siegel, Director.
General email, access@kennedy-center.org
Web, www.vsarts.org

Initiates and supports research and program development providing arts training and programming for persons with disabilities to make classrooms and communities more inclusive. Provides technical assistance and training to VSA Arts state organizations; acts as an information clearinghouse for arts and persons with disabilities.

Office of Personnel Management (OPM), *Veterans Services,* 1900 E St. N.W., #7439, 20415; (202) 606-3602. Fax, (202) 606-6017. Hakeem Basheerud-Deen, Director.
Web, www.opm.gov/policy-data-oversight/veterans-services

Provides outreach to colleges and universities on Schedule A hiring authorities for people with disabilities.

Smithsonian Institution, *Accessibility Program,* 14th St. and Constitution Ave. N.W., #1050, 20013-7012 (mailing address: P.O. Box 37012, NMAH, MRC 607, Washington, DC 20013-7012); (202) 633-2921. Fax, (202) 633-4352. Elizabeth (Beth) Ziebarth, Director. Information, (888) 783-0001.
General email, access@si.edu
Web, www.si.edu/accessibility

Coordinates the Smithsonian's efforts to improve accessibility of its programs and facilities to visitors and staff with disabilities. Serves as a resource for museums and individuals nationwide.

▶**CONGRESS**

For a listing of relevant congressional committees and subcommittees, please see page 164 or the Appendix.

Library of Congress, *National Library Service for the Blind and Physically Handicapped,* 1291 Taylor St. N.W., 20542 (mailing address: Library of Congress, Washington, DC 20542); (202) 707-5100. Fax, (202) 707-0712. Karen Keninger, Director. Toll-free, (800) 424-8567. TTY, (202) 707-0744.
General email, nls@loc.gov
Braille email, braille@loc.gov
Web, www.loc.gov/nls

Administers a national program of free library services for persons with physical disabilities in cooperation with regional and subregional libraries. Produces and distributes full-length books and magazines in recorded form and in Braille. Reference section answers questions relating to blindness and physical disabilities and on library services available to persons with disabilities.

▶**NONGOVERNMENTAL**

Assn. for Education and Rehabilitation of the Blind and Visually Impaired, 1703 N. Beauregard St., #440, Alexandria, VA 22311; (703) 671-4500. Fax, (703) 671-6391. Louis M. Tutt, Executive Director. Toll-free, (877) 492-2708.
General email, aer@aerbvi.org
Web, www.aerbvi.org

Membership: professionals who work in all phases of education and rehabilitation of children and adults who are blind and visually impaired. Provides support and professional development opportunities through conferences, continuing education, and publications. Issues professional recognition awards and student scholarships. Monitors legislation and regulations.

Assn. of University Centers on Disabilities (AUCD), *1100 Wayne Ave., #1000, Silver Spring, MD 20910; (301) 588-8252. Fax, (301) 588-2842. Andrew J. Imparato, Executive Director.*
General email, aucdinfo@aucd.org
Web, www.aucd.org and Twitter, @AUCDNews

Network of facilities that diagnose and treat the developmentally disabled. Trains graduate students and professionals in the field; helps state and local agencies develop services. Interests include interdisciplinary training and services, early screening to prevent developmental disabilities, and development of equipment and programs to serve persons with disabilities.

Council for Exceptional Children (CEC), *2900 Crystal Dr., #1000, Arlington, VA 22202-3557; (703) 620-3660. Fax, (703) 264-9494. Alexander T. Graham, Executive Director. Toll-free, (888) 232-7733. TTY, (866) 915-5000.*
General email, service@cec.sped.org
Web, www.cec.sped.org and Twitter, @CECMembership

Membership association that acts as advocate on behalf of children with disabilities and gifts and talents as well as special educators. Sets professional standards for the field; publishes books, journals, newsletters, and other resources; and offers professional development for teachers and administrators, including an annual convention. Sponsors the Yes I Can! Awards for children with disabilities who excel. Monitors legislation and regulations.

Council for Opportunity in Education, *1025 Vermont Ave. N.W., #900, 20005-3516; (202) 347-7430. Fax, (202) 347-0786. Maureen Hoyler, President.*
General email, beth.hogan@coenet.us
Web, www.coenet.us and Twitter, @COETalk

Membership: more than 1,000 colleges and agencies. Works in conjunction with colleges and agencies that host the federally funded TRIO programs, designed to help low-income, first-generation immigrants, students with disabilities, and veterans enroll in and graduate from college.

Gallaudet University, *800 Florida Ave. N.E., 20002-3695; (202) 651-5000. Roberta (Bobbi) Cordano, President, (202) 651-5005.*
Web, www.gallaudet.edu and Twitter, @GallaudetU

Offers undergraduate, graduate, and doctoral degree programs for deaf, hard of hearing, and hearing students. Conducts research; maintains the Laurent Clerc National Deaf Education Center and demonstration preschool, elementary (Kendall Demonstration Elementary School), and secondary (Model Secondary School for the Deaf) programs. Sponsors the Center for Global Education, National Deaf Education Network and Clearinghouse, and the Cochlear Implant Education Center. Links to each department's video phone are at www.gallaudet.edu/about_gallaudet/contact_us.html.

National Assn. of Private Special Education Centers, *601 Pennsylvania Ave. N.W., South Bldg., #900, 20004; (202) 434-8225. Fax, (202) 434-8224. Sherry L. Kolbe, Executive Director.*

General email, napsec@napsec.org
Web, www.napsec.org

Membership: private special education programs at the preschool, elementary, and secondary levels and postsecondary levels, as well as adult programs. Acts as advocate for greater education opportunities for children, youth, and adults with disabilities.

National Assn. of State Directors of Special Education, *225 Reinkers Lane, #420, Alexandria, VA 22314; (703) 519-3800. Fax, (703) 519-3808. Bill East, Executive Director.*
General email, nasdse@nasdse.org
Web, www.nasdse.org

Membership: state directors of special education and others interested in special education policy. Monitors legislation, regulations, policy, and research affecting special education.

Minorities and Women

▶**AGENCIES**

Bureau of Indian Education (BIE) *(Interior Dept.), 1849 C St. N.W., MS 4657-MIB, 20240; (202) 208-6123. Fax, (202) 208-3312. Charles M Roessel, Director.*
Web, www.bie.edu/WhoWeAre/BIE/index.htm

Operates schools and promotes school improvement for Native Americans, including people with disabilities. Provides assistance to Native American pupils in public schools. Aids Native American college students. Sponsors adult education programs designed specifically for Native Americans.

Civil Rights Division *(Justice Dept.), Educational Opportunities, 601 D St. N.W., #4300, 20530; (202) 514-4092. Fax, (202) 514-8337. Shaheena Simons, Chief, Acting. Toll-free, (877) 292-3804.*
General email, education@usdoj.gov
Web, www.justice.gov/crt/educational-opportunities-section

Initiates litigation to ensure equal opportunities in public education; enforces laws dealing with civil rights in public education.

Education Dept., *Civil Rights, 400 Maryland Ave. S.W., #4E313, 20202-1100; (202) 453-5900. Fax, (202) 453-6012. Catherine Lhamon, Assistant Secretary, (202) 453-7240. Toll-free, (800) 421-3481. TTY, (800) 877-8339.*
General email, ocr@ed.gov
Web, www2.ed.gov/ocr

Enforces laws prohibiting use of federal funds for education programs or activities that discriminate on the basis of race, color, sex, national origin, age, or disability; authorized to discontinue funding.

Education Dept., *Elementary and Secondary Education, Indian Education Programs, 400 Maryland Ave. S.W., #3E205, 20202-6335; (202) 260-3774. Fax, (202) 260-7779. Joyce Silverthorne, Director, (202) 401-0767.*

General email, indian.education@ed.gov

Web, www2.ed.gov/about/offices/list/oese/oie

Aids local school districts with programs for Native American and Alaska Native students.

Education Dept., *Elementary and Secondary Education, Migrant Education, 400 Maryland Ave. S.W., #3E317, LBJ, 20202-6135; (202) 260-1164. Fax, (202) 205-0089. Lisa Ramirez, Director.*

Web, www2.ed.gov/about/offices/list/oese/ome

Administers programs that fund education (preschool through postsecondary) for children of migrant workers.

Education Dept., *Elementary and Secondary Education, State Support, 400 Maryland Ave. S.W., #3W202, FB-6, 20202-6132; (202) 260-0826. Fax, (202) 260-7764. Patrick Rooney, Director, Acting.*

Web, www2.ed.gov/about/offices/list/oese/oss

Administers Title I, Part A grants to local educational agencies along with several other major programs, including Title II, Title III, The School Improvement Grants, Race To The Top, the State Assessment Grant program, and the Enhanced Assessment Grant program.

Education Dept., *Postsecondary Education, Higher Education Programs, Institutional Service, 1990 K St. N.W., 6th Floor, 20006; (202) 502-7549. Fax, (202) 502-7699. Leonard L. Haynes III, Senior Director, (202) 502-7549.*

General email, OPE_Institutional_Development@ed.gov

Web, www2.ed.gov/about/offices/list/ope/idues

Provides financial and administrative support for limited resource institutions serving minority and financially disadvantaged students. Administers programs authorized under the Higher Education Act of 1965 and its subsequent amendments. Title III programs include support for Historically Black Colleges and Universities, American Indian Tribally Controlled Colleges and Universities, and Minority Science and Engineering Improvement Program. Title V programs strengthen institutions serving Hispanic and other low-income students. Title VII supports the implementation and evaluation of and shares findings of innovative educational reform ideas.

Education Dept., *Postsecondary Education, Higher Education Programs, Student Service, 1990 K St. N.W., 7th Floor, 20006-8510; (202) 502-7600. Fax, (202) 502-7857. Linda Byrd-Johnson, Director.*

General email, OPE_TRIO@ed.gov

Web, www2.ed.gov/about/offices/list/ope/trio

Administers grant programs for low-income, potential first-generation students and individuals with disabilities from middle school to graduate school, in addition to programs focused on college readiness, campus-based child care, and graduate fellowships. Programs include Educational Opportunity Centers, Upward Bound, Upward Bound Math and Science, Talent Search, Student Support Services, Ronald E. McNair Post-Baccalaureate Achievement Program, TRIO training program, and Veterans Upward Bound.

Education Dept., *White House Initiative on American Indian and Alaska Natives Education, 400 Maryland Ave. S.W., #4W116, 20202; (202) 453-6600. Fax, (202) 453-5635. William Mendoza, Executive Director, (202) 260-0513. Web, http://sites.ed.gov/whiaiane*

Supports activities that expand and improve educational opportunities for American Indians and Alaska Native students. Interests include reducing the student dropout rate, strengthening tribal colleges and universities, and helping students acquire industry-recognized credentials for job attainment and advancement. Supports teaching native languages and histories at all educational levels.

Education Dept., *White House Initiative on Asian Americans and Pacific Islanders, 550 12th St. S.W., 10th Floor, 20202; (202) 245-6418. Fax, (202) 245-7166. Doua Thor, Executive Director. Press, (202) 245-6353.*

General email, whitehouseaapi@ed.gov

Web, http://sites.ed.gov/whieeaa and Twitter, @whitehouseAAPI

Works to increase Asian American and Pacific Islander participation in federal education programs. Supports institutions of higher education through two-year grants to improve academic programs, institutional management, and fiscal stability.

Education Dept., *White House Initiative on Educational Excellence for African Americans, 400 Maryland Ave. S.W., #4W106, 20202; (202) 205-9853. David J. Johns, Executive Director.*

General email, WHIEEAA@ed.gov

Web, http://sites.ed.gov/whieeaa and Twitter, @afameducation

Promotes high-quality education for African Americans by improving access to learning opportunities for educators and administrators, supporting efforts to increase the number of African American teachers and administrators, enhancing investments in early care and education programs, reinforcing connections to rigorous K–12 courses and increasing access to critical supports, and helping to increase the number of African American students applying to, persisting in, and successfully completing college.

Education Dept., *White House Initiative on Educational Excellence for Hispanics, 400 Maryland Ave. S.W., #4W108, 20202-3601; (202) 401-1411. Fax, (202) 401-8377. Alejandra (Alex) Ceja, Executive Director.*

General email, whieeh@ed.gov

Web, http://sites.ed.gov/hispanic-initiative and Twitter, @HispanicEd

Promotes high-quality education for Hispanic communities and the participation of Hispanics in federal education programs. Disseminates information on educational resources. Promotes parental involvement, engagement of the business community, early learning programs, and enrollment in college. Works directly with communities nationwide in public-private partnerships.

Education Dept., *White House Initiative on Historically Black Colleges and Universities,* 400 Maryland Ave. S.W., #4C128, 20202; (202) 453-5634. Fax, (202) 453-5632. Ivory Toldson, Executive Director, (202) 453-5627. General email, oswhi-hbcu@ed.gov

Web, http://sites.ed.gov/whhbcu

Seeks to expand the participation of the black college community in the programs of the federal government and to engage the private sector to help achieve this objective. Hosts annual conference. Provides information about federal contracts, grants, scholarships, fellowships, and other resources available to historically black colleges and universities.

U.S. Commission on Civil Rights, *Civil Rights Evaluation,* 1331 Pennsylvania Ave. N.W., #1150, 20425; (202) 376-7700. Fax, (202) 376-7754. Maureen Rudolf, Chief, Acting. Complaints Unit hotline, (202) 376-8513. Web, www.usccr.gov

Researches federal policy on education, including desegregation. Library open to the public.

▶ **CONGRESS**

For a listing of relevant congressional committees and subcommittees, please see page 164 or the Appendix.

▶ **NONGOVERNMENTAL**

American Assn. of University Women (AAUW), 1111 16th St. N.W., 20036-4873; (202) 785-7700. Fax, (202) 872-1425. Linda D. Hallman, Chief Executive Officer. Toll-free, (800) 326-2289. TTY, (202) 785-7777. General email, connect@aauw.org

Web, www.aauw.org

Membership: graduates of accredited colleges, universities, and recognized foreign institutions. Interests include equity for women and girls in education, the workplace, health care, and the family.

American Indian Higher Education Consortium, 121 Oronoco St., Alexandria, VA 22314; (703) 838-0400. Fax, (703) 838-0388. Carrie L. Billy, President. General email, info@aihec.org

Web, www.aihec.org and Twitter, @aihec

Membership: tribal colleges and universities (TCUs). Objectives include increased financial support for TCUs, equitable participation in the land grant system, expanded technology programs in Indian Country, and development of an accrediting body for postsecondary institutions that serve American Indians.

Assn. of American Colleges and Universities (AACU), 1818 R St. N.W., 20009; (202) 387-3760. Fax, (202) 265-9532. Carol Geary Schneider, President. Web, www.aacu.org, Twitter, @aacu and Facebook, www.facebook.com/Association-of-American-Colleges-and-Universities-48308128458

Serves as clearinghouse for information on women professionals in higher education. Interests include women's studies, women's centers, and women's leadership and professional development.

Assn. of Public and Land-Grant Universities, *Office for Access and Success: The Advancement of Public Black Colleges and Hispanic Serving Institutions,* 1307 New York Ave. N.W., #400, 20005-4722; (202) 478-6040. Fax, (202) 478-6046. Rosusan Bartee, Vice President, Acting. Web, www.aplu.org

Seeks to improve equity, access, and successful outcomes at all public and land-grant universities with a special focus on underserved students and minority-serving institutions. Conducts research, provides advocacy, implements programs, and provides capacity-building for such institutions; acts as a liaison between these institutions, the federal government, and private associations. Monitors legislation and regulations.

Clare Booth Luce Policy Institute, 112 Elden St., Suite P, Herndon, VA 20170; (703) 318-0730. Fax, (703) 318-8867. Michelle Easton, President. Toll-free, (888) 891-4288. General email, info@cblpi.org

Web, www.cblpi.org and Twitter, @CBLPI

Seeks to engage young women through student programs promoting conservative values and leadership. Offers mentoring, internship, and networking opportunities for young women.

Council for Opportunity in Education, 1025 Vermont Ave. N.W., #900, 20005-3516; (202) 347-7430. Fax, (202) 347-0786. Maureen Hoyler, President. General email, beth.hogan@coenet.us

Web, www.coenet.us and Twitter, @COETalk

Membership: more than 1,000 colleges and agencies. Works in conjunction with colleges and agencies that host the federally funded TRIO programs, designed to help low-income, first-generation immigrants, students with disabilities, and veterans enroll in and graduate from college.

Hispanic Assn. of Colleges and Universities, *Washington Office,* 1 Dupont Circle N.W., #430, 20036; (202) 833-8361. (202) 467-0893. Fax, (202) 496-9177. Antonio R. Flores, President. General email, hnip@hacu.net

Web, www.hacu.net/hacu/default.asp

Membership: Hispanic-serving institutions (HSIs) and other higher education institutions committed to improving the quality of schools for Hispanics in the United States, Puerto Rico, Latin America, and Spain. Focuses on increased federal funding for HSIs; partnerships with government agencies and industry; faculty development and research; technological assistance; and financial aid and internships for Hispanic students. (Headquarters in San Antonio, Tex.)

Institute for Responsible Citizenship, 1227 25th St. N.W., 6th Floor, 20037; (202) 660-2501. William A. Keyes, President. Web, www.theinstitute.net

Offers grants, internships, and leadership courses for African American men scholars. Academic areas for internships include art, business, finance, philanthropy, education, government, science, law, public relations, medicine, journalism, and religion.

League of United Latin American Citizens, *1133 19th St. N.W., #1000, 20036; (202) 833-6130. Fax, (202) 833-6135. Brent Wilkes, Executive Director. Toll-free, (877) LULAC-01. General email, info@lulac.org*

Web, www.lulac.org

Seeks to increase the number of minorities, especially Hispanics, attending postsecondary schools; supports legislation to increase educational opportunities for Hispanics and other minorities; provides scholarship funds and educational and career counseling.

The Links Inc., *1200 Massachusetts Ave. N.W., 20005-4501; (202) 842-8686. Fax, (202) 842-4020. Glenda Newell-Harris, President.*

Web, www.linksinc.org, Facebook, www.facebook.com/thelinksinc and Twitter, @linksinc

Predominantly African American women's service organization that works to enrich, sustain, and ensure the culture and economic survival of African Americans and other persons of African ancestry. Areas of focus are: services to youth, the arts, national trends and service, international trends and services, and health and human services. Programs are implemented via sharing of public information, education, economic development, and public policy campaigns.

NAACP Legal Defense and Educational Fund, Inc., *Washington Office, 1444 Eye St. N.W., 10th Floor, 20005; (202) 682-1300. Fax, (202) 682-1312. Leslie M. Proll, Director.*

Web, www.naacpldf.org

Civil rights litigation group that provides legal information about civil rights and advice on educational discrimination against women and minorities; monitors federal enforcement of civil rights laws. Not affiliated with the NAACP. (Headquarters in New York.)

National Alliance of Black School Educators, *310 Pennsylvania Ave. S.E., 20003; (202) 608-6310. Fax, (202) 608-6319. Marietta English, Executive Director, Acting. Toll-free, (800) 221-2654.*

Web, www.nabse.org

Seeks to increase the academic achievement of all children, in particular those of African American descent, by developing and recommending educational policy. Provides professional development, networking, advocacy, and research and development opportunities for educators and school administrators, including workshops and conferences. Disseminates new instructional and learning strategies.

National Assn. for Equal Opportunity in Higher Education (NAFEO), *209 3rd St. S.E., 20003; (202) 552-3300. Fax, (202) 552-3330. Lezli Baskerville, President.*

Web, www.nafeo.org

Membership: historically and predominantly black colleges and universities, including public, private, land-grant, two-year, four-year, graduate, and professional schools. Represents and acts as advocate on behalf of its member institutions and the students, faculty, and alumni they serve. Operates a national research and resource center on blacks in higher education.

National Assn. for the Advancement of Colored People (NAACP), *Washington Bureau, 1156 15th St. N.W., #915, 20005; (202) 463-2940. Fax, (202) 463-2953. Hilary O. Shelton, Director. General email, washingtonbureau@naacpnet.org*

Web, www.naacp.org

Membership: persons interested in civil rights for all minorities. Works for equal opportunity for minorities in all areas, including education; seeks to ensure a high-quality desegregated education for all through litigation and legislation. (Headquarters in Baltimore, Md.)

National Assn. of Colored Women's and Youth Clubs Inc. (NACWYC), *1601 R St. N.W., 20009-6420; (202) 667-4080. Fax, (202) 667-2574. Sharon R. Bridgeforth, President. General email, cearly@nacwcya.org*

Web, www.nacwc.org

Seeks to promote education, protect and enforce civil rights, raise the standard of family living, promote interracial understanding, and enhance leadership development. Awards scholarships; conducts programs in education, social service, and philanthropy.

National Clearinghouse for English Language Acquisition (NCELA), *Language Instruction Educational Programs, 8757 Georgia Ave., #460, Silver Spring, MD 20910; (866) 347-6864. Kathy Zantal-Wiener, Project Director. General email, askncela@leedmci.com*

Web, www.ncela.us

Collects, analyzes, and disseminates information relating to the effective education of linguistically and culturally diverse learners in the United States. Supports the Office of English Language Acquisition, Language Enhancement, and Academic Achievement for Limited English Proficient Students (OELA) in its mission to respond to Title III educational needs, and implement No Child Left Behind (NCLB) as it applies to English language learners. Supports networking among state-level administrators of Title III programs. Serves other stakeholders involved in English learner education, including teachers and other practitioners, parents, university faculty, administrators and federal policymakers. Authorized under Title III of the No Child Left Behind Act of 2001 (NCLB).

National Council of La Raza, *1126 16th St. N.W., #600, 20036-4845; (202) 785-1670. Fax, (202) 776-1792. Janet Murguía, President. General email, info@nclr.org*

Web, www.nclr.org, Twitter, @NCLR and Facebook, www.facebook.com/Nationalcouncilofularaza

Provides research, policy analysis, and advocacy on educational status and needs of Hispanics; promotes education reform benefiting Hispanics; develops and tests community-based models for helping Hispanic students succeed in school. Interests include counseling, testing, and bilingual, vocational, preschool through postsecondary, and migrant education.

National Council of Women's Organizations, *714 G St. S.E., #200, 20003; (202) 293-4505. Fax, (202) 293-4507. Shireen Mitchell, Chair.*
General email, ncwo@ncwo-online.org
Web, www.ncwo-online.org

Membership: local and national women's organizations. Engages in policy work and grassroots activism to address issues of concern to women, including workplace and economic equity, education and job training, affirmative action, Social Security, child care, reproductive freedom, health, and global women's equality. Monitors legislation and regulations.

National Hispanic Foundation for the Arts (NHFA), *Washington Square, 1050 Connecticut Ave. N.W., 5th Floor, #500, 20036; (202) 293-8330. Fax, (202) 772-3101. Felix Sanchez, Chair.*
General email, info@hispanicarts.org
Web, www.hispanicarts.org

Strives to increase the presence of Hispanics in the media, telecommunications, entertainment industries, and performing arts, and to increase programming for the U.S. Latino community. Provides scholarships for Hispanic students to pursue graduate study in the arts.

National Indian Education Assn. (NIEA), *1514 P St. N.W., Suite B, 20005; (202) 544-7290. Fax, (202) 544-7293. Ahniwake Rose, Executive Director.*
General email, niea@niea.org
Web, www.niea.org, Twitter, @WereNIEA and Facebook, www.facebook.com/NIEAFanPage

Represents American Indian, Alaska Native, and Native Hawaiian educators and students. Seeks to improve educational opportunities and resources for those groups nationwide while preserving their traditional cultures and values. Monitors legislation and regulations.

National Society of Black Engineers, *205 Daingerfield Rd., Alexandria, VA 22314; (703) 549-2207. Fax, (703) 683-5312. Karl Reid, Executive Director.*
General email, info@nsbe.org
Web, www.nsbe.org

Membership: college students studying engineering. Offers academic excellence programs, scholarships, leadership training, and professional and career development opportunities. Activities include tutorial programs, group study sessions, high school/junior high outreach programs, technical seminars and workshops, career fairs, and an annual convention.

National Women's Law Center, *11 Dupont Circle N.W., #800, 20036; (202) 588-5180. Fax, (202) 588-5185.*

Nancy Duff Campbell, Co-President; Marcia D. Greenberger, Co-President.
General email, info@nwlc.org
Web, www.nwlc.org

Works to protect and advance the rights of women and girls at work, in school, and beyond. Maintains programs that focus on enforcing Title IX's provisions for equal treatment in education and narrowing the gender gap in athletics and the technology-oriented workplace. Other interests include equal pay and benefits, sexual harassment laws, the right to family leave, child care and early learning, poverty and income support, and the preservation of diversity in the workplace.

Operation Understanding DC, *3000 Connecticut Ave. N.W., #335, 20008; (202) 234-6832. Fax, (202) 234-6669. Aaron Jenkins, Executive Director.*
General email, info@oudc.org
Web, www.oudc.org

African American and Jewish youth education program promoting leadership and antidiscrimination.

United Negro College Fund (UNCF), *1805 7th St. N.W., 20001 (mailing address: P.O. Box 10444, Fairfax, VA 22031-0444); (202) 810-0200. Fax, (202) 810-0224. Michael L. Lomax, President. Toll-free, (800) 331-2244.*
Web, www.uncf.org

Membership: private colleges and universities with historically black enrollment. Raises money for member institutions; monitors legislation and regulations.

Younger Women's Task Force, *1111 16th St. N.W., 20036; (202) 785-7700. Fax, (202) 872-1425. Linda Hallman, Executive Director, (202) 785-7713. Toll-free, (800) 326-2289. TTY, (202) 785-7777.*
General email, ywtf@aauw.org
Web, www.aauw.org/membership/ywtf/ and Twitter, @ywtf

Grassroots organization that encourages young women to engage in political activism on issues directly affecting them. Provides leadership training and a local and national network for peer mentoring; runs financial literacy programs. (Sponsored by the American Assn. of University Women.)

SPECIAL TOPICS IN EDUCATION

Bilingual and Multicultural

▶**AGENCIES**

Bureau of Educational and Cultural Affairs *(State Dept.), English Language Programs, 2200 C St. N.W., #4-B16/SA-5, 20520; (202) 632-9281. Kerri Hannan, Director.*
General email, english@state.gov
Web, http://eca.state.gov/about-bureau-0/organizational-structure/office-english-language-programs

Promotes the learning and teaching of American English around the world in order to foster mutual understanding between the people of other countries and the people of the United States.

Education Dept., *English Language Acquisition, Language Enhancement and Academic Achievement for Limited English Proficient Students, 400 Maryland Ave. S.W., #5E106, 20202-6510; (202) 401-4300. Fax, (202) 205-1229. Libia Gil, Assistant Deputy Secretary. NCELA helpline, (866) 347-6864.*
Web, www2.ed.gov/about/offices/list/oela/index.html

Provides grants for the professional development of teachers of English learners and administers the Native American/Alaska-Native Children in School Program and National Professional Development Discretionary Grant Programs.

Education Dept., *Postsecondary Education, International and Foreign Language Education, 1990 K St. N.W., 6th Floor, 20006; (202) 502-7700. Mohamed Abdel-Kader, Deputy Assistant Secretary.*
Web, www2.ed.gov/about/offices/list/ope/iegps

Advises the Assistant Secretary for Postsecondary Education on matters affecting postsecondary, international, and foreign language education. Responsible for encouraging and promoting the study of foreign languages and cultures of other countries at the elementary, secondary, and postsecondary levels in the United States. Administers programs that increase expertise in foreign languages and area or international studies, and coordinates with related international and foreign language education programs of other federal agencies.

▶**NONGOVERNMENTAL**

National Assn. for Bilingual Education, *c/o Ana G. Mendez University System, 11006 Veirs Mills Rd., Wheaton, MD 20902; (240) 450-3700. Fax, (240) 450-3799. Santiago V. Wood, National Executive Director. General email, nabe@nabe.org*
Web, www.nabe.org

Membership: educators, policymakers, paraprofessionals, parents, personnel, students, and researchers. Works to strengthen educational programs for non-English-speaking students and to promote foreign language education among American students. Conducts annual conference and workshops; publishes research.

National Research Council (NRC), *Testing and Assessment Board, Keck Center, 500 5th St. N.W., 20001; (202) 334-2000. Patricia Morison, Director, Acting; David J. Francis, Chair. General email, bota@nas.edu*
Web, http://sites.nationalacademies.org/dbasse/bota

Seeks to ensure fairness and accuracy in the testing of students with disabilities and English learners.

Teachers of English to Speakers of Other Languages Inc. (TESOL), *1925 Ballenger Ave., #550, Alexandria, VA 22314-6820; (703) 836-0774. Fax, (703) 836-7864,*

Rosa Aronson, Executive Director, ext. 505. Information, (888) 891-0041. General email, info@tesol.org
Web, www.tesol.org

Provides professional development programs and career services for teachers of English to speakers of other languages. Sponsors professional development programs and provides career management services.

World Learning, *International Exchange Programs, 1015 15th St. N.W., 7th Floor, 20005-2065; (202) 408-5420. Fax, (202) 408-5397. Carol Jenkins, President, International Development and Exchange Programs, (202) 464-6643. TTY, (202) 464-5530. Toll-free, (800) 858-0292. General email, development@worldlearning.org*
Web, www.worldlearning.org and Twitter, @WorldLearning

Provides training for English language teachers and other education professionals. Increases access to and the quality of basic education. Administered by World Learning's Division of International Development and Exchange Programs. Administers field-based study abroad programs, which offer semester and summer programs for high school, college, and graduate students.

Citizenship Education

▶**NONGOVERNMENTAL**

American Press Institute (API), *4401 Wilson Blvd., #900, Arlington, VA 22203; (571) 366-1200. Fax, (703) 620-5814. Thomas (Tom) Rosenstiel, Executive Director, (571) 366-1035. General email, hello@pressinstitute.org*
Web, www.americanpressinstitute.org and Twitter, @AmPress

Supports student programs that focus on newspaper readership and an appreciation of the First Amendment as ways of developing engaged and literate citizens.

Close Up Foundation, *1330 Braddock Pl., #400, Alexandria, VA 22314-1952; (703) 706-3300. Fax, (703) 706-0001. Timothy S. Davis, President. Toll-free, (800) 256-7387. General email, info@closeup.org*
Web, www.closeup.org and Twitter, @CloseUp_DC

Sponsors week-long programs on American government in Washington, D.C., for middle and high school students.

Horatio Alger Assn. of Distinguished Americans, *99 Canal Center Plaza, #320, Alexandria, VA 22314; (703) 684-9444. Fax, (703) 548-3822. Terrence J. Giroux, Executive Director. General email, association@horatioalger.org*
Web, www.horatioalger.org

Educates young people about the economic and personal opportunities available in the American free enterprise system. Conducts seminars on careers in public and community service; operates internship program. Presents the Horatio Alger Youth Award to outstanding high school students and the Horatio Alger Award to professionals who have overcome adversity to achieve success in their respective fields. Awards college scholarships to individuals who have overcome adversity.

League of Women Voters Education Fund (LWV), *1730 M St. N.W., #1000, 20036-4508; (202) 429-1965. Fax, (202) 429-0854. Wylecia Wiggs Harris, Executive Director. General email, lwv@lwv.org*

Web, www.lwv.org/education-fund

Education and research organization established by the League of Women Voters of the United States. Promotes citizen knowledge of and involvement in representative government; conducts citizen education on current public policy issues; seeks to increase voter registration and turnout; sponsors candidate forums and debates.

National 4-H Council, *7100 Connecticut Ave., Chevy Chase, MD 20815-4999; (301) 961-2800. Fax, (301) 961-2894. Jennifer L. Sirangelo, President, (301) 961-2820. Press, (301) 961-2973.*

Web, www.4-h.org, Twitter, @4H and Facebook, www.facebook.com/4-h

4-H membership: young people across America learning leadership, citizenship, and life skills. National 4-H Council strengthens and complements the 4-H youth development program of the Agricultural Dept.'s cooperative extension system of state land-grant universities. Interests include 4-H afterschool, healthy lifestyle, science engineering and technology, food security, and citizenship in governance.

Washington Workshops Foundation, *1250 24th St. N.W., #300, 20037; (202) 965-3434. Fax, (202) 965-1018. Tom Crossan, President. Information, (800) 368-5688. General email, info@workshops.org*

Web, www.workshops.org and Twitter, @WorkshopsWire

Educational foundation that provides introductory seminars on American government and politics to junior and senior high school students, including the congressional seminars for high school students.

Consumer Education

▶AGENCIES

Agriculture Dept. (USDA), *Research, Education, and Economics, 1400 Independence Ave. S.W., #214W, MS 0110, 20250-0110; (202) 720-5923. Fax, (202) 690-2842. Catherine E. Woteki, Under Secretary, (202) 720-1542. Web, www.ree.usda.gov*

Coordinates agricultural research, extension, and teaching programs in the food and agricultural sciences, including human nutrition, home economics, consumer services, agricultural economics, environmental quality, natural and renewable resources, forestry and range management, animal and plant production and protection, aquaculture, and the production, distribution, and utilization of food

and agricultural products. Oversees the National Institute of Food and Agriculture.

Consumer Product Safety Commission (CPSC), *Communications, 4330 East-West Hwy., #717, Bethesda, MD 20814-4408; (301) 504-7908. Fax, (301) 504-0862. Scott J. Wolfson, Director, (301) 504-7051. Product safety hotline, (800) 638-2772. TTY, (800) 638-8270. General email, info@cpsc.gov*

Web, www.cpsc.gov

Provides information concerning consumer product safety; works with local and state governments, school systems, and private groups to develop product safety information and education programs. Toll-free hotline accepts consumer complaints on hazardous products and injuries associated with a product and offers recorded information on product recalls and CPSC safety recommendations.

Federal Trade Commission (FTC), *Bureau of Consumer Protection, Consumer and Business Education, 400 7th Ave. S.W., CC-10402, 20024; (202) 326-3650. Fax, (202) 326-3574. Nat Wood, Associate Director. Consumer Response Center, (877) FTC-HELP. Web, www.business.ftc.gov and www.ftc.gov/about-ftc/bureaus-offices/bureau-consumer-protection/our-divisions/division-consumer business*

Develops educational material about FTC activities in order to inform consumers about their rights and to alert businesses about their compliance responsibilities.

Food and Drug Administration (FDA) *(Health and Human Services Dept.), External Affairs, 10903 New Hampshire Ave., Bldg. 32, #5360, Silver Spring, MD 20993; (301) 796-4540. Fax, (301) 827-8030. Lisa Turner, Associate Commissioner. Consumer inquiries, (888) 463-6332. Web, www.fda.gov/AboutFDA/CentersOffices/OC/OfficeofExternalAffairs/default.htm*

Responds to inquiries on issues related to the FDA. Conducts consumer health education programs for specific groups, including women, older adults, and the educationally and economically disadvantaged. Serves as liaison with national health and consumer organizations.

Food Safety and Inspection Service *(Agriculture Dept.), 1400 Independence Ave. S.W., #331E, 20250-3700; (202) 720-7025. Fax, (202) 205-0158. Alfred Almanza, Deputy Under Secretary. Press, (202) 720-9113. Consumer inquiries, (800) 535-4555. TTY, (800) 877-8339. Web, www.usda.gov/fsis*

Sponsors food safety educational programs to inform the public about measures to prevent foodborne illnesses; sponsors lectures, publications, and public service advertising campaigns. Toll-free hotline answers food safety questions.

▶NONGOVERNMENTAL

American Assn. of Family and Consumer Sciences, *400 N. Columbus St., #202, Alexandria, VA 22314; (703) 706-4600. Fax, (703) 706-4663. Carolyn W. Jackson, Executive Director. Toll-free, (800) 424-8080.*

General email, staff@aafcs.org

Web, www.aafcs.org

Membership: professional home economists. Supports family and consumer sciences education; develops accrediting standards for undergraduate family and consumer science programs; trains and certifies family and consumer science professionals. Monitors legislation and regulations concerning family and consumer issues.

Family, Career, and Community Leaders of America, *1910 Association Dr., Reston, VA 20191-1584; (703) 476-4900. Fax, (703) 439-2662. Sandy Spavone, Executive Director. Toll-free, (800) 234-4425.*

General email, inbox@fcclainc.org

Web, www.fcclainc.org and Twitter, @NationalFCCLA

National vocational student organization that helps young men and women address personal, family, work, and social issues through family and consumer sciences education.

JumpStart Coalition for Personal Finance Literacy, *1001 Connecticut Ave. N.W., #640, 20036; (202) 846-6780. Laura Levine, President.*

General email, info@jumpstart.org

Web, www.jumpstart.org

Coalition of organizations that promote financial literacy for pre-K–12 and college-aged students. Offers teacher training programs and online educational materials. Holds annual conferences for financial education professionals. Produces an annual publication that outlines financial education curriculum and topics.

Literacy, Basic Skills

▶AGENCIES

AmeriCorps *(Corp. for National and Community Service), Volunteers in Service to America (VISTA), 250 E St. S.W., 20024-3208; (202) 606-5000. Fax, (202) 565-2789. Max Finberg, Director. Volunteer recruiting information, (800) 942-2677. TTY, (800) 833-3722.*

General email, questions@americorps.gov

Web, www.americorps.gov/programs/americorps/ americorps-vista and Twitter, @nationalservice

Assigns volunteers to local and state education departments, to public agencies, and to private nonprofit organizations that have literacy programs. Other activities include tutor recruitment and training and the organization and expansion of local literacy councils, workplace literacy programs, and intergenerational literacy programs.

Education Dept., *Career, Technical, and Adult Education, Adult Education and Literacy, 550 12th St. S.W., 11th Floor, 20202-7100 (mailing address: 400 Maryland Ave. S.W., P-OCTAE, DAEL, Washington, DC 20202); (202) 245-7720. Fax, (202) 245-7838. Cheryl L. Keenan, Director.*

Web, www2.ed.gov/about/offices/list/ovae/pi/AdultEd/ index.html

Provides state and local education agencies and the general public with information on establishing, expanding, improving, and operating adult education and literacy programs. Emphasizes basic and life skills attainment, English literacy, and high school completion. Awards grants to state education agencies for adult education and literacy programs, including workplace and family literacy.

▶CONGRESS

For a listing of relevant congressional committees and subcommittees, please see page 164 or the Appendix.

Library of Congress, *Center for the Book, James Madison Memorial Bldg., 101 Independence Ave. S.E., #LM 650, 20540; (202) 707-5221. Fax, (202) 707-0269. John Y. Cole, Director.*

General email, cfbook@loc.gov

Web, www.read.gov/cfb

Promotes family and adult literacy; encourages the study of books and stimulates public interest in books, reading, and libraries; sponsors publication of a directory describing national organizations that administer literacy programs. Affiliated state centers sponsor projects and hold events that call attention to the importance of literacy.

Library of Congress, *Young Readers Center, Thomas Jefferson Bldg., 10 1st St. S.E., #LJ G29, 20540; (202) 707-1950. Fax, (202) 707-0269. Karen Jaffe, Head.*

General email, yrc@loc.gov

Web, http://read.gov/yrc

Promotes books, reading, literacy, libraries, and the scholarly study of books through affiliates and promotional programs. Places special emphasis on young readers through reading and writing contests.

▶NONGOVERNMENTAL

AFL-CIO Working for America Institute, *815 16th St. N.W., 20005; (202) 508-3717. Fax, (202) 508-3719. Jane McDonald, Assistant to the President. Office Manager, (202) 637-5251.*

General email, info@workingforamerica.org

Web, www.workingforamerica.org

Provides labor unions, employers, education agencies, and community groups with technical assistance for workplace education programs focusing on adult literacy, basic skills, and job training. Interests include new technologies and workplace innovations.

Assn. for Talent Development (ATD), *1640 King St., 3rd Floor, Alexandria, VA 22314; (703) 683-8100. Fax, (703) 683-1523. Tony Bingham, Chief Executive Officer. Toll-free, (800) 628-2783.*

General email, customercare@astd.org

Web, www.astd.org, Twitter, @atd and Facebook, www.facebook.com/ATD

Membership: trainers and human resource development specialists. Publishes information on workplace literacy.

Center for Applied Linguistics, *4646 40th St. N.W., #200, 20016-1859; (202) 362-0700. Fax, (202) 362-3740. Terrence Wiley, President. General email, info@cal.org*

Web, www.cal.org

Research and technical assistance organization that serves as a clearinghouse on application of linguistics to practical language problems. Interests include English as a second language (ESL), teacher training and material development, language education, language proficiency test development, bilingual education, and sociolinguistics.

First Book, *1319 F St. N.W., #1000, 20004-1155; (202) 393-1222. Fax, (202) 628-1258. Kyle Zimmer, President. Toll-free, (866) 732-3669. General email, staff@firstbook.org*

Web, www.firstbook.org and Twitter, @FirstBook

Donates and sells books to programs serving children of low-income families. Organizes fundraisers to support and promote literacy programs.

General Federation of Women's Clubs, *1734 N St. N.W., 20036-2990; (202) 347-3168. Fax, (202) 835-0246. Rosemary Thomas, Chief Operating Officer. Toll-free, (800) 443-4392. General email, gfwc@gfwc.org*

Web, www.gfwc.org and Twitter, @GFWCHQ

Nondenominational, nonpartisan international organization of women volunteers. Develops literacy projects in response to community needs; sponsors tutoring.

National Coalition for Literacy, *P.O. Box 2932, 20013-2932; (484) 443-8457. Jeff Carter, President. General email, ncl@ncladvocacy.org*

Web, www.national-coalition-literacy.org and Twitter, @NCLAdvocacy

Members: national organizations concerned with adult education. Promotes adult education, family literacy, and English language acquisition in the United States.

Reading Is Fundamental, *1730 Rhode Island Ave. N.W., #1100, 20036; (202) 536-3400. Fax, (202) 536-3518. Carol H. Rasco, President. Information, 877-RIF-READ. Press, (202) 536-3458. General email, contactus@rif.org*

Web, www.rif.org and Twitter, @RIFWEB

Conducts programs and workshops to motivate young people to read. Provides young people in low-income neighborhoods with free books and parents with services to encourage reading at home.

Science and Mathematics Education

▶ **AGENCIES**

Education Dept., *Postsecondary Education, Institutional Service, Minority Science and Engineering Improvement Program, 1990 K St. N.W., 6th Floor, MS K-OPE-6-6055,* *20006-8512; (202) 453-7913. Fax, (202) 502-7861. Bernadette Hence, Senior Program Manager. General email, OPE.MSEIP@ed.gov*

Web, www2.ed.gov/programs/iduesmsi/index.html

Provides grants to effect long-range improvement in science and engineering education at predominantly minority institutions and to increase the flow of underrepresented ethnic minorities, particularly minority women, into science and engineering careers.

National Aeronautics and Space Administration (NASA), *Education, 300 E St. S.W., 4th Floor, 20546; (202) 358-0103. Fax, (202) 358-7097. Donald G. James, Associate Administrator, Acting. General email, education@nasa.gov*

Web, http://education.nasa.gov

Coordinates NASA's education programs and activities to meet national educational needs and ensure a sufficient talent pool to preserve U.S. leadership in aeronautical technology and space science.

National Institute of Biomedical Imaging and Bioengineering *(National Institutes of Health), 9000 Rockville Pike, Bldg. 31, #1C14, Bethesda, MD 20892; (301) 496-8859. Fax, (301) 480-0679. Dr. Roderic I. Pettigrew, Director. General email, info@nibib.nih.gov*

Web, www.nibib.nih.gov, Twitter, @NIBIBgov and Facebook, www.facebook.com/nibibgov

Offers multidisciplinary training programs for scientists and engineers at all stages of their careers in bioimaging and bioengineering.

National Oceanic and Atmospheric Administration (NOAA) *(Commerce Dept.), National Sea Grant College Program, 1315 East-West Hwy., SSMC-3, 11th Floor, Silver Spring, MD 20910; (301) 734-1066. Fax, (301) 713-0799. Vacant, Director; Nikola Garber, Deputy Director. General email, brooke.carney@noaa.gov*

Web, www.seagrant.noaa.gov

Provides grants, primarily to colleges and universities, for marine resource development; sponsors undergraduate and graduate education and the training of technicians at the college level.

National Science Foundation (NSF), *Education and Human Resources Directorate, 4201 Wilson Blvd., #805N, Arlington, VA 22230; (703) 292-8600. Fax, (703) 292-9179. Joan E. Ferrini-Mundy, Assistant Director. Web, www.nsf.gov/dir/index.jsp?org=ehr*

Develops and supports programs to strengthen science and mathematics (STEM) education. Provides fellowships and grants for graduate research and teacher education, instructional materials, and studies on the quality of existing science and mathematics programs. Participates in international studies.

National Science Foundation (NSF), *National Center for Science and Engineering Statistics, 4201 Wilson Blvd.,*

#965S, Arlington, VA 22230; (703) 292-8780. Fax, (703) 292-9092. John R. Gawalt, Director.
Web, www.nsf.gov/statistics

Develops and analyzes U.S. and international statistics on training, use, and characteristics of scientists, engineers, and technicians.

National Science Foundation (NSF), *Undergraduate Education Division, 4201 Wilson Blvd., Room 435N, Arlington, VA 22230; (703) 292-8670. Fax, (703) 292-9015. Susan R. Singer, Director.*
Web, www.nsf.gov/div/index.jsp?div=DUE

Promotes education in science, technology, engineeringm and mathematics (STEM) at two-year and four-year colleges and universities.

Office of Science and Technology Policy (OSTP) *(Executive Office of the President), Science, Eisenhower Executive Office Bldg., 1650 Pennsylvania Ave. N.W., 20504; (202) 456-4444. Fax, (202) 456-6027. Jo Handelsman, Associate Director; Vacant, Principal Assistant Director for Science.*
General email, info@ostp.gov
Web, www.ostp.gov

Advises the president and others within the EOP on the impact of science and technology on domestic and international affairs; coordinates executive office and federal agency actions related to these issues. Evaluates the effectiveness of science education programs, which include environment, life sciences, physical sciences and engineering, and social, behavioral, and educational sciences. Provides technical support to Homeland Security Dept.

▶ **NONGOVERNMENTAL**

American Assn. for the Advancement of Science (AAAS), *Education and Human Resources Programs, 1200 New York Ave. N.W., 20005; (202) 326-6670. Fax, (202) 371-9849. Main phone is voice and TTY accessible. Shirley M. Malcom, Director, (202) 326-6720.*
General email, ehr@aaas.org
Web, www.aaas.org/program/education-and-human-resources

Membership: scientists, scientific organizations, and others interested in science and technology education. Works to increase and provide information on the status of women, minorities, and people with disabilities in the sciences and in engineering; focuses on expanding science education opportunities for women, minorities, and people with disabilities.

American Assn. of Physics Teachers, *1 Physics Ellipse, College Park, MD 20740-3845; (301) 209-3311. Fax, (301) 209-0845. Beth Cunningham, Executive Officer, (301) 209-3311.*
General email, eo@aapt.org
Web, www.aapt.org

Membership: physics teachers and others interested in physics education. Seeks to advance the institutional and cultural role of physics education. Sponsors seminars and conferences; provides educational information and materials. (Affiliated with the American Institute of Physics.)

American Society for Engineering Education, *1818 N St. N.W., #600, 20036-2479; (202) 331-3500. Fax, (202) 265-8504. Norman L. Fortenberry, Executive Director, (202) 331-3545. Press, (202) 331-3537.*
Web, www.asee.org

Membership: engineering faculty and administrators, professional engineers, government agencies, and engineering colleges, corporations, and professional societies. Conducts research, conferences, and workshops on engineering education. Monitors legislation and regulations.

Assn. of Science-Technology Centers, *818 Connecticut Ave. N.W., 7th Floor, 20006-2734; (202) 783-7200. Fax, (202) 783-7207. Anthony (Bud) F. Rock, President.*
General email, info@astc.org
Web, www.astc.org and Twitter, @ScienceCenters

Membership: more than 600 science centers, science museums, and similar operations in forty-seven countries. Strives to enhance the ability of its members to engage visitors in science activities and explorations of scientific phenomena. Sponsors conferences and informational exchanges on interactive exhibits, hands-on science experiences, and educational programs for children, families, teachers, and older audiences; publishes journal; compiles statistics; provides technical assistance for museums; speaks for science centers before Congress and federal agencies.

Challenger Center for Space Science Education, *422 1st St. S.E., 3rd Floor, 20003; (202) 827-1580. Fax, (202) 827-0031. Lance Bush, President. Toll-free, (800) 969-5747. General email, info@challenger.org*
Web, www.challenger.org and Twitter, @ChallengerCtr

Educational organization designed to stimulate interest in science, math, and technology among middle school and elementary school students. Students participate in interactive mission simulations that require training and classroom preparation. Sponsors Challenger Learning Centers across the United States, Canada, the United Kingdom, and Korea.

EarthEcho International, *2101 L St. N.W., #800, 20037; (202) 350-3190. Fax, (202) 857-3977. Philippe Cousteau, President. Press, (202) 870-1818. General email, education@earthecho.org*
Web, www.earthecho.org

Education resource center that helps students identify environmental issues in their communities and take action to solve them. Holds expeditions to South Florida to investigate the impact of human activity on its natural ecosystems. Provides teachers with learning materials to engage students with real-world data. Specializes in dead zones.

Entomological Society of America, *3 Park Pl., #307, Annapolis, MD 21401-3722; (301) 731-4535. Fax, (301) 731-4538. David Gammel, Executive Director.*
General email, esa@entsoc.org
Web, www.entsoc.org and Twitter, @EntsocAmerica

Membership: entomology researchers, teachers, extension service personnel, administrators, marketing representatives, research technicians, consultants, students, and hobbyists. Sponsors symposia, conferences, journals, and continuing education seminars.

Mathematical Assn. of America, *1529 18th St. N.W., 20036-1358; (202) 387-5200. Fax, (202) 265-2384. Michael Pearson, Executive Director. Information, (800) 741-9415.*
General email, maahq@maa.org
Web, www.maa.org

Membership: mathematics professors and individuals worldwide with a professional interest in mathematics. Seeks to improve the teaching of collegiate mathematics. Conducts professional development programs.

National Assn. of Biology Teachers, *11 Main St., Suite D, Warrenton, VA 20186 (mailing address: P.O. Box 3363, Warrenton, VA 20188); (703) 264-9696. Fax, (703) 435-4390. Jaclyn Reeves-Pepin, Executive Director. Information, (888) 501-6228.*
General email, office@nabt.org
Web, www.nabt.org

Membership: biology teachers and others interested in life sciences education at the elementary, secondary, and collegiate levels. Provides professional development opportunities through its publication program, summer workshops, conventions, and national award programs. Interests include teaching standards, science curriculum, and issues affecting biology and life sciences education.

National Council of Teachers of Mathematics, *1906 Association Dr., Reston, VA 20191-1502; (703) 620-9840. Fax, (703) 476-2970. Robert M. Doucette, Executive Director. Toll-free, (800) 235-7566.*
General email, nctm@nctm.org
Web, www.nctm.org, Twitter, @NCTM and Facebook, www.facebook.com/TeachersofMathematics

Membership: mathematics educators, researchers, students, and other interested persons. Works for the improvement of classroom instruction at all levels. Serves as forum and information clearinghouse on issues related to mathematics education. Offers educational materials and conferences. Monitors legislation and regulations.

National Geographic Society, *1145 17th St. N.W., 20036-4688; (202) 857-7000. Fax, (202) 775-6141. Gary E. Knell, President. Library, (202) 857-7783. Press, (202) 857-7027. Publication information, (800) 647-5463. Publication information TTY, (800) 548-9797.*
Web, www.nationalgeographic.com, Twitter, @NatGeo and Facebook, www.facebook.com/natgeo

Educational and scientific organization. Publishes *National Geographic, National Geographic Adventure, National Geographic Traveler, National Geographic Kids,* and *National Geographic Little Kids* magazines; produces maps, books, and films; maintains a museum; offers film-lecture series; produces television specials and the National Geographic Channel. Library open to the public.

National Research Council (NRC), *Life Sciences Board, Keck Center, 500 5th St. N.W., 6th Floor, 20001; (202) 334-2187. Fax, (202) 334-1289. Fran Sharples, Director; James P. Collins, Chair.*
General email, bls@nas.edu
Web, http://dels.nas.edu/bls

Oversees studies on undergradute level biology education.

National Research Council (NRC), *Science Education Board, Keck Center, 500 5th St. N.W., 20001; (202) 334-2164. Heidi Schweingruber, Director, (202) 334-2009; Adam Gamoran, Chair.*
General email, bose@nas.edu
Web, http://nas.edu/bose

Promotes science education in schools and informal learning environments, such as science museums, aquariums, nature centers, and social networks. Provides guidance in federal legislation, particularly as it relates to STEM education.

National Science Foundation (NSF), *Graduate Education Division, 4201 Wilson Blvd., #875S, Arlington, VA 22230; (703) 292-8630. Fax, (703) 292-9048. Dean Evasius, Division Director. TTY, (800) 281-8749.*
Web, www.nsf.gov/div/index.jsp?div=dge

Supports activities to strengthen the education of research scientists and engineers; promotes career development.

National Science Teachers Assn., *1840 Wilson Blvd., Arlington, VA 22201-3000; (703) 243-7100. Fax, (703) 243-7177. David L. Evans, Executive Director.*
Web, www.nsta.org

Membership: science teachers from elementary through college levels. Seeks to improve science education; provides forum for exchange of information. Monitors legislation and regulations.

Smithsonian Science Education Center, *901 D St. S.W., #704-B, 20024; (202) 633-2972. Fax, (202) 287-2070. Carol L. O'Donnell, Director, (202) 633-2972.*
General email, ssecinfo@si.edu
Web, www.ssec.si.edu

Works to establish effective science programs for all students. Disseminates research information; develops curriculum materials; seeks to increase public support for change of science education through the development of strategic partnerships.

Society for Science & the Public, *1719 N. N.W., 20036; (202) 785-2255. Fax, (202) 785-3751. Maya Ajmera, Chief Executive Officer.*
Web, www.societyforscience.org

Promotes understanding and appreciation of science and the role it plays in human advancement. Sponsors science competitions and other science education programs in schools; awards scholarships. Publishes *Science News* and *Science News for Kids.* Provides funds and training to select U.S. science and math teachers who serve under-resourced students.

World Future Society, *1875 Connecticut Ave. N.W., 10th Floor, 20009; (301) 656-8274. Fax, (301) 951-0394. Julie Friedman Steele, Chair. Toll-free, (800) 989-8274.*
General email, info@wfs.org

Web, www.wfs.org and Washington, D.C. Chapter, www.natcapwfs.org

Scientific and educational organization interested in future social and technological developments on a global scale. Publishes books, a magazine, and a journal. (Headquarters in Chicago, Ill.)

Vocational and Adult

▶AGENCIES

Education Dept., *Career, Technical, and Adult Education, 550 12th St. S.W., 11th Floor, 20202-7100 (mailing address: 400 Maryland Ave. S.W., P-OCTAE, Washington, DC 20202-7100); (202) 245-7700. Fax, (202) 245-7838. John Uvin, Assistant Secretary, Acting, (202) 245-7898.*
General email, ovae@ed.gov

Web, www2.ed.gov/ovae

Administers programs pertaining to adult education and literacy, career and technical education, and community colleges.

Education Dept., *Career, Technical, and Adult Education, Academic and Technical Education, 550 12th St. S.W., #11059, 20202-7100 (mailing address: 400 Maryland Ave. S.W., P-OCTAE, DATE, Washington, DC 20202-7100); (202) 245-7311. Fax, (202) 245-7170. Sharon Miller, Director, (202) 245-7846.*
Web, www2.ed.gov/about/offices/list/ovae/pi/cte/index.html

Establishes national initiatives that help states implement career and technical education programs. Administers state formula and discretionary grant programs under the Carl D. Perkins Career and Technical Education Act.

▶NONGOVERNMENTAL

Accrediting Commission of Career Schools and Colleges, *2101 Wilson Blvd., #302, Arlington, VA 22201; (703) 247-4212. Fax, (703) 247-4533. Michale S. McComis, Executive Director.*
General email, info@accsc.org

Web, www.accsc.org

Serves as the national accrediting agency for private postsecondary institutions offering occupational and vocational programs. Sponsors workshops and meetings on academic excellence and ethical practices in career education.

Accrediting Council for Continuing Education and Training (ACCET), *1722 N St. N.W., 20036; (202) 955-1113. Fax, (202) 955-1118. William B. Larkin, Executive Director.*
General email, info@accet.org

Web, www.accet.org

Peer-reviewed accrediting agency for noncollegiate continuing education and training institutions. Seeks to identify, evaluate, and enhance the delivery of continuing education and training programs. Offers professional development through workshops, conferences, and Webinars.

American Assn. for Adult and Continuing Education (AAACE), *10111 Martin Luther King Jr. Hwy., #200C, Bowie, MD 20720; (301) 459-6261. Fax, (301) 459-6241. Cle Anderson, Association Manager.*
General email, office@aaace.org

Web, www.aaace.org

Membership: adult and continuing education professionals. Acts as an information clearinghouse; evaluates adult and continuing education programs; sponsors conferences, seminars, and workshops. (Headquarters in Atlanta, Ga.)

Assn. for Career and Technical Education (ACTE), *1410 King St., Alexandria, VA 22314; (703) 683-3111. Fax, (703) 683-7424. LeAnn Wilson, Executive Director. Information, (800) 826-9972.*
General email, acte@acteonline.org

Web, www.acteonline.org and Twitter, @actecareertech

Membership: teachers, students, supervisors, administrators, and others working or interested in career and technical education (middle school through postgraduate). Interests include the impact of high school graduation requirements on career and technical education; private sector initiatives; and the improvement of the quality and image of career and technical education. Offers an annual convention and other professional development opportunities. Monitors legislation and regulations.

Assn. of Private Sector Colleges and Universities (APSCU), *1101 Connecticut Ave. N.W., #900, 20036; (202) 336-6700. Fax, (202) 336-6828. Steve Gunderson, President. Toll-free, (866) 711-8574.*
General email, apscu@apscu.org

Web, www.career.org and Twitter, @apscunow

Acts as an information clearinghouse on trade and technical schools. (Formerly Career College Assn.)

Covenant House, *Washington Office, 2001 Mississippi Ave S.E., 20020; (202) 610-9600. Madye Henson, President. TTY, (800) 786-2929.*
Web, http://covenanthousedc.org

Protects young people suffering from homelessness, abuse, and neglect. Provides services including transitional housing, GED and adult education, and job readiness. (Affiliated with Covenant House International.)

Distance Education and Accrediting Council (DEAC), *1101 17th St. N.W., #808, 20036; (202) 234-5100. Fax, (202) 332-1386. Leah K. Matthews, Executive Director.*
General email, info@deac.org

Web, www.deac.org

Membership: accredited distance education and online institutions. Accredits distance education and online institutions that offer high school diplomas, postsecondary education programs, and degree programs through to the doctoral level. Recognized by the U.S. Department of Education and the Council for Higher Education Accreditation.

International Assn. for Continuing Education and Training (IACET), *12100 Sunset Hills Rd., #130, Reston, VA 20190; (703) 234-4065. Fax, (703) 435-4390. Sara Meier, Executive Director.*
General email, info@iacet.org

Web, www.iacet.org

Membership: education and training organizations and individuals who use the Continuing Education Unit. (The C.E.U. is defined as ten contact hours of participation in an organized continuing education program that is noncredit.) Authorizes organizations that issue the C.E.U.; develops criteria and guidelines for use of the C.E.U.

International Technology and Engineering Educators Assn., *1914 Association Dr., #201, Reston, VA 20191-1539; (703) 860-2100. Fax, (703) 860-0353. Steven A. Barbato, Executive Director.*
General email, iteea@iteea.org

Web, www.iteea.org

Membership: technology education teachers, supervisors, teacher educators, and individuals studying to be technology education teachers (elementary school through university level). Technology education includes the curriculum areas of manufacturing, construction, communications, transportation, robotics, energy, design, and engineering.

National Assn. of State Directors of Career Technical Education Consortium, *8484 Georgia Ave., #320, Silver*

Spring, MD 20910; (301) 588-9630. Fax, (301) 588-9631. Kimberly A. Green, Executive Director.
General email, info@careertech.org

Web, www.careertech.org

Membership: state career education agency heads, senior staff, and business, labor, and other education officials. Advocates state and national policy to strengthen career technical education and workforce development. Monitors legislation and regulations.

SkillsUSA, *14001 SkillsUSA Way, Leesburg, VA 20176; (703) 777-8810. Fax, (703) 777-8999.*
Timothy W. Lawrence, Executive Director, ext. 601.
General email, anyinfo@skillsusa.org

Web, www.skillsusa.org

Membership: students, teachers, and administrators of trade, industrial, technical, and health occupations programs at public high schools, vocational schools, and two-year and four-year colleges. Promotes strong work skills, workplace ethics, understanding of free enterprise, and lifelong education. (Formerly Vocational Industrial Clubs of America.)

University Professional & Continuing Education Assn. (UPCEA), *1 Dupont Circle N.W., #615, 20036; (202) 659-3130. Fax, (202) 785-0374. Robert J. Hansen, Chief Executive Officer.*
Web, www.upcea.edu

Membership: higher education institutions and nonprofit organizations involved in postsecondary continuing education. Prepares statistical analyses and produces data reports for members; recognizes accomplishments in the field. Monitors legislation and regulations.

6

Employment and Labor

GENERAL POLICY AND ANALYSIS

Basic Resources

▶AGENCIES

Labor Dept. (DOL), *200 Constitution Ave. N.W., 20210; (202) 693-6000. Fax, (202) 693-6111. Thomas E. Perez, Secretary; Christopher P. Lu, Deputy Secretary. Library, (202) 693-6600. Toll-free, (866) 487-2365. TTY, (877) 889-5627.*
Web, www.dol.gov, Twitter, @USDOL and Facebook, www.facebook.com/departmentoflabor

Promotes and develops the welfare of U.S. wage earners; administers federal labor laws; acts as principal adviser to the president on policies relating to wage earners, working conditions, and employment opportunities. Library open to the public, 8:15 a.m.–4:45 p.m.

Labor Dept. (DOL), *Administrative Law Judges, 800 K St. N.W., #400N, 20001-8002; (202) 693-7300. Fax, (202) 693-7365. Stephen R. Henley, Chief Administrative Law Judge; Yvonne Washington, Chief Docket Clerk; P.J. Soto, Director, Program Operations, (202) 693-7399.*
General email, OALJ-Questions@dol.gov
Web, www.oalj.dol.gov

Presides over formal hearings to determine violations of minimum wage requirements, overtime payments, compensation benefits, employee discrimination, grant performance, alien certification, employee protection, the Sarbanes-Oxley Act, and health and safety regulations set forth under numerous statutes, executive orders, and regulations. With few exceptions, hearings are required to be conducted in accordance with the Administrative Procedure Act.

Labor Dept. (DOL), *Administrative Review Board, 200 Constitution Ave. N.W., #N5404, 20210 (mailing address: 200 Constitution Ave. N.W., #S5220, Washington, DC 20210); (202) 693-6200. Fax, (202) 693-6220. Paul M. Igasaki, Chair; Frank W. Clubb, Administrative Officer, (202) 693-6234.*
Web, www.dol.gov/arb

Issues final decisions for the secretary of labor on appeals from decisions of the administrator of the Wage and Hour Division and the Office of Administrative Law Judges under a broad range of federal labor laws, including nuclear, environmental, safety and security, financial, and transportation whistleblower protection provisions; contract compliance laws; child labor laws; immigration laws; migrant and seasonal agricultural worker protection laws; the McNamara O'Hara Service Contract Act; and the Davis-Bacon Act.

▶CONGRESS

For a listing of relevant congressional committees and subcommittees, please see page 206 or the Appendix.

Government Accountability Office (GAO), *Education, Workforce, and Income Security, 441 G St. N.W., #5928,* 20548; (202) 512-7215. Barbara D. Bovbjerg, Managing Director.
Web, www.gao.gov/careers/ewis.html

Independent nonpartisan agency in the legislative branch. Audits, analyzes, and evaluates federal education and employment programs; makes reports available to the public.

▶NONGOVERNMENTAL

AFL-CIO (American Federation of Labor-Congress of Industrial Organizations), *815 16th St. N.W., 20006; (202) 637-5000. Fax, (202) 637-5058. Richard L. Trumka, President.*
Web, www.aflcio.org

Voluntary federation of national and international labor unions in the United States. Represents members before Congress and other branches of government. Each member union conducts its own contract negotiations. Library (located in Silver Spring, Md.) open to the public.

American Enterprise Institute (AEI), *1150 17th St. N.W., 20036; (202) 862-5800. Fax, (202) 862-7177. Arthur C. Brooks, President. Press, (202) 862-5829.*
Web, www.aei.org

Research and educational organization that studies trends in employment, earnings, the environment, health care, and income in the United States.

American Staffing Assn., *277 S. Washington St., #200, Alexandria, VA 22314-3675; (703) 253-2020. Fax, (703) 253-2053. Richard A. Wahlquist, President.*
General email, usa@americanstaffing.net
Web, https://americanstaffing.net and Twitter, @StaffingTweets

Membership: companies supplying other companies with workers on a temporary or permanent basis, with outsourcing, with human resources, and with professional employer organizations (PEOs) arrangements. Monitors legislation and regulations. Encourages the maintenance of high ethical standards and provides public relations and educational support to members.

Campaign for America's Future, *1825 K St. N.W., #400, 20006; (202) 955-5665. Fax, (202) 955-5606. Robert L. Borosage, Co-Director; Roger Hickey, Co-Director.*
Web, www.ourfuture.org and Twitter, @OurFuture

Operates the Campaign for America's Future and the Institute for America's Future. Advocates policies to help working people. Supports improved employee benefits, including health care, child care, and paid family leave; promotes lifelong education and training of workers. Seeks full employment, higher wages, and increased productivity. Monitors legislation and regulations.

Center for Economic and Policy Research (CEPR), *1611 Connecticut Ave. N.W., #400, 20009; (202) 293-5380. Fax, (202) 588-1356. Dean Baker, Co-Director; Mark Weisbrot, Co-Director.*
General email, info@cepr.net
Web, www.cepr.net and Twitter, @ceprdc

EMPLOYMENT AND LABOR RESOURCES IN CONGRESS

For a complete listing of congressional committees, including their full contact information, leadership, membership, and jurisdictions, please refer to the Appendix on pages 779–896.

HOUSE:

House Agriculture Committee, (202) 225-2171.
Web, agriculture.house.gov
  Subcommittee on Biotechnology, Horticulture, and Research, (202) 225-2171.
House Appropriations Committee, (202) 225-2771.
Web, appropriations.house.gov
  Subcommittee on Labor, Health and Human Services, Education, and Related Agencies, (202) 225-3508.
House Armed Services Committee, (202) 225-4151.
Web, armedservices.house.gov
  Subcommittee on Military Personnel, (202) 225-7560.
House Education and the Workforce Committee, (202) 225-4527.
Web, edworkforce.house.gov
  Subcommittee on Health, Employment, Labor, and Pensions, (202) 225-4527.
  Subcommittee on Higher Education and Workforce Training, (202) 225-4527.
  Subcommittee on Workforce Protections, (202) 225-4527.
House Judiciary Committee, (202) 225-3951.
Web, judiciary.house.gov
  Subcommittee on Immigration and Border Security, (202) 225-3926.
House Oversight and Government Reform Committee, (202) 225-5074.
Web, oversight.house.gov
  Subcommittee on Transportation and Public Assets, (202) 225-5074.
House Small Business Committee, (202) 225-5821.
Web, smallbusiness.house.gov
  Subcommittee on Contracting and Workforce, (202) 225-5821.
House Veterans' Affairs Committee, (202) 225-3527.
Web, veterans.house.gov
  Subcommittee on Economic Opportunity, (202) 226-5491.
House Ways and Means Committee, (202) 225-3625.
Web, waysandmeans.house.gov
  Subcommittee on Human Resources, (202) 225-1025.
  Subcommittee on Social Security, (202) 225-9263.

JOINT:

Joint Economic Committee, (202) 224-5171.
Web, jec.senate.gov

SENATE:

Senate Agriculture, Nutrition, and Forestry Committee, (202) 224-2035.
Web, ag.senate.gov
  Subcommittee on Rural Development and Energy, (202) 224-2035.
Senate Appropriations Committee, (202) 224-7363.
Web, appropriations.senate.gov
  Subcommittee on Labor, Health and Human Services, Education, and Related Agencies, (202) 224-9145.
Senate Finance Committee, (202) 224-4515.
Web, finance.senate.gov
  Subcommittee on International Trade, Customs, and Global Competitiveness, (202) 224-4515.
  Subcommittee on Social Security, Pensions and Family Policy, (202) 224-4515.
  Subcommittee on Taxation and IRS Oversight, (202) 224-4515.
Senate Health, Education, Labor, and Pensions Committee, (202) 224-5375.
Web, help.senate.gov
  Subcommittee on Employment and Workplace Safety, (202) 228-1455.
  Subcommittee on Primary Health and Retirement Security, (202) 224-5480.
Senate Homeland Security and Governmental Affairs Committee, (202) 224-2627.
Web, hsgac.senate.gov
  Permanent Subcommittee on Investigations, (202) 224-4462.
  Subcommittee on Efficiency and Effectiveness of Federal Programs and the Federal Workforce, (202) 224-4462.
Senate Judiciary Committee, (202) 224-7703.
Web, judiciary.senate.gov
  Subcommittee on Immigration and the National Interest, (202) 224-7572.
Senate Small Business and Entrepreneurship Committee, (202) 224-5175.
Web, sbc.senate.gov
Senate Special Committee on Aging, (202) 224-5364.
Web, aging.senate.gov

Researches economic and social issues and the impact of related public policies. Presents findings to the public with the goal of better preparing citizens to choose among various policy options. Promotes democratic debate and voter education. Areas of interest include health care, trade, financial reform, Social Security, taxes, housing, and the labor market.

Employment Policies Institute, *1090 Vermont Ave. N.W., #800, 20005-4605; (202) 463-7650. Fax, (202) 463-7107. Richard Berman, Executive Director.*
General email, info@epionline.org
Web, www.epionline.org

Sponsors and conducts research on public policy and employment. Opposes raising the minimum wage. Monitors legislation and regulations.

Good Jobs First, *1616 P St. N.W., #210, 20036; (202) 232-1616. Greg LeRoy, Executive Director.*
General email, info@goodjobsfirst.org
Web, www.goodjobsfirst.org

Promotes corporate and government accountability in economic development incentives; primary focus is on state and local job subsidies with emerging work on federal development programs and federal regulatory violations data. Maintains Subsidy Tracker database. Includes Good Jobs New York and the Corporate Research Project.

HR Policy Assn., *1100 13th St. N.W., #850, 20005-4090; (202) 789-8670. Fax, (202) 789-0064. Daniel V. Yager, President.*
General email, info@hrpolicy.org
Web, www.hrpolicy.org

Membership: corporate vice presidents in charge of employee relations. Promotes research in employee relations, particularly in federal employment policy and implementation. Interests include international labor issues, including immigration and child labor.

Institute for Credentialing Excellence, *2025 M St. N.W., #800, 20036-3309; (202) 367-1165. Fax, (202) 367-2165. Denise Roosendaal, Executive Director.*
General email, info@credentialingexcellence.org
Web, www.credentialingexcellence.org

Membership: certifying agencies and other groups that issue credentials for professions and occupations. Promotes public understanding of competency assurance certification programs. Oversees commission that establishes certification program standards. Monitors regulations.

National Assn. of Professional Employer Organizations, *707 N. Saint Asaph St., Alexandria, VA 22314; (703) 836-0466. Fax, (703) 836-0976. Pat Cleary, President.*
General email, info@napeo.org
Web, www.napeo.org

Membership: professional employer organizations. Provides code of ethics. Conducts research; sponsors seminars and conferences for members. Monitors legislation and regulations.

National Whistleblowers Center (NWC), *P.O. Box 25074, 20027; (202) 342-1903. Stephen M. Kohn, Executive Director.*
General email, contact@whistleblowers.org
Web, www.whistleblowers.org

Protects employees who legally disclose information about illegal activities of employers. Advocates policy reform for whistleblowers. Educates the public on whistleblower rights and assist whistleblowers in finding attorneys. Coordinates a speakers bureau.

Society for Human Resource Management, *1800 Duke St., Alexandria, VA 22314-3499; (703) 548-3440. Fax, (703) 535-6490. Henry (Hank) G. Jackson, President. Information, (800) 283-7476. Press, (703) 535-6260. TTY, (703) 548-6999.*
General email, shrm@shrm.org
Web, www.shrm.org

Membership: human resource management professionals. Provides Human Resource training and certification exams. Monitors legislation and regulations concerning recruitment, training, and employment practices; occupational safety and health; compensation and benefits; employee and labor relations; and equal employment opportunity. Sponsors seminars and conferences.

Urban Institute, Center on Labor, Human Services, and Population, *2100 M St. N.W., 20037; (202) 833-7200. Fax, (202) 463-8522. Elizabeth Peters, Director.*
Web, www.urban.org/center/lhp

Analyzes employment and income trends, studies how the U.S. population is growing, and evaluates programs dealing with homelessness, child welfare, and job training. Other areas of interest include immigration, mortality, sexual and reproductive health, adolescent risk behavior, child care, domestic violence, and youth development.

U.S. Chamber of Commerce, *Economic Policy, 1615 H St. N.W., 20062-2000; (202) 463-5620. Fax, (202) 463-3174. Martin A. Regalia, Chief Economist.*
Web, www.uschamber.com/economic-policy

Monitors legislation and regulations affecting the business community, including employee benefits, health care, legal and regulatory affairs, transportation and telecommunications infrastructure, defense conversion, and equal employment opportunity.

International Issues

▶AGENCIES

Bureau of Democracy, Human Rights, and Labor *(State Dept.), International Labor Affairs, 1800 G St. N.W., #2422, 20006; (202) 216-5882. Bruce Levine, Director; Sarah Fox, Special Representative for International Labor Affairs.*
Web, www.state.gov/j/drl/ila

Works with organized labor, nongovernmental organizations, international organizations, and corporations to monitor and promote worker rights throughout the

Labor Department

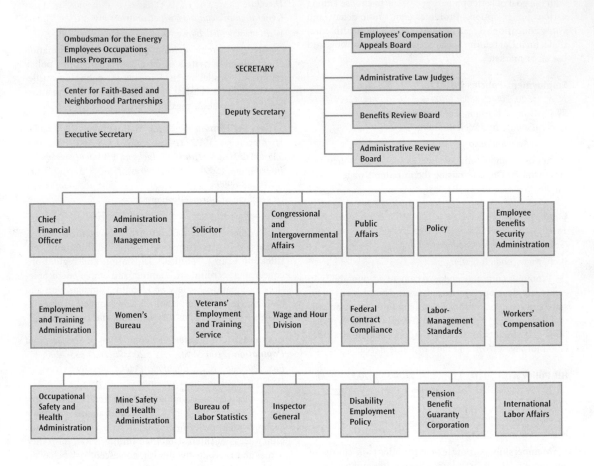

world. Contributes to U.S. foreign policy goals related to democracy promotion, trade, development, and human rights.

Bureau of International Labor Affairs (ILAB) *(Labor Dept.), 200 Constitution Ave. N.W., #S2235, 20210; (202) 693-4770. Fax, (202) 693-4780. Carol Pier, Deputy Under Secretary; Mark A. Mittelhauser, Associate Deputy Under Secretary; Eric Biel, Associate Deputy Under Secretary. General email, Contact-ILAB@dol.gov*

Web, www.dol.gov/ilab

Assists in formulating international economic and trade policies affecting American workers. Represents the United States in trade negotiations. Helps administer the United States labor attaché program. Carries out overseas technical assistance projects. Represents the United States in various international organizations. Houses the Office of Trade Agreement Implementation, which is responsible for overseeing the implementation of the labor provisions of free trade agreements.

Bureau of International Labor Affairs (ILAB) *(Labor Dept.), International Relations, 200 Constitution Ave. N.W., #S5317, 20210; (202) 693-4855. Fax, (202) 693-4860. Robert B. Shepard, Director.*

General email, Contact-OIR@dol.gov

Web, www.dol.gov/ilab/about/offices/#oir

Provides administrative support for U.S. participation in the International Labor Organization (ILO) and Asian Pacific Economic Cooperation (APEC) and at the Paris-based Organisation for Economic Co-operation and Development (OECD). Provides research on labor and employment in other countries. Facilitates information-sharing between Labor Dept. and other countries.

Bureau of International Labor Affairs (ILAB) *(Labor Dept.), International Visitors Program, 200 Constitution Ave. N.W., #S5303, 20210; (202) 693-4793. Fax, (202) 693-4784. Patricia Butler, International Program Specialist. General email, butler.patricia@dol.gov*

Web, www.dol.gov/ilab/diplomacy/fvp.htm

Works with the State Dept., the Agency for International Development, and other agencies in arranging visits and training programs for foreign officials interested in U.S. labor and trade laws and practices, worker training programs, and employment services.

Bureau of International Labor Affairs (ILAB) *(Labor Dept.), Trade and Labor Affairs, 200 Constitution Ave.*

N.W., #S5317, 20210; (202) 693-4802. Fax, (202) 693-4851. Matthew Levin, Director.
Web, www.dol.gov/ilab

Coordinates international technical cooperation in support of the labor provisions in free trade agreements. Provides services, information, expertise, and technical cooperation programs that support the Labor Dept.'s foreign policy objectives. Administers the U.S. government's responsibilities under the North American Free Trade Agreement on Labor Cooperation and labor chapters of U.S. regional and bilateral free trade agreements. Provides technical assistance for post-conflict reconstruction and reintegration activities in countries key to U.S. security. Provides technical assistance globally to help countries observe international labor standards. Supports HIV/AIDS workplace preventive education in countries around the world.

Employment and Training Administration *(Labor Dept.), Trade Adjustment Assistance, 200 Constitution Ave. N.W., N-5428, 20210; (202) 693-3560. Fax, (202) 693-3584. Norris T. Tyler III, Administrator, Acting. Toll-free, (888) 365-6822.*
Web, www.doleta.gov/tradeact

Assists American workers who are totally or partially unemployed because of increased imports or a shift in production; offers training, job search and relocation assistance, weekly benefits at state unemployment insurance levels, and other reemployment services.

President's Committee on the International Labor Organization *(Labor Dept.), 200 Constitution Ave. N.W., 20210; (202) 693-4770. Fax, (202) 693-4780. Thomas E. Perez, Secretary of Labor; Carol Pier, Deputy Under Secretary for International Affairs.*
Web, www.dol.gov/ilab/diplomacy/pc-ilo-page1.htm

Advisory committee that directs U.S. participation in the International Labor Organization; composed of government, employer, and worker representatives, including secretaries of labor, commerce, and state, the president's national security adviser, the president's national economic adviser, and the presidents of the AFL-CIO and the U.S. Council of International Business. Formulates and coordinates policy on the International Labor Organization (ILO); advises the president and the secretary of labor.

►**CONGRESS**

For a listing of relevant congressional committees and subcommittees, please see page 206 or the Appendix.

►**INTERNATIONAL ORGANIZATIONS**

International Labor Organization (ILO), *Washington Office, 1801 Eye St. N.W., 9th Floor, 20006; (202) 617-3952. Fax, (202) 617-3960. Nancy A. Donaldson, Director. General email, washington@ilo.org*
Web, www.ilo.org/washington

Works toward advancing social justice through the promotion of international labor standards, employment,

social protection, and social dialogue. Carries out research and technical cooperation and advisory services under these four major themes and related subthemes, including labor statistics, wages, occupational safety and health and other working conditions, social security, eradication of child labor and forced labor, equality of treatment in employment and occupation, freedom of association, and bargaining rights. Liaison office for the United States and multilateral organizations in Washington, D.C. (Headquarters in Geneva.)

World Bank, *Human Development Network, 1818 H St. N.W., 20433; (202) 473-1000. Keith Hanson, Vice President; Melanie Mayhew, Media Contact, (202) 458-7891.*
Web, www.worldbank.org

Assists developing countries in delivering effective and affordable health care, education, and social services. Interests include poverty reduction, income protection, nutrition, jobs access, health coverage, and basic education.

►**NONGOVERNMENTAL**

Immigration Works USA, *737 8th St. S.E., #201, 20003; (202) 506-4541. Fax, (202) 595-8962. Tamar Jacoby, President. General email, info@immigrationworksusa.org*
Web, www.immigrationworksusa.org

Coalition of business owners that seeks to educate the public about the benefits of immigration and build support for bringing immigration policy in line with the country's labor needs. Monitors legislation and regulations.

International Labor Rights Forum, *1634 Eye St. N.W., #1001, 20006; (202) 347-4100. Fax, (202) 347-4885. Judy Gearheart, Executive Director, ext. 106. General email, laborrights@ilrf.org*
Web, www.laborrights.org

Promotes the enforcement of international labor rights through policy advocacy; acts as advocate for better protection of workers. Concerns include child labor, sweatshops, and exploited workers. Monitors legislation and regulations on national and international levels.

NumbersUSA, *Capitol Hill Office, 17 D St. S.E., 1st Floor, 20003; 1400 Crystal Dr., #240, Arlington, VA 22209; (202) 543-1341. Fax, (202) 543-3147. Roy Beck, Executive Director. Donations, (703) 816-8820. General email, info@numbersusa.com*
Web, www.numbersusa.com

Public policy organization that favors immigration reduction as a way of promoting economic justice for American workers. Monitors legislation and regulations.

Solidarity Center, *888 16th St. N.W., #400, 20006; (202) 974-8383. Fax, (202) 974-8384. Shawna Bader-Blau, Executive Director. Media, (202) 974-8360. General email, information@solidaritycenter.org*
Web, www.solidaritycenter.org

Provides assistance to free and democratic trade unions worldwide. Provides trade union leadership courses in collective bargaining, union organization, trade integration, labor-management cooperation, union administration, and political theories. Sponsors social and community development projects; focus includes child labor, human and worker rights, and the role of women in labor unions. (Affiliated with the AFL-CIO.)

U.S. Chamber of Commerce, *Labor, Immigration, and Employee Benefits,* 1615 H St. N.W., 20062-2000; (202) 463-5522. Fax, (202) 463-3194. Fax, (202) 463-5901. *Randel K. Johnson, Senior Vice President. General email, laborpolicy@uschamber.com*

Web, www.uschamber.com/labor-immigration-and-employee-benefits, ADA information, www.uschamber.com/health-reform and Immigration news, http://immigration.uschamber.com

Formulates and analyzes Chamber policy in the areas of labor law, immigration, pension, and health care. Monitors legislation and regulations affecting labor-management relations, employee benefits, and immigration issues.

Labor Standards and Practices

▶**AGENCIES**

Bureau of Labor Statistics (BLS) *(Labor Dept.),* *Compensation and Working Conditions,* 2 Massachusetts Ave. N.E., #4130, 20212; (202) 691-6300. Fax, (202) 691-6310. Vacant, Associate Commissioner. *Web, www.bls.gov*

Conducts annual survey of occupational requirements, including the physical demands, environmental conditions, training requirements, and cognitive requirements of work.

Housing and Urban Development Dept. (HUD), *Labor Standards and Enforcement,* 451 7th St. S.W., #2124, 20410; (202) 708-0370. Fax, (202) 619-8022. *Robert B. Morton, Executive Director. Web, http://portal.hud.gov/hudportal/HUD?src=/program_offices/labor_standards_enforcement*

Seeks to ensure that laborers on HUD-assisted construction projects are paid prevailing wages by contractors. Administers and enforces labor standards provisions within the Davis-Bacon and related acts, the Copeland Act, and Contract Work Hours and Safety Standards Act, and the maintenance wage requirements of the U.S. Housing Act of 1937.

Labor Dept. (DOL), *Federal Contract Compliance Programs,* 200 Constitution Ave. N.W., #C3325, 20210; (202) 693-0101. Fax, (202) 693-1304. Patricia A. Shiu, Director; Thomas Dowd, Deputy Director. Toll-free, (800) 397-6251. TTY, (202) 693-1337. *General email, OFCCP-Public@dol.gov*

Web, www.dol.gov/ofccp

Monitors and enforces government contractors' compliance with federal laws and regulations on equal employment opportunities and affirmative action, including employment rights of minorities, women, persons with disabilities, and disabled and Vietnam-era veterans.

Labor Dept. (DOL), *Wage and Hour Division,* 200 Constitution Ave. N.W., #S3502, 20210; (202) 693-0051. Fax, (202) 693-1406. David Weil, Administrator; Laura A. Fortman, Principal Deputy Administrator. Press, (202) 693-4676. TTY, (877) 889-5627. *Web, www.dol.gov/whd*

Enforces the minimum-wage, overtime pay, record keeping, and child labor requirements of the Fair Labor Standards Act, the Migrant and Seasonal Agricultural Worker Protection Act, the Employee Polygraph Protection Act, the Family and Medical Leave Act, and a number of employment standards and worker protections as provided in several immigration-related statutes. Also enforces the wage garnishment provisions of the Consumer Credit Protection Act; and the prevailing wage requirements of the Davis-Bacon Act, the Service Contract Act, and other statutes applicable to federal contracts for construction and the provision of goods and services.

Labor Dept. (DOL), *Wage and Hour Division, Enforcement Policy, Child Labor and Fair Labor Standards Act Enforcement,* 200 Constitution Ave. N.W., #3516, 20210; (202) 693-0067. Fax, (202) 693-1387. Derrick J. Witherspoon, Division Chief. Press, (202) 693-0185. Toll-free, (866) 487-9243. *Web, www.dol.gov/whd*

Issues interpretations and rulings of the Fair Labor Standards Act of 1938.

Labor Dept. (DOL), *Wage and Hour Division, Enforcement Policy, Family and Medical Leave,* 200 Constitution Ave. N.W., #S3502, 20210; (202) 693-0066. Fax, (202) 693-1387. Helen M. Applewhaite, Branch Chief. Press, (202) 693-4676. *Web, www.dol.gov/whd*

Authorizes subminimum wages under the Fair Labor Standards Act for certain categories of workers, including full-time students, student learners, and workers with disabilities. Administers the Fair Labor Standards Act restrictions on working at home in certain industries and enforces child labor laws.

Labor Dept. (DOL), *Wage and Hour Division, Enforcement Policy, Farm and Labor and Immigration Team,* 200 Constitution Ave. N.W., #S3520, 20210; (202) 693-0070. Fax, (202) 693-1387. James Kessler, Branch Chief. Toll-free, (866) 487-9243. *Web, www.dol.gov/whd*

Enforces certain provisions under the Immigration and Nationality Act (INA), including labor standards protections for certain temporary nonimmigrant workers and inspection for compliance with the employment eligibility record keeping requirements.

Labor Dept. (DOL), *Wage and Hour Division, Enforcement Policy, Government Contracts Enforcement,* 200 Constitution Ave. N.W., #S3006, 20210; (202) 693-0064. Fax, (202) 693-1087. Amy DeBisshop, Branch Chief. Toll-free, (866) 487-9243. *Web, www.dol.gov/whd*

Enforces the Davis-Bacon Act, the Walsh-Healey Public Contracts Act, the Contract Work Hours and Safety Standards Act, the Service Contract Act, and other related government contract labor standards statutes.

Labor Dept. (DOL), *Wage and Hour Division, Wage Determination, Service Contracts,* 200 Constitution Ave. N.W., #S3028, 20210; (202) 693-0571. Sandra W. Hamlett, Branch Chief.
Web, www.dol.gov/whd

Issues prevailing wage determinations under the Service Contract Act of 1965 and other regulations pertaining to wage determination.

▶**CONGRESS**

For a listing of relevant congressional committees and subcommittees, please see page 206 or the Appendix.

▶**NONGOVERNMENTAL**

Fair Labor Assn. (FLA), *1111 19th St. N.W., #401, 20036; (202) 898-1000. Fax, (202) 898-9050. Sharon Waxman, President.*
General email, info@fairlabor.org
Web, www.fairlabor.org and Twitter, @FairLaborAssoc

Membership: consumer, human, and labor rights groups; apparel and footwear manufacturers and retailers; and colleges and universities. Seeks to protect the rights of workers in the United States and worldwide. Concerns include sweatshop practices, forced labor, child labor, and worker health and benefits. Monitors workplace conditions and reports findings to the public. Develops capacity for sustainable labor compliance.

Statistics and Information

▶**AGENCIES**

Bureau of Labor Statistics (BLS) *(Labor Dept.),* 2 Massachusetts Ave. N.E., #4040, 20212-0001; (202) 691-5200. Fax, (202) 691-7890. Erica Lynn Groshen, Commissioner, (202) 691-7800. Press, (202) 691-5902. TTY, (800) 877-8339.
General email, blsdata_staff@bls.gov
Web, www.bls.gov and Twitter, @BLS_gov

Collects, analyzes, and publishes data on labor economics, including employment, unemployment, hours of work, wages, employee compensation, prices, consumer expenditures, labor-management relations, productivity, technological developments, occupational safety and health, and structure and growth of the economy. Publishes reports on these statistical trends, including the *Consumer Price Index,* the *Producer Price Index,* and *Employment and Earnings.*

Bureau of Labor Statistics (BLS) *(Labor Dept.),* **Compensation and Working Conditions, Compensation Levels and Trends,** 2 Massachusetts Ave. N.E., #4175, 20212; (202) 691-6199. Fax, (202) 691-6647.

Philip M. Doyle, Assistant Commissioner. TTY, (202) 691-5200.
Web, www.bls.gov/ncs/summary.htm

Compiles data on wages and benefits. Develops the National Compensation Survey. Analyzes, distributes, and disseminates information on occupational earnings, benefits, and compensation trends.

Bureau of Labor Statistics (BLS) *(Labor Dept.),* **Current Employment Analysis,** 2 Massachusetts Ave. N.E., #4675, 20212; (202) 691-6405. Fax, (202) 691-6459.
Julie Hatch Maxfield, Assistant Commissioner, (202) 691-5473. Press, (202) 691-5902. Current Population Survey, (202) 691-6378. Local area unemployment statistics, (202) 691-6392.
General email, lausinfo@bls.gov
Web, www.bls.gov/lau

Issues labor force and unemployment statistics for states, counties, metropolitan statistical areas, cities with populations of 25,000 or more, and the United States as a whole.

Bureau of Labor Statistics (BLS) *(Labor Dept.),* **Current Employment Statistics, National,** 2 Massachusetts Ave. N.E., #4860, 20212-0001; (202) 691-6555. Fax, (202) 691-6641. Kirk Mueller, Chief.
General email, cesinfo@bls.gov
Web, www.bls.gov/ces

Surveys business and government agencies and publishes detailed industry data on employment, hours, and earnings of workers on nonfarm payrolls. Estimates are produced for the nation.

Bureau of Labor Statistics (BLS) *(Labor Dept.),* **Current Employment Statistics, State and Area,** 2 Massachusetts Ave. N.E., #4170, 20212; (202) 691-6559. Chris Manning, Chief.
Web, www.bls.gov/sae

Surveys business agencies and publishes detailed industry data on employment, hours, and earnings of workers on nonfarm payrolls. Estimates are produced for states and selected metropolitan areas.

Bureau of Labor Statistics (BLS) *(Labor Dept.),* **Employment and Unemployment Statistics,** 2 Massachusetts Ave. N.E., #4945, 20212-0022; (202) 691-6400. Fax, (202) 691-6425. Michael W. Horrigan, Associate Commissioner. Press, (202) 691-5902.
General email, labstathelpdesk@bls.gov
Web, www.bls.gov/bls/employment.htm

Monitors employment and unemployment trends on national and local levels; compiles data on worker and industry employment and earnings.

Bureau of Labor Statistics (BLS) *(Labor Dept.),* **Industry Employment Statistics,** 2 Massachusetts Ave. N.E., #4860, 20212; (202) 691-5440. Fax, (202) 691-5745.
Kenneth W. Robertson, Assistant Commissioner.
General email, ep-info@bls.gov
Web, www.bls.gov/emp

Personnel Offices at Federal Departments and Agencies

Job seekers interested in additional information can explore federal government career opportunities through the government's official employment information system; Web, www.usajobs.gov.

DEPARTMENTS

Agriculture, (202) 720-8732

Commerce, (202) 482-4807

Defense Logistics Agency, (703) 767-6445

Education, (202) 453-7942

Energy, (202) 586-8734

Health and Human Services, (202) 690-6191

  Food and Drug Administration, (240) 402-4500

  Health Resources and Services Administration, (301) 443-5895

  National Institutes of Health, (301) 496-2404

Homeland Security, (202) 282-8000

  Coast Guard, (703) 872-6338

  Federal Emergency Management Agency, (866) 896-8003

  Transportation Security Administration, (877) 872-7990

Housing and Urban Development, (202) 402-2018

Interior, (800) 336-4562

Justice, (202) 514-4350

Labor, (202) 693-7600

State, (703) 302-6812

Transportation, (202) 366-1298

Treasury, (202) 927-4800

Veterans Affairs, (202) 461-7750

AGENCIES

Administrative Office of the U.S. Courts, (202) 502-3800

Commodity Futures Trading Commission, (202) 418-5009

Consumer Product Safety Commission, (301) 504-7925

Corporation for National and Community Service, (202) 606-5000

Environmental Protection Agency, (202) 564-4606

Equal Employment Opportunity Commission, (202) 663-4306

Export-Import Bank, (202) 565-3300

Farm Credit Administration, (703) 883-4200

Federal Communications Commission, (202) 418-0130

Federal Deposit Insurance Corporation, (877) 275-3342

Federal Election Commission, (202) 694-1080

Federal Labor Relations Authority, (202) 218-7979

Federal Mediation and Conciliation Service, (202) 606-5460

Federal Reserve Board, (202) 452-3880

Federal Trade Commission, (202) 326-3633

General Services Administration, (202) 501-0398

Government Accountability Office, (202) 512-5811

Government Printing Office, (202) 512-1308

National Aeronautics and Space Administration, (202) 358-1998

National Archives and Records Administration, (301) 837-3710

National Credit Union Administration, (703) 518-6510

National Endowment for the Arts, (202) 682-5405

National Endowment for the Humanities, (202) 606-8415

National Labor Relations Board, (202) 273-3801

National Mediation Board, (202) 692-5010

National Science Foundation, (703) 292-8180

National Transportation Safety Board, (202) 314-6239; Toll-free, (800) 573-0937

Nuclear Regulatory Commission, (301) 415-7400

Office of Personnel Management, (202) 606-1800

Peace Corps, (202) 692-1040

Securities and Exchange Commission, (202) 551-7500

Small Business Administration, (202) 205-6600

Smithsonian Institution, (202) 633-6370

Social Security Administration, (800) 772-1213; TTY, (800) 325-0778

U.S. International Trade Commission, (202) 205-2651

U.S. Postal Service, (877) 477-3273

Produces monthly employment statistics, quarterly wage data, business employment dynamics statistics, and job openings and labor turnover statistics.

Bureau of Labor Statistics (BLS) *(Labor Dept.), Productivity and Technology,* 2 Massachusetts Ave. N.E., #2150, 20212-0001; (202) 691-5600. Fax, (202) 691-5664. Lucy Eldridge, Associate Commissioner. TTY, (202) 691-5618.
General email, dipsweb@bls.gov
Web, www.bls.gov/bls/productivity.htm

Develops and analyzes productivity measures for the U.S. business economy and industries, and conducts research on factors affecting productivity.

Employment and Training Administration *(Labor Dept.), Unemployment Insurance,* 200 Constitution Ave. N.W., #S4524, 20210; (202) 693-3032. Fax, (202) 693-3229. Gay M. Gilbert, Administrator.
Web, www.ows.doleta.gov/unemploy

Provides guidance and oversight with respect to federal and state unemployment compensation. Compiles statistics on state unemployment insurance programs. Studies unemployment issues related to benefits.

Occupational Safety and Health Administration (OSHA) *(Labor Dept.), Statistics,* 200 Constitution Ave. N.W., #N3507, 20210; (202) 693-1886. Fax, (202) 693-1631. *Dave Schmidt, Director.* *Web, www.osha.gov/dts/osa and www.osha.gov/oshstats*

Compiles and provides all statistical data for OSHA, such as occupational injury and illness records, which are used in setting standards and making policy.

▶**CONGRESS**

For a listing of relevant congressional committees and subcommittees, please see page 206 or the Appendix.

Unemployment Benefits

▶**AGENCIES**

Employment and Training Administration *(Labor Dept.), Trade Adjustment Assistance,* 200 Constitution Ave. N.W., N-5428, 20210; (202) 693-3560. Fax, (202) 693-3584. *Norris T. Tyler III, Administrator, Acting. Toll-free, (888) 365-6822.* *Web, www.doleta.gov/tradeact*

Assists American workers who are totally or partially unemployed because of increased imports or a shift in production; offers training, job search and relocation assistance, weekly benefits at state unemployment insurance levels, and other reemployment services.

Employment and Training Administration *(Labor Dept.), Unemployment Insurance,* 200 Constitution Ave. N.W., #S4524, 20210; (202) 693-3032. Fax, (202) 693-3229. *Gay M. Gilbert, Administrator.* *Web, www.ows.doleta.gov/unemploy*

Directs and reviews the state-administered system that provides income support for unemployed workers nationwide; advises state and federal employment security agencies on wage-loss, worker dislocation, and adjustment assistance compensation programs.

▶**CONGRESS**

For a listing of relevant congressional committees and subcommittees, please see page 206 or the Appendix.

▶**NONGOVERNMENTAL**

National Assn. of State Workforce Agencies, 444 N. Capitol St. N.W., #142, 20001; (202) 434-8020. Fax, (202) 434-8033. *Scott Sanders, Executive Director. Press, (202) 434-8023.* *General email, mkatz@naswa.org* *Web, www.naswa.org*

Membership: state workforce agency administrators. Informs members of employment training programs, unemployment insurance programs, employment services, labor market information, and legislation. Provides unemployment insurance and workforce development professionals with opportunities for networking and information exchange.

EMPLOYMENT AND TRAINING PROGRAMS

General

▶**AGENCIES**

Education Dept., *Career, Technical, and Adult Education, Academic and Technical Education,* 550 12th St. S.W., #11059, 20202-7100 (mailing address: 400 Maryland Ave. S.W., P-OCTAE, DATE, Washington, DC 20202-7100); (202) 245-7311. Fax, (202) 245-7170. *Sharon Miller, Director, (202) 245-7846.* *Web, www2.ed.gov/about/offices/list/ovae/pi/cte*

Establishes national initiatives that help states implement career and technical education programs. Administers state formula and discretionary grant programs under the Carl D. Perkins Career and Technical Education Act.

Employment and Training Administration *(Labor Dept.),* 200 Constitution Ave. N.W., #S2307, 20210; (202) 693-2700. *Portia Wu, Assistant Secretary. Press, (215) 861-5100. Toll-free employment and training hotline, 877-US2-JOBS. TTY, (877) 889-5627.* *General email, etapagemaster@dol.gov* *Web, www.doleta.gov*

Administers federal government job training and worker dislocation programs, federal grants to states for public employment service programs, and unemployment insurance benefits, primarily through state and local workforce development systems.

Employment and Training Administration *(Labor Dept.), Adult Services,* 200 Constitution Ave. N.W., #S4209, 20210; (202) 693-3046. Fax, (202) 693-3817. *Christine D. K. Ollis, Chief.* *Web, www.doleta.gov/etainfo/wrksys/WIAdultServices.cfm*

Responsible for adult training and services for dislocated workers funded under the Workforce Investment Act; examines training initiatives. Provides targeted job training services for migrant and seasonal farm workers, Native Americans, older workers, veterans, and the disabled. Aims to increase the employment, job retention, earnings, and career advancement of U.S. workers.

Employment and Training Administration *(Labor Dept.), Workforce Investment,* 200 Constitution Ave. N.W., #C4526, 20210; (202) 693-3045. Fax, (202) 693-3981. *Amanda Ahlstrand, Administrator.* *Web, www.doleta.gov/etainfo/WrkSys/WIOffice.cfm*

Provides workers with information, job search assistance, and training. Helps employers acquire skilled workers. Provides national leadership, oversight, policy guidance, and technical assistance under the Workforce

Innovation and Opportunity Act. Oversees programs administered through the One-Stop delivery system assisting communities, businesses, and job seekers, including dislocated and transitioning workers, disadvantaged youth, veterans, individuals with disabilities, migrant and seasonal farmworkers, and Native Americans, in a changing global economy.

Employment and Training Administration *(Labor Dept.), Workforce Investment, Division of Strategic Investment, 200 Constitution Ave. N.W., #C4518, 20210; (202) 693-3949. Fax, (202) 693-3890. Robin Fernkas, Division Chief.*
General email, divisionofstrategicinvestment@dol.gov
Web, www.doleta.gov

Serves as liaison between business and industry and the workforce investment system, a network of state and local resources that connects workers to job opportunities and helps businesses recruit, train, and maintain a skilled workforce. Manages the High Growth Job Training Initiative with the goal of preparing workers for high-growth and high-demand jobs. Targeted industries include advanced manufacturing, aerospace, biotechnology, health care, and information technology, construction, hospitality, transportation, and energy.

Employment and Training Administration *(Labor Dept.), Workforce Investment, National Programs, Tools, and Technical Assistance, 200 Constitution Ave. N.W., #C4510, 20210-3945; (202) 693-3045. Fax, (202) 693-3015. Kim Vitelli, Chief, (202) 693-3639.*
Web, www.doleta.gov/etainfo/wrksys/dinap.cfm#DNPTTA

Oversees and provides support for implementation of employment and training services to targeted populations, including National Farmworker Jobs Program; migrant and seasonal farmworker Monitor Advocate activities; and services for individuals with disabilities, including the Disability Employment Initiative; Work Opportunity Tax Credit; and Senior Community Service Employment Program. Provides workers and businesses with labor market information and online career information to help connect skilled workers to businesses. Oversees and provides support for grants to states to produce labor market information; oversees the agency's technical assistance platform for use by workforce development professionals, www.workforce3one.org.

Housing and Urban Development Dept. (HUD), *Labor Standards and Enforcement, 451 7th St. S.W., #2124, 20410; (202) 708-0370. Fax, (202) 619-8022. Robert B. Morton, Executive Director.*
Web, http://portal.hud.gov/hudportal/HUD?src=/program_offices/labor_standards_enforcement

Partnership between HUD and the Labor Dept. that assists low-income housing residents in obtaining job training and employment.

▶**CONGRESS**

For a listing of relevant congressional committees and subcommittees, please see page 206 or the Appendix.

▶**NONGOVERNMENTAL**

AFL-CIO Working America, *815 16th St. N.W., 20006; (202) 637-5137. Fax, (202) 508-6900. Karen Nussbaum, Executive Director.*
General email, info@workingamerica.org
Web, www.workingamerica.org

Acts as advocate on behalf of nonunion workers at the community, state, and national levels. Seeks to secure better jobs, health care, education, and retirement benefits for these workers. Monitors legislation and regulations. (A community affiliate of the AFL-CIO.)

AFL-CIO Working for America Institute, *815 16th St. N.W., 20005; (202) 508-3717. Fax, (202) 508-3719. Jane McDonald, Assistant to the President. Office Manager, (202) 637-5251.*
General email, info@workingforamerica.org
Web, www.workingforamerica.org

Provides technical assistance to labor unions, employers, education agencies, and community groups for workplace programs focusing on dislocated workers, economically disadvantaged workers, and skill upgrading. Interests include new technologies and workplace innovations.

Assn. for Talent Development (ATD), *1640 King St., 3rd Floor, Alexandria, VA 22314; (703) 683-8100. Fax, (703) 683-1523. Tony Bingham, Chief Executive Officer. Toll-free, (800) 628-2783.*
General email, customercare@astd.org
Web, www.astd.org, Twitter, @atd and Facebook, www.facebook.com/ATD

Membership: trainers and human resource development specialists. Promotes workplace training programs and human resource development. Interests include productivity, leadership development, and employee retraining and performance improvement. Holds conferences; publishes information about employee learning and development; provides online training. (Formerly American Society for Training and Development.)

D.C. Central Kitchen, *425 2nd St. N.W., 20001; (202) 234-0707. Fax, (202) 986-1051. Mike Curtin, Chief Executive Officer, (202) 266-2018.*
Email, www.dccentralkitchen.org

Administers the Culinary Jobs Training program for unemployed, homeless, or formerly incarcerated men and women.

Graduate School USA, *Center for Leadership Management, 600 Maryland Ave. S.W., 20024-2520; (202) 314-3300. Cynthia Hawkins, Director. Toll-free, (866) 329-4723. TTY, (888) 744-2717.*
General email, customersupport@graduateschool.edu
Web, www.graduateschool.edu

Trains federal employees with managerial potential for executive positions in the government. Leadership programs serve employees at levels from GS4 through SES.

National Assn. of State Workforce Agencies, *444 N. Capitol St. N.W., #142, 20001; (202) 434-8020.*

Fax, (202) 434-8033. Scott Sanders, Executive Director.
Press, (202) 434-8023.
General email, mkatz@naswa.org

Web, www.naswa.org

Membership: state employment security administrators. Informs members of federal legislation on job placement, veterans' affairs, and employment and training programs. Distributes labor market information; trains new state administrators and executive staff. Provides employment and training professionals with opportunities for networking and information exchange.

National Assn. of Workforce Boards (NAWB), 1155
15th St. N.W., #350, 20005; (202) 857-7900. Fax, (202) 857-7955. Ron Painter, Chief Executive Officer.
General email, nawb@nawb.org

Web, www.nawb.org

Membership: private industry councils and state job training coordinating councils established under the Job Training Partnership Act of 1982 (renamed Workforce Boards under the Workforce Investment Act). Interests include job training opportunities for youth and unemployed, economically disadvantaged, and dislocated workers; and private sector involvement in federal employment and training policy. Provides members with technical assistance; holds conferences and seminars.

**National Assn. of Workforce Development
Professionals (NAWDP),** 1155 15th St. N.W., #350, 20005;
(202) 589-1790. Fax, (202) 589-1799. Bridget Brown,
Executive Director.
General email, info@nawdp.org

Web, www.nawdp.org

Membership: professionals and policymakers in the employment and training field. Promotes professionalism, information exchange, networking, and professional growth in the workforce development field.

National Center on Education and the Economy (NCEE),
2121 K St. N.W., #700, 20037; (202) 379-1800. Fax, (202)
293-1560. Marc S. Tucker, President.
General email, info@ncee.org

Web, www.ncee.org

Partnership of states, school districts, corporations, foundations, and nonprofit organizations that provides tools and technical assistance for school districts to improve education and training for the workplace.

National Governors Assn. (NGA), Center for Best
Practices, Economic, Human Services, and Workforce
Programs, 444 N. Capitol St. N.W., #267, 20001-1512;
(202) 624-5345. Fax, (202) 624-7829. Jeff Bates, Director,
Acting.
Web, www.nga.org/cms/center/ehsw

Provides information, research, policy analysis, technical assistance, and resource development for governors and their staff across a range of policy issues. Promotes economic development and innovation; workforce development focused on industry-based strategies; pathways to employment and populations with special needs; and

human services for children, youth, low-income families and people with disabilities.

The Telework Coalition (TelCoa), 204 E. St. N.E., 20002;
(202) 266-0046. Fax, (202) 465-3776. Chuck Wilsker,
President.
General email, info@telcoa.org

Web, www.telcoa.org

Promotes telework and access to broadband services to increase productivity and provide employment opportunities for disabled, rural, and older workers, while reducing vehicular travel and energy use. Monitors legislation and regulations.

U.S. Chamber of Commerce, Center for Education and
Workforce, 1615 H St. N.W., 20062-2000; (202) 463-5525.
Fax, (202) 887-3424. Cheryl A. Oldham, Senior Vice
President.
General email, education@uschamber.com

Web, www.uschamberfoundation.org

Works with U.S. Chamber of Commerce members on workforce development issues, including educational reform, human resources, and job training.

U.S. Conference of Mayors, Workforce Development
Council, 1620 Eye St. N.W., 4th Floor, 20006; (202) 293-7330. Fax, (202) 293-2352. Kathleen (Kathy) Wiggins,
Assistant Executive Director for Jobs, Education, and the
Workforce Development Council, (202) 861-6723;
Ida Mukendi, Administrative Assistant, (202) 861-6724.
Web, www.usmayors.org/workforce

Offers technical assistance to members participating in federal job training programs; monitors related legislation; acts as an information clearinghouse on employment and training programs.

Aliens

▶AGENCIES

Administration for Children and Families (ACF) (Health
and Human Services Dept.), Refugee Resettlement, 330
C St. S.W., 20201; (202) 401-9246. Fax, (202) 401-0981.
Robert Carey, Director.
Web, www.acf.hhs.gov/programs/orr

Provides states and nonprofit agencies with grants for refugee social services such as English and employment training.

Employment and Training Administration (Labor
Dept.), Foreign Labor Certification, 375 E St., #12-200,
20210 (mailing address: 200 Constitution Ave. N.W.,
#12-200, Washington, DC 20210); (202) 693-3010.
Fax, (202) 693-2768. William W. Thompson III,
Administrator, Acting.
Web, www.foreignlaborcert.doleta.gov

Sets national policies and guidelines for carrying out the responsibilities of the secretary of labor pursuant to the Immigration and Nationality Act regarding the admission of foreign workers to the United States for both temporary and permanent employment; certifies whether U.S. workers are available for positions for which admission of foreign workers is sought and whether employment of foreign nationals will adversely affect the wages and working conditions of similarly employed U.S. workers.

Apprenticeship Programs

▶AGENCIES

Employment and Training Administration *(Labor Dept.), National Office of Apprenticeship, 200 Constitution Ave. N.W., #N5311, 20210-0001; (202) 693-2796. Fax, (202) 693-3799. John V. Ladd, Administrator. General email, oa.administrator@dol.gov*

Web, www.doleta.gov/apprenticeship

Advises the secretary of labor on the role of apprenticeship programs in employment training and on safety standards for those programs; encourages sponsors to include these standards in planning apprenticeship programs. Promotes establishment of apprenticeship programs in private industry and the public sector.

Employment and Training Administration *(Labor Dept.), Workforce Investment, Youth Services, 200 Constitution Ave. N.W., #N4508, 20210; (202) 693-3030. Fax, (202) 693-3861. Jen Troke, Director. General email, youthservices@dol.gov*

Web, www.doleta.gov/youth_services

Administers youth grant programs designed to enhance youth education, encourage school completion, and provide career and apprenticeship opportunities. Oversees the Going Home: Serious and Violent Offender Reentry Initiative and YouthBuild.

Dislocated Workers

▶AGENCIES

Employment and Training Administration *(Labor Dept.), Adult Services, 200 Constitution Ave. N.W., #S4209, 20210; (202) 693-3046. Fax, (202) 693-3817. Christine D. K. Ollis, Chief. Web, www.doleta.gov/etainfo/wrksys/WIAdultServices.cfm*

Responsible for adult training and services for dislocated workers funded under the Workforce Investment Act; examines training initiatives. Provides targeted job training services for migrant and seasonal farm workers, Native Americans, older workers, veterans, and the disabled. Aims to increase the employment, job retention, earnings, and career advancement of U.S. workers.

Employment and Training Administration *(Labor Dept.), Workforce Investment, 200 Constitution Ave. N.W., #C4526, 20210; (202) 693-3045. Fax, (202) 693-3981. Amanda Ahlstrand, Administrator. Web, www.doleta.gov/etainfo/WrkSys/WIOffice.cfm*

Provides workers with information, job search assistance, and training. Oversees programs administered

through the One-Stop delivery system assisting job seekers including dislocated and transitioning workers.

▶NONGOVERNMENTAL

National Assn. of Workforce Boards (NAWB), *1155 15th St. N.W., #350, 20005; (202) 857-7900. Fax, (202) 857-7955. Ron Painter, Chief Executive Officer. General email, nawb@nawb.org*

Web, www.nawb.org

Membership: private industry councils and state job training coordinating councils established under the Job Training Partnership Act of 1982 (renamed Workforce Boards under the Workforce Investment Act). Interests include job training opportunities for youth and unemployed, economically disadvantaged, and dislocated workers; and private sector involvement in federal employment and training policy. Provides members with technical assistance; holds conferences and seminars.

National Governors Assn. (NGA), *Center for Best Practices, Economic, Human Services, and Workforce Programs, 444 N. Capitol St. N.W., #267, 20001-1512; (202) 624-5345. Fax, (202) 624-7829. Jeff Bates, Director, Acting. Web, www.nga.org/cms/center/ehsw*

Provides technical assistance to members participating in employment and training activities for dislocated workers.

Migrant and Seasonal Farm Workers

▶AGENCIES

Employment and Training Administration *(Labor Dept.), Workforce Investment, 200 Constitution Ave. N.W., #C4526, 20210; (202) 693-3045. Fax, (202) 693-3981. Amanda Ahlstrand, Administrator. Web, www.doleta.gov/etainfo/WrkSys/WIOffice.cfm*

Provides workers with information, job search assistance, and training. Oversees programs administered through the One-Stop delivery system assisting job seekers including migrant and seasonal farmworkers.

Employment and Training Administration *(Labor Dept.), Workforce Investment, National Farmworker Jobs Program, 200 Constitution Ave. N.W., #C4311, 20210-3945; (202) 693-3045. Fax, (202) 693-3015. Juan Regalado, Unit Chief, Acting. General email, NFJP@dol.gov*

Web, www.doleta.gov/farmworker/html/NFJP.cfm

Provides funds for programs that help migrant and seasonal farm workers and their families find better jobs in agriculture and other areas. Services include occupational training, education, and job development and placement. Partners with states to provide services. Provides grants to assist with permanent and temporary housing.

Labor Dept. (DOL), *Wage and Hour Division, Enforcement Policy, Farm and Labor and Immigration Team, 200 Constitution Ave. N.W., #S3520, 20210; (202) 693-0070. Fax, (202) 693-1387. James Kessler,*

Selected Internships and Other Opportunities in the Washington Metropolitan Area

For congressional internships, contact members' offices. For opportunities at federal agencies, visit www.usajobs gov/StudentsAndGrads. For information on changes to the federal internship program, see www.opm.gov/policy-data-oversight/hiring-authorities/students-recent-graduates.

American Assn. for the Advancement of Science, Caroline Seaback, (202) 326-6479; www.aaas.org

American Civil Liberties Union, Adina Ellis, (202) 544-1681; www.aclu.org

American Farm Bureau Federation, Marty Tatman, (202) 406-3682; www.fb.org

American Federation of Teachers, Donna Kimbrue, (202) 879-4439; www.aft.org

American Red Cross, Internship Coordinator, (202) 303-5214; www.redcross.org

Americans for the Arts, Terry Cangelosi, (202) 371-2830; www.americansforthearts.org

Amnesty International, Internship Coordinator, (202) 544-0200; www.amnestyusa.org

B'nai B'rith International, Eric Fusfield, (202) 857-6613; www.bnaibrith.org

Carnegie Institution of Washington, Loronda Lee, (202) 939-1113; www.carnegiescience.edu

Center for Responsive Politics, Internship Coordinator, (202) 857-0044; www.opensecrets.org

Center for Science in the Public Interest, Colleen O. Day, (202) 332-9110; www.cspinet.org

Children's Defense Fund, Yvonne Darpoh, (202) 662-3511; www.childrensdefense.org

Common Cause, Internship Coordinator, (202) 736-5710; www.commoncause.org

Council on Hemispheric Affairs, Larry Birns, (202) 223-4975; www.coha.org

C-SPAN, (202) 737-3220; www.c-span.org

Democratic National Committee, Malbert Smith IV, (202) 863-8000; www.democrats.org

Friends of the Earth, (202) 783-7400; www.foe.org

Inter-American Dialogue, (202) 822-9002; www.thedialogue.org

International Assn. of Chief of Police, Ryan Daugirda, (800) 843-4227, ext. 851; www.theiacp.org

Middle East Institute, Carly Puzniak, (202) 785-1141, ext. 206; www.mei.edu

Motion Picture Assn. of America, (202) 293-1966; www.mpaa.org

National Academy of Sciences, (202) 334-2000; www.nasonline.org

National Assn. for Equal Opportunity in Higher Education, Internship Coordinator, (202) 552-3300; www.nafeo.org

National Assn. for the Advancement of Colored People, Adam Lee, (202) 463-2940; www.naacpdc.org

National Assn. of Broadcasters, Theresa Bates, (202) 429-3928; www.nab.org

National Center for Missing & Exploited Children, Carly Johnson, (877) 446-2632; www.missingkids.com

National Geographic Society, Internship Coordinator, (202) 862-8638; www.nationalgeographic.com

National Governors Assn., Deborah Lately, (202) 624-5300; www.nga.org

National Head Start Assn., Julie Antoniou, (703) 739-0875; www.nhsa.org

National Law Center on Homelessness and Poverty, Janelle Fernandez, (202) 638-2535; www.nlchp.org

National Organization for Women, Elise Coletta, (202) 628-8669; www.now.org

National Public Radio, (202) 513-2000; www.npr.org

National Trust for Historic Preservation, (202) 588-6000; www.preservationnation.org

National Wildlife Federation, Courtney Cochran, (703) 438-6265; www.nwf.org

The Nature Conservancy, (703) 841-5300; www.nature.org

Points of Light Institute, Joselyn Cassidy, (404) 979-2913; www.pointsoflight.org

Radio Free Europe/Radio Liberty, (202) 457-6900; www.rferl.org

Republican National Committee, Internship Coordinator, (202) 863-8630; www.gop.com

Special Olympics International, Andrea Cahn, (202) 628-3630; www.specialolympics.org

United Negro College Fund, (202) 810-0258; www.uncf.org

U.S. Chamber of Commerce, (202) 659-6000; www.uschamber.com

Branch Chief. Toll-free, (866) 487-9243.
Web, www.dol.gov/whd

Administers and enforces the Migrant and Seasonal Agricultural Worker Protection Act, which protects migrant and seasonal agricultural workers from substandard labor practices by farm labor contractors, agricultural employers, and agricultural associations. Also enforces the provisions of the Immigration and Nationality Act that pertain to the employment of H-2A visa workers and U.S. workers in corresponding employment; the temporary labor camp and field sanitation standards of the Occupational Safety and Health Act; and the standards pertaining to employment in agriculture of the Fair Labor Standards Act.

▶**NONGOVERNMENTAL**

Assn. of Farmworker Opportunity Programs, *1120 20th St. N.W., #3005, 20036; (202) 828-6006. Fax, (202) 828-6005. Daniel Sheehan, Executive Director.*
General email, rcrumley@afop.org
Web, www.afop.org and Twitter, @AFOPNational

Represents state-level organizations that provide job training and other services and support to migrant and seasonal farm workers. Monitors legislation and conducts research.

Migrant Legal Action Program, *1001 Connecticut Ave. N.W., #915, 20036-5524; (202) 775-7780. Fax, (202) 775-7784. Roger C. Rosenthal, Executive Director. General email, mlap@mlap.org*

Web, www.mlap.org

Supports and assists local legal services, migrant education, migrant health issues, and other organizations and private attorneys with respect to issues involving the living and working conditions of migrant farm workers. Monitors legislation and regulations.

Older Workers

►**AGENCIES**

Employment and Training Administration *(Labor Dept.), Senior Community Service Employment Program, 200 Constitution Ave. N.W., #C4510, 20210; (202) 693-3842. Fax, (202) 693-3817. Kim Vitelli, Federal Program Officer for the D.C. area. Web, www.doleta.gov/seniors*

Provides funds for part-time community service work-training programs; the programs pay minimum wage and are operated by national sponsoring organizations and state and territorial governments. The program is aimed at unemployed economically disadvantaged persons age fifty-five and over.

►**NONGOVERNMENTAL**

Experience Works, Inc., *4401 Wilson Blvd., #1100, Arlington, VA 22203; (703) 522-7272. Fax, (703) 522-0141. Sally Boofer, Chief Executive Officer. Toll-free, (866) 397-9757.*

Web, www.experienceworks.org and Twitter, @experienceworks

Trains and places older adults in the workforce. Seeks to increase awareness of issues affecting older workers and build support for policies and legislation benefiting older adults. Maintains a help line for those unemployed who are fifty five and older.

National Council on Aging, *Senior Community Service Employment Program, 251 18th St. South, #500, Arlington, VA 22202; (571) 527-3900. Fax, (571) 527-3901. Tim Hamre, Director. General email, info@ncoa.org*

Web, www.ncoa.org/economic-security/matureworkers/scsep

Operates a grant through funding from the U.S. Labor Dept. under the authority of the Older Americans Act to provide workers age fifty-five and over with community service employment and training opportunities in their resident communities.

Workers with Disabilities

►**AGENCIES**

Education Dept., *Special Education and Rehabilitative Services, Rehabilitation Services Administration, 400 Maryland Ave. S.W., 20202-7100; (202) 245-7468. Fax, (202) 245-7591. Janet L. LaBreck, Commissioner. Web, www2.ed.gov/about/offices/list/osers/rsa*

Coordinates and directs federal services for eligible persons with physical or mental disabilities, with emphasis on programs that promote employment opportunities. Provides vocational training and job placement; supports projects with private industry; administers grants for the establishment of supported-employment programs.

Employment and Training Administration *(Labor Dept.), Workforce Investment, 200 Constitution Ave. N.W., #C4526, 20210; (202) 693-3045. Fax, (202) 693-3981. Amanda Ahlstrand, Administrator. Web, www.doleta.gov/etainfo/WrkSys/WIOffice.cfm*

Provides workers with information, job search assistance, and training. Oversees programs administered through the One-Stop delivery system assisting job seekers including individuals with disabilities.

Equal Employment Opportunity Commission (EEOC), *131 M St. N.E., 20507; (202) 663-4001. Fax, (202) 663-4110. Jenny R. Yang, Chair. Toll-free information, (800) 669-4000. TTY, (202) 663-4494. Toll-free TTY, (800) 669-6820. Training Institute, (703) 291-0880. Training Institute toll-free, (866) 446-0940. Training Institute TTY, (800) 828-1120. Library, (202) 663-4630. General email, info@eeoc.gov*

Training Institute email, eeoc.traininginstitute@eeoc.gov Web, www.eeoc.gov

Works for increased employment of persons with disabilities, affirmative action by the federal government, and an equitable work environment for employees with mental and physical disabilities.

Labor Dept. (DOL), *Disability Employment Policy, 200 Constitution Ave. N.W., #S1303, 20210; (202) 693-7880. Fax, (202) 693-7888. Jennifer Sheehy, Deputy Assistant Secretary. Toll-free, 866-ODEP-DOL (633-7365). TTY, (877) 889-5627. General email, odep@dol.gov*

Web, www.dol.gov/odep

Influences disability employment policy by developing and promoting the use of evidence-based disability employment policies and practices, building collaborative partnerships, and delivering data on employment of people with disabilities.

Labor Dept. (DOL), *Wage and Hour Division, Enforcement Policy, Family and Medical Leave, 200 Constitution Ave. N.W., #S3502, 20210; (202) 693-0066. Fax, (202) 693-1387. Helen M. Applewhaite, Branch Chief. Press, (202) 693-4676. Web, www.dol.gov/whd*

Administers certification of special lower minimum wage rates for workers with disabilities and impaired earning capacity; wage applies in industry, sheltered workshops, hospitals, institutions, and group homes.

Office of Personnel Management (OPM), *Veterans Services,* 1900 E St. N.W., #7439, 20415; (202) 606-3602. Fax, (202) 606-6017.
Hakeem Basheerud-Deen, Director.
Web, www.opm.gov/policy-data-oversight/veterans-services

Provides federal employees and transitioning military service members and their families, federal human resources professionals, and hiring managers with information on employment opportunities with the federal government. Administers the Disabled Veterans Affirmative Action Program.

U.S. AbilityOne Commission, 1401 S. Clark St., Arlington, VA 22202; (703) 603-7740. Fax, (703) 603-0655.
Tina Ballard, Executive Director.
General email, info@abilityone.gov
Web, www.abilityone.gov

Presidentially appointed committee. Determines which products and services are suitable for federal procurement from qualified nonprofit agencies that employ people who are blind or have other significant disabilities; seeks to increase employment opportunities for these individuals. (Formerly Committee for Purchase from People Who Are Blind or Severely Disabled.)

▶**NONGOVERNMENTAL**

Business Leadership Network (USBLN), 1310 Braddock Pl., #101, Alexandria, VA 22314; (800) 706-2710.
Fax, (800) 706-1335. Jill Houghton, Executive Director.
General email, info@usbln.org
Web, www.usbln.org

Advocates inclusion of people with disabilities in the workplace, supply chain, and marketplaces; provides information on disability inclusion business practices.

Center for Workers with Disabilities, 1133 19th St. N.W., #400, 20036; (202) 682-0100. Fax, (202) 204-0071.
Nanette Relave, Director.
Web, http://cwd.aphsa.org/content/CWD/en/home.html

Technical assistance center for states enhancing or developing employment infrastructure and supports for working persons with disabilities. (Affiliated with the American Public Human Services Association.)

Youth

▶**AGENCIES**

Employment and Training Administration *(Labor Dept.), Workforce Investment, Youth Services,* 200 Constitution Ave. N.W., #N4508, 20210; (202) 693-3030. Fax, (202) 693-3861. Jen Troke, Director.

General email, youthservices@dol.gov
Web, www.doleta.gov/youth_services

Administers youth grant programs designed to enhance youth education, encourage school completion, and provide career and apprenticeship opportunities. Oversees the Going Home: Serious and Violent Offender Reentry Initiative and YouthBuild.

Forest Service *(Agriculture Dept.), Youth Conservation Corps,* 201 14th St. S.W., 20024 (mailing address: 1400 Independence Ave. S.W., MS 1125, Washington, DC 20250-1125); (202) 205-0650. Fax, (703) 605-5131.
Merlene Maczyk, Manager. Toll-free, (800) 832-1355.
General email, mmaczyk@fs.fed.us
Web, http://youthgo.gov

Administers, with the National Park Service and the Fish and Wildlife Service, the Youth Conservation Corps, a summer employment and training public works program for youths ages fifteen to eighteen. The program is conducted in national parks, in national forests, and on national wildlife refuges.

Labor Dept. (DOL), *Job Corps,* 200 Constitution Ave. N.W., #N4463, 20210; (202) 693-3000. Fax, (202) 693-2767. Lenita Jacobs-Simmons, Administrator. Information, (800) 733-5627. TTY, (877) 889-5627.
General email, national_office@jobcorps.gov
Web, www.jobcorps.gov/home.aspx and Facebook, www.facebook.com/doljobcorps

Provides job training for disadvantaged youth at residential centers. Most of the centers are managed and operated by corporations and nonprofit organizations.

Labor Dept. (DOL), *Wage and Hour Division, Enforcement Policy, Child Labor and Fair Labor Standards Act Enforcement,* 200 Constitution Ave. N.W., #3516, 20210; (202) 693-0067. Fax, (202) 693-1387.
Derrick J. Witherspoon, Division Chief. Press, (202) 693-0185. Toll-free, (866) 487-9243.
Web, www.dol.gov/whd

Administers and enforces child labor, special minimum wage, and other provisions of Section 14 of the Fair Labor Standards Act.

▶**NONGOVERNMENTAL**

The Corps Network, 1275 K St. N.W., #1050, 20005; (202) 737-6272. Fax, (202) 737-6277. Mary Ellen Sprenkel, President.
Web, www.corpsnetwork.org and Twitter, @TheCorpsNetwork

Membership: youth corps programs. Produces publications and workshops on starting and operating youth corps and offers technical assistance programs. Holds annual conference. Monitors legislation and regulations.

Covenant House, *Washington Office,* 2001 Mississippi Ave S.E., 20020; (202) 610-9600. Madye Henson, President. TTY, (800) 786-2929.
Web, http://covenanthousedc.org

Equal Employment Opportunity Commission

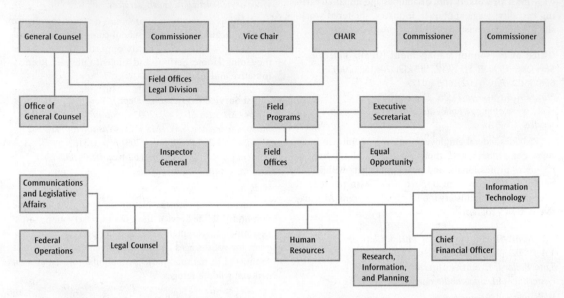

Protects young people suffering from homelessness, abuse, and neglect. Provides services including transitional housing, GED and adult education, and job readiness. (Affiliated with Covenant House International.)

EQUAL EMPLOYMENT OPPORTUNITY

General

Civil Rights Division *(Justice Dept.)*, *Employment Litigation,* *601 D St. N.W., #4040, 20579; (202) 514-3831. Fax, (202) 514-1005. Delora L. Kennebrew, Chief. Library, (202) 514-3775. TTY, (202) 514-6780.*
Web, www.justice.gov/crt/about/emp

Investigates, negotiates, and litigates allegations of employment discrimination by public schools, universities, state and local governments, and federally funded employers; has enforcement power. Enforces the Uniform Services Employment and Reemployment Rights Act. Members of the public are asked to contact the library with questions about access.

Equal Employment Opportunity Commission (EEOC), *131 M St. N.E., 20507; (202) 663-4001. Fax, (202) 663-4110. Jenny R. Yang, Chair. Toll-free information, (800) 669-4000. TTY, (202) 663-4494. Toll-free TTY, (800) 669-6820. Training Institute, (703) 291-0880. Training Institute toll-free, (866) 446-0940. Training Institute TTY, (800) 828-1120. Library, (202) 663-4630.*
General email, info@eeoc.gov
Training Institute email, eeoc.traininginstitute@eeoc.gov
Web, www.eeoc.gov

Works to end job discrimination by private and government employers based on race, color, religion, sex, national origin, disability, or age. Works to protect employees against reprisal for protest of employment practices alleged to be unlawful in hiring, promotion, firing, wages, and other terms and conditions of employment. Works for increased employment of persons with disabilities, affirmative action by the federal government, and an equitable work environment for employees with mental and physical disabilities. Enforces Title VII of the Civil Rights Act of 1964, as amended, which includes the Pregnancy Discrimination Act; Americans with Disabilities Act; Age Discrimination in Employment Act; Equal Pay Act; and, in the federal sector, rehabilitation laws. Receives charges of discrimination; attempts conciliation or settlement; can bring court action to force compliance; has review and appeals responsibility in the federal sector. Library open to the public by appointment only.

Equal Employment Opportunity Commission (EEOC), *Field Programs, 131 M St. N.E., 5th Floor, 20507; (202) 663-4801. Fax, (202) 663-7190. Nicholas Inzeo, Director. Web, www.eeoc.gov/field/index.cfm*

Provides guidance and technical assistance through 15 district offices to employees who suspect discrimination and to employers who are working to comply with equal employment laws.

Labor Dept. (DOL), *Federal Contract Compliance Programs, 200 Constitution Ave. N.W., #C3325, 20210; (202) 693-0101. Fax, (202) 693-1304. Patricia A. Shiu, Director; Thomas Dowd, Deputy Director. Toll-free, (800) 397-6251. TTY, (202) 693-1337.*
General email, OFCCP-Public@dol.gov
Web, www.dol.gov/ofccp

Monitors and enforces government contractors' compliance with federal laws and regulations on equal

Equal Employment Opportunity Contacts at Federal Departments and Agencies

DEPARTMENTS

Agriculture, Joe Leonard Jr., (202) 720-3808

Commerce, Suzan J. Aramaki, (202) 482-0625

Defense, Clarence A. Johnson, (703) 571-9319

  Air Force, James H. Carlock Jr., (240) 612-4113

  Army, James Braxton Sr., (202) 761-8707

  Marine Corps, Paula E. Bedford, (703) 784-2946

  Navy, Celina Kline, (202) 685-6466

Education, Michael A. Chew, (202) 401-0691

Energy, Neil Schuldenfrei, (202) 586-8212

Health and Human Services, Cynthia Richardson Crooks, (202) 690-6555

Homeland Security, Tamara Kessler, (202) 254-8200

  Coast Guard, Deborah Gant, (202) 372-4500

Housing and Urban Development, John P. Benison, (202) 708-3362

Interior, John W. Burden, (202) 208-5693

Justice, Lee J. Lofthus, (202) 514-3101

Labor, Naomi M. Barry-Perez, (202) 693-6500

State, John M. Robinson, (202) 647-9295

Transportation, Leslie Proll, (202) 366-4648

Treasury, Mariam G. Harvey, (202) 622-0316

Veterans Affairs, Georgia Coffey, (202) 461-4131

AGENCIES

Commission on Civil Rights, Martin R. Castro, (202) 376-7700

Commodity Futures Trading Commission, Lorena McElwain, (202) 418-5935

Consumer Product Safety Commission, Kathleen Buttrey, (301) 504-7904

Corporation for National and Community Service, Tasha Stewart, (202) 606-6791

Environmental Protection Agency, Velveta Golightly-Howell, (202) 564-7272

Equal Employment Opportunity Commission, Jenny R. Yang, (202) 663-4900

Export-Import Bank, Patrease Jones-Brown, (202) 565-3591

Farm Credit Administration, Thais Burlew, (703) 883-4290

Federal Communications Commission, Linda Miller, (202) 418-1799

Federal Deposit Insurance Corporation, Anthony Pagano, (703) 562-6062

Federal Election Commission, Kevin Salley, (202) 694-1229

Federal Emergency Management Agency, Willisa Donald, (202) 646-4122

Federal Energy Regulatory Commission (FERC), Madeline H. Lewis, (202) 502-8120

Federal Labor Relations Authority, Gina Grippando, (202) 218-7740

Federal Maritime Commission, Howard F. Jimenez, (202) 523-5859

Federal Mediation and Conciliation Service, Denise Patterson McKinney, (202) 606-5448

Federal Reserve Board, Sheila Clark, (202) 452-2883

Federal Trade Commission, Kevin D. Williams, (202) 326-2196

General Services Administration, Madeline Caliendo, (202) 501-0767

Merit Systems Protection Board, Jerry Beat, (202) 254-4405

National Aeronautics and Space Administration, Brenda R. Manuel, (202) 358-2167

National Credit Union Administration, S. Denise Hendricks, (703) 518-6326

National Endowment for the Humanities, Margaret Plympton, (202) 606-8310

National Labor Relations Board, Brenda V. Harris, (202) 273-3891

National Science Foundation, Rhonda J. Davis, (703) 292-8020

National Transportation Safety Board, Fara D. Guest, (202) 314-6190

Nuclear Regulatory Commission, Joel Kravetz, (301) 415-0503

Occupational Safety and Health Review Commission, Anthony Pellegrino, (202) 606-5390

Office of Personnel Management, Veronica Villalobos, (202) 606-2460

Peace Corps, Janet Bernal, (202) 692-2113

Securities and Exchange Commission, Alta G. Rodriguez, (202) 551-6040

Small Business Administration, Trinisha Agramonte, (202) 205-6750

Smithsonian Institution, Rudy D. Watley, (202) 633-6430

Social Security Administration, Kojuan Almond, (410) 965-4149

U.S. International Trade Commission, Altivia Jackson, (202) 205-2239

U.S. Postal Service, Eloise Lance, (202) 268-3820

employment opportunities and affirmative action, including employment rights of minorities, women, persons with disabilities, and disabled and Vietnam-era veterans.

Office of Personnel Management (OPM), *Veterans Services, 1900 E St. N.W., #7439, 20415; (202) 606-3602. Fax, (202) 606-6017. Hakeem Basheerud-Deen, Director. Web, www.opm.gov/policy-data-oversight/veterans-services*

Administers the Disabled Veterans Affirmative Action Program.

U.S. Commission on Civil Rights, *Civil Rights Evaluation, 1331 Pennsylvania Ave. N.W., #1150, 20425; (202) 376-7700. Fax, (202) 376-7754. Maureen Rudolf, Chief, Acting. Complaints Unit hotline, (202) 376-8513. Web, www.usccr.gov*

Researches federal policy in areas of equal employment and job discrimination; monitors the economic status of minorities and women, including their employment and earnings. Library open to the public.

►**CONGRESS**

For a listing of relevant congressional committees and subcommittees, please see page 206 or the Appendix.

►**NONGOVERNMENTAL**

Center for Equal Opportunity, *7700 Leesburg Pike, #231, Falls Church, VA 22043; (703) 442-0066. Fax, (703) 442-0449. Roger Clegg, President; Linda Chavez, Chair. General email, comment@ceousa.org*

Web, www.ceousa.org and Twitter, @ceousa

Research organization concerned with issues of race, ethnicity, and assimilation; opposes racial preferences in employment or education, contracting, and other areas. Monitors legislation and regulations.

Equal Employment Advisory Council, *1501 M St. N.W., #400, 20005; (202) 629-5650. Fax, (202) 629-5651. Joseph S. Lakis, President. General email, info@eeac.org*

Web, www.eeac.org

Membership: principal equal employment officers and lawyers. Files amicus curiae (friend of the court) briefs; conducts research and provides information on equal employment law and policy. Monitors legislation and regulations.

NAACP Legal Defense and Educational Fund, Inc., *Washington Office, 1444 Eye St. N.W., 10th Floor, 20005; (202) 682-1300. Fax, (202) 682-1312. Leslie M. Proll, Director. Web, www.naacpldf.org*

Civil rights litigation group that provides legal information about civil rights legislation and advice on employment discrimination against women and minorities; monitors federal enforcement of equal opportunity rights laws. Not affiliated with the NAACP. (Headquarters in New York.)

Minorities

►**AGENCIES**

Bureau of Indian Affairs (BIA) *(Interior Dept.),* **Indian Energy and Economic Development,** *1951 Constitution Ave. N.W., MS 20, 20245; (202) 219-0740. Fax, (202) 208-4564. Jack Stevens, Chief. Web, www.bia.gov*

Develops policies and programs to promote the achievement of economic goals for members of federally recognized tribes who live on or near reservations. Provides job training; assists those who have completed job training programs in finding employment; provides loan guarantees; enhances contracting opportunities for individuals and tribes; assists with environmentally responsible exploration, development, and management of energy and mineral resources to generate new jobs.

Education Dept., *White House Initiative on Asian Americans and Pacific Islanders, 550 12th St. S.W., 10th Floor, 20202; (202) 245-6418. Fax, (202) 245-7166. Doua Thor, Executive Director. Press, (202) 245-6353. General email, whitehouseaapi@ed.gov*

Web, http://sites.ed.gov/whieeaa and Twitter, @whitehouseAAPI

Works to expand Asian American and Pacific Islander federal employment opportunities. Ensures that workers' rights are protected and upheld.

Employment and Training Administration *(Labor Dept.),* **Workforce Investment, Indian and Native American Programs,** *200 Constitution Ave. N.W., #S4209, 20210; (202) 693-3841. Fax, (202) 693-3817. Athena Brown, Program Manager. Web, www.doleta.gov/dinap*

Administers grants for training and employment-related programs to promote employment opportunity; provides unemployed, underemployed, and economically disadvantaged Native Americans and Alaska and Hawaiian Natives with funds for training, job placement, and support services.

►**NONGOVERNMENTAL**

AFL-CIO, *Asian Pacific American Labor Alliance (APALA), 815 16th St. N.W., 20006; (202) 508-3733. Fax, (202) 508-3716. Gregory Cendana, Executive Director. General email, apala@apalanet.org*

Web, www.apalanet.org

Membership: Asian Pacific American (APA) union members. Represents regional Asian Pacific American labor activists in a national scope and assists in union member issues. Interests include gender analysis, youth participation, and civil rights within the APA community.

American Assn. for Access, Equity, and Diversity (AAAED), *1701 Pennsylvania Ave. N.W., #206, 20006; (202) 349-9855. Fax, (202) 355-1399. Shirley J. Wilcher, Executive Director. Toll-free, (800) 252-8952.*

General email, execdir@aaaed.org

Web, www.aaaed.org

Membership: professional managers in the areas of affirmative action, equal opportunity, diversity, and human resources. Sponsors education, research, and training programs. Acts as a liaison with government agencies involved in equal opportunity compliance. Maintains ethical standards for the profession. (Formerly the American Assn. for Affirmative Action.)

Coalition of Black Trade Unionists, *1155 Connecticut Ave. N.W., #500, 20036 (mailing address: P.O. Box 66268, Washington DC 20035); (202) 778-3318. Fax, (202) 419-1486. Terrence L. Melvin, President.*

General email, cbtu@hotmail.com

Web, www.cbtu.org

Monitors legislation affecting African American and other minority trade unionists. Focuses on equal employment opportunity, unemployment, and voter education and registration.

Labor Council for Latin American Advancement, *815 16th St. N.W., 3rd Floor, 20006; (202) 508-6919. Fax, (202) 508-6922. Hector E. Sanchez, Executive Director.*

General email, headquarters@lclaa.org

Web, www.lclaa.org, Twitter, @LCLAA and Facebook, www.facebook.com/LCLAA

Membership: Hispanic trade unionists. Encourages equal employment opportunity, voter registration, and participation in the political process. (Affiliated with the AFL-CIO and the Change to Win Federation.)

Mexican American Legal Defense and Educational Fund, *National Public Policy, 1016 16th St. N.W., #100, 20036; (202) 293-2828. Andrea Senteno, Legislative Staff Attorney; Vacant, Regional Counsel.*

Web, www.maldef.org/about/offices/washington_dc

Provides Mexican Americans and other Hispanics with high-impact litigation in the areas of employment, education, immigration rights, and voting rights. Monitors legislation and regulations. (Headquarters in Los Angeles, Calif.)

National Assn. for the Advancement of Colored People (NAACP), *Washington Bureau, 1156 15th St. N.W., #915, 20005; (202) 463-2940. Fax, (202) 463-2953. Hilary O. Shelton, Director.*

General email, washingtonbureau@naacpnet.org

Web, www.naacp.org

Membership: persons interested in civil rights for all minorities. Advises individuals with employment discrimination complaints. Seeks to eliminate job discrimination and to bring about full employment for all Americans through legislation and litigation. (Headquarters in Baltimore, Md.)

National Assn. of Hispanic Federal Executives, Inc., *P.O. Box 23270, 20026-3270; (202) 309-9027. Al Gallegos, National President.*

General email, president@nahfe.org

Web, www.nahfe.org

Works to ensure that the needs of the Hispanic American community are addressed in the policymaking levels of the federal government by promoting career and learning opportunities for qualified Hispanics in the federal GS/GM-12/15 grade levels and the Senior Executive Service policymaking positions.

National Assn. of Negro Business and Professional Women's Clubs Inc., *1806 New Hampshire Ave. N.W., 20009; (202) 483-4206. Fax, (202) 462-7253. Robin M. Waley, Executive Director.*

General email, executivedirector@nanbpwc.org

Web, www.nanbpwc.org

Promotes and protects the interests of business and professional women, serves as advisors to young people seeking to enter business and the professions, provides scholarship support for secondary education, sponsors workshops, and works to improve the quality of life in local and global communities to foster good fellowship. Monitors legislation and regulations.

National Council of La Raza, *1126 16th St. N.W., #600, 20036-4845; (202) 785-1670. Fax, (202) 776-1792. Janet Murguía, President.*

General email, info@nclr.org

Web, www.nclr.org, Twitter, @NCLR and Facebook, www.facebook.com/Nationalcounciloflaraza

Provides research, policy analysis, and advocacy on Hispanic employment status and programs; provides Hispanic community-based groups with technical assistance to help develop effective employment programs with strong educational components. Works to promote understanding of Hispanic employment needs in the private sector. Interests include women in the workplace, affirmative action, equal opportunity employment, and youth employment. Monitors federal employment legislation and regulations.

National Urban League, *Washington Bureau, 2901 14th St. N.W., 20009; (202) 265-8200. George H. Lambert Jr., Affiliate Chief Executive Officer.*

Web, http://nul.iamempowered.com/affiliate/greater-washington-urban-league

Federal advocacy division of social service organization concerned with the social welfare of African Americans and other minorities. Testifies before congressional committees and federal agencies on equal employment; studies and evaluates federal enforcement of equal employment laws and regulations. (Headquarters in New York.)

Washington Government Relations Group, *1325 G St. N.W., #500, 20005; (202) 449-7651. Fax, (202) 449-7701. Marcus Sebastian Mason, President.*

General email, info@wgrginc.org

Web, www.wgrginc.org

Works to enrich the careers and leadership abilities of African American government relations professionals working in business, financial institutions, law firms, trade associations, and nonprofit organizations. Increases dialogue between members and senior-level policymakers to produce public policy solutions.

Older Adults

▶NONGOVERNMENTAL

AARP, *601 E St. N.W., 20049; (202) 434-2277. Jo Ann C. Jenkins, Chief Executive Officer. Press, (202) 434-2560. Library, (202) 434-6233. TTY, (877) 434-7598. Toll-free, (888) 687-2277. Membership, (202) 434-3525.*
General email, member@aarp.org
Web, www.aarp.org

Membership: people fifty years of age and older. Promotes a multigenerational workforce and seeks to prevent age discrimination in the workplace.

National Caucus and Center on Black Aging, Inc., *1220 L St. N.W., #800, 20005-2407; (202) 637-8400. Fax, (202) 347-0895. Karyne Jones, President.*
General email, support@ncba-aged.org
Web, www.ncba-aged.org

Concerned with issues that affect older Black Americans and other minorities. Sponsors employment and housing programs for older adults and education and training for professionals in gerontology. Monitors legislation and regulations.

Women

▶AGENCIES

Women's Bureau *(Labor Dept.), 200 Constitution Ave. N.W., #S3002, 20210; (202) 693-6710. Fax, (202) 693-6725. Latifa Lyles, Director. Information, (800) 827-5335.*
General email, womens.bureau@dol.gov
Web, www.dol.gov/wb

Monitors women's employment issues. Promotes employment opportunities for women; sponsors workshops, job fairs, symposia, demonstrations, and pilot projects. Offers technical assistance; conducts research and provides publications on issues that affect working women; represents working women in international forums.

▶NONGOVERNMENTAL

Business and Professional Women's Foundation, *1718 M St. N.W., #148, 20036; (202) 293-1100. Fax, (202) 861-0298. Roslyn Ridgeway, Chair.*
General email, foundation@bpwfoundation.org
Web, www.bpwfoundation.org and Twitter, @WomenMisbehavin

Works to eliminate barriers to the full participation of women in the workplace. Interests include pay equity, work-life balance, women veterans, and green jobs for women. Conducts research; provides issue briefs and other publications; monitors legislation and regulations.

Coalition of Labor Union Women, *815 16th St. N.W., 2nd Floor South, 20006-1119; (202) 508-6969. Fax, (202) 508-6968. Connie Leak, President; Carol S. Rosenblatt, Executive Director.*
General email, getinfo@cluw.org
Web, www.cluw.org and Twitter, @CLUWNational

Seeks to make unions more responsive to the needs of women in the workplace; advocates affirmative action and the active participation of women in unions. Monitors legislation and regulations.

Federally Employed Women, *455 Massachusetts Ave. N.W., P.O. Box 306, 20001; (202) 898-0994. Fax, (202) 898-1535. Michelle Crockett, President.*
General email, few@few.org
Web, www.few.org

Membership: women and men who work for the federal government. Works to eliminate sex discrimination in government employment and to increase job opportunities for women; offers training programs. Monitors legislation and regulations.

Institute for Women's Policy Research (IWPR), *1200 18th St. N.W., #301, 20036; (202) 785-5100. Fax, (202) 833-4362. Heidi Hartmann, President.*
General email, iwpr@iwpr.org
Web, www.iwpr.org

Public policy research organization that focuses on women's issues, including family and work balance, employment and wages, the status of women in the United States, and discrimination based on gender, race, or ethnicity.

National Assn. of Women Business Owners, *601 Pennsylvania Ave. N.W., South Bldg., #900, 20004; (202) 609-9817. Fax, (202) 403-3788. Jen Earle, Chief Executive Officer. Toll-free, (800) 556-2926.*
General email, national@nawbo.org
Web, www.nawbo.org

Promotes the economic, social, and political interests of women business owners through networking, leadership and business development training, and advocacy.

National Council of Women's Organizations, *714 G St. S.E., #200, 20003; (202) 293-4505. Fax, (202) 293-4507. Shireen Mitchell, Chair.*
General email, ncwo@ncwo-online.org
Web, www.ncwo-online.org

Membership: local and national women's organizations. Engages in policy work and grassroots activism to address issues of concern to women, including workplace and economic equity, education and job training, affirmative action, Social Security, child care, reproductive freedom, health, and global women's equality. Monitors legislation and regulations.

National Labor Relations Board

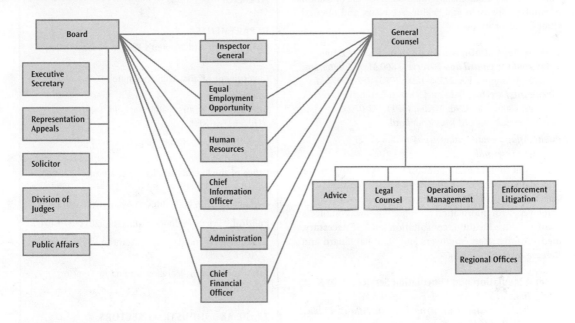

National Partnership for Women and Families, 1875 Connecticut Ave. N.W., #650, 20009-5731; (202) 986-2600. Fax, (202) 986-2539. Debra L. Ness, President.
General email, info@nationalpartnership.org

Web, www.nationalpartnership.org

Advocacy organization that promotes fairness in the workplace, access to high-quality health care, and policies that help women and men meet the demands of work and family. Publishes and disseminates information in print and on the Web to heighten awareness of work and family issues. Monitors legislative activity and pending Supreme Court cases and argues on behalf of family issues before Congress and in the courts.

National Women's Law Center, 11 Dupont Circle N.W., #800, 20036; (202) 588-5180. Fax, (202) 588-5185. Nancy Duff Campbell, Co-President; Marcia D. Greenberger, Co-President.
General email, info@nwlc.org

Web, www.nwlc.org

Works to protect and advance the rights of women and girls at work, in school, and beyond. Maintains programs that focus on enforcing Title IX's provisions for equal treatment in education and narrowing the gender gap in athletics and the technology-oriented workplace. Other interests include equal pay and benefits, sexual harassment laws, the right to family leave, child care and early learning, poverty and income support, and the preservation of diversity in the workplace.

Wider Opportunities for Women, 1001 Connecticut Ave. N.W., #930, 20036-5504; (202) 464-1596. Fax, (202) 354-4631. Amanda Andere, President.

General email, info@WOWonline.org

Web, www.WOWonline.org

Promotes equal employment opportunities for women through equal access to jobs and training, equal incomes, and an equitable workplace. Monitors public policy relating to jobs, affirmative action, vocational education, training opportunities, and welfare reform.

LABOR-MANAGEMENT OPPORTUNITY

General

▶AGENCIES

Bureau of Labor Statistics (BLS) *(Labor Dept.),* *Compensation and Working Conditions,* 2 Massachusetts Ave. N.E., #4130, 20212; (202) 691-6300. Fax, (202) 691-6310. Vacant, Associate Commissioner.
Web, www.bls.gov

Conducts quarterly surveys of wages and benefits; data used for the quarterly *Employment Cost Index*, the quarterly *Employer Costs for Employee Compensation*, and annual reports on the incidence and provisions of employee benefits.

Criminal Division *(Justice Dept.), Organized Crime and Gang Section,* 1301 New York Ave. N.W., #700, 20005; (202) 514-3594. Fax, (202) 514-3601. James Trusty, Chief. General email, criminaldivision@us.doj.gov

Web, www.justice.gov/criminal-ocgs

Reviews and advises on prosecutions of criminal violations involving labor-management relations, the operation of employee pension and health care plans, and internal affairs of labor unions.

Defense Dept. (DoD), *National Committee for Employer Support of the Guard and Reserve, 4800 Mark Center Dr., #03E25, Arlington, VA 22350-1200; (703) 882-3747. M. Alex Baird, Director; Ted Fessel, Deputy Executive Director. Toll-free, (800) 336-4590. Media, (571) 372-0705. General email, osd.USERRA@mail.mil*

Public Affairs email, osd.esgr-pa@mail.mil, Web, www.esgr.mil

Works to gain and maintain employer support for National Guard and Reserve service by recognizing outstanding support and providing service members and employers with information on applicable law. Volunteers provide free education, consultation, and, if necessary, mediation between employers and National Guard and Reserve service members.

Federal Mediation and Conciliation Service, *2100 K St. N.W., 20427; (202) 606-8100. Fax, (202) 606-4251. Alison Beck, Director; John Arnold, Public Affairs. Public Affairs, (202) 606-5442. Web, www.fmcs.gov*

Assists labor and management representatives in resolving disputes in collective bargaining contract negotiation through voluntary mediation and arbitration services; awards competitive grants to joint labor-management initiatives; trains other federal agencies in mediating administrative disputes and formulating rules and regulations under the Administrative Dispute Resolution Act of 1996 and the Negotiated Rulemaking Act of 1996; provides training to unions and management in cooperative processes. Operates 10 district offices and more than 60 field offices.

Labor Dept. (DOL), *Labor-Management Standards, 200 Constitution Ave. N.W., #N1519, 20210; (202) 693-0122. Fax, (202) 693-1206. Michael J. Hayes, Director. Press, (202) 693-4676. Information, (202) 693-0123. General email, olms-public@dol.gov*

Web, www.dol.gov/olms

Administers and enforces the Labor-Management Reporting and Disclosure Act of 1959 (Landrum-Griffin Act), which guarantees union members certain rights; sets rules for electing union officers, handling union funds, and using trusteeships; requires unions, union officers and employees, employers, and labor consultants to file financial and other reports with the Labor Dept. Administers relevant sections of the Civil Service Reform Act of 1978 and the Foreign Service Act of 1980. Administers the employee protection provisions of the Federal Transit law.

National Labor Relations Board (NLRB), *1015 Half St. S.E., 20570-0001; (202) 208-3000. Fax, (202) 208-3013. Mark G. Pearce, Chair; Richard F. Griffin Jr., General Counsel; Gary Shinners, Executive Secretary. Library, (202)*

273-3720. *Press and public information, (202) 273-1991. Toll-free, (866) 667-6572. TTY, (866) 315-6572. Web, www.nlrb.gov*

@NLRB

Administers the National Labor Relations Act. Works to prevent and remedy unfair labor practices by employers and labor unions; conducts elections among employees to determine whether they wish to be represented by a labor union for collective bargaining purposes. Complaints may be filed in field offices by calling the toll-free line. Library open to the public.

National Mediation Board, *1301 K St. N.W., #250E, 20005-7011; (202) 692-5000. Fax, (202) 692-5082. Nicholas Geale, Chair. Information, (202) 692-5050. TTY, (202) 692-5001. General email, infoline@nmb.gov*

Web, www.nmb.gov

Mediates labor disputes in the railroad and airline industries; determines and certifies labor representatives for those industries. Library open by appointment.

AFL-CIO

DEPARTMENTS

Civil, Human, and Women's Rights, Rosalyn Pelles, Director, (202) 637-5270

Government Affairs, William Samuel, Director, (202) 637-5320

International Affairs, Cathy Feingold, Director, (202) 637-5050

Legal Dept., Craig Becker, General Counsel, (202) 637-5053

Office of the President, Richard L. Trumka, President, (202) 637-5231

Organizing, Lynn Rodenhuis, Director, (202) 639-6289

Political, Michael Podhorzer, Director, (202) 637-5101

Public Affairs, Eric Hauser, Assistant to the President, (202) 637-5393

Safety and Health, Margaret Seminario, Director, (202) 637-5366

TRADE AND INDUSTRIAL SECTORS

Building and Construction Trades, Sean McGarvey, President, (202) 347-1461

Maritime Trades, Michael Sacco, President, (202) 628-6300

Metal Trades, Ronald Ault, President, (202) 508-3705

Professional Employees, Paul E. Almeida, President, (202) 638-0320

Transportation Trades, Edward Wytkind, President, (202) 628-9262

Union Label and Service Trades, Richard Kline, President, (202) 508-3700

▶CONGRESS

For a listing of relevant congressional committees and sub-committees, please see page 206 or the Appendix.

▶NONGOVERNMENTAL

AFL-CIO (American Federation of Labor-Congress of Industrial Organizations), *815 16th St. N.W., 20006; (202) 637-5000. Fax, (202) 637-5058. Richard L. Trumka, President.*
Web, www.aflcio.org

Voluntary federation of national and international labor unions in the United States. Represents members before Congress and other branches of government. Each member union conducts its own contract negotiations. Library (located in Silver Spring, Md.) open to the public.

AFL-CIO, *Asian Pacific American Labor Alliance (APALA), 815 16th St. N.W., 20006; (202) 508-3733. Fax, (202) 508-3716. Gregory Cendana, Executive Director.*
General email, apala@apalanet.org
Web, www.apalanet.org

Membership: Asian Pacific American (APA) union members. Represents regional Asian Pacific American labor activists in a national scope and assists in union member issues. Trains union members in areas including organization, development, and political advocacy.

American Arbitration Assn., *Government Relations, 1120 Connecticut Ave., #490, 20036; (202) 223-4263. Fax, (202) 223-7095. S. Pierre Paret, Vice President.*
General email, paretp@adr.org
Web, www.adr.org

Provides alternative dispute resolution services to governments and the private sector. (Headquarters in New York.)

American Federation of Musicians, *Government Relations, 5335 Wisconsin Ave. N.W., #440, 20015; (202) 274-4756. Fax, (202) 274-4759. Alfonso Pollard, Director.*
General email, apollard@afm.org
Web, www.afm.org

Seeks to improve the working conditions and salary of musicians. Monitors legislation and regulations affecting musicians and the arts. (Headquarters in New York.)

American Foreign Service Assn. (AFSA), *2101 E St. N.W., 20037; (202) 338-4045. Fax, (202) 338-6820. Ian Houston, Executive Director. Press, (202) 944-5508. Toll-free (within the U.S.), (800) 704-2372.*
General email, member@afsa.org
Web, www.afsa.org

Membership: active and retired foreign service employees of federal agencies. Represents active duty foreign service personnel in labor-management negotiations; seeks to ensure adequate resources for foreign service operations and personnel. Monitors legislation and regulations related to foreign service personnel and retirees.

The Center for Union Facts, *1090 Vermont Ave. N.W., #800, 20005; (202) 463-7106. Fax, (202) 463-7107. Richard Berman, Executive Director.*
Web, www.unionfacts.com

Seeks to educate businesses, union members, and the public about the labor movement's political activities, specifically those of union officials. Interests include management of union dues. Monitors legislation and regulations.

Coalition of Black Trade Unionists, *1155 Connecticut Ave. N.W., #500, 20036 (mailing address: P.O. Box 66268, Washington DC 20035); (202) 778-3318. Fax, (202) 419-1486. Terrence L. Melvin, President.*
General email, cbtu@hotmail.com
Web, www.cbtu.org

Monitors legislation affecting African American and other minority trade unionists. Focuses on equal employment opportunity, unemployment, and voter education and registration.

Coalition of Labor Union Women, *815 16th St. N.W., 2nd Floor South, 20006-1119; (202) 508-6969. Fax, (202) 508-6968. Connie Leak, President; Carol S. Rosenblatt, Executive Director.*
General email, getinfo@cluw.org
Web, www.cluw.org and Twitter, @CLUWNational

Seeks to make unions more responsive to the needs of women in the workplace; advocates affirmative action and the active participation of women in unions. Monitors legislation and regulations.

Communications Workers of America (CWA), *501 3rd St. N.W., 20001; (202) 434-1100. Fax, (202) 434-1279. Christopher M. Shelton, President.*
Web, www.cwa-union.org and Twitter, @CWAUnion

Membership: approximately 700,000 workers in telecommunications, journalism, publishing, cable television, electronics, and other fields. Interests include workplace democracy and restoring bargaining rights. Represents members in contract negotiations and grievances; conducts training programs and workshops. Monitors legislation and regulations. (Affiliated with the AFL-CIO.)

International Assn. of Bridge, Structural, Ornamental, and Reinforcing Iron Workers, *1750 New York Ave. N.W., #400, 20006; (202) 383-4800. Fax, (202) 638-4856. Eric Dean, President.*
General email, iwmagazine@iwintl.org
Web, www.ironworkers.org

Membership: approximately 140,000 iron workers. Helps members negotiate pay, benefits, and better working conditions; conducts training programs and workshops. Monitors legislation and regulations. (Affiliated with the AFL-CIO.)

International Assn. of Fire Fighters, *1750 New York Ave. N.W., #300, 20006-5395; (202) 737-8484. Fax, (202) 737-8418. Harold A. Schaitberger, General President.*
General email, pr@iaff.org
Web, www.iaff.org

Membership: more than 298,000 professional firefighters and emergency medical personnel. Assists members with contract negotiation and grievances; conducts training programs and workshops. Monitors legislation and regulations. (Affiliated with the AFL-CIO and the Canadian Labour Congress.)

International Assn. of Heat and Frost Insulators and Allied Workers, *9602 Martin Luther King Hwy., Lanham, MD 20706-1839; (301) 731-9101. Fax, (301) 731-5058. James McCourt, General President.*
General email, hfi@insulators.org
Web, www.insulators.org

Membership: approximately 18,000 workers in insulation industries. Helps members negotiate pay, benefits, and better working conditions; conducts training programs and workshops. Monitors legislation and regulations. (Affiliated with the AFL-CIO.)

International Assn. of Machinists and Aerospace Workers, *9000 Machinists Pl., Upper Marlboro, MD 20772-2687; (301) 967-4500. Fax, (301) 967-4588. Robert Martinez, International President. Information, (301) 967-4520. TTY, (800) 201-7165.*
General email, websteward@iamaw.org
Web, www.goiam.org

Membership: machinists in more than 200 industries. Helps members negotiate pay, benefits, and better working conditions; conducts training programs and workshops. Monitors legislation and regulations. (Affiliated with the AFL-CIO, the Canadian Labour Congress, the International Metalworkers Federation, the International Transport Workers' Federation, and the Railway Labor Executives Assn.)

International Assn. of Machinists and Aerospace Workers, *Transportation Communications Union, 3 Research Pl., Rockville, MD 20850-3279; (301) 948-4910. Fax, (301) 948-1369. Robert A. Scardelletti, President.*
General email, websteward@tcunion.org
Web, www.goiam.org/index.php/tcunion

Membership: approximately 46,000 railway workers. Assists members with contract negotiation and grievances; conducts training programs and workshops. Monitors legislation and regulations. (Affiliated with the AFL-CIO and Canadian Labour Congress.)

International Brotherhood of Boilermakers, Iron Ship Builders, Blacksmiths, Forgers, and Helpers, *Government Affairs, 1750 New York Ave. N.W., #335, 20006; (202) 756-2868. Fax, (202) 756-2869. Bridget P. Martin, Director, Political Affairs; Cecile Conroy, Director, Government Affairs.*
General email, cconroy@boilermakers.org
Web, www.boilermakers.org

Membership: approximately 80,000 workers in construction, repair, maintenance, manufacturing, and related industries in the United States and Canada. Helps members negotiate pay, benefits, and better working conditions; conducts training programs and workshops.

Monitors legislation and regulations. (Headquarters in Kansas City, Kans; affiliated with the AFL-CIO.)

International Brotherhood of Electrical Workers (IBEW), *900 7th St. N.W., 20001; (202) 833-7000. Fax, (202) 728-7676. Lonnie Stephenson, President; Salvatore J. Chilia, Secretary-Treasurer.*
General email, webmaster@ibew.org
Web, www.ibew.org

Helps members negotiate pay, benefits, and better working conditions; conducts training programs and workshops. Monitors legislation and regulations. (Affiliated with the AFL-CIO.)

International Brotherhood of Teamsters, *25 Louisiana Ave. N.W., 20001-2198; (202) 624-6800. Fax, (202) 624-6918. James P. Hoffa, General President; Christy Bailey, Director, Federal Legislation and Regulation. Press, (202) 624-6911.*
General email, communications@teamster.org
Web, www.teamster.org

Membership: more than 1.4 million workers in the transportation and construction industries, factories, offices, hospitals, warehouses, and other workplaces. Helps members negotiate pay, benefits, and better working conditions; conducts training programs and workshops. Monitors legislation and regulations.

International Longshore and Warehouse Union (ILWU), *Washington Office, 1025 Connecticut Ave. N.W., #507, 20036; (202) 463-6265. Fax, (202) 467-4875. Lindsay McLaughlin, Legislative Director.*
General email, bianca.blomquist@ilwu.org
Web, www.ilwu.org

Membership: approximately 60,000 longshore and warehouse personnel. Helps members negotiate pay, benefits, and better working conditions; conducts training programs and workshops. Monitors legislation and regulations. (Headquarters in San Francisco, Calif.)

International Longshoremen's Assn., *Washington Office, 1101 17th St. N.W., #400, 20036-4704; (202) 955-6304. Fax, (202) 955-6048. John Bowers Jr., Executive Director.*
General email, iladc@aol.com
Web, www.ilaunion.org

Membership: approximately 65,000 longshore personnel. Helps members negotiate pay, benefits, and better working conditions; conducts training programs and workshops. Monitors legislation and regulations. (Headquarters in New Jersey; affiliated with the AFL-CIO.)

International Union of Bricklayers and Allied Craftworkers, *620 F St. N.W., 20004; (202) 783-3788. Fax, (202) 393-0219. James Boland, President. Toll-free, (888) 880-8222.*
General email, askbac@bacweb.org
Web, www.bacweb.org

Membership: bricklayers, stonemasons, and other skilled craftworkers in the building industry. Helps members negotiate pay, benefits, and better working conditions; conducts training programs and workshops. Monitors legislation and regulations. (Affiliated with the AFL-CIO and the International Masonry Institute.)

International Union of Operating Engineers, *1125 17th St. N.W., 20036; (202) 429-9100. Fax, (202) 778-2613. James T. Callahan, General President.*
Web, www.iuoe.org

Membership: approximately 400,000 operating engineers, including heavy equipment operators, mechanics, and surveyors in the construction industry, and stationary engineers, including operations and building maintenance staff. Represents members in negotiating pay, benefits, and better working conditions; conducts training programs and workshops. Monitors legislation and regulations. (Affiliated with the AFL-CIO.)

International Union of Painters and Allied Trades, *7234 Parkway Dr., Hanover, MD 21076; (410) 564-5900. Fax, (866) 656-4124. Kenneth Rigmaiden, General President. General email, mail@iupat.org*
Web, www.iupat.org

Membership: more than 140,000 painters, glaziers, floor covering installers, signmakers, show decorators, and workers in allied trades in the United States and Canada. Helps members negotiate pay, benefits, and better working conditions, conducts training programs and workshops. Monitors legislation and regulations. (Affiliated with the AFL-CIO.)

Labor Council for Latin American Advancement, *815 16th St. N.W., 3rd Floor, 20006; (202) 508-6919. Fax, (202) 508-6922. Hector E. Sanchez, Executive Director. General email, headquarters@lclaa.org*
Web, www.lclaa.org, Twitter, @LCLAA and Facebook, www.facebook.com/LCLAA

Membership: Hispanic trade unionists. Encourages equal employment opportunity, voter registration, and participation in the political process. (Affiliated with the AFL-CIO and the Change to Win Federation.)

Laborers' International Union of North America, *905 16th St. N.W., 20006-1765; (202) 737-8320. Fax, (202) 737-2754. Terry O'Sullivan, President.*
Web, www.liuna.org, Twitter, @LIUNA and Facebook, www.facebook.com/LaborersInternationalUnionofNorthAmerica

Membership: more than 500,000 construction workers; federal, state, and local government employees; health care professionals; mail handlers; custodial service personnel; shipbuilders; and hazardous waste handlers. Helps members negotiate pay, benefits, and better working conditions; conducts training programs and workshops. Monitors legislation and regulations. (Affiliated with the AFL-CIO.)

National Assn. of Letter Carriers, *AFL-CIO, 100 Indiana Ave. N.W., 20001-2144; (202) 393-4695. Fax, (202) 737-1540. Fredric V. Rolando, President.*
Web, www.nalc.org

Membership: more than 270,000 city letter carriers working for, or retired from, the U.S. Postal Service. Assists members with contract negotiation and grievances; conducts training programs and workshops. Monitors legislation and regulations. (Affiliated with the AFL-CIO and the Union Network International.)

National Assn. of Manufacturers (NAM), *Human Resources Policy, 733 10th St. N.W., #700, 20001; (202) 637-3127. Fax, (202) 637-3182. Joe Trauger, Vice President. Alternate phone, (202) 637-3000.*
Web, www.nam.org

Provides information on corporate industrial relations, including collective bargaining, labor standards, international labor relations, productivity, employee benefits, health care, and other current labor issues; monitors legislation and regulations.

National Right to Work Committee, *8001 Braddock Rd., #500, Springfield, VA 22160; (703) 321-9820. Fax, (703) 321-7342. Mark Mix, President. Information, (800) 325-7892. General email, info@nrtwc.org*
Web, www.nrtwc.org

Citizens' organization opposed to compulsory union membership. Supports right-to-work legislation.

National Right to Work Legal Defense and Education Foundation, *8001 Braddock Rd., #600, Springfield, VA 22160; (703) 321-8510. Fax, (703) 321-9613. Mark Mix, President. Toll-free, (800) 336-3600. General email, info@nrtw.org*
Web, www.nrtw.org

Provides free legal aid for employees in cases of compulsory union membership abuses.

Public Service Research Council, *320 D Maple Ave. East, Vienna, VA 22180-4747; (703) 242-3575. Fax, (703) 242-3579. David Y. Denholm, President. General email, info@prsconline.org*
Web, www.psrconline.org

Independent nonprofit research and educational organization. Studies labor unions and labor issues with emphasis on employment in the public sector. Monitors legislation and regulations.

Service Employees International Union, *1800 Massachusetts Ave. N.W., 20036; (202) 730-7000. Fax, (202) 429-5563. Mary Kay Henry, President. Press, (202) 730-7162. Toll-free, (800) 424-8592. General email, media@seiu.org*
Web, www.seiu.org

Membership: approximately 2.2 million members in Canada, the United States, and Puerto Rico among health care, public services, and property services employees. Promotes better wages, health care, and job security for workers. Monitors legislation and regulations.

UNITE HERE, *Washington Office, 1775 K St. N.W., #620, 20006-1530; (202) 393-4373. Fax, (202) 223-6213. Fax, (202) 342-2929. Vacant, Political Director; D. Taylor, President.*
Web, www.unitehere.org

Membership: more than 270,000 workers in the United States and Canada who work in the hospitality, gaming, food service, manufacturing, textile, laundry, and airport industries. Assists members with contract negotiation and grievances; conducts training programs and workshops. Monitors legislation and regulations. (Headquarters in New York. Formed by the merger of the former Union of Needletrades, Textiles and Industrial Employees and the Hotel Employees and Restaurant Employees International Union.)

United Auto Workers (UAW), *Washington Office, 1757 N St. N.W., 20036; (202) 828-8500. Fax, (202) 293-3457. Josh Nassar, Legislative Director.*
Web, www.uaw.org

Membership: approximately 390,000 active and 600,000 retired North American workers in aerospace, automotive, defense, manufacturing, steel, technical, and other industries. Assists members with contract negotiations and grievances; conducts training programs and workshops. Monitors legislation and regulations. (Headquarters in Detroit, Mich.)

United Electrical, Radio, and Machine Workers of America, *Washington Office, P.O. Box 10031, Alexandria, VA 22310-0031; (703) 341-9446. Chris Townsend, Political Action Director. Information, (412) 471-8919.*
General email, uewashingtonoffice@gmail.com
Web, www.ueunion.org

Membership: manufacturing assembly workers, plastic injection molders, tool and die makers, electrical workers, sheet metal workers, truck and bus drivers, warehouse workers, custodians, clerical workers, graduate instructors, graduate researchers, scientists, librarians, social workers, and day care workers. (Headquarters in Pittsburgh, Pa.)

United Food and Commercial Workers International Union (UFCW), *1775 K St. N.W., 20006-1598; (202) 223-3111. Fax, (202) 728-1803. Marc Perrone, President.*
Web, www.ufcw.org and Twitter, @UFCW

Membership: approximately 1.3 million workers primarily in the retail, meatpacking, food processing, and poultry industries. Interests include health care reform, living wages, retirement security, safe working conditions, and the right to unionize. Monitors legislation and regulations.

United Mine Workers of America, *18354 Quantico Gateway Dr., #200, Triangle, VA 22172-1779; (703) 291-2400. Cecil E. Roberts, President.*
Web, www.umwa.org

Membership: coal miners and other mining workers. Represents members in collective bargaining with industry. Conducts educational, housing, and health and safety training programs; monitors federal coal mining safety programs.

United Steelworkers, *1155 M St. N.W., #500, 20036; (202) 778-4384. Fax, (202) 419-1486. Holly Hart, Legislative Director.*
Web, www.usw.org

Membership: more than one million workers in the steel, paper, rubber, energy, chemical, pharmaceutical, and allied industries. Helps members negotiate pay, benefits, and better working conditions; conducts training programs and workshops. Monitors legislation and regulations. (Affiliated with the AFL-CIO; headquarters in Pittsburgh, Pa.)

United Transportation Union, *Washington Office, 304 Pennsylvania Ave. S.E., 20003; (202) 543-7714. Fax, (202) 544-3024. John Risch III, National Legislative Director; Gregory Hynes, Alternate National Legislative Director. General email, nld@smart-union.org*
Web, www.utu.org

Membership: approximately 125,000 workers and retirees in the transportation industry. Helps members negotiate pay, benefits, and better working conditions; conducts training programs and workshops. Monitors legislation and regulations. (Headquarters in Cleveland, Ohio.)

U.S. Chamber of Commerce, *Labor, Immigration, and Employee Benefits, 1615 H St. N.W., 20062-2000; (202) 463-5522. Fax, (202) 463-3194. Fax, (202) 463-5901. Randel K. Johnson, Senior Vice President. General email, laborpolicy@uschamber.com*
Web, www.uschamber.com/labor-immigration-and-employee-benefits and ADA information, www.uschamber.com/health-reform
Immigration news, http://immigration.uschamber.com

Formulates and analyzes Chamber policy in the areas of labor law, immigration, pension, and health care. Monitors legislation and regulations affecting labor-management relations, employee benefits, and immigration issues.

Utility Workers Union of America, *815 16th St. N.W., 20006; (202) 974-8200. Fax, (202) 974-8201. Ed Good, Legislative Director, (740) 312-8411; Mike Coleman, National Secretary-Treasurer. General email, webmaster@uwua.net*
Web, www.uwua.net

Labor union representing approximately 50,000 workers in utilities and related industries. Helps members negotiate pay, benefits, and better working conditions; conducts training programs and workshops. Monitors legislation and regulations. (Affiliated with the AFL-CIO.)

PENSIONS AND BENEFITS

General

▶AGENCIES

Advisory Council on Employee Welfare and Pension Benefit Plans (ERISA Advisory Council) *(Labor Dept.), 200 Constitution Ave. N.W., #N5623, 20210; (202) 693-8668. Fax, (202) 219-8141. Larry Good, Executive Secretary. Web, www.dol.gov/ebsa/aboutebsa/erisa_advisory_council.html*

Advises and makes recommendations to the secretary of labor under the Employee Retirement Income Security Act of 1974 (ERISA).

Occupational Safety and Health Administration

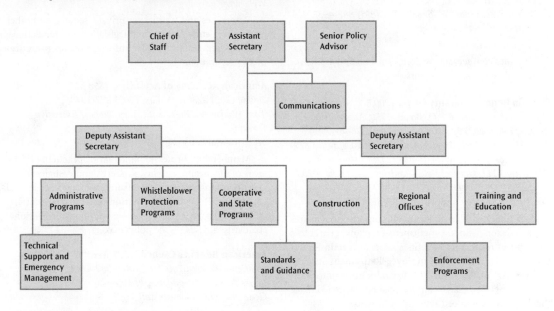

Bureau of Labor Statistics (BLS) *(Labor Dept.),*
Compensation and Working Conditions, 2 Massachusetts
Ave. N.E., #4130, 20212; (202) 691-6300. Fax, (202) 691-
6310. Vacant, Associate Commissioner.
Web, www.bls.gov

Conducts quarterly surveys of wages and benefits;
data used for the quarterly *Employment Cost Index,* the
quarterly *Employer Costs for Employee Compensation,*
and annual reports on the incidence and provisions of
employee benefits.

Bureau of Labor Statistics (BLS) *(Labor Dept.),*
*Compensation and Working Conditions, Compensation
Levels and Trends,* 2 Massachusetts Ave. N.E., #4175, 20212;
(202) 691-6199. Fax, (202) 691-6647. Philip M. Doyle,
Assistant Commissioner. TTY, (202) 691-5200.
Web, www.bls.gov/ncs/summary.htm

Compiles data on wages and benefits. Develops the
National Compensation Survey. Analyzes, distributes, and
disseminates information on occupational earnings, benefits, and compensation trends.

Criminal Division *(Justice Dept.), Organized Crime and
Gang Section,* 1301 New York Ave. N.W., #700, 20005;
(202) 514-3594. Fax, (202) 514-3601. James Trusty, Chief.
General email, criminaldivision@us.doj.gov

Web, www.justice.gov/criminal-ocgs

Reviews and advises on prosecutions of criminal violations concerning the operation of employee benefit plans
in the private sector.

Employee Benefits Security Administration *(Labor
Dept.),* 200 Constitution Ave. N.W., #S2524, 20210; (202)
693-8300. Fax, (202) 219-5526. Phyllis C. Borzi, Assistant
Secretary. Toll-free, (866) 444-3272.
Web, www.dol.gov/ebsa

Administers, regulates, and enforces private employee
benefit plan standards established by the Employee
Retirement Income Security Act of 1974 (ERISA), with
particular emphasis on fiduciary obligations; receives and
maintains required reports from employee benefit plan
administrators pursuant to ERISA.

Federal Retirement Thrift Investment Board, 77 K St.
N.W., #1000, 20002; (202) 942-1600. Gregory T. Long,
Executive Director. Toll-free, (877) 968-3778. TTY, (877)
847-4385.
Web, www.frtib.gov

Administers the Thrift Savings Plan, a tax-deferred,
defined contribution plan that permits federal employees
and members of the uniformed services to save for additional retirement security under a program similar to
private 401(k) plans.

Joint Board for the Enrollment of Actuaries, 1111
Constitution Ave. N.W., SE: RPO, REFM, Park 4, 4th Floor,
Internal Revenue Service, 20224; Fax, (703) 414-2225.
Patrick McDonough, Executive Director.
General email, nhqjbea@irs.gov

Web, www.irs.gov/tax-professionals/enrolled-actuaries

Joint board, with members from the departments of
Labor and Treasury and the Pension Benefit Guaranty
Corp., established under the Employee Retirement Income
Security Act of 1974 (ERISA). Promulgates regulations for
the enrollment of pension actuaries; examines applicants
and grants certificates of enrollment; disciplines enrolled
actuaries who have engaged in misconduct in the discharge of duties under ERISA.

Office of Personnel Management (OPM), *Retirement
Operations,* 1900 E St. N.W., #2H28, 20415; (724) 794-
2005. Fax, (724) 794-4323. Nick Ashendon, Deputy

Associate Director, (724) 794-2005, ext. 3214;
Kenneth J. Zawodny Jr., Associate Director, (724) 794-7759. Toll-free, (888) 767-6738. TTY, (855) 887-4957.
General email, retire@opm.gov

Web, www.opm.gov/retire

Provides civil servants with information and assistance on federal retirement payments.

Pension Benefit Guaranty Corp., 1200 K St. N.W., 20005-4026 (mailing address: P.O. Box 151750, Alexandria, VA 22315-1750); (202) 326-4000. Fax, (202) 326-4047.
Alice Maroni, Chief Management Officer. TTY, (800) 877-8339, ask to connect to (800) 400-7242. Customer Service, (800) 400-7242. General legal inquiries, (202) 326-4020.
Locator, (202) 326-4110.
Web, www.pbgc.gov and Twitter, @USPBGC

Self-financed U.S. government corporation. Insures private-sector defined benefit pension plans; guarantees payment of retirement benefits subject to certain limitations established in the Employee Retirement Income Security Act of 1974 (ERISA). Provides insolvent multiemployer pension plans with financial assistance to enable them to pay guaranteed retirement benefits.

State Dept., *Administration Bureau, Allowances,* 2401 E St. N.W., #L314/SA-1, 20522-0103; (202) 261-8700. Fax, (202) 261-8707. Robert L. Kingman, Director, (202) 261-8700.
General email, AllowancesO@state.gov

Web, http://aoprals.state.gov

Develops and coordinates policies, regulations, standards, and procedures to administer the governmentwide allowances and benefits program abroad under the State Dept. Standardized Regulations. Compiles statistics of living costs, hardship differentials, and danger pay allowances to compensate U.S. government civilian employees while on assignments abroad.

▶ **CONGRESS**

For a listing of relevant congressional committees and subcommittees, please see page 206 or the Appendix.

Government Accountability Office (GAO), *Education, Workforce, and Income Security,* 441 G St. N.W., #5928, 20548; (202) 512-7215. Barbara D. Bovbjerg, Managing Director.
Web, www.gao.gov/careers/ewis.html

Independent nonpartisan agency in the legislative branch. Audits, analyzes, and evaluates federal agency and private sector pension programs; makes reports available to the public.

▶ **NONGOVERNMENTAL**

AARP, 601 E St. N.W., 20049; (202) 434-2277.
Jo Ann C. Jenkins, Chief Executive Officer. Press, (202) 434-2560. Library, (202) 434-6233. TTY, (877) 434-7598.
Toll-free, (888) 687-2277. Membership, (202) 434-3525.

General email, member@aarp.org

Web, www.aarp.org

Researches and testifies on private, federal, and other government employee pension legislation and regulations; conducts seminars; provides information on preretirement preparation.

American Academy of Actuaries, 1850 M St. N.W., #300, 20036; (202) 223-8196. Fax, (202) 872-1948.
Tom Wildsmith, President; Mary Downs, Executive Director.
Web, www.actuary.org

Membership: professional actuaries practicing in the areas of life, health, liability, property, and casualty insurance; pensions; government insurance plans; and general consulting. Provides information on actuarial matters, including insurance and pensions; develops professional standards; advises public policymakers.

American Benefits Council, 1501 M St. N.W., #600, 20005; (202) 289-6700. Fax, (202) 289-4582.
James A. Klein, President.
General email, info@abcstaff.org

Web, www.americanbenefitscouncil.org

Membership: employers, consultants, banks, and service organizations. Informs members of employee benefits, including private pension benefits, health benefits, and compensation.

American Society of Pension Professionals and Actuaries, 4245 N. Fairfax Dr., #750, Arlington, VA 22203-1648; (703) 516-9300. Fax, (703) 516-9308.
Brian H. Graff, Chief Executive Officer.
General email, asppa@asppa.org

Web, www.asppa.org

Membership: administrators, actuaries, advisers, lawyers, accountants, and other financial services professionals who provide consulting and administrative services for employee-based retirement plans. Sponsors educational conferences, webcasts, and credentialing programs for retirement professionals. Monitors legislation and regulations.

The Brookings Institution, *Retirement Security Project,* 1775 Massachusetts Ave. N.W., 20036; (202) 797-6000.
William Gale, Director, (202) 797-6105. Press, (202) 797-6105.
Web, www.brookings.edu/about/projects/retirementsecurity

Promotes policy solutions for improving retirement income and financial security for middle-income and low-income workers who do not have access to employer-sponsored retirement savings plans or traditional pensions.

Coalition to Preserve Retirement Security, 112 S. Pitt St., Alexandria, VA 22314; (703) 684-5236. Fax, (703) 684-3417. Thomas Lussier, Administrator.
General email, tlussier@lgva.net

Web, www.retirementsecurity.org

Coalition of current public employees and retirees. Supports the voluntary participation of state and local employees in the Social Security system. Opposes all legislation that would compel public employees into participation in the system.

Employee Benefit Research Institute, 1100 13th St. N.W., #878, 20005; (202) 659-0670. Fax, (202) 775-6312. Harry Conaway, President.
General email, info@ebri.org
Web, www.ebri.org

Research organization serving as an employee benefits information source on health, welfare, and retirement issues. Does not lobby and does not take public policy positions.

Employers Council on Flexible Compensation, 1444 Eye St. N.W., #700, 20005; (202) 659-4300. Fax, (202) 216-9646. Martin Trussell, Executive Director.
General email, info@ecfc.org
Web, www.ecfc.org

Advocates tax-advantaged, private employer benefit programs. Supports the preservation and expansion of employee choice in savings and pension plans. Monitors legislation and regulations. Interests include cafeteria plans and 401(k) plans.

ERISA Industry Committee, 1400 L St. N.W., #350, 20005; (202) 789-1400. Fax, (202) 789-1120. Annette Guarisco Fildes, President, (202) 627-1910.
General email, eric@eric.org
Web, www.eric.org

Membership: major U.S. employers. Advocates members' positions on employee retirement, health care coverage, and welfare benefit plans. Monitors legislation and regulations.

National Assn. of Manufacturers (NAM), *Human Resources Policy,* 733 10th St. N.W., #700, 20001; (202) 637-3127. Fax, (202) 637-3182. Joe Trauger, Vice President. Alternate phone, (202) 637-3000.
Web, www.nam.org

Interests include health care, cost containment, mandated benefits, Medicare, and other federal programs that affect employers. Opposed to government involvement in health care and proposed expansion of health care liability.

National Institute on Retirement Security, 1612 K St. N.W., #500, 20006; (202) 457-8190. Diane Oakley, Executive Director.
General email, info@nirsonline.org
Web, www.nirsonline.org

Researches retirement security policies and educates the public and policymakers about the positive impact of benefit pension plans. Advocates broader, more defined retirement plans.

Pension Rights Center, 1350 Connecticut Ave. N.W., #206, 20036; (202) 296-3776. Karen W. Ferguson, Director. Toll-free, (888) 420-6550.
General email, kgarrett@pensionrights.org
Web, www.pensionrights.org

Works to preserve and expand pension rights; provides information and technical assistance on pension law.

ProtectSeniors.Org, 601 Pennsylvania Ave., South Bldg., #900, 20004; (202) 434-8193. Fax, (540) 439-9570. Jim Casey, President; Paul Miller, Executive Director. Toll-free, (800) 398-3044.
General email, info@protectseniors.org
Web, www.protectseniors.org and Twitter, @ProtectSeniors

Aims to illegalize the corporate discontinuation of promised health care benefits after employees have retired. Acts as advocate against pension stripping. Monitors legislation and regulation.

United Mine Workers of America, *Health and Retirement Funds,* 2121 K St. N.W., #350, 20037-1801; (202) 521-2200. Fax, (202) 521-2394. Lorraine Lewis, Executive Director. Call Center, (800) 291-1425.
General email, health1@umwafunds.org
Web, www.umwafunds.org

Labor/management trust fund that provides health and retirement benefits to coal miners. Health benefits are provided to pensioners, their dependents, and, in some cases, their survivors.

Urban Institute, *Center on Income and Benefits Policy,* 2100 M St. N.W., 20037; (202) 833-7200. Fax, (202) 833-4388. Gregory Acs, Director.
Web, www.urban.org/center/ibp
Retirement policy, http://urban.org/retirement_policy

Studies how public policy influences behavior and the economic well-being of families, particularly the disabled, the elderly, and those with low incomes.

Women's Institute for a Secure Retirement (WISER), 1140 19th St. N.W., #550, 20036; (202) 393-5452. Fax, (202) 393-5890. Cindy Hounsell, President.
General email, info@wiserwomen.org
Web, www.wiserwomen.org and Twitter, @WISERWomen

Provides information on women's retirement issues. Monitors legislation and regulations.

WORKPLACE SAFETY AND HEALTH

General

▶AGENCIES

Bureau of Labor Statistics (BLS) *(Labor Dept.),* *Compensation and Working Conditions,* 2 Massachusetts Ave. N.E., #4130, 20212; (202) 691-6300. Fax, (202) 691-6310. Vacant, Associate Commissioner.
Web, www.bls.gov

Compiles data on occupational safety and health.

Environment, Health, Safety, and Security *(Energy Dept.),* 1000 Independence Ave. S.W., #7G040, 20585; (202) 586-4399. Fax, (202) 586-5605. Matthew Moury, Associate Under Secretary.
General email, AVusersupport@hq.doe.gov
Web, http://energy.gov/ehss/environment-health-safety-security

Develops policy and establishes standards to ensure safety and health protection in all department activities. Coordinates and integrates health, safety, environment, and security enforcement and independent oversight programs at the Energy Dept. Responsible for policy development, technical assistance, safety analysis, education, and training.

Federal Mine Safety and Health Review Commission, *1331 Pennsylvania Ave. N.W., #520N, 20004-1710; (202) 434-9905. Fax, (202) 434-9906. Lisa Boyd, Executive Director; Mary Lu Jordan, Chair. TTY, (202) 434-4000 ext. 293.*
General email, fmshrc@fmshrc.gov
Web, www.fmshrc.gov

Independent agency established by the Federal Mine Safety and Health Act of 1977. Holds fact-finding hearings and issues orders affirming, modifying, or vacating the labor secretary's enforcement actions regarding mine safety and health. Reading room open to the public by appointment.

Mine Safety and Health Administration *(Labor Dept.),* *201 12th St. S., Arlington, VA 22202; (202) 693-9400. Fax, (202) 693-9801. Joseph A. Main, Assistant Secretary.*
General email, ASKMSHA@dol.gov
Web, www.msha.gov

Administers and enforces the health and safety provisions of the Federal Mine Safety and Health Act of 1977.

National Institute for Occupational Safety and Health (NIOSH) *(Centers for Disease Control and Prevention),* *395 E St. S.W., Patriots Plaza 1, #9200, 20201; (202) 245-0625. Dr. John Howard, Director. Information, (800) 232-4636.*
General email, cdcinfo@cdc.gov
Web, www.cdc.gov/niosh

Entity within the Centers for Disease Control and Prevention in Atlanta. Supports and conducts research on occupational safety and health issues; provides technical assistance and training; develops recommendations for the Labor Dept. Operates an occupational safety and health bibliographic database.

Occupational Safety and Health Administration (OSHA) *(Labor Dept.), 200 Constitution Ave. N.W., #S2315, 20210; (202) 693-2000. Fax, (202) 693-1659. David M. Michaels, Assistant Secretary. Emergency hotline, (800) 321-6742. TTY, (877) 889-5627.*
Web, www.osha.gov

Sets and enforces rules and regulations for workplace safety and health. Implements the Occupational Safety and Health Act of 1970. Provides federal agencies and private industries with compliance guidance and assistance. Website has a Spanish-language link.

Occupational Safety and Health Administration (OSHA) *(Labor Dept.), Communications, 200 Constitution Ave. N.W., #N3647, 20210; (202) 693-1999. Fax, (202) 693-1635. Francis Meilinger, Director. Emergency hotline, 800-321-OSHA (6742).*
Web, www.osha.gov/as

Develops strategies, products, and materials to promote public understanding of OSHA standards, regulations, guidelines, policies, and activities to improve the safety and health of employees.

Occupational Safety and Health Administration (OSHA) *(Labor Dept.), Construction, 200 Constitution Ave. N.W., #N3468, 20210; (202) 693-2020. Fax, (202) 693-1689. Jim Maddux, Director.*
Web, www.osha.gov/doc

Provides technical expertise to OSHA's enforcement personnel; initiates studies to determine causes of construction accidents; works with the private sector to promote construction safety and training and to identify, reduce, and eliminate construction-related hazards.

Occupational Safety and Health Administration (OSHA) *(Labor Dept.), Cooperative and State Programs, 200 Constitution Ave. N.W., #N3700, 20210; (202) 693-2200. Fax, (202) 693-1671. Douglas Kalinowski, Director.*
Web, www.osha.gov/dcsp

Implements OSHA's cooperative programs, coordinates the agency's compliance assistance and outreach activities, coordinates the agency's relations with state plan states; oversees OSHA international issues; and coordinates small business assistance outreach.

Occupational Safety and Health Administration (OSHA) *(Labor Dept.), Enforcement Programs, 200 Constitution Ave. N.W., #N3119, 20210; (202) 693-2100. Fax, (202) 693-1681. Thomas Galassi, Director; Dionne Williams, Director, Health Enforcement, (202) 693-2190; Arthur Buchanan, Director, General Industry and Agriculture Enforcement, (202) 893-1850. TTY, (877) 889-5627. Emergency, (800) 321-6742. Whistleblower hotline, (800) 321-6742. Whistleblower protection, (202) 693-2199.*
Web, www.osha.gov/dep/enforcement/dep_offices.html

Develops, interprets, and provides guidance for compliance safety standards for agency field personnel, private employees, and employers.

Occupational Safety and Health Administration (OSHA) *(Labor Dept.), Standards and Guidance, 200 Constitution Ave. N.W., #N3718, 20210; (202) 693-1950. Fax, (202) 693-1678. William Perry, Director.*
Web, www.osha.gov/dsg

Develops new or revised occupational health standards for toxic, hazardous, and carcinogenic substances; biological and safety hazards; or other harmful physical agents, such as vibration, noise, and radiation.

Occupational Safety and Health Review Commission, *1120 20th St. N.W., 9th Floor, 20036-3457; (202) 606-5100. Fax, (202) 606-5050. Thomasina V. Rogers, Chair, (202) 606-5370. TTY, (877) 889-5627.*
Web, www.oshrc.gov

Independent executive branch agency that adjudicates disputes between private employers and the Occupational Safety and Health Administration arising under the Occupational Safety and Health Act of 1970.

►CONGRESS

For a listing of relevant congressional committees and sub-committees, please see page 206 or the Appendix.

►NONGOVERNMENTAL

American Industrial Hygiene Assn., *3141 Fairview Park Dr., #777, Falls Church, VA 20042-4507; (703) 849-8888. Fax, (703) 207-3561. Peter O'Neil, Executive Director, ext. 760.*
General email, infonet@aiha.org
Web, www.aiha.org

Membership: scientists and engineers who practice industrial hygiene in government, labor, academic institutions, and independent organizations. Promotes health and safety standards in the workplace and the community; conducts research to identify potential dangers; educates workers about job-related risks; monitors safety regulations. Interests include international standards and information exchange.

Fair Labor Assn. (FLA), *1111 19th St. N.W., #401, 20036; (202) 898-1000. Fax, (202) 898-9050. Sharon Waxman, President.*
General email, info@fairlabor.org
Web, www.fairlabor.org and Twitter, @FairLaborAssoc

Membership: consumer, human, and labor rights groups; apparel and footwear manufacturers and retailers; and colleges and universities. Seeks to protect the rights of workers in the United States and worldwide. Concerns include sweatshop practices, forced labor, child labor, and worker health and benefits. Monitors workplace conditions and reports findings to the public. Develops capacity for sustainable labor compliance.

Institute for a Drug-Free Workplace, *10701 Parkridge Blvd., #300, Reston, VA 20191; (703) 391-7222. Fax, (703) 391-7223. Mark A. de Bernardo, Executive Director.*
General email, institute@drugfreeworkplace.org
Web, www.drugfreeworkplace.org

Coalition of businesses, business organizations, and individuals. Seeks to increase productivity, improve safety, and control insurance costs through detection and treatment of drug and alcohol abuse. Promotes fair and consistent implementation of drug abuse prevention programs; supports the right of employers to test for drugs. Monitors legislation and regulations.

International Safety Equipment Assn. (ISEA), *1901 N. Moore St., #808, Arlington, VA 22209-1702; (703) 525-1695. Fax, (703) 528-2148. Daniel K. Shipp, President.*
General email, isea@safetyequipment.org
Web, www.safetyequipment.org

Trade organization that drafts industry standards for employees' and emergency responders' personal safety and protective equipment; encourages development and use of proper equipment to deal with workplace hazards; participates in international standards activities, especially in North America. Monitors legislation and regulations.

National Assn. of Manufacturers (NAM), *Human Resources Policy, 733 10th St. N.W., #700, 20001; (202) 637-3127. Fax, (202) 637-3182. Joe Trauger, Vice President. Alternate phone, (202) 637-3000.*
Web, www.nam.org

Conducts research, develops policy, and informs members of toxic injury compensation systems, and occupational safety and health legislation, regulations, and standards internationally. Offers mediation service to business members.

Public Citizen, *Health Research Group, 1600 20th St. N.W., 20009-1001; (202) 588-1000. Fax, (202) 588-7798. Michael Carome, Director.*
General email, hrg1@citizen.org
Web, www.citizen.org/hrg and Twitter, @CitizenHRG

Citizens' interest group that studies and reports on occupational diseases; monitors the Occupational Safety and Health Administration and participates in OSHA enforcement proceedings.

Workers' Compensation

►AGENCIES

Bureau of Labor Statistics (BLS) *(Labor Dept.), Compensation and Working Conditions, Occupational Safety and Health Statistics, 2 Massachusetts Ave. N.E., #3180, 20212-0001; (202) 691-6170. Fax, (202) 691-6196. Hilery Simpson, Assistant Commissioner.*
General email, iif-staff@bls.gov
Web, www.bls.gov/iif

Compiles and publishes statistics on occupational injuries, illnesses, and fatalities.

Labor Dept. (DOL), *Benefits Review Board, 200 Constitution Ave. N.W., #N5101, 20210 (mailing address: 200 Constitution Ave. N.W., #S5220, Washington, DC 20210); (202) 693-6300. Fax, (202) 693-6310. Betty Jean Hall, Chair; Frank W. Clubb, Administrative Officer, (202) 693-6234.*
Web, www.dol.gov/brb/welcome.html

Reviews appeals of workers seeking benefits under the Longshore and Harbor Workers' Compensation Act and its extensions, including the District of Columbia Workers' Compensation Act, and Title IV (Black Lung Benefits Act) of the Federal Coal Mine Health and Safety Act.

Labor Dept. (DOL), *Employees' Compensation Appeals Board, 200 Constitution Ave. N.W., #N5101, 20210 (mailing address: 200 Constitution Ave. N.W., #S5220, Washington, DC 20210); (202) 693-6420. Fax, (202) 693-6367. Christopher James Godfrey, Chair; Frank W. Clubb, Administrative Officer, (202) 693-6234. Case inquiries, (866) 487-2365.*
Web, www.dol.gov/ecab/welcome.html

Reviews and determines appeals of final determinations of benefit claims made by the Office of Workers' Compensation Programs under the Federal Employees' Compensation Act.

Labor Dept. (DOL), *Workers' Compensation Programs (OWCP),* 200 Constitution Ave. N.W., #S3524, 20210; (202) 343-5580. Fax, (202) 693-1378. Leonard J. Howie III, Director.
Web, www.dol.gov/owcp

Administers four federal workers' compensation programs: the Federal Employees' Compensation Program, the Longshore and Harbor Workers' Compensation Program, the Black Lung Benefits Program, and the Energy Employees Occupational Illness Compensation Program.

Workers Compensation (OWCP) *(Labor Dept.), Coal Mine Workers' Compensation,* 200 Constitution Ave. N.W., #S3524, 20210; (202) 693-0036. Fax, (202) 693-1378. Michael A. Chance, Director, (202) 693-0046. Toll-free, (800) 638-7072.
General email, DCMWC-public@dol.gov

Web, www.dol.gov/owcp/dcmwc

Provides direction for administration of the black lung benefits program. Adjudicates all black lung claims; certifies benefit payments and maintains black lung beneficiary rolls.

▶**NONGOVERNMENTAL**

American Insurance Assn., *2101 L St. N.W., #400, 20037; (202) 828-7100. Fax, (202) 293-1219. Leigh Ann Pusey, President.*
General email, info@aiadc.org
Web, www.aiadc.org and Twitter, @AIADC

Membership: companies providing property and casualty insurance. Offers information on workers' compensation legislation and regulations; conducts educational activities.

National Assn. of Manufacturers (NAM), *Human Resources Policy,* 733 10th St. N.W., #700, 20001; (202) 637-3127. Fax, (202) 637-3182. Joe Trauger, Vice President. Alternate phone, (202) 637-3000.
Web, www.nam.org

Conducts research, develops policy, and informs members of workers' compensation law; provides feedback to government agencies.

7 Energy

GENERAL POLICY AND ANALYSIS

Basic Resources

▶AGENCIES

Census Bureau *(Commerce Dept.)*, *Special Reimbursable Surveys Branch*, *4600 Silver Hill Rd., 7th Floor, Suitland, MD 20746 (mailing address: change city, state, and zip code to Washington, DC 20233); (301) 763-4639. Mary Susan Bucci, Chief.*
Web, www.census.gov

Collects and tabulates data for the Manufacturing Energy Consumption Survey for the Energy Dept. concerning combustible and noncombustible energy resources for the U.S. manufacturing sector. Collects data on quarterly plant capacity utilization within the manufacturing and printing sector.

Defense Logistics Agency *(Defense Dept.)*, *Energy*, *8725 John Jay Kingman Rd., #4950, Fort Belvoir, VA 22060-6222; (703) 767-9706. Fax, (703) 767-9690. Brig. Gen. Mark M. McLeod (USAF), Commander. Toll-free, (877) 352-2255. Public Affairs, (703) 767-4108.*
Web, www.dla.mil/Energy.aspx

Provides the Defense Dept. and other federal agencies with products and services to meet energy-related needs; facilitates the cycle of storage and deployment of fuels and other energy sources, including petroleum, electricity, water, and natural gas, as well as space and missile propellants. Provides information on alternative fuels and renewable energy and serves as the executive agent for the Defense Dept.'s bulk petroleum supply chain.

Energy Dept. (DOE), *Advanced Research Projects Agency*, *1000 Independence Ave. S.W., 20585; (202) 287-1005. Fax, (202) 287-5450. Ellen Williams, Director.*
General email, ARPA-E@hq.doe.gov
Web, www.arpa-e.energy.gov and Twitter, @ARPAE

Seeks to advance energy technologies that are too early for private-sector investment yet have the potential to radically improve U.S. economic prosperity, national security, and environmental well-being. Provides energy researchers with funding, technical assistance, and market readiness through a competitive project selection process and active program management.

Energy Dept. (DOE), *Deputy Secretary*, *1000 Independence Ave. S.W., #7B252, 20585; (202) 586-5500. Fax, (202) 586-7210. Elizabeth Sherwood-Rondall, Deputy Secretary. Press, (202) 586-4940. Locator, (202) 586-5000.*
Web, www.energy.gov

Serves as chief operations officer. Manages departmental programs in conservation and renewable energy, fossil energy, energy research, the Energy Information Administration, nuclear energy, civilian radioactive waste management, and the power marketing administrations.

Energy Dept. (DOE), *Economic Impact and Diversity*, *1000 Independence Ave. S.W., #5B110, 20585; (202) 586-8383. Fax, (202) 586-3075. LaDoris G. (Dot) Harris, Director.*
Web, www.doe.gov/diversity

Advises the secretary on the impacts of energy policies, programs, regulations, and other departmental actions on underrepresented communities; minority educational institutions; and minority, small, and women-owned business enterprises.

Energy Dept. (DOE), *Energy Efficiency, Advanced Manufacturing, Research and Development*, *1000 Independence Ave. S.W., #5F065, MS EE5A, 20585-0121; (202) 586-9488. Fax, (202) 586-9234. Mark Johnson, Director.*
General email, amo_communication@ee.doe.gov
Web, www.energy.gov/eere/amo/advanced-manufacturing-office

Offers financial and technical support to small businesses and individual inventors for establishing technical performance and conducting early development of innovative ideas and inventions that have a significant energy-saving impact and future commercial market potential.

Energy Dept. (DOE), *Energy Policy and Systems Analysis*, *1000 Independence Ave. S.W., #7C034, 20585; (202) 586-4800. Fax, (202) 586-0900. Melanie Kenderdine, Director.*
Web, www.energy.gov/epsa

Principal energy policy adviser to the secretary and deputy secretary on domestic energy policy development and implementation, as well as Energy Dept. policy analysis and activities. Supports the Energy Dept. White House interagency process, providing data collection, analysis, stakeholder engagement, and data synthesis.

Energy Dept. (DOE), *Energy Policy and Systems Analysis, Energy Security*, *1000 Independence Ave. S.W., #7D034, PI40, 20585; (202) 586-4800. Fax, (202) 586-0900. Carmine Difiglio, Deputy Director for Energy Security.*
Web, www.energy.gov/office-energy-policy-and-systems-analysis

Serves as principal adviser to the secretary, deputy secretary, and under secretary in formulating and evaluating departmental policy. Reviews programs, budgets, regulations, and legislative proposals to ensure consistency with departmental policy.

Energy Dept. (DOE), *Secretary*, *1000 Independence Ave. S.W., #7A257, 20585; (202) 586-6210. Fax, (202) 586-4403. Ernest J. Moniz, Secretary. Press, (202) 586-4940. Locator, (202) 586-5000. TTY, (800) 877-8339.*
General email, thesecretary@hq.doe.gov
Web, www.energy.gov

Decides major energy policy issues and acts as principal adviser to the president on energy matters, including strategic reserves and nuclear power; acts as principal spokesperson for the department.

Energy Dept. (DOE), *Under Secretary for Management and Performance,* 1000 Independence Ave. S.W., #7A219, 20585; (202) 586-7700. Fax, (202) 586-0148. David Klaus, Deputy Under Secretary. Press, (202) 586-4940. Locator, (202) 586-5000.
Web, www.energy.gov

Responsible for all administration and management matters and for regulatory and information programs, as well as overseeing the legacy waste of the Cold War.

Energy Dept. (DOE), *Under Secretary for Science and Energy,* 1000 Independence Ave. S.W., 20585; (202) 586-0505. Franklin M. Orr Jr., Under Secretary for Science and Energy.
Web, http://energy.gov/office-under-secretary-science-and-energy

Responsible for driving transformative science and technology solutions through planning and management oversight of the department's science and energy programs.

Energy Information Administration (EIA) *(Energy Dept.),* 1000 Independence Ave. S.W., #2H027, 20585; (202) 586-4361. Fax, (202) 586-0329. Adam E. Sieminski, Administrator. Information, (202) 586-8800.
General email, infoctr@eia.doe.gov
Web, www.eia.gov

Collects and publishes data on national and international energy reserves, financial status of energy-producing companies, production, demand, consumption, and other areas; provides long- and short-term analyses of energy trends and data.

Energy Information Administration (EIA) *(Energy Dept.), Energy Analysis,* 1000 Independence Ave. S.W., #2H-073, 20585; (202) 586-2222. Fax, (202) 586-3045. John J. Conti, Assistant Administrator.
Web, www.eia.gov

Analyzes and forecasts alternative energy futures. Develops, applies, and maintains modeling systems for analyzing the interactions of demand, conversion, and supply for all energy sources and their economic and environmental impacts. Concerned with emerging energy markets and U.S. dependence on petroleum imports.

Energy Information Administration (EIA) *(Energy Dept.), Energy Consumption and Efficiency Statistics,* 1000 Independence Ave. S.W., #2F073, 20585; (202) 586-3548. Thomas Leckey, Director.
Web, www.eia.gov

Conducts national energy consumption surveys and publishes energy consumption data and analysis.

Energy Information Administration (EIA) *(Energy Dept.), Energy Statistics,* 1000 Independence Ave. S.W., #2G020, 20585; (202) 586-6012. Fax, (202) 586-9739. Stephen J. Harvey, Assistant Administrator.
General email, infoctr@eia.doe.gov
Web, www.eia.gov

Conducts survey, statistical methods, and integration activities related to energy consumption and efficiency; electricity; nuclear and renewable energy; oil, gas, and coal supply; and petroleum and biofuels. Manages EIA data collection program and the quality control for statistical reports.

Environment, Health, Safety, and Security *(Energy Dept.),* 1000 Independence Ave. S.W., #7G040, 20585; (202) 586-4399. Fax, (202) 586-5605. Matthew Moury, Associate Under Secretary.
General email, AVusersupport@hq.doe.gov
Web, www.energy.gov/ehss/environment-health-safety-security

Develops policy and establishes standards to ensure safety and health protection in all department activities. Coordinates and integrates health, safety, environment, and security enforcement and independent oversight programs at the Energy Dept. Responsible for policy development, technical assistance, safety analysis, education, and training.

Federal Energy Regulatory Commission (FERC) *(Energy Dept.),* 888 1st St. N.E., 20426; (202) 502-6088. Fax, (202) 502-8612. Norman C. Bay, Chair, (202) 502-8000. Toll-free, (866) 208-3372. TTY, (202) 502-8659. Press, (202) 502-8680. eLibrary questions, (202) 502-6652. Enforcement hotline, (202) 502-8390. Enforcement toll-free, (888) 889-8030.
General email, customer@ferc.gov
Web, www.ferc.gov

Independent agency that regulates the interstate transmission of electricity, natural gas, and oil, including approving rates and charges. Reviews proposals to build liquefied natural gas terminals and interstate natural gas pipelines and approves siting. Licenses and inspects nonfederal hydroelectric projects. Regulates the sale of natural gas for resale in interstate commerce and wholesale interstate sales of electricity. Ensures the reliability of high-voltage interstate transmission systems. Establishes accounting and financial reporting requirements for regulated utilities. Studies and recommends policies and regulations.

Interior Dept. (DOI), *Land and Minerals Management,* 1849 C St. N.W., MS 6628, 20240; (202) 208-6734. Fax, (202) 208-3619. Janice M. Schneider, Assistant Secretary.
Web, www.doi.gov

Directs and supervises the Bureau of Land Management; the Bureau of Ocean Energy Management, Regulation, and Enforcement; and the Office of Surface Mining and Reclamation Enforcement. Supervises programs associated with land-use planning, onshore and offshore minerals, surface mining reclamation and enforcement, and Outer Continental Shelf minerals management.

National Institute of Standards and Technology (NIST) *(Commerce Dept.), Special Programs Office,* 100 Bureau Dr., MS 1000, Gaithersburg, MD 20899-1000; (301) 975-4447. Fax, (301) 975-8972. Richard R. Cavanagh, Director. General information, (301) 975-2756.
Web, www.nist.gov/director/spo

ENERGY RESOURCES IN CONGRESS

For a complete listing of congressional committees, including their full contact information, leadership, membership, and jurisdictions, please refer to the Appendix on pages 779–896.

HOUSE:

House Appropriations Committee, (202) 225-2771.
Web, appropriations.house.gov

    Subcommittee on Energy and Water Development and Related Agencies, (202) 225-3421.

    Subcommittee on Interior, Environment, and Related Agencies, (202) 225-3081.

House Armed Services Committee, (202) 225-4151.
Web, armedservices.house.gov

    Subcommittee on Readiness, (202) 226-8979.

House Education and the Workforce Committee, (202) 225-4527.
Web, edworkforce.house.gov

    Subcommittee on Workforce Protections, (202) 225-4527.

House Energy and Commerce Committee, (202) 225-2927.
Web, energycommerce.house.gov

    Subcommittee on Commerce, Manufacturing, and Trade, (202) 225-2927.

    Subcommittee on Energy and Power, (202) 225-2927.

House Foreign Affairs Committee, (202) 225-5021.
Web, foreignaffairs.house.gov

House Natural Resources Committee, (202) 225-2761.
Web, naturalresources.house.gov

    Subcommittee on Energy and Mineral Resources, (202) 225-9297.

    Subcommittee on Water, Power, and Oceans, (202) 225-8331.

House Science, Space, and Technology Committee, (202) 225-6371.
Web, science.house.gov

    Subcommittee on Energy, (202) 225-6371.

House Small Business Committee, (202) 225-5821.
Web, smallbusiness.house.gov

    Subcommittee on Agriculture, Energy, and Trade, (202) 225-5821.

House Transportation and Infrastructure Committee, (202) 225-9446.
Web, transportation.house.gov

    Subcommittee on Railroads, Pipelines, and Hazardous Materials, (202) 226-0727.

    Subcommittee on Water Resources and Environment, (202) 225-4360.

House Ways and Means Committee, (202) 225-3625.
Web, waysandmeans.house.gov

    Subcommittee on Trade, (202) 225-6649.

JOINT:

Joint Committee on Taxation, (202) 225-3621.
Web, www.jct.gov

Fosters collaboration among government, military, academia, professional, and private organizations to respond to critical national needs through science-based standards and technology innovation, including energy concerns.

National Nuclear Security Administration *(Energy Dept.), Emergency Operations, 1000 Independence Ave. S.W., #GH060, 20585; (202) 586-9892. Fax, (202) 586-3904. Debrah Wilber, Associate Administrator.*
Web, www.nnsa.energy.gov/aboutus/ourprograms/emergencyoperationscounterterrorism/operationscenter

Works to ensure coordinated Energy Dept. responses to energy-related emergencies. Recommends policies to mitigate the effects of energy supply crises on the United States; recommends government responses to energy emergencies.

Office of Management and Budget (OMB) *(Executive Office of the President), Energy, Science, and Water, 725 17th St. N.W., #8002, 20503; (202) 395-3404. Fax, (202) 395-3049. John Pasquantino, Deputy Associate Director. Press, (202) 395-7254.*
Web, www.whitehouse.gov/omb

Advises and assists the president in preparing the budget for energy programs; coordinates OMB energy policy and programs.

Office of Science *(Energy Dept.), 1000 Independence Ave. S.W., #7B058, 20585; (202) 586-5430. Fax, (202) 586-4120. Cherry Murray, Director; Patricia M. Dehmer, Deputy Director of Science Programs.*
Web, www.science.energy.gov

Advises the secretary on the department's physical science research and energy research and development programs; the use of multipurpose laboratories (except weapons laboratories); and education and training for basic and applied research activities. Manages the department's high-energy and nuclear physics programs and the fusion energy program. Conducts environmental and health-related research and development programs, including studies of energy-related pollutants and hazardous materials.

▶ **CONGRESS**

For a listing of relevant congressional committees and subcommittees, please see pages 240–241 or the Appendix.

Joint Economic Committee, (202) 224-5171.
Web, jec.senate.gov/public

SENATE:

Senate Agriculture, Nutrition, and Forestry
Committee, (202) 224-2035.
Web, ag.senate.gov
Subcommittee on Rural Development and
Energy, (202) 224-2035.
Senate Appropriations Committee, (202) 224-7363.
Web, appropriations.senate.gov
Subcommittee on Energy and Water
Development, (202) 224-8119.
Subcommittee on Interior, Environment, and
Related Agencies, (202) 228-0774.
Senate Commerce, Science, and Transportation
Committee, (202) 224-0411.
Web, commerce.senate.gov
Subcommittee on Oceans, Atmosphere, Fisheries,
and the Coast Guard, (202) 224-4912.
Subcommittee on Science, Space, and
Competitiveness, (202) 224-0415.
Senate Energy and Natural Resources Committee,
(202) 224-4971.
Web, energy.senate.gov
Subcommittee on Energy, (202) 224-4971.
Subcommittee on Water and Power,
(202) 224-4971.

Senate Environment and Public Works Committee,
(202) 224-8832.
Web, epw.senate.gov
Subcommittee on Clean Air and Nuclear Safety,
(202) 224-8832.
Subcommittee on Fisheries, Water, and Wildlife,
(202) 224-8832.
Senate Finance Committee, (202) 224-4515.
Web, finance.senate.gov
Subcommittee on Energy, Natural
Resources, and Infrastructure,
(202) 224-4515.
Senate Foreign Relations Committee,
(202) 224-4651.
Web, foreign.senate.gov
Subcommittee on Multilateral International
Development, Multilateral Institutions,
and International Economic, Energy,
and Environmental Policy,
(202) 224-4651.
Senate Health, Education, Labor, and Pensions
Committee, (202) 224-5375.
Web, help.senate.gov
Subcommittee on Employment and Workplace
Safety, (202) 228-1455.
Senate Homeland Security and Governmental Affairs
Committee, (202) 224-2627.
Web, hsgac.senate.gov

Government Accountability Office (GAO), *Natural
Resources and Environment, 441 G St. N.W., #2057,
20548 (mailing address: 441 G St. N.W., #2T23A,
Washington, DC 20548); (202) 512-3841. Fax, (202) 512-
8774. Mark Gaffigan, Managing Director.
Web, www.gao.gov/careers/nre.html*

Independent nonpartisan agency in the legislative
branch. Audits, analyzes, and reports on efficiency and
effectiveness of the Defense, Energy, and Interior Depts.
Addresses governmentwide science issues and the production, regulation, and consumption of energy.

▶ **NONGOVERNMENTAL**

American Assn. of Blacks in Energy (AABE), *1625 K St.
N.W., #405, 20006; (202) 371-9530. Fax, (202) 371-9218.
Paula Jackson, President.
General email, info@aabe.org
Web, www.aabe.org*

Encourages participation of African Americans and
other minorities in energy research and in formulating
energy policy. Provides financial aid and scholarships

to African American students who pursue careers in
energy-related fields. Promotes greater awareness in private and public sectors of the impacts of energy policy
on minority communities.

American Boiler Manufacturers Assn., *8221 Old
Courthouse Rd., #380, Vienna, VA 22182; (703) 356-7172.
Fax, (703) 356-4543. Scott Lynch, President;
Robert Stemen, Chair.
Web, www.abma.com*

Membership: manufacturers of boiler systems and
boiler-related products, including fuel-burning systems.
Interests include energy and environmental issues.

Aspen Institute, *1 Dupont Circle N.W., #700, 20036-7133;
(202) 736-5800. Fax, (202) 467-0790. Walter Isaacson,
President. Press, (202) 736-3849.
General email, info@aspeninstitute.org
Web, www.aspeninstitute.org and Twitter,
@AspenInstitute*

Educational and policy studies organization. Promotes
consideration of the public good in a wide variety of policy
areas, including energy, the environment, international

Energy Department

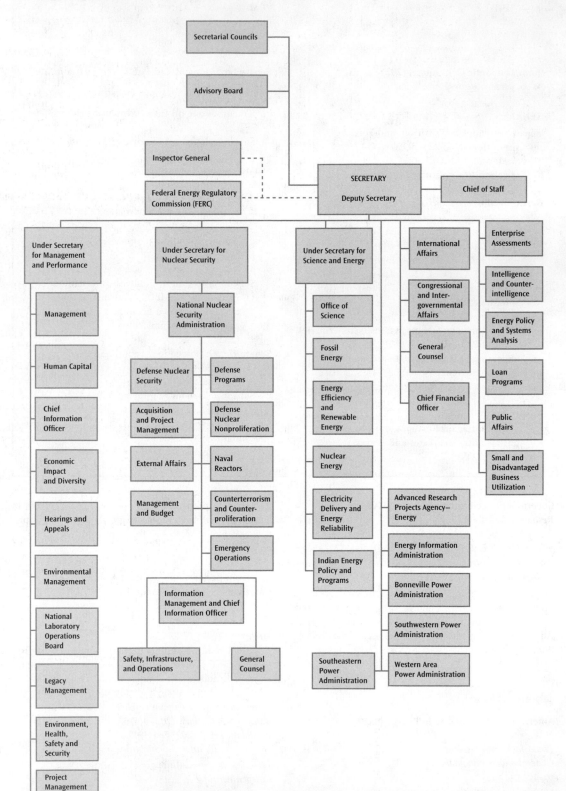

- - - - - - - Indicates a support or advisory relationship with the unit rather than a direct reporting relationship

relations, and homeland security. Working with international partners, offers educational seminars, nonpartisan policy forums, public conferences and events, and leadership development initiatives.

Building Codes Assistance Project, *1850 M St. N.W., #610, 20036; (202) 530-2211. Maureen Guttman, President.*
General email, info@bcapcodes.org
Web, www.bcap-energy.org and Twitter, @BCAPOCEAN

Advocacy group that supports and enforces national building energy codes. Assists cities, states, and countries in complying with federal energy efficient codes, including planning, technical assistance, and training. Provides outreach and coordination activities to provide information about current code data and cost analysis to policymakers. International interests include India, the Asia–Pacific region, Ukraine, and arid regions.

CECA Solutions, *2737 Devonshire Pl., #102, 20008; (202) 468-8440. Fax, (202) 318-0831. Ellen Berman, Chief Executive Officer.*
General email, info@cecarf.org
Web, www.cecarf.org

Analyzes economic and social effects of energy policies and advances interests of residential and small business consumers. Builds consensus on energy policy issues among public- and private-sector organizations, state and local groups, businesses, utilities, consumers, environmentalists, government agencies, and others. Interests include clean and sustainable fuels, distributed generation of electricity, and reliable electric systems. Conducts consumer education campaigns concerning fuel choices, energy conservation, and legislative and regulatory developments. (Formerly the Consumer Energy Council of America.)

Diesel Technology Forum, *5291 Corporate Dr., #102, Frederick, MD 21703-2875; (301) 668-7230. Fax, (301) 668-7234. Allen Schaeffer, Executive Director; Kristen Gifford, Communications.*
General email, dtf@dieselforum.org
Web, www.dieselforum.org

Represents diesel interests, with a focus on environmental protection. Advocates use of diesel engines. Supports energy research and advises policymakers. Monitors legislation and regulations.

Energy Bar Assn., *2000 M St. N.W., #715, 20036; (202) 223-5625. Fax, (202) 833-5596. Lisa A. Levine, Executive Director.*
General email, admin@eba-net.org
Web, www.eba-net.org

Membership: lawyers interested in all areas of energy law. Interests include administration of laws covering production, development, conservation, transmission, and economic regulation of energy.

Energy Future Coalition, *1750 Pennsylvania Ave. N.W., #300, 20006; (202) 463-1947. Reid Detchon, Executive Director.*
General email, info@energyfuturecoalition.org
Web, www.energyfuturecoalition.org

Nonpartisan public policy alliance that seeks to bridge the differences among business, labor, and environmental groups and identify energy policy options with broad political support. Interests include development of a national electricity transmission plan to bring renewable resources to market, and reduction of energy waste. Receives support from the United Nations Foundation.

Industrial Energy Consumers of America, *1776 K St. N.W., #720, 20006; (202) 223-1420. Paul N. Cicio, President, (202) 223-1661.*
Web, www.ieca-us.com

National trade association that represents the manufacturing industry and advocates on energy, environmental, and public policy issues. Advocates greater diversity of and lower costs for energy. Monitors legislation and regulations.

National Assn. of Energy Service Companies, *1615 M St. N.W., #800, 20036-3213; (202) 822-0950. Terry E. Singer, Executive Director.*
General email, info@naesco.org
Web, www.naesco.org

Membership: companies that design, manufacture, finance, and install energy efficiency and renewable energy equipment; energy efficiency and renewable energy services companies; and government officials. Advocates and serves as a clearinghouse on energy efficiency strategies. Monitors legislation and regulations.

National Assn. of Regulatory Utility Commissioners, *1101 Vermont Ave. N.W., #200, 20005-3521; (202) 898-2200. Fax, (202) 898-2213. Greg White, Executive Director.*
General email, admin@naruc.org
Web, www.naruc.org

Membership: members of federal, state, municipal, and international regulatory commissions that have jurisdiction over utilities and carriers. Interests include electricity, natural gas, and nuclear power.

National Assn. of State Energy Officials (NASEO), *2107 Wilson Blvd., #850, Arlington, VA 22201; (703) 299-8800. Fax, (703) 299-6208. David Terry, Executive Director.*
General email, energy@naseo.org
Web, www.naseo.org

Represents governor-designated energy officials from each state and territory. Seeks to improve energy programs, provide policy analysis, and act as an information clearinghouse. Interests include efficiency, renewables, building codes, emergency preparedness, and fuel production and distribution.

National Governors Assn. (NGA), *Center for Best Practices, Environment, Energy, and Transportation Division, 444 N. Capitol St. N.W., #267, 20001-1512; (202) 624-5300. Fax, (202) 624-7829. Sue Gander, Director.*

General email, webmaster@nga.org

Web, www.nga.org/cms/center/eet

Identifies best practices for energy, land use, environment, and transportation issues and shares these with the states.

National Governors Assn. (NGA), *Natural Resources Committee,* 444 N. Capitol St. N.W., #267, 20001-1512; (202) 624-5300. Fax, (202) 624-7814. Alex Whitaker, Director.
General email, webmaster@nga.org

Web, www.nga.org/cms/center/eet

Monitors legislation and regulations and makes recommendations on agriculture, energy, environment, and natural resource issues to ensure governors' views and priorities are represented in federal policies and regulations.

National Research Council (NRC), *Energy and Environmental Systems Board,* Keck Center, 500 5th St. N.W., #W917, 20001; (202) 334-1378. James Zucchetto, Board Director, (202) 334-3222.
Web, http://sites.nationalacademies.org/DEPS/BEES

Conducts studies in order to advise the federal government and the private sector about issues in energy and environmental technology, and related public policy. Focuses on energy supply and demand technologies and systems, including resource extraction through mining and drilling, energy conversion, distribution and delivery, and efficiency of use; environmental consequences of energy related activities; environmental systems and controls in areas related to fuels production, energy conversion, transmission, and use; and other issues relating to national security and defense. Sponsors studies, workshops, symposia, and a variety of information dissemination activities.

RAND Corporation, *Washington Office,* 1200 S. Hayes St., Arlington, VA 22202-5050; (703) 413-1100. Fax, (703) 413-8111. Richard M. Moore, Director, ext. 5399; Anita Chandra, Director, Justice, Infrastructure, and Environment, ext. 5323.
Web, www.rand.org

Analyzes the effects of existing and proposed energy policies on the environment. (Headquarters in Santa Monica, Calif.)

U.S. Chamber of Commerce, *Environment, Technology, and Regulatory Affairs,* 1615 H St. N.W., 20062-2000; (202) 463-5533. Fax, (202) 887-3445. William L. Kovacs, Senior Vice President.
General email, environment@uschamber.com

Web, www.uschamber.com/etra

Develops policy on all issues affecting energy, including alternative energy, emerging technologies, regulatory affairs, energy taxes, telecommunications, and onshore and offshore mining of energy resources.

Energy Conservation

▶**AGENCIES**

Energy Efficiency and Renewable Energy *(Energy Dept.),* 1000 Independence Ave. S.W., #6A013, MS EE1, 20585; (202) 586-9220. Fax, (202) 586-8177. David Danielson, Assistant Secretary. Information, (877) 337-3463. Press, (202) 586-4940.
General email, eereic@ee.doe.gov

Web, www.energy.gov/eere/office-energy-efficiency-renewable-energy

Develops and manages programs to improve markets for renewable energy sources, including solar, biomass, wind, geothermal, and hydropower, and to increase efficiency of energy use among residential, commercial, transportation, utility, and industrial users. Administers financial and technical assistance for state energy programs, weatherization for low-income households, and implementation of energy conservation measures by schools, hospitals, local governments, and public care institutions and federal facilities.

Energy Efficiency and Renewable Energy *(Energy Dept.),* **Advanced Manufacturing, Research, and Development,** 1000 Independence Ave. S.W., #5F065, EE5A, 20585; (202) 586-9488. Fax, (202) 586-9234. Mark Johnson, Director.
General email, AMO_Communication@ee.doe.gov

Web, www.energy.gov/eere/advanced-manufacturing-office

Conducts research and disseminates information to increase energy end-use efficiency, promote renewable energy use and industrial applications, and reduce the volume of industrial and municipal waste.

Energy Efficiency and Renewable Energy *(Energy Dept.),* **Building Technologies (BTP),** 1000 Independence Ave. S.W., MS EE5B, 20585; (202) 586-9127. Fax, (202) 586-4617. Roland Risser, Director.
Web, www.energy.gov/eere/buildings/building-technologies-office

Funds research to reduce commercial and residential building energy use. Programs include research and development, equipment standards and analysis, and technology validation and market introduction.

Energy Efficiency and Renewable Energy *(Energy Dept.),* **Federal Energy Management Program (FEMP),** 1000 Independence Ave. S.W., MS EE2L, 20585; (202) 586-5772. Fax, (202) 586-3000. Timothy Unruh, Director.
Web, http://energy.gov/eere/femp/federal-energy-management-program

Provides federal agencies with information and technology services to implement energy conservation measures. Areas include finance and contract assistance, purchase of energy-efficient products, design and operation of buildings, and vehicle fleet management.

Energy Efficiency and Renewable Energy *(Energy Dept.),* **Vehicle Technologies,** 1000 Independence Ave.

S.W., #5G030, 20585; (202) 586-8055. Fax, (202) 586-7409.
David Howell, Program Manager, Acting.
Web, www1.eere.energy.gov/vehiclesandfuels

Works with the motor vehicle industry to develop
technologies for improved vehicle fuel efficiency and
cleaner fuels.

Energy Efficiency and Renewable Energy (*Energy
Dept.*), *Weatherization and Intergovernmental
Programs*, 1000 Independence Ave. S.W., MS EE2K, 20585;
(202) 287-1518. Fax, (202) 586-1233. Anna Garcia,
Director, (202) 287-1858. Information, (202) 586-1510.
Web, www.eere.energy.gov/wip

Supports private and government efforts to improve
the energy efficiency of buildings and transportation. Promotes accelerated market penetration of energy efficiency
and renewable energy technologies. Provides funding and
technical assistance to state and local governments and
Indian tribes. Administers weatherization assistance program that assists elderly and low-income persons to make
their homes energy efficient. Reviews building codes that
promote energy efficiency in buildings.

Energy Information Administration (EIA) (*Energy
Dept.*), *Energy Consumption and Efficiency Analysis*,
1000 Independence Ave. S.W., 20585; (202) 586-1762.
James Turnure, Director
Web, www.eia.gov

Collects and provides data on energy consumption in
the residential, commercial, and industrial sectors. Pre
pares analyses on energy consumption by sector and fuel
type, including the impact of conservation measures.

Housing and Urban Development Dept. (HUD),
*Community Planning and Development, Environment
and Energy*, 451 7th St. S.W., #7250, 20410; (202) 708-
2894. Fax, (202) 708-3363. Danielle Schopp, Director, (202)
402-4442.
Web, http://portal.hud.gov/hudportal/HUD?src=/
program_offices/comm_planning/library/energy

Develops policies promoting energy efficiency, conservation, and renewable sources of supply in housing and
community development programs.

National Institute of Standards and Technology (NIST)
(*Commerce Dept.*), *Engineering Laboratory*, 100 Bureau
Dr., MS 8600, Gaithersburg, MD 20899-8600; (301) 975-
5900. Fax, (301) 975-4032. Howard H. Harary, Director.
General email, el@nist.gov
Web, www.nist.gov/el

Develops measurement techniques, test methods, and
mathematical models to encourage energy conservation
in large buildings. Interests include refrigeration, lighting,
infiltration and ventilation, heating and air conditioning,
indoor air quality, and heat transfer in the building envelope.

▶ **CONGRESS**

*For a listing of relevant congressional committees and sub-
committees, please see pages 240–241 or the Appendix.*

▶ **NONGOVERNMENTAL**

Alliance to Save Energy, 1850 M St. N.W., #600, 20036;
(202) 857-0666. Fax, (202) 331-9588. Kateri Callahan,
President.
General email, info@ase.org
Web, www.ase.org

Coalition of business, government, environmental,
and consumer leaders who promote the efficient and
clean use of energy to benefit consumers, the environment, the economy, and national security. Conducts programs addressing energy efficiency in commercial and
residential buildings, utilities, appliances, and equipment, industry, and education. International programs
provide technical and financial assistance to national and
local partners.

**American Council for an Energy-Efficient Economy
(ACEEE),** 529 14th St. N.W., #600, 20045-1000; (202) 507-
4000. Fax, (202) 429-2248. Steven Nadel, Executive
Director, (202) 507-4011.
General email, aceeeinfo@aceee.org
Web, www.aceee.org

Independent research organization concerned with
energy policy, technologies, and conservation. Interests
include consumer information, energy efficiency in buildings and appliances, improved transportation efficiency,
industrial efficiency, utility issues, and conservation in
developing countries.

Breakthrough Technologies Institute (BTI), 1100 H St.
N.W., #800, 20005; (202) 785-4222. Fax, (202) 785-4313.
Robert Rose, Executive Director.
General email, info@fuelcells.org
Web, www.btionline.org

Supports technologies that contribute to energy conservation and environmental sustainability. Analyzes
emerging technologies and publishes reports. Sponsors
briefings and workshops for policymakers, private organizations, and the public on transportation and energy
efficiency issues.

Energy Action Coalition, 1875 Connecticut Ave. N.W.,
10th Floor, 20009; (855) 593-9675. Lydia Avila, Executive
Director. Press, (202) 670-9448.
General email, theteam@energyactioncoalition.org
Web, www.energyactioncoalition.org and Twitter,
@energyaction

Membership: youth-based organizations that support
sustainable energy. Trains youth leaders to have a larger
impact on their local communities. Campaigns for clean
energy bills. Holds conferences on climate change and
sustainable energy options. Interests include activism on
college campuses and environmental justice.

Environmental Defense Fund, *Washington Office*,
1875 Connecticut Ave. N.W., #600, 20009-5728; (202)
387-3500. Fax, (202) 234-6049. Fred Krupp, President;
Felice Stradler, Director, U.S. Climate and Political

Affairs. Information, (800) 684-3322. Press, (202) 572-3396.

Web, www.edf.org and Twitter, @EnvDefenseFund

Citizens' interest group staffed by lawyers, economists, and scientists. Provides information on energy issues and advocates energy conservation measures. Interests include China and the Amazon rain forest. Provides utilities and environmental organizations with research and guidance on energy conservation. (Headquarters in New York.)

Friends of the Earth (FOE), 1101 15th St. N.W., 11th Floor, 20005; (202) 783-7400. Fax, (202) 783-0444. Erich Pica, President. Toll-free, (877) 843-8687.
General email, foe@foe.org

Web, www.foe.org and Twitter, @foe_us

Environmental advocacy group. Interests include climate disruption, renewable energy resources, and air and water pollution. Specializes in federal budget and tax issues related to the environment, including the Keystone XL pipeline, World Bank, and U.S. Export-Import Bank.

National Insulation Assn. (NIA), 12100 Sunset Hills Rd., #330, Reston, VA 20190-3233; (703) 464-6422. Fax, (703) 464-5896. Michele M. Jones, Executive Vice President, ext. 119.
General email, niainfo@insulation.org

Web, www.insulation.org

Membership: open-shop and union contractors, distributors, laminators, fabricators, and manufacturers that provide thermal insulation, insulation accessories, and components to the commercial, mechanical, and industrial markets. Provides information to members on industry trends and technologies, and offers service contacts for consumers. Monitors legislation and regulations.

North American Insulation Manufacturers Assn.,
11 Canal Center Plaza, #103, Alexandria, VA 22314; (703) 684-0084. Fax, (703) 684-0427. Curt Rich, President.
General email, insulation@naima.org

Web, www.naima.org

Membership: manufacturers of insulation products for use in homes, commercial buildings, and industrial facilities. Provides information on the use of insulation for thermal efficiency, sound control, and fire safety; monitors research in the industry. Interests include energy efficiency and sustainability. Monitors legislation and regulations.

Resources for the Future, 1616 P St. N.W., 20036-1400; (202) 328-5000. Fax, (202) 939-3460. Philip R. Sharp, President, (202) 328-5077. Library, (202) 328-5089. Press, (202) 328-5168.
General email, info@rff.org

Web, www.rff.org and Twitter, @RFF_org

Research organization that conducts independent studies on economic and policy aspects of energy, environment, conservation, and natural resource management issues worldwide. Interests include climate change, energy, natural resource issues in developing countries, and public health.

Sierra Club, *Legislative Office,* 50 F St. N.W., 8th Floor, 20001; (202) 547-1141. Fax, (202) 547-6009. Debbie Sease, Legislative Director; Bob Bingaman, National Organizing Director, (202) 675-7904; Shanice Penn, Operations Manager. Press, (202) 675-6698.
General email, information@sierraclub.org

Web, www.sierraclub.org

Citizens' interest group that promotes protection and responsible use of the Earth's ecosystems and its natural resources. Focuses on combating global warming/greenhouse effect through energy conservation, efficient use of renewable energy resources, auto efficiency, and constraints on deforestation. Monitors federal, state, and local legislation relating to the environment and natural resources. (Headquarters in San Francisco, Calif.)

Union of Concerned Scientists, *Strategy and Policy,* 1825 K St. N.W., #800, 20006-1232; (202) 223-6133. Fax, (202) 223-6162. Alden Meyer, Director.
General email, ucs@ucsusa.org

Web, www.ucsusa.org

Independent group of scientists and citizens who advocate safe and sustainable international, national, and state energy policies. Conducts research, advocacy, and educational outreach focusing on market-based strategies for developing renewable energy and alternative fuels, transportation policy, climate change policy, and energy efficiency. (Headquarters in Cambridge, Mass.)

Worldwatch Institute, 1400 16th St. N.W., #430, 20036; (202) 745-8092. Fax, (202) 478-2534. Ed Groark, President, Acting.
General email, worldwatch@worldwatch.org

Web, www.worldwatch.org and Twitter, @worldwatch

Focuses on an interdisciplinary approach to solving global environmental problems. Interests include energy conservation, renewable resources, solar power, and energy use in developing countries.

International Trade and Cooperation

▶**AGENCIES**

Bureau of Economic Analysis *(Commerce Dept.),* *International Economic Accounts, Balance of Payments,* 1441 L St. N.W., 20230; (202) 606-9561. Fax, (202) 606-5314. Paul Farello, Chief. Press, (202) 606-2649.
General email, customerservice@bea.gov

Web, www.bea.gov/international

Provides statistics on U.S. balance of trade, including figures on energy commodities. Produces monthly joint release with the U.S. Census.

Bureau of Energy Resources *(State Dept.),* 2201 C St. N.W., #4428, 20520; (202) 647-8543. Mary Warlick, Principal Deputy Assistant Secretary; Amos J. Hochstein, Special Envoy and Coordinator for International Energy Affairs.
Web, www.state.gov/e/enr and Twitter, @EnergyAtState

Manages the global energy economy through diplomacy between energy producers and consumers, and stimulates the market forces toward the advancement of sustainable, renewable energy sources.

Bureau of Energy Resources *(State Dept.), Policy Analysis and Public Diplomacy,* 2201 C St. N.W., #4422, 20520; (202) 647-2879. Fax, (202) 647-7431. *Richard Westerdale, Director.*
Web, www.state.gov

Seeks to put energy security interests at the forefront of U.S. foreign policy. Objectives include increasing energy diplomacy with major producers and consumers; stimulating market forces toward energy development and reconstruction, with an emphasis on alternative energies and electricity; and promoting good governance and increased transparency to improve commercially viable and environmentally sustainable access to people without energy services.

Bureau of International Security and Nonproliferation *(State Dept.), Nuclear Energy, Safety, and Security Affairs,* 2201 C St. N.W., #3320, 20520; (202) 647-4413. Fax, (202) 647-0775. *Richard K. Stratford, Director.*
Web, www.state.gov/t/isn/58378

Coordinates and supervises international nuclear energy policy for the State Dept.; promotes adherence to technical conventions regarding peaceful uses of nuclear energy.

Census Bureau *(Commerce Dept.), International Trade Management,* 4600 Silver Hill Rd., #6K032, Suitland, MD 20746 (mailing address: 4600 Silver Hill Rd., #6K032, Washington, DC 20233-6700); (301) 763-2255. Fax, (301) 763-6638. *Dale C. Kelly, Chief. International trade helpline, (800) 549-0595.*
Web, www.census.gov/trade

Provides detailed statistics on all U.S. imports and exports, including petroleum, advanced technology products, and agricultural products; organizes this information by commodity, country, state, district, and port.

Energy Dept. (DOE), *Energy Policy and Systems Analysis, Energy Security,* 1000 Independence Ave. S.W., #7D034, PI40, 20585; (202) 586-4800. Fax, (202) 586-0900. *Carmine Difiglio, Deputy Director for Energy Security.*
Web, www.energy.gov/office-energy-policy-and-systems-analysis

Advises the assistant secretary and Energy Dept. leadership on energy demand and supply, energy efficiency, energy research and development, and the environment, including air quality and climate. Provides analysis for the development of domestic and international energy policy. Responds to energy market disruptions and emergencies. Recommends science and technology policies.

Energy Dept. (DOE), *International Affairs,* 1000 Independence Ave. S.W., #7C016, MS IA1, 20585; (202) 586-8660. Fax, (202) 586-0861. *Jonathan Elkind, Assistant Secretary.*
Web, www.energy.gov/ia/office-international-affairs

Advises the Energy Dept. leadership in the development of a national policy concerning domestic and international energy matters. Coordinates the varied interests of the department's divisions and other government organizations. Negotiates and manages international energy agreements. Develops and promotes international partnerships for deployment of greenhouse gas abatement technologies.

Energy Information Administration (EIA) *(Energy Dept.), Integrated and International Energy Analysis,* 1000 Independence Ave. S.W., MS EI35, 20585; (202) 586-1284. Fax, (202) 586-3045. *Paul D. Holtberg, Team Leader.*
Web, www.eia.gov

Compiles, interprets, and reports international energy statistics and U.S. energy data for international energy organizations. Analyzes international energy markets; makes projections concerning world prices and trade for energy sources, including oil, natural gas, coal, and electricity; monitors world petroleum market to determine U.S. vulnerability.

International Trade Administration (ITA) *(Commerce Dept.), Industry and Analysis, Energy and Environmental Industries,* 1400 Constitution Ave. N.W., #4053, 20230; (202) 482-5225. *Adam O'Malley, Director,* (202) 482-4850.
Web, www.trade.gov/td/energy

Promotes global competitiveness of U.S. energy and environmental companies. Conducts analyses of these two sectors and of overseas trade and investment opportunities and trade barriers affecting them. Develops strategies for removing foreign trade barriers and improving investment conditions. Organizes conferences and workshops.

National Nuclear Security Administration *(Energy Dept.), Emergency Operations,* 1000 Independence Ave. S.W., #GH060, 20585; (202) 586-9892. Fax, (202) 586-3904. *Debrah Wilber, Associate Administrator.*
Web, www.nnsa.energy.gov/aboutus/ourprograms/emergencyoperationscounterterrorism/operationscenter

Monitors international energy situations as they affect domestic market conditions; recommends policies on and government responses to energy emergencies; represents the United States in the International Energy Agency's emergency programs and NATO civil emergency preparedness activities.

National Nuclear Security Administration *(Energy Dept.), Nuclear Nonproliferation and International Security,* 1000 Independence Ave. S.W., #7F075, 20585; (202) 586-0645. Fax, (202) 586-0862. *Anne M. Harrington, Deputy Administrator.*
Web, www.nnsa.energy.gov/aboutus/ourprograms/dnn

Seeks to develop and implement policy and technical solutions to eliminate proliferation-sensitive materials and limit or prevent the spread of materials, technology, and expertise related to nuclear and radiological weapons and programs around the world. Collaborates with the International Atomic Energy Agency (IAEA) to ensure the secure and safe expansion of global nuclear energy and other peaceful uses of the atom.

Nuclear Energy *(Energy Dept.), International Nuclear Energy Policy and Cooperation, 1000 Independence Ave. S.W., #5A-143, 20585; (202) 586-5253. Fax, (202) 586-8353. Edward G. McGinnis, Deputy Assistant Secretary. Web, www.energy.gov/ne/nuclear-reactor-technologies/ international-nuclear-energy-policy-and-cooperation*

Responsible for the Energy Dept.'s international civilian nuclear energy activities, including research, development and demonstration cooperation, international framework and partnership development, and international nuclear energy policy.

Nuclear Regulatory Commission, *International Programs, 11555 Rockville Pike, MS 04E21, Rockville, MD 20852; (301) 415-2344. Fax, (301) 415-2400. Nader Marnish, Director, (301) 415-1780. Web, www.nrc.gov/about-nrc/organization/ oipfuncdesc.html*

Coordinates application review process for exports and imports of nuclear materials, facilities, and components. Makes recommendations on export-import licensing upon completion of review process. Conducts related policy reviews.

Office of Science *(Energy Dept.), 1000 Independence Ave. S.W., #7B058, 20585; (202) 586-5430. Fax, (202) 586-4120. Cherry Murray, Director; Patricia M. Dehmer, Deputy Director of Science Programs. Web, www.science.energy.gov*

Coordinates energy research, science, and technology programs among producing and consuming nations; analyzes existing international research and development activities; pursues international collaboration in research and in the design, development, construction, and operation of new facilities and major scientific experiments; participates in negotiations for international cooperation activities.

Treasury Dept., *International Affairs, Environment and Energy, 1500 Pennsylvania Ave N.W., 20220; (202) 622-0139. Leonardo Martinez, Deputy Assistant Secretary. Web, www.treasury.gov/about/organizational-structure/ offices/Pages/Environment-and-Energy.aspx*

Develops, coordinates, and executes the Treasury Dept.'s role in domestic and international environment and energy policy. Assists the United States on finance issues at United Nations climate negotiations and leads the department's engagement on energy and climate finance efforts in the G-20.

Treasury Dept., *International Affairs, Middle East and North Africa, 1500 Pennsylvania Ave. N.W., #3218A, 20220; (202) 622-2129. Fax, (202) 622-0431. Eric Meyers, Deputy Assistant Secretary; Francisco Parodi, Director. Web, www.treasury.gov/about/organizational-structure/ offices/Pages/-Middle-East-and-North-Africa.aspx*

Represents the department in the World Bank, International Monetary Fund, and other international institutions that address economic, financial, development, and energy matters. Provides economic analyses of the Middle East (including Turkey) and North Africa.

U.S. International Trade Commission, *Natural Resources and Energy, 500 E St. S.W., #511F, 20436; (202) 205-3419. Fax, (202) 205-2217. Robert Carr, Chief, (202) 205-3042. General email, cynthia.foreso@usitc.gov Web, www.usitc.gov*

Advisory fact-finding agency on tariffs, commercial policy, and foreign trade matters. Analyzes data on oil, crude petroleum, petroleum products, natural gas and its products, and coal and its products (including all forms of coke) traded internationally; investigates effects of tariffs on certain chemical and energy imports.

U.S. Trade Representative *(Executive Office of the President), 600 17th St. N.W., #205, 20508; (202) 395-6890. Fax, (202) 395-4549. Amb. Michael Froman, U.S. Trade Representative. Press, (202) 395-3230. General email, correspondence@ustr.eop.gov Web, www.ustr.gov*

Serves as principal adviser to the president and primary trade negotiator on international trade policy. Develops and coordinates energy trade matters among government agencies.

▶CONGRESS

For a listing of relevant congressional committees and subcommittees, please see pages 240–241 or the Appendix.

▶INTERNATIONAL ORGANIZATIONS

European Union, *Delegation to the United States of America, 2175 K St. N.W., 20037; (202) 862-9500. Fax, (202) 429-1766. David O'Sullivan, Ambassador. General email, delegation-usa-info@eeas.europa.eu Web, www.euintheus.org and Twitter, @EUintheUS*

Provides information on European Union energy policy, initiatives, research activities, and selected statistics. (Headquarters in Brussels.)

▶NONGOVERNMENTAL

Atlantic Council, *Global Energy Center, 1101 15th St. N.W., 10th Floor, 20005-5503; (202) 463-7226. Fax, (202) 463-4590. Richard Morningstar, Director. Press, (202) 778-4967. General email, mcarstei@atlanticcouncil.org Web, www.atlanticcouncil.org*

Seeks to create common understanding of critical energy and environmental issues through nonpartisan policy analysis and recommendations. Studies and makes policy recommendations on the economic, political, and security aspects of energy supply and international environment issues.

The Brookings Institution, *Economic Studies,* *1775 Massachusetts Ave. N.W., 20036-2188; (202) 797-6000. Fax, (202) 797-6181. Ted Gayer, Director. Press, (202) 797-6105. General email, escomment@brookings.edu*

Web, www.brookings.edu/economics

Promotes environmentally sound and economically efficient climate policy, with a focus on the economics of domestic cap-and-trade approaches and global agreement.

U.S. Energy Assn., *1300 Pennsylvania Ave. N.W., #550, Mailbox 142, 20004-3022; (202) 312-1230. Fax, (202) 682-1682. Barry K. Worthington, Executive Director. General email, reply@usea.org*

Web, www.usea.org and Twitter, @USEnergyAssn

Membership: energy-related organizations, including professional, trade, and government groups. Participates in the World Energy Council (headquartered in London). Sponsors seminars and conferences on energy resources, policy management, technology, utilization, and conservation.

Winrock International, *2121 Crystal Dr., #500, Arlington, VA 22202; (703) 302-6500. Fax, (703) 302-6512. Rodney Ferguson, President. General email, information@winrock.org*

Web, www.winrock.org and Twitter, @WinrockIntl

Works to sustain natural resources and protect the environment. Matches innovative approaches in agriculture, natural resource management, clean energy, and leadership development with the unique needs of its partners. (Headquarters in Little Rock, Ark.)

Statistics

▶**AGENCIES**

Bureau of Labor Statistics (BLS) *(Labor Dept.),* *Industrial Prices and Price Index, 2 Massachusetts Ave. N.E., #3840, 20212-0001; (202) 691-7700. Fax, (202) 691-7754. Jayson Pollock, Manager, Energy and Chemical Team; David M. Friedman, Assistant Commissioner. General email, ppi-info@bls.gov*

Web, www.bls.gov/ppi

Compiles statistics on energy for the Producer Price Index; analyzes movement of prices for natural gas, petroleum, coal, and electric power in the primary commercial and industrial markets. Records changes over time in the prices domestic producers receive.

Energy Information Administration (EIA) *(Energy Dept.), National Energy Information Center, 1000 Independence Ave. S.W., #1E210, EI30, 20585; (202) 586-6537. Gina Pearson, Assistant Administrator for Communications. General email, infoctr@eia.doe.gov*

Web, www.eia.gov/neic/neicservices.htm

Serves as the information point of contact for federal, state, and local governments; academia, businesses, and industry; foreign governments and international organizations; the news media; and the public. Manages and oversees the Energy Information Administration's public Web site, printed publications, and a customer contact center.

▶**NONGOVERNMENTAL**

American Gas Assn., *Statistics, 400 N. Capitol St. N.W., #450, 20001-1535; (202) 824-7133. Fax, (202) 824-7115. Paul Pierson, Manager. Web, www.aga.org*

Issues statistics on the gas utility industry, including supply and reserves.

American Petroleum Institute, *Statistics, 1220 L St. N.W., 20005-4070; (202) 682-8000. Fax, (202) 962-4730. Hazem Arafa, Director. Toll-free, (800) 854-7179. General email, apidata@api.org*

Web, www.api.org

Provides basic statistical information on petroleum industry operations, market conditions, and environmental, health, and safety performance. Includes data on supply and demand of crude oil and petroleum products, exports and imports, refinery operations, drilling activities and costs, environmental expenditures, injuries, illnesses and fatalities, oil spills, and emissions.

Edison Electric Institute, *Business Information, 701 Pennsylvania Ave. N.W., 20004-2696; (202) 508-5000. Fax, (202) 508-5599. Christopher Eisenbrey, Manager; David K. Owens, Executive Vice President, Business Operations. Press, (202) 508-5659. General email, ceisenbrey@eei.org*

Web, www.eei.org/resourcesandmedia/products

Provides statistics on electric utility operations, including the *Statistical Yearbook of the Electric Utility Industry,* which contains data on the capacity, generation, sales, customers, revenue, and finances of the electric utility industry.

National Mining Assn., *Communications, 101 Constitution Ave. N.W., #500E, 20001-2133; (202) 463-2600. Fax, (202) 463-2666. Rich Nolan, Senior Vice President, Government and Political Affairs. Web, www.nma.org*

Collects, analyzes, and distributes statistics on the mining industry, including statistics on the production, transportation, and consumption of coal and hard rock minerals.

ELECTRICITY

General

▶**AGENCIES**

Energy Dept. (DOE), *Power Marketing Liaison Office, 1000 Independence Ave. S.W., #8G037, 20585; (202) 586-5581. Fax, (202) 586-6261. Michael D. McElhany, Assistant Administrator. Web, www.wapa.gov*

Federal Energy Regulatory Commission

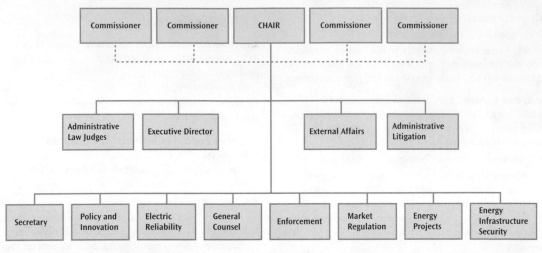

------- Signifies members of the governing body

Serves as a liaison among the Southeastern, Southwestern, and Western area power administrations; other federal agencies; and Congress. Coordinates marketing of electric power from federally owned hydropower projects.

Energy Information Administration (EIA) *(Energy Dept.), Electricity, Coal, Nuclear, and Renewable Analysis, 1000 Independence Ave. S.W., #2H073, EI50, 20585; (202) 586-2432. Jim Diefenderfer, Director.*
Web, www.eia.gov

Prepares analyses and forecasts on electric power supplies, including the effects of government policies and regulatory actions on capacity, consumption, finances, and rates. Publishes statistics on electric power industry.

National Institute of Standards and Technology (NIST) *(Commerce Dept.), Smart Grid, 100 Bureau Dr., MS 8200, Gaithersburg, MD 20899-8200; (301) 975-5987. Fax, (301) 975-4091. Chris Greer, Director.*
General email, smartgrid@nist.gov
Web, www.nist.gov/smartgrid

Develops interoperable standards to govern operations and future growth of the national Smart Grid, a planned electricity system that will add digital technology to electricity grids throughout the United States to channel their electric currents at an anticipated lower cost and higher efficiency. Works with manufacturers, consumers, energy providers, and regulators to ensure cohesion throughout the Smart Grid infrastructure.

Tennessee Valley Authority, *Government Affairs, 1 Massachusetts Ave. N.W., #300, 20444; (202) 898-2999. Fax, (202) 898-2998. Nick Pearson, Director.*
General email, tvainfo@tva.gov
Web, www.tva.gov

Federal corporation that coordinates resource conservation, development, and land-use programs in the Tennessee River Valley. Uses fossil fuel, nuclear, and hydropower sources to generate and supply wholesale power to municipal and cooperative electric systems, federal installations, and some industries.

▶CONGRESS

For a listing of relevant congressional committees and subcommittees, please see pages 240–241 or the Appendix.

▶NONGOVERNMENTAL

American Coalition for Clean Coal Electricity, *1152 15th St. N.W., #400, 20005; (202) 459-4800. Fax, (202) 459-4897. Robert M. (Mike) Duncan, President.*
General email, info@americaspower.org
Web, www.americaspower.org

Membership: coal, railroad, and electric utility companies and suppliers. Educates the public and policymakers about economic, technological, and scientific research on energy resources employed in generating electricity. Promotes the use of coal in generating electricity and supports development of carbon-sequestration and clean-coal technologies for minimizing coal's environmental impacts.

Assn. of Electrical Equipment and Medical Imaging Manufacturers (NEMA), *1300 N. 17th St., #900, Rosslyn, VA 22209-3801; (703) 841-3200. Fax, (703) 841-5900. Kevin Cosgriff, President. Press, (703) 841-3241.*
Web, www.nema.org and Twitter, @NEMAupdates

Membership: manufacturers of products used in the generation, transmission, distribution, control, and end-use of electricity, including manufacturers of medical diagnostic imaging equipment. Develops technical standards; collects, analyzes, and disseminates industry data. Interests include Smart Grid, high-performance building, carbon footprint, energy storage, and an intelligence portal. Monitors legislation, regulations, and international trade activities.

Electric Power Supply Assn., *1401 New York Ave. N.W., #1230, 20005; (202) 628-8200. Fax, (202) 628-8260. John Shelk, President. Web, www.epsa.org*

Membership: power generators active in U.S. and global markets, power marketers, and suppliers of goods and services to the industry. Promotes competition in the delivery of electricity to consumers.

Electricity Consumers Resource Council (ELCON), *1101 K St. N.W., #700, 20005; (202) 682-1390. John Hughes, President. General email, elcon@elcon.org Web, www.elcon.org*

Membership: large industrial users of electricity. Promotes development of coordinated federal, state, and local policies concerning electrical supply for industrial users; studies rate structures and their impact on consumers.

National Electrical Contractors Assn., *3 Bethesda Metro Center, #1100, Bethesda, MD 20814; (301) 657-3110. Fax, (301) 215-4500. John M. Grau, Chief Executive Officer. Web, www.necanet.org, Twitter, @necanet and Facebook, www.facebook.com/NECANET*

Membership: electrical contractors who build and service electrical wiring and equipment, including high-voltage construction and service. Represents members in collective bargaining with union workers; sponsors research and educational programs.

National Hydropower Assn., *25 Massachusetts Ave. N.W., #450, 20001; (202) 682-1700. Fax, (202) 682-9478. Linda Church Ciocci, Executive Director. General email, help@hydro.org Web, www.hydro.org*

Membership: investor-owned utilities and municipal and independent companies that generate hydroelectric power and power from new water technologies; consulting, engineering, and law firms; and equipment suppliers and manufacturers. Focus includes regulatory relief, public affairs, and coalition building. Monitors legislation and regulations.

Public Utilities

▶**AGENCIES**

Federal Energy Regulatory Commission (FERC) *(Energy Dept.), Electric Reliability, 888 1st St. N.E., #9M-01, 20426; (202) 502-8600. Fax, (202) 219-2836. Michael A. Bardee, Director. Web, www.ferc.gov/about/offices/oer.asp*

Oversees the reliability and security of the nation's bulk power system. Establishes and ensures compliance with reliability and security standards for users, owners, and operators of the bulk power system.

Federal Energy Regulatory Commission (FERC) *(Energy Dept.), Energy Market Regulation, 888 1st St. N.E., #8A-01, 20426; (202) 502-6700. Fax, (202) 208-0193.*

Jamie L. Simler, Director. Web, www.ferc.gov/about/offices/oemr.asp

Advises the Commission and processes caseloads related to the economic regulation of the electric utility, natural gas, and oil industries. Concerns include energy markets, tariffs, and pipeline rates relating to electric utility and natural gas and oil pipeline facilities and services. Analyzes applications for electric public utility corporate transactions, including public utility mergers, issuance of securities, or the assumption of liabilities, to determine if the proposed transactions are consistent with the public interest.

Federal Energy Regulatory Commission (FERC) *(Energy Dept.), Energy Policy and Innovation, 888 1st St. N.E., #7A-01, 20426; (202) 502-8693. Fax, (202) 219-1274. J. Arnold Quinn, Director. Web, www.ferc.gov/about/offices/oepi.asp*

Seeks to identify emerging issues affecting wholesale and interstate energy markets. Undertakes outreach to other regulators and industry, conducts studies and makes recommendations for Commission action with state and federal agencies and the energy industry, taking into account energy and environmental concerns. Interests include renewable energy, efficiency, smart grid technology, transmission issues, electric vehicles, carbon and greenhouse gas issues.

Federal Energy Regulatory Commission (FERC) *(Energy Dept.), Energy Projects, 888 1st St. N.E., #6A-01, 20426; (202) 502-8700. Fax, (202) 219-0205. Ann F. Miles, Director. Web, www.ferc.gov/about/offices/oep.asp*

Focuses on the engineering and environmental aspects of siting and development of new gas pipeline projects; authorizes and monitors hydroelectric projects for compliance and to safeguard the public.

Federal Energy Regulatory Commission (FERC) *(Energy Dept.), Infrastructure Security, 888 1st St. N.E., #9M-13, 20426; (202) 502-8867. Fax, (202) 219-2836. Joseph H. McClelland, Director. Web, www.ferc.gov/about/offices/oeis.asp*

Seeks to identify risk and vulnerability to potential physical and cyber attacks and to coordinate collaborative mitigation actions. Formulates and makes recommendations for Commission action with state and federal agencies and the energy industry.

Rural Development *(Agriculture Dept.), Rural Utilities Service, 1400 Independence Ave. S.W., #5135-S, MS 1510, 20250-1510; (202) 720-9540. Fax, (202) 720-1725. Brandon McBride, Administrator. Information, (202) 720-1255. Web, www.rd.usda.gov/about-rd/agencies/rural-utilities-service*

Makes loans and loan guarantees to provide electricity, telecommunication systems, and water and waste disposal services to rural areas.

▶ **NONGOVERNMENTAL**

American Public Power Assn., *2451 Crystal Dr., #1000, Arlington, VA 22202; (202) 467-2900. Fax, (202) 467-2910. Susan Kelly, President.*
Web, www.publicpower.org and Twitter, @APPAnews

Membership: local, municipally owned electric utilities nationwide. Represents industry interests before Congress, federal agencies, and the courts; provides educational programs; collects and disseminates information; funds energy research and development projects.

Edison Electric Institute, *701 Pennsylvania Ave. N.W., 20004-2696; (202) 508-5000. Fax, (202) 508-5096. Thomas R. Kuhn, President. Library, (202) 508-5603.*
General email, feedback@eei.org
Web, www.eei.org

Membership: investor-owned electric power companies. Interests include electric utility operation and concerns, including conservation and energy management, energy analysis, generation and transmission facilities, fuel resources, the environment, cogeneration and renewable energy resources, safety, reliability, taxes, and regulation matters. Provides information and statistics relating to electric energy; aids member companies in generating and selling electric energy; and conducts information forums. Library open to the public by appointment.

National Assn. of Regulatory Utility Commissioners, *1101 Vermont Ave. N.W., #200, 20005-3521; (202) 898-2200. Fax, (202) 898-2213. Greg White, Executive Director.*
General email, admin@naruc.org
Web, www.naruc.org

Membership: members of federal, state, municipal, and international regulatory commissions that have jurisdiction over utilities. Interests include electric utilities.

National Assn. of State Utility Consumer Advocates (NASUCA), *8380 Colesville Rd., #101, Silver Spring, MD 20910-6267; (301) 589-6313. Fax, (301) 589-6380. David Springe, Executive Director.*
General email, nasuca@nasuca.org
Web, www.nasuca.org

Membership: public advocate offices authorized by states to represent ratepayer interests before state and federal utility regulatory commissions. Monitors legislation and regulatory agencies with jurisdiction over electric utilities, telecommunications, natural gas, and water; conducts conferences.

National Rural Electric Cooperative Assn. (NRECA), *4301 Wilson Blvd., Arlington, VA 22203-1860; (703) 907-5500. Fax, (703) 907-5511. Jo Ann Emerson, Chief Executive Officer; Tracy Warren, Media Relations, (703) 907-5746.*
Web, www.nreca.org

Membership: rural electric cooperative systems and public power and utility districts. Provides members with legislative, legal, and regulatory services. Supports energy and environmental research and offers technical advice and assistance to developing countries.

Utility Workers Union of America, *815 16th St. N.W., 20006; (202) 974-8200. Fax, (202) 974-8201. Ed Good, Legislative Director, (740) 312-8411; Mike Coleman, National Secretary-Treasurer.*
General email, webmaster@uwua.net
Web, www.uwua.net

Labor union representing approximately 50,000 workers in utilities and related industries. Helps members negotiate pay, benefits, and better working conditions; conducts training programs and workshops. Monitors legislation and regulations. (Affiliated with the AFL-CIO.)

Research and Development

▶ **AGENCIES**

National Institute of Standards and Technology (NIST) (Commerce Dept.), Quantum Measurement Division, *100 Bureau Dr., MS 8420, Gaithersburg, MD 20899-8420; (301) 975-2220. Fax, (301) 990-3038. Carl J. Williams, Chief.*
General email, carl.williams@nist.gov
Web, www.nist.gov/pml/div684

Conducts research to characterize and define performance parameters of electrical/electronic systems, components, and materials; applies research to advance measurement instrumentation and the efficiency of electric power transmission and distribution; develops and maintains national electrical reference standards, primarily for power, energy, and related measurements, to assist in the development of new products and promote international competitiveness.

Office of Science *(Energy Dept.), Fusion Energy Sciences, 19901 Germantown Rd., #SC24, Germantown, MD 20874-1290 (mailing address: Germantown Bldg., 1000 Independence Ave. S.W., #SC24, Washington, DC 20585); (301) 903-4941. Fax, (301) 903-8584. Edmund J. Synakowski, Associate Director.*
Web, http://science.energy.gov/fes

Conducts research and development on fusion energy for electric power generation.

▶ **NONGOVERNMENTAL**

Electric Power Research Institute (EPRI), *Washington Office, 1325 G St. N.W., #1080, 20005; (202) 293-7518. Fax, (202) 296-5436. Barbara Bauman Tyran, Director, (202) 293-7513.*
General email, askepri@askepri.com
Web, www.epri.com

Membership: investor-owned and municipally owned electric utilities and rural cooperatives. Conducts research and development in power generation and delivery technologies, including fossil fuel, nuclear, and renewable energy sources used by electric utilities. Studies energy management and utilization, including conservation and environmental issues. (Headquarters in Palo Alto, Calif.)

FOSSIL FUELS

General

Energy Information Administration (EIA) *(Energy Dept.), Oil, Gas, and Coal Supply Statistics,* 1000 Independence Ave. S.W., #BE072, 20585; (202) 586-1831. Douglas M. MacIntyre, Director, Acting.
General email, infoctr@eia.doe.gov
Web, www.eia.gov/about/eia_offices.cfm

Collects and publishes weekly, monthly, and annual estimates of domestic natural gas, coal, and upstream oil. Performs analyses of the natural gas, coal, and upstream oil industries, including consumption, prices, and storage levels.

Fossil Energy *(Energy Dept.),* 1000 Independence Ave. S.W., #4G084, 20585-1290; (202) 586-6660. Fax, (202) 586-7847. Christopher A. Smith, Assistant Secretary; Julio Friedman, Principal Deputy.
Web, www.fe.doe.gov,
http://energy.gov/fe/office-fossil-energy and Twitter, @fossilenergygov

Responsible for policy and management of high-risk, long-term research and development in recovering, converting, and using fossil energy, including coal, petroleum, oil shale, and unconventional sources of natural gas. Handles the petroleum reserve and the naval petroleum and oil shale reserve programs; oversees the Clean Coal Program to design and construct environmentally clean coal-burning facilities.

U.S. Geological Survey (USGS) *(Interior Dept.), Energy Resources,* 12201 Sunrise Valley Dr., MS 913, Reston, VA 20192 (mailing address: 913 National Center, Reston, VA 20192); (703) 648-6470. Fax, (703) 648-5464. Vito Nuccio, Program Coordinator, Acting.
General email, gd-energyprogram@usgs.gov
Web, http://energy.usgs.gov

Conducts research on geologically based energy resources of the United States and the world, including assessments of the quality, quantity, and geographic locations of natural gas, oil, gas hydrates, geothermal, and coal resources. Estimates energy resource availability and recoverability, including hydraulic fracturing ("fracking"); and conducts research on the deleterious environmental impacts of energy resource occurence and use.

▶CONGRESS

For a listing of relevant congressional committees and subcommittees, please see pages 240–241 or the Appendix.

Coal

▶AGENCIES

Bureau of Land Management (BLM) *(Interior Dept.), Solid Minerals,* 20 M St. S.E., 20003 (mailing address: 1849 C St. N.W., WO 320, Washington, DC 20240); (202) 912-7112. Fax, (202) 912-7199. Mitchell Leverette, Chief.
General email, mitchell_leverette@blm.gov and mleveret@blm.gov
Web, www.blm.gov/wo/st/en/info/directory/WO-320_dir.html

Evaluates and classifies coal resources on federal lands; develops and administers leasing programs. Supervises coal-mining operations on federal lands; oversees pre- and postlease operations, including production phases of coal development. Oversees implementation of the Mining Law of 1872 and the Mineral Materials Act of 1955.

Energy Information Administration (EIA) *(Energy Dept.), Electricity, Coal, Nuclear, and Renewable Analysis,* 1000 Independence Ave. S.W., #2H073, EI-50, 20585; (202) 586-2432. Jim Diefenderfer, Director.
Web, www.eia.gov

Collects data, compiles statistics, and prepares analyses and forecasts on domestic coal supply, including availability, production, costs, processing, transportation, and distribution. Publishes data on the export and import of coal; makes forecasts and provides analyses on coal imports and exports.

Federal Mine Safety and Health Review Commission, 1331 Pennsylvania Ave. N.W., #520N, 20004-1710; (202) 434-9905. Fax, (202) 434-9906. Lisa Boyd, Executive Director; Mary Lu Jordan, Chair. TTY, (202) 434-4000, ext. 293.
General email, fmshrc@fmshrc.gov
Web, www.fmshrc.gov

Independent agency established by the Federal Mine Safety and Health Act of 1977. Holds fact-finding hearings and issues orders affirming, modifying, or vacating the labor secretary's enforcement actions regarding mine safety and health. Reading room open to the public by appointment.

Interior Dept. (DOI), *Surface Mining Reclamation and Enforcement,* 1951 Constitution Ave. N.W., #233, 20240; (202) 208-4006. Fax, (202) 219-3106. Joseph G. Pizarchik, Director. Press, (202) 208-2565. TTY, (202) 208-2694.
General email, getinfo@osmre.gov
Web, www.osmre.gov

Administers the Surface Mining Control and Reclamation Act of 1977. Establishes and enforces national standards for the regulation and reclamation of surface coal mining and the surface effects of underground coal mining; oversees state implementation of these standards.

Mine Safety and Health Administration *(Labor Dept.),* 201 12th St. South, Arlington, VA 22202; (202) 693-9400. Fax, (202) 693-9801. Joseph A. Main, Assistant Secretary.

General email, ASKMSHA@dol.gov

Web, www.msha.gov

Administers and enforces the health and safety provisions of the Federal Mine Safety and Health Act of 1977. Monitors underground mining and processing operations of minerals, including minerals used in construction materials; produces educational materials in engineering; and assists with rescue operations following mining accidents.

▶NONGOVERNMENTAL

American Coal Foundation, 101 Constitution Ave. N.W., #500 East, 20001-2133; (202) 463-9785. Fax, (202) 463-9786. Alma Paty, Executive Director.

General email, info@teachcoal.org

Web, www.teachcoal.org

Provides coal-related educational materials designed for elementary school teachers and students. Web site provides free coal sample kits. Supported by coal producers and manufacturers of mining equipment and supplies.

American Coke and Coal Chemicals Institute, 25 Massachusetts Ave. N.W., #800, 20001; (724) 772-1167. Fax, (866) 422-7794. David C. Ailor, President.

General email, information@accci.org

Web, www.accci.org

Membership: producers of metallurgical coke and coal; tar distillers and coal chemical producers; coke and coal brokers; equipment, materials, and service suppliers to the coke industry; builders of coke ovens and coke byproduct plants. Maintains committees on coke, coal chemicals, manufacturing, environment, safety and health, human resources, quality, governmental relations, and international affairs.

Assn. of Bituminous Contractors, Inc., 2401 Pennsylvania Ave., #350, 20037; (202) 522-8700. Fax, (202) 331-8049. William H. Howe, General Counsel.

Membership: independent and general contractors that build coal mines. Represents members before the Federal Mine Safety and Health Review Commission and in collective bargaining with the United Mine Workers of America.

Bituminous Coal Operators' Assn., 1776 Eye St. N.W., #245, 20006; (202) 783-3195. Michael O. McKown, President.

General email, lpatrickbcoa@aol.com

Membership: firms that mine bituminous coal. Represents members in collective bargaining with the United Mine Workers of America.

Coal Technologies Associates, P.O. Box 1130, Louisa, VA 23093; (540) 603-2022. Barbara A. Sakkestad, President, (240) 751-0900.

General email, barbarasak@aol.com

Web, www.coaltechnologies.com

Membership: business professionals interested in energy (coal technology), economic, and environmental policies and regulations. Seeks to improve coal utilization technologies and to develop coal-cleaning technologies. Facilitates the exchange of technical information on coal technologies through annual international conference.

National Coal Council, 1101 Pennsylvania Ave. N.W., #600, 20004; (202) 756-4524. Fax, (202) 756-7323. Janet Gellici, Chief Executive Officer.

General email, info@ncc1.org

Web, www.nationalcoalcouncil.org

Membership: individuals appointed by the secretary of energy. Represents coal consumers and producers, transporters, engineering firms, equipment and supply vendors, academics, consultants, NGOs, and public officials. Monitors federal policies.

National Mining Assn., 101 Constitution Ave. N.W., #500 East, 20001-2133; (202) 463-2600. Fax, (202) 463-2666. Harold P. Quinn Jr., President. Press, (202) 463-2642.

General email, webmaster@nma.org

Web, www.nma.org

Membership: coal producers, coal sales and transportation companies, equipment manufacturers, consulting firms, coal resource developers and exporters, coal-burning electric utility companies, and other energy companies. Collects, analyzes, and distributes industry statistics; conducts special studies of competitive fuels, coal markets, production and consumption forecasts, and industry planning. Interests include exports, coal leasing programs, coal transportation, environmental issues, health and safety, national energy policy, slurry pipelines, and research and development, including synthetic fuels. Monitors legislation and regulation. (Merged with Coal Exporters Assn. of the United States.)

United Mine Workers of America, 18354 Quantico Gateway Dr., #200, Triangle, VA 22172-1779; (703) 291-2400. Cecil E. Roberts, President.

Web, www.umwa.org

Membership: coal miners and other mining workers. Represents members in collective bargaining with industry. Conducts educational, housing, and health and safety training programs; monitors federal coal-mining safety programs.

Oil and Natural Gas

▶AGENCIES

Bureau of Land Management (BLM) *(Interior Dept.),* *Fluid Minerals,* 20 M St. S.E., 20003 (mailing address: 20 M St. S.E., #2134LM, Washington, DC 20003); (202) 912-7162. Fax, (202) 912-7194. Steven Wells, Division Chief.

Web, www.blm.gov/wo/st/en/info/directory/WO-310_dir.html

Evaluates and classifies oil, natural gas, and geothermal resources on federal lands; develops and administers leasing programs. Supervises extraction of oil (including from oil shale deposits), natural gas, and geothermal energy resources on federal lands; oversees prelease and postlease operations, including production phases of oil and natural gas development; oversees federal land-leasing reforms.

Bureau of Ocean Energy Management (BOEM) *(Interior Dept.), Strategic Resources, 1849 C St. N.W., MS DM5238, 20240; (202) 208-3515. Fax, (202) 513-0775. L. Renee Orr, Chief, (202) 208-3515.*
General email, boempublicaffairs@boem.gov

Web, www.boem.gov

Develops and implements the Five-Year Outer Continental Shelf (OCS) Oil and Natural Gas Leasing Program; oversees assessments and inventories of the oil, gas, and other mineral resources. Conveys access to marine minerals; maintains official maps and geographic data; conducts economic evaluations that ensure fair market value for OCS leases. Leads efforts to identify and mitigate the financial risks associated with offshore lease activities.

Bureau of Safety and Environmental Enforcement (BSEE) *(Interior Dept.), 1849 C St. N.W., MS DM5438, 20240-0001; (202) 208-3985. Fax, (202) 208-3968. Brian Salerno, Director.*
General email, bseepublicaffairs@bsee.gov

Web, www.bsee.gov and Twitter, @BSEEgov

Responsible for inspections, enforcement, and safety of offshore oil and gas operations. Functions include the development and enforcement of safety and environmental regulations, research, inspections, offshore regulatory and compliance programs, oil spill response, and training of inspectors and industry professionals.

Bureau of Safety and Environmental Enforcement (BSEE) *(Interior Dept.), Offshore Regulatory Programs, 1849 C St. N.W., MS DM5438, 20240-0001; (202) 208-3985. Fax, (202) 208-3968. Douglas Morris, Chief.*
General email, bseepublicaffairs@bsee.gov

Web, www.bsee.gov

Develops standards, regulations, and compliance programs governing Outer Continental Shelf oil, gas, and minerals exploration and operations. Purview includes safety management programs, safety and pollution prevention research, technology assessments, standards for inspections and enforcement policies, and accident investigation practices.

Energy Information Administration (EIA) *(Energy Dept.), Petroleum and Biofuel Statistics, 1000 Independence Ave. S.W., #BG041, 20585; (202) 586-1831. Douglas M. MacIntyre, Director.*
General email, infoctr@eia.doe.gov

Web, www.eia.gov/about/eia_offices.cfm

Collects, compiles, interprets, and publishes data on domestic production, distribution, and prices of crude oil and refined petroleum products; analyzes and projects availability of petroleum supplies.

Fossil Energy *(Energy Dept.), Oil and Natural Gas, 1000 Independence Ave. S.W., #3E028, 20585; (202) 586-5600. Fax, (202) 586-6221. Guido DeHoratiis, Associate Deputy Assistant Secretary.*
Web, www.fe.doe.gov

Responsible for research and development programs in oil and gas exploration, production, processing, and storage; studies ways to improve efficiency of oil recovery in depleted reservoirs; coordinates and evaluates research and development among government, universities, and industrial research organizations.

Fossil Energy *(Energy Dept.), Petroleum Reserves, Forrestal Bldg., 1000 Independence Ave. S.W., FE-40, 20585; (202) 586-4410. Robert Corbin, Deputy Assistant Secretary, (202) 586-9460.*
Web, www.energy.gov/fe/services/petroleum-reserves

Manages programs that provide the United States with strategic and economic protection against disruptions in oil supplies, including the Strategic Petroleum Reserves, the Northeast Home Heating Oil Reserve, and the Naval Petroleum and the Northeast Gasoline Supply Reserve.

Internal Revenue Service (IRS) *(Treasury Dept.), Passthroughs and Special Industries, Excise Tax Branch, 1111 Constitution Ave. N.W., #5314, 20224; (202) 317-3100. Stephanie Bland, Chief.*
Web, www.irs.gov

Administers excise tax programs, including taxes on diesel, gasoline, and special fuels. Advises district offices, internal IRS offices, and general inquirers on tax policy, rules, and regulations.

▶ **NONGOVERNMENTAL**

Air-Conditioning, Heating, and Refrigeration Institute (AHRI), *2111 Wilson Blvd., #500, Arlington, VA 22201; (703) 524-8800. Fax, (703) 562-1942. Stephen R. Yurek, President.*
General email, ahri@ahrinet.org

Web, www.ahrinet.org

Represents manufacturers of central air conditioning and commercial refrigeration equipment. Develops product performance rating standards and administers programs to verify manufacturers' certified ratings.

American Fuel & Petrochemical Manufacturers, *1667 K St. N.W., #700, 20006-1605; (202) 457-0480. Fax, (202) 457-0486. Chet Thompson, President.*
General email, info@afpm.org

Web, www.afpm.org

Membership: petroleum, petrochemical, and refining companies. Interests include allocation, imports, refining technology, petrochemicals, and environmental regulations.

American Gas Assn., *400 N. Capitol St. N.W., #450, 20001-1535; (202) 824-7000. Fax, (202) 824-7115. Dave McCurdy, President. Press, (202) 824-7027.*
Web, www.aga.org

Membership: natural gas utilities and pipeline companies. Interests include all technical and operational aspects of the gas industry. Publishes comprehensive statistical record of the gas industry; conducts national standard testing for gas appliances. Advocates policies that are favorable to increased supplies and lower prices. Monitors legislation and regulations.

American Petroleum Institute, *1220 L St. N.W., 12th Floor, 20005-4070; (202) 682-8000. Fax, (202) 682-8110. Jack N. Gerard, President. Press, (202) 682-8114. Web, www.api.org and Twitter, @EnegyTomorrow*

Membership: producers, refiners, marketers, pipeline operators, and transporters of oil, natural gas, and related products such as gasoline. Provides information on the industry, including data on exports and imports, taxation, transportation, weekly refinery operations and inventories, and drilling activity and costs; conducts research on petroleum and publishes statistical and drilling reports. Develops equipment and operating standards. Certifies compliance of equipment manufacturing and of environmental and occupational safety and health management systems.

American Public Gas Assn. (APGA), *201 Massachusetts Ave. N.E., #C4, 20002-4988; (202) 464-2742. Fax, (202) 464-0246. Bert Kalisch, President. General email, apga@apga.org Web, www.apga.org and Twitter, @APGA*

Membership: municipally owned gas distribution systems. Provides information on federal developments affecting natural gas. Promotes efficiency and works to protect the interests of public gas systems. Sponsors workshops and conferences.

Center for Liquefied Natural Gas, *1620 Eye St. N.W., #700, 20006; (202) 289-2253. Fax, (202) 962-4753. Charlie Riedl, Executive Director. Web, www.LNGfacts.org and Twitter, @LNGfacts*

Membership: liquefied natural gas producers, shippers, terminal operators and developers, and energy trade associations. Provides general and technical information on liquefied natural gas. Monitors legislation and regulations.

Compressed Gas Assn., *14501 George Carter Way, #103, Chantilly, VA 20151; (703) 788-2700. Fax, (703) 961-1831. Michael Tiller, President. General email, cga@cganet.com Web, www.cganet.com*

Membership: all segments of the compressed gas industry, including producers and distributors of compressed and liquefied gases. Promotes and coordinates technical development and standardization of the industry. Monitors legislation and regulations.

Gas Technology Institute (GTI), *Policy and Regulatory Affairs, 655 15th St. N.W., #420, 20005-3355; (202) 661-8650. Richard Kaelin, Executive Director, Washington Operations. Alternate phone, (847) 768-0511.*

General email, washingtonops@gastechnology.org Web, www.gastechnology.org and Twitter, @GasTechnology

Membership: all segments of the natural gas industry, including producers, pipelines, and distributors. Conducts research and develops new technology for gas customers and the industry. (Headquarters in Des Plaines, Ill.)

Independent Petroleum Assn. of America, *1201 15th St. N.W., #300, 20005-2842; (202) 857-4722. Fax, (202) 857-4799. Barry Russell, President. Web, www.ipaa.org*

Membership: independent oil and gas producers; land and royalty owners; and others with interests in domestic exploration, development, and production of oil and natural gas. Interests include leasing, prices and taxation, foreign trade, environmental restrictions, and improved recovery methods.

International Assn. of Drilling Contractors (IADC), *Government and Regulatory Affairs, 1667 K St. N.W., #420, 20006; (202) 293-0670. Fax, (202) 872-0047. Elizabeth Craddock, Vice President. General email, info@iadc.org Web, www.iadc.org*

Membership: drilling contractors, oil and gas producers, and others in the industry worldwide. Promotes safe exploration and production of hydrocarbons, advances in drilling technology, and preservation of the environment. Monitors legislation and regulations. (Headquarters in Houston, Tex.)

International Liquid Terminals Assn. (ILTA), *1005 N. Glebe Rd., #600, Arlington, VA 22201; (703) 875-2011. Fax, (703) 875-2018. Melinda Whitney, President. General email, info@ilta.org Web, www.ilta.org*

Membership: commercial operators of for-hire bulk liquid terminals and tank storage facilities, including those for crude oil and petroleum. Promotes the safe and efficient handling of various types of bulk liquid commodities. Sponsors workshops and seminars and publishes directories. Monitors legislation and regulations.

National Ocean Industries Assn., *1120 G St. N.W., #900, 20005; (202) 347-6900. Fax, (202) 347-8650. Randall Luthi, President. General email, noia@noia.org Web, www.noia.org*

Membership: manufacturers, producers, suppliers, and support and service companies involved in marine, offshore, and ocean work. Interests include offshore oil and gas supply and production, pursuit of offshore renewable-energy opportunities, environmental safeguards, equipment supply, gas transmission, navigation, research and technology, and shipyards.

National Petroleum Council, *1625 K St. N.W., #600, 20006-1656; (202) 393-6100. Fax, (202) 331-8539. Marshall W. Nichols, Executive Director; Charles D. Davidson, Chair.*

General email, info@npc.org

Web, www.npc.org

Federally chartered, privately funded advisory committee to the secretary of energy on matters relating to the petroleum industry, including oil and natural gas. Publishes reports concerning technical aspects of the oil and gas industries.

National Propane Gas Assn., *1899 L St. N.W., #350, 20036-4623; (202) 466-7200. Fax, (202) 466-7205. Richard R. Roldan, President, (202) 355-1388.*

General email, info@npga.org

Web, www.npga.org

Membership: retail marketers, producers, wholesale distributors, appliance and equipment manufacturers, equipment fabricators, and distributors and transporters of liquefied petroleum gas. Conducts research, safety, and educational programs; provides statistics on the industry.

National Research Council (NRC), *Gulf Research Program, Keck Center, 500 5th St. N.W., 20001; (202) 334-2000. Chris Elfring, Executive Director.*

Web, nationalacademies.org/gulf

Promotes oil system safety and the protection of human health and the environment in the Gulf of Mexico and other U.S. outer continental shelf areas.

Natural Gas Supply Assn., *1620 Eye St. N.W., #700, 20006; (202) 326-9300. Fax, (202) 326-9308. Dena Wiggins, President.*

Web, www.ngsa.org

Membership: major and independent producers of domestic natural gas. Interests include the production, consumption, marketing, and regulation of natural gas. Monitors legislation and regulations.

NGVAmerica (Natural Gas Vehicles for America), *400 N. Capitol St. N.W., 20001; (202) 824-7360. Fax, (202) 824-9160. Matthew Godlewski, President; Paul Kerkhoven, Director, Government Affairs.*

General email, pkerkhoven@ngvamerica.org

Web, www.ngvamerica.org

Membership: natural gas distributors and producers; automobile and engine manufacturers; natural gas vehicle product and service suppliers; research and development organizations; enviromental groups; and state and local government agencies. Advocates installation of natural gas and biomethane fuel stations and development of industry standards. Helps market new products and equipment related to compressed natural gas (CNG), liquefied natural gas (LNG), and biomethane-powered vehicles.

Oil Change International, *714 G St. S.E., #202, 20003; (202) 518-9029. Fax, (202) 330-5952. Stephen Kretzmann, Executive Director. Press, (202) 316-3499.*

General email, info@priceofoil.org

Web, www.priceofoil.org

Advocates national and global clean energy policies with a focus on fossil fuels. Researches the fossil fuel industry and publishes reports aimed to debate the use of oil, gas, and coal. Campaigns against fossil fuel developments.

Petroleum Marketers Assn. of America (PMAA), *1901 N. Fort Myer Dr., #500, Arlington, VA 22209-1604; (703) 351-8000. Fax, (703) 351-9160. Rob Underwood, President.*

General email, info@pmaa.org

Web, www.pmaa.org

Membership: state and regional associations representing independent branded and nonbranded marketers of petroleum products. Provides information on all aspects of petroleum marketing. Monitors legislation and regulations.

Service Station Dealers of America and Allied Trades, *1532 Pointer Ridge Pl., Suite G, Bowie, MD 20716; (301) 390-4405. Fax, (301) 390-3161. Billy Hillmulth, Vice President, (301) 390-0900.*

General email, mgates@wmda.net

Web, www.ssda-at.com

Membership: state associations of gasoline retailers, repair facilities, car washes, and convenience stores. Interests include environmental issues, retail marketing, oil allocation, imports and exports, prices, and taxation. Monitors legislation and regulations.

Society of Independent Gasoline Marketers of America (SIGMA), *3930 Pender Dr., #340, Fairfax, VA 22030-0985; (703) 709-7000. Fax, (703) 709-7007. Ryan McNutt, Chief Executive Officer.*

General email, sigma@sigma.org

Web, www.sigma.org

Membership: marketers and wholesalers of brand and nonbrand gasoline. Seeks to ensure adequate supplies of gasoline at competitive prices. Monitors legislation and regulations affecting gasoline supply and price.

Pipelines

▶ **AGENCIES**

Federal Energy Regulatory Commission (FERC) *(Energy Dept.), Energy Market Regulation, 888 1st St. N.E., #8A-01, 20426; (202) 502-6700. Fax, (202) 208-0193. Jamie L. Simler, Director.*

Web, www.ferc.gov/about/offices/oemr.asp

Establishes and enforces maximum rates and charges for oil and natural gas pipelines; establishes oil pipeline operating rules; issues certificates for and regulates construction, sale, and acquisition of natural gas pipeline facilities. Ensures compliance with the Natural Gas Policy Act, the Natural Gas Act, and other statutes.

National Transportation Safety Board (NTSB), *Railroad, Pipeline, and Hazardous Materials Investigations, 490 L'Enfant Plaza East S.W., 20594; (202) 314-6463. Fax, (202) 688-2569. Robert Hall, Director. Press, (202) 314-6100.*

Web, www.ntsb.gov/about/organization/RPHM

Nuclear Regulatory Commission

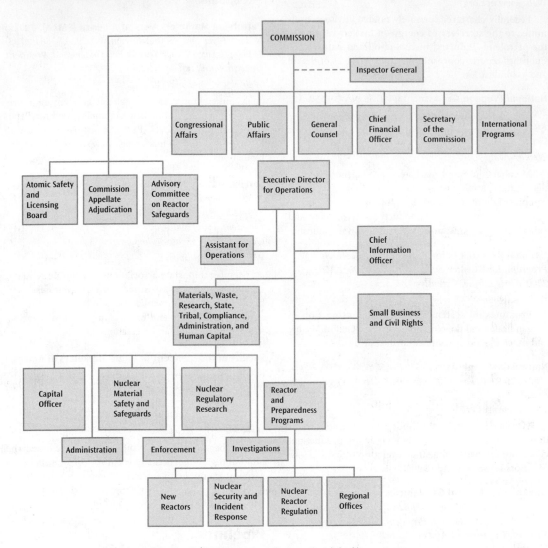

– – – Indicates a support or advisory relationship with the unit rather than a direct reporting relationship

Investigates hazardous materials and petroleum pipeline accidents.

Pipeline and Hazardous Materials Safety Administration *(Transportation Dept.), Hazardous Materials Safety, 1200 New Jersey Ave. S.E., #E21-317, 20590; (202) 366-0656. Fax, (202) 366-5713. Magdy A. El-Sibaie, Associate Administrator. Hazardous Materials Information Center, (800) 467-4922.*
General email, phmsa.hmhazmatsafety@dot.gov

Web, http://hazmat.dot.gov

Designates fuels, chemicals, and other substances as hazardous materials and regulates their transportation in interstate commerce. Provides technical assistance on hazardous waste materials transportation safety and security to state and local governments. Gathers and analyzes incident data from carriers transporting hazardous materials.

Pipeline and Hazardous Materials Safety Administration *(Transportation Dept.), Pipeline Safety, 1200 New Jersey Ave. S.E., E24-455, 20590; (202) 366-4595. Fax, (202) 366-4566. Jeffery D. Wiese, Associate Administrator.*
General email, phmsa.pipelinesafety@dot.gov

Web, http://phmsa.dot.gov

Issues and enforces federal regulations for oil, natural gas, and petroleum products pipeline safety. Inspects pipelines and oversees risk management by pipeline operators.

▶ **NONGOVERNMENTAL**

Assn. of Oil Pipe Lines (AOPL), *1808 Eye St. N.W., #300, 20006; (202) 408-7970. Fax, (202) 280-1949. Andrew J. Black, President.*

General email, aopl@aopl.org

Web, www.aopl.org

Membership: owners and operators of oil pipelines. Analyzes industry statistics. Monitors legislation and regulations.

Interstate Natural Gas Assn. of America, *20 F St. N.W., #450, 20001; (202) 216-5900. Donald F. Santa Jr., President. Press, (202) 216-5913.*

Web, www.ingaa.org

Membership: U.S. interstate, Canadian, and Mexican interprovincial natural gas pipeline companies. Commissions studies and provides information on the natural gas pipeline industry.

NUCLEAR ENERGY

General

▶AGENCIES

Energy Information Administration (EIA) *(Energy Dept.), Electricity, Coal, Nuclear, and Renewable Analysis, 1000 Independence Ave. S.W., #2H073, EI50, 20585; (202) 586-2432. Jim Diefenderfer, Director.*

Web, www.eia.gov

Prepares analyses and forecasts on the availability, production, prices, processing, transportation, and distribution of nuclear energy, both domestically and internationally. Collects and publishes data concerning the uranium supply and market.

Nuclear Regulatory Commission, *11555 Rockville Pike, MS 016G4, Rockville, MD 20852; (301) 415-7000. Fax, (301) 415-3504. Stephen G. Burns, Chair; Victor M. McCree, Executive Director for Operations; Hubert T. Bell, Inspector General; Eugene Dacus, Director, Congressional Affairs; Eliot Bremer, Director, Public Affairs, (301) 415-8200. Press, (301) 415-8200. Toll-free, (800) 368-5642. TTY, (301) 415-5575. Public Document Room, (301) 397-1209. 24-hour emergency, (301) 816-5100. Fraud, waste, and abuse hotline, (800) 233-3497. Safety & Security, (800) 695-7403.*

General email, opa@nrc.gov

Web, www.nrc.gov

Regulates commercial uses of nuclear energy; responsibilities include licensing, inspection, and enforcement; monitors and regulates the imports and exports of nuclear material and equipment.

Nuclear Regulatory Commission, *Public Affairs, 11555 Rockville Pike, MS 016D3, Rockville, MD 20852-2738; (301) 415-8200. Fax, (301) 415-3716. Eliot B. Brenner, Director.*

General email, opa.resource@nrc.gov

Web, www.nrc.gov/about-nrc/public-affairs.html

Provides the public and the news media with information about the Nuclear Regulatory Commission's programs, policy decisions, and activities, primarily through social media and by issuing news releases and distributing commission speeches, fact sheets, and brochures. Follows news coverage of the agency and responds to media and public inquiries.

Tennessee Valley Authority, *Government Affairs, 1 Massachusetts Ave. N.W., #300, 20444; (202) 898-2999. Fax, (202) 898-2998. Nick Pearson, Director.*

General email, tvainfo@tva.gov

Web, www.tva.gov

Coordinates resource conservation, development, and land-use programs in the Tennessee River Valley. Produces and supplies wholesale power to municipal and cooperative electric systems, federal installations, and some industries; interests include nuclear power generation.

▶CONGRESS

For a listing of relevant congressional committees and subcommittees, please see pages 240–241 or the Appendix.

▶NONGOVERNMENTAL

American Physical Society, *Washington Office, 529 14th St. N.W., #1050, 20045-2065; (202) 662-8700. Fax, (202) 662-8711. Michael Lubell, Director, Public Affairs. Press Secretary, (202) 662-8702.*

General email, opa@aps.org

Web, www.aps.org and Twitter, @APSphysics

Scientific and educational society of educators, students, citizens, and scientists, including industrial scientists. Sponsors studies on issues of public concern related to physics, such as reactor safety and energy use. Informs members of national and international developments. (Headquarters in College Park, Md.)

Nuclear Energy Institute, *1201 F St. N.W., #1100, 20004; (202) 739-8000. Fax, (202) 785-4019. Marvin S. Fertel, President.*

General email, NEIGA_Nuclearenergy@nei.org

Media email, media@nei.org

Web, www.nei.org

Membership: utilities; industries; labor, service, and research organizations; law firms; universities; and government agencies interested in peaceful uses of nuclear energy, including the generation of electricity. Acts as a spokesperson for the nuclear power industry; provides information on licensing and plant siting, research and development, safety and security, waste disposal, and legislative and policy issues.

Nuclear Information and Resource Service, *6930 Carroll Ave., #340, Takoma Park, MD 20912-4446; (301) 270-6477. Fax, (301) 270-4291. Timothy Judson, Executive Director.*

General email, nirsnet@nirs.org

Web, www.nirs.org

Information and networking clearinghouse for environmental activists and other individuals concerned about nuclear power plants, radioactive waste, and radiation and sustainable energy issues. Initiates large-scale organizing and public education campaigns and provides technical and strategic expertise to environmental groups. Library open to the public by appointment.

Public Citizen, *Energy Program,* 215 Pennsylvania Ave. S.E., 20003-1155; (202) 546-4996. Tyson Slocum, Director. General email, energy@citizen.org

Web, www.citizen.org/cmep

Public interest group that promotes energy efficiency and renewable energy technologies; opposes nuclear energy. Interests include nuclear plant safety and energy policy issues.

Union of Concerned Scientists, *Global Security,* 1825 K St. N.W., #800, 20006-1232; (202) 223-6133. Fax, (202) 223-6162. David Wright, Co-Director; Lisbeth Gronlund, Co-Director. General email, ucs@ucsusa.org

Web, www.ucsusa.org

An independent public interest group of scientists and citizens concerned with U.S. energy policy, including nuclear energy economics and power plant safety and security. Monitors the performance of nuclear power plants and their regulators; evaluates the economics of nuclear power relative to other low-carbon energy resources. (Headquarters in Cambridge, Mass.)

Licensing and Plant Siting

▶AGENCIES

Federal Emergency Management Agency (FEMA) *(Homeland Security Dept.), Protection and National Preparedness, Technological Hazards,* 1800 S. Bell St., MS 3025, Arlington, VA 22202; (202) 646-3158. Fax, (703) 308-0324. Timothy Greten, Director, Acting, (202) 646-2618. Web, www.fema.gov/technological-hazards-division

Reviews off-site preparedness for commercial nuclear power facilities; evaluates emergency plans before plant licensing and submits findings to the Nuclear Regulatory Commission.

Nuclear Regulatory Commission, *New Reactors,* 11545 Rockville Pike, MS T6F15, Rockville, MD 20852; (301) 415-1897. Fax, (301) 415-6323. Jennifer Uhle, Director. Web, www.nrc.gov/about-nrc/organization/ nrofuncdesc.html

Licenses and regulates nuclear power plants that use new designs; approves siting of new plants.

Nuclear Regulatory Commission, *Nuclear Material Safety and Safeguards (NMSS),* 11555 Rockville Pike, Rockville, MD 20852; (301) 415-7000. Fax, (301) 415-0020. Scott Moore, Director, Acting. Web, www.nrc.gov/about-nrc/organization/ nmssfuncdesc.html

Licenses all nuclear facilities and materials except power reactors; directs principal licensing and regulation activities for the management of nuclear waste.

Nuclear Regulatory Commission, *Nuclear Reactor Regulation,* 11555 Rockville Pike, MS O13H16M, Rockville, MD 20852; (301) 415-1270. Fax, (301) 415-8333. William Dean, Director. Web, www.nrc.gov/about-nrc/organization/ nrrfuncdesc.html

Licenses nuclear power plants and operators.

Research and Development

▶AGENCIES

Nuclear Energy *(Energy Dept.),* 1000 Independence Ave. S.W., #5A143, E-1, 20585; (202) 586-2240. Fax, (202) 586-0544. John Kotek, Assistant Secretary, Acting. Web, www.nuclear.energy.gov/ne/office-nuclear-energy

Responsible for nuclear technology research and development, management of the Energy Dept.'s nuclear technology infrastructure, uranium activities, and fuel cycle issues. Supports nuclear education, including university reactor instrumentation and equipment upgrades and general support to nuclear engineering programs at U.S. universities. Leads U.S. participation in the Global Nuclear Energy Partnership, which seeks to demonstrate a more proliferation-resistant closed fuel cycle and increase the safety and security of nuclear energy.

Nuclear Energy *(Energy Dept.), International Nuclear Energy Policy and Cooperation,* 1000 Independence Ave. S.W., #5A-143, 20585; (202) 586-5253. Fax, (202) 586-8353. Edward G. McGinnis, Deputy Assistant Secretary. Web, www.energy.gov/ne/nuclear-reactor-technologies/ international-nuclear-energy-policy-and-cooperation

Responsible for the Energy Dept.'s international civilian nuclear energy activities, including research, development and demonstration cooperation, international framework and partnership development, and international nuclear energy policy.

Nuclear Regulatory Commission, *Nuclear Regulatory Research,* 11555 Rockville Pike, 2 White Flat, Rockville, MD 20952; (301) 251-7400. Fax, (301) 251-7426. Michael F. Weber, Director. Web, www.nrc.gov/about-nrc/organization/ resfuncdesc.html

Plans, recommends, and implements nuclear regulatory research, standards development, and resolution of safety issues for nuclear power plants and other facilities regulated by the Nuclear Regulatory Commission; develops and promulgates all technical regulations.

Office of Science *(Energy Dept.), Fusion Energy Sciences,* 19901 Germantown Rd., #SC24, Germantown, MD 20874-1290 (mailing address: Germantown Bldg., 1000 Independence Ave. S.W., #SC24, Washington, DC 20585); (301) 903-4941. Fax, (301) 903-8584. Edmund J. Synakowski, Associate Director. Web, http://science.energy.gov/fes

Conducts research and development on fusion energy for electric power generation.

▶NONGOVERNMENTAL

National Research Council (NRC), *Nuclear and Radiation Studies Board,* Keck Center, 500 5th St. N.W., 20001; (202) 334-3066. Fax, (202) 334-3077. Kevin Crowley, Senior Board Director; Robert C. Dynes, Chair.
General email, nrsb@nas.edu

Web, http://dels.nas.edu/nrsb

Oversees studies on safety, security, technical efficacy, and other policy and societal issues arising from the application of nuclear and radiation-based technologies, including exposure to radiation; generation, use, remediation, and disposition of nuclear materials and radioactive wastes; malevolent uses of nuclear and radiation-based technologies; and risks and benefits of nuclear and radiation-based applications, including medical applications.

Safety, Security, and Waste Disposal

▶AGENCIES

Defense Nuclear Facilities Safety Board, 625 Indiana Ave. N.W., #700, 20004-2901; (202) 694-7080. Fax, (202) 208-6518. Joyce L. Connery, Chair; Jessie H. Roberson, Vice Chair. Information, (202) 694-7000.
General email, mailbox@dnfsb.gov

Web, www.dnfsb.gov

Independent board created by Congress and appointed by the president to provide external oversight of Energy Dept. defense nuclear weapons production facilities and make recommendations to the secretary of energy regarding public health and safety.

Energy Information Administration (EIA) *(Energy Dept.), Electricity, Coal, Nuclear, and Renewable Analysis,* 1000 Independence Ave. S.W., #2H073, EI-50, 20585; (202) 586-2432. Jim Diefenderfer, Director.
Web, www.eia.gov

Directs collection of spent fuel data and validation of spent nuclear fuel discharge data for the Civilian Radioactive Waste Management Office.

Environment, Health, Safety, and Security *(Energy Dept.),* 1000 Independence Ave. S.W., #7G040, 20585; (202) 586-4399. Fax, (202) 586-5605. Matthew Moury, Associate Under Secretary.
General email, AVusersupport@hq.doe.gov

Web, www.energy.gov/ehss/environment-health-safety-security

Develops policy and establishes standards to ensure safety and health protection in all department activities. Coordinates and integrates health, safety, environment, and security enforcement and independent oversight programs at the Energy Dept. Responsible for policy development, technical assistance, safety analysis, education, and training.

Environment, Health, Safety, and Security *(Energy Dept.), Environmental Protection, Sustainability*

Support, and Corporate Safety Analysis, 1000 Independence Ave. S.W., #6B-128, 20585; (202) 586-5680. Fax, (202) 586-7330. Dr. Michael Silverman, Director, Acting.
Web, www.energy.gov/ehss/office-environmental-protection-sustainability-support-and-corporate-safety-analysis

Establishes policies and guidance for environmental protection and compliance; provides technical assistance to departmental program and field offices in complying with environmental requirements.

Environment, Health, Safety, and Security *(Energy Dept.), Health and Safety,* 1000 Independence Ave. S.W., HS-10-GTN, 20585; (301) 903-5926. Fax, (301) 903-3445. Patricia R. Worthington, Director.
Web, http://energy.gov/ehss/organizational-chart/office-health-and-safety

Establishes hazardous material worker safety and health requirements and expectations for the Energy Dept. and assists in their implementation. Conducts and supports domestic and international hazardous material health studies and programs. Supports the Labor Dept. in the implementation of the Energy Employees Occupational Illness Compensation Program Act (EEOICPA).

Environmental Management *(Energy Dept.), Disposal Operations,* 1000 Independence Ave. S.W., #EM-31, 20585; (301) 903-7212. Fax, (301) 903-7236. Douglas Tonkay, Director. DOE switchboard, (202) 586-5000. Office of Environmental Management, (202) 586-7709.
General email, douglas.tonkay.em.does.gov

Web, www.em.doe.gov

Manages Energy Dept. programs that treat, stabilize, and dispose of radioactive waste, including that generated from the decontamination and decommissioning of Energy Dept. facilities and sites. Works to develop a reliable national system for low-level waste management and techniques for treatment and immobilization of waste from former nuclear weapons complex sites. Provides technical assistance to states and Regional Disposal Compacts on the safe and effective management of commercially generated wastes.

Environmental Protection Agency (EPA), *Air and Radiation, Radiation and Indoor Air,* 1200 Pennsylvania Ave. N.W., #5426, MC 6608T, 20460; (202) 343-9320. Fax, (202) 564-1408. Mike P. Flynn, Director.
Web, www2.epa.gov/aboutepa/about-office-air-and-radiation-oar#oria

Establishes standards to regulate the amount of radiation discharged into the environment from uranium mining and milling projects, and other activities that result in radioactive emissions; and to ensure the safe disposal of radioactive waste. Fields a Radiological Emergency Response Team to respond to radiological incidents. Oversees the National Air and Radiation Environmental Laboratory in Montgomery, Ala.

Federal Emergency Management Agency (FEMA) *(Homeland Security Dept.),* 500 C St. S.W., 20472; (202) 646-3900. Fax, (202) 212-5889. W. Craig Fugate,

Administrator; Rafael Lemaitre, Public Affairs. Press, (202) 646-3272. Locator, (202) 646-2500. FEMA helpline, (800) 621-3362. TTY, (800) 462-7585. Toll-free, (800) 621-FEMA. Disaster TTY, (800) 427-5593.
General email, femaopa@dhs.gov
Web, www.fema.gov

Assists state and local governments responding to and recovering from natural, technological, and attack-related emergencies, including in communities where accidents at nuclear power facilities have occurred and communities surrounding accidents involving transportation of radio-active materials; operates the National Emergency Training Center. Coordinates emergency preparedness, mitigation, response, and recovery activities, and planning for all federal agencies and departments.

National Transportation Safety Board (NTSB), *Railroad, Pipeline, and Hazardous Materials Investigations, 490 L'Enfant Plaza East S.W., 20594; (202) 314-6463. Fax, (202) 688-2569. Robert Hall, Director. Press, (202) 314-6100.*
Web, www.ntsb.gov/about/organization/RPHM

Investigates accidents involving the transportation of hazardous materials.

Nuclear Energy *(Energy Dept.), Fuel Cycle Research Technologies, 1000 Independence Ave. S.W., #5A-107, 20585; (202) 586-8105. Fax, (202) 586-0541. John Herczeg, Deputy Assistant Secretary; John Dickson, Assistant Administrator.*
Web, www.energy/gov/ne/nuclear-reactor-technologies

Organizes and conducts research and development through five initiatives: Fuel Cycle Options; Advanced Fuels; Separations and Waste Forms; Used Fuel Disposition; and Material Protection, Control, and Accountability Technologies. Seeks to implement safe strategies for management, storage, and permanent disposal solutions.

Nuclear Regulatory Commission, *Advisory Committee on Reactor Safeguards, 11545 Rockville Pike, Rockville, MD 20852 (mailing address: Nuclear Regulatory Commission, MS T2E26, Washington, DC 20555-0001); (301) 415-7360. Fax, (301) 415-5589. Andrea Valentin, Executive Director.*
Web, www.nrc.gov/about-nrc/organization/ acrsfuncdesc.html

Advises the commission on the licensing and operation of production and utilization facilities and related safety issues, the adequacy of proposed reactor safety standards, and technical and policy issues related to the licensing of evolutionary and passive plant designs. Reports on the NRC Safety Research Program. Reviews Energy Dept. nuclear activities and facilities and provides technical advice to the Energy Dept.'s Nuclear Safety Board upon request.

Nuclear Regulatory Commission, *Enforcement, 11555 Rockville Pike, MS O4A 15A, Rockville, MD 20852; (301) 415-2741. Fax, (301) 415-3431. Patricia Holahan, Director. Toll-free hotline, (800) 695-7403. 24-hour operations, (301) 816-5100.*

General email, allegation@nrc.gov
Web, www.nrc.gov/about-nrc/regulatory/enforcement.html

Oversees the development and implementation of policies and programs that enforce the commission's procedures concerning public health and safety. Identifies and takes action against violators.

Nuclear Regulatory Commission, *Investigations, 11555 Rockville Pike, MS O3F1, Rockville, MD 20852; (301) 415-2373. Fax, (301) 415-2370. Kevin Fowler, Director, Acting.*
Web, www.nrc.gov/about-nrc/organization/ oifuncdesc.html

Develops policy, procedures, and standards for investigations of licensees, applicants, and their contractors or vendors concerning wrongdoing. Refers substantiated criminal cases to the Justice Dept. Informs the commission's leadership about investigations concerning public health and safety.

Nuclear Regulatory Commission, *Nuclear Material Safety and Safeguards (NMSS), 11555 Rockville Pike, Rockville, MD 20852; (301) 415-7000. Fax, (301) 415-0020. Scott Moore, Director, Acting.*
Web, www.nrc.gov/about-nrc/organization/ nmssfuncdesc.html

Regulates commercial nuclear reactors; storage, transportation and disposal of high-level radioactive waste and spent nuclear fuel; and the transportation of radioactive materials regulated under the Atomic Energy Act. Develops and implements policies for uranium recovery, conversion, and enrichment activities; fuel fabrication and development; and transportation of nuclear materials, including certification of transport containers and reactor spent fuel storage.

Nuclear Regulatory Commission, *Nuclear Reactor Regulation, 11555 Rockville Pike, MS O13H16M, Rockville, MD 20852; (301) 415-1270. Fax, (301) 415-8333. William Dean, Director.*
Web, www.nrc.gov/about-nrc/organization/ nrrfuncdesc.html

Conducts safety inspections of nuclear reactors. Regulates nuclear materials used or produced at nuclear power plants.

Nuclear Regulatory Commission, *Nuclear Regulatory Research, 11555 Rockville Pike, 2 White Flat, Rockville, MD 20952; (301) 251-7400. Fax, (301) 251-7426. Michael F. Weber, Director.*
Web, www.nrc.gov/about-nrc/organization/ resfuncdesc.html

Plans, recommends, and implements resolution of safety issues for nuclear power plants and other facilities regulated by the Nuclear Regulatory Commission.

Nuclear Regulatory Commission, *Nuclear Security and Incident Response, 11601 Landsdown St., #3WFN09D20, N. Bethesda, MD 20852; (301) 287-3734. Fax, (301) 287-9351. Brian Holian, Director. Emergency, (301) 816-5100. Nonemergency, (800) 695-7403.*

Web, www.nrc.gov/about-nrc/organization/
nsirfuncdesc.html

Evaluates technical issues concerning security at nuclear facilities. Develops and directs the commission's response to incidents. Serves as point of contact with Homeland Security Dept., Energy Dept., Federal Emergency Management Agency, and intelligence and law enforcement offices and other agencies.

Nuclear Waste Technical Review Board, *2300 Clarendon Blvd., #1300, Arlington, VA 22201-3367; (703) 235-4473. Fax, (703) 235-4495. Nigel Mote, Executive Director.*
General email, info@nwtrb.gov

Web, www.nwtrb.gov

Independent board of scientists and engineers nominated by the Academy of Sciences and appointed by the president to review, evaluate, and report on Energy Dept. development of waste disposal systems and repositories for spent fuel and high-level radioactive waste. Oversees siting, packaging, and transportation of waste, in accordance with the amendments to the Nuclear Waste Policy Act of 1987.

Pipeline and Hazardous Materials Safety Administration *(Transportation Dept.), Hazardous Materials Safety, 1200 New Jersey Ave. S.E., #E21-317, 20590; (202) 366-0656. Fax, (202) 366-5713. Magdy A. El-Sibaie, Associate Administrator. Hazardous Materials Information Center, (800) 467-4922.*
General email, phmsa.hmhazmatsafety@dot.gov

Web, http://hazmat.dot.gov

Issues safety regulations and exemptions for the transportation of hazardous materials; works with the International Atomic Energy Agency on standards for international shipments of radioactive materials.

RENEWABLE ENERGIES, ALTERNATIVE FUELS

General

▶**AGENCIES**

Bureau of Energy Resources *(State Dept.), 2201 C St. N.W., #4428, 20520; (202) 647-8543. Mary Warlick, Principal Deputy Assistant Secretary; Amos J. Hochstein, Special Envoy and Coordinator for International Energy Affairs.*
Web, www.state.gov/e/enr and Twitter, @EnergyAtState

Manages the global energy economy through diplomacy between energy producers and consumers, and stimulates the market forces toward the advancement of sustainable, renewable energy sources.

Bureau of Land Management (BLM) *(Interior Dept.), Energy, Minerals, and Realty Management, 1849 C St. N.W., #5625, 20240; (202) 208-4201. Fax, (202) 208-4800. Michael Nedd, Assistant Director.*

General email, mnedd@blm.gov

Web, www.blm.gov/wo/st/en/info/directory/WO_300_dir.html

Develops and administers policy, guidance, and performance oversight for the renewable energy program, including wind, solar, and geothermal energy; the fluid minerals program, including oil, gas, and helium; the solid minerals programs, including mining law, coal, oil shale, and salable minerals; the lands and realty programs; and the Public Land Survey System. Provides national leadership and develops national partnerships with organizations interested in energy, minerals, and realty management. Provides leadership to the Bureau of Land Management's trust management for Indian minerals operations, surveys, and trust patent preparation.

Energy Efficiency and Renewable Energy *(Energy Dept.), 1000 Independence Ave. S.W., #6A013, MS EE1, 20585; (202) 586-9220. Fax, (202) 586-8177. David Danielson, Assistant Secretary. Information, (877) 337-3463. Press, (202) 586-4940.*
General email, eereic@ee.doe.gov

Web, www.energy.gov/eere/office-energy-efficiency-renewable-energy

Develops and manages programs to improve markets for renewable energy sources, including solar, biomass, wind, geothermal, and hydropower, and to increase efficiency of energy use among residential, commercial, transportation, utility, and industrial users. Administers financial and technical assistance for state energy programs, weatherization for low-income households, and implementation of energy conservation measures by schools, hospitals, local governments, and public care institutions and federal facilities.

Energy Information Administration (EIA) *(Energy Dept.), Electricity, Coal, Nuclear, and Renewable Analysis, 1000 Independence Ave. S.W., #2H073, EI50, 20585; (202) 586-2432. Jim Diefenderfer, Director.*
Web, www.eia.gov

Prepares analyses on the availability, production, costs, processing, transportation, and distribution of uranium and alternative energy supplies, including biomass, solar, wind, waste, wood, and alcohol.

Office of Science *(Energy Dept.), Basic Energy Sciences, 19901 Germantown Rd., #SC22, Germantown, MD 20874-1290 (mailing address: Germantown Bldg., 1000 Independence Ave. S.W., #SC22, Washington, DC 20585); (301) 903-3081. Fax, (301) 903-6594. Harriet Kung, Director.*
General email, sc.bes@science.doe.gov

Web, http://science.energy.gov/bes

Supports research to understand, predict, and control matter and energy at electronic, atomic, and molecular levels to provide foundations for new energy technology.

Office of Science *(Energy Dept.), Biological and Environmental Research, Biological Systems Science Division, 19901 Germantown Rd., #SC23.2, Germantown, MD 20874-1290 (mailing address: Germantown Bldg.,*

1000 Independence Ave. S.W., #SC23.2, Washington, DC 20585); (301) 903-5469. Fax, (301) 903-0567.
Todd Anderson, Director.
Web, http://science.energy.gov/ber/research/bssd

Supports research and technology development to achieve predictive systems-level understanding of complex biological systems, including redesign of microbes and plants for sustainable biofuel production, improved carbon storage, and containment remediation.

Office of Science (Energy Dept.), **Biological and Environmental Research, Climate and Environmental Sciences Division,** 19901 Germantown Rd., #SC23.1, Germantown, MD 20874-1290 (mailing address: Germantown Bldg., 1000 Independence Ave. S.W., #SC23.1, Washington, DC 20585); (301) 903-4775.
Gerald Geernaert, Director.
Web, http://science.energy.gov/ber/research/cesd

Supports research on atmospheric systems, terrestrial ecosystems, and subsurface biogeochemistry as well as Earth system modeling and regional and global climate change modeling to improve predictive understanding of Earth's climate and environmental systems in order to inform development of sustainable solutions to energy challenges.

►CONGRESS

For a listing of relevant congressional committees and subcommittees, please see pages 240–241 or the Appendix.

►NONGOVERNMENTAL

American Council on Renewable Energy (ACORE), 1600 K St. N.W., #650, 20006 (mailing address: P.O. Box 33518, Washington, DC 20003); (202) 393-0001. Fax, (202) 393-0606. Gregory Wetstone, President. Media, (202) 777-7584.
General email, info@acore.org

Web, www.acore.org

Membership: professional service firms, government officials, universities, financial institutions, nonprofits, and renewable energy industries and associations. Publishes research to educate the media and the public about renewable electricity, hydrogen, and fuels. Interests include solar power, wind power, biofuels, biomass, geothermal power, marine energy, hydroelectric power, waste-to-energy, and waste heat-to-power.

Biomass Thermal Energy Council (BTEC), 1211 Connecticut Ave. N.W., #650, 20036-2701; (202) 596-3974. Fax, (202) 223-5537. Jeff Serfass, Executive Director.
General email, info@biomassthermal.org

Web, www.biomassthermal.org and Twitter, @BiomassThermal

Membership: biomass fuel producers, appliance manufacturers and distributors, supply chain companies, and nonprofit organizations that seek to advance the use of biomass for heat and other thermal energy applications. Conducts research, public education, and advocacy for the biomass thermal energy industry. Monitors legislation and regulations.

Bipartisan Policy Center, 1225 Eye St. N.W., #1000, 20005-5977; (202) 204-2400. Fax, (202) 318-0876. Jason S. Grumet, President; Julie Anderson, Executive Director.
General email, bipartisaninfo@energycommission.org

Web, www.energycommission.org and Twitter, @BPC_Bipartisan

Researches and acts as advocate for a reduction of oil consumption in the United States. Evaluates policy options and makes recommendations to lawmakers. Monitors legislation and regulations.

Breakthrough Technologies Institute (BTI), 1100 H St. N.W., #800, 20005; (202) 785-4222. Fax, (202) 785-4313. Robert Rose, Executive Director.
General email, info@fuelcells.org

Web, www.btionline.org

Supports technologies that contribute to alternative energies. Works with policymakers to promote alternative fuels for environmental sustainability. Programs include Fuel Cells 2000, Sustainable Transportation, and the Clean Air Institute.

Electric Power Supply Assn., 1401 New York Ave. N.W., #1230, 20005; (202) 628-8200. Fax, (202) 628-8260. John Shelk, President.
Web, www.epsa.org

Membership: companies that generate electricity, steam, and other forms of energy using a broad spectrum of fossil fuel–fired and renewable technologies.

Fuel Cell and Hydrogen Energy Assn., 1211 Connecticut Ave. N.W., #650, 20036; (202) 261-1337.
Morry Markowitz, President.
General email, info@fchea.org

Web, www.fchea.org and Twitter, @FCHEA_News

Membership: industry, small businesses, universities, government agencies, and nonprofit organizations. Promotes use of hydrogen as an energy carrier; fosters the development and application of fuel cell and hydrogen technologies.

Institute for the Analysis of Global Security, 7811 Montrose Rd., #505, Potomac, MD 20854-3363; Gal Luft, Co-Director; Anne Korin, Co-Director. Toll-free, (866) 713-7527.
General email, info@iags.org

Web, www.iags.org

Seeks to promote public awareness of the link between energy and security; explores options for strengthening the world's energy security, including approaches to reducing the strategic importance of oil. Conducts and publishes research; hosts conferences; monitors legislation and regulations.

SRI International, *Washington Office,* 1100 Wilson Blvd., #2800, Arlington, VA 22209; (703) 524-2053. Fax, (703) 247-8569. Peter Kant, Executive Director, (703) 247-8424.
Web, www.sri.com

Conducts energy-related research and development. Interests include power generation, fuel and solar cells, clean energy storage, and advanced batteries. (Headquarters in Menlo Park, Calif.)

Biofuels

▶AGENCIES

Alcohol and Tobacco Tax and Trade Bureau (TTB)
(Treasury Dept.), Regulations and Rulings, 1310 G St. N.W., #200 East, Box 12, 20005; (202) 453-2265. Amy Greenburg, Director.
General email, regulations@ttb.treas.gov
Web, www.ttb.gov

Develops guidelines for regional offices responsible for issuing permits for producing gasohol and other ethyl alcohol fuels, whose uses include heating and operating machinery. Writes and interprets regulations for distilleries that produce ethyl alcohol fuels.

Energy Efficiency and Renewable Energy *(Energy Dept.), Fuel Cells Technologies, 1000 Independence Ave. S.W., #5G082, 20585; (202) 586-3388. Fax, (202) 586-2373. Sunita Satyapal, Director, (202) 586-2336.*
General email, fuelcells@ee.doe.gov
Web, www1.eere.energy.gov/hydrogenandfuelcells

Works with industry, academia, nonprofit institutions, national labs, government agencies, and other Energy Dept. offices to promote the use of fuel cells and related technologies.

Energy Information Administration (EIA) *(Energy Dept.), Petroleum and Biofuel Statistics, 1000 Independence Ave. S.W., #BG041, 20585; (202) 586-1831. Douglas M. MacIntyre, Director.*
General email, infoctr@eia.doe.gov
Web, www.eia.gov/about/eia_offices.cfm

Collects, compiles, interprets, and publishes data on domestic production, distribution, and prices of crude oil and refined petroleum products; analyzes and projects availability of petroleum supplies.

National Institute of Food and Agriculture (NIFA) *(Agriculture Dept.), Institute of Bioenergy, Climate, and Environment, 800 9th St. S.W., #3231, 20024 (mailing address: 1400 Independence Ave. S.W., MS 2210, Washington, DC 20250-2215); (202) 720-4926. Luis Tupas, Deputy Director.*
Web, www.nifa.usda.gov/office/institute-bioenergy-climate-and-environment

Administers programs to address national science priorities that advance energy independence and help agricultural, forest, and range production systems adapt to climate change variables. Provides grants to support the development of sustainable bioenergy production systems, agricultural production systems, and natural resource management activities that are adapted to climate variation and activities that otherwise support sustainable natural resource use.

Office of Science *(Energy Dept.), Biological and Environmental Research, 19901 Germantown Rd., #SC23, Germantown, MD 20874-1290 (mailing address: Germantown Bldg., 1000 Independence Ave. S.W., #SC23, Washington, DC 20585); (301) 903-3251. Fax, (301) 903-5051. Sharlene Weatherwax, Associate Director.*
General email, sc.ber@science.doe.gov
Web, http://science.energy.gov/ber

Advances biological and environmental research and provides scientific user facilities to support innovation in energy security and environmental responsibility.

Office of Science *(Energy Dept.), Biological and Environmental Research, Biological Systems Science Division, 19901 Germantown Rd., #SC23.2, Germantown, MD 20874-1290 (mailing address: Germantown Bldg., 1000 Independence Ave. S.W., #SC23.2, Washington, DC 20585); (301) 903-5469. Fax, (301) 903-0567. Todd Anderson, Director.*
Web, http://science.energy.gov/ber/research/bssd

Supports research and technology development to achieve predictive systems-level understanding of complex biological systems, including redesign of microbes and plants for sustainable biofuel production, improved carbon storage, and contaminent remediation.

Office of Science *(Energy Dept.), Biological and Environmental Research, Biological Systems Science Division, Genomic Science Program, 19901 Germantown Rd., #SC72, Germantown, MD 20874-1290; (301) 903-1239. Joseph Graber, Program Manager.*
Web, http://genomicscience.energy.gov

Supports research using microbial and plant genomic data, high-throughput technologies, and modeling and simulation to develop predictive understanding of biological systems behavior relevent to solving energy and environmental challenges.

Rural Development *(Agriculture Dept.), Business–Cooperative Service, Business Programs, 1400 Independence Ave. S.W., #5803-S, MS 3201, 20250-3201; (202) 690-4730. William Smith, Deputy Administrator. Press, (202) 690-4737.*
Web, www.rd.usda.gov/about-rd/agencies/rural-business-cooperative-service

Makes loan guarantees to rural businesses, including those seeking to develop alcohol fuels production facilities.

▶NONGOVERNMENTAL

Biomass Thermal Energy Council (BTEC), *1211 Connecticut Ave. N.W., #650, 20036-2701; (202) 596-3974. Fax, (202) 223-5537. Jeff Serfass, Executive Director.*
General email, info@biomassthermal.org
Web, www.biomassthermal.org and Twitter, @BiomassThermal

Membership: biomass fuel producers, appliance manufacturers and distributors, supply chain companies, and nonprofit organizations that seek to advance the use of biomass for heat and other thermal energy applications.

Conducts research, public education, and advocacy for the biomass thermal energy industry. Monitors legislation and regulations.

Hearth, Patio, and Barbecue Assn. (HPBA), *1901 N. Moore St., #600, Arlington, VA 22209-1708; (703) 522-0086. Fax, (703) 522-0548. Jack Goldman, President. General email, hpbamail@hpba.org*

Web, www.hpba.org

Membership: all sectors of the hearth products industry. Provides industry training programs to its members on the safe and efficient use of alternative fuels and appliances. Works with the Hearth Education Foundation, which certifies gas hearth, fireplace, pellet stove, and wood stove appliances and venting design specialists.

Methanol Institute, *225 Reinekers Lane, #205, Alexandria, VA 22314; (703) 248-3636. Fax, (703) 248-3997. Greg Dolan, Chief Executive Officer. General email, mi@methanol.org*

Web, www.methanol.org

Membership: global methanol producers and related industries. Encourages use of methanol fuels and development of chemical-derivative markets. Monitors legislation and regulations.

Renewable Fuels Assn., *425 3rd St. S.W., #1150, 20024; (202) 289-3835. Fax, (202) 289-7519. Bob Dinneen, President. General email, info@ethanolrfa.org*

Web, www.ethanolrfa.org and Twitter, @EthanolRFA

Membership: companies and state governments involved in developing the domestic ethanol industry. Distributes publications on ethanol performance. Monitors legislation and regulations.

Geothermal Energy

▶**AGENCIES**

Energy Efficiency and Renewable Energy *(Energy Dept.), Geothermal Technologies, 1000 Independence Ave. S.W., MS EE066, 20585; (202) 287-1818. Susan Hamm, Director, Acting. General email, geothermal@ee.doe.gov*

Web, www.energy.gov/eere/geothermal

Responsible for research and technology development of geothermal energy resources. Conducts outreach to state energy offices and consumers.

U.S. Geological Survey (USGS) *(Interior Dept.), Volcano Hazards, 12201 Sunrise Valley Dr., MS 904, Reston, VA 20192; (703) 648-4773. Fax, (703) 648-5483. Charles W. Mandeville, Program Coordinator. Web, http://volcanoes.usgs.gov*

Provides staff support to the U.S. Geological Survey through programs in volcano hazards.

▶**NONGOVERNMENTAL**

Geothermal Energy Assn., *209 Pennsylvania Ave. S.E., 20003; (202) 454-5261. Fax, (202) 454-5265. Karl Gawell, Executive Director. Web, www.geo-energy.org*

Membership: American companies who promote the national and global advancement of geothermal energy. Represents and supports energy policies that improve the geothermal energy industry. Holds a forum to discuss geothermal issues and advancing geothermal technologies. Researches geothermal industry statistics and provides educational outreach to the public.

Solar, Ocean, and Wind Energy

▶**AGENCIES**

Bureau of Ocean Energy Management (BOEM) *(Interior Dept.), Renewable Energy Programs, 45600 Woodland Rd., MS VAM-OREP, Sterling, VA 20166; (703) 787-1300. Fax, (703) 787-1708. James Bennett, Chief. General email, boempublicaffairs@boem.gov*

Web, www.boem.gov/Renewable-Energy

Grants leases, easements, and rights-of-way for orderly, safe, and environmentally responsible renewable energy development activities on the Outer Continental Shelf, including offshore wind and hydrokinetic projects.

Energy Efficiency and Renewable Energy *(Energy Dept.), Solar Energy Technologies, SunShot Initiative, 950 L'Enfant Plaza, 6th Floor, 20585 (mailing address: 1000 Independence Ave. S.W., Washington, DC 20585); (202) 287-1862. Fax, (202) 586-8148. Lidija Sekaric, Director, Acting. General email, solar@ee.doe.gov*

Web, www.energy.gov/eere/sunshot/sunshot-initiative

Supports research and development of solar technologies of all types through national laboratories and partnerships with industries and universities. Seeks to make solar energy cost-effective through research, manufacturing, and market solutions.

Energy Efficiency and Renewable Energy *(Energy Dept.), Wind and Water Power Technologies, 1000 Independence Ave. S.W., #5H072, MS EE2B, 20585; (202) 586-5348. Fax, (202) 586-5124. Jose Zayas, Director. Web, www.wind.energy.gov and www.water.energy.gov*

Conducts research on wind and water power technologies. Works with U.S. industries to develop hydropower and wind technologies.

▶**CONGRESS**

For a listing of relevant congressional committees and subcommittees, please see pages 240–241 or the Appendix.

► NONGOVERNMENTAL

American Wind Energy Assn., *1501 M St. N.W., #1000, 20005-1700; (202) 383-2500. Fax, (202) 383-2505. Tom Kieman, Chief Executive Officer.*
General email, windmail@awea.org

Web, www.awea.org and Twitter, @AWEA

Membership: manufacturers, developers, operators, and distributors of wind machines; utility companies; and others interested in wind energy. Advocates wind energy as an alternative energy source; makes industry data available to the public and to federal and state legislators. Promotes export of wind energy technology.

National Ocean Industries Assn., *1120 G St. N.W., #900, 20005; (202) 347-6900. Fax, (202) 347-8650. Randall Luthi, President.*
General email, noia@noia.org

Web, www.noia.org

Membership: manufacturers, producers, suppliers, and support and service companies involved in marine, offshore, and ocean work. Interests include ocean thermal energy and new energy sources.

Solar Electric Light Fund, *1612 K St. N.W., #300, 20006; (202) 234-7265. Fax, (202) 328-9512. Robert A. Freling, Executive Director.*
General email, info@self.org

Web, http://self.org

Promotes and develops solar rural electrification and energy self-sufficiency in developing countries. Assists developing world communities and governments in acquiring and installing decentralized household and community solar electric systems.

Solar Energy Industries Assn., *600 14th St. N.W., 20005; (202) 682-0556. Fax, (202) 682-0559. Rhone Resch, Chief Executive Officer; Heather Whitpan, Government Affairs, (202) 556-2871. Press, (202) 556-2885.*
General email, info@seia.org

Web, www.seia.org

Membership: industries with interests in the production and use of solar energy. Promotes growth of U.S. and international markets. Interests include photovoltaic, solar thermal power, and concentrating solar power. Conducts conferences. Monitors legislation and regulations.

8

Environment and Natural Resources

GENERAL POLICY AND ANALYSIS

Basic Resources

▶AGENCIES

Council on Environmental Quality *(Executive Office of the President)*, 730 Jackson Pl. N.W., 20503; (202) 395-5750. Fax, (202) 456-6546. Christina Goldfuss, Managing Director.
Web, www.whitehouse.gov/administration/eop/ceq and Twitter, @WhiteHouseCEQ

Develops environmental priorities; advises and assists the President on national and international environmental policy; evaluates, coordinates, and mediates federal activities on the environment; prepares the President's yearly environmental quality report to Congress.

Environment and Natural Resources Division *(Justice Dept.)*, 950 Pennsylvania Ave. N.W., #2143, 20530-0001; (202) 514-2701. Fax, (202) 514-5331. John C. Cruden, Assistant Attorney General. Press, (202) 514-2008.
General email, press@usdoj.gov
Web, www.justice.gov/enrd

Handles civil suits involving the federal government in all areas of the environment and natural resources; handles some criminal suits involving pollution control, wildlife protection, stewardship of public lands, and natural resources.

Environmental Protection Agency (EPA), *1200 Pennsylvania Ave. N.W., #3000, MC 1101A, 20460; (202) 564-4700. Fax, (202) 501-1450. Gina McCarthy, Administrator; A. Stanley Meiburg, Deputy Administrator, Acting. EPA switchboard, (202) 272-0167. Press, (202) 564-4355. TTY, (800) 877-8339.*
Web, www.epa.gov/aboutepa

Administers federal environmental policies, research, and regulations; provides information on environmental subjects, including water pollution, pollution prevention, hazardous and solid waste disposal, air and noise pollution, pesticides and toxic substances, and radiation.

Environmental Protection Agency (EPA), *Children's Health Protection,* 1301 Constitution Ave., #1144, MC 1107T, 20460; (202) 564-2188. Fax, (202) 564-2733. Dr. Ruth A Etzel, Director.
Web, www2.epa.gov/aboutepa/about-office-childrens-health-protection-ochp and www2.epa.gov/children

Supports and facilitates the EPA's efforts to protect children's health from environmental risks, both domestically and internationally. Provides leadership on interagency Healthy Homes Work Group and Healthy School Environments Initiative. Offers grants through the Office of Children's Health Protection and Environmental Education (OCHPEE).

Environmental Protection Agency (EPA), *Enforcement and Compliance Assurance, Criminal Enforcement, Forensics, and Training,* 1200 Pennsylvania Ave. N.W., #2231A, 20460; (202) 564-2480. Henry Barnet, Director.

Web, www.epa.gov/aboutepa/about-office-enforcement-and-compliance-assurance-oeca

Investigates violations of environmental laws and provides technical and forensic services for civil and criminal investigations and council for legal and policy matters.

Environmental Protection Agency (EPA), *Enforcement and Compliance Assurance, Environmental Justice,* 1200 Pennsylvania Ave. N.W., #2201A, 20460; (202) 564-2515. Matthew Tejada, Director.
Web, www.epa.gov/aboutepa/about-office-enforcement-and-compliance-assurance-oeca

Works to protect human health and the environment in communities overburdened with environmental pollution by implementing justice programs, policies, and activities.

Environmental Protection Agency (EPA), *Policy,* 1200 Pennsylvania Ave. N.W., #1804A, 20460; (202) 564-4332. Fax, (202) 501-1688. Laura Vaught, Associate Administrator.
General email, policyoffice@epa.gov
Web, www.epa.gov/aboutepa/forms/contact-epas-office-policy

Coordinates agency policy development and standard-setting activities through four divisions: Regulatory Policy and Management, the National Center for Environmental Economics, Strategic Environmental Management, and Sustainable Communities.

Environmental Protection Agency (EPA), *Research and Development,* 1200 Pennsylvania Ave. N.W., #41222, MC 8101R, 20460; (202) 564 6620. Fax, (202) 565-2430. Lek Kadeli, Principal Deputy Assistant Administrator.
Web, www2.epa.gov/aboutepa/about-office-research-and-development-ord

Develops scientific data and methods to support EPA standards and regulations. Conducts exposure and risk assessments. Researches applied and long-term technologies to reduce risks from pollution.

Environmental Protection Agency (EPA), *Research and Development, National Center for Environmental Assessment,* 2 Potomac Yard, North Bldg., 7th Floor, 2733 Crystal Dr., Arlington, VA 22202 (mailing address: 1200 Pennsylvania Ave. N.W., MC 8601P, Washington, DC 20460); (703) 347-8600. Fax, (703) 347-8699. Kenneth Olden, Director.
Web, www.epa.gov/aboutepa/about-national-center-environmental-assessment-ncea

Evaluates animal and human health data to define environmental health hazards and estimate risk to humans. Conducts research and prepares reports and assessments.

Environmental Protection Agency (EPA), *Science Advisory Board,* 1300 Pennsylvania Ave. N.W., #31150, 20004 (mailing address: 1200 Pennsylvania Ave. N.W., MC 1400R, Washington, DC 20460); (202) 564-2221. Fax, (202) 565-2098. Thomas Carpenter, Designated Federal Officer, (202) 564-4885; Christopher Zarba, Director, (202) 564-2074.
General email, sab@epa.gov

ENVIRONMENTAL RESOURCES IN CONGRESS

For a complete listing of congressional committees, including their full contact information, leadership, membership, and jurisdictions, please refer to the Appendix on pages 779–896.

HOUSE:

House Agriculture Committee, (202) 225-2171.
Web, agriculture.house.gov
> Subcommittee on Biotechnology, Horticulture, and Research, (202) 225-2171.
> Subcommittee on Conservation and Forestry, (202) 225-2171.
> Subcommittee on Livestock and Foreign Agriculture, (202) 225-2171.

House Appropriations Committee, (202) 225-2771.
Web, appropriations.house.gov
> Subcommittee on Agriculture, Rural Development, Food and Drug Administration, and Related Agencies, (202) 225-2638.
> Subcommittee on Commerce, Justice, Science, and Related Agencies, (202) 225-3351.
> Subcommittee on Energy and Water Development, and Related Agencies, (202) 225-3421.
> Subcommittee on Interior, Environment, and Related Agencies, (202) 225-3081.

House Energy and Commerce Committee, (202) 225-2927.
Web, energycommerce.house.gov
> Subcommittee on Environment and the Economy, (202) 225-2927.

House Natural Resources Committee, (202) 225-2761.
Web, naturalresources.house.gov

> Subcommittee on Energy and Mineral Resources, (202) 225-9297.
> Subcommittee on Federal Lands, (202) 226-7736.
> Subcommittee on Indian, Insular, and Alaska Native Affairs, (202) 226-9725.
> Subcommittee on Oversight and Investigation, (202) 225-7107.
> Subcommittee on Water, Power, and Oceans, (202) 225-8331.

House Science, Space, and Technology Committee, (202) 225-6371.
Web, science.house.gov
> Subcommittee on Environment, (202) 225-6371.
> Subcommittee on Research and Technology, (202) 225-6371.

House Small Business Committee, (202) 225-5821.
Web, smallbusiness.house.gov

House Transportation and Infrastructure Committee, (202) 225-9446.
Web, transportation.house.gov
> Subcommittee on Coast Guard and Maritime Transportation, (202) 226-3552.
> Subcommittee on Railroads, Pipelines, and Hazardous Materials, (202) 226-0727.
> Subcommittee on Water Resources and Environment, (202) 225-4360.

SENATE:

Senate Agriculture, Nutrition, and Forestry Committee, (202) 224-2035.
Web, ag.senate.gov

Web, www.epa.gov/sab and www.epa.gov/aboutepa/about-science-advisory-board-sab-and-sab-staff-office

Coordinates nongovernment scientists and engineers who advise the administrator on scientific and technical aspects of environmental problems and issues. Evaluates EPA research projects, the technical basis of regulations and standards, and policy statements.

Federal Highway Administration (FHWA)
(Transportation Dept.), Planning, Environment, and Realty, 1200 New Jersey Ave. S.E., #E76-306, 20590; (202) 366-0116. Fax, (202) 366-3713. Gloria M. Shepherd, Associate Administrator.
Web, www.fhwa.dot.gov/real_estate

Works with developers and municipalities to ensure conformity with the National Environmental Policy Act (NEPA) project development process.

Housing and Urban Development Dept. (HUD),
Community Planning and Development, Environment and Energy, 451 7th St. S.W., #7250, 20410; (202)

708-2894. Fax, (202) 708-3363. Danielle Schopp, Director, (202) 402-4442.
Web, http://portal.hud.gov/hudportal/HUD?src=/program_offices/comm_planning/library/energy

Issues policies and sets standards for environmental and land-use planning and environmental management practices. Oversees HUD implementation of requirements on environment, historic preservation, archaeology, flood plain management, wetlands protection, environmental justice (ensuring that the environment and human health are fairly protected for all people/Executive Order 12898), coastal zone management, sole source aquifers, farmland protection, endangered species, airport clear zones, explosive hazards, and noise.

Interior Dept. (DOI), 1849 C St. N.W., MS 6628, 20240; (202) 208-7351. Fax, (202) 208-6956. Hon. Sally Jewell, Secretary; Michael L. Connor, Deputy Secretary. Information, (202) 208-3100. Library, (202) 208-5815. Press, (202) 208-6416.

Subcommittee on Conservation, Forestry, and Natural Resources, (202) 224-2035.

Subcommittee on Livestock, Marketing, and Agriculture Security, (202) 224-2035.

Subcommittee on Rural Development and Energy, (202) 224-2035.

Senate Appropriations Committee, (202) 224-7363.

Web, appropriations.senate.gov

Subcommittee on Agriculture, Rural Development, Food and Drug Administration, and Related Agencies, (202) 224-8090.

Subcommittee on Commerce, Justice, Science, and Related Agencies, (202) 224-5202.

Subcommittee on Energy and Water Development, (202) 224-8119.

Subcommittee on Interior, Environment, and Related Agencies, (202) 228-0774.

Senate Commerce, Science, and Transportation Committee, (202) 224-0411.

Web, commerce.senate.gov

Subcommittee on Oceans, Atmosphere, Fisheries, and the Coast Guard, (202) 224-4912.

Senate Energy and Natural Resources Committee, (202) 224-4971.

Web, energy.senate.gov

Subcommittee on Energy, (202) 224-4971.

Subcommittee on National Parks, (202) 224-4971.

Subcommittee on Public Lands, Forests, and Mining, (202) 224-4971.

Subcommittee on Water and Power, (202) 224-4971.

Senate Environment and Public Works Committee, (202) 224-8832.

Web, epw.senate.gov

Subcommittee on Clean Air and Nuclear Safety, (202) 224-8832.

Subcommittee on Fisheries, Water, and Wildlife, (202) 224-8832.

Subcommittee on Superfund, Waste Management, and Regulatory Oversight, (202) 224-8832.

Subcommittee on Transportation and Infrastructure, (202) 224-8832.

Senate Finance Committee, (202) 224-4515.

Web, finance.senate.gov

Subcommittee on Energy, Natural Resources, and Infrastructure, (202) 224-4515.

Senate Foreign Relations Committee, (202) 224-4651.

Web, foreign.senate.gov

Subcommittee on Mulitlateral International Development, Multilateral Institutions, and International Economic, Energy, and Environmental Policy, (202) 224-4651.

Senate Indian Affairs Committee, (202) 224-2251.

Web, indian.senate.gov

Senate Small Business and Entrepreneurship Committee, (202) 224-5175.

Web, sbc.senate.gov

General email, feedback@ios.doi.gov

Web, www.doi.gov

Principal U.S. conservation agency. Manages most federal land; responsible for conservation and development of mineral and water resources; responsible for conservation, development, and use of fish and wildlife resources; operates recreation programs for federal parks, refuges, and public lands; preserves and administers the nation's scenic and historic areas; reclaims arid lands in the West through irrigation; administers Native American lands and develops relationships with tribal governments.

Interior Dept. (DOI), *Communications,* 1849 C St. N.W., #6312, 20240; (202) 208-6416. Fax, (202) 208-5133. *Blake Androff, Director. Employee Directory, (202) 208-3100.*

General email, interior_press@ios.doi.gov

Web, http://doi.gov/news

Issues press releases about Interior Dept. events and announcements. Provides information to the general public, tourists, businesses, Native Americans, governments, and others.

Interior Dept. (DOI), *Environmental Policy and Compliance,* 1849 C St. N.W., MS 2462, 20240; (202) 208-3891. *Mary Josie Blanchard, Director, Acting.*

Web, www.doi.gov/oepc

Provides leadership on a national and regional level for environmental policies and compliance for U.S. resource management and conservation; ensures compliance with the National Environmental Policy Act (NEPA), regulations, and reporting requirements; manages funding for long-term cleanup of hazardous materials; oversees Interior Dept.'s protection and recovery activities for natural and cultural resources and historic properties during emergency response efforts.

Interior Dept. (DOI), *Policy Analysis,* 1849 C St. N.W., MS 3530, 20240; (202) 208-5978. Fax, (202) 208-4867. *Joel Clement, Director.*

Web, www.doi.gov/ppa

Provides cross-cutting policy planning and analysis to support decision making and policies across the department; makes recommendations and develops policy options for resolving natural resource problems.

National Institute of Environmental Health Sciences (National Institutes of Health), Washington Office, 31 Center Dr., #B1C02, MSC 2256, Bethesda, MD 20892-2256; (301) 496-3511. Fax, (301) 496-0563. Linda S. Birnbaum, Director; Jed R. Bullock, Legislative Liaison. Information, (919) 541-4794.
General email, webcenter@niehs.nih.gov
Web, www.niehs.nih.gov, Facebook, www.facebook.com/ NIH.NIEHS and Twitter, @NIEHS

Conducts and supports research on the human effects of various environmental exposures, expanding the scientific basis for making public health decisions based on the potential toxicity of environmental agents. (Most operations located in Research Triangle, N.C.)

National Institute of Standards and Technology (NIST) (Commerce Dept.), Special Programs Office, 100 Bureau Dr., MS 1000, Gaithersburg, MD 20899-1000; (301) 975-4447. Fax, (301) 975-8972. Richard R. Cavanagh, Director. General information, (301) 975-2756.
Web, www.nist.gov/director/spo

Fosters collaboration among government, military, academia, professional, and private organizations to respond to critical national needs through science-based standards and technology innovation, including environmental concerns.

National Oceanic and Atmospheric Administration (NOAA) (Commerce Dept.), National Environmental Satellite, Data, and Information Service, 1335 East-West Hwy., SSMC1, 8th Floor, Silver Spring, MD 20910; (301) 713-3578. Fax, (301) 713-1249. Stephen Volz, Assistant Administrator. Press, (301) 713-0214.
General email, john.leslie@noaa.gov
Web, www.nesdis.noaa.gov

Provides satellite observations of the environment by operating polar orbiting and geostationary satellites; develops satellite techniques; increases the utilization of satellite data in environmental services.

National Oceanic and Atmospheric Administration (NOAA) (Commerce Dept.), Program Planning and Integration, 1315 East-West Hwy., SSMC3, Silver Spring, MD 20910; (301) 713-1632. Fax, (301) 713-0585. Kristen Tronvig, Director, Acting.
General email, PPI.NEPA@noaa.gov
Web, www.ppi.noaa.gov

Develops NOAA's strategic plan. Manages designated programs and fosters strategic management throughout NOAA offices and advisory panels.

Natural Resources and Environment (Agriculture Dept.), 1400 Independence Ave. S.W., #240E, 20250-0108; (202) 720-7173. Fax, (202) 720-0632. Robert Bonnie, Under Secretary; Jason Weller, Chief, Natural Resources Conservation, (202) 720-7246; Thomas Tidwell, Chief,

Forest Service. Toll-free Forest Service, (800) 832-1355. Web, www.usda.gov and www.fs.fed.us

Formulates and promulgates policy relating to environmental activities and management of natural resources. Oversees the Forest Service and the Natural Resources Conservation Service.

Office of Science and Technology Policy (OSTP) (Executive Office of the President), National Science and Technology Council, Eisenhower Executive Office Bldg., 1650 Pennsylvania Ave. N.W., 20504; (202) 456-4444. Fax, (202) 456-6021. Afua Bruce, Executive Director.
General email, info@ostp.gov
Web, www.ostp.gov

Coordinates research and development activities and programs that involve more than one federal agency. Activities concern earth sciences, materials, forestry research, and radiation policy.

U.S. Geological Survey (USGS) (Interior Dept.), 12201 Sunrise Valley Dr., MS 100, Reston, VA 20192-0002; (703) 648-4000. Fax, (703) 648-4454. Suzette M. Kimball, Director, (703) 648-7412. Information, 888-ASK-USGS. Library, (703) 648-7182. Press, (703) 648-4460.
General email, servicedesk@usgs.gov
Web, www.usgs.gov and Twitter, @USGS

Provides reports, maps, and databases that describe and analyze water, energy, biological, and mineral resources; the land surface; and the underlying geological structure and dynamic processes of the Earth.

►**CONGRESS**

For a listing of relevant congressional committees and subcommittees, please see pages 270–271 or the Appendix.

Government Accountability Office (GAO), Natural Resources and Environment, 441 G St. N.W., #2057, 20548 (mailing address: 441 G St. N.W., #2T23A, Washington, DC 20548); (202) 512-3841. Fax, (202) 512-8774. Mark Gaffigan, Managing Director.
Web, www.gao.gov/careers/nre.html

Independent nonpartisan agency in the legislative branch that audits the Agriculture Dept. and analyzes and reports on its handling of agriculture issues and food safety.

►**NONGOVERNMENTAL**

Aspen Institute, 1 Dupont Circle N.W., #700, 20036-7133; (202) 736-5800. Fax, (202) 467-0790. Walter Isaacson, President. Press, (202) 736-3849.
General email, info@aspeninstitute.org
Web, www.aspeninstitute.org and Twitter, @AspenInstitute

Educational and policy studies organization. Promotes consideration of the public good in a wide variety of policy areas, including energy and the environment. Working with international partners, offers educational seminars,

Environmental Protection Agency

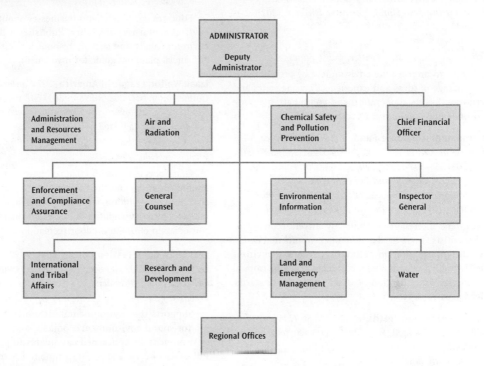

nonpartisan policy forums, public conferences and events, and leadership development initiatives.

The Conservation Fund, *1655 N. Fort Myer Dr., #1300, Arlington, VA 22209-3199; (703) 525-6300. Fax, (703) 525 4610. Lawrence A. Selzer, President.*
General email, webmaster@conservationfund.org
Web, www.conservationfund.org and Twitter, @ConservationFun

Creates partnerships with the private sector, nonprofit organizations, and public agencies to promote land and water conservation. Operates land trusts, identifies real estate for conservation, and runs loan programs.

Earth Share, *7735 Old Georgetown Rd., #900, Bethesda, MD 20814; (240) 333-0300. Fax, (240) 333-0301.*
Deb Furry, President, Acting. Information, (800) 875-3863.
General email, info@earthshare.org
Web, www.earthshare.org

Federation of environmental and conservation organizations. Works with government and private payroll contribution programs to solicit contributions to member organizations for environmental research, education, and community programs. Provides information on establishing environmental giving options in the workplace.

Edison Electric Institute, *701 Pennsylvania Ave. N.W., 20004-2696; (202) 508-5000. Fax, (202) 508-5096.*
Thomas R. Kuhn, President. Library, (202) 508-5603.
General email, feedback@eei.org
Web, www.eei.org

Membership: investor-owned electric power companies. Interests include electric utility operation and concerns, including conservation and energy management, energy analysis, resources and environment, cogeneration and renewable energy resources, safety, reliability, taxes, and regulation matters. Library open to the public by appointment.

Environment America, *Federal Advocacy Office, 218 D St. S.E., 2nd Floor, 20003; (202) 683-1250. Fax, (202) 543-6489. Anna Aurilio, Director, ext. 317.*
Web, www.environmentamerica.org

Coordinates grassroots efforts to advance environmental and consumer protection laws; conducts research on environmental issues, including global warming, clean energy, preservation and conservation, clean water and air, and toxic pollution; compiles reports and disseminates information on such issues; drafts and monitors environmental laws; testifies on behalf of proposed environmental legislation. (Headquarters in Boston.)

Environmental and Energy Study Institute (EESI), *1112 16th St. N.W., #300, 20036-4819; (202) 628-1400. Fax, (202) 204-5244. Carol Werner, Executive Director, (202) 662-1881.*
General email, info@eesi.org
Web, www.eesi.org and Twitter, @eesionline

Nonpartisan policy education and analysis group established by members of Congress to foster informed debate on environmental and energy issues. Interests include policies for sustainable development, energy, sustainable bioenergy, climate change, agriculture, transportation, and fiscal policy reform.

Environmental Council of the States, 50 F St. N.W., #350, 20001; (202) 266-4920. Fax, (202) 266-4937. Alexandra Dapolito Dunn, Executive Director, (202) 266-4929.
General email, ecos@ecos.org
Web, www.ecos.org and Twitter, @ECOStates

Works to improve the environment by providing for the exchange of ideas and experiences among states and territories; fosters cooperation and coordination among environmental management professionals.

Environmental Defense Fund, *Washington Office,* 1875 Connecticut Ave. N.W., #600, 20009-5728; (202) 387-3500. Fax, (202) 234-6049. Fred Krupp, President; Felice Stradler, Director, U.S. Climate and Political Affairs.
Information, (800) 684-3322. Press, (202) 572-3396.
Web, www.edf.org and Twitter, @EnvDefenseFund

Citizens' interest group staffed by lawyers, economists, and scientists. Takes legal action on environmental issues; provides information on pollution prevention, environmental health, wetlands, toxic substances, acid rain, tropical rain forests, and litigation of water pollution standards. (Headquarters in New York.)

Environmental Law Institute, 1730 M St. N.W., #700, 20036; (202) 939-3800. Fax, (202) 939-3868. Scott Fulton, President.
General email, law@eli.org
Web, www.eli.org and Twitter, @eli.org

Conducts policy studies on the environment and sustainability. Publishes materials on environmental issues, sponsors education and training courses and conferences on environmental law, issues policy recommendations, and provides technical assistance in the United States and abroad.

Environmental Working Group, 1436 U St. N.W., #100, 20009-3987; (202) 667-6982. Fax, (202) 232-2592. Kenneth A. Cook, President.
General email, generalinfo@ewg.org
Web, www.ewg.org and Twitter, @ewg

Research and advocacy organization that studies and reports on the presence of herbicides and pesticides in food and drinking water. Monitors legislation and regulations.

Friends of the Earth (FOE), 1101 15th St. N.W., 11th Floor, 20005; (202) 783-7400. Fax, (202) 783-0444. Erich Pica, President. Toll-free, (877) 843-8687.
General email, foe@foe.org
Web, www.foe.org and Twitter, @foe_us

Environmental advocacy group. Interests include climate and energy, oceans and water, food and emerging technology, and economic drivers of environmental degradation. Specializes in federal budget and tax issues related to the environment, sustainable food systems, corporate power, and natural resources.

Green America, 1612 K St. N.W., #600, 20006; (202) 872-5307. Fax, (202) 331-8166. Alisa Gravitz, President. Information, (800) 584-7336. Press, (202) 872-5310.
General email, info@greenamerica.org
Web, www.greenamerica.org

Educates consumers and businesses about social and environmental responsibility. Publishes a directory of environmentally and socially responsible businesses and a financial planning guide for investment.

Izaak Walton League of America, 707 Conservation Lane, Gaithersburg, MD 20878-2983; (301) 548-0150. Fax, (301) 548-0146. Scott Kovarovics, Executive Director. Toll-free, (800) 453-5463.
General email, info@iwla.org
Web, www.iwla.org

Grassroots organization that promotes conservation of natural resources and the environment. Interests include air and water pollution, farmland conservation, clean and renewable energy, wildlife habitat protection, and instilling conservation ethics in outdoor recreationists.

League of Conservation Voters (LCV), 1920 L St. N.W., #800, 20036; (202) 785-8683. Fax, (202) 835-0491. Gene Karpinski, President.
Web, www.lcv.org

Supports the environmental movement by advocating for sound environmental policies and helping elect environmentally concerned candidates to public office. Publishes the National Environmental Scorecard and Presidential Report Card.

National Audubon Society, *Public Policy,* 1200 18th St. N.W., #500, 20036; (202) 861-2242. Fax, (202) 861-4290. Mike Daulton, Vice President, Government Relations, (202) 861-2242, ext. 3030.
General email, audubonaction@audubon.org
Web, www.audubon.org and Twitter, @audobonsociety

Citizens' interest group that promotes environmental conservation and education, focusing on birds and their habitats. Provides information on bird science, water resources, public lands, rangelands, forests, parks, wildlife conservation, and the National Wildlife Refuge System. Operates state offices, local chapters, and nature centers nationwide. (Headquarters in New York.)

National Ecological Observatory Network, Inc. (NEON), *Washington Office,* 1100 Jefferson Dr. S.W., #3123, MRC 705, 20560-0001; (202) 370-7891. Fax, (202) 204-0128. Brian Wee, Chief of Strategic Alliances; Gene Kelly, Chief Executive Officer, Acting. Press, (720) 746-4936.
General email, bwee@neoninc.org
Web, www.neoninc.org, Twitter, @NEONInc and Facebook, www.facebook.com/NEONInc

Collects data across the United States on the impact of climate change, land-use change, and invasive species on natural resources and biodiversity, with the goal of detecting and forecasting ecological change on a continental scale over multiple decades. Works with various government agencies to develop standards for environmental observations and data interoperability; expected to become fully operational by 2017. Funded by the National Science Foundation in partnership with NEON. (Visitors note: Co-located in the Smithsonian's S. Dillon Ripley Center.) (Headquarters in Boulder, Colo.)

National Governors Assn. (NGA), *Center for Best Practices, Environment, Energy, and Transportation Division,* 444 N. Capitol St. N.W., #267, 20001-1512; (202) 624-5300. Fax, (202) 624-7829. Sue Gander, Director.
General email, webmaster@nga.org
Web, www.nga.org/cms/center/eet

Identifies best practices for energy, land use, environment, and transportation issues and shares these with the states.

National Governors Assn. (NGA), *Natural Resources Committee,* 444 N. Capitol St. N.W., #267, 20001-1512; (202) 624-5300. Fax, (202) 624-7814. Alex Whitaker, Director.
General email, webmaster@nga.org
Web, www.nga.org/cms/center/eet

Monitors legislation and regulations and makes recommendations on agriculture, energy, environment, and natural resource issues to ensure governors' views and priorities are represented in federal policies and regulations.

National Research Council (NRC), *Energy and Environmental Systems Board,* Keck Center, 500 5th St. N.W., #W917, 20001; (202) 334-1378. James Zucchetto, Board Director, (202) 334-3???
Web, http://sites.nationalacademies.org/DEPS/BEES

Conducts studies in order to advise the federal government and the private sector about issues in energy and environmental technology, and related public policy. Focuses on energy supply and demand technologies and systems, including resource extraction through mining and drilling, energy conversion, distribution and delivery, and efficiency of use; environmental consequences of energy related activities; environmental systems and controls in areas related to fuels production, energy conversion, transmission, and use; and other issues relating to national security and defense. Sponsors studies, workshops, symposia, and a variety of information dissemination activities.

National Research Council (NRC), *Environmental Change and Society Board,* Keck Center, 500 5th St. N.W., 20001; (202) 334-3005. Fax, (202) 334-3751.
Mary Ellen O'Connell, Director, Acting, (202) 334-2607; Richard H. Moss, Chair.
General email, BECS@nas.edu
Web, http://sites.nationalacademies.org/DBASSE/BECS

Conducts research on the interactions between human activities and the environment, including climate variation, resource use and decion making, adaptation to change, and risk and resilience.

National Sustainable Agriculture Coalition, 110 Maryland Ave. N.E., #209, 20002-5622; (202) 547-5754. Fax, (202) 547-1837. Ferd Hoefner, Policy Director; Jeremy Emmi, Managing Director.
General email, info@sustainableagriculture.net
Web, www.sustainableagriculture.net

National alliance of farm, rural, and conservation organizations. Advocates federal policies that promote environmentally sustainable agriculture, natural resources management, and rural community development. Monitors legislation and regulations.

Natural Resources Defense Council, *Washington Office,* 1152 15th St. N.W., #300, 20005; (202) 289-6868.
Fax, (202) 289-1060. Wesley Warren, Director, Policy Advocacy; David Goldston, Director, Government Affairs.
General email, nrdcinfo@nrdc.org
Web, www.nrdc.org

Environmental organization staffed by lawyers and scientists who conduct litigation and research. Interests include air, water, land use, forests, toxic materials, natural resources management and conservation, preservation of endangered plant species, and ozone pollution. Web site has a Spanish-language link. (Headquarters in New York.)

Nature Conservancy, 4245 N. Fairfax Dr., #100, Arlington, VA 22203-1606; (703) 841-5300. Fax, (703) 841-1283. Mark Tercek, President; Bill Ginn, Executive Vice President of Global Conservation Initiatives.
Information, (800) 628-6860. Press, (703) 841-3939.
General email, comment@tnc.org
Press email, ghenrich-koenis@tnc.org
Web, www.nature.org

Maintains an international system of natural sanctuaries; acquires land to protect endangered species and habitats. Collaborates with other conservation organizations, country and local governments, corporations, indigenous peoples and communities, and individuals such as fishermen, ranchers, and farmers to create management plans for natural areas.

Pew Environment Group, 901 E St. N.W., 20004-2008; (202) 552-2000. Fax, (202) 552-2299. Josh Reichert, Executive Vice President.
General email, bkramer@pewtrusts.org
Web, www.pewenvironment.org

Identifies and publicizes environmental issues at the international, national, and local levels, with the goal of strengthening environmental policies and practices. Interests include climate change, clean air, endangered species, global warming, hazardous chemicals, national park pollution, and campaign finance reform. Opposes efforts to weaken environmental laws. Monitors legislation and regulations.

Pinchot Institute for Conservation, 1616 P St. N.W., #100, 20036; (202) 797-6580. Fax, (202) 797-6583.
William C. Price, President, Acting.
Web, www.pinchot.org

Seeks to advance forest conservation and sustainable natural resources management nationally through research and analysis, education and technical assistance, and development of conservation leaders.

Public Employees for Environmental Responsibility (PEER), 2000 P St. N.W., #240, 20036; (202) 265-7337.
Fax, (202) 265-4192. Jeff Ruch, Executive Director.

General email, info@peer.org

Web, www.peer.org and *Twitter, @PEERorg*

Service organization for public citizens and employees of federal, state, and local resource management agencies. Defends legal rights of public employees who speak out concerning natural resource management and environmental protection issues. Monitors enforcement of environmental protection laws.

Resources for the Future, *1616 P St. N.W., 20036-1400; (202) 328-5000. Fax, (202) 939-3460. Philip R. Sharp, President, (202) 328-5077. Library, (202) 328-5089. Press, (202) 328-5168.*

General email, info@rff.org

Web, www.rff.org and *Twitter, @RFF_org*

Engages in research and education on environmental and natural resource issues, including forestry, multiple use of public lands, costs and benefits of pollution control, endangered species, environmental risk management, energy and national security, and climate resources. Interests include hazardous waste, the Superfund, and biodiversity. Publishes research findings; offers academic fellowships. Library open to the public by appointment.

Sierra Club, *Legislative Office, 50 F St. N.W., 8th Floor, 20001; (202) 547-1141. Fax, (202) 547-6009. Debbie Sease, Legislative Director; Bob Bingaman, National Organizing Director, (202) 675-7904; Shanice Penn, Operations Manager. Press, (202) 675-6698.*

General email, information@sierraclub.org

Web, www.sierraclub.org

Citizens' interest group that promotes protection of natural resources. Interests include the Clean Air Act; the Arctic National Wildlife Refuge; protection of national forests, parks, and wilderness; toxins; global warming; promotion of responsible international trade; and international development lending reform. Monitors legislation and regulations. (Headquarters in San Francisco, Calif.)

U.S. Chamber of Commerce, *Environment, Technology, and Regulatory Affairs, 1615 H St. N.W., 20062-2000; (202) 463-5533. Fax, (202) 887-3445. William L. Kovacs, Senior Vice President.*

General email, environment@uschamber.com

Web, www.uschamber.com/etra

Monitors operations of federal departments and agencies responsible for environmental programs, policies, regulatory issues, and food safety. Analyzes and evaluates legislation and regulations that affect the environment.

Union of Concerned Scientists, *Strategy and Policy, 1825 K St. N.W., #800, 20006-1232; (202) 223-6133. Fax, (202) 223-6162. Alden Meyer, Director.*

General email, ucs@ucsusa.org

Web, www.ucsusa.org

Membership: scientists and citizens who advocate a comprehensive approach to resolving global environmental and resource issues. Educates and mobilizes citizens on the linkages between resource depletion, environmental degradation, climate changes, and consumption patterns. (Headquarters in Cambridge, Mass.)

The Wilderness Society, *1615 M St. N.W., 20036; (202) 833-2300. Fax, (202) 429-3958. Jamie Williams, President. Toll-free, (800) 843-9453.*

General email, action@tws.org

Web, www.wilderness.org and *Twitter, @wilderness*

Promotes preservation of wilderness and the responsible management of federal lands, including national parks and forests, wilderness areas, wildlife refuges, and land administered by the Interior Dept.'s Bureau of Land Management.

Global Warming and Climate Change

▶**AGENCIES**

Bureau of Oceans and International Environmental and Scientific Affairs *(State Dept.), Global Climate Change, 2201 C St. N.W., #2480, 20520; (202) 647-3984. Christo Artusio, Director.*

Web, www.state.gov/e/oes/climate

Addresses climate change challenges through international policy, agreements, and partnerships.

Economic Research Service *(Agriculture Dept.), 355 E St. S.W., 20024-8221; (202) 694-5000. Fax, (202) 245-5467. Mary Bohman, Administrator; Greg Pompelli, Associate Administrator.*

General email, service@ers.usda.gov

Web, www.ers.usda.gov

Provides research and economic information to the USDA. Interests include economic and policy issues involving food, farm practices and management, natural resources, and rural development. Web site offers a briefing room on global climate change and other environmental topics.

Environmental Protection Agency (EPA), *Air and Radiation, Atmospheric Programs, Climate Change Division, 1200 Pennsylvania Ave. N.W., #5426, MC 6207A, 20460; (202) 343-9876. Fax, (202) 343-2342. Paul M. Gunning, Director.*

General email, hargrove.anne@epa.gov

Web, www.epa.gov/aboutepa/about-office-air-and-radiation-oar#oap and *www.epa.gov/climatechange*

Works to address global climate change and the associated risks to human health and the environment. Implements voluntary programs to reduce non–carbon dioxide emissions. Analyzes greenhouse gas emissions and reduction options. Educates the public on climate change and provides climate analysis and strategies to policymakers, experts, and U.S. climate negotiators.

National Oceanic and Atmospheric Administration (NOAA) *(Commerce Dept.), Climate Program Office, 1315 East-West Hwy., SSMC-3, Room 12124, Silver Spring, MD*

20910; (301) 734-1263. Fax, (301) 713-0515.
Wayne Higgins, Director.
General email, oar.cpo.office@noaa.gov
Web, www.cpo.noaa.gov

Manages NOAA-funded research programs that focus on climate science and assessments on a regional, national, and international scale.

National Oceanic and Atmospheric Administration (NOAA) *(Commerce Dept.), Ocean Acidification Program,* 1315 East-West Hwy., #10356, Silver Spring, MD 20910; (301) 734-1075. Libby Jewett, Director.
General email, noaa.oceanacidification@noaa.gov
Web, www.oceanacidification.noaa.gov

Monitors changes in ocean chemistry due to the continued acidification of the oceans and Great Lakes, and assesses the socioeconomic impacts. Maintains relationships with scientists, resource managers, stakeholders, policymakers, and the public to implement adaptation strategies and monitor the biological responses of ecologically and economically important species. Operates from NOAA's Office of Oceanic and Atmospheric Research.

Office of Science *(Energy Dept.), Biological and Environmental Research, Climate and Environmental Sciences Division,* 19901 Germantown Rd., #SC23.1, Germantown, MD 20874-1290 (mailing address: Germantown Bldg., 1000 Independence Ave. S.W., #SC23.1, Washington, DC 20585); (301) 903-4775. Gerald Geernaert, Director.
Web, http://science.energy.gov/ber/research/cesd

Supports research on atmospheric systems, terrestrial ecosystems, and subsurface biogeochemistry as well as Earth system modeling and regional and global climate change modeling to improve predictive understanding of Earth's climate and environmental systems in order to inform development of sustainable solutions to energy challenges.

U.S. Geological Survey (USGS) *(Interior Dept.), Climate and Land Use Change,* 12201 Sunrise Valley Dr., MS 516, Reston, VA 20192; (703) 648-4215. Fax, (703) 648-7031. Virginia Burkett, Associate Director for Climate and Land Use Change.
Web, www.usgs.gov/climate_landuse

Researches the effects of climate and land-use change on natural resources. Methods include monitoring, modeling, and forecasting. Operates the Landsat satellites. Provides coordination, technical support, and funding for existing research programs. Provides research products to policymakers, natural resources managers, and the general public.

▶ CONGRESS

For a listing of relevant congressional committees and subcommittees, please see pages 270–271 or the Appendix.

▶ NONGOVERNMENTAL

The Brookings Institution, *Climate and Energy Economics Project,* 1775 Massachusetts Ave. N.W., 20036; (202) 797-6000. Warwick McKibbin, Co-Director; Pete Wilcoxen, Co-Director. Press, (202) 797-6105.
Web, www.brookings.edu/about/projects/climate-energy-economics

Promotes economically efficient approaches to mitigating human impacts on climate change, including cap-and-trade.

The Brookings Institution, *Economic Studies,* 1775 Massachusetts Ave. N.W., 20036-2188; (202) 797-6000. Fax, (202) 797-6181. Ted Gayer, Director. Press, (202) 797-6105.
General email, escomment@brookings.edu
Web, www.brookings.edu/economics

Promotes environmentally sound and economically efficient climate policy, with a focus on the economics of domestic cap-and-trade approaches and global agreement.

Center for Climate and Energy Solutions, 2101 Wilson Blvd., #550, Arlington, VA 22201; (703) 516-4146. Fax, (703) 516-9551. Bob Perciasepe, President.
Web, www.c2es.org and Twitter, @C2ES_org

Independent organization that issues information and promotes discussion by policymakers on the science, economics, and policy of climate change.

Climate Institute, 1400 16th St. N.W., #430, 20036; (202) 552-0163. John C. Topping, President.
General email, info@climate.org
Web, www.climate.org

Educates the public and policymakers on climate change, the greenhouse effect, global warming, and the depletion of the ozone layer. Assesses climate change risks and develops strategies on mitigating climate change in developing countries and in North America.

The Climate Reality Project, 750 9th St. N.W., #520, 20001; (202) 567-6800. Fax, (202) 628-1445. Ken Berlin, President.
General email, info@climatereality.com
Web, www.climaterealityproject.org and Twitter, @ClimateReality

Aims to reduce carbon emissions, supports taxing oil and coal companies that emit large amounts of carbon, and educates the public on climate change and its relation to carbon pollution.

George C. Marshall Institute, 1601 N. Kent St., #802, Arlington, VA 22209; (571) 970-3180. Fax, (571) 970-3192. William O'Keefe, Chief Executive Officer.
General email, info@marshall.org
Web, www.marshall.org and Twitter, @Marshall_Instit

Analyzes the technical and scientific aspects of public policy and defense issues; produces publications on environmental science, space, national security, energy issues, and technology policy. Interests include climate change, space, defense policy, and cyber policy.

Global Green USA, *Washington Office, 322 4th St. N.E., 20002; (202) 380-3440. Chris Weiss, Director, Environmental Security and Sustainability.*
General email, cweiss@globalgreen.org

Web, www.globalgreen.org

Offers research and community-based projects to educate people about the environment and encourage improved environmental policy. Interests include climate change solutions, green building for affordable housing and schools, energy efficiency, and clean energy, protection of natural resources, and recycling. (Headquarters in Santa Monica, Calif.) (U.S. national affiliate of Mikhail Gorbachev's Green Cross International.)

National Council for Science and the Environment, *1101 17th St. N.W., #250, 20036; (202) 530-5810. Fax, (202) 628-4311. Michelle Wyman, Executive Director, (202) 207-0002.*
General email, ncse@ncseonline.org

Web, www.ncseonline.org and Facebook, www.facebook .com/ncseonline

Coordinates programs that bring together individuals, institutions, and communities to discuss environmental education, research, and public policy decisions affecting the environment.

National Ecological Observatory Network, Inc. (NEON), *Washington Office, 1100 Jefferson Dr. S.W., #3123, MRC 705, 20560-0001; (202) 370-7891. Fax, (202) 204-0128. Brian Wee, Chief of Strategic Alliances; Gene Kelly, Chief Executive Officer, Acting. Press, (720) 746-4936.*
General email, bwee@neoninc.org

Web, www.neoninc.org, Twitter, @NEONInc and Facebook, www.facebook.com/NEONInc

Collects data across the United States on the impact of climate change, land-use change, and invasive species on natural resources and biodiversity, with the goal of detecting and forecasting ecological change on a continental scale over multiple decades. Works with various government agencies to develop standards for environmental observations and data interoperability; expected to become fully operational by 2017. Funded by the National Science Foundation in partnership with NEON. (Visitors note: Co-located in the Smithsonian's S. Dillon Ripley Center.) (Headquarters in Boulder, Colo.)

National Research Council (NRC), *Atmospheric Sciences and Climate Board, Keck Center, 500 5th St. N.W., #602, 20001; (202) 334-3512. Fax, (202) 334-3825. Amanda Staudt, Director; A. R. Ravishankara, Chair.*
General email, basc@nas.edu

Web, http://nas.edu/basc

Supports research on climate change, air pollution, and severe weather in order to address environmental policies, human health, emergency management, energy choices, manufacturing decisions, construction codes, and agricultural methods.

Physicians for Social Responsibility (PSR), *1111 14th St. N.W., #700, 20005; (202) 667-4260. Fax, (202) 667-4201. Dr. Catherine Thomasson, Executive Director.*
General email, psrnatl@psr.org

Web, www.psr.org

Membership: doctors, nurses, health scientists, and concerned citizens. Works to slow, stop, and reverse global warming and degradation of the environment. Conducts public education programs, monitors policy, and serves as a liaison with other concerned groups.

Resources for the Future, *1616 P St. N.W., 20036-1400; (202) 328-5000. Fax, (202) 939-3460. Philip R. Sharp, President, (202) 328-5077. Library, (202) 328-5089. Press, (202) 328-5168.*
General email, info@rff.org

Web, www.rff.org and Twitter, @RFF_org

Research organization that conducts independent studies on economic and policy aspects of energy, environment, conservation, and natural resource management issues worldwide. Interests include climate change, energy, natural resource issues in developing countries, and public health.

Union of Concerned Scientists, *Climate and Energy Program, 1825 K St. N.W., #800, 20006-1232; (202) 223-6133. Fax, (202) 223-6162. Angela Ledford Anderson, Director.*
General email, ucs@ucsusa.org

Web, www.ucsusa.org

Promotes clean energy and global warming emissions reduction. Advocates international policy responses to the threat of global climate change.

Union of Concerned Scientists, *Strategy and Policy, 1825 K St. N.W., #800, 20006-1232; (202) 223-6133. Fax, (202) 223-6162. Alden Meyer, Director.*
General email, ucs@ucsusa.org

Web, www.ucsusa.org

Membership: scientists and citizens who advocate a comprehensive approach to resolving global environmental and resource issues. Educates and mobilizes citizens on the linkages between resource depletion, environmental degradation, climate changes, and consumption patterns. (Headquarters in Cambridge, Mass.)

International Issues

▶**AGENCIES**

Bureau of Oceans and International Environmental and Scientific Affairs *(State Dept.), 2201 C St. N.W., #3880, 20520-7818; (202) 647-3950. Fax, (202) 647-0217. Judith G. Garber, Assistant Secretary, Acting.*
Web, www.state.gov/e/oes and Twitter, @StateDeptOES

Concerned with foreign policy as it affects natural resources and the environment, human health, the global climate, energy production, and oceans and fisheries.

Bureau of Oceans and International Environmental and Scientific Affairs *(State Dept.), Conservation and Water,* 2201 C St. N.W., #2657, 20520; (202) 647-4683. Fax, (202) 647-1052. Christine Dawson, Director.
General email, waterteam@state.gov

Web, www.state.gov/e/oes/ecw

Represents the United States in international affairs relating to ecology and conservation issues. Interests include wildlife, tropical forests, and biological diversity.

Bureau of Oceans and International Environmental and Scientific Affairs *(State Dept.), Environmental Quality and Transboundary Issues,* 2201 C St. N.W., #2726, 20520; (202) 647-9831. Fax, (202) 647-1052. Deborah Klepp, Director.
Web, www.state.gov/e/oes/eqt

Advances U.S. interests internationally regarding multilateral environmental organizations, chemical and hazardous waste and other pollutants, and bilateral and regional environmental policies.

Bureau of Oceans and International Environmental and Scientific Affairs *(State Dept.), Policy and Public Outreach,* 2201 C St. N.W., #2880, 20520; (202) 647-4658. Susan Cleary, Director.
Web, www.state.gov/e/oes/policy

Integrates oceans, environment, polar, science, technology, and health issues into U.S. foreign policy, and works to address these issues in the media, NGOs, the private sector, and Congress.

Environmental Protection Agency (EPA), *International and Tribal Affairs,* 1200 Pennsylvania Ave. N.W., #31106, MC 2610R, 20460; (202) 564-6600. Fax, (202) 565-2407. Vacant, Assistant Administrator.
General email, oiainternet-comments@epa.gov

Web, www2.epa.gov/aboutepa/about-office-international-and-tribal-affairs-oita

Coordinates the agency's work on international environmental issues and programs, including management of bilateral agreements and participation in multilateral organizations and negotiations. Works to strengthen public health and environmental programs on tribal lands, emphasizing helping tribes administer their own environment programs.

Interior Dept. (DOI), *International Affairs,* 1849 C St. N.W., MS 3559, 20240; (202) 208-3048. Fax, (202) 513-7728. Karen Senhadji, Director.
Web, www.doi.gov/intl

Focuses on international conservation and management of wildlife and natural resources, protection of cultural resources, cooperation on indigenous affairs, and monitoring of natural hazards including volcanoes and earthquakes.

International Trade Administration (ITA) *(Commerce Dept.), Industry and Analysis, Energy and Environmental Industries,* 1400 Constitution Ave. N.W., #4053, 20230; (202) 482-5225. Adam O'Malley, Director, (202) 482-4850.
Web, www.trade.gov/td/energy

Works to facilitate and increase export of U.S. environmental technologies, including goods and services. Conducts market analysis, business counseling, and trade promotion.

Treasury Dept., *International Affairs, Environment and Energy,* 1500 Pennsylvania Ave N.W., 20220; (202) 622-0139. Leonardo Martinez, Deputy Assistant Secretary.
Web, www.treasury.gov/about/organizational-structure/offices/Pages/Environment-and-Energy.aspx

Develops, coordinates, and executes the Treasury Dept.'s role in domestic and international environment and energy policy. Assists the United States on finance issues at United Nations climate negotiations and leads the department's engagement on energy and climate finance efforts in the G-20.

►**CONGRESS**

For a listing of relevant congressional committees and subcommittees, please see pages 270–271 or the Appendix.

►**INTERNATIONAL ORGANIZATIONS**

International Joint Commission, *United States and Canada, U.S. Section,* 2000 L St. N.W., #615, 20036; (202) 736-9000. Fax, (202) 632-2007. Lana Pollack, Chair; Frank Bevacqua, Public Information Officer, (202) 736-9024.
General email, bevacquaf@washington.ijc.org

Web, www.ijc.org

Prevents and resolves disputes between the United States and Canada on transboundary water and air resources. Investigates issues upon request of the governments of the United States and Canada. Reviews applications for water resource projects. (Canadian section in Ottawa; Great Lakes regional office in Windsor, Ontario.)

International Union for the Conservation of Nature, *U.S. Office,* 1630 Connecticut Ave. N.W., 3rd Floor, 20009; (202) 387-4826. Fax, (202) 387-4823. Frank Hawkins, Director.
General email, deborah.good@iucn.org

Web, www.iucn.org/usa

Membership: world governments, their environmental agencies, and nongovernmental organizations. Studies conservation issues from local to global levels. Helps provide links for members and partners around the world to key U.S.-based institutions, such as the U.S. government and its agencies, the World Bank, the Global Environment Facility, the Inter-American Development Bank, the United Nations, and other organizations. Interests include protected areas, forests, oceans, polar regions, biodiversity, species survival, environmental law, sustainable use of resources, and the impact of trade on the environment. Hosts a number of IUCN staff, programs, and initiatives concerned with global conservation and sustainable development issues. (Headquarters in Gland, Switzerland.)

Organization of American States (OAS), *Sustainable Development,* 1889 F St. N.W., #710, 20006; (202) 458-3567. Fax, (202) 458-3560. Cletus Springer, Director.

General email, sustainable_dev@oas.org

Web, www.oas.org/en/sedi/dsd

Promotes integrated and sustainable development of natural resources in OAS member states through the design and implementation of policies, programs, and partnerships. Interests include integrated management of shared water resources, hazard risk management, sustainable cities, biodiversity protection, sustainable energy, and environmental law.

▶ **NONGOVERNMENTAL**

Antarctic and Southern Ocean Coalition, *1320 19th St. N.W., 5th Floor, 20036; (202) 234-2480. Claire Christian, Executive Director, Acting.*

General email, secretariat@asoc.org

Web, www.asoc.org and Twitter, @AntarcticaSouth

Promotes effective implementation of the Antarctic Treaty System; works to protect the fragile environment and biodiversity of the Antarctic continent, including krill conservation, in the Southern Ocean.

Conservation International, *2011 Crystal Dr., #500, Arlington, VA 22202; (703) 341-2400. Fax, (703) 553-0654. Peter Seligmann, Chief Executive Officer. Toll-free, (800) 429-5660.*

General email, community@conservation.org

Web, www.conservation.org and Twitter, @ConservationOrg

Works to conserve tropical rain forests through economic development; promotes exchange of debt relief for conservation programs that involve local people and organizations. Interests include fresh water, food, biodiversity, climate, health, and cultural services. Provides private groups and governments with information and technical advice on conservation efforts and collaborates with business and government in these efforts; supports conservation data gathering in the Americas, Europe, Africa, Asia, and the Caribbean, as well as the oceans.

Environmental Investigation Agency (EIA), *P.O. Box 53343, 20009; (202) 483-6621. Fax, (202) 986-8626. Alexander (Sascha) von Bismarck, Director.*

General email, info@eia-global.org

Web, www.eia-global.org and Twitter, @EIAEnvironment

Works to expose international environmental crime, including illegal trade of wildlife, illegal logging, and sale of ozone-depleting substances. Monitors legislation and regulations. Also maintains an office in London.

Greenpeace USA, *702 H St. N.W., #300, 20001; (202) 462-1177. Fax, (202) 462-4507. Annie Leonard, Executive Director.*

General email, info@wdc.greenpeace.org

Web, www.greenpeace.org

Seeks to expose global environmental problems and to promote solutions through nonviolent direct action, lobbying, and creative communication. Interests include forests, oceans, toxins, global warming, nuclear energy,

disarmament, and genetic engineering. (International office in Amsterdam, Netherlands.)

International Conservation Caucus Foundation (ICCF), *25786 Georgetown Station, 20027; (202) 471-4222. John B. Gantt Jr., President.*

General email, hq@iccfoundation.us

Web, www.iccfoundation.us

Seeks to improve U.S. efforts in international conservation. Coordinates between policymakers and conservationists to address ecosystem issues. Holds the International Conservation Gala and congressional briefing series. Administers awards to activists. Manages the Ocean Caucus Foundation to protect sea life.

Species Survival Network (SSN), *2100 L St. N.W., 20037; (301) 548-7769. Fax, (301) 258-3080. Will Travers, President.*

General email, info@ssn.org

Web, www.ssn.org

Coalition of organizations seeking to enforce the Convention on International Trade in Endangered Species of Wild Fauna and Flora (CITES). Acts as advocate against exploitation, injury, cruel treatment, and possible extinction of native animals and plants caused by global trade. Researches and analyzes policies to educate the public on their potential impact on the environment.

Winrock International, *2121 Crystal Dr., #500, Arlington, VA 22202; (703) 302-6500. Fax, (703) 302-6512. Rodney Ferguson, President.*

General email, information@winrock.org

Web, www.winrock.org and Twitter, @WinrockIntl

Works to sustain natural resources and protect the environment. Matches innovative approaches in agriculture, natural resource management, clean energy, and leadership development with the unique needs of its partners. (Headquarters in Little Rock, Ark.)

World Resources Institute, *10 G St. N.E., #800, 20002; (202) 729-7600. Fax, (202) 729-7610. Andrew Steer, President. Press, (202) 729-7684.*

Web, www.wri.org and Twitter, @worldresources

Conducts research on environmental problems and studies the interrelationships of natural resources, economic growth, and human needs. Interests include forestry and land use, renewable energy, fisheries, and sustainable agriculture. Assesses environmental policies of aid agencies.

World Wildlife Fund (WWF), *1250 24th St. N.W., 20037-1193 (mailing address: P.O. Box 97180, Washington, DC 20090-7180); (202) 293-4800. Fax, (202) 293-9211. Carter S. Roberts, President.*

Web, www.worldwildlife.org and Twitter, @World_Wildlife

Conducts scientific research and analyzes policy on environmental and conservation issues, including pollution reduction, land use, forestry and wetlands management, parks, soil conservation, and sustainable development. Supports projects to promote biological diversity and to save endangered species and their habitats, including tropical forests in Latin America, Asia, and Africa. Awards grants and provides technical assistance to local conservation groups.

Worldwatch Institute, *1400 16th St. N.W., #430, 20036; (202) 745-8092. Fax, (202) 478-2534. Ed Groark, President, Acting.*
General email, worldwatch@worldwatch.org
Web, www.worldwatch.org and Twitter, @worldwatch

Focuses on an interdisciplinary approach to solving global environmental problems. Interests include energy conservation, renewable resources, solar power, and energy use in developing countries.

ANIMALS AND PLANTS

General

▶**AGENCIES**

Animal and Plant Health Inspection Service (APHIS) *(Agriculture Dept.), Investigative and Enforcement Services, 4700 River Rd., Unit 85, Riverdale, MD 20737-1234; (301) 851-2948. Fax, (301) 734-4328. Vacant, Director.*
Web, www.aphis.usda.gov/aphis/ourfocus/business-services/ies

Provides investigative and enforcement services and leadership, direction, and support for compliance activities within the service.

Animal and Plant Health Inspection Service (APHIS) *(Agriculture Dept.), Plant Protection and Quarantine, 1400 Independence Ave. S.W., #302E, 20250; (202) 799-7163. Fax, (202) 690-0472. Osama El-Lissy, Deputy Administrator. Anti-smuggling hotline, (800) 877-3835.*
General email, aphis.web@aphis.usda.gov
Web, www.aphis.usda.gov/plant_health

Encourages compliance with regulations that safeguard agriculture and natural resources from the risks associated with the entry, establishment, or spread of animal and plant pests and noxious weeds. Methods include requirements for the import and export of plants and plant products; partnership agreements with industry groups, community organizations, and government entities; and public education and outreach.

National Science Foundation (NSF), *Molecular and Cellular Biosciences Division, 4201 Wilson Blvd. Arlington, VA 22230; (703) 292-8440. Fax, (703) 292-9061. Linda Hyman, Division Director, (703) 292-7132.*
Web, www.nsf.gov/div/index.jsp?div=MCB

Supports research and understanding of complex living systems at cellular levels.

National Zoological Park *(Smithsonian Institution), 3001 Connecticut Ave. N.W., 20008 (mailing address: DEVS, P.O. Box 37012, MRC 5516, Washington, DC 20013-7012); (202) 633-4888 (recorded information line). Fax, (202) 673-4836. Dennis W. Kelly, Executive Director.*
Library, (202) 633-1031. Press, (202) 633-3055. Friends of the Zoo, (202) 633-3038. TTY, (202) 673-7800. Zoo police, (202) 633-4134.
Web, www.nationalzoo.si.edu

Maintains a public zoo. Conducts research on animal behavior, ecology, nutrition, reproductive physiology, pathology, and veterinary medicine; operates an annex near Front Royal, Va., for the propagation and study of endangered species. Houses a unit of the Smithsonian Institution library open to qualified researchers by appointment. Interlibrary loans available.

U.S. Customs and Border Protection *(Homeland Security Dept.), Agricultural Program and Trade Liaison Office, 1300 Pennsylvania Ave. N.W., #2.5B, 20229; (202) 344-3298. Fax, (202) 344-1442. Kevin Harriger, Executive Director.*
Web, www.cbp.gov

Responsible for safeguarding the nation's animal and natural resources from pests and disease through inspections at ports of entry and beyond.

▶**CONGRESS**

For a listing of relevant congressional committees and subcommittees, please see pages 270–271 or the Appendix.

▶**NONGOVERNMENTAL**

American Herbal Products Assn., *8630 Fenton St., #918, Silver Spring, MD 20910; (301) 588-1171. Fax, (301) 588-1174. Michael McGuffin, President.*
General email, ahpa@ahpa.org
Web, www.ahpa.org

Membership: U.S. companies and individuals that grow, manufacture, and distribute botanicals and herbal products, including foods, beverages, dietary supplements, and personal care products; associates in education, law, media, and medicine. Supports research; promotes quality standards, consumer access, and self-regulation in the industry. Monitors legislation and regulations.

Animal Health Institute, *1325 G St. N.W., #700, 20005-3104; (202) 637-2440. Fax, (202) 393-1667. Alexander S. Mathews, President.*
Web, www.ahi.org

Membership: manufacturers of drugs and other products (including vaccines, pesticides, and vitamins) for pets and food-producing animals. Interests include pet health, livestock health, and disease outbreak prevention. Monitors legislation and regulations.

National Research Council (NRC), *Agriculture and Natural Resources Board, Keck Center, 500 5th St. N.W., #WS632, 20001; (202) 334-3062. Fax, (202) 334-1978. Robin Schoen, Director.*
General email, banr@nas.edu
Web, http://dels.nas.edu/banr

Promotes and oversees research on the environmental impact of agriculture and food sustainability, including forestry, fisheries, wildlife, and the use of land, water, and other natural resources.

Animal Rights and Welfare

▶AGENCIES

Animal and Plant Health Inspection Service (APHIS) *(Agriculture Dept.), Animal Care, 4700 River Rd., Unit 84, Riverdale, MD 20737-1234; (301) 851-3751. Fax, (301) 734-4978. Bernadette Juarez, Deputy Administrator, Acting.*
General email, ace@aphis.usda.gov
Web, www.aphis.usda.gov/animal_welfare

Administers laws for the breeding, exhibition, and care of animals raised for sale and research and transported commercially. Enforces the Animal Welfare Act and Horse Protection Act.

Animal and Plant Health Inspection Service (APHIS) *(Agriculture Dept.), Center for Animal Welfare, 4700 River Rd., #84, Riverdale, MD 20737; (301) 851-3751. Fax, (301) 734-4978. Nora Wineland, Director.*
General email, ace@aphis.usda.gov
Web, www.aphis.usda.gov/aphis/ourfocus/animalwelfare/CAW

Provides guidance on policy development and analysis, education and outreach, and scientific research related to animal welfare issues, especially in support of the Animal Welfare Act and the Horse Protection Act.

National Agricultural Library *(Agriculture Dept.), Animal Welfare Information Center, 10301 Baltimore Ave., #118, Beltsville, MD 20705; (301) 504-6212. Fax, (301) 504-5181. Kristina Adams, Coordinator.*
General email, awic@ars.usda.gov
Web, http://awic.nal.usda.gov

Provides information for improved animal care and use in research, testing, teaching, and exhibition.

National Institutes of Health (NIH) *(Health and Human Services Dept.), Animal Care and Use, 31 Center Dr., Bldg. 31, #B1C37, MSC 2252, Bethesda, MD 20892-2252; (301) 496-5424. Fax, (301) 480-8298. Terri Clark, Director.*
General email, secoacu@od.nih.gov
Web, http://oacu.od.nih.gov

Provides guidance for the humane care and use of animals in the intramural research program at NIH.

National Institutes of Health (NIH) *(Health and Human Services Dept.), Laboratory Animal Welfare, 6705 Rockledge Dr., RLK1, #360, MSC 7982, Bethesda, MD 20892-7982; (301) 496-7163. Fax, (301) 480-3394. Patricia A. Brown, Director.*
General email, olaw@mail.nih.gov
Web, http://grants.nih.gov/grants/olaw/olaw.htm

Develops and monitors policy on the humane care and use of animals in research conducted by any public health service entity.

Washington Humane Society, *1201 New York Ave N.E., 20002; (202) 576-6664. Claudia Roll, Director, Operations. Press, (202) 375-7750. 24-hour animal cruelty and emergency hotline, (202) 723-5730.*
General email, adopt@washhumane.org
Press email, matt.williams@warl.org
Web, http://support.washhumane.org

Congressionally chartered animal welfare agency and open-access animal shelter. Promotes pet adoption; offers low-cost spay and neuter services and trap-and-neuter programs.

▶CONGRESS

For a listing of relevant congressional committees and sub-committees, please see pages 270–271 or the Appendix.

▶NONGOVERNMENTAL

Alley Cat Allies, *7920 Norfolk Ave., #600, Bethesda, MD 20814-2525; (240) 482-1980. Fax, (240) 482-1990. Becky Robinson, President.*
General email, info@alleycat.org
Web, www.alleycat.org

Clearinghouse for information on feral and stray cats. Advocates the trap-neuter-return method to reduce feral cat populations.

American Humane Assn., *1400 16th St. N.W., #360, 20036; (202) 841-6080. Fax, (202) 450-2335. Mark Stubis, Chief Communications Officer, (202) 677-4227. Toll-free, (800) 227-4645.*
General email, info@americanhumane.org and marks@americanhumane.org
Web, www.americanhumane.org and Twitter, @AmericanHumane

Membership: animal shelters, humane organizations, child protection agencies, government agencies, and individuals. Prepares model state legislation on child abuse and its prevention; publishes surveys on child and animal abuse and state abuse laws.

Americans for Medical Progress, *444 N. Capitol St. N.W., #417, 20001; (202) 624-8810. Paula Clifford, Executive Director.*
General email, amp@amprogress.org
Web, www.amprogress.org and Twitter, @CureDisease

Promotes and protects animal-based medical research. Serves as a media resource by fact-checking claims of animal rights groups. Conducts public education campaigns on the link between animal research and medical advances.

Animal Welfare Institute, *900 Pennsylvania Ave. S.E., 20003 (mailing address: P.O. Box 3650, Washington, DC 20027); (202) 337-2332. Fax, (202) 446-2131. Cathy Liss, President.*
General email, awi@awionline.org
Web, www.awionline.org

Works to improve conditions for animals in laboratories, on farms, in commerce, in homes, and in the wild.

Promotes efforts to end horse slaughter. Monitors legislation and regulations. (Merged with the Society for Animal Protective Legislation.)

Compassion Over Killing, *6930 Carroll Ave., #910, Tacoma Park, MD 20912 (mailing address: P.O. Box 9773, Washington, DC 20016); (301) 891-2458. Fax, (301) 891-6815. Erica Meier, Executive Director.*
General email, info@cok.net

Web, www.cok.net and Twitter, @TryVeg

Animal rights organization that focuses primarily on cruelty to animals in agriculture. Promotes vegetarianism.

Doris Day Animal League, *2100 L St. N.W., 20037; (202) 452-1100. Holly Hazard, Executive Director.*
General email, info@ddal.org

Web, www.ddal.org

Seeks to reduce the inhumane treatment of animals through legislative initiatives, education, and programs. Works with all levels of government to pass new protection laws and strengthen existing ones. (Affiliated with the Humane Society of the United States.)

Farm Animal Rights Movement (FARM), *10101 Ashburton Lane, Bethesda, MD 20817-1729; (301) 530-1737. Fax, (301) 530-5683. Michael A. Weberman, Executive Director; Alex Hershaft, President. Toll-free, 888-FARM-USA.*
General email, info@farmusa.org

Web, www.farmusa.org, www.livevegan.org and Twitter, @FARMUSA

Works to end use of animals for food. Interests include animal protection, consumer health, agricultural resources, and environmental quality. Conducts national educational campaigns, including World Farm Animals Day, the Live Vegan program, and the Great American Meatout. Monitors legislation and regulations.

Humane Farm Animal Care, *P.O. Box 727, Herndon, VA 20172-0727; (703) 435-3883. Fax, (703) 435-3981. Adele Douglass, Executive Director.*
General email, info@certifiedhumane.org

Web, www.certifiedhumane.org

Seeks to improve the welfare of farm animals by providing viable, duly monitored standards for humane food production. Administers the Certified Humane Raised and Handled program for meat, poultry, eggs, and dairy products.

Humane Society Legislative Fund, *2100 L St. N.W., #310, 20037; (202) 676-2314. Fax, (202) 676-2300. Michael Markarian, President. Press, (301) 548-7778.*
General email, humanesociety@hslf.org

Web, www.hslf.org

Works to pass state and federal laws protecting animals from cruelty and suffering. (Lobbying arm of the Humane Society of the United States.)

Humane Society of the United States, *2100 L St. N.W., 20037; (202) 452-1100. Fax, (202) 778-6132. Wayne Pacelle, President.*
Web, www.humanesociety.org

Citizens' interest group that sponsors programs in pet and equine protection, disaster preparedness and response, wildlife and habitat protection, animals in research, and farm animal welfare. Interests include legislation to protect pets, provide more humane treatment for farm animals, strengthen penalties for illegal animal fighting, and curb abusive sport hunting practices such as trophy hunting, baiting, and hounding.

National Assn. for Biomedical Research, *1100 Vermont Ave. N.W., #1100, 20005; (202) 857-0540. Fax, (202) 659-1902. Frankie L. Trull, President.*
General email, info@nabr.org

Web, www.nabr.org

Membership: scientific and medical professional societies, academic institutions, and research-oriented corporations involved in the use of animals in biomedical research. Supports the humane use of animals in medical research, education, and product-safety assessment. Monitors legislation and regulations.

National Research Council (NRC), *Institute for Laboratory Animal Research, Keck Center, 500 5th St. N.W., #645, 20001; (202) 334-2187. Fax, (202) 334-1687. Fran Sharples, Director, Acting.*
Web, www.dels.nas.edu/ilar

Develops and makes available scientific and technical information on laboratory animals and other biological research resources for the scientific community, institutional animal care and use committees, the federal government, science educators and students, and the public.

Physicians Committee for Responsible Medicine (PCRM), *5100 Wisconsin Ave. N.W., #400, 20016; (202) 686-2210. Fax, (202) 686-2216. Neal Barnard, President.*
General email, pcrm@pcrm.org

Web, www.pcrm.org

Membership: health care professionals, medical students, and laypersons interested in preventive medicine, nutrition, and higher standards in research. Investigates alternatives to animal use in medical research experimentation, product testing, and education.

Fish

▶AGENCIES

Atlantic States Marine Fisheries Commission, *1050 N. Highland St., #200 A-N, Arlington, VA 22201; (703) 842-0740. Fax, (703) 842-0741. Robert E. Beal, Executive Director.*
General email, info@asmfc.org

Web, www.asmfc.org

Interstate compact commission of marine fisheries representatives from fifteen states along the Atlantic seaboard. Assists states in developing joint fisheries programs; works with other fisheries organizations and the federal government on environmental, natural resource, and conservation issues.

Environmental Protection Agency (EPA), *Water,* *1200 Pennsylvania Ave. N.W., MC 4101M, 20460; (202) 564-5700. Joel Beauvais, Deputy Assistant Administrator.*
Web, www.epa.gov/aboutepa/about-office-water#wetlands

Monitors water pollution to promote healthy fish habitats. Issues fish and shellfish advisories and promotes safe eating guidelines.

Interior Dept. (DOI), *Fish, Wildlife, and Parks, 1849 C St. N.W., #7256, 20240; (202) 208-4416. Fax, (202) 208-4684. Michael Bean, Principal Deputy Assistant Secretary.*
Web, www.doi.gov

Responsible for programs associated with the development, conservation, and use of fish, wildlife, recreational, historical, and national park system resources. Coordinates marine environmental quality and biological resources programs with other federal agencies.

Justice Dept. (DOJ), *Environmental Crimes, 601 D St. N.W., 2nd Floor, 20004 (mailing address: P.O. Box 7611, Washington, DC 20044); (202) 305-0321. Deborah L. Harris, Chief.*
Web, www.justice.gov/environmental-crimes-section

Supervises criminal cases under federal maritime law and other laws protecting marine fish and mammals. Focuses on smugglers and black market dealers of protected wildlife.

Justice Dept. (DOJ), *Wildlife and Marine Resources, 601 D St. N.W., 3rd Floor, 20004 (mailing address: P.O. Box 7415, Ben Franklin Station, Washington, DC 20044-7369); (202) 305-0210. Fax, (202) 305-0275. Seth M. Barsky, Section Chief.*
Web, www.justice.gov/enrd/wildlife-and-marine-resources-section

Supervises civil cases under federal maritime law and other laws protecting marine fish and mammals.

National Oceanic and Atmospheric Administration (NOAA) *(Commerce Dept.), 1401 Constitution Ave. N.W., #5128, 20230; (202) 482-3436. Fax, (202) 408-9674. Kathryn D. Sullivan, Under Secretary. Library, (301) 713-2600. Press, (202) 482-6090.*
Web, www.noaa.gov

Conducts research in marine and atmospheric sciences; surveys resources of the sea; analyzes economic aspects of fisheries operations; develops and implements policies on international fisheries; provides states with grants to conserve coastal zone areas; protects marine mammals; provides colleges and universities with grants for research, education, and marine advisory services.

National Oceanic and Atmospheric Administration (NOAA) *(Commerce Dept.), National Marine Fisheries Service, 1315 East-West Hwy., SSMC3, Silver Spring, MD 20910; (301) 427-8000. Fax, (301) 713-1940. Eileen Sobeck, Assistant Administrator. Press, (301) 427-8003.*
Web, www.nmfs.noaa.gov

Administers marine fishing regulations, including offshore fishing rights and international agreements; conducts marine resources research; studies use and management of these resources; administers the Magnuson-Stevens Fishery Conservation and Management Act; manages and protects marine resources, especially endangered species and marine mammals, within the exclusive economic zone.

U.S. Fish and Wildlife Service *(Interior Dept.), 1849 C St. N.W., #3358, 20240; (202) 208-4717. Fax, (202) 208-6965. Daniel M. Ashe, Director. Press, (703) 358-2220. Toll-free, (800) 344-9453.*
Web, www.fws.gov

Works with federal and state agencies and nonprofits to conserve, protect, and enhance fish and wildlife and their habitats for the continuing benefit of the American people.

U.S. Fish and Wildlife Service *(Interior Dept.), Endangered Species, 5275 Leesburg Pike, Falls Church, VA 22041; (703) 358-2171. Fax, (202) 208-5618. Bridget Fahey, Chief.*
Web, www.fws.gov/endangered and *Twitter, @USFWSEndsp*

Administers federal policy on fish and wildlife under the Endangered Species Act, Marine Mammal Protection Act, Fish and Wildlife Coordination Act, Oil Pollution Act, and other environmental laws. Reviews all federal and federally licensed projects to determine environmental effects on fish and wildlife. Responsible for maintaining the endangered species list and for protecting and restoring species to healthy numbers.

U.S. Fish and Wildlife Service *(Interior Dept.), Fisheries and Aquatic Conservation, 5275 Leesburg Pike, MS FAC-3C018A, Falls Church, VA 22041; (703) 358-1792. Fax, (703) 358-2847. David Hoskins, Assistant Director, Acting.*
General email, michael_derosa@fws.gov
Web, www.fws.gov/fisheries

Develops, manages, and protects interstate and international fisheries, including fisheries of the Great Lakes, fisheries on federal lands, aquatic ecosystems, endangered species of fish, and anadromous species. Administers the National Fish Hatchery System and the National Fish and Wildlife Resource Management Offices, as well as the Habitat and Conservation and Environmental Quality Divisions.

U.S. Geological Survey (USGS) *(Interior Dept.), Ecosystems, 12201 Sunrise Valley Dr., MS 300, Reston, VA 20192; (703) 648-4050. Fax, (703) 648-7031. Anne E. Kinsinger, Associate Director, (703) 648-4051.*
Web, www.usgs.gov/ecosystems

Conducts research and monitoring to develop and convey an understanding of ecosystem function and distributions, physical and biological components, and trophic dynamics for freshwater, terrestrial, and marine ecosystems and the human, fish, and wildlife communities they support. Subject areas include invasive species, endangered species and habitats, genetics and genomics, and microbiology.

▶CONGRESS

For a listing of relevant congressional committees and sub-committees, please see pages 270–271 or the Appendix.

▶NONGOVERNMENTAL

American Fisheries Society (AFS), *5410 Grosvenor Lane, #110, Bethesda, MD 20814-2199; (301) 897-8616. Fax, (301) 897-8096. Douglas Austen, Executive Director. General email, main@fisheries.org*

Web, www.fisheries.org

Membership: biologists and other scientists interested in fisheries. Promotes the fisheries profession, the advancement of fisheries science, and conservation of renewable aquatic resources. Monitors legislation and regulations.

Assn. of Fish and Wildlife Agencies, *1100 1st St. N.E., #825, 20001; (202) 838-3474. Fax, (202) 624-7891. Ron Regan, Executive Director. General email, info@fishwildlife.org*

Web, www.fishwildlife.org, Twitter, @fishwildlife and Facebook, www.facebook.com/FishWildlifeAgencies

Membership: state, provincial, and territorial fish and wildlife management agencies in the United States, Canada, and Mexico. Encourages balanced, research-based fish and wildlife resource management. Monitors legislation and regulations.

Grocery Manufacturers Assn. (GMA), *1350 Eye St. N.W., #300, 20005-3377; (202) 639-5900. Fax, (202) 639-5932. Pamela Bailey, President. Press, (202) 295-3957. General email, info@gmaonline.org*

Web, www.gmaonline.org

Membership: manufacturers and suppliers of processed and packaged food, drinks, and juice. Serves as industry liaison between seafood processors and the federal government.

National Fisheries Institute, *7918 Jones Branch Dr., #700, McLean, VA 22102; (703) 752-8882. John Connelly, President. Press, (703) 752-8891. General email, contact@nfi.org*

Web, www.aboutseafood.com and Twitter, @NFImedia

Membership: vessel owners and distributors, processors, wholesalers, importers, traders, and brokers of fish and shellfish. Monitors legislation and regulations on fisheries. Advocates eating seafood for health benefits.

Ocean Conservancy, *1300 19th St. N.W., 8th Floor, 20036; (202) 429-5609. Fax, (202) 872-0619. Janis Jones, President. Toll-free, (800) 519-1541. General email, membership@oceanconservancy.org*

Web, www.oceanconservancy.org

Works to prevent the overexploitation of living marine resources, including fisheries, and to restore depleted marine wildlife populations through research, education, and science-based advocacy.

Trout Unlimited, *1777 N. Kent St., #100, Arlington, VA 22209; (703) 522-0200. Fax, (703) 284-9400. Chris Wood, President, (703) 284-9403. Toll-free, (800) 834-2419. Web, www.tu.org*

Membership: individuals interested in the protection and restoration of cold-water fish and their habitat. Sponsors research projects with federal and state fisheries agencies; administers programs for water-quality surveillance and cleanup of streams and lakes. Monitors legislation and regulations.

Wildlife and Marine Mammals

▶AGENCIES

Animal and Plant Health Inspection Service (APHIS) (Agriculture Dept.), Wildlife Services, *1400 Independence Ave. S.W., #1624S, 20250-3402; 4700 River Rd. Riverdale, MD 20737; (202) 799-7095. Fax, (202) 690-0053. William H. Clay, Deputy Administrator. Web, www.aphis.usda.gov/wildlife_damage*

Works to minimize damage caused by wildlife to crops and livestock, natural resources, and human health and safety. Removes or eliminates predators and nuisance birds. Interests include aviation safety and coexistence of people and wildlife in suburban areas. Oversees the National Wildlife Research Center in Ft. Collins, Colo.

Forest Service (Agriculture Dept.), Watershed, Fish, Wildlife, Air, and Rare Plants, *201 14th St. S.W., 35C, 20024 (mailing address: 1400 Independence Ave. S.W., MS 1121, Washington, DC 20250-1121); (202) 205-1671. Fax, (202) 703-1544. Robert (Rob) Harper, Director. General email, switt01@fs.fed.us*

Web, www.fs.fed.us/biology

Provides national policy direction and management for watershed, fish, wildlife, air, and rare plants programs on lands managed by the Forest Service.

Interior Dept. (DOI), Fish, Wildlife, and Parks, *1849 C St. N.W., #7256, 20240; (202) 208-4416. Fax, (202) 208-4684. Michael Bean, Principal Deputy Assistant Secretary. Web, www.doi.gov*

Responsible for programs associated with the development, conservation, and use of fish, wildlife, recreational, historical, and national park system resources. Coordinates marine environmental quality and biological resources programs with other federal agencies.

Justice Dept. (DOJ), Environmental Crimes, *601 D St. N.W., 2nd Floor, 20004 (mailing address: P.O. Box 7611, Washington, DC 20044); (202) 305-0321. Deborah L. Harris, Chief. Web, www.justice.gov/environmental-crimes-section*

Supervises criminal cases under federal maritime law and other laws protecting marine fish and mammals. Focuses on smugglers and black market dealers of protected wildlife.

Justice Dept. (DOJ), *Wildlife and Marine Resources,* 601 D St. N.W., 3rd Floor, 20004 (mailing address: P.O. Box 7415, Ben Franklin Station, Washington, DC 20044-7369); (202) 305-0210. Fax, (202) 305-0275. Seth M. Barsky, Section Chief.
Web, www.justice.gov/enrd/wildlife-and-marine-resources-section

Responsible for criminal enforcement and civil litigation under federal fish and wildlife conservation statutes, including protection of wildlife, fish, and plant resources within U.S. jurisdiction, and management and restoration of Florida Everglades. Monitors interstate and foreign commerce of these resources.

Marine Mammal Commission, 4340 East-West Hwy., #700, Bethesda, MD 20814; (301) 504-0087. Fax, (301) 504-0099. Rebecca Lent, Executive Director.
General email, mmc@mmc.gov

Web, www.mmc.gov

Established by Congress to ensure protection and conservation of marine mammals and the ecosystems of which they are a part. Supports research and makes recommendations to federal agencies to ensure that their activities are consistent with the provisions of the Marine Mammal Protection Act.

Migratory Bird Conservation Commission, 5275 Leesburg Pike, Falls Church, VA 22041-3803 (mailing address: 5275 Leesburg Pike, MS 3N053, Falls Church, VA 22041-3803); (703) 358-1716. Fax, (703) 358-2223. A. Eric Alvarez, Secretary.
General email, mbcc@fws.gov

Web, www.fws.gov/refuges/realty/mbcc.html

Established by the Migratory Bird Conservation Act of 1929. Decides which areas to purchase for use as migratory bird refuges and the price at which they are acquired.

National Oceanic and Atmospheric Administration (NOAA) *(Commerce Dept.),* 1401 Constitution Ave. N.W., #5128, 20230; (202) 482-3436. Fax, (202) 408-9674. Kathryn D. Sullivan, Under Secretary. Library, (301) 713-2600. Press, (202) 482-6090.
Web, www.noaa.gov

Conducts research in marine and atmospheric sciences; surveys resources of the sea; analyzes economic aspects of fisheries operations; develops and implements policies on international fisheries; provides states with grants to conserve coastal zone areas; protects marine mammals; provides colleges and universities with grants for research, education, and marine advisory services.

National Oceanic and Atmospheric Administration (NOAA) *(Commerce Dept.), Protected Resources,* 1315 East-West Hwy., 13th Floor, Silver Spring, MD 20910; (301) 427-8400. Fax, (301) 713-0376. Donna Wieting, Director.
General email, pr.webmaster@noaa.gov

Web, www.nmfs.noaa.gov/pr

Administers the Endangered Species Act and the Marine Mammal Protection Act. Provides guidance on the conservation and protection of marine mammals, threatened and endangered marine and anadromous species, and their habitat. Develops national guidelines and policies for the implementation of the Acts, including recovery of protected species, review and issuance of permits and authorization under the Acts, and consultations with other agencies on federal actions that may affect protected species or their habitat. Prepares and reviews management and recovery plans and environmental impact analysis.

U.S. Fish and Wildlife Service *(Interior Dept.),* 1849 C St. N.W., #3358, 20240; (202) 208-4717. Fax, (202) 208-6965. Daniel M. Ashe, Director. Press, (703) 358-2220. Toll-free, (800) 344-9453.
Web, www.fws.gov

Works with federal and state agencies and nonprofits to conserve, protect, and enhance fish and wildlife and their habitats for the continuing benefit of the American people.

U.S. Fish and Wildlife Service *(Interior Dept.), Bird Habitat Conservation,* 5275 Leesburg Pike, MS MB, Falls Church, VA 22041; (703) 358-1784. Fax, (703) 358-2282. Sarah Pearson Mott, Division Chief, (703) 358-1910; Rachel F. Levin, Communications Coordinator, (703) 358-2405.
Web, www.fws.gov/birds

Coordinates U.S. activities with Canada and Mexico to protect waterfowl habitats, restore waterfowl populations, and set research priorities under the North American Waterfowl Management Plan.

U.S. Fish and Wildlife Service *(Interior Dept.), Endangered Species,* 5275 Leesburg Pike, Falls Church, VA 22041; (703) 358-2171. Fax, (202) 208-5618. Bridget Fahey, Chief.
Web, www.fws.gov/endangered and Twitter, @USFWSEndsp

Administers federal policy on fish and wildlife under the Endangered Species Act, Marine Mammal Protection Act, Fish and Wildlife Coordination Act, Oil Pollution Act, and other environmental laws. Reviews all federal and federally licensed projects to determine environmental effects on fish and wildlife. Responsible for maintaining the endangered species list and for protecting and restoring species to healthy numbers.

U.S. Fish and Wildlife Service *(Interior Dept.), National Wildlife Refuge System,* 4401 N. Fairfax Dr., Arlington, VA 22203; (703) 358-2517. Fax, (703) 358-1973. Cynthia Martinez, Chief.
Web, www.fws.gov/refuges and Twitter, @USFWSRefuges

Determines policy for the management of wildlife. Manages the National Wildlife Refuge System and land acquisition for wildlife refuges.

U.S. Geological Survey (USGS) *(Interior Dept.), Ecosystems,* 12201 Sunrise Valley Dr., MS 300, Reston, VA 20192; (703) 648-4050. Fax, (703) 648-7031. Anne E. Kinsinger, Associate Director, (703) 648-4051.
Web, www.usgs.gov/ecosystems

Conducts research and monitoring to develop and convey an understanding of ecosystem function and distributions, physical and biological components, and trophic dynamics for freshwater, terrestrial, and marine ecosystems and the human, fish, and wildlife communities they support. Subject areas include invasive species, endangered species and habitats, genetics and genomics, and microbiology.

►CONGRESS

For a listing of relevant congressional committees and subcommittees, please see pages 270–271 or the Appendix.

►NONGOVERNMENTAL

Animal Welfare Institute, *900 Pennsylvania Ave. S.E., 20003 (mailing address: P.O. Box 3650, Washington, DC 20027); (202) 337-2332. Fax, (202) 446-2131. Cathy Liss, President.*
General email, awi@awionline.org
Web, www.awionline.org

Works to preserve species threatened with extinction and protect wildlife from inhumane means of capture. Promotes efforts to end whaling and shark finning. Programs include preserving American wild horses and promoting nonlethal wildlife management solutions. Monitors legislation and regulations. (Merged with the Society for Animal Protective Legislation.)

Assn. of Fish and Wildlife Agencies, *1100 1st St. N.E., #825, 20001; (202) 838-3474. Fax, (202) 624-7891. Ron Regan, Executive Director.*
General email, info@fishwildlife.org
Web, www.fishwildlife.org, Twitter, @fishwildlife and Facebook, www.facebook.com/FishWildlifeAgencies

Membership: state, provincial, and territorial fish and wildlife management agencies in the United States, Canada, and Mexico. Encourages balanced, research-based fish and wildlife resource management. Monitors legislation and regulations.

Defenders of Wildlife, *1130 17th St. N.W., 20036; (202) 682-9400. Fax, (202) 682-1331. Jamie Rappaport Clark, President. Toll-free, (800) 385-9712.*
General email, defenders@mail.defenders.org
Web, www.defenders.org

Advocacy group that works to protect wild animals, marine life, and plant life in their natural communities. Interests include endangered species and biodiversity. Monitors legislation and regulations.

Ducks Unlimited, *Governmental Affairs, 1301 Pennsylvania Ave. N.W., #402, 20004; (202) 347-1530. Fax, (202) 347-1533. Margaret Everson, Director.*
Web, www.ducks.org

Promotes waterfowl and other wildlife conservation through activities aimed at developing and restoring natural nesting and migration habitats. (Headquarters in Memphis, Tenn.)

Humane Society of the United States, *2100 L St. N.W., 20037; (202) 452-1100. Fax, (202) 778-6132. Wayne Pacelle, President.*
Web, www.humanesociety.org

Works for the humane treatment and protection of animals. Interests include protecting endangered wildlife and marine mammals and their habitats and ending inhumane or cruel conditions in zoos.

Jane Goodall Institute, *1595 Spring Hill Rd., #550, Vienna, VA 22182; (703) 682-9220. Fax, (703) 682-9312. Mary Humphrey, Chief Operating Officer.*
Web, www.janegoodall.org

Seeks to increase primate habitat conservation, expand noninvasive primate research, and promote activities that ensure the well-being of primates. (Affiliated with Jane Goodall Institutes in Canada, Europe, Asia, and Africa.)

National Fish and Wildlife Foundation, *1133 15th St. N.W., #1100, 20005; (202) 857-0166. Fax, (202) 857-0162. Jeff Trandahl, Executive Director.*
General email, info@nfwf.org
Web, www.nfwf.org, Twitter, @NFWFnews and Facebook, www.facebook.com/FishandWildlife

Forges partnerships between the public and private sectors in support of national and international conservation activities that identify and root out causes of environmental problems that affect fish, wildlife, and plants.

National Wildlife Federation, *11100 Wildlife Center Dr., Reston, VA 20190-5362 (mailing address: P.O. Box 1583, Merrifield, VA 22116-1583); (703) 438-6000. Fax, (703) 438-3570. Collin O'Mara, President. Information, (800) 822-9919.*
General email, info@nwf.org
Web, www.nwf.org

Promotes conservation of natural resources; provides information on the environment and resource management; takes legal action on environmental issues.

National Wildlife Refuge Assn., *1001 Connecticut Ave. N.W., #905, 20036; (202) 417-3803. David Houghton, President, ext. 12; Caroline Brouwer, Government Affairs.*
General email, nwra@refugeassociation.org
Web, www.refugeassociation.org

Works to improve management and protection of the National Wildlife Refuge System by providing information to administrators, Congress, and the public. Advocates adequate funding and improved policy guidance for the Refuge System; assists individual refuges with particular needs.

Ocean Conservancy, *1300 19th St. N.W., 8th Floor, 20036; (202) 429-5609. Fax, (202) 872-0619. Janis Jones, President. Toll-free, (800) 519-1541.*
General email, membership@oceanconservancy.org
Web, www.oceanconservancy.org

Works to conserve the diversity and abundance of life in the oceans and coastal areas, to prevent the overexploitation of living marine resources and the degradation of marine ecosystems, and to restore depleted marine wildlife populations and their ecosystems.

Wildlife Habitat Council, *8737 Colesville Rd., #800, Silver Spring, MD 20910; (301) 588-8994. Fax, (301) 588-4629. Margaret O'Gorman, President, (301) 588-4219. General email, whc@wildlifehc.org*
Web, www.wildlifehc.org and Twitter, @WildlifeHC

Membership: corporations, conservation groups, local governments, and academic institutions. Seeks to increase the quality and amount of wildlife habitat on corporate, private, and public lands. Builds partnerships between corporations and conservation groups to find solutions that balance economic growth with a healthy, biodiverse, and sustainable environment. Provides technical assistance and educational programs; fosters collaboration among members.

The Wildlife Society, *5410 Grosvenor Lane, #200, Bethesda, MD 20814-2144; (301) 897-9770. Fax, (301) 530-2471. Kenneth Williams, Executive Director. General email, tws@wildlife.org*
Web, www.wildlife.org and Twitter, @wildlifesociety

Membership: wildlife biologists and resource management specialists. Provides information on management techniques, sponsors conferences, maintains list of job opportunities for members.

World Wildlife Fund (WWF), *1250 24th St. N.W., 20037-1193 (mailing address: P.O. Box 97180, Washington, DC 20090-7180); (202) 293-4800. Fax, (202) 293-9211. Carter S. Roberts, President. Web, www.worldwildlife.org and Twitter, @World_Wildlife*

International conservation organization that supports and conducts scientific research and conservation projects to promote biological diversity and to save endangered species and their habitats. Awards grants for habitat protection.

POLLUTION AND TOXINS

General

▶**AGENCIES**

Environmental Protection Agency (EPA), *Chemical Safety and Pollution Prevention, Pollution Prevention and Toxics, 1200 Pennsylvania Ave. N.W., #4146, MC 7401M, 20460; (202) 564-3810. Fax, (202) 564-0575. Wendy Cleland-Hamnet, Director. Toxic substance hotline, (202) 554-1404. Web, www.epa.gov/aboutepa/about-office-chemical-safety-and-pollution-prevention-ocspp and www.epa.gov/aboutepa/organization-chart-office-chemical-safety-and-pollution-prevention-ocspp*

Manages programs on pollution prevention and new and existing chemicals in the marketplace such as asbestos, lead, mercury, formaldehyde, PFOAs, and PCBs.

Programs include the High Production Volume Challenge Program, Sustainable Futures, the Green Chemistry Program, Green Suppliers Network, the High Production Volume Challenge Program, Design for the Environment, and the Chemical Right-to-Know Initiative. Selects and implements control measures for new and existing chemicals that present a risk to human health and the environment. Oversees and manages regulatory evaluation and decision-making processes. Evaluates alternative remedial control measures under the Toxic Substances Control Act and makes recommendations concerning the existence of unreasonable risk from exposure to chemicals, including pesticides and fungicides. Develops generic and chemical-specific rules for new chemicals. Operates the toxic substance hotline.

Environmental Protection Agency (EPA), *Enforcement and Compliance Assurance, 1200 Pennsylvania Ave. N.W., #3204, MC 2201A, 20460; (202) 564-2440. Fax, (202) 501-3842. Cynthia J. Giles, Assistant Administrator. Web, www2.epa.gov/aboutepa/about-office-enforcement-and-compliance-assurance-oeca*

Enforces laws that protect public health and the environment from hazardous materials, pesticides, and toxic substances. Implements the Clean Air Act, Clean Water Act, Comprehensive Environmental Response, Compensation and Liability Act, Emergency Planning and Community Right-to-Know Act, Federal Insecticide, Fungicide, and Rodenticide Act, Marine Protection, Research, and Sanctuaries Act, National Environmental Policy Act, Oil Pollution Act, Resource Conservation and Recovery Act, Safe Drinking Water Act, and Toxic Substances Control Act.

Environmental Protection Agency (EPA), *Land and Emergency Management, Federal Facilities Restoration and Reuse, 1 Potomac Yard, 2777 S. Crystal Dr., Arlington, VA 22202 (mailing address: 1200 Pennsylvania Ave. N.W., #5106R, Washington, DC 20460); (202) 564-2307. Charlotte Bertrand, Director, Acting. Web, www.epa.gov/fedfac/restoration-and-reuse-federal-facilities*

Works with the Defense Dept., Energy Dept., and other federal offices for more effective and less costly cleanup and reuse of federal facilities.

Environmental Protection Agency (EPA), *Land and Emergency Management, Resource Conservation and Recovery, 1 Potomac Yard, 2777 S. Crystal Dr., Arlington, VA 22202 (mailing address: 1200 Pennsylvania Ave. N.W., #5301P, Washington, DC 20460); (703) 308-8895. Barnes Johnson, Director. Web, www.epa.gov/aboutepa/about-office-land-and-emergency-management-olem*

Protects human health and the environment by ensuring responsible national management of hazardous and nonhazardous waste. Administers the Resource Conservation and Recovery Act.

Justice Dept. (DOJ), *Environmental Crimes, 601 D St. N.W., 2nd Floor, 20004 (mailing address: P.O. Box 7611,*

Washington, DC 20044); (202) 305-0321.
Deborah L. Harris, Chief.
Web, www.justice.gov/environmental-crimes-section

Conducts criminal enforcement actions on behalf of the United States for all environmental protection statutes, including air, water, pesticides, hazardous waste, wetland matters investigated by the Environmental Protection Agency, and other criminal environmental enforcement.

Justice Dept. (DOJ), *Environmental Defense, 601 D St. N.W., #8000, 20004 (mailing address: P.O. Box 7611, Washington, DC 20044); (202) 514-2219. Fax, (202) 514-8865. Letitia J. Grishaw, Chief.*
Web, www.justice.gov/environmental-crimes-section

Conducts litigation on air, water, noise, pesticides, solid waste, toxic substances, Superfund, and wetlands in cooperation with the Environmental Protection Agency; represents the EPA in suits involving judicial review of EPA actions; represents the U.S. Army Corps of Engineers in cases involving dredge-and-fill activity in navigable waters and adjacent wetlands; represents the Coast Guard in oil and hazardous spill cases; defends all federal agencies in environmental litigation.

Justice Dept. (DOJ), *Environmental Enforcement, 601 D St. N.W., #2121, 20004 (mailing address: P.O. Box 7611, Ben Franklin Station, Washington, DC 20044-7611); (202) 514-2750. Fax, (202) 514-0097. W. Benjamin Fisherow, Chief.*
Web, www.justice.gov/enrd

Conducts civil enforcement actions on behalf of the United States for all environmental protection statutes, including air, water, pesticides, hazardous waste, wetland matters investigated by the Environmental Protection Agency, and other civil environmental enforcement.

► **CONGRESS**

For a listing of relevant congressional committees and subcommittees, please see pages 270–271 or the Appendix.

► **NONGOVERNMENTAL**

American Academy of Environmental Engineers & Scientists, *147 Old Solomons Island Rd., #303, Annapolis, MD 20141; (410) 266-3311. Fax, (410) 266-7653. Burk Kalweit, Executive Director.*
General email, info@aaees.org
Web, www.aaees.org

Membership: state-licensed environmental engineers and scientists who have passed examinations in environmental engineering and/or science specialties, including general environment, air pollution control, solid waste management, hazardous waste management, industrial hygiene, radiation protection, water supply, environmental sustainability, and wastewater.

National Research Council (NRC), *Environmental Studies and Toxicology Board, Keck Center, 500 5th St. N.W., 20001; (202) 334-3982. James J. Riesa, Director, (202) 334-3060; Rogene F. Henderson, Chair.*

General email, best@nas.edu
Web, http://dels.nas.edu/best

Conducts research on environmental pollution problems affecting human health, human impacts on the environment, and the assessment and management of related risks to human health and the environment. Seeks to improve environmental decision making and public understanding of environmental issues.

Physicians for Social Responsibility (PSR), *1111 14th St. N.W., #700, 20005; (202) 667-4260. Fax, (202) 667-4201. Dr. Catherine Thomasson, Executive Director.*
General email, psrnatl@psr.org
Web, www.psr.org

Membership: doctors, nurses, health scientists, and concerned citizens. Works to protect the public and environment from toxic chemicals. Conducts public education programs, monitors policy, and serves as a liaison with other concerned groups.

Air Pollution

► **AGENCIES**

Environmental Protection Agency (EPA), *Air and Radiation, 1200 Pennsylvania Ave. N.W., #5426, MC 6101A, 20460; (202) 564-7400. Fax, (202) 564-1408. Janet McCabe, Assistant Administrator, Acting; Elizabeth Shaw, Deputy Assistant Administrator.*
Web, www.epa.gov/aboutepa/about-office-air-and-radiation-oar and www3.epa.gov/air

Administers air quality standards and planning programs of the Clean Air Act Amendment of 1990. Operates the Air and Radiation Docket and Information Center. Supervises the Office of Air Quality Planning and Standards in Durham, N.C., which develops air quality standards and provides information on air pollution control issues, including industrial air pollution. Administers the Air Pollution Technical Information Center in Research Triangle Park, N.C., which collects and provides technical literature on air pollution.

Environmental Protection Agency (EPA), *Air and Radiation, Atmospheric Programs, 1200 Pennsylvania Ave. N.W., #5426, MC 6201A, 20460; (202) 343-9140. Fax, (202) 343-2210. Sarah W. Dunham, Director.*
Web, www.epa.gov/aboutepa/about-office-air-and-radiation-oar#oap

Responsible for acid rain and global protection programs. Examines strategies for preventing atmospheric pollution and mitigating climate change. Administers public-private partnerships, such as ENERGY STAR.

Environmental Protection Agency (EPA), *Air and Radiation, Transportation and Air Quality, 1200 Pennsylvania Ave. N.W., #5426, MC 6401A, 20460; (202) 564-1682. Fax, (202) 564-1408. Christopher Grundler, Director.*
General email, otaq@epa.gov
Web, www3.epa.gov/otaq and NVFEL, www3.epa.gov/nvfel

Promotes reduction of air pollution and greenhouse gas emissions from automobiles, trucks, buses, farm and construction equipment, lawn and garden equipment, marine engines, aircraft, and locomotives. Establishes national air quality standards for on-road and nonroad mobiles and develops fuel efficiency programs. Supervises the National Vehicle and Fuel Emissions Laboratory (NVFEL) in Ann Arbor, Mich., which provides emissions testing services to aid the development of certifications, enforcement actions, test procedures, and rulemaking.

Environmental Protection Agency (EPA), *Enforcement and Compliance Assurance, Monitoring, Assistance, and Media Programs, 1200 Pennsylvania Ave. N.W., #7138, MC 2223A, 20460; (202) 564-1191. Fax, (202) 564-0050. Edward Messina, Director; Rafael Sánchez, EPA Contact, (202) 564-7028.*
Web, www.epa.gov/aboutepa/oeca.html#oc

Responsible for development and implementation of a national program of compliance concerning lead regulations and matters related to the Clean Air Act, Clean Water Act, Resource Conservation and Recovery Act, and Oil Pollution Act.

Federal Aviation Administration (FAA) *(Transportation Dept.), Policy, International Affairs, and Environment, Environment and Energy Research and Development, 800 Independence Ave. S.W., #900W, 20591; (202) 267-3576. Fax, (202) 267-5594. Lourdes Maurice, Executive Director. Web, www.faa.gov/about/office_org/headquarters_offices/apl/research*

Develops government standards for aircraft noise and emissions.

U.S. Geological Survey (USGS) *(Interior Dept.), Energy Resources, 12201 Sunrise Valley Dr., MS 913, Reston, VA 20192 (mailing address: 913 National Center, Reston, VA 20192); (703) 648-6470. Fax, (703) 648-5464. Vito Nuccio, Program Coordinator, Acting.*
General email, gd-energyprogram@usgs.gov
Web, http://energy.usgs.gov

Conducts research on geologically based energy resources of the United States and the world; estimates energy resource availability and recoverability; anticipates and mitigates deleterious environmental impacts of energy resource extraction and use.

▶**CONGRESS**

For a listing of relevant congressional committees and subcommittees, please see pages 270–271 or the Appendix.

▶**NONGOVERNMENTAL**

Alliance for Responsible Atmospheric Policy, *2111 Wilson Blvd., #850, Arlington, VA 22201; (703) 243-0344. Fax, (703) 243-2874. Kevin Fay, Executive Director. General email, info@arap.org*
Web, www.arap.org

Coalition of users and producers of chlorofluorocarbons (CFCs). Seeks further study of the ozone depletion theory.

American Lung Assn., *1301 Pennsylvania Ave. N.W., #800, 20004-1725; (202) 785-3355. Fax, (202) 452-1805. Harold Wimmer, President; Paul Billings, Vice President of Advocacy and Education.*
Web, www.lung.org and Twitter, @LungAssociation

Promotes improved lung health and the prevention of lung disease through research, education, and advocacy. Interests include antismoking campaigns; lung-related biomedical research; air pollution; and all lung diseases, including asthma, COPD, and lung cancer. (Headquarters in Chicago, Ill.)

Center for Auto Safety, *1825 Connecticut Ave. N.W., #330, 20009-5708; (202) 328-7700. Fax, (202) 387-0140. Clarence Ditlow, Executive Director.*
General email, accounts@autosafety.org
Web, www.autosafety.org

Public interest organization that conducts research on air pollution caused by auto emissions; monitors fuel economy regulations.

Center for Clean Air Policy, *750 1st St. N.E., #940, 20002; (202) 408-9260. Fax, (202) 408-8896. Bill Tyndall, Chief Executive Officer.*
General email, general@ccap.org or tassistant@ccap.org
Web, www.ccap.org and Twitter, @CleanAirPolicy

Membership: international policymakers, climate negotiators, corporations, environmentalists, and academicians. Analyzes economic and environmental effects of air pollution and related environmental problems. Serves as a liaison among government, corporate, community, and environmental groups.

Climate Institute, *1400 16th St. N.W., #430, 20036; (202) 552-0163. John C. Topping, President.*
General email, info@climate.org
Web, www.climate.org

Educates the public and policymakers on climate change, the greenhouse effect, global warming, and the depletion of the ozone layer. Assesses climate change risks and develops strategies on mitigating climate change in developing countries and in North America.

The Climate Reality Project, *750 9th St. N.W., #520, 20001; (202) 567-6800. Fax, (202) 628-1445. Ken Berlin, President.*
General email, info@climatereality.com
Web, www.climaterealityproject.org and Twitter, @ClimateReality

Aims to reduce carbon emissions, supports taxing oil and coal companies that emit large amounts of carbon, and educates the public on climate change and its relation to carbon pollution.

Environmental Defense Fund, *Washington Office, 1875 Connecticut Ave. N.W., #600, 20009-5728; (202) 387-3500. Fax, (202) 234-6049. Fred Krupp, President; Felice Stradler, Director, U.S. Climate and Political Affairs. Information, (800) 684-3322. Press, (202) 572-3396. Web, www.edf.org and Twitter, @EnvDefenseFund*

Citizens' interest group staffed by lawyers, economists, and scientists. Conducts research and provides information on pollution prevention, environmental health, and the Clean Air Act. (Headquarters in New York.)

Manufacturers of Emission Controls Assn., *2200 Wilson Blvd., #310, Arlington, VA 22201; (202) 296-4797. Joseph E. Kubsh, Executive Director. Web, www.meca.org*

Membership: manufacturers of motor vehicle emission control equipment. Provides information on emission technology and industry capabilities.

National Assn. of Clean Air Agencies (NACAA), *444 N. Capitol St. N.W., #307, 20001; (202) 624-7864. Fax, (202) 624-7863. Bill Becker, Executive Director. General email, 4cleanair@4cleanair.org Web, www.4cleanair.org*

Membership: air pollution control agencies nationwide. Seeks to improve effective management of air resources by encouraging the exchange of information among air pollution control officials. Monitors federal regulations; publishes reports and analyses; develops model rules for states and localities.

National Research Council (NRC), *Atmospheric Sciences and Climate Board, Keck Center 500 5th St. N.W., #602, 20001; (202) 334-3512. Fax, (202) 334-3825. Amanda Staudt, Director; A.R. Ravishankara, Chair. General email, basc@nas.edu Web, http://nas.edu/basc*

Supports research on climate change, air pollution, and severe weather in order to address environmental policies, human health, emergency management, energy choices, manufacturing decisions, construction codes, and agricultural methods.

Hazardous Materials

▶**AGENCIES**

Agency for Toxic Substances and Disease Registry (ATSDR) *(Health and Human Services Dept.), Washington Office, 1200 Pennsylvania Ave. N.W., MC 5202P, 20460; (703) 603-8729. Steve A. Jones, Regional Director. Press, (770) 488-0700. Web, www.atsdr.cdc.gov/dro/hq.html*

Works with federal, state, and local agencies to minimize or eliminate adverse effects of exposure to toxic substances at spill and waste disposal sites. Maintains a registry of persons exposed to hazardous substances and of diseases and illnesses resulting from exposure to hazardous or toxic substances. Maintains inventory of hazardous substances and registry of sites closed or restricted because of contamination by hazardous material. (Headquarters in Atlanta, Ga.)

Defense Dept. (DoD), *Energy, Installations, and Environment, 3400 Defense Pentagon, #5C646, 20301-3400; (703) 695-2880. Fax, (703) 693-2659. John Conger,*

Assistant Secretary, Acting. Web, www.acq.osd.mil/eie

Oversees and offers policy guidance for all Defense Dept. energy, installations, and environmental programs.

Environmental Protection Agency (EPA), *Chemical Safety and Pollution Prevention, 1200 Pennsylvania Ave. N.W., #4146, MC 7101M, 20460; (202) 564-2902. Fax, (202) 564-0801. James J. Jones, Assistant Administrator. Web, www2.epa.gov/aboutepa/about-office-chemical-safety-and-pollution-prevention-ocspp*

Studies and makes recommendations for regulating chemical substances under the Toxic Substances Control Act. Compiles list of chemical substances subject to the act. Registers, controls, and regulates use of pesticides and toxic substances. Manages the Endocrine Disruptor Screening Program.

Environmental Protection Agency (EPA), *Chemical Safety and Pollution Prevention, Pollution Prevention and Toxics, 1200 Pennsylvania Ave. N.W., #4146, MC 7401M, 20460; (202) 564-3810. Fax, (202) 564-0575. Wendy Cleland-Hamnet, Director. Toxic substance hotline, (202) 554-1404. Web, www.epa.gov/aboutepa/about-office-chemical-safety-and-pollution-prevention-ocspp and www.epa.gov/aboutepa/organization-chart-office-chemical-safety-and-pollution-prevention-ocspp*

Assesses the health and environmental hazards of existing chemical substances and mixtures; collects information on chemical use, exposure, and effects; maintains inventory of existing chemical substances; reviews new chemicals and regulates the manufacture, distribution, use, and disposal of harmful chemicals. Implements the Toxic Substances Control Act and the Pollution Prevention Act. Selects and implements control measures for new and existing chemicals that present a risk to human health and the environment. Oversees and manages regulatory evaluation and decision-making processes. Evaluates alternative remedial control measures under the Toxic Substances Control Act and makes recommendations concerning the existence of unreasonable risk from exposure to chemicals, including pesticides and fungicides. Develops generic and chemical-specific rules for new chemicals. Operates the toxic substance hotline.

Environmental Protection Agency (EPA), *Emergency Management, 1200 Pennsylvania Ave. N.W., MC 5104A, 20460; (202) 564-8600. Reggie Cheatham, Director, Acting; Dana S. Tulis, Deputy Director. Toll-free call center, (800) 424-8802. TTY, (800) 553-7672. Web, www.epa.gov/emergency-response*

Develops and administers chemical emergency preparedness and prevention programs; reviews effectiveness of programs; prepares community right-to-know regulations. Provides guidance materials, technical assistance, and training. Implements the preparedness and community right-to-know provisions of the Superfund Amendments and Reauthorization Act of 1986.

Environmental Protection Agency (EPA), *Enforcement and Compliance Assurance,* 1200 Pennsylvania Ave. N.W., #3204, MC 2201A, 20460; (202) 564-2440. Fax, (202) 501-3842. Cynthia J. Giles, Assistant Administrator. Web, www2.epa.gov/aboutepa/about-office-enforcement-and-compliance-assurance-oeca

Enforces laws that protect public health and the environment from hazardous materials, pesticides, and toxic substances. Implements the Clean Air Act, Clean Water Act, Comprehensive Environmental Response, Compensation and Liability Act, Emergency Planning and Community Right-to-Know Act, Federal Insecticide, Fungicide, and Rodenticide Act, Marine Protection, Research, and Sanctuaries Act, National Environmental Policy Act, Oil Pollution Act, Resource Conservation and Recovery Act, Safe Drinking Water Act, and Toxic Substances Control Act.

Environmental Protection Agency (EPA), *Enforcement and Compliance Assurance, Site Remediation Enforcement,* 1200 Pennsylvania Ave. N.W., #2271A, 20460; (202) 564-5110. Cyndy Mackey, Director. Web, www.epa.gov/aboutepa/about-office-enforcement-and-compliance-assurance-oeca

Requires those responsible for hazardous waste sites to clean up or reimburse the EPA for cleanup. Enforces national hazardous waste cleanup programs, including Superfund programs, Resource Conservation and Recovery Act, Oil Pollution Act, and underground storage tank systems.

Environmental Protection Agency (EPA), *Land and Emergency Management,* 1200 Pennsylvania Ave. N.W., MC 5101T, 20460; (202) 272-0167. Fax, (202) 566-0207. Mathy V. Stanislaus, Assistant Administrator, (202) 566-0200. National Response Center, (800) 424-8802. Superfund information hotline, (800) 424-9346. Local, (703) 412-9810. Web, www2.epa.gov/aboutepa/about-office-land-and-emergency-management-olem

Administers and enforces the Superfund act and manages the handling, cleanup, and disposal of hazardous wastes.

Environmental Protection Agency (EPA), *Land and Emergency Management, Brownfields and Land Revitalization,* 1300 Pennsylvania Ave. N.W., #5105T, 20460; (202) 566-2777. David Lloyd, Director. Web, www.epa.gov/land-revitalization and www.epa.gov/brownfields

Provides grants and technical assistance to communities, states, tribes, and other stakeholders needing resources to prevent, assess, safely clean up, and sustainably reuse brownfields and formerly contaminated properties.

Environmental Protection Agency (EPA), *Land and Emergency Management, Superfund Remediation and Technology Innovation,* 1 Potomac Yard, 2777 S. Crystal Dr., Arlington, VA 22202 (mailing address: 1200 Pennsylvania Ave. N.W., #5201P, Washington, DC 20460); (703) 603-8960. Jim Woolford, Director. Web, www.epa.gov/superfund

Responsible for Superfund and contaminated land cleanup; responds to environmental emergencies, oil spills, and natural disasters.

Housing and Urban Development Dept. (HUD), *Lead Hazard Control and Healthy Homes,* 451 7th St. S.W., #8236, 20410; (202) 708-0310. Fax, (202) 708-0014. Matthew Amon, Director. Web, http://portal.hud.gov/hudportal/HUD?src=/program_offices/healthy_homes

Advises HUD offices, other agencies, health authorities, and the housing industry on lead poisoning prevention. Develops regulations for lead-based paint; conducts research; makes grants to state and local governments for lead hazard reduction and inspection of housing.

Interior Dept. (DOI), *Natural Resource Damage Assessment and Restoration Program,* 1849 C St. N.W., MS 3558, 20240; (202) 208-4863. Fax, (202) 208-2681. Web, www.doi.gov/restoration

Works to restore natural resources that have been compromised as a result of oil spills or hazardous substances released into the environment.

Justice Dept. (DOJ), *Environmental Enforcement,* 601 D St. N.W., #2121, 20004 (mailing address: P.O. Box 7611, Ben Franklin Station, Washington, DC 20044-7611); (202) 514-2750. Fax, (202) 514-0097. W. Benjamin Fisherow, Chief. Web, www.justice.gov/enrd

Represents the United States in civil cases under environmental laws that involve the handling, storage, treatment, transportation, and disposal of hazardous waste. Recovers federal money spent to clean up hazardous waste sites or sues defendants to clean up sites under Superfund.

Pipeline and Hazardous Materials Safety Administration *(Transportation Dept.),* 1200 New Jersey Ave. S.E., #E27-300, 20590; (202) 366-4433. Fax, (202) 366-3666. Marie Therese Dominguez, Administrator. Hazardous Materials Information Center, (800) 467-4922. To report an incident, (800) 424-8802. General email, phmsa.administrator@dot.gov

Web, www.phmsa.dot.gov and Twitter, @PHMSA_DOT

Oversees the safe and secure movement of hazardous materials to industry and consumers by all modes of transportation, including pipelines. Works to eliminate transportation-related deaths and injuries. Promotes transportation solutions to protect communities and the environment.

Pipeline and Hazardous Materials Safety Administration *(Transportation Dept.),* **Hazardous Materials Safety,** 1200 New Jersey Ave. S.E., #E21-317, 20590; (202) 366-0656. Fax, (202) 366-5713. Magdy A. El-Sibaie, Associate Administrator. Hazardous Materials Information Center, (800) 467-4922. General email, phmsa.hmhazmatsafety@dot.gov

Web, http://hazmat.dot.gov

Interior Department

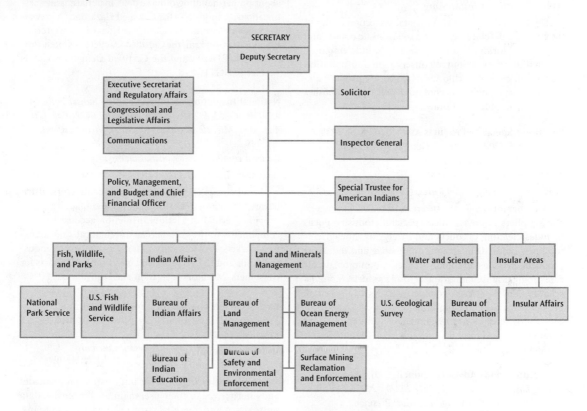

Designates substances as hazardous materials and regulates their transportation in interstate commerce; coordinates international standards regulations.

Pipeline and Hazardous Materials Safety Administration *(Transportation Dept.), Pipeline Safety, 1200 New Jersey Ave. S.E., E24-455, 20590; (202) 366-4595. Fax, (202) 366-4566. Jeffery D. Wiese, Associate Administrator.*
General email, phmsa.pipelinesafety@dot.gov

Web, http://phmsa.dot.gov

Issues and enforces federal regulations for hazardous liquids pipeline safety.

U.S. Coast Guard (USCG) *(Homeland Security Dept.), National Response Center, 2100 2nd St. S.W., #2111B, 20593-0001; (202) 267-2180. Fax, (202) 267-1322. Syed M. Qadir, Director, (202) 372-2440. TTY, (202) 267-4477. Hotline, (800) 424-8802. Local, (202) 267-2675. General email, NRC@uscg.mil*

Web, www.nrc.uscg.mil

Maintains 24-hour hotline for reporting oil spills, hazardous materials accidents, and chemical releases. Notifies appropriate federal officials to reduce the effects of accidents.

▶**CONGRESS**

For a listing of relevant congressional committees and sub-committees, please see pages 270–271 or the Appendix.

▶**NONGOVERNMENTAL**

Alliance of Hazardous Materials Professionals, *9650 Rockville Pike, Bethesda, MD 20814; (301) 634-7430. Fax, (301) 634-7431. A. Cedric Calhoun, Executive Director. Toll-free, (800) 437-0137.*
General email, info@ahmpnet.org

Web, www.ahmpnet.org

Membership: professionals who work with hazardous materials and environmental, health, and safety issues. Offers professional development and networking opportunities to members. Members must be certified by the Institute of Hazardous Materials Management (IHMM).

Center for Health, Environment, and Justice, *105 Rowell Court, 1st Floor, Falls Church, VA 22046 (mailing address: P.O. Box 6806, Falls Church, VA 22040-6806); (703) 237-2249. Fax, (703) 237-8389. Laura Barrett, Executive Director. General email, chej@chej.org*

Web, www.chej.org and Twitter, @chej

Provides citizens' groups, individuals, and municipalities with support and information on solid and hazardous waste. Sponsors workshops, a speakers bureau, on-site training and leadership development conference, and convention. Maintains toxicity files on the environmental and health effects of common chemical compounds.

Chlorine Institute Inc., *1300 Wilson Blvd., #525, Arlington, VA 22209; (703) 894-4140. Fax, (703) 894-4130. Frank Reiner, President.*

General email, info@cl2.com

Web, www.chlorineinstitute.org

Safety, health, and environmental protection center of the chlor-alkali (chlorine, caustic soda, caustic potash, and hydrogen chloride) industry. Interests include employee health and safety, resource conservation and pollution abatement, control of chlorine emergencies, product specifications, and public and community relations. Publishes technical pamphlets and drawings.

Consumer Specialty Products Assn., *1667 K St. N.W., #300, 20006; (202) 872-8110. Fax, (202) 223-2636. Christopher Cathcart, President.*

General email, info@cspa.org

Web, www.cspa.org and Twitter, @The_CSPA

Membership: manufacturers, marketers, packagers, and suppliers in the chemical specialties industry. Focus includes cleaning products and detergents, nonagricultural pesticides, disinfectants, automotive and industrial products, polishes and floor finishes, antimicrobials, air care products and candles, and aerosol products. Monitors scientific developments; conducts surveys and research; provides chemical safety information and consumer education programs; sponsors National Inhalants and Poisons Awareness and Aerosol Education Bureau. Monitors legislation and regulations.

Dangerous Goods Advisory Council, *7501 Greenway Center Dr., #760, Greenbelt, MD 20770; (202) 289-4550. Fax, (202) 289-4074. Vaughn Arthur, President.*

General email, info@dgac.org

Web, www.dgac.org

Membership: shippers, carriers, container manufacturers and conditioners, emergency response and spill cleanup companies, and trade associations. Promotes safety in the domestic and international transportation of hazardous materials. Provides information and educational services; sponsors conferences, workshops, and seminars. Advocates uniform hazardous materials regulations.

Environmental Technology Council, *1112 16th St. N.W., #420, 20036; (202) 783-0870. Fax, (202) 737-2038. David R. Case, Executive Director. Press, (202) 783-0870, ext. 202.*

General email, mail@etc.org

Web, www.etc.org

Membership: environmental service firms. Interests include the recycling, detoxification, and disposal of hazardous and industrial waste and cleanup of contaminated industrial sites; works to encourage permanent and technology-based solutions to environmental problems. Provides the public with information.

Institute of Hazardous Materials Management (IHMM), *11900 Parklawn Dr., #450, Rockville, MD 20852; (301) 984-8969. Fax, (301) 984-1516. Jeffrey Greenwald, Executive Director.*

General email, info@ihmm.org

Web, www.ihmm.org

Seeks to educate professionals and the general public about proper handling of hazardous materials; issues certifications. Administers the Certified Hazardous Materials Manager program, the Certified Hazardous Materials Practitioner program, the Certified Dangerous Goods Professsional (CDGP), and the Certified Dangerous Goods Trainer (CDGT).

National Insulation Assn. (NIA), *12100 Sunset Hills Rd., #330, Reston, VA 20190-3233; (703) 464-6422. Fax, (703) 464-5896. Michele M. Jones, Executive Vice President, ext. 119.*

General email, niainfo@insulation.org

Web, www.insulation.org

Membership: open-shop and union contractors, distributors, laminators, fabricators, and manufacturers that provide thermal insulation, insulation accessories, and components to the commercial, mechanical, and industrial markets. Provides information to members on industry trends and technologies, and offers service contacts for consumers. Monitors legislation and regulations.

Rachel Carson Council Inc., *8600 Irvington Ave., Bethesda, MD 20817; (301) 214-2400. Robert Musil, President, (301) 493-4571.*

General email, office@rachelcarsoncouncil.org

Web, www.rachelcarsoncouncil.org

Acts as a clearinghouse for information on pesticides and alternatives to their use; maintains extensive data on toxicity and the effects of pesticides on humans, domestic animals, and wildlife. Library open to the public by appointment.

Radiation Protection

▶ **AGENCIES**

Environmental Protection Agency (EPA), *Air and Radiation, Radiation and Indoor Air,* 1200 Pennsylvania Ave. N.W., #5426, MC 6608T, 20460; (202) 343-9320. Fax, (202) 564-1408. Mike P. Flynn, Director.

Web, www2.epa.gov/aboutepa/about-office-air-and-radiation-oar#oria

Establishes standards to regulate the amount of radiation discharged into the environment from uranium mining and milling projects and other activities that result in radioactive emissions; and to ensure safe disposal of radioactive waste. Fields a Radiological Emergency Response Team. Administers the nationwide Environmental Radiation Ambient Monitoring System (RadNet), which analyzes environmental radioactive contamination. Oversees the National Air and Radiation Environmental Laboratory in Montgomery, Ala.

Food and Drug Administration (FDA) *(Health and Human Services Dept.), Center for Devices and Radiological Health,* 10903 New Hampshire Ave., W066,

Silver Spring, MD 20993; (301) 796-5900. Fax, (301) 847-8510. Jeffrey E. Shuren, Director.
General email, jeff.shuren@fda.hhs.gov

Web, www.fda.gov/medicaldevices and www.fda.gov/AboutFDA/CentersOffices/OfficeofMedicalProductsand Tobacco/CDRH/default.htm

Administers national programs to control exposure to radiation; establishes standards for emissions from consumer and medical products; conducts factory inspections. Accredits and certifies mammography facilities and personnel; provides physicians and consumers with guidelines on radiation-emitting products. Conducts research, training, and educational programs.

▶ NONGOVERNMENTAL

Institute for Science and International Security, 440 1st St. N.W., #800, 20001; (202) 547-3633. David Albright, President.
General email, isis@isis-online.org

Web, www.isis-online.org

Analyzes scientific and policy issues affecting national and international security, including the problems of war, regional and global arms races, the spread of nuclear weapons, and the environmental, health, and safety hazards of nuclear weapons production.

National Council on Radiation Protection and Measurements (NCRP), 7910 Woodmont Ave., #400, Bethesda, MD 20814-3095; (301) 657-2652. Fax, (301) 907-8768. David A. Smith, Executive Director; John D. Boice Jr., President.
General email, ncrp@ncrponline.org

Web, www.ncrponline.org and Twitter, @NCRP_Bethesda

Nonprofit organization chartered by Congress that collects and analyzes information and provides recommendations on radiation protection and measurement. Studies radiation emissions from household items and from office and medical equipment. Holds annual conference; publishes reports on radiation protection and measurement.

National Research Council (NRC), Nuclear and Radiation Studies Board, Keck Center, 500 5th St. N.W., 20001; (202) 334-3066. Fax, (202) 334-3077. Kevin Crowley, Senior Board Director; Robert C. Dynes, Chair.
General email, nrsb@nas.edu

Web, http://dels.nas.edu/nrsb

Oversee studies on safety, security, technical efficacy, and other policy and societal issues arising from the application of nuclear and radiation-based technologies, including exposure to radiation; generation, use, remediation, and disposition of nuclear materials and radioactive wastes; malevolent uses of nuclear and radiation-based technologies; and risks and benefits of nuclear and radiation-based applications, including medical applications.

Recycling and Solid Waste

▶ AGENCIES

Environmental Protection Agency (EPA), Land and Emergency Management, 1200 Pennsylvania Ave. N.W., MC 5101T, 20460; (202) 272-0167. Fax, (202) 566-0207. Mathy V. Stanislaus, Assistant Administrator, (202) 566-0200. National Response Center, (800) 424-8802. Superfund information hotline, (800) 424-9346. Local, (703) 412-9810.
Web, www2.epa.gov/aboutepa/about-office-land-and-emergency-management-olem

Administers and enforces the Resource Conservation and Recovery Act and the Brownfields Program and Superfund.

▶ CONGRESS

For a listing of relevant congressional committees and sub-committees, please see pages 270–271 or the Appendix.

▶ NONGOVERNMENTAL

American Chemistry Council, 700 2nd St. N.E., 20002; (202) 249-7000. Fax, (202) 249-6100. Calvin M. (Cal) Dooley, President.
Web, www.americanchemistry.com

Membership: manufacturers of basic industrial chemicals. Seeks to increase plastics recycling; conducts research on disposal of plastic products; sponsors research on waste-handling methods, incineration, and degradation; supports programs that test alternative waste management technologies. Monitors legislation and regulations.

Assn. of State and Territorial Solid Waste Management Officials (ASTSWMO), 1101 17th St. N.W., #707, 20036; (202) 640-1060. Fax, (202) 331-3254. Dania Rodriguez, Executive Director.
Web, www.astswmo.org and Twitter, @ASTSWMO

Membership: state and territorial solid waste management officials. Works with the Environmental Protection Agency to develop policy affecting waste, materials management, and remediation.

Energy Recovery Council, 2200 Wilson Blvd., #310, Arlington, VA 22201; (202) 467-6240. Edward (Ted) Michaels, President.
General email, info@energyrecoverycouncil.org

Web, www.energyrecoverycouncil.org

Membership: companies that design, build, and operate resource recovery facilities. Promotes integrated solutions to municipal solid waste management issues. Encourages the use of waste-to-energy technology.

EPS Industry Alliance, 1298 Cronson Blvd., #201, Crofton, MD 21114; (410) 451-8340. Fax, (410) 451-8343. Betsy Steiner, Executive Director. Toll-free, (800) 607-3772. General email, info@epspackaging.org

Web, www.epspackaging.org

Membership: companies that recycle foam packaging material (expanded polystyrene). Coordinates national network of collection centers for postconsumer foam packaging products; helps to establish new collection centers.

Foodservice Packaging Institute (FPI), *7700 Leesburg Pike, #421, Falls Church, VA 22043; (703) 592-9889. Fax, (703) 592-9864. Lynn Dyer, President, (571) 255-4211. General email, fpi@fpi.org*

Web, www.fpi.org and Twitter, @FPIHQ

Membership: manufacturers, suppliers, and distributors of disposable products used in food service, packaging, and consumer products. Promotes the use of disposables for commercial and home use.

Glass Packaging Institute, *1220 N. Fillmore St., #400, Arlington, VA 22201; (703) 684-6359. Fax, (703) 546-0588. Lynn Bragg, President. General email, info@gpi.org*

Web, www.gpi.org

Membership: manufacturers of glass containers and their suppliers. Promotes industry policies to protect the environment, conserve natural resources, and reduce energy consumption; conducts research; monitors legislation affecting the industry. Interests include glass recycling.

Institute for Local Self-Reliance, *1710 Connecticut Ave. N.W., 4th Floor, 20009; (202) 898-1610. Fax, (202) 898-1612. Neil N. Seldman, President. General email, info@ilsr.org*

Web, www.ilsr.org

Conducts research and provides technical assistance on environmentally sound economic development for government, small businesses, and community organizations. Advocates the development of a materials policy at local, state, and regional levels to reduce per capita consumption of raw materials and to shift from dependence on fossil fuels to reliance on renewable resources.

Institute of Scrap Recycling Industries, Inc., *1615 L St. N.W., #600, 20036-5610; (202) 662-8500. Fax, (202) 626-0900. Robin K. Wiener, President. General email, isri@isri.org*

Web, www.isri.org

Represents processors, brokers, and consumers of scrap and recyclable paper, glass, plastic, textiles, rubber, ferrous and nonferrous metals, and electronics.

National Recycling Coalition, Inc., *1220 L St. N.W., #100-155, 20005; (202) 618-2107. Bob Gedert, President; Laura Flagg, Communications. General email, info@nrcrecycles.org*

Web, http://nrcrecycles.org

Membership: public officials; community recycling groups; local, state, and national agencies; environmentalists; waste haulers; solid waste disposal consultants; and private recycling companies. Encourages recycling to reduce waste, preserve resources, and promote economic development.

National Waste and Recycling Assn., *4301 Connecticut Ave. N.W., #300, 20008-2304; (202) 244-4700. Fax, (202) 966-4824. Sharon H. Kneiss, President. Toll-free, (800) 424-2869. General email, skneiss@wasterecycling.org*

Web, https://wasterecycling.org

Membership: organizations engaged in refuse collection, processing, and disposal. Provides information on solid and hazardous waste recycling and waste equipment, organics and composting, waste-based energy, and emerging technologies; sponsors workshops. A merger of Environmental Industry Assns. and its sub-associations, the National Solid Waste Management Assn. and the Waste Equipment Technology Assn.

PaintCare Inc., *1500 Rhode Island Ave. N.W., 20005; (855) 724-6809. Fax, (855) 358-2020. Marjaneh Zarrehparvar, Executive Director, (202) 719-3683. Press, (415) 606-3211. General email, info@paintcare.org*

Web, www.paintcare.org

Assists paint manufacturers in planning programs to help recycle or dispose of unneeded paint. Organizes paint drop-off locations. Supports statewide paint stewardship laws.

Secondary Materials and Recycled Textiles Assn. (SMART), *3465 Box Hill Corp. Center Dr., Suite H, Abingdon, MD 21009; (443) 640-1050. Fax, (443) 640-1086. Jackie King, Executive Director, ext. 105. General email, smartinfo@kingmgmt.org*

Web, www.smartasn.org and Twitter, @SMARTTextile

Membership: organizations and individuals involved in producing, shipping, and distributing recycled textiles and other textile products. Sponsors educational programs; publishes newsletters. Monitors legislation and regulations.

Solid Waste Assn. of North America (SWANA), *1100 Wayne Ave., #650, Silver Spring, MD 20910-7219; (301) 585-2898. Fax, (301) 589-7068. David Biderman, Executive Director. Toll-free, (800) 467-9262. General email, membership@swana.org*

Web, www.swana.org

Membership: government and private industry officials who manage municipal solid waste programs. Interests include waste reduction, collection, recycling (including of electronics), combustion, and disposal. Conducts training and certification programs. Operates solid waste information clearinghouse. Monitors legislation and regulations.

U.S. Conference of Mayors, *Municipal Waste Management Assn., 1620 Eye St. N.W., 4th Floor, 20006; (202) 293-7330. Fax, (202) 429-2352. Jubi Headley, Managing Director, (202) 861-6798; Judy Sheahan, Assistant Executive Director for Environmental Policy, (202) 861-6775. General email, info@usmayors.org*

Web, www.usmayors.org/mwma

Membership: mayors of cities with populations of 30,000 or more, local governments, and private companies involved in planning and developing solid waste management programs, including pollution prevention, waste-to-energy, and recycling. Interests include Superfund, brownfields, air and water quality, and waste-to-energy technologies. Assists communities with financing, environmental assessments, and associated policy implementation.

Water Pollution

▶AGENCIES

Bureau of Safety and Environmental Enforcement (BSEE) *(Interior Dept.), Offshore Regulatory Programs,* *1849 C St. N.W., MS DM 5438, 20240-0001; (202) 208-3985. Fax, (202) 208-3968. Douglas Morris, Chief.*
General email, bseepublicaffairs@bsee.gov
Web, www.bsee.gov

Develops standards, regulations, and compliance programs governing Outer Continental Shelf oil, gas, and minerals exploration and operations. Purview includes safety management programs, safety and pollution prevention research, technology assessments, standards for inspections and enforcement policies, and accident investigation practices.

Environmental Protection Agency (EPA), *Land and Emergency Management, Underground Storage Tanks,* *1300 Pennsylvania Ave N.W., 7th Floor, 20460 (mailing address: 1200 Pennsylvania Ave. N.W., #5401R, Washington, DC 20460); (202) 564-0663.*
Carolyn Hoskinson, Director.
Web, www.epa.gov/ust

Carries out regulations for underground storage tank systems storing petroleum and certain hazardous substances to prevent groundwater contamination.

Environmental Protection Agency (EPA), *Water,* *1200 Pennsylvania Ave. N.W., MC 4101M, 20460; (202) 564-5700. Joel Beauvais, Deputy Assistant Administrator.*
Web, www.epa.gov/aboutepa/about-office-water#wetlands

Implements the Clean Water Act and portions of the Ocean Dumping Ban Act, Marine Plastics Pollution Research and Control Act, London Dumping Convention, and the International Convention for the Prevention of Pollution from Ships.

Environmental Protection Agency (EPA), *Water, Ground Water and Drinking Water,* *1200 Pennsylvania Ave. N.W., #2104, MC 4601M, 20460; (202) 564-3750. Fax, (202) 564-3753. Peter C. Grevatt, Director, (202) 564-8954. Toll-free hotline, (800) 426-4791.*
General email, ogwdw.web@epa.gov
Web, www2.epa.gov/aboutepa/about-office-water#ground

Develops standards for the quality of drinking water supply systems; regulates underground injection of waste and protection of groundwater wellhead areas under the Safe Drinking Water Act; provides information on public water supply systems.

Environmental Protection Agency (EPA), *Water, Science and Technology,* *1200 Pennsylvania Ave. N.W., #5231, MC 4301M, 20460; (202) 566-0430. Fax, (202) 566-0441. Elizabeth (Betsy) Southerland, Director, (202) 566-0328.*
General email, ost.comments@epa.gov
Web, www2.epa.gov/aboutepa/about-office-water#science

Develops and coordinates water pollution control programs for the Environmental Protection Agency. Assists state and regional agencies in establishing water quality standards and planning local water resources management. Develops guidelines for industrial and municipal wastewater discharge. Provides grants for water quality monitoring and swimming advisories at recreational coastal and Great Lakes beaches. Formulates shellfish protection policies and issues fish advisories.

Environmental Protection Agency (EPA), *Water, Wastewater Management,* *1200 Pennsylvania Ave. N.W., #7116A, MC 4201M, 20460; (202) 564-0748. Fax, (202) 501-2238. Andrew Sawyers, Director, (202) 564-5668.*
General email, owm.comments@epa.gov
Web, www2.epa.gov/aboutepa/about-office-water#wastewater

Oversees the issuance of water permits. Responsible for the Pretreatment Program regulating industrial discharges to local sewage treatment. Oversees the State Revolving Funds Program, which provides assistance for the construction of wastewater treatment plants. Implements programs for prevention of water pollution, including the Clean Watersheds Needs Survey, National Pollutant Discharge Elimination System (NPDES), U.S.–Mexico Border Water Infrastructure Grant Program, and WaterSense.

Environmental Protection Agency (EPA), *Water, Wastewater Management, Municipal Support,* *1200 Pennsylvania Ave. N.W., #7119A, MC 4204M, 20460; (202) 564-5385. Fax, (202) 501-2346. Raffael Stein, Director.*
Web, www2.epa.gov/aboutepa/about-office-water#wastewater

Directs programs to assist in the design and construction of municipal sewage systems. Develops programs to ensure efficient operation and maintenance of municipal wastewater treatment facilities.

National Drinking Water Advisory Council, *1200 Pennsylvania Ave. N.W., #4100T, MC 4061M, 20460; (202) 564-7374. Michelle Schutz, Designated Federal Officer.*
Web, http://water.epa.gov/drink/ndwac

Membership: members of the general public, state and local agencies, and private groups. Advises the EPA administrator on activities, functions, and policies relating to implementation of the Safe Drinking Water Act.

National Oceanic and Atmospheric Administration (NOAA) *(Commerce Dept.), Coastal Management,* *1305 East-West Hwy., 10th Floor, SSMC4, Silver Spring, MD*

20910; (301) 713-3156. Fax, (301) 713-4012.
Jeffrey L. Payne, Director, Acting.
Web, www.coast.noaa.gov

Administers the National Coastal Zone Management
Program to help states prevent and control pollution
runoff.

**National Oceanic and Atmospheric Administration
(NOAA)** *(Commerce Dept.), Response and Restoration,*
1305 East-West Hwy., 10th Floor, Bldg. 4, Silver Spring,
MD 20910; (301) 713-3038. Fax, (301) 713-4389.
David Westerholm, Director.
General email, orr.webmaster@noaa.gov

Web, http://response.restoration.noaa.gov

Provides information on damage to marine ecosystems
caused by pollution and debris. Offers information on spill
trajectory projections and chemical hazard analyses.
Researches trends of toxic contamination on U.S. coastal
regions.

U.S. Coast Guard (USCG) *(Homeland Security Dept.),
Marine Environmental Response Policy,* 2703 Martin
Luther King Jr. Ave. S.E., CG-721, 20593; (202) 372-2234.
Fax, (202) 372-2905. Edward Bock, Chief.
Web, http://homeport.uscg.mil

Oversees cleanup operations after spills of oil and
other hazardous substances in U.S. waters, on the Outer
Continental Shelf, and in international waters. Reviews
coastal zone management and enforces international standards for pollution prevention and response.

U.S. Coast Guard (USCG) *(Homeland Security Dept.),
National Pollution Funds Center,* 2703 Martin Luther
King Jr. Ave. S.E., MS 7605, 20593; (703) 872-6000.
William Grawe, Director, Acting.
Web, www.uscg.mil/npfc

Certifies pollution liability coverage for vessels and
companies involved in oil exploration and transportation
in U.S. waters and on the Outer Continental Shelf. Ensures
adequacy of funds to respond to oil spills and deters future
spills by managing the Oil Spill Liability Trust Fund.

▶CONGRESS

*For a listing of relevant congressional committees and sub-
committees, please see pages 270–271 or the Appendix.*

▶NONGOVERNMENTAL

Assn. of Clean Water Administrators, 1634 Eye St. N.W.,
#750, 20006; (202) 756-0605. Fax, (202) 793-2600.
Julia Anastasio, Executive Director.
General email, memberservices@acwa-us.org

Web, www.acwa-us.org and Twitter, @cleanwaterACWA

Membership: state and interstate water quality regulators. Represents the states' concerns on implementation,
funding, and reauthorization of the Clean Water Act.
Monitors legislation and regulations.

Clean Water Action, 1444 Eye St. N.W., #400, 20005; (202)
895-0420. Fax, (202) 895-0438. Robert (Bob) Wendelgass,
Chief Executive Officer.
General email, cwa@cleanwater.org

Web, www.cleanwateraction.org and Twitter,
@cleanh2oaction

Citizens' organization interested in clean, safe, and
affordable water. Works to influence public policy through
education, technical assistance, and grassroots organizing. Interests include toxins and pollution, drinking
water, water conservation, sewage treatment, pesticides,
mass burn incineration, bay and estuary protection,
and consumer water issues. Monitors legislation and
regulations.

Clean Water Network, 218 D St. S.E., 20003; (202) 461-
2441. Kimberly Williams, Coordinator.
Web, www.clean-water-network.org and Twitter,
@CleanWaterNet

Advocacy coalition of local and national groups
that support clean waterways. Provides resources for
organizers to protect waterways against human-caused
pollution.

National Assn. of Clean Water Agencies, 1816 Jefferson
Pl. N.W., 20036; (202) 833-2672. Fax, (888) 267-9505.
Adam Krantz, Chief Executive Officer.
General email, info@nacwa.org

Web, www.nacwa.org

Represents public wastewater treatment works, public
and private organizations, law firms representing public
clean water agencies, and nonprofit or academic organizations. Interests include water quality and watershed
management. Sponsors conferences. Monitors legislation
and regulations.

Ocean Conservancy, 1300 19th St. N.W., 8th Floor, 20036;
(202) 429-5609. Fax, (202) 872-0619. Janis Jones, President.
Toll-free, (800) 519-1541.
General email, membership@oceanconservancy.org

Web, www.oceanconservancy.org

Works to protect the health of oceans and seas. Advocates policies that restrict discharge of pollutants harmful
to marine ecosystems.

Water Environment Federation, 601 Wythe St.,
Alexandria, VA 22314-1994; (703) 684-2400. Fax, (703)
684-2492. Eileen O'Neill, Executive Director, (703) 684-
2430. Toll-free, (800) 666-0206.
General email, inquiry@wef.org

Web, www.wef.org and Twitter, @WEForg

Membership: civil and environmental engineers, wastewater treatment plant operators, scientists, government
officials, and others concerned with water quality. Works
to preserve and improve water quality worldwide. Provides
the public with technical information and educational
materials. Monitors legislation and regulations.

RESOURCES MANAGEMENT

General

▶AGENCIES

Bureau of Land Management (BLM) *(Interior Dept.),* **Resources and Planning,** *1849 C St. N.W., #5644, 20240; (202) 208-4896. Fax, (202) 208-5010. Michael Tupper, Assistant Director, Acting.*
General email, mtupper@blm.gov
Web, www.blm.gov/wo/st/en/info/directory.html

Develops and implements natural resource programs for renewable resources use and protection, including management of forested land, rangeland, wild horses and burros, wildlife habitats, endangered species, soil and water quality, recreation, and cultural programs.

Bureau of Safety and Environmental Enforcement (BSEE) *(Interior Dept.), 1849 C St. N.W., MS DM 5438, 20240-0001; (202) 208-3985. Fax, (202) 208-3968. Brian Salerno, Director.*
General email, bseepublicaffairs@bsee.gov
Web, www.bsee.gov and Twitter, @BSEEgov

Responsible for inspections, enforcement, and safety of offshore oil and gas operations. Functions include the development and enforcement of safety and environmental regulations, research, inspections, offshore regulatory and compliance programs, oil spill response, and training of inspectors and industry professionals.

Environmental Protection Agency (EPA), *Land and Emergency Management, Resource Conservation and Recovery, 1 Potomac Yard, 2777 S. Crystal Dr., Arlington, VA 22202 (mailing address: 1200 Pennsylvania Ave. N.W., #5301P, Washington, DC 20460); (703) 308-8895. Barnes Johnson, Director.*
Web, www.epa.gov/aboutepa/about-office-land-and-emergency-management-olem

Protects human health and the environment by ensuring responsible national management of hazardous and nonhazardous waste. Administers the Resource Conservation and Recovery Act.

Interior Dept. (DOI), *1849 C St. N.W., MS 6628, 20240; (202) 208-7351. Fax, (202) 208-6956. Hon. Sally Jewell, Secretary; Michael L. Connor, Deputy Secretary. Information, (202) 208-3100. Library, (202) 208-5815. Press, (202) 208-6416.*
General email, feedback@ios.doi.gov
Web, www.doi.gov

Manages most federal land through its component agencies. Responsible for conservation and development of mineral, water, and fish and wildlife resources. Operates recreation programs for federal parks, refuges, and public lands. Preserves and administers scenic and historic areas. Administers Native American lands and develops relationships with tribal governments.

Office of Science *(Energy Dept.), Biological and Environmental Research, Biological Systems Science Division, 19901 Germantown Rd., #SC23.2, Germantown, MD 20874-1290 (mailing address: Germantown Bldg., 1000 Independence Ave. S.W., #SC23.2, Washington, DC 20585); (301) 903-5469. Fax, (301) 903-0567. Todd Anderson, Director.*
Web, http://science.energy.gov/ber/research/bssd

Supports research and technology development to achieve predictive systems-level understanding of complex biological systems, including redesign of microbes and plants for sustainable biofuel production, improved carbon storage, and contaminent remediation.

Tennessee Valley Authority, *Government Affairs, 1 Massachusetts Ave. N.W., #300, 20444; (202) 898-2999. Fax, (202) 898-2998. Nick Pearson, Director.*
General email, tvainfo@tva.gov
Web, www.tva.gov

Coordinates resource conservation, development, and land-use programs in the Tennessee River Valley. Activities include forestry and wildlife development.

U.S. Fish and Wildlife Service *(Interior Dept.), Bird Habitat Conservation, 5275 Leesburg Pike, MS MB, Falls Church, VA 22041; (703) 358-1784. Fax, (703) 358-2282. Sarah Pearson Mott, Division Chief, (703) 358-1910; Rachel F. Levin, Communications Coordinator, (703) 358-2405.*
Web, www.fws.gov/birds

Membership: government and private-sector conservation experts. Works to protect, restore, and manage wetlands and other habitats for migratory birds and other animals and to maintain migratory bird and waterfowl populations.

▶NONGOVERNMENTAL

National Assn. of Conservation Districts (NACD), *509 Capitol Court N.E., 20002-4937; (202) 547-6223. Fax, (202) 547-6450. Jeremy Peters, Chief Executive Officer.*
General email, bethany-shively@nacdet.org
Web, www.nacdnet.org

Membership: conservation districts (local subdivisions of state government). Works to promote the conservation of land, forests, and other natural resources. Interests include erosion and sediment control; water quality; forestry, water, flood plain, and range management; rural development; and urban and community conservation.

National Audubon Society, *Public Policy, 1200 18th St. N.W., #500, 20036; (202) 861-2242. Fax, (202) 861-4290. Mike Daulton, Vice President, Government Relations, (202) 861-2242, ext. 3030.*
General email, audubonaction@audubon.org
Web, www.audubon.org and Twitter, @audubonsociety

Citizens' interest group that promotes environmental conservation and education, focusing on birds and their habitats. Provides information on bird science, water resources, public lands, rangelands, forests, parks, wildlife conservation, and the National Wildlife Refuge System. Operates state offices, local chapters, and nature centers nationwide. (Headquarters in New York.)

National Research Council (NRC), Agriculture and Natural Resources Board, Keck Center, 500 5th St. N.W., #WS632, 20001; (202) 334-3062. Fax, (202) 334-1978. Robin Schoen, Director.
General email, banr@nas.edu
Web, http://dels.nas.edu/banr

Promotes and oversees research on the environmental impact of agriculture and food sustainability, including forestry, fisheries, wildlife, and the use of land, water, and other natural resources.

National Wildlife Federation, 11100 Wildlife Center Dr., Reston, VA 20190-5362 (mailing address: P.O. Box 1583, Merrifield, VA 22116-1583); (703) 438-6000. Fax, (703) 438-3570. Collin O'Mara, President. Information, (800) 822-9919.
General email, info@nwf.org
Web, www.nwf.org

Promotes conservation of natural resources; provides information on the environment and resource management; takes legal action on environmental issues.

Renewable Natural Resources Foundation, 6010 Executive Blvd., 5th Floor, N. Bethesda, MD 20852-3827; (301) 770-9101. Fax, (301) 770-9104. Robert D. Day, Executive Director.
General email, info@rnrf.org
Web, www.rnrf.org

Consortium of professional, scientific, and education organizations working to advance scientific and public education in renewable natural resources. Encourages the application of sound scientific practices to resource management and conservation. Fosters interdisciplinary cooperation among its member organizations.

U.S. Chamber of Commerce, Environment, Technology, and Regulatory Affairs, 1615 H St. N.W., 20062-2000; (202) 463-5533. Fax, (202) 887-3445. William L. Kovacs, Senior Vice President.
General email, environment@uschamber.com
Web, www.uschamber.com/etra

Develops policy on all issues affecting the production, use, and conservation of natural resources, including fuel and nonfuel minerals, timber, water, public lands, onshore and offshore energy, wetlands, and endangered species.

Winrock International, 2121 Crystal Dr., #500, Arlington, VA 22202; (703) 302-6500. Fax, (703) 302-6512. Rodney Ferguson, President.
General email, information@winrock.org
Web, www.winrock.org and Twitter, @WinrockIntl

Works with communities and governments to foster fair resource use, incentives for sustainable land use, and alternative income strategies to reduce pressure on natural resources. (Headquarters in Little Rock, Ark.)

Forests and Rangelands

▶AGENCIES

Forest Service (Agriculture Dept.), 201 14th St. S.W., 20024 (mailing address: 1400 Independence Ave. S.W., MS 1144, Washington, DC 20250-0003); (202) 205-1661. Fax, (202) 205-1765. Thomas (Tom) Tidwell, Chief. Press, (202) 205-1134. Toll-free, (800) 832-1355.
Web, www.fs.fed.us

Manages national forests and grasslands for outdoor recreation and sustained yield of renewable natural resources, including timber, water, forage, fish, and wildlife. Cooperates with state and private foresters; conducts forestry research.

Forest Service (Agriculture Dept.), International Programs, 1 Thomas Circle N.W., #400, 20005; (202) 644-4600. Fax, (202) 644-4603. Valdis E. Mezainis, Director, (202) 644-4621.
Web, www.fs.fed.us/global

Responsible for the Forest Service's involvement in international forest conservation efforts. Analyzes international resource issues; promotes information exchange; provides planning and technical assistance. Interested in sustainable forest management, covering illegal logging, climate change, migratory species.

Forest Service (Agriculture Dept.), National Forest System, 201 14th St. S.W., 5th Floor, 20024; (202) 205-1523. Fax, (202) 649-1180. Leslie A. C. Weldon, Deputy Chief.
Web, www.fs.fed.us

Manages 193 million acres of forests and rangelands. Products and services from these lands include timber, water, forage, wildlife, minerals, and recreation.

Forest Service (Agriculture Dept.), Research and Development, 201 14th St. S.W., #2NW, 20024 (mailing address: 1400 Independence Ave. S.W., Washington, DC 20250); (202) 205-1665. Fax, (202) 205-1530. Vacant, Deputy Chief. Toll-free, (800) 832-1355.
Web, www.fs.fed.us/research

Conducts biological, physical, and economic research related to forestry, including studies on harvesting methods, acid deposition, international forestry, the effects of global climate changes on forests, and forest products. Provides information on the establishment, improvement, and growth of trees, grasses, and other forest vegetation. Works to protect forest resources from fire, insects, diseases, and animal pests. Examines the effect of forest use activities on water quality, soil erosion, and sediment production. Conducts continuous forest survey and analyzes outlook for future supply and demand.

Forest Service (Agriculture Dept.), State and Private Forestry, 201 14th St. S.W., #3NW, 20024 (mailing address: 1400 Independence Ave. S.W., MS 1109, Washington, DC 20250-1109); (202) 205-1657. Fax, (202) 205-1174. James E. Hubbard, Deputy Chief.
Web, www.fs.fed.us

Assists state and private forest owners with the protection and management of 574 million acres of forest and associated watershed lands. Assistance includes fire control, protecting forests from insects and diseases, land-use planning, developing multiple-use management, and improving practices in harvesting, processing, and marketing of forest products.

Forest Service *(Agriculture Dept.), Youth Conservation Corps, 201 14th St. S.W., 20024 (mailing address: 1400 Independence Ave. S.W., MS 1125, Washington, DC 20250-1125); (202) 205-0650. Fax, (703) 605-5131. Merlene Maczyk, Manager. Toll-free, (800) 832-1355. General email, mmaczyk@fs.fed.us*

Web, http://youthgo.gov

Administers, with the National Park Service and the Fish and Wildlife Service, the Youth Conservation Corps, a summer employment and training public works program for youths ages fifteen to eighteen. The program is conducted in national parks, in national forests, and on national wildlife refuges.

►CONGRESS

For a listing of relevant congressional committees and subcommittees, please see pages 270–271 or the Appendix.

►NONGOVERNMENTAL

American Forest and Paper Assn., *Government Affairs, 1101 K St. N.W., #700, 20005; (202) 463-2700. Fax, (202) 463-2471. Elizabeth Bartheld, Vice President, Government Affairs; Donna Harman, President. General email, info@afandpa.org*

Web, www.afandpa.org

Membership: pulp, paper, and paper-based product manufacturers and those in related associations. Interests include tax, housing, environmental, international trade, sustainability, and land-use issues that affect the forest products industry.

American Forests, *1220 L St. N.W., #750, 20005; (202) 737-1944. Fax, (202) 737-2457. Scott Steen, Chief Executive Officer. Media, (202) 370-4517. General email, info@amfor.org*

Web, www.americanforests.org

Citizens' interest group that promotes protection and responsible management of forests and natural resources. Provides information on conservation, public land policy, and urban forestry. Promotes an international tree-planting campaign to help mitigate global warming.

Forest Resources Assn., *1901 Pennsylvania Ave. N.W., #303, 20006; (202) 296-3937. Fax, (202) 296-0562. Deb Hawkinson, President. General email, fra@forestresources.org*

Web, www.forestresources.org and Twitter, @forestresources

Membership: suppliers, brokers, transporters, and consumers of unprocessed wood products, as well as businesses that serve the forest products supply chain. Provides information on the safe, efficient, and sustainable harvest of forest products and their transport from woods to mill; works to ensure continued access to the timberland base. Monitors legislation and regulations.

International Wood Products Assn., *4214 King St. West, Alexandria, VA 22302; (703) 820-6696. Fax, (703) 820-8550. Cindy L. Squires, Executive Director. General email, info@iwpawood.org*

Web, www.iwpawood.org

Membership: companies that handle imported wood products. Encourages environmentally responsible forest management and international trade in wood products. Sponsors research and environmental education on tropical forestry.

National Assn. of State Foresters, *444 N. Capitol St. N.W., #540, 20001; (202) 624-5415. Fax, (202) 624-5407. Jay Farrell, Executive Director. General email, nasf@stateforesters.org*

Web, www.stateforesters.org

Membership: directors of state forestry agencies from all states, the District of Columbia, and U.S. territories. Interests include forest management, employment generated by forestry and forest products, and climate change. Monitors legislation and regulations.

National Lumber and Building Material Dealers Assn., *2025 M St. N.W., #800, 20036-3309; (202) 367-1169. Fax, (202) 367-2169. Jonathan M. Paine, President. General email, info@dealer.org*

Web, www.dealer.org

Membership: federated associations of retailers in the lumber and building material industries. Supports forest conservation programs and environmental safety. Monitors legislation and regulations.

Pinchot Institute for Conservation, *1616 P St. N.W., #100, 20036; (202) 797-6580. Fax, (202) 797-6583. William C. Price, President, Acting. Web, www.pinchot.org*

Seeks to advance forest conservation and sustainable natural resources management nationally through research and analysis, education and technical assistance, and development of conservation leaders.

Save America's Forests, *4 Library Court S.E., 20003; (202) 544-9219. Fax, (202) 544-7462. Carl Ross, Executive Director. General email, info@saveamericasforests.org*

Web, www.saveamericasforests.org

Coalition of environmental and public interest groups, scientists, businesses, and individuals. Advocates comprehensive nationwide laws and international policies to prevent deforestation and to protect forest ecosystems and indigenous rights.

Society of American Foresters, *10100 Laureate Way, Bethesda, MD 20814; (301) 897-8720. Fax, (301) 897-3690,*

Matt E. Menashes, Chief Executive Officer. Toll-free, (866) 897-8720.
General email, info@safnet.org
Web, www.safnet.org

Association of forestry professionals. Provides technical information on forestry, accredits forestry programs in universities and colleges, and publishes scientific forestry journals.

Sustainable Forestry Initiative, 2121 K St. N.W., #750, 20037; (202) 596-3450. Fax, (202) 596-3451.
Kathy Abusow, President.
General email, info@sfiprogram.org
Web, www.sfiprogram.org

Works to ensure protection of forests while continuing to produce wood and paper products as needed by the economy. Encourages perpetual growing and harvesting of trees and protection of wildlife, plants, soil, water, and air quality. Seeks to mitigate illegal logging. Interests include the economic, environmental, cultural, and legal issues related to forestry.

Land Resources

▶AGENCIES

Bureau of Land Management (BLM) *(Interior Dept.),* 1849 C St. N.W., #5665, 20240; (202) 208-3801. Fax, (202) 208-5242. Neil Kornze, Director. Press, (202) 208-6913.
General email, director@blm.gov
Web, www.blm.gov and Twitter, @BLMNational

Manages public lands and federally owned mineral resources, including oil, gas, and coal. Resources managed and leased include wildlife habitats, timber, minerals, open space, wilderness areas, forage, and recreational resources. Surveys federal lands and maintains public land records.

Bureau of Land Management (BLM) *(Interior Dept.),* **Lands, Realty, and Cadastral Survey,** 20 M St. S.E., 20003 (mailing address: 1849 C St. N.W., 2134LM, Washington, DC 20240); (202) 912-7088. Fax, (202) 912-7199.
Michael G. Stiewig, Division Chief.
Web, www.blm.gov/wo/st/en/info/directory/WO-350_dir.html

Oversees use, acquisition, and disposal of public lands. Conducts the Public Lands Survey; authorizes rights-of-way on public lands for uses that include roads, power lines, and wind and solar facilities.

Bureau of Reclamation *(Interior Dept.),* 1849 C St. N.W., MS 7069, 20240-0001; (202) 513-0501. Fax, (202) 513-0309. Estevan Lopez, Commissioner. Press, (202) 513-0575.
Web, www.usbr.gov and Twitter, @usbr

Manages, develops, and protects water and related resources in seventeen western states, in partnership with states, tribes, and water and power customers. Water resource development projects include dams, power plants, and canals.

Interior Dept. (DOI), *Board of Land Appeals,* 801 N. Quincy St., #300, Arlington, VA 22203; (703) 235-3750. Fax, (703) 235-8349. Eileen Jones, Chief Administrative Judge.
Web, www.doi.gov/oha/ibla

Adjunct office of the interior secretary that decides appeals from decisions rendered by the Bureau of Land Management; the Bureau of Ocean Energy Management, Regulation, and Enforcement; the Office of Surface Mining and Reclamation Enforcement; and the Bureau of Indian Affairs concerning the use and disposition of public lands and minerals. Issues final decisions concerning the Surface Mining Control and Reclamation Act of 1977. Is separate and independent from bureaus and offices whose decisions it reviews.

Interior Dept. (DOI), *Land and Minerals Management,* 1849 C St. N.W., MS 6628, 20240; (202) 208-6734. Fax, (202) 208-3619. Janice M. Schneider, Assistant Secretary.
Web, www.doi.gov

Directs and supervises the Bureau of Land Management; the Bureau of Ocean Energy Management, Regulation, and Enforcement; and the Office of Surface Mining and Reclamation Enforcement. Supervises programs associated with land-use planning, onshore and offshore minerals, surface mining reclamation and enforcement, and Outer Continental Shelf minerals management.

Interior Dept. (DOI), *Surface Mining Reclamation and Enforcement,* 1951 Constitution Ave. N.W., #233, 20240; (202) 208-4006. Fax, (202) 219-3106. Joseph G. Pizarchik, Director. Press, (202) 208-2565. TTY, (202) 208-2694.
General email, getinfo@osmre.gov
Web, www.osmre.gov

Regulates surface mining of coal and surface effects of underground coal mining. Responsible for reclamation of abandoned coal mine lands.

Interior Dept. (DOI), *Wildland Fire,* 1849 C St. N.W., MS 2660, 20240; (202) 208-7754. Jim Douglas, Director; Bryan Rice, Co-Director.
Web, www.doi.gov/pmb/owf

Oversees all wildland fire management programs, policies, budgets, and information technology in order to manage risk to firefighters, communities, and landscapes.

Natural Resources Conservation Service *(Agriculture Dept.),* 1400 Independence Ave. S.W., #5105AS, 20250 (mailing address: P.O. Box 2890, Washington, DC 20013-2890); (202) 720-4525. Fax, (202) 720-7690. Jason Weller, Chief, (202) 720-7246. Public Affairs, (202) 720-5776.
General email, nrcsdistributioncenter@ia.usda.gov
Web, www.nrcs.usda.gov

Responsible for soil and water conservation programs, including watershed protection, flood prevention, river basin surveys, and resource conservation and development. Provides landowners, operators, state and local units of government, and community groups with technical assistance in carrying out local programs. Web site has a Spanish-language link.

Tennessee Valley Authority, *Government Affairs,*
1 Massachusetts Ave. N.W., #300, 20444; (202) 898-2999.
Fax, (202) 898-2998. Nick Pearson, Director.
General email, tvainfo@tva.gov
Web, www.tva.gov

Coordinates resource conservation, development, and land-use programs in the Tennessee River Valley. Provides information on land usage in the region.

▶**CONGRESS**

For a listing of relevant congressional committees and sub-committees, please see pages 270–271 or the Appendix.

▶**NONGOVERNMENTAL**

American Geosciences Institute, *4220 King St.,*
Alexandria, VA 22302-1502; (703) 379-2480. Fax, (703) 379-7563. P. Patrick Leahy, Executive Director.
General email, agi@americangeosciences.org
Web, www.agiweb.org

Membership: earth science societies and associations. Provides education and outreach. Maintains computerized database of the world's geoscience literature (available to the public for a fee).

American Resort Development Assn., *1201 15th St.*
N.W., #400, 20005; (202) 371-6700. Fax, (202) 289-8544. Howard Nusbaum, President.
Web, www.arda.org

Membership: U.S. and international developers, builders, financiers, marketing companies, and others involved in resort, recreational, and community development. Serves as an information clearinghouse; monitors federal and state legislation affecting land, time share, and community development industries.

Land Trust Alliance, *1660 L St. N.W., #1100, 20036; (202) 638-4725. Fax, (202) 638-4730. Rand Wentworth, President, (202) 800-2249.*
General email, info@lta.org
Web, www.landtrustalliance.org and Twitter, @italliance

Membership: organizations and individuals who work to conserve land resources. Serves as a forum for the exchange of information; conducts research and public education programs. Monitors legislation and regulations.

National Assn. of Conservation Districts (NACD), *509 Capitol Court N.E., 20002-4937; (202) 547-6223. Fax, (202) 547-6450. Jeremy Peters, Chief Executive Officer.*
General email, bethany-shively@nacdet.org
Web, www.nacdnet.org

Membership: conservation districts (local subdivisions of state government). Works to promote the conservation of land, forests, and other natural resources. Interests include erosion and sediment control; water quality; forestry, water, flood plain, and range management; rural development; and urban and community conservation.

Public Lands Council, *1301 Pennsylvania Ave. N.W., #300, 20004-1701; (202) 347-0228. Fax, (202) 638-0607. Brenda Richards, President; Ethan Lane, Executive Director, ext. 126.*
Web, www.publiclandscouncil.org and Twitter, @PLCranching

Membership: cattle and sheep ranchers who hold permits and leases to graze livestock on public lands. (Affiliated with the National Cattlemen's Beef Association and the American Sheep Industry Association, and the Association of National Grasslands.)

Scenic America, *1307 New Hampshire Ave. N.W., 3rd Floor, 20036; (202) 463-1294. Fax, (202) 463-1299. Mary Tracy, President.*
General email, ashburn@scenic.org
Web, www.scenic.org and Twitter, @ScenicAmerica

Membership: national, state, and local groups concerned with land-use control, growth management, and landscape protection. Works to enhance the scenic quality of America's communities and countryside. Provides information and technical assistance on scenic byways, tree preservation, economics of aesthetic regulation, billboard and sign control, scenic areas preservation, and growth management.

Wallace Genetic Foundation, *4910 Massachusetts Ave. N.W., #221, 20016; (202) 966-2932. Fax, (202) 966-3370. Patricia M. Lee, Co-Executive Director; Carolyn H. Sand, Co Executive Director.*
General email, wgfdn@aol.com
Web, www.wallacegenetic.org

Supports national and international nonprofits in the areas of agricultural research, preservation of farmland, reduction of environmental toxins, conservation, biodiversity protection, global climate issues, and sustainable development.

The Wilderness Society, *1615 M St. N.W., 20036; (202) 833-2300. Fax, (202) 429-3958. Jamie Williams, President. Toll-free, (800) 843-9453.*
General email, action@tws.org
Web, www.wilderness.org and Twitter, @wilderness

Promotes preservation of wilderness and the responsible management of federal lands, including national parks and forests, wilderness areas, wildlife refuges, and land administered by the Interior Dept.'s Bureau of Land Management.

Metals and Minerals

▶**AGENCIES**

Bureau of Land Management (BLM) *(Interior Dept.),*
Energy, Minerals, and Realty Management, 1849 C St. N.W., #5625, 20240; (202) 208-4201. Fax, (202) 208-4800. Michael Nedd, Assistant Director.
General email, mnedd@blm.gov
Web, www.blm.gov/wo/st/en/info/directory/WO_300_dir.html

Develops and administers policy, guidance, and performance oversight for the renewable energy program, including wind, solar, and geothermal energy; the fluid minerals program, including oil, gas, and helium; the solid minerals programs, including mining law, coal, oil shale, and salable minerals; the lands and realty programs; and the Public Land Survey System. Provides national leadership and develops national partnerships with organizations interested in energy, minerals, and realty management. Provides leadership to the Bureau of Land Management's trust management for Indian minerals operations, surveys, and trust patent preparation.

Bureau of Safety and Environmental Enforcement (BSEE) *(Interior Dept.), Offshore Regulatory Programs, 1849 C St. N.W., MS DM 5438, 20240-0001; (202) 208-3985. Fax, (202) 208-3968. Douglas Morris, Chief. General email, bseepublicaffairs@bsee.gov*

Web, www.bsee.gov

Develops standards, regulations, and compliance programs governing Outer Continental Shelf oil, gas, and minerals exploration and operations. Purview includes safety management programs, safety and pollution prevention research, technology assessments, standards for inspections and enforcement policies, and accident investigation practices.

Interior Dept. (DOI), *Board of Land Appeals, 801 N. Quincy St., #300, Arlington, VA 22203; (703) 235-3750. Fax, (703) 235-8349. Eileen Jones, Chief Administrative Judge.*

Web, www.doi.gov/oha/ibla

Adjunct office of the interior secretary that decides appeals from decisions rendered by the Bureau of Land Management; the Bureau of Ocean Energy Management, Regulation, and Enforcement; the Office of Surface Mining and Reclamation Enforcement; and the Bureau of Indian Affairs concerning the use and disposition of public lands and minerals. Issues final decisions concerning the Surface Mining Control and Reclamation Act of 1977. Is separate and independent from bureaus and offices whose decisions it reviews.

Interior Dept. (DOI), *Land and Minerals Management, 1849 C St. N.W., MS 6628, 20240; (202) 208-6734. Fax, (202) 208-3619. Janice M. Schneider, Assistant Secretary. Web, www.doi.gov*

Directs and supervises the Bureau of Land Management; the Bureau of Ocean Energy Management, Regulation, and Enforcement; and the Office of Surface Mining and Reclamation Enforcement. Supervises programs associated with land-use planning, onshore and offshore minerals, surface mining reclamation and enforcement, and Outer Continental Shelf minerals management.

Interior Dept. (DOI), *Natural Resources Revenue, Washington Office, 1849 C St. N.W., MS 4211, 20240; (202) 513-0603. Fax, (202) 513-0682. Gregory J. (Greg) Gould, Director. Press, (202) 513-0600. Web, www.onrr.gov*

Manages revenues associated with federal offshore and federal and American Indian onshore mineral leases, as well as revenues received through offshore renewable energy efforts. Collects and disburses all natural resources revenues.

U.S. Geological Survey (USGS) *(Interior Dept.), Mineral Resources Program, 12201 Sunrise Valley Dr., MS 913, Reston, VA 20192; (703) 648-6110. Fax, (703) 648-6057. Lawrence Meinert, Program Coordinator, (703) 648-6100. General email, minerals@usgs.gov*

Web, www.minerals.usgs.gov

Coordinates mineral resource activities for the Geological Survey, including research and information on U.S. and international mineral resources, baseline information on earth materials, and geochemical and geophysical instrumentation and applications.

▶**CONGRESS**

For a listing of relevant congressional committees and subcommittees, please see pages 270–271 or the Appendix.

▶**NONGOVERNMENTAL**

Aluminum Assn., *1400 Crystal Dr., #430, Arlington, VA 22202; (703) 358-2960. Fax, (703) 358-2961. Heidi Biggs Brock, President. Press, (703) 358-2977. Web, www.aluminum.org*

Represents the aluminum industry. Develops voluntary standards and technical data; compiles statistics concerning the industry. Monitors legislation and regulations.

American Iron and Steel Institute (AISI), *Washington Office, 25 Massachusetts Ave. N.W., #800, 20001; (202) 452-7100. Fax, (202) 463-6573. Thomas Gibson, President. Press, (202) 452-7116. General email, steelnews@steel.org*

Web, www.steel.org and Twitter, @aisisteel

Represents the iron and steel industry. Publishes statistics on iron and steel production; promotes the use of steel; conducts research. Monitors legislation and regulations. (Maintains offices in Southfield, Mich., and Pittsburgh, Pa.)

Mineralogical Society of America, *3635 Concorde Pkwy., #500, Chantilly, VA 20151-1110; (703) 652-9950. Fax, (703) 652-9951. Rebecca A. Lange, President. General email, business@minsocam.org*

Web, www.minsocam.org

Membership: mineralogists, petrologists, crystallographers, geochemists, educators, students, and others interested in mineralogy. Conducts research; sponsors educational programs; promotes industrial application of mineral studies.

National Mining Assn., *101 Constitution Ave. N.W., #500 East, 20001-2133; (202) 463-2600. Fax, (202) 463-2666. Harold P. Quinn Jr., President. Press, (202) 463-2642. General email, webmaster@nma.org*

Web, www.nma.org

Membership: domestic producers of coal and industrial-agricultural minerals and metals; manufacturers of mining equipment; engineering and consulting firms; and financial institutions. Interests include mine-leasing programs, mine health and safety, research and development, public lands, and minerals availability. Monitors legislation and regulations.

Native American Trust Resources

▶AGENCIES

Administration for Native Americans *(Health and Human Services Dept.),* 330 C St. S.W., 20201; (202) 690-7776. Fax, (202) 690-7441. Lillian A. Sparks, Commissioner. Toll-free, (877) 922-9262.
General email, ana@acf.hhs.gov
Web, www.acf.hhs.gov/programs/ana

Awards grants to assist tribes with resources to develop legal and organizational capacities to protect their natural environments.

Bureau of Indian Affairs (BIA) *(Interior Dept.),* **Trust Services,** 1849 C St. N.W., MS 4620-MIB, 20240; (202) 208-5831. Fax, (202) 219-1255. Helen Riggs, Deputy Bureau Director.
Web, www.bia.gov/WhoWeAre/BIA/OTS/index.htm

Assists in developing and managing bureau programs involving Native American trust resources (agriculture, forestry, wildlife, water, irrigation, real property management probate, and title records).

Environmental Protection Agency (EPA), *Water,* 1200 Pennsylvania Ave. N.W., MC 4101M, 20460; (202) 564-5700. Joel Beauvais, Deputy Assistant Administrator.
Web, www.epa.gov/aboutepa/about-office-water#wetlands

Works with American Indian tribes to implement the Safe Drinking Water Act and improve access to safe drinking water on tribal lands.

Interior Dept. (DOI), 1849 C St. N.W., MS 6628, 20240; (202) 208-7351. Fax, (202) 208-6956. Hon. Sally Jewell, Secretary; Michael L. Connor, Deputy Secretary. Information, (202) 208-3100. Library, (202) 208-5815. Press, (202) 208-6416.
General email, feedback@ios.doi.gov
Web, www.doi.gov

Principal U.S. conservation agency. Manages most federal land, including Native American lands; develops relationships with tribal governments.

Interior Dept. (DOI), *Natural Resources Revenue,* **Washington Office,** 1849 C St. N.W., MS 4211, 20240; (202) 513-0603. Fax, (202) 513-0682.
Gregory J. (Greg) Gould, Director. Press, (202) 513-0600.
Web, www.onrr.gov

Manages revenues associated with federal offshore and federal and American Indian onshore mineral leases, as well as revenues received through offshore renewable energy efforts. Collects and disburses all natural resources revenues.

Interior Dept. (DOI), *Office of the Solicitor, Indian Affairs,* 1849 C St. N.W., MS 6511, 20240; (202) 208-3401.

Fax, (202) 219-1791. Jody Cummings, Associate Solicitor.
Web, www.doi.gov

Advises the Bureau of Indian Affairs and the secretary of the interior on all legal matters, including its trust responsibilities toward Native Americans and their natural resources.

Justice Dept. (DOJ), *Indian Resources,* 601 D St. N.W., #3507, 20004 (mailing address: P.O. Box 7611, L'Enfant Plaza, Washington, DC 20044); (202) 305-0269. Fax, (202) 305-0275. S. Craig Alexander, Chief.
Web, www.justice.gov/Indian-resources-section

Represents the United States in suits, including trust violations, brought on behalf of individual Native Americans and Native American tribes against the government. Also represents the United States as trustee for Native Americans in court actions involving protection of Native American land and resources.

▶CONGRESS

For a listing of relevant congressional committees and subcommittees, please see pages 270–271 or the Appendix.

▶NONGOVERNMENTAL

Native American Rights Fund, *Washington Office,* 1514 P St. N.W., Suite D, Rear entrance, 20005; (202) 785-4166. Fax, (202) 822-0068. John E. Echohawk, Executive Director; Richard Guest, Managing Attorney.
Web, www.narf.org

Provides Native Americans and Alaska Natives with legal assistance in land claims, water rights, hunting, and other areas. Practices federal Indian law. (Headquarters in Boulder, Colo.)

Ocean Resources

▶AGENCIES

Bureau of Oceans and International Environmental and Scientific Affairs *(State Dept.),* **Marine Conservation,** 2201 C St. N.W., #2758, 20520; (202) 647-2335. William Gibbons-Fry, Director.
Web, www.state.gov/e/oes/ocns/fish

Handles the management, conservation, and restoration of living marine resources. Seeks to maintain a healthy and productive marine environment and ecosystems.

Environmental Protection Agency (EPA), *Water,* 1200 Pennsylvania Ave. N.W., MC 4101M, 20460; (202) 564-5700. Joel Beauvais, Deputy Assistant Administrator.
Web, www.epa.gov/aboutepa/about-office-water#wetlands

Restores and maintains oceans, watersheds, and their aquatic ecosystems. Implements the Clean Water Act and portions of the Coastal Zone Act, Ocean Dumping Ban Act, Marine Protection Act, Shore Protection Act, Marine Plastics Pollution Research and Control Act, and the International Convention for the Prevention of Pollution from Ships.

National Oceanic and Atmospheric Administration (NOAA) *(Commerce Dept.), Coastal Management, 1305 East-West Hwy., 10th Floor, SSMC4, Silver Spring, MD 20910; (301) 713-3156. Fax, (301) 713-4012. Jeffrey L. Payne, Director, Acting.*
Web, www.coast.noaa.gov

Provides training, data, and tools for coastal managers, implements environmental research projects and local science-based training initiatives for estuarine reserves, provides data needed to preserve, restore, and sustain coral reefs, helps fund state and local governments' purchases of threatened coastal and estuarine land for conservation, and provides training and education to local officials and citizens. Administers the National Coastal Zone Management Program, focusing on state and federal policy, state assistance to prevent and control pollution runoff, and state incentives to enhancement of coastal management programs.

National Oceanic and Atmospheric Administration (NOAA) *(Commerce Dept.), Marine and Aviation Operations, 8403 Colesville Rd., #500, Silver Spring, MD 20910-3282; (301) 713-1045. Fax, (301) 713-1541. Rear Adm. David A. Score, Director. Press, (301) 713-7671.*
Web, www.omao.noaa.gov

Uniformed service of the Commerce Dept. that operates and manages NOAA's fleet of atmospheric, hydrographic, oceanographic, and fisheries research ships and aircraft. Supports NOAA's scientific programs.

National Oceanic and Atmospheric Administration (NOAA) *(Commerce Dept.), National Environmental Satellite, Data, and Information Service, 1335 East-West Hwy., SSMC1, 8th Floor, Silver Spring, MD 20910; (301) 713-3578. Fax, (301) 713-1249. Stephen Volz, Assistant Administrator. Press, (301) 713-0214.*
General email, john.leslie@noaa.gov
Web, www.nesdis.noaa.gov

Disseminates worldwide environmental data through a system of meteorological, oceanographic, geophysical, and solar-terrestrial data centers.

National Oceanic and Atmospheric Administration (NOAA) *(Commerce Dept.), National Marine Sanctuaries, 1305 East-West Hwy., 11th Floor, Silver Spring, MD 20910; (301) 713-3125. Fax, (301) 713-0404. Daniel J. Basta, Director.*
General email, sanctuaries@noaa.gov
Web, www.sanctuaries.noaa.gov and Twitter, @santuaries

Administers the National Marine Sanctuary Program, which seeks to protect the ecology and the recreational and cultural resources of marine and Great Lakes waters.

National Oceanic and Atmospheric Administration (NOAA) *(Commerce Dept.), National Ocean Service, 1305 East-West Hwy., SSMC4, #9149, Silver Spring, MD 20910; (301) 713-3074. Fax, (301) 713-4269. Russell Callender, Assistant Administrator, Acting. Press, (301) 713-3066.*
General email, nos.info@noaa.gov
Web, www.oceanservice.noaa.gov

Manages charting and geodetic services, oceanography and marine services, coastal resource coordination, and marine survey operations; conducts environmental cleanup of coastal pollution.

National Oceanic and Atmospheric Administration (NOAA) *(Commerce Dept.), National Sea Grant College Program, 1315 East-West Hwy., SSMC-3, 11th Floor, Silver Spring, MD 20910; (301) 734-1066. Fax, (301) 713-0799. Vacant, Director; Nikola Garber, Deputy Director.*
General email, brooke.carney@noaa.gov
Web, www.seagrant.noaa.gov

Provides institutions with grants for marine research, education, and advisory services; provides marine environmental information.

National Oceanic and Atmospheric Administration (NOAA) *(Commerce Dept.), Ocean Acidification Program, 1315 East-West Hwy., #10356, Silver Spring, MD 20910; (301) 734-1075. Libby Jewett, Director.*
General email, noaa.oceanacidification@noaa.gov
Web, www.oceanacidification.noaa.gov

Monitors changes in ocean chemistry due to the continued acidification of the oceans and Great Lakes, and assesses the socioeconomic impacts. Maintains relationships with scientists, resource managers, stakeholders, policymakers, and the public to implement adaptation strategies and monitor the biological responses of ecologically and economically important species. Operates from NOAA's Office of Oceanic and Atmospheric Research.

National Oceanic and Atmospheric Administration (NOAA) *(Commerce Dept.), Oceanic and Atmospheric Research, 1315 East-West Hwy., Silver Spring, MD 20910; (301) 713-2458. Craig N. McLean, Assistant Administrator.*
Web, http://research.noaa.gov and Twitter, @NOAAResearch

Researches weather and water information in order to provide better forecasts and earlier warnings for natural disasters. Works to protect, restore, and manage coastal and ocean resources through ecosystem-based management. Promotes the understanding of climate change and variability.

U.S. Geological Survey (USGS) *(Interior Dept.), Coastal and Marine Geology Program, 12201 Sunrise Valley Dr., MS 905, Reston, VA 20192; (703) 648-6422. Fax, (703) 648-5464. John W. Haines, Program Coordinator.*
Web, http://marine.usgs.gov

Handles resource assessment, exploration research, and marine geologic and environmental studies on U.S. coastal regions and the Outer Continental Shelf.

▶ **CONGRESS**

For a listing of relevant congressional committees and subcommittees, please see pages 270–271 or the Appendix.

▶ **NONGOVERNMENTAL**

Blue Frontier Campaign, *1530 P St. N.W., 20005 (mailing address: P.O. Box 19367, Washington, DC 20036); (202)*

387-8030. Fax, (202) 234-5176. David Helvarg, Executive Director.
General email, info@bluefront.org

Web, www.bluefront.org and Twitter, @Blue_Frontier

Promotes ocean conservation. Seeks to strengthen unity among ocean conservationists and encourage public awareness at the local, regional, and national levels.

Coastal States Organization, *444 N. Capitol St. N.W., #638, 20001; (202) 508-3860. Fax, (202) 508-3843. Mary Munson, Executive Director.*
General email, cso@coastalstates.org

Web, www.coastalstates.org

Nonpartisan organization that represents governors of thirty-five U.S. coastal states, territories, and commonwealths on management of coastal, Great Lakes, and marine resources. Interests include ocean dumping, coastal pollution, wetlands preservation and restoration, national oceans policy, and the Outer Continental Shelf. Gathers and analyzes data to assess state coastal needs; sponsors and participates in conferences and workshops.

Joint Ocean Commission Initiative, *c/o Meridian Institute, 1800 M St. N.W., #400N, 20036; (202) 354-6444. Fax, (202) 354-6441. Laura Cantral, Director.*
General email, lcantral@merid.org

Web, www.jointoceancommission.org

Provides policy information on ocean conservation and releases Ocean Policy Report Cards that analyze the effectiveness of policy initiatives on ocean and coast protection. (Formed by the U.S. Commission on Ocean Policy and the Pew Oceans Commission.)

Marine Technology Society, *1100 H St. N.W., #LL-100, 20005; (202) 717-8705. Fax, (202) 347-4302. Chris Barrett, Executive Director, Acting.*
General email, membership@mtsociety.org

Web, www.mtsociety.org

Membership: scientists, engineers, technologists, and others interested in marine science, technology, and education.

National Ocean Industries Assn., *1120 G St. N.W., #900, Washington, DC 20005; (202) 347-6900. Fax, (202) 347-8650. Randall Luthi, President.*
General email, noia@noia.org

Web, www.noia.org

Membership: manufacturers, producers, suppliers, and support and service companies involved in marine, offshore, and ocean work. Interests include offshore oil and gas supply and production, deep-sea mining, ocean thermal energy, and new energy sources.

National Research Council (NRC), *Gulf Research Program, Keck Center, 500 5th St. N.W., 20001; (202) 334-2000. Chris Elfring, Executive Director.*
Web, nationalacademies.org/gulf

Promotes oil system safety and the protection of human health and the environment in the Gulf of Mexico and other U.S. outer continental shelf areas.

National Research Council (NRC), *Ocean Studies Board, Keck Center, 500 5th St. N.W., MS 607, 20001; (202) 334-2714. Fax, (202) 334-2885. Susan Roberts, Director; Larry A. Mayer, Chair.*
General email, osbfeedback@nas.edu

Web, http://dels.nas.edu/osb

Conducts research to understand, manage, and conserve coastal and marine environments. Areas of interest include the ocean's role in the global climate system, technology and infrastructure needs for ocean research, ocean-related aspects of national security; fisheries, science and management, and ocean education.

Oceana, *1350 Connecticut Ave. N.W., 5th Floor, 20036; (202) 833-3900. Fax, (202) 833-2070. Andrew F. Sharpless, Chief Executive Officer. Toll-free, (877) 7-OCEANA.*
General email, info@oceana.org

Web, www.oceana.org and www.usa.oceana.org

Promotes ocean conservation both nationally and internationally; pursues policy changes to reduce pollution and protect fish, marine mammals, and other forms of sea life. Conducts specific scientific, legal, policy, and advocacy campaigns. Monitors legislation and regulations.

Parks and Recreation Areas

▶**AGENCIES**

Bureau of Land Management (BLM) *(Interior Dept.), Cultural, Paleontological Resources, and Tribal Consultation, 20 M St. S.E., #2134, 20003; (202) 912-7208. Fax, (202) 245-0015. Byron Loosle, Division Chief.*
General email, bloosle@blm.gov

Web, www.blm.gov/wo/st/en/prog/more/CRM.html

Identifies and manages cultural heritage and recreation programs on public lands.

Bureau of Land Management (BLM) *(Interior Dept.), Recreation and Visitor Services, 20 M St. S.E., 6th Floor, 20003 (mailing address: 1849 C St. N.W., MS 2134, Washington, DC 20240); (202) 912-7256. Fax, (202) 912-7362. Andy Tenney, Division Chief.*
Web, www.blm.gov/wo/st/en/prog/Recreation.html

Develops recreation opportunities on public lands.

Bureau of Reclamation *(Interior Dept.), 1849 C St. N.W., MS 7069, 20240-0001; (202) 513-0501. Fax, (202) 513-0309. Estevan Lopez, Commissioner. Press, (202) 513-0575.*
Web, www.usbr.gov and Twitter, @usbr

Responsible for acquisition, administration, management, and disposal of lands in seventeen western states associated with bureau water resource development projects. Provides overall policy guidance for land-use, including agreements with public agencies for outdoor recreation, fish and wildlife enhancement, and land-use authorizations such as leases, licenses, permits, and rights of way. Interests include increasing water-based outdoor recreation facilities and opportunities.

Forest Service *(Agriculture Dept.), Recreation, Heritage, and Volunteer Resources,* 201 14th St. S.W., 5SW, 20024 *(mailing address: 1400 Independence Ave. S.W., MS 1125, Washington, DC 20250-0003); (202) 205-1706. Fax, (703) 605-5105. Joe Meade, Director.*
Web, www.fs.fed.us/recreation

Develops policy and sets guidelines on administering national forests and grasslands for recreational purposes. (The Forest Service administers some of the lands designated as national recreation areas.)

Interior Dept. (DOI), *Fish, Wildlife, and Parks,* 1849 C St. N.W., #7256, 20240; (202) 208-4416. Fax, (202) 208-4684. *Michael Bean, Principal Deputy Assistant Secretary.*
Web, www.doi.gov

Responsible for programs associated with the development, conservation, and use of fish, wildlife, recreational, historical, and national park system resources. Coordinates marine environmental quality and biological resources programs with other federal agencies.

National Park Service (NPS) *(Interior Dept.),* 1849 C St. N.W., #3115, 20240; (202) 208-3818. Fax, (202) 208-7889. *Jonathan B. Jarvis, Director. Press, (202) 208-6843.*
General email, asknps@nps.gov
Web, www.nps.gov and Twitter, @NatlParkService

Administers national parks, monuments, historic sites, and recreation areas. Oversees coordination, planning, and financing of public outdoor recreation programs at all levels of government. Conducts recreation research surveys; administers financial assistance program to states for planning and development of outdoor recreation programs. (Some lands designated as national recreation areas are not under NPS jurisdiction.)

National Park Service (NPS) *(Interior Dept.), Policy,* 1201 Eye St. N.W., 7th Floor, 20005 *(mailing address: 1849 C St. N.W., Washington, DC 20240); (202) 354-3950. Fax, (202) 371-5189. Alma Ripps, Chief.*
Web, www.nps.gov/policy

Researches and develops management policy on matters relating to the National Park Service; makes recommendations on the historical significance of national trails and landmarks.

Tennessee Valley Authority, *Government Affairs,* 1 Massachusetts Ave. N.W., #300, 20444; (202) 898-2999. Fax, (202) 898-2998. Nick Pearson, Director.
General email, tvainfo@tva.gov
Web, www.tva.gov

Operates Land Between the Lakes, a national recreation and environmental education area located in western Kentucky and Tennessee.

U.S. Fish and Wildlife Service *(Interior Dept.), National Wildlife Refuge System,* 4401 N. Fairfax Dr., Arlington, VA 22203; (703) 358-2517. Fax, (703) 358-1973. *Cynthia Martinez, Chief.*
Web, www.fws.gov/refuges and Twitter, @USFWSRefuges

Manages the National Wildlife Refuge System. Most refuges are open to public use; activities include bird and wildlife watching, fishing, hunting, and environmental education.

▶**CONGRESS**

For a listing of relevant congressional committees and subcommittees, please see pages 270–271 or the Appendix.

▶**NONGOVERNMENTAL**

American Hiking Society, 8605 2nd Ave., Silver Spring, MD 20910; (301) 565-6704. Fax, (301) 565-6714. *Gregory Miller, President. Toll-free, (800) 972-8608.*
General email, info@americanhiking.org
Web, www.americanhiking.org

Membership: individuals and clubs interested in preserving America's trail system and protecting the interests of trail users. Provides information on outdoor volunteer opportunities on public lands.

American Recreation Coalition, 1200 G St. N.W., #650, 20005; (202) 682-9530. Fax, (202) 682-9529. *Derrick A. Crandall, President.*
General email, arc@funoutdoors.com
Web, www.funoutdoors.com and Twitter, @AmerRecreation

Membership: recreation industry associations, recreation enthusiast groups, and leading corporations in the recreation products and services sectors. Promotes health and well-being through outdoor recreation.

National Park Foundation, 1110 Vermont Ave. N.W., #200, 20005; (202) 796-2500. Fax, (202) 796-2509. *Will Shafroth, President; Hon. Sally Jewell, Chair.*
General email, ask-npf@nationalparks.org
Web, www.nationalparks.org

Encourages private-sector support of the national park system; provides grants and sponsors educational and cultural activities. Chartered by Congress and chaired by the Interior secretary.

National Park Trust, 401 E. Jefferson St., #203, Rockville, MD 20850; (301) 279-7275. Fax, (301) 279-7211. *Grace K. Lee, Executive Director.*
General email, npt@parktrust.org
Web, www.parktrust.org

Protects national parks, wildlife refuges, and historic monuments. Uses funds to purchase private land within or adjacent to existing parks and land suitable for new parks; works with preservation organizations to manage acquired resources.

National Parks Conservation Assn., 777 6th St. N.W., #700, 20001-3723; (202) 223-6722. Fax, (202) 454-3333. *Theresa Pierno, President. Information, (800) 628-7275.*
General email, npca@npca.org
Web, www.npca.org

Citizens interest group that seeks to protect national parks and other park system areas.

National Recreation and Park Assn., *22377 Belmont Ridge Rd., Ashburn, VA 20148-4501; (703) 858-0784. Fax, (703) 858-0794. Barbara Tulipane, Chief Executive Officer, (703) 858-2144. Toll-free, (800) 626-6772. General email, customerservice@nrpa.org*

Web, www.nrpa.org

Membership: park and recreation professionals and interested citizens. Promotes support and awareness of park, recreation, and leisure services; advances environmental and conservation efforts; facilitates development, expansion, and management of resources; provides technical assistance for park and recreational programs; and provides professional development to members. Monitors legislation and regulations.

Rails-to-Trails Conservancy, *2121 Ward Court N.W., 5th Floor, 20037; (202) 331-9696. Fax, (202) 223-9257. Keith Laughlin, President.*

Web, www.railstotrails.org and Twitter, @railstotrails

Promotes the conversion of abandoned railroad corridors into hiking and biking trails for public use. Provides public education programs and technical and legal assistance. Publishes trail guides. Monitors legislation and regulations.

Scenic America, *1307 New Hampshire Ave. N.W., 3rd Floor, 20036; (202) 463 1291. Fax, (202) 463-1299. Mary Tracy, President. General email, ashburn@scenic.org*

Web, www.scenic.org and Twitter, @ScenicAmerica

Membership: national, state, and local groups concerned with land-use control, growth management, and landscape protection. Works to enhance the scenic quality of America's communities and countryside. Provides information and technical assistance on scenic byways, tree preservation, economics of aesthetic regulation, billboard and sign control, scenic areas preservation, and growth management.

Student Conservation Assn., *4245 N. Fairfax Dr., #825, Arlington, VA 22203; (703) 524-2441. Jaime Berman Matyas, President. General email, DCinfo@thesca.org*

Web, www.thesca.org

Service organization that provides youth and adults with opportunities for training and work experience in natural resource management and conservation. Volunteers serve in national parks, forests, wildlife refuges, and other public lands.

The Wilderness Society, *1615 M St. N.W., 20036; (202) 833-2300. Fax, (202) 429-3958. Jamie Williams, President. Toll-free, (800) 843-9453. General email, action@tws.org*

Web, www.wilderness.org and Twitter, @wilderness

Promotes preservation of wilderness and the responsible management of federal lands, including national parks and forests, wilderness areas, wildlife refuges, and land administered by the Interior Dept.'s Bureau of Land Management.

World Wildlife Fund (WWF), *1250 24th St. N.W., 20037-1193 (mailing address: P.O. Box 97180, Washington, DC 20090-7180); (202) 293-4800. Fax, (202) 293-9211. Carter S. Roberts, President.*

Web, www.worldwildlife.org and Twitter, @World_Wildlife

International conservation organization that provides funds and technical assistance for establishing and maintaining parks.

Water Resources

▶**AGENCIES**

Army Corps of Engineers *(Defense Dept.), 441 G St. N.W., #3K05, 20314-1000; (202) 761-0001. Fax, (202) 761-4463. Lt. Gen. Thomas P. Bostick (USA), Chief of Engineers. Press, (202) 761-0011. General email, hq-publicaffairs@usace.army.mil*

Web, www.usace.army.mil and Twitter, @USACEHQ

Provides local governments with disaster relief, flood control, navigation, and hydroelectric power services.

Bureau of Reclamation *(Interior Dept.), 1849 C St. N.W., MS 7069, 20240-0001; (202) 513-0501. Fax, (202) 513-0309. Estevan Lopez, Commissioner. Press, (202) 513-0575. Web, www.usbr.gov and Twitter, @usbr*

Administers federal programs for water and power resource development and management in seventeen western states; oversees municipal and industrial water supplies, hydroelectric power generation, irrigation, flood control, water quality improvement, river regulation, fish and wildlife enhancement, and outdoor recreation.

Environmental Protection Agency (EPA), *Water, 1200 Pennsylvania Ave. N.W., MC 4101M, 20460; (202) 564-5700. Joel Beauvais, Deputy Assistant Administrator.*

Web, www.epa.gov/aboutepa/about-office-water#wetlands

Monitors drinking water safety and restores and maintains oceans, watersheds, and their aquatic ecosystems. Implements the Clean Water Act and Safe Drinking Water Act.

Environmental Protection Agency (EPA), *Water, Wetlands, Oceans, and Watersheds, 1200 Pennsylvania Ave. N.W., #7301, MC 4501T, 20004; (202) 566-1146. Fax, (202) 566-1147. Benita Best-Wong, Director, (202) 566-1155. General email, ow-owow-internet-comments@epa.gov*

Web, www2.epa.gov/aboutepa/about-office-water#wetlands

Coordinates federal policies affecting marine and freshwater ecosystems, including watersheds, coastal ecosystems, and wetlands. Regulates and monitors ocean dumping and seeks to minimize polluted runoff and restore impaired waters. Manages dredge-and-fill program under section 404 of the Clean Water Act. Promotes public awareness of resource preservation and management.

Interior Dept. (DOI), *Water and Science, 1849 C St. N.W., #6358, MS 6341, 20240; (202) 208-3186. Fax, (202) 208-6948. Jennifer Gimbel, Principal Deputy Assistant Secretary. Web, www.doi.gov*

Administers departmental water, scientific, and research activities. Directs and supervises the Bureau of Reclamation and the U.S. Geological Survey.

Interstate Commission on the Potomac River Basin, *30 W. Gude Dr., #450, Rockville, MD 20850; (301) 984-1908. Carlton Haywood, Executive Director.*
General email, info@icprb.org
Web, www.potomacriver.org

Nonregulatory interstate compact commission established by Congress to control and reduce water pollution and to restore and protect living resources in the Potomac River and its tributaries. Monitors water quality; assists metropolitan water utilities; seeks innovative methods to solve water supply and land resource problems. Provides information and educational materials on the Potomac River basin.

National Research Council (NRC), *Water Science and Technology Board,* *Keck Bldg., 500 5th St. N.W., #607, 20001; (202) 334-3422. Fax, (202) 334-1961. George M. Hornberger, Chair; Elizabeth Eide, Director, Acting.*
General email, wstb@nas.edu
Web, http://dels.nas.edu/wstb

Supports science, engineering, economics, and policy research for the efficient management and use of water resources.

Office of Management and Budget (OMB) *(Executive Office of the President), Water and Power, 725 17th St. N.W., #8002, 20503; (202) 395-4590. Fax, (202) 395-4817. Kelly Colyar, Chief. Press, (202) 395-7254.*
Web, www.whitehouse.gov/omb

Reviews all plans and budgets related to federal or federally assisted water power and related land resource projects.

Rural Development *(Agriculture Dept.), Rural Utilities Service, 1400 Independence Ave. S.W., #5135-S, MS 1510, 20250-1510; (202) 720-9540. Fax, (202) 720-1725. Brandon McBride, Administrator. Information, (202) 720-1255.*
Web, www.rd.usda.gov/about-rd/agencies/rural-utilities-service

Makes loans and provides technical assistance for development, repair, and replacement of water and waste disposal systems in rural areas.

Smithsonian Environmental Research Center *(Smithsonian Institution), 647 Contees Wharf Rd., Edgewater, MD 21037 (mailing address: P.O. Box 28, Edgewater, MD 21037-0028); (443) 482-2200. Fax, (443) 482-2380. Anson H. Hines, Director, (443) 482-2208. Press, (443) 482-2325.*
Web, www.serc.si.edu

Serves as a research center on water ecosystems in the coastal zone.

Tennessee Valley Authority, *Government Affairs,* *1 Massachusetts Ave. N.W., #300, 20444; (202) 898-2999. Fax, (202) 898-2998. Nick Pearson, Director.*
General email, tvainfo@tva.gov
Web, www.tva.gov

Coordinates resource conservation, development, and land-use programs in the Tennessee River Valley. Operates the river control system; projects include flood control, navigation development, and multiple-use reservoirs.

U.S. Geological Survey (USGS) *(Interior Dept.), Water, 12201 Sunrise Valley Dr., MS 150, Reston, VA 20192; (703) 648-4557. Fax, (703) 648-7031. Don Cline, Associate Director, (703) 648-4557.*
Web, http://water.usgs.gov

Administers the Water Resources Research Act of 1990. Monitors and assesses the quantity and quality of the nation's freshwater resources; collects, analyzes, and disseminates data on water use and the effect of human activity and natural phenomena on hydrologic systems; assesses sources and behavior of contaminants in the water environment, and develops tools to improve management and understanding of water resources. Provides federal agencies, state and local governments, international organizations, and foreign governments with scientific and technical assistance.

▶**CONGRESS**

For a listing of relevant congressional committees and subcommittees, please see pages 270–271 or the Appendix.

▶**NONGOVERNMENTAL**

American Rivers, *1101 14th St. N.W., #1400, 20005; (202) 347-7550. Fax, (202) 347-9240. William Robert (Bob) Irvin, President.*
General email, outreach@americanrivers.org
Web, www.americanrivers.org and Twitter, @americanrivers

Works to preserve and protect the nation's river systems through public information and advocacy. Collaborates with grassroots river and watershed groups, other conservation groups, sporting and recreation groups, businesses, local citizens, and various federal, state, and tribal agencies. Monitors legislation and regulations.

American Water Works Assn., *Government Affairs,* *1300 Eye St. N.W., #701W, 20005; (202) 628-8303. Fax, (202) 628-2846. G. Tracy Mehan III, Executive Director.*
General email, custsvc@awwa.org
Web, www.awwa.org

Membership: municipal water utilities, manufacturers of equipment for water industries, water treatment companies, and individuals. Provides information on drinking water treatment and trends and issues affecting water safety; publishes voluntary standards for the water industry; issues policy statements on water supply matters. Monitors legislation and regulations. (Headquarters in Denver, Colo.)

Assn. of State Drinking Water Administrators (ASDWA), *1401 Wilson Blvd., #1225, Arlington, VA 22209; (703) 812-9505. Fax, (703) 812-9506. James D. Taft, Executive Director.*
General email, info@asdwa.org
Web, www.asdwa.org and Twitter, @ASTSWMO

Membership: state officials responsible for the drinking water supply and enforcement of safety standards. Monitors legislation and regulations.

Environmental Defense Fund, *Washington Office, 1875 Connecticut Ave. N.W., #600, 20009-5728; (202) 387-3500. Fax, (202) 234-6049. Fred Krupp, President; Felice Stradler, Director, U.S. Climate and Political Affairs. Information, (800) 684-3322. Press, (202) 572-3396. Web, www.edf.org and Twitter, @EnvDefenseFund*

Citizens interest group staffed by lawyers, economists, and scientists. Takes legal action on environmental issues; provides information on pollution prevention, environmental health, water resources, water marketing, and sustainable fishing. (Headquarters in New York.)

Irrigation Assn., *8280 Willow Oaks Corporate Dr., #400, Fairfax, VA 22031; (703) 536-7080. Fax, (703) 536-7019. Deborah Hamlin, Executive Director. General email, info@irrigation.org Web, www.irrigation.org*

Membership: companies and individuals involved in irrigation, drainage, and erosion control worldwide. Promotes efficient and effective water management through training, education, and certification programs. Interests include economic development and environmental enhancement.

Izaak Walton League of America, *707 Conservation Lane, Gaithersburg, MD 20878-2983; (301) 548-0150. Fax, (301) 548-0146. Scott Kovarovics, Executive Director. Toll-free, (800) 453-5463. General email, info@iwla.org Web, www.iwla.org*

Grassroots organization that promotes conservation of natural resources and the environment. Coordinates a citizen action program to monitor and improve the condition of local streams.

National Assn. of Conservation Districts (NACD), *509 Capitol Court N.E., 20002-4937; (202) 547-6223. Fax, (202) 547-6450. Jeremy Peters, Chief Executive Officer. General email, bethany-shively@nacdnet.org Web, www.nacdnet.org*

Membership: conservation districts (local subdivisions of state government). Develops national policies and works to promote the conservation of water resources. Interests include erosion and sediment control and control of nonpoint source pollution.

National Assn. of Flood and Stormwater Management Agencies (NAFSMA), *1333 H St. N.W., West Tower, 10th Floor, 20005 (mailing address: P.O. Box 56764, Washington, DC 20040); (202) 289-8625. Fax, (202) 530-3389. Susan Gilson, Executive Director. General email, sgilson@nafsma.org Web, www.nafsma.org*

Membership: state, county, and local governments, and special flood management districts concerned with management of water resources. Interests include stormwater management, disaster assistance, flood insurance, and federal flood management policy. Monitors legislation and regulations.

National Assn. of Regulatory Utility Commissioners, *1101 Vermont Ave. N.W., #200, 20005-3521; (202) 898-2200. Fax, (202) 898-2213. Greg White, Executive Director. General email, admin@naruc.org Web, www.naruc.org*

Membership: members of federal, state, municipal, and international regulatory commissions that have jurisdiction over utilities. Interests include water.

National Assn. of Water Companies (NAWC), *2001 L St. N.W., #850, 20036; (202) 833-8383. Fax, (202) 331-7442. Michael Deane, Executive Director. General email, carlos@nuwc.com Web, www.nawc.org*

Membership: privately owned, regulated water companies. Provides members with information on legislative and regulatory issues and other subjects.

National Water Resources Assn. (NWRA), *4 E St. S.E., 20003; (202) 698-0693. Fax, (202) 698-0694. Dave Koland, President; Robert Johnson, Executive Vice President. General email, nwra@nwra.org Web, http://nwra.org*

Membership: conservation and irrigation districts, municipalities, and others interested in water resources. Works for the development and maintenance of water resources and a sustainable water supply. Represents interests of members before Congress and regulatory agencies.

Rural Community Assistance Partnership (RCAP), *1701 K St. N.W., #700, 20006; (202) 408-1273. Fax, (202) 408-8165. Robert Stewart, Executive Director. Toll-free, (800) 321-7227. General email, info@rcap.org Web, www.rcap.org*

Provides expertise to rural communities on wastewater disposal, protection of groundwater supply, and access to safe drinking water. Targets communities with predominantly low-income or minority populations. Offers outreach policy analysis, training, and technical assistance to elected officials and other community leaders, utility owners and operators, and residents.

Water Environment Federation, *601 Wythe St., Alexandria, VA 22314-1994; (703) 684-2400. Fax, (703) 684-2492. Eileen O'Neill, Executive Director, (703) 684-2430. Toll-free, (800) 666-0206. General email, inquiry@wef.org Web, www.wef.org and Twitter, @WEForg*

Membership: civil and environmental engineers, wastewater treatment plant operators, scientists, government officials, and others concerned with water quality. Works to preserve and improve water quality worldwide. Provides the public with technical information and educational materials. Monitors legislation and regulations.

9  Government Operations

GENERAL POLICY AND ANALYSIS

Basic Resources

▶AGENCIES

Administrative Conference of the United States (ACUS), *1120 20th St. N.W., #706, 20036; (202) 480-2080. Vacant, Chair; Matthew L. Weiner, Executive Director, (202) 480-2104; Shawne C. McGibbon, General Counsel, (202) 480-2088.*
General email, info@acus.gov
Web, www.acus.gov

Independent federal agency consisting of federal officials and experts from the private sector and academia; promotes efficiency and fairness in government procedures, regulatory programs, and grant and benefit administration. Conference committees include the Committee on Adjudication, Committee on Administration and Management, Committee on Collaborative Governance, Committee on Judicial Review, Committee on Regulation, and Committee on Rulemaking.

Domestic Policy Council *(Executive Office of the President), The White House, 20502; (202) 456-5594. Fax, (202) 456-3342. Cecilia Muñoz, Director.*
Web, www.whitehouse.gov/dpc

Comprises cabinet officials and staff members. Coordinates the domestic policymaking process to facilitate the implementation of the president's domestic agenda throughout federal agencies in such major domestic policy areas as agriculture, education, energy, environment, health, housing, labor, and veterans affairs.

Executive Office of the President, *Intergovernmental Affairs, 1600 Pennsylvania Ave. N.W., 20502; (202) 456-1097. Fax, (202) 456-1641. Jerry Abramson, Director. TTY, (202) 456-6213.*
Web, www.whitehouse.gov/administration/eop/iga

Seeks to build relationships with constituents and to connect citizens with their elected officials.

Executive Office of the President, *Public Engagement, Dwight D. Eisenhower Executive Office Bldg., #110, 20502; (202) 456-1097. Fax, (202) 456-1641. Paulette Aniskoff, Director. TTY, (202) 456-6213.*
Web, www.whitehouse.gov/engage

Promotes presidential priorities through outreach to concerned constituencies and public interest groups.

General Services Administration (GSA), *1800 F St. N.W., 20405; (202) 501-0800. Denise Turner Roth, Administrator; Adam Neufeld, Deputy Administrator; Carol Ochoa Jr., Inspector General, (202) 501-0450.*
Web, www.gsa.gov and Twitter, @usgsa

Establishes policies for managing federal government property, including construction and operation of buildings and procurement and distribution of supplies and equipment; manages transportation and telecommunications.

Manages disposal of surplus federal property. Responsible for www.USA.gov.

General Services Administration (GSA), *Citizen Services and Innovative Technologies, 1800 F St. N.W., 2nd Floor, 20405; (202) 501-0705. Fax, (202) 357-0077. Phaedra S. Chrousos, Associate Administrator.*
Web, www.gsa.gov

Identifies and applies new technologies to improve the way the federal government provides the public with access to information and services. Administers the Web site www.USA.gov, a comprehensive search engine of government information; call (800) FED-INFO for information by phone.

General Services Administration (GSA), *Government-wide Policy, 1800 F St. N.W., 20405; (202) 501-8880. Fax, (202) 208-1224. Troy Cribb, Associate Administrator.*
Web, www.gsa.gov/ogp

Coordinates GSA policymaking activities, including areas of personal and real property, travel and transportation, acquisition (internal GSA and governmentwide), information technology, regulatory information, and use of federal advisory committees; promotes collaboration between government and the private sector in developing policy and management techniques; works to integrate acquisition, management, and disposal of government property.

General Services Administration (GSA), *Government-wide Policy, Acquisition Policy, 1800 F St. N.W., 20405; (202) 501-4755. Fax, (202) 357-0038. Jeffrey A. (Jeff) Koses, Senior Procurement Executive.*
General email, askacquisition@gsa.gov and far.sec@gsa.gov
Web, www.gsa.gov/portal/category/101099

Develops and implements federal government acquisition policies and procedures; administers Federal Acquisition Regulation (FAR) for civilian agencies. Manages several GSA-specific and governmentwide acquisition database systems. Conducts pre-award and post-award contract reviews; suspends and debars contractors for unsatisfactory performance; coordinates and promotes governmentwide career management and training programs for contracting personnel.

General Services Administration (GSA), *USAGov, 1800 F St. N.W., 20405; (202) 501-1794. Fax, (202) 357-0078. Sarah Crane, Director. Toll-free, (844) 872-4681.*
Web, www.publications.usa.gov, Web, www.gobiernoUSA .gov and www.gsa.gov/portal/category/101011

Manages the portal site to U.S. government information, www.usa.gov. Manages kids.gov, a resource that provides government information to younger Americans. Distributes free and low-cost federal publications of consumer interest via the Internet at www.publications.usa.gov, or when callers dial (888) 878-3256 for a catalog. Publishes the *Consumer Action Handbook*, a free resource that can be used online at http://consumeraction.gov or obtained when callers dial (888) 8-PUEBLO. Assists people with questions about American government agencies, programs, and services via telephone, (800) FED-INFO

GOVERNMENT OPERATIONS RESOURCES IN CONGRESS

For a complete listing of congressional committees, including their full contact information, leadership, membership, and jurisdictions, please refer to the Appendix on pages 779–896.

HOUSE:

House Administration Committee, (202) 225-8281.
Web, cha.house.gov

House Appropriations Committee, (202) 225-2771.
Web, appropriations.house.gov

    Subcommittee on Commerce, Justice, Science, and Related Agencies, (202) 225-3351.

    Subcommittee on Financial Services and General Government, (202) 225-7245.

    Subcommittee on Legislative Branch, (202) 226-7252.

House Budget Committee, (202) 226-7270.
Web, budget.house.gov

House Education and the Workforce Committee, (202) 225-4527.
Web, edworkforce.house.gov

    Subcommittee on Workforce Protections, (202) 225-4527.

House Energy and Commerce Committee, (202) 225-2927.
Web, energycommerce.house.gov

    Subcommittee on Oversight and Investigations, (202) 225-2927.

House Ethics Committee, (202) 225-7103.
Web, ethics.house.gov

House Financial Services Committee, (202) 225-7502.
Web, financialservices.house.gov

    Subcommittee on Oversight and Investigations, (202) 225-7502.

House Homeland Security Committee, (202) 226-8417.
Web, homeland.house.gov

    Subcommittee on Oversight and Management Efficiency, (202) 226-8417.

House Judiciary Committee, (202) 225-3951.
Web, judiciary.house.gov

    Subcommittee on the Constitution and Civil Justice, (202) 225-2825.

House Oversight and Government Reform Committee, (202) 225-5074.
Web, oversight.house.gov

    Subcommittee on Government Operations, (202) 225-5074.

    Subcommittee on Health Care, Benefits, and Administrative Rules, (202) 225-5074.

    Subcommittee on Interior, (202) 225-5074.

House Rules Committee, (202) 225-9191.
Web, rules.house.gov

House Science, Space, and Technology Committee, (202) 225-6371.
Web, science.house.gov

    Subcommittee on Oversight, (202) 225-6371.

House Small Business Committee, (202) 225-5821.
Web, smallbusiness.house.gov

([800] 333-4636), or Web site, http://answers.usa.gov. Operates a contact center to provide information in English or Spanish on all federal government agencies, programs, and services via toll-free telephone, e-mail, and chat. Operated under contract by Sykes in Pennsylvania and Florida. Responds to inquiries about federal programs and services. Gives information about or referrals to appropriate offices. (Formerly Federal Citizen Information Center.)

Office of Administration *(Executive Office of the President),* 725 17th St. N.W., #240, 20503; (202) 456-2861. *Catherine (Beth) Sullivan, Director.*
Web, www.whitehouse.gov/oa/administration/eop/oa

Provides administrative support services to the Executive Office of the President, including financial management and information technology support, human resources management, library and research assistance, facilities management, procurement, printing and graphics support, security, and mail and messenger operations.

Office of Management and Budget (OMB) *(Executive Office of the President),* 725 17th St. N.W., 20503; (202) 395-3080. Fax, (202) 395-3888. *Shaun Donovan, Director.*

Press, (202) 395-7254.
Web, www.whitehouse.gov/omb

Works with other federal agencies to develop and maintain the Web site ExpectMore.gov, which uses the Program Assessment Rating Tool (PART) to gauge the effectiveness of federal programs. Holds programs accountable for improving their performance and management.

Office of Management and Budget (OMB) *(Executive Office of the President), Federal Procurement Policy,* 725 17th St. N.W., #9013, 20503; (202) 395-5802. *Anne Rung, Administrator; Matthew Beck, Assistant to Ms. Rung. Press, (202) 395-7254.*
Web, www.whitehouse.gov/omb/procurement

Oversees and coordinates government procurement policies, regulations, and procedures. Responsible for cost accounting rules governing federal contractors and subcontractors. Interests include effective use of competition, cost-effective contracting for vehicles, and managing a useful information technology system for federal procurement managers.

Office of Management and Budget (OMB) *(Executive Office of the President), Information and Regulatory Affairs,* 725 17th St. N.W., #10236, 20503; (202) 395-5897.

Subcommittee on Investigations, Oversight, and Regulations, (202) 225-5821.

House Veterans' Affairs Committee, (202) 225-3527.
Web, veterans.house.gov

Subcommittee on Oversight and Investigations, (202) 225-3569.

House Ways and Means Committee, (202) 225-3625.
Web, waysandmeans.house.gov

Subcommittee on Oversight, (202) 225-5522.

SENATE:

Senate Appropriations Committee, (202) 224-7363.
Web, appropriations.senate.gov

Subcommittee on Commerce, Justice, Science, and Related Agencies, (202) 224-5202.

Subcommittee on Financial Services and General Government, (202) 224-1133.

Subcommittee on Legislative Branch, (202) 224-7256.

Senate Budget Committee, (202) 224-0642.
Web, www.budget.senate.gov

Senate Environment and Public Works Committee, (202) 224-8832.
Web, epw.senate.gov

Subcommittee on Superfund, Waste Management, and Regulatory Oversight, (202) 224-8832.

Subcommittee on Transportation and Infrastructure, (202) 224-8832.

Senate Finance Committee, (202) 224-4515.
Web, finance.senate.gov

Subcommittee on Fiscal Responsibility and Economic Growth, (202) 224-4515.

Senate Homeland Security and Governmental Affairs Committee, (202) 224-2627.
Web, hsgac.senate.gov

Permanent Subcommittee on Investigations, (202) 224-4462.

Subcommittee on Federal Spending, Oversight, and Emergency Management, (202) 224-4462.

Subcommittee on Regulatory Affairs and Federal Management, (202) 224-4462.

Senate Judiciary Committee, (202) 224-7703.
Web, judiciary.senate.gov

Subcommittee on Oversight, Agency Action, Federal Rights, and Federal Courts, (202) 224-5972.

Senate Rules and Administration Committee, (202) 224-6352.
Web, rules.senate.gov

Senate Select Committee on Ethics, (202) 224-2981.
Web, ethics.senate.gov

Senate Small Business and Entrepreneurship Committee, (202) 224-5175.
Web, sbc.senate.gov

Fax, (202) 395-6102. Harold Shelanski, Administrator.
Press, (202) 395-7254.
Web, www.whitehouse.gov/omb/inforeg_infopoltech

Oversees development of federal regulatory programs. Supervises agency information management activities in accordance with the Paperwork Reduction Act of 1995, as amended; reviews agency analyses of the effect of government regulatory activities on the U.S. economy.

Office of Management and Budget (OMB) *(Executive Office of the President), Performance and Personnel Management, 725 17th St. N.W., #7236, 20503; (202) 395-5017. Fax, (202) 395-5738. Dustin Brown, Deputy Assistant Director. Press, (202) 395-7254.*
Web, www.whitehouse.gov/omb/performance

Examines, evaluates, and suggests improvements for agencies and programs within the Office of Personnel Management and the Executive Office of the President.

Office of Management and Budget (OMB) *(Executive Office of the President), Statistical and Science Policy, 725 17th St. N.W., #10201, 20503; (202) 395-3093. Fax, (202) 395-7245. Katherine K. Wallman, Chief. Press, (202) 395-7254.*
Web, www.whitehouse.gov/omb

Carries out the statistical policy and coordination functions under the Paperwork Reduction Act of 1995; develops long-range plans for improving federal statistical programs; develops policy standards and guidelines for statistical data collection, classification, and publication; evaluates statistical programs and agency performance.

Regulatory Information Service Center *(General Services Administration), 1800 F St. N.W., #2219F, 20405; (202) 482-7340. Fax, (202) 482-7360. John C. Thomas, Executive Director.*
General email, risc@gsa.gov
Web, www.gsa.gov/risc

Provides the president, Congress, and the public with information on federal regulatory policies and their effects on society; recommends ways to make regulatory information more accessible to government officials and the public. Publishes the Unified Agenda of Federal Regulatory and Deregulatory Actions. See www.reginfo.gov for information about government regulations.

► **CONGRESS**

For a listing of relevant congressional committees and subcommittees, please see pages 314–315 or the Appendix.

White House Offices

OFFICE OF THE PRESIDENT
President, Barack Obama

>1600 Pennsylvania Ave. N.W., 20500; (202) 456-1414,
>   Fax (202) 456-2461
>Web, www.whitehouse.gov
>Email, president@whitehouse.gov

Chief of Staff, Denis McDonough, (202) 456-1414.
Deputy Chiefs of Staff, Anita Decker Breckenridge,
and Kristie Canegallo, (202) 456-1414

Advance and Operations, Michael Brush, Director,
(202) 456-4709

Cabinet Secretary, Broderick D. Johnson, Director,
(202) 456-2572

Communications, Jennifer Psaki, Director, (202) 456-1414

Correspondence, Fiona O. Reeves, Director, (202) 456-1414

Counsel, John Podesta, White House Counsel,
(202) 456-1414

Faith-Based and Neighborhood Partnerships, Melissa
Rogers, Director, (202) 456-3394

House Liaison, Alejandro Perez, Deputy Assistant to the
President, (202) 456-6620

Intergovernmental Affairs and Public Engagement,
Valerie B. Jarrett, Senior Advisor to the President,
(202) 456-1414

Legislative Affairs, Katie Beirne Fallon, Assistant to the
President, (202) 456-1414

Management and Administration, Katy Kale, Assistant to
the President, (202) 456-5400

Media Affairs, Jennifer Palmieri, Director, (202) 456-6238

National AIDS Policy, Douglas M. Brooks, Director,
(202) 456-7320

National Intelligence, James R. Clapper, Director,
(703) 733-8600

National Security Advisor, Susan Rice, (202) 456-9491

New Media, Jesse C. Lee, Director, (202) 456-6238

Presidential Personnel, Valerie Green, Assistant to the
President, (202) 456-9713

Press Secretary, Josh Earnest, Press Secretary,
(202) 456-2580

Public Engagement, Paulette Aniskoff, Director,
(202) 456-1414

Scheduling and Advance, Chase Cushman, Director,
(202) 456-5325

Speechwriting, Cody Keenan, Director, (202) 456-1414

Staff Secretary, Joani Walsh, (202) 456-2702

U.S. Secret Service (Homeland Security), Joseph Clancy,
Director, (202) 406-5708

White House Fellows, Jennifer Yeager Kaplan,
(202) 395-4522

White House Military Office, Emmett Beliveau, Director,
(202) 757-2151

OFFICE OF THE FIRST LADY
First Lady, Michelle Obama

>1600 Pennsylvania Ave. N.W., 20500;
>   (202) 456-7064; www.whitehouse.gov/firstlady
>   Email, first.lady@whitehouse.gov

Chief of Staff, Christina Tchen, Chief of Staff,
(202) 456-7064

Communications, Caroline Adler, Director,
Hannah August, Press Secretary, (202) 456-6313

OFFICE OF THE VICE PRESIDENT
Vice President, Joseph R. Biden Jr.

>1600 Pennsylvania Ave. N.W., 20500,
>   www.whitehouse.gov/vicepresident
>   Email, vice.president@whitehouse.gov

Chief of Staff, Steve Ricchetti, Chief of Staff, (202) 456-2423

Communications, Kate Bedingfield, Director,
(202) 456-1414

Wife of the Vice President, Dr. Jill Biden, (202) 456-1414

Government Accountability Office (GAO), *441 G St.
N.W., 20548; (202) 512-5500. Fax, (202) 512-5507.
Gene L. Dodaro, Comptroller General. Information, (202)
512-3000. Publications and Documents, (202) 512-6000.
Congressional Relations, (202) 512-4400.
Web, www.gao.gov*

Independent, nonpartisan agency in the legislative
branch. Serves as the investigating agency for Congress;
carries out legal, accounting, auditing, and claims settlement functions; makes recommendations for more effective government operations; publishes monthly lists of
reports available to the public.

Government Accountability Office (GAO), *Financial
Markets and Community Investment, 441 G St N.W.,
#2440B, 20548; (202) 512-8678. Joan Holloway,*

*Staff Assistant.
Web, www.gao.gov/careers/fmci.html*

Supports congressional efforts to ensure that U.S.
financial markets function smoothly and effectively, identify fraud and abuse, and promote sound, sustainable
community investment by assessing the effectiveness of
federal initiatives aimed at small businesses, state, and
local governments, and communities.

Library of Congress, *Federal Research Division, John
Adams Bldg., 101 Independence Ave. S.E., #LA 5281,
20540-4840; (202) 707-3900. Fax, (202) 707-3920.
Mukta Ohri, Chief.
General email, frds@loc.gov
Web, www.loc.gov/rr/frd*

The Cabinet of Barack Obama

The president's cabinet includes the vice president and the heads of fifteen executive departments. In addition, every president has discretion to elevate any number of other government officials to cabinet-rank status. The cabinet is primarily an advisory group.

VICE PRESIDENT

Joseph R. Biden Jr., Vice President, (202) 456-1414;
Web, www.whitehouse.gov/vicepresident
Email, vice.president@whitehouse.gov

EXECUTIVE DEPT. CABINET MEMBERS

Agriculture Dept., Thomas J. Vilsack, Secretary,
(202) 720-3631; Web, www.usda.gov

Commerce Dept., Penny Pritzker, Secretary, (202) 482-2000;
Web, www.commerce.gov; Email, TheSec@doc.gov

Defense Dept., Chuck Hagel, Secretary, (703) 571-3343;
Web, www.defense.gov

Education Dept., John King (Acting), Secretary,
(202) 401-3000; Web, www.ed.gov

Energy Dept., Ernest Moniz, Secretary, (202) 586-6210;
Web, www.energy.gov

Health and Human Services Dept., Sylvia Matthews
Burwell, Secretary, (202) 690-7000; Web, www.hhs.gov

Homeland Security Dept., Jeh Johnson, Secretary,
(202) 282-8000; Web, www.dhs.gov

Housing and Urban Development Dept., Julián Castro,
Secretary, (202) 708-0417; Web, www.hud.gov

Interior Dept., Sally Jewell, Secretary, (202) 208-3100;
Web, www.doi.gov

Justice Dept., Loretta Lynch, Attorney General,
(202) 514-2000; Web, www.justice.gov

Labor Dept., Thomas E. Perez, Secretary, (202) 693-6000;
Web, www.dol.gov

State Dept., John Kerry, Secretary, (202) 647-5291;
Web, www.state.gov

Transportation, Anthony Foxx, Secretary, (202) 366-9201;
Web, www.dot.gov

Treasury Dept., Jack Lew, Secretary, (202) 622-2000;
Web, www.treasury.gov

Veterans Affairs Dept., Robert McDonald, Secretary,
(202) 461-4800; Web, www.va.gov

OTHER CABINET-RANK OFFICIALS

Council of Economic Advisors, Jason Furman, Chair
(202) 456-1414; Web, www.whitehouse.gov/cea

Environmental Protection Agency, Gina McCarthy,
Administrator, (202) 564-4700; Web, www.epa.gov

Office of Management and Budget, Shaun L.S. Donovan,
Director, (202) 395-3080;
Web, www.whitehouse.gov/omb

Office of the White House Chief of Staff, Denis McDonough,
Chief of Staff, (202) 456-1414; Web, www.whitehouse.gov

Small Business Administration, Maria Contreras-Sweet,
Administrator, (202) 205-6708; Web, www.sba.gov

U.S. Trade Representative, Michael Froman, Ambassador,
(202) 395-6890; Web, www.ustr.gov

United States Mission to the United Nations, Samantha
Power, Ambassador, (212) 415-4050

Provides research and analytical support to federal agencies and authorized federal contractors.

▶ NONGOVERNMENTAL

American Political Science Assn. (APSA), *1527 New Hampshire Ave. N.W., 20036-1206; (202) 483-2512. Fax, (202) 483-2657. Steven Rathgeb Smith, Executive Director. General email, apsa@apsanet.org*

Web, www.apsanet.org and Twitter, @APSAtweets

Membership: political scientists, primarily college and university professors. Promotes scholarly inquiry into all aspects of political science, including international affairs and comparative government. Works to increase public understanding of politics; provides services to facilitate and enhance research, teaching, and professional development of its members. Acts as liaison with federal agencies, Congress, and the public. Seeks to improve the status of women and minorities in the profession. Offers congressional fellowships, workshops, and awards. Provides information on political science issues.

The Brookings Institution, *1775 Massachusetts Ave. N.W., 20036; (202) 797-6000. Fax, (202) 797-6004.*

Strobe Talbott, President. Press, (202) 797-6105. General email, communications@brookings.edu

Web, www.brookings.edu and Twitter, @Brookingsinst

Public policy research organization that seeks to improve the performance of American institutions, the effectiveness of government programs, and the quality of public policy through research and analysis. Sponsors lectures, debates, and policy forums.

The Brookings Institution, *Governance Studies, 1755 Massachusetts Ave. N.W., 20036; (202) 797-6090. Fax, (202) 797-6144. Darrell M. West, Director, (202) 797-6481. Information, (202) 797-6000. Press, (202) 797-6105. Web, www.brookings.edu/governance*

Explores the formal and informal political institutions of democratic governments to assess how they govern, how their practices compare, and how citizens and government servants can advance sound government.

Center for Plain Language, *21 E. Main St., Richmond, VA 23219; (301) 219-1731. Rebecca Gholson, Executive Director. General email, centerforplainlanguage@gmail.com*

Web, www.centerforplainlanguage.org and Twitter, @plain_language

Government Accountability Office

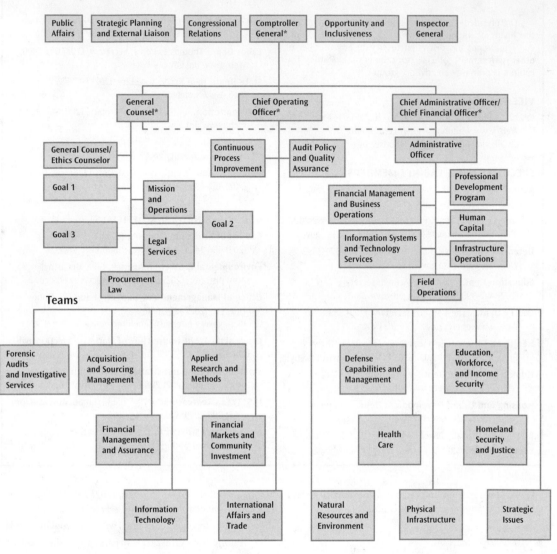

- - - - Indicates a support or advisory relationship with the teams/units rather than a direct reporting relationship
*The Executive Committee

Advocates plain-language/reader-focused writing through education and training within government, the private sector, and academia.

Center for Regulatory Effectiveness (CRE), 1601
Connecticut Ave. N.W., #500, 20009; (202) 265-2383.
Fax, (202) 939-6969. James J. Tozzi, Executive Director.
General email, comments@thecre.com

Web, www.thecre.com

Clearinghouse for methods to improve the federal regulatory process and public access to data and information used to develop federal regulations. Conducts analyses of the activities of the OMB Office of Information and Regulatory Affairs and serves as a regulatory watchdog over executive branch agencies. Acts as advocate on regulatory issues.

Center for the Study of the Presidency and Congress,
601 13th St. N.W., #1050N, 20005; (202) 872-9800.
Fax, (202) 872-9811. Maximillian Angerholtzer III,
President.
General email, ann.packo@thepresidency.org

Web, www.thepresidency.org

Membership: college students, government officials, and business leaders interested in the presidency, government, and politics. Conducts conferences, lectures, and symposiums on domestic, economic, and foreign policy issues. Publishes papers, essays, books, and reports on various aspects of the presidency and Congress.

Federal Managers Assn., 1641 Prince St., Alexandria, VA
22314-2818; (703) 683-8700. Fax, (703) 683-8707.
Patricia J. Niehaus, National President; Todd Wells,

Executive Director, ext. 102.
General email, info@fedmanagers.org
Web, www.fedmanagers.org

Seeks to improve the effectiveness of federal supervisors and managers and the operations of the federal government. Interests include cost-effective government restructuring, competitive civil service pay and benefits, and maintaining the core values of the civil service.

Federation of American Scientists (FAS), *Project on Government Secrecy,* 1725 DeSales St. N.W., #600, 20036; (202) 546-3300. Fax, (202) 675-1010. Steven Aftergood, Project Director. Press, (202) 454-4694.
General email, fas@fas.org

Web, www.fas.org/issues/government-secrecy

Promotes public access to government information and fosters development of rational information security policies. Works to reduce the scope of government secrecy, including national security classification and declassification policies. Publishes hard-to-find government documents online.

Partnership for Public Service, 1100 New York Ave. N.W., #200E, 20005; (202) 775-9111. Fax, (202) 775-8885. Max Stier, President.
Web, www.ourpublicservice.org

Membership: large corporations and private businesses, including financial and information technology organizations. Seeks to improve government efficiency, productivity, and management through a cooperative effort of the public and private sectors.

Buildings and Services

▶**AGENCIES**

Federal Protective Service (FPS) *(Homeland Security Dept.),* 800 N. Capitol St., 5th Floor, 20002; Fax, (202) 732-8109. L. Eric Patterson, Director. Switchboard, (202) 282-8000.
Web, www.dhs.gov/about-federal-protective-service

Works to ensure that appropriate levels of security are in place in General Services Administration-managed facilities throughout the United States. Conducts assessments on all GSA-controlled facilities to evaluate threats and tailor appropriate security countermeasures. Has enforcement capability to detain and arrest people, seize goods or conveyances, obtain arrest and search warrants, respond to incidents and emergency situations, provide protection during demonstrations or civil unrest, and be deputized for law enforcement response in special situations.

General Services Administration (GSA), *Asset and Transportation Management,* 1275 1st St. N.E., 20417; (202) 501-1777. Fax, (202) 273-4670. Carolyn Austin-Diggs, Principal Deputy Administrator.
Web, www.gsa.gov/portal/category/21400

Seeks to improve the management and control of procured transportation services governmentwide, promoting regulatory flexibility and business incentives and tools.

General Services Administration (GSA), *Federal Acquisition Institute,* 9830 Flagler Rd., Bldg. 270, Ft. Belvoir, VA 22060-5565 (mailing address: 9820 Belvoir Rd., Bldg. 270, Ft. Belvoir, VA 22060); (703) 805-2333. Fax, (703) 805-2111. Melissa Starinksy, Director.
General email, contact@fai.gov

Web, www.fai.gov and www.gsa.gov/portal/content/118227

Fosters development of a professional acquisition workforce governmentwide; collects and analyzes acquisition workforce data; helps agencies identify and recruit candidates for the acquisitions field; develops instructional materials; evaluates training and career development programs.

General Services Administration (GSA), *Federal Acquisition Service,* 2200 Crystal Dr., 11th Floor, Arlington, VA 22202; (703) 605-5400. Fax, (703) 605-9955. Thomas A. Sharpe Jr., Commissioner. National Customer Service Center (NCSC), (800) 488-3111 and NCSCcustomer.service@gsa.gov.
General email, contactfas@gsa.gov

Web, www.gsa.gov/portal/content/105080

Responsible for providing federal agencies with common-use goods and nonpersonal services and for procurement and supply, transportation and travel management, disposal of surplus personal property and motor vehicle management.

General Services Administration (GSA), *National Capital Region,* 301 7th St. S.W., #7022, 20407; (202) 708-9100. Fax, (202) 708-9966. Julia E. Hudson, Regional Administrator.
Web, www.gsa.gov/ncr

Provides federal agencies with office space and property management services, supplies, telecommunications, transportation, construction services, energy conservation and recycling services, and information technology support; has equal status with regional offices.

General Services Administration (GSA), *Portfolio Management,* 1800 F St. N.W., #7300, 20405-0001; (202) 501-0638. Fax, (202) 208-0033. Martha Benson, Assistant Commissioner, (202) 208-7176.
Web, www.gsa.gov/portal/category/22181

Develops, promotes, and assesses compliance with management policies and regulations for the effective and efficient stewardship of federal real property assets and alternative workplaces. Provides oversight and guidance for governmentwide real property asset management plans and related activities, including the use and disposal of excess real property.

General Services Administration (GSA), *Public Buildings Services,* 1800 F St. N.W., #6459, 20405; (202) 501-1100. Norman Dong, Commissioner.
Web, www.gsa.gov/pbs

Administers the acquisition, construction, maintenance, and operation of buildings owned or leased by the federal government. Manages and disposes of federal real estate.

Ethics in Government

▶AGENCIES

Administrative Conference of the United States (ACUS), *1120 20th St. N.W., #706, 20036; (202) 480-2080. Vacant, Chair; Matthew L. Weiner, Executive Director, (202) 480-2104; Shawne C. McGibbon, General Counsel, (202) 480-2088.*
General email, info@acus.gov

Web, www.acus.gov

Independent federal agency consisting of federal officials and experts from the private sector and academia; promotes efficiency and fairness in government procedures, regulatory programs, and grant and benefit administration. Conference committees include the Committee on Adjudication, Committee on Administration and Management, Committee on Collaborative Governance, Committee on Judicial Review, Committee on Regulation, and Committee on Rulemaking.

U.S. Office of Government Ethics, *1201 New York Ave. N.W., #500, 20005-3917; (202) 482-9300. Fax, (202) 482-9237. Walter M. Shaub Jr., Director. TTY, (800) 877-8339.*
General email, contactoge@oge.gov

Web, www.oge.gov

Ensures that executive branch ethics programs are in compliance with applicable ethics laws and regulations. Administers executive branch policies relating to financial disclosure, employee conduct, and conflict-of-interest laws. Works to prevent conflicts of interest on the part of federal employees and to resolve those that do occur. Provides educational materials and training; conducts outreach to the general public, the private sector, and civil society; shares model practices with and provides technical assistance to state, local, and foreign governments and international organizations; manages email list service to notify federal ethics officials of changes in law and regulations.

U.S. Office of Special Counsel, *1730 M St. N.W., #218, 20036-4505; (202) 254-3600. Fax, (202) 254-3711. Carolyn N. Lerner, Special Counsel; Adam Miles, Deputy Special Counsel, Policy and Congressional Affairs; Nick Schwellenbach, Senior Communications Specialist; Catherine McMullen, Chief, Disclosure Unit. Issues relating to the Hatch Act, (800) 854-2824. TTY, (800) 877-8339. Prohibited personnel practices, (800) 872-9855. Whistleblower disclosure hotline, (800) 572-2249.*
Web, www.osc.gov

Investigates allegations of prohibited personnel practices and prosecutes individuals who violate federal statutes and regulations governing federal employees, military veterans, and reservists. Receives and refers federal employee disclosures of waste, fraud, inefficiency, mismanagement, and other violations in the federal government. Enforces the Hatch Act, which limits political activity by most federal and District of Columbia employees.

▶CONGRESS

For a listing of relevant congressional committees and subcommittees, please see pages 314–315 or the Appendix.

Government Accountability Office (GAO), *Forensic Audits and Investigative Service, 441 G St. N.W., 20548; (202) 512-6722. Web, www.gao.gov/careers/fais.html*

Provides Congress with forensic audits and investigations of fraud, waste, and abuse; manages FraudNet.

▶NONGOVERNMENTAL

Citizens Against Government Waste, *1301 Pennsylvania Ave. N.W., #1075, 20004; (202) 467-5300. Fax, (202) 467-4253. Thomas A. Schatz, President.*
General email, membership@cagw.org

Web, www.cagw.org and Twitter, @GovWaste

Taxpayer watchdog group that monitors government spending to identify how waste, mismanagement, and inefficiency in government can be eliminated. Has created criteria to identify pork-barrel spending. Publishes the annual *Congressional Pig Book*, which lists the names of politicians and their pet pork-barrel projects. Monitors legislation and regulations.

Citizens for Responsibility and Ethics in Washington (CREW), *455 Massachusetts Ave. N.W., 6th Floor, 20001; (202) 408-5565. Fax, (202) 588-5020. Noah Bookbinder, Executive Director.*
General email, info@citizensforethics.org

Web, www.citizensforethics.org and Twitter, @CREWcrew

Promotes ethics and accountability in government and public life. Investigates, reports, and litigates government misconduct. Seeks to enforce government disclosure of information.

Fund for Constitutional Government (FCG), *122 Maryland Ave. N.E., 20002; (202) 546-3799. Fax, (202) 543-3156. Conrad Martin, Executive Director.*
General email, info@fcgonline.org

Web, www.fcgonline.org

Promotes an open and accountable government. Seeks to expose and correct corruption in the federal government and private sector through research and public education. Sponsors the Electronic Privacy Information Center, the Government Accountability Project, the Project on Government Oversight, and OpenTheGovernment.org

Government Accountability Project, *1612 K St. N.W., #1100, 20006; (202) 457-0034. Fax, (202) 457-0059. Anna Myers, Executive Director; Louis Clark, President.*
General email, info@whistleblower.org

Web, www.whistleblower.org

Membership: federal employees, union members, professionals, and interested citizens. Provides legal and strategic counsel to employees in the public and private sectors who seek to expose corporate and government actions that are illegal, wasteful, or repressive; aids such employees in personnel action taken against them; assists grassroots organizations investigating corporate

wrongdoing, government inaction, or corruption. Promotes policy and legal reforms of whistle-blower laws.
(Formerly the National Whistle-blower Center.)

Project on Government Oversight, *1100 G St. N.W.,
#500, 20005-3806; (202) 347-1122. Fax, (202) 347-1116.
Danielle Brian, Executive Director.*
General email, info@pogo.org
Web, www.pogo.org

Public interest organization that works to expose
waste, fraud, abuse, and conflicts of interest in all aspects
of federal spending.

Sunlight Foundation, *1818 N St. N.W., #300, 20036; (202)
742-1520. Fax, (202) 742-1524. John Wonderlich, Executive
Director, Acting.*
Web, www.sunlightfoundation.com

Utilizes new information technology to make government more transparent and accountable. Projects include
Sunlight Labs, Sunlight Reporting Group, http://Political-
PartyTime.org, and http://influenceexplorer.com. Offers
"OpenGov grants" for innovative projects that liberate
or use municipal government data and tutorials for media
and citizens on the role of money in politics.

Executive Reorganization

▶**AGENCIES**

Office of Management and Budget (OMB) *(Executive
Office of the President),* **President's Management
Council,** *Dwight D. Eisenhower Executive Office Bldg.,
#216, 20503; (202) 395-5020. Fax, (202) 395-6102.
Beth Cobert, Deputy Director; Adam Niefeld, Assistant,
(202) 395-5020.*
Web, www.whitehouse.gov/omb and www.qsa.gov/portal/
content/133811

Membership: chief operating officers of federal government departments and agencies. Responsible for implementing the management improvement initiatives of
the administration. Develops and oversees improved governmentwide management and administrative systems;
formulates long-range plans to promote these systems;
works to resolve interagency management problems and
to implement reforms.

▶**CONGRESS**

*For a listing of relevant congressional committees and sub-
committees, please see pages 314–315 or the Appendix.*

Government Accountability Office (GAO), *Information
Technology, 441 G St. N.W., #4T21B, 20548; (202) 512-
6408. Joel C. Willemssen, Managing Director.*
Web, www.gao.gov

Seeks to make the federal government more effective in
its information management by improving performance
and reducing costs. Assesses best practices in the public
and private sectors; makes recommendations to government agencies. Interests include information security.

CENSUS, POPULATION DATA

General

▶**AGENCIES**

Census Bureau *(Commerce Dept.), 4600 Silver Hill Rd.,
#8H001, Suitland, MD 20746 (mailing address: 4600 Silver
Hill Rd., #8H001, Washington, DC 20233-0100); (301) 763-
2135. Fax, (301) 763-3761. John H. Thompson, Director.
Information, (800) 923-8282. Press, (301) 763-3030.
Library, (301) 763-2511. TTY, (800) 877-8339.*
General email, pio@census.gov
Web, www.census.gov and Twitter, @uscensusbureau

Conducts surveys and censuses (including the decennial
census of population, the American Community Survey,
the economic census, and census of governments); collects
and analyzes demographic, social, economic, housing,
foreign trade, and data on governmental data; publishes
statistics for use by federal, state, and local governments,
Congress, businesses, planners, and the public. Provides
online resources and data analysis tools. Library open to
the public Monday through Friday, 9:30 a.m.–3:30 p.m.

Census Bureau *(Commerce Dept.), Decennial Census,
4600 Silver Hill Rd., #3H160, Suitland, MD 20746 (mailing
address: 4600 Silver Hill Rd., #H160, Washington, DC
20233-7000); (301) 763-8050. Fax, (301) 763-8867.
Lisa M. Blumerman, Associate Director.*
Web, www.census.gov

Provides data from the decennial census (including
general plans and procedures); economic, demographic,
and population statistics; and information on trends.
Conducts preparation for the next census.

Census Bureau *(Commerce Dept.), Population, 4600
Silver Hill Rd., #6H174, Suitland, MD 20746 (mailing
address: 4600 Silver Hill Rd., #6H174, Washington, DC
20233-8800); (301) 763-2071. Fax, (301) 763-2516.
Karen Humes, Division Chief.*
General email, pop@census.gov
Web, www.census.gov/popest

Prepares population estimates and projections for
national, state, and local areas and congressional districts.
Provides data on demographic and social statistics in the
following areas: families and households, marital status
and living arrangements, farm population, migration and
mobility, population distribution, ancestry, fertility, child
care, race and ethnicity, language patterns, school enrollment, educational attainment, and voting.

Census Bureau *(Commerce Dept.), Social, Economic,
and Housing Statistics, 4600 Silver Hill Rd., #7H174,
Suitland, MD 20746 (mailing address: 4600 Silver Hill Rd.,
#H174, Washington, DC 20233-8500); (301) 763-3234.
Fax, (301) 763-3232. Victoria A. Velkoff, Chief.*
Web, www.census.gov/housing

Develops statistical programs for the decennial census,
the American Community Survey, and for other surveys
on housing, income, poverty, and the labor force. Collects

Financial Officers for Federal Departments and Agencies

DEPARTMENTS

Agriculture, Jon Holladay (Acting), (202) 720-0727

Commerce, Ellen Herbst, (202) 482-4951

Defense, Michael McCord, (703) 571-3343

   Air Force, Hon. Ricardo A. Aguilera, (703) 697-1974

   Army, Hon. Robert M. Speer, (703) 614-4356

   Navy, Susan J. Rabern, (703) 697-2325

Education, Thomas Skelly, (202) 401-0287

Energy, Joe Hezir, (202) 586-4171

Health and Human Services, Ellen Murray, (202) 690-6396

Homeland Security, Chip Fulgham, (202) 447-5751

   Coast Guard, Rear Adm. Todd A. Sokalzuk, (202) 372-3470

Housing and Urban Development, Vacant, (202) 401-6765

Interior, Doug Glenn, (202) 208-4246

Justice, Lee Lofthus, (202) 307-0623

Labor, Karen Tekleberhan, (202) 693-6800

State, Christopher Flaggs, (202) 647-4000

Transportation, Shoshana M. Lew, (202) 366-9191

Treasury, Deputy Chief Financial Officer, Dorrice Roth, (202) 622-0410. Comptroller of the Currency, David Lebryk, (202) 649-6400

Veterans Affairs, Helen Tierney, (202) 461-6703

AGENCIES

Advisory Council on Historic Preservation, Ralston Cox, (202) 606-8528

Agency for International Development, Reginald Mitchell, (702) 567-5219

Central Intelligence Agency, Vacant, (703) 482-0623

Commission on Civil Rights, Tinalousie Martin, (202) 376-8364

Commodity Futures Trading Commission, Mary Jean Buhler, (202) 418-5477

Consumer Product Safety Commission, Jay Hoffman, (301) 504-7207

Corporation for National and Community Service, Jeffrey Page (Acting), (202) 606-6649

Corporation for Public Broadcasting, William P. Tayman, (202) 879-9600

Environmental Protection Agency, David Bloom (Acting), (202) 564-1151

Equal Employment Opportunity Commission, (800) 669-4000

Export-Import Bank, David M. Sena, (202) 565-3952

Farm Credit Administration, Stephen G. Smith, (703) 883-4200

Federal Bureau of Investigation, Richard L. Haley II, (202) 324-3000

Federal Communications Commission, Mark Stephens, (202) 418-0817

Federal Deposit Insurance Corporation, Steven O. App, (202) 898-8732

Federal Election Commission, Judy Berning (Acting), (202) 694-1315

Federal Emergency Management Agency, Thomas Lowry, (800) 621-3362

Federal Energy Regulatory Commission, William Douglas Foster Jr., (202) 502-6118

Federal Home Loan Mortgage Corporation (Freddie Mac), James G. Mackey, (703) 903-2000

Federal Maritime Commission, Karon E. Douglass, (202) 523-5770

---

and explains the proper use of economic, social, and demographic data. Responsible for the technical planning, analysis, and publication of data from current surveys, including the decennial census, the American Community Survey, the American Housing Survey, the Current Population Survey, and the Survey of Income and Program Participation.

▶ CONGRESS

For a listing of relevant congressional committees and subcommittees, please see pages 314–315 or the Appendix.

▶ NONGOVERNMENTAL

Population Assn. of America, *8630 Fenton St., #722, Silver Spring, MD 20910; (301) 565-6710. Fax, (301) 565-*

7850. Danielle Staudt, Executive Director; Judith Seltzer, President.
Web, www.populationassociation.org

   Membership: university, government, and industry researchers in demography. Publishes newsletters, monitors legislation and related government activities, and supports collaboration of demographers. Holds annual technical sessions to present papers on domestic and international population issues and statistics.

Population Reference Bureau, *1875 Connecticut Ave. N.W., #520, 20009-5728; (202) 483-1100. Fax, (202) 328-3937. Jeffrey Jordan, President. Toll-free, (800) 877-9881. Media, (202) 939-5407.*
General email, popref@prb.org
Web, www.prb.org and Twitter, @PRBdata

Federal Mediation and Conciliation Service, Fran Leonard, (202) 606-3661

Federal National Mortgage Association (Fannie Mae), David Benson, (202) 752-7000

Federal Trade Commission, David Rebich, (202) 326-2116

General Services Administration, Gerard Badorrek, (202) 501-1721

Government Accountability Office, Karl Maschino, (202) 512-5800

International Bank for Reconstruction and Development (World Bank), Joaquim Levy, (202) 473-1000

John F. Kennedy Center for the Performing Arts, Lynne Pratt, (202) 416-8000

Merit Systems Protection Board, Kevin J. Nash, (202) 653-7263

National Academy of Sciences, Mary Didi Salmon, (202) 334-2000

National Aeronautics and Space Administration, David Radzanowski, (202) 358-0001

National Archives and Records Administration, Micah Cheatham, (301) 837-2992

National Credit Union Administration, Rendell L. Jones, (703) 518-6570

National Endowment for the Arts, Winona H. Varnon (Deputy), (202) 682-5534

National Endowment for the Humanities, Larry Meyers, (202) 606-8336

National Labor Relations Board, Ronald E. Crupi, (202) 273-3884

National Mediation Board, Samantha T. Jones (Assistant), (202) 692-5010

National Railroad Passenger Corporation (Amtrak), Gerald Sokol Jr., (202) 906-3369

National Science Foundation, Martha A. Rubenstein, (703) 292-8200

National Transportation Safety Board, Edward Benthall, (202) 314-6210

Nuclear Regulatory Commission, Maureen Wylie, (301) 415-7322

Occupational Safety and Health Review Commission, Angela Tyler, (202) 606-5370

Office of Management and Budget, Shaun Donovan, (202) 395-3080

Office of Personnel Management, Daniel Marella (Acting), (202) 606-2638

Overseas Private Investment Corporation, Allan Villabroza, (202) 336-8400

Peace Corps, Joseph Hepp, (202) 692-1606

Pension Benefit Guaranty Corporation, Patricia Kelly, (202) 326-4008

Postal Regulatory Commission, (202) 789 6010

Securities and Exchange Commission, Kenneth Johnson, (202) 551-7840

Small Business Administration, Tami Perriello, (202) 205-6449

Smithsonian Institution, Albert G. Horvath, (202) 633-5149

Social Security Administration, Peter D. Spencer, (410) 965-3148

U.S. International Trade Commission, John Ascienzo, (202) 205-3098

U.S. Postal Service, Joseph R. Corbett, (202) 268-5272

Educational organization engaged in information dissemination, training, and policy analysis on domestic and international population trends and issues. Interests include international development and family planning programs, the environment, and U.S. social and economic policy.

Urban Institute, *Center on Labor, Human Services, and Population, 2100 M St. N.W., 20037; (202) 833-7200. Fax, (202) 463-8522. Elizabeth Peters, Director. Web, www.urban.org/center/lhp*

Analyzes employment and income trends, studies how the U.S. population is growing, and evaluates programs dealing with homelessness, child welfare, and job training. Other areas of interest include immigration, mortality, sexual and reproductive health, adolescent risk behavior, child care, domestic violence, and youth development.

CIVIL SERVICE

General

▶AGENCIES

National Archives and Records Administration (NARA), *Information Security Oversight (ISOO), 700 Pennsylvania Ave. N.W., #100, 20408-0001; (202) 357-5250. Fax, (202) 357-5907. William A. Cira, Director, Acting, (202) 357-5323.*
General email, isoo@nara.gov
Web, www.archives.gov/isoo

Receiving guidance from the National Security Council, oversees policy on security classification on documents for the federal government and industry; monitors performance of all security classification/declassification programs for the federal government and industry; develops policies and procedures for sensitive unclassified information. Evaluates implementation, advises department and agency heads of corrective actions, and prepares an annual report to the president.

Office of Personnel Management (OPM), *1900 E St. N.W., #5A09, 20415-0001; (202) 606-1800. Fax, (202) 606-2573. Beth Cobert, Director, Acting. Press, (202) 606-2402. TTY, (800) 877-8339.*
Web, www.opm.gov

Administers civil service rules and regulations; sets policy for personnel management, labor-management relations, workforce effectiveness, and employment within the executive branch; manages federal personnel activities, including recruitment, pay comparability, and benefit programs.

Office of Personnel Management (OPM), *Data Analysis Group, 1900 E St. N.W., #2449, 20415-0001; (202) 606-0821. Fax, (202) 606-1719. David Weisman, Group Co-Manager, Acting, (202) 606-0821; Bob Heim, Group Co-Manager, Acting, (202) 606-1909.*
General email, fedstats@opm.gov
Web, www.opm.gov/feddata

Official government source of statistics on the government workforce. Produces information and analyses for the Office of Personnel Management, Congress, and the public on statistical aspects of the federal civilian workforce, including trends in composition, grade levels, minority employment, sizes of agencies, and salaries.

Office of Personnel Management (OPM), *Veterans Services, 1900 E St. N.W., #7439, 20415; (202) 606-3602. Fax, (202) 606-6017. Hakeem Basheerud-Deen, Director.*
Web, www.opm.gov/policy-data-oversight/veterans-services

Monitors federal agencies' personnel practices and develops policies and programs for veterans.

U.S. Office of Special Counsel, *1730 M St. N.W., #218, 20036-4505; (202) 254-3600. Fax, (202) 254-3711. Carolyn N. Lerner, Special Counsel; Adam Miles, Deputy Special Counsel, Policy and Congressional Affairs; Nick Schwellenbach, Senior Communications Specialist; Catherine McMullen, Chief, Disclosure Unit. Issues relating to the Hatch Act, (800) 854-2824. TTY, (800) 877-8339. Prohibited personnel practices, (800) 872-9855. Whistle-blower disclosure hotline, (800) 572-2249.*
Web, www.osc.gov

Interprets federal laws, including the Hatch Act, concerning political activities allowed by certain federal employees; investigates allegations of Hatch Act violations and conducts prosecutions. Investigates and prosecutes complaints under the Whistle-blower Protection Act.

▶**CONGRESS**

For a listing of relevant congressional committees and subcommittees, please see pages 314–315 or the Appendix.

▶**NONGOVERNMENTAL**

American Federation of Government Employees (AFGE), *80 F St. N.W., 20001; (202) 737-8700. Fax, (202) 639-6490. J. David Cox, President, (202) 639-6435. Press, (202) 639-6419. Membership, (202) 639-6410.*
General email, comments@afge.org
Web, www.afge.org

Membership: approximately 670,000 federal and District of Columbia government employees. Provides legal services to members; assists members with contract negotiations and grievances. Monitors legislation and regulations. (Affiliated with the AFL-CIO.)

Blacks in Government, *3005 Georgia Ave. N.W., 20001-3807; (202) 667-3280. Fax, (202) 667-3705. Darlene H. Young, President.*
General email, bignational@bignet.org
Web, www.bignet.org

Advocacy organization for public employees. Promotes equal opportunity and career advancement for African American government employees; provides career development information; seeks to eliminate racism in the federal workforce; sponsors programs, business meetings, and social gatherings; represents interests of African American government workers to Congress and the executive branch; promotes voter education and registration.

Federal Managers Assn., *1641 Prince St., Alexandria, VA 22314-2818; (703) 683-8700. Fax, (703) 683-8707. Patricia J. Niehaus, National President; Todd Wells, Executive Director, ext. 102.*
General email, info@fedmanagers.org
Web, www.fedmanagers.org

Seeks to improve the effectiveness of federal supervisors and managers and the operations of the federal government. Interests include cost-effective government restructuring, competitive civil service pay and benefits, and maintaining the core values of the civil service.

Federally Employed Women, *455 Massachusetts Ave. N.W., (mailing address: P.O. Box 306, Washington, DC 20001); (202) 898-0994. Fax, (202) 898-1535. Michelle Crockett, President.*
General email, few@few.org
Web, www.few.org

Membership: women and men who work for the federal government. Works to eliminate sex discrimination in government employment and to increase job opportunities for women; offers training programs. Monitors legislation and regulations.

Senior Executives Assn., *77 K St. N.E., #2600, 20002; (202) 971-3300. Fax, (202) 971-3317. Jason A. Brietel, President, Acting.*
General email, action@seniorexecs.org
Web, www.seniorexecs.org

Professional association representing Senior Executive Service members and other federal career executives.

Sponsors professional education. Interests include management improvement. Monitors legislation and regulations.

Dismissals and Disputes

▶AGENCIES

Merit Systems Protection Board, *1615 M St. N.W., 5th Floor, 20419; (202) 653-7200. Fax, (202) 653-7130. Susan Tsui Grundmann, Chair; William D. Spencer, Clerk of the Board. Toll-free, (800) 209-8960. MSPB Inspector General hotline, (800) 424-9121. TTY, (800) 877-8339. General email, mspb@mspb.gov*

Web, www.mspb.gov

Independent quasi-judicial agency that handles hearings and appeals involving federal employees; protects the integrity of federal merit systems and ensures adequate protection for employees against abuses by agency management. Library open to the public by appointment.

Merit Systems Protection Board, *Appeals Counsel, 1615 M St. N.W., 20419; (202) 653-7200. Fax, (202) 653-7130. Susan Swafford, Director. General email, mspb@mspb.gov*

Web, www.mspb.gov

Analyzes and processes petitions for review of appeals decisions from the regional offices; prepares opinions and orders for board consideration; analyzes and processes cases that are reopened and prepares proposed depositions.

Merit Systems Protection Board, *Policy and Evaluations, 1615 M St. N.W., 20419; (202) 653-7200. Fax, (202) 653-7211. James M. Read, Director, (202) 254-4464; James Tsugawa, Deputy Director, (202) 254-4506. Information, (202) 254-4496. TTY, (800) 877-8339. General email, studies@mspb.gov*

Web, www.mspb.gov

Conducts studies on the civil service and other executive branch merit systems; reports to the president and Congress on whether federal employees are adequately protected against political abuses and prohibited personnel practices. Conducts annual oversight review of the Office of Personnel Management.

Merit Systems Protection Board, *Washington Regional Office, 1901 S. Bell St., #950, Arlington, VA 22202; (703) 756-6250. Fax, (703) 756-7112. Hon. Jeremiah Cassidy, Regional Director. General email, washingtonregionaloffice@mspb.gov*

Web, www.mspb.gov

Hears and decides appeals of adverse personnel actions (such as removals, suspensions for more than fourteen days, and reductions in grade or pay), retirement, and performance-related actions for federal civilian employees who work in the Washington, D.C., area, Virginia, North Carolina, or in overseas areas not covered by other regional board offices. Federal civilian employees who work outside Washington should contact the Merit Systems Protection Board regional office in their area.

Office of Personnel Management (OPM), *Employee Services, Partnership and Labor Relations, Employee Accountability, 1900 E St. N.W., #7H28H, 20415-0001; (202) 606-2930. Fax, (202) 606-2613. Debra Buford, Manager. General email, er@opm.gov*

Web, www.opm.gov/er

Develops, implements, and interprets policy on governmentwide employee relations. Intervenes in or seeks reconsideration of erroneous third-party decisions.

Office of Personnel Management (OPM), *General Counsel, 1900 E St. N.W., #7347, 20415-0001; (202) 606-1700. Fax, (202) 606-2609. Robin Jacobsohn, General Counsel. Web, www.opm.gov/about-us/our-people-organization/office-of-the-general-counsel*

Represents the federal government before the Merit Systems Protection Board, other administrative tribunals, and the courts.

U.S. Office of Special Counsel, *1730 M St. N.W., #218, 20036-4505; (202) 254-3600. Fax, (202) 254-3711. Carolyn N. Lerner, Special Counsel; Adam Miles, Deputy Special Counsel, Policy and Congressional Affairs; Nick Schwellenbach, Senior Communications Specialist; Catherine McMullen, Chief, Disclosure Unit. Issues relating to the Hatch Act, (800) 854-2824. TTY, (800) 877-8339, Prohibited personnel practices, (800) 872-9855. Whistleblower disclosure hotline, (800) 572-2249. Web, www.osc.gov*

Investigates allegations of prohibited personnel practices, including reprisals against whistle-blowers (federal employees who disclose waste, fraud, inefficiency, and wrongdoing by supervisors of federal departments and agencies). Initiates necessary corrective or disciplinary action. Enforces the Hatch Act, which limits political activity by most federal and District of Columbia employees.

▶JUDICIARY

U.S. Court of Appeals for the Federal Circuit, *717 Madison Pl. N.W., 20439; (202) 275-8000. Fax, (202) 275-9678. Sharon Prost, Chief Judge; Daniel E. O'Toole, Clerk, (202) 272-8020. Help Desk, (202) 275-8036. Mediation, (202) 275-8120. Web, www.cafc.uscourts.gov*

Reviews decisions of the Merit Systems Protection Board.

Hiring, Recruitment, and Training

▶AGENCIES

Office of Personnel Management (OPM), *Classification and Assessment Policy, 1900 E St. N.W., #6500, 20415-0001; (202) 606-3600. Fax, (202) 606-4891. April Davis, Manager. General email, fedclass@opm.gov*

Web, www.opm.gov/fedclass

Develops job classification standards for occupations in the general schedule and federal wage system.

Inspectors General for Federal Departments and Agencies

Departmental and agency inspectors general are responsible for identifying and reporting program fraud and abuse, criminal activity, and unethical conduct in the federal government. In the legislative branch the Government Accountability Office also has fraud and abuse hotlines: (202) 512-7470. Check www.ignet.gov for additional listings.

DEPARTMENTS

Agriculture, Hon. Phyllis Fong, (202) 720-8001;
  Hotline, (800) 424-9121

Commerce, David Smith (Acting), (202) 482-4661;
  Hotline, (800) 482-5197

Defense, Glenn Fine, (703) 604-8300;
  Hotline, (800) 424-9098

Education, Hon. Kathleen Tighe, (202) 245-6900;
  Hotline, (800) 647-8733

Energy, Ricky Haas (Acting), (202) 586-4393;
  Hotline, (800) 541-1625

Health and Human Services, Hon. Daniel Levinson,
  (202) 619-3148;
  Hotline, (800) 447-8477

Homeland Security and FEMA, Hon. John Roth,
  (202) 254-4100;
  Hotline, (800) 323-8603

Housing and Urban Development, Hon. David A.
  Montoya, (202) 708-0430;
  Hotline, (800) 347-3735

Interior, Mary L. Kendall (Acting), (202) 208-5745;
  Hotline, (800) 424-5081

Justice, Hon. Michael E. Horowitz, (202) 514-3435;
  Hotline, (800) 869-4499

Labor, Hon. Scott Dahl, (202) 693-5100;
  Hotline, (800) 347-3756

State, Hon. Steve Linick, (202) 663-0340;
  Hotline, (800) 409-9926

Transportation, Hon. Calvin L. Scovel III, (202) 366-1959;
  Hotline, (800) 424-9071

Treasury, Hon. Eric M. Thorson, (202) 622-1090;
  Hotline, (800) 359-3898

Veterans Affairs, Linda Halliday (Acting), (202) 461-4720;
  Hotline, (800) 488-8244

AGENCIES

Agency for International Development, Catherine M.
  Trujillo (Acting), (202) 712-1150;
  Hotline, (202) 712-1023

Appalachian Regional Commission, Hubert Sparks,
  (202) 884-7675;
  Hotline, (800) 532-4611

Board of Governors of the Federal Reserve System,
  Mark Bialek, (202) 973-5000;
  Hotline, (800) 827-3340

Central Intelligence Agency, Christopher R. Sharpley
  (Acting), (703) 874-2553;
  Hotline, (703) 874-2600

Commodity Futures Trading Commission, A. Roy Lavik,
  (202) 418-5110;
  Hotline, (202) 418-5510

Consumer Financial Protection Bureau, Mark Bialek,
  (202) 973-5000;
  Hotline, (800) 827-3340

Consumer Product Safety Commission, Christoper W.
  Dentel, (301) 504-7644;
  Hotline, (301) 504-7906

Defense Intelligence Agency, Kristi Waschull,
  (202) 231-1010;
  Hotline, (202) 231-1000

Elections Assistance Commission, Patricia Layfield,
  (301) 734-3104;
  Hotline, (866) 552-0004

Environmental Protection Agency,
  Hon. Arthur A. Elkins Jr., (202) 566-0847;
  Hotline, (888) 546-8740

Equal Employment Opportunity Commission,
  Milton Mayo, (202) 663-4327;
  Hotline, (800) 849-4230

Export-Import Bank of the United States, Mike McCarthy
  (Acting), (202) 565-3908;
  Hotline, (888) 644-3946

Farm Credit Administration, Elizabeth Dean,
  (703) 883-4083;
  Hotline, (800) 437-7322

Federal Communications Commission, David L. Hunt,
  (202) 418-0470;
  Hotline, (888) 863-2244

Federal Election Commission, Lynne A. McFarland,
  (202) 694-1015;
  Hotline, (800) 964-3342

Federal Deposit Insurance Corporation, Fred W. Gibson
  (Acting), (703) 562-2166;
  Hotline, (800) 964-3342

Federal Housing Finance Agency, Hon. Laura S.
  Wertheimer, (202) 730-0881;
  Hotline, (800) 793-7724

Federal Labor Relations Authority, Dana Rooney-Fisher,
  (202) 218-7744;
  Hotline, (800) 331-3572

Federal Maritime Commission, Jon Hatfield,
  (202) 523-5863;
  Hotline, (202) 523-5865

Federal Trade Commission, Roslyn A. Mazer,
(202) 326-3527;
Hotline, (202) 326-2800

General Services Administration, Hon. Carol Fortine
Ochoa, (202) 501-0450;
Hotline, (800) 424-5210

Government Accountability Office, Michael Raponi,
(202) 512-0039;
Hotline, (800) 743-7574

Legal Services Corporation, Jeffrey E. Schanz,
(202) 295-1660;
Hotline, (800) 678-8868

National Aeronautics and Space Administration, Hon.
Paul K. Martin, (202) 358-1220;
Hotline, (800) 424-9183

National Credit Union Administration, James Hagen,
(703) 528-6350;
Hotline, (703) 518-6357

National Geospatial-Intelligence Agency, Joseph
Composto;
Hotline, (800) 380-7729

National Labor Relations Board, David Berry,
(202) 273-1960;
Hotline, (800) 736-2983

National Reconnaissance Office, Robin Walmsley (Acting),
(703) 808-1830;
Hotline, (703) 808-1644

National Science Foundation, Allison Lerner, (703) 292-7100;
Hotline, (800) 428-2189

National Security Agency, George Ellard,
(301) 688-6327

Nuclear Regulatory Commission, Hon. Hubert T. Bell,
(301) 415-5930;
Hotline, (800) 233-3497

Office of Personnel Management, Norbert Vint (Acting),
(202) 606-1200;
Hotline, (202) 418-3300

**Office of the Inspector General of the Intelligence
Community,** Hon. I. Charles McCullough III,
(571) 204-8149;
Hotline, (855) 731-3260

Pension Benefit Guaranty Corporation, Robert
Westbrooks, (202) 326-4000, ext. 3437;
Hotline, (800) 303-9737

Postal Regulatory Commission, Jack Callender,
(202) 789-6817;
Hotline, (202) 789-6817

Securities and Exchange Commission, Carl Hoecker,
(202) 551-6061;
Hotline, (877) 442-0854

Small Business Administration, Hon. Peggy E. Gustafson,
(202) 205-6586;
Hotline, (800) 767-0385

Social Security Administration, Hon. Patrick P. O'Carroll,
(410) 966-8385;
Hotline, (800) 269-0271

**Special Inspector General for Afghanistan
Reconstruction,** John F. Sopko, (703) 545-6000;
Hotline, (866) 329-8893

**Special Inspector General for the Troubled Asset Relief
Program,** Hon. Christy Goldsmith Romero,
(202) 622-1419;
Hotline, (877) 744-2009

Treasury Inspector General for Tax Administration,
Hon. J. Russell George, (202) 622-6500;
Hotline, (800) 366-4484

U.S. International Trade Commission, Philip M.
Heneghan, (202) 205-2210;
Hotline, (800) 358-8530

U.S. Postal Service, Tammy Whitcomb (Acting),
(703) 248-2300;
Hotline, (888) 877-7644

OTHER FEDERAL AGENCIES

Amtrak, Tom Howard, (202) 906-4600;
Hotline, (800) 468-5469

Architect of the Capitol, Kevin Mulshine,
(202) 593-1948;
Hotline, (877) 827-3340

Corporation for National and Community Service,
Hon. Deborah Jeffrey, (202) 606-9390;
Hotline, (800) 452-8210

Corporation for Public Broadcasting, Mary Mitchelson,
(202) 879-9660;
Hotline, (800) 599-2170

Government Printing Office, Michael Raponi,
(202) 512-0039;
Hotline, (800) 743-7574

Library of Congress, Kurt W. Hyde, (202) 707-6314;
Hotline, (202) 707-6306

National Archives, James E. Springs, (301) 837-3000;
Hotline, (800) 786-2551

National Endowment for the Arts, Michael J. Binder
(Acting), (202) 682-5402;
Hotline, (877) 535-7448

National Endowment for the Humanities, Laura Davis,
(202) 606-8350;
Hotline, (877) 786-7598

Peace Corps, Kathy A. Buller, (202) 692-2900;
Hotline, (800) 233-5874

Smithsonian Institution, Cathy Helm,
(202) 633-7050;
Hotline, (202) 252-0321

U.S. Capitol Police, Fay F. Ropella, (202) 593-4555;
Hotline, (866) 358-8530

Office of Personnel Management (OPM), *Federal Investigative Services,* *1900 E St. N.W., #2H31, 20415-0001; (202) 606-1800. Fax, (202) 606-2390. Merton W. Miller, Associate Director, (202) 606-2173. TTY, (202) 606-2532. General email, FISinquiries@opm.gov*

Web, www.opm.gov/investigations

Initiates and conducts investigations of new federal employees.

Office of Personnel Management (OPM), *Human Resources Solutions,* *1900 E St. N.W., #2469F, 20415-1000; (202) 606-0900. Fax, (202) 606-9200. Joseph S. Kennedy, Associate Director.*

Web, www.opm.gov/about-us/our-people-organization/ program-divisions/human-resources-solutions

Manages federal human resources policy, including staffing, compensation, benefits, labor relations, and position classification.

Office of Personnel Management (OPM), *Merit System Accountability and Compliance,* *1900 E St. N.W., #6484, 20415-5100; (202) 606-2980. Fax, (202) 606-5056. Mark W. Lambert, Associate Director.*

Web, www.opm.gov/about-us/our-people-organization/ program-divisions/merit-system-accountability-and-compliance

Responsible for training and curriculum development programs for government executives and supervisors.

Office of Personnel Management (OPM), *Veterans Services,* *1900 E St. N.W., #7439, 20415; (202) 606-3602. Fax, (202) 606-6017. Hakeem Basheerud-Deen, Director. Web, www.opm.gov/policy-data-oversight/veterans-services*

Provides federal employees and transitioning military service members and their families, federal human resources professionals, and hiring managers with information on employment opportunities with the federal government.

Office of Personnel Management (OPM), *Veterans Services, Intergovernmental Personnel Act Mobility Program,* *1900 E St. N.W., #7463, 20415-0001; (202) 606-1155. Fax, (202) 606-4430. Gregory Snowden, Program Head. General email, ipa@opm.gov*

Web, www.opm.gov/programs/ipa

Implements temporary personnel exchanges between federal agencies and nonfederal entities, including state and local governments, institutions of higher education, and other organizations.

Labor-Management Relations

▶AGENCIES

Federal Labor Relations Authority, *1400 K St. N.W., 20424-0001; (202) 218-7770. Fax, (202) 482-6526. Carol Waller Pope, Chair; Sarah Whittle Spooner, Executive Director, (202) 218-7791. Press, (202) 218-7776. Web, www.flra.gov*

Oversees the federal labor-management relations program; administers the law that protects the right of non-postal federal employees to organize, bargain collectively,

and participate through labor organizations of their own choosing.

Federal Service Impasses Panel *(Federal Labor Relations Authority),* *1400 K St. N.W., #200, 20424-0001; (202) 218-7790. Fax, (202) 482-6674. H. Joseph Schimansky, Executive Director; Mary E. Jacksteit, Chair. Web, www.flra.gov/fsip*

Assists in resolving contract negotiation impasses over conditions of employment between federal agencies and labor organizations representing federal employees.

Office of Personnel Management (OPM), *Employee Services, Partnership and Labor Relations,* *1900 E St. N.W., #7H28, 20415-0001; (202) 606-2930. Fax, (202) 606-2613. Tim F. Curry, Deputy Associate Director. Web, www.opm.gov/about-us/our-people-organization/ program-divisions/employee-services*

Develops policy for government agencies and unions regarding employee-management and labor-management relations.

Office of Personnel Management (OPM), *General Counsel,* *1900 E St. N.W., #7347, 20415-0001; (202) 606-1700. Fax, (202) 606-2609. Robin Jacobsohn, General Counsel. Web, www.opm.gov/about-us/our-people-organization/ office-of-the-general-counsel*

Advises the government on law and legal policy relating to federal labor-management relations; represents the government before the Merit Systems Protection Board.

▶NONGOVERNMENTAL

National Alliance of Postal and Federal Employees (NAPFE), *1640 11th St. N.W., #102, 20001; (202) 939-6325. Fax, (202) 939-6392. Wilbur Duncan, President. General email, headquarters@napfe.org Web, www.napfe.com*

Membership: approximately 70,000 postal and federal employees. Helps members negotiate pay, benefits, equal opportunity, and better working conditions; conducts training programs and workshops. Monitors legislation and regulations.

National Assn. of Government Employees (NAGE), *Washington Office,* *901 N. Pitt St., #100, Alexandria, VA 22314; (703) 519-0300. Fax, (703) 519-0311. David J. Holway, National President. Toll-free, (866) 412-7790. Web, www.nage.org*

Membership: approximately 200,000 federal government employees. Helps members negotiate pay, benefits, and better working conditions; conducts training programs and workshops. Monitors legislation and regulations. (Affiliated with Service Employees International Union. Headquarters in Quincy, Mass.)

National Federation of Federal Employees, *1212 New York Ave. N.W., #450, 20005; (202) 216-4420. Fax, (202) 898-1861. William R. Dougan, National President. General email, nffenews@nffe.org Web, www.nffe.org*

Office of Personnel Management

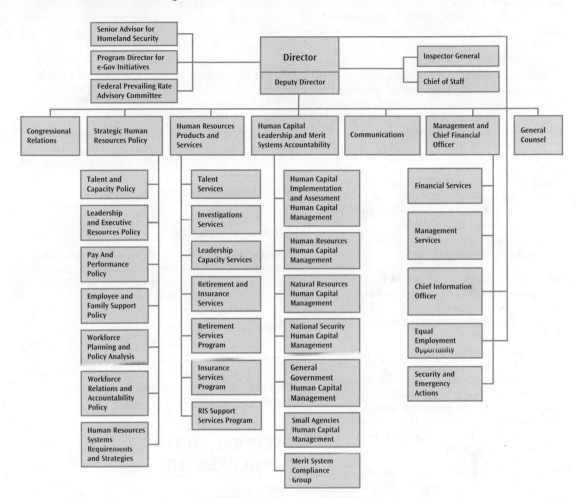

Membership: approximately 100,000 employees throughout various agencies within the federal government. Helps members negotiate pay, benefits, and better working conditions; conducts training programs and workshops. Monitors legislation and regulations. (Affiliated with International Assn. of Machinists & Aerospace Workers, AFL-CIO.)

National Treasury Employees Union (NTEU), *1750 H St. N.W., 20006; (202) 572-5500. Fax, (202) 572-5644. Tony Reardon, President.*
General email, nteu-pr@nteu.org

Web, www.nteu.org

Membership: approximately 150,000 employees from the Treasury Dept. and thirty other federal agencies and departments. Helps members negotiate pay, benefits, and better working conditions; conducts training programs and workshops. Monitors legislation and regulations.

Public Service Research Council, *320 D Maple Ave. East, Vienna, VA 22180-4747; (703) 242-3575. Fax, (703) 242-3579. David Y. Denholm, President.*

General email, info@psrconline.org
Web, www.psrconline.org

Independent nonprofit research and educational organization. Studies labor unions and labor issues with emphasis on employment in the public sector. Monitors legislation and regulations.

Pay and Employee Benefits

▶ AGENCIES

Labor Dept. (DOL), *Federal Employees' Compensation, 200 Constitution Ave. N.W., #S3229, 20210; (202) 693-0040. Douglas C. Fitzgerald, Director. Toll-free, (866) 692-7487 (customers should contact their district office first, www.dol.gov/owcp/dfec/regs/compliance/wc.htm). TTY, (877) 889-5627.*
Web, www.dol.gov/owcp/dfec

Administers the Federal Employees Compensation Act, which provides disability compensation for federal employees, including wage replacement benefits, medical treatment, vocational rehabilitation, and other benefits.

Office of Personnel Management (OPM), *Employee Services,* 1900 E St. N.W., #7460 MM, 20415; (202) 606-7400. Mark D. Reinhold, Associate Director, (202) 606-2520.
Web, www.opm.gov/about-us/our-people-organization/program-divisions/employee-services

Develops federal human resource systems for pay and leave, employee development, staffing, recruiting, hiring, Factor Evaluation System (FES) policy, and labor and employee relations, senior executive services, veterans' services, and performance management.

Office of Personnel Management (OPM), *Federal Prevailing Rate Advisory Committee,* 1900 E St. N.W., #5H27, 20415; (202) 606-9400. Fax, (202) 606-2573. Sheldon Friedman, Chair, (202) 606-1712.
Web, www.opm.gov/policy-data-oversight/pay-leave/pay-systems/federal-wage-system#url=FPRAC

Advises OPM on the governmentwide administration of Federal Wage System employees.

Office of Personnel Management (OPM), *Healthcare and Insurance, Federal Employee Insurance Operations,* 1900 E St. N.W., #3425, 20415; (202) 606-4995. Fax, (202) 606-4640. Alan Spielman, Assistant Director.
Web, www.opm.gov/insure

Administers group life insurance for federal employees and retirees; negotiates rates and benefits with health insurance carriers; settles disputed claims. Administers the Federal Employees' Health Benefits (FEHB), the Federal Employees' Group Life Insurance (FEGLI), the Federal Long Term Care Insurance (FLTCIP), Federal Employee Dental and Vision Benefits (FEDVIP), and the Flexible Spending Accounts (FSA) programs.

Office of Personnel Management (OPM), *Pay and Leave,* 1900 E St. N.W., #7H31, 20415; (202) 606-2838. Fax, (202) 606-4264. Brenda Roberts, Deputy Associate Director.
General email, pay-leave-policy@opm.gov
Web, www.opm.gov/policy-data-oversight/pay-leave

Develops and maintains governmentwide agency regulations pertaining to pay and leave. Responsible for the General Schedule and locality pay adjustment process for white-collar federal workers. Supports the Federal Salary Council and the president's "pay agent" (composed of the directors of OPM and the Office of Management and Budget and the secretary of labor). Annual report of the pay agent and General Schedule pay rates are available on OPM's Web site. Supports the Federal Prevailing Rate Advisory Committee and provides regulations and policies for the administration of the federal wage system for blue-collar federal employees.

Office of Personnel Management (OPM), *Retirement Operations,* 1900 E St. N.W., #2H28, 20415; (724) 794-2005. Fax, (724) 794-4323. Nick Ashendon, Deputy Associate Director, (724) 794-2005, ext. 3214; Kenneth J. Zawodny Jr., Associate Director, (724) 794-7759. Toll-free, (888) 767-6738. TTY, (855) 887-4957.
General email, retire@opm.gov
Web, www.opm.gov/retire

Administers the civil service and federal employees' retirement systems; responsible for monthly annuity payments and other benefits; organizes and maintains retirement records; distributes information on retirement and on insurance programs for annuitants.

Office of Personnel Management (OPM), *Work-Life,* 1900 E St. N.W., #7456, 20415-2000; (202) 606-0846. Julie Brill, Manager.
General email, worklife@opm.gov
Web, www.opm.gov/policy-data-oversight/worklife

Sets policy and guidelines for federal agencies in establishing and maintaining programs on the federal telework program, employee assistance programs, the Federal Child Care Subsidy Program, and health and wellness.

▶**NONGOVERNMENTAL**

National Active and Retired Federal Employees Assn. (NARFE), 606 N. Washington St., Alexandria, VA 22314; (703) 838-7760. Fax, (703) 838-7785. Richard Thissen, President. Member relations, (800) 456-8410.
General email, hq@narfe.org
Web, www.narfe.org

Works to preserve the integrity of the federal employee retirement systems. Provides members with information about benefits for retired federal employees and for survivors of deceased federal employees. Monitors legislation and regulations.

FEDERAL CONTRACTS AND PROCUREMENT

General

▶**AGENCIES**

Defense Health Agency (DHA) *(Defense Dept.),* **Small Business Programs,** 7700 Arlington Blvd., #5101, Falls Church, VA 22042-5101; (703) 681-4614. Cassandra W. Martin, Director.
Web, http://health.mil/Military-Health-Topics/Acquisition-Procurement-and-Small-Business/Small-Business-Programs

Seeks to ensure that small businesses have a fair opportunity to compete and be selected for DHA contracts, both at the prime and subcontract levels. Provides information on agency purchases and the contracting process through forums, mentoring programs, and written materials.

General Services Administration (GSA), *Civilian Board of Contract Appeals,* 1800 M St. N.W., 6th Floor, South Tower, 20036; 1800 F St. N.W., 20405; (202) 606-8800. Fax, (202) 606-0019. J. Gregory Parks, Chief Counsel; Stephen M. Daniels, Chair.
General email, stephendaniels@cbca.gov
Web, www.cbca.gov

Procurement Officers for Federal Departments and Agencies

DEPARTMENTS

Agriculture, Lisa M. Wilusz, (202) 720-9448

Commerce, Barry Berkowitz, (202) 482-4248

Defense, Althea Coetzee (Acting), (571) 256-7008

Education, Jim Ropelewski, (202) 245-6221

Energy, Paul Bosco, (202) 586-3524

Health and Human Services, Anglea Billups, (202) 260-6187

Homeland Security, Soraya Correa, (202) 447-5300

Housing and Urban Development, Keith W. Surber (Acting), (202) 402-2909

Interior, Debra E. Sonderman, (202) 254-5501

Justice, Michael H. Allen, (202) 514-3101

Labor, Edward Hugler, (202) 693-4040

State, Corey Rindner, (703) 516-1689

Transportation, Willie Smith, (202) 366-5613

Treasury, Iris B. Cooper, (202) 622-1039

Veterans Affairs, Jan R. Frye, (202) 461-6920

AGENCIES

Consumer Product Safety Commission, Donna M. Hutton, (301) 504-7009

Corporation for National and Community Service, William Anderson, (202) 606-6980

Environmental Protection Agency, John Bashista, (202) 564-4310

Export-Import Bank, Mark Pitra, (202) 565-3338

Farm Credit Administration, Stephen G. Smith, (703) 883-4378

Federal Communications Commission, Keith K. Nakasone, (202) 418-1933

Federal Deposit Insurance Corporation, Michael J. Rubino, (703) 562-2192

Federal Emergency Management Agency, Bobby McCane, (202) 646-3355

Federal Maritime Commission, Michael Kilby, (202) 523-5900

Federal Mediation and Conciliation Service, Cynthia Washington, (202) 606-5477

Federal Reserve System, Vacant, (202) 452-2767

Federal Trade Commission, John Isgrigg III, (202) 326-2307

General Services Administration, Jeff Koses, (703) 605-5535

National Aeronautics and Space Administration, William P. McNally, (202) 358-2090

National Labor Relations Board, Gloria Joseph, (202) 273-3890

National Mediation Board, June D.W. King, (202) 692-5010

National Science Foundation, Jeffery Lupis, (703) 292-7944

Nuclear Regulatory Commission, James C. Corbett, (301) 415-8725

Office of Personnel Management, Nina M. Ferraro, (202) 606-4519

Securities and Exchange Commission, Julie Basile, (202) 551-8699

Small Business Administration, Tami Perriello, (202) 205-7521

Social Security Administration, Seth Binstock, (410) 965-9538

U.S. International Trade Commission, Debra Bridge, (202) 205-2004

U.S. Postal Service, Susan Brownell, (202) 268-4040

Presides over various disputes involving Federal executive branch agencies. Resolves contract disputes between government contractors and agencies under the Contract Dispute Act.

General Services Administration (GSA), *Federal Procurement Data System–Next Generation (FPDS-NG),* *10780 Parkridge Blvd., #300, Reston, VA 20191; (800) 488-3111. Mary Searcy, Director.*
General email, mashelpdesk@gsa.gov
Web, www.fpds.gov and www.gsa.gov/portal/content/157105

Service contracted out by GSA that collects procurement data from all federal government contracts and disseminates these data via the Internet. Reports include agency identification, products or services purchased, dollar obligation, principal place of performance, and contractor identification; also provides socioeconomic indicators such as business size and business ownership type.

General Services Administration (GSA), *Government-wide Policy, 1800 F St. N.W., 20405; (202) 501-8880. Fax, (202) 208-1224. Troy Cribb, Associate Administrator.*
Web, www.gsa.gov/ogp

Coordinates GSA policymaking activities, including areas of personal and real property, travel and transportation, acquisition (internal GSA and governmentwide), information technology, regulatory information, and use of federal advisory committees; promotes collaboration between government and the private sector in developing policy and management techniques; works to integrate acquisition, management, and disposal of government property.

General Services Administration (GSA), *Government-wide Policy, Acquisition Policy, 1800 F St. N.W., 20405; (202) 501-4755. Fax, (202) 357-0038. Jeffrey A. (Jeff) Koses, Senior Procurement Executive.*

General email, askacquisition@gsa.gov and far.sec@gsa.gov

Web, www.gsa.gov/portal/category/101099

Develops and implements federal government acquisition policies and procedures; administers Federal Acquisition Regulation (FAR) for civilian agencies. Manages several GSA-specific and governmentwide acquisition database systems. Conducts pre-award and post-award contract reviews; suspends and debars contractors for unsatisfactory performance; coordinates and promotes governmentwide career management and training programs for contracting personnel.

General Services Administration (GSA), *Small Business Utilization, 1275 1st St. N.E., 20417; (202) 208-5938. Fax, (202) 501-2590. Jerome Fletcher II, Associate Administrator, (202) 969-7089.*
General email, smallbusiness@gsa.gov

Web, www.gsa.gov/osbu and Twitter, @GSAOSBU

Works to increase small business access to government contract procurement opportunities. Provides policy guidance and direction for GSA Regional Small Business Offices, which offer advice and assistance to businesses interested in government procurement.

Minority Business Development Agency *(Commerce Dept.), 1401 Constitution Ave. N.W., #5053, 20230; (202) 482-2332. Fax, (202) 501-4698. Alejandra Castillo, Director.*
Web, www.mbda.gov

Assists minority business owners in obtaining federal loans and contract awards; produces an annual report on federal agencies' performance in procuring from minority-owned businesses. Assists minority entrepreneurs one-on-one with financial planning, marketing, management, and technical assistance. Focuses on promoting wealth in minority communities.

U.S. AbilityOne Commission, *1401 S. Clark St., Arlington, VA 22202; (703) 603-7740. Fax, (703) 603-0655. Tina Ballard, Executive Director.*
General email, info@abilityone.gov

Web, www.abilityone.gov

Presidentially appointed committee. Determines which products and services are suitable for federal procurement from qualified nonprofit agencies that employ people who are blind or have other significant disabilities; seeks to increase employment opportunities for these individuals. (Formerly Committee for Purchase from People Who Are Blind or Severely Disabled.)

► CONGRESS

For a listing of relevant congressional committees and subcommittees, please see pages 314–315 or the Appendix.

Government Accountability Office (GAO), *Acquisition and Sourcing Management, 441 G St. N.W., 20548; (202) 512-4841. Michelle Mackin, Director.*
Web, www.gao.gov/careers/asm.html

Advises Congress and governmental agencies about federal spending and maximizing investments related to acquisitions, procurements, and contracting.

Government Accountability Office (GAO), *Procurement Law Division, 441 G St. N.W., #7494, 20548; (202) 512-8278. Fax, (202) 512-9749. Ralph O. White, Managing Associate General Counsel.*
Web, www.gao.gov

Considers and rules on the proposed or actual award of a government contract upon receipt of a written protest.

► NONGOVERNMENTAL

Coalition for Government Procurement, *1990 M St. N.W., #450, 20036; (202) 331-0975. Fax, (202) 822-9788. Roger D. Waldron, President.*
General email, info@thecgp.org

Web, www.thecgp.org and Twitter, @TheCGPOrg

Alliance of business firms that sell to the federal government. Seeks equal opportunities for businesses to sell to the government; monitors practices of the General Services Administration and government procurement legislation and regulations.

National Contract Management Assn. (NCMA), *21740 Beaumeade Circle, #125, Ashburn, VA 20147; (571) 382-0082. Fax, (703) 448-0939. Michael Fischetti, Executive Director, (571) 382-1123. Toll-free, (800) 344-8096.*
General email, wearelistening@ncmahq.org

Web, www.ncmahq.org, Twitter, @NCMA and Facebook, www.facebook.com/NCMAHQ

Membership: individuals concerned with administering, procuring, negotiating, and managing government and commercial contracts and subcontracts. Sponsors the Certified Professional Contracts Manager Program and various educational and professional programs.

NIGP: The Institute for Public Procurement, *2411 Dulles Corner Park, #350, Herndon, VA 20171; (703) 736-8900. Fax, (703) 736-9644. Rick Grimm, Chief Executive Officer, ext. 240. Information, (800) 367-6447.*
Web, www.nigp.org

Membership: governmental purchasing departments, agencies, and organizations at the federal, state, and local levels in the United States, Canada, and internationally. Provides public procurement officers with technical assistance and information, training seminars, and professional certification. (Formerly the National Institute of Governmental Purchasing.)

Professional Services Council (PSC), *4401 Wilson Blvd., #1110, Arlington, VA 22203; (703) 875-8059. Fax, (703) 875-8922. David Berteau, President.*
Web, www.pscouncil.org

Membership: associations and firms that provide local, state, federal, and international governments with professional, engineering, and technical services. Analyzes the process by which the government awards contracts to private firms. Monitors legislation and regulations.

POSTAL SERVICE

General

▶AGENCIES

U.S. Postal Service (USPS), *475 L'Enfant Plaza S.W., 20260-0001; (202) 268-2000. Fax, (202) 268-5211. Megan J. Brennan, Postmaster General. Library, (202) 268-2906. Press, (202) 268-6524. Locator, (202) 268-2000. General information, (800) 275-8777. Web, www.usps.com*

Offers postal service throughout the country as an independent establishment of the executive branch. Library open to the public by appointment.

U.S. Postal Service (USPS), *Inspection Service, 475 L'Enfant Plaza S.W., #3301, 20260-2100; (202) 268-4264. Fax, (202) 268-7316. Guy Cottrell, Chief Postal Inspector. Fraud and abuse hotline, (877) 876-2455. Press, (202) 268-3700. Web, http://postalinspectors.uspis.gov*

Investigates violations of postal laws, such as theft of mail or posted valuables, assaults on postal employees, organized crime in postal-related matters, and prohibited mailings. Conducts internal audits; investigates postal activities to determine effectiveness of procedures; monitors compliance of individual post offices with postal regulations.

▶CONGRESS

For a listing of relevant congressional committees and subcommittees, please see pages 314–315 or the Appendix.

Consumer Services

▶AGENCIES

Postal Regulatory Commission, *Public Affairs and Government Relations, 901 New York Ave. N.W., #200, 20268; (202) 789-6800. Fax, (202) 789-6891. Ann C. Fisher, Director. General email, prc-pagr@prc.gov Web, www.prc.gov/offices/pagr*

Supports public outreach and education and media relations; provides information for consumers and responds to their inquiries. Informal complaints regarding individual rate and service inquiries are referred to the Consumer Advocate of the Postal Service.

U.S. Postal Service (USPS), *Consumer and Industry Affairs, 475 L'Enfant Plaza S.W., 20260; (202) 268-4910. Fax, (202) 268-6251. James A. Nemec, Vice President. Web, www.usps.com*

Develops policies, plans, and programs for commercial mailers to improve customer satisfaction. Directs the Business Partners program. Activities include local postal customer councils, the National Postal Forum, and the Mailers' Technical Advisory Committee.

U.S. Postal Service (USPS), *Office of the Consumer Advocate, 475 L'Enfant Plaza S.W., #4100, 20260-0004; (202) 268-6308. Fax, (202) 636-5344. James A. Nemec, Vice President and Consumer Advocate, (202) 268-2681. Inquiries, (800) ASK-USPS or (800) 275-8777. TTY, (877) 889-2457. General email, usps_ca_response@usps.gov Web, www.usps.com*

Provides information to consumers on USPS services and products. Receives and attempts to settle consumer grievances.

Employee and Labor Relations

▶AGENCIES

U.S. Postal Service (USPS), *Employee Resource Management, 475 L'Enfant Plaza S.W., #9840, 20260-4200; (202) 268-3783. Fax, (202) 268-5605. Nancy L. Rettinhouse, Vice President. Web, www.usps.com*

Drafts and implements employment policies and practices and safety and health guidelines.

U.S. Postal Service (USPS), *Labor Relations, 475 L'Enfant Plaza S.W., #9014, 20260-4100; (202) 268-7447. Fax, (202) 268-3074. Douglas A. Tulino, Vice President. Web, www.usps.com*

Handles collective bargaining and contract administration for the U.S. Postal Service.

▶NONGOVERNMENTAL

American Postal Workers Union (APWU), *1300 L St. N.W., 20005; (202) 842-4200. Fax, (202) 842-4297. Mark Dimondstein, President, (202) 842-4250. Web, www.apwu.org and Twitter, @APWUnational*

Membership: more than 200,000 postal employees and retirees, including clerks, motor vehicle operators, maintenance operators, and retirees. Assists members with contract negotiation and grievances; conducts training programs and workshops. Monitors legislation and regulations. (Affiliated with the Postal, Telegraph, and Telephone International and the AFL-CIO.)

National Alliance of Postal and Federal Employees (NAPFE), *1640 11th St. N.W., #102, 20001; (202) 939-6325. Fax, (202) 939-6392. Wilbur Duncan, President. General email, headquarters@napfe.org Web, www.napfe.com*

Membership: approximately 70,000 postal and federal employees. Helps members negotiate pay, benefits, equal opportunity, and better working conditions; conducts training programs and workshops. Monitors legislation and regulations.

National Assn. of Letter Carriers, AFL-CIO, *100 Indiana Ave. N.W., 20001-2144; (202) 393-4695. Fax, (202) 737-1540. Fredric V. Rolando, President.*
Web, www.nalc.org

Membership: more than 270,000 city letter carriers working for, or retired from, the U.S. Postal Service. Assists members with contract negotiation and grievances; conducts training programs and workshops. Monitors legislation and regulations. (Affiliated with the AFL-CIO and the Union Network International.)

National Assn. of Postal Supervisors, *1727 King St., #400, Alexandria, VA 22314-2753; (703) 836-9660. Fax, (703) 836-9665. Louis Atkins, President.*
General email, napshq@naps.org
Web, www.naps.org

Membership: more than 35,000 present and retired postal supervisors, managers, and postmasters. Management association that cooperates with other postal management associations, unions, and the U.S. Postal Service to improve the efficiency of the postal service; promotes favorable working conditions and broader career opportunities for all postal employees; provides members with information on current functions and legislative issues of the postal service.

National Assn. of Postmasters of the United States, *8 Herbert St., Alexandria, VA 22305-2600; (703) 683-9027. Fax, (703) 683-0923. David Ravenelle, Executive Director.*
General email, napusinfo@napus.org
Web, www.napus.org

Membership: present and former postmasters and postal managers of the United States. Promotes the postal service and the welfare of its members. Assists postmasters facing discipline or other adverse actions. Monitors legislation and regulations.

National League of Postmasters, *1 Beltway Center, 5904 Richmond Hwy., #500, Alexandria, VA 22303-1864; (703) 329-4550. Fax, (703) 329-0466. Gregory Sean Acord, President.*
General email, information@postmasters.org
Web, www.postmasters.org

Represents postmasters in labor negotiations with the U.S. Postal Service and in legislative matters of concern. Works to improve the salaries, working hours, and working conditions of postmasters.

National Rural Letter Carriers' Assn., *1630 Duke St., Alexandria, VA 22314-3467; (703) 684-5545. Fax, (703) 518-0677. Jeanette P. Dwyer, President.*
Web, www.nrlca.org

Membership: more than 100,000 rural letter carriers working for, or retired from, the U.S. Postal Service. Seeks to improve rural mail delivery. Negotiates labor agreements affecting members; conducts training programs and workshops. Monitors legislation and regulations.

National Star Route Mail Contractors Assn., *324 E. Capitol St. N.E., 20003-3897; (202) 543-1661. Fax, (202) 543-8863. John V. Maraney, Executive Director. Toll-free, (800) 543-1661.*
General email, twilliams@starroutecontractors.org
Web, www.starroutecontractors.org

Membership: contractors for highway mail transport and selected rural route deliverers. Acts as liaison between contractors and the U.S. Postal Service, the Transportation Dept., the Labor Dept., and Congress concerning contracts, wages, and other issues. Monitors legislation and regulations.

Mail Rates and Classification

▶**AGENCIES**

Postal Regulatory Commission, *901 New York Ave. N.W., #200, 20268-0001; (202) 789-6800. Fax, (202) 789-6891. Robert G. Taub, Chair, Acting.*
General email, prc-dockets@prc.gov
Web, www.prc.gov

Independent agency with regulatory oversight over the U.S. Postal Service. Develops and maintains regulations concerning postal rates; consults with the Postal Service on delivery service standards and performance measures; consults with the State Dept. on international postal policies; prevents anticompetitive postal practices; and adjudicates complaints.

U.S. Postal Service (USPS), *Mail Entry, 475 L'Enfant Plaza S.W., #2P836, 20260; (202) 268-8081. Fax, (202) 268-8273. Pritha Mehra, Vice President, (202) 268-8091.*
Web, www.usps.com and *Business services, www.usps.com/business*

Implements policies governing the acceptance and verification of business mail by the U.S. Postal Service.

U.S. Postal Service (USPS), *Pricing, 475 L'Enfant Plaza S.W., #4012, 20260-5014; (202) 268-8116. Fax, (202) 268-6251. Sharon Owens, Vice President.*
Web, www.usps.com

Sets prices for U.S. Postal Service product lines using competitive pricing methods.

U.S. Postal Service (USPS), *Product Classification, 475 L'Enfant Plaza S.W., #4446, 20260-5015; (202) 268-3789. Fax, (202) 268-3888. Lizbeth (Liz) Dobbins, Manager.*
Web, www.usps.com

Issues policy statements on domestic mail classification matters. Ensures the accuracy of policies developed by the Postal Regulatory Commission with respect to domestic mail classification schedules.

▶**NONGOVERNMENTAL**

Alliance of Nonprofit Mailers, *1211 Connecticut Ave. N.W., #610, 20036-2705; (202) 462-5132. Fax, (202) 462-0423. Stephen Kearney, Executive Director.*

General email, alliance@nonprofitmailers.org

Web, www.nonprofitmailers.org

Works to maintain reasonable mail rates for nonprofit organizations. Represents member organizations before Congress, the U.S. Postal Service, the Postal Regulatory Commission, and the courts on nonprofit postal rate and mail classification issues.

Assn. for Postal Commerce (POSTCOM), *1800 Diagonal Rd., #320, Alexandria, VA 22314-2862; (703) 524-0096. Fax, (703) 997-2414. Gene A. Del Polito, President.*

General email, info@postcom.org

Web, www.postcom.org and Twitter, @PostCom2

Membership: companies and organizations interested in mail as a medium for advertising and product delivery. Provides members with information about postal news worldwide, postal policy, postal rates, and legislation regarding postal regulations. Monitors legislation and regulations.

DMA Nonprofit Federation, *1615 L St. N.W., #1100, 20036; (202) 861-2498. Fax, (202) 628-4383. Xenia Boone, General Counsel. Alternate phone, (202) 861-2427.*

General email, uosgood@the-dma.org

Web, www.nonprofitfederation.org

Membership: nonprofit organizations and their suppliers that rely on nonprofit mail and other marketing channels, including digital, email, and telephone, to reach donors. Serves as a liaison between members and the U.S. Postal Service; represents members' interests before regulatory agencies; monitors legislation and regulations. Hosts conferences on fund-raising across marketing channels.

EPICOMM—Assn. for Leaders in Print, Mail, Fulfillment, and Marketing Services, *1800 Diagonal Rd., #320, Alexandria, VA 22314-2806; (703) 836-9200. Fax, (703) 548-8204. Ken Garner, President.*

General email, info@epicomm.org

Web, www.epicomm.org and Twitter, @EpicommAssoc

Membership: companies in the graphic communications industry in North America. Provides advocacy and management training. (Formed by merger of Assn. of Marketing Service Providers and National Assn. for Printing Leadership.)

Parcel Shippers Assn. (PSA), *P.O. Box 450, Oxon Hill, MD 20750; (571) 257-7617. Fax, (301) 749-8684. Richard Porras, President.*

General email, psa@parcelshippers.org

Web, www.parcelshippers.org

Voluntary organization of business firms concerned with the shipment of parcels. Works to improve parcel post rates and service; represents members before the Postal Regulatory Commission in matters regarding parcel post rates. Monitors legislation and regulations.

Stamps, Postal History

▶**AGENCIES**

National Postal Museum *(Smithsonian Institution), 2 Massachusetts Ave. N.E., 20002 (mailing address: P.O. Box 37012, Washington, DC 20013); (202) 633-5555. Fax, (202) 633-9393. Allen Kane, Director. Tours and education, (202) 633-5534. Press, (202) 633-5518.*

Web, http://postalmuseum.si.edu

Exhibits postal history and stamp collections; provides information on world postal and stamp history.

U.S. Postal Service (USPS), *Citizens' Stamp Advisory Committee, 475 L'Enfant Plaza S.W., #3300, 20260-3501; (202) 268-3875. Fax, (202) 268-4965. Janet Klug, Chair.*

Web, http://about.usps.com/who-we-are/leadership/stamp-advisory-committee.htm

Reviews stamp subject nominations, which are open to the public. Develops the annual Stamp Program and makes subject and design recommendations to the Postmaster General.

U.S. Postal Service (USPS), *Stamp Development, 475 L'Enfant Plaza S.W., #3300, 20260-3501; (202) 268-5141. Fax, (202) 268-4965. Mary Anne Penner, Director, Acting.*

Web, www.usps.com

Manages the stamp selection function; develops the basic stamp pre-production design; manages relationship with stamp collecting community.

PUBLIC ADMINISTRATION

General

▶**AGENCIES**

Office of Management and Budget (OMB) *(Executive Office of the President), President's Management Council, Dwight D. Eisenhower Executive Office Bldg., #216, 20503; (202) 395-5020. Fax, (202) 395-6102. Beth Cobert, Deputy Director; Adam Niefeld, Assistant, (202) 395-5020.*

Web, www.whitehouse.gov/omb and www.qsa.gov/portal/content/133811

Membership: chief operating officers of federal government departments and agencies. Responsible for implementing the management improvement initiatives of the administration. Develops and oversees improved governmentwide management and administrative systems; formulates long-range plans to promote these systems; works to resolve interagency management problems and to implement reforms.

President's Commission on White House Fellowships, *712 Jackson Pl. N.W., 20503; (202) 395-4522. Fax, (202) 395-6179. Jennifer Yeager Kaplan, Director.*

General email, whitehousefellows@whf.eop.gov

Web, www.whitehouse.gov/about/fellows

Nonpartisan commission that provides professionals from all sectors of national life with the opportunity to observe firsthand the processes of the federal government. Fellows work for one year as special assistants to cabinet members or to principal members of the White House staff. Qualified applicants have demonstrated superior accomplishments early in their careers and have a commitment to leadership and public service.

►CONGRESS

For a listing of relevant congressional committees and subcommittees, please see pages 314–315 or the Appendix.

Government Accountability Office (GAO), *Education, Workforce, and Income Security, 441 G St. N.W., #5928, 20548; (202) 512-7215. Barbara D. Bovbjerg, Managing Director.*
Web, www.gao.gov/careers/ewis.html

Independent nonpartisan agency in the legislative branch. Responsible for intergovernmental relations activities. Reviews the effects of federal grants and regulations on state and local governments. Works to reduce intergovernmental conflicts and costs. Seeks to improve the allocation and targeting of federal funds to state and local governments through changes in federal funding formulas.

►NONGOVERNMENTAL

American Society for Public Administration, *1730 Rhode Island Ave. N.W., #500, 20036; (202) 393-7878. Fax, (202) 638-4952. William P. Shields Jr., Executive Director.*
General email, info@aspanet.org
Web, www.aspanet.org and Twitter, @ASPANational

Membership: government administrators, public officials, educators, researchers, and others interested in public administration. Presents awards to distinguished professionals in the field; sponsors workshops and conferences; disseminates information about public administration. Promotes high ethical standards for public service.

Assn. of Government Accountants, *2208 Mount Vernon Ave., Alexandria, VA 22301; (703) 684-6931. Fax, (703) 548-9367. Ann M. Ebberts, Chief Executive Officer. Toll-free, (800) 242-7211.*
General email, agamembers@agacgfm.org
Web, www.agacgfm.org and Twitter, @AGACGFM

Membership: professionals engaged in government accounting, auditing, budgeting, and information systems. Sponsors education, research, and conferences; administers certification program.

Federally Employed Women, *455 Massachusetts Ave. N.W., (mailing address: P.O. Box 306, Washington, DC, 20001); (202) 898-0994. Fax, (202) 898-1535. Michelle Crockett, President.*
General email, few@few.org
Web, www.few.org

Membership: women and men who work for the federal government. Works to eliminate sex discrimination in government employment and to increase job opportunities for women; offers training programs. Monitors legislation and regulations.

International City/County Management Assn. (ICMA), *777 N. Capitol St. N.E., #500, 20002-4201; (202) 289-4262. Fax, (202) 962-3500. Robert J. O'Neill, Executive Director, ext. 3528. Member services and information, (202) 962-3680. Toll-free, (800) 745-8780.*
General email, membership@icma.org
Web, www.icma.org

Membership: appointed managers and administrators of cities, towns, counties, and other local governments around the world; local government employees; academics; and other individuals with an interest in local government. Provides member support, publications, data and information, peer and results-oriented assistance, and training and professional development to members and others to help build sustainable communities. Sponsors workshops, regional summits, and an annual conference. Publishes resources for local government management professionals.

International Public Management Assn. for Human Resources (IPMA-HR), *1617 Duke St., Alexandria, VA 22314; (703) 549-7100. Fax, (703) 684-0948. Neil Reichenberg, Executive Director.*
General email, ipma@ipma-hr.org
Web, www.ipma-hr.org

Membership: personnel professionals from federal, state, and local governments. Provides information on training procedures, management techniques, and legislative developments on the federal, state, and local levels.

National Academy of Public Administration, *1600 K St. N.W., #400, 20006; (202) 347-3190. Fax, (202) 223-0823. Dan G. Blair, President.*
General email, academy@napawash.org
Web, www.napawash.org

Membership: scholars and administrators in public management. Chartered by Congress to assist federal, state, and local government agencies, public officials, and foundations with government and management challenges.

National Foundation for Women Legislators, *1727 King St., #300, Alexandria, VA 22314; (703) 518-7931. Jody Thomas, Executive Director.*
General email, nfwl@womenlegislators.org
Web, www.womenlegislators.org, Twitter, @ElectedWomen and Facebook, www.facebook.com/electedwomen

Provides leadership development and networking resources to women leaders at the city, state, and federal levels of government.

National Women's Political Caucus, *1001 Connecticut Ave., #1020, 20005 (mailing address: P.O. Box 50476, Washington, DC 20091); (202) 785-1100. Donna Lent, President; Diedre Malone, Communications.*
General email, info@nwpc.org
Web, www.nwpc.org

Seeks to increase the number of women in policy-making positions in federal, state, and local government. Identifies, recruits, trains, and supports pro-choice women candidates for public office. Monitors agencies and provides names of qualified women for high-level and mid-level appointments.

Network of Schools of Public Policy, Affairs, and Administration (NASPAA), *1029 Vermont Ave. N.W., #1100, 20005-3517; (202) 628-8965. Fax, (202) 626-4978. Laurel McFarland, Executive Director.*
General email, naspaa@naspaa.org

Web, www.naspaa.org

Serves as a clearinghouse for information on education in public administration, public policy, and public affairs programs in colleges and universities.

Women in Government Relations, *8400 Westpark Dr., 2nd Floor, McLean, VA 22102; (703) 610-9030. Fax, (703) 995-0528. Emily Bardach, Executive Director.*
General email, info@wgr.org

Web, www.wgr.org and Twitter, @WGRDC

Membership: professionals in business, trade associations, and government whose jobs involve governmental relations at the federal, state, or local level. Serves as a forum for exchange of information among its members.

STATE AND LOCAL GOVERNMENT

General

▶AGENCIES

General Services Administration (GSA), *Catalog of Federal Domestic Assistance (CFDA),* 2200 Crystal City Dr., Crystal Park 1, Arlington, VA 22202; 1800 F St. N.W., 20405-0001; (703) 605-3427. Priscilla Owens, Director, (703) 605-3408. Help Desk, (866) 606-8220.
Web, www.cfda.gov

Disseminates information on federal domestic assistance programs through the CFDA Web site. Information includes all types of federal aid and explains types of assistance, eligibility requirements, application processes, and suggestions for writing proposals. Catalog may be downloaded from the CFDA Web site. Printed version may be ordered from the Superintendent of Documents, U.S. Government Printing Office, Washington, DC 20402; (202) 512-1800, or toll-free, (866) 512-1800; or online at http://bookstore.gpo.gov.

Housing and Urban Development Dept. (HUD), *Policy Development and Research,* 451 7th St. S.W., #8100, 20410-6000; (202) 708-1600. Fax, (202) 619-8000. Katherine M. O'Regan, Assistant Secretary.
Web, www.huduser.org

Assesses and maintains information on housing needs, market conditions, and programs; conducts research on housing and community development issues such as building technology, economic development, and urban planning.

Multistate Tax Commission, *444 N. Capitol St. N.W., #425, 20001-1538; (202) 650-0300. Gregory S. Matson, Director.*
General email, mtc@mtc.gov

Web, www.mtc.gov

Membership: state governments that have enacted the Multistate Tax Compact. Promotes fair, effective, and efficient state tax systems for interstate and international commerce; works to preserve state tax sovereignty. Encourages uniform state tax laws and regulations for multistate and multinational enterprises. Maintains three regional audit offices that monitor compliance with state tax laws and encourage uniformity in taxpayer treatment. Administers program to identify businesses that do not file tax returns with states.

Office of Management and Budget (OMB) *(Executive Office of the President),* **Federal Financial Management,** 725 17th St. N.W., #6025, 20503; (202) 395-3895. Fax, (202) 395-3952. Dave Mader, Controller. Press, (202) 395-7254.
Web, www.whitehouse.gov/omb/financial_default

Facilitates exchange of information on financial management standards, techniques, and processes among officers of state and local governments.

▶CONGRESS

For a listing of relevant congressional committees and subcommittees, please see pages 314–315 or the Appendix.

▶NONGOVERNMENTAL

American Legislative Exchange Council (ALEC), *2900 Crystal Dr., #600, Arlington, VA 22202; (703) 373-0933. Fax, (703) 373-0927. Lisa B. Nelson, Chief Executive Officer. Media, (703) 373-5030.*
General email, membership@alec.org

Web, www.alec.org and Twitter, @ALEC_states

Nonpartisan educational and research organization for state legislators. Conducts research and provides information and model state legislation on public policy issues. Supports the development of state policies to limit government, expand free markets, promote economic growth, and preserve individual liberty.

The Brookings Institution, *Metropolitan Policy Program,* 1755 Massachusetts Ave. N.W., 20036; (202) 797-6000. Fax, (202) 797-2965. Amy Liu, Director. Press, (202) 797-6105.
General email, metro@brookings.edu

Web, www.brookings.edu/metro

Helps U.S. cities and metropolitan areas study and reform their economic, fiscal, and social policies. Conducts research at the national, state, and local levels.

Coalition of Northeastern Governors (CONEG), *Policy Research Center, Inc.,* 400 N. Capitol St. N.W., #382,

20001; (202) 624-8450. Fax, (202) 624-8463.
Anne D. Stubbs, Executive Director.
General email, coneg@sso.org

Web, www.coneg.org

Membership: governors of seven northeastern states (Connecticut, Maine, Massachusetts, New Hampshire, New York, Rhode Island, and Vermont). Addresses shared interests in regional energy, economic development, transportation, and the environment; serves as an information clearinghouse on regional and federal issues; facilitates joint action among member states. Secretariat to the New England Governors & Eastern Canadian Premiers and to the Northeast Committee on Environment.

Council of State Governments (CSG), *Washington Office, 444 N. Capitol St. N.W., #401, 20001; (202) 624-5460. Fax, (202) 624-5452. David Adkins, Executive Director (Ky.); Andy Karellis, Director, Federal Affairs. Media, (859) 244-8246.*
General email, membership@csg.org

Web, www.csg.org, www.csgdc.org and Twitter, @CGGovts

Membership: governing bodies of states, commonwealths, and territories, and various affiliated national organizations of state officials. Promotes interstate, federal-state, and state-local cooperation; interests include education, transportation, human services, housing, natural resources, and economic development. Provides services to affiliates and associated organizations, including the National Assn. of State Treasurers, National Assn. of Government Labor Officials, and other state administrative organizations in specific fields. Monitors legislation and executive policy. (Headquarters in Lexington, Ky.)

Government Finance Officers Assn. (GFOA), *Federal Liaison Center, 1301 Pennsylvania Ave., #309, 20004-1714; (202) 393-8020. Fax, (202) 393-0780. Dustin McDonald, Director.*
General email, federalliaison@gfoa.org

Web, www.gfoa.org

Membership: state and local government finance managers. Offers training and publications in public financial management. Conducts research in public fiscal management, design and financing of government programs, and formulation and analysis of government fiscal policy. (Headquarters in Chicago, Ill.)

International Municipal Lawyers Assn. (IMLA), *7910 Woodmont Ave., #1440, Bethesda, MD 20814; (202) 466-5424. Fax, (202) 785-0152. Chuck Thompson, General Counsel, ext. 7110.*
General email, info@imla.org

Web, www.imla.org

Membership: local government attorneys and public law practitioners. Acts as a research service for members in all areas of municipal law; participates in litigation of municipal and constitutional law issues.

National Assn. of Bond Lawyers, *601 13th St., #800-S, 20005-3875; (202) 503-3300. Fax, (202) 637-0217. Linda H. Wyman, Chief Operating Officer.*

Local Government in the Washington Metropolitan Area

DISTRICT OF COLUMBIA

Executive Office of the Mayor,
Muriel Bowser, Mayor
John A. Wilson Bldg.
1350 Pennsylvania Ave. N.W., #316, 20004;
  (202) 727-6300, Fax: (202) 727-0505
Email, eom@dc.gov
Web, mayor.dc.gov

MARYLAND

Montgomery County,
Ike Leggett, County Executive
101 Monroe St., 2nd Floor, Rockville, MD 20850;
  (240) 777-0311, Fax: (240) 777-2544
Email, countyexecutive@co.pg.md.us or
ocemail@montgomerycountymd.gov
Web, www.montgomerycountymd.gov/exec/

Prince George's County,
Rushern L. Baker III, County Executive
14741 Gov. Oden Bowie Dr., Upper Marlboro, MD 20772;
  (301) 952-4131, Fax: (301) 952-5148
Email, countyexecutive@co.pg.md.us
Web, www.princegeorgescountymd.gov

VIRGINIA

Arlington County,
Mark Schwartz, County Manager
2100 Clarendon Blvd., Arlington, VA 22201,
  (703) 228-3120, Fax:, (703) 228-4611
Email, countymanager@arlingtonva.us
Web, www.arlingtonva.us

City of Alexandria,
Allison Silberberg, Mayor
301 King St., Room 1900, Alexandria, VA 22314;
  (703) 746-4357, Fax, (703) 838-6426
Email, alexvamayor@aol.com
Web, www.alexandriava.gov

City of Falls Church,
Wyatt Shields, City Manager
300 Park Ave., #303 E, Falls Church, VA 22046;
  (703) 248-5004, Fax: (703) 248-5146
Email, city-manager@fallschurchva.gov
Web, www.fallschurchva.gov

Fairfax County,
Edward L. Long Jr., County Executive
12000 Government Center Pkwy., #552, Fairfax, VA 22035;
  (703) 324-2531, Fax: (703) 324-3956
Email, coexec@fairfaxcounty.gov
Web, www.fairfaxcounty.gov

General email, nabl@nabl.org

Web, www.nabl.org

Membership: state and municipal finance lawyers. Educates members and others on the law relating to state and municipal bonds and other obligations. Provides advice and comment at the federal, state, and local levels on legislation, regulations, rulings, and court and administrative proceedings regarding public obligations.

National Assn. of Counties (NACo), *25 Massachusetts Ave. N.W., #500, 20001-2028; (202) 393-6226. Fax, (202) 393-2630. Matthew D. Chase, Executive Director. Press, (202) 942-4220. Toll-free, (888) 407-6226.*

Web, www.naco.org

Membership: county governments and county officials and their staffs through NACo's affiliates. Conducts research, supplies information, and provides technical and public affairs assistance on issues affecting counties. Interests include homeland security, drug abuse, access to health care, and public-private partnerships. Monitors legislation and regulations.

National Assn. of Regional Councils (NARC), *777 N. Capitol St. N.E., #305, 20002; (202) 618-6363. Leslie Wollack, Executive Director.*

General email, info@narc.org

Web, www.narc.org

Membership: regional councils of local governments, councils of government, and metropolitan planning organizations. Works to improve local governments' intergovernmental planning and coordination at the regional level. Interests include transportation, economic and community development, workforce development, housing, aging, energy, environment, public safety, and emergency management.

National Assn. of Secretaries of State, *444 N. Capitol St. N.W., #401, 20001; (202) 624-3525. Fax, (202) 624-3527. Leslie Reynolds, Executive Director.*

General email, nass@sso.org

Web, www.nass.org

Organization of secretaries of state and lieutenant governors or other comparable state officials from the fifty states, the District of Columbia, Guam, Puerto Rico, and the U.S. Virgin Islands. Interests include budget and finance, elections and voting, state business services and licensing, e-government, and state heritage, including a digital archives initiative.

National Assn. of State Auditors, Comptrollers, and Treasurers, *Washington Office, 444 N. Capitol St. N.W., #234, 20001; (202) 624-5451. Fax, (202) 624-5473. Cornelia Chebinou, Washington Director.*

Web, www.nasact.org

Membership: elected and appointed state and territorial officials who deal with the financial management of state government. Provides information on financial best practices and research. Monitors legislation and regulations. (Headquarters in Lexington, Ky.)

National Assn. of State Budget Officers, *444 N. Capitol St. N.W., #642, 20001-1511; (202) 624-5382. Fax, (202) 624-7745. Stacey Mazer, Executive Director, Acting.*

General email, nasbo-direct@nasbo.org

Web, www.nasbo.org

Membership: state budget and financial officers. Publishes research reports on budget-related issues; shares best practices; provides training and technical assistance. (Affiliate of the National Governors Assn.)

National Assn. of Towns and Townships (NATaT), *1130 Connecticut Ave. N.W., #300, 20036; (202) 454-3954. Fax, (202) 331-1598. Jennifer Imo, Federal Director. Toll-free, (866) 830-0008.*

General email, info@natat.org

Web, www.natat.org

Membership: towns, townships, small communities, and others interested in supporting small-town government. Provides local government officials from small jurisdictions with technical assistance, educational services, and public policy support; conducts research and coordinates training for local government officials nationwide. Interests include tax benefits for local public service volunteers, local economic development, water and wastewater infrastructure, transportation improvements, and allocation of federal resources. (Affiliated with National Center for Small Communities.)

National Black Caucus of Local Elected Officials (NBC/ LEO), *National League of Cities, 1301 Pennsylvania Ave. N.W., 20004-1763; (202) 626-3000. Priscilla Tyson, President. General information, (877) 827-2385.*

General email, constituencygroups@nlc.org

Web, www.nlc.org

Membership: Black elected officials at the local level and other interested individuals. Seeks to increase Black participation on the National League of Cities' steering and policy committees. Informs members on issues, and plans strategies to achieve objectives through legislation and direct action. Interests include cultural diversity, local government and community participation, housing, economics, job training, the family, and human rights.

National Black Caucus of State Legislators, *444 N. Capitol St. N.W., #622, 20001; (202) 624-5457. Fax, (202) 508-3826. LaKimba DeSadier, Executive Director.*

Web, www.nbcsl.org

Membership: Black state legislators. Promotes effective leadership among Black state legislators through education, research, and training; serves as an information network and clearinghouse for members.

National Conference of State Legislatures, *Washington Office, 444 N. Capitol St. N.W., #515, 20001; (202) 624-5400. Fax, (202) 737-1069. Neal Osten, Director; Molly Ramsdell, Director.*

General email, info@ncsl.org

Web, www.ncsl.org

Coordinates and represents state legislatures at the federal level; conducts research, produces videos, and publishes reports in areas of interest to state legislatures; conducts an information exchange program on intergovernmental relations; sponsors seminars for state legislators and their staffs. Interests include unfunded federal mandates, state-federal law conflict, and fiscal integrity. Monitors legislation and regulations. (Headquarters in Denver, Colo.)

National Foundation for Women Legislators, *1727 King St., #300, Alexandria, VA 22314; (703) 518-7931. Jody Thomas, Executive Director.*
General email, nfwl@womenlegislators.org

Web, www.womenlegislators.org, Twitter, @ElectedWomen and Facebook, www.facebook.com/ electedwomen

Provides leadership development and networking resources to women leaders at the city, state, and federal levels of government.

National Governors Assn. (NGA), *444 N. Capitol St. N.W., #267, 20001-1512; (202) 624-5300. Scott Pattison, Executive Director. Press, (202) 624-5313.*
General email, webmaster@nga.org

Web, www.nga.org

Membership: governors of states, commonwealths, and territories. Provides members with policy and technical assistance. Makes policy recommendations to Congress and the president on community and economic development; education; international trade and foreign relations; energy and the environment; health care and welfare reform; agriculture; transportation, commerce, and technology; communications; criminal justice; public safety; and workforce development.

National League of Cities, *1301 Pennsylvania Ave. N.W., #550, 20004; (202) 626-3000. Fax, (202) 626-3043. Clarence Anthony, Executive Director. Toll-free, (877) 827-2385.*
General email, info@nlc.org

Web, www.nlc.org

Membership: cities and state municipal leagues. Provides city leaders with training, technical assistance, and publications; investigates needs of local governments in implementing federal programs that affect cities. Holds two annual conferences; conducts research; sponsors awards. Monitors legislation and regulations. (Affiliates include National Black Caucus of Local Elected Officials.)

NIGP: The Institute for Public Procurement, *2411 Dulles Corner Park, #350, Herndon, VA 20171; (703) 736-8900. Fax, (703) 736-9644. Rick Grimm, Chief Executive Officer, ext. 240. Information, (800) 367-6447.*
Web, www.nigp.org

Membership: governmental purchasing departments, agencies, and organizations at the federal, state, and local levels in the United States, Canada, and internationally. Provides public procurement officers with technical assistance and information, training seminars, and professional certification. (Formerly the National Institute of Governmental Purchasing.)

Public Risk Management Assn. (PRIMA), *700 S. Washington St., #218, Alexandria, VA 22314; (703) 528-7701. Fax, (703) 739-0200. Marshall W. Davies, Executive Director, (703) 253-1265.*
General email, info@primacentral.org

Web, www.primacentral.org

Membership: state and local governments and their risk management practitioners, including benefits and insurance managers, and private sector organizations. Develops and teaches cost-effective management techniques for handling public liability issues; promotes professional development of its members. Gathers and disseminates information about risk management to public and private sectors.

Public Technology Institute (PTI), *1420 Prince St., #200, Alexandria, VA 22314-2815; (202) 626-2400. Alan R. Shark, Executive Director, (202) 626-2445. Press, (202) 626-2432.*
General email, info@pti.org

Web, www.pti.org and Twitter, @Public_Tech

Cooperative research, development, and technology-transfer organization of cities and counties in North America. Assists local governments in increasing efficiency, reducing costs, improving services, and developing public enterprise programs to help local officials create revenues and serve citizens. Participates in international conferences.

Southern Governors' Assn., *444 N. Capitol St. N.W., #388, 20001-1585; (202) 624-5897. Fax, (202) 624-7797. Diane Duff, Executive Director.*
General email, sga@sso.org

Web, www.southerngovernors.org

Membership: governors of sixteen southern states, plus the territories of Puerto Rico and the U.S. Virgin Islands, and corporate affiliates. Provides a regional, bipartisan forum for governors to help formulate and implement national policy; works to enhance the region's competitiveness nationally and internationally, to explore common problems, and to coordinate regional initiatives.

Stateline.org, *901 E St. N.W., 7th Floor, 20004; (202) 552-2000. Fax, (202) 552-2299. Scott Greenberger, Executive Editor.*
General email, editor@stateline.org

Web, www.stateline.org

Independent online news site and forum. Encourages debate on state-level issues such as health care, tax and budget policy, the environment, and immigration. (Part of the Pew Charitable Trust.)

U.S. Conference of Mayors, *1620 Eye St. N.W., 4th Floor, 20006; (202) 293-7330. Fax, (202) 293-2352. J. Thomas Cochran, Executive Director.*

General email, info@usmayors.org

Web, www.usmayors.org

Membership: mayors of cities with populations of 30,000 or more. Promotes city-federal cooperation; publishes reports and conducts meetings on federal programs, policies, and initiatives that affect urban and suburban interests. Serves as a clearinghouse for information on urban and suburban problems. (Approximately 1,400 U.S. cities.)

Western Governors' Assn., *Washington Office,* 400 N. Capitol St. N.W., #376, 20001; (202) 624-5402. Fax, (202) 624-7707. James (Jim) Ogsbury, Executive Director, (303) 623-9378.

Web, www.westgov.org and Twitter, @westgov

Independent, nonpartisan organization of governors from nineteen western states, two Pacific territories, and one commonwealth. Identifies and addresses key policy and governance issues in natural resources, clean energy and alternative transportation fuels, the environment, radioactive waste transportation, human services, economic development, international relations, and public management. (Headquarters in Denver, Colo.)

Women In Government, 1319 F St. N.W., #710, 20004; (202) 333-0825. Fax, (202) 333-0875. Dyan Alexander, Executive Director.

Web, www.womeningovernment.org and Twitter, @WomenInGovt

Membership: women state legislators. Seeks to enhance the leadership role of women policymakers by providing issue education and leadership training. Sponsors seminars and conducts educational research.

Washington Area

▶CONGRESS

For a listing of relevant congressional committees and subcommittees, please see pages 314–315 or the Appendix.

▶NONGOVERNMENTAL

Metropolitan Washington Council of Governments, 777 N. Capitol St. N.E., #300, 20002-4239; (202) 962-3200. Fax, (202) 962-3203. Chuck Bean, Executive Director. Press, (202) 962-3250. TTY, (202) 962-3213.

General email, ccogdtp@mwcog.org

Web, www.mwcog.org

Membership: local governments in the Washington area, plus members of the Maryland and Virginia legislatures and the U.S. Congress. Analyzes and develops regional responses to issues such as the environment, affordable housing, economic development, health, population growth, human and social services, public safety, and transportation.

Walter E. Washington Convention Center Authority, 801 Mt. Vernon Pl. N.W., 20001; (202) 249-3000. Fax, (202) 249-3133. Gregory A. O'Dell, Chief Executive Officer. Information, (800) 368-9000. Press, (202) 249-3217.

Web, www.dcconvention.com and Twitter, @ConventionsDC

Promotes national and international conventions, meetings, and trade shows; hosts sports, entertainment, and special events; fosters redevelopment of downtown Washington.

10

Health

GENERAL POLICY AND ANALYSIS

Basic Resources

►AGENCIES

Agency for Health Care Research and Quality (AHCRQ) *(Health and Human Services Dept.), Communication and Knowledge Transfer,* 5600 Fishers Lane, Rockville, MD 20857; (301) 427-1364. Fax, (301) 427-1873. Howard Holland, Director, (301) 427-1104. Public inquiries, (301) 427-1104.
General email, info@ahrq.gov
Web, www.ahrq.gov/about/ockt/ocktmiss.htm

Works to improve the quality, safety, effectiveness, and efficiency of health care in the United States. Promotes improvements in clinical practices and in organizing, financing, and delivering health care services. Conducts and supports comparative effectiveness research, demonstration projects, evaluations, and training; disseminates information on a wide range of activities.

Assistant Secretary for Health *(Health and Human Services Dept.),* 200 Independence Ave. S.W., #716G, 20201; (202) 690-7694. Dr. Karen B. DeSalvo, Assistant Secretary, Acting.
General email, ASH@hhs.gov
Web, www.hhs.gov/ash

Develops public health policy recommendations across Health and Human Services Dept offices. Oversees the Office of the Surgeon General and Commissioned Corps of the U.S. Public Health Service.

Assistant Secretary for Health *(Health and Human Services Dept.), Disease Prevention and Health Promotion,* 1101 Wootton Pkwy., #LL100, Rockville, MD 20852; (240) 453-8280. Fax, (240) 453-8282. Dr. Donald Wright, Director.
General email, odphpinfo@hhs.gov
Web, www.health.gov

Develops national policies for disease prevention, clinical preventive services, and health promotion; assists the private sector and agencies with disease prevention, clinical preventive services, and health promotion activities.

Assistant Secretary for Health *(Health and Human Services Dept.), National Health Information Center,* 1100 Wootton Pwky., #LL100, Rockville, MD 20852 (mailing address: P.O. Box 1133, Washington, DC 20013-1133); (240) 453-8280. Fax, (301) 984-4256. Dr. Donald Wright, Project Manager.
General email, healthfinder@nhic.org and *info@nhic.org*
Web, www.health.gov/nhic and *www.healthfinder.gov*

A project of the Office of Disease Prevention and Health Promotion; provides referrals on health topics and resources. Maintains a calendar of National Health Observances.

Assistant Secretary for Health *(Health and Human Services Dept.), Surgeon General,* Tower Bldg., 1101 Wootton Pkwy., Plaza Level 1, #100, Rockville, MD 20852 (mailing address: Tower Bldg., Plaza Level 1, #100, 1101 Wootton Pkwy., Rockville, MD 20852); (240) 276-8853. Fax, (240) 453-6141. Vice Adm. (Dr.) Vivek Murthy, Surgeon General. Media, (202) 202-0143.
Web, www.surgeongeneral.gov

Directs activities of the Office of the Assistant Secretary for Health. Serves as the secretary's principal adviser on health concerns; exercises specialized responsibilities in various health areas, including domestic and global health. Advises the public on smoking, AIDS, immunization, diet, nutrition, disease prevention, and other general health issues, including responses to bioterrorism. Oversees activities of all members of the Commissioned Corps of the U.S. Public Health Service.

Bureau of Oceans and International Environmental and Scientific Affairs *(State Dept.), International Health and Biodefense,* 2201 C St. N.W., #2734, 20520; (202) 647-1318. Lynette Poulton, Director.
Web, www.state.gov/e/oes/intlhealthbiodefense

Advances the Global Health Security Agenda and focuses on issues including pandemic preparedness, new outbreaks of disease, new international policy discussions, and the impact of science and technology, medicine, and public health.

Centers for Disease Control and Prevention (CDC) *(Health and Human Services Dept.), Washington Office,* 395 E St. S.W., #9100, 20201; (202) 245-0600. Fax, (202) 245-0602. Dr. Thomas R. Frieden, Director; Dena Morris, Director, Washington Office. Public inquiries, (800) 232-4636. TTY, (888) 232-6348.
General email, cdinfo@cdc.gov
Web, www.cdc.gov/washington and *Twitter, @CDCgov*

Collaborates with state and local health departments to further health promotion; prevention of disease, injury, and disability; and preparedness for new health threats. Monitors the health of individuals, detects and investigates health problems, conducts research to enhance prevention, develops and acts as advocate for public health policies, implements prevention strategies, promotes healthy behaviors, fosters safe and healthful environments, and provides leadership and training. (Headquarters in Atlanta, Ga.)

Federal Trade Commission (FTC), *Bureau of Consumer Protection, Advertising Practices,* 400 7th Ave. S.W., #10418, 20024; (202) 326-3090. Fax, (202) 326-3259. Mary Engle, Associate Director.
Web, www.ftc.gov/about-ftc/bureaus-offices/bureau-consumer-protection/our-divisions/division-advertising-practices

Protects consumers from deceptive and unsubstantiated advertising through law enforcement, public reports, and industry outreach. Evaluates the nutritional and health benefits of foods and the effectiveness of dietary supplements, drugs, and medical devices, particularly as they relate to weight loss.

HEALTH RESOURCES IN CONGRESS

For a complete listing of congressional committees, including their full contact information, leadership, membership, and jurisdictions, please refer to the Appendix on pages 779–896.

HOUSE:

House Agriculture Committee, (202) 225-2171.
Web, agriculture.house.gov
    Subcommittee on Nutrition, (202) 225-2171.
House Appropriations Committee, (202) 225-2771.
Web, appropriations.house.gov
    Subcommittee on Agriculture, Rural Development, Food and Drug Administration, and Related Agencies, (202) 225-2638.
    Subcommittee on Labor, Health and Human Services, Education, and Related Agencies, (202) 225-3508.
House Armed Services Committee, (202) 225-4151.
Web, armedservices.house.gov
    Subcommittee on Military Personnel, (202) 225-7560.
House Budget Committee, (202) 226-7270.
Web, budget.house.gov
House Education and the Workforce Committee, (202) 225-4527.
Web, edworkforce.house.gov
    Subcommittee on Health, Employment, Labor, and Pensions, (202) 225-4527.
    Subcommittee on Workforce Protections, (202) 225-4527.
House Energy and Commerce Committee, (202) 225-2927.
Web, energycommerce.house.gov
    Subcommittee on Environment and the Economy, (202) 225-2927.
    Subcommittee on Health, (202) 225-2927.

House Foreign Affairs Committee, (202) 225-5021.
Web, foreignaffairs.house.gov
    Subcommittee on Africa, Global Health, Global Human Rights, and International Organizations, (202) 225-5021.
House Natural Resources Committee, (202) 225-2761.
Web, naturalresources.house.gov
House Oversight and Government Reform Committee, (202) 225-5074.
Web, oversight.house.gov
    Subcommittee on Health Care, Benefits, and Administrative Rules, (202) 225-5074.
House Science, Space, and Technology Committee, (202) 225-6371.
Web, science.house.gov
    Subcommittee on Research and Technology, (202) 225-6371.
House Small Business Committee, (202) 225-5821.
Web, smallbusiness.house.gov
    Subcommittee on Health and Technology, (202) 225-5821.
House Veterans' Affairs Committee, (202) 225-3527.
Web, veterans.house.gov
    Subcommittee on Health, (202) 225-9154.
House Ways and Means Committee, (202) 225-3625.
Web, waysandmeans.house.gov
    Subcommittee on Health, (202) 225-3943.

Food and Drug Administration (FDA) *(Health and Human Services Dept.),* 10903 New Hampshire Ave., Silver Spring, MD 20993; (888) 463-6332. Fax, (301) 847-3536. Dr. Stephen Ostroff, Commissioner, Acting. Main Library (White Oak in Silver Spring), (301) 796-2039. Press, (301) 796-4540.
Web, www.fda.gov and Twitter, @US_FDA

Protects public health by assessing the safety, effectiveness, and security of human and veterinary drugs, vaccines, and other biological products. Protects the safety and security of the nation's food supply, cosmetics, diet supplements, and products emitting radiation. Regulates tobacco products. Develops labeling and packaging standards; conducts inspections of manufacturers; issues orders to companies to recall and/or cease selling or producing hazardous products; enforces rulings and recommends action to Justice Dept. when necessary. Libraries open to the public; 24-hour advance appointment required.

Food and Drug Administration (FDA) *(Health and Human Services Dept.), International Programs,* 10903 New Hampshire Ave., Bldg. 31/32, Silver Spring, MD 20993; (301) 796-4600. Fax, (301) 595-7937. Mary Lou Valdez, Associate Commissioner.
Web, www.fda.gov/internationalprograms and www.fda.gov/AboutFDA/CentersOffices/OfficeofGlobalRegulatoryOperationsandPolicy/OfficeofInternationalPrograms/default.htm

Serves as FDA's liaison with foreign counterpart agencies, international organizations, and the U.S. diplomatic corps. Gathers and assesses information to inform decisions about FDA-regulated product imports. Seeks to advance global public health through distribution of health information, coordination of public health strategies, and promotion of public safety. Seeks to harmonize regulatory standards. Provides technical assistance.

Food and Drug Administration (FDA) *(Health and Human Services Dept.), Regulatory Affairs,* 10903

SENATE:

Senate Agriculture, Nutrition, and Forestry Committee, (202) 224-2035.
Web, ag.senate.gov
    Subcommittee on Rural Development and Energy, (202) 224-2035.
    Subcommittee on Nutrition, Specialty Crops, and Agricultural Research, (202) 224-2035.
Senate Appropriations Committee, (202) 224-7363.
Web, appropriations.senate.gov
    Subcommittee on Agriculture, Rural Development, Food and Drug Administration, and Related Agencies, (202) 224-8090.
    Subcommittee on Labor, Health and Human Services, Education, and Related Agencies, (202) 224-7363.
Senate Armed Services Committee, (202) 224-3871.
Web, armed-services.senate.gov
    Subcommittee on Personnel, (202) 224-3871.
Senate Banking, Housing, and Urban Affairs Committee, (202) 224-7391.
Web, banking.senate.gov
Senate Budget Committee, (202) 224-0642.
Web, budget.senate.gov
Senate Commerce, Science, and Transportation Committee, (202) 224-0411.
Web, commerce.senate.gov
    Subcommittee on Consumer Protections, Product Safety, Insurance, and Data Security, (202) 224-0411.

Senate Environment and Public Works Committee, (202) 224-8832.
Web, epw.senate.gov
    Subcommittee on Clean Air and Nuclear Safety, (202) 224-8832.
    Subcommittee on Superfund, Waste Management, and Regulatory Oversight, (202) 224-8832.
    Subcommittee on Transportation and Infrastructure, (202) 224-8832.
Senate Finance Committee, (202) 224-4515.
Web, finance.senate.gov
    Subcommittee on Health Care, (202) 224-4515.
Senate Health, Education, Labor, and Pensions Committee, (202) 224-5375.
Web, help.senate.gov
    Subcommittee on Children and Families, (202) 224-5375.
    Subcommittee on Employment and Workplace Safety, (202) 228-1455.
    Subcommittee on Primary Health and Retirement Security, (202) 224-5480.
Senate Indian Affairs Committee, (202) 224-2251.
Web, indian.senate.gov
Senate Judiciary Committee, (202) 224-7703.
Web, judiciary.senate.gov
    Subcommittee on Crime and Terrorism, (202) 224-6971.
Senate Small Business and Entrepreneurship Committee, (202) 224-5175.
Web, sbc.senate.gov
Senate Special Committee on Aging, (202) 224-5364.
Web, aging.senate.gov

New Hampshire Ave., WO31-3528, Silver Spring, MD 20993; (301) 796-8800. Fax, (301) 847-8544. Melinda K. Plaisier, Associate Commissioner. Web, www.fda.gov/aboutfda/centersoffices/officeofglobalregulatoryoperationsandpolicy/ora/default.htm

Directs and coordinates the FDA's compliance activities; manages field offices; advises FDA commissioner on domestic and international regulatory policies.

Health and Human Services Dept. (HHS), *200 Independence Ave. S.W., 20201; (202) 690-7000. Fax, (202) 690-7203. Sylvia Burwell, Secretary; Mary K. Wakefield, Deputy Secretary, Acting, (202) 690-6133. Press, (202) 690-6343. Press, (202) 690-6139. Toll-free, (877) 696-6775. TTY, (800) 877-8339. Web, www.hhs.gov*

Acts as principal adviser to the president on health and welfare plans, policies, and programs of the federal government. Encompasses the Centers for Medicare and Medicaid Services, the Administration for Children and Families, the Public Health Service, and the Centers for Disease Control and Prevention.

Health and Human Services Dept. (HHS), *National Committee on Vital and Health Statistics, 3311 Toledo Rd., Hyattsville, MD 20782; (301) 458-4715. Fax, (301) 458-4022. Rebecca Hines, Executive Secretary. Web, www.ncvhs.hhs.gov*

Statutory public advisory body on health data statistics and national health information policy. Serves as a national forum on health data. Aims to accelerate the evolution of public and private health information systems toward more uniform, shared data standards within the context of privacy and security concerns.

Health and Human Services Dept. (HHS), *National Coordinator for Health Information Technology, 200 Independence Ave. S.W., #729-D, 20201; (202) 690-7151.*

Fax, (202) 690-6079. Karen B. DeSalvo, National Coordinator.
General email, onc.request@hhs.gov
Web, www.healthit.gov

Coordinates nationwide efforts to implement information technology that allows for electronic use and exchange of health information. Goals include ensuring security for patient health information, improving health care quality, and reducing health care costs.

Health and Human Services Dept. (HHS), *Planning and Evaluation, 200 Independence Ave. S.W., #415F, 20201; (202) 690-7858. Fax, (202) 690-7383. Richard Frank, Assistant Secretary.*
Web, https://aspe.hhs.gov

Advises the secretary on policy development in health, disability, human services, data, and science, and provides advice and analysis on economic policy. Manages strategic and legislative planning and reviews regulations. Conducts research and evaluation studies, develops policy analyses, and estimates the cost and benefits of policy alternatives under consideration by the department or Congress.

Health and Human Services Dept. (HHS), *Preparedness and Response, 200 Independence Ave. S.W., #638-G, 20201; (202) 205-2882. Dr. Nicole Lurie, Assistant Secretary.*
Web, www.phe.gov

Serves as the secretary's principal adviser on matters relating to bioterrorism and public health emergencies. Directs activities of HHS relating to the protection of the civilian population from acts of bioterrorism and other public health emergencies.

Health and Human Services Dept. (HHS), *President's Commission for the Study of Bioethical Issues, 1425 New York Ave. N.W., #C100, 20005; (202) 233-3960. Fax, (202) 233-3990. Amy Gutmann, Chair; Lisa M. Lee, Executive Director.*
General email, info@bioethics.gov
Web, www.bioethics.gov

Advisory panel of the nation's leaders in medicine, science, ethics, religion, law, and engineering. Advises the President on bioethical issues arising from advances in biomedicine and related areas of science and technology. Seeks to identify and promote policies and practices that ensure that scientific research, healthcare delivery, and technological innovation are conducted in a socially and ethically responsible manner.

Health Resources and Services Administration *(Health and Human Services Dept.), 5600 Fishers Lane, #13N192, Rockville, MD 20857; (301) 443-2216. Fax, (301) 443-1246. Jim Macrae, Administrator, Acting. Information, (301) 443-3376. TTY, (877) 897-9910.*
General email, askhrsa.gov
Web, www.hrsa.gov

Administers federal health service programs related to access, quality, equity, and cost of health care. Supports state and community efforts to deliver care to underserved areas and groups with special health needs. Oversees organ, bone marrow, and cord blood donation; compensates individuals harmed by vaccination; and maintains databases that protect against health care malpractice, waste, fraud, and abuse.

Health Resources and Services Administration *(Health and Human Services Dept.), Rural Health Policy, 5600 Fishers Lane, #17W45, Rockville, MD 20857; (301) 443-0835. Fax, (301) 443-2803. Tom Morris, Associate Administrator.*
General email, tmorris@hrsa.gov
Web, www.ruralhealth.hrsa.gov

Works with federal agencies, states, and the private sector to develop solutions to health care problems in rural communities. Administers grants to rural communities and supports rural health services research. Studies the effects of Medicare and Medicaid programs on rural access to health care.

Homeland Security Dept. (DHS), *Health Affairs, 650 Massachusetts Ave. N.W., MS 0020, 20528; (202) 254-6479. Alexander Garza, Assistant Secretary.*
General email, healthaffairs@dhs.gov
Web, www.dhs.gov/office-health-affairs

Guides DHS leaders on medical and public health issues related to national security; analyzes data and monitors biological and chemical threats and responses to pandemics.

National Aeronautics and Space Administration (NASA), *Chief Health and Medical Officer, 300 E St. S.W., 20546; (202) 358-2390. Fax, (202) 358-3349. Dr. Richard S. Williams, Chief Health and Medical Officer.*
Web, www.hq.nasa.gov/office/chmo

Ensures the health and safety of NASA employees in space and on the ground. Develops health and medical policy, establishes guidelines for health and medical practices, oversees health care delivery, and monitors human and animal research standards within the agency.

National Center for Health Statistics *(Centers for Disease Control and Prevention), 3311 Toledo Rd., #7204, Hyattsville, MD 20782; (301) 458-4800. Fax, (301) 458-4020. Charles J. Rothwell, Director. Information, (800) 232-4636.*
Web, www.cdc.gov/nchs

Compiles, analyzes, and disseminates national statistics on population health characteristics, health facilities and human resources, health costs and expenditures, and health hazards. Interests include international health statistics.

National Institute for Occupational Safety and Health (NIOSH) *(Centers for Disease Control and Prevention), 395 E St. S.W., Patriots Plaza 1, #9200, 20201; (202) 245-0625. Dr. John Howard, Director. Information, (800) 232-4636.*
General email, cdcinfo@cdc.gov
Web, www.cdc.gov/niosh

Supports and conducts research on occupational safety and health issues; provides technical assistance and training; organizes international conferences and symposia; develops recommendations for the Labor Dept. Operates occupational safety and health bibliographic databases; publishes documents on occupational safety and health.

National Institute of Standards and Technology (NIST) *(Commerce Dept.), Special Programs Office, 100 Bureau Dr., MS 1000, Gaithersburg, MD 20899-1000; (301) 975-4447. Fax, (301) 975-8972. Richard R. Cavanagh, Director. General information, (301) 975-2756.*
Web, www.nist.gov/director/spo

Fosters collaboration among government, military, academia, professional, and private organizations to respond to critical national needs through science-based standards and technology innovation, including areas of health.

National Institutes of Health (NIH) *(Health and Human Services Dept.), 1 Center Dr., Bldg. 1, #344, MSC 0188, Bethesda, MD 20892-0148; (301) 496-4000. Fax, (301) 496-0017. Dr. Francis S. Collins, Director; Dr. Lawrence A. Tabak, Deputy Director. Press, (301) 496-5787.*
Web, www.nih.gov

Supports and conducts biomedical research into the causes and prevention of diseases and furnishes information to health professionals and the public. Comprises research institutes and other components (the National Library of Medicine, the National Center for Advancing Translational Sciences, the John E. Fogarty International Center, and 27 institutes, including the National Cancer Institute; the National Institute of Allergy and Infectious Diseases; the National Heart, Lung, and Blood Institute; and the National Institute of Diabetes and Digestive and Kidney Diseases). All institutes are located in Bethesda, except the National Institute of Environmental Health Sciences, P.O. Box 12233, Research Triangle Park, N.C. 27709.

National Institutes of Health (NIH) *(Health and Human Services Dept.), Science Policy, 6705 Rockledge Dr., MSC 7985, Bethesda, MD 20892-7985; (301) 496-9838. Fax, (301) 496-9839. Carrie D. Wolinetz, Associate Director. General email, sciencepolicy@od.nih.gov*
Web, http://osp.od.nih.gov

Advises the NIH director on science policy issues affecting the medical research community. Participates in the development of new policy and program initiatives. Monitors and coordinates agency planning and evaluation activities. Plans and implements a comprehensive science education program. Develops and implements NIH policies and procedures for the safe conduct of recombinant DNA and other biotechnology activities.

National Research Council (NRC), *Health and Medicine Division, Keck Center, 500 5th St. N.W., 20001; (202) 334-2352. Victor Dzau, Chair.*
General email, HMD-NASEM@nas.edu
Web, www.nationalacademies.org/hmd

Advises the government and public sector on matters relating to medical research, care, and education; examines policy matters relating to health care and public health.

State Dept., *Medical Services, 2401 E St. N.W., #L218, 20522-0102; (202) 663-1649. Fax, (202) 663-1613. Dr. Charles Rosenfarb, Medical Director.*
Web, www.state.gov/m/med

Operates a worldwide primary health care system for U.S. citizen employees, and eligible family members, of participating U.S. government agencies. Conducts physical examinations of Foreign Service officers and candidates; provides clinical services; assists with medical evacuation of patients overseas.

► CONGRESS

For a listing of relevant congressional committees and subcommittees, please see pages 344–345 or the Appendix.

Government Accountability Office (GAO), *Health Care, 441 G St. N.W., #5A21, 20548; (202) 512-7114. Angela A. Bascetta, Managing Director.*
Web, www.gao.gov/careers/healthcare.html

Independent nonpartisan agency in the legislative branch. Audits all federal government health programs, including those administered by the departments of Defense, Health and Human Services, and Veterans Affairs.

► INTERNATIONAL ORGANIZATIONS

Consortium of Universities for Global Health, *1608 Rhode Island Ave. N.W., #211B, 20036; (202) 974-6363. Fax, (202) 833-5078. Keith Martin, Executive Director. General email, info@cugh.org*
Web, www.cugh.org and Twitter, @CUGHnews

Assists universities in sharing resources and research on global health challenges. Coordinates academic partnerships between national universities and international educational institutions in developing countries. Develops national and global health centers.

Pan American Health Organization, *525 23rd St. N.W., 20037; (202) 974-3000. Fax, (202) 974-3663. Dr. Carissa F. Etienne, Director.*
Web, www.paho.org

Works to extend health services to underserved populations of its member countries and to control or eradicate communicable diseases; promotes cooperation among governments to solve public health problems. (Regional Office for the Americas of the World Health Organization, which is headquartered in Geneva, Switzerland.)

World Bank, *Human Development Network, 1818 H St. N.W., 20433; (202) 473-1000. Keith Hanson, Vice President; Melanie Mayhew, Media Contact, (202) 458-7891. Web, www.worldbank.org*

Assists developing countries in delivering effective and affordable health care, education, and social services. Interests include poverty reduction, income protection, nutrition, jobs access, health coverage, and basic education.

▶**NONGOVERNMENTAL**

American Clinical Laboratory Assn., *1100 New York Ave. N.W., #725 West, 20005; (202) 637-9466. Fax, (202) 637-2050. Alan Mertz, President.*
General email, info@acla.com
Web, www.acla.com

Membership: laboratories and laboratory service companies. Advocates laws and regulations that recognize the role of laboratory services in cost-effective health care. Works to ensure the confidentiality of patient test results. Provides education, information, and research materials to members.

American Public Health Assn., *800 Eye St. N.W., 20001-3710; (202) 777-2742. Fax, (202) 777-2534. Dr. Georges Benjamin, Executive Director. TTY, (202) 777-2500.*
General email, comments@apha.org
Web, www.apha.org and Twitter, @PublicHealth

Membership: health providers, educators, environmentalists, policymakers, and health officials at all levels working both within and outside of governmental organizations and educational institutions. Works to protect communities from serious, preventable health threats. Strives to ensure that community-based health promotion and disease prevention activities and preventive health services are universally accessible in the United States. Develops standards for scientific procedures in public health.

American Red Cross, *Government Relations, 2025 E St. N.W., 20006-5009; (202) 303-4371. Cherae Bishop, Senior Vice President, Government Relations.*
General email, governmentrelations@redcross.org
Web, www.redcross.org/about-us/governance/government-relations

Works to create, through legislative and regulatory initiatives, a pubic policy environment that will forward the mission and objectives of the American Red Cross.

Assn. of State and Territorial Health Officials, *2231 Crystal Dr., #450, Arlington, VA 22202; (202) 371-9090. Fax, (571) 527-3189. Sharon Moffatt, Executive Director, Acting.*
Web, www.astho.org, www.statepublichealth.org and Twitter, @astho

Membership: executive officers of state and territorial health departments. Serves as legislative review agency and information source for members.

The Brookings Institution, *Economic Studies, 1775 Massachusetts Ave. N.W., 20036-2188; (202) 797-6000. Fax, (202) 797-6181. Ted Gayer, Director. Press, (202) 797-6105.*
General email, escomment@brookings.edu
Web, www.brookings.edu/economics

Studies federal health care issues and health programs, including Medicare, Medicaid, and long-term care.

Center for Economic and Policy Research (CEPR), *1611 Connecticut Ave. N.W., #400, 20009; (202) 293-5380. Fax, (202) 588-1356. Dean Baker, Co-Director; Mark Weisbrot, Co-Director.*
General email, info@cepr.net
Web, www.cepr.net and Twitter, @ceprdc

Researches economic and social issues and the impact of related public policies. Presents findings to the public with the goal of better preparing citizens to choose among various policy options. Promotes democratic debate and voter education. Areas of interest include health care, trade, financial reform, Social Security, taxes, housing, and the labor market.

Global Health Council, *1875 Connecticut Ave. N.W., 10th Floor, 20009; 1199 N. Fairfax St., Alexandria, VA 22314; (703) 717-5251. Fax, (703) 717-5215. Christina Sow, Executive Director.*
General email, membership@globalhealth.org
Web, www.globalhealth.org

Membership: students, health care professionals, NGOs, foundations, corporations, and academic institutions. Works to secure the information and resources for improved global health.

Grantmakers in Health, *1100 Connecticut Ave. N.W., #1200, 20036; (202) 452-8331. Fax, (202) 452-8340. Faith Mitchell, President.*
General email, info@gih.org
Web, www.gih.org and Twitter, @GIHealth

Seeks to increase the capacity of health foundations and giving programs to enhance public health. Fosters information exchange among grantmakers. Publications include a bulletin on current news in health and human services.

Health Policy Institute *(Georgetown University), 3300 Whitehaven St. N.W., #5000, Box 571444, 20057-1485; (202) 687-0880. Fax, (202) 687-3110. Toni McRae, Administrative Assistant.*
Web, http://ihcrp.georgetown.edu

Research branch of Georgetown University's Public Policy Institute. Interests include quality of care, cost effectiveness, outcomes research, structure and impact of managed care, health privacy, and access to care.

Healthcare Leadership Council, *750 9th St. N.W., #500, 20001; (202) 452-8700. Fax, (202) 296-9561. Mary R. Grealy, President; Michael Freeman, Executive Vice President.*
General email, mfreeman@hlc.org
Web, www.hlc.org

Membership: health care leaders who examine major health issues, including access and affordability. Works to implement new public policies.

Henry J. Kaiser Family Foundation, *Washington Office, 1330 G St. N.W., 20005; (202) 347-5270. Fax, (202) 347-5274. Drew Altman, President.*
Web, www.kff.org

Health and Human Services Department

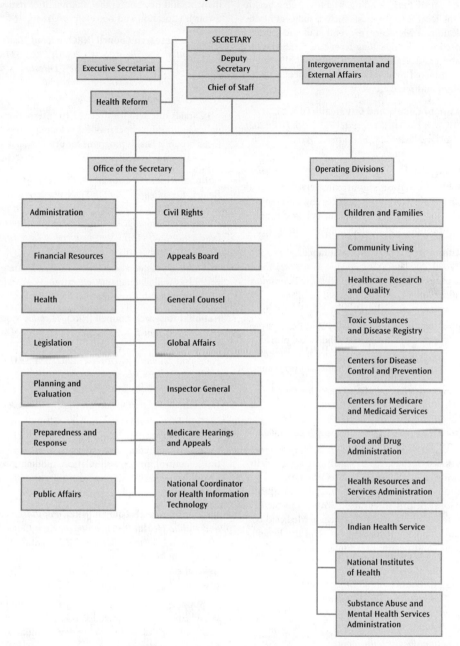

Offers information on major health care issues. Conducts research and communications programs. Monitors legislation and regulations. (Headquarters in Menlo Park, Calif. Not affiliated with Kaiser Permanente or Kaiser Industries.)

International Epidemiology Institute, *1455 Research Blvd., #550, Rockville, MD 20850; (301) 424-1054. Fax, (301) 424-1053. William J. Blot, Chief Executive Officer; Vacant, President.*
General email, info@iei.us

Web, www.iei.us

Investigates biomedical problems and environmental health issues for the public and private sectors, universities, and other institutions. Conducts studies and clinical trials. Helps identify potential risks and benefits associated with new medicines and new medical devices, including implants. (Affiliated with Vanderbilt University in Nashville, Tenn.)

National Assn. of Counties (NACo), *25 Massachusetts Ave. N.W., #500, 20001-2028; (202) 393-6226. Fax, (202) 393-2630. Matthew D. Chase, Executive Director. Press, (202) 942-4220. Toll-free, (888) 407-6226.*
Web, www.naco.org

Promotes federal understanding of county governments' role in providing, funding, and overseeing health services at the local level. Interests include indigent health care, Medicaid and Medicare, prevention of and services for HIV infection and AIDS, long-term care, mental health, maternal and child health, and traditional public health programs conducted by local health departments. Monitors legislation and regulations.

National Assn. of County and City Health Officials, *1100 17th St. N.W., 7th Floor, 20036; (202) 783-5550. Fax, (202) 783-1583. LaMar Hasbrouck, Executive Director.*
General email, info@naccho.org

Web, www.naccho.org

Represents the nation's approximately 2,800 local health departments. Develops resources and programs to support local public health practices and systems. Submits health policy proposals to the federal government.

National Committee for Quality Assurance, *1100 13th St. N.W., #1000, 20005; (202) 955-3500. Fax, (202) 955-3599. Margaret E. O'Kane, President. Toll-free information on health plans and accreditation, (888) 275-7585.*
Web, www.ncqa.org

Provides information on the quality of health care provided by health care institutions and individual providers. Assesses and reports on managed care plans through accreditation and performance measurement programs.

National Governors Assn. (NGA), *Center for Best Practices, Health Division, 444 N. Capitol St. N.W., #267, 20001-1512; (202) 624-5343. Fax, (202) 624-7825. Frederick Isasi, Director. Information, (202) 624-5300.*
Web, www.nga.org/cms/center/health

Covers issues in the areas of health care service delivery and reform, including payment reform, health workforce planning, quality improvement, and public health and behavioral health integration within the medical delivery system. Other focus areas include Medicaid cost containment, state employee and retiree health benefits, maternal and child health, prescription drug abuse prevention, and health insurance exchange planning.

National Health Council, *1730 M St. N.W., #500, 20036-4561; (202) 785-3910. Fax, (202) 785-5923. Marc M. Boutin, Chief Executive Officer.*
General email, info@nhcouncil.org

Web, www.nationalhealthcouncil.org

Membership: voluntary health agencies, associations, and business, insurance, and government groups interested in health. Conducts research on health and health-related issues. Monitors legislation and regulations.

National Quality Forum, *1030 15th St. N.W., #800, 20005; (202) 783-1300. Fax, (202) 783-3434. Christine Cassel, President. Press, (202) 478-9326.*
General email, info@qualityforum.org

Web, www.qualityforum.org

Works to improve the quality of health care in the United States by setting national priorities and goals for performance improvement, endorsing national consensus

standards for measuring and publicly reporting on performances, and promoting the attainment of national goals through education and outreach programs.

National Research Council (NRC), *Global Health Board, Keck Center, 500 5th St. N.W., 20001; (202) 334-2352. Fax, (202) 334-3861. Patrick Kelley, Director.*
General email, HMD-NASEM@nas.edu

Web, www.nationalacademies.org/hmd

Carries out activities related to international health policy and health concerns of developing countries; main focus is public health programs for prevention and control of disease and disability.

National Research Council (NRC), *Health Care Services Board, Keck Center, 500 5th St. N.W., 20001; (202) 334-3168. Fax, (202) 334-2862. Sharyl Nass, Board Director.*
Web, www.nationalacademies.org/hmd/About-HMD/Leadership-Staff/HMD-Staff-Leadership-Boards/Board-on-Health-Care-Services.aspx

Advises policymakers about the healthcare system in general as well as financing, effectiveness, workforce, and delivery of health care.

National Research Council (NRC), *Human-Systems Integration Board, Keck Center, 500 5th St. N.W., 11th Floor, 20001; (202) 334-2678. Fax, (202) 334-2210. Poornima Madhavan, Director, (202) 334-3357; Nancy J. Cooke, Chair.*
General email, bohsi@nas.edu

Web, http://sites.nationalacademies.org/dbasse/bohsi

Conducts studies on human factors and human-systems integration. Areas of research include virtual reality, human-computer interaction, nuclear safety, air traffic control, military simulation, modeling social networks, home health care, and disability and rehabilitation research.

National Research Council (NRC), *Population Health and Public Health Practice Board, Keck Center, 500 5th St. N.W., 20001; (202) 334-2383. Fax, (202) 334-2939. Rose Marie Martinez, Director.*
General email, iom_hpdp@nas.edu

Web, www.nationalacademies.org/hmd

Supports research on public health, including vaccine safety, pandemic preparedness issues, smoking cessation, health disparities, and reducing environmental and occupational hazards.

National Vaccine Information Center, *21525 Ridgetop Circle, #100, Sterling, VA 20166; (703) 938-0342. Fax, (571) 313-1268. Barbara Loe Fisher, President, (703) 938-0342.*
General email, contactnvic@gmail.com

Web, www.nvic.org

Educational organization that supports informed vaccination decisions, including the option to forgo vaccination. Provides assistance to parents of children who have experienced vaccine reactions and publishes information on diseases and vaccines. Monitors vaccine research, legislation, and regulations.

Partnership for Prevention, *200 M St. N.W. #400, 20036; (202) 828-5100. Fax, (202) 728-9469. Elissa Matulis Meyers, President. General email, info@prevent.org*

Web, www.prevent.org

Seeks to make prevention a priority in national health policy and practice. Coordinates the prevention-oriented efforts of federal health agencies, corporations, states, and nonprofit organizations in order to achieve the Healthy People 2020 national prevention goals. (A division of the Center for Prevention at Altarum.)

Public Citizen, *Health Research Group, 1600 20th St. N.W., 20009-1001; (202) 588-1000. Fax, (202) 588-7798. Michael Carome, Director. General email, hrg1@citizen.org*

Web, www.citizen.org/hrg and Twitter, @CitizenHRG

Citizens' interest group that conducts policy-oriented research on health care issues. Interests include hospital quality and costs, doctors' fees, physician discipline and malpractice, state administration of Medicare programs, workplace safety and health, unnecessary surgery, comprehensive health planning, dangerous drugs, carcinogens, and medical devices. Favors a single-payer (Canadian-style) comprehensive health program.

RAND Corporation, *Health Unit, Washington Office, 1200 S. Hayes St., Arlington, VA 22202-5050; (703) 413-1100. Fax, (703) 413-8111. Jeffrey Wasserman, Director, ext. 6693. General email, rand_health@rand.org*

Web, www.rand.org/health and Twitter, @RANDHealth

Research organization that assesses health issues, including alternative reimbursement schemes for health care. Interests include health care costs and quality, military health, obesity, chronic disease prevention, and public health preparedness. Monitors national and international trends. (Headquarters in Santa Monica, Calif.)

Regulatory Affairs Professionals Society, *5635 Fishers Lane, #550, Rockville, MD 20852; (301) 770-2920 ext. 200. Fax, (301) 841-7956. Sherry Keramidas, Executive Director. General email, raps@raps.org*

Web, www.raps.org and Twitter, @RAPSorg

Membership: regulatory professionals in the medical device, pharmaceutical, and biotechnology product sectors worldwide. Promotes the safety and effectiveness of health care products. Supports the regulatory profession with resources, including education and certification. Monitors legislation and regulations.

Urban Institute, *Health Policy Center, 2100 M St. N.W., 20037; (202) 833-7200. Fax, (202) 223-1149. Genevieve Kenney, Director; Stephen Zuckerman, Director. Web, http://healthpolicycenter.org*

Analyzes trends and underlying causes of changes in health insurance, coverage access to care, and use of health care services by the U.S. population. Researches and analyzes select health issues, including private insurance; the uninsured; Medicaid, Medicare, and the State Children's Health Insurance Program (SCHIP); disability and long-term care; vulnerable populations; and health care reform.

Health Insurance, Managed Care

►AGENCIES

Centers for Medicare and Medicaid Services (CMS) *(Health and Human Services Dept.), Center for Consumer Information and Insurance Oversight, 200 Independence Ave. S.W., #739H, 20001; (202) 260-6090. Fax, (202) 690-6518. Kevin Counihan, Director. Affordable care hotline, (888) 393-2789. General email, healthins@hhs.gov*

Web, http://cciio.cms.gov

Assists states in reviewing insurance rates, including oversight of administrative costs as a percentage of expenditures for medical care (medical loss ratio); provides guidance and oversight for state-based insurance exchanges; administers the pre-existing condition insurance plan, the temporary high-risk pool program, and the early retiree reinsurance program; compiles and maintains data for an Internet portal providing information on insurance options.

Centers for Medicare and Medicaid Services (CMS) *(Health and Human Services Dept.), Center for Medicare, 7500 Security Blvd., C5-01-14, Baltimore, MD 21244; (410) 786-0550. Fax, (410) 786-0192. Sean Cavanaugh, Director, (410) 786-3350. Information, (410) 786-3000. Web, www.cms.gov/medicare/medicare.html*

Manages the traditional fee-for-service Medicare program, which includes the development of payment policy and management of Medicare fee-for-service contractors.

►CONGRESS

For a listing of relevant congressional committees and subcommittees, please see pages 344–345 or the Appendix.

Congressional Budget Office, *Health, Retirement, and Long-Term Analysis, FHOB, 2nd and D Sts. S.W., 4th Floor, 20515-6925; (202) 226-2666. Fax, (202) 225-3149. Linda Bilheimer, Assistant Director. Web, www.cbo.gov*

Analyzes federal programs and policies concerning health care and retirement, including Medicare, Medicaid, subsidies to be provided through health insurance exchanges, and Social Security. Responsible for long-term budget protection and analyses of long-term effects of proposed legislation. Prepares reports to Congress.

►NONGOVERNMENTAL

Alliance for Health Reform, *1444 Eye St. N.W., #910, 20005-6573; (202) 789-2300. Fax, (202) 789-2233. Sarah Dash, Co-President; Marilyn Ferafini, Co-President.*

General email, info@allhealth.org

Web, www.allhealth.org

Nonpartisan organization that advocates health care reform, including cost containment and coverage for all. Sponsors conferences and seminars for journalists, business leaders, policymakers, and the public.

America's Health Insurance Plans, *601 Pennsylvania Ave. N.W., South Bldg., #500, 20004; (202) 778-3200. Fax, (202) 331-7487. Marilyn Tavenner, President. Press, (202) 778-8494.*

General email, ahip@ahip.org

Web, www.ahip.org

Membership: companies providing medical expense, long-term care, disability income, dental, supplemental, and stop-loss insurance and reinsurance to consumers, employers, and public purchasers. Advocates evidence-based medicine, targeted strategies for giving all Americans access to health care, and health care cost savings through regulatory, legal, and other reforms. Provides educational programs and legal counsel. Monitors legislation and regulations. (Merger of the American Assn. of Health Plans and Health Insurance Assn. of America.)

American Medical Assn. (AMA), *Government Relations, 25 Massachusetts Ave. N.W., #600, 20001-7400; (202) 789-7400. Fax, (202) 789-7485. Richard Deem, Senior Vice President of Advocacy.*

Web, www.ama-assn.org

Membership: physicians, residents, and medical students. Interests include the cost, quality, and access to health care; and physician payment and delivery innovation. Monitors legislation and regulations. (Headquarters in Chicago, Ill.)

Autism Speaks, *Washington Office, 1990 K St. N.W., 2nd Floor, 20006; (202) 955-3111. Angela Geiger, President. Toll-free, (888) 288-4762.*

Web, www.autismspeaks.org

Advocates insurance reform to maximize coverage for evidence-based treatments for autism and autism spectrum disorders.

Blue Cross and Blue Shield Assn., *Washington Office, 1310 G St. N.W., 20005; (202) 626-4780. Fax, (202) 626-4833. Scott Serota, President. Press, (202) 626-8625.*

Web, www.bcbs.com

Owns the Blue Cross and Blue Shield names and marks (brands) and grants several types of licenses to use them; also conducts trade association activities and operates businesses to support its license holders. (Headquarters in Chicago, Ill.)

Council for Affordable Health Coverage, *1101 14th St. N.W., #700, 20005; (202) 559-0205. Joel White, President.*

Web, http://cahc.net

Coalition of insurers, employers, patients, consumers, and pharmaceutical manufacturers and providers working to lower the cost of health care by educating health care consumers, promoting competitive and transparent

markets, expanding affordable coverage options, and supporting incentives for prevention.

Employee Benefit Research Institute, *1100 13th St. N.W., #878, 20005; (202) 659-0670. Fax, (202) 775-6312. Harry Conaway, President.*

General email, info@ebri.org

Web, www.ebri.org

Research organization serving as an employee benefits information source on health, welfare, and retirement issues. Does not lobby and does not take public policy positions.

Employers Council on Flexible Compensation, *1444 Eye St. N.W., #700, 20005; (202) 659-4300. Fax, (202) 216-9646. Martin Trussell, Executive Director.*

General email, info@ecfc.org

Web, www.ecfc.org

Represents employers who have or are considering flexible compensation plans. Supports the preservation and expansion of employee choice in health insurance coverage. Monitors legislation and regulations.

Galen Institute, *P.O. Box 320010, Alexandria, VA 22320; (703) 299-8900. Fax, (703) 299-0721. Grace-Marie Turner, President.*

General email, galen@galen.org

Web, www.galen.org

Provides ideas and information on health care financing, and the use of tax policy to advance consumer choice. Advocates health savings accounts, competition among private plans in Medicare, and other free-market health reform ideas.

The HSA Coalition, *1747 Pennsylvania Ave., 20006; (202) 271-3959. Dan Perrin, President.*

Web, www.hsacoalition.org

Analyzes health savings accounts' policies and issues. Monitors and regulates legislation to protect and expand the number of Americans who could choose to have a health savings account (HSA).

National Academy of Social Insurance, *1200 New Hampshire Ave. N.W., #830, 20036; (202) 452-8097. Fax, (202) 452-8111. William J. Arnone, Chair.*

General email, nasi@nasi.org

Web, www.nasi.org

Promotes research and education on Social Security, Medicare, health care financing, and related public and private programs; assesses social insurance programs and their relationship to other programs; supports research and leadership development. Acts as a clearinghouse for social insurance information.

National Assn. of Health Underwriters, *1212 New York Ave. N.W., #1100, 20005; (202) 552-5060. Fax, (202) 747-6820. Janet Trautwein, Executive Vice President. Press, (202) 595-0724.*

General email, info@nahu.org

Web, www.nahu.org

Membership: licensed health insurance agents, brokers, consultants, and benefit professionals. Offers continuing education programs as well as business-development tools. Promotes private sector health insurance. Monitors legislation and regulations.

National Assn. of Manufacturers (NAM), *Human Resources Policy,* 733 10th St. N.W., #700, 20001; (202) 637-3127. Fax, (202) 637-3182. Joe Trauger, Vice President. Alternate phone, (202) 637-3000.
Web, www.nam.org

Interests include health care, Social Security, employee benefits, cost containment, mandated benefits, Medicare, and other federal programs that affect employers. Opposed to government involvement in health care.

National Business Group on Health, 20 F St. N.W., #200, 20001-6705; (202) 558-3000. Fax, (202) 628-9244. Brian Marcotte, President, (202) 558-3005.
General email, info@businessgrouphealth.org
Web, www.businessgrouphealth.org

Membership: large corporations with an interest in health care benefits. Interests include reimbursement policies, disease prevention and health promotion, hospital cost containment, health care planning, corporate education, Medicare, and retiree medical costs. Monitors legislation and regulations.

National Coalition on Health Care, 1825 K St. N.W., #411, 20005; (202) 638-7151. John Rother, Chief Executive Officer.
Web, www.nchc.org

Membership: insurers, labor organizations, large and small businesses, consumer groups, and healthcare providers. Advocates for affordable high quality health care. Monitors legislation and regulations.

National Health Care Anti-Fraud Assn., 1220 L St. N.W., #600, 20005; (202) 659-5955. Fax, (202) 785-6764. Louis Saccoccio, Chief Executive Officer.
General email, nhcaa@nhcaa.org
Web, www.nhcua.org

Membership: health insurance companies and regulatory and law enforcement agencies. Members work to identify, investigate, and prosecute individuals and groups defrauding health care reimbursement systems. Offers education and training for fraud investigators, including medical identity theft. Sponsors the Institute for Health Care Fraud Prevention.

ProtectSeniors.Org, 601 Pennsylvania Ave., South Bldg., #900, 20004; (202) 434-8193. Fax, (540) 439-9570. Jim Casey, President; Paul Miller, Executive Director. Toll-free, (800) 398-3044.
General email, info@protectseniors.org
Web, www.protectseniors.org and Twitter, @ProtectSeniors

Aims to illegalize the corporate discontinuation of promised health care benefits after employees have retired. Acts as advocate against pension stripping. Monitors legislation and regulation.

Society of Professional Benefit Administrators, 2 Wisconsin Circle, #670, Chevy Chase, MD 20815; (301) 718-7722. Fax, (301) 718-9440. Anne Lennan, President. General email, info@spbatpa.org
Web, www.spbatpa.org

Membership: third-party administration firms that manage employee benefit plans for client employers. Interests include health care regulations, employee benefits, revision of Medicare programs, and health care cost containment. Monitors industry trends, government compliance requirements, and developments in health care financing.

Hospitals

▶AGENCIES

Centers for Medicare and Medicaid Services (CMS) (Health and Human Services Dept.), Survey and Certification Group, 7500 Security Blvd., C2-21-16, Baltimore, MD 21244-1850; (410) 786-9493. Fax, (410) 786-0194. Thomas Hamilton, Director; Jan Tarantino, Deputy Director, (410) 786-0905.
Web, www.cms.gov/medicare/medicare.html

Enforces health care and safety standards for hospitals, nursing homes, and other health care facilities.

▶CONGRESS

For a listing of relevant congressional committees and subcommittees, please see pages 344–345 or the Appendix.

▶NONGOVERNMENTAL

America's Essential Hospitals, 401 Ninth St. N.W. #900, 20004; (202) 585-0100. Fax, (202) 585-0101. Dr. Bruce Siegel, Chief Executive Officer.
General email, info@essentialhospitals.org
Web, www.essentialhospitals.org

Membership: city and county public hospitals, state universities, and hospital districts and authorities. Interests include Medicaid patients and vulnerable populations, including AIDS patients, the homeless, the mentally ill, and non-English-speaking patients. Holds annual regional meetings. Monitors legislation and regulations. (Formerly National Assn. of Public Hospitals and Health Systems.)

American Hospital Assn., *Washington Office,* Two City Center, #400, 800 10th St. N.W., 20001; (202) 638-1100. Fax, (202) 626-2303. Richard J. (Rick) Pollack, President, (202) 626-2363. Information, (800) 424-4301.
Web, www.aha.org

Membership: hospitals, other inpatient care facilities, outpatient centers, Blue Cross plans, areawide planning agencies, regional medical programs, hospital schools of nursing, and individuals. Conducts research and education projects in such areas as provision of comprehensive care, hospital economics, hospital facilities and design,

Centers for Medicare and Medicaid Services

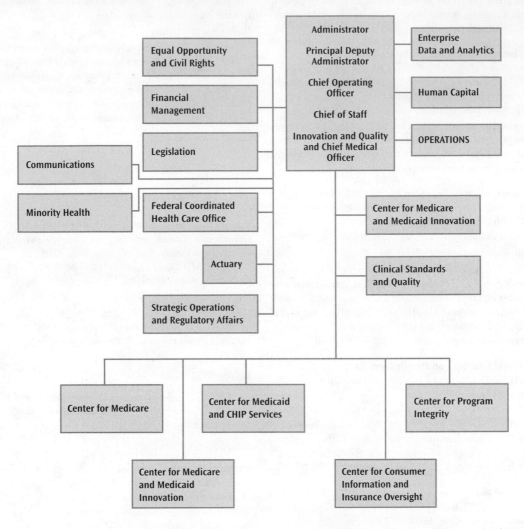

and community relations; participates with other health care associations in establishing hospital care standards. Monitors legislation and regulations. (Headquarters in Chicago, Ill.)

American Medical Rehabilitation Providers Assn. (AMRPA), *1710 N St. N.W., 20036; (202) 223-1920. Fax, (202) 223-1925. Carolyn Zollar, Executive Vice President, Government Relations. Toll-free, (888) 346-4624. Web, www.amrpa.org*

Association representing a membership of free-standing rehabilitation hospitals and rehabilitation units of general hospitals, outpatient rehabilitation facilities, skilled nursing facilities, and others. Provides leadership, advocacy, and resources to develop medical rehabilitation services and supports for persons with disabilities and others in need of services. Acts as a clearinghouse for information to members on the nature and availability of services. Monitors legislation and regulations.

Assn. of Academic Health Centers, *1400 16th St. N.W., #720, 20036; (202) 265-9600. Fax, (202) 265-7514. Dr. Steven Wartman, President. Web, www.aahcdc.org and Twitter, @aahcdc*

Membership: academic health centers (composed of a medical school, a teaching hospital, and at least one other health professional school or program). Participates in studies and public debates on health professionals' training and education, patient care, and biomedical research.

Children's Hospital Association, *Washington Office, 600 13th St. N.W., #500, 20005; (202) 753-5500. Fax, (202) 347-5147. Mark Weitecha, President. Web, www.childrenshospitals.org, Twitter, @hospitals4kids and Facebook, www.facebook.com/childrenshospitals*

Membership: more than 220 children's hospitals nationwide. Acts as a resource for pediatric data and analytics for clinical and operational performance. Monitors state and federal issues on clinical care, education, research, and advocacy. (Merger of the Child Health Corporation of America, National Assn. of Children's Hospitals and Related Institutions, and National Assn. of Children's Hospitals.)

Federation of American Hospitals, *750 9th St. N.W., #600, 20001-4524; (202) 624-1500. Fax, (202) 737-6462. Charles N. Kahn III, President. Press, (202) 624-1527. General email, info@fah.org*

Web, www.fah.org and Twitter, @FedAmerHospital

Membership: investor-owned or federally owned or managed community hospitals and health systems. Interests include national health care issues, such as cost containment, Medicare and Medicaid, the tax code, and the hospital workforce. Monitors legislation and regulations.

Medicaid and Medicare

▶AGENCIES

Centers for Medicare and Medicaid Services (CMS) *(Health and Human Services Dept.), 200 Independence Ave. S.W., #314G, 20201; (202) 690-6726. Fax, (202) 690-6262. Andy Slavitt, Administrator, Acting; Dr. Mandy Cohen, Chief of Staff. Information, (410) 786-3000. Toll-free, (877) 267-2323. TTY, (866) 226-1819. Web, www.cms.gov*

Administers Medicare (a health insurance program for persons with disabilities or age sixty-five or older who are eligible to participate) and Medicaid (a health insurance program for persons judged unable to pay for health services).

Centers for Medicare and Medicaid Services (CMS) *(Health and Human Services Dept.), Center for Medicaid and CHIP Services, 7500 Security Blvd., #C5-21-17, Baltimore, MD 21244; (410) 786-3871. Fax, (410) 786-0025. Victoria (Vikki) Wachino, Director; Tim Hill, Deputy Director. Web, www.cms.gov/About-CMS/Agency-Information/ CMSLeadership/office_CMCSC.html and www.medicaid.gov*

Administers and monitors Medicaid programs to ensure program quality and financial integrity; promotes beneficiary awareness and access to services.

Centers for Medicare and Medicaid Services (CMS) *(Health and Human Services Dept.), Center for Medicare, 7500 Security Blvd., C5-01-14, Baltimore, MD 21244; (410) 786-0550. Fax, (410) 786-0192. Sean Cavanaugh, Director, (410) 786-3350. Information, (410) 786-3000. Web, www.cms.gov/medicare/medicare.html*

Manages the contractual framework for the Medicare program; establishes and enforces performance standards for contractors who process and pay Medicare claims. Issues regulations and guidelines for administration of the Medicare program.

Centers for Medicare and Medicaid Services (CMS) *(Health and Human Services Dept.), Center for Medicare and Medicaid Innovation, 2810 Lord Baltimore Dr., Baltimore, MD 21244; (410) 786-3000.*

Dr. Patrick Conway, Deputy Administrator, Innovation and Quality. General email, innovate@cms.hhs.gov

Web, www.innovations.cms.gov and Twitter, @CMSInnovates

Established pursuant to the Affordable Care Act of 2010 to explore innovative approaches to Medicare, Medicaid, and CHIP health care delivery and administration, with the goal of improving health outcomes and lowering costs. Solicits input from health care providers, the business community, patients and families, and other interested parties in order to indentify best practices. Funds state demonstration projects to evaluate integrated care and payment approaches.

Centers for Medicare and Medicaid Services (CMS) *(Health and Human Services Dept.), Chronic Care Management, 7500 Security Blvd., C5-05-27, Baltimore, MD 21244; (410) 786-4533. Fax, (410) 786-0765. Janet P. Samen, Director, (410) 786-4533. TTY, (866) 226-1819. Web, www.cms.gov/medicare/medicare.html*

Administers coverage policy and payment for Medicare patients with end-stage renal disease and psychiatric inpatient and outpatient services for the severely mentally ill.

Centers for Medicare and Medicaid Services (CMS) *(Health and Human Services Dept.), Clinical Standards and Quality, 7500 Security Blvd., S3-02-01, Baltimore, MD 21244; (410) 786-6841. Fax, (410) 786-6857. Dr. Kate Goodrich, Director; Dr. Patrick Conway, Deputy Administrator. Web, www.cms.gov/About-CMS/Agency-Information/ CMSLeadership/Office_CCSQ.html*

Develops, establishes, and enforces standards that regulate the quality of care of hospitals and other health care facilities under Medicare and Medicaid programs. Administers operations of survey and peer review organizations that enforce health care standards, primarily for institutional care.

Centers for Medicare and Medicaid Services (CMS) *(Health and Human Services Dept.), Disabled and Elderly Health Programs Group, 7500 Security Blvd., S2-14-26, Baltimore, MD 21244; (410) 786-0325. Fax, (410) 786-9004. Michael Nardone, Director. Web, www.medicaid.gov*

Reviews all benefit and pharmacy state plan amendments for all Medicaid populations, Medicaid managed-care delivery systems, home-based and community-based services, and long-term services. Supports transformation grant programs, including Money Follows the Person and the Balancing Incentive Program.

Centers for Medicare and Medicaid Services (CMS) *(Health and Human Services Dept.), Enterprise Information, 7500 Security Blvd., C5-02-00, Baltimore, MD 21244; (410) 786-5544. Fax, (410) 786-1810. David Nelson, Director, (410) 786-5246. Web, www.cms.gov*

Serves as primary federal statistical office for disseminating economic data on Medicare and Medicaid.

Health Resources and Services Administration *(Health and Human Services Dept.), Rural Health Policy,* 5600 Fishers Lane, #17W45, Rockville, MD 20857; (301) 443-0835. Fax, (301) 443-2803. Tom Morris, Associate Administrator.
General email, tmorris@hrsa.gov

Web, www.ruralhealth.hrsa.gov

Studies the effects of Medicare and Medicaid programs on rural access to health care.

▶**NONGOVERNMENTAL**

Federation of American Hospitals, 750 9th St. N.W., #600, 20001-4524; (202) 624-1500. Fax, (202) 737-6462. Charles N. Kahn III, President. Press, (202) 624-1527.
General email, info@fah.org

Web, www.fah.org and Twitter, @FedAmerHospital

Membership: investor-owned, for-profit hospitals and health care systems. Studies Medicaid and Medicare reforms. Maintains speakers bureau; compiles statistics on investor-owned hospitals. Monitors legislation and regulations.

Medicare Rights Center, 1825 K St. N.W., #400, 20006; (202) 637-0961. Fax, (202) 637-0962. Joe Baker, President. Press, (212) 201-6286. Helpline, (800) 333-4114.
General email, info@medicarerights.org

Web, www.medicarerights.org

Advocates affordable health care for seniors and people with disabilities. Educates the public on medicare rights and benefits. Provides free Medicare counseling, as well as courses and training to health care professionals. Monitors legislation and regulations.

National Committee to Preserve Social Security and Medicare, 10 G St. N.E., #600, 20002-4215; (202) 216-0420. Fax, (202) 216-0446. Max Richtman, President. Press, (202) 216-8378. Senior hotline/Legislative updates, (800) 998-0180.
General email, webmaster@ncpssm.org

Web, www.ncpssm.org, Twitter, @NCPSSM and Facebook, www.facebook.com/NationalCommittee

Educational and advocacy organization that focuses on Social Security and Medicare programs and on related income security and health issues. Interests include retirement income protection, health care reform, and the quality of life of seniors. Monitors legislation and regulations.

Medical Devices and Technology

▶**AGENCIES**

Access Board, 1331 F St. N.W., #1000, 20004-1111; (202) 272-0080. Fax, (202) 272-0081. David M. Capozzi, Executive Director, (202) 272-0010. Toll-free technical assistance, (800) 872-2253. TTY, (202) 272-0082. Toll-free TTY, (800) 993-2822.

General email, info@access-board.gov

Web, www.access-board.gov

Develops and maintains accessibility requirements for buildings, transit vehicles, telecommunications equipment, medical diagnostic equipment, and electronic and information technology. Provides technical assistance and training on these guidelines and standards. Enforces access standards for federally funded facilities through the Architectural Barriers Act.

Armed Forces Radiobiology Research Institute *(Defense Dept.),* 8901 Wisconsin Ave., Bldg. 42, Bethesda, MD 20889-5603; (301) 295-0530. Fax, (301) 295-9477. Col. L. Andrew Huff (USAF, MC), Director. Public Affairs, (301) 295-1214.
Web, www.usuhs.edu/afrri

Serves as the principal ionizing radiation radiobiology research laboratory under the jurisdiction of the Uniformed Services University of the Health Sciences. Educates and trains radiation biologists. Participates in international conferences and projects.

Food and Drug Administration (FDA) *(Health and Human Services Dept.), Center for Devices and Radiological Health,* 10903 New Hampshire Ave., W066, Silver Spring, MD 20993; (301) 796-5900. Fax, (301) 847-8510. Jeffrey E. Shuren, Director.
General email, jeff.shuren@fda.hhs.gov

Web, www.fda.gov/medicaldevices and www.fda.gov/AboutFDA/CentersOffices/OfficeofMedicalProductsandTobacco/CDRH

Evaluates safety, efficacy, and labeling of medical devices; classifies devices; establishes performance standards; assists in legal actions concerning medical devices; coordinates research and testing; conducts training and educational programs. Maintains an international reference system to facilitate trade in devices. Library open to the public.

Food and Drug Administration (FDA) *(Health and Human Services Dept.), Combination Products,* W032 Hub/Mail Room #5129, 10903 New Hampshire Ave., Silver Spring, MD 20993; (301) 796-8930. Fax, (301) 847-8619. Thinh X. Nguyen, Director.
General email, combination@fda.gov

Web, www.fda.gov/oc/CombinationProducts

Seeks to streamline the processing of complex drug-device, drug-biologic, and device-biologic combination products. Responsibilities cover the entire regulatory lifecycle of combination products, including jurisdiction decisions as well as the timeliness and effectiveness of pre-market review, and the consistency and appropriateness of post-market regulation. Responsible for the classification of medical or biological products.

Food and Drug Administration (FDA) *(Health and Human Services Dept.), Industry and Consumer Education,* 10903 New Hampshire Ave., Silver Spring, MD 20993; (301) 796-7100. Fax, (301) 847-8149. Elias Mallis, Director, (301) 796-6216. Toll-free, (800) 638-2041.

General email, DICE@fda.hhs.gov

Web, www.fda.gov/MedicalDevices/
DeviceRegulationandGuidance/ContactUs–
DivisionofIndustryandConsumerEducation

Serves as liaison between small-business manufacturers of medical devices and the FDA. Assists manufacturers in complying with FDA regulatory requirements;
sponsors seminars.

**National Institute of Biomedical Imaging and
Bioengineering** *(National Institutes of Health)*, 9000
Rockville Pike, Bldg. 31, #1C14, Bethesda, MD 20892; (301)
496-8859. Fax, (301) 480-0679. Dr. Roderic I. Pettigrew,
Director.
General email, info@nibib.nih.gov

Web, www.nibib.nih.gov, Twitter, @NIBIBgov and
Facebook, www.facebook.com/nibibgov

Conducts and supports research and development of
biomedical imaging and bioengineering techniques and
devices to improve the prevention, detection, and treatment of disease.

National Library of Medicine *(National Institutes of
Health)*, **Lister Hill National Center for Biomedical
Communications**, 8600 Rockville Pike, Bldg. 38A,
#07N707, Bethesda, MD 20894; (301) 496-4441.
Dr. Clement McDonald, Director. Visitor's Center, (301)
496-7771.
Web, http://lhncbc.nlm.nih.gov

A research and development division of the National
Library of Medicine. Conducts and supports research and
development in the dissemination of high-quality imagery, medical language processing, high-speed access to
biomedical information, intelligent database systems
development, multimedia visualization, knowledge management, data mining, machine-assisted indexing, termi-
nology, and data structure and standards for exchanging
clinical data.

▶NONGOVERNMENTAL

Advanced Medical Technology Assn., 701 Pennsylvania
Ave. N.W., #800, 20004-2654; (202) 783-8700. Fax, (202)
783-8750. Vincent Forlenza, President.
General email, info@advamed.org

Web, www.advamed.org

Membership: manufacturers of medical devices, diagnostic products, and health care information systems.
Interests include safe and effective medical devices; conducts educational seminars. Monitors legislation, regulations, and international issues.

American Assn. for Homecare, 1707 L St. N.W., #350,
20036; (202) 372-0107. Fax, (202) 835-8306. Thomas Ryan,
President. Toll-free, (866) 289-0492.
General email, info@aahomecare.org

Web, www.aahomecare.org

Membership: home medical equipment manufacturers
and home health care service providers. Works to serve
the medical needs of Americans who require oxygen
equipment and therapy, mobility assistive technologies,
medical supplies, inhalation drug therapy, home infusion,
and other home medical services. Provides members with
education, training, and information about industry trends.
Monitors legislation and regulations.

American College of Radiology, Washington Office, 505
9th St. N.W., #910, 20004; 1891 Preston White Dr., Reston,
VA 20191-4326; (703) 648-8900. Fax, (703) 295-6773.
Cynthia Moran, Senior Director, Government Relations,
(202) 223-1670; Dr. William Thorwarth Jr., Chief Executive
Officer. Toll-free, (800) 227-5463.
General email, info@acr.org

Web, www.acr.org

Membership: certified radiologists and medical physicists in the United States and Canada. Develops programs
in radiation protection, technologist training, practice
standards, and health care insurance; maintains a placement service for radiologists; participates in international
conferences.

American Institute of Ultrasound in Medicine, 14750
Sweitzer Lane, #100, Laurel, MD 20707-5906; (301) 498-
4100. Fax, (301) 498-4450. Carmine Valente, Chief
Executive Officer. Toll-free, (800) 638-5352.
General email, admin@aium.org

Web, www.aium.org and Twitter, @AIUM_Ultrasound

Membership: medical professionals who use ultrasound technology in their practices. Promotes multidisciplinary research and education on safe and effective use of
diagnostic ultrasound through conventions and educational programs. Develops guidelines for accreditation.
Monitors international research.

American Medical Informatics Assn., 4720 Montgomery
Lane, #500, Bethesda, MD 20814; (301) 657-1291.
Fax, (301) 657-1296. Dr. Douglas Fridsma, President;
Karen Greenwood, Chief Operating Officer.
General email, mail@amia.org

Web, www.amia.org and Twitter, @AMIAinformatics

Membership: medical professionals and students interested in informatics. Studies and pursues effective uses of
biomedical data, information, and knowledge for scientific
inquiry, problem solving, and decision making to improve
human health. Applications include basic and applied
research, clinical services, consumer services, and public
health.

American Orthotic and Prosthetic Assn., 330 John
Carlyle St., #200, Alexandria, VA 22314-5760; (571) 431-
0876. Fax, (571) 431-0899. Tom Fise, Executive Director,
(571) 431-0802.
General email, info@aopanet.org

Web, www.aopanet.org and Twitter, @AmericanOandP

Membership: companies that manufacture or supply
artificial limbs and braces, and patient care professionals
who fit and supervise their use.

American Roentgen Ray Society, 44211 Slatestone Court,
Leesburg, VA 20176-5109; (703) 729-3353.

Fax, (703) 729-4839. Susan B. Cappitelli, Executive Director. Toll-free, (866) 940-2777.
General email, info@arrs.org
Web, www.arrs.org and Twitter, @ARRS_Radiology

Membership: physicians and researchers in radiology and allied sciences. Publishes research; conducts conferences; presents scholarships and awards; monitors international research.

Health Industry Distributors Assn., *310 Montgomery St., Alexandria, VA 22314-1516; (703) 549-4432. Fax, (703) 549-6495. Matthew Rowan, President.*
General email, hida@hida.org
Web, www.hida.org

Membership: medical products distributors. Sponsors and conducts trade shows and training seminars. Monitors legislation and regulations.

National Research Council (NRC), *Nuclear and Radiation Studies Board, Keck Center, 500 5th St. N.W., 20001; (202) 334-3066. Fax, (202) 334-3077. Kevin Crowley, Senior Board Director; Robert C. Dynes, Chair.*
General email, nrsb@nas.edu
Web, http://dels.nas.edu/nrsb

Oversee studies on safety, security, technical efficacy, and other policy and societal issues arising from the application of nuclear and radiation-based technologies, including exposure to radiation; generation, use, remediation, and disposition of nuclear materials and radioactive wastes; malevolent uses of nuclear and radiation-based technologies; and risks and benefits of nuclear and radiation-based applications, including medical applications.

The Optical Society, *2010 Massachusetts Ave. N.W., 20036; (202) 223-8130. Fax, (202) 223-1096. Elizabeth Rogan, Chief Executive Officer.*
General email, info@osa.org
Web, www.osa.org

Membership: global optics and photonic scientists, engineers, educators, students, technicians, business professionals, and others interested in optics and photonics worldwide. Promotes research and information exchange; conducts conferences; publishes a scientific journal; sponsors technical groups and programming as well as outreach and educational activities.

Program for Appropriate Technology in Health (PATH), *Washington Office, 455 Massachusetts Ave. N.W., #1000, 20001; (202) 822-0033. Fax, (202) 457-1466. Steve Davis, President.*
General email, info@path.org
Web, www.path.org

Develops, tests, and implements health technologies and strategies for low-resource countries. Works with community groups, other nongovernmental organizations, governments, companies, and UN agencies to expand the most successful programs. Interests include reproductive health, immunization, maternal-child health, emerging and epidemic diseases, and nutrition. (Headquarters in Seattle, Wash.)

Nursing Homes and Hospices

▶ **AGENCIES**

Centers for Medicare and Medicaid Services (CMS) *(Health and Human Services Dept.), Continuing Care Providers, 7500 Security Blvd., C2-21-16, Baltimore, MD 21244-1850; (410) 786-4857. Fax, (410) 786-0194. Peggye Wilkerson, Director.*
Web, www.cms.gov

Monitors compliance with government standards of psychiatric hospitals and long-term and intermediate care facilities, including residential treatment facilities, community mental health centers, intermediate care facilities for mental retardation, outpatient rehabilitation facilities, home health care, hospice care, portable X-ray units, dialysis facilities, and outpatient physical, language, and speech therapy facilities. Focus includes quality of care, environmental conditions, and participation in Medicaid and Medicare programs. Coordinates health care programs for the mentally challenged.

Centers for Medicare and Medicaid Services (CMS) *(Health and Human Services Dept.), Nursing Homes, 7500 Security Blvd., C2-21-16, Baltimore, MD 21244; (410) 786-7818. Fax, (410) 786-0194. Karen Tritz, Director.*
Web, www.cms.gov

Monitors compliance of nursing homes with government standards. Focus includes quality of care, environmental conditions, and participation in Medicaid and Medicare programs.

Centers for Medicare and Medicaid Services (CMS) *(Health and Human Services Dept.), Survey and Certification Group, 7500 Security Blvd., C2-21-16, Baltimore, MD 21244-1850; (410) 786-9493. Fax, (410) 786-0194. Thomas Hamilton, Director; Jan Tarantino, Deputy Director, (410) 786-0905.*
Web, www.cms.gov/medicare/medicare.html

Enforces health care and safety standards for nursing homes and other long-term care facilities.

▶ **NONGOVERNMENTAL**

AARP, *Federal Affairs Health and Family, 601 E St. N.W., 20049; (202) 434-3770. Fax, (202) 434-3745. Ariel Gonzalez, Director of Health and Family Advocacy. Main switchboard, (202) 434-2277.*
Web, www.aarp.org

Maintains the Legal Counsel for the Elderly, which acts as advocate on behalf of older residents of the District of Columbia who reside in nursing homes and board and care homes. Monitors legislation and regulations.

American College of Health Care Administrators, *1321 Duke St., #400, Alexandria, VA 22314; (202) 536-5120. Fax, (866) 874-1585. Cecilia Sepp, President.*
General email, info@achca.org
Web, www.achca.org

Membership: administrators of long-term health care organizations and facilities, including home health care programs, hospices, day care centers for the elderly, nursing and hospital facilities, retirement communities, assisted living communities, and mental health care centers. Conducts research on statistical characteristics of nursing home and other medical administrators; conducts seminars and workshops; offers education courses; provides certification for administrators.

American Health Care Assn., *1201 L St. N.W., 20005; (202) 842-4444. Fax, (202) 842-3860. Mark Parkinson, President. Publication orders, (800) 321-0343. Press, (202) 898-3165.*
General email, help@hctrendtracker.com
Web, www.ahcancal.org

Association of facility-based long-term and post-acute care providers and affiliates of state health organizations. Advocates high-quality care and services for frail, elderly, and disabled Americans, communicating with government, business leaders, and the general public. Provides information, education, and administrative tools. Monitors legislation and regulations.

Argentum, *1650 King St., #602, Alexandria, VA 22314; (703) 894-1805. Fax, (703) 894-1831. James Balda, President. Press, (703) 562-1185.*
General email, info@alfa.org
Web, www.alfa.org

Represents operators of communities for seniors, including independent-living, assisted-living, and Alzheimer's care facilities, but not including nursing homes or hospices. Promotes the development of standards and increased awareness for the senior living industry. Provides members with information on policy, funding access, and quality of care. Interests include informed choice, safe environments, caring and competent staff, and funding alternatives to increase accessibility to senior communities. Monitors legislation and regulations. (Formerly Assisted Living Federation of America.)

CCAL – Advancing Person-Centered Living, *2342 Oak St., Falls Church, VA 22046; (703) 533-3225. Jackie Pinkowitz, Chair; Karen Love, Founder.*
General email, info@ccal.org
Web, www.ccal.org

Educates consumers, trains professionals, and acts as advocate on assisted living issues, and home and community services.

Hospice Foundation of America, *1710 Rhode Island Ave. N.W., #400, 20036; (202) 457-5811. Fax, (202) 457-5815. Amy Tucci, President. Toll-free, (800) 854-3402.*
General email, hfaoffice@hospicefoundation.org
Web, www.hospicefoundation.org

Acts as an advocate for the hospice style of health care through ongoing programs of public education and training, information dissemination, and research.

National Assn. for Home Care and Hospice, *228 7th St. S.E., 20003; (202) 547-7424. Fax, (202) 547-3540. Val J. Halamandaris, President.*

General email, info@nahc.org
Web, www.nahc.org

Membership: hospice, home care, and private-duty providers and other community service organizations assisting those with chronic health problems or life-threatening illness. Works to educate and provide information for the public on hospice and home care. Interests include Medicare, Medicaid, and other insurance for home care and hospice. Monitors legislation and regulations.

National Center for Assisted Living, *1201 L St. N.W., 20005; (202) 842-4444. Fax, (202) 842-3860. Lindsay Schwartz, Director, Workforce and Quality Improvement Programs. Public Affairs, (202) 898-2825.*
General email, lgluckstern@ncal.org
Web, www.ahcancal.org/ncal

Membership: assisted living professionals. Provides networking opportunities and professional development; hosts educational seminars and an annual convention. Provides free resources for consumers looking into assisted living and other long-term care resources. Monitors legislation and regulations. (Affiliated with American Health Care Assn.)

National Consumer Voice for Quality Long-Term Care (NCCNHR), *1001 Connecticut Ave. N.W., #425, 20036; (202) 332-2275. Fax, (866) 230-9789. Lori O. Smetanka, Executive Director, Acting; Amanda Overall Laib, National Long-Term Care Ombudsman Resource Center Director, Acting.*
General email, info@theconsumervoice.org
Web, www.theconsumervoice.org and Facebook, www.facebook.com/theconsumervoice

Advocates high-quality care and quality of life for consumers in all long-term care settings. Promotes citizen participation in all aspects of nursing homes; acts as clearinghouse for nursing home advocacy. Hosts National Long-Term Care Ombudsman Resource Center.

National Hospice and Palliative Care Organization, *1731 King St., Alexandria, VA 22314; (703) 837-1500. Fax, (703) 837-1233. J. Donald (Don) Schumacher, President; Amanda Bow, Communications. Press, (703) 837-3139. Toll-free consumer information and referral helpline, (800) 658-8898.*
General email, nhpco_info@nhpco.org
Web, www.nhpco.org, Twitter, @NHPCO_news and Facebook, www.facebook.com/NHPCO

Membership: institutions and individuals providing hospice and palliative care and other interested organizations and individuals. Promotes supportive care for the terminally ill and their families; sets hospice program standards; provides information on hospices. Monitors legislation and regulations. Consumer Web site can be found at www.caringinfo.org.

National Long-Term Care Ombudsman Resource Center, *1001 Connecticut Ave. N.W., #425, 20036; (202) 332-2275, ext. 222. Fax, (202) 332-2949. Lori O. Smetanka, Director.*

General email, ombudcenter@theconsumervoice.org

Web, www.ltcombudsman.org

Provides technical assistance, management guidance, policy analysis, and program development information on behalf of state and substate ombudsman programs. (Affiliate of the National Consumer Voice for Quality Long-Term Care.)

Pharmaceuticals

▶**AGENCIES**

Federal Trade Commission (FTC), *Bureau of Consumer Protection, Advertising Practices, 400 7th Ave. S.W., #10418, 20024; (202) 326-3090. Fax, (202) 326-3259. Mary Engle, Associate Director.*

Web, www.ftc.gov/about-ftc/bureaus-offices/bureau-consumer-protection/our-divisions/division-advertising-practices

Protects consumers from deceptive and unsubstantiated advertising through law enforcement, public reports, and industry outreach. Evaluates the nutritional and health benefits of foods and the effectiveness of dietary supplements, drugs, and medical devices, particularly as they relate to weight loss.

Food and Drug Administration (FDA) *(Health and Human Services Dept.), Center for Drug Evaluation and Research, 10903 New Hampshire Ave., W051, #6133, Silver Spring, MD 20993; (301) 796-5400. Fax, (301) 595-7910. Dr. Janet Woodcock, Director. Press, (301) 796-3700.*

Web, www.fda.gov/drugs and www.fda.gov/AboutFDA/CentersOffices/OfficeofMedicalProductsandTobacco/CDER

Reviews and approves applications to investigate and market new drugs; monitors prescription drug advertising; works to harmonize drug approval internationally.

Food and Drug Administration (FDA) *(Health and Human Services Dept.), Center for Drug Evaluation and Research, Biostatistics, White Oak Bldg. 21, 10903 New Hampshire Ave., #3554, Silver Spring, MD 20993; (301) 796-1700. Fax, (301) 796-9734. Lisa LaVange, Director.*

Web, www.fda.gov/aboutfda/centersoffices/officeofmedicalproductsandtobacco/cder/ucm166250.htm

Conducts research and provides information on statistical methodology for drug regulation and development.

Food and Drug Administration (FDA) *(Health and Human Services Dept.), Center for Drug Evaluation and Research, Generic Drugs, 10903 New Hampshire Ave., Bldg. 75, #1692, Silver Spring, MD 20993; (240) 402-7920. Fax, (301) 595-1147. Dr. Kathleen Uhl, Director, (240) 402-7921.*

General email, genericdrugs@fda.hhs.gov

Web, www.fda.gov/AboutFDA/CentersOffices/Officeof MedicalProductsandTobacco/CDER /ucm119100.htm

Oversees generic drug review process to ensure the safety and effectiveness of approved drugs.

Food and Drug Administration (FDA) *(Health and Human Services Dept.), Center for Drug Evaluation and Research, New Drugs, 10903 New Hampshire Ave., Bldg 22, #6300, Silver Spring, MD 20993; (301) 796-0700. Fax, (301) 796-9856. John Jenkins, Director.*

Web, www.fda.gov/AboutFDA/CentersOffices/Officeof MedicalProductsandTobacco/CDER/ucm184426.htm

Provides regulatory oversight for investigational studies during drug development; makes decisions regarding marketing approval for new innovator and non-generic drugs, including decisions related to changes to already marketed products.

Food and Drug Administration (FDA) *(Health and Human Services Dept.), Center for Drug Evaluation and Research, Pharmaceutical Quality, 10903 New Hampshire Ave., WO Bldg. 21, Silver Spring, MD 20993; (301) 796-1900. Fax, (301) 796-9748. Michael Kopcha, Director, (301) 796-1436.*

Web, www.fda.gov/AboutFDA/CentersOffices/OfficeofMedicalProductsandTobacco/CDER

Reviews the critical quality attributes and manufacturing processes of new drugs, establishes quality standards to ensure safety and efficacy, and facilitates new drug development.

Food and Drug Administration (FDA) *(Health and Human Services Dept.), Orphan Products Development, 10903 New Hampshire Ave., Bldg. 32, #5271, Silver Spring, MD 20993-0002; (301) 796-8660. Fax, (301) 847-8621. Dr. Gayatri R. Rao, Director.*

General email, orphan@fda.hhs.gov

Web, www.fda.gov/ForIndustry/DevelopingProductsforRareDiseasesConditions

Promotes the development of drugs, devices, and alternative medical food therapies for rare diseases or conditions. Coordinates activities on the development of orphan drugs among federal agencies, manufacturers, and organizations representing patients.

Food and Drug Administration (FDA) *(Health and Human Services Dept.), Prescription Drug Promotion, 10903 New Hampshire Ave., Bldg. 51, #3203, Silver Spring, MD 20993-0002; (301) 796-1200. Fax, (301) 847-8444. Thomas W. Abrams, Director.*

Web, www.fda.gov/aboutfda/centersoffices/officeofmedicalproductsandtobacco/cder/ucm090142.htm

Monitors prescription drug advertising and labeling; investigates complaints; conducts market research on health care communications and drug issues.

National Institutes of Health (NIH) *(Health and Human Services Dept.), Dietary Supplements, 6100 Executive Blvd., #3B01, MSC-7517, Bethesda, MD 20892-7517; (301) 435-2920. Fax, (301) 480-1845. Paul M. Coates, Director.*

General email, ods@nih.gov

Web, http://ods.od.nih.gov

Reviews scientific evidence on the safety and efficacy of dietary supplements. Conducts, promotes, and coordinates scientific research within the NIH relating to dietary supplements. Conducts and supports conferences,

Food and Drug Administration

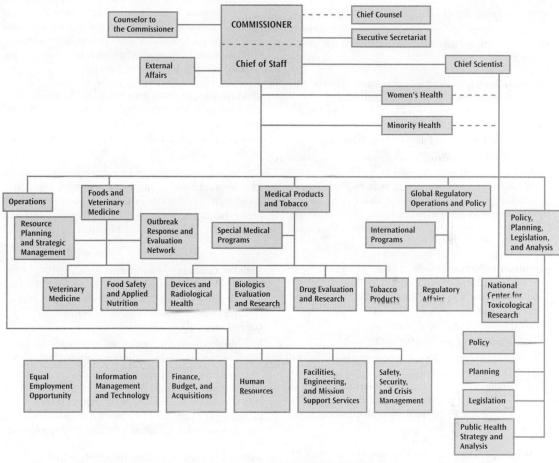

- - - - Indicates a support or advisory relationship with the unit rather than a direct reporting relationship

workshops, and symposia and publishes research results on scientific topics related to dietary supplements.

▶NONGOVERNMENTAL

American Assn. of Colleges of Pharmacy, *1727 King St., Alexandria, VA 22314-2700; (703) 739-2330. Fax, (703) 836-8982. Lucinda L. Maine, Executive Vice President. General email, mail@aacp.org*

Web, www.aacp.org

Represents and acts as advocate for pharmacists in the academic community. Conducts programs and activities in cooperation with other national health and higher education associations.

American Assn. of Pharmaceutical Scientists, *2107 Wilson Blvd., #700, Arlington, VA 22201-3042; (703) 243-2800. Fax, (703) 243-9650. Walt Marlowe, Executive Director. Public Relations, (703) 248-4740.*

General email, aaps@aaps.org

Web, www.aaps.org

Membership: pharmaceutical scientists from biomedical, biotechnological, and health care fields. Promotes pharmaceutical sciences as an industry. Represents scientific interests within academia and public and private institutions. Provides forums for scientists to engage in dialogue, networking, and career development. Monitors legislation and regulations.

American Pharmacists Assn., *2215 Constitution Ave. N.W., 20037-2985; (202) 628-4410. Fax, (202) 783-2351. Thomas Menighan, Chief Executive Officer, (202) 429-7567. Information, (800) 237-2742. Library, (202) 429-7524. Web, www.pharmacist.com and Twitter, @pharmacists*

Membership: practicing pharmacists, pharmaceutical scientists, and pharmacy students. Promotes professional education and training; publishes scientific journals and handbooks on nonprescription drugs; monitors international research. Library open to the public by appointment.

American Society for Pharmacology and Experimental Therapeutics, *9650 Rockville Pike, Bethesda, MD 20814-3995; (301) 634-7060. Fax, (301) 634-7061. Judith Siuciak, Executive Officer.*
General email, info@aspet.org
Web, www.aspet.org and Twitter, @ASPET

Membership: researchers and teachers involved in basic and clinical pharmacology primarily in the United States and Canada.

American Society of Health-System Pharmacists (ASHP), *7272 Wisconsin Ave., Bethesda, MD 20814; (301) 657-3000. Fax, (301) 657-1251. Paul W. Abramowitz, Chief Executive Officer. Toll-free, (888) 279-0681.*
Web, www.ashp.org and Twitter, @ASHPOfficial

Membership: pharmacists who practice in organized health care settings such as hospitals, health maintenance organizations, and long-term care facilities. Publishes reference materials and provides educational programs and conferences. Accredits pharmacy residency and pharmacy technician training programs. Monitors legislation and regulations.

Consumer Healthcare Products Assn., *1625 Eye St. N.W., #600, 20006; (202) 429-9260. Fax, (202) 223-6835. Patrick Lockwood-Taylor, Chair; Scott Melville, President. Press and public affairs, (202) 429-3520.*
General email, mtringale@chpa.org
Web, www.chpa.org and Twitter, @CHPA

Membership: manufacturers and marketers of nonprescription medicines and nutritional supplements; associate members include suppliers, advertising agencies, research and testing laboratories, and others. Promotes the role of self-medication in health care. Monitors legislation and regulations.

Drug Policy Alliance, *National Affairs, 925 15th St. N.W., 2nd Floor, 20005; (202) 683-2030. Fax, (202) 216-0803. Ethan Nadelmann, Executive Director.*
General email, dc@drugpolicy.org
Web, www.drugpolicy.org

Seeks to broaden debate on drug policy to include considering alternatives to incarceration, expanding maintenance therapies, and restoring constitutional protections. Studies drug policy in other countries. Monitors legislation and regulations. (Headquarters in New York.)

Generic Pharmaceutical Assn., *777 6th St. N.W., #510, 20001; (202) 249-7100. Fax, (202) 249-7105. Chester (Chip) Davis Jr., President.*
General email, info@gphaonline.org
Web, www.gphaonline.org and Twitter, @GPhA

Membership: manufacturers and distributors of generic pharmaceuticals and pharmaceutical chemicals and suppliers of goods and services to the generic pharmaceutical industry. Monitors legislation and regulations. Attempts to increase availability and public awareness of safe, effective generic medicines.

Healthcare Distribution Management Assn., *901 N. Glebe Rd., #1000, Arlington, VA 22203; (703) 787-0000. Fax, (703) 812-5282. John Gray, President.*
Web, www.healthcaredistribution.org

Membership: distributors of pharmaceutical and health-related products and information. Serves as a forum on major industry issues. Researches and disseminates information on distribution issues and management practices. Monitors legislation and regulations. (Formerly the National Wholesale Druggists' Assn.)

National Assn. of Chain Drug Stores, *1776 Wilson Blvd., #200, Arlington, VA 22209; (703) 549-3001. Fax, (703) 836-4869. Steven Anderson, President.*
General email, contactus@nacds.org
Web, www.nacds.org

Membership: chain drug retailers; associate members include manufacturers, suppliers, publishers, and advertising agencies. Provides information on the pharmacy profession, community pharmacy practice, and retail prescription drug economics. Monitors legislation and regulations.

National Community Pharmacists Assn., *100 Daingerfield Rd., Alexandria, VA 22314; (703) 683-8200. Fax, (703) 683-3619. B. Douglas Hoey, Chief Executive Officer, ext. 2648. Membership, (800) 544-7447.*
General email, info@ncpanet.org
Web, www.ncpanet.org, Twitter, @Commpharmacy and Facebook, www.facebook.com/commpharmacy?ref=nf

Membership: independent pharmacy owners, including independent pharmacies, independent pharmacy franchises, and independent chains. Promotes the interests of independent community pharmacists to compete in the health care market. Monitors legislation and regulations.

National Council on Patient Information and Education, *200-A Monroe St., #212, Rockville, MD 20850-4448; (301) 340-3940. Fax, (301) 340-3944. Paul W. Abramowitz, Executive Vice President.*
General email, ncpie@ncpie.info
Web, www.talkaboutrx.org, www.bemedicinesmart.org, and www.recoveryopensdoors.org, Twitter, @TweetNCPIE and Facebook, www.facebook.com/NCPIE

Membership: organizations of health care professionals, pharmaceutical manufacturers, federal agencies, voluntary health organizations, and consumer groups. Works to improve communication between health care professionals and patients about the appropriate use of medicines; produces educational resources; conducts public affairs programs; sponsors awards program. Additional information can be found at www.bemedwise.org and www.mustforseniors.org (medication use safety training for seniors).

National Pharmaceutical Council, *1717 Pennsylvania Ave., #800, 20006; (202) 827-2100. Fax, (202) 827-0314. Dan Leonard, President, (202) 827-2080.*

General email, info@npcnow.org

Web, www.npcnow.org

Membership: pharmaceutical manufacturers that research and produce trade-name prescription medication and other pharmaceutical products. Sponsors and conducts scientific analyses of the use of pharmaceuticals and the clinical and economic value of innovation.

Parenteral Drug Assn. (PDA), 4350 East-West Hwy., #150, Bethesda, MD 20814; (301) 656-5900. Fax, (301) 986-0296. Richard Johnson, President.

General email, info@pda.org

Web, www.pda.org

Membership: scientists involved in the development, manufacture, quality control, and regulation of pharmaceuticals/biopharmaceuticals and related products. Provides science, technology, and regulatory information and education to the pharmaceutical and biopharmaceutical community. Influences FDA regulatory process.

Pharmaceutical Care Management Assn., 325 7th St. N.W. 9th Floor, 20004; (202) 756-5700. Fax, (202) 756-5708. Mark Merritt, President.

General email, info@pcmanet.org

Web, www.pcmanet.org

Membership: companies providing managed care pharmacy and pharmacy benefits management. Promotes legislation, research, education, and practice standards that foster high-quality, affordable pharmaceutical care.

Pharmaceutical Research and Manufacturers of America, 950 F St. N.W., #300, 20004; (202) 835-3400. Steve Ubl, President. Media, (202) 835-3460.

Web, www.phrma.org

Membership: research-based pharmaceutical and biotechnology companies that orginate, develop, and manufacture prescription drugs. Advocates public policies that encourage discovery of new medicines. Provides consumer information on drug abuse, the safe and effective use of prescription medicines, and developments in important areas, including the treatment of HIV/AIDS.

U.S. Pharmacopeial Convention, 12601 Twinbrook Pkwy., Rockville, MD 20852-1790; (301) 881-0666. Fax, (301) 816-8148. Ronald Piervincenzi, Chief Executive Officer. Toll-free, (800) 227-8772.

Web, www.usp.org

Establishes and revises standards for drug strength, quality, purity, packaging, labeling, and storage of prescription and over-the-counter medications. Publishes drug use information, official drug quality standards, patient education materials, and consumer drug references. Interests include international standards. (Offices in Switzerland, India, China, and Brazil.)

HEALTH PROFESSIONS

General

▶**AGENCIES**

Aerospace Medical Assn., 320 S. Henry St., Alexandria, VA 22314-3579; (703) 739-2240. Fax, (703) 739-9652. Jeffery Sventek, Executive Director.

General email, inquiries@asma.org

Web, www.asma.org

Membership: physicians, flight surgeons, aviation medical examiners, flight nurses, scientists, technicians, and specialists in clinical, operational, and research fields of aerospace medicine. Promotes programs to improve aerospace medicine and maintain safety in aviation by examining and monitoring the health of aviation personnel; members may consult in aircraft investigation and cockpit design.

Assistant Secretary for Health (Health and Human Services Dept.), Surgeon General, Commissioned Corps of the U.S. Public Health Service (PHS), Division of Commissioned Corps Personnel and Readiness (DCCPR), 1101 Wootton Pkwy., Plaza Level, #100, Rockville, MD 20852; (240) 453-6000. Fax, (240) 453-6109. Rear Adm. Scott F. Giberson, Director; Cmdr. Christopher Dunbar, Director, Recruitment. Recruitment, (800) 279-1605.

General email, CCHelpDesk@hhs.gov

Recruitment email, Corpsrecruitment@hhs.gov, and Web, www.usphs.gov and http://dcp.psc.gov/ccmis

Responsible for the overall force management, operations, and deployment readiness and response of the Commissioned Corps of the U.S. Public Health Service, uniformed service health professionals with a wide range of specialties who respond to emergencies, conduct research, and care for patients in underserved communities through federal agencies such as the National Institutes of Health, the Centers for Disease Control and Prevention, the Indian Health Service, and the Bureau of Prisons.

Centers for Medicare and Medicaid Services (CMS) (Health and Human Services Dept.), Clinical Standards and Quality, 7500 Security Blvd., S3-02-01, Baltimore, MD 21244; (410) 786-6841. Fax, (410) 786-6857. Dr. Kate Goodrich, Director; Dr. Patrick Conway, Deputy Administrator.

Web, www.cms.gov/About-CMS/Agency-Information/CMSLeadership/Office_CCSQ.html

Oversees professional review and other medical review programs; establishes guidelines; prepares issue papers relating to legal aspects of professional review and quality assurance.

Education Dept., Health Education Assistance Loan Program, 830 1st St. N.E., #44B, 20202; (844) 509-8957. Tawana Lewis, Supervisor.

General email, heal@ed.gov

Web, www.ifap.ed.gov/HEALInfo/HEALInfo.html

Insures loans provided by private lenders to students attending eligible health professions schools under the Public Health Service Act. New loans to student borrowers have been discontinued. Refinancing has been terminated.

Health Resources and Services Administration *(Health and Human Services Dept.), Bureau of Health Workforce, 5600 Fishers Lane, #11 West Wing, Rockville, MD 20857; (301) 443-5794. Fax, (301) 443-0463. Luis Pidilla, Associate Administrator, Acting. Web, www.hrsa.gov/about/organization/bureaus/bhw*

Supports primary care and public health education and practice. Supports recruitment of health care professionals, including nursing and allied health professionals, for underserved populations. Administers categorical training programs, scholarship and loan programs, and minority and disadvantaged assistance programs. Oversees National Practitioner Data Bank.

Health Resources and Services Administration *(Health and Human Services Dept.), Bureau of Health Workforce, National Practitioner Data Bank, 15036 Conference Center Dr., Chantilly, VA 10832; (301) 443-2300. Fax, (703) 803-1964. Ernia Hughes, Division Director, Acting, (301) 443-2300. Information, (800) 767-6732. General email, help@npdb.hrsa.gov*

Web, www.npdb-hipdb.hrsa.gov

Provides information on reports of malpractice payments, adverse state licensure, clinical privileges, and society membership actions (only to eligible entities, including state licensing boards, hospitals, and other health care entities) about physicians, dentists, and other licensed health care practitioners.

Health Resources and Services Administration *(Health and Human Services Dept.), National Health Service Corps, 5600 Fishers Lane, #8-05, Rockville, MD 20857; (301) 594-4130. Fax, (301) 443-2080. Kimberly Kleine, Associate Administrator, Acting. Toll-free, (800) 221-9393. Web, www.nhsc.hrsa.gov*

Supplies communities experiencing a shortage of health care personnel with doctors and other medical professionals.

Health Resources and Services Administration *(Health and Human Services Dept.), National Health Service Corps, Clinician Recruitment and Services, 5600 Fishers Lane, Rockville, MD 20857; (301) 594-4400. Fax, (301) 594-4981. Mary Wakefield, Director. Toll-free, (800) 221-9393. Web, www.nhsc.hrsa.gov and Twitter, @NHSCorps*

Supplies communities experiencing a shortage of health care personnel with doctors and other medical professionals. Provides educational financial aid incentives for service.

National Institute of Biomedical Imaging and Bioengineering *(National Institutes of Health), 9000 Rockville Pike, Bldg. 31, #1C14, Bethesda, MD 20892; (301)* 496-8859. Fax, (301) 480-0679. Dr. Roderic I. Pettigrew, Director.

General email, info@nibib.nih.gov

Web, www.nibib.nih.gov, Twitter, @NIBIBgov and Facebook, www.facebook.com/nibibgov

Offers multidisciplinary training programs for scientists and engineers at all stages of their careers in bioimaging and bioengineering.

National Institute of General Medical Sciences *(National Institutes of Health), Training, Workforce Development, and Diversity, 45 Center Dr., Bldg. 45, #2AS37, MSC 6200, Bethesda, MD 20892-6200; (301) 594-3900. Fax, (301) 480-2753. Dr. Alison Gammie, Director, Acting.*

Web, http://nigms.nih.gov/training

Administers research and research training programs aimed at increasing the number of minority biomedical scientists. Funds grants, fellowships, faculty development awards, and development of research facilities.

Uniformed Services University of the Health Sciences *(Defense Dept.), 4301 Jones Bridge Rd., Bethesda, MD 20814-4799; (301) 295-3013. Fax, (301) 295-1960. Dr. Charles L. Rice, President. Toll-free information, (800) 515-5257. Registrar, (301) 295-3199. General email, president@usuhs.edu*

Web, www.usuhs.mil

An accredited four-year medical and dental school under the auspices of the Defense Dept. Awards doctorates and master's degrees in health-related and science-related fields. The Graduate School of Nursing awards a master of science and a doctoral degree in nursing.

►CONGRESS

For a listing of relevant congressional committees and subcommittees, please see pages 344–345 or the Appendix.

►NONGOVERNMENTAL

AFT Healthcare, *555 New Jersey Ave. N.W., 20001; (202) 879-4400. Fax, (202) 879-4545. Randi Weingarten, President. General email, afthealthcare@aft.org*

Web, www.aft.org/healthcare

Membership: teachers, public employees, and nurses and other health care workers. Assists members with contract negotiation and grievances; conducts training programs and workshops. Monitors legislation and regulations. (Division of the American Federation of Teachers.)

Alliance for Academic Internal Medicine, *330 John Carlyle St., #610, Alexandria, VA 22314; (703) 341-4540. Fax, (703) 519-1893. Bergitta E. Cotroneo, Executive Vice President. General email, aaim@im.org*

Web, www.im.org

Membership: program directors, clerkship directors, administrators, and chairs of internal medicine departments at all U.S. medical schools and several affiliated teaching hospitals. Provides services, training, and educational opportunities for leaders in internal medicine departments. Monitors legislation and regulations.

American Assn. of Colleges of Pharmacy, *1727 King St., Alexandria, VA 22314-2700; (703) 739-2330. Fax, (703) 836-8982. Lucinda L. Maine, Executive Vice President.*
General email, mail@aacp.org

Web, www.aacp.org

Membership: teachers and administrators representing colleges of pharmacy accredited by the American Council on Pharmaceutical Education. Sponsors educational programs; conducts research; provides career information; helps administer the Pharmacy College Admissions Test.

American College of Health Care Administrators, *1321 Duke St., #400, Alexandria, VA 22314; (202) 536-5120. Fax, (866) 874-1585. Cecilia Sepp, President.*
General email, info@achca.org

Web, www.achca.org

Membership: administrators of long-term health care organizations and facilities, including home health care programs, hospices, day care centers for the elderly, nursing and hospital facilities, retirement communities, assisted living communities, and mental health care centers. Conducts research on statistical characteristics of nursing home and other medical administrators; conducts seminars and workshops; offers education courses; provides certification for administrators.

American College of Radiology, *Washington Office, 505 9th St. N.W., #910, 20004; 1891 Preston White Dr., Reston, VA 20191-4326; (703) 648-8900. Fax, (703) 295-6773. Cynthia Moran, Senior Director, Government Relations, (202) 223-1670; Dr. William Thorwarth Jr., Chief Executive Officer. Toll-free, (800) 227-5463.*
General email, info@acr.org

Web, www.acr.org

Membership: certified radiologists and medical physicists in the United States and Canada. Develops programs in radiation protection, technologist training, practice standards, and health care insurance; maintains a placement service for radiologists; participates in international conferences.

American Health Lawyers Assn., *1620 Eye St. N.W., 6th Floor, 20006-4010; (202) 833-1100. Fax, (202) 833-1105. David Cade, Chief Executive Officer, (202) 833-0777.*
General email, info@healthlawyers.org

Web, www.healthlawyers.org

Membership: corporate, institutional, and government lawyers interested in the health field; law students; and health professionals. Serves as an information clearinghouse on health law; sponsors health law educational programs and seminars.

American Institute of Ultrasound in Medicine, *14750 Sweitzer Lane, #100, Laurel, MD 20707-5906; (301) 498-4100. Fax, (301) 498-4450. Carmine Valente, Chief Executive Officer. Toll-free, (800) 638-5352.*
General email, admin@aium.org

Web, www.aium.org and Twitter, @AIUM_Ultrasound

Membership: medical professionals who use ultrasound technology in their practices. Promotes multidisciplinary research and education on safe and effective use of diagnostic ultrasound through conventions and educational programs. Develops guidelines for accreditation. Monitors international research.

American Medical Athletic Assn., *4405 East-West Hwy., #405, Bethesda, MD 20814-4535; (301) 913-9517. Fax, (301) 913-9520. David Watt, Executive Director, ext. 13. Toll-free, (800) 776-2732.*
General email, amaa@americanrunning.org

Web, www.amaasportsmed.org

Membership: sports medicine and allied health professionals. Assists members in promoting running and physical fitness to their patients and in developing their own physical fitness programs. Promotes and reports on sports medicine research and discussion. (Sister organization to American Running Assn.)

American Medical Group Assn., *One Prince St., Alexandria, VA 22314-3318; (703) 838-0033. Fax, (703) 548-1890. Donald W. Fisher, President.*
Web, www.amga.org and Twitter, @theAMGA

Membership: medical group and health system organizations. Compiles statistics on group practice and clinical best practices. Sponsors a foundation for research and education programs. Advocates the multispecialty group practice model of health care delivery. Provides educational and networking programs and publications, benchmarking data services, and financial and operations assistance. Monitors legislation and regulations.

American Running Assn., *4405 East-West Hwy., #405, Bethesda, MD 20814-4535; (301) 913-9517. Fax, (301) 913-9520. David Watt, Executive Director. Toll-free, (800) 776-2732.*
General email, milerun@americanrunning.org

Web, www.americanrunning.org

Membership: athletes, health clubs, physicians, businesses, and individuals. Promotes proper nutrition and regular exercise. Provides members with medical advice and referrals, fitness information, and assistance in developing fitness programs. (Sister organization to American Medical Athletic Assn.)

American Society of Consultant Pharmacists (ASCP), *1321 Duke St., 4th Floor, Alexandria, VA 22314-3563; (703) 739-1300. Fax, (703) 739-1321. Frank Grosso, Executive Director. Toll-free, (800) 355-2727. Toll-free fax, (800) 220-1321.*
General email, info@ascp.com

Web, www.ascp.com and Twitter, @ASCPharm

Membership: dispensing and clinical pharmacists with expertise in therapeutic medication management for geriatric patients; provides services to long-term care facilities, institutions, and hospices as well as older adults in assisted living and home-based care. Monitors legislation and regulations.

American Speech-Language-Hearing Assn. (ASHA), *2200 Research Blvd., Rockville, MD 20850-3289; (301) 296-5700. Fax, (301) 296-8580. Arlene Pietranton, Executive Director. Press, (301) 296-8732. Toll-free for Action Center, (800) 498-2071 (voice and TTY accessible). Toll-free for non-members, (800) 638-8255.*
General email, actioncenter@asha.org

Web, www.asha.org and Twitter, @ASHAWeb

Membership: specialists in speech-language pathology and audiology. Sponsors professional education programs; acts as accrediting agent for graduate programs; certifies audiologists and speech-language pathologists. Advocates the rights of the communicatively disabled; provides information on speech, hearing, and language problems. Provides referrals to speech-language pathologists and audiologists. Interests include national and international standards for bioacoustics and noise.

Assn. for Healthcare Philanthropy, *313 Park Ave., #400, Falls Church, VA 22046; (703) 532-6243. Fax, (703) 532-7170. Steven W. Churchill, President.*
General email, ahp@ahp.org

Web, www.ahp.org and Twitter, @AHPIntl

Membership: hospital and health care executives who manage fundraising activities and organizations and individuals who provide consulting services for such activities. Acts as a clearinghouse on philanthropy and offers programs, services, and publications and e-communications to members.

Assn. for Prevention Teaching and Research, *1001 Connecticut Ave. N.W., #610, 20036; (202) 463-0550. Fax, (202) 463-0555. Allison L. Lewis, Executive Director. Toll-free, (866) 520-2787.*
General email, info@aptrweb.org

Web, www.aptrweb.org and Twitter, @APTRupdate

Membership: faculty, researchers, residents, and students within schools of medicine, schools of public health, schools of nursing, schools of pharmacy, physician assistant programs, graduate programs for public health, and health agencies. Works to advance population-based and public health education, research, and service by linking supporting members from the academic prevention community. Develops curricular resources and professional development programs. (Formerly the Assn. of Teachers of Preventive Medicine.)

Assn. for Professionals in Infection Control and Epidemiology (APIC), *1275 K St. N.W., #1000, 20005; (202) 789-1890. Katrina Crist, Chief Executive Officer, (202) 789-1890. Toll-Free, (800) 650-9570.*
General email, info@apic.org

Web, www.apic.org

Professional association for infection prevention health practitioners, including nurses, physicians, public health professionals, epidemiologists, microbiologists, and medical technologists. Monitors legislation and regulations.

Assn. of Accredited Naturopathic Medical Colleges, *818 18th St. N.W., #250, 20006; (800) 345-7454. Dr. JoAnn Yanez, Executive Director.*
General email, info@aanmc.org

Web, www.aanmc.org and Twitter, @AANMC

Membership: accredited schools of naturopathic medicine. Promotes naturopathic and medical education, research, and teaching. Provides database of practicing naturopathic physicians and information on how to become a licensed naturopathic doctor.

Assn. of Reproductive Health Professionals, *1300 19th St. N.W., #200, 20036; (202) 466-3825. Fax, (202) 466-3826. Wayne C. Shields, President, (202) 378-8289.*
General email, arhp@arhp.org

Web, www.arhp.org and Twitter, @ARHP_ORG

Membership: obstetricians, gynecologists, other physicians, researchers, educators, and advanced practice clinicians, including nurse practioners, physician assistants, and certified nurse midwives. Educates health professionals and the public on reproductive health issues, including family planning, contraception, HIV/AIDS and other sexually transmitted diseases, abortion, menopause, infertility, and cancer prevention and detection. Monitors legislation and regulations.

Assn. of Schools and Programs of Public Health, *1900 M St. N.W., #710, 20036; (202) 296-1099. Fax, (202) 296-1252. Dr. Harrison C. Spencer, President.*
General email, info@aspph.org

Web, www.aspph.org and Twitter, @ASPPHtweets

Membership: deans, faculty, and students of accredited graduate schools of public health. Promotes improved education and training of professional public health personnel; interests include disease prevention, health promotion, and international health.

Assn. of Schools of Allied Health Professions, *122 C St. N.W., #650, 20001; (202) 237-6481. Fax, (202) 237-6485. John Colbert, Executive Director.*
General email, thomas@asahp.org

Web, www.asahp.org and Twitter, @ASAHPDC

Membership: two-year and four-year colleges and academic health science centers with allied health professional training programs; administrators, educators, and practitioners; and professional societies. Serves as information resource; works with the Health and Human Services Dept. to conduct surveys of allied health education programs. Interests include health promotion and disease prevention, ethics in health care, and the participation of women and persons with disabilities in allied health. Monitors legislation and regulations.

Assn. of University Programs in Health Administration (AUPHA), 2000 14th St. North, #780, Arlington, VA 22201; (703) 894-0940. Fax, (703) 894-0941. Gerald Glandon, President.
General email, aupha@aupha.org

Web, www.aupha.org and Twitter, @AUPHA

Membership: university-based educational programs, faculty, practitioners, and provider organizations. Works to improve the field of health care management and practice by educating entry-level professional managers.

Council on Education for Public Health, 1010 Wayne Ave., #220, Silver Spring, MD 20910; (202) 789-1050. Fax, (202) 789-1895. Laura Rasar King, Executive Director.
Web, www.ceph.org

Accredits schools of public health and undergraduate and graduate programs in public health. Works to strengthen public health programs through research and other means.

Health Volunteers Overseas, 1900 L St. N.W., #310, 20036; (202) 296-0928. Fax, (202) 296-8018. Nancy A. Kelly, Executive Director.
General email, info@hvousa.org

Web, www.hvousa.org

Operates training programs in developing countries for health professionals who wish to teach low-cost health care delivery practices.

Healthcare Financial Management Assn., Washington Office, 1825 K St. N.W., #900, 20006; (202) 296-2920. Fax, (202) 238-3456. Richard Gundling, Senior Vice President. Information, (800) 252-4362.
Web, www.hfma.org

Membership: health care financial management specialists. Offers educational programs; provides information on financial management of health care. (Headquarters in Westchester, Ill.)

Hispanic-Serving Health Professions Schools, 2639 Connecticut Ave. N.W., #203, 20008; (202) 290-1186. Fax, (202) 290-1339. Maureen Lichtveld, President.
General email, hshps@hshps.org

Web, www.hshps.org

Seeks to increase representation of Hispanics in all health care professions through academic development, initiatives, and training. Monitors legislation and regulations.

National Assn. of County and City Health Officials, 1100 17th St. N.W., 7th Floor, 20036; (202) 783-5550. Fax, (202) 783-1583. LaMar Hasbrouck, Executive Director.
General email, info@naccho.org

Web, www.naccho.org

Membership: city, county, and district health officers. Provides members with information on national, state, and local health developments. Works to develop the technical competence, managerial capacity, and leadership potential of local public health officials.

National Assn. of Healthcare Access Management, 2025 M St. N.W., #800, 20036-3309; (202) 367-1125. Fax, (202) 367-2125. Mike Copps, Executive Director.
General email, info@naham.org

Web, www.naham.org

Promotes professional growth and recognition of health care patient access managers, who handle hospital patient admissions, registration, finance, and patient relations; provides instructional videotapes; sponsors educational programs.

National Center for Homeopathy, 7918 Jones Branch Dr., #300, McLean, VA 22102; (703) 506-7667. Fax, (703) 506-3266. Alison Teitelbaum, Executive Director.
General email, info@nationalcenterforhomeopathy.org

Web, www.nationalcenterforhomeopathy.org and Twitter, @NCHHomeopathy

Educational organization for professionals, groups, associations, and individuals interested in homeopathy. Promotes health through homeopathy; conducts education programs; holds annual conference; publishes quarterly magazine and monthly newsletter.

North American Spine Assn., Washington Office, 300 New Jersey Ave N.W., 20001; (630) 230-3671. Christopher Bono, President, (617) 732-7238. Toll-free, (888) 960-6277.
Web, www.spine.org

Membership: physicians, nurse practitioners, nurses, physician assistants, chiropractors, physical therapists, researchers, other health care professionals with an interest in the spine. Monitors legislation and regulations.

Physicians for Human Rights, Washington Office, 1110 Vermont Ave. N.W., 5th Floor, 20005; (202) 728-5335. Fax, (202) 728-3053. Andrea Gittleman, Director, U.S. Policy Acting, Vacant, Washington Director.
General email, phrusa@phrusa.org

Web, www.physiciansforhumanrights.org

Mobilizes doctors, nurses, health specialists, scientists, and others to promote health and human rights globally. Investigates and seeks to end human rights abuses. Issues reports and press releases; conducts training programs on health and human rights issues; acts as advocate before policymakers. (Headquarters in New York City.)

Society of Health and Physical Educators (SHAPE) America, 1900 Association Dr., Reston, VA 20191-1598; (703) 476-3400. Fax, (703) 476-9527. E. Paul Roetert, Chief Executive Officer. Toll-free, (800) 213-7193. Press, (703) 476-1461.
General email, info@shapeamerica.org

Web, www.shapeamerica.org

Membership: health educators and allied health professionals in community and volunteer health agencies, educational institutions, and businesses. Develops health education programs; monitors legislation.

Chiropractors

▶NONGOVERNMENTAL

American Chiropractic Assn., *1701 Clarendon Blvd., #200, Arlington, VA 22209; (703) 276-8800. Fax, (703) 243-2593. Richard (Rick) Miller, Executive Vice President, Acting. Media, (703) 812-0211.*
General email, memberinfo@amerchiro.org
Web, www.acatoday.org

Association of chiropractic physicians. Promotes standards of care. Interests include health care coverage, sports injuries, physical fitness, internal disorders, and orthopedics. Supports foundation for chiropractic education and research. Maintains a legal action fund to sue on behalf of patients whose insurers deny them coverage of chiropractic services. Monitors legislation and regulations.

Foundation for the Advancement of Chiropractic Tenets and Science, *6400 Arlington Blvd., #800, Falls Church, VA 22042; (703) 528-5000. Fax, (703) 528-5023. George Curry, President. Toll-free, (800) 423-4690.*
General email, chiro@chiropractic.org
Web, www.chiropractic.org

Offers financial aid for education and research programs in colleges and independent institutions; studies chiropractic services in the United States; provides international relief and development programs. (Affiliate of the International Chiropractors Assn.)

International Chiropractors Assn., *6400 Arlington Blvd., #800, Falls Church, VA 22042; (703) 528-5000. Fax, (703) 528-5023. Ron Hendrickson, Executive Director. Toll-free, (800) 423-4690.*
General email, chiro@chiropractic.org
Web, www.chiropractic.org

Membership: chiropractors, students, educators, and laypersons. Seeks to increase public awareness of chiropractic care. Supports research on health issues; administers scholarship program; monitors legislation and regulations.

North American Spine Assn., *Washington Office, 300 New Jersey Ave N.W., 20001; (630) 230-3671. Christopher Bono, President, (617) 732-7238. Toll-free, (888) 960-6277.*
Web, www.spine.org

Membership: physicians, nurse practitioners, nurses, physician assistants, chiropractors, physical therapists, researchers, other health care professionals with an interest in the spine. Monitors legislation and regulations.

Dental Care

▶AGENCIES

National Institute of Dental and Craniofacial Research *(National Institutes of Health), 31 Center Dr., Bldg. 31, #2C39, MS 2290, Bethesda, MD 20892-2190; (301) 496-3571 Fax, (301) 402-2185. Martha J. Somerman, Director.*

Toll-free, (866) 232-4528.
General email, nidcrinfo@mail.nih.gov
Web, www.nidcr.nih.gov

Conducts and funds clinical research and promotes training and career development in oral, dental, and craniofacial health. Monitors international research and evaluates its implications for public policy.

Veterans Health Administration (VHA) *(Veterans Affairs Dept.), Dentistry, 810 Vermont Ave. N.W., 10NC7, 20005; (202) 461-6947. Dr. Patricia Arola, Assistant Under Secretary.*
Web, www.va.gov/dental

Administers and coordinates VA oral health care programs; dental care delivered in a VA setting; administration of oral research, education, and training for VA oral health personnel; delivery of care to VA patients in private practice settings.

▶NONGOVERNMENTAL

American College of Dentists, *839 Quince Orchard Blvd., Suite J, Gaithersburg, MD 20878-1614; (301) 977-3223. Fax, (301) 977-3330. Stephen A. Ralls, Executive Director.*
General email, office@acd.org
Web, www.acd.org

Honorary society of dentists. Fellows are elected based on their contributions to education, research, dentistry, and community and civic organizations. Organizes ethics seminars, award programs, online courses on leadership and dental ethics, and speaker series.

American Dental Assn. (ADA), *Government Relations, 1111 14th St. N.W., #1100, 20005; (202) 898-2400. Fax, (202) 898-2437. Michael Graham, Managing Director.*
General email, govtpol@ada.org
Web, www.ada.org

Conducts research, provides dental education materials, compiles statistics on dentistry and dental care. Monitors legislation and regulations. (Headquarters in Chicago, Ill.)

American Dental Education Assn., *655 K St., #800, 20001; (202) 289-7201. Fax, (202) 289-7204. Dr. Richard W. Valachovic, President.*
General email, adea@adea.org and frontdesk@adea.org
Web, www.adea.org

Membership: U.S. and Canadian dental schools; advanced, hospital, and allied dental education programs; corporations; and faculty and students. Works to influence education, research, and the delivery of oral health care for the improvement of public health. Provides information on dental teaching and research and on admission requirements of U.S. dental schools; publishes a monthly journal and newsletter.

Children's Dental Health Project (CDHP), *1020 19th St. N.W., #400, 20036; (202) 833-8288. Meg Booth, Executive Director, (202) 833-8288. Media, (202) 417-3600.*

General email, info@cdhp.org

Web, www.cdhp.org and Twitter, @Teeth_Matter

Coalition comprising policymakers, dental care professionals, and individuals seeking innovated and cost-effective solutions to improve children's dental health. Provides information to policymakers, oral health care providers, and media about dental care provisions of the Affordable Care Act; monitors Medicaid and other insurance programs; promotes prevention strategies.

Dental Trade Alliance, 4350 N. Fairfax Dr., #220, Arlington, VA 22203; (703) 379-7755. Fax, (703) 931-9429. Gary W. Price, Chief Executive Officer.
General email, contact@dentaltradealliance.org

Web, www.dentaltradealliance.org

Membership: dental laboratories and distributors and manufacturers of dental equipment and supplies. Collects and disseminates statistical and management information; conducts studies, programs, and projects of interest to the industry; acts as liaison with government agencies. (Formerly the American Dental Trade Assn.)

International Assn. for Dental Research, 1619 Duke St., Alexandria, VA 22314-3406; (703) 548-0066. Fax, (703) 548-1883. Dr. Christopher H. Fox, Executive Director; Carolyn Mullen, Director, Government Affairs.
General email, research@iadr.org

Web, www.dentalresearch.org

Membership: professionals engaged in dental research worldwide. Conducts annual convention, conferences, and symposia.

National Dental Assn., 6411 Ivy Lane, #703, Greenbelt, MD 20770; (240) 241-4448. Fax, (240) 297-9181. LaVette C. Henderson, Deputy Executive Director.
General email, lhenderson@ndaonline.org

Web, www.ndaonline.org

Promotes the interests of ethnic minority dentists through recruitment, educational and financial services, and federal legislation and programs.

Medical Researchers

▶AGENCIES

National Institutes of Health (NIH) *(Health and Human Services Dept.),* **Intramural Training and Education,** 2 Center Dr., Bldg. 2, #2E04, MSC 0230, Bethesda, MD 20892-0240; (301) 496-2427. Fax, (301) 594-9606. Sharon Milgram, Director.
General email, trainingwww@mail.nih.gov

Web, www.training.nih.gov

Administers programs and initiatives to recruit and develop individuals who participate in research training activities on the NIH's campuses. Maintains an interactive Web site for the various research training programs. Supports the training mission of the NIH Intramural Research Program through placement, retention, support, and tracking of trainees at all levels, as well as program delivery and evaluation. Administers the NIH Academy, the Summer Internship Program, the Undergraduate Scholarship Program, the Graduate Partnerships Program, and the Postbac and Technical Intramural Research Training Award programs.

▶NONGOVERNMENTAL

Alliance for Regenerative Medicine, 525 2nd St. N.E., 20002; (202) 568-6240. Michael Werner, Executive Director; Lyndsey Scull, Communications Director.
General email, info@alliancerm.org

Web, www.alliancerm.org

Membership: nationally recognized patient advocacy organizations, academic research institutions, companies, health insurers, financial institutions, foundations, and individuals with life-threatening illnesses and disorders. Acts as advocate for research and technologies in regenerative medicine, including stem cell research and somatic cell nuclear transfer; seeks to increase public understanding. (Formerly Coalition for the Advancement of Medical Research.)

American Assn. for Clinical Chemistry, 900 7th St. N.W., 20001; (202) 857-0717. Fax, (202) 887-5093. Janet Kreizman, Chief Executive Officer. Toll-free, (800) 892-1400.
General email, info@aacc.org

Web, www.aacc.org

International society of chemists, physicians, and other scientists specializing in clinical chemistry. Provides educational and professional development services; presents awards for outstanding achievement. Monitors legislation and regulations.

American Assn. of Immunologists, 9650 Rockville Pike, Bethesda, MD 20814-3994; (301) 634-7178. Fax, (301) 634-7887. M. Michele Hogan, Executive Director.
General email, infoaai@aai.org

Web, www.aai.org

Membership: scientists working in virology, bacteriology, biochemistry, genetics, immunology, and related disciplines. Conducts training courses and workshops; compiles statistics; participates in international conferences; publishes *The Journal of Immunology*. Monitors legislation and regulations.

American Medical Writers Assn., 30 W. Gude Dr., #525, Rockville, MD 20850-4347; (240) 238-0940. Fax, (301) 294-9006. Susan Krug, Executive Director.
General email, amwa@amwa.org

Web, www.amwa.org and Twitter, @AmMedWriters

Provides professional education and additional services to writers, editors, and others in the field of biomedical communication.

American Society for Clinical Laboratory Science, 1861 International Dr., #200, Tysons Corner, VA 22102; (571) 748-3770. Elissa Passiment, Executive Vice President.
General email, ascls@ascls.org

Web, www.ascls.org

Membership: clinical laboratory scientists. Conducts continuing education programs for clinical laboratory scientists and laboratory practitioners. Monitors legislation and regulations.

American Society for Clinical Pathology, *Washington Office, 1225 New York Ave. N.W., #350, 20005-6156; (202) 347-4450. Fax, (202) 347-4453. Jeff Jacobs, Senior Vice President. Customer service for members, (800) 267-2727.*
General email, info@ascp.org
Web, www.ascp.org

Membership: pathologists, residents, and other physicians; clinical scientists; registered certified medical technologists; and technicians. Promotes continuing education, educational standards, and research in pathology. Monitors legislation, regulations, and international research. (Headquarters in Chicago, Ill.)

Assn. of Public Health Laboratories, *8515 Georgia Ave., #700, Silver Spring, MD 20910; (240) 485-2745. Fax, (240) 485-2700. Scott J. Becker, Executive Director, (240) 485-2747. Press, (240) 485-2793.*
General email, info@aphl.org
Web, www.aphl.org and Twitter, @APHL

Membership: state and local public health, environmental, agricultural, and food safety laboratories. Offers technical assistance to member laboratories; sponsors educational programs for public health and clinical laboratory practitioners; develops systems for electronic exchange of lab data; develops laboratory system in under-resourced countries. Works with the CDC, FDA, EPA, and other federal partners to support disease detection and surveillance, laboratory response to health crises, quality drinking water, and other public health services.

Board of Registered Polysomnographic Technologists, *8400 Westpark Dr., 2nd Floor, McLean, VA 22102; (703) 610-9020. Fax, (703) 610-0229. Jim Magruder, Executive Director.*
General email, info@brpt.org
Web, www.brpt.org

Provides credentialing and certification for polysomnographic technologists. Offers continuing education programs and education opportunities.

Society of Research Administrators International (SRA International), *1560 Wilson Blvd., #310, Arlington, VA 22209; (703) 741-0140. Fax, (703) 741-0142. Elliott Kulakowski, Executive Director, ext. 215.*
General email, info@srainternational.org
Web, www.srainternational.org

Membership: scientific and medical research administrators in the United States and other countries. Educates the public about the profession; offers professional development services; sponsors mentoring and awards programs.

Society of Toxicology, *1821 Michael Faraday Dr., #300, Reston, VA 20190; (703) 438-3115. Fax, (703) 438-3113. Clarissa Russell Wilson, Executive Director.*
General email, sothq@toxicology.org
Web, www.toxicology.org

Membership: scientists from academic institutions, government, and industry worldwide who work in toxicology. Promotes professional development, exchange of information, and research to advance toxicological science.

Nurses and Physician Assistants

▶**AGENCIES**

National Institute of Nursing Research *(National Institutes of Health), 31 Center Dr., Bldg. 31, #5B05A, MSC 2178, Bethesda, MD 20892-2178; (301) 496-0207. Fax, (301) 496-8845. Patricia A. Grady, Director, (301) 496-8230.*
Web, www.ninr.nih.gov and Twitter, @NINR

Provides grants and awards for nursing research and research training. Research focus includes health promotion and disease prevention, quality of life, health disparities, and end-of-life issues.

▶**NONGOVERNMENTAL**

AFT Healthcare, *555 New Jersey Ave. N.W., 20001; (202) 879-4400. Fax, (202) 879-4545. Randi Weingarten, President.*
General email, afthealthcare@aft.org
Web, www.aft.org/healthcare

Membership: teachers, public employees, and nurses and other health care workers. Assists members with contract negotiation and grievances; conducts training programs and workshops. Monitors legislation and regulations. (Division of the American Federation of Teachers.)

American Academy of Physician Assistants (AAPA), *2318 Mill Rd., #1300, Alexandria, VA 22314-1552; (703) 836-2272. Fax, (703) 684-1924. Jenna Dorn, Chief Executive Officer.*
General email, aapa@aapa.org
Web, www.aapa.org

Membership: physician assistants and physician assistant students. Sponsors continuing medical education programs for recertification of physician assistants; offers malpractice insurance. Interests include health care reform, quality of care, research, and laws and regulations affecting physician assistant practice and patients. Monitors legislation and regulations.

American Assn. of Colleges of Nursing, *1 Dupont Circle N.W., #530, 20036-1120; (202) 463-6930. Fax, (202) 785-8320. Jennifer Butlin, Executive Director, (202) 887-6791.*
General email, info@aacn.nche.edu
Web, www.aacn.nche.edu

Promotes high-quality baccalaureate and graduate nursing education; works to secure federal support of nursing education, nursing research, and student financial assistance; operates databank providing information on enrollments, graduations, salaries, and other conditions in nursing higher education. Interests include international practices.

American College of Nurse-Midwives, *8403 Colesville Rd., #1550, Silver Spring, MD 20910-6374; (240) 485-1800. Fax, (240) 485-1818. Lorrie Kaplan, Chief Executive Officer, (240) 485-1810. Press, (240) 485-1826.*
General email, info@acnm.org

Web, www.midwife.org

Membership: certified nurse-midwives and certified midwives who preside at deliveries and provide postnatal care or primary gynecological care. Establishes clinical practice studies. Interests include preventive health care for women.

American Nurses Assn., *8515 Georgia Ave., #400, Silver Spring, MD 20910; (301) 628-5000. Fax, (301) 628-5001. Marla Weston, Chief Executive Officer. Toll-free, (800) 274-4262.*
General email, info@ana.org

Web, www.nursingworld.org and Twitter, @ANANursingWorld

Membership: registered nurses. Promotes high standards of nursing practice, the rights of nurses in the workplace, and a positive and realistic view of nursing. Affiliated organizations include the American Nurses Foundation, the American Academy of Nursing, and the American Nurses Credentialing Center. Monitors legislation and regulations.

National Assn. of Nurse Practitioners in Women's Health, *505 C St. N.E., 20002; (202) 543-9693. Fax, (202) 543-9858. Gay Johnson, Chief Executive Officer.*
General email, info@npwh.org

Web, www.npwh.org

Develops standards for nurse practitioner training and practices. Sponsors and provides accreditation of women's health nurse practitioner continuing education programs. Provides the public and government with information on nurse practitioner education, practice, and women's health issues.

National Black Nurses Assn., *8630 Fenton St., #330, Silver Spring, MD 20910-3803; (301) 589-3200. Fax, (301) 589-3223. Millicent Gorham, Executive Director.*
Web, www.nbna.org

Membership: Black nurses from the United States, the eastern Caribbean, and Africa. Fosters improvement in the level of care available to minorities, conducts continuing education programs, and builds relationships with public and private agencies and organizations to exert influence on laws and programs. Conducts and publishes research.

Physical and Occupational Therapy

▶NONGOVERNMENTAL

American Occupational Therapy Assn., *4720 Montgomery Lane, #200, Bethesda, MD 20814-3449; (301) 652-6611. Fax, (301) 652-7711. Fred Somers, Executive Director. TTY, (800) 377-8555.*
Web, www.aota.org and Twitter, @AOTAInc

Membership: occupational therapists, occupational therapy assistants, and students. Associate members include businesses and organizations supportive of occupational therapy. Accredits educational programs and credentials occupational therapists. Supports research and sponsors scholarships, grants, and fellowships.

American Physical Therapy Assn., *1111 N. Fairfax St., Alexandria, VA 22314-1488; (703) 684-2782. Fax, (703) 684-7343. Michael Bowers, Chief Executive Officer. Information, (800) 999-2782. TTY, (703) 683-6748.*
General email, memberservices@apta.org

Web, www.apta.org and Twitter, @APTAtweets

Membership: physical therapists, assistants, and students. Establishes professional standards and accredits physical therapy programs; seeks to improve physical therapy education, practice, and research.

Physicians

▶NONGOVERNMENTAL

American Academy of Dermatology, *Government Affairs, 1445 New York Ave. N.W., #800, 20005; (202) 842-3555. Fax, (202) 842-4355. Barbara Greenan, Senior Director.*
Web, www.aad.org

Membership: practicing dermatologists. Promotes the science and art of medicine and surgery related to the skin, hair, and nails. Advocates high-quality dermatologic care and for higher standards of care. Monitors legislation and regulations.

American Academy of Family Physicians, *Washington Office, 1133 Connecticut Ave. N.W., #1100, 20036-4342; (202) 232-9033. Fax, (202) 232-9044. R. Shawn Martin, Vice President for Practice Advancement and Advocacy. Toll-free, (888) 794-7481.*
General email, fp@aafp.org

Web, www.aafp.org

Membership: family physicians, family practice residents, and medical students. Sponsors continuing medical education programs; promotes family practice residency programs. Monitors legislation and regulations. (Headquarters in Leawood, Kans.)

American Academy of Orthopaedic Surgeons, *Washington Office, 317 Massachusetts Ave. N.E., #100, 20002; (202) 546-4430. Fax, (202) 546-5051. Graham H. Newson, Executive Director; William Shaffer, Medical Director.*
General email, dc@aaos.org

Web, www.aaos.org and Twitter, @AAOSAdvocacy

Membership: orthopaedic surgeons and musculoskeletal care professionals. Offers continuing education activities; publishes scientific and medical journals and electronic resources. Engages in health policy and advocates on behalf of orthopaedic surgeons and patients. (Headquarters in Rosemont, Ill.)

American Academy of Otolaryngology—Head and Neck Surgery, *1650 Diagonal Rd., Alexandria, VA 22314-2857; (703) 836-4444. Fax, (703) 683-5100.*
Dr. Sujana S. Chandrase Khar, President;
Dr. James Denneny III, Chief Executive Officer. Press, (703) 535-3762.
Web, www.entnet.org

Membership: otolaryngologists—head and neck surgeons. Supports the advancement of scientific medical research. Provides continuing medical education for members. Monitors legislation, regulations, and international research.

American Assn. of Colleges of Osteopathic Medicine, *5550 Friendship Blvd., #310, Chevy Chase, MD 20815-7231; (301) 968-4100. Fax, (301) 968-4101.*
Stephen C. Shannon, President.
Web, www.aacom.org

Administers a centralized application service for osteopathic medical colleges; supports an increase in the number of minority and economically disadvantaged students in osteopathic colleges; maintains an information database; sponsors recruitment programs. Monitors legislation and regulations.

American Assn. of Naturopathic Physicians, *818 18th St. N.W., #250, 20006; (202) 237-8150. Fax, (202) 237-8152.*
Jaclyn Chasse, President; Ryan Cliche, Executive Director. Toll-free, (866) 538-2267.
General email, member.services@naturopathic.org
Web, www.naturopathic.org

Promotes naturopathic physician education and acceptance of naturopathic medicine in the nation's health care system.

American Assn. of Neurological Surgeons, *725 15th St. N.W., #800, 20005; (202) 628-2072. Fax, (202) 628-5264.*
Kathleen T. Craig, Executive Director, (847) 378-0537.
General email, info@aans.org
Web, www.aans.org

Research and education association dedicated to advancing the specialty of neurological surgery; advocates neurosurgeons' interests in public policy. Publishes the *Journal of Neurosurgery* and other publications and resources. (Headquarters in Rolling Meadows, Ill.)

American College of Cardiology, *2400 N St. N.W., 20037; (202) 375-6000. Fax, (202) 375-7000. Shai Jacobovitz, Chief Executive Officer. Press, (202) 375-6476. Toll-free, (800) 253-4636.*
General email, resource@acc.org
Web, www.acc.org

Membership: physicians, surgeons, and scientists specializing in cardiovascular health care. Sponsors programs in continuing medical education; collaborates with national and international cardiovascular organizations.

American College of Emergency Physicians, *Public Affairs, 2121 K St. N.W., #325, 20037-1801; (202) 728-0610, ext. 3011. Fax, (202) 728-0617. Dean Wilkerson, Executive Director. Toll-free, (860) 320-0610, ext. 3011.*

General email, pr@acep.org
Public Affairs email, publicaffairs@acep.org
Web, www.acep.org

Membership: physicians, residents, and interns. Interests include health care reform, Medicare and Medicaid legislation and regulations, medical liability, overcrowding in emergency departments, access to emergency care, bioterrorism and terrorism preparedness, managed care, and adult and pediatric emergencies. Disseminates public education materials. (Headquarters in Dallas, Texas.)

American College of Obstetricians and Gynecologists, *409 12th St. S.W., 20024-2188 (mailing address: P.O. Box 70620, Washington, DC 20024-9998); (202) 638-5577. Fax, (202) 488-3983. Dr. Hal C. Lawrence III, Executive Vice President. Press, (202) 484-3321. Toll-free, (800) 673-8444.*
Web, www.acog.org

Membership: medical specialists in obstetrics and gynecology. Disseminates standards of clinical practice and promotes patient involvement in medical care. Monitors legislation, regulations, and international research on maternal and child health care.

American College of Oral and Maxillofacial Surgeons (ACOMS), *2025 M St. N.W., #800, 20036; (202) 367-1182. Fax, (202) 367-2182. Steven C. Kemp, Executive Director. Web, www.acoms.org and Twitter, @theACOMS*

Professional association serving the specialty of oral and maxillofacial surgery, the surgical arm of dentistry. Publishes the journal *Oral Surgery, Oral Medicine, Oral Pathology, Oral Radiology.* (Headquarters in Rosemont, Ill.)

American College of Osteopathic Surgeons, *123 N. Henry St., Alexandria, VA 22314-2903; (703) 684-0416. Fax, (703) 684-3280. Linda Ayers, Executive Director, (571) 551-2005. Toll-free, (800) 888-1312.*
General email, info@facos.org
Web, www.facos.org

Membership: osteopathic surgeons in disciplines of neurosurgery, thoracic surgery, cardiovascular surgery, urology, plastic surgery, and general surgery. Offers members continuing surgical education programs and use of the ACOS-sponsored coding and reimbursement online database. Monitors legislation and regulations.

American College of Preventive Medicine, *455 Massachusetts Ave. N.W., #200, 20001; (202) 466-2044. Fax, (202) 466-2662. Michael Barry, Executive Director.*
General email, info@acpm.org
Web, www.acpm.org

Membership: physicians in general preventive medicine, public health, international health, occupational medicine, and aerospace medicine. Provides educational opportunities; advocates public policies consistent with scientific principles of the discipline; supports the investigation and analysis of issues relevant to the field.

American College of Surgeons, *Washington Office, 20 F St. N.W., #1000, 20001; (202) 337-2701. Fax, (202) 337-4271. Christian Shalgian, Director, Advocacy and Health Policy, (202) 337-2701.*

General email, cshalgian@facs.org

Web, www.facs.org

Monitors legislation and regulations concerning surgery; conducts continuing education programs and sponsors scholarships for graduate medical education. Interests include hospital cancer programs, trauma care, hospital accreditation, and international research. (Headquarters in Chicago, Ill.)

American Health Quality Assn., *7918 Jones Branch Dr., #300, McLean, VA 22102; (202) 331-5790. Colleen Delaney Eubanks, Executive Director. General email, info@ahqa.org*

Web, www.ahqa.org

National network of private Quality Improvement Organizations (QIOs) that seek to improve health care provider performance through quality improvement, technical assistance, provider performance measurement feedback, teaching self-assessment techniques, responding to consumer complaints and appeals, and initiating community-based quality improvement programs. Monitors legislation and regulations.

American Medical Assn. (AMA), *Government Relations, 25 Massachusetts Ave. N.W., #600, 20001-7400; (202) 789-7400. Fax, (202) 789-7485. Richard Deem, Senior Vice President of Advocacy* Web, www.ama-assn.org

Membership: physicians, residents, and medical students. Provides information on the medical profession and health care; cooperates in setting standards for medical schools and hospital intern and residency training programs; offers physician placement service and counseling on management practices; provides continuing medical education. Interests include international research and peer review. Monitors legislation and regulations. (Headquarters in Chicago, Ill.)

American Osteopathic Assn., *Advocacy Center, 1090 Vermont Ave. N.W., #500, 20005; (202) 349-6740. Fax, (202) 544-3525. Ray Quintero, Senior Vice President, Public Policy. Toll-free, (800) 962-9008. General email, info@osteopathic.org*

Web, www.osteopathic.org

Membership: osteopathic physicians. Promotes public health, education, and research; accredits osteopathic educational institutions. Monitors legislation and regulations. (Headquarters in Chicago, Ill.)

American Podiatric Medical Assn., *9312 Old Georgetown Rd., Bethesda, MD 20814; (301) 581-9200. Fax, (301) 530-2752. Dr. James R. Christina, Executive Director. Web, www.apma.org and Twitter, @APMAtweets*

Membership: podiatrists in affiliated and related societies. Interests include advocacy in legislative affairs, health policy and practice, scientific meetings, and public education.

American Psychiatric Assn., *1000 Wilson Blvd., #1825, Arlington, VA 22209-3901; (703) 907-7300. Fax, (703) 907-1085. Dr. Saul Levin, Medical Director. Press, (703) 907-8640.*

Publishing, (703) 907-7322. Toll-free, (888) 357-7924. General email, apa@psych.org

Web, www.psychiatry.org and Twitter, @APAPsychiatric

Membership: psychiatrists. Promotes availability of high-quality psychiatric care; provides the public with information; assists state and local agencies; conducts educational programs for professionals and students in the field; participates in international meetings and research. Library open to members.

American Roentgen Ray Society, *44211 Slatestone Court, Leesburg, VA 20176-5109; (703) 729-3353. Fax, (703) 729-4839. Susan B. Cappitelli, Executive Director. Toll-free, (866) 940-2777. General email, info@arrs.org*

Web, www.arrs.org and Twitter, @ARRS_Radiology

Membership: physicians and researchers in radiology and allied sciences. Publishes research; conducts conferences; presents scholarships and awards; monitors international research.

American Society of Addiction Medicine, *4601 N. Park Ave., Upper Arcade, #101, Chevy Chase, MD 20815-4520; (301) 656-3920. Fax, (301) 656-3815. Penny Mills, Executive Vice President, (301) 547-4105. General email, email@asam.org*

Web, www.asam.org and Twitter, @ASAMorg

Membership: physicians and medical students. Supports the study and provision of effective treatment and care for people with alcohol and drug dependencies; educates physicians. Monitors legislation and regulations.

American Society of Nuclear Cardiology (ASNC), *4340 East-West Hwy., #1120, Bethesda, MD 20814; (301) 215-7575. Fax, (301) 215-7113. Kathleen Flood, Chief Executive Officer. General email, info@asnc.org*

Web, www.asnc.org

Membership: physicians, scientists, technologists, and other professionals engaged in nuclear cardiology practice or research. Provides professional education programs; establishes standards and guidelines for training and practice; promotes research worldwide. Works with agreement states to monitor user-licensing requirements of the Nuclear Regulatory Commission.

American Society of Transplant Surgeons, *2461 S. Clark St., #640, Arlington, VA 22202; (703) 414-7870. Fax, (703) 414-7874. Kim Gifford, Executive Director. General email, asts@asts.org*

Web, www.asts.org

Promotes education and research on organ and tissue transplantation for patients with end-stage organ failure. Provides information for policy decisions affecting the practice of transplantation. Offers professional development for transplant colleagues.

Assn. of American Medical Colleges (AAMC), *655 K St. N.W., #100, 20001-2399; (202) 828-0400. Fax, (202) 828-1125. Dr. Darrell G. Kirch, President.*

General email, aacas@aamc.org

Web, www.aamc.org and Twitter, @AAMCtoday

Membership: accredited U.S. and Canadian schools of medicine, teaching hospitals, health systems, academic and scientific societies, medical students and faculty, and residents and resident physicians. Administers Medical College Admission Test.

Clerkship Directors in Internal Medicine, *330 John Carlyle St., #610, Alexandria, VA 22314; (703) 341-4540. Fax, (703) 519-1893. Bergitta E. Cotroneo, Executive Vice President.*

General email, aaimonline@im.org

Web, www.im.org/p/cm/ld/fid=235

Membership: directors of third-year and fourth-year internal medicine clerkships at U.S. and Canadian medical schools. (Affiliated with Alliance for Academic Internal Medicine.)

College of American Pathologists, *Advocacy Division, 1350 Eye St. N.W., #590, 20005-3305; (202) 354-7100. Fax, (202) 354-8101. John Scott, Vice President. Information, (800) 392-9994.*

Web, www.cap.org and Twitter, @Pathologists

Membership: physicians who are board certified in clinical or anatomic pathology. Accredits laboratories and provides them with proficiency testing programs; promotes the practice of pathology and laboratory medicine worldwide. Monitors legislation and regulations. (Headquarters in Northfield, Ill.)

National Medical Assn., *8403 Colesville Rd., #820, Silver Spring, MD 20910; (202) 347-1895. Martin Hamlette, Executive Director.*

Web, www.nmanet.org

Membership: physicians of African descent. Supports increased participation of minorities in the health professions, especially medicine.

Physician Hospitals of America, *2025 M St. N.W., #800, 20036; (202) 367-1113. Fax, (202) 367-2113. John Richardson, Executive Director.*

General email, info@physicianhospitals.org

Web, www.physicianhospitals.org

Membership organization advocating the physician-owned hospital industry; provides networking and continuing education opportunities.

Physicians Committee for Responsible Medicine (PCRM), *5100 Wisconsin Ave. N.W., #400, 20016; (202) 686-2210. Fax, (202) 686-2216. Neal Barnard, President.*

General email, pcrm@pcrm.org

Web, www.pcrm.org

Membership: health care professionals, medical students, and laypersons interested in preventive medicine, nutrition, and higher standards in research. Conducts clinical research, educational programs, and public information campaigns; advocates more effective and compassionate health-related policies in government and in public and private institutions.

Society of Thoracic Surgeons, *Advocacy, 20 F St. N.W., #310C, 20001; (202) 787-1230. Fax, (202) 280-1477. Natalie Boden, Director, Communications, (312) 202-5819.*

General email, advocacy@sts.org

Web, www.sts.org

Membership: surgeons, researchers, and allied health care professionals in cardiothoracic surgery. Monitors legislation and regulations. (Headquarters in Chicaco, Ill.)

Veterinarians

▶**AGENCIES**

Food and Drug Administration (FDA) *(Health and Human Services Dept.), Center for Veterinary Medicine, 7519 Standish Pl., HFV-1, Rockville, MD 20855-0001; (240) 402-7002. Fax, (240) 276-9001. Dr. Bernadette Dunham, Director.*

General email, askcvm@fda.hhs.gov

Web, www.fda.gov/animalveterinary

Regulates the manufacture and distribution of drugs, food additives, feed, and devices for livestock and pets. Conducts research; works to ensure animal health and the safety of food derived from animals.

▶**NONGOVERNMENTAL**

American Veterinary Medical Assn., *Governmental Relations, 1910 Sunderland Pl. N.W., 20036-1642; (202) 789-0007. Fax, (202) 842-4360. Dr. Mark Lutschaunig, Director. Toll-free, (800) 321-1473.*

General email, avmagrd@avma.org

Web, www.avma.org

Monitors legislation and regulations that influence animal and human health and advance the veterinary medical profession. (Headquarters in Schaumburg, Ill.)

Assn. of American Veterinary Medical Colleges (AAVMC), *1101 Vermont Ave. N.W., #301, 20005-3536; (202) 371-9195. Fax, (202) 842-0773. Dr. Andrew T. Maccabe, Executive Director.*

Web, www.aavmc.org and Twitter, @AAVMC

Membership: U.S., Canadian, and international schools and colleges of veterinary medicine, departments of comparative medicine, and departments of veterinary science in agricultural colleges. Produces veterinary reports; provides information about scholarships and continuing education programs and sponsors conferences on veterinary medical issues.

National Zoological Park *(Smithsonian Institution), 3001 Connecticut Ave. N.W., 20008 (mailing address: DEVS, P.O. Box 37012, MRC 5516, Washington, DC 20013-7012); (202) 633-4888 (recorded information line). Fax, (202) 673-4836. Dennis W. Kelly, Executive Director. Library, (202) 633-1031. Press, (202) 633-3055. Friends of the Zoo, (202) 633-3038. TTY, (202) 673-7800. Zoo police, (202) 633-4134.*

Web, www.nationalzoo.si.edu

Conducts research on animal behavior, ecology, nutrition, reproductive physiology, pathology, and veterinary medicine.

Vision Care

▶AGENCIES

National Eye Institute *(National Institutes of Health),* *31 Center Dr., #6A32, MSC 2510, Bethesda, MD 20892-2510; (301) 496-5248. Fax, (301) 402-1065.* *Dr. Paul A. Sieving, Director. Information, (301) 496-5248.* *General email, 2020@nei.nih.gov*

Web, www.nei.nih.gov and Twitter, @NatEyeInstitute

Conducts and supports research, training, health information dissemination, and other programs with respect to blinding eye diseases, visual disorders, mechanisms of visual function, preservation of sight, and the special health problems and requirements of the blind.

▶NONGOVERNMENTAL

American Academy of Ophthalmology, *Governmental Affairs, 20 F St. N.W., #400, 20001-6701; (202) 737-6662. Fax, (202) 737-7061. Cathy G. Cohen, Vice President.* *General email, politicalaffairs@aaodc.org*

Web, www.aao.org

Membership: eye physicians and surgeons. Provides information on eye diseases. Monitors legislation, regulations, and international research. (Headquarters in San Francisco, Calif.)

American Board of Opticianry and National Contact Lens Examiners Board, *6506 Loisdale Rd., #209, Springfield, VA 22150; (703) 719-5800. Fax, (703) 719-9144. James Morris, Executive Director. Toll-free, (800) 296-1379.* *General email, mail@abo-ncle.org*

Web, www.abo-ncle.org

Establishes standards for opticians who dispense eyeglasses and contact lenses. Administers voluntary professional exams and awards certification to opticians and ophthalmic professionals; maintains registry of certified eyeglass and contact lens dispensers. Adopts and enforces continuing education requirements; assists state licensing boards; approves educational offerings for recertification requirements.

American Optometric Assn., *Washington Office, 1505 Prince St., #300, Alexandria, VA 22314-2874; (703) 739-9200. Fax, (703) 739-9497. Jon Hymes, Executive Director. Information, (800) 365-2219.* *General email, jfhymes@aoa.org*

Web, www.aoa.org and Twitter, @AOAConnect

Membership: optometrists, optometry students, and paraoptometric assistants and technicians in a federation of state, student, and armed forces optometric associations. Sets professional standards and provides research and information on eye care to the public. Monitors

legislation and regulations and acts as liaison with international optometric groups and government optometrists; conducts continuing education programs for optometrists and provides information on eye care. (Headquarters in St. Louis, Mo.)

American Society of Cataract and Refractive Surgery, *4000 Legato Rd., #700, Fairfax, VA 22033; (703) 591-2220. Fax, (703) 591-0614. David Karcher, Executive Director.* *Web, www.ascrs.org and Twitter, @ASCRStweets*

Membership: more than 9,000 ophthalmologists who specialize in cataract and refractive surgery. Offers educational programs and services to its members. Monitors regulations affecting ophthalmic practices. Sponsors independent research. Maintains a foundation dedicated to improving public understanding of ophthalmology and providing eye care to underserved parts of the world.

Assn. for Research in Vision and Ophthalmology (ARVO), *1801 Rockville Pike, #400, Rockville, MD 20852-5622; (240) 221-2900. Fax, (240) 221-0370. Iris M. Rush, Executive Director.* *General email, arvo@arvo.org*

Web, www.arvo.org and Twitter, @ARVOinfo

Promotes eye and vision research; issues awards for significant research and administers research grant program.

Assn. of Schools and Colleges of Optometry, *6110 Executive Blvd., #420, Rockville, MD 20852; (301) 231-5944. Fax, (301) 770-1828. Dawn Mancuso, Executive Director.* *General email, cdoyle@opted.org*

Web, www.opted.org and Twitter, @OptometricED

Membership: U.S. and Puerto Rican optometry schools and colleges and foreign affiliates. Provides information about the Optometry College Admission Test to students. Supports the international development of optometric education. Monitors legislation and regulations.

Eye Bank Assn. of America, *1015 18th St. N.W., #1010, 20036-5504; (202) 775-4999. Fax, (202) 429-6036. Kevin P. Corcoran, President.* *General email, info@restoresight.org*

Web, www.restoresight.org

Membership: eye banks in Brazil, Canada, England, Japan, Saudi Arabia, Taiwan, and the United States. Sets and enforces medical standards for processing, storing, evaluating, and distributing ocular and corneal tissue for transplantation; seeks to increase donations to eye, tissue, and organ banks; conducts training and certification programs for eye bank technicians; compiles statistics; accredits eye banks.

International Eye Foundation, *10801 Connecticut Ave., Kensington, MD 20895; (240) 290-0263. Fax, (240) 290-0269. Victoria M. Sheffield, President.* *General email, ief@iefusa.org*

Web, www.iefusa.org

Operates blindness prevention programs focusing on cataracts, trachoma, "river blindness," and childhood blindness, including vitamin A deficiency. Provides affordable ophthalmic instruments, equipment, and supplies to eye hospitals in developing countries to help lower surgical costs. Works to strengthen management and financial sustainability of eye hospitals and clinics in developing countries. Works with the World Health Organization, ministries of health, and international and indigenous organizations in Africa, Asia, Latin America, and eastern Europe to promote eye care.

Lab Division, *225 Reinekers Lane, #700, Alexandria, VA 22314; (703) 548-4580. Fax, (703) 548-4580. R. Michael Daley, Chief Executive Officer; Steve Sutherlin, Lab Division Liaison. Toll-free, (866) 826-0290. General email, info@thevisioncouncil.org*

Web, www.thevisioncouncil.org/members/optical-lab-division

Membership: optical laboratories. Promotes the eyewear industry; collects and disseminates lab performance data; sponsors conferences. Monitors legislation and regulations. (Affiliated with The Vision Council.)

The Vision Council, *225 Reinekers Lane, #700, Alexandria, VA 22314; (703) 548-4560. Fax, (703) 548-4580. Mike Daley, Chief Executive Officer. Toll-free, (866) 826-0290. General email, info@thevisioncouncil.org*

Web, www.thevisioncouncil.org and Twitter, @opticalindustry

Sponsors trade shows and public relations programs for the ophthalmic industry. Educates the public on developments in the optical industry. Represents manufacturers and distributors of optical products and equipment.

HEALTH SERVICES FOR SPECIAL GROUPS

General

▶AGENCIES

Administration for Children and Families (ACF) *(Health and Human Services Dept.),* *330 C St. S.W., 20201 (mailing address: 370 L'Enfant Promenade S.W., Washington, DC 20447); (202) 401-2337. Mark Greenberg, Assistant Secretary, Acting. Public Affairs, (202) 401-9215. Web, www.acf.hhs.gov*

Administers and funds programs for Native Americans, children, youth, low-income families, and those with intellectual and developmental disabilities. Responsible for Social Services Block Grants to the states. Provides agencies with technical assistance; administers Head Start program; funds the National Runaway Safe Line, (800) RUNAWAY (786-2929), the Domestic Violence Hotline, (800) 799-7233, the National Teen Dating Abuse Help Line, (866) 331-9474, and programs for abused children.

Centers for Medicare and Medicaid Services (CMS) *(Health and Human Services Dept.),* *Continuing Care Providers, 7500 Security Blvd., C2-21-16, Baltimore, MD 21244-1850; (410) 786-4857. Fax, (410) 786-0194. Peggye Wilkerson, Director.*

Web, www.cms.gov

Monitors compliance with government standards of psychiatric hospitals and long-term and intermediate care facilities, including residential treatment facilities, community mental health centers, intermediate care facilities for mental retardation, outpatient rehabilitation facilities, home health care, hospice care, portable X-ray units, dialysis facilities, and outpatient physical, language, and speech therapy facilities. Focus includes quality of care, environmental conditions, and participation in Medicaid and Medicare programs. Coordinates health care programs for the mentally challenged.

Education Dept., *Special Education and Rehabilitative Services, Rehabilitative Services Administration, 400 Maryland Ave. S.W., 20202-7100; (202) 245-7468. Fax, (202) 245-7591. Janet L. LaBreck, Commissioner. Web, www2.ed.gov/about/offices/list/osers/rsa*

Allocates funds to state agencies and nonprofit organizations for programs serving eligible physically and mentally disabled persons; services provided by these funds include medical and psychological treatment as well as establishment of supported-employment and independent-living programs.

Eunice Kennedy Shriver National Institute of Child Health and Human Development *(National Institutes of Health), National Center for Medical Rehabilitation Research, 6100 Executive Blvd., Bldg. 6100, #2A-03, MSC 7510, Bethesda, MD 20892; (301) 402-2242. Fax, (301) 402-0832. Dr. Alison Cernich, Director. Web, www.nichd.nih.gov/about/org/ncmrr*

Fosters the development of scientific knowledge needed to enhance the health, productivity, independence, and quality of life of persons with disabilities. Supports a program of basic and applied research promoting tissue plasticity, assistive technology and devices, improved outcomes, and increased patient participation.

Health Resources and Services Administration *(Health and Human Services Dept.), Bureau of Primary Health Care, 5600 Fishers Lane, #16W29, Rockville, MD 20857; (301) 594-4110. Fax, (301) 594-4072. Tonya Bowers, Associate Administrator, Acting. Web, www.bphc.hrsa.gov*

Advocates improving the health of racial and ethnic minority populations and others who experience difficulty in accessing health care, through the development of health policies and programs that will increase access and eliminate health disparities.

Health Resources and Services Administration *(Health and Human Services Dept.), Policy Program and Development, 5600 Fishers Lane, #17C-26, Rockville, MD 20857; (301) 594-4300. Fax, (301) 594-4997. Jennifer Joseph, Director. Web, www.bphc.hrsa.gov*

Awards grants to public and nonprofit migrant, community, and health care centers to provide direct health care services in areas that are medically underserved. Provides staff support for National Advisory Council on Migrant Health. Administers Consolidated Health Centers Program and other bureau-funded programs.

Immigration and Customs Enforcement (ICE)
(Homeland Security Dept.), ICE Health Service Corps, 500 12th St. S.W., 2nd Floor, 20536; (202) 732-4600. Vacant, Assistant Director, (202) 732-3047. Web, www.ice.gov/about/offices/enforcement-removal-operations/ihs

Consists of U.S. Public Health Service commissioned officers, federal civil servants, and contract support staff. Administers ICE's detainee health care program, providing direct care to detained aliens at designated facilities and overseeing medical care at other detention facilities.

Indian Health Service *(Health and Human Services Dept.), 5600 Fishers Lane, Rockville, MD 20857; (202) 857-3293. Roger G. McSwain, Principal Deputy Director. Information, (301) 443-3593. TTY, (301) 443-6394. Web, www.ihs.gov*

Acts as the health advocate for and operates hospitals and health centers that provide preventive, curative, and community health care for Native Americans and Alaska Natives. Provides and improves sanitation and water supply systems in Native American and Alaska Native communities.

National Institute on Deafness and Other Communication Disorders *(National Institutes of Health), 31 Center Dr., #3C02, MSC-2320, Bethesda, MD 20892-2320; (301) 496-7243. Fax, (301) 402-0018. Dr. James F. Battey Jr., Director. Toll-free, (800) 241-1044. TTY, (800) 241-1055. Interpreter service, (301) 496-1807. Evenings and weekends, (301) 496-3315. General email, nidcdinfo@nidcd.nih.gov*

Web, www.nidcd.nih.gov

Conducts and supports research and research training and disseminates information on hearing disorders and other communication processes, including diseases that affect hearing, balance, smell, taste, voice, speech, and language. Monitors international research.

National Institute on Minority Health and Health Disparities (NIMHD) *(National Institutes of Health), 2 Democracy Plaza, 6707 Democracy Blvd., #800, MSC-5465, Bethesda, MD 20892-5465; (301) 402-1366. Fax, (301) 480-4049. Yvonne T. Maddox, Director, Acting. General email, nimhdinfor@nimhd.nih.gov*

Web, www.nimhd.nih.gov

Promotes minority health and leads, coordinates, supports, and assesses the NIH's effort to eliminate health disparities. Conducts and supports basic clinical, social, and behavioral research; promotes research infrastructure and training; fosters emerging programs; disseminates information; and reaches out to minority and other communities suffering from health disparities.

▶ CONGRESS

For a listing of relevant congressional committees and subcommittees, please see pages 344–345 or the Appendix.

▶ NONGOVERNMENTAL

Assn. of Clinicians for the Underserved (ACU), *1420 Spring Hill Rd., #600, Tysons Corner, VA 22102; (844) 422-8247. Fax, (703) 562-8801. Craig Kennedy, Executive Director. General email, acu@clinicians.org*

Web, www.clinicians.org and Twitter, @ACUunderserved

Membership: clinicians, advocates, and health care organizations. Works to improve the health of underserved populations and eliminate health disparities in the United States. Educates and supports health care clinicians serving these populations. Interests include health care access, transdisciplinary approaches to health care, workforce development and diversity, pharmaceutical access, and health information technology.

Catholic Health Assn. of the United States, *1875 Eye St. N.W., #1000, 20006; (202) 296-3993. Fax, (202) 296-3997. Sister Carol Keehan, President. Web, www.chausa.org and Twitter, @TheCHAUSA*

Concerned with the health care needs of the poor and disadvantaged. Promotes health care reform, including universal insurance coverage, and more cost-effective, affordable health care.

Easter Seals, *Washington Region Office, 1420 Spring St., Silver Spring, MD 20910; (301) 588-8700. Fax, (301) 920-9770. Lisa Reeves, Executive Officer. Toll-free, (800) 886 3771. Web, www.easterseals.com/DCMDVA*

Promotes equal opportunity for people with disabilities or special needs. Interests include child development, early childhood education, adult medical daycare services, and services aimed to aid military veterans and their families as they reenter their communities. (Headquarters in Chicago, Ill.)

National Assn. of Community Health Centers, *7501 Wisconsin Ave., #1100W, Bethesda, MD 20814; (301) 347-0400. Fax, (301) 347-0459. Tom Van Coverden, President. General email, shansen@nachc.com*

Web, www.nachc.com

Membership: community, migrant, public housing, and homeless health centers. Represents America's federally qualified health centers. Seeks to ensure the continued development of community health care programs through policy analysis, research, technical assistance, publications, education, and training.

National Health Law Program, *Washington Office, 1444 Eye St. N.W., #1105, 20005; (202) 289-7661. Fax, (202) 289-7724. Elizabeth G. Taylor, Executive Director. General email, nhelpdc@healthlaw.org*

Web, www.healthlaw.org

Organization of lawyers representing the economically disadvantaged and minorities. Offers technical assistance, workshops, seminars, and training for health law specialists. Issues include health care reform, Medicaid, child and adolescent health, and disability and reproductive rights.

Rehabilitation Engineering and Assistive Technology Society of North America (RESNA), *1700 N. Moore St., #1540, Arlington, VA 22209-1903; (703) 524-6686. Fax, (703) 524-6630. Michael Birogioli, Executive Director. General email, info@resna.org*

Web, www.resna.org and Twitter, @RESNAorg

Membership: engineers, health professionals, assistive technologists, persons with disabilities, and others. Promotes and supports developments in rehabilitation engineering and technology; acts as an information clearinghouse. (RESNA stands for Rehabilitation Engineering and Assistive Technology Society of North America.)

Minority Health

▶**AGENCIES**

Agency for Health Care Research and Quality (AHCRQ) *(Health and Human Services Dept.), Communication and Knowledge Transfer, 5600 Fishers Lane, Rockville, MD 20857; (301) 427-1364. Fax, (301) 427-1873. Howard Holland, Director, (301) 427-1104. Public inquiries, (301) 427-1104. General email, info@ahrq.gov*

Web, www.ahrq.gov/about/ockt/ocktmiss.htm

Researches health care quality among minorities. Identifies and devises solutions for disparities in access to care, diagnosis, and treatment of illness. Provides health care professionals with research on minority health.

Assistant Secretary for Health *(Health and Human Services Dept.), Minority Health, 1101 Wootton Pkwy., #600, Rockville, MD 20852; (240) 453-2882. Fax, (240) 453-2883. Dr. J. Nadine Gracia, Deputy Assistant Secretary. Information, (800) 444-6472. General email, info@minorityhealth.gov*

Web, http://minorityhealth.hhs.gov and Twitter, @MinorityHealth

Oversees the implementation of the secretary's Task Force on Black and Minority Health and legislative mandates; develops programs to meet the health care needs of minorities; awards grants to coalitions of minority community organizations.

Centers for Medicare and Medicaid Services (CMS) *(Health and Human Services Dept.), Minority Health, 7500 Security Blvd., S2-12-17, Baltimore, MD 21244; (410) 786-6842. Cara V. James, Director, (410) 786-2773. Web, www.cms.gov/About-CMS/Agency-Information/Office-of-Minority-Health*

Seeks to reduce inequalities in health outcomes of racial and ethnic minority populations. Manages disparities data and evaluates impact; coordinates minority health initiatives within the agency; serves as the liaison to other agency offices of minority health.

Education Dept., *White House Initiative on Asian Americans and Pacific Islanders, 550 12th St. S.W., 10th Floor, 20202; (202) 245-6418. Fax, (202) 245-7166. Doua Thor, Executive Director. Press, (202) 245-6353. General email, whitehouseaapi@ed.gov*

Web, http://sites.ed.gov/whieeaa and Twitter, @whitehouseAAPI

Works to increase Asian American and Pacific Islander participation in federal health programs. Interests include reducing health risks, improving access to high-quality health care, and promoting healthy living.

Food and Drug Administration (FDA) *(Health and Human Services Dept.), Minority Health, 10903 New Hampshire Ave., Silver Spring, MD 20993; (240) 402-5084. Fax, (301) 847-3536. Jonca Bull, Director, (301) 796-8000. General email, omh@fda.hhs.gov*

Web, www.fda.gov/aboutfda/centersoffices/oc/officeofminorityhealth/default.htm, www.fda.gov/forconsumers/byaudience/minorityhealth/default.htm and Twitter, @FDAOMH

Serves as the principal advisor to the Commissioner on minority health and health disparities. Provides leadership and direction in identifying agency actions that can help reduce health disparities, including the coordination of efforts across the agency. Promotes effective communication and the dissemination of information to the public, particularly underserved, vulnerable populations.

Health and Human Services Dept. (HHS), *Civil Rights, 200 Independence Ave. S.W., #515F, 20201; (202) 619-0403. Fax, (202) 619-3437. Jocelyn Samuels, Director. TTY, (800) 537-7697. General email, OCRMail@hhs.gov*

Web, www.hhs.gov/ocr

Administers and enforces laws prohibiting discrimination on the basis of race, color, sex, national origin, religion, age, or disability in programs receiving federal funds from the department; authorized to discontinue funding. Responsible for health information privacy under the Health Insurance Portability and Accountability Act.

Health and Human Services Dept. (HHS), *Minority Health, 1101 Wootton Pkwy., #600, Rockville, MD 20852; (240) 453-2882. Fax, (240) 453-2883. Dr. Nadine Gracia, Deputy Assistant Secretary. Information, (800) 444-6472. TTY, (301) 251-1432. General email, info@minorityhealth.hhs.gov*

Web, http://minorityhealth.hhs.gov

Promotes improved health among racial and ethnic minority populations. Advises the Health and Human Services Dept. secretary and the Office of Public Health and

National Institutes of Health

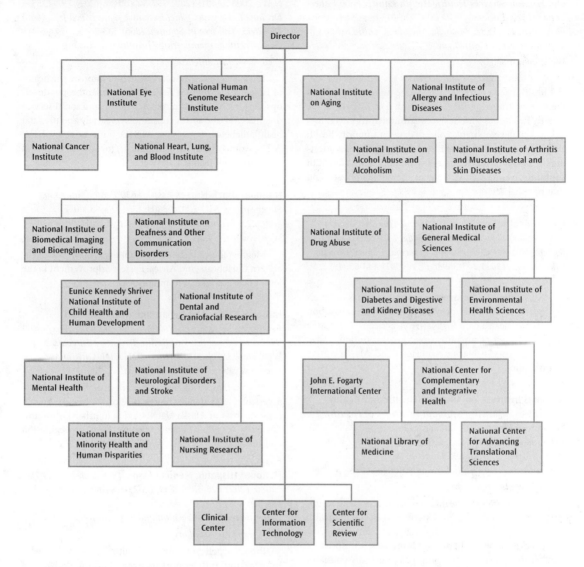

Science on public health program activities affecting American Indian and Alaska Native, Black/African American, Asian American, Pacific Islander, Native Hawaiian, and Hispanic populations. Awards grants to programs and projects that address minority health issues, including prevention projects to administer health promotion, education, and disease prevention programs.

Health and Human Services Dept. (HHS), *Minority Health Resource Center, 8400 Corporate Dr., #500, Landover, MD 20785 (mailing address: P.O. Box 37337, Washington, DC 20013-7337); (301) 251-1797. Fax, (301) 251-2160. Michelle Loosli, Director. Information, (800) 444-6472. TTY, (301) 251-1432.*
General email, info@minorityhealth.hhs.gov
Web, www.minorityhealth.hhs.gov

Serves as a national resource and referral service on minority health issues. Distributes information on health

topics such as substance abuse, cancer, heart disease, violence, diabetes, HIV/AIDS, and infant mortality. Provides free services, including customized database searches, publications, mailing lists, and referrals regarding American Indian and Alaska Native, African American, Asian American and Pacific Islander, and Hispanic populations.

Health Resources and Services Administration *(Health and Human Services Dept.), Bureau of Primary Health Care, 5600 Fishers Lane, #16W29, Rockville, MD 20857; (301) 594-4110. Fax, (301) 594-4072. Tonya Bowers, Associate Administrator, Acting.*
Web, www.bphc.hrsa.gov

Advises the associate administrator for primary care on public health activities affecting ethnic, racial, and other minority groups, including migrant and seasonal farmworkers, homeless persons, persons living in public housing, older adults, and women.

Health Resources and Services Administration *(Health and Human Services Dept.), Health Equity, 5600 Fishers Lane, #1270, Rockville, MD 20857; (301) 443-2964. Fax, (301) 443-7853. Michelle Allender-Smith, Director. General email, ask@hrsa.gov*

Web, www.hrsa.gov

Sponsors programs and activities that address the special health needs of racial and ethnic minorities. Advises the administrator on minority health issues affecting the Health Resources and Services Administration (HRSA) and policy development; collects data on minority health activities within HRSA; represents HRSA programs affecting the health of racial and ethnic minorities to the health community and organizations in the public, private, and international sectors.

Indian Health Service *(Health and Human Services Dept.), 5600 Fishers Lane, Rockville, MD 20857; (202) 857-3293. Roger G. McSwain, Principal Deputy Director. Information, (301) 443-3593. TTY, (301) 443-6394. Web, www.ihs.gov*

Acts as the health advocate for and operates hospitals and health centers that provide preventive, curative, and community health care for Native Americans and Alaska Natives. Provides and improves sanitation and water supply systems in Native American and Alaska Native communities.

National Institute on Minority Health and Health Disparities (NIMHD) *(National Institutes of Health), 2 Democracy Plaza, 6707 Democracy Blvd., #800, MSC-5465, Bethesda, MD 20892-5465; (301) 402-1366. Fax, (301) 480-4049. Yvonne T. Maddox, Director, Acting. General email, nimhdinfor@nimhd.nih.gov*

Web, www.nimhd.nih.gov

Promotes minority health and leads, coordinates, supports, and assesses the NIH's effort to eliminate health disparities. Conducts and supports basic clinical, social, and behavioral research; promotes research infrastructure and training; fosters emerging programs; disseminates information; and reaches out to minority and other communities suffering from health disparities.

▶ **NONGOVERNMENTAL**

Asian and Pacific Islander American Health Forum, *Government Relations, 1629 K St. N.W., #400, 20006; (202) 466-7772. Fax, (202) 296-0610. Amina Abbas, Director, Government Relations. General email, info@apiahf.org*

Web, www.apiahf.org and Twitter, @apiahf

Works to improve the health status of and access to care by Asian Americans and Pacific Islanders and to address health disparities, including disability and mental health, HIV/AIDS, smoking, and cancer. Monitors legislation in the areas of health, politics, and social and economic issues that affect Asian Americans, native Hawaiians, and Pacific Islanders.

National Alliance for Hispanic Health, *1501 16th St. N.W., 20036-1401; (202) 387-5000. Fax, (202) 797-4353. Dr. Jane L. Delgado, Chief Executive Officer. Toll-free, (866) 783-2645. Toll-free in Spanish, (866) 783-2645. General email, membership@healthyamericas.org*

Web, www.hispanichealth.org

Advocates and conducts research to improve the health of Hispanics; promotes research and philanthropy; develops capacity of community-based health and social service organizations. Educates consumers on family and prenatal health, diabetes, depression, ADHD, immunization, HIV/AIDS, women's health, osteoporosis, tobacco control, and environmental health.

National Black Nurses Assn., *8630 Fenton St., #330, Silver Spring, MD 20910-3803; (301) 589-3200. Fax, (301) 589-3223. Millicent Gorham, Executive Director. Web, www.nbna.org*

Membership: Black nurses from the United States, the eastern Caribbean, and Africa. Fosters improvement in the level of care available to minorities.

National Council of Urban Indian Health, *924 Pennsylvania Ave. S.E., 20003; (202) 544-0344. Fax, (202) 544-9394. Maurice (Mo) Smith, Executive Director. Web, www.ncuih.org, Twitter, @NCUIH_Official and Facebook, www.facebook.com/NCUIH*

Membership: Indian health care providers. Supports accessible, high-quality health care programs for American Indians and Alaska Natives living in urban communities. Provides education and training. Monitors legislation and funding.

National Hispanic Medical Assn., *1920 L St. N.W., #725, 20036; (202) 628-5895. Fax, (202) 628-5898. Dr. Elena V. Rios, President. General email, nhma@nhmamd.org*

Web, www.nhmamd.org

Provides policymakers and health care providers with information and support to strengthen the delivery of health care to Hispanic communities in the United States. Areas of interest include high-quality care and increased opportunities in medical education for Latinos. Works with federal officials, other Hispanic advocacy groups, and Congress to eliminate disparities in health care for minorities.

National Minority AIDS Council (NMAC), *1000 Vermont Ave. N.W., #200, 20005; (202) 483-6622. Fax, (202) 483-1135. Paul A. Kawata, Executive Director. General email, communications@nmac.org*

Web, www.nmac.org

Works to build the capacity of small faith- and community-based organizations delivering HIV/AIDS services in communities of color. Holds national conferences; administers treatment and research programs and training; disseminates electronic and printed resource materials; conducts public policy advocacy.

Older Adults

► **AGENCIES**

Centers for Medicare and Medicaid Services (CMS) *(Health and Human Services Dept.), Nursing Homes,* 7500 Security Blvd., C2-21-16, Baltimore, MD 21244; (410) 786-7818. Fax, (410) 786-0194. Karen Tritz, Director. Web, www.cms.gov

Monitors compliance of nursing homes with government standards. Focus includes quality of care, environmental conditions, and participation in Medicaid and Medicare programs.

National Institute on Aging *(National Institutes of Health),* 31 Center Dr., Bldg. 31, #5C27, MSC 2292, Bethesda, MD 20892-2292; (301) 496-9265. Fax, (301) 496-2525. Dr. Richard J. Hodes, Director. Communications and Public Liaison, (301) 496-1752. Information Center, (800) 222-2225. TTY, (800) 222-4225. Alzheimer's Disease Education and Referral Center, (800) 438-4380. General email, niaic@nih.gov

Web, www.nia.nih.gov

Conducts and supports biomedical, social, and behavioral research and training related to the aging process and the diseases and special problems of the aged. Manages the Alzheimer's Disease Education and Referral Center (www.alzheimers.nia.nih.gov).

Veterans Health Administration (VHA) *(Veterans Affairs Dept.), Geriatrics and Extended Care,* 810 Vermont Ave. N.W., #10P4G, 20420; (202) 461-6750. Fax, (202) 465-6195. Dr. Richard M. Allman, Chief Consultant. Web, www.va.gov/geriatrics

Administers research, educational, and clinical health care programs in geriatrics at VA and community nursing homes, personal care homes, VA domiciliaries, state veterans' homes, and in home-based and other noninstitutional care.

► **NONGOVERNMENTAL**

AARP, 601 E St. N.W., 20049; (202) 434-2277. Jo Ann C. Jenkins, Chief Executive Officer. Press, (202) 434-2560. Library, (202) 434-6233. TTY, (877) 434-7598. Toll-free, (888) 687-2277. Membership, (202) 434-3525. General email, member@aarp.org

Web, www.aarp.org

Membership: people fifty years of age and older. Conducts educational and counseling programs in areas concerning older adults, such as widowed persons services, health promotion, housing, and consumer protection.

AARP, *Federal Affairs Health and Family,* 601 E St. N.W., 20049; (202) 434-3770. Fax, (202) 434-3745. Ariel Gonzalez, Director of Health and Family Advocacy. Main switchboard, (202) 434-2277. Web, www.aarp.org

Maintains the Legal Counsel for the Elderly, which acts as advocate on behalf of older residents of the District of Columbia who reside in nursing homes and board and care homes. Monitors legislation and regulations.

AARP Foundation, 601 E St. N.W., 20049; (202) 434-6200. Fax, (202) 434-6593. Lisa Marsh Ryerson, Executive Director. Press, (202) 434-2560. Toll-free, (888) 687-2277. General email, foundation@aarp.org

Web, www.aarp.org/foundation

Seeks to educate the public on aging issues; sponsors conferences and produces publications on age-related concerns. Interests include aging and living environments for older persons. Funds age-related research, educational grants, legal hotlines, senior employment programs, and reverse mortgage projects. (Affiliated with AARP.)

Alliance for Aging Research, 1700 K St. N.W., #740, 20006; (202) 293-2856. Fax, (202) 955-8394. Sue Peschin, Executive Director. General email, info@agingresearch.org

Web, www.agingresearch.org

Membership: senior corporate and foundation executives, science leaders, and congressional representatives. Citizen advocacy organization that seeks to improve the health and independence of older Americans through public and private research.

Alliance for Retired Americans, 815 16th St. N.W., 4th Floor North, 20006-4104; (202) 637-5399. Fax, (202) 637-5398. Robert Roach, President. Membership, (800) 333-7212. Web, www.retiredamericans.org

Supports expansion of Medicare, improved health programs, national health care, and reduced cost of drugs. Nursing Home Information Service provides information on nursing home standards and regulations. Monitors legislation and regulations. (Affiliate of the AFL-CIO.)

Alzheimer's Assn., *Advocacy and Public Policy,* 1212 New York Ave., #800, 20005-6105; (202) 393-7737. Fax, (866) 865-0270. Robert J. Egge, Chief Public Policy Officer. Toll-free, (800) 272-3900. General email, advocate@alz.org

Web, www.alz.org

Offers family support services and educates the public about Alzheimer's disease, a neurological disorder mainly affecting the brain tissue in older adults. Promotes research and long-term care protection; maintains liaison with Alzheimer's associations abroad. Monitors legislation and regulations. (Headquarters in Chicago, Ill.)

American Assn. for Geriatric Psychiatry, 6728 Old McLean Village Dr., McLean, VA 22101; (703) 556-9222. Fax, (703) 556-8729. Christopher N. Wood, Executive Officer, (703) 556-9222, ext. 142. General email, main@aagponline.org

Web, www.aagponline.org

Works to improve the practice of geriatric psychiatry and knowledge about it through education, research, and advocacy. Monitors legislation and regulations.

Gerontological Society of America, *1220 L St. N.W., #901, 20005-4018; (202) 842-1275. Fax, (202) 587-5860. James Appleby, Executive Director, (202) 587-2821.*
General email, geron@geron.org

Web, www.geron.org

Scientific organization of researchers, educators, and professionals in the field of aging. Promotes the study of aging and the application of research to public policy. Interests include health and civic engagement.

Leading Age, *2519 Connecticut Ave. N.W., 20008-1520; (202) 783-2242. Fax, (202) 783-2255. Katie Smith Sloan, Chief Executive Officer.*
General email, info@leadingage.org

Web, www.leadingage.org

Membership: nonprofit nursing homes, housing, and health-related facilities for the elderly sponsored by religious, fraternal, labor, private, and governmental organizations. Conducts research on long-term care for the elderly; sponsors institutes and workshops on accreditation, financing, and institutional life. Monitors legislation and regulations.

National Assn. for Home Care and Hospice, *228 7th St. S.E., 20003; (202) 547-7424. Fax, (202) 547-3540. Val J. Halamandaris, President.*
General email, info@nahc.org

Web, www.nahc.org

Membership: hospice, home care, and private-duty providers. Advocates the rights of the aged, disabled, and ill to remain independent in their own homes as long as possible. Monitors legislation and regulations.

National Caucus and Center on Black Aging, Inc., *1220 L St. N.W., #800, 20005-2407; (202) 637-8400. Fax, (202) 347-0895. Karyne Jones, President.*
General email, support@ncba-aged.org

Web, www.ncba-aged.org

Concerned with issues that affect older Black Americans and other minorities. Sponsors employment and housing programs for older adults and education and training for professionals in gerontology. Monitors legislation and regulations.

National Consumer Voice for Quality Long-Term Care (NCCNHR), *1001 Connecticut Ave. N.W., #425, 20036; (202) 332-2275. Fax, (866) 230-9789. Lori O. Smetanka, Executive Director, Acting; Amanda Overall Laib, National Long-Term Care Ombudsman Resource Center Director, Acting.*
General email, info@theconsumervoice.org

Web, www.theconsumervoice.org and Facebook, www.facebook.com/theconsumervoice

Advocates high-quality care and quality of life for consumers in all long-term care settings. Promotes citizen participation in all aspects of nursing homes; acts as clearinghouse for nursing home advocacy. Hosts National Long-Term Care Ombudsman Resource Center.

National Council on Aging, *251 18th St. South, #500, Arlington, VA 22202; (571) 527-3900. Fax, (571) 527-3901. James P. Firman, President. Press, (571) 527-3914. Eldercare locator, (800) 677-1116.*
General email, info@ncoa.org

Web, www.ncoa.org, Twitter, @NCOAging and Facebook, www.facebook.com/NCOAging

Promotes the physical, mental, and emotional health of older persons and studies adult day care and community-based long-term care. Monitors legislation and regulations.

National Hispanic Council on Aging, *Walker Bldg., 734 15th St. N.W., #1050, 20005; (202) 347-9733. Fax, (202) 347-9735. Yanira Cruz, President.*
General email, nhcoa@nhcoa.org

Web, www.nhcoa.org

Membership: senior citizens, health care workers, professionals in the field of aging, and others in the United States and Puerto Rico who are interested in topics related to Hispanics and aging. Provides research training, policy analysis, consulting, and technical assistance; sponsors seminars, workshops, and management internships.

National Long-Term Care Ombudsman Resource Center, *1001 Connecticut Ave. N.W., #425, 20036; (202) 332-2275, ext. 222. Fax, (202) 332-2949. Lori O. Smetanka, Director.*
General email, ombudcenter@theconsumervoice.org

Web, www.ltcombudsman.org

Provides technical assistance, management guidance, policy analysis, and program development information on behalf of state and substate ombudsman programs. (Affiliate of the National Consumer Voice for Quality Long-Term Care.)

Prenatal, Maternal, and Child Health Care

▶**AGENCIES**

Assistant Secretary for Health *(Health and Human Services Dept.), Adolescent Health, 1101 Wootton Pkwy., #700, Rockville, MD 20852; (240) 453-2846. Evelyn Kappeler, Director.*
General email, oah.gov@hhs.gov

Web, www.hhs.gov/ash/oah

Supports and evaluates teen pregnancy prevention programs; implements the Pregnancy Assistance Fund; coordinates HHS efforts related to adolescent health promotion and disease prevention.

Centers for Medicare and Medicaid Services (CMS) *(Health and Human Services Dept.), Center for Medicaid and CHIP Services, 7500 Security Blvd., #C5-21-17, Baltimore, MD 21244; (410) 786-3871. Fax, (410) 786-0025. Victoria (Vikki) Wachino, Director; Tim Hill, Deputy Director.*

Web, www.cms.gov/About-CMS/Agency-Information/ CMSLeadership/office_CMCSC.html and www.medicaid.gov

Develops health care policies and programs for needy children under Medicaid; works with the Public Health Service and other related agencies to coordinate the department's child health resources.

Environmental Protection Agency (EPA), *Children's Health Protection, 1301 Constitution Ave., #1144, MC 1107T, 20460; (202) 564-2188. Fax, (202) 564-2733. Dr. Ruth A. Etzel, Director.*
Web, www2.epa.gov/aboutepa/about-office-childrens-health-protection-ochp and www2.epa.gov/children

Supports and facilitates the EPA's efforts to protect children's health from environmental risks, both domestically and internationally. Provides leadership on interagency Healthy Homes Work Group and Healthy School Environments Initiative. Offers grants through the Office of Children's Health Protection and Environmental Education (OCHPEE).

Eunice Kennedy Shriver National Institute of Child Health and Human Development *(National Institutes of Health), 31 Center Dr., Bldg. 31, #2A03, MSC 2425, Bethesda, MD 20892-2425 (mailing address: NICHD Information Resource Center, P.O. Box 3006, Rockville, MD 20847); (301) 496-1848. Fax, (301) 402-1104. Dr. Catherine Y. Spong, Director, Acting. Toll-free, (800) 370-2943. Toll-free fax, (866) 760-5947. Media, (301) 496-5133. General email, nichdinformationresourcecenter@ mail.nih.gov*
Web, www.nichd.nih.gov

Supports and conducts research in biomedical, behavioral, and social sciences related to child and maternal health, medical rehabilitation, and reproductive sciences. Interests include demography, social sciences, and population dynamics; male/female fertility and infertility; developing and evaluating contraceptive methods; safety and efficacy of pharmaceuticals for pregnant women, infants, and children; HIV/AIDS infection, transmission, and associated infections; pediatric growth and endocrine research; child development and behavior; developmental biology, typical and atypical development; intellectual and developmental disabilities; gynecologic health conditions, including pelvic floor disorders; pregnancy, labor, and delivery; fetal and infant health; sudden infant death syndrome (SIDS); childhood injury and critical illness; genetics, genomics, and rare diseases; epidemiology and biostatistics; health behavior; medical rehabilitation, including brain injury, stroke, and spinal cord injury.

Eunice Kennedy Shriver National Institute of Child Health and Human Development *(National Institutes of Health), Division of Extramural Research, Child Development and Behavior Branch, 6100 Executive Blvd., #4B05H, MSC 7510, Bethesda, MD 20892-7510; (301) 435-6879. Lisa Freund, Branch Chief.*
Web, www.nichd.nih.gov/about/org/der/branches/cdbb

Develops scientific initiatives and supports research and research training relevant to the psychological,

neurobiological, language, behavioral, and educational development and health of children. Major research areas include behavioral pediatrics, cognitive development, behavioral neuroscience, psychobiology, early learning and school readiness, language and bilingualism, math and science cognition, learning disabilities, and social and emotional development.

Eunice Kennedy Shriver National Institute of Child Health and Human Development *(National Institutes of Health), Division of Extramural Research, Developmental Biology and Structural Variation Branch, 6100 Executive Blvd., #4B01E, MSC 7510, Bethesda, MD, 20892-7510; (301) 496-5541. Fax, (301) 480-0303. Dr. Arthur Tyl Hewitt, Branch Chief.*
Web, www.nichd.nih.gov/about/org/der/branches/dbsvb

Supports basic and clinical research on normal and abnormal development that relates to the causes and prevention of structural birth defects, as well as research training in relevant academic and medical areas. Research focuses on elucidating the biochemical, molecular biologic, genetic, and cellular mechanisms of embryonic development.

Eunice Kennedy Shriver National Institute of Child Health and Human Development *(National Institutes of Health), Division of Extramural Research, Maternal and Pediatric Infectious Disease Branch, 6100 Executive Blvd., #4B11, MSC 7510, Bethesda, MD 20892-7510; (301) 435-6868. Rohan Hazra, Branch Chief.*
Web, www.nichd.nih.gov/about/org/der/branches/mpidb

Supports and conducts research into the epidemiology, natural history, pathogenesis, transmission, treatment, and prevention of infectious diseases, including congenital infections such as cytomegalovirus and toxoplasmosis; tropical diseases specifically affecting children and pregnant women; and vaccine-preventable disease in infants, children, adolescents, and women.

Eunice Kennedy Shriver National Institute of Child Health and Human Development *(National Institutes of Health), Division of Extramural Research, Obstetric and Pediatric Pharmacology and Therapeutics Branch, 6100 Executive Blvd., #4A01B, MSC 7510, Bethesda, MD 20892-7510; (301) 435-6865. Fax, (301) 480-2897. Anne Zajicek, Branch Chief.*
Web, www.nichd.nih.gov/about/org/der/branches/opptb

Promotes basic, translational, and clinical research to improve the safety and efficacy of therapeutics, primarily pharmaceuticals, and to ensure centralization and coordination of research, clinical trials, and drug development activities for obstetric and pediatric populations. Develops and supports an understanding of how to appropriately treat disease during pregnancy, infancy, childhood, and adolescence using therapeutic approaches, including medications that are appropriately tested within their target populations.

Eunice Kennedy Shriver National Institute of Child Health and Human Development *(National Institutes of Health), Division of Extramural Research, Pediatric Growth and Nutrition Branch, 6100 Executive Blvd.,*

#4B05K, MSC 7510, Bethesda, MD 20892-7510; (301) 496-5593. Fax, (301) 480-9791. Gilman Drew Grave, Branch Chief.
Web, www.nichd.nih.gov/about/org/der/branches/pgnb

Supports research aimed at understanding the mechanisms of growth and development at the gene-molecular level and at higher levels of cell and organ function. Determines the role of nutrition throughout the life cycle, with an emphasis on the needs of women of reproductive age, including pregnant and lactating women, preterm and term infants, and children through adolescence, to promote health, optimal growth and development, and to prevent disease. Explores the role of nutrients in reproduction, immune function, cognition and behavioral development.

Eunice Kennedy Shriver National Institute of Child Health and Human Development *(National Institutes of Health), Division of Extramural Research, Pediatric Trauma and Critical Illness Branch, 6100 Executive Blvd., #8B05F, MSC 7510, Bethesda, MD 20892-7510; (301) 496-1514. Valerie Maholmes, Branch Chief.*
Web, www.nichd.nih.gov/about/org/der/branches/ptcib

Supports research and research training in pediatric trauma, injury, and critical illness across the continuum of care. Researches the prevention, treatment, management, and outcomes of physical and psychological trauma and the surgical, medical, psychosocial, and systems interventions needed to improve outcomes for critically ill and injured children and youth.

Eunice Kennedy Shriver National Institute of Child Health and Human Development *(National Institutes of Health), Division of Extramural Research, Pregnancy and Perinatology Branch, 6100 Executive Blvd., #4B03E, MSC 7510, Bethesda, MD 20892-7510; (301) 402-1872. Tonse Raju, Branch Chief.*
Web, www.nichd.nih.gov/about/org/der/branches/ppb

Supports research to improve the health of women before, during, and after pregnancy to reduce the number of preterm births and other birth complications, increase infant survival free from disease and disability, and ensure the long-term health of mothers and their children.

Food And Drug Administration (FDA) *(Health and Human Services Dept.), Pediatric Therapeutics, White Oak Bldg. 32, 10903 New Hampshire Ave., Silver Spring, MD 20993-0002; (301) 796-8659. Fax, (301) 847-8640. Mary Dianne Murphy, Director.*
General email, opt@fda.hhs.gov

Web, www.fda.gov/AboutFDA/CentersOffices/OfficeofMedicalProductsandTobacco/OfficeofScienceandHealthCoordination/ucm2018186.htm

Works to provide timely access to medical products proven to be safe and effective for children. Designs clinical studies that expand the knowledge of pediatrics.

Health Resources and Services Administration *(Health and Human Services Dept.), Maternal and Child Health Bureau, 5600 Fishers Lane, #18W, Rockville, MD 20857; (301) 443-2170. Fax, (301) 480-1312. Aaron Lopata, Chief Medical Officer; Michael C. Lu, Associate Administrator.*
Web, www.mchb.hrsa.gov

Administers programs for prenatal, maternal, and child health care. Funds block grants to states for mothers and children and for children with special health needs; awards funding for research training, genetic disease testing, counseling and information dissemination, hemophilia diagnostic and treatment centers, and demonstration projects to improve the health of mothers and children. Interests also include emergency medical services for children, universal newborn hearing screening, and traumatic brain injury.

Health Resources and Services Administration *(Health and Human Services Dept.), National Vaccine Injury Compensation Program, 5600 Fishers Lane, Parklawn Bldg., #11C-26, Rockville, MD 20857; (800) 338-2382. Dr. Avril Houston, Director, Acting.*
Web, www.hrsa.gov/vaccinecompensation

Provides no-fault compensation to individuals thought to be injured by certain childhood vaccines; including rotavirus vaccine; diphtheria and tetanus toxoids and pertussis vaccine; measles, mumps, and rubella vaccine; varicella, hepatitis A and B, HiB vaccine; oral polio and inactivated polio vaccines; and influenza, pneumococcal conjugate, meningococcal, and human papillomavirus vaccines.

▶ **NONGOVERNMENTAL**

American Academy of Child and Adolescent Psychiatry, *3615 Wisconsin Ave. N.W., 20016-3007; (202) 966-7300. Fax, (202) 966-2891. Dr. Gregory K. Fitz, President.*
Web, www.aacap.org

Membership: child and adolescent psychiatrists trained to promote healthy development and to evaluate, diagnose, and treat children, adolescents, and families affected by mental illness. Sponsors annual meeting and review for medical board examinations. Provides information on child and adolescent development and mental illnesses. Monitors international research and U.S. legislation concerning children with mental illness.

American Academy of Pediatrics, *Federal Affairs, 601 13th St. N.W., #400N, 20005; (202) 347-8600. Fax, (202) 393-6137. Karen Remley, Executive Director. Information, (800) 336-5475.*
General email, kids1st@aap.org
Web, www.aap.org

Advocates maternal and child health legislation and regulations. Interests include increased access and coverage for persons under age twenty-one, immunizations, injury prevention, environmental hazards, child abuse, emergency medical services, biomedical research, Medicaid, disabilities, pediatric AIDS, substance abuse, and nutrition. (Headquarters in Elk Grove Village, Ill.)

American College of Nurse-Midwives, *8403 Colesville Rd., #1550, Silver Spring, MD 20910-6374; (240) 485-1800. Fax, (240) 485-1818. Lorrie Kaplan, Chief Executive Officer, (240) 485-1810. Press, (240) 485-1826.*
General email, info@acnm.org
Web, www.midwife.org

Membership: certified nurse-midwives and certified midwives who preside at deliveries and provide postnatal care or primary gynecological care. Establishes clinical practice studies. Interests include preventive health care for women.

American College of Obstetricians and Gynecologists, *409 12th St. S.W., 20024-2188 (mailing address: P.O. Box 70620, Washington, DC 20024-9998); (202) 638-5577. Fax, (202) 488-3983. Dr. Hal C. Lawrence III, Executive Vice President. Press, (202) 484-3321. Toll-free, (800) 673-8444.*
Web, www.acog.org

Membership: medical specialists in obstetrics and gynecology. Disseminates standards of clinical practice and promotes patient involvement in medical care. Monitors legislation, regulations, and international research on maternal and child health care.

Assn. of Maternal and Child Health Programs (AMCHP), *2030 M St. N.W., #350, 20036; (202) 775-0436. Fax, (202) 775-0061. Lori Tremmel Freeman, Chief Executive Officer. General email, info@amchp.org*

Web, www.amchp.org and Twitter, @DC_AMCHP

Membership: state public health leaders and others. Works to improve the health and well-being of women, children, and youth, including those with special health care needs and their families.

Assn. of Women's Health, Obstetric, and Neonatal Nurses (AWHONN), *2000 L St. N.W., #740, 20036; (202) 261-2400. Fax, (202) 728-0575. Lynn Erdman, Chief Executive Officer. Toll-free, (800) 673-8499. Customer Service, (800) 354-2268.*
General email, customerservice@awhonn

Web, www.awhonn.org and Twitter, @AWHONN

Promotes the health of women and newborns. Provides nurses with information and support. Produces educational materials and legislative programs.

Children's Defense Fund, *25 E St. N.W., 20001; (202) 628-8787. Fax, (202) 662-3510. Marian Wright Edelman, President. Toll-free, (800) 233-1200.*
General email, cdfinfo@childrensdefense.org

Web, www.childrensdefense.org and Twitter, @ChildDefender

Advocacy group concerned with programs for children and youth. Assesses adequacy of the Early and Periodic Screening, Diagnosis, and Treatment Program for Medicaid-eligible children. Promotes adequate prenatal care for adolescent and lower-income women; works to prevent adolescent pregnancy.

Children's Dental Health Project (CDHP), *1020 19th St. N.W., #400, 20036; (202) 833-8288. Meg Booth, Executive Director, (202) 833-8288. Media, (202) 417-3600. General email, info@cdhp.org*

Web, www.cdhp.org and Twitter, @Teeth_Matter

Coalition comprised of policymakers, dental care professionals, and individuals seeking innovated and cost-effective solutions to improve children's dental health.

Provides information to policymakers, oral health care providers, and media about dental care provisions of the Affordable Care Act; monitors Medicaid and other insurance programs; promotes prevention strategies.

Children's Hospital Association, *Washington Office, 600 13th St. N.W., #500, 20005; (202) 753-5500. Fax, (202) 347-5147. Mark Weitecha, President.*
Web, www.childrenshospitals.org, Twitter, @hospitals4kids and Facebook, www.facebook.com/childrenshospitals

Promotes education and research on child health care related to more than 220 children's hospitals in the United States and internationally; compiles statistics and provides information on pediatric hospitalizations. (Merger of the Child Health Corporation of America, National Assn. of Children's Hospitals and Related Institutions, and National Assn. of Children's Hospitals.)

Guttmacher Institute, *Public Policy, 1301 Connecticut Ave. N.W., #700, 20036-3902; (202) 296-4012. Fax, (202) 223-5756. Rachel Benson Gold, Vice President for Public Policy; Susan Cohen, Vice President for Public Policy. Toll-free, (877) 823-0262.*
General email, policyinfo@guttmacher.org

Web, www.guttmacher.org

Conducts research, policy analysis, and public education in reproductive health issues, including maternal and child health. (Headquarters in New York.)

Healthy Teen Network, *1501 St. Paul St., #124, Baltimore, MD 21202; (410) 685-0410. Fax, (410) 685-0481. Pat Paluzzi, President.*
General email, info@healthyteennetwork.org

Web, www.healthyteennetwork.org

Membership: health and social work professionals, community and state leaders, and individuals. Promotes services to prevent and resolve problems associated with adolescent sexuality, pregnancy, and parenting. Helps to develop stable and supportive family relationships through program support and evaluation. Monitors legislation and regulations.

Lamaze International, *2025 M St. N.W., #800, 20036-3309; (202) 367-1128. Fax, (202) 367-2128. Linda Harmon, Executive Director. Information, (800) 368-4404. General email, info@lamaze.org*

Web, www.lamaze.org, Twitter, @LamazeOnline and Facebook, www.facebook.com/LamazeChildbirth

Membership: supporters of the Lamaze philosophy of childbirth, including parents, physicians, childbirth educators, and other health professionals. Trains and certifies Lamaze educators. Provides referral service for parents seeking Lamaze classes.

March of Dimes, *Government Affairs, 1401 K St. N.W., 9th Floor, 20005; (202) 659-1800. Fax, (202) 296-2964. Cynthia Pellegrini, Senior Vice President for Public Policy and Government Affairs.*
Web, www.marchofdimes.org/advocacy-and-government-affairs-issues-and-advocacy-priorities.aspx

Works to prevent birth defects, low birth weight, and infant mortality. Awards grants for research and provides funds for treatment of birth defects. Medical services grantees provide prenatal counseling. Monitors legislation and regulations. (Headquarters in White Plains, N.Y.)

The National Alliance to Advance Adolescent Health, *1615 M St. N.W., #290, 20036; (202) 223-1500. Fax, (202) 429-9357. Margaret A. McManus, President.*
General email, dbeck@thenationalalliance.org
Web, www.thenationalalliance.org

Seeks to increase adolescents' access to integrated physical, behavioral, and sexual health care to reduce health risk behaviors, identify health problems earlier, and equip adolescents to manage their health conditions. Promotes expanded comprehensive clinical and community prevention health strategies for adolescents.

National Assn. of School Psychologists, *4340 East-West Hwy., #402, Bethesda, MD 20814; (301) 657-0270. Fax, (301) 657-0275. Susan Gorin, Executive Director, (301) 347-1640. Toll-free, (866) 331-6277.*
General email, kcowan@naspweb.org
Web, www.nasponline.org

Membership: graduate education students and professors, school psychologists, supervisors of school psychological services, and others who provide mental health services for children in school settings. Provides professional education and development to members. Provides school safety and crisis response direct services. Fosters information exchange; advises local, state, and federal policymakers and agencies that develop children's mental health educational services. Develops professional ethics and standards.

National Center for Education in Maternal and Child Health, *2115 Wisconsin Ave. N.W., #601, 20007-2292 (mailing address: Georgetown University, Box 571272, Washington, DC 20057-1272); (877) 624-1935. Fax, (202) 784-9777. Rochelle Mayer, Director, (202) 784-9552; Olivia Pickett, Director of Library Services.*
General email, mchgroup@georgetown.edu
Web, www.ncemch.org and Twitter, @MCH_Library

Collects and disseminates information about maternal and child health to health professionals and the general public. Carries out special projects for the U.S. Maternal and Child Health Bureau. Library open to the public by appointment. (Affiliated with McCourt School of Public Policy, Georgetown University.)

National Organization on Fetal Alcohol Syndrome, *1200 Eton Court N.W., 3rd Floor, 20007; (202) 785-4585. Fax, (202) 466-6456. Tom Donaldson, President, ext. 100. Information, (800) 666-6327.*
General email, information@nofas.org
Web, www.nofas.org

Works to eradicate fetal alcohol syndrome and alcohol-related birth defects through public education, conferences, medical school curricula, and partnerships with federal programs interested in fetal alcohol syndrome.

Zero to Three: National Center for Infants, Toddlers, and Families, *1255 23rd St. N.W., #350, 20037; (202) 638-1144. Fax, (202) 638-0851. Matthew Melmed, Executive Director. Publications, (800) 899-4301.*
General email, 0to3@presswarehouse.com
Web, www.zerotothree.org and Twitter, @zerotothree

Works to improve infant health, mental health, and development. Sponsors training programs for professionals, offers fellowships, and publishes books, curricula, assessment tools, videos, and practical guidebooks. Provides private and government organizations with information on early childhood development issues.

Women's Health

▶**AGENCIES**

Assistant Secretary for Health *(Health and Human Services Dept.), Women's Health, 200 Independence Ave. S.W., #712E, 20201; (202) 690-7650. Fax, (202) 205-2631. Dr. Nancy C. Lee, Deputy Assistant Secretary. Information, (800) 994-9662. TTY, (888) 220-5446.*
General email, womenshealth@hhs.gov
Web, www.womenshealth.gov/owh or www.womenshealth. gov, www.girlshealth.gov and Twitter, @womenshealth

Promotes better health for girls and women as well as health equity through sex/gender-specific approaches. Methods include educating health professionals and motivating behavior change in consumers through the dissemination of health information.

Eunice Kennedy Shriver National Institute of Child Health and Human Development *(National Institutes of Health), Division of Extramural Research, Gynecologic Health and Disease Branch, 6100 Executive Blvd., #8B01, Bethesda, MD 20892-7510; (301) 594-8429. Fax, (301) 480-1972. Lisa Halvorson, Branch Chief, (301) 480-1646.*
Web, www.nichd.nih.gov/about/org/der/branches/ghdb

Supports basic, translational, and clinical programs related to gynecologic health throughout the reproductive lifespan, beginning at puberty and extending through early menopause. Areas of interest include studies on menstrual disorders, uterine fibroids, endometriosis, ovarian cysts and polycystic ovary syndrome, and pelvic floor disorders, as well as studies of the mechanisms underlying chronic pelvic pain, vulvodynia, and dysmenorrhea. Promotes research in gynecological health through grants, cooperative agreements, and contracts; supports research training and career development programs for investigators interested in women's reproductive health.

Eunice Kennedy Shriver National Institute of Child Health and Human Development *(National Institutes of Health), Division of Extramural Research, Pediatric Growth and Nutrition Branch, 6100 Executive Blvd., #4B05K, MSC 7510, Bethesda, MD 20892-7510; (301) 496-5593. Fax, (301) 480-9791. Gilman Drew Grave, Branch Chief.*
Web, www.nichd.nih.gov/about/org/der/branches/pgnb

Information Sources on Women's Health

AIDSinfo (NIH), (800) 448-0440, TTY, (888) 480-3739; www.aidsinfo.nih.gov

American College of Nurse-Midwives, (240) 485-1800; www.midwife.org

American College Of Obstetricians and Gynecologists, (202) 638-5577; www.acog.org

American Society for Reproductive Medicine, (202) 978-5000; www.asrm.org

Assn. of Maternal and Child Health Programs, (202) 775-0436; www.amchp.org

Assn. of Reproductive Health Professionals, (202) 466-3825; www.arhp.org

Assn. of Women's Health, Obstetric, and Neonatal Nurses, (202) 261-2400; Toll-free, (800) 673-8499; www.awhonn.org

Breast Cancer Network of Strength, After Breast Cancer Diagnosis, (414) 977-1780; www.abcdbreastcancersupport.org

Guttmacher Institute, (202) 296-4012; Toll-free, (877) 823-0262; www.guttmacher.org

Healthfinder (HHS), www.healthfinder.gov

Health Resources and Services Administration (HRSA), Maternal and Child Health (HHS), (800) 311-2229; www.mchb.hrsa.gov

Lamaze International, (202) 367-1128; Toll-free, (800) 368-4404; www.lamaze.org

Medem Network, (877) 599-5123; www.medfusion.com

Medline (NIH), www.nlm.nih.gov/medlineplus/women.html

National Abortion Federation, (202) 667-5881; hotline, (800) 772-9100; www.prochoice.org

National Breast Cancer Coalition, (202) 296-7477; Toll-free, (800) 622-2838; www.breastcancerdeadline2020.org

National Cancer Institute (NIH), (800) 422-6237; www.cancer.gov

National Center for Education in Maternal and Child Health (Georgetown Univ.), (202) 784-9770; www.ncemch.org

National Coalition for Women With Heart Disease, (202) 728-7199; www.womenheart.org

National Family Planning and Reproductive Health Assn., (202) 293-3114; www.nationalfamilyplanning.org

National Institute of Aging (NIH), Information Center, (800) 222-2225, TTY, (800) 222-4225; www.nia.nih.gov

National Institute of Allergy and Infectious Diseases (NIH), AIDS, (301) 496-5717, Toll-free hotline, (866) 284-4107; www.niaid.nih.gov

National Institute of Child Health and Human Development (NIH), (800) 370-2943, TTY, (888) 320-6942; www.nichd.nih.gov

National Osteoporosis Foundation, (202) 223-2226; Toll-free, (800) 231-4222; www.nof.org

National Research Center for Women and Families, (202) 223-4000; www.center4research.org

National Women's Health Information Center (HHS), (800) 994-9662; www.womenshealth.gov

National Women's Health Network, (202) 682-2640; www.nwhn.org

Office of Research on Women's Health (NIH), (301) 402-1770; http://orwh.od.nih.gov

Planned Parenthood Federation of America, (202) 973-4800; www.plannedparenthood.org

Society for Women's Health Research, (202) 223-8224; www.swhr.org

U.S. National Library of Medicine (NIH), Communications, (301) 594-5983; www.nlm.nih.gov

Women's Mental Health Consortium, National Institute of Mental Health (NIH), (866) 615-6464; www.nimh.nih.gov; www.womensmentalhealthconsortium.net

---

Supports research aimed at understanding the mechanisms of growth and development at the gene-molecular level and at higher levels of cell and organ function. Determines the role of nutrition throughout the life cycle, with an emphasis on the needs of women of reproductive age, including pregnant and lactating women, preterm and term infants, and children through adolescence, to promote health, optimal growth and development, and to prevent disease. Explores the role of nutrients in reproduction, immune function, cognition and behavioral development.

Food and Drug Administration (FDA) *(Health and Human Services Dept.), Women's Health, 10903 New Hampshire Ave., WO32-2333, Silver Spring, MD 20993; (301) 796-9440. Fax, (301) 847-8604. Marsha B. Henderson, Assistant Commissioner, (202) 796-9439.*

General email, marsha.henderson@fda.hhs.gov
Web, www.fda.gov/AboutFDA/CentersOffices/OC/OfficeofWomensHealth

Supports scientific research on women's health and collaborates with other government agencies and national organizations to sponsor scientific and consumer outreach on women's health issues. Interests include breast cancer, cardiovascular disease, diabetes, pregnancy, menopause, and the safe use of medications.

Health Resources and Services Administration *(Health and Human Services Dept.), Women's Health, 5600 Fishers Lane, Rockville, MD 20857; (301) 443-8664. Sabrina Matoff-Stepp, Director. Toll-free, (800) 221-9393.*
Web, www.hrsa.gov/about/organization/bureaus/owh

Works to improve health care by reducing sex-and gender-based disparities. Support dissemination of information on topics related to women's health, including health insurance and violence prevention.

National Heart, Lung, and Blood Institute *(National Institutes of Health), Cardiovascular Sciences Division, Women's Health Initiative,* 2 Rockledge Center, 6701 Rockledge Dr., #9192, MS 7913, Bethesda, MD 20892-7935; (301) 435-6667. Fax, (301) 480-5158. Shari Ludlam, Branch Chief, Acting. Information, (301) 592-8573. Press, (301) 496-4236.
Web, www.nhlbi.nih.gov/whi

Supports clinical trials and observational studies to improve understanding of the causes and prevention of major diseases affecting the health of women. Interests include cardiovascular disease, cancer, fractures, and hormone therapy.

National Institutes of Health (NIH) *(Health and Human Services Dept.), Research on Women's Health,* 6707 Democracy Blvd., #400, MSC 5484, Bethesda, MD 20892-5484; (301) 402-1770. Fax, (301) 402-1798. Dr. Janine Austin Clayton, Director.
Web, http://orwh.od.nih.gov

Collaborates with NIH institutes and centers to establish NIH goals and policies for research related to women's health and sex-based or gender-based studies of the differences between women and men. Supports expansion of research on diseases, conditions, and disorders that affect women; monitors inclusion of women and minorities in clinical research; develops opportunities and support for recruitment and advancement of women in biomedical careers.

▶ **NONGOVERNMENTAL**

Assn. of Women's Health, Obstetric, and Neonatal Nurses (AWHONN), 2000 L St. N.W., #740, 20036; (202) 261-2400. Fax, (202) 728-0575. Lynn Erdman, Chief Executive Officer. Toll-free, (800) 673-8499. Customer Service, (800) 354-2268.
General email, customerservice@awhonn

Web, www.awhonn.org and Twitter, @AWHONN

Promotes the health of women and newborns. Provides nurses with information and support. Produces educational materials and legislative programs.

Black Women's Health Imperative, 55 M St. S.E., #940, 20003; (202) 548-4000. Fax, (202) 543-9743. Linda Goler Blount, President.
General email, imperative@bwhi.org

Web, www.bwhi.org and Twitter, @blkwomenshealth

Provides the tools and information for African American women to prevent health problems, to recognize symptoms and early warning signs, and to understand all of the options available for their specific health situations. Achieves these ends through community outreach, advocacy, resources and research, education, and mobilization. (Formerly the National Black Women's Health Project.)

Eating Disorders Coalition for Research, Policy, and Action, P.O. Box 96503-98807, 20090; (202) 543-9570. Fax, (646) 417-6378. David Jaffe, Executive Director.
General email, manager@eatingdisorderscoalition.org

Web, www.eatingdisorderscoalition.org

Seeks greater national and federal recognition of eating disorders. Promotes recognition of eating disorders as a public health priority and the implementation of more accessible treatment and more effective prevention programs. Monitors legislation and regulations.

Institute for Women's Policy Research (IWPR), 1200 18th St. N.W., #301, 20036; (202) 785-5100. Fax, (202) 833-4362. Heidi Hartmann, President.
General email, iwpr@iwpr.org

Web, www.iwpr.org

Public policy research organization that focuses on women's issues, including health care and comprehensive family and medical leave programs.

National Center for Health Research, 1001 Connecticut Ave. N.W., #1100, 20036; (202) 223-4000. Fax, (202) 223-4242. Diana Zuckerman, President; Paul Brown, Government Relations.
General email, info@center4research.org

Web, www.center4research.org

Utilizes scientific and medical research to improve the quality of women's lives and the lives of family members. Seeks to educate policymakers about medical and scientific research through hearings, meetings, and publications. Affiliated with the Cancer Prevention and Treatment Fund.

National Women's Health Network, 1413 K St. N.W., 4th Floor, 20005; (202) 682-2640. Fax, (202) 682-2648. Cynthia Pearson, Executive Director. Health information, (202) 682-2646.
General email, nwhn@nwhn.org and healthquestions@nwhn.org

Web, www.nwhn.org

Acts as an information clearinghouse on women's health issues; monitors federal health policies and legislation. Interests include older women's health issues, sexual and reproductive health, contraception, menopause, abortion, unsafe drugs, AIDS, breast cancer, and universal health.

Society for Women's Health Research, 1025 Connecticut Ave. N.W., #601, 20036; (202) 223-8224. Fax, (202) 833-3472. Phyllis Greenberger, President.
General email, info@swhr.org

Web, www.swhr.org

Promotes public and private funding for women's health research and changes in public policies affecting women's health. Seeks to advance women as leaders in the health professions and to inform policymakers, educators, and the public of research outcomes. Sponsors meetings; produces reports; conducts educational campaigns.

WomenHeart: National Coalition for Women With Heart Disease, *1100 17th St. N.W., #500, 20036; (202) 728-7199. Fax, (202) 728-7238. Mary McGowan, Chief Executive Officer.*
General email, mail@womenheart.org

Web, www.womenheart.org and Twitter, @WomenHeartOrg

Patient-centered organization that seeks to advance women's heart health through advocacy, community education, and patient support. Composed of patients and their families, health care providers, advocates, and interested consumers.

HEALTH TOPICS: RESEARCH AND ADVOCACY

General

▶AGENCIES

Assistant Secretary for Health *(Health and Human Services Dept.),* **Human Research Protections,** *Tower Bldg., 1101 Wootton Pkwy., #200, Rockville, MD 20852; (240) 453-6900. Fax, (240) 453-6909. Dr. Jerry Menikoff, Director. Toll-free, (866) 447-4777.*
General email, ohrp@hhs.gov

Web, www.hhs.gov/ohrp

Promotes the rights, welfare, and well-being of subjects involved in research conducted or supported by the Health and Human Services Dept.; helps to ensure that research is carried out in accordance with federal regulations by providing clarification and guidance, developing educational programs and materials, and maintaining regulatory oversight.

Consumer Product Safety Commission (CPSC), *Health Sciences, 4330 East-West Hwy., #600, Bethesda, MD 20814-4408; (301) 987-2240. Fax, (978) 967-8401. Alice Thaler, Associate Executive Director.*
Web, www.cpsc.gov

Evaluates potential health effects and hazards of consumer products and their foreseeable uses and misuses, and performs exposure and risk assessments for product-related hazards.

Eunice Kennedy Shriver National Institute of Child Health and Human Development *(National Institutes of Health),* **Division of Extramural Research,** *6100 Executive Blvd., #4A05, MSC 7510, Bethesda, MD 20892-7510; (301) 496-8535. Dr. Della Hann, Director.*
Web, www.nichd.nih.gov/about/org/der

Develops, implements, and coordinates cross-cutting, multidisciplinary research activities that focus on demography, social sciences, and population dynamics; male and female fertility and infertility; developing and evaluating contraceptive methods; improving the safety and efficacy of pharmaceuticals for use in pregnant women, infants, and children; HIV infection and transmission, AIDS, and associated infections; pediatric growth and endocrine research; child development and behavior; developmental biology and typical and atypical development; intellectual and developmental disabilities; gynecologic health conditions, including pelvic floor disorders; and childhood injury and critical illness. Coordinates research and training grant programs.

Fogarty International Center *(National Institutes of Health), 31 Center Dr., MSC 2220, Bethesda, MD 20892-2220; (301) 496-1415. Fax, (301) 402-2173. Dr. Roger I. Glass, Director.*
General email, ficinfo@nih.gov

Web, www.fic.nih.gov and Twitter, @fogarty_NIH

Promotes and supports international scientific research and training to reduce disparities in global health. Leads formulation and implementation of international biomedical research and policy. Supports the conduct of research in high-priority global health areas, including infectious diseases such as HIV/AIDS, and helps build research capacity in the developing world.

Health Resources and Services Administration *(Health and Human Services Dept.),* **Healthcare Systems Bureau, Organ Donation and Transplantation,** *5600 Fishers Lane, #8W, Rockville, MD 20857; (301) 443-7577. Fax, (301) 594-6095. Melissa Greenwald, Director, Acting.*
General email, donation@hrsa.gov

Web, www.organdonor.gov

Implements provisions of the National Organ Transplant Act. Provides information on federal programs involved in transplantation; supports the national network for deceased donor organ procurement and matching; maintains information on transplant recipients; awards grants to increase organ donation and transplantation. Administers the C.W. Bill Young Cell Transplantation Program and the National Cord Blood Inventory.

Mark O. Hatfield Clinical Research Center *(National Institutes of Health), 10 Center Dr., Bethesda, MD 20892; (301) 496-4000. Dr. John I. Gallin, Director. Patient Recruitment, (800) 411-1222. Admissions, (301) 496-3315.*
Web, http://clinicalcenter.nih.gov

Provides inpatient and outpatient care and conducts clinical research. Promotes the application of scientific laboratory research to benefit patient health and medical care. With the Warren Grant Magnuson Clinical Center, forms the NIH Clinical Center.

National Heart, Lung, and Blood Institute *(National Institutes of Health), 31 Center Dr., Bldg. 31, #5A48, MSC 2486, Bethesda, MD 20892-2486; (301) 592-8573. Fax, (301) 402-0818. Dr. Gary H. Gibbons, Director, (301) 496-5166. Press, (301) 496-4236.*
General email, nhlbiinfo@nhlbi.nih.gov

Web, www.nhlbi.nih.gov, Twitter, @nih_nhlbi and Facebook, www.facebook.com/NHLBI

Collects and disseminates information on diseases of the heart, lungs, and blood, with an emphasis on disease prevention. Works with patients, families, health care professionals, scientists, community organizations, and the media to promote the application of research results to address public health needs. Promotes international collaboration in its educational programs for scientists and clinicians.

National Institute of General Medical Sciences *(National Institutes of Health),* 45 Center Dr., #3AN44E, MSC 6200, Bethesda, MD 20892-6200; (301) 496-7301. Fax, (301) 402-0156. Jon R. Lorsch, Director. General email, info@nigms.nih.gov

Web, www.nigms.nih.gov, Twitter, @NIGMS and Facebook, www.facebook.com/nigms.nih.gov

Primarily supports basic biomedical research and training that lays the foundation for advances in disease diagnosis, treatment, and prevention. Areas of special interest include bioinformatics, cell biology, developmental biology, physiology, biological chemistry genetics, and computational biology.

National Institute of General Medical Sciences *(National Institutes of Health), Training, Workforce Development, and Diversity,* 45 Center Dr., Bldg. 45, #2AS37, MSC 6200, Bethesda, MD 20892-6200; (301) 594-3900. Fax, (301) 480-2753. Dr. Alison Gammie, Director, Acting.
Web, http://nigms.nih.gov/training

Administers research and research training programs aimed at increasing the number of minority biomedical scientists. Funds grants, fellowships, faculty development awards, and development of research facilities.

National Institutes of Health (NIH) *(Health and Human Services Dept.),* 1 Center Dr., Bldg. 1, #344, MSC 0188, Bethesda, MD 20892-0148; (301) 496-4000. Fax, (301) 496-0017. Dr. Francis S. Collins, Director; Dr. Lawrence A. Tabak, Deputy Director. Press, (301) 496-5787.
Web, www.nih.gov

Supports and conducts biomedical research on the causes and prevention of diseases; furnishes health professionals and the public with information.

National Institutes of Health (NIH) *(Health and Human Services Dept.), Center for Information Technology,* 10401 Fernwood Rd., Bethesda, MD 20817; (301) 496-5703. Fax, (301) 402-1754. Andrea T. Norris, Director.
Web, http://cit.nih.gov

Responsible for incorporating computers into biomedical research information, technology, security, and administrative procedures of the NIH. Serves as the primary scientific and technological resource for the NIH in the areas of high performance computing, database applications, mathematics, statistics, laboratory automation, engineering, computer science and technology, telecommunications, and information resources management.

National Institutes of Health (NIH) *(Health and Human Services Dept.), Center for Scientific Review,* 6701 Rockledge Dr., #3030, MSC 7768, Bethesda, MD 20892-7776; (301) 435-1115. Fax, (301) 480-3965. Richard K. Nakamura, Director, (301) 480-3965.
Web, www.csr.nih.gov

Conducts scientific merit review of research grant and fellowship applications submitted to the NIH. Participates in formulating grant and award policies.

National Institutes of Health (NIH) *(Health and Human Services Dept.), National Center for Advancing Translational Sciences (NCATS),* 1 Democracy Plaza, 9th Floor, #900, 6701 Democracy Blvd., MSC 4874, Bethesda, MD 20892-4874 (mailing address: Use zip code 20817 for express mail.); (301) 435-0888. Dr. Christopher P. Austin, Director.
General email, info@ncats.nih.gov

Web, www.ncats.nih.gov

Works in partnership with regulatory, academic, nonprofit, and private sectors to identify and overcome hurdles that slow the development of effective treatments and cures.

National Institutes of Health (NIH) *(Health and Human Services Dept.), National Center for Complementary and Integrative Health (NICCIH),* 31 Center Dr., Bldg. 31, #2B11, MSC 2182, Bethesda, MD 20892-2182; (301) 435-6826. Fax, (301) 402-4741. Dr. Josephine P. Briggs, Director. Information, (888) 644-6226. TTY, (866) 464-3615.
General email, info@nccih.nih.gov

Web, www.nccih.nih.gov

Conducts and supports research on complementary and alternative medicine; trains researchers and disseminates information to practitioners and the public.

National Library of Medicine *(National Institutes of Health),* 8600 Rockville Pike, Bldg. 38, #2E17, MSC 3808, Bethesda, MD 20894; (301) 496-6308. Fax, (301) 402-1384. Betsy L. Humphreys, Director, Acting. Local and International, (301) 594-5983. TTY, (800) 735-2258.
General email, custserv@nlm.nih.gov

Web, www.nlm.nih.gov and PubMed Central, www.ncbi.nlm.nih.gov/pmc

Offers medical library services and computer-based reference service to the public, health professionals, libraries in medical schools and hospitals, and research institutions. Operates a toxicology information service for the scientific community, industry, and federal agencies. Assists medical libraries through the National Network of Libraries of Medicines. Assists in the improvement of basic library resources. Reading room open to the public Monday through Friday, 8:30 a.m.–5:00 p.m.

National Library of Medicine *(National Institutes of Health), Health Information Programs Development,* 8600 Rockville Pike, Bldg. 38, #2S20, MSC 12, Bethesda, MD 20894; (301) 496-2311. Fax, (301) 496-4450. Michael F. Huerta, Director.
General email, custserv@nlm.nih.gov

Web, www.nlm.nih.gov

Facilitates worldwide use of the library's medical databases through agreements with individual nations, international organizations, and commercial vendors. Helps the library acquire and share international biomedical literature.

National Library of Medicine *(National Institutes of Health), National Center for Biotechnology Information,* 8600 Rockville Pike, Bldg. 38A, 8th Floor, Bethesda, MD 20892; (301) 496-2475. Fax, (301) 480-4559.
Dr. David J. Lipman, Director.
General email, info@ncbi.nlm.nih.gov

Web, www.ncbi.nlm.nih.gov and Pub Med Central, www.pubmedcentral.nih.gov

Creates automated systems for storing and analyzing knowledge of molecular biology and genetics. Develops new information technologies to aid in understanding the molecular processes that control human health and disease. Conducts basic research in computational molecular biology. Sponsors PubMed Central, a publicly accessible digital archive of life sciences journal literature.

Naval Medical Research Center *(Defense Dept.),* 503 *Robert Grant Ave., #1W28, Silver Spring, MD 20910-7500;* (301) 319-7403. Fax, (301) 319-7424.
Capt. Jacqueline D. Rychnovsky, Commanding Officer.
General email, svc.pao.nmrc@med.navy.mil

Web, www.med.navy.mil/sites/nmrc

Performs basic and applied biomedical research in areas of military importance, including infectious diseases, hyperbaric medicine, wound repair enhancement, environmental stress, and immunobiology. Provides support to field laboratories and naval hospitals; monitors research internationally.

NIH Clinical Center *(National Institutes of Health),* 10 Center Dr., #6-2551, Bethesda, MD 20892-1504; (301) 496-4000. Fax, (301) 402-2984. Dr. John I. Gallin, Director. Communications, (301) 496-2563.
Web, www.cc.nih.gov

Serves as a clinical research center for the NIH; patients are referred by physicians and self-referred throughout the United States and overseas.

Walter Reed Army Institute of Research *(Defense Dept.),* 503 Robert Grant Ave., Silver Spring, MD 20910-7500; (301) 319-9000. Fax, (301) 319-9549. Col. (Dr.) Dana K. Renta, Commander. Public Affairs Officer, (301) 319-9471. Reference librarian, (301) 319-9555. General email, usarmy.detrick.medcom-wrair.mbx.public-affairs@mail.mil

Web, www.wrair.army.mil and Twitter, @wrair

Provides research, education, and training in support of the Defense Dept.'s health care system. Develops vaccines and drugs to prevent and treat infectious diseases. Other research efforts include surveillance of naturally occurring infectious diseases of military importance and study of combat casualty care (blood loss, resuscitation, and brain and other organ system trauma), battle casualties, operational stress, sleep deprivation, and medical countermeasures against biological and chemical agents.

▶ **CONGRESS**

For a listing of relevant congressional committees and subcommittees, please see pages 344–345 or the Appendix.

▶ **NONGOVERNMENTAL**

Academy Health, *1150 17th St. N.W., #600, 20036; (202) 292-6700. Fax, (202) 292-6800. Dr. Lisa A. Simpson, Chief Executive Officer.*
Web, www.academyhealth.org

Membership: individuals and organizations with an interest in health services research, including health policymakers, universities, private research organizations, professional associations, consulting firms, advocacy organizations, insurers, managed care companies, health care systems, and pharmaceutical companies. Serves as an information clearinghouse on health services research and policy; communicates with policymakers concerning state and federal health policies; works to increase public and private funding for health services research, including comparative effectiveness and public health systems and services research. Offers professional development and training programs for health services researchers and policymakers. Monitors legislation and regulations. (Formerly Academy for Health Services Research and Health Policy.)

American Physiological Society, *9650 Rockville Pike, 3rd Floor, Bethesda, MD 20814-3991; (301) 634-7164. Fax, (301) 634-7245. Martin Frank, Executive Director.*
Web, www.the-aps.org and Twitter, @APSPhysiology

Researches how the body and its organ systems function. Promotes scientific research, education, and dissemination of information through publication of peer-reviewed journals; monitors international research. Offers travel fellowships for scientific meetings; encourages minority participation in physiological research. Works to establish standards for the humane care and use of laboratory animals. Publishes fourteen scientific journals and a newsletter.

American Public Health Assn., *800 Eye St. N.W., 20001-3710; (202) 777-2742. Fax, (202) 777-2534. Dr. Georges Benjamin, Executive Director. TTY, (202) 777-2500.*
General email, comments@apha.org

Web, www.apha.org and Twitter, @PublicHealth

Membership: health providers, educators, environmentalists, policymakers, and health officials at all levels working both within and outside of governmental organizations and educational institutions. Works to protect communities from serious, preventable health threats. Strives to ensure that community-based health promotion and disease prevention activities and preventive health services are universally accessible in the United States. Develops standards for scientific procedures in public health.

American Trauma Society, *201 Park Washington Court, Falls Church, VA 22046; (703) 538-3544. Fax, (703) 241-5603. Ian Weston, Executive Director. Toll-free, (800) 556-7890.*

General email, info@amtrauma.org

Web, www.amtrauma.org and Twitter, @ATSTrauma

Seeks to prevent trauma and improve its treatment. Coordinates programs aimed at reducing the incidence and severity of trauma; sponsors research; provides training to nurses and others involved in the trauma field. Provides support to trauma survivors. Monitors legislation and regulations.

Center for Applied Proteomics and Molecular Medicine *(George Mason University), 10920 George Mason Circle, MS 1A9, Manassas, VA 20110; (703) 993-9526. Fax, (703) 993-8606. Lance Liotta, Co-Director; Emanuel Petricoin III, Co-Director.*

General email, phackett@gmu.edu

Web, http://capmm.gmu.edu

Researches blood-based protein biomarker discovery and molecular analysis of tissue in order to tailor treatment to individual patients. Participates in clinical trials.

Foundation for the National Institutes of Health, *9650 Rockville Pike, Bethesda, MD 20814-3999; (301) 402-5311. Fax, (301) 480-2752. Maria C. Freire, President, (301) 443-1811.*

General email, foundation@fnih.org

Web, www.fnih.org

Established by Congress to support the NIH's mission of developing new knowledge through biomedical research. Works to foster collaborative relationships in education, research, and related activities between the NIH, industry, academia, and nonprofit organizations; supports basic and clinical research to advance medical knowledge; supports training and advanced education programs for future researchers; and invests in educational programs related to medical research.

Howard Hughes Medical Institute, *4000 Jones Bridge Rd., Chevy Chase, MD 20815-6789; (301) 215-8500. Fax, (301) 215-8863. Robert Tjian, President.*

Web, www.hhmi.org

Conducts biomedical research programs in major academic medical centers, hospitals, and universities. Areas of research include cell biology, computational biology, genetics, immunology, neuroscience, and structural biology. Maintains a grants program in science education, including precollege, undergraduate, graduate, and postgraduate levels. Supports selected biomedical researchers in foreign countries.

Institute for Alternative Futures (IAF), *2331 Mill Rd., #100, Alexandria, VA 22314; (703) 684-5880. Fax, (703) 684-0640. Jonathan Peck, President.*

General email, futurist@altfutures.org

Web, www.altfutures.org

Research and educational organization that explores the implications of future developments in various fields and facilitates planning efforts. Works with state and local governments, Congress, international organizations, federal government, and regional associations; conducts seminars. Interests include pharmaceutical research, health

care, telecommunications, artificial intelligence, energy, the environment, and sustainability.

Institute of Medicine, *500 5th St. N.W., 20001; (202) 334-2352. Victor Dzau, President, (202) 334-3300. Library, (202) 334-2125. Press, (202) 334-2138.*

General email, iomwww@nas.edu

Web, www.iom.edu

Seeks to improve health nationally; provides evidence-based advice to policymakers, health professionals, the private sector, and the public. National Academy of Sciences George E. Brown Jr. Library open to researchers by appointment.

Johns Hopkins University Applied Physics Laboratory, *Research and Exploratory Development, 11100 Johns Hopkins Rd., Laurel, MD 20723-6099; (240) 228-5000. Jim Schatz, Head.*

Web, www.jhuapl.edu/ourwork/red

Research and development laboratory that seeks to improve warfighter survivability, sustainment, and performance through battlefield trauma prevention and mitigation, along with medical device evaluation and development. Programs include improvement of soldier protection equipment, the development of a neurally integrated upper extremity prosthetic, and blast-related traumatic brain injury research.

National Center for Healthy Housing, *10320 Little Patuxent Pkwy., #500, Columbia, MD 21044; (410) 992-0712. Fax, (443) 539-4150. Nancy Rockett Eldridge, Executive Director.*

General email, info@nchh.org

Web, www.nchh.org

Collects, analyzes, and distributes information on creating and maintaining safe and healthful housing. Provides technical assistance and training to public health, housing, and environmental professionals. Interests include aging in place for older adults, radon, allergens, pest management, and lead poisoning.

National Institute of Environmental Health Sciences *(National Institutes of Health), Washington Office, 31 Center Dr., #B1C02, MSC 2256, Bethesda, MD 20892-2256; (301) 496-3511. Fax, (301) 496-0563. Linda S. Birnbaum, Director; Jed R. Bullock, Legislative Liaison. Information, (919) 541-4794.*

General email, webcenter@niehs.nih.gov

Web, www.niehs.nih.gov, Twitter, @NIEHS and Facebook, www.facebook.com/NIH.NIEHS

Conducts and supports research on the human effects of various environmental exposures, expanding the scientific basis for making public health decisions based on the potential toxicity of environmental agents. (Most operations located in Research Triangle, N.C.)

Research!America, *1101 King St., #520, Alexandria, VA 22314-2960; (703) 739-2577. Fax, (703) 739-2372. Mary Woolley, President. Information, (800) 366-2873.*

General email, info@researchamerica.org

Web, www.researchamerica.org and Twitter, @ResearchAmerica

Membership: academic institutions, professional societies, voluntary health organizations, corporations, and individuals interested in promoting medical research. Provides information on the benefits of medical and health research and seeks to increase funding for research. Monitors legislation and regulations.

Science Communication Network, 4833 West Lane, Bethesda, MD 20814; (301) 654-6665. Amy Kostant, Executive Director.
General email, info@sciencecom.org

Web, www.sciencecommunicationnetwork.org

Conducts educational workshops to give scientists and other health professionals the media tools to enable their work to be accurately reported to the public. Focuses on environmental health science, green chemistry, and science integrity issues.

SRI International, Washington Office, 1100 Wilson Blvd., #2800, Arlington, VA 22209; (703) 524-2053. Fax, (703) 247-8569. Peter Kant, Executive Director, (703) 247-8424.
Web, www.sri.com

Research and consulting organization. Conducts studies on biotechnology, genetic engineering, drug metabolism, cancer, toxicology, disease control systems, and other areas of basic and applied research; monitors international research. (Headquarters in Menlo Park, Calif.)

Alternative Medicine

▶AGENCIES

Food and Drug Administration (FDA) (Health and Human Services Dept.), Center for Food Safety and Applied Nutrition, 5100 Paint Branch Pkwy., HFS-009, College Park, MD 20740-3835; (240) 402-1600. Fax, (301) 436-2668. Susan T. Mayne, Director.
General email, consumer@fda.gov

Web, www.fda.gov/AboutFDA/CentersOffices/OfficeofFoods/CFSAN/default.htm

Develops standards for dietary supplements taken as part of alternative medicine treatments. Conducts research about dietary supplements and nutrition in general.

National Institutes of Health (NIH) (Health and Human Services Dept.), National Center for Complementary and Integrative Health (NICCIH), 31 Center Dr., Bldg. 31, #2B11, MSC-2182, Bethesda, MD 20892-2182; (301) 435-6826. Fax, (301) 402-4741. Dr. Josephine P. Briggs, Director. Information, (888) 644-6226. TTY, (866) 464-3615.
General email, info@nccih.nih.gov

Web, www.nccih.nih.gov

Works with the Food and Drug Administration (FDA) to develop regulations for the research and use of alternative medicine.

▶NONGOVERNMENTAL

Alliance for Natural Health USA, 6931 Arlington Rd., #304, Bethesda, MD 20814; (202) 467-1985. Fax, (202) 315-5837. Gretchen DuBeau, Executive and Legal Director. Toll-free, (800) 230-2762. Press, (202) 803-5123.
General email, office@anh-usa.org

Web, www.anh-usa.org

Acts as advocate on behalf of natural health care consumers and practitioners, and the dietary supplements industry. Promotes an integrative approach to health and natural health care choices for both physicians and patients. Monitors legislation and regulations. (The American Assn. for Health Freedom merged with the Alliance for Natural Health in December 2009.)

American Assn. of Naturopathic Physicians, 818 18th St. N.W., #250, 20006; (202) 237-8150. Fax, (202) 237-8152. Jaclyn Chasse, President; Ryan Cliche, Executive Director. Toll-free, (866) 538-2267.
General email, member.services@naturopathic.org

Web, www.naturopathic.org

Membership: naturopathic physicians who are licensed as primary health care providers. Promotes the combination of modern medicine and natural and traditional therapies, including therapeutic nutrition, botanical medicine, homeopathy, and natural childbirth.

American Music Therapy Assn., 8455 Colesville Rd., #1000, Silver Spring, MD 20910; (301) 589-3300. Fax, (301) 589-5175. Andrea Farbman, Executive Director.
General email, info@musictherapy.org

Web, www.musictherapy.org and Twitter, @AMTAInc

Promotes the therapeutic use of music by approving degree programs and clinical training sites, establishing professional competencies and clinical practice standards for music therapists, and conducting research in the music therapy field.

Assn. of Accredited Naturopathic Medical Colleges, 818 18th St. N.W., #250, 20006; (800) 345-7454.
Dr. JoAnn Yanez, Executive Director.
General email, info@aanmc.org

Web, www.aanmc.org and Twitter, @AANMC

Membership: accredited schools of naturopathic medicine. Promotes naturopathic and medical education, research, and teaching. Provides database of practicing naturopathic physicians and information on how to become a licensed naturopathic doctor.

National Center for Homeopathy, 7918 Jones Branch Dr., #300, McLean, VA 22102; (703) 506-7667. Fax, (703) 506-3266. Alison Teitelbaum, Executive Director.
General email, info@nationalcenterforhomeopathy.org

Web, www.nationalcenterforhomeopathy.org and Twitter, @NCHHomeopathy

Promotes health through homeopathy. Seeks to educate the public about homeopathic medicine and increase its availability in the United States.

Arthritis, Bone Diseases

▶AGENCIES

National Institute of Arthritis and Musculoskeletal and Skin Diseases *(National Institutes of Health), 31 Center Dr., Bldg. 31, #4C32, MS 2350, Bethesda, MD 20892-2350; (301) 496-4353. Fax, (301) 402-3607. Dr. Stephen I. Katz, Director. TTY, (301) 565-2966. Health information, (877) 226-4267.*
General email, niamsinfo@mail.nih.gov
Web, www.niams.nih.gov

Conducts and funds research on arthritis, rheumatic, skin, muscle, and bone diseases and musculoskeletal disorders. Funds national arthritis centers.

National Institute of Arthritis and Musculoskeletal and Skin Diseases *(National Institutes of Health), Information Clearinghouse, 1 AMS Circle, Bethesda, MD 20892-3675; (301) 495-4484. Fax, (301) 718-6366. Vacant, Project Manager. Toll-free, (877) 226-4267. TTY, (301) 565-2966.*
General email, niamsinfo@mail.nih.gov
Web, www.niams.nih.gov

Supports medical research into the causes, treatment, and prevention of diseases of the bones, muscles, joints, and skin. Provides general information on health conditions and referrals to organizations.

National Institutes of Health (NIH) *(Health and Human Services Dept.), Osteoporosis and Related Bone Diseases, 2 AMS Circle, Bethesda, MD 20892; (202) 223-0344. Fax, (202) 293-2356. Dr. Stephen Katz, Director, (301) 496-4353. TTY, (800) 624-2663.*
General email, NIHBoneInfo@mail.nih.gov
Web, www.bones.nih.gov

Provides patients, health professionals, and the public with resources and information on metabolic bone diseases, including osteoporosis, Paget's disease of bone, and osteogenesis imperfecta. Seeks to increase the awareness, knowledge, and understanding of the prevention, early detection, and treatment of osteoporosis and related bone diseases.

▶NONGOVERNMENTAL

National Osteoporosis Foundation, *251 18th St., #630, Arlington, VA 22202; (703) 647-3000. Fax, (703) 414-3742. Amy Porter, Executive Director. Toll-free, (800) 231-4222.*
General email, info@nof.org
Web, www.nof.org

Volunteer health organization that seeks to prevent osteoporosis and related bone fractures, to promote lifelong bone health, to improve the lives of those affected by osteoporosis, and to find a cure through programs of awareness, advocacy, and public health education and research. Monitors legislation and international research.

Osteogenesis Imperfecta Foundation, *804 W. Diamond Ave., #210, Gaithersburg, MD 20878; (301) 947-0083.*
Fax, (301) 947-0456. Tracy Smith Hart, Chief Executive Officer. Toll-free, (844) 889-7579.
General email, bonelink@oif.org
Web, www.oif.org and Twitter, @OIFoundation

Provides healthcare professionals and patients with information about osteogenesis imperfecta (OI), also known as brittle bone disease; offers research grants; promotes public policy that supports people living with OI.

Blood, Bone Marrow

▶AGENCIES

Health Resources and Services Administration *(Health and Human Services Dept.), Healthcare Systems Bureau, Organ Donation and Transplantation, 5600 Fishers Lane, #8W, Rockville, MD 20857; (301) 443-7577. Fax, (301) 594-6095. Melissa Greenwald, Director, Acting.*
General email, donation@hrsa.gov
Web, www.organdonor.gov

Administers the National Marrow Donor Program, which maintains a registry of potential unrelated bone marrow donors.

National Heart, Lung, and Blood Institute *(National Institutes of Health), Blood Diseases and Resources Division, 6701 Rockledge Dr., #9030, MSC 7950, Bethesda, MD 20892-7950; (301) 435-0080. Fax, (301) 480-0867. Dr. W. Keith Hoots, Director. Public Affairs, (301) 496-4236.*
Web, www.nhlbi.nih.gov/about/org/dbdr

Supports research and training on the causes, diagnosis, treatment, and prevention of non-malignant blood diseases and research in transfusion medicine and blood banking, stem cell biology, and blood supply adequacy and safety. Provides biospecimens and cellular resources to the scientific community.

National Heart, Lung, and Blood Institute *(National Institutes of Health), Blood Diseases and Resources Division, Blood Epidemiology and Clinical Therapeutics Branch, 6701 Rockledge Dr., #9142, MSC 7950, Bethesda, MD 20892-7950; (301) 435-0065. Fax, (301) 480-1046. Dr. Simone Glynn, Branch Chief.*
Web, www.nhlbi.nih.gov/about/org/dbdr

Responsible for oversight, support, and stimulation of epidemiologic, clinical, and implementation research throughout the spectrum of blood science. Branch responsibilities include: oversight, support, and stimulation of epidemiologic health services and observational clinical research; oversight, support, and stimulation of therapeutic and interventional clinical trials (T2 Research); acquisition and maintenance of expertise in clinical study and trial design and administration on behalf of the Division; oversight, support, and stimulation of implementation science and research (T3 Research); training of blood science workforce; and scientific liaison for epidemiologic, clinical, and implementation research across the Division, NHLBI, NIH, and partner federal agencies.

National Heart, Lung, and Blood Institute *(National Institutes of Health), Blood Diseases and Resources Division, Molecular, Cellular, and Systems Blood Science Branch,* 6701 Rockledge Dr., #90930, 20892-7950; (301) 435-0070. Fax, (301) 480-1016. *Yu-Chang Yang, Branch Chief.*
Web, www.nhlbi.nih.gov/about/org/dbdr

Provides oversight, support, and stimulation of fundamental basic research and early stage laboratory translation of the biology of blood, the blood forming elements, and the interface between each of the latter with other cellular and organ systems. Branch responsibilities include: oversight, support, and stimulation of discovery science focused on the explication of the physiology and pathophysiology of blood, bone marrow, and blood vessels; oversight support and stimulation of systems of biological approaches to understanding the critical role of blood/bone marrow/vascular endothelium in animal and human organs and organisms; oversight, support, and stimulation of the application of fundamental genetics, proteomic and metabolomics tools to understanding hematologic physiology and pathophysiology; administration of and liaison to the HNLBI/NIH resources related to basic research in non-neoplastic hematology; and fostering scientific communication across the Division, NHLBI, NIH, and partner federal agencies.

National Heart, Lung, and Blood Institute *(National Institutes of Health), Health Information Center,* 31 Center Dr., Bldg. 31, Bethesda, MD 20892-2480 (mailing address: P.O. Box 30105, Bethesda, MD 20824-0105); (301) 592-8573. *Lenora Johnson, Director,* (301) 496-4236.
General email, nhlbiInfo@nhlbi.nih.gov
Web, www.nhlbi.nih.gov/health/contact

Provides public and patient education materials on the prevention and treatment of heart, lung, and blood diseases.

National Institute of Diabetes and Digestive and Kidney Diseases *(National Institutes of Health), Kidney, Urologic, and Hematologic Diseases,* 2 Democracy Plaza, 6707 Democracy Blvd., #625, MSC 5458, Bethesda, MD 20892; (301) 496-6325. Fax, (301) 480-3510.
Dr. Robert A. Star, Director. Press, (301) 496-3583. *Information,* (800) 891-5390.
Web, www.niddk.nih.gov

Funds research on the prevention, diagnosis, and treatment of renal disorders. Conducts research and reviews grant proposals concerning maintenance therapy for persons with chronic kidney, urologic, and renal diseases. Supports basic research on and clinical studies of the states of blood cell formation, mobilization, and release. Interests include anemia associated with chronic diseases, iron and white blood cell metabolism, and genetic control of hemoglobin.

Warren Grant Magnuson Clinical Center *(National Institutes of Health), Transfusion Medicine,* 10 Center Dr., Bldg. 10, #1C711, MSC 1184, Bethesda, MD 20892-1184; (301) 496-4506. Fax, (301) 402-1360. *Dr. Harvey G. Klein, Chief,* (301) 496-9702. *Press,* (301) 496-2563.
Web, http://clinicalcenter.nih.gov/dtm

Supplies blood and blood components for research and patient care. Provides training programs and conducts research in the preparation and transfusion of blood and blood products. Research topics include hepatitis, automated cell separation, immunohematology, and AIDS transmittal through transfusions.

▶**NONGOVERNMENTAL**

AABB, 8101 Glenbrook Rd., Bethesda, MD 20814-2749; (301) 907-6977. Fax, (301) 907-6895. *Miriam A. Markowitz, Chief Executive Officer. Press,* (301) 215-6526. *General email, aabb@aabb.org*
Web, www.aabb.org

Membership: hospital and community blood centers, transfusion and transplantation services, and individuals involved in transfusion and transplantation medicine and related biological therapies. Develops and implements standards, accreditation and educational programs, and services that optimize patient and donor care and safety. Encourages the voluntary donation of blood and other tissues and organs through education and public information. (Formerly the American Assn. of Blood Banks.)

American Red Cross, *National Headquarters,* 2025 E St. N.W., 20006-5009; (202) 303-5000. *Gail J. McGovern, President. Press,* (202) 303-5551. *Toll-free,* 800-RED-CROSS (733-2767).
Web, www.redcross.org and Twitter, @RedCross

Humanitarian relief and health education organization chartered by Congress; provides services in the United States and internationally, when requested. Collects blood and maintains blood centers; conducts research; operates the national bone marrow registry and a rare-donor registry. Serves as U.S. member of the International Federation of Red Cross and Red Crescent Societies, headquartered in Geneva, Switzerland.

American Society for Bone and Mineral Research, 2025 M St. N.W., #800, 20036-3309; (202) 367-1161. Fax, (202) 367-2161. *Ann Elderkin, Executive Director.*
General email, asbmr@asbmr.org
Web, www.asbmr.org

Membership: scientists and physicians who study bone and mineral metabolism. Promotes public awareness of bone diseases. Publishes the *Journal of Bone and Mineral Research* and the *Primer on the Metabolic Bone Diseases and Disorders of Mineral Metabolism.* Awards grants for member research.

Cancer

▶**AGENCIES**

National Cancer Institute *(National Institutes of Health),* 31 Center Dr., Bldg. 31, #11A48, Bethesda, MD 20892; (301) 496-5615. Fax, (301) 402-0338.
Dr. Douglas Lowy, Director, Acting. Press, (301) 496-6641. *Toll-free,* (800) 422-6237.
Web, www.cancer.gov

Conducts and funds research on the causes, diagnosis, treatment, prevention, control, and biology of cancer and the rehabilitation of cancer patients; administers the National Cancer Program; coordinates international research activities. Sponsors regional and national cancer information services.

National Cancer Institute *(National Institutes of Health), Cancer Prevention, 9609 Medical Center Dr., Bethesda, MD 20892; (240) 276-7120. Dr. Sheldon Kramer, Director.*
Web, http://prevention.cancer.gov

Seeks to plan, direct, implement, and monitor cancer research focused on early detection, cancer risk, chemoprevention, and supportive care. Focuses on intervention in the process of carcinogenesis to prevent development into invasive cancer. Supports various approaches, from pre-clinical discovery and development of biomarkers and chemoprevention agents, including pharmaceuticals and micronutrients, to Phase III clinical testing. Programs are carried out with other National Cancer Institute divisions, NIH institutes, and federal and state agencies.

National Cancer Institute *(National Institutes of Health), Communications and Public Liaison, 9609 Medical Center Dr., #2E-532, Bethesda, MD 20892-9760; (240) 276-6600. Fax, (240) 276-7680. Peter Garrett, Director.*
General email, ncioce@mail.nih.gov
Web, www.cancer.gov.aboutnci/organization/ocpi

Collects and disseminates scientific information on cancer biology, etiology, screening, prevention, treatment, and supportive care. Evaluates and develops new media formats for cancer information.

National Cancer Institute *(National Institutes of Health), Translational Research Program, 9609 Medical Center Dr., Bethesda, MD 20892; (240) 276-5730. Fax, (240) 276-7881. Dr. Toby T. Hecht, Associate Director.*
General email, ncitrp-r@mail.nih.gov
Web, http://trp.cancer.gov

Administers SPORE grants (the Specialized Programs of Research Excellence). Encourages the study of organ-specific cancers, blood malignancies, and other cancers. Promotes and funds interdisciplinary research and information exchange between basic and clinical science to move basic research findings from the laboratory to applied settings involving patients and populations. Encourages laboratory and clinical scientists to work collaboratively to plan, design, and implement research programs on cancer prevention, detection, diagnosis, treatment, and control.

President's Cancer Panel, *c/o National Cancer Institute, 9000 Rockville Pike, Bldg. 31, B2B37, MSC 2590, Bethesda, MD 20892; (301) 451-9399. Fax, (301) 451-5909. Dr. Abby Sandler, Executive Secretary.*
General email, prescancerpanel@nih.gov
Web, http://deuinfo.nci.nih.gov/advisory/pcp

Presidentially appointed committee that monitors and evaluates the National Cancer Program; reports to the president and Congress.

▶**NONGOVERNMENTAL**

American Cancer Society, *Cancer Action Network, 555 11th St. N.W., #300, 20004; (202) 661-5700. Fax, (202) 661-5750. Christopher W. Hansen, President.*
Web, www.acscan.org

Supports evidence-based policy and legislation designed to eliminate cancer as a major health problem; works to encourage elected officials and candidates to make cancer a top national priority. Monitors legislation and regulations. (Headquarters in Atlanta, Ga.)

American Childhood Cancer Organization, *10920 Connecticut Ave., Suite A, Kensington, MD 20895 (mailing address: P.O. Box 498, Kensington, MD 20895-0498); (301) 962-3520. Fax, (301) 962-3521. Ruth I. Hoffman, Executive Director. Information, (855) 858-2226.*
General email, staff@acco.org
Web, www.acco.org

Membership: families of children with cancer, survivors of childhood cancer, and health and education professionals. Serves as an information and educational network; sponsors self-help groups for parents of children and adolescents with cancer. Monitors legislation and regulations.

American Institute for Cancer Research, *1759 R St. N.W., 20009-2583; (202) 328-7744. Fax, (202) 328-7226. Marilyn Gentry, President. Information, (800) 843-8114.*
General email, aicrweb@aicr.org
Web, www.aicr.org and Twitter, @aicrtweets

Funds research on relationship of nutrition, physical activity, and weight management to cancer risk. Interprets scientific literature; sponsors education programs on cancer prevention.

American Society for Radiation Oncology (ASTRO), *8280 Willow Oaks Corporate Dr., #500, Fairfax, VA 22031; (703) 502-1550. Fax, (703) 502-7852. Laura Thevenot, Chief Executive Officer, (703) 839-7302. Toll-free, (800) 962-7876.*
General email, information@astro.org
Web, www.astro.org and Twitter, @ASTRO_org

Radiation oncology, biology, and physics organization that seeks to improve patient care through education, clinical practice, the advancement of science, and advocacy.

American Society of Clinical Oncology, *2318 Mill Rd., #800, Alexandria, VA 22314; (571) 483-1300. Fax, (703) 299-0255. Dr. Allen S. Lichter, Chief Executive Officer. Toll-free, (888) 282-2552.*
General email, asco@asco.org
Web, www.asco.org and Twitter, @ASCO

Membership: physicians and scientists specializing in cancer prevention, treatment, education, and research. Promotes exchange of information in clinical research and patient care relating to all stages of cancer; monitors international research.

Assn. of Community Cancer Centers, *11600 Nebel St., #201, Rockville, MD 20852-2557; (301) 984-9496. Fax, (301) 770-1949. Christian G. Downs, Executive Director. Web, www.accc-cancer.org and Twitter, @ACCCBuzz*

Membership: individuals from community hospitals involved in multidisciplinary cancer programs, including physicians, administrators, nurses, medical directors, pharmacists, and other members of the cancer care team. Supports comprehensive cancer care for all. Monitors legislation and regulations.

Cancer Support Community, *1050 17th St. N.W., #500, 200336; (202) 659-9709. Fax, (202) 974-7999. Kim Thiboldeaux, Chief Executive Officer; Linda House, President. TTY, (888) 793-9355. General email, help@cancersupportcommunity.org Web, www.cancersupportcommunity.org*

Research and advocacy organization providing support services to those facing cancer. Research and Training Institute supports cancer-related psychosocial, behavioral, and surviorship research.

Leukemia and Lymphoma Society, *National Capital Area Chapter, 3601 Eisenhower Ave., #450, Alexandria, VA 22304; (703) 399-2900. Fax, (703) 399-2901. Beth Gorman, Executive Director. Information, (800) 955-4572. Web, www.lls.org, Twitter, @LLSusa and Facebook, www.facebook.com/LLSNatCap*

Voluntary health organization that funds blood cancer research, education, and patient services. Seeks to find cures for leukemia, lymphoma, Hodgkin's disease, and myeloma, and to improve the quality of life of patients and their families. Local chapters provide blood cancer patients with disease and treatment information, financial assistance, counseling, and referrals. (Headquarters in White Plains, New York.)

Lung Cancer Alliance, *1700 K St. N.W., #660, 20006; (202) 463-2080. Laurie Fenton Ambrose, President. Press, (202) 742-1422. Toll-free helpline, (800) 298-2436. General email, info@lungcanceralliance.org Web, www.lungcanceralliance.org*

Advocates lung cancer research and access to screenings, treatments, diagnostics, and testing. Provides information about lung cancer risks and early detection.

National Breast Cancer Coalition, *1010 Vermont Ave. N.W., #900, 20005; (202) 296-7477. Fax, (202) 265-6854. Frances M. Visco, President. Toll-free, (800) 622-2838. Press, (202) 973-0593. General email, info@breastcancerdeadline2020.org Web, www.breastcancerdeadline2020.org*

Membership: organizations, local coalitions, and individuals. Supports increasing funding for breast cancer research; monitors how funds are spent; seeks to expand access to quality health care for all; and ensures that trained advocates influence all decision making that impacts breast cancer.

National Coalition for Cancer Survivorship, *1010 Wayne Ave., #315, Silver Spring, MD 20910-5600; (301) 650-9127. Fax, (301) 565-9670. Shelley Fuld Nasso, Chief Executive Officer. Toll-free information and publications, (877) 622-7937. General email, info@canceradvocacy.org Web, www.canceradvocacy.org, Twitter, @CancerAdvocacy and Facebook, www.facebook.com/cancersurvivorship*

Membership: survivors of cancer (newly diagnosed, in treatment, and living beyond cancer), their families and friends, health care providers, and support organizations. Distributes information, including the Cancer Survival Toolbox, about living with cancer diagnosis and treatment; offers free publications and resources that help enable individuals to take charge of their own care or the care of others.

Ovarian Cancer National Alliance, *1101 14th St., #850, 20005; (202) 331-1332. Fax, (202) 331-2292. Audra Moran, President and Chief Executive Officer. Toll-free, (866) 399-6262. General email, ocna@ovariancancer.org Web, www.ovariancancer.org*

Acts as an advocate at the federal and state levels for adequate and sustained funding for ovarian cancer research and awareness programs. Promotes legislation that would improve the quality of life and access to care for all cancer patients. Provides information and resources for survivors, women at risk, and health providers.

Diabetes, Digestive Diseases

▶**AGENCIES**

National Diabetes Information Clearinghouse *(National Institutes of Health), 1 Information Way, Bethesda, MD 20892-3560; (800) 860-8747. Fax, (301) 634-0716. Dr. Griffin P. Rodgers, Director; Justin Gray, Senior Information Specialist. TTY, (866) 569-1162. General email, ndic@info.niddk.nih.gov Web, www.diabetes.niddk.nih.gov*

Provides health professionals and the public with information on the symptoms, causes, treatments, and general nature of diabetes.

National Digestive Diseases Information Clearinghouse *(National Institutes of Health), 1 Information Way, Bethesda, MD 20892-3570; (800) 860-8747. Fax, (301) 634-0716. Dr. Griffin P. Rodgers, Director; Justin Gray, Senior Information Specialist. TTY, (866) 569-1162. General email, nddic@info.niddk.nih.gov Web, www.digestive.niddk.nih.gov*

Provides health professionals and the public with information on the symptoms, causes, treatments, and general nature of digestive diseases and ailments.

National Institute of Diabetes and Digestive and Kidney Diseases *(National Institutes of Health), 31 Center Dr., Bldg. 31, #9A52, MS 2560, Bethesda, MD 20892-2560; (301) 496-5741. Fax, (301) 402-2125. Dr. Griffin P. Rodgers, Director. Press, (301) 496-3583. Web, www.niddk.nih.gov, Twitter, @NIDDKgov and Facebook, www.facebook.com/National-Institute-of-Diabetes-and-Digestive-and-Kidney-Diseases-NIDDK-159778759845*

Conducts and supports basic and clinical research and research training on diabetes and other endocrine and metabolic diseases, digestive diseases, nutrition, obesity, and kidney, urologic, and hematologic diseases. Web site provides evidence-based health information.

National Institute of Diabetes and Digestive and Kidney Diseases *(National Institutes of Health), Diabetes, Endocrinology, and Metabolic Diseases, 2 Democracy Plaza, 6707 Democracy Blvd., #683, MSC 2560, Bethesda, MD 20892; (301) 496-7349. Fax, (301) 480-3503. Judith E. Fradkin, Director. Press, (301) 496-3583. Web, www.niddk.nih.gov*

Provides research funding and support for basic and clinical research in the areas of type 1 and type 2 diabetes and other metabolic disorders, including cystic fibrosis; endocrinology and endocrine disorders; obesity, neuroendocrinology, and energy balance; and development, metabolism, and basic biology of liver, fat, and endocrine tissues.

National Institute of Diabetes and Digestive and Kidney Diseases *(National Institutes of Health), Digestive Diseases and Nutrition, 2 Democracy Plaza, 6707 Democracy Blvd., #677, MSC 5450, Bethesda, MD 20892-5450; (301) 594-7680. Fax, (301) 480-8300. Stephen P. James, Director. Press, (301) 496-3583. Web, www.niddk.nih.gov*

Awards grants and contracts to support basic and clinical research related to digestive diseases and nutrition, as well as training and career development. Conducts and supports research concerning liver and biliary diseases; pancreatic diseases; gastrointestinal disease, including neuroendocrinology, motility, immunology, absorption, and transport in the gastrointestinal tract; nutrient metabolism; obesity; and eating disorders.

▶**NONGOVERNMENTAL**

American Diabetes Assn. (ADA), *1701 N. Beauregard St., Alexandria, VA 22311; (703) 549-1500. Fax, (703) 549-5995. Devin Hagan, Chief Executive Officer. Toll-free, (800) 342-2383. Web, www.diabetes.org*

Works to improve access to quality care and to eliminate discrimination against people because of their diabetes. Provides local affiliates with education, information, and referral services. Conducts and funds research on diabetes. Monitors international research. Monitors legislation and regulations.

American Gastroenterological Assn., *4930 Del Ray Ave., Bethesda, MD 20814; (301) 654-2055. Fax, (301) 654-*

5920. Tom Serena, Executive Vice President. Press, (301) 941-2620. General email, member@gastro.org Web, www.gastro.org

Membership: 17,000 gastroenterology clinicians, scientists, health care professionals, and educators. Sponsors scientific research on digestive diseases; disseminates information on new methods of prevention and treatment. Monitors legislation and regulations. (Affiliated with the Foundation of Digestive Health and Nutrition.)

Endocrine Society, *2055 L St. N.W., #600, 20036; (202) 971-3636. Fax, (202) 736-9705. Lisa H. Fish, President; Henry M. Kronenberg, President-elect. Toll-free, (888) 363-6274. General email, societyservices@endocrine.org Web, www.endocrine.org*

Membership: scientists, doctors, health care educators, clinicians, nurses, and others interested in endocrine glands and their disorders. Promotes endocrinology research and clinical practice; sponsors seminars and conferences; gives awards and travel grants.

JDRF, *Advocacy, 1400 K St. N.W., #1212, 20005; (202) 371-9746. Fax, (202) 371-2760. Cynthia Rice, Senior Vice President, Advocacy and Policy. Toll-free, (800) 533-1868. General email, advocacy@jdrf.org Web, www.jdrf.org*

Conducts research, education, and public awareness programs aimed at improving the lives of people with type 1 (juvenile) diabetes and finding a cure for diabetes and its related complications. Monitors legislation and regulations. (Formerly the Juvenile Diabetes Research Foundation.) (Headquarters in New York.)

Family Planning and Population

▶**AGENCIES**

Agency for International Development (USAID), *Global Health, Population and Reproductive Health, 1300 Pennsylvania Ave. N.W., #3.06-011, 20523-3600; (202) 712-4120. Fax, (202) 216-3485. Jennifer Adams, Deputy Assistant Administrator. Press, (202) 712-4320. General email, pi@usaid.gov Web, www.usaid.gov/what-we-do/global-health/family-planning*

Advances and supports family planning and reproductive health programs in more than 45 countries.

Assistant Secretary for Health *(Health and Human Services Dept.), Adolescent Health, 1101 Wootton Pkwy., #700, Rockville, MD 20852; (240) 453-2846. Evelyn Kappeler, Director. General email, oah.gov@hhs.gov Web, www.hhs.gov/ash/oah*

Supports and evaluates teen pregnancy prevention programs; implements the Pregnany Assistance Fund;

coordinates HHS efforts related to adolescent health promotion and disease prevention.

Assistant Secretary for Health *(Health and Human Services Dept.), Population Affairs, 200 Independence Ave. S.W., 20201; (240) 453-2800. Fax, (240) 453-2801. Susan B. Moskosky, Director, Acting.*
General email, opa@hhs.gov

Web, www.hhs.gov/opa and Twitter, @opa1

Responsible for Title X Family Planning Program, which provides family planning services, health screening services, and screening for STDs (including HIV) to all who want and need them, with priority given to low-income persons; the Title XX Adolescent Family Life Program, including demonstration projects to develop, implement, and evaluate program interventions to promote abstinence from sexual activity among adolescents and to provide comprehensive health care, education, and social services to pregnant and parenting adolescents; and for planning, monitoring, and evaluating population research.

Census Bureau *(Commerce Dept.), Fertility and Family Statistics, 4600 Silver Hill Rd., #7H371, Suitland, MD 20746-8500 (mailing address: change city, state, and zip code to Washington, DC 20233); (301) 763-2416. Fax, (301) 763-3232. Rose Kreider, Branch Chief.*
Web, www.census.gov/hhes/fertility and www.census.gov/hhes/families

Provides data and statistics on fertility and family composition. Conducts census and survey research on the number of children, household composition, and living arrangements of women in the United States, especially working mothers. Conducts studies on child care and child well-being.

Eunice Kennedy Shriver National Institute of Child Health and Human Development *(National Institutes of Health), Division of Extramural Research, Contraceptive Research Branch, 6100 Executive Blvd., #4AOSC, MSC 7510, Bethesda, MD 20892-7510; (301) 496-5577. Fax, (301) 480-1972. Dr. Caroline Signore, Branch Chief, Acting.*
Web, www.nichd.nih.gov/about/org/der/brunches/crb

Develops and supports research and research training programs in contraceptive development and other areas of reproductive health. Major research areas include new contraceptive methods; mechanisms of action and effects of contraceptive and reproductive hormones, drugs, devices, and procedures; as well as optimal formulations and dosages of contraceptive agents and spermicidal microbicides.

Eunice Kennedy Shriver National Institute of Child Health and Human Development *(National Institutes of Health), Division of Extramural Research, Fertility and Infertility Branch, (301) 435-6970. Fax, (301) 480-0289. Louis DePaolo, Branch Chief.*
Web, www.nichd.nih.gov/about/org/der/branches/fi

Encourages, enables, and supports scientific research aimed at alleviating human infertility, discovering new ways to control fertility, and expanding knowledge of processes that underlie human reproduction. Provides funds for basic and clinical studies that enhance understanding of normal reproduction and reproductive pathophysiology, as well as enable the development of more effective strategies for the diagnosis, management, and prevention of conditions that compromise fertility.

Eunice Kennedy Shriver National Institute of Child Health and Human Development *(National Institutes of Health), Division of Extramural Research, Population Dynamics Branch, 6100 Executive Blvd., #8B07H, MSC 7510, Bethesda, MD 20892-7510; (301) 496-1174. Fax, (301) 496-0962. Rebecca L. Clark, Branch Chief.*
Web, www.nichd.nih.gov/about/org/der/branches/pdb

Conducts research and research training in demography, reproductive health, and population health. Major focus is human populations, including fertility, mortality and morbidity, migration, population distribution, nuptiality, family demography, population growth and decline, and the causes and consequences of demographic change. Supports behavioral and social science research on sexually transmitted diseases, HIV/AIDS, family planning, and infertility. Collects data on human health, productivity, behavior, and development at the population level using methods including inferential statistics, natural experiments, policy experiments, statistical modeling, and gene/environment interaction studies.

▶**NONGOVERNMENTAL**

Advocates for Youth, *2000 M St. N.W., #750, 20036; (202) 419-3420. Fax, (202) 419-1448. Debra Hauser, President.*
General email, information@advocatesforyouth.org

Web, www.advocatesforyouth.org

Seeks to reduce the incidence of unintended teenage pregnancy and AIDS through public education, training and technical assistance, research, and media programs.

American Society for Reproductive Medicine, *J. Benjamin Younger Office of Public Affairs, 409 12th St. S.W., 20024-2188; (202) 863-2494. Sean B. Tipton, Public Affairs Director.*
General email, advocacy@asrm.dc.org

Web, www.asrm.org

Membership: obstetrician/gynecologists, urologists, reproductive endocrinologists, embryologists, mental health professionals, internists, nurses, practice administrators, laboratory technicians, pediatricians, research scientists, and veterinarians. Seeks to educate health care professionals, policymakers, and the public on the science and practice of reproductive medicine and associated legal and ethical issues. Monitors legislation and regulations. (Headquarters in Birmingham, Ala.).

Guttmacher Institute, *Public Policy, 1301 Connecticut Ave. N.W., #700, 20036 3902; (202) 296-4012. Fax, (202) 223-5756. Rachel Benson Gold, Vice President for Public Policy; Susan Cohen, Vice President for Public Policy. Toll-free, (877) 823-0262.*
General email, policyinfo@guttmacher.org

Web, www.guttmacher.org

Conducts research, policy analysis, and public education in reproductive health, fertility regulation, population, and related areas of U.S. and international health. (Headquarters in New York.)

National Abortion Federation (NAF), *1660 L St. N.W., #450, 20036; (202) 667-5881. Fax, (202) 667-5890. Vicki Saporta, President. NAF hotline, (800) 772-9100. General email, naf@prochoice.org*

Web, www.prochoice.org

Professional association of abortion providers in the United States, Canada, and Mexico City. Offers information on medical, legal, and social aspects of abortion; sets quality standards for abortion care. Conducts training and accredited continuing medical education. Runs a toll-free hotline for women seeking information or referrals. Monitors legislation and regulations.

National Campaign to Prevent Teen and Unplanned Pregnancy, *1776 Massachusetts Ave. N.W., #200, 20036; (202) 478-8500. Fax, (202) 478-8588. Ginny Ehrlich, Chief Executive Officer. General email, campaign@thenc.org*

Web, www.thenationalcampaign.org and Twitter, @TheNC

Nonpartisan initiative that seeks to reduce the U.S. teen and unplanned pregnancy rates. Provides education and information regarding contraception.

National Family Planning and Reproductive Health Assn., *1627 K St. N.W., 12th Floor, 20006-1702; (202) 293-3114. Fax, (202) 293-1990. Clare Coleman, President. General email, info@nfprha.org*

Web, www.nfprha.org

Represents family planning providers, including nurses, nurse practitioners, administrators, and other health care professionals nationwide. Provides advocacy, education, and training for those in the family planning and reproductive health care field. Interests include family planning for the low-income and uninsured, and reducing rates of unintended pregnancy.

Planned Parenthood Federation of America, *Public Policy, 1110 Vermont Ave. N.W., #300, 20005; (202) 973-4800. Fax, (202) 296-3242. Cecile Richards, President. Media, (202) 261-4433.*

Web, www.plannedparenthood.org

Educational, research, and medical services organization. Washington office conducts research and monitors legislation on health care topics, including reproductive health, women's health, contraception, family planning, abortion, and global health. (Headquarters in New York accredits affiliated local centers, which offer medical services, birth control, and family planning information.)

Population Action International, *1300 19th St. N.W., #200, 20036; (202) 557-3400. Fax, (202) 728-4177. Suzanne Ehlers, President. General email, info@pai.org*

Web, www.pai.org

Promotes population stabilization through public education and universal access to voluntary family planning. Library open to the public by appointment.

Population Connection, *2120 L St. N.W., #500, 20037; (202) 332-2200. Fax, (202) 332-2302. John Seager, President. Toll-free, (800) 767-1956. General email, info@populationconnection.org*

Web, www.populationconnection.org

Membership: persons interested in sustainable world populations. Promotes the expansion of domestic and international family planning programs; supports a voluntary population stabilization policy and women's access to abortion and family planning services; works to protect the earth's resources and environment. (Formerly Zero Population Growth.)

Population Institute, *107 2nd St. N.E., 20002; (202) 544-3300. Fax, (202) 544-0068. Robert Walker, President. General email, info@populationinstitute.org*

Web, www.populationinstitute.org

Promotes voluntary family planning and reproductive health services. Seeks to increase public awareness of social, economic, and environmental consequences of rapid population growth. Advocates a balance between global population and natural resources to policymakers in developing and industrialized nations. Recruits and trains population activists.

Population Reference Bureau, *1875 Connecticut Ave. N.W., #520, 20009-5728; (202) 483-1100. Fax, (202) 328-3937. Jeffrey Jordan, President. Toll-free, (800) 877-9881. Media, (202) 939-5407. General email, popref@prb.org*

Web, www.prb.org and Twitter, @PRBdata

Educational organization engaged in information dissemination, training, and policy analysis on domestic and international population trends and issues. Interests include international development and family planning programs, the environment, and U.S. social and economic policy.

Genetics, Genetic Disorders

▶ **AGENCIES**

Eunice Kennedy Shriver National Institute of Child Health and Human Development *(National Institutes of Health), Division of Extramural Research, Intellectual and Developmental Disabilities Branch, 6100 Executive Blvd., #4B09G, MSC 7510, Bethesda, MD 20892-7510; (301) 496-1383. Melissa Ann Parisi, Branch Chief.*
Web, www.nichd.nih.gov/about/org/der/branches/iddb

Provides support for research projects, training programs, and research centers dedicated to promoting the well-being of individuals with intellectual and developmental disabilities. Major research foci include chromosome abnormalities, genetic and genomic syndromes, epigenetic disorders, cellular and molecular biology, family and community relations, newborn and population screenings, Fragile X syndrome and associated disorders, rare diseases, muscular dystrophy, and autism spectrum disorders.

Health Resources and Services Administration *(Health and Human Services Dept.), Maternal and Child Health Bureau, 5600 Fishers Lane, #18W, Rockville, MD 20857; (301) 443-2170. Fax, (301) 480-1312. Aaron Lopata, Chief Medical Officer; Michael C. Lu, Associate Administrator.*
Web, www.mchb.hrsa.gov

Awards funds, including demonstration grants, to develop or enhance regional, local, and state genetic screening, diagnostic, counseling, and follow-up programs; assists states in their newborn screening programs; provides funding for regional hemophilia treatment centers; and supports comprehensive care for individuals and families with Cooley's anemia and those with sickle cell anemia identified through newborn screening.

National Heart, Lung, and Blood Institute *(National Institutes of Health), Blood Diseases and Resources Division, Translational Blood Science and Resource Branch, 6701 Rockledge Dr., #90930, Bethesda, MD 20892-7950; (301) 435-0050. Fax, (301) 480-1046. Traci Heath Mondoro, Branch Chief. Press, (301) 496-4236.*
Web, www.nhlbi.nih.gov/about/org/dbdr

Provides oversight, support, and stimulation of translational research throughout the spectrum of blood science, as well as the resources required to support heart, lung, blood, and sleep research. Branch responsibilities include oversight, support, and stimulation of post-discovery science, preclinical research, and early phase clinical studies and trials (TI, T2 Research); oversight, support, and stimulation of SBIR/STTR initiatives in the blood sciences; administration of and liaison to NHLBI resources related to translational research; training of the blood science workforce; and scientific liaison for translation research across the Division, NHLBI, NIH, and partner federal agencies.

National Human Genome Research Institute *(National Institutes of Health), 31 Center Dr., Bldg. 31, #4B09, MSC 2152, Bethesda, MD 20892-2152; (301) 496-0844. Fax, (301) 402-4831. Dr. Eric D. Green, Director. Information, (301) 496-0844.*
Web, www.genome.gov and Facebook, www.facebook.com/genome.gov

Conducts and funds a broad range of studies aimed at understanding the structure and function of the human genome and its role in health and disease. Supports the development of resources and technology that will accelerate genome research and its application to human health. Studies the ethical, legal, and social implications of genome research, and supports the training of investigators, as well as the dissemination of genome information to the public and to health professionals.

National Institute of Allergy and Infectious Diseases *(National Institutes of Health), Allergy, Immunology, and Transplantation, 5601 Fishers Lane, #7C13, MS 9828,*

Rockville, MD 20852; (301) 496-1886. Fax, (301) 402-0175. Dr. Daniel Rotrosen, Director.
Web, www.niaid.nih.gov/about/organization/dait

Supports extramural basic and clinical research to increase understanding of the causes and mechanisms that lead to the development of immunologic diseases and to expand knowledge that can be applied to developing improved techniques of diagnosis, treatment, and prevention. Interests include lupus; allergic diseases, such as asthma, hay fever, and contact dermatitis; and acute and chronic inflammatory disorders.

National Institute of General Medical Sciences *(National Institutes of Health), Genetics and Developmental Biology, 45 Center Dr., #2AS25K, MSC 6200, Bethesda, MD 20892-6200; (301) 594-0943. Fax, (301) 480-2228. Dorit Zuk, Director.*
Web, www.nigms.nih.gov/about/overview/Pages/GDB.aspx

Supports research and research training in genetics. Maintains Human Genetic Cell Repository; distributes cell lines and DNA samples to research scientists.

National Institutes of Health (NIH) *(Health and Human Services Dept.), Biotechnology Activities, 6705 Rockledge Dr., #750, MSC 7985, Bethesda, MD 20892-7985; (301) 196-9030. Fax, (301) 496-9839. Lyric Jorgenson, Director, Acting.*
General email, oba-osp@od.nih.gov
Web, http://osp.od.nih.gov/office-biotechnology-activities/oba

Reviews requests submitted to the NIH involving genetic testing, recombinant DNA technology, xenotransplantation, and biosecurity; develops and implements research guidelines for safe conduct of DNA-related research. Monitors scientific progress in human genetics.

▶ **NONGOVERNMENTAL**

Center for Sickle Cell Disease *(Howard University), 1840 7th St. N.W., 20001; (202) 865-8292. Fax, (202) 232-6719. Juan Saloman-Andonie, Administrative Director.*
Web, www.sicklecell.howard.edu and www.sicklecelltransition.org/#!about-atp/mainPage

Screens and tests for sickle cell disease; conducts research; promotes public education and community involvement; provides counseling, patient care, and transition support from pediatric to adult care services.

Cystic Fibrosis Foundation, *6931 Arlington Rd., 2nd Floor, Bethesda, MD 20814; (301) 951-4422. Fax, (301) 951-6378. Dr. Preston W. Campbell III, President. Information, (800) 344-4823.*
General email, info@cff.org
Web, www.cff.org

Conducts research on cystic fibrosis, a genetic disease affecting the respiratory and digestive systems. Focuses on medical research to identify a cure and to improve quality of life for those living with cystic fibrosis.

Genetic Alliance, *4301 Connecticut Ave. N.W., #404, 20008-2369; (202) 966-5557. Fax, (202) 966-8553. Sharon Terry, President.*
General email, info@geneticalliance.org

Web, www.geneticalliance.org and Twitter, @GeneticAlliance

Coalition of government, industry, advocacy organizations, and private groups that seeks to advance genetic research and its applications. Promotes increased funding for research, improved access to services, and greater support for emerging technologies, tests, and treatments. Acts as an advocate on behalf of individuals and families living with genetic conditions.

Genetics Society of America, *9650 Rockville Pike, Bethesda, MD 20814-3998; (301) 634-7300. Fax, (301) 634-7079. Adam Fagen, Executive Director. Toll-free, (866) 486-4363.*
General email, society@genetics-gsa.org

Web, www.genetics-gsa.org and Twitter, @GeneticsGSA

Facilitates professional cooperation among persons conducting research in and teaching genetics. Advocates research funding; sponsors meetings; and publishes scholarly research journals.

Kennedy Institute of Ethics *(Georgetown University), Healy Hall, 37th and O Sts. N.W., 4th Floor, 20057; (202) 687-0360. Fax, (202) 687-8089. Margaret Little, Director. Library, (202) 687-3885.*
General email, kennedyinstitute@georgetown.edu

Web, https://kennedyinstitute.georgetown.edu, Twitter, @kieatgu and Facebook, www.facebook.com/KennedyInstituteofEthics

Carries out teaching and research on medical ethics, including legal and ethical definitions of death, allocation of health resources, and recombinant DNA and human gene therapy. Sponsors the annual Intensive Bioethics Course. Conducts international programs. Serves as the home of the Bioethics Research Library at Georgetown University (http://bioethics.georgetown.edu) and the National Information Resource on Ethics and Human Genetics (http://genthx.georgetown.edu). Provides free reference assistance and bibliographic databases covering all ethical issues in health care, genetics, and biomedical research. Publishes the *Kennedy Institute of Ethics Journal.* Library open to the public.

March of Dimes, *Government Affairs, 1401 K St. N.W., 9th Floor, 20005; (202) 659-1800. Fax, (202) 296-2964. Cynthia Pellegrini, Senior Vice President for Public Policy and Government Affairs.*
Web, www.marchofdimes.org/advocacy-and-government-affairs-issues-and-advocacy-priorities.aspx

Works to prevent and treat birth defects. Awards grants for research and provides funds for treatment of birth defects. Monitors legislation and regulations. (Headquarters in White Plains, N.Y.)

Osteogenesis Imperfecta Foundation, *804 W. Diamond Ave., #210, Gaithersburg, MD 20878; (301) 947-0083.*
Fax, (301) 947-0456. Tracy Smith Hart, Chief Executive Officer. Toll-free, (844) 889-7579.
General email, bonelink@oif.org

Web, www.oif.org and Twitter, @OIFoundation

Provides healthcare professionals and patients with information about osteogenesis imperfecta (OI), also known as brittle bone disease; offers research grants; promotes public policy that supports people living with OI.

Heart Disease, Strokes

▶AGENCIES

National Heart, Lung, and Blood Institute *(National Institutes of Health), Cardiovascular Sciences Division, 6701 Rockledge Dr., #8128, Bethesda, MD 20892; (301) 435-0422. Fax, (301) 480-7971. Dr. George Mensah, Director, Acting. Press, (301) 496-4236.*
General email, lauerm@nhlbi.nih.gov

Web, www.nhlbi.nih.gov/about/org/dcvs#DCVS

Supports basic, clinical, population, and health services research on the causes, prevention, and treatment of cardiovascular disease and technology development. Interests include disease and risk factor patterns in populations; clinical trials of interventions; and genetic, behavioral, sociocultural, environmental, and health-systems factors of disease risk and outcomes.

National Heart, Lung, and Blood Institute *(National Institutes of Health), Health Information Center, 31 Center Dr., Bldg. 31, Bethesda, MD 20892-2480 (mailing address: P.O. Box 30105, Bethesda, MD 20824-0105); (301) 592-8573. Lenora Johnson, Director, (301) 496-4236.*
General email, nhlbilnfo@nhlbi.nih.gov

Web, www.nhlbi.nih.gov/health/contact

Acquires, maintains, and disseminates information on cholesterol, high blood pressure, heart attack awareness, and asthma to the public and health professionals.

National Institute of Neurological Disorders and Stroke *(National Institutes of Health), 31 Center Dr., Bldg. 31, #8A52, MS 2540, Bethesda, MD 20824; (301) 496-5751. Fax, (301) 402-2186. Dr. Walter J. Koroshetz, Director. Information, (301) 496-5751. Toll-free, (800) 352-9424.*
Web, www.ninds.nih.gov, Twitter, @NINDSnews and Facebook, www.facebook.com/NINDSandPartners

Conducts research and disseminates information on the causes, prevention, diagnosis, and treatment of neurological disorders and stroke; supports basic and clinical research in related scientific areas. Provides research grants to public and private institutions and individuals. Operates a program of contracts for the funding of research and research-support efforts.

▶NONGOVERNMENTAL

American Heart Assn., *Federal Advocacy, 1150 Connecticut Ave. N.W., #300, 20036; (202) 785-7900.*

Fax, (202) 785-7955. Retha Sherrod, Director, Media Advocacy.
Web, www.heart.org

Membership: physicians, scientists, and other interested individuals. Supports research, patient advocacy, treatment, and community service programs that provide information about heart disease and stroke; participates in international conferences and research. Monitors legislation and regulations. (Headquarters in Dallas, Texas.)

WomenHeart: National Coalition for Women With Heart Disease, *1100 17th St. N.W., #500, 20036; (202) 728-7199. Fax, (202) 728-7238. Mary McGowan, Chief Executive Officer.*
General email, mail@womenheart.org
Web, www.womenheart.org and Twitter, @WomenHeartOrg

Patient-centered organization that seeks to advance women's heart health through advocacy, community education, and patient support. Composed of patients and their families, health care providers, advocates, and interested consumers.

HIV and AIDS

▶**AGENCIES**

Assistant Secretary for Health *(Health and Human Services Dept.), HIV/AIDS and Infectious Disease Policy, 200 Independence Ave. S.W., #443H, 20201; (202) 690-5560. Fax, (202) 690-7560. Richard Wolitski, Director, Acting.*
Web, www.hhs.gov/ash/ohaidp/index.html
HIV/AIDS information, http://aids.gov and Twitter, @AIDSgov

Advises the Assistant Secretary for Health and senior Health and Human Services officials on the implementation and development of policies, programs, and activities related to HIV/AIDS, viral hepatitis, other infectious diseases of public health signicance, and blood safety and availability.

Assistant Secretary for Health *(Health and Human Services Dept.), Minority Health, 1101 Wootton Pkwy., #600, Rockville, MD 20852; (240) 453-2882. Fax, (240) 453-2883. Dr. J. Nadine Gracia, Deputy Assistant Secretary. Information, (800) 444-6472.*
General email, info@minorityhealth.gov
Web, http://minorityhealth.hhs.gov and Twitter, @MinorityHealth

Awards grants to minority AIDS education and prevention projects.

Centers for Disease Control and Prevention (CDC) *(Health and Human Services Dept.), Washington Office, 395 E St. S.W., #9100, 20201; (202) 245-0600. Fax, (202) 245-0602. Dr. Thomas R. Frieden, Director; Dena Morris, Director, Washington Office. Public inquiries, (800) 232-4636. TTY, (888) 232-6348.*

General email, cdinfo@cdc.gov
Web, www.cdc.gov/washington and Twitter, @CDCgov

Conducts research to prevent and control acquired immune deficiency syndrome (AIDS); promotes public awareness through guidelines for health care workers, educational packets for schools, and monthly reports on incidences of AIDS. (Headquarters in Atlanta, Ga.)

Eunice Kennedy Shriver National Institute of Child Health and Human Development *(National Institutes of Health), Division of Extramural Research, Maternal and Pediatric Infectious Disease Branch, 6100 Executive Blvd., #4B11, MSC 7510, Bethesda, MD 20892-7510; (301) 435-6868. Rohan Hazra, Branch Chief.*
Web, www.nichd.nih.gov/about/org/der/branches/mpidb

Supports and conduct domestic and international research related to the epidemiology, diagnosis, clinical manifestations, pathogenesis, transmission, treatment, and prevention of HIV infection and its complications in infants, children, adolescents, and preganant and nonpregnant women. Investigates the effects of HIV and other infectious agents and their therapies on pregnant women, pregnancy outcomes, fetuses, and children, and the impact of pregnancy on the course of HIV disease and other infectious diseases.

Food and Drug Administration (FDA) *(Health and Human Services Dept.), Center for Biologics Evaluation and Research, 10903 New Hampshire Ave., W071, Silver Spring, MD 20993; (240) 402-8010. Fax, (301) 595-1310. Dr. Peter Marks, Director. Press and publications, (301) 827-2000.*
Web, www.fda.gov/AboutFDA/CentersOffices/OfficeofMedicalProductsandTobacco/CBER/default.htm

Develops testing standards for vaccines, blood supply, and blood products and derivatives to prevent transmission of the human immunodeficiency virus (HIV); regulates biological therapeutics; helps formulate international standards. Serves as the focus for AIDS activities within the FDA.

Food and Drug Administration (FDA) *(Health and Human Services Dept.), Center for Drug Evaluation and Research, 10903 New Hampshire Ave., W051, #6133, Silver Spring, MD 20993; (301) 796-5400. Fax, (301) 595-7910. Dr. Janet Woodcock, Director. Press, (301) 796-3700.*
Web, www.fda.gov/drugs and www.fda.gov/AboutFDA/CentersOffices/OfficeofMedicalProductsandTobacco/CDER/default.htm

Approves new drugs for AIDS and AIDS-related diseases. Reviews and approves applications to investigate and market new drugs; works to harmonize drug approval internationally.

Health Resources and Services Administration *(Health and Human Services Dept.), HIV/AIDS Bureau, 5600 Fishers Lane, #09W37, Rockville, MD 20857; (301) 443-1993. Laura Cheever, Associate Administrator.*
Web, www.hab.hrsa.gov

Administers grants to support health care programs for AIDS patients, including those that reimburse low-income patients for drug expenses. Provides patients with AIDS and HIV-related disorders with ambulatory and community-based care. Conducts AIDS/HIV education and training activities for health professionals.

National Institute of Allergy and Infectious Diseases *(National Institutes of Health), HIV/AIDS,* 5601 Fishers Lane, #8D33, MS 9831, Rockville, MD 20852; (301) 496-9112. Fax, (301) 402-1505. Carl W. Dieffenbach, Director.
Web, www.niaid.nih.gov/about/organization/daids

Supports extramural basic and clinical research to better understand HIV and how it causes disease; find new tools to prevent HIV infection, including a preventative vaccine; develop new and more effective treatments for people infected with HIV; and work toward a cure.

National Institutes of Health (NIH) *(Health and Human Services Dept.), AIDS Research,* 5635 Fishers Lane, #4000, MSC 9310, Rockville, MD 20892-9310; (301) 496-0357. Fax, (301) 496-2119. Richard W. Eisinger, Director, Acting. General email, oartemp1@od31em1.od.nih.gov
Web, www.oar.nih.gov

Responsible for the scientific, budgetary, legislative, and policy elements of the NIH AIDS research program. Plans, coordinates, evaluates, and funds all NIH AIDS research.

State Dept., *U.S. Global AIDS Coordinator,* 1800 G St. N.W., SA-22 #10300, 20037; (202) 663-2440. Fax, (202) 663-2979. Deborah L. Birx, Ambassador, (202) 633-2579. Press, (202) 663-1151.
General email, SGACPublicAffairs@state.gov
Web, www.pepfar.gov

Oversees and coordinates all U.S. international HIV/AIDS activities, including implementation of the President's Emergency Plan for AIDS Relief.

Walter Reed Army Institute of Research *(Defense Dept.), U.S. Military HIV Research Program,* 6720A Rockledge Dr., #400, Bethesda, MD 20817; (301) 500-3600. Fax, (301) 500-3666. Col. Nelson L. Michael, Director. General email, info@hivresearch.org
Web, www.hivresearch.org and Twitter, @MHRPinfo

Conducts HIV research, encompassing vaccine development, prevention, disease surveillance, and care and treatment options.

Warren Grant Magnuson Clinical Center *(National Institutes of Health), Transfusion Medicine,* 10 Center Dr., Bldg. 10, #1C711, MSC 1184, Bethesda, MD 20892-1184; (301) 496-4506. Fax, (301) 402-1360. Dr. Harvey G. Klein, Chief, (301) 496-9702. Press, (301) 496-2563.
Web, http://clinicalcenter.nih.gov/dtm

Supplies blood and blood components for patient care and research. Conducts research on diseases transmissible by blood, primarily AIDS and hepatitis.

▶**NONGOVERNMENTAL**

The AIDS Institute, 1705 DeSales St. N.W., 20036; (202) 835-8373. Fax, (202) 835-8368. Michael Ruppal, Executive Director.
General email, info@theaidsinstitute.org
Web, www.theaidsinstitute.org

Conducts research and disseminates information on health care and HIV issues. Develops and promotes policy aimed at improving the health and welfare of children, youth, and families affected by HIV. Provides training and technical assistance to health care providers and consumers. Program office is in Tampa, Florida.

AIDS United, 1424 K St. N.W., #200, 20005; (202) 408-4848. Fax, (202) 408-1818. Michael Kaplan, President; Carl Baloney Jr., Director, Government Affairs.
General email, aidsaction@aidsaction.org
Web, www.aidsunited.org

Channels resources to community-based organizations to fight HIV/AIDS at the local level. Provides grants and other support to nearly 400 organizations, principally for prevention efforts.

American Red Cross, *National Headquarters,* 2025 E St. N.W., 20006-5009; (202) 303-5000. Gail J. McGovern, President. Press, (202) 303-5551. Toll-free, 800-RED-CROSS (733-2767).
Web, www.redcross.org and Twitter, @RedCross

Humanitarian relief and health education organization chartered by Congress. Conducts public education campaigns on HIV/AIDS. Operates worldwide vaccination program. Serves as U.S. member of the international Red Cross and Red Crescent Societies, headquartered in Geneva, Switzerland.

Children's AIDS Fund, 1329 Shepard Dr., #7, Sterling, VA 20164 (mailing address: P.O. Box 16433, Washington, DC 20041); (703) 433-1560. Fax, (703) 433-1561. Anita M. Smith, President.
General email, info@childrensaidsfund.org
Web, www.childrensaidsfund.org

Provides care, services, resources, referrals, and education to children and their families affected by HIV disease. Focuses on children from birth through age 24 who are infected with HIV, have been orphaned by HIV, or will potentially be orphaned by HIV.

DKT International, 1701 K St. N.W., #900, 20006; (202) 223-8780. Fax, (202) 223-8786. Christopher H. Purdy, President. Press, (713) 721-4774.
General email, info@dktinternational.org
Web, www.dktinternational.org and Twitter, @dktchangeslives

Supports HIV/AIDS prevention by managing international social marketing campaigns for contraceptives. Assists in family planning and providing safe abortions. Interests include high-risk populations in developing countries.

The Foundation for AIDS Research (amfAR), *Public Policy, 1150 17th St. N.W., #406, 20036-4622; (202) 331-8600. Fax, (202) 331-8606. Gregorio Millett, Vice President and Director.*
Web, www.amfar.org

Supports funding for basic biomedical and clinical AIDS research; promotes AIDS prevention education worldwide; advocates effective AIDS-related public policy. Monitors legislation, regulations, and international research. (Headquarters in New York.)

Human Rights Campaign (HRC), *1640 Rhode Island Ave. N.W., 20036; (202) 216-1500. Fax, (202) 347-5323. Chad Griffin, President. Toll-free, (800) 777-4723. TTY, (202) 216-1572.*
General email, hrc@hrc.org
Web, www.hrc.org

Promotes legislation to fund HIV/AIDS research and educates the LGBT community and our allies about the realities of HIV prevention, treatment, and care.

National Minority AIDS Council (NMAC), *1000 Vermont Ave. N.W., #200, 20005; (202) 483-6622. Fax, (202) 483-1135. Paul A. Kawata, Executive Director.*
General email, communications@nmac.org
Web, www.nmac.org

Works to build the capacity of small faith- and community-based organizations delivering HIV/AIDS services in communities of color. Holds national conferences; administers treatment and research programs and training; disseminates electronic and printed resource materials; conducts public policy advocacy.

Infectious Diseases, Allergies

▶**AGENCIES**

Eunice Kennedy Shriver National Institute of Child Health and Human Development *(National Institutes of Health), Division of Extramural Research, Maternal and Pediatric Infectious Disease Branch, 6100 Executive Blvd., #4B11, MSC 7510, Bethesda, MD 20892-7510; (301) 435-6868. Rohan Hazra, Branch Chief.*
Web, www.nichd.nih.gov/about/org/der/branches/mpidb

Supports and conducts research into the epidemiology, natural history, pathogenesis, transmission, treatment, and prevention of infectious diseases, including congenital infections such as cytomegalovirus and toxoplasmosis; tropical diseases specifically affecting children and pregnant women; and vaccine-preventable disease in infants, children, adolescents, and women.

Health and Human Services Dept. (HHS), *National Vaccine Program, 200 Independence Ave. S.W., #715H, 20201; (202) 690-5566. Bruce Gellin, Director.*
General email, nvpo@hhs.gov
Web, www.hhs.gov/nvpo and www.vaccines.gov

Coordinates with federal offices about vaccine and immunization activities. Carries out National Vaccine Plan goals to prevent infections diseases.

National Institute of Allergy and Infectious Diseases *(National Institutes of Health), 5601 Fishers Lane, MSC 9806, Bethesda, MD 20892-9806; (301) 496-5717. Fax, (301) 402-3573. Dr. Anthony S. Fauci, Director. Toll-free health and research information, (866) 284-4107. TTY health and research information, (800) 877-8339. Press, (301) 402-1663.*
Web, www.niaid.nih.gov, Twitter, @NIAIDNews and Facebook, www.facebook.com/niaid.nih

Conducts research and supports research worldwide on the causes of infectious and immune-mediated diseases to develop better means of prevention, diagnosis, and treatment.

National Institute of Allergy and Infectious Diseases *(National Institutes of Health), Microbiology and Infectious Diseases, 5601 Fishers Lane, #7G51, MS 9826, Rockville, MD 20892; (301) 496-1884. Fax, (301) 480-4528. Carole A. Heilman, Director.*
Web, www.niaid.nih.gov/about/organization/dmid

Supports extramural basic and clinical research to control and prevent diseases caused by virtually all human infectious agents except HIV by providing funding and resources for researchers.

▶**NONGOVERNMENTAL**

Allergy and Asthma Network, *8229 Boone Blvd., #260, Vienna, VA 22182-2661; (703) 641-9595. Fax, (703) 288-5271. Tonya Winders, President. Information, (800) 878-4403.*
Web, www.allergyasthmanetwork.org

Membership: families dealing with asthma and allergies. Works to eliminate suffering and death due to asthma, allergies, and related conditions through education, advocacy, and community outreach.

Asthma and Allergy Foundation of America (AAFA), *8201 Corporate Dr., #1000, Landover, MD 20785; (202) 466-7643. Fax, (202) 466-8940. Cary Sennett, President. Information, (800) 727-8462.*
General email, info@aafa.org
Web, www.aafa.org and Twitter, @AAFANational

Provides information on asthma and allergies; awards research grants to asthma and allergic disease professionals; offers in-service training to allied health professionals, child care providers, and others.

Food Allergy Research and Education (FARE), *7925 Jones Branch Dr., #1100, McLean, VA 22102; (703) 691-3179. Fax, (703) 691-2713. James R. Baker Jr., Chief Executive Officer. Toll-free, (800) 929-4040.*
General email, faan@foodallergy.org
Web, www.foodallergy.org and Twitter, @FoodAllergy

Membership: dietitians, nurses, physicians, school staff, government representatives, members of the food and pharmaceutical industries, and food-allergy patients and their families. Provides information and educational resources on food allergies and allergic reactions. Offers research grants.

National Center for Biodefense and Infectious Diseases *(George Mason University), 10650 Pyramid Pl., Manassas, VA 20110; (703) 993-4265. Fax, (703) 993-4280. Charles Bailey, Executive Director. General email, cbailey2@gmu.edu*

Web, http://ncbid.gmu.edu and http://cos.gmu.edu

Researches and develops diagnostics and treatments for emerging infectious diseases as well as those pathogens that could be used as terrorist weapons that require special containment. Manages a graduate education program.

National Foundation for Infectious Diseases, *7201 Wisconsin Ave., #750, Bethesda, MD 20814; (301) 656-0003. Fax, (301) 907-0878. Marla Dalton, Executive Director. General email, info@nfid.org*

Web, www.nfid.org, Twitter, @NFIDvaccines and Facebook, www.facebook.com/nfidvaccines

Works to educate the public and health care professionals about the causes, treatment, and prevention of infectious diseases.

National Institute of Allergy and Infectious Diseases *(National Institutes of Health), Allergy, Immunology, and Transplantation, 5601 Fishers Lane, #7C13, MS 9828, Rockville, MD 20852; (301) 496-1886. Fax, (301) 402-0175. Dr. Daniel Rotrosen, Director. Web, www.niaid.nih.gov/about/organization/dait*

Supports extramural basic and clinical research to increase understanding of the causes and mechanisms that lead to the development of immunologic diseases and to expand knowledge that can be applied to developing improved techniques of diagnosis, treatment, and prevention. Interests include lupus; allergic diseases, such as asthma, hay fever, and contact dermatitis; and acute and chronic inflammatory disorders.

Kidney Disease

►AGENCIES

Centers for Medicare and Medicaid Services (CMS) *(Health and Human Services Dept.), Chronic Care Management, 7500 Security Blvd., C5-05-27, Baltimore, MD 21244; (410) 786-4533. Fax, (410) 786-0765. Janet P. Samen, Director, (410) 786-4533. TTY, (866) 226-1819. Web, www.cms.gov/medicare/medicare.html*

Administers coverage policy and payment for Medicare patients with end-stage renal disease and psychiatric inpatient and outpatient services for the severely mentally ill.

National Institute of Diabetes and Digestive and Kidney Diseases *(National Institutes of Health), 31 Center Dr., Bldg. 31, #9A52, MS 2560, Bethesda, MD*

20892-2560; (301) 496-5741. Fax, (301) 402-2125. Dr. Griffin P. Rodgers, Director. Press, (301) 496-3583. Web, www.niddk.nih.gov, Twitter, @NIDDKgov and Facebook, www.facebook.com/National-Institute-of-Diabetes-and-Digestive-and-Kidney-Diseases-NIDDK-159778759845

Conducts and supports basic and clinical research and research training on diabetes and other endocrine and metabolic diseases, digestive diseases, nutrition, obesity, and kidney, urologic, and hematologic diseases. Web site provides evidence-based health information.

National Institute of Diabetes and Digestive and Kidney Diseases *(National Institutes of Health), Kidney, Urologic, and Hematologic Diseases, 2 Democracy Plaza, 6707 Democracy Blvd., #625, MSC 5458, Bethesda, MD 20892; (301) 496-6325. Fax, (301) 480-3510. Dr. Robert A. Star, Director. Information, (800) 891-5390. Press, (301) 496-3583. Web, www.niddk.nih.gov*

Funds research on the prevention, diagnosis, and treatment of renal disorders. Conducts research and reviews grant proposals concerning maintenance therapy for persons with chronic kidney, urologic, and renal diseases. Supports basic research on and clinical studies of the states of blood cell formation, mobilization, and release. Interests include anemia associated with chronic diseases, iron and white blood cell metabolism, and genetic control of hemoglobin.

National Institute of Diabetes and Digestive and Kidney Diseases *(National Institutes of Health), National Kidney and Urologic Diseases Information Clearinghouse, 3 Information Way, Bethesda, MD 20892-3580; (301) 654-4415. Fax, (703) 738-4929. Jody Nurik, Project Manager. Information, (800) 860-8747. Press, (301) 496-3583. TTY, (866) 569-1162. General email, nkudic@info.niddk.nih.gov*

Web, www.niddk.nih.gov/health-information/health-communication-programs/niddk-information-clearinghouses

Supplies health care providers and the public with information on the symptoms, causes, treatments, and general nature of kidney and urologic diseases.

►NONGOVERNMENTAL

American Kidney Fund, *11921 Rockville Pike, #300, Rockville, MD 20852; (301) 881-3052. Fax, (240) 514-3510. LaVarne A. Burton, Chief Executive Officer. Toll-free, (800) 638-8299. Helpline, (866) 300-2900. General email, helpline@kidneyfund.org*

Web, www.kidneyfund.org and Twitter, @KidneyFund

Provides direct financial support to dialysis and kidney transplant patients in need; supports health education and kidney disease prevention efforts.

American Society of Nephrology (ASN), *1510 H St. N.W., #800, 20005; (202) 640-4660. Fax, (202) 637-9793. Dr. Raymond C. Harris, President.*

General email, email@asn-online.org

Web, www.asn-online.org

Membership: health professionals who specialize in kidney disease. Holds the annual Kidney Week meeting for members to share research. Advocates awareness of kidney disease. Publishes the *Journal of the American Society of Nephrology* and the *Clinical Journal of the American Society of Nephrology*. Offers online courses and information on training programs for nephrologists. Awards grants and fellowships to members who conduct research on kidney disease treatment and prevention.

National Kidney Foundation, *Government Relations,* 5335 Wisconsin Ave. N.W., #300, 20015-2078; (202) 244-7900. Fax, (202) 244-7405. Michele Anthony, Executive Director. Information, (800) 622-9010.

General email, infowdc@kidney.org

Web, www.kidney.org; www.kidneywdc.org

Supports funding for kidney dialysis and other forms of treatment for kidney disease; provides information on detection and screening of kidney diseases; supports organ transplantation programs. Monitors legislation, regulations, and international research. (Headquarters in New York.)

Lung Disease

▶AGENCIES

National Heart, Lung, and Blood Institute *(National Institutes of Health), Health Information Center,* 31 Center Dr., Bldg. 31, Bethesda, MD 20892-2480 (mailing address: P.O. Box 30105, Bethesda, MD 20824-0105); (301) 592-8573. Lenora Johnson, Director, (301) 496-4236.

General email, nhlbilnfo@nhlbi.nih.gov

Web, www.nhlbi.nih.gov/health/contact

Acquires, maintains, and disseminates information on asthma and other lung ailments.

National Heart, Lung, and Blood Institute *(National Institutes of Health), Lung Diseases Division,* 2 Rockledge Center, 6701 Rockledge Dr., #10042, MS 7952, Bethesda, MD 20892; (301) 435-0233. Fax, (301) 480-3547. James P. Kiley, Director.

Web, www.nhlbi.nih.gov/about/org/dld

Plans, implements, and monitors research and training programs in lung diseases and sleep disorders, including research on causes, diagnosis, treatments, prevention, and health education. Interests include COPD, genetics, cystic fibrosis, asthma, bronchopulmonary dysplasia, immunology, respiratory neurobiology, sleep-disordered breathing, critical care and acute lung injury, developmental biology and pediatric pulmonary diseases, immunologic and fibrotic pulmonary disease, rare lung disorders, pulmonary vascular disease, and pulmonary complications of AIDS and tuberculosis.

▶NONGOVERNMENTAL

American Lung Assn., 1301 Pennsylvania Ave. N.W., #800, 20004-1725; (202) 785-3355. Fax, (202) 452-1805. Harold Wimmer, President; Paul Billings, Vice President of Advocacy and Education.

Web, www.lung.org and Twitter, @LungAssociation

Promotes improved lung health and the prevention of lung disease through research, education, and advocacy. Interests include antismoking campaigns; lung-related biomedical research; air pollution; and all lung diseases, including asthma, COPD, and lung cancer. (Headquarters in Chicago, Ill.)

Cystic Fibrosis Foundation, 6931 Arlington Rd., 2nd Floor, Bethesda, MD 20814; (301) 951-4422. Fax, (301) 951-6378. Dr. Preston W. Campbell III, President. Information, (800) 344-4823.

General email, info@cff.org

Web, www.cff.org

Conducts research on cystic fibrosis, a genetic disease affecting the respiratory and digestive systems. Focuses on medical research to identify a cure and to improve quality of life for those living with cystic fibrosis.

Lung Cancer Alliance, 1700 K St. N.W., #660, 20006; (202) 463-2080. Laurie Fenton Ambrose, President. Press, (202) 742-1422. Toll-free helpline, (800) 298-2436.

General email, info@lungcanceralliance.org

Web, www.lungcanceralliance.org

Advocates lung cancer research and access to screenings, treatments, diagnostics, and testing. Provides information about lung cancer risks and early detection.

Neurological and Muscular Disorders

▶AGENCIES

Eunice Kennedy Shriver National Institute of Child Health and Human Development *(National Institutes of Health), Division of Extramural Research, Intellectual and Developmental Disabilities Branch,* 6100 Executive Blvd., #4B09G, MSC 7510, Bethesda, MD 20892-7510; (301) 496-1383. Melissa Ann Parisi, Branch Chief.

Web, www.nichd.nih.gov/about/org/der/branches/iddb

Provides support for research projects, training programs, and research centers dedicated to promoting the well-being of individuals with intellectual and developmental disabilities. Major research foci include chromosome abnormalities, genetic and genomic syndromes, epigenetic disorders, cellular and molecular biology, family and community relations, newborn and population screenings, Fragile X syndrome and associated disorders, rare diseases, muscular dystrophy, and autism spectrum disorders.

National Institute of Neurological Disorders and Stroke *(National Institutes of Health),* 31 Center Dr., Bldg. 31,

#8A52, MS 2540, Bethesda, MD 20824; (301) 496-5751. Fax, (301) 402-2186. Dr. Walter J. Koroshetz, Director. Information, (301) 496-5751. Toll-free, (800) 352-9424. Web, www.ninds.nih.gov, Twitter, @NINDSnews and Facebook, www.facebook.com/NINDSandPartners

Conducts research and disseminates information on the causes, prevention, diagnosis, and treatment of neurological disorders and stroke; supports basic and clinical research in related scientific areas. Provides research grants to public and private institutions and individuals. Operates a program of contracts for the funding of research and research-support efforts.

▶**NONGOVERNMENTAL**

Alzheimer's Assn., *Advocacy and Public Policy,*
1212 New York Ave., #800, 20005-6105; (202) 393-7737. Fax, (866) 865-0270. Robert J. Egge, Chief Public Policy Officer. Toll-free, (800) 272-3900.
General email, advocate@alz.org
Web, www.alz.org

Offers family support services and educates the public about Alzheimer's disease, a neurological disorder mainly affecting the brain tissue in older adults. Promotes research and long-term care protection; maintains liaison with Alzheimer's associations abroad. Monitors legislation and regulations. (Headquarters in Chicago, Ill.)

American Academy of Orthopaedic Surgeons,
Washington Office, 317 Massachusetts Ave. N.E., #100, 20002; (202) 546-4430. Fax, (202) 546-5051. Graham H. Newson, Executive Director; William Shaffer, Medical Director.
General email, dc@aaos.org
Web, www.aaos.org and Twitter, @AAOSAdvocacy

Membership: orthopaedic surgeons and musculoskeletal care professionals. Offers continuing education activities; publishes scientific and medical journals and electronic resources. Engages in health policy and advocates on behalf of orthopaedic surgeons and patients. (Headquarters in Rosemont, Ill.)

Autism Speaks, *Washington Office, 1990 K St. N.W., 2nd Floor, 20006; (202) 955-3111. Angela Geiger, President. Toll-free, (888) 288-4762.*
Web, www.autismspeaks.org

Science and advocacy organization that funds biomedical research to determine the causes, prevention, treatments, and cure for autism.

Brain Injury Assn. of America, *1608 Spring Hill Rd., #110, Vienna, VA 22182; (703) 761-0750. Fax, (703) 761-0755. Susan H. Connors, President. Information, (800) 444-6443.*
General email, info@biausa.org
Web, www.biausa.org and Twitter, @biaamerica

Works to improve the quality of life for persons with traumatic brain injuries and for their families. Promotes the prevention of head injuries through public awareness and education programs. Offers state-level support services for individuals and their families. Monitors legislation and regulations.

Epilepsy Foundation, *8301 Professional Pl. East, #200, Landover, MD 20785-2353; (301) 459-3700. Fax, (301) 577-2684. Phillip Gattone, Chief Executive Officer. Information, (800) 332-1000. Spanish language, (866) 748-8008.*
General email, contactus@efa.org
Web, www.epilepsyfoundation.org and Twitter, @EpilepsyFdn

Promotes research and treatment of epilepsy; makes research grants; disseminates information and educational materials. Affiliates provide direct services for people with epilepsy and make referrals when necessary.

Foundation for the Advancement of Chiropractic Tenets and Science, *6400 Arlington Blvd., #800, Falls Church, VA 22042; (703) 528-5000. Fax, (703) 528-5023. George Curry, President. Toll-free, (800) 423-4690.*
General email, chiro@chiropractic.org
Web, www.chiropractic.org

Offers financial aid for education and research programs in colleges and independent institutions; studies chiropractic services in the United States; provides international relief and development programs. (Affiliate of the International Chiropractors Assn.)

National Multiple Sclerosis Society, *Washington Chapter, 1800 M St. N.W., #B50 South, 20036; (202) 296-5363. Fax, (202) 296-3425. Chartese Berry, Chapter President. Toll-free, (800) 344-4867.*
General email, info-dcmd@nmss.org
Web, www.msandyou.org

Seeks to advance medical knowledge of multiple sclerosis, a disease of the central nervous system; disseminates information worldwide. Patient services include individual and family counseling, exercise programs, equipment loans, medical and social service referrals, transportation assistance, back-to-work training programs, and inservice training seminars for nurses, homemakers, and physical and occupational therapists. (Headquarters in New York.)

Society for Neuroscience, *1121 14th St. N.W., #1010, 20005; (202) 962-4000. Fax, (202) 962-4941. Marty Saggese, Executive Director.*
General email, info@sfn.org
Web, www.sfn.org

Membership: scientists and physicians worldwide who research the brain, spinal cord, and nervous system. Interests include the molecular and cellular levels of the nervous system; systems within the brain, such as vision and hearing; and behavior produced by the brain. Promotes education in the neurosciences and the application of research to treat nervous system disorders.

Spina Bifida Assn., *1600 Wilson Blvd., #800, Arlington, VA 22209 (mailing address: P.O. Box 17427, Arlington, VA 22216); (202) 944-3285. Fax, (202) 944-3295. Sara Struwe, Chief Executive Officer, ext. 12. Information, (800) 621-3141.*

General email, sbaa@sbaa.org
Web, www.spinabifidaassociation.org

Membership: individuals with spina bifida, their supporters, and concerned professionals. Offers educational programs, scholarships, and support services; acts as a clearinghouse; provides referrals and information about treatment and prevention. Serves as U.S. member of the International Federation for Hydrocephalus and Spina Bifida, which is headquartered in Geneva, Switzerland. Monitors legislation and regulations.

United Cerebral Palsy (UCP), *1825 K St. N.W., #600, 20006; (202) 776-0406. Fax, (202) 776-0414. Stephen Bennett, President. Information, (800) 872-5827. Web, www.ucp.org and Twitter, @UCPnational*

National network of state and local affiliates that assists individuals with cerebral palsy and other developmental disabilities and their families. Provides parent education, early intervention, employment services, family support and respite programs, therapy, assistive technology, and vocational training.

Nutrition

▶**AGENCIES**

Center for Nutrition Policy and Promotion *(Agriculture Dept.), 3101 Park Center Dr., 10th Floor, Alexandria, VA 22302-1594; (703) 305-7600. Fax, (703) 305-3300. Angela Tagtow, Executive Director. Newsroom, (703) 305-7600.*
Web, www.cnpp.usda.gov

Defines and coordinates nutrition education policy, promotes food and nutrition guidance, and develops nutrition information materials for consumers, policymakers, and professionals in health, education, industry, and media.

Eunice Kennedy Shriver National Institute of Child Health and Human Development *(National Institutes of Health), Division of Extramural Research, Pediatric Growth and Nutrition Branch, 6100 Executive Blvd., #4B05K, MSC 7510, Bethesda, MD 20892-7510; (301) 496-5593. Fax, (301) 480-9791. Gilman Drew Grave, Branch Chief.*
Web, www.nichd.nih.gov/about/org/der/branches/pgnb

Supports research aimed at understanding the mechanisms of growth and development at the gene-molecular level and at higher levels of cell and organ function. Determines the role of nutrition throughout the life cycle, with an emphasis on the needs of women of reproductive age, including pregnant and lactating women, preterm and term infants, and children through adolescence, to promote health, optimal growth and development, and to prevent disease. Explores the role of nutrients in reproduction, immune function, cognition and behavioral development.

National Agricultural Library *(Agriculture Dept.), Food and Nutrition Information Center, 10301 Baltimore Ave., #108, Beltsville, MD 20705-2351; (301) 504-5414.*

Fax, (301) 504-6409. Wendy Davis, Nutrition and Food Safety Program Leader.
General email, fnic@ars.usda.gov
Web, http://fnic.nal.usda.gov

Serves primarily educators, health professionals, and consumers seeking information about nutrition assistance programs and general nutrition. Serves as an online provider of science-based information about food and nutrition and links to such information. Lends books and audiovisual materials for educational purposes through interlibrary loan; maintains a database of food and nutrition software and multimedia programs; provides reference services; develops resource lists of health and nutrition publications. Library open to the public.

National Institute of Diabetes and Digestive and Kidney Diseases *(National Institutes of Health), Digestive Diseases and Nutrition, 2 Democracy Plaza, 6707 Democracy Blvd., #677, MSC 5450, Bethesda, MD 20892-5450; (301) 594-7680. Fax, (301) 480-8300. Stephen P. James, Director. Press, (301) 496-3583.*
Web, www.niddk.nih.gov

Awards grants and contracts to support basic and clinical research related to digestive diseases and nutrition, as well as training and career development. Conducts and supports research concerning liver and biliary diseases; pancreatic diseases; gastrointestinal disease, including neuroendocrinology, motility, immunology, absorption, and transport in the gastrointestinal tract; nutrient metabolism; obesity; and eating disorders.

National Institute of Diabetes and Digestive and Kidney Diseases *(National Institutes of Health), Nutrition Research, 2 Democracy Plaza, 6707 Democracy Blvd., #677, MS 5450, Bethesda, MD 20892; (301) 594-8822. Fax, (301) 480-3768. Dr. Stephen P. James, Director, Acting, (301) 594-7680.*
Web, www.niddk.nih.gov/about-niddk/offices-divisions/office-nutrition-research

Supports research on nutritional requirements, dietary fiber, obesity, eating disorders, energy regulation, clinical nutrition, trace minerals, and basic nutrient functions.

National Institute of Food and Agriculture (NIFA) *(Agriculture Dept.), Institute of Food Safety and Nutrition, 1400 Independence Ave. S.W., MS 2225, 20250-2225; (202) 702-5004. Fax, (202) 401-4888. Denise Riordan Eblen, Deputy Director.*
Web, www.nifa.usda.gov/office/institute-food-safety-and-nutrition

Works toward safe food supply by reducing foodborne illness. Addresses causes of microbial contamination and antimicrobial resistance; educates consumer and food safety professionals; and develops food processing technologies. Promotes programs to improve citizens' health through better nutrition, reducing childhood obesity, and improving food quality.

National Institutes of Health (NIH) *(Health and Human Services Dept.), Dietary Supplements, 6100 Executive*

Blvd., #3B01, MSC 7517, Bethesda, MD 20892-7517; (301) 435-2920. Fax, (301) 480-1845. Paul M. Coates, Director.

General email, ods@nih.gov

Web, http://ods.od.nih.gov

Reviews scientific evidence on the safety and efficacy of dietary supplements. Conducts, promotes, and coordinates scientific research within the NIH relating to dietary supplements. Conducts and supports conferences, workshops, and symposia and publishes research results on scientific topics related to dietary supplements.

▶**NONGOVERNMENTAL**

Academy of Nutrition and Dietetics, *Washington Office, 1120 Connecticut Ave. N.W., #460, 20036-3989; (202) 775-8277. Fax, (202) 775-8284. Jeanne Blankenship, Vice President. Toll-free, (800) 877-0877.*

General email, govaffairs@eatright.org

Media email, media@eatright.org

Web, www.eatright.org

Membership: dietitians and other nutrition professionals. Promotes public health and nutrition; accredits academic programs in clinical nutrition and food service management; sets standards of professional practice. Sponsors the National Center for Nutrition and Dietetics. (Headquarters in Chicago, Ill.)

American Society for Nutrition, *9211 Corporate Blvd., #300, Rockville, MD 20850; (240) 428-3650. Fax, (240) 404-6797. John Courtney, Executive Officer.*

General email, info@nutrition.org

Web, www.nutrition.org

Membership: nutritional research scientists and practioners, including clinical nutritionists. Supports and advocates research on the role of human nutrition in health and disease; encourages undergraduate and graduate nutrition education; offers awards for research. (Merger of the American Society for Clinical Nutrition and the American Society for Nutritional Sciences.)

American Society for Parenteral and Enteral Nutrition (ASPEN), *8630 Fenton St., #412, Silver Spring, MD 20910-3805; (301) 587-6315. Fax, (301) 587-2365. Debra BenAvram, Executive Director, ext. 126. Toll-free, (800) 727-4567.*

General email, aspen@nutr.org

Web, www.nutritioncare.org and Twitter, @ASPENWEB

Membership: health care professionals who provide patients with intravenous nutritional support during hospitalization and rehabilitation at home. Develops nutrition guidelines; provides educational materials; conducts annual meetings.

Eating Disorders Coalition for Research, Policy, and Action, *P.O. Box 96503-98807, 20090; (202) 543-9570. Fax, (646) 417-6378. David Jaffe, Executive Director.*

General email, manager@eatingdisorderscoalition.org

Web, www.eatingdisorderscoalition.org

Seeks greater national and federal recognition of eating disorders. Promotes recognition of eating disorders as a public health priority and the implementation of more accessible treatment and more effective prevention programs. Monitors legislation and regulations.

Obesity Society, *8757 Georgia Ave., #1320, Silver Spring, MD 20910; (301) 563-6526. Fax, (301) 563-6595. Francesca Dea, Executive Director.*

Web, www.obesity.org

Promotes research, education, and advocacy to better understand, prevent, and treat obesity. Informs the medical community and the public of new advances.

Skin Disorders

▶**AGENCIES**

National Institute of Arthritis and Musculoskeletal and Skin Diseases *(National Institutes of Health), 31 Center Dr., Bldg. 31, #4C32, MS 2350, Bethesda, MD 20892-2350; (301) 496-4353. Fax, (301) 402-3607. Dr. Stephen I. Katz, Director. TTY, (301) 565-2966. Health information, (877) 226-4267.*

General email, niamsinfo@mail.nih.gov

Web, www.niams.nih.gov

Supports research on the causes and treatment of skin diseases, including psoriasis, eczema, and acne.

▶**NONGOVERNMENTAL**

American Academy of Facial Plastic and Reconstructive Surgery, *310 S. Henry St., Alexandria, VA 22314; (703) 299-9291. Fax, (703) 299-8898. Stephen C. Duffy, Executive Vice President.*

General email, info@aafprs.org

Web, www.aafprs.org

Membership: facial plastic and reconstructive surgeons and other board-certified surgeons whose focus is surgery of the face, head, and neck. Promotes research and study in the field. Helps train residents in facial plastic and reconstructive surgery; offers continuing medical education. Sponsors scientific and medical meetings, international symposia, fellowship training program, seminars, and workshops. Provides videotapes on facial plastic and reconstructive surgery.

Melanoma Research Foundation, *1411 K St. N.W., #800, 20005; (202) 347-9675. Fax, (202) 347-9678. Timothy Turnham, Executive Director. Toll-Free, (800) 673-1290. Helpline, (877) 673-6460.*

Web, www.melanoma.org

Educates patients, caregivers, and physicians about the diagnosis, prevention, and treatment of melanoma; advocates medical research for effective treatments.

Sleep Disorders

▶**AGENCIES**

National Heart, Lung, and Blood Institute *(National Institutes of Health), Lung Diseases Division, National Center on Sleep Disorders Research (NCSDR), 6701*

Rockledge Dr., #10170, MS 7952, Bethesda, MD 20892; (301) 435-0199. Fax, (301) 480-3451. Michael J. Twery, Program Director, Acting.
Web, www.nhlbi.nih.gov/about/org/ncsdr

Supports research and training related to sleep and circadian rhythm risks contributing to heart, lung, and blood disorders. Serves as a point of contact and coordination for sleep research and education across NIH, several federal agencies, and outside organizations.

▶NONGOVERNMENTAL

American Sleep Apnea Assn., 1717 Pennsylvania Ave N.W., #1025, 20006; (888) 293-3650. Fax, (888) 293-3650. Darrel Drobnich, President.
General email, asaa@sleepapnea.org
Web, www.sleepapnea.org

Promotes continuing improvements in treatments for sleep apnea and advocates on behalf of sleep apnea patients. Monitors legislation and regulations.

Circadian Sleep Disorders Network, 4619 Woodfield Rd., Bethesda, MD 20814; Peter Mansbach, President.
General email, csd-n@csd-n.org
Web, www.circadiansleepdisorders.org

Seeks to increase awareness of circadian sleep disorders among the medical community and general public. Advocates for accommodation of patients in education and employment.

National Sleep Foundation, 1010 N. Glebe Rd., #420, Arlington, VA 22201; (703) 243-1697. Fax, (202) 347-3472. David Cloud, Chief Executive Officer.
General email, nsf@sleepfoundation.org
Web, www.sleepfoundation.org

Supports sleep-related public education and research to understand sleep problems and sleep disorders, including insomnia, sleep apnea, and narcolepsy. Works to prevent sleep-related accidents, especially those that involve driving. Monitors legislation and regulations related to sleep, alertness, and safety, such as hours-of-service rules for commercial drivers.

National Sleep Foundation, Sleep for Kids, 1010 N. Glebe Rd., #310, Arlington, VA 22201;
General email, nsf@sleepfoundation.org
Web, www.sleepforkids.org

Provides information about the importance of sleep for children and sleep disorders, and tips for parents and teachers to help school-aged children develop good sleep habits.

Substance Abuse

▶AGENCIES

Centers for Disease Control and Prevention (CDC) (Health and Human Services Dept.), Smoking and Health, 395 E St. S.W., #9100, 20201; (202) 245-0550.

Fax, (202) 245-0554. Simon McNabb, Senior Policy Adviser. Information, (800) 232-4636.
General email, tobaccoinfo@cdc.gov
Web, www.cdc.gov/tobacco and Twitter, @CDCTobaccoFree

Develops, conducts, and supports strategic efforts to protect the public's health in the area of tobacco prevention and control. Funds, trains, and provides technical assistance to states, territories, tribal support centers, and national networks (e.g., National Tobacco Control Program); increases awareness and education about tobacco (e.g., publications, CDC's Smoking & Tobacco Use Web site, Tips from Former Smokers campaign, earned and digital media); conducts and supports national and international surveillance (e.g., National Youth Tobacco Survey, Global Tobacco Surveillance System).

Education Dept., Elementary and Secondary Education, Safe and Healthy Students, 400 Maryland Ave. S.W., #3E328, 20202-6135; (202) 453-6777. Fax, (202) 453-6742. David Esquith, Director.
General email, osdfs.safeschl@ed.gov
Web, www2.ed.gov/about/offices/list/oese

Develops policy for the department's drug and violence prevention initiatives for students in elementary and secondary schools and institutions of higher education. Provides financial assistance for drug and violence prevention activities. Coordinates education efforts in drug and violence prevention with those of other federal departments and agencies.

Health Resources and Services Administration (Health and Human Services Dept.), Policy Program and Development, 5600 Fishers Lane, #17C-26, Rockville, MD 20857; (301) 594-4300. Fax, (301) 594-4997. Jennifer Joseph, Director.
Web, www.bphc.hrsa.gov

Provides grants to health centers to expand services to include behavioral health and substance abuse services.

National Institute on Alcohol Abuse and Alcoholism (National Institutes of Health), 5635 Fishers Lane, MSC 9304, Bethesda, MD 20892-9304; (301) 443-3860. Fax, (301) 443-7043. Dr. George F. Koob, Director. Press, (301) 443-2857.
General email, niaaaweb-r@exchange.nih.gov
Web, www.niaaa.nih.gov

Supports basic and applied research on preventing and treating alcoholism and alcohol-related problems; conducts research and disseminates findings on alcohol abuse and alcoholism. Participates in U.S. and international research.

National Institute on Drug Abuse (National Institutes of Health), 6001 Executive Blvd., #5274, MSC 9561, Bethesda, MD 20892-9581; (301) 443-1124. Fax, (301) 480-2485. Nora Volkow, Director. Press, (301) 443-6245.
Web, www.drugabuse.gov

Conducts and sponsors research on the prevention, effects, and treatment of drug abuse. Monitors international policy and research.

Office of National Drug Control Policy (ONDCP) *(Executive Office of the President), 750 17th St. N.W., 20503; (202) 395-6700. Fax, (202) 395-6708. Michael Botticelli, Director. Web, www.whitehouse.gov/ondcp and Twitter, @DrugPolicyReform*

Establishes policies and oversees the implementation of a national drug control strategy with the goal of reducing illicit drug use, manufacturing, trafficking, and drug-related crimes, violence, and health consequences. Coordinates the international and domestic antidrug efforts of executive branch agencies and ensures that such efforts sustain and complement state and local antidrug activities. Advises the president and the National Security Council on drug control policy. (Clearinghouse address: P.O. Box 6000, Rockville, MD 20849-6000.)

Substance Abuse and Mental Health Services Administration (SAMHSA) *(Health and Human Services Dept.), 5600 Fishers Lane, Rockville, MD 20852; (240) 276-2000. Fax, (240) 276-2010. Kana Enomoto, Administrator, Acting. Information, (877) 726-4727. TTY, (800) 487-4889. Hotline, (800) 662-4357. General email, samhsainfo@samhsa.hhs.gov Web, www.samhsa.gov*

Provides and manages block grants and special programmatic funding aimed at reducing the impact of substance abuse and mental illness on communities. Provides states, providers, communities, and the public with information about behavioral health issues and prevention/treatment approaches. Administers substance abuse and mental health treatment referral service: (800) 662-4357 or www.samhsa.gov/treatment. Offers behavioral health publications and other resources: http://store.samhsa .gov/home or P.O. Box 2345, Rockville, MD 20847.

Substance Abuse and Mental Health Services Administration (SAMHSA) *(Health and Human Services Dept.), Center for Substance Abuse Prevention, 5600 Fishers Lane, Rockville, MD 20852; (240) 276-2420. Fax, (240) 276-2430. Frances M. Harding, Director. TTY, (800) 487-4889. Information, (877) 726-4727. Workplace helpline, 800-WORKPLACE; (800) 967-5752. Web, www.samhsa.gov/about-us/who-we-are/offices-centers/csap*

Demonstrates, evaluates, and disseminates strategies for preventing alcohol and drug abuse. Operates the National Clearinghouse for Alcohol and Drug Information, which provides information, publications, and grant applications for programs to prevent substance abuse. (Clearinghouse address: http://store.samhsa.gov or P.O. Box 2345, Rockville, MD 20847; toll-free phone, (800) 729-6686.)

Substance Abuse and Mental Health Services Administration (SAMHSA) *(Health and Human Services Dept.), Center for Substance Abuse Treatment, 5600*

Fishers Lane, Rockville, MD 20852; (240) 276-1660. Fax, (240) 276-1670. Kimberly Johnson, Director. Treatment referral, (800) 662-4357. Publications, (800) 729-6686. TTY, (800) 487-4889. Information, (877) 726-4727. Web, www.samhsa.gov/about-us/who-we-are/offices-centers/csat

Develops and supports policies and programs that improve and expand treatment services for alcoholism, substance abuse, and addiction. Administers grants that support private and public addiction prevention and treatment services. Evaluates alcohol treatment programs and other drug treatment programs and delivery systems.

▶**INTERNATIONAL ORGANIZATIONS**

International Commission for the Prevention of Alcoholism and Drug Dependency, *12501 Old Columbia Pike, Silver Spring, MD 20904; (301) 680-6719. Fax, (301) 680-6707. Dr. Peter N. Landless, Executive Director; Katia Reinart, Director, North American Region. General email, the_icpa@hotmail.com Web, http://icpaworld.org*

Membership: health officials, physicians, educators, clergy, and judges worldwide. Promotes scientific research on prevention of alcohol and drug dependencies; provides information about medical effects of alcohol and drugs; conducts world congresses. (Health Ministries Dept. of the General Conference of Seventh-Day Adventists.)

▶**NONGOVERNMENTAL**

American Society of Addiction Medicine, *4601 N. Park Ave., Upper Arcade, #101, Chevy Chase, MD 20815-4520; (301) 656-3920. Fax, (301) 656-3815. Penny Mills, Executive Vice President, (301) 547-4105. General email, email@asam.org Web, www.asam.org and Twitter, @ASAMorg*

Membership: physicians and medical students. Supports the study and provision of effective treatment and care for people with alcohol and drug dependencies; educates physicians. Monitors legislation and regulations.

Assn. for Addiction Professionals (NAADAC), *1001 N. Fairfax St., #201, Alexandria, VA 22314; (703) 741-7686. Fax, (800) 377-1136. Cynthia Moreno Tuohy, Executive Director. Information, (800) 548-0497. General email, naadac2@naadac.org Web, www.naadac.org and Twitter, @NAADACorp*

Membership: professionals in the addiction field. Supports professional development by providing educational resources, certification programs, workshops, and conferences for treatment professionals. (Formerly National Assn. of Alcoholism and Drug Abuse Counselors.)

Drug Strategies, *2101 L St. N.W., #800, 20037; (415) 638-6600. Mathea Falco, President. General email, drugstrategies@gmail.com Web, www.drugstrategies.com*

Researches effectiveness of drug abuse prevention, treatment, and education. Supports effective practices and educates the public on treating substance abuse. Special interests include teenagers and prescription pill abuse.

Employee Assistance Professionals Assn., *4350 N. Fairfax Dr., #740, Arlington, VA 22203; (703) 387-1000. Fax, (703) 522-4585. Lucy Henry, President. General email, info@eapassn.org*

Web, www.eapassn.org

Membership: professionals in the workplace who assist employees and their family members with personal and behavioral problems, including health, marital, family, financial, alcohol, drug, legal, emotional, stress, or other personal problems that adversely affect employee job performance and productivity.

Mothers Against Drunk Driving (MADD), *Government Affairs, 1025 Connecticut Ave. N.W., #1210, 20036-5415; (202) 688-1193. Fax, (972) 869-2206. J.T. Griffin, Chief Government Affairs Officer; Frank Harris, State Legislative Affairs Manager, (202) 688-1194. Toll-free, (877) 275-6233. 24-hour helpline, 877-MADD-HELP. Web, www.madd.org, Twitter, @MADDOnline and Facebook, www.facebook.com/MADD.Official*

Advocacy group that seeks to stop drunk driving and prevent underage drinking. Monitors legislation and regulations. (Headquarters in Irving, Tex.)

National Assn. of State Alcohol and Drug Abuse Directors (NASADAD), *1025 Connecticut Ave. N.W., #605, 20036-5430; (202) 293-0090. Fax, (202) 293-1250. Rob Morrison, Executive Director. General email, dcoffice@nasadad.org*

Web, www.nasadad.org

Provides information on drug abuse treatment and prevention; contracts with federal and state agencies for design of programs to fight and prevent drug abuse.

Treatment Communities of America (TCA), *1875 Eye St. N.W., #574, 20006; (202) 518-5475. Patricia Beauchemin, Executive Director. General email, tca.office@verizon.net*

Web, www.treatmentcommunitiesofamerica.org

Membership: nonprofit organizations that provide substance abuse and mental health treatment and rehabilitation. Provides policy analysis and educates the public on substance abuse and treatment issues. Promotes the interests of therapeutic communities, their clients, and staffs. Monitors legislation and regulations.

Truth Initiative, *900 G St. N.W., 4th Floor, 20036; (202) 454-5755. Fax, (202) 454-5599. Robin Koval, President. General email, press@truthinitiative.org*

Web, www.truthinitiative.org and Twitter, @Truthinitiative

Develops programs to disseminate information on the health effects of tobacco. Provides prevention and cessation services through grants, technical training and assistance, youth activism, partnerships, and community outreach. (Formerly the American Legacy Foundation.)

MENTAL HEALTH

General

►AGENCIES

Centers for Medicare and Medicaid Services (CMS) *(Health and Human Services Dept.), Chronic Care Management, 7500 Security Blvd., C5-05-27, Baltimore, MD 21244; (410) 786-4533. Fax, (410) 786-0765. Janet P. Samen, Director, (410) 786-4533. TTY, (866) 226-1819.*

Web, www.cms.gov/medicare/medicare.html

Administers coverage policy and payment for Medicare patients with end-stage renal disease and psychiatric inpatient and outpatient services for the severely mentally ill.

National Institute of Mental Health *(National Institutes of Health), 6001 Executive Blvd., #6200, MSC 9663, Bethesda, MD 20892-9663; (301) 443-4513. Fax, (301) 443-4279. Dr. Bruce N. Cuthbert, Director, Acting, (301) 443-3673. Toll-free, (866) 615-6464. Toll-free TTY, (866) 415-8051. TTY, (301) 443-8431. General email, nimhinfo@nih.gov*

Web, www.nimh.nih.gov, Twitter, @NIMHgov and Facebook, www.facebook.com/nimhgov

Conducts research on the cause, diagnosis, treatment, and prevention of mental disorders; provides information on mental health problems and programs. Participates in international research.

National Institute of Mental Health *(National Institutes of Health), Neuroscience and Basic Behavioral Science, 6001 Executive Blvd., #7204, MSC 9645, Rockville, MD 20892; (301) 443-3563. Fax, (301) 443-1731. Linda S. Brady, Director.*

Web, www.nimh.nih.gov/about/organization/dnbbs

Supports research programs in the areas of basic neuroscience, genetics, basic behavioral science, research training, resource development, drug discovery, and research dissemination. Responsible for ensuring that relevant basic science knowledge is generated to create improved diagnosis, treatment, and prevention of mental and behavioral disorders.

National Institute of Mental Health *(National Institutes of Health), Research on Disparities and Global Mental Health, 6001 Executive Blvd., #7213, MSC 9659, Bethesda, MD 20892; (301) 443-2847. Fax, (301) 443-9877. Dr. Pamela Y. Collins, Director.*

Web, ww.nimh.nih.gov/about/organization/gmh

Funds and oversees research to identify trends and gaps in the areas of mental health disparities, women's mental health, and global mental health. Supports research training for minorities in the mental health field; supports development of the mental health research workforce in low- and middle-income countries.

National Institute of Mental Health *(National Institutes of Health), Translational Research, 6001 Executive Blvd., #7120, MSC 9632, Bethesda, MD 20892; (301) 443-3673. Fax, (301) 480-4415. Dr. Sarah H. Lisanby, Director. Web, www.nimh.nih.gov/about/organization/dtr*

Directs, plans, and supports programs of research and research training that translate knowledge from basic science to discover the etiology, pathophysiology, and trajectory of mental disorders and develops effective interventions for children and adults. Supports integrative, multidisciplinary research on the following areas: the phenotype characterization and risk factors for psychiatric disorders; neurobehavioral mechanisms of psychopathology; trajectories of risk and resilience based on the interactive influences of genetics, brain development, environment, and experience; and design and testing of innovative psychosocial, psychopharmacologic, and somatic treatment interventions.

National Institutes of Health (NIH) *(Health and Human Services Dept.), Behavioral and Social Sciences Research, 31 Center Dr., Bldg. 31, #B1C19, Bethesda, MD 20892-0183; (301) 402-1146. Fax, (301) 402-1150. William Riley, Director, Acting. Web, http://obssr.od.nih.gov*

Works to advance behavioral and social sciences training, to integrate a biobehavioral perspective across the NIH, and to improve communication among scientists and with the public. Develops funding initiatives for research and training. Sets priorities for research. Provides training and career development opportunities for behavioral and social scientists. Links minority students with mentors. Organizes cultural workshops and lectures.

Substance Abuse and Mental Health Services Administration (SAMHSA) *(Health and Human Services Dept.), 5600 Fishers Lane, Rockville, MD 20852; (240) 276-2000. Fax, (240) 276-2010. Kana Enomoto, Administrator, Acting. Information, (877) 726-4727. TTY, (800) 487-4889. Hotline, (800) 662-4357. General email, samhsainfo@samhsa.hhs.gov Web, www.samhsa.gov*

Provides and manages block grants and special programmatic funding aimed at reducing the impact of substance abuse and mental illness on communities. Provides states, providers, communities, and the public with information about behavioral health issues and prevention/treatment approaches. Administers substance abuse and mental health treatment referral service: (800) 662-4357 or www.samhsa.gov/treatment. Offers behavioral health publications and other resources: http://store.samhsa .gov/home or P.O. Box 2345, Rockville, MD 20847.

Substance Abuse and Mental Health Services Administration (SAMHSA) *(Health and Human Services Dept.), Center for Mental Health Services, 5600 Fishers Lane, Rockville, MD 20852; (240) 276-1310. Fax, (240) 276-1320. Paolo del Vecchio, Director. Information, (877) 726-4727. TTY, (800) 487-4889. Treatment referral, (800) 662-4357.*

Web, www.samhsa.gov/about-us/who-we-are/offices-centers/cmhs

Works with federal agencies, tribal entities and territories, and state and local governments to demonstrate, evaluate, and disseminate service delivery models to treat mental illness, promote mental health, and prevent the developing or worsening of mental illness. Operates the National Mental Health Information Center.

Veterans Health Administration (VHA) *(Veterans Affairs Dept.), Mental Health Services, 810 Vermont Ave. N.W., MS 10P4M, 20420; (202) 461-4170. Fax, (202) 495-5933. Marsden McGuire, Deputy Chief Consultant; Vashtie Reedy, Management Program Analyst. Web, www.mentalhealth.va.gov*

Develops ambulatory and inpatient psychiatry and psychology programs for the mentally ill and for drug and alcohol abusers; programs are offered in VA facilities and twenty-one Veterans Integrated Service Networks. Incorporates special programs for veterans suffering from post-traumatic stress disorders, serious mental illness, addictive disorders, and homelessness.

▶ **CONGRESS**

For a listing of relevant congressional committees and subcommittees, please see pages 344–345 or the Appendix.

▶ **NONGOVERNMENTAL**

Active Minds, *2001 S St. N.W., #450, 20009; (202) 332-9595. Alison Malmon, Executive Director, (202) 332-9595 ext. 101. Press, (202) 332-9595 ext. 109. Web, www.activeminds.org*

Supports student-run chapters nationwide to help promote youth mental health awareness on college campuses. Offers mental health and mental illness information and resources.

American Academy of Child and Adolescent Psychiatry, *3615 Wisconsin Ave. N.W., 20016-3007; (202) 966-7300. Fax, (202) 966-2891. Dr. Gregory K. Fitz, President. Web, www.aacap.org*

Membership: child and adolescent psychiatrists trained to promote healthy development and to evaluate, diagnose, and treat children, adolescents, and families affected by mental illness. Sponsors annual meeting and review for medical board examinations. Provides information on child and adolescent development and mental illnesses. Monitors international research and U.S. legislation concerning children with mental illness.

American Assn. of Pastoral Counselors, *9504A Lee Hwy., Fairfax, VA 22031-2303; (703) 385-6967. Fax, (703) 352-7725. Douglas M. Ronsheim, Executive Director. General email, info@aapc.org Web, www.aapc.org*

Membership: mental health professionals with training in both religion and the behavioral sciences. Nonsectarian organization that accredits pastoral counseling centers, certifies pastoral counselors, and approves training programs.

American Assn. of Suicidology, *5221 Wisconsin Ave. N.W., 20015; (202) 237-2280. Fax, (202) 237-2282. Amy J. Kulp, Executive Director, Acting. Suicide prevention lifeline, 800-273-TALK (8255).*
General email, info@suicidology.org

Web, www.suicidology.org

Membership: educators, researchers, suicide prevention centers, school districts, volunteers, and survivors affected by suicide. Works to understand and prevent suicide; provides suicide prevention training, serves as an information clearinghouse.

American Bar Assn. (ABA), *Commission on Disability Rights, 1050 Connecticut Ave. N.W., #400, 20036; (202) 662-1570. Fax, (202) 442-3439. Mark D. Agrast, Chair; Amy L. Allbright, Director.*
General email, cdr@americanbar.org

Web, www.americanbar.org/disabilityrights

Promotes the rule of law for persons with mental, physical, and sensory disabilities and their full and equal participation in the legal profession. Offers online resources, publications, and continuing education opportunities on disability law topics and engages in national initiatives to remove barriers to the education, employment, and advancement of lawyers with disabilities.

American Foundation for Suicide Prevention, *940 1st St N W., #300, 20001; (202) 449-3600. Fax, (202) 449-3601. John Madigan, Senior Director of Public Policy. National Suicide Prevention Lifeline, (800) 273-8255.*
General email, jmadigan@afsp.org

Web, www.afsp.org

Seeks to understand and prevent suicide through research, education, and advocacy. Provides programs and resources for survivors of suicide loss and people at risk, funds scientific research, offers educational programs for professionals, educates the public about mood disorders and suicide prevention, and promotes policies that impact suicide and prevention. Monitors legislation and regulations. (Headquarters in New York, NY.)

American Mental Health Counselors Assn., *675 N. Washinton St., #470, Alexandria, VA 22314; (703) 548-6002. Fax, (703) 548-4775. Joel E. Miller, Executive Director. Toll-free, (800) 326-2642.*
Web, www.amhca.org and Twitter, @AMHCA1

Membership: professional counselors and graduate students in the mental health field. Sponsors leadership training and continuing education programs for professionals in the field of mental health counseling; holds annual conference. Monitors legislation and regulations.

American Psychiatric Assn., *1000 Wilson Blvd., #1825, Arlington, VA 22209-3901; (703) 907-7300. Fax, (703) 907-1085. Dr. Saul Levin, Medical Director. Press, (703) 907-8640. Publishing, (703) 907-7322. Toll-free, (888) 357-7924.*
General email, apa@psych.org

Web, www.psychiatry.org and Twitter, @APAPsychiatric

Membership: psychiatrists. Promotes availability of high-quality psychiatric care; provides the public with information; assists state and local agencies; conducts educational programs for professionals and students in the field; participates in international meetings and research. Library open to members.

American Psychological Assn., *750 1st St. N.E., 20002-4242; (202) 336-5500. Fax, (202) 336-5502. Cynthia Belar, Chief Executive Officer, Acting. Library, (202) 336-5640. Toll-free, (800) 374-2721. TTY, (202) 336-6123.*
Web, www.apa.org and Twitter, @APA

Membership: professional psychologists, educators, and behavioral research scientists. Supports research, training, and professional services; works toward improving the qualifications, competence, and training programs of psychologists. Monitors international research and U.S. legislation on mental health. Library open to the public by appointment.

American Psychosomatic Society, *6728 Old McLean Village Dr., McLean, VA 22101-3906; (703) 556-9222. Fax, (703) 556-8729. Laura E. Degnon, Executive Director.*
General email, info@psychosomatic.org

Web, www.psychosomatic.org and Twitter, @connectAPS

Advances and disseminates scientific understanding of relationships among biological, psychological, social, and behavioral factors in medicine through publications, annual meetings, conferences, and interest groups.

Anxiety and Depression Assn. of America, *8701 Georgia Ave., #412, Silver Spring, MD 20910; (240) 485-1001. Fax, (240) 485-1035. Susan K. Gurley, Executive Director, Acting. Press, (240) 485-1016.*
General email, jteichroew@adaa.org

Web, www.adaa.org and Twitter, @Got_Anxiety

Membership: clinicians and researchers who treat and study anxiety and depression disorders; individuals with these disorders and their families; and other interested individuals. Promotes prevention, treatment, and cure of anxiety and depression disorders by disseminating information, linking individuals to treatment, and encouraging research and advancement of scientific knowledge.

Assn. of Black Psychologists, *7119 Allentown Rd., #203, Ft. Washington, MD 20744; (301) 449-3082. Fax, (301) 449-3084. Anisha N. Lewis, Executive Director.*
General email, abpsi@abpsi.org

Web, www.abpsi.org

Membership: psychologists, psychology students, and others in the mental health field. Develops policies and resources to foster mental health in the African American community; holds annual convention.

Bazelon Center for Mental Health Law, *1101 15th St. N.W., #1212, 20005; (202) 467-5730. Fax, (202) 223-0409. Robert Bernstein, President.*
General email, communications@bazelon.org

Web, www.bazelon.org and Twitter, @BazelonCenter

Public interest law firm. Works to establish and advance the legal rights of children and adults with mental disabilities and ensure their equal access to services and resources needed for full participation in community life.

Provides technical support to lawyers and other advocates. Conducts test case litigation to defend rights of persons with mental disabilities. Conducts policy analysis, builds coalitions, issues advocacy alerts, publishes handbooks, and maintains advocacy resources online. Monitors legislation and regulations.

CHADD: The National Resource on ADHD, *4601 Presidents Dr., #300, Lanham, MD 20706; (301) 306-7070. Fax, (301) 306-7090. Michael MacKay, President. Toll-free, (800) 233-4050. Web, www.chadd.org*

Membership: healthcare and mental health professionals, educators, and individuals with ADHD or ADHD-related symptoms. Conducts advocacy and outreach to policymakers at the state and federal levels in areas including healthcare reform, bullying in schools, and mental health parity. The affiliated National Research Center is a CDC-funded clearinghouse for evidence-based information about ADHD.

Eating Disorders Coalition for Research, Policy, and Action, *P.O. Box 96503-98807, 20090; (202) 543-9570. Fax, (646) 417-6378. David Jaffe, Executive Director. General email, manager@eatingdisorderscoalition.org Web, www.eatingdisorderscoalition.org*

Seeks greater national and federal recognition of eating disorders. Promotes recognition of eating disorders as a public health priority and the implementation of more accessible treatment and more effective prevention programs. Monitors legislation and regulations.

Mental Health America, *2000 N. Beauregard St., 6th Floor, Alexandria, VA 22311; (703) 684-7722. Fax, (703) 684-5968. Paul Gionfriddo, President. Information, (800) 969-6642. General email, info@mentalhealthamerica.net Web, www.mentalhealthamerica.net*

Works to increase accessible and appropriate care for adults and children with mental disorders. Informs and educates public about mental illnesses and available treatment. Supports research on illnesses and services.

National Action Alliance for Suicide Prevention, *1025 Thomas Jefferson St. N.W., #700, 20007; (202) 572-3784. Fax, (202) 223-4059. Robert W. Turner, Co-Chair; Dr. Carolyn M. Clancy, Co-Chair. Press, (617) 618-2457. General email, info@actionallianceforsuicideprevention.org Web, www.actionallianceforsuicideprevention.org*

Seeks to advance the National Strategy for Suicide Prevention (NSSP) and reduce the rate of suicide. Advocates health care reform to include suicide prevention methods and improve data on suicide.

National Alliance on Mental Illness (NAMI), *3803 N. Fairfax Dr., #100, Arlington, VA 22203; (703) 524-7600. Fax, (703) 524-9094. Mary Giliberti, Chief Executive Officer. Toll-free, (800) 950-6264. General email, info@nami.org Web, www.nami.org*

Membership: mentally ill individuals and their families and caregivers. Works to eradicate mental illness and improve the lives of those affected by brain disorders; sponsors public education and advocacy. Monitors legislation and regulations.

National Assn. of Psychiatric Health Systems, *900 17th St. N.W., #420, 20006-2507; (202) 393-6700. Fax, (202) 783-6041. Mark Covall, President. General email, naphs@naphs.org Web, www.naphs.org*

Membership: behavioral health care systems that provide inpatient, residential, and outpatient treatment and prevention and care programs for children, adolescents, adults, and older adults with mental and substance use disorders.

National Assn. of School Psychologists, *4340 East-West Hwy., #402, Bethesda, MD 20814; (301) 657-0270. Fax, (301) 657-0275. Susan Gorin, Executive Director, (301) 347-1640. Toll-free, (866) 331-6277. General email, kcowan@naspweb.org Web, www.nasponline.org*

Membership: graduate education students and professors, school psychologists, supervisors of school psychological services, and others who provide mental health services for children in school settings. Provides professional education and development to members. Provides school safety and crisis response direct services. Fosters information exchange; advises local, state, and federal policymakers and agencies that develop children's mental health educational services. Develops professional ethics and standards.

National Assn. of State Mental Health Program Directors, *66 Canal Center Plaza, #302, Alexandria, VA 22314-1591; (703) 739-9333. Fax, (703) 548-9517. Brian Hepburn, Executive Director. Web, www.nasmhpd.org*

Membership: officials in charge of state mental health agencies. Compiles data on state mental health programs. Fosters collaboration among members; provides technical assistance and consultation. Maintains research institute. Operates under a cooperative agreement with the National Governors Association. (Affiliated with NASMHPD Research Institute, Inc., Falls Church, Va.)

National Council for Behavioral Health, *1400 K St. N.W., #400, 20006; (202) 684-7457. Fax, (202) 386-9391. Linda Rosenberg, President. General email, communications@thenationalcouncil.org Web, www.TheNationalCouncil.org, Twitter, @nationalcouncil and Facebook, www.facebook.com/ TheNationalCouncil*

Membership: community mental health agencies and state community mental health associations. Conducts research on community mental health activities; provides information, technical assistance, and referrals. Operates a job bank; publishes newsletters and a membership directory. Monitors legislation and regulations affecting community mental health facilities. (Formerly National Council for Community Behavioral Healthcare.)

National Register of Health Service Psychologists, *1200 New York Ave. N.W., #800, 20005; (202) 783-7663. Fax, (202) 347-0550. Morgan T. Sammons, Executive Director.*
Web, www.nationalregister.org

Credentials and promotes health service psychologists that meet the National Register's requirements. Conducts biannual investigations of ethical behavior of health service psychologists. Maintains a database of licensed and accredited health service psychologists. Sponsors free continuing education programs. Monitors legislation and regulations related to health care reform.

Psychiatric Rehabilitation Assn., *7918 Jones Branch Dr., #300, McLean, VA 22101; (703) 442-2078. Fax, (703) 506-3266. Tom Gibson, Chief Executive Officer, Acting.*
General email, info@psychrehabassociation.org
Web, www.uspra.org and Twitter, @PsychRehab

Membership: agencies, mental health practitioners, researchers, policymakers, family groups, and consumer organizations. Supports the community adjustment of persons with psychiatric disabilities. Promotes the role of rehabilitation in mental health systems; opposes discrimination based on mental disability. Certifies psychosocial rehabilitation practitioners.

The Treatment Advocacy Center, *200 N. Glebe Rd., #801, Arlington, VA 22203; (703) 294-6001. Fax, (703) 294-6010. John Snook, Executive Director. Press, (703) 294-6003.*
General email, info@treatmentadvocacycenter.org
Web, www.treatmentadvocacycenter.org

Works to eliminate legal and other barriers to treatment of severe mental illness.

Treatment Communities of America (TCA), *1875 Eye St. N.W., #574, 20006; (202) 518-5475. Patricia Beauchemin, Executive Director.*
General email, tca.office@verizon.net
Web, www.treatmentcommunitiesofamerica.org

Membership: nonprofit organizations that provide substance abuse and mental health treatment and rehabilitation. Provides policy analysis and educates the public on substance abuse and treatment issues. Promotes the interests of therapeutic communities, their clients, and staffs. Monitors legislation and regulations.

11

Housing and Development

GENERAL POLICY AND ANALYSIS

Basic Resources

▶AGENCIES

Economic Development Administration *(Commerce Dept.),* *1401 Constitution Ave. N.W., #78006, 20230; (202) 482-5081. Fax, (202) 273-4781. Jay Williams, Assistant Secretary.*
Web, www.eda.gov

Advises the commerce secretary on domestic economic development. Administers development assistance programs that provide financial and technical aid to economically distressed areas to stimulate economic growth and create jobs. Awards public works and technical assistance grants to public institutions, nonprofit organizations, and Native American tribes; assists state and local governments with economic adjustment problems caused by long-term or sudden economic dislocation.

General Services Administration (GSA), *Catalog of Federal Domestic Assistance (CFDA), 2200 Crystal City Dr., Crystal Park 1, Arlington, VA 22202; 1800 F St. N.W., 20405-0001; (703) 605-3427. Priscilla Owens, Director, (703) 605-3408. Help desk, (866) 606-8220.*
Web, www.cfda.gov

Disseminates information on federal domestic assistance programs through the CFDA Web site. Information includes all types of federal aid and explains types of assistance, eligibility requirements, application processes, and suggestions for writing proposals. Catalog may be downloaded from the CFDA Web site. Printed version may be ordered from the Superintendent of Documents, U.S. Government Printing Office, Washington, DC 20402; (202) 512-1800, or toll-free, (866) 512-1800; or online at http://bookstore.gpo.gov.

Housing and Urban Development Dept. (HUD), *451 7th St. S.W., #10000, 20410; (202) 708-0417. Fax, (202) 619-8257. Julian Castro, Secretary; Nani A. Coloretti, Deputy Secretary, (202) 708-0123. Information, (202) 708-1112. Congressional and intergovernmental relations, (202) 708-0005. Locator, (202) 401-0388. TTY, (202) 708-1455.*
Web, www.hud.gov

Responsible for federal programs concerned with housing needs, fair housing opportunities, and improving and developing the nation's urban and rural communities. Administers mortgage insurance, rent subsidy, preservation, rehabilitation, and antidiscrimination in housing programs. Advises the president on federal policy and makes legislative recommendations on housing and community development issues.

Housing and Urban Development Dept. (HUD), *HUD USER, P.O. Box 23268, 20026-3268; (800) 245-2691. Fax, (703) 742-7889. Jennie Bray, Project Manager, (703) 742-7881, ext. 211. TTY, (800) 927-7589.*
General email, helpdesk@huduser.gov
Web, www.huduser.org

Research information service and clearinghouse for HUD research reports. Provides information on past and current HUD research; maintains HUD USER, an in-house database. Extensive collection of publications and documents available online.

Housing and Urban Development Dept. (HUD), *Policy Development and Research, 451 7th St. S.W., #8100, 20410-6000; (202) 708-1600. Fax, (202) 619-8000. Katherine M. O'Regan, Assistant Secretary.*
Web, www.huduser.org

Studies ways to improve the effectiveness and equity of HUD programs; analyzes housing and urban issues, including national housing goals, the operation of housing financial markets, the management of housing assistance programs, and statistics on federal and housing insurance programs; conducts the American Housing Survey; develops policy recommendations to improve federal housing programs. Works to increase the affordability of rehabilitated and newly constructed housing through technological and regulatory improvements.

Housing and Urban Development Dept. (HUD), *Program Evaluation Division, 451 7th St. S.W., #8120, 20410; (202) 402-6139. Carol S. Star, Director.*
General email, carol.s.star@hud.gov
Web, www.hud.gov

Conducts research, program evaluations, and demonstrations for all HUD housing, community development, and fair housing and equal opportunity programs.

Office of Management and Budget (OMB) *(Executive Office of the President), Housing, 725 17th St. N.W., #9226, 20503; (202) 395-4610. Fax, (202) 395-1307. Michelle Enger, Chief. Press, (202) 395-7254.*
Web, www.whitehouse.gov/omb

Assists and advises the OMB director in budget preparation, reorganizations, and evaluations of Housing and Urban Development Dept. programs.

Rural Development *(Agriculture Dept.), Legislative and Public Affairs, 1400 Independence Ave. S.W., 20250-0705; (202) 720-1019. David Sandretti, Director. Press, (202) 690-0498.*
Web, www.rd.usda.gov/about-rd/offices/legislative-public-affairs

Disseminates information to the media and general public about policy matters related to housing and rural development.

▶CONGRESS

For a listing of relevant congressional committees and subcommittees, please see page 420 or the Appendix.

▶NONGOVERNMENTAL

APPA: Leadership in Educational Facilities, *1643 Prince St., Alexandria, VA 22314-2818; (703) 684-1446. Fax, (703) 549-2772. E. Lander Medlin, Executive Vice President.*
General email, info@appa.org
Web, www.appa.org and Twitter, @APPA_facilities

HOUSING AND DEVELOPMENT RESOURCES IN CONGRESS

For a complete listing of congressional committees, including their full contact information, leadership, membership, and jurisdictions, please refer to the Appendix on pages 779–896.

HOUSE:

House Agriculture Committee, (202) 225-2171.
Web, agriculture.house.gov
  Subcommittee on Commodity Exchanges, Energy, and Credit, (202) 225-2171.
  Subcommittee on Conservation and Forestry, (202) 225-2171.
House Appropriations Committee, (202) 225-2771.
Web, appropriations.house.gov
  Subcommittee on Agriculture, Rural Development, Food and Drug Administration, and Related Agencies, (202) 225-2638.
  Subcommittee on Financial Services and General Government, (202) 225-7245.
  Subcommittee on Transportation, HUD, and Related Agencies, (202) 225-2141.
House Budget Committee, (202) 226-7270.
Web, budget.house.gov
House Financial Services Committee, (202) 225-7502.
Web, financialservices.house.gov
  Subcommittee on Capital Markets, and Government Sponsored Enterprises, (202) 225-7502.
  Subcommittee on Financial Institutions and Consumer Credit, (202) 225-7502.
  Subcommittee on Housing and Insurance, (202) 225-7502.
  Subcommittee on Monetary Policy and Trade, (202) 225-7502.
  Subcommittee on Oversight and Investigations, (202) 225-7502.
House Small Business Committee, (202) 225-5821.
Web, smallbusiness.house.gov
  Subcommittee on Agriculture, Energy, and Trade, (202) 225-5821.
House Transportation and Infrastructure Committee, (202) 225-9446.
Web, transportation.house.gov
  Subcommittee on Economic Development, Public Buildings, and Emergency Management, (202) 225-3014.
House Ways and Means Committee, (202) 225-3625.
Web, waysandmeans.house.gov
  Subcommittee on Oversight, (202) 225-5522.

SENATE:

Senate Agriculture, Nutrition, and Forestry Committee, (202) 224-2035.
Web, ag.senate.gov
  Subcommittee on Rural Development and Energy, (202) 224-2035.
Senate Appropriations Committee, (202) 224-7363.
Web, appropriations.senate.gov
  Subcommittee on Agriculture, Rural Development, Food and Drug Administration, and Related Agencies, (202) 224-8090.
  Subcommittee on Financial Services and General Government, (202) 224-1133.
  Subcommittee on Transportation, HUD, and Related Agencies, (202) 224-7281.
Senate Banking, Housing, and Urban Affairs Committee, (202) 224-7391.
Web, banking.senate.gov
  Subcommittee on Economic Policy, (202) 224-3753.
  Subcommittee on Financial Institutions and Consumer Protection, (202) 224-2315.
  Subcommittee on Housing, Transportation, and Community Development, (202) 224-4744.
  Subcommittee on Securities, Insurance, and Investment, (202) 224-4642.
Senate Budget Committee, (202) 224-0642.
Web, budget.senate.gov
Senate Environment and Public Works Committee, (202) 224-8832.
Web, epw.senate.gov
Senate Finance Committee, (202) 224-4515.
Web, finance.senate.gov
Senate Homeland Security and Governmental Affairs Committee, (202) 224-2627.
Web, hsgac.senate.gov
Senate Indian Affairs Committee, (202) 224-2251.
Web, indian.senate.gov
Senate Judiciary Committee, (202) 224-7703.
Web, judiciary.senate.gov
  Subcommittee on the Constitution, (202) 224-7840.
Senate Small Business and Entrepreneurship Committee, (202) 224-5175.
Web, sbc.senate.gov
Senate Special Committee on Aging, (202) 224-5364.
Web, aging.senate.gov

Housing and Urban Development Department

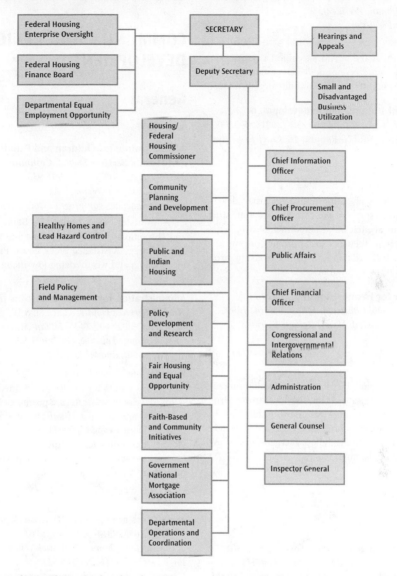

Membership: professionals involved in the administration, maintenance, planning, and development of buildings and facilities used by colleges and universities, K–12 private and public schools, museums, libraries, and other educational institutions. Interests include maintenance and upkeep of housing facilities. Provides information on campus energy management programs and campus accessibility for people with disabilities. (Formerly the Assn. of Higher Education Facilities Officers.)

Center for Economic and Policy Research (CEPR), *1611 Connecticut Ave. N.W., #400, 20009; (202) 293-5380. Fax, (202) 588-1356. Dean Baker, Co-Director; Mark Weisbrot, Co-Director.*
General email, info@cepr.net

Web, www.cepr.net and Twitter, @ceprdc

Researches economic and social issues and the impact of related public policies. Presents findings to the public with the goal of better preparing citizens to choose among various policy options. Promotes democratic debate and voter education. Areas of interest include health care, trade, financial reform, Social Security, taxes, housing, and the labor market.

Housing and Development Law Institute, *630 Eye St. N.W., 20001-3736; (202) 289-3400. Fax, (202) 289-3401. Lisa L. Walker, Chief Executive Officer.*
General email, hdli@hdli.org

Web, www.hdli.org

Membership organization that assists agencies and developers in public and affordable housing and community development in addressing common legal concerns and problems; publishes a quarterly compilation of nationwide case law affecting housing agencies; conducts seminars on legal issues and practices in the housing and community development field.

Institute for Local Self-Reliance, *1710 Connecticut Ave. N.W., 4th Floor, 20009; (202) 898-1610. Fax, (202) 898-1612. Neil N. Seldman, President.*
General email, info@ilsr.org

Web, www.ilsr.org

Conducts research and provides technical assistance on environmentally sound economic development for government, small businesses, and community organizations.

National Assn. of Housing and Redevelopment Officials, *630 Eye St. N.W., 20001-3736; (202) 289-3500. Fax, (202) 289-8181. Saul N. Ramirez Jr., Chief Executive. Toll-free, (877) 866-2476.*
General email, nahro@nahro.org

Web, www.nahro.org

Membership: housing, community, and urban development practitioners and organizations, and state and local government agencies and personnel. Works with federal government agencies to improve community development and affordable and public housing programs; conducts training programs.

National Center for Healthy Housing, *10320 Little Patuxent Pkwy., #500, Columbia, MD 21044; (410) 992-0712. Fax, (443) 539-4150. Nancy Rockett Eldridge, Executive Director.*
General email, info@nchh.org

Web, www.nchh.org

Collects, analyzes, and distributes information on creating and maintaining safe and healthful housing. Provides technical assistance and training to public health, housing, and environmental professionals. Interests include aging in place for older adults, radon, allergens, pest management, and lead poisoning.

Statistics

▶AGENCIES

Census Bureau *(Commerce Dept.), Social, Economic, and Housing Statistics, 4600 Silver Hill Rd., #7H174, Suitland, MD 20746 (mailing address: 4600 Silver Hill Rd. #7H174, Washington, DC 20233-8500); (301) 763-3234. Fax, (301) 763-3232. Victoria A. Velkoff, Chief.*
Web, www.census.gov/housing

Publishes decennial census of housing and the American Housing Survey, which describe housing inventory characteristics. Also publishes a quarterly survey of market absorption. Survey on housing vacancy is available on the Web site.

Housing and Urban Development Dept. (HUD), *Economic Affairs, 451 7th St. S.W., #8204, 20410-6000; (202) 402-5899. Fax, (202) 708-1159. Kurt Usowski, Deputy Assistant Secretary.*
Web, www.hud.gov

Assembles data on housing markets and subsidized housing programs; conducts housing statistical surveys, analyzes housing finance markets; analyzes economic effects of HUD regulations; gathers local housing market intelligence; and conducts other economic research.

COMMUNITY AND REGIONAL DEVELOPMENT

General

▶AGENCIES

Administration for Children and Families (ACF) *(Health and Human Services Dept.), Community Services, 330 C St. S.W., 20201; (202) 401-9333. Fax, (202) 401-4694. Jeannie Chaffin, Director.*
Web, www.acf.hhs.gov/programs/ocs

Administers the Community Services Block Grant and Discretionary Grant programs and the Low-Income Home Energy Assistance Block Grant Program for heating, cooling, and weatherizing low-income households.

Administration for Native Americans *(Health and Human Services Dept.), 330 C. St. S.W., 20201; (202) 690-7776. Fax, (202) 690-7441. Lillian A. Sparks, Commissioner. Toll-free, (877) 922-9262.*
General email, ana@acf.hhs.gov

Web, www.acf.hhs.gov/programs/ana

Awards grants for locally determined social and economic development strategies; promotes Native American economic and social self-sufficiency; funds tribes and Native American and Native Hawaiian organizations; provides grant funding for community development projects. Commissioner chairs the Intradepartmental Council on Indian Affairs, which coordinates Native American-related programs.

Army Corps of Engineers *(Defense Dept.), 441 G St. N.W., #3K05, 20314-1000; (202) 761-0001. Fax, (202) 761-4463. Lt. Gen. Thomas P. Bostick (USA), Chief of Engineers. Press, (202) 761-0011.*
General email, hq-publicaffairs@usace.army.mil

Web, www.usace.army.mil and Twitter, @USACEHQ

Provides local governments with disaster relief, flood control, navigation, and hydroelectric power services.

Community Development Financial Institutions Fund *(Treasury Dept.), 1801 L St. N.W., 6th Floor, 20036 (mailing address: 1500 Pennsylvania Ave. N.W., Washington, DC 20220); (202) 653-0300. Annie Donovan, Director.*
General email, cdfihelp@cdfi.treas.gov

Web, www.cdfifund.gov

Provides funds and tax credits to financial institutions to build private markets, create healthy local tax revenues, and expand the availability of credit, investment capital, affordable housing, and financial services in low-income urban, rural, and Native communities.

Defense Dept. (DoD), *Economic Adjustment,* 2231 Crystal Dr., #520, Arlington, VA 22202-4704; (703) 697-2130. Fax, (703) 607-0170. Patrick J. O'Brien, Director. Web, www.oea.gov

Civilian office that helps community officials develop strategies and coordinate plans to alleviate the economic effect of major defense program changes, including base closings (BRAC) and contract cutbacks. Assists communities where defense activities are being expanded. Serves as the staff for the Economic Adjustment Committee, an interagency group that coordinates federal technical and financial transition assistance to localities.

Education Dept., *White House Initiative on Asian Americans and Pacific Islanders,* 550 12th St. S.W., 10th Floor, 20202; (202) 245-6418. Fax, (202) 245-7166. Doua Thor, Executive Director. Press, (202) 245-6353. General email, whitehouseaapi@ed.gov

Web, http://sites.ed.gov/whieeaa and Twitter, @whitehouseAAPI

Works to increase Asian American and Pacific Islander participation in federal housing and community development programs. Interests include creating sustainable communities by connecting housing to jobs and helping to build clean energy communities.

Housing and Urban Development Dept. (HUD), *Community Planning and Development,* 451 7th St. S.W., #7100, 20410; (202) 708-2690. Fax, (202) 708-3336. Harriet Tregoning, Principal Deputy Assistant Secretary; Clifford Taffet, General Deputy Assistant Secretary. Web, http://portal.hud.gov/hudportal/HUD?src=/program_offices/comm_planning

Provides cities and states with community and economic development and housing assistance, including community development block grants. Encourages public-private partnerships in urban development and private sector initiatives. Oversees enterprise zone development program.

Housing and Urban Development Dept. (HUD), *Community Planning and Development, Block Grant Assistance,* 451 7th St. S.W., #7286, 20410; (202) 708-3587. Fax, (202) 401-2044. Stan Gimont, Director. Web, http://portal.hud.gov/hudportal/HUD?src=/program_offices/comm_planning/communitydevelopment

Provides grants on a formula basis to states, cities, and urban counties to be used for a wide range of eligible activities selected by the grantee.

Housing and Urban Development Dept. (HUD), *Community Planning and Development, Block Grant Assistance, States and Small Cities Division,* 451 7th St. S.W., #7184, 20410; (202) 708-1322. Fax, (202) 401-2044. Pamela Glekas Spring, Director. Web, www.hud.gov/offices/cpd/communitydevelopment/programs

Provides states with grants for distribution to small cities (fewer than 50,000 persons) and small counties (fewer than 200,000 persons) that do not receive funding

through the Entitlement Community Development Block Grant Program. Funds benefit low-income and moderate-income persons, eliminate slums and blighted conditions, or meet other urgent community development needs. All states (except Hawaii), plus Puerto Rico, receive State Community Development Block Grant (CDBG) program funding. In Hawaii, HUD provides funding directly to the local governments. A separate program also provides funding to the Insular Areas.

Housing and Urban Development Dept. (HUD), *Community Planning and Development, Economic Resilience,* 451 7th St. S.W., #10180, 20410; (202) 402-3097. Fax, (202) 708-0465. Danille Arigoni, Director, Acting. General email, EconomicResilience@hud.gov

Web, http://portal.hud.gov/hudportal/HUD?src=/program_offices/economic_resilience and Twitter, @HudResilience

Works to connect housing to jobs, helping to build a clean energy economy. Fosters local innovation and coordinated federal housing and transportation. Awards grants for affordable housing development and transportation-related issues, as well as green and sustainable energy practices.

Housing and Urban Development Dept. (HUD), *Community Planning and Development, Environment and Energy,* 451 7th St. S.W., #7230, 20410; (202) 708-2894. Fax, (202) 708-3363. Danielle Schopp, Director, (202) 402-4442. Web, http://portal.hud.gov/hudportal/HUD?src=/program_offices/comm_planning/library/energy

Issues policies and sets standards for environmental and land-use planning and for environmental management practices. Develops policies promoting energy efficiency, conservation, and renewable sources of supply in housing and community development programs.

Housing and Urban Development Dept. (HUD), *Community Planning and Development, Technical Assistance and Management,* 451 7th St. S.W., #7228, 20410; (202) 708-3176. David Enzel, Director. Web, http://portal.hud.gov/hudportal/HUD?src=/program_offices/comm_planning

Develops program policies and designs and implements technical assistance plans for state and local governments for use in community planning and development programs.

Housing and Urban Development Dept. (HUD), *Field Policy and Management,* 451 7th St. S.W., #7108, 20410; (202) 708-2426. Fax, (202) 708-1558. Mary McBride, Assistant Deputy Secretary. Web, http://portal.hud.gov/hudportal/HUD?src=/program_offices/field_policy_mgt

Acts as liaison and coordinates all activities between the Office of Community Planning and Development and regional and field offices; evaluates the performance of regional and field offices. Conducts policy analyses and evaluations of community planning and development programs, including the Community Development Block Grant Program, the Empowerment Zones/Enterprise Communities Program, and the McKinney Act programs.

►CONGRESS

For a listing of relevant congressional committees and sub-committees, please see page 420 or the Appendix.

►NONGOVERNMENTAL

American Planning Assn., *1030 15th St. N.W., #750W, 20005; (202) 872-0611. Fax, (202) 872-0643. James Drinan, Executive Director; Jason Jordan, Director of Governmental Affairs.*
Web, www.planning.org and Twitter, @APA_Planning

Membership: professional planners and others interested in urban, suburban, and rural planning. Serves as a clearinghouse for planners. Sponsors professional development workshops conducted by the American Institute of Certified Planners. Prepares studies and technical reports; conducts seminars and conferences. (Headquarters in Chicago, Ill.)

American Resort Development Assn., *1201 15th St. N.W., #400, 20005; (202) 371-6700. Fax, (202) 289-8544. Howard Nusbaum, President.*
Web, www.arda.org

Membership: U.S. and international developers, builders, financiers, marketing companies, and others involved in resort, recreational, and community development. Serves as an information clearinghouse; monitors federal and state legislation affecting land, time share, and community development industries.

Center for Community Change, *1536 U St. N.W., 20009; (202) 339-9300. Fax, (202) 387-4892. Deepak Bhargava, Executive Director.*
General email, info@communitychange.org
Web, www.communitychange.org and Twitter, @communitychange

Works to strengthen grassroots organizations that help low-income people, working-class people, and minorities develop skills and resources to improve their communities and change the policies and institutions that affect their lives. Monitors legislation and regulations.

Center for Neighborhood Enterprise, *1625 K St. N.W., #1200, 20006; (202) 518-6500. Fax, (202) 588-0314. Robert L. Woodson Sr., President. Information, (866) 518-1263.*
General email, info@cneonline.org
Web, www.cneonline.org and Twitter, @cneonline

Provides community and faith-based organizations with training, technical assistance, and additional sources of support. Addresses issues such as youth violence, substance abuse, teen pregnancy, homelessness, joblessness, poor education, and deteriorating neighborhoods.

Council of State Community Development Agencies, *1825 K St. N.W., #515, 20006; (202) 293-5820. Fax, (202) 293-2820. Dianne E. Taylor, Executive Director.*
General email, info@coscda.org
Web, www.coscda.org

Membership: directors and staff of state community development agencies. Promotes common interests among the states, including community and economic development, housing, homelessness, infrastructure, and state and local planning.

Institute for Sustainable Communities, Washington Office, *888 17th St. N.W., #610, 20006; (202) 777-7575. Fax, (202) 777-7577. George Hamilton, President; Debra Perry, U.S. Senior Program Manager.*
General email, isc@iscvt.org
Web, www.iscvt.org

Provides training and technical assistance to communities to engage citizens in developing and implementing plans for a sustainable future. (Headquarters in Montpelier, Vt.)

International Information on Site Planning, *715 G St. S.E., 20003; (202) 546-2322. Fax, (202) 546-2722. Beatriz de Winthuysen Coffin, Director.*
General email, iisitep@aol.com
Web, www.iisp-insitu.com

Directs research and provides information on site planning development and design of sites and buildings; conducts study and travel programs.

KaBOOM!, *4301 Connecticut Ave N.W., #ML-1, 20008; (202) 659-0215. Fax, (202) 659-0210. Darell Hammond, Chief Executive Officer. Press, (202) 528-1691.*
General email, webmaster@kaboom.org
Web, www.kaboom.org, Twitter, @kaboom and Facebook, www.facebook.com/kaboom

Offers grants to develop and manage playgrounds in low-income communities. Publishes research on public policy and the impact of play areas in neighborhoods.

Land Trust Alliance, *1660 L St. N.W., #1100, 20036; (202) 638-4725. Fax, (202) 638-4730. Rand Wentworth, President, (202) 800-2249.*
General email, info@lta.org
Web, www.landtrustalliance.org and Twitter, @italliance

Membership: organizations and individuals who work to conserve land resources. Serves as a forum for the exchange of information; conducts research and public education programs. Monitors legislation and regulations.

Local Initiatives Support Corp., Washington Office, *1825 K St. N.W., #1100, 20006; (202) 739-9284. Fax, (202) 785-4850. Oramenta Newsome, Executive Director; Matt Josephs, Senior Vice President, Policy.*
Web, www.liscdc.org

Provides community development corporations and nonprofit organizations with financial and technical assistance to build affordable housing and revitalize distressed neighborhoods. (Headquarters in New York.)

National Assn. of Conservation Districts (NACD), *509 Capitol Court N.E., 20002-4937; (202) 547-6223. Fax, (202) 547-6450. Jeremy Peters, Chief Executive Officer.*
General email, bethany-shively@nacdet.org
Web, www.nacdnet.org

Membership: conservation districts (local subdivisions of state government). Works to promote the conservation of land, forests, and other natural resources. Interests include erosion and sediment control; water quality; forestry, water, flood plain, and range management; rural development; and urban and community conservation.

National Assn. of Counties (NACo), *Community and Economic Development, 25 Massachusetts Ave. N.W., #500, 20001; (202) 393-6226. Fax, (202) 942-4281. Daria Daniel, Associate Legislative Director.*
Web, www.naco.org/programs/csd/pages/communityeconomicdevelopment.aspx

Membership: county governments. Conducts research and provides information on community development block grants, assisted low-income housing, and other housing and economic development programs. Monitors legislation and regulations.

National Assn. of Development Organizations, *400 N. Capitol St. N.W., #390, 20001; (202) 624-7806. Fax, (202) 624-8813. Joe McKinney, Executive Director, (202) 624-5947.*
General email, info@nado.org
Web, www.nado.org

Membership: organizations interested in regional, local, and rural economic development. Provides information on federal, state, and local development programs and revolving loan funds; sponsors conferences and training.

National Assn. of Regional Councils (NARC), *777 N. Capitol St. N.E., #305, 20002; (202) 618-6363. Leslie Wollack, Executive Director.*
General email, info@narc.org
Web, www.narc.org

Membership: regional councils of local governments and metropolitan planning organizations. Works with member local governments to encourage areawide economic growth and cooperation between public and private sectors, with emphasis on community development.

National Community Development Assn., *177 Eye St. N.W., #1150, 20006; (202) 587-2772. Fax, (202) 887-5546. Vicki Watson, Executive Director.*
Web, www.ncdaonline.org

Membership: local governments that administer federally supported community and economic development, housing, and human service programs.

National Trust for Historic Preservation, *2600 Virginia Ave. N.W., #1000, 20037; (202) 588-6000. Fax, (202) 588-6038. Stephanie Meeks, President; Robin Scullin, Public Affairs. Toll-free, (800) 944-6847.*
General email, info@savingplaces.org
Web, www.preservationnation.org

Conducts seminars, workshops, and conferences on topics related to preservation, including neighborhood conservation, main street revitalization, rural conservation, and preservation law; offers financial assistance through loan and grant programs; provides advisory services; operates historic house sites, which are open to the public; and publishes quarterly magazine and e-newsletters.

Partners for Livable Communities, *1429 21st St. N.W., 20036; (202) 887-5990. Robert H. McNulty, President. General email, fkoleszar@livable.org*
Web, www.livable.org

Promotes working partnerships among public, private, and governmental sectors to improve the quality of life and economic development at local and regional levels. Conducts conferences and workshops; maintains referral clearinghouse; provides technical assistance.

Scenic America, *1307 New Hampshire Ave. N.W., 3rd Floor, 20036; (202) 463-1294. Fax, (202) 463-1299. Mary Tracy, President.*
General email, ashburn@scenic.org
Web, www.scenic.org and Twitter, @ScenicAmerica

Membership: national, state, and local groups concerned with land-use control, growth management, and landscape protection. Works to enhance the scenic quality of America's communities and countryside. Provides information and technical assistance on scenic byways, tree preservation, economics of aesthetic regulation, billboard and sign control, scenic areas preservation, and growth management.

Smart Growth America, *1707 L St. N.W., #250, 20036; (202) 207-3355. Fax, (202) 207-3349. Geoffrey Anderson, President.*
General email, info@smartgrowthamerica.org
Web, www.smartgrowthamerica.org

Coalition of advocacy groups that supports citizen-driven planning that coordinates development, transportation, revitalization of older areas, and preservation of open space and the environment.

Rural Areas

▶ **AGENCIES**

Farm Service Agency (FSA) *(Agriculture Dept.), Farm Loan Programs, 1400 Independence Ave. S.W., #3605S, MS 0520, 20250-0520; (202) 720-4671. Fax, (202) 690-3573. James F. Radintz, Deputy Administrator.*
Web, www.fsa.usda.gov

Supports rural development through farm program loans, including real estate, farm production, and emergency loans.

National Agricultural Library *(Agriculture Dept.), Rural Information Center, 10301 Baltimore Ave., #123, Beltsville, MD 20705-2351; (800) 633-7701. Fax, (301) 504-5181. Louise Reynnells, Coordinator.*
General email, ric@ars.usda.gov
Web, http://ric.nal.usda.gov

Provides services for rural communities, local officials, organizations, businesses, and rural citizens in the interest of maintaining rural areas. Interests include community development, tourism promotion, water quality, recycling, and technology transfer.

Rural Development *(Agriculture Dept.), 1400 Independence Ave. S.W., #206W, 20250-0107; (202) 720-4581. Fax, (202) 720-2080. Lisa Mensah, Under Secretary. Web, www.rd.usda.gov and Twitter, @usdaRD*

Acts as chief adviser to the secretary on agricultural credit and related matters; coordinates rural development policies and programs throughout the federal government; supervises the Rural Utilities Service, Rural Housing Service, and Rural Business-Cooperative Service.

Rural Development *(Agriculture Dept.), Business–Cooperative Service, Business Programs, 1400 Independence Ave. S.W., #5803-S, MS 3201, 20250-3201; (202) 690-4730. William Smith, Deputy Administrator. Press, (202) 690-4737. Web, www.rd.usda.gov/about-rd/agencies/rural-business-cooperative-service*

Promotes rural economic development by providing financial assistance and business planning to community businesses.

Rural Development *(Agriculture Dept.), Rural Housing Service, Housing Programs, 1400 Independence Ave. S.W., #5014, MS 0701, 20250-0701; (202) 690-1533. Fax, (202) 690-0500. Tony Hernandez, Administrator. Web, www.rd.usda.gov/about-rd/agencies/rural-housing-service*

Offers financial assistance to apartment dwellers and homeowners in rural areas; provides funds to construct or improve single-family and multifamily housing and community facilities.

Rural Development *(Agriculture Dept.), Rural Utilities Service, 1400 Independence Ave. S.W., #5135-S, MS 1510, 20250-1510; (202) 720-9540. Fax, (202) 720-1725. Brandon McBride, Administrator. Information, (202) 720-1255. Web, www.rd.usda.gov/about-rd/agencies/rural-utilities-service*

Makes loans and loan guarantees to rural electric and telephone companies providing service in rural areas. Administers the Rural Telephone Bank, which provides supplemental financing from federal sources. Makes loans for economic development and creation of jobs in rural areas, for water and waste disposal, and for distance learning and telemedicine.

▶**CONGRESS**

For a listing of relevant congressional committees and subcommittees, please see page 420 or the Appendix.

▶**NONGOVERNMENTAL**

Farm Credit Council, *50 F St. N.W., #900, 20001-1530; (202) 626-8710. Fax, (202) 626-6718. Ken Auer, President, (202) 879 0843*

General email, auer@fccouncil.com

Web, www.fccouncil.com and Twitter, @thefccouncil

Represents the Farm Credit System, a national financial cooperative that makes loans to agricultural producers, rural homebuyers, farmer cooperatives, and rural utilities. Finances the export of U.S. agricultural commodities.

Housing Assistance Council, *1025 Vermont Ave. N.W., #606, 20005-3516; (202) 842-8600. Fax, (202) 347-3441. Moises Loza, Executive Director.*

General email, hac@ruralhome.org

Web, www.ruralhome.org

Provides low-income housing development groups in rural areas with seed money loans and technical assistance; assesses programs designed to respond to rural housing needs; makes recommendations for federal and state involvement; publishes technical guides and reports on rural housing issues.

Irrigation Assn., *8280 Willow Oaks Corporate Dr., #400, Fairfax, VA 22031; (703) 536-7080. Fax, (703) 536-7019. Deborah Hamlin, Executive Director.*

General email, info@irrigation.org

Web, www.irrigation.org

Membership: companies and individuals involved in irrigation, drainage, and erosion control worldwide. Promotes efficient and effective water management through training, education, and certification programs. Interests include economic development and environmental enhancement.

National Cooperative Business Assn., CLUSA International (NCBA CLUSA), *1775 Eye St. N.W., #800, 20006; (202) 638-6222. Fax, (202) 638-1374. Judy Ziewacz, President.*

General email, info@ncba.coop

Web, www.ncba.coop, Twitter, @NCBACLUSA and Facebook, www.facebook.com/NCBACLUSA

Alliance of cooperatives, businesses, and state cooperative associations. Provides information about starting and managing agricultural cooperatives in the United States and in developing nations. Monitors legislation and regulations.

National Council of Farmer Cooperatives (NCFC), *50 F St. N.W., #900, 20001-1530; (202) 626-8700. Fax, (202) 626-8722. Charles F. Conner, President.*

General email, info@ncfc.org

Web, www.ncfc.org

Membership: cooperative businesses owned and operated by farmers. Encourages research on agricultural cooperatives; provides statistics and analyzes trends. Monitors legislation and regulations on agricultural trade, transportation, energy, and tax issues.

National Rural Electric Cooperative Assn. (NRECA), *4301 Wilson Blvd., Arlington, VA 22203-1860; (703) 907-5500. Fax, (703) 907-5511. Jo Ann Emerson, Chief Executive Officer; Tracy Warren, Media Relations, (703) 907-5746. Web, www.nreca.org*

Membership: rural electric cooperative systems and public power and utility districts. Provides members with legislative, legal, and regulatory services. Supports energy and environmental research and offers technical advice and assistance to developing countries.

National Rural Housing Coalition, *1331 G St. N.W., 10th Floor, 20005; (202) 393-5229. Fax, (202) 393-3034. Robert A. Rapoza, Executive Secretary. General email, nrhc@ruralhousingcoalitions.org*

Web, www.ruralhousingcoalition.org

Advocates improved housing for low-income rural families; works to increase public awareness of rural housing problems; administers the Self-Help Housing Fund, Farm Worker Housing Fund, Rural Community Assistance Fund, and HUD Task Force. Monitors legislation and regulations.

National Sustainable Agriculture Coalition, *110 Maryland Ave. N.E., #209, 20002-5622; (202) 547-5754. Fax, (202) 547-1837. Ferd Hoefner, Policy Director; Jeremy Emmi, Managing Director. General email, info@sustainableagriculture.net*

Web, www.sustainableagriculture.net

National alliance of farm, rural, and conservation organizations. Advocates federal policies that promote environmentally sustainable agriculture, natural resources management, and rural community development. Monitors legislation and regulations.

National Telecommunications Cooperative Assn. (NTCA), *4121 Wilson Blvd., #1000, Arlington, VA 22203-1801; (703) 351-2000. Fax, (703) 351-2001. Shirley Bloomfield, Chief Executive Officer. General email, pubrelations@ntca.org*

Web, www.ntca.org

Membership: locally owned and controlled telecommunications cooperatives and companies serving rural and small-town areas. Offers educational seminars, workshops, publications, technical assistance, and various employee benefits programs to members. Monitors legislation and regulations.

Rural Coalition, *1029 Vermont Ave., #601, 20005; (202) 628-7160. Fax, (202) 393-1816. Lorette Picciano, Executive Director. General email, ruralco@ruralco.org*

Web, www.ruralco.org and Twitter, @RuralCo

Alliance of organizations that develop public policies benefiting rural communities. Collaborates with community-based groups on agriculture and rural development issues, including health and the environment, minority farmers, farm workers, Native Americans' rights, and rural community development. Provides rural groups with technical assistance.

Rural Community Assistance Partnership (RCAP), *1701 K St. N.W., #700, 20006; (202) 408-1273. Fax, (202) 408-8165. Robert Stewart, Executive Director. Toll-free, (800) 321-7227.*

General email, info@rcap.org

Web, www.rcap.org

Provides expertise to rural communities on wastewater disposal, protection of groundwater supply, and access to safe drinking water. Targets communities with predominantly low-income or minority populations. Offers outreach policy analysis, training, and technical assistance to elected officials and other community leaders, utility owners and operators, and residents.

Specific Regions

▶**AGENCIES**

Appalachian Regional Commission, *1666 Connecticut Ave. N.W., #700, 20009-1068; (202) 884-7700. Fax, (202) 884-7691. Scott T. Hamilton, Executive Director; Earl F. Gohl, Federal Co-Chair. Press, (202) 884-7771. General email, info@arc.gov*

Web, www.arc.gov

Federal-state-local partnership for economic development of the region, including West Virginia and parts of Alabama, Georgia, Kentucky, Maryland, Mississippi, New York, North Carolina, Ohio, Pennsylvania, South Carolina, Tennessee, and Virginia. Plans and provides technical and financial assistance and coordinates federal and state efforts for economic development of Appalachia.

Bureau of Reclamation *(Interior Dept.), 1849 C St. N.W., MS 7069, 20240-0001; (202) 513-0501. Fax, (202) 513-0309. Estevan Lopez, Commissioner. Press, (202) 513-0575.*

Web, www.usbr.gov and Twitter, @usbr

Administers federal programs for water and power resource development and management in seventeen western states; oversees municipal and industrial water supplies, hydroelectric power generation, irrigation, flood control, water quality improvement, river regulation, fish and wildlife enhancement, and outdoor recreation.

Interstate Commission on the Potomac River Basin, *30 W. Gude Dr., #450, Rockville, MD 20850; (301) 984-1908. Carlton Haywood, Executive Director. General email, info@icprb.org*

Web, www.potomacriver.org

Nonregulatory interstate compact commission established by Congress to control and reduce water pollution and to restore and protect living resources in the Potomac River and its tributaries. Monitors water quality; assists metropolitan water utilities; seeks innovative methods to solve water supply and land resource problems. Provides information and educational materials on the Potomac River basin.

National Capital Planning Commission, *401 9th St. N.W., North Lobby, #500, 20004; (202) 482-7200. Fax, (202) 482-7272. Marcel Acosta, Executive Director.*

General email, info@ncpc.gov

Web, www.ncpc.gov

Central planning agency for the federal government in the national capital region, which includes the District of Columbia and suburban Maryland and Virginia. Reviews and approves plans for the physical growth and development of the national capital area, using environmental, historic, and land-use criteria.

Tennessee Valley Authority, *Government Affairs,* *1 Massachusetts Ave. N.W., #300, 20444; (202) 898-2999. Fax, (202) 898-2998. Nick Pearson, Director.*

General email, tvainfo@tva.gov

Web, www.tva.gov

Federal corporation that coordinates resource conservation, development, and land-use programs in the Tennessee River Valley. Uses fossil fuel, nuclear, and hydropower sources to generate and supply wholesale power to municipal and cooperative electric systems, federal installations, and some industries.

►**NONGOVERNMENTAL**

Greater Washington Board of Trade, *800 Connecticut Ave., #10001, 20006; (202) 857-5900. Fax, (202) 223-2648. James C. (Jim) Dinegar, President.*

General email, info@bot.org and danielflores@bot.org

Web, www.bot.org

Promotes and plans economic growth for the capital region. Supports business-government partnerships, technological training, and transportation planning; promotes international trade; works to increase economic viability of the city of Washington. Monitors legislation and regulations at local, state, and federal levels.

New England Council, *Washington Office, 331 Constitution Ave. N.E., 20002; (202) 547-0048. Fax, (202) 547-9149. James T. Brett, President; Peter Phipps, Vice President of Federal Affairs.*

General email, necouncil@newenglandcouncil.com

Web, https://newenglandcouncil.com

Provides information on business and economic issues concerning New England; serves as liaison between the New England congressional delegations and business community. (Headquarters in Boston, Mass.)

Northeast–Midwest Institute, *50 F St. N.W., #950, 20001; (202) 544-5200. Fax, (202) 544-0043. Michael Goff, President.*

General email, info@nemw.org

Web, www.nemw.org

Public policy research organization that promotes the economic vitality and environmental sustainability of the northeast and midwest regions. Interests include distribution of federal funding to regions, economic development, human resources, energy, and natural resources.

Urban Areas

►**AGENCIES**

General Services Administration (GSA), *Urban Development/Good Neighbor Program, 1800 F St. N.W., #3341, 20405-0001; (202) 501-1856. Fax, (202) 501-3393. Frank Giblin, Program Manager.*

General email, frank.giblin@gsa.gov

Web, www.gsa.gov/portal/content/104461 and Twitter, @GSA_urbder

Advises on locations, designs, and renovations of federal facilities in central business areas, historic districts, and local redevelopment areas where they can anchor or promote community development. Collaborates with local and national civic and other organizations. Serves as clearinghouse for good practices.

Housing and Urban Development Dept. (HUD), *Community Planning and Development, Affordable Housing Programs, 451 7th St. S.W., #7164, 20410; (202) 708-2684. Fax, (202) 708-1744. Virginia Sardone, Director, Acting.*

Web, www.hud.gov/hudportal/HUD?src=/program_offices/comm_planning/affordablehousing

Coordinates with cities to convey publicly owned, abandoned property to low-income families in exchange for their commitment to repair, occupy, and maintain the property.

Housing and Urban Development Dept. (HUD), *Community Planning and Development, Economic Development, 451 7th St. S.W., #7136, 20410; (202) 708-4091. Fax, (202) 401-2231. Valerie Piper, Deputy Assistant Secretary, (202) 402-4445.*

Web, http://portal.hud.gov/hudportal/HUD?src=/program_offices/comm_planning/economicdevelopment

Manages economic development programs, including Empowerment Zones/Renewal Communities, Rural Housing and Economic Development, and Brownfields Economic Development Initiatives. Encourages private-public partnerships for development through neighborhood development corporations. Formulates policies and legislative proposals on economic development.

NeighborWorks America, *999 N. Capitol St. N.E., #900, 20002; (202) 760-4000. Fax, (202) 376-2600. Paul Weech, President.*

General email, editor@nw.org

Web, www.nw.org

Chartered by Congress to assist localities in developing and operating local neighborhood-based programs designed to reverse decline in urban residential neighborhoods and rural communities. Oversees the National NeighborWorks Network, an association of local nonprofit organizations concerned with urban and rural development.

▶NONGOVERNMENTAL

International Downtown Assn., *1025 Thomas Jefferson St. N.W., #500W, 20007; (202) 393-6801. Fax, (202) 393-6869. David T. Downey, President, (202) 798-5922.*
General email, question@ida-downtown.org

Web, www.ida-downtown.org

Membership: organizations, corporations, public agencies, and individuals interested in the development and management of city downtown areas. Supports cooperative efforts between the public and private sectors to revitalize downtowns and adjacent neighborhoods; provides members with information, technical assistance, and advice.

International Economic Development Council, *734 15th St. N.W., #900, 20005; (202) 223-7800. Fax, (202) 223-4745. Jeffrey Finkle, President; Akia Garnett. Press, (703) 942-9474.*
General email, mail@iedconline.org

Web, www.iedconline.org

Membership: public economic development directors, chamber of commerce staff, utility executives, academicians, and others who design and implement development programs. Provides information to members on job creation, attraction, and retention.

Milton S. Eisenhower Foundation, *1875 Connecticut Ave N.W., #410, 20009-5728; (202) 234-8104. Fax, (202) 234-8484. Alan Curtis, President.*
General email, info@eisenhowerfoundation.org

Web, www.eisenhowerfoundation.org

Strives to help urban communities combat violence by supporting programs with proven records of success. Provides funding, technical assistance, evaluation, and supervision to communities wishing to replicate successful programs.

National Assn. for the Advancement of Colored People (NAACP), *Washington Bureau, 1156 15th St. N.W., #915, 20005; (202) 463-2940. Fax, (202) 463-2953. Hilary O. Shelton, Director.*
General email, washingtonbureau@naacpnet.org

Web, www.naacp.org

Membership: persons interested in civil rights for all minorities. Works to eliminate discrimination in housing and urban affairs. Interests include programs for urban redevelopment, urban homesteading, and low-income housing. Supports programs that make affordable rental housing available to minorities and that maintain African American ownership of urban and rural land. (Headquarters in Baltimore, Md.)

National Assn. of Neighborhoods, *1300 Pennsylvania Ave. N.W., #700, 20004; (202) 332-7766. Fax, (202) 789-7349. Ricardo C. Byrd, Executive Director.*
General email, info@nanworld.org

Web, www.nanworld.org

Federation of neighborhood groups that provides technical assistance to local governments, neighborhood groups, and businesses. Seeks to increase influence of grassroots groups on decisions affecting neighborhoods; sponsors training workshops promoting neighborhood awareness.

National League of Cities, *1301 Pennsylvania Ave. N.W., #550, 20004; (202) 626-3000. Fax, (202) 626-3043. Clarence Anthony, Executive Director. Toll-free, (877) 827-2385.*
General email, info@nlc.org

Web, www.nlc.org

Membership: cities and state municipal leagues. Aids city leaders in developing programs; investigates needs of local governments in implementing federal community development programs.

National Urban League, *Washington Bureau, 2901 14th St. N.W., 20009; (202) 265-8200. George H. Lambert Jr., Affiliate Chief Executive Officer.*
Web, http://nul.iamempowered.com/affiliate/greater-washington-urban-league

Federal advocacy division of social service organization concerned with the social welfare of African Americans and other minorities. Conducts legislative and policy analysis on housing and urban affairs. Operates a job network. (Headquarters in New York.)

Urban Institute, *Center for Metropolitan Housing and Communities Policy, 2100 M St. N.W., 20037; (202) 833-7200. Fax, (202) 872-8154. Rolf Pendall, Director.*
Web, www.urban.org/center/met

Research center that deals with urban problems. Researches federal, state, and local policies; focus includes community development block grants, neighborhood rehabilitation programs, and housing issues.

Urban Land Institute, *1025 Thomas Jefferson St. N.W., #500W, 20007-5201; (202) 624-7000. Fax, (202) 624-7140. Patrick L. Phillips, Global Chief Executive Officer, (202) 624-7163. Information, (800) 321-5011. Library, (202) 624-7137.*
Web, www.uli.org

Membership: land developers, planners, state and federal agencies, financial institutions, home builders, consultants, and Realtors. Provides responsible leadership in the use of land to enhance the total environment; monitors trends in new community development.

U.S. Conference of Mayors, *1620 Eye St. N.W., 4th Floor, 20006; (202) 293-7330. Fax, (202) 293-2352. J. Thomas Cochran, Executive Director.*
General email, info@usmayors.org

Web, www.usmayors.org

Membership: mayors of cities with populations of 30,000 or more. Promotes city-federal cooperation; publishes reports and conducts meetings on federal programs, policies, and initiatives that affect urban and suburban interests. Serves as a clearinghouse for information on urban and suburban problems. (Approximately 1,400 U.S. cities.)

CONSTRUCTION

General

▶ AGENCIES

General Services Administration (GSA), *Public Buildings Services, 1800 F St. N.W., #6459, 20405; (202) 501-1100. Norman Dong, Commissioner.*
Web, www.gsa.gov/pbs

Administers the acquisition, construction, maintenance, and operation of buildings owned or leased by the federal government. Manages and disposes of federal real estate.

National Research Council (NRC), *Infrastructure and the Constructed Environment Board, Keck Center, 500 5th St. N.W., #WS938, 20001; (202) 334-3505. Fax, (202) 334-3718. Rear Adm. David J. Nash (USN, Ret.), Chair.*
General email, bice@nas.edu
Web, http://sites.nationalacademies.org/deps

Advises the government, private sector, and the public on technology, science, and public policy related to the design, construction, operations, maintenance, security, and evaluation of buildings, facilities, and infrastructure systems; the relationship between the constructed and natural environments and their interaction with human activities; the effects of natural and manmade hazards on constructed facilities and infrastructure; and the interdependencies of infrastructure systems, including power, water, transportation, telecommunications, wastewater, buildings.

Veterans Affairs Dept. (VA), *Construction and Facilities Management, 425 Eye St., N.W., 6th Floor, 20001 (mailing address: 810 Vermont Ave. N.W., MS 003C, Washington, DC 20420); (202) 632-4607. Stella S. Fiotes, Executive Director.*
General email, cfm@va.gov
Web, www.cfm.va.gov

Principal construction and real estate arm of the Veterans Administration. Manages all major VA construction and leasing projects.

▶ NONGOVERNMENTAL

American Public Works Assn., *Washington Office, 1275 K St. N.W., #750, 20005; (202) 408-9541. Fax, (202) 408-9542. Larry Frevatt, Executive Director, Acting; Andrea Eales, Director, Government Affairs.*
General email, apwa.dc@apwa.net
Web, www.apwa.net and Twitter, @APWATweets

Membership: engineers, architects, and others who maintain and manage public works facilities and services. Conducts research and education and promotes exchange of information on transportation and infrastructure-related issues. (Headquarters in Kansas City, Mo.)

American Subcontractors Assn., *1004 Duke St., Alexandria, VA 22314-3588; (703) 684-3450. Fax, (703) 836-3482. Colette Nelson, Chief Advocacy Officer.*
General email, asaoffice@asa-hq.com
Web, www.asaonline.com and Twitter, @ASAupdate

Membership: construction subcontractors, specialty contractors, and their suppliers. Addresses business, contract, and payment issues affecting all subcontractors. Interests include procurement laws, payment practices, and lien laws. Monitors legislation and regulations.

Associated Builders and Contractors, *440 1st St. N.W., #200, 20001; (202) 595-1505. Michael Bellaman, President.*
General email, gotquestion@abc.org
Web, www.abc.org and Twitter, @ABCNational

Membership: construction contractors engaged primarily in nonresidential construction, subcontractors, and suppliers. Sponsors apprenticeship, safety, and training programs. Provides labor relations information; compiles statistics. Monitors legislation and regulations.

Associated General Contractors of America, *2300 Wilson Blvd., #300, Arlington, VA 22201; (703) 548-3118. Fax, (703) 548-3119. Stephen E. Sandherr, Chief Executive Officer.*
General email, info@agc.org
Web, www.agc.org and Twitter, @AGCofA

Membership: general contractors engaged primarily in nonresidential construction; subcontractors; suppliers; accounting; insurance and bonding; and law firms. Conducts training programs, conferences, seminars, and market development activities for members. Produces position papers on construction issues. Monitors legislation and regulations.

Construction Management Assn. of America (CMAA), *7926 Jones Branch Dr., #800, McLean, VA 22102-3303; (703) 356-2622. Fax, (703) 356-6388. Bruce D'Agostino, President.*
General email, info@cmaanet.org
Web, www.cmaanet.org and Twitter, @CMAA_HQ

Promotes the development of construction management as a profession through publications, education, a certification program, and an information network. Serves as an advocate for construction management in the legislative, executive, and judicial branches of government.

Construction Specifications Institute (CSI), *110 S. Union St., #100, Alexandria, VA 22314; (800) 689-2900. Fax, (703) 236-4600. Mark Dorsey, Executive Director.*
General email, csi@csinet.org
Web, http://csinet.org and Twitter, @CSIConstruction

Membership: architects, engineers, contractors, and others in the construction industry. Promotes construction technology; publishes reference materials to help individuals prepare construction documents; sponsors certification programs for construction specifiers and manufacturing representatives.

Mechanical Contractors Assn. of America, *1385 Piccard Dr., Rockville, MD 20850; (301) 869-5800. Fax, (301) 990-9690. John R. Gentille, Chief Executive Officer.*
Web, www.mcaa.org

Membership: mechanical contractors and members of related professions. Seeks to improve building standards and codes. Provides information, publications, and training programs; conducts seminars and annual convention. Monitors legislation and regulations.

National Assn. of Home Builders (NAHB), *1201 15th St. N.W., 20005-2800; (202) 266-8200. Fax, (202) 266-8400. Gerald M. Howard, Chief Executive Officer. Press, (202) 266-8254. Toll-free, (800) 368-5242.*
General email, info@nahb.org
Web, www.nahb.org

Membership: contractors, builders, architects, engineers, mortgage lenders, and others interested in home building and residential real estate construction. Participates in updating and developing building codes and standards; offers technical information. Interests include policies to stimulate the housing market; and taxation, financing, environmental, and land-use policies. Monitors legislation and regulations.

National Assn. of Minority Contractors, *910 17th St. N.W., #413, 20006; (202) 296-1600. Fax, (202) 296-1644. Wendell Stemley, National President; Vacant, National Executive Director.*
General email, info@namcnational.org
Web, www.namcnational.org

Membership: minority businesses and related firms, women contractors, strategic alliances, and individuals serving those businesses in the construction industry. Advises members on commercial and government contracts; provides technical assistance and industry-specific training; provides bid information on government contracts. Monitors legislation and regulations. Advocates for legislative changes.

National Assn. of Plumbing-Heating-Cooling Contractors, *180 S. Washington St., #100, Falls Church, VA 22046; (703) 237-8100. Fax, (703) 237-7442. Michael Copp, Executive Vice President. Information, (800) 533-7694.*
General email, naphcc@naphcc.org
Web, www.phccweb.org

Provides education and training for plumbing, heating, and cooling contractors and their employees. Offers career information, internships, and scholarship programs for business and engineering students to encourage careers in the plumbing and mechanical contracting field.

National Electrical Contractors Assn., *3 Bethesda Metro Center, #1100, Bethesda, MD 20814; (301) 657-3110. Fax, (301) 215-4500. John M. Grau, Chief Executive Officer. Web, www.necanet.org, Twitter, @necanet and Facebook, www.facebook.com/NECANET*

Membership: electrical contractors who build and service electrical wiring and equipment, including high-voltage construction and service. Represents members in collective bargaining with union workers; sponsors research and educational programs.

National Utility Contractors Assn. (NUCA), *3925 Chain Bridge Rd., #300, Fairfax, VA 22030; (703) 358-9300. Fax, (703) 358-9307. Bill Hillman, Chief Executive Officer. General email, nuca@nuca.com*
Web, www.nuca.com

Membership: contractors who perform water, sewer, and other underground utility construction. Sponsors conferences; conducts surveys. Monitors public works legislation and regulations.

Sheet Metal and Air Conditioning Contractors' National Assn., *4201 Lafayette Center Dr., Chantilly, VA 20151-1219; Capitol Hill Office, 305 4th St. N.E., 20002; (703) 803-2980. Fax, (703) 803-3732. Vincent R. Sandusky, Chief Executive Officer. Capitol Hill, (202) 547-8202.*
General email, info@smacna.org
Web, www.smacna.org

Membership: unionized sheet metal and air conditioning contractors. Provides information on standards and installation and fabrication methods. Interests include energy efficiency and sustainability.

Society for Marketing Professional Services, *123 N. Pitt St., #400, Alexandria, VA 22314; (703) 549-6117. Fax, (703) 549-2498. Michael V. Geary, Chief Executive Officer, ext. 221. Information, (800) 292-7677.*
General email, info@smps.org
Web, www.smps.org

Membership: individuals who provide professional services to the building industry. Assists individuals who market design services in the areas of architecture, engineering, planning, interior design, landscape architecture, and construction management. Provides seminars, workshops, and publications for members. Maintains job banks.

Sustainable Buildings Industry Council, *1090 Vermont Ave. N.W., #700, 20005-4950; (202) 289-7800. Fax, (202) 289-1092. Ryan Colker, Director.*
General email, rcolker@nibs.org
Web, www.nibs.org/?page=sbic

Membership: building industry associations, corporations, small businesses, and independent professionals. Provides information on all aspects of sustainable design and construction: energy efficiency, renewable technologies, daylighting, healthy indoor environments, sustainable building materials and products, and resource conservation. (Affiliated with the National Institute of Building Sciences.)

U.S. Green Building Council, *2101 L St. N.W., #500, 20037; (202) 742-3792. Fax, (202) 828-5110. S. Richard Fedrizzi, Chief Executive Officer. Toll-free, (800) 795-1747.*
General email, LEEDinfo@usgbc.org
Web, www.usgbc.org

Promotes buildings that are environmentally responsible, profitable, and healthy. Rates green buildings in order to accelerate implementation of environmentally friendly design practices.

Architecture and Design

▶AGENCIES

General Services Administration (GSA), *Design and Construction, Office of the Chief Architect, 1800 F St. N.W., #3300, 20405-0001; (202) 501-1888. Fax, (202) 501-3393. Leslie Shepherd, Chief Architect, (202) 501-2289.*
General email, les.shepherd@gsa.gov
Web, www.gsa.gov/portal/content/104549

Administers the Art in Architecture Program, which commissions publicly scaled works of art for government buildings and landscapes, and the Fine Arts Program, which manages the GSA's collection of fine artwork that has been commissioned for use in government buildings. Administers the historic preservation of Historic Federal Buildings, and the Design Excellence Program, which reviews designs of Federal Buildings and courthouses.

▶NONGOVERNMENTAL

American Institute of Architects, *1735 New York Ave. N.W., 20006-5292; (202) 626-7300. Fax, (202) 626-7547. Robert Ivy, Chief Executive Officer. Press, (202) 626-7467. Toll-free, (800) 242-3837. Government Advocacy, (202) 626-7507.*
General email, infocentral@aia.org
Web, www.aia.org and Twitter, @AIANational

Membership: licensed American architects, interns, architecture faculty, engineers, planners, and those in government, manufacturing, or other fields in a capacity related to architecture. Works to advance the standards of architectural education, training, and practice. Promotes the aesthetic, scientific, and practical efficiency of architecture, urban design, and planning; monitors international developments. Offers continuing and professional education programs; sponsors scholarships, internships, and awards. Houses archival collection, including documents and drawings of American architects and architecture. Library open to the public by appointment. Monitors legislation and regulations.

American Society of Interior Designers, *718 7th St. N.W., 4th Floor, 20001; (202) 546-3480. Fax, (202) 546-3240. Randy Fiser, Chief Executive Officer.*
General email, asid@asid.org
Web, www.asid.org and Twitter, @asid

Offers certified professional development courses addressing the technical, professional, and business needs of designers; bestows annual scholarships, fellowships, and awards; supports licensing efforts at the state level.

American Society of Landscape Architects, *636 Eye St. N.W., 20001-3736; (202) 898-2444. Fax, (202) 898-1185.*

Nancy Somerville, Executive Vice President. Toll-free, (888) 999-2752.
General email, info@asla.org
Web, www.asla.org and Twitter, @landarchitects

Membership: professional landscape architects. Advises government agencies on land-use policy and environmental matters. Accredits university-level programs in landscape architecture; conducts professional education seminars for members.

AmericanHort, *Government Relations, 525 9th St. N.W., #800, 20004 (mailing address: 2130 Stella Court, Columbus, OH 43215); (202) 789-2900. Fax, (202) 789-1893. David Savoia, President, Acting.*
General email, hello@AmericanHort.org
Web, www.AmericanHort.org and Twitter, @American_Hort

Serves as an information clearinghouse on the technical aspects of nursery and landscape business and design.

Assn. of Collegiate Schools of Architecture, *1735 New York Ave. N.W., 3rd Floor, 20006; (202) 785-2324. Fax, (202) 628-0448. Michael J. Monti, Executive Director.*
General email, info@acsa-arch.org
Web, www.acsa-arch.org and Twitter, @ACSAUpdate

Membership: U.S. and Canadian institutions that offer at least one accredited architecture degree program. Conducts workshops and seminars for architecture school faculty; presents awards for student and faculty excellence in architecture; publishes a guide to architecture schools in North America.

Industrial Designers Society of America, *555 Grove St., #200, Herndon, VA 20170; (703) 707-6000. Fax, (703) 787-8501. Daniel Martinage, Executive Director.*
General email, idsa@idsa.org
Web, www.idsa.org

Membership: designers of products, equipment, instruments, furniture, transportation, packages, exhibits, information services, and related services, and educators of industrial design. Provides the Bureau of Labor Statistics with industry information. Monitors legislation and regulations.

Landscape Architecture Foundation, *1129 20th St. N.W., #202, 20036; (202) 331-7070. Fax, (202) 331-7079. Barbara Deutsch, Executive Director.*
General email, laf@lafoundation.org
Web, https://lafoundation.org, Twitter, @lafoundation and Facebook, www.facebook.com/Landscape.Architecture.Foundation

Conducts research and provides educational and scientific information on sustainable landscape architecture and development and related fields. Awards scholarships and fellowships.

National Architectural Accrediting Board Inc., *1101 Connecticut Ave. N.W., #410, 20036; (202) 783-2007. Fax, (202) 783-2822. Andrea S. Rutledge, Executive Director.*

General email, info@naab.org

Web, www.naab.org

Accredits Bachelor, Master, and Doctor of Architecture degree programs in the United States; assists organizations in other countries to develop accreditation standards.

National Assn. of Landscape Professionals, *950 Herndon Pkwy., #450, Herndon, VA 20170; (703) 736-9666. Fax, (703) 736-9668. Sabeena Hickman, Chief Executive Officer. Toll-free, (800) 395-2522.*
General email, info@landscapeprofessionals.org

Web, www.landscapeprofessionals.org

Membership: lawn care professionals, exterior maintenance contractors, installation/design/building professionals, and interiorscapers. Provides members with education, business management and marketing tools, and networking opportunities. Offers certification program. Focus is the green industry. Monitors legislation.

National Assn. of Schools of Art and Design, *11250 Roger Bacon Dr., #21, Reston, VA 20190-5248; (703) 437-0700. Fax, (703) 437-6312. Karen Moynahan, Executive Director.*
General email, info@arts-accredit.org

Web, http://nasad.arts-accredit.org

Specialized professional accrediting agency for postsecondary programs in art and design. Conducts and shares research and analysis on topics pertinent to art and design programs and fields of art and design. Offers professional development opportunities for executives of art and design programs.

National Council of Architectural Registration Boards (NCARB), *1801 K St. N.W., #700-K, 20006-1310; (202) 783-6500. Fax, (202) 783-0290. Michael J. Armstrong, Chief Executive Officer. Customer Service, (202) 879-0520.*
Web, www.ncarb.org

Membership: state architectural registration boards. Develops examinations used in the United States and its territories for licensing architects; certifies architects.

Codes, Standards, and Research

▶ **AGENCIES**

Access Board, *1331 F St. N.W., #1000, 20004-1111; (202) 272-0080. Fax, (202) 272-0081. David M. Capozzi, Executive Director, (202) 272-0010. Toll-free technical assistance, (800) 872-2253. TTY, (202) 272-0082. Toll-free TTY, (800) 993-2822.*
General email, info@access-board.gov

Web, www.access-board.gov

Develops and maintains accessibility requirements for buildings, transit vehicles, telecommunications equipment, medical diagnostic equipment, and electronic and information technology. Provides technical assistance and training on these guidelines and standards. Enforces access standards for federally funded facilities through the Architectural Barriers Act.

Energy Efficiency and Renewable Energy *(Energy Dept.),* **Building Technologies (BTP),** *1000 Independence Ave. S.W., MS EE-5B, 20585; (202) 586-9127. Fax, (202) 586-4617. Roland Risser, Director.*
Web, www.energy.gov/eere/buildings/building-technologies-office

Funds research to reduce commercial and residential building energy use. Programs include research and development, equipment standards and analysis, and technology validation and market introduction.

Environmental Protection Agency (EPA), *Air and Radiation, Radiation and Indoor Air, 1200 Pennsylvania Ave. N.W., #5426, MC 6608T, 20460; (202) 343-9320. Fax, (202) 564-1408. Mike P. Flynn, Director.*
Web, www2.epa.gov/aboutepa/about-office-air-and-radiation-oar#oria

Establishes standards for measuring radon. Develops model building codes for state and local governments. Provides states and building contractors with technical assistance and training on radon detection and mitigation. Oversees the Radiation and Indoor Environments Laboratory in Las Vegas, Nev. Administers the Clean Air Act.

Federal Housing Administration (FHA) *(Housing and Urban Development Dept.),* **Manufactured Housing Programs,** *451 7th St. S.W., #9102, 20410-8000; (202) 402-7112. Fax, (202) 708-4213. Pamela Danner, Administrator. Consumer complaints, (800) 927-2891.*
General email, mhs@hud.gov

Web, http://portal.hud.gov/hudportal/HUD?src=/program_offices/housing/rmra/mhs/mhshome

Establishes and maintains standards for selection of new materials and methods of construction; evaluates technical suitability of products and materials; develops uniform, preemptive, and mandatory national standards for manufactured housing; enforces standards through design review and quality control inspection of factories; administers a national consumer protection program. Handles dispute resolution.

Housing and Urban Development Dept. (HUD), *Lead Hazard Control and Healthy Homes, 451 7th St. S.W., #8236, 20410; (202) 708-0310. Fax, (202) 708-0014. Matthew Amon, Director.*
Web, http://portal.hud.gov/hudportal/HUD?src=/program_offices/healthy_homes

Advises HUD offices, other agencies, health authorities, and the housing industry on lead poisoning prevention. Develops regulations for lead-based paint; conducts research; makes grants to state and local governments for lead hazard reduction and inspection of housing.

National Institute of Building Sciences, *1090 Vermont Ave. N.W., #700, 20005-4950; (202) 289-7800. Fax, (202) 289-1092. Henry L. Green, President.*
General email, nibs@nibs.org

Web, www.nibs.org

Public-private partnership authorized by Congress to improve the regulation of building construction, facilitate the safe introduction of innovative building technology, and disseminate performance criteria and other technical information.

National Institute of Standards and Technology (NIST) *(Commerce Dept.), Engineering Laboratory, 100 Bureau Dr., MS 8600, Gaithersburg, MD 20899-8600; (301) 975-5900. Fax, (301) 975-4032. Howard H. Harary, Director.*
General email, el@nist.gov

Web, www.nist.gov/el

Performs analytical, laboratory, and field research in the area of building technology and its applications for building usefulness, safety, and economy; produces performance criteria and evaluation, test, and measurement methods for building owners, occupants, designers, manufacturers, builders, and federal, state, and local regulatory authorities. Researches architecture, materials construction, energy production and distribution, and manufacturing to develop recommendations for constructing buildings that maximize safety, withstand earthquakes and other natural disasters, and are energy efficient. Contributes standards and codes development; provides performance metrics, measurement and testing methods, and protocols; and evaluates systems and practices.

National Institute of Standards and Technology (NIST) *(Commerce Dept.), Public Affairs, 100 Bureau Dr., Stop 1070, Gaithersburg, MD 20899-1070; (301) 975-6478. Fax, (301) 926-1630. Gail Porter, Director. TTY, (800) 877-8339.*
General email, inquiries@nist.gov

Web, www.nist.gov

Provides services to support National Safety Construction Team Act investigations to assess building performance, emergency response, and evacuation procedures.

U.S. Fire Administration *(Federal Emergency Management Agency), 16825 S. Seton Ave., Emmitsburg, MD 21727-8998; (301) 447-1000. Fax, (301) 447-1270. Ernest Mitchell Jr., Administrator, (202) 646-4223. Press, (301) 447-1853.*
Web, www.usfa.fema.gov

Conducts research and collects, analyzes, and disseminates data on combustion, fire-prevention, firefighter safety, and the management of fire prevention organizations; studies and develops arson-prevention programs and fire-prevention codes; maintains the National Fire Incident Reporting System.

▶**NONGOVERNMENTAL**

American Society of Civil Engineers (ASCE), *1801 Alexander Bell Dr., Reston, VA 20191-4400; Washington Office, 101 Constitution Ave., #375E, 20001; (202) 789-7850. Fax, (202) 789-7859. Thomas W. Smith III, Executive Director. Toll-free, (800) 548-2723. Press, (703) 295-6406.*
Web, www.asce.org and Twitter, @ascetweets

Membership: professionals and students in civil engineering. Develops standards by consensus for construction documents and building codes, and standards for civil engineering education, licensure, and ethics. Organizes international conferences; maintains technical and

professional reference materials; hosts e-learning sites. Advocates improvements in public infrastructure; monitors legislation and regulations.

American Society of Heating, Refrigerating, and Air Conditioning Engineers (ASHRAE), *Government Affairs, 1828 L St. N.W., #810, 20036-5104; (202) 833-1830. Fax, (202) 833-0118. Vacant, Director; Mark Ames, Manager.*
General email, washdc@ashrae.org

Web, www.ashrae.org

Membership: engineers and others involved with the heating, ventilation, air conditioning, and refrigeration industry in the United States and abroad, including students. Sponsors research, meetings, and educational activities. Develops industry standards; publishes technical data. Monitors legislation and regulations.

Assn. of Pool and Spa Professionals, *2111 Eisenhower Ave., #500, Alexandria, VA 22314-4698; (703) 838-0083. Fax, (703) 549-0493. Rich Gottwald, President.*
General email, MemberServices@apsp.org

Web, www.apsp.org and Twitter, @TheAPSP

Membership: manufacturers, dealers and retailers, service companies, builders, and distributors of pools, spas, and hot tubs. Promotes the industry; provides educational programs for industry professionals; establishes standards for construction and safety. Monitors legislation and regulations.

Center for Auto Safety, *1825 Connecticut Ave. N.W., #330, 20009-5708; (202) 328-7700. Fax, (202) 387-0140. Clarence Ditlow, Executive Director.*
General email, accounts@autosafety.org

Web, www.autosafety.org

Monitors Federal Trade Commission warranty regulations and HUD implementation of federal safety and construction standards for manufactured mobile homes.

Home Innovation Research Labs, *400 Prince George's Blvd., Upper Marlboro, MD 20774; (301) 249-4000. Fax, (301) 430-6180. Michael Luzier, President. Toll-free, (800) 638-8556.*
Web, www.homeinnovation.com

Conducts contract research and product labeling and certification for U.S. industry, government, and trade associations related to home building and light commercial industrial building. Interests include energy conservation, new technologies, international research, public health issues, affordable housing, special needs housing for the elderly and persons with disabilities, building codes and standards, land development, and environmental issues. (Independent subsidiary of the National Assn. of Home Builders [NAHB].)

International Code Council, *500 New Jersey Ave. N.W., 6th Floor, 20001-2070; (202) 370-1800. Fax, (202) 783-2348. Dominic Sims, Chief Executive Officer. Toll-free, (888) 422-7233.*
General email, webmaster@iccsafe.org

Web, www.iccsafe.org

Membership association dedicated to building safety and sustainability. Develops codes used to construct residential and commercial buildings, including homes and schools. Offers "green" standards accreditation for businesses providing energy-efficient and sustainable infrastructure.

National Fire Protection Assn., *Government Affairs,* *1401 K St. N.W., #500, 20005; (202) 898-0222. Fax, (202) 898-0044. Gregory B. Cade, Government Affairs Division Director. Toll-free, (800) 344-3555.*
General email, wdc@nfpa.org
Web, www.nfpa.org, Twitter, @NFPA and Facebook, www.facebook.com/theNFPA

Membership: individuals and organizations interested in fire protection. Develops and updates fire protection codes and standards; sponsors technical assistance programs; collects fire data statistics. Monitors legislation and regulations. (Headquarters in Quincy, Mass.)

Materials and Labor

▶ **NONGOVERNMENTAL**

American Coatings Assn., *1500 Rhode Island Ave. N.W., 20005; (202) 462-6272. Fax, (202) 462-8549. J. Andrew Doyle, President, (202) 462-3932.*
General email, aca@paint.org
Web, www.paint.org

Membership: paint and coatings manufacturers, raw materials suppliers, distributors, and other industry professionals. Provides educational and public outreach programs for the industry; interests include health, safety, and the environment. Monitors legislation and regulations.

American Forest and Paper Assn., *Government Affairs,* *1101 K St. N.W., #700, 20005; (202) 463-2700. Fax, (202) 463-2471. Elizabeth Bartheld, Vice President, Government Affairs; Donna Harman, President.*
General email, info@afandpa.org
Web, www.afandpa.org

Membership: wood and specialty products manufacturers and those in related associations. Interests include tax, housing, environmental, international trade, natural resources, and land-use issues that affect the wood and paper products industry.

Architectural Woodwork Institute, *46179 Westlake Dr., #120, Potomac Falls, VA 20165-5874; (571) 323-3636. Fax, (571) 323-3630. Philip Duvic, Executive Vice President.*
General email, info@awinet.org
Web, www.awinet.org and Twitter, @ArchWoodworking

Membership: architectural woodworkers, suppliers, design professionals, and students. Promotes the use of architectural woodworking; establishes industry standards; conducts seminars and workshops.

Asphalt Roofing Manufacturers Assn., *529 14th St. N.W., #750, 20045; (202) 591-2450. Fax, (202) 591-2445. Reed Hitchcock, Executive Vice President.*
General email, info@asphaltroofing.org
Web, www.asphaltroofing.org

Membership: manufacturers of bitumen-based roofing products. Assists in developing local building codes and standards for asphalt roofing products. Provides technical information; supports research. Monitors legislation and regulations.

Assn. of the Wall and Ceiling Industries, *513 W. Broad St., #210, Falls Church, VA 22046-3257; (703) 538-1600. Fax, (703) 534-8307. Steven A. Etkin, Executive Vice President.*
Web, www.awci.org and Twitter, @AWCI_INFO

Membership: contractors and suppliers working in the wall and ceiling industries. Sponsors conferences and seminars. Monitors legislation and regulations.

The Brick Industry Assn., *1850 Centennial Park Dr., #301, Reston, VA 20191-1542; (703) 620-0010. Fax, (703) 620-3928. Raymond W. Leonhard, President, (703) 674-1537.*
General email, brickinfo@bia.org
Web, www.gobrick.com and Twitter, @BrickIndustry

Membership: manufacturers and distributors of clay brick. Provides technical expertise and assistance; promotes bricklaying vocational education programs; maintains collection of technical publications on brick masonry construction. Monitors legislation and regulations.

Building Systems Councils of the National Assn. of Home Builders, *1201 15th St. N.W., 7th Floor, 20005-2800; Fax, (202) 266-8141. John Lingerfelt, Director, (202) 266-8357. Toll-free, (800) 368-5242, ext. 8576.*
Web, www.nahb.org and Twitter, @NAHBhome

Membership: manufacturers and suppliers of home building products and services. Represents all segments of the industry. Assists in developing National Assn. of Home Builders policies regarding building codes, legislation, and government regulations affecting manufacturers of model-code-compliant, factory-built housing (includes concrete, log, modular, and panelized); sponsors educational programs; conducts plant tours of member operations.

Composite Panel Assn., *19465 Deerfield Ave., #306, Leesburg, VA 20176; (703) 724-1128. Fax, (703) 724-1588. Jackson Morrill, President.*
General email, admin@decorativesurfaces.org
Web, www.CompositePanel.com

Membership: manufacturers of particleboard, medium-density fiberboard, and hardboard engineered wood-siding/trim, and decorative surfaces in North America. Promotes use of these materials; conducts industry education; offers a certification program for recycled and low emitting products (Eco-Certified Composite [ECC] Sustainability and Certification Program). Monitors legislation and regulations.

Door and Hardware Institute, *14150 Newbrook Dr., #200, Chantilly, VA 20151-2232; (703) 222-2010. Fax, (703) 222-2410. Jerry S. Heppes, Chief Executive Officer.*
General email, info@dhi.org
Web, www.dhi.org

Membership: companies and individuals that manufacture or distribute doors and related fittings. Promotes the industry. Interests include building security, life safety and exit devices, and compliance with the Americans with Disabilities Act. Monitors legislation and regulations.

Gypsum Assn., *6525 Belcrest Rd., #480, Hyattsville, MD 20782; (301) 277-8686. Fax, (301) 277-8747. Stephen H. Meima, Executive Director.*
General email, info@gypsum.org
Web, www.gypsum.org

Membership: manufacturers of gypsum wallboard and plaster. Assists members, code officials, builders, designers, and others with technical problems and building code questions; publishes *Fire Resistance Design Manual* referenced by major building codes; conducts safety programs for member companies. Monitors legislation and regulations.

Hardwood Plywood and Veneer Assn., *1825 Michael Faraday Dr., Weston, VA 20190; (703) 435-2900. Fax, (703) 435-2537. Clifford (Kip) Howlett, President.*
General email, innovate@hpva.org
Web, www.hpva.org

Membership: manufacturers, distributors, wholesalers, suppliers, and sales agents of hardwood, plywood, veneer, and laminated wood floor. Disseminates business information; sponsors workshops and seminars; issues certifications; conducts research.

International Assn. of Bridge, Structural, Ornamental, and Reinforcing Iron Workers, *1750 New York Ave. N.W., #400, 20006; (202) 383-4800. Fax, (202) 638-4856. Eric Dean, President.*
General email, iwmagazine@iwintl.org
Web, www.ironworkers.org

Membership: approximately 140,000 iron workers. Helps members negotiate pay, benefits, and better working conditions; conducts training programs and workshops. Monitors legislation and regulations. (Affiliated with the AFL-CIO.)

International Assn. of Heat and Frost Insulators and Allied Workers, *9602 Martin Luther King Hwy., Lanham, MD 20706-1839; (301) 731-9101. Fax, (301) 731-5058. James McCourt, General President.*
General email, hfi@insulators.org
Web, www.insulators.org

Membership: approximately 18,000 workers in insulation industries. Helps members negotiate pay, benefits, and better working conditions; conducts training programs and workshops. Monitors legislation and regulations. (Affiliated with the AFL-CIO.)

International Brotherhood of Boilermakers, Iron Ship Builders, Blacksmiths, Forgers, and Helpers, *Government Affairs, 1750 New York Ave. N.W., #335, 20006; (202) 756-2868. Fax, (202) 756-2869. Bridget P. Martin, Director, Political Affairs; Cecile Conroy, Director, Government Affairs.*
General email, cconroy@boilermakers.org
Web, www.boilermakers.org

Membership: approximately 80,000 workers in construction, repair, maintenance, manufacturing, and related industries in the United States and Canada. Helps members negotiate pay, benefits, and better working conditions; conducts training programs and workshops. Monitors legislation and regulations. (Headquarters in Kansas City, Kans.; affiliated with the AFL-CIO.)

International Brotherhood of Electrical Workers (IBEW), *900 7th St. N.W., 20001; (202) 833-7000. Fax, (202) 728-7676. Lonnie Stephenson, President; Salvatore J. Chilia, Secretary-Treasurer.*
General email, webmaster@ibew.org
Web, www.ibew.org

Helps members negotiate pay, benefits, and better working conditions; conducts training programs and workshops. Monitors legislation and regulations. (Affiliated with the AFL-CIO.)

International Brotherhood of Teamsters, *25 Louisiana Ave. N.W., 20001-2198; (202) 624-6800. Fax, (202) 624-6918. James P. Hoffa, General President; Christy Bailey, Director, Federal Legislation and Regulation. Press, (202) 624-6911.*
General email, communications@teamster.org
Web, www.teamster.org

Membership: more than 1.4 million workers in the transportation and construction industries, factories, offices, hospitals, warehouses, and other workplaces. Helps members negotiate pay, benefits, and better working conditions; conducts training programs and workshops. Monitors legislation and regulations.

International Union of Bricklayers and Allied Craftworkers, *620 F St. N.W., 20004; (202) 783-3788. Fax, (202) 393-0219. James Boland, President. Toll-free, (888) 880-8222.*
General email, askbac@bacweb.org
Web, www.bacweb.org

Membership: bricklayers, stonemasons, and other skilled craftworkers in the building industry. Helps members negotiate pay, benefits, and better working conditions; conducts training programs and workshops. Monitors legislation and regulations. (Affiliated with the AFL-CIO and the International Masonry Institute.)

International Union of Operating Engineers, *1125 17th St. N.W., 20036; (202) 429-9100. Fax, (202) 778-2613. James T. Callahan, General President.*
Web, www.iuoe.org

Membership: approximately 400,000 operating engineers, including heavy equipment operators, mechanics, and surveyors in the construction industry, and stationary engineers, including operations and building maintenance staff. Represents members in negotiating pay, benefits, and better working conditions; conducts training programs and workshops. Monitors legislation and regulations. (Affiliated with the AFL-CIO.)

International Union of Painters and Allied Trades, 7234 Parkway Dr., Hanover, MD 21076; (410) 564-5900. Fax, (866) 656-4124. Kenneth Rigmaiden, General President.
General email, mail@iupat.org

Web, www.iupat.org

Membership: more than 140,000 painters, glaziers, floor covering installers, signmakers, show decorators, and workers in allied trades in the United States and Canada. Helps members negotiate pay, benefits, and better working conditions; conducts training programs and workshops. Monitors legislation and regulations. (Affiliated with the AFL-CIO.)

Kitchen Cabinet Manufacturers Assn., 1899 Preston White Dr., Reston, VA 20191-5435; (703) 264-1690. Fax, (703) 620-6530. C. Richard Titus, Executive Vice President.
General email, info@kcma.org

Web, www.kcma.org and Twitter, @KCMAorg

Represents cabinet manufacturers and suppliers to the industry. Provides government relations, management statistics, marketing information, and plant tours. Administers cabinet testing and certification programs.

National Concrete Masonry Assn., 13750 Sunrise Valley Dr., Herndon, VA 20171-4662; (703) 713-1900. Fax, (703) 713-1910. Robert D. Thomas, President.
General email, info@ncma.org

Web, www.ncma.org, Twitter, @ConcreteMasonry and Facebook, www.facebook.com/
NationalConcreteMasonryAssociation

Membership: producers of concrete masonry and suppliers of related goods and services. Conducts research; provides members with technical, marketing, government relations, and communications assistance.

National Glass Assn. (NGA), 1945 Old Gallows Rd., #750, Vienna, VA 22182; (703) 442-4890. Fax, (703) 442-0630. Nicole Harris, President. Toll-free, (866) 342-5642.
Web, www.glass.org and Twitter, @NatGlassAssoc

Membership: companies in the flat (architectural and automotive) glass industry. Provides education and training programs to promote quality workmanship, ethics, and safety standards in the architectural, automotive, and window and door glass industries. Acts as a clearinghouse for information and links professionals with job listings, suppliers, and technical support. Monitors legislation and regulations.

National Insulation Assn. (NIA), 12100 Sunset Hills Rd., #330, Reston, VA 20190-3233; (703) 464-6422. Fax, (703)

464-5896. Michele M. Jones, Executive Vice President, ext. 119.
General email, niainfo@insulation.org

Web, www.insulation.org

Membership: open-shop and union contractors, distributors, laminators, fabricators, and manufacturers that provide thermal insulation, insulation accessories, and components to the commercial, mechanical, and industrial markets. Provides information to members on industry trends and technologies, and offers service contacts for consumers. Monitors legislation and regulations.

National Lumber and Building Material Dealers Assn., 2025 M St. N.W., #800, 20036-3309; (202) 367-1169. Fax, (202) 367-2169. Jonathan M. Paine, President.
General email, info@dealer.org

Web, www.dealer.org

Membership: federated associations of retailers in the lumber and building material industries. Provides statistics training and networking opportunities to members. Monitors legislation and regulations.

North American Insulation Manufacturers Assn., 11 Canal Center Plaza, #103, Alexandria, VA 22314; (703) 684-0084. Fax, (703) 684-0427. Curt Rich, President.
General email, insulation@naima.org

Web, www.naima.org

Membership: manufacturers of insulation products for use in homes, commercial buildings, and industrial facilities. Provides information on the use of insulation for thermal efficiency, sound control, and fire safety; monitors research in the industry. Interests include energy efficiency and sustainability. Monitors legislation and regulations.

Operative Plasterers' and Cement Masons' International Assn. of the United States and Canada, 11720 Beltsville Dr., #700, Beltsville, MD 20705; (301) 623-1000. Fax, (301) 623-1032. Patrick D. Finley, President.
General email, opcmiaintl@opcmia.org

Web, www.opcmia.org

Membership: approximately 58,000 cement masons and plasterers. Helps members negotiate pay, benefits, and better working conditions; conducts training programs and workshops. Monitors legislation and regulations. (Affiliated with the AFL-CIO.)

Portland Cement Assn., 1150 Connecticut Ave. N.W., #500, 20036-4104; (202) 408-9494. Fax, (202) 408-0877. James G. Toscas, President.
Web, www.cement.org

Membership: producers of portland cement. Monitors legislation and regulations. (Headquarters in Skokie, Ill.)

Roof Coatings Manufacturers Assn., 529 14th St. N.W., #750, 20045; (202) 591-2452. Fax, (202) 591-2445. John Ferraro, Executive Director, (202) 207-0919.
General email, questions@roofcoatings.org

Web, www.roofcoatings.org

Membership: firms, partnerships, and corporations that manufacture or supply cold-applied protective roof coatings. Provides guidance on building codes and standards and technical developments. Affiliated with the Reflective Roof Coatings Institute.

Sheet Metal, Air, Rail, and Transportation Workers (SMART), *1750 New York Ave. N.W., 6th Floor, 20006; (202) 662-0880. Joseph Sellers Jr., General President. Toll-free, 800-662 0800.*
General email, info@smart-union.org
Web, http://smart-union.org

Membership: U.S., Puerto Rican, and Canadian workers in the building and construction trades, manufacturing, and the railroad and shipyard industries. Assists members with contract negotiation and grievances; conducts training programs and workshops. Monitors legislation and regulations. (Affiliated with the Sheet Metal and Air Conditioning Contractors' Assn., the AFL-CIO, and the Canadian Labour Congress.)

FIRE PREVENTION AND CONTROL

General

▶AGENCIES

Forest Service *(Agriculture Dept.), Fire and Aviation Management, 201 14th St. S.W., 3rd Floor, 3 Central, 20024 (mailing address: 1400 Independence Ave. S.W., MS 1107, Washington, DC 20250-0003); (202) 205-1483. Fax, (202) 205-1401. Tom Harbour, Director.*
Web, www.fs.fed.us/fire

Responsible for aviation and fire management programs, including fire control planning and prevention, suppression of fires, and the use of prescribed fires. Provides state foresters with financial and technical assistance for fire protection in forests and on rural lands.

Interior Dept. (DOI), *Wildland Fire, 1849 C St. N.W., MS 2660, 20240; (202) 208-7754. Jim Douglas, Director; Bryan Rice, Co-Director.*
Web, www.doi.gov/pmb/owf

Oversees all wildland fire management programs, policies, budgets, and information technology in order to manage risk to firefighters, communities, and landscapes.

National Institute of Standards and Technology (NIST) *(Commerce Dept.), Engineering Laboratory, 100 Bureau Dr., MS 8600, Gaithersburg, MD 20899-8600; (301) 975-5900. Fax, (301) 975-4032. Howard H. Harary, Director.*
General email, el@nist.gov
Web, www.nist.gov/el

Conducts basic and applied research on fire and fire resistance of construction materials; develops testing methods, standards, design concepts, and technologies for fire protection and prevention.

U.S. Fire Administration *(Federal Emergency Management Agency), 16825 S. Seton Ave., Emmitsburg, MD 21727-8998; (301) 447-1000. Fax, (301) 447-1270. Ernest Mitchell Jr., Administrator, (202) 646-4223. Press, (301) 447-1853.*
Web, www.usfa.fema.gov

Conducts research and collects, analyzes, and disseminates data on combustion, fire-prevention, firefighter safety, and the management of fire prevention organizations; studies and develops arson-prevention programs and fire-prevention codes; maintains the National Fire Incident Reporting System.

U.S. Fire Administration *(Federal Emergency Management Agency), National Fire Academy, 16825 S. Seton Ave., Emmitsburg, MD 21727-8998; (301) 447-1035. Fax, (301) 447-1441. Kirby Kiefer, Deputy Superintendent.*
General email, usfa-webmaster@fema.dhs.gov
Web, www.usfa.dhs.gov/training/nfa

Trains fire officials and related professionals in fire-prevention and management, current firefighting technologies, and the administration of fire prevention organizations.

▶NONGOVERNMENTAL

International Assn. of Fire Chiefs, *4025 Fair Ridge Dr., #300, Fairfax, VA 22033-2868; (703) 273-0911. Fax, (703) 273-9363. Mark Light, Executive Director.*
Web, www.iafc.org

Membership: fire service chiefs and chief officers. Conducts research on fire control; testifies before congressional committees. Monitors legislation and regulations affecting fire safety codes.

International Assn. of Fire Fighters, *1750 New York Ave. N.W., #300, 20006-5395; (202) 737-8484. Fax, (202) 737-8418. Harold A. Schaitberger, General President.*
General email, pr@iaff.org
Web, www.iaff.org

Membership: more than 298,000 professional firefighters and emergency medical personnel. Assists members with contract negotiation and grievances; conducts training programs and workshops. Monitors legislation and regulations. (Affiliated with the AFL-CIO and the Canadian Labour Congress.)

National Fire Protection Assn., *Government Affairs, 1401 K St. N.W., #500, 20005; (202) 898-0222. Fax, (202) 898-0044. Gregory B. Cade, Government Affairs Division Director. Toll-free, (800) 344-3555.*
General email, wdc@nfpa.org
Web, www.nfpa.org, Twitter, @NFPA and Facebook, www.facebook.com/theNFPA

Membership: individuals and organizations interested in fire protection. Develops and updates fire protection codes and standards; sponsors technical assistance programs; collects fire data statistics. Monitors legislation and regulations. (Headquarters in Quincy, Mass.)

HOUSING

General

▶ **AGENCIES**

Federal Housing Administration (FHA) *(Housing and Urban Development Dept.), Housing Assistance and Grant Administration,* 451 7th St. S.W., #6134, 20410-8000; (202) 708-3000. Fax, (202) 708-3104. *Catherine Brennan, Director. Web, http://portal.hud.gov/hudportal/HUD?src=/ program_offices/housing/mfh/hsgmfbus/abouthaga*

Directs and oversees the housing assistance and grant programs, including project-based Section 8 housing assistance, Section 202/811 capital advance and project rental assistance programs, the Assisted-Living Conversion Program (ALCP), rent supplements, service coordinator, and congregate housing services grant programs.

Federal Housing Administration (FHA) *(Housing and Urban Development Dept.), Housing Assistance Contract Administration Oversight,* 451 7th St. S.W., #6151, 20410-8000; (202) 708-2677. Fax, (202) 708-1300. *Kerry Hickman, Director; Lewis Suiter, Deputy Director. Web, http://portal.hud.gov/hudportal/HUD?src=/ program_offices/housing/mfh/hsgmfbus/abouthacao*

Administers Section 8 contracts and other rental subsidy programs. Ensures that Section 8 subsidized properties meet the department's goal of providing decent, safe, and sanitary housing to low income families.

Federal Housing Administration (FHA) *(Housing and Urban Development Dept.), Multifamily Housing,* 451 7th St. S.W., #6106, 20410; (202) 708-2495. Fax, (202) 708-2583. *Benjamin T. Metcalf, Deputy Assistant Secretary. Web, http://portal.hud.gov/hudportal/HUD?src=/ program_offices/housing/mfh/hsgmfbus/aboutdas*

Determines risk and administers programs associated with government-insured mortgage programs, architectural procedures, and land development programs for multifamily housing. Administers the Rural Rental Housing Program and the development of congregate housing facilities that provide affordable housing, adequate space for meals, and supportive services.

Federal Housing Administration (FHA) *(Housing and Urban Development Dept.), Single Family Housing,* 451 7th St. S.W., #9282, 20410; (202) 708-3175. Fax, (202) 708-2582. *Kathleen Zadareky, Deputy Assistant Secretary. Web, http://portal.hud.gov/hudportal/HUD?src=/ program_offices/housing/sfh*

Determines risk and administers programs associated with government-insured mortgage programs for single family housing. Administers requirements to obtain and maintain federal government approval of mortgages.

Housing and Urban Development Dept. (HUD), *Community Planning and Development, Block Grant Assistance, Entitlement Communities Division,* 451 7th St. S.W., #7282, 20410; (202) 708-1577. Fax, (202) 401-2044. *Steve Johnson, Director. Web, www.hud.gov*

Provides entitled cities and counties with block grants to provide housing, community, revitalization, and economic opportunity for low-income and moderate-income people.

Housing and Urban Development Dept. (HUD), *Community Planning and Development, Rural Housing and Economic Development,* 451 7th St. S.W., #7136, 20410; (202) 402-2290. Fax, (202) 708-7543. *Jackie Williams, Director. TTY, (202) 708-1455. Web, http://portal.hud.gov/hudportal/HUD?src=/ program_offices/comm_planning*

Promotes decent housing and economic opportunities for low-income and middle-income individuals; offers rental, homebuyer, and homeowner assistance and resources for homeless persons, youth, and veterans.

Housing and Urban Development Dept. (HUD), *Housing Office,* 451 7th St. S.W., #9100, 20410; (202) 708-2601. Fax, (202) 708-1403. *Edward Golding, Assistant Secretary. TTY, (202) 708-1455. Web, http://portal.hud.gov/hudportal/HUD?src=/ program_offices/housing*

Administers housing programs, including the production, financing, and management of housing; directs preservation and rehabilitation of the housing stock; manages regulatory programs.

Rural Development *(Agriculture Dept.), Rural Housing Service, Housing Programs,* 1400 Independence Ave. S.W., #5014, MS 0701, 20250-0701; (202) 690-1533. Fax, (202) 690-0500. *Tony Hernandez, Administrator. Web, www.rd.usda.gov/about-rd/agencies/rural-housing-service*

Makes loans and grants in rural communities (population under 20,000) to low-income borrowers, including the elderly and persons with disabilities, for buying, building, or improving single-family houses. Makes grants to communities for rehabilitating single-family homes.

▶ **CONGRESS**

For a listing of relevant congressional committees and subcommittees, please see page 420 or the Appendix.

▶ **NONGOVERNMENTAL**

Center for Housing Policy, 1900 M St. N.W., #200, 20036; (202) 466-2121. Fax, (202) 466-2122. *Chris Estes, President. General email, nhc@nhc.org Web, www.nhc.org and Twitter, @NHCandCenter*

Researches and develops fundamentals of housing policy. Seeks to create new policies that integrate housing into overall social and economic goals. Sponsors educational forums and publishes reports (available online). (Research affiliate of the National Housing Conference.)

Enterprise Community Partners, *70 Corporate Center, 11000 Broken Land Pkwy., #700, Columbia, MD 21044; (410) 964-1230. Fax, (410) 964-1376. Terry L. Ludwig, Chief Executive Officer. Toll-free, (800) 624-4298.*
Web, www.enterprisecommunity.org

Works with local groups to help provide decent, affordable housing for low-income individuals and families, including green affordable housing. Works to link public transit to affordable housing.

Habitat for Humanity International, *Government Relations and Advocacy, 1424 K St. N.W., #600, 20005-2429; (202) 628-9171. Fax, (202) 628-9169. Chris Vincent, Vice President, Advocacy and Government Relations.*
General email, advocacy@habitat.org
Web, www.habitat.org

Christian ministry that seeks to eliminate poverty housing. Helps people attain housing through home construction, rehabilitation and repairs, and increased access to improved shelter through programs. Offers housing support services that enable low-income families to make improvements on their homes. Works in more than 70 countries.

Housing Assistance Council, *1025 Vermont Ave. N.W., #606, 20005-3516; (202) 842-8600. Fax, (202) 347-3441. Moises Loza, Executive Director.*
General email, hac@ruralhome.org
Web, www.ruralhome.org

Operates in rural areas and in cities of fewer than 25,000 citizens. Advises low-income and minority groups seeking federal assistance for improving rural housing and community facilities; studies and makes recommendations for state and local housing policies; makes low-interest loans for housing programs for low-income and minority groups living in rural areas, including Native Americans and farm workers.

National Community Stabilization Trust (NCST), *910 17th St. N.W., #1030, 20006; (202) 223-3237. Robert Grossinger, President. Press, (214) 710-3411.*
General email, info@stabilizationtrust.org
Web, www.stabilizationtrust.com

Assists local housing providers in acquiring foreclosed properties from financial institutions to build new affordable living properties. Manages funds for community stabilization programs from public and private investors. Coordinates management and rehabilitation of foreclosed properties. Works with housing organizations to solve policy issues.

National Housing and Rehabilitation Assn., *1400 16th St. N.W., #420, 20036; (202) 939-1750. Fax, (202) 265-4435. Peter H. Bell, President, (202) 939-1741; Thom Amdur, Executive Director, (202) 939-1753. General email, info@housingonline.com*
Web, www.housingonline.com

Membership: historic rehabilitation businesses, development firms and organizations, and city, state, and local agencies concerned with affordable multifamily housing. Monitors government policies affecting multifamily development and rehabilitation.

National Housing Conference (NHC), *1900 M St. N.W., #200, 20036; (202) 466-2121. Chris Estes, President; Lisa Sturtevant, Vice President, Research; Ethan Handelman, Vice President, Policy and Advocacy. General email, info@nhc.org*
Web, www.nhc.org and Twitter, @NHCandCenter

Membership: state and local housing officials, community development specialists, builders, bankers, lawyers, civic leaders, tenants, architects and planners, labor and religious groups, and national housing and housing-related organizations. Mobilizes public support for community development and affordable housing programs; conducts educational sessions. Supports the Center for Housing Policy, NHC's research affiliate.

National Leased Housing Assn., *1900 L St. N.W., #300, 20036; (202) 785-8888. Fax, (202) 785-2008. Denise B. Muha, Executive Director.*
General email, info@hudnlha.com
Web, www.hudnlha.com

Membership: public and private organizations and individuals concerned with multifamily low and moderate income and government-assisted housing programs. Conducts training seminars. Monitors legislation and regulations.

National Low Income Housing Coalition, *1000 Vermont Ave., #500, 20005; (202) 662-1530. Fax, (202) 393-1973. Sheila Crowley, President, ext. 224.*
General email, info@nlihc.org
Web, www.nlihc.org

Membership: organizations and individuals that support low-income housing. Works to end the affordable housing crisis in America. Interests include the needs of the lowest-income people and those who are homeless. Monitors legislation.

Fair Housing, Special Groups

▶**AGENCIES**

Civil Rights Division *(Justice Dept.), 950 Pennsylvania Ave. N.W., #5643, 20530; (202) 514-4609. Fax, (202) 514-0293. Vanita Gupta, Assistant Attorney General, Acting, (202) 514-2151. Press, (202) 514-2007. TTY, (202) 514-0716. General email, complaint@usdoj.gov*
Web, www.justice.gov/crt and Twitter, @TheJusticeDept

Enforces federal civil rights laws prohibiting discrimination on the basis of race, color, religion, sex, disability, age, or national origin in housing, public accommodations and facilities, and credit and federally assisted programs.

Federal Housing Administration (FHA) *(Housing and Urban Development Dept.), Asset Management and Portfolio Oversight,* 451 7th St. S.W., #6162, 20410; (202) 402-2472. Fax, (202) 708-3104. Nancie-Ann Bodell, Director, Acting.
Web, http://portal.hud.gov/hudportal/HUD?src=/program_offices/housing/mfh/hsgmfbus/aboutam

Oversees HUD management, ownership, and sale of properties, which HUD owns by virtue of default and foreclosure or for which HUD is mortgagee-in-possession.

Housing and Urban Development Dept. (HUD), *Community Planning and Development, Housing Opportunities for Persons with AIDS Program,* 451 7th St. S.W., #7248, 20410; (202) 402-5374. Rita Flegel, Director.
General email, HOPWA@hud.gov
Web, www.hudexchange.info/programs/hopwa

Makes grants to local communities, states, and nonprofit organizations for projects that benefit low-income persons living with HIV/AIDS and their families.

Housing and Urban Development Dept. (HUD), *Fair Housing and Equal Opportunity,* 451 7th St. S.W., #5100, 20410-2000; (202) 708-4252. Fax, (202) 708-4483. Gustavo Velasquez, Assistant Secretary. Housing discrimination hotline, (800) 669-9777
Web, http://portal.hud.gov/hudportal/HUD?src=/program_offices/fair_housing_equal_opp

Monitors compliance with legislation requiring equal opportunities in housing for minorities, persons with disabilities, and families with children. Monitors compliance with construction codes to accommodate people with disabilities in multifamily dwellings. Hotline answers inquiries about housing discrimination.

Housing and Urban Development Dept. (HUD), *Fair Housing Initiative Programs,* 451 7th St. S.W., #5222, 20410; (202) 402-7095. Fax, (202) 708-4886. Myron P. Newry, Director.
Web, http://portal.hud.gov/hudportal/HUD?src=/program_offices/fair_housing_equal_opp/12fhiphome

Awards grants to public and private organizations and to state and local agencies. Funds projects that educate the public about fair housing rights; investigates housing discrimination complaints. Programs are designed to prevent or eliminate discriminatory housing practices.

Public and Indian Housing *(Housing and Urban Development Dept.), Native American Programs,* 451 7th St. S.W., #4126, 20410-5000; (202) 401-7914. Fax, (202) 401-7909. Rodger J. Boyd, Deputy Assistant Secretary, (202) 402-4141.
Web, http://portal.hud.gov/hudportal/HUD?src=/program_offices/public_indian_housing/ih

Administers federal assistance for Native American tribes. Assistance programs focus on housing and community and economic development through competitive and formula grants. Funds for approved activities are provided directly to tribes or Alaska Native villages or to a tribally designated housing authority.

Rural Development *(Agriculture Dept.), Civil Rights,* 1400 Independence Ave. S.W., #1341, MS 0703, 20250-0703; (202) 692-0252. Fax, (202) 692-0279. Angilla Denton, Director. Toll-free, (800) 787-8821.
General email, rd.civilrights@wdc.usda.gov
Web, www.rd.usda.gov/about-rd/offices/civil-rights

Processes Equal Employment Opportunity complaints for Rural Development employees, former employees, and applicants. Enforces compliance with the Equal Credit Opportunity Act, which prohibits discrimination on the basis of sex, marital status, race, color, religion, disability, or age in rural housing, utilities, and business programs. Provides civil rights training to Rural Development's national, state, and field staffs.

▶**NONGOVERNMENTAL**

American Seniors Housing Assn., 5225 Wisconsin Ave. N.W., #502, 20015; (202) 237-0900. Fax, (202) 237-1616. General email, info@seniorshousing.org
Web, www.seniorshousing.org

Membership: development, finance, and operation professionals working in seniors apartments, independent and assisted living communities, and retirement communities. Promotes the advancement of quality seniors housing and health care through research, education, and monitoring legislation and regulations.

B'nai B'rith International, *Center for Senior Services,* 1120 20th St. N.W., #300N, 20036; (202) 857-6535. Fax, (202) 857-6531. Mark D. Olshan, Director. Toll-free, (866) 999-6596.
General email, seniors@bnaibrith.org
Web, www.bnaibrith.org

Acts as an advocate on behalf of the aging population in America. Works with local groups to sponsor federally assisted housing for independent low-income senior citizens and persons with disabilities, regardless of race or religion.

Leading Age, 2519 Connecticut Ave. N.W., 20008-1520; (202) 783-2242. Fax, (202) 783-2255. Katie Smith Sloan, Chief Executive Officer.
General email, info@leadingage.org
Web, www.leadingage.org

Membership: nonprofit nursing homes, housing, and health-related facilities for the elderly. Provides research and technical assistance for providers of long-term care for the elderly. Monitors legislation and regulations.

National American Indian Housing Council, 900 2nd St. N.E., #107, 20002; (202) 789-1754. Fax, (202) 789-1758. Pamela M. Silas, Executive Director. Toll-free, (800) 284-9165.
General email, info@naihc.net
Web, www.naihc.net

Membership: Native American housing authorities. Clearinghouse for information on Native American housing issues; works for safe and sanitary dwellings for Native American and Alaska Native communities; monitors policies of the Housing and Urban Development Dept. and housing legislation; provides members with training and technical assistance in managing housing assistance programs.

National Assn. for the Advancement of Colored People (NAACP), *Washington Bureau, 1156 15th St. N.W., #915, 20005; (202) 463-2940. Fax, (202) 463-2953.*
Hilary O. Shelton, Director.
General email, washingtonbureau@naacpnet.org
Web, www.naacp.org

Membership: persons interested in civil rights for all minorities. Works to eliminate discrimination in housing and urban affairs. Supports programs that make affordable rental housing available to minorities and that maintain African American ownership of land. (Headquarters in Baltimore, Md.)

National Assn. of Real Estate Brokers, *9831 Greenbelt Rd., #309, Lanham, MD 20706; (301) 552-9340. Fax, (301) 552-9216. Ronald Cooper, President; Michelle Savoy, Office Manager.*
General email, info@nareb.com
Web, www.nareb.com

Membership: minority real estate brokers, appraisers, contractors, property managers, and salespersons. Works to prevent discrimination in housing policies and practices; conducts seminars on contracting and federal policy.

National Caucus and Center on Black Aging, Inc., *1220 L St. N.W., #800, 20005-2407; (202) 637-8400. Fax, (202) 347-0895. Karyne Jones, President.*
General email, support@ncba-aged.org
Web, www.ncba-aged.org

Concerned with issues that affect older Black Americans and other minorities. Sponsors employment and housing programs for older adults and education and training for professionals in gerontology. Monitors legislation and regulations.

National Council of La Raza, *1126 16th St. N.W., #600, 20036-4845; (202) 785-1670. Fax, (202) 776-1792. Janet Murguía, President.*
General email, info@nclr.org
Web, www.nclr.org, Twitter, @NCLR and Facebook, www.facebook.com/Nationalcounciloflaraza

Helps Hispanic community-based groups obtain funds, develop and build low-income housing and community facilities, and develop and finance community economic development projects; conducts research and provides policy analysis on the housing status and needs of Hispanics; monitors legislation on fair housing and government funding for low-income housing.

National Council on Aging, *251 18th St. South, #500, Arlington, VA 22202; (571) 527-3900. Fax, (571) 527-3901. James P. Firman, President. Press, (571) 527-3914. Eldercare locator, (800) 677-1116.*
General email, info@ncoa.org
Web, www.ncoa.org, Twitter, @NCOAging and Facebook, www.facebook.com/NCOAging

Serves as an information clearinghouse on aging. Works to ensure quality housing for older persons. Monitors legislation and regulations.

National Fair Housing Training Academy, *600 Maryland Ave. S.W., #027, 20024; (202) 314-3422. Patricia Roberts Harris, Director.*
General email, Support@nfhta.org
Web, www.nfhta.org

Provides fair housing and civil rights training and education to federal, state, and local agencies, educators, attorneys, advocates, and other fair housing professionals. (Sponsored and funded by the Housing and Urban Development Dept.)

National Multifamily Housing Council, *1850 M St. N.W., #540, 20036-5803; (202) 974-2300. Fax, (202) 775-0112. Douglas Bibby, President.*
General email, info@nmhc.org
Web, www.nmhc.org

Membership: owners, financiers, managers, and developers of multifamily housing. Serves as a clearinghouse on rent control, condominium conversion, taxes, fair housing, and environmental issues.

National Rural Housing Coalition, *1331 G St. N.W., 10th Floor, 20005; (202) 393-5229. Fax, (202) 393-3034. Robert A. Rapoza, Executive Secretary.*
General email, nrhc@ruralhousingcoalitions.org
Web, www.ruralhousingcoalition.org

Advocates improved housing for low-income rural families; works to increase public awareness of rural housing problems; administers the Self-Help Housing Fund, Farm Worker Housing Fund, Rural Community Assistance Fund, and HUD Task Force. Monitors legislation and regulations.

Public and Subsidized Housing

▶**AGENCIES**

Public and Indian Housing *(Housing and Urban Development Dept.), 451 7th St. S.W., #4100, 20410-0800; (202) 708-0950. Fax, (202) 619-8478. Lourdes Castro Ramirez, Principal Deputy Assistant Secretary.*
General email, daniella.d.mungo@hud.gov
Web, http://portal.hud.gov/hudportal/HUD?src=/program_offices/public_indian_housing

Seeks to ensure that safe, decent, and affordable housing is available to low-income and Native American families, the elderly, and persons with disabilities.

Public and Indian Housing *(Housing and Urban Development Dept.), Housing Voucher Management and Operations, 451 7th St. S.W., #4208, 20410; (202) 708-0477. Fax, (202) 708-0690. Milan M. Ozdinec, Deputy Assistant Secretary, (202) 708-1380.*
Web, http://portal.hud.gov/hudportal/HUD?src=/program_offices/public_indian_housing

Administers certificate and housing voucher programs and moderate rehabilitation authorized by Section 8 of the Housing Act of 1937, as amended. Provides rental subsidies to lower-income families.

Public and Indian Housing *(Housing and Urban Development Dept.), Public Housing and Voucher Programs,* 451 7th St. S.W., #4130, 20410-5000; (202) 708-2815. Fax, (202) 708-0690. Milan M. Ozdinec, Deputy Assistant Secretary. Section 8, (202) 708-0477. Information Service, (202) 708-0744.
Web, http://portal.hud.gov/hudportal/HUD?src=/program_offices/public_indian_housing

Establishes policies and procedures for low-income public housing and rental assistance programs, including special needs for the elderly and disabled, standards for rental and occupancy, utilities and maintenance engineering, and financial management.

Public and Indian Housing *(Housing and Urban Development Dept.), Public Housing Investments,* 451 7th St. S.W., #4130, 20410-0050; (202) 401-8812. Fax, (202) 401-2370. Dominique Blom, Deputy Assistant Secretary.
Web, http://portal.hud.gov/hudportal/HUD?src=/program_offices/public_indian_housing

Establishes development policies and procedures for low-income housing programs, including criteria for site approval and construction standards; oversees administration of the Capital Fund for modernizing existing public housing, the Choice Neighborhood Program, and the Moving to Work demonstration program for public housing authorities. Administers the HOPE VI Program and manages the Special Applications Center.

►NONGOVERNMENTAL

Council of Large Public Housing Authorities, 455 Massachusetts Ave. N.W., #425, 20001; (202) 638-1300. Fax, (202) 638-2364. Sunia Zaterman, Executive Director. General email, clpha@clpha.org
Web, www.clpha.org

Works to preserve and improve public housing through advocacy, research, policy analysis, and public education.

Public Housing Authorities Directors Assn., 511 Capitol Court N.E., #200, 20002-4937; (202) 546-5445. Fax, (202) 546-2280. Timothy G. Kaiser, Executive Director.
Web, www.phada.org

Membership: executive directors of public housing authorities. Serves as liaison between members and the Housing and Urban Development Dept. and Congress; conducts educational seminars and conferences. Monitors legislation and regulations.

Urban Institute, *Center for Metropolitan Housing and Communities Policy,* 2100 M St. N.W., 20037; (202) 833-7200. Fax, (202) 872-8154. Rolf Pendall, Director.
Web, www.urban.org/center/met

Research center that deals with urban problems. Researches housing policy problems, including housing management, public housing programs, finance, and rent control.

REAL ESTATE

General

►AGENCIES

Federal Emergency Management Agency (FEMA) *(Homeland Security Dept.), Federal Insurance and Mitigation Administration,* 1800 S. Bell St., MS 3020, Arlington, VA 22202; (202) 646-2781. Fax, (202) 646-7970. Vacant, Associate Administrator.
Web, www.fema.gov/what-mitigation/federal-insurance-mitigation-administration

Administers federal flood insurance programs, including the National Flood Insurance Program. Makes low-cost flood insurance available to eligible homeowners.

Federal Highway Administration (FHWA) *(Transportation Dept.), Planning, Environment, and Realty,* 1200 New Jersey Ave. S.E., #E76-306, 20590; (202) 366-0116. Fax, (202) 366-3713. Gloria M. Shepherd, Associate Administrator.
Web, www.fhwa.dot.gov/real_estate

Works with developers and municipalities to ensure conformity with the National Environmental Policy Act (NEPA) project development process.

General Services Administration (GSA), *Public Buildings Services,* 1800 F St. N.W., #6459, 20405; (202) 501-1100. Norman Dong, Commissioner.
Web, www.gsa.gov/pbs

Administers the acquisition, construction, maintenance, and operation of buildings owned or leased by the federal government. Manages and disposes of federal real estate.

Housing and Urban Development Dept. (HUD), *Community Planning and Development, Affordable Housing Programs,* 451 7th St. S.W., #7164, 20410; (202) 708-2684. Fax, (202) 708-1744. Virginia Sardone, Director, Acting.
Web, www.hud.gov/hudportal/HUD?src=/program_offices/comm_planning/affordablehousing

HOME program helps to expand the supply of decent, affordable housing for low- and very-low-income families by providing grants to states and local governments to help renters, new home buyers, or existing homeowners. SHOP program provides funds for nonprofit organizations to purchase home sites and develop or improve the infrastructure needed to facilitate sweat equity and volunteer-based homeownership programs for low-income families.

►CONGRESS

For a listing of relevant congressional committees and subcommittees, please see page 420 or the Appendix.

►NONGOVERNMENTAL

American Land Title Assn., 1800 M St. N.W., #300S, 20036; (202) 296-3671. Fax, (202) 223-5843. Michelle L. Korsmo, Chief Executive Officer. Toll-free, (800) 787-2582.

General email, service@alta.org

Web, www.alta.org and Twitter, @ALTAonline

Membership: land title insurance underwriting companies, abstracters, lawyers, and title insurance agents. Searches, reviews, and insures land titles to protect real estate investors, including home buyers and mortgage lenders; provides industry information. Monitors legislation and regulations.

American Resort Development Assn., *1201 15th St. N.W., #400, 20005; (202) 371-6700. Fax, (202) 289-8544. Howard Nusbaum, President.*

Web, www.arda.org

Membership: U.S. and international developers, builders, financiers, marketing companies, and others involved in resort, recreational, and community development. Serves as an information clearinghouse; monitors federal and state legislation.

American Society of Appraisers (ASA), *11107 Sunset Hills Rd., #310, Reston, VA 20190; (703) 478-2228. Fax, (703) 742-8471. Jim Hirt, Chief Executive Officer, (703) 733-2112. Toll-free, (800) 272-8258.*

General email, asainfo@appraisers.org

Web, www.appraisers.org and Twitter, @ASAappraisers

Membership: accredited appraisers of real property, including land, houses, and commercial buildings; business valuation; machinery and technical specialties; yachts; aircraft; public utilities; personal property, including antiques, fine art, residential contents; gems and jewelry. Affiliate members include students and professionals interested in appraising. Provides technical information; accredits appraisers; provides consumer information programs.

Appraisal Foundation, *1155 15th St. N.W., #1111, 20005; (202) 347-7722. Fax, (202) 347-7727. David S. Bunton, President.*

General email, info@appraisalfoundation.org

Web, www.appraisalfoundation.org and Twitter, @uspap

Ensures that appraisers are qualified to offer their services by promoting uniform appraisal standards and establishing education, experience, and examination requirements.

Appraisal Institute, *Government Relations, 440 1st St. N.W., #880, 20001; (202) 298-6449. Fax, (202) 298-5547. William (Bill) Garber, Director of Government and External Relations.*

General email, insidethebeltway@appraisalinstitute.org

Web, www.appraisalinstitute.org

Provides Congress, regulatory agencies, and the executive branch with information on appraisal matters. (Headquarters in Chicago, Ill.)

Assn. of Foreign Investors in Real Estate, *1300 Pennsylvania Ave. N.W., 20004-3020; (202) 312-1400. Fax, (202) 312-1401. James A. Fetgatter, Chief Executive.*

General email, afireinfo@afire.org

Web, www.afire.org

Represents foreign institutions that are interested in the laws, regulations, and economic trends affecting the U.S. real estate market. Informs the public and the government of the contributions foreign investment makes to the U.S. economy. Examines current issues and organizes seminars for members.

International Real Estate Federation (FIABCI), *U.S. Chapter, 1050 Connecticut Ave. N.W., #500, 20036; (202) 772-3308. Bill Endsley, President.*

General email, info@fiabci-usa.com

Web, www.fiabci.com

Membership: real estate professionals in the fields of appraisal, brokerage, counseling, development, financing, and property management. Sponsors seminars, workshops, and conferences. (International headquarters in Paris.)

Manufactured Housing Institute, *1655 N. Ft. Meyer Dr., #104, Arlington, VA 22209; (703) 558-0400. Fax, (703) 558-0401. Richard A. Jennison, President.*

General email, info@mfghome.org

Web, www.manufacturedhousing.org

Represents community owners and developers, financial lenders, and builders, suppliers, and retailers of manufactured and modular homes. Provides information on manufactured and modular home construction standards, finance, site development, property management, and marketing.

National Assn. of Home Builders (NAHB), *1201 15th St. N.W., 20005-2800; (202) 266-8200. Fax, (202) 266-8400. Gerald M. Howard, Chief Executive Officer. Press, (202) 266-8254. Toll-free, (800) 368-5242.*

General email, info@nahb.org

Web, www.nahb.org

Membership: contractors, builders, architects, engineers, mortgage lenders, and others interested in home building and residential real estate construction. Offers educational programs and information on housing policy and mortgage finance in the United States.

National Assn. of Real Estate Brokers, *9831 Greenbelt Rd., #309, Lanham, MD 20706; (301) 552-9340. Fax, (301) 552-9216. Ronald Cooper, President; Michelle Savoy, Office Manager.*

General email, info@nareb.com

Web, www.nareb.com

Membership: minority real estate brokers, appraisers, contractors, property managers, and salespersons. Works to prevent discrimination in housing policies and practices; conducts seminars on contracting and federal policy.

National Assn. of Real Estate Investment Trusts, *1875 Eye St. N.W., #600, 20006-5413; (202) 739-9400. Fax, (202) 739-9401. Steven Wechsler, President. Toll-free, (800) 362-7348.*

Web, www.reit.com

Membership: real estate investment trusts and corporations, partnerships, and individuals interested in real estate securities and the industry. Interests include federal

Federal Housing Finance Agency

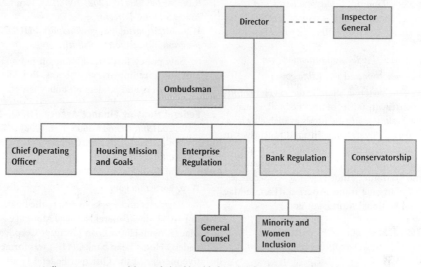

- - - - - Indicates a support or advisory relationship with the unit rather than a direct reporting relationship

taxation, securities regulation, financial standards and reporting standards and ethics, and housing and education, compiles industry statistics. Monitors federal and state legislation and regulations.

National Assn. of Realtors, *Government Affairs, 500 New Jersey Ave. N.W., 11th Floor, 20001-2020; (202) 383-1000. Fax, (202) 383-7580. Jerry Giovaniello, Senior Vice President. Toll-free, (800) 874-6500.*
Web, www.realtor.org

Sets professional standards, trademark regulations, and code of ethics for the real estate business; promotes education, research, and exchange of information. Interests include housing markets, property rights, and federal housing finance and insurance programs and agencies. Monitors legislation and regulations. (Headquarters in Chicago, Ill.)

The Real Estate Roundtable, *801 Pennsylvania Ave. N.W., #720, 20004; (202) 639-8400. Fax, (202) 639-8442. Jeffrey D. DeBoer, President.*
General email, info@rer.org
Web, www.rer.org

Membership: real estate owners, advisers, builders, investors, lenders, and managers. Serves as forum for public policy issues, including taxes, energy, homeland security, the environment, capital, credit, and investments.

Society of Industrial and Office Realtors, *1201 New York Ave., #350, 20005-6126; (202) 449-8200. Fax, (202) 216-9325. Richard Hollander, Executive Vice President, (202) 449 8202.*
General email, admin@sior.com
Web, www.sior.com

Membership: commercial and industrial real estate brokers worldwide. Certifies brokers; sponsors seminars and conferences; mediates and arbitrates business disputes for members; sponsors a speakers bureau. (Affiliated with the National Assn. of Realtors.)

Mortgages and Finance

▶AGENCIES

Comptroller of the Currency *(Treasury Dept.),* **Chief Counsel,** *Constitution Center, 400 7th St. S.W., 20506; (202) 649-5400. Fax, (202) 649-6077. Amy S. Friend, Senior Deputy Comptroller and Chief Counsel.*
Web, www.occ.gov

Enforces and oversees compliance by nationally chartered banks with laws prohibiting discrimination in credit transactions on the basis of sex or marital status. Enforces regulations concerning bank advertising; may issue cease-and-desist orders.

Consumer Financial Protection Bureau (CFPB), *1275 1st St. N.E., 20002; (202) 435-7000. Fax, (855) 237-2392. Richard Cordray, Director. Toll-free, (855) 411-2372. RESPA enquiries, (855) 411-2372. TTY, (855) 729-2372.*
General email, info@consumerfinance.gov
RESPA email, cfpb_respaenquiries@consumerfinance.gov
Web, www.consumerfinance.gov and Twitter, @cfpb

Responsible for helping home buyers become better shoppers for settlement services and eliminating kickbacks and referral fees that unnecessarily increase the costs of certain settlement services. Administers mortgage regulations including the Ability-to-Repay/Qualified Mortgage rule, which prohibits certain predatory lending practices and requires mortgage creditors to make a reasonable and good-faith effort to verify a borrower's ability to repay a loan.

Fannie Mae *(Federal Housing Finance Agency),* 3900 Wisconsin Ave. N.W., 20016-2892; (202) 752-7000. Fax, (240) 699-3893. Timothy J. Mayopoulos, Chief Executive Officer. Information for consumers, (800) 732-6643. Mortgage Help Network, (800) 732-6643. Press, (202) 752-7351.
General email, andrew_j_wilson@fanniemae.com
Web, www.fanniemae.com and www.fhfa.gov

Congressionally chartered, shareholder-owned corporation under conservatorship of the Federal Housing Finance Agency. Makes mortgage funds available by buying conventional and government-insured mortgages in the secondary mortgage market; raises capital through sale of short-term and long-term obligations, mortgages, and stock; issues and guarantees mortgage-backed securities; administers the mortgage fraud program. (Fannie Mae stands for Federal National Mortgage Assn.)

Farmer Mac, 1999 K St. N.W., 4th Floor, 20036; (202) 872-7700. Fax, (800) 999-1814. Timothy Buzby, President. Toll-free, (800) 879-3276.
Web, www.farmermac.com

Private corporation chartered by Congress to provide a secondary mortgage market for farm and rural housing loans. Guarantees principal and interest repayment on securities backed by farm and rural housing loans. (Farmer Mac stands for Federal Agricultural Mortgage Corp.)

Federal Housing Administration (FHA) *(Housing and Urban Development Dept.),* 451 7th St. S.W., #9100, 20410; (202) 708-2601. Fax, (202) 708-1624. Vacant, Assistant Secretary for Housing.
Web, http://portal.hud.gov/hudportal/HUD?src=/program_offices/housing/fhahistory

Provides mortage insurance on loans made by approved lenders for single and multifamily homes and hospitals.

Federal Housing Administration (FHA) *(Housing and Urban Development Dept.),* *Multifamily Housing Production,* 451 7th St. S.W., #6136, 20410-8000; (202) 708-1142. Fax, (202) 708-3104. Theodore K. Toon, Director. TTY, (202) 708-1455.
Web, http://portal.hud.gov/hudportal/HUD?src=/program_offices/housing/mfh/hsgmfbus/aboutmfd

Establishes procedures for the origination of FHA-insured mortgages for multifamily housing. Administers the mortgage insurance programs for rental, cooperative, and condominium housing, nursing homes, and assisted living systems.

Federal Housing Administration (FHA) *(Housing and Urban Development Dept.),* *Single Family Program Development,* 451 7th St. S.W., #9278, 20410-8000; (202) 708-2121. Fax, (202) 708-4308. Elissa Saunders, Director.
Web, http://portal.hud.gov/hudportal/HUD?src=/program_offices/housing/sfh

Establishes procedures for mortgage insurance programs related to the purchase or rehabilitation of single family homes.

Federal Housing Administration (FHA) *(Housing and Urban Development Dept.),* *Title I Insurance,* 451 7th St. S.W., #9266, 20410; (202) 708-2121. Fax, (202) 708-4308. Kevin Stevens, Director.
Web, http://portal.hud.gov/hudportal/HUD?src=/program_offices/housing/sfh/title

Sets policy for Title I loans on manufactured home and property improvement loans. Provides information to borrowers and lenders on policy issues.

Federal Housing Finance Agency (FHFA), 400 7th St. S.W., 20219; (202) 649-3800. Fax, (202) 649-1071. Melvin L. Watt, Director. Ombudsman, (888) 665-1474. Media, (202) 649-3700.
General email, fhfainfo@fhfa.gov
Web, www.fhfa.gov

Regulates and works to ensure the financial soundness of Fannie Mae (Federal National Mortgage Assn.), Freddie Mac (Federal Home Loan Mortgage Corp.), and the eleven Federal Home Loan banks. FHFA was formed by a legislative merger of the Office of Federal Housing Enterprise Oversight (OFHEO), the Federal Housing Finance Board, and HUD's Government-sponsored Enterprise (GSE) mission team.

Federal Housing Finance Agency (FHFA), *Enterprise Regulation,* 400 7th St. S.W., 20219; (202) 649-3809. Fax, (202) 777-1206. Nina Nichols, Deputy Director.
General email, DeputyDirector-Enterprises@FHFA.gov
Web, www.fhfa.gov

Responsible for ensuring that Fannie Mae and Freddie Mac are adequately capitalized and operate in a safe and sound manner. Supervision includes programs for accounting and disclosure, capital adequacy, examination, financial analysis, and supervision infrastructure.

Federal Housing Finance Agency (FHFA), *Federal Home Loan Bank Regulation (FHLBank Regulation),* 400 7th St. S.W., 20219; (202) 649-3808. Fax, (202) 649-3500. Fred C. Graham, Deputy Director.
General email, DeputyDirector-FHLBanks@FHFA.gov
Web, www.fhfa.gov

Responsible for ensuring that the Federal Home Loan Banks operate in a fiscally sound manner, have adequate capital, and are able to raise funds in capital markets. Conducts safety and soundness examinations, Affordable Housing Program examinations, examination and supervisory policy and program development, FHLBank analysis, risk modeling, risk monitoring and information management, and risk analysis and research.

Freddie Mac *(Federal Housing Finance Agency),* 8200 Jones Branch Dr., McLean, VA 22102-3110; (703) 903-2000. Fax, (703) 903-3495. Donald H. Layton, Chief Executive Officer. Press, (703) 903-3933. Toll-free, (800) 424-5401. Homeowners hotline, (800) 373-3343.
Web, www.freddiemac.com and www.fhfa.gov

Chartered by Congress to support homeownership and rental housing by increasing the flow of funds for residential mortgages and mortgage-related securities.

Resources for Mortgage Financing and Other Housing Assistance

The following agencies and organizations offer consumer information pertaining to mortgages and other housing issues.

Center for Responsible Lending, Washington, DC, office, (202) 349-1850; www.responsiblelending.org

Center on Budget and Policy Priorities, (202) 408-1080; www.cbpp.org

Consumer Federation of America, (202) 387-6121; www.consumerfed.org

Council for Affordable and Rural Housing, (703) 837-9001; www.carh.org

Fannie Mae, (202) 752-7000; www.fanniemae.com

Freddie Mac, (703) 903-2000; www.freddiemac.com

Housing and Urban Development Dept., (202) 708-1112; www.hud.gov

Housing Assistance Council, (202) 842-8600; www.ruralhome.org

Mortgage Bankers Assn., (202) 557-2700; www.mbaa.org

National Assn. of Development Companies, (202) 349-0070; www.nadco.org

National Assn. of Home Builders, (800) 368-5242; www.nahb.org

National Assn. of Local Housing Finance Agencies, (202) 367-1197; www.nalhfa.org

National Assn. of Realtors, (800) 874-6500; www.realtor.org

National Council of State Housing Agencies, (202) 624-7710; www.ncsha.org

National Housing Conference, (202) 466-2121; www.nhc.org

National Housing Trust, (202) 333-8931; www.nhtinc.org

National Leased Housing Assn., (202) 785-8888; www.hudnlha.com

National Low Income Housing Coalition, (202) 662-1530; www.nlihc.org

National Reverse Mortgage Lenders Assn., (202) 939-1760; www.reversemortgage.org or www.nrmlaonline.org

NeighborhoodWorks America, (202) 760-4000; www.nw.org

Smart Growth America, (202) 207-3355, www.smartgrowthamerica.org

Urban Institute, (202) 833-7200; www.urban.org

Purchases loans from lenders to replenish their supply of funds so they may make more mortgage loans to borrowers. (Freddie Mac stands for Federal Home Loan Mortgage Corp.)

Ginnie Mae *(Housing and Urban Development Dept.),* 550 12th St. S.W., 3rd Floor, 20024 (mailing address: 451 7th St. S.W., #B-133, Washington, DC 20410); (202) 708-0926. Fax, (202) 485-0206. Theodore W. Tozer, President; Mary K. Kinney, Executive Vice President. Hotline, (888) 446-6434.
Web, www.ginniemae.gov *and Twitter,* @GinnieMaeGov

Supports government housing objectives by expanding affordable housing finance via secondary markets for multi-family and single-family residential, hospital, and nursing home mortgages. The wholly owned government corporation serves as a vehicle for channeling funds from domestic and global capital markets into the U.S. mortgage market through mortgage-backed securities programs and helps to increase the supply of credit available for housing. Guarantees privately issued securities backed by Federal Housing Administration, Veterans Affairs Dept., USDA Rural Development, and HUD's Office of Public and Indian Housing mortgages. (Ginnie Mae stands for Government National Mortgage Assn.)

Housing and Urban Development Dept. (HUD), *Housing Office,* 451 7th St. S.W., #9100, 20410; (202) 708-2601. Fax, (202) 708-1403. Edward Golding, Assistant Secretary. TTY, (202) 708-1455.

Web, http://portal.hud.gov/hudportal/HUD?src=/ program_offices/housing

Administers all Federal Housing Administration (FHA) mortgage insurance programs; approves and monitors all lending institutions that conduct business with HUD.

Small Business Administration (SBA), *Disaster Assistance,* 409 3rd St. S.W., #6050, 20416; (202) 205-6734. Fax, (202) 205-7728. James Rivera, Associate Administrator. Service Center, (800) 659-2955. TTY, (800) 877-8339.
Web, www.sba.gov/offices/headquarters/oda

Provides victims of physical disasters with disaster and economic injury loans for homes, businesses, and personal property. Lends funds for uncompensated losses incurred from any disaster declared by the president of the United States or the administrator of the SBA. Lends funds to individual homeowners, business concerns of all sizes, and nonprofit institutions to repair or replace damaged structures and furnishings, business machinery, equipment, and inventory. Provides economic injury loans to small businesses for losses to meet necessary operating expenses, provided the business could have paid these expenses prior to the disaster.

Veterans Benefits Administration (VBA) *(Veterans Affairs Dept.),* *Loan Guaranty Service,* 810 Vermont Ave. N.W., #525, 20420; (202) 632-8862. Fax, (202) 495-5798. Michael L. (Mike) Frueh, Director.
Web, www.benefits.va.gov/homeloans

Guarantees private institutional financing of home loans (including manufactured home loans) for veterans; provides disabled veterans with direct loans and grants for specially adapted housing; administers a direct loan program for Native American veterans living on trust land.

►CONGRESS

For a listing of relevant congressional committees and subcommittees, please see page 420 or the Appendix.

►NONGOVERNMENTAL

American Bankers Assn. (ABA), *1120 Connecticut Ave. N.W., 20036; (202) 663-5000. Fax, (202) 663-7578. Rob Nichols, President. Information, 800-BANKERS. General email, custserv@aba.com*

Web, www.aba.com

Membership: insured depository institutions involved in finance, including community banking. Provides information on issues that affect the industry. Monitors economic issues affecting savings institutions; publishes real estate lending survey. Monitors legislation and regulations. (America's Community Bankers merged with the American Banking Assn.)

Center for Responsible Lending, *Washington Office, 910 17th St. N.W., #500, 20006; (202) 349-1850. Fax, (202) 289-9009. Michael Calhoun, President. Web, www.responsiblelending.org and Twitter, @CRLONLINE*

Seeks to protect homeownership and family wealth by working to eliminate abusive financial practices. Conducts studies on lending practices, assists consumer attorneys, and provides information to policymakers. Provides a Web-based archive of information for public use. Monitors legislation and regulations at state and federal levels.

Mortgage Bankers Assn., *1919 M St. N.W., 5th Floor, 20036; (202) 557-2700. Fax, (202) 408-4961. David H. Stevens, President. Information, (800) 793-6222. Web, www.mba.org, Twitter, @MBAMortgage and Facebook, www.facebook.com/mbamortgage*

Membership: institutions involved in real estate finance. Maintains School of Mortgage Banking; collects statistics on the industry. Conducts seminars and workshops in specialized areas of mortgage finance. Monitors legislation and regulations.

National Assn. of Affordable Housing Lenders, *1667 K St. N.W., #210, 20006; (202) 293-9850. Benson Roberts, President. General email, naahl@naahl.org*

Web, www.naahl.org

Membership: lenders who specialize in providing private capital for affordable housing and community development in low-income and moderate-income areas.

National Assn. of Consumer Advocates, *1215 17th St. N.W., 5th Floor, 20036; (202) 452-1989. Fax, (202) 452-0099. Ira J. Rheingold, Executive Director. General email, info@consumeradvocates.org*

Web, www.consumeradvocates.org

Membership: consumer advocate attorneys. Seeks to protect the rights of consumers from fraudulent, abusive, and predatory business practices. Provides consumer law training through conferences and publications. Monitors legislation and regulations on banking, credit, and housing laws.

National Assn. of Local Housing Finance Agencies, *2025 M St. N.W., #800, 20036-3309; (202) 367-1197. Fax, (202) 367-2197. Jason Boehlert, Executive Director. General email, info@nalhfa.org*

Web, www.nalhfa.org

Membership: professionals of city and county governments that finance affordable housing. Provides professional development programs in new housing finance and other areas. Monitors legislation and regulations.

National Council of State Housing Agencies, *444 N. Capitol St. N.W., #438, 20001; (202) 624-7710. Fax, (202) 624-5899. Barbara J. Thompson, Executive Director. General email, info@ncsha.org*

Web, www.ncsha.org, Twitter, @HomeEverything and Facebook, www.facebook.com/National-Council-of-State-Housing-Agencies-NCSHA-73339029343

Membership: state housing finance agencies. Promotes greater opportunities for lower-income people to rent or buy affordable housing.

National Reverse Mortgage Lenders Assn., *1400 16th St. N.W., #420, 20036; (202) 939-1760. Fax, (202) 265-4435. Peter H. Bell, President, (202) 939-1741. General email, dhicks@dworbell.com*

Web, www.nrmlaonline.org

National trade association for firms that originate, service, and invest in reverse mortgages. Monitors legislation and regulations.

Property Management

►AGENCIES

Bureau of Land Management (BLM) *(Interior Dept.), Lands, Realty, and Cadastral Survey, 20 M St. S.E., 20003 (mailing address: 1849 C St. N.W., 2134LM, Washington, DC 20240); (202) 912-7088. Fax, (202) 912-7199. Michael G. Stiewig, Division Chief. Web, www.blm.gov/wo/st/en/info/directory/WO-350_dir.html*

Oversees use, acquisition, and disposal of public lands. Conducts the Public Lands Survey; authorizes rights-of-way on public lands for uses that include roads, power lines, and wind and solar facilities.

Federal Housing Administration (FHA) *(Housing and Urban Development Dept.), Asset Management and Portfolio Oversight,* 451 7th St. S.W., #6162, 20410; (202) 402-2472. Fax, (202) 708-3104. Nancie-Ann Bodell, Director, Acting.
Web, http://portal.hud.gov/hudportal/HUD?src=/program_offices/housing/mfh/hsgmfbus/aboutam

Oversees HUD management, ownership, and sale of properties, which HUD owns by virtue of default and foreclosure or for which HUD is mortgagee-in-possession.

Federal Housing Administration (FHA) *(Housing and Urban Development Dept.), Procurement Management,* 451 7th St. S.W., #2222, 20410; (202) 402-7127. Amelia McCormick, Director.
Web, http://portal.hud.gov

Develops and implements policies and procedures and conducts contract administration for the Office of Housing and the Federal Housing Administration headquarters' procurement actions.

Real Estate Assessment Center *(Housing and Urban Development Dept.),* 550 12th St. S.W., #100, 20410; (202) 475-7949. Fax, (202) 485-0286. Donald J. Lavoy, Deputy Assistant Secretary. Toll-free, (888) 245-4860.
General email, reac_tac@hud.gov
Web, www.hud.gov/reac

Conducts physical inspections and surveys of resident satisfaction in publicly owned, insured, or subsidized housing. Assesses financial condition and management operations of public housing agencies.

▶ **NONGOVERNMENTAL**

Building Owners and Managers Assn. International, 1101 15th St. N.W., #800, 20005; (202) 408-2662. Fax, (202) 326-6377. Henry Chamberlain, President.
General email, info@boma.org
Web, www.boma.org and Twitter, @BOMAIntl

Membership: office building owners and managers. Reviews changes in model codes and building standards; conducts seminars and workshops on building operation and maintenance issues; sponsors educational and training programs. Monitors legislation and regulations.

Community Associations Institute, 6402 Arlington Blvd., #500, Falls Church, VA 22042; (703) 970-9220. Fax, (703) 970-9558. Tom Skiva, Chief Executive Officer. Toll-free, (888) 224-4321.
General email, cai-info@ACIonline.org
Web, www.caionline.org and Twitter, @CAIsocial

Membership: homeowner associations, builders, lenders, owners, managers, Realtors, insurance companies, and public officials. Provides members with information on creating, financing, and maintaining common facilities and services in condominiums and other planned developments.

NAIOP Commercial Real Estate Development Assn., 2201 Cooperative Way, #300, Herndon, VA 20171-3034;
(703) 904-7100. Fax, (703) 904-7942. Thomas J. Bisacquino, President.
Web, www.naiop.org

Membership: developers, planners, designers, builders, financiers, and managers of industrial and office properties. Provides research and continuing education programs. Monitors legislation and regulations on capital gains, real estate taxes, impact fees, growth management, environmental issues, and hazardous waste liability.

National Apartment Assn., 4300 Wilson Blvd., #400, Arlington, VA 22203; (703) 518-6141. Fax, (703) 248-9440. Doug Culkin, President.
General email, webmaster@naahq.org
Web, www.naahq.org

Membership: state and local associations of owners, managers, investors, developers, and builders of apartment houses or other rental properties. Conducts educational and professional certification programs. Monitors legislation and regulations.

National Assn. of Home Builders (NAHB), 1201 15th St. N.W., 20005-2800; (202) 266-8200. Fax, (202) 266-8400. Gerald M. Howard, Chief Executive Officer. Press, (202) 266-8254. Toll-free, (800) 368-5242.
General email, info@nahb.org
Web, www.nahb.org

Membership: contractors, builders, architects, engineers, mortgage lenders, and others interested in home building and residential real estate construction.

National Assn. of Housing and Redevelopment Officials, 630 Eye St. N.W., 20001-3736; (202) 289-3500. Fax, (202) 289-8181. Saul N. Ramirez Jr., Chief Executive. Toll-free, (877) 866-2476.
General email, nahro@nahro.org
Web, www.nahro.org

Membership: housing, community, and urban development practitioners and organizations, and state and local government agencies and personnel. Conducts studies and provides training and certification in the operation and management of rental housing.

National Assn. of Housing Cooperatives, 1444 Eye St. N.W., #700, 20005-6542; (202) 737-0797. Fax, (202) 216-9646. Mitch Dvorak, Executive Director.
General email, info@nahc.coop
Web, www.coophousing.org

Membership: housing cooperative professionals and organizations that provide services to housing cooperatives. Promotes housing cooperatives; provides technical assistance in all phases of cooperative housing; sponsors educational programs and on-site training; provides legal service referrals; monitors legislation; maintains an information clearinghouse on housing cooperatives. Online resources include a directory of financial, legal, and management services experts in the housing cooperative community.

National Center for Housing Management, *447 Carlisle Dr., Suite A, Herndon, VA 20170; (800) 368-5625. Fax, (703) 435-9775. W. Glenn Stevens, President. General email, service@nchm.org*

Web, www.nchm.org

Private corporation created by executive order to meet housing management and training needs. Conducts research, demonstrations, and educational and training programs in all types of multifamily housing management. Develops and implements certification systems for housing management programs.

National Cooperative Business Assn., CLUSA International (NCBA CLUSA), *1775 Eye St. N.W., #800, 20006; (202) 638-6222. Fax, (202) 638-1374. Judy Ziewacz, President. General email, info@ncba.coop*

Web, www.ncba.coop, Twitter, @NCBACLUSA and Facebook, www.facebook.com/NCBACLUSA

Alliance of cooperatives, businesses, and state cooperative associations. Provides information about starting and managing housing cooperatives. Monitors legislation and regulations.

National Multifamily Housing Council, *1850 M St. N.W., #540, 20036-5803; (202) 974-2300. Fax, (202) 775-0112. Douglas Bibby, President. General email, info@nmhc.org*

Web, www.nmhc.org

Membership: owners, financiers, managers, and developers of multifamily housing. Advocates policies and programs at the federal, state, and local levels to increase the supply and quality of multifamily units in the United States; serves as a clearinghouse on rent control, condominium conversion, taxes, fair housing, and environmental issues.

Property Management Assn., *7508 Wisconsin Ave., 4th Floor, Bethesda, MD 20814; (301) 657-9200. Fax, (301) 907-9326. Carole Worley, Executive Director. General email, info@pma-dc.org*

Web, www.pma-dc.org

Membership: property managers and firms that offer products and services needed in the property management field. Promotes information exchange on property management practices.

12 🌐

International Affairs

GENERAL POLICY AND ANALYSIS

Basic Resources

▶AGENCIES

Agency for International Development (USAID), *Conflict Management and Mitigation, 1300 Pennsylvania Ave. N.W., #7.7131, 20523; (202) 712-0121. Neil Levine, Director. General email, conflict@usaid.gov*

Web, www.usaid.gov/who-we-are/organization/bureaus/ bureau-democracy-conflict-and-humanitarian-assistance/ office-0

Supports USAID's work as it relates to conflict management, fragility, political instability, and extremism. Applies best practices of conflict management to areas such as democracy and governance, economic growth, natural resource management, and peace-building efforts.

Agency for International Development (USAID), *Economic Growth, Education, and Environment, 1300 Pennsylvania Ave. N.W., #3.9, 20523-3900; (202) 712-0670. Fax, (202) 216-3239. Charles North, Senior Deputy Assistant Administrator. Web, www.usaid.gov/who-we-are/organization/bureaus/ bureau-economic-growth-education-and-environment*

Assists with the economic growth of developing countries by providing policy, technical, and financial assistance for cost-effective, reliable energy programs and other infrastructure. Focuses on the Clean Energy Initiative, energy efficiency and conservation, public-private partnerships, increased access to energy, technology innovation, and training of officials in developing countries.

Bureau of Consular Affairs *(State Dept.), 2201 C St. N.W., #6826, 20520-4818; (202) 647-9584. Fax, (202) 647-9622. Michele T. Bond, Assistant Secretary, Acting. National Passport Information Center (fees are charged for calls to this number, [877] 487-2778 with credit card). Assistance to U.S. citizens overseas, (888) 407-4747 in United States and Canada or (202) 501-4444 if overseas during business hours or (202) 647-4000 after hours. Press, (202) 485-6150. Web, http://travel.state.gov and Twitter, @TravelGov*

Issues passports to U.S. citizens and visas to immigrants and nonimmigrants seeking to enter the United States. Provides protection, assistance, and documentation for U.S. citizens abroad.

Bureau of Democracy, Human Rights, and Labor *(State Dept.), International Religious Freedom, 2201 C St. N.W., #2428, Washington, DC; (202) 647-3607. David N. Saperstein, Ambassador at Large. Web, www.state.gov/j/drl/irf*

Monitors religious persecution and discrimination worldwide, recommends and implements regional policies, and develops programs to promote religious freedom.

Bureau of Intelligence and Research *(State Dept.), 2201 C St. N.W., #6468, 20520-6531; (202) 647-9177. Fax, (202) 736-4688. Daniel B. Smith, Assistant Secretary. Web, www.state.gov/s/inr*

Coordinates foreign policy-related research, analysis, and intelligence programs for the State Dept. and other federal agencies.

Bureau of International Organization Affairs *(State Dept.), 2201 C St. N.W., #6323, 20520-6319; (202) 647-9600. Fax, (202) 647-9722. Bathsheba N. Crocker, Assistant Secretary. Press, (202) 647-6899. General email, io-bureau@state.gov*

Web, www.state.gov/p/io and Twitter, @State_IO

Coordinates and develops policy guidelines for U.S. participation in the United Nations and in other international organizations and conferences.

Bureau of Oceans and International Environmental and Scientific Affairs *(State Dept.), International Health and Biodefense, 2201 C St. N.W., #2734, 20520; (202) 647-1318. Lynette Poulton, Director. Web, www.state.gov/e/oes/intlhealthbiodefense*

Advances the Global Health Security Agenda and focuses on issues including pandemic preparedness, new outbreaks of disease, new international policy discussions, and the impact of science and technology, medicine, and public health.

Bureau of Oceans and International Environmental and Scientific Affairs *(State Dept.), Policy and Public Outreach, 2201 C St. N.W., #2880, 20520; (202) 647-4658. Susan Cleary, Director. Web, www.state.gov/e/oes/policy*

Integrates oceans, environment, polar, science, technology, and health issues into U.S. foreign policy, and works to address these issues in the media, NGOs, the private sector, and Congress.

Defense Dept. (DoD), *International Security Affairs, 2000 Defense Pentagon, #3C889, 20301-2000; (703) 697-2788. Fax, (703) 697-3279. Elissa B. Slotkin, Assistant Secretary, Acting; Kenneth B. Handelman, Principal Deputy Assistant Secretary, Acting. Web, http://policy.defense.gov/OUSDPOffices/ ASDforInternationalSecurityAffairs.aspx*

Advises the secretary of defense and recommends policies on regional security issues in the Middle East, Africa, Russia/Eurasia, and Europe/NATO.

National Security Staff (NSS) *(Executive Office of the President), International Economic Affairs, The White House, 20504; (202) 456-9281. Fax, (202) 456-9280. Wally Adeyemo, Deputy National Security Adviser. Web, www.whitehouse.gov/administration/eop/nsc*

Advises the president, the National Security Council, and the National Economic Council on all aspects of U.S. foreign policy dealing with U.S. international economic policies.

National Security Staff (NSS) *(Executive Office of the President), Strategic Communications and Speechwriting, Dwight D. Eisenhower Executive Office Bldg., #302, 20500; (202) 456-9271. Fax, (202) 456-9270. Benjamin J. (Ben) Rhodes, Deputy National Security Adviser. Administrative office, (202) 456-9301. Web, www.whitehouse.gov/administration/eop/nsc*

Advises U.S. government agencies on the direction and theme of the president's message. Assists in the development and coordination of communications programs that disseminate consistent and accurate messages about the U.S. government and policies to the global audience.

President's Intelligence Advisory Board and Intelligence Oversight Board (*Executive Office of the President*), *New Executive Office Bldg., #5020, 20502; (202) 156 2352. Fax, (202) 395-3403. Shirley Jackson, Co-Chair; Jami Miscik, Co-Chair.*
Web, www.whitehouse.gov/administration/eop/piab

Members appointed by the president. Assesses the quality, quantity, and adequacy of foreign intelligence collection and of counterintelligence activities by all government agencies; advises the president on matters concerning intelligence and national security.

State Dept., *2201 C St. N.W., 20520; (202) 647-4000. Fax, (202) 647-3344. John F. Kerry, Secretary, (202) 647-9572; Antony J. Blinken, Deputy Secretary, (202) 647-5505. Press, (202) 647-2492.*
Web, www.state.gov and Twitter, @StateDept

Directs and coordinates U.S. foreign relations and interdepartmental activities of the U.S. government overseas.

State Dept., Civilian Security, Democracy, and Human Rights, *2201 C St. N.W., #7261, 20520; (202) 647-6240. Fax, (202) 647-0753. Sarah B. Sewall, Under Secretary.*
Web, www.state.gov/j

Advises the secretary on transnational issues. Divisions include Democracy, Human Rights, and Labor; International Narcotics and Law Enforcement; Conflict and Stabilization Operations; Population, Refugees, and Migration; Counterterrorism; Global Criminal Justice; and Monitor and Combat Trafficking in Persons.

State Dept., Policy Planning, *2201 C St. N.W., #7311, 20520; (202) 647-2972. Fax, (202) 647-0844. David McKean, Director.*
Web, www.state.gov/s/p

Advises the secretary and other State Dept. officials on foreign policy matters.

State Dept., Religion and Global Affairs, *2201 C St. N.W., 20520; (202) 647-0704. Shaun Casey, Special Representative.*
General email, RGAOffice@state.gov
Web, www.state.gov/s/rga and Twitter, @SpecialRepCasey

Advises the Secretary on policy matters as they relate to religion; supports State Dept. posts and bureaus in their efforts to access religious dynamics and engage religious actors; serves as point of entry for individuals who would like to engage the State Dept. on matters of religion and global affairs.

State Dept., Under Secretary for Management, *2201 C St. N.W., #7207, 20520; (202) 647-1500. Fax, (202) 647-0168. Patrick F. Kennedy, Under Secretary.*
Web, www.state.gov/m

Serves as principal adviser to the secretary on management matters, including budgetary, administrative, and personnel policies of the department and the Foreign Service.

State Dept., Under Secretary for Political Affairs, *2201 C St. N.W., #7250, 20520; (202) 647-0995. Fax, (202) 647-4780. Wendy R. Sherman, Under Secretary.*
Web, www.state.gov/p

Manages regional and bilateral policy issues and assists in the overall direction of the department. Oversees the Africa, East Asia and the Pacific, Europe and Eurasia, Near East, South and Central Asia, Western Hemisphere, and International Organizations bureaus.

State Dept., Under Secretary for Public Diplomacy and Public Affairs, *2201 C St. N.W., #5932, 20520; (202) 647-9199. Fax, (202) 647-9140. Richard Stengel, Under Secretary.*
Web, www.state.gov/r

Seeks to broaden public affairs discussion on foreign policy with U.S. citizens, media, and institutions. Divisions include Education and Cultural Affairs, International Information Programs, Public Affairs, Strategic Counterterrorism Communications, and Policy, Planning, and Resources.

▶ **CONGRESS**

For a listing of relevant congressional committees and subcommittees, please see pages 454–455 or the Appendix.

Government Accountability Office (GAO), *International Affairs and Trade,* *441 G St. N.W., #4T21, 20548; (202) 512-4128. Loren Yager, Managing Director.*
Web, www.gao.gov/careers/iat.html

Independent nonpartisan agency in the legislative branch. Audits, analyzes, and evaluates international programs; makes unclassified reports available to the public.

House Democracy Partnership Commission, *227 CHOB, 20515; (202) 225-4561. Fax, (202) 225-1166. Rep. Peter Roskam, Chair; Jeff Billman, Staff Director.*
General email, jeff.billman@mail.house.gov
Web, http://hdac.house.gov

Provides advice to members and staff of parliaments of select countries that have established or are developing democratic governments.

Library of Congress, Serial and Government Publications, *James Madison Memorial Bldg., 101 Independence Ave. S.E., #LM 133, 20540-4760; (202) 707-5690. Teri Sierra, Chief. Reference desk, (202) 707-5208. Current periodical reading room, (202) 707-5691.*
Web, www.loc.gov/rr/news

Collects and maintains information on governmental and nongovernmental organizations that are domestically or internationally based, financed, and sponsored. Responds to written or telephone requests to provide information on the history, structure, operation, and activities of these organizations. Collects and maintains domestic

INTERNATIONAL AFFAIRS RESOURCES IN CONGRESS

For a complete listing of congressional committees, including their full contact information, leadership, membership, and jurisdictions, please refer to the Appendix on pages 779–896.

HOUSE:

House Appropriations Committee, (202) 225-2771. Web, appropriations.house.gov
    Subcommittee on Commerce, Justice, Science, and Related Agencies, (202) 225-3351.
    Subcommittee on Interior, Environment, and Related Agencies, (202) 225-3081.
    Subcommittee on State, Foreign Operations, and Related Programs, (202) 225-2041.

House Armed Services Committee, (202) 225-4151. Web, armedservices.house.gov
    Subcommittee on Strategic Forces, (202) 225-1967.

House Energy and Commerce Committee, (202) 225-2927. Web, energycommerce.house.gov
    Subcommittee on Commerce, Manufacturing, and Trade, (202) 225-2927.

House Financial Services Committee, (202) 225-7502. Web, financialservices.house.gov
    Subcommittee on Monetary Policy and Trade, (202) 225-7502.

House Foreign Affairs Committee, (202) 225-5021. Web, foreignaffairs.house.gov
    Subcommittee on Africa, Global Health, Global Human Rights, and International Organizations, (202) 225-5021.
    Subcommittee on Asia and the Pacific, (202) 225-5021.
    Subcommittee on Europe, Eurasia, and Emerging Threats, (202) 225-5021.
    Subcommittee on Terrorism, Nonproliferation, and Trade, (202) 225-5021.
    Subcommittee on the Middle East and North Africa, (202) 225-5021.
    Subcommittee on the Western Hemisphere, (202) 225-5021.

House Homeland Security Committee, (202) 226-8417. Web, homeland.house.gov
    Subcommittee on Border and Maritime Security, (202) 226-8417.

House Judiciary Committee, (202) 225-3951. Web, judiciary.house.gov
    Subcommittee on Crime, Terrorism, Homeland Security, and Investigations, (202) 225-5727.
    Subcommittee on Immigration and Border Security, (202) 225-3926.

House Natural Resources Committee, (202) 225-2761. Web, naturalresources.house.gov
    Subcommittee on Water, Power, and Oceans, (202) 225-8331.

House Oversight and Government Reform Committee, (202) 225-5074. Web, oversight.house.gov
    Subcommittee on National Security, (202) 225-5074.

House Permanent Select Committee on Intelligence, (202) 225-4121. Web, intelligence.house.gov

House Science, Space, and Technology Committee, (202) 225-6371. Web, science.house.gov
    Subcommittee on Research and Technology, (202) 225-6371.
    Subcommittee on Space, (202) 225-6371.

House Small Business Committee, (202) 225-5821. Web, smallbusiness.house.gov
    Subcommittee on Agriculture, Energy, and Trade, (202) 225-5821.
    Subcommittee on Economic Growth, Tax, and Capital Access, (202) 225-5821.

and foreign newspapers and periodicals. Some microfilm materials are available for interlibrary loan through the Library of Congress CALM Division.

▶ INTERNATIONAL ORGANIZATIONS

European Parliament Liaison Office, *2175 K St. N.W., 10th Floor, 20037; (202) 862-4730. Antione Ripoll, Director, (202) 862-4731.*
General email, epwashington@ep.europarl.eu
Web, www.europarl.europa.eu/us

Acts as the contact point between the European Parliament and the U.S. Congress. Seeks to intensify working relations between the European Parliament and the U.S.

Congress at all levels, particularly between corresponding committees of jurisdiction, and between European Parliament lawmakers and U.S. regulators. Represents the Parliament's viewpoint to the U.S. administration and Congress.

European Union, *Delegation to the United States of America, 2175 K St. N.W., 20037; (202) 862-9500. Fax, (202) 429-1766. David O'Sullivan, Ambassador. General email, delegation-usa-info@eeas.europa.eu*
Web, www.euintheus.org and Twitter, @EUintheUS

Provides information on European Union energy policy, initiatives, research activities, and selected statistics. (Headquarters in Brussels.)

House Transportation and Infrastructure Committee, (202) 225-9446.
Web, transportation.house.gov
Subcommittee on Coast Guard and Maritime Transportation, (202) 226-3552.
House Ways and Means Committee, (202) 225-3625.
Web, waysandmeans.house.gov
Subcommittee on Trade, (202) 225-6649.

JOINT:

Joint Economic Committee, (202) 224-5171.
Web, jec.senate.gov/public or jec.senate.gov/republicans/public

SENATE:

Senate Appropriations Committee, (202) 224-7363.
Web, appropriations.senate.gov
Subcommittee on State, Foreign Operations, and Related Programs, (202) 224-7363.
Senate Armed Services Committee, (202) 224-3871.
Web, armed-services.senate.gov
Subcommittee on Seapower, (202) 224-3871.
Senate Banking, Housing, and Urban Affairs Committee, (202) 224-7391.
Web, banking.senate.gov
Subcommittee on National Security and International Trade and Finance, (202) 224-2023.
Senate Commerce, Science, and Transportation Committee, (202) 224-0411.
Web, commerce.senate.gov
Subcommittee on Oceans, Atmosphere, Fisheries, and the Coast Guard, (202) 224-4912.
Senate Energy and Natural Resources Committee, (202) 224-4971.
Web, energy.senate.gov
Senate Finance Committee, (202) 224-4515.
Web, finance.senate.gov

Subcommittee on International Trade, Customs, and Global Competitiveness, (202) 224-4515.
Senate Foreign Relations Committee, (202) 224-4651.
Web, foreign.senate.gov
Subcommittee on Africa and Global Health Policy, (202) 224-4651.
Subcommittee on East Asia, the Pacific, and International Cybersecurity Policy, (202) 224-4651.
Subcommittee on Europe and Regional Security Cooperation, (202) 224-4651.
Subcommittee on Multilateral International Development, Multilateral Institutions, and International Economic, Energy, and Environmental Policy, (202) 224-4651.
Subcommittee on Near East, South Asia, Central Asia, and Counterterrorism, (202) 224-4651.
Subcommittee on State Department and USAID Management, International Operations, and Bilateral International Development, (202) 224-4651.
Subcommittee on Western Hemisphere, Transnational Crime, Civilian Security, Democracy, Human Rights, and Global Women's Issues, (202) 224-4651.
Senate Homeland Security and Governmental Affairs Committee, (202) 224-2627.
Web, hsgac.senate.gov
Senate Judiciary Committee, (202) 224-7703.
Web, judiciary.senate.gov
Subcommittee on Crime and Terrorism, (202) 224-6791.
Subcommittee on Immigration and the National Interest, (202) 224-7572.
Subcommittee on Privacy, Technology, and the Law, (202) 228-4280.

International Monetary Fund (IMF), *700 19th St. N.W., 20431; (202) 623-7000. Fax, (202) 623-4661. Christine Lagarde, Managing Director; Matthew Haarsager, U.S. Executive Director. Web, www.imf.org*

International organization of 188 member countries that promotes policies for financial stability and economic growth, works to prevent financial crises, and helps members solve balance-of-payments problems through loans funded by member contributions.

Organisation for Economic Co-operation and Development (OECD), *Washington Center, 1776 Eye St. N.W. #450, 20006; (202) 785-6323. Fax, (202) 315-2508. Carol Guthrie, Head of Center.*

General email, washington.contact@oecd.org
Web, www.oecd.org/washington

Membership: thirty-four nations, including Australia, Canada, Japan, Mexico, New Zealand, the United States, and western European nations. Serves as a forum for government officials to exchange information on their countries' policies. (Headquarters in Paris.)

Organization for Economic Cooperation and Development (OECD), *Washington Center, 1776 Eye St. N.W., #450, 20006; (202) 785-6323. Fax, (202) 785-0350. Carol Guthrie, Head of Center; Miguel Gorman, Media Officer. General email, washington.contact@oecd.org Web, www.oecd.org/washington*

State Department

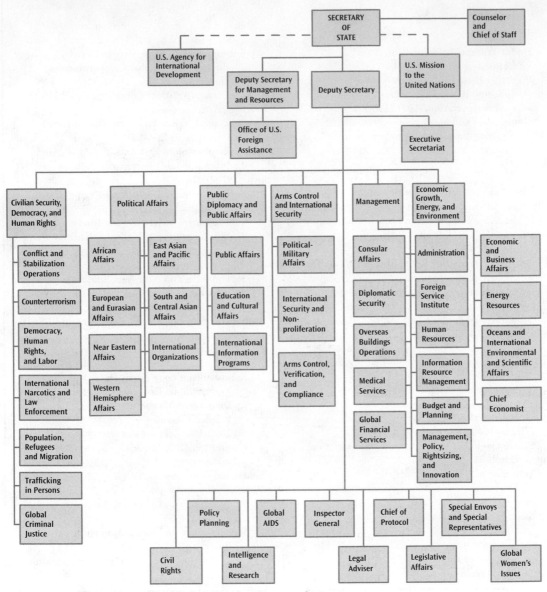

- - - Denotes independent agencies that receive guidance from the secretary of state

Supports research to understand economic, social, and environmental change; measures productivity and global flows of trade and investment. Acts as a liaison to the United States and Canada, working with government and the legislature as well as with regional contacts and leaders in business, labor, civil society, academia, and the media, to promote and provide the OECD's analysis, testimony, and data. Washington Center assists public with access to OECD publications, research, and policy work. (Headquarters in Paris.)

Organization of American States (OAS), *17th St. and Constitution Ave. N.W., 20006; Administration Bldg., 19th and Constitution N.W., 20006; General Secretariat Bldg.,*

1889 F St. N.W., 20006; (202) 370-5000. Fax, (202) 458-3967. Luis Almagro Lemes, Secretary General.
Library, (202) 458-6041.
General email, ai@oas.org
Web, www.oas.org

Membership: the United States, Canada, and all independent Latin American and Caribbean countries. Funded by quotas paid by member states and by contributions to special multilateral funds. Works to promote democracy, eliminate poverty, and resolve disputes among member nations. Provides member states with technical and advisory services in cultural, educational, scientific, social, and economic areas. Library open to the public (at 19th and Constitution).

Quota International, *1420 21st St. N.W., 20036; (202) 331-9694. Fax, (202) 331-4395. Barbara Schreiber, Executive Director.*
General email, staff@quota.org
Web, www.quota.org, https://quotainternational.org and Twitter, @QuotaIntl

International service organization that links members in twelve countries in a worldwide network of service and friendship. Interests include deaf, hard-of-hearing, and speech-impaired individuals and disadvantaged women and children. Maintains the We Share Foundation, a charitable organization.

United Nations Information Center, *1775 K St. N.W., #400, 20006-1500; (202) 331-8670. Fax, (202) 331-9191. Robert Skinner, Director.*
General email, unicdc@unic.org
Web, www.unicwash.org

Lead United Nations (UN) office in Washington. Serves as a resource for information and materials about the United Nations. Houses a collection of UN official documents (which includes General Assembly, Economic & Social Council, and Security Council documents), which can be accessed on a case-by-case basis by contacting the office. Library open by appointment only.

▶ **NONGOVERNMENTAL**

American Enterprise Institute (AEI), *Foreign and Defense Policy Studies, 1150 17th St. N.W., #1100, 20036; (202) 862-5800. Fax, (202) 862-7177. Danielle Pletka, Vice President, (202) 862-5943.*
Web, www.aei.org

Research and educational organization that conducts conferences, seminars, and debates and sponsors research on international affairs.

American Foreign Policy Council, *509 C St. N.E., 20002; (202) 543-1006. Fax, (202) 543-1007. Herman Pirchner Jr., President.*
General email, afpc@afpc.org
Web, www.afpc.org

Provides policymakers with information on foreign policy issues and options. Assists international leaders in establishing democracies. Holds meetings between congressional officials and officials in other countries. Publishes articles on current foreign affairs. Interests include terrorism in Europe and Asia, the Russia–China alliance, and nuclear weapons.

Aspen Institute, *1 Dupont Circle N.W., #700, 20036-7133; (202) 736-5800. Fax, (202) 467-0790. Walter Isaacson, President. Press, (202) 736-3849.*
General email, info@aspeninstitute.org
Web, www.aspeninstitute.org and Twitter, @AspenInstitute

Educational and policy studies organization. Promotes consideration of the public good in a wide variety of policy areas, including international relations and homeland security, business and economic development, education, energy, and the environment. Working with international partners, offers educational seminars, nonpartisan policy forums, public conferences and events, and leadership development initiatives.

Atlantic Council, *1030 15th St. N.W., 12th Floor, 20005; (202) 463-7226. Fax, (202) 463-7241. Frederick Kempe, President.*
General email, info@atlanticcouncil.org
Web, www.atlanticcouncil.org and Twitter, @ATLANTICCOUNCIL

Conducts studies and makes policy recommendations on U.S. foreign security and international economic policies in the Atlantic and Pacific communities; sponsors conferences and educational exchanges.

The Brookings Institution, *Foreign Policy Studies, 1775 Massachusetts Ave. N.W., 20036; (202) 797-6000. Fax, (202) 797-6004. Bruce Jones, Director. Press, (202) 797-6105.*
Web, www.brookings.edu/foreign-policy

Conducts studies on foreign policy, national security, regional and global affairs, and economic policies. Includes five policy centers: Center for Middle East Policy, the Center for East Asia Policy Studies, the Center on the United States and Europe, Center for 21st Century Security and Intelligence, and the John L. Thornton China Center.

The Brookings Institution, *Project on International Order and Strategy, 1775 Massachusetts Ave. N.W., 20036; (202) 540-7759. Thomas Wright, Director, (202) 797-6072. Press, (202) 797-6103.*
Web, www.brookings.edu/about/projects/international-order-strategy

Fosters research, policy engagement, and debate on international order and strategy. Interests include the rise of new powers on the international stage, the diffusion of political and military power, Western economic difficulties, challenges in the Middle East, and territorial disputes in Asia.

Carnegie Endowment for International Peace, *1779 Massachusetts Ave. N.W., 20036-2103; (202) 483-7600. Fax, (202) 483-1840. William Burns, President.*
General email, info@carnegieendowment.org
Web, www.carnegieendowment.org and Twitter, @CarnegieEndow

Global network of policy research centers in Russia, China, Europe, the Middle East, and the United States. Conducts research on international affairs and U.S. foreign policy. Program activities cover a broad range of military, political, and economic issues; sponsors panel discussions.

Center for International Policy, *2000 M St. N.W., #720, 20036; (202) 232-3317. Fax, (202) 232-3440. William Goodfellow, Executive Director.*
General email, cip@ciponline.org
Web, www.ciponline.org and Twitter, @CIPonline

Research and educational organization concerned with peace and security worldwide. Special interests include military spending, U.S. intelligence policy, and U.S. policy toward Asia, Colombia, and Cuba. Publishes the *International Policy Report*.

Center for National Policy, *1250 Eye St., #500, 20005; (202) 216-9723. Fax, (202) 682-1818. Scott Bates, President.*
General email, info@cnponline.org

Web, www.cnponline.org

Public policy research and educational organization that serves as a forum for development of national policy alternatives. Leads discussion and advances policies aimed at promoting U.S. global engagement and leadership in the 21st century. Focus on issues such as cybersecurity and defense energy. (Partner of the Truman National Security Project.)

Center for Strategic and International Studies, *1616 Rhode Island Ave. N.W., 20036; (202) 887-0200. Fax, (202) 775-3199. John J. Hamre, Chief Executive Officer.*
Web, www.csis.org

A bipartisan organization that seeks to advance global security and prosperity by providing strategic insights and practical policy solutions to decision makers. Expertise includes defense and international security, emerging global issues, and regional transformation.

Center for the Advanced Study of Language *(University of Maryland), 7005 52nd Ave., College Park, MD 20742; (301) 226-8900. Fax, (301) 226-8811. Michael May, Executive Director.*
General email, info@casl.umd.edu

Web, www.casl.umd.edu

Conducts research in language and cognition that supports national security; collaborates with government agencies; works to improve the performance of foreign language professionals in the federal government, specifically intelligence. Joint venture with the Department of Defense.

Center for the National Interest, *1025 Connecticut Ave. N.W., #1200, 20036-5651; (202) 887-1000. Fax, (202) 887-5222. Dimitri K. Simes, President; Paul J. Saunders, Executive Director.*
General email, info@cftni.org

Web, www.cftni.org and Twitter, @CFTNI

Works to develop new principles for U.S. global engagement and security; energy security and climate change; immigration and national security; and U.S. relations with China, Japan, Mexico, and Russia. Publishes a bimonthly magazine.

Center of Concern, *1225 Otis St. N.E., 20017; (202) 635-2757. Lester A. Myers, President, (202) 421-1181.*
General email, coc@coc.org

Web, www.coc.org and Twitter, @CenterofConcern

Independent, interdisciplinary organization that conducts social analysis, theological reflection, policy advocacy, and public education on issues of international justice and peace from the perspective of a Catholic social tradition.

Citizens for Global Solutions, *420 7th St. S.E., 20003; (202) 546-3950. Earl James, Chief Executive Officer.*
General email, info@globalsolutions.org

Web, www.globalsolutions.org and Twitter, @GlobalSolutions

Encourages U.S. global engagement on a broad range of foreign policy issues, including UN reform, international law and justice, health and the environment, international institutions, and peace and security.

Council on Foreign Relations, *Washington Office, 1777 F St. N.W., 20006; (202) 509-8400. Fax, (202) 509-8490. Richard Haass, President; James Lindsay, Senior Vice President.*
General email, communications@cfr.org

Web, www.cfr.org and Twitter, @CFR_org

Promotes understanding of U.S. foreign policy and international affairs. Awards research grants through its International Affairs Fellowship Program. Publishes *Foreign Affairs* bimonthly. (Headquarters in New York.)

Cultivating New Frontiers in Agriculture (CNFA), *1828 L St. N.W., #710, 20036; (202) 296-3920. Fax, (202) 296-3948. Sylvain Roy, President.*
General email, info@cnfa.org

Web, www.cnfa.org

International development organization that has worked in over 42 countries to provide agricultural solutions to stimulate economic growth and improve livelihoods by cultivating entrepreneurship.

David S. Wyman Institute for Holocaust Studies, *1200 G St. N.W., #800, 20005; (202) 434-8994. Rafael Medoff, Director.*
General email, info@wymaninstitute.org

Web, www.wymaninstitute.org

Educates the public about U.S. response to Nazism and the Holocaust through scholarly research, public events and exhibits, publications, conferences, and educational programs.

Eisenhower Institute, *818 Connecticut Ave. N.W., 8th Floor, 20006; (202) 628-4444. Fax, (202) 628-4445. Jeffrey M. Blavatt, Executive Director; Susan Eisenhower, Chair Emeritus.*
General email, eiadmin@gettysburg.edu

Web, www.eisenhowerinstitute.org

Nonpartisan research and educational organization modeled on President Eisenhower's legacy of public policy formation and leadership, stressing pursuit of facts, respectful dialogue, and a focus on the future. Provides scholarships, fellowships, internships, and other sponsored opportunities for students to participate in dialogue with prominent figures and to pursue study of public policy and related fields. (Affiliated with Gettysburg College in Gettysburg, Pa.)

Freedom House, *1850 M St. N.W., 11th Floor, 20036; (202) 296-5101. Fax, (202) 293-2840. Mark P. Lagon, President. Press, (202) 747-7035.*

General email, info@freedomhouse.org

Web, www.freedomhouse.org and *Twitter, @FreedomHouseDC*

Promotes civil society; democratic governance; women's rights; LGBTI rights; elections; intergovernmental bodies; free markets; the rule of law; independent media, including Internet freedom; and U.S. engagement in international affairs through education, advocacy, and training initiatives. Collects and analyzes data on political rights and civil liberties worldwide; publishes comparative surveys and reports; sponsors conferences and training programs.

Friends Committee on National Legislation (FCNL), *245 2nd St. N.E., 20002-5795; (202) 547-6000. Fax, (202) 547-6019. Diane Randall, Executive Secretary. Toll-free, (800) 630-1330. Recorded information, (202) 547-4343.*

General email, fcnl@fcnl.org

Web, www.fcnl.org

Seeks to broaden public interest and affect legislation and policy concerning regional and global institutions, peace processes, international development, and the work of the United Nations. (Affiliated with the Religious Society of Friends [Quakers].)

Institute for Foreign Policy Analysis, *1725 DeSales St. N.W., #402, 20036; (202) 463-7942. Fax, (202) 785-2785. Robert L. Pfaltzgraff Jr., President.*

General email, dcmail@ifpa.org

Web, www.ifpa.org

Trains policy analysts in the fields of foreign policy and national security. Sponsors research and workshops.

Institute for Policy Studies, *1301 Connecticut Ave. N.W., #600, 20036; (202) 234-9382. Fax, (202) 387-7915. John Cavanagh, Director.*

General email, info@ips-dc.org

Web, www.ips-dc.org

Research and educational organization. Interests include foreign policy, peace, the economy, and the environment.

Institute of International Education, *National Security Education Program, 1101 Wilson Blvd., #1210, Arlington, VA 22209 (mailing address: P.O. Box 20010, Arlington, VA 22209); (571) 256-0711. Fax, (703) 696-5667. Michael Nugent, Director. Information, (800) 618-6737.*

General email, nsep@nsep.gov

Web, www.nsep.gov

Administers Boren Awards and Language Flagship programs; provides scholarships, fellowships, and institutional grants to students and academics with an interest in foreign affairs and national security.

Institute of World Politics, *1521 16th St. N.W., 20036-1464; (202) 462-2101. Fax, (202) 464-0335. John Lenczowski, President. Toll-free, (888) 566-9497.*

General email, info@iwp.edu

Web, www.iwp.edu

Offers master's degree and professional education in national security, statescraft, and international affairs.

International Center, *1001 North Carolina Ave. S.E., 20003 (mailing address: P.O. Box 41720, Arlington, VA 22204); (202) 285-4328. Virginia Foote, President.*

General email, theinternationalcenter@theintlcenter.org

Web, www.theintlcenter.org

Research, advocacy, and aid organization concerned with U.S. foreign policy in developing countries. Project arms include trade and investment between the United States and Vietnam, reforestation and agroforestry training in Central America and the Caribbean, rehabilitation services and equipment for Cambodians with disabilities, land-mine clearance and school upgrades in Vietnam, and youth sports exchange programs.

International Foundation for Electoral Systems (IFES), *2011 Crystal Dr., 10th Floor, Arlington, VA 22202; (202) 350-6700. Fax, (202) 350-6701. William R. (Bill) Sweeney, President.*

General email, media@ifes.org

Web, www.ifes.org

Nonpartisan organization providing professional support to electoral democracies, both emerging and mature. Through field work and applied research and advocacy, strives to promote citizen participation, transparency, and accountability in political life and civil society.

International Republican Institute (IRI), *1225 Eye St. N.W., #700, 20005-3987; (202) 408-9450. Fax, (202) 408-9462. Mark Green, President.*

General email, info@iri.org

Web, www.iri.org

Created under the National Endowment for Democracy Act. Fosters democratic self-rule through closer ties and cooperative programs with political parties and other nongovernmental institutions overseas.

Just Foreign Policy, *4410 Massachusetts Ave. N.W., #290, 20016; (202) 448-2898. Robert Naiman, Policy Director.*

General email, info@justforeignpolicy.org

Web, www.justforeignpolicy.org

Nonpartisan membership organization that seeks to influence U.S. foreign policy through education, organization, and mobilization of citizens. Advocates cooperation, international law, and diplomacy as means to achieve a just foreign policy.

National Democratic Institute for International Affairs (NDI), *455 Massachusetts Ave. N.W., 8th Floor, 20001-2621; (202) 728-5500. Kenneth Wollack, President. Toll-free fax, (888) 875-2887.*

General email, contactndi@ndi.org

Web, www.ndi.org, Twitter, @NDI and *Facebook, www.facebook.com/National.Democratic.Institute*

Conducts nonpartisan international programs to help maintain and strengthen democratic institutions worldwide. Focuses on party building, governance, and electoral systems.

National Endowment for Democracy, *1025 F St. N.W., #800, 20004; (202) 378-9700. Fax, (202) 378-9407.*

Carl Gershman, President; J. William (Bill) Leonard, Chief Operating Officer; Jane Riley Jacobsen, Public Affairs.
General email, info@ned.org

Web, www.ned.org, Twitter, @NEDemocracy and Facebook, www.facebook.com/National.Endowment.for.Democracy

Grant-making organization that receives funding from Congress. Awards grants to private organizations involved in democratic development abroad, including the areas of democratic political processes; pluralism; and education, culture, and communications.

National Security Archive (*George Washington University*), Gelman Library, 2130 H St. N.W., #701, 20037; (202) 994-7000. Fax, (202) 994-7005.
Thomas Blanton, Director.
General email, nsarchive@gwu.edu

Web, www.nsarchive.org

Research institute and library that provides information on U.S. foreign and economic policy and national security affairs. Maintains and publishes collection of declassified and unclassified documents obtained through the Freedom of Information Act. Archive open to the public by appointment. Web site has a Russian-language link.

Partnership for a Secure America (PSA), 1775 K St. N.W., #400, 20006; (202) 293-8580. Andrew K. Semmel, Executive Director.
General email, info@psaonline.org

Web, www.psaonline.org

Supports a bipartisan approach to national security policies and issues. Researches and publishes reports on national security threats such as terrorism. Organizes conferences for political parties to debate and develop consensus on issues.

Paul H. Nitze School of Advanced International Studies, 1740 Massachusetts Ave. N.W., 20036; (202) 663-5700. Fax, (202) 663-5647. Vali Nasr, Dean. Press, (202) 663-5620.
Web, www.sais-jhu.edu

Offers graduate and nondegree programs in international relations, economics, public policy, regional and functional studies, and foreign languages. Sponsors the Johns Hopkins Foreign Policy Institute and several other research centers. (Affiliated with Johns Hopkins University.)

Pew Research Center, *Global Attitudes and Trends Project,* 1615 L St. N.W., #700, 20036; (202) 419-4400. Fax, (202) 419-4399. Richard Wike, Director.
General email, info@pewglobal.org

Web, www.pewglobal.org

Conducts public opinion surveys about world affairs and makes results available to journalists, academics, policymakers, and the public. Attempts to gauge attitudes in every region of the world toward globalization, democracy, trade, terrorism and other key issues. (A Pew Research Center project.)

Truman National Security Project, 1250 Eye St. N.W., #500, 20005; (202) 216-9723. Fax, (202) 289-4199.
Mike Breen, President.
General email, info@trumanproject.org

Web, http://trumanproject.org and Twitter, @TrumanProject

Membership: veterans and policy and political leaders. Forum for development of national policy alternatives. Promotes national security policy coordination, strengthening the U.S. military and intelligence, foreign affairs and diplomacy, democracy, and open trade. (Partner of the Center for National Policy.)

U.S. Conference of Catholic Bishops (USCCB), *International Justice and Peace,* 3211 4th St. N.E., 20017-1194; (202) 541-3160. Fax, (202) 541-3339.
Stephen Colecchi, Director.
General email, jphdmail@usccb.org

Web, www.usccb.org/about/international-justice-and-peace

Works with the U.S. State Dept., foreign government offices, and international organizations on issues of peace, justice, and human rights.

U.S. Global Leadership Coalition (USGLC), 1129 20th St. N.W., #600, 20036; (202) 689-8911. Fax, (202) 689-8910.
Liz Schrayer, President. Press, (202) 730-4163.
General email, info@usglc.org

Web, www.usglc.org

Advocates strengthening the International Affairs Budget. Seeks to combat global terrorism, diseases, and poverty. Interests include emerging world markets, developing countries, and humanitarian aid. Holds summits and publishes annual reports on global policy issues and proposals.

Women in International Security, 1779 Massachusetts Ave. N.W., #510, 20036; (202) 552-5401. Chantal de Jonge Oudraat, President.
General email, info@wiisglobal.org

Web, www.wiisglobal.org and Twitter, @WIISGlobal

Seeks to advance the role of women in international relations and international peace and security. Maintains a database of women foreign and defense policy specialists worldwide; organizes conferences in the United States and elsewhere; disseminates information on jobs, internships, and fellowships. Has chapters in the United States and international affiliates. (Affiliated with SIPRI North America.)

Women's Foreign Policy Group, 1615 M St. N.W., #210, 20036; (202) 429-2692. Fax, (202) 429-2630. Patricia Ellis, President.
General email, programs@wfpg.org

Web, www.wfpg.org and Twitter, @wfpg

Promotes women's leadership and women's interests in international affairs professions. Conducts policy programs, mentoring, and research.

World Affairs Councils of America, *1200 18th St. N.W., #902, 20036; (202) 833-4557. Fax, (202) 833-4555. Bill Clifford, President.*
General email, waca@worldaffairscouncils.org
Web, www.worldaffairscouncils.org and Twitter, @WACAmerica

Nonpartisan network that supports and represents local councils dedicated to educating the public on international issues at a grassroots level. Holds a national annual conference for member councils of each state. Coordinates expert speaker arrangements for small communities and provides fellowships for international business leaders. Supports programs that educate high school students on global affairs.

Diplomats and Foreign Agents

▶AGENCIES

Bureau of Diplomatic Security *(State Dept.), 2201 C St. N.W., #6316, 20520; (571) 345-2502. Fax, (571) 345-2527. Gregory B. Starr, Assistant Secretary.*
General email, DSPublicAffairs@state.gov
Web, www.state.gov/m/ds

Provides a secure environment for conducting U.S. diplomacy and promoting American interests abroad and in the United States.

Bureau of Diplomatic Security *(State Dept.), Diplomatic Security Service, 1801 N. Lynn St., 23rd Floor, Rosslyn, VA 22209; (571) 345-2502. Fax, (202) 647-0122. Bill A. Miller, Director. Diplomatic Service Command Center, (571) 345-3146.*
Web, www.state.gov

Oversees the safety and security of all U.S. government employees at U.S. embassies and consulates abroad. Responsible for the safety of the secretary of state and all foreign dignitaries below head of state level who are visiting the United States. Conducts background investigations of potential government employees, investigates passport and visa fraud, and warns government employees of any counterintelligence dangers they might encounter.

Foreign Service Institute *(State Dept.), 4000 Arlington Blvd., Arlington, VA 22204-1500 (mailing address: U.S. Department of State, Washington, DC 20522-4201); (703) 302-6729. Fax, (703) 302-7227. Nancy McEldowney, Director. Student messages and course information, (703) 302-7144.*
Web, www.state.gov/m/fsi

Provides training for U.S. government personnel involved in foreign affairs agencies, including employees of the State Dept., USAID, and the Defense Dept. Includes the Schools of Applied Information Technology, Language Studies, Leadership and Management, and Professional and Area Studies as well as the Transition Center and the Assn. for Diplomatic Studies and Training.

Justice Dept. (DOJ), *Foreign Agents Registration Unit, 600 E St. N.W., #1301, 20004; (202) 233-0776; (202) 233-0777. Fax, (202) 233-2147. Heather H. Hunt, Chief.*
General email, fara.public@usdoj.gov
Web, www.fara.gov

Receives and maintains the registration of agents representing foreign countries, companies, organizations, and individuals. Compiles semiannual report on foreign agent registrations. Foreign agent registration files are open for public inspection.

State Dept., *Administration Bureau, Overseas Schools, 2401 E St. N.W., #H328, 20037; (202) 261-8200. Fax, (202) 261-8224. Keith D. Miller, Director.*
General email, OverseasSchools@state.gov
Web, www.state.gov/m/a/os

Promotes high-quality educational opportunities at the elementary and secondary school levels for dependents of American citizens carrying out the programs and interests of the U.S. government abroad.

State Dept., *Foreign Missions, 3507 International Pl. N.W., 20008-3025; (202) 895-3500. Fax, (202) 736-4145. Gentry O. Smith, Director.*
General email, ofminfo@state.gov
Web, www.state.gov/ofm

Regulates the benefits, privileges, and immunities granted to foreign missions and their personnel in the United States on the basis of the treatment accorded U.S. missions abroad and considerations of national security and public safety.

State Dept., *Human Resources Bureau, 2201 C St. N.W., #6218, 20520; (202) 647-9898. Fax, (202) 647-5080. Arnold A. Chacón, Director.*
Web, www.state.gov/m/dghr

Directs human resource policies of the State Dept. and Foreign Service.

State Dept., *Human Resources Bureau, Career Development and Assignments, 2121 Virginia Ave. N.W., #4100, 20522 (mailing address: HR/CDA, Washington, DC 20520-6258); (202) 663-0779. Fax, (202) 663-0994. Geeta Pasi, Director.*
Web, www.state.gov

Coordinates programs related to the professional development of American members of the Foreign Service, including career development and assignment counseling programs, training, and presidential appointments and resignations.

State Dept., *Human Resources Bureau, Family Liaison, 2201 C St. N.W., #1239, 20520-0108; (202) 647-1076. Fax, (202) 647-1670. Susan Frost, Director.*
General email, flo@state.gov
Web, www.state.gov/m/dghr/flo

Works to improve the quality of life of U.S. government employees and their family members assigned to, or returning from, a U.S. embassy or consulate abroad. Areas of interest are education and youth, family member employment, and support services for personal and past crises, including evacuations. Manages the worldwide Community Liaison Office program.

State Dept., *Medical Services,* *2401 E St. N.W., #L218, 20522-0102; (202) 663-1649. Fax, (202) 663-1613. Dr. Charles Rosenfarb, Medical Director. Web, www.state.gov/m/med*

Operates a worldwide primary health care system for U.S. citizen employees, and eligible family members, of participating U.S. government agencies. Conducts physical examinations of Foreign Service officers and candidates; provides clinical services; assists with medical evacuation of patients overseas.

State Dept., *Office of the Chief of Protocol,* *2201 C St. N.W., #1238, 20520; (202) 647-2663 during business hours, (202) 647-1512 after business hours. Fax, (202) 647-3980. Peter Selfridge, Chief. Press, (202) 647-2681. Web, www.state.gov/s/cpr*

Serves as principal adviser to the president, vice president, the secretary, and other high-ranking government officials on matters of diplomatic procedure governed by law or international customs and practice.

▶**CONGRESS**

For a listing of relevant congressional committees and subcommittees, please see pages 454–455 or the Appendix.

▶**NONGOVERNMENTAL**

American Foreign Service Assn. (AFSA), *2101 E St. N.W., 20037; (202) 338-4045. Fax, (202) 338-6820. Ian Houston, Executive Director. Press, (202) 944-5508. Toll-free (within the United States), (800) 704-2372. General email, member@afsa.org*

Web, www.afsa.org

Membership: active and retired foreign service employees of the State Dept., International Broadcasting Board, Agency for International Development, Foreign Commercial Service, and the Foreign Agricultural Service. Offers scholarship programs; maintains club for members; represents active duty foreign service personnel in labor-management negotiations. Seeks to ensure adequate resources for foreign service operations and personnel. Conducts outreach programs to educate the public on diplomacy. Interests include business-government collaboration and international trade. Monitors legislation and regulations related to foreign service personnel and retirees.

Council of American Ambassadors, *888 17th St. N.W., #306, 20006-3312; (202) 296-3757. Fax, (202) 296-0926. Timothy A. Chorba, President; Carolyn M. Gretzinger, Executive Director. General email, council@americanambassadors.org*

Web, www.americanambassadors.org

Membership: U.S. ambassadors. Seeks to educate the public on foreign policy issues affecting the national interest. Hosts discussions, lectures, and conferences. Offers fellowships for students and foreign service personnel.

Executive Council on Diplomacy, *818 Connecticut Ave. N.W., #1200, 20006-2702; (202) 466-5199. Fax, (202) 872-8696. Solveig Spielmann, Executive Director. General email, ecd@diplomacycouncil.org*

Web, www.diplomacycouncil.org

Brings foreign diplomats from international organizations such as the United Nations and World Bank into contact with their U.S. counterparts. Provides a forum for discussion on issues such as agriculture, international trade, education, and the arts.

Institute for the Study of Diplomacy *(Georgetown University),* *1316 36th St. N.W., 20007; (202) 965-5735. Fax, (202) 965-5652. Barbara Bodine, Director. Web, http://isd.georgetown.edu*

Part of the Edmund A. Walsh School of Foreign Service. Focuses on the practical implementation of foreign policy objectives; draws on academic research and the concrete experience of diplomats and other members of the policy community.

Humanitarian Aid

▶**AGENCIES**

Administration for Children and Families (ACF) *(Health and Human Services Dept.),* **Refugee Resettlement,** *330 C St. S.W., 20201; (202) 401-9246. Fax, (202) 401-0981. Robert Carey, Director. Web, www.acf.hhs.gov/programs/orr*

Directs a domestic resettlement program for refugees; reimburses states for costs incurred in giving refugees monetary and medical assistance; awards funds to voluntary resettlement agencies for providing refugees with monetary assistance and case management.

Agency for International Development (USAID), *Democracy, Conflict, and Humanitarian Assistance, 1300 Pennsylvania Ave. N.W., #8.6-84, 20523-8601; (202) 712-0100. Thomas Staal, Assistant Administrator. Web, www.usaid.gov/who-we-are/organization/bureaus/ bureau-democracy-conflict-and-humanitarian-assistance*

Manages U.S. foreign disaster assistance, emergency and developmental food aid, democracy programs, conflict management programs, and programs to assist countries transitioning out of crises. Assists U.S. voluntary organizations, schools, and hospitals abroad. Serves as USAID's liaison to the U.S. military.

Agency for International Development (USAID), *Farmer-to-Farmer Program, 1424 K St. N.W., #700, 20007; (202) 712-4086. Gary E. Alex, Program Manager. General email, galex@usaid.gov*

Web, www.usaid.gov/what-we-do/agriculture-and-food-security/supporting-agricultural-capacity-development/ john-ogonowski

Promotes sustainable improvements in food security and agricultural processing, production, and marketing. Provides voluntary assistance to farmers, farm groups, and agribusinesses in developing countries, benefitting

International Disaster Relief Organizations

Action Against Hunger, (212) 967-7800; www.actionagainsthunger.org

American Jewish Joint Distribution Committee, (212) 687-6200; www.jdc.org

American Red Cross, (800) 733-2767 or (202) 303-5214; www.redcross.org

AmeriCares, (800) 486-4357; www.americares.org

CARE, (202) 595-2800; www.care.org

Catholic Relief Services, (888) 277-7575; www.crs.org

Child Fund, (800) 776-6767; www.childfund.org

Church World Service, (800) 297-1516 or (574) 264-3102; www.cwsglobal.org

Direct Relief International, (805) 964-4767; www.directrelief.org

Episcopal Relief and Development, (855) 312-4325; www.episcopalrelief.org

Health Right International, (212) 226-9890; www.healthright.org

InterAction, (202) 667-8227; www.interaction.org

International Federation of Red Cross/Red Crescent, (212) 338-0161; www.ifrc.org

International Medical Corps, (310) 826-7800; internationalmedicalcorps.org

International Rescue Committee, (212) 551-3000; www.rescue.org

Islamic Relief USA, (855) 447-1001; www.irusa.org

Lutheran World Relief, (800) 597-5972; www.lwr.org

Mercy Corps, (800) 292-3355; www.mercycorps.org

Operation USA, (800) 678-7255; www.opusa.org

Oxfam America, (800) 776-9326; www.oxfamamerica.org

Pan American Health Organization, (202) 974-3000, www.paho.org/disasters

Save the Children, (800) 728-3843 or (202) 640-6600; www.savethechildren.org

UNICEF, (800) 367-5437; www.unicefusa.org

World Food Programme (UN), (202) 653-0010; www.wfp.org

World Vision, (888) 511-6548; www.worldvision.org

approximately one million farmer families in over 80 countries. Formally the John Ogonowski and Doug Bereuter Farmer-to-Farmer Program.

Agency for International Development (USAID), *Global Health,* *1300 Pennsylvania Ave. N.W., #3.64, 20523-3100; (202) 712-4120. Fax, (202) 216 3485. Ariel Pablos-Méndez, Assistant Administrator.*
Web, www.usaid.gov/what-we-do/global-health

Participates in global efforts to stabilize world population growth and support women's reproductive rights. Focus includes family planning; reproductive health care; infant, child, and maternal health; and prevention of sexually transmitted diseases, especially AIDS. Conducts demographic and health surveys; educates girls and women.

Agency for International Development (USAID), *Transition Initiatives,* *1300 Pennsylvania Ave. N.W., #B3.06-124, 20523-8602; (202) 712-0914. Stephen Lennon, Director, (202) 712-1409.*
General email, DCHA.OTIOutreachMailList@usaid.gov
Web, www.usaid.gov/political-transition-initiatives and Twitter, @USAIDOTI

Provides efficient short-term assistance to countries in crisis in order to stabilize their governments.

Agency for International Development (USAID), *U.S. Foreign Disaster Assistance,* *1300 Pennsylvania Ave. N.W., 8th Floor, 20523-8602; (202) 712-0841. Fax, (202) 216-3191. Carol Chan, Director, Acting.*
General email, ofdainquiries@ofda.gov

Web, www.usaid.gov/who-we-are/organization/bureaus/bureau-democracy-conflict-and-humanitarian-assistance

Office within the Democracy, Conflict, and Humanitarian Assistance Bureau. Administers disaster relief and preparedness assistance to foreign countries to save lives and alleviate human suffering. Aids displaced persons in disaster situations and helps other countries manage natural disasters and complex emergencies.

Assistant Secretary for Health *(Health and Human Services Dept.), Global Health Affairs,* *200 Independence Ave. S.W., #639H, 20201; (202) 690-6174. (202) 260-0399. Fax, (202) 690-7127. Amb. Jimmy J. Kolker, Assistant Secretary.*
General email, globalhealth@hhs.gov
Web, www.globalhealth.gov

Represents the Health and Human Services Dept. before other governments, U.S. government agencies, international organizations, and the private sector on international and refugee health issues. Promotes international cooperation; provides health-related humanitarian and developmental assistance.

Bureau of Conflict and Stabilization Operations *(State Dept.),* *2121 Virginia Ave. N.W., #7100, 20522; (202) 663-0323. Dolores M. Brown, Assistant Secretary, Acting.*
General email, csopublic@state.gov
Web, www.state.gov/j/cso and Twitter, @StateCSO

Advances U.S. national security by working with partners in select countries to mitigate and prevent violent conflict. Conducts conflict analysis to identify factors contributing to mass violence or instability; develops prioritized strategies to address these factors; provides experienced leadership and technical experts to operationalize U.S. government and host-nation plans. Provides funding and training.

Bureau of Population, Refugees, and Migration *(State Dept.), 2201 C St. N.W., #6825, 20520-5824; (202) 647-7360. Fax, (202) 647-8162. Anne C. Richard, Assistant Secretary.*
Web, www.state.gov/j/prm and Twitter, @StatePRM

Develops and implements policies and programs on matters relating to international refugees, internally displaced persons, and victims of conflict, including repatriation and resettlement programs; funds and monitors overseas relief, assistance, and repatriation programs; manages refugee admission to the United States.

State Dept., *U.S. Foreign Assistance Resources, 2201 C St. N.W., #5927, 20520; (202) 647-2527. Fax, (202) 647-2529. Hari Sastry, Director.*
Web, www.state.gov/f

Works to ensure the strategic and effective allocation, management, and use of foreign assistance resources.

▶CONGRESS

For a listing of relevant congressional committees and subcommittees, please see pages 454–455 or the Appendix.

▶INTERNATIONAL ORGANIZATIONS

The Global Fund for Children, *1101 14th St. N.W., #420, 20005; (202) 331-9003. Fax, (202) 331-9004. Susan Goodell, Chief Executive Officer.*
General email, info@globalfundforchildren.org
Web, www.globalfundforchildren.org

Funds grassroots organizations that help impoverished, abused, and refugee children in foreign countries. Assists in management, planning, and networking between other organizations. Holds workshops for grantees to share knowledge, experience, and practices aimed at helping vulnerable children.

International Assn. for Human Values, *Washington Office, 2401 15th St. N.W., 20009; (202) 250-3405. Fax, (202) 747-6543. Filiz Odabas-Geldiay, Executive Director.*
General email, usa@iahv.org
Web, www.iahv.org/us-en

Humanitarian organization offering programs to promote nonviolence and service projects. Interests include youth empowerment, leadership, disaster relief and rehabilitation, sustainable rural and community development, women's empowerment, veterans' trauma relief, and prisoner reform programs.

International Committee of the Red Cross (ICRC), *Washington Office, 1100 Connecticut Ave. N.W., #500, 20036; (202) 587-4600. Fax, (202) 587-4696. François Stamm, Head, U.S. and Canadian Delegation. Press, (202) 587-4604.*

General email, washington_was@icrc.org
Web, www.icrc.org

Serves as the ICRC's main point of contact with U.S. authorities on issues concerning operations and international humanitarian law. Supports efforts internationally. Visits people held by the U.S. government in Guantánamo Bay, Cuba. (Headquarters in Geneva.)

International Organization for Migration (IOM), *Washington Office, 1752 N St. N.W., #700, 20036; (202) 862-1826. Fax, (202) 862-1879. Luca Dall'Oglio, Chief of Mission, ext. 229; William Lacy Swing, Director General.*
General email, iomwashington@iom.int
Web, www.iom.int/countries/united-states-america

Nonpartisan organization that plans and operates resource mobilization functions (RMF), including refugee resettlement, national migration, and humanitarian assistance to displaced populations at the request of its member governments. Advises governments on migration policies, supports victims of human trafficking, assists returning migrants, and raises awareness about the benefits of migration. Recruits skilled professionals for developing countries. (Headquarters in Geneva.)

Pan American Health Organization, *525 23rd St. N.W., 20037; (202) 974-3000. Fax, (202) 974-3663. Dr. Carissa F. Etienne, Director.*
Web, www.paho.org

Works to extend health services to underserved populations of its member countries and to control or eradicate communicable diseases; promotes cooperation among governments to solve public health problems. (Regional Office for the Americas of the World Health Organization, which is headquartered in Geneva, Switzerland.)

U.S. Fund for the United Nations Children's Fund (UNICEF), *Public Policy and Advocacy, 1775 K St. N.W., #360, 20006; (202) 296-4242. Fax, (202) 296-4060. Martin S. Rendón, Vice President; Mark Engman, Director, (202) 802-9102.*
General email, washington@unicefusa.org
Web, www.unicefusa.org/campaigns/public-policy-advocacy

Serves as the information reference service on UNICEF; advocates policies to advance the well-being of the world's children. Interests include international humanitarian assistance, U.S. volunteerism, child survival, and international health. (Headquarters in New York.)

United Nations High Commissioner for Refugees, *Washington Office, 1800 Massachusetts Ave. N.W., #500, 20036; (202) 296-5191. Fax, (202) 296-5660. Shelly Pitterman, Regional Representative.*
General email, usawa@unhcr.org
Web, www.unhcrwashington.org

Works with governments and voluntary organizations to protect and assist refugees worldwide. Promotes long-term alternatives to refugee camps, including voluntary repatriation, local integration, and resettlement overseas. (Headquarters in Geneva.)

▶ **NONGOVERNMENTAL**

American Red Cross, *National Headquarters, 2025 E St. N.W., 20006-5009; (202) 303-5000. Gail J. McGovern, President. Press, (202) 303-5551. Toll-free, 800-RED-CROSS (733-2767).*
Web, www.redcross.org and Twitter, @RedCross

Humanitarian organization chartered by Congress to provide domestic and international disaster relief and to act as a medium of communication between the U.S. armed forces and their families in time of war and personnel emergencies. Provides shelter, food, emotional support, supplies, funds, and technical assistance for relief in domestic and major international disasters through the International Federation of Red Cross and Red Crescent Societies, headquartered in Geneva.

Bikes for the World, *1408 N. Fillmore St., #11, Arlington, VA 22201; (703) 740-7856. Fax, (703) 525-0931. Keith Oberg, Executive Director.*
General email, office@bikesfortheworld.org
Web, www.bikesfortheworld.org and Twitter, @bikeftworld

Collects unwanted bicycles and related paraphernalia in the United States and delivers them to low-cost community development programs assisting the poor in developing countries.

Center for Civilians in Conflict, *1850 M St., #350, 20036; (202) 558-6958. Fax, (623) 321-7076. Federico Borello, Executive Director.*
General email, info@civiliansinconflict.org
Web, www.civiliansinconflict.org

Advocates to national governments and militaries for recognition, compensation, and other assistance to civilians they have harmed in armed conflicts.

ChildFund International, *Washington Office, 1200 18th St. N.W., #718, 20036; (804) 756-2700. Fax, (202) 682-3481. Anne Lynam Goddard, President; Sarah Bouchie, Vice President of Program Development. Toll-free, (800) 776-6767.*
General email, questions@childfund.org
Web, www.childfund.org and Twitter, @ChildFund

Nonsectarian international humanitarian organization that promotes improved child welfare standards and services worldwide by supporting long-term sustainable development. Provides children in emergency situations brought on by war, natural disaster, and other circumstances with education, medical care, food, clothing, and shelter. Provides aid and promotes the development potential of children of all backgrounds. (Headquarters in Richmond, Va.)

Christian Relief Services, *8301 Richmond Hwy., #900, Alexandria, VA 22309; (703) 317-9086. Fax, (703) 317-9690. Paul Krizek, Executive Director. Information, (800)-33-RELIEF.*
General email, info@christianrelief.org
Web, www.christianrelief.org

Promotes economic development and the alleviation of poverty in urban areas of the United States, Appalachia, Native American reservations, Haiti, Mexico, Honduras, Lithuania, the Czech Republic, and Africa. Donates medical supplies and food; administers housing, hospital, and school construction programs; provides affordable housing for low-income individuals and families.

Disability Rights International, *1666 Connecticut Ave. N.W., #325, 20009; (202) 296-0800. Fax, (202) 697-5422. Eric Rosenthal, Executive Director; Priscila Rodriguez, Spanish-language contact.*
General email, info@driadvocacy.org
Web, www.driadvocacy.org and Twitter, @DRI_advocacy

Challenges discrimination of and abuse faced by people with disabilities worldwide, with special attention to protecting the rights of children living in orphanages or other institutions. Documents conditions, publishes reports, and trains grassroots advocates.

Evangelical Lutheran Church in America, *Advocacy, 122 C St. N.W., #125, 20001; (202) 783-7507. Stacy Martin, Director. Toll-free, (800) 638-3522.*
General email, washingtonoffice@elca.org
Web, www.elca.org/advocacy and Twitter, @ELCA

Lutheran Immigration and Refugee Service responds to people caught in conflict and facing persecution, advocates for their needs and interests, helps people access resources for basic human needs, works with foster care programs for minors, offers legal assistance, and develops new and innovative service programs and partnerships. (Headquarters in Chicago, Ill.)

Health Volunteers Overseas, *1900 L St. N.W., #310, 20036; (202) 296-0928. Fax, (202) 296-8018. Nancy A. Kelly, Executive Director.*
General email, info@hvousa.org
Web, www.hvousa.org

Operates training programs in developing countries for health professionals who wish to teach low-cost health care delivery practices.

International Rescue Committee, *Public Policy and Advocacy, 1730 M St. N.W., #505, 20036; (202) 822-0166. Fax, (202) 822-0089. Nazanin Ash, Vice President.*
General email, advocacy@theIRC.org
Web, www.rescue.org

Provides worldwide emergency aid, protection, resettlement services, educational support, and advocacy for refugees, displaced persons, and victims of oppression and violent conflict; recruits volunteers. (Headquarters in New York.)

Jesuit Refugee Service / USA, *1016 16th St. N.W., #500, 20036; (202) 462-0400. Fax, (202) 328-9212. Mitzi Schroeder, Policy Director; Armando Borja, National Director.*
General email, jrsusa@jesuit.org
Web, www.jrsusa.org

U.S. Jesuit organization that aids refugees and other forcibly displaced persons worldwide, through accompaniment, advocacy, and service. Mobilizes the U.S. Jesuit response to forced displacement; provides advocacy and funding support to programs throughout the world. Monitors refugee and immigration legislation. (International headquarters in Rome.)

Latino Resource and Justice Center (CARECEN), *1460 Columbia Rd. N.W., #C-1, 20009; (202) 328-9799. Fax, (202) 328-7894. Abel Nuñez, Executive Director. General email, info@carecendc.org*

Web, http://carecendc.org, Twitter, @CarecenDC and Facebook, www.facebook.com/CARECEN.DC

Helps Central American and Latino immigrants obtain and maintain legal status. Seeks to address the legal and social service needs of Latinos in the Washington area; to facilitate Latinos' transition to life in the United States; and to provide Latinos with the resources and leadership skills necessary to promote the community's development. Works closely with other community-based agencies.

National Council of Churches, *110 Maryland Ave. N.E., #108, 20002-5603; (202) 544-2350. Fax, (202) 543-1297. Jim Winkler, President. General email, info@nationalcouncilofchurches.us*

Web, www.nationalcouncilofchurches.us, Twitter, @ncccusa and Facebook, www.facebook.com/ nationalcouncilofchurches

Works to foster cooperation among Christian congregations across the nation in programs concerning poverty, racism, family, environment, and international humanitarian objectives.

Oxfam America, *Policy and Campaigns, 1101 17th St. N.W. #1300, 20036-4710; (202) 496-1180. Fax, (202) 496-1190. Raymond C. Offenheiser, President; Paul O'Brien, Vice President for Policy and Campaigns. Information, (800) 776-9326. Press, (202) 496-1169. General email, info@oxfamamerica.org*

Web, www.oxfamamerica.org and Twitter, @OxfamAmerica

Funds disaster relief and long-term development programs internationally. Organizes grassroots support in the United States for issues affecting global poverty, including climate change, aid reform, and corporate transparency. (Headquarters in Boston, Mass.)

Program for Appropriate Technology in Health (PATH), *Washington Office, 455 Massachusetts Ave. N.W., #1000, 20001; (202) 822-0033. Fax, (202) 457-1466. Steve Davis, President. General email, info@path.org*

Web, www.path.org

Develops, tests, and implements health technologies and strategies for low-resource countries. Works with community groups, other nongovernmental organizations, governments, companies, and United Nations agencies to expand the most successful programs. Interests include reproductive health, immunization, maternal-child health,

emerging and epidemic diseases, and nutrition. (Headquarters in Seattle, Wash.)

Refugees International, *2001 S St. N.W., #700, 20009; (202) 828-0110. Fax, (202) 828-0819. Michel Gabaudan, President. Toll-free, (800) 733-8433. General email, ri@refugeesinternational.org*

Web, www.refugeesinternational.org and Twitter, @RefugeesIntl

Advocates assistance and protection for displaced people worldwide. Conducts field studies to identify basic needs and makes recommendations to policymakers and aid agencies.

Salvation Army Disaster Service, *2626 Pennsylvania Ave. N.W., 20037-1618; (202) 756-2600. Fax, (202) 464-7203. Maj. Andrew Wiley, Divisional Secretary. Web, www.disaster.salvationarmyusa.org and Twitter, @SalArmyEDS*

Provides U.S. and international disaster victims and rescuers with emergency support, including food, clothing, and counseling services.

U.S. Committee for Refugees and Immigrants, *2231 Crystal Dr., #350, Arlington, VA 22202-3794; (703) 310-1130. Fax, (703) 769-4241. Lavinia Limón, President. Press, (703) 310-1166. General email, uscri@uscridc.org*

Web, www.refugees.org

Defends rights of refugees in the United States and abroad. Helps immigrants and refugees adjust to American society; assists in resettling recently arrived immigrants and refugees; offers information, counseling services, and temporary living accommodations through its member agencies nationwide; issues publications on refugees and refugee resettlement; collects and disseminates information on refugee issues. Monitors legislation and regulations.

U.S. Conference of Catholic Bishops (USCCB), *Migration and Refugee Services, 3211 4th St. N.E., 20017; (202) 541-3352. Fax, (202) 541-3399. Bill Canny, Executive Director, (202) 541-3169. General email, mrs@usccb.org*

Web, www.usccb.org/mrs

Acts as advocate for immigrants, refugees, migrants, and victims of human trafficking. Works with legislative and executive branches of the U.S. government and with national and international organizations such as the U.N. High Commissioner for Refugees to promote fair and responsive immigration and refugee policy.

Women for Women International, *2000 M St. N.W., #200, 20036; (202) 737-7705. Fax, (202) 737-7709. Jennifer L. Windsor, Chief Executive Officer. General email, general@womenforwomen.org*

Web, www.womenforwomen.org and Twitter, @WomenforWomen

Helps women in war-torn regions rebuild their lives through financial and emotional support, job skills training, rights education, access to capital, and assistance for small business development.

World Vision, *Advocacy,* *300 Eye St. N.E., 20002; (202) 572-6300. Fax, (202) 572-6480. Kent R. Hill, Senior Vice President, International Programs; Michael Worsley, Engagement Officer, Washington, D.C., (202) 635-7600. Press, (202) 679-1620.*
General email, usprograms@worlddivision.org
Web, www.worldvision.org and Washington, D.C., www.worldvisionusprograms.org/national_capital.php

Christian humanitarian and development organization that works with children, their families, and their communities worldwide. Interests include social injustice and the causes of poverty. Provides emergency disaster relief and long-term development programs domestically and abroad. (Headquarters in Seattle, Wash.)

Information and Exchange Programs

▶**AGENCIES**

Broadcasting Board of Governors, *330 Independence Ave. S.W., #3300, 20237; (202) 203-4545. Fax, (202) 203-4585. Vacant, Executive Director. Press, (202) 203-4400. Locator, (202) 203-4000.*
General email, publicaffairs@bbg.gov
Web, www.bbg.gov and Twitter, @BBGov

Established by Congress to supervise all U.S. government nonmilitary international broadcasting, including Voice of America, Radio and TV Martí, Radio Free Europe/Radio Liberty, Radio Free Asia, and the Middle East Broadcasting Networks (MBN). Assesses the quality and effectiveness of broadcasts with regard to U.S. foreign policy objectives; reports annually to the president and to Congress.

Bureau of Educational and Cultural Affairs *(State Dept.), 2200 C St. N.W., #SA-5, 20522; (202) 632-6445. Fax, (202) 632-2701. Evan Ryan, Assistant Secretary. Press, (202) 632-6452.*
Web, www.eca.state.gov and Twitter, @ECAatState

Seeks to promote mutual understanding between the people of the United States and other countries through international educational and training programs. Promotes personal, professional, and institutional ties between private citizens and organizations in the United States and abroad; presents U.S. history, society, art, and culture to overseas audiences.

Bureau of Educational and Cultural Affairs *(State Dept.), Academic Exchange Programs, 2200 C St. N.W., #4-B06/SA-5, 20520; (202) 632-3234. Mary Kirk, Director.*
Web, http://eca.state.gov/about-bureau-0/organizational-structure/office-academic-exchanges

Provides opportunities for international study and research from the undergraduate through postdoctoral and professional levels. Works with the Fulbright Program, Critical Language Scholarship Program, Global Undergraduate Exchange Program, Edmund S. Muskie Graduate Fellowship Program, and Study of the United States Institutes.

Bureau of Educational and Cultural Affairs *(State Dept.), Citizen Exchange Programs, 2200 C St. N.W., #3-B16/SA-5, 20520; (202) 632-6062. Bruce Armstrong, Director.*
Web, www.eca.state.gov/about-bureau-0/organizational-structure/office-citizen-exchanges

Provides professional, youth, cultural, and sports exchange opportunities for U.S. and foreign participants.

Bureau of Educational and Cultural Affairs *(State Dept.), English Language Programs, 2200 C St. N.W., #4-B16/SA-5, 20520; (202) 632-9281. Kerri Hannan, Director.*
General email, english@state.gov
Web, http://eca.state.gov/about bureau-0/organizational-structure/office-english-language-programs

Promotes the learning and teaching of American English around the world in order to foster mutual understanding between the people of other countries and the people of the United States.

Bureau of Educational and Cultural Affairs *(State Dept.), Global Educational Programs, 2200 C St. N.W., #4-CC17/SA-5, 20520; (202) 632-6345. Anthony D. Koliha, Director.*
Web, http://eca.state.gov/about-bureau-0/organizational-structure/office-global-educational-programs

Monitors the flow of international students to the United States and of U.S. students to other countries. Administers the Hubert H. Humphrey Fellowship Program, the Community College Initiative Program, and the Benjamin A. Gilman International Scholarship Program.

Bureau of Educational and Cultural Affairs *(State Dept.), International Visitors, 2200 C St. N.W., #3-B06/SA-5, 20520; (202) 632-3303. Vacant, Director; Susan Schultz, Deputy Director.*
Web, http://eca.state.gov/about-bureau-0/organizational-structure/office-international-visitors

Seeks to build mutual understanding between the United States and other nations through short-term visits to the United States for current and emerging foreign leaders.

Bureau of Educational and Cultural Affairs *(State Dept.), Private Sector Exchange, 2200 C St. N.W., #5-BB11/SA-5, 20520; (202) 632-9386. Robin Lerner, Director.*
General email, jvisas@state.gov
Web, http://eca.state.gov/about-bureau-0/organizational-structure/office-private-sector-exchange

Administers the Exchange Visitor Program to allow nonimmigrants to participate in work-based and study-based exchange programs in the United States.

National Institute of Standards and Technology (NIST) *(Commerce Dept.), International and Academic Affairs, 100 Bureau Dr., MS 1090, Gaithersburg, MD 20899-1090; (301) 975-3069. Fax, (301) 975-3530. Claire M. Saundry, Director. TTY, (301) 975-8295.*

General email, inquiries@nist.gov

Web, www.nist.gov/iaao

Represents the institute in international functions involving science and technology; coordinates programs with foreign institutions; assists scientists from foreign countries who visit the institute for consultation. Administers a postdoctoral research associates program and oversees NIST's cooperation with academic institutions and researchers.

Voice of America *(International Broadcasting Bureau),* *330 Independence Ave. S.W., #3300, 20237; (202) 203-4959. Fax, (202) 203-4960. Kelu Chao, Director, Acting.*

General email, askvoa@voanews.com

Web, www.voanews.com and Twitter, @VOABuzz

A multimedia international broadcasting service funded by the U.S. government through the Broadcasting Board of Governors. Broadcasts news, information, educational, and cultural programming to an estimated worldwide audience of more than 134 million people weekly. Programs are produced in forty-four languages.

▶**NONGOVERNMENTAL**

Alliance for International Exchange, *1828 L St. N.W., #1150, 20036; (202) 293-6141. Fax, (202) 293-6144. Ilir Zherka, Executive Director.*

General email, merber@alliance-exchange.org

Web, www.alliance-exchange.org

Promotes public policies that support the growth of international exchange between the United States and other countries. Provides professional representation, resource materials, publications, and public policy research for those involved in international exchanges.

American Bar Assn. (ABA), *International Legal Exchange Program (ILEX), 1050 Connecticut Ave. N.W., #400, 20036; (202) 662-1660. Fax, (202) 662-1669. Christina Heid, Director, (202) 662-1034.*

General email, intilex@staff.abanet.org

Web, www.americanbar.org/groups/international_law

Facilitates entry into the United States for foreign lawyers offered training in U.S. law firms. Serves as designated U.S. government overseer for the J-1 visa and accepts applications from foreign lawyers. Houses the International Legal Resource Center.

American Council of Young Political Leaders, *2131 K St. N.W., #400, 20037; (202) 857-0999. Fax, (202) 857-0027. Linda Rotunno, Chief Executive Officer, (202) 448-9320.*

General email, lrotunno@acypl.org

Web, www.acypl.org

Bipartisan political education organization that promotes understanding among young elected leaders and political professionals around the world. Designs and manages international educational exchanges.

American Councils for International Education: ACTR/ ACCELS, *1828 L St. N.W., #1200, 20036; (202) 833-7522. Fax, (202) 833-7523. Dan E. Davidson, President.*

General email, general@americancouncils.org

Web, www.americancouncils.org

Conducts educational exchanges for high school, university, and graduate school students as well as scholars with the countries of Africa, eastern Europe, Eurasia, southeast Europe, and the Middle East.

Atlas Corps, *641 S St. N.W., #202, 20001; (202) 391-0694. Scott Beale, Chief Executive Officer.*

General email, info@atlascorps.org

Web, www.atlascorps.org

Provides U.S. fellowships to international leaders in public service and leaders of social issues in order to globally promote innovation in the nonprofit sector.

Business–Higher Education Forum, *2025 M St. N.W., #800, 20036; (202) 367-1189. Fax, (202) 367-2100. Brian K. Fitzgerald, Chief Executive Officer.*

General email, info@bhef.com

Web, www.bhef.com and Twitter, @BHEF

Membership: chief executive officers of major corporations, museums, colleges, and universities. Promotes the development of industry-university alliances around the world. Provides countries in central and eastern Europe with technical assistance in enterprise development, management training, market economics, education, and infrastructure development.

Center for Intercultural Education and Development *(Georgetown University), 3300 Whitehaven St. N.W., #1000, 20007 (mailing address: P.O. Box 579400, Washington, DC 20007); (202) 687-1400. Fax, (202) 687-2555. Chantal Santelices, Executive Director, (202) 687-1918.*

General email, cied@georgetown.edu

Web, http://cied.georgetown.edu

Designs and administers programs aimed at improving the quality of lives of economically disadvantaged people; provides technical education, job training, leadership skills development, and business management training; runs programs in Central America, the Caribbean, Central Europe, and Southeast Asia.

Council for International Exchange of Scholars, *1400 K St. N.W., #700, 20005; (202) 686-4000. Fax, (202) 686-4029. Maria de los Angeles Crummett, Executive Director, (202) 686-4001.*

General email, scholars@iie.org

Web, www.cies.org

Cooperates with the U.S. government in administering Fulbright grants for university teaching and advanced research abroad. (A division of the Institute of International Education.)

English-Speaking Union, *Washington Office, 4000 Cathedral Ave. N.W., #803B, 20016; (202) 244-6140. Fax, (202) 333-8258. Bonnie McCabe, President.*

General email, washingtondc@esuus.org
Web, www.esuus.org/washingtondc

International educational and cultural organization that promotes exchange programs with countries in which English is a major language; presents programs on the culture and history of the English-speaking world; sponsors annual Shakespeare competition among Washington metropolitan area schools. (National headquarters in New York.)

Global Ties U.S., *1250 H St. N.W., #305, 20005; (202) 842-1414. Fax, (202) 289-4625. Jennifer Clinton, President.*
General email, info@globaltiesus.org
Web, www.globaltiesus.org *and Twitter, @GlobalTiesUS*

Members coordinate international exchange programs and bring international visitors to communities throughout the United States. Provides its members, from 44 states and 13 countries, with connections, leadership development, and professional resources. (Formerly National Council for International Visitors.)

Graduate School USA, *International Institute, 600 Maryland Ave. S.W., #320, 20024-2520; (202) 314-3500. Fax, (202) 479-6806. David Simpson, Director. TTY, (888) 744-2717.*
General email, intlinst@graduateschool.edu
Web, www.graduateschool.edu/ii

Offers professional training and educational services to the public, including employees of foreign governments, international organizations, nongovernmental agencies, and employees of U.S. agencies engaged in international activities. Provides tailored programs in the areas of capacity building, professional and educational exchanges, governance, and health.

Institute of International Education, *Washington Office, 1400 K St. N.W., #700, 20005-2403; (202) 898-0600. Fax, (202) 326-7754. Allan Goodman, President.*
Web, www.iie.org/Offices/Washington-DC

Educational exchange, technical assistance, and training organization that arranges professional programs for international visitors; conducts training courses in energy, environment, journalism, human resource development, educational policy and administration, and business-related fields; provides developing countries with short-term and long-term technical assistance in human resource development; arranges professional training and support for staff of human rights organizations; sponsors fellowships and applied internships for midcareer professionals from developing countries; manages programs sending U.S. teachers, undergraduate and graduate students, and professionals abroad; implements contracts and cooperative agreements for the State Dept., the U.S. Agency for International Development, foreign governments, philanthropic foundations, multilateral banks, and other organizations. (Headquarters in New York.)

International Arts and Artists, *9 Hillyer Court N.W., 20008; (202) 338-0680. Fax, (202) 333-0758. David Furchgott, President.*

General email, info@artsandartists.org
Web, www.artsandartists.org

Collects multicultural art and plans art exhibits for museums. Offers affordable print and digital services to artists and organizations. Assists international artists and institutions in obtaining visas. Provides international internships and training programs. Offers an exchange program for artists to travel and complete international art-related internships. Local gallery, the Hillyer Arts Space, exhibits contemporary art.

International Research and Exchanges Board (IREX), *1275 K St. N.W., #600, 20005; (202) 628-8188. Fax, (202) 628-8189. Kristin Lord, President.*
General email, irex@irex.org
Web, www.irex.org

Provides programs, grants, and consulting expertise in more than 100 countries to improve the quality of education, strengthen independent media, and foster pluralistic civil society development.

Meridian International Center, *1630 Crescent Pl. N.W., 20009; (202) 667-6800. Fax, (202) 667-1475. Amb. Stuart Holliday, President. Toll-free, (800) 424-2974.*
General email, info@meridian.org
Web, www.meridian.org

Conducts international educational and cultural programs; provides foreign visitors and diplomats in the United States with services, including cultural orientation, seminars, and language assistance. Offers international exhibitions for Americans.

NAFSA: Assn. of International Educators, *1307 New York Ave. N.W., 8th Floor, 20005-4701; (202) 737-3699. Fax, (202) 737-3657. Marlene M. Johnson, Executive Director. Publications, (866) 538-1927.*
General email, inbox@nafsa.org
Web, www.nafsa.org

Membership: individuals engaged in the field of international education and exchange at the postsecondary level. Promotes educational opportunities across national boundaries. Sets and upholds standards of good practice and provides professional education and training.

Radio Free Asia, *2025 M St. N.W., #300, 20036; (202) 530-4900. Libby Liu, President. Press, (202) 530-4976.*
General email, contact@rfa.org
Web, www.rfa.org *and Twitter, @RadioFreeAsia*

Independent radio, Internet, and television service funded by federal grants to promote and support democracy where public access to free press is restricted. Broadcasts programs to East Asian countries, including China, Tibet, North Korea, Vietnam, Cambodia, Laos, and Burma; programming includes news, analysis, and specials on political developments, as well as cultural programs.

Radio Free Europe/Radio Liberty, *Washington Office, 1201 Connecticut Ave. N.W., #400, 20036; (202) 457-6900. Fax, (202) 457-6992. Nejad Pejic, Chief Executive Officer, Acting. Press, (202) 457-6948.*

General email, zvanersm@rferl.org

Web, www.rferl.org and Twitter, @RFERL

Independent radio, Internet, and television service funded by federal grants to promote and support democracy. Broadcasts programs to 23 countries, including Russia, Afghanistan, Pakistan, Iraq, Iran, and the republics of Central Asia; programming includes news, analysis, and specials on political developments, as well as cultural programs. Research materials available to the public by appointment. (Headquarters in Prague, Czech Republic.)

Sister Cities International, *915 15th St. N.W., 4th Floor, 20005; (202) 347-8630. Fax, (202) 393-6524.*
Mary D. Kane, President.
General email, info@sister-cities.org
Web, www.sister-cities.org

A network of 2,000 partnerships between U.S. and foreign cities. Promotes global cooperation at the municipal level, cultural understanding, and economic stimulation through exchanges of citizens, ideas, and materials. Serves as information clearinghouse for economic and sustainability issues and as program coordinator for trade missions. Sponsors youth programs.

World Learning, *International Exchange Programs, 1015 15th St. N.W., 7th Floor, 20005-2065; (202) 408-5420. Fax, (202) 408-5397. Carol Jenkins, President, International Development and Exchange Programs, (202) 464-6643. TTY, (202) 464-5530. Toll-free, (800) 858-0292.*
General email, development@worldlearning.org
Web, www.worldlearning.org and Twitter, @WorldLearning

Assists public and private organizations engaged in international cooperation and business. Works with governments and private counterparts to support foreign professional exchanges. Develops tailored technical training programs for midcareer professionals. Provides technical expertise, management support, travel, and business development services. Administers programs that place international exchange students in U.S. colleges and universities. Implements youth exchanges focused on leadership, current issues, and peacebuilding. Administered by World Learning's Division of International Development and Exchange Programs. Administers field-based study abroad programs, which offer semester and summer programs for high school, college, and graduate students.

Youth for Understanding USA, *641 S St. N.W., #200, 20001; (240) 744-5200. Fax, (240) 588-7571. Michael E. Hill, President. Teen information, (800) 833-6243.*
General email, admissions@yfu.org
Web, www.yfuusa.org and Twitter, @yfu_usa

Educational organization that administers international exchange programs, primarily for high school students. Administers scholarship programs that sponsor student exchanges.

War, Conflict, and Peacekeeping

▶**AGENCIES**

Bureau of Political-Military Affairs *(State Dept.),* **Plans and Initiatives,** *2401 E St. N.W., #1038, 20520; (202) 663-3040. Fax, (202) 632-3391. Michael Smith, Director.*
Web, www.state.gov/t/pm/ppa

Facilitates training and equipping of international peacekeepers; addresses counterpiracy; provides diplomatic perspectives to Defense Dept. strategic planning.

State Dept., *Policy Planning, 2201 C St. N.W., #7311, 20520; (202) 647-2972. Fax, (202) 647-0844. David McKean, Director.*
Web, www.state.gov/s/p

Advises the secretary and other State Dept. officials on foreign policy matters, including international peacekeeping and peace enforcement operations.

U.S. Institute of Peace, *2301 Constitution Ave. N.W., 20037; (202) 457-1700. Fax, (202) 429-6063. Stephen J. Hadley, Chair; Nancy Lindborg, President. Press, (202) 429-3869.*
General email, info@usip.org
Web, www.usip.org

Independent, nonpartisan institution established by Congress. Aims to prevent and resolve violent international conflicts, promote post-conflict stability, and increase peace-building capacity, tools, and intellectual capital worldwide.

▶**CONGRESS**

For a listing of relevant congressional committees and subcommittees, please see pages 454–455 or the Appendix.

▶**NONGOVERNMENTAL**

Act Now to Stop War and End Racism (ANSWER) Coalition, *617 Florida Ave. N.W., Lower Level, 20001; (202) 265-1948. Fax, (202) 280-1022. Sarah Sloan, National Staff Coordinator. Press, (202) 265-1948.*
General email, info@answercoalition.org
Web, www.answercoalition.org

Works to end war and conflict, with current emphasis on ending the occupation in Iraq, Afghanistan, and Pakistan. Conducts demonstrations with other peace and anti-war groups, especially ethnic and cultural identity groups concerned with ending racism.

Center for Advanced Defense Studies, *1100 H St. N.W., #750, 20005; (202) 289-3332. Fax, (202) 789-2786. David Johnson, Executive Director.*
General email, info@c4ads.org
Web, www.c4ads.org and Twitter, @C4ADS

Analyzes global data and publishes reports on international conflict and security concerns. Conducts field research in conflict areas.

Conflict Solutions International, 1629 K St. N.W., #300, 20006; (202) 349-3972. George d'Angelo, President.
General email, info@csiorg.org

Web, www.conflictsolution.org

All-volunteer nonpartisan organization that reviews and analyzes global issues to support ending violent conflict. Holds forums to educate the public and increase awareness of religious movements, civil conflict, and independence groups. Interests include relations between the United States and Cuba, including negotiations to release political prisoners.

Fourth Freedom Forum, *Washington Office,* 1101 14th St. N.W., #900, 20005; (202) 464-6009. Fax, (202) 238-9604. Alistair Millar, Executive Director.
General email, amillar@fourthfreedom.org

Web, www.fourthfreedom.org

Conducts research and training to advance global cooperation to address transnational threats, including terrorism, nuclear proliferation, and drug trafficking. (Headquarters in Goshen, Ind.)

Fund for Peace, 1101 14th St. N.W., #1020, 20005; (202) 223-7940. Fax, (202) 223-7947. J.J. Messner, Executive Director.
Web, www.global.fundforpeace.org

Promotes international sustainable security. Produces the Failed States Index and the Conflict Assessment System Tool (CAST) that gathers information for determining conflict risk. Works with policymakers, government agencies, nonprofits, journalists, and private organizations to advocate nonviolent conflict resolution. Interests include early warning, election violence, and preventing violence against women.

International Center on Nonviolent Conflict (ICNC), P.O. Box 27606, 20038; (202) 416-4720. Fax, (202) 466-5918. Hardy Merriman, President.
General email, icnc@nonviolent-conflict.org

Web, www.nonviolent-conflict.org

Advocates nonviolent methods to protect international human rights and democracy. Supports research and education to broaden these methods. Holds seminars on successful nonviolent conflict practices.

International Crisis Group, *Washington Office,* 1629 K St. N.W., #450, 20006; (202) 785-1601. Fax, (202) 785-1630. Mark L. Schneider, Senior Vice President.
General email, washington@crisisgroup.org

Web, www.crisisgroup.org

Private, multinational organization that seeks to prevent international conflict. Writes and distributes reports and raises funds. (Headquarters in Brussels.)

International Peace and Security Institute (IPSI), 1720 N St. N.W., 20036; (202) 375-7764. Fax, (202) 330-5376. Cameron M. Chisholm, President.
General email, info@ipsinstitute.org

Web, www.ipsinstitute.org

Researches and analyzes global conflict. Holds educational symposiums and offers training programs to promote peacebuilding skills. Publishes weekly reports on international conflict management and current affairs.

International Stability Operations Assn. (ISOA), 8221 Old Courthouse Rd., #200, Vienna, VA 22182 (mailing address: 1714 Corwin Dr., Silver Spring, MD 20910); (703) 596-9417. Fax, (571) 282-4800. Ado Machida, President.
General email, isoa@stability-operations.org

Web, www.stability-operations.org

Membership: private-sector service companies involved in all sectors of peace and stability operations around the world, including mine clearance, logistics, security, training, and emergency humanitarian aid. Works to institute standards and codes of conduct. Monitors legislation.

Refugees International, 2001 S St. N.W., #700, 20009; (202) 828-0110. Fax, (202) 828-0819. Michel Gabaudan, President. Toll-free, (800) 733-8433.
General email, ri@refugeesinternational.org

Web, www.refugeesinternational.org and Twitter, @RefugeesIntl

Advocates assistance and protection for displaced people worldwide. Conducts field studies to identify basic needs and makes recommendations to policymakers and aid agencies.

Search for Common Ground (SFCG), 1601 Connecticut Ave. N.W., 20009; (202) 265-4300. Fax, (202) 232-6718. Shamil Idriss, President.
Web, www.sfcg.org and Twitter, @SFCG_

International nonprofit that seeks to end global violent conflict at a grassroots level. Provides mediation services and training for youth and women activists. Produces print and video media to encourage discussions on how to solve issues nonviolently. Supports theatre and sports programs for youth in politically disadvantaged areas.

United to End Genocide, 1010 Vermont Ave. N.W., #1100, 20005; (202) 556-2100. Fax, (202) 833-1479. Thomas H. (Tom) Andrews, President.
General email, info@endgenocide.org

Web, www.endgenocide.org

Seeks to prevent and end genocide and mass atrocities by advocacy to elected officials and civil society leaders worldwide. Goals include accountability for perpetrators and justice for victims. Monitors warning signs of genocide. Organizes Diaspora and human rights advocates. Promotes grassroots actions. Monitors legislation. (Formerly the Save Darfur Coalition/Genocide Awareness Network.)

Win Without War, 2000 M St. N.W., #720, 20036; (202) 232-3317. Fax, (202) 232-3440. Angela Miller, Program Director, (202) 232-3317, ext. 110.

General email, info@winwithoutwar.org

Web, www.winwithoutwar.org and *Twitter, @winwithoutwar*

Coalition of national organizations promoting international cooperation and agreements as the best means for securing peace. Encourages U.S. foreign policies of counterterrorism and weapons nonproliferation, but opposes unilateral military preemption. (Affiliated with the Center for International Policy.)

IMMIGRATION AND NATURALIZATION

General

►AGENCIES

Administration for Children and Families (ACF) *(Health and Human Services Dept.), Refugee Resettlement, 330 C St. S.W., 20201; (202) 401-9246. Fax, (202) 401-0981. Robert Carey, Director.*
Web, www.acf.hhs.gov/programs/orr

Directs a domestic resettlement program for refugees; reimburses states for costs incurred in giving refugees monetary and medical assistance; awards funds to voluntary resettlement agencies for providing refugees with monetary assistance and case management.

Bureau of Consular Affairs *(State Dept.), Visa Services, 2401 E St. N.W., #6811, 20522-0106; (202) 647-9584. Edward J. Ramotowski, Deputy Assistant Secretary. National Visa Center, (603) 334-0700.*
Web, http://travel.state.gov/content/visas/en.html

Supervises visa issuance system, which is administered by U.S. consular offices abroad.

Civil Division *(Justice Dept.), Immigration Litigation, 450 5th St. N.W., 20539 (mailing address: P.O. Box 878, Ben Franklin Station, Washington, DC 20044); (202) 616-4930. Fax, (202) 307-8837. David M. McConnell, Director.*
Web, www.justice.gov/civil/office-immigration-litigation

Handles most civil litigation arising under immigration and nationality laws.

Executive Office for Immigration Review *(Justice Dept.), 950 Pennsylvania Ave. N.W., Falls Church, VA 20530-0001; (703) 305-0169. Juan P. Osuna, Director. TTY, (800) 828-1120. Legislative and Public Affairs, (703) 305-0289. Case Information System, (800) 898-7180. Employer Sanctions and Antidiscrimination Cases, (703) 305-0864. Justice Dept., (202) 514-2000.*
Web, www.justice.gov/eoir

Quasi-judicial body that includes the Board of Immigration Appeals and offices of the chief immigration judge and the chief administration hearing officer. Interprets immigration laws; conducts hearings and hears appeals on immigration issues.

U.S. Citizenship and Immigration Services (USCIS) *(Homeland Security Dept.), 20 Massachusetts Ave. N.W., 20529; (800) 375-5283. León Rodríguez, Director. Press, (202) 272-1200. TTY, (800) 767-1833.*
Web, www.uscis.gov

Responsible for the administration of immigration and naturalization adjudication functions and establishing immigration services policies and priorities.

U.S. Coast Guard (USCG) *(Homeland Security Dept.), Law Enforcement, CG-MLE, 2703 Martin Luther King Jr. Ave. S.E., MS 7516, 20593-7516; (202) 372-2183. Capt. Phil Welzant, Chief.*
Web, www.uscg.mil/hq/cg5/cg531

Oversees enforcement of federal laws and treaties and other international agreements to which the United States is party on, over, and under the high seas and waters subject to the jurisdiction of the United States.

►CONGRESS

For a listing of relevant congressional committees and subcommittees, please see pages 454–455 or the Appendix.

►INTERNATIONAL ORGANIZATIONS

International Catholic Migration Commission (ICMC), *Washington Office, 3211 4th St. N.E., #141, 20017-1194; (202) 541-3389. Johan Ketelers, Secretary General; Jane Bloom, Head, U.S. Liaison Office.*
General email, bloom@icmc.net
Web, www.icmc.net

Supports ICMC's worldwide programs by liaising with the U.S. government, nongovernmental organizations, and the American public. Works with refugees, internally displaced persons, migrants, asylum seekers, and trafficking victims. Responds to refugees' immediate needs while working for return to and reintegration in their home country, local integration, or resettlement in a third country. (Headquarters in Geneva.)

International Organization for Migration (IOM), *Washington Office, 1752 N St. N.W., #700, 20036; (202) 862-1826. Fax, (202) 862-1879. Luca Dall'Oglio, Chief of Mission, ext. 229; William Lacy Swing, Director General.*
General email, iomwashington@iom.int
Web, www.iom.int/countries/united-states-america

Nonpartisan organization that plans and operates resource mobilization functions (RMF), including refugee resettlement, national migration, and humanitarian assistance to displaced populations at the request of its member governments. Advises governments on migration policies, supports victims of human trafficking, assists returning migrants, and raises awareness about the benefits of migration. Recruits skilled professionals for developing countries. (Headquarters in Geneva.)

▶ NONGOVERNMENTAL

American Immigration Lawyers Assn., *1331 G St. N.W., #300, 20005-3142; (202) 507-7600. Fax, (202) 783-7853. Benjamin Johnson, Executive Director.*
Web, www.aila.org

Association for lawyers interested in immigration law. Provides information and continuing education programs on immigration law and policy; offers workshops and conferences. Monitors legislation and regulations.

Center for Immigration Studies, *1629 K St. N.W., #600, 20006; (202) 466-8185. Fax, (202) 466-8076. Mark Krikorian, Executive Director.*
General email, center@cis.org
Web, www.cis.org and Twitter, @wwwCISorg

Nonpartisan organization that conducts research and policy analysis of the economic, social, demographic, and environmental impact of immigration on the United States. Sponsors symposiums.

Ethiopian Community Development Council, Inc., *901 S. Highland St., Arlington, VA 22204; (703) 685-0510. Fax, (703) 685-0529. Tsehaye Teferra, President.*
General email, info@ecdcus.org
Web, www.ecdcinternational.org and Twitter, @ECDC_ACC_WMA

Seeks to improve quality of life for African immigrants and refugees in the United States through local and national programs. Interests include the resettlement and acculturation of refugees, health education, and cultural outreach for communities. Also provides business loans and management training for minority-owned and women-owned businesses in the Washington metropolitan area.

Federation for American Immigration Reform (FAIR), *25 Massachusetts Ave. N.W., #330, 20001; (202) 328-7004. Fax, (202) 387-3447. Daniel A. Stein, President. Toll-free, (877) 627-3247.*
General email, fair@fairus.org
Web, www.fairus.org and Twitter, @FAIRImmigration

Organization of individuals interested in immigration reform. Monitors immigration laws and policies.

Immigration Works USA, *737 8th St. S.E., #201, 20003; (202) 506-4541. Fax, (202) 595-8962. Tamar Jacoby, President.*
General email, info@immigrationworksusa.org
Web, www.immigrationworksusa.org

Coalition of business owners that seeks to educate the public about the benefits of immigration and build support for bringing immigration policy in line with the country's labor needs. Monitors legislation and regulations.

Institute for the Study of International Migration *(Georgetown University), 3300 Whitehaven St. N.W., 3rd Floor, 20007; (202) 687-2258. Fax, (202) 687-2541. B. Lindsay Lowell, Executive Director, Acting.*
General email, isim@georgetown.edu
Web, http://isim.georgetown.edu/about

Researches international migration policy, cause, and conflict. Specializes in forced migration of people for political or militant reasons. Publishes the *International Migration Journal.* Administers academic certificates to students in subjects such as Refugee and Humanitarian Emergencies and International Migration. Offers scholarship programs for international researchers and students to study independent topics.

Lutheran Immigration and Refugee Service, *Advocacy, 122 C St. N.W., #125, 20001-2172; (202) 783-7509. Fax, (202) 783-7502. Brittney Nystrom, Director of Advocacy.*
General email, dc@lirs.org
Web, www.lirs.org, Twitter, @LIRSorg and Facebook, www.facebook.com/LIRSorg

Resettles refugees and provides them with case management, job training, English language, and legal assistance. Provides specialized foster care services for unaccompanied refugee youth and facilitates the reunification of unaccompanied immigrant children in federal custody with their parents or relatives. Funds and provides technical assistance to local projects that offer social and legal services to immigrants and refugees, particularly those in immigration detention. (Headquarters in Baltimore, Md.)

Migration Policy Institute, *1400 16th St. N.W., #300, 20036; (202) 266-1940. Fax, (202) 266-1900. Michael Fix, President.*
General email, info@migrationpolicy.org
Web, www.migrationpolicy.org

Nonpartisan think tank that studies the movement of people within the United States and worldwide. Provides analysis, development, and evaluation of migration, integration, and refugee policies at local, national, and international levels.

National Council of La Raza, *1126 16th St. N.W., #600, 20036-4845; (202) 785-1670. Fax, (202) 776-1792. Janet Murguía, President.*
General email, info@nclr.org
Web, www.nclr.org, Twitter, @NCLR and Facebook, www.facebook.com/Nationalcounciloflaraza

Provides research, policy analysis, and advocacy relating to immigration policy and programs. Monitors federal legislation on immigration, legalization, employer sanctions, employment discrimination, and eligibility of immigrants for federal benefit programs. Assists community-based groups involved in immigration and education services and educates employers about immigration laws.

National Immigration Forum, *50 F St. N.W., #300, 20001; (202) 347-0040. Fax, (202) 347-0058. Ali Noorani, Executive Director. Press, (202) 383-5987.*
General email, media@immigrationforum.org
Web, www.immigrationforum.org, Twitter, @NatImmForum and Facebook, www.facebook.com/NationalImmigrationForum

Pro-immigration advocacy organization that provides policy analysis, research, and updates on immigration policy developments to members and allies across the country. Monitors legislation and regulations related to immigrants and immigration. Works in coalition with broad cross-section of immigrant advocacy, immigrant-serving, religious, business, and labor organizations to advance policies welcoming to immigrants.

NumbersUSA, *Capitol Hill Office, 17 D St. S.E., 1st Floor, 20003; 1400 Crystal Dr., #240, Arlington, VA 22209; (202) 543-1341. Fax, (202) 543-3147. Roy Beck, Executive Director. Donations, (703) 816-8820.*
General email, info@numbersusa.com
Web, www.numbersusa.com

Public policy organization that favors immigration reduction as a way of promoting economic justice for American workers. Monitors legislation and regulations.

Pew Research Center, *Hispanic Trends Project, 1615 L St. N.W., #700, 20036; (202) 419-3600. Fax, (202) 419-3608. Mark Hugo Lopez, Director. Information, (202) 419-3606. Press, (202) 419-4372.*
Web, www.pewhispanic.org

Seeks to improve understanding of the U.S. Hispanic population and its impact on the nation, as well as explore Latino views on a range of social matters and public policy issues, including public opinion, identity, and trends in voting, immigration, work, and education. Conducts public opinion surveys and other studies that are made available to the public. (A project of the Pew Research Center.)

U.S. Committee for Refugees and Immigrants, *2231 Crystal Dr., #350, Arlington, VA 22202-3794; (703) 310-1130. Fax, (703) 769-4241. Lavinia Limón, President. Press, (703) 310-1166.*
General email, uscri@uscridc.org
Web, www.refugees.org

Defends rights of refugees in the United States and abroad. Helps immigrants and refugees adjust to American society; assists in resettling recently arrived immigrants and refugees; offers information, counseling services, and temporary living accommodations through its member agencies nationwide; issues publications on refugees and refugee resettlement; collects and disseminates information on refugee issues. Monitors legislation and regulations.

U.S. Conference of Catholic Bishops (USCCB), *Migration and Refugee Services, 3211 4th St. N.E., 20017; (202) 541-3352. Fax, (202) 541-3399. Bill Canny, Executive Director, (202) 541-3169.*
General email, mrs@usccb.org
Web, www.usccb.org/mrs

Acts as advocate for immigrants, refugees, migrants, and victims of human trafficking. Works with legislative and executive branches of the U.S. government and with national and international organizations such as the U.N. High Commissioner for Refugees to promote fair and responsive immigration and refugee policy.

INTERNATIONAL LAW AND AGREEMENTS

General

▶**AGENCIES**

Bureau of Political-Military Affairs *(State Dept.), Security Negotiations and Agreements, 2201 C St. N.W., #3242, 20037; (202) 647-0622. Chris Spigelmire, Deputy Director.*
Web, www.state.gov/t/pm/c17194.htm

Negotiates and oversees implementation of international security agreements, including defense cooperation agreements, burden-sharing and facilities access agreements, transit and overflight arrangements, and state flights agreements, in order to facilitate the deployment and movement of U.S. forces and materiel abroad and provide protections for U.S. service members operating overseas.

Federal Bureau of Investigation (FBI) *(Justice Dept.), International Operations Division, 935 Pennsylvania Ave. N.W., #7825, 20535; (202) 324-5904. Fax, (202) 324-5292. John Boles, Assistant Director.*
Web, www.fbi.gov/about-us/international_operations

Supports FBI involvement in international investigations; oversees liaison offices in U.S. embassies abroad. Maintains contacts with other federal agencies, Interpol, foreign police and security officers based in Washington, D.C., and national law enforcement associations.

Securities and Exchange Commission (SEC), *International Affairs, 100 F St. N.E., MS 1004, 20549; (202) 551-6690. Fax, (202) 772-9281. Paul A. Leder, Director.*
Web, www.sec.gov/oia#.ux83foxfmar

Promotes investor protection, cross-border securities transactions, and fair, efficient, and transparent markets by advancing international regulatory and enforcement cooperation, promoting the adoption of high regulatory standards worldwide, and formulating technical assistance programs to strengthen the regulatory structure in global finance markets. Works with a global network of securities regulators and law enforcement authorities to facilitate cross-border regulatory compliance and help ensure that international borders are not used to escape detection and prosecution of fraudulent securities activities. Provides the commission and SEC staff with advice and assistance in international enforcement and regulatory efforts.

State Dept., *Global Criminal Justice, 2201 C St. N.W., #7419A, 20520; (202) 647-5072. Fax, (202) 736-4495. Todd F. Buchwald, Special Coordinator.*
Web, www.state.gov/j/gcj and Twitter, @StateDept_GCJ

Oversees U.S. stance on the creation of courts and other judicial mechanisms to bring perpetrators of crimes under international law to justice. Engages in diplomacy with foreign governments whose nationals have been captured in the war on terrorism. Has primary responsibility for policy on Iraqi war crimes.

State Dept., *Office of the Legal Adviser,* 2201 C St. N.W., #6421, 20520-6310; (202) 647-5036. Mary McLeod, Legal Adviser, Acting.
Web, www.state.gov/s/l

Provides the secretary and the department with legal advice on domestic and international problems; participates in international negotiations; represents the U.S. government in international litigation and in international conferences related to legal issues.

State Dept., *Office of the Legal Advisor, International Claims and Investment Disputes,* 2430 E St. N.W., #207, 20520; (202) 776-8360. Fax, (202) 776-8389. Lisa J. Grosh, Assistant Legal Adviser.
Web, www.state.gov/s/l/c3433

Handles claims by foreign governments and their nationals against the U.S. government, as well as claims against the State Dept. for negligence under the Federal Tort Claims Act. Administers the Iranian claims program and negotiates agreements with other foreign governments on claims settlements.

State Dept., *Office of the Legal Advisor, Law Enforcement and Intelligence,* 2201 C St. N,W,, #5419, 20520, (202) 647-5111. Fax, (202) 647-4802. Thomas Heinemann, Assistant Legal Adviser.
Web, www.state.gov

Negotiates extradition treaties, legal assistance treaties in criminal matters, and other agreements relating to international criminal matters.

State Dept., *Office of the Legal Advisor, Treaty Affairs,* 2201 C St. N.W., #5420, 20520; (202) 647-1092. Fax, (202) 647-9844. Michael Mattler, Assistant Legal Adviser for Treaty Affairs, (202) 647-1092.
General email, treatyoffice@state.gov
Web, www.state.gov/s/l/treaty

Provides legal advice on treaties and other international agreements, including constitutional questions, drafting, negotiation, and interpretation of treaties; maintains records of treaties and executive agreements.

Transportation Dept. (DOT), *International Aviation,* 1200 New Jersey Ave. S.E., #W86-316, 20590; (202) 366-2423. Fax, (202) 366-3694. Paul L. Gretch, Director.
Web, www.dot.gov/policy/aviation-policy/office-international-aviation

Responsible for international aviation regulation and negotiations, including fares, tariffs, and foreign licenses; represents the United States at international aviation meetings.

►CONGRESS

For a listing of relevant congressional committees and subcommittees, please see pages 454–455 or the Appendix.

►INTERNATIONAL ORGANIZATIONS

INTERPOL Washington *(Justice Dept.),* INTERPOL Washington, U.S. Dept. of Justice, 20530-0001; (202) 616-9000. Fax, (202) 616-8400. Geoffrey S. Shank, Director.
Web, www.justice.gov/interpol-washington

U.S. representative to INTERPOL; participates in international investigations on behalf of U.S. police; coordinates the exchange of investigative information on crimes, including drug trafficking, counterfeiting, missing persons, and terrorism. Coordinates law enforcement requests for investigative assistance in the United States and abroad. Assists with extradition processes. Serves as liaison between foreign and U.S. law enforcement agencies at federal, state, and local levels. (Headquarters in Lyons, France.)

►NONGOVERNMENTAL

American Arbitration Assn., *Government Relations,* 1120 Connecticut Ave., #490, 20036; (202) 223-4263. Fax, (202) 223-7095. S. Pierre Paret, Vice President.
General email, paretp@adr.org
Web, www.adr.org

Provides dispute resolution services and information. Administers international arbitration and mediation systems. (Headquarters in New York.)

American Bar Assn. (ABA), *International Law,* 1050 Connecticut Ave. N.W., 20036; (202) 662-1660. Fax, (202) 662-1669. Leanne Pfautz, Section Director, (202) 662-1661.
General email, intlaw@americanbar.org
Web, www.americanbar.org/intlaw

Monitors and makes recommendations concerning developments in the practice of international law that affect ABA members and the public. Conducts programs, including International Legal Exchange, and produces publications covering the practice of international law.

American Bar Assn. (ABA), *Rule of Law Initiative,* 1050 Connecticut Ave. N.W., #450, 20036; (202) 662-1950. Fax, (202) 662-1597. Elizabeth Anderson, Director.
General email, rol@americanbar.org
Web, www.americanbar.org/rol

Promotes the rule of law and specific legal reforms in developing countries throughout the world; recruits volunteer legal professionals from the United States and western Europe. Interests include human rights, anticorruption initiatives, criminal law, efforts against human trafficking, judicial reform, legal education reform, civic education, reforming the legal profession, and women's rights.

American Society of International Law, 2223 Massachusetts Ave. N.W., 20008-2864; (202) 939-6000. Fax, (202) 797-7133. Mark D. Agrast, Executive Director. Library, (202) 939-6017.
Web, www.asil.org and Twitter, @asilorg

Membership: lawyers, academics, corporate counsel, judges, representatives of government and nongovernmental organizations, international civil servants, students, and others interested in international law. Conducts research and study programs on international law. Holds an annual meeting on current issues in international law. Library open to the public, 9:00 a.m.–4:00 p.m.

Antarctic and Southern Ocean Coalition, *1320 19th St. N.W., 5th Floor, 20036; (202) 234-2480. Claire Christian, Executive Director, Acting.*
General email, secretariat@asoc.org

Web, www.asoc.org and Twitter, @AntarcticaSouth

Promotes effective implementation of the Antarctic Treaty System; works to protect the fragile environment and biodiversity of the Antarctic continent, including krill conservation, in the Southern Ocean.

Codex Alimentarius Commission, *U.S. Codex Office, 1400 Independence Ave. S.W., South Bldg., #4861, 20250-3700; (202) 205-7760. Fax, (202) 720-3157. Mary Frances Lowe, U.S. Codex Manager; Paulo Almeida, U.S. Associate Manager. Toll-free TTY, (800) 877-8339. Meat and Poultry Hotline, (888) 674-6854.*
General email, uscodex@fsis.usda.gov

Web, www.fsis.usda.gov/codex and Twitter, @USDAFoodSafety

Operates within the Food and Agricultural Organization (FAO) and the World Health Organization (WHO) to establish international food and food safety standards and to ensure fair trade practices. Convenes committees in member countries to address specific commodities and issues including labeling, additives in food and veterinary drugs, pesticide residues and other contaminants, and systems for food inspection. (Located in the USDA Food Safety and Inspection Service; international headquarters in Rome at the UN's Food and Agricultural Organization.)

Inter-American Bar Assn., *1889 F St. N.W., #355, 20006; (202) 466-5944. Fax, (202) 466-5946. Maria Caroline Obarrio, Secretary General.*
General email, iaba@iaba.org

Web, www.iaba.org

Membership: lawyers and bar associations in the Western Hemisphere with associate members in Europe. Works to promote uniformity of national and international laws; holds conferences; makes recommendations to national governments and organizations. Library open to the public.

World Jurist Assn., *7910 Woodmont Ave., #1440, Bethesda, MD 20814; (202) 466-5428. Fax, (202) 452-8540. Franklin Hoet-Linares, President; Garry E. Hunter, Executive Vice President.*
General email, wja@worldjurist.org

Web, www.worldjurist.org and Twitter, @worldjurist

Membership: lawyers, law professors, judges, law students, and nonlegal professionals worldwide. Conducts research; promotes world peace through adherence to international law; holds annual conference and biennial congresses. (Affiliates, at same address, include World Assn. of Judges, World Assn. of Law Professors, World Assn. of Lawyers, and World Business Associates.)

World Justice Project (WJP), *1025 Vermont Ave. N.W., #1200, 20005; (202) 407-9330. Fax, (202) 747-5816. Juan Carlos Botero, Executive Director.*
General email, wjp@worldjusticeproject.org

Web, www.worldjusticeproject.org and Twitter, @TheWJP

Supports the international rule of law in order to enforce civil and criminal justice, open government, and absence of corruption. Publishes journals and researches the rule of law and its influence on international economies and politics. Produces the annual Rule of Law Index, which measures countries' effectiveness at practicing the rule of law. Holds conferences and other outreach activities to advance practical solutions to strengthen the rule of law.

Americans Abroad

▶**AGENCIES**

Bureau of Consular Affairs *(State Dept.), Children's Issues, 600 19th St. N.W., 9th Floor, 20006; (202) 501-4444. Henry Hand, Director. Toll-free, (888) 407-4747.*
General email, AskCI@state.gov

Web, http://travel.state.gov/content/childabduction/en.html

Assists with consular aspects of children's services and fulfills U.S. treaty obligations relating to the abduction of children. Advises foreign service posts on international parental child abduction and intercountry adoption.

Bureau of Consular Affairs *(State Dept.), Fraud Prevention, 600 19th St. N.W., #8-206, 20006; (202) 485-6754. Josh Glazeroff, Director.*
Web, http://travel.state.gov/content/travel/en/about/organization.html

Provides resources, tool, and information to consular officials in order to identify and prevent passport and visa fraud.

Bureau of Consular Affairs *(State Dept.), Overseas Citizens Services, 600 19th St. N.W., 10th Floor, #SA17, 20006; (888) 407-4747. Fax, (202) 647-3732. Michelle Bernier-Toth, Director. From overseas, (202) 501-4444.*
Web, http://travel.state.gov

Handles matters involving protective services for Americans abroad, including arrests, assistance in death cases, loans, medical emergencies, welfare and whereabouts inquiries, travel warnings and consular information, nationality and citizenship determination, document issuance, judicial and notarial services, estates, property claims, third-country representation, and disaster assistance.

Bureau of Consular Affairs *(State Dept.), Overseas Citizens Services, Legal Affairs, 600 19th St. N.W., SA-17A, 20037; (202) 501-4444. Fax, (202) 485-8033. Corrin Ferber, Director of Legal Affairs. Recorded consular* information, (202) 647-5225. Toll-free, (888) 407-4747. General email, ask-ocs-l-attyreplies@state.gov

Web, http://travel.state.gov

Offers guidance concerning the administration and enforcement of laws on citizenship and on the appropriate documentation of Americans traveling and residing abroad; gives advice on legislative matters, including implementation of new laws, and on treaties and agreements; reconsiders the acquisition and loss of U.S. citizenship in complex cases; and administers the overseas federal benefits program.

Bureau of Consular Affairs *(State Dept.), Passport Services,* 600 19 St. N.W., #6826, 20006; (202) 647-9584. Brenda Sprague, Deputy Assistant Secretary. National Passport Information Center, (877) 487-2778.
National Passport Information Center email, NPIC@state .gov

Web, http://travel.state.gov/content/travel/en/about/ organization.html and https://travel.state.gov/content/ passports/en/passports.html

Creates passports and provides information and resources to citizens about how to obtain, replace, and change a U.S. passport.

Bureau of Consular Affairs *(State Dept.), Special Issuance Agency,* 600 19th St. N.W., #3.200, 20006; (202) 485-8244. Christine Harold-Aluyen, Director. National passport information, (877) 487-2778.
Web, http://travel.state.gov/content/passports/en/passports/ information/where-to-apply/agencies/special-issuance-agency.html

Administers passport laws and issues passports. (Most branches of the U.S. Postal Service and most U.S. district and state courts are authorized to accept applications and payment for passports and to administer the required oath to U.S. citizens. Completed applications are sent from the post office or court to the nearest State Dept. regional passport office for processing.) Maintains a variety of records received from the Overseas Citizens Services, including consular certificates of witness to marriage and reports of birth and death. (Individuals wishing to apply for a U.S. passport may seek additional information via the phone number or Web address listed above.)

Foreign Claims Settlement Commission of the United States *(Justice Dept.),* 600 E St. N.W., #6002, 20579; (202) 616-6975. Fax, (202) 616-6993. Anuj C. Desai, Commissioner; Sylvia Becker, Commissioner.
General email, info.fcsc@usdoj.gov

Web, www.justice.gov/fcsc

Processes claims by U.S. nationals against foreign governments for property losses sustained.

National Security Division *(Justice Dept.), Justice for Victims of Overseas Terrorism,* 950 Pennsylvania Ave. N.W., 20530; (202) 514-7941. Fax, (202) 514-8714. Heather Cartwright, Director.
General email, nsd.public@usdoj.gov

Web, www.justice.gov/nsd-ovt

Monitors the investigation and prosecution of terrorist attacks against U.S. citizens abroad; works with other Justice Dept. offices to ensure that the rights of victims are respected. Responsible for establishing a Joint Task Force with the State Dept. in the event of a terrorist incident against U.S. citizens overseas. Responds to congressional and citizens' inquiries on the department's response to such attacks.

State Dept., *Office of the Legal Advisor, International Claims and Investment Disputes,* 2430 E St. N.W., #207, 20520; (202) 776-8360. Fax, (202) 776-8389. Lisa J. Grosh, Assistant Legal Adviser.
Web, www.state.gov/s/l/c3433

Handles claims by U.S. government and citizens against foreign governments; handles claims by owners of U.S. flag vessels for reimbursements of fines, fees, licenses, and other direct payments for illegal seizures by foreign governments in international waters under the Fishermen's Protective Act.

Boundaries

▶**AGENCIES**

Bureau of Western Hemisphere Affairs *(State Dept.), Mexican Affairs,* 2201 C St. N.W., #3924, 20520-6258; (202) 647-8766. Fax, (202) 647-5752. Kevin O'Reilly, Director.
Web, www.state.gov/p/wha

Advises the secretary on Mexican affairs. Acts as liaison between the United States and Mexico in international boundary and water matters as defined by binational treaties and agreements. Also involved with border health and environmental issues, new border crossings, and significant modifications to existing crossings.

Saint Lawrence Seaway Development Corp.
(Transportation Dept.), 1200 New Jersey Ave. S.E., #W32-300, 20590; (202) 366-0091. Fax, (202) 366-7147. Betty Sutton, Administrator. Toll-free, (800) 785-2779.
General email, slsc@dot.gov

Web, www.seaway.dot.gov

Operates and maintains the Saint Lawrence Seaway within U.S. territorial limits; conducts development programs and coordinates activities with its Canadian counterpart.

▶**INTERNATIONAL ORGANIZATIONS**

International Boundary Commission, *United States and Canada, U.S. Section,* 2000 L St. N.W., #615, 20036; (202) 736-9102. Fax, (202) 632-2008. Kyle K. Hipsley, Commissioner, (202) 736-9102.
General email, hipsleyk@ibcusca.org

Web, www.internationalboundarycommission.org

Defines and maintains the international boundary line between the United States and Canada. Rules on applications for approval of projects affecting boundary or transboundary waters. Assists the United States and Canada in protecting the transboundary environment. Alerts the governments to emerging issues that may give rise to bilateral disputes. Jointly reports to the U.S. and Canadian governments on an annual basis. (Canadian section in Ottawa.)

International Joint Commission, *United States and Canada, U.S. Section,* 2000 L St. N.W., #615, 20036; (202) 736-9000. Fax, (202) 632-2007. Lana Pollack, Chair; Frank Bevacqua, Public Information Officer, (202) 736-9024. General email, bevacquaf@washington.ijc.org

Web, www.ijc.org

Handles disputes concerning the use of boundary waters; negotiates questions dealing with the rights, obligations, and interests of the United States and Canada along the border; establishes procedures for the adjustment and settlement of questions. (Canadian section in Ottawa; Great Lakes regional office in Windsor, Ontario.)

Extradition

▶**AGENCIES**

Justice Dept. (DOJ), *International Affairs,* 1301 New York Ave. N.W., #800, 20005; (202) 514-0000. Fax, (202) 514-0080. Vaughn A. Ary, Director. Citizen phone line, (202) 353-4641. General email, criminal.division@usdoj.gov

Web, www.justice.gov/criminal/oia

Performs investigations necessary for extradition of fugitives from the United States and other nations. Handles U.S. and foreign government requests for mutual legal assistance, including documentary evidence.

State Dept., *Office of the Legal Advisor, Law Enforcement and Intelligence,* 2201 C St. N.W., #5419, 20520; (202) 647-5111. Fax, (202) 647-4802. Thomas Heinemann, Assistant Legal Adviser. Web, www.state.gov

Negotiates and approves extradition of fugitives between the United States and other nations.

▶**NONGOVERNMENTAL**

Center for National Security Studies, 1730 Pennsylvania Ave. N.W., 7th Floor, 20006; (202) 721-5650. Fax, (202) 530-0128. Kate A. Martin, Director. General email, cnss@cnss.org

Web, www.cnss.org

Monitors and conducts research on extradition, intelligence, national security, and civil liberties.

Fishing, Law of the Sea

▶**AGENCIES**

Bureau of Oceans and International Environmental and Scientific Affairs *(State Dept.), Marine Conservation,* 2201 C St. N.W., #2758, 20520; (202) 647-2335. William Gibbons-Fry, Director. Web, www.state.gov/e/oes/ocns/fish

Promotes food security through sustainable fisheries.

Bureau of Oceans and International Environmental and Scientific Affairs *(State Dept.), Oceans and Polar Affairs,* 2201 C St. N.W., #2665, 20520; (202) 647-3262. Fax, (202) 647-4353. Evan T. Blooms, Director. Web, www.state.gov/e/oes/ocns/opa

Promotes U.S. interests in ocean and polar affairs through implementation of the Law of the Sea Convention, participation in international conferences, and negotiation of formal agreements.

National Oceanic and Atmospheric Administration (NOAA) *(Commerce Dept.), National Marine Fisheries Service,* 1315 East-West Hwy., SSMC3, Silver Spring, MD 20910; (301) 427-8000. Fax, (301) 713-1940. Eileen Sobeck, Assistant Administrator. Press, (301) 427-8003. Web, www.nmfs.noaa.gov

Administers marine fishing regulations, including offshore fishing rights and international agreements.

U.S. Coast Guard (USCG) *(Homeland Security Dept.), Law Enforcement,* CG-MLE, 2703 Martin Luther King Jr. Ave. S.E., MS 7516, 20593-7516; (202) 372-2183. Capt. Phil Welzant, Chief. Web, www.uscg.mil/hq/cg5/cg531

Oversees enforcement of federal laws and treaties and other international agreements to which the United States is party on, over, and under the high seas and waters subject to the jurisdiction of the United States. Enforces domestic fisheries laws and international fisheries agreements.

▶**CONGRESS**

For a listing of relevant congressional committees and subcommittees, please see pages 454–455 or the Appendix.

Human Rights

▶**AGENCIES**

Bureau of Democracy, Human Rights, and Labor *(State Dept.),* 2201 C St. N.W., #7827, 20520-7812; (202) 647-2126. Fax, (202) 647-5283. Tom Malinowski, Assistant Secretary. Web, www.state.gov/j/drl and Twitter, @State_DRL

Implements U.S. policies relating to human rights, labor, and religious freedom; prepares annual review of human rights worldwide; provides the U.S. Citizenship and Immigration Services with advisory opinions regarding asylum petitions.

Bureau of Democracy, Human Rights, and Labor *(State Dept.), International Labor Affairs,* 1800 G St. N.W., #2422, 20006; (202) 216-5882. Bruce Levine, Director; Sarah Fox, Special Representative for International Labor Affairs. Web, www.state.gov/j/drl/ila

Works with organized labor, nongovernmental organizations, international organizations, and corporations to monitor and promote worker rights throughout the

U.S. Customs and Border Protection

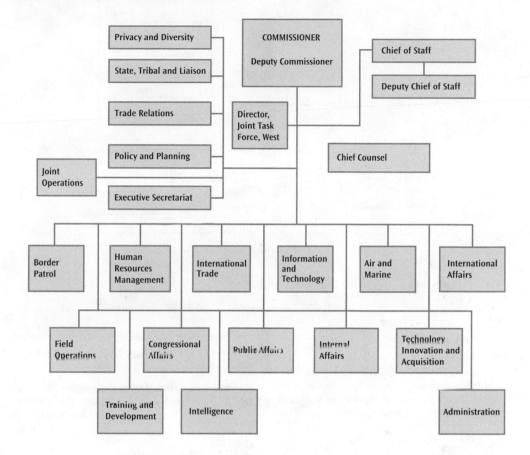

world. Contributes to U.S. foreign policy goals related to democracy promotion, trade, development, and human rights.

Bureau of Democracy, Human Rights, and Labor *(State Dept.), Multilateral and Global Affairs, Business and Human Rights Team,* 2401 E St. N.W., 20037; (202) 663-2935. Jason Pielemeier, Section Chief.
General email, BHR@state.gov

Web, www.humanrights.gov

Works with companies, nongovernmental organizations, and governments to provide corporate contributions to global prosperity while ensuring companies operate in a manner that protects against human rights abuses.

Justice Dept. (DOJ), *Human Rights and Special Prosecutions,* 1301 New York Ave. N.W., John C. Keeney Bldg., #200, 20530; (202) 616-2492. Fax, (202) 616-2491. Teresa McHenry, Chief; Eli M. Rosenbaum, Director, Strategy and Policy.
Web, www.justice.gov/criminal/hrsp

Tracks war criminals within the United States with connections to world genocidal conflicts. Handles legal action to ensure denaturalization and/or deportation.

State Dept., *Global Women's Issues,* 2201 C St. N.W., #7532, 20520; (202) 647-7285. Fax, (202) 647-7288. Catherine M. Russell, Ambassador at Large for Global Women's Issues.
Web, www.state.gov/s/gwi

Works to promote the human rights of women within U.S. foreign policy. Participates in international organizations and conferences; advises other U.S. agencies; disseminates information.

State Dept., *Monitor and Combat Trafficking in Persons,* 1800 G St. N.W., #2201, 20520; (202) 312-9639. Fax, (202) 312-9637. Susan Coppedge, Ambassador-at-Large.
General email, tipoutreach@state.gov

Web, www.state.gov/g/tip and Twitter, @JTIP_State

Combats trafficking in persons domestically and internationally. Publishes annual *Trafficking in Persons Report,* which assesses the progress of other governments, analyzes best practices and new data, and summarizes U.S. efforts to combat human trafficking at home. Funds programs that provide related law enforcement training, comprehensive victim services, and raise public awareness.

U.S. Commission on International Religious Freedom, 732 N. Capitol St. N.W., #A714, 20401; (202) 523-3240. Fax, (202) 523-5020. Paul Liben, Executive Director.

International Trade Administration

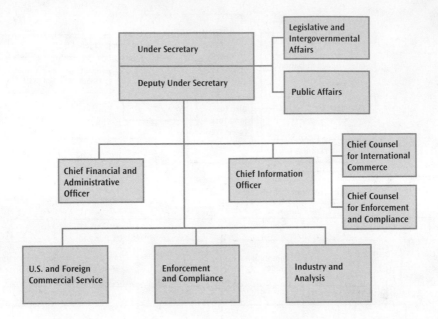

- Under Secretary
- Deputy Under Secretary
- Legislative and Intergovernmental Affairs
- Public Affairs
- Chief Financial and Administrative Officer
- Chief Information Officer
- Chief Counsel for International Commerce
- Chief Counsel for Enforcement and Compliance
- U.S. and Foreign Commercial Service
- Enforcement and Compliance
- Industry and Analysis

General email, media@uscirf.gov

Web, www.uscirf.gov and Twitter, @USCIRF

Agency created by the International Religious Freedom Act of 1998 to monitor religious freedom worldwide and to advise the president, the secretary of state, and Congress on how best to promote it.

►CONGRESS

For a listing of relevant congressional committees and subcommittees, please see pages 454–455 or the Appendix.

Congressional–Executive Commission on China,
243 FHOB, 20515; (202) 226-3766. Fax, (202) 226-3804. Rep. Christopher H. Smith, Co-Chair; Sen. Marco Rubio, Co-Chair; Paul B. Protic, Staff Director, (202) 226-3798. General email, infocecc@mail.house.gov

Web, www.cecc.gov and Twitter, @CECCgov

Independent agency created by Congress. Membership includes individuals from the executive and legislative branches. Monitors human rights and the development of the rule of law in the People's Republic of China. Submits an annual report to the president and Congress.

►NONGOVERNMENTAL

American Bar Assn. (ABA), *Rule of Law Initiative, 1050 Connecticut Ave. N.W., #450, 20036; (202) 662-1950. Fax, (202) 662-1597. Elizabeth Anderson, Director. General email, rol@americanbar.org*

Web, www.americanbar.org/rol

Promotes the rule of law and specific legal reforms in developing countries throughout the world; recruits volunteer legal professionals from the United States and western Europe. Interests include human rights, anti-corruption initiatives, criminal law, efforts against human trafficking, judicial reform, legal education reform, civic education, reforming the legal profession, and women's rights.

Amnesty International USA, *Washington National Office, 600 Pennsylvania Ave. S.E., 5th Floor, 20003; (202) 544-0200. Fax, (202) 546-7142. Michael O'Reilly, Managing Director. Toll-free, 800-AMNESTY. Media, (202) 509-8194. General email, aiusa@aiusa.org*

Web, www.amnestyusa.org and Twitter, @amnesty

International organization that investigates, exposes, and responds to human rights abuses. Works for the release of men and women imprisoned anywhere in the world for their beliefs, political affiliation, color, ethnic origin, sex, language, or religion, provided they have neither used nor advocated violence. Opposes torture and the death penalty; urges fair and prompt trials for all political prisoners. (U.S. headquarters in New York.)

Center for Human Rights and Humanitarian Law,
4300 Nebraska Ave. N.W., 20016; (202) 274-4180. Macarena Saez, Executive Director. General email, humlaw@wcl.american.edu

Web, www.wclcenterforhr.org and Twitter, @humanrts

Seeks to promote human rights and humanitarian law. Establishes training programs for judges, lawyers, and law schools; assists emerging democracies and other nations in developing laws and institutions that protect human rights; organizes conferences with public and private institutions. (Affiliated with the Washington College of Law at American University.)

Free the Slaves, *1320 19th St. N.W., #600, 20036; (202) 775-7480. Fax, (202) 775-7485. Maurice Middleberg, Executive Director.*

General email, info@freetheslaves.net

Web, http://freetheslaves.net and Twitter, @FreeTheSlaves

Conducts field operations in India, Nepal, Haiti, Ghana, Congo, and Brazil to liberate slaves and help them rebuild their lives and advocacy initiatives in the United States and overseas to change the economic, legal, and social conditions that allow modern slavery to exist. Partners with governments, international institutions, faith communities, and the business community to engage their assistance in creating an enabling environment for antislavery projects. Develops new monitoring and evaluation methods to establish slavery prevalence and programmatic impact.

Genocide Watch *(George Mason University),* School of Conflict Analysis, 3351 N. Fairfax Dr., MS 4D3, Arlington, VA 22201; (202) 643-1405. Fax, (703) 993-1302. Gregory Stanton, President.

General email, communications@genocidewatch.org

Web, www.genocidewatch.net and Twitter, @genocide_watch

Educates the public and policymakers about the causes, processes, and warning signs of genocide; seeks to create the institutions and the political will to prevent and stop genocide and to bring perpetrators of genocide to justice. (Coordinator of the Alliance Against Genocide.)

GoodWeave USA, *1111 14th St. N.W., #820, 20005; (202) 234-9050. Fax, (202) 234-9056. Nina Smith, Executive Director.*

General email, info@goodweave.org

Web, www.goodweave.org

International human rights organization working to end child labor in Indian, Nepalese, and Afghanistani handmade carpet industries. Inspects and certifies workplace conditions. Runs schools and rehabilitation centers for former child workers.

Human Rights First, *Washington Office, 805 15th St. N.W., #900, 20005-2207; (202) 547-5692. Fax, (202) 543-5999. Elisa Massimino, President. Press, (202) 370-3323.*

General email, perezsantiago@humanrightsfirst.org

Web, www.humanrightsfirst.org

Promotes human rights as guaranteed by the International Bill of Human Rights. Mobilizes activists and the legal community to pressure the U.S. government and private companies to respect human rights and the rule of the law. Advocates American leadership to secure core freedoms worldwide.

Human Rights Watch, *Washington Office, 1630 Connecticut Ave. N.W., #500, 20009; (202) 612-4321. Fax, (202) 612-4333. Sarah Margon, Washington Director, U.S. Foreign Policy.*

General email, hrwdc@hrw.org

Web, www.hrw.org

International, nonpartisan human rights organization that monitors human rights violations worldwide, subdivided into five regional concentrations—Africa, Americas, Asia, Europe and Central Asia, and the Middle East and North Africa. Coordinates thematic projects on women's rights, LGBT rights, arms, children's rights, health and disability rights, business and human rights, counterterrorism, and international justice. Conducts fact-finding missions in more than 90 countries around the world; publicizes violations and encourages international protests; maintains file on human rights violations. (Headquarters in New York.)

International Assn. of Official Human Rights Agencies (IAOHRA), *444 N. Capitol St. N.W., #536, 20001; (202) 624-5410. Fax, (202) 624-8185. Jean M. Kelleher, President; Melody Fowler-Green, Executive Director.*

General email, iaohra@sso.org

Web, www.iaohra.org

Works with government and human rights agencies worldwide to promote civil and human rights, including elimination of unlawful discrimination in employment, housing, education, and public accommodations. Offers management training for human rights executives and civil rights workshops for criminal justice agencies; develops training programs in investigative techniques, settlement and conciliation, and legal theory. Serves as an information clearinghouse on human rights laws and enforcement.

International Justice Mission, *P.O. Box 58147, 20037-8147; (703) 465-5495. Fax, (703) 465-5499. Sean Litton, President.*

General email, contact@ijm.org

Web, www.ijm.org

Seeks to help people suffering injustice and oppression who cannot rely on local authorities for relief. Documents and monitors conditions of abuse and oppression, educates churches and the public about abuses, and mobilizes intervention on behalf of victims.

Jubilee Campaign USA, *9689-C Main St., Fairfax, VA 22031; (703) 503-0791. Fax, (703) 503-0792. Ann Buwalda, Executive Director. TTY, (877) 654-4331.*

General email, jubilee@jubileecampaign.org

Web, www.jubileecampaign.org

Promotes human rights and religious liberty for ethnic and religious minorities in countries that oppress them. Advocates the release of prisoners of conscience and revising laws to achieve this. Especially interested in ending the exploitation of children.

Physicians for Human Rights, *Washington Office, 1110 Vermont Ave. N.W., 5th Floor, 20005; (202) 728-5335. Fax, (202) 728-3053. Andrea Gittleman, Director, U.S. Policy, Acting; Vacant, Washington Director.*

General email, phrusa@phrusa.org

Web, www.physiciansforhumanrights.org

Mobilizes doctors, nurses, health specialists, scientists, and others to promote health and human rights globally. Investigates and seeks to end human rights abuses. Issues reports and press releases; conducts training programs on health and human rights issues;

acts as advocate before policymakers. (Headquarters in New York City.)

Polaris Project, *P.O. Box 65323, 20035; (202) 745-1001. Fax, (202) 745-1119. Bradley Myles, Chief Executive Officer. 24-hour hotline, (888) 373-7888.*
General email, info@polarisproject.org
Web, www.polarisproject.org and Twitter, @Polaris_Project

Fights human trafficking at the local, national, and international levels with an emphasis on policy advocacy and survivor support. Operates the 24-hour National Human Trafficking Resource Center Hotline for victims, law enforcement agencies, and others.

Robert F. Kennedy Center for Justice and Human Rights, *1300 19th St. N.W., #750, 20036-1651; (202) 463-7575. Fax, (202) 463-6606. Kerry Kennedy, President. Media, (917) 284-6356.*
General email, info@rfkhumanrights.org
Web, www.rfkcenter.org and Twitter, @RFKHumanRights

Presents annual book, journalism, and human rights awards and carries out programs that support the work of the human rights award laureates in their countries. Investigates and reports on human rights; campaigns to heighten awareness of these issues, stop abuses, and encourage governments, international organizations, and corporations to adopt policies that ensure respect for human rights. Provides training for human rights advocates.

Torture Abolition and Survivors Support Coalition International (TASSC), *4121 Harewood Rd. N.E., Suite B, 20017-1597; (202) 529-2991. Fax, (202) 529-8334. Gizachew Emiru, Director.*
General email, info@tassc.org
Web, www.tassc.org

Coalition of torture survivors seeking to end torture through public education and political advocacy. Provides resources and information to survivors of torture and their families.

Narcotics Trafficking

▶**AGENCIES**

Bureau of International Narcotics and Law Enforcement Affairs *(State Dept.), 2201 C St. N.W., #7826, 20520-7512; (202) 647-8464. William R. Brownfield, Assistant Secretary.*
Web, www.state.gov/j/inl and Twitter, @StateINL

Coordinates efforts to establish and facilitate stable criminal justice systems in order to strengthen international law enforcement and judicial effectiveness, bolster cooperation in legal affairs, and support the rule of law, while respecting human rights. Seeks to disrupt the overseas production and trafficking of illicit drugs by means of counterdrug and anticrime assistance and coordination with foreign nations and international organizations.

Defense Dept. (DoD), *Counternarcotics and Global Threats, 2500 Defense Pentagon, #5C653, 20301-2900; (703) 697-7202. Fax, (703) 692-6947. Caryn Hollis, Deputy Assistant Secretary, Acting.*
Web, http://policy.defense.gov/OUSDPOffices/ASDforSpecialOperationsLowIntensityConflict/CounternarcoticsandGlobalThreats.aspx

Coordinates and monitors Defense Dept. support of civilian drug law enforcement agencies and interagency efforts to detect and monitor the maritime and aerial transit of illegal drugs into the United States. Represents the secretary on drug control matters outside the department.

Drug Enforcement Administration (DEA) *(Justice Dept.), 700 Army-Navy Dr., Arlington, VA 22202 (mailing address: 8701 Morrissette Dr., MS AES, Springfield, VA 22152); Fax, (202) 307-4540. Chuck Rosenberg, Administrator, Acting. Phone (Command Center), (202) 307-8000. Press, (202) 307-7977. General information, (202) 307-1000.*
Web, www.dea.gov

Assists foreign narcotics agents; cooperates with the State Dept., embassies, the Agency for International Development, and international organizations to strengthen narcotics law enforcement and to reduce supply and demand in developing countries; trains and advises narcotics enforcement officers in developing nations.

U.S. Coast Guard (USCG) *(Homeland Security Dept.), Law Enforcement, CG-MLE, 2703 Martin Luther King Jr. Ave. S.E., MS 7516, 20593-7516; (202) 372-2183. Capt. Phil Welzant, Chief.*
Web, www.uscg.mil/hq/cg5/cg531

Oversees enforcement of federal laws and treaties and other international agreements to which the United States is party on, over, and under the high seas and waters subject to the jurisdiction of the United States jurisdiction. Combats smuggling of narcotics and other drugs into the United States via the Atlantic and Pacific Oceans and the Gulf of Mexico. Works with U.S. Customs and Border Protection on drug law enforcement.

U.S. Customs and Border Protection *(Homeland Security Dept.), Border Patrol, 1300 Pennsylvania Ave. N.W., #6.5E, 20229; (202) 344-2050. Fax, (202) 344-3140. Ronald D. Vitiello, Chief, Acting.*
Web, www.cbp.gov/border-security/along-us-borders/overview

Mobile uniformed law enforcement arm of the Homeland Security Dept. Primary mission is to detect and prevent the illegal trafficking of people and contraband across U.S. borders.

U.S. Customs and Border Protection *(Homeland Security Dept.), Field Operations, 1300 Pennsylvania Ave. N.W., #2.4A, 20229; (202) 344-1620. Fax, (202) 344-2777. Todd Owen, Assistant Commissioner. Press, (202) 344-1700.*
Web, www.cbp.gov/border-security/ports-entry

Interdicts and seizes contraband, including narcotics and other drugs, at the U.S. border.

INTERNATIONAL TRADE AND DEVELOPMENT

General

▶AGENCIES

Antitrust Division *(Justice Dept.), Foreign Commerce,* 450 5th St. N.W., #1100, 20530; (202) 514-2464. Fax, (202) 514-4508. Edward T. Hand, Chief.
Web, www.justice.gov/atr

Acts as the division's liaison with foreign governments and international organizations, including the European Union, regarding antitrust enforcement and competition issues. Works with the State Dept. to exchange information with foreign governments concerning investigations involving foreign corporations and nationals.

Bureau of Economic Analysis *(Commerce Dept.), Direct Investment,* 1441 L St. N.W., 20230; (202) 606-9591. Fax, (202) 606-5311. Patricia (Sally) Abaroa, Chief.
General email, internationalaccounts@bea.gov
Web, www.bea.gov

Compiles statistics on foreign direct investment in the United States and U.S. direct investment abroad.

Bureau of Economic and Business Affairs *(State Dept.),* 2201 C St. N.W., #4932, 20520-5820; (202) 647-7971. Fax, (202) 647-5713. Charles H. Rivkin, Assistant Secretary.
Web, www.state.gov/e/eb and Twitter, @EconEngage

Formulates and implements policies related to U.S. economic relations with foreign countries, including international business practices, communications and information, trade, finance, investment, development, natural resources, energy, and transportation.

Bureau of Economic and Business Affairs *(State Dept.), Agriculture Policy,* 2201 C St. N.W., #4686, 20520-0002; (202) 647-3090. Fax, (202) 647-1894. Eric W. Luftman, Director, (202) 647-0133.
Web, www.state.gov/e/eb/tpp/agp

Develops agricultural trade policy; handles questions pertaining to international negotiations on all agricultural products covered by the World Trade Organization (WTO) and bilateral trade agreements. Oversees the distribution of biotechnology outreach funds to promote international acceptance of the technology.

Bureau of Economic and Business Affairs *(State Dept.), Commercial and Business Affairs,* 2201 C St. N.W., #5820, 20520-5820; (202) 647-1625. Fax, (202) 647-3953. Vacant, Special Representative; Caryn R. McClelland, Deputy Special Representative.
General email, cbaweb@state.gov
Web, www.state.gov/e/eb/cba

Serves as primary contact in the State Dept. for U.S. businesses. Coordinates efforts to facilitate U.S. business interests abroad, ensures that U.S. business interests are given sufficient consideration in foreign policy, and provides assistance to firms with problems overseas (such as claims and trade complaints). Oversees the Global Entrepreneurship Program.

Bureau of Economic and Business Affairs *(State Dept.), Investment Affairs,* 2201 C St. N.W., #4820, 20520-5820; (202) 736-4907. Fax, (202) 647-0320. Michael Tracton, Director.
General email, eb-a-oia-dl@state.gov
Web, www.state.gov/e/eb/ifd/oia

Develops U.S. investment policy. Makes policy recommendations regarding multinational enterprises and the expropriation of and compensation for U.S. property overseas. Negotiates bilateral and multilateral investment agreements. Coordinates the State Dept.'s position with respect to the Committee for Foreign Investments in the United States.

Bureau of Economic and Business Affairs *(State Dept.), Sanctions Policy and Implementation,* 2201 C St. N.W., #4657, 20520; (202) 647-7489. Fax, (202) 647-4064. Julie H. Nutter, Deputy Assistant Secretary.
Web, www.state.gov/e/eb/tfs/spi

Develops and implements U.S. economic sanctions of embargoed countries. Coordinates U.S. participation in multilateral strategic trade control and revisions related to the export of strategically critical high-technology goods. Cooperates with the Commerce, Defense, and Treasury Depts. regarding export controls.

Bureau of Economic and Business Affairs *(State Dept.), Trade Policy and Programs,* 2201 C St. N.W., #4652, EB/TPP, 20520-5820; (202) 647-5968. Fax, (202) 647-1825. William E. Craft, Deputy Assistant Secretary.
General email, ebtpp@state.gov
Web, www.state.gov/e/eb/tpp

Develops and administers policies and programs on international trade, including trade negotiations and agreements, import relief, unfair trade practices, trade relations with developing countries, export development, and export controls (including controls imposed for national security or foreign policy purposes).

Bureau of Industry and Security *(Commerce Dept.),* 14th St. and Constitution Ave. N.W., #3898, 20230; (202) 482-1455. Fax, (202) 482-2387. Eric L. Hirschhorn, Under Secretary. Press, (202) 482-2721. Export licensing information, (202) 482-4811.
Web, www.bis.doc.gov and Twitter, @BISgov

Administers Export Administration Act; coordinates export administration programs of federal departments and agencies; maintains control lists and performs export licensing for the purposes of national security, foreign policy, and short supply. Monitors impact of foreign boycotts on the United States; ensures availability of goods and services essential to industrial performance on contracts for national defense. Assesses availability of foreign products and technology to maintain control lists and licensing.

Census Bureau *(Commerce Dept.), International Trade Management,* 4600 Silver Hill Rd., #6K032, Suitland, MD 20746 (mailing address: 4600 Silver Hill Rd., #6K032,

Washington, DC 20233-6700); (301) 763-2255. Fax, (301) 763-6638. Dale C. Kelly, Chief. International trade helpline, (800) 549-0595.
Web, www.census.gov/trade

Provides data on all aspects of foreign trade in commodities. Compiles information for 240 trading partners, including China, Japan, and Mexico, through all U.S. states and ports. Publishes the monthly economic indicator, U.S. International Trade in Goods and Services, in conjunction with the U.S. Bureau of Economic Analysis.

Committee on Foreign Investment in the United States (Treasury Dept.), 1500 Pennsylvania Ave. N.W., #5221, 20220; (202) 622-1860. Fax, (202) 622-0391.
Stephen (Steve) Hanson, Staff Chair.
General email, cfius@treasury.gov
Web, www.treasury.gov/cfius

Reviews foreign acquisition of U.S. companies and determines whether they pose national security threats. Conducts investigations into such acquisitions.

Export-Import Bank of the United States, 811 Vermont Ave. N.W., 20571; (202) 565-3946. Fax, (202) 565-3380. Fred P. Hochberg, Chair. Press, (202) 565-3200. Toll-free hotline, (800) 565-3946. TTY, (202) 565-3377.
Web, www.exim.gov

Independent agency of the U.S. government with 12 regional offices. Aids in financing exports of U.S. goods and services; guarantees export loans made by commercial lenders, working capital guarantees, and export credit insurance; conducts an intermediary loan program. National Contact Center advises businesses in using U.S. government export programs.

Federal Trade Commission (FTC), International Affairs, 600 Pennsylvania Ave. N.W., #H494, 20580; (202) 326-2600. Fax, (202) 326-2873. Randolph W. Tritell, Director, (202) 326-3051.
Web, www.ftc.gov/about-ftc/bureaus-offices/office-international-affairs

Assists in the enforcement of antitrust laws and consumer protection by arranging appropriate cooperation and coordination with foreign governments in international cases. Negotiates bilateral and multilateral antitrust and consumer protection agreements and represents the United States in international antitrust policy forums. Assists developing countries in moving toward market-based economies.

International Trade Administration (ITA) (Commerce Dept.), 1401 Constitution Ave. N.W., #3850, 20230; (202) 482-2867. Fax, (202) 482-4821. Stefan M. Selig, Under Secretary. Press, (202) 482-3809. Publications, (202) 482-5487. Trade information, (800) 872-8723.
Web, www.trade.gov

Seeks to strengthen the competitiveness of U.S. industry, promote trade and investment, and ensure fair trade and compliance with trade law and agreements.

International Trade Administration (ITA) (Commerce Dept.), Enforcement and Compliance, 1401 Constitution

Ave. N.W., #3099B, 20230; (202) 482-0063. Fax, (202) 482-0947. Paul Piquado, Assistant Secretary; Ronald K. Lorentzen, Deputy Assistant Secretary.
General email, ECcommunications@trade.gov
Web, http://trade.gov/enforcement

Safeguards and enhances the competitive strength of U.S. industries against unfair trade through the enforcement of U.S. antidumping duty (AD) and countervailing duty (CVD) trade laws and ensures compliance with trade agreements negotiated on behalf of U.S. industries. Promotes the creation and maintenance of U.S. jobs and economic growth by supporting the negotiation of international trade agreements to open foreign markets. Works in close coordination with the President's Interagency Trade Enforcement Center on a variety of trade-related issues. Administers the Foreign Trade Zones program and certain sector-specific agreements and programs, such as the Steel Import Monitoring and Analysis licensing program.

International Trade Administration (ITA) (Commerce Dept.), Global Markets, 1401 Constitution Ave. N.W., #31032, 20230; (202) 482-3022. Fax, (202) 482-5444. Holly Vineyard, Deputy Assistant Secretary.
Web, www.trade.gov/markets

Develops and implements trade and investment policies affecting countries, regions, or international organizations to improve U.S. market access abroad. Provides information and analyses of foreign market barriers and economic conditions to the U.S. private sector; monitors foreign compliance with trade agreements signed with the United States.

International Trade Administration (ITA) (Commerce Dept.), Global Markets and U.S. and Foreign Commercial Service, 1401 Constitution Ave. N.W., #3868, 20230; (202) 482-5777. Arun Kumar, Assistant Secretary.
Web, www.trade.gov

Promotes the export of U.S. goods and services; protects and advocates U.S. business interests abroad; provides counseling and information on overseas markets, international contacts, and trade promotion.

International Trade Administration (ITA) (Commerce Dept.), Global Markets, North and Central America, 1401 Constitution Ave. N.W., #3024, 20230; (202) 482-6452. Fax, (202) 482-5013. Geri Word, Director.
Web, www.trade.gov/markets

Coordinates Commerce Dept. activities and assists U.S. business regarding export to Mexico, Canada, Central America, and the Caribbean. Helps negotiate and ensures compliance with U.S. free trade agreements, including NAFTA (North American Free Trade Agreement) and the Dominican Republic–Central American Free Trade Agreement (CAFTA-DR).

International Trade Administration (ITA) (Commerce Dept.), Global Markets, SelectUSA, 1401 Constitution Ave. N.W., #1235, 20230-0001; (202) 482-0829. Fax, (202) 482-3643. Vinai K. Thummalapally, Executive Director. Call Center, (202) 482-6800.

General email, info@selectusa.gov

Web, http://selectusa.gov

Manages foreign direct investment promotion and encourages U.S. companies to expand, add new facilities, and bring back jobs from abroad. Facilitates investor inquiries, conducts outreach to foreign investors, provides support for state and local governments' investment promotion efforts, and serves as an ombudsman in Washington, D.C., for the international investment community. Web site available in eight languages.

International Trade Administration (ITA) *(Commerce Dept.), Industry and Analysis,* 1401 Constitution Ave. N.W., #2854, 20230; (202) 482-1461. Fax, (202) 482-5697. *Marcus Jadotte, Assistant Secretary; Maureen Smith, Deputy Assistant Secretary.*

Web, www.trade.gov/industry

Seeks to strengthen the international competitiveness of U.S. businesses; coordinates export promotion programs and trade missions; compiles and analyzes trade data. Divisions focus on basic industries, service industries and finance, technology and aerospace, consumer goods, tourism, and environmental technologies exports.

International Trade Administration (ITA) *(Commerce Dept.), Industry and Analysis, Trade Policy and Analysis,* 1401 Constitution Ave. N.W., #21028, 20230, (202) 482-3177. Fax, (202) 482-4614. *Praveen Dixit, Deputy Assistant Secretary, (202) 482-6232.*

Web, www.trade.gov/mas/ian/otpahome

Monitors and analyzes U.S. international trade and competitive performance, foreign direct investment in the United States, and international economic factors affecting U.S. trade; identifies future trends and problems.

International Trade Administration (ITA) *(Commerce Dept.), Industry and Analysis, Trade Promotion Programs and Strategic Partnerships,* Ronald Reagan Bldg., 1401 Constitution Ave. N.W., #800-RRB, 20230; (202) 482-4501. Fax, (202) 482-7800. *Anne Grey, Executive Director, Trade Promotion Programs; Jamie Merriman, Director, Strategic Partnerships.*

Web, http://trade.gov/industry and http://export.gov/cspartners

Supports the entry of U.S. industries into new markets by establishing domestic forums to showcase U.S. goods for foreign purchasers through the International Buy Program (IBP), and certifying international forums to connect U.S. exporters with overseas clients through the Trade Fair Certification Program. Creates opportunities for U.S. firms to meet on a one-to-one basis with foreign industry executives and government officials to establish sales channels through the Trade Missions Program. The Strategic Partnership Program works in conjunction with private corporations, trade associations, and educational institutions to leverage combined resources to further U.S. exports.

National Institute of Food and Agriculture (NIFA) *(Agriculture Dept.), Center for International Programs,* 800 9th St. S.W., #2436, 20024 (mailing address: 1400 Independence Ave. S.W., MS 2203, Washington, DC 20250-2203); (202) 720-3801. Fax, (202) 690-2355. *Michael McGirr, Division, Acting.*

Web, www.nifa.usda.gov/office/center-international-programs

Promotes science education in developing economies and shares research to enhance food production and stabilize economies. Interests include agricultural extension, teaching, and research.

National Institute of Standards and Technology (NIST) *(Commerce Dept.), Standards Services,* 100 Bureau Dr., MS 2100, Gaithersburg, MD 20899; (301) 975-4000. Fax, (301) 975-4715. *Nancy Evans, Director.*

General email, standardsinfo@nist.gov

Web, http://gsi.nist.gov/global

Monitors and participates in industries' development of federal and global standards and standard-enforcement mechanisms. Conducts standards-related research and training and holds workshops for domestic and international audiences. Provides information on industry standards and specifications, conformity assessment, test methods, domestic and international technical regulations, codes, and recommended practices.

Overseas Private Investment Corp., 1100 New York Ave. N.W., 20527; (202) 336-8400. Fax, (202) 336-7949. *Elizabeth L. Littlefield, President. Press, (202) 336-8514. Anticorruption hotline, (202) 336-8400.*

General email, info@opic.gov

Web, www.opic.gov

Provides assistance through political risk insurance, direct loans, and loan guarantees to qualified U.S. private investors to support their investments in emerging markets. Offers preinvestment information and counseling. Provides insurance against the risks of expropriation, political violence, and inconvertibility of local currency.

President's Export Council *(Commerce Dept.),* 14th St. and Constitution Ave. N.W., #4043, 20230; (202) 482-1124. Fax, (202) 482-4452. *Tricia Van Orden, Executive Secretariat.*

Web, www.trade.gov/pec

Advises the president on all aspects of export trade, including export controls, promotion, and expansion. Composed of up to 28 private-sector leaders in business, agriculture, and federal, state, and local government.

Small Business Administration (SBA), *International Trade,* 409 3rd St. S.W., #2400, 20416; (202) 205-6720. Fax, (202) 205-7272. *Eileen Sánchez, Associate Administrator. TTY, (800) 877-8339.*

Web, www.sba.gov/offices/headquarters/oit

Offers instruction, assistance, and information on exporting through counseling and conferences. Helps businesses gain access to export financing through loan guarantee programs.

State Dept., *Economic Growth, Energy, and the Environment,* 2201 C St. N.W., #7256, 20520-7512; (202)

647-7575. Fax, (202) 647-9763. Catherine (Cathy) Novelli, Under Secretary.
Web, www.state.gov/e

Advises the secretary on formulation and implementation of international economic policies and programs, including international monetary and financial affairs, trade, telecommunications, energy, agriculture, commodities, investments, and international transportation issues. Coordinates economic summit meetings.

Trade Promotion Coordinating Committee, *14th St. and Constitution Ave. N.W., #31027, 20230; (202) 482-5455. Fax, (202) 482-4137. Penny Pritzker, Secretary of Commerce; Patrick Kirwan, Director.*
Web, www.export.gov/advocacy/eg_main_022762.asp

Coordinates all export promotion and export financing activities of the U.S. government. Composed of heads of the departments of Commerce, State, Treasury, Defense, Homeland Security, Interior, Agriculture, Labor, Transportation, and Energy, OMB, U.S. Trade Representative, National Security Council/National Economic Council, EPA, Small Business Administration, AID, Export-Import Bank, Overseas Private Investment Corporation, and the U.S. Trade and Development Agency. Secretary of Commerce is the chair.

Treasury Dept., *International Affairs, African Nations, 1500 Pennsylvania Ave. N.W., 20220; Eric Meyer, Deputy Assistant Secretary. Press, (202) 622-2960.*
Web, www.treasury.gov/about/organizational-structure/offices/Pages/--Africa.aspx

Develops and guides economic policy and loan and development programs toward 49 sub-Saharan African economies.

Treasury Dept., *International Affairs, East Asia, 1500 Pennsylvania Ave. N.W., 20220; (202) 622-7222. Robert Dohner, Deputy Assistant Secretary.*
Web, www.treasury.gov/about/organizational-structure/offices/Pages/East-Asia.aspx

Provides economic analysis of countries in East Asia, including Australia, China, Hong Kong, Japan, the Koreas, Mongolia, New Zealand, the Pacific Islands, and Taiwan. Plays a role in managing the U.S.–China Strategic and Economic Dialogue and U.S. engagement with Asian regional initiatives.

Treasury Dept., *International Affairs, Europe and Eurasia, 1500 Pennsylvania Ave N.W., 20220; (202) 622-2722. Daleep Singh, Deputy Assistant Secretary.*
Web, www.treasury.gov/about/organizational-structure/offices/Pages/--Europe-and-Eurasia.aspx

Guides and develops economic policies toward 50 economies in Europe and Eurasia.

Treasury Dept., *International Affairs, International Trade, 1500 Pennsylvania Ave. N.W., #5204, 20220; (202) 622-1733. Fax, (202) 622-1731. Brad McDonald, Director.*
Web, www.treasury.gov/about/organizational-structure/offices/International-Affairs/Pages/trade.aspx

Formulates Treasury Dept. foreign trade policies and coordinates them with other agencies through the U.S. Trade Representative.

Treasury Dept., *International Affairs, Investment Security, 1500 Pennsylvania Ave. N.W., #5221, 20220; (202) 622-1860. Fax, (202) 622-9212. Aimen Mir, Deputy Assistant Secretary; Sephen Hanson, Director.*
General email, cifius@do.treas.gov
Web, www.treasury.gov/about/organizational-structure/offices/Pages/-Investment-Security.aspx

Oversees foreign investment and U.S. open investment policy.

Treasury Dept., *Terrorism and Financial Intelligence, Foreign Assets Control, 1500 Pennsylvania Ave. N.W., Treasury Annex, 20220; (202) 622-2490. Fax, (202) 622-1657. Adam Szubin, Under Secretary, Acting. Fax-on-demand, (202) 622-0077. Hotline, (800) 540-6322.*
General email, ofac_feedback@do.treas.gov
Web, www.treasury.gov/about/organizational-structure/offices/Pages/Office-of-Foreign-Assets-Control.aspx

Administers and enforces economic and trade sanctions against targeted foreign countries and regimes, terrorists, international narcotics traffickers, transnational criminal organizations, and those engaged in activities related to the proliferation of weapons of mass destruction. Acts under presidential wartime and national emergency powers, as well as under authority granted by specific legislation, to impose controls on transactions and freeze foreign assets under U.S. jurisdiction.

U.S. Customs and Border Protection *(Homeland Security Dept.), 1300 Pennsylvania Ave. N.W., #4.4A, 20229; (202) 325-8000. Fax, (202) 344-1380. R. Gil Kerlikowske, Commissioner. Information, (877) 227-5511. Press, (202) 344-1700. TTY, (866) 880-6582.*
Web, www.cbp.gov

Assesses and collects duties and taxes on imported merchandise; processes persons and baggage entering the United States; collects import and export data for international trade statistics; controls export carriers and goods to prevent fraud and smuggling. Library open to the public by appointment.

U.S. Customs and Border Protection *(Homeland Security Dept.), Commercial Targeting and Enforcement, 1300 Pennsylvania Ave. N.W., #L-14, 20229; (202) 863-6548. Fax, (202) 863-6060. Troy Riley, Executive Director.*
Web, www.cbp.gov

Enforces compliance with all commercial import requirements; collects import statistics.

U.S. Foreign Trade Zones Board *(Commerce Dept.), 1401 Constitution Ave. N.W., #21013, 20230; (202) 482-2862. Fax, (202) 482-0002. Andrew McGilvray, Executive Secretary.*
Web, www.trade.gov/ftz

Authorizes public and private corporations to establish foreign trade zones to which foreign and domestic goods can be brought without being subject to customs duties.

U.S. International Trade Commission, *500 E St. S.W., 20436; (202) 205-2000. Fax, (202) 708-2431. Meredith Broadbent, Chair, (202) 205-2250. Reference Library, (202) 205-2630. TTY, (202) 205-1810. Press, (202) 205-1819. Web, www.usitc.gov*

Provides Congress, the president, and the U.S. trade representative with technical information and advice on trade and tariff matters. Determines the impact of imports on U.S. industries in antidumping and countervailing duty investigations. Directs actions against certain unfair trade practices, such as intellectual property infringement. Investigates and reports on U.S. industries and the global trends that affect them. Publishes the Harmonized Tariff Schedule of the United States. Library open to the public.

U.S. Trade and Development Agency, *1000 Wilson Blvd., #1600, Arlington, VA 22209-3901; (703) 875-4357. Fax, (703) 875-4009. Leocadia I. Zak, Director. General email, info@ustda.gov*

Web, www.ustda.gov

Assists U.S. companies exporting to developing and middle-income countries. Provides grants for feasibility studies. Offers technical assistance and identifies commercial opportunities in these countries.

U.S. Trade Representative *(Executive Office of the President), 600 17th St. N.W., #205, 20508; (202) 395-6890. Fax, (202) 395-4549. Amb. Michael Froman, U.S. Trade Representative. Press, (202) 395-3230. General email, correspondence@ustr.eop.gov*

Web, www.ustr.gov

Serves as principal adviser to the president and primary trade negotiator on international trade policy. Develops and coordinates U.S. trade policy, including commodity and direct investment matters, import remedies, East-West trade policy, U.S. export expansion policy, and the implementation of MTN (Multilateral Trade Negotiations) agreements. Conducts international trade negotiations and represents the United States in World Trade Organization (WTO) matters.

U.S. Trade Representative *(Executive Office of the President), Intergovernmental Affairs and Public Engagement (IAPE), 600 17th St. N.W., #107, 20508; (202) 395-6120. Fax, (202) 395-3692. Oman Khan, Assistant U.S. Trade Representative. Web, www.ustr.gov*

Leads the U.S. Trade Representatives's public outreach efforts to state and local governments; business and agricultural communities; and labor, environmental, and consumer groups. Oversees the U.S. Trade Advisory Committee system.

►CONGRESS

For a listing of relevant congressional committees and subcommittees, please see pages 454–455 or the Appendix.

►INTERNATIONAL ORGANIZATIONS

Food and Agriculture Organization of the United Nations (FAO), *Liaison Office in Washington, 2121 K St. N.W., #800B, 20037-0001; (202) 653-2400. Fax, (202) 653-5760. Ajay Markanday, Director. General email, faolow@fao.org*

Web, www.fao.org/north-america/en, www.worldfood dayusa.org and Twitter, @WorldFoodDayUSA

Offers development assistance; collects, analyzes, and disseminates information; provides policy and planning advice to governments; acts as an international forum for debate on food and agricultural issues, including animal health and production, fisheries, and forestry; encourages sustainable agricultural development and a long-term strategy for the conservation and management of natural resources. Coordinates World Food Day. (International headquarters in Rome.)

Inter-American Development Bank, *1300 New York Ave. N.W., 20577; (202) 623-1000. Fax, (202) 623-3096. Luis Alberto Moreno, President; Mark Ropes, U.S. Executive Director. Library, (202) 623-3211. Press, (202) 623-1555. Web, www.iadb.org*

Promotes, through loans and technical assistance the investment of public and private capital in member countries of Latin America and the Caribbean for social and economic development purposes. Facilitates economic integration of the Latin American region, operating the Inter-American Investment Corporation and the Multilateral Investment Fund. Library open to the public by appointment.

International Centre for Settlement of Investment Disputes (ICSID), *1818 H St. N.W., MS J2-200, 20433; (202) 458-1534. Fax, (202) 522-2615. Meg Kinnear, Secretary General, (202) 473-5531. General email, ICSIDsecretariat@worldbank.org*

Web, www.worldbank.org/icsid

Handles the conciliation and arbitration of investment disputes between contracting states and foreign investors. Has more than 140 member states and is affiliated with the World Bank.

International Development Assn., *1818 H St. N.W., MSN MCG5-501, 20433; (202) 473-1000. Fax, (202) 477-0169. Lisa Finneran, Director, (202) 473-1468. Web, www.worldbank.org/ida*

Affiliate of the World Bank funded by membership contributions and transfers of funds from the World Bank. Provides long-term, low-interest, and interest-free loans and grants to the poorest countries.

International Monetary Fund (IMF), *Statistics, 700 19th St. N.W., 20431; (202) 623 7123. Louis Marc Ducharme, Director. Publications, (202) 623-7430. General email, statisticsquery@imf.org and publications@imf.org*

Web, www.elibrary-data.imf.org and www.imf.org/external/data.htm

Publishes monthly *International Financial Statistics (IFS)*, which includes comprehensive financial data for most countries, and *Direction of Trade Statistics*, a quarterly publication, which includes the distribution of exports and imports for 1692 countries. Annual statistical publications include the *Balance of Payments Statistics Yearbook, Direction of Trade Statistics Yearbook, Government Finance Statistics Yearbook*, and *International Financial Statistics Yearbook*. Free online and paid print subscriptions available to the public. All four publications are available on CD-ROM and on the Web site.

Organisation for Economic Co-operation and Development (OECD), *Washington Center, 1776 Eye St. N.W. #450, 20006; (202) 785-6323. Fax, (202) 315-2508. Carol Guthrie, Head of Center.*
General email, washington.contact@oecd.org
Web, www.oecd.org/washington

Membership: thirty-four nations, including Australia, Canada, Japan, Mexico, New Zealand, the United States, and western European nations. Funded by membership contributions. Serves as a forum for members to exchange information and coordinate their economic policies; compiles statistics. Washington Center sells OECD publications and software; maintains a reference library that is open to the public. (Headquarters in Paris.)

Organization of American States (OAS), *Economic Development, 1889 F St. N.W., #750, 20006; (202) 370-9953. Fax, (202) 458-3561. Maryse Robert, Director.*
General email, mrobert@oas.org
Web, www.oas.org/en/sedi/desd

Responsible for matters related to economic development in the hemisphere, with a focus on micro, small, and medium-sized enterprises. Works to promote economic growth, social inclusion, competition, and innovation.

The SEEP Network (The Small Enterprise Education and Promotion Network), *1611 N. Kent St., #610, Arlington, VA 22209; (202) 534-1400. Fax, (703) 276-1433. Sharon D'Onofrio, Executive Director. Press, (202) 534-1402.*
General email, seep@seepnetwork.org
Web, www.seepnetwork.org and Twitter, @TheSEEPNetwork

Membership: international organizations seeking to end poverty. Promotes inclusive markets and financial systems to improve impoverished areas. Conducts research on industry trends, opinions, and practices in developing countries. Interests include financial services and business development.

World Bank, *1818 H St. N.W., 20433; (202) 473-1000. Fax, (202) 477-6391. Hon. Jim Yong Kim, President; Matthew McGuire, U.S. Executive Director. Press, (202) 473-7660. Bookstore, (202) 458-4500. Publications, (800) 645-7247 or (703) 661-1580. Anticorruption hotline, (202) 458-7677.*
General email, Cunit1@worldbank.org
Web, www.worldbank.org and Twitter, @worldbank

International development institution funded by government membership subscriptions and borrowings on private capital markets. Aims to end extreme poverty and advance education, health, and economies. Finances economic development projects in agriculture, environmental protection, education, public utilities, telecommunications, water supply, sewerage, public health, and other areas.

▶**JUDICIARY**

U.S. Court of Appeals for the Federal Circuit, *717 Madison Pl. N.W., 20439; (202) 275-8000. Fax, (202) 275-9678. Sharon Prost, Chief Judge; Daniel E. O'Toole, Clerk, (202) 272-8020. Help Desk, (202) 275-8036. Mediation, (202) 275-8120.*
Web, www.cafc.uscourts.gov

Reviews decisions concerning the International Trade Commission.

▶**NONGOVERNMENTAL**

Assn. of Foreign Investors in Real Estate, *1300 Pennsylvania Ave. N.W., 20004-3020; (202) 312-1400. Fax, (202) 312-1401. James A. Fetgatter, Chief Executive.*
General email, afireinfo@afire.org
Web, www.afire.org

Represents foreign institutions that are interested in the laws, regulations, and economic trends affecting the U.S. real estate market. Informs the public and the government of the contributions foreign investment makes to the U.S. economy. Examines current issues and organizes seminars for members.

Assn. of Women in International Trade, *100 M St. S.E., #600, 20003; (630) 352-2216. Fax, (630) 352-2301. Elizabeth Schumacher, Executive Director.*
General email, info@wiit.org
Web, www.wiit.org

Membership: women and men from all sectors concerned with international trade, including import-export firms, government, corporations, and nonprofit organizations. Provides members with opportunities for professional development. Maintains job bank and sponsors mentoring program.

The Brookings Institution, *Global Economy and Development Studies, 1775 Massachusetts Ave. N.W., 20036; (202) 797-6000. Fax, (202) 797-6004. Kemal Dervis, Director. Communications, (202) 797-6421.*
General email, globalmedia@brookings.edu
Web, www.brookings.edu/global

Facilitates international policy debate on globalization, poverty reduction, global economy, and public goods.

Center for Global Development, *2055 L St. N.W., #500, 20036; (202) 416-4000. Fax, (202) 416-4050. Nancy Birdsall, President.*
General email, info@cgdev.org
Web, www.cgdev.org and Twitter, @CGDev

Works to reduce global poverty and inequality through policy-oriented research and active engagement on development issues with policymakers and the public. Conducts independent research to develop practical ideas for global prosperity.

Center for International Private Enterprise, *1211 Connecticut Ave. N.W., #700, 20036; (202) 721-9200. Fax, (202) 721-9250. Andrew Wilson, Executive Director, Acting.*
General email, info@cipe.org
Web, www.cipe.org and Twitter, @CIPEglobal

Promotes global democratic development through private enterprise and market-oriented reform. Supported by the National Endowment for Democracy, works with business leaders, policymakers, and journalists to build civic institutions. Key program areas include anticorruption, access to information, the informal sector and property rights, and women and youth. (Affiliated with the U.S. Chamber of Commerce.)

Coalition for Employment Through Exports, *1625 K St. N.W., #200, 20006; (202) 296-6107. Fax, (202) 296-9709. John Hardy Jr., President.*
General email, info@usaexport.org
Web, www.usaexport.org

Membership: major U.S. exporters and banks. Works to ensure adequate lending authority for the Export-Import Bank and other trade finance facilities as well as competitive export financing policies for the United States.

Economic Strategy Institute, *3050 K St. N.W., #220, 20007; (202) 965-9484. Clyde V. Prestowitz Jr., President.*
General email, info@econstrat.org
Web, www.econstrat.org

Works to increase U.S. economic competitiveness through research on domestic and international economic policies, industrial and technological developments, and global security issues. Testifies before Congress and government agencies.

Emergency Committee for American Trade, *900 17th St. N.W., #1150, 20006; (202) 659-5147. Fax, (202) 659-1347. Calman J. Cohen, President.*
General email, ecattrade@ecattrade.com
Web, www.ecattrade.com

Membership: U.S. corporations interested in international trade and investment. Supports liberalized trade and investment and opposes restrictions on U.S. exports and imports.

Federation of International Trade Assns., *11654 Plaza America Dr., #120, Reston, VA 20190; (703) 634-3482. Kimberly Park, President.*
General email, info@fita.org
Web, www.fita.org

Membership: local, regional, and national trade associations throughout North America that have an international mission. Works to increase North American exports.

Global Business Dialogue, *1140 Connecticut Ave. N.W., #950, 20036; (202) 463-5074. Fax, (202) 463-7075. R.K. Morris, President.*
General email, comments@gbdinc.org
Web, www.gbdinc.org

Promotes discussion of trade and investment within the global business community.

Institute for Sustainable Communities, *Washington Office, 888 17th St. N.W., #610, 20006; (202) 777-7575. Fax, (202) 777-7577. George Hamilton, President; Debra Perry, Senior Program Manager, U.S..*
General email, isc@iscvt.org
Web, www.iscvt.org

Provides training and technical assistance to communities to engage citizens in developing and implementing plans for a sustainable future. (Headquarters in Montpelier, Vt.)

International Business Ethics Institute, *1776 Eye St. N.W., 9th Floor, 20006; (202) 296-6938. Fax, (202) 296-5897. Lori Tansey Martens, President.*
General email, info@business-ethics.org
Web, www.business-ethics.org

Nonpartisan educational organization that promotes business ethics and corporate responsibility. Works to increase public awareness and dialogue about international business ethics issues through various educational resources and activities. Works with companies to assist them in establishing effective international ethics programs.

International Executive Service Corps (IESC), *1900 M St. N.W., #500, 20036; (202) 589-2600. Fax, (202) 326-0289. Thomas Miller, President.*
General email, iesc@iesc.org
Web, www.iesc.org

Promotes self-sustainable economic growth in developing countries. Implements financial and management programs to improve trade, technology, and tourism. Includes the Geekcorps division to assist in managing technical programs.

National Assn. of Manufacturers (NAM), *International Economic Affairs, 733 10th St. N.W., #700, 20001; (202) 637-3144. Fax, (202) 637-3182. Linda Dempsey, Vice President.*
Web, www.nam.org

Represents manufacturing business interests on international economic issues, including trade, international investment, export financing, and export controls.

National Customs Brokers and Forwarders Assn. of America, *1200 18th St. N.W., #901, 20036; (202) 466-0222. Fax, (202) 466-0226. Barbara Reilly, Executive Vice President.*
General email, recep@ncbfaa.org
Web, www.ncbfaa.org

Membership: customs brokers and freight forwarders in the United States. Fosters information exchange within the industry. Monitors legislation and regulations.

National Foreign Trade Council, *1625 K St. N.W., #200, 20006-1604; (202) 887-0278. Fax, (202) 452-8160. William A. Reinsch, President.*
General email, nftcinformation@nftc.org
Web, www.nftc.org, Twitter, @NFTC and Facebook, www.facebook.com/National-Foreign-Trade-Council-105955409792

Membership: U.S. companies engaged in international trade and investment. Advocates open international trading, export expansion, and policies to assist U.S. companies competing in international markets. Provides members with information on international trade topics. Sponsors seminars and conferences.

Organization for International Investment, *1225 19th St. N.W., #501, 20036; (202) 659-1903. Fax, (202) 659-2293. Nancy McLernon, President.*
General email, jsamford@ofii.org; ralexander@ofii.org
Web, www.ofii.org

Membership: U.S. subsidiaries of international companies. Provides data on international investment in the United States, including reports on exports, tax revenue, and job creation. Monitors legislation and regulations concerning the business operations of U.S. subsidiaries.

Peterson Institute for International Economics (IIE), *1750 Massachusetts Ave. N.W., 20036-1903; (202) 328-9000. Fax, (202) 659-3225. Adam Posen, President.*
General email, comments@piie.com
Web, www.petersoninstitute.org

Conducts studies and makes policy recommendations on international economic issues, including monetary affairs, trade, investment, energy, exchange rates, commodities, and North–South and East–West economic relations.

U.S. Chamber of Commerce, *International Affairs Division, 1615 H St. N.W., 20062-2000; (202) 463-5460. Fax, (202) 463-3114. Myron Brilliant, Executive Vice President.*
Web, www.uschamber.com/international

Provides liaison with network of U.S. chambers of commerce abroad; administers bilateral business councils; responsible for international economic policy development; informs members of developments in international affairs, business economics, and trade; sponsors seminars and conferences. Monitors legislation and regulations.

United States Council for International Business, *Policy and Government Affairs, 1400 K St. N.W., #450, 20005; (202) 371-1316. Fax, (202) 371-8249. Robert Mulligan, Senior Vice President, (202) 682-7375.*
General email, info@uscib.org
Web, www.uscib.org

Membership: multinational corporations, service companies, law firms, and business associations. Represents U.S. business positions before intergovernmental bodies, foreign governments, and business communities. Promotes an open system of world trade, finance, and investment. (Headquarters in New York.)

Urban Institute, *Center on International Development and Governance, 2100 M St. N.W., 20037; (202) 833-7200. Fax, (202) 466-3982. Charles Cadwell, Director.*
General email, idginfo@urban.org
Web, www.urban.org/center/idg

Promotes economic and democratic development in developing and transition countries. Conducts research and works with government officials, international development agencies, and international financial institutions to provide technical assistance toward local governance, service delivery, and public finance.

Washington International Trade Assn., *1300 Pennsylvania Ave. N.W., #G-329, 20004-3014; (202) 312-1600. Fax, (202) 312-1601. Ken Levinson, Executive Director.*
General email, wita@wita.org
Web, https://wita.org

Membership: trade professionals. Conducts programs and provides neutral forums to discuss international trade issues. Monitors legislation and regulations.

Women Thrive Worldwide, *1875 Connecticut Ave. N.W., #405, 20009; (202) 999-4500. Fax, (202) 999-4455. Patricia T. Morris, President.*
General email, thrive@womenthrive.org
Web, www.womenthrive.org and Twitter, @WomenThrive

Advocates international economic policies and human rights that support women worldwide in ending poverty. Researches and develops economic trade policies that reduce poverty, illiteracy, illness, and violence in developing countries.

World Cocoa Foundation, *1411 K St. N.W., 500, 20005; (202) 737-7870. Fax, (202) 737-7832. Timothy S. McCoy, President, Acting.*
General email, wcf@worldcocoa.org
Web, www.worldcocoafoundation.org and Twitter, @WorldCocoa

Promotes a sustainable cocoa economy through economic and social development and environmental conservation in cocoa-growing communities. Helps raise funds for cocoa farmers and increases their access to modern farming practices.

World Shipping Council, *1156 15th St. N.W., #300, 20005; (202) 589-1230. Fax, (202) 589-1231. John W. Butler, President.*
General email, info@worldshipping.org
Web, www.worldshipping.org

Membership association representing the liner shipping industry. Works with policymakers and other industry groups interested in international transportation issues, including maritime security, regulatory policy, tax issues, safety, the environment, harbor dredging, and trade infrastructure. Monitors legislation and regulations.

Development Assistance

►AGENCIES

Agency for International Development (USAID),
*Economic Growth, Education, and Environment, 1300
Pennsylvania Ave. N.W., #3.9, 20523-3900; (202) 712-0670.
Fax, (202) 216-3239. Charles North, Senior Deputy
Assistant Administrator.
Web, www.usaid.gov/who-we-are/organization/bureaus/
bureau-economic-growth-education-and-environment*

Works to foster increased capability of foreign missions to collaborate with governments, entrepreneurs, and other local institutions and individuals to encourage country-based assistance programs. Divisions focus on economic growth, including business, microenterprise development, and institutional reform; the environment and energy use; human capacity development, including education and training; and women in development.

Agency for International Development (USAID),
*Education, 1300 Pennsylvania Ave. N.W., #3.9-37, 20523-3901; (202) 712-1873. Fax, (202) 216-3229. James Peters,
Director, Acting.
Web, www.usaid.gov/who-we-are/organization/bureaus/
bureau-economic-growth-education-and-environment*

Provides field support, technical leadership, and research to help foreign missions and countries manage and develop their human resources. Improves the means of basic and higher education as well as training. Administers the AID Participant Training Program, which provides students and midcareer professionals from developing countries with academic and technical training, and the Entrepreneur International Initiative, a short-term training/trade program that matches developing country entrepreneurs with American counterparts to familiarize them with American goods, services, and technology.

Foreign Agricultural Service (FAS) *(Agriculture Dept.),
1400 Independence Ave. S.W., #5071S, MS 1001, 20250-1001; (202) 720-3935. Fax, (202) 690-2159.
Philip (Phil) Karsting, Administrator. Public Affairs, (202)
720-7115. TTY, (202) 720-1786.
Web, www.fas.usda.gov and Twitter, USDAForeignAg*

Administers the U.S. foreign food aid program with the U.S. Agency for International Development. Responsible for the Food for Progress program, and the McGovern-Dole International Food for Education and Child Nutrition Program.

Millennium Challenge Corp., *1099 14th St. N.W., #700,
20005-3550; (202) 521-3600. Fax, (202) 521-3700.
Dana J. Hyde, Chief Executive Officer.
General email, web@mcc.gov
Web, www.mcc.gov*

Government corporation that provides financial assistance to developing nations that encourage economic freedom. Funds are used for agricultural development, education, enterprise and private-sector development, governance, health, and building trade capacity. Monitors legislation and regulations.

Peace Corps, *1111 20th St. N.W., 20526; (202) 692-1040.
Fax, (202) 692-8400. Carrie Hessler-Radelet, Director.
Information, (855) 855-1961. Press, (202) 692-2230.
Web, www.peacecorps.gov and Twitter, @PeaceCorps*

Promotes world peace, friendship, and mutual understanding between the United States and developing nations. Administers volunteer programs to assist developing countries in education, the environment, health (particularly HIV awareness and prevention), small business development, agriculture, and urban youth development.

State Dept., *Global Food Security, 2201 C St. N.W.,
#5323, 20520; (202) 647-4027. Nancy Stetson, Special
Representative.
Web, www.state.gov/s/globalfoodsecurity/index.htm*

Supports country-driven approaches to address the root causes of hunger and poverty, and helps countries transform their own agricultural sectors to grow enough food to sustainably feed their people.

Treasury Dept., *International Affairs, Development
Policy and Debt, 1500 Pennsylvania Ave. N.W., #5417,
20220; (202) 622-9124. Fax, (202) 622-0664.
Alexia Latortue, Deputy Assistant Secretary.
Web, www.treasury.gov/about/organizational-structure/
offices/Pages/Development-Policy-and-Debt.aspx*

Leads economic growth and poverty reduction efforts in developing countries by providing funds to multilateral development banks; advises the department and the department banks on reforms and innovative financing proposals; formulates the U.S. position on issues facing debtor countries.

►INTERNATIONAL ORGANIZATIONS

TechnoServe, *1120 19th St. N.W., 8th Floor, 20036; (202)
785-4515. Fax, (202) 785-4544. Will Warshauer, President.
Press, (202) 650-5713. Donor Support, (800) 999-6757.
General email, info@technoserve.org
Web, www.technoserve.org*

International nonprofit that assists entrepreneurs in poor and developing countries. Provides access to technology, information, and resources that connect business owners to suppliers and industry networks to increase their revenue. Specializes in farming and agricultural enterprises.

United Nations Development Programme (UNDP),
*Washington Office, 1775 K St. N.W., #420, 20006; (202)
331-9130. Fax, (202) 331-9363. Helen Clark,
Administrator; Paul Clayman, Director.
General email, undp.washington@undp.org
Web, www.undp.org and Twitter, @UNDPDC*

Funded by voluntary contributions from national governments. Administers United Nations' support for economic and social development in developing countries, democratic governance, poverty reduction, crisis prevention and recovery, energy and the environment, and HIV/AIDS. (Headquarters in New York.)

United Way Worldwide, *701 N. Fairfax St., Alexandria, VA 22314-2045; (703) 836-7112. Fax, (703) 519-0097. Brian A. Gallagher, President.*
Web, www.unitedway.org

Membership: independent United Way organizations in 41 countries and territories, including 1,300 in the United States. Provides staff training; fund-raising, planning, and communications assistance; resource management; and national public service advertising. Activities support education, financial stability, and health.

Women for Women International, *2000 M St. N.W., #200, 20036; (202) 737-7705. Fax, (202) 737-7709. Jennifer L. Windsor, Chief Executive Officer.*
General email, general@womenforwomen.org
Web, www.womenforwomen.org and Twitter, @WomenforWomen

Helps women in war-torn regions rebuild their lives through financial and emotional support, job skills training, rights education, access to capital, and assistance for small business development.

World Bank, *Human Development Network, 1818 H St. N.W., 20433; (202) 473-1000. Keith Hanson, Vice President; Melanie Mayhew, Media Contact, (202) 458-7891.*
Web, www.worldbank.org

Assists developing countries in delivering effective and affordable health care, education, and social services. Interests include poverty reduction, income protection, nutrition, jobs access, health coverage, and basic education.

▶**NONGOVERNMENTAL**

ACDI/VOCA, *50 F St. N.W., #1000, 20001-1530; (202) 469-6000. Fax, (202) 469-6257. William Polidoro, President.*
General email, webmaster@acdivoca.org
Web, www.acdivoca.org

Recruits professionals for voluntary, short-term technical assistance to cooperatives, environmental groups, and agricultural enterprises in developing countries and emerging democracies. Interests include poverty reduction, community stabilization, and market integration. Promotes rural finance for micro-sized to medium-sized enterprises.

Adventist Development and Relief Agency, *12501 Old Columbia Pike, Silver Spring, MD 20904; (301) 680-6380. Fax, (301) 680-6370. Jonathan Duffy, President. Toll-free, (800) 424-2372.*
General email, response@adra.org
Web, www.adra.org

Worldwide humanitarian agency of the Seventh-day Adventist Church. Works to alleviate poverty in developing countries and responds to disasters. Sponsors activities that improve health, foster economic and social well-being, and build self-reliance.

American Jewish World Service, *Government Affairs, 1001 Connecticut Ave. N.W., #1200, 20036-3405; (202) 379-4300. Fax, (202) 379-4310. Timi Gerson, Director of Advocacy, (301) 379-4270. Information, (800) 889-7146.*
Web, www.ajws.org and Twitter, @ajws

International development organization that works to alleviate poverty, hunger, and disease. Provides grants to grassroots organizations; offers volunteer services, advocacy, and education for society building, sustainable development, and protection of human rights. Promotes global citizenship within the Jewish community. (Headquarters in New York.)

Ashoka: Innovators for the Public, *1700 N. Moore St., #2000, Arlington, VA 22209; (703) 527-8300. Fax, (703) 527-8383. Bill Drayton, Chief Executive Officer.*
General email, info@ashoka.org
Web, www.ashoka.org and Twitter, @Ashoka

Supports fellowships for individuals with ideas for social change in seventy developing nations. Provides fellows with research support, organizational networking, legal counseling, economic support, and business consulting. Seeks to educate the public about the developing world and the work of its fellows.

CARE, *Washington Office, 1899 L St. N.W., #500, 20036; (202) 595-2800. Fax, (202) 296-8695. David Ray, Head of Policy and Advocacy. Toll-free, (800) 422-7385.*
General email, info@care.org
Web, www.care.org and Twitter, @CARE

Assists the developing world's poor through emergency assistance and community self-help programs that focus on sustainable development, agriculture, agroforestry, water and sanitation, health, family planning, and income generation. Community-based efforts are centered on providing resources to poor women. (U.S. headquarters in Atlanta, Ga.; international headquarters in Geneva.)

Center for Intercultural Education and Development *(Georgetown University), 3300 Whitehaven St. N.W., #1000, 20007 (mailing address: P.O. Box 579400, Washington, DC 20007); (202) 687-1400. Fax, (202) 687-2555. Chantal Santelices, Executive Director, (202) 687-1918.*
General email, cied@georgetown.edu
Web, http://cied.georgetown.edu

Designs and administers programs aimed at improving the quality of lives of economically disadvantaged people; provides technical education, job training, leadership skills development, and business management training; runs programs in Central America, the Caribbean, Central Europe, and Southeast Asia.

Development Gateway, *1110 Vermont Ave. N.W., #500, Washington, DC 20005; (202) 572-9200. Jean-Louis Sarbib, Chief Executive Officer.*
General email, info@developmentgateway.org
Web, www.developmentgateway.org

Provides international and grassroots development organizations with visual translations of data and analysis. Assists in applying data-based solutions to policies. Seeks to improve evaluation, decision making, and management of international development efforts.

Global Communities, *8601 Georgia Ave., #800, Silver Spring, MD 20910-3440; (301) 587-4700. Fax, (301) 587-7315. David Weiss, President.*
General email, mailbox@globalcommunities.org
Web, www.globalcommunities.org

Works under contract with the Agency for International Development, United Nations, and World Bank to strengthen local government housing departments abroad.

Institute for State Effectiveness, *600 New Hampshire Ave. N.W., 20037; (202) 298-5959. Fax, (202) 298-5564. Claire Lockhart, President.*
General email, info@effectivestates.org
Web, www.effectivestates.org

Aims to improve international government accountability by creating policies and educating local leaders and citizens on successful accountability practices. Studies how nations build accountable governments and creates similar tools for developing countries and leaders.

InterAction, *1400 16th St. N.W., #210, 20036; (202) 667-8227. Fax, (202) 667-8236. Samuel A. Worthington, Chief Executive Officer. Communications, (202) 552-6561.*
General email, ia@interaction.org
Web, www.interaction.org

Alliance of more than 190 U.S.-based international development and humanitarian nongovernmental organizations. Provides a forum for exchange of information on development assistance issues, including food aid and other relief services, migration, and refugee affairs. Monitors legislation and regulations.

International Center for Research on Women, *1120 20th St. N.W., #500N, 20036; (202) 797-0007. Fax, (202) 797-0020. Sarah Degnan Kambou, President. Press, (202) 742-1263.*
General email, info@icrw.org
Web, www.icrw.org

Advances gender equality and human rights, fights poverty, and promotes sustainable economic and social development through research, program implementation, information-gathering, publications, and strategic media outreach. Conducts empirical research and promotes practical, evidence-based solutions that enable women to control their own lives and fully participate in their societies.

Leadership Initiatives, *4410 Massachusetts Ave., #236, 20016; (202) 465-4796. Fax, (202) 280-1221. Marshall Bailly, Executive Director.*
General email, info@lichange.org
Web, www.lichange.org

Offers entrepreneurship training and leadership courses to individuals in developing countries. Connects students to international leaders to solve local business issues. Interests include mentoring orphans and youth. Focuses on communities in Nigeria, Namibia, and the Philippines.

National Peace Corps Assn., *1900 L St. N.W., #610, 20036-5002; (202) 293-7728. Fax, (202) 293-7554. Glenn Blumhorst, President.*
General email, ncpa@peacecorpsconnect.org
Web, www.peacecorpsconnect.org

Membership: returned Peace Corps volunteers, staff, and interested individuals. Promotes a global perspective in the United States; seeks to educate the public about the developing world; supports Peace Corps programs; maintains network of returned volunteers.

Oxfam America, *Policy and Campaigns, 1101 17th St. N.W., #1300, 20036-4710; (202) 496-1180. Fax, (202) 496-1190. Raymond C. Offenheiser, President; Paul O'Brien, Vice President for Policy and Campaigns. Information, (800) 776-9326. Press, (202) 496-1169.*
General email, info@oxfamamerica.org
Web, www.oxfamamerica.org and Twitter, @OxfamAmerica

Funds disaster relief and long-term development programs internationally. Organizes grassroots support in the United States for issues affecting global poverty, including climate change, aid reform, and corporate transparency. (Headquarters in Boston, Mass.)

Partners for Livable Communities, *1429 21st St. N.W., 20036; (202) 887-5990. Robert H. McNulty, President.*
General email, fkoleszar@livable.org
Web, www.livable.org

Promotes working partnerships among public, private, and governmental sectors to improve the quality of life and economic development at local and regional levels. Conducts conferences and workshops; maintains referral clearinghouse; provides technical assistance.

PYXERA Global, *1030 15th St. N.W., #730E, 20005; (202) 872-0933. Fax, (202) 872-0923. Deirdre White, Chief Executive Officer.*
General email, info@pyxeraglobal.org
Web, www.pyxeraglobal.org and Twitter, @PYXERAGlobal

Recruits and coordinates public, private, and volunteer resources to strengthen small and medium-sized businesses and the institutions, governments, and industries that drive economic growth in emerging markets through five practice areas: global citizenship and volunteerism, supply chain development, tourism development, security and economic recovery, and access to finance for development. (Formerly CDC Development Solutions.)

Salvation Army World Service Office, *615 Slaters Lane, Alexandria, VA 22314 (mailing address: P.O. Box 1428, Alexandria, VA 22313); (703) 684-5528. Fax, (703) 684-5536. Lt. Col. Thomas Bowers, National Secretary; Lt. Col. Jacalyn Bowers, Assistant National Secretary.*
General email, sawso@usn.salvationarmy.org
Web, www.sawso.org

Works in Eastern Europe, Latin America, the Caribbean, Africa, Asia, and the South Pacific to provide technical assistance to local Salvation Army programs of health services, vocational and business training, literacy, microenterprise, and relief and reconstruction assistance. (International headquarters in London.)

Vital Voices Global Partnership, *1625 Massachusetts Ave. N.W., #300, 20036; (202) 861-2625. Fax, (202) 296-4142. Alyse Nelson, Chief Executive Officer.*
General email, info@vitalvoices.org

Web, www.vitalvoices.org and Twitter, @VitalVoices

Worldwide organization of volunteers with governmental, corporate, or other leadership expertise that trains and mentors emerging women leaders in Asia, Africa, Eurasia, Latin America, and the Middle East. Seeks to expand women's political participation and representation, increase women's entrepreneurship and business leadership, and combat human rights violations affecting women.

World Learning, *International Exchange Programs,*
1015 15th St. N.W., 7th Floor, 20005-2065; (202) 408-5420. Fax, (202) 408-5397. Carol Jenkins, President, International Development and Exchange Programs, (202) 464-6643. TTY, (202) 464-5530. Toll-free, (800) 858-0292. General email, development@worldlearning.org

Web, www.worldlearning.org and Twitter, @WorldLearning

Partners with nongovernmental organizations, government institutions, schools, universities, and others to strengthen local capacity and performance. Develops training programs that prepare local organizations to lead development initiatives. Provides technical assistance, mentoring, and small grant funding. Administered by World Learning's Division of International Development and Exchange Programs.

Finance, Monetary Affairs

►AGENCIES

Bureau of Economic Analysis *(Commerce Dept.),*
International Economic Accounts, Balance of Payments,
1441 L St. N.W., 20230; (202) 606-9561. Fax, (202) 606-5314. Paul Farello, Chief. Press, (202) 606-2649. General email, customerservice@bea.gov

Web, www.bea.gov/international

Compiles, analyzes, and publishes quarterly and annual statistics on the U.S. international transactions accounts and the U.S. international investment position accounts. Publishes a monthly release with U.S. Census Bureau on U.S. trade in goods and services. Conducts research and analysis on the international economic accounts.

Bureau of Economic and Business Affairs *(State Dept.),*
International Finance and Development, *2201 C St. N.W., #4880, 20520; (202) 647-4632. Fax, (202) 647-7453. Lisa J. Kubiske, Principal Deputy Assistant Secretary. Web, www.state.gov/e/eb/ifd*

Formulates and implements policies related to multinational investment and insurance; activities of the World Bank and regional banks in the financial development of various countries; bilateral aid; international monetary reform; international antitrust cases; and international debt, banking, and taxation.

Bureau of Economic and Business Affairs *(State Dept.),*
Monetary Affairs, *2201 C St. N.W., #4880, 20520; (202) 647-9497. Fax, (202) 647-7453. Samuel Watson, Director. General email, eb-a-oma-dl@state.gov*

Web, www.state.gov/e/eb/ifd/oma

Monitors global macroeconomic developments and identifies financial trends and potential crises in countries affecting U.S. interests. Formulates debt relief policies and negotiates debt relief agreements.

Federal Reserve System, *International Finance, 20th and C Sts. N.W., #B1242C, 20551-0001; (202) 452-3770. Fax, (202) 452-6424. Steven B. Kamin, Director; Michelle Smith, Press Contact. Press, (202) 452-3799. Web, www.federalreserve.gov/econresdata/ifstaff.htm*

Provides the Federal Reserve's board of governors with economic analyses of international developments. Compiles data on exchange rates.

Treasury Dept., *International Affairs, 1500 Pennsylvania Ave. N.W., #3432, 20220; (202) 622-1270. Fax, (202) 622-0417. Nathan Sheets, Under Secretary. Press, (202) 622-2920. Web, www.treasury.gov/about/organizational-structure/offices/Pages/Office-Of-International-Affairs.aspx*

Coordinates and implements U.S. international economic and financial policy in cooperation with other government agencies. Works to improve the international monetary and investment system; monitors international gold and foreign exchange operations; coordinates development lending; coordinates Treasury Dept. participation in foreign investment in the United States; studies international monetary, economic, and financial issues; analyzes data on international transactions.

Treasury Dept., *International Affairs, Trade Finance and Investment Negotiations, 1500 Pennsylvania Ave. N.W., #5419, 20220; (202) 622-1749. Fax, (202) 622-0967. Anthony Ieronmo, Director.*
Web, www.treasury.gov/about/organizational-structure/offices/Pages/-Trade-and-Investment-Policy.aspx

Heads the U.S. delegation to the Participants and Working Party on Export Credits and Credit Guarantees of the Organization for Economic Cooperation and Development, negotiating agreements to reduce subsidies in export credit support. Negotiates bilateral investment treaties (BITs) and the investment portion of free trade agreements (FTAs) with foreign governments.

►CONGRESS

For a listing of relevant congressional committees and sub-committees, please see pages 454–455 or the Appendix.

►INTERNATIONAL ORGANIZATIONS

International Finance Corp., *2121 Pennsylvania Ave. N.W., 20433; (202) 473-1000. Philippe Le Houérou, Executive Vice President. Press, (202) 473-8764. Web, www.ifc.org*

A member of the World Bank Group that lends to private sector companies and financial institutions. Works with the private sector to encourage entrepreneurship and build sustainable businesses: advising them on a wide range of issues, including environmental, social, and governance standards, energy and efficiency, and supply chains. Helps expand access to critical finance for individuals and micro, small, and medium enterprises through its work with financial intermediary clients.

International Monetary Fund (IMF), *700 19th St. N.W., 20431; (202) 623-7000. Fax, (202) 623-4661. Christine Lagarde, Managing Director; Matthew Haarsager, U.S. Executive Director. Web, www.imf.org*

International organization of 188 member countries that promotes policies for financial stability and economic growth, works to prevent financial crises, and helps members solve balance-of-payment problems through loans funded by member contributions.

Multilateral Investment Guarantee Agency, *1818 H St. N.W., 20433; (202) 458-2538. Fax, (202) 522-0316. Keiko Honda, Executive Vice President. Press, (202) 473-0844. General email, migainquiry@worldbank.org Web, www.miga.org*

World Bank affiliate that encourages foreign investment in developing countries. Provides guarantees against losses due to currency transfer, expropriation, war, civil disturbance, breach of contract, and the nonhonoring of a sovereign financial obligation. Provides dispute resolution services for guaranteed investments to prevent disruptions to developmentally beneficial projects. Membership open to World Bank member countries.

World Bank, *1818 H St. N.W., 20433; (202) 473-1000. Fax, (202) 477-6391. Hon. Jim Yong Kim, President; Matthew McGuire, U.S. Executive Director. Press, (202) 473-7660. Bookstore, (202) 458-4500. Publications, (800) 645-7247 or (703) 661-1580. Anticorruption hotline, (202) 458-7677. General email, Cunit1@worldbank.org Web, www.worldbank.org and Twitter, @worldbank*

International organization encouraging the flow of public and private foreign investment into developing countries through low-interest loans, credits, and grants; collects data on selected economic indicators, world trade, and external public debt. Consists of The International Bank for Reconstruction and Development, The International Development Assn., The International Finance Corporation, The Multilateral Investment Guarantee Agency, and The International Centre for Settlement of Investment Dispute.

▶**NONGOVERNMENTAL**

BAFT, *1120 Connecticut Ave. N.W., 5th Floor, 20036-3902; (202) 663-7575. Fax, (202) 663-5538. Tod R. Burwell, Chief Executive Officer.*

General email, info@baft-ifsa.com Web, www.baft.org

Membership: international financial services providers, including U.S. and non-U.S. commercial banks, financial services companies, and suppliers with major international operations. Interests include international trade, trade finance, payments, compliance, asset servicing, and transaction banking. Monitors and acts as advocate globally on activities that affect the business of commercial and international banks and nonfinancial companies. (Formerly Bankers' Assn. for Financial Trade.)

Bretton Woods Committee, *1726 K St. N.W., #950, 20006; (202) 331-1616. Fax, (202) 785-9423. Randy S. Rodgers, Executive Director. General email, info@brettonwoods.org Web, www.brettonwoods.org and Twitter, @BrettonWoodsCom*

Works to increase public understanding of the World Bank, the regional development institutions, the International Monetary Fund, and the World Trade Organization.

Center for International Policy, *Financial Transparency Coalition, 2000 M St. N.W., #720, 20036; (202) 232-3317. Fax, (202) 232-3440. Porter McConnell, Director. General email, info@financialtransparency.org Web, www.financialtransparency.org*

Research and educational organization concerned with improving international financial transparency in order to decrease illicit financial flows. Encourages multinational corporations to report their profits and taxes, create open information sources on beneficial ownership, and automatic tax information exchange.

Global Financial Integrity (GFI), *1100 17th St. N.W., #505, 20036; (202) 293-0740. Fax, (202) 293-1720. Raymond Baker, President, (202) 293-0740, ext. 226. Press, (202) 293-0740, ext. 231. General email, gfi@gfintegrity.org Web, www.gfintegrity.org*

Nonprofit that researches and advocates against illicit financial flows between foreign countries. Publishes reports that analyze illegal monetary transfers around the world. Assists developing countries in applying policies to prevent illicit transactions due to drug trafficking, political corruption, money laundering, and terrorist funding.

Institute of International Finance, *1333 H St. N.W., #800 East, 20005; (202) 857-3600. Fax, (202) 775-1430. Timothy D. Adams, President. General email, info@iif.com Web, www.iif.com*

Global association of financial institutions. Provides analysis and research on emerging markets. Identifies and analyzes regulatory, financial, and economic policy issues. Promotes the development of sound financial systems with particular emphasis on emerging markets.

Intercontinental Exchange, *Washington Office,* *801 Pennsylvania Ave. N.W., #630, 20004-2685; (202) 347-4300. Fax, (202) 347-4372. Alex Albert, Vice President. Web, www.intercontinentalexchange.com*

Provides information about risk management services to market participants around the world. Washington office monitors legislation and regulations. (Headquarters in Atlanta, Ga.)

Microcredit Summit Campaign, *1101 15th St. N.W., #1200, 20005; (202) 637-9600. Fax, (202) 452-9356. Larry Reed, Director. General email, info@microcreditsummit.org*

Web, www.microcreditsummit.org

Membership: microfinance institutions, organizations, practitioners, and advocates aiming to provide international poor families with credit for self-employment and financial and business services. Specializes in helping women in poor families become financially self-sustainable. Holds annual summits to discuss successful microfinance practices that combat global poverty.

Transparency International USA, *1023 15th St. N.W., #300, 20005; (202) 589-1616. Fax, (202) 589-1512. Claudia J. Damas, President. General email, administration@transparency-usa.org*

Web, www.transparency-usa.org

Seeks to curb corruption in international transactions. Promotes reform of government, business, and development assistance transactions through effective anti-corruption laws and policies. (Headquarters in Berlin, Germany.)

REGIONAL AFFAIRS

See also Foreign Embassies, U.S. Ambassadors, and Country Desk Offices (Appendix).

Africa

For North Africa, see Near East and South Asia.

▶**AGENCIES**

African Development Foundation (ADF), *1400 Eye St. N.W., #1000, 20005-2248; (202) 673-3916. Fax, (202) 673-3810. Shari Berenbach, President. Press, (202) 673-3916, ext. 8811. General email, info@usadf.gov*

Web, www.usadf.gov

Established by Congress to work with and fund organizations and individuals involved in community-based development projects in Africa. Gives preference to projects involving extensive participation by local Africans. Work focuses on conflict and postconflict areas.

Agency for International Development (USAID), *Africa Bureau, 1300 Pennsylvania Ave. N.W., #4.08C, 20523-4801; (202) 712-4810. Fax, (202) 216-3008. Tom Delaney, Senior Deputy Assistant Administrator. Press, (202) 712-4320.*

Web, www.usaid.gov/who-we-are/organization/bureaus/bureau-africa

Advises the AID administrator on U.S. policy toward developing countries in Africa.

Bureau of African Affairs *(State Dept.), 2201 C St. N.W., #6234A, 20520-3430; (202) 647-2530. Fax, (202) 647-6301. Linda Thomas-Greenfield, Assistant Secretary, (202) 647-0444.*

Web, www.state.gov/p/af and Twitter, @StateAfrica

Advises the secretary on U.S. policy toward sub-Saharan Africa. Directors, assigned to different regions in Africa, aid the assistant secretary.

Bureau of African Affairs *(State Dept.), Central African Affairs, 2201 C St. N.W., #4244, 20520-2902; (202) 647-2080. Fax, (202) 647-1726. Richard C. Paschall, Director, (202) 647-6491.*

Web, www.state.gov/p/af

Includes Burundi, Cameroon, Central African Republic, Chad, the Democratic Republic of Congo, the Republic of Congo, Equatorial Guinea, Gabon, Rwanda, and São Tomé and Príncipe.

Bureau of African Affairs *(State Dept.), East African Affairs, 2201 C St. N.W., #4248, 20520; (202) 647-4066. Fax, (202) 647-0810. Nancy A. Cohen, Director.*

Web, www.state.gov/p/af

Includes Comoros, Djibouti, Eritrea, Ethiopia, Kenya, Madagascar, Mauritius, Seychelles, Somalia, Tanzania, and Uganda.

Bureau of African Affairs *(State Dept.), Southern African Affairs, 2201 C St. N.W., #4236, 20520; (202) 647-9836. Fax, (202) 647-5007. Christine A. Elder, Director.*

Web, www.state.gov/p/af

Includes Angola, Botswana, Lesotho, Malawi, Mozambique, Namibia, South Africa, Swaziland, Zambia, and Zimbabwe.

Bureau of African Affairs *(State Dept.), Special Envoy for the Sudans and South Sudan, 2201 C St. N.W., #5819, 20520; (202) 647-4531. Fax, (202) 647-4553. Donald E. Booth, Special Envoy.*

Web, www.state.gov/s/sudan

Represents the U.S. government's interests in Sudan and Darfur/South Sudan.

Bureau of African Affairs *(State Dept.), West African Affairs, 2201 C St. N.W., #4246, 20520-3430; (202) 647-3395. Fax, (202) 647-4855. David D. Reimer, Director.*

Web, www.state.gov/p/af

Includes Benin, Burkina Faso, Cape Verde, Côte d'Ivoire, the Gambia, Ghana, Guinea, Guinea-Bissau, Liberia, Mali, Mauritania, Niger, Nigeria, Senegal, Sierra Leone, and Togo.

Defense Dept. (DoD), *International Security Affairs, 2000 Defense Pentagon, #3C889, 20301-2000; (703) 697-2788. Fax, (703) 697-3279. Elissa B. Slotkin, Assistant*

Secretary, Acting; Kenneth B. Handelman, Principal Deputy Assistant Secretary, Acting.
Web, http://policy.defense.gov/OUSDPOffices/ASDforInternationalSecurityAffairs.aspx

Advises the secretary of defense and recommends policies on regional security issues in the Middle East, Africa, Russia/Eurasia, and Europe/NATO.

Defense Dept. (DoD), *International Security Affairs, Africa,* 2000 Defense Pentagon, 20301-2000; (703) 697-2788. Amanda J. Dory, Deputy Assistant Secretary; Todd Coker, Principal Director.
Web, www.defense.gov

Advises the assistant secretary for international security affairs on matters dealing with Africa.

►CONGRESS

For a listing of relevant congressional committees and subcommittees, please see pages 454–455 or the Appendix.

Library of Congress, *African and Middle Eastern Division,* Thomas Jefferson Bldg., 101 Independence Ave. S.E., #LJ 220, 20540; (202) 707-7937. Fax, (202) 252-3180. Mary-Jane Deeb, Chief. Reading room, (202) 707-4188.
General email, amed@loc.gov
Web, www.loc.gov/rr/amed

Maintains collections of African, Near Eastern, and Hebraic material. Prepares bibliographies and special studies relating to Africa and the Middle East. Reference service and reading rooms available to the public. (Need reader's card to use.)

►INTERNATIONAL ORGANIZATIONS

World Bank, *Africa,* 1818 H St. N.W., 20433; (202) 473-1000. Makhtar Diop, Vice President; Aby Toure, Media Contact, (202) 473-8302.
General email, africateam@worldbank.org
Web, www.worldbank.org/en/region/afr

Aims to reduce poverty in middle-income countries and creditworthy poorer countries by promoting sustainable development through low-interest loans, zero to low-interest credits, grants, guarantees, risk management products, and analytical and advisory services. Priorities in Africa include education, health, public administration, infrastructure, financial and private sector development, agriculture, and environmental and natural resource management.

►NONGOVERNMENTAL

Africa Faith and Justice Network (AFJN), 3025 4th St. N.E., #122, 20017; (202) 817-3670. Fax, (202) 817-3671. Rev. Aniedi Okure OP, Executive Director.
General email, afjn@afjn.org
Web, www.afjn.org

Acts as advocate with Catholic missionary congregations and Africa-focused coalitions for U.S. economic and political policies that benefit Africa. Promotes the Catholic view of peace building, human rights, and social justice. Interests include ending armed conflict, equitable trade with and investment in Africa, and sustainable development.

Africare, 440 R St. N.W., 20001-1935; (202) 462-3614. Fax, (202) 464-0867. Robert Mallett, President.
General email, info@africare.org
Web, www.africare.org

Seeks to improve the quality of life in rural Africa through development of water resources, increased food production, and delivery of health services.

The Brookings Institution, *Global Economy and Development Studies, Africa Growth Initiative,* 1775 Massachusetts Ave. N.W., 20036; (202) 797-6000. Fax, (202) 797-6004. Amadou Sy, Director.
General email, AGI@Brookings.edu
Web, www.brookings.edu/about/projects/africa-growth

Conducts policy research and analysis focusing on sustainable economic growth in Africa. Interests include financial development, risks to growth including climate change and epidemics, trade and regional integration, governance transparency, reduction of gender barriers, and youth employment.

Corporate Council on Africa, 1100 17th St. N.W., #1000, 20036; (202) 835-1115. Fax, (202) 835-1117. Stephen Hayes, President.
General email, cca@africacncl.org
Web, www.africacncl.org and Twitter, @CorpCnclAfrica

Membership: American corporations working with African agriculture, energy, finance, health, trade, communication technology, and security industries. Promotes business relations between the United States and Africa. Facilitates government and business advancements in Africa's trade industry. Monitors legislation and regulations that impact African commercial relations.

Lubuto Library Partners, 5614 Connecticut Ave N.W., #368, 20015; (202) 558-5609. Jane Kinney Meyers, Director.
General email, webmail@lubuto.org
Web, www.lubuto.org

Works with public and private libraries and other partners to construct an open-access library collection and accessible services for children and youth in Africa. Sponsors library programs to foster education in the arts and technology; offers services for children with disabilities.

Sudan Sunrise, 11404 Summer House Court, Reston, VA 20194; (202) 499-6984. Tom Prichard, Executive Director.
General email, info@sudansunrise.org
Web, www.sudansunrise.org

Supports schools and education programs for children of various religions, tribes, and communities in Sudan and South Sudan.

East Asia and Pacific

▶ **AGENCIES**

Agency for International Development (USAID), *Asia Bureau,* 1300 Pennsylvania Ave. N.W., 20523-4900; (202) 712-0200. Fax, (202) 216-3386. Jonathon Stivers, Assistant Administrator. Press, (202) 712-4320.
Web, www.usaid.gov/who-we-are/organization/bureaus/bureau-asia

Advises the AID administrator on U.S. economic development policy in Asia.

Bureau of East Asian and Pacific Affairs *(State Dept.),* 2201 C St. N.W., #6205, 20520-6205; (202) 647-6600. Daniel Russel, Assistant Secretary. Press, (202) 647-2538.
Web, www.state.gov/p/eap and Twitter, @USAsiaPacific

Advises the secretary on U.S. policy toward East Asian and Pacific countries. Directors assigned to specific countries within the bureau aid the assistant secretary.

Bureau of East Asian and Pacific Affairs *(State Dept.), Australia, New Zealand, and Pacific Island Affairs,* 2201 C St. N.W., #4318, 20520; (202) 736-4741. Fax, (202) 647-0118. Steven Schwartz, Director, (202) 736-4659.
Web, www.state.gov/p/eap

Bureau of East Asian and Pacific Affairs *(State Dept.), Chinese and Mongolian Affairs,* 2201 C St. N.W., #4318, 20520; (202) 647-6787. Fax, (202) 736-7809.
Peter M. Haymond, Director.
Web, www.state.gov/p/eap

Bureau of East Asian and Pacific Affairs *(State Dept.), Japanese Affairs,* 2201 C St. N.W., #4206, 20520; (202) 647-2913. Fax, (202) 647-4402. Joe Young, Director.
Web, www.state.gov/p/eap

Bureau of East Asian and Pacific Affairs *(State Dept.), Korean Affairs,* 2201 C St. N.W., #4206, 20520; (202) 647-7717. Fax, (202) 647-7388. Mark Lambert, Director.
Web, www.state.gov/p/eap

Bureau of East Asian and Pacific Affairs *(State Dept.), Mainland Southeast Asia Affairs,* 2201 C St. N.W., #5206, 20520-6310; (202) 647-0064. Fax, (202) 647-3069.
Pepper Richhart, Director.
Web, www.state.gov

Includes Burma, Cambodia, Laos, Thailand, and Vietnam.

Bureau of East Asian and Pacific Affairs *(State Dept.), Maritime Southeast Asia Affairs,* 2201 C St. N.W., #5210, 20520; (202) 647-1221. Fax, (202) 736-4559.
James Carouso, Director.
Web, www.state.gov

Includes Brunei, East Timor, Indonesia, Malaysia, the Philippines, and Singapore.

Bureau of East Asian and Pacific Affairs *(State Dept.), North Korea Affairs,* 2201 C St. N.W., #5209, 20520-5209; (202) 647-4611. Amb. Robert R. King, Special Envoy.
Web, www.state.gov/p/eap/ci/kn

Bureau of East Asian and Pacific Affairs *(State Dept.), Taiwan Coordination,* 2201 C St. N.W., #4312, 20520; (202) 647-7711. Fax, (202) 736-7818. Christian Castro, Director.
Web, www.state.gov/p/eap

Defense Dept. (DoD), *Asian and Pacific Security Affairs,* 2700 Defense Pentagon, #5D688, 20301-2400; (703) 695-4175. David Shear, Assistant Secretary; Kelly E. Magsamen, Principal Deputy Assistant Secretary. Press, (703) 697-5131.
Web, http://policy.defense.gov/OUSDPOffices/ASDforAsianandPacificSecurityAffairs.aspx

Advises the under secretary of defense on matters dealing with Asia and the Pacific.

Defense Dept. (DoD), *East Asia Security Affairs,* 2700 Defense Pentagon, #5D688, 20301-2700; (703) 695-4175. Abraham M. Denmark, Deputy Assistant Secretary.
Web, http://policy.defense.gov/OUSDPOffices/ASDforAsianandPacificSecurityAffairs.aspx

Advises the under secretary of defense on matters dealing with China, Japan, Mongolia, North and South Korea, and Taiwan.

Japan–United States Friendship Commission, *1201 15th St. N.W., #330, 20005-2842; (202) 653-9800. Fax, (202) 653-9802. Paige Cottingham-Streater, Executive Director. General email, jusfc@jusfc.gov*
Web, www.jusfc.gov

Independent agency established by Congress that makes grants and administers funds and programs promoting educational and cultural exchanges between Japan and the United States.

U.S.–China Economic and Security Review Commission, *444 N. Capitol St. N.W., #602, 20001; (202) 624-1407. Fax, (202) 624-1406. Michael R. Danis, Executive Director. General email, contact@uscc.gov*
Web, www.uscc.gov

Investigates the national security implications of the bilateral trade and economic relationship between China and the United States. Makes recommendations to Congress based on its findings.

▶ **CONGRESS**

For a listing of relevant congressional committees and subcommittees, please see pages 454–455 or the Appendix.

Congressional–Executive Commission on China, *243 FHOB, 20515; (202) 226-3766. Fax, (202) 226-3804. Rep. Christopher H. Smith, Co-Chair; Sen. Marco Rubio, Co-Chair; Paul B. Protic, Staff Director, (202) 226-3798. General email, infocecc@mail.house.gov*
Web, www.cecc.gov and Twitter, @CECCgov

Independent agency created by Congress. Membership includes individuals from the executive and legislative branches. Monitors human rights and the development of the rule of law in the People's Republic of China. Submits an annual report to the president and Congress.

Library of Congress, *Asian Division,* Thomas Jefferson Bldg., 101 Independence Ave. S.E., #LJ 150, 20540; (202) 707-3766. Fax, (202) 252-3336. Dongfang Shao, Chief. Reading room, (202) 707-5426.
Web, www.loc.gov/rr/asian

Maintains collections of Asian-American Pacific, Chinese, Korean, Japanese, Southeast Asian, South Asian, and Tibetan and Mongolian material. Reference service is provided in the Asian Reading Room, room #150.

▶INTERNATIONAL ORGANIZATIONS

World Bank, *East Asia and Pacific,* 1818 H St. N.W., 20433; (202) 473-1000. Victoria Kwakwa, Vice President; Carl Hanlon, Media Contact, (202) 473-8087.
Web, www.worldbank.org

Works to fight poverty and improve the living standards of low- and middle-income people in the countries of East Asia and the Pacific by providing loans, policy advice, technical assistance, and knowledge-sharing services. Areas of interest include finance, economic development, education, water supply, agriculture, public health, and environmental protection.

▶NONGOVERNMENTAL

American Institute in Taiwan, 1700 N. Moore St., #1700, Arlington, VA 22209-1385; (703) 525-8474. Fax, (703) 841-1385. Kin W. Moy, Director; Amb. Raymond Burghardt, Chair.
Web, www.ait.org.tw/en/home/html

Chartered by Congress to coordinate commercial, cultural, and other activities between the people of the United States and Taiwan. Represents U.S. interests and maintains offices in Taiwan.

Asia Foundation, *Washington Office,* 1779 Massachusetts Ave. N.W., #815, 20036; (202) 588-9420. Fax, (202) 588-9409. Nancy Yuan, Director.
General email, info@asiafound-dc.org
Web, www.asiafoundation.org

Provides grants and technical assistance in Asia and the Pacific Islands (excluding the Middle East). Seeks to strengthen legislatures, legal and judicial systems, market economies, the media, and nongovernmental organizations. (Headquarters in San Francisco, Calif.)

Asia Policy Point (APP), 1730 Rhode Island Ave. N.W., #414, 20036; (202) 822-6040. Fax, (202) 822-6044. Mindy Kotler, Director.
General email, asiapolicyhq@gmail.com
Web, www.jiaponline.org
Blog, http://newasiapolicypoint.blogspot.com

Studies Japanese and Northeast Asian security and public policies as they relate to the United States. Researches and analyzes issues affecting Japan's relationship with the West. (Formerly the Japan Information Access Project.)

Asia Society Policy Institute, 1300 Eye St. N.W., #400E, 20005; (202) 833-2742. Fax, (202) 833-0189. Wendy Cutler, Managing Director.
General email, asiadc@asiasociety.org
Web, www.asiasociety.org

Membership: individuals, organizations, and corporations interested in Asia and the Pacific (excluding the Middle East). Focuses on United States and Asia foreign policy issues. Sponsors seminars and lectures on political, economic, and cultural issues. (Headquarters in New York.)

East–West Center, *Washington Office,* 1819 L St. N.W., #600, 20036; (202) 293-3995. Fax, (202) 293-1402. Satu P. Limaye, Director.
General email, washington@eastwestcenter.org
Web, www.eastwestcenter.org

Promotes strengthening of relations and understanding among countries and peoples of Asia, the Pacific, and the United States. Plans to undertake substantive programming activities, including collaborative research, training, seminars, and outreach; publications; and congressional study groups. (Headquarters in Honolulu, Hawaii.)

Formosan Assn. for Public Affairs, 552 7th St, S.E., 20003; (202) 547-3686. Fax, (202) 543-7891. Mark L. Kao, President.
General email, home@fapa.org
Web, www.fapa.org

Political group that advocates the independence of Taiwan and promotes democracy. Seeks to improve relations between the United States and Taiwan. Educates the public, policymakers, and the media about current issues in Taiwan. Monitors legislation and regulations related to Taiwan's relationship with the United States.

Heritage Foundation, *Asian Studies Center,* 214 Massachusetts Ave. N.E., 20002-4999; (202) 546-4400. Fax, (202) 675-1779. Walter Lohman, Director. Press, (202) 675-1761.
General email, info@heritage.org
Web, www.heritage.org/about/staff/departments/asian-studies-center?ac=1

Conducts research and provides information on U.S. policies in Asia and the Pacific. Interests include economic and security issues in the Asia Pacific region. Hosts speakers and visiting foreign policy delegations; sponsors conferences.

Japan–America Society of Washington, 1819 L St. N.W., Level B2, 20036-3807; (202) 833-2210. Amb. John R. Malott, President.
General email, info@jaswdc.org
Web, www.jaswdc.org

Conducts programs on U.S.–Japan political, security, and economic issues. Cultural programs include lectures, a Japanese-language school, and assistance to Japanese performing artists. Maintains library for members. Participates in National Cherry Blossom Festival.

Taipei Economic and Cultural Representative Office (TECRO), *4201 Wisconsin Ave. N.W., 20016; (202) 895-1800. Fax, (202) 966-0825. Lyushun Shen, Representative. Press, (202) 895-1850.*
General email, tecroinfodc@tecro.us
Web, www.taiwanembassy.org/US

Represents political, economic, and cultural interests of the government of the Republic of China (Taiwan) in the United States.

U.S. Campaign for Burma, *1001 Connecticut Ave. N.W., #740, 20036; (202) 234-8022. Fax, (202) 234-8044. Simon Billenness, Executive Director, (617) 596-6158.*
General email, info@uscampaignforburma.org
Web, www.uscampaignforburma.org and Twitter, @USCB

Advocacy group that works at a grassroots level to promote human rights, justice, and democracy in Burma. Reviews policies relating to Burma. Educates policymakers and business leaders about current affairs and issues. Provides aid to refugees and encourages awareness of political prisoners.

U.S.–Asia Institute, *232 E. Capitol St. N.E., 20003; (202) 544-3181. Fax, (202) 747-5889. Mary Sue Bissell, Executive Director.*
General email, usai@usasiainstitute.org
Web, www.usasiainstitute.org

Organization of individuals interested in Asia. Encourages dialogue among political and business leaders in the United States and Asia. Interests include foreign policy, international trade, Asian and American cultures, education, and employment. Conducts research and sponsors conferences and workshops in cooperation with the State Dept. to promote greater understanding between the United States and Asian nations.

U.S.–China Business Council, *1818 N St. N.W., #200, 20036-2470; (202) 429-0340. Fax, (202) 775-2476. John Frisbie, President.*
General email, info@uschina.org
Web, www.uschina.org

Member-supported organization that represents U.S. companies engaged in business relations with the People's Republic of China. Participates in U.S. policy issues relating to China and other international trade. Publishes research reports. (Maintains offices in Beijing and Shanghai.)

United States–Indonesia Society, *1625 Massachusetts Ave. N.W., #550, 20036-2260; (202) 232-1400. Fax, (202) 232-7300. Dave Merrill, President.*
General email, usindo@usindo.org
Web, www.usindo.org

Seeks to strengthen relations between the United States and Indonesia. Educates and holds forums on the economic and political trends in Indonesia. Grants scholarships and fellowships to students and professionals to travel from or to the United States and Indonesia. Assists in rebuilding educational systems in communities impacted by the 2004 tsunami.

Europe

(Includes the Baltic states)

▶**AGENCIES**

Agency for International Development (USAID), *Europe and Eurasia Bureau, 301 4th St. S.W., #247, 20523 (mailing address: 1300 Pennsylvania Ave. N.W., Washington, DC 20521); (202) 567-4020. Fax, (202) 567-4256. Susan Kosinski Fritz, Assistant Administrator, Acting.*
Web, www.usaid.gov/who-we-are/organization/bureaus/bureau-europe-and-eurasia

Advises the AID administrator on U.S. economic development policy in Europe and Eurasia.

Bureau of European and Eurasian Affairs *(State Dept.), 2201 C St. N.W., #6226, 20520; (202) 647-9626. Fax, (202) 647-5716. Victoria Nuland, Assistant Secretary, (202) 647-9626. Press, (202) 647-6575.*
Web, www.state.gov/p/eur

Advises the secretary on U.S. policy toward European and Eurasian countries. Directors assigned to specific countries within the bureau aid the assistant secretary.

Bureau of European and Eurasian Affairs *(State Dept.), Central European Affairs, 2201 C St. N.W., #4230, 20520; (202) 647-1484. Fax, (202) 647-5117. Aubrey A. Carlson, Director.*
Web, www.state.gov/p/eur

Includes Austria, Bulgaria, Czech Republic, Hungary, Liechtenstein, Poland, Romania, Slovak Republic, Slovenia, and Switzerland.

Bureau of European and Eurasian Affairs *(State Dept.), European Security and Political Affairs, 2201 C St. N.W., #6511, 20520; (202) 647-1626. Fax, (202) 647-1369. Joe Manso, Director.*
Web, www.state.gov/p/eur

Coordinates and advises, with the Defense Dept. and other agencies, the U.S. mission to NATO and the U.S. delegation to the Organization for Security and Cooperation in Europe regarding political, military, and arms control matters.

Bureau of European and Eurasian Affairs *(State Dept.), European Union and Regional Affairs, 2201 C St. N.W., #5424, 20520; (202) 647-2469. Fax, (202) 647-9959. Gregory Burton, Director.*
Web, www.state.gov/p/eur

Handles all matters concerning the European Union, with emphasis on trade issues. Monitors export controls and economic activities for the North Atlantic Treaty Organization and the Organization for Security and Cooperation in Europe.

Bureau of European and Eurasian Affairs *(State Dept.), Nordic and Baltic Affairs, 2201 C St. N.W., #5428, 20520; (202) 647-5669. Fax, (202) 736-4170. Nathaniel Dean, Director.*
Web, www.state.gov/p/eur

Includes Denmark, Estonia, Finland, Iceland, Latvia, Lithuania, Norway, and Sweden.

Bureau of European and Eurasian Affairs *(State Dept.), South Central European Affairs,* 2201 C St. N.W., #5219, 20520; (202) 647-0608. Fax, (202) 647-1838. *Thomas K. Yazdgerdi, Director.*
Web, www.state.gov/p/eur

Includes Albania, Bosnia-Herzegovina, Croatia, Kosovo, Macedonia, Serbia, and Montenegro.

Bureau of European and Eurasian Affairs *(State Dept.), Southern European Affairs,* 2201 C St. N.W., #5511, 20520; (202) 647-6112. Fax, (202) 647-5087. *Philip S. Kosnett, Director.*
Web, www.state.gov/p/eur

Includes Cyprus, Greece, and Turkey.

Bureau of European and Eurasian Affairs *(State Dept.), Special Envoy for Holocaust Issues,* 2201 C St. N.W., #6219, 20520-6219; (202) 647-8287. *Nicholas Dean, Special Envoy.*
Web, www.state.gov/r/pa/ei/biog/231276.htm

Bureau of European and Eurasian Affairs *(State Dept.), Western European Affairs,* 2201 C St. N.W., #5218, 20520; (202) 647-1469. Fax, (202) 647-3459. *Robin S. Quinville, Director.*
Web, www.state.gov/p/eur

Includes Andorra, Belgium, Bermuda, France, Ireland, Italy, Luxembourg, Malta, Monaco, the Netherlands, Portugal, San Marino, Spain, the United Kingdom, and the Vatican.

Defense Dept. (DoD), *International Security Affairs,* 2000 Defense Pentagon, #3C889, 20301-2000; (703) 697-2788. Fax, (703) 697-3279. *Elissa B. Slotkin, Assistant Secretary, Acting; Kenneth B. Handelman, Principal Deputy Assistant Secretary, Acting.*
Web, http://policy.defense.gov/OUSDPOffices/ ASDforInternationalSecurityAffairs.aspx

Advises the secretary of defense and recommends policies on regional security issues in the Middle East, Africa, Russia/Eurasia, and Europe/NATO.

Defense Dept. (DoD), *International Security Affairs, European and NATO Policy,* 2000 Defense Pentagon, #5B652, 20301-2000; (703) 695-5553. Fax, (703) 571-9637. *Jim J. Townsend, Deputy Assistant Secretary; Rachel Ellehuus, Principal Director.*
Web, www.defense.gov

Advises the assistant secretary for international security affairs on matters dealing with Europe and NATO.

▶**CONGRESS**

For a listing of relevant congressional committees and subcommittees, please see pages 454–455 or the Appendix.

Library of Congress, *European Division,* Thomas Jefferson Bldg., 101 Independence Ave. S.E., #LJ 249, 20540;

(202) 707-5414. Fax, (202) 707-8482. *Georgette M. Dorn, Chief, Acting. Reference desk, (202) 707-4515.*
Web, www.loc.gov/rr/european

Provides reference service on the library's European collections (except collections on Spain, Portugal, and the British Isles). Prepares bibliographies and special studies relating to European countries, including Russia and the other states of the former Soviet Union and eastern bloc. Maintains current unbound Slavic language periodicals and newspapers, which are available at the European Reference Desk. Recommends materials for acquisition.

▶**INTERNATIONAL ORGANIZATIONS**

European Union, *Delegation to the United States of America,* 2175 K St. N.W., 20037; (202) 862-9500. Fax, (202) 429-1766. *David O'Sullivan, Ambassador. General email, delegation-usa-info@eeas.europa.eu*
Web, www.euintheus.org and Twitter, @EUintheUS

Information and public affairs office in the United States for the European Union. Provides social policy data on the European Union and provides statistics and information on member countries, including those related to energy, economics, development and cooperation, commerce, agriculture, industry, and technology. (Headquarters in Brussels.)

World Bank, *Europe and Central Asia,* 1818 H St. N.W., 20433; (202) 473-1000. *Cyril Muller, Vice President; Elena Karaban, Media Contact, (202) 458-2736.*
Web, www.worldbank.org

Works to fight poverty and improve the living standards of low- and middle-income people in the countries of eastern Europe by providing loans, policy advice, technical assistance, and knowledge-sharing services. Areas of interest include finance, economic development, education, water supply, agriculture, public health, and environmental protection.

▶**NONGOVERNMENTAL**

American Hellenic Institute, *1220 16th St. N.W., 20036-3202; (202) 785-8430. Fax, (202) 785-5178. Nick Larigakis, President. General email, info@ahiworld.org*
Web, www.ahiworld.org

Works to strengthen relations between Greece and Cyprus and the United States and within the American Hellenic community.

British American Security Information Council (BASIC), *1725 DeSales St. N.W., #600, 20036; Paul Ingram, Executive Director. General email, basicuk@basicint.org*
Web, www.basicint.org and Twitter, @basic_int

Independent analysis and advocacy organization that researches global security issues, including nuclear policies, military strategies, armaments, and disarmament. Assists in the development of global security policies, promotes public awareness, and facilitates exchange of information on both sides of the Atlantic. (UK office is in London.)

British–American Business Assn., *P.O. Box 16482, 20041; (202) 293-0010. Fax, (202) 296-3332. Eamonn Cooney, President.*
General email, info@babawashington.org
Web, www.babawashington.org and Twitter, @BABADC

Organization dedicated to the development of business relations between the United Kingdom and the United States.

Center for European Policy Analysis, *1225 19th St. N.W., #450, 20036; (202) 551-9200. A. Wess Mitchell, President.*
General email, info@cepa.org
Web, www.cepa.org and Twitter, @cepa

Researches public policy in Central and Eastern European countries and seeks to improve their relations with the United States Holds conferences on issues affecting transnational business, economy, security, and energy resources.

European Institute, *1001 Connecticut Ave. N.W., #220, 20036; (202) 895-1670. Fax, (202) 362-1088. Joelle Attinger, President.*
General email, info@europeaninstitute.org
Web, www.europeaninstitute.org and Twitter, @EPWashingtonDC

Membership: governments and multinational corporations. Provides an independent forum for business leaders, government officials, journalists, academics, and policy experts. Organizes seminars and conferences. Interests include international finance, economics, energy, telecommunications, defense and procurement policies, the integration of central Europe into the European Union and NATO, and relations with Asia and Latin America.

German American Business Council, *2000 M St. N.W., #335, 20036; (202) 955-5595. Ulrich Gamerdinger, Executive Director.*
General email, info@gabcwashington.com
Web, http://gabcwashington.com

Promotes closer ties between Germany and the United States through improved communication between embassies, industry, governments, and academia.

German Marshall Fund of the United States, *1744 R St. N.W., 20009; (202) 683-2650. Fax, (202) 265-1662. Karen Donfried, President.*
General email, info@gmfus.org
Web, www.gmfus.org and Twitter, @gmfus

American institution created by a gift from Germany as a permanent memorial to Marshall Plan aid. Seeks to stimulate exchange of ideas and promote transatlantic cooperation. Awards grants to promote the study of international and domestic policies; supports comparative research and debate on key issues.

Irish National Caucus, *P.O. Box 15128, 20003-0849; (202) 544-0568. Fax, (202) 488-7537. Fr. Sean McManus, President.*
General email, support@irishnationalcaucus.org
Web, www.irishnationalcaucus.org

Educational organization concerned with protecting human rights in Northern Ireland. Seeks to end anti-Catholic discrimination in Northern Ireland through implementation of the McBride Principles, initiated in 1984. Advocates nonviolence and supports the peace process in Northern Ireland. Monitors legislation and regulations.

Joint Baltic American National Committee (JBANC), *400 Hurley Ave., Rockville, MD 20850; (301) 340-1954. Fax, (301) 309-1405. Karl Altau, Managing Director.*
General email, jbanc@jbanc.org
Web, www.jbanc.org and Twitter, @JBANCchatter

Washington representative of the Estonian, Latvian, and Lithuanian American communities in the United States; acts as a representative on issues affecting the Baltic states.

Transatlantic Business Council, *919 18th St. N.W., #220, 20006; (202) 828-9104. Fax, (202) 828-9106. Tim Bennett, Director General.*
General email, dnunnery@transatlanticbusiness.org
Web, www.transatlanticbusiness.org

Membership: American companies with operations in Europe and European companies with operations in the United States. Promotes a barrier-free transatlantic market that contributes to economic growth, innovation, and security.

Latin America, Canada, and the Caribbean

▶AGENCIES

Agency for International Development (USAID), *Latin America and the Caribbean Bureau, 1300 Pennsylvania Ave. N.W., #5.09, 20523-5900; (202) 712-4760. Fax, (202) 216-3012. Elizabeth (Beth) Hogan, Assistant Administrator, Acting. Press, (202) 712-5952.*
Web, www.usaid.gov/who-we-are/organization/bureaus/bureau-latin-america-and-caribbean

Advises the AID administrator on U.S. policy toward developing Latin American and Caribbean countries. Designs and implements assistance programs for developing nations.

Bureau of Western Hemisphere Affairs *(State Dept.), 2201 C St. N.W., #6262, 20520; (202) 647-5780. Fax, (202) 647-0834. Roberta S. Jacobson, Assistant Secretary. Press, (202) 647-8042.*
Web, www.state.gov/p/wha and Twitter, @WHAAsstSecty

Advises the secretary on U.S. policy toward North, Central, and South America. Directors assigned to specific regions within the bureau aid the assistant secretary.

Bureau of Western Hemisphere Affairs *(State Dept.),* **Andean Affairs,** *2201 C St. N.W., #1332, 20520; (202) 647-1715. William Duncan, Director.*
Web, www.state.gov/p/wha

Includes Bolivia, Colombia, Ecuador, Peru, and Venezuela.

Bureau of Western Hemisphere Affairs *(State Dept.),* **Brazilian and Southern Cone Affairs,** *2201 C St. N.W., #4258, 20520; (202) 647-1926. Fax, (202) 736-7825. William A. Ostick, Director, (202) 647-3403.*
Web, www.state.gov/p/wha

Includes Argentina, Brazil, Chile, Paraguay, and Uruguay.

Bureau of Western Hemisphere Affairs *(State Dept.),* **Canadian Affairs,** *2201 C St. N.W., #3918, 20520; (202) 647-2170. Fax, (202) 647-4088. Karen Choe-Fichte, Director, Acting.*
Web, www.state.gov/p/wha

Bureau of Western Hemisphere Affairs *(State Dept.),* **Caribbean Affairs,** *2201 C St. N.W., #4262, 20520-6258; (202) 647-5088. Fax, (202) 647-2901. John Dinkelman, Director.*
Web, www.state.gov/p/wha

Includes Antigua and Barbuda, Aruba, Bahamas, Barbados, Dominica, Dominican Republic, Grenada, Guyana, Jamaica, Netherlands Antilles, St. Kitts and Nevis, St. Lucia, St. Vincent and the Grenadines, Suriname, and Trinidad and Tobago.

Bureau of Western Hemisphere Affairs *(State Dept.),* **Central American Affairs,** *2201 C St. N.W., #5906, 20520; (202) 647-0087. Fax, (202) 647-2597. Ian Brownlee, Director.*
Web, www.state.gov

Includes Belize, Costa Rica, El Salvador, Guatemala, Honduras, Nicaragua, and Panama.

Bureau of Western Hemisphere Affairs *(State Dept.),* **Cuban Affairs,** *2201 C St. N.W., #3234, 20520; (202) 647-9272. Fax, (202) 647-7095. Mark A. Wells, Coordinator.*
Web, www.state.gov/p/wha

Bureau of Western Hemisphere Affairs *(State Dept.),* **Haiti Special Coordinator,** *2201 C St. N.W., 12B63, 20520-6258; (202) 647-9510. Fax, (202) 647-8900. Kenneth Merten, Special Coordinator for Haiti.*
General email, HaitiSpecialCoordinator@state.gov
Web, www.state.gov/p/wha/ci/ha/hsc

Coordinates assistance to Haiti. Oversees U.S. government engagement with Haiti, including implementation of a reconstruction strategy in partnership with the Haitian government.

Bureau of Western Hemisphere Affairs *(State Dept.),* **Mexican Affairs,** *2201 C St. N.W., #3924, 20520-6258; (202) 647-8766. Fax, (202) 647-5752. Kevin O'Reilly, Director.*
Web, www.state.gov/p/wha

Bureau of Western Hemisphere Affairs *(State Dept.),* **U.S. Mission to the Organization of American States,** *2201 C St. N.W., #5914, 20520-6258; (202) 647-9422. Fax, (202) 647-0911. Michael J. Fitzpatrick, U.S. Permanent Representative, Acting.*
Web, www.state.gov/p/wha

Formulates U.S. policy and represents U.S. interests at the Organization of American States (OAS).

Defense Dept. (DoD), *International Security Affairs,* **Western Hemisphere,** *2000 Defense Pentagon, #3E806, 20301-2000; (703) 697-7200. Fax, (703) 697-6602. Rebecca B. Chavez, Deputy Assistant Secretary; John Kreul, Principal Director.*
Web, www.defense.gov

Advises the assistant secretary for international security affairs on inter-American matters; aids in the development of U.S. policy toward Latin America.

Inter-American Foundation, *1331 Pennsylvania Ave. N.W., #1200, 20004; (202) 360-4530. Robert N. Kaplan, President.*
General email, inquiries@iaf.gov
Web, www.iaf.gov

Supports small-scale Latin American and Caribbean social and economic development efforts through grassroots development programs, grants, and fellowships.

International Trade Administration (ITA) *(Commerce Dept.),* **Global Markets, North and Central America,** *1401 Constitution Ave. N.W., #3024, 20230; (202) 482-6452. Fax, (202) 482-5013. Geri Word, Director.*
Web, www.trade.gov/markets

Coordinates Commerce Dept. activities and assists U.S. business regarding export to Mexico, Canada, Central America, and the Caribbean. Helps negotiate and ensures compliance with U.S. free trade agreements, including NAFTA (North American Free Trade Agreement) and the Dominican Republic–Central American Free Trade Agreement (CAFTA-DR).

►CONGRESS

For a listing of relevant congressional committees and subcommittees, please see pages 454–455 or the Appendix.

Library of Congress, *Hispanic Division,* *Thomas Jefferson Bldg., 101 Independence Ave. S.E., #LJ 240, 20540; (202) 707-5400. Fax, (202) 707-2005. Georgette M. Dorn, Chief. Reference staff and reading room, (202) 707-5397.*
Web, www.loc.gov/rr/hispanic

Orients researchers and scholars in the area of Iberian, Latin American, Caribbean, and U.S. Latino studies. All major subject areas are represented with emphasis on history, literature, and the social sciences. Primary and secondary source materials are available in the library's general collections for the study of all periods, from pre-Columbian to the present. The collection includes the "Archive of Hispanic Literature on Tape" with recordings of nearly 700 authors reading their own material, available in the reading room and with a select number of recordings available for streaming online as the collection is being digitized.

▶INTERNATIONAL ORGANIZATIONS

Inter-American Development Bank, *1300 New York Ave. N.W., 20577; (202) 623-1000. Fax, (202) 623-3096. Luis Alberto Moreno, President; Mark Ropes, U.S. Executive Director. Library, (202) 623-3211. Press, (202) 623-1555. Web, www.iadb.org*

Promotes, through loans and technical assistance, the investment of public and private capital in member countries of Latin America and the Caribbean for social and economic development purposes. Facilitates economic integration of the Latin American region, operating the Inter-American Investment Corporation and the Multilateral Investment Fund. Library open to the public by appointment.

Inter-American Telecommunication Commission (CITEL) *(Organization of American States), 1889 F St. N.W., 6th Floor, 20006; (202) 370-4713. Fax, (202) 458-6854. Oscar Léon, Executive Secretary. General email, citel@oas.org*

Web, www.citel.oas.org

Membership: OAS member states and associate members from the telecommunications, Internet, electronic, and media industries, and others. Works with the public and private sectors to facilitate the development of universal telecommunications in the Americas.

Organization of American States (OAS), *17th St. and Constitution Ave. N.W., 20006; Administration Bldg., 19th and Constitution N.W., 20006; General Secretariat Bldg., 1889 F St. N.W., 20006; (202) 370-5000. Fax, (202) 458-3967. Luis Almagro Lemes, Secretary General. Library, (202) 458-6041. General email, ai@oas.org*

Web, www.oas.org

Membership: the United States, Canada, and all independent Latin American and Caribbean countries. Funded by quotas paid by member states and by contributions to special multilateral funds. Works to promote democracy, eliminate poverty, and resolve disputes among member nations. Provides member states with technical and advisory services in cultural, educational, scientific, social, and economic areas. Library open to the public (at 19th and Constitution).

United Nations Economic Commission for Latin America and the Caribbean (CEPAL), *Washington Office, 1825 K St. N.W., #1120, 20006-1210; (202) 596-3713. Fax, (202) 296-0826. Inés Bustillo, Director. General email, eclacwash@eclac.org*

Web, www.cepal.org/en/headquarters-and-offices/eclac-washington-dc

Membership: Latin American, Caribbean, and some industrially developed Western nations. Seeks to strengthen economic relations between countries both within and outside Latin America through research and analysis of socioeconomic problems, training programs, and advisory services to member governments. (Headquarters in Santiago, Chile.)

World Bank, *Latin America and the Caribbean, 1818 H St. N.W., 20433; (202) 473-1000. Jorge Familiar, Vice President; Ricardo A. Vargas Gomez, Media Contact, (202) 458-0777. Web, www.worldbank.org/lac*

Works to fight poverty and improve the living standards of poor and middle-income people in the countries of Latin America and the Caribbean by providing loans, policy advice, technical assistance, and knowledge-sharing services. Areas of interest include finance, economic development, education, water supply, agriculture, and infrastructure, public health, and environmental protection.

▶NONGOVERNMENTAL

Caribbean–Central American Action, *1625 K St. N.W., #200, 20006; (202) 464-2031. Fax, (202) 452-8160. Sally Yearwood, Executive Director. General email, info@c-caa.org*

Web, www.c-caa.org and Twitter, @CCAA_Updates

Promotes trade and investment in Caribbean Basin countries; encourages democratic public policy in member countries and works to strengthen private initiatives.

Council of the Americas/Americas Society, *Washington Office, 1615 L St. N.W., #250, 20036; (202) 659-8989. Fax, (202) 659-7755. Susan Segal, President; Eric Farnsworth, Vice President, Washington, DC. Web, www.as-coa.org and Twitter, @ASCOA*

Membership: businesses with interests and investments in Latin America. Seeks to expand the role of private enterprise in development of the region. (Headquarters in New York.)

Council on Hemispheric Affairs, *1250 Connecticut Ave. N.W., #1C, 20036; (202) 223-4975. Fax, (202) 223-4979. Larry R. Birns, Director. General email, coha@coha.org*

Web, www.coha.org and Twitter, @cohastaff

Seeks to expand interest in inter-American relations and increase press coverage of Latin America and Canada. Monitors U.S., Latin American, and Canadian relations, with emphasis on human rights, trade, growth of democratic institutions, freedom of the press, and hemispheric economic and political developments; provides educational materials and analyzes issues. Issues annual survey on human rights and freedom of the press. Publishes a biweekly newsletter.

Group of Fifty (Grupo de los Cincuenta), *1300 19th St. N.W., #200, 20036; (202) 386-9161. Andres Naim, Executive Director. General email, Contact@G-50.org*

Web, www.g-50.org

Membership: business leaders who own Latin American enterprises. Holds an annual forum to improve networking between business executives and to promote economic growth in Latin America.

Guatemala Human Rights Commission/USA, *3321 12th St. N.E., 20017-4008; (202) 529-6599. Kelsey Alford-Jones, Director.*
General email, ghrc-usa@ghrc-usa.org
Web, www.ghrc-usa.org

Provides information and collects and makes available reports on human rights violations in Guatemala; publishes a quarterly report of documented cases of specific abuses. Takes on special projects and leads delegations to further sensitize the public and the international community to human rights abuses in Guatemala.

Inter-American Dialogue, *1211 Connecticut Ave. N.W., #510, 20036-2701; (202) 822-9002. Michael Shifter, President.*
General email, iad@thedialogue.org
Web, www.thedialogue.org

Serves as a forum for communication and exchange among leaders of the Americas. Provides analyses and policy recommendations on issues of hemispheric concern. Interests include economic integration, trade, and the strengthening of democracy in Latin America. Hosts private and public exchanges; sponsors conferences and seminars; publishes daily newsletter, *Latin America Advisor.*

Latin America Working Group, *2029 P St. N.W., #301, 20036; (202) 546-7010. Fax, (202) 543-7647. Lisa Haugaard, Executive Director.*
General email, lawg@lawg.org
Web, www.lawg.org, Twitter, @lawgaction and Facebook, www.facebook.com/lawgaction

Represents more than sixty organizations concerned with Latin America. Encourages U.S. policies toward Latin America that promote human rights, justice, peace, and sustainable development.

Pan American Development Foundation, *1889 F St. N.W., 2nd Floor, 20006; (202) 458-3969. Fax, (202) 458-6316. John Sanbrailo, Executive Director.*
Web, www.padf.org and Twitter, @PADForg

Works with the public and private sectors to improve the quality of life throughout the Caribbean and Latin America. Associated with the Organization of American States (OAS).

Partners of the Americas, *1424 K St. N.W., #700, 20005-2410; (202) 628-3300. Fax, (202) 628-3306. Stephen Vetter, President.*
General email, info@partners.net
Web, www.partners.net

Membership: chapters, individuals and organizations in the United States, Latin America, Brazil, and the Caribbean. Sponsors technical assistance projects and cultural exchanges between the United States, Latin America, Brazil, and the Caribbean; supports self-help projects in

food security and agricultural development, sport for development, youth and children, climate change and environmental protection, professional leadership exchanges, civil society and governance, and women and gender equality.

U.S.–Mexico Chamber of Commerce, *6800 Versar Center, #450, Springfield, VA 22151 (mailing address: P.O. Box 14414, Washington, DC 20044); (703) 752-4751. Fax, (703) 642-1088. Albert C. Zapanta, President.*
General email, info@usmcoc.org
Web, www.usmcoc.org and Twitter, @USMCOC

Promotes trade and investment between the United States and Mexico. Provides members with information and expertise on conducting business between the two countries as pertains to NAFTA. Serves as a clearinghouse for information.

Washington Office on Latin America, *1666 Connecticut Ave. N.W., #400, 20009; (202) 797-2171. Fax, (202) 797-2172. Joy Olson, Executive Director.*
General email, wola@wola.org
Web, www.wola.org and Twitter, @WOLA_org

Acts as a liaison between government policymakers and groups and individuals concerned with human rights and U.S. policy in Latin America and the Caribbean. Serves as an information resource center; monitors legislation.

Near East and South Asia

(Includes North Africa)

▶**AGENCIES**

Agency for International Development (USAID), *Asia Bureau, 1300 Pennsylvania Ave. N.W., 20523-4900; (202) 712-0200. Fax, (202) 216-3386. Jonathon Stivers, Assistant Administrator. Press, (202) 712-4320.*
Web, www.usaid.gov/who-we-are/organization/bureaus/bureau-asia

Advises the AID administrator on U.S. economic development policy in Asia.

Agency for International Development (USAID), *Middle East Bureau, 1300 Pennsylvania Ave. N.W., 20523-4900; (202) 712-4180. Fax, (202) 216-3524. Paige Alexander, Assistant Administrator.*
Web, www.usaid.gov/who-we-are/organization/bureaus/bureau-middle-east

Advises the AID administrator on U.S. economic development policy in the Middle East.

Bureau of Near Eastern Affairs *(State Dept.), 2201 C St. N.W., #6242, 20520-6243; (202) 647-7209. Fax, (202) 736-4462. Anne W. Patterson, Assistant Secretary.*
Web, www.state.gov/p/nea

Advises the secretary on U.S. policy toward countries of the Near East and North Africa. Directors assigned to specific countries within the bureau aid the assistant secretary.

Bureau of Near Eastern Affairs *(State Dept.)*, *Arabian Peninsula Affairs*, 2201 C St. N.W., #4224, 20520-6243; (202) 647-7521. Ellen J. Germain, Director, (202) 647-6184. General email, nea-arp-dl@state.gov

Web, www.state.gov/p/nea

Includes Bahrain, Kuwait, Oman, Qatar, Saudi Arabia, United Arab Emirates, and Yemen.

Bureau of Near Eastern Affairs *(State Dept.)*, *Egypt Affairs*, 2201 C St. N.W., #5256, 20520; (202) 647-8078. Fax, (202) 482-1632. E. Candace Putnam, Director.

Web, www.state.gov/p/nea

Bureau of Near Eastern Affairs *(State Dept.)*, *Iranian Affairs*, 2201 C St. N.W., #1058, 20520; (202) 647-2520. Holly Holzer, Director.

Web, www.state.gov/p/nea

Bureau of Near Eastern Affairs *(State Dept.)*, *Iraq Affairs*, 2201 C St. N.W., #4827, 20520; (202) 647-5693. Fax, (202) 736-4464. Scott M. Oudkirk, Director.

Web, www.state.gov/p/nea

Bureau of Near Eastern Affairs *(State Dept.)*, *Israel and Palestinian Affairs*, 2201 C St. N.W., #6251, 20520; (202) 647-3672. Fax, (202) 736-4461. Christopher P. Henzel, Deputy Assistant Secretary, Acting.

Web, www.state.gov/p/nea

Bureau of Near Eastern Affairs *(State Dept.)*, *Levant Affairs*, 2201 C St. N.W., #4241, 20520-6243; (202) 647-1018. Fax, (202) 647-0989. Theresa Grencik, Director.

Web, www.state.gov/p/nea

Includes Jordan, Lebanon, and Syria.

Bureau of Near Eastern Affairs *(State Dept.)*, *Maghreb Affairs*, 2201 C St. N.W., #6811, 20520-6243; (202) 647-2365. Fax, (202) 485-2843. Gregory D. LoGerfo, Director.

Web, Theresa Grenchik

Includes Algeria, Libya, Morocco, Tunisia, and Mauritania.

Bureau of Near Eastern Affairs *(State Dept.)*, *U.S.–Middle East Partnership Initiative*, 2430 E St. N.W., 2nd Floor, 20524; (202) 776-8500. Fax, (202) 776-8445. Brian Aggeler, Director.

Web, http://mepi.state.gov and Twitter, @USMEPI

Funds programs that seek to advance democracy in the Middle East. Encourages reform in the areas of politics, economics, education, and women's rights. Offers exchange programs for U.S. and Middle East/North Africa-based students, entrepreneurs, lawmakers, and civil society leaders.

Bureau of South and Central Asian Affairs *(State Dept.)*, 2201 C St. N.W., #6254, 20520-6258; (202) 736-4325. Fax, (202) 736-4333. Nisha Desai Biswal, Assistant Secretary.

Web, www.state.gov/p/sca and Twitter, @State_SCA

Advises the secretary on U.S. policy toward South and Central Asian countries. Directors assigned to specific countries within the bureau aid the assistant secretary.

Bureau of South and Central Asian Affairs *(State Dept.)*, *Afghanistan Affairs*, 2201 C St. N.W., #1880, 20520-6258; (202) 647-5175. Fax, (202) 647-5505. John Ginkel, Director.

Web, www.state.gov/p/sca

Bureau of South and Central Asian Affairs *(State Dept.)*, *India Affairs*, 2201 C St. N.W., #5251, 20520-6243; (202) 647-1114. Fax, (202) 736-4463. Sean B. Stein, Director.

Web, www.state.gov/p/sca

Bureau of South and Central Asian Affairs *(State Dept.)*, *Nepal, Sri Lanka, Bangladesh, Bhutan, and Maldives Affairs*, 2201 C St. N.W., #5250, 20520-6243; (202) 647-1613. Fax, (202) 647-1183. Clinton S. (Tad) Brown, Director.

Web, www.state.gov/p/sca

Bureau of South and Central Asian Affairs *(State Dept.)*, *Pakistan Affairs*, 2201 C St. N.W., #1861, 20520-6258; (202) 647-9823. Fax, (202) 647-3001. David Ranz, Director.

Web, www.state.gov/p/sca

Defense Dept. (DoD), *Afghanistan, Pakistan, and Central Asia Security Affairs*, 2700 Defense Pentagon, #5D688, 20301; (703) 695-4175. Christine S. Abizaid, Deputy Assistant Secretary.

Web, http://policy.defense.gov/OUSDPOffices/ASDforAsianandPacificSecurityAffairs.aspx

Advises the under secretary of defense on matters dealing with Afghanistan, Pakistan, and Central Asia.

Defense Dept. (DoD), *International Security Affairs*, 2000 Defense Pentagon, #3C889, 20301-2000; (703) 697-2788. Fax, (703) 697-3279. Elissa B. Slotkin, Assistant Secretary, Acting; Kenneth B. Handelman, Principal Deputy Assistant Secretary, Acting.

Web, http://policy.defense.gov/OUSDPOffices/ASDforInternationalSecurityAffairs.aspx

Advises the secretary of defense and recommends policies on regional security issues in the Middle East, Africa, Russia/Eurasia, and Europe/NATO.

Defense Dept. (DoD), *International Security Affairs, Middle East*, 2000 Defense Pentagon, #5B712, 20301-2000; (703) 697-1335. Fax, (703) 693-6795. Andrew Exum, Deputy Assistant Secretary; Brig. Gen. Michael A. Fantini (USAF), Principal Director.

Web, www.defense.gov

Advises the assistant secretary for international security affairs on matters dealing with the Middle East and South Asia.

Defense Dept. (DoD), *South and Southeast Asia Security Affairs*, 2700 Defense Pentagon, #5D688, 20301-2700; (703) 695-4175. Amy Searight, Deputy Assistant Secretary.

Web, http://policy.defense.gov/OUSDPOffices/ASDforAsianandPacificSecurityAffairs.aspx

Advises the under secretary of defense on matters dealing with nations of Southeast Asia, Australia, Timor-Leste, New Zealand, Pacific Island States, and bilateral security relations with India and all other South Asian countries.

►CONGRESS

For a listing of relevant congressional committees and subcommittees, please see pages 454–455 or the Appendix.

Library of Congress, *African and Middle Eastern Division,* Thomas Jefferson Bldg., 101 Independence Ave. S.E., #LJ 220, 20540; (202) 707-7937. Fax, (202) 252-3180. Mary-Jane Deeb, Chief. Reading room, (202) 707-4188. General email, amed@loc.gov
Web, www.loc.gov/rr/amed

Maintains collections of African, Near Eastern, and Hebraic material. Prepares bibliographies and special studies relating to Africa and the Middle East. Reference service and reading rooms available to the public. (Need reader's card to use.)

Library of Congress, *Asian Division,* Thomas Jefferson Bldg., 101 Independence Ave. S.E., #LJ 150, 20540; (202) 707-3766. Fax, (202) 252-3336. Dongfang Shao, Chief. Reading room, (202) 707-5426.
Web, www.loc.gov/rr/asian

Maintains collections of Asian-American Pacific, Chinese, Korean, Japanese, Southeast Asian, South Asian, and Tibetan and Mongolian material. Reference service is provided in the Asian Reading Room, room #150.

►INTERNATIONAL ORGANIZATIONS

League of Arab States, *Washington Office,* 1100 17th St. N.W., #602, 20036; (202) 265-3210. Fax, (202) 331-1525. Amb. Mohamed Al-Hussaini Al-Sharif, Director. General email, arableague@aol.com
Web, www.arableague-us.org

Membership: Arab countries in the Near East, North Africa, and the Indian Ocean. Coordinates members' policies in political, cultural, economic, and social affairs; mediates disputes among members and between members and third parties. Washington office maintains the Arab Information Center. (Headquarters in Cairo.)

Southeast Asia Resource Action Center (SEARAC), 1628 16th St. N.W., 3rd Floor, 20009; (202) 601-2960. Fax, (202) 667-6449. Quyen Dinh, Executive Director. General email, searac@searac.org
Web, www.searac.org

Works to advance Cambodian, Hmong, Laotian, and Vietnamese refugee rights through leadership and advocacy training. Collects and analyzes data on Southeast Asian Americans; publishes reports.

World Bank, *Middle East and North Africa,* 1818 H St. N.W., 20433; (202) 473-1000. Hafez Ghanem, Vice President; Lara Saade, Media Contact, (202) 473-9887. Web, www.worldbank.org

Works to fight poverty and improve the living standards of low- and middle-income people in the countries of the Middle East and North Africa by providing loans, policy advice, technical assistance, and knowledge-sharing services. Areas of interest include finance, economic development, education, water supply, agriculture, public health, and environmental protection.

World Bank, *South Asia,* 1818 H St. N.W., 20433; (202) 473-1000. Annette Dixon, Vice President; Yann Doignan, Media Contact, (202) 473-3239.
Web, www.worldbank.org

Works to fight poverty and improve the living standards of low- and middle-income people in the countries of South Asia by providing loans, policy advice, technical assistance, and knowledge-sharing services. Areas of interest include finance, economic development, education, water supply, agriculture, public health, and environmental protection.

►NONGOVERNMENTAL

American Israel Public Affairs Committee, 251 H St. N.W., 20001-2017; (202) 639-5200. Fax, (202) 347-4889. Howard Kohr, Executive Director. General email, information@aipac.org
Web, www.aipac.org and Twitter, @AIPAC

Works to maintain and improve relations between the United States and Israel.

American Jewish Committee, Project Interchange, 1156 15th St. N.W., 20005; (202) 833-0025. Fax, (202) 331-7702. Robin S. Levenston, Executive Director. General email, townsendc@projectinterchange.org
Web, www.projectinterchange.org

Sponsors policymakers, industry, leaders, journalists, and scholars to travel to Israel to meet and take part in seminars with Israeli government officials, business leaders, and academics to learn about current developments and issues affecting education, immigration, human rights, and the economy in Israel.

American Kurdish Information Network (AKIN), 2722 Connecticut Ave. N.W., #42, 20008-5366; (202) 483-6444. Kani Xulam, Director. General email, akin@kurdistan.org
Web, www.kurdistan.org

Membership: Americans of Kurdish origin, recent Kurdish immigrants and refugees, and others. Collects and disseminates information about the Kurds, an ethnic group living in parts of Turkey, Iran, Iraq, and Syria. Monitors human rights abuses against Kurds; promotes self-determination in Kurdish homelands; fosters Kurdish American friendship and understanding.

American Near East Refugee Aid (ANERA), 1111 14th St. N.W., #400, 20005; (202) 266-9700. Fax, (202) 266-9701. William Corcoran, President. General email, anera@anera.org
Web, www.anera.org and Twitter, @ANERAorg

Works with local institutions and partner organizations to provide sustainable development, health, education, and employment programs to Palestinian communities and impoverished families throughout the Middle East.

Delivers humanitarian aid during emergencies. (Field offices in the West Bank, Gaza, and Lebanon.)

AMIDEAST, *2025 M St. N.W., #600, 20036-3363; (202) 776-9600. Fax, (202) 776-7000. Theodore H. Kattouf, President. General email, inquiries@amideast.org*

Web, www.amideast.org

Promotes understanding and cooperation between Americans and the people of the Middle East and North Africa through education, information, and development programs in the region. Produces educational material to help improve teaching about the Middle East and North Africa in American schools and colleges.

Asia Society Policy Institute, *1300 Eye St. N.W., #400E, 20005; (202) 833-2742. Fax, (202) 833-0189. Wendy Cutler, Managing Director. General email, asiadc@asiasociety.org*

Web, www.asiasociety.org

Membership: individuals, organizations, and corporations interested in Asia and the Pacific (excluding the Middle East). Focuses on United States and Asia foreign policy issues. Sponsors seminars and lectures on political, economic, and cultural issues. (Headquarters in New York.)

B'nai B'rith International, *1120 20th St. N.W., #300N, 20036; (202) 857-6600. Fax, (202) 857-2700. Daniel S. Mariaschin, Executive Vice President. Toll-free, (888) 388-4224. General email, info@bnaibrith.org*

Web, www.bnaibrith.org and Twitter, @BnaiBrith

International Jewish organization that promotes the security and continuity of the Jewish people and the State of Israel; defends human rights; combats anti-Semitism; and promotes Jewish identity through cultural activities. Interests include strengthening family life and the education and training of youth, providing broad-based services for the benefit of senior citizens, and advocacy on behalf of Jews throughout the world.

Center for Contemporary Arab Studies *(Georgetown University), 241 Intercultural Center, 37th and O St. N.W., 20057-1020; (202) 687-5793. Fax, (202) 687-7001. Osama Abi-Mershod, Director. General email, ccasinfo@georgetown.edu*

Web, http://ccas.georgetown.edu and Twitter, @ccasGU

The master's program at Georgetown University; sponsors lecture series, seminars, and conferences. Conducts a community outreach program that assists secondary school teachers in the development of instructional materials on the Middle East; promotes the study of the Arabic language in area schools.

Center for Democracy and Human Rights in Saudi Arabia, *1050 17th St. N.W., #1000, 20036; (202) 558-5552. Fax, (202) 536-5210. Ali Alyami, Executive Director, (202) 413-0084. General email, cdhr@cdhr.info*

Web, www.cdhr.info and Twitter, @CDHRSA

Monitors relations between the United States and Saudi Arabia. Promotes democratic reform of Saudi policies and studies the global impact of current events in Saudi Arabia. Interests include women's rights, religious and press freedom, secular judiciary systems, and government accountability. Holds conferences to analyze Saudi polices, international relations, current events, and strict interpretations of Islam. educates the public, policymakers, and the media on related issues.

Foundation for Middle East Peace, *1761 N St. N.W., 20036-2801; (202) 835-3650. Fax, (202) 835-3651. Matthew Duss, President. General email, info@fmep.org*

Web, www.fmep.org and Twitter, @FMEP

Educational organization that seeks to promote understanding and resolution of the Israeli-Palestinian conflict. Provides media with information; and awards grants to organizations and activities that contribute to the solution of the conflict.

Hollings Center for International Dialogue, *1310 G St. N.W., #750, 20005; (202) 833-5090. Michael Carroll, Executive Director. General email, info@hollingscenter.org*

Web, www.hollingscenter.org

Holds conferences to encourage mutual understanding and policy debate between the U.S. and Muslim-oriented regions in North Africa, the Middle East, and South Asia. Participants include younger generation leaders, academics, government officials, and business leaders. Awards grants for independent study of issues that arise between the U.S. and Muslim-dominated territories.

Institute for Palestine Studies, *Washington Office, 3501 M St. N.W., 20007-2624; (202) 342-3990. Fax, (202) 342-3927. Michelle Esposito, Executive Director. General email, ipsdc@palestine-studies.org*

Web, www.palestine-studies.org

Scholarly research institute that specializes in the history and development of the Palestine problem, the Arab–Israeli conflict, and their peaceful resolution. (Maintains offices in Beirut and Jerusalem.)

Institute of Turkish Studies *(Georgetown University), Intercultural Center, Box 571033, #305R, 20057-1033; (202) 687-0292. Fax, (202) 687-3780. Sinan Ciddi, Executive Director. General email, itsdirector@turkishstudies.org*

Web, www.turkishstudies.org

Independent grant-making organization that supports and encourages the development of Turkish studies in American colleges and universities. Awards grants to individual scholars and educational institutions in the United States.

Middle East Institute, *1761 N St. N.W., 20036-2882; (202) 785-1141. Fax, (202) 331-8861. Amb. Wendy J. Chamberlin, President. Library, (202) 785-1141, ext. 222. Press, (202) 785-1141, ext. 236. Language Dept., (202) 785-1141, ext. 226.*

General email, information@mei.edu

Web, www.mei.edu

Membership: individuals interested in the Middle East. Seeks to broaden knowledge of the Middle East through research, conferences and seminars, language classes, lectures, and exhibits. Library open to members and the press Monday through Friday 10:00 a.m.–5:00 p.m.

Middle East Media Research Institute (MEMRI), *P.O. Box 27837, 20038-7837; (202) 955-9070. Fax, (202) 955-9077. Steven Stalinsky, Executive Director.*

General email, memri@memri.org

Web, www.memri.org

Explores the Middle East through the region's media. Seeks to inform the debate over U.S. policy in the Middle East.

Middle East Policy Council, *1730 M St. N.W., #512, 20036-4505; (202) 296-6767. Fax, (202) 296-5791. Hon. Ford M. Fraker, President.*

General email, info@mepc.org

Web, www.mepc.org and Twitter, @MidEastPolicy

Encourages public discussion and understanding of issues affecting U.S. policy in the Middle East. Sponsors conferences for the policy community; conducts educational outreach program; publishes journal and an e-newsletter.

Middle East Research and Information Project, *1344 T St. N.W., #1, 20009; (202) 223-3677. Fax, (202) 223-3604. Christopher J. Toensing, Executive Director.*

General email, subscriptions@merip.org

Web, www.merip.org

Works to educate the public about the contemporary Middle East. Focuses on U.S. policy in the region and issues of human rights and social justice; publishes quarterly journal and online news analysis.

National Council on U.S.–Arab Relations, *1730 M St. N.W., #503, 20036; (202) 293-6466. Fax, (202) 293-7770. John Duke Anthony, President.*

General email, info@ncusar.org

Web, http://ncusar.org, Twitter, @NCUSAR and Facebook, www.facebook.com/NCUSAR

Educational organization that works to improve mutual understanding between the United States and the Middle East and North Africa (MENA) region. Serves as a clearinghouse on Arab issues and maintains speakers bureau. Coordinates trips for U.S. professionals and congressional delegations to the MENA region.

National U.S.–Arab Chamber of Commerce, *1101 17th St. N.W., #1220, 20036; (202) 289-5920. Fax, (202) 289-5938. David Hamod, President.*

General email, info@nusacc.org

Web, www.nusacc.org

Promotes trade between the United States and the Middle East and North Africa (MENA) region. Offers members informational publications, research and certification services, and opportunities to meet with international delegations. Operates four regional offices.

New Israel Fund, *Washington Office, 2100 M St. N.W., #619, 20037; (202) 842-0900. Fax, (202) 842-0991. Karen Paul-Stern, Washington Regional Director; Daniel Sokatch, Chief Executive Officer.*

General email, dc@nif.org

Web, www.nif.org

International philanthropic partnership of North Americans, Israelis, and Europeans. Supports activities that defend civil and human rights, promote Jewish-Arab equality and coexistence, advance the status of women, nurture tolerance, bridge social and economic gaps, encourage government accountability, and assist citizen efforts to protect the environment. Makes grants and provides capacity-building assistance to Israeli public interest groups; trains civil rights lawyers. (Headquarters in New York City.)

Project on Middle East Democracy (POMED), *1611 Connecticut Ave. N.W., #300, 20009; (202) 828-9660. Fax, (202) 828-9661. Stephen McInerney, Executive Director. Press, (202) 828-9600, ext. 23.*

General email, todd.ruffner@pomed.org

Web, www.pomed.org

Researches and publishes reports to educate policy makers on methods the United States can use to build democracies in the Middle East. Holds conferences to address United States-Middle East policy issues. Advocates democracy in the Middle East and supports pro-democracy foreign policies.

S. Daniel Abraham Center for Middle East Peace, *633 Pennsylvania Ave. N.W., 5th Floor, 20004; (202) 624-0850. Fax, (202) 624-0855. S. Daniel Abraham, Chair.*

General email, info@centerpeace.org

Web, www.centerpeace.org and Twitter, @AbrahamCenter

Membership: Middle Eastern policymakers, U.S. government officials, and international business leaders. Serves as a mediator to encourage a peaceful resolution to the Arab–Israeli conflict; sponsors travel to the region, diplomatic exchanges, and conferences for Middle Eastern and U.S. leaders interested in the peace process.

United Palestinian Appeal (UPA), *1330 New Hampshire Ave. N.W., #104, 20036-6350; (202) 659-5007. Fax, (202) 296-0224. Saleem F. Zaru, Executive Director.*

General email, contact@helpupa.org

Web, www.helpUPA.org

An American charitable organization dedicated to improving the quality of life for Palestinians in the Middle East, particularly those in the West Bank, the Gaza Strip, and refugee camps. Provides funding for community development projects, health care, education, children's services, and emergency relief. Funded by private donations from individuals and foundations in the United States and the Middle East and North Africa (MENA) region.

Washington Institute for Near East Policy, *1111 19th St. N.W., #500, 20036; (202) 452-0650. Fax, (202) 223-5364. Robert Satloff, Executive Director.*

Web, www.washingtoninstitute.org and *Twitter, @washinstitute*

Research and educational organization that seeks to improve the effectiveness of U.S. policy in the Middle East by promoting debate among policymakers, journalists, and scholars.

Russia and New Independent States

For the Baltic states, see Europe.

►AGENCIES

Agency for International Development (USAID), *Europe and Eurasia Bureau,* 301 4th St. S.W., #247, 20523 (mailing address: 1300 Pennsylvania Ave. N.W., Washington, DC 20521); (202) 567-4020. Fax, (202) 567-4256. Susan Kosinski Fritz, Assistant Administrator, Acting.
Web, www.usaid.gov/who-we-are/organization/bureaus/bureau-europe-and-eurasia

Advises the AID administrator on U.S. economic development policy in Europe and Eurasia.

Bureau of European and Eurasian Affairs *(State Dept.),* *Caucasus Affairs and Regional Conflicts,* 2201 C St. N.W., #4220, 20520-7512; (202) 647-8741. Fax, (202) 736-7915. Natasha S. Francerchi, Director.
Web, www.state.gov/p/eur

Includes Armenia, Azerbaijan, Georgia, and conflict regions.

Bureau of European and Eurasian Affairs *(State Dept.),* *Russian Affairs,* 2201 C St. N.W., #4417, 20520-7512; (202) 647-9806. Fax, (202) 647-8980. David Kostelancik, Director.
Web, www.state.gov/p/eur

Bureau of European and Eurasian Affairs *(State Dept.),* *Ukraine, Moldova, and Belarus Affairs,* 2201 C St. N.W., #4427, 20520-7512; (202) 647-6750. Fax, (202) 647-3506. Michael D. Scanlan, Director.
Web, www.state.gov/p/eur

Bureau of South and Central Asian Affairs *(State Dept.),* *Central Asian Affairs,* 2201 C St. N.W., #1880, 20520; (202) 647-6745. Fax, (202) 736-4650. Grace Shelton, Director.
Web, www.state.gov/p/sca

Includes Kazakhstan, Kyrgyzstan, Tajikistan, Turkmenistan, and Uzbekistan.

Defense Dept. (DoD), *International Security Affairs,* 2000 Defense Pentagon, #3C889, 20301-2000; (703) 697-2788. Fax, (703) 697-3279. Elissa B. Slotkin, Assistant Secretary, Acting; Kenneth B. Handelman, Principal Deputy Assistant Secretary, Acting.
Web, http://policy.defense.gov/OUSDPOffices/ASDforInternationalSecurityAffairs.aspx

Advises the secretary of defense and recommends policies on regional security issues in the Middle East, Africa, Russia/Eurasia, and Europe/NATO.

Defense Dept. (DoD), *International Security Affairs, Russia, Ukraine, and Eurasia,* 2000 Defense Pentagon, 20301-2000; (703) 697-2788. Vacant, Deputy Assistant Secretary; Laura Gross, Principal Director.
Web, www.defense.gov

Advises the assistant secretary for international security affairs on matters dealing with Russia, Ukraine, and Eurasia.

►CONGRESS

For a listing of relevant congressional committees and subcommittees, please see pages 454–455 or the Appendix.

Library of Congress, *European Division,* Thomas Jefferson Bldg., 101 Independence Ave. S.E., #LJ 249, 20540; (202) 707-5414. Fax, (202) 707-8482. Georgette M. Dorn, Chief, Acting. Reference desk, (202) 707-4515.
Web, www.loc.gov/rr/european

Provides reference service on the library's European collections (except collections on Spain, Portugal, and the British Isles). Prepares bibliographies and special studies relating to European countries, including Russia and the other states of the former Soviet Union and eastern bloc. Maintains current unbound Slavic language periodicals and newspapers, which are available at the European Reference Desk. Recommends materials for acquisition.

►INTERNATIONAL ORGANIZATIONS

World Bank, *Europe and Central Asia,* 1818 H St. N.W., 20433; (202) 473-1000. Cyril Muller, Vice President; Elena Karaban, Media Contact, (202) 458-2736.
Web, www.worldbank.org

Works to fight poverty and improve the living standards of low- and middle-income people in the countries of eastern Europe and central Asia, including states of the former Soviet Union, by providing loans, policy advice, technical assistance, and knowledge-sharing services. Interests include finance, economic development, education, water supply, agriculture, public health, and environmental protection.

►NONGOVERNMENTAL

Armenian Assembly of America, 734 15th St., #500, 20005; (202) 393-3434. Fax, (202) 638-4904. Bryan Ardouny, Executive Director.
General email, info@aaainc.org
Web, www.aaainc.org

Promotes public understanding and awareness of Armenian issues; advances research and data collection and disseminates information on the Armenian people; advocates greater Armenian American participation in the American democratic process; works to alleviate human suffering of Armenians.

Armenian National Committee of America, *1711 N St. N.W., 20036; (202) 775-1918. Fax, (202) 223-7964. Aram Hamparian, Executive Director.*
General email, anca@anca.org

Web, www.anca.org and Twitter, @ANCA_DC

Armenian American grassroots political organization. Works to advance concerns of the Armenian American community. Interests include strengthening U.S.–Armenian relations.

Center on Global Interests, *1050 Connecticut Ave. N.W., #500, 20036; (202) 973-2832. Nikolai Zlobin, President.*
General email, info@globalinterests.org

Web, www.globalinterests.org and Twitter, @CGI_DC

Research center that analyzes and publishes reports on foreign relations. Specializes in U.S. and Russian affairs. Holds international conferences to educate policymakers and the media on global challenges, economies, policies, and conflict.

Eurasia Foundation, *1350 Connecticut Ave. N.W., #1000, 20036-1730; (202) 234-7370. Fax, (202) 234-7377. Horton Beebe-Center, President.*
General email, info@eurasia.org

Web, www.eurasia.org and Twitter, @EFNetwork

Operates in Eurasia, the Middle East, and China. Provides capacity building, entrepreneurship training, advocacy education, social entrepreneurship training, and fellowship exchanges to support small business growth, local institutional performance, the responsiveness of local governments, and the leadership of young people.

Institute for European, Russian, and Eurasian Studies *(George Washington University), 1957 E St. N.W., #412, 20052-0001; (202) 994-6340. Fax, (202) 994-5436. Peter Rollberg, Director.*
General email, ieresgw@email.gwu.edu

Web, www.gwu.edu/~ieresgwu

Studies and researches European, Russian, and Eurasian affairs. Sponsors a master's program in European and Eurasian studies. (Affiliated with the George Washington University Elliott School of International Affairs.)

Jamestown Foundation, *1111 16th St. N.W., #320, 20036; (202) 483-8888. Fax, (202) 483-8337. Glen E. Howard, President.*
General email, pubs@jamestown.org

Web, www.jamestown.org

Provides policymakers with information about events and trends in societies that are strategically or tactically important to the United States and that frequently restrict access to such information. Serves as an alternative source to official or intelligence channels, especially with regard to Eurasia and terrorism. Publishes the *Militant Leadership Monitor,* covering leaders of major insurgencies and militant movements.

Kennan Institute, *1 Woodrow Wilson Plaza, 1300 Pennsylvania Ave. N.W., 20004-3027; (202) 691-4100. Fax, (202) 691-4247. Matthew Rojansky, Director.*

General email, kennan@wilsoncenter.org

Web, www.wilsoncenter.org/program/kennan-institute, Twitter, @kennaninstitute and Facebook, www.facebook.com/Kennan.Institute

Offers residential research scholarships to academic scholars and to specialists from government, media, and the private sector for studies to improve American knowledge about Russia, Ukraine, Central Asia, and the Caucasus. Sponsors lectures; publishes reports; promotes dialogue between academic specialists and policymakers. (Affiliated with the Woodrow Wilson International Center for Scholars.)

NCSEJ: National Coalition Supporting Eurasian Jewry, *1120 20th St. N.W, #300N, 20006-3413; (202) 898-2500. Fax, (202) 898-0822. Mark B. Levin, Executive Director; Daniel Rubin, Chair.*
General email, ncsj@ncsj.org

Web, www.ncsej.org

Membership: national Jewish organizations and local federations. Coordinates efforts by members to aid Jews in the former Soviet Union.

U.S.–Russia Business Council, *1110 Vermont Ave. N.W., #350, 20005; (202) 739-9180, Fax, (202) 659-5920. Daniel A. Russell, President. Press, (202) 739-9187.*
General email, info@usrbc.org

Web, www.usrbc.org

Membership: U.S. companies involved in trade and investment in Russia. Promotes commercial ties between the United States and Russia; provides business services. Monitors legislation and regulations. (Maintains office in Moscow.)

U.S.–Ukraine Foundation, *Washington Office, 1660 L St. N.W., #1000, 20036-5634; (202) 524-6555. Fax, (202) 280-1989. Nadia K. McConnell, President.*
General email, info@usukraine.org

Web, www.usukraine.org

Encourages and facilitates democratic and human rights development and free market reform in the Ukraine. Creates and sustains communications channels between the United States and Ukraine. Manages the U.S.–Ukraine Community Partnerships Project. (Maintains office in Kiev, Ukraine.)

Ukrainian National Information Service, *Washington Office, 311 Massachusetts Ave. N.E., Lower Level, 20002; (202) 547-0018. Fax, (202) 547-0019. Michael Sawkiw Jr., Director.*
General email, unis@ucca.org

Web, www.ucca.org

Information bureau of the Ukrainian Congress Committee of America in New York. Monitors U.S. policy and foreign assistance to Ukraine. Supports educational, cultural, and humanitarian activities in the Ukrainian-American community. (Headquarters in New York.)

U.S. Territories and Associated States

►AGENCIES

Interior Dept. (DOI), *Insular Areas (U.S. Territories and Freely Associated States), 1849 C St. N.W., MS 2429, 20240; (202) 208-4736. Fax, (202) 208-5226. Esther Kia'aina, Assistant Secretary, (202) 208-4709; Nikolao (Nik) Pula, Director. Web, www.doi.gov/oia*

Promotes economic, social, and political development of U.S. territories (Guam, American Samoa, the Virgin Islands, and the Commonwealth of the Northern Mariana Islands). Supervises federal programs for the Freely Associated States (Federated States of Micronesia, Republic of the Marshall Islands, and Republic of Palau).

►CONGRESS

For a listing of relevant congressional committees and subcommittees, please see pages 454–455 or the Appendix.

American Samoa's Delegate to Congress, *2422 LHOB, 20515; (202) 225-8577. Fax, (202) 225-8757. Aumua Amata Radewagen. General email, aumuaamata@mail.house.gov Web, http://radewagen.house.gov*

Represents American Samoa in Congress.

Guam's Delegate to Congress, *2441 RHOB, 20515; (202) 225-1188. Fax, (202) 226-0341. Madeleine Z. Bordallo. Web, www.house.gov/bordallo*

Represents Guam in Congress.

Northern Mariana Islands' Delegate to Congress, *423 CHOB, 20515; (202) 225-2646. Fax, (202) 226-4249. Gregorio Sablan. Toll-free, (877) 446-3465. Web, www.sablan.house.gov*

Represents the Northern Mariana Islands in Congress.

Puerto Rican Resident Commissioner, *2410 RHOB, 20515; (202) 225-2615. Fax, (202) 225-2154. Pedro Pierluisi, Resident Commissioner. Web, http://pierluisi.house.gov and Twitter, @pedropierluisi*

Represents the Commonwealth of Puerto Rico in Congress.

Virgin Islands' Delegate to Congress, *509 CHOB, 20515; (202) 225-1790. Fax, (202) 225-5517. Stacey Plaskett. Web, http://plaskett.house.gov and Twitter, @StaceyPlaskett*

Represents the Virgin Islands in Congress.

►NONGOVERNMENTAL

Commonwealth of Puerto Rico Federal Affairs Administration, *1100 17th St. N.W., #800, 20036; (202) 778-0710. Fax, (202) 778-0721. Juan E. Hernández, Executive Director. General email, info@prfaa.com Web, www.prfaa.com and Twitter, @PRFAA*

Represents the governor and the government of the Commonwealth of Puerto Rico before Congress and the executive branch; conducts research; serves as official press information center for the Commonwealth of Puerto Rico. Monitors legislation and regulations.

13 ⚖

Law and Justice

GENERAL POLICY AND ANALYSIS

Basic Resources

►AGENCIES

Executive Office for U.S. Attorneys *(Justice Dept.)*, *950 Pennsylvania Ave. N.W., #2242, 20530-0001; (202) 252-1000. Fax, (202) 252-1415. Monty Wilkinson, Director. Web, www.justice.gov/usao/eousa/director.html*

Provides the offices of U.S. attorneys with technical assistance and supervision in areas of legal counsel, personnel, and training. Publishes the *U.S. Attorneys' Manual* and *United States Attorneys' Bulletin*. Administers the Attorney General's Office of Legal Education, which conducts workshops and seminars to develop the litigation skills of the department's attorneys in criminal and civil trials. Develops and implements Justice Dept. procedures for collecting criminal fines.

Justice Dept. (DOJ), *950 Pennsylvania Ave. N.W., #4400, 20530-0001; (202) 514-2001. Fax, (202) 307-6777. Loretta Lynch, Attorney General; Stuart Delery, Associate Attorney General, Acting, (202) 514-9500; Sally Yates, Deputy Attorney General, (202) 514-2101; Melanie Newman, Public Affairs, (202) 514-2007. Information and switchboard, (202) 514-2000. Public Affairs, (202) 514-2007. Library, (202) 514-3775. Public comments, (202) 353-1555. General email, askdoj@usdoj.gov Web, www.justice.gov*

Serves as counsel for the U.S. government. Represents the government in enforcing the law in the public interest. Plays key role in protecting against criminals and subversion, in ensuring healthy competition of business in U.S. free enterprise system, in safeguarding the consumer, and in enforcing drug, immigration, and naturalization laws. Plays a significant role in protecting citizens through effective law enforcement, crime prevention, crime detection, and prosecution and rehabilitation of offenders. Conducts all suits in the Supreme Court in which the United States is concerned. Represents the government in legal matters generally, furnishing legal advice and opinions to the president, the cabinet, and the heads of executive departments, as provided by law. Justice Dept. organization includes divisions on antitrust, civil law, civil rights, criminal law, environment and natural resources, and taxes, as well as the Bureau of Alcohol, Tobacco, Firearms, and Explosives; Drug Enforcement Administration; Executive Office for Immigration Review; Federal Bureau of Investigation; Federal Bureau of Prisons; Foreign Claims Settlement Commission; Office of Justice Programs; U.S. Attorneys; U.S. Marshals Service; U.S. Parole Commission; and U.S. Trustees.

Justice Dept. (DOJ), *Access to Justice Initiative, 950 Pennsylvania Ave. N.W., #3340, 20530; (202) 514-5312. Fax, (202) 514-5326. Bob Bullock, Senior Counselor. Web, www.justice.gov/atj*

Works to improve the availability and quality of legal defense for vulnerable populations, including immigrants, juveniles, the homeless, disabled veterans, and victims of domestic and sexual violence. Identifies areas of need and effective programs, and works collaboratively with local, state, tribal, and federal participants to implement solutions. Priorities include expanding community partnerships, promoting less court-intensive solutions, and increasing resources for defender programs.

Justice Dept. (DOJ), *Legal Policy, 950 Pennsylvania Ave. N.W., #4234, 20530-0001; (202) 514-4601. Fax, (202) 514-2424. Jonathan Wroblewski, Principal Deputy Assistant Attorney General. Web, www.justice.gov/olp*

Develops and implements the Justice Dept.'s major policy initiatives, often with the cooperation of other offices within the department and among other agencies. Works with Office of Legislative Affairs to promote the department's policies in Congress.

Justice Dept. (DOJ), *Professional Responsibility, 950 Pennsylvania Ave. N.W., #3266, 20530-0001; (202) 514-3365. Fax, (202) 514-5050. Robin C. Ashton, Counsel. Web, www.justice.gov/opr*

Receives and reviews allegations of misconduct by Justice Dept. attorneys; refers cases that warrant further review to appropriate investigative agency or unit; makes recommendations to the attorney general for action on certain misconduct cases.

Justice Dept. (DOJ), *Solicitor General, 950 Pennsylvania Ave. N.W., #5143, 20530-0001; (202) 514-2203. Fax, (202) 514-9769. Donald B. Verrilli Jr., Solicitor General. Information on pending cases, (202) 514-2218. Web, www.justice.gov/osg*

Represents the federal government before the Supreme Court of the United States.

Legal Services Corp., *3333 K St. N.W., 3rd Floor, 20007-3522; (202) 295-1500. Fax, (202) 337-6797. James J. Sandman, President, (202) 295-1515. Public Reading Room, (202) 295-1502. General email, rauscherc@lsc.org Web, www.lsc.gov and Twitter, @lsctweets*

Independent federal corporation established by Congress. Awards grants to local agencies that provide the poor with legal services. Library open to the public by appointment only.

Office of Justice Programs (OJP) *(Justice Dept.)*, *810 7th St. N.W., 20531; (202) 307-5933. Fax, (202) 514-7805. Karol V. Mason, Assistant Attorney General. Press, (202) 307-0703. General email, askojp@ncjrs.gov Web, www.ojp.usdoj.gov*

Provides federal leadership, coordination, and assistance in developing the nation's capacity to prevent and control crime, administer justice, and assist crime victims. Includes the Bureau of Justice Assistance, which supports state and local criminal justice strategies; the Bureau of

Justice Statistics, which collects, analyzes, and disseminates criminal justice data; the National Institute of Justice, which is the primary research and development agency of the Justice Dept.; the Office of Juvenile Justice and Delinquency Prevention, which supports state and local efforts to combat juvenile crime and victimization; the Office of Victims of Crime, which provides support for crime victims and leadership to promote justice and healing for all crime victims; and the Community Capacity Development Office, which provides resources to support community-based anticrime efforts.

State Justice Institute, *11951 Freedom Dr., #1020, Reston, VA 20190; (571) 313-8843. Fax, (571) 313-1173. Jonathan Mattiello, Executive Director. General email, contact@sji.gov*

Web, www.sji.gov

Awards grants to state courts and to state agencies for programs that improve state courts' judicial administration. Maintains judicial information clearinghouses and establishes technical resource centers; conducts educational programs; delivers technical assistance.

►CONGRESS

For a listing of relevant congressional committees and subcommittees, please see pages 516–517 or the Appendix.

Government Accountability Office (GAO), *Homeland Security and Justice, 441 G St. N.W., #6H19, 20548; (202) 512-8777. George A. Scott, Managing Director. Web, www.gao.gov/careers/hsj.html*

Independent nonpartisan agency in the legislative branch. Audits, analyzes, and evaluates federal administration of homeland security programs and activities; makes some reports available to the public.

►JUDICIARY

Administrative Office of the U.S. Courts, *1 Columbus Circle N.E., 20544-0001; (202) 502-2600. James C. Duff, Director. Web, www.uscourts.gov/adminoff.html*

Provides administrative support to the federal courts, including the procurement of supplies and equipment; the administration of personnel, budget, and financial control services; and the compilation and publication of statistical data and reports on court business. Implements the policies of the Judicial Conference of the United States and supports its committees. Recommends plans and strategies to manage court business. Procures needed resources, legislation, and other assistance for the judiciary from Congress and the executive branch.

Federal Judicial Center, *1 Columbus Circle N.E., 20002-8003; (202) 502-4160. Fax, (202) 502-4099. Jeremy D. Fogel, Director. Library, (202) 502-4156. Public Affairs, (202) 502-4250. Web, www.fjc.gov*

Conducts research on the operations of the federal court system; develops and conducts continuing education and training programs for judges and judicial personnel; and makes recommendations to improve the administration of the courts.

Judicial Conference of the United States, *1 Columbus Circle N.E., #7430, 20544; (202) 502-2400. Fax, (202) 502-1144. John G. Roberts Jr., Chief Justice of the United States, Chair; James C. Duff, Director. Web, www.uscourts.gov*

Serves as the policymaking and governing body for the administration of the federal judicial system; advises Congress on the creation of new federal judgeships. Interests include international judicial relations.

Supreme Court of the United States, *1 1st St. N.E., 20543; (202) 479-3000. John G. Roberts Jr., Chief Justice; Kathleen Arberg, Public Information Officer, (202) 479-3211. TTY, (202) 479-3472. Visitor Info, (202) 479-3030. Web, www.supremecourtus.gov*

Highest appellate court in the federal judicial system. Interprets the U.S. Constitution, federal legislation, and treaties. Provides information on new cases filed, the status of pending cases, and admissions to the Supreme Court Bar. Library open to Supreme Court bar members only.

►NONGOVERNMENTAL

Alliance for Justice, *11 Dupont Circle N.W., 2nd Floor, 20036-1213; (202) 822-6070. Fax, (202) 822-6068. Nan Aron, President. General email, alliance@afj.org Web, www.afj.org*

Membership: public interest lawyers and advocacy, environmental, civil rights, and consumer organizations. Promotes reform of the legal system to ensure access to the courts; monitors selection of federal judges; works to preserve the rights of nonprofit organizations to advocate on behalf of their constituents. Monitors candidates for vacancies in the federal judiciary; independently reviews nominees' records; maintains statistics on the judiciary.

American Assn. for Justice, *777 6th St. N.W., #200, 20001; (202) 965-3500. Fax, (202) 342-5484. Linda Lipsen, Chief Executive Officer. Toll-free, (800) 424-2725. General email, aaj@justice.org Web, www.justice.org*

Membership: attorneys, judges, law professors, and students. Works to strengthen the civil justice system and the right to trial by jury. Interests include victims' rights, property and casualty insurance, revisions of federal rules of evidence, criminal code, jurisdictions of courts, juries, and consumer law. (Formerly the Assn. of Trial Lawyers of America.)

American Bar Assn. (ABA), *1050 Connecticut Ave. N.W., #400, 20036; (202) 662-1000. Fax, (202) 662-1099. Jack Rives, Executive Director. Information, (800) 285-2221. Library, (202) 662-1011. Web, www.americanbar.org*

Composed of the Governmental Affairs Office, Public Services Division, Government and Public Sector Lawyers

LAW AND JUSTICE RESOURCES IN CONGRESS

For a complete listing of congressional committees, including their full contact information, leadership, membership, and jurisdictions, please refer to the Appendix on pages 779–896.

HOUSE:

House Administration Committee, (202) 225-8281. Web, cha.house.gov

House Appropriations Committee, (202) 225-2771. Web, appropriations.house.gov

    Subcommittee on Commerce, Justice, Science, and Related Agencies, (202) 225-3351.

    Subcommittee on Homeland Security, (202) 225-5834.

House Education and the Workforce Committee, (202) 225-4527. Web, edworkforce.house.gov

    Subcommittee on Workforce Protections, (202) 225-4527.

House Energy and Commerce Committee, (202) 225-2927. Web, energycommerce.house.gov

    Subcommittee on Commerce, Manufacturing, and Trade, (202) 225-2927.

    Subcommittee on Energy and Power, (202) 225-2927.

    Subcommittee on Health, (202) 225-2927.

House Ethics Committee, (202) 225-7103. Web, ethics.house.gov

House Financial Services Committee, (202) 225-7502. Web, financialservices.house.gov

    Subcommittee on Financial Institutions and Consumer Credit, (202) 225-7502.

House Homeland Security Committee, (202) 226-8417. Web, homeland.house.gov

    Subcommittee on Border and Maritime Security, (202) 226-8417.

House Judiciary Committee, (202) 225-3951. Web, judiciary.house.gov

    Subcommittee on the Constitution and Civil Justice, (202) 225-2825.

    Subcommittee on Courts, Intellectual Property, and the Internet, (202) 226-7680.

    Subcommittee on Crime, Terrorism, Homeland Security, and Investigations, (202) 225-5727.

    Subcommittee on Immigration and Border Security, (202) 225-3926.

    Subcommittee on Regulatory Reform, Commercial, and Antitrust Law, (202) 226-7680.

House Natural Resources Committee, (202) 225-2761. Web, naturalresources.house.gov

    Subcommittee on Energy and Mineral Resources, (202) 225-9297.

House Oversight and Government Reform Committee, (202) 225-5074. Web, oversight.house.gov

    Subcommittee on Government Operations, (202) 225-5074.

House Small Business Committee, (202) 225-5821. Web, smallbusiness.house.gov

    Subcommittee on Health and Technology, (202) 225-5821.

House Ways and Means Committee, (202) 225-3625. Web, waysandmeans.house.gov

    Subcommittee on Human Resources, (202) 225-1025.

Division, International Law and Practice Section, Criminal Justice Section, Taxation Section, Individual Rights and Responsibilities Section, Dispute Resolution Section, Administrative Law and Regulatory Practice Section, Rule of Law Initiative, and others. (Headquarters in Chicago, Ill.)

American Bar Assn. (ABA), *Governmental Affairs, 1050 Connecticut Ave. N.W., #400, 20036; (202) 662-1760. Fax, (202) 662-1762. Thomas M. Susman, Director, (202) 662-1765.*
General email, thomas.susman@americanbar.org
Web, www.americanbar.org/poladv

Advocates before Congress, the executive branch, and other governmental entities on issues of importance to the legal profession. Publishes the *ABA Washington Letter,* a monthly online legislative analysis; and *ABA Washington Summary,* a daily online publication.

American Constitution Society for Law and Policy, *1333 H St. N.W., 11th Floor, 20005; (202) 393-6181. Fax, (202) 393-6189. Caroline Fredrickson, President.*
General email, info@acslaw.org
Web, www.acslaw.org

National association of lawyers, law students, judges, legal scholars, and policymakers that promotes a progressive vision of constitutional law and public policy. Produces issue briefs and publications. Organizes lectures, conferences, seminars, and two annual student competitions.

American Tort Reform Assn., *1101 Connecticut Ave. N.W., #400, 20036-4351; (202) 682-1163. Fax, (202) 682-1022. Sherman Joyce, President.*
Web, www.atra.org and Twitter, @AMTortReform

Membership: businesses, associations, trade groups, professional societies, and individuals interested in reforming the civil justice system in the United States.

SENATE:

Senate Agriculture, Nutrition, and Forestry Committee, (202) 224-2035.
Web, ag.senate.gov

Subcommittee on Livestock, Marketing, and Agriculture Security, (202) 224-2035.

Senate Appropriations Committee, (202) 224-7363.
Web, appropriations.senate.gov

Subcommittee on Commerce, Justice, Science, and Related Agencies, (202) 224-5202.

Subcommittee on Homeland Security, (202) 224-7363.

Senate Commerce, Science, and Transportation Committee, (202) 224-0411.
Web, commerce.senate.gov

Subcommittee on Consumer Protection, Product Safety, Insurance and Data Security, (202) 224-0411.

Subcommittee on Oceans, Atmosphere, Fisheries, and the Coast Guard, (202) 224-4912.

Senate Finance Committee, (202) 224-4515.
Web, finance.senate.gov

Subcommittee on Taxation and IRS Oversight, (202) 224-4515.

Senate Foreign Relations Committee, (202) 224-4651.
Web, foreign.senate.gov

Subcommittee on Western Hemisphere, Transnational Crime, Civilian Security, Democracy, Human Rights, and Global Women's Issues, (202) 224-4651.

Senate Health, Education, Labor, and Pensions Committee, (202) 224-5375.
Web, help.senate.gov

Subcommittee on Children and Families, (202) 224-5375.

Subcommittee on Employment and Workplace Safety, (202) 228-1455.

Senate Homeland Security and Governmental Affairs Committee, (202) 224-2627.
Web, hsgac.senate.gov

Permanent Subcommittee on Investigations, (202) 224-4462.

Senate Indian Affairs Committee, (202) 224-2251.
Web, indian.senate.gov

Senate Judiciary Committee, (202) 224-7703.
Web, judiciary.senate.gov

Subcommittee on Antitrust, Competition Policy, and Consumer Rights, (202) 224-6884.

Subcommittee on the Constitution, (202) 224-7840.

Subcommittee on Crime and Terrorism, (202) 224-6791.

Subcommittee on Immigration and the National Interest, (202) 224-7572.

Subcommittee on Oversight, Agency Action, Federal Rights, and Federal Courts, (202) 224-5972.

Subcommittee on Privacy, Technology, and the Law, (202) 228-4280.

Senate Rules and Administration Committee, (202) 224-6352.
Web, rules.senate.gov

Senate Select Committee on Ethics, (202) 224-2981.
Web, ethics.senate.gov

Senate Small Business and Entrepreneurship Committee, (202) 224-5175.
Web, sbc.senate.gov

Senate Special Committee on Aging, (202) 224-5364.
Web, aging.senate.gov

Develops model state legislation and position papers on tort liability and reform. Monitors legislation, regulations, and legal rulings.

Aspen Institute, *1 Dupont Circle N.W., #700, 20036-7133; (202) 736-5800. Fax, (202) 467-0790. Walter Isaacson, President. Press, (202) 736-3849.*
General email, info@aspeninstitute.org

Web, www.aspeninstitute.org and Twitter, @AspenInstitute

Educational and policy studies organization. Brings together individuals from diverse backgrounds to discuss how to deal with longstanding philosophical disputes and contemporary social challenges in law and justice.

Center for Study of Responsive Law, *1530 P St. N.W., 20005 (mailing address: P.O. Box 19367, Washington, DC 20036); (202) 387-8030. Fax, (202) 234-5176.*

John Richard, Administrator.
General email, info@csrl.org
Web, www.csrl.org

Consumer interest clearinghouse that conducts research and holds conferences on public interest law. Interests include white-collar crime, the environment, occupational health and safety, the postal system, banking deregulation, insurance, freedom of information policy, and broadcasting.

Federal Bar Assn., *1220 N. Fillmore St., #444, Arlington, VA 22201; (571) 481-9100. Fax, (571) 481-9090. Karen Silberman, Executive Director.*
General email, fba@fedbar.org

Web, www.fedbar.org and Twitter, @federalbar

Membership: attorneys employed by the federal government or practicing before federal courts or agencies. Conducts research and programs in fields that include tax, environment, veterans health, intellectual property,

Justice Department

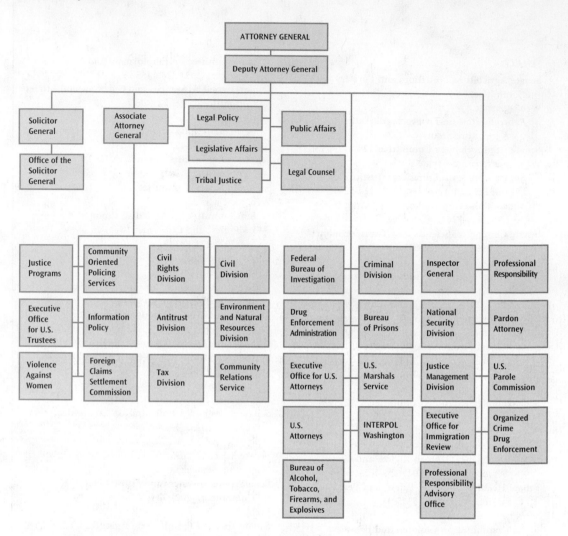

Social Security, transportation, Native American, antitrust, immigration, and international law; concerns include professional ethics, legal education (primarily continuing education), and legal services.

The Federalist Society, *1776 Eye St. N.W., #300, 20006; (202) 822-8138. Fax, (202) 296-8061. Eugene B. Meyer, President.*
General email, info@fed-soc.org
Web, www.fed-soc.org

Promotes conservative and libertarian principles among lawyers, judges, law professors, law students, and the general public. Sponsors lectures, debates, seminars, fellowships, and awards programs.

Government Accountability Project, *1612 K St. N.W., #1100, 20006; (202) 457-0034. Fax, (202) 457-0059. Anna Myers, Executive Director; Louis Clark, President.*
General email, info@whistleblower.org
Web, www.whistleblower.org

Membership: federal employees, union members, professionals, and interested citizens. Supports and represents employee whistleblowers. Works to ensure that whistleblower disclosures about improper government and industry actions that are harmful to the environment, public health, national security, food safety, the financial sector, and several other areas are defended and heard. Represents whistleblower clients in legal actions and operates attorney referral service through National Whistleblower Legal Defense and Education Fund. (Formerly the National Whistleblower Center.)

Justice at Stake, *717 D St. N.W., #203, 20004; (202) 588-9700. Fax, (202) 588-9485. Susan Liss, Executive Director. Press, (202) 588-9454.*
General email, info@justiceatstake.org
Web, www.justiceatstake.org

Advocates for a fair and impartial court system. Responds to special interest pressure in courts. Educates citizens on their legal rights. Manages programs that evaluate judges and assists in funding judicial campaigns. Monitors legislation and regulations.

Lawyers for Civil Justice, *1140 Connecticut Ave. N.W., #503, 20036-4013; (202) 429-0045. Fax, (202) 429-6982. Andrea B. Looney, Executive Director. Web, www.lfcj.com and Twitter, @LCJReform*

Membership: defense lawyers and corporate counsel. Interests include tort reform, litigation cost containment, and tort and product liability. Monitors legislation and regulations affecting civil justice reform.

National Bar Assn., *1225 11th St. N.W., 20001-4217; (202) 842-3900. Fax, (202) 315-3051. Keith Andrew Perry, Executive Director; Benjamin Crump, President. General email, nbapresident@nationalbar.org*

Web, www.nationalbar.org

Membership: primarily minority attorneys, legal professionals, judges, and law students. Interests include legal education and improvement of the judicial process. Sponsors legal education seminars in all states that require continuing legal education for lawyers.

National Center for State Courts, *Government Relations, 111 2nd St. N.E., 20002; (202) 684-2622. Fax, (202) 544-0978. Kay Farley, Executive Director. Toll-free, (866) 616-6164. General email, govrel@ncsc.org*

Web, www.ncsc.org

Works to improve state court systems through research, technical assistance, and training programs. Monitors legislation affecting court systems; interests include state-federal jurisdiction, family law, criminal justice, court administration, international agreements, and automated information systems. Serves as secretariat for eleven state court organizations, including the Conference of Chief Justices, Conference of State Court Administrators, American Judges Assn., and National Assn. for Court Management. (Headquarters in Williamsburg, Va.)

RAND Corporation, *Washington Office, 1200 S. Hayes St., Arlington, VA 22202-5050; (703) 413-1100. Fax, (703) 413-8111. Richard M. Moore, Director, ext. 5399; Anita Chandra, Director, Justice, Infrastructure, and Environment, ext. 5323. Web, www.rand.org*

Analyzes current problems of the American civil and criminal justice systems and evaluates recent and pending changes and reforms. (Headquarters in Santa Monica, Calif.)

U.S. Chamber of Commerce, *Congressional and Public Affairs, 1615 H St. N.W., 20062-2000; (202) 463-5600. Jack Howard, Senior Vice President. Web, www.uschamber.com*

Federation of individuals, firms, corporations, trade and professional associations, and local, state, and regional chambers of commerce. Monitors legislation and regulations in administrative law, antitrust policy, civil justice reform, and product liability reform.

U.S. Chamber of Commerce, *Institute for Legal Reform, 1615 H St. N.W., 20062-2000; (202) 463-5724. Fax, (202) 463-5302. Lisa A. Rickard, President. General email, ilr@uschamber.com*

Web, www.instituteforlegalreform.org

Works to reform state and federal civil justice systems. Strives to reduce excessive litigation. Hosts public forums on legal and tort reform.

Urban Institute, *Justice Policy Center, 2100 M St. N.W., 20037; (202) 833-7200. Fax, (202) 659-8985. Nancy LaVigne, Director. Web, www.urban.org/center/jpc*

Conducts research and evaluation designed to improve justice and public safety policies and practices at the national, state, and local levels. Works with practitioners, public officials, and community groups to generate evidence on effectiveness of existing programs and to provide guidance on improvements.

Washington Legal Foundation, *2009 Massachusetts Ave. N.W., 20036; (202) 588-0302. Fax, (202) 588-0386. Constance Claffey Larcher, Executive Director. General email, info@wlf.org*

Web, www.wlf.org and Twitter, @WashLglFndn

Public interest law and policy center. Seeks a legal and regulatory environment supportive of free enterprise through litigation, publishing, and communications. Interests include environmental health, safety regulations, intellectual property rights, and commercial speech.

Women's Bar Assn., *2020 Pennsylvania Ave. N.W., #446, 20006; (202) 639-8880. Fax, (202) 639-8889. Carol Montoya, Executive Director. General email, admin@wbadc.org*

Web, www.wbadc.org and Twitter, @WBADC

Membership: women and men who are judges, attorneys in the public and private sectors, law students, and lawyers at home who remain professionally active. Promotes appointment of members to positions in the judiciary and legislative policies that foster the advancement of women.

World Jurist Assn., *7910 Woodmont Ave., #1440, Bethesda, MD 20814; (202) 466-5428. Fax, (202) 452-8540. Franklin Hoet-Linares, President; Garry E. Hunter, Executive Vice President. General email, wja@worldjurist.org*

Web, www.worldjurist.org and Twitter, @worldjurist

Membership: lawyers, law professors, judges, law students, and nonlegal professionals worldwide. Conducts research; promotes world peace through adherence to international law; holds annual conference and biennial congresses. (Affiliates, at same address, include World Assn. of Judges, World Assn. of Law Professors, World Assn. of Lawyers, and World Business Associates.)

General Counsels for Federal Departments and Agencies

DEPARTMENTS

Agriculture, Jeffrey Prieto, (202) 720-3351

Commerce, Kelly R. Welsh, (202) 482-4772

Defense, Robert S. Taylor (Acting), (703) 695-3341

　Air Force, Gordon O. Tanner, (703) 697-0941

　Army, (Vacant), (703) 697-9235

　Navy, Paul L. Oostburg Sanz, (703) 614-1994

Education, James Cole Jr., (202) 401-6000

Energy, Steve Croley, (202) 586-5281

Health and Human Services, William B. Schultz, (202) 690-7741

Homeland Security, Stevan E. Bunnell, (202) 282-9822

Housing and Urban Development, Helen R. Kanovsky, (202) 708-2244

Interior, Hilary Tompkins, (202) 208-4423

Justice, Jean King, (703) 305-0470

Labor, Patricia Smith, (202) 693-5260

State, Brian J. Egan, (202) 663-0383

Transportation, Kathryn B. Thomson, (202) 366-4702

Treasury, Priya Aiyar (Acting), (202) 622-0283

Veterans Affairs, Leigh A. Bradley, (800) 488-8244

AGENCIES

Advisory Council on Historic Preservation, Javier Marques (Associate), (202) 517-0192

Agency for International Development, John Simpkins, (202) 712-0900

Central Intelligence Agency, Caroline Krass, (703) 482-1100

Commission on Civil Rights, Todd Gaziano (Chief Legal Officer), (202) 376-7700

Commodity Futures Trading Commission, Jonathan L. Marcus, (202) 418-5120

Consumer Product Safety Commission, Stephanie Tsacoumis, (301) 504-7612

Corporation for National Service, Jeremy Joseph, (202) 606-6677

Environmental Protection Agency, Avi Garbow, (202) 564-8040

Equal Employment Opportunity Commission, P. David Lopez, (202) 663-4702

Export-Import Bank, Douglas Ochs Adler, (202) 565-3451

Farm Credit Administration, Charles R. Rawls, (703) 883-4021

Federal Communications Commission, Jonathan Sallet, (202) 418-1700

Federal Deposit Insurance Corporation, Charles Yi, (877) 275-3342

Federal Election Commission, Daniel A. Petalas, (202) 694-1650

Federal Emergency Management Agency, Adrian Sevier, (800) 621-3362

Federal Energy Regulatory Commission, Max Minzner, (202) 502-6000

Federal Labor Relations Authority, Julia Akins Clark, (202) 218-7910

Dispute Resolution

▶AGENCIES

Justice Dept. (DOJ), *Community Relations Service, 600 E St. N.W., #6000, 20530; (202) 305-2935. Paul Monteiro, Director, Acting.*
General email, askcrs@usdoj.gov

Web, www.justice.gov/crs

Works with state and local governments, private and public organizations, civil rights groups, and local community leaders to promote conflict resolution for community challenges arising from differences of race, color, national origin, gender, gender identity, sexual orientation, religion and disability. Assists communities in developing local mechanisms and community capacity to prevent tension and violent hate crimes from occurring in the future.

Justice Dept. (DOJ), *Legal Policy, Interagency Alternative Dispute Resolution Working Group, 950 Pennsylvania Ave. N.W., #4529, 20530-0001; (202) 616-9471. Fax, (202) 616-9570. Joanna M. Jacobs, Director, (202) 305-4439.*
General email, ADRWeb@usdoj.gov

Web, www.adr.gov

Division of the office of the associate attorney general. Coordinates Justice Dept. activities related to dispute resolution. Responsible for alternative dispute resolution (ADR) policy and training. Manages the Interagency ADR Working Group.

Occupational Safety and Health Review Commission, *1120 20th St. N.W., 9th Floor, 20036-3457; (202) 606-5100. Fax, (202) 606-5050. Thomasina V. Rogers, Chair, (202) 606-5370. TTY, (877) 889-5627.*
Web, www.oshrc.gov

Independent executive branch agency that adjudicates disputes between private employers and the Occupational Safety and Health Administration arising under the Occupational Safety and Health Act of 1970.

▶NONGOVERNMENTAL

American Arbitration Assn., *Government Relations, 1120 Connecticut Ave., #490, 20036; (202) 223-4263. Fax, (202) 223-7095. S. Pierre Paret, Vice President.*
General email, paretp@adr.org

Web, www.adr.org

Federal Maritime Commission, Tyler J. Wood,
(202) 523-5740

Federal Mediation and Conciliation Service, Dawn E.
Starr, (202) 606-5444

Federal Reserve System, Scott G. Alvarez,
(202) 974-7008

Federal Trade Commission, Jonathan E. Nuechterlein,
(202) 326-2868

General Services Administration, Kris E. Durmer,
(202) 501-2200

**International Bank for Reconstruction and
Development (World Bank),** Anne-Marie Leroy,
(202) 473-1000

Merit Systems Protection Board, Bryan Polisuk,
(202) 653-7171

National Aeronautics and Space Administration,
Sumara M. Thompson-King,
(202) 358-2440

National Credit Union Administration, Michael T.
McKenna, (703) 518-6540

National Endowment for the Humanities, Michael
McDonald, (202) 606-8322

National Endowment for the Arts, India Pinkney,
(202) 682-5418

National Labor Relations Board, Richard F. Griffin Jr.,
(202) 273-3700

National Mediation Board, Mary L. Johnson,
(202) 692-5040

National Railroad Passenger Corporation (Amtrak),
Eleanor D. Acheson, (800) 872-7245

National Science Foundation, Lawrence Rudolph,
(703) 292-8060

National Transportation Safety Board, David Tochen
(Acting), (202) 314-6080

Nuclear Regulatory Commission, Margaret Doane,
(301) 415-1743

**Occupational Safety and Health Review
Commission,** Nadine N. Mancini,
(202) 606-5410

Office of Personnel Management, Robin Jacobsohn,
(202) 606-1700

Overseas Private Investment Corporation, Kimberly
Heimert, (202) 336-8400

Peace Corps, Vacant, (202) 692-2150

Pension Benefit Guaranty Corporation, Judith Starr,
(202) 326-4400

Postal Regulatory Commission, David A. Trissell,
(202) 789-6820

Securities and Exchange Commission, Annie K. Small,
(202) 551-5100

Small Business Administration, Melvin F. Williams Jr.,
(202) 205-7425

Smithsonian Institution, Judith Leonard,
(202) 633-5115

Social Security Administration, Andy Liu,
(404) 562-1182

U.S. International Trade Commission, David Shonka
(Acting), (404) 562-1182

U.S. Postal Service, Thomas J. Marshall,
(202) 268-2950

Provides alternative dispute resolution services to governments and the private sector. (Headquarters in New York.)

American Bar Assn. (ABA), *Dispute Resolution, 1050
Connecticut Ave. N.W., #400, 20036; (202) 662-1680.
Fax, (202) 662-1683. David Moora, Section Director,
(202) 662-1685.
General email, dispute@americanbar.org*

Web, www.americanbar.org/dispute

Provides training and resources to lawyers, law students, mediators, and arbitrators on dispute resolution.

Center for Dispute Settlement, *1666 Connecticut Ave.
N.W., #525, 20009-1039; (202) 265-9572. Fax, (202) 332-
3951. Linda R. Singer, President.
General email, admin@cdsusa.org*

Web, www.cdsusa.org and Twitter, @CdsCenter

Designs, implements, and evaluates alternative and nonjudicial methods of dispute resolution. Mediates disputes. Provides training in dispute resolution for public and private institutions, individuals, and communities.

Council of Better Business Bureaus, *Dispute Resolution,
3033 Wilson Blvd., #600, Arlington, VA 22201-3843; (703)
276-0100. Fax, (703) 525-8277. Vacant, Senior Vice
President, Enterprise Programs.
General email, contactdr@council.bbb.org*

*Web, www.bbb.org/council/bbb/dispute-handling-and-
resolution*

Administers mediation and arbitration programs through Better Business Bureaus nationwide to assist in resolving disputes between businesses and consumers. Assists with unresolved disputes between car owners and automobile manufacturers. Maintains pools of certified arbitrators nationwide. Provides mediation training.

Judicial Appointments

▶AGENCIES

Justice Dept. (DOJ), *Legal Policy, 950 Pennsylvania Ave.
N.W., #4234, 20530-0001; (202) 514-4601. Fax, (202) 514-
2424. Jonathan Wroblewski, Principal Deputy Assistant
Attorney General.
Web, www.justice.gov/olp*

Investigates and processes prospective candidates for presidential appointment (subject to Senate confirmation) to the federal judiciary.

▶CONGRESS

For a listing of relevant congressional committees and sub-committees, please see pages 516–517 or the Appendix.

▶JUDICIARY

Administrative Office of the U.S. Courts, *1 Columbus Circle N.E., 20544-0001; (202) 502-2600. James C. Duff, Director.*
Web, www.uscourts.gov/adminoff.html

Supervises all administrative matters of the federal court system, except the Supreme Court. Transmits to Congress the recommendations of the Judicial Conference of the United States concerning creation of federal judgeships and other legislative proposals.

Judicial Conference of the United States, *1 Columbus Circle N.E., #7430, 20544; (202) 502-2400. Fax, (202) 502-1144. John G. Roberts Jr., Chief Justice of the United States, Chair; James C. Duff, Director.*
Web, www.uscourts.gov

Serves as the policymaking and governing body for the administration of the federal judicial system; advises Congress on the creation of new federal judgeships. Interests include international judicial relations.

BUSINESS AND TAX LAW

Antitrust

▶AGENCIES

Antitrust Division *(Justice Dept.), 950 Pennsylvania Ave. N.W., #3109, 20530-0001; (202) 514-2401. Fax, (202) 616-2645. William J. Baer, Assistant Attorney General. Press, (202) 514-2007.*
General email, antitrust.atr@usdoj.gov
Web, www.usdoj.gov/atr

Enforces antitrust laws to prevent monopolies and unlawful restraint of trade; has civil and criminal jurisdiction; coordinates activities with the Bureau of Competition of the Federal Trade Commission.

Antitrust Division *(Justice Dept.), Antitrust Documents Group, 450 5th St. N.W., #1024, 20530; (202) 514-2481. Fax, (202) 514-3763. SueAnn Slates, Supervisor, (202) 307-1398.*
General email, atrdocsgrp@usdoj.gov
Web, www.justice.gov/atr

Maintains files and handles requests for information on federal civil and criminal antitrust cases; provides the president and Congress with copies of statutory reports prepared by the division on a variety of

competition-related issues; issues opinion letters on whether certain business activity violates antitrust laws.

Antitrust Division *(Justice Dept.), Litigation I, 450 5th St. N.W., #4100, 20530; (202) 307-0001. Fax, (202) 307-5802. Peter J. Mucchetti, Chief.*
Web, www.justice.gov/atr/about-division/litigation-i-section

Investigates and litigates cases involving health care, paper, pulp, timber, food products, cosmetics and hair care, bread, beer, appliances, and insurance.

Antitrust Division *(Justice Dept.), Litigation II, 450 5th St. N.W., #8700, 20530; (202) 307-0924. Fax, (202) 514-9033. Maribeth Petrizzi, Chief.*
Web, www.justice.gov/atr/about/lit2.html

Investigates and litigates cases involving defense, waste industries, avionics and aeronautics, road and highway construction, metals and mining, industrial equipment, and banking.

Antitrust Division *(Justice Dept.), Litigation III, 450 5th St. N.W., #4000, 20530-0001; (202) 307-0468. Fax, (202) 514-7308. David C. Kully, Chief.*
General email, ATR.LitIII.Information@usdoj.gov
Web, www.justice.gov/atr/about/lit3.html

Investigates and litigates certain antitrust cases involving such commodities as movies, radio, TV, newspapers, performing arts, sports, and credit and debit cards. Handles certain violations of antitrust laws that involve patents, copyrights, and trademarks. Deals with mergers and acquisitions.

Antitrust Division *(Justice Dept.), Networks and Technology Enforcement, 450 5th St. N.W., #7100, 20530; (202) 307-6200. Fax, (202) 616-8544. James J. Tierney, Chief.*
General email, antitrust.atr@usdoj.gov
Web, www.justice.gov/atr/about/ntes.html

Investigates and litigates certain antitrust cases involving financial services, including securities, commodity futures, and insurance firms; participates in agency proceedings and rulemaking in these areas.

Antitrust Division *(Justice Dept.), Transportation, Energy, and Agriculture, 450 5th St. N.W., #8000, 20530; (202) 307-6349. Fax, (202) 307-2784. Kathleen O'Neill, Chief.*
Web, www.justice.gov/atr/about/tea.html

Responsible for civil antitrust enforcement, competition advocacy, and competition policy in the area of domestic and international aviation, bus and leisure travel, railroads, trucking, and ocean shipping, hotels, restaurants, and travel services, electricity, oil field services, food products, crops, seeds, fish, and livestock, and agricultural biotech. Participates in proceedings before the Federal Energy Regulatory Commission, Environmental Protection Agency, Agriculture Dept., Energy Dept., State Dept., Commerce Dept., Transportation Dept., and the Federal Maritime Commission.

Federal Maritime Commission

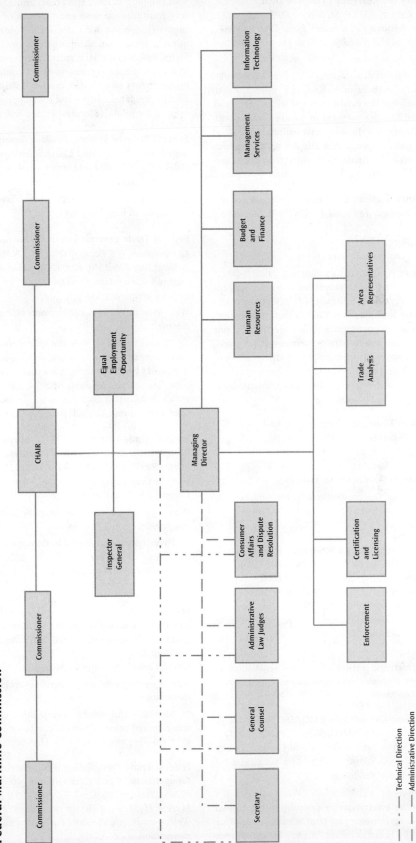

Comptroller of the Currency *(Treasury Dept.),*
Constitution Center, 400 7th St. S.W., 20219; (202) 649-
6800. Thomas J. Curry, Comptroller. Press, (202) 649-6870.
General email, publicaffairs3@occ.treas.gov

Web, www.occ.treas.gov and Twitter, @USOCC

Charters and examines operations of national banks,
federal savings associations, and U.S. operations of
foreign-owned banks; establishes guidelines for bank
examinations; handles mergers of national banks with
regard to antitrust law. Ensures that national banks and
savings associations operate in a safe and sound manner,
provide fair access to financial services, treat customers
fairly, and comply with applicable laws and regulations.

Federal Communications Commission (FCC), *Wireline*
Competition Bureau, 445 12th St. S.W., #5C343, 20554;
(202) 418-1500. Fax, (202) 418-2825.
Matthew DelNero, Chief.
Web, www.fcc.gov/wireline-competition

Regulates mergers involving common carriers (wireline facilities that furnish interstate communications
services). Creates and recommends policy goals, objectives, programs, and plans for the FCC on matters concerning wireline telecommunications. Objectives include
promoting competition in wireline services and markets,
deregulation, encouraging economically efficient investment in wireline telecommunications infrastructure,
expanding the availability of wireline telecommunications
services, and fostering economic growth.

Federal Deposit Insurance Corp. (FDIC), *Risk*
Management Supervision, 550 17th St. N.W., #5036,
20429; (202) 898-6519. Fax, (202) 898-3638.
Doreen R. Eberly, Director.
Web, www.fdic.gov/about/contact/#HQDSC

Studies and analyzes applications for mergers, consolidations, acquisitions, and assumption transactions between
insured banks.

Federal Energy Regulatory Commission (FERC) *(Energy*
Dept.), 888 1st St. N.E., 20426; (202) 502-6088. Fax, (202)
502-8612. Norman C. Bay, Chair, (202) 502-8000.
Toll-free, (866) 208-3372. TTY, (202) 502-8659. Press, (202)
502-8680. eLibrary questions, (202) 502-6652. Enforcement
hotline, (202) 502-8390. Enforcement toll-free, (888) 889-8030.
General email, customer@ferc.gov

Web, www.ferc.gov

Regulates mergers, consolidations, and acquisitions of
electric utilities; regulates the acquisition of interstate natural gas pipeline facilities.

Federal Maritime Commission (FMC), *800 N. Capitol St.*
N.W., 20573-0001; (202) 523-5725. Fax, (202) 523-0014.
Vern W. Hill, Managing Director; Mario Cordero, Chair.
TTY, (800) 877-8339. Library, (202) 523-5762.
General email, inquiries@fmc.gov

Web, www.fmc.gov

Regulates the foreign ocean shipping of the United
States; reviews agreements (on rates, services, and other
matters) filed by ocean common carriers for compliance

with shipping statutes and grants limited antitrust immunity. Monitors the laws and practices of foreign governments that could have a discriminatory or otherwise
adverse impact on shipping conditions in the United
States. Enforces special regulatory requirements applicable
to ocean common carriers owned or controlled by foreign
governments (controlled carriers). Adjudicates claims
filed by regulated entities and the shipping public. Library
open to the public (Monday–Friday, 8:00 a.m.–4:30 p.m.).

Federal Reserve System, *Banking Supervision and*
Regulation, 20th St. and Constitution Ave. N.W., 20551;
(202) 973-6999. Michael Gibson, Director, (202) 452-2495.
Web, www.federalreserve.gov/econresdata/bsrstaff.htm

Approves bank mergers, consolidations, and other
alterations in bank structure.

Federal Trade Commission (FTC), *Bureau of*
Competition, 600 Pennsylvania Ave. N.W., #CC-5422,
20580; (202) 326-3300. Fax, (202) 326-2884.
Deborah L. Feinstein, Director.
General email, antitrust@ftc.gov

Web, www.ftc.gov/about-ftc/bureaus-offices/bureau-
competition

Enforces antitrust laws and investigates possible violations, mergers and acquisitions, and anticompetitive practices; seeks voluntary compliance and pursues civil judicial
remedies; reviews premerger filings; coordinates activities
with the Antitrust Division of the Justice Dept. Library
open to the public (Monday–Friday, 8:30 a.m.–5:00 p.m.).

Federal Trade Commission (FTC), *Bureau of*
Competition, Anticompetitive Practices, 400 7th St. S.W.,
#5417, 20024; (202) 326-2641. Fax, (202) 326-3496.
Geoffrey Green, Assistant Director. Toll-free, (877) 382-4357.
General email, antitrust@ftc.gov

Web, www.ftc.gov/about-ftc/bureaus-offices/bureau-
competition

Investigates nonmerger anticompetitive practices in
real estate and a variety of other industries. Interests
include intellectual property and professional and regulatory boards.

Federal Trade Commission (FTC), *Bureau of*
Competition, Compliance, 400 7th St. S.W., #8416, 20024;
(202) 326-2526. Fax, (202) 326-3396. Daniel P. Ducore,
Assistant Director.
General email, bccompliance@ftc.gov

Web, www.ftc.gov/about-ftc/bureaus-offices/bureau-
competition

Monitors and enforces competition orders and oversees required remediations in company conduct. Investigates possible violations of the Hart-Scott-Rodino Act.

Federal Trade Commission (FTC), *Bureau of*
Competition, Health Care Division, 400 7th St. S.W.,
#7245, 20024; (202) 326-3759. Fax, (202) 326-3384.
Markus H. Meier, Assistant Director.
Web, www.ftc.gov/about-ftc/bureaus-offices/bureau-
competition

Investigates and litigates nonmerger anticompetitive practices among physicians, hospitals, and health insurers in the health care industry, including the pharmaceutical industry. Works against pay-for-delay agreements among pharmaceutical companies that insulate brand-name drugs from competition with lower cost generic drugs.

Federal Trade Commission (FTC), *Bureau of Competition, Honors Paralegal Program,* 400 7th St. S.W., #8310, 20024; (202) 326-2750. Fax, (202) 326-3496. Kimberly Burris-DoDo, Coordinator.
General email, honorsparalegals@ftc.gov
Web, www.ftc.gov/about-ftc/careers-ftc/work-ftc/honors-paralegal-program

Administers paralegal program for individuals considering a career in law, economics, business, or public service. Honors paralegals are given significant responsibility and hands-on experience while assisting attorneys and economists in the investigation and litigation of antitrust matters. Applicants are appointed for 14-month to four-year terms.

Federal Trade Commission (FTC), *Bureau of Competition, Mergers I,* 400 7th St. S.W., #6226, 20024; (202) 326-3106. Fax, (202) 326-2655. Michael Moiseyev, Assistant Director.
General email, antitrust@ftc.gov
Web, www.ftc.gov/about-ftc/bureaus-offices/bureau-competition/inside-bureau-competition

Investigates and litigates antitrust violations in mergers and acquisitions, primarily in the health care–related industries, including pharmaceutical manufacturing and distribution and medical devices. Also handles scientific, industrial, defense, and technology industries.

Federal Trade Commission (FTC), *Bureau of Competition, Mergers II,* 400 7th Ave. S.W., #7414, 20024; (202) 326-3468. Fax, (202) 326-2071. Benjamin Gris, Assistant Director.
General email, antitrust@ftc.gov
Web, www.ftc.gov/about-ftc/bureaus-offices/bureau-competition/inside-bureau-competition

Investigates and litigates antitrust violations in mergers and acquisitions in the chemicals, coal mining, technology, entertainment, and computer hardware and software industries.

Federal Trade Commission (FTC), *Bureau of Competition, Mergers III,* 400 7th Ave. S.W., #7616, 20024; (202) 326-2805. Fax, (202) 326-3383. Vacant, Assistant Director.
General email, antitrust@ftc.gov
Web, www.ftc.gov/about-ftc/bureaus-offices/bureau-competition/inside-bureau-competition

Investigates and litigates antitrust violations in mergers and acquisitions concerning the oil and gas, ethanol, industrial spray equipment, and energy industries.

Federal Trade Commission (FTC), *Bureau of Competition, Mergers IV,* 400 7th Ave. S.W., #6418,

Washinton, DC, 20024; (202) 326-2579. Fax, (202) 326-2286. Alexis Gilman, Assistant Director.
General email, antitrust@ftc.gov
Web, www.ftc.gov/about-ftc/bureaus-offices/bureau-competition/inside-bureau-competition

Investigates and litigates antitrust violations in mergers and acquisitions concerning hospitals, the grocery food product industry, the media, funeral homes, and consumer goods.

Federal Trade Commission (FTC), *Bureau of Competition, Premerger Notification,* 400 7th Ave. S.W., #5301, 20024; (202) 326-3100. Fax, (202) 326-2624. Robert L. Jones, Assistant Director, (202) 326-2740.
General email, antitrust@ftc.gov
Web, www.ftc.gov/enforcement/premerger-notification-program

Reviews premerger filings under the Hart-Scott-Rodino Act for the FTC and Justice Dept. Coordinates investigative work with federal and state agencies; participates in international projects.

Surface Transportation Board *(Transportation Dept.),* 395 E St. S.W., #1220, 20423-0001; (202) 245-0245. Fax, (202) 245-0458. Daniel Elliott III, Chair, (202) 245-0210. Library, (202) 245-0288. TTY, (800) 877-8339. Press, (202) 245-0238.
General email, STBHelp@stb.dot.gov
Web, www.stb.dot.gov

Regulates rail rate disputes, railroad consolidations, rail line construction proposals, line abandonments, and rail car service. Library open to the public.

► **CONGRESS**

For a listing of relevant congressional committees and subcommittees, please see pages 516–517 or the Appendix.

► **NONGOVERNMENTAL**

American Antitrust Institute (AAI), 1730 Rhode Island Ave., #1100, 20036; (202) 536-3408. Diana L. Moss, President. Media, (720) 233-5971.
Web, www.antitrustinstitute.org

Pro-antitrust organization that provides research and policy analysis to journalists, academic researchers, lawyers, economists, businesspeople, government officials, courts, and the general public. Seeks to educate the public on the importance of fair competition. Monitors legislation and regulations on competition-oriented policies.

Assn. of Corporate Counsel, 1025 Connecticut Ave. N.W., #200, 20036-5425; (202) 293-4103. Fax, (202) 293-4701. Veta T. Richardson, President.
Web, www.acc.com and Twitter, @ACCinhouse

Membership: practicing lawyers in corporate law departments, associations, and in legal departments of other private-sector organizations. Provides information on corporate law issues, including securities, health and safety, the environment, intellectual property, litigation, international legal affairs, pro bono work, and labor benefits. Monitors legislation and regulations, with primary focus on issues affecting in-house attorneys' ability to practice law. (Formerly American Corporate Counsel Assn.)

The Business Roundtable, *300 New Jersey Ave. N.W., #800, 20001; (202) 872-1260. Fax, (202) 466-3509. Gov. John Engler, President. Press, (202) 496-3269. General email, info@brt.org*

Web, www.businessroundtable.org and Twitter, @BizRoundtable

Membership: chief executives of the nation's largest corporations. Examines issues of concern to business, including antitrust law.

National Chamber Litigation Center, *1615 H St. N.W., 20062-2000; (202) 463-5337. Fax, (202) 463-5346. Lily Fu Claffee, Executive Vice President. General email, litigationcenter@uschamber.com*

Web, www.chamberlitigation.com

Public policy law firm of the U.S. Chamber of Commerce. Advocates businesses' positions in court on such issues as antitrust, bankruptcy, and employment, environmental, and constitutional law. Provides businesses with legal assistance and amicus support in legal proceedings before federal courts and agencies.

Bankruptcy

▶AGENCIES

Executive Office for U.S. Trustees *(Justice Dept.), 441 G St. N.W., #6150, 20530; (202) 307-1399. Fax, (202) 307-2397. Clifford J. White III, Director, (202) 307-1391. General email, ustrustee.program@usdoj.gov*

Web, www.justice.gov/ust

Handles the administration and oversight of bankruptcy and liquidation cases filed under the Bankruptcy Reform Act, including detecting and combating bankruptcy fraud. Provides individual U.S. trustee offices with administrative and management support.

Justice Dept. (DOJ), *Legal Policy, 950 Pennsylvania Ave. N.W., #4234, 20530-0001; (202) 514-4601. Fax, (202) 514-2424. Jonathan Wroblewski, Principal Deputy Assistant Attorney General.*

Web, www.justice.gov/olp

Studies and develops policy for improvement of the criminal and civil justice systems, including bankruptcy reform policy.

▶CONGRESS

For a listing of relevant congressional committees and subcommittees, please see pages 516–517 or the Appendix.

▶JUDICIARY

Administrative Office of the U.S. Courts, *Court Services Division, 1 Columbus Circle N.E., 20544-0001; (202) 502-1500. Mary Louise Mitterhoff, Chief.*

Web, www.uscourts.gov

Provides staff, policy, legal, operational, and program support for the appeals, district, and U.S. bankruptcy courts.

▶NONGOVERNMENTAL

American Bankruptcy Institute, *66 Canal Center Plaza, #600, Alexandria, VA 22314-1592; (703) 739-0800. Fax, (703) 739-1060. Samuel Gerdano, Executive Director. General email, support@abiworld.org*

Web, www.abiworld.org

Membership: lawyers, federal and state legislators, and representatives of accounting and financial services firms, lending institutions, credit organizations, and consumer groups. Provides information and educational services on insolvency, reorganization, and bankruptcy issues; sponsors conferences, seminars, and workshops.

National Assn. of Consumer Bankruptcy Attorneys, *2200 Pennsylvania Ave. N.W., 4th Floor, 20037; (800) 499-9040. Fax, (866) 408-9515. Maureen Thompson, Legislative Director; Dan Labert, Executive Director. General email, admin@nacba.org*

Web, www.nacba.org

Advocates on behalf of consumer debtors and their attorneys. Files amicus briefs on behalf of parties in the U.S. courts of appeal and Supreme Court, and provides educational programs and workshops for attorneys. Monitors legislation and regulations.

National Chamber Litigation Center, *1615 H St. N.W., 20062-2000; (202) 463-5337. Fax, (202) 463-5346. Lily Fu Claffee, Executive Vice President. General email, litigationcenter@uschamber.com*

Web, www.chamberlitigation.com

Public policy law firm of the U.S. Chamber of Commerce. Advocates businesses' positions in court on such issues as antitrust, bankruptcy, and employment, environmental, and constitutional law. Provides businesses with legal assistance and amicus support in legal proceedings before federal courts and agencies.

Tax Violations

▶AGENCIES

Internal Revenue Service (IRS) *(Treasury Dept.), Criminal Investigation, 1111 Constitution Ave. N.W., #2501, 20224; (202) 317-3200. Richard Weber, Chief. Tax fraud hotline, (800) 829-0433.*

Web, www.irs.gov

Investigates money laundering and violations of the tax law. Lends support in counterterrorism and narcotics investigations conducted in conjunction with other law enforcement agencies, both foreign and domestic.

Internal Revenue Service (IRS) *(Treasury Dept.),* *Procedures and Administration,* *1111 Constitution Ave. N.W., #5503, 20224; (202) 622-3400. Fax, (202) 317-5374. Drita Tonuzi, Associate Chief Counsel. Press, (202) 622-4000.*
Web, www.irs.gov

Oversees field office litigation of civil cases that involve underpayment of taxes when the taxpayer chooses to challenge the determinations of the IRS in the U.S. Tax Court, or when the taxpayer chooses to pay the amount in question and sue the IRS for a refund. Reviews briefs and defense letters prepared by field offices for tax cases; drafts legal advice memos; prepares tax litigation advice memoranda; coordinates litigation strategy. Makes recommendations concerning appeal and certiorari. Prepares tax regulations, rulings, and other published guidance regarding the Internal Revenue Code, as enacted.

Justice Dept. (DOJ), *Tax Division,* *950 Pennsylvania Ave. N.W., #4141, 20530; (202) 514-2901. Fax, (202) 514-5479. Caroline D. Ciraolo, Assistant Attorney General, Acting, (202) 514-2901.*
Web, www.usdoj.gov/tax

Authorizes prosecution of all criminal cases involving tax violations investigated and developed by the Internal Revenue Service (IRS); represents the IRS in civil litigation except in U.S. Tax Court proceedings; represents other agencies, including the Defense and Interior Depts., in cases with state or local tax authorities.

► CONGRESS

For a listing of relevant congressional committees and subcommittees, please see pages 516–517 or the Appendix.

► JUDICIARY

U.S. Tax Court, *400 2nd St. N.W., #134, 20217; (202) 521-0700. Michael B. Thornton, Chief Judge, (202) 521-0777.*
Web, www.ustaxcourt.gov

Tries and adjudicates disputes involving income, estate, and gift taxes and personal holding company surtaxes in cases in which deficiencies have been determined by the Internal Revenue Service.

► NONGOVERNMENTAL

American Bar Assn. (ABA), *Taxation Section,* *1050 Connecticut Ave. N.W., #400, 20036; (202) 662-8670. Fax, (202) 662-8682. Janet In, Director, (202) 662-8677. General email, tax@americanbar.org*
Web, www.americanbar.org/tax

Studies and recommends policies on taxation; provides information on tax issues; sponsors continuing legal education programs; monitors tax laws and legislation.

CIVIL RIGHTS

General

► AGENCIES

Civil Rights Division *(Justice Dept.),* *950 Pennsylvania Ave. N.W., #5643, 20530; (202) 514-4609. Fax, (202) 514-0293. Vanita Gupta, Assistant Attorney General, Acting, (202) 514-2151. Press, (202) 514-2007. TTY, (202) 514-0716.*
General email, complaint@usdoj.gov
Web, www.justice.gov/crt and Twitter, @TheJusticeDept

Enforces federal civil rights laws prohibiting discrimination on the basis of race, color, religion, sex, disability, age, or national origin in voting, education, employment, credit, housing, public accommodations and facilities, and federally assisted programs.

Civil Rights Division *(Justice Dept.), Disability Rights,* *950 Pennsylvania Ave. N.W., 20530; (202) 307-0663. Fax, (202) 307-1197. Rebecca Bond, Chief. Information and ADA specialist, (800) 514-0301. TTY, (800) 514-0383.*
Web, www.justice.gov/crt/about/drs

Litigates cases under Titles I, II, and III of the Americans with Disabilities Act, which prohibits discrimination on the basis of disability in places of public accommodation and in all activities of state and local government. Provides technical assistance to businesses and individuals affected by the law.

Civil Rights Division *(Justice Dept.), Educational Opportunities,* *601 D St. N.W., #4300, 20530; (202) 514-4092. Fax, (202) 514-8337. Shaheena Simons, Chief, Acting. Toll-free, (877) 292-3804.*
General email, education@usdoj.gov
Web, www.justice.gov/crt/educational-opportunities-section

Initiates litigation to ensure equal opportunities in public education; enforces laws dealing with civil rights in public education.

Civil Rights Division *(Justice Dept.), Employment Litigation,* *601 D St. N.W., #4040, 20579; (202) 514-3831. Fax, (202) 514-1005. Delora L. Kennebrew, Chief. Library, (202) 514-3775. TTY, (202) 514-6780.*
Web, www.justice.gov/crt/about/emp

Investigates, negotiates, and litigates allegations of employment discrimination by public schools, universities, state and local governments, and federally funded employers; has enforcement power. Enforces the Uniform Services Employment and Reemployment Rights Act. Members of the public are asked to contact the library with questions about access.

Education Dept., *Civil Rights,* *400 Maryland Ave. S.W., #4E313, 20202-1100; (202) 453-5900. Fax, (202) 453-6012. Catherine Lhamon, Assistant Secretary, (202) 453-7240. Toll-free, (800) 421-3481. TTY, (800) 877-8339.*
General email, ocr@ed.gov
Web, www2.ed.gov/ocr

Selected Minorities-Related Resources

ADVOCACY AND ANTIDISCRIMINATION

American-Arab Anti-Discrimination Committee, (202) 244-2990; www.adc.org

Anti-Defamation League, (212) 885-7700; www.adl.org

Arab American Institute, (202) 429-9210; www.aaiusa.org

Human Rights Campaign, (202) 628-4160; www.hrc.org

Japanese American Citizens League, (202) 223-1240; www.jacl.org

Mexican American Legal Defense and Education Fund, (202) 293-2828; www.maldef.org

NAACP (National Assn. For the Advancement of Colored People), (202) 463-2940; www.naacp.org

National Council of La Raza, (202) 785-1670; www.nclr.org

National Gay and Lesbian Task Force, (202) 393-5177; www.thetaskforce.org

National Organization for Women, (202) 628-8669; www.now.org

Organization of Asian Pacific Americans, (formerly the Organization of Chinese Americans), (202) 223-5500; www.ocanational.org

Rainbow/PUSH Coalition, (202) 393-7874; www.rainbowpush.org

BUSINESS AND LABOR

Business and Professional Women USA, (202) 293-1100; www.bpwfoundation.org

Center for Women's Business Research, (212) 785-7335; www.regender.org

Council of Federal EEO and Civil Rights Executives, (800) 669-4000; www.eeoc.gov

Minority Business Development Agency, (202) 482-2332; www.mbda.gov

National Assn., of Hispanic Federal Executives Inc., (202) 315-3942; www.nahfe.org

National Assn. of Minority Contractors, (202) 296-1600; www.namcnational.org

National Assn. of Women Business Owners, (800) 556-2926; www.nawbo.org

National Black Chamber of Commerce, (202) 466-6888; www.nationalbcc.org

National U.S.-Arab Chamber of Commerce, (202) 289-5920; www.nusacc.org

U.S. Hispanic Chamber of Commerce, (202) 842-1212; www.ushcc.com

U.S. Pan Asian American Chamber of Commerce, (202) 296-5221; www.uspaacc.com

EDUCATION

American Assn. for Access, Equity and Diversity (formerly the American Assn. for Affirmative Action), (202) 349-9855; www.aaaed.org

American Indian Higher Education Consortium, (703) 838-0400; www.aihec.org

Assn. of American Colleges and Universities, (202) 387-3760; www.aacu.org

---

Enforces laws prohibiting use of federal funds for education programs or activities that discriminate on the basis of race, color, sex, national origin, age, or disability; authorized to discontinue funding.

Equal Employment Opportunity Commission (EEOC), *131 M St. N.E., 20507; (202) 663-4001. Fax, (202) 663-4110. Jenny R. Yang, Chair. Toll-free information, (800) 669-4000. TTY, (202) 663-4494. Toll-free TTY, (800) 669-6820. Training Institute, (703) 291-0880. Training Institute toll-free, (866) 446-0940. Training Institute TTY, (800) 828-1120. Library, (202) 663-4630.*
General email, info@eeoc.gov

Training Institute email, eeoc.traininginstitute@eeoc.gov

Web, www.eeoc.gov

Works to end job discrimination by private and government employers based on race, color, religion, sex, national origin, disability, or age. Works to protect employees against reprisal for protest of employment practices alleged to be unlawful in hiring, promotion, firing, wages, and other terms and conditions of employment. Works for increased employment of persons with disabilities, affirmative action by the federal government, and an

equitable work environment for employees with mental and physical disabilities. Enforces Title VII of the Civil Rights Act of 1964, as amended, which includes the Pregnancy Discrimination Act; Americans with Disabilities Act; Age Discrimination in Employment Act; Equal Pay Act; and, in the federal sector, rehabilitation laws. Receives charges of discrimination; attempts conciliation or settlement; can bring court action to force compliance; has review and appeals responsibility in the federal sector. Library open to the public by appointment only.

Health and Human Services Dept. (HHS), *Civil Rights, 200 Independence Ave. S.W., #515F, 20201; (202) 619-0403. Fax, (202) 619-3437. Jocelyn Samuels, Director. TTY, (800) 537-7697.*
General email, OCRMail@hhs.gov

Web, www.hhs.gov/ocr

Administers and enforces laws prohibiting discrimination on the basis of race, color, sex, national origin, religion, age, or disability in programs receiving federal funds from the department; authorized to discontinue funding. Responsible for health information privacy under the Health Insurance Portability and Accountability Act.

Assn. of Research Libraries, (202) 296-2296; www.arl.org/diversity

National Assn. for Equal Opportunity in Higher Education, (202) 552-3300; www.nafeonation.org

GOVERNMENT, LAW, AND PUBLIC POLICY

Asian American Justice Center, (202) 296-2300; www.advancingequality.org

Blacks in Government, (202) 667-3280; www.bignet.org

Congressional Black Caucus Foundation, Inc., (202) 263-2800; www.cbcfinc.org

Congressional Hispanic Caucus Institute, (202) 543-1771; www.chci.org

Council on American-Islamic Relations, (202) 488-8787; www.cair.com

Institute for Women's Policy Research, (202) 785-5100; www.iwpr.org

Joint Center for Political and Economic Studies, (202) 789-3500; www.jointcenter.org

Leadership Conference on Civil Rights, (202) 466-3311; www.civilrights.org

National Congress on American Indians, (202) 466-7767; www.ncai.org

National Women's Law Center, (202) 588-5180; www.nwlc.org

National Women's Political Caucus, (202) 785-1100; www.nwpc.org

Society of American Indian Government Employees, www.saige.org

HEALTH

Asian and Pacific Islander American Health Forum, (202) 466-7772; www.apiahf.org

National Alliance for Hispanic Health, (202) 387-5000; www.hispanichealth.org

National Black Nurses Assn., (301) 589-3200; www.nbna.org

National Council of Urban Indian Health, (202) 544-0344; www.ncuih.org

National Hispanic Medical Assn., (202) 628-5895; www.nhmamd.org

National Minority AIDS Council, (202) 853-1846; www.nmac.org

MEDIA

Center for Digital Democracy, (202) 986-2220; www.democraticmedia.org

International Women's Media Foundation, (202) 496-1992; www.iwmf.org

Minority Media and Telecommunications Council, (202) 332-0500; www.mmtconline.org

National Assn. of Black Owned Broadcasters, (202) 463-8970; www.nabob.org

National Assn. of Hispanic Journalists, (202) 662-7145; www.nahj.org

National Lesbian and Gay Journalists Assn., (202) 588-9888; www.nlgja.org

Labor Dept. (DOL), *Civil Rights Center, 200 Constitution Ave. N.W., #N4123, 20210; (202) 693-6500. Fax, (202) 693-6505. Naomi M. Barry-Perez, Director. Library, (202) 693-6613. TTY, (800) 877-8339.*
General email, civilrightscenter@dol.gov

Web, www.dol.gov/oasam/programs/crc

Resolves complaints of discrimination on the basis of race, color, religion, sex, national origin, age, or disability in programs funded by the department. Library open to the public.

U.S. Commission on Civil Rights, *1331 Pennsylvania Ave. N.W., #1150, 20425; (202) 376-7700. Fax, (202) 376-7672. Martin R. Castro, Chair; Mauro Albert Morales, Staff Director. Press, (202) 376-8371. TTY, (202) 372-8116.*
General email, publiccomments@usccr.gov

Civil right complaints, referrals@usccr.gov

Web, www.usccr.gov and Twitter, @USCCRgov

Assesses federal laws, policies, and legal developments to determine the nature and extent of denial of equal protection under the law on the basis of race, color, religion, sex, national origin, age, or disability in employment, voting rights, education, administration of justice, and housing. Issues reports and makes recommendations to the president and Congress; serves as national clearinghouse for civil rights information; receives civil rights complaints and refers them to the appropriate federal agency for action. Library open to the public.

U.S. Commission on Civil Rights, *Public Affairs and Congressional Affairs, 1331 Pennsylvania Ave. N.W., #1150, 20425; (202) 376-8371. Fax, (202) 376-7672. Gerson Gomez, Public Affairs Officer.*
General email, publicaffairs@usccr.gov

Web, www.usccr.gov

Informs development of national civil rights policy and enforcement of federal civil rights laws. Interests include voting rights and alleged discrimination based on race, color, religion, gender, age, disability, and national origin.

▶ **CONGRESS**

For a listing of relevant congressional committees and subcommittees, please see pages 516–517 or the Appendix.

►NONGOVERNMENTAL

American Assn. for Access, Equity, and Diversity (AAAED), *1701 Pennsylvania Ave. N.W., #206, 20006; (202) 349-9855. Fax, (202) 355-1399. Shirley J. Wilcher, Executive Director. Toll-free, (800) 252-8952.*
General email, execdir@aaaed.org
Web, www.aaaed.org

Membership: professional managers in the areas of affirmative action, equal opportunity, diversity, and human resources. Sponsors education, research, and training programs. Acts as a liaison with government agencies involved in equal opportunity compliance. Maintains ethical standards for the profession. (Formerly the American Assn. for Affirmative Action.)

Appleseed, *727 15th St. N.W., 11th Floor, 20005; (202) 347-7960. Fax, (202) 347-7961. Bert Brandenburg, President.*
General email, appleseed@appleseednetwork.org
Web, www.appleseednetwork.org

Network of seventeen public interest justice centers in the United States and Mexico advocating reforms designed to provide greater access to economic opportunity, fair courts, criminal justice, housing, education, food, and accountable government.

Leadership Conference on Civil and Human Rights, *1629 K St. N.W., 10th Floor, 20006; (202) 466-3311. Fax, (202) 466-3435. Wade Henderson, President.*
General email, info@civilrights.org
Web, www.civilrights.org, Twitter, @civilrightsorg and Facebook, www.facebook.com/civilandhumanrights

Coalition of national organizations representing minorities, women, labor, older Americans, people with disabilities, and religious groups. Works for enactment and enforcement of civil rights, human rights, and social welfare legislation; acts as clearinghouse for information on civil rights legislation and regulations.

NAACP Legal Defense and Educational Fund, Inc., *Washington Office, 1444 Eye St. N.W., 10th Floor, 20005; (202) 682-1300. Fax, (202) 682-1312. Leslie M. Proll, Director.*
Web, www.naacpldf.org

Civil rights litigation group that provides legal information on civil rights issues, including employment, housing, and educational discrimination; monitors federal enforcement of civil rights laws. Not affiliated with the NAACP. (Headquarters in New York.)

National Coalition Building Institute, *Metro Plaza Bldg., 8403 Colesville Road, #1100, Silver Spring, MD 20910; (240) 638-2813. Cherie Brown, Chief Executive Officer.*
General email, info@ncbi.org
Web, www.ncbi.org

Offers national and global leadership workshops and programs that combat racism and prejudice. Publishes reports on effective practices in reducing racism in education and the workplace.

Poverty and Race Research Action Council, *1200 18th St. N.W., #200, 20036; (202) 906-8023. Fax, (202) 842-2885. Philip Tegeler, Executive Director.*
General email, info@prrac.org
Web, www.prrac.org

Facilitates cooperative links between researchers and activists who work on race and poverty issues. Publishes bimonthly *Poverty & Race* newsletter and a civil rights history curriculum guide. Policy research areas include housing, education, and health disparities.

Rainbow PUSH Coalition, *Public Policy Institute, Government Relations and Telecommunications Project, 727 15th St. N.W., #1200, 20005; (202) 393-7874. Fax, (202) 393-1495. Steve Smith, Executive Director, Government Relations; Jesse L. Jackson Sr., President; Frank Watkins, Director, Public Policy. Press, (773) 373-3366.*
General email, info@rainbowpush.org
Web, http://rainbowpush.org/pages/get_local_washington_dc# and Twitter, @RPCoalition

Independent civil rights organization concerned with public policy toward political, economic, and social justice for women, workers, and minorities. (Headquarters in Chicago, Ill.)

African Americans

►NONGOVERNMENTAL

Blacks in Government, *3005 Georgia Ave. N.W., 20001-3807; (202) 667-3280. Fax, (202) 667-3705. Darlene H. Young, President.*
General email, bignational@bignet.org
Web, www.bignet.org

Advocacy organization for public employees. Promotes equal opportunity and career advancement for African American government employees; provides career development information; seeks to eliminate racism in the federal workforce; sponsors programs, business meetings, and social gatherings; represents interests of African American government workers to Congress and the executive branch; promotes voter education and registration.

Congressional Black Caucus Foundation, *1720 Massachusetts Ave. N.W., 20036-1903; (202) 263-2800. Fax, (202) 775-0773. A. Shuanise Washington, President.*
General email, info@cbcfinc.org
Web, www.cbcfinc.org and Twitter, @CBCFInc

Conducts research and offers programs on public policy issues with the aim of improving the socioeconomic circumstances of African Americans and other underserved populations. Sponsors fellowship programs in which professionals and academic candidates work on congressional committees and subcommittees. Holds issue forums and leadership seminars. Provides elected officials, organizations, and researchers with statistical, demographic, public policy, and political information. Sponsors internship, scholarship, and fellowship programs.

Joint Center for Political and Economic Studies, *2000 H St. N.W., #422, Stuart Hall, 20052; (202) 789-3500. Fax, (202) 789-6390. Spencer Overton, President. General email, info@jointcenter.org*

Web, www.jointcenter.org

Documents and analyzes the political and economic status of African Americans, focusing on political participation, economic advancement, and health policy. Publishes *Focus Magazine* annually; disseminates information through forums and conferences.

National Assn. for the Advancement of Colored People (NAACP), *Washington Bureau, 1156 15th St. N.W., #915, 20005; (202) 463-2940. Fax, (202) 463-2953. Hilary O. Shelton, Director. General email, washingtonbureau@naacpnet.org*

Web, www.naacp.org

Membership: persons interested in civil rights for all minorities. Seeks, through legal, legislative, and direct action, to end discrimination in all areas, including discriminatory practices in the administration of justice. Studies and recommends policy on court administration and jury selection. Maintains branch offices in many state and federal prisons. (Headquarters in Baltimore, Md.)

National Assn. of Colored Women's and Youth Clubs Inc. (NACWYC), *1601 R St. N.W., 20009-6420; (202) 667-4080. Fax, (202) 667-2574. Sharon R. Bridgeforth, President. General email, cearly@nacwcya.org*

Web, www.nacwc.org

Seeks to promote education, protect and enforce civil rights, raise the standard of family living, promote interracial understanding, and enhance leadership development. Awards scholarships; conducts programs in education, social service, and philanthropy.

National Black Caucus of Local Elected Officials (NBC/LEO), *National League of Cities, 1301 Pennsylvania Ave. N.W., 20004-1763; (202) 626 3000. Priscilla Tyson, President. General information, (877) 827-2385. General email, constituencygroups@nlc.org*

Web, www.nlc.org

Membership: Black elected officials at the local level and other interested individuals. Seeks to increase Black participation on the National League of Cities' steering and policy committees. Informs members on issues, and plans strategies to achieve objectives through legislation and direct action. Interests include cultural diversity, local government and community participation, housing, economics, job training, the family, and human rights.

National Black Caucus of State Legislators, *444 N. Capitol St. N.W., #622, 20001; (202) 624-5457. Fax, (202) 508-3826. LaKimba DeSadier, Executive Director. Web, www.nbcsl.org*

Membership: Black state legislators. Interests include legislation and public policies that impact the general welfare of African American consituents within respective jurisdictions.

National Black Justice Coalition, *P.O. Box 71395, 20024; (202) 319-1552. Fax, (202) 319-7365. Sharon J. Lettman-Hicks, Chief Executive Officer. General email, info@nbjc.org*

Web, www.nbjc.org

Seeks equality for Black lesbian, gay, bisexual, and transgender people by fighting racism and homophobia through education initiatives.

National Center for Public Policy Research, *Project 21, 501 Capitol Ct. N.E., #200, 20002; (202) 507-6398 ext. 11. Fax, (202) 543-5975. Horace Cooper, Co-Chair; Cherylyn LeBon, Co-Chair; David W. Almasi, Staff Director. General email, project21@nationalcenter.org*

Web, www.nationalcenter.org/P21Index.html

Emphasizes spirit of entrepreneurship, sense of family, and traditional values among African Americans.

National Council of Negro Women, *633 Pennsylvania Ave. N.W., 20004-2605; (202) 737-0120. Fax, (202) 737-0476. Ingrid Saunders Jones, Chair; Janice Mathis, Executive Director. General email, info@ncnw.org*

Web, www.ncnw.org

Seeks to advance opportunities for African American women, their families, and communities through research, advocacy, and national and community-based programs in the United States and Africa.

National Urban League, *Washington Bureau, 2901 14th St. N.W., 20009; (202) 265-8200. George H. Lambert Jr., Affiliate Chief Executive Officer. Web, http://nul.iamempowered.com/affiliate/greater-washington-urban-league*

Federal advocacy division of social service organization concerned with the social welfare of African Americans and other minorities. Seeks elimination of racial segregation and discrimination; monitors legislation, policies, and regulations to determine impact on minorities; interests include employment, health, welfare, education, housing, and community development. (Headquarters in New York.)

Hispanics

▶**NONGOVERNMENTAL**

League of United Latin American Citizens, *1133 19th St. N.W., #1000, 20036; (202) 833-6130. Fax, (202) 833-6135. Brent Wilkes, Executive Director. Toll-free, (877) LULAC-01. General email, info@lulac.org*

Web, www.lulac.org

Seeks full social, political, economic, and educational rights for Hispanics in the United States. Programs include housing projects for the poor, employment and training for youth and women, and political advocacy on issues affecting Hispanics, including immigration. Operates National Educational Service Centers (LNESCs) and awards scholarships. Holds exposition open to the public.

Mexican American Legal Defense and Educational Fund, *National Public Policy, 1016 16th St. N.W., #100, 20036; (202) 293-2828. Andrea Senteno, Legislative Staff Attorney; Vacant, Regional Counsel.*
Web, www.maldef.org/about/offices/washington_dc

Works with Congress and the White House to promote legislative advocacy for minority groups. Interests include equal employment, voting rights, bilingual education, immigration, and discrimination. Monitors legislation and regulations. (Headquarters in Los Angeles, Calif.)

National Council of La Raza, *1126 16th St. N.W., #600, 20036-4845; (202) 785-1670. Fax, (202) 776-1792. Janet Murguía, President.*
General email, info@nclr.org
Web, www.nclr.org, Twitter, @NCLR and Facebook, www.facebook.com/Nationalcounciloflaraza

Seeks to reduce poverty of and discrimination against Hispanic Americans. Offers assistance to Hispanic community-based organizations. Conducts research and policy analysis. Interests include education, employment and training, asset development, immigration, language access issues, civil rights, and housing and community development. Monitors legislation and regulations.

National Puerto Rican Coalition, Inc., *1444 Eye St. N.W., #800, 20005; (202) 223-3915. Rafael A. Fantauzzi, President.*
General email, nprc@nprcinc.org
Web, www.nprcinc.org

Membership: Puerto Rican organizations and individuals. Analyzes and advocates for public policy that benefits Puerto Ricans; offers training and technical assistance to Puerto Rican organizations and individuals; develops national communication network for Puerto Rican community-based organizations and individuals.

U.S. Conference of Catholic Bishops (USCCB), *Cultural Diversity in the Church, Hispanic Affairs, 3211 4th St. N.E., 20017-1194; (202) 541-3150. Fax, (202) 541-5417. Alejandro Aguilera-Titus, Assistant Director; Christina Chabali, Staff Assistant.*
General email, cdha@usccb.org
Web, www.usccb.org/issues-and-action/cultural-diversity/hispanic-latino

Acts as an information clearinghouse on communications and pastoral and liturgical activities; serves as liaison for other church institutions and government and private agencies concerned with Hispanics; provides information on legislation; acts as advocate for Hispanics within the National Conference of Catholic Bishops

Lesbian, Gay, Bisexual, and Transgender People

▶**NONGOVERNMENTAL**

Dignity USA, *Washington Office, 721 8th St. S.E., 20003 (mailing address: P.O. Box 15279, Washington, DC 20003-0279); (202) 546-2235. Fax, (202) 521-3954. Daniel Barutta, President.*
General email, dignity@dignitywashington.org
Web, www.dignitywashington.org

Membership: gay, lesbian, bisexual, and transgender Catholics, their families, and friends. Works to promote spiritual development, social interaction, educational outreach, and acceptance within the Catholic community. Sponsors a Spanish language affiliate group, Grupo Latino. (Headquarters in Medford, Mass.)

Gay & Lesbian Victory Fund and Leadership Institute, *1133 15th St. N.W., #350, 20005; (202) 842-8679. Fax, (202) 289-3863. Aisha Moodie-Mills, President.*
General email, victory@victoryfund.org
Web, www.victoryfund.org and Twitter, @VictoryFund

Supports the candidacy of openly gay and lesbian individuals in federal, state, and local elections.

Gay and Lesbian Activists Alliance of Washington (GLAA), *P.O. Box 75265, 20013; (202) 667-5139. Richard (Rick) J. Rosendall, President.*
General email, equal@glaa.org
Web, www.glaa.org

Advances the rights of gays, lesbians, and transgender people within the Washington community.

Human Rights Campaign (HRC), *1640 Rhode Island Ave. N.W., 20036; (202) 216-1500. Fax, (202) 347-5323. Chad Griffin, President. Toll-free, (800) 777-4723. TTY, (202) 216-1572.*
General email, hrc@hrc.org
Web, www.hrc.org

Provides campaign support and educates the public to ensure the rights of lesbian, gay, bisexual, and transgender people at home, work, school, and in the community. Works to prohibit workplace discrimination based on sexual orientation and gender identity, combat hate crimes, and fund AIDS research, care, and prevention.

Log Cabin Republicans, *1090 Vermont Ave. N.W., #850, 20005; (202) 420-7873. Gregory T. Angelo, President.*
General email, info@logcabin.org
Web, www.logcabin.org

Membership: lesbian, gay, bisexual, transgender, and allied Republicans. Educates conservative politicians and voters on LGBT issues; disseminates information; conducts seminars for members. Promotes conservative values among members of the gay community. Raises campaign funds. Monitors legislation and regulations.

National Black Justice Coalition, *P.O. Box 71395, 20024; (202) 319-1552. Fax, (202) 319-7365. Sharon J. Lettman-Hicks, Chief Executive Officer. General email, info@nbjc.org*

Web, www.nbjc.org

Seeks equality for Black lesbian, gay, bisexual, and transgender people by fighting racism and homophobia through education initiatives.

National Center for Transgender Equality (NCTE), *1325 Massachusetts Ave. N.W., #700, 20005; (202) 903-0112. Mara Keisling, Executive Director. General email, ncte@transequality.org*

Web, www.transequality.org

Works to advance the equality of transgender people through advocacy, collaboration, and empowerment, and to make them safe from discrimination and violence. Provides resources to local efforts nationwide.

National Lesbian and Gay Journalists Assn. (NLGJA), *2120 L St. N.W., #850, 20037; (202) 588-9888. Adam Pawlus, Executive Director. General email, info@nlgja.org*

Web, www.nlgja.org

Works within the journalism industry to foster fair and accurate coverage of lesbian, gay, bisexual, and transgender issues. Opposes workplace bias against all minorities and provides professional development for its members.

National LGBTQ Task Force, *1325 Massachusetts Ave. N.W., #600, 20005-4164; (202) 393-5177. Fax, (202) 393-2241. Rea Carey, Executive Director, (202) 639-6302, rcarey@thetaskforce.org. General email, thetaskforce@thetaskforce.org*

Web, www.thetaskforce.org, Twitter, @TheTaskForce and Facebook, www.facebook.com/thetaskforce

Works toward equal rights for the lesbian, gay, bisexual, and transgender community. Trains activists working at the state and local levels. Conducts research and public policy analysis. Monitors legislation. (Formerly National Gay and Lesbian Task Force [NGLTF].)

National Organization for Women (NOW), *1100 H St. N.W., #300, 20005; (202) 628-8669. Terry O'Neill, President. TTY, (202) 331-9002. General email, now@now.org*

Web, www.now.org

Membership: women and men interested in feminist civil rights. Promotes the development and enforcement of legislation prohibiting discrimination on the basis of sexual orientation.

Parents, Families, and Friends of Lesbians and Gays (PFLAG), *1828 L St. N.W., #660, 20036; (202) 467-8180. Fax, (202) 467-8194 Jody M. Huckaby, Executive Director. General email, info@pflag.org*

Web, www.pflag.org

Promotes the health and well-being of gay, lesbian, transgender, and bisexual persons, their families, and their friends through support, education, and advocacy. Works to change public policies and attitudes toward gay, lesbian, transgender, and bisexual persons. Monitors legislation and regulations.

Supporting and Mentoring Youth Advocates and Leaders (SMYAL), *410 7th St. S.E., 20003-2707; (202) 546-5940. Fax, (202) 330-5839. Sultan Shakir, Executive Director, (202) 567-3151. TTY, (202) 464-4548. General email, supporterinfo@smyal.org*

Web, www.smyal.org

Provides support to youth who are lesbian, gay, bisexual, transgender, intersex, or who may be questioning their sexuality. Facilitates youth center and support groups; promotes HIV/AIDS awareness; coordinates public education programs about homophobia. (Formerly Sexual Minority Youth Assistance League [SMYAL].)

Woodhull Sexual Freedom Alliance (WSFA), *1400 16th St. N.W., #101, 20036; (888) 960-3332. Fax, (202) 330-5282. Ricci J. Levy, President. General email, info@woodhullalliance.org*

Web, www.woodhullalliance.org and Twitter, @woodhullsfa

Advocacy group for sexual and gender identity. Interests include reducing discrimination based on family structure. Presents awards to activists who advance sexual freedom as a human right. Holds annual summits to share experiences and solutions to current human rights issues related to sex, gender, and family. Monitors legislation and regulation on sexual freedom. (Previously the Woodhull Freedom Foundation.)

Native Americans

▶ **AGENCIES**

Administration for Native Americans *(Health and Human Services Dept.), 330 C. St. S.W., 20201; (202) 690-7776. Fax, (202) 690-7441. Lillian A. Sparks, Commissioner. Toll-free, (877) 922-9262. General email, ana@acf.hhs.gov*

Web, www.acf.hhs.gov/programs/ana

Awards grants for locally determined social and economic development strategies; promotes Native American economic and social self-sufficiency; funds tribes and Native American and Native Hawaiian organizations; provides grant funding for community development projects. Commissioner chairs the Intradepartmental Council on Indian Affairs, which coordinates Native American-related programs.

Bureau of Indian Affairs (BIA) *(Interior Dept.), 1849 C St. N.W., MS 4640-06, 20240; (202) 208-5116. Fax, (202) 208-6334. Larry Roberts, Assistant Secretary, Acting. Press, (202) 219-4150.*

Web, www.bia.gov

Works with federally recognized Indian tribal governments and Alaska Native communities in a government-to-government relationship. Encourages and supports tribes' efforts to govern themselves and to provide needed programs and services on the reservations. Manages land held in trust for Indian tribes and individuals. Funds educational benefits, road construction and maintenance, social services, police protection, economic development efforts, and special assistance to develop governmental and administrative skills.

Justice Dept. (DOJ), *Tribal Justice, 950 Pennsylvania Ave. N.W., 20530-0001; (202) 514-8812. Tracy Toulou, Director. Web, www.justice.gov/otj*

Serves as the Justice Dept.'s point of contact for communication with Indian tribes and their concerns. Collaborates with federal and other government agencies to promote consistent, informed governmentwide policies, operations, and initiatives related to Indian Tribes.

Tribal Justice and Safety *(Justice Dept.), 950 Pennsylvania Ave. N.W., 20530; Tracy Toulou, Director. Grants management hotline, (888) 549-9901, option 3. Response center, (888) 421-6770. General email, tribalgrants@usdoj.gov Web, www.justice.gov/tribal*

Represents tribal community interests, including law enforcement policy, communications, detention facilities, federal prosecution in Indian country, tribal court development, domestic violence, drug courts and substance abuse, federal litigation involving tribes, and civil rights. Coordinates assistance grant funding from across various Justice Dept. offices and agencies.

►**CONGRESS**

For a listing of relevant congressional committees and subcommittees, please see pages 516–517 or the Appendix.

►**JUDICIARY**

U.S. Court of Federal Claims, *717 Madison Pl. N.W., 20005; (202) 357-6400. Fax, (202) 357-6401. Patricia E. Campbell-Smith, Chief Judge, (202) 357-6357; Hazel Keahey, Clerk, (202) 357-6412. Web, www.uscfc.uscourts.gov*

Deals with Native American tribal claims against the government that are founded upon the Constitution, congressional acts, government regulations, and contracts. Examples include congressional reference cases; patent cases; claims for land, water, and mineral rights; and the accounting of funds held for Native Americans under various treaties.

►**NONGOVERNMENTAL**

National Congress of American Indians, *Embassy of Tribal Nations, 1516 P St. N.W., 20005; (202) 466-7767. Fax, (202) 466-7797. Jacqueline Johnson Pata, Executive Director. General email, ncai@ncai.org Web, www.ncai.org*

Membership: American Indian and Alaska Native tribal governments and individuals. Provides information and

serves as general advocate for tribes. Monitors legislative and regulatory activities affecting Native American affairs.

Native American Rights Fund, *Washington Office, 1514 P St. N.W., Suite D, Rear entrance, 20005; (202) 785-4166. Fax, (202) 822-0068. John E. Echohawk, Executive Director; Richard Guest, Managing Attorney. Web, www.narf.org*

Provides Native Americans and Alaska Natives with legal assistance in land claims, water rights, hunting, and other areas. Practices federal Indian law. (Headquarters in Boulder, Colo.)

Navajo Nation, *Washington Office, 750 1st St. N.E., #1010, 20002; (202) 682-7390. Fax, (202) 682-7391. Jackson Brossy, Executive Director; Russell Begoye, President. General email, info@nnwo.org Web, www.nnwo.org*

Monitors legislation and regulations affecting the Navajo people; serves as an information clearinghouse on the Navajo Nation. (Headquarters in Window Rock, Ariz.)

Older Adults

►**AGENCIES**

Administration for Community Living (ACL) *(Health and Human Services Dept.), Administration on Aging, 330 C St. S.W., 20201; (202) 619-0724. Edwin L. Walker, Deputy Assistant Secretary. Press, (202) 357-3507. Eldercare locator, (800) 677-1116. TTY, (800) 877-8339. General email, aclinfo@acl.hhs.gov Web, www.aoa.hhs.gov*

Advocacy agency for older Americans and their concerns. Collaborates with tribal organizations, community and national organizations, and state and area agencies to implement grant programs and services designed to improve the quality of life for older Americans, such as information and referral, adult day care, elder abuse prevention, home-delivered meals, in-home care, transportation, and services for caregivers.

►**CONGRESS**

For a listing of relevant congressional committees and subcommittees, please see pages 516–517 or the Appendix.

►**NONGOVERNMENTAL**

60 Plus, *515 King St., #315, Alexandria, VA 22314; (703) 807-2070. Fax, (703) 807-2073. James L. Martin, Chair; Amy Noone Frederick, President. General email, info@60plus.org Web, www.60plus.org*

Advocates for the rights of senior citizens. Interests include free enterprise, less government regulation, and tax reform. Works to eliminate estate taxes. Publishes rating system of members of Congress. Monitors legislation and regulations.

AARP Foundation, *Legal Advocacy, 601 E St. N.W., 20049; (202) 434-2060. William Alvarado Rivera, Senior Vice President, Litigation. Toll-free, (888) 687-2277. Toll-free TTY, (877) 434-7598.*
General email, foundation@aarp.org
Web, www.aarp.org/aarp-foundation/our-work/legal-advocacy

Advocates the legal rights of citizens age fifty years and older. Addresses age discrimination in the workplace; consumer and financial fraud and utilities issues; employee benefits, including pensions; investor protection; health including long-term services and supports, Medicaid, Medicare, and prescription drug affordability; housing, including predatory mortgage lending and livable communities; low-income benefits, including the Supplemental Nutrition Assistance Program; and voting rights.

Alliance for Retired Americans, *815 16th St. N.W., 4th Floor North, 20006-4104; (202) 637-5399. Fax, (202) 637-5398. Robert Roach, President. Membership, (800) 333-7212.*
Web, www.retiredamericans.org

Alliance of retired members of unions affiliated with the AFL-CIO, senior citizen clubs, associations, councils, and other groups. Seeks to nationalize health care services and to strengthen benefits to older adults, including improved Social Security payments, increased employment, and education and health programs. Offers prescription drug program and vision care Medicare supplement. (Affiliate of the AFL-CIO.)

Justice in Aging, *1444 Eye St. N.W., #1100, 20005; (202) 289-6976. Fax, (202) 289-7224. Kevin Prindiville, Executive Director.*
General email, nsclc@nsclc.org
Web, www.justiceinaging.org

Provides training, technical assistance, and litigation for attorneys representing the elderly poor and persons with disabilities. Represents clients before Congress and federal departments and agencies. Focus includes Social Security, Medicare, Medicaid, long-term care residents' rights, home health care, pensions, and protective services. Funded by the Administration on Aging and various charitable foundations. Formerly National Senior Citizens Law Center.

National Council on Aging, *251 18th St. South, #500, Arlington, VA 22202; (571) 527-3900. Fax, (571) 527-3901. James P. Firman, President. Press, (571) 527-3914. Eldercare locator, (800) 677-1116.*
General email, info@ncoa.org
Web, www.ncoa.org, Twitter, @NCOAging and Facebook, www.facebook.com/NCOAging

Serves as an information clearinghouse on training, technical assistance, advocacy, and research on every aspect of aging. Provides information on social services for older persons. Monitors legislation and regulations.

National Hispanic Council on Aging, *Walker Bldg., 734 15th St. N.W., #1050, 20005; (202) 347-9733. Fax, (202) 347-9735. Yanira Cruz, President.*
General email, nhcoa@nhcoa.org
Web, www.nhcoa.org

Membership: senior citizens, health care workers, professionals in the field of aging, and others in the United States and Puerto Rico who are interested in topics related to Hispanics and aging. Provides research training, policy analysis, consulting, and technical assistance; sponsors seminars, workshops, and management internships.

Seniors Coalition, *1250 Connecticut Ave. N.W., #200, 20036; (202) 261-3594. Fax, (866) 728-5450. Joseph L. Bridges, Chief Executive Officer. Toll-free, (800) 325-9891.*
General email, tsc@senior.org
Web, www.senior.org

Seeks to protect the quality of life and economic well-being of older Americans. Interests include health care, Social Security, taxes, pharmaceutical issues, and Medicare. Conducts seminars and monitors legislation and regulations.

Other Minority Groups

▶AGENCIES

Education Dept., *White House Initiative on Asian Americans and Pacific Islanders, 550 12th St. S.W., 10th Floor, 20202; (202) 245-6418. Fax, (202) 245-7166. Doua Thor, Executive Director. Press, (202) 245-6353.*
General email, whitehouseaapi@ed.gov
Web, http://sites.ed.gov/whieeaa and Twitter, @whitehouseAAPI

Ensures that Asian Americans and Pacific Islanders have equal access to federal programs and services. Methods include expanding language access and increasing enforcement efforts to combat discrimination.

▶NONGOVERNMENTAL

American–Arab Anti-Discrimination Committee (ADC), *1990 M St. N.W., #610, 20036; (202) 244-2990. Fax, (202) 333-3980. Samer E. Khalaf, President.*
General email, adc@adc.org
Web, www.adc.org and Twitter, @adctweets

Nonpartisan and nonsectarian organization that promotes and seeks to protect the human rights and cultural heritage of Americans of Arab descent. Works to combat discrimination against Arab Americans in employment, education, and political life and to prevent stereotyping of Arabs in the media. Monitors legislation and regulations.

Anti-Defamation League, *Washington Office, 1100 Connecticut Ave. N.W., #1020, 20036; (202) 452-8310. Fax, (202) 296-2371. David Friedman, Regional Director.*
General email, washington-dc@adl.org
Web, www.adl.org and Twitter, @ADL_National

Seeks to combat anti-Semitism and other forms of bigotry. Interests include discrimination in employment, housing, voting, and education; U.S. foreign policy in the

Middle East; and the treatment of Jews worldwide. Monitors legislation and regulations affecting Jewish interests and the civil rights of all Americans. (Headquarters in New York.)

Asian Americans Advancing Justice (AAJC), *1620 L St. N.W., #1050, 20036; (202) 296-2300. Fax, (202) 296-2318. Mee Moua, President.*
General email, information@advancingequality.org
Web, www.advancingequality.org and Twitter, @AAAJ_AAJC

Works to advance the human and civil rights of Asian Americans and other minority groups through advocacy, public policy, public education, and litigation. Promotes civic engagement at the local, regional, and national levels. Interests include affirmative action, hate crimes, media diversity, census, broadband and telecommunications, youth advocacy, immigrant rights, language access, and voting rights.

Japanese American Citizens League, *Washington Office, 1629 K St. N.W., #400, 20006; (202) 223-1240. Fax, (202) 296-8082. Priscilla Ouchida, Executive Director.*
General email, dc@jacl.org
Web, www.jacl.org

Monitors legislative and regulatory activities affecting the rights of Japanese Americans. Supports civil rights of all Americans, with a focus on Asian and Asian Pacific Americans. (Headquarters in San Francisco, Calif.)

OCA: Asian Pacific American Advocates, *1322 18th St. N.W., 20036-1803; (202) 223-5500. Fax, (202) 296-0540. Ken Lee, Chief Executive Officer.*
General email, oca@ocanational.org
Web, www.ocanational.org

Advocacy group seeking to advance the social, political, and economic well-being of Asian Pacific Americans in the United States.

Women

▶**NONGOVERNMENTAL**

Assn. for Women in Science, *1321 Duke St., #210, Alexandria, VA 22314; (703) 894-4490. Fax, (703) 894-4489. Janet Bandows Koster, Executive Director.*
General email, awis@awis.org
Web, www.awis.org and Twitter, @AWISNational

Promotes equal opportunity for women in scientific professions; provides career and funding information. Provides educational scholarships for women in science. Interests include international development.

Independent Women's Forum (IWF), *1875 Eye St. N.W., #500, 20006; (202) 857-3293. Fax, (202) 429-9574. Sabrina Schaeffer, Executive Director.*
General email, info@iwf.org
Web, www.iwf.org

Membership: women and men interested in advancing limited government, equality under the law, property rights, free markets, strong families, and a powerful and effective national defense and foreign policy. Publishes policy papers; makes appearances on radio and television broadcasts; maintains speakers bureau. Interests include school choice, Social Security, health care reform, and democracy promotion and women's human rights in the Middle East.

Jewish Women International, *1129 20th St. N.W., #801, 20036; (202) 857-1300. Fax, (202) 857-1380. Loribeth Weinstein, Chief Executive Officer. Toll-free, (800) 343-2823.*
General email, jwi@jwi.org
Web, www.jwi.org

Membership: Jewish women, supporters, and partners in the United States and Canada. Interests include empowerment of women and girls, ending domestic and sexual violence, financial literacy and economic security, and highlighting women's leadership at multigenerational intersections.

National Council of Women's Organizations, *714 G St. S.E., #200, 20003; (202) 293-4505. Fax, (202) 293-4507. Shireen Mitchell, Chair.*
General email, ncwo@ncwo-online.org
Web, www.ncwo-online.org

Membership: local and national women's organizations. Engages in policy work and grassroots activism to address issues of concern to women, including workplace and economic equity, education and job training, affirmative action, Social Security, child care, reproductive freedom, health, and global women's equality. Monitors legislation and regulations.

National Organization for Women (NOW), *1100 H St. N.W., #300, 20005; (202) 628-8669. Terry O'Neill, President. TTY, (202) 331-9002.*
General email, now@now.org
Web, www.now.org

Membership: women and men interested in feminist civil rights. Uses traditional and nontraditional forms of political activism, including nonviolent civil disobedience, to improve the status of all women regardless of age, income, sexual orientation, or race. Maintains liaisons with counterpart organizations worldwide.

National Partnership for Women and Families, *1875 Connecticut Ave. N.W., #650, 20009-5731; (202) 986-2600. Fax, (202) 986-2539. Debra L. Ness, President.*
General email, info@nationalpartnership.org
Web, www.nationalpartnership.org

Advocacy organization that promotes fairness in the workplace, access to high-quality health care, and policies that help women and men meet the demands of work and family. Publishes and disseminates information in print and on the Web to heighten awareness of work and family issues. Monitors legislative activity and pending Supreme

U.S. Courts

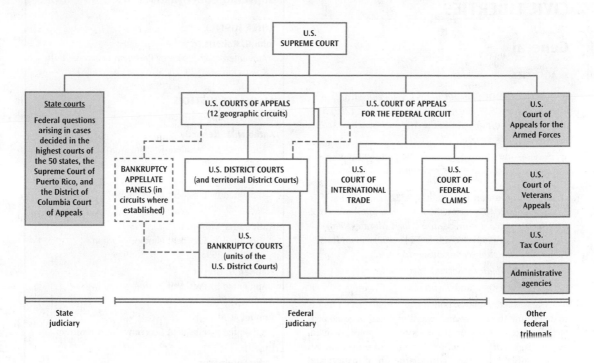

Court cases and argues on behalf of family issues before Congress and in the courts.

National Women's Law Center, *11 Dupont Circle N.W., #800, 20036; (202) 588-5180. Fax, (202) 588-5185. Nancy Duff Campbell, Co-President; Marcia D. Greenberger, Co-President. General email, info@nwlc.org*

Web, www.nwlc.org

Works to expand and protect women's legal rights through advocacy and public education. Interests include reproductive rights, health, education, employment, income security, and family support.

OWL: The Voice of Women 40+, *1627 Eye St. N.W., #600, 20006; (202) 450-8986. Fax, (202) 332-2949. Bobbie A. Brinegar, Executive Director. General email, info@owl-national.org*

Web, www.owl-national.org

Grassroots organization concerned with the status and quality of life of middle-aged and older women. Interests include health care, Social Security, pension rights, housing, employment, women as caregivers, effects of budget cuts, and issues relating to health insurance and long-term care.

Sewall-Belmont House & Museum, *144 Constitution Ave. N.E., 20002-5608; (202) 546-1210. Fax, (202) 546-3997. Page Harrington, Executive Director, ext. 20. Press, (202) 546-1210, ext. 12. General email, info@sewallbelmont.org*

Web, www.sewallbelmont.org

Maintains archives and artifacts documenting women's equality under the law. Interests include the suffragists, the National Women's Party, and the Equal Rights Amendment campaign.

Women's Research and Education Institute (WREI), *3808 Brighton Ct., Alexandria, VA 22305; (703) 837-1977. Susan Scanlan, President. General email, wrei@wrei.org*

Web, www.wrei.org

Analyzes policy-relevant information on women's issues. Educates the public through reports and conferences. Interests include women's employment and economic status; women in nontraditional occupations; military women and veterans; older women; women's health issues; and women and immigration. Library open to the public.

YWCA USA, *2025 M St. N.W., #550, 20036; (202) 467-0801. Fax, (202) 467-0802. Dara Richardson-Heron, Chief Executive Officer, (202) 835-2352. General email, info@ywca.org*

Web, www.ywca.org and Twitter, @ywcausa

Strives to empower women and girls and to eliminate racism. Provides services and programs concerning child care and youth development, economic empowerment, global awareness, health and fitness, housing and shelter, leadership development, racial justice and human rights, and violence prevention. (YWCA stands for Young Women's Christian Association.)

CONSTITUTIONAL LAW AND CIVIL LIBERTIES

General

►AGENCIES

Justice Dept. (DOJ), *Legal Counsel,* 950 Pennsylvania Ave. N.W., #5218, 20530-0001; (202) 514-2051. Fax, (202) 514-0539. Karl Thompson, Assistant Attorney General, Acting. Web, www.justice.gov/olc

Advises the attorney general, the president, and executive agencies on questions regarding constitutional law.

U.S. Commission on Civil Rights, 1331 Pennsylvania Ave. N.W., #1150, 20425; (202) 376-7700. Fax, (202) 376-7672. Martin R. Castro, Chair; Mauro Albert Morales, Staff Director. Press, (202) 376-8371. TTY, (202) 372-8116. General email, publiccomments@usccr.gov

Civil right complaints, referrals@usccr.gov

Web, www.usccr.gov and Twitter, @USCCRgov

Assesses federal laws, policies, and legal developments to determine the nature and extent of denial of equal protection under the law on the basis of race, color, religion, sex, national origin, age, or disability in employment, voting rights, education, administration of justice, and housing. Issues reports and makes recommendations to the president and Congress; serves as national clearinghouse for civil rights information; receives civil rights complaints and refers them to the appropriate federal agency for action. Library open to the public.

►CONGRESS

For a listing of relevant congressional committees and subcommittees, please see pages 516–517 or the Appendix.

►JUDICIARY

Supreme Court of the United States, 1 1st St. N.E., 20543; (202) 479-3000. John G. Roberts Jr., Chief Justice; Kathleen Arberg, Public Information Officer, (202) 479-3211. TTY, (202) 479-3472. Visitor Info, (202) 479-3030. Web, www.supremecourtus.gov

Highest appellate court in the federal judicial system. Interprets the U.S. Constitution, federal legislation, and treaties. Provides information on new cases filed, the status of pending cases, and admissions to the Supreme Court Bar. Library open to Supreme Court bar members only.

►NONGOVERNMENTAL

American Civil Liberties Union (ACLU), *National Capital Area,* 4301 Connecticut Ave. N.W., #434, 20008-2368; P.O. Box 11637, 20008; (202) 457-0800. Monica Hopkins-Maxwell, Executive Director. Web, www.aclu-nca.org

---

Supreme Court Justices

CHIEF JUSTICE

John G. Roberts Jr.
Appointed chief justice by President George W. Bush, sworn in Sept. 29, 2005.

ASSOCIATE JUSTICES
in order of appointment

Anthony M. Kennedy
Appointed by President Reagan, sworn in Feb. 18, 1988.

Clarence Thomas
Appointed by President George Bush, sworn in Oct. 23, 1991.

Ruth Bader Ginsburg
Appointed by President Clinton, sworn in Aug. 10, 1993.

Stephen G. Breyer
Appointed by President Clinton, sworn in Aug. 3, 1994.

Samuel A. Alito Jr.
Appointed by President George W. Bush, sworn in Jan. 31, 2006.

Sonia Sotomayor
Appointed by President Barack Obama, sworn in Aug. 8, 2009.

Elena Kagan
Appointed by President Barack Obama, sworn in Aug. 7, 2010.

Seeks to protect the civil liberties of the citizens, including federal employees, of the District of Columbia. Interests include First Amendment rights, privacy, and due process.

American Civil Liberties Union (ACLU), *Washington Legislative Office,* 915 15th St. N.W., 20005; (202) 544-1681. Fax, (202) 546-0738. Michael Macleod-Ball, Chief of Staff. Press, (202) 544-2312. General email, media@dcaclu.org

Web, www.aclu.org/legiupdate

Focuses on constitutional rights and civil liberties, minority and women's rights, gay and lesbian rights, and privacy; supports legalized abortion, opposes government-sponsored school prayer and legislative restrictions on television content. Washington office monitors legislative and regulatory activities and public policy. Library open to the public by appointment. (Headquarters in New York maintains docket of cases.)

American Constitution Society for Law and Policy, 1333 H St. N.W., 11th Floor, 20005; (202) 393-6181. Fax, (202) 393-6189. Caroline Fredrickson, President. General email, info@acslaw.org

Web, www.acslaw.org

National association of lawyers, law students, judges, legal scholars, and policymakers that promotes a progressive vision of constitutional law and public policy. Produces issue briefs and publications. Organizes lectures, conferences, seminars, and two annual student competitions.

Center for Individual Rights, *1233 20th St. N.W., #300, 20036; (202) 833-8400. Fax, (202) 833-8410. Terence (Terry) J. Pell, President. Toll-free, (877) 426-2665. General email, cir@cir-usa.org*

Web, www.cir-usa.org

Public interest law firm that provides free representation to individuals who cannot afford adequate legal counsel in cases raising constitutional questions of individual rights. Interests include freedom of speech and religious expression, civil rights, and Congress's enumerated powers.

The Constitution Project (TCP), *1200 18th St. N.W., #1000, 20036; (202) 580-6920. Fax, (202) 580-6929. Virginia E. Sloan, President. Press, (202) 580-6922. General email, info@constitutionproject.org*

Web, www.constitutionproject.org and *Twitter, @ConPro*

Think tank that brings together policy experts and legal practitioners from across the political and ideological spectrum to address current constitutional challenges. Interests include checks and balances, counterterrorism policies and practices, criminal discovery, data collection and privacy, the death penalty, DNA collection, government surveillance and searches, immigration, right to counsel, sentencing, and transparency and accountability. Hosts discussions and online forums; issues written reports and press releases.

Constitutional Accountability Center, *1200 18th St. N.W., #501, 20036; (202) 296-6889. Fax, (202) 296-6895. Elizabeth B. Wydra, President. General email, cac@theusconstitution.org*

Web, www.theusconstitution.org and *Twitter, @MyConstitution*

Nonprofit think tank, law firm, and advocacy group that supports constitutional rights and freedoms by working with courts, the government, and academic professionals. Publishes books and reports on constitutional issues. Manages cases related to constitutional law. Interests include civil rights, citizenship, corporations, and the environment.

Ethics and Public Policy Center, *1730 M St. N.W., #910, 20036; (202) 682-1200. Fax, (202) 408-0632. M. Edward Whelan III, President. General email, ethics@eppc.org*

Web, www.eppc.org and *Twitter, @EPPCdc*

Examines current issues of jurisprudence, especially those relating to constitutional interpretation.

First Amendment Center, *555 Pennsylvania Ave. N.W., 20001; (202) 292-6288. Fax, (202) 292-6295. Charles C. Haynes, Senior Scholar, (202) 292-6293; Ken Paulson, President, (615) 898-2195.*

General email, info@fac.org

Web, www.firstamendmentcenter.org and *Twitter, @1stAmendmentCtr*

Works to preserve and protect First Amendment freedoms through information and education. Serves as a nonpartisan forum for the study and exploration of free-expression issues, including freedom of speech, the press, religion, and the rights to assemble and to petition the government. Co-sponsors, with the Newseum, the Religious Freedom Education Project. The center is an operating program of the Freedom Forum and is associated with the Diversity Institute. Affiliated with Vanderbilt University through the Vanderbilt Institute for Public Policy Studies. Located in the Newseum.

Institute for Justice, *901 N. Glebe Rd., #900, Arlington, VA 22203; (703) 682-9320. Fax, (703) 682-9321. Scott Bullock, President. General email, general@ij.org*

Web, www.ij.org

Sponsors seminars to train law students, grassroots activists, and practicing lawyers in applying advocacy strategies in public-interest litigation. Seeks to protect individuals from arbitrary government interference in free speech, private property rights, parental school choice, and economic liberty. Litigates cases.

National Organization for Women (NOW), *1100 H St. N.W., #300, 20005; (202) 628-8669. Terry O'Neill, President. TTY, (202) 331-9002. General email, now@now.org*

Web, www.now.org

Membership: women and men interested in civil rights for women. Works to end discrimination based on gender, to preserve abortion rights, and to pass an equal rights amendment to the Constitution.

Open Society Foundations (OSF), *Washington Office, 1730 Pennsylvania Ave. N.W., 7th Floor, 20006; (202) 721-5600. Fax, (202) 530-0128. Stephen Rickard, Director, Washington Office. General email, info@osi-dc.org*

Web, www.soros.org/initiatives/washington

Addresses violations of civil liberties in the United States. Interests include criminal and civil justice reform, global economic policies, and women's rights. (Headquarters in New York. Affiliated with the Soros Foundation Network.)

Abortion and Reproductive Issues

▶ **NONGOVERNMENTAL**

Assn. of Reproductive Health Professionals, *1300 19th St. N.W., #200, 20036; (202) 466-3825. Fax, (202) 466-3826. Wayne C. Shields, President, (202) 378-8289. General email, arhp@arhp.org*

Web, www.arhp.org and *Twitter, @ARHP_ORG*

Privacy Resources

For general information and additional privacy contacts visit www.identitytheft.gov. See government agencies' individual Web sites for their privacy policies and freedom of information procedures.

AGENCIES AND CONGRESS

Federal Trade Commission, Identity Theft, www.ftc.gov/idtheft; Privacy Initiatives, www.ftc.gov/privacy; hotline, (877) 438-4338

House Judiciary Committee, Subcommittee on the Constitution and Civil Justice, (202) 225-2825; www.judiciary.house.gov

National Do-Not-Call Registry, toll-free, (888) 382-1222, TTY: (866) 290-4236; www.fcc.gov/encyclopedia/do-not-call-list

Office of Management and Budget (concerning the Privacy Act), (202) 395-3647; www.whitehouse.gov/omb/inforeg_infopoltech#pg

Senate Judiciary Committee, (202) 224-5225 (Majority), (202) 224-7703 (Minority); www.judiciary.senate.gov

U.S. Postal Service, (800) 275-8777; http://about.usps.com/who-we-are/privacy-policy/ privacy-policy-highlights.htm

NONGOVERNMENTAL

American Bar Association, Lawyer Referral Service, (202) 662-1000; www.findlegalhelp.org

American Civil Liberties Union, (202) 544-1681; www.aclu.org/technology-and-liberty

Call for Action, (240) 747-0229; www.callforaction.org

Center for Democracy and Technology, (202) 637-9800; www.cdt.org

Center for National Security Studies, (202) 721-5650; www.cnss.org

Center for Study of Responsive Law, (202) 387-8030; www.csrl.org

Consumer Data Industry Association, (202) 371-0910; www.cdiaonline.org

Consumers Union of the United States, (202) 462-6262; www.consumersunion.org

Direct Marketing Assn., Do-Not-Call Registry, (202) 955-5030; www.thedma.org

Electronic Privacy Information Center (EPIC), (202) 483-1140; www.epic.org or www.privacy.org

Health Privacy Project, (202) 637-9800; www.cdt.org/ health-privacy

National Consumers League, (202) 835-3323; www.nclnet.org

U.S. Postal Inspection Service, (877) 876-2455; postalinspectors.uspis.gov

U.S. Public Interest Research Group (USPIRG), (202) 546-9707; www.uspirg.org

---

Membership: obstetricians, gynecologists, other physicians, researchers, educators, and advanced practice clinicians, including nurse practioners, physician assistants, and certified nurse midwives. Educates health professionals and the public on reproductive health issues, including family planning, contraception, HIV/AIDS and other sexually transmitted diseases, abortion, menopause, infertility, and cancer prevention and detection. Monitors legislation and regulations.

Catholics for Choice, *1436 U St. N.W., #301, 20009-3997; (202) 986-6093. Fax, (202) 332-7995. Jon O'Brien, President. General email, cfc@catholicsforchoice.org*

Web, www.catholicsforchoice.org and Twitter, @Catholics4Choice

Works to change church positions and public policies that limit individual freedom, particularly those related to sexuality and reproduction. Provides the public, policymakers, and groups working for change with information and analysis.

Center for Law and Religious Freedom, *8001 Braddock Rd., #302, Springfield, VA 22151; (703) 894-1087. Fax, (703) 642-1075. Kimberlee W. Colby, Director. Web, www.clsnet.org/center*

Provides legal assistance and advocacy on anti-abortion and religious-freedom issues. Monitors legislation and regulations. (Affiliated with the Christian Legal Society.)

Feminists for Life of America, *P.O. Box 320667, Alexandria, VA 22320; (703) 836-3354. Serrin M. Foster, President. General email, info@feministsforlife.org*

Web, www.feministsforlife.org

Membership: women and men who are against abortion and in favor of feminism. Opposes abortion, euthanasia, and capital punishment; seeks to redress economic and social conditions that cause women to choose abortion.

March for Life Education and Defense Fund, *1317 8th St. N.W., 20001; (202) 234-3300. Fax, (202) 234-3350. Jeanne F. Monahan, President. General email, info@marchforlife.org*

Web, www.marchforlife.org and Twitter, @March_for_Life

Membership: individuals and organizations that support government action prohibiting abortion. Sponsors annual march in Washington each January 22. Monitors legislation and regulations.

NARAL Pro-Choice America, *1156 15th St. N.W., #700, 20005; (202) 973-3000. Fax, (202) 973-3096. Ilyse Hogue, President. Press, (202) 973-3032. Web, www.prochoiceamerica.org and Twitter, @NARAL*

Membership: persons who support using the political process to guarantee women a range of reproductive choices, including preventing unintended pregnancy, bearing healthy children, and choosing legal abortion. (Formerly National Abortion and Reproductive Rights Action League.)

National Abortion Federation (NAF), *1660 L St. N.W., #450, 20036; (202) 667-5881. Fax, (202) 667-5890. Vicki Saporta, President. NAF hotline, (800) 772-9100. General email, naf@prochoice.org*

Web, www.prochoice.org

Membership: abortion providers. Seeks to ensure that abortion is safe, legal, and accessible.

National Committee for a Human Life Amendment, *P.O. Box 34116, 20043; (202) 393-0703. Amy T. McInerny, Executive Director. General email, info@nchla.org*

Web, www.humanlifeactioncenter.org

Supports legislation and a constitutional amendment prohibiting abortion.

National Organization for Women (NOW), *1100 H St. N.W., #300, 20005; (202) 628-8669. Terry O'Neill, President. TTY, (202) 331-9002. General email, now@now.org*

Web, www.now.org

Membership: women and men interested in civil rights for women. Works to preserve abortion rights.

National Right to Life Committee, *512 10th St. N.W., 20004-1401; (202) 626-8800. Fax, (202) 737-9189. David N. O'Steen, Executive Director, ext. 114; Carol Tobias, President. Press, (202) 626-8825. General email, nrlc@nrlc.org; and mediarelations@nrlc.org*

Web, www.nrlc.org

Association of fifty state right-to-life organizations. Opposes abortion, infanticide, and euthanasia; supports legislation prohibiting abortion except when the life of the mother is endangered. Operates an information clearinghouse and speakers bureau. Monitors legislation and regulations.

National Women's Health Network, *1413 K St. N.W., 4th Floor, 20005; (202) 682-2640. Fax, (202) 682-2648. Cynthia Pearson, Executive Director. Health information, (202) 682-2646. General email, nwhn@nwhn.org and healthquestions@nwhn.org*

Web, www.nwhn.org

Advocacy organization interested in women's health. Seeks to preserve legalized abortion; monitors legislation and regulations; testifies before Congress.

Religious Coalition for Reproductive Choice, *1413 K St. N.W., 14th Floor, 20005; (202) 628-7700. Fax, (202) 628-7716. Rev. Harry F. Knox, President. General email, info@rcrc.org*

Web, www.rcrc.org and Twitter, @RCRChoice

Coalition of religious groups favoring birth control, sexuality education, and access to legal abortion. Opposes

constitutional amendments and federal and state legislation restricting access to abortion services in most cases. Monitors legislation and regulations.

U.S. Conference of Catholic Bishops (USCCB), *Secretariat of Pro-Life Activities, 3211 4th St. N.E., 20017-1194; (202) 541-3070. Fax, (202) 541-3054. Tom Grenchik, Executive Director. Publications, (800) 235-8722. General email, prolife@usccb.org*

Web, www.usccb.org/prolife

Provides information on the position of the Roman Catholic Church on abortion. Monitors legislation on abortion, embryonic stem-cell research, human cloning, and related issues. Promotes alternatives to abortion.

Claims against the Government

▶**AGENCIES**

Civil Division *(Justice Dept.), National Courts, 1100 L St. N.W., #12124, 20530; (202) 514-7300. Fax, (202) 307-0972. Robert E. Kirschman Jr., Director.*

Web, www.justice.gov/civil/national-courts-section-0

Represents the United States in the U.S. Court of Federal Claims. Practice areas include government contracts, constitutional claims, government pay and personnel suits, veterans and other benefits appeals, and international trade and tariff matters.

Civil Division *(Justice Dept.), Torts Branch, Aviation and Admiralty Litigation, 1425 New York Ave. N.W., #10100, 20005 (mailing address: P.O. Box 14271, Washington, DC 20044-4271); (202) 616-4100. Fax, (202) 616-4002. Barry Benson, Director.*

Web, www.justice.gov/civil/torts/aa/t-aa.html

Represents the federal government in civil suits concerning the maritime industry and aviation and admiralty incidents and accidents.

Environment and Natural Resources Division *(Justice Dept.), 950 Pennsylvania Ave. N.W., #2143, 20530-0001; (202) 514-2701. Fax, (202) 514-5331. John C. Cruden, Assistant Attorney General. Press, (202) 514-2008. General email, press@usdoj.gov*

Web, www.justice.gov/enrd

Represents the United States in the U.S. Court of Federal Claims in cases arising from acquisition of property, Indian rights and claims, and environmental challenges to federal programs and activities.

Justice Dept. (DOJ), *Indian Resources, 601 D St. N.W., #3507, 20004 (mailing address: P.O. Box 7611, L'Enfant Plaza, Washington, DC 20044), (202) 305-0269. Fax, (202) 305-0275. S. Craig Alexander, Chief.*

Web, www.justice.gov/Indian-resources-section

Represents the United States in suits, including trust violations, brought on behalf of individual Native Americans and Native American tribes against the government.

Justice Dept. (DOJ), *Tax Division, 950 Pennsylvania Ave. N.W., #4141, 20530; (202) 514-2901. Fax, (202) 514-5479. Caroline D. Ciraolo, Assistant Attorney General, Acting, (202) 514-2901.*
Web, www.usdoj.gov/tax

Represents the United States and its officers in all civil and criminal litigation arising under the internal revenue laws, other than proceedings in the US Tax Court.

State Dept., *Office of the Legal Advisor, International Claims and Investment Disputes, 2430 E St. N.W., #207, 20520; (202) 776-8360. Fax, (202) 776-8389. Lisa J. Grosh, Assistant Legal Adviser.*
Web, www.state.gov/s/l/c3433

Handles claims by U.S. government and citizens against foreign governments, as well as claims by foreign governments and their nationals against the U.S. government; negotiates international claims agreements. Handles claims against the State Dept. for negligence (under the Federal Tort Claims Act) and claims by owners of U.S. flag vessels due to illegal seizures by foreign governments in international waters (under the Fishermen's Protective Act).

▶**CONGRESS**

For a listing of relevant congressional committees and subcommittees, please see pages 516–517 or the Appendix.

▶**JUDICIARY**

U.S. Court of Federal Claims, *717 Madison Pl. N.W., 20005; (202) 357-6400. Fax, (202) 357-6401. Patricia E. Campbell-Smith, Chief Judge, (202) 357-6357; Hazel Keahey, Clerk, (202) 357-6412.*
Web, www.uscfc.uscourts.gov

Renders judgment on any nontort claims for monetary damages against the United States founded upon the Constitution, statutes, government regulations, and government contracts. Examples include compensation for taking of property, claims arising under construction and supply contracts, certain patent cases, cases involving the refund of federal taxes, and statutory claims made by foreign governments against the United States. Hears cases involving Native American claims.

Privacy

▶**AGENCIES**

Federal Trade Commission (FTC), *Bureau of Consumer Protection, Financial Practices, 400 7th Ave. S.W., CC-10416, 20024; (202) 326-3224. Fax, (202) 326-3768. Malini Maithal, Associate Director, Acting.*
Web, www.ftc.gov/about-ftc/bureaus-offices/bureau-consumer-protection/our-divisions/division-financial-practices

Enforces the Fair Credit Reporting Act, which requires credit bureaus to furnish correct and complete information to businesses evaluating credit, insurance, or job applications.

National Security Agency (NSA) *(Defense Dept.), Civil Liberties and Privacy, 9800 Savage Rd., #6272, Fort Meade, MD 20755-6000; (301) 688-6524. Rebecca Richards, Civil Liberties and Privacy Officer.*
Web, www.nsa.gov/civil_liberties/about_us/index.shtml

Advises the director of the NSA to ensure that privacy and civil liberties protections are inherent in strategic decisions, particularly in the areas of technology and processes. Seeks to increase transparency.

Office of Management and Budget (OMB) *(Executive Office of the President), Information and Regulatory Affairs, 725 17th St. N.W., #10236, 20503; (202) 395-5897. Fax, (202) 395-6102. Harold Shelanski, Administrator. Press, (202) 395-7254.*
Web, www.whitehouse.gov/omb/inforeg_infopoltech

Oversees implementation of the Privacy Act of 1974 and other privacy-related and security-related statutes. Issues guidelines and regulations.

▶**CONGRESS**

For a listing of relevant congressional committees and subcommittees, please see pages 516–517 or the Appendix.

▶**NONGOVERNMENTAL**

Assn. of Direct Response Fundraising Counsel (ADRFCO), *1612 K St. N.W., #1102, 20006-2849; (202) 293-9640. Fax, (202) 887-9699. Robert S. Tigner, General Counsel.*
General email, adrfco@msn.com
Web, www.adrfco.org

Membership: businesses in the direct response fundraising industry. Establishes standards of ethical practice in such areas as ownership of direct mail donor lists and mandatory disclosures by fundraising counsel. Educates nonprofit organizations and the public on direct response fundraising. Represents members' interests before the federal and state governments.

Call for Action, *11820 Parklawn Dr., #340, Rockville, MD 20852; (240) 747-0229. Fax, (240) 747-0239. Shirley Rooker, President; Eduard Bartholme, Executive Director.*
Web, www.callforaction.org

International network of consumer hotlines affiliated with local broadcast partners. Helps consumers resolve problems with businesses, government agencies, and other organizations through mediation. Provides information on privacy concerns.

Center for Democracy and Technology, *1401 K St. N.W., 2nd Floor, 20005; (202) 637-9800. Fax, (202) 637-0968. Nuala O'Connor, President.*
General email, info@cdt.org
Web, www.cdt.org and Twitter, @CenDemTech

Promotes and defends privacy and civil liberties on the Internet. Interests include free expression, social networking and access to the Internet, consumer protection, health information privacy and technology, and government surveillance.

Communications Workers of America (CWA), *501 3rd St. N.W., 20001; (202) 434-1100. Fax, (202) 434-1279. Christopher M. Shelton, President. Web, www.cwa-union.org and Twitter, @CWAUnion*

Membership: telecommunications, broadcast, and printing and publishing workers. Opposes electronic monitoring of productivity, eavesdropping by employers, and misuse of drug and polygraph tests.

Consumers Union of the United States, *Washington Office, 1101 17th St. N.W., #500, 20036; (202) 462-6262. Fax, (202) 265-9548. Martha Tellado, President; David Butler, Director, Acting, Washington Office. Web, www.consumersunion.org*

Consumer advocacy group active in protecting the privacy of consumers. Interests include credit report accuracy. (Headquarters in Yonkers, N.Y.)

Electronic Privacy Information Center (EPIC), *1718 Connecticut Ave. N.W., #200, 20009; (202) 483-1140. Fax, (202) 483-1248. Marc Rotenberg, President. General email, info@epic.org Web, www.epic.org*

Public interest research center. Conducts research and conferences on domestic and international civil liberties issues, including privacy, free speech, information access, computer security, and encryption; litigates cases. Monitors legislation and regulations. Operates an online bookstore.

National Assn. of State Utility Consumer Advocates (NASUCA), *8380 Colesville Rd., #101, Silver Spring, MD 20910-6267; (301) 589-6313. Fax, (301) 589-6380. David Springe, Executive Director. General email, nasuca@nasuca.org Web, www.nasuca.org*

Membership: public advocate offices authorized by states to represent ratepayer interests before state and federal utility regulatory commissions. Supports privacy protection for telephone customers.

National Consumers League, *1701 K St. N.W., #1200, 20006; (202) 835-3323. Fax, (202) 835-0747. Sally Greenberg, Executive Director. General email, info@nclnet.org Web, www.nclnet.org, Twitter, @ncl_tweets and Facebook, www.facebook.com/nationalconsumersleague*

Advocacy group concerned with privacy rights of consumers. Interests include credit and financial records, medical records, direct marketing, telecommunications, and workplace privacy.

U.S. Public Interest Research Group (USPIRG), *218 D St. S.E., 1st Floor, 20003; (202) 546-9707. Fax, (202) 543-6489. Andre Delattre, Executive Director (in Boston), (312) 544-4436, ext. 203; Ed Mierzwinski, Consumer Program Director, ext. 314. General email, uspirg@pirg.org Web, www.uspirg.org and Twitter, @uspirg*

Coordinates grassroots efforts to advance consumer protection laws. Works for the protection of privacy rights, particularly in the area of fair credit reporting. (Headquarters in Boston.)

Religious Freedom

▶**NONGOVERNMENTAL**

Americans for Religious Liberty, *P.O. Box 6656, Silver Spring, MD 20916; (301) 460-1111. Edd Doerr, President. General email, arlinc@verizon.net Web, www.arlinc.org*

Educational organization concerned with issues involving the separation of church and state. Opposes government-sponsored school prayer and tax support for religious institutions; supports religious neutrality in public education; defends abortion rights. Provides legal services in litigation cases. Maintains speakers bureau.

Americans United for Separation of Church and State, *1901 L St. N.W., #400, 20036; (202) 466-3234. Fax, (202) 466-2587. Barry W. Lynn, Executive Director. General email, americansunited@au.org Web, www.au.org and Twitter, @americansunited*

Citizens' interest group that opposes government-sponsored prayer in public schools and tax aid for parochial schools.

Center for Law and Religious Freedom, *8001 Braddock Rd., #302, Springfield, VA 22151; (703) 894-1087. Fax, (703) 642-1075. Kimberlee W. Colby, Director. Web, www.clsnet.org/center*

Provides legal assistance and advocacy on anti-abortion and religious-freedom issues. Monitors legislation and regulations. (Affiliated with the Christian Legal Society.)

Chaplain Alliance for Religious Liberty, *P.O. Box 151353, Alexandria, VA 22315; (571) 293-2427. Fax, (910) 221-2226. Col. Ron Crews (USAR, Ret.), Executive Director; Brig. Gen. Doug Lee (USAR, Ret.), President. General email, info@chaplainalliance.org Web, http://chaplainalliance.org*

Membership: military chaplains and others who support orthodox Christian doctrines. Seeks to ensure that all chaplains and those they serve may exercise their religious liberties without fear of reprisal. Interests include the conflict between official protection for gays in the military and orthodox Christian teachings. Issues press releases; grants media interviews; monitors legislation and regulations.

Christian Legal Society, *8001 Braddock Rd., #302, Springfield, VA 22151; (703) 642-1070. Fax, (703) 642-1075. David Nammo, Chief Executive Officer. General email, clshq@clsnet.org Web, www.clsnet.org and Twitter, @CLS_HQ*

Membership: Christian lawyers, judges, paralegals, law professors, law students, and others. Interests include the defense of religious freedom and the provision of legal aid to the poor.

International Religious Liberty Assn., *12501 Old Columbia Pike, Silver Spring, MD 20904-6600; (301) 680-6686. Fax, (301) 680-6695. Robert Seiple, President.*
General email, info@irla.org
Web, www.irla.org

Seeks to preserve and expand religious liberty and freedom of conscience; advocates separation of church and state; sponsors international and domestic meetings and congresses.

National Assn. of Evangelicals, *P.O. Box 23269, 20026; (202) 479-0815. Fax, (202) 379-9955. Leith Anderson, President.*
General email, info@nae.net
Web, www.nae.net

Membership: evangelical churches, organizations (including schools), and individuals. Supports religious freedom. Monitors legislation and regulations.

Separation of Powers

▶NONGOVERNMENTAL

Public Citizen, *Litigation Group, 1600 20th St. N.W., 20009-1001; (202) 588-1000. Allison Zieve, Director of Litigation. Press, (202) 588-7741.*
General email, litigation@citizen.org
Web, www.citizen.org/litigation

Conducts litigation for Public Citizen, a citizens' interest group, in cases involving separation of powers; represents individuals and groups with similar interests.

CRIMINAL LAW

General

▶AGENCIES

Criminal Division *(Justice Dept.), 950 Pennsylvania Ave. N.W., #2107, 20530-0001; (202) 514-2601. Fax, (202) 514-9412. Leslie R. Caldwell, Assistant Attorney General.*
General email, Criminal.Division@usdoj.gov
Web, www.justice.gov/criminal

Enforces all federal criminal laws except those specifically assigned to the antitrust, civil rights, environment and natural resources, and tax divisions of the Justice Dept. Supervises and directs U.S. attorneys in the field on criminal matters and litigation; supervises international extradition proceedings. Coordinates federal enforcement efforts against white-collar crime, fraud, and child pornography; handles civil actions under customs, liquor, narcotics, gambling, and firearms laws; coordinates enforcement activities against organized crime. Directs the National Asset Forfeiture Program for seizing the proceeds of criminal activity. Investigates and prosecutes criminal offenses involving public integrity and subversive activities, including treason, espionage, and sedition; Nazi

war crimes; and related criminal offenses. Handles all civil cases relating to internal security and counsels federal departments and agencies regarding internal security matters. Drafts responses on proposed and pending criminal law legislation.

Criminal Division *(Justice Dept.), Enforcement Operations, International Prisoner Transfer Program, John C. Keeney Bldg., 1301 New York Ave. N.W., 10th Floor, 20005; (202) 514-3173. Fax, (202) 514-9003. Paula A. Wolff, Chief.*
Web, www.justice.gov/criminal/oeo/international-prisoner-transfer-program

Implements prisoner transfer treaties with foreign countries.

Criminal Division *(Justice Dept.), Organized Crime and Gang Section, 1301 New York Ave. N.W., #700, 20005; (202) 514-3594. Fax, (202) 514-3601. James Trusty, Chief.*
General email, criminaldivision@us.doj.gov
Web, www.justice.gov/criminal-ocgs

Investigates and prosecutes important gang cases. Formulates violent crime and gang prosecution policy. Maintains responsibility over all domestic violent crime and firearms-related statutes within the U.S. code. Works with law enforcement to target and dismantle the most serious gang-related threats nationwide and internationally.

Federal Bureau of Investigation (FBI) *(Justice Dept.), 935 Pennsylvania Ave. N.W., #7176, 20535-0001; (202) 324-3000. James B. Comey, Director. Information, (202) 324-3000. Press, (202) 324-3691.*
Web, www.fbi.gov

Investigates all violations of federal criminal laws except those assigned specifically to other federal agencies. Exceptions include alcohol, counterfeiting, and tobacco violations (Justice Dept. and Commerce Dept.); customs violations and illegal entry of aliens (Homeland Security Dept.); and postal violations (U.S. Postal Service). Priorities include protecting the United States against terror attacks; protecting civil rights; combating public corruption at all levels, transnational/national criminal organizations and enterprises, white-collar crime, and significant violent crime; and supporting federal, state, local, and international partners. Services to other law enforcement agencies include fingerprint identifications, laboratory services, police training, and access to the National Crime Information Center (a communications network among federal, state, and local police agencies).

Justice Dept. (DOJ), *National Commission on Forensic Science, 950 Pennsylvania Ave. N.W., 20530-0001; (202) 305-3481. Sally Yates, Co-Chair; Willie E. May, Co-Chair. Programs, (301) 975-2756. Public Affairs, (202) 514-2007.*
General email, Andrew.J.Bruck@usdoj.gov
Web, www.justice.gov/ncfs

Provides recommendations for national methods and strategies for improving forensic science, including strengthening the validity and reliability of the forensic sciences; enhancing quality assurance and quality control in forensic science laboratories and units; identifying and recommending scientific guidance and protocols for evidence seizure, testing, analysis, and reporting by forensic science laboratories and units; and identifying and assessing other needs of the forensic science communities and meeting the increasing demands generated by the criminal and civil justice systems at all levels of government. In partnership with the National Institute of Standards and Technology.

Office of Justice Programs (OJP) *(Justice Dept.), National Institute of Justice, 810 7th St. N.W., 7th Floor, 20531; (202) 307-2942. Fax, (202) 307-6394. Nancy Rodriguez, Director. Press, (202) 307-0703.*
General email, ojp.ocom.@usdoj.gov
Web, www.nij.gov

Conducts research on all aspects of criminal justice, including crime prevention, enforcement, adjudication, and corrections; evaluates programs; develops model programs using new techniques. Serves as an affiliated institute of the United Nations Crime Prevention and Criminal Justice Program (UNCPCJ); studies transnational issues, especially within the Western Hemisphere. Maintains the National Criminal Justice Reference Service, which provides information on criminal justice research: (800) 851-3420; in Maryland, (301) 519-5500; Web, www .ncjrs.gov. Sponsors the National Missing and Unidentified Persons System, a clearinghouse for missing persons and unidentified decedent records: http://NamUs.gov.

►CONGRESS

For a listing of relevant congressional committees and subcommittees, please see pages 516–517 or the Appendix.

►INTERNATIONAL ORGANIZATIONS

INTERPOL Washington *(Justice Dept.), INTERPOL Washington, U.S. Dept. of Justice, 20530-0001; (202) 616-9000. Fax, (202) 616-8400. Geoffrey S. Shank, Director. Web, www.justice.gov/interpol-washington*

U.S. representative to INTERPOL; participates in international investigations on behalf of U.S. police; coordinates the exchange of investigative information on crimes, including drug trafficking, counterfeiting, missing persons, and terrorism. Coordinates law enforcement requests for investigative assistance in the United States and abroad. Assists with extradition processes. Serves as liaison between foreign and U.S. law enforcement agencies at federal, state, and local levels. (Headquarters in Lyons, France.)

►NONGOVERNMENTAL

American Bar Assn. (ABA), *Criminal Justice, 1050 Connecticut Ave. N.W., #400, 20036; (202) 662-1500. Fax, (202) 662-1501. Kevin Scruggs, Director, (202) 662-1503. General email, crimjustice@americanbar.org*
Web, www.americanbar.org/crimjust

Responsible for all matters pertaining to criminal law and procedure for the association. Studies and makes recommendations on all facets of the criminal and juvenile justice systems, including sentencing, juries, pretrial procedures, grand juries, and white-collar crime. (Headquarters in Chicago, Ill.)

Justice Policy Institute, *1012 14th St. N.W., #600, 20005; (202) 558-7974. Fax, (202) 558-7978. Marc Schindler, Executive Director.*
General email, info@justicepolicy.org
Web, www.justicepolicy.org

Research, advocacy, and policy development organization. Analyzes current and emerging adult and juvenile criminal justice problems; educates the public about criminal justice issues; provides technical assistance to communities seeking to reform incarceration policies. Interests include new prison construction, alternatives to incarceration, antigang legislation, and curfew laws.

National Assn. of Attorneys General, *2030 M St. N.W., 8th Floor, 20036; (202) 326-6000. James McPherson, Executive Director. Press, (202) 326-6047.*
General email, feedback@naag.org
Web, www.naag.org and Twitter, @NatlAssnAttysGen

Membership: attorneys general of the states, territories, and commonwealths. Fosters interstate cooperation on legal and law enforcement issues, conducts policy research and analysis, and facilitates communication between members and all levels of government.

National Assn. of Crime Victim Compensation Boards, *P.O. Box 16003, Alexandria, VA 22302; (703) 780-3200. Dan Eddy, Executive Director.*
General email, dan.eddy@nacvcb.org
Web, www.nacvcb.org

Provides state compensation agencies with training and technical assistance. Provides public information on victim compensation.

National Assn. of Criminal Defense Lawyers, *1660 L St. N.W., 12th Floor, 20036; (202) 872-8600. Fax, (202) 872-8690. Norman L. Reimer, Executive Director.*
General email, assist@nacdl.org
Web, www.nacdl.org

Volunteer bar association of criminal defense attorneys and their local, state, and international affiliates. Provides members with continuing education, a brief bank, an ethics hotline, and specialized assistance in such areas as forensic science. Offers free legal assistance to members threatened with sanctions. Interests include eliminating mandatory minimum sentencing, forensic lab reform, death penalty reform, protection of privacy rights, indigent defense reform, overcriminalization, and civil liberties. Monitors legislation and regulations.

National Center for Missing and Exploited Children, *Charles B. Wang International Children's Bldg., 699 Prince St., Alexandria, VA 22314-3175; (703) 224-2150. Fax, (703) 224-2122. John Clark, Chief Executive Officer. Toll-free hotline, (800) 843-5678.*
Web, www.missingkids.com

Private organization that assists parents and citizens' groups in locating and safely returning missing children; offers technical assistance to law enforcement agencies; coordinates public and private missing children programs; maintains database that coordinates information on missing children.

National Crime Prevention Council, *1201 Connecticut Ave. N.W., #200, 20036; (202) 466-6272. Fax, (202) 296-1356. Ann M. Harkins, President. Publications, (800) 627-2911.*
Web, www.ncpc.org, Twitter, @McGruffatNCPC and Facebook, www.ncpc.org

Educates public on crime prevention through media campaigns, supporting materials, and training workshops; sponsors McGruff public service campaign; runs demonstration programs in schools.

National District Attorneys Assn. (NDAA), *99 Canal Center Plaza, #330, Alexandria, VA 22314; (703) 549-9222. Fax, (703) 836-3195. Kay Chopard Cohen, Executive Director.*
Web, www.ndaa.org and Twitter, @ndaajustice

Membership: prosecutors. Sponsors conferences and workshops on such topics as criminal justice, district attorneys, the courts, child abuse, national traffic laws, community prosecution, violence against women, gun violence, and others. Conducts research; provides information, training, and technical assistance to prosecutors; and analyzes policies related to improvements in criminal prosecution.

Child Abuse, Domestic Violence, and Sexual Assault

►AGENCIES

Administration for Children and Families (ACF) *(Health and Human Services Dept.), Family and Youth Services, 330 C St. S.W., 20201; (202) 205-8347. William H. Bentley, Associate Commissioner.*
Web, www.acf.hhs.gov/programs/fysb

Administers federal discretionary grant programs for projects serving runaway and homeless youth and for projects that deter youth involvement in gangs. Provides youth service agencies with training and technical assistance. Monitors federal policies, programs, and legislation. Supports research on youth development issues, including gangs, runaways, and homeless youth. Operates national clearinghouse on families and youth. Issues grants and monitors abstinence education programs.

Criminal Division *(Justice Dept.), Child Exploitation and Obscenity Section, 1400 New York Ave. N.W., 6th Floor, 20005; (202) 514-5780. Fax, (202) 514-1793. Steven J. Grocki, Chief.*
Web, www.justice.gov/criminal/ceos

Enforces federal child exploitation, obscenity, and pornography laws; prosecutes cases involving violations of these laws, including international trafficking and kidnapping. Maintains collection of briefs, pleadings, and other material for use by federal, state, and local prosecutors. Assists the U.S. Attorney's Office with investigations, trials, and appeals pertaining to these offenses. Advises and trains law enforcement personnel, federal prosecutors, and Justice Dept. officials.

Defense Dept. (DoD), *Sexual Assault Prevention and Response, 4800 Mark Center Dr., #07G21, Alexandria, VA 22350; (571) 372-2657. Maj. Gen. Camille M. Nichols (USA), Director. Hotline, (877) 995-5247.*
General email, whc.mc-alex.wso.mbx.SAPRO@mail.mil
Web, www.sapr.mil and www.myduty.mil

Serves as the single point of accountability for the Defense Dept.'s sexual assault policy. Responsible for improving prevention, enhancing reporting and response, and holding perpetrators appropriately accountable.

Justice Dept. (DOJ), *Defending Childhood Initiative, 950 Pennsylvania Ave. N.W., 20530-0001; (202) 514-2007. Robert L. Listenbee, Co-Chair; Joe Torre, Co-Chair.*
Web, www.justice.gov/defendingchildhood

Seeks to address, reduce, and more fully understand childhood exposure to violence. Provides funding for research, evaluation, public awareness, and training for professional members and affiliates of national organizations

Justice Dept. (DOJ), *Elder Justice Initiative, 950 Pennsylvania Ave. N.W., 20530; Andy Mao, Coordinator.*
General email, elder.justice@usdoj.gov
Web, www.justice.gov/elderjustice and State web resources, www.justice.gov/elderjustice/support/resources.html

Provides resources for victims of elder abuse and financial exploitation and their families, practitioners, law enforcement agencies and prosecutors, and researchers of elder abuse.

Justice Dept. (DOJ), *Violence Against Women, 145 N St. N.E., #10W.121, 20530; (202) 307-6026. Fax, (202) 307-3911. Beatrice A. Hanson, Principal Deputy Director. National Domestic Violence Hotline, 800-799-SAFE. TTY, (202) 307-2277.*
General email, ovw.info@usdoj.gov
Web, www.ovw.usdoj.gov

Seeks more effective policies and services to combat domestic violence, sexual assault, stalking, and other crimes against women. Helps administer grants to states to fund shelters, crisis centers, and hotlines, and to hire law enforcement officers, prosecutors, and counselors specializing in cases of sexual violence and other violent crimes against women.

Office of Justice Programs (OJP) *(Justice Dept.), National Institute of Justice, 810 7th St. N.W., 7th Floor, 20531; (202) 307-2942. Fax, (202) 307-6394. Nancy Rodriguez, Director. Press, (202) 307-0703.*
General email, ojp.ocom.@usdoj.gov
Web, www.nij.gov

Conducts research on all aspects of criminal justice, including AIDS issues for law enforcement officials. Studies on rape and domestic violence available from the National Criminal Justice Reference Service: (800) 851-3420; in Maryland, (301) 519-5500; Web, www.ncjrs.gov.

Office of Justice Programs (OJP) *(Justice Dept.), Project Safe Childhood,* 810 7th St. N.W., 20531; Switchboard, (202) 514-2000.
General email, AskDOJ@usdoj.gov
Web, www.justice.gov/psc

Combines law enforcement efforts, community action, and public awareness to combat child exploitation, particularly in regard to child pornography, online enticement, child sex tourism, commercial sexual exploitation, and sexual exploitation in Indian Country. Offers resources and publications.

Office of Justice Programs (OJP) *(Justice Dept.), Sex Offender Sentencing, Monitoring, Apprehending, Registering, and Tracking (SMART),* 810 7th St. N.W., 20531; (202) 514-4689. Fax, (202) 616-2906.
Luis C. deBaca, Director.
General email, AskSMART@usdoj.gov
Web, http://ojp.gov/smart

Administers the standards for the Sex Offender Registration and Notification Program. Administers grant programs, including those relating to sex offender registration and notification. Works with and provides technical assistance to states, principal U.S. territories, local governments, tribal governments, and other public and private entities involved in activities related to sex offender registration or notification or to other measures for the protection of children or other members of the public from sexual abuse or exploitation

► **NONGOVERNMENTAL**

American Bar Assn. (ABA), *Center on Children and the Law,* 1050 Connecticut Ave. N.W., #400, 20036; (202) 662-1720. Fax, (202) 662-1755. Robert Horowitz, Director, Acting. Toll-free, (800) 285-2221.
General email, ctrchildlaw@americanbar.org
Web, www.americanbar.org/child

Provides state and private child welfare organizations with training and technical assistance. Interests include child abuse and neglect, adoption, foster care, and medical neglect.

National Center for Missing and Exploited Children, Charles B. Wang International Children's Bldg., 699 Prince St., Alexandria, VA 22314-3175; (703) 224-2150. Fax, (703) 224-2122. John Clark, Chief Executive Officer. Toll-free hotline, (800) 843-5678.
Web, www.missingkids.com

Private organization that assists parents and citizens' groups in locating and safely returning missing children; offers technical assistance to law enforcement agencies; coordinates public and private missing children programs; maintains database that coordinates information on missing children.

National Network to End Domestic Violence, 1400 16th St. N.W., #330, 20036; (202) 543-5566. Fax, (202)

543-5626. Kim Gandy, President. National Domestic Violence Hotline, (800) 799-7233. TTY, (800) 787-3224.
Web, www.nnedv.org

Represents state domestic violence coalitions at the federal level. Advocates for stronger legislation against domestic violence.

Rape, Abuse, and Incest National Network (RAINN), 1220 L St. N.W., #505, 20005; (202) 544-1034. Fax, (202) 544-3556. Scott Berkowitz, President. National Sexual Assault hotline, (800) 656-4673.
General email, info@rainn.org
Web, www.rainn.org and Twitter, @RAINN01

Links sexual assault victims to confidential local services through national sexual assault hotline. Operates the Defense Dept.'s sexual assault helpline. Provides extensive public outreach and education programs nationwide on sexual assault prevention, prosecution, and recovery. Promotes national policy efforts to improve services to victims.

Stop Child Predators, 5185 MacArthur Blvd., #575, 20016; (202) 248-7052. Fax, (202) 248-4427. Stacie D. Rumenap, President.
General email, info@stopchildpredators.org
Web, www.stopchildpredators.org

Advocacy organization that seeks to protect children from crime and hold their victimizers accountable. Works with victims' families, law enforcement, and decision makers to develop effective policies and solutions. Goals include establishing penalty enhancements for those who commit sexual offenses against children and creating an integrated nationwide sex offender registry.

Drug Control

► **AGENCIES**

Criminal Division *(Justice Dept.), Narcotic and Dangerous Drugs Section,* 145 N St. N.E., 20530; (202) 514-0917. Fax, (202) 514-6112. Arthur G. Wyatt, Chief; Wayne Raabe, Principal Deputy Chief. Press, (202) 514-2007.
Web, www.justice.gov/criminal/ndds

Investigates and prosecutes participants in criminal syndicates involved in the large-scale importation, manufacture, shipment, or distribution of illegal narcotics and other dangerous drugs. Trains agents and prosecutors in the techniques of major drug litigation.

Defense Dept. (DoD), *Counternarcotics and Global Threats,* 2500 Defense Pentagon, #5C653, 20301-2900; (703) 697-7202. Fax, (703) 692-6947. Caryn Hollis, Deputy Assistant Secretary, Acting.
Web, http://policy.defense.gov/OUSDPOffices/ASDforSpecialOperationsLowIntensityConflict/CounternarcoticsandGlobalThreats.aspx

Advises the secretary on Defense Dept. policies and programs in support of federal counternarcotics operations and the implementation of the president's national drug control policy.

Drug Enforcement Administration (DEA) *(Justice Dept.),*
700 Army-Navy Dr., Arlington, VA 22202 (mailing address: 8701 Morrissette Dr., MS AES, Springfield, VA 22152); Fax, (202) 307-4540. Chuck Rosenberg, Administrator, Acting. Phone (Command Center), (202) 307-8000. Press, (202) 307-7977. General information, (202) 307-1000.
Web, www.dea.gov

Enforces federal laws and statutes relating to narcotics and other dangerous drugs, including addictive drugs, depressants, stimulants, and hallucinogens; manages the National Narcotics Intelligence System in cooperation with federal, state, and local officials; investigates violations and regulates legal trade in narcotics and dangerous drugs. Provides school and community officials with drug abuse policy guidelines. Provides information on drugs and drug abuse.

Drug Enforcement Administration Museum and Visitors Center *(Justice Dept.),* *700 Army Navy Dr., Arlington, VA 22202 (mailing address: P.O. Box 2534, Springfield, VA 22152); (202) 307-3463. Fax, (202) 307-8956. Sean Fearns, Director.*
General email, staff@deamuseum.org
Web, www.deamuseum.org

Seeks to educate the public on the role and impact of federal drug law enforcement through state-of-the-art exhibits, displays, interactive stations, and outreach programs. Admission is free; groups of fifteen or more should call ahead for reservations.

Federal Bureau of Investigation (FBI) *(Justice Dept.),* *935 Pennsylvania Ave. N.W., #7176, 20535-0001; (202) 324-3000. James B. Comey, Director. Information, (202) 324-3000. Press, (202) 324-3691.*
Web, www.fbi.gov

Shares responsibility with the Drug Enforcement Administration for investigating violations of federal criminal drug laws; investigates organized crime involvement with illegal narcotics trafficking.

Food and Drug Administration (FDA) *(Health and Human Services Dept.),* *Center for Drug Evaluation and Research, 10903 New Hampshire Ave., W051, #6133, Silver Spring, MD 20993; (301) 796-5400. Fax, (301) 595-7910. Dr. Janet Woodcock, Director. Press, (301) 796-3700.*
Web, www.fda.gov/drugs and www.fda.gov/AboutFDA/CentersOffices/OfficeofMedicalProductsandTobacco/CDER

Makes recommendations to the Justice Dept.'s Drug Enforcement Administration on narcotics and dangerous drugs to be controlled.

Office of Justice Programs (OJP) *(Justice Dept.), Bureau of Justice Assistance, 810 7th St. N.W., 4th Floor, 20531; (202) 616-6500. Fax, (202) 305-1367. Denise E. O'Donnell, Director.*
General email, askbja@usdoj.gov
Web, www.bja.gov

Awards grants and provides eligible state, local, and tribal governments with training and technical assistance to enforce laws relating to narcotics and other dangerous drugs.

Office of National Drug Control Policy (ONDCP) *(Executive Office of the President), 750 17th St. N.W., 20503; (202) 395-6700. Fax, (202) 395-6708. Michael Botticelli, Director.*
Web, www.whitehouse.gov/ondcp and Twitter, @DrugPolicyReform

Establishes policies and oversees the implementation of a national drug control strategy with the goal of reducing illicit drug use, manufacturing, trafficking, and drug-related crimes, violence, and health consequences. Coordinates the international and domestic antidrug efforts of executive branch agencies and ensures that such efforts sustain and complement state and local antidrug activities. Advises the president and the National Security Council on drug control policy. (Clearinghouse address: P.O. Box 6000, Rockville, MD 20849-6000.)

U.S. Coast Guard (USCG) *(Homeland Security Dept.), Law Enforcement, CG-MLE, 2703 Martin Luther King Jr. Ave. S.E., MS 7516, 20593-7516; (202) 372-2183. Capt. Phil Welzant, Chief.*
Web, www.uscg.mil/hq/cg5/cg531

Oversees enforcement of federal laws and treaties and other international agreements to which the United States is party on, over, and under the high seas and waters subject to the jurisdiction of the United States. Combats smuggling of narcotics and other drugs into the United States via the Atlantic and Pacific Oceans and the Gulf of Mexico. Works with U.S. Customs and Border Protection on drug law enforcement.

U.S. Customs and Border Protection *(Homeland Security Dept.), Border Patrol, 1300 Pennsylvania Ave. N.W., #6.5E, 20229; (202) 344-2050. Fax, (202) 344-3140. Ronald D. Vitiello, Chief, Acting.*
Web, www.cbp.gov/border-security/along-us-borders/overview

Mobile uniformed law enforcement arm of the Homeland Security Dept. Primary mission is to detect and prevent the illegal trafficking of people and contraband across U.S. borders.

U.S. Customs and Border Protection *(Homeland Security Dept.), Field Operations, 1300 Pennsylvania Ave. N.W., #2.4A, 20229; (202) 344-1620. Fax, (202) 344-2777. Todd Owen, Assistant Commissioner. Press, (202) 344-1700.*
Web, www.cbp.gov/border-security/ports-entry

Interdicts and seizes contraband, including narcotics and other drugs, at the U.S. border.

U.S. Immigration and Customs Enforcement (ICE) *(Homeland Security Dept.), 500 12th St. S.W., 20536; (202) 732-3000. Fax, (202) 732-3080. Sarah R. Saldaña, Director. Press, (202) 732-4242. Hotline to report suspicious activity, (866) 347-2423.*
Web, www.ice.gov

Investigates narcotics smuggling, including money laundering, document and identity fraud, and immigration enforcement; interdicts flow of narcotics into the United States.

►**NONGOVERNMENTAL**

Drug Policy Alliance, *National Affairs,* 925 15th St. N.W., 2nd Floor, 20005; (202) 683-2030. Fax, (202) 216-0803. *Ethan Nadelmann, Executive Director.*
General email, dc@drugpolicy.org
Web, www.drugpolicy.org

Supports reform of current drug control policy. Advocates medical treatment to control drug abuse; opposes random drug testing. Sponsors the biennial International Conference on Drug Policy Reform. (Headquarters in New York.)

Marijuana Policy Project, P.O. Box 77492, Capitol Hill, 20013; (202) 462-5747. Fax, (202) 232-0442. *Robert D. Kampia, Executive Director.*
General email, info@mpp.org
Web, www.mpp.org, Twitter, @MarijuanaPolicy and Facebook, www.facebook.com/MarijuanaPolicyProject

Promotes reform of marijuana policies and regulations. Opposes the prohibition of responsible growing and use of marijuana by adults. Interests include allowing doctors to recommend marijuana to seriously ill patients and eliminating criminal penalties for marijuana use.

National Assn. of State Alcohol and Drug Abuse Directors (NASADAD), 1025 Connecticut Ave. N.W., #605, 20036-5430; (202) 293-0090. Fax, (202) 293-1250. *Rob Morrison, Executive Director.*
General email, dcoffice@nasadad.org
Web, www.nasadad.org

Provides information on drug abuse treatment and prevention; contracts with federal and state agencies for design of programs to fight and prevent drug abuse.

National Organization for the Reform of Marijuana Laws (NORML), 1100 H St. N.W., #830, 20005; (202) 483-5500. Fax, (202) 483-0057. *Allen St. Pierre, Executive Director; Stephen W. Dillon, Chair.*
General email, norml@norml.org
Web, www.norml.org

Works to reform federal, state, and local marijuana laws and policies. Educates the public and conducts litigation on behalf of marijuana consumers. Monitors legislation and regulations.

RAND Corporation, *Drug Policy Research Center, Washington Office,* 1200 S. Hayes St., Arlington, VA 22202-5050; (703) 413-1100. Fax, (703) 413-8111. *Beau Kilmer, Co-Director; Rosalie Liccardo Pacula, Co-Director.*
General email, dprc@rand.org
Web, www.rand.org/multi/dprc

Studies and analyzes the nation's drug problems and policies. Emphasis on empirical research and policy recommendations; interests include international and local policy, trafficking, interdiction, modeling and forecasting, prevention, and treatment. Provides policymakers with information. (Headquarters in Santa Monica, Calif.)

Gun Control

►**AGENCIES**

Bureau of Alcohol, Tobacco, Firearms, and Explosives (ATF) *(Justice Dept.),* 99 New York Ave. N.E., 20226; (202) 648-7777. Fax, (202) 648-9762. *Thomas E. Brandon, Deputy Director.* Illegal firearm activity hotline, (800) 283-4867. Firearm theft hotline, (800) 930-9275.
General email, ATFTips@atf.gov
Web, www.atf.gov and Twitter, @ATFHQ

Enforces and administers laws to eliminate illegal possession and use of firearms. Investigates criminal violations and regulates legal trade, including imports and exports. Receives reports of illegal firearms activity and firearm theft.

►**NONGOVERNMENTAL**

Brady Center to Prevent Gun Violence, 840 1st St. N.E., #400, 20002; (202) 370-8101. Fax, (202) 370-8102. *Dan Gross, President.*
Web, www.bradycampaign.org and Twitter, @Bradybuzz

Educational, research, and legal action organization that seeks to allay gun violence, especially among children. Library open to the public. Public interest organization that works for gun control legislation and serves as an information clearinghouse. Monitors legislation and regulations.

Coalition to Stop Gun Violence, 805 15th St. N.W., #700, 20005; (202) 408-0061. *Mike Beard, President Emeritus; Joshua Horwitz, Executive Director.*
General email, csgv@csgv.org
Web, www.csgv.org and Twitter, @CSGV

Membership: 47 national organizations and individual supporters. Works to reduce gun violence by fostering effective community and national action.

Educational Fund to Stop Gun Violence, 805 15th St. N.W., #700, 20005; (202) 408-7560. *Josh Horwitz, Executive Director; Vlad Everett, Communications.*
General email, efsgv@efsgv.org
Web, http://efsgv.org and Twitter, @EFSGV

Group of national organizations, including faith-based groups, child welfare advocates, public health professionals, and social justice organizations, that seeks to reduce gun violence through research and education. Monitors legislation and regulations. (Affiliated with the Coalition to Stop Gun Violence.)

Gun Owners of America, 8001 Forbes Pl., #102, Springfield, VA 22151; (703) 321-8585. Fax, (703) 321-8408. *Erich Pratt, Executive Director.*
Web, www.gunowners.org

Seeks to preserve the right to bear arms and to protect the rights of law-abiding gun owners. Administers foundation that provides gun owners with legal assistance in suits against the federal government. Monitors legislation, regulations, and international agreements.

National Rifle Assn. of America (NRA), *11250 Waples Mill Rd., Fairfax, VA 22030; (703) 267-1000. Fax, (703) 267-3976. Wayne LaPierre, Executive Vice President. Press, (703) 267-3820. Toll-free, (800) 672-3888. Web, www.nra.org*

Membership: target shooters, hunters, gun collectors, gunsmiths, police officers, and others interested in firearms. Promotes shooting sports and recreational shooting and safety; studies and makes recommendations on firearms laws. Opposes gun control legislation. (Affiliated with the Institute for Legislative Action, the NRA's lobbying arm.)

Juvenile Justice

►AGENCIES

Education Dept., *Elementary and Secondary Education, State Support,* *400 Maryland Ave. S.W., #3W202, FB-6, 20202-6132; (202) 260-0826. Fax, (202) 260-7764. Patrick Rooney, Director, Acting. Web, www2.ed.gov/about/offices/list/oese/oss*

Funds state and local institutions responsible for providing neglected or delinquent children with free public education.

Office of Justice Programs (OJP) *(Justice Dept.),* *Juvenile Justice and Delinquency Prevention,* *810 7th St. N.W., 20531; (202) 307-5911. Fax, (301) 240-5830. Robert L. Listenbee, Administrator. Clearinghouse, (800) 851-3420. Web, www.ojjdp.gov*

Administers federal programs related to prevention and treatment of juvenile delinquency; missing and exploited children; child victimization; and training, technical assistance, and research and evaluation in these areas. Coordinates with youth programs of the departments of Agriculture, Education, Housing and Urban Development, Interior, and Labor, and the Health and Human Services Administration, including the Center for Studies of Crime and Delinquency. Operates the Juvenile Justice Clearinghouse. Sponsors the National Criminal Justice Reference Service ((800) 851-3420).

►NONGOVERNMENTAL

Coalition for Juvenile Justice, *1319 F St. N.W., #402, 20004; (202) 467-0864. Fax, (202) 887-0738. Marie Williams, Executive Director, ext. 113. General email, info@juvjustice.org Web, www.juvjustice.org and Twitter, @4juvjustice*

Nationwide coalition of governor-appointed advisory groups, practitioners, and volunteers. Seeks to improve juvenile justice and to prevent children and youth from becoming involved in the courts. Issues include the removal of youth from adult jails and lockups and attention to the disproportionate number of youth of color in the juvenile justice system.

Organized Crime

►AGENCIES

Criminal Division *(Justice Dept.),* *Narcotic and Dangerous Drugs Section,* *145 N St. N.E., 20530; (202) 514-0917. Fax, (202) 514-6112. Arthur G. Wyatt, Chief; Wayne Raabe, Principal Deputy Chief. Press, (202) 514-2007. Web, www.justice.gov/criminal/ndds*

Investigates and prosecutes participants in criminal syndicates involved in the large-scale importation, manufacture, shipment, or distribution of illegal narcotics and other dangerous drugs. Trains agents and prosecutors in the techniques of major drug litigation.

Criminal Division *(Justice Dept.),* *Organized Crime and Gang Section,* *1301 New York Ave. N.W., #700, 20005; (202) 514-3594. Fax, (202) 514-3601. James Trusty, Chief. General email, criminaldivision@us.doj.gov Web, www.justice.gov/criminal-ocgs*

Enforces federal criminal laws when subjects under investigation are alleged racketeers or part of syndicated criminal operations; coordinates efforts of federal, state, and local law enforcement agencies against organized crime, including emerging international groups. Cases include extortion, murder, bribery, fraud, money laundering, narcotics, labor racketeering, and violence that disrupts the criminal justice process.

Federal Bureau of Investigation (FBI) *(Justice Dept.),* *Criminal Investigative Division, Organized Crime,* *935 Pennsylvania Ave. N.W., #3352, 20535-0001; (202) 324-5625. Fax, (202) 324-0880. Maxwell Marker, Section Chief, Eastern Hemisphere; Marlin Ritzman, Section Chief, Western Hemisphere. Web, www.fbi.gov/about-us/investigate/organizedcrime*

Coordinates all FBI organized crime investigations. Determines budget, training, and resource needs for investigations, including those related to international organized crime. Conducts undercover operations, surveillance, and multi-agency investigations, and works with international partners.

Other Violations

►AGENCIES

Bureau of Alcohol, Tobacco, Firearms, and Explosives (ATF) *(Justice Dept.),* *99 New York Ave. N.E., 20226; (202) 648-7777. Fax, (202) 648-9762. Thomas E. Brandon, Deputy Director. Illegal firearm activity hotline, (800) 283-4867. Firearm theft hotline, (800) 930-9275. General email, ATFTips@atf.gov Web, www.atf.gov and Twitter, @ATFHQ*

Performs law enforcement functions relating to alcohol (beer, wine, distilled spirits), tobacco, arson, explosives, and destructive devices; investigates criminal violations and regulates legal trade.

Criminal Division *(Justice Dept.), Asset Forfeiture and Money Laundering Section,* 1400 New York Ave. N.W., #10100, 20005; (202) 514-1263. Fax, (202) 514-5522. *M. Kendall Day, Chief.*
Web, www.justice.gov/criminal/afmls

Investigates and prosecutes money laundering and criminal and civil forfeiture offenses involving illegal transfer of funds within the United States and from the United States to other countries. Oversees and coordinates legislative policy proposals. Advises U.S. attorneys' offices in multidistrict money laundering and criminal and civil forfeiture prosecutions. Represents Justice Dept. in international anti-money laundering and criminal and civil forfeiture initiatives.

Criminal Division *(Justice Dept.), Fraud Section,* 1400 New York Ave. N.W., #4100, 20530; (202) 514-7023. Fax, (202) 514-7021. *Andrew Weissmann, Chief.*
Web, www.justice.gov/criminal-fraud

Administers federal enforcement activities related to fraud and white-collar crime. Focuses on frauds against government programs, transnational and multidistrict fraud, and cases involving the security and commodity exchanges, banking practices, and consumer victimization.

Federal Bureau of Investigation (FBI) *(Justice Dept.), Cyber Division,* 935 Pennsylvania Ave. N.W., #5835, 20535; (202) 324-7770. Fax, (202) 324-2840. *James Trainor Jr., Assistant Director.*
Web, www.fbi.gov/about-us/investigate/cyber

Coordinates the investigations of federal violations in which the Internet or computer networks are exploited for terrorist, foreign government–sponsored intelligence, or criminal activities, including copyright violations, fraud, pornography, child exploitation, and malicious computer intrusions.

Federal Bureau of Investigation (FBI) *(Justice Dept.), Economic Crimes,* 935 Pennsylvania Ave. N.W., #3925, 20535; (202) 324-6352. Fax, (202) 324-9147. *Francine Gross, Chief. Press, (202) 324-3691.*
Web, www.fbi.gov

Investigates, reduces, and prevents significant financial crimes against individuals, businesses, and industries by safeguarding the integrity and credibility of corporations, securities and commodities markets, investment vehicles, and the insurance industry. Reinforces compliance in the corporate world and promotes investor confidence in the United States' financial markets. Categorizes the frauds it investigates into four separate classifications: corporate fraud, securities and commodities fraud, insurance fraud (non-health care related), and mass marketing fraud.

Federal Bureau of Investigation (FBI) *(Justice Dept.), National Security Branch, Counterintelligence Division,* 935 Pennsylvania Ave. N.W., 20535; (202) 324-4614.

Fax, (202) 324-0848. *Randall C. Coleman, Assistant Director. National security hotline, (202) 324-3000.*
Web, www.fbi.gov/about-us/investigate/counterintelligence

Provides centralized management and oversight of all foreign counterintelligence investigations. Integrates law enforcement with intelligence efforts to investigate violations of federal laws against espionage, including economic espionage. Seeks to prevent foreign acquisition of weapons of mass destruction, penetration of the U.S. intelligence community and government agencies and contractors, and compromise of U.S. critical national assets.

Internal Revenue Service (IRS) *(Treasury Dept.), Criminal Investigation,* 1111 Constitution Ave. N.W., #2501, 20224; (202) 317-3200. *Richard Weber, Chief. Tax fraud hotline, (800) 829-0433.*
Web, www.irs.gov

Investigates money laundering and violations of the tax law. Lends support in counterterrorism and narcotics investigations conducted in conjunction with other law enforcement agencies, both foreign and domestic.

Justice Dept. (DOJ), *Human Rights and Special Prosecutions,* 1301 New York Ave. N.W., John C. Keeney Bldg., #200, 20530; (202) 616-2492. Fax, (202) 616-2491. *Teresa McHenry, Chief; Eli M. Rosenbaum, Director, Strategy and Policy.*
Web, www.justice.gov/criminal/hrsp

Tracks war criminals within the United States with connections to world genocidal conflicts. Handles legal action to ensure denaturalization and/or deportation.

National Security Division *(Justice Dept.),* 950 Pennsylvania Ave. N.W., #7339, 20530; (202) 514-1057. Fax, (202) 514-9836. *Hon. John P. Carlin, Assistant Attorney General. Press, (202) 514-2007. General email, nsd.public@usdoj.gov*
Web, www.justice.gov/nsd

Coordinates the Justice Dept.'s intelligence, counterterrorism, counterespionage, and other national security activities. Offers support for victims of overseas terrorism; provides legal assistance and advice, in coordination with the Office of Legal Counsel as appropriate, to all branches of government on matters of national security law and policy.

National Security Division *(Justice Dept.), Counterintelligence and Export Control,* 950 Pennsylvania Ave. N.W., 20530; (202) 514-1057. Fax, (202) 514-8714. *John P. Carlin, Assistant Attorney General. General email, nsd.public@usdoj.gov*
Web, www.justice.gov/nsd

Supervises the investigation and prosecution of cases affecting national security, foreign relations, and the export of military and strategic commodities and technology. Has executive responsibility for authorizing the prosecution of cases under criminal statutes relating to espionage, sabotage, neutrality, and atomic energy. Provides legal advice to U.S. Attorney's offices and investigates agencies on federal statutes concerning national security. Coordinates criminal cases involving the application of the Classified

Information Procedures Act. Administers and enforces the Foreign Agents Registration Act of 1938 and related disclosure statutes.

National Security Division *(Justice Dept.),* **Counterterrorism,** *950 Pennsylvania Ave. N.W., 20530; (202) 514-1057. Fax, (202) 514-8714. Michael J. Mullaney, Chief.*
General email, nsd.public@usdoj.gov
Web, www.justice.gov/nsd/counterrorism-section

Responsible for the design, implementation, and support of law enforcement efforts, legislative initiatives, policies, and strategies related to combating international and domestic terrorism. Seeks to assist, through investigation and prosecution, in preventing and disrupting acts of terrorism anywhere in the world that impact significant U.S. interests and persons.

National Security Division *(Justice Dept.),* **Law and Policy,** *950 Pennsylvania Ave. N.W., 20530; (202) 514-7941. Brad Wiegmann, Deputy Assistant Attorney General.*
General email, nsd.justice@usdoj.gov
Web, www.justice.gov/nsd

Develops and implements Justice Dept. policies with regard to intelligence, counterterrorism, and other national security matters. Provides legal assistance and advice on matters of national security law.

Securities and Exchange Commission (SEC), *Office of the Whistleblower, 100 F St. N.E., MS 5628, 20549; (202) 551-4790. Fax, (703) 813-9322. Sean McKessy, Chief.*
Web, www.sec.gov/whistleblower

Receives information about possible securities law violations and provides information about the whistleblower program.

U.S. Customs and Border Protection *(Homeland Security Dept.),* **Field Operations,** *1300 Pennsylvania Ave. N.W., #2.4A, 20229; (202) 344-1620. Fax, (202) 344-2777. Todd Owen, Assistant Commissioner. Press, (202) 344-1700.*
Web, www.cbp.gov/border-security/ports-entry

Combats smuggling of funds; enforces statutes relating to the processing and regulation of people, carriers, cargo, and mail into and out of the United States. Investigates counterfeiting, child pornography, commercial fraud, and Internet crimes.

U.S. Postal Service (USPS), *Inspection Service, 475 L'Enfant Plaza S.W., #3301, 20260-2100; (202) 268-4264. Fax, (202) 268-7316. Guy Cottrell, Chief Postal Inspector. Fraud and abuse hotline, (877) 876-2455. Press, (202) 268-3700.*
Web, http://postalinspectors.uspis.gov

Protects mail, postal funds, and property from criminal violations of postal laws, such as mail fraud or distribution of obscene materials.

U.S. Secret Service *(Homeland Security Dept.), 950 H St. N.W., #8000, 20223; (202) 406-5700. Fax, (202) 406-5246. Joseph P. Clancy, Director. Information, (202) 406-5708. Press, (202) 406-5708.*
Web, www.secretservice.gov

Protects the president and vice president of the United States and their immediate family members, foreign heads of state and their spouses, and other individuals as designated by the president. Investigates threats against these protectees; protects the White House, vice president's residence, and foreign missions; and plans and implements security designs for national special security events. Investigates violations of laws relating to counterfeiting of U.S. currency; financial crimes, including access device fraud, financial institution fraud, identity theft, and computer fraud; and computer-based attacks on the financial, banking, and telecommunications infrastructure.

U.S. Secret Service *(Homeland Security Dept.),* **Criminal Investigative Division,** *950 H St. N.W., #5000, 20223; (202) 406-9330. Fax, (202) 406-5016. Stuart Tryon, Special Agent-in-Charge.*
Web, www.secretservice.gov/investigation

Investigates crimes associated with financial institutions. Jurisdiction includes bank fraud, access device fraud involving credit and debit cards, telecommunications and computer crimes, fraudulent identification, fraudulent government and commercial securities, and electronic funds transfer fraud.

▶NONGOVERNMENTAL

International Anticounterfeiting Coalition, *1730 M St. N.W., #1020, 20036; (202) 223-6667. Robert Barchiesi, President.*
General email, iacc@iacc.org
Web, www.iacc.org

Works to combat counterfeiting and piracy by promoting laws, regulations, and directives to render theft of intellectual property unprofitable. Oversees anticounterfeiting programs that increase patent, trademark, copyright, service mark, trade dress, and trade secret protection. Provides information and training to law enforcement officials to help identify counterfeit and pirate products.

Stalking Resource Center, *2000 M St. N.W., #480, 20036; (202) 467-8700. Fax, (202) 467-8701. Michelle Garcia, Director.*
General email, src@ncvc.org
Web, www.victimsofcrime.org/SRC

Acts as an information clearinghouse on stalking. Works to raise public awareness of the dangers of stalking. Encourages the development and implementation of multidisciplinary responses to stalking in local communities. Offers practitioner training and technical assistance. (Affiliated with the National Center for Victims of Crime.)

Sentencing and Corrections

▶AGENCIES

Federal Bureau of Prisons *(Justice Dept.), 320 1st St. N.W., 20534; (202) 307-3198. Fax, (202) 514-6620. Thomas R. Kane Jr., Director, Acting, (202) 307-3250. Press, (202) 514-6551. Inmate locator service, (202) 307-3126.*
Web, www.bop.gov

Supervises operations of federal correctional institutions, community treatment facilities, and commitment and management of federal inmates; oversees contracts with local institutions for confinement and support of federal prisoners. Regional offices are responsible for administration; central office in Washington coordinates operations and issues standards and policy guidelines. Central office includes Federal Prison Industries, a government corporation providing prison-manufactured goods and services for sale to federal agencies, and the National Institute of Corrections, an information and technical assistance center on state and local corrections programs.

Federal Bureau of Prisons *(Justice Dept.), Health Services,* 320 1st St. N.W., #454, 20534; (202) 307-3055. Fax, (202) 514-6620. Dr. Deborah G. Schult, Assistant Director.
Web, www.bop.gov/about/agency/org_hsd.jsp

Administers health care and treatment programs for prisoners in federal institutions.

Federal Bureau of Prisons *(Justice Dept.), Industries, Education, and Vocational Training,* 400 1st St. N.W., 20534; (202) 305-3500. Fax, (202) 514-6620. Mary M. Mitchell, Assistant Director, (202) 305-3501. Customer Service, (800) 827-3168.
Web, www.unicor.gov and www.bop.gov/about/agency/org_ievt.jsp

Administers program whereby inmates in federal prisons produce goods and services that are sold to the federal government.

Federal Bureau of Prisons *(Justice Dept.), National Institute of Corrections,* 320 1st St. N.W., #5007, 20534; (202) 307-3106. Fax, (202) 514-6620. Jim Cosby, Director. Toll-free, (800) 995-6423.
Web, www.nicic.org and www.bop.gov/about/agency/org_nic.jsp

Provides training, technical assistance, information clearinghouse services, and policy/program development assistance to federal, state, and local corrections agencies.

Justice Dept. (DOJ), *Pardon Attorney,* 1425 New York Ave. N.W., #11000, 20530 (mailing address: 145 N St. N.E., #5E508, Washington, DC 20530); (202) 616-6070. Fax, (202) 616-6069. Robert A. Zauzmer, Pardon Attorney, Acting.
Web, www.justice.gov/pardon

Receives and reviews petitions to the president for all forms of executive clemency, including pardons and sentence reductions; initiates investigations and prepares the deputy attorney general's recommendations to the president on petitions.

Office of Justice Programs (OJP) *(Justice Dept.), Bureau of Justice Assistance,* 810 7th St. N.W., 4th Floor, 20531; (202) 616-6500. Fax, (202) 305-1367. Denise E. O'Donnell, Director.
General email, askbja@usdoj.gov
Web, www.bja.gov

Provides states and communities with funds and technical assistance for corrections demonstration projects.

Office of Justice Programs (OJP) *(Justice Dept.), National Institute of Justice,* 810 7th St. N.W., 7th Floor, 20531; (202) 307-2942. Fax, (202) 307-6394. Nancy Rodriguez, Director. Press, (202) 307-0703.
General email, ojp.ocom.@usdoj.gov
Web, www.nij.gov

Conducts research on all aspects of criminal justice, including crime prevention, enforcement, adjudication, and corrections. Maintains the National Criminal Justice Reference Service, which provides information on corrections research: (800) 851-3420; in Maryland, (301) 519-5500; Web, www.ncjrs.gov.

U.S. Parole Commission *(Justice Dept.),* 90 K St. N.E., 3rd Floor, 20530; (202) 346-7000. Fax, (202) 357-1085. J. Patricia Wilson Smoot, Chair.
General email, public.inquiries@usdoj.gov
Web, www.justice.gov/uspc

Makes release and revocation decisions for all federal prisoners serving sentences of more than one year for offenses committed before November 1, 1987, and for D.C. Code offenders serving parolable offenses or subject to a term of supervised release.

U.S. Sentencing Commission, 1 Columbus Circle N.E., #2-500 South Lobby, 20002-8002; (202) 502-4500. Fax, (202) 502-4699. Patti B. Saris, Chair.
General email, pubaffairs@ussc.gov
Web, www.ussc.gov

Establishes sentencing guidelines and policy for all federal courts, including guidelines prescribing the appropriate form and severity of punishment for those convicted of federal crimes. Provides training and research on sentencing-related issues. Serves as an information resource.

► JUDICIARY

Administrative Office of the U.S. Courts, 1 Columbus Circle N.E., 20544-0001; (202) 502-2600. James C. Duff, Director.
Web, www.uscourts.gov/adminoff.html

Supervises all administrative matters of the federal court system, except the Supreme Court; collects statistical data on business of the courts.

Administrative Office of the U.S. Courts, *Probation and Pretrial Services,* 1 Columbus Circle N.E., #4-300, 20544-0001; (202) 502-1600. Fax, (202) 502-1677. Matthew Rowland, Assistant Director.
Web, www.uscourts.gov

Determines the resource and program requirements of the federal and pretrial services system. Provides policy guidance, program evaluation services, management and technical assistance, and training to probation and pretrial services officers.

▶NONGOVERNMENTAL

American Bar Assn. (ABA), *Criminal Justice,* *1050 Connecticut Ave. N.W., #400, 20036; (202) 662-1500. Fax, (202) 662-1501. Kevin Scruggs, Director, (202) 662-1503.*
General email, crimjustice@americanbar.org
Web, www.americanbar.org/crimjust

Studies and makes recommendations on all aspects of the correctional system, including overcrowding in prisons and the privatization of prisons and correctional institutions. (Headquarters in Chicago, Ill.)

American Civil Liberties Union Foundation, *National Prison Project, 915 15th St. N.W., 7th Floor, 20005; (202) 393-4930. Fax, (202) 393-4931. David Fathi, Director.*
Web, www.aclu.org/prison

Litigates on behalf of prisoners through class action suits. Seeks to improve prison conditions and the penal system; serves as resource center for prisoners' rights.

American Correctional Assn. (ACA), *206 N. Washington St., #200, Alexandria, VA 22314; (703) 224-0000. Fax, (703) 224-0179. James A. Gondles Jr., Executive Director, (703) 324-0103. Information, (800) 222-5646.*
Web, www.aca.org

Membership: corrections professionals in all aspects of corrections, including juvenile and adult facilities, community facilities, and academia; affiliates include state and regional corrections associations in the United States and Canada. Conducts and publishes research; provides state and local governments with technical assistance; certifies corrections professionals. Offers professional development courses and accreditation programs. Monitors legislation and regulation. Interests include criminal justice issues, correctional standards, and accreditation programs. Library open to the public.

Amnesty International USA, *Washington National Office, 600 Pennsylvania Ave. S.E., 5th Floor, 20003; (202) 544-0200. Fax, (202) 546-7142. Michael O'Reilly, Managing Director. Toll-free, 800-AMNESTY. Media, (202) 509-8194.*
General email, aiusa@aiusa.org
Web, www.amnestyusa.org and Twitter, @amnesty

International organization that opposes retention or reinstitution of the death penalty; advocates humane treatment of all prisoners. (U.S. headquarters in New York.)

Death Penalty Information Center, *1015 18th St. N.W., #704, 20036; (202) 289-2275. Robert Dunham, Executive Director.*
General email, dpic@deathpenaltyinfo.org
Web, www.deathpenaltyinfo.org

Provides the media and public with analysis and information on issues concerning capital punishment. Conducts briefings for journalists; prepares reports; issues press releases.

Families Against Mandatory Minimums, *1100 H St. N.W., #1000, 20005; (202) 822-6700. Fax, (202) 822-6704. Julie Stewart, President.*
General email, famm@famm.org
Web, www.famm.org and Twitter, @FAMMFoundation

Seeks to repeal statutory mandatory minimum prison sentences. Works to increase public awareness of inequity of mandatory minimum sentences through grassroots efforts and media outreach programs.

NAACP Legal Defense and Educational Fund, Inc., *Washington Office, 1444 Eye St. N.W., 10th Floor, 20005; (202) 682-1300. Fax, (202) 682-1312. Leslie M. Proll, Director.*
Web, www.naacpldf.org

Civil rights litigation group that supports abolition of capital punishment; assists attorneys representing prisoners on death row; focuses public attention on race discrimination in the application of the death penalty. Not affiliated with the NAACP. (Headquarters in New York.)

National Center on Institutions and Alternatives, *7205 Rutherford Rd., Baltimore, MD 21244; (410) 265-1490. Fax, (410) 597-9656. Herbert J. Hoelter, Chair.*
General email, hhoelter@ncianet.org
Web, www.ncianet.org

Seeks to reduce incarceration as primary form of punishment imposed by criminal justice system; advocates use of extended community service, work-release, and halfway house programs; operates youth and adult residential programs; provides defense attorneys and courts with specific recommendations for sentencing and parole. (Affiliated with the Augustus Institute. Headquarters in Baltimore, Md.)

National Coalition to Abolish the Death Penalty, *1620 L St. N.W., #250, 20036; (202) 331-4090. Diann Rust-Tierney, Executive Director.*
General email, info@ncadp.org
Web, www.ncadp.org, Twitter, @ncadp and Facebook, www.facebook.com/ncadp

Membership: organizations and individuals opposed to the death penalty. Maintains collection of death penalty research. Provides training, resources, and conferences. Works with families of murder victims; tracks execution dates. Monitors legislation and regulations.

Prison Fellowship Ministries, *44180 Riverside Pkwy., Lansdowne, VA 20176; (703) 478-0100. Tim Robison, Chief Executive Officer, Acting. Toll-free, (800) 206-9764.*
Web, www.pfm.org

Religious organization that ministers to prisoners and ex-prisoners, victims, and the families involved. Offers counseling, seminars, and support for readjustment after release; works to increase the fairness and effectiveness of the criminal justice system.

The Sentencing Project, *1705 DeSales St. N.W., 8th Floor, 20036; (202) 628-0871. Fax, (202) 628-1091. Marc Mauer, Executive Director.*
General email, staff@sentencingproject.org
Web, www.sentencingproject.org

Engages in research and advocacy on criminal justice policy issues, including sentencing, incarceration, juvenile justice, racial disparity, alternatives to incarceration, and felony disenfranchisement. Publishes research.

Victim Assistance

►AGENCIES

Federal Bureau of Investigation (FBI) *(Justice Dept.),* **Victim Assistance,** *935 Pennsylvania Ave. N.W., #3329, 20535; (202) 324-1339. Fax, (202) 324-2113. Kathryn McKay Turman, Program Director. Toll-free, (866) 828-5320.*
General email, victim.assistance@ic.fbi.gov
Web, www.fbi.gov/stats-services/victim_assistance

Ensures that victims of crimes investigated by the FBI are identified, offered assistance, and given information about case events. Manages the Victim Assistance Program in the fifty-six FBI field offices as well as the FBI's international offices. Trains agents and personnel to work with victims. Coordinates resources and services to victims in cases of terrorism and crimes against citizens that occur outside the United States. Coordinates with other federal agencies on behalf of victims.

National Security Division *(Justice Dept.),* **Justice for Victims of Overseas Terrorism,** *950 Pennsylvania Ave. N.W., 20530; (202) 514-7941. Fax, (202) 514-8714. Heather Cartwright, Director.*
General email, nsd.public@usdoj.gov
Web, www.justice.gov/nsd-ovt

Monitors the investigation and prosecution of terrorist attacks against U.S. citizens abroad; works with other Justice Dept. offices to ensure that the rights of victims are respected. Responsible for establishing a Joint Task Force with the State Dept. in the event of a terrorist incident against U.S. citizens overseas. Responds to congressional and citizens' inquiries on the department's response to such attacks.

Office of Justice Programs (OJP) *(Justice Dept.),* **Victims of Crime,** *810 7th St. N.W., 8th Floor, 20531; (202) 307-5983. Fax, (202) 514-6383. Joye E. Frost, Director. Resource Center, (800) 851-3420 or TTY (301) 240-6310. Victim hotline, (800) 331-0075 or TTY, (800) 553-2508.*
General email, askovc@ojp.gov
Web, www.ovc.gov/about

Works to advance the rights of and improve services to the nation's crime victims. Supports programs and initiatives to assist other federal agencies, state and local governments, tribal governments, private nonprofit organizations, and the international community in their efforts to aid victims of violent and nonviolent crime. Provides emergency funding and services for victims of terrorism and mass violence and victims of human trafficking. Funds the development of training and technical assistance for victim service providers and other professionals through the Training and Technical Assistance Center, (866) 682-8822 or TTY (866) 682-8880. Funds demonstration projects and coordinates annual observances of National Crime Victims' Rights Week. Web site has a Spanish-language link.

►NONGOVERNMENTAL

National Assn. of Crime Victim Compensation Boards, *P.O. Box 16003, Alexandria, VA 22302; (703) 780-3200. Dan Eddy, Executive Director.*
General email, dan.eddy@nacvcb.org
Web, www.nacvcb.org

Provides state compensation agencies with training and technical assistance. Provides public information on victim compensation.

National Center for Missing and Exploited Children, *Charles B. Wang International Children's Bldg., 699 Prince St., Alexandria, VA 22314-3175; (703) 331-2150. Fax, (703) 224-2122. John Clark, Chief Executive Officer. Toll-free hotline, (800) 843-5678.*
Web, www.missingkids.com

Private organization that assists parents and citizens' groups in locating and safely returning missing children; offers technical assistance to law enforcement agencies; coordinates public and private missing children programs; maintains database that coordinates information on missing children.

National Center for Victims of Crime, *2000 M St. N.W., #480, 20036; (202) 467-8700. Fax, (202) 467-8701. Mai Fernandez, Executive Director.*
Web, www.victimsofcrime.org

Works with victims' groups and criminal justice agencies to protect the rights of crime victims through state and federal statutes and policies. Promotes greater responsiveness to crime victims through training and education; provides research and technical assistance in the development of victim-related legislation.

National Organization for Victim Assistance, *510 King St., #424, Alexandria, VA 22314; (703) 535-6682. Fax, (703) 535-5500. Richard Barajas, Executive Director. Toll-free and referral line, (800) 879-6682.*
Web, www.trynova.org

Membership: persons involved with victim and witness assistance programs, criminal justice professionals, researchers, crime victims, and others interested in victims' rights. Monitors legislation; provides victims and victim support programs with technical assistance, referrals, and program support; provides information on victims' rights.

LAW ENFORCEMENT

General

▶AGENCIES

Criminal Division *(Justice Dept.), Computer Crime and Intellectual Property Section,* 1301 New York Ave. N.W., #600, 20530; (202) 514-1026. Fax, (202) 514-6113. John Lynch, Chief.
Web, www.justice.gov/criminal-ccips

Investigates and litigates criminal cases involving computers, intellectual property, and the Internet. Administers the Computer Crime Initiative, a program designed to combat electronic penetrations, data theft, and cyberattacks on critical information systems. Provides specialized technical and legal assistance to other Justice Dept. divisions; coordinates international efforts; formulates policies and proposes legislation on computer crime and intellectual property issues.

Federal Bureau of Investigation (FBI) *(Justice Dept.), Partner Engagement,* 935 Pennsylvania Ave. N.W., #7128, 20535; (202) 324-7126. Kerry Sleeper, Assistant Director. General email, olec@leo.gov
Web, www.fbi.gov/about-us/office-of-partner-engagement/ope

Advises FBI executives on the use of state and local law enforcement and resources in criminal, cyber, and counterterrorism investigations. Coordinates the bureau's intelligence-sharing and technological efforts with state and local law enforcement. Serves as a liaison with the Homeland Security Dept. and other federal entities.

Federal Law Enforcement Training Center *(Homeland Security Dept.), Washington Operations,* 555 Eleventh St. N.W. #400, 20004; (202) 233-0260. Fax, (202) 233-0258. Connie Patrick, Director, (912) 267-2070. General email, FLETC-WashingtonOffice@dhs.gov
Web, www.fletc.gov/washington-operations-wo

Trains federal law enforcement personnel. Provides services to state, local, tribal, and international law enforcement agencies. (Headquarters in Glynco, Ga.)

Financial Crimes Enforcement Network *(Treasury Dept.),* P.O. Box 39, Vienna, VA 22183-0039; (703) 905-3591. Fax, (703) 905-3690. Jennifer Shasky Calvery, Director. Press, (703) 905-3770. Resource Center, (800) 767-2825.
General email, frc@fincen.gov
Web, www.fincen.gov

Administers an information network in support of federal, state, and local law enforcement agencies in the prevention and detection of terrorist financing, money-laundering operations, and other financial crimes. Administers the Bank Secrecy Act.

Interior Dept. (DOI), *Law Enforcement and Security,* 1849 C St. N.W., MS 3428-MIB, 20240; (202) 208-6319. Fax, (202) 208-1185. Tim Lynn, Director, Acting;

Harry Humbert, Deputy Assistant Secretary. Watch Office, (202) 208-4108.
Web, www.doi.gov/pmb/oles

Provides leadership, policy guidance, and oversight to the Interior Dept.'s law enforcement, homeland security, and security programs. Works to protect critical infrastructure facilities, national icons, and monuments; develops law enforcement staffing models; establishes departmental training requirements and monitors their implementation; oversees the hiring of key law enforcement and security personnel; and reviews law enforcement and security budgets.

Office of Justice Programs (OJP) *(Justice Dept.), Bureau of Justice Assistance,* 810 7th St. N.W., 4th Floor, 20531; (202) 616-6500. Fax, (202) 305-1367. Denise E. O'Donnell, Director.
General email, askbja@usdoj.gov
Web, www.bja.gov

Provides funds to eligible state and local governments and to nonprofit organizations for criminal justice programs, primarily those that combat drug trafficking and other drug-related crime.

Transportation Security Administration (TSA) *(Homeland Security Dept.), Office of Law Enforcement, Federal Air Marshal Service,* TSA-18, 601 S. 12th St., Arlington, VA 20598-6018; (703) 487-3400. Fax, (703) 487-3405. Colleen Callahan, Assistant Administrator, Acting. Web, www.tsa.gov/about-tsa/office-law-enforcement

Protects air security in the United States. Promotes public confidence in the U.S. civil aviation system. Deploys marshals on flights around the world to detect and deter hostile acts targeting U.S. air carriers, airports, passengers, and crews.

U.S. Marshals Service *(Justice Dept.),* 2604 Jefferson Davis Hwy., CS-3, #1200, Alexandria, VA 22301; (202) 307-9100. Fax, (703) 603-7021. Vacant, Director. Public Affairs, (202) 307-9065. TTY, (202) 307-5012. General email, us.marshals@usdoj.gov
Web, www.usmarshals.gov

Acts as the enforcement arm of the federal courts and U.S. attorney general. Responsibilities include court and witness security, prisoner custody and transportation, prisoner support, maintenance and disposal of seized and forfeited property, and special operations. Administers the Federal Witness Security Program. Apprehends fugitives, including those wanted by foreign nations and believed to be in the United States; oversees the return of fugitives apprehended abroad and wanted by U.S. law enforcement. Carries out the provisions of the Adam Walsh Child Protection and Safety Act.

▶CONGRESS

For a listing of relevant congressional committees and subcommittees, please see pages 516–517 or the Appendix.

Feminist Majority Foundation, *National Center for Women and Policing, 1600 Wilson Blvd., #801, Arlington, VA 22209; (703) 522-2214. Fax, (703) 522-2219. Eleanor Smeal, President; Margaret Moore, Director.* General email, womencops@feminist.org

Web, http://womenandpolicing.com

Seeks to increase the number of women at all ranks of policing and law enforcement. Sponsors conferences and training programs. (Headquarters in Beverly Hills, Calif.)

International Assn. of Chiefs of Police, *44 Canal Center Plaza, #200, Alexandria, VA 22314; (703) 836-6767. Fax, (703) 836-4543. Vince Talucci, Executive Director. Toll-free, (800) 843-4227.* General email, information@theiacp.org

Web, www.theiacp.org

Membership: foreign and U.S. police executives and administrators at federal, state, and local levels. Consults and conducts research on all aspects of police activity; conducts training programs and develops educational aids; conducts public education programs.

International Assn. of Chiefs of Police, *Advisory Committee for Patrol and Tactical Operations, 44 Canal Center Plaza #200, Alexandria, VA 22314; (703) 836-6767. Jenny Gargano, Staff Liaison, ext. 847. Toll-free, (800) 843-7227.* General email, kollon@theiacp.org

Web, www.theiacp.org

Membership: foreign and U.S. police executives and administrators. Maintains liaison with civil defense and emergency service agencies in the United States and other nations; prepares guidelines for police cooperation with emergency and disaster relief agencies during emergencies.

National Criminal Justice Assn., *720 7th St. N.W., 3rd Floor, 20001; (202) 628-8550. Fax, (202) 448-1723. Cabell C. Cropper, Executive Director; Bethany Broida, Communications. Press, (202) 448-1713.* General email, info@ncja.org

Web, www.ncja.org

Membership: criminal justice organizations and professionals. Provides members and interested individuals with technical assistance and information.

National Organization of Black Law Enforcement Executives, *4609 Pinecrest Office Park Dr., Suite F, Alexandria, VA 22312-1442; (703) 658-1529. Fax, (703) 658-9479. Dwayne A. Crawford, Executive Director.* General email, dcrawford@noblenatl.org

Web, www.noblenational.org

Membership: African American police chiefs and senior law enforcement executives. Works to increase community involvement in the criminal justice system and to enhance the role of African Americans in law enforcement. Provides urban police departments with assistance in police operations, community relations, and devising strategies to sensitize the criminal justice system to the problems of the African American community.

National Sheriffs' Assn., *1450 Duke St., Alexandria, VA 22314-3490; (703) 836-7827. Fax, (703) 838-5349. Jonathan Thompson, Executive Director. Toll-free, (800) 424-7827.* General email, nsamail@sheriffs.org

Web, www.sheriffs.org

Membership: sheriffs and other municipal, state, and federal law enforcement officers. Conducts research and training programs for members in law enforcement, court procedures, and corrections. Publishes *Sheriff* magazine and an e-newsletter.

Police Executive Research Forum, *1120 Connecticut Ave. N.W., #930, 20036; (202) 466-7820. Fax, (202) 466-7826. Chuck Wexler, Executive Director. TTY, (202) 466-2670.* General email, perf@policeforum.org

Web, www.policeforum.org

Membership: law enforcement executives. Conducts research on law enforcement issues and disseminates criminal justice and law enforcement information.

Police Foundation, *1201 Connecticut Ave. N.W., #200, 20036-2636; (202) 833-1460. Fax, (202) 659-9149. James Bueermann, President.* General email, info@policefoundation.org

Web, www.policefoundation.org

Research and education foundation that conducts studies to improve police procedures; provides technical assistance for innovative law enforcement strategies, including community-oriented policing.

LEGAL PROFESSIONS AND RESOURCES

General

American Bar Assn. (ABA), *International Law, 1050 Connecticut Ave. N.W., 20036; (202) 662-1660. Fax, (202) 662-1669. Leanne Pfautz, Section Director, (202) 662-1661.* General email, intlaw@americanbar.org

Web, www.americanbar.org/intlaw

Monitors and makes recommendations concerning developments in the practice of international law that affect ABA members and the public. Conducts programs, including International Legal Exchange, and produces publications covering the practice of international law.

American Health Lawyers Assn., *1620 Eye St. N.W., 6th Floor, 20006-4010; (202) 833-1100. Fax, (202) 833-1105. David Cade, Chief Executive Officer, (202) 833-0777.* General email, info@healthlawyers.org

Web, www.healthlawyers.org

Membership: corporate, institutional, and government lawyers interested in the health field; law students; and health professionals. Serves as an information clearinghouse on health law; sponsors health law educational programs and seminars.

American Immigration Lawyers Assn., *1331 G St. N.W., #300, 20005-3142; (202) 507-7600. Fax, (202) 783-7853. Benjamin Johnson, Executive Director.*
Web, www.aila.org

Association for lawyers interested in immigration law. Provides information and continuing education programs on immigration law and policy; offers workshops and conferences. Monitors legislation and regulations.

American Inns of Court Foundation, *225 Reinekers Lane, Alexandria, VA 22314; (703) 684-3590. Fax, (703) 684-3607. Brig. Gen Malinda E. Dunn, Executive Director. Toll-free, (800) 233-3590.*
General email, info@innsofcourt.org
Web, www.innsofcourt.org

Promotes professionalism, ethics, civility, and legal skills of judges, lawyers, academicians, and law students in order to improve the quality and efficiency of the legal profession.

Asian Americans Advancing Justice (AAJC), *1620 L St. N.W., #1050, 20036; (202) 296-2300. Fax, (202) 296-2318. Mee Moua, President.*
General email, information@advancingequality.org
Web, www.advancingequality.org and Twitter, @AAAJ_AAJC

Works to advance the human and civil rights of Asian Americans and other minority groups through advocacy, public policy, public education, and litigation. Promotes civic engagement at the local, regional, and national levels. Interests include affirmative action, hate crimes, media diversity, census, broadband and telecommunications, youth advocacy, immigrant rights, language access, and voting rights.

The Assn. of American Law Schools, *1614 20th St. N.W., 20009-1001; (202) 296-8851. Fax, (202) 296-8869. Judith Areen, Executive Director.*
General email, aals@aals.org
Web, www.aals.org and Twitter, @TheAALS

Membership: law schools, subject to approval. Membership criteria include high-quality academic programs, faculty, scholarship, and students; academic freedom; diversity of people and viewpoints; and emphasis on public service. Hosts meetings and workshops; publishes a directory of law teachers. Acts as advocate on behalf of legal education; monitors legislation and judicial decisions.

Assn. of Transportation Law Professionals, *P.O. Box 5407, Annapolis, MD 21403; (410) 268-1311. Fax, (410) 268-1322. Lauren Michalski, Executive Director.*
General email, info@atlp.org
Web, www.atlp.org

Membership: Transportation attorneys and company counsel, government officials, and industry practitioners.

Provides members with continuing educational development in transportation law and practice.

Christian Legal Society, *8001 Braddock Rd., #302, Springfield, VA 22151; (703) 642-1070. Fax, (703) 642-1075. David Nammo, Chief Executive Officer.*
General email, clshq@clsnet.org
Web, www.clsnet.org and Twitter, @CLS_HQ

Membership: Christian lawyers, judges, paralegals, law professors, law students, and others. Interests include the defense of religious freedom and the provision of legal aid to the poor.

Equal Employment Advisory Council, *1501 M St. N.W., #400, 20005; (202) 629-5650. Fax, (202) 629-5651. Joseph S. Lakis, President.*
General email, info@eeac.org
Web, www.eeac.org

Membership: principal equal employment officers and lawyers. Files amicus curiae (friend of the court) briefs; conducts research and provides information on equal employment law and policy. Monitors legislation and regulations.

Federal Circuit Bar Assn., *1620 Eye St. N.W., #801, 20006; (202) 466-3923. Fax, (202) 833-1061. James E. Brookshire, Executive Director, (202) 558-2421.*
General email, brookshire1@fedcirbar.org
Web, www.fedcirbar.org

Represents practitioners before the Court of Appeals for the Federal Circuit. Fosters discussion between different groups within the legal community; sponsors regional seminars; publishes a scholarly journal.

Hispanic National Bar Assn., *1020 19th St. N.W., #505, 20036; (202) 223-4777. Fax, (202) 503-3403. Robert Maldonado, President; Alba Cruz Hacker, Director.*
General email, info@hnba.com
Web, www.hnba.com

Membership: Hispanic American attorneys, judges, professors, paralegals, and law students. Seeks to increase professional opportunities in law for Hispanic Americans and to increase Hispanic American representation in law schools. (Affiliated with National Hispanic Leadership Agenda and the American Bar Assn.)

International Law Institute, *1055 Thomas Jefferson St. N.W., #M-100, 20007; (202) 247-6006. Fax, (202) 247-6010. Kim Phan, Executive Director.*
General email, info@ili.org
Web, www.ili.org

Performs scholarly research, offers training programs, and provides technical assistance in the areas of international law and economic development. Sponsors international conferences.

National Assn. of College and University Attorneys, *1 Dupont Circle N.W., #620, 20036-1182; (202) 833-8390. Fax, (202) 296-8379. Kathleen Curry Santora, Chief Executive Officer.*
General email, nacua@nacua.org
Web, www.nacua.org

Provides information on legal developments affecting postsecondary education. Operates a clearinghouse through which in-house and external legal counselors are able to network with their counterparts on current legal problems.

National Assn. of Consumer Bankruptcy Attorneys, *2200 Pennsylvania Ave. N.W., 4th Floor, 20037; (800) 499-9040. Fax, (866) 408-9515. Maureen Thompson, Legislative Director; Dan Labert, Executive Director.*
General email, admin@nacba.org

Web, www.nacba.org

Advocates on behalf of consumer debtors and their attorneys. Files amicus briefs on behalf of parties in the U.S. courts of appeal and Supreme Court, and provides educational programs and workshops for attorneys. Monitors legislation and regulations.

National Assn. of Criminal Defense Lawyers, *1660 L St. N.W., 12th Floor, 20036; (202) 872-8600. Fax, (202) 872-8690. Norman L. Reimer, Executive Director.*
General email, assist@nacdl.org

Web, www.nacdl.org

Volunteer bar association of criminal defense attorneys and their local, state, and international affiliates. Provides members with continuing education, a brief bank, an ethics hotline, and specialized assistance in such areas as forensic science. Offers free legal assistance to members threatened with sanctions. Interests include eliminating mandatory minimum sentencing, forensic lab reform, death penalty reform, protection of privacy rights, indigent defense reform, overcriminalization, and civil liberties. Monitors legislation and regulations.

National Consumer Law Center, *Washington Office, 1001 Connecticut Ave. N.W., #510, 20036-5528; (202) 452-6252. Fax, (202) 463-9462. Richard DuBois, Executive Director.*
General email, consumerlaw@nclc.org

Web, www.consumerlaw.org and www.nclc.org

Provides lawyers funded by the Legal Services Corp. with research and assistance; provides lawyers with training in consumer and energy law. (Headquarters in Boston, Mass.)

National Court Reporters Assn., *12030 Sunrise Valley Dr., #400, Reston, VA 20191; (703) 556-6272. Fax, (703) 391-0629. Michael S. Nelson, Executive Director. Toll-free, (800) 272-6272. TTY, (703) 556-6289.*
General email, msic@ncrahq.org

Web, www.ncra.org

Membership organization that offers certification and continuing education for court reporting and captioning. Acts as a clearinghouse on technology and information for and about court reporters; certifies legal video specialists. Monitors legislation and regulations.

Street Law, Inc., *1010 Wayne Ave., #870, Silver Spring, MD 20910; (301) 589-1130. Fax, (301) 589-1131. Lee Arbetman, Executive Director.*

General email, clearinghouse@streetlaw.org

Web, www.streetlaw.org

International educational organization that promotes public understanding of law, the legal system, democracy, and human rights. Provides curriculum materials, training, and technical assistance to secondary school systems, law schools, departments of corrections, juvenile justice systems, bar associations, community groups, and state, local, and foreign governments.

Data and Research

▶**AGENCIES**

Community Oriented Policing Services (COPS) *(Justice Dept.), 145 N St. N.E., 20530 (mailing address: for overnight delivery, use zip code 20002); (202) 616-2888. Fax, (202) 616-2914. Ronald L. Davis, Director, (202) 616-2888. Phone for COPS program, (202) 307-1480. Congressional Relations, (202) 514-9079. Response Center, (800) 421-6770.*
General email, askCopsRC@usdoj.gov

Web, www.cops.usdoj.gov and Twitter, @COPSOffice

Awards grants to tribal, state, and local law enforcement agencies to hire and train community policing professionals, acquire and deploy crime-fighting technologies, and develop and test policing strategies. Provides publications and other educational materials on a wide range of law enforcement concerns and community policing topics. Community policing emphasizes crime prevention through partnerships between law enforcement and citizen.

Justice Dept. (DOJ), *Elder Justice Initiative, 950 Pennsylvania Ave. N.W., 20530; Andy Mao, Coordinator.*
General email, elder.justice@usdoj.gov

Web, www.justice.gov/elderjustice and State web resources, www.justice.gov/elderjustice/support/resources.html

Provides access to a database containing bibliographic information for thousands of scientific, legal, and general elder abuse and financial exploitation articles and reviews.

Justice Dept. (DOJ), *National Criminal Justice Reference Service, P.O. Box 6000, Rockville, MD 20849-6000; (800) 851-3420. Fax, (301) 240-5830. TTY, (301) 240-6310. International callers, (301) 240-7760.*
Web, www.ncjrs.gov

Offers justice and drug-related information and resources to support research, policy, and program development. Curates the NCJRS Virtual Library.

Office of Justice Programs (OJP) *(Justice Dept.), Bureau of Justice Statistics, 810 7th St. N.W., 2nd Floor, 20531; (202) 307-0765. Fax, (202) 307-5846. William J. Sabol, Director; Cara McCarthy, Public Affairs.*
General email, askbjs@usdoj.gov

Web, www.ojp.usdoj.gov/bjs

Collects, evaluates, publishes, and provides statistics on criminal justice. Data available from the National Criminal Justice Reference Service: P.O. Box 6000, Rockville, Md., 20849-6000; toll-free, (800) 851-3420; international callers, (301) 519-5500; TTY (877) 712-9279; and from the National Archive of Criminal Justice Data in Ann Arbor, Mich., (800) 999-0960.

Office of Justice Programs (OJP) *(Justice Dept.), National Institute of Justice,* 810 7th St. N.W., 7th Floor, 20531; (202) 307-2942. Fax, (202) 307-6394. Nancy Rodriguez, Director. Press, (202) 307-0703.
General email, ojp.ocom.@usdoj.gov
Web, www.nij.gov

Conducts research on all aspects of criminal justice, including crime prevention, enforcement, adjudication, and corrections; evaluates programs; develops model programs using new techniques. Serves as an affiliated institute of the United Nations Crime Prevention and Criminal Justice Programme (UNCPCJ); studies transnational issues. Maintains the National Criminal Justice Reference Service, which provides information on criminal justice, including activities of the Office of National Drug Control Policy and law enforcement in Latin America: (800) 851-3420 or (301) 519-5500; Web, www.ncjrs.gov.

►CONGRESS

For a listing of relevant congressional committees and subcommittees, please see pages 516–517 or the Appendix.

Library of Congress, *Law Library,* James Madison Memorial Bldg., 101 Independence Ave. S.E., #LM 240, 20540; (202) 707-5065. Fax, (202) 707-1820.
Roberta I. Shaffer, Law Librarian. Reading room, (202) 707-5080. Reference, (202) 707-5079.
Web, www.loc.gov/law, Twitter, @LawLibCongress and Facebook, www.facebook.com/lawlibraryofcongress

Maintains collections of foreign, international, and comparative law texts organized jurisdictionally by country. Covers all legal systems, including common, civil, Roman, canon, religious, and ancient and medieval law. Services include a public reading room; a microtext facility, with readers and printers for microfilm and microfiche; and foreign law/rare book reading areas. Staff of legal specialists is competent in approximately forty languages; does not provide advice on legal matters.

►JUDICIARY

Administrative Office of the U.S. Courts, 1 Columbus Circle N.E., 20544-0001; (202) 502-2600. James C. Duff, Director.
Web, www.uscourts.gov/adminoff.html

Supervises all administrative matters of the federal court system, except the Supreme Court; prepares statistical data and reports on the business of the courts, including reports on juror utilization; caseloads of federal, public, and community defenders; and types of cases adjudicated.

Administrative Office of the U.S. Courts, *Data and Analysis,* 1 Columbus Circle N.E., #2-250, 20544; (202) 502-3900. Fax, (202) 502-1411. Gary Yakimob, Chief. Press, (202) 502-2600.
Web, www.uscourts.gov

Compiles information and statistics from civil, criminal, appeals, and bankruptcy cases. Publishes statistical reports on court management; juror utilization; federal offenders; equal access to justice; the Financial Privacy Act; caseloads of federal, public, and community defenders; and types of cases adjudicated.

Supreme Court of the United States, *Library,* 1 1st St. N.E., 20543; (202) 479-3037. Fax, (202) 479-3477. Linda Maslow, Librarian, (202) 479-3000.
Web, www.supremecourtus.gov

Maintains collection of Supreme Court documents dating from the mid-1800s. Records, briefs, and depository documents available for public use.

►NONGOVERNMENTAL

Justice Research and Statistics Assn., 720 7th St. N.W., 3rd Floor, 20001; (202) 842-9330. Fax, (202) 448-1723. Jeffrey Sedgwick, Executive Director.
General email, cjinfo@jrsa.org
Web, www.jrsa.org

Provides information on the collection, analysis, dissemination, and use of data concerning crime and criminal justice at the state level; serves as liaison between the Justice Dept. Bureau of Justice Statistics and the states; develops standards for states on the collection, analysis, and use of statistics. Offers courses in criminal justice and in research and evaluation methodologies in conjunction with its annual conference.

PUBLIC INTEREST LAW

General

►AGENCIES

Justice Dept. (DOJ), *Access to Justice Initiative,* 950 Pennsylvania Ave. N.W., #3340, 20530; (202) 514-5312. Fax, (202) 514-5326. Bob Bullock, Senior Counselor.
Web, www.justice.gov/atj

Works to improve the availability and quality of legal defense for vulnerable populations, including immigrants, juveniles, the homeless, disabled veterans, and victims of domestic and sexual violence. Identifies areas of need and effective programs, and works collaboratively with local, state, tribal, and federal participants to implement solutions. Priorities include expanding community partnerships, promoting less court-intensive solutions, and increasing resources for defender programs.

Legal Services Corp., 3333 K St. N.W., 3rd Floor, 20007-3522; (202) 295-1500. Fax, (202) 337-6797.
James J. Sandman, President, (202) 295-1515. Public reading room, (202) 295-1502.
General email, rauscherc@lsc.gov
Web, www.lsc.gov and Twitter, @lsctweets

Independent federal corporation established by Congress. Awards grants to local agencies that provide the poor with legal services. Library open to the public by appointment only.

► CONGRESS

For a listing of relevant congressional committees and subcommittees, please see pages 516–517 or the Appendix.

► NONGOVERNMENTAL

Alliance for Justice, *11 Dupont Circle N.W., 2nd Floor, 20036-1213; (202) 822-6070. Fax, (202) 822-6068. Nan Aron, President.*
General email, alliance@afj.org
Web, www.afj.org

Membership: public interest lawyers and advocacy, environmental, civil rights, and consumer organizations. Promotes reform of the legal system to ensure access to the courts; monitors selection of federal judges; works to preserve the rights of nonprofit organizations to advocate on behalf of their constituents. Monitors candidates for vacancies in the federal judiciary; independently reviews nominees' records; maintains statistics on the judiciary.

American Bar Assn. (ABA), *Commission on Disability Rights, 1050 Connecticut Ave. N.W., #400, 20036; (202) 662-1570. Fax, (202) 442-3439. Mark D. Agrust, Chair; Amy L. Allbright, Director.*
General email, cdr@americanbar.org
Web, www.americanbar.org/disabilityrights

Promotes the rule of law for persons with mental, physical, and sensory disabilities and their full and equal participation in the legal profession. Offers online resources, publications, and continuing education opportunities on disability law topics and engages in national initiatives to remove barriers to the education, employment, and advancement of lawyers with disabilities.

Bazelon Center for Mental Health Law, *1101 15th St. N.W., #1212, 20005; (202) 467-5730. Fax, (202) 223-0409. Robert Bernstein, President.*
General email, communications@bazelon.org
Web, www.bazelon.org and Twitter, @BazelonCenter

Public interest law firm. Works to establish and advance the legal rights of children and adults with mental disabilities and ensure their equal access to services and resources needed for full participation in community life. Provides technical support to lawyers and other advocates. Conducts test case litigation to defend rights of persons with mental disabilities. Conducts policy analysis, builds coalitions, issues advocacy alerts, publishes handbooks, and maintains advocacy resources online. Monitors legislation and regulations.

Center for Law and Education, *7101 Holly Ave., Takoma Park, MD 20912-4225; (202) 986-3000. Fax, (202) 986-6648. Paul Weckstein, Co-Director, (202) 986-3000, ext. 101; Kathleen Boundy, Co-Director (located in Boston).*
General email, cle@cleweb.org
Web, www.cleweb.org

National advocacy organization committed to improving education of low-income students. Works with students, parents, their advocates, and members of the school community to implement and effectuate school and district level changes. Focuses on school and district reform and civil rights; uses multi-forum advocacy (legislative, administrative advocacy, and litigation, as needed) on behalf of low-income individuals. (Headquarters in Boston, Mass.)

Center for Law and Social Policy (CLASP), *1200 18th St. N.W., #200, 20036; (202) 906-8000. Fax, (202) 842-2885. Olivia Golden, Executive Director.*
General email, aparker@clasp.org
Web, www.clasp.org

Public policy organization with expertise in national, state, and local policy affecting low-income Americans. Seeks to improve the economic security and educational and workforce prospects of low-income children, youth, adults, and families.

Center for Study of Responsive Law, *1530 P St. N.W., 20005 (mailing address: P.O. Box 19367, Washington, DC 20036); (202) 387-8030. Fax, (202) 234-5176. John Richard, Administrator.*
General email, info@csrl.org
Web, www.csrl.org

Consumer interest clearinghouse that conducts research and holds conferences on public interest law. Interests include white-collar crime, the environment, occupational health and safety, the postal system, banking deregulation, insurance, freedom of information policy, and broadcasting.

Institute for Justice, *901 N. Glebe Rd., #900, Arlington, VA 22203; (703) 682-9320. Fax, (703) 682-9321. Scott Bullock, President.*
General email, general@ij.org
Web, www.ij.org

Sponsors seminars to train law students, grassroots activists, and practicing lawyers in applying advocacy strategies in public-interest litigation. Seeks to protect individuals from arbitrary government interference in free speech, private property rights, parental school choice, and economic liberty. Litigates cases.

Institute for Public Representation, *600 New Jersey Ave. N.W., #312, 20001; (202) 662-9535. Fax, (202) 662-9634. Hope Babcock, Co-Director; Angela Campbell, Co-Director; Michael Kirkpatrick, Co-Director.*
General email, gulcipr@law.georgetown.edu
Web, www.law.georgetown.edu/academics/academic-programs/clinical-programs/our-clinics/institute-for-public-representation.cfm
Blog, instituteforpublicrepresentation.org

Public interest law firm funded by Georgetown University Law Center that studies federal administrative law and federal court litigation. Interests include communications law, environmental protection, and disability rights.

Lawyers' Committee for Civil Rights Under Law, *1401 New York Ave. N.W., #400, 20005-2124; (202) 662-8600. Fax, (202) 783-0857. Kristen Clarke, Executive Director. Toll-free, (888) 299-5227.*
General email, info@lawyerscommittee.org
Web, www.lawyerscommittee.org, Twitter, @LawyersComm and Facebook, www.facebook.com/ lawyerscommittee

Provides minority groups and the poor with legal assistance in such areas as voting rights, employment discrimination, education, environment, and equal access to government services and benefits.

Migrant Legal Action Program, *1001 Connecticut Ave. N.W., #915, 20036-5524; (202) 775-7780. Fax, (202) 775-7784. Roger C. Rosenthal, Executive Director.*
General email, mlap@mlap.org
Web, www.mlap.org

Provides both direct representation to farm workers and technical assistance and support to health, education, and legal services programs for migrants. Monitors legislation and regulations.

National Assn. of Consumer Bankruptcy Attorneys, *2200 Pennsylvania Ave. N.W., 4th Floor, 20037; (800) 499-9040. Fax, (866) 408-9515. Maureen Thompson, Legislative Director; Dan Labert, Executive Director.*
General email, admin@nacba.org
Web, www.nacba.org

Advocates on behalf of consumer debtors and their attorneys. Files amicus briefs on behalf of parties in the U.S. courts of appeal and Supreme Court, and provides educational programs and workshops for attorneys. Monitors legislation and regulations.

National Consumer Law Center, *Washington Office, 1001 Connecticut Ave. N.W., #510, 20036-5528; (202) 452-6252. Fax, (202) 463-9462. Richard DuBois, Executive Director.*
General email, consumerlaw@nclc.org
Web, www.consumerlaw.org and www.nclc.org

Provides lawyers funded by the Legal Services Corp. with research and assistance; researches problems of low-income consumers and develops alternative solutions. (Headquarters in Boston, Mass.)

National Health Law Program, *Washington Office, 1444 Eye St. N.W., #1105, 20005; (202) 289-7661. Fax, (202) 289-7724. Elizabeth G. Taylor, Executive Director.*
General email, nhelpdc@healthlaw.org
Web, www.healthlaw.org

Organization of lawyers representing the economically disadvantaged and minorities. Offers technical assistance, workshops, seminars, and training for health law specialists. Issues include health care reform, Medicaid, child and adolescent health, and disability and reproductive rights.

National Law Center on Homelessness and Poverty, *2000 M St. N.W., #210, 20036; (202) 638-2535. Fax, (202) 628-2737. Maria Foscarinis, Executive Director.*
General email, email@nlchp.org
Web, www.nlchp.org

Legal advocacy group that works to prevent and end homelessness through impact litigation, legislation, and education. Conducts research on homelessness issues. Acts as a clearinghouse for legal information and technical assistance. Monitors legislation and regulations.

National Legal Aid and Defender Assn., *1901 Pennsylvania Ave. N.W., #500, 20006; (202) 452-0620. Fax, (202) 872-1031. Jo-Ann Wallace, President; Bill Wright, Communications.*
General email, info@nlada.org
Web, www.nlada.org

Membership: national organizations and individuals providing indigent clients, including prisoners, with legal aid and defender services. Serves as a clearinghouse for member organizations; provides training and support services.

Public Citizen, *Litigation Group, 1600 20th St. N.W., 20009-1001; (202) 588-1000. Allison Zieve, Director of Litigation. Press, (202) 588-7741.*
General email, litigation@citizen.org
Web, www.citizen.org/litigation

Conducts litigation for Public Citizen, a consumer advocacy group, in the areas of consumer rights, access to courts, health and safety, government and corporate accountability, and separation of powers; represents other individuals and nonprofit groups with similar interests.

Public Justice Foundation, *1825 K St. N.W., #200, 20006; (202) 797-8600. Fax, (202) 232-7203. F. Paul Bland Jr., Executive Director, ext. 223; Arthur H. Bryant, Chair.*
Web, www.publicjustice.net and Twitter, @Public_Justice

Membership: consumer activists, trial lawyers, public interest lawyers, and law professors and students. Litigates to influence corporate and government decisions about products or activities adversely affecting health or safety. Interests include toxic torts, environmental protection, civil rights and civil liberties, workers' safety, consumer protection, and the preservation of the civil justice system. (Formerly Trial Lawyers for Public Justice.)

14

Military Personnel and Veterans

GENERAL POLICY AND ANALYSIS

Basic Resources

▶AGENCIES

Air Force Dept. *(Defense Dept.), Force Management,* 1400 W. Perimeter Rd., #4710, Joint Base Andrews, 20762; (240) 612-4040. Fax, (703) 604-1657. Col. Jerry Diaz, Chief.
Web, www.afpc.af.mil

Military office that oversees Air Force retention policies for officers and enlisted personnel, and provides analytical support for personnel issues.

Air Force Dept. *(Defense Dept.), Manpower Personnel and Services,* 1040 Air Force Pentagon, #4E168, 20330-1040; (703) 697-6088. Lt. Gen. Gina M. Grosso, Deputy Chief of Staff.
Web, www.afpc.af.mil

Military office that coordinates military and civilian personnel policies of the Air Force Dept.

Army Dept. *(Defense Dept.), G-1,* 300 Army Pentagon, #2E446, 20310-0300; (703) 697-8060. Fax, (703) 695-1631. Lt. Gen. James (Jim) C. McConville, Deputy Chief of Staff, G-1.
Web, www.armyg1.army.mil

Military office that coordinates military and civilian personnel policies of the Army Dept.

Army Dept. *(Defense Dept.), Manpower and Reserve Affairs,* 111 Army Pentagon, #2E460, 20310-0111; (703) 697-9253. Fax, (703) 692-9000. Debra S. Wada, Assistant Secretary.
Web, www.asamra.army.mil

Civilian office that reviews policies and programs for Army personnel and reserves; makes recommendations to the secretary of the Army. Oversees training, military preparedness, and mobilization for all civilians and active and reserve members of the Army.

Army Dept. *(Defense Dept.), My Army Benefits,* 2530 Crystal Dr., #6000, Arlington, VA 22202; (703) 286-2560. Fax, (703) 601-0057. Brig. Gen. Henry L. Huntley, Director. Toll-free, (888) 721-2769.
General email, usarmy.pentagon.hqda-des-g1.mbx.help-my-army-benefits@mail.mil
Web, http://myarmybenefits.us.army.mil

Military office that provides Army benefits information.

Defense Dept. *(DoD), Community and Public Outreach,* 1400 Defense Pentagon, 2E984, 20301-1400; (703) 693-2337. Fax, (703) 697-2577. Bryan Whitman, Deputy Assistant Secretary, Acting. Toll-free (Military OneSource), (800) 342-9647. Public Affairs, (703) 697-5131.
Web, www.defense.gov

Administers Pentagon tours; hosts Joint Civilian Orientation Conference (JCOC), enabling senior American business, education, and community leaders to engage with military personnel; replies to inquiries from the general public; serves as primary liaison to national veterans and military organizations.

Defense Dept. *(DoD), Military Personnel Policy,* 4000 Defense Pentagon, #5A678, 20301-4000; (703) 571-0116. Fax, (703) 571-0120. Rear Adm. Anthony M. Kurta (USNR, Ret.), Deputy Assistant Secretary.
Web, www.defense.gov

Military office that coordinates military personnel policies of the Defense Dept. and reviews military personnel policies of the individual services.

Defense Dept. *(DoD), Personnel and Readiness,* 4000 Defense Pentagon, #3E986, 20301-4000; (703) 695-5254. Fax, (703) 571-5363. Vacant, Under Secretary.
Web, www.defense.gov

Coordinates civilian and military personnel policies of the Defense Dept. and reviews personnel policies of the individual services. Handles equal opportunity policies; serves as focal point for all readiness issues. Administers Military OneSource, a 24/7 toll-free information and referral telephone service for matters relating to education, financial aid, relocation, housing, child care, counseling, and other employee concerns. Military OneSource is available worldwide to military personnel and their families. Toll-free, (800) 342-9647; international, (800) 3429-6477; international collect, (484) 530-5908; www.militaryonesource.mil.

Defense Dept. *(DoD), Public Affairs,* The Pentagon, #2D961, 20301-1400; (703) 571-3343. Fax, (703) 697-3501. Peter Cook, Assistant Secretary, Acting, (703) 697-9312. Press, (703) 697-5131.
Web, www.defense.gov/news

Responds to public inquiries concering Defense Dept. mission, activities, policies, and personnel.

Marine Corps *(Defense Dept.), Human Resources and Organizational Management,* U.S. Marine Corps (HQMC), Code ARHM, 3000 Marine Corps Pentagon, #2C253, 20350-3000; (703) 614-8371. William I. Whaley, Director.
General email, hromdir@usmc.mil
Web, www.hqmc.marines.mil/hrom

Develops and implements personnel and equal employment opportunity programs to recruit, develop, and maintain the workforce at Marine Corps headquarters. Develops and implements personnel and equal employment opportunity programs for civilian employees of the Marine Corps headquarters.

Marine Corps *(Defense Dept.), Manpower and Reserve Affairs,* James Wesley Marsh Center, 3280 Russell Rd., Bldg. 3280, Quantico, VA 22134; (703) 784-9007. Lt. Gen. Mark A. Brilakis (USMC), Deputy Commandant.
Web, www.manpower.usmc.mil

Oversees planning, directing, coordinating, and supervising of both active and reserve Marine Corps forces.

Navy Dept. *(Defense Dept.), Military Personnel, Plans, and Policy,* 701 S. Courthouse Rd., Arlington, VA 22204;

MILITARY PERSONNEL AND VETERANS RESOURCES IN CONGRESS

For a complete listing of congressional committees, including their full contact information, leadership, membership, and jurisdictions, please refer to the Appendix on pages 779–896.

HOUSE:

House Appropriations Committee, (202) 225-2771.
Web, appropriations.house.gov
    Subcommittee on Defense, (202) 225-2847.
    Subcommittee on Military Construction,
        Veterans Affairs, and Related Agencies,
        (202) 225-3047.
House Armed Services Committee, (202) 225-4151.
Web, armedservices.house.gov
    Subcommittee on Emerging Threats and
        Capabilities, (202) 226-2843.
    Subcommittee on Military Personnel,
        (202) 225-7560.
    Subcommittee on Oversight and Investigations,
        (202) 226-5048.
    Subcommittee on Readiness, (202) 226-8979.
    Subcommittee on Seapower and Protection
        Forces, (202) 226-8979.
    Subcommittee on Strategic Forces,
        (202) 225-1967.
    Subcommittee on Tactical Air and Land Forces,
        (202) 225-4440.
House Financial Services Committee, (202) 225-7502.
Web, financialservices.house.gov
    Subcommittee on Financial Institutions and
        Consumer Credit, (202) 225-7502.
    Subcommittee on Housing and Insurance,
        (202) 225-7502.
    Subcommittee on Oversight and Investigations,
        (202) 225-7502.
House Foreign Affairs Committee,
    (202) 225-5021.
Web, foreignaffairs.house.gov
House Oversight and Government Reform
    Committee, (202) 225-5074.
Web, oversight.house.gov
    Subcommittee on National Security,
        (202) 225-5074.
House Transportation and Infrastructure
    Committee, (202) 225-9446.
Web, transportation.house.gov
    Subcommittee on Coast Guard and Maritime
        Transportation, (202) 226-3552.

House Veterans' Affairs Committee,
    (202) 225-3527.
Web, veterans.house.gov
    Subcommittee on Disability Assistance and
        Memorial Affairs, (202) 225-9164.
    Subcommittee on Economic Opportunity,
        (202) 226-5491.
    Subcommittee on Health, (202) 225-9154.
    Subcommittee on Oversight and Investigations,
        (202) 225-3569.

SENATE:

Senate Appropriations Committee, (202) 224-7363.
Web, appropriations.senate.gov
    Subcommittee on Defense, (202) 224-6688.
    Subcommittee on Military Construction,
        Veterans Affairs, and Related Agencies,
        (202) 224-8224.
Senate Armed Services Committee,
    (202) 224-3871.
Web, armed-services.senate.gov
    Subcommittee on Airland, (202) 224-3871.
    Subcommittee on Emerging Threats and
        Capabilities, (202) 224-3871.
    Subcommittee on Personnel, (202) 224-3871.
    Subcommittee on Readiness and Management
        Support, (202) 224-3871.
    Subcommittee on Seapower, (202) 224-3871.
    Subcommittee on Strategic Forces,
        (202) 224-3871.
Senate Banking, Housing, and Urban Affairs
    Committee, (202) 224-7391.
Web, banking.senate.gov
    Subcommittee on Financial Institutions and
        Consumer Protection, (202) 224-2315.
Senate Foreign Relations Committee, (202) 224-4651.
Web, foreign.senate.gov
Senate Homeland Security and Governmental Affairs
    Committee, (202) 224-2627.
Web, hsgac.senate.gov
Senate Veterans' Affairs Committee,
    (202) 224-9126.
Web, veterans.senate.gov

---

(703) 604-6155. Fax, (703) 604-5943. Rear Adm. Robert (Fritz) Burke, Director.
Web, www.navy.mil

Military office that coordinates naval personnel policies, including promotions, professional development, and compensation, for officers and enlisted personnel.

Navy Dept. *(Defense Dept.), Naval Personnel, 701 S. Courthouse Rd., Arlington, VA 22204; (703) 604-2863.*

Fax, (703) 604-5942. Vice Adm. William F. Moran, Chief. Toll-free, (866) 827-5672. TTY, (866) 297-1971.
General email, UASKPC@navy.mil

Web, www.navy.mil/cno

Responsible for planning and programming of manpower and personnel resources, budgeting for Navy personnel, developing systems to manage total force manpower and personnel resources, and assignment of Navy personnel. (Office based in Millington, Tenn.)

Noncommissioned Officers Assn., *National Capital Office,* P.O. Box 3085, Oakton, VA 22124; (703) 549-0311. Fax, (703) 549-0245. H. Gene Overstreet, President; Jon Ostrowski, Executive Director for Government Affairs. Toll-free, (800) 662-2620.
General email, jostrowski@ncoadc.org

Web, www.ncoausa.org

Congressionally chartered fraternal organization of active duty, reserve, guard, and retired enlisted military personnel. Sponsors job fairs to assist members in finding employment. (Headquarters in Selma, Tex.)

U.S. Coast Guard (USCG) *(Homeland Security Dept.),* **Human Resources Directorate,** CG-1, MS 7907, 2703 Martin Luther King Jr. Ave. S.E., 20593; (202) 475-5000. Rear Adm. Cari B. Thomas, Assistant Commandant.
Web, www.uscg.mil/hr

Responsible for hiring, recruiting, and training all military and nonmilitary Coast Guard personnel. Administers employee benefits.

▶CONGRESS

For a listing of relevant congressional committees and subcommittees, please see page 565 or the Appendix.

▶NONGOVERNMENTAL

Air Force Assn., 1501 Lee Hwy., Arlington, VA 22209-1198; (703) 247-5800. Fax, (703) 247-5853. Larry O. Spencer, President. Toll-free, (800) 727-3337. Press, (703) 247-5850.
General email, membership@afa.org

Web, www.afa.org

Membership: civilians and active duty, reserve, retired, and cadet personnel of the Air Force. Informs members and the public of developments in the aerospace field. Monitors legislation and Defense Dept. policies. Library on aviation history open to the public by appointment.

Air Force Sergeants Assn., 5211 Auth Rd., Suitland, MD 20746; (301) 899-3500. Fax, (301) 899-8136. Robert L. Frank, Chief Executive Officer. Toll-free, (800) 638-0594.
General email, staff@hqafsa.org

Web, www.hqafsa.org

Membership: active duty, reserve, National Guard, and retired enlisted Air Force personnel. Monitors and advocates legislation and policies that promote quality of life benefits for its members.

The Enlisted Assn., *Washington Office,* 1001 N. Fairfax St., #102, Alexandria, VA 22314; (703) 684-1981. Fax, (703) 548-4876. Deirdre Parke Holleman, Executive Director. Toll-free, (800) 554-8732. VA caregiver support, (855) 260-3274.
General email, treadmin@treadc.org

Web, www.trea.org

Membership: enlisted personnel of the armed forces, including active duty, reserve, guard, and retirees. Runs scholarship, legislative, and veterans service programs. (Also known as Retired Enlisted Assn., Headquarters in Aurora, Colo.)

Fleet Reserve Assn. (FRA), 125 N. West St., Alexandria, VA 22314-2754; (703) 683-1400. Fax, (703) 549-6610. Thomas J. Snee, National Executive Director, (703) 683-1400, ext. 101. Membership/Customer service, (800) 372-1924.
General email, news-fra@fra.org

Web, www.fra.org and Twitter, @FRAHQ

Membership: current and former enlisted members of the Navy, Marine Corps, and Coast Guard. Interests include health care, pay, benefits, and quality-of-life programs for sea services personnel. Recognized by the Veterans Affairs Dept. to assist veterans and widows of veterans with benefit claims. Monitors legislation and regulations.

Marine Corps League, 8626 Lee Hwy., #201, Fairfax, VA 22031-3070 (mailing address: P.O. Box 3070, Merrifield, VA 22116); (703) 207-9588. Fax, (703) 207-0047. Thomas W. Hazlett Sr., Executive Director, Acting. Toll-free, (800) 625-1775.
Web, www.mclnational.org

Membership: active duty, retired, and reserve Marine Corps groups. Promotes the interests of the Marine Corps and works to preserve its traditions; assists veterans and their survivors. Monitors legislation and regulations.

Military Order of the World Wars, 435 N. Lee St., Alexandria, VA 22314-2301; (703) 683-4911. Fax, (703) 683-4501. Brig. Gen. Arthur B. Morrill III (USAF, Ret.), Chief of Staff. Toll-free, (877) 320-3774.
General email, chiefofstaff@moww.org

Web, www.moww.org

Membership: retired and active duty commissioned officers, warrant officers, and flight officers. Supports a strong national defense; supports patriotic education in schools; presents awards to outstanding Junior and Senior Reserve Officers Training Corps (ROTC) cadets, Boy Scouts, and Girl Scouts.

National Assn. for Uniformed Services, 5535 Hempstead Way, Springfield, VA 22151-4094; (703) 750-1342. Fax, (703) 354-4380. Maj. Gen. Thomas L. Wilkerson (USMC, Ret.), President. Information, (800) 842-3451.
General email, naus@naus.org

Web, www.naus.org

Membership: active duty, reserve, and retired officers and enlisted personnel of all uniformed services and their families and survivors. Interests include benefits of military retirees, veterans, active duty military families, and survivors. Monitors legislation and regulations. (Affiliated with the Society of Military Widows.)

Navy League of the United States, 2300 Wilson Blvd., #200, Arlington, VA 22201-5424; (703) 528-1775. Fax, (703) 528-2333. Bruce K. Butler, National Executive Director. Toll-free, (800) 356-5760.
General email, service@navyleague.org

Web, www.navyleague.org

Membership: retired and reserve military personnel and civilians interested in the U.S. Navy, Marine Corps, Coast Guard, and Merchant Marine. Distributes literature, provides speakers, and conducts seminars to promote interests of the sea services. Monitors legislation.

U.S. Army Warrant Officers Assn., *462 Herndon Pkwy., #207, Herndon, VA 20170-5235; (703) 742-7727. Fax, (703) 742-7728. Jack DuTeil, Executive Director. Toll-free, (800) 587-2962.*
General email, usawoaed@verizon.net
Web, www.usawoa.org

Membership: active duty, guard, reserve, and retired and former warrant officers. Monitors and makes recommendations to Defense Dept., Army Dept., and Congress on policies and programs affecting Army warrant officers and their families. Provides professional development programs for members.

United Service Organizations (USO), *2111 Wilson Blvd., #1200, Arlington, VA 22201 (mailing address: P.O. Box 96860, Washington, DC 20077); (703) 908-6400. Fax, (703) 908-6402. J.D. Crouch II, President. Toll-free, (888) 484-3876.*
Web, www.uso.org and Twitter, @the_USO

Voluntary civilian organization chartered by Congress. Provides military personnel and their families in the United States and overseas with social, educational, and recreational programs.

DEFENSE PERSONNEL

Chaplains

▶AGENCIES

Air Force Dept. *(Defense Dept.), Chief of Chaplains, 1380 Air Force Pentagon, 20330; (571) 256-7729. Fax, (571) 256-7642. Maj. Gen. Dondi E. Costin, Chief of Chaplains.*
General email, usaf.pentagon.af.hc.mbx.workflow@mail.mil
Web, www.chaplaincorps.af.mil

Oversees chaplains and religious services within the Air Force; maintains liaison with religious denominations.

Army Dept. *(Defense Dept.), Chief of Chaplains, 2700 Army Pentagon, #3E524, 20310-2700; (703) 695-1133. Fax, (703) 695-9834. Maj. Gen. Paul Hurley (USA), Chief of Chaplains.*
Web, www.chapnet.chaplaincorps.net

Oversees chaplains and religious services within the Army; maintains liaison with religious denominations.

Defense Dept. (DoD), *Armed Forces Chaplains Board, OUSD (P&R) MPP-AFCB, 4000 Defense Pentagon, #2E341, 20301-4000; (703) 697-9015. Fax, (703) 693-2280. Rear Adm. Margaret Kibben (USN), Chair; Capt. Jerome Hinson (USN), Executive Director.*
General email, osd.afcb5120@mail.mil
Web, http://prhome.defense.gov/MRA/MPP/AFCB

Membership: chiefs and deputy chiefs of chaplains of the armed services; works to coordinate religious policies and services among the military branches.

Marine Corps *(Defense Dept.), Chaplain, 3000 Navy Pentagon, 20350; (703) 614-4627. Fax, (703) 695-3431. Rear Adm. Brent W. Scott (USN), Chaplain.*
Web, www.hqmc.marines.mil/Agencies/HeadquartersandServiceBattalion/chaplainoffice.aspx

Oversees chaplains and religious services within the Marine Corps; maintains liaison with religious denominations.

National Guard Bureau *(Defense Dept.), Chaplain Services, 111 S. George Mason Dr., Arlington, VA 22204; (703) 607-8657. Fax, (703) 607-5295. Brig. Gen. David E. Graetz (CHC, USA), Director.*
Web, www.nationalguard.mil

Represents the Chief National Guard Bureau on all aspects of the chaplains' mission. Directs and oversees the activities and policies of the National Guard Chaplain Services. Oversees chaplains and religious services within the National Guard; maintains liaison with religious denominations.

Navy Dept. *(Defense Dept.), Chief of Chaplains, 2000 Navy Pentagon, #5E270, 20350-1000; (703) 614-4043. Fax, (703) 695-8523. Rear Adm. Margaret Grun Kibben, Chief.*
Web, www.navy.mil/local/crb and www.navy.mil/local/chaplaincorps

Oversees chaplains and religious services within the Navy; maintains liaison with religious denominations.

U.S. Coast Guard (USCG) *(Homeland Security Dept.), Chaplain, CG-00A, 2703 Martin Luther King Jr. Ave. S.E., 20593; (202) 372-4434. Fax, (202) 372-8305. Capt. Gregory N. Todd, Chaplain.*
General email, HQS-PF-fldr-CG-00A-ChaplainOffice@uscg.mil
Web, www.uscg.mil/hq/chaplain

Oversees chaplains and religious services within the Coast Guard; maintains liaison with religious denominations.

▶NONGOVERNMENTAL

Chaplain Alliance for Religious Liberty, *P.O. Box 151353, Alexandria, VA 22315; (571) 293-2427. Fax, (910) 221-2226. Col. Ron Crews (USAR, Ret.), Executive Director; Brig. Gen. Doug Lee (USAR, Ret.), President.*
General email, info@chaplainalliance.org
Web, http://chaplainalliance.org

Membership: military chaplains and others who support orthodox Christian doctrines. Seeks to ensure that all chaplains and those they serve may exercise their religious liberties without fear of reprisal. Interests include the conflict between official protection for gays in the military and orthodox Christian teachings. Issues press releases; grants media interviews; monitors legislation and regulations.

Military Chaplains Assn. of the United States of America, *5541 Lee Hwy., Arlington, VA 22207-7056 (mailing address: P.O. Box 7056, Arlington, VA*

22207-7056); (703) 533-5890. Capt. Lyman Smith (USN, Ret.), Executive Director.

General email, chaplains@mca-usa.org

Web, www.mca-usa.org

Membership: chaplains of all faiths in all branches of the armed services and chaplains of veterans affairs and civil air patrol. Provides training opportunities for chaplains and a referral service concerning chaplains and chaplaincy.

National Conference on Ministry to the Armed Forces, P.O. Box 7572, Arlington, VA 22207-9998; (703) 608-2100. Harold Robinson, Chair; Capt. John (Jack) H. Lea III (CHC, USN, Ret.), Executive Director.

General email, info@ncmaf.com

Web, www.ncmaf.com

Connects over 200 denominations and faith groups with the armed forces and Veterans Affairs chaplaincies.

Civilian Employees

►AGENCIES

Air Force Dept. (Defense Dept.), Civilian Force Policy, 1400 W. Perimeter Rd., #4770, Joint Base Andrews, 20762; (240) 612-4022. Dana Crowe, Chief.

Web, www.afpc.af.mil/main/welcome.asp

Civilian office that monitors and reviews Air Force policies, benefits and entitlements, civilian pay, career programs, and external and internal placement of staff.

Air Force Dept. (Defense Dept.), Personnel Policy, 1040 Air Force Pentagon, #4D950, 20330-1040; (703) 695-6770. John W. Snodgrass, Executive Director.

Web, www.afpc.af.mil

Implements and evaluates Air Force civilian personnel policies; serves as the principal adviser to the Air Force personnel director on civilian personnel matters and programs.

Army Dept. (Defense Dept.), Diversity and Leadership, 111 Army Pentagon, #2A332, 20310-0111; (703) 614-5284. Fax, (703) 614-5279. Vacant, Deputy Assistant Secretary; Evonne Fields, Executive Assistant, (703) 614-5332.

Web, www.asamra.army.mil/org_diversity.cfm

Civilian office that administers equal employment opportunity and civil rights programs and policies for civilian employees of the Army.

Defense Dept. (DoD), Staffing and Civilian Transition Programs, 4800 Mark Center Dr., #05F16, SCTP Division, Alexandria, VA 22350-1100; (571) 372-1528. Fax, (571) 372-1704. William Mann, Chief of Staff.

Web, www.cpms.osd.mil

Manages workforce restructuring programs for Defense Dept. civilians, including downsizing, placement, voluntary early retirement, and transition assistance programs.

Marine Corps (Defense Dept.), Human Resources and Organizational Management, U.S. Marine Corps (HQMC), Code ARHM, 3000 Marine Corps Pentagon,

#2C253, 20350-3000; (703) 614-8371. William I. Whaley, Director.

General email, hromdir@usmc.mil

Web, www.hqmc.marines.mil/hrom

Develops and implements personnel and equal employment opportunity programs to recruit, develop, and maintain the workforce at Marine Corps headquarters. Develops and implements personnel and equal employment opportunity programs for civilian employees of the Marine Corps headquarters.

Navy Dept. (Defense Dept.), Civilian Human Resources, 614 Sicard St. S.E., #100, 20374-5072; (703) 695-2633. Patricia C. Adams, Deputy Assistant Secretary. Toll-free, (800) 378-4559.

General email, donhrfaq@navy.mil

Web, www.donhr.navy.mil

Civilian office that develops and reviews Navy and Marine Corps civilian personnel and equal opportunity programs and policies.

U.S. Coast Guard (USCG) (Homeland Security Dept.), Civil Rights Directorate, Commandant, CG-00H, 2703 Martin Luther King Jr. Ave. S.E., MS 700, 20593-7000; (202) 372-4500. Terri A. Dickerson, Director.

General email, OCR@uscg.mil

Web, www.uscg.mil/hq/cg00/cg00h

Manages military and civilian internal equal employment opportunity programs.

U.S. Coast Guard (USCG) (Homeland Security Dept.), Human Resources Directorate, CG-1, MS 7907, 2703 Martin Luther King Jr. Ave. S.E., 20593; (202) 475-5000. Rear Adm. Cari B. Thomas, Assistant Commandant.

Web, www.uscg.mil/hr

Responsible for hiring, recruiting, and training all military and nonmilitary Coast Guard personnel. Administers employee benefits.

Equal Opportunity

►AGENCIES

Air Force Dept. (Defense Dept.), Equal Opportunity, 1602 California Ave., #217, Joint Base Andrews, NAF, MD 20762; (240) 612-4006. James Carlock, Program Director. Equal opportunity hotline, (800) 371-0617.

Web, www.afpc.af.mil

Office that develops and administers Air Force equal opportunity programs and policies.

Army Dept. (Defense Dept.), Diversity and Leadership, 111 Army Pentagon, #2A332, 20310-0111; (703) 614-5284. Fax, (703) 614-5279. Vacant, Deputy Assistant Secretary; Evonne Fields, Executive Assistant, (703) 614-5332.

Web, www.asamra.army.mil/org_diversity.cfm

Develops policy and conducts program reviews for the Dept. of Army Civilian Equal Employment Opportunity and Affirmative Employment Programs.

Defense Dept. (DoD), *Defense Advisory Committee on Women in the Services,* 4800 Mark Center Dr., #04J25-01, Alexandria, VA 22350-9000; (703) 697-2122. Fax, (703) 614-6233. Col. Aimee L. Kominiak (USA), Military Director.
General email, osd.pentagon.ousd-p-r.mbx.dacowits@mail.mil

Web, http://dacowits.defense.gov

Provides the DoD with advice and recommendations on matters and policies relating to the recruitment and retention, treatment, employment, integration, and well-being of highly qualified professional women in the armed forces.

Defense Dept. (DoD), *Diversity Management and Equal Opportunity,* 4000 Defense Pentagon, #5D641, 20301-4000; (703) 571-9321. Fax, (703) 571-9338. Clarence A. Johnson, Director.
Web, http://diversity.defense.gov

Formulates equal employment opportunity policy for the Defense Dept. Evaluates civil rights complaints from military personnel, including issues of sexual harassment and recruitment.

Marine Corps *(Defense Dept.),* *Equal Opportunity and Diversity Management,* HQUSMC, MNRA (MPE), 3280 Russell Rd., Quantico, VA 22134-5103; (703) 784-9371. Fax, (703) 784-9814. Alfrita Jones, Deputy.
Web, www.marines.mil

Military office that develops, monitors, and administers Marine Corps equal opportunity and diversity programs.

Navy Dept. *(Defense Dept.),* *Diversity and Inclusion,* 701 S. Courthouse Rd., #3R180, Arlington, VA 22204; (703) 604-5004. Fax, (703) 604-5943. Capt. Candace Eckert (USN), Special Assistant to Chief of Naval Personnel; Jessica Milam, Director, Women's Policy.
Web, www.public.navy.mil/bupers-npc/support/diversity

Military office that develops and administers Navy diversity programs and policies.

U.S. Coast Guard (USCG) *(Homeland Security Dept.),* *Civil Rights Directorate,* Commandant, CG-00H, 2703 Martin Luther King Jr. Ave. S.E., MS 700, 20593-7000; (202) 372-4500. Terri A. Dickerson, Director.
General email, OCR@uscg.mil

Web, www.uscg.mil/hq/cg00/cg00h

Administers equal opportunity regulations for Coast Guard military personnel.

▶NONGOVERNMENTAL

Human Rights Campaign (HRC), 1640 Rhode Island Ave. N.W., 20036; (202) 216-1500. Fax, (202) 347-5323. Chad Griffin, President. Toll-free, (800) 777-4723. TTY, (202) 216-1572.
General email, hrc@hrc.org

Web, www.hrc.org

Promotes legislation affirming the rights of lesbian, gay, bisexual, and transgender people. Focus includes discrimination in the military.

Minerva Center, 20 Granada Rd., Pasadena, MD 21122-2708; (410) 437-5379. Linda Grant DePauw, Director.
General email, lgdepauw@gmail.com

Web, www.minervacenter.com

Encourages the study of women in war and women and the military. Focus includes current U.S. servicewomen, women veterans, women in war and the military abroad, and the preservation of artifacts, oral history, and first-hand accounts of women's experience in military service.

Family Services

▶AGENCIES

Air Force Dept. *(Defense Dept.),* *Manpower Personnel and Services,* 1040 Air Force Pentagon, #4E168, 20330-1040; (703) 697-6088. Lt. Gen. Gina M. Grosso, Deputy Chief of Staff.
Web, www.afpc.af.mil

Military office that responds to inquiries concerning deceased Air Force personnel and their beneficiaries; refers inquiries to the Military Personnel Center at Randolph Air Force Base in San Antonio, Texas.

Air Force Dept. *(Defense Dept.),* *Military and Family Support Center,* 1191 Menoher Dr., Andrews AFB, MD 20762; (301) 981-7087. Fax, (301) 981-9215. Jamie-Lynn Smith, Chief.
Web, www.andrewsfss.com

Military policy office that monitors and reviews services provided to Air Force families and civilian employees with family concerns; oversees Airmen and Family Readiness Centers.

Defense Dept. (DoD), *Education Activity,* 4800 Mark Center Dr., Alexandria, VA 22350-1400; (571) 372-0590. Fax, (571) 372-5829. Thomas M. Brady, Director.
General email, dodea.director@hq.dodea.edu

Web, www.dodea.edu

Civilian office that maintains school system for dependents of all military personnel and eligible civilians in the United States and abroad. Develops uniform curriculum and educational standards; monitors student performance and school accreditation.

Defense Dept. (DoD), *Resources and Oversight,* 4000 Defense Pentagon, #2E319, 20301-4000; (703) 571-2373. Carolee Van Horn, Director.
Web, www.defense.gov

Coordinates policies related to quality of life of military personnel and their families.

Marine Corps *(Defense Dept.),* *Casualty Assistance Section,* HQUSMC, 2008 Elliott Rd., Quantico, VA 22134-5102; (703) 784-9512. Fax, (703) 784-4134. Gerald Castle,

Head; Cindy Grubb, Head of Case Management.
Toll-free, (800) 847-1597.
General email, casualty.section@usmc.mil
Web, www.mcieast.marines.mil/staffoffices/adjutant/
casualtyassistanceprogram.aspx

Confirms beneficiaries of deceased Marine Corps personnel for benefits distribution.

Marine Corps *(Defense Dept.)*, **Marine and Family Programs,** *HQUSMC, M and RA (MF), 3280 Russell Rd., Quantico, VA 22134-5103; (703) 784-9501. Fax, (703) 432-9269. Maj. Gen. Burke W. Whitman (USMC), Director.*
Web, www.usmc-mccs.org

Sponsors family service centers located on major Marine Corps installations. Oversees the administration of policies affecting the quality of life of Marine Corps military families. Administers relocation assistance programs.

Navy Dept. *(Defense Dept.)*, **Personnel Readiness and Community Support,** *701 S. Courthouse Rd., Arlington, VA 22204; (703) 604-5045. John McCloud, Liaison.*
Web, www.npc.navy.mil

Acts as liaison between D.C. area and Navy quality of life programs located in Tenn., which provide naval personnel and families being sent overseas with information and support; addresses problems of abuse and sexual assault within families; helps Navy spouses find employment; facilitates communication between Navy families and Navy officials; and assists in relocating Navy families during transition from military to civilian life.

U.S. Coast Guard (USCG) *(Homeland Security Dept.)*, **Health, Safety, and Work-Life,** *CG-11, 2703 Martin Luther King Jr. Ave. S.E., 20593; (202) 475-5130. Fax, (202) 475-5906. Rear Adm. Erica Schwartz, Director.*
General email, germaine.y.jefferson@uscg.mil
Web, www.uscg.mil/hq/cg1/cg11/default.asp

Oversees all health, safety, and work-life aspects of the Coast Guard, including individual and family support programs.

▶CONGRESS

For a listing of relevant congressional committees and subcommittees, please see page 565 or the Appendix.

▶NONGOVERNMENTAL

Air Force Aid Society Inc., *241 18th St. South, #202, Arlington, VA 22202-3409; (703) 972-2650. Fax, (703) 607-3022. Lt. Gen. John D. Hopper Jr., Chief Executive Officer. Toll-free, (800) 769-8951.*
General email, afas-hq@afas.org
Web, www.afas.org

Membership: Air Force active duty, reserve, and retired military personnel and their dependents. Provides active duty and retired Air Force military personnel with personal emergency loans for basic needs, travel, or dependents' health expenses; assists families of active duty, deceased,

or retired Air Force personnel with postsecondary education grants.

American Red Cross, *Service to the Armed Forces, 2025 E St. N.W., 2nd Floor, 20006-5009; (202) 303-5000, ext. 2. Fax, (202) 303-0216. Sherri L. Brown, Senior Vice President, (202) 303-8283. Emergency communication services, (888) 443-5722.*
Web, www.redcross.org

Provides emergency services for active duty armed forces personnel and their families, including verified communications, financial assistance, information and referral, and counseling. Mandated by Congress to contact military personnel in family emergencies; provides military personnel with verification of family situations for emergency leave applications.

Armed Forces Hostess Assn., *6604 Army Pentagon, #2E1087, 20310-6604; (703) 614-0350. Fax, (703) 697-5542. Elaine Freeman, President. Alternate phone, (703) 614-0485.*
General email, usarmy.pentagon.hqda-sptsvcs.mbx
.afha@mail.mil
Web, https://sswafha.hqda.pentagon.mil/Home.aspx

Volunteer office staffed by retirees and spouses of military personnel of all armed services. Serves as an information clearinghouse for military and civilian Defense Dept. families; maintains information on military bases in the United States and abroad; issues information handbook for families in the Washington area.

Army Distaff Foundation (Knollwood), *6200 Oregon Ave. N.W., 20015-1543; (202) 541-0400. Fax, (202) 364-2856. Maj. Gen. Stephen T. Rippe (USA, Ret.), Chief Executive Officer. Information, (800) 541-4255. Admission, (202) 541-0149.*
General email, dschrag@armydistaff.org
Web, www.armydistaff.org

Nonprofit continuing care retirement community for career military officers and their families. Provides retirement housing and health care services.

Army Emergency Relief, *200 Stovall St., #5S33, Alexandria, VA 22332; (703) 428-0000. Fax, (703) 325-7183. Lt. Gen. Robert F. Foley (USA, Ret.), Executive Director. Toll-free, (866) 878-6378.*
General email, aer@aerhq.org
Web, www.aerhq.org, Twitter, @aerhq and Facebook, www.facebook.com/AERHQ

Provides emergency financial assistance to retirees and to soldiers and family members of the U.S. Army, Army Reserves, and National Guard who are on extended active duty; provides scholarships to further the education of service members' spouses and dependents.

EX-POSE: Ex-Partners of Servicemembers for Equality, *P.O. Box 11191, Alexandria, VA 22312-0191; (703) 941-5844. Fax, (703) 212-6951. Nancy Davis, Manager.*
General email, ex-pose@juno.com
Web, www.ex-pose.org

Membership: military members, retirees, current/former spouses and their children. Educates military couples going through divorce. Provides explanation of possible legal interests and legal entitlements depending on the length of marriage. Open Tuesday and Wednesday, 10:00 a.m.–3:00 p.m.

Federal Education Assn., *1201 16th St. N.W., #117, 20036; (202) 822-7850. Fax, (202) 822-7867. Chuck McCarter, President. General email, fea@feaonline.org*

Web, www.feaonline.org

Membership: teachers and personnel of Defense Dept. schools for military dependents in the United States and abroad. Helps members negotiate pay, benefits, and better working conditions. Provides professional development through workshops and publications. Monitors legislation and regulations.

Fisher House Foundation, *111 Rockville Pike, #420, Rockville, MD 20850; (301) 294-8560. Fax, (301) 294-8562. David A. Coker, President. Toll-free, (888) 294-8560. General email, info@fisherhouse.org*

Web, www.fisherhouse.org and Twitter, @FisherHouseFdtn

Builds new houses on the grounds of major military and VA hospitals to enable families of hospitalized service members to stay within walking distance. Donates the Fisher Houses to the U.S. government. Administers the Hero Miles Program, which uses donated frequent flier miles to purchase airline tickets for hospitalized service members and their families. Provides scholarships for military children.

Freedom Alliance, *22570 Markey Court, #240, Dulles, VA 20166; (703) 444-7940. Fax, (703) 444-9893. Tom Kilgannon, President. Toll-free, (800) 475-6620. General email, info@freedomalliance.org*

Web, www.freedomalliance.org and Twitter, @FreedomAlliance

Promotes strong national defense and honors military service. Awards monetary grants to wounded troops; assists soldiers and their families with housing and travel expenses; provides active duty troops with meals, clothing, entertainment, and other comforts. Provides college scholarships to children of those killed or permanently disabled in an operations mission or training accident.

National Military Family Assn., *3601 Eisenhower Ave., #425, Alexandria, VA 22304; (703) 931-6632. Fax, (703) 931-4600. Gail McGinn, Chair; Joyce Raezer, Executive Director. General email, info@militaryfamily.org*

Web, www.militaryfamily.org

Membership: active duty and retired military, National Guard, and reserve personnel of all U.S. uniformed services, civilian personnel, families, and other interested individuals. Works to improve the quality of life for military families.

Naval Services FamilyLine, *1043 Harwood St. S.E., #100, Bldg. 154, Washington Navy Yard, DC, 20374-5067; (202)* 433-2333. *Fax, (202) 433-4622. Beth Mulloy, Chair. Toll-free, (877) 673-7773. General email, info@nsfamilyline.org*

Web, www.nsfamilyline.org

Offers support services to spouses of Navy personnel; disseminates information on all aspects of military life; fosters sense of community among sea service personnel and their families.

Navy–Marine Corps Relief Society, *875 N. Randolph St., #225, Arlington, VA 22203-1977; (703) 696-4904. Adm. Charles (Steve) S. Abbot, President. Toll-free, (800) 654-8364. General email, communications@nmcrs.org*

Web, www.nmcrs.org

Assists active duty and retired Navy and Marine Corps personnel and their families in times of need. Disburses interest-free loans and grants. Provides educational scholarships and loans; visiting nurse services; and other services, including combat casualty assistance, thrift shops, budget counseling, and volunteer training.

Our Military Kids, Inc., *6861 Elm St., #2-A, McLean, VA 22101; (703) 734-6654. Fax, (703) 734-6503. Linda Davidson, Executive Director. Toll-free, (866) 691-6654. General email, omkinquiry@ourmilitarykids.org*

Web, www.ourmilitarykids.org

Provides grants for extracurricular activities for school-aged children of deployed and severely injured soldiers, including Reserve and National Guard military personnel.

Financial Services

▶AGENCIES

Air Force Dept. *(Defense Dept.),* **Financial Management and Comptroller,** *1130 Air Force Pentagon, #4E978, 20330-1130; (703) 697-1974. Fax, (703) 695-8144. Lisa S. Disbrow, Assistant Secretary. Web, www.saffm.hq.af.mil*

Advises the secretary of the Air Force on policies relating to financial services for military and civilian personnel.

Defense Dept. (DoD), *Accounting and Finance Policy Analysis, 1100 Defense Pentagon, #3D150, 20301-1100; (703) 571-1396. Donjette Gilmore, Director. Web, www.defense.gov*

Develops accounting policy for the Defense Dept. federal management regulation.

▶CONGRESS

For a listing of relevant congressional committees and subcommittees, please see page 565 or the Appendix.

▶NONGOVERNMENTAL

Armed Forces Benefit Assn., *909 N. Washington St., Alexandria, VA 22314; (703) 549-4455. Fax, (703) 706-5961. Gen. Ralph (Ed) E. Eberhart (USAF, Ret.), President. Toll-free, (800) 776-2322.*

General email, info@afba.com

Web, www.afba.com and *Twitter, @AFBAbenefits*

Membership: active duty and retired personnel of the uniformed services, federal civilian employees, government contractors, first responders, and family members. Offers low-cost life, health, and long-term care insurance and financial, banking, and investment services worldwide.

Army and Air Force Mutual Aid Assn., *102 Sheridan Ave., Fort Myer, VA 22211-1110; (703) 707-4600. Fax, (888) 210-4882. Maj. Walt Lincoln (USA, Ret.), President. Toll-free, (800) 522-5221.*

General email, info@aafmaa.com

Web, www.aafmaa.com

Private organization that offers member and family life insurance, financial, and survivor assistance services to all ranks of Army, Air Force, Coast Guard, Marine Corps, and Navy who are active duty; Guard, Reserve, USAFA, USCGA, USMA, USMMA, and USNA cadets or midshipmen; ROTC contract/scholarship cadets; and retirees.

Army Emergency Relief, *200 Stovall St., #5S33, Alexandria, VA 22332; (703) 428-0000. Fax, (703) 325-7183. Lt. Gen. Robert F. Foley (USA, Ret.), Executive Director. Toll-free, (866) 878-6378.*

General email, aer@aerhq.org

Web, www.aerhq.org, Twitter, @aerhq and *Facebook, www.facebook.com/AERHQ*

Provides emergency financial assistance to retirees and to soldiers and family members of the U.S. Army, Army Reserves, and National Guard who are on extended active duty; provides scholarships to further the education of service members' spouses and dependents.

Defense Credit Union Council, *601 Pennsylvania Ave. N.W., South Bldg., #600, 20004-2601; (202) 638-3950. Fax, (202) 638-3410. Roland Arteaga, President.*

General email, admin@dcuc.org

Web, www.dcuc.org

Trade association of credit unions serving the Defense Dept.'s military and civilian personnel. Works with the National Credit Union Administration to solve problems concerning the operation of credit unions for the military community; maintains liaison with the Defense Dept.

Health Care

► AGENCIES

Air Force Dept. *(Defense Dept.), Surgeon General, 1780 Air Force Pentagon, #4E114, 20330-1780; (703) 692-6800. Lt. Gen. (Dr.) Mark A. Ediger, Surgeon General.*

Web, www.airforcemedicine.afms.mil

Directs the provision of medical and dental services for Air Force personnel and their beneficiaries.

Army Dept. *(Defense Dept.), Command Policy and Programs, 300 Army Pentagon, 20310-0300; (703) 692-1281. Lt. Col. David J. Deppmeier (USA), Chaplain; Lt. Col. Jerome (Jerry) Pionk (USA), Director of Public Affairs.*

Web, www.asamra.army.mil/mission.cfm

Develops policies and initiatives to enhance soldiers' health, fitness, and morale, with the goal of improving personnel readiness and institutional strength of the army. Interests include weight control and suicide prevention.

Army Dept. *(Defense Dept.), Surgeon General, 7700 Arlington Blvd., #4SW112, Falls Church, VA 22042-5140; (703) 681-3000. Fax, (703) 681-3167. Lt. Gen. (Dr.) Nadja Y. West (USA), Surgeon General.*

General email, OTSGWebPublisher@amedd.army.mil

Web, www.armymedicine.army.mil and *Twitter, @ArmyMedicine*

Directs the provision of medical and dental services for Army personnel and their dependents.

Army Dept. *(Defense Dept.), Warrior Transition Command, 200 Stovall St., #7527, Alexandria, VA 22332; (703) 428-7118. Fax, (703) 325-0291. Col. Christopher Toner, Commander. Wounded soldier and family hotline, (800) 984-8523.*

Web, www.wtc.army.mil and *Twitter, @armyWTC*

Provides leadership, command, and control for wounded soldiers' health and welfare, military administrative requirements, and readiness. Collaborates with medical providers in order to facilitate quality care, disposition, and transition. Supports the needs of wounded warriors and their families; supports the professional growth of all personnel.

Army Dept. *(Defense Dept.), Wounded Warrior Program, 200 Stovall St., #7N65, Alexandria, VA 22332-5000; (877) 393-9058. Fax, (703) 325-1516. Col. David S. Oeschger (USA), Director. Overseas, (312) 221-9113.*

General email, usarmy.pentagon.medcom-WTC.mbx .contact-center@mail.mil

Web, http://wtc.army.mil/aw2 and *Twitter, @armyWTC*

Assists and advocates for severely disabled and ill soldiers, veterans, and their families. Provides each soldier with a personal AW2 advocate. Tracks and monitors severely disabled soldiers beyond their medical retirement.

Assistant Secretary for Health *(Health and Human Services Dept.), Surgeon General, Commissioned Corps of the U.S. Public Health Service (PHS), Division of Commissioned Corps Personnel and Readiness (DCCPR), 1101 Wootton Pkwy., Plaza Level, #100, Rockville, MD 20852; (240) 453-6000. Fax, (240) 453-6109. Rear Adm. Scott F. Giberson, Director; Cmdr. Christopher Dunbar, Director, Recruitment. Recruitment, (800) 279-1605.*

General email, CCHelpDesk@hhs.gov

Recruitment email, Corpsrecruitment@hhs.gov

Web, www.usphs.gov and *http://dcp.psc.gov/ccmis*

Responsible for the overall force management, operations, and deployment readiness and response of the Commissioned Corps of the U.S. Public Health Service. Manages officer medical records and evaluations, recruitment, and calls to active duty.

Defense Dept. *(DoD), Health Affairs, Clinical Program Policy, 1200 Defense Pentagon, #3E1082, 20301-1200;*

(703) 681-1708. Fax, (703) 681-3655. Dr. Jack W. Smith, Director.
Web, www.health.mil

Develops policies for the medical benefits programs for active duty and retired military personnel and dependents in the Defense Dept.

Defense Dept. (DoD), *National Intrepid Center of Excellence, 8901 Wisconsin Ave., Bldg. 51, Bethesda, MD 20889; Capt. (Dr.) Walter M. Greenhalgh (USN), Director. 24-hour helpline, (301) 319-3600. Press, (301) 319-3619. General email, dha.bethesda.ncr-medical.mbx.nicoe@mail.mil*
Web, www.nicoe.capmed.mil

Provides evaluation, treatment planning, research, and education for service members and their families dealing with the interactions of mild traumatic brain injury and psychological health conditions. Primary patient population is active duty service members who are not responding to current therapy; provider-referral required.

Defense Health Agency (DHA) *(Defense Dept.), 7700 Arlington Blvd., #5101, Falls Church, VA 22042-5101; (703) 681-1730. Vice Adm. (Dr.) Raquel C. Bono (USN), Director. Web, www.health.mil/About-MHS/Defense-Health-Agency*

Combat support agency directing medical services for the Army, Navy, Air Force, and Marine Corps. Administers the TRICARE health plan providing medical, dental, and pharmacy programs worldwide to service members, retirees, and their families. Manages inpatient facilities and associated clinics in the national capital region.

Marine Corps *(Defense Dept.), Marine and Family Programs, HQUSMC, M and RA (MF), 3280 Russell Rd., Quantico, VA 22134-5103; (703) 784-9501. Fax, (703) 432 9269. Maj. Gen. Burke W. Whitman (USMC), Director. Web, www.usmc-mccs.org*

Military office that directs Marine Corps health care, family violence, and drug and alcohol abuse policies and programs.

Naval Medical Research Center *(Defense Dept.), 503 Robert Grant Ave., #1W28, Silver Spring, MD 20910-7500; (301) 319-7403. Fax, (301) 319-7424. Capt. Jacqueline D. Rychnovsky, Commanding Officer. General email, svc.pao.nmrc@med.navy.mil*
Web, www.med.navy.mil/sites/nmrc

Performs basic and applied biomedical research in areas of military importance, including infectious diseases, hyperbaric medicine, wound repair enhancement, environmental stress, and immunobiology. Provides support to field laboratories and naval hospitals; monitors research internationally.

Navy Dept. *(Defense Dept.), Manpower and Reserve Affairs, Health Affairs, 1000 Navy Pentagon, #4D548, 20350-1000; (703) 693-0238. Fax, (703) 697-1475. Capt. Mary Jenkins, Director. Web, www.navy.mil*

Reviews medical programs for Navy and Marine Corps military personnel and develops and reviews policies relating to these programs.

Navy Dept. *(Defense Dept.), Patient Administration/ TriCare Operations, 7700 Arlington Blvd., #5113, Falls Church, VA 22042; (703) 681-9025. Cmdr. John Kendrick, Director, Health Care Operations, (703) 681-5516; Lt. Cmdr. Noah Sperner, Patient Administration, (703) 681-9205; Lt. Christina Hyatt, TriCare Operations, (703) 681-9239. Web, www.med.navy.mil*

Military office that interprets and oversees the implementation of Navy health care policy. Assists in the development of eligibility policy for medical benefits programs for Navy and Marine Corps military personnel.

Navy Dept. *(Defense Dept.), Surgeon General, 7700 Arlington Blvd., #5113, Falls Church, VA 22042-5113; (703) 681-9025. Fax, (703) 681-9527. Vice Adm. C. Forrest Faison III, Surgeon General. Phone (after hours), (202) 714-0131. Public Affairs, (703) 681-9038. Web, www.med.navy.mil*

Directs the provision of medical and dental services for Navy and Marine Corps personnel and their dependents; oversees the Navy's Bureau of Medicine and Surgery.

U.S. Coast Guard (USCG) *(Homeland Security Dept.), Health, Safety, and Work-Life, CG-11, 2703 Martin Luther King Jr. Ave. S.E., 20593; (202) 475-5130. Fax, (202) 475-5906. Rear Adm. Erica Schwartz, Director. General email, germaine.y.jefferson@uscg.mil*
Web, www.uscg.mil/hq/cg1/cg11

Oversees all health, safety, and work-life aspects of the Coast Guard, including the operation of medical and dental clinics and sick bays on ships. Investigates Coast Guard accidents, such as the grounding of ships and downing of aircraft. Oversees all work-life-related programs, including health promotion, mess halls and galleys, and individual and family support programs.

Walter Reed Army Institute of Research *(Defense Dept.), 503 Robert Grant Ave., Silver Spring, MD 20910-7500; (301) 319-9000. Fax, (301) 319-9549. Col. (Dr.) Dana K. Renta, Commander. Public Affairs Officer, (301) 319-9471. Reference Librarian, (301) 319-9555. General email, usarmy.detrick.medcom-wrair.mbx.public-affairs@mail.mil*
Web, www.wrair.army.mil and Twitter, @wrair

Provides research, education, and training in support of the Defense Dept.'s health care system. Develops vaccines and drugs to prevent and treat infectious diseases. Other research efforts include surveillance of naturally occurring infectious diseases of military importance and study of combat casualty care (blood loss, resuscitation, and brain and other organ system trauma), battle casualties, operational stress, sleep deprivation, and medical countermeasures against biological and chemical agents.

▶**NONGOVERNMENTAL**

AMSUS – Society of Federal Health Professionals, *9320 Old Georgetown Rd., Bethesda, MD 20814-1653; (301) 897-8800. Fax, (301) 530-5446. Vice Adm. Michael L. Cowan (USN, Ret.), Executive Director. Toll-free, (800) 761-9320.*

General email, amsus@amsus.org

Web, www.amsus.org and Twitter, @AMSUS

Membership: health professionals, including nurses, dentists, pharmacists, and physicians, who work or have worked for the U.S. Public Health Service, the VA, or the Army, Navy, Air Force, Guard, and Reserves, and students. Works to improve all phases of federal health services.

CAUSE (Comfort for America's Uniformed Services), 4114 Legato Rd., Suite B, Fairfax, VA 22033; (703) 591-4965. Fax, (703) 591-4931. Theresa Rudacille, Executive Director.

General email, info@cause-usa.org

Web, www.cause-usa.org and Twitter, @HelpWarriors

Provides comfort items and organizes recreational programs for U.S. military service personnel undergoing medical treatment or recuperating in government hospitals or rehabilitation facilities.

Commissioned Officers Assn. of the U.S. Public Health Service, 8201 Corporate Dr., #200, Landover, MD 20785; (301) 731-9080. Fax, (301) 731-9084. Col. James T. Currie (USA, Ret.), Executive Director.

Web, www.coausphs.org and Twitter, @COAUSPHS

Membership: commissioned officers of the U.S. Public Health Service. Supports improvements to public health, especially through the work of the PHS Commissioned Corps. Sponsors conferences and training workshops. Monitors legislation and regulations.

Injured Marine Semper Fi Fund/Semper Fi Fund, 715 Broadway St., Quantico, VA 22134 (mailing address: Wounded Warrior Center Bldg., H49, Box 555193, Camp Pendleton, CA 92055-5193); (703) 640-0181. Fax, (703) 640-0192. Karen Guenther, President.

General email, info@semperfifund.org

Web, www.semperfifund.org

With its program America's First, provides immediate financial assistance and lifetime support to post 9/11 wounded, critically ill, and injured members of all branches of the U.S. Armed Forces and their families, ensuring that they have the resources needed during recovery and transition back to their communities.

Missing in Action, Prisoners of War

▶AGENCIES

Air Force Dept. *(Defense Dept.), Manpower Personnel and Services,* 1040 Air Force Pentagon, #4E168, 20330-1040; (703) 697-6088. Lt. Gen. Gina M. Grosso, Deputy Chief of Staff.

Web, www.afpc.af.mil

Military office that responds to inquiries about missing in action (MIA) personnel for the Air Force; refers inquiries to the Military Personnel Center at Randolph Air Force Base in San Antonio, Texas.

Bureau of East Asian and Pacific Affairs *(State Dept.), Mainland Southeast Asia Affairs,* 2201 C St. N.W., #5206,

20520-6310; (202) 647-0064. Fax, (202) 647-3069. Pepper Richhart, Director.

Web, www.state.gov

Handles issues related to Americans missing in action in Indochina; serves as liaison with Congress, international organizations, and foreign governments on developments in these countries.

Defense Dept. (DoD), *Defense POW/MIA Accounting,* 241 18th St. South, #800, Arlington, VA 22202; (703) 699-1102. Fax, (703) 602-1890. Michael S. Linnington, Director. Press, (703) 699-1420.

Web, www.dpaa.mil

Civilian office responsible for policy matters relating to prisoners of war and missing personnel issues. Represents the Defense Dept. before Congress, the media, veterans organizations, and prisoner of war and missing personnel families.

Defense Dept. (DoD), *Public Affairs,* The Pentagon, #2D961, 20301-1400; (703) 571-3343. Fax, (703) 697-3501. Peter Cook, Assistant Secretary, Acting, (703) 697-9312. Press, (703) 697-5131.

Web, www.defense.gov/news

Responds to public inquiries concerning Defense Dept. personnel.

Marine Corps *(Defense Dept.), Casualty Assistance Section,* HQUSMC, 2008 Elliott Rd., Quantico, VA 22134-5102; (703) 784-9512. Fax, (703) 784-4134. Gerald Castle, Head; Cindy Grubb, Head of Case Management. Toll-free, (800) 847-1597.

General email, casualty.section@usmc.mil

Web, www.mcieast.marines.mil/staffoffices/adjutant/casualtyassistanceprogram.aspx

Military office that acts as liaison for inquiries about missing in action (MIA) personnel for the Marine Corps and distributes information about Marine Corps MIAs to the next of kin.

Navy Dept. *(Defense Dept.), Naval Personnel,* 701 S. Courthouse Rd., Arlington, VA 22204; (703) 604-2863. Fax, (703) 604-5942. Vice Adm. William F. Moran, Chief. Toll-free, (866) 827-5672. TTY, (866) 297-1971.

General email, UASKPC@navy.mil

Web, www.navy.mil/cno

Military office that responds to inquiries about missing in action (MIA) personnel for the Navy and distributes information about Navy MIAs. (Office based in Millington, Tenn.)

▶CONGRESS

For a listing of relevant congressional committees and subcommittees, please see page 565 or the Appendix.

▶NONGOVERNMENTAL

National League of Families of American Prisoners and Missing in Southeast Asia, 5673 Columbia Pike, #100, Falls Church, VA 22041; (703) 465-7432. Fax, (703)

465-7433. Ann Mills-Griffith, Chair; Lacy Rourke,
National Coordinator.
General email, powmiafam@aol.com

Web, www.pow-miafamilies.org

Membership: family members of MIAs and POWs and returned POWs of the Vietnam War are voting members; nonvoting associate members include veterans and other interested people. Works for the release of all prisoners of war, an accounting of the missing, and repatriation of the remains of those who have died serving their country in Southeast Asia. Works to raise public awareness of these issues; maintains regional and state coordinators.

Pay and Compensation

► AGENCIES

Air Force Dept. *(Defense Dept.), Manpower Personnel and Services, Compensation and Travel Policy, 1500 Perimeter Rd., #4790, Andrews AFB, MD 20762; (240) 612-4350. Jean Love, Chief.*
Web, www.afpc.af.mil

Military office that develops and administers Air Force military personnel pay and compensation policies.

Army Dept. *(Defense Dept.), Military Compensation, 111 Army Pentagon, #2E469, 20310-0111; (703) 697-1482. Fax, (703) 693-7072. Col. Alvaro W. Lofstrom (USA), Assistant Deputy, Military Personnel Policy, (703) 695-4394; Jerilyn (Jeri) B. Busch, Director.*
Web, http://militarypay.defense.gov

Military office that provides oversight of the development and administration of and compliance with Army military personnel pay and compensation policies.

Defense Dept. (DoD), *Military Compensation, 4000 Defense Pentagon, #3D1067, 20301-4000; (703) 695-3177. Fax, (703) 697-0202. Jerilyn (Jeri) B. Busch, Director.*
Web, http://militarypay.defense.gov

Promulgates military pay and compensation policies to the uniformed services and advises the secretary of defense on military compensation policy.

Marine Corps *(Defense Dept.), Military Manpower Policy, 3280 Russell Rd., Quantico, VA 22134-5105; (703) 784-9350. Fax, (703) 784-9812. Brig. Gen. George W. Smith (USMC), Director; Lt. Col. Gary D. Rotsch (USMC), Compensation/Incentive Officer.*
General email, manpower@usmc.mil

Web, www.marines.mil

Military office that develops and administers Marine Corps personnel pay and compensation policies.

Navy Dept. *(Defense Dept.), Military Pay and Compensation Policy, 701 S. Courthouse Rd., Arlington, VA 22204; (703) 604-4718. David Haldeman, Branch Head.*
General email, nxag_n130@navy.mil

Web, www.public.navy.mil/bupers-npc/career/payand benefits

Military office that develops and administers Navy military pay, compensation, and personnel policies.

Veterans Affairs Dept. (VA), *Consumer Affairs, 810 Vermont Ave. N.W., #915, 20420; (202) 461-7383. Fax, (202) 273-5716. Shirley Williams, Program Assistant, (202) 461-7088.*
Web, www.va.gov

Responds to veterans' complaints concerning VA benefits and services. Answers questions about policy and makes referrals to other VA offices, as appropriate.

Recruitment

► AGENCIES

Air Force Dept. *(Defense Dept.), Force Management, 1400 W. Perimeter Rd., #4710, Joint Base Andrews, 20762; (240) 612-4040. Fax, (703) 604-1657. Col. Jerry Diaz, Chief.*
Web, www.afpc.af.mil

Military office that oversees Air Force retention policies for officers and enlisted personnel, and provides analytical support for personnel issues.

Defense Dept. (DoD), *Accession Policy, 4000 Defense Pentagon, #3D1066, 20301-4000; (703) 695-5525. Stephanie P. Miller, Director; Chris Arendt, Deputy Director.*
Web, www.defense.gov

Military office that monitors Defense Dept. recruiting programs and policies, including advertising, market research, and enlistment standards. Coordinates with the individual services on recruitment of military personnel.

Marine Corps *(Defense Dept.), Recruiting Command, 3280 Russell Rd., Quantico, VA 22134-5105; (703) 784-9400. Brig. Gen. Paul Kennedy (USMC), Commanding General.*
General email, mcrcpa@marines.usmc.mil

Web, www.mcrc.marines.mil

Military office that administers and executes policies for Marine Corps officer and enlisted recruitment programs.

Selective Service System, *1515 Wilson Blvd., #400, Arlington, VA 22209-2425; (703) 605-4100. Fax, (703) 605-4106. Lawrence G. Romo, Director. Locator, (703) 605-4000. Toll-free, (888) 655-1825. TTY, (800) 877-8339. TTY Espanol, (800) 845-6136.*
General email, information@sss.gov

Web, www.sss.gov

Supplies the armed forces with manpower when authorized; registers male citizens of the United States ages eighteen to twenty-five. In an emergency, would institute a draft and would provide alternative service assignments to men classified as conscientious objectors.

Retirement, Separation

▶AGENCIES

Armed Forces Retirement Home—Washington,
140 Rock Creek Church Rd. N.W., 20011-8400 (mailing address: 3700 N. Capitol St. N.W., Washington, DC 20011-8400); (800) 422-9988, (202) 541-5501. Fax, (202) 541-7519. Steven G. McManus, Chief Operating Officer.
General email, admissions@afrh.gov

Web, www.afrh.gov

Gives domiciliary and medical care to retired members of the armed services or career service personnel unable to earn a livelihood. Formerly known as U.S. Soldiers' and Airmen's Home. (Armed Forces Retirement Home in Gulfport, Miss., reopened in 2010.)

Army Dept. *(Defense Dept.), Retirement Services, 251 18th St. South, #210, Arlington, VA 22202-3531; (703) 571-7232. Fax, (703) 601-0120. Col. John W. Radke (USA, Ret.), Chief. Alternate phone, (703) 545-2637.*
General email, ArmyRSO@mail.mil

Web, https://soldierforlife.army.mil/retirement

Military office that makes retirement policy and oversees retirement programs for Army military personnel.

Defense Dept. (DoD), *Military Compensation, 4000 Defense Pentagon, #3D1067, 20301-4000; (703) 695-3177. Fax, (703) 697-0202. Jerilyn (Jeri) B. Busch, Director.*
Web, http://militarypay.defense.gov

Develops retirement policies and reviews administration of retirement programs for all Defense Dept. military personnel.

Marine Corps *(Defense Dept.), Retired Services, 3280 Russell Rd., Quantico, VA 22134-5103; (703) 784-9312. Fax, (703) 784-9834. Vincent P. Pate, Head.*
Toll-free, (800) 336-4649.
Web, www.marines.mil

Military office that administers retirement programs and benefits for Marine Corps retirees and the Marine Corps retirement community survivor benefit plan.

Marine Corps *(Defense Dept.), Separation and Retirement, 3280 Russell Rd., Quantico, VA 22134-5103; (703) 784-9304. Fax, (703) 784-9834.*
Col. Steven M. Hanscom (USMC, Ret.), Head.
Web, www.marines.mil

Military office that processes Marine Corps military personnel retirements and separations but does not administer benefits.

▶NONGOVERNMENTAL

Army Distaff Foundation (Knollwood), *6200 Oregon Ave. N.W., 20015-1543; (202) 541-0400. Fax, (202) 364-2856. Maj. Gen. Stephen T. Rippe (USA, Ret.), Chief Executive Officer. Information, (800) 541-4255. Admission, (202) 541-0149.*
General email, dschrag@armydistaff.org
Web, www.armydistaff.org

Nonprofit continuing care retirement community for career military officers and their families. Provides retirement housing and health care services.

MILITARY EDUCATION AND TRAINING

General

▶AGENCIES

Air Force Dept. *(Defense Dept.), Force Management Integration, 1660 Air Force Pentagon, #5E818, 20330-1660; (703) 614-4751. Fax, (703) 693-4244.*
Col. Dennis Curran, Deputy Assistant Secretary.

Civilian office that monitors and reviews education policies of the U.S. Air Force Academy at Colorado Springs and officer candidates' training and Reserve Officers Training Corps (ROTC) programs for the Air Force. Advises the secretary of the Air Force on education matters, including graduate education, voluntary education programs, and flight, specialized, and recruit training.

Air Force Dept. *(Defense Dept.), Personnel Policy, 1040 Air Force Pentagon, #4D950, 20330-1040; (703) 695-6770. John W. Snodgrass, Executive Director.*
Web, www.afpc.af.mil

Supervises operations and policies of all professional military education, including continuing education programs. Oversees operations and policies of Air Force service schools, including technical training for newly enlisted Air Force personnel.

Army Dept. *(Defense Dept.), Collective Training Division, 450 Army Pentagon, #2D623, 20310-0450; (703) 692-8370. Fax, (703) 692-4093. Col. Pat Hynes (USA), Chief.*
General email, usarmy.lee.tradoc.mbx.leee-cascom-doctrine@mail.mil
Web, www.army.mil

Military office that plans and monitors program resources for active duty and reserve unit training readiness programs.

Army Dept. *(Defense Dept.), Military Personnel Management, 300 Army Pentagon, #1D429, 20310-0300; (703) 695-5871. Fax, (703) 695-6012. Maj.*
Gen. Jason T. Evans (USA), Director.
Web, www.army.mil

Military office that supervises operations and policies of the U.S. Military Academy and officer candidates' training and Reserve Officers Training Corps (ROTC) programs. Advises the chief of staff of the Army on academy and education matters.

Civil Air Patrol National Capital Wing, *200 McChord St. S.W., #111, Joint Base Anacostia-Bolling, 20032; (202) 767-4405. Col. Bruce Heinlein, Wing Commander.*
General email, info@natcapwing.org
Web, www.natcapwg.cap.gov and Twitter, @NatCapWing

Official auxiliary of the U.S. Air Force. Sponsors a cadet training and education program for junior and senior high school age students. Conducts emergency services, homeland security missions, and an aerospace education program. (Headquarters at Maxwell Air Force Base, Ala.)

Defense Acquisition University *(Defense Dept.),* 9820 *Belvoir Rd., Fort Belvoir, VA 22060-5565; (703) 805-3360. Fax, (703) 805-2639. James P. Woolsey, President. Toll-free, (800) 845-7606.*
Web, www.dau.mil

Academic institution that offers courses to military and civilian personnel who specialize in acquisition and procurement. Conducts research to support and improve management of defense systems acquisition programs.

Defense Dept. (DoD), *Accession Policy,* 4000 *Defense Pentagon, #3D1066, 20301-4000; (703) 695-5525. Stephanie P. Miller, Director; Chris Arendt, Deputy Director. Web, www.defense.gov*

Reviews and develops education policies of the service academies, service schools, graduate and voluntary education programs, education programs for active duty personnel, tuition assistance programs, and officer candidates' training and Reserve Officers Training Corps (ROTC) programs for the Defense Dept. Advises the secretary of defense on education matters.

Defense Dept. (DoD), *Force Readiness and Training,* 4000 *Defense Pentagon, #1E537, 20301-4000; (703) 695-2618. Fax, (703) 692-2855. Frank C. DiGiovanni, Director.*
Web, http://prhome.defense.gov

Develops, reviews, and analyzes legislation, policies, plans, programs, resource levels, and budgets for the training of military personnel and military units. Develops the substantive-based framework, working collaboratively across the defense, federal, academic, and private sectors, for the global digital knowledge environment. Manages with other government agencies the sustainability and modernization of DoD training ranges.

Dwight D. Eisenhower School for National Security and Resource Strategy *(Defense Dept.), Fort Lesley J. McNair, 408 4th Ave. S.W., Bldg. 59, 20319-5062; (202) 685-4278. Fax, (202) 685-3920. Brig. Gen. Thomas A. Gorry (USMC), Commandant. Administration, (202) 685-4333.*
General email, university-registrar@ndu.edu
Web, http://es.ndu.edu

Division of National Defense University. Offers professional level courses for senior military officers and senior civilian government officials. Academic program focuses on management of national resources, mobilization, and industrial preparedness. (Formerly known as the Industrial College of the Armed Forces.)

Marine Corps *(Defense Dept.), Alfred M. Gray Research Center,* 2040 *Broadway St., Quantico, VA 22134; (703) 784-2240. Fax, (703) 784-4306.*

Charles P. Neimeyer, Director. Library, (703) 784-4409. Archives, (703) 784-4685.
Web, http://guides.grc.usmcu.edu/grc

Supports the professional, military, educational, and academic needs of the students and faculty of the Marine Corps University. Acts as a central research facility for marines in operational units worldwide. Houses the library and archives of the Marine Corps.

Marine Corps *(Defense Dept.), Training and Education Command,* 1019 *Elliot Rd., Quantico, VA 22134-5001; (703) 784-3730. Fax, (703) 784-0012. Maj. Gen. James W. Lukeman, Commanding General. Web, www.tecom.marines.mil*

Military office that develops and implements training and education programs for regular and reserve personnel and units.

National Defense University *(Defense Dept.), Fort Lesley J. McNair, 300 5th Ave. S.W., Bldg. 62, #305A, 20319-5066; (202) 685-4700. Fax, (202) 685-3935. Maj. Gen. Frederick M. Padilla (USMC), President. Press, (202) 685-3140.*
General email, NDUWebmaster@ndu.edu
Web, www.ndu.edu and Facebook, www.facebook.com/ndu.edu

Specialized university sponsored by the Joint Chiefs of Staff to prepare individuals for senior executive duties in the national security establishment. Offers master of science degrees in national resource strategy, national security strategy, joint campaign planning and strategy, and government information leadership; a master of arts degree in strategic security studies; and nondegree and certificate programs and courses.

National War College *(Defense Dept.), Fort Lesley J. McNair, 300 D St. S.W., Bldg. 61, 20319-5078; (202) 685-3674. Fax, (202) 685-6461. Brig. Gen. Darren (Tom) E. Hartford (USAF), Commandant. Web, http://nwc.ndu.edu*

Division of National Defense University. Offers professional level courses for senior military officers, senior civilian government officials, and foreign officers. Academic program focuses on the formulation and implementation of national security policy and military strategy.

Navy Dept. *(Defense Dept.), Manpower and Reserve Affairs,* 1000 *Navy Pentagon, #4E590, 20350-1000; (703) 695-4333. Fax, (703) 614-4103. Hon. Franklin R. Parker III, Assistant Secretary.*
Web, www.navy.mil

Civilian office that reviews policies of the U.S. Naval Academy, Navy and Marine Corps service schools, and officer candidates' training and Reserve Officer Training Corps (ROTC) programs. Advises the secretary of the Navy on education matters, including voluntary education programs.

U.S. Coast Guard (USCG) *(Homeland Security Dept.), Human Resources Directorate,* CG-1, MS 7907, 2703 *Martin Luther King Jr. Ave. S.E., 20593;*

(202) 475-5000. Rear Adm. Cari B. Thomas, Assistant Commandant.
Web, www.uscg.mil/hr

Responsible for hiring, recruiting, and training all military and nonmilitary Coast Guard personnel. Administers employee benefits.

U.S. Naval Academy (Defense Dept.), *121 Blake Rd., Annapolis, MD 21402-5000; (410) 293-1000. Fax, (410) 293-3133. Vice Adm. Walter (Ted) Carter Jr. (USN), Superintendent; Capt. Stephen B. Latta (USN, Ret.), Dean of Admissions; Col. Stephen Liszewski (USMC), Commandant of Midshipmen. Visitor information, (410) 293-8687. Admissions/Candidate guidance, (410) 293-1858. Public Affairs, (410) 293-1520.*
General email, pao@usna.edu

Web, www.usna.edu and www.usna.edu/Admissions

Provides undergraduate education for young men and women who have been nominated by members of their state's congressional delegation or, in some cases, the president or vice president of the United States. Graduates receive bachelor of science degrees and are commissioned as either an ensign in the U.S. Navy or a second lieutenant in the U.S. Marine Corps.

Uniformed Services University of the Health Sciences (Defense Dept.), *4301 Jones Bridge Rd., Bethesda, MD 20814-4799; (301) 295-3013. Fax, (301) 295-1960. Dr. Charles L. Rice, President. Toll-free information, (800) 515-5257. Registrar, (301) 295-3199.*
General email, president@usuhs.edu

Web, www.usuhs.mil

An accredited four-year medical and dental school under the auspices of the Defense Dept. Awards doctorates and master's degrees in health-related and science-related fields. The Graduate School of Nursing awards a master of science and a doctoral degree in nursing.

▶**CONGRESS**

For a listing of relevant congressional committees and subcommittees, please see page 565 or the Appendix.

▶**NONGOVERNMENTAL**

Assn. of Military Colleges and Schools of the U.S., *12332 Washington Brice Rd., Fairfax, VA 22033; (703) 272-8406. Col. Ray Rottman (USAF, Ret.), Executive Director.*
General email, amcsus@cox.net

Web, www.amcsus.org and Twitter, @militaryschools

Membership: nonfederal military colleges and universities, junior colleges, and preparatory secondary schools that emphasize character development, leadership, and knowledge. Interests include Reserve Officers Training Corps (ROTC). Publishes a newsletter; sponsors an annual meeting and outreach activities. Represents member schools before the Defense Dept., Education Dept., and the general public.

George and Carol Olmsted Foundation, *80 East Jefferson St., #300B, Falls Church, VA 22046; (703) 536-3500. Maj. Gen. Bruce K. Scott (USA, Ret.), President. Toll-free, (877) 656-7833.*
General email, scholars@olmstedfoundation.org

Web, www.olmstedfoundation.org and Twitter, @OlmstedScholars

Administers grants for two years of graduate study overseas, including foreign language study, for selected officers of the armed forces.

Military Order of the World Wars, *435 N. Lee St., Alexandria, VA 22314-2301; (703) 683-4911. Fax, (703) 683-4501. Brig. Gen. Arthur B. Morrill III (USAF, Ret.), Chief of Staff. Toll-free, (877) 320-3774.*
General email, chiefofstaff@moww.org

Web, www.moww.org

Membership: retired and active duty commissioned officers, warrant officers, and flight officers. Presents awards to outstanding Reserve Officers Training Corps (ROTC) cadets; gives awards to Boy Scouts and Girl Scouts; conducts youth leadership conferences.

National Research Council (NRC), *Air Force Studies Board, Keck Center, 500 5th St. N.W., 9th Floor, 20001; (202) 334-2000. Gen. Douglas M. Fraser (USAF, Ret.), Board Chair.*
Web, http://sites.nationalacademies.org/DEPS/AFSB

Supports activities related to the development of science and technology within the Air Force. Interests of study include fuel efficiency, acquisition processes, and assuring the future scientific and technical qualification of Air Force personnel.

Navy League of the United States, *2300 Wilson Blvd., #200, Arlington, VA 22201-5424; (703) 528-1775. Fax, (703) 528-2333. Bruce K. Butler, National Executive Director. Toll-free, (800) 356-5760.*
General email, service@navyleague.org

Web, www.navyleague.org

Sponsors Naval Sea Cadet Corps and Navy League Sea Cadet Corps for young people ages eleven through eighteen years. Graduates are eligible to enter the Navy at advanced pay grades.

Servicemembers Opportunity Colleges, *1307 New York Ave. N.W., 5th Floor, 20005-4701; (202) 667-0079. Fax, (202) 667-0622. Kathryn (Kathy) Snead, Director. Information, (800) 368-5622.*
General email, socmail@aascu.org

Web, www.soc.aascu.org

Partnership of higher education associations, educational institutions, the Defense Dept., and the military services. Offers courses for credit and degree programs to military personnel and their families stationed in the United States and around the world.

MILITARY GRIEVANCES AND DISCIPLINE

General

►AGENCIES

Air Force Dept. *(Defense Dept.), Air Force Review Boards Agency,* 1500 W. Perimeter Rd., #3700, Andrews AFB, MD 20762-7002; (240) 612-5400. Fax, (240) 612-6016. R. Philip Deavel, Director.
Web, www.af.mil/information/factsheets/factsheet.asp

Civilian office that responds to complaints from Air Force military and civilian personnel and assists in seeking corrective action.

Air Force Dept. *(Defense Dept.), Complaints Resolution Directorate,* Carpenter Bldg., 5683 Castle Ave., Joint Base Anacostia-Bolling, 20032; (202) 404-5262.
Col. John G. Payne, Director.
Web, www.af.mil/inspectorgeneralcomplaints.asp

Military office that handles complaints and requests for assistance from civilians and Air Force and other military personnel.

Army Dept. *(Defense Dept.), Army Review Boards Agency,* 251 18th St. South, #385, Arlington, VA 22202-3531; (703) 545-6900. Fax, (703) 601-0703.
Francine Blackmon, Deputy Assistant Secretary.
Web, http://arba.army.pentagon.mil

Civilian office that administers boards reviewing appeals cases. Administers the Army Grade Determination Review Board, Army Board for Correction of Military Records, Disability Rating Review Board, Discharge Review Board, Army Clemency and Parole Board, Physical Disability Review Board, and Physical Disability Appeals Board, Army Corrections Command Board, and the Army Suitability Evaluation Board.

Defense Dept. (DoD), *Diversity Management and Equal Opportunity,* 4000 Defense Pentagon, #5D641, 20301-4000; (703) 571-9321. Fax, (703) 571-9338.
Clarence A. Johnson, Director.
Web, http://diversity.defense.gov

Formulates equal employment opportunity policy for the Defense Dept. Evaluates civil rights complaints from military personnel, including issues of sexual harassment and recruitment.

Defense Dept. (DoD), *Legal Policy,* 4000 Defense Pentagon, #2C548A, 20301-4000; (703) 697-3387.
Paul Kantwill, Director; Lt. Col. Ryan Oakley, Deputy Director.
Web, www.defense.gov

Coordinates policy in a variety of personnel-related areas, including the Members Civil Relief Act, legal assistance, political activities, and corrections.

Defense Dept. (DoD), *Sexual Assault Prevention and Response,* 4800 Mark Center Dr., #07G21, Alexandria, VA 22350; (571) 372-2657. Maj. Gen. Camille M. Nichols (USA), Director. Hotline, (877) 995-5247.
General email, whc.mc-alex.wso.mbx.SAPRO@mail.mil
Web, www.sapr.mil and www.myduty.mil

Serves as the single point of accountability for the Defense Dept.'s sexual assault policy. Responsible for improving prevention, enhancing reporting and response, and holding perpetrators appropriately accountable.

Defense Legal Services Agency *(Defense Dept.), General Counsel,* 1600 Defense Pentagon, #3E788, 20301-1600; (703) 695-3341. Robert S. Taylor, General Counsel, Acting.
Web, www.dod.mil/dodgc

Provides legal guidance to the Air Force, Army, Navy, and other Defense Dept. agencies. Administers programs governing military standards and conduct.

Marine Corps *(Defense Dept.), Inspector General of the Marine Corps,* 701 S. Courthouse Rd., Bldg. 12, #1J165, Arlington, VA 22204; (703) 604-4661. Col. Rick A. Uribe Jr. (USMC), Inspector General. Complaint hotline, (866) 243-3887.
General email, ORGMB_IGMC_ADMIN@usmc.mil
Web, www.hqmc.marines.mil/igmc

Military office that investigates complaints from Marine Corps personnel and assists in seeking corrective action.

Navy Dept. *(Defense Dept.), Manpower and Reserve Affairs,* 1000 Navy Pentagon, #4E590, 20350-1000; (703) 695-4333. Fax, (703) 614-4103. Hon. Franklin R. Parker III, Assistant Secretary.
Web, www.navy.mil

Civilian office that receives complaints from Navy and Marine Corps military personnel and assists in seeking corrective action.

►CONGRESS

For a listing of relevant congressional committees and subcommittees, please see page 565 or the Appendix.

Correction of Military Records

►AGENCIES

Air Force Dept. *(Defense Dept.), Board for the Correction of Military Records,* SAF/MRBC, 1500 W. Perimeter, #3700, Joint Base Andrews, NAF, 20762; (240) 612-5379. Fax, (240) 612-5619. John Zallario, Executive Director.
Web, http://kb.defense.gov/app/answers/detail/a_id/386/~/boards-for-correction-of-military-records

Civilian board that reviews appeals for corrections to Air Force personnel records and makes recommendations to the secretary of the Air Force.

Army Dept. *(Defense Dept.)*, **Board for the Correction of Military Records**, *251 18th St. South, #385, Arlington, VA 22202-3523; (703) 545-6900. Fax, (703) 601-0703. Sarah Bercaw, Director.*
Web, http://arba.army.pentagon.mil

Civilian board that reviews appeals for corrections to Army personnel records and makes recommendations to the secretary of the Army under Section 1552 of Title 10 of the U.S. Code.

Defense Dept. (DoD), *Legal Policy, 4000 Defense Pentagon, #2C548A, 20301-4000; (703) 697-3387. Paul Kantwill, Director; Lt. Col. Ryan Oakley, Deputy Director.*
Web, www.defense.gov

Coordinates policy for armed services boards charged with correcting military records.

Navy Dept. *(Defense Dept.)*, **Board for Correction of Naval Records**, *701 S. Courthouse Rd., Bldg. 12, #1001, Arlington, VA 22204-2490; (703) 604-6884. Fax, (703) 604-3437. Scott Thompson, Executive Director.*
General email, karen.clemons@navy.mil

Applications email, BCNR_Application@navy.mil
Web, secnav.navy.mil/mra/bcnr

Civilian board that reviews appeals for corrections to Navy and Marine Corps personnel records and makes recommendations to the secretary of the Navy.

U.S. Coast Guard (USCG) *(Homeland Security Dept.)*, **Board for Correction of Military Records**, *245 Murray Lane, MS 485, 20528; (202) 447-4099. Fax, (202) 447-3111. Julia Andrews, Chair.*
General email, cgbcmr@dhs.gov
Web, www.uscg.mil/legal/BCMR.asp

Civilian board (an adjunct to the U.S. Coast Guard) that reviews appeals for corrections to Coast Guard personnel records and makes recommendations to the general counsel of the Homeland Security Dept.

Legal Proceedings

▶AGENCIES

Air Force Dept. *(Defense Dept.)*, **Judge Advocate General**, *1420 Air Force Pentagon, 20330-1420; (703) 614-5732. Lt. Gen. Christopher F. Burne, Judge Advocate General.*
Web, www.afjag.af.mil

Military office that prosecutes and defends Air Force personnel during military legal proceedings. Gives legal advice and assistance to Air Force staff.

Army Dept. *(Defense Dept.)*, **Army Clemency and Parole Board**, *Crystal Square 5, 251 18th St. South, #385, Arlington, VA 22202-3531; (703) 571-0532. Fax, (703) 601-0493. Steven L. Andraschko, Chair, (703) 571-0533.*
General email, army.arbainquiry@mail.mil
Web, http://arba.army.pentagon.mil/clemency-parole.cfm

Conducts clemency, parole, and mandatory supervised release hearings for eligible Army prisoners.

Army Dept. *(Defense Dept.)*, **Judge Advocate General**, *2200 Army Pentagon, #3E542, 20310-2200; (703) 697-5151. Fax, (703) 697-1059. Lt. Gen. Flora D. Darpino (USA), Judge Advocate General. Service desk, (703) 693-0000.*
Web, www.jagcnet.army.mil

Military policy office for the field offices that prosecute and defend Army personnel during military legal proceedings. Serves as an administrative office for military appeals court, which hears legal proceedings involving Army personnel.

Defense Dept. (DoD), *Court of Appeals for the Armed Forces, 450 E St. N.W., 20442-0001; (202) 761-1448. Fax, (202) 761-4672. William DeCicco, Clerk of the Court. Library, (202) 761-1466.*
Web, www.armfor.uscourts.gov

Serves as the appellate court for cases involving dishonorable or bad conduct discharges, confinement of a year or more, and the death penalty, and for cases certified to the court by the judge advocate general of an armed service. Less serious cases are reviewed by the individual armed services. Library open to the public.

Marine Corps *(Defense Dept.)*, **Judge Advocate**, *3000 Marine Corps Pentagon, #4D558, 20350-3000; (703) 614-8661. Fax, (703) 693-3208. Maj. Gen. John R. Ewers Jr. (USMC), Staff Judge Advocate.*
Web, www.hqmc.marines.mil/sja

Military office that administers legal proceedings involving Marine Corps personnel.

Navy Dept. *(Defense Dept.)*, **Judge Advocate General**, *1322 Patterson Ave. S.E., #3000, Washington Navy Yard, DC 20374-5066; (703) 614-7420. Fax, (703) 697-4610. Vice Adm. James W. Crawford III, Judge Advocate General. Press, (202) 685-5275.*
Web, www.jag.navy.mil

Military office that administers the Judge Advocate General's Corps, which conducts legal proceedings involving Navy and Marine Corps personnel.

Military Police and Corrections

▶AGENCIES

Army Dept. *(Defense Dept.)*, **Provost Marshal General, Operations Division**, *2800 Army Pentagon, DAPM-MPO, #MF748, 20310-2800; (703) 693-9478. Fax, (703) 693-6580. Col. Bob Willis (USA), Chief, (703) 693-9478.*
Web, www.army.mil/opmg and Twitter, @ArmyOPMG

Develops policies and supports military police and corrections programs in all branches of the U.S. Army. Operates the Military Police Management Information System (MPMIS), which automates incident reporting and tracks information on facilities, staff, and inmates, including enemy prisoners of war.

Defense Dept. (DoD), *Legal Policy,* *4000 Defense Pentagon, #2C548A, 20301-4000; (703) 697-3387. Paul Kantwill, Director; Lt. Col. Ryan Oakley, Deputy Director.* Web, www.defense.gov

Coordinates and reviews Defense Dept. policies and programs relating to deserters.

MILITARY HISTORY AND HONORS

General

▶AGENCIES

Air Force Dept. *(Defense Dept.),* **Air Force History and Museum Programs,** *AF/HO, 1190 Air Force Pentagon, #4E284, 20330-1190; (703) 697-5600. Fax, (703) 693-3496. Walter (Wult) Grudzinskas, Director. Reference, (202) 404-2264.* Web, www.airforcehistory.af.mil

Publishes histories, studies, monographs, and reference works; directs worldwide Air Force History and Museums Program and provides guidance to the Air Force Historical Research Agency at Maxwell Air Force Base in Alabama; supports Air Force Air Staff agencies and responds to inquiries from the public and the U.S. government.

Army Dept. *(Defense Dept.),* **Institute of Heraldry,** *9325 Gunston Rd., Bldg. 1466, #S122, Fort Belvoir, VA 22060-5579; (703) 806-4971. Fax, (703) 806-4964. Charles Mugno, Director.* General email, TIOHWebmaster@us.army.mil

Web, www.tioh.hqda.pentagon.mil

Furnishes heraldic services to the armed forces and other U.S. government agencies, including the Executive Office of the President. Responsible for research, design, development, and standardization of official symbolic items, including seals, decorations, medals, insignias, badges, flags, and other items awarded to or authorized for official wear or display by government personnel and agencies. Limited research and information services on these items are provided to the general public.

Army Dept. *(Defense Dept.),* **U.S. Army Center of Military History,** *Fort Lesley J. McNair, Collins Hall, 102 4th Ave., Bldg. 35, 20319-5060; (202) 685-2706. Fax, (202) 685-4570. Charles Bowrey, Executive Director. Library, (202) 685-3573.* Web, www.history.army.mil

Publishes the official history of the Army. Provides information on Army history; coordinates Army museum system and art program. Works with Army school system to ensure that history is included in curriculum. Provides Heraldic products and services in support of federal governemnt. Sponsors professional appointments, fellowships, and awards. Library open to researchers for archival research Monday through Thursday, 8:00 a.m.–4:00 p.m., and Friday 8:00 a.m.–12:00 noon; not a lending library.

Defense Dept. (DoD), *Historical Office,* *1777 N. Kent St., #5000, Arlington, VA 22209; Erin R. Mahan, Chief Historian.* Web, http://history.defense.gov

Researches and writes historical accounts of the office of the secretary of defense; coordinates historical activities of the Defense Dept. and prepares special studies at the request of the secretary.

Defense Dept. (DoD), *Joint History Office,* *9999 Defense Pentagon, #1A466, 20318-9999; (703) 695-2137. Fax, (703) 614-6243. John F. Shortal, Director.* General email, john.f.shortal.civ@mail.mil

Web, www.defense.gov

Provides historical support services to the chair of the Joint Chiefs of Staff and the Joint Staff, including research; writes the official history of the Joint Chiefs. Supervises field programs encompassing nine Unified Commands.

Marine Corps *(Defense Dept.),* **History Division,** *Marine Corps University, 3078 Upshur Ave., Quantico, VA 22134; (703) 432-4877. Fax, (703) 432-5054. Charles P. Neimeyer, Director, (703) 432-4877. Reference, (703) 432-4874. Archives, (703) 784-4685.* General email, history.division@usmc.mil

Web, www.mcu.usmc.mil/historydivision

Writes official histories of the corps for government agencies and the public; answers inquiries about Marine Corps history.

National Archives and Records Administration (NARA), *Reference Services, 8601 Adelphi Rd., #2400, College Park, MD 20740-6001; (301) 837-3510. Fax, (301) 837-1752. Richard W. Peuser, Branch Chief.* Web, www.archives.gov/frc/reference-services.html

Contains Army records from the Revolutionary War to the Vietnam War, Navy records from the Revolutionary War to the Korean War, and Air Force records from 1947 to 1954. Handles records captured from enemy powers at the end of World War II and a small collection of records captured from the Vietnamese. Conducts research in response to specific inquiries; makes records available for reproduction or examination in research room.

National Museum of American History *(Smithsonian Institution),* **Armed Forces History,** *14th St. and Constitution Ave. N.W., NMAH-4032, MRC 620, 20560-0620; (202) 633-3950. Jennifer Locke Jones, Chair.* Web, http://americanhistory.si.edu/about/departments/armed-forces-history

Maintains collections relating to the history of the U.S. armed forces, U.S. military technology, and the American flag; includes manuscripts, documents, correspondence, uniforms, small arms and weapons, and other personal memorabilia of armed forces personnel of all ranks. Research areas are open by appointment.

National Museum of Health and Medicine *(Defense Dept.),* *2460 Linden Lane, Silver Spring, MD 20910 (mailing address: 2460 Linden Lane, Bldg. 2500, Silver*

National Park Service

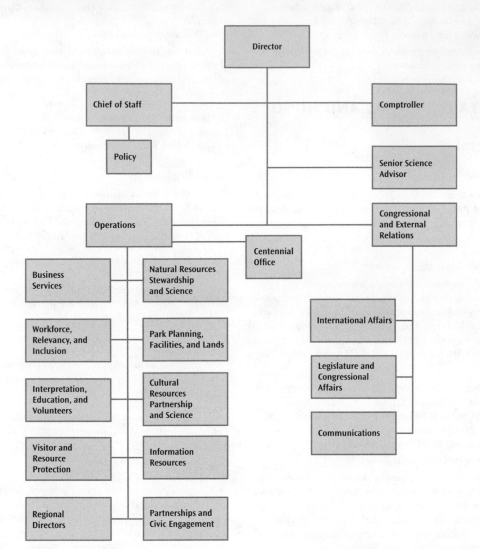

Spring, MD 20910); (301) 319-3300. Fax, (301) 319-3373. Dr. Adrianne Noe, Director. Tours, (301) 319-3312. *General email, usarmy.detrick.medcom-usamrmc.list .medical-museum@mail.mil*

Web, www.medicalmuseum.mil and *Twitter, @medicalmuseum*

Maintains exhibits related to pathology and the history of medicine, particularly military medicine during the Civil War. Open to the public 10:00 a.m.–5:30 p.m., 7 days a week. Study collection available for scholars by appointment.

Naval History and Heritage Command *(Navy Dept.),* 805 Kidder Breese St. S.E., Washington Navy Yard, DC 20374-5060; (202) 433-2210. Fax, (202) 781-0021. Rear Adm. Samuel Cox (USN, Ret.), Director. Library, (202) 433-4132. Museum, (202) 433-4882. Art Gallery, (202) 433-3815. Archives, (202) 433-4937. Press, (202) 433-7880. *General email, NHHCPublicAffairs@navy.mil*

Web, www.history.navy.mil

Produces publications on naval history. Maintains historical files on Navy ships, operations, shore installations, and aviation. Collects Navy art, artifacts, and photographs. Library, archives, museum, and gallery are open to the public.

Naval History and Heritage Command *(Navy Dept.), Navy Art Collection,* Washington Navy Yard, 822 Sicard St. S.E., Bldg. 67, 20374 (mailing address: 805 Kidder Breese St. S.E., Washington Navy Yard, DC 20374); (202) 433-3815. Gale Munro, Head. *General email, NavyArt@navy.mil*

Web, www.history.navy.mil

Holdings include more than 18,000 paintings, prints, drawings, and sculptures. Artworks depict naval ships, personnel, and action from all eras of U.S. naval history, especially the eras of World War II, the Korean War, and Desert Shield/Storm. Open to the public. Visitors without Defense Dept. or military identification must call in advance. Photo identification required.

U.S. Coast Guard (USCG) *(Homeland Security Dept.),* *Historian,* CG-09224, 2703 Martin Luther King Jr. Ave. S.E., MS 7301, 20593; (202) 372-4651. Fax, (202) 372-4984. *Robert M. Browning, Chief Historian.* *Web, www.uscg.mil/history*

Collects and maintains Coast Guard historical artifacts and documents. Archives are available to the public by appointment only.

U.S. Navy Museum *(Naval Historical Center),* Bldg. 76, 805 Kidder Breese St. S.E., Washington Navy Yard, DC 20374-5060; (202) 433-4882. Fax, (202) 433-8200. *Laura Hockensmith, Deputy Director, Education and Public Programs; James H. Bruns, Director of Museum; Rear Adm. Samuel Cox (USN, Ret.), Director of Naval History. Tours,* (202) 433-6826. *Internships,* (202) 433-6901. *General email, navymuseum@navy.mil*

Web, www.history.navy.mil/museum/NationalMuseums/ org8-1.htm

Collects, preserves, displays, and interprets historic naval artifacts and artwork. Presents a complete overview of U.S. naval history. Open to the public. Photo identification required.

▶**NONGOVERNMENTAL**

Air Force Historical Foundation, 1602 California Ave., #F-162, Joint Base Andrews, MD 20762 (mailing address: P.O. Box 790, Clinton, MD 20735-0790); (301) 736-1959. *Lt. Col. James Vertenten (USAF, Ret.), Executive Director,* (240) 691-3323. *General email, execdir@afhistoricalfoundation.org*

Web, www.afhistory.org

Membership: individuals interested in the history of the U.S. Air Force and U.S. air power. Bestows awards on Air Force Academy and Air War College students and to other active duty personnel. Funds research and publishes books on aviation and Air Force history.

Marine Corps Heritage Foundation, 3800 Fettler Park Dr., #104, Dumfries, VA 22025; (703) 640-7965. Fax, (703) 640-9546. *Lt. Gen. Robert R. Blackman Jr. (USMC, Ret.), President. Toll-free,* (800) 397-7585. *General email, info@marineheritage.org*

Web, www.marineheritage.org

Preserves and promotes Marine Corps history through education, awards, and publications. Offers funding for the study of Marine Corps history. Funds the ongoing expansion of the National Museum of the Marine Corps.

National Guard Educational Foundation, 1 Massachusetts Ave. N.W., 20001; (202) 789-0031. Fax, (202) 682-9358. *Anne Armstrong, Deputy Director,* (202) 408-5890; *Ryan Trainor, Archivist,* (202) 408-5887. *Library,* (202) 408-5890. *Toll-free,* (888) 226-4287. *General email, ngef@ngef.org*

Web, www.ngef.org

Promotes public awareness of the National Guard by providing information about its history and traditions. Museum and library open to the public.

National Museum of American Jewish Military History, 1811 R St. N.W., 20009; (202) 265-6280. Fax, (202) 462-3192. *Greg Byrne, Director. Tours,* (202) 265-6280. *General email, nmajmh@nmajmh.org*

Web, www.nmajmh.org

Collects, preserves, and displays memorabilia of Jewish men and women in the military; conducts research; sponsors seminars; provides information on the history of Jewish participation in the U.S. armed forces.

Naval Historical Foundation, 1306 Dahlgren Ave. S.E., Washington Navy Yard, DC 20374-5055 (mailing address: P.O. Box 15304, Washington, DC 20043); (202) 678-4333. Fax, (703) 580-5280. *Capt. Charles T. Creekman (USN, Ret.), Executive Director. Toll-free,* (888) 880-0102. *General email, nhfwny@navyhistory.org*

Web, www.navyhistory.org

Collects private documents and artifacts relating to naval history; maintains collection on deposit with the Library of Congress for public reference; conducts oral history and heritage speakers programs; raises funds to support the Navy Museum and historical programs.

Cemeteries and Memorials

▶**AGENCIES**

American Battle Monuments Commission, Courthouse Plaza 2, 2300 Clarendon Blvd., #500, Arlington, VA 22201-3367; (703) 696-6900. Fax, (703) 696-6666. *Max Cleland, Secretary,* (703) 696-6902. *General email, info@abmc.gov*

Web, www.abmc.gov

Manages twenty-four military cemeteries overseas and certain memorials in the United States; provides next of kin with grave site and related information.

Army Dept. *(Defense Dept.),* Arlington National Cemetery, Interment Services, Arlington, VA 22211; (877) 907-8585. *Patrick K. Hallinan, Executive Director. Fax (for documents),* (571) 256-3334. *General email for documents, arlingtoncemetery.isb@mail .mil*

Web, www.arlingtoncemetery.mil

Arranges interment services and provides eligibility information for burials at Arlington National Cemetery.

National Cemetery Administration *(Veterans Affairs Dept.),* 810 Vermont Ave. N.W., #400, 20420; (202) 461-6112. Fax, (202) 273-6709. *Ronald E. Walters, Under Secretary for Memorial Affairs, Acting. Information on burial eligibility,* (800) 827-1000. *Web, www.cem.va.gov and www.gravelocator.cem.va.gov*

Administers VA national cemeteries; furnishes markers and headstones for deceased veterans; administers state grants to establish, expand, and improve veterans' cemeteries. Provides presidential memorial certificates to next of kin.

► CONGRESS

For a listing of relevant congressional committees and subcommittees, please see page 565 or the Appendix.

► NONGOVERNMENTAL

Air Force Memorial Foundation, *1 Air Force Memorial Dr., Arlington, VA 22204; (703) 979-0674. Fax, (703) 979-0556. CMSgt. Barbara S. Taylor (USAF, Ret.), Managing Director.*
General email, afmf@airforcememorial.org
Web, www.airforcememorial.org

Oversees daily management of and directs event planning and fund-raising in support of the Air Force Memorial.

U.S. Navy Memorial Foundation, *701 Pennsylvania Ave. N.W., #123, 20004-2608; (202) 380-0710. Fax, (202) 737-2308. Vice Adm. John B. Totushek, President.*
Toll-free, (800) 821-8892.
General email, cmccalip@navymemorial.org
Web, www.navymemorial.org

Educational foundation authorized by Congress. Focuses on U.S. naval history; built and supports the national Navy memorial to honor those who serve or have served in the sea services.

Women in Military Service for America Memorial Foundation, *Dept. 560, 20042-0560; (703) 533-1155. Fax, (703) 931-4208. Maj. Gen. Dee Ann Williams (USA, Ret.), President; Ann Marie Sharratt, Executive Director. Information, (800) 222-2294.*
General email, hq@womensmemorial.org
Web, www.womensmemorial.org

Authorized by Congress to create, support, and build the national memorial to honor women who serve or have served in the U.S. armed forces from the Revolutionary War to the present. Mailing address is for donations.

Ceremonies, Military Bands

► AGENCIES

Air Force Dept. *(Defense Dept.), Air Force Bands, 1690 Air Force Pentagon, #5D1068, 20330; (703) 695-0019. Fax, (703) 693-9601. CMSgt. William E. Marr, Band Manager.*
Web, www.bands.af.mil

Disseminates information to the public regarding various Air Force bands, including their schedules and performances. Oversees policy, training, and personnel assignments for Air Force bands.

Army Dept. *(Defense Dept.), Army Field Band, 4214 Field Band Dr., #5330, Fort Meade, MD 20755-7055; (301) 677-6586. Lt. Col. Jim R. Keene (USA), Commander.*
General email, usarmyfieldband@mail.mil
Web, www.army.mil/fieldband and http://armyfieldband .com

Supports the Army by providing musical services for official military ceremonies and community events. Sponsors vocal and instrumental clinics for high school and college students.

Army Dept. *(Defense Dept.), Ceremonies and Special Events, Fort Lesley J. McNair, 45 1st Ave., Bldg. 42, 20319-5058; (202) 685-4937. Fax, (202) 685-3379. Phil Fowler, Director; Gary S. Davis, Ceremonies Chief; Tina Peck, Special Events Chief.*
Web, mdwhome.mdw.army.mil/event(s)-support/ requesting-ceremonial-support

Coordinates and schedules public ceremonies and special events, including appearances of all armed forces bands and honor guards.

Army Dept. *(Defense Dept.), The U.S. Army Band, Attn: TUSAB, 400 McNair Rd., Fort Myer, VA 22211-1306; (703) 696-3718. Fax, (703) 696-0279. Col. Timothy J. Holtan (USA), Commander. Music Library, (703) 696-3648.*
Web, www.usarmyband.com and Twitter, @thearmyband

Supports the Army by providing musical services for official military ceremonies and community events.

Defense Dept. (DoD), *Community and Public Outreach, 1400 Defense Pentagon, 2E984, 20301-1400; (703) 693-2337. Fax, (703) 697-2577. Bryan Whitman, Deputy Assistant Secretary, Acting. Toll-free (Military OneSource), (800) 342-9647. Public Affairs, (703) 697-5131.*
Web, www.defense.gov

Administers requests for ceremonial bands and other military assets for public events.

Marine Corps *(Defense Dept.), Marine Band, Marine Barracks Annex, 7th St. and K St. S.E., 20003 (mailing address: Marine Barracks Washington, 8th St. and Eye St. S.E., Washington, DC 20390); (202) 433-5809. Fax, (202) 433-4752. Lt. Col. Jason K. Fettig, Director. Concert information, (202) 433-4011. National tours, (703) 614-1405.*
General email, marineband.publicaffairs@usmc.mil
Web, www.marineband.marines.mil and Facebook, www.facebook.com/marineband

Supports the Marine Corps by providing musical services for official military ceremonies and community events.

Navy Dept. *(Defense Dept.), Navy Band, 617 Warrington Ave. S.E., Washington Navy Yard, DC 20374-5054; (202) 433-3676. Fax, (202) 433-4108. Capt. Kenneth Collins, Commanding Officer. Information, (202) 433-3366. Auditions, (202) 433-2840. Public Affairs, (202) 433-4777.*
General email, NavyBand.Public.Affairs@navy.mil
Web, www.navyband.navy.mil

Supports the Navy by providing musical services for official military ceremonies and community events.

U.S. Naval Academy *(Defense Dept.), Band, 101 Buchanan Rd., Annapolis, MD 21402-1258; (410) 293-1257. Fax, (410) 293-2116. Lt. Diane E. Nichols, Director; Stephanie Woodall, Coordinator, Music Department, (410)*

293-2439. *Concert information, (410) 293-3282. Press, (410) 293-1262.*
General email, bandrops@usna.edu
Web, www.usna.edu/USNABand

The Navy's oldest continuing musical organization. Supports the Navy by providing musical services for official military ceremonies and community events.

U.S. Naval Academy *(Defense Dept.), Drum and Bugle Corps,* U.S. Naval Academy, Alumni Hall, 675 Decatur Rd., Annapolis, MD 21402-5086; (410) 293-3602. *Fax, (410) 293-4508. Jeff Weir, Corps Director.*
General email, weir@usna.edu
Web, www.usna.edu/USNADB

One of the oldest drum and bugle corps in the United States. The all-midshipmen drum and bugle corps plays for Brigade of Midshipmen at sporting events, pep rallies, parades, and noon formations. Supports the Navy by providing musical services for official military ceremonies and community events.

RESERVES AND NATIONAL GUARD

General

▶ AGENCIES

Air Force Dept. *(Defense Dept.), Air Force Reserve,* 1150 Air Force Pentagon, #4E138, 20330-1150; (703) 695-8959. *Lt. Gen. James F. Jackson, Chief.*
Web, www.afrc.af.mil

Military office that coordinates and directs Air Force Reserve matters (excluding the Air National Guard).

Air Force Dept. *(Defense Dept.), Reserve Affairs,* 1660 Air Force Pentagon, #5D742, 20330-1660; (703) 697-6375. *Fax, (703) 695-2701. Stephanie Barna, Deputy Assistant Secretary.*
Web, www.af.mil

Civilian office that reviews and monitors Air Force Reserve and Air National Guard.

Army Dept. *(Defense Dept.), Army Reserve,* 2400 Army Pentagon, #3E562, 20310-2400; (703) 695-0031. *Lt. Gen. Jeffrey W. Talley (USA), Chief.*
Web, www.usar.army.mil and Twitter, @USArmyReserve

Military office that monitors legislative affairs as well as coordinates and directs Army Reserve matters (excluding the Army National Guard).

Army Dept. *(Defense Dept.), Manpower and Reserve Affairs,* 111 Army Pentagon, #2E460, 20310-0111; (703) 697-9253. *Fax, (703) 692-9000. Debra S. Wada, Assistant Secretary.*
Web, www.asamra.army.mil

Civilian office that reviews policies and programs for Army personnel and reserves; makes recommendations to the secretary of the Army. Oversees training, military

preparedness, and mobilization for all civilians and active and reserve members of the Army.

Defense Dept. (DoD), *Reserve Affairs,* 1500 Defense Pentagon, #2E556, 20301-1500; (703) 697-6631. *Fax, (703) 697-1682. Stephanie Barna, Assistant Secretary, Acting.*
Web, http://ra.defense.gov

Civilian office that addresses all policy matters pertaining to the seven reserve components of the military services.

Marine Corps *(Defense Dept.), Reserve Affairs,* 3280 Russell Rd., Quantico, VA 22134-5103; (703) 784-9100. *Fax, (703) 784-9805. Col. Robert T. Tobin (USMC), Director.*
Web, www.marines.mil

Military office that coordinates and directs Marine Corps Reserve matters.

National Guard Bureau *(Defense Dept.),* 1636 Defense Pentagon, #1E169, 20301; (703) 614-3087. *Fax, (703) 614-0274. Gen. Frank J. Grass (USA), Chief. Press, (703) 607-2584.*
Web, www.nationalguard.mil

Military office that oversees and coordinates activities of the Air National Guard and Army National Guard.

National Guard Bureau *(Defense Dept.), Air National Guard,* 1000 Air Force Pentagon, #4E126, 20330; (703) 614-8033. *Maj. Gen. Brian Neal (ANG), Director, Acting.*
Web, www.ang.af.mil and Facebook, www.facebook.com/AirNationalGuard

Military office that coordinates and directs Air National Guard matters.

National Guard Bureau *(Defense Dept.), Army National Guard,* 111 S. George Mason Dr., Arlington, VA 22204; (703) 607-7000. *Fax, (703) 607-7088. Lt. Gen. Timothy J. Kadavy (ARNG), Director. Public Affairs, (703) 601-6767.*
Web, www.nationalguard.mil

Military office that coordinates and directs Army National Guard matters.

National Guard Bureau *(Defense Dept.), Chaplain Services,* 111 S. George Mason Dr., Arlington, VA 22204; (703) 607-8657. *Fax, (703) 607-5295. Brig. Gen. David E. Graetz (CHC, USA), Director.*
Web, www.nationalguard.mil

Represents the Chief National Guard Bureau on all aspects of the chaplains' mission. Directs and oversees the activities and policies of the National Guard Chaplain Services. Oversees chaplains and religious services within the National Guard; maintains liaison with religious denominations.

Navy Dept. *(Defense Dept.), Navy Reserve,* 2000 Navy Pentagon, CNO-N095, #4E426, 20350-2000; (703) 693-5757. *Vice Adm. Robin R. Braun, Chief. Duty office, (757) 445-8506.*
Web, www.navy.com/about/about-reserve.html

Military office that coordinates and directs Navy Reserve matters.

Veterans Affairs Department

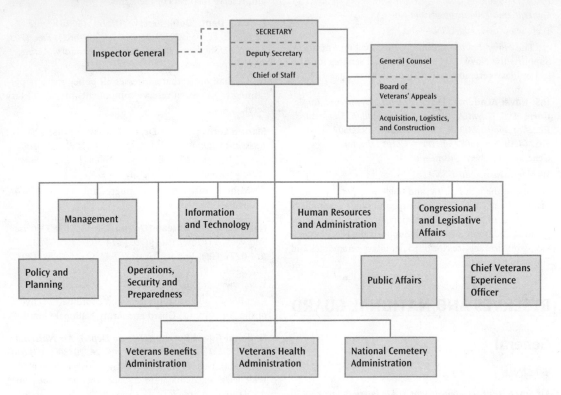

Navy Dept. *(Defense Dept.), Reserve Affairs, 1000 Navy Pentagon, #4D548, 20350-1000; (703) 614-1327. Fax, (703) 693-4959. Dennis Biddick, Deputy Assistant Secretary. Web, www.public.navy.mil/asnmra/pages*

Civilian office that reviews Navy and Marine Corps Reserve policies.

U.S. Coast Guard (USCG) *(Homeland Security Dept.), Reserve and Military Personnel, CG-13, 2703 Martin Luther King Jr. Ave. S.E., MS 7907, 20593-7097; (202) 475-5420. Rear Adm. Kurt B. Hinrichs, Director. Web, www.uscg.mil/hq/cg1/cg13*

Develops and oversees military personnel policy programs to recruit, train, and support all U.S. Coast Guard reserve and active duty forces.

▶ NONGOVERNMENTAL

Assn. of Civilian Technicians (ACT), *12620 Lake Ridge Dr., Lake Ridge, VA 22192-2354; (703) 494-4845. Fax, (703) 494-0961. Terry W. Garnett, National President. Web, www.actnat.com*

Membership: federal civil service employees of the National Guard and Title 5 federal employees. Represents members before federal agencies and Congress.

Assn. of the U.S. Navy, *1619 King St., Alexandria, VA 22314-2793; (703) 548-5800. Fax, (703) 683-3647. Vice Adm. John B. Totushek, Executive Director. Toll-free, (877) 628-9411. Web, www.ausn.org and Twitter, @AUSNTweets*

Membership: active duty and retired Navy and Navy Reserve officers and their families and persons interested in the U.S. Navy. Supports and promotes U.S. military and naval policies, particularly the interests of the Navy personnel and Navy veterans. Offers education programs, reviews of officer and enlisted records, and scholarships for the education of family members. Provides the public with information on national security issues. Assists members with Navy careers, military retirement, and veterans' benefits.

Assn. of the United States Army, *2425 Wilson Blvd., Arlington, VA 22201; (703) 841-4300. Fax, (703) 525-9039. Gen. Gordon R. Sullivan, President. Information, (800) 336-4570. Web, www.ausa.org and Twitter, @AUSAorg*

Membership: civilians and active duty and retired members of the armed forces. Conducts symposia on defense issues and researches topics that affect the military.

Enlisted Assn. of the National Guard of the United States, *3133 Mt. Vernon Ave., Alexandria, VA 22305-2640; (703) 519-3846. Fax, (703) 519-3849. Bryan Birch, Executive Director, Acting. Information, (800) 234-3264. General email, eangus@eangus.org*
Web, www.eangus.org

Membership: active duty and retired enlisted members and veterans of the National Guard. Promotes a strong national defense and National Guard. Sponsors scholarships, conducts seminars, and provides information concerning members and their families.

National Guard Assn. of the United States,
*1 Massachusetts Ave. N.W., 20001-1431; (202) 789-0031.
Fax, (202) 682-9358. Maj. Gen. Gus Hargett (ARNG, Ret.),
President, (202) 408-5894.
General email, ngaus@ngaus.org*

Web, www.ngaus.org

Membership: active duty and retired officers of the National Guard. Works to promote a strong national defense and to maintain a strong, ready National Guard.

Reserve Officers Assn. of the United States,
*1 Constitution Ave. N.E., 20002-5618; (202) 479-2200.
Fax, (202) 547-1641. Col. James R. Sweeney, President.
Information, (800) 809-9448.
General email, info@roa.org*

Web, www.roa.org and Twitter, @ReserveOfficer

Membership: active duty and inactive commissioned and noncommissioned officers of all uniformed services. Supports continuation of a reserve force to enhance national security. Monitors legislation and regulations.

Veterans of Modern Warfare, *#33107, P.O. Box 96503, 20090; Fax, (202) 596-6779. Joseph F. Morgan, President. Toll-free, (888) 445-9891. Suicide hotline, (800) 273-8255. General email, info@vmwusa.org*

Web, www.vmwusa.org and Twitter, @VMWUSA

Chapter-based membership organization. Provides information and assistance in obtaining benefits to all veterans, including active duty and National Guard and Reserve components, as well as any veteran who has served in the U.S. Armed Forces since August 2, 1990. Advocates for veterans.

VETERANS

General

▶AGENCIES

Armed Forces Retirement Home—Washington, *140 Rock Creek Church Rd. N.W., 20011-8400 (mailing address: 3700 N. Capitol St. N.W., Washington, DC 20011-8400); (800) 422-9988. (202) 541-5501. Fax, (202) 541-7519. Steven G. McManus, Chief Operating Officer. General email, admissions@afrh.gov*

Web, www.afrh.gov

Gives domiciliary and medical care to retired members of the armed services or career service personnel unable to earn a livelihood. Formerly known as U.S. Soldiers' and Airmen's Home. (Armed Forces Retirement Home in Gulfport, Miss., reopened in 2010.)

Center for Minority Veterans *(Veterans Affairs Dept.), 810 Vermont Ave. N.W., #436, MC 00M, 20420; (202) 461-6191. Fax, (202) 273-7092. Barbara Ward, Director. Web, www.va.gov/centerforminorityveterans*

Advises the secretary on adoption and implementation of policies and programs affecting minority veterans,

specifically Pacific Islander, Asian American, African American, Hispanic/Latino, and Native American, including American Indian, Alaska Native, and Native Hawaiian, veterans.

Center for Women Veterans *(Veterans Affairs Dept.), 810 Vermont Ave. N.W., #435, MC 00W, 20420; (202) 461-6193. Fax, (202) 273-7092. Betty Moseley Brown, Director, Acting. General email, oow@va.gov*

Web, www.va.gov/womenvet

Advises the secretary on policy on matters related to women veterans; seeks to ensure that women veterans receive benefits and services on par with those of male veterans.

Navy Dept. *(Defense Dept.), Council of Review Boards, 720 Kennon St. S.E., Bldg. 36, #309, Washington Navy Yard, DC 20374-5023; (202) 685-6408. Fax, (202) 685-6610. Col. Jeffrey Riehl (USMC, Ret.), Director. Web, www.public.navy.mil/ASNMRA/CORB/PEB*

Includes the Naval Clemency and Parole Board, which reviews cases of Navy and Marine Corps prisoners; the Naval Discharge Review Board, which considers former service members' less-than-honorable discharge for potential upgrade; the Physical Evaluation Board, which makes determinations about physical fitness for continuation of military service; and the Combat-Related Special Compensation Board, which makes determinations about combat-related conditions and appropriate compensation. All boards make recommendations to the secretary of the Navy.

Noncommissioned Officers Assn., National Capital Office, *P.O. Box 3085, Oakton, VA 22124; (703) 549-0311. Fax, (703) 549-0245. H. Gene Overstreet, President; Jon Ostrowski, Executive Director for Government Affairs. Toll-free, (800) 662-2620. General email, jostrowski@ncoadc.org*

Web, www.ncoausa.org

Congressionally chartered and accredited by the Veterans Affairs Dept. to assist veterans and widows of veterans with claims for benefits. (Headquarters in Selma, Tex.)

Veterans Affairs Dept. (VA), *810 Vermont Ave. N.W., MC-00, 20420; (202) 461-4800. Fax, (202) 495-5463. Robert A. McDonald, Secretary; Robert D. Snyder, Chief of Staff; Sloan D. Gibson, Deputy Secretary. Press, (202) 461-7500. Locator, (202) 273-5400. Crisis line, (800) 273-8255, option 1. Health care, (877) 222-8387. Benefits, (800) 827-1000. Web, www.va.gov*

Information System (IRIS), https://iris.va.gov

Administers programs benefiting veterans, including disability compensation, pensions, education, home loans, insurance, vocational rehabilitation, medical care at veterans' hospitals and outpatient facilities, and burial benefits.

Veterans Affairs Dept. (VA), *Construction and Facilities Management,* *425 Eye St., N.W., 6th Floor, 20001 (mailing address: 810 Vermont Ave. N.W., MS 003C, Washington, DC 20420); (202) 632-4607. Stella S. Fiotes, Executive Director.*
General email, cfm@va.gov
Web, www.cfm.va.gov

Principal construction and real estate arm of the Veterans Administration. Manages all major VA construction and leasing projects.

Veterans Affairs Dept. (VA), *Consumer Affairs,* *810 Vermont Ave. N.W., #915, 20420; (202) 461-7383. Fax, (202) 273-5716. Shirley Williams, Program Assistant, (202) 461-7088.*
Web, www.va.gov

Responds to veterans' complaints concerning VA benefits and services. Answers questions about policy and makes referrals to other VA offices, as appropriate.

Veterans Affairs Dept. (VA), *Policy and Planning,* *810 Vermont Ave. N.W., #300, MS 008, 20420; (202) 461-5800. Fax, (202) 273-5993. Linda Spoonster Schwartz, Assistant Secretary.*
General email, vacontactopp@va.gov
Web, www.va.gov/op3

Serves as the single, departmentwide repository, clearinghouse, and publication source for veterans' demographic and statistical information. Provides advice and support to the secretary in the areas of strategic planning, policy development, program analysis and management, and data governance.

Veterans Benefits Administration (VBA) *(Veterans Affairs Dept.),* *1800 G St. N.W., 20223 (mailing address: 810 Vermont Ave. N.W., #520, Washington, DC 20420); (202) 461-9300. Fax, (202) 275-3591. Danny Pummill, Under Secretary, Acting. Toll-free insurance hotline, (800) 669-8477.*
Web, www.vba.va.gov

Administers nonmedical benefits programs for veterans and their dependents and survivors. Benefits include veterans' compensation (including disability compensation) and pensions, survivors' benefits, education and rehabilitation assistance, home loan benefits, insurance coverage, and burials.

Veterans Benefits Administration (VBA) *(Veterans Affairs Dept.),* *Compensation Service,* *810 Vermont Ave. N.W., #645, MS 21, 20420; (202) 461-9700. Fax, (202) 530-9094. Thomas J. Murphy, Director. Toll-free, (800) 827-1000.*
Web, www.vba.va.gov/bln/21

Administers disability payments; handles claims for burial and plot allowances by veterans' survivors. Provides information on and assistance with benefits legislated by Congress for veterans of active military, naval, or air service.

► **CONGRESS**

For a listing of relevant congressional committees and subcommittees, please see page 565 or the Appendix.

► **NONGOVERNMENTAL**

American Legion, *1608 K St. N.W., 20006; (202) 861-2700. Fax, (202) 861-2786. Verna Jones, Executive Director, 202 263-5740. Information, (800) 433-2786.*
Web, www.legion.org and Twitter, @AmericanLegion

Membership: honorably discharged veterans who served on active duty during periods of declared military conflict. Chartered by Congress to assist veterans with claims for benefits; offers a large array of programs and services for veterans and their families. (National headquarters in Indianapolis, Ind.)

American Red Cross, *Service to the Armed Forces,* *2025 E St. N.W., 2nd Floor, 20006-5009; (202) 303-5000, ext. 2. Fax, (202) 303-0216. Sherri L. Brown, Senior Vice President, (202) 303-8283. Emergency communication services, (888) 443-5722.*
Web, www.redcross.org

Assists veterans and their dependents with claims for benefits on a limited basis; provides emergency services for active duty armed forces personnel and their families; supports medical care and rehabilitation services at military and veterans hospitals.

AMVETS (American Veterans), *4647 Forbes Blvd., Lanham, MD 20706; (301) 459-9600. Fax, (301) 459-7924. Jim King, Executive Director. Toll-free, (877) 726-8387.*
General email, amvets@amvets.org
Web, www.amvets.org and Twitter, @AMVETSNational

Membership: those who are serving or have served honorably in any branch of the military from WWII to the present. Helps members obtain benefits and services; participates in community programs; operates a volunteer service that donates time to hospitalized veterans and warrior transition programs. Monitors legislation and regulations.

Armed Forces Foundation, *16 N. Carolina Ave. S.E., 20003; (202) 547-4713. Fax, (202) 547-4712. Brian Cooke, President.*
General email, info@armedforcesfoundation.org
Web, www.armedforcesfoundation.org

Nonprofit organization that supports mental and physical health of military service members, veterans, and their families. Programs include ProCamps Worldwide, the Wounded Warrior Amputee Softball Team, and the Help Save Our Troops campaign. Operation Caring Classroom educates children about Veterans' Day and sponsors counselors. Awards funds to service members who have been injured or impacted by their service.

Blinded Veterans Assn., *125 N. West St., Alexandria, VA 22314; (202) 371-8880. Fax, (202) 371-8258. Al Avina, Executive Director. Toll-free, (800) 669-7079.*
General email, bva@bva.org

Web, www.bva.org and Twitter, @BlindedVeterans

Chartered by Congress to assist veterans with claims for benefits. Seeks out blinded veterans to make them aware of benefits and services available to them.

Catholic War Veterans U.S.A., *441 N. Lee St., Alexandria, VA 22314-2301; (703) 549-3622. Fax, (703) 684-5196. Dave Crum, Executive Director.*
General email, admin@cwv.org

Web, www.cwv.org and Twitter, @JoinCWVToday

Recognized by the Veterans Affairs Dept. to assist veterans with claims for benefits. Conducts community service programs; offers scholarships for children; supports benefits for Vietnam veterans commensurate with those received by World War II veterans.

Disabled American Veterans, *National Service and Legislative Headquarters, 807 Maine Ave. S.W., 20024-2410; (202) 554-3501. Fax, (202) 554-3581. Michael E. Dobmeier, Judge Advocate; Ron F. Hope, National Commander.*
Web, www.dav.org

Chartered by Congress to assist veterans with claims for benefits; represents veterans seeking to correct alleged errors in military records. Assists families of veterans with disabilities. (Headquarters in Cold Spring, Ky.)

The Enlisted Assn., *Washington Office, 1001 N. Fairfax St., #102, Alexandria, VA 22314; (703) 684-1981. Fax, (703) 548 4876. Deirdre Parke Holleman, Executive Director. Toll-free, (800) 554-8732. VA caregiver support, (855) 260-3274.*
General email, treadmin@treadc.org

Web, www.trea.org

Membership: enlisted personnel of the armed forces, including active duty, reserve, guard, and retirees. Runs scholarship, legislative, and veterans service programs. (Also known as Retired Enlisted Assn., Headquarters in Aurora, Colo.)

Jewish War Veterans of the U.S.A., *1811 R St. N.W., 20009; (202) 265-6280. Fax, (202) 234-5662. Herb Rosenbleeth, National Executive Director.*
General email, jwv@jwv.org

Web, www.jwv.org

Recognized by the Veterans Affairs Dept. to assist veterans with claims for benefits. Offers programs in community relations and services, foreign affairs, national defense, and veterans affairs. Monitors legislation and regulations that affect veterans.

Marine Corps League, *8626 Lee Hwy., #201, Fairfax, VA 22031-3070 (mailing address: P.O. Box 3070, Merrifield, VA 22116); (703) 207-9588. Fax, (703) 207-0047. Thomas W. Hazlett Sr., Executive Director, Acting.*

Toll-free, (800) 625-1775.
Web, www.mclnational.org

Membership: active duty, retired, and reserve Marine Corps groups. Chartered by Congress to assist veterans with claims for benefits. Operates a volunteer service program in VA hospitals.

Military Officers Assn. of America, *201 N. Washington St., Alexandria, VA 22314-2539; (703) 549-2311. Fax, (703) 838-8173. Lt. Gen. Dana Atkins (USAF, Ret.), President. Information, (800) 234-6622.*
General email, msc@moaa.org

Web, www.moaa.org

Membership: officers, former officers, and surviving spouses of officers of the uniformed services. Assists members, their dependents, and survivors with military personnel matters, including service status and retirement problems; provides employment assistance. Monitors legislation affecting active duty officers, retirees, and veterans' affairs, health, and military compensation issues.

Military Order of the Purple Heart of the U.S.A., *5413 Backlick Rd., Suite B, Springfield, VA 22151-3960; (703) 642-5360. Fax, (703) 642-1841. Ernesto P. Hernandez III (USAF, Ret.), National Adjutant. Toll-free, (888) 668-1656. General email, moph@purpleheart.org*

Web, www.purpleheart.org

Membership: veterans awarded the Purple Heart for combat wounds. Chartered by Congress to assist veterans and their families. Conducts service and welfare work on behalf of disabled and needy veterans and their families, especially those requiring claims assistance, those who are homeless, and those requiring employment assistance. Organizes volunteers to provide assistance to hospitalized veterans at VA medical facilities and State Veterans Homes.

National Coalition for Homeless Veterans, *333 1/2 Pennsylvania Ave. S.E., 20003-1148; (202) 546-1969. Fax, (202) 546-2063. Baylee Crone, Executive Director. Toll-free, (800) VET HELP.*
General email, info@nchv.org

Web, www.nchv.org

Provides technical assistance to service providers; advocates on behalf of homeless veterans.

National Veterans Legal Services Program, *1600 K St. N.W., #500, 20006 (mailing address: P.O. Box 65762, Washington, DC 20035); (202) 265-8305. Fax, (202) 328-0063. Ronald B. Abrams, Co-Executive Director; Barton F. Stichman, Co-Executive Director.*
General email, info@nvlsp.org

Web, www.nvlsp.org

Represents the interests of veterans through educational programs, advocacy, public policy programming, and litigation.

Paralyzed Veterans of America, *801 18th St. N.W., 20006-3517; (202) 872-1300. Sherman Gillums Jr., Deputy*

Executive Director. Information, (800) 424-8200. TTY, (800) 795-4327.

General email, info@pva.org

Web, www.pva.org

Congressionally chartered veterans service organization that assists veterans with claims for benefits. Distributes information on special education for paralyzed veterans; advocates for high-quality care and supports and raises funds for medical research.

Veterans for Common Sense, 900 2nd St. N.E., #216, 20002; Anthony Hardie, Director, (608) 239-4658.

General email, info@veteransforcommonsense.org

Web, www.veteransforcommonsense.org

Grassroots policy advocacy nonprofit that aims to protect veterans benefits and rights. Monitors legislation and regulations.

Veterans of Foreign Wars of the United States, 200 Maryland Ave. N.E., 20002-5724; (202) 543-2239. Fax, (202) 543-2746. John A. Biedrzycki, Commander-in-Chief; Joe Davis, Director of Public Affairs, (202) 608-8357. Helpline, (800) 839-1899.

General email, vfw@vfw.org

Web, www.vfw.org and Twitter, @VFWHQ

Chartered by Congress to assist veterans with claims for benefits, including disability compensation, education, and pensions. Inspects VA health care facilities and cemeteries. Monitors medical updates and employment practices regarding veterans. (Headquarters in Kansas City, Mo.)

Veterans of Modern Warfare, #33107, P.O. Box 96503, 20090; Fax, (202) 596-6779. Joseph F. Morgan, President. Toll-free, (888) 445-9891. Suicide hotline, (800) 273-8255.

General email, info@vmwusa.org

Web, www.vmwusa.org and Twitter, @VMWUSA

Chapter-based membership organization. Provides information and assistance in obtaining benefits to all veterans, including active duty and National Guard and Reserve components, as well as any veteran who has served in the U.S. Armed Forces since August 2, 1990. Advocates for veterans.

Vietnam Veterans of America, 8719 Colesville Rd., #100, Silver Spring, MD 20910-3710; (301) 585-4000. Fax, (301) 585-0519. John P. Rowan, President. Information, (800) 882-1316.

General email, communications@vva.org

Web, www.vva.org

Congressionally chartered membership organization that provides information on legislation that affects Vietnam-era veterans and their families. Engages in legislative and judicial advocacy in areas relevant to Vietnam-era veterans. Provides information concerning benefits and initiates programs that ensure access to education and employment opportunities. Promotes full accounting of POWs and MIAs.

Appeals of VA Decisions

▶AGENCIES

Defense Dept. (DoD), *Legal Policy,* 4000 Defense Pentagon, #2C548A, 20301-4000; (703) 697-3387. Paul Kantwill, Director; Lt. Col. Ryan Oakley, Deputy Director.

Web, www.defense.gov

Coordinates policy in a variety of personnel-related areas, including the Members Civil Relief Act, legal assistance, political activities, and corrections.

Navy Dept. *(Defense Dept.),* **Council of Review Boards,** 720 Kennon St. S.E., Bldg. 36, #309, Washington Navy Yard, DC 20374-5023; (202) 685-6408. Fax, (202) 685-6610. Col. Jeffrey Riehl (USMC, Ret.), Director.

Web, www.public.navy.mil/ASNMRA/CORB

Military office that administers boards that review appeal cases for the Navy and the Marine Corps. Composed of the Physical Evaluation Board, the Naval Discharge Review Board, the Naval Clemency and Parole Board, the Combat-Related Special Compensation (CRSC) Branch, and the Board for Decorations and Medals.

Veterans Affairs Dept. (VA), *Board of Veterans Appeals,* 425 Eye St. N.W., 20001; (800) 923-8387. Fax, (202) 343-1889. Laura H. Eskenazi, Vice Chair. Claims status, (202) 565-5436. Information, (202) 632-4603.

Web, www.bva.va.gov

Final appellate body within the department; reviews claims for veterans benefits on appeal from agencies of original jurisdiction. Decisions of the board are subject to review by the U.S. Court of Appeals for Veterans Claims.

▶JUDICIARY

U.S. Court of Appeals for the Federal Circuit, 717 Madison Pl. N.W., 20439; (202) 275-8000. Fax, (202) 275-9678. Sharon Prost, Chief Judge; Daniel E. O'Toole, Clerk, (202) 272-8020. Help Desk, (202) 275-8036. Mediation, (202) 275-8120.

Web, www.cafc.uscourts.gov

Reviews decisions concerning the Veterans' Judicial Review Provisions.

U.S. Court of Appeals for Veterans Claims, 625 Indiana Ave. N.W., #900, 20004-2950; (202) 501-5970. Fax, (202) 501-5848. Lawrence B. Hagel, Chief Judge; Gregory O. Block, Clerk.

Web, www.uscourts.cavc.gov

Independent court that reviews decisions of the VA's Board of Veterans Appeals concerning benefits. Focuses primarily on disability benefits claims.

►NONGOVERNMENTAL

American Legion, *Claims Services, Veterans Affairs, and Rehabilitation Division,* *1608 K St. N.W., 20006; (202) 861-2700. Fax, (202) 833-4452. Zack Hearn, Deputy Director.*
Web, www.legion.org

Membership: honorably discharged veterans who served during declared military conflicts. Assists veterans with appeals before the Veterans Affairs Dept. for compensation and benefits claims.

American Legion, *Discharge Review and Correction Boards Unit,* *1608 K St. N.W., 20006-2847; (202) 861-2700. Fax, (202) 861-0033. Ray Spencer, Supervisor.*
Web, www.legion.org

Membership: honorably discharged veterans who served during declared military conflicts. Represents before the Defense Dept. former military personnel seeking to upgrade less-than-honorable discharges and to correct alleged errors in military records.

Disabled American Veterans, *National Service and Legislative Headquarters,* *807 Maine Ave. S.W., 20024-2410; (202) 554-3501. Fax, (202) 554-3581. Michael E. Dobmeier, Judge Advocate; Ron F. Hope, National Commander.*
Web, www.dav.org

Oversees regional offices in assisting disabled veterans with claims, benefits, and appeals, including upgrading less-than-honorable discharges. Monitors legislation. (Headquarters in Cold Spring, Ky.)

National Veterans Legal Services Program, *1600 K St. N.W., #500, 20006 (mailing address: P.O. Box 65762, Washington, DC 20035); (202) 265-8305. Fax, (202) 328-0063. Ronald B. Abrams, Co-Executive Director; Barton F. Stichman, Co-Executive Director.*
General email, info@nvlsp.org
Web, www.nvlsp.org

Represents the interests of veterans through educational programs, advocacy, public policy programming, and litigation.

Veterans of Foreign Wars of the United States, *200 Maryland Ave. N.E., 20002-5724; (202) 543-2239. Fax, (202) 543-2746. John A. Biedrzycki, Commander-in-Chief; Joe Davis, Director of Public Affairs, (202) 608-8357. Helpline, (800) 839-1899.*
General email, vfw@vfw.org
Web, www.vfw.org and Twitter, @VFWHQ

Assists veterans and their dependents and survivors with appeals before the Veterans Affairs Dept. for benefits claims. Assists with cases in the U.S. Court of Appeals for Veterans Claims. (Headquarters in Kansas City, Mo.)

Education, Economic Opportunity

►AGENCIES

Office of Personnel Management (OPM), *Veterans Services,* *1900 E St. N.W., #7439, 20415; (202) 606-3602. Fax, (202) 606-6017. Hakeem Basheerud-Deen, Director.*
Web, www.opm.gov/policy-data-oversight/veterans-services

Provides federal employees and transitioning military service members and their families, federal human resources professionals, and hiring managers with information on employment opportunities with the federal government. Administers the Disabled Veterans Affirmative Action Program.

Small Business Administration (SBA), *Veterans Business Development,* *409 3rd St. S.W., #5700, 20416; (202) 205-6773. Fax, (202) 205-7292. Barb Carson, Associate Administrator, Acting. TTY, (800) 877-8339.*
Web, www.sba.gov/offices/headquarters/ovbd

Helps veterans use SBA loans through counseling, procurement, and training programs in entrepreneurship.

Veterans Benefits Administration (VBA) *(Veterans Affairs Dept.), Education Service,* *1800 G St. N.W., #601, 20006 (mailing address: 810 Vermont Ave. N.W., Washington, DC 20420); (202) 461-9800. Maj. Gen. Robert M. Worley II, Director. Bill information, (888) 442-4551.*
Web, www.gibill.va.gov

Administers VA's education program, including financial support for veterans' education and for spouses and dependent children of deceased and disabled veterans; provides eligible veterans and dependents with educational assistance under the G.I. Bill and Veterans Educational Assistance Program. Provides postsecondary institutions with funds, based on their enrollment of eligible veterans.

Veterans Benefits Administration (VBA) *(Veterans Affairs Dept.), Loan Guaranty Service,* *810 Vermont Ave. N.W., #525, 20420; (202) 632-8862. Fax, (202) 495-5798. Michael (Mike) L. Frueh, Director.*
Web, www.benefits.va.gov/homeloans

Guarantees private institutional financing of home loans (including manufactured home loans) for veterans; provides disabled veterans with direct loans and grants for specially adapted housing; administers a direct loan program for Native American veterans living on trust land.

Veterans Benefits Administration (VBA) *(Veterans Affairs Dept.), Vocational Rehabilitation and Employment Service,* *810 Vermont Ave. N.W., MS 28, 20420; (202) 461-9600. Fax, (202) 275-5122. Jack Kammerer, Director.*
Web, www.vba.va.gov/bln/vre

Administers VA's vocational rehabilitation and employment program, which provides service-disabled veterans with services and assistance; helps veterans to become employable and to obtain and maintain suitable employment.

Veterans' Employment and Training Service *(Labor Dept.), 200 Constitution Ave. N.W., #S1325, 20210; (202) 693-4700. Fax, (202) 693-4754. Michael H. Michaud, Assistant Secretary. Toll-free, (800) 487-2365.*
Web, www.dol.gov/vets

Works with and monitors state employment offices to see that preference is given to veterans seeking jobs; advises the secretary on veterans' issues.

► **CONGRESS**

For a listing of relevant congressional committees and subcommittees, please see page 565 or the Appendix.

► **NONGOVERNMENTAL**

Blinded Veterans Assn., *125 N. West St., Alexandria, VA 22314; (202) 371-8880. Fax, (202) 371-8258. Al Avina, Executive Director. Toll-free, (800) 669-7079.*
General email, bva@bva.org
Web, www.bva.org and Twitter, @BlindedVeterans

Provides blind and disabled veterans with vocational rehabilitation.

National Assn. of State Workforce Agencies, *444 N. Capitol St. N.W., #142, 20001; (202) 434-8020. Fax, (202) 434-8033. Scott Sanders, Executive Director. Press, (202) 434-8023.*
General email, mkatz@naswa.org
Web, www.naswa.org

Membership: state employment security administrators. Provides veterans employment and training professionals with opportunities for networking and information exchange. Monitors legislation and regulations that affect veterans' employment and training programs involving state employment security agencies.

Paralyzed Veterans of America, *801 18th St. N.W., 20006-3517; (202) 872-1300. Sherman Gillums Jr., Deputy Executive Director. Information, (800) 424-8200. TTY, (800) 795-4327.*
General email, info@pva.org
Web, www.pva.org

Congressionally chartered veterans service organization that assists veterans with claims for benefits. Promotes access to educational and public facilities and to public transportation for people with disabilities; seeks modification of workplaces.

Health Care, VA Hospitals

► **AGENCIES**

Army Dept. *(Defense Dept.), Wounded Warrior Program, 200 Stovall St., #7N65, Alexandria, VA 22332-5000; (877) 393-9058. Fax, (703) 325-1516.*

Col. David S. Oeschger (USA), Director. Overseas, (312) 221-9113.
General email, usarmy.pentagon.medcom-WTC.mbx .contact-center@mail.mil
Web, http://wtc.army.mil/aw2 and Twitter, @armyWTC

Assists and advocates for severely disabled and ill soldiers, veterans, and their families. Provides each soldier with a personal AW2 advocate. Tracks and monitors severely disabled soldiers beyond their medical retirement.

Defense Dept. (DoD), *Force Health Protection and Readiness, 7700 Arlington Blvd., Falls Church, VA 22042; (703) 681-8456. Dr. David J. Smith, Deputy Assistant Secretary.*
General email, FHPR.communications@tma.osd.mil
Web, http://fhpr.osd.mil

Advises the secretary of defense on measures to improve the health of deployed forces. Maintains communication between the Defense Dept., service members, veterans, and their families.

Veterans Health Administration (VHA) *(Veterans Affairs Dept.), 810 Vermont Ave. N.W., #800, 20420; (202) 273-5400. Fax, (202) 273-7090. Dr. David J. Shulkin, Under Secretary. Toll-free, (877) 222-8387.*
Web, www.va.gov/health and Twitter, @VeteransHealth

Oversees all health care policies for all eligible veterans. Recommends policy and administers medical and hospital services for eligible veterans. Publishes guidelines on treatment of veterans exposed to Agent Orange.

Veterans Health Administration (VHA) *(Veterans Affairs Dept.), Academic Affiliations, 810 Vermont Ave. N.W., 10A2D, 20420; (202) 461-9490. Fax, (202) 461-9855. Dr. Robert L. Jesse, Chief Officer.*
Web, www.va.gov/oaa

Administers education and training programs for health professionals, students, and residents through partnerships with affiliated academic institutions.

Veterans Health Administration (VHA) *(Veterans Affairs Dept.), Dentistry, 810 Vermont Ave. N.W., 10NC7, 20005; (202) 461-6947. Dr. Patricia Arola, Assistant Under Secretary.*
Web, www.va.gov/dental

Administers and coordinates VA oral health care programs; dental care delivered in a VA setting; administration of oral research, education, and training for VA oral health personnel; delivery of care to VA patients in private practice settings.

Veterans Health Administration (VHA) *(Veterans Affairs Dept.), Geriatrics and Extended Care, 810 Vermont Ave. N.W., #10P4G, 20420; (202) 461-6750. Fax, (202) 465-6195. Dr. Richard M. Allman, Chief Consultant.*
Web, www.va.gov/geriatrics

Administers research, educational, and clinical health care programs in geriatrics at VA and community nursing homes, personal care homes, VA domiciliaries, state veterans' homes, and in home-based and other noninstitutional care.

Veterans Health Administration (VHA) *(Veterans Affairs Dept.), Mental Health Services, 810 Vermont Ave. N.W., MS 10P4M, 20420; (202) 461-4170. Fax, (202) 495-5933. Marsden McGuire, Deputy Chief Consultant; Vashtie Reedy, Management Program Analyst.*
Web, www.mentalhealth.va.gov

Develops ambulatory and inpatient psychiatry and psychology programs for the mentally ill and for drug and alcohol abusers; programs are offered in VA facilities and twenty-one Veterans Integrated Service Networks. Incorporates special programs for veterans suffering from post-traumatic stress disorders, serious mental illness, addictive disorders, and homelessness.

Veterans Health Administration (VHA) *(Veterans Affairs Dept.), Office of the Assistant Deputy Under Secretary for Health Policy and Planning, 810 Vermont Ave. N.W., (10A5), 20420; (202) 461-7100. Fax, (202) 273-9030. Pat Vandenberg, Assistant Deputy Under Secretary.*
Web, www.va.gov/healthpolicyplanning

Coordinates and develops departmental planning to distribute funds to VA field facilities.

Veterans Health Administration (VHA) *(Veterans Affairs Dept.), Patient Care Services, 810 Vermont Ave. N.W., (10P4), MS 11, 20420; (202) 461-7800. Fax, (202) 495-5243, Dr. Maureen F. McCarthy, Assistant Deputy Under Secretary, Acting; Dr. Deepak Mandi, Deputy Chief Officer, Acting.*
Web, www.patientcare.va.gov

Manages clinical programs of the VA medical care system, including rehabilitation and recovery, diagnosis and therapy, palliative care, disease prevention, and health promotion.

Veterans Health Administration (VHA) *(Veterans Affairs Dept.), Readjustment Counseling Service, 1717 H St. N.W., #444, 20006; (202) 461-6525. Fax, (202) 495-6206. Vacant, Chief Officer. Toll-free, (877) 927-8307.*
Web, www.vetcenter.va.gov and www.va.gov

Responsible for community-based centers for veterans nationwide. Provides outreach and counseling services for war-related psychological problems and transition to civilian life. Offers bereavement counseling to surviving family members.

Veterans Health Administration (VHA) *(Veterans Affairs Dept.), Research and Development, 810 Vermont Ave. N.W., (10P9), MS 10P9, 20420; (202) 443-5600. Fax, (202) 495-6196. Kyang-Mi Chang, Chief Officer.*
General email, vha10P9ordops@va.gov
Web, www.research.va.gov

Formulates and implements policy for the research and development program of the Veterans Health Administration; advises the under secretary for health on research-related matters and on management of the VA's health care system; represents the VA in interactions with external organizations in matters related to biomedical and health services research.

Veterans Health Administration (VHA) *(Veterans Affairs Dept.), Voluntary Service, 810 Vermont Ave. N.W., (10B2A), 20420; (202) 461-7300. Fax, (202) 495-6208. Sabrina Clark, Director.*
General email, VHACO10B2AStaff@va.gov
Web, www.volunteer.va.gov

Supervises volunteer programs in VA medical centers.

▶ **CONGRESS**

For a listing of relevant congressional committees and subcommittees, please see page 565 or the Appendix.

▶ **NONGOVERNMENTAL**

National Assn. of Veterans Affairs Physicians and Dentists, *P.O. Box 15418, Arlington, VA 22215-0418; (866) 836-3520. Fax, (540) 972-1728. Dr. Samuel V. Spagnolo, President.*
General email, info@navapd.org
Web, www.navapd.org

Seeks to improve the quality of care and conditions at VA hospitals. Monitors legislation and regulations on veterans' health care.

National Conference on Ministry to the Armed Forces, Endorsers Conference for Veterans Affairs Chaplaincy, *P.O. Box 7572, Arlington, VA 22207-9998; (703) 608-2100. Rev. Wollom (Wally) A. Jensen (USN, Ret.), Chair.*
Web, www.ncmaf.org

Encourages religious ministry to veterans in all Veterans Affairs hospitals.

Paralyzed Veterans of America, *801 18th St. N.W., 20006-3517; (202) 872-1300. Sherman Gillums Jr., Deputy Executive Director. Information, (800) 424-8200. TTY, (800) 795-4327.*
General email, info@pva.org
Web, www.pva.org

Congressionally chartered veterans service organization. Consults with the Veterans Affairs Dept. on the establishment and operation of spinal cord injury treatment centers.

Vietnam Veterans of America, *Veterans Health Council, 8719 Colesville Rd., #100, Silver Spring, MD 20910-3710; (301) 585-4000, ext. 111. Fax, (301) 585-3180. Thomas (Tom) J. Berger, Executive Director. Toll-free, (800) 882-1316.*
General email, vhc@veteranshealth.org
Web, www.veteranshealth.org

Health education and information network for veterans and their families.

Spouses, Dependents, Survivors

▶ **AGENCIES**

Air Force Dept. *(Defense Dept.), Manpower Personnel and Services, 1040 Air Force Pentagon, #4E168, 20330-1040; (703) 697-6088. Lt. Gen. Gina M. Grosso, Deputy Chief of Staff.*
Web, www.afpc.af.mil

Military office that responds to inquiries concerning deceased Air Force personnel and their beneficiaries; refers inquiries to the Military Personnel Center at Randolph Air Force Base in San Antonio, Texas.

Marine Corps *(Defense Dept.), Casualty Assistance Section, HQUSMC, 2008 Elliott Rd., Quantico, VA 22134-5102; (703) 784-9512. Fax, (703) 784-4134. Gerald Castle, Head; Cindy Grubb, Head of Case Management. Toll-free, (800) 847-1597.*
General email, casualty.section@usmc.mil
Web, www.mcieast.marines.mil/staffoffices/adjutant/casualtyassistanceprogram.aspx

Confirms beneficiaries of deceased Marine Corps personnel for benefits distribution.

Veterans Health Administration (VHA) *(Veterans Affairs Dept.), Readjustment Counseling Service, Bereavement Counseling for Surviving Family Members, (202) 461-6530. Fax, (303) 216-9073. Andrew Carraway, Chief Officer.*
General email, vetcenter.bereavement@va.gov
Web, www.vetcenter.va.gov/Bereavement_Counseling.asp

Offers bereavement counseling to parents, spouses, siblings, and children of armed forces personnel who died in service to their country and to family members of reservists and those in the National Guard who died while federally activated. Services include outreach, counseling, and referrals. Counseling provided without cost at community-based Vet Centers.

▶NONGOVERNMENTAL

American Gold Star Mothers Inc., *2128 Leroy Pl. N.W., 20008-1893; (202) 265-0991. Cindy Kruge, National President.*
General email, goldstarmoms@yahoo.com
Web, www.goldstarmoms.com

Membership: mothers who have lost sons or daughters in military service. Members serve as volunteers in VA hospitals and around the country.

Army and Air Force Mutual Aid Assn., *102 Sheridan Ave., Fort Myer, VA 22211-1110; (703) 707-4600. Fax, (888) 210-4882. Maj. Walt Lincoln (USA, Ret.), President. Toll-free, (800) 522-5221.*
General email, info@aafmaa.com
Web, www.aafmaa.com

Private service organization that offers member and family insurance services to U.S. armed forces personnel. Recognized by the Veterans Affairs Dept. to assist veterans and their survivors with claims for benefits.

Army Distaff Foundation (Knollwood), *6200 Oregon Ave. N.W., 20015-1543; (202) 541-0400. Fax, (202) 364-2856. Maj. Gen. Stephen T. Rippe (USA, Ret.), Chief Executive Officer. Information, (800) 541-4255. Admission, (202) 541-0149.*
General email, dschrag@armydistaff.org
Web, www.armydistaff.org

Nonprofit continuing care retirement community for career military officers and their families. Provides retirement housing and health care services.

EX-POSE: Ex-Partners of Servicemembers for Equality, *P.O. Box 11191, Alexandria, VA 22312-0191; (703) 941-5844. Fax, (703) 212-6951. Nancy Davis, Manager.*
General email, ex-pose@juno.com
Web, www.ex-pose.org

Membership: military members, retirees, current/former spouses and their children. Educates military couples going through divorce. Provides explanation of possible legal interests and legal entitlements depending on the length of marriage. Open Tuesday and Wednesday, 10:00 a.m.–3:00 p.m.

Society of Military Widows, *5535 Hempstead Way, Springfield, VA 22151; (703) 750-1342. Fax, (703) 354-4380. Patricia Walker, President; Janet Snyder, Legislative Chair. Information, (800) 842-3451.*
General email, kara7072@aol.com
Web, www.militarywidows.org

Membership: widows of active, reserve, or veteran military personnel. Serves the interests of widows of servicemen; provides support programs and information. Monitors legislation concerning military widows' benefits. (Affiliated with the National Assn. for Uniformed Services.)

Tragedy Assistance Program for Survivors (TAPS), *3033 Wilson Blvd., #630, Arlington, VA 22201; (202) 588-8277. Fax, (571) 385-2524. Bonnie Carroll, President. Toll-free 24-hour crisis intervention hotline, (800) 959-8277.*
General email, info@taps.org
Web, www.taps.org

Offers emotional support to those who have lost a loved one in military service. Has caseworkers who act as liaisons to military and veterans agencies. Provides 24/7 resource and information help line. Hosts Good Grief camps for children, seminars for adults, and online and in-person support groups. Publishes a quarterly magazine on grief and loss.

15

National and
Homeland Security

GENERAL POLICY AND ANALYSIS

Basic Resources

▶AGENCIES

Air Force Dept. *(Defense Dept.)*, 1670 Air Force Pentagon, #4E878, 20330-1670; (703) 697-7376. Fax, (703) 695-7791. *Deborah Lee James, Secretary; Lisa S. Disbrow, Under Secretary, Acting. Press, (703) 695-0640.*
Web, www.af.mil

Civilian office that develops and reviews Air Force national security policies in conjunction with the chief of staff of the Air Force and the secretary of defense.

Air Force Dept. *(Defense Dept.)*, *Chief of Staff*, 1670 Air Force Pentagon, 20330-1670; (703) 697-9225. Fax, (703) 693-9297. *Gen. Mark A. Welsh III, Chief of Staff.*
Web, www.af.mil/information/csaf

Military office that develops and directs Air Force national security policies in conjunction with the secretary of the Air Force and the secretary of defense.

Army Dept. *(Defense Dept.)*, 101 Army Pentagon, #3E700, 20310-0101; (703) 695-1717. Fax, (703) 697-8036. *Patrick J. Murphy, Secretary, Acting.*
Web, www.army.mil and Twitter, @USArmy

Civilian office that develops and reviews Army national security policies in conjunction with the chief of staff of the Army and the secretary of defense.

Army Dept. *(Defense Dept.)*, *Chief of Staff*, 200 Army Pentagon, #3E672, 20310-0200; (703) 697-0900. Fax, (703) 614-5268. *Gen. Mark A. Milley (USA), Chief of Staff.*
Web, www.army.mil and Twitter, @GENMarkMilley

Military office that develops and administers Army national security policies in conjunction with the secretary of the Army and the secretary of defense.

Bureau of Conflict and Stabilization Operations *(State Dept.)*, 2121 Virginia Ave. N.W., #7100, 20522; (202) 663-0323. *Dolores M. Brown, Assistant Secretary, Acting. General email, csopublic@state.gov*
Web, www.state.gov/j/cso and Twitter, @StateCSO

Advances U.S. national security by working with partners in select countries to mitigate and prevent violent conflict. Conducts conflict analysis to identify factors contributing to mass violence or instability; develops prioritized strategies to address these factors; provides experienced leadership and technical experts to operationalize U.S. government and host-nation plans. Provides funding and training.

Bureau of Political-Military Affairs *(State Dept.)*, 2201 C St. N.W., #8757, 20520; (202) 647-9022. Fax, (202) 736-4779. *Tina Kaidanow, Assistant Secretary, Acting.*
Web, www.state.gov/t/pm

Liaison between the State Dept. and Defense Dept. Provides policy direction in the areas of international security, security assistance, military operations, defense strategy and policy, military use of space, and defense trade.

Defense Dept. (DoD), 1000 Defense Pentagon, #3E880, 20301-1000; (703) 692-7100. Fax, (703) 571-8951. *Ashton B. Carter, Secretary; Robert O. Work, Deputy Secretary. Information, (703) 571-3343. Pentagon operator, (703) 545-6700. Press, (703) 697-5131. Tours, (703) 697-1776.*
Web, www.defense.gov

Civilian office that develops national security policies and has overall responsibility for administering national defense; responds to public and congressional inquiries about national defense matters.

Defense Dept. (DoD), *Energy, Installations, and Environment*, 3400 Defense Pentagon, #5C646, 20301-3400; (703) 695-2880. Fax, (703) 693-2659. *John Conger, Assistant Secretary, Acting.*
Web, www.acq.osd.mil/eie

Oversees and offers policy guidance for all Defense Dept. energy, installations, and environmental programs.

Defense Dept. (DoD), *Homeland Defense and Global Security*, 2600 Defense Pentagon, #3C852A, 20301-2600; (703) 697-7728. Fax, (703) 614-2259. *Tom Atkin, Assistant Secretary, Acting.*
Web, www.defense.gov

Develops and coordinates national security and defense strategies and advises on the resources, forces, and contingency plans necessary to implement those strategies. Ensures the integration of defense strategy into the department's resource allocation and force structure development. Evaluates the capability of forces to accomplish defense strategy. Also serves as primary liaison between the Defense Dept. and the Homeland Security Dept. Supervises all Defense Dept. homeland defense activities.

Defense Dept. (DoD), *Joint Chiefs of Staff*, 9999 Defense Pentagon, #2E872, 20318-9999; (703) 697-9121. Fax, (703) 697-6002. *Gen. Joseph F. Dunford Jr. (USA), Chair.*
Web, www.jcs.mil

Joint military staff office that assists the president, the National Security Council, and the secretary of defense in developing national security policy and in coordinating operations of the individual armed services.

Defense Dept. (DoD), *Policy*, 2000 Defense Pentagon, #3E806, 20301; (703) 697-7200. Fax, (703) 697-6602. *Christine E. Wormuth, Under Secretary for Policy; Brian P. McKeon, Principal Deputy Under Secretary.*
Web, http://policy.defense.gov

Civilian office responsible for policy matters relating to international security issues and political-military affairs. Oversees such areas as arms control, foreign military sales, intelligence collection and analysis, and NATO and regional security affairs.

Defense Dept. (DoD), *Special Operations and Low-Intensity Conflict*, 2500 Defense Pentagon, #3C852A, 20301-2500; (703) 695-9667. Fax, (703) 693-6335. *Michael D. Lumpkin, Assistant Secretary.*
Web, www.defense.gov

Serves as special staff assistant and civilian adviser to the secretary of defense on matters related to special operations and international terrorism.

Defense Logistics Agency *(Defense Dept.), Energy,* *8725 John Jay Kingman Rd., #4950, Fort Belvoir, VA 22060-6222; (703) 767-9706. Fax, (703) 767-9690. Brig. Gen. Mark M. McLeod (USAF), Commander. Toll-free, (877) 352-2255. Public Affairs, (703) 767-4108.* *Web, www.dla.mil/Energy.aspx*

Provides the Defense Dept. and other federal agencies with products and services to meet energy-related needs; facilitates the cycle of storage and deployment of fuels and other energy sources, including petroleum, electricity, water and natural gas, as well as space and missile propellants. Provides information on alternative fuels and renewable energy and serves as the executive agent for the Defense Dept.'s bulk petroleum supply chain.

Homeland Security Dept. (DHS), *3801 Nebraska Ave. N.W., 20528; (202) 282-8000. Fax, (202) 282-8236. Jeh Johnson, Secretary; Alejandro Mayorkas, Deputy Secretary. Press, (202) 282-8010. Comments, (202) 282-8495.* *Web, www.dhs.gov*

Responsible for the development and coordination of a comprehensive national strategy to protect the United States against terrorist attacks and other threats and hazards. Coordinates the strategy of the executive branch with those of state and local governments and private entities to detect, prepare for, protect against, respond to, and recover from terrorist attacks and other emergencies in the United States. Administers the National Terrorism Advisory System to communicate information about terrorist threats to the public.

Homeland Security Dept. (DHS), *Science and Technology Directorate, 245 Murray Lane, 20528; (202) 254-6006. Fax, (202) 254-5704. Reginald Brothers, Under Secretary. Press, (202) 282-8010.* *Web, www.dhs.gov/st-directorate*

Responsible for oversight and coordination of the development and augmentation of homeland security technology.

Marine Corps *(Defense Dept.), Commandant, Marine Corps Headquarters, 3000 Marine Corps Pentagon, #4E734, 20350-3000; (703) 614-2500. Fax, (703) 697-7246. Gen. Robert B. Neller (USMC), Commandant. Information, 703614-2500.* *Web, www.hqmc.marines.mil/cmc/home.aspx*

Military office that develops and directs Marine Corps national security policies in conjunction with the secretary of defense and the secretary of the Navy.

National Institute of Standards and Technology (NIST) *(Commerce Dept.), Special Programs Office, 100 Bureau Dr., MS 1000, Gaithersburg, MD 20899-1000; (301) 975-4447. Fax, (301) 975-8972. Richard R. Cavanagh, Director. General information, (301) 975-2756.* *Web, www.nist.gov/director/spo*

Fosters collaboration among government, military, academia, professional, and private organizations to respond to critical national needs through science-based standards and technology innovation, including areas of homeland security and cybersecurity.

National Security Council (NSC) *(Executive Office of the President), The White House, 20504; (202) 456-9491. Susan Rice, National Security Adviser. Press, (202) 456-9271.* *Web, www.whitehouse.gov/administration/eop/nsc*

Advises the president on domestic, foreign, and military policies relating to national security.

Navy Dept. *(Defense Dept.), 1200 Navy Pentagon, #4D652, 20350-1000; (703) 695-3131. Fax, (703) 693-9545. Raymond (Ray) E. Mabus, Secretary; Thomas W. Hicks, Under Secretary, Acting. General email, secnavypa.fct@navy.mil* *Web, www.navy.mil*

Civilian office that develops and reviews Navy and Marine Corps national security policies in conjunction with the chief of naval operations, the commandant of the Marine Corps, and the secretary of defense.

Navy Dept. *(Defense Dept.), Naval Operations, 2000 Navy Pentagon, #4E658, 20350-2000; (703) 695-5661. Fax, (703) 693-9408. Adm. John Richardson, Chief.* *Web, www.navy.mil/cno*

Military office that develops Navy national security policies in conjunction with the secretary of defense and the secretary of the Navy and in cooperation with the commandant of the Marine Corps.

State Dept., *Foreign Missions, 3507 International Pl. N.W., 20008-3025; (202) 895-3500. Fax, (202) 736-4145. Gentry O. Smith, Director. General email, ofminfo@state.gov* *Web, www.state.gov/ofm*

Authorized to control the numbers, locations, and travel privileges of foreign diplomats and diplomatic staff in the United States.

U.S. Coast Guard (USCG) *(Homeland Security Dept.), 2703 Martin Luther King Jr. Ave. S.E., MS 7000, 20593-7000; (202) 372-4411. Fax, (202) 372-8302. Adm. Paul F. Zukunft, Commandant. Public Affairs, (202) 372-4600.* *Web, www.uscg.mil*

Provides homeland security for U.S. harbors, ports, and coastlines. Implements heightened security measures for commercial, tanker, passenger, and merchant vessels. Enforces federal laws on the high seas and navigable waters of the United States and its possessions; maintains a state of military readiness to assist the Navy in time of war or when directed by the president.

▶ **CONGRESS**

For a listing of relevant congressional committees and subcommittees, please see pages 598–599 or the Appendix.

NATIONAL AND HOMELAND SECURITY RESOURCES IN CONGRESS

For a complete listing of congressional committees, including their full contact information, leadership, membership, and jurisdictions, please refer to the Appendix on pages 779–896.

HOUSE:

House Appropriations Committee, (202) 225-2771.
Web, appropriations.house.gov
    Subcommittee on Defense, (202) 225-2847.
    Subcommittee on Energy and Water Development, and Related Agencies, (202) 225-3421.
    Subcommittee on Financial Services and General Government, (202) 225-7245.
    Subcommittee on Homeland Security, (202) 225-5834.
    Subcommittee on Interior, Environment, and Related Agencies, (202) 225-3081.
    Subcommittee on Military Construction, Veterans Affairs, and Related Agencies, (202) 225-3047.
    Subcommittee on State, Foreign Operations, and Related Programs, (202) 225-2041.
House Armed Services Committee, (202) 225-4151.
Web, armedservices.house.gov
    Subcommittee on Emerging Threats and Capabilities, (202) 226-2843.
    Subcommittee on Military Personnel, (202) 225-7560.
    Subcommittee on Readiness, (202) 226-8979.
    Subcommittee on Strategic Forces, (202) 225-1967.
    Subcommittee on Tactical Air and Land Forces, (202) 225-4440.
House Energy and Commerce Committee, (202) 225-2927.
Web, energycommerce.house.gov
    Subcommittee on Health, (202) 225-2927.
House Financial Services Committee, (202) 225-7502.
Web, financialservices.house.gov
    Subcommittee on Housing and Insurance, (202) 225-7502.
House Foreign Affairs Committee, (202) 225-5021.
Web, foreignaffairs.house.gov

    Subcommittee on Terrorism, Nonproliferation, and Trade, (202) 225-5021.
House Homeland Security Committee, (202) 226-8417.
Web, homeland.house.gov
    Subcommittee on Border and Maritime Security, (202) 226-8417.
    Subcommittee on Counterterrorism and Intelligence, (202) 226-8417.
    Subcommittee on Cybersecurity, Infrastructure Protection, and Security Technologies, (202) 226-8417.
    Subcommittee on Emergency Preparedness Response and Communications, (202) 226-8417.
    Subcommittee on Oversight and Management Efficiency, (202) 226-8417.
    Subcommittee on Transportation Security, (202) 226-8417.
House Judiciary Committee, (202) 225-3951.
Web, judiciary.house.gov
    Subcommittee on the Constitution and Civil Justice, (202) 225-2825.
    Subcommittee on Crime, Terrorism, Homeland Security, and Investigations, (202) 225-5727.
    Subcommittee on Immigration and Border Security, (202) 225-3926.
House Oversight and Government Reform Committee, (202) 225-5074.
Web, oversight.house.gov
    Subcommittee on National Security, (202) 225-5074.
House Permanent Select Committee on Intelligence, (202) 225-4121.
Web, intelligence.house.gov
    Subcommittee on CIA, (202) 225-4121.
    Subcommittee on Department of Defense Intelligence and Overhead Architecture, (202) 225-4121.
    Subcommittee on Emerging Threats, (202) 225-4121.

Government Publishing Office (GPO), *Security and Intelligent Documents Unit, 732 N. Capitol St. N.W., #C566, 20401; (202) 512-1000. Jim Bradley, Deputy Director.*
Web, *www.gpo.gov/customers/sid.htm*

    Works with other federal agencies to ensure the safe and secure design, production, and distribution of security and intelligence documents such as U.S. passports and other secure credentials for federal agencies.

▶**NONGOVERNMENTAL**

Air Force Assn., *1501 Lee Hwy., Arlington, VA 22209-1198; (703) 247-5800. Fax, (703) 247-5853. Larry O. Spencer, President. Toll-free, (800) 727-3337. Press, (703) 247-5850.*
General email, *membership@afa.org*
Web, *www.afa.org*

Subcommittee on NSA and Cybersecurity,
(202) 225-4121.
Subcommittee on Research and Technology,
(202) 225-6371.
House Science, Space, and Technology Committee,
(202) 225-6371.
Web, science.house.gov
House Transportation and Infrastructure
Committee, (202) 225-9446.
Web, transportation.house.gov
Subcommittee on Economic Development,
Public Buildings, and Emergency
Management, (202) 225-3014.

SENATE:
Senate Appropriations Committee,
(202) 224-7363.
Web, appropriations.senate.gov
Subcommittee on Defense, (202) 224-6688.
Subcommittee on Energy and Water
Development, (202) 224-8119.
Subcommittee on Financial Services and General
Government, (202) 224-1133.
Subcommittee on Homeland Security,
(202) 224-8244.
Subcommittee on Interior, Environment, and
Related Agencies, (202) 228-0774.
Subcommittee on Military Construction,
Veterans Affairs, and Related Agencies,
(202) 224-8224.
Subcommittee on State, Foreign Operations, and
Related Programs, (202) 224-7284.
Senate Armed Services Committee,
(202) 224-3871.
Web, armed-services.senate.gov
Subcommittee on Airland, (202) 224-3871.
Subcommittee on Emerging Threats and
Capabilities, (202) 224-3871.
Subcommittee on Personnel,
(202) 224-3871.
Subcommittee on Readiness and Management
Support, (202) 224-3871.
Subcommittee on Seapower, (202) 224-3871.

Subcommittee on Strategic Forces,
(202) 224-3871.
Senate Banking, Housing, and Urban Affairs
Committee, (202) 224-7391.
Web, banking.senate.gov
Subcommittee on National Security and
International Trade and Finance,
(202) 224-2023.
Senate Environment and Public Works Committee,
(202) 224-8832.
Web, epw.senate.gov
Subcommittee on Clean Air and Nuclear Safety,
(202) 224-8832.
Subcommittee on Transportation and
Infrastructure, (202) 224-8832.
Senate Foreign Relations Committee,
(202) 224-4651.
Web, foreign.senate.gov
Subcommittee on Western Hemisphere,
Transnational Crime, Civilian Security,
Democracy, Human Rights, and Global
Women's Issues, (202) 224-4651.
Senate Homeland Security and Governmental Affairs
Committee, (202) 224-2627.
Web, hsgac.senate.gov
Permanent Subcommittee on Investigations,
(202) 224-4462.
Subcommittee on Federal Spending,
Oversight, and Emergency Management,
(202) 224-4462.
Subcommittee on Regulatory Affairs and Federal
Management, (202) 224-4462.
Senate Judiciary Committee, (202) 224-7703.
Web, judiciary.senate.gov
Subcommittee on the Constitution,
(202) 224-7840.
Subcommittee on Crime and Terrorism,
(202) 224-6791.
Subcommittee on Immigration and the National
Interest, (202) 224-7572.
Senate Select Committee on Intelligence,
(202) 224-1700.
Web, intelligence.senate.gov

Membership: civilians and active duty, reserve, retired, and cadet personnel of the Air Force. Informs members and the public of developments in the aerospace field. Monitors legislation and Defense Dept. policies. Library on aviation history open to the public by appointment.

American Assn. for the Advancement of Science (AAAS), *Center for Science, Technology, and Security Policy, 1200 New York Ave. N.W., 20005; (202) 326-6493. Fax, (202) 289-1846. Norman P. Neureiter, Director. Press, (202) 326-6431.*

General email, cstspinfo@aaas.org
Web, http://aaas.org/program/center-science-technology-and-security-policy

Encourages the integration of science and public policy to enhance national and international security. Facilitates communication among academic centers, policy institutions, and policymakers. (Supported by the Science, Technology, and Security Initiative of the MacArthur Foundation.)

American Conservative Union (ACU), *1331 H St. N.W.,* *#500, 20005; (202) 347-9388. Fax, (202) 347-9389.* *Dan Schneider, Executive Director.* *General email, acu@conservative.org*

Web, www.conservative.org

Legislative interest organization concerned with national defense policy, legislation related to nuclear weapons, U.S. strategic position vis-à-vis the former Soviet Union, missile defense programs, U.S. troops under UN command, and U.S. strategic alliance commitments.

American Enterprise Institute (AEI), *Foreign and Defense Policy Studies, 1150 17th St. N.W., #1100, 20036; (202) 862-5800. Fax, (202) 862-7177. Danielle Pletka, Vice President, (202) 862-5943.* *Web, www.aei.org*

Research and educational organization that conducts conferences, seminars, and debates and sponsors research on national security, defense policy, and arms control.

American Security Council Foundation, *1250 24th St. N.W., #300, 20037; (202) 263-3661. Fax, (202) 263-3662. Gary James, Director of Operations.* *General email, info@ascfusa.org*

Press email, press@ascfusa.org

Web, www.ascfusa.org

Nonpartisan organization that promotes developing and maintaining military, economic, and diplomatic strength to preserve national security. Monitors legislation and conducts educational activities.

American Security Project, *1100 New York Ave. N.W., #710, 20005; (202) 347-4267. Fax, (202) 470-6631. Brig. Gen. Stephen A. Cheney, Chief Executive Officer.* *General email, press@americansecurityproject.org*

Web, www.americansecurityproject.org

Nonprofit, nonpartisan organization that educates the public on the advancement of national security. Distributes research on security issues to the media, publications, and events. Promotes action and holds meetings to discuss new national security strategies.

Aspen Institute, *1 Dupont Circle N.W., #700, 20036-7133; (202) 736-5800. Fax, (202) 467-0790. Walter Isaacson, President. Press, (202) 736-3849.* *General email, info@aspeninstitute.org*

Web, www.aspeninstitute.org and Twitter, @AspenInstitute

Educational and policy studies organization. Promotes consideration of the public good in a wide variety of policy areas, including international relations homeland security. Working with international partners, offers educational seminars, nonpartisan policy forums, public conferences and events, and leadership development initiatives.

Assn. of the United States Army, *2425 Wilson Blvd., Arlington, VA 22201; (703) 841-4300. Fax, (703) 525-9039. Gen. Gordon R. Sullivan, President. Information, (800) 336-4570.* *Web, www.ausa.org and Twitter, @AUSAorg*

Membership: civilians and active duty and retired members of the armed forces. Conducts symposia on defense issues and researches topics that affect the military.

Atlantic Council, *1030 15th St. N.W., 12th Floor, 20005; (202) 463-7226. Fax, (202) 463-7241. Frederick Kempe, President.* *General email, info@atlanticcouncil.org*

Web, www.atlanticcouncil.org and Twitter, @ATLANTICCOUNCIL

Conducts studies and makes policy recommendations on U.S. foreign security and international economic policies in the Atlantic and Pacific communities; sponsors conferences and educational exchanges.

The Brookings Institution, *Foreign Policy Studies, 1775 Massachusetts Ave. N.W., 20036; (202) 797-6000. Fax, (202) 797-6004. Bruce Jones, Director. Press, (202) 797-6105.* *Web, www.brookings.edu/foreign-policy*

Research and educational organization that focuses on major national security topics, including U.S. armed forces, weapons decisions, terrorism threats, employment policies, and the security aspects of U.S. foreign relations.

Business Executives for National Security (BENS), *1030 15th St. N.W., #200 East, 20005; (202) 296-2125. Fax, (202) 296-2490. Gen. Norton A. Swartz (USAF, Ret.), Chief Executive Officer; Henry (Butch) Hinton, Chief Operating Officer.* *General email, bens@bens.org*

Web, www.bens.org and Twitter, @BENS_org

Monitors legislation on national security issues from a business perspective; holds conferences, congressional forums, and other meetings on national security issues; works with other organizations on defense policy issues.

Center for Advanced Defense Studies, *1100 H St. N.W., #750, 20005; (202) 289-3332. Fax, (202) 789-2786. David Johnson, Executive Director.* *General email, info@c4ads.org*

Web, www.c4ads.org and Twitter, @C4ADS

Analyzes global data and reports on international conflict and security challenges. Conducts field research in conflict areas. Awards annual fellowships to experts in weapons trafficking, conflict prevention, terrorism, and global crime.

Center for National Policy, *1250 Eye St., #500, 20005; (202) 216-9723. Fax, (202) 682-1818. Scott Bates, President.* *General email, info@cnponline.org*

Web, www.cnponline.org

Public policy research and educational organization that serves as a forum for development of national policy alternatives. Leads discussion and advances policies aimed at promoting U.S. global engagement and leadership in the 21st century. Focus on issues such as cybersecurity and defense energy. (Partner of the Truman National Security Project.)

Defense Department

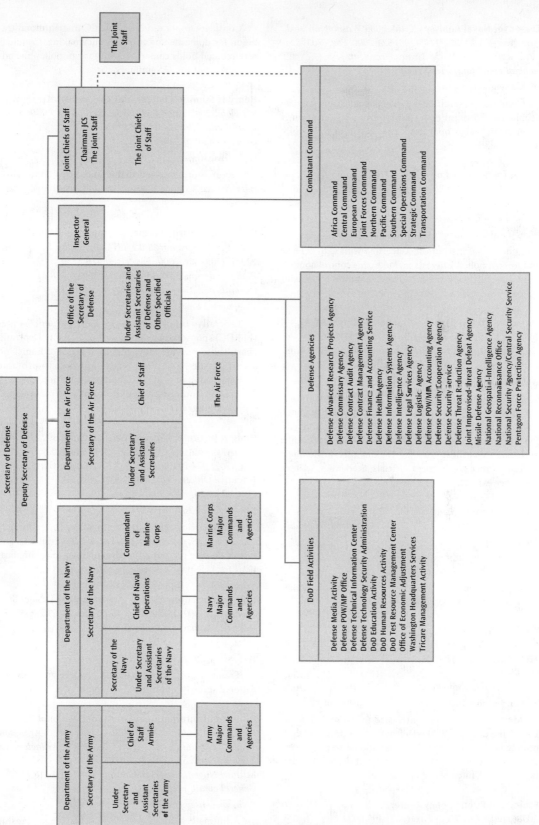

- - - - - - - - - Indicates a support or advisory relationship with the unit rather than a direct reporting relationship

Center for Naval Analyses (CNA), *3003 Washington Blvd., Arlington, VA 22201-2117; (703) 824-2000. Fax, (703) 824-2942. Katherine A.W. McGrady, President.*
General email, inquiries@cna.org

Web, www.cna.org and Twitter, @CNA_org

Conducts research on weapons acquisitions, tactical problems, and naval operations. Parent organization is CNA, which also operates CNA Institute for Public Research

Center for Security Policy, *1901 Pennsylvania Ave. N.W., #201, 20006-3439; (202) 835-9077. Fax, (202) 835-9066. Frank J. Gaffney Jr., President, (202) 835-9077, ext. 1006.*
General email, info@securefreedom.org

Web, www.centerforsecuritypolicy.org

Educational institution concerned with U.S. defense and foreign policy. Interests include arms control compliance and verification policy, and technology transfer policy.

Committee on the Present Danger, *P.O. Box 33249, 20033-3249; (202) 207-0190. Fax, (202) 207-0191. George P. Shultz, Co-Chair; R. James Woolsey, Co-Chair.*
General email, commpresdanger@aol.com

Web, www.committeeonthepresentdanger.org

International, nonpartisan educational organization concerned with militant Islamist regimes, movements, and organizations around the world. Supports policies that use various means, including military, economic, political, social means, to address this threat. Members include former government officials, academics, writers, and other experts.

The Conservative Caucus (TCC), *92 Main St., #202-8, Warrenton, VA 20816; (540) 219-4536. Peter J. Thomas, Chair.*
General email, info@conservativeusa.org

Web, www.conservativeusa.org

Legislative interest organization that promotes grassroots activity on national defense and foreign policy.

Defense Orientation Conference Assn. (DOCA), *9245 Old Keene Mill Rd., #100, Burke, VA 22015-4202; (703) 451-1200. Fax, (703) 451-1201. Vicki E. Churchwood, President.*
General email, doca@doca.org

Web, www.doca.org

Membership: citizens interested in national defense. Under the auspices of the Defense Dept., promotes continuing education of members on national security issues through visits to embassies and tours of defense installations in the United States and abroad.

Ethics and Public Policy Center, *1730 M St. N.W., #910, 20036; (202) 682-1200. Fax, (202) 408-0632. M. Edward Whelan III, President.*
General email, ethics@eppc.org

Web, www.eppc.org and Twitter, @EPPCdc

Considers implications of Judeo-Christian moral tradition for domestic and foreign policymaking. Conducts research and holds conferences on foreign policy, including the role of the U.S. military abroad.

Henry L. Stimson Center, *1211 Connecticut Ave. N.W., 8th Floor, 20036; (202) 223-5956. Fax, (202) 238-9604. Brian Finlay, President.*
General email, info@stimson.org

Web, www.stimson.org

Research organization that studies arms control and international security, focusing on policy, technology, and politics.

Homeland Security Studies and Analysis Institute (HSSAI), *5275 Leesburg Pike, #N-5000, Falls Church, VA 22041; (703) 416-2000. Fax, (703) 416-3530. Philip Anderson, Director. Toll-free, (800) 368-4173.*
General email, homelandsecurity@hsi.dhs.gov

Web, www.homelandsecurity.org

Federally funded research development center (FFRDC) sponsored by the Homeland Security Dept. and chartered to provide independent analysis of homeland security issues. Conducts research, works to promote dialogue, and provides executive education through workshops, conferences, publications and reports, and outreach programs.

Hudson Institute, *National Security Studies, 1201 Pennsylvania Ave. N.W., 4th Floor, 20004; (202) 974-2400. Fax, (202) 974-2410. Kenneth R. Weinstein, Chief Executive Officer. Press, (202) 974-6456.*
General email, info@hudson.org

Web, www.hudson.org

Public policy research organization that conducts studies on U.S. overseas bases, U.S.-NATO relations, and missile defense programs. Focuses on long-range implications for U.S. national security.

Institute for Foreign Policy Analysis, *1725 DeSales St. N.W., #402, 20036; (202) 463-7942. Fax, (202) 785-2785. Robert L. Pfaltzgraff Jr., President.*
General email, dcmail@ifpa.org

Web, www.ifpa.org

Trains policy analysts in the fields of foreign policy and national security. Sponsors research and workshops.

Institute of International Education, *National Security Education Program, 1101 Wilson Blvd., #1210, Arlington, VA 22209 (mailing address: P.O. Box 20010, Arlington, VA 22209); (571) 256-0711. Fax, (703) 696-5667. Michael Nugent, Director. Information, (800) 618-6737.*
General email, nsep@nsep.gov

Web, www.nsep.gov

Administers Boren Awards and Language Flagship programs; provides scholarships, fellowships, and institutional grants to students and academics with an interest in foreign affairs and national security.

Homeland Security Department

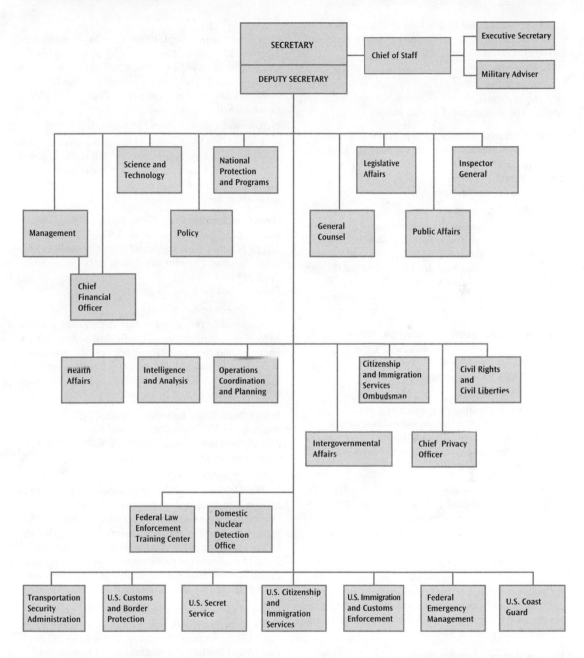

Jewish Institute for National Security Affairs (JINSA),
1101 14th St. N.W., #1110, 20005; (202) 667-3900.
Fax, (202) 403-2268. Michael Makovsky,
Executive Director.
General email, info@jinsa.org
Web, www.jinsa.org

Seeks to educate the public about the importance of effective U.S. defense capability and inform the U.S. defense and foreign affairs community about Israel's role in Mediterranean and Middle Eastern affairs. Sponsors lectures and conferences; facilitates dialogue between

security policymakers, military officials, diplomats, and the general public.

Marine Corps League, *8626 Lee Hwy., #201, Fairfax, VA 22031-3070 (mailing address: P.O. Box 3070, Merrifield, VA 22116); (703) 207-9588. Fax, (703) 207-0047. Thomas W. Hazlett Sr., Executive Director, Acting. Toll-free, (800) 625-1775.*
Web, www.mclnational.org

Membership: active duty, retired, and reserve Marine Corps groups. Promotes the interests of the Marine Corps and works to preserve its traditions; assists veterans and their survivors. Monitors legislation and regulations.

National Institute for Public Policy, *9302 Lee Hwy., #750, Fairfax, VA 22031-1214; (703) 293-9181. Fax, (703) 293-9198. Keith B. Payne, President.*
Web, www.nipp.org

Studies public policy and its relation to national security. Interests include arms control, strategic weapons systems and planning, and foreign policy.

National Security Archive *(George Washington University), Gelman Library, 2130 H St. N.W., #701, 20037; (202) 994-7000. Fax, (202) 994-7005. Thomas Blanton, Director.*
General email, nsarchiv@gwu.edu
Web, www.nsarchive.org

Research institute and library that provides information on U.S. foreign and economic policy and national security affairs. Maintains and publishes collection of declassified and unclassified documents obtained through the Freedom of Information Act. Archive open to the public by appointment. Web site has a Russian-language link.

Partnership for a Secure America (PSA), *1775 K St. N.W., #400, 20006; (202) 293-8580. Andrew K. Semmel, Executive Director.*
General email, info@psaonline.org
Web, www.psaonline.org

Supports a bipartisan approach to national security policies and issues. Researches and publishes reports on national security threats such as terrorism. Organizes conferences for political parties to debate and develop consensus on issues.

RAND Corporation, *Washington Office, 1200 S. Hayes St., Arlington, VA 22202-5050; (703) 413-1100. Fax, (703) 413-8111. Richard M. Moore, Director, ext. 5399; Anita Chandra, Director, Justice, Infrastructure, and Environment, ext.5323.*
Web, www.rand.org

Conducts research on national security issues, including political/military affairs of the former Soviet Union and U.S. strategic policy. Research focuses on citizen preparedness, defense strategy, and military force planning. (Headquarters in Santa Monica, Calif.)

Truman National Security Project, *1250 Eye St. N.W., #500, 20005; (202) 216-9723. Fax, (202) 289-4199. Mike Breen, President.*
General email, info@trumanproject.org
Web, http://trumanproject.org and Twitter, @TrumanProject

Membership: veterans and policy and political leaders. Forum for development of national policy alternatives. Promotes national security policy coordination, strengthening the U.S. military and intelligence, foreign affairs and diplomacy, democracy, and open trade. (Partner of the Center for National Policy.)

Civil Rights and Liberties

▶AGENCIES

Homeland Security Dept. (DHS), *Civil Rights and Civil Liberties, 245 Murray Lane S.W., Bldg. 410, MS 0190, 20528-0190; (202) 401-1474. Fax, (202) 401-4708. Megan H. Mack, Civil Rights and Civil Liberties Officer. Toll-free, (866) 644-8360. Toll-free TTY, (866) 644-8361. General email, crcl.eeo@hq.dhs.gov*
Web, www.dhs.gov/topic/civil-rights-and-civil-liberties

Provides legal and policy advice to the secretary and senior officers of the department on civil rights and civil liberties issues; maintains dialogue with minority communities; investigates and resolves complaints filed by members of the public.

Homeland Security Dept. (DHS), *Privacy Office, 245 Murray Lane, Bldg. 110, 20528-0655; Fax, (202) 343-4010. Megan H. Mack, Civil Rights and Civil Liberties Officer; Karen Neuman, Chief Privacy Officer. DHS switchboard, (202) 282-8000.*
General email, privacy@dhs.gov
Web, www.dhs.gov/privacy

Responsible for ensuring that department policies and use of technology sustain individual privacy. Makes annual report to Congress and enforces the provisions of the 1974 Privacy Act and evaluates legislative and regulatory proposals involving collection, use, and disclosure of personal information by the federal government.

Justice Dept. (DOJ), *Information Policy, 1425 New York Ave. N.W., #11050, 20530; (202) 514-3642. Fax, (202) 514-1009. Melanie Ann Pustay, Director. Information, (202) 514-2000. General email, doj.oip.foia@usdoj.gov*
Web, www.justice.gov/oip

Provides federal agencies with advice and policy guidance on matters related to implementing and interpreting the Freedom of Information Act (FOIA). Processes FOIA requests on behalf of the Department's Senior Leadership Offices; adjudicates administrative appeals from Justice Department denials of public requests for access to documents; litigates selected FOIA and Privacy Act cases; conducts FOIA training for government agencies.

Office of Management and Budget (OMB) *(Executive Office of the President), Information and Regulatory Affairs, 725 17th St. N.W., #10236, 20503; (202) 395-5897. Fax, (202) 395-6102. Harold Shelanski, Administrator. Press, (202) 395-7254.*
Web, www.whitehouse.gov/omb/inforeg_infopoltech

Oversees development of federal regulatory programs. Supervises agency information management activities in accordance with the Paperwork Reduction Act of 1995, as amended; reviews agency analyses of the effect of government regulatory activities on the U.S. economy.

▶CONGRESS

For a listing of relevant congressional committees and subcommittees, please see pages 598–599 or the Appendix.

▶NONGOVERNMENTAL

American Civil Liberties Union (ACLU), *Washington Legislative Office,* 915 15th St. N.W., 20005; (202) 544-1681. Fax, (202) 546-0738. Michael Macleod-Ball, Chief of Staff. Press, (202) 544-2312.
General email, media@dcaclu.org

Web, www.aclu.org/legiupdate

Advocates legislation to guarantee constitutional rights and civil liberties. Monitors agency compliance with the Privacy Act and other access statutes. Produces publications. (Headquarters in New York maintains docket of cases.)

American Society of Access Professionals, 1444 Eye St. N.W., #700, 20005; (202) 712-9054. Fax, (202) 216-9646. Claire Shanley, Executive Director.
General email, asap@bostrom.com

Web, www.accesspro.org and Twitter, @ASAPAccessPro

Membership: federal employees, attorneys, journalists, and others working with or interested in access-to-information laws. Seeks to improve the administration of the Freedom of Information Act, the Privacy Act, and other access statutes.

Center for Democracy and Technology, 1401 K St. N.W., 2nd Floor, 20005; (202) 637-9800. Fax, (202) 637-0968. Nuala O'Connor, President.
General email, info@cdt.org

Web, www.cdt.org and Twitter, @CenDemTech

Promotes civil liberties and democratic values in computer and communications media, both in the United States and abroad. Interests include free speech, privacy, and open access to the Internet. Monitors legislation and regulations.

Center for National Security Studies, 1730 Pennsylvania Ave. N.W., 7th Floor, 20006; (202) 721-5650. Fax, (202) 530-0128. Kate A. Martin, Director.
General email, cnss@cnss.org

Web, www.cnss.org

Human rights and civil liberties organization specializing in national security, access to government information, government secrecy, government surveillance, intelligence oversight, and detentions.

Electronic Privacy Information Center (EPIC), 1718 Connecticut Ave. N.W., #200, 20009; (202) 483-1140. Fax, (202) 483-1248. Marc Rotenberg, President.
General email, info@epic.org

Web, www.epic.org

Public interest research center. Conducts research and conferences on domestic and international civil liberties issues, including privacy, free speech, information access, computer security, and encryption; litigates cases. Monitors legislation and regulations. Operates an online bookstore.

Radio Television Digital News Assn., 529 14th St. N.W., #1240, 20045; (202) 659-6510. Fax, (202) 223-4007. Mike Cavender, Executive Director, (770) 622-7011.
Web, www.rtdna.org and Twitter, @RTDNA

Membership: electronic journalists in radio, television, and all digital media. Sponsors and promotes education and advocacy concerning First Amendment issues, freedom of information, and government secrecy issues; ethics in reporting; improving coverage; implementing technology; and other news industry issues. Radio and Television News Directors Foundation (RTNDF) is the educational arm of the association.

Reporters Committee for Freedom of the Press, 1156 15th St. N.W., #1250, 20005; (202) 795-9300. Fax, (202) 795-9310. Bruce D. Brown, Executive Director, (202) 795-9301. Legal defense hotline, (800) 336-4243.
General email, info@rcfp.org and hotline@rcpf.org

Web, www.rcfp.org

Committee of reporters, news editors, publishers, and lawyers from the print and broadcast media. Maintains a legal defense and research fund for members of the news media involved in freedom of the press court cases; interests include access to information and privacy issues faced by journalists covering antiterrorism initiatives and military actions abroad.

Defense and Homeland Security Budgets

▶AGENCIES

Defense Contract Audit Agency *(Defense Dept.),* 8725 John Jay Kingman Rd., #2135, Fort Belvoir, VA 22060-6219; (703) 767-3200. Fax, (703) 767-3267. Anita Dales, Director. Media, (703) 693-6858.
Web, www.dcaa.mil

Performs all contract audits for the Defense Dept. Provides Defense Dept. personnel responsible for procurement and contract administration with accounting and financial advisory services regarding the negotiation, administration, and settlement of contracts and subcontracts.

Defense Dept. (DoD), *Comptroller,* 1100 Defense Pentagon, #3E770, 20301-1100; (703) 695-3237. Fax, (703) 693-0582. Mike McCord, Comptroller.
Web, http://comptroller.defense.gov

Supervises and reviews the preparation and implementation of the defense budget. Advises the secretary of defense on fiscal matters. Collects and distributes information on the department's management of resources.

Homeland Security Dept. (DHS), *Chief Financial Officer,* 7th and D Sts. S.W., 20528; (202) 447-5751. Chip Fulghum, Chief Financial Officer.
Web, www.dhs.gov/office-chief-financial-officer

Responsible for the Homeland Security Dept.'s budget, budget justifications, supplemental spending bill figures, and five-year financial blueprint.

Homeland Security Dept. (DHS), *Management Directorate,* 3801 Nebraska Ave. N.W., 20528; 245 Murray

Lane, MS 04401, 20528; (202) 447-3400. Fax, (202) 447-3713. Russell C. Deyo, Under Secretary.
Web, www.dhs.gov/about-directorate-management

Responsible for Homeland Security Dept. budget, operations, appropriations, expenditure of funds, accounting and finance, procurement, human resources and personnel, information technology systems, facilities, property, equipment and all material resources, and performance measurement.

Office of Management and Budget (OMB) *(Executive Office of the President), Homeland Security,* 725 17th St. N.W., #9208, 20503; (202) 395-5090. Fax, (202) 395-0850. (202) 395-4892. James Holm, Chief. Press, (202) 395-7254. phone, (202) 395-4892.
Web, www.whitehouse.gov/omb

Assists and advises the OMB director on budget preparation, proposed legislation, and evaluations of Homeland Security Dept. programs, policies, and activities.

Office of Management and Budget (OMB) *(Executive Office of the President), National Security,* 725 17th St. N.W., #10001, 20503; (202) 395-3884. Fax, (202) 395-3307. Jonathan Lachman, Associate Director.
Press, (202) 395-7254.
Web, www.whitehouse.gov/omb

Supervises preparation of the Defense Dept., intelligence community, and veterans affairs portions of the federal budget.

▶**CONGRESS**

For a listing of relevant congressional committees and subcommittees, please see pages 598–599 or the Appendix.

Government Accountability Office (GAO), *Defense Capabilities and Management,* 441 G St. N.W., #4440B, 20548; (202) 512-4300. Cathleen Berrick, Managing Director.
Web, www.gao.gov/careers/dcm.html

Independent nonpartisan agency in the legislative branch. Audits, analyzes, and evaluates defense spending programs; makes unclassified reports available to the public.

Government Accountability Office (GAO), *Homeland Security and Justice,* 441 G St. N.W., #6H19, 20548; (202) 512-8777. George A. Scott, Managing Director.
Web, www.gao.gov/careers/hsj.html

Independent nonpartisan agency in the legislative branch. Audits, analyzes, and evaluates federal administration of homeland security programs and initiatives related to national preparedness. Makes some reports available to the public.

▶**NONGOVERNMENTAL**

Center for Strategic and Budgetary Assessments (CSBA), 1667 K St. N.W., #900, 20006-1659; (202) 331-7990. Fax, (202) 331-8019. Thomas Mahnken, President.

General email, info@csbaonline.org
Web, www.csbaonline.org and Twitter, @CSBA_

Think tank that promotes deliberation of national security strategy, the future of the U.S. military, and defense investment options. Conducts analyses of defense budget and programmatic analysis. Compares the relative strengths and weaknesses of the United States and potential military competitors. Conducts seminar-style wargames to analyze the operational and strategic levels of conflict, as well as strategy and investment alternatives. Anticipates future military trends, based on analysis of historical trends.

Institute for Policy Studies, *Foreign Policy in Focus,* 1301 Connecticut Ave. N.W., #600, 20036; (202) 234-9382. Fax, (202) 387-7915. John Feffer, Co-Director.
General email, fpif@ips-dc.org
Web, www.fpif.org

Think tank that provides analysis of U.S. foreign policy and international affairs and recommends progressive policy alternatives. Publishes reports; organizes briefings for the public, media, and policymakers. Interests include climate change, global poverty, nuclear weapons, terrorism, and military conflict.

National Campaign for a Peace Tax Fund, 2121 Decatur Pl. N.W., 20008-1923; (202) 483-3751. Jack McHale, Executive Director. Toll-free, (888) 732-2382.
General email, info@peacetaxfund.org
Web, www.peacetaxfund.org

Supports legislation permitting taxpayers who are conscientiously opposed to military expenditures to have the military portion of their income tax money placed in a separate, nonmilitary fund.

Women's Action for New Directions (WAND), *Washington Office,* 322 4th St. N.E., 20002; (202) 544-5055. Fax, (202) 544-7612. Adzi Vokhiwa, Senior Associate; Kathy Crandall Robinson, Senior Public Policy Director.
General email, peace@wand.org
Web, www.wand.org and Twitter, @WomensAction

Seeks to redirect federal spending priorities from military spending toward domestic needs; works to develop citizen expertise through education and political involvement; provides educational programs and material about nuclear and conventional weapons; monitors defense legislation, budget policy legislation, and legislation affecting women. (Headquarters in Arlington, Mass.)

Military Aid and Peacekeeping

▶**AGENCIES**

Bureau of European and Eurasian Affairs *(State Dept.), European Security and Political Affairs,* 2201 C St. N.W., #6511, 20520; (202) 647-1626. Fax, (202) 647-1369. Joe Manso, Director.
Web, www.state.gov/p/eur

Coordinates and advises, with the Defense Dept. and other agencies, the U.S. mission to NATO and the U.S. delegation to the Organization for Security and Co-operation in Europe regarding political, military, and arms control matters.

Bureau of International Organization Affairs *(State Dept.), United Nations Political Affairs,* 2201 C St. N.W., #1828, 20520-6319; (202) 647-2393. Fax, (202) 647-0039. *Robert Faucher, Director.*
Web, www.state.gov/p/io

Deals with UN political and institutional matters and international security affairs.

Bureau of Political-Military Affairs *(State Dept.), Security Assistance,* 2401 E St. N.W., 20037; (202) 647-7775. *Kevin O'Keefe, Director.*
Web, www.state.gov/t/pm/sa

Administers funding for security assistance and capacity-building programs in foreign countries.

Defense Dept. (DoD), *International Security Affairs,* 2000 Defense Pentagon, #3C889, 20301-2000; (703) 697-2788. Fax, (703) 697-3279. *Elissa B. Slotkin, Assistant Secretary, Acting; Kenneth B. Handelman, Principal Deputy Assistant Secretary, Acting.*
Web, http://policy.defense.gov/OUSDPOffices/ASDforInternationalSecurityAffairs.aspx

Advises the secretary of defense and recommends policies on regional security issues in the Middle East, Africa, Russia/Eurasia, and Europe/NATO.

Defense Dept. (DoD), *International Security Affairs, European and NATO Policy,* 2000 Defense Pentagon, #5B652, 20301 2000; (703) 695-5553. Fax, (703) 571-9637. *Jim J. Townsend, Deputy Assistant Secretary; Rachel Ellehuus, Principal Director.*
Web, www.defense.gov

Advises the assistant secretary for international security affairs on matters dealing with Europe and NATO.

Defense Security Cooperation Agency *(Defense Dept.),* 2800 Defense Pentagon, 20301-2800; (703) 601-1646. *Vice Adm. Joseph W. Rixey (USN), Director; Jennifer Zakriski, Deputy Director. Public Affairs, (703) 604-6617.*
General email, dsca.ncr.lmo.mbx.info@mail.mil
Web, www.dsca.mil

Administers programs providing defense articles and services, military training and education, humanitarian assistance, and landmine removal to international partners in furtherance of U.S. policies and strategic objectives.

State Dept., *Arms Control and International Security,* 2201 C St. N.W., #7208, 20520-7512; (202) 647-4226. *Rose Gottemoeller, Under Secretary, (202) 647-1049.*
Web, www.state.gov/t

Works with the secretary of state to develop policy on foreign security assistance programs, technology transfer, and arms control.

▶CONGRESS

For a listing of relevant congressional committees and sub-committees, please see pages 598–599 or the Appendix.

Government Accountability Office (GAO), *Defense Capabilities and Management,* 441 G St. N.W., #4440B, 20548; (202) 512-4300. *Cathleen Berrick, Managing Director.*
Web, www.gao.gov/careers/dcm.html

Independent nonpartisan agency in the legislative branch. Audits, analyzes, and evaluates international programs, including U.S. participation in international peacekeeping and peace enforcement operations; makes unclassified reports available to the public.

▶INTERNATIONAL ORGANIZATIONS

Inter-American Defense Board, 2600 16th St. N.W., 20441-0002; (202) 939-6041. Fax, (202) 319-2791. *Vice Adm. Gonzalo Rios Polastri, Chair (in Peru). Inter-American Defense College, (202) 646-1337.*
General email, jid@jid.org
Web, www.iadb.jid.org

Membership: military officers from twenty-six countries of the Western Hemisphere. Plans for the collective self-defense of the American continents. Develops procedures for standardizing military organization and operations; operates the Inter-American Defense Board and Inter-American Defense College. Advises the Organization of American States on military and defense matters.

▶NONGOVERNMENTAL

International Stability Operations Assn. (ISOA), 8221 Old Courthouse Rd., #200, Vienna, VA 22182 (mailing address: 1714 Corwin Dr., Silver Spring, MD 20910); (703) 596-9417. Fax, (571) 282-4800. *Ado Machida, President.*
General email, isoa@stability-operations.org
Web, www.stability-operations.org

Membership: private-sector service companies involved in all sectors of peace and stability operations around the world, including mine clearance, logistics, security, training, and emergency humanitarian aid. Works to institute standards and codes of conduct. Monitors legislation.

ARMS CONTROL, DISARMAMENT, AND THREAT REDUCTION

General

▶AGENCIES

Arms Control and Nonproliferation *(Executive Office of the President),* Dwight D. Eisenhower Executive Office Bldg., #379, 20506; (202) 456-9181. Fax, (202) 456-9180. *Laura Holgate, Special Assistant for the White House.*

Responsible for policies concerning arms proliferation and control in the context of homeland security.

Bureau of Arms Control, Verification, and Compliance
(State Dept.), 2201 C St. N.W., #5950, 20520; (202) 647-7811. Frank A. Rose, Assistant Secretary, (202) 647-5315.
Web, www.state.gov/t/avc

Leads development of U.S. arms control, missile defense, and space policies, including negotiation and implementation of international nonproliferation and disarmament agreements.

Bureau of Arms Control, Verification, and Compliance
(State Dept.), Emerging Security Challenges, 2201 C St. N.W., #5725, 20520; (202) 647-9325. Eric E. Desautels, Director.
Web, www.state.gov/t/avc/c21764.htm

Provides research and recommendations on all policy and threat issues related to missile defense systems and cooperation, outer space security issues and transparency, cyberstability, and Arctic and Antarctic security issues.

Bureau of Arms Control, Verification, and Compliance
(State Dept.), Euro-Atlantic Security Affairs, 2201 C St. N.W., #5724, 20520; (202) 647-9170. Richard A. Davis, Director.
Web, www.state.gov/t/avc/cca

Handles matters relating to existing and prospective European and Euro-Atlantic arms control, nonproliferation, disarmament agreements, and security arrangements.

Bureau of Arms Control, Verification, and Compliance
(State Dept.), Multilateral and Nuclear Affairs, 2201 C St. N.W., #5751, 20520; (202) 647-2792. Jeffrey L. Eberhart, Director.
Web, www.state.gov/t/avc/c23757.htm

Coordinates U.S. policy on bilateral and multilateral nuclear arms control and disarmament agreements and commitments, verification, and compliance issues.

Bureau of Arms Control, Verification, and Compliance
(State Dept.), Strategic Stability and Deterrence, 2201 C St. N.W., #5758, 20520; (202) 736-4467. Wade Boese, Director.
Web, www.state.gov/t/avc/c23758.htm

Promotes stability and reduces nuclear threats through policy development, negotiation, and implementation of arms control to ensure U.S. security.

Bureau of Arms Control, Verification, and Compliance
(State Dept.), Verification and Transparency Technologies, 2201 C St. N.W., #5871, 20520; (202) 647-2408. Brian Nordman, Director.
Web, www.state.gov/t/avc/vtt

Identifies and prioritizes emerging verification and compliance issues, and recommends the appropriate use of the Bureau's resources for both current and future arms control challenges, including the application of technological and analytical solutions.

Bureau of Economic and Business Affairs *(State Dept.), Threat Finance Countermeasures, 2210 C St. N.W., #3843, 20520; (202) 647-5763. Fax, (202) 647-7407. Andrew J. Weinschenk, Director.*
Web, www.state.gov/e/eb/tfs/tfc

Seeks to minimize the funding available to groups and individuals that prove a threat to domestic, international, and regional security.

Bureau of International Security and Nonproliferation
(State Dept.), 2201 C St. N.W., #3932, 20520; (202) 647-9868. Fax, (202) 736-4863. Thomas M. Countryman, Assistant Secretary, (202) 647-9612.
Web, www.state.gov/t/isn and Twitter, @ISNAsstScy

Leads U.S. efforts to prevent the spread of weapons of mass destruction (WMD, including nuclear, chemical, and biological weapons) and their delivery systems; spearheads efforts to promote international consensus on WMD proliferation; supports efforts of foreign partners to prevent, protect against, and respond to the threat or use of WMD by terrorists.

Bureau of International Security and Nonproliferation
(State Dept.), Multilateral Nuclear and Security Affairs, 2201 C St. N.W., #5821, 20520; (202) 647-9644. James Wayman, Director.
Web, www.state.gov/t/isn/offices/c55402.htm

Leads development and implementation of U.S. policies related to global nuclear nonproliferation, including international treaties, protocols, and nuclear-related security assurances. Coordinates U.S. policy regarding International Atomic Energy Agency safeguards.

Defense Dept. (DoD), *Chemical and Biological Defense Program, 3050 Defense Pentagon, #5B1064, 20301-3050; (703) 693-9410. Fax, (703) 695-0476. Dr. David (Chris) Christian Hassell, Deputy Assistant, Acting.*
Web, www.acq.osd.mil/cp

Coordinates, integrates, and provides oversight for the Joint Services Chemical and Biological Defense Program.

Defense Dept. (DoD), *Homeland Defense and Global Security, 2600 Defense Pentagon, #3C852A, 20301-2600; (703) 697-7728. Fax, (703) 614-2259. Tom Atkin, Assistant Secretary, Acting.*
Web, www.defense.gov

Advises the secretary on reducing and countering nuclear, biological, chemical, and missile threats to the United States and its forces and allies; arms control negotiations, implementation, and verification policy; nuclear weapons policy, denuclearization, threat reduction, and nuclear safety and security; and technology transfer and cyber security.

Defense Dept. (DoD), *Plans, 2000 Defense Pentagon, #5E384, 20032; (703) 614-0462. Fax, (703) 695-7230. Elizabeth Cordray, Deputy Assistant Secretary. Press, (703) 697-5131.*
Web, www.defense.gov

Formulates national policies to prevent and counter the proliferation of nuclear, chemical, and biological weapons; missiles; and conventional technologies. Devises arms control agreements, export controls, technology transfer policies, and military planning policies.

Defense Threat Reduction Agency *(Defense Dept.), 8725 John Jay Kingman Rd., MS 6201, Fort Belvoir, VA*

22060-6201; (703) 767-4883. Kenneth A. Myers III, Director. Press, (703) 767-5870.
General email, dtra.belvoir.JO.mbx.dtra-publicaffairs@mail.mil
Web, www.dtra.mil

Seeks to reduce, eliminate, and counter the threat to the United States and its allies from weapons of mass destruction; conducts technology security activities, cooperative threat reduction programs, arms control treaty monitoring, and on-site inspection; provides technical support on weapons of mass destruction matters to the Defense Dept. components.

Joint Improvised-Threat Defeat Agency *(Defense Dept.),* 5000 Army Pentagon, 20310; (703) 995-6900. Lt. Gen Michael H. Shields, Director. Operational Support, (703) 995-5553. Media, (703) 995-6536 ext. 5045.
General email, jida.ncr.j3.mbx.operational-support@mail.mil
Web, https://jieddo.mil

Combat support agency handling actions to counter improvised threats, especially improvised explosive devices (IEDs).

State Dept., *Nuclear Risk Reduction Center (NRRC),* 2201 C St. N.W., #5635, 20520; (202) 647-0027. Deborah C. Schneider, Director.
Web, www.state.gov/t/avc/nrrc

Supports implementation of arms control and security agreements with foreign governments by operating government-to-government communications systems.

▶**CONGRESS**

For a listing of relevant congressional committees and subcommittees, please see pages 598–599 or the Appendix.

▶**NONGOVERNMENTAL**

Arms Control Assn., *1313 L St. N.W., #130, 20005; (202) 463-8270. Fax, (202) 463-8273. Daryl G. Kimball, Executive Director.*
General email, aca@armscontrol.org
Web, www.armscontrol.org and Twitter, @ArmsControlNow

Nonpartisan organization that seeks to broaden public understanding and support for effective arms control and disarmament in national security policy through education and media programs. Publishes *Arms Control Today.*

Center for Arms Control and Nonproliferation, *322 4th St. N.E., 20002; (202) 546-0795. John Isaac, Executive Director, Acting, ext. 2222.*
Web, http://armscontrolcenter.org

Advocates reducing nuclear weapon arsenals, preventing the spread of nuclear weapons, and minimizing the risk of nuclear war by educating the public and policymakers about arms control through policy analysis and research.

Council for a Livable World, *322 4th St. N.E., 20002-5824; (202) 543-4100. John Tierney, Executive Director; James McKeon, Communications Manager.*
General email, advocacy@clw.org
Web, http://livableworld.org and Twitter, @Livableworld

Citizens' interest group that supports nuclear arms control treaties, strengthened biological and chemical weapons conventions, reduced military spending, peacekeeping, and tight restrictions on international arms sales.

Federation of American Scientists (FAS), *1725 DeSales St. N.W., #600, 20036; (202) 546-3300. Fax, (202) 675-1010. Charles D. Ferguson, President.*
General email, fas@fas.org
Web, www.fas.org and Twitter, @FAScientists

Opposes the global arms race and supports nuclear disarmament and limits on government secrecy. Promotes learning technologies and conducts studies and monitors legislation on U.S. weapons policy; provides the public with information on arms control and related issues.

Friends Committee on National Legislation (FCNL), *245 2nd St. N.E., 20002-5795; (202) 547-6000. Fax, (202) 547-6019. Diane Randall, Executive Secretary. Toll-free, (800) 630-1330. Recorded information, (202) 547-4343.*
General email, fcnl@fcnl.org
Web, www.fcnl.org

Supports world disarmament; international cooperation; domestic, economic, peace, and social justice issues; and improvement in relations between the United States and the former Soviet Union. Opposes conscription. Affiliated with the Religious Society of Friends (Quakers).

GlobalSecurity.org, *300 N. Washington St., #B-100, Alexandria, VA 22314-2540; (703) 548-2700. Fax, (703) 548-2424. John E. Pike, Director.*
General email, info@globalsecurity.org
Web, www.globalsecurity.org

Provides background information and covers developing news stories on the military, weapons proliferation, space, homeland security, and intelligence. Offers profiles of agencies, systems, facilities, and current operations as well as a library of primary documentation.

High Frontier, *500 N. Washington St., Alexandria, VA 22314-2314; (703) 535-8774. Henry (Hank) Cooper, Chair.*
General email, info@highfrontier.org
Web, www.highfrontier.org

Educational organization that provides information on missile defense programs and proliferation. Advocates development of a single-stage-to-orbit space vehicle, a moon base program, and a layered missile defense system. Operates speakers bureau; monitors defense legislation.

Nonproliferation Policy Education Center (NPEC), *1600 Wilson Blvd., #1400, Arlington, VA 22209; (571) 970-3187. Henry D. Sokolski, Executive Director.*
General email, info@npolicy.org
Web, www.npolicy.org

Conducts and publishes research on strategic weapons proliferation issues and makes it available to the press, congressional and executive branch staff, foreign officials, and international organizations.

Nuclear Threat Initiative (NTI), *1747 Pennsylvania Ave. N.W., 7th Floor, 20006; (202) 296-4810. Fax, (202) 296-4811. Joan Rohlfing, President; Sam Nunn, Corporate Executive Officer.*
General email, contact@nti.org

Web, www.nti.org

Works to reduce threats from nuclear, biological, and chemical weapons; publishes monthly and quarterly e-newsletters.

Peace Action, *8630 Fenton St., #524, Silver Spring, MD 20910-5642; (301) 565-4050. Fax, (301) 565-0850. Kevin Martin, Executive Director. Press, (301) 565-4050 ext. 316.*
Web, www.peace-action.org

Grassroots organization that supports a negotiated comprehensive test ban treaty. Seeks a reduction in the military budget and a transfer of those funds to nonmilitary programs. Works for an end to international arms trade.

Physicians for Social Responsibility (PSR), *1111 14th St. N.W., #700, 20005; (202) 667-4260. Fax, (202) 667-4201. Dr. Catherine Thomasson, Executive Director.*
General email, psrnatl@psr.org

Web, www.psr.org

Membership: doctors, nurses, health scientists, and concerned citizens. Works toward the elimination of nuclear weapons and use of nuclear power. Conducts public education programs, monitors policy, and serves as a liaison with other concerned groups.

Union of Concerned Scientists, *Global Security, 1825 K St. N.W., #800, 20006-1232; (202) 223-6133. Fax, (202) 223-6162. David Wright, Co-Director; Lisbeth Gronlund, Co-Director.*
General email, ucs@ucsusa.org

Web, www.ucsusa.org

Combines technical analysis, education and advocacy, and engagement with the public and scientific community to promote policies that enhance national and international security. Focuses on technical issues, including verified reductions of nuclear arsenals, fissile material controls, missile defense, and space security. Plays a role in increasing the number of independent scientists and technical analysts working professionally on security issues worldwide. (Headquarters in Cambridge, Mass.)

Nuclear Weapons and Power

▶ **AGENCIES**

Bureau of International Security and Nonproliferation *(State Dept.), Nuclear Energy, Safety, and Security Affairs, 2201 C St. N.W., #3320, 20520; (202) 647-4413. Fax, (202) 647-0775. Richard K. Stratford, Director.*
Web, www.state.gov/t/isn/58378

Advises the secretary on policy matters relating to nonproliferation and export controls, nuclear technology and safeguards, and nuclear safety. Negotiates bilateral and multilateral agreements pertaining to nuclear trade, safety, and physical protection.

Defense Nuclear Facilities Safety Board, *625 Indiana Ave. N.W., #700, 20004-2901; (202) 694-7080. Fax, (202) 208-6518. Joyce L. Connery, Chair; Jessie H. Roberson, Vice Chair. Information, (202) 694-7000.*
General email, mailbox@dnfsb.gov

Web, www.dnfsb.gov

Independent board created by Congress and appointed by the president to provide external oversight of Energy Dept. defense nuclear weapons production facilities and make recommendations to the secretary of energy regarding public health and safety.

Energy Dept. (DOE), *Under Secretary for Nuclear Security, 1000 Independence Ave. S.W., #7A049, 20585; (202) 586-5555. Fax, (202) 586-4892. Frank Klotz, Under Secretary for Nuclear Security. Toll-free, (800) 342-5363.*
Web, http://nnsa.energy.gov

Maintains the safety, security, and effectiveness of the U.S. nuclear weapons stockpile without nuclear testing; provides the U.S. Navy with safe and effective nuclear propulsion; provides the nation with nuclear counterterrorism and incident response capability.

Homeland Security Dept. (DHS), *Domestic Nuclear Detection, 3801 Nebraska Ave. N.W., 20528; (202) 254-7000. Huban Gowadia, Director, Acting.*
Web, www.dhs.gov/domestic-nuclear-detection-office

Seeks to improve the nation's capability to detect and report unauthorized attempts to import, possess, store, develop, or transport nuclear or radiological material for use against the nation, as well as integration of federal nuclear forensics programs. Oversees the development of an integrated global and domestic nuclear detection program with partners from federal, state, local, and international governments and the private sector, and the deployment of a nuclear detection system.

National Nuclear Security Administration *(Energy Dept.), Defense Programs, 1000 Independence Ave. S.W., #4A019, 20585; (202) 586-2179. Fax, (202) 586-5670. Brig. Gen. Stephen Davis (USAF), Deputy Administrator, Acting.*
Web, www.nnsa.energy.gov/aboutus/ourprograms/defenseprograms

Responsible for nuclear weapons research, development, and engineering; performs laser fusion research and development.

National Nuclear Security Administration *(Energy Dept.), Nuclear Nonproliferation and International Security, 1000 Independence Ave. S.W., #7F075, 20585; (202) 586-0645. Fax, (202) 586-0862. Anne M. Harrington, Deputy Administrator.*
Web, www.nnsa.energy.gov/aboutus/ourprograms/dnn

Seeks to develop and implement policy and technical solutions to eliminate proliferation-sensitive materials and limit or prevent the spread of materials, technology, and expertise related to nuclear and radiological weapons and programs around the world. Collaborates with the International Atomic Energy Agency (IAEA) to ensure the secure and safe expansion of global nuclear energy and other peaceful uses of the atom.

National Security Staff (NSS) *(Executive Office of the President), Defense Policy and Strategy,* The White House, 20504; (202) 456-9191. Fax, (202) 456-9190. (202) 456-9301. Troy Thomas, Senior Director. phone, (202) 456-9301.
Web, www.whitehouse.gov/administration/eop/nsc

Advises the assistant to the president for national security affairs on matters concerning defense policy.

Navy Dept. *(Defense Dept.), Naval Reactors, Naval Nuclear Propulsion Program,* 1240 Isaac Hull Ave. S.E., MS 8037, Washington Navy Yard, DC 20376-8037; (202) 781-6172. Fax, (202) 781-6403. Adm. James F. Caldwell Jr., Director; Tom Dougan, Public Affairs, (202) 781-5818.
Web, www.navy.mil and *http://nnsa.energy.gov/aboutus/ourprograms/powernavy2/aboutnr*

Responsible for naval nuclear propulsion.

► **CONGRESS**

For a listing of relevant congressional committees and subcommittees, please see pages 598–599 or the Appendix.

► **NONGOVERNMENTAL**

Fourth Freedom Forum, *Washington Office,* 1101 14th St. N.W., #900, 20005; (202) 464-6009. Fax, (202) 238-9604. Alistair Millar, Executive Director.
General email, amillar@fourthfreedom.org
Web, www.fourthfreedom.org

Conducts research and training to advance global cooperation to address transnational threats, including terrorism, nuclear proliferation, and drug trafficking. (Headquarters in Goshen, Ind.)

Institute for Science and International Security, 440 1st St. N.W., #800, 20001; (202) 547-3633. David Albright, President.
General email, isis@isis-online.org
Web, www.isis-online.org

Conducts research and analysis on nuclear weapons production and nonproliferation issues.

BORDERS, CUSTOMS, AND IMMIGRATION

General

► **AGENCIES**

Federal Law Enforcement Training Center *(Homeland Security Dept.), Washington Operations,* 555 Eleventh St. N.W. #400, 20004; (202) 233-0260. Fax, (202) 233-0258. Connie Patrick, Director, (912) 267-2070.
General email, FLETC-WashingtonOffice@dhs.gov
Web, www.fletc.gov/washington-operations-wo

Trains law enforcement personnel. Provides services to state, local, tribal, and international law enforcement agencies. (Headquarters in Glynco, Ga.)

Homeland Security Dept. (DHS), *Citizenship and Immigration Services Ombudsman,* MS 0180, 20528-0180; (202) 357-8100. Fax, (202) 357-0042. Maria Odom, Ombudsman. Toll-free, (855) 882-8100.
General email, cisombudsman@hq.dhs.gov
Web, www.dhs.gov/cisombudsman

Assists individuals and employers in resolving problems with the U.S. Citizenship and Immigration Services (USCIS); proposes changes in the administrative practices of USCIS in an effort to mitigate identified problems.

U.S. Citizenship and Immigration Services (USCIS) *(Homeland Security Dept.),* 20 Massachusetts Ave. N.W., 20529; (800) 375-5283. León Rodríguez, Director. Press, (202) 272-1200. TTY, (800) 767-1833.
Web, www.uscis.gov

Responsible for the delivery of immigration and citizenship services. Priorities include the promotion of national security and the implementation of measures to improve service delivery.

U.S. Customs and Border Protection *(Homeland Security Dept.),* 1300 Pennsylvania Ave. N.W., #4.4A, 20229; (202) 325-8000. Fax, (202) 344-1380. R. Gil Kerlikowske, Commissioner. Information, (877) 227-5511. Press, (202) 344-1700. TTY, (866) 880-6582.
Web, www.cbp.gov

Assesses and collects duties and taxes on imported merchandise; processes persons and baggage entering the United States; collects import and export data for international trade statistics; controls export carriers and goods to prevent fraud and smuggling. Library open to the public by appointment.

U.S. Customs and Border Protection *(Homeland Security Dept.), Agricultural Program and Trade Liaison Office,* 1300 Pennsylvania Ave. N.W., #2.5B, 20229; (202) 344-3298. Fax, (202) 344-1442. Kevin Harriger, Executive Director.
Web, www.cbp.gov

Responsible for safeguarding the nation's animal and natural resources from pests and disease through inspections at ports of entry and beyond.

U.S. Customs and Border Protection *(Homeland Security Dept.), Border Patrol,* 1300 Pennsylvania Ave. N.W., #6.5E, 20229; (202) 344-2050. Fax, (202) 344-3140. Ronald D. Vitiello, Chief, Acting.
Web, www.cbp.gov/border-security/along-us-borders/overview

Mobile uniformed law enforcement arm of the Homeland Security Dept. Primary mission is to detect and prevent the illegal trafficking of people and contraband across U.S. borders.

U.S. Immigration and Customs Enforcement (ICE) *(Homeland Security Dept.),* 500 12th St. S.W., 20536; (202) 732-3000. Fax, (202) 732-3080. Sarah R. Saldaña, Director. Press, (202) 732-4242. Hotline to report suspicious activity, (866) 347-2423.
Web, www.ice.gov

Enforces immigration and customs laws within the United States. Focuses on the protection of specified federal buildings and on air and marine enforcement. Undertakes investigations and conducts interdictions.

►CONGRESS

For a listing of relevant congressional committees and subcommittees, please see pages 598–599 or the Appendix.

DEFENSE TRADE AND TECHNOLOGY

General

►AGENCIES

Bureau of Industry and Security *(Commerce Dept.),* *14th St. and Constitution Ave. N.W., #3898, 20230; (202) 482-1455. Fax, (202) 482-2387. Eric L. Hirschhorn, Under Secretary. Press, (202) 482-2721. Export licensing information, (202) 482-4811.* *Web, www.bis.doc.gov and Twitter, @BISgov*

Administers Export Administration Act; maintains control lists and performs export licensing for the purposes of national security, foreign policy, and prevention of short supply.

Bureau of Industry and Security *(Commerce Dept.),* *Export Enforcement, 14th St. and Constitution Ave. N.W., #3723, 20230; (202) 482-3618. Fax, (202) 482-4173. David W. Mills, Assistant Secretary; Richard R. Majaukas, Deputy Assistant Secretary; Douglas Hassebrock, Director, (202) 482-1208. Export enforcement hotline, (800) 424-2980.* *Web, www.bis.doc.gov/index.php/enforcement/oee/7-enforcement*

Enforces dual-use export controls on exports of U.S. goods and technology for purposes of national security, nonproliferation, counterterrorism, foreign policy, and short supply. Enforces the antiboycott provisions of the Export Administration Regulations.

Bureau of Political-Military Affairs *(State Dept.),* *Defense Trade Controls, 2401 E St. N.W., SA-1, #H1200, 20037 (mailing address: PM/DDTC, SA-1, 12th Floor, Bureau of Political Military Affairs, Washington, DC 20522-0112); (202) 663-2980. Fax, (202) 261-8199. Brian H. Nilsson, Deputy Assistant Secretary.* *Web, www.pmddtc.state.gov*

Controls the commercial export of defense articles, services, and related technical data; authorizes the permanent export and temporary import of such items.

Defense Dept. (DoD), *Defense Technology Security Administration, 4800 Mark Center Dr., #03D08, Alexandria, VA 22350-1600; (571) 372-2301. Fax, (571) 372-2583. Beth M. McCormick, Director; Michael Laychak, Deputy Director.* *Web, www.dtsa.mil*

Develops and implements technology security policy for international transfers of defense-related goods, services, and technologies. Participates in interagency and international activities and regimes that monitor, control, and prevent transfers that could threaten U.S. national security interests.

Defense Dept. (DoD), *International Cooperation, 3070 Defense Pentagon, #5A1062B, 20301-3070; (703) 697-4172. Fax, (703) 693-2026. Keith Webster, Director.* *Web, www.acq.osd.mil/ic*

Advises the under secretary of defense for Acquisitions, Technology, and Logistics on cooperative research and development, production, procurement, and follow-up support programs with foreign nations; monitors the transfer of secure technologies to foreign nations.

National Institute of Standards and Technology (NIST) *(Commerce Dept.), National Security Standards Program, 100 Bureau Dr., MS 8102, Gaithersburg, MD 20898-8102; (301) 975-8610. William Billotte, Program Manager.* *Web, www.nist.gov/national-security-standards*

Develops technical standards related to national security through federal, state, local and private sector, and international engagement. Focuses on standards for Chemical/Biological/Radiological/Nuclear/Explosive (CBRNE) detection as well as personal protective equipment (PPE), physical infrastructure resilience, and security.

National Nuclear Security Administration *(Energy Dept.), Nuclear Nonproliferation and International Security, 1000 Independence Ave. S.W., #7F075, 20585; (202) 586-0645. Fax, (202) 586-0862. Anne M. Harrington, Deputy Administrator.* *Web, www.nnsa.energy.gov/aboutus/ourprograms/dnn*

Seeks to develop and implement policy and technical solutions to eliminate proliferation-sensitive materials and limit or prevent the spread of materials, technology, and expertise related to nuclear and radiological weapons and programs around the world. Collaborates with the International Atomic Energy Agency (IAEA) to ensure the secure and safe expansion of global nuclear energy and other peaceful uses of the atom.

National Security Staff (NSS) *(Executive Office of the President), International Economic Affairs, The White House, 20504; (202) 456-9281. Fax, (202) 456-9280. Wally Adeyemo, Deputy National Security Adviser.* *Web, www.whitehouse.gov/administration/eop/nsc*

Advises the president, the National Security Council, and the National Economic Council on all aspects of U.S. foreign policy dealing with U.S. international economic policies.

Nuclear Regulatory Commission, *International Programs, 11555 Rockville Pike, MS 04E21, Rockville, MD 20852; (301) 415-2344. Fax, (301) 415-2400. Nader Marnish, Director, (301) 415-1780.* *Web, www.nrc.gov/about-nrc/organization/oipfuncdesc.html*

Immigration Reform and Advocacy Resources

The following agencies, organizations, blogs, and hotlines offer information pertaining to immigrant and refugee advocacy and immigration reform.

ADVOCACY

American Immigration Lawyers Assn., (202) 507-7600; www.aila.org

Amnesty International, (202) 544-0200; www.amnestyusa.org

Ayuda, (202) 387-4848; www.ayuda.com

Break the Chain Campaign (Institute for Policy Studies), (202) 234-9382; www.ips-dc.org

Capital Area Immigrants' Rights (CAIR) Coalition, (202) 331-3320; www.caircoalition.org

Catholic Legal Immigration Network, Inc., (301) 565-4800; http://cliniclegal.org

Center for Community Change, (202) 339-9300; www.communitychange.org

Commission on Immigration at the American Bar Assn., (202) 662-1000; www.americanbar.org/groups/public_services/immigration.html

Detention Watch Network, (202) 350-9055; www.detentionwatchnetwork.org

United Nations High Commissioner for Refugees Regional Office, (855) 808-6427; www.unrefugees.org

U.S. Committee for Refugees and Immigrants, (703) 310-1130; www.refugees.org

U.S. Conference of Catholic Bishops, Migration, and Refugee Services, (202) 541-3352; www.usccb.org/mrs

Young Professionals in Foreign Policy Refugee Assistance Program, http://www.ypfp.org/refugees

REFORM

America's Voice, (202) 724-6397; www.americasvoice.org

Center for Immigration Studies, (202) 466-8185; www.cis.org

Federation for American Immigration Reform (FAIR), (202) 328-7004; www.fairus.org

Immigration Equality Action Fund, Press (212) 714-2904; www.immigrationequality.org

Immigration Policy Center at the American Immigration Council, (202) 507-7500; www.immigrationpolicy.org

Immigration Reform Law Institute, (202) 232-5590; www.irli.org

Immigration Solutions Group, PLLC, (202) 234-0899; www.immigrationsolutions.com

ImmigrationWorks USA, (202) 506-4541; www.immigrationworksusa.org

Migration Policy Institute, (202) 266-1940; www.migrationpolicy.org

National Council of La Raza, (202) 785-1670; www.nclr.org

National Immigration Forum, (202) 347-0040; https://immigrationforum.org

SOCIAL MEDIA AND BLOGS

Borderlines Blog, Transborder Project, CIP Senior Analyst Tom Barry (575) 313-4544; http://borderlinesblog.blogspot.com

Center for Immigration Studies Blog, http://cis.org/ImmigrationBlog

Immigration Equality Action Fund Blog, http://www.immigrationequality.org/blog

Progressives for Immigration Reform Blog, www.progressivesforimmigrationreform.org/blog

Reform Immigration for America Blog, http://reformimmigrationforamerica.org/on-our-blog

HOTLINES

Asylee Information and Hotline, (800) 354-0365

Office of Special Counsel for Immigration-Related Unfair Employment Practices, U.S. Department of Justice, Civil Rights Division, Worker hotline, (800) 255-7688; Employer hotline, (800) 255-8155; TTY, (800) 237-2515

U.S. Immigration and Customs Enforcement (ICE), Detainees' Hotline, (855) 448-6903

U.S. Citizenship and Immigration Services National Customer Service Center, (800) 375-5283

Coordinates application review process for exports and imports of nuclear materials, facilities, and components. Makes recommendations on export-import licensing upon completion of review process. Conducts related policy reviews.

Treasury Dept., *Terrorism and Financial Intelligence, Foreign Assets Control, 1500 Pennsylvania Ave. N.W., Treasury Annex, 20220; (202) 622-2490. Fax, (202) 622-1657. Adam Szubin, Under Secretary, Acting. Fax-on-demand, (202) 622-0077. Hotline, (800) 540-6322.*

General email, ofac_feedback@do.treas.gov

Web, www.treasury.gov/about/organizational-structure/offices/Pages/Office-of-Foreign-Assets-Control.aspx

Authorized under the Enemy Act, the International Emergency Economic Powers Act, and United Nations Participation Act, and other relevant statutory authorities to control financial and commercial dealings with certain countries and their foreign nationals in times of war or emergencies. Regulations involving foreign assets control, narcotics, nonproliferation, and commercial transactions

Air Force Department

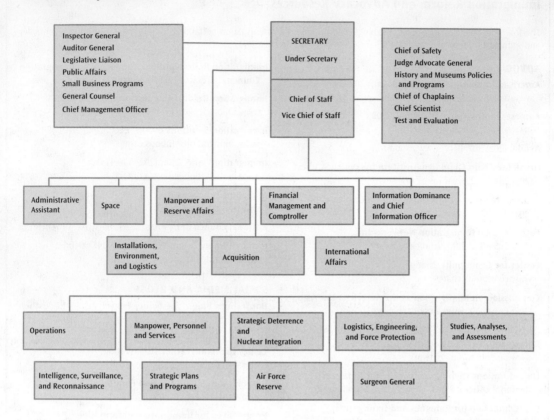

currently apply in varying degrees to the Balkans, Belarus, Burma, Côte d'Ivoire, Cuba, Iran, Iraq, Lebanon, Libya, North Korea, Somalia, Sudan, Syria, Yemen, and Zimbabwe, as well as terrorists wherever located and transnational criminal organizations.

►CONGRESS

For a listing of relevant congressional committees and subcommittees, please see pages 598–599 or the Appendix.

Research and Development

►AGENCIES

Air Force Dept. *(Defense Dept.), Acquisition, 1060 Air Force Pentagon, #4E962, 20330-1060; (703) 697-6361. Fax, (703) 693-6400. Lt. Gen. William LaPlante, Air Force Service Acquisition Executive.*
Web, ww3.safaq.hq.af.mil

Air Force office that directs and reviews Air Force research, development, and acquisition of weapons systems.

Air Force Dept. *(Defense Dept.), Scientific Research, 875 N. Randolph St., #3112, Arlington, VA 22203-1768; (703) 696-7551. Fax, (703) 696-9556. Thomas F. Christian, Director.*
Web, www.afosr.af.mil

Sponsors and sustains basic research; assists in the transfer of research results to the war fighter; supports Air Force goals of control and maximum utilization of air and space.

Army Corps of Engineers *(Defense Dept.), Research and Development, 441 G St. N.W., #3417, 20314-1000; (202) 761-1839. Fax, (202) 761-0907. Jeffery P. Holland, SES, Director.*
Web, www.usace.army.mil

Supports the research and development efforts of the corps by providing strategic planning and strategic direction and oversight, developing policy and doctrine, developing national program integration, and advising the chief of engineers on science and technology issues.

Army Dept. *(Defense Dept.), Acquisition, Logistics, and Technology, 103 Army Pentagon, #2E532, 20310-0103; (703) 695-6154. Fax, (703) 697-4003. Heidi Shyu, Assistant Secretary. Press, (703) 697-7592.*
Web, www.army.mil/asaalt

Civilian office that directs Army acquisition research and development of weapons systems and missiles.

Army Dept. *(Defense Dept.), Research and Technology, 103 Army Pentagon, #2E533, 20310-0103; (703) 692-1837. Mary Miller, Director.*
Web, www.army.mil

Sponsors and supports basic research at Army laboratories, universities, and other public and private organizations; assists in the transfer of research and technology to the field.

Bureau of Intelligence and Research *(State Dept.), 2201 C St. N.W., #6468, 20520-6531; (202) 647-9177. Fax, (202) 736-4688. Daniel B. Smith, Assistant Secretary.*
Web, www.state.gov/s/inr

Coordinates foreign policy–related research, analysis, and intelligence programs for the State Dept. and other federal agencies.

Defense Advanced Research Projects Agency *(Defense Dept.), 675 N. Randolph St., Arlington, VA 22203-2114; (703) 696-2400. Arati Prabhakar, Director; Richard Weiss, External Relations, (571) 218-4988.*
Web, www.darpa.mil

Sponsors basic and applied research to maintain U.S. technological superiority and prevent strategic surprise by adversaries.

Defense Dept. (DoD), *Research and Engineering, 3030 Defense Pentagon, #3E272, 20301-3030; (703) 695-9604. Stephen Welby, Assistant Secretary.*
Web, www.acq.osd.mil/chieftechnologist/index.html

Civilian office responsible for policy, guidance, and oversight for the Defense Dept.'s Science and Technology Program. Serves as focal point for in-house laboratories, university research, and other science and technology matters.

Defense Technical Information Center *(Defense Dept.), 8725 John Jay Kingman Rd., #1948, Fort Belvoir, VA 22060-6218; (703) 767-9100. Christopher E. Thomas, Administrator. Registration, (703) 767-8273. Toll-free, (800) 225-3842.*
Web, www.dtic.mil

Acts as a central repository for the Defense Dept.'s collection of current and completed research and development efforts in all fields of science and technology. Disseminates research and development information to contractors, grantees, and registered organizations working on government research and development projects, particularly for the Defense Dept. Users must register with the center.

Marine Corps *(Defense Dept.), Systems Command, 2200 Lester St., Quantico, VA 22134-6050; (703) 432-1800. Fax, (703) 432-3535. Brig. Gen. Joseph Shrader (USMC), Commanding General.*
Web, www.marcorsyscom.usmc.mil

Military office that directs Marine Corps research, development, and acquisition.

Missile Defense Agency *(Defense Dept.), 5700 18th St., Bldg. 245, Fort Belvoir, VA 22060-5573; (571) 231-8006. Fax, (571) 231-8090. Vice Adm. James D. Syring (USN), Director, Maj. Gen. Ole A. Knudson (USA), Deputy Director. Fraud, waste, and abuse hotline, (800) 424-9098. General email, mda.info@mda.mil*
Web, www.mda.mil

Manages and directs the ballistic missile defense acquisition and research and development programs. Seeks to deploy improved theater missile defense systems and to develop options for effective national missile defenses while increasing the contribution of defensive systems to U.S. and allied security.

National Communications System *(Homeland Security Dept.), President's National Security Telecommunications Advisory Committee, 245 Murray Lane, MS 0615, Arlington, VA 20598-0615; Mark McLaughlin, Chair. DHS switchboard, (202) 282-8000. General email, NSTAC@hq.dhs.gov*
Web, www.dhs.gov/national-security-telecommunications-advisory-committee

Advises the president, the National Security Council, the Office of Science and Technology Policy, and the Office of Management and Budget on specific measures to improve telecommunications for the federal government. Areas of major focus include strengthening national security, enhancing cybersecurity, maintaining the global communications infrastructure, assuring communications for disaster response, and addressing infrastructure interdependencies and dependencies.

Naval Research Laboratory *(Defense Dept.), Research. 4555 Overlook Ave. S.W., 20375-5320; (202) 767-3301. Fax, (202) 404-2676. Capt. Mark Bruington, Commanding Officer; John A. Montgomery, Director. Press, (202) 767-2541. Personnel locator, (202) 767-3200.*
Web, www.nrl.navy.mil

Conducts scientific research and develops advanced technology for the Navy. Areas of research include radar systems, radiation technology, tactical electronic warfare, and weapons guidance systems.

Navy Dept. *(Defense Dept.), Naval Research, 875 N. Randolph St., #1425, Arlington, VA 22203-1995; (703) 696-5031. Fax, (703) 696-5940. Rear Adm. Mat Winter, Chief.*
Web, www.onr.navy.mil

Oversees the offices of Naval Research, Naval Technology, and Advanced Technology; works to ensure transition of research and technology to the fleet; sponsors and supports basic research at Navy laboratories, universities, and other public and private organizations.

Navy Dept. *(Defense Dept.), Research, Development, and Acquisition, 1000 Navy Pentagon, #4E665, 20350-1000; (703) 695-6315. Fax, (703) 697-0172. Sean J. Stackley, Assistant Secretary; Rear Adm. Matthew Klunder, Director, (703) 695-0611; Cmdr. Thurraya Kent, Director, Public Affairs, (703) 695-0611.*
Web, www.secnav.navy.mil/rda/pages/default/aspx

Civilian office that directs and reviews Navy and Marine Corps research and development of weapons systems.

Office of Science and Technology Policy (OSTP) *(Executive Office of the President), Eisenhower Executive Office Bldg., 1650 Pennsylvania Ave. N.W., 20504; (202) 456-4444. Fax, (202) 456-6021. John P. Holdren, Director.*

Army Department

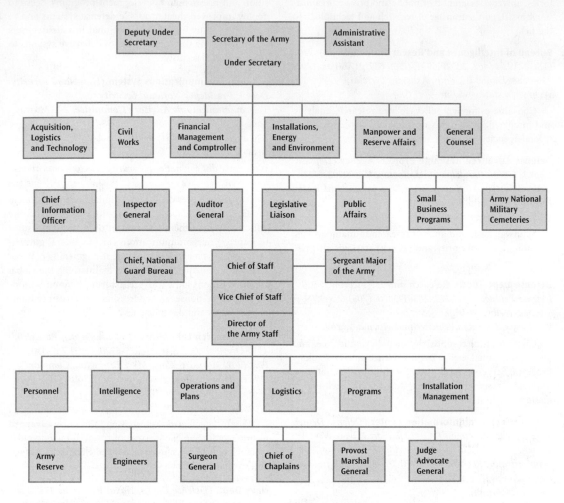

General email, info@ostp.gov

Web, www.ostp.gov

Advises the president on science and technology matters as they affect national security; coordinates science and technology initiatives at the interagency level. Interests include nuclear materials, security, nuclear arms reduction, and counterterrorism.

U.S. Coast Guard (USCG) (Homeland Security Dept.),
Engineering and Logistics, CG4, 2703 Martin Luther King Jr. Ave. S.E., MS 7714, 20593; (202) 475-5554. Fax, (202) 475-5957. Rear Adm. Bruce D. Baffer, Assistant Commandant; Albert Curry Jr., Deputy Assistant Commandant.
Web, www.uscg.mil/hq/cg4

Develops and maintains engineering standards for the building of ships, aircraft, shore infrastructure, and Coast Guard facilities.

►CONGRESS

For a listing of relevant congressional committees and subcommittees, please see pages 598–599 or the Appendix.

►NONGOVERNMENTAL

AFCEA (Armed Forces Communications and Electronics Assn.), *4400 Fair Lakes Court, Fairfax, VA 22033-3899; (703) 631-6100. Fax, (703) 631-6169.*
Lt. Gen. Robert M. Shea (USMC, Ret.), President.
Toll-free, (800) 336-4583.
General email, service@afcea.org

Web, www.afcea.org

Membership: industrial organizations, scientists, and military and government personnel in the fields of communications, electronics, computers, and electrical engineering. Consults with the Defense Dept. and other federal agencies on design and maintenance of command, control, communications, computer, and intelligence systems; holds events displaying latest communications products.

American Society of Naval Engineers (ASNE), *1452 Duke St., Alexandria, VA 22314-3458; (703) 836-6727. Fax, (703) 836-7491. Leigh McCue, Executive Director.*
General email, asnehq@navalengineers.org

Web, www.navalengineers.org

Navy Department

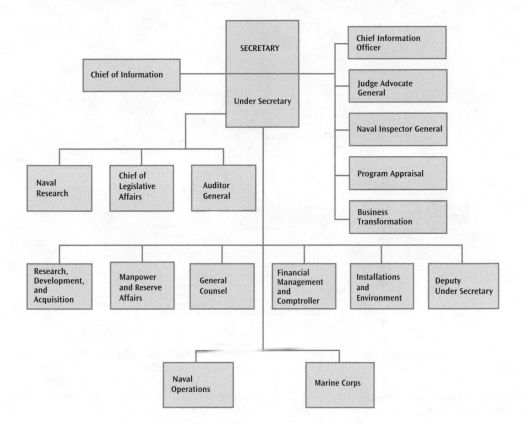

Membership: civilian, active duty, and retired naval engineers. Provides forum for an exchange of information between industry and government involving all phases of naval engineering.

Analytic Services Inc., *5275 Leesburg Pike, #N5000, Falls Church, VA 22041; (703) 416-2000. Carmen J. Spencer, President. Toll-free, (877) 339-4389.*
Web, www.anser.org

Systems analysis organization funded by government contracts. Conducts weapons systems analysis.

Institute for Defense Analyses (IDA), *4850 Mark Center Dr., Alexandria, VA 22311-1882; (703) 845-2000. Fax, (703) 845-2588. David Chu, President. Library, (703) 845-2087. General email, info-sac@ida.org*
Web, www.ida.org

Federally funded research and development center that focuses on national security and defense. Conducts research, systems evaluation, and policy analysis for Defense Dept. and other agencies.

Johns Hopkins University Applied Physics Laboratory, *11100 Johns Hopkins Rd., Laurel, MD 20723-6099; (240) 228-5000. Fax, (240) 228-5995. Ralph D. Semmel, Director. Public Affairs, (240) 228-5020.*
Web, www.jhuapl.edu

Research and development organization that conducts research for the Defense Dept. and other federal agencies. Interests include defense, national security, and space technologies.

Johns Hopkins University Applied Physics Laboratory, *Research and Exploratory Development, 11100 Johns Hopkins Rd., Laurel, MD 20723-6099; (240) 228-5000. Jim Schatz, Head.*
Web, www.jhuapl.edu/ourwork/red

Research and development laboratory that seeks to improve warfighter survivability, sustainment, and performance through battlefield trauma prevention and mitigation, along with medical device evaluation and development. Programs include improvement of soldier protection equipment, the development of a neurally integrated upper extremity prosthetic, and blast-related traumatic brain injury research.

LMI, *7940 Jones Branch Dr., Tysons, VA 22102; (703) 917-9800. Fax, (703) 917-7591. Nelson M. Ford, President. Toll-free, (800) 213-4817.*
Web, www.lmi.org

Conducts research on military and nonmilitary logistics, including transportation, supply and maintenance, force management, weapons support, acquisition, health systems, international programs, energy and environment, mathematical modeling, installations, operations, and

U.S. Coast Guard

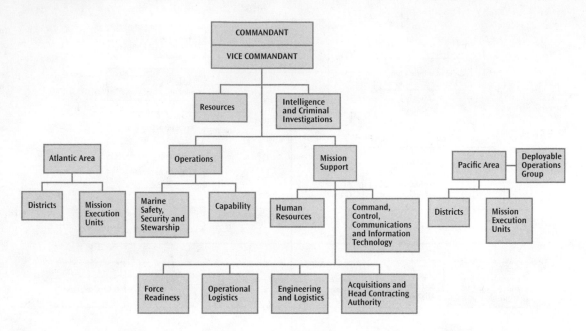

information systems. (Formerly Logistics Management Institute.)

Military Operations Research Society (MORS),
2111 Wilson Blvd., #700, Alexandria, VA 22201; (703) 933-9070. Fax, (703) 933-9066. Susan Reardon, Chief Executive Officer.
General email, morsoffice@mors.org
Web, www.mors.org

Membership: professional analysts of military operations. Fosters information exchange; promotes professional development and high ethical standards; educates members on emerging issues, analytical techniques, and applications of research.

National Research Council (NRC), *Air Force Studies Board,* *Keck Center, 500 5th St. N.W., 9th Floor, 20001; (202) 334-2000. Gen. Douglas M. Fraser (USAF, Ret.), Board Chairman.*
Web, http://sites.nationalacademies.org/DEPS/AFSB

Supports activities related to the development of science and technology within the Air Force. Interests of study include fuel efficiency, acquisition processes, and assuring the future scientific and technical qualification of Air Force personnel.

National Research Council (NRC), *Army Science and Technology Board,* *500 5th St. N.W., 9th Floor, 20001; (202) 334-3118. Gen. David M. Maddox (USA, Ret.), Chair.*
Web, http://sites.nationalacademies.org/DEPS/BAST

Supports activities and and advises the Secretary of the Army about policies related to the development of science and technology within the Army.

National Research Council (NRC), *Human-Systems Integration Board,* *Keck Center, 500 5th St. N.W., 11th Floor, 20001; (202) 334-2678. Fax, (202) 334-2210. Poornima Madhavan, Director, (202) 334-3357; Nancy J. Cooke, Chair.*
General email, bohsi@nas.edu
Web, http://sites.nationalacademies.org/dbasse/bohsi

Conducts studies on human factors and human-systems integration. Areas of research include virtual reality, human-computer interaction, nuclear safety, air traffic control, military simulation, modeling social networks, home health care, and disability and rehabilitation research.

National Research Council (NRC), *Naval Studies Board,* *Keck Center, 500 5th St. N.W., 9th Floor, 20001; (202) 334-3523. Fax, (202) 334-3695. Hon. Paul A. Schneider, Chair; Charles F. Draper, Director.*
General email, nsb@nas.edu
Web, http://sites.nationalacademies.org/DEPS/nsb

Conducts research and supports activites that help provide scientific and technical planning advice to the Navy.

Society of American Military Engineers, *607 Prince St., Alexandria, VA 22314-3117; (703) 549-3800. Fax, (703) 684-0231. Brig. Gen. Joseph Schroedel (USA, Ret.), Executive Director, ext. 110. Press, (703) 548-6153.*
General email, editor@same.org
Web, www.same.org

Membership: military and civilian engineers, architects, and construction professionals. Conducts workshops and conferences on subjects related to military engineering.

SRI International, Washington Office, 1100 Wilson Blvd., #2800, Arlington, VA 22209; (703) 524-2053. Fax, (703) 247-8569. Peter Kant, Executive Director, (703) 247-8424. Web, www.sri.com

Research organization supported by government and private contracts. Conducts research on military technology, including lasers and computers. Other interests include strategic planning and armed forces interdisciplinary research. (Headquarters in Menlo Park, Calif.)

EMERGENCY PREPAREDNESS AND RESPONSE

General

▶AGENCIES

Army Corps of Engineers (Defense Dept.), Contingency Operations and Office of Homeland Security, 441 G St. N.W., 20314-1000; (202) 761-4601. Fax, (202) 761-5096. Karen L. Durham-Aguilera, SES, Director. Web, www.usace.army.mil

Assists military combatant commands, as well as federal, state, and local emergency management and emergency response organizations, with mitigation, planning, training, and exercises to build and sustain capabilities to protect from and respond to any emergency or disaster, including natural disasters and terrorist attacks involving weapons of mass destruction.

Civil Air Patrol National Capital Wing, 200 McChord St. S.W., #111, Joint Base Anacostia-Bolling, 20032; (202) 767-4405. Col. Bruce Heinlein, Wing Commander. General email, info@natcapwing.org

Web, www.natcapwg.cap.gov and Twitter, @NatCapWing

Official auxiliary of the U.S. Air Force. Conducts search-and-rescue missions for the Air Force; participates in emergency airlift and disaster relief missions. (Headquarters at Maxwell Air Force Base, Ala.)

Federal Emergency Management Agency (FEMA) (Homeland Security Dept.), 500 C St. S.W., 20472; (202) 646-3900. Fax, (202) 212-5889. W. Craig Fugate, Administrator; Rafael Lemaitre, Public Affairs. Press, (202) 646-3272. Locator, (202) 646-2500. FEMA helpline, (800) 621-3362. TTY, (800) 462-7585. Toll-free, 800-621-FEMA. Disaster TTY, (800) 427-5593. General email, femaopa@dhs.gov

Web, www.fema.gov

Manages federal response and recovery efforts following natural disasters, terrorist attacks, and all other kinds of national emergencies. Initiates mitigation activities; works with state and local emergency managers; manages the National Flood Insurance Program.

Federal Emergency Management Agency (FEMA) (Homeland Security Dept.), Federal Insurance and Mitigation Administration, 1800 S. Bell St., MS 3020, Arlington, VA 22202; (202) 646-2781. Fax, (202) 646-7970.

Vacant, Associate Administrator. Web, www.fema.gov/what-mitigation/federal-insurance-mitigation-administration

Administers federal flood insurance programs, including the National Flood Insurance Program. Makes low-cost flood insurance available to eligible homeowners.

Federal Emergency Management Agency (FEMA) (Homeland Security Dept.), Grant Programs, 800 K St. N.W., North Tower, 20001; (800) 368-6498. Brian E. Kamoie, Assistant Administrator. General email, askcsid@fema.gov

Web, www.fema.gov/grants

Administers and manages non-disaster grants to states, local communities, regional authorities, and tribal jurisdictions to mitigate hazards and to prevent, deter, respond to, and recover from terrorism and other threats to national security.

Federal Emergency Management Agency (FEMA) (Homeland Security Dept.), Protection and National Preparedness, 800 K St. N.W., 20002; (202) 646-3100. Fax, (202) 786-0851. Timothy W. Manning, Deputy Administrator. Disaster Assistance, (800) 621-FEMA. TTY, (800) 462-7585. NIMS email, FEMA-NIMS@dhs.gov

Web, www.fema.gov/protection-and-national-preparedness, www.fema.gov/national-incident-management-system and www.fema.gov/fema-regional-nims-contacts

Coordination of preparedness and protection-related activities throughout FEMA, including grants, planning, training, exercises, individual and community preparedness, assessments, lessons learned, continuity of government, and national capital region coordination. Includes the following offices and components: Counterterrorism and Security Preparedness, Preparedness Integration and Coordination, and Strategic Resource Management. Oversees the National Incident Management System (NIMS). Integrates federal, state, local, and tribal emergency response and preparedness practices into a national framework. Promotes standardized structures and procedures and interoperable communications systems. Operates ten regional offices.

Federal Emergency Management Agency (FEMA) (Homeland Security Dept.), Protection and National Preparedness, National Continuity Programs, 500 C St. S.W., #524, 20472; (202) 646-4145. Fax, (202) 646-3921. Damon C. Penn, Assistant Administrator. Web, www.fema.gov/national-continuity-programs

Responsible for the coordination of all Federal Emergency Management Agency national security programs. Manages Integrated Public Alert Warning System (IPAWS).

Federal Emergency Management Agency (FEMA) (Homeland Security Dept.), Protection and National Preparedness, Technological Hazards, 1800 S. Bell St., MS 3025, Arlington, VA 22202; (202) 646-3158. Fax, (703) 308-0324. Timothy Greten, Director, Acting, (202) 646-2618. Web, www.fema.gov/technological-hazards-division

Helps FEMA prepare to respond to disasters and incidents of all kinds. Coordinates and develops plans, resources, assessments, and national standards for emergency response operations. Oversees standards for emergency response operations. Oversees community response plans for chemical and nuclear hazards. Develops and delivers grant opportunities and education and training programs for the emergency management and first responder communities.

Federal Emergency Management Agency (FEMA)
(Homeland Security Dept.), Response and Recovery,
Federal Disaster Coordination, *500 C St. S.W., 20472;*
(202) 212-1946. Fax, (202) 212-1002.
Elizabeth Zimmerman, Associate Administrator.
Web, www.fema.gov/office-response-and-recovery

Responsible for coordination of the president's disaster relief program.

Health and Human Services Dept. (HHS), *National*
Disaster Medical System, 200 Independence Ave. S.W,
#638G, 20201; (202) 205-7978. Dr. Andrew Garrett,
Director. Public Affairs, (202) 205-8114.
Web, http://phe.gov/ndms

Provides local, state, and tribal governments with medical response, patient movement, and the definitive care of victims of major emergencies and presidentially declared disasters, including those resulting from natural, technological, and human-caused hazards, such as transportation accidents and acts of terrorism involving chemical, biological, radiological, nuclear, and explosive weapons. Maintains a national capability to provide medical, veterinary, and mortuary teams, supplies, and equipment at the sites of disasters, and in transit from the impacted area into participating definitive care facilities.

Homeland Security Dept. (DHS), *Cybersecurity and*
Communications, 245 Murray Lane S.W., Bldg. 410, MS
8570, 20528-8570; Andy Ozment, Assistant Secretary. DHS
switchboard, (202) 282-8000. Press, (202) 282-8010. TTY,
(202) 282-8000.
Web, www.dhs.gov/office-cybersecurity-and-
communications

Works with other federal agencies in developing comprehensive plans to prevent and mitigate cyber-based attacks. Works with the public and private sectors as well as international partners to enhance the security of the nation's cyber and communications infrastructure. Identifies security vulnerabilities and coordinates warning and response procedures.

Homeland Security Dept. (DHS), *Infrastructure*
Protection, 1310 N. Courthouse Rd., Arlington, VA 22201;
(703) 235-8110. Fax, (202) 235-9757. Caitlin Durkovich,
Assistant Secretary.
Web, www.dhs.gov/about-office-infrastructure-protection

Identifies and assesses threats to the nation's physical and informational structure from acts of terrorism or natural disasters. Coordinates programs to respond to and quickly recover from attacks or other emergencies.

Homeland Security Dept. (DHS), *National Protection*
and Programs Directorate, 3801 Nebraska Ave., Bldg. 5,
20528; Fax, (202) 295-0870. Suzanne Spaulding, Under
Secretary, Acting. DHS switchboard, (202) 282-8000.
Web, www.dhs.gov/national-protection-and-programs-
directorate

Identifies and assesses threats to the nation's physical and cyber infrastructure; issues warnings to prevent damage.

Interior Dept. (DOI), *Emergency Management, 1849 C St.*
N.W., MS 6628, 20240; (202) 208-4679. Fax, (202) 219-
3421. Lisa Branum, Director. Watch Office (24/7), (202)
208-4108. Toll-free, (877) 246-1373.
General email, DOI_Watch_Office@ios.doi.gov
Web, www.doi.gov/emergency

Establishes and disseminates policy and coordinates the development of Interior Dept. programs for emergency prevention, planning, response, and recovery that affects federal and tribal lands, facilities, infrastructure, and resources. Provides assistance to other units of government under federal laws, executive orders, interagency emergency response plans such as the National Response Framework, and other agreements.

National Nuclear Security Administration *(Energy*
Dept.), Emergency Operations, 1000 Independence Ave.
S.W., #GH060, 20585; (202) 586-9892. Fax, (202) 586-
3904. Debrah Wilber, Associate Administrator.
Web, www.nnsa.energy.gov/aboutus/ourprograms/
emergencyoperationscounterterrorism/operationscenter

Works to ensure coordinated Energy Dept. responses to energy-related emergencies. Recommends policies to mitigate the effects of energy supply crises on the United States; recommends government responses to energy emergencies.

Small Business Administration (SBA), *Disaster*
Assistance, 409 3rd St. S.W., #6050, 20416; (202) 205-6734.
Fax, (202) 205-7728. James Rivera, Associate
Administrator. Service Center, (800) 659-2955. TTY,
(800) 877-8339.
Web, www.sba.gov/offices/headquarters/oda

Provides victims of physical disasters with disaster and economic injury loans for homes, businesses, and personal property. Lends funds for uncompensated losses incurred from any disaster declared by the president of the United States or the administrator of the SBA. Lends funds to individual homeowners, business concerns of all sizes, and nonprofit institutions to repair or replace damaged structures and furnishings, business machinery, equipment, and inventory. Provides economic injury loans to small businesses for losses to meet necessary operating expenses, provided the business could have paid these expenses prior to the disaster.

U.S. Coast Guard (USCG) *(Homeland Security Dept.),*
Counterterrorism and Defense Policy, 2100 2nd St. S.W.,
MS 7363, 20593; (202) 372-2101. Fax, (202) 372-2911.
Robert Irvine, Chief.
Web, www.uscg.mil/hq/cg5/cg532

Ensures that the Coast Guard can mobilize effectively during national emergencies, including those resulting from enemy military attack.

U.S. Coast Guard (USCG) *(Homeland Security Dept.),* **National Response Center,** *2100 2nd St. S.W., #2111B, 20593-0001; (202) 267-2180. Fax, (202) 267-1322. Syed M. Qadir, Director, (202) 372-2440. TTY, (202) 267-4477. Hotline, (800) 424-8802. Local, (202) 267-2675. General email, NRC@uscg.mil*

Web, www.nrc.uscg.mil

Maintains 24-hour hotline for reporting oil spills, hazardous materials accidents, and chemical releases. Notifies appropriate federal officials to reduce the effects of accidents.

U.S. Coast Guard (USCG) *(Homeland Security Dept.),* **Response Policy,** *CG-53, 2100 2nd St. S.W., 20593-7516; (202) 372-2010. Rear Adm. Peter Brown, Director. Web, www.uscg.mil*

Conducts search-and-rescue and polar and domestic ice-breaking operations. Regulates waterways under U.S. jurisdiction. Operates the Coast Guard National Response Center; participates in defense operations and homeland security; assists with law enforcement/drug interdictions.

U.S. Fire Administration *(Federal Emergency Management Agency),* *16825 S. Seton Ave., Emmitsburg, MD 21727-8998; (301) 447-1000. Fax, (301) 447-1270. Ernest Mitchell Jr., Administrator, (202) 646-4223. Press, (301) 447-1853. Web, www.usfa.fema.gov*

Provides public education, first responder training, technology, and data initiatives in an effort to prevent losses due to fire and related emergencies. Administers the Emergency Management Institute and the National Fire Academy for firefighters and emergency management personnel.

►**CONGRESS**

For a listing of relevant congressional committees and subcommittees, please see pages 598–599 or the Appendix.

►**NONGOVERNMENTAL**

American Red Cross, *Disaster Preparedness and Response, 2025 E St. N.W., 20006-5009; (202) 303-5000, ext. 1. Gail J. McGovern, President. Press, (202) 303-5551. Donations, 800-RED-CROSS. Toll-free, (800) 733-2767. Web, www.redcross.org and Disaster Preparedness, www.redcross.org/training*

Chartered by Congress to administer disaster relief. Provides disaster victims with food, shelter, first aid, medical care, and access to other available resources. Feeds emergency workers; handles inquiries from concerned family members outside the disaster area; helps promote disaster preparedness and prevention through training.

National Assn. of State EMS Officials (NASEMSO), *201 Park Washington Ct., Falls Church, VA 22046-4527;*

(703) 538-1799. Fax, (703) 241-5603. Elizabeth B. Armstrong, Executive Vice President. General email, info@nasemso.org

Web, www.nasemso.org

Supports development of effective emergency medical services (EMS) systems at the local, state, and regional levels. Works to formulate national EMS policy and foster communication and sharing among state EMS officials.

National Emergency Management Assn., *Washington Office, 444 N. Capitol St. N.W., #401, 20001-1557; (202) 624-5460. Fax, (202) 624-5452. Alexa Noruk, Government Relations Director. Web, www.nemaweb.org*

Professional association of state emergency managers. Promotes improvement of emergency management through strategic partnerships and innovative programs. (Headquarters in Lexington, Ky.; member of the Council of State Governments.)

National Research Council (NRC), *Disasters Roundtable, Keck Center, 500 5th St. N.W., 20001; (202) 334-2243. Fax, (202) 334-1393. Ells M. Stanley Sr., Chair. General email, dr@nas.edu*

Web, http://dels.nas.edu/global/dr

Facilitates the exchange of ideas among scientists, practitioners, and policymakers concerned with issues related to natural, technological, and other disasters. Roundtable workshops are held three times a year in Washington, D.C.

Salvation Army Disaster Service, *2626 Pennsylvania Ave. N.W., 20037-1618; (202) 756-2600. Fax, (202) 464-7203. Maj. Andrew Wiley, Divisional Secretary. Web, www.disaster.salvationarmyusa.org and Twitter, @SalArmyEDS*

Provides U.S. and international disaster victims and rescuers with emergency support, including food, clothing, and counseling services.

Coordination and Partnerships

►**AGENCIES**

Federal Bureau of Investigation (FBI) *(Justice Dept.),* **National Joint Terrorism Task Force,** *935 Pennsylvania Ave. N.W., 20535-0001; (571) 280-5688. Fax, (571) 280-6922. William Callahan, Unit Chief. Web, www.fbi.gov/washingtondc/about-us/our-partnerships/partners and www.fbi.gov/about-us/investigate/terrorism/national-joint-terrorism-task-force*

Group of more than fifty agencies from the fields of intelligence, public safety, and federal, state, and local law enforcement that collects terrorism information and intelligence and funnels it to the more than five hundred JTTFs (teams of local, state, and federal agents based at FBI field offices), various terrorism units within the FBI, and partner agencies. Helps the FBI with terrorism investigations.

Federal Emergency Management Agency (FEMA)
(Homeland Security Dept.), Emergency Management Institute, 16825 S. Seton Ave., Emmitsburg, MD 21727; (301) 447-1000. Fax, (301) 447-1658. Tony Russell, Superintendent, (301) 447-1286.
Web, www.training.fema.gov/EMI

Provides federal, state, tribal, and local government personnel and some private organizations engaged in emergency management with technical, professional, and vocational training. Educational programs include hazard mitigation, emergency preparedness, and disaster response.

Federal Emergency Management Agency (FEMA)
(Homeland Security Dept.), Grant Programs, 800 K St. N.W., North Tower, 20001; (800) 368-6498. Brian E. Kamoie, Assistant Administrator.
General email, askcsid@fema.gov
Web, www.fema.gov/grants

Administers and manages non-disaster grants to states, local communities, regional authorities, and tribal jurisdictions to mitigate hazards and to prevent, deter, respond to, and recover from terrorism and other threats to national security.

Federal Emergency Management Agency (FEMA)
(Homeland Security Dept.), Individual and Community Preparedness, Techworld Bldg., 800 K St. N.W., #5127, 20472-3630; (202) 786-9557. Helen Lowman, Director. Flood insurance information, (888) 379-9531. Storm shelter information, (866) 222-3580.
General email, citizencorps@dhs.gov
Web, www.ready.gov/citizen-corps

Conducts research on individual, business, and community preparedness. Administers Citizen Corps, a national network of state, territory, tribal, and local councils that coordinate with local first responders to develop community-specific public education, outreach, training, and volunteer opportunities that address community preparedness and resiliency.

Federal Emergency Management Agency (FEMA)
(Homeland Security Dept.), Protection and National Preparedness, 800 K St. N.W., 20002; (202) 646-3100. Fax, (202) 786-0851. Timothy W. Manning, Deputy Administrator. Disaster assistance, (800) 621-FEMA. TTY, (800) 462-7585.
NIMS email, FEMA-NIMS@dhs.gov
Web, www.fema.gov/protection-and-national-preparedness, www.fema.gov/national-incident-management-system and www.fema.gov/fema-regional-nims-contacts

Coordination of preparedness and protection-related activities throughout FEMA, including grants, planning, training, exercises, individual and community preparedness, assessments, lessons learned, continuity of government, and national capital region coordination. Includes the following offices and components: Counterterrorism and Security Preparedness, Preparedness Integration and Coordination, and Strategic Resource Management. Oversees the National Incident Management System (NIMS). Integrates federal, state, local, and tribal emergency response and preparedness practices into a national framework. Promotes standardized structures and procedures and interoperable communications systems. Operates ten regional offices.

Homeland Security Dept. (DHS), *Bombing Prevention, 3801 Nebraska Ave. N.W., 20528; (703) 235-9382. Fax, (703) 235-9711. Patrick Starke, Director.*
General email, obp@hq.dhs.gov
Web, www.dhs.gov/obp

Coordinates national efforts to detect, prevent, and respond to terrorist improvised explosive device (IED) threats and leads the Homeland Security Dept. efforts to implement the National Counter-IED policy. Works with federal agencies, state and local governments, and the private sector to promote information sharing and IED awareness. Maintains database on equipment, training, and assets required for effective response to IED threats. Sponsors Technical Resource for Incident Prevention (TRIPwire), an online information-sharing network for bomb technicians and other law enforcement officials.

Homeland Security Dept. (DHS), *Operations Coordination, 3801 Nebraska Ave. N.W., Bldg. 3, #01107, 20528; (202) 282-9580. Fax, (202) 282-9811. Richard Chavez, Director.*
Web, www.dhs.gov/office-operations-coordination

Collects and fuses intelligence and enforcement activities information that may have a terrorist nexus from a variety of federal, state, territorial, tribal, local, and private sector partners to continually monitor the nation's threat environment. Coordinates incident management activities within the department and with state governors, homeland security advisors, law enforcement partners, and critical infrastructure operators in all states and major urban areas nationwide.

Homeland Security Dept. (DHS), *Policy Office, Private Sector, 3801 Nebraska Ave. N.W., Bldg. 81, #17, 20528; (202) 282-8484. Fax, (202) 282-8679. James J. Dinneen, Assistant Secretary, Acting. Press, (202) 282-8010.*
General email, private.sector@dhs.gov
Web, www.dhs.gov

Works to facilitate outreach to industry and flow of information between industry and the department on security topics ranging from protecting critical infrastructure from sabotage to securing computer networks from hackers. Adminsters the Loaned Executive Program to partner with executive-level experts on a volunteer basis for specific needs.

Transportation Dept. (DOT), *Intelligence, Security, and Emergency Response, 1200 New Jersey Ave. S.E., #56125, 20590; (202) 366-6525. Fax, (202) 366-7261. Michael Lowder, Director, (202) 366-6530.*
Web, www.dot.gov/mission/administrations/intelligence-security-emergency-response

Advises the secretary on transportation intelligence and security policy. Develops, coordinates, and reviews transportation emergency preparedness programs for use in emergencies affecting national defense and in

Federal Emergency Management Agency

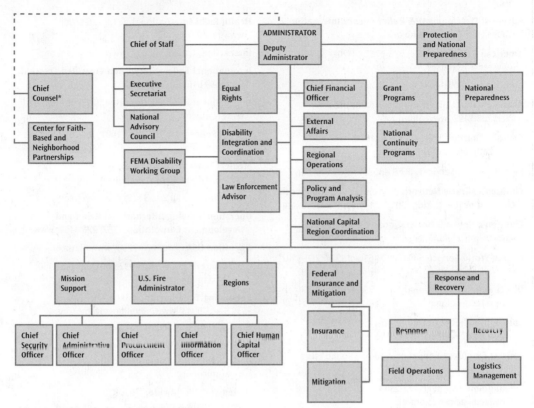

* Department of Homeland Security Direct Reports

– – – Indicates a support or advisory relationship with the unit rather than a direct reporting relationship

emergencies caused by natural and man-made disasters and crisis situations.

► CONGRESS

For a listing of relevant congressional committees and subcommittees, please see pages 598–599 or the Appendix.

► INFORMATION SHARING AND ANALYSIS CENTERS

A 1998 decision directive issued by President Bill Clinton defined various infrastructure industries critical to the national economy and public well-being. The directive proposed the creation of Information Sharing and Analysis Centers (ISACs), which would be established by each critical infrastructure industry to communicate with its members, its government partners, and other ISACs about threat indications, vulnerabilities, and protection strategies. Each ISAC is led by a government agency or private entity. ISACs led by Washington-area agencies or companies are listed below.

Communications ISAC *(Homeland Security Dept.), c/o National Coordinating Center for Communications, 245 Murray Lane, MS 0615, 20520; (703) 235-5080. John O'Connor, Manager, National Coordinating Center for Communications; Rear Adm. Ronald T. Hewitt*

(USCG), Director, Office of Emergency Communications. General email, ncc@hq.dhs.gov

Web, www.dhs.gov/national-coordinating-center-communications

Communications network that links federal civilian, military, diplomatic, and intelligence agencies with private sector cyber and telecommunications providers to protect the nation's telecommunications infrastructure and restore it from disruptions caused by attacks or natural disasters. Includes the National Cybersecurity and Communications Integration Center, a 24/7 center for protection of computer and communications across federal, state, and local governments; intelligence and law enforcement agencies; and the private sector.

Emergency Management and Response-ISAC, *16825 S. Seton Ave., Emmitsburg, MD 21727-8920; (301) 447-1325. Fax, (301) 447-1034. Rick Ziebart, Emergency Response Support Branch Chief, USFA, (301) 447-1821; Ernie Mitchell Jr., U.S. Fire Administrator, (202) 646-4223. General email, fema-nfirshelp@fema.dhs.gov*

Web, www.usfa.fema.gov/operations/ops_cip.html

Collects, analyzes, and disseminates information to support the critical infrastructure protection and resilience efforts of the nation's emergency services sector. Researches current physical and cyber protection issues,

Domestic Disaster Relief Organizations

Adventist Development & Relief Agency International, (800) 424-2372; www.adra.org

American Red Cross, (800) 733-2767 or (202) 303-5214; www.redcross.org

AmeriCares, (800) 486-4357; www.americares.org

Ananda Marga Universal Relief Team, Inc., (301) 738-7122; www.amurt.net

Catholic Charities USA, (713) 526-4611; www.catholiccharitiesusa.org

Catholic Relief Services, (877) 435-7277; www.crs.org

Children's Miracle Network (Osmond Foundation for the Children of the World), (801) 214-7400; www.cmn.org

Children's Network International, (888) 818-4483; www.helpthechildren.org

Church World Service, (800) 297-1516 or (574) 264-3102; www.cwsglobal.org

Direct Relief International, (805) 964-4767; www.directrelief.org

Episcopal Relief & Development, (855) 312-4325; www.episcopalrelief.org

Federal Employee Education and Assistance Fund (FEEA), (303) 933-7580; www.feea.org

Feeding America, (800) 771-2303; www.feedingamerica.org

Feed the Children, (800) 627-4556; www.feedthechildren.org

Habitat for Humanity International, (800) 422-4828; www.habitat.org

Health Right International, (212) 226-9890; www.healthright.org

InterAction, (202) 667-8227; www.interaction.org

International Federation of Red Cross/Red Crescent, (212) 338-0161; www.ifrc.org

International Rescue Committee, (212) 551-3000; www.rescue.org

Islamic Relief USA, (855) 447-1001 or (703) 370-7202; www.irusa.org

Medical Teams International, (800) 959-4325 or (503) 624-1000; www.medicalteams.org

Mercy Corps, (800) 292-3355; www.mercycorps.org

Operation Blessing International Relief and Development Corporation, (757) 226-3401; www.ob.org

Operation USA, (800) 678-7255; www.opusa.org

Oxfam America, (800) 776-9326 or (202) 496-1180; www.oxfamamerica.org

Rebuilding Together, Inc., (800) 473-4229 or (202) 483-9083; www.rebuildingtogether.org

Save the Children, (800) 728-3843; www.savethechildren.org

United Methodist Committee on Relief, (800) 554-8583; www.umcor.org

United Way Worldwide, (703) 836-7112; www.unitedway.org

World Health Organization (Pan American Health Organization), (202) 974-3000; www.who.int/en or www.paho.org

World Vision, (888) 511-6548; www.worldvision.org

---

operates an information center, issues alerts and messages, and prepares instructional materials relevant to the emergency services community.

Financial Services ISAC (FS-ISAC), *12020 Sunrise Valley Dr., #230, Reston, VA 20191; (877) 612-2622. Fax, (301) 579-6106. William (Bill) Nelson, President.*
General email, admin@fsisac.com

Web, www.fsisac.com

Provides a confidential venue for sharing security vulnerabilities and solutions, including data obtained from such sources as other ISACs, law enforcement agencies, technology providers, and security associations. Works to facilitate trust, cooperation, and information sharing among its participants and assesses proactive means of mitigating cybersecurity risks.

Surface Transportation Information Sharing and Analysis Center (ISAC), *c/o EWA Information and Infrastructure Technologies, Inc., 13873 Park Center Rd., #200, Herndon, VA 20171-5406; (703) 478-7600. Fax, (703) 478-7647. Paul G. Wolfe, Director, (703) 478-7656.*

Toll-free, (866) 784-7221.
General email, st-isac@surfacetransportationisac.org

Web, www.surfacetransportationisac.org

Protects physical and electronic infrastructure of surface transportation and public transit carriers. Collects, analyzes, and distributes critical security and threat information from worldwide resources; shares best security practices and provides 24/7 immediate physical and cyberthreat warnings.

WaterISAC, *1620 Eye St. N.W., #500, 20006-4027; (202) 331-0479. Diane VanDe Hei, Executive Director. Toll-free, (866) 426-4722.*
General email, info@waterisac.org

Web, www.waterisac.org

Gathers, analyzes, and disseminates threat information concerning the water community from utilities' security incident reports and agencies of the federal government. Provides the water community with access to sensitive information and resources about cyber, physical, and contamination threats.

International Assn. of Chiefs of Police, *Advisory Committee for Patrol and Tactical Operations, 44 Canal Center Plaza, #200, Alexandria, VA 22314; (703) 836-6767. Jenny Gargano, Staff Liaison, ext. 847. Toll-free, (800) 843-7227.*
General email, kollon@theiacp.org

Web, www.theiacp.org

Membership: foreign and U.S. police executives and administrators. Maintains liaison with civil defense and emergency service agencies in the United States and other nations; prepares guidelines for police cooperation with emergency and disaster relief agencies during emergencies.

National Governors Assn. (NGA), *Center for Best Practices, Homeland Security and Public Safety Division, 444 N. Capitol St. N.W., #267, 20001-1512; (202) 624-5300. Fax, (202) 624-5313. Jeffrey McLeod, Division Director.*
Web, www.nga.org/cms/center/hsps

Provides support to governors in responding to the challenges of homeland security through technical assistance and policy research, and by facilitating their participation in national discussion and initiatives. Current issues include cybersecurity, prescription drug abuse, public safety broadband, sentencing and corrections reform, homeland security grant reform, justice information-sharing, and public health preparedness.

National Voluntary Organizations Active in Disaster (NVOAD), *615 Slaters Lane, Alexandria, VA 22314 (mailing address: P.O. Box 26125, Alexandria, VA 22313); (703) 778-5088. Fax, (703) 778-5091. Bill Driscoll Jr., President; Katherine Clements, Director of Operations.*
General email, info@nvoad.org

Web, www.nvoad.org

Seeks to promote communication, cooperation, coordination, and collaboration among voluntary agencies that participate in disaster response, relief, and recovery nationally.

Emergency Communications

Air Force Dept. *(Defense Dept.), Office of Information Dominance and Chief Information Officer, 1800 Air Force Pentagon, #4E1050, 20330-1800; (703) 695-6829. Fax, (703) 692-7512. Lt. Gen. William J. Bender, Chief Warfighting Integration and Information Officer. Press, (703) 695-0640.*
General email, safxc.workflow@pentagon.af.mil

Web, www.safxc.af.mil

Responsible for policymaking, planning, programming, and evaluating performance of the Air Force's command, control, communications, and computer (C-4) system.

Army Dept. *(Defense Dept.), Chief Information Officer / G-6, 107 Army Pentagon, #3E608, 20310-0107; (703) 695-4366. Fax, (703) 695-3091. Lt. Gen. Robert S. Ferrell (USA),* Chief Information Officer.
Web, http://ciog6.army.mil and Twitter, @ArmyCIOG6

Oversees policy and budget for the Army's information systems and programs.

Defense Dept. (DoD), *Chief Information Officer, 6000 Defense Pentagon, #3E1030, 20301-6000; (703) 695-0348. Fax, (703) 614-8060. Terry Halvorsen, Chief Information Officer.*
Web, http://dodcio.defense.gov

Civilian office with policy oversight for all command, control, and communications matters.

Defense Dept. (DoD), *Command, Control, Communications, and Computers/Cyber, 8000 Joint Staff Pentagon, #1E1044, 20318-6000; (703) 695-3562. Fax, (703) 614-2945. Lt. Gen. Mark S. Bowman, Director.*
Web, www.jcs.mil/Directorates/J6%7CC4Cyber.aspx

Advises the secretary of defense on policy for command, control, communications, and computer/cyber matters throughout the Defense Dept.

Defense Dept. (DoD), *White House Communications Agency, U.S. Naval Station, Anacostia Annex, 2743 Defense Blvd. S.W., #220, 20373-5815; (202) 757-5530. Fax, (202) 757-5529. Col. Cleophus Thomas Jr., Director.*
Web, www.disa.mil/whca

Responsible for presidential communications.

Federal Communications Commission (FCC), *Emergency Alert System, 445 12th St. S.W., #7-A807, 20554; (202) 418-1228. Fax, (202) 418-2790. Bonnie Gay, EAS Coordinator. FCC 24/7 Operations Center, (202) 418-1122.*
General email, eas@fcc.gov

FCC 24/7 Operations Center, FCCOPCenter@fcc.gov

Web, www.fcc.gov/pshs/services/eas and www.fcc.gov/encyclopedia/emergy-alert-system-eas

Develops rules and regulations for the Emergency Alert System, which is the national warning system the president would use to communicate with the public during a national emergency in the event that access to normal media outlets becomes unavailable. It is also used by state and local officials for weather-related and man-made emergencies.

Federal Communications Commission (FCC), *Public Safety and Homeland Security Bureau, 445 12th St. S.W., #7C732, 20554; (202) 418-1300. Fax, (202) 418-2817. Rear Adm. David G. Simpson (USN, Ret.), Chief. Press, (202) 418-0503. 24-Hour Operations Center, (202) 418-1122.*
General email, pshsbinfo@fcc.gov

Web, www.fcc.gov/public-safety-homeland-security

Develops, recommends, and administers the FCC's policies pertaining to public safety communications issues, including 911 and E911. Responsible for the operability and interoperability of public safety communications, communications infrastructure protection and disaster response, and network security and reliability. Administers the Emergency Response Interoperability Network (ERIC), establishing and maintaining a broadband public safety wireless network, including authentication and encryption.

Homeland Security Dept. (DHS), *Emergency Communications,* 245 Murray Lane, MS 0615, Arlington, VA 20528-0615; (703) 235-3660. Fax, (703) 235-4981. Ron Hewitt, Director. Press, (703) 235-4965.
General email, oec@dhs.gov

Web, www.dhs.gov/office-emergency-communications

Ensures that the federal government has the necessary communications capabilities to permit its continued operation during a national emergency; provides emergency responders and government officials with communications support as it directs the nation's recovery from a major disaster; provides training, coordination, tools, and guidance to help federal, state, local, tribal, territorial, and industry partners develop their emergency communications capabilities.

National Communications System *(Homeland Security Dept.), President's National Security Telecommunications Advisory Committee,* 245 Murray Lane, MS 0615, Arlington, VA 20598-0615; Mark McLaughlin, Chair. DHS switchboard, (202) 282-8000.
General email, NSTAC@hq.dhs.gov

Web, www.dhs.gov/national-security-telecommunications-advisory-committee

Advises the president, the National Security Council, the Office of Science and Technology Policy, and the Office of Management and Budget on specific measures to improve telecommunications for the federal government. Areas of major focus include strengthening national security, enhancing cybersecurity, maintaining the global communications infrastructure, assuring communications for disaster response, and addressing infrastructure interdependencies and dependencies.

U.S. Coast Guard (USCG) *(Homeland Security Dept.), National Response Center,* 2100 2nd St. S.W., #2111B, 20593-0001; (202) 267-2180. Fax, (202) 267-1322. Syed M. Qadir, Director, (202) 372-2440. TTY, (202) 267-4477. Hotline, (800) 424-8802. Local, (202) 267-2675.
General email, NRC@uscg.mil

Web, www.nrc.uscg.mil

Maintains 24-hour hotline for reporting oil spills, hazardous materials accidents, and chemical releases. Notifies appropriate federal officials to reduce the effects of accidents.

Industrial and Military Planning and Mobilization

▶**AGENCIES**

Bureau of Industry and Security *(Commerce Dept.), Strategic Industries and Economic Security,* 14th St. and Constitution Ave. N.W., #3876, 20230; (202) 482-4506. Fax, (202) 482-5650. Michael Vaccaro, Director, (202) 482-8232.

General email, petrina.bean@bis.doc.gov

Web, www.bis.doc.gov/index.php/other-areas/strategic-industries-and-economic-security-sies

Administers the Defense Production Act and provides industry with information on the allocation of resources falling under the jurisdiction of the act.

Defense Logistics Agency *(Defense Dept.), Logistics Operations,* 8725 John Jay Kingman Rd., Fort Belvoir, VA 22060-6221; (703) 767-1600. Fax, (703) 767-1588. Rear Adm. Vincent L. Griffith (USN), Director. Press, (703) 767-6200.
Web, www.dla.mil/HQ/LogisticsOperations.aspx

Oversees management, storage, and distribution of items used to support logistics for the military services and federal agencies. Synchronizes the Defense Logistics Agency's capabilities with the combatant commands, military services, the joint staff, other combat support defense agencies, and designated federal agencies. Provides logistics policy, with an emphasis on modernizing business systems and maximizing readiness and combat logistics support.

Maritime Administration *(Transportation Dept.), Sealift Operations and Emergency Preparedness,* West Bldg., 1200 New Jersey Ave. S.E., W23-302, 20590; (202) 366-1031. Fax, (202) 366-5904. Russell Krause, Deputy Director, Acting.
Web, www.marad.dot.gov/ports/maritime-emergency-preparedness-and-response

Plans for the transition of merchant shipping from peacetime to wartime operations under the direction of the National Shipping Authority. Participates in interagency planning and policy development for maritime security-related directives. Coordinates port personnel and the military for deployments through the commercial strategic seaports. Represents the United States at the NATO Planning Board for Ocean Shipping. (The National Shipping Authority is a stand-by organization that is activated upon the declaration of a war or other national emergency.)

Maritime Administration *(Transportation Dept.), Ship Operations,* West Bldg., 1200 New Jersey Ave. S.E., MAR-610, MS 2-W25-336, 20590; (202) 366-1875. Fax, (202) 366-3954. William H. Cahill, Director.
Web, www.marad.dot.gov

Maintains the National Defense Reserve Fleet, a fleet of older vessels traded in by U.S. flag operators that are called into operation during emergencies; manages and administers the Ready Reserve Force, a fleet of ships available for operation within four to twenty days, to meet the nation's sealift readiness requirements.

Maritime Administration *(Transportation Dept.), Strategic Sealift,* West Bldg., 1200 New Jersey Ave. S.E., Mar-600, MS 1, W25-330, 20590; (202) 366-5400. Fax, (202) 366-5904. Kevin M. Tokarski, Associate Administrator.
Web, www.marad.dot.gov/ships_shipping_landing_page/national_security/national_security.htm

Administers strategic sealift programs for the Maritime Administration and ensures that merchant shipping is available in times of war or national emergency.

►CONGRESS

For a listing of relevant congressional committees and subcommittees, please see pages 598–599 or the Appendix.

►NONGOVERNMENTAL

National Defense Industrial Assn. (NDIA), *2111 Wilson Blvd., #400, Arlington, VA 22201-3061; (703) 522-1820. Fax, (703) 522-1885. Gen. Craig R. McKinley (USAF, Ret.), President.*
Web, www.ndia.org, Twitter, @NDIAToday and Facebook, www.facebook.com/NDIAMembership

Membership: U.S. citizens and businesses interested in national security. Also open to individuals and businesses in nations that have defense agreements with the United States. Provides information and expertise on defense preparedness issues; works to increase public awareness of national defense preparedness through education programs; serves as a forum for dialogue between the defense industry and the government.

National Defense Transportation Assn. (NDTA), *50 S. Pickett St., #220, Alexandria, VA 22304; (703) 751-5011. Fax, (703) 823-8761. Rear Adm. Mark H. Buzby (USN, Ret.), President.*
Web, www.ndtahq.com

Membership: transportation service companies. Maintains liaison with the Defense Dept., the Transportation Dept., and the Transportation Security Administration to prepare emergency transportation plans.

Infrastructure Protection

►AGENCIES

Energy Dept. (DOE), *Electricity Delivery and Energy Reliability, 1000 Independence Ave. S.W., #8H033, 20585; (202) 586-1411. Fax, (202) 586-5860. Patricia Hoffman, Assistant Secretary.*
Web, http://energy.gov/oe/office_electricity_delivery_and_energy_reliability

Leads the federal response to energy emergencies, guides technology research and development on the security and reliability of the nation's energy systems, provides training and support for stakeholders, and works to assess and mitigate energy system vulnerabilities. Works in conjunction with the Homeland Security Dept. and other DOE programs, federal groups, state and local governments, and private industry.

Federal Bureau of Investigation (FBI) *(Justice Dept.), Cyber Division, 935 Pennsylvania Ave. N.W., #5835, 20535; (202) 324-7770. Fax, (202) 324-2840. James Trainor Jr., Assistant Director.*
Web, www.fbi.gov/about-us/investigate/cyber

Coordinates the investigations of federal violations in which the Internet or computer networks are exploited for terrorist, foreign government-sponsored intelligence, or criminal activities, including copyright violations, fraud, pornography, child exploitation, and malicious computer intrusions.

Federal Protective Service (FPS) *(Homeland Security Dept.), 800 N. Capitol St., 5th Floor, 20002; Fax, (202) 732-8109. L. Eric Patterson, Director. Switchboard, (202) 282-8000.*
Web, www.dhs.gov/about-federal-protective-service

Works to ensure that appropriate levels of security are in place in General Services Administration–managed facilities throughout the United States. Conducts assessments on all GSA-controlled facilities to evaluate threats and tailor appropriate security countermeasures. Has enforcement capability to detain and arrest people, seize goods or conveyances, obtain arrest and search warrants, respond to incidents and emergency situations, provide protection during demonstrations or civil unrest, and be deputized for law enforcement response in special situations.

Homeland Security Dept. (DHS), *Cybersecurity and Communications, 245 Murray Lane S.W., Bldg. 410, MS 8570, 20528-8570; Andy Ozment, Assistant Secretary. DHS switchboard, (202) 282-8000. Press, (202) 282 8010. TTY, (202) 282-8000.*
Web, www.dhs.gov/office-cybersecurity-and-communications

Works with other federal agencies in developing comprehensive plans to prevent and mitigate cyber-based attacks. Works with the public and private sectors as well as international partners to enhance the security of the nation's cyber and communications infrastructure. Identifies security vulnerabilities and coordinates warning and response procedures.

Homeland Security Dept. (DHS), *Infrastructure Protection, 1310 N. Courthouse Rd., Arlington, VA 22201; (703) 235-8110. Fax, (202) 235-9757. Caitlin Durkovich, Assistant Secretary.*
Web, www.dhs.gov/about-office-infrastructure-protection

Coordinates the collection and analysis of intelligence and information pertaining to threats against U.S. infrastructure and leads related programs and policy efforts; identifies and assesses vulnerabilities, takes preventive action, and issues timely warnings. Develops partnerships and communication lines with state and local governments and the private sector.

National Aeronautics and Space Administration (NASA), *Protective Services, 300 E St. S.W., #6T39, 20546; (202) 358-2010. Fax, (202) 358-3238. Joseph Mahaley, Assistant Administrator; Charles Lombard, Deputy Assistant Administrator.*
Web, www.hq.nasa.gov/hq/security.html

Serves as the focal point for policy formulation, oversight, coordination, and management of NASA's security, counterintelligence, counterterrorism, emergency preparedness and response, and continuity of operations programs.

National Institute of Standards and Technology (NIST)
(Commerce Dept.), Computer Security, 100 Bureau Dr.,
MS 8930, Gaithersburg, MD 20899-8930; (301) 975-8443.
Fax, (301) 975-8670. Matthew Scholl, Chief.
General email, inquiries@nist.gov
Web, www.nist.gov/itl/csd

Works to improve information systems security by
raising awareness of information technology risks, vulnerabilities, and protection requirements; researches and
advises government agencies of risks; devises measures for
cost-effective security and privacy of sensitive federal
systems.

Pentagon Force Protection Agency, 9000 Defense
Pentagon, 20301; (703) 695-0412. Fax, (703) 695-0681.
Steven E. Calvery, Director. Emergency line, (703)
697-5555.
General email, pfpa.pentagon.cco.mbx.general@mail.mil
Web, www.pfpa.mil

Civilian agency providing protection for Pentagon
occupants, visitors, and infrastructure, including law
enforcement, security, surveillance, and crisis prevention.

Transportation Security Administration (TSA)
(Homeland Security Dept.), TSA-1, 601 S. 12th St.,
7th Floor, Arlington, VA 20598-6001; (571) 227-1536.
Fax, (571) 227-1398. Peter Neffenger, Administrator.
Press, (571) 227-2829. TSA Contact Center, (866)
289-9673.
General email, TSA-ContactCenter@tsa.dhs.gov
Web, www.tsa.gov/public

Responsible for aviation, rail, land, and maritime transportation security. Programs and interests include the
stationing of federal security directors and federal passenger screeners at airports, the Federal Air Marshal
Program, improved detection of explosives, and enhanced
port security.

Transportation Security Administration (TSA)
(Homeland Security Dept.), Freedom Center, 13555 EDS
Dr., Herndon VA 20171 (mailing address: TSOC Annex,
601 S. 12th St., Arlington, VA 22202); (866) 655-7023.
William Stuckey, Manager.
Web, www.tsa.gov

Operations center that provides continual federal,
state, and local coordination, communications, and domain
awareness for all of the Homeland Security Dept.'s transportation-related security activities worldwide. Transportation domains include highway, rail, shipping, and
aviation.

Treasury Dept., *Domestic Finance, Critical*
Infrastructure Protection and Compliance Policy, 1500
Pennsylvania Ave. N.W., 20220; (202) 622-5071. Fax, (202)
622-2310. Brian J. Peretti, Esq., Director, Acting.
General email, OCIP@do.treas.gov
Web, www.treasury.gov/about/organizational-structure/
offices/Pages/–Office-of-Critical-Infrastructure-Protection-
and-Compliance-Policy.aspx

Works with the private sector to protect the nation's
financial infrastructure. Maintains privacy protections for
personal financial information. Develops regulations
against money laundering and terrorism financing. Serves
as the department's principal liaison with the Homeland
Security Dept. on infrastructure protection issues.

U.S. Coast Guard (USCG) *(Homeland Security Dept.),*
Deputy for Operations Policy and Capabilities, CG-
DCO-D, 2703 Martin Luther King Jr. Ave. S.E., MS 7318,
20593; (202) 372-1001. Fax, (202) 372-2900. Rear
Adm. Vincent B. Atkins, Deputy.
Web, www.uscg.mil/hq/cg5

Establishes and enforces regulations for port safety;
environmental protection; vessel safety, inspection, design,
documentation, and investigation; licensing of merchant
vessel personnel; and shipment of hazardous materials.

U.S. Computer Emergency Readiness Team (US-CERT)
(Homeland Security Dept.), 245 Murray Lane S.W., Bldg.
410, MS 0635, 20598; (888) 282-0870. Fax, (703) 235-5110.
Vacant, Director. Press, (202) 282-8010.
General email, info@us-cert.gov
Web, www.us-cert.gov

Leads and coordinates efforts to improve the nation's
cybersecurity capabilities; promotes cyber information
sharing; and manages cyber risks to the nation through
detection, analysis, communication, coordination, and
response activities.

U.S. Secret Service *(Homeland Security Dept.), Criminal*
Investigative Division, 950 H St. N.W., #5000, 20223;
(202) 406-9330. Fax, (202) 406-5016. Stuart Tryon,
Special Agent-in-Charge.
Web, www.secretservice.gov/investigation

Investigates crimes associated with financial institutions. Jurisdiction includes bank fraud, access device fraud
involving credit and debit cards, telecommunications and
computer crimes, fraudulent identification, fraudulent
government and commercial securities, and electronic
funds transfer fraud.

▶**CONGRESS**

For a listing of relevant congressional committees and sub-
committees, please see pages 598–599 or the Appendix.

▶**NONGOVERNMENTAL**

SANS Institute, 8120 Woodmont Ave., #310, Bethesda,
MD 20814-2784; (301) 951-7267. Fax, (301) 951-0140.
Alan Paller, Director.
General email, info@sans.org
Web, www.sans.org and Twitter, @SANSInstitute

Develops, maintains, and makes available at no cost
the largest collection of research documents about information security. Operates Internet Storm Center, the
Internet's early warning system. (Also known as SysAd-
min, Audit, Network, Security Institute.)

Public Health and Environment

►AGENCIES

Bureau of Oceans and International Environmental and Scientific Affairs *(State Dept.), International Health and Biodefense, 2201 C St. N.W., #2734, 20520; (202) 647-1318. Lynette Poulton, Director.*
Web, www.state.gov/e/oes/intlhealthbiodefense

Advances the Global Health Security Agenda and focuses on issues including pandemic preparedness, new outbreaks of disease, new international policy discussions, and the impact of science and technology, medicine, and public health.

Centers for Disease Control and Prevention (CDC) *(Health and Human Services Dept.), Washington Office, 395 E St. S.W., #9100, 20201; (202) 245-0600. Fax, (202) 245-0602. Dr. Thomas R. Frieden, Director; Dena Morris, Director, Washington Office. Public inquiries, (800) 232-4636. TTY, (888) 232-6348.*
General email, cdinfo@cdc.gov

Web, www.cdc.gov/washington and Twitter, @CDCgov

Supports the CDC's Bioterrorism and Preparedness and Response Program, which develops federal, state, and local capacity to respond to bioterrorism. (Headquarters in Atlanta, Ga.)

Environmental Protection Agency (EPA), *Emergency Management, 1200 Pennsylvania Ave. N.W., MC 5104A, 20460; (202) 564-8600. Reggie Cheatham, Director, Acting; Dana S. Tulis, Deputy Director. Toll-free call center, (800) 424-8802, TTY, (800) 553-7672.*
Web, www.epa.gov/emergency-response

Responsible for planning for and responding to the harmful effects of the release or dissemination of toxic chemicals. Areas of responsibility include helping state and local responders plan for emergencies, coordinating with key federal partners, training first responders, and providing resources in the event of a terrorist incident. Carries out preparedness and response activities for intentional and accidental CBRN (Chemical, Biological, Radiation, and Nuclear) events.

Health and Human Services Dept. (HHS), *National Disaster Medical System, 200 Independence Ave. S.W, #638G, 20201; (202) 205-7978. Dr. Andrew Garrett, Director. Public Affairs, (202) 205-8114.*
Web, http://phe.gov/ndms

Federally coordinated program that collaborates with other federal agencies; tribal, state, and local governments; private businesses; and civilian volunteers to ensure the delivery of medical resources following a disaster.

Health and Human Services Dept. (HHS), *Preparedness and Response, 200 Independence Ave. S.W., #638-G, 20201; (202) 205-2882. Dr. Nicole Lurie, Assistant Secretary.*
Web, www.phe.gov

Responsible for coordinating U.S. medical and public health preparedness and response to emergencies, including natural disasters, pandemic and emerging infectious disease, and acts of biological, chemical, and nuclear terrorism. Manages advanced research and development of medical countermeasures. Oversees the hospital preparedness grant program, which provides funding to state governments.

Homeland Security Dept. (DHS), *Health Affairs, 650 Massachusetts Ave. N.W., MS 0020, 20528; (202) 254-6479. Alexander Garza, Assistant Secretary. General email, healthaffairs@dhs.gov*
Web, www.dhs.gov/office-health-affairs

Guides DHS leaders on medical and public health issues related to national security; analyzes data and monitors biological and chemical threats and responses to pandemics.

National Institute of Allergy and Infectious Diseases *(National Institutes of Health), 5601 Fishers Lane, MSC 9806, Bethesda, MD 20892-9806; (301) 496-5717. Fax, (301) 402-3573. Dr. Anthony S. Fauci, Director. Toll-free health and research information, (866) 284-4107. TTY health and research information, (800) 877-8339. Press, (301) 402-1663.*
Web, www.niaid.nih.gov, Twitter, @NIAIDNews and Facebook, www.facebook.com/niaid.nih

Responsible for coordinating and administering a medical program to counter radiological and nuclear threats. Works with the National Cancer Institute and other federal agencies, academia, and industry to develop medical measures to assess, diagnose, and care for civilians exposed to radiation.

►CONGRESS

For a listing of relevant congressional committees and subcommittees, please see pages 598–599 or the Appendix.

►NONGOVERNMENTAL

American Red Cross, *Disaster Preparedness and Response, 2025 E St. N.W., 20006-5009; (202) 303-5000, ext. 1. Gail J. McGovern, President. Press, (202) 303-5551. Donations, 800-RED-CROSS. Toll-free, (800) 733-2767.*
Web, www.redcross.org and Disaster Preparedness, www.redcross.org/training

Chartered by Congress to administer disaster relief. Provides disaster victims with food, shelter, first aid, medical care, and access to other available resources. Feeds emergency workers; handles inquiries from concerned family members outside the disaster area; helps promote disaster preparedness and prevention through training.

National Assn. of State EMS Officials (NASEMSO), *201 Park Washington Ct., Falls Church, VA 22046-4527; (703) 538-1799. Fax, (703) 241-5603. Elizabeth B. Armstrong, Executive Vice President.*

General email, info@nasemso.org

Web, www.nasemso.org

Supports development of effective emergency medical services (EMS) systems at the local, state, and regional levels. Works to formulate national EMS policy and foster communication and sharing among state EMS officials.

National Center for Biodefense and Infectious Diseases
(George Mason University), *10650 Pyramid Pl., Manassas, VA 20110; (703) 993-4265. Fax, (703) 993-4280. Charles Bailey, Executive Director.*
General email, cbailey2@gmu.edu

Web, http://ncbid.gmu.edu and http://cos.gmu.edu

Researches and develops diagnostics and treatments for emerging infectious diseases as well as those pathogens that could be used as terrorist weapons that require special containment. Manages a graduate education program.

National Research Council (NRC), *Global Health Board, Keck Center, 500 5th St. N.W., 20001; (202) 334-2352. Fax, (202) 334-3861. Patrick Kelley, Director.*
General email, HMD-NASEM@nas.edu

Web, www.nationalacademies.org/hmd

Carries out activities related to international health policy and health concerns of developing countries; main focus is public health programs for prevention and control of disease and disability.

National Research Council (NRC), *Population Health and Public Health Practice Board, Keck Center, 500 5th St. N.W., 20001; (202) 334-2383. Fax, (202) 334-2939. Rose Marie Martinez, Director.*
General email, iom_hpdp@nas.edu

Web, www.nationalacademies.org/hmd

Supports research on public health, including vaccine safety, pandemic preparedness issues, smoking cessation, health disparities, and reducing environmental and occupational hazards.

National Vaccine Information Center, *21525 Ridgetop Circle, #100, Sterling, VA 20166; (703) 938-0342. Fax, (571) 313-1268. Barbara Loe Fisher, President, (703) 938-0342.*
General email, contactnvic@gmail.com

Web, www.nvic.org

Educates the public and provides research on vaccination safety procedures and effectiveness; supports reform of the vaccination system; publishes information on diseases and vaccines; and monitors legislation and regulations.

Selective Service

▶**AGENCIES**

Selective Service System, *1515 Wilson Blvd., #400, Arlington, VA 22209-2425; (703) 605-4100. Fax, (703) 605-4106. Lawrence G. Romo, Director.*

Locator, (703) 605-4000. Toll-free, (888) 655-1825. TTY, (800) 877-8339. TTY Espanol, (800) 845-6136.
General email, information@sss.gov

Web, www.sss.gov

Supplies the armed forces with manpower when authorized; registers male citizens of the United States ages eighteen to twenty-five. In an emergency, would institute a draft and would provide alternative service assignments to men classified as conscientious objectors.

▶**CONGRESS**

For a listing of relevant congressional committees and subcommittees, please see pages 598–599 or the Appendix.

Strategic Stockpiles

▶**AGENCIES**

Defense Dept. (DoD), *Manufacturing and Industrial Base Policy, 3330 Defense Pentagon, #3B854, 20301-3300; (703) 697-0051. Fax, (703) 695-4885. André J. Gudger, Deputy Assistant Secretary, Acting.*
General email, MIBT@osd.mil

Web, www.acq.osd.mil/mibp

Develops and oversees strategic, industrial, and critical materials policies, including oversight of the National Defense Stockpile.

Defense Logistics Agency *(Defense Dept.), Strategic Materials, 8725 John Jay Kingman Rd., #3229, Fort Belvoir, VA 22060-6223; (703) 767-5500. Fax, (703) 767-3316. Ronnie Favors, Administrator; Vacant, Deputy Administrator. Press, (703) 767-6479.*
Web, www.dla.mil/HQ/Acquisition/Strategicmaterials.aspx

Manages the national defense stockpile of strategic and critical materials. Purchases strategic materials, including beryllium and newly developed high-tech alloys. Disposes of excess materials, including tin, silver, industrial diamond stones, tungsten, and vegetable tannin.

Fossil Energy *(Energy Dept.), Petroleum Reserves, Forrestal Bldg., 1000 Independence Ave. S.W., FE-40, 20585; (202) 586-4410. Robert Corbin, Deputy Assistant Secretary, (202) 586-9460.*
Web, www.energy.gov/fe/services/petroleum-reserves

Manages programs that provide the United States with strategic and economic protection against disruptions in oil supplies, including the Strategic Petroleum Reserves, the Northeast Home Heating Oil Reserve, and the Naval Petroleum and the Northeast Gasoline Supply Reserve.

▶**CONGRESS**

For a listing of relevant congressional committees and subcommittees, please see pages 598–599 or the Appendix.

INTELLIGENCE AND COUNTERTERRORISM

General

► AGENCIES

Army Dept. *(Defense Dept.), Intelligence, 1000 Army Pentagon, #2E408, 20310-1000; (703) 695-3033. Fax, (703) 697-7605. Lt. Gen. Mary A. Legere (USA), Deputy Chief of Staff. Web, www.army.mil*

Military office that directs Army intelligence activities and coordinates activities with other intelligence agencies.

Bureau of Counterterrorism *(State Dept.), 2201 C St. N.W., #2509, 20520; (202) 647-9892. Fax, (202) 647-9256. Justin Siberell, Coordinator, Acting. Press, (202) 647-1845. Web, www.state.gov/j/ct*

Implements U.S. counterterrorism policy and coordinates activities with foreign governments; responds to terrorist acts; works to promote a stronger counterterrorism stance worldwide.

Bureau of Diplomatic Security *(State Dept.), 2201 C St. N.W., #6316, 20520; (571) 345-2502. Fax, (571) 345-2527. Gregory D. Starr, Assistant Secretary. General email, DSPublicAffairs@state.gov Web, www.state.gov/m/ds*

Conducts the Antiterrorism Assistance Program, which provides training to foreign governments fighting terrorism.

Bureau of Intelligence and Research *(State Dept.), 2201 C St. N.W., #6468, 20520-6531; (202) 647-9177. Fax, (202) 736-4688. Daniel B. Smith, Assistant Secretary. Web, www.state.gov/s/inr*

Coordinates foreign policy–related research, analysis, and intelligence programs for the State Dept. and other federal agencies.

Central Intelligence Agency (CIA), *CIA Headquarters, 930 Dolley Madison Blvd., McLean, VA 20505 (mailing address: CIA Headquarters, Washington, DC 20505); (703) 482-0623. Fax, (571) 204-3800. John O. Brennan, Director; David S. Cohen, Deputy Director. Web, www.cia.gov and Twitter, @CIA*

Gathers and evaluates foreign intelligence to assist the president and senior U.S. government policymakers in making foreign policy and national security decisions. Reports directly to the Office of National Intelligence, which coordinates intelligence functions of all government agencies involved with homeland security.

Defense Dept. (DoD), *Chief Information Officer, 6000 Defense Pentagon, #3E1030, 20301-6000; (703) 695-0348. Fax, (703) 614-8060. Terry Halvorsen, Chief Information Officer. Web, http://dodcio.defense.gov*

Civilian office with policy oversight for all command, control, and communications matters.

Defense Dept. (DoD), *Intelligence, 5000 Defense Pentagon, #3E834, 20301-5000; (703) 695-0971. Fax, (703) 693-5706. Marcel Lettre, Under Secretary. Web, www.defense.gov*

Responsible for ensuring the secretary of defense's access to intelligence information.

Defense Dept. (DoD), *Intelligence Oversight, 7200 Defense Pentagon, #2E1052, 20301-7200; (703) 695-9542. Fax, (703) 697-2974. Michael T. Mahar, Senior Intelligence Oversight Official. General email, osd.pentagon.odcmo.list.dod-sioo-iod@mail.mil Web, dodsioo.defense.gov*

Responsible for the independent oversight of all Defense Dept. intelligence, counterintelligence, and related activities, and for the formulation of intelligence oversight policy; reviews intelligence operations and investigates and reports on possible violations of federal law or regulations.

Defense Dept. (DoD), *Special Operations and Low-Intensity Conflict, 2500 Defense Pentagon, #3C852A, 20301-2500; (703) 695-9667. Fax, (703) 693-6335, Michael D. Lumpkin, Assistant Secretary. Web, www.defense.gov*

Serves as special staff assistant and civilian adviser to the secretary of defense on matters related to special operations and international terrorism.

Defense Information Systems Agency *(Defense Dept.), 6910 Cooper Ave., Fort Meade, MD 20755; (703) 607-6001. Fax, (301) 225-0535. Lt. Gen. Alan R. Lynn Jr. (USA), Director. Web, www.disa.mil*

The Defense Dept. agency responsible for information technology and the central manager for major portions of the defense information infrastructure. Units include the White House Communications Agency.

Defense Intelligence Agency *(Defense Dept.), 200 MacDill Blvd., 20340; (202) 231-5554. Fax, (202) 231-0851. Maj. Gen. Vincent R. Stewart (USMC), Director. General email, DIA-PAO@dia.mil Web, www.dia.mil*

Collects and evaluates foreign military–related intelligence information to satisfy the requirements of the secretary of defense, Joint Chiefs of Staff, selected components of the Defense Dept., Office of National Intelligence, and other authorized agencies.

Energy Dept. (DOE), *Intelligence and Counterintelligence, 1000 Independence Ave. S.W., #8F089, 20585; (202) 586-2610. Fax, (202) 287-5999. Steven K. Black, Director; Charles Durant, Deputy Director of Counterintelligence; Kevin Kremer, Principal Deputy Director of Intelligence. Web, www.energy.gov/office-intelligence-and-counterintelligence*

Counterterrorism Resources and Contacts

The following agencies, organizations, and hotlines offer information pertaining to terrorism and counterterrorism issues.

AGENCIES

Bureau of Industry and Security, Eric L. Hirschhorn, Under Secretary, (202) 482-1455; toll free (800) 424-2980, (Commerce Department)

Central Intelligence Agency, John O. Brennan, Director, (703) 482-1100, (Justice Department)

Defence Intelligence Agency, Lt. Gen. Vincent Stewart, Director, (202) 231-5554, (Defense Department)

FBI Counterterrorism Division, Michael B. Steinbach, Asst. Director, (202) 324-3691, (Justice Department)

Homeland Security Council, Lisa Monaco, Assistant to the President for Counterterrorism and Homeland Security, (202) 456-6317, (Executive Office of the President)

Homeland Security Dept., Jeh Charles Johnson, Secretary, (202) 282-8010

INTERPOL, United States Central Bureau, Geoffrey S. Shank, Director, (202) 616-9000, (Justice Department)

National Counterterrorism Center, Nicholas J. Rasmussen, Director

National Nuclear Security Administration, Jay Tilden, (202) 586-5555, (Energy Department)

National Security Agency/Central Security Service, Michael S. Rogers, Director, (301) 688-6524, (Defense Department)

National Security Council, Ambassador Susan Rice, National Security Advisor, (202) 456-9491, (Executive Office of the President)

National Security Division, Counterterrorism and Espionage, John P. Carlin, Asst. Attorney General, (202) 514-1057, (Justice Department)

Office of Counterterrorism and Emergency Coordination (FDA), Rosemary Roberts, Director, (301) 796-2210, (Health and Human Services Department)

Office of Foreign Assets Control, Adam J. Szubin, Director, (202) 622-2510, (Treasury Department)

Office of Nuclear Security and Incident Response, Brian Holian, Director, (301) 415-8003

Office of Terrorism and Financial Intelligence, David S. Cohen, Under Secretary, (202) 622-8260, (Treasury Department)

Office of the Coordinator for Counterterrorism, Michael A. Sheehan, Coordinator and Ambassador at Large, (202) 647-9892, (State Department)

Office of the Director of National Intelligence, James R. Clapper Jr., Director, (703) 733-8600

Transportation Security Administration, Peter Neffenger, Administrator, (866) 289-9673, (Homeland Security Department)

U.S. Immigration and Customs Enforcement, Sarah Saldaña, Director, (202) 732-4200

U.S. Secret Service, Joseph P. Clancy, Director, (202) 406-8000, (Homeland Security Department)

ORGANIZATIONS

Foundation for Defense of Democracies, Mark Dubowitz, Director, (202) 207-0190

International Center for Terrorism Studies, Yonah Alexander, Director, (703) 525-0770

RAND Homeland Security and Defense Center, Henry Willis, Director, (412) 683-2300 ext. 4560

HOTLINES

Federal Bureau of Investigation, (202) 324-3000

Office of Foreign Assets Control, (800) 540-6322

Transportation Security Administration, (866) 289-9673

U.S. Immigration and Customs Enforcement, (866) 347-2423

Identifies and deters intelligence threats directed at Energy Dept. facilities, personnel, information, and technology. Protects nuclear weapons secrets and other sensitive scientific projects.

Federal Bureau of Investigation (FBI) *(Justice Dept.), Critical Incident Response Group, Strategic Information and Operations Center, 935 Pennsylvania Ave. N.W., #5712, 20535; (202) 323-3300. Fax, (202) 323-2212. Martin Culbreth, Section Chief, (202) 323-2015. Press, (202) 324-3691. Toll-free, (877) 324-6324. Secure line, (202) 323-2214.*
General email, sioc@ic.fbi.gov
Web, www.fbi.gov/about-us/cirg/sioc

Serves as a twenty-four-hour crisis management and information processing center. Coordinates initial and crisis response investigations of violations of federal law relating to terrorism, sabotage, espionage, treason, sedition, and other matters affecting national security.

Federal Bureau of Investigation (FBI) *(Justice Dept.), National Joint Terrorism Task Force, 935 Pennsylvania Ave. N.W., 20535-0001; (571) 280-5688. Fax, (571) 280-6922. William Callahan, Unit Chief.*
Web, www.fbi.gov/washingtondc/about-us/our-partnerships/partners and www.fbi.gov/about-us/investigate/terrorism/national-joint-terrorism-task-force

Group of more than fifty agencies from the fields of intelligence, public safety, and federal, state, and local law enforcement that collects terrorism information and intelligence and funnels it to the more than five hundred JTTFs (teams of local, state, and federal agents based at FBI field offices), various terrorism units within the FBI, and partner agencies. Helps the FBI with terrorism investigations.

Federal Bureau of Investigation (FBI) *(Justice Dept.),* **National Security Branch, Counterterrorism Division,** *935 Pennsylvania Ave. N.W., #4204, 20535; (571) 280-5000. Fax, (202) 324-7050. Michael Steinbach, Assistant Director. Press, (202) 324-3691. National security hotline, (202) 324-3000.*
Web, www.fbi.gov/about-us/investigate/terrorism

Collects, analyzes, and shares information and intelligence with authorities to combat international terrorism operations within the United States and in support of extraterritorial investigations, domestic terrorism operations, and counterterrorism. Maintains the Joint Terrorism Task Force, which includes representatives from the Defense Dept., Energy Dept., Federal Emergency Management Agency, CIA, U.S. Customs and Border Protection, U.S. Secret Service, and Immigration and Customs Enforcement.

Federal Bureau of Investigation (FBI) *(Justice Dept.),* **National Security Branch, Terrorist Screening Center,** *935 Pennsylvania Ave. N.W., 20535; (571) 350-5678. Christopher M. Piehota, Director. Toll-free, (866) 872-5678. Press, (571) 350-6397.*
General email, tsc@tsc.gov
Press email, media@tsc.gov
Web, www.fbi.gov/about-us/nsb/tsc

Coordinates access to terrorist watch lists from multiple agencies. Provides operational support to federal screeners and state and local law enforcement officials.

Homeland Security Council *(Executive Office of the President),* *The White House, 20500; (202) 456-6317. Lisa O. Monaco, Assistant to the President for Homeland Security and Counterterrorism.*
Web, www.whitehouse.gov/administration/eop/nsc

Advises the president on combating global terrorism and homeland security policy.

Homeland Security Dept. (DHS), *3801 Nebraska Ave. N.W., 20528; (202) 282-8000. Fax, (202) 282-8236. Jeh Johnson, Secretary; Alejandro Mayorkas, Deputy Secretary. Press, (202) 282-8010. Comments, (202) 282-8495.*
Web, www.dhs.gov

Responsible for the development and coordination of a comprehensive national strategy to protect the United States against terrorist attacks and other threats and hazards. Coordinates the strategy of the executive branch with those of state and local governments and private entities to detect, prepare for, protect against, respond to, and recover from terrorist attacks and other emergencies in the United States. Administers the National Terrorism Advisory System to communicate information about terrorist threats to the public.

Homeland Security Dept. (DHS), *Intelligence and Analysis,* *3801 Nebraska Ave. N.W., Bldg. 19, 20528; (202) 447-4154. Francis Taylor, Under Secretary.*
Web, www.dhs.gov/office-intelligence-and-analysis

Uses intelligence from multiple sources to identify and assess current and future threats to the United States; provides guidance to the secretary on homeland security issues.

Marine Corps *(Defense Dept.),* **Intelligence,** *3000 Marine Corps Pentagon, #1A262B, 20350-3000; (703) 614-2522. Fax, (703) 614-5888. Brig. Gen. Michael S. Groen (USMC), Director.*
Web, www.hqmc.marines.mil/intelligence

Military office that directs Marine Corps intelligence policy and coordinates activities with other intelligence agencies.

National Aeronautics and Space Administration (NASA), **Protective Services,** *300 E St. S.W., #6T39, 20546; (202) 358-2010. Fax, (202) 358-3238. Joseph Mahaley, Assistant Administrator; Charles Lombard, Deputy Assistant Administrator.*
Web, www.hq.nasa.gov/hq/security.html

Serves as the focal point for policy formulation, oversight, coordination, and management of NASA's security, counterintelligence, counterterrorism, emergency preparedness and response, and continuity of operations programs.

National Geospatial-Intelligence Agency *(Defense Dept.),* *7500 Geoint Dr., Springfield, VA 22150-7500; 4600 Sangamore Rd., Bethesda, MD 20816-5003; (571) 557-5400. Fax, (571) 558-3169. Robert Cardillo, Director. Maps and imagery products, (571) 557-5400.*
General email, publicaffairs@nga.mil
Web, www.nga.mil, Twitter, @NGA_GEOINT and Facebook, www.facebook.com/NatlGEOINTAgency

Combat support agency that develops imagery and map-based intelligence in support of national defense objectives.

National Reconnaissance Office *(Defense Dept.),* *14675 Lee Rd., Chantilly, VA 20151-1715; (703) 808-1198. Fax, (703) 808-1171. Betty J. Sapp, Director.*
General email, publicaffairs@nro.mil
Web, www.nro.gov

Researches, develops, and operates intelligence satellites. Gathers intelligence for various purposes, including indications and warnings, monitoring of arms control agreements, military operations and exercises, and monitoring of natural disasters and other environmental issues.

National Security Agency (NSA) *(Defense Dept.),* *9800 Savage Rd., Fort Meade, MD 20755-6000; (301) 688-6524. Fax, (301) 688-6198. Gen. Michael S. Rogers (USN), Director; Richard H. Ledgett Jr., Deputy Director. FOIA Public Liaison Office, (301) 688-6527. Public Affairs and Media, (301) 688-6524.*
General email, nsapao@nsa.gov
Web, www.nsa.gov

Office of the Director of National Intelligence

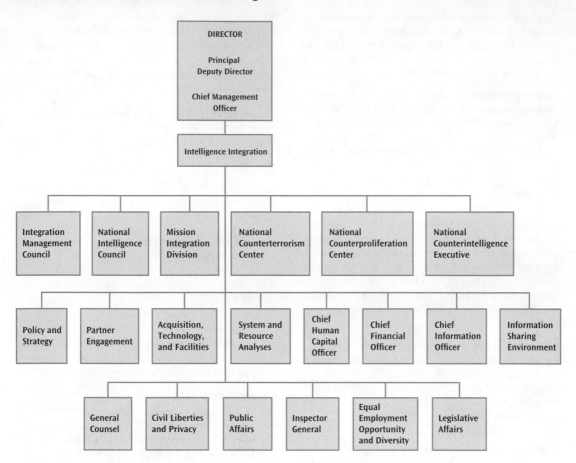

Provides technology, products, and services to secure information and information infrastructure critical to U.S. national security interests. Organizes and controls all foreign signals collection and processing activities of the United States in accordance with requirements established by the Defense Dept., the Office of the Director of National Intelligence, and by national policies with the advice of the National Foreign Intelligence Board.

National Security Division *(Justice Dept.), 950 Pennsylvania Ave. N.W., #7339, 20530; (202) 514-1057. Fax, (202) 514-9836. Hon. John P. Carlin, Assistant Attorney General. Press, (202) 514-2007. General email, nsd.public@usdoj.gov*

Web, www.justice.gov/nsd

Coordinates the Justice Dept.'s intelligence, counterterrorism, counterespionage, and other national security activities; offers support for victims of overseas terrorism.

National Security Division *(Justice Dept.), Counterintelligence and Export Control, 950 Pennsylvania Ave. N.W., 20530; (202) 514-1057. Fax, (202) 514-8714. John P. Carlin, Assistant Attorney General. General email, nsd.public@usdoj.gov*

Web, www.justice.gov/nsd

Supervises the investigation and prosecution of cases affecting national security, foreign relations, and the export of military and strategic commodities and technology. Has executive responsibility for authorizing the prosecution of cases under criminal statutes relating to espionage, sabotage, neutrality, and atomic energy. Provides legal advice to U.S. Attorney's offices and investigates agencies on federal statutes concerning national security. Coordinates criminal cases involving the application of the Classified Information Procedures Act. Administers and enforces the Foreign Agents Registration Act of 1938 and related disclosure statutes.

National Security Division *(Justice Dept.), Counterterrorism, 950 Pennsylvania Ave. N.W., 20530; (202) 514-1057. Fax, (202) 514-8714. Michael J. Mullaney, Chief. General email, nsd.public@usdoj.gov*

Web, www.justice.gov/nsd/counterterrorism-section

Responsible for the design, implementation, and support of law enforcement efforts, legislative initiatives, policies, and strategies related to combating international and domestic terrorism. Seeks to assist, through investigation and prosecution, in preventing and disrupting acts of terrorism anywhere in the world that impact significant U.S. interests and persons.

National Security Division *(Justice Dept.), Intelligence,* 950 Pennsylvania Ave. N.W., 20530; (202) 514-7941. Fax, (202) 514-8714. Stuart Evans, Deputy Assistant Attorney General.
General email, nsd.public@usdoj.gov

Web, www.justice.gov/nsd/office-intelligence

Seeks to ensure that Intelligence Community agencies have the legal authorities necessary to conduct intelligence operations, particularly operations involving the Foreign Intelligence Surveillance Act (FISA). Oversees various national security activities of Intelligence Community agencies; participates in FISA-related litigation.

National Security Division *(Justice Dept.), Law and Policy,* 950 Pennsylvania Ave. N.W., 20530; (202) 514-7941. Brad Wiegmann, Deputy Assistant Attorney General.
General email, nsd.justice@usdoj.gov

Web, www.justice.gov/nsd

Develops and implements Justice Dept. policies with regard to intelligence, counterterrorism, and other national security matters. Provides legal assistance and advice on matters of national security law.

Office of the Director of National Intelligence (DNI), Washington, DC 20511; (703) 733-8600. James R. Clapper Jr., Director of National Intelligence, (703) 275-2012; Stephanie L. O'Sullivan, Principal Deputy Director; Brian Hale, Public Affairs. Press and public affairs, (703) 275-3637.
Web, www.dni.gov

Leads a unified intelligence community and serves as the principal adviser to the president on intelligence matters. Orders the collection of new intelligence to ensure the sharing of information among agencies and to establish common standards for the intelligence community's personnel. Responsible for determining the annual budgets for all national intelligence agencies and for directing how these funds are spent.

Office of the Director of National Intelligence (DNI), *National Counterintelligence and Security Center,* LX/ICC-B, 20511; (301) 227-8529. Fax, (301) 227-8586. William Evanina, National Counterintelligence Executive.
Web, www.ncsc.gov

Conducts foreign intelligence threat assessments; promotes collaboration and information sharing throughout the U.S. counterintelligence community through conferences and other outreach and training activities; makes recommendations to decision makers concerning national counterintelligence strategy.

Office of the Director of National Intelligence (DNI), *National Counterterrorism Center,* Liberty Crossing, 20505; (571) 280-6160. Fax, (571) 280-5551. Nicholas Rasmussen, Director; Eugene Barlow, Public Affairs. Public Affairs, (571) 280-6153.
General email, nctcpao@nctc.gov

Web, www.nctc.gov

Serves as a hub for terrorism threat-related information collected domestically and abroad. Responsible for assessing, integrating, and disseminating terrorist threat information and all-source analysis; maintains U.S. government's central database on known and suspected terrorists; and identifies collection requirements related to the terrorist threat. Participates in strategic planning for counterterrorism activities.

Office of the Director of National Intelligence (DNI), *National Intelligence Council,* CIA Headquarters, Langley, VA 20505; (703) 482-6724. Fax, (703) 482-8652. Gregory Treverton, Chair.
Web, www.dni.gov/nic

Supports the director of national intelligence and serves as the intelligence community's center for mid- and long-term strategic thinking. Provides a focal point for policymakers' inquiries and needs. Establishes contacts with private sector and academic experts in the intelligence field.

President's Intelligence Advisory Board and Intelligence Oversight Board *(Executive Office of the President),* New Executive Office Bldg., #5020, 20502; (202) 456-2352. Fax, (202) 395-3403. Shirley Jackson, Co-Chair; Jami Miscik, Co-Chair.
Web, www.whitehouse.gov/administration/eop/piab

Members appointed by the president. Assesses the quality, quantity, and adequacy of foreign intelligence collection and of counterintelligence activities by all government agencies; advises the president on matters concerning intelligence and national security.

State Dept., *Center for Strategic Counterterrorism Communications (CSCC),* 2201 C St. N.W., #2429, 20520; (202) 736-7548. Rashad Hussain, Coordinator.
Web, www.state.gov.r/cscc

Works to coordinate, orient, and inform government-wide foreign communications activities targeted against terrorism and violent extremism.

Transportation Dept. (DOT), *Intelligence, Security, and Emergency Response,* 1200 New Jersey Ave. S.E., #56125, 20590; (202) 366-6525. Fax, (202) 366-7261. Michael Lowder, Director, (202) 366-6530.
Web, www.dot.gov/mission/administrations/intelligence-security-emergency-response

Advises the secretary on transportation intelligence and security policy. Acts as liaison with the intelligence community, federal agencies, corporations, and interest groups; administers counterterrorism strategic planning processes.

Transportation Security Administration (TSA) *(Homeland Security Dept.), Intelligence and Analysis,* TSA-10, 601 S. 12th St., 6th Floor, Arlington, VA 22202-4220; (703) 601-3100. Fax, (703) 601-3290. Thomas L. Bush, Assistant Administrator, Acting.
Web, www.tsa.gov

Oversees TSA's intelligence gathering and information sharing as they pertain to national security and the safety of the nation's transportation systems.

Treasury Dept., *Terrorism and Financial Intelligence,* *1500 Pennsylvania Ave. N.W., #4316, 20220; (202) 622-8260. Fax, (202) 622-1914. David S. Cohen, Under Secretary. Press, (202) 622-2960.*
Web, www.treasury.gov/about/organizational-structure/offices/Pages/Office-of-Terrorism-and-Financial-Intelligence.aspx

Manages the Treasury Dept.'s efforts against financial networks supporting global terrorism and other national security threats.

Treasury Dept., *Terrorism and Financial Intelligence, Terrorist Financing and Financial Crime, 1500 Pennsylvania Ave. N.W., 20220; (202) 622-1655. Fax, (202) 622-3915. Daniel L. Glaser, Assistant Secretary. Press, (202) 622-2960.*
Web, www.treasury.gov/about/organizational-structure/offices/Pages/Office-of-Terrorist-Financing-and-Financial-Crimes.aspx

Sets strategy and policy for combating the financing of terrorism both domestically and abroad.

U.S. Coast Guard (USCG) *(Homeland Security Dept.),* *Intelligence and Criminal Investigations, 2703 Martin Luther King Jr. Ave. S.E., 20593; (202) 372-2700. Fax, (202) 372-2956. Rear Adm. Christopher J. Tomney, Assistant Commandant.*
Web, www.uscg.mil

Manages all Coast Guard intelligence activities and programs. Conducts internal and external criminal investigations.

U.S. Customs and Border Protection *(Homeland Security Dept.), Intelligence and Investigative Liaison, 1300 Pennsylvania Ave. N.W., #7.3D, 20229; (202) 344-1150. David Glawe, Assistant Commissioner.*
Web, www.cbp.gov/about/leadership/assistant-commissioners-office/intelligence-investigative-liaison

Coordinates the effort to prevent the introduction of weapons of mass destruction into the United States and to prevent international terrorists from obtaining weapons of mass destruction materials, technologies, arms, funds, and other support.

►CONGRESS

For a listing of relevant congressional committees and subcommittees, please see pages 598–599 or the Appendix.

►NONGOVERNMENTAL

Assn. of Former Intelligence Officers (AFIO), *7700 Leesburg Pike, #324, Falls Church, VA 22043; (703) 790-0320. Fax, (703) 991-1278. Elizabeth A. Bancroft, Executive Director.*
General email, afio@afio.com
Web, www.afio.com

Membership: current and former military and civilian intelligence officers. Encourages public support for intelligence agencies; supports increased intelligence education in colleges and universities; and provides guidance to students seeking careers in intelligence.

Center for National Security Studies, *1730 Pennsylvania Ave. N.W., 7th Floor, 20006; (202) 721-5650. Fax, (202) 530-0128. Kate A. Martin, Director.*
General email, cnss@cnss.org
Web, www.cnss.org

Monitors and conducts research on civil liberties and intelligence and national security, including activities of the Central Intelligence Agency and the Federal Bureau of Investigation.

Foundation for Defense of Democracies (FDD), *P.O. Box 33249, 20033-0249; (202) 207-0190. Fax, (202) 207-0191. Clifford D. May, President; Mark Dubowitz, Executive Director.*
General email, info@defenddemocracy.org
Web, www.defenddemocracy.org and Twitter, @followFDD

Conducts research and education related to the war on terrorism and the promotion of democracy.

Fourth Freedom Forum, *Washington Office, 1101 14th St. N.W., #900, 20005; (202) 464-6009. Fax, (202) 238-9604. Alistair Millar, Executive Director.*
General email, amillar@fourthfreedom.org
Web, www.fourthfreedom.org

Conducts research and training to advance global cooperation to address transnational threats, including terrorism, nuclear proliferation, and drug trafficking. (Headquarters in Goshen, Ind.)

Potomac Institute for Policy Studies, *International Center for Terrorism Studies (ICTS), 901 N. Stuart St., #1200, Arlington, VA 22203-1821; (703) 525-0770. Fax, (703) 525-0299. Michael S. Swetnam, Chief Executive Officer; Yonah Alexander, Director.*
General email, webmaster@potomacinstitute.org
Web, www.potomacinstitute.org

Public policy research institute that conducts studies on key science and technology issues. The ICTS focuses on all forms of terrorism and the potential for terrorism, including biological, chemical, or nuclear violence, as well as information warfare and cyberterrorism.

Internal (Agency) Security

►AGENCIES

Air Force Dept. *(Defense Dept.), Special Investigations, 27130 Telegraph Rd., Quantico, VA 22134; (571) 305-8028. Brig. Gen. Keith M. Givens, Commander.*
Web, www.osi.af.mil

Develops and implements policy on investigations of foreign intelligence, terrorism, and other crimes as they relate to Air Force security.

Army Dept. *(Defense Dept.), Counterintelligence, Foreign Disclosure, and Security,* 1000 Army Pentagon, #2D350, 20310-1000; (703) 695-1007. Fax, (703) 695-3149. *Gerry B. Turnbow, Director.*
Web, www.army.mil

Responsible for foreign disclosure, policy formation, planning, programming, oversight, and representation for counterintelligence, human intelligence, and security countermeasures of the Army.

Bureau of Diplomatic Security *(State Dept.), Countermeasures,* 1801 N. Lynn St., #23L04, Rosslyn, VA 22209; (571) 345-3836. *Wayne B. Ashbery, Deputy Assistant Secretary.*
Web, www.state.gov

Oversees Physical Security, Security Technology, and Diplomatic Courier programs for the State Dept.

Bureau of Diplomatic Security *(State Dept.), Diplomatic Security Service,* 1801 N. Lynn St., 23rd Floor, Rosslyn, VA 22209; (571) 345-2502. Fax, (202) 647-0122. *Bill A. Miller, Director. Diplomatic Service Command Center, (571) 345-3146.*
Web, www.state.gov

Oversees the safety and security of all U.S. government employees at U.S. embassies and consulates abroad; warns government employees of any counterintelligence dangers they might encounter.

Bureau of Diplomatic Security *(State Dept.), Security Infrastructure,* 1801 N. Lynn St., 23rd Floor, Rosslyn, VA 22209; (571) 345-3791. Fax, (571) 345-3792. *Donald R. Reid, Senior Coordinator.*
Web, www.state.gov/m/ds

Manages matters relating to security infrastructure in the functional areas of information security, computer security, and personnel security and suitability.

Defense Dept. (DoD), *Counterintelligence and Security,* 5000 Defense Pentagon, #3C1088, 20301-5000; (703) 697-5216. Fax, (703) 695-8217. *Toby Sullivan, Director.*
Web, www.defense.gov

Oversees counterintelligence policy and oversight to protect against espionage and other foreign intelligence activities, sabotage, international terrorist activities, and assassination efforts of foreign powers, organizations, or persons directed against the Defense Dept.

Defense Security Service *(Defense Dept.),* 27130 Telegraph Rd., Quantico, VA 22134; (571) 305-6083. Fax, (571) 305-6869. *James J. Kern, Director, Acting. Press, (571) 305-6562.*
Web, www.dss.mil

Administers programs to protect classified government information and resources, including the National Industrial Security Program (NISP). Serves the Defense Dept. and other executive departments and agencies. Operates the Center for Development and Security Excellence to educate, train, and enhance awareness of security matters.

Energy Dept. (DOE), *Intelligence and Counterintelligence,* 1000 Independence Ave. S.W., #8F089, 20585; (202) 586-2610. Fax, (202) 287-5999. *Steven K. Black, Director; Charles Durant, Deputy Director of Counterintelligence; Kevin Kremer, Principal Deputy Director of Intelligence.*
Web, www.energy.gov/office-intelligence-and-counterintelligence

Identifies and deters intelligence threats directed at Energy Dept. facilities, personnel, information, and technology. Protects nuclear weapons secrets and other sensitive scientific projects.

INTERPOL Washington *(Justice Dept.),* INTERPOL Washington, U.S. Dept. of Justice, 20530-0001; (202) 616-9000. Fax, (202) 616-8400. *Geoffrey S. Shank, Director.*
Web, www.justice.gov/interpol-washington

U.S. representative to INTERPOL; interacts in international investigations of terrorism on behalf of U.S. police. Serves as liaison between foreign and U.S. law enforcement agencies. Headquarters office sponsors forums enabling foreign governments to discuss counterterrorism policy. (Headquarters in Lyons, France.)

National Archives and Records Administration (NARA), *Information Security Oversight (ISOO),* 700 Pennsylvania Ave. N.W., #100, 20408-0001; (202) 357-5250. Fax, (202) 357-5907. *William A. Cira, Director, Acting, (202) 357-5323.*
General email, isoo@nara.gov
Web, www.archives.gov/isoo

Receiving guidance from the National Security Council, administers governmentwide security classification program under which information is classified, declassified, and safeguarded for national security purposes. Develops policies and procedures for sensitive unclassified information.

National Security Agency (NSA) *(Defense Dept.),* 9800 Savage Rd., Fort Meade, MD 20755-6000; (301) 688-6524. Fax, (301) 688-6198. *Gen. Michael S. Rogers (USN), Director; Richard H. Ledgett Jr., Deputy Director. FOIA Public Liaison Office, (301) 688-6527. Public Affairs and Media, (301) 688-6524.*
General email, nsapao@nsa.gov
Web, www.nsa.gov

Maintains and operates the Defense Dept.'s Computer Security Center; ensures communications and computer security within the government.

Navy Dept. *(Defense Dept.), Naval Criminal Investigative Service,* 27130 Telegraph Rd., Quantico, VA 22134; (571) 305-9000. Fax, (571) 305-9115. *Andrew Traver, Director. Hotline, (877) 579-3648. fax, (571) 305-9115.*
Web, www.navy.mil/local/ncis

Handles felony criminal investigations, counterintelligence, counterterrorism, and security for the Navy Dept., working with federal, state, local, and foreign agencies to investigate crimes; processes security clearances for the Navy Dept.

MILITARY INSTALLATIONS

General

▶AGENCIES

Army Dept. *(Defense Dept.), Installations, Energy, and Environment,* 110 Army Pentagon, #3E464, 20310-0110; (703) 692-9800. Fax, (703) 692-9808. Katherine Hammack, Assistant Secretary.
General email, asaie.webmaster@hqda.army.mil
Web, www.asaie.army.mil/asaiee

Civilian office that establishes policy, provides strategic direction and supervises all matters pertaining to infrastructure, Army installations and contingency bases, energy, and environmental programs to enable global Army operations.

Defense Dept. (DoD), *Energy, Installations, and Environment,* 3400 Defense Pentagon, #5C646, 20301-3400; (703) 695-2880. Fax, (703) 693-2659. John Conger, Assistant Secretary, Acting.
Web, www.acq.osd.mil/eie

Oversees and offers policy guidance for all Defense Dept. energy, installations, and environmental programs.

Defense Dept. (DoD), *International Security Affairs,* 2000 Defense Pentagon, #3C889, 20301-2000; (703) 697-2788. Fax, (703) 697-3279. Elissa B. Slotkin, Assistant Secretary, Acting; Kenneth B. Handelman, Principal Deputy Assistant Secretary, Acting.
Web, http://policy.defense.gov/OUSDPOffices/ASDforInternationalSecurityAffairs.aspx

Advises the secretary of defense and recommends policies on regional security issues in the Middle East, Africa, Russia/Eurasia, and Europe/NATO.

▶CONGRESS

For a listing of relevant congressional committees and subcommittees, please see pages 598–599 or the Appendix.

Base Closings, Economic Impact

▶AGENCIES

Air Force Dept. *(Defense Dept.), Base Realignment and Closure,* 1665 Air Force Pentagon, #4B941, 20330-1665; (703) 697-6492. Col. Joe Morganti, Director.
Web, www.safie.hq.af.mil/library

Military office that provides management oversight for implementing base closings and base realignment under the Base Realignment Act (BRAC).

Air Force Dept. *(Defense Dept.), Installations,* 1665 Air Force Pentagon, #4B941, SAF/IEI, 20330-1665; (703) 695-3592. Fax, (703) 693-7568. Jennifer Miller, Deputy Assistant Secretary.

General email, safiei.workflow@pentagon.af.mil
Web, www.safie.hq.af.mil

Civilian office that plans and reviews the building, repairing, renovating, and closing of Air Force bases.

Army Dept. *(Defense Dept.), Employment Policy,* 6010 6th St., #200, Bldg. 1465, Ft. Belvoir, VA 22060-5595; (703) 806-3846. Fax, (703) 806-2345. Anna Miller, Chief, (703) 806-3202.
Web, www.army.mil

Military office responsible for employment policies to assist civilian personnel in cases of Defense Dept. program changes, including base closings.

Defense Dept. (DoD), *Economic Adjustment,* 2231 Crystal Dr., #520, Arlington, VA 22202-4704; (703) 697-2130. Fax, (703) 607-0170. Patrick J. O'Brien, Director.
Web, www.oea.gov

Civilian office that helps community officials develop strategies and coordinate plans to alleviate the economic effect of major defense program changes, including base closings (BRAC) and contract cutbacks. Assists communities where defense activities are being expanded. Serves as the staff for the Economic Adjustment Committee, an interagency group that coordinates federal technical and financial transition assistance to localities.

Defense Dept. (DoD), *Staffing and Civilian Transition Programs,* 4800 Mark Center Dr., #05F16, SCTP Division, Alexandria, VA 22350-1100; (571) 372-1528. Fax, (571) 372-1704. William Mann, Chief of Staff.
Web, www.cpms.osd.mil

Manages workforce restructuring programs for Defense Dept. civilians, including downsizing, placement, voluntary early retirement, and transition assistance programs.

Marine Corps *(Defense Dept.), Installation Command, Installation and Logistics Facilities Directorate,* 3000 Marine Corps Pentagon, #2D153A, 20350-3000; (703) 695-8202. Fax, (703) 695-8550. Capt. Scott D. Loeschke (USN), Director.
Web, www.mcicom.marines.mil

Military office that reviews studies on base closings under the Base Realignment Act (BRAC).

Commissaries, PXs, and Service Clubs

▶AGENCIES

Defense Commissary Agency *(Defense Dept.),* 1300 E Ave., Fort Lee, VA 23801-1800; (703) 571-7185. Fax, (703) 571-9297. Thomas C. Owens, Director, Washington Office. Alternate phone, (804) 734-8000.
Web, www.commissaries.com

Serves as a representative for the Defense Commissary Agency in the Pentagon and the Washington, D.C. area. Monitors legislation and regulations.
(Headquarters in Fort Lee, Va.)

Defense Dept. (DoD), *Army and Air Force Exchange, Washington Office,* 2530 Crystal Dr., #4158, Arlington, VA 22202; (703) 602-8975. Thomas C. Shull, Director. Web, www.aafes.com/about-exchange *and* www.shopmyexchange.com

Delivers goods and services to the military community at competitively low prices. Returns earnings to Army and Air Force to support morale, welfare, and recreation programs. (Headquarters in Dallas, Tex.)

Navy Dept. *(Defense Dept.),* **Manpower and Reserve Affairs,** 1000 Navy Pentagon, #4E590, 20350-1000; (703) 695-4333. Fax, (703) 614-4103. Hon. Franklin R. Parker III, Assistant Secretary. Web, www.navy.mil

Civilian office that develops policies for Navy and Marine Corps commissaries, exchanges, and service clubs and reviews their operations.

Navy Dept. *(Defense Dept.),* **Navy Exchange Service Command,** 701 S. Courthouse Rd., Arlington, VA 22204; (757) 631-4170. Andy Howell, Washington Liason. Navy Exchange, (757) 631-4170. Web, www.mynavyexchange.com

Civilian office that serves as a liaison among the Navy Exchange Service Command, the Navy Supply Systems Command, Congress, and the Defense Dept. (Headquarters in Virginia Beach, Va.)

►CONGRESS

For a listing of relevant congressional committees and subcommittees, please see pages 598 599 or the Appendix.

►NONGOVERNMENTAL

American Logistics Assn., 1101 Vermont Ave. N.W., #1002, 20005; (202) 466-2520. Fax, (202) 823-9181. Patrick B. Nixon, President. General email, info@ala-national.org

Web, www.ala-national.org

Membership: suppliers of military commissaries and exchanges. Acts as liaison between the Defense Dept. and service contractors; monitors legislation and testifies on issues of interest to members.

United Service Organizations (USO), 2111 Wilson Blvd., #1200, Arlington, VA 22201 (mailing address: P.O. Box 96860, Washington, DC 20077); (703) 908-6400. Fax, (703) 908-6402. J.D. Crouch II, President. Toll-free, (888) 484-3876. Web, www.uso.org *and Twitter,* @the_USO

Voluntary civilian organization chartered by Congress. Provides military personnel and their families in the United States and overseas with social, educational, and recreational programs.

Construction, Housing, and Real Estate

►AGENCIES

Air Force Dept. *(Defense Dept.),* **Housing Operations and Management,** 1260 Air Force Pentagon, #4C1057, 20330-1260; (703) 693-4193. Sheila Schwartz, Branch Chief. Web, www.housing.af.mil

Military office that manages the operation of Air Force housing on military installations in the United States and overseas.

Air Force Dept. *(Defense Dept.),* **Installations,** 1665 Air Force Pentagon, #4B941, SAF/IEI, 20330-1665; (703) 695-3592. Fax, (703) 693-7568. Jennifer Miller, Deputy Assistant Secretary. General email, safiei.workflow@pentagon.af.mil

Web, www.safie.hq.af.mil

Civilian office that plans and reviews construction policies and programs of Air Force military facilities (including the Military Construction Program), basing of major weapons systems and units, housing programs, and real estate buying, selling, and leasing in the United States.

Air Force Dept. *(Defense Dept.),* **Office of Civil Engineers,** 1260 Air Force Pentagon, 20330; (703) 693-4301. Fax, (703) 693-4893. Maj. Gen. Tim Green, Director. Web, www.afcec.af.mil

Military office that plans and directs construction of Air Force facilities in the United States and overseas. Oversees the Civil Engineer Center in San Antonio, Texas.

Army Corps of Engineers *(Defense Dept.),* 441 G St. N.W., #3K05, 20314-1000; (202) 761-0001. Fax, (202) 761-4463. Lt. Gen. Thomas P. Bostick (USA), Chief of Engineers. Press, (202) 761-0011. General email, hq-publicaffairs@usace.army.mil

Web, www.usace.army.mil *and Twitter,* @USACEHQ

Military office that establishes policy and designs, directs, and manages civil works and military construction projects of the Army Corps of Engineers; directs the Army's real estate leasing and buying for military installations and civil works projects.

Defense Dept. (DoD), *Facilities Investment and Management,* 3400 Defense Pentagon, #5C646, 20301-3400; (703) 697-6195. Fax, (703) 693-2659. Michael McAndrew, Director. Web, www.acq.osd.mil/eie/FIM/FIM_index.html

Responsible for military construction and facility-related legislative proposals and policies to manage worldwide defense installations and to acquire, construct, maintain, modernize, and dispose of defense facilities. Prepares the department's annual military construction budget; manages military construction, real property maintenance, and base operations; oversees host nation programs for facilities; and develops procedures for measuring the effect of defense facilities on military readiness.

Marine Corps *(Defense Dept.)*, **Installation and Environment,** *3250 Catlin Ave., #235, Quantico, VA 22134-5001; (703) 784-2557. Fax, (703) 784-2332. Kirk Nelson, Director.*
Web, www.quantico.marines.mil/OfficesStaff/GFInstallationandEnvironment.aspx

Control point for the Marine Corps divisions of public works, family housing, and natural resources and environmental affairs.

Marine Corps *(Defense Dept.)*, **Installation Command, Installation and Logistics Facilities Directorate,** *3000 Marine Corps Pentagon, #2D153A, 20350-3000; (703) 695-8202. Fax, (703) 695-8550. Capt. Scott D. Loeschke (USN), Director.*
Web, www.mcicom.marines.mil

Military office responsible for military construction and the acquisition, management, and disposal of Marine Corps real property.

Navy Dept. *(Defense Dept.)*, **Energy, Installations, and Environment,** *1000 Navy Pentagon, #4E731, 20350-1000; (703) 693-4530. Fax, (703) 693-1165. Vice Adm. Dennis V. McGinn (USN. Ret.), Principal Deputy Assistant Secretary.*
Web, www.secnav.navy.mil/eie/pages

Civilian office that monitors and reviews construction of Navy military facilities and housing and the buying and leasing of real estate in the United States and overseas. Interests include environmental planning, protection and restoration; conservation of natural resources.

Navy Dept. *(Defense Dept.)*, **Naval Facilities Engineering Command,** *1322 Patterson Ave. S.E., #100, Washington Navy Yard, DC 20374-5065; (202) 685-9499. Fax, (202) 685-1463. Rear Adm. Bret Mullenberg, Commander. Press and public affairs, (202) 685-9232.*
Web, www.navy.mil/local/navfachq

Military command that plans, designs, and constructs facilities for Navy and other Defense Dept. activities around the world and manages Navy public works, utilities, environmental programs, and real estate.

Navy Dept. *(Defense Dept.)*, **Real Estate,** *1000 Navy Pentagon, #4A674, Washington Navy Yard, DC 20350; (703) 614-5848. Fax, (703) 693-4528. Jim Omans, Director.*
Web, www.navfac.navy.mil/products_and_services/real_estate.html

Military office that directs the Navy's real estate leasing, buying, and disposition for military installations.

U.S. Coast Guard (USCG) *(Homeland Security Dept.)*, **Housing Programs,** *CG-1333, 2703 Martin Luther King Jr. Ave. S.E., MS 7097, 20593-7097; (202) 475-5407. Fax, (202) 475-5927. Melissa Fredrickson, Chief.*
Web, http://uscg.mil/hr/cg133/housing

Provides housing and management for uniformed Coast Guard personnel.

▶CONGRESS

For a listing of relevant congressional committees and sub-committees, please see pages 598–599 or the Appendix.

PROCUREMENT, ACQUISITION, AND LOGISTICS

General

▶AGENCIES

Air Force Dept. *(Defense Dept.)*, **Acquisition,** *1060 Air Force Pentagon, #4E962, 20330-1060; (703) 697-6361. Fax, (703) 693-6400. Lt. Gen. William LaPlante, Air Force Service Acquisition Executive.*
Web, ww3.safaq.hq.af.mil

Air Force office that directs and reviews Air Force procurement policies and programs.

Air Force Dept. *(Defense Dept.)*, **Contracting,** *1060 Air Force Pentagon, #700, 20330-1060; (571) 256-2397. Maj. Gen Casey D. Blake, Deputy Assistant Secretary.*
Web, ww3.safaq.hq.af.mil/contracting

Develops, implements, and enforces contracting policies on Air Force acquisitions worldwide, including research and development services, weapons systems, logistics services, and operational contracts.

Air Force Dept. *(Defense Dept.)*, **Global Power Programs,** *1060 Air Force Pentagon, #4A122, 20330; (571) 256-0191. Fax, (571) 256-0280. Maj. Gen. Jon M. Norman, Director.*
Web, www.af.mil/publicwebsites/sitecmd

Military office that directs Air Force acquisition and development programs within the tactical arena.

Army Dept. *(Defense Dept.)*, **Procurement,** *103 Army Pentagon, #2D528, 20310-0103; (703) 695-2488. Harry Hallock, Deputy Assistant Secretary.*
Web, www.army.mil

Directs and reviews Army procurement policies.

Defense Acquisition University *(Defense Dept.)*, *9820 Belvoir Rd., Fort Belvoir, VA 22060-5565; (703) 805-3360. Fax, (703) 805-2639. James P. Woolsey, President. Toll-free, (800) 845-7606.*
Web, www.dau.mil

Academic institution that offers courses to military and civilian personnel who specialize in acquisition and procurement. Conducts research to support and improve management of defense systems acquisition programs.

Defense Contract Audit Agency *(Defense Dept.)*, *8725 John Jay Kingman Rd., #2135, Fort Belvoir, VA 22060-6219; (703) 767-3200. Fax, (703) 767-3267. Anita Dales, Director. Media, (703) 693-6858.*
Web, www.dcaa.mil

Performs all contract audits for the Defense Dept. Provides Defense Dept. personnel responsible for procurement and contract administration with accounting and financial advisory services regarding the negotiation, administration, and settlement of contracts and subcontracts.

Defense Contract Management Agency *(Defense Dept.),* *14501 George Carter Way, 2nd Floor, Chantilly, VA 20151; (571) 521-1600. Lt. Gen. Wendy M. Masiello (USAF), Director.*
Web, www.dcma.mil

Ensures the integrity of the contracting process, and provides a broad range of contract-procurement management services, including cost and pricing, quality assurance, contract administration and termination, and small business support.

Defense Dept. (DoD), *Acquisition, Technology, and Logistics, 3010 Defense Pentagon, #3E1010, 20301-3010; (703) 697-7021. Fax, (703) 697-5471. Frank Kendall III, Under Secretary; Alan Estevez, Deputy Under Secretary.*
Web, www.acq.osd.mil

Formulates and directs policy relating to the department's purchasing system, research and development, logistics, advanced technology, international programs, environmental security, industrial base, and nuclear, biological, and chemical programs. Oversees all defense procurement and acquisition programs.

Defense Dept. (DoD), *Armed Services Board of Contract Appeals, 5109 Leesburg Pike, Skyline 6, 7th Floor, Falls Church, VA 22041-3208; (703) 681-8500. Fax, (703) 681-8535. Mark Stempler, Chair, Acting; Catherine A. Stanton, General Counsel.*
General email, asbca.recorder@mail.mil
Web, www.asbca.mil

Adjudicates disputes arising under Defense Dept. contracts.

Defense Dept. (DoD), *Defense Acquisition Regulations System (DARS) Directorate and DARS Council, 3060 Defense Pentagon, #3B941, 20301-3060; (571) 372-6176. Fax, (571) 372-6101. Linda Neilson, Deputy Director.*
Web, www.acq.osd.mil/dpap/dars

Develops procurement regulations and manages changes to procurement regulations for the Defense Dept.

Defense Dept. (DoD), *Defense Procurement and Acquisition Policy, 3060 Defense Pentagon, #3C152, 20301-3060; (571) 256-7003. Fax, (571) 256-7004. Claire M. Grady, Director.*
Web, www.acq.osd.mil/dpap

Responsible for all acquisition and procurement policy matters for the Defense Dept. Serves as principal adviser to the under secretary of defense for acquisition, technology, and logistics on strategies relating to all major weapon systems programs, major automated information systems programs, and services acquisitions.

Defense Dept. (DoD), *Logistics and Materiel Readiness, 3500 Defense Pentagon, #1E518, 20301-3500;*

(703) 697-1369. Fax, (703) 693-0555. Hon. David J. Berteau, Assistant Secretary. General email, osd.pentagon.ousd-atl.mxb@mail.mil Web, www.acq.osd.mil/log

Formulates and implements department policies and programs for the conduct of logistics, maintenance, materiel readiness, strategic mobility, and sustainable support.

Defense Dept. (DoD), *Operational Test and Evaluation, 1700 Defense Pentagon, #3E1088, 20301-1700; (703) 697-3655. Fax, (703) 693-5248. J. Michael (Mike) Gilmore, Director. Press, (703) 697-5331.*
Web, www.dote.osd.mil

Ensures that major acquisitions, including weapons systems, are operationally effective and suitable prior to full-scale investment. Provides the secretary of defense and Congress with independent assessment of these programs.

Defense Logistics Agency *(Defense Dept.), 8725 John Jay Kingman Rd., #2533, Fort Belvoir, VA 22060-6221; (703) 767-5200. Fax, (703) 767-5207. Lt. Gen. Andrew E. Busch, Director. Press, (703) 767-6200.*
Web, www.dla.mil

Administers defense contracts; acquires, stores, and distributes food, clothing, medical, and other supplies used by the military services and other federal agencies; administers programs related to logistical support for the military services; and assists military services with developing, acquiring, and using technical information and defense materiel and disposing of materiel no longer needed.

Marine Corps *(Defense Dept.), Contracts, 701 S. Courthouse Rd., #2000, Arlington, VA 22204; (703) 604-3584. Fax, (703) 604-6675. Linda S. Becker, Deputy Director.*
Web, www.iandl.marines.mil/divisions/contracts(LB).aspx

Military office that directs Marine Corps procurement programs.

Navy Dept. *(Defense Dept.), Acquisition and Procurement, 1000 Navy Pentagon, #BF992A, 20350-1000; (703) 614-9445. Fax, (703) 614-9394. Elliott Branch, Deputy Assistant Secretary; Capt. John Couture, Executive Director, Acting.*
Web, www.sec.navy.mil/rda/pages/DASN_AP

Directs and reviews Navy acquisition and procurement policy.

Navy Dept. *(Defense Dept.), Military Sealift Command, Bldg. 210, Washington Navy Yard, DC 20398-5540; (202) 685-5007. Fax, (202) 685-5020. Rear Adm. Thomas K. Shannon, Commander. Press, (202) 685-5055.*
Web, www.msc.navy.mil

Provides sea transportation of equipment, fuel, supplies, and ammunition to sustain U.S. forces.

U.S. Coast Guard (USCG) *(Homeland Security Dept.), Acquisition, 2703 Martin Luther King Jr. Ave. S.E., MS*

7816, 20593; (202) 475-3000. Fax, (202) 372-8432. Rear Adm. Joseph M. Vojvodich, Assistant Commandant.
General email, acquisitionweb@uscg.mil

Web, www.uscg.mil/acquisition

Administers all procurement made through the Acquisition Contract Support Division.

U.S. Coast Guard (USCG) *(Homeland Security Dept.),*
Engineering and Logistics, *CG-44, 2703 Martin Luther King Jr. Ave. S.E., MS 7714, 20593; (202) 475-5554. Fax, (202) 475-8406. Capt. Brenda Kerr, Chief.*
Web, www.uscg.mil/hq/cg4/default.asp

Sets policy and procedures for the procurement, distribution, maintenance, and replacement of materiel and personnel for the Coast Guard.

► CONGRESS

For a listing of relevant congressional committees and subcommittees, please see pages 598–599 or the Appendix.

Government Accountability Office (GAO), *Defense Capabilities and Management, 441 G St. N.W., #4440B, 20548; (202) 512-4300. Cathleen Berrick, Managing Director.*
Web, www.gao.gov/careers/dcm.html

Independent nonpartisan agency in the legislative branch. Audits, analyzes, and evaluates Defense Dept. acquisition programs; makes unclassified reports available to the public.

► NONGOVERNMENTAL

CompTIA, *Public Advocacy, 515 2nd St. N. E., 20002; (202) 682-9110. Fax, (202) 682-9111.*
Todd Thibodeaux, President; Elizabeth (Liz) Hyman, Executive Vice President, Public Advocacy.
Press, (202) 682-4458.
General email, techvoice@comptia.org

Web, www.comptia.org

Membership: companies providing information technology and electronics products and services to government organizations at the federal, state, and local levels. Provides information on governmental affairs, business intelligence, industry trends, and forecasts. Monitors legislation and regulation on federal procurement of technology products and services. (Headquarters in Downers Grove, Ill.)

National Defense Transportation Assn. (NDTA),
50 S. Pickett St., #220, Alexandria, VA 22304; (703) 751-5011. Fax, (703) 823-8761. Rear Adm. Mark H. Buzby (USN, Ret.), President.
Web, www.ndtahq.com

Membership: transportation users, manufacturers, and mode carriers; information technology firms; and related military, government, and civil interests worldwide. Promotes a strong U.S. transportation capability through coordination of private industry, government, and the military.

16
Science and Technology

GENERAL POLICY AND ANALYSIS

Basic Resources

▶AGENCIES

National Institute of Standards and Technology (NIST) *(Commerce Dept.), Special Programs Office,* 100 Bureau Dr., MS 1000, Gaithersburg, MD 20899-1000; (301) 975-4447. Fax, (301) 975-8972. Richard R. Cavanagh, Director. General information, (301) 975-2756.
Web, www.nist.gov/director/spo

Fosters collaboration among government, military, academia, professional, and private organizations to respond to critical national needs through science-based standards and technology innovation, including areas of forensic science and information technology.

National Institutes of Health (NIH) *(Health and Human Services Dept.), Science Policy,* 6705 Rockledge Dr., MSC 7985, Bethesda, MD 20892-7985; (301) 496-9838. Fax, (301) 496-9839. Carrie D. Wolinetz, Associate Director. General email, sciencepolicy@od.nih.gov
Web, http://osp.od.nih.gov

Advises the NIH director on science policy issues affecting the medical research community. Participates in the development of new policy and program initiatives. Monitors and coordinates agency planning and evaluation activities. Plans and implements a comprehensive science education program. Develops and implements NIH policies and procedures for the safe conduct of recombinant DNA and other biotechnology activities.

National Science Foundation (NSF), 4201 Wilson Blvd., Arlington, VA 22230; (703) 292-5111. Fax, (703) 292-9232. France A. Córdova, Director. Library, (703) 292-7830. Publications, (703) 292-7827. Government Affairs, (703) 292-8070. TTY, (703) 292-5090. Toll-free TTY, (800) 281-8749.
General email, info@nsf.gov
Web, www.nsf.gov

Sponsors scientific and engineering research; develops and helps implement science and engineering education programs; fosters dissemination of scientific information; promotes international cooperation within the scientific community; and assists with national science policy planning.

National Science Foundation (NSF), *Human Resource Development Division,* 4201 Wilson Blvd., #815N, Arlington, VA 22230; (703) 292-8640. Fax, (703) 292-9018. Sylvia James, Division Director.
Web, www.nsf.gov/div/index.jsp?div=hrd

Supports and encourages participation in scientific and engineering (STEM) education and research by women, minorities, and people with disabilities. Awards grants and scholarships.

National Science Foundation (NSF), *National Center for Science and Engineering Statistics,* 4201 Wilson Blvd.,

#965S, Arlington, VA 22230; (703) 292-8780. Fax, (703) 292-9092. John R. Gawalt, Director.
Web, www.nsf.gov/statistics

Compiles, analyzes, and disseminates quantitative information about domestic and international resources devoted to science, engineering, and technology. Provides information to other federal agencies for policy formulation.

National Science Foundation (NSF), *National Science Board,* 4201 Wilson Blvd., #1225N, Arlington, VA 22230; (703) 292-7000. Fax, (703) 292-9008. Michael L. Van Woert, Director; Nadine Lymn, Communications, (703) 292-2490. TTY, (800) 281-8749.
General email, NationalScienceBrd@nsf.gov
Web, www.nsf.gov/nsb

Formulates policy for the National Science Foundation; advises the president on national science policy.

Office of Management and Budget (OMB) *(Executive Office of the President), Energy, Science, and Water,* 725 17th St. N.W., #8002, 20503; (202) 395-3404. Fax, (202) 395-3049. John Pasquantino, Deputy Associate Director. Press, (202) 395-7254.
Web, www.whitehouse.gov/omb

Assists and advises the OMB director in budget preparation; analyzes and evaluates programs in space and science, including the activities of the National Science Foundation and the National Aeronautics and Space Administration; coordinates OMB science, energy, and space policies and programs.

Office of Science *(Energy Dept.),* 1000 Independence Ave. S.W., #7B058, 20585; (202) 586-5430. Fax, (202) 586-4120. Cherry Murray, Director; Patricia M. Dehmer, Deputy Director of Science Programs.
Web, www.science.energy.gov

Advises the secretary on the department's physical science and energy research and development programs; the management of the nonweapons multipurpose laboratories; and education and training activities required for basic and applied research. Manages the department's high-energy physics, nuclear physics, fusion energy sciences, basic energy sciences, health and environmental research, and computational and technology research. Provides and operates the large-scale facilities required for research in the physical and life sciences.

Office of Science and Technology Policy (OSTP) *(Executive Office of the President),* Eisenhower Executive Office Bldg., 1650 Pennsylvania Ave. N.W., 20504; (202) 456-4444. Fax, (202) 456-6021. John P. Holdren, Director. Press, (202) 456-6124.
General email, info@ostp.gov
Web, www.ostp.gov

Provides the president with policy analysis on scientific and technological matters as they relate to domestic and international affairs; coordinates executive office and federal agency responses to these issues; evaluates the effectiveness of scientific and technological programs.

Office of Science and Technology Policy (OSTP)
(Executive Office of the President), Science, Eisenhower Executive Office Bldg., 1650 Pennsylvania Ave. N.W., 20504; (202) 456-4444. Fax, (202) 456-6027. Jo Handelsman, Associate Director; Vacant, Principal Assistant Director for Science.
General email, info@ostp.gov

Web, www.ostp.gov

Analyzes policies and advises the president and others within the EOP on biological, physical, social, and behavioral sciences and on engineering; coordinates executive office and federal agency actions related to these issues. Evaluates the effectiveness of government science programs.

Office of Science and Technology Policy (OSTP)
(Executive Office of the President), Technology and Innovation, Eisenhower Executive Office Bldg., 1650 Pennsylvania Ave. N.W., 20504; (202) 456-4444. Fax, (202) 456-6021. Vacant, Associate Director and Chief Technology Officer of the President.
General email, info@ostp.gov

Web, www.ostp.gov

Analyzes policies and advices the president on technology and related issues of physical, computational, and space sciences; coordinates executive office and federal agency actions related to these issues. Issues include: national broadband access, advancing health IT; modernizing public safety communications; and clean manufacturing.

►CONGRESS

For a listing of relevant congressional committees and subcommittees, please see pages 646–647 or the Appendix.

►NONGOVERNMENTAL

American Assn. for Laboratory Accreditation (A2LA), *5202 Presidents Court, Frederick, MD 21703; (301) 644-3248. Fax, (240) 454-9449.* Peter S. Unger, President, (301) 644-3212.
General email, info@a2la.org

Web, www.a2la.org

Monitors and accredits laboratories that test construction materials and perform acoustics and vibration, biological, calibration, chemical, electrical, environmental, geotechnical, mechanical, nondestructive, and thermal testing. Offers laboratory-related training and programs for accreditation of inspection bodies, proficiency testing providers, and reference material producers.

American Assn. for the Advancement of Science (AAAS), *1200 New York Ave. N.W., 12th Floor, 20005; (202) 326-6400. Fax, (202) 371-9526.* Rush D. Holt, Chief Executive Officer, (202) 326-6640. Press, (202) 326-6440.
General email, ehr@aaas.org

Web, www.aaas.org

Membership: scientists, affiliated scientific organizations, and individuals interested in science. Promotes science education; the increased participation of women, minorities, and the disabled in the science and technology workforce; the responsible use of science in public policy; international cooperation in science; and the increased public engagement with science and technology. Sponsors national and international symposia, workshops, and meetings; publishes *Science* magazine.

American Assn. for the Advancement of Science (AAAS), *Scientific Responsibility, Human Rights, and Law Program, 1200 New York Ave. N.W., 8th Floor, 20005; (202) 326-6600. Fax, (202) 289-4950.* Mark S. Frankel, Director.
Web, http://aaas.org/srhrl

Engages policymakers and the general public on the ethical, legal, and human-rights issues related to the conduct and application of science and technology. Defends the freedom to engage in scientific inquiry; promotes responsible research practices; advances the application of science and technology to document human rights violations.

American Council of Independent Laboratories (ACIL), *1875 Eye St. N.W., #500, 20006; (202) 887-5872. Fax, (202) 887-0021.* Milton Bush, Chief Executive Officer.
General email, info@acil.org

Web, www.acil.org

Membership: independent commercial scientific and engineering firms. Promotes professional and ethical business practices in providing analysis, testing, and research in engineering, food sciences, analytical chemistry, and environmental geosciences.

Assn. for Women in Science, *1321 Duke St., #210, Alexandria, VA 22314; (703) 894-4490. Fax, (703) 894-4489.* Janet Bandows Koster, Executive Director.
General email, awis@awis.org

Web, www.awis.org and Twitter, @AWISNational

Promotes equal opportunity for women in scientific professions; provides career and funding information. Provides educational scholarships for women in science. Interests include international development.

Council of Scientific Society Presidents, *1155 16th St. N.W., 20036; (202) 872-6230.* Madeleine Jacobs, President.
General email, info@sciencepresidents.org

Web, www.cssp.us

Membership: presidents, presidents-elect, and immediate past presidents of professional scientific societies and federations. Supports professional science education. Serves as a forum for discussion of emerging scientific issues, formulates national science policy, and develops the nation's scientific leadership.

Federation of American Scientists (FAS), *1725 DeSales St. N.W., #600, 20036; (202) 546-3300. Fax, (202) 675-1010.* Charles D. Ferguson, President.
General email, fas@fas.org

Web, www.fas.org and Twitter, @FAScientists

Conducts studies and monitors legislation on issues and problems related to science and technology, especially

SCIENCE AND TECHNOLOGY RESOURCES IN CONGRESS

For a complete listing of congressional committees, including their full contact information, leadership, membership, and jurisdictions, please refer to the Appendix on pages 779–896.

HOUSE:

House Administration Committee, (202) 225-8281.
Web, cha.house.gov

House Agriculture Committee, (202) 225-2171.
Web, agriculture.house.gov

    Subcommittee on Biotechnology, Horticulture, and Research, (202) 225-2171.

    Subcommittee on Conservation and Forestry, (202) 225-2171.

House Appropriations Committee, (202) 225-2771.
Web, appropriations.house.gov

    Subcommittee on Commerce, Justice, Science, and Related Agencies, (202) 225-3351.

    Subcommittee on Interior, Environment, and Related Agencies, (202) 225-3081.

    Subcommittee on Labor, Health and Human Services, Education, and Related Agencies, (202) 225-3508.

House Armed Services Committee, (202) 225-4151.
Web, armedservices.house.gov

    Subcommittee on Emerging Threats and Capabilities, (202) 226-2843.

House Education and the Workforce Committee, (202) 225-4527.
Web, edworkforce.house.gov

    Subcommittee on Early Childhood, Elementary, and Secondary Education, (202) 225-4527.

    Subcommittee on Higher Education and Workforce Training, (202) 225-4527.

House Energy and Commerce Committee, (202) 225-2927.
Web, energycommerce.house.gov

    Subcommittee on Communications and Technology, (202) 225-2927.

House Homeland Security Committee, (202) 226-8417.
Web, homeland.house.gov

    Subcommittee on Cybersecurity, Infrastructure Protection, and Security Technologies, (202) 226-8417.

House Judiciary Committee, (202) 225-3951.
Web, judiciary.house.gov

    Subcommittee on Courts, Intellectual Property, and the Internet, (202) 226-7680.

House Natural Resources Committee, (202) 225-2761.
Web, naturalresources.house.gov

    Subcommittee on Energy and Mineral Resources, (202) 225-9297.

    Subcommittee on Federal Lands, (202) 226-7736.

    Subcommittee on Oversight and Investigations, (202) 225-7107.

    Subcommittee on Water, Power, and Oceans, (202) 225-8331.

House Science, Space, and Technology Committee, (202) 225-6371.
Web, science.house.gov

    Subcommittee on Energy, (202) 225-6371.

    Subcommittee on Oversight, (202) 225-6371.

    Subcommittee on Research and Technology, (202) 225-6371.

    Subcommittee on Space, (202) 225-6371.

U.S. nuclear arms policy, energy, arms transfer, and civil aerospace issues.

George C. Marshall Institute, *1601 N. Kent St., #802, Arlington, VA 22209; (571) 970-3180. Fax, (571) 970-3192. William O'Keefe, Chief Executive Officer.*
General email, info@marshall.org

Web, www.marshall.org and Twitter, @Marshall_Instit

Analyzes the technical and scientific aspects of public policy issues; produces publications on environmental science, space, national security, cyberthreats, and technology policy.

Government-University-Industry Research Roundtable (GUIRR), *500 5th St. N.W., Keck 549, 20001; (202) 334-3486. Fax, (202) 334-1369. Susan Sauer Sloan, Director.*
General email, guirr@nas.edu

Web, http://sites.nationalacademies.org/pga/guirr

Forum sponsored by the National Academy of Sciences, National Academy of Engineering, and Institute of Medicine. Provides scientists, engineers, and members of government, academia, and industry with an opportunity to discuss ways to catalyze productive cross-sector collaboration, take action on scientific matters of national importance, and improve the infrastructure for science and technology research.

Information Technology and Innovation Foundation, *1101 K St. N.W., #610, 20005; (202) 449-1351. Fax, (202) 638-4922. Robert D. Atkinson, President. Press, (202) 626-5744.*
General email, mail@itif.org

Web, www.itif.org

Nonprofit think tank that supports the advancement of technology. Studies and publishes reports on policy. Holds forums for policymakers to discuss issues affecting technological innovation.

Knowledge Ecology International (KEI), *1621 Connecticut Ave. N.W., #500, 20009; (202) 332-2670. Fax, (202) 332-2673. James Love, Director.*
Web, www.keionline.org

House Small Business Committee, (202) 225-5821.
Web, smallbusiness.house.gov
  Subcommittee on Health and Technology,
    (202) 225-5821.

SENATE:

Senate Agriculture, Nutrition, and Forestry
  Committee, (202) 224-2035.
Web, ag.senate.gov
  Subcommittee on Nutrition, Specialty Crops, and
    Agricultural Research, (202) 224-2035.
Senate Appropriations Committee,
  (202) 224-7363.
Web, appropriations.senate.gov
  Subcommittee on Commerce, Justice, Science,
    and Related Agencies, (202) 224-5202.
  Subcommittee on Interior, Environment, and
    Related Agencies, (202) 228-0774.
  Subcommittee on Labor, Health and Human
    Services, Education, and Related Agencies,
    (202) 224-9145.
Senate Armed Services Committee,
  (202) 224-3871.
Web, armed-services.senate.gov
  Subcommittee on Emerging Threats and
    Capabilities, (202) 224-3871.
  Subcommittee on Strategic Forces,
    (202) 224-3871.
Senate Commerce, Science, and Transportation
  Committee, (202) 224-0411.
Web, commerce.senate.gov

Subcommittee on Aviation Operations, Safety,
    and Security, (202) 224-9000.
  Subcommittee on Communications, Technology,
    Innovation, and the Internet,
    (202) 224-9340.
  Subcommittee on Consumer Protection, Product
    Safety, Insurance, and Data Security,
    (202) 224-0411.
  Subcommittee on Oceans, Atmosphere,
    Fisheries, and the Coast Guard,
    (202) 224-4912.
  Subcommittee on Science, Space and
    Competitiveness, (202) 224-0415.
  Subcommittee on Surface Transportation and
    Merchant Marine Infastructure, Safety, and
    Security, (202) 224-9000.
Senate Energy and Natural Resources Committee,
  (202) 224-4971.
Web, energy.senate.gov
  Subcommittee on Energy, (202) 224-4971.
  Subcommittee on Public Lands, Forests, and
    Mining, (202) 224-4971.
  Subcommittee on Water and Power,
    (202) 224-4971.
Senate Environment and Public Works Committee,
  (202) 224-8832.
Web, epw.senate.gov
  Subcommittee on Clean Air and Nuclear Safety,
    (202) 224-8832.
  Subcommittee on Fisheries, Water, and Wildlife,
    (202) 224-8832.

Advocates consumer access to health care, electronic commerce, competition policy, and information regarding intellectual property rights. (Formerly the Consumer Project on Technology.)

Laboratory Products Assn., *5618 Ox Rd., Suite C, Fairfax, VA 22039 (mailing address: P.O. Box 428, Fairfax, VA 22038); (703) 836-1360. Fax, (703) 836-6644. Clark Mulligan, President.*
General email, aerrera@lpanet.org
Web, www.lpanet.org

Membership: manufacturers and distributors of laboratory products and optical instruments. (Affiliated with the Optical Imaging Assn.)

National Geographic Society, *Committee for Research and Exploration, 1145 17th St. N.W., 20036-4688; (202) 862-8264. Fax, (202) 429-5729. Peter H. Raven, Chair. TTY, (800) 548-9797.*
General email, cre@ngs.org
Web, www.nationalgeographic.com/explorers

Sponsors basic research grants in the sciences, including anthropology, archaeology, astronomy, biology, botany, ecology, physical and human geography, geology, oceanography, paleontology, and zoology. To apply for grants, see Web site.

National Research Council (NRC), *Keck Center, 500 5th St. N.W., 20001; (202) 334-2000. Fax, (202) 334-2419. Ralph J. Cicerone, Chair; C.D. (Dan) Mote Jr., Chair; Victor J. Dzau, Chair; Bruce B. Darling, Executive Director. Library, (202) 334-2125. Press, (202) 334-2138. Publications, (800) 624-6242.*
General email, news@nas.edu

Web, www.nationalacademies.org, Twitter, @theNASciences and Facebook, www.facebook.com/ theNASciences

Serves as the principal operating agency of the National Academy of Sciences, National Academy of Engineering, and the National Academy of Medicine. Program units focus on physical, social, and life sciences; applications of science, including medicine, transportation, and education; international affairs; and U.S. government policy. Library open to the public by appointment.

National Research Council (NRC), *Disasters Roundtable,* Keck Center, 500 5th St. N.W., 20001; (202) 334-2243. Fax, (202) 334-1393. Ells M. Stanley Sr., Chair.
General email, dr@nas.edu

Web, http://dels.nas.edu/global/dr

Facilitates the exchange of ideas among scientists, practitioners, and policymakers concerned with issues related to natural, technological, and other disasters. Roundtable workshops are held three times a year in Washington, D.C.

Science Communication Network, *4833 West Lane,* Bethesda, MD 20814; (301) 654-6665. Amy Kostant, Executive Director.
General email, info@sciencecom.org

Web, www.sciencecommunicationnetwork.org

Conducts educational workshops to give scientists and other health professionals the media tools to enable their work to be accurately reported to the public. Focuses on environmental health science, green chemistry, and science integrity issues.

Society for Science & the Public, *1719 N St., N.W.,* 20036; (202) 785-2255. Fax, (202) 785-3751. Maya Ajmera, Chief Executive Officer.
Web, www.societyforscience.org

Promotes understanding and appreciation of science and the role it plays in human advancement. Sponsors science competitions and other science education programs in schools; awards scholarships. Publishes *Science News* and *Science News for Kids.* Provides funds and training to select U.S. science and math teachers who serve under-resourced students.

Union of Concerned Scientists, *Strategy and Policy,* 1825 K St. N.W., #800, 20006-1232; (202) 223-6133. Fax, (202) 223-6162. Alden Meyer, Director.
General email, ucs@ucsusa.org

Web, www.ucsusa.org

Provides oversight and guidance for advocacy on energy, transportation, agriculture, and arms control issues. (Headquarters in Cambridge, Mass.)

Union of Concerned Scientists, *Washington Office,* 1825 K St. N.W., #800, 20006; (202) 223-6133. Fax, (202) 223-6162. Alden Meyer, Director, Strategy and Policy.
Web, www.ucsusa.org, Twitter, @UCSUSA and Facebook, www.facebook.com/unionofconcernedscientists

Science advocacy organization with interests in the areas of clean energy, clean vehicles, food and agriculture, global warming, nuclear power, and nuclear weapons. (Headquarters in Cambridge, Mass.)

Data, Statistics, and References

▶**AGENCIES**

Dibner Library of the History of Science and Technology *(Smithsonian Institution),* 14th St. and Constitution Ave. N.W., NMAH 1041, MRC 672, 20560 (mailing address: P.O. Box 37012, MRC 154, Washington, D.C. 20013-7012); (202) 633-3872. Lilla Vekerdy, Head of Special Collections. Press, (202) 633-1522.
General email, Dibnerlibrary@si.edu

Web, www.library.si.edu/libraries/dibner-library-history-science-and-technology

Collection includes major holdings in the history of science and technology dating from the fifteenth century to the nineteenth century. Extensive collections in engineering, transportation, chemistry, mathematics, physics, electricity, and astronomy. Open to the public by appointment.

National Aeronautics and Space Administration (NASA), *Goddard Space Flight Center, Science Proposal Support Office,* 8800 Greenbelt Rd., Code 605, Greenbelt, MD 20771; (301) 286-0807. Fax, (301) 286-1772. David Leisawitz, Chief.
General email, spso@gsfc.nasa.gov

Web, http://science.gsfc.nasa.gov/spso

Supports the writing of proposals for NASA, within the Goddard Space Flight Center.

National Aeronautics and Space Administration (NASA), *Goddard Space Flight Center, Solar System Exploration Data Services,* 8800 Greenbelt Rd., Code 690.1, Greenbelt, MD 20771; (301) 286-1743. Fax, (301) 286-1683. Thomas (Tom) Morgan, Program Manager, Planetary Data System.
General email, request@nssdc.gsfc.nasa.gov

Web, http://ssedso.gsfc.nasa.gov

Coordinates data management and archiving plans within NASA's Science Mission. Operates the National Space Science Data Center (NSSDC) as a permanent archive for data associated with NASA's missions; the Crustal Dynamics Data Information System (CDDIS); and the Planetary Data System (PDS).

National Institute of Standards and Technology (NIST) *(Commerce Dept.), Information Services, Research Library,* 100 Bureau Dr., MS 2500, Gaithersburg, MD 20899-2500; (301) 975-3052. Fax, (301) 975-6793. Mary-Deirdre Coraggio, Director.
General email, library@nist.gov

Web, www.nist.gov/nvl

Creates and maintains a virtual knowledge base that supports research and administrative needs for the institute. Includes material on engineering, chemistry, physics, mathematics, materials science, and computer science. Home to NIST museum and history program. Publication and information services available to the public.

National Institute of Standards and Technology (NIST) *(Commerce Dept.), Information Technology Lab, Statistical Engineering, 100 Bureau Dr., Bldg. 222, #A-247, MS 8980, Gaithersburg, MD 20899-8980; (301) 975-2839. Fax, (301) 975-3144. William F. Guthrie, Chief, Acting.*
Web, www.nist.gov/itl/sed

Promotes the use of effective statistical techniques for planning analysis of experiments in the physical sciences within industry and government; interprets experiments and data collection programs. Offers training courses and workshops in methods and techniques.

National Institute of Standards and Technology (NIST) *(Commerce Dept.), Material Measurement Laboratory, 100 Bureau Dr., Bldg. 227, #A311, MS 8300, Gaithersburg, MD 20899-8300; (301) 975-8300. Fax, (301) 975-3845. Laurie E. Locasio, Director.*
General email, mmlinfo@nist.gov

Web, www.nist.gov/mml

Serves as the national reference laboratory for measurements in the chemical, biological, and material sciences. Researches industrial, biological, and environmental materials and processes to support development in manufacturing, nanotechnology, electronics, energy, health care, law enforcement, food safety, and other areas. Disseminates reference measurement procedures, certified reference materials, and best-practice guides.

National Institute of Standards and Technology (NIST) *(Commerce Dept.), Physical Measurement Laboratory, 100 Bureau Dr., Bldg. 221, #B160, MS 8400, Gaithersburg, MD 20899-8400; (301) 975-4200. Fax, (301) 975-3038. James K. Olthoff, Director.*
Web, www.nist.gov/pml

Develops and disseminates national standards of measurement for length, mass, force, acceleration, time, wavelength, frequency, humidity, and radiation. Conducts molecular and atomic research and research on physics, electromagnetics, and the properties of solids, liquids, and radio waves. Collaborates with industries, universities, and professional and standards-setting organizations. Develops and disseminates national standards of measurement for length, mass, force, acceleration, time, wavelength, frequency, humidity, and radiation.

National Institute of Standards and Technology (NIST) *(Commerce Dept.), Standard Reference Data, 100 Bureau Dr., MS 2300, Gaithersburg, MD 20899-2300; (301) 975-2200. Fax, (301) 975-4553. Cindy McKneely, Supervisory Measurement Services Product Specialist.*
General email, data@nist.gov

Web, www.nist.gov/srd

Collects and disseminates critically evaluated physical, chemical, and materials properties data in the physical sciences and engineering for use by industry, government, and academic laboratories. Develops databases in a variety of formats, including disk, CD-ROM, and online.

National Museum of American History *(Smithsonian Institution), Library, 14th St. and Constitution Ave. N.W., R5016, MRC 630, 20560-0630 (mailing address: #5016 Smithsonian Institution, P.O. Box 37012, MRC 360, Washington, DC 20013-7012); (202) 633-3865. Fax, (202) 633-3427. William Baxter, Head Librarian.*
General email, askalibrarian@si.edu

Web, www.library.si.edu/libraries/national-museum-american-history-library

Collection includes materials on the history of science and technology, with concentrations in engineering, transportation, and applied science. Maintains collection of trade catalogs and materials about expositions and world fairs. Open to the public by appointment. All library holdings are listed in the online catalog at http://siris-libraries.si.edu/ipac20/ipac.jsp?profile=liball.

National Oceanic and Atmospheric Administration (NOAA) *(Commerce Dept.), Central Library, Library and Information Services, 1315 East-West Hwy., SSMC3, 2nd Floor, Silver Spring, MD 20910; (301) 713-2600. Fax, (301) 713-4598. Stanley Elswick, Director, Acting. Reference service, (301) 713-2600, ext. 157. TTY, (301) 713-2779.*
General email, library.reference@noaa.gov

Web, www.lib.noaa.gov

Collection includes electronic NOAA documents, reports, and videos; electronic and print journals; the NOAA Photo Library; bibliographic database of other NOAA libraries; and climate data. Makes interlibrary loans; library open to the public, with two forms of photo ID, Monday through Friday, 9:00 a.m.–4:00 p.m.

National Oceanic and Atmospheric Administration (NOAA) *(Commerce Dept.), National Centers for Environmental Information, 1315 East-West Hwy., SSMC3, 4th Floor, Silver Spring, MD 20910-3282; (301) 713-3277. Fax, (301) 713-3302. Margarita Conkright Gregg, Director, (301) 713-4840.*
General email, nodc.services@noaa.gov

Web, www.nodc.noaa.gov

Responsible for hosting and providing access to comprehensive oceanic, atmospheric, and geophysical data. Provides world's largest collection of freely available oceanographic data, including water temperatures dating back to the late 1700s and measuring thousands of meters deep, scientific journals, rare books, historical photo collections, and maps through the NOAA Central Library, and data management expertise and training. Merger of NOAA's three data centers: National Climatic Data Center, National Geophysical Data Center, and National Oceanographic Data Center, which includes the National Coastal Data Development Center.

National Oceanic and Atmospheric Administration (NOAA) *(Commerce Dept.), National Environmental Satellite, Data, and Information Service, 1335 East-West Hwy., SSMC1, 8th Floor, Silver Spring, MD 20910; (301) 713-3578. Fax, (301) 713-1249. Stephen Volz, Assistant Administrator. Press, (301) 713-0214.*

General email, john.leslie@noaa.gov

Web, www.nesdis.noaa.gov

Acquires and disseminates global environmental (marine, atmospheric, solid earth, and solar-terrestrial) satellite data. Maintains comprehensive data and information referral service.

National Technical Information Service (NTIS) *(Commerce Dept.),* 5301 Shawnee Rd., Alexandria, VA 22312; (703) 605-6000. Fax, (703) 605-6900. Bruce Borzino, Director, (703) 605-6400. Toll-free, (800) 553-6847. Bookstore, (703) 605-6040. TTY, (703) 487-4639. Customer support, (703) 605-6050. Toll-free customer support, (888) 584-8332.

General email, customerservice@ntis.gov

Web, www.ntis.gov

Collects and organizes technical, scientific, engineering, and business-related information generated by U.S. and foreign governments and makes it available for commercial use in the private sector. Makes available approximately 3 million works covering research and development, current events, business and management studies, translations of foreign open source reports, foreign and domestic trade, general statistics, environment and energy, health and social sciences, and hundreds of other areas. Provides computer software and computerized data files in a variety of formats, including Internet downloads. Houses the Homeland Security Information Center, a centralized source on major security concerns for health and medicine, food and agriculture, and biochemical war.

Smithsonian Institution, *Office of the Director, Libraries,* 10th St. and Constitution Ave. N.W., National Museum of Natural History, 20560 (mailing address: P.O. Box 37012, MRC 154, Washington, DC 20013-7012); (202) 633-2240. Fax, (202) 786-2866. Nancy E. Gwinn, Director.

Web, http://library.si.edu

Maintains collection of general reference, biographical, and interdisciplinary materials; serves as an information resource on institution libraries, a number of which have collections in scientific subjects, including horticulture, botany, science and technology, and anthropology.

U.S. Geological Survey (USGS) *(Interior Dept.), Library Services,* 950 National Center, #1D100, Reston, VA 20192 (mailing address: 12201 Sunrise Valley Dr., #1D100, MS 950, Reston, VA 20192); (703) 648-4301. Fax, (703) 648-6373. Cate Canevari, Director, (703) 648-7182.

General email, library@usgs.gov

Web, http://library.usgs.gov

Maintains collection of books, periodicals, serials, maps, and technical reports on geology, mineral and water resources, mineralogy, paleontology, petrology, soil and environmental sciences, biology, and physics and chemistry as they relate to natural sciences. Open to the public; makes interlibrary loans.

▶ **CONGRESS**

For a listing of relevant congressional committees and subcommittees, please see pages 646–647 or the Appendix.

Government Accountability Office (GAO), *Publications and Dissemination,* 441 G St. N.W., #1T61B, 20548; (202) 512-3992. Leo Barbour, Director.

General email, info@gao.gov

Web, www.gao.gov

Provides information to the public on federal programs, reports, and testimonies. GAO publications and information about GAO publications are available upon request in print or online.

Library of Congress, *Science, Technology, and Business,* John Adams Bldg., 101 Independence Ave. S.E., #LA 508, 20540; (202) 707-5639. Fax, (202) 707-1925. Ron Bluestone, Chief. Business Reference Services, (202) 707-7934. Science Reference Services, (202) 707-6401. Technical reports, (202) 707-5655.

Web, www.loc.gov/rr/scitech

Offers reference service by telephone, by correspondence, and in person. Maintains a collection of more than 3 million reports on science, technology, business management, and economics.

▶ **NONGOVERNMENTAL**

American Statistical Assn., 732 N. Washington St., Alexandria, VA 22314-1943; (703) 684-1221. Fax, (703) 684-2037. Ronald Wasserstein, Executive Director. Toll-free, (888) 231-3473.

General email, asainfo@amstat.org

Web, www.amstat.org

Membership: statistical practitioners in industry, government, and academia. Supports excellence in the development, application, and dissemination of statistical science through meetings, publications, membership services, education, accreditation, and advocacy.

Statistical Assessment Service (STATS), 933 N. Kenmore St., #405, Arlington, VA 22201; (571) 319-0029. Fax, (202) 872-4014. S. Robert Lichter, President; Rebecca Goldin, Director.

Web, www.stats.org

Research and resource organization. Interests include improving the quality of scientific and statistical information in public discourse. Acts as a resource for journalists and policymakers on scientific issues and controversies. (Affiliated with George Mason University.)

International Programs

▶ **AGENCIES**

Bureau of International Organization Affairs *(State Dept.), Specialized and Technical Agencies,* 2401 E St., Room L-409, 20037 (mailing address: 2201 C St. N.W.,

#SA1, Washington, DC 20037); (202) 663-2648. Fax, (202) 647-8902. Vacant, Director.
Web, www.state.gov

Oversees U.S. participation in international specialized and technical organizations, including the International Atomic Energy Agency; the United Nations Environment Programme; and the Commission on Sustainable Development. Works to ensure that United Nations agencies follow United Nations Conference on Environment and Development recommendations on sustainable growth.

Bureau of Oceans and International Environmental and Scientific Affairs *(State Dept.)*, 2201 C St. N.W., #3880, 20520-7818; (202) 647-3950. Fax, (202) 647-0217. Judith G. Garber, Assistant Secretary, Acting.
Web, www.state.gov/e/oes and Twitter, @StateDeptOES

Formulates and implements policies and proposals for U.S. international scientific, technological, environmental, oceanic and marine, Arctic and Antarctic, and space programs; coordinates international science and technology policy with other federal agencies.

Bureau of Oceans and International Environmental and Scientific Affairs *(State Dept.)*, *International Health and Biodefense*, 2201 C St. N.W., #2734, 20520; (202) 647-1318. Lynette Poulton, Director.
Web, www.state.gov/e/oes/intlhealthbiodefense

Advances the Global Health Security Agenda and focuses on issues including pandemic preparedness, new outbreaks of disease, new international policy discussions, and the impact of science and technology, medicine, and public health.

Bureau of Oceans and International Environmental and Scientific Affairs *(State Dept.)*, *Science and Technology Cooperation*, 1800 G St. N.W., #10100, 20006; (202) 663-2623. Lisa Brodey, Director.
Web, www.state.gov/e/oes/stc

Advances U.S. foreign policy through science and technology, and fosters a global environment that supports innovation and transparency in government.

International Trade Administration (ITA) *(Commerce Dept.)*, *Industry and Analysis, Manufacturing*, 1401 Constitution Ave. N.W., #28004, 20230; (202) 482-1872. Fax, (202) 482-0856. Scott Kennedy, Deputy Assistant Secretary, Acting.
Web, www.trade.gov/td/manufacturing and www.manufacturing.gov

Conducts analyses and competitive assessments of high-tech industries, including aerospace, automotive, industrial machinery, medical devices, and the pharmaceutical industry. Develops trade policies for these industries, negotiates market access for U.S. companies, assists in promoting exports through trade missions, shows, and fairs in major overseas markets.

National Institute of Standards and Technology (NIST) *(Commerce Dept.)*, *International and Academic Affairs*, 100 Bureau Dr., MS 1090, Gaithersburg, MD 20899-1090;

(301) 975-3069. Fax, (301) 975-3530. Claire M. Saundry, Director. TTY, (301) 975-8295.
General email, inquiries@nist.gov
Web, www.nist.gov/iaao

Represents the institute in international functions involving science and technology; coordinates programs with foreign institutions; assists scientists from foreign countries who visit the institute for consultation. Administers a postdoctoral research associates program and oversees NIST's cooperation with academic institutions and researchers.

National Oceanic and Atmospheric Administration (NOAA) *(Commerce Dept.)*, *National Environmental Satellite, Data, and Information Service*, 1335 East-West Hwy., SSMC1, 8th Floor, Silver Spring, MD 20910; (301) 713-3578. Fax, (301) 713-1249. Stephen Volz, Assistant Administrator. Press, (301) 713-0214.
General email, john.leslie@noaa.gov
Web, www.nesdis.noaa.gov

Acquires and disseminates global environmental satellite data: marine, atmospheric, solid earth, and solar-terrestrial. Participates, with the National Meteorological Center, in the United Nations World Weather Watch Programme developed by the World Meteorological Organization. Manages U.S. civil earth-observing satellite systems and atmospheric, oceanographic, geophysical, and solar data centers. Provides the public, businesses, and government agencies with environmental data and information products and services.

National Oceanic and Atmospheric Administration (NOAA) *(Commerce Dept.)*, *National Weather Service, National Centers for Environmental Prediction*, 5830 University Research Court, College Park, MD 20740; (301) 683-1314. Fax, (301) 683-1325. Bill Lapenta, Director.
Web, www.ncep.noaa.gov

The National Center for Environmental Prediction and the National Environmental Satellite, Data, and Information Service are part of the World Weather Watch Programme developed by the United Nations World Meteorological Organization. Collects and exchanges data with other nations; provides other national weather service offices, private meteorologists, and government agencies with products, including forecast guidance products.

National Science Foundation (NSF), *International Science and Engineering*, 4201 Wilson Blvd., #11-1155, Arlington, VA 22230; (703) 292-8710. Fax, (703) 292-9067. Rebecca L. Keiser, Section Head.
Web, www.nsf.gov/dir/index.jsp?org=OISE

Serves as the foundation's focal point for international scientific and engineering activities; promotes new partnerships between U.S. scientists and engineers and their foreign colleagues; provides support for U.S. participation in international scientific organizations from three overseas offices (Paris, Tokyo, and Beijing).

Smithsonian Institution, *International Relations,* *1100 Jefferson Dr. S.W., #3123, 20560 (mailing address: P.O. Box 37012, Quad MRC 705, Washington, DC 20013-7012); (202) 633-4795. Fax, (202) 786-2557. Molly Fannon, Director.*
General email, global@si.edu

Web, www.smithsonianofi.com/sors-index/office-of-international-relations.oir

Fosters the development and coordinates the international aspects of Smithsonian scientific activities; facilitates basic research in the natural sciences and encourages international collaboration among individuals and institutions.

► INTERNATIONAL ORGANIZATIONS

InterAcademy Partnership, *Washington Office,* *500 5th St. N.W., #528, 20001; (202) 334-2804. Fax, (202) 334-2139. Tom Arrison, U.S. contact, (202) 334-3755.*
General email, iap@twas.org

Web, www.interacademies.net

Membership: academies of science in countries worldwide. Promotes communication among leading authorities in the natural and social sciences; establishes regional networks of academies to identify critical issues, thereby building capacity for advice to governments and international organizations. Interests include science education, the engagement of women in science, and sustainable management of water, energy, and other resources. (National Academy of Sciences is U.S. member. Headquarters is in Trieste, Italy.)

► NONGOVERNMENTAL

American Assn. for the Advancement of Science (AAAS), *International Office,* *1200 New York Ave. N.W., 11th Floor, 20005; (202) 326-6650. Fax, (202) 289-4958. Tom Wang, Chief International Officer.*
Web, www.aaas.org

Promotes international cooperation among scientists. Helps build scientific infrastructure in developing countries. Works to improve the quality of scientific input in international discourse.

National Research Council (NRC), *Policy and Global Affairs,* *Keck Center, 500 5th St. N.W., #528, 20001; (202) 334-3847. Fax, (202) 334-2139. Richard E. Bissell, Executive Director.*
General email, pga@nas.edu

Web, http://sites.nationalacademies.org/pga

Serves the international interests of the National Research Council, National Academy of Sciences, National Academy of Engineering, and Institute of Medicine. Promotes effective application of science and technology to the economic and social problems of industrialized and developing countries, and advises U.S. government agencies.

Research Applications

► AGENCIES

Defense Technical Information Center *(Defense Dept.),* *8725 John Jay Kingman Rd., #1948, Fort Belvoir, VA 22060-6218; (703) 767-9100. Christopher E. Thomas, Administrator. Registration, (703) 767-8273. Toll-free, (800) 225-3842.*
Web, www.dtic.mil

Acts as a central repository for the Defense Dept.'s collection of current and completed research and development efforts in all fields of science and technology. Disseminates research and development information to contractors, grantees, and registered organizations working on government research and development projects, particularly for the Defense Dept. Users must register with the center.

Justice Dept. (DOJ), *National Commission on Forensic Science,* *950 Pennsylvania Ave. N.W., 20530-0001; (202) 305-3481. Sally Yates, Co-Chair; Willie E. May, Co-Chair. Programs, (301) 975-2756. Public Affairs, (202) 514-2007.*
General email, Andrew.J.Bruck@usdoj.gov

Web, www.justice.gov/ncfs

Provides recommendations for national methods and strategies for improving forensic science, including strengthening the validity and reliability of the forensic sciences; enhancing quality assurance and quality control in forensic science laboratories and units; identifying and recommending scientific guidance and protocols for evidence seizure, testing, analysis, and reporting by forensic science laboratories and units; and identifying and assessing other needs of the forensic science communities and meeting the increasing demands generated by the criminal and civil justice systems at all levels of government. In partnership with the National Institute of Standards and Technology.

National Aeronautics and Space Administration (NASA), *Science Mission Directorate,* *300 E St. S.W., #3J28, 20546; (202) 358-3889. Fax, (202) 358-3092. John Grunsfeld, Associate Administrator.*
General email, science@hq.nasa.gov

Web, http://science.nasa.gov/about-us/organization-and-leadership

Seeks to understand the origins, evolution, and structure of the solar system and the universe; to understand the integrated functioning of the earth and the sun; and to ascertain the potential for life elsewhere. Administers space mission programs and mission-enabling programs, including suborbital missions. Sponsors scientific research and analysis. Exchanges information with the international science community. Primary areas of study are astronomy and astrophysics, earth sciences, heliophysics, and planetary science.

National Institute of Standards and Technology (NIST) *(Commerce Dept.),* *100 Bureau Dr., Bldg. 101, #A1134, Gaithersburg, MD 20899-1000 (mailing address: 100*

Bureau Dr., MS 1000, Gaithersburg, MD 20899); (301) 975-2300. Fax, (301) 869-8972. Willie E. May, Director. TTY, (800) 877-8339.
General email, director@nist.gov
Web, www.nist.gov/director

Nonregulatory agency that serves as national reference and measurement laboratory for the physical and engineering sciences. Works with industry, government agencies, and academia; promotes U.S. innovation and industrial competitiveness. Research interests include advanced manufacturing, information technology and cybersecurity, energy, health care, environment and consumer safety, and physical infrastructure.

National Institutes of Health (NIH) *(Health and Human Services Dept.), Intramural Research, Technology Transfer,* 6011 Executive Blvd., #325, MSC-7660, Rockville, MD 20852-3804; (301) 496-7057. Fax, (301) 402-0220. Richard Rodriguez, Director, Acting.
General email, nihott@mail.nih.gov
Web, http://ott.nih.gov

Evaluates, protects, monitors, and manages the NIH invention portfolio. Oversees patent prosecution, negotiates and monitors licensing agreements, and provides oversight and central policy review of cooperative research and development agreements. Also manages the patent and licensing activities for the Food and Drug Administration (FDA). Responsible for the central development and implementation of technology transfer policies for three research components of the Public Health Service—the NIH, the FDA, and the Centers for Disease Control and Prevention.

National Science Foundation (NSF), *National Nanotechnology Initiative,* 4201 Wilson Blvd., #505N, Arlington, VA 22230; (703) 292-8300. Fax, (703) 292-9013. Mihail C. Roco, Senior Adviser, (703) 292-7032.
General email, info@nnco.nano.gov
Web, www.nsf.gov/crssprgm/nano

Coordinates multiagency efforts in understanding nanoscale phenomena and furthering nanotechnology research and development.

▶NONGOVERNMENTAL

American National Standards Institute (ANSI), 1899 L St. N.W., 11th Floor, 20036; (202) 293-8020. Fax, (202) 293-9287. Joe Bhatia, President, (202) 331-3605.
Web, www.ansi.org

Administers and coordinates the voluntary U.S. private sector–led consensus standards and conformity assessment system. Serves as the official U.S. representative to the International Organization of Standardization (ISO) and, via the U.S. National Committee, the International Electrotechnical Commission (IEC), and is a U.S. representative to the International Accreditation Forum (IAF).

The Brookings Institution, *Center for Technology Innovation,* 1775 Massachusetts Ave. N.W., 20036; (202) 797-6090. Darrell M. West, Director, (202) 797-6481.
Web, www.brookings.edu/about/centers/techinnovation

Research center promoting policymaking and public debate about technology innovation, including digital infrastructure, the mobile economy, e-governance, digital media and entertainment, cybersecurity and privacy, digital medicine, and virtual education.

The Brookings Institution, *Governance Studies,* 1755 Massachusetts Ave. N.W., 20036; (202) 797-6090. Fax, (202) 797-6144. Darrell M. West, Director, (202) 797-6481. Information, (202) 797-6000. Press, (202) 797-6105.
Web, www.brookings.edu/governance

Promotes public debate on technology innovation and develops data-driven scholarship to understand the legal, economic, social, and governance impact of technology.

Institute for Alternative Futures (IAF), 2331 Mill Rd., #100, Alexandria, VA 22314; (703) 684-5880. Fax, (703) 684-0640. Jonathan Peck, President.
General email, futurist@altfutures.org
Web, www.altfutures.org

Research and educational organization that explores the implications of future developments in various fields and facilitates planning efforts. Works with state and local governments, Congress, international organizations, federal government, and regional associations; conducts seminars. Interests include pharmaceutical research, health care, telecommunications, artificial intelligence, energy, the environment, and sustainability.

National Center for Advanced Technologies (NCAT), 1000 Wilson Blvd., #1700, Arlington, VA 22209-3901; (703) 358-1000. Fax, (703) 358-1012. Don Forest, President.
General email, ncat@ncat.com
Web, www.ncat.com

Encourages U.S. competition in the world market by uniting government, industry, and university efforts to develop advanced technologies. (Affiliated with the Aerospace Industries Assn. of America.)

National Research Council (NRC), *Behavioral, Cognitive, and Sensory Sciences Board,* Keck Center, 500 5th St. N.W., 11th Floor, 20001; (202) 334-2678. Fax, (202) 334-3584. Barbara A. Wanchisen, Director, (202) 334-2394; Susan T. Fiske, Chair.
General email, BBCSS@nas.edu
Web, http://nas.edu/bbcss

Membership: experts in the fields of cognition, human development, sensory sciences, social psychology, cognitive neuroscience, behavioral neuroscience, social neuroscience, medical ethics, evolutionary and economic anthropology, and health psychology. Advises government agencies on policies relating to the behavioral, cognitive, and sensory sciences.

Public Technology Institute (PTI), 1420 Prince St., #200, Alexandria, VA 22314 2815; (202) 626-2400. Alan R. Shark, Executive Director, (202) 626-2445. Press, (202) 626-2432.
General email, info@pti.org
Web, www.pti.org and Twitter, @Public_Tech

Cooperative research, development, and technology-transfer organization of cities and counties in North America. Applies available technological innovations and develops other methods to improve public services.

RAND Corporation, *Washington Office, 1200 S. Hayes St., Arlington, VA 22202-5050; (703) 413-1100. Fax, (703) 413-8111. Richard M. Moore, Director, ext. 5399; Anita Chandra, Director, Justice, Infrastructure, and Environment, ext.5323.*
Web, www.rand.org

Research organization. Interests include energy, emerging technologies and critical systems, space and transportation, technology policies, international cooperative research, water resources, ocean and atmospheric sciences, and other technologies in defense and nondefense areas. (Headquarters in Santa Monica, Calif.)

SRI International, *Washington Office, 1100 Wilson Blvd., #2800, Arlington, VA 22209; (703) 524-2053. Fax, (703) 247-8569. Peter Kant, Executive Director, (703) 247-8424.*
Web, www.sri.com

Research and consulting organization that conducts basic and applied research for government, industry, and business. Interests include engineering, physical and life sciences, and international research. (Headquarters in Menlo Park, Calif.)

Scientific Research Practices

▶**AGENCIES**

Assistant Secretary for Health *(Health and Human Services Dept.), Human Research Protections, Tower Bldg., 1101 Wootton Pkwy., #200, Rockville, MD 20852; (240) 453-6900. Fax, (240) 453-6909. Dr. Jerry Menikoff, Director. Toll-free, (866) 447-4777.*
General email, ohrp@hhs.gov
Web, www.hhs.gov/ohrp

Promotes the rights, welfare, and well-being of subjects involved in research conducted or supported by the Health and Human Services Dept.; helps to ensure that research is carried out in accordance with federal regulations by providing clarification and guidance, developing educational programs and materials, and maintaining regulatory oversight.

Assistant Secretary for Health *(Health and Human Services Dept.), Research Integrity, Tower Bldg., 1101 Wootton Pkwy., #750, Rockville, MD 20852; (240) 453-8200. Fax, (301) 443-5351. Kathy Partin, Director.*
General email, askori@hhs.gov
Web, www.ori.hhs.gov

Seeks to promote the quality of Public Health Service extramural and intramural research programs. (Extramural programs provide funding to research institutions that are not part of the federal government. Intramural programs provide funding for research conducted within federal government facilities.) Provides oversight of

institutional inquiries and investigations of research misconduct and technical assistance to institutions during these proceedings; reviews institutional findings and process and proposes administrative actions to the Health and Human Services Dept. when the Office of Research Integrity makes a finding of research misconduct; sponsors educational programs and activities for professionals interested in research integrity; sponsors grants for conferences and basic research on research integrity; administers institutional assurance program; and coordinates with institutions to protect from retaliation individuals involved in research misconduct matters.

Education Dept., *Chief Financial Officer, Financial Management Operations, 550 12th St. S.W., 6th Floor, 20005; (202) 245-8118. Fax, (202) 205-0765. Gary Wood, Director.*
General email, gary.wood@ed.gov
Web, www2.ed.gov/about/offices/list/ocfo/humansub.html

Advises grantees and applicants for department-supported research on regulations for protecting human subjects. Provides guidance to the Education Dept. on the requirements for complying with the regulations. Serves as the primary Education Dept. contact for matters concerning the protection of human subjects in research.

Food and Drug Administration (FDA) *(Health and Human Services Dept.), Good Clinical Practice, 10903 New Hampshire Ave., #WO32-5103, Silver Spring, MD 20993; (301) 796-8340. Joanne Less, Director.*
General email, gcp.questions@fda.hhs.gov
Web, www.fda.gov/AboutFDA/CentersOffices/OfficeofMedicalProductsandTobacco/OfficeofScienceandHealthCoordination/ucm2018191.htm

Provides information to the FDA Commissioner about clinical human research trials and impacts on policy.

Health and Human Services Dept. (HHS), *President's Commission for the Study of Bioethical Issues, 1425 New York Ave. N.W., #C100, 20005; (202) 233-3960. Fax, (202) 233-3990. Amy Gutmann, Chair; Lisa M. Lee, Executive Director.*
General email, info@bioethics.gov
Web, www.bioethics.gov

Advisory panel of the nation's leaders in medicine, science, ethics, religion, law, and engineering. Advises the president on bioethical issues arising from advances in biomedicine and related areas of science and technology. Seeks to identify and promote policies and practices that ensure that scientific research, healthcare delivery, and technological innovation are conducted in a socially and ethically responsible manner.

National Aeronautics and Space Administration (NASA), *Chief Health and Medical Officer, 300 E St. S.W., 20546; (202) 358-2390. Fax, (202) 358-3349. Dr. Richard S. Williams, Chief Health and Medical Officer.*
Web, www.hq.nasa.gov/office/chmo

Monitors human and animal research and clinical practice to ensure that NASA adheres to appropriate medical and ethical standards and satisfies all regulatory and statutory requirements.

National Institutes of Health (NIH) *(Health and Human Services Dept.), Animal Care and Use,* 31 Center Dr., Bldg. 31, #B1C37, MSC 2252, Bethesda, MD 20892-2252; (301) 496-5424. Fax, (301) 480-8298. *Terri Clark, Director.*
General email, secoacu@od.nih.gov

Web, http://oacu.od.nih.gov

Provides guidance for the humane care and use of animals in the intramural research program at NIH.

National Institutes of Health (NIH) *(Health and Human Services Dept.), Human Research Protections Program,* 9000 Rockville Pike, Clinical Center, Bldg. 10, #2C146, MSC 1154, Bethesda, MD 20892-1154; (301) 402-3444. Fax, (301) 402-3443. *Dr. Lynnette Nieman, Director.*
Web, http://ohsr.od.nih.gov

Helps NIH investigators understand and comply with ethical principles and regulatory requirements involved in human subjects research. Assists NIH components in administering and regulating human subjects research activities.

National Institutes of Health (NIH) *(Health and Human Services Dept.), Laboratory Animal Welfare,* 6705 Rockledge Dr., RLK1, #360, MSC 7982, Bethesda, MD 20892-7982; (301) 496-7163. Fax, (301) 480-3394. *Patricia A. Brown, Director.*
General email, olaw@mail.nih.gov

Web, http://grants.nih.gov/grants/olaw/olaw.htm

Develops and monitors policy on the humane care and use of animals in research conducted by any public health service entity.

Office of Science *(Energy Dept.), Biological and Environmental Research, Biological Systems Science Division, Human Subjects Protection Program,* 19901 Germantown Rd., #SC23.2, Germantown, MD 20874-1290 (mailing address: Germantown Bldg., 1000 Independence Ave. S.W., #SC23.2, Washington, DC 20585); (301) 903-7693. Fax, (301) 903-0567. *Elizabeth (Libby) White, Program Manager.*
General email, humansubjects@science.doe.gov

Web, http://humansubjects.energy.gov

Works to protect the rights and welfare of human subject research volunteers by establishing guidelines and enforcing regulations on scientific research that uses human subjects, including research that involves identifiable or high-risk data, worker populations or subgroups; humans testing devices, products, or materials; and bodily materials. Acts as an educational and technical resource to investigators, administrators, and institutional research boards.

▶NONGOVERNMENTAL

American Assn. for the Advancement of Science (AAAS), *Scientific Responsibility, Human Rights, and Law Program,* 1200 New York Ave. N.W., 8th Floor, 20005; (202) 326-6600. Fax, (202) 289-4950. *Mark S. Frankel, Director.*
Web, http://aaas.org/srhrl

Engages policymakers and the general public on the ethical, legal, and human-rights issues related to the conduct and application of science and technology. Defends the freedom to engage in scientific inquiry; promotes responsible research practices; advances the application of science and technology to document human rights violations.

Humane Society of the United States, *Animal Research Issues,* 700 Professional Dr., Gaithersburg, MD 20879; (202) 452-1100. Fax, (301) 258-7760. *Katy Conlee, Vice President.*
General email, ari@humanesociety.org

Web, www.humanesociety.org/about/departments/animals_research.html

Seeks to end the suffering of animals in research. Promotes the use of alternatives that replace, refine, or reduce the use of animals in scientific research, education, and consumer product testing. Conducts outreach programs aimed toward the public and the scientific community.

National Assn. for Biomedical Research, 1100 Vermont Ave. N.W., #1100, 20005; (202) 857-0540. Fax, (202) 659-1902. *Frankie L. Trull, President.*
General email, info@nabr.org

Web, www.nabr.org

Membership: scientific and medical professional societies, academic institutions, and research-oriented corporations involved in the use of animals in biomedical research. Supports the humane use of animals in medical research, education, and product-safety assessment. Monitors legislation and regulations.

National Research Council (NRC), *Laboratory Assessments Board,* Keck Center, 500 5th St. N.W., #W900, 20001; (202) 334-3311. Fax, (202) 334-2791. *James P. McGee, Director.*
General email, lab@nas.edu

Web, http://sites.nationalacademies.org/deps/lab

Reviews and assesses the quality of internal research conducted at NRC laboratories, including those established by federal agencies at national laboratories and at government-owned, contractor-operated facilities.

Society of Research Administrators International (SRA International), 1560 Wilson Blvd., #310, Arlington, VA 22209; (703) 741-0140. Fax, (703) 741-0142. *Elliott Kulakowski, Executive Director, ext. 215.*
General email, info@srainternational.org

Web, www.srainternational.org

Membership: scientific and medical research administrators in the United States and other countries. Educates the public about the profession; offers professional development services; sponsors mentoring and awards programs.

BIOLOGY AND LIFE SCIENCES

General

▶AGENCIES

National Aeronautics and Space Administration (NASA), *Human Space Flight Capability Division, 300 E St. S.W., #7V20, 20546; (202) 358-2320. Fax, (202) 358-3091.* Benjamin J. Neumann, Division Director. Web, www.hq.nasa.gov

Conducts NASA's life sciences research.

National Institute of General Medical Sciences *(National Institutes of Health), 45 Center Dr., #3AN44E, MSC 6200, Bethesda, MD 20892-6200; (301) 496-7301. Fax, (301) 402-0156. Jon R. Lorsch, Director.* General email, info@nigms.nih.gov

Web, www.nigms.nih.gov, Twitter, @NIGMS and Facebook, www.facebook.com/nigms.nih.gov

Primarily supports basic biomedical research and training that lays the foundation for advances in disease diagnosis, treatment, and prevention. Areas of special interest include bioinformatics, cell biology, developmental biology, physiology, biological chemistry genetics, and computational biology.

National Museum of Natural History *(Smithsonian Institution), 10th St. and Constitution Ave. N.W., 20560-0106 (mailing address: P.O. Box 37012, MRC 106, Washington, DC 20013-7012); (202) 633-2664. Fax, (202) 633-0169. Kirk Johnson, Director. Library, (202) 633-1680. Press, (202) 633-2950. TTY, (202) 633-5285. General Smithsonian information, (202) 633-1000.* General email, naturalexperience@si.edu

Web, www.mnh.si.edu and Twitter, @NMNH

Conducts research and maintains exhibitions and collections relating to the natural sciences. Collections are organized into seven research and curatorial departments: anthropology, botany, entomology, invertebrate zoology, mineral sciences, paleobiology, and vertebrate zoology.

National Museum of Natural History *(Smithsonian Institution), Library, 10th St. and Constitution Ave. N.W., East Court, 1st Floor, 20560-0154 (mailing address: P.O. Box 37012, MRC 154, Washington, DC 20013-7012); (202) 633-1680. Gil Taylor, Head, Acting.* General email, askalibrarian@si.edu

Web, www.library.si.edu/libraries/national-museum-natural-history-library

Maintains reference collections covering anthropology, biodiversity, biology, botany, ecology, entomology, ethnology, mineral sciences, paleobiology, and zoology; permits on-site use of the collections. Open to the public by appointment; makes interlibrary loans.

National Oceanic and Atmospheric Administration *(NOAA) (Commerce Dept.), National Marine Fisheries Service, 1315 East-West Hwy., SSMC3, Silver Spring, MD 20910; (301) 427-8000. Fax, (301) 713-1940. Eileen Sobeck, Assistant Administrator. Press, (301) 427-8003.* Web, www.nmfs.noaa.gov

Conducts research and collects data on marine ecology and biology; collects, analyzes, and provides information through the Marine Resources Monitoring, Assessment, and Prediction Program. Administers the Magnuson-Stevens Fishery Conservation and Management Act and marine mammals and endangered species protection programs. Works with the Army Corps of Engineers on research into habitat restoration and conservation.

National Science Foundation (NSF), *Biological Sciences Directorate, 4201 Wilson Blvd., #605N, Arlington, VA 22230; (703) 292-8400. Fax, (703) 292-9154. James L. Olds, Assistant Director.* Web, www.nsf.gov/dir/index.jsp?org=bio

Serves as a forum for addressing biology research issues, sharing information, identifying gaps in scientific knowledge, and developing consensus among concerned federal agencies. Facilitates continuing cooperation among federal agencies on topical issues.

National Science Foundation (NSF), *Environmental Biology Division, 4201 Wilson Blvd., Room 635N, Arlington, VA 22230; (703) 292-8480. Fax, (703) 292-9064. Paula Mabee, Director.* Web, www.nsf.gov/bio/deb/about.jsp

Supports research on populations, species, communities, and ecosystems, including biodiversity, phylogenetic systematics, molecular evolution, life history evolution, natural selection, ecology, biogeography, ecosystem services, conservation biology, global change, and biogeochemical cycles.

Office of Science *(Energy Dept.), Biological and Environmental Research, 19901 Germantown Rd., #SC23, Germantown, MD 20874-1290 (mailing address: Germantown Bldg., 1000 Independence Ave. S.W., #SC23, Washington, DC 20585); (301) 903-3251. Fax, (301) 903-5051. Sharlene Weatherwax, Associate Director.* General email, sc.ber@science.doe.gov

Web, http://science.energy.gov/ber

Advances biological and environmental research and provides scientific user facilities to support innovation in energy security and environmental responsibility.

Office of Science *(Energy Dept.), Biological and Environmental Research, Biological Systems Science Division, Genomic Science Program, 19901 Germantown Rd., #SC72, Germantown, MD 20874-1290; (301) 903-1239. Joseph Graber, Program Manager.* Web, http://genomicscience.energy.gov

Supports research using microbial and plant genomic data, high-throughput technologies, and modeling and simulation to develop predictive understanding of biological systems behavior relevent to solving energy and environmental challenges.

U.S. Geological Survey (USGS) *(Interior Dept.), Ecosystems, 12201 Sunrise Valley Dr., MS 300, Reston, VA*

20192; (703) 648-4050. Fax, (703) 648-7031. Anne E. Kinsinger, Associate Director, (703) 648-4051. Web, www.usgs.gov/ecosystems

Conducts research and monitoring to develop and convey an understanding of ecosystem function and distributions, physical and biological components, and trophic dynamics for freshwater, terrestrial, and marine ecosystems and the human, fish, and wildlife communities they support. Subject areas include invasive species, endangered species and habitats, genetics and genomics, and microbiology.

▶ **NONGOVERNMENTAL**

American Institute of Biological Sciences, 1800 Alexander Bell Dr., #400, Reston, VA 20191; (703) 674-2500. Fax, (703) 674-2509. Scott Glisson, Director, Acting; Robert Gropp, Director, Acting. Web, www.aibs.org

Membership: biologists, biology educators, and biological associations. Promotes interdisciplinary cooperation among members engaged in biological research and education; conducts educational programs for members; reviews projects supported by government grants. Monitors legislation and regulations.

American Society for Biochemistry and Molecular Biology, 11200 Rockville Pike, #302, Bethesda, MD 20852-3110; (240) 283-6600. Fax, (301) 881-2080. Barbara A. Gordon, Executive Director. General email, asbmb@asbmb.org

Web, www.asbmb.org and Twitter, @ASBMB

Professional society of biological chemists. Participates in International Union of Biochemistry and Molecular Biology. Monitors legislation and regulations.

American Society for Cell Biology, 8120 Woodmont Ave., #750, Bethesda, MD 20814-2762; (301) 347-9300. Fax, (301) 347-9310. Cynthia Godes, Executive Director, Acting. General email, ascbinfo@ascb.org

Web, www.ascb.org and Twitter, @ASCBiology

Membership: scientists who have education or research experience in cell biology or an allied field. Promotes scientific exchange worldwide; organizes courses, workshops, and symposia. Monitors legislation and regulations.

American Society for Microbiology, 1752 N St. N.W., 20036-2904; (202) 737-3600. Fax, (202) 942-9279. Stefano Bertuzzi, Executive Director. Press, (202) 942-9297. General email, service@asmusa.org

Web, www.asm.org

Membership: microbiologists. Encourages education, training, scientific investigation, and application of research results in microbiology and related subjects; participates in international research.

American Type Culture Collection, 10801 University Blvd., Manassas, VA 20110-2209 (mailing address: P.O. Box 1549, Manassas, VA 20108); (703) 365-2700.

Fax, (703) 365-2750. Raymond H. Cypress, Chief Executive Officer. Toll-free, (800) 638-6597. General email, sales@atcc.org

Web, www.atcc.org

Provides research and development tools, reagents, and related biological material management services to government agencies, academic institutions, and private industry worldwide. Serves as a bioresource center of live cultures and genetic material.

AOAC International, 2275 Research Blvd., #300, 20850-3250; (301) 924-7077. Fax, (301) 924-7089. E. James Bradford, Executive Director. Information, (800) 379-2622. General email, aoac@aoac.org

Web, www.aoac.org

International association of analytical science professionals, companies, government agencies, nongovernmental organizations, and institutions. Promotes voluntary consensus standards development for analytical methodology, fit-for-purpose methods, and quality measurements in the analytical sciences.

Biophysical Society, 11400 Rockville Pike, #800, Rockville, MD 20852; (240) 290-5600. Fax, (240) 290-5555. Rosalba Kampman, Executive Officer. General email, society@biophysics.org

Web, www.biophysics.org and Twitter, @BiophysicalSoc

Membership: scientists, professors, and researchers engaged in biophysics or related fields. Encourages development and dissemination of knowledge in biophysics through meetings, publications, and outreach activities.

Carnegie Institute for Science, 1530 P St. N.W., 20005-1910; (202) 387-6400. Fax, (202) 387-8092. Matthew P. Scott, President. Web, www.carnegiescience.edu and Twitter, @carnegiescience

Conducts research in plant science biology, genetic and developmental biology, earth and planetary sciences, astronomy, and global ecology and matter at extreme states at the Carnegie Institution's six research departments: Dept. of Embryology (Baltimore, Md.); Geophysical Laboratory (Washington, D.C.); Dept. of Global Ecology (Stanford, Calif.); Dept. of Plant Biology (Stanford, Calif.); Dept. of Terrestrial Magnetism (Washington, D.C.); and The Observatories (Pasadena, Calif., and Las Campanas, Chile).

Ecological Society of America, 1990 M St. N.W., #700, 20036; (202) 833-8773. Fax, (202) 833-8775. Katherine S. McCarter, Executive Director. General email, esahq@esa.org

Web, www.esa.org

Promotes research in ecology and the scientific study of the relationship between organisms and their past, present, and future environments. Interests include biotechnology; management of natural resources, habitats, and ecosystems to protect biological diversity; and ecologically sound public policies.

Federation of American Societies for Experimental Biology (FASEB), *9650 Rockville Pike, Bethesda, MD 20814-3998; (301) 634-7000. Fax, (301) 634-7001. Guy C. Fogleman, Executive Director, (301) 634-7090. Toll-free, (800) 433-2732.*
General email, info@faseb.org
Web, www.faseb.org, Twitter, @FASEBopa

Advances biological science through collaborative advocacy for research policies that promote scientific progress and education and lead to improvements in human health. Provides educational meetings and publications to disseminate biological research results. Represents 27 scientific societies and more than 120,000 biomedical researchers around the world.

National Ecological Observatory Network, Inc. (NEON), *Washington Office, 1100 Jefferson Dr. S.W., #3123, MRC 705, 20560-0001; (202) 370-7891. Fax, (202) 204-0128. Brian Wee, Chief of Strategic Alliances; Gene Kelly, Chief Executive Officer, Acting. Press, (720) 746-4936.*
General email, bwee@neoninc.org
Web, www.neoninc.org, Twitter, @NEONInc and Facebook, www.facebook.com/NEONInc

Collects data across the United States on the impact of climate change, land use change, and invasive species on natural resources and biodiversity, with the goal of detecting and forecasting ecological change on a continental scale over multiple decades. Works with various government agencies to develop standards for environmental observations and data interoperability; expected to become fully operational by 2017. Funded by the National Science Foundation in partnership with NEON. (Visitors note: Co-located in the Smithsonian's S. Dillon Ripley Center.) (Headquarters in Boulder, Colo.)

National Research Council (NRC), *Life Sciences Board, Keck Center, 500 5th St. N.W., 6th Floor, 20001; (202) 334-2187. Fax, (202) 334-1289. Fran Sharples, Director; James P. Collins, Chair.*
General email, bls@nas.edu
Web, http://dels.nas.edu/bls

Supports technical and policy research in the life sciences, including bioterrorism, genomics, biodiversity conservation, and basic biomedical research, such as stem cells.

Biotechnology

▶**AGENCIES**

Environmental Protection Agency (EPA), *Chemical Safety and Pollution Prevention, 1200 Pennsylvania Ave. N.W., #4146, MC 7101M, 20460; (202) 564-2902. Fax, (202) 564-0801. James J. Jones, Assistant Administrator.*
Web, www2.epa.gov/aboutepa/about-office-chemical-safety-and-pollution-prevention-ocspp

Studies and makes recommendations for regulating chemical substances under the Toxic Substances Control Act. Compiles list of chemical substances subject to the act. Registers, controls, and regulates use of pesticides and toxic substances. Manages the Endocrine Disruptor Screening Program.

National Institutes of Health (NIH) *(Health and Human Services Dept.), Biotechnology Activities, 6705 Rockledge Dr., #750, MSC 7985, Bethesda, MD 20892-7985; (301) 496-9838. Fax, (301) 496-9839. Lyric Jorgenson, Director, Acting.*
General email, oba-osp@od.nih.gov
Web, http://osp.od.nih.gov/office-biotechnology-activities/oba

Reviews requests submitted to the NIH involving genetic testing, recombinant DNA technology, xenotransplantation, and biosecurity; develops and implements research guidelines for safe conduct of DNA-related research. Monitors scientific progress in human genetics.

National Library of Medicine *(National Institutes of Health), National Center for Biotechnology Information, 8600 Rockville Pike, Bldg. 38A, 8th Floor, Bethesda, MD 20892; (301) 496-2475. Fax, (301) 480-4559. Dr. David J. Lipman, Director.*
General email, info@ncbi.nlm.nih.gov
Web, www.ncbi.nlm.nih.gov and Pub Med Central, www.pubmedcentral.nih.gov

Creates automated systems for storing and analyzing knowledge of molecular biology and genetics. Develops new information technologies to aid in understanding the molecular processes that control human health and disease. Conducts basic research in computational molecular biology. Sponsors PubMed Central, a publicly accessible digital archive of life sciences journal literature.

National Science Foundation (NSF), *Molecular and Cellular Biosciences Division, 4201 Wilson Blvd., Arlington, VA 22230; (703) 292-8440. Fax, (703) 292-9061. Linda Hyman, Division Director, (703) 292-7132.*
Web, www.nsf.gov/div/index.jsp?div=MCB

Supports research and understanding of complex living systems at cellular levels.

▶**NONGOVERNMENTAL**

Biotechnology Innovation Organization, *1201 Maryland Ave. S.W., #900, 20024; (202) 962-9200. Fax, (202) 488-6301. James C. Greenwood, President.*
General email, info@bio.org
Web, www.bio.org and Twitter, @IAmBiotech

Membership: U.S. and international companies engaged in biotechnology. Monitors government activities at all levels; promotes educational activities; conducts workshops.

Friends of the Earth (FOE), *1101 15th St. N.W., 11th Floor, 20005; (202) 783-7400. Fax, (202) 783-0444. Erich Pica, President. Toll-free, (877) 843-8687.*
General email, foe@foe.org
Web, www.foe.org and Twitter, @foe_us

Monitors legislation and regulations on issues related to seed industry consolidation and patenting laws and on business developments in genetic engineering and synthetic biology and their effect on farming, food production, genetic resources, and the environment.

Genetic Alliance, *4301 Connecticut Ave. N.W., #404, 20008-2369; (202) 966-5557. Fax, (202) 966-8553. Sharon Terry, President.*
General email, info@geneticalliance.org
Web, www.geneticalliance.org and Twitter, @GeneticAlliance

Coalition of government, industry, advocacy organizations, and private groups that seeks to advance genetic research and its applications. Promotes increased funding for research, improved access to services, and greater support for emerging technologies, tests, and treatments. Acts as an advocate on behalf of individuals and families living with genetic conditions.

J. Craig Venter Institute, *9714 Medical Center Dr., Rockville, MD 20850; (301) 795-7000. J. Craig Venter, Chief Executive Officer.*
Web, www.jcvi.org

Research institute that analyzes genomes and gene products for medical, nutritional, and agricultural uses; studies genomic sciences and their ethical, legal, and economic implications for society. Produces reports; offers courses, workshops, and internships.

Kennedy Institute of Ethics *(Georgetown University), Healy Hall, 37th and O Sts. N.W., 4th Floor, 20057; (202) 687-0360. Fax, (202) 687-8089. Margaret Little, Director. Library, (202) 687-3885.*
General email, kennedyinstitute@georgetown.edu
Web, https://kennedyinstitute.georgetown.edu, Facebook, www.facebook.com/KennedyInstituteofEthics and Twitter, @kieatgu

Carries out teaching and research on medical ethics, including legal and ethical definitions of death, allocation of health resources, and recombinant DNA and human gene therapy. Sponsors the annual Intensive Bioethics Course. Conducts international programs. Serves as the home of the Bioethics Research Library at Georgetown University (http://bioethics.georgetown.edu) and the National Information Resource on Ethics and Human Genetics (http://genthx.georgetown.edu). Provides free reference assistance and bibliographic databases covering all ethical issues in health care, genetics, and biomedical research. Publishes the *Kennedy Institute of Ethics Journal.* Library open to the public.

National Research Council (NRC), *Health Sciences Policy Board, Keck Center, 500 5th St. N.W., 20001; (202) 334-1888. Fax, (202) 334-1329. Andrew Pope, Director.*
Web, www.nationalacademies.org/hmd

Oversees research and activities related to basic biomedical and clinical research, including the role of science in policy and decisionmaking; the education of health and research professionals and the general public, the preparedness, resilience, and sustainability of communities; biomedical ethics.

Botany

▶AGENCIES

National Arboretum *(Agriculture Dept.), 3501 New York Ave. N.E., 20002-1958; (202) 245-2726. Fax, (202) 245-4575. Richard T. Olsen, Director.*
Web, www.usna.usda.gov

Maintains public display of plants on 446 acres; provides information and makes referrals concerning cultivated plants (exclusive of field crops and fruits); conducts plant breeding and research; maintains herbarium.

National Arboretum *(Agriculture Dept.), Floral and Nursery Plants Research, 3501 New York Ave. N.E., #100, 20002; (202) 245-2701. Fax, (202) 245-5973. Ramon Jordan, Associate Director.*
Web, www.ars.usda.gov/main/site_main.htm?modecode=80-20-05-05

Supports research and implementation of new technologies in florist and nursery industries. Areas of research include development of new floral, nursery, and turf plants; detection and control of pathogens in ornamental plants; ornamental plant taxonomy; improvement of nursery production systems; and curation of woody landscape plant germplasm as part of the National Plant Germplasm System.

National Museum of Natural History *(Smithsonian Institution), Botany, 10th St. and Constitution Ave. N.W., 20560-0166 (mailing address: P.O. Box 37012, MRC 166, Washington, DC 20013-7012); (202) 633-0920. Fax, (202) 786-2563. Warren L. Wagner, Department Chair. Library, (202) 633-1680.*
Web, www.botany.si.edu

Seeks to discover and describe the diversity of plant life in terrestrial and marine environments, interpret the origins of diversity, and explain the processes responsible for diversity. Research includes systematics, phylogenetics, anatomy, morphology, biogeography, and ecology. Studies how humans are affected by, and have altered, plant diversity. Works to manage, grow, and conserve the collection in the United States National Herbarium (more than 5 million specimens) as a global plant resource. Library open to the public Monday through Friday, 10:00 a.m.–4:00 p.m., by appointment only.

Smithsonian Institution, *Botany and Horticulture Library, 10th St. and Constitution Ave. N.W., #W422, 20560-0166 (mailing address: P.O. Box 37012, MRC 154, Washington, DC 20013-7012); (202) 633-1685. Fax, (202) 786-2866. Robin Everly, Branch Librarian.*
General email, askalibrarian@si.edu
Web, www.library.si.edu/libraries/botany

Collections include taxonomic botany, plant morphology, general botany, history of botany, grasses, and algae. Permits on-site use of collections (9:00 a.m.–4:30 p.m.;

appointment necessary); makes interlibrary loans. (Housed at the National Museum of Natural History.)

► CONGRESS

For a listing of relevant congressional committees and sub-committees, please see pages 646–647 or the Appendix.

U.S. Botanic Garden, *100 Maryland Ave. S.W., 20001 (mailing address: 245 1st St. S.W., Washington, DC 20024); (202) 225-8333. Fax, (202) 225-1561. Ari Novy, Executive Director, (202) 225-6670. Horticulture hotline, (202) 226-4785. Program registration information, (202) 225-1116. Special events, (202) 226-7674. Tour line, (202) 226-2055. Press, (202) 226-4145.*
General email, usbg@aoc.gov
Web, www.usbg.gov

Collects, cultivates, and grows various plants for public display and study.

► NONGOVERNMENTAL

American Society for Horticultural Science (ASHS), *1018 Duke St., Alexandria, VA 22314; (703) 836-4606. Fax, (703) 836-2024. Michael W. Neff, Executive Director, ext. 106.*
General email, webmaster@ashs.org
Web, www.ashs.org and Twitter, @ASHA_Hort

Membership: educators, government workers, firms, associations, and individuals interested in horticultural science. Promotes scientific research and education in horticulture, including international exchange of information.

American Society of Plant Biologists, *15501 Monona Dr., Rockville, MD 20855-2768; (301) 251-0560. Fax, (301) 279-2996. Crispin Taylor, Executive Director.*
General email, info@aspb.org
Web, http://my.aspb.org

Membership: plant physiologists, plant biochemists, and molecular biologists. Seeks to educate and promote public interest in the plant sciences. Publishes journals; provides job listings for members; sponsors awards, annual conference, meetings, courses, and seminars.

National Assn. of Plant Patent Owners, *525 9th St. N.W., #800, 20004; (202) 789-2900. Fax, (202) 789-1893. Craig Regelbrugge, Administrator.*
Web, www.americanhort.org

Membership: owners of patents on newly propagated horticultural plants. Informs members of plant patents issued, provisions of patent laws, and changes in practice. Promotes the development, protection, production, and distribution of new varieties of horticultural plants. Works with international organizations of plant breeders on matters of common interest. (Affiliated with AmericanHort, formerly the American Nursery and Landscape Assn.)

Zoology

► AGENCIES

National Museum of Natural History *(Smithsonian Institution), Entomology, 10th St. and Constitution Ave. N.W., 20560-0105 (mailing address: P.O. Box 37012, MRC 187, #CE-723, Washington, DC 20013-7012); (202) 633-1016. Fax, (202) 786-2894. Sean G. Brady, Chair, (202) 633-0997. Library, (202) 633-1680.*
Web, http://entomology.si.edu

Conducts worldwide research in entomology. Maintains the national collection of insects; lends insect specimens to specialists for research and classification; conducts scholarly training and lectures; publishes research; and maintains databases. Library open to the public by appointment.

National Museum of Natural History *(Smithsonian Institution), Invertebrate Zoology, 10th St. and Constitution Ave. N.W., 20560-0163 (mailing address: P.O. Box 37012, MRC 163, Washington, DC 20013-7012); (202) 633-1740. Fax, (202) 633-0182. Jon L. Norenburg, Chair. Library, (202) 633-1680.*
Web, http://invertebrates.si.edu

Conducts research on the identity, morphology, histology, life history, distribution, classification, and ecology of marine, terrestrial, and freshwater invertebrate animals (except insects); maintains the national collection of invertebrate animals; aids exhibit and educational programs; conducts predoctoral and postdoctoral fellowship programs; provides facilities for visiting scientists in the profession.

National Museum of Natural History *(Smithsonian Institution), Paleobiology, 10th St. and Constitution Ave. N.W., 20560-0121 (mailing address: P.O. Box 37012, MRC 121, Washington, DC 20013-7012); (202) 633-1328. Fax, (202) 786-2832. Hans Dieter-Sues, Chair.*
General email, paleodept@si.edu
Loans and visiting the collections, paleovisits@si.edu
Web, http://paleobiology.si.edu

Conducts research worldwide on invertebrate paleontology, paleobotany, sedimentology, and vertebrate paleontology; provides information on paleontology, paleoclimatology, paleoceanography, ecosystem dynamics, and processes of evolution and extinction. Maintains national collection of fossil organisms and sediment samples.

National Museum of Natural History *(Smithsonian Institution), Vertebrate Zoology, 10th St. and Constitution Ave. N.W., 20560-0159 (mailing address: P.O. Box 37012, MRC 163, Washington, DC 20013-7012); (202) 633-0790. Fax, (202) 633-0182. Gary R. Graves, Chair. Library, (202) 633-1680.*
Web, http://vertebrates.si.edu

Conducts research worldwide on the systematics, ecology, evolution, zoogeography, and behavior of mammals, birds, reptiles, amphibians, and fish; maintains the national collection of specimens.

►NONGOVERNMENTAL

Assn. of Zoos and Aquariums, *8403 Colesville Rd., #710, Silver Spring, MD 20910-3314; (301) 562-0777. Fax, (301) 562-0888. Jim Maddy, President.*
General email, generalinquiry@aza.org
Web, www.aza.org and Twitter, @zoos_aquariums

Membership: interested individuals and professionally run zoos and aquariums in North America. Administers professional accreditation program; participates in worldwide conservation, education, and research activities.

Entomological Society of America, *3 Park Pl., #307, Annapolis, MD 21401-3722; (301) 731-4535. Fax, (301) 731-4538. David Gammel, Executive Director.*
General email, esa@entsoc.org
Web, www.entsoc.org and Twitter, @EntsocAmerica

Scientific association that promotes the science of entomology and the interests of professionals in the field, with branches throughout the United States. Advises on crop protection, food chain, and individual and urban health matters dealing with insect pests.

Jane Goodall Institute, *1595 Spring Hill Rd., #550, Vienna, VA 22182; (703) 682-9220. Fax, (703) 682-9312. Mary Humphrey, Chief Operating Officer.*
Web, www.janegoodall.org

Seeks to increase primate habitat conservation, expand noninvasive primate research, and promote activities that ensure the well-being of primates. (Affiliated with Jane Goodall Institutes in Canada, Europe, Asia, and Africa.)

ENGINEERING

General

►AGENCIES

National Institute of Standards and Technology (NIST) *(Commerce Dept.), Center for Nanoscale Science and Technology, 100 Bureau Dr., MS 6200, Gaithersburg, MD 20899-6200; (301) 975-8001. Fax, (301) 975-8026. Robert J. Celotta, Director.*
General email, cnst@nist.gov
Web, www.nist.gov/cnst

Provides nanoscale measurement and fabrication methods and access to nanoscale construction technologies to NIST labs, universities, and industries. Offers researchers training and use of in-house nanotechnology tools. Researches nanoscale measurement instruments and methods, and promotes collaboration and shared use.

National Institute of Standards and Technology (NIST) *(Commerce Dept.), Engineering Laboratory, 100 Bureau Dr., MS 8600, Gaithersburg, MD 20899-8600; (301) 975-5900. Fax, (301) 975-4032. Howard H. Harary, Director.*
General email, el@nist.gov
Web, www.nist.gov/el

Performs analytical, laboratory, and field research in the area of building technology and its applications for building usefulness, safety, and economy; produces performance criteria and evaluation, test, and measurement methods for building owners, occupants, designers, manufacturers, builders, and federal, state, and local regulatory authorities.

National Science Foundation (NSF), *Engineering Directorate, 4201 Wilson Blvd., #505N, Arlington, VA 22230; (703) 292-8300. Fax, (703) 292-9013. Pramid Khargonekar, Assistant Director.*
Web, www.nsf.gov/dir/index.jsp?org=eng

Directorate that supports fundamental research and education in engineering through grants and special equipment awards. Programs are designed to enhance international competitiveness and to improve the quality of engineering in the United States.

►NONGOVERNMENTAL

American Assn. of Engineering Societies, *1801 Alexander Bell Dr., Reston, VA 20191; (202) 296-2237. Fax, (202) 296-1151. Wendy B. Cowan, Executive Director. Toll-free, (888) 400-2237.*
Web, www.aaes.org

Federation of engineering societies; member associations are in industry, construction, government, academia, and private practice. Advances the knowledge, understanding, and practice of engineering. Serves as delegate to the World Federation of Engineering Organizations.

American Council of Engineering Companies, *1015 15th St. N.W., 8th Floor, 20005-2605; (202) 347-7474. Fax, (202) 898-0068. David A. Raymond, President.*
General email, acec@acec.org
Web, www.acec.org

Membership: practicing consulting engineering firms and state, local, and regional consulting engineers councils. Serves as an information clearinghouse for member companies in such areas as legislation, legal cases, marketing, management, professional liability, business practices, and insurance. Monitors legislation and regulations.

American Society for Engineering Education, *1818 N St. N.W., #600, 20036-2479; (202) 331-3500. Fax, (202) 265-8504. Norman L. Fortenberry, Executive Director, (202) 331-3545. Press, (202) 331-3537.*
Web, www.asee.org

Membership: engineering faculty and administrators, professional engineers, government agencies, and engineering colleges, corporations, and professional societies. Conducts research, conferences, and workshops on engineering education. Monitors legislation and regulations.

American Society of Civil Engineers (ASCE), *1801 Alexander Bell Dr., Reston, VA 20191-4400; Washington Office, 101 Constitution Ave., #375E, 20001; (202) 789-7850. Fax, (202) 789-7859. Thomas W. Smith III, Executive Director. Toll-free, (800) 548-2723. Press, (703) 295-6406.*
Web, www.asce.org and Twitter, @ascetweets

Membership: professionals and students in civil engineering. Develops standards by consensus for construction documents and building codes, and standards for civil engineering education, licensure, and ethics. Organizes international conferences; maintains technical and professional reference materials; hosts e-learning sites. Advocates improvements in public infrastructure; monitors legislation and regulations.

American Society of Mechanical Engineers (ASME), *Government Relations,* 1828 L St. N.W., #810, 20036-5104; (202) 785-3756. Fax, (202) 429-9417.
Kathryn Holmes, Director, Government Relations, (202) 785-7390.
General email, grdept@asme.org
Web, www.asme.org and Twitter, @ASMEdotorg

Serves as a clearinghouse for sharing of information between the federal government and the engineering profession. Monitors legislation and regulations. (Headquarters in New York.)

Geoprofessional Business Assn., 1300 Piccard Dr., #LL14, Rockville, MD 20850; (301) 565-2733. Fax, (301) 589-2017.
Gordon Matheson, Executive Director; Joel G. Carson, President.
General email, info@geoprofessional.org
Web, www.asfe.org and Twitter, @GBAssn

Membership: geoprofessional service firms, including firms that perform geotechnical and infrastructure engineering, environmental services, and construction materials engineering and testing. Conducts seminars and a peer review program on quality control policies and procedures in geoprofessional service firms. (Formerly the Assn. of Soil and Foundation Engineers.)

Institute of Electrical and Electronics Engineers–USA (IEEE-USA), *Washington Office,* 2001 L St. N.W., #700, 20036; (202) 785-0017. Fax, (202) 785-0835.
Chris Brantley, Managing Director.
General email, ieeeusa@ieee.org
Web, www.ieeeusa.org

U.S. arm of an international technological and professional organization concerned with all areas of electrotechnology policy, including aerospace, computers, communications, biomedicine, electric power, and consumer electronics. (Headquarters in New York.)

International Test and Evaluation Assn., 4400 Fair Lakes Court, #104, Fairfax, VA 22033-3801; (703) 631-6220. Fax, (703) 631-6221. James M. Gaidry, Executive Director, ext. 204.
General email, info@itea.org
Web, www.itea.org

Membership: engineers, scientists, managers, and other industry, government, and academic professionals interested in testing and evaluating products and complex systems. Provides a forum for information exchange; monitors international research.

National Academy of Engineering, 500 5th St. N.W., 20001; (202) 334-3200. Fax, (202) 334-2158. C.D. Mote Jr., President.
Web, www.nae.edu and Twitter, @NAE_DC

Society whose members are elected in recognition of important contributions to the field of engineering and technology. Shares responsibility with the National Academy of Sciences for examining questions of science and technology at the request of the federal government; promotes international cooperation. (Affiliated with the National Academy of Sciences.)

National Research Council (NRC), *Infrastructure and the Constructed Environment Board,* Keck Center, 500 5th St. N.W., #WS938, 20001; (202) 334-3505. Fax, (202) 334-3718. Rear Adm. David J. Nash (USN, Ret.), Chair.
General email, bice@nas.edu
Web, http://sites.nationalacademies.org/deps

Advises the government, private sector, and the public on technology, science, and public policy related to the design, construction, operations, maintenance, security, and evaluation of buildings, facilities, and infrastructure systems; the relationship between the constructed and natural environments and their interaction with human activities; the effects of natural and manmade hazards on constructed facilities and infrastructure; and the interdependencies of infrastructure systems, including power, water, transportation, telecommunications, wastewater, buildings.

National Research Council (NRC), *National Material and Manufacturing Board,* Keck Center, 500 5th St. N.W., #WS921, 20001; (202) 334-3505.
Fax, (202) 334-3575. James Lancaster, Director; Robert Schafrik, Chair.
General email, nmmb@nas.edu
Web, http://sites.nationalacademies.org/DEPS/NMMB

Conducts research on materials and manufacturing, including at the atomic, molecular, and nano scales, and innovative applications of new and existing materials, including pilot-scale and large-scale manufacturing, the design of new devices, and disposal.

National Society of Black Engineers, 205 Daingerfield Rd., Alexandria, VA 22314; (703) 549-2207. Fax, (703) 683-5312. Karl Reid, Executive Director.
General email, info@nsbe.org
Web, www.nsbe.org

Membership: college students studying engineering. Offers academic excellence programs, scholarships, leadership training, and professional and career development opportunities. Activities include tutorial programs, group study sessions, high school/junior high outreach programs, technical seminars and workshops, career fairs, and an annual convention.

National Society of Professional Engineers (NSPE), 1420 King St., Alexandria, VA 22314-2794; (703) 684-2800.

Fax, (703) 836-4875. Mark Golden, Executive Director.
Member services, (888) 285-6773.
General email, memserv@nspe.org

Web, www.nspe.org

Membership: U.S.-licensed professional engineers from all disciplines. Holds engineering seminars; operates an information center.

ENVIRONMENTAL AND EARTH SCIENCES

General

▶AGENCIES

National Aeronautics and Space Administration (NASA),
Science Mission Directorate, 300 E St. S.W., #3J28, 20546;
(202) 358-3889. Fax, (202) 358-3092. John Grunsfeld,
Associate Administrator.
General email, science@hq.nasa.gov

Web, http://science.nasa.gov/about-us/organization-and-leadership

Seeks to understand the integrated functioning of the earth and the sun. Administers space mission programs and mission-enabling programs, including sub-orbital missions. Sponsors scientific research and analysis. Exchanges information with the international science community. Interests include earth climate and environmental change.

National Oceanic and Atmospheric Administration
(NOAA) *(Commerce Dept.), Central Library, Library and*
Information Services, 1315 East-West Hwy., SSMC3, 2nd
Floor, Silver Spring, MD 20910; (301) 713-2600.
Fax, (301) 713-4598. Stanley Elswick, Director, Acting.
Reference service, (301) 713-2600, ext. 157. TTY, (301)
713-2779.
General email, library.reference@noaa.gov

Web, www.lib.noaa.gov

Collection includes electronic NOAA documents, reports, and videos; electronic and print journals; the NOAA Photo Library; bibliographic database of other NOAA libraries; and climate data. Makes interlibrary loans; library open to the public, with two forms of photo ID, Monday through Friday, 9:00 a.m.–4:00 p.m.

National Oceanic and Atmospheric Administration
(NOAA) *(Commerce Dept.), National Centers for*
Environmental Information, 1315 East-West Hwy.,
SSMC3, 4th Floor, Silver Spring, MD 20910-3282; (301)
713-3277. Fax, (301) 713-3302. Margarita Conkright
Gregg, Director, (301) 713-4840.
General email, nodc.services@noaa.gov

Web, www.nodc.noaa.gov

Responsible for hosting and providing access to comprehensive oceanic, atmospheric, and geophysical data. Provides world's largest collection of freely available oceanographic data, including water temperatures dating back to the late 1700s and measuring thousands of meters deep, scientific journals, rare books, historical photo collections, and maps through the NOAA Central Library, and data management expertise and training. Merger of NOAA's three data centers: National Climatic Data Center, National Geophysical Data Center, and National Oceanographic Data Center, which includes the National Coastal Data Development Center.

National Science Foundation (NSF), *Geosciences*
Directorate, 4201 Wilson Blvd., #705N, Arlington, VA
22230; (703) 292-8500. Fax, (703) 292-9042.
Roger Wakimoto, Assistant Director.
Web, www.nsf.gov/div/index.jsp?org=geo

Directorate that supports research about the earth, including its atmosphere, continents, oceans, and interior. Works to improve the education and human resource base for the geosciences; participates in international and multidisciplinary activities, especially to study changes in the global climate.

National Science Foundation (NSF), *Polar Programs*
Division, 4201 Wilson Blvd., #755S, Arlington, VA 22230;
(703) 292-8030. Fax, (703) 292-9081. Kelly K. Falkner,
Director.
Web, www.nsf.gov/div/index.jsp?div=plr

Funds and manages U.S. activity in Antarctica; provides grants for arctic programs in polar biology and medicine, earth sciences, atmospheric sciences, meteorology, ocean sciences, and glaciology. The Polar Information Program serves as a clearinghouse for polar data and makes referrals on specific questions.

Smithsonian Environmental Research Center
(Smithsonian Institution), *647 Contees Wharf Rd.,*
Edgewater, MD 21037 (mailing address: P.O. Box 28,
Edgewater, MD 21037-0028); (443) 482-2200. Fax, (443)
482-2380. Anson H. Hines, Director, (443) 482-2208.
Press, (443) 482-2325.
Web, www.serc.si.edu

Performs laboratory and field research that measures physical, chemical, and biological interactions to determine the mechanisms of environmental responses to humans' use of air, land, and water. Evaluates properties of the environment that affect the functions of living organisms. Maintains research laboratories, public education program, facilities for controlled environments, and estuarine and terrestrial lands. Wildlife sanctuary open to the public Monday through Saturday, 9:00 a.m.–4:30 p.m., except federal holidays.

U.S. Geological Survey (USGS) *(Interior Dept.), 12201*
Sunrise Valley Dr., MS 100, Reston, VA 20192-0002; (703)
648-4000. Fax, (703) 648-4454. Suzette M. Kimball,
Director, (703) 648-7412. Information, 888-ASK-USGS.
Library, (703) 648-7182. Press, (703) 648-4460.
General email, servicedesk@usgs.gov

Web, www.usgs.gov and Twitter, @USGS

Provides reports, maps, and databases that describe and analyze water, energy, biological, and mineral resources; the land surface; and the underlying geological structure and dynamic processes of the Earth.

U.S. Geological Survey (USGS) *(Interior Dept.), Climate and Land Use Change, 12201 Sunrise Valley Dr., MS 516, Reston, VA 20192; (703) 648-4215. Fax, (703) 648-7031. Virginia Burkett, Associate Director for Climate and Land Use Change.*
Web, www.usgs.gov/climate_landuse

Researches the effects of climate and land use change on natural resources. Methods include monitoring, modeling, and forecasting. Operates the Landsat satellites. Provides coordination, technical support, and funding for existing research programs. Provides research products to policymakers, natural resources managers, and the general public.

U.S. Geological Survey (USGS) *(Interior Dept.), Library Services, 950 National Center, #1D100, Reston, VA 20192 (mailing address: 12201 Sunrise Valley Dr., #1D100, MS 950, Reston, VA 20192); (703) 648-4301. Fax, (703) 648-6373. Cate Canevari, Director, (703) 648-7182.*
General email, library@usgs.gov
Web, http://library.usgs.gov

Maintains collection of books, periodicals, serials, maps, and technical reports on geology, mineral and water resources, mineralogy, paleontology, petrology, soil and environmental sciences, biology, and physics and chemistry as they relate to natural sciences. Open to the public; makes interlibrary loans.

United States Arctic Research Commission, *4350 N. Fairfax Dr., #510, Arlington, VA 22203; (703) 525-0111. Fax, (703) 525-0114. John W. Farrell, Executive Director, (703) 525-0113.*
General email, info@arctic.gov
Web, www.arctic.gov

Presidential advisory commission that develops policy for arctic research; assists the interagency Arctic Research Policy Committee in implementing a national plan of arctic research; recommends improvements in logistics, data management, and dissemination of arctic information.

► **CONGRESS**

For a listing of relevant congressional committees and subcommittees, please see pages 646–647 or the Appendix.

► **NONGOVERNMENTAL**

American Geophysical Union, *2000 Florida Ave. N.W., 20009-1277; (202) 462-6900. Fax, (202) 328-0566. Christine McEntee, Executive Director; Margaret Leinen, President. Information, (800) 966-2481.*
General email, service@agu.org
Web, www.agu.org

Membership: scientists and technologists who study the environments and components of the earth, sun, and solar system. Promotes international cooperation; disseminates information.

National Research Council (NRC), *Polar Research Board, Keck Center, 500 5th St. N.W., #602, 20001; (202) 334-3479. Fax, (202) 334-3825. Julie Brigham-Grette, Chair; Amanda Staudt, Director, (202) 334-3512.*
General email, prb@nas.edu
Web, http://dels.nas.edu/prb

Promotes polar science and provides scientific guidance to federal agencies and the nation on issues in the Arctic, the Antarctic, and cold regions in general.

Atmospheric Sciences

► **AGENCIES**

National Oceanic and Atmospheric Administration (NOAA) *(Commerce Dept.), 1401 Constitution Ave. N.W., #5128, 20230; (202) 482-3436. Fax, (202) 408-9674. Kathryn D. Sullivan, Under Secretary. Library, (301) 713-2600. Press, (202) 482-6090.*
Web, www.noaa.gov

Conducts research in marine and atmospheric sciences; issues weather forecasts and warnings vital to public safety and the national economy; maintains a national environmental center with data from satellite observations and other sources, including meteorological, oceanic, geodetic, and seismological data centers; provides colleges and universities with grants for research, education, and marine advisory services; prepares and provides nautical and aeronautical charts and maps.

National Oceanic and Atmospheric Administration (NOAA) *(Commerce Dept.), Climate Program Office, 1315 East-West Hwy., SSMC-3, Room. 12124, Silver Spring, MD 20910; (301) 734-1263. Fax, (301) 713-0515. Wayne Higgins, Director.*
General email, oar.cpo.office@noaa.gov
Web, www.cpo.noaa.gov

Manages NOAA-funded research programs that focus on climate science and assessments on a regional, national, and international scale.

National Oceanic and Atmospheric Administration (NOAA) *(Commerce Dept.), National Weather Service, 1325 East-West Hwy., #18150, Silver Spring, MD 20910; (301) 713-9095. Fax, (301) 713-0610. Louis W. Uccellini, Assistant Administrator. Library, (301) 683-1307. National Weather Service forecast office, (703) 260-0101.*
Web, www.weather.gov

Issues warnings of hurricanes, severe storms, and floods; provides weather forecasts and services for the general public and for aviation and marine interests.

National Oceanic and Atmospheric Administration (NOAA) *(Commerce Dept.), National Weather Service, Climate Prediction Center, 5830 University Research*

Court, College Park, MD 20740; (301) 683-3427.
Mike S. Halpert, Deputy Director.
Web, www.cpc.ncep.noaa.gov

Provides climate forecasts, assesses the impact of short-term climate variability, and warns of potentially extreme climate-related events.

National Oceanic and Atmospheric Administration (NOAA) *(Commerce Dept.), National Weather Service, National Centers for Environmental Prediction, 5830 University Research Court, College Park, MD 20740; (301) 683-1314. Fax, (301) 683-1325. Bill Lapenta, Director.*
Web, www.ncep.noaa.gov

The National Center for Environmental Prediction and the National Environmental Satellite, Data, and Information Service are part of the World Weather Watch Programme developed by the United Nations World Meteorological Organization. Collects and exchanges data with other nations; provides other national weather service offices, private meteorologists, and government agencies with products, including forecast guidance products.

National Oceanic and Atmospheric Administration (NOAA) *(Commerce Dept.), Oceanic and Atmospheric Research, 1315 East-West Hwy., Silver Spring, MD 20910; (301) 713-2458. Craig N. McLean, Assistant Administrator.*
Web, http://research.noaa.gov and Twitter, @NOAAResearch

Researches weather and water information in order to provide better forecasts and earlier warnings for natural disasters. Works to protect, restore, and manage coastal and ocean resources through ecosystem-based management. Promotes the understanding of climate change and variability.

National Science Foundation (NSF), *Atmospheric and Geospace Sciences Division, 4201 Wilson Blvd., #775S, Arlington, VA 22230; (703) 292-8520. Fax, (703) 292-9022. Paul B. Shepson, Division Director.*
Web, www.nsf.gov/div/index.jsp?div=ags

Supports research on the earth's atmosphere and the sun's effect on it, including studies of the physics, chemistry, and dynamics of the earth's upper and lower atmospheres and its space environment; climate processes and variations; and the natural global cycles of gases and particles in the earth's atmosphere.

Office of Science *(Energy Dept.), Biological and Environmental Research, Climate and Environmental Sciences Division, 19901 Germantown Rd., #SC23.1, Germantown, MD 20874-1290 (mailing address: Germantown Bldg., 1000 Independence Ave. S.W., #SC23.1, Washington, DC 20585); (301) 903-4775. Gerald Geernaert, Director.*
Web, http://science.energy.gov/ber/research/cesd

Supports research on atmospheric systems, terrestrial ecosystems, and subsurface biogeochemistry as well as Earth system modeling and regional and global climate change modeling to improve predictive understanding of Earth's climate and environmental systems in order to inform development of sustainable solutions to energy challenges.

▶**NONGOVERNMENTAL**

Alliance for Responsible Atmospheric Policy, *2111 Wilson Blvd., #850, Arlington, VA 22201; (703) 243-0344. Fax, (703) 243-2874. Kevin Fay, Executive Director.*
General email, info@arap.org
Web, www.arap.org

Coalition of users and producers of chlorofluorocarbons (CFCs). Seeks further study of the ozone depletion theory.

Climate Institute, *1400 16th St. N.W., #430, 20036; (202) 552-0163. John C. Topping, President.*
General email, info@climate.org
Web, www.climate.org

Educates the public and policymakers on climate change, the greenhouse effect, global warming, and the depletion of the ozone layer. Assesses climate change risks and develops strategies on mitigating climate change in developing countries and in North America.

National Research Council (NRC), *Atmospheric Sciences and Climate Board, Keck Center, 500 5th St. N.W., #602, 20001; (202) 334-3512. Fax, (202) 334-3825. Amanda Staudt, Director; A.R. Ravishankara, Chair.*
General email, basc@nas.edu
Web, http://nas.edu/basc

Supports research on climate change, air pollution, and severe weather in order to address environmental policies, human health, emergency management, energy choices, manufacturing decisions, construction codes, and agricultural methods.

Geology and Earth Sciences

▶**AGENCIES**

National Museum of Natural History *(Smithsonian Institution), Mineral Sciences, 10th St. and Constitution Ave. N.W., 4th Floor, East Wing, 20560 (mailing address: P.O. Box 37012, MRC 119, Washington, DC 20013-7012); (202) 633-1860. Fax, (202) 357-2476. Jeffrey Post, Chair. Library, (202) 633-1680.*
Web, www.mineralsciences.si.edu

Conducts research on gems, minerals, meteorites, rocks, and ores. Interests include mineralogy, petrology, volcanology, and geochemistry. Maintains the Global Volcanism Network, which reports worldwide volcanic and seismic activity. Library open to the public by appointment.

National Museum of Natural History *(Smithsonian Institution), Paleobiology, 10th St. and Constitution Ave. N.W., 20560-0121 (mailing address: P.O. Box 37012, MRC 121, Washington, DC 20013-7012); (202) 633 1328. Fax, (202) 786-2832. Hans Dieter-Sues, Chair.*
General email, paleodept@si.edu
Loans and visiting the collections, paleovisits@si.edu
Web, http://paleobiology.si.edu

Conducts research worldwide on invertebrate paleontology, paleobotany, sedimentology, and vertebrate paleontology; provides information on paleontology, paleoclimatology, paleoceanography, ecosystem dynamics, and processes of evolution and extinction. Maintains national collection of fossil organisms and sediment samples.

National Science Foundation (NSF), *Earth Sciences Division, 4201 Wilson Blvd., #785, Arlington, VA 22230; (703) 292-8550. Fax, (703) 292-9025. Carol Frost, Division Director.*
Web, www.nsf.gov/div/index.jsp?div=ear

Provides grants for research in geology, geophysics, geochemistry, and related fields, including tectonics, hydrologic sciences, and continental dynamics.

Office of Science *(Energy Dept.), Biological and Environmental Research, Climate and Environmental Sciences Division, 19901 Germantown Rd., #SC23.1, Germantown, MD 20874-1290 (mailing address: Germantown Bldg., 1000 Independence Ave. S.W., #SC23.1, Washington, DC 20585); (301) 903-4775. Gerald Geernaert, Director.*
Web, http://science.energy.gov/ber/research/cesd

Supports research on atmospheric systems, terrestrial ecosystems, and subsurface biogeochemistry as well as Earth system modeling and regional and global climate change modeling to improve predictive understanding of Earth's climate and environmental systems in order to inform development of sustainable solutions to energy challenges.

U.S. Geological Survey (USGS) *(Interior Dept.), Earthquake Hazards, 12201 Sunrise Valley Dr., MS905, Reston, VA 20192 (mailing address: 905 National Center, Reston, VA 20192); (703) 648-6786. Fax, (703) 648-6717. William Leith, Senior Science Advisor.*
Web, http://earthquake.usgs.gov

Manages geologic, geophysical, and engineering investigations, including assessments of hazards from earthquakes; conducts research on the mechanisms and occurrences of earthquakes worldwide and their relationship to the behavior of the crust and upper mantle; develops methods for predicting the time, place, and magnitude of earthquakes; conducts engineering and geologic studies on ground failures.

U.S. Geological Survey (USGS) *(Interior Dept.), Geological Mapping, 12201 Sunrise Valley Dr., MS 908, Reston, VA 20192; (703) 648-6943. Fax, (703) 648-6937. Peter T. Lyttle, Program Coordinator.*
Web, http://ncgmp.usgs.gov

Funds the production of geologic maps in the United States. Provides geologic mapping data from across North America to public and private organizations.

U.S. Geological Survey (USGS) *(Interior Dept.), Global Seismographic Network, 12201 Sunrise Valley Dr., MS 905, Reston, VA 20192; (703) 648-6714. Fax, (703) 648-6717. Cicily Wolfe, Associate Program Coordinator.*
Web, http://earthquake.usgs.gov/monitoring/gsn

Monitors and researches seismic activity globally through a network of seismological and geophysical sensors.

U.S. Geological Survey (USGS) *(Interior Dept.), Land Change Science Program, 12201 Sunrise Valley Dr., MS 516, Reston, VA 20192; (703) 648-4516. Fax, (703) 648-5542. Jonathan H. Smith, Program Coordinator.*
Web, http://usgs.gov/climate_landuse/lcs

Collects, analyzes, and disseminates information about natural and human-induced changes to the Earth's surface to better understand the causes and consequences of land cover change. Develops methods and processes for the use of land-surface science in public policy.

U.S. Geological Survey (USGS) *(Interior Dept.), Volcano Hazards, 12201 Sunrise Valley Dr., MS 904, Reston, VA 20192; (703) 648-4773. Fax, (703) 648-5483. Charles W. Mandeville, Program Coordinator.*
Web, http://volcanoes.usgs.gov

Manages geologic, geophysical, and engineering investigations, including assessments of hazards from volcanoes; conducts research worldwide on the mechanisms of volcanoes and on igneous and geothermal systems. Issues warnings of potential volcanic hazards.

▶**NONGOVERNMENTAL**

American Geosciences Institute, *4220 King St., Alexandria, VA 22302-1502; (703) 379-2480. Fax, (703) 379-7563. P. Patrick Leahy, Executive Director.*
General email, agi@americangeosciences.org
Web, www.agiweb.org

Membership: earth science societies and associations. Maintains a computerized database with worldwide information on geology, engineering and environmental geology, oceanography, and other geological fields (available to the public for a fee).

National Research Council (NRC), *Earth Sciences and Resources Board, Keck Center, 500 5th St. N.W., #616, 20001; (202) 334-2744. Fax, (202) 334-1377. Elizabeth A. Eide, Director; Gene Whitney, Chair.*
General email, besr@nas.edu
Web, http://dels.nas.edu/besr

Coordinates activities, oversees research, and advises policymakers on solid-earth sciences issues. Interests include geography, geological and geotechnical engineering, mapping, and seismology and geodynamics.

Oceanography

▶**AGENCIES**

National Museum of Natural History *(Smithsonian Institution), Botany, 10th St. and Constitution Ave. N.W., 20560-0166 (mailing address: P.O. Box 37012, MRC 166, Washington, DC 20013-7012); (202) 633-0920. Fax, (202) 786-2563. Warren L. Wagner, Department Chair. Library, (202) 633-1680.*
Web, www.botany.si.edu

Investigates the biology, evolution, and classification of tropical and subtropical marine algae and seagrasses. Acts as curator of the national collection in this field. Develops and participates in scholarly programs. Library open to the public Monday through Friday, 10:00 a.m.–4:00 p.m., by appointment only.

National Museum of Natural History *(Smithsonian Institution), Invertebrate Zoology, 10th St. and Constitution Ave. N.W., 20560-0163 (mailing address: P.O. Box 37012, MRC 163, Washington, DC 20013-7012); (202) 633-1740. Fax, (202) 633-0182. Jon L. Norenburg, Chair. Library, (202) 633-1680.*
Web, http://invertebrates.si.edu

Conducts research on the identity, morphology, histology, life history, distribution, classification, and ecology of marine, terrestrial, and freshwater invertebrate animals (except insects); maintains the national collection of invertebrate animals; aids exhibit and educational programs; conducts predoctoral and postdoctoral fellowship programs; provides facilities for visiting scientists in the profession.

National Museum of Natural History *(Smithsonian Institution), Library, 10th St. and Constitution Ave. N.W., East Court, 1st Floor, 20560-0154 (mailing address: P.O. Box 37012, MRC 154, Washington, DC 20013-7012); (202) 633-1680. Gil Taylor, Head, Acting.*
General email, askalibrarian@si.edu
Web, www.library.si.edu/libraries/national-museum-natural-history-library

Maintains reference collections covering anthropology, biodiversity, biology, botany, ecology, entomology, ethnology, mineral sciences, paleobiology, and zoology; permits on-site use of the collections. Open to the public by appointment; makes interlibrary loans.

National Museum of Natural History *(Smithsonian Institution), Vertebrate Zoology, 10th St. and Constitution Ave. N.W., 20560-0159 (mailing address: P.O. Box 37012, MRC 163, Washington, DC 20013-7012); (202) 633-0790. Fax, (202) 633-0182. Gary R. Graves, Chair. Library, (202) 633-1680.*
Web, http://vertebrates.si.edu

Processes, sorts, and distributes to scientists specimens of marine vertebrates; engages in taxonomic sorting, community analysis, and specimen and sample data management.

National Oceanic and Atmospheric Administration (NOAA) *(Commerce Dept.), 1401 Constitution Ave. N.W., #5128, 20230; (202) 482-3436. Fax, (202) 408-9674. Kathryn D. Sullivan, Under Secretary. Library, (301) 713-2600. Press, (202) 482-6090.*
Web, www.noaa.gov

Conducts research in marine and atmospheric sciences; issues weather forecasts and warnings vital to public safety and the national economy; maintains a national environmental center with data from satellite observations and other sources, including meteorological, oceanic, geodetic, and seismological data centers; provides colleges and universities with grants for research, education, and marine advisory services; prepares and provides nautical and aeronautical charts and maps.

National Oceanic and Atmospheric Administration (NOAA) *(Commerce Dept.), Marine and Aviation Operations, 8403 Colesville Rd., #500, Silver Spring, MD 20910-3282; (301) 713-1045. Fax, (301) 713-1541. Rear Adm. David A. Score, Director. Press, (301) 713-7671.*
Web, www.omao.noaa.gov

Uniformed service of the Commerce Dept. that operates and manages NOAA's fleet of atmospheric, hydrographic, oceanographic, and fisheries research ships and aircraft. Supports NOAA's scientific programs.

National Oceanic and Atmospheric Administration (NOAA) *(Commerce Dept.), National Ocean Service, 1305 East-West Hwy., SSMC4, #9149, Silver Spring, MD 20910; (301) 713-3074. Fax, (301) 713-4269. Russell Callender, Assistant Administrator, Acting. Press, (301) 713-3066.*
General email, nos.info@noaa.gov
Web, www.oceanservice.noaa.gov

Manages charting and geodetic services, oceanography and marine services, coastal resource coordination, and marine survey operations; conducts environmental cleanup of coastal pollution.

National Science Foundation (NSF), *Ocean Sciences Division, 4201 Wilson Blvd., #725N, Arlington, VA 22230; (703) 292-8580. Fax, (703) 292-9085. Richard W. Murray, Director.*
Web, www.nsf.gov/div/index.jsp?div=oce

Awards grants and contracts for acquiring, upgrading, and operating oceanographic research facilities that lend themselves to shared usage. Facilities supported include ships, submersibles, and shipboard and shorebased data logging and processing equipment. Supports development of new drilling techniques and systems.

U.S. Geological Survey (USGS) *(Interior Dept.), Coastal and Marine Geology Program, 12201 Sunrise Valley Dr., MS 905, Reston, VA 20192; (703) 648-6422. Fax, (703) 648-5464. John W. Haines, Program Coordinator.*
Web, http://marine.usgs.gov

Surveys the continental margins and the ocean floor to provide information on the mineral resources potential of submerged lands.

▶ **NONGOVERNMENTAL**

Marine Technology Society, *1100 H St. N.W., #LL-100, 20005; (202) 717-8705. Fax, (202) 347-4302. Chris Barrett, Executive Director, Acting.*
General email, membership@mtsociety.org
Web, www.mtsociety.org

Membership: scientists, engineers, technologists, and others interested in marine science and technology. Provides information on marine science, technology, and education.

National Ocean Industries Assn., *1120 G St. N.W., #900, 20005; (202) 347-6900. Fax, (202) 347-8650. Randall Luthi, President.*
General email, noia@noia.org
Web, www.noia.org

Membership: manufacturers, producers, suppliers, and support and service companies involved in marine, offshore, and ocean work. Interests include offshore oil and gas supply and production, deep-sea mining, ocean thermal energy, and new energy sources.

National Research Council (NRC), *Ocean Studies Board, Keck Center, 500 5th St. N.W., MS 607, 20001; (202) 334-2714. Fax, (202) 334-2885. Susan Roberts, Director; Larry A. Mayer, Chair.*
General email, osbfeedback@nas.edu
Web, http://dels.nas.edu/osb

Conducts research to understand, manage, and conserve coastal and marine environments. Areas of interest include the ocean's role in the global climate system, technology and infrastructure needs for ocean research, ocean-related aspects of national security; fisheries science and management, and ocean education.

MATHEMATICAL, COMPUTER, AND PHYSICAL SCIENCES

General

▶AGENCIES

National Institute of Standards and Technology (NIST) *(Commerce Dept.), 100 Bureau Dr., Bldg. 101, #A1134, Gaithersburg, MD 20899-1000 (mailing address: 100 Bureau Dr., MS 1000, Gaithersburg, MD 20899); (301) 975-2300. Fax, (301) 869-8972. Willie E. May, Director. TTY, (800) 877-8339.*
General email, director@nist.gov
Web, www.nist.gov/director/index.cfm

Nonregulatory agency that serves as national reference and measurement laboratory for the physical and engineering sciences. Works with industry, government agencies, and academia; promotes U.S. innovation and industrial competitiveness. Research interests include advanced manufacturing, information technology and cybersecurity, energy, health care, environment and consumer safety, and physical infrastructure.

National Institute of Standards and Technology (NIST) *(Commerce Dept.), Information Technology Lab, 100 Bureau Dr., Bldg. 225, #B264, MS 8900, Gaithersburg, MD 20899-8900; (301) 975-2900. Fax, (301) 975-2378. Charles (Chuck) H. Romine, Director.*
General email, itl_inquiries@nist.gov
Web, www.nist.gov/itl

Collaborates in mathematical, statistical, and computer sciences with other institute laboratories, other federal agencies, the U.S. private sector, standards development organizations, and other national and international stakeholders; provides consultations, methods, and research supporting the institute's scientific and engineering projects.

National Institutes of Health (NIH) *(Health and Human Services Dept.), Center for Information Technology, 10401 Fernwood Rd., Bethesda, MD 20817; (301) 496-5703. Fax, (301) 402-1754. Andrea T. Norris, Director.*
Web, http://cit.nih.gov

Serves as the primary scientific and technological resource for the NIH in the areas of high performance computing, database applications, mathematics, statistics, laboratory automation, engineering, computer science and technology, telecommunications, and information resources management.

National Science Foundation (NSF), *Mathematical and Physical Sciences Directorate, 4201 Wilson Blvd., #1005N, Arlington, VA 22230; (703) 292-8800. Fax, (703) 292-9151. F. Fleming Crim, Assistant Director.*
Web, www.nsf.gov/dir/index.jsp?org=mps

Directorate that supports research in the mathematical and physical sciences; divisions focus on physics, chemistry, materials research, mathematical sciences, and astronomical sciences. Works to improve the education and human resource base for these fields; participates in international and multidisciplinary activities.

Office of Science *(Energy Dept.), Basic Energy Sciences, 19901 Germantown Rd., #SC22, Germantown, MD 20874-1290 (mailing address: Germantown Bldg., 1000 Independence Ave. S.W., #SC22, Washington, DC 20585); (301) 903-3081. Fax, (301) 903-6594. Harriet Kung, Director.*
General email, sc.bes@science.doe.gov
Web, http://science.energy.gov/bes

Supports research to understand, predict, and control matter and energy at electronic, atomic, and molecular levels to provide foundations for new energy technology.

▶NONGOVERNMENTAL

Carnegie Institute for Science, *1530 P St. N.W., 20005-1910; (202) 387-6400. Fax, (202) 387-8092. Matthew P. Scott, President.*
Web, www.carnegiescience.edu and Twitter, @carnegiescience

Conducts research in plant science biology, genetic and developmental biology, earth and planetary sciences, astronomy, and global ecology and matter at extreme states at the Carnegie Institution's six research departments: Dept. of Embryology (Baltimore, Md.); Geophysical Laboratory (Washington, D.C.); Dept. of Global Ecology (Stanford, Calif.); Dept. of Plant Biology (Stanford, Calif.); Dept. of Terrestrial Magnetism (Washington, D.C.); and The Observatories (Pasadena, Calif., and Las Campanas, Chile).

National Research Council (NRC), *Human-Systems Integration Board,* Keck Center, 500 5th St. N.W., 11th Floor, 20001; (202) 334-2678. Fax, (202) 334-2210. Poornima Madhavan, Director, (202) 334-3357; Nancy J. Cooke, Chair.
General email, bohsi@nas.edu

Web, http://sites.nationalacademies.org/dbasse/bohsi

Conducts studies on human factors and human-systems integration. Areas of research include virtual reality, human-computer interaction, nuclear safety, air traffic control, military simulation, modeling social networks, home health care, and disability and rehabilitation research.

Chemistry

▶AGENCIES

National Institute of Standards and Technology (NIST) *(Commerce Dept.), Center for Neutron Research,* 100 Bureau Dr., Bldg. 235, MS 6100, Gaithersburg, MD 20899-8100; (301) 975-6210. Fax, (301) 869-4770. Robert Dimeo, Director.
General email, ncnr@nist.gov

Web, www.nist.gov/ncnr/index.cfm

Provides neutron measurement capabilities to the U.S. research community, universities, and industry.

National Science Foundation (NSF), *Chemistry Division,* 4201 Wilson Blvd., #1055, Arlington, VA 22230; (703) 292-8840. Fax, (703) 292-9037. Carol Bessel, Director, Acting.
Web, www.nsf.gov/div/index.jsp?div=che

Awards grants to research programs in organic and macromolecular chemistry, experimental and theoretical physical chemistry, analytical and surface chemistry, and inorganic, bioinorganic, and organometallic chemistry; provides funds for instruments needed in chemistry research; coordinates interdisciplinary programs. Monitors international research.

National Science Foundation (NSF), *Materials Research Division,* 4201 Wilson Blvd., #1065N, Arlington, VA 22230; (703) 292-8810. Fax, (703) 292-9035. Linda Sapochak, Director, Acting, (703) 292-8562.
Web, www.nsf.gov/div/index.jsp?div=dmr

Provides grants for research in condensed matter physics; solid-state and materials, chemistry, polymers, metallic materials and nanostructures, ceramics, electronic and photonic materials and condensed matter and materials theory. Supports multidisciplinary research in these areas through Materials Research Science and Engineering Centers (MRSEC) and national facilities such as the National High Magnetic Field Laboratory (NHMFL) and Synchrotron Radiation Center (SRC); funds major instrumentation projects as well as the acquisition and development of instrumentation for research to create new or advance current capabilities; and encourages international collaboration to positively impact the global advancement of materials research.

▶NONGOVERNMENTAL

American Assn. for Clinical Chemistry, 900 7th St. N.W., 20001; (202) 857-0717. Fax, (202) 887-5093. Janet Kreizman, Chief Executive Officer. Toll-free, (800) 892-1400.
General email, info@aacc.org

Web, www.aacc.org

International society of chemists, physicians, and other scientists specializing in clinical chemistry. Provides educational and professional development services; presents awards for outstanding achievement. Monitors legislation and regulations.

American Chemical Society, 1155 16th St. N.W., 20036; (202) 872-4600. Fax, (202) 872-4615. Thomas M. Connelly, Executive Director. Information, (800) 227-5558. Library, (202) 872-4513. Press, (202) 872-6042.
General email, help@acs.org

Web, www.acs.org

Membership: professional chemists and chemical engineers. Maintains educational programs, including those that evaluate college chemistry departments and high school chemistry curricula. Administers grants and fellowships for basic research; sponsors international exchanges; presents achievement awards. Library open to the public by appointment.

American Chemical Society, *Petroleum Research Fund,* 1155 16th St. N.W., 20036; (202) 872-4481. Fax, (202) 872-6319. Dean A. Dunn, Administrator, (202) 872-4083.
General email, prfinfo@acs.org

Web, www.acsprf.org

Makes grants to nonprofit institutions for advanced scientific education and fundamental research related to the petroleum industry in chemistry, geology, and engineering.

American Chemistry Council, 700 2nd St. N.E., 20002; (202) 249-7000. Fax, (202) 249-6100. Calvin (Cal) M. Dooley, President.
Web, www.americanchemistry.com

Membership: manufacturers of basic industrial chemicals. Provides members with technical research, communications services, and legal affairs counseling. Sponsors research on chemical risk assessments, biomonitoring, and nanotechnology. Interests include environmental safety and health, transportation, energy, and international trade and security. Monitors legislation and regulations.

AOAC International, 2275 Research Blvd., #300, 20850-3250; (301) 924-7077. Fax, (301) 924-7089. E. James Bradford, Executive Director. Information, (800) 379-2622.
General email, aoac@aoac.org

Web, www.aoac.org

International association of analytical science professionals, companies, government agencies, nongovernmental organizations, and institutions. Supports the standards and method development, evaluation, and publication of reliable chemical and biological methods of analysis for foods, drugs, feed, fertilizers, pesticides, water, and other substances.

National Research Council (NRC), *Chemical Sciences and Technology Board,* *Keck Center, 500 5th St. N.W., 20001; (202) 334-2156. Fax, (202) 334-1393. Teresa Fryberger, Director.*
General email, bcst@nas.edu
Web, http://dels.nas.edu/bcst

Advises policymakers and decisionmakers about matters related to chemistry and chemical engineering.

Society of Chemical Manufacturers and Affiliates (SOCMA), *1850 M St. N.W., #700, 20036-5810; (202) 721-4100. Fax, (202) 296-8120. Lawrence (Larry) D. Sloan, President.*
General email, info@socma.com
Web, www.socma.com

Membership: companies that manufacture, distribute, and market organic chemicals; producers of chemical components; and providers of custom chemical services. Interests include international trade, environmental and occupational safety, chemical security, and health issues; conducts workshops and seminars. Promotes commercial opportunities for members. Monitors legislation and regulations.

Computer Sciences

▶**AGENCIES**

National Coordination Office for Networking and Information Technology Research and Development, *4121 Wilson Blvd., #II-405, Arlington, VA 22230 (mailing address: 4201 Wilson Blvd., #II-405, Arlington, VA 22230); (703) 292-4873. Fax, (703) 292-9097. Keith Marzullo, Director.*
General email, nco@nitrd.gov
Web, www.nitrd.gov

Coordinates multi-agency research and development projects that involve computing, communications, and technology research and development. Reports to the National Science and Technology Council; provides information to Congress, U.S. and foreign organizations, and the public.

National Institute of Standards and Technology (NIST) (Commerce Dept.), *Information Technology Lab, 100 Bureau Dr., Bldg. 225, #B264, MS 8900, Gaithersburg, MD 20899-8900; (301) 975-2900. Fax, (301) 975-2378. Charles (Chuck) H. Romine, Director.*
General email, itl_inquiries@nist.gov
Web, www.nist.gov/itl

Collaborates with other institute laboratories, other federal agencies, the U.S. private sector, standards development organizations, and other national and international stakeholders in the development and application of new information technologies to help meet national priorities; develops and deploys standards, tests, and metrics to assure

secure, reliable, and interoperable information systems; collaborates to develop cybersecurity standards, guidelines, and techniques for federal agencies and U.S. industry; conducts research in computer science and technology.

National Science Foundation (NSF), *Advanced Cyberinfrastructure Division, 4201 Wilson Blvd., #1145S, Arlington, VA 22230; (703) 292-8970. Fax, (703) 292-9060. Irene Qualters, Director.*
Web, www.nsf.gov/div/index.jsp?div=aci

Supports the development of computing and information infrastructure and helps advance all science and engineering domains. Infrastructure is made accessible to researchers and educators nationwide. Interests include computing and communication, network systems, cyberinfrastructure, and information and intelligent systems.

National Science Foundation (NSF), *Computer and Information Science and Engineering Directorate, 4201 Wilson Blvd., #1105N, Arlington, VA 22230; (703) 292-8900. Fax, (703) 292-9074. James Kurose, Assistant Director.*
Web, www.nsf.gov/dir/index.jsp?org=cise

Supports investigator-initiated research in computer science and engineering. Promotes the use of advanced computing, communications, and information systems. Provides grants for research and education.

National Science Foundation (NSF), *Computer and Network Systems Division, 4201 Wilson Blvd., #1175N, Arlington, VA 22230; (703) 292-8950. Fax, (703) 292-9010. Peter Arsberger, Director, Acting.*
Web, www.nsf.gov/div/index.jsp?div=CNS

Supports research and education activities that strive to create new computing and networking technologies and that explore new ways to utilize existing technologies. Seeks to foster the creation of better abstractions and tools for designing, building, analyzing, and measuring future systems. Supports the computing infrastructure that is required for experimental computer science and coordinates cross-divisional activities that foster integration of research and education and broadening of participation in the computer, information science, and engineering (CISE) workforce. Awards grants.

National Science Foundation (NSF), *Computing and Communication Foundations Division, 4201 Wilson Blvd., #1115N, Arlington, VA 22230; (703) 292-8910. Fax, (703) 292-9059. S. Rao Kosaraju, Division Director.*
Web, www.nsf.gov/div/index.jsp?div=ccf

Supports research and educational activities exploring the foundations of computing and communication devices and their usage. Seeks advances in computing and communication theory, algorithms for computer and computational sciences, and architecture and design of computers and software. Awards grants.

National Science Foundation (NSF), *Information and Intelligent Systems Division, 4201 Wilson Blvd., #1125S, Arlington, VA 22230; (703) 292-8930. Fax, (703) 292-9073. Lynne E. Parker, Director.*
Web, www.nsf.gov/div/index.jsp?div=iis

Supports research and education that develops new knowledge about the role people play in the design and use of information technology; advances the ability to represent, collect, store, organize, visualize, and communicate about data and information; and advances knowledge about how computational systems can perform tasks autonomously, robustly, and with flexibility. Awards grants.

Office of Science *(Energy Dept.), Advanced Scientific Computing Research,* 19901 Germantown Rd., #SC21, Germantown, MD 20874-1290 (mailing address: Germantown Bldg., 1000 Independence Ave. S.W., #SC21, Washington, DC 20585); (301) 903-7486. Fax, (301) 903-4846. J. Steve Binkley, Associate Director.
General email, sc.ascr@science.doe.gov

Web, http://science.energy.gov/ascr

Supports mathematical, computational, and computer science research on behalf of the Energy Dept.

▶ **NONGOVERNMENTAL**

American Council for Technology and Industry Advisory Council (ACT/IAC), 3040 Williams Dr., #500, Fairfax, VA 22031; (703) 208-4800. Fax, (703) 208-4805. Kenneth Allen, Executive Director.
General email, act-iac@actgov.org

Web, www.actgov.org

Brings government and industry IT executives together to enhance government's ability to use information technologies. Activities include conferences, white papers, professional development programs, and other events to foster education, the exchange of information, and collaboration.

Center for Strategic and International Studies, *Strategic Technologies Program,* 1616 Rhode Island Ave. N.W., 20036; (202) 775-3175. Fax, (202) 775-3199. James A. Lewis, Director.
General email, techpolicy@csis.org

Web, www.csis.org/program/technology-and-public-policy

Conducts and publishes research on emerging technologies, intelligence reform, and space and globalization programs.

CompTIA, *Public Advocacy,* 515 2nd St. N. E., 20002; (202) 682-9110. Fax, (202) 682-9111. Todd Thibodeaux, President; Elizabeth (Liz) Hyman, Executive Vice President, Public Advocacy. Press, (202) 682-4458.
General email, techvoice@comptia.org

Web, www.comptia.org

Trade association for technology companies offering hardware, software, electronics, telecommunications, and information technology products and services. Offers business services and networking programs to members. Monitors legislation and regulations. (Headquarters in Downers Grove, Ill.)

Computer and Communications Industry Assn. (CCIA), 900 17th St. N.W., #1100, 20006; (202) 783-0070.

Fax, (202) 783-0534. Edward J. Black, President; Heather Greenfield, Director of Communications.
General email, hgreenfield@ccianet.org

Web, www.ccianet.org and Twitter, @ccianet

Membership: Internet service providers, software providers, and manufacturers and suppliers of computer data processing and communications-related products and services. Interests include Internet freedom, privacy and neutrality, government electronic surveillance, telecommunications policy, tax policy, federal procurement policy, communications and computer industry standards, intellectual property policies, encryption, international trade, and antitrust reform.

Information Technology Industry Council (ITI), 1101 K St. N.W., #610, 20005; (202) 737-8888. Fax, (202) 638-4922. Dean C. Garfield, President. Press, (202) 524-5543.
General email, info@itic.org

Web, www.itic.org and Twitter, @ITI_TechTweets

Membership: providers of information and communications technology products and services. Acts as advocate for member companies in the areas of privacy, immigration reform, cybersecurity, intellectual property, tax reform, telecommunications, STEM education, trade, accessibility, voluntary standards, sustainability, and internet governance

Institute of Electrical and Electronics Engineers–USA (IEEE-USA), *Washington Office,* 2001 L St. N.W., #700, 20036; (202) 785-0017. Fax, (202) 785-0835. Chris Brantley, Managing Director.
General email, ieeeusa@ieee.org

Web, www.ieeeusa.org

U.S. arm of an international technological and professional organization. Interests include computing and information technology and promoting career and technology policy interests of members. (Headquarters in New York.)

National Research Council (NRC), *Computer Science and Telecommunications Board,* Keck Center, 500 5th St. N.W., 20001; (202) 334-2605. Fax, (202) 334-2318. Farnam Jahanian, Chair, (412) 268-3363; Jon Eisenberg, Director, (202) 334-2605.
General email, cstb@nas.edu

Web, http://sites.nationalacademies.org/CSTB

Advises the federal government on technical and public policy issues relating to computing and communications. Research includes computer science, cybersecurity, privacy, the Internet, and electronic voting and voter registration.

Society for Imaging Science and Technology, 7003 Kilworth Lane, Springfield, VA 22151; (703) 642-9090. Fax, (703) 642-9094. Suzanne E. Grinnan, Executive Director.
General email, info@imaging.org

Web, www.imaging.org

Membership: individuals and companies worldwide in fields of imaging science and technology, including digital printing, electronic imaging, color science, image preservation, photo finishing, prepress technology, and hybrid imaging. Gathers and disseminates technical information; fosters professional development.

Software and Information Industry Assn. (SIIA), *1090 Vermont Ave. N.W., 6th Floor, 20005; (202) 289-7442. Fax, (202) 289-7097. Kenneth (Ken) Wasch, President, (202) 789-4440.*
Web, www.siia.net

Membership: software and digital content companies. Promotes the industry worldwide; conducts antipiracy program and other intellectual property initiatives; sponsors conferences, seminars, and other events. Monitors legislation and regulations.

Mathematics

▶AGENCIES

National Institute of Standards and Technology (NIST) *(Commerce Dept.), Information Technology Lab, 100 Bureau Dr., Bldg. 225, #B264, MS 8900, Gaithersburg, MD 20899-8900; (301) 975-2900. Fax, (301) 975-2378. Charles (Chuck) H. Romine, Director.*
General email, itl_inquiries@nist.gov
Web, www.nist.gov/itl/index.cfm

Seeks to develop applied and computational mathematics to solve problems arising in measurement science and engineering applications; collaborates with NIST and external scientists; disseminates related reference data and software; develops and applies statistical and probabilistic methods and techniques supporting research in measurement science, technology, and the production of standard reference materials.

National Science Foundation (NSF), *Mathematical and Physical Sciences Directorate, 4201 Wilson Blvd., #1005N, Arlington, VA 22230; (703) 292-8800. Fax, (703) 292-9151. F. Fleming Crim, Assistant Director.*
Web, www.nsf.gov/dir/index.jsp?org=mps

Provides grants for research in the mathematical sciences in the following areas: classical and modern analysis, geometric analysis, topology and foundations, algebra and number theory, applied and computational mathematics, and statistics and probability. Maintains special projects program, which supports scientific computing equipment for mathematics research and several research institutes. Sponsors conferences, workshops, and postdoctoral research fellowships. Monitors international research.

National Science Foundation (NSF), *Mathematical Sciences Division, 4201 Wilson Blvd., Room 1025N, Arlington, VA 22230; (703) 292-8870. Fax, (703) 292-9032. Michael Vogelius, Director.*
Web, www.nsf.gov/div/index.jsp?org=DMS

Supports research on the properties and applications of mathematical structures

▶NONGOVERNMENTAL

American Statistical Assn., *732 N. Washington St., Alexandria, VA 22314-1943; (703) 684-1221. Fax, (703) 684-2037. Ronald Wasserstein, Executive Director. Toll-free, (888) 231-3473.*
General email, asainfo@amstat.org
Web, www.amstat.org

Membership: statistical practitioners in industry, government, and academia. Supports excellence in the development, application, and dissemination of statistical science through meetings, publications, membership services, education, accreditation, and advocacy.

Conference Board of the Mathematical Sciences, *1529 18th St. N.W., 20036; Ronald C. Rosier, Director.*
Web, www.cbmsweb.org

Membership: presidents of seventeen mathematical sciences professional societies. Serves as a forum for discussion of issues of concern to the mathematical sciences community.

Mathematical Assn. of America, *1529 18th St. N.W., 20036-1358; (202) 387-5200. Fax, (202) 265-2384. Michael Pearson, Executive Director. Information, (800) 741-9415.*
General email, maahq@maa.org
Web, www.maa.org

Membership: mathematics professors and individuals worldwide with a professional interest in mathematics. Seeks to improve the teaching of collegiate mathematics. Conducts professional development programs.

National Research Council (NRC), *Mathematical Sciences and their Applications Board, Keck Center, 500 5th St. N.W., #K974, 20001; (202) 334-2421. Fax, (202) 334-2422. Scott T. Weidman, Director; Donald Saari, Chair.*
General email, bmsa@nas.edu
Web, http://sites.nationalacademies.org/DEPS/BMSA

Leads NRC mathematical sciences activities. Main interests include, core mathematics, applied mathematics, statistics, operations research, scientific computing, and financial and risk analysis.

Physics

▶AGENCIES

National Science Foundation (NSF), *Materials Research Division, 4201 Wilson Blvd., #1065N, Arlington, VA 22230; (703) 292-8810. Fax, (703) 292-9035. Linda Sapochak, Director, Acting, (703) 292-8562.*
Web, www.nsf.gov/div/index.jsp?div=dmr

Provides grants for research in condensed matter physics; solid-state and materials, chemistry, polymers, metallic materials and nanostructures, ceramics, electronic and photonic materials and condensed matter and materials theory. Supports multidisciplinary research in these areas through Materials Research Science and Engineering Centers (MRSEC) and national facilities such as the National High Magnetic Field Laboratory (NHMFL) and Synchrotron Radiation Center (SRC); funds major instrumentation projects as well as the acquisition and development of instrumentation for research to create new or advance current capabilities; and encourages international collaboration to positively impact the global advancement of materials research.

National Science Foundation (NSF), *Physics Division,* *4201 Wilson Blvd., #1015N, Arlington, VA 22230; (703) 292-8890. Fax, (703) 292-9078. Denise Caldwell, Director, (703) 292-7371.*
Web, www.nsf.gov/div/index.jsp?div=phy

Awards grants for research and special programs in atomic, molecular, and optical physics; elementary particle physics; and nuclear, theoretical, and gravitational physics.

Office of Science *(Energy Dept.),* *High Energy Physics,* *Germantown Bldg., 1000 Independence Ave. S.W., #SC25, 20585; (301) 903-3624. Fax, (301) 903-2597. James L. Siegrist, Associate Director.*
General email, sc.hep@science.doe.gov
Web, http://science.energy.gov/hep

Provides grants and facilities for research in high energy (or particle) physics. Constructs, operates, and maintains particle accelerators used in high energy research.

Office of Science *(Energy Dept.),* *Nuclear Physics, 19901 Germantown Rd., #SC26, Germantown, MD 20874-1290 (mailing address: Germantown Bldg., 1000 Independence Ave. S.W., #SC26, Washington, DC 20585); (301) 903-3613. Fax, (301) 903-3833. Timothy J. Hallman, Associate Director.*
General email, sc.np@science.doe.gov
Web, http://science.energy.gov/np

Provides grants and facilities for research in nuclear physics. Manages the nuclear data program. Develops, constructs, and operates accelerator facilities and detectors used in nuclear physics research.

▶ **NONGOVERNMENTAL**

American Institute of Physics, *1 Physics Ellipse, College Park, MD 20740-3843; (301) 209-3100. Fax, (301) 209-3133. Robert G. W. Brown, Executive Director, (301) 209-3131.*
Web, www.aip.org

Fosters cooperation within the physics community; improves public understanding of science; disseminates information on scientific research.

American Institute of Physics, *Center for History of Physics, 1 Physics Ellipse, College Park, MD 20740-3843; (301) 209-3100. Fax, (301) 209-0882. Gregory Good, Director. Library, (301) 209-3177.*
General email, chp@aip.org
Web, www.aip.org/history-programs

Records and preserves the history of modern physics and allied fields, including astronomy, meteorological studies, and optics. Maintains a documentation program containing interviews, unpublished data, and historical records and photographs. Manages the Niels Bohr Library, which is open to the public.

American Physical Society, *Washington Office, 529 14th St. N.W., #1050, 20045-2065; (202) 662-8700. Fax, (202) 662-8711. Michael Lubell, Director, Public Affairs. Press Secretary, (202) 662-8702.*
General email, opa@aps.org
Web, www.aps.org and Twitter, @APSphysics

Scientific and educational society of educators, students, citizens, and scientists, including industrial scientists. Sponsors studies on issues of public concern related to physics, such as reactor safety and energy use. Informs members of national and international developments. (Headquarters in College Park, Md.)

National Research Council (NRC), *Physics and Astronomy Board, Keck Center, 500 5th St. N.W., 20001; (202) 334-3520. Fax, 202-34-3575. Michael S. Witherell, Chair; James Lancaster, Director.*
General email, bpa@nas.edu
Web, http://sites.nationalacademies.org/BPA

Provides information to the government and public on scientific matters relating to physics and astronomy, including atomic, molecular, and optical sciences, astronomy and astrophysics, plasma science, radio frequencies, and condensed matter and materials.

The Optical Society, *2010 Massachusetts Ave. N.W., 20036; (202) 223-8130. Fax, (202) 223-1096. Elizabeth Rogan, Chief Executive Officer.*
General email, info@osa.org
Web, www.osa.org

Membership: global optics and photonic scientists, engineers, educators, students, technicians, business professionals, and others interested in optics and photonics worldwide. Promotes research and information exchange; conducts conferences; publishes a scientific journal; sponsors technical groups and programming as well as outreach and educational activities.

Weights and Measures, Metric System

▶ **AGENCIES**

National Institute of Standards and Technology (NIST) *(Commerce Dept.), Material Measurement Laboratory, 100 Bureau Dr., Bldg. 227, #A311, MS 8300, Gaithersburg, MD 20899-8300; (301) 975-8300. Fax, (301) 975-3845. Laurie E. Locasio, Director.*
General email, mmlinfo@nist.gov
Web, www.nist.gov/mml

Serves as the national reference laboratory for measurements in the chemical, biological, and material sciences. Researches industrial, biological, and environmental materials and processes to support development in manufacturing, nanotechnology, electronics, energy, health care, law enforcement, food safety, and other areas.

Disseminates reference measurement procedures, certified reference materials, and best-practice guides.

National Institute of Standards and Technology (NIST) *(Commerce Dept.), Physical Measurement Laboratory,* *100 Bureau Dr., Bldg. 221, #B160, MS 8400, Gaithersburg, MD 20899-8400; (301) 975-4200. Fax, (301) 975-3038. James K. Olthoff, Director.*
Web, www.nist.gov/pml

Develops and disseminates national standards of measurement for length, mass, force, acceleration, time, wavelength, frequency, humidity, and radiation.

National Institute of Standards and Technology (NIST) *(Commerce Dept.), Quantum Measurement Division,* *100 Bureau Dr., MS 8420, Gaithersburg, MD 20899-8420; (301) 975-2220. Fax, (301) 990-3038. Carl J. Williams, Chief. General email, carl.williams@nist.gov*
Web, www.nist.gov/pml/div684

Applies research to advance measurement instrumentation and the efficiency of electric power transmission and distribution; develops and maintains national electrical reference standards, primarily for power, energy, and related measurements.

National Institute of Standards and Technology (NIST) *(Commerce Dept.), Weights and Measures, 100 Bureau Dr., MS 2600, Gaithersburg, MD 20899-2600; (301) 975-4004. Fax, (301) 975-8091. Carol Hockert, Chief; Barbara Turner, Public Relations. General email, owm@nist.gov*
Web, www.nist.gov/pml/wmd

Promotes uniformity in weights and measures law and enforcement. Provides weights and measures agencies with training and technical assistance; assists state and local agencies in adapting their weights and measures to meet national standards; conducts research; sets uniform standards and regulations. As the U.S. representative to the International Organization of Legal Metrology, works to harmonize international standards and regulatory practices.

National Institute of Standards and Technology (NIST) *(Commerce Dept.), Weights and Measures, Laws and Metric Group, 100 Bureau Dr., MS 2600, Gaithersburg, MD 20899-2600; (301) 975-4004. Fax, (301) 975-8091. Kenneth S. Butcher, Group Leader. General email, owm@nist.gov*
Web, www.nist.gov/metric

Coordinates federal metric conversion transition to ensure consistency in the interpretation and enforcement of packaging, labeling, net content, and other laws; provides the public with technical and general information about the metric system; assists state and local governments, businesses, and educators with metric conversion activities.

▶**CONGRESS**

For a listing of relevant congressional committees and subcommittees, please see pages 646–647 or the Appendix.

SOCIAL SCIENCES

General

▶**AGENCIES**

National Institutes of Health (NIH) *(Health and Human Services Dept.), Behavioral and Social Sciences Research,* *31 Center Dr., Bldg. 31, #B1C19, Bethesda, MD 20892-0183; (301) 402-1146. Fax, (301) 402-1150. William Riley, Director, Acting.*
Web, http://obssr.od.nih.gov

Works to advance behavioral and social sciences training, to integrate a biobehavioral perspective across the NIH, and to improve communication among scientists and with the public. Develops funding initiatives for research and training. Sets priorities for research. Provides training and career development opportunities for behavioral and social scientists. Links minority students with mentors. Organizes cultural workshops and lectures.

National Museum of Natural History *(Smithsonian Institution), Anthropology, 10th St. and Constitution Ave. N.W., 20560-0112 (mailing address: P.O. Box 37012, MRC 112, Washington, DC 20013-7012); (202) 633-1920. Fax, (202) 357-2208. Torrey Rick, Director. Library, (202) 633-1680. General Smithsonian information, (202) 633-1000.*
Web, http://anthropology.si.edu

Studies humanity, past and present. Research tools include human-environmental interactions, population migrations, origins of domestication and agriculture, endangered languages and knowledge, and physical and forensic anthropology. Maintains archaeological, ethnographic, and skeletal biology collections; the National Anthropological Archive; the Human Studies Film Archives; and public exhibitions of human cultures.

National Museum of Natural History *(Smithsonian Institution), Library, 10th St. and Constitution Ave. N.W., East Court, 1st Floor, 20560-0154 (mailing address: P.O. Box 37012, MRC 154, Washington, DC 20013-7012); (202) 633-1680. Gil Taylor, Head, Acting. General email, askalibrarian@si.edu*
Web, www.library.si.edu/libraries/national-museum-natural-history-library

Maintains reference collections covering anthropology, biodiversity, biology, botany, ecology, entomology, ethnology, mineral sciences, paleobiology, and zoology; permits on-site use of the collections. Open to the public by appointment; makes interlibrary loans.

National Science Foundation (NSF), *Social, Behavioral, and Economic Sciences Directorate, 4201 Wilson Blvd., #905N, Arlington, VA 22230; (703) 292-8700. Fax, (703) 292-9083. Fay Cook, Assistant Director.*
Web, www.nsf.gov/dir/index.jsp?org=SBE

Directorate that awards grants for research in behavioral and cognitive sciences, social and economic sciences, science resources studies, and international programs. Provides support for workshops, symposia, and conferences.

▶NONGOVERNMENTAL

American Anthropological Assn., *2300 Claredon Blvd., #1301, Arlington, VA 22201; (703) 528-1902. Fax, (703) 528-3546. Edward Liebow, Executive Director.*
Web, www.aaanet.org

Membership: anthropologists, educators, students, and others interested in anthropological studies. Publishes research studies of member organizations, sponsors workshops, and disseminates to members information concerning developments in anthropology worldwide.

American Institutes for Research, *1000 Thomas Jefferson St. N.W., 20007; (202) 403-5000. Fax, (202) 403-5001. David Myers, President. TTY, (877) 334-3499. Media, (202) 403-6043.*
General email, inquiry@air.org
Web, www.air.org and Twitter, @AIR_Info

Conducts behavioral and social science research and provides technical assistance both domestically and internationally in the areas of education, health, and workforce productivity.

American Psychological Assn., *750 1st St. N.E., 20002-4242; (202) 336-5500. Fax, (202) 336-5502. Cynthia Belar, Chief Executive Officer, Acting. Library, (202) 336-5640. Toll-free, (800) 374-2721. TTY, (202) 336-6123.*
Web, www.apa.org and Twitter, @APA

Membership: professional psychologists, educators, and behavioral research scientists. Supports research, training, and professional services; works toward improving the qualifications, competence, and training programs of psychologists. Monitors international research and U.S. legislation on mental health. Library open to the public by appointment.

American Psychosomatic Society, *6728 Old McLean Village Dr., McLean, VA 22101-3906; (703) 556-9222. Fax, (703) 556-8729. Laura E. Degnon, Executive Director.*
General email, info@psychosomatic.org
Web, www.psychosomatic.org and Twitter, @connectAPS

Advances and disseminates scientific understanding of relationships among biological, psychological, social, and behavioral factors in medicine through publications, annual meetings, conferences, and interest groups.

American Sociological Assn., *1430 K St. N.W., #600, 20005; (202) 383-9005. Fax, (202) 638-0882. Sally T. Hillsman, Executive Officer. TTY, (202) 638-0981.*
General email, customer@asanet.org
Web, www.asanet.org

Membership: sociologists, social scientists, and others interested in research, teaching, and application of sociology in the United States and internationally. Sponsors professional development program, teaching resources center, and education programs; offers congressional fellowships for sociologists with a PhD or substantial work experience, and predoctoral sociology fellowships for minorities.

The Brookings Institution, *1775 Massachusetts Ave. N.W., 20036; (202) 797-6000. Fax, (202) 797-6004. Strobe Talbott, President. Press, (202) 797-6105.*
General email, communications@brookings.edu
Web, www.brookings.edu and Twitter, @Brookingsinst

Public policy research organization that seeks to improve the performance of American institutions, the effectiveness of government programs, and the quality of public policy through research and analysis. Sponsors lectures, debates, and policy forums.

Consortium of Social Science Assns., *1701 K St. N.W., #1150, 20006; (202) 842-3525. Fax, (202) 842-2788. Wendy A. Naus, Executive Director.*
General email, cossa@cossa.org
Web, www.cossa.org and Twitter, @COSSADC

Consortium of more than 100 associations, scientific societies, universities, research centers, and institutions in the fields of criminology, economics, history, political science, psychology, sociology, statistics, geography, linguistics, law, and social science. Advocates support for research and monitors federal funding in the social and behavioral sciences; conducts seminars; publishes a biweekly electronic newsletter.

Human Resources Research Organization (HumRRO), *66 Canal Center Plaza, #700, Alexandria, VA 22314-1578; (703) 549-3611. Fax, (703) 549-9025. William J. Strickland, President.*
Web, www.humrro.org

Studies, designs, develops, surveys, and evaluates personnel systems, chiefly in the workplace. Interests include personnel selection and promotion, career progression, performance appraisal, training, program evaluation, leadership assessment, and human capital analytics.

Institute for the Study of Man, *P.O. Box 34143, 20043; (202) 266-9908. Fax, (202) 371-1523. Roger Pearson, Executive Director.*
General email, iejournal@aol.com
Web, www.jies.org

Publishes the *Journal of Indo-European Studies* and other academic journals, books, and monographs in areas related to Indo-European anthropology, archaeology, linguistics, cultural history, and mythology. Sponsors seminars.

National Research Council (NRC), *Behavioral, Cognitive, and Sensory Sciences Board, Keck Center, 500 5th St. N.W., 11th Floor, 20001; (202) 334-2678. Fax, (202) 334-3584. Barbara A. Wanchisen, Director, (202) 334-2394; Susan T. Fiske, Chair.*
General email, BBCSS@nas.edu
Web, http://nas.edu/bbcss

Membership: experts in the fields of cognition, human development, sensory sciences, social psychology, cognitive neuroscience, behavioral neuroscience, social neuroscience, medical ethics, evolutionary and economic anthropology, and health psychology. Advises government

National Aeronautics and Space Administration

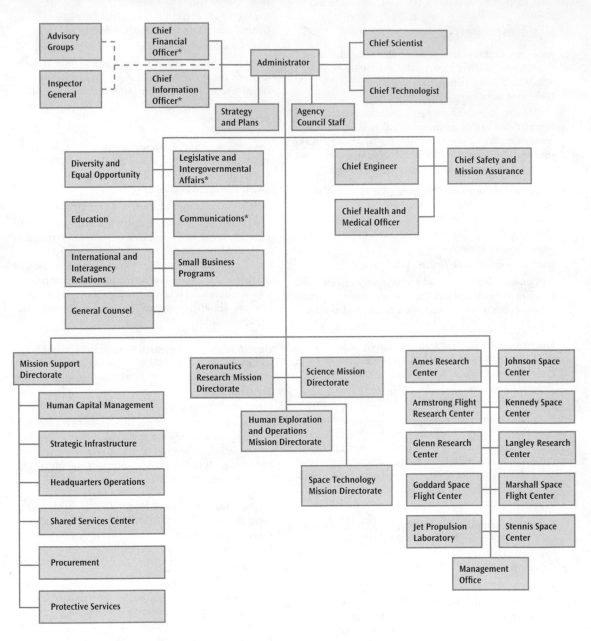

* Center functional office directors report to Agency Associate Administrator. Deputy and below report to center leadership.
– – – – Operate Independently

agencies on policies relating to the behavioral, cognitive, and sensory sciences.

National Research Council (NRC), *Children, Youth, and Families Board,* Keck Center, 500 5th St. N.W., 20001; (202) 334-2300. Fax, (202) 334-2201. Angela Diaz, Chair; Natacha Blain, Director.
General email, bcyf@nas.edu
Web, http://sites.nationalacademies.org/dbasse/bcyf

Interdiscipinary scientific body seeking to analyze the challenges and critical issues facing children, youth, and families. Interests include the intersection of poverty, education, and life expectancy.

Pew Research Center, 1615 L St. N.W., #700, 20036; (202) 419-4300. Fax, (202) 419-4349. Michael Dimock, President. Media, (202) 419-4372.
General email, info@pewresearch.org
Web, www.pewresearch.org

Nonpartisan research organization that studies issues of public interest in America and around the world. Conducts public opinion polling and social science research; reports news; analyzes news coverage; and holds forums and briefings.

Pew Research Center, *Social and Demographic Trends Project,* *1615 L St. N.W., #700, 20036; (202) 419-4372. Fax, (202) 419-4349. Kim Parker, Director. Media, (202) 419-4372.*
Web, www.pewsocialtrends.org

Studies behaviors and attitudes of Americans in key realms of their daily lives, using original survey research and analysis of government data. Topics of study include the racial wealth gap, the millennial generation, population geography, demographics, immigration, and marriage and family needs.

Geography and Mapping

►**AGENCIES**

Bureau of Intelligence and Research *(State Dept.),* *Office of the Geographer and Global Issues, 2201 C St. N.W., #6722, 20520; (202) 647-2021. Lee R. Schwartz, Director.*
Web, www.state.gov

Advises the State Dept. and other federal agencies on geographic and cartographic matters. Furnishes technical and analytical research and advice in the field of geography.

Census Bureau *(Commerce Dept.), Geography, 4600 Silver Hill Rd., 4th Floor, Suitland, MD 20746 (mailing address: 4600 Silver Hill Rd., 4th Floor, Washington, DC 20233-7400); (301) 763-1128. Fax, (301) 763-4710. Timothy F. Trainor, Chief.*
General email, geo.geography@census.gov
Web, www.census.gov/geo

Manages the MAF TIGER system, a nationwide geographic and address database; prepares maps for use in conducting censuses and surveys and for showing their results geographically; determines names and current boundaries of legal geographic units; defines names and boundaries of selected statistical areas; develops geographic code schemes; maintains computer files of area measurements, geographic boundaries, and map features with address ranges.

National Archives and Records Administration (NARA), *Cartographic and Architectural Unit, 8601 Adelphi Rd., #3320, College Park, MD 20740-6001; (301) 837-3200. Fax, (301) 837-3622. Deborah Lelansky, Cartographic Supervisor, (301) 837-1911.*
General email, carto@nara.gov
Web, www.archives.gov/dc-metro/college-park/researcher-info.html#cartographic

Makes information available on federal government cartographic records, architectural drawings, and aerial mapping films; prepares descriptive guides and inventories

of records. Research room open to the public. Records may be reproduced for a fee.

National Geospatial-Intelligence Agency *(Defense Dept.), 7500 Geoint Dr., Springfield, VA 22150-7500; 4600 Sangamore Rd., Bethesda, MD 20816-5003; (571) 557-5400. Fax, (571) 558-3169. Robert Cardillo, Director. Maps and imagery products, (571) 557-5400.*
General email, publicaffairs@nga.mil
Web, www.nga.mil, Twitter, @NGA_GEOINT and Facebook, www.facebook.com/NatlGEOINTAgency

Combat support agency that develops imagery and map-based intelligence in support of national defense objectives.

National Oceanic and Atmospheric Administration (NOAA) *(Commerce Dept.), National Geodetic Survey, 1315 East-West Hwy., SSMC-3, #9340, Silver Spring, MD 20910-3282; (301) 713-3242. Fax, (301) 713-4172. Juliana P. Blackwell, Director.*
General email, ngs.infocenter@noaa.gov
Web, http://geodesy.noaa.gov

Develops and maintains the National Spatial Reference System, a national geodetic reference system that serves as a common reference for latitude, longitude, height, scale, orientation, and gravity measurements. Maps the nation's coastal zone and waterways; conducts research and development programs to improve the collection, distribution, and use of spatial data; coordinates the development and application of new surveying instrumentation and procedures.

National Oceanic and Atmospheric Administration (NOAA) *(Commerce Dept.), National Ocean Service, Coast Survey, 1315 East-West Hwy., #6147, SSMC3, Silver Spring, MD 20910-3282; (301) 713-2770. Fax, (301) 713-4019. Rear Adm. Gerd F. Glang, Director. Toll-free, (888) 990-6622.*
Web, www.nauticalcharts.noaa.gov and Twitter, @NOAAcharts

Directs programs and conducts research to support fundamental scientific and engineering activities and resource development for safe navigation of the nation's waterways and territorial seas. Prints on demand and distributes nautical charts.

U.S. Board on Geographic Names, *12201 Sunrise Valley Dr., MS 523, Reston, VA 20192-0523 (mailing address: 523 National Center, Reston, VA 20192); (703) 648-4552. Fax, (703) 648-4549. Louis (Lou) Yost, Executive Secretary.*
General email, bgnexec@usgs.gov
Web, http://geonames.usgs.gov

Interagency organization established by Congress to standardize geographic names used by the U.S. government. Board members are representatives from the departments of Agriculture, Commerce, Defense, Homeland Security, Interior, and State; the Central Intelligence Agency; the Government Printing Office; the Library of Congress; and the U.S. Postal Service. Sets policy governing the use of both domestic and foreign geographic names as well as underseas feature names and Antarctic feature names. (Affiliated with the U.S. Geological Survey.)

U.S. Geological Survey (USGS) *(Interior Dept.), 12201 Sunrise Valley Dr., MS 100, Reston, VA 20192-0002; (703) 648-4000. Fax, (703) 648-4454. Suzette M. Kimball, Director, (703) 648-7412. Information, 888-ASK-USGS. Library, (703) 648-7182. Press, (703) 648-4460. General email, servicedesk@usgs.gov*

Web, www.usgs.gov and Twitter, @USGS

Provides reports, maps, and databases that describe and analyze water, energy, biological, and mineral resources; the land surface; and the underlying geological structure and dynamic processes of the Earth.

U.S. Geological Survey (USGS) *(Interior Dept.), Geological Mapping, 12201 Sunrise Valley Dr., MS 908, Reston, VA 20192; (703) 648-6943. Fax, (703) 648-6937. Peter T. Lyttle, Program Coordinator. Web, http://ncgmp.usgs.gov*

Funds the production of geologic maps in the United States. Provides geologic mapping data from across North America to public and private organizations.

U.S. Geological Survey (USGS) *(Interior Dept.), National Geospatial Program, 12201 Sunrise Valley Dr., MS 511, Reston, VA 20192 (mailing address: 511 National Center, Reston, VA 20192); (703) 648-4725. Fax, (703) 648-4722. Michael Tischler, Director. Web, www.usgs.gov/ngpo*

Plans and coordinates information dissemination activities.

► **CONGRESS**

For a listing of relevant congressional committees and sub-committees, please see pages 646–647 or the Appendix.

Library of Congress, Geography and Map Division, *James Madison Memorial Bldg., 101 Independence Ave. S.E., #LM B01, 20540; (202) 707-8530. Fax, (202) 707-8531. Ralph Ehrenberg, Chief. Reading room, (202) 707-6277. Web, www.loc.gov/rr/geogmap*

Maintains cartographic collection of maps, atlases, globes, and reference books. Reference service provided; reading room open to the public. Interlibrary loans available through the library's loan division. Restricted copying privelages. Free copies may be made for personal use only (self-service).

► **NONGOVERNMENTAL**

Assn. of American Geographers, *1710 16th St. N.W., 20009-3198; (202) 234-1450. Fax, (202) 234-2744. Douglas Richardson, Executive Director. General email, gaia@aag.org*

Web, www.aag.org and Twitter, @theAAG

Membership: educators, students, business executives, government employees, and scientists in the field of geography. Seeks to advance professional studies in geography

and encourages the application of geographic research in education, government, and business.

National Geographic Maps, *1145 17th St. N.W., 20036-4688; (202) 857-7000. Juan Valdés, Director, Editorial and Cartographic Research. Toll-free and map orders, (800) 962-1643. Toll-free fax, (800) 626-8676. General email, maps@ngs.org*

Web, www.natgeomaps.com

Produces and sells to the public political, physical, and thematic maps, atlases, and globes. (Affiliated with the National Geographic Society.)

National Society of Professional Surveyors, *5119 Pegasus Ct., Suite Q, Frederick, MD 21704; (240) 439-4615. Fax, (240) 439-4952. Curtis W. Sumner, Executive Director, (240) 439-4615, ext. 106. General email, info@nsps.org*

Web, www.nsps.us.com

Membership: professionals working worldwide in surveying, cartography, geodesy, and geographic/land information systems (computerized mapping systems used in urban, regional, and environmental planning). Sponsors workshops and seminars for surveyors and mapping professionals; participates in accreditation of college and university surveying and related degree programs; grants scholarships; develops and administers certification programs for hydrographers and survey technicians. Monitors legislation and regulations.

SPACE SCIENCES

General

► **AGENCIES**

Air Force Dept. *(Defense Dept.), Space Command, 1670 Air Force Pentagon, 4C855, 20330-1640; (703) 693-5799. Fax, (703) 695-4028. Gen. John E. Hyten, Commander. Web, www.afspc.af.mil*

Manages the planning, programming, and acquisition of space systems for the Air Force and other military services.

Bureau of Oceans and International Environmental and Scientific Affairs *(State Dept.), Space and Advanced Technology, 1800 G St. N.W., #10100, 20006; (202) 663-2400. Kenneth D. Hodgkins, Director. Web, www.state.gov/e/oes/sat*

Works with U.S. space policies and multilateral science activities to support U.S. foreign policy objectives in order to enhance U.S. space and technological competitiveness.

Federal Aviation Administration (FAA) *(Transportation Dept.), Commercial Space Transportation, 800 Independence Ave. S.W., #331, AST-1, 20591; (202) 267-7793. Fax, (202) 267-5450. George Nield, Associate Administrator. Web, www.faa.gov/about/office_org/headquarters_offices/ast*

Promotes and facilitates the operation of commercial expendable space launch vehicles by the private sector; licenses and regulates these activities.

National Aeronautics and Space Administration (NASA), *300 E St. S.W., 20024-3210 (mailing address: 300 E St. S.W., Washington, DC 20546-0001); (202) 358-1010. Fax, (202) 358-2810. Charles F. Bolden Jr., Administrator. Information, (202) 358-0000. TTY, (800) 877-8339. Library, (202) 358-0168.*
General email, public-inquiries@hq.nasa.gov

Web, www.nasa.gov and Library, www.hq.nasa.gov/office/hqlibrary

Develops, manages, and has oversight of the agency's programs and missions. Interacts with Congress and state officials and responds to national and international inquiries. Serves as the administrative office for the agency. Library open to the public Monday through Friday, 7:30 a.m.–5:00 p.m.

National Aeronautics and Space Administration (NASA), *Aeronautics Research Mission Directorate, 300 E St. S.W., #6B27, 20546; (202) 358-4600. Fax, (202) 358-3640. Jaiwon Shin, Associate Administrator.*
Web, www.aeronautics.nasa.gov

Conducts research in aerodynamics, materials, structures, avionics, propulsion, high-performance computing, human factors, aviation safety, and space transportation in support of national space and aeronautical research and technology goals. Manages the following NASA research centers: Ames (Moffett Field, Calif.); Dryden (Edwards, Calif.); Langley (Hampton, Va.); and Glenn (Cleveland, Ohio).

National Aeronautics and Space Administration (NASA), *Chief Engineer, 300 E St. S.W., #6N19, 20546; (202) 358-1823. Fax, (202) 358-3296. Ralph R. Roe Jr., Chief Engineer, (757) 864-2400.*
Web, http://oce.nasa.gov

Serves as the agency's principal adviser on matters pertaining to the technical readiness and execution of programs and projects.

National Aeronautics and Space Administration (NASA), *Chief Health and Medical Officer, 300 E St. S.W., 20546; (202) 358-2390. Fax, (202) 358-3349. Dr. Richard S. Williams, Chief Health and Medical Officer. Web, www.hq.nasa.gov/office/chmo*

Ensures the health and safety of NASA employees in space and on the ground. Develops health and medical policy, establishes guidelines for health and medical practices, oversees health care delivery, and monitors human and animal research standards within the agency.

National Aeronautics and Space Administration (NASA), *Education, 300 E St. S.W., 4th Floor, 20546; (202) 358-0103. Fax, (202) 358-7097. Donald G. James, Associate Administrator, Acting. General email, education@nasa.gov*
Web, http://education.nasa.gov

Coordinates NASA's education programs and activities to meet national educational needs and ensure a sufficient talent pool to preserve U.S. leadership in aeronautical technology and space science.

National Aeronautics and Space Administration (NASA), *Goddard Space Flight Center, 8800 Greenbelt Rd., Code 130, Greenbelt, MD 20771; (301) 286-5121. Fax, (301) 286-1714. Christopher J. Scolese, Director. Information, (301) 286-2000. Visitor Center, (301) 286-8981.*
Web, www.nasa.gov/centers/goddard

Conducts space and earth science research; develops and operates flight missions; maintains spaceflight tracking and data acquisition networks; develops technology and instruments; develops and maintains advanced information systems for the display, analysis, archiving, and distribution of space and earth science data; and develops National Oceanic and Atmospheric Administration (NOAA) satellite systems that provide environmental data for forecasting and research.

National Aeronautics and Space Administration (NASA), *Goddard Space Flight Center, Heliophysics Science Division, 8800 Greenbelt Rd., Code 670, Greenbelt, MD 20771; (301) 286-6418. Fax, (301) 286-5348. Michael Hesse, Director. Web, http://hsd.gsfc.nasa.gov*

Provides scientific expertise necessary to achieve NASA's strategic science goals in solar physics, heliospheric physics, geospace physics, and space weather. Houses the Solar Physics Laboratory, the Heliospheric Physics Laboratory, the Geospace Physics Laboratory, and the Space Weather Laboratory.

National Aeronautics and Space Administration (NASA), *Goddard Space Flight Center, National Space Science Data Center, 8800 Greenbelt Rd., Code 690.1, Greenbelt, MD 20771; (301) 286-6695. Fax, (301) 286-1635. Edwin Grayzeck, Head. General email, nssdc-request@lists.nasa.gov*
Web, http://nssdc.gsfc.nasa.gov

Permanent archive for NASA space science mission data. Acquires, catalogs, and distributes NASA mission data to the international space science community, including research organizations and scientists, universities, and other interested organizations worldwide. Teams with NASA's discipline-specific space science "active archives," which provide researchers and, in some cases, the general public with access to data. Provides software tools and network access, including online information databases about NASA and non-NASA data, to promote collaborative data analysis. (Mail data requests to above address, attention: NSSDC Code 690.1/Request Coordination Office.)

National Aeronautics and Space Administration (NASA), *Goddard Space Flight Center, Sciences and Exploration Directorate, 8800 Greenbelt Rd., Code 600, Greenbelt, MD 20771; (301) 286-6066. Fax, (301) 286-1772. Colleen Hartman, Director.*
Web, http://science.gsfc.nasa.gov

Plans, organizes, implements, and evaluates a broad system of theoretical and experimental scientific research in the study of the earth-sun system, the solar system and the origins of life, and the birth and evolution of the universe. Activities include modeling and basic research, flight experiment development, and data analysis.

National Aeronautics and Space Administration (NASA), Goddard Space Flight Center, Solar System Exploration Data Services, 8800 Greenbelt Rd., Code 690.1, Greenbelt, MD 20771; (301) 286-1743. Fax, (301) 286-1683. Thomas (Tom) Morgan, Program Manager, Planetary Data System.
General email, request@nssdc.gsfc.nasa.gov
Web, http://ssedso.gsfc.nasa.gov

Coordinates data management and archiving plans within NASA's Science Mission. Operates the National Space Science Data Center (NSSDC) as a permanent archive for data associated with NASA's missions; the Crustal Dynamics Data Information System (CDDIS); and the Planetary Data System (PDS).

National Aeronautics and Space Administration (NASA), Human Exploration and Operations Directorate, 300 E St. S.W., #7K39, 20546; (202) 358-2015. Fax, (202) 358-2838. William H. Gerstenmaier, Associate Administrator. Information, (202) 358-0000.
Web, www.nasa.gov/directorates/heo

Responsible for space operations related to human and robotic exploration, including launch, transport, and communications. Manages the International Space Station, commercial space transportation, and research and development in space life sciences.

National Aeronautics and Space Administration (NASA), NASA Advisory Council, 300 E St. S.W., #2V79, 20546; (202) 358-4510. Fax, (202) 358-3030. Steven W. Squyres, Chair; Diane Rausch, Executive Director.
Web, www.nasa.gov/offices/nac

Advises the administrator on programs and issues of importance to NASA. The council consists of nine committees: Aeronautics; Audit, Finance, and Analysis; Commercial Space; Education and Public Outreach; Exploration; Information Technology Infrastructure; Science; Space Operations; and Technology and Innovation.

National Aeronautics and Space Administration (NASA), Protective Services, 300 E St. S.W., #6T39, 20546; (202) 358-2010. Fax, (202) 358-3238. Joseph Mahaley, Assistant Administrator; Charles Lombard, Deputy Assistant Administrator.
Web, www.hq.nasa.gov/hq/security.html

Serves as the focal point for policy formulation, oversight, coordination, and management of NASA's security, counterintelligence, counterterrorism, emergency preparedness and response, and continuity of operations programs.

National Aeronautics and Space Administration (NASA), Safety and Mission Assurance, 300 E St. S.W., #5A42, 20546; (202) 358-2406. Fax, (202) 358-2699,

Terrence W. Wilcutt, Chief; Bill Loewy, GIDEP Program Manager.
General email, nasa-sma@mail.nasa.gov
Web, www.hq.nasa.gov/office/codeq

Evaluates the safety and reliability of NASA systems and programs. Alerts officials to technical execution and physical readiness of NASA projects.

National Aeronautics and Space Administration (NASA), Science Mission Directorate, 300 E St. S.W., #3J28, 20546; (202) 358-3889. Fax, (202) 358-3092. John Grunsfeld, Associate Administrator.
General email, science@hq.nasa.gov
Web, http://science.nasa.gov/about-us/organization-and-leadership

Seeks to understand the origins, evolution, and structure of the solar system and the universe; to understand the integrated functioning of the earth and the sun; and to ascertain the potential for life elsewhere. Administers space mission programs and mission-enabling programs, including suborbital missions. Sponsors scientific research and analysis.

National Air and Space Museum (Smithsonian Institution), 6th St. and Independence Ave. S.W., 20560; (202) 633-2214. Fax, (202) 633-8174. Gen. J.R. (Jack) Dailey (USMC, Ret.), Director. TTY, (202) 633-5285. Education Office, (202) 633-2540. Library, (202) 633-2320. Tours, (202) 633-2563.
General email, nasmvisitorservices@si.edu
Web, www.airandspace.si.edu

Collects, preserves, and exhibits astronautical objects and equipment of historical interest, including aircraft, spacecraft, and communications and weather satellites. Library open to the public by appointment.

National Oceanic and Atmospheric Administration (NOAA) (Commerce Dept.), Space Commercialization, 1401 Constitution Ave. N.W., #2518, 20230; (202) 482-6125. Fax, (202) 482-4429. Mark Paese, Director, Acting.
General email, space.commerce@noaa.gov
Web, www.space.commerce.gov

The principal unit for space commerce within NOAA and the Commerce Dept. Promotes economic growth and technological advancement of U.S. commercial space industry focusing on sectors including satellite navigation, satellite imagery, space transportation, and entrepreneurial space business. Participates in discussions of national space policy.

Steven F. Udvar-Hazy Center (Smithsonian Institution), National Air and Space Museum, 14390 Air and Space Museum Pkwy., Chantilly, VA 20151; (703) 572-4118. Gen. John R. Dailey, Director. Public Affairs, (202) 633-1000. TTY, (202) 633-5285.
General email, nasm-visitorservices@si.edu
Web, www.airandspace.si.edu/visit/udvar-hazy-center

Displays and preserves a collection of historical aviation and space artifacts, including the B-29 Superfortress, Enola Gay, the Lockheed SR-71 Blackbird, the prototype of the Boeing 707, the space shuttle Discovery, and the Concord. Provides a center for research into the history, science, and technology of aviation and space flight. Open to the public daily 10:00 a.m.–5:30 p.m., except December 25.

►CONGRESS

For a listing of relevant congressional committees and subcommittees, please see pages 646–647 or the Appendix.

►INTERNATIONAL ORGANIZATIONS

European Space Agency (ESA), *Washington Office, 1201 F St. N.W., #470, 20004; (202) 488-4158. Fax, (202) 488-4930. Micheline Tabache, Head.*
Web, www.esa.int

Intergovernmental agency that promotes international collaboration in space research and development and the use of space technology for peaceful purposes. Members include Austria, Belgium, Czech Republic, Denmark, Estonia, Finland, France, Germany, Greece, Ireland, Italy, Luxembourg, the Netherlands, Norway, Poland, Portugal, Romania, Spain, Sweden, Switzerland, and the United Kingdom; Canada participates in some programs; Hungary, Estonia, Latvia, and Slovenia are European Cooperating States. (Headquarters in Paris.)

►NONGOVERNMENTAL

Aerospace Industries Assn. (AIA), *1000 Wilson Blvd., #1700, Arlington, VA 22209-3928; (703) 358-1000. Fax, (703) 358-1012. David Melcher, President. Press, (703) 358-1076.*
General email, aia@aia-aerospace.org
Web, www.aia-aerospace.org

Represents manufacturers of commercial, military, and business aircraft; helicopters; aircraft engines; missiles; spacecraft; and related components and equipment. Interests include international standards and trade.

American Astronautical Society, *6352 Rolling Mill Pl., #102, Springfield, VA 22152-2370; (703) 866-0020. Fax, (703) 866-3526. James R. Kirkpatrick, Executive Director.*
General email, aas@astronautical.org
Web, www.astronautical.org

Scientific and technological society of researchers, scientists, astronauts, and other professionals in the field of astronautics and spaceflight engineering. Organizes national and local meetings and symposia; promotes international cooperation.

American Institute of Aeronautics and Astronautics (AIAA), *12700 Sunrise Valley Dr., #200, Reston, VA 20191-5807; (703) 264-7500. Fax, (703) 264-7551. Sandy Magnus, Executive Director. Information, (800) 639-2422.*
General email, custserv@aiaa.org
Web, www.aiaa.org and Twitter, @aiaa

Membership: engineers, scientists, and students in the fields of aeronautics and astronautics. Holds workshops on aerospace technical issues for congressional subcommittees; sponsors international conferences. Offers computerized database through its Technical Information Service.

National Research Council (NRC), *Aeronautics and Space Engineering Board, Keck Center, 500 5th St. N.W., #W932, 9th Floor, 20001; (202) 334-3477. Fax, (202) 334-3701. Michael Moloney, Director.*
General email, aseb@nas.edu
Web, www.nationalacademies.org/aseb

Membership: aeronautics and space experts. Advises government agencies on aeronautics and space engineering research, technology, experiments, international programs, and policy. Library open to the public by appointment.

National Research Council (NRC), *Space Studies Board, Keck Center, 500 5th St. N.W., 9th Floor, 20001; (202) 334-3477. Fax, (202) 334-3701. Michael Moloney, Director, (202) 334-2142; David N. Spengel, Chair.*
General email, ssb@nas.edu
Web, www.nationalacademies.org/ssb

Provides advice to the government on space policy issues and issues concerning space science activities, including space-based astrophysics, heliophysics, solar system exploration, earth science, and microgravity life and physical sciences. Produces discipline-based "Decadal Surveys," which set priorities for government investments over ten-year time periods.

National Space Society, *12100 Sunset Hills Rd., #130, Reston, VA 220190 (mailing address: P.O. Box 98106, Washington, DC 20090-8106); (202) 429-1600. Fax, (703) 435-3490. Bruce Pittman, Executive Director, Acting.*
General email, nsshq@nss.org
Web, www.nss.org

Membership: individuals interested in space programs and applications of space technology. Provides information on NASA, commercial space activities, and international cooperation; promotes public education on space exploration and development; conducts conferences and workshops; publishes quarterly magazine. Monitors legislation and regulations.

Resources for the Future, *1616 P St. N.W., 20036-1400; (202) 328-5000. Fax, (202) 939-3460. Philip R. Sharp, President, (202) 328-5077. Library, (202) 328-5089. Press, (202) 328-5168.*
General email, info@rff.org
Web, www.rff.org and Twitter, @RFF_org

Examines the economic aspects of U.S. space policy, including policy on communications satellites and space debris. Focuses on the role of private business versus that of government.

Space Policy Institute *(George Washington University), 1957 E St. N.W., #403, 20052; (202) 994-7292. Fax, (202) 994-1639. Scott Pace, Director.*
General email, spi@gwu.edu
Web, www.gwu.edu/~spi

Conducts research on space policy issues; organizes seminars, symposia, and conferences. Focuses on civilian space activities, including competitive and cooperative interactions on space between the United States and other countries.

Astronomy

► AGENCIES

National Aeronautics and Space Administration (NASA), *Science Mission Directorate, 300 E St. S.W., #3J28, 20546; (202) 358-3889. Fax, (202) 358-3092. John Grunsfeld, Associate Administrator.*
General email, science@hq.nasa.gov
Web, http://science.nasa.gov/about-us/organization-and-leadership

Seeks to understand the origins, evolution, and structure of the solar system and the universe; to understand the integrated functioning of the earth and the sun; and to ascertain the potential for life elsewhere. Administers space mission programs and mission-enabling programs, including suborbital missions. Sponsors scientific research and analysis.

National Science Foundation (NSF), *Astronomical Sciences Division, 4201 Wilson Blvd., #1045S, Arlington, VA 22230; (703) 292-8820. Fax, (703) 292-9034. James S. Ulvestad, Division Director.*
Web, www.nsf.gov/div/index.jsp?div=ast

Provides grants for ground-based astronomy and astronomical research on planetary astronomy, stellar astronomy and astrophysics, galactic astronomy, extragalactic astronomy and cosmology, and advanced technologies and instrumentation. Maintains astronomical facilities; participates in international projects.

U.S. Naval Observatory *(Defense Dept.), 3450 Massachusetts Ave. N.W., 20392-5420; (202) 762-1467. Fax, (202) 762-1489. Capt. Brian Connon, Superintendent. Public Affairs, (202) 762-1438.*
General email, USNO_PAO@navy.mil
Web, www.usno.navy.mil/USNO

Determines the precise positions and motions of celestial bodies. Operates the U.S. master clock. Provides the U.S. Navy and Defense Dept. with astronomical and timing data for navigation, precise positioning, and command, control, and communications. Maintains a library, with the catalog available on the Web site.

► NONGOVERNMENTAL

American Astronomical Society, *2000 Florida Ave. N.W., #300, 20009-1231; (202) 328-2010. Fax, (202) 234-2560. Joel Parriott, Director, Public Policy.*
General email, aas@aas.org
Web, www.aas.org

Membership: astronomers and other professionals interested in the advancement of astronomy in North America and worldwide. Publishes technical journals; holds scientific meetings; participates in international organizations; awards prizes for outstanding scientific achievements.

American Geophysical Union, *2000 Florida Ave. N.W., 20009-1277; (202) 462-6900. Fax, (202) 328-0566. Christine McEntee, Executive Director; Margaret Leinen, President. Information, (800) 966-2481.*
General email, service@agu.org
Web, www.agu.org

Membership: scientists and technologists who study the environments and components of the earth, sun, and solar system. Promotes international cooperation; disseminates information.

Assn. of Universities for Research in Astronomy (AURA), *1212 New York Ave. N.W., #450, 20005; (202) 483-2101. Fax, (202) 483-2106. Matt Mountain, President.*
Web, www.aura-astronomy.org and Twitter, @AURADC

Consortium of universities. Manages four ground-based observatories and the international Gemini Project for the National Science Foundation and manages the Space Telescope Science Institute for the National Aeronautics and Space Administration.

Carnegie Institute for Science, *1530 P St. N.W., 20005-1910; (202) 387-6400. Fax, (202) 387-8092. Matthew P. Scott, President.*
Web, www.carnegiescience.edu and Twitter, @carnegiescience

Conducts research in plant science biology, genetic and developmental biology, earth and planetary sciences, astronomy, and global ecology and matter at extreme states at the Carnegie Institution's six research departments: Dept. of Embryology (Baltimore, Md.); Geophysical Laboratory (Washington, D.C.); Dept. of Global Ecology (Stanford, Calif.); Dept. of Plant Biology (Stanford, Calif.); Dept. of Terrestrial Magnetism (Washington, D.C.); and The Observatories (Pasadena, Calif., and Las Campanas, Chile).

National Research Council (NRC), *Physics and Astronomy Board, Keck Center, 500 5th St. N.W., 20001; (202) 334-3520. Fax, 202-34-3575. Michael S. Witherell, Chair; James Lancaster, Director.*
General email, bpa@nas.edu
Web, http://sites.nationalacademies.org/BPA

Provides information to the government and public on scientific matters relating to physics and astronomy, including atomic, molecular, and optical sciences, astronomy and astrophysics, plasma science, radio frequencies, and condensed matter and materials.

17

Social Services and Disabilities

GENERAL POLICY AND ANALYSIS

Basic Resources

▶ AGENCIES

Administration for Children and Families (ACF) *(Health and Human Services Dept.),* 330 C St. S.W., 20201 *(mailing address: 370 L'Enfant Promenade S.W., Washington, DC 20447); (202) 401-2337. Mark Greenberg, Assistant Secretary, Acting. Public Affairs, (202) 401-9215.*
Web, www.acf.hhs.gov

Administers and funds programs for Native Americans, low-income families and individuals, and persons with disabilities. Responsible for Social Services Block Grants to the states; coordinates Health and Human Services Dept. policy and regulations on child protection, day care, foster care, adoption services, child abuse and neglect, and special services for those with disabilities. Administers the Head Start program and funds the National Runaway Safe Line, (800) 786-2929, and the Domestic Violence Hotline, (800) 799-7233; TTY, (800) 787-3224.

Administration for Children and Families (ACF) *(Health and Human Services Dept.), Refugee Resettlement,* 330 C St. S.W., 20201; (202) 401-9246. Fax, (202) 401-0981. *Robert Carey, Director.*
Web, www.acf.hhs.gov/programs/orr

Provides benefits and services to refugees, Cuban and Haitian entrants, asylees, trafficking and torture victims, repatriated U.S. citizens, and unaccompanied alien children. Seeks to help individuals achieve economic self-sufficiency and social adjustment within the shortest time possible following arrival to the United States.

Administration for Community Living (ACL) *(Health and Human Services Dept.),* 330 C St. S.W., 20201; (202) 401-4634. *Kathy Greenlee, Administrator.*
General email, aclinfo@acl.hhs.gov
Web, www.acl.gov

Oversees programs that provide assistance to older adults, persons with disabilities, and family caregivers. Represents and advocates for individuals with disabilities and older adults throughout the federal government, seeking to ensure that these individuals are as involved as appropriate in the development and implementation of policies, programs, and regulations related to community living.

Administration for Native Americans *(Health and Human Services Dept.),* 330 C. St. S.W., 20201; (202) 690-7776. Fax, (202) 690-7441. *Lillian A. Sparks, Commissioner. Toll-free, (877) 922-9262.*
General email, ana@acf.hhs.gov
Web, www.acf.hhs.gov/programs/ana

Awards grants for locally determined social and economic development strategies; promotes Native American economic and social self-sufficiency; funds tribes and Native American and Native Hawaiian organizations; provides grant funding for community development projects.

Commissioner chairs the Intradepartmental Council on Indian Affairs, which coordinates Native American–related programs.

AmeriCorps *(Corp. for National and Community Service), Volunteers in Service to America (VISTA),* 250 E St. S.W., 20024-3208; (202) 606-5000. Fax, (202) 565-2789. *Max Finberg, Director. Volunteer recruiting information, (800) 942-2677. TTY, (800) 833-3722.*
General email, questions@americorps.gov
Web, www.americorps.gov/programs/americorps/americorps-vista and Twitter, @nationalservice

Assigns full-time volunteers to public and private nonprofit organizations for one year to alleviate poverty in local communities. Volunteers receive a living allowance, health care, and other benefits and their choice of a post-service stipend or education award.

Bureau of Indian Affairs (BIA) *(Interior Dept.), Indian Services,* 1849 C St. N.W., MS 4513-MIB, 20240; (202) 513-7640. Fax, (202) 208-5113. *Hankie Ortiz, Deputy Bureau Director. Public Affairs, (202) 208-3710.*
Web, www.bia.gov/WhoWeAre/bia/ois/index.htm

Gives assistance, in accordance with state payment standards, to American Indians and Alaska Natives of federally recognized tribes living on or near reservations and in tribal service areas, and provides family and individual counseling and child welfare services. Assists tribal and Indian landowners with managing natural and energy trust resources; builds and maintains housing, transportation, energy, and irrigation infrastructure; and provides law enforcement protection, corrections, and administration of justice services on federal Indian lands.

Corporation for National and Community Service, 250 E St. N.W., 20525; (202) 606-5000. Fax, (202) 606-3460. *Wendy M. Spencer, Chief Executive Officer, (202) 606-5000, ext. 6735. Press, (202) 606-6775. Volunteer recruiting information, (800) 942-2677. TTY, (800) 833-3722.*
General email, info@cns.gov
Web, www.nationalservice.gov and Twitter, @nationalservice

Independent corporation that administers federally sponsored domestic volunteer programs that provide disadvantaged citizens with services, including AmeriCorps, AmeriCorps-VISTA (Volunteers in Service to America), AmeriCorps-NCCC (National Civilian Community Corps), and the Senior Corps.

Food and Nutrition Service *(Agriculture Dept.),* 3101 Park Center Dr., #906, Alexandria, VA 22302-1500; (703) 305-2060. Fax, (703) 305-2908. *Audrey Rowe, Administrator. Information, (703) 305-2286.*
Web, www.fns.usda.gov and Twitter, @USDANutrition

Administers all Agriculture Dept. domestic food assistance, including the distribution of funds and food for school breakfast and lunch programs (preschool through secondary) to public and nonprofit private schools; the Supplemental Nutrition Assistance Program (SNAP, formerly the food stamp program); and a supplemental nutrition program for women, infants, and children (WIC).

SOCIAL SERVICES AND DISABILITIES RESOURCES IN CONGRESS

For a complete listing of congressional committees, including their full contact information, leadership, membership, and jurisdictions, please refer to the Appendix on pages 779–896.

HOUSE:

House Agriculture Committee, (202) 225-2171.
Web, agriculture.house.gov
  Subcommittee on Nutrition, (202) 225-2171.
House Appropriations Committee, (202) 225-2771.
Web, appropriations.house.gov
  Subcommittee on Agriculture, Rural Development, Food and Drug Administration, and Related Agencies, (202) 225-2638.
  Subcommittee on Financial Services and General Government, (202) 225-7245.
  Subcommittee on Labor, Health and Human Services, Education, and Related Agencies, (202) 225-3508.
  Subcommittee on Military Construction, Veterans Affairs, and Related Agencies, (202) 225-3047.
  Subcommittee on Transportation, HUD, and Related Agencies, (202) 225-2141.
House Education and the Workforce Committee, (202) 225-4527.
Web, edworkforce.house.gov
  Subcommittee on Early Childhood, Elementary, and Secondary Education, (202) 225-4527.
  Subcommittee on Health, Employment, Labor, and Pensions, (202) 225-4527.
  Subcommittee on Higher Education and Workforce Training, (202) 225-4527.
House Energy and Commerce Committee, (202) 225-2927.
Web, energycommerce.house.gov
  Subcommittee on Health, (202) 225-2927.
House Small Business Committee, (202) 225-5821.
Web, smallbusiness.house.gov
  Subcommittee on Health and Technology, (202) 225-5821.
House Veterans' Affairs Committee, (202) 225-3527.
Web, veterans.house.gov

  Subcommittee on Disability Assistance and Memorial Affairs, (202) 225-9164.
House Ways and Means Committee, (202) 225-3625.
Web, waysandmeans.house.gov
  Subcommittee on Health, (202) 225-3943.
  Subcommittee on Social Security, (202) 225-9263.

SENATE:

Senate Agriculture, Nutrition, and Forestry Committee, (202) 224-2035.
Web, ag.senate.gov
  Subcommittee on Nutrition, Specialty Crops, and Agricultural Research, (202) 224-2035.
Senate Appropriations Committee, (202) 224-7363.
Web, appropriations.senate.gov
  Subcommittee on Agriculture, Rural Development, Food and Drug Administration, and Related Agencies, (202) 224-8090.
  Subcommittee on Labor, Health and Human Services, Education, and Related Agencies, (202) 224-9145.
  Subcommittee on Transportation, HUD, and Related Agencies, (202) 224-7281.
Senate Finance Committee, (202) 224-4515.
Web, finance.senate.gov
  Subcommittee on Health Care, (202) 224-4515.
  Subcommittee on Social Security, Pensions, and Family Policy, (202) 224-4515.
Senate Health, Education, Labor, and Pensions Committee, (202) 224-5375.
Web, help.senate.gov
  Subcommittee on Children and Families, (202) 224-5375.
  Subcommittee on Primary Health and Retirement Security, (202) 224-5480.
Senate Special Committee on Aging, (202) 224-5364.
Web, aging.senate.gov
Senate Veterans' Affairs Committee, (202) 224-9126.
Web, veterans.senate.gov

Food and Nutrition Service *(Agriculture Dept.), Food Distribution, 3101 Park Center Dr., #504, Alexandria, VA 22302-1500; (703) 305-2680. Fax, (703) 305-2964. Laura Castro, Director.*
General email, fdd-pst@fns.usda.gov
Web, www.fns.usda.gov/fdd

Administers the purchasing and distribution of food to state agencies for child care centers, public and private schools, public and nonprofit charitable institutions, and summer camps. Coordinates the distribution of special commodities, including surplus cheese and butter. Administers the National Commodity Processing Program, which

facilitates distribution, at reduced prices, of processed foods to state agencies.

Food and Nutrition Service *(Agriculture Dept.), Supplemental Nutrition Assistance Program (SNAP), 3101 Park Center Dr., #808, Alexandria, VA 22302-1500; (703) 305-2026. Fax, (703) 305-2454. Jessica Shahin, Associate Administrator, (703) 305-2022.*
Web, www.fns.usda.gov/snap

Administers SNAP through state welfare agencies to provide needy persons with Electronic Benefit Transfer cards to increase food purchasing power. Provides matching funds to cover half the cost of EBT card issuance.

Health and Human Services Dept. (HHS), *200 Independence Ave. S.W., 20201; (202) 690-7000. Fax, (202) 690-7203. Sylvia Burwell, Secretary; Mary K. Wakefield, Deputy Secretary, Acting, (202) 690-6133. Press, (202) 690-6343. Press, (202) 690-6139. Toll-free, (877) 696-6775. TTY, (800) 877-8339.*
Web, www.hhs.gov

Acts as principal adviser to the president on health and welfare plans, policies, and programs of the federal government. Encompasses the Centers for Medicare and Medicaid Services, the Administration for Children and Families, the Public Health Service, and the Centers for Disease Control and Prevention.

Health and Human Services Dept. (HHS), *Disability, Aging, and Long-Term Care Policy, 200 Independence Ave. S.W., #424E, 20201; (202) 690-6443. Fax, (202) 401-7733. Linda Elam, Deputy Assistant Secretary.*
Web, http://aspe.hhs.gov/office_specific/daltcp.cfm

Responsible for developing, evaluating, and coordinating HHS policies and programs that support the independence, productivity, health, and long-term care needs of children, working-age adults, and older persons with disabilities. Operates regionally within ten HHS offices.

Health and Human Services Dept. (HHS), *Planning and Evaluation, Human Services Policy, Economic Support for Families, 200 Independence Ave. S.W., #404E.5, 20201; (202) 690-7409. Fax, (202) 690-6562. John Tambornino, Director.*
Web, www.aspe.hhs.gov/office-human-services-policy

Collects and disseminates information on human services programs that provide nonelderly populations, including families with children, with cash, employment, training, and related assistance.

▶CONGRESS

For a listing of relevant congressional committees and subcommittees, please see page 685 or the Appendix.

Government Accountability Office (GAO), *Education, Workforce, and Income Security, 441 G St. N.W., #5928, 20548; (202) 512-7215. Barbara D. Bovbjerg, Managing Director.*
Web, www.gao.gov/careers/ewis.html

Independent nonpartisan agency in the legislative branch. Audits, analyzes, and evaluates Health and Human Services Dept. and Corporation for National and Community Service programs; makes reports available to the public.

▶NONGOVERNMENTAL

American Public Human Services Assn., *1133 19th St. N.W., #400, 20036; (202) 682-0100. Fax, (202) 289-6555. Tracy Wareing Evans, Executive Director, ext. 231.*
General email, memberservice@aphsa.org
Web, www.aphsa.org

Membership: state and local human services administrators. Works toward an integrated human services

system to improve the health and well-being of individuals and communities. Exchanges knowledge and best practices through conferences and publications; implements policies in partnership with government, businesses, and community organizations; monitors legislation and regulations.

Catholic Charities USA, *2050 Ballenger Ave., #400, Alexandria, VA 22314; (703) 549-1390. Fax, (703) 549-1656. Sister Donna Markham, President.*
General email, info@catholiccharitiesusa.org
Web, www.catholiccharitiesusa.org and Twitter, @CCharitiesUSA

Member agencies and institutions provide assistance to persons of all backgrounds; community-based services include day care, counseling, food, and housing. National office provides members with advocacy and professional support, including networking, training and consulting, program development, and financial benefits. Represents the Catholic community in times of domestic disaster.

Center for Community Change, *1536 U St. N.W., 20009; (202) 339-9300. Fax, (202) 387-4892. Deepak Bhargava, Executive Director.*
General email, info@communitychange.org
Web, www.communitychange.org and Twitter, @communitychange

Works to strengthen grassroots organizations that help low-income people, working-class people, and minorities develop skills and resources to improve their communities and change the policies and institutions that affect their lives. Monitors legislation and regulations.

Center for Law and Social Policy (CLASP), *1200 18th St. N.W., #200, 20036; (202) 906-8000. Fax, (202) 842-2885. Olivia Golden, Executive Director.*
General email, aparker@clasp.org
Web, www.clasp.org

Public policy organization with expertise in national, state, and local policy affecting low-income Americans. Seeks to improve the economic security and educational and workforce prospects of low-income children, youth, adults, and families.

Center for the Study of Social Policy, *1575 Eye St. N.W., #500, 20005-3922; (202) 371-1565. Fax, (202) 371-1472. Frank Farrow, Director.*
General email, info@cssp.org
Web, www.cssp.org and Twitter, @CtrSocialPolicy

Assists states and communities in organizing, financing, and delivering human services, with a focus on children and families. Helps build capacity for local decision making; helps communities use informal supports in the protection of children; promotes nonadversarial approach to class action litigation on behalf of dependent children.

Center on Budget and Policy Priorities, *820 1st St. N.E., #510, 20002; (202) 408-1080. Fax, (202) 408-1056. Robert Greenstein, President.*
General email, center@cbpp.org
Web, www.cbpp.org and Twitter, @CenterOnBudget

Research group that analyzes changes in federal and state programs, such as tax credits, Medicaid coverage, and food stamps, and their effect on low-income and moderate-income households.

Christian Relief Services, *8301 Richmond Hwy., #900, Alexandria, VA 22309; (703) 317-9086. Fax, (703) 317-9690. Paul Krizek, Executive Director. Information, (800)-33-RELIEF.*
General email, info@christianrelief.org
Web, www.christianrelief.org

Promotes economic development and the alleviation of poverty in urban areas of the United States, Appalachia, Native American reservations, Haiti, Mexico, Honduras, Lithuania, the Czech Republic, and Africa. Donates medical supplies and food; administers housing, hospital, and school construction programs; provides affordable housing for low-income individuals and families.

Coalition on Human Needs, *1120 Connecticut Ave. N.W., #312, 20036; (202) 223-2532. Fax, (202) 223-2538. Deborah Weinstein, Executive Director.*
General email, mroark@chn.org
Web, www.chn.org and Twitter, @CoalitiononHN

Promotes public policies that address the needs of low-income Americans. Members include civil rights, religious, labor, and professional organizations and service providers concerned with the well-being of children, women, the elderly, and people with disabilities.

Community Action Partnership, *1140 Connecticut Ave. N.W., #1210, 20036; (202) 265-7546. Fax, (202) 265-5048. Denise Harlowe, Chief Executive Officer, (202) 595-0660. General email, info@communityactionpartnership.com*
Web, www.communityactionpartnership.com

Provides community action agencies with information, training, and technical assistance; advocates, at all levels of government, for low-income people.

Council on Social Work Education, *1701 Duke St., #200, Alexandria, VA 22314-3457; (703) 683-8080. Fax, (703) 683-8099. Darla Spence Coffey, President.*
General email, info@cswe.org
Web, www.cswe.org

Membership: educational and professional institutions, social welfare agencies, and private citizens. Promotes high-quality education in social work. Accredits social work programs.

Food Research and Action Center (FRAC), *1200 18th St. N.W., #400, 20036; (202) 986-2200. Fax, (202) 986-2525. James D. Weill, President.*
General email, comments@frac.org
Web, www.frac.org and Twitter, @fractweets

Public interest advocacy center that works to end hunger and undernutrition in the United States. Offers organizational aid, training, and information to groups seeking to improve or expand federal food programs, including food stamp, child nutrition, and WIC (women, infants, and children) programs; conducts studies relating to hunger and poverty; coordinates network of antihunger organizations. Monitors legislation and regulations.

Foundation for International Community Assistance (FINCA), *1201 15th St. N.W., 8th Floor, 20005; (202) 682-1510. Fax, (202) 682-1535. Rupert Scofield, President. General email, info@finca.org*
Web, www.finca.org and Twitter, @FINCA

Provides financial services to low-income entrepreneurs outside the United States in order to create jobs, build assets, and improve standards of living. Delivers microfinance products and services through a network of wholly owned programs in Africa, Eurasia, the Middle East, and Latin America, operating on commercial principals of performance and sustainability. Focuses efforts on those living on less than $2.50/day, with a loan portfolio of approximately $1 billion estimated to reach about one million people worldwide.

Goodwill Industries International, *15810 Indianola Dr., Rockville, MD 20855; (301) 530-6500. Fax, (301) 530-1516. Jim Gibbons, President. Toll-free, (800) 466-3945. General email, contactus@goodwill.org*
Web, www.goodwill.org

Serves people with disabilities, low-wage workers, and others by providing education and career services as well as job placement opportunities and post-employment support. Helps people become independent, tax-paying members of their communities.

Grameen Foundation, *1101 15th St. N.W., 3rd Floor, 20005; (202) 628-3560. Fax, (202) 628-2341. Steve Hollingworth, President.*
Web, www.grameenfoundation.org

Seeks to eliminate poverty by providing microfinance and technology products and services in sub-Saharan Africa, Asia, the Middle East and North Africa (MENA) region, Latin America, and the Caribbean. Develops mobile phone–based solutions that address "information poverty" among the poor, providing tools, information, and services in the fields of health, agriculture, financial services, and livelihood creation. Focuses on assistance to women seeking to start or expand their own businesses.

Institute for Women's Policy Research (IWPR), *1200 18th St. N.W., #301, 20036; (202) 785-5100. Fax, (202) 833-4362. Heidi Hartmann, President.*
General email, iwpr@iwpr.org
Web, www.iwpr.org

Public policy research organization that focuses on women's issues, including family and work balance, employment and wages, the status of women in the United States, and discrimination based on gender, race, or ethnicity.

Jewish Federations of North America, *Washington Office, 1720 Eye St. N.W., 20006; (202) 785-5900. Fax, (202) 785-4937. William Daroff, Director.*
General email, dc@JewishFederations.org
Web, www.jewishfederations.org

Acts as advocate for the 153 Jewish federations across the United States on issues of concern, including long-term care, families at risk, and naturally occurring retirement communities. Offers marketing, communications, and public relations support; coordinates a speakers bureau. (Headquarters in New York.)

National Assn. for the Advancement of Colored People (NAACP), *Washington Bureau,* 1156 15th St. N.W., #915, 20005; (202) 463-2940. Fax, (202) 463-2953. *Hilary O. Shelton, Director.*
General email, washingtonbureau@naacpnet.org
Web, www.naacp.org

Membership: persons interested in civil rights for all minorities. Interests include welfare reform and related social welfare matters. Administers programs that create employment and affordable housing opportunities and that improve health care. Monitors legislation and regulations. (Headquarters in Baltimore, Md.)

National Assn. of Social Workers, 750 1st St. N.E., #800, 20002-4241; (202) 408-8600. Fax, (202) 336-8313. *Angelo McClain, Chief Executive Officer; Darrell Wheeler, President. Press, (202) 336-8324.*
General email, membership@naswdc.org
Web, www.socialworkers.org

Membership: graduates of accredited social work education programs and students in accredited programs. Promotes the interests of social workers and their clients; promotes professional standards; offers professional development opportunities; certifies members of the Academy of Certified Social Workers; conducts research. Monitors legislation and regulations.

National Community Action Foundation (NCAF), 400 N. Capitol St. N.W., #G80, 20001 (mailing address: P.O. Box 78214, Washington, DC 20013); (202) 842-2092. Fax, (202) 842-2095. *David A. Bradley, Executive Director.*
General email, info@ncaf.org
Web, www.ncaf.org

Organization for community action agencies concerned with issues that affect the poor. Provides information on Community Services Block Grants, low-income energy assistance, employment and training, weatherization of low-income housing, nutrition, and the Head Start program.

National Human Services Assembly, 1101 14th St. N.W., #600, 20005; (202) 347-2080. Fax, (202) 393-4517. *Irv Katz, President, Acting.*
General email, info@nassembly.org
Web, www.nassembly.org

Membership: national nonprofit health and human service organizations. Provides collective leadership in the areas of health and human service. Provides members' professional staff and volunteers with a forum to share information. Supports public policies, programs, and resources that advance the effectiveness of health and human service organizations and their service delivery.

National Urban League, *Washington Bureau,* 2901 14th St. N.W., 20009; (202) 265-8200. *George H. Lambert Jr., Affiliate Chief Executive Officer.*

Web, http://nul.iamempowered.com/affiliate/greater-washington-urban-league

Federal advocacy division of social service organization concerned with the social welfare of African Americans and other minorities. (Headquarters in New York.)

Poverty and Race Research Action Council, 1200 18th St. N.W., #200, 20036; (202) 906-8023. Fax, (202) 842-2885. *Philip Tegeler, Executive Director.*
General email, info@prrac.org
Web, www.prrac.org

Facilitates cooperative links between researchers and activists who work on race and poverty issues. Publishes bimonthly *Poverty & Race* newsletter and a civil rights history curriculum guide. Policy research areas include housing, education, and health disparities.

Public Welfare Foundation, 1200 U St. N.W., 20009-4443; (202) 965-1800. Fax, (202) 265-8851. *Mary E. McClymont, President. Media, ext. 242.*
General email, info@publicwelfare.org
Web, www.publicwelfare.org and Twitter, @PublicWelfare

Seeks to assist disadvantaged populations overcome barriers to full participation in society. Works to end over-incarceration of adults and juveniles. Awards grants to nonprofits in the following areas: criminal and juvenile justice and workers' rights.

Salvation Army, 615 Slaters Lane, Alexandria, VA 22314 (mailing address: P.O. Box 269, Alexandria, VA 22313-0269); (703) 684-5500. Fax, (703) 684-3478. *David Jeffrey, National Commander.*
Web, www.salvationarmyusa.org and Twitter, @SalvationArmyUS

International Christian social welfare organization that provides food, clothing, shelter, and social services to the homeless, the elderly, children, and persons with illness or disabilities. (International headquarters in London.)

Stalking Resource Center, 2000 M St. N.W., #480, 20036; (202) 467-8700. Fax, (202) 467-8701. *Michelle Garcia, Director.*
General email, src@ncvc.org
Web, www.victimsofcrime.org/SRC

Acts as an information clearinghouse on stalking. Works to raise public awareness of the dangers of stalking. Encourages the development and implementation of multidisciplinary responses to stalking in local communities. Offers practitioner training and technical assistance. (Affiliated with the National Center for Victims of Crime.)

U.S. Conference of City Human Services Officials, 1620 Eye St. N.W., 4th Floor, 20006; (202) 293-7330. Fax, (202) 293-2352. *Crystal D. Swann, Assistant Executive Director for Children, Health, and Human Services, (202) 861-6707.*
General email, info@usmayors.org
Web, www.usmayors.org/humanservices

Promotes improved social services for specific urban populations through meetings, technical assistance, and training programs for members; fosters information exchange among federal, state, and local governments, human services experts, and other groups concerned with human services issues. (Affiliate of the U.S. Conference of Mayors.)

Urban Institute, *2100 M St. N.W., 20037; (202) 833-7200. Fax, (202) 467-5775. Sarah Rosen Wartell, President. Public Affairs, (202) 261-5709. General email, publicaffairs@urban.org*

Web, www.urban.org

Nonpartisan public policy research and education organization. Interests include states' use of federal funds; delivery of social services to specific groups, including children of mothers in welfare reform programs; retirement policy, income, and community-based services for the elderly; job placement and training programs for welfare recipients; health care cost containment and access; food stamps; child nutrition; the homeless; housing; immigration; justice policy and prisoner reentry; federal, state, and local tax policy; and education policy.

Urban Institute, *Center on Income and Benefits Policy, 2100 M St. N.W., 20037; (202) 833-7200. Fax, (202) 833-4388. Gregory Acs, Director. Web, www.urban.org/center/ibp Web, retirement policy, http://urban.org/retirement_policy*

Studies how public policy influences behavior and the economic well-being of families, particularly the disabled, the elderly, and those with low incomes.

Urban Institute, *Center on Labor, Human Services, and Population, 2100 M St. N.W., 20037; (202) 833-7200. Fax, (202) 463-8522. Elizabeth Peters, Director. Web, www.urban.org/center/lhp*

Analyzes employment and income trends, studies how the U.S. population is growing, and evaluates programs dealing with homelessness, child welfare, and job training. Other areas of interest include immigration, mortality, sexual and reproductive health, adolescent risk behavior, child care, domestic violence, and youth development.

CHILDREN AND FAMILIES

General

▶**AGENCIES**

Administration for Children and Families (ACF) *(Health and Human Services Dept.), 330 C St. S.W., 20201 (mailing address: 370 L'Enfant Promenade S.W., Washington, DC 20447); (202) 401-2337. Mark Greenberg, Assistant Secretary, Acting. Public Affairs, (202) 401-9215. Web, www.acf.hhs.gov*

Plans, manages, and coordinates national assistance programs that promote stability, economic security, responsibility, and self-support for families; supervises programs and the use of funds to provide the most needy with aid and to increase alternatives to public assistance. Programs include Temporary Assistance to Needy Families, Child

Welfare, Head Start, Child Support Enforcement, Low-Income Home Energy Assistance, Community Services Block Grant, and Refugee Resettlement Assistance.

Administration for Children and Families (ACF) *(Health and Human Services Dept.), Child Support Enforcement, 330 C St. S.W., 20201 (mailing address: 370 L'Enfant Promenade S.W., Washington, DC 20447); (202) 401-9369. Fax, (202) 401-5655. Vicki Turetsky, Commissioner. Information, (202) 401-9373. Web, www.acf.hhs.gov/programs/cse*

Helps states develop, manage, and operate child support programs. Maintains the Federal Parent Locator Service, which provides state and local child support agencies with information for locating absent parents. State enforcement agencies locate absent parents, establish paternity, establish and enforce support orders, and collect child support payments.

Administration for Children and Families (ACF) *(Health and Human Services Dept.), Children's Bureau, 330 C St. S.W., 20201; (202) 401-6947. Joe Bock, Associate Commissioner. Web, www.acf.hhs.gov/programs/cb*

Works with state and local agencies to develop programs that focus on preventing the abuse of children in troubled families, protecting children from further abuse, and finding permanent placements for those who cannot safely return to their homes. Administers grants.

Administration for Children and Families (ACF) *(Health and Human Services Dept.), Family and Youth Services, 330 C St. S.W., 20201; (202) 205-8347. William H. Bentley, Associate Commissioner. Web, www.acf.hhs.gov/programs/fysb*

Administers federal discretionary grant programs for projects serving runaway and homeless youth and for projects that deter youth involvement in gangs. Provides youth service agencies with training and technical assistance. Monitors federal policies, programs, and legislation. Supports research on youth development issues, including gangs, runaways, and homeless youth. Operates national clearinghouse on families and youth. Issues grants and monitors abstinence education programs.

Administration for Children and Families (ACF) *(Health and Human Services Dept.), Family Assistance, 330 C St. S.W., 20201; (202) 401-9275. Nisha Patel, Director. Web, www.acf.hhs.gov/programs/ofa*

Provides leadership, direction, and technical guidance to the states and territories on administration of the TANF (Temporary Assistance to Needy Families) Block Grant. Focuses efforts to increase economic independence and productivity for families. Provides direction and guidance in collection and dissemination of performance and other data for these programs.

Assistant Secretary for Health *(Health and Human Services Dept.), Adolescent Health, 1101 Wootton Pkwy., #700, Rockville, MD 20852; (240) 453-2846. Evelyn Kappeler, Director.*

General email, oah.gov@hhs.gov

Web, www.hhs.gov/ash/oah

Implements the Pregnany Assistance Fund to assist states and tribes with support services for expecting and parenting teens and their families including student services at high schools, higher education institutions, and community centers and services for pregnant women who are victims of domestic abuse and sexual violence.

Eunice Kennedy Shriver National Institute of Child Health and Human Development *(National Institutes of Health), 31 Center Dr., Bldg. 31, #2A03, MSC 2425, Bethesda, MD 20892-2425 (mailing address: NICHD Information Resource Center, P.O. Box 3006, Rockville, MD 20847); (301) 496-1848. Fax, (301) 402-1104. Dr. Catherine Y. Spong, Director, Acting. Toll-free, (800) 370-2943. Toll-free fax, (866) 760-5947. Media, (301) 496-5133.*

General email, nichdinformationresourcescenter@ mail.nih.gov

Web, www.nichd.nih.gov

Supports and conducts research in biomedical, behavioral, and social sciences related to child and maternal health, medical rehabilitation, and reproductive sciences. Interests include demography, social sciences, and population dynamics; male/female fertility and infertility; developing and evaluating contraceptive methods; safety and efficacy of pharmaceuticals for pregnant women, infants, and children; HIV/AIDS infection, transmission, and associated infections; pediatric growth and endocrine research; child development and behavior; developmental biology, typical and atypical development; intellectual and developmental disabilities; gynecologic health conditions, including pelvic floor disorders; pregnancy, labor, and delivery; fetal and infant health; sudden infant death syndrome (SIDS); childhood injury and critical illness; genetics, genomics, and rare diseases; epidemiology and biostatistics; health behavior; medical rehabilitation, including brain injury, stroke, and spinal cord injury.

Food and Nutrition Service *(Agriculture Dept.), Child Nutrition, 3101 Park Center Dr., #640, Alexandria, VA 22302-1500; (703) 305-2590. Fax, (703) 305-2879. Cindy Long, Deputy Administrator, (703) 305-2054. Press, (202) 720-4623.*

General email, cndinternet@fns.usda.gov

Web, www.fns.usda.gov/school-meals/child-nutrition-programs

Administers the transfer of funds to state agencies for the National School Lunch Program; the School Breakfast Program; the Special Milk Program, the Child and Adult Care Food Program, and the Summer Food Service Program. These programs help fight hunger and obesity by reimbursing organizations such as schools, child care centers, and after-school programs for providing healthy meals to children.

Food and Nutrition Service *(Agriculture Dept.), National School Lunch Program, 3101 Park Center Dr.,*

#926, Alexandria, VA 22302; (703) 305-2590. Cindy Long, Deputy Administrator. Communications, (703) 305-2281.

Web, www.fns.usda.gov/nslp/national-school-lunch-program-nslp

Administers the federal assistance meal program operating in public and nonprofit private schools and residential child care institutions. Provides daily nutritionally balanced, low-cost or free lunches to children.

Food and Nutrition Service *(Agriculture Dept.), Policy Support, 3101 Park Center Dr., #1014, Alexandria, VA 22302-1500; (703) 305-2017. Fax, (703) 305-2576. Richard Lucas, Deputy Associate Administrator.*

General email, oaneweb@fns.usda.gov

Web, www.fns.usda.gov/ora

Evaluates federal nutrition assistance programs; provides results to policymakers and program administrators. Funds demonstration grants for state and local nutrition assistance projects.

Food and Nutrition Service *(Agriculture Dept.), Special Supplemental Nutrition Program for Women, Infants, and Children (WIC), 3101 Park Center Dr., #528, Alexandria, VA 22302-1594; (703) 305-2746. Fax, (703) 305-2196. Sarah Widor, Director.*

Web, www.fns.usda.gov/wic

Provides health departments and agencies with federal funding for food supplements and administrative expenses to make food, nutrition education, and health services available to infants, young children, and pregnant, nursing, and postpartum women.

Health and Human Services Dept. (HHS), *Head Start, 330 C St. S.W., 8th Floor, 20201; (202) 205-8573. Blanca Enriquez, Director.*

Web, www.acf.hhs.gov/programs/ohs

Awards grants to nonprofit and for-profit organizations and local governments for operating community Head Start programs (comprehensive development programs for children, ages three to five, of low-income families); manages a limited number of parent and child centers for families with children up to age five. Conducts research and manages demonstration programs, including those under the Comprehensive Child Care Development Act of 1988; administers the Child Development Associate scholarship program, which trains individuals for careers in child development, often as Head Start teachers.

Health and Human Services Dept. (HHS), *Planning and Evaluation, Human Services Policy, Children and Youth Policy, 200 Independence Ave. S.W., #405F, 20201; (202) 690-7409. Fax, (202) 690-6562. Cheryl Hoffman, Director.*

Web, www.aspe.hhs.gov/office-human-services-policy

Develops policies and procedures for programs that benefit children, youth, and families. Interests include child protection, domestic violence, family support, gang violence, child care and development, and care for drug-exposed, runaway, and homeless children and their families.

Justice Dept. (DOJ), *Violence Against Women,* 145 N St. N.E., #10W.121, 20530; (202) 307-6026. Fax, (202) 307-3911. Beatrice A. Hanson, Principal Deputy Director. National Domestic Violence Hotline, (800) 799-SAFE. TTY, (202) 307-2277.
General email, ovw.info@usdoj.gov
Web, www.ovw.usdoj.gov

Seeks more effective policies and services to combat domestic violence, sexual assault, stalking, and other crimes against women. Helps administer grants to states to fund shelters, crisis centers, and hotlines, and to hire law enforcement officers, prosecutors, and counselors specializing in cases of sexual violence and other violent crimes against women.

National Institute of Food and Agriculture (NIFA) *(Agriculture Dept.),* **Institute of Youth, Family, and Community,** 800 9th St. S.W., #4343, 20024 (mailing address: 1400 Independence Ave. S.W., MS 2250, Washington, DC 20250-2225); (202) 720-5305. Fax, (202) 720-3945. Muquarrab Qureshi, Deputy Director.
Web, www.nifa.usda.gov/office/institute-youth-family-and-community

Provides grants and programmatic training to support youth and family development; partners with county governments, the private sector, and state land-grant universities. Program areas include food and agricultural science education, particularly in minority-serving institutions; childhood nutrition; community food projects; and community service. Includes divisions of Community Education, Family and Consumer Sciences, and Youth and 4-H.

Office of Justice Programs (OJP) *(Justice Dept.),* **Juvenile Justice and Delinquency Prevention,** 810 7th St. N.W., 20531; (202) 307-5911. Fax, (301) 240-5830. Robert L. Listenbee, Administrator. Clearinghouse, (800) 851-3420.
Web, www.ojjdp.gov

Administers federal programs related to prevention and treatment of juvenile delinquency; missing and exploited children; child victimization; and training, technical assistance, and research and evaluation in these areas. Coordinates with youth programs of the departments of Agriculture, Education, Housing and Urban Development, Interior, and Labor, and the Health and Human Services Administration, including the Center for Studies of Crime and Delinquency. Operates the Juvenile Justice Clearinghouse. Sponsors the National Criminal Justice Reference Service ([800] 851-3420).

► **CONGRESS**

For a listing of relevant congressional committees and subcommittees, please see page 685 or the Appendix.

► **NONGOVERNMENTAL**

Active Minds, 2001 S St. N.W., #450, 20009; (202) 332-9595. Alison Malmon, Executive Director, (202) 332-9595, ext. 101. Press, (202) 332-9595 ext. 109.
Web, www.activeminds.org

Supports student-run chapters nationwide to help promote youth mental health awareness on college campuses. Offers mental health and mental illness information and resources.

Alliance for Strong Families and Communities, *Public Policy,* 1020 19th St. N.W., #500, 20036; (202) 429-0364. Marlo Nash, Senior Vice President, Public Policy, (202) 429-0638.
General email, policy@alliance1.org
Web, www.alliance1.org

Provides resources and leadership to more than 300 nonprofit child-serving and family-serving organizations in the United States and Canada. Works to strengthen community-based programs and services to families, children, and communities. Monitors legislation.

American Assn. for Marriage and Family Therapy, 112 S. Alfred St., Alexandria, VA 22314-3061; (703) 838-9808. Fax, (703) 838-9805. Tracy Todd, Executive Director.
General email, central@aamft.org
Web, www.aamft.org

Membership: professional marriage and family therapists. Promotes professional standards in marriage and family therapy through training programs; provides the public with educational material and online referral service for marriage and family therapy.

American Bar Assn. (ABA), *Center on Children and the Law,* 1050 Connecticut Ave. N.W., #400, 20036; (202) 662-1720. Fax, (202) 662-1755. Robert Horowitz, Director, Acting. Toll-free, (800) 285-2221.
General email, ctrchildlaw@americanbar.org
Web, www.americanbar.org/child

Works to increase lawyer representation of children; sponsors speakers and conferences; monitors legislation. Interests include child sexual abuse and exploitation, missing and runaway children, parental kidnapping, child support, foster care, and adoption of children with special needs.

American Humane Assn., 1400 16th St. N.W., #360, 20036; (202) 841-6080. Fax, (202) 450-2335. Mark Stubis, Chief Communications Officer, (202) 677-4227. Toll-free, (800) 227-4645.
General email, info@americanhumane.org and marks@americanhumane.org
Web, www.americanhumane.org and Twitter, @AmericanHumane

Membership: animal shelters, humane organizations, child protection agencies, government agencies, and individuals. Prepares model state legislation on child abuse and its prevention; publishes surveys on child and animal abuse and state abuse laws.

America's Promise Alliance, 1110 Vermont Ave. N.W., #900, 20005; (202) 657-0600. Fax, (202) 657-0601. Alma Johnson Powell, Chair; John Gomperts, President.
Web, www.americaspromise.org

Works with national and local organizations to support America's youth. Interests include adult mentoring, safe environments, physical and psychological health, effective education, and opportunities to help others. Seeks to reduce the high school dropout rate.

Boys and Girls Clubs of America, *Government Relations,* *1707 L St. N.W., #670, 20036; (202) 507-6670.* *Kevin McCartney, Senior Vice President, (202) 507-6671.* *General email, info@bgca.org*

Web, www.bgca.org

National network of neighborhood-based facilities that provide programs for underserved children six to eighteen years old, conducted by professional staff. Programs emphasize leadership development, education and career exploration, financial literacy, health and life skills, the arts, sports, fitness and recreation, and family outreach. (Headquarters in Atlanta, Ga.)

The Brookings Institution, *Economic Studies, 1775* *Massachusetts Ave. N.W., 20036-2188; (202) 797-6000.* *Fax, (202) 797-6181. Ted Gayer, Director.* *Press, (202) 797-6105.* *General email, escomment@brookings.edu*

Web, www.brookings.edu/economics

Studies policies for the well-being of children and families to address poverty, inequality, and lack of opportunity.

Caregiver Action Network, *1130 Connecticut Ave. N.W., #300, 20036; (202) 454-3970. John Schall, Chief* *Executive Officer.* *General email, info@caregiveraction.org*

Web, www.caregiveraction.org and Twitter, *@CaregiverAction*

Seeks to increase the quality of life of family caregivers by providing support and information; works to raise public awareness of caregiving through educational activities. (Formerly National Family Caregivers Assn.)

Child Welfare League of America, *1726 M St. N.W., #500, 20036-4522; (202) 688-4200. Fax, (202) 833-1689.* *Christine L. James-Brown, President.* *General email, cwla@cwla.org*

Web, www.cwla.org and Twitter, @theCWLA

Membership: public and private child welfare agencies. Develops standards for the field; provides information on adoption, early childhood education, foster care, group home services, child protection, residential care for children and youth, services to pregnant adolescents and young parents, and other child welfare issues. Monitors and advocates on federal children and family legislation.

ChildFund International, *Washington Office, 1200 18th* *St. N.W., #718, 20036; (804) 756-2700. Fax, (202) 682-3481. Anne Lynam Goddard, President; Sarah Bouchie, Vice President of Program Development. Toll-free, (800) 776-6767.* *General email, questions@childfund.org*

Web, www.childfund.org and Twitter, @ChildFund

Works internationally to ensure the survival, protection, and development of children. Promotes the improvement in quality of life of children within the context of family, community, and culture. Helps children in unstable situations brought on by war, natural disasters, and other high-risk circumstances. (Headquarters in Richmond, Va.)

Children's Defense Fund, *25 E St. N.W., 20001; (202) 628-8787. Fax, (202) 662-3510. Marian Wright Edelman, President. Toll-free, (800) 233-1200.* *General email, cdfinfo@childrensdefense.org*

Web, www.childrensdefense.org and Twitter, *@ChildDefender*

Advocacy group concerned with programs and policies for children and youth, particularly poor and minority children. Interests include health care, child welfare and mental health, early childhood development, education and youth development, child care, job training and employment, and family support. Works to ensure educational and job opportunities for youth.

Children's Home Society and Family Services, *Washington Office, 8555 16th St., #600, Silver Spring, MD 20910; (301) 562-6500. Fax, (301) 587-3869.* *Jodi Harpstead, Director. Toll-free, (888) 904-2229.* *General email, inquire@chsfs.org*

Web, www.chsfs.org and Twitter, @CHLSSAdoption

Provides information on international adoption; sponsors seminars and workshops for adoptive and prospective adoptive parents. (Headquarters in St. Paul, Minn.)

Children's Rights Council (CRC), *1296 Cronson Blvd., #3086, Crofton, MD 21114; 720 Eye St. S.E., 20003; (301) 459-1220. Lisa Britt, Chief Executive Officer.* *General email, info@crckids.org*

Web, www.crckids.org

Membership: parents and professionals. Works to strengthen families through education and advocacy. Supports family formation and preservation. Conducts conferences and serves as an information clearinghouse. Interests include children whose parents are separated, unwed, or divorced.

Congressional Coalition on Adoption Institute (CCAI), *311 Massachusetts Ave. N.E., 20002; (202) 544-8500.* *Fax, (202) 544-8501. Becky Weichhand, Executive Director.* *General email, info@ccainstitute.org*

Web, www.ccainstitute.org and Twitter, @CCAInstitute

Promotes awareness of children without families. Educates policymakers about foster care and adoption issues.

Council for Professional Recognition, *2460 16th St.* *N.W., 20009-3547; (202) 265-9090. Fax, (202) 265-9161.* *Valora Washington, Chief Executive Officer.* *Toll-free, (800) 424-4310.* *CDA Candidates email, cdafeedback@cda.org* *Web, www.cdacouncil.org and Twitter, @cdacouncil*

Promotes high standards for early childhood teachers. Awards credentials to family day care, preschool, home visitor, and infant-toddler caregivers. Administers the Child Development Associate National Credentialing Program, designed to assess and credential early childhood education professionals.

Cradle of Hope, 8630 Fenton St., #310, Silver Spring, MD 20910; (301) 587-4400. Fax, (301) 588-3091. Linda Perilstein, Executive Director.
General email, frontdesk@cradlehope.org

Web, www.cradlehope.org

International adoption center specializing in the placement of children from China. Offers preadoption and postadoption support services. Sponsors the Bridge of Hope program, a summer camp where older Chinese children meet and spend time with potential host families, in several U.S. locations, including the Washington, D.C., metro region.

Every Child Matters, 1023 15th St. N.W., #401, 20005; (202) 223-8177. Fax, (202) 223-8499. Brian Ahlberg, President.
General email, info@everychildmatters.org

Web, www.everychildmatters.org and Twitter, @VotingforKids

Works to make children's needs a political priority through public education activities. Interests include prevention of child abuse and neglect, improvement of the health of low-income children, solutions in child care, early childhood education, and after-school programs.

FAIR Girls, 2100 M St. N.W., #170-254, 20037-1233; (202) 265-1505. Andrea Powell, Executive Director. Crisis hotline, (855) 900-3247. National trafficking hotline, (888) 373-7888.
General email, info@fairgirls.org

Web, www.fairgirls.org

Advocates against sex trafficking of young girls and transgender victims. Researches sex trafficking prevention and public policies that help protect at-risk women. Supports survivors of human trafficking by offering workshops aimed to educate survivors on health, finding jobs, managing stress, and communication. Operates in Bosnia, Afghanistan, Serbia, Russia, Uganda, and the United States.

Family and Home Network, P.O. Box 492, Merrifield, VA 22116; 3110 Landover St., Alexandria, VA 22305; (703) 304-3982. Catherine Myers, Executive Director.
General email, cmyers@familyandhome.org

Web, www.familyandhome.org and Twitter, @familyhomeorg

Provides information and support for parents who stay home, or who would like to stay home (full or part time), to raise their children, in the United States and abroad. Monitors legislation and regulations relating to family issues.

Foster Care to Success, 21351 Gentry Dr., #130, Sterling, VA 20166; (571) 203-0270. Fax, (571) 203-0273. Eileen McCaffrey, Executive Director; Tina Raheem, Director, Scholarships and Grants.
General email, info@fc2success.org

Web, www.fc2success.org and Twitter, @FC2Success

Advocates for orphaned, abandoned, and homeless teenage youths. Provides scholarships, research, information, emergency cash grants, volunteer programs, guidance, and support. Interests include the rights of orphaned children, transition from youth foster care to young adult independence, and breaking the welfare cycle. Learning center provides training and educational materials. (Formerly Orphan Foundation of America.)

Generations United, 25 E St. N.W., 3rd Floor, 20001; (202) 289-3979. Fax, (202) 289-3952. Donna M. Butts, Executive Director.
General email, gu@gu.org

Web, www.gu.org and Twitter, @GensUnited

Membership organization that promotes intergenerational programs and public policies. Focuses on the economic, social, and personal benefits of intergenerational cooperation. Encourages collaboration between organizations that represent different age groups.

Girl Scouts of the U.S.A., *Public Policy and Advocacy,* 816 Connecticut Ave. N.W., 3rd Floor, 20006; (202) 659-3780. Fax, (202) 331-8065. Anna Maria Chavez, Chief Executive Officer.
General email, advocacy@girlscouts.org

Web, www.girlscouts.org

Educational service organization for girls ages five to seventeen that promotes personal development through social action, leadership, and other projects. Areas of advocacy include girls' healthy living, increasing girls' participation in STEM (science, technology, engineering, and math) fields, financial literacy, career education, and supporting girls in underserved communities. (Headquarters in New York.)

Kidsave, 4622 Wisconsin Ave. N.W., #202, 20016; (202) 503-3100. Fax, (202) 503-3131. Terry Baugh, President.
General email, info@kidsave.org

Web, www.kidsave.org, Twitter, @Kidsave_Intl and Facebook, www.facebook.com/KidsaveInternational

Maintains programs that provide children age eight and older in orphanages and foster care the opportunity for weekend visits and short stays with families in the community with the goal of permanent adoption or long-term mentoring. Monitors child welfare legislation and regulations worldwide.

National 4-H Council, 7100 Connecticut Ave., Chevy Chase, MD 20815-4999; (301) 961-2800. Fax, (301) 961-2894. Jennifer L. Sirangelo, President, (301) 961-2820. Press, (301) 961-2973.
Web, www.4-h.org, Twitter, @4H and Facebook, www.facebook.com/4-h

4-H membership: young people across the United States engaged in hands-on learning activities in leadership, citizenship, life skills, science, healthy living, and food security. National 4-H Council is a national, private-sector partner of the 4-H Youth Development Program and its parent, the Cooperative Extension System of the Agriculture Dept. In the United States, 4-H programs are implemented by 109 land-grant universities and more than 3,000 cooperative extension offices. Outside the United States, 4-H programs operate through independent, country-led organizations in more than 50 countries.

National Assn. for the Education of Young Children, *1313 L St. N.W., #500, 20005; (202) 232-8777. Fax, (202) 328-1846. Rhian Allvin, Executive Director. Information, (800) 424-2460.*
General email, naeyc@naeyc.org

Web, www.naeyc.org

Membership: early childhood teachers, administrators, college faculty, and directors of early childhood programs at the state and local levels. Works to improve the quality of early childhood care and education. Administers national accreditation system for early childhood programs. Maintains information service.

National Black Child Development Institute, *1313 L St. N.W., #110, 20005-4110; (202) 833-2220. Fax, (202) 833-8222. Tobeka G. Green, President. Toll-free, (800) 556-2234.*
General email, moreinfo@nbcdi.org

Web, www.nbcdi.org and Twitter, @NBCDI

Advocacy group for Black children, youth, and families. Interests include child care, adoption, and health, and early childhood education. Provides information on government policies that affect Black children, youth, and families.

National Campaign to Prevent Teen and Unplanned Pregnancy, *1776 Massachusetts Ave. N.W., #200, 20036; (202) 478-8500. Fax, (202) 478-8588. Ginny Ehrlich, Chief Executive Officer.*
General email, campaign@thenc.org

Web, www.thenationalcampaign.org and Twitter, @TheNC

Nonpartisan initiative that seeks to reduce the U.S. teen and unplanned pregnancy rates. Provides education and information regarding contraception.

National Child Support Enforcement Assn., *7918 Jones Branch Dr., #300, McLean, VA 22102; (703) 506-2880. Fax, (703) 506-3266. Ann Marie Ruskin, Executive Director, Acting.*
General email, customerservice@ncsea.org

Web, www.ncsea.org

Promotes enforcement of child support obligations and educates social workers, attorneys, judges, and other professionals on child support issues. Fosters exchange of ideas among child support professionals. Monitors legislation and regulations.

National Coalition Against Domestic Violence, *Public Policy, 2000 M St. N.W., #480, 20036; (202) 467-8714. Fax, (202) 785-8576. Ruth M. Glenn, Executive Director, (303) 839-1852, ext. 105. TTY, (202) 787-3224. National Domestic Violence Hotline, (800) 799-7233 (SAFE).*
General email, publicpolicy@ncadv.org

Web, www.ncadv.org, Twitter, @NCADV and Facebook, www.facebook.com/SupportNCADV

Monitors legislation and public policy initiatives concerning victims and survivors of domestic violence. Work includes empowering victims, promoting and coordinating direct services, and educating the public about domestic violence. Offers the Cosmetic & Reconstructive Support Program to survivors. (Headquarters in Denver, Colo.)

National Collaboration for Youth, *1101 14th St. N.W., #600, 20005; (202) 347-2080. Fax, (202) 393-4517. Irv Katz, President, Acting.*
General email, policy@nassembly.org

Web, www.collab4youth.org

Membership: national youth-serving organizations. Works to improve members' youth development programs through information exchange and other support. Raises public awareness of youth issues. Monitors legislation and regulations. (Affiliate of the National Human Services Assembly.)

National Council for Adoption, *225 N. Washington St., Alexandria, VA 22314-2561; (703) 299-6633. Fax, (703) 299-6004. Charles (Chuck) Johnson, Chief Executive Officer. Press, (301) 751-3750.*
General email, ncfa@adoptioncouncil.org

Web, www.adoptioncouncil.org, Twitter, @AdoptionCouncil and Facebook, www.facebook.com/AdoptionCouncil

Organization of individuals, national and international agencies, and corporations interested in adoption. Supports adoption through legal, ethical agencies; advocates the right to confidentiality in adoption. Conducts research and holds conferences; provides information; supports pregnancy counseling, maternity services, and counseling for infertile couples. Monitors legislation and regulations.

National Fatherhood Initiative, *12410 Milestone Center Dr., #600, Germantown, MD 20876; (301) 948-0599. Fax, (301) 948-6776. Christopher (Chris) Brown, President. Information, (301) 948-4325.*
General email, info@fatherhood.org

Web, www.fatherhood.org, Twitter, @NFUDC and Facebook, www.facebook.com/nationalfatherhoodinitiative

Works to improve the well-being of children by increasing the proportion of children growing up with involved, responsible, and committed fathers. Provides curricula, training, and assistance to state and community fatherhood initiatives. Conducts public awareness campaigns and research. Monitors legislation.

National Head Start Assn., *1651 Prince St., Alexandria, VA 22314; (703) 739-0875. Fax, (703) 739-0878. Yasmina S. Vinci, Executive Director. Toll-free, (866) 677-8724.*
Web, www.nhsa.org

Membership: organizations that represent Head Start children, families, and staff. Recommends strategies on issues affecting Head Start programs; provides training and professional development opportunities. Monitors legislation and regulations.

National Network for Youth (NN4Y), *741 8th St. S.E., 20003; (202) 783-7949. Darla Bardine, Executive Director. National Runaway Safeline, (800) 786-2929.*
General email, info@nn4youth.org

Web, www.nn4youth.org

Membership: providers of services related to runaway and homeless youth. Offers technical assistance to new and existing youth projects. Monitors legislation and regulations.

National PTA, *1250 N. Pitt St., Alexandria, VA 22314; (703) 518-1200. Fax, (703) 836-0942. Nathan R. Monell, Executive Director; Elizabeth Rorick, Government Affairs and Communications. Toll-free, (800) 307-4782.*
General email, info@pta.org
Web, www.pta.org

Membership: parent-teacher associations at the preschool, elementary, and secondary levels. Supports school breakfast and lunch programs; works as an active member of the Child Nutrition Forum, which supports federally funded nutrition programs for children.

National Urban League, *Washington Bureau, 2901 14th St. N.W., 20009; (202) 265-8200. George H. Lambert Jr., Affiliate Chief Executive Officer.*
Web, http://nul.iamempowered.com/affiliate/greater-washington-urban-league

Federal advocacy division of social service organization concerned with the social welfare of African Americans and other minorities. Youth Development division provides local leagues with technical assistance for youth programs and seeks training opportunities for youth within Urban League programs. (Headquarters in New York.)

Rape, Abuse, and Incest National Network (RAINN), *1220 L St. N.W., #505, 20005; (202) 544-1034. Fax, (202) 544-3556. Scott Berkowitz, President. National sexual assault hotline, (800) 656-4673.*
General email, info@rainn.org
Web, www.rainn.org and Twitter, @RAINN01

Links sexual assault victims to confidential local services through national sexual assault hotline. Operates the Defense Dept.'s sexual assault helpline. Provides extensive public outreach and education programs nationwide on sexual assault prevention, prosecution, and recovery. Promotes national policy efforts to improve services to victims.

Share Our Strength, *1030 15th St. N.W., #1100W, 20005; (202) 393-2925. Fax, (202) 347-5868. Bill Shore, Executive Director. Toll-free, (800) 969-4767.*
General email, contactus@strength.org
Web, www.nokidhungry.org

Works to alleviate and prevent hunger and poverty for children in the United States. Provides food assistance; treats malnutrition; seeks long-term solutions to hunger and poverty through fund-raising, partnerships with corporations and nonprofit organizations, grants, and educational programs.

Urban Institute, *Low-Income Working Families Initiative, 2100 M St. N.W., 20037; (202) 833-7200. Fax, (202) 833-4388. Margaret Simms, Director.*
Web, www.urban.org/center/lwf

Studies low-income families, identifies factors that contribute to poor outcomes, and develops public policy solutions. Interests include economic security, the public programs safety net, better life chances for children, and racial and ethnic disparities.

Youth Advocate Program International, *4000 Albermarle St. N.W., #401, 20016; (202) 244-6410. Mubarak E. Awad, Director.*
General email, whe@peaceandyouth.org
Web, www.yapi.org

Supports the development and operation of community-based services for at-risk youth and their families. (Formerly the Youth Advocate Program International, Inc.)

Older Adults

▶**AGENCIES**

Administration for Community Living (ACL) *(Health and Human Services Dept.), Administration on Aging, 330 C St. S.W., 20201; (202) 619-0724. Edwin L. Walker, Deputy Assistant Secretary. Press, (202) 357-3507. Eldercare locator, (800) 677-1116. TTY, (800) 877-8339.*
General email, aclinfo@acl.hhs.gov
Web, www.aoa.hhs.gov

Advocacy agency for older Americans and their concerns. Collaborates with tribal organizations, community and national organizations, and state and area agencies to implement grant programs and services designed to improve the quality of life for older Americans, such as information and referral, adult day care, elder abuse prevention, home-delivered meals, in-home care, transportation, and services for caregivers.

Senior Corps *(Corporation for National and Community Service), Retired and Senior Volunteer Program, Foster Grandparent Program, and Senior Companion Program, 1201 New York Ave. N.W., 20525; (202) 606-5000. Erwin Tan, Director, (202) 606-3237. National service information hotline, (800) 942-2677. TTY, (800) 833-3722.*
General email, info@cns.gov
Web, www.seniorcorps.gov

Network of programs that help older Americans find service opportunities in their communities, including the Retired and Senior Volunteer Program, which encourages older citizens to use their talents and experience in community service; the Foster Grandparent Program, which gives older citizens opportunities to work with exceptional children and children with special needs; and the Senior Companion Program, which recruits older citizens to help homebound adults, especially seniors, with special needs.

▶**CONGRESS**

For a listing of relevant congressional committees and subcommittees, please see page 685 or the Appendix.

Resources for Older Adults

ADVOCACY

AARP, (888) OUR-AARP or (877) 342-2277 (Spanish); www.aarp.org

AARP, Legal Services Network, (886) 330-0753

Alliance for Retired Americans, (202) 637-5399; www.retiredamericans.org

Gray Panthers, (800) 280-5362 or (202) 737-6637

National Caucus and Center on Black Aged, Inc., (202) 637-8400; www.ncba-aged.org

National Committee to Preserve Social Security and Medicare, (800) 966-1935 or (202) 216-0420; www.ncpssm.org

National Consumers League, (202) 835-3323; www.nclnet.org or www.sosrx.org

National Hispanic Council on Aging, (202) 347-9733; www.nhcoa.org

Seniors Coalition, (202) 261-3594; www.senior.org

60 Plus, (703) 807-2070; www.60plus.org

AGENCIES

Administration on Aging (AoA), (202) 619-0724; www.aoa.gov

Centers for Medicare and Medicaid Services (CMS), (877) 267-2323; www.cms.gov

Employment and Training Administration, Older Worker Program, (877) 872-5627; www.doleta.gov/seniors

National Assn. of Area Agencies on Aging, Eldercare Locator, (202) 872-0888; www.n4a.org

National Institute on Aging (NIA), (301) 496-1752; www.nia.nih.gov

National Institutes of Health (NIH), Senior Health, nihseniorhealth.gov

Social Security Administration (SSA), (800) 772-1213; www.ssa.gov

Veterans Affairs Dept., (800) 827-1000; www.va.gov

HEALTH

Alliance for Aging Research, (202) 293-2856; www.agingresearch.org

Alzheimer's Assn., (800) 272-3900; www.alz.org

Families USA, (202) 628-3030; www.familiesusa.org

Geriatric Mental Health Foundation, (formerly the American Assn. for Geriatric Psychiatry), (703) 556-9222; www.gmhfonline.org

National Osteoporosis Foundation, (800) 231-4222 or (703) 647-3000; www.nof.org

HOUSING, NURSING HOMES, ASSISTED LIVING

Armed Forces Retirement Home, Washington, (202) 541-7501; www.afrh.gov

Army Distaff Foundation, (800) 541-4255 or (202) 541-0400; www.armydistaff.org

B'nai B'rith International, Center for Senior Services, (866) 999-6596; www.bnaibrith.org/seniors.html

Consumer Consortium on Assisted Living, (732) 212-9036; www.ccal.org

National Consumer Voice for Quality Long-term Care, (202) 332-2275; www.theconsumervoice.org

SERVICES, COMMUNITY SERVICE

American Veterans (AMVETS), (877) 726-8387; www.amvets.org

Jewish Council for the Aging of Greater Washington, (301) 255-4200; www.accessjca.org

National Council on the Aging, (571) 527-3900; www.ncoa.org

National Senior Service Corps, (800) 424-8867; www.seniorcorps.org

Senior Community Service Employment Program, (877) 872-5627; www.doleta.gov/seniors

---

▶**NONGOVERNMENTAL**

AARP, *601 E St. N.W., 20049; (202) 434-2277. Jo Ann C. Jenkins, Chief Executive Officer. Press, (202) 434-2560. Library, (202) 434-6233. TTY, (877) 434-7598. Toll-free, (888) 687-2277. Membership, (202) 434-3525. General email, member@aarp.org*

Web, www.aarp.org

Membership: people fifty years of age and older. Conducts educational and counseling programs in areas concerning older adults, such as widowed persons services, health promotion, housing, and consumer protection.

Alliance for Retired Americans, *815 16th St. N.W., 4th Floor North, 20006-4104; (202) 637-5399. Fax, (202)* 637-5398. Robert Roach, President. Membership, (800) 333-7212.
Web, www.retiredamericans.org

Seeks to strengthen benefits to the elderly, including improved Social Security payments, increased employment, and education and health programs. (Affiliate of the AFL-CIO.)

American Seniors Housing Assn., *5225 Wisconsin Ave. N.W., #502, 20015; (202) 237-0900. Fax, (202) 237-1616. General email, info@seniorshousing.org*
Web, www.seniorshousing.org

Membership: development, finance, and operation professionals working in seniors apartments, independent and assisted living communities, and retirement communities. Promotes the advancement of quality seniors housing and health care through research, education, and monitoring legislation and regulations.

The Brookings Institution, *Economic Studies, 1775 Massachusetts Ave. N.W., 20036-2188; (202) 797-6000. Fax, (202) 797-6181. Ted Gayer, Director. Press, (202) 797-6105.*
General email, escomment@brookings.edu
Web, www.brookings.edu/economics

Promotes efforts to make retirement saving easier and improve retirement income prospects for American workers.

Experience Works, Inc., *4401 Wilson Blvd., #1100, Arlington, VA 22203; (703) 522-7272. Fax, (703) 522-0141. Sally Boofer, Chief Executive Officer. Toll-free, (866) 397-9757.*
Web, www.experienceworks.org and Twitter, @experienceworks

Trains and places older adults in the workforce. Seeks to increase awareness of issues affecting older workers and build support for policies and legislation benefiting older adults. Maintains a help line for those unemployed who are 55 and older.

Families USA, *1201 New York Ave. N.W., #1100, 20005; (202) 628-3030. Fax, (202) 347-2417. Ron Pollack, Executive Director.*
General email, info@familiesusa.org
Web, www.familiesusa.org and Twitter, @FamiliesUSA

Interests include health care, the Affordable Care Act, Social Security, Medicare, and Medicaid. Offers Enrollment Assistant Resource Centers to help consumers and businesses obtain high-quality, affordable health care. Monitors legislation and regulations affecting the elderly. Focuses on communities of color.

Jewish Council for the Aging of Greater Washington, *12320 Parklawn Dr., Rockville, MD 20852-1726; (301) 255-4200. Fax, (301) 231-9360. David N. Gamse, Chief Executive Officer. TTY, (301) 881-5263.*
General email, seniorhelpline@accessjca.org
Web, www.accessjca.org

Nonsectarian organization that provides programs and services throughout the metropolitan D.C. area to help older people continue living independent lives. Offers employment services, computer training, adult day care, social day care, transportation, information services and referrals for transportation and in-home services, and volunteer opportunities.

National Assn. of Area Agencies on Aging, *1730 Rhode Island Ave. N.W., #1200, 20036; (202) 872-0888. Fax, (202) 872-0057. Sandy Markwood, Chief Executive Officer.*
General email, info@n4a.org
Web, www.n4a.org

Works to establish an effective national policy on aging; provides local agencies on aging and Native American aging programs with training and technical assistance; disseminates information to these agencies and the public. Monitors legislation and regulations.

National Assn. of Area Agencies on Aging, *Eldercare Locator, 1730 Rhode Island Ave. N.W., #1200, 20036; (202) 872-0888. Fax, (202) 872-0057. Patrice Earnest, Program Manager. Toll-free, (800) 677-1116.*
General email, eldercarelocator@n4a.org
Web, www.eldercare.gov

National toll-free directory assistance service that connects older people and caregivers with local support resources, including meal services, home care, transportation, housing alternatives, home repair, recreation, social activities, and legal services. Language interpretation service for 150 languages available 9:00 a.m.–8:00 p.m. at the toll-free number. (Provided by the U.S. Administration on Aging and administered by the National Assn. of Area Agencies on Aging.)

National Assn. of States United for Aging and Disabilities, *1201 15th St. N.W., #350, 20005-2842; (202) 898-2578. Fax, (202) 898-2583. Martha Roherty, Executive Director.*
General email, info@nasuad.org
Web, www.nasuad.org

Membership: state and territorial governmental units that deal with older adults, people with disabilities, and their caregivers. Provides members with information, technical assistance, and professional training. Monitors legislation and regulations.

National Caucus and Center on Black Aging, Inc., *1220 L St. N.W., #800, 20005-2407; (202) 637-8400. Fax, (202) 347-0895. Karyne Jones, President.*
General email, support@ncba-aged.org
Web, www.ncba-aged.org

Concerned with issues that affect older Black Americans and other minorities. Sponsors employment and housing programs for older adults and education and training for professionals in gerontology. Monitors legislation and regulations.

National Council on Aging, *251 18th St. South, #500, Arlington, VA 22202; (571) 527-3900. Fax, (571) 527-3901. James P. Firman, President. Press, (571) 527-3914. Eldercare locator, (800) 677-1116.*
General email, info@ncoa.org
Web, www.ncoa.org, Twitter, @NCOAging and Facebook, www.facebook.com/NCOAging

Serves as an information clearinghouse on training, technical assistance, advocacy, and research on every aspect of aging. Provides information on social services for older persons. Monitors legislation and regulations.

National Hispanic Council on Aging, *Walker Bldg., 734 15th St. N.W., #1050, 20005; (202) 347-9733. Fax, (202) 347-9735. Yanira Cruz, President.*
General email, nhcoa@nhcoa.org
Web, www.nhcoa.org

Membership: senior citizens, health care workers, professionals in the field of aging, and others in the United States and Puerto Rico who are interested in topics related to Hispanics and aging. Provides research training, policy analysis, consulting, and technical assistance; sponsors seminars, workshops, and management internships.

DISABILITIES

General

▶AGENCIES

Access Board, *1331 F St. N.W., #1000, 20004-1111; (202) 272-0080. Fax, (202) 272-0081. David M. Capozzi, Executive Director, (202) 272-0010. Toll-free technical assistance, (800) 872-2253. TTY, (202) 272-0082. Toll-free TTY, (800) 993-2822.*
General email, info@access-board.gov
Web, www.access-board.gov

Develops and maintains accessibility requirements for buildings, transit vehicles, telecommunications equipment, medical diagnostic equipment, and electronic and information technology. Provides technical assistance and training on these guidelines and standards. Enforces access standards for federally funded facilities through the Architectural Barriers Act.

Administration for Community Living (ACL) *(Health and Human Services Dept.), National Institute on Disability, Independent Living, and Rehabilitation Research, 330 C St. S.W., 20201 (mailing address: 400 Maryland Ave. S.W., MS 2700, Washington, DC 20202-7100); (202) 245-7640. Fax, (202) 245-7323. John Tschida, Director. Press, (202) 245-6721.*
General email, nidrr-mailbox@ed.gov
Web, www.acl.gov/Programs/NIDILRR

Supports applied research, training, and development to improve the lives of individuals with disabilities from birth to adulthood. Generates new knowledge and promotes its effective use to improve the abilities of people with disabilities to perform activities of their choice in the community, and also to expand society's capacity to provide full opportunities and accommodations for its citizens with disabilities. Awards grants for rehabilitation research programs and scientific, technical, and methodological research; coordinates federal rehabilitation research programs; offers field research fellowships.

Civil Rights Division *(Justice Dept.), Disability Rights, 950 Pennsylvania Ave. N.W., 20530; (202) 307-0663. Fax, (202) 307-1197. Rebecca Bond, Chief. Information and ADA specialist, (800) 514-0301. TTY, (800) 514-0383.*
Web, www.justice.gov/crt/about/drs

Litigates cases under Titles I, II, and III of the Americans with Disabilities Act, which prohibits discrimination on the basis of disability in places of public accommodation and in all activities of state and local government. Provides technical assistance to businesses and individuals affected by the law.

Education Dept., *Special Education and Rehabilitative Services, 550 12th St S W., 5th Floor, 20202-7100 (mailing address: 400 Maryland Ave. S.W., Washington, DC 20202-7000); (202) 245-7468. Fax, (202) 245-7638. Main phone is voice and TTY accessible. Michael Yudin, Assistant Secretary.*
Web, www2.ed.gov/about/offices/list/osers

Provides information on federal legislation and programs and national organizations concerning individuals with disabilities.

Education Dept., *Special Education and Rehabilitative Services, Rehabilitation Services Administration, 400 Maryland Ave. S.W., 20202-7100; (202) 245-7468. Fax, (202) 245-7591. Janet L. LaBreck, Commissioner.*
Web, www2.ed.gov/about/offices/list/osers/rsa

Coordinates and directs major federal programs for eligible physically and mentally disabled persons. Administers distribution of grants for training and employment programs and for establishing supported-employment and independent-living programs. Provides vocational training and job placement.

Equal Employment Opportunity Commission (EEOC), *Legal Counsel, Americans with Disabilities Act Policy Division, 131 M St. N.E., 20507; (202) 653-4665. Fax, (202) 653-6034. Christopher J. Kuczynski, Assistant Legal Counsel. TTY, (202) 663-7026.*
Web, www.eeoc.gov

Provides interpretations, opinions, and technical assistance on the ADA provisions relating to employment.

Eunice Kennedy Shriver National Institute of Child Health and Human Development *(National Institutes of Health), National Center for Medical Rehabilitation Research, 6100 Executive Blvd., Bldg. 6100, #2A-03, MSC 7510, Bethesda, MD 20892; (301) 402-2242. Fax, (301) 402-0832. Dr. Alison Cernich, Director.*
Web, www.nichd.nih.gov/about/org/ncmrr

Fosters the development of scientific knowledge needed to enhance the health, productivity, independence, and quality of life of persons with disabilities. Supports a program of basic and applied research promoting tissue plasticity, assistive technology and devices, improved outcomes, and increased patient participation.

John F. Kennedy Center for the Performing Arts, *VSA and Accessibility, 2700 F St. N.W., 20566 (mailing address: P.O. Box 101510, Arlington, VA 22210); (202) 416-8898. Fax, (202) 416-4840. Betty Siegel, Director.*
General email, access@kennedy-center.org
Web, www.vsarts.org

Initiates and supports research and program development providing arts training and programming for persons with disabilities to make classrooms and communities more inclusive. Provides technical assistance and training to VSA Arts state organizations; acts as an information clearinghouse for arts and persons with disabilities.

Labor Dept. (DOL), *Disability Employment Policy, 200 Constitution Ave. N.W., #S1303, 20210; (202) 693-7880.*

Fax, (202) 693-7888. Jennifer Sheehy, Deputy Assistant Secretary. Toll-free, (866) ODEP-DOL (633-7365). TTY, (877) 889-5627.
General email, odep@dol.gov
Web, www.dol.gov/odep

Seeks to eliminate physical and psychological barriers to the disabled through education and information programs; promotes education, training, rehabilitation, and employment opportunities for people with disabilities.

National Council on Disability, 1331 F St. N.W., #850, 20004-1107; (202) 272-2004. Fax, (202) 272-2022. Rebecca Cokely, Executive Director. TTY, (202) 272-2074.
General email, ncd@ncd.gov
Web, www.ncd.gov and Facebook, www.facebook.com/NCDgov

Independent federal agency providing advice to the president, Congress, and executive branch agencies to promote policies and programs that ensure equal opportunity for individuals with disabilities and enable individuals with disabilities to achieve self-sufficiency and full integration into society.

Smithsonian Institution, *Accessibility Program,* 14th St. and Constitution Ave. N.W., #1050, 20013-7012 (mailing address: P.O. Box 37012, NMAH, MRC 607, Washington, DC 20013-7012); (202) 633-2921. Fax, (202) 633-4352. Elizabeth (Beth) Ziebarth, Director. Information, (888) 783-0001.
General email, access@si.edu
Web, www.si.edu/accessibility

Coordinates the Smithsonian's efforts to improve accessibility of its programs and facilities to visitors and staff with disabilities. Serves as a resource for museums and individuals nationwide.

Social Security Administration (SSA), *Disability Determinations,* 3570 Annex Bldg., 6401 Security Blvd., Baltimore, MD 21235; (410) 965-1170. Fax, (410) 965-6503. Ann Roberts, Associate Commissioner. Information, (800) 772-1213. TTY, (800) 325-0778.
Web, www.ssa.gov/disability

Administers and regulates the disability insurance program and disability provisions of the Supplemental Security Income (SSI) program.

Workers Compensation (OWCP) *(Labor Dept.),* *Coal Mine Workers' Compensation,* 200 Constitution Ave. N.W., #S3524, 20210; (202) 693-0036. Fax, (202) 693-1378. Michael A. Chance, Director, (202) 693-0046. Toll-free, (800) 638-7072.
General email, DCMWC-public@dol.gov
Web, www.dol.gov/owcp/dcmwc

Provides direction for administration of the black lung benefits program. Adjudicates all black lung claims; certifies benefit payments and maintains black lung beneficiary rolls.

►**CONGRESS**

For a listing of relevant congressional committees and subcommittees, please see page 685 or the Appendix.

Library of Congress, *National Library Service for the Blind and Physically Handicapped,* 1291 Taylor St. N.W., 20542 (mailing address: Library of Congress, Washington, DC 20542); (202) 707-5100. Fax, (202) 707-0712. Karen Keninger, Director. Toll-free, (800) 424-8567. TTY, (202) 707-0744.
General email, nls@loc.gov
Braille email, braille@loc.gov
Web, www.loc.gov/nls

Administers a national program of free library services for persons with physical disabilities in cooperation with regional and subregional libraries. Produces and distributes full-length books and magazines in recorded form and in Braille. Reference section answers questions relating to blindness and physical disabilities and on library services available to persons with disabilities.

►**NONGOVERNMENTAL**

American Assn. of People with Disabilities (AAPD), 2013 H St. N.W., 5th Floor, 20006; (202) 457-0046. Helen Berger, President. Toll-free, (800) 840-8844.
General email, communications@aapd.com
Web, www.aapd.com

Works to organize the disability community to affect political, economic, and social change through programs on employment, independent living, and assistive technology. Seeks to educate the public and policymakers on issues affecting persons with disabilities. Works in coalition with other organizations toward full enforcement of disability and antidiscrimination laws.

American Bar Assn. (ABA), *Commission on Disability Rights,* 1050 Connecticut Ave. N.W., #400, 20036; (202) 662-1570. Fax, (202) 442-3439. Mark D. Agrast, Chair; Amy L. Allbright, Director.
General email, cdr@americanbar.org
Web, www.americanbar.org/disabilityrights

Promotes the rule of law for persons with mental, physical, and sensory disabilities and their full and equal participation in the legal profession. Offers online resources, publications, and continuing education opportunities on disability law topics and engages in national initiatives to remove barriers to the education, employment, and advancement of lawyers with disabilities.

American Counseling Assn., *Rehabilitation,* 6101 Stevenson Ave., Alexandria, VA 22304-3300; (703) 823-9800. Fax, (703) 823-0252. Richard Yep, Executive Director. Toll-free, (800) 347-6647. TTY, (703) 823-6862.
General email, ryep@counseling.org
Web, www.counseling.org

Membership: counselors, counselor educators, and graduate students in the rehabilitation field, and other interested persons. Establishes counseling and research standards; encourages establishment of rehabilitation facilities; conducts leadership training and continuing education programs; serves as a liaison between counselors and clients. Monitors legislation and regulations.

American Medical Rehabilitation Providers Assn. (AMRPA), *1710 N St. N.W., 20036; (202) 223-1920. Fax, (202) 223-1925. Carolyn Zollar, ExecutiveVice President, Government Relations. Toll-free, (888) 346-4624. Web, www.amrpa.org*

Association representing a membership of freestanding rehabilitation hospitals and rehabilitation units of general hospitals, outpatient rehabilitation facilities, skilled nursing facilities, and others. Provides leadership, advocacy, and resources to develop medical rehabilitation services and supports for persons with disabilities and others in need of services. Acts as a clearinghouse for information to members on the nature and availability of services. Monitors legislation and regulations.

American Network of Community Options and Resources (ANCOR), *1101 King St., #380, Alexandria, VA 22314; (703) 535-7850. Fax, (703) 535-7860. Barbara Merrill, Chief Executive Officer. General email, ancor@ancor.org*

Web, www.ancor.org and Twitter, @communitya

Membership: privately operated agencies and corporations that provide support and services to people with disabilities. Advises and works with regulatory and consumer agencies that serve people with disabilities; provides information and sponsors seminars and workshops. Monitors legislation and regulations.

American Occupational Therapy Assn., *4720 Montgomery Lane, #200, Bethesda, MD 20814-3449; (301) 652-6611. Fax, (301) 652-7711. Fred Somers, Executive Director. TTY, (800) 377-8555. Web, www.aota.org and Twitter, @AOTAInc*

Membership: occupational therapists, occupational therapy assistants, and students. Associate members include businesses and organizations supportive of occupational therapy. Accredits educational programs and credentials occupational therapists. Supports research and sponsors scholarships, grants, and fellowships.

American Orthotic and Prosthetic Assn., *330 John Carlyle St., #200, Alexandria, VA 22314-5760; (571) 431-0876. Fax, (571) 431-0899. Tom Fise, Executive Director, (571) 431-0802. General email, info@aopanet.org*

Web, www.aopanet.org and Twitter, @AmericanOandP

Membership: companies that manufacture or supply artificial limbs and braces, and patient care professionals who fit and supervise their use.

American Physical Therapy Assn., *1111 N. Fairfax St., Alexandria, VA 22314-1488; (703) 684-2782. Fax, (703) 684-7343. Michael Bowers, Chief Executive Officer. Information, (800) 999-2782. TTY, (703) 683-6748. General email, memberservices@apta.org*

Web, www.apta.org and Twitter, @APTAtweets

Membership: physical therapists, assistants, and students. Establishes professional standards and accredits physical therapy programs; seeks to improve physical therapy education, practice, and research.

American Speech-Language-Hearing Assn. (ASHA), *2200 Research Blvd., Rockville, MD 20850-3289; (301) 296-5700. Fax, (301) 296-8580. Arlene Pietranton, Executive Director. Press, (301) 296-8732. Toll-free for Action Center, (800) 498-2071 (voice and TTY accessible). Toll-free for nonmembers, (800) 638-8255. General email, actioncenter@asha.org*

Web, www.asha.org and Twitter, @ASHAWeb

Membership: specialists in speech-language pathology and audiology. Sponsors professional education programs; acts as accrediting agent for graduate programs; certifies audiologists and speech-language pathologists. Advocates the rights of the communicatively disabled; provides information on speech, hearing, and language problems. Provides referrals to speech-language pathologists and audiologists. Interests include national and international standards for bioacoustics and noise.

Assn. of People Supporting Employment First (APSE), *414 Hungerford Dr., #224, Rockville, MD 20850; (301) 279-0060. Fax, (301) 279-0075. Allison Wohl, Executive Director. General email, cesp@apse.org*

Web, www.apse.org

Advocates opportunities for equitable employment for those with disabilities. Monitors legislation and regulations.

Assn. of University Centers on Disabilities (AUCD), *1100 Wayne Ave., #1000, Silver Spring, MD 20910; (301) 588-8252. Fax, (301) 588-2842. Andrew J. Imparato, Executive Director. General email, aucdinfo@aucd.org*

Web, www.aucd.org and Twitter, @AUCDNews

Network of facilities that diagnose and treat the developmentally disabled. Trains graduate students and professionals in the field; helps state and local agencies develop services. Interests include interdisciplinary training and services, early screening to prevent developmental disabilities, and development of equipment and programs to serve persons with disabilities.

Brain Injury Assn. of America, *1608 Spring Hill Rd., #110, Vienna, VA 22182; (703) 761-0750. Fax, (703) 761-0755. Susan H. Connors, President. Information, (800) 444-6443. General email, info@biausa.org*

Web, www.biausa.org and Twitter, @biaamerica

Works to improve the quality of life for persons with traumatic brain injuries and for their families. Promotes the prevention of head injuries through public awareness and education programs. Offers state-level support services for individuals and their families. Monitors legislation and regulations.

Center for Workers with Disabilities, *1133 19th St. N.W., #400, 20036; (202) 682-0100. Fax, (202) 204-0071. Nanette Relave, Director. Web, http://cwd.aphsa.org/content/CWD/en/home.html*

Technical assistance center for states enhancing or developing employment infrastructure and supports for working persons with disabilities. (Affiliated with the American Public Human Services Association.)

Consortium for Citizens with Disabilities (CCD), 1825 K St. N.W., #1200, 20006; (202) 783-2229. Fax, (202) 783-8250. Kim Mustteno, Chair.
General email, info@c-c-d.org
Web, www.c-c-d.org

Coalition of national disability organizations. Advocates for a national public policy that ensures the self-determination, independence, empowerment, and integration in all aspects of society for children and adults with disabilities.

Disabled American Veterans, *National Service and Legislative Headquarters,* 807 Maine Ave. S.W., 20024-2410; (202) 554-3501. Fax, (202) 554-3581.
Michael E. Dobmeier, Judge Advocate; Ron F. Hope, National Commander.
Web, www.dav.org

Chartered by Congress to assist veterans with claims for benefits; represents veterans seeking to correct alleged errors in military records. Assists families of veterans with disabilities. (Headquarters in Cold Spring, Ky.)

Disabled Sports USA, 451 Hungerford Dr., #100, Rockville, MD 20850; (301) 217-0960. Fax, (301) 217-0968.
Kirk M. Bauer, Executive Director, (301) 217-9838.
General email, info@dsusa.org
Web, www.dsusa.org and www.disabledsportsusa.org

Offers nationwide sports rehabilitation programs in more than forty summer and winter sports; promotes independence, confidence, and fitness through programs for people with permanent disabilities, including wounded service personnel; conducts workshops and competitions through community-based chapters; participates in world championships.

Easter Seals, *Washington Region Office,* 1420 Spring St., Silver Spring, MD 20910; (301) 588-8700. Fax, (301) 920-9770. Lisa Reeves, Executive Officer.
Toll-free, (800) 886-3771.
Web, www.easterseals.com/DCMDVA

Promotes equal opportunity for people with disabilities or special needs. Interests include child development, early childhood education, adult medical daycare services, and services aimed to aid military veterans and their families as they reenter their communities. (Headquarters in Chicago, Ill.)

Epilepsy Foundation, 8301 Professional Pl. East, #200, Landover, MD 20785-2353; (301) 459-3700. Fax, (301) 577-2684. Phillip Gattone, Chief Executive Officer.
Information, (800) 332-1000. Spanish language, (866) 748-8008.
General email, contactus@efa.org
Web, www.epilepsyfoundation.org and Twitter, @EpilepsyFdn

Promotes research and treatment of epilepsy; makes research grants; disseminates information and educational materials. Affiliates provide direct services for people with epilepsy and make referrals when necessary.

Girl Scouts of the U.S.A., *Public Policy and Advocacy,* 816 Connecticut Ave. N.W., 3rd Floor, 20006; (202) 659-3780. Fax, (202) 331-8065. Anna Maria Chavez, Chief Executive Officer.
General email, advocacy@girlscouts.org
Web, www.girlscouts.org

Educational service organization for girls ages five to seventeen. Promotes personal development through social action, leadership, and such programs as Girl Scouting for Handicapped Girls. (Headquarters in New York.)

Goodwill Industries International, 15810 Indianola Dr., Rockville, MD 20855; (301) 530-6500. Fax, (301) 530-1516. Jim Gibbons, President. Toll-free, (800) 466-3945.
General email, contactus@goodwill.org
Web, www.goodwill.org

Serves people with disabilities, low-wage workers, and others by providing education and career services, as well as job placement opportunities and post-employment support. Helps people become independent, tax-paying members of their communities.

Helen A. Kellar Institute for Human Disabilities *(George Mason University),* 4400 University Blvd., MS 1F2, Fairfax, VA 22030; (703) 993-3670. Fax, (703) 993-3681. Michael M. Behrmann, Director.
Web, http://kihd.gmu.edu

Combines resources from local, state, national, public, and private affiliations to develop products, services, and programs for persons with disabilities.

International Code Council, 500 New Jersey Ave. N.W., 6th Floor, 20001-2070; (202) 370-1800. Fax, (202) 783-2348. Dominic Sims, Chief Executive Officer.
Toll-free, (888) 422-7233.
General email, webmaster@iccsafe.org
Web, www.iccsafe.org

Provides review board for the American National Standards Institute accessibility standards, which ensure that buildings are accessible to persons with physical disabilities.

National Assn. of Councils on Developmental Disabilities, 1825 K St. N.W., #600, 20006; (202) 506-5813. Fax, (202) 506-5846. Donna A. Meltzer, Chief Executive Officer.
General email, info@nacdd.org
Web, www.nacdd.org

Membership: state and territorial councils authorized by the Developmental Disabilities Act. Promotes the interests of people with developmental disabilities. Interests include services, supports, and equal opportunity. Monitors legislation and regulations.

National Assn. of States United for Aging and Disabilities, 1201 15th St. N.W., #350, 20005-2842; (202) 898-2578. Fax, (202) 898-2583. Martha Roherty, Executive Director.

General email, info@nasuad.org

Web, www.nasuad.org

Membership: state and territorial governmental units that deal with older adults, people with disabilities, and their caregivers. Provides members with information, technical assistance, and professional training. Monitors legislation and regulations.

National Council on Independent Living, *2013 H St. N.W., 6th Floor, 20006; (202) 207-0334. Fax, (202) 207-0341. Kelly Buckland, Executive Director. Toll-free, (877) 525-3400.*

General email, ncil@ncil.org

Web, www.ncil.org, Twitter, @NCILAdvocacy and Facebook, www.facebook.com/ NationalCouncilonIndependentLiving

Membership: independent living centers, individuals with disabilities, and organizations that advocate for the human and civil rights of people with disabilities. Assists member centers in building their capacity to promote social change, eliminate disability-based discrimination, and create opportunities for people with disabilities to participate in the legislative process. Offers members training programs, conducts an annual conference, and disseminates related news and research. Monitors legislation and regulations.

National Disability Institute, *1667 K St. N.W., #640, 20006; (202) 296-2040. Michael Morris, Executive Director.*
General email, info@realeconomicimpact.org

Web, www.realeconomicimpact.org

Advocates public policies that address the economic interests of those with disabilities and their families. Interests include tax education and preparation, asset development, financial education, and employment programs.

National Multiple Sclerosis Society, *Washington Chapter, 1800 M St. N.W., #B50 South, 20036; (202) 296-5363. Fax, (202) 296-3425. Chartese Berry, Chapter President. Toll-free, (800) 344-4867.*
General email, info-dcmd@nmss.org

Web, www.msandyou.org

Seeks to advance medical knowledge of multiple sclerosis, a disease of the central nervous system; disseminates information worldwide. Patient services include individual and family counseling, exercise programs, equipment loans, medical and social service referrals, transportation assistance, back-to-work training programs, and inservice training seminars for nurses, homemakers, and physical and occupational therapists. (Headquarters in New York.)

National Rehabilitation Assn., *8400 Corporate Dr., #500, Landover, MD 20785 (mailing address: P.O. Box 150235, Alexandria, VA 22315); (703) 836-0850. Fax, (703) 836-0848. Fred Schroeder, Executive Director. Toll-free, (888) 258-4295. TTY, (703) 836-0849.*
General email, info@nationalrehab.org

Web, www.nationalrehab.org

Membership: administrators, counselors, therapists, disability examiners, vocational evaluators, instructors, job placement specialists, disability managers in the corporate sector, and others interested in rehabilitation of the physically and mentally disabled. Sponsors conferences and workshops. Monitors legislation and regulations.

National Rehabilitation Information Center (NARIC), *8400 Corporate Dr., #500, Landover, MD 20785; (301) 459-5900. Fax, (301) 459-4263. Mark Odum, Director. Information, (800) 346-2742. TTY, (301) 459-5984.*
General email, naricinfo@heitechservices.com

Web, http://naric.com

Provides information on disability and rehabilitation research. Acts as referral agency for disability and rehabilitation facilities and programs. Web site has a Spanish-language link.

Paralyzed Veterans of America, *801 18th St. N.W., 20006-3517; (202) 872-1300. Sherman Gillums Jr., Deputy Executive Director. Information, (800) 424-8200. TTY, (800) 795-4327.*
General email, info@pva.org

Web, www.pva.org

Congressionally chartered veterans service organization that assists veterans with claims for benefits. Distributes information on special education for paralyzed veterans; advocates for high-quality care and supports and raises funds for medical research.

Rehabilitation Engineering and Assistive Technology Society of North America (RESNA), *1700 N. Moore St., #1540, Arlington, VA 22209-1903; (703) 524-6686. Fax, (703) 524-6630. Michael Birogioli, Executive Director.*
General email, info@resna.org

Web, www.resna.org and Twitter, @RESNAorg

Membership: engineers, health professionals, assistive technologists, persons with disabilities, and others. Promotes and supports developments in rehabilitation engineering and technology; acts as an information clearinghouse. (RESNA stands for Rehabilitation Engineering and Assistive Technology Society of North America.)

Special Olympics International Inc., *1133 19th St. N.W., 20036-3604; (202) 628-3630. Fax, (202) 824-0354. Mary Davis, Chief Executive Officer, Acting; Timothy P. Shriver, Chair. Toll-free, (800) 700-8585.*
General email, info@specialolympics.org

Web, www.specialolympics.org

Offers individuals with intellectual disabilities opportunities for year-round sports training; sponsors athletic competition for 4 million athletes worldwide in twenty-two individual and Olympic-type team sports.

Spina Bifida Assn., *1600 Wilson Blvd., #800, Arlington, VA 22209 (mailing address: P.O. Box 17427, Arlington, VA 22216); (202) 944-3285. Fax, (202) 944-3295. Sara Struwe, Chief Executive Officer, ext. 12. Information, (800) 621-3141.*
General email, sbaa@sbaa.org

Web, www.spinabifidaassociation.org

Membership: individuals with spina bifida, their supporters, and concerned professionals. Offers educational programs, scholarships, and support services; acts as a clearinghouse; provides referrals and information about treatment and prevention. Serves as U.S. member of the International Federation for Hydrocephalus and Spina Bifida, which is headquartered in Geneva. Monitors legislation and regulations.

TASH, *2013 H St. N.W., 20006; (202) 540-9020. Fax, (202) 540-9019. Barb Trader, Executive Director, (202) 540-9020. Press, (202) 540-8014.*
General email, info@tash.org
Web, www.tash.org

International human rights advocacy group for people with disabilities. Educates the public and policymakers on issues such as equal education, employment, and community living for people with disabilities. Publishes journals and conducts research to improve living practices for severely disabled people. Monitors legislation and regulations on antidiscrimination measures.

United Cerebral Palsy (UCP), *1825 K St. N.W., #600, 20006; (202) 776-0406. Fax, (202) 776-0414. Stephen Bennett, President. Information, (800) 872-5827.*
Web, www.ucp.org and Twitter, @UCPnational

National network of state and local affiliates that assists individuals with cerebral palsy and other developmental disabilities and their families. Provides parent education, early intervention, employment services, family support and respite programs, therapy, assistive technology, and vocational training. Promotes research on cerebral palsy; supports the use of assistive technology and community-based living arrangements for persons with cerebral palsy and other developmental disabilities.

Blind and Visually Impaired

▶CONGRESS

For a listing of relevant congressional committees and subcommittees, please see page 685 or the Appendix.

Library of Congress, *National Library Service for the Blind and Physically Handicapped, 1291 Taylor St. N.W., 20542 (mailing address: Library of Congress, Washington, DC 20542); (202) 707-5100. Fax, (202) 707-0712. Karen Keninger, Director. Toll-free, (800) 424-8567. TTY, (202) 707-0744.*
General email, nls@loc.gov
Braille email, braille@loc.gov
Web, www.loc.gov/nls

Administers a national program of free library services for persons with physical disabilities in cooperation with regional and subregional libraries. Produces and distributes full-length books and magazines in recorded form and in Braille. Reference section answers questions relating to blindness and physical disabilities and on library services available to persons with disabilities.

▶NONGOVERNMENTAL

American Council of the Blind (ACB), *2200 Wilson Blvd., #650, Arlington, VA 22201; (202) 467-5081. Fax, (703) 465-5085. Eric Bridges, Executive Director. Toll-free, (800) 424-8666.*
General email, info@acb.org
Web, www.acb.org

Membership organization serving blind and visually impaired individuals. Interests include telecommunications, rehabilitation services, and transportation. Provides blind individuals with information and referral services; advises state organizations and agencies serving the blind; sponsors scholarships for the blind and visually impaired. Provides information to the public.

American Foundation for the Blind, *Public Policy Center, 1660 L St. N.W., #513, 20036; (202) 469-6831. Fax, (646) 478-9260. Paul W. Schroeder, Vice President, Programs and Policy.*
General email, afbgov@afb.net
Web, www.afb.org

Advocates equality of access and opportunity for the blind and visually impaired. Conducts research and provides consulting; develops and implements public policy and legislation. Maintains the Helen Keller Archives and M.C. Migel Memorial Library at its headquarters in New York.

Assn. for Education and Rehabilitation of the Blind and Visually Impaired, *1703 N. Beauregard St., #440, Alexandria, VA 22311; (703) 671-4500. Fax, (703) 671-6391. Louis M. Tutt, Executive Director. Toll-free, (877) 492-2708.*
General email, aer@aerbvi.org
Web, www.aerbvi.org

Membership: professionals who work in all phases of education and rehabilitation of children and adults who are blind and visually impaired. Provides support and professional development opportunities through conferences, continuing education, and publications. Issues professional recognition awards and student scholarships. Monitors legislation and regulations.

Blinded Veterans Assn., *125 N. West St., Alexandria, VA 22314; (202) 371-8880. Fax, (202) 371-8258. Al Avina, Executive Director. Toll-free, (800) 669-7079.*
General email, bva@bva.org
Web, www.bva.org and Twitter, @BlindedVeterans

Chartered by Congress to assist veterans with claims for benefits. Seeks out blinded veterans to make them aware of benefits and services available to them.

National Federation of the Blind, *200 E. Wells St., Baltimore, MD 21230 (mailing address: P.O. Box 29141, Washington, DC 20017); (410) 659-9314. Fax, (410) 685-5653. Shawn M. Callaway, President, (202) 352-1511.*
General email, nfb@nfb.org
Web, https://nfb.org

Membership organization providing support networks for the blind and information about blindness and vision loss, assistive technologies, education and employment services.

National Industries for the Blind (NIB), *1310 Braddock Pl., Alexandria, VA 22314-1691; (703) 310-0500. Kevin A. Lynch, Chief Executive Officer. General email, communications@nib.org*

Web, www.nib.org, Twitter, @NatIndBlind and Facebook, www.facebook.com/NatIndBlind

Works to develop and improve opportunities for evaluating, training, employing, and advancing people who are blind and visually disabled. Develops business opportunities in the federal, state, and commercial marketplaces for organizations employing people who are blind or visually impaired.

Prevention of Blindness Society of Metropolitan Washington, *1775 Church St. N.W., 20036; (202) 234-1010. Fax, (202) 234-1020. Michele Hartlove, Executive Director. General email, mail@youreyes.org*

Web, www.youreyes.org

Conducts preschool and elementary school screening program and glaucoma screening; provides information and referral service on eye health care; assists low-income persons in obtaining eye care and provides eyeglasses for a nominal fee to persons experiencing financial stress; conducts macular degeneration support group.

Deaf and Hard of Hearing

▶AGENCIES

General Services Administration (GSA), *Federal Relay Service (FedRelay), 10304 Eaton Pl., Fairfax, VA 22030; (703) 306-6308. Angela Officer, Program Manager, Acting, (703) 689-5654. Customer service, (800) 877-0996 (Voice/ TTY, ASCII, Spanish). TTY/ASCII, (800) 877-8339. VCO (Voice Carry Over), (877) 877-6280. Speech-to-Speech, (877) 877-8982. Voice, (866) 377-8642. TeleBraille, (866) 893-8340.*

General email, ITCSC@gsa.gov

Web, www.gsa.gov/fedrelay

Provides telecommunications services for conducting official business with and within the federal government to individuals who are deaf, hard of hearing, or have speech disabilities. Federal Relay Service features are Voice, TTY, HCO, Speech-to-Speech, Spanish, Telebraille, Captioned Telephone Service (CTS), IP Relay, Video Relay Service (VRS), Internet Relay (FRSO), and Relay Conference Captioning (RCC). For those with limited English proficiency, contact fas.car@gsa.gov, as services are available in Spanish, Vietnamese, Russian, Portuguese, Polish, Haitian, Creole, and Arabic.

National Institute on Deafness and Other Communication Disorders *(National Institutes of Health), 31 Center Dr., #3C02, MSC 2320, Bethesda, MD 20892-2320; (301) 496-7243. Fax, (301) 402-0018.*

Dr. James F. Battey Jr., Director. Toll-free, (800) 241-1044. TTY, (800) 241-1055. Interpreter service, (301) 496-1807. Evenings and weekends, (301) 496-3315. General email, nidcdinfo@nidcd.nih.gov

Web, www.nidcd.nih.gov

Conducts and supports research and research training and disseminates information on hearing disorders and other communication processes, including diseases that affect hearing, balance, smell, taste, voice, speech, and language. Monitors international research.

▶NONGOVERNMENTAL

Alexander Graham Bell Assn. for the Deaf and Hard of Hearing, *3417 Volta Pl. N.W., 20007-2778; (202) 337-5220. Fax, (202) 337-8314. Emilio Alonso-Mendoza, Chief Executive Officer. TTY, (202) 337-5221. General email, info@agbell.org*

Web, nc.agbell.org

Provides hearing-impaired children in the United States and abroad with information and special education programs; works to improve employment opportunities for deaf persons; acts as a support group for parents of deaf persons.

American Academy of Audiology, *11480 Commerce Park Dr., #220, Reston, VA 20191 (mailing address: Capitol Hill Office: 312 Massachusetts Ave. N.E., Washington, DC 20002); (703) 790-8466. Fax, (703) 790-8631. Tanya Tolpegin, Executive Director. Toll-free, (800) 222-2336. General email, infoaud@audiology.org*

Web, www.audiology.org

Membership: more than 11,000 audiologists. Provides consumer information on testing and treatment for hearing loss and balance care; sponsors research and continuing education for audiologists. Monitors legislation and regulations.

American Speech-Language-Hearing Assn. (ASHA), *2200 Research Blvd., Rockville, MD 20850-3289; (301) 296-5700. Fax, (301) 296-8580. Arlene Pietranton, Executive Director. Press, (301) 296-8732. Toll-free for Action Center, (800) 498-2071 (voice and TTY accessible). Toll-free for nonmembers, (800) 638-8255. General email, actioncenter@asha.org*

Web, www.asha.org and Twitter, @ASHAWeb

Membership: specialists in speech-language pathology and audiology. Sponsors professional education programs; acts as accrediting agent for graduate programs; certifies audiologists and speech-language pathologists. Advocates the rights of the communicatively disabled; provides information on speech, hearing, and language problems. Provides referrals to speech-language pathologists and audiologists. Interests include national and international standards for bioacoustics and noise.

Better Hearing Institute, *1444 Eye St. N.W., #700, 20005; (202) 449-1100. Fax, (202) 216-9646. Carole M. Rogin, President. Hearing helpline, (800) 327-9355.*

General email, mail@betterhearing.org

Web, www.betterhearing.org and Twitter, @better_hearing

Educational organization that conducts national public information programs on hearing loss, hearing aids, and other treatments. (Affiliated with the Hearing Loss Assn. of America.)

Gallaudet University, 800 Florida Ave. N.E., 20002-3695; (202) 651-5000. Roberta (Bobbi) Cordano, President, (202) 651-5005.

Web, www.gallaudet.edu and Twitter, @GallaudetU

Offers undergraduate, graduate, and doctoral degree programs for deaf, hard-of-hearing, and hearing students. Conducts research; maintains the Laurent Clerc National Deaf Education Center and demonstration preschool, elementary (Kendall Demonstration Elementary School), and secondary (Model Secondary School for the Deaf) programs. Sponsors the Center for Global Education, National Deaf Education Network and Clearinghouse, and the Cochlear Implant Education Center. Links to each department's video phone are at www.gallaudet.edu/about_gallaudet/contact_us.html.

Hearing Industries Assn., 1444 Eye St. N.W., #700, 20005; (202) 449-1090. Fax, (202) 216-9646. Andy Bopp, Executive Director.

General email, mjones@bostrom.com

Web, www.hearing.org

Membership: hearing aid manufacturers and companies that supply hearing aid components.

Hearing Loss Assn. of America, 7910 Woodmont Ave., #1200, Bethesda, MD 20814; (301) 657-2248. Fax, (301) 913-9413. Barbara Kelley, Executive Director, Acting.

Web, www.hearingloss.org

Promotes understanding of the nature, causes, and remedies of hearing loss. Provides hearing-impaired people with support and information. Seeks to educate the public about hearing loss and the problems of the hard of hearing. Provides travelers with information on assistive listening devices in museums, theaters, and places of worship. (Formerly Self-Help for Hard-of-Hearing People.)

Laurent Clerc National Deaf Education Center, *Planning, Development, and Dissemination,* 800 Florida Ave. N.E., 20002-3695; (202) 651-5340, Voice and TTY. Fax, (202) 651-5708. Edward Bosso, Vice President. Toll-free, (800) 526-9105. Cochlear Implant Education Center, (202) 651-5638.

Web, www.gallaudet.edu/clerc-center, Twitter, @ClercCenter and Facebook, www.facebook.com/InsideClercCenter

Provides information on topics dealing with hearing loss and deafness for children and young adults up to age twenty-one, and operates elementary and secondary demonstration schools. Houses the Cochlear Implant Education Center and serves as a clearinghouse for information on questions related to deafness. (Affiliated with Gallaudet University.)

National Assn. of the Deaf, 8630 Fenton St., #820, Silver Spring, MD 20910-3819; (301) 587-1788. Fax, (301) 587-1791. Howard A. Rosenblum, Chief Executive Officer. TTY, (301) 587-1789.

Web, www.nad.org and Twitter, @NADtweets

Membership: state associations, affiliate organizations, and individuals that promote, protect, and preserve the civil, human, and linguistic rights of deaf and hard-of-hearing individuals in the United States. Provides advocacy and legal expertise in the areas of early intervention, education, employment, health care, technology and telecommunications. Provides youth leadership training. Represents the United States to the World Federation of the Deaf (WFD).

National Captioning Institute, 3725 Concorde Pkwy., #100, Chantilly, VA 20151; Fax, (703) 917-9853. Gene Chao, Chief Executive Officer. Phone/TTY, (703) 917-7600.

General email, mail@ncicap.org

Web, www.ncicap.org

Captions television programs for the deaf and hard of hearing and produces audio descriptions for the blind on behalf of public and commercial broadcast television networks, cable networks, syndicators, program producers, government agencies, advertisers, and home video distributors. Offers subtitling and language translation services. Produces and disseminates information about the national closed-captioning service and audio-description services.

Registry of Interpreters for the Deaf, 333 Commerce St., Alexandria, VA 22314; (703) 838-0030. Fax, (703) 838-0454. Anna Witter-Merithew, Executive Director, Acting. TTY, (703) 838-0459.

General email, RIDinfo@rid.org

Web, www.rid.org and Twitter, @RID_Inc

Membership: professional interpreters, transliterators, interpretation students, and educators. Trains, tests, and certifies interpreters; maintains registry of certified interpreters; establishes certification standards. Sponsors training workshops and conferences; publishes professional development literature.

TDI, 8630 Fenton St., #121, Silver Spring, MD 20910-3803; Claude L. Stout, Executive Director. Phone (voice/video), (301) 563-9112.

General email, info@TDIforaccess.org

Web, www.TDIforaccess.org

Membership: individuals, organizations, and businesses that advocate equal access to telecommunications, media, and information technologies for Americans who are deaf and hard of hearing. Interests include closed captioning for television, movies, DVDs, and online videos; emergency access (911); and TTY and Telecommunications Relays Services. Publishes a quarterly magazine and an annual resource directory. Monitors legislation and regulations.

Intellectual and Developmental Disabilities

▶AGENCIES

Administration for Community Living (ACL) *(Health and Human Services Dept.), Administration on Intellectual and Developmental Disabilities,* 330 C St. S.W., 20201; (202) 401-4541. Fax, (202) 357-3555. Aaron Bishop, Commissioner.
General email, info@acl.gov

Web, www.acl.gov/Programs/AIDD

Administers the Intellectual and Developmental Disabilities Assistance and Bill of Rights Act of 2000, providing grants for state protection and advocacy systems for people with intellectual and developmental disabilities; state councils on intellectual and developmental disabilities; university centers for intellectual and developmental disabilities education, research, and services; and projects of national significance that must be addressed on a local level affecting people with intellectual and developmental disabilities and their families. Also administers the disability provisions in the Help America Vote Act.

Eunice Kennedy Shriver National Institute of Child Health and Human Development *(National Institutes of Health), Division of Extramural Research, Intellectual and Developmental Disabilities Branch,* 6100 Executive Blvd., #4B09G, MSC 7510, Bethesda, MD 20892-7510; (301) 496-1383. Melissa Ann Parisi, Branch Chief.
Web, www.nichd.nih.gov/about/org/der/branches/iddb

Provides support for research projects, training programs, and research centers dedicated to promoting the well-being of individuals with intellectual and developmental disabilities. Major research foci include chromosome abnormalities, genetic and genomic syndromes, epigenetic disorders, cellular and molecular biology, family and community relations, newborn and population screenings, Fragile X syndrome and associated disorders, rare diseases, muscular dystrophy, and autism spectrum disorders.

▶NONGOVERNMENTAL

American Assn. on Intellectual and Developmental Disabilities (AAIDD), 501 3rd St. N.W., #200, 20001-2760; (202) 387-1968. Fax, (202) 387-2193. Margaret Nygren, Executive Director.
Web, www.aaidd.org

Association for professionals who work in the field of intellectual and developmental disabilities. Promotes progressive policy, sound research, effective practices, and human rights for people with intellectual and developmental disabilities. Sponsors conferences and training workshops. Monitors legislation and regulations.

The Arc, 1825 K St. N.W., #1200, 20006; (202) 534-3700. Fax, (202) 534-3731. Peter V. Berns, Chief Executive Officer. Information, (800) 433-5255.
General email, info@thearc.org

Web, www.thearc.org and Twitter, @thearc

Membership: individuals assisting people with intellectual and developmental disability. Provides oversight and technical assistance for local groups that provide services and support.

The Arc, *Governmental Affairs,* 1825 K St. N.W., #1200, 20006; (202) 783-2229. Fax, (202) 534-3731. Marty Ford, Senior Executive Officer.
General email, info@thearc.org

Web, www.thearc.org/what-we-do/public-policy

Membership: people with intellectual and developmental disabilities and their service providers. Provides services and support for individuals with disabilities, their families, and The Arc's state and local chapters nationwide. Monitors federal legislation, regulations, and legal decisions.

Autism Society of America, 4340 East-West Hwy., #350, Bethesda, MD 20814; (301) 657-0881. Fax, (301) 657-0869. Scott Badesch, President. Information, (800) 328-8476.
General email, info@autism-society.org

Web, www.autism-society.org and Twitter, @AutismSociety

Monitors legislation and regulations affecting support, education, training, research, and other services for individuals with autism. Offers referral service and information to the public.

Best Buddies International, *Capitol Region,* 131 E. Broad St., #205, Falls Church, VA 22046; (703) 533-9420. Fax, (703) 533-9423. Karen Glasser, Regional Director. Information, (800) 892-8339.
Web, www.bestbuddies.org/capitolregion and Twitter, @BestBuddies

Volunteer organization that provides companionship, integrated employment, and leadership development programs to people with intellectual disabilities worldwide. (Headquarters in Miami, Fla.)

Joseph P. Kennedy Jr. Foundation, 1133 19th St. N.W., 12th Floor, 20036-3604; (202) 393-1250. Fax, (202) 824-0351. Steve Eidelman, Executive Director.
General email, eidelman@jpkf.org

Web, www.jpkf.org

Seeks to enhance the quality of life of persons with intellectual disabilities and their families through public policy advocacy. Provides information and training on the policymaking process.

National Assn. of State Directors of Developmental Disabilities Services (NASDDDS), 301 N. Fairfax St., #101, Alexandria, VA 22314-2633; (703) 683-4202. Fax, (703) 684-1395. Mary Fay, Executive Director.
Web, www.nasddds.org

Membership: chief administrators of state intellectual and developmental disability programs. Coordinates exchange of information on intellectual and developmental disability programs among the states; provides technical assistance to members and information on state programs.

National Children's Center, 6200 2nd St. N.W., 20011; (202) 722-2300. Fax, (202) 722-2383. Jesse M. Chancellor, President.
Web, www.nccinc.org

Provides educational, social, and clinical services to infants, children, and adults with intellectual and other developmental disabilities. Services provided through a 24-hour intensive treatment program, group homes and independent living programs, educational services, adult treatment programs, and early intervention programs for infants with disabilities or infants at high risk. Operates a child development center for children with and without disabilities.

National Disability Rights Network, 820 1st St. N.E., #740, 20002; (202) 408-9514. Fax, (202) 408-9520. Curtis L. (Curt) Decker, Executive Director, ext. 107. TTY, (202) 408-9521.
General email, info@ndrn.org
Web, http://ndrn.org/index.php

Membership: agencies working for people with disabilities. Provides state agencies with training and technical assistance; maintains an electronic mail network. Monitors legislation and regulations. (Formerly the National Assn. of Protection and Advocacy Systems and Client Assistance Programs [P&A/CAP]).

Psychiatric Rehabilitation Assn., 7918 Jones Branch Dr., #300, McLean, VA 22101; (703) 442-2078. Fax, (703) 506-3266. Tom Gibson, Chief Executive Officer, Acting.
General email, info@psychrehabassociation.org
Web, www.uspra.org and Twitter, @PsychRehab

Membership: agencies, mental health practitioners, researchers, policymakers, family groups, and consumer organizations. Supports the community adjustment of persons with psychiatric disabilities. Promotes the role of rehabilitation in mental health systems; opposes discrimination based on mental disability. Certifies psychosocial rehabilitation practitioners.

HOMELESSNESS

General

▶**AGENCIES**

Education Dept., Career, Technical, and Adult Education; Adult Education and Literacy, 550 12th St. S.W., 11th Floor, 20202-7100 (mailing address: 400 Maryland Ave. S.W., P-OCTAE, DAEL, Washington, DC 20202); (202) 245-7720. Fax, (202) 245-7838. Cheryl L. Keenan, Director.
Web, www2.ed.gov/about/offices/list/ovae/pi/AdultEd

Provides state and local agencies and community-based organizations with assistance in establishing education programs for homeless adults.

Education Dept., Title I Office, Education for Homeless Children and Youth Program, 400 Maryland Ave. S.W., #3C130, FB-6, 20202-6132; (202) 401-0962. Fax, (202) 260-7764. John McLaughlin, Program Specialist.
General email, HomelessEd@ed.gov
Web, www2.ed.gov/programs/homeless

Provides formula grants to education agencies in the states, Puerto Rico, and through the Bureau of Indian Affairs to Native Americans to educate homeless children and youth and to establish an office of coordinator of education for homeless children and youth in each jurisdiction.

Emergency Food and Shelter National Board Program, 701 N. Fairfax St., #310, Alexandria, VA 22314-2064; (703) 706-9660. Fax, (703) 706-9677. Randall D. Kinder, Chief.
General email, efsp@unitedway.org
Web, www.efsp.unitedway.org

Public/private partnership that administers the Emergency Food and Shelter Program under the McKinney-Vento Act. Gives supplemental assistance to more than 14,000 human service agencies. Does not provide direct assistance to the public.

Housing and Urban Development Dept. (HUD), Community Planning and Development, 451 7th St. S.W., #7100, 20410; (202) 708-2690. Fax, (202) 708-3336. Harriet Tregoning, Principal Deputy Assistant Secretary; Clifford Taffet, General Deputy Assistant Secretary.
Web, http://portal.hud.gov/hudportal/HUD?src=/program_offices/comm_plunning

Gives supplemental assistance to facilities that aid the homeless; awards grants for innovative programs that address the needs of homeless families with children.

Housing and Urban Development Dept. (HUD), Community Planning and Development, Community Assistance Division, 451 7th St. S.W., #7262, 20410; (202) 708-1234. Fax, (202) 401-0053. Brian Fitzmaurice, Deputy Director.
Web, www.hud.gov

Advises and represents the secretary on homelessness matters; promotes cooperation among federal agencies on homelessness issues; coordinates assistance programs for the homeless under the McKinney Act. Trains HUD field staff in administering homelessness programs. Distributes funds to eligible nonprofit organizations, cities, counties, tribes, and territories for shelter, care, transitional housing, and permanent housing for the disabled homeless. Programs provide for acquisition and rehabilitation of buildings, prevention of homelessness, counseling, and medical care. Administers the Federal Surplus Property Program and spearheads the initiative to lease HUD-held homes to the homeless.

▶**NONGOVERNMENTAL**

Covenant House, Washington Office, 2001 Mississippi Ave. S.E., 20020; (202) 610-9600. Madye Henson, President. TTY, (800) 786-2929.
Web, http://covenanthousedc.org

Social Security Administration

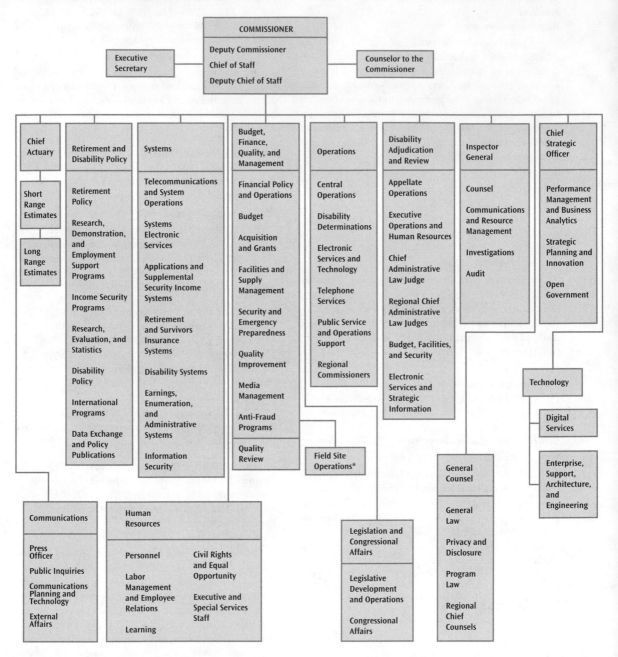

COMMISSIONER
Deputy Commissioner
Chief of Staff
Deputy Chief of Staff

Executive Secretary

Counselor to the Commissioner

Chief Actuary
- Short Range Estimates
- Long Range Estimates

Retirement and Disability Policy
- Retirement Policy
- Research, Demonstration, and Employment Support Programs
- Income Security Programs
- Research, Evaluation, and Statistics
- Disability Policy
- International Programs
- Data Exchange and Policy Publications

Systems
- Telecommunications and System Operations
- Systems Electronic Services
- Applications and Supplemental Security Income Systems
- Retirement and Survivors Insurance Systems
- Disability Systems
- Earnings, Enumeration, and Administrative Systems
- Information Security

Budget, Finance, Quality, and Management
- Financial Policy and Operations
- Budget
- Acquisition and Grants
- Facilities and Supply Management
- Security and Emergency Preparedness
- Quality Improvement
- Media Management
- Anti-Fraud Programs
- Quality Review

Operations
- Central Operations
- Disability Determinations
- Electronic Services and Technology
- Telephone Services
- Public Service and Operations Support
- Regional Commissioners

Disability Adjudication and Review
- Appellate Operations
- Executive Operations and Human Resources
- Chief Administrative Law Judge
- Regional Chief Administrative Law Judges
- Budget, Facilities, and Security
- Electronic Services and Strategic Information

Inspector General
- Counsel
- Communications and Resource Management
- Investigations
- Audit

Chief Strategic Officer
- Performance Management and Business Analytics
- Strategic Planning and Innovation
- Open Government

Technology
- Digital Services
- Enterprise, Support, Architecture, and Engineering

Field Site Operations*

Communications
- Press Officer
- Public Inquiries
- Communications Planning and Technology
- External Affairs

Human Resources
- Personnel
- Labor Management and Employee Relations
- Learning
- Civil Rights and Equal Opportunity
- Executive and Special Services Staff

Legislation and Congressional Affairs
- Legislative Development and Operations
- Congressional Affairs

General Counsel
- General Law
- Privacy and Disclosure
- Program Law
- Regional Chief Counsels

*Field Site Operations reports to Quality Review

Protects young people suffering from homelessness, abuse, and neglect. Provides services including transitional housing, GED and adult education, and job readiness. (Affiliated with Covenant House International.)

D.C. Central Kitchen, *425 2nd St. N.W., 20001; (202) 234-0707. Fax, (202) 986-1051. Mike Curtin, Chief Executive Officer, (202) 266-2018.*
Web, www.dccentralkitchen.org

Distributes food to D.C.-area homeless shelters, transitional homes, low-income schoolchildren, and corner store "food deserts."

Housing Assistance Council, *1025 Vermont Ave. N.W., #606, 20005-3516; (202) 842-8600. Fax, (202) 347-3441. Moises Loza, Executive Director.*
General email, hac@ruralhome.org
Web, www.ruralhome.org

Provides low-income housing development groups in rural areas with seed money loans and technical assistance; assesses programs designed to respond to rural housing needs; makes recommendations for federal and state involvement; publishes technical guides and reports on rural housing issues.

National Alliance to End Homelessness, *1518 K St. N.W., #410, 20005; (202) 638-1526. Fax, (202) 638-4664. Nan Roman, President. General email, info@naeh.org*

Web, www.endhomelessness.org

Policy, research, and capacity-building organization that works to prevent, alleviate, and end problems of the homeless. Provides data and research to policymakers and the public; encourages public-private collaboration for stronger programs to reduce the homeless population, and works with communities to improve assistance programs for the homeless.

National Coalition for Homeless Veterans, *333 1/2 Pennsylvania Ave. S.E., 20003-1148; (202) 546-1969. Fax, (202) 546-2063. Baylee Crone, Executive Director. Toll-free, (800) VET-HELP. General email, info@nchv.org*

Web, www.nchv.org

Provides technical assistance to service providers; advocates on behalf of homeless veterans.

National Coalition for the Homeless, *2201 P St. N.W., 20037-1033; (202) 462-4822. Megan Hustings, Director, Acting. General email, info@nationalhomeless.org*

Web, www.nationalhomeless.org, Facebook, www.facebook.com/NationalCoalitionfortheHomeless and Twitter, @Ntl_Homeless

Advocacy network of persons who are or have been homeless, state and local coalitions, other activists, service providers, housing developers, and others. Seeks to create the systemic and attitudinal changes necessary to end homelessness. Works to meet the needs of persons who are homeless or at risk of becoming homeless.

National Law Center on Homelessness and Poverty, *2000 M St. N.W., #210, 20036; (202) 638-2535. Fax, (202) 628-2737. Maria Foscarinis, Executive Director. General email, email@nlchp.org*

Web, www.nlchp.org

Legal advocacy group that works to prevent and end homelessness through impact litigation, legislation, and education. Conducts research on homelessness issues. Acts as a clearinghouse for legal information and technical assistance. Monitors legislation and regulations.

Salvation Army, *615 Slaters Lane, Alexandria, VA 22314 (mailing address: P.O. Box 269, Alexandria, VA 22313-0269); (703) 684-5500. Fax, (703) 684-3478. David Jeffrey, National Commander. Web, www.salvationarmyusa.org and Twitter, @SalvationArmyUS*

International religious social welfare organization that provides the homeless with residences and social services, including counseling, emergency help, and employment services. (International headquarters in London.)

U.S. Conference of Mayors, *Task Force on Hunger and Homelessness, 1620 Eye St. N.W., 4th Floor, 20006; (202) 293-7330. Fax, (202) 293-2352. Eugene T. Lowe, Assistant Director for Community Development and Housing, (202) 861-6710. Web, www.usmayors.org*

Tracks trends in hunger, homelessness, and community programs that address homelessness and hunger in U.S. cities; issues reports. Monitors legislation and regulations.

SOCIAL SECURITY

General

▶**AGENCIES**

Social Security Administration (SSA), *6401 Security Blvd., Baltimore, MD 21235; (410) 965-3120. Fax, (410) 966-1463. Carolyn Colvin, Commissioner, Acting; Michelle King, Deputy Commissioner, Acting. Information, (800) 772-1213. Press, (410) 965-8904. TTY, (800) 325-0778. Web, www.ssa.gov*

Administers national Social Security programs and the Supplemental Security Income program.

Social Security Administration (SSA), *Central Operations, 1500 Woodlawn Dr., Baltimore, MD 21241; (410) 966-7000. Fax, (410) 966-6005. Janice G. Roushee, Associate Commissioner. Information, (800) 772-1213.*

Reviews and authorizes claims for benefits under the disability insurance program and all claims for beneficiaries living abroad; certifies benefits payments; maintains beneficiary rolls.

Social Security Administration (SSA), *Disability Adjudication and Review, 5107 Leesburg Pike, #1600, Falls Church, VA 22041-3255; (703) 605-8200. Fax, (703) 605-8201. Theresa L. Gruber, Deputy Commissioner. Web, www.ssa.gov/disability*

Administers a nationwide system of administrative law judges who conduct hearings and decide appealed cases concerning benefits provisions. Reviews decisions for appeals council action, if necessary, and renders the secretary's final decision. Reviews benefits cases on disability, retirement and survivors' benefits, and supplemental security income.

Social Security Administration (SSA), *Disability Determinations, 3570 Annex Bldg., 6401 Security Blvd., Baltimore, MD 21235; (410) 965-1170. Fax, (410) 965-6503. Ann Roberts, Associate Commissioner. Information, (800) 772-1213. TTY, (800) 325-0778. Web, www.ssa.gov/disability*

Provides direction for administration of the disability insurance program, which is paid out of the Social Security Trust Fund. Administers disability and blindness provisions of the Supplemental Security Income (SSI) program. Responsible for claims filed under black lung benefits program before July 1, 1973.

Social Security Administration (SSA), *Income Security Programs,* 6401 Security Blvd., #252, Altmeyer Bldg., Baltimore, MD 21235; Fax, (410) 965-8582. (410) 966-0607. Samara Richardson, Associate Commissioner, Acting.
Web, www.ssa.gov

Develops policies and procedures for administering the Retirement and Survivors' Insurance (RSI) programs and the Supplemental Security Income (SSI) program for the elderly, blind, and disabled. Develops agreements with the states and other agencies that govern state supplementation programs, Medicaid eligibility, food stamps, and fiscal reporting processes.

Social Security Administration (SSA), *Operations,* 6401 Security Blvd., West High Rise, #1204, Baltimore, MD 21235; (410) 965-3145. Fax, (410) 966-7941.
Nancy A. Berryhill, Deputy Commissioner.
Information, (800) 772-1213. TTY, (800) 325-0778.
Web, www.ssa.gov

Issues Social Security numbers, maintains earnings and beneficiary records, authorizes claims, certifies benefits, and makes post-adjudicative changes in beneficiary records for retirement, survivors and disability insurance, and black lung claims. Maintains toll-free number for workers who want information on future Social Security benefits.

Social Security Administration (SSA), *Research, Evaluation, and Statistics,* 500 E St. S.W., #922, 20254; (202) 358-6020. Fax, (202) 358-6187. John W. R. Phillips, Associate Commissioner. Publications, (202) 358-6405.
Web, www.ssa.gov/policy/about/ORES.html

Compiles statistics on beneficiaries; conducts research on the economic status of beneficiaries and the relationship between Social Security, the American people, and the economy; analyzes the effects of proposed Social Security legislation, especially on lower-income and middle-income individuals and families; disseminates results of research and statistical programs through publications.

Workers Compensation (OWCP) *(Labor Dept.), Coal Mine Workers' Compensation,* 200 Constitution Ave. N.W., #S3524, 20210; (202) 693-0036. Fax, (202) 693-1378. Michael A. Chance, Director, (202) 693-0046.
Toll-free, (800) 638-7072.
General email, DCMWC-public@dol.gov
Web, www.dol.gov/owcp/dcmwc

Provides direction for administration of the black lung benefits program. Adjudicates all black lung claims; certifies benefit payments and maintains black lung beneficiary rolls.

►**CONGRESS**

For a listing of relevant congressional committees and subcommittees, please see page 685 or the Appendix.

Government Accountability Office (GAO), *Education, Workforce, and Income Security,* 441 G St. N.W., #5928, 20548; (202) 512-7215. Barbara D. Bovbjerg, Managing Director.
Web, www.gao.gov/careers/ewis.html

Independent nonpartisan agency in the legislative branch that audits, analyzes, and evaluates programs within the Dept. of Health and Human Services, including Social Security; makes reports available to the public.

►**NONGOVERNMENTAL**

AARP, 601 E St. N.W., 20049; (202) 434-2277. Jo Ann C. Jenkins, Chief Executive Officer. Press, (202) 434-2560. Library, (202) 434-6233. TTY, (877) 434-7598. Toll-free, (888) 687-2277. Membership, (202) 434-3525.
General email, member@aarp.org
Web, www.aarp.org

Membership: people fifty years of age and older. Works to address members' needs and interests through education, advocacy, and service. Monitors legislation and regulations and disseminates information on issues affecting older Americans, including issues related to Social Security. (Formerly the American Assn. of Retired Persons.)

National Academy of Social Insurance, 1200 New Hampshire Ave. N.W., #830, 20036; (202) 452-8097. Fax, (202) 452-8111. William J. Arnone, Chair.
General email, nasi@nasi.org
Web, www.nasi.org

Promotes research and education on Social Security, Medicare, health care financing, and related public and private programs; assesses social insurance programs and their relationship to other programs; supports research and leadership development. Acts as a clearinghouse for social insurance information.

National Committee to Preserve Social Security and Medicare, 10 G St. N.E., #600, 20002-4215; (202) 216-0420. Fax, (202) 216-0446. Max Richtman, President. Press, (202) 216-8378. Senior hotline/Legislative updates, (800) 998-0180.
General email, webmaster@ncpssm.org
Web, www.ncpssm.org, Twitter, @NCPSSM and Facebook, www.facebook.com/NationalCommittee

Educational and advocacy organization that focuses on Social Security and Medicare programs and on related income security and health issues. Interests include retirement income protection, health care reform, and the quality of life of seniors. Monitors legislation and regulations.

18

Transportation

GENERAL POLICY AND ANALYSIS

Basic Resources

▶AGENCIES

Access Board, *1331 F St. N.W., #1000, 20004-1111; (202) 272-0080. Fax, (202) 272-0081. David M. Capozzi, Executive Director, (202) 272-0010. Toll-free technical assistance, (800) 872-2253. TTY, (202) 272-0082. Toll-free TTY, (800) 993-2822.*
General email, info@access-board.gov
Web, www.access-board.gov

Develops and maintains accessibility requirements for buildings, transit vehicles, telecommunications equipment, medical diagnostic equipment, and electronic and information technology. Provides technical assistance and training on these guidelines and standards. Enforces access standards for federally funded facilities through the Architectural Barriers Act.

National Transportation Safety Board (NTSB), *490 L'Enfant Plaza East S.W., 20594-2000; (202) 314-6000. Fax, (202) 314-6018. Christopher A. Hart, Chair; Kelly Nantel, Public Affairs; Susan Kantrowitz, Director of Administration. Information, (202) 314-6000. Press, (202) 314-6100.*
Web, www.ntsb.gov

Promotes transportation safety through independent investigations of accidents and other safety problems. Makes recommendations for safety improvement. Operates three regional offices.

National Transportation Safety Board (NTSB), *Research and Engineering, 490 L'Enfant Plaza East S.W., 20594-2000; (202) 314-6501. Fax, (240) 752-6247. Joseph M. Kolly, Director.*
Web, www.ntsb.gov/about/organization/RE

Evaluates effectiveness of federal, state, and local safety programs. Identifies transportation safety issues not being addressed by government or industry. Conducts studies on specific safety problems. Provides technical support to accident investigations. Operates in four divisions: Safety Research and Statistical Analysis; Vehicle Performance; Vehicle Recorder; and Materials Laboratory.

National Transportation Safety Board (NTSB), *Safety Recommendations and Advocacy, 490 L'Enfant Plaza East S.W., 20594-2000; (202) 314-6100. Fax, (240) 752-6247. Joseph M. Kolly, Director, Acting.*
Web, www.ntsb.gov

Makes transportation safety recommendations to federal and state agencies on all modes of transportation. Produces the annual "Most Wanted" list of critical transportation safety projects.

Office of Management and Budget (OMB) *(Executive Office of the President), Transportation, 725 17th St. N.W., #9002, 20503; (202) 395-6138. Fax, (202) 395-4797. Vacant, Chief. Press, (202) 395-7254.*
Web, www.whitehouse.gov/omb

Assists and advises the OMB director on budget preparation, proposed legislation, and evaluations of Transportation Dept. programs, policies, and activities.

Office of the Assistant Secretary of Research and Technology *(Transportation Dept.), 1200 New Jersey Ave. S.E., 20590; (202) 366-4000. Fax, (202) 366-3759. Gregory D. Winfree, Assistant Secretary. DOT library, (800) 853-1351.*
General email, ritainfo@dot.gov
Web, www.rita.dot.gov

Coordinates and manages the department's research portfolio and expedites implementation of innovative technologies. Oversees the Bureau of Transportation Statistics, Volpe National Transportation Systems Center (in Cambridge, Mass.), and the Transportation Safety Institute (in Oklahoma City).

Office of the Assistant Secretary of Research and Technology *(Transportation Dept.), Bureau of Transportation Statistics, 1200 New Jersery Ave. S.E., #E34-314, 20590; (202) 366-1270. Patricia S. Hu, Director. Information, (800) 853-1351. Media, (202) 366-5568.*
General email, ritainfo@dot.gov
Web, www.rita.dot.gov/bts

Works to improve public awareness of the nation's transportation systems. Collects, analyzes, and publishes a comprehensive, cross-modal set of transportation statistics.

Office of the Assistant Secretary of Research and Technology *(Transportation Dept.), Research, Development, and Technology, 1200 New Jersey Ave. S.E., #E33-304, 20590-0001; (202) 366-5447. Fax, (202) 366-3671. Kevin Womack, Director.*
Web, www.rita.dot.gov/rdt

Supports transportation innovation research, engineering, education, and safety training. Focus includes intermodal transportation; partnerships among government, universities, and industry; and economic growth and competitiveness through use of new technologies. Monitors international research.

Pipeline and Hazardous Materials Safety Administration *(Transportation Dept.), 1200 New Jersey Ave. S.E., #E27-300, 20590; (202) 366-4433. Fax, (202) 366-3666. Marie Therese Dominguez, Administrator. Hazardous Materials Information Center, (800) 467-4922. To report an incident, (800) 424-8802.*
General email, phmsa.administrator@dot.gov
Web, www.phmsa.dot.gov and Twitter, @PHMSA_DOT

Oversees the safe and secure movement of hazardous materials to industry and consumers by all modes of transportation, including pipelines. Works to eliminate transportation-related deaths and injuries. Promotes transportation solutions to protect communities and the environment.

Pipeline and Hazardous Materials Safety Administration *(Transportation Dept.), Hazardous Materials Safety, 1200 New Jersey Ave. S.E., #E21-317, 20590; (202) 366-0656. Fax, (202) 366-5713.*

TRANSPORTATION RESOURCES IN CONGRESS

For a complete listing of congressional committees, including their full contact information, leadership, membership, and jurisdictions, please refer to the Appendix on pages 779–896.

HOUSE:

House Appropriations Committee,
(202) 225-2771.
Web, appropriations.house.gov
   Subcommittee on Energy and Water Development, and Related Agencies, (202) 225-3421.
   Subcommittee on Financial Services and General Government, (202) 225-7245.
   Subcommittee on Homeland Security, (202) 225-5834.
   Subcommittee on Transportation, HUD, and Related Agencies, (202) 225-2141.
House Energy and Commerce Committee, (202) 225-2927.
Web, energycommerce.house.gov
   Subcommittee on Commerce, Manufacturing, and Trade, (202) 225-2927.
House Homeland Security Committee, (202) 226-8417.
Web, homeland.house.gov
   Subcommittee on Border and Maritime Security, (202) 226-8417.
   Subcommittee on Transportation Security, (202) 226-8417.
House Natural Resources Committee, (202) 225-2761.
Web, naturalresources.house.gov
   Subcommittee on Water, Power, and Oceans, (202) 225-8331.
House Science, Space, and Technology Committee, (202) 225-6371.
Web, science.house.gov
   Subcommittee on Research and Technology, (202) 225-6371.
   Subcommittee on Space, (202) 225-6371.
House Transportation and Infrastructure Committee, (202) 225-9446.
Web, transportation.house.gov
   Subcommittee on Aviation, (202) 226-3220.
   Subcommittee on Coast Guard and Maritime Transportation, (202) 226-3552.
   Subcommittee on Economic Development, Public Buildings, and Emergency Management, (202) 225-3014.
   Subcommittee on Highways and Transit, (202) 225-6715.
   Subcommittee on Railroads, Pipelines, and Hazardous Materials, (202) 226-0727.
   Subcommittee on Water Resources and Environment, (202) 225-4360.

SENATE:

Senate Appropriations Committee, (202) 224-7363.
Web, appropriations.senate.gov
   Subcommittee on Transportation, HUD, and Related Agencies, (202) 224-7281.
Senate Banking, Housing, and Urban Affairs Committee, (202) 224-7391.
Web, banking.senate.gov
   Subcommittee on Housing, Transportation and Community Development, (202) 224-4744.
Senate Commerce, Science, and Transportation Committee, (202) 224-0411.
Web, commerce.senate.gov
   Subcommittee on Aviation Operations, Safety, and Security, (202) 224-9000.
   Subcommittee on Surface Transportation and Merchant Marine Infastructure, Safety, and Security, (202) 224-9000.
Senate Environment and Public Works Committee, (202) 224-8832.
Web, epw.senate.gov
   Subcommittee on Transportation and Infrastructure, (202) 224-8832.
Senate Finance Committee, (202) 224-4515.
Web, finance.senate.gov
   Subcommittee on Energy, Natural Resources, and Infrastructure, (202) 224-4515.

Magdy A. El-Sibaie, Associate Administrator. Hazardous Materials Information Center, (800) 467-4922.
General email, phmsa.hmhazmatsafety@dot.gov
Web, http://hazmat.dot.gov

Federal safety authority for the transportation of hazardous materials by air, rail, highway, and water. Works to reduce dangers of hazardous materials transportation. Issues regulations for classifications, communications, shipper and carrier operations, training and security requirements, and packaging and container specifications.

Pipeline and Hazardous Materials Safety Administration *(Transportation Dept.), Pipeline Safety, 1200 New Jersey Ave. S.E., E24-455, 20590; (202) 366-4595. Fax, (202) 366-4566. Jeffery D. Wiese, Associate Administrator.*
General email, phmsa.pipelinesafety@dot.gov
Web, http://phmsa.dot.gov

Issues and enforces federal regulations for oil, natural gas, and petroleum products pipeline safety. Inspects pipelines and oversees risk management by pipeline operators.

Transportation Department

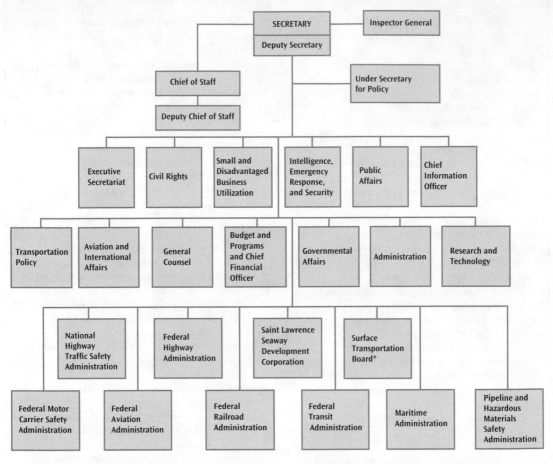

*The Surface Transportation Board is decisionally independent, although it is administratively affiliated with the Department of Transportation.

Surface Transportation Board *(Transportation Dept.),* *Public Assistance, Governmental Affairs, and* *Compliance,* 395 E St. S.W., #1202, 20423-0001; (202) 245-0238. Fax, (202) 245-0461. Lucille L. Marvin, Director. Press, (202) 245-0238. Toll-free, (866) 254-1792. TTY, (800) 877-8339.
General email, stbhelp@stb.dot.gov
Web, www.stb.dot.gov/stb/about/office_ocps.html

Informs members of Congress, the public, and the media of board actions. Prepares testimony for hearings; comments on proposed legislation; assists the public in matters involving transportation regulations.

Transportation Dept. (DOT), 1200 New Jersey Ave. S.E., 20590; (202) 366-4000. Anthony Foxx, Secretary; Victor M. Mendez, Deputy Secretary. Press, (202) 366-4570. TTY, (800) 877-8339.
Web, www.transportation.gov

Responsible for shaping and administering policies and programs to protect and enhance the transportation system and services. Includes the Federal Aviation Administration, Federal Highway Administration, Federal Motor

Carrier Safety Administration, Federal Railroad Administration, Maritime Administration, National Highway Traffic Safety Administration, Pipeline and Hazardous Materials Safety Administration, Federal Transit Administration, and the Saint Lawrence Seaway Development Corp. The Surface Transportation Board is also administratively affiliated, but decisionally independent.

Transportation Dept. (DOT), *Aviation and International* *Affairs,* 1200 New Jersey Ave. S.E., #W88-322, 20590; (202) 366-8822. Fax, (202) 493-2005. Susan Kurland, Assistant Secretary. Press, (202) 366-4570. TTY, (800) 877-8339.
Web, www.dot.gov/policy/assistant-secretary-aviation-international-affairs

Develops and implements public policy related to the airline industry and international civil aviation. Administers laws and regulations over a range of aviation trade issues, including U.S. and foreign carrier economic authority to engage in air transportation, small community transportation, the establishment of mail rates within Alaska and in the international market, and access at U.S. airports.

Transportation Dept. (DOT), *Intelligence, Security, and Emergency Response,* *1200 New Jersey Ave. S.E., #56125, 20590; (202) 366-6525. Fax, (202) 366-7261. Michael Lowder, Director, (202) 366-6530.* Web, www.dot.gov/mission/administrations/intelligence-security-emergency-response

Advises the secretary on transportation intelligence and security policy. Acts as liaison with the intelligence community, federal agencies, corporations, and interest groups; administers counterterrorism strategic planning processes.

Transportation Dept. (DOT), *Safety, Energy, and Environment,* *1200 New Jersey Ave. S.E., #W84-310, 20590; (202) 366-4416. Fax, (202) 366-0263. Barbara McCann, Director. TTY, (800) 877-8339.* Web, www.dot.gov/policy/office-safety-energy-environment

Develops, coordinates, and evaluates public policy with respect to safety, environmental, energy, and accessibility issues affecting all aspects of transportation. Assesses the economic and institutional implications of domestic transportation matters. Oversees legislative and regulatory proposals affecting transportation. Provides advice on research and development requirements. Develops policy proposals to improve the performance, safety, and efficiency of the transportation system.

Transportation Security Administration (TSA) *(Homeland Security Dept.), TSA-1, 601 S. 12th St., 7th Floor, Arlington, VA 20598-6001; (571) 227-1536. Fax, (571) 227-1398. Peter Neffenger, Administrator. Press, (571) 227-2829. TSA Contact Center, (866) 289-9673. General email, TSA-ContactCenter@tsa.dhs.gov* Web, www.tsa.gov/public

Protects the nation's transportation systems to ensure freedom of movement for people and commerce.

Transportation Security Administration (TSA) *(Homeland Security Dept.), Acquisition, TSA-25, 601 S. 12th St., Arlington, VA 20598-6025; (571) 227-2161. Fax, (571) 227-2911. Latetia Anderson, Assistant Administrator.* Web, www.tsa.gov

Administers contract grants, cooperative agreements, and other transactions in support of TSA's mission. Develops acquisitions strategies, policies, programs, and processes.

Transportation Security Administration (TSA) *(Homeland Security Dept.), Contact Center, 601 S. 12th St., 7th Floor, Arlington, VA 20598; (866) 289-9673. Michelle Cartagena, Program Manager. General email, tsa-contactcenter@tsa.dhs.gov* Web, www.tsa.gov

Answers questions and collects concerns from the public regarding travel security.

Transportation Security Administration (TSA) *(Homeland Security Dept.), Freedom Center, 13555 EDS Dr., Herndon, VA 20171 (mailing address: TSOC Annex,* *601 S. 12th St., Arlington, VA 22202); (866) 655-7023. William Stuckey, Manager.* Web, www.tsa.gov

Operations center that provides continual federal, state, and local coordination, communications, and domain awareness for all of the Homeland Security Dept.'s transportation-related security activities worldwide. Transportation domains include highway, rail, shipping, and aviation.

Transportation Security Administration (TSA) *(Homeland Security Dept.), Intelligence and Analysis, TSA-10, 601 S. 12th St., 6th Floor, Arlington, VA 22202-4220; (703) 601-3100. Fax, (703) 601-3290. Thomas L. Bush, Assistant Administrator, Acting.* Web, www.tsa.gov

Conducts a range of programs designed to ensure that known or suspected terrorists do not gain access to sensitive areas of the nation's transportation system, including the Alien Flight, Registered Traveler, Secure Flight, and Transportation Worker Identification Credential programs and Hazmat Materials Truck Drivers Background Checks.

Transportation Security Administration (TSA) *(Homeland Security Dept.), Legislative Affairs, TSA-5, 601 S. 12th St., Arlington, VA 20598-6001; (571) 227-2717. Peter Harding, Assistant Administrator, Acting.* Web, www.tsa.gov

Serves as the TSA's primary point of contact for Congress. Coordinates responses to congressional inquiries, verifies hearings and witnesses, and delivers testimony related to the nation's transportation security.

Transportation Security Administration (TSA) *(Homeland Security Dept.), Security Policy and Industry Engagement, TSA-28, 601 S. 12th St., Arlington, VA 20598-6028; (571) 227-1417. Fax, (571) 227-2932. Eddie Mayenschein, Assistant Administrator.* Web, www.tsa.gov

Formulates policy and shares information related to security in various segments of the transportation industry, including commercial airports, commercial airlines, general aviation, mass transit and passenger rail, freight rail, maritime, highway and motor carrier, pipeline and air cargo. Coordinates with the U.S. Coast Guard.

Transportation Security Administration (TSA) *(Homeland Security Dept.), Strategic Communications and Public Affairs, TSA-4, 601 S. 12th St., Arlington, VA 20598-6028; (571) 227-2829. Fax, (571) 227-2552. David Castelvete, Assistant Administrator, Acting. General email, tsamedia@tsa.dhs.gov* Web, www.tsa.gov/press

Responsible for TSA's communications and public information outreach, both externally and internally.

▶ **CONGRESS**

For a listing of relevant congressional committees and sub-committees, please see page 713 or the Appendix.

Transportation Security Administration

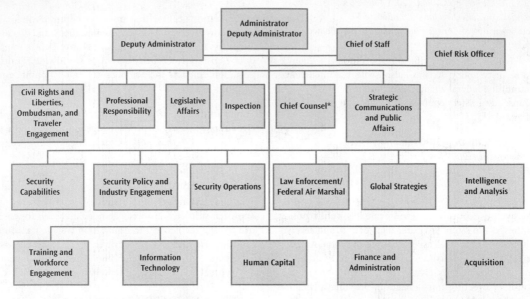

*General Counsel has oversight of the Chief Counsel.

Government Accountability Office (GAO), *Physical Infrastructure,* 441 G St. N.W., #2063, 20548 (mailing address: 441 G St. N.W., #2T23B, Washington, DC 20548); (202) 512-2834. Phil Herr, Managing Director. Web, www.gao.gov/careers/physicalinfrastructure.html

Independent nonpartisan agency in the legislative branch. Audits, analyzes, and evaluates performance of the Transportation Dept. and its component agencies; makes reports available to the public.

▶ NONGOVERNMENTAL

American Concrete Pavement Assn. (ACPA), *Washington Office,* 500 New Jersey Ave. N.W., 7th Floor, 20001; (202) 638-2272. Fax, (202) 638-2688. Gerald F. Voigt, President. Web, www.acpa.org

Represents the concrete pavement industry. Promotes use of concrete for airport, highway, street, and local road pavements. Provides members with project assistance, educational workshops, and training programs. Researches concrete pavement design, construction, and rehabilitation. (Headquarters in Rosemont, Ill.)

American Public Works Assn., *Washington Office,* 1275 K St. N.W., #750, 20005; (202) 408-9541. Fax, (202) 408-9542. Larry Frevatt, Executive Director, Acting; Andrea Eales, Director, Government Affairs. General email, apwa.dc@apwa.net

Web, www.apwa.net and Twitter, @APWATweets

Membership: engineers, architects, and others who maintain and manage public works facilities and services. Conducts research and education and promotes exchange of information on transportation and infrastructure-related issues. (Headquarters in Kansas City, Mo.)

Americans for Transportation Mobility Coalition, U.S. Chamber of Commerce, 1615 H St. N.W., 20062; (202) 463-5842. Ed Mortimer, Executive Director. General email, mobility@uschamber.com

Web, www.fasterbettersafer.org

Advocates increased dedicated federal and private sector funding for roads, bridges, and public transportation systems. Members include associations involved in designing, building, or maintaining transportation infrastructure. Monitors legislation. (Affiliated with the U.S. Chamber of Commerce.)

Assn. for Safe International Road Travel (ASIRT), 12320 Parklawn Dr., Rockville, MD 20852; (240) 249-0100. Fax, (301) 230-0411. Cathy Silberman, Executive Director. General email, asirt@asirt.org

Web, www.asirt.org and Facebook, www.facebook.com/ASIRT.org

Promotes road safety through education and advocacy with governments in the United States and abroad. Serves as information resource for governments, study abroad programs, travel organizations, nongovernmental organizations, and individual travelers.

Assn. of Metropolitan Planning Organizations, 444 N. Capitol St., #345, 20001; (202) 624-3680. Fax, (202) 624-3685. DeLania Hardy, Executive Director. Web, www.ampo.org and Twitter, @ASSOC_MPOS

Membership: more than 385 metropolitan councils of elected officials and transportation professionals responsible for planning local transportation systems. Provides a forum for professional and organizational development; sponsors conferences and training programs.

Assn. of Transportation Law Professionals, *P.O. Box 5407, Annapolis, MD 21403; (410) 268-1311. Fax, (410) 268-1322. Lauren Michalski, Executive Director.*
General email, info@atlp.org

Web, www.atlp.org

Membership: Transportation attorneys and company counsel, government officials, and industry practitioners. Interests include railroad, motor, energy, pipeline, antitrust, labor, logistics, safety, environmental, air, and maritime matters.

Diesel Technology Forum, *5291 Corporate Dr., #102, Frederick, MD 21703-2875; (301) 668-7230. Fax, (301) 668-7234. Allen Schaeffer, Executive Director; Kristen Gifford, Communications.*
General email, dtf@dieselforum.org

Web, www.dieselforum.org

Membership: vehicle and engine manufacturers, component suppliers, petroleum refineries, and emissions control device makers. Advocates use of diesel engines. Provides information on diesel power technology use and efforts to improve fuel efficiency and emissions control. Monitors legislation and regulations.

Eno Center for Transportation, *1710 Rhode Island Ave. N.W., #500, 20005; (202) 879-4700. Emil Franker, President, Acting, (202) 879-4711.*
General email, publicaffairs@enotrans.org

Web, www.enotrans.org

Nonpartisan think tank that seeks continuous improvement in transportation and its public and private leadership in order to increase the system's mobility, safety, and sustainability. Offers professional development programs, policy forums, and publications.

Institute of Navigation, *8551 Rixlew Lane, #360, Manassas, VA 20109; (703) 366-2723. Fax, (703) 366-2724. Lisa Beaty, Executive Director.*
General email, membership@ion.org

Web, www.ion.org

Membership: individuals and organizations interested in navigation and position-determining systems. Encourages research in navigation and establishment of uniform practices in navigation operations and education; conducts symposia on air, space, marine, and land navigation, as well as position determination.

Institute of Transportation Engineers (ITE), *1627 Eye St. N.W., #600, 20006; (202) 785-0060. Fax, (202) 785-0609. Philip J. Caruso, Deputy Executive Director, ext. 126.*
General email, ite_staff@ite.org

Web, www.ite.org

Membership: international professional transportation engineers. Conducts research, seminars, and training sessions; provides professional and scientific information on transportation standards and recommended practices.

International Brotherhood of Teamsters, *25 Louisiana Ave. N.W., 20001-2198; (202) 624-6800. Fax, (202) 624-6918. James P. Hoffa, General President; Christy Bailey,*

Director, Federal Legislation and Regulation.
Press, (202) 624-6911.
General email, communications@teamster.org

Web, www.teamster.org

Membership: more than 1.4 million workers in the transportation and construction industries, factories, offices, hospitals, warehouses, and other workplaces. Helps members negotiate pay, benefits, and better working conditions; conducts training programs and workshops. Monitors legislation and regulations.

National Defense Transportation Assn. (NDTA), *50 S. Pickett St., #220, Alexandria, VA 22304; (703) 751-5011. Fax, (703) 823-8761. Rear Adm. Mark H. Buzby (USN, Ret.), President.*
Web, www.ndtahq.com

Membership: transportation users, manufacturers, and mode carriers; information technology firms; and related military, government, and civil interests worldwide. Promotes a strong U.S. transportation capability through coordination of private industry, government, and the military.

National Governors Assn. (NGA), *Center for Best Practices, Environment, Energy, and Transportation Division, 444 N. Capitol St. N.W., #267, 20001-1512; (202) 624-5300. Fax, (202) 624-7829. Sue Gander, Director.*
General email, webmaster@nga.org

Web, www.nga.org/cms/center/eet

Identifies best practices for energy, land use, environment, and transportation issues and shares these with the states.

National Research Council (NRC), *Transportation Research Board, Keck Center, 500 5th St. N.W., 7th Floor, 20001; (202) 334-2934. Fax, (202) 334-2003. Neil J. Pedersen Jr., Executive Director. Library, (202) 334-2947. Press, (202) 334-3134.*
Web, www.trb.org

Promotes research in transportation systems planning and administration and in the design, construction, maintenance, and operation of transportation facilities. Provides information to state and national highway and transportation departments; operates research information services; conducts studies, conferences, and workshops; publishes technical reports. Library open to the public by appointment.

National Research Council (NRC), *Transportation Research Board Library, Keck Center, 500 5th St. N.W., #439, 20001; (202) 334-2989. Fax, (202) 334-2527. H. Aryeah Cohen, Senior Librarian. Press, (202) 334-3252.*
General email, TRBlibrary@nas.edu

Web, www.trb.org/library

Primary archive for the Transportation Research Board, Highway Research Board, Strategic Highway Research Program, and Marine Board. Subject areas include transportation, aviation, engineering, rail, roads, and transit. Provides information to transportation-related federal agencies. Library open to the public by appointment.

Sheet Metal, Air, Rail, and Transportation Workers (SMART), *1750 New York Ave. N.W., 6th Floor, 20006; (202) 662-0880. Joseph Sellers Jr., General President. Toll-free, (800) 662 0800.*
General email, info@smart-union.org
Web, http://smart-union.org

Membership: United States, Puerto Rican, and Canadian workers in the building and construction trades, manufacturing, and the railroad and shipyard industries. Assists members with contract negotiation and grievances; conducts training programs and workshops. Monitors legislation and regulations. (Affiliated with the Sheet Metal and Air Conditioning Contractors' Assn., the AFL-CIO, and the Canadian Labour Congress.)

Surface Transportation Information Sharing and Analysis Center (ISAC), *c/o EWA Information and Infrastructure Technologies, Inc., 13873 Park Center Rd., #200, Herndon, VA 20171-5406; (703) 478-7600. Fax, (703) 478-7647. Paul G. Wolfe, Director, (703) 478-7656. Toll-free, (866) 784-7221.*
General email, st-isac@surfacetransportationisac.org
Web, www.surfacetransportationisac.org

Protects physical and electronic infrastructure of surface transportation and public transit carriers. Collects, analyzes, and distributes critical security and threat information from worldwide resources; shares best security practices and provides 24/7 immediate physical and cyberthreat warnings.

United Transportation Union, *Washington Office, 304 Pennsylvania Ave. S.E., 20003; (202) 543-7714. Fax, (202) 544-3024. John Risch III, National Legislative Director; Gregory Hynes, Alternate National Legislative Director.*
General email, nld@smart-union.org
Web, www.utu.org

Membership: approximately 125,000 workers and retirees in the transportation industry. Helps members negotiate pay, benefits, and better working conditions; conducts training programs and workshops. Monitors legislation and regulations. (Headquarters in Cleveland, Ohio.)

Freight and Intermodalism

▶AGENCIES

Federal Railroad Administration *(Transportation Dept.), Public Engagement, West Bldg., 1200 New Jersey Ave. S.E., MS 10, 20590; (202) 493-6405. Fax, (202) 493-6009. Timothy Barkley Sr., Director, (202) 493-1305.*
General email, frapa@dot.gov
Web, www.fra.dot.gov/page/p0030

Plans, coordinates, and administers activities related to railroad economics, finance, traffic and network analysis, labor management, and transportation planning, as well as intermodal, environmental, emergency response, and international programs.

Maritime Administration *(Transportation Dept.), Port Infrastructure Development and Congestion Mitigation, West Bldg., 1200 New Jersey Ave. S.E., MAR-510, #W21-308, 20590; (202) 366-5076. Fax, (202) 366-6988. Robert Bouchard, Director.*
Web, www.marad.dot.gov/ports/office-of-port-infrastructure-development-and-congestion-mitigation

Provides coordination and management of port infrastructure projects; provides leadership in national congestion mitigation efforts that involve waterway and port issues; promotes the development and improved utilization of ports and port facilities, including intermodal connections, terminals, and distribution networks; and provides technical information and advice to other agencies and organizations concerned with intermodal development. Information and advice include the analysis of intermodal economics, the development of applicable information systems, investigation of institutional and regulatory impediments, and the application of appropriate transportation management systems.

Surface Transportation Board *(Transportation Dept.), 395 E St. S.W., #1220, 20423-0001; (202) 245-0245. Fax, (202) 245-0458. Daniel Elliott III, Chair, (202) 245-0210. Library, (202) 245-0288. TTY, (800) 877-8339. Press, (202) 245-0238.*
General email, STBHelp@stb.dot.gov
Web, www.stb.dot.gov

Regulates rates for water transportation and intermodal connections in noncontiguous domestic trade (between the mainland and Alaska, Hawaii, or U.S. territories). Library open to the public.

▶NONGOVERNMENTAL

American Moving and Storage Assn. (AMSA), *1611 Duke St., Alexandria, VA 22314-3406; (703) 683-7410. Fax, (703) 683-7527. Scott Michael, President, (703) 683-7418. Information, (888) 849-2672.*
General email, info@moving.org
Web, www.promover.org and Twitter, @AMSAProMover

Represents members' views before the Transportation Dept. and other government agencies. Conducts certification and training programs. Provides financial support for research on the moving and storage industry.

Intermodal Assn. of North America, *11785 Beltsville Dr., #1100, Calverton, MD 20705-4048; (301) 982-3400. Fax, (301) 982-4815. Joanne F. (Joni) Casey, President, ext. 349.*
General email, info@intermodal.org
Web, www.intermodal.org

Membership: railroads, stacktrain operators, water carriers, motor carriers, marketing companies, and suppliers to the intermodal industry. Promotes intermodal transportation of freight. Monitors legislation and regulations.

National Assn. of Chemical Distributors (NACD), *1560 Wilson Blvd., #1100, Arlington, VA 22209; (703) 527-6223. Fax, (703) 527-7747. Eric Byer, President.*

Federal Aviation Administration

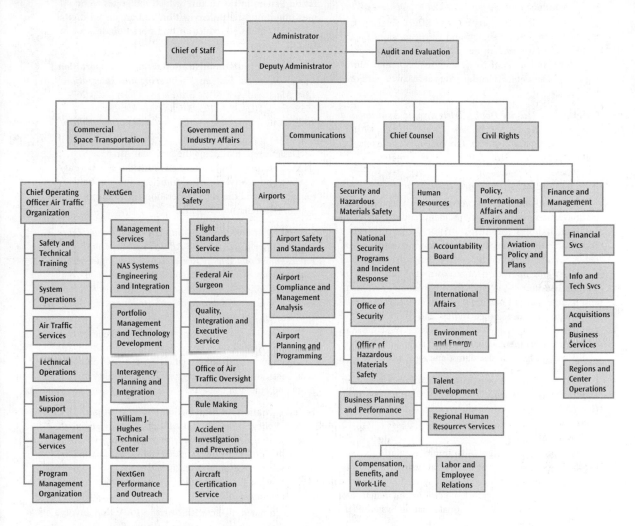

General email, nacdpublicaffairs@nacd.com

Web, www.nacd.com

Membership: firms involved in purchasing, processing, blending, storing, transporting, and marketing of chemical products. Provides members with information on such topics as training, safe handling and transport of chemicals, liability insurance, and environmental issues. Manages the NACD Chemical Educational Foundation. Monitors legislation and regulations.

National Customs Brokers and Forwarders Assn. of America, *1200 18th St. N.W., #901, 20036; (202) 466-0222. Fax, (202) 466-0226. Barbara Reilly, Executive Vice President.*

General email, recep@ncbfaa.org

Web, www.ncbfaa.org

Membership: customs brokers and freight forwarders in the United States. Fosters information exchange within the industry. Monitors legislation and regulations.

National Industrial Transportation League, *1700 N. Moore St., #1900, Arlington, VA 22209-1904; (703) 524-5011. Fax, (703) 524-5017. Bruce J. Carlton, President.*

General email, info@nitl.org

Web, www.nitl.org

Membership: air, water, and surface shippers and receivers, including industries, corporations, chambers of commerce, and trade associations. Monitors legislation and regulations.

AIR TRANSPORTATION

General

▶ AGENCIES

Civil Air Patrol National Capital Wing, *200 McChord St. S.W., #111, Joint Base Anacostia-Bolling, 20032; (202) 767-4405. Col. Bruce Heinlein, Wing Commander.*

General email, info@natcapwing.org

Web, www.natcapwg.cap.gov and Twitter, @NatCapWing

Official civilian auxiliary of the U.S. Air Force. Primary function is to conduct search-and-rescue missions for the Air Force. Maintains an aerospace education program for adults and a cadet program for junior and senior high school students. (Headquarters at Maxwell Air Force Base, Ala.)

Civil Division *(Justice Dept.), Torts Branch, Aviation and Admiralty Litigation,* 1425 New York Ave. N.W., #10100, 20005 (mailing address: P.O. Box 14271, Washington, DC 20044-4271); (202) 616-4100. Fax, (202) 616-4002. Barry Benson, Director.
Web, www.justice.gov/civil/torts/aa/t-aa.html

Represents the federal government in civil suits arising from aviation and admiralty incidents and accidents. In aviation, handles tort litigation for the government's activities in the operation of the air traffic control system, regulation of air commerce, weather services, aeronautical charting, and operation of its own civil and military aircraft. In admiralty, defends the government's placement and maintenance of maritime navigational aids, its nautical charting and dredging activities, and its operation and maintenance of U.S. and contract-operated vessels. Brings cases for government cargo damage, pollution cleanups, and damage to U.S. locks, dams, and navaids.

Federal Aviation Administration (FAA) *(Transportation Dept.),* 800 Independence Ave. S.W., 20591; (202) 267-3111. Fax, (202) 267-7887. Michael P. Huerta, Administrator. Press, (202) 267-3883. Toll-free, (866) 835-5322.
Web, www.faa.gov

Regulates air commerce to improve aviation safety; promotes development of a national system of airports; develops and operates a common system of air traffic control and air navigation for both civilian and military aircraft; prepares the annual National Aviation System Plan.

Federal Aviation Administration (FAA) *(Transportation Dept.), Airport Planning and Environment,* 800 Independence Ave. S.W., #619, APP-400, 20591-0001; (202) 267-3263. Fax, (202) 267-5383. Michael Hines, Manager. Aviation safety, (202) 267-3131.
Web, www.faa.gov/about/office_org/headquarters_offices/ arp/offices/app/app400

Leads the FAA's strategic policy and planning efforts, coordinates the agency's reauthorization before Congress, and is responsible for national aviation policies and strategies in the environment and energy arenas, including aviation activity forecasts, economic analyses, aircraft noise and emissions research and policy, environmental policy, and aviation insurance.

Federal Aviation Administration (FAA) *(Transportation Dept.), NextGen,* 800 Independence Ave. S.W., 20591; (202) 267-7111. Fax, (202) 267-5621. Jim Eck, Assistant Administrator.
General email, nextgen@faa.gov

Web, www.faa.gov/about/office_org/headquarters_ offices/ang

Plans and develops the Next Generation Air Transportation System infrastructure, which integrates technologies inluding satellite navigation and advanced digital communications, to reduce air transportation delays, save fuel, and lower carbon emissions.

Federal Aviation Administration (FAA) *(Transportation Dept.), NextGen, Systems Engineering and Integration,* 1250 Maryland Ave. S.W., 3rd Floor, 20024; (202) 267-6559. Fax, (202) 385-7105. Michele Merkle, Director.
Web, www.faa.gov/about/office_org/headquarters_offices/ ang/offices

Designs and maintains the National Airspace System (NAS) Enterprise Architecture and provides systems engineering and safety expertise to bridge the gap between today's NAS and the Next Generation Air Transportation System (NextGen).

Federal Aviation Administration (FAA) *(Transportation Dept.), Policy, International Affairs, and Environment; Environment and Energy Research and Development,* 800 Independence Ave. S.W., #900W, 20591; (202) 267-3576. Fax, (202) 267-5594. Lourdes Maurice, Executive Director.
Web, www.faa.gov/about/office_org/headquarters_offices/ apl/research

Responsible for environmental affairs and energy conservation for aviation, including implementation and administration of various aviation-related environmental acts. Seeks to improve energy efficiency while reducing noise and emission impacts.

Federal Aviation Administration (FAA) *(Transportation Dept.), Policy, International Affairs, and Environment; International Affairs,* 600 Independence Ave. S.W., #10B, 6th Floor East, API-1, 20591; (202) 267-1000. Fax, (202) 267-7198. Carey Fagan, Executive Director.
Web, www.faa.gov/about/office_org/headquarters_offices/ apl/international_affairs

Coordinates all activities of the FAA that involve foreign relations; acts as liaison with the State Dept. and other agencies concerning international aviation; provides other countries with technical assistance on civil aviation problems; formulates international civil aviation policy for the United States.

International Trade Administration (ITA) *(Commerce Dept.), Industry and Analysis, Transportation and Machinery,* 1401 Constitution Ave. N.W., #38032, 20230-0001; (202) 482-1474. Fax, (202) 482-0674. Scott Kennedy, Director.
Web, http://trade.gov/td/otm

Promotes the export of U.S. aerospace, automotive, and machinery products; compiles and analyzes industry data; seeks to secure a favorable position for the U.S. aerospace, auto, and machinery industries in global markets through policy and trade agreements.

National Aeronautics and Space Administration (NASA), Aeronautics Research Mission Directorate, 300 E St. S.W., #6B27, 20546; (202) 358-4600. Fax, (202) 358-3640. Jaiwon Shin, Associate Administrator.
Web, www.aeronautics.nasa.gov

Conducts research in aerodynamics, materials, structures, avionics, propulsion, high-performance computing, human factors, aviation safety, and space transportation in support of national space and aeronautical research and technology goals. Manages the following NASA research centers: Ames (Moffett Field, Calif.); Dryden (Edwards, Calif.); Langley (Hampton, Va.); and Glenn (Cleveland, Ohio).

National Air and Space Museum *(Smithsonian Institution)*, *6th St. and Independence Ave. S.W., 20560; (202) 633-2214. Fax, (202) 633-8174. Gen. J. R. (Jack) Dailey (USMC, Ret.), Director. TTY, (202) 633-5285. Education office, (202) 633-2540. Library, (202) 633-2320. Tours, (202) 633-2563.*
General email, nasmvisitorservices@si.edu

Web, www.airandspace.si.edu

Maintains exhibits and collections on aeronautics, pioneers of flight, and early aircraft through modern air technology. Library open to the public by appointment.

National Mediation Board, *1301 K St. N.W., #250E, 20005-7011; (202) 692-5000. Fax, (202) 692-5082. Nicholas Geale, Chair. Information, (202) 692-5050. TTY, (202) 692-5001.*
General email, infoline@nmb.gov

Web, www.nmb.gov

Mediates labor disputes in the airline industry; determines and certifies labor representatives for the industry.

Office of the Assistant Secretary of Research and Technology *(Transportation Dept.), Bureau of Transportation Statistics, Airline Information, 1200 New Jersey Ave. S.E., #E-34, RTS 42, 20590; (202) 366-4373. Fax, (202) 366-3383. William Chadwick, Director.*
General email, ritainfo@dot.gov

Web, www.rita.dot.gov/bts/sites/rita.dot.gov.bts/files/subject_areas/airline_information/index.html

Develops, interprets, and enforces accounting and reporting regulations for all areas of the aviation industry; issues air carrier reporting instructions, waivers, and due-date extensions.

Steven F. Udvar-Hazy Center *(Smithsonian Institution), National Air and Space Museum, 14390 Air and Space Museum Pkwy., Chantilly, VA 20151; (703) 572-4118. Gen. John R. Dailey, Director. Public Affairs, (202) 633-1000. TTY, (202) 633-5285.*
General email, nasm-visitorservices@si.edu

Web, www.airandspace.si.edu/visit/udvar-hazy-center

Displays and preserves a collection of historical aviation and space artifacts, including the B-29 Superfortress, Enola Gay, the Lockheed SR-71 Blackbird, the prototype of the Boeing 707, the space shuttle Discovery, and the Concord. Provides a center for research into the history, science, and technology of aviation and space flight. Open to the public daily 10:00 a.m.–5:30 p.m., except December 25.

Transportation Dept. (DOT), *Aviation Analysis, 1200 New Jersey Ave. S.E., #W86-481, 20590; (202) 366-5903.*

Fax, (202) 366-7638. Todd M. Homan, Director. Press, (202) 366-4570. TTY, (800) 877-8339.
Web, www.dot.gov/policy/aviation-policy/office-aviation-analysis

Analyzes essential air service needs of communities; directs subsidy policy and programs; guarantees air service to small communities; conducts research for the department on airline mergers, international route awards, and employee protection programs; administers the air carrier fitness provisions of the Federal Aviation Act; registers domestic air carriers; enforces charter regulations for tour operators.

Transportation Dept. (DOT), *Aviation Consumer Protection, 1200 New Jersey Ave. S.E., 20590; (202) 366-2220. Norman Strickman, Director, (202) 366-5960. Air Travelers With Disabilities hotline, (800) 778-4838. TTY, (202) 366-0511.*
Web, www.dot.gov/airconsumer

Addresses complaints about airline service and consumer-protection matters. Conducts investigations, provides assistance, and reviews regulations affecting air carriers.

Transportation Dept. (DOT), *International Aviation, 1200 New Jersey Ave. S.E., #W86-316, 20590; (202) 366-2423. Fax, (202) 366-3694. Paul L. Gretch, Director.*
Web, www.dot.gov/policy/aviation-policy/office-international-aviation

Responsible for international aviation regulation and negotiations, including fares, tariffs, and foreign licenses; represents the United States at international aviation meetings.

▶**CONGRESS**

For a listing of relevant congressional committees and subcommittees, please see page 713 or the Appendix.

▶**NONGOVERNMENTAL**

Aeronautical Repair Station Assn., *121 N. Henry St., Alexandria, VA 22314-2903; (703) 739-9543. Fax, (703) 739-9488. Sarah MacLeod, Executive Director.*
General email, arsa@arsa.org

Web, www.arsa.org

Membership: repair stations that have Federal Aviation Administration certificates or comparable non-U.S. certification; associate members are suppliers and distributors of components and parts. Works to improve relations between repair stations and manufacturers. Interests include establishing uniformity in the application, interpretation, and enforcement of FAA regulations. Monitors legislation and regulations.

Aerospace Industries Assn. (AIA), *1000 Wilson Blvd., #1700, Arlington, VA 22209-3928; (703) 358-1000. Fax, (703) 358-1012. David Melcher, President. Press, (703) 358-1076.*
General email, aia@aia-aerospace.org

Web, www.aia-aerospace.org

Represents manufacturers of commercial, military, and business aircraft; helicopters; aircraft engines; missiles; spacecraft; and related components and equipment. Interests include international standards and trade.

Air Line Pilots Assn., International, *1625 Massachusetts Ave. N.W., 20036; (703) 689-2270. Tim Canoll, President. Press, (703) 481-4440. Toll-free, (888) 359-2572.*
General email, alpaemail@alpa.org

Web, www.alpa.org

Membership: airline pilots in the United States and Canada. Promotes air travel safety; assists investigations of aviation accidents. Monitors legislation and regulations. (Affiliated with the AFL-CIO and the Canadian Labour Conference.)

Aircraft Owners and Pilots Assn. (AOPA), *Legislative Affairs, 421 Aviation Way, Frederick, MD 21701; (301) 695-2000. Fax, (301) 695-2375. Mark Parker, President. Toll-free for members, (800) 872-2672.*
Web, www.aopa.org

Membership: owners and pilots of general aviation aircraft. Washington office monitors legislation and regulations. Headquarters office provides members with a variety of aviation-related services; issues airport directory and handbook for pilots; sponsors the Air Safety Foundation. (Headquarters in Frederick, Md.)

Airlines for America, *1275 Pennsylvania Ave. N.W., #1300, 20004; (202) 626-4000. Fax, (202) 626-4166. Nicholas Calio, President. Press, (202) 626-4034.*
General email, a4a@airlines.org

Web, www.airlines.org

Membership: U.S. scheduled air carriers. Promotes aviation safety and the facilitation of air transportation for passengers and cargo. Collects data on trends in airline operations. Monitors legislation and regulations.

American Helicopter Society (AHS International), *2701 Prosperity Ave., #210, Fairfax, VA 22031; (703) 684-6777. Fax, (703) 739-9279. Michael Hirschberg, Executive Director.*
General email, staff@vtol.org

Web, www.vtol.org

Membership: individuals and organizations interested in vertical flight. Acts as an information clearinghouse for technical data on helicopter design improvement, aerodynamics, and safety. Awards the Vertical Flight Foundation Scholarship to college students interested in helicopter technology.

American Institute of Aeronautics and Astronautics (AIAA), *12700 Sunrise Valley Dr., #200, Reston, VA 20191-5807; (703) 264-7500. Fax, (703) 264-7551. Sandy Magnus, Executive Director. Information, (800) 639-2422.*
General email, custserv@aiaa.org

Web, www.aiaa.org and Twitter, @aiaa

Membership: engineers, scientists, and students in the fields of aeronautics and astronautics. Holds workshops on aerospace technical issues for congressional subcommittees; sponsors international conferences.

Offers computerized database through its Technical Information Service.

Assn. of Flight Attendants–CWA, *501 3rd St. N.W., 20001-2797; (202) 434-1300. Fax, (202) 434-1319. Sara Nelson, President. Press, (202) 434-0586. Toll-free, (800) 424-2401.*
General email, info@afacwa.org

Web, www.afanet.org and Twitter, @afa_cwa

Membership: approximately 60,000 flight attendants. Helps members negotiate pay, benefits, and better working conditions; conducts training programs and workshops. Monitors legislation and regulations. (Affiliated with the AFL-CIO.)

Cargo Airline Assn., *1620 L St. N.W., #610, 20036-2438; (202) 293-1030. Fax, (202) 293-4377. Stephen A. Alterman, President.*
General email, info@cargoair.org

Web, www.cargoair.org

Membership: cargo airlines and other firms interested in the development and promotion of air freight.

Coalition of Airline Pilots Assns. (CAPA), *444 N. Capitol St., #532, 20001; (202) 624-3535. Fax, (202) 624-3536. Maryanne DeMarco, Executive Director, (202) 624-3538.*
General email, info@capapilots.org

Web, www.capapilots.org and Twitter, @CAPApilots

Trade association of more than 28,000 professional pilots. Addresses safety, security, legislative, and regulatory issues affecting flight deck crew members, as well as domestic and international policy issues regarding aviation safety and security.

General Aviation Manufacturers Assn. (GAMA), *1400 K St. N.W., #801, 20005-2485; (202) 393-1500. Fax, (202) 842-4063. Peter J. (Pete) Bunce, President.*
General email, bforan@gama.aero

Web, www.gama.aero

Membership: manufacturers of business, commuter, and personal aircraft and manufacturers of engines, avionics, and related equipment. Monitors legislation and regulations; sponsors safety and public information programs.

Helicopter Assn. International, *1920 Ballenger Ave., Alexandria, VA 22314-2898; (703) 683-4646. Fax, (703) 683-4745. Matthew Zuccaro, President.*
General email, rotor@rotor.org

Web, www.rotor.com

Membership: owners, manufacturers, and operators of helicopters and affiliated companies in the civil helicopter industry. Provides information on use and operation of helicopters; offers business management and aviation safety courses; sponsors annual industry exposition. Monitors legislation and regulations.

National Aeronautic Assn., *Reagan National Airport, Hangar 7, #202, 20001-6015; (703) 416-4888. Fax, (703) 416-4877. Jonathan Gaffney, President.*
General email, naa@naa.aero

Web, www.naa.aero

Membership: persons interested in development of general and sporting aviation, including skydiving, commercial and military aircraft, and spaceflight. Supervises sporting aviation competitions; administers awards in aviation; oversees and approves official U.S. aircraft, aeronautics, and space records. Serves as U.S. representative to the International Aeronautical Federation in Lausanne, Switzerland.

National Agricultural Aviation Assn., *1440 Duke St., Alexandria, VA 22314; (202) 546-5722. Fax, (202) 546-5726. Andrew D. Moore, Executive Director.*
General email, information@agaviation.org
Web, www.agaviation.org

Membership: agricultural pilots; operating companies that seed, fertilize, and spray land by air; and allied industries. Monitors legislation and regulations. (Affiliated with National Agricultural Aviation Research and Education Foundation.)

National Air Carrier Assn., *1000 Wilson Blvd., #1700, Arlington, VA 22209-3928; (703) 358-8060. Fax, (703) 358-8070. A. Oakley Brooks, President.*
Web, www.naca.cc

Membership: U.S. air carriers certified for nonscheduled and scheduled operations for passengers and cargo in the United States and abroad. Monitors legislation and regulations.

National Air Transportation Assn., *818 Connecticut Ave. N.W., #900, 20006; (202) 774-1535. Fax, (202) 452-0837. Thomas L. Hendricks, President. Information, (800) 808-6282.*
Web, www.nata.aero

Membership: companies that provide on-demand air charter, flight training, maintenance and repair, avionics, and other services. Manages an education foundation; compiles statistics; provides business assistance programs. Monitors legislation and regulations. (Affiliated with the National Air Transportation Foundation.)

National Assn. of State Aviation Officials, *8400 Westpark Dr., 2nd Floor, McLean, VA 22102; (703) 454-0649. Fax, (703) 995-0837. Greg Principato, President.*
General email, info@nasao.org
Web, www.nasao.org

Membership: state and territorial aeronautics agencies that deal with aviation issues, including regulation. Seeks uniform aviation laws; manages an aviation research and education foundation.

National Business Aviation Assn. (NBAA), *1200 G St. N.W., #1100, 20005; (202) 783-9000. Fax, (202) 331-8364. Ed Bolen, President. Toll-free, (800) 394-6222.*
General email, info@nbaa.org
Web, www.nbaa.org

Membership: companies owning and operating aircraft for business use, suppliers, and maintenance and air fleet service companies. Conducts seminars and workshops in business aviation management. Sponsors annual civilian aviation exposition. Monitors legislation and regulations.

National Research Council (NRC), *Human-Systems Integration Board, Keck Center, 500 5th St. N.W., 11th Floor, 20001; (202) 334-2678. Fax, (202) 334-2210. Poornima Madhavan, Director, (202) 334-3357; Nancy J. Cooke, Chair.*
General email, bohsi@nas.edu
Web, http://sites.nationalacademies.org/dbasse/bohsi

Conducts studies on human factors and human-systems integration. Areas of research include virtual reality, human-computer interaction, nuclear safety, air traffic control, military simulation, modeling social networks, home health care, and disability and rehabilitation research.

Regional Airline Assn., *2025 M St. N.W., #800, 20036-3309; (202) 367-1170. Fax, (202) 367-2170. Faye Malarkey Black, President.*
General email, raa@raa.org
Web, www.raa.org

Membership: regional airlines that provide passenger, scheduled cargo, and mail service. Issues an annual report on the industry and hosts an annual convention. Monitors legislation and regulation.

RTCA Inc., *1150 18th St. N.W., #910, 20036; (202) 833-9339. Fax, (202) 833-9434. Margaret T. Jenny, President.*
General email, info@rtca.org
Web, www.rtca.org and Twitter, @RTCAInc

Membership: federal agencies, aviation organizations, and commercial firms interested in aeronautical systems. Develops and publishes standards for aviation, including minimum operational performance standards for equipment; conducts research, makes recommendations to FAA, and issues reports on the field of aviation electronics and telecommunications.

Airports

► **AGENCIES**

Animal and Plant Health Inspection Service (APHIS) (Agriculture Dept.), Wildlife Services, *1400 Independence Ave. S.W., #1624S, 20250-3402; 4700 River Rd., Riverdale, MD 20737; (202) 799-7095. Fax, (202) 690-0053. William H. Clay, Deputy Administrator.*
Web, www.aphis.usda.gov/wildlife_damage

Works to minimize damage caused by wildlife to human health and safety. Interests include aviation safety; works with airport managers to reduce the risk of bird strikes. Oversees the National Wildlife Research Center in Ft. Collins, Colo.

Bureau of Land Management (BLM) (Interior Dept.), Lands, Realty, and Cadastral Survey, *20 M St. S.E., 20003 (mailing address: 1849 C St. N.W., 2134LM, Washington, DC 20240); (202) 912-7088. Fax, (202) 912-7199. Michael G. Stiewig, Division Chief.*

Web, www.blm.gov/wo/st/en/info/directory/WO-350_ dir.html

Operates the Airport Lease Program, which leases public lands for use as public airports.

Federal Aviation Administration (FAA) *(Transportation Dept.), Airports, 800 Independence Ave. S.W., #600E, ARP-1, 20591; (202) 267-8738. Fax, (202) 267-5301. Eduardo Angeles, Associate Administrator. Web, www.faa.gov/about/office_org/headquarters_ offices/arp*

Makes grants for development and improvement of publicly operated and owned airports and some privately owned airports; inspects and certifies safety design standards for airports; administers the congressional Airport Improvement Program and Passenger Facility Charges Program; ensures that airports receiving federal funding comply with federal regulations. Questions about local airports are usually referred to a local FAA field office.

Maryland Aviation Administration, *P.O. Box 8766, Terminal Bldg., 3rd Floor, BWI Airport, MD 21240-0766; (410) 859-7100. Fax, (410) 850-4729. Paul J. Wiedefeld, Chief Executive Officer. Information, (800) 435-9294. Press, (410) 859-7027. TTY, (410) 859-7227. General email, maa@mdot.state.md.us Web, www.marylandaviation.com and www.bwiairport.com*

Responsible for aviation operations, planning, instruction, and safety in Maryland; operates Baltimore/Washington International Thurgood Marshall Airport (BWI) and Martin State Airport.

Metropolitan Washington Airports Authority, *1 Aviation Circle, 20001-6000; (703) 417-8600. Fax, (703) 417-8949. John E. Potter, President. Press, (703) 417-8370. Web, www.mwaa.com*

Independent interstate agency created by Virginia and the District of Columbia with the consent of Congress; operates Washington Dulles International Airport and Ronald Reagan Washington National Airport.

▶NONGOVERNMENTAL

Airports Council International (ACI), *1615 L St. N.W., #300, 20036; (202) 293-8500. Fax, (202) 331-1362. Kevin Burke, President. Toll-free, (888) 424-7767. General email, postmaster@aci-na.org Web, www.aci-na.org*

Membership: authorities, boards, commissions, and municipal departments operating public airports. Serves as liaison with government agencies and other aviation organizations; works to improve passenger and freight facilitation; acts as clearinghouse on engineering and operational aspects of airport development. Monitors legislation and regulations.

American Assn. of Airport Executives, *601 Madison St., #400, Alexandria, VA 22314; (703) 824-0504. Fax, (703) 820-1395. Todd Hauptli, President, (703) 578-2514. Web, www.aaae.org*

Membership: airport managers, superintendents, consultants, government officials, authorities and commissioners, and others interested in the construction, management, and operation of airports. Conducts examination for and awards the professional designation of Accredited Airport Executive.

Aviation Safety and Security

▶AGENCIES

Federal Aviation Administration (FAA) *(Transportation Dept.), Accident Investigation and Prevention, 800 Independence Ave. S.W., #840, AVP-1, 20591; (202) 267-9612. Fax, (202) 267-3265. Wendell Griffin, Director. Web, www.faa.gov/about/office_org/headquarters_offices/ avs/offices/avp*

Investigates aviation accidents and incidents to detect unsafe conditions and trends in the national airspace system and to coordinate corrective action.

Federal Aviation Administration (FAA) *(Transportation Dept.), Air Traffic Organization, 800 Independence Ave. S.W., #1018A, AJA-O, 20591; (202) 267-7224. Fax, (202) 267-5085. Teri L. Bristol, Chief Operating Officer. FAA communications, (202) 267-3883. Web, www.faa.gov/about/office_org/headquarters_ offices/ato*

Operates the national air traffic control system; employs air traffic controllers at airport towers, terminal radar approach controls, en route air traffic control centers, and flight service stations in Alaska; maintains the William J. Hughes Technical Center for aviation research, testing, and evaluation.

Federal Aviation Administration (FAA) *(Transportation Dept.), Air Traffic Organization, Air Traffic Services, 600 Independence Ave. S.W., #FOB 10-B, #3E1500, 20591; (202) 267-0634. Fax, (202) 493-4306. Tim Arel, Vice President. Web, www.faa.gov/about/office_org/headquarters_offices/ ato/service_units/air_traffic_services*

Provides safe, secure, and efficient management for the National Airspace System and international airspace assigned to U.S. control. Responsible for Airport Traffic Control Towers (federal and contract), Terminal Radar Approach facilities, Air Route Traffic Control Centers, and Combined Center Radar Approach Control facilities to guide aircraft through their various phases of flight.

Federal Aviation Administration (FAA) *(Transportation Dept.), Air Traffic Organization, Technical Operations, 800 Independence Ave. S.W., #700E-10A, 20591; (202) 267-3366. Fax, (202) 267-6060. Vaughn Turner, Vice President. Web, www.faa.gov/about/office_org/headquarters_offices/ ato/service_units/techops*

Conducts research and development programs aimed at providing procedures, facilities, and devices needed for a safe and efficient system of air navigation and air traffic control.

Federal Aviation Administration (FAA) *(Transportation Dept.), Air Traffic Safety Oversight Service,* 800 Independence Ave. S.W., 20591; (202) 267-5202. Anthony Ferrante, Director.
Web, www.faa.gov/about/office_org/headquarters_offices/avs/offices/aov

Establishes safety standards and provides independent oversight of the Air Traffic Organization.

Federal Aviation Administration (FAA) *(Transportation Dept.), Aviation Safety, Aerospace Medicine,* 800 Independence Ave. S.W., #800W, AAM-1, 20591; (202) 267-3535. Fax, (202) 267-5399. James R. Fraser, Federal Air Surgeon.
Web, www.faa.gov/about/office_org/headquarters_offices/avs/offices/aam

Responsible for the medical activities and policies of the FAA; designates, through regional offices, aviation medical examiners who conduct periodic medical examinations of all air personnel; regulates and oversees drug and alcohol testing programs for pilots, air traffic controllers, and others who hold safety-sensitive positions; maintains a Civil Aerospace Medical Institute in Oklahoma City.

Federal Aviation Administration (FAA) *(Transportation Dept.), Aviation Safety, Aircraft Certification Service,* 800 Independence Ave. S.W., #800E, AIR-1, 20591-0004; (202) 267-8235. Fax, (202) 267-5364. Dorenda Baker, Director. Aviation safety, (202) 267-3131.
Web, www.faa.gov/about/office_org/field_offices/avs/offices/air

Certifies all aircraft for airworthiness; approves designs and specifications for new aircraft, aircraft engines, propellers, and appliances; supervises aircraft manufacturing and testing. Directs a fuels program and an international division.

Federal Aviation Administration (FAA) *(Transportation Dept.), Aviation Safety, Flight Standards Service,* 800 Independence Ave. S.W., #821, AFS-1, 20591; (202) 267-8237. Fax, (202) 267-5230. John Duncan, Director. Press, (202) 267-3883.
Web, www.faa.gov/about/office_org/headquarters_offices/avs/offices/afs

Sets certification standards for air carriers, commercial operators, air agencies, and air personnel (except air traffic control tower operators); directs and executes certification and inspection of flight procedures, operating methods, air personnel qualification and proficiency, and maintenance aspects of airworthiness programs; manages the registry of civil aircraft and all official air personnel records; supports law enforcement agencies responsible for drug interdiction.

Federal Aviation Administration (FAA) *(Transportation Dept.), Security and Hazardous Materials Safety,* 800 Independence Ave. S.W., #300, 20591; (202) 267-7211. Fax, (202) 267-8496. Claudio Manno, Associate Administrator.
Web, www.faa.gov/about/office_org/headquarters_offices/ash

Seeks to ensure air transportation safety by preventing hazardous materials accidents aboard aircraft and protecting FAA employees and facilities from criminal and terrorist acts.

Federal Bureau of Investigation (FBI) *(Justice Dept.), Criminal Investigative Division,* 935 Pennsylvania Ave. N.W., #3012, 20535; (202) 324-4260. Fax, (202) 324-0027. Joseph S. Campbell, Assistant Director.
Web, www.fbi.gov

Investigates cases of aircraft hijacking, destruction of aircraft, and air piracy. Works with TSA and FAA to ensure security of national air carrier systems in areas of violent crime, organized crime, civil rights, corruption, and financial crimes.

Federal Communications Commission (FCC), *Enforcement Bureau,* 445 12th St. S.W., 3rd Floor, #7C723, 20554; (202) 418-7450. Fax, (202) 418-2810. Travis LeBlanc, Chief. Media Relations, (202) 418-0500. Toll-free, (888) 225-5322.
Web, www.fcc.gov/enforcement-bureau

Provides technical services to aid the Federal Aviation Administration in locating aircraft in distress; provides interference resolution for air traffic control radio frequencies.

National Transportation Safety Board (NTSB), *Aviation Safety,* 490 L'Enfant Plaza East S.W., #5400, 20594-0001; (202) 314-6344. Fax, (240) 752-6257. John DeLisi, Director. Information, (202) 314-6540. Press, (202) 314-6100.
Web, www.ntsb.gov/about/organization/AS

Responsible for management, policies, and programs in aviation safety and for aviation accident investigations. Manages programs on special investigations, safety issues, and safety objectives. Acts as U.S. representative in international investigations.

Transportation Security Administration (TSA) *(Homeland Security Dept.),* TSA-1, 601 S. 12th St., 7th Floor, Arlington, VA 20598-6001; (571) 227-1536. Fax, (571) 227-1398. Peter Neffenger, Administrator. Press, (571) 227-2829. TSA Contact Center, (866) 289-9673. General email, TSA-ContactCenter@tsa.dhs.gov
Web, www.tsa.gov/public

Protects the nation's transportation system. Performs and oversees airport security, including passenger and baggage screeners, airport federal security directors, and air marshals. Questions and concerns regarding travel can be submitted toll-free to the TSA Contact Center.

Transportation Security Administration (TSA) *(Homeland Security Dept.), Office of Law Enforcement, Federal Air Marshal Service,* TSA-18, 601 S. 12th St., Arlington, VA 20598-6018; (703) 487-3400. Fax, (703) 487-3405. Colleen Callahan, Assistant Administrator, Acting.
Web, www.tsa.gov/about-tsa/office-law-enforcement

Protects air security in the United States. Promotes public confidence in the U.S. civil aviation system. Deploys marshals on flights around the world to detect and deter

National Transportation Safety Board

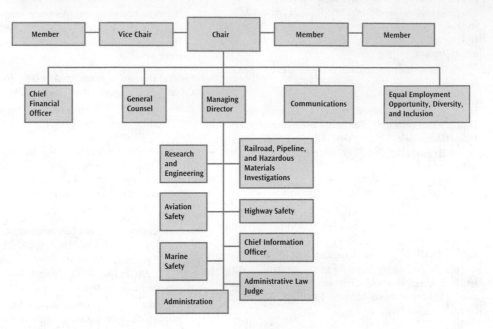

hostile acts targeting U.S. air carriers, airports, passengers, and crews.

▶NONGOVERNMENTAL

Aerospace Medical Assn., *320 S. Henry St., Alexandria, VA 22314-3579; (703) 739-2240. Fax, (703) 739-9652. Jeffery Sventek, Executive Director.*
General email, inquiries@asma.org

Web, www.asma.org

Membership: physicians, flight surgeons, aviation medical examiners, flight nurses, scientists, technicians, and specialists in clinical, operational, and research fields of aerospace medicine. Promotes programs to improve aerospace medicine and maintain safety in aviation by examining and monitoring the health of aviation personnel; members may consult in aircraft investigation and cockpit design.

Air Traffic Control Assn., *1101 King St., #300, Alexandria, VA 22314-2963; (703) 299-2430. Fax, (703) 299-2437. Peter F. Dumont, President.*
General email, info@atca.org

Web, www.atca.org

Membership: air traffic controllers, flight service station specialists, pilots, aviation engineers and manufacturers, and others interested in air traffic control systems. Compiles and publishes information and data concerning air traffic control; provides information to members, Congress, and federal agencies.

American Assn. of Airport Executives, *601 Madison St., #400, Alexandria, VA 22314; (703) 824-0504. Fax, (703) 820-1395. Todd Hauptli, President, (703) 578-2514.*
Web, www.uuue.org

Maintains the Transportation Security Clearinghouse, which matches fingerprints and other personal information from airport and airline employees against FBI databases.

Flight Safety Foundation, *701 N. Fairfax St., #400, Alexandria, VA 22314-1774; (703) 739-6700. Fax, (703) 739-6708. Ken Hylander, Chair; Jon Beatty, Chief Executive Officer. Press, (703) 739-6700, ext. 116.*
General email, info@flightsafety.org

Web, www.flightsafety.org and Twitter, @flightsafety

Membership: aerospace manufacturers, domestic and foreign airlines, energy and insurance companies, educational institutions, and organizations and corporations interested in flight safety. Sponsors seminars, publishes literature, and conducts studies and safety audits on air safety for governments and industries. Administers award programs that recognize achievements in air safety.

International Society of Air Safety Investigators (ISASI), *107 E. Holly Ave., #11, Sterling, VA 20164-5405; (703) 430-9668. Fax, (703) 430-4970. Frank S. Del Gandio, President; Ann Schull, International Office Manager.*
General email, isasi@erols.com

Web, www.isasi.org

Membership: specialists who investigate and seek to define the causes of aircraft accidents. Encourages improvement of air safety and investigative procedures through information exchange and educational seminars.

National Air Traffic Controllers Assn., *1325 Massachusetts Ave. N.W., 20005; (202) 628-5451. Fax, (202) 628-5767. Paul Rinaldi, President. Toll-free, (800) 266-0895.*
Web, www.natca.org

Seeks to increase air traffic controller staffing levels, improve working conditions, and encourage procurement of more modern, reliable equipment. Concerned with airport safety worldwide.

Professional Aviation Safety Specialists, *1200 G St. N.W., #750, 20005; (202) 293-7277. Fax, (202) 293-7727. Mike Perrone, President.*
Web, www.passnational.org

Membership: FAA and DoD employees who install, maintain, support and certify air traffic control and national defense equipment, inspect and oversee the commercial and general aviation industries, develop flight procedures, and perform quality analyses of complex aviation systems used in air traffic control and national defense in the United States and abroad.

MARITIME TRANSPORTATION

General

▶**AGENCIES**

Army Corps of Engineers *(Defense Dept.),* *441 G St. N.W., #3K05, 20314-1000; (202) 761-0001. Fax, (202) 761-4463. Lt. Gen. Thomas P. Bostick (USA), Chief of Engineers. Press, (202) 761-0011.*
General email, hq-publicaffairs@usace.army.mil
Web, www.usace.army.mil and Twitter, @USACEHQ

Provides local governments with navigation, flood control, disaster relief, and hydroelectric power services.

Civil Division *(Justice Dept.), Torts Branch, Aviation and Admiralty Litigation, 1425 New York Ave. N.W., #10100, 20005 (mailing address: P.O. Box 14271, Washington, DC 20044-4271); (202) 616-4100. Fax, (202) 616-4002. Barry Benson, Director.*
Web, www.justice.gov/civil/torts/aa/t-aa.html

Represents the federal government in civil suits concerning the maritime industry, including ships, shipping, and merchant marine personnel. Handles civil cases arising from admiralty incidents and accidents, including oil spills.

Federal Maritime Commission (FMC), *800 N. Capitol St. N.W., 20573-0001; (202) 523-5725. Fax, (202) 523-0014. Vern W. Hill, Managing Director; Mario Cordero, Chair. TTY, (800) 877-8339. Library, (202) 523-5762.*
General email, inquiries@fmc.gov
Web, www.fmc.gov

Regulates the foreign ocean shipping of the United States; enforces maritime shipping laws and regulations regarding rates and charges, freight forwarding, passengers, and port authorities. Library open to the public (Monday–Friday, 8:00 a.m.–4:30 p.m.).

Federal Maritime Commission (FMC), *Certification and Licensing, 800 N. Capitol St. N.W., #970, 20573-0001; (202) 523-5787. Fax, (202) 566-0011. Sandra L. Kusumoto, Director.*

General email, blc@fmc.gov
Web, www.fmc.gov/bureaus_offices/bureau_of_ certification_and_licensing.aspx

Licenses ocean freight forwarders and non-vessel-operating common carriers. Issues certificates of financial responsibility to ensure that cruise lines refund fares and meet their liability in case of death, injury, or nonperformance. Library open to the public (Monday–Friday, 8:00 a.m.–4:30 p.m.).

Federal Maritime Commission (FMC), *Trade Analysis, 800 N. Capitol St. N.W., #940, 20573-0001; (202) 523-5796. Fax, (202) 523-4372. Florence A. Carr, Director. Library, (202) 523-5762.*
General email, tradeanalysis@fmc.gov
Web, www.fmc.gov/bureaus_offices/bureau_of_trade_ analysis.aspx

Analyzes and monitors agreements between terminal operators and shipping companies and agreements among ocean common carriers. Reviews and analyzes service contracts, monitors rates of government-owned controlled carriers, reviews carrier-published tariff systems under the accessibility and accuracy standards, and responds to inquiries or issues that arise concerning service contracts or tariffs. Conducts competition and market analysis to detect activity that is substantially anti-competitive. Library open to the public (Monday–Friday, 8:00 a.m.–4:30 p.m.).

Maritime Administration *(Transportation Dept.), West Bldg., 1200 New Jersey Ave. S.E., 20590; (202) 366-1719. Fax, (202) 366-3890. Capt. Paul N. Jaenichen Sr., Administrator; Michael J. Rodriguez, Deputy Administrator. Press, (202) 366-5807.*
Web, www.marad.dot.gov and Facebook, www.facebook. com/DOTMARAD

Conducts research on shipbuilding and operations; provides financing guarantees and a tax-deferred fund for shipbuilding; promotes the maritime industry; operates the U.S. Merchant Marine Academy in Kings Point, New York.

Maritime Administration *(Transportation Dept.), Business and Finance Development, West Bldg., 1200 New Jersey Ave. S.E., MAR-750, 20590; (202) 366-9595. Owen J. Doherty, Associate Administrator.*
Web, www.marad.dot.gov

Works with shipyards, ship owners, operations and labor to aid growth of modern shipyards. Functions include financial approval, marine financing, cargo preference and domestic trade, workforce development and shipyard and marine engineering.

Maritime Administration *(Transportation Dept.), Cargo and Commercial Sealift, West Bldg., 1200 New Jersey Ave. S.E., MAR-620, MS 2, 20590; (202) 366-4610. Fax, (202) 366-5522. William H. Cahill, Director, Acting.*
General email, cargo.marad@dot.gov
Web, www.marad.dot.gov/ships-and-shipping/cargo-preference

Enforces cargo preference laws and regulations. Promotes and monitors the use of U.S. flag vessels in the movement of cargo on international waters.

Maritime Administration *(Transportation Dept.),* **Environment and Compliance,** *West Bldg., 1200 New Jersey Ave. S.E., W28-342, 20590; (202) 366-1931. Fax, (202) 366-6988. John P. Quinn, Associate Administrator.*
Web, www.marad.dot.gov/environment-and-safety/associate-administrator-for-environment-and-compliance

Focuses on environmental stewardship, maritime safety, and maritime security; maritime research and development; and maritime international and domestic rules, regulations, and standards. Provides environmental support for America's Marine Highway Program and ensures compliance with the National Environmental Policy Act. Advises Maritime Administrator on domestic and international environmental policies that affect maritime transportation.

Maritime Administration *(Transportation Dept.),* **International Activities,** *West Bldg., 1200 New Jersey Ave. S.E., W28-312, 20590; (202) 366-5493.*
Lonnie Kishiyama, Director.
Web, www.marad.dot.gov

Formulates the agency's position on international issues affecting the U.S. maritime industry with the goal of reducing or eliminating international barriers to trade and improving market access.

Maritime Administration *(Transportation Dept.),* **Labor and Workforce Development,** *West Bldg., 1200 New Jersey Ave. S.E., MAR-750, W23-314, 20590; (202) 366-5469. Anne Wehde, Director. Workforce Development, (202) 493-0029.*
General email, careersafloat@dot.gov
Web, www.marad.dot.gov

Administers programs for the U.S. Merchant Marine Academy and State Academies. Promotes maritime workforce development.

Maritime Administration *(Transportation Dept.),* **Marine Financing,** *West Bldg., 1200 New Jersey Ave. S.E., 2nd Floor, 20590; (202) 366-2118. Fax, (202) 366-7901. David Gilmore, Director.*
Web, www.marad.dot.gov/ships_shipping_landing_page/title_xi_home/title_xi_home.htm

Provides ship financing guarantees for ship construction and shipyard modernization; administers the Capital Construction Fund Program; deals with the Federal Ship Financing Program (part of Title XI).

Maritime Administration *(Transportation Dept.),* **Policy and Plans,** *West Bldg., 1200 New Jersey Ave. S.E., MAR-232, 20590; (202) 366-2145. Fax, (202) 366-3890. Douglas McDonald, Director.*
Web, www.marad.dot.gov/about_us_landing_page/policy_initiatives/Policy_Initiatives.htm

Supports the agency's policy development process with research, analysis, and documentation. Assesses the effects of legislative and regulatory proposals on maritime programs and maritime industries. Investigates the effects of national and global events on maritime policy and operations.

Maritime Administration *(Transportation Dept.),* **Strategic Sealift,** *West Bldg., 1200 New Jersey Ave. S.E., Mar-600, MS 1, W25-330, 20590; (202) 366-5400. Fax, (202) 366-5904. Kevin M. Tokarski, Associate Administrator.*
Web, www.marad.dot.gov/ships_shipping_landing_page/national_security/national_security.htm

Administers strategic sealift programs for the Maritime Administration and ensures that merchant shipping is available in times of war or national emergency.

Navy Dept. *(Defense Dept.),* **Military Sealift Command,** *Bldg. 210, Washington Navy Yard, DC 20398-5540; (202) 685-5007. Fax, (202) 685-5020. Rear Adm. Thomas K. Shannon, Commander. Press, (202) 685-5055.*
Web, www.msc.navy.mil

Provides sea transportation of equipment, fuel, supplies, and ammunition to sustain U.S. forces.

U.S. Coast Guard (USCG) *(Homeland Security Dept.),* *2703 Martin Luther King Jr. Ave. S.E., MS 7000, 20593-7000; (202) 372-4411. Fax, (202) 372-8302. Adm. Paul F. Zukunft, Commandant. Public Affairs, (202) 372-4600.*
Web, www.uscg.mil

Carries out search-and-rescue missions in and around navigable waters and on the high seas; enforces federal laws on the high seas and navigable waters of the United States and its possessions; conducts marine environmental protection programs; administers boating safety programs; inspects and regulates construction, safety, and equipment of merchant marine vessels; establishes and maintains a system of navigation aids; carries out domestic icebreaking activities; maintains a state of military readiness to assist the Navy in time of war or when directed by the president.

U.S. Coast Guard (USCG) *(Homeland Security Dept.),* **Engineering and Logistics,** *CG4, 2703 Martin Luther King Jr. Ave. S.E., MS 7714, 20593; (202) 475-5554. Fax, (202) 475-5957. Rear Adm. Bruce D. Baffer, Assistant Commandant; Albert Curry Jr., Deputy Assistant Commandant.*
Web, www.uscg.mil/hq/cg4

Develops and maintains engineering standards for the building of ships, aircraft, shore infrastructure, and Coast Guard facilities.

U.S. Coast Guard (USCG) *(Homeland Security Dept.),* **Investigations and Casualty Analysis,** *CG-545, 2100 2nd St. S.W., 20593-7581; (202) 372-1029. Fax, (202) 372-1907. Capt. Jason Nuebauer, Chief.*
Web, www.uscg.mil/hq/cg5/cg545

Handles disciplinary proceedings for merchant marine personnel. Compiles and analyzes records of marine casualties. Focuses on marine safety and environmental protection through marine inspection activities, including investigation of spills and drug and alcohol testing.

U.S. Coast Guard (USCG) *(Homeland Security Dept.),* *Strategic Analysis,* *CG-0951, 2703 Martin Luther King Jr. Ave. S.E., MS 7104, 20593-7104; (202) 372-2695. Fax, (202) 372-4976. Capt. Steven (Rob) Wittrock, Chief.* *Web, www.uscg.mil/strategy/default.asp*

Identifies and analyzes emerging geopolitical, economic, and environmental issues and trends; develops specific recommendations to improve the strategic and operational posture of the U.S. Coast Guard.

▶**CONGRESS**

For a listing of relevant congressional committees and subcommittees, please see page 713 or the Appendix.

▶**NONGOVERNMENTAL**

American Maritime Congress, *444 N. Capitol St. N.W., #800, 20001-1570; (202) 347-8020. Fax, (202) 347-1550. James E. Caponiti, President.* *General email, diannelauer@americanmaritime.org* *Web, www.americanmaritime.org*

Organization of U.S.-flag carriers engaged in oceanborne transportation. Conducts research, education, and advocacy on behalf of the U.S.-flag merchant marine.

Boat U.S. (Boat Owners Assn. of the United States), *880 S. Pickett St., Alexandria, VA 22304-4606; (703) 461-2878. Fax, (703) 461-2847. Margaret Podlich, President.* *General email, govtaffairs@boatus.com* *Web, www.boatus.com and Twitter, @BoatUS*

Membership: owners of recreational boats. Represents boat-owner interests before the federal, state, and local governments.

Chamber of Shipping of America, *1730 Rhode Island Ave. N.W., #702, 20036-4517; (202) 775-4399. Fax, (202) 659-3795. Kathy J. Metcalf, President.* *Web, www.knowships.org*

Represents U.S.-based companies that own, operate, or charter oceangoing tankers, container ships, and other merchant vessels engaged in domestic and international trade and companies that maintain a commercial interest in the operation of such oceangoing vessels.

Marine Engineers' Beneficial Assn. (MEBA), *444 N. Capitol St. N.W., #800, 20001-1570; (202) 638-5355. Fax, (202) 638-5369. Marshall Ainley, President.* *Web, www.mebaunion.org*

Maritime labor union. Represents engineers and deck officers, domestically and internationally. Monitors legislation and regulation.

Maritime Institute for Research and Industrial Development, *1025 Connecticut Ave. N.W., #507, 20036-5412; (202) 463-6505. Fax, (202) 223-9093. C. James (Jim) Patti, President.* *General email, jpatti@miraid.org*

Membership: U.S.-flagship operators. Promotes the development of the U.S. merchant marine. Interests include the use of private commercial merchant vessels by the Defense Dept., enforcement of cargo preference (Jones Act) laws for U.S.-flagships, and maintenance of cabotage laws.

National Marine Manufacturers Assn., *Government Relations, 650 Massachusetts Ave. N.W., #520, 20001; (202) 737-9750. Fax, (202) 628-4716. Nicole Vasilaros, Vice President, (202) 737-9763.* *Web, www.nmma.org/government/default*

Membership: recreational marine equipment manufacturers. Promotes boating safety and the development of boating facilities. Monitors legislation and regulations. (Headquarters in Chicago, Ill.)

National Research Council (NRC), *Marine Board, Keck Center, 500 5th St. N.W., 20001; (202) 334-2000. Vice Adm. James C. Card (USCG, Ret.), Chair.* *Web, www.trb.org/MarineBoard/MarineBoard.aspx*

Supports research and provides information relating to new technologies, laws and regulations, economics, the environment, and other issues affecting the marine transportation system, port operations, coastal engineering, and marine governance.

Shipbuilders Council of America, *20 F St. N.W., #500, 20001; (202) 737-3234. Fax, (202) 478-1241. Matt Paxton, President.* *Web, http://shipbuilders.org*

Membership: U.S. shipyards that repair and build commercial ships and naval and other government vessels; and allied industries and associations. Monitors legislation and regulations.

Transportation Institute, *5201 Auth Way, Camp Springs, MD 20746-4211; (301) 423-3335. Fax, (301) 423-0634. James L. Henry, President.* *General email, info@trans-inst.org* *Web, www.trans-inst.org*

Membership: U.S.-flag maritime shipping companies. Conducts research on freight regulation and rates, government subsidies and assistance, domestic and international maritime matters, maritime safety, ports, Saint Lawrence Seaway, shipbuilding, and regulation of shipping.

World Shipping Council, *1156 15th St. N.W., #300, 20005; (202) 589-1230. Fax, (202) 589-1231. John W. Butler, President.* *General email, info@worldshipping.org* *Web, www.worldshipping.org*

Membership association representing the liner shipping industry. Works with policymakers and other industry groups interested in international transportation issues, including maritime security, regulatory policy, tax issues, safety, the environment, harbor dredging, and trade infrastructure. Monitors legislation and regulations.

Maritime Safety

▶AGENCIES

Maritime Administration *(Transportation Dept.),* *Environment and Compliance, Security Office,* West Bldg., 1200 New Jersey Ave. S.E., W28-340, 20590; (202) 366-1883. Cameron T. Naron, Director.
Web, www.marad.dot.gov/ports_landing_page/port_ cargo_security/port_cargo_security.htm

Promotes security throughout the maritime transportation system through data support, maritime warnings, and advisories for American vessels by using information technology.

National Oceanic and Atmospheric Administration (NOAA) *(Commerce Dept.), National Ocean Service, Coast Survey,* 1315 East-West Hwy., #6147, SSMC3, Silver Spring, MD 20910-3282; (301) 713-2770. Fax, (301) 713-4019. Rear Adm. Gerd F. Glang, Director. Toll-free, (888) 990-6622.
Web, www.nauticalcharts.noaa.gov and *Twitter, @NOAAcharts*

Directs programs and conducts research to support fundamental scientific and engineering activities and resource development for safe navigation of the nation's waterways and territorial seas. Prints on demand and distributes nautical charts.

National Transportation Safety Board (NTSB), *Marine Safety,* 490 L'Enfant Plaza East S.W., #6300, 20594-0001; (202) 314-6456. Fax, (202) 459-9299. Brian Curtis, Director, Acting.
Web, www.ntsb.gov/about/organization/MS

Investigates selected marine transportation accidents, including major marine accidents that involve U.S. Coast Guard operations or functions. Determines the facts upon which the board establishes probable cause; makes recommendations on matters pertaining to marine transportation safety and accident prevention.

Occupational Safety and Health Administration (OSHA) *(Labor Dept.), Maritime and Agriculture,* 200 Constitution Ave. N.W., #N3609, 20210-0001; (202) 693-2222. Fax, (202) 693-1663. Amy Wangdahl, Office Director.
Web, www.osha.gov/dts/maritime/mission.html

Writes occupational safety and health standards and guidance products for the maritime industry and agriculture.

Occupational Safety and Health Administration (OSHA) *(Labor Dept.), Maritime Enforcement,* 200 Constitution Ave. N.W., #N3610, 20210-0001; (202) 693-2399. Fax, (202) 693-2369. Stephen Butler, Director.
Web, www.osha.gov/dts/maritime/dir_maritime.html

Administers occupational safety and health enforcement program for the maritime industries. Provides comprehensive program guidelines, policies, procedures, technical assistance, and information dissemination.

U.S. Coast Guard (USCG) *(Homeland Security Dept.), Boating Safety,* CG-BSX-2, 2703 Martin Luther King Jr. Ave. S.E., MS 7501, 20593; (202) 372-1062. Fax, (202) 372-1908. Jeffrey Hoedt, Chief.
Web, www.uscgboating.org

Tracks and analyzes boating accidents; writes and enforces safety regulations for recreational boats and associated equipment; sets boater education standards; coordinates public awareness and information programs; awards grants to states and nongovernmental organizations to improve safety.

U.S. Coast Guard (USCG) *(Homeland Security Dept.), Deputy for Operations Policy and Capabilities,* CG-DCO-D, 2703 Martin Luther King Jr. Ave. S.E., MS 7318, 20593; (202) 372-1001. Fax, (202) 372-2900. Rear Adm. Vincent B. Atkins, Deputy.
Web, www.uscg.mil/hq/cg5

Establishes and enforces regulations for port safety; environmental protection; vessel safety, inspection, design, documentation, and investigation; licensing of merchant vessel personnel; and shipment of hazardous materials.

U.S. Coast Guard (USCG) *(Homeland Security Dept.), Design and Engineering Standards,* CG-ENG, 2703 Martin Luther King Jr. Ave. S.E., MS 7509, 20593; (202) 372-1352. Fax, (202) 372-1925. Capt. John W. Mauger, Chief.
Web, www.uscg.mil/hq/cg5/cg521

Develops standards; responsible for general vessel arrangements, naval architecture, vessel design and construction, and transport of bulk dangerous cargoes. Supports national advisory committees and national professional organizations to achieve industry standards.

U.S. Coast Guard (USCG) *(Homeland Security Dept.), Investigations and Casualty Analysis,* CG-545, 2100 2nd St. S.W., 20593-7581; (202) 372-1029. Fax, (202) 372-1907. Capt. Jason Nuebauer, Chief.
Web, www.uscg.mil/hq/cg5/cg545

Compiles and analyzes records of accidents involving commercial vessels that result in loss of life, serious injury, or substantial damage.

U.S. Coast Guard (USCG) *(Homeland Security Dept.), Marine Safety Center,* 2703 Martin Luther King Jr. Ave. S.E., 20593; (202) 795-6729. Capt. John Nadeau, Commanding Officer.
General email, msc@uscg.mil
Web, www.uscg.mil/hq/msc and *http://homeport.uscg.mil*

Reviews and approves commercial vessel plans and specifications to ensure technical compliance with federal safety and pollution abatement standards.

U.S. Coast Guard (USCG) *(Homeland Security Dept.), National Response Center,* 2100 2nd St. S.W., #2111B, 20593-0001; (202) 267-2180. Fax, (202) 267-1322. Syed M. Qadir, Director, (202) 372-2440. TTY, (202) 267-4477. Hotline, (800) 424-8802. Local, (202) 267-2675.
General email, NRC@uscg.mil
Web, www.nrc.uscg.mil

Maintains 24-hour hotline for reporting oil spills, hazardous materials accidents, and chemical releases. Notifies appropriate federal officials to reduce the effects of accidents.

U.S. Coast Guard (USCG) *(Homeland Security Dept.),* *Response Policy,* CG-53, 2100 2nd St. S.W., 20593-7516; (202) 372-2010. *Rear Adm. Peter Brown, Director.*
Web, www.uscg.mil

Conducts search-and-rescue and polar and domestic ice-breaking operations. Regulates waterways under U.S. jurisdiction. Operates the Coast Guard National Response Center; participates in defense operations and homeland security; assists with law enforcement/drug interdictions.

▶**NONGOVERNMENTAL**

Cruise Lines International Assn., *1201 F St. N.W., #250, 20004; (202) 759-9370. Fax, (202) 759-9344. Cindy D'Aoust, President, Acting.*
General email, info@cruising.org
Web, www.cruising.org

Membership: more than sixty cruise lines as well as other cruise industry professionals. Advises domestic and international regulatory organizations on shipping policy. Works with U.S. and international agencies to promote safety, public health, security, medical facilities, environmental awareness, and passenger protection. Monitors legislation and regulations.

National Maritime Safety Assn., *919 18th St. N.W., #901, Washington, DC 20006; (202) 587-4801. John E. Crowley, Executive Director.*
General email, mlo@nmsa.us
Web, www.nmsa.us

Represents the marine cargo handling industry in safety and health matters arising under various statutes, including the Occupational Safety and Health Act. Serves as a clearinghouse on information to help reduce injuries and illnesses in the marine cargo handling workplace. Monitors legislation and regulations.

Ports and Waterways

▶**AGENCIES**

Army Corps of Engineers *(Defense Dept.), Civil Works,* 441 G St. N.W., 20314-1000; (202) 761-0099. Fax, (202) 761-0559. *Steven L. Stockton, SES, Director; Maj. Gen. Donald E. Jackson Jr. (USA), Deputy Commanding General for Civil and Emergency Operations.*
Web, www.usace.army.mil

Coordinates field offices that oversee harbors, dams, levees, waterways, locks, reservoirs, and other construction projects designed to facilitate transportation, flood control, and environmental restoration projects. Major projects include the Mississippi, Missouri, and Ohio Rivers; Bay Delta in California; the Great Lakes; the Chesapeake Bay; the Everglades in Florida; and the Gulf of Mexico.

Maritime Administration *(Transportation Dept.), Intermodal System Development,* West Bldg., 1200 New Jersey Ave. S.E., MAR-500, W21-320, 20590; (202) 366-0678. Fax, (202) 366-6988. *Lauren K. Brand, Associate Administrator.*
Web, www.marad.dot.gov/about-us/key-personnel/ associate-administrator-for-intermodal-systems- development

Responsible for direction and administration of port and intermodal transportation development and port readiness for national defense.

Saint Lawrence Seaway Development Corp. *(Transportation Dept.),* 1200 New Jersey Ave. S.E., #W32-300, 20590; (202) 366-0091. Fax, (202) 366-7147. *Betty Sutton, Administrator. Toll-free, (800) 785-2779.*
General email, slsc@dot.gov
Web, www.seaway.dot.gov

Operates and maintains the Saint Lawrence Seaway within U.S. territorial limits; conducts development programs and coordinates activities with its Canadian counterpart.

Tennessee Valley Authority, *Government Affairs,* 1 Massachusetts Ave. N.W., #300, 20444; (202) 898-2999. Fax, (202) 898-2998. *Nick Pearson, Director.*
General email, tvainfo@tva.gov
Web, www.tva.gov

Coordinates resource conservation, development, and land-use programs in the Tennessee River Valley. Operates the river control system; projects include flood control, navigation development, and multiple-use reservoirs.

U.S. Coast Guard (USCG) *(Homeland Security Dept.),* 2703 Martin Luther King Jr. Ave. S.E., MS 7000, 20593-7000; (202) 372-4411. Fax, (202) 372-8302. *Adm. Paul F. Zukunft, Commandant. Public Affairs, (202) 372-4600.*
Web, www.uscg.mil

Enforces rules and regulations governing the safety and security of ports and anchorages and the movement of vessels in U.S. waters. Supervises cargo transfer operations, storage, and stowage; conducts harbor patrols and waterfront facility inspections; establishes security zones and monitors vessel movement.

▶**NONGOVERNMENTAL**

American Assn. of Port Authorities (AAPA), *1010 Duke St., Alexandria, VA 22314-3589; (703) 684-5700. Fax, (703) 684-6321. Kurt J. Nagle, President.*
General email, info@aapa-ports.org
Web, www.aapa-ports.org

Membership: public port authorities in the Western Hemisphere. Provides technical and economic information on port finance, environmental issues, construction, operation, and security.

American Waterways Operators, *801 N. Quincy St., #200, Arlington, VA 22203-1708; (703) 841-9300. Fax, (703) 841-0389. Thomas A. Allegretti, President.*
Web, www.americanwaterways.com

Membership: operators of barges, tugboats, and tow-boats on navigable coastal and inland waterways. Acts as liaison with Congress, the U.S. Coast Guard, the Army Corps of Engineers, and other federal agencies. Establishes safety standards and conducts training for efficient, environmentally responsible transportation. Monitors legislation and regulations.

International Longshore and Warehouse Union (ILWU), *Washington Office,* 1025 Connecticut Ave. N.W., #507, 20036; (202) 463-6265. Fax, (202) 467-4875. *Lindsay McLaughlin, Legislative Director. General email, bianca.blomquist@ilwu.org Web, www.ilwu.org*

Membership: approximately 60,000 longshore and warehouse personnel. Helps members negotiate pay, benefits, and better working conditions; conducts training programs and workshops. Monitors legislation and regulations. (Headquarters in San Francisco, Calif.)

International Longshoremen's Assn., *Washington Office,* 1101 17th St. N.W., #400, 20036-4704; (202) 955-6304. Fax, (202) 955-6048. *John Bowers Jr., Executive Director. General email, iladc@aol.com Web, www.ilaunion.org*

Membership: approximately 65,000 longshore personnel. Helps members negotiate pay, benefits, and better working conditions; conducts training programs and workshops. Monitors legislation and regulations. (Headquarters in New Jersey; affiliated with the AFL-CIO.)

National Assn. of Waterfront Employers, 1200 19th St. N.W., 3rd Floor, 20036; (202) 587-4800. Fax, (202) 587-4888. *John E. Crowley, Executive Director. General email, mto@nawe.us Web, www.nawe.us*

Membership: private sector stevedore companies and marine terminal operators, their subsidiaries, and other waterfront-related employers. Legislative interests include trade, shipping, antitrust issues, insurance, port security, and user-fee issues. Monitors legislation and regulations.

National Research Council (NRC), *Marine Board,* Keck Center, 500 5th St. N.W., 20001; (202) 334-2000. *Vice Adm. James C. Card (USCG, Ret.), Chair. Web, www.trb.org/MarineBoard/MarineBoard.aspx*

Supports research and provides information relating to new technologies, laws and regulations, economics, the environment, and other issues affecting the marine transportation system, port operations, coastal engineering, and marine governance.

National Waterways Conference, 1100 N. Glebe Rd., #1010, Arlington, VA 22201; (703) 224-8007. Fax, (866) 371-1390. *Amy W. Larson, President, (703) 224-8007. General email, info@waterways.org Web, www.waterways.org*

Membership: petroleum, coal, chemical, electric power, building materials, iron and steel, and grain companies; port authorities; water carriers; and others interested or involved in waterways. Sponsors educational programs on waterways. Monitors legislation and regulations.

Passenger Vessel Assn., 103 Oronoco St., #200, Alexandria, VA 22314; (703) 518-5005. Fax, (703) 518-5151. *John R. Groundwater, Executive Director. Toll-free, (800) 807-8360. General email, pvainfo@passengervessel.com Web, www.passengervessel.com*

Membership: owners, operators, and suppliers for U.S. and Canadian passenger vessels and international vessel companies. Interests include insurance, safety and security, and U.S. congressional impact upon dinner and excursion boats, car and passenger ferries, overnight cruise ships, and riverboat casinos. Monitors legislation and regulations.

Transportation Institute, 5201 Auth Way, Camp Springs, MD 20746-4211; (301) 423-3335. Fax, (301) 423-0634. *James L. Henry, President. General email, info@trans-inst.org Web, www.trans-inst.org*

Membership: U.S.-flag maritime shipping companies. Conducts research on freight regulation and rates, government subsidies and assistance, domestic and international maritime matters, maritime safety, ports, Saint Lawrence Seaway, shipbuilding, and regulation of shipping.

Waterways Council, Inc., 499 S. Capitol St. S.W., #401, 20003; (202) 765-2166. Fax, (202) 765-2167. *Michael Toohey, President. Press email, dcalhoun@waterwayscouncil.org, Web, www.waterwayscouncil.org and Twitter, @WaterwaysCouncil*

Membership: port authorities, waterways carriers, shippers, shipping associations, and waterways advocacy groups. Advocates for a modern and well-maintained system of inland waterways and port infrastructure. Monitors legislation and regulations.

MOTOR VEHICLES

General

▶AGENCIES

Federal Highway Administration (FHWA) *(Transportation Dept.),* 1200 New Jersey Ave. S.E., 20590-0001; (202) 366-4000. Fax, (202) 366-3244. *Jeffrey F. Paniati, Executive Director, (202) 366-2242. Press and public affairs, (202) 366-0660. Web, www.fhwa.dot.gov*

Administers federal-aid highway programs with money from the Highway Trust Fund; works to improve highway and motor vehicle safety; coordinates research and development programs on highway and traffic safety, construction costs, and the environmental impact of highway transportation; administers regional and territorial highway building programs and the highway beautification program.

Federal Motor Carrier Safety Administration
(Transportation Dept.), Bus and Truck Standards and Operations, 1200 New Jersey Ave. S.E., #N64-330, 20590; (202) 366-5370. Fax, (202) 366-8842. Chuck Horan, Director, (202) 366-2362.
Web, www.fmcsa.dot.gov/safety/look-you-book/look-you-book

Regulates motor vehicle size and weight on federally aided highways; conducts studies on issues relating to motor carrier transportation; promotes uniformity in state and federal motor carrier laws and regulations.

►CONGRESS

For a listing of relevant congressional committees and subcommittees, please see page 713 or the Appendix.

►NONGOVERNMENTAL

American Assn. of Motor Vehicle Administrators
(AAMVA), 4301 Wilson Blvd., #700, Arlington, VA 22203-1753; (703) 522-4200. Fax, (703) 522-1553. Anne S. Ferro, President. Press, (703) 908-5891.
General email, info@aamva.org
Web, www.aamva.org

Membership: officials responsible for administering and enforcing motor vehicle and traffic laws in the United States and Canada. Promotes uniform laws and regulations for vehicle registration, driver's licenses, and motor carrier services.

American Automobile Assn. (AAA), *Washington Office,*
607 14th St. N.W., #200, 20005-4798; (202) 942-2050. Fax, (202) 783-4788. Jill Ingrassia, Managing Director of Government Relations and Traffic Safety Advocacy; Kathleen Bower, Vice President, Public Affairs.
General email, jingrassia@national.AAA.com
Web, www.aaa.com

Membership: state and local automobile associations. Conducts public outreach and offers publications through the AAA Foundation for Traffic Safety. Interests include all aspects of highway transportation, travel and tourism, safety, drunk driving, and legislation that affects motorists. (Headquarters in Heathrow, Fla.)

American Bus Assn.,
111 K St. N.E., 9th Floor, 20002; (202) 842-1645. Fax, (202) 842-0850. Peter J. Pantuso, President, (202) 218-7229. Toll-free, (800) 283-2877.
General email, abainfo@buses.org
Web, www.buses.org

Membership: privately owned intercity bus companies, state associations, travel/tourism businesses, bus manufacturers, and those interested in the bus industry. Monitors legislation and regulations.

American Trucking Assns.,
950 N. Glebe Rd., #210, Arlington, VA 22203-4181 (mailing address: Washington Office, 430 1st St. S.E., #100, Washington, DC 20003); (703)

838-1700. Fax, (703) 838-1936. William P. (Bill) Graves, President. Press, (703) 838-1873. Legislative Affairs, (202) 544-6245.
General email, media@trucking.org
Web, www.trucking.org and Twitter, @TRUCKINGdotORG

Membership: state trucking associations, individual trucking and motor carrier organizations, and related supply companies. Maintains departments on industrial relations, law, management systems, research, safety, traffic, state laws, taxation, communications, legislation, economics, and engineering.

Electric Drive Transportation Assn. (EDTA), 1250 Eye St.,
#902, 20005; (202) 408-0774. Fax, (202) 408-7610. Brian P. Wynne, President. Press, (202) 408-0774, ext. 312.
General email, info@electricdrive.org
Web, www.electricdrive.org

Membership: automotive and other equipment manufacturers, utilities, technology developers, component suppliers, and government agencies. Conducts public policy advocacy, education, industry networking, and international conferences in the areas of battery, hybrid, and fuel cell electric drive technologies and infrastructures.

Highway Loss Data Institute, 1005 N. Glebe Rd., #700,
Arlington, VA 22201; (703) 247-1600. Fax, (703) 247-1588. Adrian Lund, President.
Web, www.iihs.org

Research organization that gathers, processes, and publishes data on the ways in which insurance losses vary among different kinds of vehicles. (Affiliated with Insurance Institute for Highway Safety.)

International Parking Institute, 1330 Braddock Pl.,
#350, Alexandria, VA 22314; (571) 699-3011. Fax, (703) 566-2267. Shawn D. Conrad, Chief Executive Officer.
General email, ipi@parking.org
Web, www.parking.org

Membership: operators, designers, and builders of parking lots and structures. Provides leadership to the parking industry; supports professional development; works with transportation and related fields.

Motorcycle Industry Council, *Government Relations,*
1235 South Clark St., #600, Arlington, VA 22202; (703) 416-0444. Fax, (703) 416-2269. Kathy Van Kleeck, Senior Vice President.
Web, www.mic.org

Membership: manufacturers and distributors of motorcycles, mopeds, and related parts, accessories, and equipment. Monitors legislation and regulations. (Headquarters in Irvine, Calif.)

Motorcycle Riders Foundation, 1325 G St. N.W., #500,
20005; (202) 546-0983. Fax, (202) 546-0986. Kirk Willard, President.
General email, mrfoffice@mrf.org
Web, www.mrf.org

Lobby and advocacy group that supports motorcyclist rights. Sponsors seminars for activists. Interests include motorcycle safety, training, and licensing. Monitors legislation and regulations.

National Assn. of Regulatory Utility Commissioners, *1101 Vermont Ave. N.W., #200, 20005-3521; (202) 898-2200. Fax, (202) 898-2213. Greg White, Executive Director.*
General email, admin@naruc.org

Web, www.naruc.org

Membership: members of federal, state, municipal, and international regulatory commissions that have jurisdiction over motor and common carriers. Interests include motor carriers.

National Institute for Automotive Service Excellence, *101 Blue Seal Dr. S.E., #101, Leesburg, VA 20175; (703) 669-6600. Fax, (703) 669-6122. Timothy Zilke, President. Toll-free, (800) 390-6789.*
General email, contactus@ase.com

Web, www.ase.com and Facebook, www.facebook.com/ASEtests

Administers program for testing and certifying automotive technicians; researches methods to improve technician training.

National Motor Freight Traffic Assn., *1001 N. Fairfax St., #600, Alexandria, VA 22314-1798; (703) 838-1810. Fax, (703) 683-6296. Paul Levine, Executive Director. Toll-free, (866) 411-6632.*
General email, customerservice@nmfta.org

Web, www.nmfta.org

Membership: motor carriers of general goods in interstate and intrastate commerce. Publishes *National Motor Freight Classification.*

National Parking Assn., *1112 16th St. N.W., #840, 20036-4880; (202) 296-4336. Fax, (202) 296-3102. Christine Banning, President, (202) 470-6299. Toll-free, (800) 647-7275.*
General email, info@weareparking.org

Web, www.npapark.org

Membership: parking garage operators, parking consultants, universities, municipalities, medical centers, and vendors. Offers information and research services; sponsors seminars and educational programs on garage design and equipment. Monitors legislation and regulations.

National Private Truck Council, *950 N. Glebe Rd., #2300, Arlington, VA 22203-4183; (703) 683-1300. Fax, (703) 683-1217. Gary F. Petty, President, (703) 838-8898.*
General email, memberservice@nptc.org

Web, www.nptc.org

Membership: manufacturers, retailers, distributors, wholesalers, and suppliers that operate their own private truck fleets in conjunction with their nontransportation businesses. Interests include standards, best practices, benchmarking, federal regulatory compliance, peer-to-peer networking, and business economics. Supports economic deregulation of the trucking industry and uniformity

in state taxation of the industry. NPTC Institute supports continuing education and certification programs.

National Tank Truck Carriers (NTTC), *950 N. Glebe Rd., #520, Arlington, VA 22203-4183; (703) 838-1960. Fax, (703) 838-8860. Dan Furth, President.*
General email, nttcstaff@tanktruck.org

Web, www.tanktruck.org

Focuses on issues of the tank truck industry and represents the industry before Congress and federal agencies.

NATSO, Inc., *1300 Braddock Pl., #501, Alexandria, VA 22314; (703) 549-2100. Lisa J. Mullings, President.*
General email, editor@natso.com

Web, www.natso.com

Membership: travel plaza and truck stop operators and suppliers to the truck stop industry. Provides credit information and educational training programs. Monitors legislation and regulations. Operates the NATSO Foundation, which promotes highway safety.

NGVAmerica (Natural Gas Vehicles for America), *400 N. Capitol St. N.W., 20001; (202) 824-7360. Fax, (202) 824-9160. Matthew Godlewski, President; Paul Kerkhoven, Director, Government Affairs.*
General email, pkerkhoven@ngvamerica.org

Web, www.ngvamerica.org

Membership: natural gas distributors and producers; automobile and engine manufacturers; natural gas vehicle product and service suppliers; research and development organizations; enviromental groups; and state and local government agencies. Advocates installation of natural gas and biomethane fuel stations and development of industry standards. Helps market new products and equipment related to compressed natural gas (CNG), liquefied natural gas (LNG), and biomethane-powered vehicles.

Truckload Carriers Assn., *555 E. Braddock Rd., Alexandria, VA 22314; (703) 838-1950. Fax, (703) 836-6610. John Lyboldt, President.*
General email, tca@truckload.org

Web, www.truckload.org

Membership: truckload carriers and industry suppliers. Provides information and educational programs to members. Represents intercity common and contract trucking companies before Congress, federal agencies, courts, and the media.

Union of Concerned Scientists, *Clean Vehicles Program, 1825 K St. N.W., #800, 20006-1232; (202) 223-6133. Fax, (202) 223-6162. Michelle Robinson, Director.*
General email, ucs@ucsusa.org

Web, www.ucsusa.org

Develops and promotes strategies to reduce U.S. consumption of oil, including increasing fuel efficiency of cars and trucks, as well as promoting advanced vehicle technology including battery-electric, hybrid-electric, and fuel cell vehicles, and next-generation biofuels. (Headquarters in Cambridge, Mass.)

Highways

►AGENCIES

Federal Highway Administration (FHWA)
(Transportation Dept.), Infrastructure, 1200 New Jersey Ave. S.E., #E75-312, 20590; (202) 366-0371. Fax, (202) 493-0099. Walter C. (Butch) Waidelich Jr., Associate Administrator.
Web, www.fhwa.dot.gov/infrastructure

Provides guidance and oversight for planning, design, construction, and maintenance operations relating to federal aid, direct federal construction, and other highway programs; establishes design guidelines and specifications for highways built with federal funds.

Federal Highway Administration (FHWA)
(Transportation Dept.), National Highway Institute, 1310 N. Courthouse Rd., Arlington, VA 22201-1555; (703) 235-0500. Fax, (703) 235-0593. Valerie Briggs, Director. Toll-free, (877) 558-6873.
Web, www.nhi.fhwa.dot.gov

Develops and administers, in cooperation with state highway departments, technical training programs for agency, state, and local highway department employees.

Federal Highway Administration (FHWA)
(Transportation Dept.), Planning, Environment, and Realty, 1200 New Jersey Ave. S.E., #E76-306, 20590; (202) 366-0116. Fax, (202) 366-3713. Gloria M. Shepherd, Associate Administrator.
Web, www.fhwa.dot.gov/real_estate

Works with developers and municipalities to ensure conformity with the National Environmental Policy Act (NEPA) project development process.

Federal Highway Administration (FHWA)
(Transportation Dept.), Policy and Governmental Affairs, 1200 New Jersey Ave. S.E., #E87-312, 20590-0001; (202) 366-8169. Fax, (202) 366-3590. David Kim, Associate Administrator, (202) 366-0585.
Web, www.fhwa.dot.gov/policy

Develops policy and administers the Federal Highway Administration's international programs. Conducts policy studies and analyzes legislation; makes recommendations; compiles and reviews highway-related data. Represents the administration at international conferences; administers foreign assistance programs.

Federal Highway Administration (FHWA)
(Transportation Dept.), Research, Development, and Technology, 6300 Georgetown Pike, #T306, McLean, VA 22101-2296; (202) 493-3999. Fax, (202) 493-3170. Michael Trentacoste, Associate Administrator, (202) 493-3259. Library, (202) 493-3058.
General email, hiwot.abdi@dot.gov
Web, www.fhwa.dot.gov/research

Conducts highway research and development programs; studies safety, location, design, construction, operation, and maintenance of highways; cooperates with state and local highway departments in utilizing results of research. Library access via public library exchange.

U.S. Coast Guard (USCG) *(Homeland Security Dept.), 2703 Martin Luther King Jr. Ave. S.E., MS 7000, 20593-7000; (202) 372-4411. Fax, (202) 372-8302. Adm. Paul F. Zukunft, Commandant. Public Affairs, (202) 372-4600.*
Web, www.uscg.mil

Regulates the construction, maintenance, and operation of bridges across U.S. navigable waters.

►NONGOVERNMENTAL

American Assn. of State Highway and Transportation Officials (AASHTO), *444 N. Capitol St. N.W., #249, 20001-1512; (202) 624-5800. Fax, (202) 624-5806. Frederick G. (Bud) Wright, Executive Director, (202) 624-5811.*
General email, info@aashto.org
Web, www.transportation.org

Membership: the transportation departments of the 50 states, the District of Columbia, and Puerto Rico, and affiliated agencies, including the U.S. Department of Transportation as a nonvoting ex officio member. Maintains committees on all modes of transportation and departmental affairs.

American Road and Transportation Builders Assn. (ARTBA), *1219 28th St. N.W., 20007-3389; (202) 289-4434. Fax, (202) 289-4435. T. Peter Ruane, President.*
General email, general@artba.org
Web, www.artba.org and Twitter, @ARTBA

Membership: highway and transportation contractors; federal, state, and local engineers and officials; construction equipment manufacturers and distributors; and others interested in the transportation construction industry. Serves as liaison with government; provides information on highway engineering and construction developments.

Intelligent Transportation Society of America, *1100 New Jersey Ave. S.E., #850, 20003; (202) 484-4847. Fax, (202) 484-3483. Regina Hopper, President; Quentin Kelly, Legislative Affairs, (202) 721-4212. Toll-free, (800) 374-8472.*
General email, info@itsa.org
Web, www.itsa.org

Advocates application of electronic, computer, and communications technology to make surface transportation more efficient and to improve safety, security, and environmental sustainability. Coordinates research, development, and implementation of intelligent transportation systems by government, academia, and industry.

International Bridge, Tunnel and Turnpike Assn., *1146 19th St. N.W., #600, 20036-3725; (202) 659-4620. Fax, (202) 659-0500. Patrick D. Jones, Executive Director, ext. 21; Neil Gray, Director, Government Affairs, ext. 14.*
General email, ibtta@ibtta.org
Web, www.ibtta.org

Membership: public and private operators of toll facilities and associated industries. Conducts research; compiles statistics.

International Road Federation (IRF), *Madison Pl., 500 Montgomery St., 5th Floor, Alexandria, VA 22314; (703) 535-1001. Fax, (703) 535-1007. C. Patrick Sankey, President.*
General email, info@irfnews.org
Web, www.irfnews.org

Membership: contractors, consultants, equipment manufacturers, researchers, and others involved in the road building industry. Administers fellowship program that allows foreign engineering students to study at U.S. graduate schools. Maintains interest in roads and highways worldwide.

The Road Information Program (TRIP), *3000 Connecticut Ave. N.W., #208, 20008; (202) 466-6706. William M. Wilkins, Executive Director.*
General email, wilkins@tripnet.org
Web, www.tripnet.org and Twitter, @TRIP_Inc

Organization of transportation specialists; conducts research on economic and technical transportation issues; promotes consumer awareness of the condition of the national road and bridge system.

Manufacturing and Sales

▶**AGENCIES**

Energy Efficiency and Renewable Energy *(Energy Dept.),* **Vehicle Technologies,** *1000 Independence Ave. S.W., #5G030, 20585; (202) 586-8055. Fax, (202) 586-7409. David Howell, Program Manager, Acting.*
Web, www1.eere.energy.gov/vehiclesandfuels

Works with the motor vehicle industry to develop technologies for improved vehicle fuel efficiency and cleaner fuels.

International Trade Administration (ITA) *(Commerce Dept.),* **Industry and Analysis, Transportation and Machinery,** *1401 Constitution Ave. N.W., #38032, 20230-0001; (202) 482-1474. Fax, (202) 482-0674. Scott Kennedy, Director.*
Web, http://trade.gov/td/otm

Promotes the export of U.S. aerospace, automotive, and machinery products; compiles and analyzes industry data; seeks to secure a favorable position for the U.S. aerospace, auto, and machinery industries in global markets through policy and trade agreements.

▶**NONGOVERNMENTAL**

Alliance of Automobile Manufacturers, *803 7th St. N.W., 20001; (202) 326-5500. Fax, (202) 326-5598. Mitch Bainwol, President.*
Web, www.autoalliance.org

Trade association of thirteen major automakers. Provides advocacy on automotive issues focusing primarily on environment, energy, and safety. Seeks to harmonize global automotive standards.

American Automotive Leasing Assn., *675 N. Washington St., #410, Alexandria, VA 22314-1939; (703) 548-0777. Fax, (703) 548-1925. Pamela Sederholm, Executive Director.*
General email, sederholm@aalafleet.com
Web, www.aalafleet.com

Membership: automotive commercial fleet leasing and management companies. Monitors legislation and regulations.

American International Automobile Dealers Assn., *500 Montgomery St., #800, Alexandria, VA 22314; (703) 519-7800. Fax, (703) 519-7810. Cody Lusk, President. Toll-free, (800) 462-4232.*
General email, goaiada@aiada.org
Web, www.aiada.org and Twitter, @AIADA_News

Promotes a favorable market for international nameplate automobiles in the United States through education of policymakers and the general public. Monitors legislation and regulations concerning tariffs, quotas, taxes, fuel economy, and clean air initiatives.

Assn. of Global Automakers, *1050 K St. N.W., #650, 20001; (202) 650-5555. John Bozzella, President.*
General email, info@globalautomakers.org
Web, www.globalautomakers.org and Twitter, @GlobalAutomkrs

Membership: automobile manufacturers and parts suppliers. Monitors legislation and regulations.

Auto Care Assn., *7101 Wisconsin Ave., #1300, Bethesda, MD 20814-3415; (301) 654-6664. Fax, (301) 654-3299. Bill Hanvey, President.*
General email, info@autocare.org
Web, www.autocare.org and Twitter, @AutoCareOrg

Membership: domestic and international manufacturers, manufacturers' representatives, retailers, and distributors in the automotive aftermarket industry, which involves service of a vehicle after it leaves the dealership. Offers educational programs, conducts research, and provides members with technical and international trade services; acts as liaison with government; sponsors annual marketing conference and trade shows. (Formerly Automotive Aftermarket Industry Assn.)

Automotive Parts Remanufacturers Assn., *7250 Heritage Village Pl., #20, Gainsville, VA 20155; (703) 968-2772. Fax, 703-9753-2445. Joe Kripli, President.*
General email, mail@apra.org
Web, www.apra.org and Twitter, @guyreman

Membership: rebuilders and remanufacturers of automotive parts. Conducts educational programs on transmission, brake, clutch, water pump, air conditioning, electrical parts, heavy-duty brake, and carburetor rebuilding.

Automotive Recyclers Assn. (ARA), *9113 Church St., Manassas, VA 20110-5456; (571) 208-0428.*

Fax, (571) 208-0430. Michael E. Wilson, Chief Executive Officer. Toll-free, (888) 385-1005.

General email, staff@a-r-a.org

Web, www.a-r-a.org and Twitter, @AutoRecyclers

Membership: retail and wholesale firms involved in the dismantling and sale of used motor vehicle parts. Works to increase the efficiency of businesses in the automotive recycling industry. Cooperates with public and private agencies to encourage further automotive recycling efforts.

Certified Automotive Parts Assn., 1000 Vermont Ave. N.W., #1010, 20005; (202) 737-2212. Fax, (202) 737-2214. Jack Gillis, Executive Director.

General email, info@CAPAcertified.org

Web, www.capacertified.org

Provides certification of automotive parts used for collision repairs. Evaluates products based on quality standards for fit, materials, and resistance to corrosion. Encourages a competitive market to reduce the price of automobile accident repairs.

Coalition for Auto Repair Equality, 105 Oronoco St., #115, Alexandria, VA 22314-2015; (703) 519-7555. Fax, (703) 519-7747. Sandy Bass-Cors, Executive Director. Toll-free, (800) 229-5380.

General email, care@careauto.org

Web, www.careauto.org

Works to promote greater competition in the automotive aftermarket repair industry in order to protect consumers. Monitors state and federal legislation that impacts motorists and the automotive aftermarket repair industry.

Japan Automobile Manufacturers Assn. (JAMA), Washington Office, 1050 17th St. N.W., #410, 20036; (202) 296-8537. Fax, (202) 872-1212. Ronald Bookbinder, General Director.

General email, info@jama.org

Web, www.jama.org

Membership: Japanese motor vehicle manufacturers. Interests include energy, market, trade, and environmental issues. (Headquarters in Tokyo.)

National Automobile Dealers Assn. (NADA), 8400 Westpark Dr., Tysons, VA 22102-3591; (703) 821-7000. Fax, (703) 821-7075. Peter K. Welch, President; Michael Harrington, Vice President, Legislative Affairs; Jonathan Collegio, Senior Vice President, Public Affairs. Press, (703) 821-7121. Toll-free, (800) 252-6232.

Web, www.nada.org

Membership: domestic and imported franchised new car and truck dealers. Publishes the National Automobile Dealers Used Car Guide (Blue Book).

Recreation Vehicle Dealers Assn. of North America (RVDA), 3930 University Dr., Fairfax, VA 22030-2515; (703) 591-7130. Fax, (703) 359-0152. Phil Ingrassia, President.

General email, info@rvda.org

Web, www.rvda.org and Twitter, @RVLearningCtr

Membership: recreation vehicle dealers. Interests include government regulation of safety, trade, warranty, and franchising; provides members with educational services, certification programs, and conventions; works to improve service standards for consumers. Monitors legislation and regulations.

Recreation Vehicle Industry Assn. (RVIA), 1896 Preston White Dr., Reston, VA 20191-4363 (mailing address: P.O. Box 2999, Reston, VA 20195-0999); (703) 620-6003. Fax, (703) 620-5071. Frank Hugelmeyer, President, ext. 335.

Web, www.rvia.org

Membership: manufacturers of recreation vehicles and their suppliers. Compiles shipment statistics and other technical data; provides consumers and the media with information on the industry. Assists members' compliance with American National Standards Institute requirements for recreation vehicles. Monitors legislation and regulations.

Tire Industry Assn., 1532 Pointer Ridge Pl., Suite G, Bowie, MD 20716-1883; (301) 430-7280. Fax, (301) 430-7283. Glen Nicholson, President. Toll-free, (800) 876-8372.

General email, info@tireindustry.org

Web, www.tireindustry.org

Membership: all segments of the tire industry, including those that manufacture, repair, recycle, sell, service, or use new or retreaded tires and also suppliers that furnish equipment or services to the industry. Interests include environmental and small-business issues. Monitors legislation and regulations.

Truck Renting and Leasing Assn., 675 N. Washington St., #410, Alexandria, VA 22314-1939; (703) 299-9120. Fax, (703) 299-9115. Jake Jacoby, President.

Web, www.trala.org

Membership: vehicle renting and leasing companies and suppliers to the industry. Acts as liaison with state and federal legislative bodies and regulatory agencies. Interests include truck security and safety, tort reform, operating taxes and registration fees, insurance, and environmental issues. Monitors state and federal legislation and regulations.

Truck Trailer Manufacturers Assn. (TTMA), 7001 Heritage Village Plaza, #220, Gainsville, VA 20155; (703) 549-3010. Jeff Sims, President.

General email, ttma@erols.com

Web, www.ttmanet.org

Membership: trailer manufacturing and supply companies. Serves as liaison between its members and government agencies. Publishes technical and industry news reports.

UNITE HERE, Washington Office, 1775 K St. N.W., #620, 20006-1530; (202) 393-4373. Fax, (202) 223-6213, (202) 342-2929. Vacant, Political Director; D. Taylor, President.

Web, www.unitehere.org

Membership: more than 270,000 workers in the United States and Canada who work in the hospitality, gaming, food service, manufacturing, textile, laundry, and airport industries. Assists members with contract negotiation and grievances; conducts training programs and workshops. Monitors legislation and regulations. (Headquarters in New York. Formed by the merger of the former Union of Needletrades, Textiles and Industrial Employees and the Hotel Employees and Restaurant Employees International Union.)

United Auto Workers (UAW), *Washington Office, 1757 N St. N.W., 20036; (202) 828-8500. Fax, (202) 293-3457. Josh Nassar, Legislative Director.*
Web, www.uaw.org

Membership: approximately 390,000 active and 600,000 retired North American workers in aerospace, automotive, defense, manufacturing, steel, technical, and other industries. Assists members with contract negotiations and grievances; conducts training programs and workshops. Monitors legislation and regulations. (Headquarters in Detroit, Mich.)

Traffic Safety

▶AGENCIES

Federal Highway Administration (FHWA)
(Transportation Dept.), Operations, 1200 New Jersey Ave. S.E., #E86-205, 20590-0001; (202) 366-8753. Fax, (202) 366-3225. Jeffrey A. Lindley, Associate Administrator, (202) 366-9210. Toll-free helpline, (866) 367-7487. Press, (202) 366-4650.
Web, www.ops.fhwa.dot.gov

Fosters the efficient management and operation of the highway system. Responsible for congestion management, pricing, ITS deployment, traffic operations, emergency management, and freight management. Includes offices of Transportation Management, Freight Management and Operations, and Transportation Operations.

Federal Motor Carrier Safety Administration
(Transportation Dept.), 1200 New Jersey Ave. S.E., #W60-300, 20590; (855) 368-4200. Fax, (202) 366-3224. T.F. Scott Darling III, Administrator, Acting. Toll-free information, (800) 832-5660. Toll-free hotline, (888) 327-4236. Consumer complaints, (888) 368-7238. TTY, (800) 877-8339.
Web, www.fmcsa.dot.gov

Partners with federal, state, and local enforcement agencies, the motor carrier industry, safety groups, and organized labor in efforts to reduce bus- and truck-related crashes.

Federal Motor Carrier Safety Administration
(Transportation Dept.), Bus and Truck Standards and Operations, 1200 New Jersey Ave. S.E., #N64-330, 20590; (202) 366-5370. Fax, (202) 366-8842. Chuck Horan, Director, (202) 366-2362.
Web, www.fmcsa.dot.gov/safety/look-you-book/look-you-book

Interprets and disseminates national safety regulations regarding commercial drivers' qualifications, maximum hours of service, accident reporting, and transportation of hazardous materials. Sets minimum levels of financial liability for trucks and buses. Responsible for Commercial Driver's License Information Program.

National Highway Traffic Safety Administration
(Transportation Dept.), West Bldg., 1200 New Jersey Ave. S.E., #42300, 20590; (202) 366-1836. Fax, (202) 366-2106. Mark R. Rosekind, Administrator. Press, (202) 366-9550. Toll-free 24-hour hotline, (888) 327-4236. TTY, (800) 424-9153.
Web, www.nhtsa.gov and www.safercar.gov

Implements motor vehicle safety programs; issues federal motor vehicle safety standards; conducts testing programs to determine compliance with these standards; rates vehicles under the 5-star government rating program for crashworthiness and antirollover stability; maintains the Web site www.safercar.gov, a consumer auto safety information site; funds local and state motor vehicle and driver safety programs; conducts research on motor vehicle safety and equipment, and human factors relating to auto and traffic safety. The Auto Safety Hotline and the Web site provide safety information and handle consumer problems and complaints involving safety-related defects and noncompliance matters.

National Highway Traffic Safety Administration
(Transportation Dept.), National Driver Register, 1200 New Jersey Ave. S.E., #W55-123, 20590-0001; (202) 366-4800. Fax, (202) 366-2746. Sean H. McLaurin, Chief. Toll-free, (888) 851-0436.
Web, www.nhtsa.gov/Data/National+Driver+Register +(NDR)

Maintains and operates the National Driver Register, a program in which states exchange information on motor vehicle driving records to ensure that drivers with suspended licenses in one state cannot obtain licenses in any other state.

National Transportation Safety Board (NTSB), *490 L'Enfant Plaza East S.W., 20594-2000; (202) 314-6000. Fax, (202) 314-6018. Christopher A. Hart, Chair; Kelly Nantel, Public Affairs; Susan Kantrowitz, Director of Administration. Information, (202) 314-6000. Press, (202) 314-6100.*
Web, www.ntsb.gov

Promotes transportation safety through independent investigations of accidents and other safety problems. Makes recommendations for safety improvement. Operates three regional offices.

National Transportation Safety Board (NTSB), *Highway Safety, 490 L'Enfant Plaza East S.W., 20594-0001; (202) 314-6471. Fax, (202) 459-9334. Robert Molloy, Director, Acting. Press, (202) 314-6100.*
Web, www.ntsb.gov/about/organization/HS

In cooperation with states, investigates selected highway transportation accidents to compile the facts upon which the board determines probable cause; works to prevent similar recurrences; makes recommendations on matters pertaining to highway safety and accident prevention.

►NONGOVERNMENTAL

AAA Foundation for Traffic Safety, *607 14th St. N.W., #201, 20005; (202) 638-5944. Fax, (202) 638-5943. J. Peter Kissinger, President. To order educational materials, (800) 305-7233.*
General email, info@aaafoundation.org
Web, www.aaafoundation.org

Sponsors "human factor" research on traffic safety issues, including bicycle, pedestrian, and road safety; supplies traffic safety educational materials to elementary and secondary schools, commercial driving schools, law enforcement agencies, motor vehicle administrations, and programs for older drivers.

Advocates for Highway and Auto Safety, *750 1st St. N.E., #1130, 20002-8007; (202) 408-1711. Fax, (202) 408-1699. Jacqueline Gillan, President.*
General email, advocates@saferoads.org
Web, www.saferoads.org

Coalition of insurers, citizens' groups, and public health and safety organizations. Advocates public policy designed to reduce deaths, injuries, and economic costs associated with motor vehicle crashes and fraud and theft involving motor vehicles. Interests include safety belts and child safety seats, drunk driving abuse, motorcycle helmets, vehicle crashworthiness, and speed limits. Monitors legislation and regulations.

American Highway Users Alliance, *1920 L St. N.W., #525, 20036; (202) 857-1200. Fax, (202) 857-1220. Gregory M. Cohen, President.*
General email, info@highways.org
Web, www.highways.org

Membership: companies and associations representing major industry and highway user groups. Develops information, analyzes public policy, and advocates legislation to improve roadway safety and efficiency and to increase the mobility of the American public. (Affiliated with the Roadway Safety Foundation.)

American Trucking Assns., *Policy and Regulatory Affairs, 950 N. Glebe Rd., #210, Arlington, VA 22203; (703) 838-1996. Fax, (703) 838-1748. David J. Osiecki, Senior Vice President. Press, (703) 838-1873.*
Web, www.trucking.org

Membership: state trucking associations, individual trucking and motor carrier organizations, and related supply companies. Provides information on safety for the trucking industry. Monitors legislation and regulations.

Center for Auto Safety, *1825 Connecticut Ave. N.W., #330, 20009-5708; (202) 328-7700. Fax, (202) 387-0140. Clarence Ditlow, Executive Director.*
General email, accounts@autosafety.org
Web, www.autosafety.org

Public interest organization that receives written consumer complaints against auto manufacturers; monitors federal agencies responsible for regulating and enforcing auto and highway safety rules.

Commercial Vehicle Safety Alliance (CVSA), *6303 Ivy Lane, #310, Greenbelt, MD 20770-6319 (mailing address: Policy and Government Affairs: 444 N. Capitol St. N.W., #722, Washington, DC 20001-1534); (301) 830-6143. Fax, (301) 830-6144. Collin Mooney, Executive Director; Adrienne L. Gildea, Deputy Executive Director.*
General email, cvsahq@cvsa.org
Web, www.cvsa.org and Twitter, @CVSA

Membership: local, state, provincial, territorial, and federal motor carrier safety officials and industry representatives from the United States, Canada, and Mexico. Promotes improved methods of highway and terminal inspection of commercial vehicles, drivers, and cargo; and uniformity and reciprocity of inspection criteria and enforcement across jurisdictions.

Governors Highway Safety Assn., *444 N. Capitol St. N.W., #722, 20001-1534; (202) 789-0942. Fax, (202) 789-0946. Jonathan Adkins, Executive Director.*
General email, headquarters@ghsa.org
Web, www.ghsa.org

Membership: state officials who manage highway safety programs. Interprets technical data concerning highway safety. Represents the states in policy debates on national highway safety issues.

Institute of Transportation Engineers (ITE), *1627 Eye St. N.W., #600, 20006; (202) 785-0060. Fax, (202) 785-0609. Philip J. Caruso, Deputy Executive Director, ext. 126. General email, ite_staff@ite.org*
Web, www.ite.org

Membership: international professional transportation engineers. Interests include safe and efficient surface transportation; provides professional and scientific information on transportation standards and recommended practices.

Insurance Institute for Highway Safety, *1005 N. Glebe Rd., #800, Arlington, VA 22201; (703) 247-1500. Fax, (703) 247-1588. Adrian Lund, President. Highway Loss Data Institute, (703) 247-1600. Vehicle Research Center, (434) 985-4600.*
Web, www.iihs.org

Membership: property and casualty insurance associations and individual insurance companies. Conducts research and provides data on highway safety; seeks ways to reduce losses from vehicle crashes. (Operates with Highway Loss Data Institute and the Vehicle Research Center.)

Mothers Against Drunk Driving (MADD), *Government Affairs, 1025 Connecticut Ave. N.W., #1210, 20036-5415; (202) 688-1193. Fax, (972) 869-2206. J.T. Griffin, Chief Government Affairs Officer; Frank Harris, State Legislative Affairs Manager, (202) 688-1194. Toll-free, (877) 275-6233. 24-hour helpline, 877-MADD HELP.*
Web, www.madd.org, Twitter, @MADDOnline and Facebook, www.facebook.com/MADD.Official

Advocacy group that seeks to stop drunk driving and prevent underage drinking. Monitors legislation and regulations. (Headquarters in Irving, Tex.)

National School Transportation Assn. (NSTA), *122 S. Royal St., Alexandria, VA 22314; (703) 684-3200. Fax, (703) 684-3212. Ronna Weber, Executive Director. General email, info@yellowbuses.org*

Web, www.yellowbuses.org

Membership: private owners who operate school buses on contract, bus manufacturers, and allied companies. Primary area of interest and research is school bus safety.

Network of Employers for Traffic Safety, *344 Maple Ave. West, #357, Vienna, VA 22180; (703) 755-5350. Jack Hanley, Executive Director. General email, sgillies@trafficsafety.org*

Web, www.trafficsafety.org

Dedicated to reducing the human and economic cost associated with automobile and highway crashes. Helps employers develop and implement workplace traffic and highway safety programs. Provides technical assistance.

Roadway Safety Foundation, *1101 14th St. N.W., #750, 20005; (202) 857-1228. Fax, (202) 857-1220. Gregory M. Cohen, Executive Director. General email, info@roadwaysafety.org*

Web, www.roadwaysafety.org and Twitter, @roadway_safety

Conducts highway safety programs to reduce automobile-related crashes and deaths. (Affiliated with American Highway Users Alliance.)

Rubber Manufacturers Assn., *1400 K St. N.W., #900, 20005; (202) 682-4800. Fax, (202) 682-4854. Anne Forristall Luke, President. General email, info@rma.org*

Web, www.rma.org and Twitter, @BeTireSmart

Membership: American tire manufacturers. Provides consumers with information on tire care and safety. Develops safety standards for passenger, light truck, and commercial truck tires. Monitors legislation and regulations.

United Motorcoach Assn. (UMA), *113 S. West St., 4th Floor, Alexandria, VA 22314-2824; (703) 838-2929. Fax, (703) 838-2950. Victor S. Parra, Chief Executive Officer. Toll-free, (800) 424-8262. General email, info@uma.org*

Web, www.uma.org

Membership: professional bus and motorcoach companies and suppliers and manufacturers in the industry. Provides information, offers technical assistance, conducts research, and monitors legislation. Interests include insurance, safety programs, and credit.

RAIL TRANSPORTATION

General

▶**AGENCIES**

Federal Railroad Administration *(Transportation Dept.), 1200 New Jersey Ave. S.E., 3rd Floor, 20590;*
(202) 493-6014. Fax, (202) 493-6481. Sarah Feinberg, Administrator, Acting. Public Affairs, (202) 493-6024. General email, frapa@dot.gov

Web, www.fra.dot.gov

Develops national rail policies; enforces rail safety laws; administers financial assistance programs available to states and the rail industry; conducts research and development on improved rail safety. Operates eight regional offices.

Federal Railroad Administration *(Transportation Dept.), Public Engagement, West Bldg., 1200 New Jersey Ave. S.E., MS 10, 20590; (202) 493-6405. Fax, (202) 493-6009. Timothy Barkley Sr., Director, (202) 493-1305. General email, frapa@dot.gov*

Web, www.fra.dot.gov/page/p0030

Plans, coordinates, and administers activities related to railroad economics, finance, traffic and network analysis, labor management, and transportation planning, as well as intermodal, environmental, emergency response, and international programs.

Federal Railroad Administration *(Transportation Dept.), Railroad Policy and Development, 1200 New Jersey Ave. S.E., 3rd Floor, 20590; (202) 493-6381. Fax, (202) 493-6330. Paul W. Nissenbaum, Associate Administrator. General email, OfficeofRPD@dot.gov*

Web, www.fra.dot.gov/page/p0031

Administers federal assistance programs for national, regional, and local rail services, including freight service assistance, service continuation, and passenger service. Conducts research on and development of new rail technologies.

Federal Railroad Administration *(Transportation Dept.), Railroad Safety, 1200 New Jersey Ave. S.E., 3rd Floor, 20590; (202) 493-6014. Fax, (202) 493-6216. Robert C. Lauby, Associate Administrator. General email, rrswebinquiries@dot.gov*

Web, www.fra.dot.gov/page/p0032

Administers and enforces federal laws and regulations that promote railroad safety, including track maintenance, inspection and equipment standards, operating practices, and transportation of explosives and other hazardous materials. Conducts inspections and reports on railroad equipment facilities and accidents. All safety and/or security issues, such as bomb threats or biochemical threats, are managed by security specialists.

National Mediation Board, *1301 K St. N.W., #250E, 20005-7011; (202) 692-5000. Fax, (202) 692-5082. Nicholas Geale, Chair. Information, (202) 692-5050. TTY, (202) 692-5001. General email, infoline@nmb.gov*

Web, www.nmb.gov

Mediates labor disputes in the railroad industry; determines and certifies labor representatives for the industry.

National Railroad Passenger Corp. (Amtrak), *60 Massachusetts Ave. N.E., 20002; (202) 906-3000. Joseph H. Boardman, President. Press, (202) 906-3860. Reservations, (800) 872-7245. Emergency, (800) 331-0008. TTY, (800) 523-6590. Web, www.amtrak.com*

Quasi-public corporation created by the Rail Passenger Service Act of 1970 to improve and develop intercity passenger rail service.

Railroad Retirement Board, *Legislative Affairs, 1310 G St. N.W., #500, 20005-3004; (202) 272-7742. Fax, (202) 272-7728. Margaret Stanley, Director, (202) 272-7742. Toll-free, (877) 772-5772. General email, ola@rrb.gov/org/ogc/ola.asp Web, www.rrb.gov/org/ogc/ola.asp*

Assists congressional offices with inquiries on retirement, spouse, survivor, unemployment, and sickness benefits for railroad employees and retirees. Assists with legislation. (Headquarters in Chicago, Ill.)

Surface Transportation Board *(Transportation Dept.), 395 E St. S.W., #1220, 20423-0001; (202) 245-0245. Fax, (202) 245-0458. Daniel Elliott III, Chair, (202) 245-0210. Library, (202) 245-0288. TTY, (800) 877-8339. Press, (202) 245-0238. General email, STBHelp@stb.dot.gov Web, www.stb.dot.gov*

Regulates rail rate disputes, railroad consolidations, rail line construction proposals, line abandonments, and rail car service. Library open to the public.

Surface Transportation Board *(Transportation Dept.), Public Assistance, Governmental Affairs, and Compliance, 395 E St. S.W., #1202, 20423-0001; (202) 245-0238. Fax, (202) 245-0461. Lucille L. Marvin, Director. Press, (202) 245-0238. Toll-free, (866) 254-1792. TTY, (800) 877-8339. General email, stbhelp@stb.dot.gov Web, www.stb.dot.gov/stb/about/office_ocps.html*

Informs members of Congress, the public, and the media of board actions. Administers the Rail Customer and Public Assistance Program.

U.S. Coast Guard (USCG) *(Homeland Security Dept.), 2703 Martin Luther King Jr. Ave. S.E., MS 7000, 20593-7000; (202) 372-4411. Fax, (202) 372-8302. Adm. Paul F. Zukunft, Commandant. Public Affairs, (202) 372-4600. Web, www.uscg.mil*

Regulates the construction, maintenance, and operation of bridges across U.S. navigable waters, including railway bridges.

▶**CONGRESS**

For a listing of relevant congressional committees and subcommittees, please see page 713 or the Appendix.

▶**NONGOVERNMENTAL**

American Short Line and Regional Railroad Assn. (ASLRRA), *50 F St. N.W., #7020, 20001-1564; (202) 628-4500. Fax, (202) 628-6430. Linda Bauer Darr, President, (202) 585-3440. General email, aslrra@aslrra.org Web, www.aslrra.org*

Membership: independently owned short line and regional railroad systems as well as companies that supply goods and services to short line railroads. Assists members with technical and legal questions; compiles information on laws, regulations, and other matters affecting the industry.

Assn. of American Railroads, *425 3rd St. S.W., #1000, 20024; (202) 639-2100. Fax, (202) 639-2886. Edward R. Hamberger, President. Press, (202) 639-2345. General email, info@aar.org Web, www.aar.org and Twitter, @AAR_FreightRail*

Membership: major freight railroads in the United States, Canada, and Mexico, as well as Amtrak. Provides information on freight railroad operations, safety and maintenance, economics and finance, management, and law and legislation; conducts research; issues statistical reports.

Brotherhood of Maintenance of Way Employees, *International Brotherhood of Teamsters, National Legislation, 25 Louisiana Ave. N.W., 7th Floor, 20001; (202) 508-6445. Fax, (202) 508-6450. Freddie N. Simpson, President; Charlie Hogue, Director, Government Affairs. General email, bmwe-dc@bmwewash.org Web, www.bmwe.org and Twitter, @BMWEDIBT*

Membership: rail industry workers and others. Assists members with contract negotiation and grievances; conducts training programs and workshops. Monitors legislation and regulations. (Headquarters in Novi, Mich.)

International Assn. of Machinists and Aerospace Workers, *Transportation Communications Union, 3 Research Pl., Rockville, MD 20850-3279; (301) 948-4910. Fax, (301) 948-1369. Robert A. Scardelletti, President. General email, websteward@tcunion.org Web, www.goiam.org/index.php/tcunion*

Membership: approximately 46,000 railway workers. Assists members with contract negotiation and grievances; conducts training programs and workshops. Monitors legislation and regulations. (Affiliated with the AFL-CIO and Canadian Labour Congress.)

National Assn. of Railroad Passengers, *505 Capital Court N.E., #300, 20002-7706; (202) 408-8362. Fax, (202) 408-8287. Jim Mathews, Chief Executive Officer. General email, narp@narprail.org Web, www.narprail.org*

Education and advocacy organization. Works to expand and improve U.S. intercity and commuter rail passenger service, increase federal funds for mass transit, and address environmental concerns pertaining to mass transit. Works with Amtrak on scheduling, new services, and fares.

National Assn. of Regulatory Utility Commissioners, *1101 Vermont Ave. N.W., #200, 20005-3521; (202) 898-2200. Fax, (202) 898-2213. Greg White, Executive Director. General email, admin@naruc.org*

Web, www.naruc.org

Membership: members of federal, state, municipal, and international regulatory commissions that have jurisdiction over motor and common carriers. Interests include railroads.

National Railroad Construction and Maintenance Assn., *500 New Jersey Ave. N.W., #400, 20001; (202) 715-1264. Fax, (202) 318-0867. Chuck Baker, President. General email, info@nrcma.org*

Web, www.nrcma.org

Membership: railroad suppliers and contractors. Supports government funding for rail and transit systems. Holds conferences on industry practices, safety, and policy issues.

National Railway Labor Conference, *251 18th St. South, Arlington, VA 22202; (571) 336-7600. Ken Gradia, Chair. Web, www.nrlc.ws*

Assists member railroad lines with labor matters; negotiates with railroad labor representatives.

Railway Supply Institute (RSI), *425 3rd St. S.W., #920, 20024; (202) 347-4664. Fax, (202) 347-0047. Thomas D. Simpson, President. Web, www.rsiweb.org and Twitter, @Railway_Supply*

Membership: railroad and rail rapid transit suppliers. Conducts research on safety and new technology; monitors legislation.

TRANSIT SYSTEMS

General

▶AGENCIES

Federal Transit Administration *(Transportation Dept.), 1200 New Jersey Ave. S.E., #E57-310, 20590; (202) 366-4043. Fax, (202) 366-9854. Therese W. McMillan, Administrator, Acting; Carolyn Flowers, Senior Advisor. Information and press, (202) 366-4043. TTY, (800) 877-8339. Toll-free, (866) 377-8642. Web, www.fta.dot.gov and Twitter, @FTA_DOT*

Responsible for developing improved public transportation facilities, equipment, techniques, and methods; assists state and local governments in financing public transportation systems; oversees the safety of U.S. public transit.

Federal Transit Administration *(Transportation Dept.), Budget and Policy, 1200 New Jersey Ave. S.E., #E52-326, 20590; (202) 366-4050. Fax, (202) 366-7116. Robert Tuccillo, Associate Administrator. Press, (202) 366-4043. Web, www.fta.dot.gov*

Develops budgets, programs, legislative proposals, and policies for the federal transit program; evaluates program proposals and their potential impact on local communities; coordinates private sector initiatives of the agency.

Federal Transit Administration *(Transportation Dept.), Program Management, 1200 New Jersey Ave. S.E., 4th Floor, 20590; (202) 366-4020. Fax, (202) 366-7951. Henrika Buchanan-Smith, Associate Administrator. Information and press, (202) 366-4043. Web, www.fta.dot.gov*

Administers capital planning and operating assistance grants and loan activities; monitors transit projects in such areas as environmental impact, special provisions for the elderly and people with disabilities, efficiency, and investment.

Federal Transit Administration *(Transportation Dept.), Research, Demonstration, and Innovation, 1200 New Jersey Ave. S.E., #E43-431, 20590; (202) 366-4052. Fax, (202) 366-3765. Vincent Valdes, Associate Administrator. Information and press, (202) 366-4043. Web, www.fta.dot.gov*

Provides industry and state and local governments with contracts, cooperative agreements, and grants for testing, developing, and demonstrating methods of improved mass transportation service and technology.

Maryland Transit Administration, *6 St. Paul St., Baltimore, MD 21202-1614; (410) 539-5000. Fax, (410) 333-0893. Paul Comfort, Chief Executive Officer. Information, 866-RIDE-MTA. Press, (410) 767-3936. Mobility/Paratransit, (410) 764-8181. TTY, (410) 539-3497. Web, http://mta.maryland.gov*

Responsible for mass transit programs in Maryland; provides MARC commuter rail service for Baltimore, Washington, and suburbs in Maryland and West Virginia.

Surface Transportation Board *(Transportation Dept.), 395 E St. S.W., #1220, 20423-0001; (202) 245-0245. Fax, (202) 245-0458. Daniel Elliott III, Chair, (202) 245-0210. Library, (202) 245-0288. TTY, (800) 877-8339. Press, (202) 245-0238. General email, STBHelp@stb.dot.gov*

Web, www.stb.dot.gov

Regulates mergers and through-route requirements for the intercity bus industry. Library open to the public.

Virginia Railway Express (VRE), *1500 King St., #202, Alexandria, VA 22314; (703) 684-1001. Fax, (703) 684-1313. Doug Allen, Chief Executive Officer. Press, (703) 838-5416. Toll-free, (800) 743-3873. TTY, (703) 684-0551. General email, gotrains@vre.org*

Web, www.vre.org and Twitter, @VaRailXpress

Regional transportation partnership that provides commuter rail service from Fredericksburg and Manassas, Va., to Washington, D.C.

Washington Metropolitan Area Transit Authority (Metro), *600 5th St. N.W., 20001; (202) 962-1234. Fax, (202) 962-1133. Paul J. Wiedefeld, General Manager. Information, (202) 637-7000. Metro access (for those with* *disabilities), (800) 523-7009. Lost and found, (202) 962-1195. TTY (Administration), (202) 962-1000. TTY (Metro access), (301) 588-7535.*

Web, www.wmata.com and Twitter, @wmata

Provides bus and rail transit service to Washington, D.C., and neighboring Maryland and Virginia communities; assesses and plans for transportation needs. Provides fare, schedule, and route information; promotes accessibility for persons with disabilities and the elderly.

▶ CONGRESS

For a listing of relevant congressional committees and subcommittees, please see page 713 or the Appendix.

▶ NONGOVERNMENTAL

Amalgamated Transit Union (ATU), *10000 New Hampshire Ave., Silver Spring, MD 20903; (301) 431-7100. Fax, (301) 431-7117. Lawrence J. Hanley, President. Toll-free, (888) 240-1196.*
General email, mreza@atu.org

Web, www.atu.org

Membership: transit workers in the United States and Canada, including bus, van, ambulance, subway, and light rail operators; clerks, baggage handlers, and maintenance employees in urban transit, over-the-road, and school bus industries; and municipal workers. Assists members with contract negotiations and grievances; conducts training programs and seminars. Monitors legislation and regulations. (Affiliated with the AFL-CIO.)

American Bus Assn., *111 K St. N.E., 9th Floor, 20002; (202) 842-1645. Fax, (202) 842-0850. Peter J. Pantuso, President, (202) 218-7229. Toll-free, (800) 283-2877.*
General email, abainfo@buses.org

Web, www.buses.org

Membership: privately owned intercity bus companies, state associations, travel/tourism businesses, bus manufacturers, and those interested in the bus industry. Monitors legislation and regulations.

American Public Transportation Assn. (APTA), *1300 Eye St. N.W., #1200 East, 20006-1215; (202) 496-4800. Fax, (202) 496-4324. Michael Melaniphy, President. Press, (202) 496-4816.*
General email, apta@apta.com

Web, www.apta.com and Twitter, @APTA_Info

Membership: rapid rail and motor bus systems and manufacturers, suppliers, and consulting firms. Represents all modes of public transportation. Compiles data on the industry; promotes research. Monitors legislation and regulations.

Community Transportation Assn. of America, *1341 G St. N.W., 10th Floor, 20005; Fax, (202) 737-9197. Scott Bogren, Executive Director. Toll-free, (800) 891-0590.*
Web, www.ctaa.org and Twitter, @CTMag1

Works to improve mobility for the elderly, the poor, and persons with disabilities; concerns include rural, small-city, and specialized transportation.

National Assn. of Railroad Passengers, *505 Capital Court N.E., #300, 20002-7706; (202) 408-8362. Fax, (202) 408-8287. Jim Mathews, Chief Executive Officer.*
General email, narp@narprail.org

Web, www.narprail.org

Education and advocacy organization. Works to expand and improve U.S. intercity and commuter rail passenger service, increase federal funds for mass transit, and address environmental concerns pertaining to mass transit. Works with Amtrak on scheduling, new services, and fares.

National Research Council (NRC), *Infrastructure and the Constructed Environment Board, Keck Center, 500 5th St. N.W., #WS938, 20001; (202) 334-3505. Fax, (202) 334-3718. Rear Adm. David J. Nash (USN, Ret.), Chair.*
General email, bice@nas.edu

Web, http://sites.nationalacademies.org/deps

Advises the government, private sector, and the public on technology, science, and public policy related to the design, construction, operations, maintenance, security, and evaluation of buildings, facilities, and infrastructure systems; the relationship between the constructed and natural environments and their interaction with human activities; the effects of natural and manmade hazards on constructed facilities and infrastructure; and the interdependencies of infrastructure systems, including power, water, transportation, telecommunications, wastewater, buildings.

United Motorcoach Assn. (UMA), *113 S. West St., 4th Floor, Alexandria, VA 22314-2824; (703) 838-2929. Fax, (703) 838-2950. Victor S. Parra, Chief Executive Officer. Toll-free, (800) 424-8262.*
General email, info@uma.org

Web, www.uma.org

Membership: professional bus and motorcoach companies and suppliers and manufacturers in the industry. Provides information, offers technical assistance, conducts research, and monitors legislation. Interests include insurance, safety programs, and credit.

19

U.S. Congress and Politics

ACCESS TO CONGRESSIONAL INFORMATION

Basic Resources

▶ AGENCIES

National Archives and Records Administration (NARA), *Center for Legislative Archives, 700 Pennsylvania Ave. N.W., #8E, 20408; (202) 357-5350. Fax, (202) 357-5911. Richard H. Hunt, Director.*
Web, www.archives.gov/legislative

Collects and maintains records of congressional committees and legislative files from 1789 to the present. Publishes inventories and guides to these records.

National Archives and Records Administration (NARA), *Federal Register, 800 N. Capitol St. N.W., #700, 20001 (mailing address: NF, 8601 Adelphi Rd., College Park, MD 20740-6001); (202) 741-6000. Fax, (202) 741-6012. Oliver Potts, Director. TTY, (202) 741-6086.*
General email, fedreg.info@nara.gov
Web, www.archives.gov/federal_register/the-federal-register

Assigns public law numbers to enacted legislation, executive orders, and proclamations. Responds to inquiries on public law numbers. Assists inquirers in finding presidential signing or veto messages in the *Daily Compilation of Presidential Documents* and the *Public Papers of the Presidents.* Compiles slip laws and annual United States Statutes at Large; compiles indexes for finding statutory provisions. Operates Public Law Electronic Notification System (PENS), which provides information by email on new legislation. Coordinates the functions of the Electoral College and the constitutional amendment process. Publications available from the U.S. Government Printing Office.

▶ CONGRESS

For a listing of relevant congressional committees and subcommittees, please see page 746 or the Appendix.

Clerk of the U.S. House of Representatives, *H154 CAP, 20515-6601; (202) 225-7000. Karen L. Haas, Clerk. Communications, (202) 225-1908.*
General email, info.clerkweb@mail.house.gov
Web, http://clerk.house.gov

Maintains and distributes House bills, reports, public laws, and documents to members' offices, committee staffs, and the general public. Provides daily schedules, when the House is in session, on Web site. Provides legislative history of all measures reported by House and Senate committees. Provides additional materials in the *Congressional Record* (also available from the Contact Center, Government Printing Office, Washington, D.C., [202] 512-1800 or in electronic format at www.gpoaccess .gov). Provides video coverage of House floor proceedings through http://houselive.gov.

Government Publishing Office (GPO), *Contact Center, 732 N. Capitol St. N.W., 20401; (202) 512-1800. Fax, (202) 512-2104. Esther Edmonds, Manager. Toll-free, (866) 512-1800.*
General email, contactcenter@gpo.gov
Web, www.gpo.gov

The federal government's official digital secure resource for producing, procuring, cataloging, indexing, authenticating, disseminating, and preserving the official information products of the U.S. government. Responsible for the production and distribution of information products and services for all three branches of the federal government, including U.S. passports for the Department of State as well as the official publications of Congress, the White House, and other federal agencies in digital and print formats. Provides for free permanent public access to federal government information through the Federal Digital System (www.fdsys.gov), partnerships with approximately 1,200 libraries nationwide participating in the Federal Depository Library Program, and a secure online bookstore.

Senate Executive Clerk, *S138 CAP, 20510; (202) 224-4341. Jennifer Gorham, Executive Clerk.*

Maintains and distributes copies of treaties submitted to the Senate for ratification; provides information on submitted treaties and nominations. (Shares distribution responsibility with Senate Printing and Document Services, [202] 224-7701.)

Senate Historical Office, *201 SHOB, 20510; (202) 224-6900. Betty K. Koed, Historian.*
General email, historian@sec.senate.gov
Web, www.senate.gov/artandhistory/history/common/generic/Senate_Historical_Office.htm

Serves as an information clearinghouse on Senate history, traditions, and members. Collects, organizes, and distributes to the public unpublished Senate documents; collects and preserves photographs and pictures related to Senate history; conducts an oral history program; advises senators and Senate committees on the disposition of their noncurrent papers and records. Produces publications on the history of the Senate.

Senate Office of Conservation and Preservation, *S416 CAP, 20510; (202) 224-4550. Leona Faust, Director, Acting, (202) 224-5730.*

Develops and coordinates programs related to the conservation and preservation of Senate records and materials for the secretary of the Senate.

Senate Printing and Document Services, *B04 SHOB, 20510-7106; (202) 224-7701. Fax, (202) 228-2815. Karen Moore, Director.*
General email, orders@sec.senate.gov
Web, www.senate.gov/legislative/common/generic/Doc_Room.htm

Maintains and distributes Senate bills, reports, public laws, and documents. To obtain material send a self-addressed mailing label or fax with request. Documents and information may be accessed on the Web site.

U.S. CONGRESS AND POLITICS RESOURCES IN CONGRESS

For a complete listing of congressional committees, including their full contact information, leadership, membership, and jurisdictions, please refer to the Appendix on pages 779–896.

HOUSE:

House Administration Committee, (202) 225-8281.
Web, cha.house.gov
House Appropriations Committee, (202) 225-2771.
Web, appropriations.house.gov
  Subcommittee on Financial Services and General Government, (202) 225-7245.
  Subcommittee on Legislative Branch, (202) 226-7252.
House Ethics Committee, (202) 225-7103.
Web, ethics.house.gov
House Judiciary Committee, (202) 225-3951.
Web, judiciary.house.gov
  Subcommittee on the Constitution and Civil Justice, (202) 225-2825.
House Oversight and Government Reform Committee, (202) 225-5074.
Web, oversight.house.gov
  Subcommittee on Government Operations, (202) 225-5074.
  Subcommittee on Interior, (202) 225-5074.
House Rules Committee, (202) 225-9191.
Web, rules.house.gov
  Subcommittee on Rules and Organization of the House, (202) 225-9191.
  Subcommittee on the Legislative and Budget Process, (202) 225-9191.
House Transportation and Infrastructure Committee, (202) 225-9446.
Web, transportation.house.gov
  Subcommittee on Economic Development, Public Buildings, and Emergency Management, (202) 225-3014.
House Ways and Means Committee, (202) 225-3625.
Web, waysandmeans.house.gov

JOINT:

Joint Committee on Printing, (202) 225-2061.
Web, cha.house.gov/jointcommittees/joint-committee-on-printing
Joint Committee on the Library of Congress, (202) 225-8281.
Web, cha.house.gov/jointcommittees/joint-committee-library

SENATE:

Senate Appropriations Committee, (202) 224-7363.
Web, appropriations.senate.gov
  Subcommittee on Financial Services and General Government, (202) 224-1133.
  Subcommittee on Legislative Branch, (202) 224-7256.
Senate Finance Committee, (202) 224-4515.
Web, finance.senate.gov
Senate Homeland Security and Governmental Affairs Committee, (202) 224-2627.
Web, hsgac.senate.gov
  Permanent Subcommittee on Investigations, (202) 224-4462.
  Subcommittee on Federal Spending, Oversight, and Emergency Management, (202) 224-4462.
  Subcommittee on Regulatory Affairs and Federal Management, (202) 224-4462.
Senate Judiciary Committee, (202) 224-7703.
Web, judiciary.senate.gov
  Subcommittee on the Constitution, (202) 224-7840.
Senate Rules and Administration Committee, (202) 224-6352.
Web, rules.senate.gov
Senate Select Committee on Ethics, (202) 224-2981.
Web, ethics.senate.gov

U.S. House of Representatives, *Office of Art and Archives, B53 CHOB, 20515; (202) 226-1300. Fax, (202) 226-4635. Farar P. Elliott, Chief, Art and Archives.*
General email, art@mail.house.gov
Archives email, archives@mail.house.gov
Office of the Historian email, history@mail.house.gov
Web, http://history.house.gov

Works with the Office of the Historian to provide access to published documents and historical records of the House. Advises members on the disposition of their records and papers; maintains information on manuscript collections of former members; maintains biographical files on former members; houses photographs and artifacts

of former members. Produces publications on Congress and its members.

U.S. House of Representatives, *Office of the Historian, B53 CHOB, 20515; (202) 226-1300. Matthew A. Wasniewski, House Historian.*
General email, history@mail.house.gov
Web, http://history.house.gov

Works with the Office of Art and Archives to provide access to published documents and historical records of the House. Conducts historical research. Advises members on the disposition of their records and papers; maintains information on manuscript collections of former members; maintains biographical files on former members. Produces publications on Congress and its members.

►NEWS SERVICES

CQ Press, 2600 Virginia Ave. N.W. #600, 20037; (202) 729-1900. Fax, (805) 375-5291. Blaise R. Simqu, President. Toll-free, (866) 818-7243.
General email, customerservice@cqpress.com
Web, www.cqpress.com

Publishes books, directories, periodicals, and Web products on U.S. government, history, and politics. Products include *U.S. Political Stats, CQ Press Encyclopedia of American Government,* and *CQ Researcher.* (An imprint of SAGE Publishing; Headquarters in Thousand Oaks, Calif.)

Washington Post, 1301 K St. N.W., 20071; (202) 334-6000. Frederick J. Ryan Jr., Publisher; Marty Baron, Executive Editor. Toll-free, (800) 627-1150.
Web, www.washingtonpost.com and Twitter, @washingtonpost

Provides news and analysis of congressional activities.

►NONGOVERNMENTAL

White House Correspondents' Assn., 600 New Hampshire Ave. N.W., #800, 20037; (202) 266-7453. Fax, (202) 266-7454. Julia Whiston, Executive Director
General email, whca@starpower.net
Web, www.whca.net and Twitter, @whca

Membership: reporters with permanent White House press credentials. Acts as a liaison between reporters and White House staff. Sponsors annual WHCA Journalism Awards and Scholarships fund-raising dinner.

Congressional Record

The Congressional Record, *published daily when Congress is in session, is a printed account of proceedings on the floor of the House and Senate. A Daily Digest section summarizes the day's action on the floor and in committees and lists committee meetings scheduled for the following day. An index is published biweekly and at the close of sessions of Congress. Since January 1995, House members have not been allowed to edit their remarks before they appear in the Record, but senators retain this privilege. Material not spoken on the floor may be inserted through unanimous consent to revise or extend a speech and is published in a distinctive typeface. Grammatical, typographical, and technical corrections are also permitted.*

►CONGRESS

For a listing of relevant congressional committees and subcommittees, please see page 746 or the Appendix.

Government Publishing Office (GPO), *Main Bookstore, Congressional Order Desk,* 732 N. Capitol St. N.W., 20401; (202) 512-1800. Fax, (202) 512-2104. Esther Edmonds,

Manager, (202) 512-1694. Bookstore, (202) 512-0312. Bookstore Contact Center, (866) 512-1800.
General email, ContactCenter@gpo.gov
Web, http://bookstore.gpo.gov

Sells copies of and subscriptions to the *Congressional Record.* Expert help from government information librarians is available at http://govtinfo.org. Orders may be placed on Web site. The *Congressional Record* from 1994 to the present is available online at www.fdsys.gov.

Library of Congress, *Law Library,* James Madison Memorial Bldg., 101 Independence Ave. S.E., #LM 240, 20540; (202) 707-5065. Fax, (202) 707-1820.
Roberta I. Shaffer, Law Librarian. Reading room, (202) 707-5080. Reference, (202) 707-5079.
Web, www.loc.gov/law, Twitter, @LawLibCongress and Facebook, www.facebook.com/lawlibraryofcongress

Copies of the *Congressional Record* are available for reading. Terminals in the reading room provide access to a computer system containing bill digests from the 93rd Congress to date. The *Congressional Record* can also be accessed online at www.congress.gov.

►NONGOVERNMENTAL

Martin Luther King Jr. Memorial Library, 901 G St. N.W., 20001-4599; (202) 727-0321. Fax, (202) 727-1129. Richard Reyes-Gavilan, Director. Circulation, (202) 727-1579. TTY, (202) 727-2255.
General email, mlkjrlibrary@dc.gov
Web, www.dclibrary.org/mlk

Maintains collection of the *Congressional Record* from 1879 to the present, available in various formats (bound volumes, microfilm, microfiche, and electronic).

Schedules, Status of Legislation

Information can also be obtained from the Congressional Record *(Daily Digest) and from individual congressional committees (see 114th Congress, p. 779).*

►CONGRESS

For a listing of relevant congressional committees and subcommittees, please see page 746 or the Appendix.

Clerk of the U.S. House of Representatives, H154 CAP, 20515-6601; (202) 225-7000. Karen L. Haas, Clerk. Communications, (202) 225-1908.
General email, info.clerkweb@mail.house.gov
Web, http://clerk.house.gov

Maintains and distributes House bills, reports, public laws, and documents to members' offices, committee staffs, and the general public. Provides daily schedules, when the House is in session, on Web site. Provides legislative history of all measures reported by House and Senate committees. Provides additional materials in the *Congressional Record* (also available from the Contact Center, Government Printing Office, Washington, D.C.,

[202] 512-1800 or in electronic format at www.gpoaccess .gov). Provides video coverage of House floor proceedings through http://houselive.gov.

House Democratic Cloakroom, *H222 CAP, 20515; (202) 225-7330. Robert Fischer, Manager. House floor action, (202) 225-7400. Legislative program, (202) 225-1600.*

Provides information about House floor proceedings.

House Republican Cloakroom, *H223 CAP, 20515; (202) 225-7350. Fax, (202) 225-8247. Jarod Eichorn, Manager. Legislative program, (202) 225-2020.*
Web, http://repcloakroom.house.gov and Twitter, @repcloakroom

Provides information about House floor proceedings.

Senate Democratic Cloakroom, *S225 CAP, 20510; (202) 224-4691. Nicole Catucci-Brockmeyer, Assistant; Danica Daneshforonz Rodman, Assistant; Stephanie Paone, Assistant; Daniel Tinsley, Assistant; Brad Watt, Assistant. Senate floor action, (202) 224-8541.*
Provides information about Senate floor proceedings.

Senate Republican Cloakroom, *S226 CAP, 20510; (202) 224-6191. Fax, (202) 224-2860. Laura Dove, Secretary. Senate floor action, (202) 224-8601.*
Web, Repcloakroom.house.gov

Provides information about Senate floor proceedings.

U.S. House of Representatives, *Legislative Resource Center,* *135 CHOB, 20515; Fax, (202) 226-5208. Ronald (Dale) Thomas, Chief. Bill status, (202) 226-5200. General email, info.clerkweb@mail.house.gov*
Web, http://clerk.house.gov/about/offices_lrc.aspx

Provides legislative information, records and registration, historical information, and library services to the House and the public. Reading room contains computer terminals where collections may be viewed or printed out. Collections include House and Senate journals (1st Congress to present); *Congressional Record* and its predecessors (1st Congress to present); House reports, documents, bills, resolutions, and hearings; Senate reports and documents; U.S. statutes, treaties, the *Federal Register*, U.S. codes, and numerous other documents. (See Web site or call for a complete list of collections.)

► **NEWS SERVICES**

Associated Press, *Washington Bureau, 1100 13th St. N.W., #500, 20005-4076; (202) 641-9000. Fax, (202) 263-8800. Sally Buzbee, Bureau Chief. General email, info@ap.org*
Web, www.ap.org and Twitter, @AP

Publishes daybook that lists congressional committee meetings and hearings and their location and subject matter. Fee for services. (Headquarters in New York.)

CQ Roll Call, *77 K St. N.E., 20002-4681; (202) 650-6500. Keith White, Managing Director. Subscriptions and demonstrations, (202) 650-6599. Editorial newsroom, (202) 650-6455. Toll-free, (800) 432-2250.*
Web, www.cqrollcall.com

Provides nonpartisan online congressional news and analysis, including legislative summaries, votes, testimony, and archival and reference materials. Provides hearing and markup schedules, including time and location, meeting agendas, and full witness listings. Fee for services. (Merger of Congressional Quarterly, Roll Call, and Capitol Advantage; subsidiary of the Economist Group.)

United Press International (UPI), *1133 19th St., N.W., 20036; (202) 898-8000. Fax, (202) 898-8048. Nicholas Chiaia, President.*
Web, www.upi.com and Twitter, @UPI

Wire service that lists congressional committee meetings and hearings, locations, and subject matter. Fee for services.

CAMPAIGNS AND ELECTIONS

General

► **AGENCIES**

Election Assistance Commission, *1335 East-West Hwy., #4300, Silver Spring, MD 20910; (301) 563-3919. Fax, (301) 734-3108. Brian D. Newby, Executive Director. Toll-free, (866) 747-1471.*
General email, HAVAinfo@eac.gov
Web, www.eac.gov

Serves as national information clearinghouse on the administration of federal elections. Responsible for adopting voting system guidelines. Tests and certifies voting system hardware and software. Studies election technology and voting accessibility. Reports data from the states for each federal election and maintains the National Mail Voter registration form.

Federal Communications Commission (FCC), *Media Bureau, Policy Division,* *445 12th St. S.W., 20554; (202) 418-1450. Fax, (202) 418-1069. Martha Heller, Chief.*
Web, www.fcc.gov/media/policy/policy-division

Handles complaints and inquiries concerning the equal time rule, which requires equal broadcast opportunities for all legally qualified candidates for the same office, and other political broadcast, cable, and satellite rules. Interprets and enforces related Communications Act provisions, including the requirement for sponsorship identification of all paid political broadcast, cable, and satellite announcements and the requirement for broadcasters to furnish federal candidates with reasonable access to broadcast time for political advertising. Administers Equal Employment Opportunity (EEO) matters.

Federal Election Commission (FEC), *999 E St. N.W., 20463; (202) 694-1000. Matthew S. Petersen, Chair. Press, (202) 694-1220. Public Records, (202) 694-1120. Information, (202) 694-1100. Toll-free information, (800) 424-9530. TTY, (202) 219-3336.*
General email, info@fec.gov
Web, www.fec.gov

Federal Election Commission

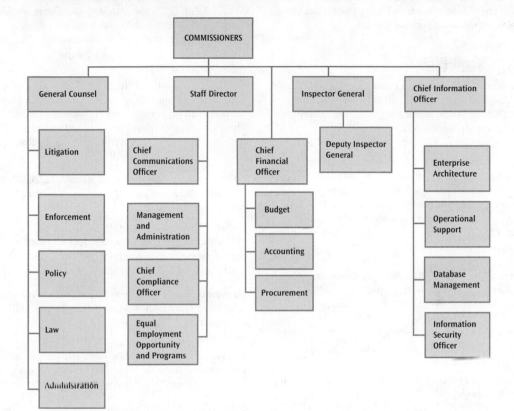

Formulates, administers, and enforces policy with respect to the Federal Election Campaign Act of 1971 as amended, including campaign disclosure requirements, contribution and expenditure limitations, and public financing of presidential nominating conventions and campaigns. Receives campaign finance reports; makes rules and regulations; conducts audits and investigations. Makes copies of campaign finance reports available for inspection.

Federal Election Commission (FEC), *Public Disclosure and Media Relations,* 999 E St. N.W., 20463; (202) 694-1120. Fax, (202) 501-0693. Judy Ingram, Director. Information, (800) 424-9530. TTY, (202) 219-3336. General email, pubrec@fec.gov
Web, www.fec.gov/about/offices/press/press.shtml

Makes available for public inspection and copying the detailed campaign finance reports on contributions and expenditures filed by candidates for federal office, their supporting political committees, and individuals and committees making expenditures on behalf of a candidate. Maintains copies of all reports and statements filed since 1972.

Justice Dept. (DOJ), *Election Crimes,* 1400 New York Ave. N.W., #12100, 20005; (202) 514-1412. Richard Pilger, Director, (202) 514-1178. Press, (202) 514-2007. Web, www.justice.gov

Supervises enforcement of federal criminal laws related to campaigns and elections. Oversees investigation of deprivation of voting rights; intimidation and coercion of voters; denial or promise of federal employment or other benefits; illegal political contributions, expenditures, and solicitations; and all other election violations referred to the division.

▶ CONGRESS

For a listing of relevant congressional committees and subcommittees, please see page 746 or the Appendix.

House Commission on Congressional Mailing Standards (Franking Commission), 1309 LHOB, 20515-6328; (202) 225-8281. Rep. Candice S. Miller, Chair; Sean Moran, Majority Staff Director; Matt DeFreitas, Minority Staff Director.
Web, http://cha.house.gov/franking-commission

Issues regulations governing mass mailings by members' offices. Receives complaints, conducts investigations, and issues decisions on disputes arising from the alleged abuse of franked mail by House members.

U.S. House of Representatives, *Legislative Resource Center, Records and Registration,* 135 CHOB, 20515-6612; (202) 226-5200. Fax, (202) 226-5169. Steve Pingeton, Manager.
Web, http://clerk.house.gov

Receives personal financial disclosure reports for members of the House, candidates for the House, and certain employees. Open for public inspection.

▶ NONGOVERNMENTAL

American Assn. of Political Consultants, *8400 Westpark Dr., 2nd Floor, McLean, VA 22102; (703) 245-8020. Fax, (703) 995-0628. Alana Joyce, Executive Director.*
General email, info@theaapc.org
Web, www.theaapc.org

Membership: political consultants, media specialists, campaign managers, corporate public affairs officers, pollsters, public officials, academicians, fund-raisers, lobbyists, college students, and congressional staffers. Focuses on ethics of the profession; provides members with opportunities to meet industry leaders and learn new techniques and emerging technologies.

American Bar Assn. (ABA), *Standing Committee on Election Law, 1050 Connecticut Ave. N.W., #400, 20036; (202) 662-1691. Fax, (202) 638-3844. Elizabeth M. Yang, Director.*
General email, election@americanbar.org
Web, www.americanbar.org/groups/public_services/election_law.html

Studies ways to improve the U.S. election and campaign process.

Campaign Finance Institute, *1425 K St. N.W., #350, 20005; (202) 969-8890. Fax, (202) 969-5612. Michael J. Malbin, Executive Director.*
General email, info@CFInst.org
Web, www.cfinst.org and Twitter, @cfinst_org

Conducts objective research and educates about campaign financing. Makes recommendations for policy changes in campaign financing.

The Campaign Legal Center, *1411 K St. N.W., #1400, 20005; (202) 736-2200. Fax, (202) 736-2222. J. Gerald Hebert, Executive Director.*
General email, info@campaignlegalcenter.org
Web, www.campaignlegalcenter.org and Twitter, @CampaignLegal

Dedicated to improving the elections process by promoting voluntary, realistic standards of campaign conduct.

Commission on Presidential Debates, *1200 New Hampshire Ave. N.W., #445, 20036; (202) 872-1020. Fax, (202) 783-5923. Frank J. Fahrenkopf Jr., Co-Chair; Michael McCurry, Co-Chair; Janet H. Brown, Executive Director.*
General email, comments@debates.org
Web, www.debates.org and Twitter, @debates

Independent nonpartisan organization established to sponsor general election presidential and vice presidential debates and to undertake educational and research activities related to the debates.

Common Cause, *805 15th St. N.W., #800, 20005; (202) 833-1200. Fax, (202) 659-3716. Miles Rapoport, President, (202) 736-5740. Press, (202) 736-5788.*
General email, mrapoport@commoncause.org
Web, www.commoncause.org and Twitter, @CommonCause

Nonpartisan national citizens' lobby on behalf of open, honest, and accountable government. Through 400,000 members and supporters, works in Washington and state capitals in support of limits on contributions and spending, high ethical standards in government, voting rights, media reform, and economic justice.

CQ Political MoneyLine, *77 K St. N.E., 8th Fl., 20002-4681; (202) 650-6500. Kent Cooper, Editor; Tony Raymond, Editor.*
General email, questions@cq.com
Web, www.politicalmoneyline.com

Monitors and reports on money as it is used in campaigns, political action committees, 527s, political parties, and by lobbyists. (Affiliated with CQ-Roll Call.)

Electionline.org, *2630 Adams Mill Rd. N.W., #208, 20009; (202) 588-7332. Mindy Moretti, Editor.*
General email, info@electionline.org
Web, www.electionline.org

Online resource providing news and analysis on election reform. (Receives support from Hewlett Fund and Democracy Fund.)

Every Voice Center, *1211 Connecticut Ave. N.W., #600, 20036; (202) 640-5600. Fax, (202) 640-5601. David Donnelly, President, (202) 895-2357.*
General email, info@everyvoice.org
Web, www.everyvoice.org and Twitter, @EveryVoice

National grassroots organization interested in campaign finance reform. Supports the Fair Election model of campaign finance under which candidates who accept only small donations receive additional money from a public fund sufficient to run a competitive campaign.

OpenSecrets.org/Center for Responsive Politics, *1101 14th St. N.W., #1030, 20005-5635; (202) 857-0044. Fax, (202) 857-7809. Sheila Krumholz, Executive Director; Viveca Novak, Editorial and Communications Director. Press, (202) 354-0111.*
General email, info@crp.org; press@crp.org
Web, www.opensecrets.org

Conducts research on federal campaign finance and lobbying in connection with congressional and presidential elections.

Election Statistics and Apportionment

▶ AGENCIES

Census Bureau *(Commerce Dept.), Census Redistricting Data, 4600 Silver Hill Rd., #8H019, Suitland, MD 20746 (mailing address: 4600 Silver Hill Rd., #8H019,*

Washington, DC 20233-0100); (301) 763-4039. Fax, (301) 763-4348. James Whitehorne, Chief, Acting.
General email, RDO@census.gov

Web, www.census.gov/rdo

Provides state legislatures with population figures for use in legislative redistricting.

Census Bureau *(Commerce Dept.), Customer Liaison and Marketing Services,* 4600 Silver Hill Rd., North Bldg., #8H180, Suitland, MD 20746 (mailing address: Customer Service, Bureau of the Census, MS 0801, Washington, DC 20233-0500); (301) 763-4636. Fax, (301) 763-6831. Kim Collier, Chief, Acting. Press, (301) 763-3030. Orders, (800) 923-8282.
General email, clmso.call.center.help@census.gov

Web, www.census.gov/clo/www/clo.html

Main contact for information about the Census Bureau's products and services. Census data and maps on counties, municipalities, and other small areas are available on the Web site and in libraries.

Census Bureau *(Commerce Dept.), Population,* 4600 Silver Hill Rd., #6H174, Suitland, MD 20746 (mailing address: 4600 Silver Hill Rd., #H174, Washington, DC 20233-8800); (301) 763-2071. Fax, (301) 763-2516. Karen Humes, Division Chief.
General email, pop@census.gov

Web, www.census.gov/popest

Computes every ten years the population figures that determine the number of representatives each state may have in the House of Representatives.

▶CONGRESS

For a listing of relevant congressional committees and sub-committees, please see page 746 or the Appendix.

Clerk of the U.S. House of Representatives, H154 CAP, 20515-6601; (202) 225-7000. Karen L. Haas, Clerk. Communications, (202) 225-1908.
General email, info.clerkweb@mail.house.gov

Web, http://clerk.house.gov

Publishes biennial compilation of statistics on congressional and presidential elections.

▶NONGOVERNMENTAL

Common Cause, *State Organization,* 805 15th St. N.W., #800, 20005; (202) 833-1200. Fax, (202) 659-3716. Jenny Rose Flanagan, Vice President for State Operations, (303) 842-1515. Press, (202) 736-5788.
Web, www.commoncause.org

Nonpartisan citizens' lobby on behalf of open, honest, and accountable government. Offices in Washington, D.C., and 35 states. Supports independent redistricting commissions to draw congressional and state legislative districts. Works for laws strengthening voting rights and modern voting equipment.

Voting, Political Participation

▶NONGOVERNMENTAL

America Votes, 1155 Connecticut Ave. N.W., #600, 20036; (202) 962-7240. Fax, (202) 962-7241. Greg Speed, President.
Web, www.americavotes.org

Coalition that seeks to increase voter registration, education, and participation in electoral politics.

Arab American Institute, 1600 K St. N.W., #601, 20006; (202) 429-9210. Fax, (202) 429-9214. James J. Zogby, President.
General email, communications@aaiusa.org

Web, www.aaiusa.org and Twitter, @AAIUSA

Fosters civic and political empowerment of Americans of Arab descent through research, policy formation, and political activism.

Clare Booth Luce Policy Institute, 112 Elden St., Suite P, Herndon, VA 20170; (703) 318-0730. Fax, (703) 318-8867. Michelle Easton, President. Toll-free, (888) 891-4288.
General email, info@cblpi.org

Web, www.cblpi.org and Twitter, @CBLPI

Seeks to engage young women through student programs promoting conservative values and leadership. Offers mentoring, internship, and networking opportunities for young women.

Coalition of Black Trade Unionists, 1155 Connecticut Ave. N.W., #500, Washington, DC, 20036 (mailing address: P.O. Box 66268, Washington, DC 20035); (202) 778-3318. Fax, (202) 419-1486. Terrence L. Melvin, President.
General email, cbtu@hotmail.com

Web, www.cbtu.org

Monitors legislation affecting African American and other minority trade unionists. Focuses on equal employment opportunity, unemployment, and voter education and registration.

Democracy 21, 2000 Massachusetts Ave. N.W., 20036; (202) 355-9600. Fax, (202) 355-9606. Fred Wertheimer, President.
General email, info@Democracy21.org

Web, www.democracy21.org

Focuses on using the communications revolution to strengthen democracy and on eliminating the influence of big money in American politics.

Democratic National Committee (DNC), *Campaign Division,* 430 S. Capitol St. S.E., 20003; (202) 863-8000. Rep. Debbie Wasserman Schultz, Chair. Press, (202) 863-8148. Contributions, (877) 336-7200.
General email, dncpress@dnc.org

Web, www.democrats.org

Responsible for electoral activities at the federal, state, and local levels; sponsors workshops to recruit Democratic candidates and to provide instruction in campaign techniques; conducts party constituency outreach programs; coordinates voter registration; plans the party's quadrennial presidential nominating convention.

Resources for Political Participation

NATIONWIDE CAMPAIGNS

Democratic Congressional Campaign Committee,
(202) 863-1500; www.dccc.org

Democratic Governors Assn., (202) 772-5600;
www.democraticgovernors.org

Democratic National Committee (DNC), (202) 863-8000;
www.democrats.org

Democratic Senatorial Campaign Committee,
(202) 224-2447; www.dscc.org

FairVote-The Center for Voting and Democracy,
(301) 270-4616; www.fairvote.org

Fieldworks, (202) 667-4400; www.fieldworks.com

Green Party of the United States, (202) 319-7191;
www.gp.org

League of Women Voters (LWV), (202) 429-1965;
www.lwv.org

Libertarian Party, (202) 333-0008; www.lp.org

Mobilize, (202) 400-3848; www.mobilize.org

National Republican Congressional Committee,
(202) 479-7000; www.nrcc.org

National Republican Senatorial Committee,
(202) 675-6000; www.nrsc.org

Republican Governors Assn., (202) 662-4140;
www.rga.org

Republican National Committee (RNC), (202) 863-8500;
www.gop.com

Rock the Vote, (202) 780-0644; www.rockthevote.com

IN MARYLAND, VIRGINIA, AND WASHINGTON, D.C.

DC Vote, (202) 462-6000; www.dcvote.org

District of Columbia Board of Elections and Ethics,
(202) 727-2525; www.dcboee.org

Maryland State Board of Elections, (800) 222-8683
or (410) 269-2840; www.elections.state.md.us

Virginia State Board of Elections, (800) 552-9745
or (804) 864-8901; www.elections.virginia.gov

Volunteer on Election Day in Maryland,
www.elections.state.md.us/get_involved

FairVote, *6930 Carroll Ave., #610, Takoma Park, MD 20912; (301) 270-4616. Fax, (301) 270-4133. Robert Richie, Executive Director.*
General email, info@fairvote.org
Web, www.fairvote.org and Twitter, @fairvote

Studies how voting systems affect participation, representation, and governance both domestically and internationally. Advocates for a national popular vote for president, American forms of proportional representation, instant runoff voting, a constitutionally protected right to vote, and universal voter registration. (Formerly the Center for Voting and Democracy.)

Internet Education Foundation, *1401 K St. N.W., #200, 20005; (202) 638-4370. Fax, (202) 637-0968. Tim Lordan, Executive Director.*
General email, tlordan@neted.org
Web, www.neted.org

Sponsors educational initiatives promoting the Internet as a valuable medium for democratic participation, communications, and commerce. Funds the Congressional Internet Caucus Advisory Committee, which works to inform Congress of important Internet-related policy issues. Monitors legislation and regulations.

Joint Center for Political and Economic Studies, *2000 H St. N.W., #422, Stuart Hall, 20052; (202) 789-3500. Fax, (202) 789-6390. Spencer Overton, President.*
General email, info@jointcenter.org
Web, www.jointcenter.org

Documents and analyzes the political and economic status of African Americans, focusing on political

participation, economic advancement, and health policy. Publishes *Focus Magazine* annually; disseminates information through forums and conferences.

Labor Council for Latin American Advancement, *815 16th St. N.W., 3rd Floor, 20006; (202) 508-6919. Fax, (202) 508-6922. Hector E. Sanchez, Executive Director.*
General email, headquarters@lclaa.org
Web, www.lclaa.org, Facebook, www.facebook.com/ LCLAA and Twitter, @LCLAA

Membership: Hispanic trade unionists. Encourages equal employment opportunity, voter registration, and participation in the political process. (Affiliated with the AFL-CIO and the Change to Win Federation.)

League of Women Voters (LWV), *1730 M St. N.W., #1000, 20036-4508; (202) 429-1965. Fax, (202) 429-0854. Elisabeth MacNamara, President; Wylecia Wiggs Harris, Executive Director.*
General email, lwv@lwv.org
Web, www.lwv.org, Twitter, @LWV and Facebook, www.facebook.com/leagueofwomenvoters

Membership: women and men interested in nonpartisan political action and study. Works to increase participation in government; provides information on voter registration and balloting. Interests include social policy, natural resources, international relations, and representative government.

National Assn. of Latino Elected and Appointed Officials Educational Fund, *Washington Office, 600 Pennsylvania Ave. S.E., #480, 20003; (202) 546-2536. Arturo Vargas, Executive Director.*

General email, jgarcia@naleo.org

Web, www.naleo.org

Research and advocacy group that provides civic affairs information and assistance on legislation affecting Latinos. Encourages Latino participation in local, state, and national politics. Interests include health care and social, economic, and educational issues. (Headquarters in Los Angeles, Calif.)

National Black Caucus of Local Elected Officials (NBC/LEO), *National League of Cities, 1301 Pennsylvania Ave. N.W., 20004-1763; (202) 626-3000. Priscilla Tyson, President. General information, (877) 827-2385.*

General email, constituencygroups@nlc.org

Web, www.nlc.org

Membership: Black elected officials at the local level and other interested individuals. Seeks to increase Black participation on the National League of Cities' steering and policy committees. Informs members on issues, and plans strategies to achieve objectives through legislation and direct action. Interests include cultural diversity, local government and community participation, housing, economics, job training, the family, and human rights.

National Black Caucus of State Legislators, *444 N. Capitol St. N.W., #622, 20001; (202) 624-5457. Fax, (202) 508-3826. LaKimba DeSadier, Executive Director.*

Web, www.nbcsl.org

Membership: Black state legislators. Promotes effective leadership among Black state legislators through education, research, and training; serves as an information network and clearinghouse for members.

National Coalition on Black Civic Participation, *1050 Connecticut Ave. N.W., 5th Floor, #500, 20036; (202) 659-4929. Fax, (202) 659-5025. Melanie L. Campbell, President.*

General email, ncbcp@ncbcp.org

Web, www.ncbcp.org and Facebook, www.facebook.com/The-National-Coalition-on-Black-Civic-Participation-149636419244

Seeks to increase Black voter civic participation to eliminate barriers to political participation for Black Americans. Sponsors a variety of voter education, registration, and get-out-the-vote and protect-the-vote activities, including Operation Big Vote, Black Youth Vote, Black Women's Roundtable, the Information Resource Center, Civic Engagement, Voices of the Electorate, and the Unity Black Voter Empowerment Campaign. Monitors legislation and regulations.

National Congress of Black Women, *1250 4th St. S.W., #WG-1, 20024; (202) 678-6788. E. Faye Williams, President.*

General email, info@nationalcongressbw.org

Web, www.nationalcongressbw.org

Nonpartisan political organization that encourages Black American women to participate in the political process. Advocates nonpartisan voter registration and encourages Black American women to engage in other political activities. Develops positions and participates in platform development and strategies that address the needs of communities at every level of government.

National Women's Political Caucus, *1001 Connecticut Ave., #1020, 20005 (mailing address: P.O. Box 50476, Washington, DC 20091); (202) 785-1100. Donna Lent, President; Diedre Malone, Communications.*

General email, info@nwpc.org

Web, www.nwpc.org

Advocacy group that seeks greater involvement of women in politics. Seeks to identify, recruit, and train women for elective and appointive political office, regardless of party affiliation; serves as an information clearinghouse on women in politics, particularly during election campaigns; publishes directory of women holding federal and state offices.

Republican National Committee (RNC), *Political, 310 1st St. S.E., 20003; (202) 863-8500. Fax, (202) 863-8773. Chris Carr, Political Director; Reince Priebus, Chair. Press, (202) 863-8614.*

General email, ecampaign@gop.com

Web, www.gop.com

Responsible for electoral activities at the federal, state, and local levels; operates party constituency outreach programs; coordinates voter registration.

U.S. Student Assn., *1211 Connecticut Ave. N.W., #406, 20036; (202) 640-6570. Fax, (202) 223-4005. Alexandra Flores-Quilty, President.*

General email, manager@usstudents.org

Web, www.usstudents.org

Represents postsecondary students, student government associations, and state student lobby associations. Monitors legislation and regulations. Organizes students to participate in the political process through congressional testimony, letter-writing campaigns, and lobbying visits. Represents students in various coalitions, including the Committee for Education Funding, the Student Aid Alliance, the Generational Alliance, and the Leadership Conference on Civil Rights.

USAction, *1101 17th St. N.W., #1220, 20036; (202) 263-4520. Fax, (202) 262-4530. Fred Azcarate, Executive Director. Press, (202) 263-4567.*

General email, info@usaction.org

Web, www.usaction.org

Provides funding and training to register, educate, and mobilize voters to influence federal and state issues, based on progressive priorities. Has affiliates in 21 states.

Voter Participation Center, *1707 L St. N.W., #300, 20036; (202) 659-9570. Fax, (202) 659-9585. Page S. Gardner, Founder; Katie Whelan, Executive Director, Acting.*

General email, info@voterparticipation.org

Web, www.voterparticipation.org and Twitter, @VoterCenter

Nonpartisan organization that seeks to increase voter participation, especially of unmarried women (single, widowed, divorced, or separated), people of color, and 18-to-29-year-old citizens. (Formerly Women's Voices, Women Vote.)

Younger Women's Task Force, *1111 16th St. N.W., 20036; (202) 785-7700. Fax, (202) 872-1425. Linda Hallman, Executive Director, (202) 785-7713. Toll-free, (800) 326-2289. TTY, (202) 785-7777.*
General email, ywtf@aauw.org

Web, www.aauw.org/membership/ywtf and Twitter, @ywtf

Grassroots organization that encourages young women to engage in political activism on issues directly affecting them. Provides leadership training and a local and national network for peer mentoring; runs financial literacy programs. (Sponsored by the American Assn. of University Women.)

CAPITOL

Capitol switchboard, (202) 224-3121, and Federal Relay Service (TTY), (800) 877-8339. See also 114th Congress (p. 779) for each member's office.

General

▶**CONGRESS**

Architect of the Capitol, *SB15 CAP, 20515; (202) 228-1793. Fax, (202) 228-1893. Stephen T. Ayers, Architect. Flag Office, (202) 228-4239.*
Web, www.aoc.gov and Twitter, @uscapitol

Maintains the Capitol and its grounds, the House and Senate office buildings, Capitol power plant, Robert A. Taft Memorial, Thurgood Marshall Federal Judiciary Building, Capitol Police headquarters, and buildings and grounds of the Supreme Court and the Library of Congress; operates the Capitol Visitor Center, and the Botanic Garden and Senate restaurants. Acquires property and plans and constructs buildings for Congress, the Supreme Court, and the Library of Congress. Assists the Congress in deciding which artwork, historical objects, and exhibits are to be accepted for display in the Capitol and is responsible for their care and repair, as well as the maintenance and restoration of murals and architectural elements throughout the Capitol campus. Arranges inaugural ceremonies and other ceremonies held in the buildings or on the grounds. Flag office flies American flags over the Capitol at legislators' request.

Senate Commission on Art, *S411 CAP, 20510; (202) 224-2955. Melinda K. Smith, Curator of the Senate.*
General email, curator@sec.senate.gov

Web, www.senate.gov/pagelayout/art/one_item_and_teasers/Explore_Senate_Art.htm

Accepts artwork and historical objects for display in Senate office buildings and the Senate wing of the Capitol. Maintains and exhibits Senate collections (paintings, sculptures, furniture, and manuscripts); oversees and maintains old Senate and Supreme Court chambers.

Superintendent of the House Office Buildings, *B341 RHOB, 20515; (202) 225-4141. William M. Weidemeyer, Superintendent.*
Web, www.aoc.gov

Oversees construction, maintenance, and operation of House office buildings; assigns office space to House members under rules of procedure established by the Speaker's office and the House Office Building Commission.

Superintendent of the Senate Office Buildings, *G245 SDOB, 20510; (202) 224-5023. Takis Tzamaras, Superintendent.*
Web, www.aoc.gov

Oversees construction, maintenance, and operation of Senate office buildings.

U.S. Botanic Garden, *100 Maryland Ave. S.W., 20001 (mailing address: 245 1st St. S.W., Washington, DC 20024); (202) 225-8333. Fax, (202) 225-1561. Ari Novy, Executive Director, (202) 225-6670. Horticulture hotline, (202) 226-4785. Program registration information, (202) 225-1116. Special events, (202) 226-7674. Tour line, (202) 226-2055. Press, (202) 226-4145.*
General email, usbg@aoc.gov

Web, www.usbg.gov

Collects, cultivates, and grows various plants for public display and study.

U.S. Capitol Police, *119 D St. N.E., 20510; (202) 224-9806. Fax, (202) 228-2592. Kim C. Dine, Chief. Public information, (202) 224-1677.*
General email, ASKUSCP@uscp.gov

Web, www.uscapitolpolice.gov

Responsible for security for the Capitol, House and Senate office buildings, and Botanic Garden; approves demonstration permits.

▶**NONGOVERNMENTAL**

U.S. Capitol Historical Society, *200 Maryland Ave. N.E., 20002; (202) 543-8919. Fax, (202) 544-8244. Ronald A. Sarasin, President; William C. diGiacomantonio, Chief Historian. Information, (800) 887-9318.*
General email, uschs@uschs.org

Web, www.uschs.org

Membership: members of Congress, individuals, and organizations interested in the preservation of the history and traditions of the U.S. Capitol. Conducts historical research; offers tours, lectures, workshops, and films; holds events involving members of Congress; publishes an annual historical calendar.

Tours and Events

▶**CONGRESS**

The House and Senate public galleries are open when Congress is in session. The House galleries are also open when the House is not in session. Free gallery passes are available from any congressional office.

Architect of the Capitol, *Congressional Accessibility Services,* Crypt of The Capitol, 20510; (202) 224-4048. Fax, (202) 228-4679. David Hauck, Director. TTY, (202) 224-4049.
Web, www.aoc.gov/accessibility-services

Office works to make the Capitol and its grounds and buildings accessible to members of Congress, staff, and the public.

Sergeant at Arms and Doorkeeper of the U.S. Senate, S151 CAP, 20510-7200; (202) 224-2341. Frank J. Larkin, Sergeant at Arms and Doorkeeper.
Web, www.senate.gov/reference/office/sergeant_at_arms.htm

Enforces rules and regulations of the Senate public gallery. Responsible for security of the Capitol and Senate buildings. Approves visiting band performances on the Senate steps. (To arrange for performances, contact your senator.)

Sergeant at Arms of the U.S. House of Representatives, H124 CAP, 20515-6611; (202) 225-2456. Fax, (202) 225-3233. Paul D. Irving, Sergeant at Arms.
Web, www.house.gov/content/learn/officers_and_organizations/sergeant_at_arms.php

Enforces rules and regulations of the House public gallery. Responsible for the security of the Capitol and House buildings. Approves visiting band performances on the House steps. (To arrange for performances, contact your representative.)

U.S. Capitol Visitor Center, The Capitol, 20510; (202) 593-1816. Fax, (202) 593-1832. Beth Plemmons, Chief Executive Officer for Visitor Services. Press, (202) 593-1833. Visitor information, (202) 225-6827; (202) 226-8000. TTY, (202) 224-4049.
Web, www.visitthecapitol.gov

Offers the general public free guided tours of the interior of the U.S. Capitol. Provides accommodations for visitors with special needs.

U.S. Capitol Historical Society, 200 Maryland Ave. N.E., 20002; (202) 543-8919. Fax, (202) 544-8244. Ronald A. Sarasin, President; William C. diGiacomantonio, Chief Historian. Information, (800) 887-9318.
General email, uschs@uschs.org
Web, www.uschs.org

Offers tours, lectures, films, publications, and merchandise; maintains information centers in the Capitol.

CONGRESS AT WORK

See 114th Congress (p. 779) for members' offices and committee assignments and for rosters of congressional committees and subcommittees.

General

►CONGRESS

For a listing of relevant congressional committees and subcommittees, please see page 746 or the Appendix.

House Recording Studio, B310 RHOB, 20515; (202) 225-3941. Fax, (202) 225-0707. Patrick Hirsch, Director.
Assists House members in making tape recordings. Provides daily gavel-to-gavel television coverage of House floor proceedings.

Interparliamentary Affairs, HC4 CAP, 20515; (202) 226-1766. Janice Robinson, Director.
Assists the House Speaker with international travel and the reception of foreign legislators.

Interparliamentary Services, 808 SHOB, 20510; (202) 224-3047. Sally Walsh, Director.
Provides support to senators participating in interparliamentary conferences and other international travel. Responsible for financial, administrative, and protocol functions.

Office of Photography, *U.S. House of Representatives,* B302 RHOB, 20515; (202) 225-2840. Fax, (202) 225-5896. Jeff Blakley, Director.
Provides House members with photographic assistance.

Parliamentarian of the U.S. House of Representatives, H209 CAP, 20515; (202) 225-7373. Thomas J. Wickham Jr., Parliamentarian.
Advises presiding officers on parliamentary procedures and committee jurisdiction over legislation; prepares and maintains a compilation of the precedents of the House.

Parliamentarian of the U.S. Senate, S133 CAP, 20510; (202) 224-6128. Elizabeth C. MacDonough, Parliamentarian.
Advises presiding officers on parliamentary procedures and committee jurisdiction over legislation; prepares and maintains a compilation of the precedents of the Senate.

Senate Democratic Policy and Communications Center, S318 CAP, 20510; (202) 224-2939. Fax, (202) 228-5576. Sen. Charles E. Schumer, Chair; Matthew House, Chief Spokesperson, (202) 224-2939.
Web, www.democrats.senate.gov
Offers radio, television, and Internet services to Senate Democrats and their staffs to more effectively disseminate information to constituents at home.

Sergeant at Arms and Doorkeeper of the U.S. Senate, *Senate Photo Studio,* G85 SDOB, 20510; (202) 224-6000. Bill Allen, Manager.
Provides Senate members with photographic assistance.

Sergeant at Arms of the U.S. House of Representatives, *Emergency Management Division,* 192 FHOB, 20515-6462; (202) 226-0950. Fax, (202) 226-6598. Bob Dohr, Senior Assistant Sergeant at Arms.

Liaises between the House and the Homeland Security Dept., the U.S. Capitol Police, and other responders in the coordination of response to emergency situations.

Leadership

▶HOUSE

See House Leadership and Partisan Committees (p. 803).

House Democratic Caucus, *1420 LHOB, 20515; (202) 225-1400. Rep. Xavier Becerra, Chair; Rep. Joseph Crowley, Vice Chair; Fabiola Rodriguez-Ciampoli, Executive Director.*
General email, democratic.caucus@mail.house.gov
Web, www.dems.gov

Membership: House Democrats. Selects Democratic leadership; formulates party rules and floor strategy; considers caucus members' recommendations on major issues; votes on the Democratic Steering and Policy Committee's recommendations for Democratic committee assignments.

House Democratic Steering and Policy Committee, *233 CHOB, 20515-6527; (202) 225-4965. Fax, (202) 225-4188. Rep. Rosa L. DeLauro, Co-Chair;*
Rep. Donna Edwards, Co-Chair.

Makes recommendations to the Democratic leadership on party policy and priorities and participates in decision making with the leadership.

House Republican Conference, *202A CHOB, 20515; (202) 225-5107. Rep. Cathy Ann McMorris Rodgers, Chair; Rep. Lynn Jenkins, Vice Chair; Jeremy Deutsch, Staff Contact.*
Web, www.gop.gov

Membership: House Republicans. Selects Republican leadership; formulates party rules and floor strategy, and considers party positions on major legislation; votes on the Republican Committee on Committees' recommendations for House committee chairs and Republican committee assignments; publishes Weekly Floor Briefing and Daily Floor Briefing, which analyze pending legislation.

House Republican Policy Committee, *202A CHOB, 20515-6549; (202) 225-3021. Fax, (202) 225-3382. Rep. Luke Messer, Chair; Jerry White, Staff Contact. General email, policycommittee@mail.house.gov*
Web, http://policy.house.gov

Studies legislation and makes recommendations on House Republican policies and positions on proposed legislation.

Majority Leader of the U.S. House of Representatives, *H107 CAP, 20515-6503; (202) 225-4000. Fax, (202) 226-1115. Rep. Kevin McCarthy, Majority Leader; Tim Berry, Chief of Staff.*
Web, www.majorityleader.gov

Serves as chief strategist and floor spokesperson for the majority party in the House.

Majority Whip of the U.S. House of Representatives, *H329 CAP, 20004; (202) 225-0197. Fax, (202) 226-0781. Rep. Steve Scalise, Majority Whip; Brett Horton, Chief of Staff.*
Web, http://majoritywhip.house.gov

Serves as assistant majority leader in the House; helps marshal majority forces in support of party strategy.

Minority Leader of the U.S. House of Representatives, *H204 CAP, 20515-6537; (202) 225-0100. Fax, (202) 225-8259. Rep. Nancy Pelosi, Minority Leader; Nadeam Elshami, Chief of Staff.*
Web, http://democraticleader.gov

Serves as chief strategist and floor spokesperson for the minority party in the House.

Minority Whip of the U.S. House of Representatives, *H148 CAP, 20515; (202) 225-3130. Fax, (202) 226-0663. Rep. Steny H. Hoyer, Minority Whip; Alexis Covey-Brandt, Chief of Staff.*
Web, http://democraticwhip.gov

Serves as assistant minority leader in the House; helps marshal minority forces in support of party strategy.

Speaker of the U.S. House of Representatives, *Speaker's Office, H232 CAP, 20515; (202) 225-0600. Fax, (202) 225-5117. Rep. Paul Ryan, Speaker; Dave Hoppe, Chief of Staff. Web, www.speaker.gov*

Presides over the House while in session; preserves decorum and order; announces vote results; recognizes members for debate and introduction of bills, amendments, and motions; refers bills and resolutions to committees; decides points of order; appoints House members to conference committees; votes at own discretion.

▶SENATE

See Senate Leadership and Partisan Committees (p. 876).

Democratic Policy and Communication Center, *419 SHOB, 20510; (202) 224-3232. Fax, (202) 228-3432. Sen. Charles E. Schumer, Chair.*
Web, www.dpcc.senate.gov

Studies and makes recommendations to the Democratic leadership on legislation for consideration by the Senate; prepares policy papers and develops Democratic policy initiatives.

Democratic Steering and Outreach Committee, *SHOB712, 20510; (202) 224-9048. Fax, (202) 224-5476. Sen. Amy Klobuchar, Chair.*
General email, steering@dsoc.senate.gov
Web, www.dsoc.senate.gov

Makes Democratic committee assignments subject to approval by the Senate Democratic Conference. Develops and maintains relationships with leaders and organizations outside of Congress.

Majority Leader of the U.S. Senate, *317 SROB, 20510-1702; (202) 224-2541. Fax, (202) 224-2499. Sen. Mitch McConnell, Majority Leader; Sharon Soderstrom, Chief of Staff.*
Web, www.mcconnell.senate.gov

Serves as chief strategist and floor spokesperson for the majority party in the Senate.

Majority Whip of the U.S. Senate, *517 SHOB, 20510-4305; (202) 224-2934. Fax, (202) 228-2856. Sen. John Cornyn, Majority Whip; Beth Jafari, Chief of Staff.*
Web, www.cornyn.senate.gov

Serves as assistant majority leader in the Senate; helps marshal majority forces in support of party strategy.

Minority Leader of the U.S. Senate, *522 SHOB, 20510; (202) 224-3542. Fax, (202) 228-2856. Sen. Harry M. Reid, Minority Leader; Drew Willison, Chief of Staff.*
Web, www.reid.senate.gov

Serves as chief strategist and floor spokesperson for the minority party in the Senate.

Minority Whip of the U.S. Senate, *711 SHOB, 20510-1304; (202) 224-2152. Fax, (202) 228-0400. Sen. Richard J. Durbin, Minority Whip; Patrick J. Souders, Chief of Staff.*

Serves as assistant minority leader in the Senate; helps marshal minority forces in support of party strategy.

President Pro Tempore of the U.S. Senate, *104 SHOB, 20510-4402; (202) 224-5251. Fax, (202) 224-6351. Sen. Orrin G. Hatch, President Pro Tempore.*

Presides over the Senate in the absence of the vice president.

Senate Democratic Conference, *S309 CAP, 20510; (202) 224-3735. Sen. Harry M. Reid, Chair; Sen. Charles E. Schumer, Vice Chair; Sen. Patty Murray, Secretary.*
Web, www.democrats.senate.gov

Membership: Democratic senators. Selects Democratic leadership; formulates party rules and floor strategy and considers party positions on major legislation; votes on the Democratic Steering Committee's recommendations for Democratic committee assignments.

Senate Republican Conference, *405 SHOB, 20510; (202) 224-2764. Fax, (202) 224-4276. Sen. John Thune, Chair; Rep. Roy Blunt, Vice Chair.*
Web, http://republican.senate.gov

Membership: Republican senators. Serves as caucus and central coordinating body of the party. Organizes and elects Senate Republican leadership; votes on Republican Committee on Committees' recommendations for Senate committee chairs and Republican committee assignments. Staff provides various support and media services for Republican members.

Senate Republican Policy Committee, *347 SROB, 20510; (202) 224-2946. Fax, (202) 228-2628. Sen. John Barrasso, Chair; Dan Kunsiman, Director.*
Web, http://rpc.senate.gov

Studies and makes recommendations to the Republican leader on the priorities and scheduling of legislation on the Senate floor; prepares policy papers and develops Republican policy initiatives.

Vice President of the United States, *President of the Senate,* *The White House, 20500; (202) 224-2424.*

Joseph R. Biden Jr., President of the Senate; Lorea Stallard, Associate Director for Legislative Affairs.
General email, vice.president@whitehouse.gov
Web, www.whitehouse.gov/administration/vice-president-biden and Twitter, @VP

Presides over the Senate while in session; preserves decorum and order; announces vote results; recognizes members for debate and introduction of bills, amendments, and motions; decides points of order; votes only in the case of a tie. (President pro tempore of the Senate presides in the absence of the vice president.)

Officers

▶ **HOUSE**

Chaplain of the U.S. House of Representatives, *HB25 CAP, 20515; (202) 225-2509. Fax, (202) 226-4928. Rev. Patrick J. Conroy, S.J., Chaplain.*
General email, chaplainoffice@mail.house.gov
Web, http://chaplain.house.gov

Opens each day's House session with a prayer and offers other religious services and study groups to House members, their families, and staffs. (Prayer sometimes offered by visiting chaplain.)

Chief Administrative Officer of the U.S. House of Representatives, *HB26 CAP, 20515; (202) 226-6660. Will Plaster, Chief Administrative Officer*
Web, www.cao.house.gov

Responsible for House member and staff payrolls; computer system; internal mail, office furnishings and supplies; telecommunications; tour guides; nonlegislative functions of the House printing services, recording studio, and records office; and other administrative areas.

Clerk of the U.S. House of Representatives, *H154 CAP, 20515-6601; (202) 225-7000. Karen L. Haas, Clerk. Communications, (202) 225-1908.*
General email, info.clerkweb@mail.house.gov
Web, http://clerk.house.gov

Responsible for direction of duties of House employees; receives lobby registrations and reports of campaign expenditures and receipts of House candidates; disburses funds appropriated for House expenditures; responsible for other activities necessary for the continuing operation of the House.

General Counsel of the U.S. House of Representatives, *219 CHOB, 20515; (202) 225-9700. Kerry W. Kircher, General Counsel.*
General email, www.ogc.house.gov

Advises House members and committees on legal matters.

House Legislative Counsel, *H2-337 FHOB, 20515-6721; (202) 225-6060. Fax, (202) 225-3437. Sandra Strokoff, Legislative Counsel.*
General email, legcoun@mail.house.gov
Web, www.legcouncil.house.gov

Assists House members and committees in drafting legislation.

Inspector General of the U.S. House of Representatives, *386 FHOB, 20515; (202) 226-1250. Fax, (202) 225-4240. Theresa M. Grafenstine, Inspector General; Debbie B. Hunter, Deputy Inspector General; Michael Ptasienski, Deputy Inspector General. General email, HouseIG@mail.house.gov*

Web, www.house.gov/content/learn/officers_and_organizations/inspector_general.php

Conducts periodic audits of the financial and administrative functions of the House and joint entities.

Sergeant at Arms of the U.S. House of Representatives, *H124 CAP, 20515-6611; (202) 225-2456. Fax, (202) 225-3233. Paul D. Irving, Sergeant at Arms. Web, www.house.gov/content/learn/officers_and_organizations/sergeant_at_arms.php*

Maintains order on the House floor; executes orders from the Speaker of the House. Serves on the Capitol Police Board and Capitol Guide Board; oversees Capitol security (with Senate Sergeant at Arms) and protocol.

Speaker of the U.S. House of Representatives, *Floor Assistant, H232 CAP, 20515; (202) 225-0600. Fax, (202) 225-5117. Sarah Coyle, Floor Assistant; Ryan O'Toole, Floor Assistant.*

Assists the majority leadership and members on legislative matters.

►SENATE

Chaplain of the U.S. Senate, *S332 CAP, 20510-7002; (202) 224-2510. Fax, (202) 224-9686. Barry C. Black, Chaplain. Web, www.senate.gov/reference/office/chaplain.htm*

Opens each day's Senate session with a prayer and offers other religious services to Senate members, their families, and staffs. (Prayer sometimes offered by visiting chaplain.)

Legislative Counsel of the Senate, *668 SDOB, 20510-7250; (202) 224-6461. Fax, (202) 224-0567. Gary Endicott, Legislative Counsel. Web, www.slc.senate.gov*

Assists Senate members and committees in drafting legislation.

Majority Secretary of the U.S. Senate, *S337 CAP, 20510-7024; (202) 224-3835. Fax, (202) 224-2860. Laura Dove, Secretary; Robert Duncan, Assistant Secretary. Web, www.senate.gov/senators/leadership.htm*

Assists the majority leader and majority party in the Senate.

Minority Secretary of the U.S. Senate, *S309 CAP, 20510-7014; (202) 224-3735. Gary B. Myrick, Secretary; Tim Mitchell, Assistant Secretary. Web, www.senate.gov/senators/leadership.htm*

Assists the minority leader and the minority party in the Senate.

Secretary of the U.S. Senate, *S312 CAP, 20510; (202) 224-3622. Julie E. Adams, Secretary of the Senate. Web, www.senate.gov/reference/office/secretary_of_senate.htm*

Chief legislative, financial, and administrative officer of the Senate. Responsible for direction of duties of Senate employees and administration of oaths; receives lobby registrations and reports of campaign expenditures and receipts of Senate candidates; responsible for other day-to-day Senate activities.

Senate Legal Counsel, *642 SHOB, 20510-7250; (202) 224-4435. Fax, (202) 224-3391. Morgan J. Frankel, Legal Counsel.*

Advises Senate members and committees on legal matters.

Sergeant at Arms and Doorkeeper of the U.S. Senate, *S151 CAP, 20510-7200; (202) 224-2341. Frank J. Larkin, Sergeant at Arms and Doorkeeper. Web, www.senate.gov/reference/office/sergeant_at_arms.htm*

Oversees the Senate wing of the Capitol; doormen; Senate pages; and telecommunication, photographic, supply, and janitorial services. Maintains order on the Senate floor and galleries; oversees Capitol security (with House Sergeant at Arms); sits on the Capitol Police Board and Capitol Guide Board.

Pay and Perquisites

►CONGRESS

For a listing of relevant congressional committees and subcommittees, please see page 746 or the Appendix.

Attending Physician of Congress, *H166 CAP, 20515-8907; (202) 225-5421. Dr. Brian Monahan, Attending Physician; Keith A. Pray, Chief of Staff.*

Provides members with primary care, first aid, emergency care, and environmental/occupational health services; provides House and Senate employees, visiting dignitaries, and tourists with first-aid and emergency care.

Clerk of the U.S. House of Representatives, *H154 CAP, 20515-6601; (202) 225-7000. Karen L. Haas, Clerk. Communications, (202) 225-1908. General email, info.clerkweb@mail.house.gov*

Web, http://clerk.house.gov

Prepares and submits quarterly reports covering the receipts and expenditures of the House, including disbursements by each committee and each member's office and staff. Reports available from the Legislative Resource Center.

House Commission on Congressional Mailing Standards (Franking Commission), *1309 LHOB, 20515-6328; (202) 225-8281. Rep. Candice S. Miller, Chair; Sean Moran, Majority Staff Director; Matt DeFreitas, Minority Staff Director. Web, http://cha.house.gov/franking-commission*

Oversight of the use of franked mail by House members.

Secretary of the U.S. Senate, *S312 CAP, 20510; (202) 224-3622. Julie E. Adams, Secretary of the Senate. Web, www.senate.gov/reference/office/secretary_of_senate.htm*

Prepares and submits semiannual reports covering the receipts and expenditures of the Senate, including data on each committee and each member's office and staff. Reports available from the Government Printing Office.

▶NONGOVERNMENTAL

National Taxpayers Union, *Communications, 25 Massachusetts Ave. N.W., #140, Alexandria, VA 20001; (703) 683-5700. Peter Sepp, President; Nan Swift, Federal Affairs. General email, ntu@ntu.org*

Web, www.ntu.org

Citizens' interest group that publishes reports on congressional pay and perquisites, including pensions and the franking privilege.

Standards of Conduct

▶AGENCIES

Justice Dept. (DOJ), *Public Integrity, 1400 New York Ave. N.W., #12000, 20005; (202) 514-1412. Raymond Hulser, Chief. Web, www.justice.gov/criminal/pin*

Conducts investigations of wrongdoing in selected cases that involve alleged corruption of public office or violations of election law by public officials, including members of Congress.

▶CONGRESS

For a listing of relevant congressional committees and subcommittees, please see page 746 or the Appendix.

Secretary of the U.S. Senate, *Public Records, Ethics, 232 SHOB, 20510; (202) 224-0758. Dana K. McCallum, Superintendent of Public Records. General email, lobby@sec.senate.gov*

Web, www.senate.gov/legislative/opr.htm

Receives and maintains the financial disclosure records of Senate members, officers, employees, candidates, and legislative organizations. Receives reports from committee chairs on foreign travel by senators and staff. Records open for public inspection, 9:00 a.m.–5:30 p.m.

U.S. House of Representatives, *Legislative Resource Center, Records and Registration, 135 CHOB, 20515-6612; (202) 226-5200. Fax, (202) 226-5169. Steve Pingeton, Manager. Web, http://clerk.house.gov*

Receives and maintains the financial disclosure records of House members, officers, employees, candidates, and certain legislative organizations. Receives reports from committee chairs on foreign travel by members and staff. Records open for public inspection.

CONGRESSIONAL SUPPORT GROUPS

General

▶CONGRESS

For a listing of relevant congressional committees and subcommittees, please see page 746 or the Appendix.

Congressional Budget Office, *FHOB, 2nd and D Sts. S.W., 4th Floor, 20515-6925; (202) 226-2602. Fax, (202) 225-7509. Keith Hall, Director. Information, (202) 226-2600. Publications, (202) 226-2809. Web, www.cbo.gov and Twitter, @USCBO*

Nonpartisan office that provides the House and Senate with analyses needed for economic and budget decisions, and with the information and estimates required for the congressional budget process.

Government Accountability Office (GAO), *441 G St. N.W., 20548; (202) 512-5500. Fax, (202) 512-5507. Gene L. Dodaro, Comptroller General. Information, (202) 512-3000. Publications and Documents, (202) 512-6000. Congressional Relations, (202) 512-4400. Web, www.gao.gov*

Independent, nonpartisan agency in the legislative branch. Serves as the investigating agency for Congress; carries out legal, accounting, auditing, and claims settlement functions; makes recommendations for more effective government operations; publishes monthly lists of reports available to the public.

House Legislative Counsel, *H2-337 FHOB, 20515-6721; (202) 225-6060. Fax, (202) 225-3437. Sandra Strokoff, Legislative Counsel. General email, legcoun@mail.house.gov*

Web, www.legcouncil.house.gov

Assists House members and committees in drafting legislation.

Law Revision Counsel, *H2-308 FHOB, 20515-6711; (202) 226-2411. Fax, (202) 225-0010. Ralph V. Seep, Law Revision Counsel. General email, uscode@mail.house.gov*

Web, http://uscode.house.gov and Twitter, @uscode

Develops and updates an official classification of U.S. laws. Codifies, cites, and publishes the U.S. Code.

Library of Congress, *Congressional Research Service, James Madison Memorial Bldg., 101 Independence Ave. S.E., #LM 203, 20540; (202) 707-5775. Fax, (202) 707-6745. Mary B. Mazanec, Director. Information, (202) 707-5700. Web, www.loc.gov/crsinfo*

Provides confidential policy and legal research and analysis exclusively to committees and members of the House and Senate, regardless of party affiliation. Using multiple disciplines and research methodologies, assists at every stage of the legislative process, from early considerations that precede bill drafting, through committee

3

hearings and floor debate, to the oversight of enacted laws and various agency activities.

Senate Legal Counsel, *642 SHOB, 20510-7250; (202) 224-4435. Fax, (202) 224-3391. Morgan J. Frankel, Legal Counsel.*

Advises Senate members and committees on legal matters.

Liaison Offices

▶**CONGRESS**

For a listing of relevant congressional committees and subcommittees, please see page 746 or the Appendix.

Agriculture Dept. (USDA), *Congressional Relations, 1400 Independence Ave. S.W., #219-A, 20250; (202) 720-7095. Todd Batta, Assistant Secretary, (202) 205-4380. Web, www.usda.gov/wps/portal/usda/usdahome?navid=OCR*

Advises Congress on agriculture legislation and budget proposals.

Animal and Plant Health Inspection Service (APHIS) *(Agriculture Dept.), Legislative and Public Affairs, South Bldg., 1400 Independence Ave. S.W., #1147, 20250; (202) 799-7030. Abbey Fretz, Legislative Director. Web, www.aphis.usda.gov/aphis/banner/contactus/sa_aphis_contacts/ct_contact_lpa*

Advises Congress on legislation related to agriculture, food, natural resources, and wildlife.

Census Bureau *(Commerce Dept.), Congressional and Intergovernmental Affairs, 4600 Silver Hill Rd., Suitland, MD 20746; (301) 763-6100. Fax, (301) 763-3780. Rene Munoz, Chief. General email, cao@census.gov Web, www.census.gov/about/cong-gov-affairs.html*

Advises Congress on census policies and programs; provides Census data to Congress.

Commerce Dept., *Legislative and Intergovernmental Affairs, Herbert C. Hoover Bldg., 1401 Constitution Ave. N.W., 20230; (202) 482-3663. Fax, (202) 482-4420. Margaret Cummisky, Assistant Secretary. Web, www.commerce.gov/os/office-legislative-and-intergovernmental-affairs*

Advises Congress on legislation related to job creation, economic growth, sustainable development, and improved standards of living.

Education Dept., *Legislative and Congressional Affairs, 400 Maryland Ave. S.W., #6W315, 20202-3500; (202) 401-0020. Lloyd Horwich, Assistant Secretary, Acting. General email, olca@ed.gov Web, www2.ed.gov/about/offices/list/olca*

Advises Congress on policy and legislation related to education.

Energy Dept. (DOE), *Congressional and Intergovernmental Affairs, 1000 Independence Ave. S.W., #7B138, 20585; (202) 586-5450. Fax, (202) 586-4891. Brad Crowell, Assistant Secretary. Toll-free, (800) 342-5363. General email, robert.tuttle@hq.doe.gov Web, www.energy.gov/congressional/office-congressional-and-intergovernmental-affairs*

Advises Congress on energy-related policies, programs, and initiatives.

Equal Employment Opportunity Commission (EEOC), *Legislative Affairs, 131 M St. N.E., Room 6NE25J, 20507; (202) 663-4191. Fax, (202) 663-4912. Patricia Crawford, Directory, Acting. General email, Legis.Affairs@eeoc.gov Web, www.eeoc.gov/eeoc/legislative*

Advises Congress on policy and legislation related to equal employment and discrimination in the workplace; coordinates department testimony before congressional hearings.

Federal Bureau of Investigation (FBI) *(Justice Dept.), Congressional Affairs, 935 Pennsylvania Ave. N.W., #7240, 20535; (202) 324-5051. Fax, (202) 324-6490. Stephen D. Kelly, Assistant Director. Web, www.fbi.gov*

Advises Congress about FBI activities.

Food and Nutrition Service *(Agriculture Dept.), Communications and Governmental Affairs, 3101 Park Center Dr., #926, Alexandria, VA 22302; (703) 305-2281. Fax, (703) 305-2312. Bruce Alexander, Director. Web, www.fns.usda.gov/cga*

Advises Congress on policy and legislation related to food and nutrition programs; coordinates department testimony before congressional hearings.

Homeland Security Dept. (DHS), *Legislative Affairs, MS 0020, 20528; (202) 447-5890. Fax, (202) 447-5437. M. Tia Johnson, Assistant Secretary. Web, www.dhs.gov/about-office-legislative-affairs*

Advises Congress about national threat and hazard response as well as safe and secure borders.

Interior Dept. (DOI), *Congressional and Legislative Affairs, 1849 C St. N.W., 20240; (202) 208-7693. Fax, (202) 208-7619. Sarah Neimeyer, Director. Web, www.doi.gov/ocl*

Advises Congress on policy and legislation related to natural resources and tribal communities; coordinates department testimony before congressional hearings.

International Trade Administration *(Commerce Dept.), Legislative and Intergovernmental Affairs, 1401 Constitution Ave. N.W., 20230; (202) 482-3015. Fax, (202) 482-0900. Jordan Haas, Director. Web, http://trade.gov/olia*

Advises Congress on legislation and policies related to international trade matters and export opportunities.

Justice Dept. (DOJ), *Legislative Affairs, 950 Pennsylvania Ave. N.W., 20530-0001; (202) 514-2141. Peter J. Kadzik, Assistant Attorney General.*
Web, www.justice.gov/ola

Advises Congress on Justice Dept. initiatives; coordinates department testimony before congressional hearings; participates in the Senate confirmation process for federal judges and Justice Dept. nominees.

Labor Dept. (DOL), *Congressional and Intergovernmental Affairs, 200 Constitution Ave. N.W., 20210; (202) 693-4600. Adri Jayaratne, Assistant Secretary, Acting.*
Web, www.dol.gov/ocia

Advises Congress on policy and legislation related to federal labor matters.

National Institute of Standards and Technology (NIST) *(Commerce Dept.), Congressional and Legislative Affairs, 100 Bureau Dr., MS 1051, Gaithersburg, MD 20899-1051; (301) 975-5675. Fax, (301) 926-2569. Jim Schufreider, Director, (301) 922-1366.*
Web, www.nist.gov/director/ocla

Advises Congress on policy related to technology, measurements, and standards; coordinates agency testimony before congressional hearings.

National Marine Manufacturers Assn., *Government Relations, 650 Massachusetts Ave. N.W., #520, 20001; (202) 737-9750. Fax, (202) 628-4716. Nicole Vasilaros, Vice President, (202) 737-9763.*
Web, www.nmma.org/government/default

Advises Congress on matters related to boating safety and the development of boating facilities.

National Oceanic and Atmospheric Administration (NOAA) *(Commerce Dept.), Legislative and Intergovernmental Affairs, 1401 Constitution Ave. N.W., #5128, 20230; (202) 482-4981. Coby Dolan, Director; Hannah Mellman, Legislative Affairs Specialist, (202) 482-5597.*
Web, www.legislative.noaa.gov

Advises Congress on legislation and policy related to climate change, marine commerce, and ocean and coastal resources; coordinates agency testimony before congressional hearings.

Office of Personnel Management (OPM), *Congressional, Legislative, and Intergovernmental Affairs, 1900 E St. N.W., #6316G, 20415 (mailing address: Constituent Services, B332 RHOB, Washington, DC 20515); (202) 606-1300. Fax, (202) 606-1344. Jason Levine, Director. Constituent services, (202) 225-4955.*
Web, www.opm.gov/about-us/our-people-organization/congressional-legislative-intergovernmental-affairs

Advises Congress on federal civil service matters, especially those pertaining to federal employment, retirement, and health benefits programs.

Pension Benefit Guaranty Corporation (PBGC), *Legislative Affairs, 1200 K St. N.W., 20005-4026; (202) 326-4000. Fax, (202) 326-4224. Alice Maroni, Chief*

Management Officer. Phone for members and staff, (202) 326-4223.
General email, congressionals@pbgc.gov
Web, www.pbgc.gov/news/pbgc-legislative-affairs.html

Advises Congress on policy and legislation related to pension benefits and private-sector retirement benefit plans.

Postal Regulatory Commission, *Public Affairs and Government Relations, 901 New York Ave. N.W., #200, 20268; (202) 789-6800. Fax, (202) 789-6891. Ann C. Fisher, Director.*
General email, prc-pagr@prc.gov
Web, www.prc.gov/offices/pagr

Advises Congress on policy related to the Postal Service; coordinates commission testimony before congressional hearings.

Rural Development *(Agriculture Dept.), Legislative and Public Affairs, 1400 Independence Ave. S.W., 20250-0705; (202) 720-1019. David Sandretti, Director. Press, (202) 690-0498.*
Web, www.rd.usda.gov/about-rd/offices/legislative-public-affairs

Advises Congress on legislation and policy related to housing, lending, and rural development; coordinates agency testimony before congressional hearings.

Securities and Exchange Commission (SEC), *Investor Advocate, 100 F St. N.E., 20549; (202) 551-3302. Rick Fleming, Director.*
Web, www.sec.gov/investorad

Submits reports to Congress concerning SEC activities.

Transportation Dept. (DOT), *Government Affairs, 1200 New Jersey Ave. S.E., 20590; (202) 366-4573. Dana Gresham, Assistant Secretary.*
Web, www.transportation.gov/government-affairs

Advises Congress on policy and legislation related to transportation and transportation systems; coordinates department testimony before congressional hearings.

Treasury Dept., *Legislative Affairs, 1500 Pennsylvania Ave. N.W., 20220; (202) 622-2000. Anne Wall, Assistant Secretary.*
Web, www.treasury.gov/about/organizational-structure/offices/Pages/Legislative-Affairs.aspx

Advises Congress on legislation and policies related to economics, finance, and financial security; coordinates department testimony before congressional hearings.

U.S. Commission on Civil Rights, *Public Affairs and Congressional Affairs, 1331 Pennsylvania Ave. N.W., #1150, 20425; (202) 376-8371. Fax, (202) 376-7672. Gerson Gomez, Public Affairs Officer.*
General email, publicaffairs@usccr.gov
Web, www.usccr.gov

Advises Congress on legisation and policy related to civil rights issues.

U.S. House of Representatives

U.S.–China Economic and Security Review Commission, *444 N. Capitol St. N.W., #602, 20001; (202) 624-1407. Fax, (202) 624-1406. Michael R. Danis, Executive Director.*
General email, contact@uscc.gov

Web, www.uscc.gov

Investigates the national security implications of the bilateral trade and economic relationship between China and the United States. Makes recommendations to Congress based on its findings.

▶ **HOUSE**

Air Force Legislative Liaison, *B322 RHOB, 20515-0001; (202) 225-6656. Fax, (202) 685-2592. Col. Wesley Hallman, Director. Alternate phone, (202) 685-4531.*
General email, usaf@mail.house.gov

Provides House members with services and information on all matters related to the U.S. Air Force.

Army Liaison, *B325 RHOB, 20515; (202) 685-2676. Fax, (202) 685-2674. Col. David M. Hamilton (USA), Chief; Maj. Gen. Laura J. Richardson (USA), Chief Legislative Liaison.*
Web, http://ocll.hqda.pentagon.mil

Provides House members with services and information on all matters related to the U.S. Army.

Navy–Marine Corps Liaison, *B324 RHOB, 20515; Fax, (202) 685-6077. Capt. Todd Flannery, Navy Director, House; Lt. Col. Joe Jones, Marine Corps Director, House. Navy (House), (202) 225-7126. Marine Corps (House), (202) 225-7124.*

Provides House members with services and information on all matters related to the U.S. Navy and the U.S. Marine Corps.

State Dept., *Capitol Hill House Liason, B330 RHOB, 20515; (202) 226-4642. Julia E. Frifield, Assistant Secretary. Web, www.state.gov/s/h/c26762.htm*

Advises House members on foreign policy and legislation; provides services related to consular affairs and travel by members of Congress.

U.S. Coast Guard House Liaison, *B320 RHOB, 20515; (202) 225-4775. Fax, (202) 426-6081. Cmdr. Jo-Ann Burdian, Chief.*

Provides House members with services and information on all matters related to the U.S. Coast Guard.

Veterans Affairs Dept., *Congressional Liaison Service, B328 RHOB, 20515; (202) 225-2280. Fax, (202) 453-5225. Ron Maurer, Director, House and Senate.*
General email, ocla-cls@va.gov

Web, www.va.gov

Provides House members with services and information on all matters related to veterans' benefits and services.

White House Legislative Affairs, *White House, 1600 Pennsylvania Ave. N.W., 20502; (202) 456-2230. Fax, (202) 456-3343. Amy Rosenbaum Fallon, Assistant to the President for Legislative Affairs; Alejandro Perez, Deputy Director, House Liaison.*
Web, www.whitehouse.gov

Serves as a liaison between the president and the House of Representatives.

▶ **SENATE**

Air Force Legislative Liaison, *182 SROB, 20510; (202) 224-2481. Fax, (202) 685-2575. Col. John Allen, Director. General email, SAFLLS@pentagon.af.mil*

Provides senators with services and information on all matters related to the U.S. Air Force.

Army Liaison, *183 SROB, 20510; (202) 224-2881. Col. Scott Jackson (USA), Chief; Maj. Gen. Laura J. Richardson (USA), Chief Legislative Liaison.*
Web, http://ocll.hqda.pentagon.mil

Provides senators with services and information on all matters related to the U.S. Army.

Navy–Marine Corps Liaison, *SR-182, 20510; Fax, (202) 685-6005. Capt. Sara Joyner, Navy Director, Senate; Col. Kyle Ellison, Marine Corps Director, Senate. Navy*

(Senate), (202) 224-4682. Marine Corps (Senate), (202) 224-4681.

Provides senators with services and information on all matters related to the U.S. Navy and the U.S. Marine Corps.

State Dept., *Capitol Hill Senate Liaison, B189 SROB, 20002; (202) 228-1602/1603. Julia E. Frifield, Assistant Secretary.*
Web, www.state.gov/s/h/c26762.htm

Advises Senate members on foreign policy and legislation; provides services related to consular affairs and travel by members of Congress.

U.S. Coast Guard Senate Liaison, *183 SROB, 20510; (202) 224-2913. Fax, (202) 755-1695. Cmdr. Brian LeFebvre, Chief.*

Provides senators with services and information on all matters related to the U.S. Coast Guard.

Veterans Affairs Dept., *Congressional Liaison Service, 189 SROB, 20510; (202) 224-5351. Fax, (202) 453-5218. Ron Maurer, Director, House and Senate. General email, ocla-cls@va.gov*

Provides senators with services and information on all matters related to veterans' benefits and services.

White House Legislative Affairs, *White House, 1600 Pennsylvania Ave. N.W., 20502; (202) 456-2230. Fax, (202) 456-3343. Amy Rosenbaum Fallon, Assistant to the President for Legislative Affairs; Martin Paone, Deputy Director, Senate Liaison. Web, www.whitehouse.gov*

Serves as a liaison between the Senate and the president.

Libraries
▶CONGRESS

For a listing of relevant congressional committees and subcommittees, please see page 746 or the Appendix.

Library of Congress, *Congressional Research Service, James Madison Memorial Bldg., 101 Independence Ave. S.E., #LM 203, 20540; (202) 707-5775. Fax, (202) 707-6745. Mary B. Mazanec, Director. Information, (202) 707-5700. Web, www.loc.gov/crsinfo*

Provides members of Congress and committees with research and reference assistance.

Library of Congress, *Law Library, James Madison Memorial Bldg., 101 Independence Ave. S.E., #LM 240, 20540; (202) 707-5065. Fax, (202) 707-1820. Roberta I. Shaffer, Law Librarian. Reading room, (202) 707-5080. Reference, (202) 707-5079. Web, www.loc.gov/law, Twitter, @LawLibCongress and Facebook, www.facebook.com/lawlibraryofcongress*

Maintains collections of foreign, international, and comparative law texts organized jurisdictionally by country. Covers all legal systems, including common, civil, Roman, canon, religious, and ancient and medieval law.

Services include a public reading room; a microtext facility, with readers and printers for microfilm and microfiche; and foreign law/rare book reading areas. Staff of legal specialists is competent in approximately forty languages; does not provide advice on legal matters.

Library of the Senate, *B15 SROB, 20510; (202) 224-7106. Fax, (202) 229-0879. Leona Faust, Librarian.*

Maintains special collection for Senate private use of primary source legislative materials, including reports, hearing transcripts, prints, documents, and debate proceedings. (Not open to the public.)

U.S. House of Representatives, *Legislative Resource Center, Library Services, 135 CHOB, 20515; (202) 225-9000. Fax, (202) 226-5204. Rae Ellen Best, House Librarian. Web, http://library.clerk.house.gov*

Serves as the statutory and official depository of House reports, hearings, prints, and documents for the clerk of the House. Includes the divisions of Library Services, Public Information, Records and Registration, and the House Document Room.

Pages
▶CONGRESS

For a listing of relevant congressional committees and subcommittees, please see page 746 or the Appendix.

Senate Page School, *U.S. Senate, 20510-7248; (202) 224-3927. Nicka Thompson, Principal.*

Provides education for pages of the Senate.

Sergeant at Arms and Doorkeeper of the U.S. Senate, *Senate Page Program, Webster Hall, #11, 20510; (202) 228-1291. Elizabeth Roach, Director.*

Oversees and enforces rules and regulations concerning Senate pages after they have been appointed.

Staff
▶CONGRESS

Human Resources, *House Vacancy Announcement and Placement Service, H2-102 FHOB, 20515-6201; (202) 225-2926. Fax, (202) 226-7514. Jason Hite, Chief Human Resources Officer. Web, www.house.gov/content/jobs/members_and_committees.php*

Holds résumés and provides as requested by House committees.

Senate Placement Office, *116 SHOB, 20510; (202) 224-9167. Brian Bean, Administrator. TTY, (202) 224-4215. General email, placementofficeinfo@saa.senate.gov Web, www.senate.gov/visiting/common/generic/placement_office.htm*

U.S. Senate

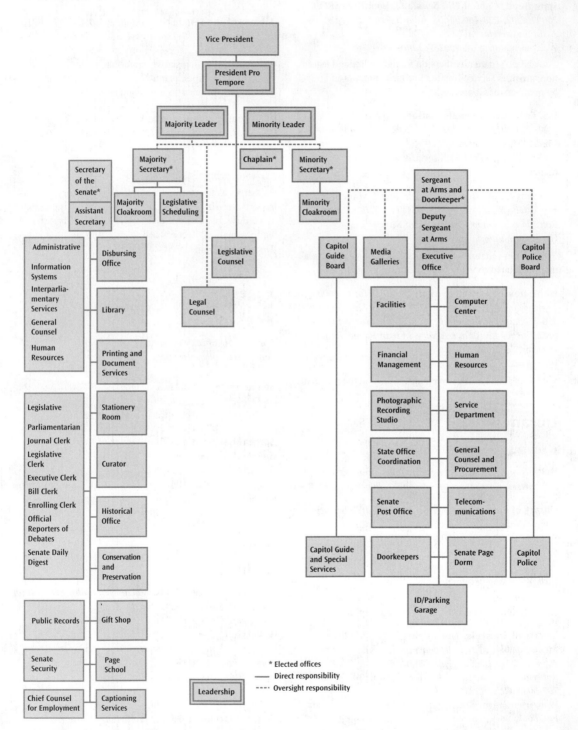

Provides members, committees, and administrative offices of the Senate with placement and referral services. Compiles Senate Employment Bulletin, an online listing of available jobs.

▶NONGOVERNMENTAL

Congressional Management Foundation, *710 E St. S.E., 20003; (202) 546-0100. Fax, (202) 547-0936. Brad Fitch, President.*
General email, cmf@congressfoundation.org
Web, www.congressfoundation.org and Twitter, @CongressFdn

Nonpartisan organization that provides members of Congress and their staffs with management information and services through seminars, consultation, research, and publications.

Federal Bar Assn., *1220 N. Fillmore St., #444, Arlington, VA 22201; (571) 481-9100. Fax, (571) 481-9090. Karen Silberman, Executive Director.*
General email, fba@fedbar.org
Web, www.fedbar.org and Twitter, @federalbar

Organization of bar members who are present or former staff members of the House, Senate, Library of Congress, Supreme Court, Government Accountability Office, or Government Printing Office, or attorneys in legislative practice before federal courts or agencies.

House Chiefs of Staff Assn., *2211 RHOB, 20515; (202) 225-6411. Fax, (202) 226-0778. Drew Kent, Chief of Staff.*
Sponsors professional development programs and social activities for current chiefs of staff and staff directors. Promotes bipartisanship.

POLITICAL ADVOCACY

General

▶CONGRESS

For a listing of relevant congressional committees and subcommittees, please see page 746 or the Appendix.

U.S. House of Representatives, *Legislative Resource Center, Records and Registration, 135 CHOB, 20515-6612; (202) 226-5200. Fax, (202) 226-5169. Steve Pingeton, Manager.*
Web, http://clerk.house.gov

Receives and maintains lobby registrations and quarterly financial reports of lobbyists. Administers the statutes of the Federal Regulation of Lobbying Act of 1995 and counsels lobbyists. Receives and maintains agency filings made under the requirements of Section 319 of the Interior Dept. and Related Agencies Appropriations Act for fiscal 1990 (known as the Byrd Amendment). Open for public inspection.

▶NONGOVERNMENTAL

Assn. of Government Relations Professionals, *444 N. Capitol St. N.W., #237, 20001; (202) 508-3833. Jim Hickey Jr., President.*
General email, info@agrp.org
Web, www.agrp.org

Membership: lobbyists and government relations and public affairs professionals. Works to improve the skills, ethics, and public image of lobbyists. Monitors lobby legislation; conducts educational programs on public issues, lobbying techniques, and other topics of interest to membership.

Charles F. Kettering Foundation, *Washington Office, 444 N. Capitol St. N.W., #434, 20001-1512; (202) 393-4478. Fax, (202) 393-7644. David Mathews, President.*
Web, www.kettering.org and Twitter, @KetteringFdn

Works to understand democracy and its processes and improve the domestic policymaking process through citizen deliberation. Supports international programs focusing on unofficial, citizen-to-citizen diplomacy. Encourages greater citizen involvement in formation of public policy. Interests include public education and at-risk youths. (Headquarters in Dayton, Ohio.)

Citizens United, *1006 Pennsylvania Ave. S.E., 20003-2142; (202) 547-5420. Fax, (202) 547-5421. David N. Bossie, President.*
General email, info@citizensunited.org
Web, www.citizensunited.org

Advocates for key elements of the conservative legislative and policy agenda.

Public Citizen, *1600 20th St. N.W., 20009; (202) 588-1000. Fax, (202) 588-7798. Robert Weissman, President.*
General email, pcmail@citizen.org
Web, www.citizen.org and Twitter, @Public_Citizen

Public interest consumer advocacy organization comprising the following programs: Congress Watch, Health Research Group, Energy Program, Litigation Group, Global Trade Watch, Democracy for People Project, and Commercial Alert Program.

Women & Politics Institute *(American University), 4400 Massachusetts Ave. N.W., #237, 20016; (202) 885-2903. Fax, (202) 885-2967. Jennifer Lawless, Director, (202) 885-6452.*
General email, wpi@american.edu
Web, www.american.edu/spa/wpi and Twitter, @wpiatau

Research center that encourages women to participate in politics and addresses women's issues. Administers graduate and undergraduate certificates to academics studying women, policy, and political leadership. Sponsors the annual 5k Race to Representation to promote awareness of the gender gap in political leadership. Assists women in securing employment in the political sphere through leadership training programs.

Ethnic Group Advocacy

▶NONGOVERNMENTAL

American Polish Advisory Council, *2025 O St. N.W., 20036; (202) 630-1714. Fax, (202) 827-7916. Darek Barcikowski, Executive Director. Web, www.americanpolishadvisorycouncil.org*

Promotes Polish Americans' involvement in politics, public affairs, service, and policymaking. Educates Polish Americans about the American governmental system and voting. Researches political, economic, and civil issues facing Polish American communities. Holds an annual conference to discuss the current and future role of Poland's relationship with the United States.

American–Arab Anti-Discrimination Committee (ADC), *1990 M St. N.W., #610, 20036; (202) 244-2990. Fax, (202) 333-3980. Samer E. Khalaf, President. General email, adc@adc.org Web, www.adc.org and Twitter, @adctweets*

Nonpartisan and nonsectarian organization that promotes and seeks to protect the human rights and cultural heritage of Americans of Arab descent. Works to combat discrimination against Arab Americans in employment, education, and political life and to prevent stereotyping of Arabs in the media. Monitors legislation and regulations.

Arab American Institute, *1600 K St. N.W., #601, 20006; (202) 429-9210. Fax, (202) 429-9214. James J. Zogby, President. General email, communications@aaiusa.org Web, www.aaiusa.org and Twitter, @AAIUSA*

Fosters civic and political empowerment of Americans of Arab descent through research, policy formation, and political activism.

Armenian National Committee of America, *1711 N St. N.W., 20036; (202) 775-1918. Fax, (202) 223-7964. Aram Hamparian, Executive Director. General email, anca@anca.org Web, www.anca.org and Twitter, @ANCA_DC*

Armenian American grassroots political organization. Works to advance concerns of the Armenian American community. Interests include strengthening U.S.–Armenian relations.

Asian Americans Advancing Justice (AAJC), *1620 L St. N.W., #1050, 20036; (202) 296-2300. Fax, (202) 296-2318. Mee Moua, President. General email, information@advancingequality.org Web, www.advancingequality.org and Twitter, @AAAJ_AAJC*

Works to advance the human and civil rights of Asian Americans and other minority groups through advocacy, public policy, public education, and litigation. Promotes civic engagement at the local, regional, and national levels. Interests include affirmative action, hate crimes, media diversity, census, broadband and telecommunications, youth advocacy, immigrant rights, language access, and voting rights.

B'nai B'rith International, *1120 20th St. N.W., #300N, 20036; (202) 857-6600. Fax, (202) 857-2700. Daniel S. Mariaschin, Executive Vice President. Toll-free, (888) 388-4224. General email, info@bnaibrith.org Web, www.bnaibrith.org and Twitter, @BnaiBrith*

Advocates policies in support of Jews and the State of Israel.

Japanese American Citizens League, *Washington Office, 1629 K St. N.W., #400, 20006; (202) 223-1240. Fax, (202) 296-8082. Priscilla Ouchida, Executive Director. General email, dc@jacl.org Web, www.jacl.org*

Monitors legislative and regulatory activities affecting the rights of Japanese Americans. Supports civil rights of all Americans, with a focus on Asian and Asian Pacific Americans. (Headquarters in San Francisco, Calif.)

Labor Council for Latin American Advancement, *815 16th St. N.W., 3rd Floor, 20006; (202) 508-6919. Fax, (202) 508-6922. Hector E. Sanchez, Executive Director. General email, headquarters@lclaa.org Web, www.lclaa.org, Twitter, @LCLAA and Facebook, www.facebook.com/LCLAA*

Membership: Hispanic trade unionists. Encourages equal employment opportunity, voter registration, and participation in the political process. (Affiliated with the AFL-CIO and the Change to Win Federation.)

League of United Latin American Citizens, *1133 19th St. N.W., #1000, 20036; (202) 833-6130. Fax, (202) 833-6135. Brent Wilkes, Executive Director. Toll-free, (877) LULAC-01. General email, info@lulac.org Web, www.lulac.org*

Seeks to increase the number of minorities, especially Hispanics, attending postsecondary schools; supports legislation to increase educational opportunities for Hispanics and other minorities; provides scholarship funds and educational and career counseling. Seeks full social, political, economic, and educational rights for Hispanics in the United States. Programs include housing projects for the poor, employment and training for youth and women, and political advocacy on issues affecting Hispanics, including immigration. Operates National Educational Service Centers (LNESCs) and awards scholarships. Holds exposition open to the public.

Mexican American Legal Defense and Educational Fund, *National Public Policy, 1016 16th St. N.W., #100, 20036; (202) 293-2828. Andrea Senteno, Legislative Staff Attorney; Vacant, Regional Counsel. Web, www.maldef.org/about/offices/washington_dc*

Provides Mexican Americans and other Hispanics with high-impact litigation in the areas of employment, education, immigration rights, and voting rights. Monitors legislation and regulations. (Headquarters in Los Angeles,

Calif.) Works with Congress and the White House to promote legislative advocacy for minority groups. Interests include equal employment, voting rights, bilingual education, immigration, and discrimination. Monitors legislation and regulations. (Headquarters in Los Angeles, Calif.)

National Assn. of Latino Elected and Appointed Officials Educational Fund, *Washington Office,* 600 *Pennsylvania Ave. S.E., #480, 20003; (202) 546-2536. Arturo Vargas, Executive Director. General email, jgarcia@naleo.org Web, www.naleo.org*

Research and advocacy group that provides civic affairs information and assistance on legislation affecting Latinos. Encourages Latino participation in local, state, and national politics. Interests include health care and social, economic, and educational issues. (Headquarters in Los Angeles, Calif.)

National Congress of American Indians, *Embassy of Tribal Nations, 1516 P St. N.W., 20005; (202) 466-7767. Fax, (202) 466-7797. Jacqueline Johnson Pata, Executive Director. General email, ncai@ncai.org Web, www.ncai.org*

Membership: American Indian and Alaska Native tribal governments and individuals. Provides information and serves as general advocate for tribes. Monitors legislative and regulatory activities affecting Native American affairs.

National Italian American Foundation, *1860 19th St. N.W., 20009; (202) 387-0600. Fax, (202) 387-0800. John Viola, Chief Operating Officer, (202) 939-3115. Media, (202) 939-3106. General email, information@niaf.org Web, www.niaf.org*

Represents the interests of Italian Americans before Congress.

National Puerto Rican Coalition, Inc., *1444 Eye St. N.W., #800, 20005; (202) 223-3915. Rafael A. Fantauzzi, President. General email, nprc@nprcinc.org Web, www.nprcinc.org*

Membership: Puerto Rican organizations and individuals. Analyzes and advocates for public policy that benefits Puerto Ricans; offers training and technical assistance to Puerto Rican organizations and individuals; develops national communication network for Puerto Rican community-based organizations and individuals.

OCA: Asian Pacific American Advocates, *1322 18th St. N.W., 20036-1803; (202) 223-5500. Fax, (202) 296-0540. Ken Lee, Chief Executive Officer. General email, oca@ocanational.org Web, www.ocanational.org*

Advocacy group seeking to advance the social, political, and economic well-being of Asian Pacific Americans in the United States.

Orthodox Union, *Advocacy Center, 820 1st St. N.E., #730, 20002; (202) 513-6484. Fax, (202) 513-6497. Nathan Diament, Executive Director. General email, info@ouadvocacy.org Web, www.ou.org/public_affairs*

Works to protect Orthodox Jewish interests and freedoms through dissemination of policy briefings to government officials. Encourages Jewish law and a traditional perspective on public policy issues. Coordinates grassroots activities. (Headquarters in New York.)

Southeast Asia Resource Action Center (SEARAC), *1628 16th St. N.W., 3rd Floor, 20009; (202) 601-2960. Fax, (202) 667-6449. Quyen Dinh, Executive Director. General email, searac@searac.org Web, www.searac.org*

Works to advance Cambodian, Hmong, Laotian, and Vietnamese refugee rights through leadership and advocacy training. Collects and analyzes data on Southeast Asian Americans; publishes reports.

Political Action Committees and 527s

The following are some key political action committees (PACs) based in Washington.

▶ **LABOR**

Active Ballot Club *(United Food and Commercial Workers International Union, AFL-CIO), 1775 K St. N.W., 20006; (202) 223-3111. Fax, (202) 728-1830. Anthony M. (Marc) Perrone, President; Patrick J. O'Neill, Treasurer. Web, www.ufcwaction.org/abc*

Air Line Pilots Assn. PAC, *1625 Massachusetts Ave. N.W., 8th Floor, 20036; (703) 689-2270. Fax, (202) 797-4030. Tim Canoll, President; W. Randolph Helling, Treasurer. Web, www.alpa.org*

Amalgamated Transit Union—COPE (Committee on Political Education), *10000 New Hampshire Ave., Silver Spring, MD 20903; (301) 431-7100. Fax, (301) 431-7117. Oscar Owens, Treasurer. Web, www.atu.org*

American Federation of State, County, and Municipal Employees (AFSCME), *1625 L St. N.W., 20036-5687; (202) 429-1000. Fax, (202) 429-1293. Lee A. Saunders, President. Press, (202) 429-1145. TTY, (202) 659-0446. Web, www.afscme.org*

American Federation of Teachers (AFT), *Political Dept., 555 New Jersey Ave. N.W., 20001; (202) 879-4436. Fax, (202) 393-6375. John Ost, Political Director;*

Ratings of Members of Congress

The following organizations either publish voting records on selected issues or regularly rate members of Congress.

AFL-CIO, 815 16th St. N.W., 20006; (202) 637-5018; www.aflcio.org

American Conservative Union, 1331 H St. N.W., #500, 20005; (202) 347-9388, Fax: (202) 347-9389; www.conservative.org

American Farm Bureau Federation, 600 Maryland Ave. S.W., #1000W, 20024; (202) 406-3600; www.fb.org

Americans for Democratic Action, 1629 K St. N.W., #300, 20006; (202) 600-7762, Fax: (202) 204-8637; www.adaction.org

Americans for Tax Reform, 722 12th St. N.W., #400, 20005; (202) 785-0266, Fax: (202) 785-0261; www.atr.org

Citizens Against Government Waste, 1301 Pennsylvania Ave. N.W., #1075, 20004; (202) 467-5300, Fax: (202) 467-4253; www.cagw.org

Citizens for Responsibility and Ethics in Washington, 455 Massachusetts Ave. N.W., 6th Floor, 20001; (202) 408-5565. www.citizensforethics.org

The Club for Growth, 2001 L St. N.W., #600, 20036; (202) 955-5500, Fax: (202) 955-9466; www.clubforgrowth.org

Drum Major Institute for Public Policy, 3041 Broadway, 4th Floor, Auburn Hall, New York, NY 10027; (212) 203-9219; www.drummajorinst.org

Human Rights Campaign, 1640 Rhode Island Ave. N.W., 20036-3278; (800) 777-4723 or (202) 628-4160, Fax: (202) 347-5323, TTY: (202) 216-1572; www.hrc.org

Leadership Conference on Civil Rights, 1629 K St. N.W., 10th Floor, 20006; (202) 466-3311; www.civilrights.org

League of Conservation Voters, 1920 L St. N.W., #800, 20036; (202) 785-8683, Fax: (202) 835-0491; www.lcv.org

NAACP (National Assn. for the Advancement of Colored People), 4805 Mt. Hope D. Baltimore, MD 21215; (410) 580-5777; www.naacp.org

NARAL Pro-Choice America, 1156 15th St. N.W., #700, 20005; (202) 973-3000, Fax: (202) 973-3096; www.prochoiceamerica.org

National Assn. of Social Workers-PACE (Political Action for Candidate Election), 750 1st St. N.E., #700, 20002; (202) 408-8600; www.socialworkers.org/pace

National Education Assn., 1201 16th St. N.W., 20036-3290; (202) 833-4000, Fax: (202) 822-7974; www.nea.org

National Federation of Independent Business, 1201 F St. N.W., #200, 20004-1221; (202) 554-9000; www.nfib.com

National Right to Life Committee, 512 10th St. N.W., 20004; (202) 626-8800; www.nrlc.org

National Taxpayers Union, 25 Massachusetts Ave. N.W., #140, 20001; (703) 683-5700; www.ntu.org

Population Connection, 2120 L St. N.W., #500, 20037; (202) 332-2200, Fax: (202) 332-2302; www.populationconnection.org

Public Citizen, Congress Watch, 215 Pennsylvania Ave. S.E., 20003; (202) 546-4996; www.citizen.org

U.S. Chamber of Commerce, Congressional Affairs, 1615 H St. N.W., 20062; (202) 659-6000; www.uschamber.com

U.S. Student Assn., 1211 Connecticut Ave. N.W., #406, 20036; (202) 640-6570, Fax: (202) 223-4005; www.usstudents.org

Lorretta Johnson, Secretary-Treasurer, (202) 879-4400. Press, (202) 879-4458. Web, www.aft.org

Committee on Letter Carriers Political Education (*National Assn. of Letter Carriers, AFL-CIO*), 100 Indiana Ave. N.W., 20001-2144; (202) 393-4695. Fax, (202) 756-7400. Fredric V. Rolando, President; Tim O'Malley, Executive Vice President. Legislation information, (202) 662-2833. General email, nalcinf@nalc.org Web, www.nalc.org and Twitter, @NALC_National

Committee on Political Action of the American Postal Workers Union, *AFL-CIO,* 1300 L St. N.W., 20005; (202) 842-4210. Fax, (202) 682-2528. John L. Marcotte, Director. Web, www.apwu.org

CWA-COPE Political Contributions Committee (*Communications Workers of America, AFL-CIO*), 501 3rd St. N.W. 20001-2797; (202) 434-1100. Fax, (202)

434-1279. Chris Shelton, President. Web, www.cwa-union.org

International Assn. of Sheet Metal, Air, Rail, and Transportation Workers, Political Action League, 1750 New York Ave. N.W., 6th Floor, 20006-5386; (202) 662-0800. Fax, (202) 662-0880. Steve Dodd, Political Director; Joe Sellers, President. Press, (202) 662-0812. General email, info@smart-union.org Web, http://smart-union.org

International Brotherhood of Electrical Workers Political Action Committee, 900 7th St. N.W., 20001; (202) 728-6046. Fax, (202) 728-6144. Sherilyn Wright, Director, Political and Legislative Affairs. Press, (202) 728-6014. General email, ibewpoliticaldept@ibew.org Web, www.ibew.org

International Brotherhood of Teamsters, *Federal Legislation and Regulation,* 25 Louisiana Ave. N.W., 20001-2194; (202) 624-8741. Fax, (202) 624-8973.

Christy Bailey, Director; Ken Hall, General Secretary–Treasurer. Press, (202) 624-6911.
General email, drive@teamster.org

Web, www.teamster.org

Ironworkers Political Action League, 1750 New York Ave. N.W., #400, 20006; (202) 383-4800. Fax, (202) 638-4856. Dave Kolbe, Political and Legislative Representative; Ron Piksa, General Treasurer.
General email, iwmagazine@wintl.org

Web, www.ironworkers.org

Laborers' Political League of Laborers' International Union of North America, 905 16th St. N.W., 20006-1765; (202) 942-2272. Fax, (202) 942-2307. David Mallino, Legislative and Political Director; Armand E. Sabitoni, General Secretary-Treasurer.
General email, dmallino@liuna.org

Web, www.liuna.org

Machinists Non-Partisan Political League
(International Assn. of Machinists and Aerospace Workers, AFL-CIO), 9000 Machinists Pl., Upper Marlboro, MD 20772-2687; (301) 967-4575. Fax, (301) 967-4595. Rick de la Fuente, Political Action Director; Hasan Solomon, Legislative Director; Dora Cerventes, General Secretary-Treasurer.
Web, www.goiam.org/index.php/mnpl

National Air Traffic Controllers Assn. PAC, 1325 Massachusetts Ave. N.W., 20005; (202) 628-5451. Fax, (202) 628-5767. Patricia Gilbert, Treasurer.
General email, mfevola@natcadc.org

Web, www.natca.org

National Education Assn., *Government Relations,* 1201 16th St. N.W., #510, 20036-3290; (202) 822-7300. Fax, (202) 822-7309. Mary Kusler, Director.
General email, educationvotes@nea.org

Web, www.nea.org

Professional Aviation Safety Specialists PAC, 1200 G St. N.W., #750, 20005; (202) 293-7277. Fax, (202) 293-7727. Abby Bernstein, Legislative Director.
Web, www.passnational.org/about-us/national-office

Seafarers International Union of North America, 5201 Auth Way, Camp Springs, MD 20746-4275; (301) 899-0675. Fax, (301) 899-7355. Michael Sacco, President. Press, (301) 899-0675, ext. 4300.
Web, www.seafarers.org and Twitter, @SeafarersUnion
    Represents U.S. merchant mariners.

United Mine Workers of America, *Coal Miners PAC,* 18354 Quantico Gateway Dr., #200, Triangle, VA 22172; (703) 291-2400. Daniel J. Kane, Treasurer.
General email, mdelbalzo@umwa.org

Web, www.umwa.org

▶**NONCONNECTED**

America Votes, 1155 Connecticut Ave. N.W., #600, 20036; (202) 962-7240. Fax, (202) 962-7241. Greg Speed, President.
Web, www.americavotes.org
    Seeks to mobilize Americans to register and vote around critical issues.

American Sugarbeet Growers Assn. PAC, 1156 15th St. N.W., #1101, 20005; (202) 833-2398. Fax, (240) 235-4291. Ruth Ann Geib, Vice President.
Web, www.americansugarbeet.org

Automotive Free International Trade PAC, 1625 Prince St., #225, Alexandria, VA 22314-2889; (703) 684-8880. Fax, (703) 684-8920. Mary Hanagan, Executive Director. Toll-free, (800) 234-8748.
General email, information@afitpac.com

Web, www.afitpac.com

Black America's PAC, 1325 GSt. N.W., #500, 20005; (202) 552-7422. Fax, (202) 552-7421. Alvin Williams, President.
General email, www.bampac.org/bampac_contact form.org

Web, www.bampac.org and Twitter, @BAM_PAC

Club for Growth, 2001 L St. N.W., #600, 20036, (202) 955-5500. Fax, (202) 955-9466. David McIntosh, President.
General email, www.clubforgrowth.org/contact

Web, www.clubforgrowth.org
    Promotes mainly Republican candidates with conservative economic policies and voting records.

Council for a Livable World, 322 4th St. N.E., 20002-5824; (202) 543-4100. John Tierney, Executive Director; James McKeon, Communications Mgr.
General email, advocacy@clw.org

Web, http://livableworld.org and Twitter, @Livableworld
    Supports congressional candidates who advocate arms control and progressive national security policy.

Deloitte and Touche LLP Federal PAC, 701 Pennsylvania Ave. N.W., #530, 20004; (202) 734-3180. Cindy M. Stevens, Treasurer.
General email, deloittepac@deloitte.com

Web, www.deloittepac.com

EMILY's List, 1800 M St., #375N, 20036; (202) 326-1400. Fax, (202) 326-1415. Stephanie Schriock, President; Jess McIntosh, Communications. Toll-free, 800-68-EMILY.
Web, www.emilyslist.org
    Raises money to support pro-choice Democratic women candidates for political office.

Gay & Lesbian Victory Fund and Leadership Institute, 1133 15th St. N.W., #350, 20005; (202) 842-8679. Fax, (202) 289-3863. Aisha Moodie-Mills, President.
General email, victory@victoryfund.org

Web, www.victoryfund.org and Twitter, @VictoryFund
    Identifies, trains, and supports open lesbian, gay, bisexual, and transgender candidates and officials at the local,

state, and federal levels of government. Raises funds for endorsed candidates.

GOPAC, *2300 Clarendon Blvd., #1305, Arlington, VA 22201; (703) 566-0376. David Avella, Chair.*
General email, contact@gopac.org
Web, www.gopac.org

Recruits and trains conservative Republican candidates for local and state office.

KPMG PAC, *1801 K St. N.W., #12000, 20006 (mailing address: P.O. Box 18254, Washington, DC 20036-9998); (202) 533-5816. Fax, (202) 533-8516. Stephen E. Allis, Treasurer.*
Web, www.kpmg.com and Twitter, @ kpmg_us

KPMG is a global network of firms providing audit, tax, and advisory services to businesses.

PricewaterhouseCoopers PAC, *600 13th St. N.W., #1000, 20005; (202) 414-1000. Fax, (202) 414-1301. Laura Cox Kaplan, Principal-in-Charge of U.S. Government Regulatory Affairs and Public Policy; Gary Price, Chief Administrative Officer.*
Web, http://pwc.com

Progressive Majority, *1825 K St. N.W., #450, 20006; (202) 248-5639. Fax, (202) 429-0755. Gloria A. Totten, President.*
General email, manager@progressivemajority.org
Web, www.progressivemajority.org

Identifies, trains, and supports progressive candidates for public office at the state and local levels. Prioritizes recruitment of candidates of color and people new to the political process.

▶TRADE, MEMBERSHIP, AND HEALTH

Action Committee for Rural Electrification *(National Rural Electric Cooperative Assn.), 4301 Wilson Blvd., Arlington, VA 22203-1860; (703) 907-5500. Fax, (703) 907-5516. Michael Whelan, Director.*
General email, mike.whelan@nreca.coop
Web, www.nreca.coop/political-action/acre

Represents national interests of cooperative electric utility companies and their consumers.

American Assn. for Justice PAC, *777 6th St. N.W., #200, 20001; (202) 965-3500. Fax, (202) 338-8709. Tara Pinto, Associate Director. Toll-free, (800) 424-2725.*
General email, outreach@justice.org
Web, www.justice.org
(Formerly the Assn. of Trial Lawyers of America.)

American Bankers Assn. BankPAC, *1120 Connecticut Ave. N.W., 8th Floor, 20036; (202) 663-5113. Fax, (202) 663-7544. John Hall, Treasurer.*
General email, gfields@aba.com
Web, www.aba.com

American Health Care Assn. Political Action Committee (AHCA-PAC), *1201 L St. N.W., 20005-4015; (202) 898-2844. Fax, (202) 842-3860. Jennifer Knorr Hahs, Political Action Director.*
Web, www.ahcancal.org

American Medical Assn. Political Action Committee (AMPAC), *25 Massachusetts Ave. N.W., #600, 20001; (202) 789-7400. Fax, (202) 789-7469. Kevin Walker, Executive Director.*
Web, www.ampaconline.org

BUILD PAC of the National Assn. of Home Builders, *1201 15th St. N.W., 20005-2800; (202) 266-8259. Fax, (202) 266-8400. Meghan Everngam, Vice President.*
Web, www.nahb.org/buildpac

Membership: includes building contractors, remodelers, and others who support candidates and issues affecting the home-building industry.

Credit Union Legislative Action Council, *601 Pennsylvania Ave. N.W., #600, South Bldg., 20004-2601; (202) 638-5777. Fax, (202) 638-7734. Trey Hawkins, Political Affairs Director. Toll-free, (800) 356-9655, ext. 4077.*
General email, thawkins@cuna.coop
Web, www.cuna.org/culac

Dealers Election Action Committee of the National Automobile Dealers Assn., *412 1st St. S.E., 1st Floor, 20003; (202) 627-6755. Fax, (703) 556-8571. Peter K. Welch, President. Information, (703) 821-7000.*
General email, help@nada.org
Web, www.nada.org/advocacy&outreach

Human Rights Campaign PAC (HRC), *1640 Rhode Island Ave. N.W., 20036; (202) 216-1545. Fax, (202) 347-5323. Mike Mings, Director. TTY, (202) 216-1572.*
General email, hrc@hrc.org
Web, www.hrc.org/issues/pages/federal-pac

Supports pro-equality candidates for state and federal office who favor lesbian, gay, bisexual, and transgender equality.

Independent Insurance Agents and Brokers of America Political Action Committee (InsurPac), *20 F St. N.W., #610, 20001; (202) 863-7000. Fax, (202) 863-7015. Nathan Riedel, Vice President of Political Affairs.*
General email, InsurPac@iiaba.net
Web, www.independentagent.com/governmentaffairs/insurPac/default.aspx

Insurance and Financial Advisors PAC, *2901 Telestar Court, Falls Church, VA 22042-1205; (703) 770-8100. Fax, (703) 770-8151. Magenta Ishak, Vice President for Political Affairs.*
General email, mishak@naifa.org
Web, www.naifa.org/advocacy/ifapac and Twitter, @NAIFA

National Active and Retired Federal Employees PAC (NARFE), *606 N. Washington St., Alexandria, VA 22314; (703) 838-7760. Fax, (703) 838-7785. John Hatton, Deputy Legislative Director. Member relations, (800) 456-8410.*

General email, leg@narfe.org

Web, www.narfe.org/legislation/articles.cfm?ID=1778

National Assn. of Broadcasters Television and Radio Political Action Committee, 101 Constitution Ave. N.W., #L-110, 20001; (202) 341-3780. Fax, (202) 478-0342. Geoff Ziebert, Executive Director.
General email, nabpac@nabpac.org

Web, www.nabpac.org

National Assn. of Social Workers Political Action for Candidate Election, 750 1st St. N.E., #800, 20002-4241; (202) 408-8600. Fax, (202) 336-8311. Brian Dautch, Senior Political Affairs Associate.
Web, www.naswdc.org/pace

National Beer Wholesalers Assn. PAC, 1101 King St., #600, Alexandria, VA 22314-2944; (703) 683-4300. Fax, (703) 683-8965. Linda Auglis, Director.
General email, info@nbwa.org

Web, www.nbwa.org

National Committee to Preserve Social Security and Medicare PAC, 10 G St. N.E., #600, 20002-4215; (202) 216-0420. Fax, (202) 216-0445. Phillip Rotondi, Administrator. Press, (202) 216-8378.
Web, www.ncpssm.org

Physical Therapy Political Action Committee (PT-PAC), 1111 N. Fairfax St., Alexandria, VA 22314-1488; (703) 706-3163. Fax, (703) 706-3246. Michael Matlack, Director.
Web, www.ptpac.org

Planned Parenthood Action Fund, 1110 Vermont Ave. N.W., #300, 20005; (202) 973-4800. Fax, (202) 296-3242. Cecile Richards, President.
General email, actionfund@ppfa.org

Web, www.ppaction.org

Nonpartisan organization that supports candidates who advocate for reproductive health care, including sex education, health care reform for women, birth control, and legal abortion access in the United States. Seeks to influence voters through grassroots organization and education. Monitors legislation and regulations.

Seniors Housing Political Action Committee, 5225 Wisconsin Ave. N.W., #502, 20015; (202) 237-0900. Fax, (202) 237-1616. Jeanne McGlynn Delgado, Vice President, Public Affairs.
Web, www.seniorshousing.org/sh-pac.php

Solar Energy Industries Assn. PAC, 600 14th St. N. W., 20005; (202) 682-0556. Fax, (202) 682-0559. Suzanne Farris, Director, (202) 556-2881.
General email, pac@seia.org

Web, www.seia.org/cs/solarPAC

Seeks to raise awareness of solar energy and supports congressional candidates who promote solar technologies in the global marketplace.

Women's Campaign Fund, 718 7th St. N.W., 2nd Floor, 20001; (202) 796-8259. Betsy Mullins, President.

General email, info@wcfonline.org

Web, www.wcfonline.org and Twitter, @WCFonline

Nonpartisan organization that seeks to increase the number of women in elected office who support reproductive health choices.

Super Political Action Committees

Independent expenditure-only committees, commonly known as SuperPACs, are organizations registered with the Federal Election Commission that may raise unlimited funds from individuals, corporations, businesses, and others to advocate for or against specific candidates for public office. Direct contributions to candidates' campaigns are prohibited.

▶**NONCONNECTED**

American Crossroads, P.O. Box 34413, 20043; (202) 559-6428. Jo Ann Davidson, Chair; Steven Law, President.
General email, info@americancrossroads.org

Web, www.americancrossroads.org

Promotes Republican candidates who support strong defense, free enterprise, and limited government. Targets voters through television ads, mailings, and phone campaigns.

American Dental Assn. PAC, 1111 14th St. N.W., #1100, 20005; (202) 898-2400. (202) 898-2424. Fax, (202) 898-2437. Sarah Milligan, Director of Political Affairs.
General email, govtpol@ada.org

Web, www.ada.org

Nonpartisan organization that promotes congressional candidates who advocate for dentists, oral health, and oral health's connection to overall health. Provides educational resources to dentists interested in seeking public office at local, state, or national levels.

Club for Growth Action, 2001 L St. N.W., #600, 20036; (202) 955-5500. Fax, (202) 955-9466. David McIntosh, President.
Web, www.clubforgrowth.org

Promotes fiscally conservative congressional candidates during Republican primary and general campaigns. Interests include limited government, low taxes, estate tax repeal, social security reform, free trade, tax code reform, school choice, and deregulation.

National Realtors Assn. Political Action Committee, 500 New Jersey Ave. N.W., 20001-2020; (202) 383-1000. Walt Witek, Senior Vice President, Political Affairs. Toll-free, (800) 874-6500.
Web, www.realtor.org/topics/rpac

Nonpartisan organization that promotes federal, state, and local candidates who advocate for private property rights and free enterprise. (Headquarters in Chicago.)

United Mine Workers of America, *Power PAC,* 18354 Quantico Gateway Dr., #200, Triangle, VA 22172-1779; (703) 291-2400. Daniel J. Kane, Treasurer.

General email, mdelbalzo@umwa.org

Web, www.umwa.org

Women Vote! – EMILY's List, *1800 M St. N.W., #375N, 20036; (202) 326-1400. Melissa Williams, Senior Director.* Web, http://emilyslist.org/pages/entry/women-vote

Seeks to influence women to vote for pro-choice Democratic women candidates and other Democratic candidates. Targets candidates opposed to these positions.

Working for Us PAC, *888 16th St. N.W., #650, 20006; (202) 499-7420. Steve Rosenthal, President.* General email, info@workingforuspac.org

Web, www.workingforuspac.org

Promotes candidates focused on job creation, health care reform, and expanding public services. Campaigns against candidates opposed to these principles. (Affiliated with The Organizing Group.)

Political Interest Groups

▶NONGOVERNMENTAL

American Conservative Union (ACU), *1331 H St. N.W., #500, 20005; (202) 347-9388. Fax, (202) 347-9389. Dan Schneider, Executive Director.* General email, acu@conservative.org

Web, www.conservative.org

Legislative interest organization that focuses on defense, foreign policy, economics, the national budget, taxes, and legal and social issues. Monitors legislation and regulations.

American Family Voices, *1250 Eye St. N.W., #250, 20005; (202) 393-4352. Fax, (202) 331-0131. Michael Lux, President.* General email, admin@americanfamilyvoices.org

Web, www.americanfamilyvoices.org

Advocates on behalf of middle-class and low-income families dealing with economic, health care, and consumer issues.

Americans for Democratic Action, *1629 K St. N.W., #300, 20006; (202) 600-7762. Fax, (202) 204-8637. Don Kusler, Executive Director.* General email, info@adaction.org

Web, www.adaction.org and Twitter, @ADAction

Legislative interest organization that seeks to strengthen civil, constitutional, women's, family, workers', and human rights, and promotes grassroots activism. Interests include education, health care, immigration, peace, tax reform, and voter access.

Americans for Prosperity, *1310 N. Courthouse Rd., #700, Arlington, VA 22201; (703) 224-3200. Fax, (703) 224-3201. Tim Phillips, President. Toll-free, (866) 730-0150.* General email, info@AFPhq.org

Web, www.americansforprosperity.org

Grassroots organization that seeks to educate citizens about economic policy and encourage their participation

in the public policy process. Supports limited government and free markets on the local, state, and federal levels. Specific interests include Social Security, trade, and taxes. Monitors legislation and regulations.

Americans United For Change, *1250 Eye St. N.W., #250, 20005 (mailing address: P.O. Box 34606, Washington, DC 20043); (202) 470-6954. Fax, (202) 331-0131. Caroline Ciccone, Executive Director. Press, (202) 470-5878.* Web, http://americansunitedforchange.org and Twitter, @AU4Change

Conducts national campaigns that utilize grassroots organizing, polling, and message development; earned and paid media; online organizing; and paid and volunteer phonework to advance the progressive agenda. Interests include Medicare, Medicaid, Social Security, health care reform, gun violence prevention, clean energy, and economic fairness and security.

Campaign for America's Future, *1825 K St. N.W., #400, 20006; (202) 955-5665. Fax, (202) 955-5606. Robert L. Borosage, Co-Director; Roger Hickey, Co-Director.* Web, www.ourfuture.org and Twitter, @OurFuture

Operates the Campaign for America's Future and the Institute for America's Future. Advocates policies to help working people. Supports improved employee benefits, including health care, child care, and paid family leave; promotes lifelong education and training of workers. Seeks full employment, higher wages, and increased productivity. Monitors legislation and regulations.

Cato Institute, *1000 Massachusetts Ave. N.W., 20001-5403; (202) 842-0200. Fax, (202) 842-3490. Peter Goettler, President. Press, (202) 842-0200, ext. 800.* General email, pr@cato.org

Web, www.cato.org and Twitter, @CatoInstitute

Public policy research organization that advocates limited government and individual liberty. Interests include privatization and deregulation, low and simple taxes, and reduced government spending. Encourages voluntary solutions to social and economic problems.

Center for American Progress, *1333 H St. N.W., 10th Floor, 20005; (202) 682-1611. Fax, (202) 682-1867. Neera Tanden, President.* General email, progress@americanprogress.org

Web, www.americanprogress.org and Twitter, @amprog

Nonpartisan research and educational institute that strives to ensure opportunity for all Americans. Advocates policies to create sustained economic growth and new opportunities. Supports fiscal discipline, shared prosperity, and investments in people through education, health care, and workforce training.

Center for Public Justice, *1115 Massachusetts Ave. N.W., 3rd Floor, 20005 (mailing address: P.O. Box 48368, Washington, DC 20002-0368); (202) 695-2667. Stephanie Summers, Chief Executive Officer.* General email, inquiries@cpjustice.org

Web, www.cpjustice.org and Twitter, @cpjustice

Christian think tank advocating biblical-based solutions to policymakers. Interests include education reform, foreign affairs, welfare policy, and religious freedom.

Christian Coalition of America, *P.O. Box 37030, 20013-7030; (202) 479-6900. Fax, (202) 479-4262. Roberta Combs, President. Press, (202) 549-6257.*
General email, coalition@cc.org
Web, www.cc.org and Twitter, @ccoalition

Membership: individuals who support traditional, conservative Christian values. Represents members' views to all levels of government and to the media.

Christian Science Committee on Publication, *Federal Office, 1001 G St., #1000 West, 20001 (mailing address: P.O. Box 15726, Washington, DC 20003); (202) 296-2190. Fax, (202) 296-2426. Gary Jones, Manager.*
General email, federal@christianscience.com
Web, www.christianscience.com/member-resources/committee-on-publications

Public service organization that provides information on the religious convictions and practices of Christian Scientists; works with Congress and regulatory agencies to ensure that the interests of Christian Science are not adversely affected by law or regulations.

Common Cause, *805 13th St. N.W., #800, 20005; (202) 833-1200. Fax, (202) 659-3716. Miles Rapoport, President, (202) 736-5740. Press, (202) 736-5788.*
General email, mrapoport@commoncause.org
Web, www.commoncause.org and Twitter, @CommonCause

Nonpartisan citizens' lobby that works for reform in federal and state government and politics. Advocates national and state limits on political spending, small donor-based public financing of election campaigns, high ethical standards and tough ethics enforcement for public officials, strong voting rights laws and modern voting equipment, and free exchange of ideas online.

Concerned Women for America, *1015 15th St. N.W., #1100, 20005; (202) 488-7000. Fax, (202) 488-0806. Penny Young Nance, Chief Executive Officer.*
Web, www.cwfa.org and Twitter, @CWforA

Educational organization that seeks to protect the rights of the family and preserve Judeo-Christian values. Monitors legislation affecting family and religious issues.

Concord Coalition, *1011 Arlington Blvd., #300, Arlington, VA 22209; (703) 894-6222. Fax, (703) 894-6231. Robert L. Bixby, Executive Director.*
General email, concordcoalition@concordcoalition.org
Web, www.concordcoalition.org and Twitter, @ConcordC

Nonpartisan grassroots organization dedicated to educating the public about the causes and consequences of federal budget deficits, the long-term challenges facing America's unsustainable entitlement programs, how to build a sound foundation for economic growth, and ensuring that Social Security, Medicare, and Medicaid are secure for all generations.

The Conservative Caucus (TCC), *92 Main St., #202-8, Warrenton, VA 20816; (540) 219-4536. Peter J. Thomas, Chair.*
General email, info@conservativeusa.org
Web, www.conservativeusa.org

Legislative interest organization that promotes grassroots activity on issues such as national defense and economic and tax policy. The Conservative Caucus Research, Analysis, and Education Foundation studies public issues including Central American affairs, defense policy, and federal funding of political advocacy groups.

Eagle Forum, *Washington Office, 316 Pennsylvania Ave. S.E., #203, 20003; (202) 544-0353. Fax, (202) 547-6996. Glyn Wright, Executive Director.*
General email, glyn@eagleforum.org
Web, www.eagleforum.org

Supports conservative, pro-family policies at all levels of government. Promotes traditional marriage, pro-life policies, limited government, and American sovereignty. Other concerns include education, national defense, and taxes. (Headquarters in Alton, Ill.)

English First, *8001 Forbes Pl., #102, Springfield, VA 22151-2205; (703) 321-8818. Fax, (703) 321-8408. Frank McGlynn, Executive Director.*
Web, www.englishfirst.org

Seeks to make English the official language of the United States. Advocates policies that make English education available to all children. Monitors legislation and regulations. Opposes multilingual education and governmental policies, including Clinton Executive Order 13166.

Family Research Council, *801 G St. N.W., 20001-3729; (202) 393-2100. Fax, (202) 393-2134. Tony Perkins, President. Toll-free, (800) 225-4008.*
Web, www.frc.org

Legislative interest organization that analyzes issues affecting the family and seeks to ensure that the interests of the family are considered in the formulation of public policy.

Feminist Majority, *1600 Wilson Blvd., #801, Arlington, VA 22209-2505; (703) 522-2214. Fax, (703) 522-2219. Eleanor Smeal, President; Alice Cohan, Political Director.*
General email, feedback@feminist.org
Web, www.feministmajority.org and Twitter, @femmajority

Legislative interest group that seeks to increase the number of feminists running for public office; promotes a national feminist agenda.

Food Policy Action, *1436 U St. N.W., #200, 20009; (202) 631-6362. Claire Benjamin, Executive Director, (202) 631-6362.*
General email, info@foodpolicyaction.org
Web, http://foodpolicyaction.org

Promotes policies that support healthy food options; works to reduce hunger and improve food access; publishes a congressional vote and legislation scorecard.

Free Congress Research and Education Foundation (FCF), *901 N. Washington, #206, Alexandria, VA 22314; (703) 837-0030. Fax, (703) 837-0031. James Gilmore, President.*
General email, contact@freecongress.org

Web, www.freecongress.org and Twitter, @freecongress

Conservative political think tank that promotes traditional values. Studies economic and transportation policy. Trains citizens to participate in a democracy.

FreedomWorks, *400 N. Capitol St. N.W., #765, 20001; (202) 783-3870. Fax, (202) 942-7649. Adam Brandon, President. Toll-free, (888) 564-6273.*
Web, www.freedomworks.org and Twitter, @FreedomWorks

Recruits, educates, trains, and mobilizes citizens to promote lower taxes, less government, and greater economic freedom. Maintains scorecards on members of the Senate and House based on adherence to FreedomWorks positions.

Frontiers of Freedom, *4094 Majestic Lane, #380, Fairfax, VA 22033; (703) 246-0110. Fax, (703) 246-0129. George C. Landrith, President.*
General email, info@ff.org

Web, www.ff.org

Seeks to increase personal freedom through a reduction in the size of government. Interests include property rights, regulatory and tax reform, global warming, national missile defense, Internet regulation, school vouchers, and Second Amendment rights. Monitors legislation and regulations.

The Heritage Foundation, *214 Massachusetts Ave. N.E., 20002-4999; (202) 546-4400. Fax, (202) 546-8328. Jim DeMint, President. Press, (202) 675-1761.*
General email, info@heritage.org

Web, www.heritage.org

Conservative public policy research organization that conducts research and analysis and sponsors lectures, debates, and policy forums advocating individual freedom, limited government, the free market system, and a strong national defense.

Log Cabin Republicans, *1090 Vermont Ave. N.W., #850, 20005; (202) 420-7873. Gregory T. Angelo, President.*
General email, info@logcabin.org

Web, www.logcabin.org

Membership: lesbian, gay, bisexual, transgender and allied Republicans. Educates conservative politicians and voters on LGBT issues; disseminates information; conducts seminars for members. Promotes conservative values among members of the gay community. Raises campaign funds. Monitors legislation and regulations.

Millennium Institute, *1875 Eye St. N.W., #549, 20006; (202) 857-5204. Fax, (202) 383-6209. Hans R. Herren, President.*
General email, info@millennium-institute.org

Web, www.millennium-institute.org

Research and development organization that provides computer modeling services for planning and building a sustainable economic and ecological future.

National Center for Policy Analysis, *600 Pennsylvania Ave. S.E., #310, 20003; (202) 830-0177. Allen West, Executive Director; Brian Williams, Legislative Director.*
General email, governmentrelations@ncpa.org

Media email, media@ncpa.org

Web, www.ncpa.org

Nonpartisan public policy research organization. Disseminates research on health care, energy, national security, taxes, retirement, small business, and the environment. Develops policies that promote private, free-market alternatives to government regulation and control. (Headquarters in Dallas, Tex.)

National Jewish Democratic Council, *P.O. Box 65683, 20035; (202) 216-9060. Delores Henderson, Administrator.*
General email, njdc@njdc.org

Web, www.njdc.org

Encourages Jewish involvement in the Democratic party and its political campaigns. Monitors and analyzes domestic and foreign policy issues that concern the American Jewish community.

National Organization for Marriage, *2029 K St. N.W., #300, 20006; (888) 894-3604. Brian S. Brown, President.*
General email, contact@nationformarriage.org

Web, www.nationformarriage.org

Supports marriage-related initiatives at state and local levels, with an emphais on the Northeast and West Coast. Opposes same-sex marriage. Monitors legislation.

National Organization for Women (NOW), *1100 H St. N.W., #300, 20005; (202) 628-8669. Terry O'Neill, President. TTY, (202) 331-9002.*
General email, now@now.org

Web, www.now.org

Membership: women and men interested in feminist civil rights. Acts through demonstrations, court cases, and legislative efforts to improve the status of all women. Interests include increasing the number of women in elected and appointed office, improving women's economic status and health coverage, ending violence against women, preserving abortion rights, and abolishing discrimination based on gender, race, age, and sexual orientation.

National Taxpayers Union, *Communications, 25 Massachusetts Ave. N.W., #140, Alexandria, VA 20001; (703) 683-5700. Peter Sepp, President; Nan Swift, Federal Affairs.*
General email, ntu@ntu.org

Web, www.ntu.org

Citizens' interest group that promotes tax and spending reduction at all levels of government. Supports constitutional amendments to balance the federal budget and limit taxes.

NDN (New Democrat Network), *1200 18th St. N.W., 7th Floor, 20036; (202) 544-9200. Simon Rosenberg, President.*
General email, info@ndn.org
Web, www.ndn.org

Studies progressive politics as it relates to the rise in conservatism, changing voter trends, and new media strategies for campaigns.

NETWORK (National Catholic Social Justice Lobby), *25 E St. N.W., #200, 20001-1630; (202) 347-9797. Fax, (202) 347-9864. Sr. Simone Campbell, Executive Director.*
General email, networkupdate@networklobby.org
Web, www.networklobby.org

Catholic social justice lobby that coordinates political activity and promotes economic and social justice. Monitors legislation and regulations.

New America Foundation, *740 15th St., #900, 20036; (202) 986-2700. Fax, (202) 986-3696. Anne-Marie Slaughter, President; Eric Schmidt, Chair.*
Web, www.newamerica.org

Public policy institute that seeks to bring innovative policy ideas to the fore and nurture the next generation of public policy intellectuals. Sponsors research, writing, conferences, and events. Funds studies of government programs. Seeks to stimulate more informed reporting and analyses of government activities.

No Labels, *1130 Connecticut Ave. N.W., #325, 20036; (202) 588-1990. Fax, (202) 588-7383. Margaret Kimbrell, Executive Director.*
General email, backoffice@nolabels.org
Web, www.nolabels.org

Promotes a bipartisan approach to improving issues such as unemployment, social security and Medicare, the federal budget, and securing energy.

People for the American Way (PFAW), *1101 15th St. N.W., #600, 20005-5002; (202) 467-4999. Fax, (202) 293-2672. Michael B. Keegan, President. Toll-free, (800) 326-7329.*
General email, pfaw@pfaw.org
Web, www.pfaw.org

Nonprofit organization that promotes public policies that reflect the values of freedom, fairness, and equal opportunity; advocates for constitutional protections and civil rights, and for strong democratic institutions, including a federal judiciary that upholds individual rights. Conducts leadership development programs for college students, African American religious leaders, and young elected officials.

Public Affairs Council, *2121 K St. N.W., #900, 20037; (202) 787-5950. Fax, (202) 787-5942. Douglas G. Pinkham, President.*
General email, pac@pac.org
Web, www.pac.org

Membership: public affairs professionals. Informs and counsels members on public affairs programs. Sponsors conferences on election issues, government relations, and political trends. Sponsors the Foundation for Public Affairs.

Public Citizen, *Congress Watch, 215 Pennsylvania Ave. S.E., 20003; (202) 546-4996. Lisa Gilbert, Director.*
General email, action@citizen.org
Web, www.citizen.org/congress

Citizens' interest group engaged in public education, research, media outreach, and citizen activism. Interests include campaign finance reform, consumer protection, financial services, public health and safety, government reform, trade, and the environment.

Rainbow PUSH Coalition, *Public Policy Institute, Government Relations and Telecommunications Project, 727 15th St. N.W., #1200, 20005; (202) 393-7874. Fax, (202) 393-1495. Steve Smith, Executive Director, Government Relations; Jesse L. Jackson Sr., President; Frank Watkins, Directory, Public Policy. Press, (773) 373-3366.*
General email, info@rainbowpush.org
Web, http://rainbowpush.org/pages/get_local_washington_dc# and Twitter, @RPCoalition

Independent civil rights organization concerned with foreign policy and public policy toward political, economic, and social justice for women, workers, and minorities. Interests include poverty and hunger, peace and justice, gun violence, corporate diversity, and voter registration. (Headquarters in Chicago, Ill.)

Republican Jewish Coalition, *50 F St. N.W., #100, 20001; (202) 638-6688. Fax, (202) 638-6694. Matthew Brooks, Executive Director; David M. Flaum, National Chair.*
General email, rjc@rjchq.org
Web, www.rjchq.org and Twitter, @RJC

Legislative interest group that works to build support among Republican party decision makers on issues of concern to the Jewish community; studies domestic and foreign policy issues affecting the Jewish community; supports a strong relationship between the United States and Israel. Monitors legislation and regulations.

Taxpayers for Common Sense, *651 Pennsylvania Ave. S.E., 20003; (202) 546-8500. Ryan Alexander, President.*
General email, info@taxpayer.net
Web, www.taxpayer.net

Nonpartisan organization that works with Congress, the media, and grassroots organizations to reduce government waste and increase accountability for federal expenditures. Disseminates research results to the public via media and Web outreach.

Third Way, *1025 Connecticut Ave. N.W., #501, 20036; (202) 384-1700. Fax, (202) 775-0430. Jonathan Cowan, President.*
General email, contact@thirdway.org
Web, www.thirdway.org

Think tank that works with moderate and progressive legislators to develop modern solutions to economic, cultural, and national security issues. Conducts studies and polls; develops policy papers and strategy documents.

Traditional Values Coalition, *Washington Office,* 139 C St. S.E., 20003; (202) 547-8570. Fax, (202) 546-6403. Andrea S. Lafferty, President. General email, mail@traditionalvalues.org

Web, www.traditionalvalues.org

Legislative interest group that supports religious liberties and traditional, conservative Judeo-Christian values. Interests include anti-abortion issues, pornography, decreased federal funding for the arts, parental rights, and the promotion of school prayer. Opposes gay rights legislation. (Headquarters in Anaheim, Calif.)

U.S. Chamber of Commerce, *Political Affairs and Federation Relations,* 1615 H St. N.W., 20062-2000; (202) 463-5560. Robert Engstrom, Senior Vice President. Web, www.uschamber.com/political-affairs-and-federation-relations

Federation that works to enact pro-business legislation; tracks election law legislation; coordinates the chamber's candidate endorsement program and its grassroots lobbying activities.

Urban Institute, 2100 M St. N.W., 20037; (202) 833-7200. Fax, (202) 467-5775. Sarah Rosen Wartell, President. Public Affairs, (202) 261-5709. General email, publicaffairs@urban.org

Web, www.urban.org

Nonpartisan research and education organization. Investigates U.S. social and economic problems; encourages discussion on solving society's problems, improving and implementing government decisions, and increasing citizens' awareness of public choices.

Veterans of Foreign Wars of the United States, *National Legislative Service,* 200 Maryland Ave. N.E., 20002-5724; (202) 543-2239. Fax, (202) 543-2746. Robert E. Wallace, Executive Director. Web, www.vfw.org/VFW-in-DC/National-Legislative-Service

Represents members before Congress and participates in congressional hearings, with a focus on health and quality of life issues. Manages the VFW Action Corps grassroots organization. Monitors legislation and regulations.

Washington Government Relations Group, 1325 G St. N.W., #500, 20005; (202) 449-7651. Fax, (202) 449-7701. Marcus Sebastian Mason, President. General email, info@wgrginc.org

Web, www.wgrginc.org

Works to enrich the careers and leadership abilities of African American government relations professionals working in business, financial institutions, law firms, trade associations, and nonprofit organizations. Increases

dialogue between members and senior-level policymakers to produce public policy solutions.

Women Legislators' Lobby (WiLL), *Policy and Programs,* 322 4th St. N.E., 20002; (202) 544-5055. Fax, (202) 544-7612. Adzi Vokhiwa, Senior Program Associate. Web, www.willwand.org and Twitter, @WomenLegisLobby

Bipartisan group of women state legislators. Sponsors conferences, training workshops, issue briefings, and seminars; provides information and action alerts on ways federal policies affect states. Interests include federal budget priorities, national security, and arms control. Monitors related legislation and regulations. (National office in Arlington, Mass. Affiliated with Women's Action for New Directions.)

Women's Action for New Directions (WAND), *Washington Office,* 322 4th St. N.E., 20002; (202) 544-5055. Fax, (202) 544-7612. Adzi Vokhiwa, Senior Associate; Kathy Crandall Robinson, Senior Public Policy Director. General email, peace@wand.org

Web, www.wand.org and Twitter, @WomensAction

Seeks to empower women to act politically to reduce violence and militarism and redirect excessive military resources toward unmet human and environmental needs. Monitors legislation on federal budget priorities. (Headquarters in Arlington, Mass.)

Women's Policy, Inc., 409 12th St. S.W., #600, 20024; (202) 554-2323. Fax, (202) 554-2346. Cynthia A. Hall, President. General email, webmaster@womenspolicy.org

Web, www.womenspolicy.org and Twitter, @WomensPolicyInc

Nonpartisan organization that provides legislative analysis and information services on congressional actions affecting women and their families. Works with congressional women's caucus leaders at federal, state, and local levels, as well as other groups, to provide information pertaining to women's issues. Sponsors Congressional Fellowships on Women and Public Policy for graduate students who are placed in congressional offices from January through August to work on policy issues affecting women.

Women's Research and Education Institute (WREI), 3808 Brighton Court, Alexandria, VA 22305; (703) 837-1977. Susan Scanlan, President. General email, wrei@wrei.org

Web, www.wrei.org

Analyzes policy-relevant information on women's issues. Educates the public through reports and conferences. Interests include women's employment and economic status; women in nontraditional occupations; military women and veterans; older women; women's health issues; and women and immigration. Library open to the public.

POLITICAL PARTY ORGANIZATIONS

Democratic

▶NONGOVERNMENTAL

Democratic Congressional Campaign Committee,
430 S. Capitol St. S.E., 20003-4024; (202) 863-1500.
Fax, (202) 485-3412. Rep. Ben Ray Luján, Chair.
General email, dccc@dccc.org
Web, www.dccc.org

Provides Democratic House candidates with financial and other campaign services.

Democratic Governors Assn., *1225 Eye St. N.W., #1100,*
20005; (202) 772-5600. Fax, (202) 772-5602. Dan Malloy,
Chair; Elisabeth Pearson, Executive Director.
General email, dga@dga.net
Web, www.democraticgovernors.org

Serves as a liaison between governors' offices and Democratic Party organizations; assists Democratic gubernatorial candidates.

Democratic National Committee (DNC), *430 S. Capitol St.*
S.E., 20003; (202) 863-8000. Fax, (202) 863-8063.
Rep. Debbie Wasserman Schultz, Chair. Press, (202)
863-8148.
General email, info@democrats.org
Web, www.democrats.org

Formulates and promotes Democratic Party policies and positions; assists Democratic candidates for state and national office; organizes national political activities; works with state and local officials and organizations.

Democratic National Committee (DNC), *Assn. of State*
Democratic Chairs, 430 S. Capitol St. S.E., 20003;
(202) 863-8000. Raymond Buckley, President. Press,
(202) 863-8148.
General email, info@democrats.org
Web, http://asdc.democrats.org

Acts as a liaison between state parties and the DNC; works to strengthen state parties for national, state, and local elections; conducts fund-raising activities for state parties.

Democratic National Committee (DNC),
Communications, 430 S. Capitol St. S.E., 20003; (202) 863-
8148. Luis Miranda, Director.
General email, DNCPress@dnc.org
Web, www.democrats.org

Assists federal, state, and local Democratic candidates and officials in delivering a coordinated message on current issues; works to improve and expand relations with the press and to increase the visibility of Democratic officials and the Democratic Party.

Democratic National Committee (DNC), *Finance,*
430 S. Capitol St. S.E., 20003; (202) 863-8000.
Fax, (202) 572-7819. Jordan Kaplan, Director.
Press, (202) 863-8148.
General email, info@democrats.org
Web, www.democrats.org

Responsible for developing the Democratic Party's financial base. Coordinates fund-raising efforts for and gives financial support to Democratic candidates in national, state, and local campaigns.

Democratic National Committee (DNC), *Research, 430 S.*
Capitol St. S.E., 20003; (202) 863-8000. Lauren Dillon,
Director. Press, (202) 863-8148.
General email, info@democrats.org
Web, www.democrats.org

Provides Democratic elected officials, candidates, state party organizations, and the general public with information on Democratic Party policy and programs.

Democratic Senatorial Campaign Committee,
120 Maryland Ave. N.E., 20002-5610; (202) 224-2447.
Sen. Jon Tester, Chair; Tom Lopach, Executive Director.
General email, info@dscc.org
Web, www.dscc.org

Provides Democratic senatorial candidates with financial, research, and consulting services.

Woman's National Democratic Club, *Committee on*
Public Policy, 1526 New Hampshire Ave. N.W., 20036;
(202) 232-7363. Fax, (202) 328-8772. Karen Pataky, Chair.
General email, info@democraticwoman.org
Web, www.democraticwoman.org

Studies issues and presents views to congressional committees, the Democratic Party Platform Committee, Democratic leadership groups, elected officials, and other interested groups.

Republican

▶NONGOVERNMENTAL

College Republican National Committee, *1500 K St.*
N.W., #325, 20005; (202) 608-1411. Fax, (202) 608-1429.
Alex Smith, National Chair; Gus Portela, Executive
Director. Information, (888) 765-3564.
General email, team@crnc.org
Web, www.crnc.org

Membership: Republican college students. Promotes grassroots support for the Republican Party and provides campaign assistance.

National Federation of Republican Women, *124 N.*
Alfred St., Alexandria, VA 22314; (703) 548-9688.
Fax, (703) 548-9836. Carrie Almond, President.
General email, mail@nfrw.org
Web, www.nfrw.org

Organizes volunteers for support of Republican candidates for national, state, and local offices; encourages candidacy of Republican women; sponsors campaign management schools. Recruits Republican women candidates for office.

National Republican Congressional Committee, *320 1st St. S.E., 20003-1838; (202) 479-7000. Fax, (202) 863-0693. Rep. Greg Walden, Chair; Rob Simms, Executive Director. Press, (202) 479-7070.*
General email, website@nrcc.org

Web, www.nrcc.org

Provides Republican House candidates with campaign assistance, including financial, public relations, media, and direct mail services.

National Republican Senatorial Committee (NRSC), *425 2nd St. N.E., 20002-4914; (202) 675-6000. Sen. Roger F. Wicker, Chair; Ward Baker, Executive Director.*
General email, info@nrsc.org

Web, www.nrsc.org

Provides Republican senatorial candidates with financial and public relations services.

Republican Governors Assn., *1747 Pennsylvania Ave. N.W., #250, 20006; (202) 662-4140. Fax, (202) 662-4924. Gov. Bill Haslam, Chair; Paul Bennecke, Executive Director.*
General email, info@rga.org

Web, www.rga.org and Twitter, @The_RGA

Serves as a liaison between governors' offices and Republican Party organizations; assists Republican candidates for governor.

Republican Main Street Partnership, *325 7th St. N.W., #610, 20004; (202) 393-4353. Fax, (202) 393-4354. Sarah Chamberlain, President.*
Web, www.republicanmainstreet.org and Twitter, @MainStreetGOP

Membership: centrist Republican Party members of Congress. Develops and promotes moderate Republican policies.

Republican National Committee (RNC), *310 1st St. S.E., 20003; (202) 863-8500. Fax, (202) 863-8820. Reince Priebus, Chair; Sharon Day, Co-Chair. Press, (202) 863-8614.*
General email, ecampaign@gop.com

Web, www.gop.com and Twitter, @GOP

Develops and promotes Republican Party policies and positions; assists Republican candidates for state and national office; sponsors workshops to recruit Republican candidates and provide instruction in campaign techniques; organizes national political activities; works with state and local officials and organizations.

Republican National Committee (RNC), *Communications, 310 1st St. S.E., 20003; (202) 863-8614. Fax, (202) 863-8773. Sean M. Spicer, Director; Allison Moore, Press Secretary.*
General email, RNcommunications@gop.com

Web, www.gop.com

Assists federal, state, and local Republican candidates and officials in delivering a coordinated message on current issues; works to improve and expand relations with the press and to increase the visibility of Republican officials and the Republican message.

Republican National Committee (RNC), *Counsel, 310 1st St. S.E., 20003; (202) 863-8638. Fax, (202) 863-8654. John Phillippe, Chief Counsel; John Ryder, General Counsel. Press, (202) 863-8614.*
General email, counsel@gop.com

Web, www.gop.com

Responsible for legal affairs of the RNC, including equal time and fairness cases before the Federal Communications Commission. Advises the RNC and state parties on redistricting and campaign finance law compliance.

Republican National Committee (RNC), *Finance, 310 1st St. S.E., 20003; (202) 863-8720. Fax, (202) 863-8690. Cara Mason, Director.*
General email, finance@gop.com

Web, www.gop.com

Responsible for developing the Republican Party's financial base. Coordinates fund-raising efforts for and gives financial support to Republican candidates in national, state, and local campaigns.

Ripon Society, *1155 15th St. N.W., #550, 20005; (202) 216-1008. James K. Conzelman, Chief Executive Officer.*
General email, info@riponsociety.org

Web, www.riponsociety.org and Twitter, @RiponSociety

Membership: moderate Republicans. Works for the adoption of moderate policies within the Republican party.

Other Political Parties

▶**NONGOVERNMENTAL**

Green Party of the United States, *6411 Orchard Ave., #101, Takoma Park, MD 20912 (mailing address: P.O. Box 75075, Washington, DC 20013); (202) 319-7191. Cynthia Joseph, Office Manager. Press, (202) 904-7614.*
General email, office@gp.org

Web, www.gp.org

Committed to environmentalism, nonviolence, social justice, and grassroots organizing.

Libertarian Party, *1444 Duke St., Alexandria, VA 22314; (202) 333-0008. Fax, (202) 333-0072. Wes Benedict, Executive Director. Press, (202) 333-0008, ext. 225. Toll-free, (800) 353-2887.*
General email, info@lp.org

Web, www.lp.org

Nationally organized political party. Seeks to bring libertarian ideas into the national political debate. Believes in the primacy of the individual over government; supports property rights, free trade, and eventual elimination of taxes.

114th Congress

Delegations to the 114th Congress

Following are the senators and representatives of state delegations for the 114th Congress. This information is current as of April 25, 2016. Senators are presented first and listed according to seniority. Representatives follow, listed by district. Freshman members appear in italics and "AL" indicates at-large members. # indicates new senators who served in the House of Representatives in the 113th Congress. $ indicates members of the House of Representatives who were elected on November 4, 2014, both to finish the 113th Congress and for a full term in the 114th Congress; they are italicized with the true freshmen members.

ALABAMA

Richard Shelby (R)
Jeff A. Sessions (R)
1. Bradley Byrne (R)
2. Martha Roby (R)
3. Mike Rogers (R)
4. Robert B. Aderholt (R)
5. Mo Brooks (R)
6. *Gary Palmer (R)*
7. Terri A. Sewell (D)

ALASKA

Lisa Murkowski (R)
Dan Sullivan (R)
AL Don A. Young (R)

AMERICAN SAMOA (NON-VOTING DELEGATE)

AL *Amata Coleman Radewagen (R)*

ARIZONA

John McCain (R)
Jeff Flake (R)
1. Ann Kirkpatrick (D)
2. *Martha McSally (R)*
3. Raúl M. Grijalva (D)
4. Paul Gosar (R)
5. Matt Salmon (R)
6. David Schweikert (R)
7. *Ruben Gallego (D)*
8. Trent Franks (R)
9. Kyrsten Sinema (D)

ARKANSAS

John Boozman (R)
Tom Cotton (R) #
1. Rick Crawford (R)
2. *French Hill (R)*
3. Steve Womack (R)
4. *Bruce Westerman (R)*

CALIFORNIA

Dianne Feinstein (D)
Barbara Boxer (D)
1. Doug LaMalfa (R)
2. Jared Huffman (D)
3. John Garamendi (D)
4. Tom McClintock (R)
5. Mike Thompson (D)
6. Doris Matsui (D)
7. Ami Bera (D)
8. Paul Cook (R)
9. Jerry McNerney (D)
10. Jeff Denham (R)
11. *Mark DeSaulnier (D)*
12. Nancy Pelosi (D)
13. Barbara Lee (D)
14. Jackie Speier (D)
15. Eric Swalwell (D)
16. Jim Costa (D)
17. Mike Honda (D)
18. Anna G. Eshoo (D)
19. Zoe Lofgren (D)
20. Sam Farr (D)
21. David G. Valadao (R)
22. Devin Nunes (R)
23. Kevin McCarthy (R)
24. Lois Capps (D)
25. *Steve Knight (R)*
26. Julia Brownley (D)
27. Judy Chu (D)
28. Adam Schiff (D)
29. Tony Cárdenas (D)
30. Brad Sherman (D)
31. *Pete Aguilar (D)*
32. Grace F. Napolitano (D)
33. *Ted Lieu (D)*
34. Xavier Becerra (D)
35. *Norma Torres (D)*
36. Raul Ruiz (D)
37. Karen Bass (D)
38. Linda Sánchez (D)
39. Edward R. Royce (R)
40. Lucille Roybal-Allard (D)
41. Mark Takano (D)
42. Ken Calvert (R)
43. Maxine Waters (D)
44. *Mimi Walters (R)*
45. Janice Hahn (D)
46. Loretta Sánchez (D)
47. Alan Lowenthal (D)
48. Dana Rohrabacher (R)
49. Darrell Issa (R)
50. Duncan Hunter (R)
51. Juan Vargas (D)
52. Scott H. Peters (D)
53. Susan Davis (D)

COLORADO

Michael F. Bennet (D)
Cory Gardner (R) #
1. Diana DeGette (D)
2. Jared Polis (D)
3. Scott Tipton (R)
4. *Ken Buck (R)*
5. Doug Lamborn (R)
6. Mike Coffman (R)
7. Ed Perlmutter (D)

CONNECTICUT

Richard Blumenthal (D)
Chris Murphy (D)
1. John B. Larson (D)
2. Joe Courtney (D)
3. Rosa L. DeLauro (D)
4. James A. Himes (D)
5. Elizabeth Esty (D)

DELAWARE

Tom Carper (D)
Christopher Coons (D)
AL John Carney (D)

DISTRICT OF COLUMBIA (NON-VOTING DELEGATE)

AL Eleanor Holmes Norton (D)

FLORIDA

Bill J. Nelson (D)
Marco Rubio (R)
1. Jeff Miller (R)
2. *Gwen Graham (D)*
3. Ted Yoho (R)
4. Ander Crenshaw (R)
5. Corrine Brown (D)
6. Ron DeSantis (R)
7. John Mica (R)
8. Bill Posey (R)
9. Alan Grayson (D)
10. Daniel Webster (R)
11. Richard Nugent (R)
12. Gus Bilirakis (R)
13. David W. Jolly (R)
14. Kathy Castor (D)
15. Dennis A. Ross (R)
16. Vern Buchanan (R)
17. Thomas J. Rooney (R)
18. Patrick Murphy (D)
19. *Curt Clawson (R)* $
20. Alcee L. Hastings (D)
21. Ted Deutch (D)
22. Lois Frankel (D)
23. Debbie Wasserman
    Schultz (D)
24. Frederica S. Wilson (D)
25. Mario Diaz-Balart (R)
26. *Carlos Curbelo (R)*
27. Ileana Ros-Lehtinen (R)

GEORGIA

Johnny Isakson (R)
David Perdue (R)
1. *Buddy Carter (R)*
2. Sanford D. Bishop
   Jr. (D)
3. Lynn Westmoreland (R)
4. Henry C. (Hank) Johnson
   Jr. (D)
5. John Lewis (D)
6. Tom Price (R)
7. Rob Woodall (R)
8. Austin Scott (R)
9. Doug Collins (R)
10. *Jody Hice (R)*
11. *Barry Loudermilk (R)*
12. *Rick Allen (R)*
13. David Scott (D)
14. Tom Graves (R)

GUAM (NON-VOTING DELEGATE)

AL Madeleine Z. Bordallo (D)

HAWAII

Brian Schatz (D)
Mazie K. Hirono (D)
1. *Mark Takai (D)*
2. Tulsi Gabbard (D)

IDAHO

Mike Crapo (R)
James E. Risch (R)
1. Raúl Labrador (R)
2. Mike Simpson (R)

ILLINOIS

Richard J. Durbin (D)
Mark Kirk (R)
1. Bobby L. Rush (D)
2. Robin Kelly (D)
3. Daniel Lipinski (D)
4. Luis V. Gutierrez (D)
5. Mike Quigley (D)
6. Peter Roskam (R)
7. Danny K. Davis (D)
8. Tammy Duckworth (D)
9. Jan Schakowsky (D)
10. *Bob Dold (R)*
11. Bill Foster (D)
12. *Mike Bost (R)*
13. Rodney Davis (R)
14. Randy Hultgren (R)
15. John Shimkus (R)
16. Adam Kinzinger (R)
17. Cheri Bustos (D)
18. *Darin LaHood (R)*

INDIANA

Dan Coats (R)
Joe Donnelly (D)
1. Pete Visclosky (D)
2. Jackie Walorski (R)
3. Marlin Stutzman (R)
4. Todd Rokita (R)
5. Susan W. Brooks (R)
6. Luke Messer (R)
7. André Carson (D)
8. Larry Bucshon (R)
9. Todd Young (R)

IOWA

Chuck Grassley (R)
Joni Ernst (R)
1. *Rod Blum (R)*
2. Dave Loebsack (D)
3. *David Young (R)*
4. Steve King (R)

KANSAS

Pat Roberts (R)
Jerry Moran (R)
1. Tim Huelskamp (R)
2. Lynn Jenkins (R)
3. Kevin Yoder (R)
4. Mike Pompeo (R)

KENTUCKY

Mitch McConnell (R)
Rand Paul (R)
1. Ed Whitfield (R)
2. Brett Guthrie (R)
3. John Yarmuth (D)
4. Thomas Massie (R)
5. Hal Rogers (R)
6. Andy Barr (R)

LOUISIANA

David Vitter (R)
Bill Cassidy (R) #
1. Steve Scalise (R)
2. Cedric Richmond (D)
3. Charles W. Boustany Jr. (R)
4. John Fleming (R)
5. *Ralph Abraham (R)*
6. *Garret Graves (R)*

MAINE

Susan Collins (R)
Angus King (I)
1. Chellie Pingree (D)
2. *Bruce Poliquin (R)*

MARYLAND

Barbara Mikulski (D)
Benjamin L. Cardin (D)
1. *Andy Harris (R)*
2. C. A. (Dutch) Ruppersberger
   (D)
3. John Sarbanes (D)
4. Donna F. Edwards (D)
5. Steny Hoyer (D)
6. John Delaney (D)
7. Elijah E. Cummings (D)
8. Chris Van Hollen (D)

MASSACHUSETTS

Elizabeth Warren (D)
Edward J. Markey (D)
1. Richard E. Neal (D)
2. Jim McGovern (D)
3. Niki Tsongas (D)
4. Joe Kennedy III (D)

5. Katherine Clark (D)
6. *Seth Moulton (D)*
7. Michael E. Capuano (D)
8. Stephen F. Lynch (D)
9. Bill Keating (D)

MICHIGAN

Debbie A. Stabenow (D)
Gary Peters (D) #
    1. Dan Benishek (R)
    2. Bill Huizenga (R)
    3. Justin Amash (R)
    4. *John Moolenaar (R)*
    5. Dan Kildee (D)
    6. Fred Upton (R)
    7. Tim Walberg (R)
    8. *Mike Bishop (R)*
    9. Sandy Levin (D)
    10. Candice S. Miller (R)
    11. *Dave Trott (R)*
    12. *Deborah Dingell (D)*
    13. John Conyers Jr. (D)
    14. *Brenda Lawrence (D)*

MINNESOTA

Amy Klobuchar (D)
Al Franken (D)
    1. Tim Walz (D)
    2. John Kline (R)
    3. Erik Paulsen (R)
    4. Betty McCollum (D)
    5. Keith Ellison (D)
    6. *Tom Emmer (R)*
    7. Collin C. Peterson (D)
    8. Rick Nolan (D)

MISSISSIPPI

Thad A. Cochran (R)
Roger Wicker (R)
    1. *Trent Kelly (R)*
    2. Bennie Thompson (D)
    3. Gregg Harper (R)
    4. Steven Palazzo (R)

MISSOURI

Claire McCaskill (D)
Roy Blunt (R)
    1. Wm. Lacy Clay (D)
    2. Ann Wagner (R)
    3. Blaine Luetkemeyer (R)
    4. Vicky Hartzler (R)
    5. Emanuel Cleaver (D)
    6. Sam Graves (R)
    7. Billy Long (R)
    8. Jason Smith (R)

MONTANA

Jon Tester (D)
Steve Daines (R) #
AL *Ryan Zinke (R)*

NEBRASKA

Deb Fischer (R)
Ben Sasse (R)
    1. Jeff Fortenberry (R)
    2. *Brad Ashford (D)*
    3. Adrian Smith (R)

NEVADA

Harry Reid (D)
Dean Heller (R)
    1. Dina Titus (D)
    2. Mark Amodei (R)
    3. Joe Heck (R)
    4. *Cresent Hardy (R)*

NEW HAMPSHIRE

Jeanne Shaheen (D)
Kelly Ayotte (R)
    1. *Frank Guinta (R)*
    2. Ann McLane Kuster (D)

NEW JERSEY

Bob Menéndez (D)
Cory Booker (D)
    1. *Donald Norcross (D) $*
    2. Frank LoBiondo (R)
    3. *Tom MacArthur (R)*
    4. Chris Smith (R)
    5. Scott Garrett (R)
    6. Frank Pallone Jr. (D)
    7. Leonard Lance (R)
    8. Albio Sires (D)
    9. Bill Pascrell Jr. (D)
    10. Donald M. Payne Jr. (D)
    11. Rodney Frelinghuysen (R)
    12. *Bonnie Watson Coleman (D)*

NEW MEXICO

Tom Udall (D)
Martin Heinrich (D)
    1. Michelle Lujan Grisham (D)
    2. Steve Pearce (R)
    3. Ben Ray Luján (D)

NEW YORK

Charles E. Schumer (D)
Kirsten Gillibrand (D)
    1. *Lee Zeldin (R)*
    2. Pete King (R)
    3. Steve Israel (D)
    4. *Kathleen Rice (D)*
    5. Gregory W. Meeks (D)
    6. Grace Meng (D)
    7. Nydia M. Velázquez (D)
    8. Hakeem S. Jeffries (D)
    9. Yvette D. Clarke (D)
    10. Jerrold Nadler (D)
    11. Dan Donovan *(R)*
    12. Carolyn B. Maloney (D)
    13. Charles B. Rangel (D)
    14. Joseph Crowley (D)
    15. José E. Serrano (D)
    16. Eliot L. Engel (D)
    17. Nita Lowey (D)
    18. Sean Patrick Maloney (D)
    19. Chris P. Gibson (R)
    20. Paul D. Tonko (D)
    21. *Elise Stefanik (R)*
    22. Richard Hanna (R)
    23. Tom Reed (R)
    24. *John Katko (R)*
    25. Louise M. Slaughter (D)
    26. Brian Higgins (D)
    27. Chris Collins (R)

NORTH CAROLINA

Richard Burr (R)
Thom Tillis (R)
    1. G. K. Butterfield (D)
    2. Renee Ellmers (R)
    3. Walter B. Jones (R)
    4. David E. Price (D)
    5. Virginia Foxx (R)
    6. *Bradley Walker (R)*
    7. *David Rouzer (R)*
    8. Richard Hudson (R)
    9. Robert Pittenger (R)
    10. Patrick McHenry (R)
    11. Mark Meadows (R)
    12. *Alma Adams (D) $*
    13. George Holding (R)

NORTH DAKOTA

John Hoeven (R)
Heidi Heitkamp (D)
AL Kevin Cramer (R)

NORTHERN MARIANA ISLANDS (NON-VOTING DELEGATE)

AL Gregorio Kilili Camacho Sablan (D)

OHIO

Sherrod Brown (D)
Rob Portman (R)
  1. Steve Chabot (R)
  2. Brad Wenstrup (R)
  3. Joyce Beatty (D)
  4. Jim Jordan (R)
  5. Bob Latta (R)
  6. Bill Johnson (R)
  7. Bob Gibbs (R)
  8. Vacant
  9. Marcy Kaptur (D)
  10. Mike Turner (R)
  11. Marcia L. Fudge (D)
  12. Patrick J. Tiberi (R)
  13. Tim Ryan (D)
  14. David Joyce (R)
  15. Steve Stivers (R)
  16. Jim Renacci (R)

OKLAHOMA

James M. Inhofe (R)
James Lankford (R) #
  1. Jim Bridenstine (R)
  2. Markwayne Mullin (R)
  3. Frank Lucas (R)
  4. Tom Cole (R)
  5. *Steve Russell (R)*

OREGON

Ron Wyden (D)
Jeff Merkley (D)
  1. Suzanne Bonamici (D)
  2. Greg Walden (R)
  3. Earl Blumenauer (D)
  4. Peter DeFazio (D)
  5. Kurt Schrader (D)

PENNSYLVANIA

Robert P. Casey Jr. (D)
Pat Toomey (R)
  1. Robert Brady (D)
  2. Chaka Fattah (D)
  3. Mike Kelly (R)
  4. Scott Perry (R)
  5. Glenn (GT) Thompson (R)
  6. *Ryan Costello (R)*
  7. Pat Meehan (R)
  8. Mike Fitzpatrick (R)
  9. Bill Shuster (R)
  10. Tom Marino (R)
  11. Lou Barletta (R)
  12. Keith Rothfus (R)
  13. *Brendan Boyle (D)*
  14. Michael Doyle Jr. (D)
  15. Charlie Dent (R)
  16. Joe Pitts (R)
  17. Matt Cartwright (D)
  18. Tim Murphy (R)

PUERTO RICO (NON-VOTING DELEGATE)

AL Pedro Pierluisi (D)

RHODE ISLAND

Jack D. Reed (D)
Sheldon Whitehouse (D)
  1. David Cicilline (D)
  2. Jim Langevin (D)

SOUTH CAROLINA

Lindsey Graham (R)
Tim Scott (R)
  1. Mark Sanford (R)
  2. Joe Wilson (R)
  3. Jeff Duncan (R)
  4. Trey Gowdy (R)
  5. Mick Mulvaney (R)
  6. James E. Clyburn (D)
  7. Tom Rice (R)

SOUTH DAKOTA

John Thune (R)
Mike Rounds (R)
AL Kristi Noem (R)

TENNESSEE

Lamar Alexander (R)
Bob Corker (R)
  1. Phil Roe (R)
  2. John J. Duncan Jr. (R)
  3. Chuck Fleischmann (R)
  4. Scott DesJarlais (R)
  5. Jim Cooper (D)
  6. Diane Black (R)
  7. Marsha Blackburn (R)
  8. Stephen Fincher (R)
  9. Steve Cohen (D)

TEXAS

John Cornyn (R)
Ted Cruz (R)
  1. Louie Gohmert (R)
  2. Ted Poe (R)
  3. Sam Johnson (R)
  4. *John Ratcliffe (R)*
  5. Jeb Hensarling (R)
  6. Joe Barton (R)
  7. John Culberson (R)
  8. Kevin Brady (R)
  9. Al Green (D)
  10. Michael McCaul (R)
  11. Mike Conaway (R)
  12. Kay Granger (R)
  13. Mac Thornberry (R)
  14. Randy Weber (R)
  15. Rubén Hinojosa (D)
  16. Beto O'Rourke (D)
  17. Bill Flores (R)
  18. Sheila Jackson Lee (D)
  19. Randy Neugebauer (R)
  20. Joaquin Castro (D)
  21. Lamar Smith (R)
  22. Pete Olson (R)
  23. *Will Hurd (R)*
  24. Kenny Marchant (R)
  25. Roger Williams (R)
  26. Michael C. Burgess (R)
  27. Blake Farenthold (R)
  28. Henry Cuellar (D)
  29. Gene Green (D)
  30. Eddie Bernice Johnson (D)
  31. John Carter (R)
  32. Pete Sessions (R)
  33. Marc Veasey (D)
  34. Filemon Vela (D)
  35. Lloyd Doggett (D)
  36. *Brian Babin (R)*

UTAH

Orrin G. Hatch (R)
Mike Lee (R)
  1. Rob Bishop (R)
  2. Chris Stewart (R)
  3. Jason Chaffetz (R)
  4. *Mia Love (R)*

VERMONT

Patrick P. Leahy (D)
Bernie Sanders (I)
AL Peter Welch (D)

VIRGIN ISLANDS (NON-VOTING DELEGATE)

AL *Stacey Plaskett (D)*

VIRGINIA

Mark R. Warner (D)
Tim Kaine (D)
  1. Robert J. Wittman (R)
  2. Scott Rigell (R)
  3. Robert C. (Bobby) Scott (D)
  4. J. Randy Forbes (R)
  5. Robert Hurt (R)
  6. Bob Goodlatte (R)
  7. *David Brat (R) $*

8. *Don Beyer (D)*
9. H. Morgan Griffith (R)
10. *Barbara Comstock (R)*
11. Gerald E. Connolly (D)

WASHINGTON

Patty Murray (D)
Maria Cantwell (D)
    1. Suzan DelBene (D)
    2. Rick Larsen (D)
    3. Jaime Herrera Beutler (R)
    4. *Dan Newhouse (R)*
    5. Cathy McMorris Rodgers (R)
    6. Derek Kilmer (D)
    7. Jim McDermott (D)
    8. Dave Reichert (R)

9. Adam Smith (D)
10. Denny Heck (D)

WEST VIRGINIA

Joe Manchin (D)
Shelley Moore Capito (R) #
    1. David R. McKinley (R)
    2. *Alex Mooney (R)*
    3. *Evan Jenkins (R)*

WISCONSIN

Ron Johnson (R)
Tammy Baldwin (D)
    1. Paul Ryan (R)
    2. Mark Pocan (D)

3. Ron Kind (D)
4. Gwen Moore (D)
5. Jim Sensenbrenner (R)
6. *Glenn Grothman (R)*
7. Sean Duffy (R)
8. Reid Ribble (R)

WYOMING

Mike Enzi (R)
John Barrasso (R)
AL Cynthia Lummis (R)

House Committees

The standing and select committees of the U.S. House of Representatives follow. Each listing includes the room number, office building, zip code, telephone and fax numbers, Web address, minority Web address if available, key majority and minority staff members, jurisdiction for each full committee, and party ratio. Subcommittees are listed under the full committees. Members are listed in order of seniority on the committee or subcommittee. Many committees and subcommittees may be contacted via Web-based email forms found on their Web sites.

Republicans, the current majority, are shown in roman type; Democrats, in the minority, appear in italic. The top name in the italicized list is the Ranking Minority Member. Vacancy indicates that a committee or subcommittee seat had not been filled as of April 25, 2016. The partisan committees of the House are listed on page 803. The area code for all phone and fax numbers is (202). A phone number and/or office number next to either the Majority or Minority Staff Director indicates a change from the full committee's office number and/or phone number. If no numbers are listed, the individual's office number and phone number are the same as for the full committee.

AGRICULTURE

Office: 1301 LHOB 20515-6001
Phone: 225-2171   **Fax:** 225-0917
Web: agriculture.house.gov
Minority Web: democrats.agriculture.house.gov
Majority Staff Director: Scott Graves
Minority Staff Director: Rob Larew, 225-0317, 1010 LHOB
Jurisdiction: (1) adulteration of seeds, insect pests, and protection of birds and animals in forest reserves; (2) agriculture generally; (3) agricultural and industrial chemistry; (4) agricultural colleges and experiment stations; (5) agricultural economics and research; (6) agricultural education extension services; (7) agricultural production and marketing, and stabilization of prices of agricultural products and commodities (not including distribution outside of the United States); (8) animal industry and diseases of animals; (9) commodities exchanges; (10) crop insurance and soil conservation; (11) dairy industry; (12) entomology and plant quarantine; (13) extension of farm credit and farm security; (14) livestock inspection, poultry inspection, meat and meat products inspection, and seafood and seafood products inspection; (15) forestry in general, and forest reserves other than those created from the public domain; (16) human nutrition and home economics; (17) plant industry, soils, and agricultural engineering; (18) rural electrification; (19) rural development; (20) water conservation related to activities of the Department of Agriculture.
Party Ratio: R 26-D 19

Mike Conaway, Tex., Chair	*Collin C. Peterson, Minn.*
Bob Goodlatte, Va.	*David Scott, Ga.*
Frank Lucas, Okla.	*Jim Costa, Calif.*
Steve King, Iowa	*Tim Walz, Minn.*
Randy Neugebauer, Tex.	*Marcia L. Fudge, Ohio*
Mike Rogers, Ala.	*Jim McGovern, Mass.*
Glenn (GT) Thompson, Pa.	*Suzan DelBene, Wash.*
Bob Gibbs, Ohio	*Filemon Vela, Tex.*
Austin Scott, Ga.	*Michelle Lujan Grisham,*
Rick Crawford, Ark.	*N.M.*
Scott DesJarlais, Tenn.	*Ann McLane Kuster, N.H.*
Chris P. Gibson, N.Y.	*Rick Nolan, Minn.*
Vicky Hartzler, Mo.	*Cheri Bustos, Ill.*
Dan Benishek, Mich.	*Sean Patrick Maloney, N.Y.*
Jeff Denham, Calif.	*Ann Kirkpatrick, Ariz.*
Doug LaMalfa, Calif.	*Pete Aguilar, Calif.*
Rodney Davis, Ill.	*Stacey Plaskett, Virgin Is.*
Ted Yoho, Fla.	*Alma Adams, N.C.*
Jackie Walorski, Ind.	*Gwen Graham, Fla.*
Rick Allen, Ga.	*Brad Ashford, Neb.*
Mike Bost, Ill.	
David Rouzer, N.C.	
Ralph Abraham, La.	
John Moolenaar, Mich.	
Dan Newhouse, Wash.	
Trent Kelly, Miss.	

Subcommittees

Biotechnology, Horticulture, and Research
Office: 1301 LHOB 20515   **Phone:** 225-2171
   Rodney Davis (Chair), Glenn (GT) Thompson, Austin Scott, Chris P. Gibson, Jeff Denham, Ted Yoho, John Moolenaar, Dan Newhouse
   Suzan DelBene (Ranking Minority Member), Marcia L. Fudge, Jim McGovern, Ann McLane Kuster, Gwen Graham

Commodity Exchanges, Energy, and Credit
Office: 1301 LHOB 20515   **Phone:** 225-2171
   Austin Scott (Chair), Bob Goodlatte, Frank Lucas, Randy Neugebauer, Mike Rogers, Doug LaMalfa, Rodney Davis, Trent Kelly
   David Scott (Ranking Minority Member), Filemon Vela, Sean Patrick Maloney, Ann Kirkpatrick, Pete Aguilar

Conservation and Forestry
Office: 1301 LHOB 20515   **Phone:** 225-2171
   Glenn (GT) Thompson (Chair), Frank Lucas, Steve King, Scott DesJarlais, Chris P. Gibson, Dan Benishek, Rick Allen, Mike Bost
   Michelle Lujan Grisham (Ranking Minority Member), Ann McLane Kuster, Rick Nolan, Suzan DelBene, Ann Kirkpatrick

AGRICULTURE (continued)

General Farm Commodities and Risk Management
Office: 1301 LHOB 20515   **Phone:** 225-2171

Rick Crawford (Chair), Frank Lucas, Randy Neugebauer, Mike Rogers, Bob Gibbs, Austin Scott, Jeff Denham, Doug LaMalfa, Jackie Walorski, Rick Allen, Mike Bost, Ralph Abraham

Tim Walz (Ranking Minority Member), Cheri Bustos, Gwen Graham, Brad Ashford, David Scott, Jim Costa, Sean Patrick Maloney, Ann Kirkpatrick

Livestock and Foreign Agriculture
Office: 1301 LHOB 20515   **Phone:** 225-2171

David Rouzer (Chair), Bob Goodlatte, Steve King, Scott DesJarlais, Vicky Hartzler, Ted Yoho, Dan Newhouse, Trent Kelly

Jim Costa (Ranking Minority Member), Stacey Plaskett, Filemon Vela, Rick Nolan, Cherie Bustos

Nutrition
Office: 1301 LHOB 20515   **Phone:** 225-2171

Jackie Walorski (Chair), Randy Neugebauer, Glenn (GT) Thompson, Bob Gibbs, Rick Crawford, Vicky Hartzler, Dan Benishek, Rodney Davis, Ted Yoho, David Rouzer, Ralph Abraham, John Moolenaar

Jim McGovern (Ranking Minority Member), Marcia L. Fudge, Alma Adams, Michelle Lujan Grisham, Pete Aguilar, Stacey Plaskett, Brad Ashford, Suzan DelBene

APPROPRIATIONS

Office: H-305 CAP 20515-6015
Phone: 225-2771   **Fax:** 225-5078
Web: appropriations.house.gov
Minority Web: democrats.appropriations.house.gov
Majority Staff Director: William E. Smith
Minority Staff Director: David Pomerantz, 225-3481, 1016 LHOB
Jurisdiction: (1) appropriation of the revenue for the support of the Government; (2) rescissions of appropriations contained in appropriations acts; (3) transfers of unexpected balances; (4) bills and joint resolutions reported by other Committees that provide new entitlement authority as defined in Section 3(9) of the Congressional Budget Act of 1974 and referred to the Committee under Clause 4(a)(2); (5) bills and joint resolutions that provide new budget authority, limitation on the use of funds, or other authority relating to new direct loan obligations and new loan guarantee commitments referencing section 504(b) of the Congressional Budget Act of 1974.
Party Ratio: R 30-D 21

Hal Rogers, Ky., Chair	*Nita Lowey, N.Y.*
Rodney Frelinghuysen, N.J.	*Marcy Kaptur, Ohio*
Robert B. Aderholt, Ala.	*Pete Visclosky, Ind.*
Kay Granger, Tex.	*José E. Serrano, N.Y.*
Mike Simpson, Idaho	*Rosa L. DeLauro, Conn.*
John Culberson, Tex.	*David E. Price, N. C.*
Ander Crenshaw, Fla.	*Lucille Roybal-Allard, Calif.*
John Carter, Tex.	*Sam Farr, Calif.*

Ken Calvert, Calif.	*Chaka Fattah, Pa.*
Tom Cole, Okla.	*Sanford D. Bishop Jr., Ga.*
Mario Diaz-Balart, Fla.	*Barbara Lee, Calif.*
Charlie Dent, Pa.	*Mike Honda, Calif.*
Tom Graves, Ga.	*Betty McCollum, Minn.*
Kevin Yoder, Kans.	*Steve Israel, N.Y.*
Steve Womack, Ark.	*Tim Ryan, Ohio*
Jeff Fortenberry, Neb.	*C.A. (Dutch)*
Thomas J. Rooney, Fla.	*Ruppersberger, Md.*
Chuck Fleischmann, Tenn.	*Debbie Wasserman Schultz,*
Jaime Herrera Beutler, Wash.	*Fla.*
David Joyce, Ohio	*Henry Cuellar, Tex.*
David G. Valadao, Calif.	*Chellie Pingree, Maine*
Andy Harris, Md.	*Mike Quigley, Ill.*
Martha Roby, Ala.	*Derek Kilmer, Wash.*
Mark Amodei, Nev.	
Chris Stewart, Utah	
Scott Rigell, Va.	
David W. Jolly, Fla.	
David Young, Iowa	
Evan Jenkins, W. Va.	
Steven Palazzo, Mo.	

Subcommittees
Agriculture, Rural Development, Food and Drug Administration, and Related Agencies
Office: 2362A RHOB 20515   **Phone:** 225-2638

Robert B. Aderholt (Chair), Kevin Yoder, Thomas J. Rooney, David G. Valadao, Andy Harris, David Young, Steven Palazzo

Sam Farr (Ranking Minority Member), Rosa L. DeLauro, Sanford D. Bishop Jr., Chellie Pingree

Commerce, Justice, Science, and Related Agencies
Office: H-310 CAP 20515   **Phone:** 225-3351

John Culberson (Chair), Robert B. Aderholt, John Carter, Jaime Herrera Beutler, Martha Roby, David W. Jolly, Steven Palazzo

Chaka Fattah (Ranking Minority Member), Mike Honda, José E. Serrano, Derek Kilmer

Defense
Office: H-405 CAP 20515   **Phone:** 225-2847

Rodney Frelinghuysen (Chair), Kay Granger, Ander Crenshaw, Ken Calvert, Tom Cole, Steve Womack, Robert B. Aderholt, John Carter, Mario Diaz-Balart, Tom Graves

Pete Visclosky (Ranking Minority Member), Betty McCollum, Steve Israel, Tim Ryan, C.A. (Dutch) Ruppersberger, Marcy Kaptur

Energy and Water Development, and Related Agencies
Office: 2362B RHOB 20515   **Phone:** 225-3421

Mike Simpson (Chair), Rodney Frelinghuysen, Ken Calvert, Chuck Fleischmann, Jeff Fortenberry, Kay Granger, Jaime Herrera Beutler, David G. Valadao

Marcy Kaptur (Ranking Minority Member), Pete Visclosky, Mike Honda, Lucille Roybal-Allard

Financial Services and General Government
Office: B300 RHOB 20515   **Phone:** 225-7245

Ander Crenshaw (Chair), Tom Graves, Kevin Yoder, Steve Womack, Jaime Herrera Beutler, Mark Amodei, Scott Rigell

José E. Serrano (Ranking Minority Member), Mike Quigley, Chaka Fattah, Sanford D. Bishop Jr.

Homeland Security
Office: B307 RHOB 20515   **Phone:** 225-5834

John Carter (Chair), John Culberson, Rodney Frelinghuysen, Chuck Fleischmann, Andy Harris, Chris Stewart, David Young

Lucille Roybal-Allard (Ranking Minority Member), David E. Price, Henry Cuellar, Marcy Kaptur

Interior, Environment, and Related Agencies
Office: B308 RHOB 20515   **Phone:** 225-3081

Ken Calvert (Chair), Mike Simpson, Tom Cole, David Joyce, Chris Stewart, Mark Amodei, Evan Jenkins

Betty McCollum (Ranking Minority Member), Chellie Pingree, Derek Kilmer, Steve Israel

Labor, Health and Human Services, Education, and Related Agencies
Office: 2358B RHOB 20515   **Phone:** 225-3508

Tom Cole (Chair), Mike Simpson, Steve Womack, Chuck Fleischmann, Andy Harris, Martha Roby, Charlie Dent, Scott Rigell

Rosa L. DeLauro (Ranking Minority Member), Lucille Roybal-Allard, Barbara Lee, Chaka Fattah

Legislative Branch
Office: HT-2 CAP 20515   **Phone:** 226-7252

Tom Graves (Chair), Mark Amodei, Scott Rigell, Evan Jenkins, Steven Palazzo

Debbie Wasserman Schultz (Ranking Minority Member), Sam Farr, Betty McCollum

Military Construction, Veterans Affairs, and Related Agencies
Office: HVC-227 CAP 20515   **Phone:** 225-3047

Charlie Dent (Chair), Jeff Fortenberry, Thomas J. Rooney, Martha Roby, David G. Valadao, David Joyce, David W. Jolly

Sanford D. Bishop Jr. (Ranking Minority Member), Sam Farr, David E. Price, Barbara Lee

State, Foreign Operations, and Related Programs
Office: HT-2 CAP 20515   **Phone:** 225-2041

Kay Granger (Chair), Mario Diaz-Balart, Charlie Dent, Ander Crenshaw, Thomas J. Rooney, Jeff Fortenberry, Chris Stewart

Nita Lowey (Ranking Minority Member), Barbara Lee, C.A. (Dutch) Ruppersberger, Debbie Wasserman Schultz, José E. Serrano

Transportation, Housing and Urban Development, and Related Agencies
Office: 2358A RHOB 20515   **Phone:** 225-2141

Mario Diaz-Balart (Chair), David Joyce, John Culberson, Kevin Yoder, David W. Jolly, David Young, Evan Jenkins

David E. Price (Ranking Minority Member), Mike Quigley, Tim Ryan, Henry Cuellar

ARMED SERVICES

Office: 2216 RHOB 20515-6035
Phone: 225-4151   **Fax:** 225-9077
Web: armedservices.house.gov
Minority Web: democrats.armedservices.house.gov
Majority Staff Director: Robert L. Simmons
Minority Staff Director: Paul Arcangeli

Jurisdiction: (1) ammunition depots, forts, arsenals, Army, Navy and Air Force reservations and establishments; (2) common defense generally; (3) conservation, development, and use of naval petroleum reserves and oil shale reserves; (4) the Department of Defense generally, including the Departments of the Army, Navy, and Air Force generally; (5) interoceanic canals generally, including measures relating to the maintenance, operation, and administration of interoceanic canals; (6) Merchant Marine Academy and State Merchant Marine Academies; (7) military applications of nuclear energy; (8) tactical intelligence and intelligence-related activities of the Department of Defense; (9) national security aspects of the merchant marine, including financial assistance for the construction and operation of vessels, the maintenance of the U.S. shipbuilding and ship repair industrial base, cabotage (trade or transport in coastal waters or air space, or between two points within a country), cargo preference and merchant marine personnel as these matters relate to the national security; (10) pay, promotion, retirement, and other benefits and privileges of members of the armed services; (11) scientific research and development in support of the armed services; (12) selective service; (13) size and composition of the Army, Navy, Marine Corps, and Air Force; (14) soldiers' and sailors' homes; (15) strategic and critical materials necessary for the common defense; (16) cemeteries administered by the Department of Defense.
Party Ratio: R 36-D 27

Mac Thornberry, Tex., Chair	*Adam Smith, Wash.*
Walter B. Jones, N.C.	*Loretta Sánchez, Calif.*
J. Randy Forbes, Va.	*Robert Brady, Pa.*
Jeff Miller, Fla.	*Susan Davis, Calif.*
Joe Wilson, S.C.	*Jim Langevin, R.I.*
Frank LoBiondo, N.J.	*Rick Larsen, Wash.*
Rob Bishop, Utah	*Jim Cooper, Tenn.*
Mike Turner, Ohio	*Madeleine Z. Bordallo, Guam*
John Kline, Minn.	*Joe Courtney, Conn.*
Mike Rogers, Ala.	*Niki Tsongas, Mass.*
Trent Franks, Ariz.	*John Garamendi, Calif.*
Bill Shuster, Pa.	*Hank Johnson, Ga.*
Mike Conaway, Tex.	*Jackie Speier, Calif.*
Doug Lamborn, Colo.	*Joaquín Castro, Tex.*
Robert J. Wittman, Va.	*Tammy Duckworth, Ill.*
Duncan Hunter, Calif.	*Scott H. Peters, Calif.*
John Fleming, La.	*Marc Veasey, Tex.*
Mike Coffman, Colo.	*Tulsi Gabbard, Hawaii*
Chris P. Gibson, N.Y.	*Tim Walz, Minn.*
Vicky Hartzler, Mo.	*Beto O'Rourke, Tex.*
Joe Heck, Nev.	*Donald Norcross, N.J.*
Austin Scott, Ga.	*Ruben Gallego, Ariz.*
Mo Brooks, Ala.	*Mark Takai, Hawaii*

ARMED SERVICES (continued)

Richard Nugent, Fla.
Paul Cook, Calif.
Jim Bridenstine, Okla.
Brad Wenstrup, Ohio
Jackie Walorski, Ind.
Bradley Byrne, Ala.
Sam Graves, Mo.
Ryan Zinke, Mont.
Elise Stefanik, N.Y.
Martha McSally, Ariz.
Steve Knight, Calif.
Tom MacArthur, N.J.
Steve Russell, Okla.

Gwen Graham, Fla.
Brad Ashford, Neb.
Seth Moulton, Mass.
Pete Aguilar, Calif.

Subcommittees

Emerging Threats and Capabilities
Office: 2340 RHOB 20515   **Phone:** 226-2843
Joe Wilson (Chair), John Kline, Bill Shuster, Duncan Hunter, Richard Nugent, Ryan Zinke, Trent Franks, Doug Lamborn, Mo Brooks, Bradley Byrne, Elise Stefanik
Jim Langevin (Ranking Minority Member), Jim Cooper, John Garamendi, Joaquín Castro, Marc Veasey, Donald Norcross, Brad Ashford, Pete Aguilar

Military Personnel
Office: 2340 RHOB 20515   **Phone:** 225-7560
Joe Heck (Chair), Walter B. Jones, John Kline, Mike Coffman, Tom MacArthur, Elise Stefanik, Paul Cook, Steve Knight
Susan Davis (Ranking Minority Member), Robert Brady, Niki Tsongas, Jackie Speier, Tim Walz, Beto O'Rourke

Oversight and Investigations
Office: 2117 RHOB 20515   **Phone:** 226-5048
Vicky Hartzler (Chair), Jeff Miller, Mike Conaway, Joe Heck, Austin Scott, Martha McSally
Jackie Speier (Ranking Minority Member), Jim Cooper, Hank Johnson, Gwen Graham

Readiness
Office: 2340 RHOB 20515   **Phone:** 226-8979
Robert J. Wittman (Chair), Rob Bishop, Vicky Hartzler, Austin Scott, Elise Stefanik, Frank LoBiondo, Mike Rogers, Chris P. Gibson, Richard Nugent, Brad Wenstrup, Sam Graves, Steve Russell
Madeleine Z. Bordallo (Ranking Minority Member), Susan Davis, Joe Courtney, Joaquín Castro, Tammy Duckworth, Scott H. Peters, Tulsi Gabbard, Beta O'Rourke, Ruben Gallego

Seapower and Projection Forces
Office: 2340 RHOB 20515   **Phone:** 226-8979
J. Randy Forbes (Chair), Mike Conaway, Bradley Byrne, Robert J. Wittman, Duncan Hunter, Vicky Hartzler, Paul Cook, Jim Bridenstine, Jackie Walorski, Ryan Zinke, Steve Knight, Steven Russell
Joe Courtney (Ranking Minority Member), Jim Langevin, Rick Larsen, Madeleine Z. Bordallo, Hank Johnson, Scott H. Peters, Tulsi Gabbard, Gwen Graham, Seth Moulton

Strategic Forces
Office: 2340 RHOB 20515   **Phone:** 225-1967
Mike Rogers (Chair), Trent Franks, Doug Lamborn, Mike Coffman, Mo Brooks, Jim Bridenstine, Randy Forbes, Rob Bishop, Mike Turner, John Fleming
Jim Cooper (Ranking Minority Member), Loretta Sánchez, Rick Larsen, John Garamendi, Mark Takai, Brad Ashford, Pete Aguilar

Tactical Air and Land Forces
Office: 2340 RHOB 20515   **Phone:** 225-4440
Mike Turner (Chair), Frank LoBiondo, John Fleming, Chris P. Gibson, Paul Cook, Brad Wenstrup, Jackie Walorski, Sam Graves, Martha McSally, Steve Knight, Tom MacArthur, Walter B. Jones, Joe Wilson
Loretta Sánchez (Ranking Minority Member), Niki Tsongas, Hank Johnson, Tammy Duckworth, Marc Veasey, Tim Walz, Donald Norcross, Ruben Gallego, Mark Takai, Gwen Graham, Seth Moulton

BUDGET

Office: 207 CHOB 20515-6065
Phone: 226-7270   **Fax:** 226-7174
Web: budget.house.gov
Minority Web: democrats.budget.house.gov
Majority Staff Director: Richard May
Minority Staff Director: Thomas S. Kahn, 226-7200, 134 CHOB
Jurisdiction: (1) concurrent resolutions on the budget (as defined in section 3(4) of the Congressional Budget Act of 1974), other matters required to be referred to the committee under titles III and IV of that Act, and other measures setting forth appropriate levels of budget totals for the U.S. government; (2) budget process generally; (3) establishment, extension, and enforcement of special controls over the Federal budget, including the budgetary treatment of off-budget Federal agencies and measures providing exemption from reduction under any order issued under part C of the Balanced Budget and Emergency Deficit Control Act of 1985; (4) study on a continuing basis the effect on budget outlays of relevant existing and proposed legislation and report the results of such studies to the House on a recurring basis; (5)(a) review on a continuing basis the conduct by the Congressional Budget Office of its functions and duties; (b) hold hearings and receive testimony from Members, Senators, Delegates, the Resident Commissioner, and such appropriate representatives of Federal departments and agencies, the general public, and national organizations as it considers desirable in developing concurrent resolutions on the budget for each fiscal year; (c) make all reports required of it by the Congressional Budget Act of 1974; (d) study on a continuing basis those provisions of law that exempt Federal agencies or any of their activities or outlays from inclusion in the Budget of the U.S. government, and report to the House from time to time its recommendations for terminating or modifying such provisions; (e) study on a continuing basis proposals designed to improve and facilitate the congressional budget process, and report to the House

from time to time the results of such studies, together with its recommendations; (f) request and evaluate continuing studies of tax expenditures, devise methods of coordinating tax expenditures, policies, and programs with direct budget outlays, and report the results of such studies to the House on a recurring basis.
Party Ratio: R 22-D 14

Tom Price, Ga., Chair	Chris Van Hollen, Md.
Scott Garrett, N.J.	John Yarmuth, Ky.
Mario Diaz-Balart, Fla.	Bill Pascrell Jr., N.J.
Tom Cole, Okla.	Tim Ryan, Ohio
Tom McClintock, Calif.	Gwen Moore, Wisc.
Diane Black, Tenn.	Kathy Castor, Fla.
Todd Rokita, Ind.	Jim McDermott, Wash.
Rob Woodall, Ga.	Barbara Lee, Calif.
Marsha Blackburn, Tenn.	Mark Pocan, Wisc.
Vicky Hartzler, Mo.	Michelle Lujan Grisham,
Marlin Stutzman, Ind.	N.M.
Mark Sanford, S.C.	Debbie Dingell, Mich.
Steve Womack, Ariz.	Ted Lieu, Calif.
Dave Brat, Va.	Donald Norcross, N.J.
Rod Blum, Iowa	Seth Moulton, Mass.
Alex Mooney, W. Va.	
Glenn Grothman, Wisc.	
Gary Palmer, Ala.	
John Moolenaar, Mich.	
Bruce Westerman, Ark.	
Jim Renacci, Ohio	
Bill Johnson, Ohio	

EDUCATION AND THE WORKFORCE

Office: 2181 RHOB 20515-6100
Phone: 225-4527 **Fax:** 225-9571
Web: edworkforce.house.gov
Minority Web: democrats.edworkforce.house.gov
Majority Staff Director: Juliane Sullivan
Minority Staff Director: Denise Forte, 225-3725, 2101 RHOB

Jurisdiction: (1) elementary and secondary education initiatives including the No Child Left Behind Act, school choice for low-income families, special education (the Individuals with Disabilities Education Act), and teacher quality and training; (2) higher education programs, including the Higher Education Act, which supports college access for low- and middle-income students and helps families pay for college; (3) job training, adult education, and workforce development initiatives, including those under the Workforce Investment Act (WIA), which help local communities train and retrain workers; (4) early childhood care and preschool education programs, including Head Start and the Child Care and Development Block Grant; (5) career and technical education programs; (6) school lunch and child nutrition programs; (7) programs for the care and treatment of at-risk youth, child abuse prevention, and adoption; (8) programs for older Americans; (9) educational research and improvement; (10) work requirements under the Temporary Assistance for Needy Families (TANF) program created in the 1996 welfare reform law; (11) anti-poverty programs, including the Community Services Block Grant Act and the Low Income Home Energy Assistance Program (LIHEAP); (12) pensions, health care, and other employer-sponsored benefits covered by the Employee Retirement Income Security Act (ERISA); (13) application of the National Labor Relations Act (NLRA) to collective bargaining and union representation; (14) occupational safety and health and mine safety; (15) unpaid, job-protected leave as outlined in the Family Medical Leave Act (FMLA), as well as "comp time" or family friendly work schedules; (16) equal employment opportunity and civil rights in employment, including the Americans with Disabilities Act (ADA); (17) various temporary worker programs under the Immigration and Nationality Act; (18) wage and hour requirements under the Fair Labor Standards Act (FLSA); (19) prevailing wage requirements for federal contractors under the Davis-Bacon Act and the Service Contract Act; (20) workers' compensation for federal employees, energy employees, longshore and harbor employees, and individuals affected by black lung disease; (21) matters dealing with employer and employee relations, as well as union transparency (the Labor-Management Reporting and Disclosure Act).
Party Ratio: R 22-D 16

John Kline, Minn., Chair	Robert C. (Bobby) Scott, Va.
Joe Wilson, S.C.	Rubén Hinojosa, Tex.
Virginia Foxx, N.C.	Susan Davis, Calif.
Duncan Hunter, Calif.	Raúl M. Grijalva, Ariz.
Phil Roe, Tenn.	Joe Courtney, Conn.
Glenn (GT) Thompson, Pa.	Marcia L. Fudge, Ohio
Tim Walberg, Mich.	Jared Polis, Colo.
Matt Salmon, Ariz.	Gregorio Kilili
Brett Guthrie, Ky.	Camacho Sablan,
Todd Rokita, Ind.	Northern Mariana Is.
Lou Barletta, Pa.	Frederica S. Wilson, Fla.
Joe Heck, Nev.	Suzanne Bonamici, Ore.
Luke Messer, Ind.	Mark Pocan, Wisc.
Bradley Byrne, Ala.	Mark Takano, Calif.
Dave Brat, Va.	Hakeem S. Jeffries, N.Y.
Buddy Carter, Ga.	Katherine Clark, Mass.
Mike Bishop, Mich.	Alma Adams, N.C.
Glenn Grothman, Wisc.	Mark DeSaulnier, Calif.
Steve Russell, Okla.	
Carlos Curbelo, Fla.	
Elise Stefanik, N.Y.	
Rick Allen, Ga.	

Subcommittees

Early Childhood, Elementary, and Secondary Education
Office: 2181 RHOB 20515 **Phone:** 225-4527
Todd Rokita (Chair), Duncan Hunter, Glenn (GT) Thompson, Dave Brat, Buddy Carter, Mike Bishop, Glen Grothman, Steve Russell, Carlos Curbelo
Marcia L. Fudge (Ranking Minority Member), Susan Davis, Raúl M. Grijalva, Gregorio Kilili Camacho Sablan, Suzanne Bonamici, Mark Takano, Katherine Clark

EDUCATION AND THE WORKFORCE
(continued)

Health, Employment, Labor, and Pensions
Office: 2181 RHOB 20515   **Phone:** 225-4527

Phil Roe (Chair), Joe Wilson, Virginia Foxx, Tim Walberg, Matt Salmon, Brett Guthrie, Lou Barletta, Joe Heck, Luke Messer, Bradley Byrne, Buddy Carter, Glenn Grothman, Rick Allen

Jared Polis (Ranking Minority Member), Joe Courtney, Mark Pocan, Rubén Hinojosa, Gregorio Kilili Camacho Sablan, Frederica S. Wilson, Suzanne Bonamici, Mark Takano, Hakeem S. Jeffries, Robert C. (Bobby) Scott

Higher Education and Workforce Training
Office: 2181 RHOB 20515   **Phone:** 225-4527

Virginia Foxx (Chair)Phil Roe, Matt Salmon, Brett Guthrie, Lou Barletta, Joe Heck, Luke Messer, Bradley Byrne, Carlos Curbelo, Elise Stefanik, Rick Allen

Rubén Hinojosa (Ranking Minority Member), Hakeem S. Jeffries, Alma Adams, Mark DeSaulnier, Susan Davis, Raúl M. Grijalva, Joe Courtney, Jared Polis

Workforce Protections
Office: 2181 RHOB 20515   **Phone:** 225-4527

Tim Walberg (Chair), Duncan Hunter, Glenn (GT) Thompson, Todd Rokita, Dave Brat, Mike Bishop, Steve Russell, Elise Stefanik

Frederica S. Wilson (Ranking Minority Member), Mark Pocan, Katherine Clark, Alma Adams, Mark DeSaulnier, Marcia L. Fudge

ENERGY AND COMMERCE

Office: 2125 RHOB 20515-6115
Phone: 225-2927   **Fax:** 225-1919
Web: energycommerce.house.gov
Minority Web: democrats.energycommerce.house.gov
Majority Staff Director: Gary Andres
Minority Staff Director: Jeffrey Carroll, 225-3641, 2322-A RHOB

Jurisdiction: (1) biomedical research and development; (2) consumer affairs and consumer protection; (3) health and health facilities (except health care supported by payroll deductions); (4) interstate energy compacts; (5) interstate and foreign commerce generally; (6) exploration, production, storage, supply, marketing, pricing, and regulation of energy resources, including all fossil fuels, solar energy, and other unconventional or renewable energy resources; (7) conservation of energy resources; (8) energy information generally; (9) the generation and marketing of power (except by federally chartered or Federal regional power marketing authorities); the reliability and interstate transmission of, and ratemaking for, all power, and siting of generation facilities, except the installation of interconnections between government water power projects; (10) general management of the Department of Energy and management and all functions of the Federal Energy Regulatory Commission; (11) national energy policy generally; (12) public health and quarantine; (13) regulation of the domestic nuclear energy industry, including regulation of research and development reactors and nuclear regulatory

research; (14) regulation of interstate and foreign communications; (15) travel and tourism. The committee shall have the same jurisdiction with respect to regulation of nuclear facilities and of use of nuclear energy as it has with respect to regulation of nonnuclear facilities and of use of nonnuclear energy.
Party Ratio: R 31-D 23

Fred Upton, Mich., Chair	*Frank Pallone Jr., N.J.*
Joe Barton, Tex.	*Bobby L. Rush, Ill.*
Ed Whitfield, Ky.	*Anna G. Eshoo, Calif.*
John Shimkus, Ill.	*Eliot L. Engel, N.Y.*
Joe Pitts, Pa.	*Gene Green, Tex.*
Greg Walden, Ore.	*Diana DeGette, Colo.*
Tim Murphy, Pa.	*Lois Capps, Calif.*
Michael C. Burgess, Tex.	*Michael Doyle Jr., Pa.*
Marsha Blackburn, Tenn.	*Jan Schakowsky, Ill.*
Steve Scalise, La.	*G. K. Butterfield, N.C.*
Bob Latta, Ohio	*Doris Matsui, Calif.*
Cathy McMorris Rodgers, Wash.	*Kathy Castor, Fla.*
Gregg Harper, Miss.	*John Sarbanes, Md.*
Leonard Lance, N.J.	*Jerry McNerney, Calif.*
Brett Guthrie, Ky.	*Peter Welch, Vt.*
Pete Olson, Tex.	*Ben Ray Luján, N.M.*
David McKinley, W. Va.	*Paul D. Tonko, N.Y.*
Mike Pompeo, Kans.	*John Yarmuth, Ky.*
Adam Kinzinger, Ill.	*Yvette D. Clarke, N.Y.*
Morgan Griffith, Va.	*Dave Loebsack, Iowa*
Gus Bilirakis, Fla.	*Kurt Schrader, Ore.*
Bill Johnson, Ohio	*Joe Kennedy III, Mass.*
Billy Long, Mo.	*Tony Cárdenas, Calif.*
Renee Ellmers, N.C.	
Larry Bucshon, Ind.	
Bill Flores, Tex.	
Susan W. Brooks, Ind.	
Markwayne Mullin, Okla.	
Richard Hudson, N.C.	
Chris Collins, N.Y.	
Kevin Cramer, N.D.	

Subcommittees

Commerce, Manufacturing, and Trade
Office: 2125 RHOB 20515   **Phone:** 225-2927

Michael C. Burgess (Chair), Leonard Lance, Marsha Blackburn, Gregg Harper, Brett Guthrie, Pete Olson, Mike Pompeo, Adam Kinzinger, Gus Bilirakis, Susan W. Brooks, Markwayne Mullin, Fred Upton (ex officio)

Jan Schakowsky (Ranking Minority Member), Yvette D. Clarke, Joe Kennedy III, Tony Cárdenas, Bobby L. Rush, G.K. Butterfield, Peter Welch, Frank Pallone Jr. (ex officio)

Communications and Technology
Office: 2125 RHOB 20515   **Phone:** 225-2927

Greg Walden (Chair), Bob Latta, John Shimkus, Marsha Blackburn, Steve Scalise, Leonard Lance, Brett Guthrie, Pete Olson, Mike Pompeo, Adam Kinzinger, Gus Bilirakis, Bill Johnson, Billy Long, Renee Ellmers, Chris Collins, Kevin Cramer, Joe Barton, Fred Upton (ex officio)

Anna G. Eshoo (Ranking Minority Member), Michael Doyle Jr., Doris Matsui, Peter Welch, John Yarmuth, Yvette

D. Clarke, David Loebsack, Bobby L. Rush, Diana DeGette, G. K. Butterfield, Jerry McNerney, Ben Ray Luján, Frank Pallone Jr. (ex officio)

Energy and Power
Office: 2125 RHOB 20515　**Phone:** 225-2927

Ed Whitfield (Chair), Pete Olson, John Shimkus, Joe Pitts, Bob Latta, Gregg Harper, David McKinley, Mike Pompeo, Adam Kinzinger, Morgan Griffith, Bill Johnson, Billy Long, Renee Ellmers, Bill Flores, Markwayne Mullin, Richard Hudson, Joe Barton, Fred Upton (ex officio)

Bobby L. Rush (Ranking Minority Member), Jerry McNerney, Paul D. Tonko, Eliot L. Engel, Gene Green, Lois Capps, Michael Doyle Jr., Kathy Castor, John Sarbanes, Peter Welch, John Yarmuth, David Loebsack, Frank Pallone Jr. (ex officio)

Environment and the Economy
Office: 2125 RHOB 20515　**Phone:** 225-2927

John Shimkus (Chair), Gregg Harper, Ed Whitfield, Joe Pitts, Tim Murphy, Bob Latta, David McKinley, Bill Johnson, Larry Bucshon, Bill Flores, Richard Hudson, Kevin Cramer, Fred Upton (ex officio)

Paul D. Tonko (Ranking Minority Member), Kurt Schrader, Gene Green, Diana DeGette, Lois Capps, Michael Doyle Jr., Jerry McNerney, Tony Cárdenas, Frank Pallone Jr. (ex officio)

Health
Office: 2125 RHOB 20515　**Phone:** 225-2927

Joe Pitts (Chair), Brett Guthrie, Ed Whitfield, John Shimkus, Tim Murphy, Michael C. Burgess, Marsha Blackburn, Cathy McMorris Rodgers, Leonard Lance, Morgan Griffith, Gus Bilirakis, Billy Long, Renee Ellmers, Larry Bucshon, Susan W. Brooks, Chris Collins, Joe Barton, Fred Upton (ex officio)

Gene Green (Ranking Minority Member), Eliot L. Engel, Lois Capps, Jan Schakowsky, G.K. Butterfield, Kathy Castor, John Sarbanes, Doris Matsui, Ben Ray Luján, Kurt Schrader, Joe Kennedy III, Tony Cárdenas, Frank Pallone Jr. (ex officio)

Oversight and Investigations
Office: 2125 RHOB 20515　**Phone:** 225-2927

Tim Murphy (Chair), David McKinley, Michael C. Burgess, Marsha Blackburn, Morgan Griffith, Larry Bucshon, Bill Flores, Susan W. Brooks, Markwayne Mullin, Richard Hudson, Chris Collins, Kevin Cramer, Joe Barton, Fred Upton (ex officio)

Diana DeGette (Ranking Minority Member), Jan Schakowsky, Kathy Castor, Paul D. Tonko, John Yarmuth, Yvette D. Clarke, Joe Kennedy III, Gene Green, Peter Welch, Frank Pallone Jr. (ex officio)

ETHICS

Office: 1015 LHOB 20515-6328
Phone: 225-7103　**Fax:** 225-7392
Web: ethics.house.gov
Majority Staff Director: Tom Rust
Counsel to the Ranking Minority Member: Dan Taylor

Jurisdiction: (1) recommend administrative actions to establish or enforce standards of official conduct; (2) investigate alleged violations of the Code of Official Conduct or of any applicable rules, laws, or regulations governing the performance of official duties or the discharge of official responsibilities. Such investigations must be made in accordance with Committee rules; (3) report to appropriate federal or state authorities substantial evidence of a violation of any law applicable to the performance of official duties that may have been disclosed in a Committee investigation. Such reports must be approved by the House or by an affirmative vote of two-thirds of the Committee; (4) render advisory opinions regarding the propriety of any current or proposed conduct of a Member, officer, or employee, and issue general guidance on such matters as necessary; (5) consider requests for written waivers of the gift rule (clause 5 of House Rule XXV).
Party Ratio: R 5-D 5

Charlie Dent, Pa., Chair	Linda Sánchez, Calif.
Patrick Meehan, Pa.	Michael E. Capuano, Mass.
Trey Gowdy, S.C.	Yvette D. Clarke, N.Y.
Susan W. Brooks, Ind.	Ted Deutch, Fla.
Kenny Marchant, Tex.	John B. Larson

FINANCIAL SERVICES

Office: 2129 RHOB 20515-6050
Phone: 225-7502　**Fax:** 226-0471
Web: financialservices.house.gov
Minority Web: democrats.financialservices.house.gov
Majority Staff Director: Shannon McGahn
Minority Staff Director: Charla Ouertatani, 225-4247, 4340 OHOB
Jurisdiction: (1) banks and banking, including deposit insurance and federal monetary policy; (2) economic stabilization, defense production, renegotiation, and control of the price of commodities, rents, and services; (3) financial aid to commerce and industry (other than transportation); (4) insurance generally; (5) international finance; (6) international financial and monetary organizations; (7) money and credit, including currency and the issuance of notes and redemption thereof; gold and silver, including the coinage thereof; valuation and revaluation of the dollar; (8) public and private housing; (9) securities and exchanges; (10) urban development.
Party Ratio: R 34-D 26

Jeb Hensarling, Tex., Chair	Maxine Waters, Calif.
Pete King, N.Y.	Carolyn B. Maloney, N.Y.
Edward R. Royce, Calif.	Nydia M. Velázquez, N.Y.
Frank Lucas, Okla.	Brad Sherman, Calif.
Scott Garrett, N.J.	Gregory W. Meeks, N.Y.
Randy Neugebauer, Tex.	Michael E. Capuano, Mass.
Patrick McHenry, N.C.	Rubén Hinojosa, Tex.
Stevan Pearce, N.M.	Wm. Lacy Clay, Mo.
Bill Posey, Fla.	Stephen F. Lynch, Mass.
Mike Fitzpatrick, Pa.	David Scott, Ga.
Lynn Westmoreland, Ga.	Al Green, Tex.
Blaine Luetkemeyer, Mo.	Emanuel Cleaver, Mo.

FINANCIAL SERVICES (continued)

Bill Huizenga, Mich.
Sean Duffy, Wisc.
Robert Hurt, Va.
Steve Stivers, Ohio
Stephen Fincher, Tenn.
Marlin Stutzman, Ind.
Mick Mulvaney, S.C.
Randy Hultgren, Ill.
Dennis A. Ross, Fla.
Robert Pittenger, N.C.
Ann Wagner, Mo.
Andy Barr, Ky.
Keith Rothfus, Pa.
Luke Messer, Ind.
David Schweikert, Ariz.
Frank Guinta, N.H.
Scott Tipton, Colo.
Roger Williams, Tex.
Bruce Poliquin, Maine
Mia Love, Utah
French Hill, Ark.
Tom Emmer, Minn.

Gwen Moore, Wisc.
Keith Ellison, Minn.
Ed Perlmutter, Colo.
James A. Himes, Conn.
John Carney, Del.
Terri Sewell, Ala.
Bill Foster, Ill.
Dan Kildee, Mich.
Patrick Murphy, Fla.
John Delaney, Md.
Kyrsten Sinema, Ariz.
Joyce Beatty, Ohio
Denny Heck, Wash.
Juan Vargas, Calif.

Subcommittees

Capital Markets and Government Sponsored Enterprises
Office: 2129 RHOB 20515   **Phone:** 225-7502
Scott Garrett (Chair), Robert Hurt, Pete King, Edward R. Royce, Randy Neugebauer, Patrick T. McHenry, Bill Huizenga, Sean Duffy, Steve Stivers, Stephen Fincher, Randy Hultgren, Dennis A. Ross, Ann Wagner, Luke Messer, David Schweikert, Bruce Poliquin, French Hill, Jeb Hensarling (ex officio)
Carolyn B. Maloney (Ranking Minority Member), Brad Sherman, Rubén Hinojosa, Stephen F. Lynch, Ed Perlmutter, David Scott, James A. Himes, Keith Ellison, Bill Foster, Gregory W. Meeks, John Carney, Terri Sewell, Patrick Murphy, Maxine Waters (ex officio)

Financial Institutions and Consumer Credit
Office: 2129 RHOB 20515   **Phone:** 225-7502
Randy Neugebauer (Chair), Stevan Pearce, Frank Lucas, Bill Posey, Mike Fitzpatrick, Lynn Westmoreland, Blaine Luetkemeyer, Marlin Stutzman, Mick Mulvaney, Robert Pittenger, Andy Barr, Keith Rothfus, Frank Guinta, Scott Tipton, Roger Williams, Mia Love, Tom Emmer, Jeb Hensarling (ex officio)
Wm. Lacy Clay (Ranking Minority Member), Gregory W. Meeks, Rubén Hinojosa, David Scott, Carolyn B. Maloney, Nydia M. Velázquez, Brad Sherman, Stephen F. Lynch, Michael E. Capuano, John Delaney, Denny Heck, Kyrsten Sinema, Juan Vargas, Maxine Waters (ex officio),

Housing and Insurance
Office: 2129 RHOB 20515   **Phone:** 225-7502
Blaine Luetkemeyer (Chair), Edward R. Royce, Scott Garrett, Lynn Westmoreland, Stevan Pearce, Robert Hurt, Steve Stivers, Dennis A. Ross, Andy Barr, Keith Rothfus, Bill Posey, Roger Williams, Jeb Hensarling (ex officio),

Emanuel Cleaver (Ranking Minority Member), Nydia M. Velázquez, Michael E. Capuano, Wm. Lacy Clay, Al Green, Gwen Moore, Keith Ellison, Joyce Beatty, Daniel Kildee, Maxine Waters (ex officio)

Monetary Policy and Trade
Office: 2129 RHOB 20515   **Phone:** 225-7502
Bill Huizenga (Chair), Mick Mulvaney, Frank Lucas, Stevan Pearce, Lynn Westmoreland, Marlin Stutzman, Robert Pittenger, Luke Messer, David Schweikert, Frank Guinta, Mia Love, Tom Emmer, Jeb Hensarling (ex officio)
Gwen Moore (Ranking Minority Member), Bill Foster, Ed Perlmutter, James A. Himes, John Carney, Terri Sewell, Patrick Murphy, Dan Kildee, Denny Heck, Maxine Waters (ex officio)

Oversight and Investigations
Office: 2129 RHOB 20515   **Phone:** 225-7502
Sean Duffy (Chair), Mike Fitzpatrick, Pete King, Patrick McHenry, Robert Hurt, Stephen Fincher, Mick Mulvaney, Randy Hultgren, Ann Wagner, Scott Tipton, Bruce Poliquin, French Hill, Jeb Hensarling (ex officio)
Al Green (Ranking Minority Member), Michael E. Capuano, Emanuel Cleaver, Keith Ellison, John Delaney, Joyce Beatty, Denny Heck, Kyrsten Sinema, Juan Vargas, Maxine Waters (ex officio)

Task Force to Investigate Terrorism Financing
Office: 2129 RHOB 20515 **Phone**: 225-7502
Mike Fitzpatrick, (Chair), Pete King, Steve Stivers, Dennis A. Ross, Ann Wagner, Andy Barr, Keith Rothfus, David Schweikert, Roger Williams, French Hill, Jeb Hensarling (ex officio)
Stephen F. Lynch (Ranking Member), Brad Sherman, Gregory W. Meeks, Al Green, Keith Ellison, James A. Himes, Bill Foster, Dan Kildee, Kyrsten Sinema, Maxine Waters (ex officio)

FOREIGN AFFAIRS

Office: 2170 RHOB 20515-6050
Phone: 225-5021   **Fax:** 225-5394
Web: foreignaffairs.house.gov
Minority Web: democrats.foreignaffairs.house.gov
Majority Staff Director: Thomas Sheehy
Minority Staff Director: Jason Steinbaum, 226-8467, B360 RHOB
Jurisdiction: (1) foreign assistance (including development assistance, Millennium Challenge Corporation, the Millennium Challenge Account, HIV/AIDS in foreign countries, security assistance, and Public Law 480 programs abroad); (2) the Peace Corps; (3) national security developments affecting foreign policy; (4) strategic planning and agreements; (5) war powers, treaties, executive agreements, and the deployment and use of U.S. Armed Forces; (6) peacekeeping, peace enforcement, and enforcement of UN or other international sanctions; (7) arms control and disarmament issues; (8) the U.S. Agency for International Development; (9) activities and policies of the State, Commerce and Defense Departments and

other agencies related to the Arms Export Control Act, and the Foreign Assistance Act including export and licensing policy for munitions items and technology and dual-use equipment and technology; (10) international law; (11) promotion of democracy; (12) international law enforcement issues, including narcotics control programs and activities; (13) Broadcasting Board of Governors; (14) embassy security; (15) international broadcasting; (16) public diplomacy, including international communication, information policy, international education, and cultural programs.
Party Ratio: R 25-D 19

Edward R. Royce, Calif., Chair	Eliot L. Engel, N.Y.
	Brad Sherman, Calif.
Chris Smith, N.J.	Gregory W. Meeks, N.Y.
Ileana Ros-Lehtinen, Fla.	Albio Sires, N.J.
Dana Rohrabacher, Calif.	Gerald E. Connolly, Va.
Steve Chabot, Ohio	Ted Deutch, Fla.
Joe Wilson, S.C.	Brian Higgins, N.Y.
Michael McCaul, Tex.	Karen Bass, Calif.
Ted Poe, Tex.	Bill Keating, Mass.
Matt Salmon, Ariz.	David Cicilline, R.I.
Darrell Issa, Calif.	Alan Grayson, Fla.
Tom Marino, Pa.	Ami Bera, Calif.
Jeff Duncan, S.C.	Alan Lowenthal, Calif.
Mo Brooks, Ala.	Grace Meng, N.Y
Paul Cook, Calif.	Lois Frankel, Fla.
Randy Weber, Tex.	Tulsi Gabbard, Hawaii
Scott Perry, Pa.	Joaquín Castro, Tex.
Ron DeSantis, Fla.	Robin Kelly, Ill.
Mark Meadows, N.C.	Brendan Boyle, Pa.
Ted Yoho, Fla.	
Curt Clawson, Fla.	
Scott DesJarlais, Tenn.	
Reid Ribble, Wisc.	
Dave Trott, Mich.	
Lee Zeldin, N.Y.	
Dan Donovan, N.Y.	

Subcommittees

Africa, Global Health, Global Human Rights, and International Organizations
Office: 5210 OHOB 20515   **Phone:** 225-5021
Chris Smith (Chair), Mark Meadows, Curt Clawson, Scott DesJarlais, Dan Donovan
Karen Bass (Ranking Minority Member), David Cicilline, Ami Bera

Asia and the Pacific
Office: 5190 OHOB 20515   **Phone:** 225-5021
Matt Salmon (Chair), Dana Rohrabacher, Steve Chabot, Tom Marino, Jeff Duncan, Mo Brooks, Scott Perry, Scott DesJarlais
Brad Sherman (Ranking Minority Member), Ami Bera, Tulsi Gabbard, Alan Lowenthal, Gerald E. Connolly, Grace Meng

Europe and Eurasia, and Emerging Threats
Office: 5210 OHOB 20515   **Phone:** 225-5021

Dana Rohrabacher (Chair), Ted Poe, Tom Marino, Mo Brooks, Paul Cook, Randy Weber, Reid Ribble, Dave Trott
Gregory W. Meeks (Ranking Minority Member), Albio Sires, Theodore Deutch, Bill Keating, Lois Frankel, Tulsi Gabbard

Middle East and North Africa
Office: 5220 OHOB 20515   **Phone:** 225-5021
Ileana Ros-Lehtinen (Chair), Steve Chabot, Joe Wilson, Darrel Issa, Randy Weber, Ron DeSantis, Mark Meadows, Ted Yoho, Curt Clawson, Dave Trott, Lee Zeldin
Ted Deutch (Ranking Minority Member), Gerald E. Connolly, Brian Higgins, David Cicilline, Alan Grayson, Grace Meng, Lois Frankel, Brendan Boyle

Terrorism, Nonproliferation, and Trade
Office: 5100 OHOB 20515   **Phone:** 225-5021
Ted Poe (Chair), Joe Wilson, Darrell Issa, Paul Cook, Scott Perry, Reid Ribble, Lee Zeldin
Bill Keating (Ranking Minority Member), Brad Sherman, Brian Higgins, Joaquín Castro, Robin Kelly

Western Hemisphere
Office: 5100 OHOB 20515   **Phone:** 225-5021
Jeff Duncan (Chair), Chris Smith, Ileana Ros-Lehtinen, Matt Salmon, Ron DeSantis, Ted Yoho, Dan Donovan
Albio Sires (Ranking Minority Member), Joaquín Castro, Robin Kelly, Gregory W. Meeks, Alan Grayson, Alan Lowenthal

HOMELAND SECURITY

Office: H2-176 FHOB 20515-6480
Phone: 226-8417   **Fax:** 226-3399
Web: homeland.house.gov
Minority Web: chsdemocrats.house.gov
Majority Staff Director: Brendan Shields
Minority Staff Director: Darek Newby, 226-2616, H2-117 FHOB
   Jurisdiction: (1) overall homeland security policy; (2) organization and administration of the Department of Homeland Security; (3) functions of the Department of Homeland Security relating to the following: (a) border and port security (except immigration policy and non-border enforcement); (b) customs (except customs revenue); (c) integration, analysis, and dissemination of homeland security information; (d) domestic preparedness for and collective response to terrorism; (e) research and development; (f) transportation security.
Party Ratio: R 18-D 12

Michael McCaul, N.Y., Chair	Bennie Thompson, Miss.
	Loretta Sánchez, Calif.
Lamar Smith, Tex.	Sheila Jackson Lee, Tex.
Pete King, Calif.	Jim Langevin, R.I.
Mike Rogers, Ala.	Brian Higgins, N.Y.
Candice S. Miller, Mich.	Cedric Richmond, La.
Jeff Duncan, S.C.	Bill Keating, Mass.
Tom Marino, Pa.	Donald M. Payne Jr., N.J.
Lou Barletta, Pa.	Filemon Vela, Tex.
Scott Perry, Pa.	

HOMELAND SECURITY (continued)

Curt Clawson, Fla.
John Katko, N.Y.
Will Hurd, Tex.
Buddy Carter, Ga.
Mark Walker, N.C.
Barry Loudermilk, Ga.
Martha McSally, Ariz.
John Ratcliffe, Tex.
Dan Donovan, N.Y.

Bonnie Watson Coleman, N.J.
Kathleen Rice, N.Y.
Norma Torres, Calif.

Subcommittees

Border and Maritime Security
Office: H2-176 FHOB 20515   **Phone:** 226-8417
   Candice S. Miller (Chair), Lamar Smith, Mike Rogers, Jeff Duncan, Lou Barletta, Will Hurd, Martha McSally
   Filemon Vela (Ranking Minority Member), Loretta Sánchez, Sheila Jackson Lee, Brian Higgins, Norma J. Torres

Counterterrorism and Intelligence
Office: H2-176 FHOB 20515   **Phone:** 226-8417
   Pete King (Chair), Candice S. Miller, Lou Barletta, John Katko, Will Hurd
   Brian Higgins (Ranking Minority Member), Bill Keating, Filemon Vela

Cybersecurity, Infrastructure Protection, and Security Technologies
Office: H2-176 FHOB 20515   **Phone:** 226-8417
   John Ratcliffe (Chair), Pete King, Tom Marino, Scott Perry, Curt Clawson, Dan Donovan
   Cedric Richmond (Ranking Minority Member), Loretta Sánchez, Sheila Jackson Lee, Jim Langevin

Emergency Preparedness, Response, and Communications
Office: H2-176 FHOB 20515   **Phone:** 226-8417
   Martha McSally (Chair), Tom Marino, Mark Walker, Barry Loudermilk, Dan Donovan
   Donald M. Payne Jr. (Ranking Minority Member), Bonnie Watson Coleman, Kathleen Rice

Oversight and Management Efficiency
Office: H2-176 FHOB 20515   **Phone:** 226-8417
   Scott Perry (Chair), Jeff Duncan, Curt Clawson, Buddy Carter, Barry Loudermilk
   Bonnie Watson Coleman (Ranking Minority Member), Cedric Richmond, Norma J. Torres

Transportation Security
Office: H2-176 FHOB 20515   **Phone:** 226-8417
   John Katko (Chair), Mike Rogers, Buddy Carter, Mark Walker, John Ratcliffe, Michael McCaul (ex officio)
   Kathleen Rice (Ranking Minority Member), Bill Keating, Donald M. Payne Jr., Bennie Thompson (ex officio)

HOUSE ADMINISTRATION

Office: 1309 LHOB 20515-6157
Phone: 225-8281   **Fax:** 225-9957
Web: cha.house.gov

Minority Web: democrats.cha.house.gov
Majority Staff Director: Sean Moran
Minority Staff Director: Jamie Fleet, 225-2061, 1307 LHOB
   Jurisdiction: (1) appropriations from accounts for committee salaries and expenses (except for the Committee on Appropriations), House Information Resources, and allowances and expenses of Members, Delegates, the Resident Commissioner, House Officers and administrative offices of the House; (2) auditing and settling of all accounts described in (1), above; (3) employment of persons by the House, including staff for Members, Delegates, the Resident Commissioner, and committees; and reporters of debates, subject to rule VI; (4) except as provided in clause 1(q)(11), matters relating to the Library of Congress, including management thereof, statuary and pictures, acceptance or purchase of works of art for the U.S. Capitol, the U.S. Botanic Garden, and purchase of books and manuscripts; (5) The Smithsonian Institution and the incorporation of similar institutions (except as provided in paragraph (q)(11)); (6) expenditure of accounts described in (1), above; (7) Franking Commission; (8) printing and correction of the Congressional Record; (9) accounts of the House generally; (10) assignment of office space for Members, Delegates, the Resident Commissioner, and committees; (11) disposition of useless executive papers; (12) election of the President, Vice President, and Members of the House of Representatives, Senators, Delegates, or the Resident Commissioner; corrupt practices, contested elections, credentials and qualifications, and federal elections generally; (13) services to the House, including the House Restaurant, parking facilities and administration of the House Office Buildings and of the House wing of the U.S. Capitol; (14) travel of Members of the House of Representatives, Delegates, and the Resident Commissioner; (15) raising, reporting and use of campaign contributions for candidates for office of Representative in the House of Representatives, Delegate to the House of Representatives, and of Resident Commissioner; (16) compensation, retirement and other benefits of the Members, Delegates, the Resident Commissioner, officers, and employees of the Congress.
Party Ratio: R 6-D 3

Candice S. Miller, Mich., Chair
Gregg Harper, Miss.
Richard Nugent, Fla.
Rodney Davis, Ill.
Barbara Comstock, Va.
Mark Walker, N.C.

Robert Brady, Pa.
Zoe Lofgren, Calif.
Juan Vargas, Calif.

JUDICIARY

Office: 2138 RHOB 20515-6216
Phone: 225-3951   **Fax:** 226-7680
Web: judiciary.house.gov
Minority Web: democrats.judiciary.house.gov
Majority Chief of Staff: Shelly Husband
Minority Staff Director: Perry H. Apelbaum, 225-6906, B351 RHOB

Jurisdiction: (1) judiciary and judicial proceedings, civil and criminal; (2) administrative practice and procedure; (3) apportionment of Representatives; (4) bankruptcy, mutiny, espionage, and counterfeiting; (5) civil liberties; (6) constitutional amendments; (7) criminal law enforcement; (8) federal courts and judges, and local courts in the Territories and possessions; (9) immigration policy and non-border enforcement; (10) interstate compacts generally; (11) claims against the United States; (12) members of Congress, attendance of members, Delegates, and the Resident Commissioner; and their acceptance of incompatible offices; (13) national penitentiaries; (14) patents, the Patent and Trademark Office, copyrights, and trademarks; (15) presidential succession; (16) protection of trade and commerce against unlawful restraints and monopolies; (17) revision and codification of the Statutes of the United States; (18) state and territorial boundary lines; (19) subversive activities affecting the internal security of the United States.

Party Ratio: R 23-D 16

Bob Goodlatte, Va., Chair	*John Conyers Jr., Mich.*
Jim Sensenbrenner, Wisc.	*Jerrold Nadler, NY.*
Lamar Smith, Tex.	*Zoe Lofgren, Calif.*
Steve Chabot, Ohio	*Sheila Jackson Lee, Tex.*
Darrell Issa, Calif.	*Steve Cohen, Tenn.*
J. Randy Forbes, Va.	*Hank Johnson, Ga.*
Steve King, Iowa	*Pedro Pierluisi, P.R.*
Trent Franks, Ariz.	*Judy Chu, Calif.*
Louie Gohmert, Tex.	*Ted Deutch, Fla.*
Jim Jordan, Ohio	*Luis V. Gutierrez, Ill.*
Ted Poe, Tex.	*Karen Bass, Calif.*
Jason Chaffetz, Utah	*Cedric Richmond, La.*
Tom Marino, Pa.	*Suzan DelBene, Wash.*
Trey Gowdy, S.C.	*Hakeem S. Jeffries, N.Y.*
Rául Labrador, Idaho	*David Cicilline, R.I.*
Blake Farenthold, Tex.	*Scott H. Peters, Calif.*
Doug Collins, Ga.	
Ron DeSantis, Fla.	
Mimi Walters, Calif.	
Ken Buck, Colo.	
John Ratcliffe, Tex.	
Dave Trott, Mich.	
Mike Bishop, Mich.	

Subcommittees

The Constitution and Civil Justice
Office: H2-362 FHOB 20515   **Phone:** 225-2825
Trent Franks (Chair), Ron DeSantis, Steve King, Louie Gohmert, Jim Jordan
Steve Cohen (Ranking Minority Member), Jerrold Nadler, Ted Deutch

Courts, Intellectual Property, and the Internet
Office: 6310 OHOB 20024   **Phone:** 226-7680
Darrell Issa (Chair), Doug Collins, Jim Sensenbrenner, Lamar Smith, Steve Chabot, J. Randy Forbes, Trent Franks, Jim Jordan, Ted Poe, Jason Chaffetz, Tom Marino, Blake Farenthold, Ron DeSantis, Mimi Walters
Jerrold Nadler (Ranking Minority Member), Judy Chu, Ted Deutch, Karen Bass, Cedric Richmond, Suzan DelBene,

Hakeem S. Jeffries, David Cicilline, Scott H. Peters, Zoe Lofgren, Steve Cohen, Hank Johnson

Crime, Terrorism, Homeland Security, and Investigations
Office: 6340 OHOB 20024   **Phone:** 225-5727
Jim Sensenbrenner (Chair), Louie Gohmert, Steve Chabot, J. Randy Forbes, Ted Poe, Jason Chaffetz, Trey Gowdy, Rául Labrador, Ken Buck, Mike Bishop
Sheila Jackson Lee (Ranking Minority Member), Pedro Pierluisi, Judy Chu, Luis V. Gutierrez, Karen Bass, Cedric Richmond

Immigration and Border Security
Office: 6320 OHOB 20024   **Phone:** 225-3926
Trey Gowdy (Chair), Rául Labrador, Lamar Smith, Steve King, Ken Buck, John Ratcliffe, Dave Trott
Zoe Lofgren (Ranking Minority Member), Luis V. Gutierrez, Sheila Jackson Lee, Pedro Pierluisi

Regulatory Reform, Commercial and Antitrust Law
Office: 6240 OHOB 20024   **Phone:** 226-7680
Tom Marino (Chair), Blake Farenthold, Darrell Issa, Doug Collins, Mimi Walters, John Ratcliffe, Dave Trott, Mike Bishop
Hank Johnson (Ranking Minority Member), Suzan DelBene, Hakeem S. Jeffries, David Cicilline, Scott H. Peters

NATURAL RESOURCES

Office: 1324 LHOB 20515-6201
Phone: 225-2761   **Fax:** 225-5929
Web: naturalresources.house.gov
Minority Web: democrats.naturalresources.house.gov
Majority Staff Director: Jason Knox
Minority Staff Director: David Watkins, 225-6065, 1329 LHOB
Jurisdiction: (1) fisheries and wildlife, including research, restoration, refuges, and conservation; (2) forest reserves and national parks created from the public domain; (3) Forfeiture of land grants and alien ownership, including alien ownership of mineral lands; (4) Geological Survey; (5) international fishing agreements; (6) interstate compacts relating to apportionment of waters for irrigation purposes; (7) irrigation and reclamation, including water supply for reclamation projects and easements of public lands for irrigation projects; and acquisition of private lands when necessary to complete irrigation projects; (8) Native Americans generally, including the care and allotment of Native American lands and general and special measures relating to claims that are paid out of Native American funds; (9) insular possessions of the United States generally (except those affecting the revenue and appropriations); (10) military parks and battlefields, national cemeteries administered by the Secretary of the Interior, parks within the District of Columbia, and the erection of monuments to the memory of individuals; (11) mineral land laws and claims and entries thereunder; (12) mineral resources of public lands; (13) mining interests generally; (14) mining schools and experimental stations; (15) marine affairs, including coastal zone management

NATURAL RESOURCES (continued)

(except for measures relating to oil and other pollution of navigable waters); (16) oceanography; (17) petroleum conservation on public lands and conservation of the radium supply in the United States; (18) preservation of prehistoric ruins and objects of interest on the public domain; (19) public lands generally, including entry, easements, and grazing thereon; (20) relations of the United States with Native Americans and Native American tribes; (21) Trans-Alaska Oil Pipeline (except ratemaking).

Party Ratio: R 26-D 18

Rob Bishop, Utah, Chair	Raúl M. Grijalva, Ariz.
Don A. Young, Alaska	Grace F. Napolitano, Calif.
Louie Gohmert, Tex.	Madeleine Z. Bordallo,
Doug Lamborn, Colo.	Guam
Robert J. Wittman, Va.	Jim Costa, Calif.
John Fleming, La.	Gregorio Kilili
Tom McClintock, Calif.	Camacho Sablan,
Glenn (GT) Thompson, Pa.	Northern Mariana Is.
Cynthia Lummis, Wyo.	Niki Tsongas, Mass.
Dan Benishek, Mich.	Pedro Pierluisi, P.R.
Jeff Duncan, S.C.	Jared Huffman, Calif.
Paul Gosar, Ariz.	Raúl Ruiz, Calif.
Raúl Labrador, Idaho	Alan Lowenthal, Calif.
Doug LaMalfa, Calif.	Matt Cartwright, Pa.
Jeff Denham, Calif.	Don Beyer, Va.
Paul Cook, Calif.	Norma Torres, Calif.
Bruce Westerman, Ark.	Debbie Dingell, Mich.
Garrett Graves, La.	Ruben Gallego, Calif.
Dan Newhouse, Wash.	Lois Capps, Calif.
Ryan Zinke, Mont.	Jared Polis, Colo.
Jody Hice, Ga.	Wm. Lacy Clay, Mo.
Amata Coleman	
Radewagen, Am. Samoa	
Tom MacArthur, N.J.	
Alex Mooney, W. Va.	
Cresent Hardy, Nev.	
Darin LaHood, Ill.	

Subcommittees

Energy and Mineral Resources
Office: 1333 LHOB 20515 **Phone:** 225-9297
Doug Lamborn (Chair), Louie Gohmert, Robert J. Wittman, John Fleming, Glenn (GT) Thompson, Cynthia Lummis, Dan Benishek, Jeff Duncan, Paul Gosar, Raúl Labrador, Paul Cook, Garret Graves, Ryan Zinke, Alex Mooney, Cresent Hardy, Rob Bishop (ex officio)
Alan Lowenthal (Ranking Minority Member), Jim Costa, Niki Tsongas, Matt Cartwright, Don Beyer, Ruben Gallego, Lois Capps, Jared Polis, Raúl M. Grijalva (ex officio)

Federal Lands
Office: 1332 LHOB 20515 **Phone:** 226-7736
Tom McClinktock (Chair), Don A. Young, Louie Gohmert, Glenn (GT) Thompson, Cynthia Lummis, Raúl Labrador, Doug LaMalfa, Bruce Westerman, Dan Newhouse, Ryan Zinke, Jody Hice, Tom MacArthur, Cresent Hardy, Darin LaHood, Rob Bishop (ex officio)

Niki Tsongas (Ranking Minority Member), Matt Cartwright, Don Beyer, Pedro Pierluisi, Jared Huffman, Alan Lowenthal, Debbie Dingell, Lois Capps, Jared Polis, Raúl M. Grijalva (ex officio)

Indian, Insular and Alaska Native Affairs
Office: 4450 OHOB 20515 **Phone:** 226-9725
Don A. Young (Chair), Dan Benishek, Paul Gosar, Doug LaMalfa, Jeff Denham, Paul Cook, Amata Coleman Radewagen, Rob Bishop (ex officio)
Raúl Ruiz (Ranking Minority Member), Madeleine Z. Bordallo, Gregorio Kilili, Camacho Sablan, Pedro Pierluisi, Norma Torres, Raúl M. Grijalva (ex officio)

Oversight and Investigations
Office: 4170 OHOB 20515 **Phone:** 225-7107
Louie Gohmert (Chair), Doug Lamborn, Raúl Labrador, Bruce Westerman, Jody Hice, Amata Coleman Radewagen, Alex Mooney, Darin LaHood, Rob Bishop (ex officio)
Debbie Dingell (Ranking Minority Member), Jared Huffman, Ruben Gallego, Jared Polis, Raúl M. Grijalva (ex officio)

Water, Power, and Oceans
Office: 1522 LHOB 20515 **Phone:** 225-8331
John Fleming (Chair), Don A. Young, Robert J. Wittman, Tom McClintock, Cynthia Lummis, Jeff Duncan, Paul Gosar, Doug LaMalfa, Garret Graves, Jeff Denham, Dan Newhouse, Tom MacArthur, Rob Bishop (ex officio)
Jared Huffman (Ranking Minority Member), Grace Napolitano, Jim Costa, Ruben Gallego, Madeleine Z. Bordallo, Gregorio Kilili Camacho Sablan, Raúl Ruiz, Alan Lowenthal, Norma Torres, Debbie Dingell, Raúl M. Grijalva (ex officio)

OVERSIGHT AND GOVERNMENT REFORM

Office: 2157 RHOB 20515-6143
Phone: 225-5074 **Fax:** 225-3974
Web: oversight.house.gov
Minority Web: democrats.oversight.house.gov
Majority Staff Director: Jennifer Hemingway
Minority Staff Director: David Rapallo, 225-5051, 2471 RHOB

Jurisdiction: (1) federal civil service, including intergovernmental personnel; and the status of officers and employees of the United States, including their compensation, classification, and retirement; (2) municipal affairs of the District of Columbia in general (other than appropriations); (3) federal paperwork reduction; (4) government management and accounting measures generally; (5) holidays and celebrations; (6) overall economy, efficiency, and management of government operations and activities, including federal procurement; (7) national archives; (8) population and demography generally, including the Census; (9) Postal Service generally, including transportation of the mails; (10) public information and records; (11) relationship of the federal government to the states

and municipalities generally; (12) reorganizations in the executive branch of the government.
Party Ratio: R 25-D 18

Jason Chaffetz, Utah, Chair	Elijah E. Cummings, Md.
Blake Farenthold, Tex.	Carolyn B. Maloney, N.Y.
Cynthia Lummis, Wyo.	Eleanor Holmes Norton,
Buddy Carter, Ga.	D.C.
Gary Palmer, Ala.	Wm. Lacy Clay, Mo.
Jim Jordan, Ohio	Stephen F. Lynch, Mass.
Jody Hice, Ga.	Jim Cooper, Tenn.
John J. Duncan Jr., Tenn.	Gerald E. Connolly, Va.
John Mica, Fla.	Matt Cartwright, Pa.
Justin Amash, Mich.	Tammy Duckworth, Ill.
Mark Meadows, N.C.	Robin Kelly, Ill.
Mike Turner, Ohio	Brenda Lawrence, Mich.
Ken Buck, Colo.	Ted Lieu, Calif.
Mark Walker, N.C.	Bonnie Watson Coleman,
Paul Gosar, Ariz.	N.J.
Mick Mulvaney, S.C.	Michelle Lujan Grisham,
Rod Blum, Iowa	N.M.
Ron DeSantis, Fla.	Peter Welch, Vt.
Scott DesJarlais, Tenn.	Stacey Plaskett, Virgin Is.
Thomas Massie, Ky.	Mark DeSaulnier, Calif.
Tim Walberg, Mich.	Brendan Boyle, Pa.
Trey Gowdy, S.C.	
Steve Russell, Okla.	
Glenn Grothman, Wisc.	
Will Hurd, Tex.	

Subcommittees

Government Operations
Office: 6460 OHOB 20515   **Phone:** 225-5074
Mark Meadows (Chair), Tim Walberg, Buddy Carter, Glenn Grothman, Jim Jordan, Ken Buck, Mick Mulvaney, Thomas Massie, Trey Gowdy
Gerald E. Connolly (Ranking Minority Member), Carolyn B. Maloney, Eleanor Holmes Norton, Stacey Plaskett, Stephen F. Lynch, Wm. Lacy Clay

Health Care, Benefits, and Administrative Rules
Office: 6450 OHOB 20515   **Phone:** 225-5074
Jim Jordan (Chair), Mick Mulvaney, Buddy Carter, Cynthia Lummis, Jody Hice, Mark Meadows, Mark Walker, Ron DeSantis, Scott DesJarlais, Tim Walberg, Trey Gowdy
Matt Cartwright (Ranking Minority Member), Bonnie Watson Coleman, Brendan Boyle, Eleanor Holmes Norton, Jim Cooper, Mark DeSaulnier, Michelle Lujan Grisham

Information Technology
Office: 6470 OHOB 20515   **Phone:** 225-5074
William Hurd (Chair), Blake Farenthold, Mark Walker, Paul Gosar, Rod Blum
Robin Kelly (Ranking Minority Member), Gerald E. Connolly, Tammy Duckworth, Ted Lieu

Interior
Office: 6430 OHOB 20515   **Phone:** 225-5074
Cynthia Lummis (Chair), Ken Buck, Blake Farenthold, Gary Palmer, Paul Gosar, Steve Russell
Brenda Lawrence (Ranking Minority Member), Matt Cartwright, Stacey Plaskett

National Security
Office: 6440 OHOB 20515   **Phone:** 225-5074
Ron DeSantis (Chair), Steve Russell, Jody Hice, John J. Duncan Jr., John Mica, William Hurd
Stephen F. Lynch (Ranking Minority Member), Brenda Lawrence, Robin Kelly, Ted Lieu,

Transportation and Public Assets
Office: 6470 OHOB 20515   **Phone:** 225-5074
John Mica (Chair), Glenn Grothman, John J. Duncan Jr., Justin Amash, Mike Turner, Thomas Massie
Tammy Duckworth (Ranking Minority Member), Bonnie Watson Coleman, Brendan Boyle, Mark DeSaulnier

RULES

Office: H-312 CAP 20515-6269
Phone: 225-9191   **Fax:** 225-6763
Web: rules.house.gov
Minority Web: democrats.rules.house.gov
Majority Staff Director: Hugh Halpern
Minority Staff Director: Miles M. Lackey, 225-9091, 1116 LHOB
Jurisdiction: (1) the rules and joint rules (other than rules or joint rules relating to the Code of Official Conduct), and order of business of the House; (2) recesses and final adjournments of Congress.
Party Ratio: R 9-D 4

Pete Sessions, Tex., Chair	Louise M. Slaughter, N.Y.
Virginia Foxx, N.C.	Jim McGovern, Mass.
Tom Cole, Okla.	Alcee L. Hastings, Fla.
Rob Woodall, Ga.	Jared Polis, Colo.
Michael C. Burgess, Tex.	
Steve Stivers, Ohio	
Doug Collins, Ga.	
Bradley Byrne, Ala.	
Dan Newhouse, Wash.	

Subcommittees

Legislative and Budget Process
Office: H-312 CAP 20515   **Phone:** 225-9191
Rob Woodall (Chair), Michael C. Burgess, Bradley Byrne, Dan Newhouse, Virginia Foxx
Alcee L. Hastings (Ranking Minority Member), Jared Polis

Rules and Organization of the House
Office: H-312 CAP 20515   **Phone:** 225-9191
Steve Stivers (Chair), Bradley Byrne, Dan Newhouse, Pete Sessions, Doug Collins
Louise M. Slaughter (Ranking Minority Member), Jim McGovern

SCIENCE, SPACE, AND TECHNOLOGY

Office: 2321 RHOB 20515-6301
Phone: 225-6371   **Fax:** 226-0113
Web: science.house.gov
Minority Web: democrats.science.house.gov
Majority Chief of Staff: Jennifer Brown

SCIENCE, SPACE, AND TECHNOLOGY
(continued)

Minority Chief of Staff: Richard Obermann, 225-6375, 394 FHOB

Jurisdiction: (1) all energy research, development, and demonstration, and projects therefor, and all federally owned or operated non-military energy laboratories; (2) astronautical research and development, including resources, personnel, equipment, and facilities; civil aviation research and development; (3) environmental research and development; (4) marine research; commercial application of energy technology; (5) National Institute of Standards and Technology, standardization of weights and measures and the metric system; (6) National Aeronautics and Space Administration; (7) National Science Foundation; (8) National Weather Service; (9) outer space, including exploration and control thereof; (10) science scholarships; scientific research, development, and demonstration, and projects therefor.

Party Ratio: R 22-D 17

Lamar Smith, Tex., Chair	Eddie Bernice Johnson, Tex.
Jim Sensenbrenner, Wisc.	Zoe Lofgren, Calif.
Dana Rohrabacher, Calif.	Daniel Lipinski, Ill.
Frank Lucas, Okla.	Donna F. Edwards, Md.
Randy Neugebauer, Tex.	Suzanne Bonamici, Ore.
Michael McCaul, Tex.	Eric Swalwell, Calif.
Ralph Abraham, La.	Alan Grayson, Fla.
Mo Brooks, Ala.	Ami Bera, Calif.
Randy Hultgren, Ill.	Elizabeth Esty, Conn.
Bill Posey, Fla.	Marc Veasey, Tex.
Thomas Massie, Ky.	Katherine Clark, Mass.
Jim Bridenstine, Okla.	Don Beyer, Va.
Randy Weber, Tex.	Ed Perlmutter, Colo.
John Moolenaar, Mich.	Paul D. Tonko, N.Y.
Steve Knight, Calif.	Mark Takano, Calif.
Brian Babin, Tex.	Bill Foster, Ill.
Bruce Westerman, Ark.	Vacancy
Barbara Comstock, Va.	
Darin LaHood, Ill.	
Gary Palmer, Ala.	
Barry Loudermilk, Ga.	

Subcommittees

Energy
Office: 2319 RHOB 20515   **Phone:** 225-6371
Randy Weber (Chair), Dana Rohrabacher, Randy Neugebauer, Mo Brooks, Randy Hultgren, Thomas Massie, Barbara Comstock, Steve Knight, Barry Loudermilk
Alan Grayson (Ranking Minority Member), Eric Swalwell, Marc Veasey, Dan Lipinski, Katherine Clark, Ed Perlmutter

Environment
Office: 2319 RHOB 20515   **Phone:** 225-6371
Jim Bridenstein (Chair), Jim Sensenbrenner, Randy Neugebauer, Randy Weber, John Moolenaar, Brian Babin, Bruce Westerman, Ralph Abraham, Gary Palmer

Suzanne Bonamici (Ranking Minority Member), Donna F. Edwards, Alan Grayson, Ami Bera, Mark Takano, Bill Foster

Oversight
Office: 2321 RHOB 20515   **Phone:** 225-6371
Barry Loudermilk (Chair), Jim Sensenbrenner, Bill Posey, Thomas Massie, Darin LaHood, Vacancy
Don Beyer (Ranking Minority Member), Alan Grayson, Zoe Lofgren

Research and Technology
Office: 4220 OHOB 20515   **Phone:** 225-6371
Barbara Comstock (Chair), Frank Lucas, Michael McCaul, Ralph Abraham, Randy Hultgren, John Moolenaar, Darin LaHood, Bruce Westerman, Gary Palmer
Dan Lipinski (Ranking Minority Member), Elizabeth Esty, Katherine Clark, Paul D. Tonko, Suzanne Bonamici, Eric Swalwell

Space
Office: 4220 OHOB 20515   **Phone:** 225-6371
Brian Babin (Chair), Dana Rohrabacher, Frank Lucas, Michael McCaul, Mo Brooks, Bill Posey, Steve Knight, Jim Bridenstine, Vacancy
Donna F. Edwards (Ranking Minority Member), Ami Bera, Zoe Lofgren, Ed Perlmutter, Marc Veasey, Don Beyer

SMALL BUSINESS

Office: 2361 RHOB 20515-6315
Phone: 225-5821   **Fax:** 226-5276
Web: smallbusiness.house.gov
Minority Web: democrats.smallbusiness.house.gov
Majority Staff Director: Kevin Fitzpatrick
Minority Staff Director: Michael Day, 225-4038, B-343C RHOB

Jurisdiction: (1) assistance to and protection of small business, including financial aid, regulatory flexibility, and paperwork reduction; (2) participation of small-business enterprises in federal procurement and government contracts; (3) The Committee on Small Business shall study and investigate on a continuing basis the problems of all types of small business.

Party Ratio: R 13-D 10

Steve Chabot, Ohio, Chair	Nydia M. Velázquez, N.Y.
Steve King, Iowa	Yvette D. Clarke, N.Y.
Blaine Luetkemeyer, Mo.	Judy Chu, Calif.
Richard Hanna, N.Y.	Janice Hahn, Calif.
Tim Huelskamp, Kans.	Donald M. Payne Jr., N.J.
Chris P. Gibson, N.Y.	Grace Meng, N.Y.
Dave Brat, Va.	Brenda Lawrence, Mich.
Amata Coleman	Alma Adams, N.C.
Radewagen, Am. Samoa	Seth Moulton, Mass.
Steve Knight, Calif.	Mark Takai, Hawaii
Carlos Curbelo, Fla.	
Cresent Hardy, Nev.	
Trent Kelly, Miss.	
Vacancy	

Subcommittees

Agriculture, Energy and Trade
Office: 2361 RHOB 20515   **Phone:** 225-5821
Carlos Curbelo (Chair), Steve King, Blaine Luetkemeyer, Tim Huelskamp, Chris P. Gibson, Dave Brat
Grace Meng (Ranking Minority Member), Brenda Lawrence, Mark Takai, Vacancy

Contracting and Workforce
Office: 2361 RHOB 20515   **Phone:** 225-5821
Richard Hanna (Chair), Steve King, Chris P. Gibson, Steve Knight, Cresent Hardy, Trent Kelly
Mark Takai (Ranking Minority Member), Judy Chu, Brenda Lawrence, Yvette D. Clarke

Economic Growth, Tax, and Capital Access
Office: 2361 RHOB 20515   **Phone:** 225-5821
Tim Huelskamp (Chair), Richard Hanna, Dave Brat, Amata Coleman Radewagen, Trent Kelly
Judy Chu (Ranking Minority Member), Janice Hahn, Donald M. Payne Jr., Yvette D. Clarke

Health and Technology
Office: 2361 RHOB 20515   **Phone:** 225-5821
Amata Coleman Radewagen (Chair), Blaine Luetkemeyer, Carlos Curbelo, Mike Bost, Vacancy, Vacancy
Seth Moulton (Ranking Minority Member), Judy Chu, Vacancy, Vacancy

Investigations, Oversight, and Regulations
Office: 2361 RHOB 20515   **Phone:** 225-5821
Cresent Hardy (Chair), Steve Knight, Mike Bost, Vacancy, Vacancy
Alma Adams (Ranking Minority Member), Vacancy, Vacancy, Vacancy

TRANSPORTATION AND INFRASTRUCTURE

Office: 2251 RHOB 20515-6256
Phone: 225-9446   **Fax:** 225-6782
Web: transportation.house.gov
Minority Web: democrats.transportation.house.gov
Majority Chief of Staff: Chris Bertram
Minority Staff Director: Katherine Dedrick, 225-4472, 2164 RHOB
Jurisdiction: (1) Coast Guard, including lifesaving service, lighthouses, lightships, ocean derelicts, and the Coast Guard Academy; (2) federal management of emergencies and natural disasters; (3) flood control and improvement of rivers and harbors; (4) inland waterways; (5) inspection of merchant marine vessels, lights and signals, lifesaving equipment, and fire protection on such vessels; (6) navigation and laws relating thereto, including pilotage; (7) registering and licensing of vessels and small boats; (8) rules and international arrangements to prevent collisions at sea; (9) the Capitol Building, the Senate and House Office Buildings; (10) constructions or maintenance of roads and post roads (other than appropriations therefore); (11) construction or reconstruction, maintenance, and care of buildings and grounds of the Botanic Garden, the Library of Congress, and the Smithsonian Institution; (12) merchant marine (except for national security aspects thereof);

(13) purchase of sites and construction of post offices, customhouses, federal courthouses, and government buildings within the District of Columbia; (14) oil and other pollution of navigable waters, including inland, costal, and ocean waters; (15) marine affairs, including coastal zone management, as they relate to oil and other pollution of navigable waters; (16) public buildings and occupied or improved grounds of the United States generally; (17) public works for the benefit of the benefit of navigation, including bridges and dams (other than international bridges and dams); (18) related transportation regulatory agencies (except the Transportation Security Administration); (19) roads and the safety thereof; (20) transportation, including civil aviation, railroads, water transportation, transportation safety (except automobile safety and transportation security functions of the Department of Homeland Security), transportation infrastructure, transportation labor, and railroad retirement and unemployment (except revenue measures related thereto); (21) water power.
Party Ratio: R 34-D 25

Bill Shuster, Pa., Chair	*Peter DeFazio, Ore.*
Don A. Young, Alaska	*Eleanor Holmes Norton,*
John J. Duncan Jr., Tenn.	*D.C.*
John Mica, Fla.	*Jerrold Nadler, N.Y.*
Frank LoBiondo, N.J.	*Corrine Brown, Fla.*
Sam Graves, Mo.	*Eddie Bernice Johnson, Tex.*
Candice S. Miller, Mich.	*Elijah E. Cummings, Md.*
Duncan Hunter, Calif.	*Rick Larsen, Wash.*
Rick Crawford, Ark.	*Michael E. Capuano, Mass.*
Lou Barletta, Pa.	*Grace F. Napolitano, Calif.*
Blake Farenthold, Tex.	*Daniel Lipinski, Ill.*
Bob Gibbs, Ohio	*Steve Cohen, Tenn.*
Richard Hanna, N.Y.	*Albio Sires, N.J.*
Daniel Webster, Fla.	*Donna F. Edwards, Md.*
Jeff Denham, Calif.	*John Garamendi, Calif.*
Reid Ribble, Wisc.	*André Carson, Ind.*
Thomas Massie, Ky.	*Janice Hahn, Calif.*
Mark Meadows, N.C.	*Rick Nolan, Minn.*
Scott Perry, Pa.	*Ann Kirkpatrick, Ariz.*
Rodney Davis, Ill.	*Dina Titus, Nev.*
Mark Sanford, S.C.	*Sean Patrick Maloney, N.Y.*
Rob Woodall, Ga.	*Elizabeth Esty, Conn.*
Todd Rokita, Ind.	*Lois Frankel, Fla.*
John Katko, N.Y.	*Cheri Bustos, Ill.*
Brian Babin, Tex.	*Jared Huffman, Calif.*
Cresent Hardy, Nev.	*Julia Brownley, Calif.*
Ryan Costello, Pa.	
Garret Graves, S.C.	
Mimi Walters, Calif.	
Barbara Comstock, Va.	
Carlos Curbelo, Fla.	
David Rouzer, N.C.	
Lee Zeldin, N.Y.	
Mike Bost, Ill.	

Subcommittees

Aviation
Office: 2251 RHOB 20515   **Phone:** 226-3220
Frank LoBiondo (Chair), Don Young, John J. Duncan Jr., John Mica, Sam Graves, Candice S. Miller, Blake

TRANSPORTATION AND INFRASTRUCTURE

(continued)

Farenthold, Richard Hanna, Reid Ribble, Mark Meadows, Rodney Davis, Mark Sanford, Rob Woodall, Todd Rokita, Ryan Costello, Mimi Walters, Barbara Comstock, Carlos Curbelos, Lee Zeldin, Bill Shuster (ex officio)

Rick Larsen (Ranking Minority Member), Eleanor Holmes Norton, Eddie Bernice Johnson, Daniel Lipinski, Andre Carson, Ann Kirkpatrick, Dina Titus, Sean Patrick Maloney, Cheri Bustos, Julia Brownley, Michael E. Capuano, Steve Cohen, Rick Nolan, John Garamendi, Peter A. DeFazio (ex officio)

Coast Guard and Maritime Transportation

Office: 507 FHOB 20515   **Phone:** 226-3552

Duncan Hunter (Chair), Don Young, Frank LoBiondo, Bob Gibbs, Mark Sanford, Garret Graves, Carlos Curbelo, David Rouzer, Lee Zeldin, Bill Shuster (ex officio)

John Garamendi (Ranking Minority Member), Elijah E. Cummings, Corrine Brown, Janice Hahn, Lois Frankel, Julia Brownley, Peter DeFazio (ex officio)

Economic Development, Public Buildings, and Emergency Management

Office: 586 FHOB 20515   **Phone:** 225-3014

Lou Barletta (Chair), Rick Crawford, Thomas Massie, Mark Meadows, Scott Perry, Ryan Costello, Barbara Comstock, Carlos Curbelo, David Rouzer, Bill Shuster (ex officio)

André Carson (Ranking Minority Member), Eleanor Holmes Norton, Albio Sires, Donna F. Edwards, Dina Titus, Peter DeFazio (ex officio)

Highways and Transit

Office: 2251 RHOB 20515   **Phone:** 225-6715

Sam Graves (Chair), Don A. Young, John J. Duncan Jr., John Mica, Frank LoBiondo, Duncan Hunter, Rick Crawford, Lou Barletta, Blake Farenthold, Bob Gibbs, Richard Hanna, Daniel Webster, Jeff Denham, Reid Ribble, Thomas Massie, Mark Meadows, Scott Perry, Rodney Davis, Rob Woodall, John Katko, Brian Babin, Cresent Hardy, Ryan Costello, Garret Graves, Mimi Walters, Barbara Comstock, Mike Bost, Bill Shuster (ex officio)

Eleanor Holmes Norton (Ranking Minority Member), Jerrold Nadler, Eddie Bernice Johnson, Steve Cohen, Albio Sires, Donna F. Edwards, Janice Hahn, Rick Nolan, Ann Kirkpatrick, Dina Titus, Sean Patrick Maloney, Elizabeth Esty, Lois Frankel, Cheri Bustos, Jared Huffman, Julia Brownley, Michael E. Capuano, Grace Napolitano, Corrine Brown, Daniel Lipinski, Peter DeFazio (ex officio)

Railroads, Pipelines, and Hazardous Materials

Office: B329 RHOB 20515   **Phone:** 226-0727

Jeff Denham (Chair), John J. Duncan Jr., John Mica, Sam Graves, Candice S. Miller, Lou Barletta, Blake Farenthold, Richard Hanna, Daniel Webster, Scott Perry, Todd Rokita, John Katko, Brian Babin, Cresent Hardy, Mimi Walters, Lee Zeldin, Mike Bost, Bill Shuster (ex officio)

Michael E. Capuano (Ranking Minority Member), Corrine Brown, Daniel Lipinski, Jerrold Nadler, Elijah E. Cummings, Rick Larsen, Steve Cohen, Albio Sires, Rick Nolan, Elizabeth Esty, Grace Napolitano, Janice Hahn, Peter DeFazio (ex officio)

Water Resources and Environment

Office: 585 FHOB 20515   **Phone:** 225-4360

Bob Gibbs (Chair), Candice S. Miller, Duncan Hunter, Rick Crawford, Daniel Webster, Jeff Denham, Reid Ribble, Thomas Massie, Rodney Davis, Mark Sanford, Todd Rokita, John Katko, Brian Babin, Cresent Hardy, Garret Graves, David Rouzer, Mike Bost, Bill Shuster (ex officio)

Grace Napolitano (Ranking Minority Member), Donna F. Edwards, John Garamendi, Lois Frankel, Jared Huffman, Eddie Bernice Johnson, Ann Kirkpatrick, Dina Titus, Sean Patrick Maloney, Elizabeth Esty, Eleanor Holmes Norton, Rick Nolan, Peter DeFazio (ex officio)

VETERANS' AFFAIRS

Office: 335 CHOB 20515-6335
Phone: 225-3527   **Fax:** 225-5486
Web: veterans.house.gov
Minority Web: democrats.veterans.house.gov
Majority Staff Director: Jon Towers
Minority Staff Director: Don Phillips, 225-9756, 333 CHOB

Jurisdiction: (1) veterans' measures generally; (2) pensions of all the wars of the United States, general and special; (3) life insurance issued by the government on account of service in the Armed Forces; (4) compensation, vocational rehabilitation, and education of veterans; (5) veterans' hospitals, medical care, and treatment of veterans; (6) Soldiers' and Sailors' Civil Relief; (7) readjustment of servicemen to civilian life; (8) national cemeteries.
Party Ratio: R 14-D 10

Jeff Miller, Fla., Chair.	*Corrine Brown, Fla.*
Doug Lamborn, Colo.	*Mark Takano, Calif.*
Gus Bilirakis, Fla.	*Julia Brownley, Calif.*
Phil Roe, Tenn.	*Dina Titus, Nev.*
Dan Benishek, Mich.	*Raúl Ruiz, Calif.*
Tim Huelskamp, Kans.	*Ann McLane Kuster, N.H.*
Mike Coffman, Colo.	*Beto O'Rourke, Tex.*
Brad Wenstrup, Ohio	*Kathleen Rice, N.Y.*
Jackie Walorski, Ind.	*Jerry McNerney, Calif.*
Ralph Abraham, La.	*Tim Walz, Minn.*
Lee Zeldin, N.Y.	
Ryan Costello, Pa.	
Amata	
Coleman Radewagen, Am. Samoa	
Mike Bost, Ill.	

Subcommittees

Disability Assistance and Memorial Affairs

Office: 337 CHOB 20515   **Phone:** 225-9164

Ralph Abraham (Chair), Doug Lamborn, Lee M. Zeldin, Ryan Costello, Mike Bost

Dina Titus (Ranking Minority Member), Julia Brownley, Raúl Ruiz

Economic Opportunity

Office: 335 CHOB 20515   **Phone:** 226-5491

Brad Wenstrup (Chair), Lee Zeldin, Amata Coleman Radewagen, Ryan Costello, Mike Bost

Mark Takano (Ranking Minority Member), Dina Titus, Kathleen Rice, Jerry McNerney

Health

Office: 337 CHOB 20515   **Phone:** 225-9154

Dan Benishek (Chair), Gus Bilirakis, Phil Roe, Tim Huelskamp, Mike Coffman, Brad Wenstrup, Ralph Abraham

Julia Brownley (Ranking Minority Member), Mark Takano, Raúl Ruiz, Ann McLane Kuster, Beto O'Rourke

Oversight and Investigations

Office: 337A CHOB 20515   **Phone:** 225-3569

Mike Coffman (Chair), Doug Lamborn, Phil Roe, Dan Benishek, Tim Huelskamp, Jackie Walorski

Ann McLane Kuster (Ranking Minority Member), Beto O'Rourke, Kathleen Rice, Tim Walz

WAYS AND MEANS

Office: 1102 LHOB 20515-6348

Phone: 225-3625   **Fax:** 225-2610

Web: waysandmeans.house.gov

Minority Web: democrats.waysandmeans.house.gov

Majority Staff Director: David Stewart

Minority Chief Counsel: Janice A. Mays, 225-4021, 1106 LHOB

Jurisdiction: (1) customs revenue, collection districts, and ports of entry and delivery; (2) reciprocal trade agreements; (3) revenue measures generally; (4) revenue measures relating to insular possessions; (5) bonded debt of the United States, subject to the last sentence of clause 4(f). Clause 4(f) requires the Committee on Ways and Means to include in its annual report to the Committee on the Budget a specific recommendation, made after holding public hearings, as to the appropriate level of the public debt that should be set forth in the concurrent resolution on the budget; (6) deposit of public monies; (7) transportation of dutiable goods; (8) tax exempt foundations and charitable trusts; (9) National Social Security (except health care and facilities programs that are supported from general revenues as opposed to payroll deductions and except work incentive programs).

Party Ratio: R 24-D 15

Kevin Brady, Tex., Chair	*Sandy Levin, Mich.*
Sam Johnson, Tex.	*Charles B. Rangel, N.Y.*
Kevin Brady, Tex.	*Jim McDermott, Wash.*
Devin Nunes, Calif.	*John Lewis, Ga.*
Patrick J. Tiberi, Ohio	*Richard E. Neal, Mass.*
Dave Reichert, Wash.	*Xavier Becerra, Calif.*
Charles W. Boustany Jr., La.	*Lloyd Doggett, Tex.*
Peter Roskam, Ill.	*Mike Thompson, Calif.*
Tom Price, Ga.	*John B. Larson, Conn.*
Vern Buchanan, Fla.	*Earl Blumenauer, Ore.*
Adrian Smith, Neb.	*Ron Kind, Wisc.*
Lynn Jenkins, Kans.	*Bill Pascrell Jr., N.J.*
Erik Paulsen, Minn.	*Joseph Crowley, N.Y.*
Kenny Marchant, Tex.	*Danny K. Davis, Ill.*
Diane Black, Tenn.	*Linda Sánchez, Calif.*
Tom Reed, N.Y.	
Todd Young, Ind.	
Mike Kelly, Pa.	
Jim Renacci, Ohio	
Patrick Meehan, Pa.	
Kristi Noem, S.D.	
George Holding, N.C.	
Jason Smith, Mo.	
Bob Dold, Ill.	
Tom Rice, S.C.	

Subcommittees

Health

Office: 1135 LHOB 20515   **Phone:** 225-3943

Patrick J. Tiberi (Chair), Sam Johnson, Devin Nunes, Peter Roskam, Tom Price, Vern Buchanan, Adrian Smith, Lynn Jenkins, Kenny Marchant, Diane Black, Erik Paulsen

Jim McDermott (Ranking Minority Member), Mike Thompson, Ron Kind, Earl Blumenauer, Bill Pascrell Jr., Danny K. Davis, John Lewis

Human Resources

Office: 1129 LHOB 20515   **Phone:** 225-1025

Vern Buchanan (Chair), Tom Reed, Kristi Noem, Bob Dold, Tom Rice, Dave Reichert

Lloyd Doggett (Ranking Minority Member), John Lewis, Joseph Crowley, Danny K. Davis

Oversight

Office: B318 RHOB 20515   **Phone:** 225-5522

Peter Roskam (Chair), Kenny Marchant, Patrick Meehan, George Holding, Jason Smith, Tom Reed

Tom Rice, John Lewis (Ranking Minority Member), Joseph Crowley, Charles B. Rangel, Danny K. Davis

Social Security

Office: B317 RHOB 20515   **Phone:** 225-9263

Sam Johnson (Chair), Bob Dold, Vern Buchanan, Adrian Smith, Mike Kelly, Jim Renacci, Tom Rice

Xavier Becerra (Ranking Minority Member), John B. Larson, Earl Blumenauer, Jim McDermott

Tax Policy

Office: 1136 LHOB 20515   **Phone:** 225-5522

Charles W. Boustany Jr. (Chair), Dave Reichert, Patrick J. Tiberi, Tom Reed, Todd Young, Mike Kelly, Jim Renacci, Kristi Noem, George Holding

Richard E. Neal (Ranking Minority Member), John B. Larson, Linda Sánchez, Mike Thompson, Lloyd Doggett

Trade

Office: 1104 LHOB 20515   **Phone:** 225-6649

Dave Reichert (Chair), Devin Nunes, Adrian Smith, Lynn Jenkins, Charles W. Boustany Jr., Erik Paulsen, Kenny Marchant, Todd Young, Mike Kelly, Patrick Meehan

Charles B. Rangel (Ranking Minority Member), Richard E. Neal, Earl Blumenauer, Ron Kind, Bill Pascrell Jr., Lloyd Doggett

PERMANENT SELECT INTELLIGENCE

Office: HVC-304 CAP 20515-6415
Phone: 225-4121 **Fax:** 225-1991
Web: intelligence.house.gov
Minority Web: democrats.intelligence.house.gov
Majority Staff Director: Jeffrey Shockey
Minority Staff Director: Michael Bahar, 225-7690
   Jurisdiction: There shall be referred to the select committee proposed legislation, messages, petitions, memorials and other matters relating to the following: (1) the Central Intelligence Agency, the Director of National Intelligence and the National Intelligence Program as defined in section 3(6) of the National Security Act of 1947; (2) intelligence and intelligence-related activities of all other departments and agencies of the government, including the tactical intelligence and intelligence-related activities of the Department of Defense; (3) the organization or reorganization of the government to the extent that the organization or reorganization relates to a function or activity involving intelligence or intelligence-related activities; (4) authorizations for appropriations, both direct and indirect, for the following: (a) the Central Intelligence Agency, the Director of National Intelligence, and the National Intelligence Program as defined in section 3(6) of the National Security Act of 1947; (b) intelligence and intelligence-related activities of all other departments and agencies of the Government, including the tactical intelligence and intelligence-related activities of the Department of Defense; (c) a department, agency, subdivision or program that is a successor to an agency or program named to or referred to in (a) or (b).
Party Ratio: R 13-D 9

Devin Nunes, Calif., Chair	*Adam Schiff, Calif.*
Jeff Miller, Fla.	*Luis V. Gutierrez, Ill.*
Mike Conaway, Tex.	*James A. Himes, Conn.*
Pete King, N.Y.	*Terri Sewell, Ala.*
Frank LoBiondo, N.J.	*Andre Carson, Ind.*
Lynn Westmoreland, Ga.	*Jackie Speier, Calif.*
Thomas J. Rooney, Fla.	*Mike Quigley, Ill.*
Joe Heck, Nev.	*Eric Swalwell, Calif.*
Mike Pompeo, Kans.	*Patrick Murphy, Fla.*
Ileana Ros-Lehtinen, Fla.	
Mike Turner, Ohio	
Brad Wenstrup, Ohio	
Chris Stewart, Utah	

Subcommittees

CIA
Office: HVC-304 CAP 20515 **Phone:** 225-4121
   Frank LoBiondo (Chair), Mike Conaway, Pete King, Lynn Westmoreland, Thomas J. Rooney, Mike Pompeo
   Eric Swalwell (Ranking Minority Member), Luis V. Gutierrez, James A. Himes, Andre Carson

Department of Defense Intelligence and Overhead Architecture
Office: HVC-304 CAP 20515 **Phone:** 225-4121
   Joe Heck (Chair), Jeff Miller, Ileana Ros-Lehtinen, Mike Turner, Brad Wenstrup, Chris Stewart
   Terri Sewell (Ranking Minority Member), Luis V. Gutierrez, Eric Swalwell, Patrick Murphy

Emerging Threats
Office: HVC-304 CAP 20515 **Phone:** 225-4121
   Thomas J. Rooney (Chair), Frank LoBiondo, Joe Heck, Mike Turner, Brad Wenstrup, Chris Stewart
   Mike Quigley (Ranking Minority Member), Terri Sewell, Andre Carson, Jackie Speier

NSA and Cybersecurity
Office: HVC-304 CAP 20515 **Phone:** 225-4121
   Lynn Westmoreland (Chair), Jeff Miller, Mike Conaway, Pete King, Mike Pompeo, Ileana Ros-Lehtinen
   James A. Himes (Ranking Minority Member), Jackie Speier, Mike Quigley, Patrick Murphy

SELECT ON BENGHAZI

Office: 1036 LHOB 20515
Phone: 226-7100 **Fax:** 226-3883
Web: benghazi.house.gov
Minority Web: democrats.benghazi.house.gov
Majority Staff Director: Philip Kiko
Minority Staff Director: Susanne Sachsman Grooms, 225-7100
   Jurisdiction: Authorized and directed to conduct a full and complete investigation and study and issue a final report of its findings to the House regarding: (1) all policies, decisions, and activities that contributed to the attacks on U.S. facilities in Benghazi, Libya, on September 11, 2012, as well as those that affected the ability of the United States to prepare for the attacks; (2) all policies, decisions, and activities to respond to and repel the attacks on U.S. facilities in Benghazi, Libya, on September 11, 2012, including efforts to rescue U.S. personnel; (3) internal and public executive branch communications about the attacks on U.S. facilities in Benghazi, Libya, on September 11, 2012; (4) accountability for policies and decisions related to the security of facilities in Benghazi, Libya, and the response to the attacks, including individuals and entities responsible for those policies and decisions; (5) executive branch authorities' efforts to identify and bring to justice the perpetrators of the attacks on U.S. facilities in Benghazi, Libya, on September 11, 2012; (6) executive branch activities and efforts to comply with congressional inquiries into the attacks on U.S. facilities in Benghazi, Libya, on September 11, 2012; (7) recommendations for improving executive branch cooperation and compliance with congressional oversight and investigations; (8) information related to lessons learned from the attacks and executive branch activities and efforts to protect U.S. facilities and personnel abroad; (9) any other relevant issues relating to the attacks, the response to the attacks, or the investigation by the House of Representatives into the attacks.
Party Ratio: R 7-D 5

Trey Gowdy, S.C., Chair	*Elijah E. Cummings, Md.*
Lynn Westmoreland, Ga.	*Adam Smith, Wash.*
Jim Jordan, Ohio	*Adam Schiff, Calif.*
Peter Roskam, Ill.	*Linda Sánchez, Calif.*
Mike Pompeo, Kans.	*Tammy Duckworth, Ill.*
Martha Roby, Ala.	
Susan W. Brooks, Ind.	

HOUSE LEADERSHIP AND PARTISAN COMMITTEES

REPUBLICAN LEADERS

Speaker of the House: Paul Ryan, Wisc.
Majority Leader: Kevin McCarthy, Calif.
Majority Whip: Steve Scalise, La.
Chief Deputy Majority Whip: Patrick McHenry, N.C.

REPUBLICAN PARTISAN COMMITTEES

National Republican Congressional Committee
Office: 320 1st St. S.E. 20003-1838
Phone: 479-7000 **Fax:** 863-0693
Web: www.nrcc.org
Email: website@nrcc.org
Greg Walden, Ore., Chair

Other Leadership (in alphabetical order)

Megan Cummings, Financial Director
Jessica Furst-Johnson, General Counsel
Rob Jentgens, Director of the Treasury
Todd Johnson, Research Director
Katie Martin Prill, Communications Director
Jess McGowan, Strategic Director
Tom Newhouse, Digital Director
John Rogers, Political Director
Rob Simms, Executive Director

Republican Conference
Office: 202A CHOB 20515
Phone: 225-5107 **Fax:** 226-0154
Web: www.gop.gov
Email: GOP@mail.house.gov
Cathy McMorris Rodgers, Wash., Chair
Lynn Jenkins, Kans., Vice Chair
Virginia Foxx, N.C., Secretary

Republican Policy Committee
Office: 202A CHOB 20515-6549
Phone: 225-3021 **Fax:** 225-4656
Web: policy.house.gov
Luke Messer, Ind., Chair

Republican Steering Committee
Office: H-232 CAP 20515-3508
Phone: 225-6200 **Fax:** 225-5117
Web: speaker.house.gov
Paul Ryan, Wisc., Speaker of the House
Kevin McCarthy, Calif., Majority Leader

DEMOCRATIC LEADERS

Minority Leader: Nancy Pelosi, Calif.
Minority Whip: Steny Hoyer, Md.
Assistant Democratic Leader: James E. Clyburn, S.C.

DEMOCRATIC PARTISAN COMMITTEES

Democratic Congressional Campaign Committee
Office: 430 S. Capitol St. S.E. 20003-4024
Phone: 863-1500 **Fax:** 485-3412
Web: www.dccc.org
Email: dccc@dccc.org
Ben Ray Luján, N.M., Chair

Other Leadership (in alphabetical order)

Don Beyer, Va., National Finance Chair
James E. Clyburn, S.C., National Mobilization Chair
Denny Heck, Wash., Recruitment Chair
Dan Kildee, Mich., Frontline Program Chair
Richard E. Neal, Mass., Business Council Co-Chair
Gary Peters, Mich., Recruitment Vice Chair
Jan Schakowsky, Ill., Candidate Services National Chair
Terri Sewell, Ala., Business Council Co-Chair

Democratic Caucus
Office: 1420 LHOB 20515
Phone: 225-1400 **Fax:** 226-4412
Web: www.dems.gov
Email: democratic.caucus@mail.house.gov
Xavier Becerra, Calif., Chair
Joseph Crowley, N.Y., Vice Chair

Democratic Steering and Policy Committee
Office: 235 CHOB 20515
Phone: 225-4965 **Fax:** 224-4188
Nancy Pelosi, Chair
Rosa L. DeLauro, Conn., Co-Chair
Karen Bass, Calif., Chair of Organization, Study, and Review

Democratic Policy and Communications Center
Office: 419 SHOB 20515
Phone: 224-3232
Web: www.dpcc.senate.gov
Email: dpcc@dpcc.senate.gov
Chuck Schumer, N.Y., Chair
Debbie Stabenow, Mich., Vice Chair
Elizabeth Warren, Mass., Policy Advisor

House Members' Offices

Listed below are House members and their party, state, and district affiliation, followed by the address and telephone number for their Washington office. The area code for all Washington, D.C., numbers is 202. The top administrative aide, Web address, Facebook page, and Twitter account for each member are also provided, when available. Most members may be contacted via the Web-based email forms found on their Web sites. These are followed by the address, telephone and fax numbers, and name of a key aide in the member's district office(s). Each listing concludes with the representative's committee assignments. For partisan committee assignments, see page 803.

As of April 25, 2016, there were 246 Republicans, 188 Democrats, 0 Independents, 1 vacancy (Ohio District 8), and 6 non-voting members in the House of Representatives.

Abraham, Ralph, R-La. (5)

Capitol Hill Office: 417 CHOB 20515-1805; 225-8490; Fax: 225-5639; *Chief of Staff:* Luke Letlow
Web: abraham.house.gov
Facebook: www.facebook.com/CongressmanRalphAbraham
Twitter: @RepAbraham
District Offices: 1434 Dorchester Dr., Suite E; 318-445-0818; Fax: 318-445-3776; *Office Manager:* Donna Howe
426 DeSiard St., Monroe, LA 71201; 318-322-3500; Fax: 318-322-3577; *Scheduler:* Emma Herrock
Committee Assignments: Agriculture; Science, Space, and Technology; Veterans' Affairs

Adams, Alma, D-N.C. (12)

Capitol Hill Office: 222 CHOB 20515-3312; 225-1510; Fax: 225-1512; *Chief of Staff:* Rhonda Foxx
Web: adams.house.gov
Facebook: www.facebook.com/CongresswomanAdams
Twitter: @RepAdams
District Offices: 321 W. 11th St., #100 and #200, Charlotte, NC 28202; 704-344-9950; Fax: 704-344-9971; *Deputy Chief of Staff:* Keith Kelly
1600 E. Wendover Ave., Suite I; 336-275-9950; Fax: 336-379-9951; *Deputy Chief of Staff:* Keith Kelly
Committee Assignments: Agriculture; Education and the Workforce; Joint Economic; Small Business

Aderholt, Robert B., R-Ala. (4)

Capitol Hill Office: 235 CHOB 20515; 225-4876; Fax: 225-5587; *Chief of Staff:* Brian Rell
Web: aderholt.house.gov
Facebook: www.facebook.com/RobertAderholt
Twitter: @robert_aderholt
District Offices: 205 4th Ave. N.E., #104, Cullman, AL 35055-1965; 256-734-6043; Fax: 256-737-0885; *Director of Constituent Services:* Jennifer Butler-Taylor
Federal Bldg., 600 Broad St., #107, Gadsden, AL 35901-3745; 256-546-0201; Fax: 256-546-8778; *Field Rep.:* James Manasco
Carl Elliott Federal Bldg., 1710 Alabama Ave., #247, Jasper, AL 35501-5400; 205-221-2310; Fax: 205-221-9035; *District Field Director:* Paul Housel

1011 George Wallace Blvd., #146, Tuscumbia, AL 35674; 256-381-3450; Fax: 256-381-7659; *Field Rep.:* Kreg Kennedy
Committee Assignments: Appropriations; Commission on Security and Cooperation in Europe

Aguilar, Pete, D-Calif. (31)

Capitol Hill Office: 1223 LHOB 20515-0531; 225-3201; Fax: 226-6962; *Chief of Staff:* Boris Medzhibovsky
Web: aguilar.house.gov
Facebook: www.facebook.com/reppeteaguilar
Twitter: @reppeteaguilar
District Office: 685 E. Carnegie Dr., #100, San Bernadino, CA 92408; 909-890-4445; Fax: 909-980-1651; *Scheduler:* Danielle Giulino
Committee Assignments: Agriculture; Armed Services

Allen, Rick, R-Ga. (12)

Capitol Hill Office: 513 CHOB 20515-1012; 225-2823; Fax: 225-3377; *Chief of Staff:* Tim Baker
Web: allen.house.gov
Facebook: www.facebook.com/CongressmanRickAllen
Twitter: @reprickallen
District Offices: 2743 Perimeter Pkwy., Bldg. 200, #225, Augusta, GA 30909; 706-228-1980; Fax: 706-228-1954; *District Director:* Brinsley Thigpin
101 N. Jefferson St., Dublin, GA 31021; 478-272-4030; Fax: 478-277-0113; *Scheduler:* Heath Wheat
50 E. Main St., Statesboro, GA 30458; 912-243-9452; Fax: 912-243-9453; *Comm. Director:* Madison Fox
Committee Assignments: Agriculture, Education and the Workforce

Amash, Justin, R-Mich. (3)

Capitol Hill Office: 114 CHOB 20515-2203; 225-3831; Fax: 225-5144; *Chief of Staff:* Poppy Nelson
Web: amash.house.gov
Facebook: www.facebook.com/repjustinamash
Twitter: @repjustinamash
District Office: 110 Michigan St. N.W., #460, Grand Rapids, MI 49503-2313; 616-451-8383; Fax: 616-454-5630; *District Director:* Jordan Bush

Satellite Office: 70 W. Michigan Ave., #212, Battle Creek, MI 49017; 269-205-3823; *District Director:* Jordan Bush

Committee Assignments: Joint Economic; Oversight and Government Reform

Amodei, Mark, R-Nev. (2)

Capitol Hill Office: 332 CHOB 20515; 225-6155; Fax: 225-5679; *Chief of Staff:* Bruce Miller

Web: amodei.house.gov

Facebook: www.facebook.com/MarkAmodeiNV2

Twitter: @markamodeinv2

District Offices: 905 Railroad St., #104 D, Elko, NV 89801; 775-777-7705; Fax: 775-753-9984; *Rural Rep.:* Martin Paris

5310 Kietzke Lane, #103, Reno, NV 89511; 775-686-5760; Fax: 775-686-5711; *District Director:* Stacy Parobek

Committee Assignment: Appropriations

Ashford, Brad, D-Neb. (2)

Capitol Hill Office: 107 CHOB 20515-2702; 225-4155; Fax: 226-5452; *Chief of Staff:* Jeremy Nordquist

Web: ashford.house.gov

Facebook: www.facebook.com/repbradashford

Twitter: @RepBradAshford

District Office: 7126 Pacific St., Omaha, NE 68106; 402-916-5678; Fax: 402-502-7092 *Staff Asst.:* Zac Andrews

Committee Assignments: Agriculture; Armed Services

Babin, Brian, R-Tex. (36)

Capitol Hill Office: 316 CHOB 20515-4336; 225-1555; Fax: 226-0396; *Chief of Staff:* Stuart Burns

Web: babin.house.gov

Facebook: www.facebook.com/RepBrianBabin

Twitter: @RepBrianBabin

District Offices: 203 Ivy Ave., #600, Deer Park, TX 77536; 832-780-0966; Fax: 832-780-0964; *District Director:* Kelly Waterman

420 Green Ave., Orange, TX 77630-5803; 409-883-8075; Fax: 409-886-9918; *Director of Community Relations:* Steve Janushkowsky

Satellite Office: 100 W. Bluff Dr., #100, Woodville, TX 75979; 844-303-8934; *Director of Community Relations:* Rachel Iglesias

Committee Assignments: Science, Space and Technology; Transportation and Infrastructure

Barletta, Lou, R-Pa. (11)

Capitol Hill Office: 115 CHOB 20515; 225-6511; Fax: 226-6250; *Chief of Staff:* Andrea Waldock

Web: barletta.house.gov

Facebook: www.facebook.com/CongressmanLouBarletta

Twitter: @reploubarletta

District Offices: 59 W. Louther St., Carlisle, PA 17013; 717-249-0190; Fax: 717-218-0190; *Field Rep.:* Leah Sailhamer

4813 Jonestown Rd., #101, Harrisburg, PA 17109; 717-525-7002; Fax: 717-695-6794; *Director of Constituent Services:* Bruce Krell

1 S. Church St., #100, Hazleton, PA 18201-6200; 570-751-0050; Fax: 570-751-0054; *Director of Constituent Services/Field Rep.:* Pat Rogan

106 Arch St., Sunbury, PA 17801; 570-988-7801; Fax: 570-988-7805; *Director of Constituent Services/Field Rep.:* Peggy Reichenbach

Committee Assignments: Education and the Workforce; Homeland Security; Transportation and Infrastructure

Barr, Andy, R-Ky. (6)

Capitol Hill Office: 1432 LHOB 20515; 225-4706; Fax: 225-2122; *Chief of Staff:* Mary Rosado

Web: barr.house.gov

Facebook: www.facebook.com/RepAndyBarr

Twitter: @RepAndyBarr

District Office: 2709 Old Rosebud Rd., Lexington, KY 40509; 859-219-1366; Fax: 859-219-3437; *District Director:* Tyler White

Committee Assignment: Financial Services

Barton, Joe, R-Tex. (6)

Capitol Hill Office: 2107 RHOB 20515; 225-2002; Fax: 225-3052; *Chief of Staff:* Ryan Thompson

Web: joebarton.house.gov

Facebook: www.facebook.com/RepJoeBarton

Twitter: @RepJoeBarton

District Offices: 6001 W. I-20, #200, Arlington, TX 76017; 817-543-1000; Fax: 817-548-7029; *Constituent Liaison:* Deborah Rollins

2106-A W. Ennis Ave., Ennis, TX 75119-3624; 972-875-8488; Fax: 972-875-1907; *Deputy District Director:* Linda Gillespie

Committee Assignment: Energy and Commerce

Bass, Karen, D-Calif. (37)

Capitol Hill Office: 408 CHOB 20515-0533; 225-7084; Fax: 225-2422; *Chief of Staff:* Carrie Kohns

Web: bass.house.gov

Facebook: www.facebook.com/RepKarenBass

Twitter: @RepKarenBass

District Office: 4929 Wilshire Blvd., #650, Los Angeles, CA 90010-3820; 323-965-1422; Fax: 323-965-1113; *Deputy Chief of Staff:* Darryn Harris

Committee Assignments: Foreign Affairs; Judiciary

Beatty, Joyce, D-Ohio (3)

Capitol Hill Office: 133 CHOB 20515; 225-4324; Fax: 225-1984; *Chief of Staff:* Kimberly Ross

Web: beatty.house.gov

Facebook: www.facebook.com/RepJoyceBeatty

Twitter: @RepBeatty

District Office: 471 E. Broad St., #1100, Columbus, OH 43215; 614-220-0003; Fax: 614-220-5640; *Deputy District Director:* Ron McGuire

Committee Assignment: Financial Services

Becerra, Xavier, D-Calif. (34)

Capitol Hill Office: 1226 LHOB 20515-0531; 225-6235; Fax: 225-2202; *Chief of Staff:* Sean McCluskie
Web: becerra.house.gov
Facebook: www.facebook.com/XavierBecerra
Twitter: @repbecerra
District Office: 350 S. Bixel St., #120, Los Angeles, CA 90017; 213-481-1425; Fax: 213-481-1427; *District Director:* Liz Saldivar
Committee Assignment: Ways and Means

Benishek, Dan, R-Mich. (1)

Capitol Hill Office: 514 CHOB 20515-2201; 225-4735; Fax: 225-4710; *Chief of Staff:* John Billings
Web: benishek.house.gov
Facebook: www.facebook.com/CongressmanDan
Twitter: @congressmandan
District Offices: 454 W. Baldwin St., Alpena, MI 49707; 989-340-1634; Fax: 989-340-1636; *Deputy District Director:* Jesse Osmer
500 S. Stephenson Ave., #500, Iron Mountain, MI 49801-3420; 906-828-2114; Fax: 906-828-2116; *District Director:* Traci Jahnke
307 S. Front St., #120, Marquette, MI 49855-4613; 906-273-2074; Fax: 906-273-2076; *Special Asst.:* Kevin Flohe
3301 Veterans Dr., #106, Traverse City, MI 49684; 231-421-5599; Fax: 231-421-8036; *Constituent Services Rep.:* Luke Londo
Committee Assignments: Agriculture; Natural Resources; Veterans' Affairs

Bera, Ami, D-Calif. (7)

Capitol Hill Office: 1535 LHOB 20515; 225-5716; Fax: 226-1298; *Chief of Staff:* Chad Obermiller
Web: bera.house.gov
Facebook: www.facebook.com/RepAmiBera
Twitter: @RepBera
District Office: 8950 Cal Center Dr., Bldg. 3, #100, Sacramento, CA 95826; 916-635-0505; Fax: 916-635-0514; *District Director:* Faith Whitmore
Committee Assignments: Foreign Affairs; Science, Space, and Technology

Beyer, Don, D-Va. (8)

Capitol Hill Office: 431 CHOB 20515-4608; 225-4376; Fax: 225-0017; *Chief of Staff:* Ann O'Hanlon
Web: beyer.house.gov
Facebook: www.facebook.com/RepDonBeyer
Twitter: @RepDonBeyer
District Office: 5285 Shawnee Rd., #250, Alexandria, VA 22312; 703-658-5403; Fax: 703-658-5408; *District Director:* Susie Warner
Committee Assignments: Joint Economic; Natural Resources; Science, Space, and Technology

Bilirakis, Gus, R-Fla. (12)

Capitol Hill Office: 2112 RHOB 20515-0909; 225-5755; Fax; 225-4085; *Chief of Staff:* Elizabeth Hittos

Web: bilirakis.house.gov
Facebook: www.facebook.com/GusBilirakis
Twitter: @RepGusBilirakis
District Offices: 7132 Little Rd., New Port Richey, FL 34654; 727-232-2921; Fax: 727-232-2923; *Director of Casework:* Kristen Sellas
600 Klosterman Rd., Room BB-038, Tarpon Springs, FL 34689-1299; 727-940-5860; Fax: 727-940-5861; *Scheduler:* Daniel Paash
5901 Argerian Dr., #102, Wesley Chapel, FL 33545-4220; 813-501-4942; Fax: 813-501-4944; *Deputy Chief of Staff:* Summer Robertson
Committee Assignments: Energy and Commerce; Veterans' Affairs

Bishop, Mike, R-Mich. (8)

Capitol Hill Office: 428 CHOB 20515-2208; 225-4872; Fax: 225-5820; *Chief of Staff:* Allan Filip
Web: mikebishop.house.gov
Facebook: www.facebook.com/RepMikeBishop
Twitter: @MikeBishopMI
District Office: 711 E. Grand River Ave., Suite A, Brighton, MI 48116; 810-227-8600; Fax: 810-227-8628; *District Director:* Katherine Vantiem
Committee Assignments: Education and the Workforce; Judiciary

Bishop, Rob, R-Utah (1)

Capitol Hill Office: 123 CHOB 20515-4401; 225-0453; Fax: 225-5857; *Chief of Staff:* Scott B. Parker
Web: robbishop.house.gov
Facebook: www.facebook.com/RepRobBishop
Twitter: @RepRobBishop
District Office: Federal Bldg., 324 25th St., #1017, Ogden UT 84401; 801-625-0107; Fax: 801-625-0124; *District Director:* Peter Jenks
Satellite Office: 6 N. Main St., Brigham City, UT 84302-2116; 435-734-2270; Fax: 435-734-2290
Committee Assignments: Armed Services; Natural Resources, Chair

Bishop, Sanford D., Jr., D-Ga. (2)

Capitol Hill Office: 2407 RHOB 20515-1002; 225-3631; Fax: 225-2203; *Chief of Staff:* Michael Reed
Web: bishop.house.gov
Facebook: www.facebook.com/sanfordbishop
Twitter: @sanfordbishop
District Offices: Albany Towers, 235 W. Roosevelt Ave., #114, Albany, GA 31701-2662; 229-439-8067; Fax: 229-436-2099; *District Director:* Kenneth Cutts
18 Ninth St., #201, Columbus, GA 31901-2778; 706-320-9477; Fax: 706-320-9479; *Constituent Services:* Harry Crawford
682 Cherry St., City Hall Annex, #302, Macon, GA 31201; 478-803-2631; Fax: 478-803-2637; *Field Rep.:* Michelle Sands
Committee Assignment: Appropriations

Black, Diane, R-Tenn. (6)

Capitol Hill Office: 1131 LHOB 20515-4206; 225-4231; Fax: 225-6887; *Chief of Staff:* Teresa Koeberlein
Web: black.house.gov
Facebook: www.facebook.com/DianeBlackTN06
Twitter: @RepDianeBlack
District Offices: 321 E. Spring St., #301, Cookeville, TN 38501-4168; 931-854-0069; Fax: 615-206-8980; *Caseworker:* Bonny Warren
355 N. Belvedere Dr., #308, Gallatin, TN 37066-5410; 615-206-8204; Fax: 615-206-8980; *District Director:* Charles Schneider
Committee Assignments: Budget; Ways and Means

Blackburn, Marsha, R-Tenn. (7)

Capitol Hill Office: 2226 RHOB 20515-4207; 225-2811; Fax: 225-3004; *Chief of Staff:* Michael R. Platt
Web: blackburn.house.gov
Facebook: www.facebook.com/marshablackburn
Twitter: @MarshaBlackburn
District Offices: 128 N. 2nd St., #202, Clarksville, TN 37040; 931-503-0391; Fax: 931-503-0393; *Constituent Outreach:* Steve Allbrooks
305 Public Square, #212, Franklin, TN 37062; 615-591-5161; Fax: 615-599-2916; *District Director:* Darcy Anderson
Committee Assignments: Budget; Energy and Commerce

Blum, Rod, R-Iowa. (1)

Capitol Hill Office: 213 CHOB 20515-1501; 225-2911; Fax: 225-6666; *Chief of Staff:* Paul Smith
Web: blum.house.gov
Facebook: www.facebook.com/congressmanrodblum
Twitter: @RepRodBlum
District Offices: 1050 Main St., Dubuque, IA 52001; 563-557-7789; *District Director:* John Ferland
310 3rd St. S.E., Cedar Rapids, IA 52401; 319-364-2288; Fax: 319-364-2994; *Staff Director:* Alexah Rogge
515 Main St., Suite D, Cedar Falls, IA 50613; 319-266-6925; *Staff Asst.:* Justin Jensen
Committee Assignments: Budget; Oversight and Government Reform

Blumenauer, Earl, D-Ore. (3)

Capitol Hill Office: 1111 LHOB 20515; 225-4811; Fax: 225-8941; *Deputy Chief of Staff:* David Gillman
Web: blumenauer.house.gov
Facebook: www.facebook.com/blumenauer
Twitter: @repblumenauer
District Office: 911 N.E. 11th Ave., #200, Portland, OR 97232; 503-231-2300; Fax: 5032305413; *Chief of Staff:* Julia Pomeroy
Committee Assignment: Ways and Means

Bonamici, Suzanne, D-Ore. (1)

Capitol Hill Office: 439 CHOB 20515; 225-0855; Fax: 225-9497; *Chief of Staff:* Rachael Bornstein
Web: bonamici.house.gov

Facebook: www.facebook.com/suzannebonamici
Twitter: @RepBonamici
District Office: 12725 S.W. Millikan Way, #220, Beaverton, OR 97005; 503-469-6010; Fax: 503-469-6018; *District Director:* Sarah Baessler
Committee Assignments: Education and the Workforce; Science, Space, and Technology

Bordallo, Madeleine Z., D-Guam (At Large)

Capitol Hill Office: 2441 RHOB 20515-5301; 225-1188; Fax: 226-0341; *Chief of Staff:* Matthew Herrmann
Web: bordallo.house.gov.gov
Facebook: www.facebook.com/madeleine.bordallo
District Office: 120 Father Duenas Ave., #107, Hagåtña, GU 96910-5058; 671-477-4272; Fax: 671-477-2587; *District Director:* Jon Junior Calvo
Committee Assignments: Armed Services; Natural Resources

Bost, Mike, R-Ill. (12)

Capitol Hill Office: 1440 LHOB 20515-1312; 225-5661; Fax: 225-0285; *Chief of Staff:* Matt McCullough
Web: bost.house.gov
Facebook: www.facebook.com/RepBost
Twitter: @RepBost
District Offices: 23 Public Sq., #404, Belleville, IL 62220; 618-233-8026; Fax: 618-233-8765; *District Director:* Matt Rice
300 E. Main St., Carbondale, IL 62901; 618-457-5787; Fax: 618-457-2990
Mt. Vernon City Hall, 1100 Main St., Mt. Vernon, IL 62864; 618-513-5294
Committee Assignments: Agriculture, Veterans' Affairs

Boustany, Charles W., Jr., R-La. (3)

Capitol Hill Office: 1431 LHOB 20515-1807; 225-2031; Fax: 225-5724; *Chief of Staff:* Terri Fish
Web: boustany.house.gov
Facebook: www.facebook.com/RepBoustany
Twitter: @Repboustany
District Offices: 800 Lafayette St., #1400, Lafayette, LA 70501-6800; 337-235-6322; Fax: 337-235-6072; *District Director:* Joan Finley
Capital One Tower, One Lakeshore Dr., #1775, Lake Charles, LA 70629-0114; 337-433-1747; Fax: 337-433-0974; *Constituent Services Rep.:* Theresa Martin
Committee Assignment: Ways and Means

Boyle, Brendan, D-Pa. (13)

Capitol Hill Office: 118 CHOB 20515-3813; 225-6111; Fax: 226-0611; *Chief of Staff:* Daniel Lodise
Web: boyle.house.gov
Facebook: www.facebook.com/CongressmanBoyle
Twitter: @RepBrendanBoyle
District Offices: 115 E. Glenside Ave., #1, Glenside, PA 19038; 215-517-6572; Fax: 215-277-7225; *Constiuent Rep.:* Michele Lockman

2375 Woodward St., #105, Philadelphia, PA 19115; 215-335-3355; Fax: 215-856-3734; *District Director:* James Kennedy

Committee Assignments: Foreign Affairs; Oversight and Government Reform

Brady, Kevin, R-Tex. (8)

Capitol Hill Office: 301 CHOB 20515-4308; 225-4901; Fax: 225-5524; *Chief of Staff:* Lori Harju
Web: kevinbrady.house.gov
Facebook: www.facebook.com/kevinbrady
Twitter: @RepKevinBrady
District Offices: 200 River Pointe Dr., #304, Conroe, TX 77304-2817; 936-441-5700; Fax: 936-441-5757; *District Director:* Todd Stephens
1300 11th St., #400, Huntsville, TX 77340; 936-439-9532; Fax: 936-439-9546; *Field Rep.:* Vita Swares
Committee Assignments: Joint Economic, Chair; Joint Taxation; Ways and Means

Brady, Robert, D-Pa. (1)

Capitol Hill Office: 102 CHOB 20515-3801; 225-4731; Fax: 225-0088; *Chief of Staff:* Stanley V. White
Web: brady.house.gov
Facebook: www.facebook.com/RepRobertBrady
Twitter: @RepBrady
District Offices: 1350 Edgmont Ave., #2575, Chester, PA 19013; 610-874-7094; Fax: 484-816-0029; *Office Manager:* Susie Kirkland
2637 E. Clearfield St., Philadelphia, PA 19134-5023; 267-519-2252; Fax: 267-519-2262; *District Director:* Tom Johnson
1909 S. Broad St., Philadelphia, PA 19148-2216; 215-389-4627; Fax: 215-389-4636; *District Director:* Thomas Blackwell
Satellite Office: 2630 Memphis St., Philadelphia, PA 19125-2344; 215-426-4616; Fax: 215-426-7741; *Community Liaison:* Peg Rzepski
Committee Assignments: Armed Services; House Administration, Ranking Minority Member; Joint Library; Joint Printing

Brat, Dave, R-Va. (7)

Capitol Hill Office: 330 CHOB 20515-4607; 225-2815; Fax: 225-0011; *Chief of Staff:* Phil Rapp
Web: brat.house.gov
Facebook: www.facebook.com/RepDaveBrat
Twitter: @RepDaveBrat
District Offices: 4201 Dominion Blvd., #110, Glen Allen, VA 23060; 804-747-4073; Fax: 804-747-5308; *District Director:* Lloyd Lenhart
9104 Courthouse Rd., P.O. Box 99, Spotsylvania, VA 22553; 540-507-7216; Fax: 540-507-7019; *District Director:* Chris Snider
Committee Assignments: Budget; Education and the Workforce; Small Business

Bridenstine, Jim, R-Okla. (1)

Capitol Hill Office: 216 CHOB 20515-3601; 225-2211; Fax: 225-9187; *Chief of Staff:* Joseph Kaufman

Web: bridenstine.house.gov
Facebook: www.facebook.com/CongressmanJimBridenstine
Twitter: @RepJBridenstine
District Office: 2448 E. 81st St., #5150, Tulsa, OK 74137; 918-935-3222; Fax: 918-935-2716; *District Director:* Gabe Sherman
Committee Assignments: Armed Services; Science, Space, and Technology

Brooks, Mo, R-Ala. (5)

Capitol Hill Office: 1230 LHOB 20515; 225-4801; Fax: 225-4392; *Chief of Staff Legis. Director:* Mark Pettitt
Web: brooks.house.gov
Facebook: www.facebook.com/pages/RepMoBrooks
Twitter: @RepMoBrooks
District Offices: 302 Lee St., Room 86, Decatur, AL 35601-1926; 256-355-9400; Fax: 256-355-9406; *Field Rep.:* Johnny Turner
102 S. Court St., #310, Florence, AL 35630; 256-718-5155; Fax: 256-718-5156; *Field Rep.:* Laura Smith
2101 W. Clinton Ave., #302, Huntsville, AL 35805-3109; 256-551-0190; Fax: 256-551-0194; *District Director:* Tiffany Noel
Committee Assignments: Armed Services; Foreign Affairs; Science, Space, and Technology

Brooks, Susan W., R-Ind. (5)

Capitol Hill Office: 1505 LHOB 20515; 225-2276; Fax: 225-0016; *Chief of Staff:* Mel Raines
Web: susanwbrooks.house.gov
Facebook: www.facebook.com/CongresswomanSusanWBrooks
Twitter: @SusanWBrooks
District Offices: 11611 N. Meridian St., #415, Carmel, IN 46032; 317-848-0201; Fax: 317-846-7306; *District Director:* Karen Glaser
120 E. 8th St., #101, Anderson, IN 46016; 765-640-5115; Fax: 765-640-5116; *Deputy District Director:* Kevin Sulc
Committee Assignments: Energy and Commerce; Ethics; Select on Benghazi

Brown, Corrine, D-Fla. (5)

Capitol Hill Office: 2111 RHOB 20515; 225-0123; Fax: 225-2256; *Chief of Staff:* Ronnie Simmons
Web: corrinebrown.house.gov
Facebook: www.facebook.com/congresswomanbrown
Twitter: @RepCorrineBrown
District Offices: 101 E. Union St., #202, Jacksonville, FL 32202-6002; 904-354-1652; Fax: 904-354-2721; *District Director:* Glenel Bowden
455 N. Garland Ave., #414, Orlando FL 32801; 407-872-2208; Fax: 407-872-5763; *Area Director:* Ronita Sanders
Committee Assignments: Transportation and Infrastructure; Veterans' Affairs, Ranking Minority Member

Brownley, Julia, D-Calif. (26)

Capitol Hill Office: 1019 LHOB 20515; 225-5811; Fax: 225-1100; *Chief of Staff:* Lenny Young

Web: juliabrownley.house.gov
Facebook: www.facebook.com/RepJuliaBrownley
Twitter: @JuliaBrownley26
District Offices: 300 E. Esplanade Dr., #470, Oxnard, CA 93036; 805-379-1779; Fax: 805-379-1799; *District Director:* Carina Armenta
223 E. Thousand Oaks Blvd., #411, Thousand Oaks, CA 91360; 805-379-1779; Fax: 805-379-1799; *Field Rep.:* Sheri Orgel
Committee Assignments: Transportation and Infrastructure; Veterans' Affairs

Buchanan, Vern, R-Fla. (16)

Capitol Hill Office: 2104 RHOB 20515; 225-5015; Fax: 226-0828; *Chief of Staff:* Dave Karvelas
Web: buchanan.house.gov
Facebook: www.facebook.com/CongressmanBuchanan
Twitter: @vernbuchanan
District Offices: 1051 Manatee Ave. West, #305, Bradenton, FL 34205-4954; 941-747-9081; Fax: 941-748-1564; *Field Rep.:* Gary Tibbetts
111 S. Orange Ave., Floor 2R, #202W, Sarasota, FL 34236-5806; 941-951-6643; Fax: 941-951-2972; *District Director:* Sally Tibbetts
Committee Assignment: Ways and Means

Buck, Ken, R-Colo. (4)

Capitol Hill Office: 416 CHOB 20515-0604; 225-4676; Fax: 225-5870; *Chief of Staff:* Greg Brophy
Web: buck.house.gov
Facebook: www.facebook.com/repkenbuck
Twitter: @RepKenBuck
District Offices: 900 Castleton Rd., #112, Castle Rock, CO 80109; 720-639-9165; *District Director:* Laurie Bratten
1122 9th St., #204, Greeley, CO 80631; 970-702-2136; Fax: 970-702-2951; *Area Rep.:* Molly Ford
302 N. 3rd St., Sterling, CO 80751; 970-762-0109; Fax: 970-552-0915; *Area Rep.:* Josh Sonnenberg
Committee Assignments: Judiciary; Oversight and Government Reform

Bucshon, Larry, R-Ind. (8)

Capitol Hill Office: 1005 LHOB 20515; 225-4636; Fax: 225-3284; *Chief of Staff:* Teresa Buckley
Web: bucshon.house.gov
Facebook: www.facebook.com/RepLarryBucshon
Twitter: @RepLarryBucshon
District Offices: 420 Main St., #1402, Evansville, IN 47708; 812-465-6484; Fax: 812-422-4761; *District Director:* Carol Jones
901 Wabash Ave., #140, Terre Haute, IN 47807-3232; 812-232-0523; Fax: 812-232-0526; *Field Rep.:* Joey Montgomery
Satellite Offices: 610 Main St., 2nd Floor, Jasper, IN 47547; 812-482-4255; *Field Director:* Larry Ordner
1500 N. Chestnut St., Vincennes, IN 47591; 855-519-1629
Committee Assignment: Energy and Commerce

Burgess, Michael C., R-Tex. (26)

Capitol Hill Office: 2336 RHOB 20515; 225-7772; Fax: 225-2919; *Chief of Staff:* Kelle Strickland
Web: burgess.house.gov
Facebook: www.facebook.com/michaelcburgess
Twitter: @michaelcburgess
District Office: 2000 S. Stemmons Fwy., #200, Lake Dallas, TX 75065; 940-497-5031; Fax: 940-497-5067; *District Director:* Erik With
Committee Assignments: Commission on Security and Cooperation in Europe; Energy and Commerce; Rules

Bustos, Cheri, D-Ill. (17)

Capitol Hill Office: 1009 LHOB 20515; 225-5905; Fax: 225-5396; *Chief of Staff:* Jon Pyatt
Web: bustos.house.gov
Facebook: www.facebook.com/RepCheri
Twitter: @RepCheri
District Offices: 3100 N. Knoxville Ave., #205, Peoria, IL 61603; 309-966-1813; *Constituent Advocate:* Laura Glesing
119 N. Church St., #207-208, Rockford, IL 61101; 815-968-8011; *Constituent Advocate:* Tiana McCall
2401 4th Ave., Rock Island, IL 61201; 309-786-3406; Fax: 309-786-3720; *District Director:* Chris Shallow
Committee Assignments: Agriculture; Transportation and Infrastructure

Butterfield, G. K., D-N.C. (1)

Capitol Hill Office: 2305 RHOB 20515-3301; 225-3101; Fax: 225-3354; *Chief of Staff:* Troy G. Clair
Web: butterfield.house.gov
Facebook: www.facebook.com/congressmangkbutterfield
Twitter: @GKButterfield
District Offices: 411 W. Chapel Hill St., #905, Durham, NC 27701; 919-908-0164; Fax: 919-908-0169; *Director of Constituent Affairs/Northwest District Outreach:* Dollie Burwell
216 Nash St. N.E., Suite B, Wilson, NC 27893-3802; 252-237-9816; Fax: 252-291-0356; *District Director:* Reginald Speight
Committee Assignment: Energy and Commerce

Byrne, Bradley, R-Ala. (1)

Capitol Hill Office: 119 CHOB 20515-0101; 225-4931; Fax: 225-0562; *Chief of Staff:* Alex Schriver
Web: byrne.house.gov
Facebook: www.facebook.com/RepByrne
Twitter: @RepByrne
District Offices: 502 W. Lee Ave., Summerdale, AL 36580; 251-989-2664; Fax: 251-989-2669; *Constituent Services Rep.:* Allison Clark
11 N. Water St., #15290, Mobile, AL 36602; 251-690-2811; Fax: 251-690-2815; *District Director:* Elizabeth Roney
Committee Assignments: Armed Services; Education and the Workforce; Rules

Calvert, Ken, R-Calif. (42)

Capitol Hill Office: 2269 RHOB 20515-0544; 225-1986;
Fax: 225-2004; *Chief of Staff:* Dave Ramey
Web: calvert.house.gov
Facebook: www.facebook.com/CalvertforCongress
Twitter: @KenCalvert
District Office: 4160 Temescal Canyon Rd., #214, Corona,
CA 92883-4624; 951-277-0042; Fax: 951-277-0420;
District Director: Jolyn Murphy
Committee Assignment: Appropriations

Capps, Lois, D-Calif. (24)

Capitol Hill Office: 2231 RHOB 20515-0523; 225-3601;
Fax: 225-5632; *Chief of Staff:* Sarah Rubinfield
Web: capps.house.gov
Facebook: www.facebook.com/loiscapps
Twitter: @RepLoisCapps
District Offices: 1411 Marsh St., #205, San Luis Obispo,
CA 93401-2923; 805-546-8348; Fax: 805-546-8368;
District Rep.: Greg Haas
301 E. Carrillo St., Suite A, Santa Barbara, CA 93101-1410;
805-730-1710; Fax: 805-730-9153; *District Director:*
Vianey Lopez
1101 S. Broadway St., Suite A, Santa Maria, CA 93454; 805-
349-3832; Fax: 805-361-0895; *Field Rep.:*
Blanca Figueroa
Committee Assignment: Energy and Commerce

Capuano, Michael E., D-Mass. (7)

Capitol Hill Office: 1414 LHOB 20515-2108; 225-5111;
Fax: 225-9322; *Chief of Staff:* Robert E. Primus
Web: house.govcapuano
Facebook: www.facebook.com/RepMichaelCapuano
Twitter: @mikecapuano
District Office: 110 1st St., Cambridge, MA 02141-2109;
617-621-6208; Fax: 617-621-8628; *District Director:*
Jon Lenicheck
Satellite Offices: Roxbury Community College, Campus
Library, Room 211, Boston, MA 02120; 617-621-
6208; Fax: 617-621-8628; *District Rep.:*
Candace Sealey
Stetson Hall, 6 S. Main St., Room 124, Randolph, MA
02368; 617-621-6208; Fax: 617-621-8628; *District Rep.:*
Kate Chang
Committee Assignments: Ethics; Financial Services;
Transportation and Infrastructure

Cárdenas, Tony, D-Calif. (29)

Capitol Hill Office: 1510 LHOB 20515; 225-6131;
Fax: 225-0819; *Chief of Staff:* Sam Jammal
Web: cardenas.house.gov
Facebook: www.facebook.com/repcardenas
Twitter: @repcardenas
District Office: 8134 Van Nuys Blvd., #206, Panorama
City, CA 91402; 818-781-7407; Fax: 818-781-7462;
District Director: Gabriela Marquez
Committee Assignment: Energy and Commerce

Carney, John, D-Del. (At Large)

Capitol Hill Office: 1406 LHOB 20515; 225-4165;
Fax: 225-2291; *Chief of Staff:* Sheila Grant
Web: johncarney.house.gov
Facebook: www.facebook.com/JohnCarneyDE
Twitter: @johncarneyde
District Offices: 33 The Circle, Georgetown, DE 19947;
302-854-0667; Fax: 302-854-0669; *Kent and Sussex
County Coord.:* Drew Slater
233 N. King St., #200, Wilmington, DE 19801-2521; 302-691-
7333; Fax: 302-428-1950; *State Director:* Molly Magarik
Committee Assignment: Financial Services

Carson, André, D-Ind. (7)

Capitol Hill Office: 2453 RHOB 20515-1407; 225-4011;
Fax: 225-5633; *Chief of Staff:* Kimberly Rudolph
Web: carson.house.gov
Facebook: www.facebook.com/CongressmanAndreCarson
Twitter: @repandrecarson
District Office: Julia M. Carson Government Center,
E. Fall Creek Pkwy. N. Dr., #300, Indianapolis, IN
46205-4258; 317-283-6516; Fax: 317-283-6567; *District
Director:* Megan Sims
Committee Assignments: Permanent Select Intelligence;
Transportation and Infrastructure

Carter, Buddy, R-Ga. (1)

Capitol Hill Office: 432 CHOB 20515-1001; 225-5831;
Fax: 226-2269; *Chief of Staff:* Chris Crawford
Web: buddycarter.house.gov
Facebook: www.facebook.com/CongressmanBuddyCarter
Twitter: @repBuddyCarter
District Offices: 1510 Newcastle St., #200, Brunswick, GA
31520; 912-265-9010; Fax: 912-265-9013; *Community
Liaison:* Nick Schemmel
6602 Abercorn St., #105B, Savannah, GA 31405; 912-352-
0101; Fax: 912-352-0105; *Staff Asst.:* Reagan Gresham
Committee Assignments: Education and the Workforce;
Homeland Security; Oversight and Government Reform

Carter, John, R-Tex. (31)

Capitol Hill Office: 2110 RHOB 20515-4331; 225-3864;
Fax: 225-5886; *Chief of Staff:* Jonas Miller
Web: carter.house.gov
Facebook: www.facebook.com/judgecarter
Twitter: @JudgeCarter
District Offices: One Financial Center, 1717 N. Hwy. 35,
#303, Round Rock, TX 78664; 512-246-1600; Fax: 512-
246-1620; *Texas Chief of Staff:* Jonas Miller
6544 S. General Bruce Dr., Suite B, Temple, TX 76502-
5811; 254-933-1392; Fax: 254-933-1650; *Constituent
Liaison:* Cheryl Hassmann
Committee Assignment: Appropriations

Cartwright, Matt, D-Pa. (17)

Capitol Hill Office: 1419 LHOB 20515; 225-5546;
Fax: 226-0996; *Chief of Staff:* Hunter Ridgway
Web: cartwright.house.gov

Facebook: www.facebook.com/
    CongressmanMattCartwright
Twitter: @RepCartwright
District Offices: 121 Progress Ave., #310, Pottsville, PA
    17901; 570-624-0140; Fax: 570-622-2902; *Caseworker:*
    Sabrina McLaughlin
226 Wyoming Ave., Scranton, PA 18503; 570-341-1050;
    Fax: 570-341-1055; *District Director:* Bob Morgan
400 Northampton St., #307, Easton, PA 18042; 484-546-
    0776; Fax: 610-252-3257; *Field Rep.:* Anne Lauritzen
Satellite Office: 20 N. Pennsylvania Ave., #201, Wilkes-
    Barre, PA 18711; 570-371-0317; *Caseworker:*
    Christa Mecadon
Committee Assignments: Natural Resources; Oversight
    and Government Reform

Castor, Kathy, D-Fla. (14)

Capitol Hill Office: 205 CHOB 20515-0911; 225-3376;
    Fax: 225-5652; *Chief of Staff:* Clay Phillips
Web: castor.house.gov
Facebook: www.facebook.com/USRepKathyCastor
Twitter: @USRepKCastor
District Office: 4144 N. Armenia Ave., #300, Tampa, FL
    33607-6435; 813-871-2817; Fax: 813-871-2864; *Press
    Secretary:* Marcia Mejia
Satellite Office: University of South Florida-St. Pete
    Williams House; 511 2nd St. South, St. Petersburg, FL
    33701; 727-873-2817; *Field Rep.:* Marcia Mejia
Committee Assignments: Budget; Energy and Commerce

Castro, Joaquin, D-Tex. (20)

Capitol Hill Office: 212 CHOB 20515; 225-3236; Fax: 225-
    1915; *Chief of Staff:* Carlos Sanchez
Web: castro.house.gov
Facebook: www.facebook.com/JoaquinCastroTX
Twitter: @JoaquinCastrotx
District Office: 727 E. Cesar E. Chavez Blvd., #B-128, San
    Antonio, TX 78206; 210-348-8216; Fax: 210-979-0737;
    District Director: Toni Serna
Committee Assignments: Armed Services; Foreign Affairs

Chabot, Steve, R-Ohio (1)

Capitol Hill Office: 2371 RHOB 20515; 225-2216;
    Fax: 225-3012; *Chief of Staff:* Stacy Barton
Web: chabot.house.gov
Facebook: www.facebook.com/RepSteveChabot
Twitter: @repstevechabot
District Offices: 441 Vine St., Room 3003, Cincinnati, OH
    45202-3003; 513-684-2723; Fax: 513-421-8722; *District
    Director:* Michael Cantwell
11 S. Broadway, Lebanon, OH 45036; 513-421-8704;
    Fax: 513-421-8722; *Field Rep.:* David McCandless;
    Deputy District Director: Alyssa Heim
Committee Assignments: Foreign Affairs; Judiciary; Small
    Business, Chair

Chaffetz, Jason, R-Utah (3)

Capitol Hill Office: 2236 RHOB 20515; 225-7751;
    Fax: 225-5629; *Chief of Staff:* Fred Ferguson

Web: chaffetz.house.gov
Facebook: www.facebook.com/
    CongressmanJasonChaffetz
Twitter: @jasoninthehouse
District Office: 51 S. University Ave., #318, Provo, UT
    84601-4491; 801-851-2500; Fax: 801-851-2509; *District
    Director:* Wade Garrett
Committee Assignments: Judiciary; Oversight and
    Government Reform, Chair

Chu, Judy, D-Calif. (27)

Capitol Hill Office: 1520 LHOB 20515-0532; 225-5464;
    Fax: 225-5467; *Chief of Staff:* Linda Shim
Web: chu.house.gov
Facebook: www.facebook.com/Chu4Congress
Twitter: @RepJudyChu
District Offices: 527 S. Lake Ave., #106, Pasadena, CA
    91101; 626-304-0110; Fax: 626-304-0132; *District
    Director:* Becky Cheng
415 W. Foothill Blvd., #122, Claremont, CA 91711; 909-
    625-5394; Fax: 909-399-0198; *Field Rep.:*
    Enrique Robles
Committee Assignments: Judiciary; Small Business

Cicilline, David, D-R.I. (1)

Capitol Hill Office: 2244 RHOB 20515-3901; 225-4911;
    Fax: 225-3290; *Chief of Staff:* Peter Karafotas
Web: cicilline.house.gov
Facebook: www.facebook.com/
    CongressmanDavidCicilline
Twitter: @repcicilline
District Office: 1070 Main St., #300, Pawtucket, RI 02860-
    2134; 401-729-5600; Fax: 401-729-5608; *District
    Director:* Arianne Corrente
Committee Assignments: Foreign Affairs; Judiciary

Clark, Katherine, D-Mass. (5)

Capitol Hill Office: 1721 LHOB 20515-2107; 225-2836;
    Fax: 226-0092; *Chief of Staff:* Brooke Scannell
Web: katherineclark.house.gov
Facebook: www.facebook.com/CongresswomanClark
Twitter: @KatherineClark
District Office: 701 Concord Ave., #101, Cambridge, MA
    02138; 617-354-0292; Fax: 617-354-1456; *District
    Director:* Christian Lobue
Satellite Office: 116 Concord St., #1, Framingham, MA
    01702; 508-319-9757; *District Counsel:*
    Wade Blackman
Committee Assignments: Education and the Workforce;
    Science, Space, and Technology

Clarke, Yvette D., D-N.Y. (9)

Capitol Hill Office: 2351 RHOB 20515; 225-6231;
    Fax: 226-0112; *Chief of Staff:* Shelley Davis
Web: clarke.house.gov
Facebook: www.facebook.com/repyvettedclarke
Twitter: @YvetteClarke

District Office: 222 Lenox Rd., #1 & 2, Brooklyn, NY 11226-3302; 718-287-1142; Fax: 718-287-1223; *District Director:* Anita Taylor

Committee Assignments: Energy and Commerce; Ethics; Small Business

Clawson, Curt, R-Fla. (19)

Capitol Hill Office: 228 CHOB 20515-0919; 225-2536; Fax: 226-0439; *Chief of Staff:* Pat Cauley

Web: clawson.house.gov

Facebook: www.facebook.com/ClawsonTheOutsider

Twitter: @repcurtclawson

District Offices: 3299 Tamiami Trail East, #105, Naples, FL 34112; 239-252-6225; *District Director:* Rochelle C. Dudley

804 Nicholas Pkwy. East, #1, Cape Coral, FL 33990; 239-573-5837; *District Rep.:* Rickey Nelson

Committee Assignments: Foreign Affairs; Homeland Security

Clay, Wm. Lacy, D-Mo. (1)

Capitol Hill Office: 2428 RHOB 20515-2501; 225-2406; Fax: 226-3717; *Chief of Staff:* Yvette Cravins

Web: lacyclay.house.gov

Facebook: www.facebook.com/lacy.clay.3

Twitter: @LacyClayMO1

District Offices: 111 S. 10th St., #24.344, St. Louis, MO 63102; 314-367-1970; Fax: 314-367-1341; *Community Outreach Coord.:* Jasmina Hadzic

6830 Gravois, St. Louis, MO 63116; 314-669-9393; 314-669-9398; *Communications Director; Press Secretary:* Steve Engelhardt

Committee Assignments: Financial Services; Natural Resources; Oversight and Government Reform

Cleaver, Emanuel, D-Mo. (5)

Capitol Hill Office: 2335 RHOB 20515; 225-4535; Fax: 225-4403; *Chief of Staff:* John H. Jones

Web: cleaver.house.gov

Facebook: www.facebook.com/emanuelcleaverii

Twitter: @repcleaver

District Offices: 211 W. Maple Ave., Independence, MO 64050-2815; 816-833-4545; Fax: 816-833-2991; *Community Affairs Liaison:* Breanna Cameron

101 W. 31st St., Kansas City, MO 64108-3318; 816-842-4545; Fax: 816-471-5215; *District Director:* Geoff Jolley

1923 Main St., Higginsville, MO 64037; 660-584-7373; Fax: 660-584-7227; *Rural Development Coordinator:* Kelli Montgomery

Committee Assignment: Financial Services

Clyburn, James E., D-S.C. (6)

Capitol Hill Office: 242 CHOB 20515; 225-3315; Fax: 225-2313; *Chief of Staff:* Yelberton R. Watkins

Web: clyburn.house.gov

Facebook: www.facebook.com/jameseclyburn

Twitter: @clyburn

District Offices: 1225 Lady St., #200, Columbia, SC 29201-3210; 803-799-1100; Fax: 803-799-9060; *District Director:* Robert Nance

130 W. Main St., Kingstree, SC 29556; 843-355-1211; Fax: 843-355-1232; *Caseworker:* Kenneth Barnes

176 Brooks Blvd., Santee, SC 29142; 803-854-4700; Fax: 803-854-4900; *District Director:* Robert Nance

Assistant to the Democratic Leader

Coffman, Mike, R-Colo. (6)

Capitol Hill Office: 2443 RHOB 20515; 225-7882; Fax: 226-4623; *Communications Director:* Cinamon Watson

Web: coffman.house.gov

Facebook: www.facebook.com/repmikecoffman

Twitter: @RepMikeCoffman

District Office: 3300 S. Parker Rd., Cherry Creek P. IV, #305, Aurora, CO 80014; 720-748-7514; Fax: 720-748-7680; *Chief of Staff:* Ben Stein

Committee Assignments: Armed Services; Veterans' Affairs

Cohen, Steve, D-Tenn. (9)

Capitol Hill Office: 2404 RHOB 20515; 225-3265; Fax: 225-5663; *Chief of Staff:* Marilyn Dillihay

Web: cohen.house.gov

Facebook: www.facebook.com/CongressmanSteveCohen

Twitter: @repcohen

District Office: Clifford Davis/Odell Horton Federal Bldg., 167 N. Main St., #369, Memphis, TN 38103-1822; 901-544-4131; Fax: 901-544-4329; *District Director:* Marzie Thomas

Committee Assignments: Commission on Security and Cooperation in Europe; Judiciary; Transportation and Infrastructure

Cole, Tom, R-Okla. (4)

Capitol Hill Office: 2467 RHOB 20515-3604; 225-6165; Fax: 225-3512; *Chief of Staff:* Sean P. Murphy

Web: cole.house.gov

Facebook: www.facebook.com/TomColeOK04

Twitter: @tomcoleok04

District Offices: 100 E. 13th St., #213, Ada, OK 74820-6548; 580-436-5375; Fax: 580-436-3512; *Field Rep.:* Coty Dildine

711 D Ave. S.W., #201, Lawton, OK 73501-4561; 580-357-2131; Fax: 580-357-7477; *Field Rep.:* Debe Homer

2424 Springer Dr., #201, Norman, OK 73069-3965; 405-329-6500; Fax: 405-321-7369; *District Director:* Jess Peters

Committee Assignments: Appropriations; Budget; Joint Library; Rules

Collins, Chris, R-N.Y. (27)

Capitol Hill Office: 1117 LHOB 20515; 225-5265; Fax: 225-5910; *Chief of Staff:* Michael Hook

Web: chriscollins.house.gov

Facebook: www.facebook.com/RepChrisCollins

Twitter: @RepChrisCollins

District Offices: 128 Main St., #2, Geneseo, NY 14454; 585-519-4002; Fax: 585-519-4009; *Field Rep.:* Chris Catt
2813 Wehrle Dr., #13, Williamsville, NY 14221; 716-634-2324; Fax: 716-631-7610; *District Director:* Michael Kracker
Committee Assignment: Energy and Commerce

Collins, Doug, R-Ga. (9)

Capitol Hill Office: 1504 LHOB 20515; 225-9893; Fax: 226-1224; *Chief of Staff:* Brendan Belair
Web: dougcollins.house.gov
Facebook: www.facebook.com/RepresentativeDougCollins
Twitter: @RepDougCollins
District Office: 210 Washington St. N.W., #202, Gainesville, GA 30501; 770-297-3388; Fax: 770-297-3390; *District Director:* Joel Katz
Committee Assignments: Judiciary; Rules

Comstock, Barbara, R-Va. (10)

Capitol Hill Office: 226 CHOB 20515-4610; 225-5136; Fax: 225-0437; *Chief of Staff:* Susan Falconer
Web: comstock.house.gov
Facebook: www.facebook.com/RepBarbaraComstock
Twitter: @RepComstock
District Office: 21430 Cedar Dr., #218, Sterling, VA 20164; 703-404-6903 Fax: 703-404-6906; *Director of Constituent Services:* Lucy Norment
117 E. Piccadilly St., Winchester, VA 22601; 540-773-3600; *Community Liaison:* Dave Stegmaier
Committee Assignments: House Administration; Science, Space and Technology; Transportation and Infrastructure

Conaway, Mike, R-Tex. (11)

Capitol Hill Office: 2430 RHOB 20515-4311; 225-3605; Fax: 225-1783; *Chief of Staff:* Mark Williams
Web: conaway.house.gov
Facebook: www.facebook.com/mike.conaway
Twitter: @ConawayTX11
District Offices: Brownwood City Hall, 501 Center Ave., Brownwood, TX 76801-2809; 325-646-1950; Fax: 325-646-2979; *Field Rep.:* Hilary Stegemoller
County Annex, 104 W. Sandstone St., Llano, TX 78643-2319; 325-247-2826; Fax: 325-247-2676; *Field Rep.:* Nancy Watson
6 Desta Dr., #2000, Midland, TX 79705-5520; 432-687-2390; Fax: 432-687-0277; *District Director:* Evan Thomas
City Hall, 411 W. 8th St., 5th Floor, Odessa, TX 79761-4422; 432-331-9667; Fax: 432-332-6538; *Field Rep.:* Gloria Apolinario
O.C. Fisher Federal Bldg., 33 E. Twohig Ave., #307, San Angelo, TX 76903-6451; 325-659-4010; Fax: 325-659-4014; *Regional Director:* Joanne Powell
Committee Assignments: Agriculture, Chair; Armed Services; Permanent Select Intelligence

Connolly, Gerald E., D-Va. (11)

Capitol Hill Office: 2238 RHOB 20515-4611; 225-1492; Fax: 225-3071; *Chief of Staff:* James Walkinshaw

Web: connolly.house.gov
Facebook: www.facebook.com/CongressmanGerryConnolly
Twitter: @gerryconnolly
District Offices: 4115 Annandale Rd., #103, Annandale, VA 22003-2500; 703-256-3071; Fax: 703-354-1284; *District Director:* Sharon Stark
2241D Tacketts Mill Dr., Woodbridge, VA 22192-5307; 571-408-4407; Fax: 703-670-6042; *Prince William County Director:* Brianna Sewell
Committee Assignments: Foreign Affairs; Oversight and Government Reform

Conyers, John, Jr., D-Mich. (13)

Capitol Hill Office: 2426 RHOB 20515-2214; 225-5126; Fax: 225-0072; *Chief of Staff; Legis. Counsel, Black Caucus, Korean Caucus:* Cynthia Martin
Web: conyers.house.gov
Facebook: www.facebook.com/CongressmanConyers
Twitter: @repjohnconyers
District Offices: 231 W. Lafayette Blvd., #669, Detroit, MI 48226-2766; 313-961-5670; Fax: 313-226-2085; *District Director:* Yolonda Lipsey
33300 Warren Rd., #13, Westland, MI 48185-9620; 734-675-4084; Fax: 734-675-4218; *Caseworker:* Katie Gorno
Committee Assignment: Judiciary, Ranking Member

Cook, Paul, R-Calif. (8)

Capitol Hill Office: 1222 LHOB 20515; 225-5861; Fax: 225-6498; *Chief of Staff:* John Sobel
Web: cook.house.gov
Facebook: www.facebook.com/electpaulcook
Twitter: @RepPaulCook
District Offices: 14955 Dale Evans Pkwy., Apple Valley, CA 92307; 760-247-1815; Fax: 760-247-8073; *District Director:* Matt Knox
34282 Yucaipa Blvd., Yucaipa, CA 92399; 909-797-4900; Fax: 909-797-4997; *Field Rep.:* Jan Leja
Committee Assignments: Armed Services; Foreign Affairs; Natural Resources

Cooper, Jim, D-Tenn. (5)

Capitol Hill Office: 1536 LHOB 20515-4205; 225-4311; Fax: 226-1035; *Chief of Staff:* Lisa Quigley
Web: cooper.house.gov
Facebook: www.facebook.com/JimCooper
Twitter: @repjimcooper
District Office: 605 Church St., Nashville, TN 37219-2314; 615-736-5295; Fax: 615-736-7479; *District Director:* Kathy Buggs
Committee Assignments: Armed Services; Oversight and Government Reform

Costa, Jim, D-Calif. (16)

Capitol Hill Office: 1314 LHOB 20515-0520; 225-3341; Fax: 225-9308; *Chief of Staff; Ethics:* Juan Lopez
Web: costa.house.gov
Facebook: www.facebook.com/RepJimCosta
Twitter: @RepJimCosta

District Offices: 855 M St., #940, Fresno, CA 93721-2757; 559-495-1620; Fax: 559-495-1027; *District Director:* Vacant

2222 M St., #305, Merced, CA 95340; 209-384-1620; Fax: 209-304-1629 *Field Rep.:* Daniel Martinez, Matthew Wainwright

Committee Assignments: Agriculture; Natural Resources

Costello, Ryan, R-Pa. (6)

Capitol Hill Office: 427 CHOB 20515-3806; 225-4315; Fax: 225-8440; *Chief of Staff:* Lauryn Schothorst
Web: costello.house.gov
Facebook: www.facebook.com/ CongressmanRyanCostello
Twitter: @RepRyanCostello
District Offices: 840 N. Park Rd., Wyomissing, PA 19610; 610-376-7630; Fax: 610-376-7633; *Communications Director:* Johanna Persing

21 W. Market St., #105, West Chester, PA 19382; 610-696-2982; Fax: 610-696-2985; *Scheduler:* Kathryn Ercole

Committee Assignments: Transporation and Infrastructure; Veterans' Affairs

Courtney, Joe, D-Conn. (2)

Capitol Hill Office: 2348 RHOB 20515; 225-2076; Fax: 225-4977; *Chief of Staff:* Neil McKiernan
Web: courtney.house.gov
Facebook: www.facebook.com/joecourtney
Twitter: @repjoecourtney
District Offices: 77 Hazard Ave., Suite J, Enfield, CT 06082-3890; 860-741-6011; Fax: 860-741-6036; *Field Rep.:* Matthew Reutter

55 Main St., #250, Norwich, CT 06360; 860-886-0139; Fax: 860-886-2974; *District Director:* Ayanti Grant

Committee Assignments: Armed Services; Education and Workforce

Cramer, Kevin, R-N.D. (At Large)

Capitol Hill Office: 1032 LHOB 20515; 225-2611; Fax: 226-0893; *Chief of Staff:* Mark Gruman
Web: cramer.house.gov
Facebook: www.facebook.com/CongressmanKevinCramer
Twitter: @RepKevinCramer
District Offices: 220 East Rosser Ave., 328 Federal Bldg. Bismarck, ND 58501-3869; 701-224-0355; Fax: 701-224-0431; *Scheduler:* Kris Cramer

3217 Fiechtner Dr., Suite D, Fargo, ND 58103; 701-356-2216; Fax: 701-356-2217; *State Director:* Lisa Gibbens

4200 James Ray Dr., #600, Grand Forks, ND 58202; 701-738-4880; *Field Rep.:* Randy Richards

315 Main St., #203, Minot, ND 58701; 701-839-0255; *Field Rep.:* Kaitlyn Kline

Committee Assignment: Energy and Commerce

Crawford, Rick, R-Ark. (1)

Capitol Hill Office: 1711 LHOB 20515; 225-4076; Fax: 225-5602; *Chief of Staff:* Jonah Shumate
Web: crawford.house.gov
Facebook: www.facebook.com/RepRickCrawford

Twitter: @reprickcrawford
District Offices: 112 S. 1st St., Cabot, AR 72023-3007; 501-843-3043; Fax: 501-843-4955; *Field Rep.:* Jay Sherrod

2400 E. Highland Dr., #300, Jonesboro, AR 72401-6229; 870-203-0540; Fax: 870-203-0542; *District Director:* Andrea Allen

1001 Hwy. 62 E., #9, Mountain Home, AR 72653; 870-424-2075; Fax: 870-424-3149; *Field Rep.:* Joseph Didden

Committee Assignments: Agriculture; Transportation and Infrastructure

Crenshaw, Ander, R-Fla. (4)

Capitol Hill Office: 2161 RHOB 20515-0904; 225-2501; Fax: 225-2504; *Chief of Staff:* Erica Striebel
Web: crenshaw.house.gov
Facebook: www.facebook.com/pages/Congressman-Ander-Crenshaw-200388204657
Twitter: @AnderCrenshaw
District Office: 1061 Riverside Ave., #100, Jacksonville, FL 32204-4151; 904-598-0481; Fax: 904-598-0486; *District Director:* Jacquelyn Smith

Committee Assignment: Appropriations

Crowley, Joseph, D-N.Y. (14)

Capitol Hill Office: 1436 LHOB 20515; 225-3965; Fax: 225-1909; *Chief of Staff:* Kate Keating
Web: crowley.house.gov
Facebook: www.facebook.com/repjoecrowley
Twitter: @repjoecrowley
District Offices: 2800 Bruckner Blvd., #201, Bronx, NY 10465-1907; 718-931-1400; Fax: 718-931-1340; *District Chief of Staff:* Anne Marie Anzalone

82-11 37th Ave., #402, Queens, NY 11372; 718-779-1400; Fax: 718-505-0156; *Deputy District Director:* Alex Florez

Committee Assignment: Ways and Means

Cuellar, Henry, D-Tex. (28)

Capitol Hill Office: 2209 RHOB 20515; 225-1640; Fax: 225-1641; *Chief of Staff:* Cynthia Gaona
Web: cuellar.house.gov
Facebook: www.facebook.com/pages/repcuellar
Twitter: @RepCuellar
District Offices: 602 E. Calton Rd., #2, Laredo, TX 78041-3693; 956-725-0639; Fax: 956-725-2647; *Grants Coord.:* Juan Sanchez

117 E. Tom Landry St., Mission, TX 78572-4160; 956-424-3942; Fax: 956-424-3936; *Constituent Services Coordinator:* Narda Terrones

100 N. F.M. 3167, Rio Grande City, TX 78582; 956-487-5603; Fax: 956-488-0952; *Outreach Coordinator:* Nicole Hernandez

615 E. Houston St., #563, San Antonio, TX 78205-2048; 210-271-2851; Fax: 210-277-6671; *Outreach Coord.:* Gilbert La Fuente

Committee Assignment: Appropriations

Culberson, John, R-Tex. (7)

Capitol Hill Office: 2372 RHOB 20515-4307; 225-2571; Fax: 225-4381; *Chief of Staff:* Jamie Gahun

Web: culberson.house.gov
Facebook: www.facebook.com/john.culberson.5
Twitter: @congculberson
District Office: 10000 Memorial Dr., #620, Houston, TX 77024; 713-682-8828; Fax: 713-680-8070; *District Director:* Cynthia Dannenbrink
Committee Assignment: Appropriations

Cummings, Elijah E., D-Md. (7)

Capitol Hill Office: 2230 RHOB 20515-2007; 225-4741; Fax: 225-3178; *Chief of Staff:* Vernon Simms
Web: cummings.house.gov
Facebook: www.facebook.com/elijahcummings
Twitter: @RepCummings
District Offices: 1010 Park Ave., #105, Baltimore, MD 21201-5600; 410-685-9199; Fax: 410-685-9399; *District Director:* Francine Allen
754 Frederick Rd., Catonsville, MD 21228-4504; 410-719-8777; Fax: 410-455-0110; *Special Asst.:* Katie Malone
8267 Main St., #102, Ellicott City, MD 21043-9903; 410-465-8259; Fax: 410-465-8740; *Special Asst.:* Amy Stratton
Committee Assignments: Oversight and Government Reform, Ranking Member; Select on Benghazi, Ranking Member; Transportation and Infrastructure

Curbelo, Carlos, R-Fla. (26)

Capitol Hill Office: 1429 LHOB 20515-0926; 225-2778; Fax: 226-0346; *Chief of Staff:* Roy Schultheis
Web: curbelo.house.gov
Facebook: www.facebook.com/carloslcurbelo
Twitter: @RepCurbelo
District Offices: 12851 SW 42nd St., #131, Miami, FL 33175; 305-222-0160; Fax: 305-228-9397; *District Director:* Chris Miles
1100 Simonton St., #1-213; Key West, FL 33040; 305-292-4485; Fax: 305-292-4486; *District Director:* Nicole Rapanos
404 W. Palm Dr., Florida City, FL 33034; 305-247-1234; *Community Outreach Liaison:* Alana Collante
Committee Assignments: Education and the Workforce; Small Business; Transportation and Infrastructure

Davis, Danny K., D-Ill. (7)

Capitol Hill Office: 2159 RHOB 20515-1307; 225-5006; Fax: 225-5641; *Chief of Staff:* Yul Edwards
Web: davis.house.gov
Facebook: www.facebook.com/CongressmanDKDavis
Twitter: @DannyKDavis
District Office: 2746 W. Madison St., Chicago, IL 60612-2040; 773-533-7520; Fax: 773-533-7530; *District Director:* Cherita Logan
Committee Assignment: Ways and Means

Davis, Rodney, R-Ill. (13)

Capitol Hill Office: 1740 LHOB 20515; 225-2371; Fax: 226-0791; *Chief of Staff:* Jen Daulby
Web: rodneydavis.house.gov
Facebook: www.facebook.com/RepRodneyDavis

Twitter: @RodneyDavis
District Offices: 2004 Fox Dr., Champaign, IL 61820; 217-403-4690; Fax: 217-403-4691; *District Director:* Helen Albert
243 S. Water St., #100, Decatur, IL 62523; 217-791-6224; Fax: 217-791-6168; *Community Outreach:* Candice Trees
9 Junction Dr., #9, Glen Carbon, IL 62034; 618-205-8660; Fax: 618-205-8662; *Grants and Projects Coord.:* Phillip Lasseigne
108 E. Market, Taylorville, IL 62568; 217-824-5117; Fax: 217-824-5121; *Constituent Services Rep.:* Margaret Kettelkamp
Satellite Offices: 2833 S. Grand Ave., Suite E., Springfield, IL 62703; 217-791-6224; Fax: 217-791-6168 *Community Outreach:* Candice Trees
104 W. North St., Normal, IL 61761; 309-252-8834; *Casework Director:* Jennifer White
Committee Assignments: Agriculture; House Administration; Transportation and Infrastructure

Davis, Susan, D-Calif. (53)

Capitol Hill Office: 1214 LHOB 20515-0553; 225-2040; Fax: 225-2948; *Chief of Staff:* Lisa Sherman
Web: susandavis.house.gov
Facebook: www.facebook.com/RepSusanDavis
Twitter: @RepSusanDavis
District Office: 2700 Adams Ave., #102, San Diego, CA 92116; 619-280-5353; Fax: 619-280-5311; *District Director:* Jessica Poole
Committee Assignments: Armed Services; Education and the Workforce

DeFazio, Peter, D-Ore. (4)

Capitol Hill Office: 2134 RHOB 20515-3704; 225-6416; *Chief of Staff:* Kristie Greco
Web: defazio.house.gov
Facebook: www.facebook.com/RepPeterDeFazio
Twitter: @RepPeterDeFazio
District Offices: 405 E. 8th Ave., #2030, Eugene, OR 97401-2706; 541-465-6732; Fax: 541-465-6458; *District Director:* Nick Batz
612 S.E. Jackson St., #9, Roseburg, OR 97470-4956; 541-440-3523; Fax: 541-440-3713; *Field Rep.:* Christine Conroy
Committee Assignment: Transportation and Infrastructure, Ranking Minority Member

DeGette, Diana, D-Colo. (1)

Capitol Hill Office: 2368 RHOB 20515; 225-4431; Fax: 225-5657; *Chief of Staff:* Lisa B. Cohen
Web: degette.house.gov
Facebook: www.facebook.com/DianaDeGette
Twitter: @RepDianaDeGette
District Office: 600 Grant St., #202, Denver, CO 80203-3525; 303-844-4988; Fax: 303-844-4996; *Acting District Director:* Andrea Aotobeu-Trujillo
Committee Assignment: Energy and Commerce

Delaney, John, D-Md. (6)

Capitol Hill Office: 1632 LHOB 20515; 225-2721;
    Fax: 225-2193; *Chief of Staff:* Justin Schall
Web: delaney.house.gov
Facebook: www.facebook.com/congressmanjohndelaney
Twitter: @RepJohnDelaney
District Offices: 9801 Washingtonian Blvd., #330,
    Gaithersburg, MD 20878; 301-926-0300; Fax: 301-926-
    0324; *District Director:* Kevin Mack
38 S. Potomac St., #205, Hagerstown, MD 21740; 301-733-
    2900; *District Director:* Sonny Holding
Committee Assignments: Financial Services; Joint
    Economic

DeLauro, Rosa L., D-Conn. (3)

Capitol Hill Office: 2413 RHOB 20515-0703; 225-3661;
    Fax: 225-4890; *Chief of Staff:* Beverly Aimaro Pheto
Web: delauro.house.gov
Facebook: www.facebook.com/CongresswomanRosa
    DeLauro
Twitter: @rosadelauro
District Office: 59 Elm St., #205, New Haven, CT 06510-
    2036; 203-562-3718; Fax: 203-772-2260; *District
    Director:* Jennifer Lamb
Satellite Offices: Valley Regional Planning Agency,
    Conference Room, 12 Main St., Derby, CT 06418-1931;
    203-735-5005; *District Director:* Jennifer Lamb
Municipal Bldg., 245 DeKoven Dr., #B-20, Middletown,
    CT 06457-3460; 860-344-1159; *District Director:*
    Jennifer Lamb
Municipal Bldg., 229 Church St., Mayors Conference
    Room, 4th Floor, Naugatuck, CT 06770-4145; 203-729-
    0204; *District Director:* Jennifer Lamb
Committee Assignment: Appropriations

DelBene, Suzan, D-Wash. (1)

Capitol Hill Office: 318 CHOB 20515; 225-6311; Fax: 226-
    1606; *Chief of Staff:* Aaron Schmidt
Web: delbene.house.gov
Facebook: www.facebook.com/RepDelBene
Twitter: @RepDelBene
District Offices: 22121 17th Ave. S.E., Bldg. E, #220,
    Bothell, WA 98021; 425-485- 0085; Fax: 425-485-0083;
    District Director: Matt Isenhower
204 W. Montgomery St., Mount Vernon, WA 98273; 360-
    416-7879; *Outreach Coordinator:* Karlee Deatherage
Committee Assignments: Agriculture; Judiciary

Denham, Jeff, R-Calif. (10)

Capitol Hill Office: 1730 LHOB 20515; 225-4540;
    Fax: 225-3402; *Chief of Staff:* Jason G. Larrabee
Web: denham.house.gov
Facebook: www.facebook.com/RepJeffDenham
Twitter: @RepJeffDenham
District Office: 4701 Sisk Rd., #202, Modesto, CA 95356;
    209-579-5458; Fax: 209-579-5028; *District Director:*
    Bob Rucker
Committee Assignments: Agriculture; Natural Resources;
    Transportation and Infrastructure

Dent, Charlie, R-Pa. (15)

Capitol Hill Office: 2455 RHOB 20515; 225-6411;
    Fax: 226-0778; *Chief of Staff:* Drew Kent
Web: dent.house.gov
Facebook: www.facebook.com/congressmandent
Twitter: @dentforcongress
District Offices: 3900 Hamilton Blvd., #207, Allentown,
    PA 18103-6122; 610-770-3490; Fax: 610-770-3498;
    District Director: Vincent O'Domski
250 W. Chocolate Ave., #2, Hershey, PA 17033; 717-533-
    3959; Fax: 717-533-3979; *Dawson County
    Coordinator:* Alicia Hain
61 N. 3rd St., Hamburg, PA 19526; 610-562-4281;
    Fax: 610-562-4352; *District Director:*
    Vincent O'Domski
342 W. Main St., Annville, PA 17003; 717-867-1026;
    Fax: 717-867-1540; *Lebanon County Coordinator:*
    Brian Craig
Committee Assignments: Appropriations; Ethics, Chair

DeSantis, Ron, R-Fla. (6)

Capitol Hill Office: 308 CHOB 20515; 225-2706; Fax: 226-
    6299; *Chief of Staff:* Dustin Carmack
Web: desantis.house.gov
Facebook: www.facebook.com/RepDeSantis
Twitter: @RepDeSantis
District Offices: 1000 City Center Circle, Port Orange, FL
    32129; 386-756-9798; Fax: 386-756-9903; *District Rep.:*
    Naomi D'antonio
3940 Lewis Speedway, #2104, St. Augustine, FL 32084; 904-
    827-1101; Fax: 904-827-1114; *District Director:*
    Robert Mons
Committee Assignments: Foreign Affairs; Judiciary;
    Oversight and Government Reform

DeSaulnier, Mark, D-Calif. (11)

Capitol Hill Office: 327 CHOB 20515-0511; 225-2095;
    Fax: 225-5609; *Chief of Staff:* Betsy Arnold Marr
Web: desaulnier.house.gov
Facebook: www.facebook.com/RepMarkDeSaulnier
Twitter: @RepDeSaulnier
District Offices: 440 Civic Center Plaza, 2nd Floor,
    Richmond, CA 94804; 510-620-1000; Fax: 510-620-
    1005; *District Director:* Shanelle Preston Scales
101 Ygnacio Valley Rd., #210, Walnut Creek, CA 94598;
    925-933-2660; Fax: 925-933-2677; *District Director:*
    Shanelle Preston Scales
Committee Assignments: Education and the Workforce;
    Oversight and Government Reform

DesJarlais, Scott, R-Tenn. (4)

Capitol Hill Office: 413 CHOB 20515-4204; 225-6831;
    Fax: 226-5172; *Chief of Staff:* Richard Vaughn
Web: desJarlais.house.gov
Facebook: www.facebook.com/ScottDesJarlaisTN04
Twitter: @DesJarlaisTN04
District Offices: 711 N. Garden St., Columbia, TN 38401-
    3262; 931-381-9920; Fax: 931-381-9945; *Constituent
    Services Coord.:* Becky Moon

305 W. Main St., Murfreesboro, TN 37130; 615-896-1986; Fax: 615-896-8218; *Field Rep.:* Tina Jones

Satellite Offices: 301 Keith St., #212, Cleveland, TN 37311; 423-472-7500; Fax: 423-472-7800; *Field Rep.:* Shirley Pond

Federal Bldg., 200 S. Jefferson St., #311, Winchester, TN 37398; 931-962-3180; Fax: 931-962-3435; *District Rep.:* Isiah Robinson

Committee Assignments: Agriculture; Foreign Affairs; Oversight and Government Reform

Deutch, Ted, D-Fla. (21)

Capitol Hill Office: 2447 RHOB 20515-0919; 225-3001; Fax: 225-5974; *Chief of Staff:* Joshua Rogin

Web: deutch.house.gov

Facebook: www.facebook.com/CongressmanTedDeutch

Twitter: @repteddeutch

District Offices: 7900 Glades Rd., #250, Boca Raton, FL 33434; 561-470-5440; Fax: 561-470-5446; *District Director:* Wendi Lipsich

Margate City Hall, 5790 Margate Blvd., Margate, FL 33063-3614; 954-972-6454; Fax: 954-974-3191; *District Rep.:* Theresa Brier

1300 Coral Springs Dr., Coral Springs, FL 33071; 954-255-8336; *District Rep.:* Theresa Brier

Committee Assignments: Ethics; Foreign Affairs; Judiciary

Diaz-Balart, Mario, R-Fla. (25)

Capitol Hill Office: 440 CHOB 20515-0921; 225-4211; Fax: 225-8576; *Chief of Staff:* Cesar A. Gonzalez

Web: mariodiazbalart.house.gov

Facebook: www.facebook.com/mdiazbalart

Twitter: @mariodb

District Offices: 8669 36th St. N.W., #100, Doral, FL 33166-6640; 305-470-8555; Fax: 305-470-8575; *Deputy Chief of Staff:* Miguel Otero

4715 Golden Gate Pkwy., #1, Naples, FL 34116; 239-348-1620; Fax: 239-348-3569; *Congressional Aide:* Enrique Padron

Committee Assignments: Appropriations; Budget

Dingell, Debbie, D-Mich. (12)

Capitol Hill Office: 116 CHOB 20515-2212; 225-4071; Fax: 226-0371; *Chief of Staff:* Peter Chandler

Web: debbiedingell.house.gov

Facebook: www.facebook.com/RepDebbieDingell

Twitter: @RepDebDingell

District Offices: 301 W. Michigan Ave., #400, Ypsilanti, MI 48197; 734-481-1100; *Caseworker:* Jannine Kadri

19855 W. Outer Dr., #103-E, Dearborn, MI 48124; 313-278-2936; Fax: 313-278-3914; *District Director:* Kevin Hrit

Committee Assignments: Budget; Natural Resources

Doggett, Lloyd, D-Tex. (35)

Capitol Hill Office: 2307 RHOB 20515-4325; 225-4865; Fax: 225-3073; *Chief of Staff:* Michael J. Mucchetti

Web: doggett.house.gov

Facebook: www.facebook.com/lloyddoggett

Twitter: @replloyddoggett

District Offices: Federal Bldg., 300 E. 8th St., #763, Austin, TX 78701-3224; 512-916-5921; Fax: 512-916-5108; *Deputy District Director:* Lee Ann Calaway

217 W. Travis St., San Antonio, TX 78205; 210-704-1080; Fax: 210-299-1442; *District Director:* Maryellen Beliz

Committee Assignment: Ways and Means

Dold, Bob, R-Ill. (10)

Capitol Hill Office: 221 CHOB 20515-1310; 225-4835; Fax: 225-0837; *Chief of Staff:* David Stern

Web: dold.house.gov

Facebook: www.facebook.com/RepDold

Twitter: @RepDold

District Office: 300 Village Green, #235, Lincolnshire, IL 60069; 847-793-8400; Fax: 847-793-8499; *District Director:* Phillipe Melin

Satellite Office: 442 N. Cedar Lake Rd., Round Lake, IL 60073; 847-309-6627; Fax: 847-793-8499; *Staff:* Vacant

Committee Assignment: Ways and Means

Donovan, Dan, R-N.Y. (11)

Capitol Hill Office: 1725 LHOB 20515-3213; 225-3371; *Chief of Staff:* Chris Berardini

Web: donovan.house.gov

Facebook: www.facebook.com/RepDanDonovan

Twitter: @dandonovan_ny

District Offices: 7308 13th Ave., Brooklyn, NY 11228-2011; 718-630-5277; Fax: 718-630-5388; *Brooklyn Staff Director:* Fran Vella-Marrone

265 New Dorp Lane, 2nd Floor, Staten Island, NY 10306-3005; 718-351-1062; Fax: 718-980-0768; *District Director:* Nick Curran

Committee Assignments: Foreign Affairs; Homeland Security

Doyle, Michael, Jr., D-Pa. (14)

Capitol Hill Office: 239 CHOB 20515; 225-2135; Fax: 225-3084; *Chief of Staff:* David G. Lucas

Web: doyle.house.gov

Facebook: www.facebook.com/usrepmikedoyle

Twitter: @usrepmikedoyle

District Offices: 627 Lysle Blvd., McKeesport, PA 15132; 412-664-4049; Fax: 412-664-4053; *Economic Development Rep.:* Janie O'Grady

11 Duff Rd., Penn Hills, PA 15235; 412-241-6055; Fax: 412-241-6820; *Caseworker:* John Jones

2637 E. Carson St., Pittsburgh, PA 15203-5109; 412-390-1499; Fax: 412-390-2118; *District Director:* Paul D'Alesandro

Satellite Offices: 1350 5th Ave., Coraopolis, PA 15108-2024; 412-264-3460; *Community Development Rep.:* Joseph Heffley

Committee Assignment: Energy and Commerce

Duckworth, Tammy, D-Ill. (8)

Capitol Hill Office: 104 CHOB 20515; 225-3711; Fax: 225-7830; *Chief of Staff:* Kalina Bakalov

Web: duckworth.house.gov

Facebook: www.facebook.com/CongresswomanTammy Duckworth
Twitter: @repduckworth
District Office: 1701 E. Woodfield Rd., #704, Schaumburg, IL 60173; 847-413-1959; *District Director:* Marina Saz-Huppert
Committee Assignments: Armed Services; Oversight and Government Reform; Select on Benghazi

Duffy, Sean, R-Wisc. (7)

Capitol Hill Office: 1208 LHOB 20515-4907; 225-3365; Fax: 225-3240; *Chief of Staff:* Pete Meachum
Web: duffy.house.gov
Facebook: www.facebook.com/RepSeanDuffy
Twitter: @RepSeanDuffy
District Office: 502 2nd St., #202, Hudson, WI 54016; 715-808-8160; Fax: 715-808-8167; *District Director:* Jesse Garza
Satellite Offices: 823 Belknap St., #225, Superior, WI 54880-2974; 715-392-3984; Fax: 715-392-3999; *Regional Rep.:* Jesse Garza
208 Grand Ave., Wausau, WI 54403-6217; 715-298-9344; Fax: 715-298-9348; *District Director:* Jesse Garza
Committee Assignments: Financial Services; Joint Economic

Duncan, Jeff, R-S.C. (3)

Capitol Hill Office: 106 CHOB 20515-4003; 225-5301; Fax: 225-3216; *Chief of Staff:* Lance Williams
Web: jeffduncan.house.gov
Facebook: www.facebook.com/RepJeffDuncan
Twitter: @RepJeffDuncan
District Offices: 303 W. Beltline Blvd., Anderson, SC 29625-1505; 864-224-7401; Fax: 864-225-7049; *District Director:* Rick Adkins
200 Courthouse Public Square, P.O. Box 471, Laurens, SC 29360; 864-681-1028; Fax: 864-681-1030; *Field Rep.:* Jan Harman
Committee Assignments: Foreign Affairs; Homeland Security; Natural Resources

Duncan, John J., Jr., R-Tenn. (2)

Capitol Hill Office: 2207 RHOB 20515-4202; 225-5435; Fax: 225-6440; *Deputy Chief of Staff; Transportation and Infrastructure Committee:* Don Walker
Web: duncan.house.gov
Facebook: www.facebook.com/CongressmanDuncan
Twitter: @RepJohnDuncanJr
District Offices: 800 Market St., #110, Knoxville, TN 37902-2303; 865-523-3772; Fax: 865-544-0728; *Office Manager:* Jenny Stansberry
331 Court St., Maryville, TN 37804; 865-984-5464; Fax: 865-984-0521; *Office Manager:* Vickie Flynn
Committee Assignments: Oversight and Government Reform; Transportation and Infrastructure

Edwards, Donna F., D-Md. (4)

Capitol Hill Office: 2445 RHOB 20515; 225-8699; Fax: 225 8714; *Chief of Staff:* Adrienne Christian

Web: donnaedwards.house.gov
Facebook: www.facebook.com/ CongresswomanDonnaFEdwards
Twitter: @repdonnaedwards
District Office: 5001 Silver Hill Rd., #106, Suitland, MD 20746-5208; 301-516-7601; Fax: 301-516-7608; *District Director:* Betty Horton-Hodge
Committee Assignments: Science, Space, and Technology; Transportation and Infrastructure

Ellison, Keith, D-Minn. (5)

Capitol Hill Office: 2263 RHOB 20515; 225-4755; Fax: 225-4886; *Chief of Staff:* Kari Moe
Web: ellison.house.gov
Facebook: www.facebook.com/Keith.Ellison
Twitter: @keithellison
District Office: 2100 Plymouth Ave. North, Minneapolis, MN 55411-3675; 612-522-1212; Fax: 612-522-9915; *District Director:* Jamie Long
Committee Assignment: Financial Services

Ellmers, Renee, R-N.C. (2)

Capitol Hill Office: 1210 LHOB 20515; 225-4531; Fax: 225-5662; *Chief of Staff:* Al Lytton
Web: ellmers.house.gov
Facebook: www.facebook.com/reneeellmers
Twitter: @RepReneeEllmers
District Offices: 222 Sunset Ave., #101, Asheboro, NC 27203; 336-626-3060; Fax: 336-629-7819; *Field Rep.:* Cindy Wilkins; *Constituent Services Director:* Rebecca Briles
406 W. Broad St., Dunn, NC 28334-4808; 910-230-1910; Fax: 910-230-1940; *District Director:* Pat Fitzgerald
Committee Assignment: Energy and Commerce

Emmer, Tom, R-Minn. (6)

Capitol Hill Office: 503 CHOB 20515-2306; 225-2331; Fax: 225-6475; *Chief of Staff:* David Fitzsimmons
Web: emmer.house.gov
Facebook: www.facebook.com/RepTomEmmer
Twitter: @reptomemmer
District Office: 9201 Quaday Ave. N.E., #206, Otsego, MN 55330; 763-241-6848; Fax: 763-241-7955; *Staff Asst.:* Caitlin Fontaine
Committee Assignment: Financial Services

Engel, Eliot L., D-N.Y. (16)

Capitol Hill Office: 2462 RHOB 20515-3217; 225-2464; Fax: 225-5513; *Chief of Staff:* Ned Michalek
Web: engel.house.gov
Facebook: www.facebook.com/RepEliotEngel
Twitter: @RepEliotEngel
District Offices: 3655 Johnson Ave., Bronx, NY 10463-1671; 718-796-9700; Fax: 718-796-5134; *Chief of Staff:* Bill Weitz
6 Gramatan Ave., #205, Mount Vernon, NY 10550-3208; 914-699-4100; Fax: 914-699-3646; *Staff Asst.:* Cynthia Miller

177 Dreiser Loop, Room 3, Bronx, NY 10475; 718-320-2314; Fax: 718-320-2047 *Staff Asst.:* Maxine Sullivan
Committee Assignments: Energy and Commerce; Foreign Affairs, Ranking Minority Member

Eshoo, Anna G., D-Calif. (18)

Capitol Hill Office: 241 CHOB 20515; 225-8104; Fax: 225-8890; *Exec. Asst.; Scheduler:* Jena Gross
Web: eshoo.house.gov
Facebook: www.facebook.com/RepAnnaEshoo
Twitter: @RepAnnaEshoo
District Office: 698 Emerson St., Palo Alto, CA 94301-1609; 650-323-2984; Fax: 650-323-3498; *District Chief of Staff:* Karen Chapman
Committee Assignment: Energy and Commerce

Esty, Elizabeth, D-Conn. (5)

Capitol Hill Office: 405 CHOB 20515; 225-4476; *Chief of Staff:* Tony Baker
Web: esty.house.gov
Facebook: www.facebook.com/RepEsty
Twitter: @RepEsty
District Office: 114 W. Main St., #206, New Britain, CT 06051-4223; 860-223-8412; Fax: 860-225-7289; *District Director:* Stephanie Podewell
Committee Assignments: Science, Space, and Technology; Transportation and Infrastructure

Farenthold, Blake, R-Tex. (27)

Capitol Hill Office: 1027 LHOB 20515; 225-7742; Fax: 226-1134; *Chief of Staff:* Bob Haueter
Web: www.farenthold.house.gov
Facebook: www.facebook.com/BlakeFarenthold
Twitter: @farenthold
District Offices: 101 N. Shoreline Blvd., #300, Corpus Christi, TX 78401-2837; 361-884-2222; Fax: 361-884-2223; *Deputy District Director:* J.D. Kennedy
5606 N. Navarro St., #203, Victoria, TX 77904; 361-894-6446; Fax: 361-894-6460; *Constituent Liaison:* Shawna Mitchell
Committee Assignments: Judiciary; Oversight and Government Reform; Transportation and Infrastructure

Farr, Sam, D-Calif. (20)

Capitol Hill Office: 1126 LHOB 20515-0517; 225-2861; Fax: 225-6791; *Chief of Staff:* Rochelle S. Dornatt
Web: www.farr.house.gov
Facebook: www.facebook.com/RepSamFarr
Twitter: @repsamfarr
District Offices: 100 W. Alisal St., Salinas, CA 93901; 831-424-2229; Fax: 831-424-7099; *District Director:* Alec Arago
701 Ocean St., #318C, Santa Cruz, CA 95060-4027; 831-429-1976; Fax: 831-429-1458; *Congressional Aide:* Ryan Simon
Committee Assignment: Appropriations

Fattah, Chaka, D-Pa. (2)

Capitol Hill Office: 2301 RHOB 20515-3802; 225-4001; Fax: 225-5392; *Chief of Staff:* Roger Jackson
Web: www.fattah.house.gov
Facebook: www.facebook.com/repfattah
Twitter: @chakafattah
District Office: 2401 N. 54th St., Philadelphia, PA 19131; 215-871-4455; Fax: 215-871-4456; *Office Manager:* Dolores Ridley
Committee Assignment: Appropriations

Fincher, Stephen, R-Tenn. (8)

Capitol Hill Office: 2452 RHOB 20515-4208; 225-4714; Fax: 225-1765; *Chief of Staff:* Jessica Carter
Web: www.fincher.house.gov
Facebook: www.facebook.com/RepFincherTN08
Twitter: @repfinchertn08
District Offices: 100 S. Main St., #1, Dyersburg, TN 38024-4662; 731-285-0910; Fax: 731-285-5008; *Field Rep.:* Ivy Fultz
117 N. Liberty St., Jackson, TN 38301-6205; 731-423-4848; Fax: 731-427-1537; *Deputy Chief of Staff:* Scott Golden
406 Lindell St. South, Suite C, Martin, TN 38237-2481; 731-588-5190; *Field Rep.:* Heather Waggoner
12015 Walker St, Arlington, TN 38002; 901-581-4718; *Caseworker:* Debbie Shires
5384 Poplar Ave., #410, Memphis, TN 38119; 901-682-4422; *Caseworker:* Kelly Hankins
Committee Assignment: Financial Services

Fitzpatrick, Mike, R-Pa. (8)

Capitol Hill Office: 2400 RHOB 20515; 225-4276; Fax: 225-9511; *Chief of Staff:* Paul Ritacco
Web: www.fitzpatrick.house.gov
Facebook: www.facebook.com/RepFitzpatrick
Twitter: @RepFitzpatrick
District Office: 1717 Langhorne Newtown Rd., #400, Langhorne, PA 19047-1086; 215-579 8102; Fax: 215-579-8109; *District Director:* Stacey Mulholland
Committee Assignment: Financial Services

Fleischmann, Chuck, R-Tenn. (3)

Capitol Hill Office: 230 CHOB 20515; 225-3271; Fax: 225-3494; *Chief of Staff:* Jim Hippe
Web: fleischmann.house.gov
Facebook: www.facebook.com/repchuck
Twitter: @repchuck
District Offices: 6 E. Madison Ave., Athens, TN 37303; 423-745-4671; Fax: 423-745-6025; *Field Rep.:* Maxine O'Dell-Gernert
900 Georgia Ave., #126, Chattanooga, TN 37402-2282; 423-756-2342; Fax: 423-756-6613; *District Director:* Bob White
200 Administration Rd., #100, Oak Ridge, TN 37830-8823; 865-576-1976; Fax: 865-576-3221; *Field Rep.:* Cindy Boshears
Committee Assignment: Appropriations

Fleming, John, R-La. (4)

Capitol Hill Office: 2182 RHOB 20515-1804; 225-2777; Fax: 225-8039; *Chief of Staff:* Dana G. Gartzke
Web: fleming.house.gov
Facebook: www.facebook.com/RepJohnFleming
Twitter: @RepFleming
District Offices: 103 N. 3rd St., Leesville, LA 71446-4013; 337-238-0778; Fax: 337-238-0566; *District Director, Southern Region:* Lee Turner
6425 Youree Dr., #350, Shreveport, LA 71105-4634; 318-798-2254; Fax: 318-798-2063; *District Director:* John Barr
Committee Assignments: Armed Services; Natural Resources

Flores, Bill, R-Tex. (17)

Capitol Hill Office: 1030 LHOB 20515; 225-6105; Fax: 225-0350; *Chief of Staff:* Jeff Morhouse
Web: www.flores.house.gov
Facebook: www.facebook.com/RepBillFlores
Twitter: @RepBillFlores
District Offices: 3000 Briarcrest Dr., #406, Bryan, TX 77802; 979-703-4037; Fax: 979-703-8845; *Deputy District Director:* James Edge
400 Austin Ave., #302, Waco, TX 76701-2139; 254-732-0748; Fax: 254-732-1755; *District Director:* Jana Hickson
Committee Assignment: Energy and Commerce

Forbes, J. Randy, R-Va. (4)

Capitol Hill Office: 2135 RHOB 20515; 225-6365; Fax: 226-1170; *Chief of Staff:* Dee Gilmore
Web: www.forbes.house.gov
Facebook: www.facebook.com/randyforbes
Twitter: @randy_forbes
District Offices: 505 Independence Pkwy., #104, Chesapeake, VA 23320-5178; 757-382-0080; Fax: 757-382-0780; *District Director:* Curtis Byrd
9401 Courthouse Rd., #202, Chesterfield, VA 23832; 804-318-1363; Fax: 804-318-1013; *District Director, Western Region:* Nicole Bunce
Committee Assignments: Armed Services; Judiciary

Fortenberry, Jeff, R-Neb. (1)

Capitol Hill Office: 1514 LHOB 20515-2701; 225-4806; Fax: 225-5686; *Chief of Staff:* Margo Matter
Web: www.fortenberry.house.gov
Facebook: www.facebook.com/jefffortenberry
Twitter: @JeffFortenberry
District Offices: 301 S. 13th St., #100, Lincoln, NE 68508-2532; 402-438-1598; Fax: 402-438-1604; *District Director:* Todd Wiltgen
125 S. 4th St., #101, Norfolk, NE 68701-5200; 402-379-2064; Fax: 402-379-2101; *Field Rep.:* Nate Blum
Satellite Office: 641 N. Broad St., P.O. Box 377, Fremont, NE 68026-4932; 402-727-0888; Fax: 402-727-9130; *Field Rep.:* Nate Blum
Committee Assignment: Appropriations

Foster, Bill, D-Ill. (11)

Capitol Hill Office: 1224 LHOB 20515; 225-3515; Fax: 225-9420; *Chief of Staff:* Adam Elias
Web: www.foster.house.gov
Facebook: www.facebook.com/CongressmanBillFoster
Twitter: @RepBillFoster
District Offices: 2711 E. New York St., #204, Aurora, IL 60502; 630-585-7672; Fax: 630-585-7689; *District Director:* Carole Cheney
195 Springfield Ave., #102, Joliet, IL 60435; 815-280-5876; Fax: 815-582-4342; *Constituent Services Director; Deputy District Director:* Chastity Wells-Armstrong
Committee Assignments: Financial Services; Science, Space, and Technology

Foxx, Virginia, R-N.C. (5)

Capitol Hill Office: 2350 RHOB 20515; 225-2071; Fax: 225-2995; *Chief of Staff:* Brandon Renz
Web: www.foxx.house.gov
Facebook: www.facebook.com/RepVirginiaFoxx
Twitter: @virginiafoxx
District Offices: 400 Shadowline Dr., #205, Boone, NC 28607-4291; 828-265-0240; Fax: 828-265-0390; *District Director:* Adam Whitener
3540 Clemmons Rd., #125, Clemmons, NC 27012-8775; 336-778-0211; Fax: 336-778-2290; *Office Manager:* Patricia Bandy
Committee Assignments: Education and the Workforce; Rules

Frankel, Lois, D-Fla. (22)

Capitol Hill Office: 1037 LHOB 20515; 225-9890; Fax: 225-1224; *Chief of Staff:* Jim Cho
Web: www.frankel.house.gov
Facebook: www.facebook.com/RepLoisFrankel
Twitter: @RepLoisFrankel
District Office: 2500 N. Military Trail, #490, Boca Raton, FL 33431; 561-998-9045; Fax: 561-998-9048; *District Director:* Felicia Goldstein
Committee Assignments: Foreign Affairs; Transportation and Infrastructure

Franks, Trent, R-Ariz. (8)

Capitol Hill Office: 2435 RHOB 20515-0302; 225-4576; Fax: 225-6328; *Chief of Staff:* Jonathon Hayes
Web: www.franks.house.gov
Facebook: www.facebook.com/TrentFranks
Twitter: @RepTrentFranks
District Office: 7121 W. Bell Rd., #200, Glendale, AZ 85308-8549; 623-776-7911; Fax: 623-776-7832; *District Director:* Dan Hay
Committee Assignments: Armed Services; Judiciary

Frelinghuysen, Rodney, R-N.J. (11)

Capitol Hill Office: 2306 RHOB 20515-3011; 225-5034; Fax: 225-3186; *Chief of Staff:* Nancy Fox
Web: www.frelinghuysen.house.gov
Facebook: www.facebook.com/rfrelinghuysen

Twitter: @USRepRodney
District Office: 30 Schuyler Pl., 2nd Floor, Morristown, NJ 07960-5128; 973-984-0711; Fax: 973-292-1569; *District Director:* Anthony Alvarez
Committee Assignment: Appropriations

Fudge, Marcia L., D-Ohio (11)

Capitol Hill Office: 2344 RHOB 20515; 225-7032; Fax: 225-1339; *Chief of Staff:* Veleter Mazyck
Web: www.fudge.house.gov
Facebook: www.facebook.com/RepMarciaLFudge
Twitter: @RepMarciaFudge
District Offices: 4834 Richmond Rd., #150, Warrensville Heights, OH 44128-5922; 216-522-4900; Fax: 216-522-4908; *Press Secretary:* Lauren Williams
1225 Lawton St., Akron, OH 44320; 330-835-4758; Fax: 330-835-4863; *Outreach Coordinator:* Ginger Baylor
Committee Assignments: Agriculture; Education and the Workforce

Gabbard, Tulsi, D-Hawaii (2)

Capitol Hill Office: 1609 LHOB 20515; 225-4906; Fax: 225-4987; *Chief of Staff:* Kainoa Penaroza
Web: gabbard.house.gov
Facebook: www.facebook.com/RepTulsiGabbard
Twitter: @tulsipress
District office: 5-104 Prince Kuhio Federal Bldg., 300 Ala Moana Blvd., Honolulu, HI 96850-0001; 808-541-1986; Fax: 808-538-0233; *District Director:* Walt Kaneakua
Committee Assignments: Armed Services; Foreign Affairs

Gallego, Rubén, D-Ariz. (7)

Capitol Hill Office: 1218 LHOB 20515-0307; 225-4065; Fax: 225-1655; *Chief of Staff:* David Montes
Web: rubengallego.house.gov
Facebook: www.facebook.com/reprubengallego
Twitter: @reprubengallego
District Office: 411 N. Central Ave., #150, Phoenix, AZ 85004; 602-256-0551; Fax: 602-257-9103; *Director of Constituent Services:* Sandra Ferniza
Committee Assignments: Armed Services; Natural Resources

Garamendi, John, D-Calif. (3)

Capitol Hill Office: 2438 RHOB 20515; 225-1880; Fax: 225-5914; *Deputy Chief of Staff:* Emily Burns
Web: garamendi.house.gov
Facebook: www.facebook.com/repgaramendi
Twitter: @RepGaramendi
District Offices: 412 G. St., Davis, CA 95616; 530-753-5301; Fax: 530-753-5614; *District Director:* John Evalle
1261 Travis Blvd., Fairfield, CA 94533-6293; 707-438-1822; Fax: 707-438-0523; *District Rep.:* Brandon Thompson
Satellite Office: 795 Plumas St., Yuba City, CA 95991; 530-329-8865; Fax: 530-763-4248; *Field Rep.:* Jeannie Klever
Committee Assignments: Armed Services; Transportation and Infrastructure

Garrett, Scott, R-N.J. (5)

Capitol Hill Office: 2232 RHOB 20515-3005; 225-4465; Fax: 225-9048; *Chief of Staff:* Amy Smith
Web: garrett.house.gov
Facebook: www.facebook.com/repscottgarrett
Twitter: @RepGarrett
District Offices: 266 Harristown Rd., #104, Glen Rock, NJ 07452-3321; 201-444-5454; Fax: 201-444-5488; *District Director:* Rob Pettet
83 Spring St., #302A, Newton, NJ 07860-2080; 973-300-2000; Fax: 973-300-1051; *Constituent Services Rep.:* Amy Nittolo
Committee Assignments: Budget; Financial Services

Gibbs, Bob, R-Ohio (7)

Capitol Hill Office: 329 CHOB 20515-3518; 225-6265; Fax: 225-3394; *Chief of Staff:* Meredith Dolan
Web: gibbs.house.gov
Facebook: www.facebook.com/RepBobGibbs
Twitter: @repbobgibbs
District Offices: 110 Cottage St., Ashland, OH 44805; 419-207-0650; Fax: 419-207-0655; *District Director:* Daryl Kick
110 Central Plaza, South Canton, OH 44702; 330-730-1631; *Field Rep.:* Jennifer Kiko
Committee Assignments: Agriculture; Transportation and Infrastructure

Gibson, Chris P., R-N.Y. (19)

Capitol Hill Office: 1708 LHOB 20515; 225-5614; Fax: 225-1168; *Chief of Staff:* Stephanie Valle
Web: gibson.house.gov
Facebook: www.facebook.com/RepChrisGibson
Twitter: @repchrisgibson
District Offices: 2 Hudson St., P.O. Box 775, Kinderhook, NY 12106; 518-610-8133; Fax: 518-610-8135; *Deputy District Director:* Ann Mueller; *District Director:* Steve Bulger
721 Broadway, Kingston, NY 12401; 845-514-2322; Fax: 845-514-2541; *Field Rep.:* George Christian
92 Sullivan Ave., P.O. Box 578, Ferndale, NY 12754; 845-747-9261; Fax: 845-747-9273; *Field Rep.:* Christine Schiff
Satellite Offices: 25 Chestnut St., Cooperstown, NY 13326; 607-282-4002; Fax: 607-282-4089; *Field Rep.:* Carol Waller
111 Main St., Delhi, NY 13753-1233; 607-746-9537; Fax: 607-746-9527; *Field Rep.:* Paula Brown
4328 Albany Post Rd., Route 9, Hyde Park, NY 12538; 845-698-0132; Fax: 845-698-0150; *Field Rep.:* Patty Hohmann
Committee Assignments: Agriculture; Armed Services; Small Business

Gohmert, Louie, R-Tex. (1)

Capitol Hill Office: 2243 RHOB 20515-4301; 225-3035; Fax: 226-1230; *Chief of Staff:* Connie Hair
Web: gohmert.house.gov

Facebook: www.facebook.com/Louie-Gohmert-50375006903

Twitter: @replouiegohmert

District Offices: 101 E. Methvin St., #302, Longview, TX 75601-7277; 903-236-8597; Fax: 903-561-7110; *Caseworker:* Shannon Crisp

300 E. Shepherd Ave., #210, Lufkin, TX 75901-3252; 936-632-3180; Fax: 903-561-7110; *District Director:* Jonna Fitzgerald

102 W. Houston St., Marshall, TX 75670-4038; 903-938-8386; Fax: 903-561-7110; *District Director:* Jonna Fitzgerald

101 W. Main St., #160, Nacogdoches, TX 75961-4830; 936-715-9514; Fax: 903-561-7110; *Caseworker:* Melinda Kartye

1121 ESE Loop 323, #206, Tyler, TX 75701-9637; 903-561-6349; Fax: 903-561-7110; *Caseworker:* Lisa Blackman

Committee Assignments: Judiciary; Natural Resources

Goodlatte, Bob, R-Va. (6)

Capitol Hill Office: 2309 RHOB 20515-4606; 225-5431; Fax: 225-9681; *Chief of Staff:* Peter Larkin

Web: goodlatte.house.gov

Facebook: www.facebook.com/BobGoodlatte

Twitter: @RepGoodlatte

District Offices: 70 N. Mason St., Harrisonburg, VA 22802; 540-432-2391; Fax: 540-432-6593; *District Rep.:* Matt Homer

916 Main St., #300, Lynchburg, VA 24504; 434-845-8306; Fax: 434-845-8245; *District Rep.:* Aaron Van Allen

10 Franklin Rd. S.E., #540, Roanoke, VA 24011; 540-885-2672; Fax: 540-857-2675; *Chief of Staff:* Pete Larkin

117 S. Lewis St., #215, Staunton, VA 24401; 540-885-3861; Fax: 540-885-3930; *District Director:* Debbie Garrett

Committee Assignments: Agriculture; Judiciary, Chair

Gosar, Paul, R-Ariz. (4)

Capitol Hill Office: 504 CHOB 20515-0301; 225-2315; Fax: 226-9739; *Chief of Staff:* Tom Van Flein

Web: gosar.house.gov

Facebook: www.facebook.com/repgosar

Twitter: @repgosar

District Offices: 122 N. Cortez St., #104, Prescott, AZ 86301; 928-445-1683; Fax: 928-445-3414; *Office Manager:* Julie Brown

6499 S. Kings Ranch Rd., #4, Gold Canyon, AZ 85118; 480-882-2697; Fax: 480-882-2698; *District Director:* Penny Pew

Satellite Office: 220 N. 4th St., Kingman, AZ 86401; *District Director:* Penny Pew

Committee Assignments: Natural Resources; Oversight and Government Reform

Gowdy, Trey, R-S.C. (4)

Capitol Hill Office: 1404 LHOB 20515; 225-6030; Fax: 226-1177; *Chief of Staff:* Cindy Crick

Web: gowdy.house.gov

Facebook: www.facebook.com/RepTreyGowdy

Twitter: @tgowdysc

District Offices: 104 S. Main St., #801, Greenville, SC 29601-2742; 864-241-0175; Fax: 864-241-0982; *Chief of Staff:* Cindy Crick

101 W. St. John St., Spartanburg, SC 29306-5179; 864-583-3264; Fax: 864-583-3926; *Office Manager:* Missy House

Committee Assignments: Ethics; Judiciary; Oversight and Government Reform; Select on Benghazi, Chair

Graham, Gwen, D-Fla. (2)

Capitol Hill Office: 1213 LHOB 20515-0902; 225-5235; Fax: 225-5615; *Chief of Staff:* Julia Woodward

Web: graham.house.gov

Facebook: www.facebook.com/RepGwenGraham

Twitter: @repgwengraham

District Offices: 840 W. 11th St., #2250, Panama City, FL 32401; 850-785-0812; Fax: 850-763-3764; *Caseworker:* Sarah Blei

300 S. Adams St., #A-3, Tallahassee, FL 32301; 850-891-8610; Fax: 850-891-8620; *District Director:* Mary Lee Kiracofe

Committee Assignments: Agriculture; Armed Services

Granger, Kay, R-Tex. (12)

Capitol Hill Office: 1026 LHOB 20515; 225-5071; Fax: 225-5683; *Chief of Staff:* William Zito

Web: kaygranger.house.gov

Facebook: www.facebook.com/RepKayGranger

Twitter: @RepKayGranger

District Office: River Plaza, 1701 River Run Rd., #407, Fort Worth, TX 76107-6548; 817-338-0909; Fax: 817-335-5852; *District Director:* Kristin Vandergriss

Committee Assignment: Appropriations

Graves, Garrett, R-La. (6)

Capitol Hill Office: 204 CHOB 20515; 225-3901; Fax: 225-7313; *Chief of Staff:* Nancy Peele

Web: garretgraves.house.gov

Facebook: www.facebook.com/congressmangarretgraves

Twitter: @repgarretgraves

District Offices: 2351 Energy Dr., #1200, Baton Rouge, LA 70808; 225-442-1731 Fax: 225-442-1736; *Staff Asst.:* Johnathon Smith

29261 Frost Rd., 2nd Floor, Livingston, LA 70754; 225-686-4413; Fax: 225-442-1736; *Staff Asst.:* Johnathon Smith

908 E. 1st St., Candies Hall, #405, Thibodaux, LA 70301; 985-448-4103-225-442-1736; *District Director:* David Cavill

Committee Assignments: Natural Resources; Transportation

Graves, Sam, R-Mo. (6)

Capitol Hill Office: 1415 LHOB 20515-2506; 225-7041; Fax: 225-8221; *Chief of Staff:* Paul Sass

Web: graves.house.gov

Facebook: www.facebook.com/ Sam-Graves-118514606128/

Twitter: @RepSamGraves

District Offices: 11724 N.W. Plaza Circle, #900, Kansas City, MO 64153; 816-792-3976; Fax: 816-792-0694; *District Director:* Tom Brown

411 Jules St., #111, St. Joseph, MO 64501-2275; 816-749-0800; Fax: 816-749-0801; *Field Rep.:* Matt Barry

Satellite Office: 906 Broadway, P.O. Box 364, Hannibal, MO 63401; 573-221-3400; *Field Rep.:* Bryan Nichols

Committee Assignments: Armed Services; Transportation and Infrastructure

Graves, Tom, R-Ga. (14)

Capitol Hill Office: 2442 RHOB 20515; 225-5211; Fax: 225-8272; *Chief of Staff:* John Donnolly

Web: tomgraves.house.gov

Facebook: www.facebook.com/reptomgraves

Twitter: @reptomgraves

District Offices: 702 S. Thornton Ave., Dalton, GA 30720-8211; 706-226-5320; Fax: 706-278-0840; *District Director:* Bud Whitmire

600 E. 1st St., #301, Rome, GA 30161; 706-290-1776; Fax: 706-232-7864; *Field Rep.:* Drew Ferguson

Committee Assignment: Appropriations

Grayson, Alan, D-Fla. (9)

Capitol Hill Office: 303 CHOB 20515; 225-9889; Fax: 225-9742; *Chief of Staff:* Julie Tagen

Web: grayson.house.gov

Facebook: www.facebook.com/alangrayson

Twitter: @AlanGrayson

District Offices: 101 N. Church St., #550, Kissimmee, FL 34741; 407-518-4983; Fax: 407-846-2087; *Field Rep.:* Liz Price

5842 S. Semoran Blvd., Orlando, FL 32822; 407-615-8889; Fax: 407-615-8890; *District Director:* Juan Lopez-Sanchez

Satellite Offices: 620 Main St., Haines City, FL 33844; 863-419-3518; *District Director:* Liz Price

401 Walnut St., Kissimmee, FL 34759; 863-427-0900; *District Director:* Liz Price

Committee Assignments: Foreign Affairs; Science, Space, and Technology

Green, Al, D-Tex. (9)

Capitol Hill Office: 2347 RHOB 20515-4309; 225-7508; Fax: 225-2947; *Chief of Staff:* Jacqueline A. Ellis

Web: algreen.house.gov

Facebook: www.facebook.com/Congressman-Al-Green-224027854297805/

Twitter: @RepAlGreen

District Office: 3003 S. Loop West, #460, Houston, TX 77054-1301; 713-383-9234; Fax: 713-383-9202; *District Manager of Administration:* Crystal Webster

Committee Assignment: Financial Services

Green, Gene, D-Tex. (29)

Capitol Hill Office: 2470 RHOB 20515-4329; 225-1688; Fax: 225-9903; *Chief of Staff:* Rhonda Jackson

Web: green.house.gov

Facebook: www.facebook.com/RepGeneGreen

Twitter: @RepGeneGreen

District Offices: 11811 I-10 East, #430, Houston, TX 77029-1974; 713-330-0761; Fax: 713-330-0807; *District Scheduler:* Sophia Gutierrez

256 N. Sam Houston Pkwy. East, #29, Houston, TX 77060-2028; 281-999-5879; Fax: 281-999-5716; *Chief of Staff, Office Manager:* Rhonda Jackson

Committee Assignment: Energy and Commerce

Griffith, Morgan, R-Va. (9)

Capitol Hill Office: 1108 LHOB 20515-4609; 225-3861; Fax: 225-0076; *Chief of Staff:* Kelly Lungren McCollum

Web: morgangriffith.house.gov

Facebook: www.facebook.com/RepMorganGriffith

Twitter: @RepMGriffith

District Offices: 323 W. Main St., Abingdon, VA 24210-2605; 276-525-1405; Fax: 276-525-1444; *District Director:* Michelle Jenkins

17 W. Main St., Christiansburg, VA 24073-3055; 540-381-5671; Fax: 540-381-5675; *Constituent Rep.: Barbara Stafford*

Committee Assignment: Energy and Commerce

Grijalva, Raul M., D-Ariz. (3)

Capitol Hill Office: 1511 LHOB 20515-0307; 225-2435; Fax: 225-1541; *Chief of Staff:* Amy Emerick

Web: grijalva.house.gov

Facebook: www.facebook.com/Rep.Grijalva

Twitter: @RepRaulGrijalva

District Offices: Rancho Santa Fe Center, 13065 W. McDowell Rd., #C-113, Avondale, AZ 85392; 623-536-3388; Fax: 623-748-0451; *District Rep.:* Jennifer Papworth

146 N. State Ave., P.O. Box 4105, Somerton, AZ 85350; 928-343-7933; Fax: 928-343-7949; *District Aide; Caseworker:* Martha Garcia

738 N. 5th Ave., #110, Tucson, AZ 85705-8485; 520-622-6788; Fax: 520-622-0198; *District Director:* Rubén Reyes

Committee Assignments: Education and the Workforce; Natural Resources, Ranking Minority Member

Grothman, Glenn, R-Wisc. (6)

Capitol Hill Office: 501 CHOB 20515-4906; 225-2476; Fax: 225-2356; *Chief of Staff:* Tyler Houlton

Web: grothman.house.gov

Facebook: www.facebook.com/RepGrothman

Twitter: @RepGrothman

District Office: 1020 S. Main St., Suite B, Fond du Lac, WI 54935; 920-907-0624; *District Director:* Al Ott

Committee Assignments: Budget; Education and the Workforce; Joint Economic; Oversight and Government Reform

Guinta, Frank, R-N.H. (1)

Capitol Hill Office: 326 CHOB 20515-2901; 225-5456; Fax: 225-5822; *Chief of Staff:* Jay Ruais

Web: guinta.house.gov

Facebook: www.facebook.com/FrankGuinta

Twitter: @frankguinta

District Office: 33 Lowell St., Manchester, NH 03101; 603-641-9536 Fax: 603-641-9561; *Director of Constituent Services:* Jennifer Smith

Committee Assignment: Financial Services

Guthrie, Brett, R-Ky. (2)

Capitol Hill Office: 2434 RHOB 20515-1702; 225-3501; Fax: 226-2019; *Chief of Staff:* Eric Bergren

Web: guthrie.house.gov

Facebook: www.facebook.com/CongressmanGuthrie

Twitter: @RepGuthrie

District Office: 996 Wilkinson Trace, #B2, Bowling Green, KY 42103; 270-842-9896; Fax: 270-842-9081; *District Director:* Mark Lord

Satellite Offices: 411 W. Lincoln Trail Blvd., Radcliff, KY 40160; *Field Rep.:* Brian Smith

2200 Airport Rd., Owensboro, KY 42301; *Field Rep.:* Suzanne Miles

Committee Assignments: Education and the Workforce; Energy and Commerce

Gutierrez, Luis V., D-Ill. (4)

Capitol Hill Office: 2408 RHOB 20515; 225-8203; Fax: 225-7810; *Chief of Staff:* Susan Collins

Web: gutierrez.house.gov

Facebook: www.facebook.com/RepGutierrez

Twitter: @LuisGutierrez

District Office: 3240 W. Fullerton Ave., Chicago, IL 60647-5429; 773-342-0774; Fax: 773-342-0776; *District Director:* Theresa Paucar

Committee Assignments: Judiciary; Permanent Select Intelligence

Hahn, Janice, D-Calif. (44)

Capitol Hill Office: 404 CHOB 20515; 225-8220; Fax: 226-7290; *Chief of Staff:* Laurie Saroff

Web: hahn.house.gov

Facebook: www.facebook.com/RepJaniceHahn

Twitter: @Rep_JaniceHahn

District Office: 140 W. 6th St., San Pedro, CA 90731; 310-831-1799; Fax: 310-831-1885; *District Director:* Lara Larramendi

Satellite Offices: 205 S. Willowbrook Ave., Compton, CA 90220; 310-605-5520; Fax: 310-761-1457; *District Director:* Lara Larramendi

544 N. Avalon Blvd., #307, Wilmington, CA 90744-5806; 310-549-8282; Fax: 310-549-8250; *Field Rep.:* Veronica Ledesma

8650 California Ave., South Gate, CA 90280; 323-563-9562; *Field Rep.:* Veronica Ledesma

701 E. Carson St., Carson, CA 90745; 310-830-7600 ext. 1038; *Deputy District Director:* Eric Boyd

Committee Assignments: Small Business; Transportation and Infrastructure

Hanna, Richard, R-N.Y. (22)

Capitol Hill Office: 319 CHOB 20515-3224; 225-3665; Fax: 225-1891; *Chief of Staff:* Justin Stokes

Web: hanna.house.gov

Facebook: www.facebook.com/reprichardhanna

Twitter: @reprichardhanna

District Offices: 49 Court St., #230, Binghamton, NY 13901; 607-723-0212; Fax: 607-723-0215; *Staff Asst.:* Kyle Fischer

258 Genesee St., Utica, NY 13502; 315-724-9740; Fax: 315-724-9746; *Director of Veterans' Outreach:* Jason Phelps

Committee Assignments: Small Business; Transportation and Infrastructure;

Hardy, Cresent, R-Nev. (4)

Capitol Hill Office: 1330 LHOB 20515-2804; 225-9894; Fax: 225-9783; *Chief of Staff:* Alan Tennille

Web: hardy.house.gov

Facebook: www.facebook.com/RepCresentHardy

Twitter: @cresenthardy

District Office: 2250 Las Vegas Blvd. North, #500, N. Las Vegas, NV 89030; 702-912-1634; Fax: 702-476-0911 *District Director:* Sonia Joya

Committee Assignments: Natural Resources; Small Business; Transportation and Infrastructure

Harper, Gregg, R-Miss. (3)

Capitol Hill Office: 307 CHOB 20515-2403; 225-5031; Fax: 225-5797; *Chief of Staff:* Michael J. Cravens

Web: harper.house.gov

Facebook: www.facebook.com/GreggHarper

Twitter: @GreggHarper

District Offices: 1901 Front St., Suite A, Meridian, MS 39301-5206; 601-693-6681; Fax: 601-693-1801; *Special Asst. Constituent Services:* Francis White

2507-A Old Brandon Rd., Pearl, MS 39208; 601-932-2410; Fax: 601-932-4647; *District Director:* Chip Reynolds

1 Research Blvd., #206, Starkville, MS 39759-8749; 662-324-0007; Fax: 662-324-0033; *Special Asst. Constituent Services:* Kyle Jordan

Satellite Office: 230 S. Whitworth St., Brookhaven, MS 39601-3343; 601-823-3400; Fax: 601-823-5512; *District Director:* Chip Reynolds

Committee Assignments: Energy and Commerce; House Administration; Joint Library, Chair; Joint Printing, Vice Chair

Harris, Andy, R-Md. (1)

Capitol Hill Office: 1533 LHOB 20515; 225-5311; Fax: 225-0254; *Chief of Staff:* John Dutton

Web: harris.house.gov

Facebook: www.facebook.com/AndyHarrisMD

Twitter: @repandyharrismd

District Offices: 15 E. Churchville Rd., #102B, Bel Air, MD 21014-3837; 410-588-5670; Fax: 410-588-5673; *Community Liaison:* Mary O'Keefe

100 Olde Point Village, #101, Chester, MD 21619; 410-643-5425; Fax: 410-643-5429; *Community Liaison:* Denise Lovelady

212 W. Main St., #204B, Salisbury, MD 21801-5026; 443-944-8624; Fax: 443-944-8625; *Constituent Liaison:* Bill Reddish

Committee Assignment: Appropriations

Hartzler, Vicky, R-Mo. (4)

Capitol Hill Office: 2235 RHOB 20515-2504; 225-2876; Fax: 225-0148; *Deputy Chief of Staff:* Shaelyn McClanahan
Web: hartzler.house.gov
Facebook: www.facebook.com/Congresswoman.Hartzler
Twitter: @rephartzler
District Offices: 2415 Carter Lane, #4, Columbia, MO 65201; 573-442-9311; Fax: 573-442-9309; *Press Secretary:* Steve Walsh
1909 N. Commercial St., Harrisonville, MO 64701-1252; 816-884-3411; Fax: 816-884-3163; *Field Rep.:* Adam Timmerman
219 N. Adams Ave., Lebanon, MO 65536-3029; 417-532-5582; Fax: 417-532-3886; *Field Rep.:* Steve Walsh
Committee Assignments: Agriculture; Armed Services; Budget

Hastings, Alcee L., D-Fla. (20)

Capitol Hill Office: 2353 RHOB 20515-0923; 225-1313; Fax: 225-1171; *Chief of Staff:* Lale M. Morrison
Web: alceehastings.house.gov
Facebook: www.facebook.com/pages/Congressman-Alcee-L-Hastings-95696782238
Twitter: @RepHastingsFL
District Offices: 2701 W. Oakland Park Blvd, #200, Fort Lauderdale, FL 33311; 954-733-2800; Fax: 954-735-9444; *Florida Chief of Staff:* Art Kennedy
Town of Mangonia Park Municipal Center; 1755 E. Tiffany Dr., Mangonia Park, FL 33407; 561-469-7048; Fax: 516-848-6940; *Staff Asst.:* Dan Liftman
Committee Assignments: Commission on Security and Cooperation in Europe; Rules

Heck, Denny, D-Wash. (10)

Capitol Hill Office: 425 CHOB 20515; 225-9740; Fax: 225-0129; *Chief of Staff:* Hart Edmonson
Web: dennyheck.house.gov
Facebook: www.facebook.com/CongressmanDennyHeck
Twitter: @RepDennyHeck
District Offices: 420 College St. S.E., #3000, Lacey, WA 98503; 360-459-8514; Fax: 360-459-8581; *District Director:* LaTasha Wortham
1432 E. 29th St., #203, Tacoma, WA 98404; 253-722-5860; *Field Rep.:* Lauren Adler
Committee Assignment: Financial Services

Heck, Joe, R-Nev. (3)

Capitol Hill Office: 132 CHOB 20515-2803; 225-3252; Fax: 225-2185; *Chief of Staff:* Greg Facchiano
Web: heck.house.gov
Facebook: www.facebook.com/RepJoeHeck
Twitter: @RepJoeHeck
District Office: 8872 S. Eastern Ave., #220, Las Vegas, NV 89123; 702-387-4941; Fax: 702-837-0728; *District Director:* Keith Hughes
Committee Assignments: Armed Services; Education and the Workforce; Permanent Select Intelligence

Hensarling, Jeb, R-Tex. (5)

Capitol Hill Office: 2228 RHOB 20515; 225-3484; Fax: 226-4888; *Chief of Staff:* Andrew Duke
Web: hensarling.house.gov
Facebook: www.facebook.com/RepHensarling
Twitter: @RepHensarling
District Offices: 810 E. Corsicana St., Suite C, Athens, TX 75751-2629; 903-675-8288; Fax: 903-675-8351; *Regional Director:* Phillip Smith
6510 Abrams Rd., #243, Dallas, TX 75231-7278; 214-349-9996; Fax: 214-349-0738; *District Director:* Mike Garcia
Committee Assignment: Financial Services, Chair

Herrera Beutler, Jaime, R-Wash. (3)

Capitol Hill Office: 1130 LHOB 20515-4703; 225-3536; Fax: 225-3478; *Chief of Staff:* Casey Bowman
Web: herrerabeutler.house.gov
Facebook: www.facebook.com/herrerabeutler
Twitter: @herrerabeutler
District Offices: 750 Anderson St., Suite B, Vancouver, WA 98661-3853; 360-695-6292; Fax: 360-695-6197; *District Director:* Sahari Hildreth
Satellite Office: 350 N. Market Blvd., Chehalis, WA 98532; 360-695-6292; *District Director:* Sahari Hildreth
Committee Assignment: Appropriations

Hice, Jody, R-Ga. (10)

Capitol Hill Office: 1516 LHOB 20515; 225-4101; Fax: 226-0776 *Chief of Staff:* David Sours
Web: hice.house.gov
Facebook: www.facebook.com/congressmanjodyhice
Twitter: @congressmanhice
District Offices: 100 Court St., Monroe, GA 30655; 770-207-1776; Fax: 770-266-6751; *District Director:* Joshua Findlay
210 Railroad St., #2401, Thomson, GA 30824; 770-207-1776; *Field Rep.:* Carolyn Dallas
3015 Heritage Rd., #6, Milledgeville, GA 31061; 478-457-0007; Fax: 478-451-2911; *Field Rep.:* Carolyn Dallas
Committee Assignments: Natural Resources; Oversight and Government Reform

Higgins, Brian, D-N.Y. (26)

Capitol Hill Office: 2459 RHOB 20515-3227; 225-3306; Fax: 226-0347; *Chief of Staff; Legis. Director:* Andrew Tantillo
Web: higgins.house.gov
Facebook: www.facebook.com/RepBrianHiggins
Twitter: @RepBrianHiggins
District Offices: 726 Exchange St., #601, Buffalo, NY 14210-1484; 716-852-3501; Fax: 716-852-3929; *District Chief of Staff:* Chuck Eaton
640 Park Pl., Niagara Falls, NY 14301; 716-282-1274; Fax: 716-282-2479; *District Director:* Suzanne Macri
Committee Assignments: Foreign Affairs; Homeland Security

Hill, French, R-Ark. (2)

Capitol Hill Office: 1229 LHOB 20515-0402; 225-2506;
Fax: 225-5903; *Chief of Staff:* Brooke Bennett
Web: hill.house.gov
Facebook: www.facebook.com/RepFrenchHill
Twitter: @RepFrenchHill
District Offices: 1501 N. University, #150, Little Rock, AR
72207; 501-324-5941; Fax: 501-324-6029; *District
Director:* Jill Cox
1105 Deer St., #12, Conway, AR 72032; 501-358-3481;
Fax: 501-358-3494; *Director of Military and Veteran's
Affairs:* Tom McNabb
Committee Assignments: Financial Services

Himes, James A., D-Conn. (4)

Capitol Hill Office: 1227 LHOB 20515-0704; 225-5541;
Fax: 225-9629; *Chief of Staff:* Mark Henson
Web: himes.house.gov
Facebook: www.facebook.com/CongressmanJimHimes
Twitter: @jahimes
District Offices: Court Exchange, 211 State St., 2nd Floor,
Bridgeport, CT 06604-4808; 866-453-0028; Fax: 203-
333-6655; *District Director:* Tyrone McClain
888 Washington Blvd., 10th Floor, Stamford, CT 06901-
2902; 203-353-9400; Fax: 203-333-6655; *Constituent
Services Rep.:* Gloria DePina
Committee Assignments: Financial Services; Permanent
Select Intelligence

Hinojosa, Ruben, D-Tex. (15)

Capitol Hill Office: 2262 RHOB 20515-4315; 225-2531;
Fax: 225-5688; *Chief of Staff:* Peter Spiro
Web: hinojosa.house.gov
Facebook: www.facebook.com/
CongressmanRubenHinojosa
Twitter: @USRepRHinojosa
District Office: 2864 W. Trenton Rd., Edinburg, TX
78539-9232; 956-682-5545; Fax: 956-682-0141; *District
Director:* Norma Brewster
Committee Assignments: Education and the Workforce;
Financial Services

Holding, George, R-N.C. (13)

Capitol Hill Office: 507 CHOB 20515; 225-3032; Fax: 225-
0181; *Chief of Staff:* Tucker Knott
Web: holding.house.gov
Facebook: www.facebook.com/CongressmanGeorgeHolding
Twitter: @RepHolding
District Office: 3725 National Dr., #101, Raleigh, NC
27612; 919-782-4400; Fax: 919-782-4490; *District
Director:* Alice McCall
Satellite Office: 120 Main St., Fremont, NC 27830; 919-
440-5247; *Field Rep.:* Debra Marm
Committee Assignment: Ways and Means

Honda, Mike, D-Calif. (17)

Capitol Hill Office: 1713 LHOB 20515-0515; 225-2631;
Fax: 225-2699; *Chief of Staff:* Jennifer Van der Heide

Web: honda.house.gov
Facebook: www.facebook.com/RepMikeHonda
Twitter: @RepMikeHonda
District Office: 900 Lafayette St., #206, Santa Clara, CA
95050; 408-436-2720; Fax: 408-436-2721; *District
Director:* Lenine Umali
Satellite Offices: Main Library, 2400 Stevenson Blvd.,
Fremont, CA 94538; 855-680-3759; *District Director:*
Lenine Umali
Newark Library, 6300 Civic Terrace Ave., Newark, CA;
855-680-3759; *District Director:* Lenine Umali
Committee Assignment: Appropriations

Hoyer, Steny, D-Md. (5)

Capitol Hill Office: 1705 LHOB 20515-2005; 225-4131;
Fax: 225-4300; *Chief of Staff:* Alexis Covey-Brandt
Web: hoyer.house.gov
Facebook: www.facebook.com/WhipHoyer
Twitter: @WhipHoyer
District Offices: U.S. District Courthouse, 6500
Cherrywood Lane, #310, Greenbelt, MD 20770-1287;
301-474-0119; Fax: 301-474-4697; *Deputy District
Director:* Terrance Taylor
401 Post Office Rd., #202, Waldorf, MD 20602-2738; 301-
843-1577; Fax: 301-843-1331; *District Director:*
Betsy Bossart
Minority Whip

Hudson, Richard, R-N.C. (8)

Capitol Hill Office: 429 CHOB 20515; 225-3715; Fax: 225-
4036; *Chief of Staff:* Pepper Natonski
Web: hudson.house.gov
Facebook: www.facebook.com/RepRichHudson
Twitter: @RepRichHudson
District Offices: 325 McGill Ave., #500, Concord, NC
28027-6194; 704-786-1612; Fax: 704-782-1004; *District
Director:* Chris Carter
1015 Fayetteville Rd., Rockingham, NC 28379; 910-997-
2070; *Constituent Liaison:* Chris Maples
Committee Assignment: Energy and Commerce

Huelskamp, Tim, R-Kans. (1)

Capitol Hill Office: 1110 LHOB 20515-1601; 225-2715;
Fax: 225-5124; *Chief of Staff:* Mark Kelly
Web: huelskamp.house.gov
Facebook: www.facebook.com/congressmanhuelskamp
Twitter: @conghuelskamp
District Offices: 100 Military Ave., #205, Dodge City, KS
67801-4945; 620-225-0172; Fax: 620-225-0297; *District
Director:* Steve Howe
1 N. Main St., #525, Hutchinson, KS 67501-5228; 620-665-
6138; Fax: 620-665-6360; *Constituent Services Rep.:*
Nathan Cox
200 S. Sante Fe, #6, Salina, KS 67401; 785-309-0572; Fax: 785-
827-6957; *Constituent Service Rep.:* Ashley Howard
Satellite Office: 727 Poyntz Ave., #10, Manhattan, KS
66502; 785-309-0572; Fax: 785-827-6957; *Constituent
Services Rep.:* Josh Powell
Committee Assignments: Small Business; Veterans' Affairs

Huffman, Jared, D-Calif. (2)

Capitol Hill Office: 1630 LHOB 20515; 225-5161;
Fax: 225-5163; *Chief of Staff:* Ben Miller
Web: huffman.house.gov
Facebook: www.facebook.com/RepHuffman
Twitter: @RepHuffman
District Offices: 317 3rd St., #1, Eureka, CA 95501; 707-
407-3585; Fax: 707-407-3559; *District Director:*
Jenny Callaway
430 N. Franklin St., P.O. Box 2208, Fort Bragg, CA 95437;
707-962-0933; Fax: 707-962-0905; *Field Rep.:*
Heather Gurewitz,
999 Fifth Ave., #290, San Rafael, CA 94901; 415-258-9657;
Fax: 415-258-9913; *Field Rep.:* Wesley Labat
206 G St., #3, Petaluma, CA 94952; 707-981-8967; *Field
Rep.:* Matt Olhausen
559 Low Gap Rd., Ukiah, CA 95482; 707-671-7449;
District Rep.: Rosaanne Ibarra
Committee Assignments: Natural Resources;
Transportation and Infrastructure

Huizenga, Bill, R-Mich. (2)

Capitol Hill Office: 1217 LHOB 20515-2202; 225-4401;
Fax: 226-0779; *Chief of Staff:* Jon DeWitte
Web: huizenga.house.gov
Facebook: www.facebook.com/rephuizenga
Twitter: @rephuizenga
District Offices: 1 S. Harbor Ave., #6B, Grand Haven, MI
49417; 616-414-5516; *District Director:*
Greg Van Woerkom
4555 Wilson Ave. S.W., #3, Grandville, MI 49418; 616-
570-0917; Fax: 616-570-0934; *District Director:*
Greg Van Woerkom
Committee Assignment: Financial Services

Hultgren, Randy, R-Ill. (14)

Capitol Hill Office: 2455 RHOB 20515; 225-2976;
Fax: 225-0697; *Chief of Staff:* Katherine McGuire
Web: hultgren.house.gov
Facebook: www.facebook.com/RepHultgren
Twitter: @rephultgren
District Office: 40W310 Lafox Rd., #F2, Campton Hills, IL
60175; 630-584-2734; Fax: 630-584-2746; *District
Director:* David Carlin
Committee Assignments: Financial Services; Science,
Space, and Technology

Hunter, Duncan, R-Calif. (50)

Capitol Hill Office: 2429 RHOB 20515-0552; 225-5672;
Fax: 225-0235; *Chief of Staff:* Joe Kasper
Web: hunter.house.gov
Facebook: www.facebook.com/DuncanHunter
District Office: 1611 N. Magnolia Ave., #310, El Cajon, CA
92020; 619-448-5201; Fax: 619-449-2251; *District
Chief of Staff:* Rick Terrazas
Satellite Office: 41000 Main St., Temecula, CA 92590;
951-695-5108; *District Chief of Staff:* Rick Terrazas
Committee Assignments: Armed Services; Education and
the Workforce; Transportation and Infrastructure

Hurd, Will, R-Tex. (23)

Capitol Hill Office: 317 CHOB 20515; 225-4511; Fax: 225-
2237; *Chief of Staff:* Stoney Burke
Web: hurd.house.gov
Facebook: www.facebook.com/hurdonthehill
Twitter: @hurdonthehill
District Offices: 17721 Rogers Ranch Pkwy, #120, San
Antonio, TX 78258; 210-921-3130; Fax: 210-927-4903;
District Director: Daniel Messa
1104 W. 10th St., Del Rio, TX 78840; 830-422-2040; *Field
Rep.:* Carmen Gutierrez
100 Monroe St., Eagle Pass, TX 78852; 210-238-4296; *Field
Rep.:* Carmen Gutierrez
124 S. Horizon, Socorro, TX 79927; 915-235-6421; *Field
Rep.:* Karina Rivera
1 University Way, #212 E & #212F, San Antonio, TX
78224; 210-784-5023; *District Director:* Daniel Messa
Committee Assignments: Homeland Security; Oversight
and Government Reform

Hurt, Robert, R-Va. (5)

Capitol Hill Office: 125 CHOB 20515; 225-4711; Fax: 225-
5681; *Chief of Staff:* Kelly Simpsom
Web: hurt.house.gov
Facebook: www.facebook.com/RepRobertHurt
Twitter: @reproberthurt
District Offices: 686 Berkmar Circle, Charlottesville, VA
22901-1464; 434-973-9631; Fax: 434-973-9635;
Outreach and Coalitions Director: Scott Leake
308 Craghead St., #102D, Danville, VA 24541-1470; 434-791-
2596; Fax: 434-791-4619; *District Director:* Linda Green
515 S. Main St., P.O. Box 0, Farmville, VA 23901; 434-395-
0120; Fax: 434-395-1248; *Office Manager:*
Lauren Andrews
Committee Assignment: Financial Services

Israel, Steve, D-N.Y. (3)

Capitol Hill Office: 2457 RHOB 20515-3202; 225-3335;
Fax: 225-4669; *Chief of Staff:* Patricia Russell
Web: israel.house.gov
Facebook: www.facebook.com/RepSteveIsrael
Twitter: @repSteveIsrael
District Office: 534 Broad Hollow Rd., #302, Melville, NY
11747; 631-777-7391; Fax: 631-777-7610; *District
Director:* Seema Bhansali
Committee Assignment: Appropriations

Issa, Darrell, R-Calif. (49)

Capitol Hill Office: 2269 RHOB 20515-0549; 225-3906;
Fax: 225-3303; *Chief of Staff:* Veronica Wong
Web: issa.house.gov
Facebook: www.facebook.com/darrellissa
Twitter: @DarrellIssa
District Offices: 1800 Thibodo Rd., #310, Vista, CA 92081-
7515; 760-599-5000; Fax: 760-599-1178; *District
Director:* Bill Christiansen
33282 Golden Lantern, #102, Dana Point, CA 92629; 949-
281-2449; *Field Rep.:* Amy Walker
Committee Assignments: Foreign Affairs; Judiciary

Jackson Lee, Sheila, D-Tex. (18)

Capitol Hill Office: 2251 RHOB 20515-4318; 225-3816;
Fax: 225-3317; *Chief of Staff:* Glenn Rushing
Web: jacksonlee.house.gov
Facebook: www.facebook.com/
CongresswomanSheilaJacksonLee
Twitter: @JacksonLeeTX18
District Offices: 1919 Smith St., #1180, Houston, TX
77002-8098; 713-655-0050; Fax: 713-655-1612;
Scheduler/Office Manager: Martha Hernandez
6719 W. Montgomery Rd., #204, Houston, TX 77091-
3105; 713-691-4882; *Caseworker/Field Rep.:*
Ivan Sanchez
420 W. 19th St., Houston, TX 77008-3914; 713-861-4070;
Caseworker/Field Rep.: Tonya Williams
4300 Lyons Ave., Houston, TX 77020; 713-227-7740;
Caseworker/Field Rep.: Stacie Keyes
Committee Assignments: Homeland Security; Judiciary

Jeffries, Hakeem S., D-N.Y. (8)

Capitol Hill Office: 1607 LHOB 20515; 225-5936;
Fax: 225-1018; *Chief of Staff:* Cedric Grant
Web: jeffries.house.gov
Facebook: www.facebook.com/RepHakeemJeffries
Twitter: @RepJeffries
District Offices: 445 Neptune Ave., 1st Floor, #2C,
Brooklyn, NY 11224; 718-373-0033; Fax: 718-373-
1333; *Field Rep.:* Larry Savinkin
55 Hanson Pl., #603, Brooklyn, NY 11217; 718-237-2211;
Fax: 718-237-2273; *District Director:* Tasia Jackson
Committee Assignments: Education and the Workforce;
Judiciary

Jenkins, Evan, R-W.V. (3)

Capitol Hill Office: 2307 RHOB 20515-4803; 225-3452;
Fax: 225-9061; *Chief of Staff:* Patrick Howell
Web: evanjenkins.house.gov
Facebook: www.facebook.com/RepEvanJenkins
Twitter: @RepEvanJenkins
District Offices: 845 5th Ave., #152, Huntington, WV
25701; 304-522-2201; Fax: 304-529-5716; *District
Director:* Michael Chirico
223 Prince St., Beckley, WV 25801; 304-250-6177;
Fax: 304-250-6179; *Field Director:* Kim McMillion
Satellite Office: 601 Federal St. #1003, Bluefield, WV
24701; 304-325-6800; *Field Director:* Kim McMillion
Committee Assignment: Appropriations

Jenkins, Lynn, R-Kans. (2)

Capitol Hill Office: 1526 LHOB 20515; 225-6601;
Fax: 225-7986; *Chief of Staff:* Pat Leopold
Web: lynnjenkins.house.gov
Facebook: www.facebook.com/replynnjenkins
Twitter: @replynnjenkins
District Offices: 1001 N. Broadway St., Suite C, Pittsburg,
KS 66762-3944; 620-231-5966; Fax: 620-231-5972;
Congressional Aide: Stephanie Lightle
3550 S.W. 5th St., Topeka, KS 66606-1998; 785-234-5966;
Fax: 785-234-5967; *District Director:* Bill Roe

120 N. 6th St., Independence, KS 67301; 620-231-5966,
Fax: 620-231-5972; *Congressional Aide:*
Stephanie Lightle
Committee Assignment: Ways and Means

Johnson, Bill, R-Ohio (6)

Capitol Hill Office: 1710 LHOB 20515; 225-5705;
Fax: 225-5907; *Chief of Staff:* Mike Smullen
Web: billjohnson.house.gov
Facebook: www.facebook.com/RepBillJohnson
Twitter: @repbilljohnson
District Offices: 116 Southgate Pkwy., Cambridge, OH
43725; 740-432-2366; Fax: 740-432-2587; *Field Rep.:*
Anthony Adornetto
202 Park Ave., Suite C, Ironton, OH 45638-1595; 740-534-
9431; Fax: 740-534-9482; *Field Rep.:* Julie Stephens
246 Front St., Marietta, OH 45750-2908; 740-376-0868;
Fax: 740-376-0886; *Field Rep.:* Dan Halliburton
192 E. State St., Salem, OH 44460-2843; 330-337-6951;
Fax: 330-337-7125; *Field Rep.:* Bianca Koup
District Director: Sarah Poulton
Committee Assignments: Budget; Energy and Commerce

Johnson, Eddie Bernice, D-Tex. (30)

Capitol Hill Office: 2468 RHOB 20515-4330; 225-8885;
Fax: 226-1477; *Chief of Staff Texas Democratic
Delegation:* Murat T. Gokcigdem
Web: ebjohnson.house.gov
Facebook: www.facebook.com/CongresswomanEBJtx30
Twitter: @RepEBJ
District Office: 3102 Maple Ave., #600, Dallas, TX 75201-
1236; 214-922-8885; Fax: 214-922-7028; *District
Director:* Esperanza Worley
Committee Assignments: Science, Space, and Technology,
Ranking Minority Member; Transportation and
Infrastructure

Johnson, Hank, Jr., D-Ga. (4)

Capitol Hill Office: 2240 RHOB 20515; 225-1605;
Fax: 226-0691; *Chief of Staff:* Arthur D. Sidney
Web: hankjohnson.house.gov
Facebook: www.facebook.com/Congressman-Hank-
Johnson-115356957005
Twitter: @rephankjohnson
District Office: 5700 Hillandale Dr., #120, Lithonia, GA
30058-4104; 770-987-2291; Fax: 770-987-8721; *District
Director:* Kathy Register
Satellite Office: Conyers, GA Area, 770-987-2291;
Fax: 770-987-8721; *Communications Director:*
Andy Phela
Committee Assignments: Armed Services; Judiciary

Johnson, Sam, R-Tex. (3)

Capitol Hill Office: 2304 RHOB 20515-4303; 225-4201;
Fax: 225-1485; *Chief of Staff/District Director:*
Lori McMahon
Web: samjohnson.house.gov
Facebook: www.facebook.com/RepSamJohnson
Twitter: @SamsPressShop

District Office: 1255 W. 15th St., #170, Plano, TX 75075; 469-304-0382; Fax: 469-304-0392; *Staff Asst.:* Meagan Talton

Committee Assignments: Joint Taxation; Ways and Means

Jolly, David W., R-Fla. (13)

Capitol Hill Office: 1728 LHOB 20515-0913; 225-5961; Fax: 225-9764; *Chief of Staff:* John David (J.D.) White

Web: jolly.house.gov

Facebook: www.facebook.com/repdavidjolly

Twitter: @USRepDavidJolly

District Offices: 9210 113th St., Seminole, FL 33772; 727-392-4100; *Constituent Services Supervisor:* Nicole Smith

425 22nd Ave. North, Suite C, St. Petersburg, FL 33704; 727-823-8900; Fax: 727-821-0484; *Sceduler:* Stephani Lavely

29275 U.S. Hwy. 19 N., Clearwater, FL 33761; 727-781-4400; Fax: 727-781-4409; *Constituent Services Rep.:* Sandy Hutton

Committee Assignment: Appropriations

Jones, Walter B., R-N.C. (3)

Capitol Hill Office: 2333 RHOB 20515-3303; 225-3415; Fax: 225-3286; *Chief of Staff:* Joshua Bowlen

Web: jones.house.gov

Facebook: www.facebook.com/Walter-Jones-15083070102

Twitter: @RepWalterJones

District Office: 1105-C Corporate Dr., Greenville, NC 27858-5968; 252-931-1003; Fax: 252-931-1002; *District Director:* Catherine Jordan

Satellite Offices: 1 Governental Ave., Havelock, NC 28532; 252-565-6846; *Congressional Aide:* William Moore

234 NW Corridor Blvd., #313B, Jacksonville, NC 28540; 252-565-6846; *Congressional Aide:* Mike Anglen

Committee Assignment: Armed Services

Jordan, Jim, R-Ohio (4)

Capitol Hill Office: 1524 LHOB 20515 3504; 225-2676; Fax: 226-0577; *Chief of Staff:* Ray Yonkura

Web: jordan.house.gov

Facebook: www.facebook.com/repjimjordan

Twitter: @Jim_Jordan

District Offices: 3121 W. Elm Plaza, Lima, OH 45805-2516; 419-999-6455; Fax: 419-999-4238; *District Director:* Cameron Warner

13B E. Main St., Norwalk, OH 44857; 419-663-1426; Fax: 419-668-3015; *Deputy District Director:* Neil Lynch

Committee Assignments: Judiciary; Oversight and Government Reform; Select on Benghazi

Joyce, David, R-Ohio (14)

Capitol Hill Office: 1124 LHOB 20515; 225-5731; Fax: 225-3307; *Chief of Staff:* Dino DiSanto

Web: joyce.house.gov

Facebook: www.facebook.com/RepDaveJoyce

Twitter: @RepDaveJoyce

District Offices: 1 Victoria Pl., #320, Painesville, OH 44077; 440-352-3939; Fax: 440-352-3622; *District Director:* Nick Ciofani

10075 Ravenna Rd., Twinsburg, OH 44087-1718; 330-425-9291; Fax: 330-425-7071; *District Director:* Nick Ciofani

Committee Assignment: Appropriations

Kaptur, Marcy, D-Ohio (9)

Capitol Hill Office: 2186 RHOB 20515-3509; 225-4146; Fax: 225-7711; *Legislative Director:* Jenny Perrino

Web: kaptur.house.gov

Facebook: www.facebook.com/RepresentativeMarcyKaptur

Twitter: @RepMarcyKaptur

District Offices: 1 Maritime Plaza, #600, Toledo, OH 43604-1853; 419-259-7500; Fax: 419-255-9623; *Chief of Staff:* Steve Katich

200 W. Erie, #310, Lorain, OH 44052; 440-288-1500; *Legislative Asst.:* Jacob Smith

17021 Lorain Ave. Cleveland, OH 44111, 216-767-5933; Fax: 419-255-9623; *Casework Director:* Susan Rowe

Committee Assignment: Appropriations

Katko, John, R-N.Y. (24)

Capitol Hill Office: 1123 LHOB 20515-3224; 225-3701; Fax: 225-4042, *Chief of Staff:* Brad Gentile

Web: katko.house.gov

Facebook: www.facebook.com/RepJohnKatko

Twitter: @repjohnkatko

District Offices: 71 Genesee St., Auburn, NY 13021; 315-253-4068; Fax: 315-253-2435; *Exec. Asst.:* Jordan D. Lane

440 S. Warren St., 7th Floor, #711, Syracuse, NY 13202; 315-423-5657; Fax: 315-423-5604; *District Director:* Thomas Connelan

Committee Assignments: Homeland Security; Transportation and Infrastructure

Keating, Bill, D-Mass. (9)

Capitol Hill Office: 315 CHOB 20515-2110; 225-3111; Fax: 225-5658; *Chief of Staff:* Garrett Donovan

Web: keating.house.gov

Facebook: www.facebook.com/Congressman.Keating

Twitter: @USRepKeating

District Offices: 297 North St., #312, Hyannis, MA 02601-5134; 508-771-0666; Fax: 508-790-1959; *District Rep.:* Anthony Morse

558 Pleasant St., #309, New Bedford, MA 02740; 508-999-6462; Fax: 508-999-6468; *Regional Director:* Ines Goncalves-Drolet

2 Court St., Plymouth, MA 02360; 508-746-9000; Fax: 508-732-0072; *District Director:* Michael Jackman

Committee Assignments: Foreign Affairs; Homeland Security

Kelly, Mike, R-Pa. (3)

Capitol Hill Office: 1519 LHOB 20515; 225-5406; Fax: 225-3103; *Chief of Staff:* Matthew Stroia

Web: kelly.house.gov

Facebook: www.facebook.com/Representative-Mike-Kelly-191056827594903
Twitter: @MikeKellyPA
District Offices: 101 E. Diamond St., #218, Butler, PA 16001; 724-282-2557; Fax: 724-282-3682; *District Scheduler:* Marci Mustello
208 E. Bayfront Pkwy., #102, Erie, PA 16507-2405; 814-454-8190; Fax: 814-454-8197; *District Director:* Brad Moore
33 Chestnut Ave., Sharon, PA 16146; 724-342-7170; Fax: 724-342-7242; *Senior Constituent Service Rep.:* Jill Burke
Committee Assignment: Ways and Means

Kelly, Robin, D-Ill. (2)

Capitol Hill Office: 1239 LHOB 20515; 225-0773; Fax: 225-4583; *Chief of Staff:* Brandon Garrett
Web: robinkelly.house.gov
Facebook: www.facebook.com/RepRobinKelly
Twitter: @RepRobinKelly
District Office: 600 Holiday Plaza Dr., #505, Matteson, IL 60443; 708-679-0078; Fax: 708-679-0216 *District Director:* Aubrey Wilson; *Director of Constituent Services:* Cynthia DeWitt
Satellite Office: 304 S. Indiana Ave., Lower Level, Kankakee, IL 60901; 708-679-0078; *Field Rep.:* Rick Bryant
Committee Assignments: Foreign Affairs; Oversight and Government Reform

Kelly, Trent, R-Miss. (1)

Capitol Hill Office: 1427 LHOB 20515; 225-4306; Fax: 225-3549; *Chief of Staff:* Ted Maness
Web: trentkelly.house.gov
Facebook: www.facebook.com/RepTrentKelly
Twitter: @RepTrentKelly
District Offices: 318 N. 7th St., Suite D, Columbus, MS 39701; 662-327-0748 Fax: 662-328-5982 *Field Rep.:* Brent Thompson
2565 Caffey St., #200, P.O. Box 218, Hernando, MS 38632; 662-449-3090; Fax: 662-449-4836; *Field Rep.:* Walt Starr
431 W. Main St., Tupelo, MS 38804; 662-841-8808; Fax: 662-841-8845; *District Director:* Paul Howell
855 S. Dunn St., Eupora, MS 39744; 662-258-7240; Fax: 662-258-7240; *Field Rep.:* Willy Weddle
Committee Assignments: Agriculture; Small Business

Kennedy, Joe, III, D-Mass. (4)

Capitol Hill Office: 306 CHOB 20515; 225-5931; Fax: 225-0182; *Chief of Staff:* Craig Mecher
Web: kennedy.house.gov
Facebook: www.facebook.com/CongressmanJoeKennedyIII
Twitter: @RepJoeKennedy
District Offices: 8 N. Main St., #200, Attleboro, MA 02703; 508-431-1110; Fax: 508-431-1101; *Field Rep.:* Lisa Nelson

29 Crafts St., #375, Newton, MA 02458-1275; 617-332-3333; Fax: 617-332- 3308; *District Director:* Nick Clemons
Committee Assignment: Energy and Commerce

Kildee, Dan, D-Mich. (5)

Capitol Hill Office: 227 CHOB 20515; 225-3611; Fax: 225-6393; *Chief of Staff:* Jennifer Cox
Web: dankildee.house.gov
Facebook: www.facebook.com/RepDanKildee
Twitter: @RepDanKildee
District Office: 111 E. Court St., #3B, Flint, MI 48502; 810-238-8627; Fax: 810-238-8658; *District Chief of Staff:* Amy Hovey
Committee Assignment: Financial Services

Kilmer, Derek, D-Wash. (6)

Capitol Hill Office: 1520 LHOB 20515; 225-5916; Fax: 226-3575; *Chief of Staff:* Jonathon Smith
Web: kilmer.house.gov
Facebook: www.facebook.com/derek.kilmer
Twitter: @RepDerekKilmer
District Offices: 345 6th St., #500, Bremerton, WA 98337; 360-373-9725; *Constituent Services Director:* Cheri Williams
950 Pacific Ave., #1230, Tacoma, WA 98402; 253-272-3515; *District Director:* Joe Dacca
Satellite Office: 332 E. 5th St., Port Angeles, WA 98632; 360-797-3623; *District Rep.:* Judith Morris
Committee Assignment: Appropriations

Kind, Ron, D-Wisc. (3)

Capitol Hill Office: 1502 LHOB 20515; 225-5506; Fax: 225-5739; *Chief of Staff:* Mike Goodman
Web: kind.house.gov
Facebook: www.facebook.com/repronkind
Twitter: @repronkind
District Offices: 131 S. Barstow St., #301, Eau Claire, WI 54701-2625; 715-831-9214; Fax: 715-831-9272; *Congressional Aide:* Mark Aumann
205 5th Ave. South, #400, La Crosse, WI 54601-4059; 608-782-2558; Fax: 608-782-4588; *District Chief of Staff:* Loren Kannenberg
Committee Assignment: Ways and Means

King, Pete, R-N.Y. (2)

Capitol Hill Office: 339 CHOB 20515-3203; 225-7896; Fax: 226-2279; *Chief of Staff:* Kevin C. Fogarty
Web: peteking.house.gov
Facebook: www.facebook.com/reppeteking
Twitter: @reppeteking
District Office: 1003 Park Blvd., Massapequa Park, NY 11762-2758; 516-541-4225; Fax: 516-541-6602; *District Director:* Anne Rosenfeld
Committee Assignments: Financial Services; Homeland Security; Permanent Select Intelligence

King, Steve, R-Iowa (4)

Capitol Hill Office: 2210 RHOB 20515; 225-4426;
Fax: 225-3193; *Chief of Staff:* Sarah Stevens
Web: steveking.house.gov
Facebook: www.facebook.com/SteveKingIA
Twitter: @SteveKingIA
District Offices: 1421 S. Bell Ave., #102, Ames, Iowa
50010; 515-232-2885; Fax: 515-232-2844; *District Rep.:*
Victoria Hurst
723 Central Ave., Fort Dodge, Iowa 50501; 515-573-2738;
Fax: 515-576-7141; *District Rep.:* Jim Oberhelman
202 1st St. S.E., #126, Mason City, Iowa, 50401; 641-201-
1624; Fax: 641-201-1523; *District Rep.:* Vacant
526 Nebraska St., Sioux City, IA 51101-1313; 712-224-
4692; Fax: 712-224-4693; *District Director:*
Sandy Hanlon
306 N. Grand Ave., P.O. Box 650, Spencer, IA 51301-4141;
712-580-7754; Fax: 712-580-3354; *District Rep.:*
Andrea Easter
Committee Assignments: Agriculture; Judiciary; Small
Business

Kinzinger, Adam, R-Ill. (16)

Capitol Hill Office: 1221 LHOB 20515-1311; 225-3635;
Fax: 225-3521; *Chief of Staff:* Austin Weatherford
Web: kinzinger.house.gov
Facebook: www.facebook.com/RepKinzinger
Twitter: @repkinzinger
District Offices: 628 Columbus St., #507, Ottawa, IL
61350; 815-431-9271; Fax: 815-431-9383; *District
Director:* Bonnie Walsh
342 W. Walnut, Watseka, IL 60970; 815-432-0580;
Scheduler: Patrick Doggett
725 N. Lyford Rd., #3, Rockford, IL 61107; 815-708-8032;
Field Rep.: John Walsh
Committee Assignment: Energy and Commerce

Kirkpatrick, Ann, D-Ariz. (1)

Capitol Hill Office: 201 CHOB 20515; 225-3361; Fax: 225-
3462; *Chief of Staff:* Carmen Gallus
Web: kirkpatrick.house.gov
Facebook: www.facebook.com/RepKirkpatrick
Twitter: @RepKirkpatrick
District Offices: 211 N. Florence St., #1, Casa Grande, AZ
85122; 520-316-0839; Fax: 520-316-0842; *Deputy
District Director:* Blanca Rubio-Varela
405 N. Beaver St., #6, Flagstaff, AZ 86001; 928-213-9977;
Fax: 928-213-9981; *District Director:* Ron Lee
11555 W. Civic Center Dr., #104A, Marana, AZ 85653;
520-382-2663; Fax: 520-382-2664; *Caseworker:*
Zak Royse
Satellite Offices: 550 N. 9th Pl., Show Low, AZ 85901;
928-537-5657; Fax: 928-537-2995; *Community
Outreach Rep.:* Sharon Adams
49 Maple St., Tuba City, AZ 86503; 928-213-9977;
Fax: 928-213-9981; *District Outreach Rep.:* Marie Nez
South State Hwy, 191, P.O. Box 1952, Chinle, AZ 86503;
923-213-9977; Fax: 928-213-9981; *District Outreach
Rep.:* Stan Robbins

1400 E. Ash, Globe, AZ 85501; 928-425-3231; Fax: 928-
402-4363; *Community Outreach Rep.:* Cathy Melvin
Committee Assignments: Agriculture; Transportation
and Infrastructure

Kline, John, R-Minn. (2)

Capitol Hill Office: 2439 RHOB 20515-2302; 225-2271;
Fax: 225-2595; *Chief of Staff:* Jean Hinz
Web: kline.house.gov
Facebook: www.facebook.com/repjohnkline
Twitter: @RepJohnKline
District Office: 350 W. Burnsville Pkwy., #135, Burnsville,
MN 55337-2572; 952-808-1213; Fax: 952-808-1261;
District Director: Brooke Dorobiala
Committee Assignments: Armed Services; Education and
the Workforce, Chair

Knight, Steve, R-Calif. (25)

Capitol Hill Office: 1023 LHOB 20515-0525; 225-1956;
Fax: 226-0683; *Chief of Staff:* David Orosco
Web: knight.house.gov
Facebook: www.facebook.com/RepresentativeSteveKnight
Twitter: @SteveKnight25
District Office: 1008 W. Ave., M-14, Suite E, Palmdale, CA
93551; 661-441-0320; Fax: 661-441-2677 *District
Director.* Lisa Moulton
26415 Carl Boyer Dr., #220, Santa Clarita, CA 91350; 661-
255-5630; Fax: 661-255-5633; *Field Rep.:* Dante Acosta
1445 E. Los Angeles Ave., #206, Simi Valley, CA 93065;
805-581-7130; 805-581-7141; *Field Rep.:*
Patricia Saraceno
Committee Assignments: Armed Services; Science, Space
and Technology; Small Business

Kuster, Ann McLane, D-N.H. (2)

Capitol Hill Office: 137 CHOB 20515; 225-5206; Fax: 225-
2946; *Chief of Staff:* Abby Curran
Web: kuster.house.gov
Facebook: www.facebook.com/
CongresswomanAnnieKuster
Twitter: @RepAnnieKuster
District Offices: 18 N. Main St., 4th Floor, Concord, NH
03301; 603-226-1002; Fax: 603-226-1010; *District
Director:* Jake Berry
70 E. Pearl St., Nashua, NH 03060; 603-595-2006;
Fax: 603-595-2016; *Constituent Outreach Coord.:*
Aseeb Miazi
33 Main St., #202, Littleton, NH 03561; 603-444-7700;
Service Coordinator: Brian Bresnahan
Committee Assignments: Agriculture; Veterans' Affairs

Labrador, Raul, R-Idaho (1)

Capitol Hill Office: 1523 LHOB 20515-1201; 225-6611;
Fax: 225-3029; *Deputy Chief of Staff:*
Mike Hunnington
Web: labrador.house.gov
Facebook: www.facebook.com/raul.r.labrador
Twitter: @Raul_Labrador

District Offices: 1250 W. Ironwood Dr., #243, Coeur d'Alene, ID 83814-2682; 208-667-0127; Fax: 208-667-0310; *Regional Director:* Judy Morbeck

313 D St., #107, Lewiston, ID 83501-1894; 208-743-1388; Fax: 208-743-0247; *Regional Director:* Scott Carlton

33 E. Broadway Ave., #251, Meridian, ID 83642-2619; 208-888-3188; Fax: 208-888-0894; *District Director:* Doug Taylor

Committee Assignments: Judiciary; Natural Resources

LaHood, Darin, R-Ill. (18)

Capitol Hill Office: 2464 RHOB 20515-1318; 225-6201; Fax: 225-9249; *Chief of Staff:* Steven Pfrang
Web: lahood.house.gov
Facebook: www.facebook.com/darinlahood
Twitter: @LaHoodDarin
District Office: 100 NE Monroe St., Room 100, Peoria, IL 61602-1047; 309-671-7027; Fax: 309-671-7309; *District Director:* Brad Stolter
Committee Assignments: Natural Resources; Science, Space and Technology

LaMalfa, Doug, R-Calif. (1)

Capitol Hill Office: 322 CHOB 20515; 225-3076; Fax: 226-0852; *Chief of Staff:* Mark Spannagel
Web: lamalfa.house.gov
Facebook: www.facebook.com/RepLaMalfa
Twitter: @RepLaMalfa
District Offices: 2862 Olive Hwy., Suite D, Oroville, CA 95966; 530-534-7100; Fax: 530-534-7800; *District Director:* Lisa Buescher
2885 Churn Creek Rd., Suite C, Redding, CA 96002; 530-223-5898; Fax: 530-223-5897; *District Rep.:* Stephanie White
2399 Rickenbacker Way, Auburn, CA 95602; 530-878-5035; Fax: 530-878-5037; *Caseworker:* Leslie Schuessler
Committee Assignments: Agriculture; Natural Resources

Lamborn, Doug, R-Colo. (5)

Capitol Hill Office: 2402 RHOB 20515; 225-4422; Fax: 226-2638; *Chief of Staff:* Adam Magary
Web: lamborn.house.gov
Facebook: www.facebook.com/CongressmanDoug Lamborn
Twitter: @RepDLamborn
District Office: 1125 Kelly Johnson Blvd., #330, Colorado Springs, CO 80920-3965; 719-520-0055; Fax: 719-520-0840; *District Director:* Dale Anderson
Satellite Office: 415 Main St., Buena Vista, CO 81211; 719-520-0055; Fax: 719-520-0840; *District Director:* Dale Anderson
Committee Assignments: Armed Services; Natural Resources; Veterans' Affairs

Lance, Leonard, R-N.J. (7)

Capitol Hill Office: 2352 RHOB 20515; 225-5361; Fax: 225-9460; *Chief of Staff:* Todd Mitchell
Web: lance.house.gov
Facebook: www.facebook.com/CongressmanLance

Twitter: @RepLanceNJ7
District Offices: 361 Route 31, #1400, Flemington, NJ 08822; 908-788-6900; Fax: 908-788-2869; *District Scheduler:* Anna Pellecchia
425 North Ave. East, Westfield, NJ 07090-1443; 908-518-7733; Fax: 908-518-7751; *District Director:* Amanda Woloshen
Committee Assignment: Energy and Commerce

Langevin, Jim, D-R.I. (2)

Capitol Hill Office: 109 CHOB 20515-3902; 225-2735; Fax: 225-5976; *Chief of Staff:* Kristin E. Nicholson
Web: langevin.house.gov
Facebook: www.facebook.com/CongressmanJimLangevin
Twitter: @jimlangevin
District Office: 300 Centerville Rd., #200 South, Warwick, RI 02886-0200; 401-732-9400; Fax: 401-737-2982; *District Director:* Seth Klaiman
Committee Assignments: Armed Services; Homeland Security

Larsen, Rick, D-Wash. (2)

Capitol Hill Office: 2113 RHOB 20515; 225-2605; Fax: 225-4420; *Chief of Staff:* Kimberly Johnston
Web: larsen.house.gov
Facebook: www.facebook.com/RepRickLarsen
Twitter: @RepRickLarsen
District Offices: 119 N. Commercial St., #1350, Bellingham, WA 98225-4452; 360-733-4500; Fax: 360-733-5144; *Community Liaison:* Thomas Boucher
Wall Street Bldg., 2930 Wetmore Ave., #9F, Everett, WA 98201-4070; 425-252-3188; Fax: 425-252-6606; *District Director:* Jill McKinnie
Committee Assignments: Armed Services; Transportation and Infrastructure

Larson, John B., D-Conn. (1)

Capitol Hill Office: 1501 LHOB 20515-0701; 225-2265; Fax: 225-1031; *Chief of Staff:* Lee Slater
Web: larson.house.gov
Facebook: www.facebook.com/RepJohnLarson
Twitter: @repjohnlarson
District Office: 221 Main St., 2nd Floor, Hartford, CT 06106-1890; 860-278-8888; Fax: 860-278-2111; *District Chief of Staff:* Kevin Brown
Committee Assignments: Ethics; Ways and Means

Latta, Bob, R-Ohio (5)

Capitol Hill Office: 2448 RHOB 20515; 225-6405; Fax: 225-1985; *Chief of Staff:* Ryan Walker
Web: latta.house.gov
Facebook: www.facebook.com/boblatta
Twitter: @boblatta
District Offices: 1045 N. Main St., #6, Bowling Green, OH 43402-1361; 419-354-8700; Fax: 419-354-8702; *District Director:* Andrew Lorenz
101 Clinton St., #1200, Defiance, OH 43512-2165; 419-782-1996; Fax: 419-784-9808; *Sr. District Rep.:* Kathy Shaver

318 Dorney Plaza, #302, Findlay, OH 45840; 419-422-7791; *District Rep.:* LuAnne Cooke
Committee Assignment: Energy and Commerce

Lawrence, Brenda L., D-Mich. (14)

Capitol Hill Office: 1609 LHOB 20515-2214; 225-5802; Fax: 226-2356; *Chief of Staff:* Duron Marshall
Web: lawrence.house.gov
Facebook: www.facebook.com/brendalawrenceforcongress
Twitter: @RepLawrence
District Office: 26700 Lahser Rd., #330, Southfield, MI 48033; 248-356-2052; Fax: 248-356-4532; *Special Assistant:* Marty Williams
Committee Assignments: Oversight and Government Reform; Small Business

Lee, Barbara, D-Calif. (13)

Capitol Hill Office: 2267 RHOB 20515-0509; 225-2661; Fax: 225-9817; *Chief of Staff:* Julie Nickson
Web: lee.house.gov
Facebook: www.facebook.com/RepBarbaraLee
Twitter: @RepBarbaraLee
District Office: 1301 Clay St., #1000N, Oakland, CA 94612-5233; 510-763-0370; Fax: 510-763-6538; *Manager of Public Outreach:* Adrienne Ursino
Satellite Offices: 300 Estudillo Ave., Suite C, San Leandro, CA 94577; *Casework Manager/Congressional Aide:* Jonathan Gast
1550 Oak St., 2nd Floor, Staff Room, Alameda, CA 94501; *Congressional Aide:* Katherine Kwong
Citizens Foundation, 1470 Fruitvale Ave., Oakland, CA 94601; *Congressional Aide:* Jose Hernandez
Committee Assignments: Appropriations; Budget

Levin, Sandy, D-Mich. (9)

Capitol Hill Office: 1236 LHOB 20515-2212; 225-4961; Fax: 226-1033; *Chief of Staff:* Hilarie Chambers
Web: levin.house.gov
Facebook: www.facebook.com/RepSandyLevin
Twitter: @repsandylevin
District Office: 27085 Gratiot Ave., Roseville, MI 48066-2947; 586-498-7122; Fax: 586-498-7123; *District Director:* Walt Herzig
Committee Assignments: Joint Taxation; Ways and Means, Ranking Minority Member

Lewis, John, D-Ga. (5)

Capitol Hill Office: 343 CHOB 20515-1005; 225-3801; Fax: 225-0351; *Chief of Staff; Floor Asst.:* Michael Collins
Web: johnlewis.house.gov
Facebook: www.facebook.com/RepJohnLewis
Twitter: @repjohnlewis
District Office: Equitable Bldg., 100 Peachtree St. N.W., #1920, Atlanta, GA 30303-1906; 404-659-0116; Fax: 404-331-0947; *District Director:* Aaron Ward
Committee Assignment: Ways and Means

Lieu, Ted, D-Calif. (33)

Capitol Hill Office: 415 CHOB 20515-0533; 225-3976; Fax: 225-4099; *Chief of Staff:* Marc Cevasco
Web: lieu.house.gov
Facebook: www.facebook.com/TedLieu
Twitter: @TedLieu
District Office: 5055 Wilshire Blvd., #310, Los Angeles, CA 90036; 323-651-1040; Fax: 323-655-0502; *Staff Asst.:* Elizabeth Arevalo
Satellite Office: 1600 Rosecrans Ave., 4th Floor, Manhattan Beach, CA 90266; 310-321-7664; Fax: 323-655-0502; *Communications:* John d'Annibale
Committee Assignments: Budget; Oversight and Government Reform

Lipinski, Daniel, D-Ill. (3)

Capitol Hill Office: 2346 RHOB 20515-1303; 225-5701; Fax: 225-1012; *Chief of Staff:* Eric L. Lausten
Web: lipinski.house.gov
Facebook: www.facebook.com/repdanlipinski
Twitter: @RepLipinski
District Offices: 6245 S. Archer Ave., Chicago, IL 60638-2609; 312-886-0481; Fax: 773-767-9395; *District Director:* Jerry Hurckes
Central Square Bldg., 222 E. 9th St., #109, Lockport, IL 60441; 815-838-1990; Fax 815-838-1993; *Communications Director:* Isaac Sancken
5309 W. 95th St., Oak Lawn, IL 60453-2444; 708-424-0853; Fax: 708-424-1855; *Congressional Aide:* Jerry Mulvihill
Orland Park Village Hall, 14700 S. Ravinia Ave., Orland Park, IL 60462; 708-403-4379; Fax: 708-403-5963; *Congressional Aide:* Marianne Chmela
Committee Assignments: Science, Space, and Technology; Transportation and Infrastructure

LoBiondo, Frank, R-N.J. (2)

Capitol Hill Office: 2427 RHOB 20515-3002; 225-6572; Fax: 225-3318; *Chief of Staff:* Mary Annie Harper
Web: lobiondo.house.gov
Facebook: www.facebook.com/FrankLoBiondo
Twitter: @RepLoBiondo
District Office: 5914 Main St., #103, Mays Landing, NJ 08330-1746; 609-625-5008; Fax: 609-625-5071; *Director of Constituent Services:* Joan Dermanoski
Committee Assignments: Armed Services; Permanent Select Intelligence; Transportation and Infrastructure

Loebsack, Dave, D-Iowa (2)

Capitol Hill Office: 1527 LHOB 20515-1502; 225-6576; Fax: 226-0757; *Chief of Staff:* Eric Witte
Web: loebsack.house.gov
Facebook: www.facebook.com/DaveLoebsack
Twitter: @daveloebsack
District Offices: 209 W. 4th St., #104, Davenport, IA 52801; 563-323-5988; Fax: 563-323-5231; *District Director:* Robert Sueppel
125 S. Dubuque St., Iowa City, IA 52240-4000; 319-351-0789; Fax: 319-351-5789; *District Rep.:* David Leshtz
Committee Assignment: Energy and Commerce

Lofgren, Zoe, D-Calif. (19)

Capitol Hill Office: 1401 LHOB 20515-0516; 225-3072; Fax: 225-3336; *Chief of Staff:* Stacey Leavandosky
Web: lofgren.house.gov
Facebook: www.facebook.com/zoelofgren
Twitter: @RepZoeLofgren
District Office: 635 N. 1st St., Suite B, San Jose, CA 95112-5110; 408-271-8700; Fax: 408-271-8714; *District Chief of Staff:* Sandra Soto
Committee Assignments: House Administration; Joint Library; Judiciary; Science, Space, and Technology

Long, Billy, R-Mo. (7)

Capitol Hill Office: 1541 LHOB 20515-2507; 225-6536; Fax: 225-5604; *Chief of Staff:* Joe Lillis
Web: long.house.gov
Facebook: www.facebook.com/Rep.Billy.Long
Twitter: @UsRepLong
District Offices: 2727 E. 32nd St., #2, Joplin, MO 64804-3155; 417-781-1041; Fax: 417-781-2832; *Field Rep.:* Jacob Heisten
3232 E. Ridgeview St., Springfield, MO 65804-4076; 417-889-1800; Fax: 417-889-4915; *District Director:* Royce Reding
Committee Assignment: Energy and Commerce

Loudermilk, Barry, R-Ga. (11)

Capitol Hill Office: 238 CHOB 20515-1011; 225-2931; Fax: 225-2944; *Chief of Staff:* Rob Adkerson
Web: loudermilk.house.gov
Facebook: www.facebook.com/barry.loudermilk
Twitter: @reploudermilk
District Offices: 9898 Hwy. 92, #100, Woodstock, GA 30188; 770-429-1776; Fax: 770-517-7427; *District Director:* Caric Martin
135 W. Cherokee Ave., #122, Cartersville, GA 30120; 770-429-1776; *District Director:* Caric Martin
600 Galleria Pkwy., #120, Atlanta, GA 30339; 770-429-1776; Fax: 678-556-5184; *Field Director:* Claire Bartlett
Committee Assignments: Homeland Security; Science, Space and Technology

Love, Mia, R-Utah (4)

Capitol Hill Office: 217 CHOB 20515-4404; 225-3011; Fax: 225-5638; *Chief of Staff:* Muffy Day
Web: love.house.gov
Facebook: www.facebook.com/miablove
Twitter: @miablove
District Office: 9067 S. 1300 West, #101, West Jordan, UT 84088; 801-996-8729; Fax: 801-987-8631; *District Director:* Laurel Price
Committee Assignments: Financial Services

Lowenthal, Alan, D-Calif. (47)

Capitol Hill Office: 108 CHOB 20515; 225-7924; Fax: 225-7926; *Chief of Staff:* Tim Hysom
Web: lowenthal.house.gov
Facebook: www.facebook.com/RepLowenthal
Twitter: @RepLowenthal
District Office: 100 W. Broadway, #600, Long Beach, CA 90802; 562-436-3828; Fax: 562-437-6434; *District Director:* Mark Pulido
Satellite Offices: 8200 Westminster Blvd., Westminster, CA 92583; 562-436-3828; Fax: 562-437-6434; *Field Rep.:* Phong Ly
11222 Garden Grove Blvd., 3rd Floor, Garden Grove, CA 92843; 562-436-3828; Fax: 562-437-6434; *Field Rep.:* Phong Ly
5275 Orange Ave., Cypress, CA 90630; 562-436-3828; Fax: 562-437-6434; *Field Rep.:* Irantzu Pujadas
7800 Katella Ave., Stanton, CA 90680; 562-436-3828; Fax: 562-437-6434; *Field Rep.:* Irantzu Pujadas
Committee Assignments: Foreign Affairs; Natural Resources

Lowey, Nita, D-N.Y. (17)

Capitol Hill Office: 2365 RHOB 20515-3218; 225-6506; Fax: 225-0546; *Chief of Staff:* Elizabeth Stanley
Web: lowey.house.gov
Facebook: www.facebook.com/RepLowey
Twitter: @NitaLowey
District Offices: 67 N. Main St., #101, New City, NY 10956; 845-639-3485; Fax: 845-634-4079; *District Rep.:* Sarah Levine
222 Mamaroneck Ave., #312, White Plains, NY 10605; 914-428-1707; Fax: 914-328-1505; *District Director:* Patricia Keegan
Committee Assignment: Appropriations, Ranking Minority Member

Lucas, Frank, R-Okla. (3)

Capitol Hill Office: 2405 RHOB 20515-3603; 225-5565; Fax: 225-8698; *Communications Director:* Andrew Witmer
Web: lucas.house.gov
Facebook: www.facebook.com/RepFrankLucas
Twitter: @RepFrankLucas
District Office: 10952 N.W. Expressway, Suite B, Yukon, OK 73099-8214; 405-373-1958; Fax: 405-373-2046; *Chief of Staff:* Stacey Glasscock
Committee Assignments: Agriculture; Financial Services; Science, Space, and Technology

Luetkemeyer, Blaine, R-Mo. (3)

Capitol Hill Office: 2440 RHOB 20515; 225-2956; Fax: 225-5712; *Chief of Staff; Legis. Director:* Seth Appleton
Web: luetkemeyer.house.gov
Facebook: www.facebook.com/BlaineLuetkemeyer
Twitter: @RepBlainePress
District Offices: 2117 Missouri Blvd., Jefferson City, MO 65109; 573-635-7232; Fax: 573-635-8347; *Deputy District Director:* Jeremy Ketterer
113 E. Pearce Blvd., Wentzville, MO 63385; 636-327-7055; Fax: 636-327-3254; *Deputy District Director:* Tanner Smith

516 Jefferson St., Washington, MO 63090-2706; 636-239-2276; Fax: 636-239-0478; *Deputy District Director:* Jim McNichols
Committee Assignments: Financial Services; Small Business

Luján, Ben Ray, D-N.M. (3)

Capitol Hill Office: 2446 RHOB 20515; 225-6190; Fax: 226-1528; *Chief of Staff:* Angela K. Ramirez
Web: lujan.house.gov
Facebook: www.facebook.com/RepBenRayLujan
Twitter: @repbenraylujan
District Offices: 800 Municipal Dr., Farmington, NM 87401-2663; 505-324-1005; Fax: 505-324-1026; *Field Rep.:* Pete Valencia
110 W. Aztec Ave., Gallup, NM 87301-6202; 505-863-0582; Fax: 505-863-0678; *Field Rep.; Navajo Nation Advisor:* Brian Lee
903 University Ave., Las Vegas, NM 87701; 505-454-3038; Fax: 505-454-3265; *Field Rep.:* Steven Salas
3200 Civic Center Circle N.E., #330, Rio Rancho, NM 87144-4503; 505-994-0499; Fax: 505-994-0550; *Constituent Liaison:* Joseph Casados
1611 Calle Lorca, Suite A, Santa Fe, NM 87505-7640; 505-984-8950; Fax: 505-986-5047; *District Director:* Jennifer Conn-Catechis
404 W. Route 66 Blvd., Tucumcari, NM 88401 3279, 573-161-0029; Fax: 575-461-3192; *Field Rep.:* Ron Wilmot
Committee Assignment: Energy and Commerce

Lujan Grisham, Michelle, D-N.M. (1)

Capitol Hill Office: 214 CHOB 20515; 225-6316; Fax: 225-4975; *Chief of Staff:* Dominic Gabello
Web: lujangrisham.house.gov
Facebook: www.facebook.com/RepLujanGrisham
Twitter: @replujangrisham
District Office: 400 Gold Ave. S.W., #680, Albuquerque, NM 87102; 505-346-6781; Fax: 505-346-6723; *District Director:* Marianna Padilla
Committee Assignments: Agriculture; Budget; Oversight and Government Reform

Lummis, Cynthia, R-Wyo. (At Large)

Capitol Hill Office: 2433 RHOB 20515-5001; 225-2311; Fax: 225-3057; *Chief of Staff:* Landon Stropko
Web: lummis.house.gov
Facebook: www.facebook.com/cynthia.lummis
Twitter: @CynthiaLummis
District Offices: 100 E. B St., #4003, Casper, WY 82602-1969; 307-261-6595; Fax: 307-261-6597; *Field Rep.:* Jackie King
2120 Capitol Ave., #8005, Cheyenne, WY 82001-3631; 307-772-2595; Fax: 307-772-2597; *Chief of Staff:* Tucker Fagan
45 E. Loucks St., #300F, Sheridan, WY 82801-6331; 307-673-4608; Fax: 307-673-4982; *Field Rep.:* Matt Jones
Committee Assignments: Natural Resources; Oversight and Government Reform

Lynch, Stephen F., D-Mass. (8)

Capitol Hill Office: 2369 RHOB 20515; 225-8273; Fax: 225-3984; *Chief of Staff:* Kevin Ryan
Web: lynch.house.gov
Facebook: www.facebook.com/repstephenlynch
Twitter: @RepStephenLynch
District Offices: 88 Black Falcon Ave., #340, Boston, MA 02210-2433; 617-428-2000; Fax: 617-428-2011; *District Director:* Bob Fowkes
Plymouth County Registry of Deeds, 155 W. Elm St., #200, Brockton, MA 02301-4326; 508-586-5555; Fax: 508-580-4692; *District Rep.:* Shaynah Barnes
1245 Hancock St., #16, Quincy, MA 02169; 617-657-6305; Fax: 617-773-0955; *District Rep.:* Joe King
Committee Assignments: Financial Services; Oversight and Government Reform

MacArthur, Tom, R-N.J. (3)

Capitol Hill Office: 1239 LHOB 20515-3003; 225-4765; Fax: 225-0778; *Chief of Staff:* Ryan Carney
Web: macarthur.house.gov
Facebook: www.facebook.com/congressmantommacarthur
Twitter: @reptommacarthur
District Offices: Township of Toms, River Hall, 33 Washington St., Toms River, NJ 08753; 732-569-6495; Fax: 732-998-8137; *District Director:* Chole Rockow
Gibson House Community Center, 535 E. Main St., Marlton, NJ 08053; 856-267-5182; Fax: 856-574-4697; *Scheduler:* Chris Griswold
Committee Assignments: Armed Services; Natural Resources

Maloney, Carolyn B., D-N.Y. (12)

Capitol Hill Office: 2308 RHOB 20515; 225-7944; Fax: 225-4709; *Chief of Staff:* Michael Iger
Web: maloney.house.gov
Facebook: www.facebook.com/CarolynMaloney
Twitter: @RepMaloney
District Offices: 31-19 Newtown Ave., Astoria, NY 11102; 718-932-1804; Fax: 718-932-1805; *District Rep.:* Edward Babor
1651 3rd Ave., #311, New York, NY 10128-3679; 212-860-0606; Fax: 212-860-0704; *New York Chief of Staff:* Minna Elias
619 Lorimer St., Brooklyn, NY 11211; 718-349-5972; Fax: 718-349-5973; *Caseworker:* Theresa Rack
Committee Assignments: Financial Services; Joint Economic; Oversight and Government Reform

Maloney, Sean Patrick, D-N.Y. (18)

Capitol Hill Office: 1529 LHOB 20515; 225-5441; Fax: 225-3289; *Chief of Staff:* Timothy Persico
Web: seanmaloney.house.gov
Facebook: www.facebook.com/repseanmaloney
Twitter: @RepSeanMaloney
District Office: 123 Grand St., 2nd Floor, Newburgh, NY 12550; 845-561-1259; Fax: 845-561-2890; *District Director:* Michael Limperopulos
Committee Assignments: Agriculture; Transportation and Infrastructure

Marchant, Kenny, R-Tex. (24)

Capitol Hill Office: 2313 RHOB 20515-4324; 225-6605; Fax: 225-0074; *Chief of Staff:* Brian Thomas
Web: marchant.house.gov
Facebook: www.facebook.com/RepKennyMarchant
Twitter: @repkenmarchant
District Office: 9901 E. Valley Ranch Pkwy., #2060, Irving, TX 75063-7186; 972-556-0162; Fax: 972-409-9704; *District Director:* Susie Miller
Committee Assignments: Ethics; Ways and Means

Marino, Tom, R-Pa. (10)

Capitol Hill Office: 410 CHOB 20515-3810; 225-3731; Fax: 225-9594; *Chief of Staff:* William Tighe
Web: marino.house.gov
Facebook: www.facebook.com/CongressmanMarino
Twitter: @RepTomMarino
District Offices: 543 Easton Turnpike, #101, Lake Ariel, PA 18436, 570-689-6024; Fax: 570-689-6028; *District Director:* David Weber
713 Bridge St., #29, Selinsgrove, PA 17870; 570-374-9469; Fax: 570-374-9589; *District Rep.:* Aimee Snyder
1020 Commerce Park Dr., #1A, Williamsport, PA 17701-5434; 570-322-3961; Fax: 570-322-3965; *Constituent Services Rep.:* Jacque Bell
Committee Assignments: Foreign Affairs; Homeland Security; Judiciary

Massie, Thomas, R-Ky. (4)

Capitol Hill Office: 314 CHOB 20515; 225-3465; Fax: 225-0003; *Chief of Staff:* Hans Hoeg
Web: massie.house.gov
Facebook: www.facebook.com/RepThomasMassie
Twitter: @RepThomasMassie
District Offices: 1700 Greenup Ave., R-505, Ashland, KY 41101-7573; 606-324-9898; *Field Rep.:* J.R. Reed
541Buttermilk Pike, #208, Crescent Springs, KY 41017-3924; 859-426-0080; Fax: 859-426-0061; *Staff Asst.:* Christina Johnson
108 W. Jefferson St., LaGrange, KY 40031; 502-265-9119; Fax: 502-265-9126; *Western District Field Rep.:* Stacey Rockaway
Committee Assignments: Oversight and Government Reform; Science, Space, and Technology; Transportation and Infrastructure

Matsui, Doris, D-Calif. (6)

Capitol Hill Office: 2311 RHOB 20515-0506; 225-7163; Fax: 225-0566; *Chief of Staff:* Julie Eddy
Web: matsui.house.gov
Facebook: www.facebook.com/doris.matsui
Twitter: @dorismatsui
District Office: Robert T. Matsui U.S. Courthouse, 501 Eye St., #12-600, Sacramento, CA 95814-4778; 916-498-5600; Fax: 916-444-6117; *District Director:* Sam Stesanki
Committee Assignment: Energy and Commerce

McCarthy, Kevin, R-Calif. (23)

Capitol Hill Office: 2421 RHOB 20515; 225-2915; Fax: 225-2908; *Chief of Staff:* James B. Min
Web: kevinmccarthy.house.gov
Facebook: www.facebook.com/CongressmanKevinMc Carthy
Twitter: @GOPLeader
District Office: 4100 Empire Dr., #150, Bakersfield, CA 93309-0409; 661-327-3611; Fax: 661-637-0867; *District Director:* Vincent Fong
Majority Leader

McCaul, Michael, R-Tex. (10)

Capitol Hill Office: 131 CHOB 20515-4310; 225-2401; Fax: 225-5955; *Chief of Staff:* Chris Alsup
Web: mccaul.house.gov
Facebook: www.facebook.com/michaeltmccaul
Twitter: @RepMcCaul
District Offices: Austin Bldg., 9009 Mountain Ridge Dr., #230, Austin, TX 78759; 512-473-2357; Fax: 512-473-0514; *District Director:* Mary Elen Williams
Rosewood Professional Bldg., 990 Village Square Dr., Suite B, Tomball, TX 77375-4269; 281-255-8372; Fax: 281-255-0034; *Constituent Liaison/Caseworker:* Sherrie Meicher
Satellite Offices: Katy Commerce Center, 1773 Westborough Dr., #223, Katy, TX 77449; 281-398-1247; *Eastern District Field Director:* Holli Davies
2000 S. Market St., #303, Brenham, TX 77833-5800; 979-830-8497; Fax: 979-830-1984; *Constituent Liaison/Caseworker:* Marita Mikeska
Committee Assignments: Foreign Affairs; Homeland Security, Chair; Science, Space, and Technology

McClintock, Tom, R-Calif. (4)

Capitol Hill Office: 2331 RHOB 20515-0504; 225-2511; Fax: 225-5444; *Chief of Staff:* Igor Birman; *Deputy Chief of Staff:* Chris Tudor
Web: mcclintock.house.gov
Facebook: www.facebook.com/Congressman-Tom-McClintock-81125319109
Twitter: @RepMcClintock
District Office: 2200A Douglas Blvd., #240, Roseville, CA 95661; 916-786-5560; Fax: 916-786-6364; *District Director:* Rocklun Deal
Committee Assignments: Budget; Natural Resources

McCollum, Betty, D-Minn. (4)

Capitol Hill Office: 2256 RHOB 20515-2304; 225-6631; Fax: 225-1968; *Chief of Staff:* Bill Harper
Web: mccollum.house.gov
Facebook: www.facebook.com/repbettymccollum
Twitter: @BettyMcCollum04
District Office: 165 Western Ave. North, #17, St. Paul, MN 55102-4613; 651-224-9191; Fax: 651-224-3056; *District Director:* Joshua Straka
Committee Assignment: Appropriations

McDermott, Jim, D-Wash. (7)

Capitol Hill Office: 1035 LHOB 20515-4707; 225-3106; Fax: 225-6197; *Chief of Staff:* Diane M. Shust
Web: mcdermott.house.gov
Facebook: www.facebook.com/CongressmanJimMcDermott
Twitter: @RepJimMcDermott
District Office: 1809 7th Ave., #409, Seattle, WA 98101-1399; 206-553-7170; Fax: 206-553-7175; *Communications Director:* Daniel Rubin
Committee Assignments: Budget; Ways and Means

McGovern, Jim, D-Mass. (2)

Capitol Hill Office: 438 CHOB 20515-2103; 225-6101; Fax: 225-5759; *Chief of Staff:* Jennifer Chandler
Web: mcgovern.house.gov
Facebook: www.facebook.com/RepJimMcGovern
Twitter: @RepMcGovern
District Offices: 24 Church St., #29, Leominster, MA 01453; 978-466-3552; Fax: 978-466-3973; *District Rep.:* Eladia Romero
94 Pleasant St., Northhampton, MA 01060; 413-341-8700; Fax: 413-584-1216; *District Rep.:* Keith Barnacle
12 E. Worcester St., #1, Worcester, MA 01604; 508-831-7356; Fax: 508-754-0982; *District Director:* Kathleen Polanowicz
Committee Assignments: Agriculture; Rules

McHenry, Patrick, R-N.C. (10)

Capitol Hill Office: 2334 RHOB 20515; 225-2576; Fax: 225-0316; *Chief of Staff:* Sean Joyce
Web: mchenry.house.gov
Facebook: www.facebook.com/CongressmanMcHenry
Twitter: @PatrickMcHenry
District Offices: 128 W. Main Ave., #115, Gastonia, NC 28053; 704-833-0096; Fax: 828-833-8311; *Regional Director:* Brett Keeter
1990 Main Ave. S.E., P.O. Box 1830, Hickory, NC 28603; 828-327-6100; Fax: 828-327-8311; *Sr. District Rep.:* Nancy Meek
Satellite Office: 160 Midland Ave., Black Mountain, NC 28711; 828-669-0600; *Regional Director:* Roger Kumpf
Committee Assignment: Financial Services

McKinley, David, R-W. Va. (1)

Capitol Hill Office: 412 CHOB 20515; 225-4172; Fax: 225-7564; *Chief of Staff:* Mike Hamilton
Web: mckinley.house.gov
Facebook: www.facebook.com/RepMcKinley
Twitter: @RepMcKinley
District Offices: 709 Beechurst Ave., #29, Morgantown, WV 26505-4689; 304-284-8506; *District Director:* Rod Rogers
425 Juliana St., #1004, Parkersburg, WV 26101-5323; 304-422-5972; *Constituent Services Rep.:* Robert Villers
Horne Bldg., 1100 Main St., #101, Wheeling, WV 26003; 304-232-3801; Fax: 304-232-3813; *Constituent Services Rep.:* Chelsea Kisner
Committee Assignment: Energy and Commerce

McMorris Rodgers, Cathy, R-Wash. (5)

Capitol Hill Office: 203 CHOB 20515; 225-2006; Fax: 225-3392; *Chief of Staff:* David Peluso
Web: mcmorris.house.gov
Facebook: www.facebook.com/mcmorrisrodgers
Twitter: @cathymcmorris
District Offices: 555 S. Main St., Colville, WA 99114-2503; 509-684-3481; Fax: 509-684-3482; *Deputy District Director:* Sheila Stalp
10 N. Post St., #625, Spokane, WA 99201-0706; 509-353-2374; Fax: 509-234-0445; *Deputy District Director:* Louise Sendrich
26 E. Main St., #2, Walla Walla, WA 99362-1925; 509-529-9358; Fax: 509-529-9379; *Constituent Relations Liaison:* Cathy Schaeffer
Committee Assignment: Energy and Commerce; Republican Leadership, Chair

McNerney, Jerry, D-Calif. (9)

Capitol Hill Office: 2265 RHOB 20515-0511; 225-1947; Fax: 225-4060; *Chief of Staff:* Nicole Alioto
Web: mcnerney.house.gov
Facebook: www.facebook.com/jerrymcnerney
Twitter: @RepMcNerney
District Offices: Antioch Community Center, 4703 Lone Tree Way, Antioch, CA 94531; 925-754e0716; Fax: 925-754-0728; *District Director:* Alisa Alva
2222 Grand Canal Blvd., #7, Stockton, CA 95207-6671; 209-476-8552; Fax: 209-476-8587; *District Scheduler:* Emily Owen
Committee Assignments: Energy and Commerce; Veterans' Affairs

McSally, Martha, R-Ariz. (2)

Capitol Hill Office: 1029 LHOB 20515-0302; 225-2542; Fax: 225-0378; *Chief of Staff:* Justin Roth
Web: mcsally.house.gov
Facebook: www.facebook.com/RepMcSally
Twitter: @ReoMcSally
District Offices: 77 Calle Portal, #B-160, Sierra Vista, AZ 85635; 520-459-3115; Fax: 520-459-5419; *Constituent Services Rep.:* Cynthia Giesecke
4400 E. Broadway Blvd., #510, Tucson, AZ 85711; 520-881-3588; Fax 520-322-9490; *Constituent Services Rep.:* Rosa Montano
Committee Assignments: Armed Services; Homeland Security

Meadows, Mark, R-N.C. (11)

Capitol Hill Office: 1024 LHOB 20515; 225-6401; Fax: 226-6422; *Chief of Staff:* Paul Fitzpatrick
Web: meadows.house.gov
Facebook: www.facebook.com/Repmarkmeadows
Twitter: @RepMarkMeadows
District Offices: 200 N. Grove St., #90, Hendersonville, NC 28792; 828-693-5660; Fax: 828-693-5603; *Office Manager:* Pamela Ward

Committee Assignments: Foreign Affairs; Oversight and Government Reform; Transportation and Infrastructure

Meehan, Patrick, R-Pa. (7)

Capitol Hill Office: 434 CHOB 20515; 225-2011; Fax: 226-0820; *Chief of Staff:* Brian Schubert
Web: meehan.house.gov
Facebook: www.facebook.com/CongressmanPatrickMeehan
Twitter: @repmeehan
District Office: 940 W. Sproul Rd., Springfield, PA 19064-1255; 610-690-7323; Fax: 610-690-7329; *District Director:* Caitlin Ganley
Committee Assignments: Ethics; Ways and Means

Meeks, Gregory W., D-N.Y. (5)

Capitol Hill Office: 2234 RHOB 20515; 225-3461; Fax: 226-4169; *Chief of Staff:* Sofia Lafargue
Web: meeks.house.gov
Facebook: www.facebook.com/gregorymeeksny05
Twitter: @GregoryMeeks
District Offices: 67-12 Rockaway Beach Blvd., Arverne, NY 11692; 347-230-4032; Fax: 347-230-4045; *District Chief of Staff:* Robert Simmons
153-01 Jamaica Ave., 2nd Floor, Jamaica, NY 11432; 718-725-6000; Fax: 718-725-9868; *Executive Director:* Joe Edwards
Committee Assignments: Financial Services; Foreign Affairs

Meng, Grace, D-N.Y. (6)

Capitol Hill Office: 1317 LHOB 20515; 225-2601; Fax: 225-1589; *Chief of Staff:* David Bagby
Web: meng.house.gov
Facebook: www.facebook.com/repgracemeng
Twitter: @RepGraceMeng
District Offices: 40-13 159th St., Flushing, NY 11358; 718-445-7860; Fax: 718-445-7868; *Deputy District Director:* Anthony Lemma
118-35 Queens Blvd., 17th Floor, Forest Hills, NY 11375; 718-358-6364; Fax: 718-445-7868; *Deputy District Director:* Anthony Lemma
Committee Assignments: Foreign Affairs; Small Business

Messer, Luke, R-Ind. (6)

Capitol Hill Office: 508 CHOB 20515; 225-3021; Fax: 225-3382; *Chief of Staff:* Doug Menorca
Web: messer.house.gov
Facebook: www.facebook.com/RepLukeMesser
Twitter: @RepLukeMesser
District Offices: 107 W. Charles St., Munice, IN 47305-2420; 765-747-5566; Fax: 765-747-5586; *District Director:* John Hatter
2 Public Square, Shelbyville, IN 46176; 317-421-0704; Fax: 317-421-0739; *Field Rep.:* Tim Hawkins
Satellite Office: 50 N. 5th St., Richmond, IN 47374-4247; 765-962-2883; Fax: 765-962-3225; *Field Rep.:* Brandon Searcy
Committee Assignments: Education and the Workforce; Financial Services

Mica, John, R-Fla. (7)

Capitol Hill Office: 2187 RHOB 20515; 225-4035; Fax: 226-0821; *Chief of Staff:* Wiley Deck
Web: mica.house.gov
Facebook: www.facebook.com/JohnMica
Twitter: @micaforcongress
District Offices: 840 Deltona Blvd., Suite G, Deltona, FL 32725; 386-860-1499; Fax: 386-860-5730; *District Rep.:* Barry Cotton
100 E. Sybelia Ave., #340, Maitland, FL 32751-4495; 407-657-8080; Fax: 407-657-5353; *District Rep.:* Leslie O'Shaughnessy
95 E. Mitchell Hammock Rd., #202, Oviedo, FL 32765; 407-366-0833; Fax: 407-366-0839; *District Rep.:* Patrick Kelly
Committee Assignments: Oversight and Government Reform; Transportation and Infrastructure

Miller, Candice S., R-Mich. (10)

Capitol Hill Office: 320 CHOB 20515; 225-2106; Fax: 226-1169; *Chief of Staff:* Salley Wood
Web: candicemiller.house.gov
Facebook: www.facebook.com/CongresswomanCandiceMiller
Twitter: @CandiceMiller
District Office: 48701 Van Dyke Ave., Shelby Township, MI 48317-2562; 586-997-5010; Fax: 586-997-5013; *District Director:* Karen Czernel
Committee Assignments: House Administration, Chair; Homeland Security; Joint Library; Joint Printing; Transportation and Infrastructure

Miller, Jeff, R-Fla. (1)

Capitol Hill Office: 336 CHOB 20515; 225-4136; Fax: 225-3414; *Chief of Staff:* Daniel F. McFaul
Web: jeffmiller.house.gov
Facebook: www.facebook.com/RepJeffMiller
Twitter: @RepJeffMiller
District Offices: 348 Miracle Strip Pkwy. S.W., #24, Fort Walton Beach, FL 32548-5263; 850-664-1266; Fax: 850-664-0851; *Field Rep.:* Bob Black
4300 Bayou Blvd., #13, Pensacola, FL 32503-2671; 850-479-1183; Fax: 850-479-9394; *District Director:* Sheilah Bowman
Committee Assignments: Armed Services; Permanent Select Intelligence; Veterans' Affairs, Chair

Moolenaar, John, R-Mich. (4)

Capitol Hill Office: 117 CHOB 20515-2204; 225-3561; Fax: 225-9679; *Chief of Staff:* Ryan Tarrant
Web: moolenaar.house.gov
Facebook: www.facebook.com/RepMoolenaar
Twitter: @repmoolenaar
District Office: 200 E. Main St., #230, Midland, MI 48640; 989-631-2552; Fax: 989-631-6271; *District Director:* Ashton Bortz
201 N. Mitchell St., #301, Cadillac, MI 49601; 231-942-5070; Fax: 231-876-9505; *Staff:* Vacant
Committee Assignments: Agriculture; Budget; Science, Space and Technology

Mooney, Alex, R-W.V. (2)

Capitol Hill Office: 1232 LHOB 20515-4802; 225-2711; Fax: 225-7856; *Chief of Staff:* Brian Chatman
Web: mooney.house.gov
Facebook: www.facebook.com/CongressmanAlexMooney
Twitter: @RepAlexMooney
District Offices: 405 Capitol St., #514, Charleston, WV 25301; 304-925-5964; Fax: 304-926-8912; *District Director:* Fred Joseph
300 Foxcroft Ave., #102, Martinsburg, WV 25401; 304-264-8810; Fax: 304-264-8815; *Eastern Panhandle Director:* Steve Smoot
Committee Assignments: Budget; Natural Resources

Moore, Gwen, D-Wisc. (4)

Capitol Hill Office: 2245 RHOB 20515-4904; 225-4572; Fax: 225-8135; *Chief of Staff:* Minh Ta
Web: gwenmoore.house.gov
Facebook: www.facebook.com/GwenSMoore
Twitter: @RepGwenMoore
District Office: 316 N. Milwaukee St., #406, Milwaukee, WI 53202-5818; 414-297-1140; Fax: 414-297-1086; *District Director:* Shirley Ellis
Committee Assignments: Budget; Financial Services

Moulton, Seth, D-Mass. (6)

Capitol Hill Office: 1408 LHOB 20515-2106; 225-8020; Fax: 225-5915; *Chief of Staff:* Roger Dean Huffstetler
Web: moulton.house.gov
Facebook: www.facebook.com/RepMoulton
Twitter: @TeamMoulton
District Office: 21 Front St., Salem, MA 01970; 978-531-1669; Fax: 978-717-5463; *District Director:* Rick Jakious
Committee Assignments: Armed Services; Budget; Small Business

Mullin, Markwayne, R-Okla. (2)

Capitol Hill Office: 1113 LHOB 20515; 225-2701; Fax: 225-3038; *Chief of Staff:* Karl Ahlgren
Web: mullin.house.gov
Facebook: www.facebook.com/RepMullin
Twitter: @RepMullin
District Offices: 1 E. Choctaw, #175, McAlester, OK 74501; 918-423-5951; Fax: 918-423-1940; *Field Rep.:* Betty Ford
3109 Azalea Park Dr., Muskogee, OK 74401-6614; 918-687-2533; Fax: 918-686-0128; *Caseworker:* Mary Bower
Committee Assignment: Energy and Commerce

Mulvaney, Mick, R-S.C. (5)

Capitol Hill Office: 2419 RHOB 20515-4005; 225-5501; Fax: 225-0464; *Chief of Staff:* Al Simpson
Web: mulvaney.house.gov
Facebook: www.facebook.com/MulvaneySC5
Twitter: @RepMickMulvaney
District Offices: 110 Railroad Ave., Gaffney, SC 29340; 864-206-6004; Fax: 864-206-6005; *Constituent Services Director:* Park Gillespie

1456 Ebenezer Rd., Rock Hill, SC 29732-2339; 803-327-1114; Fax: 803-327-4330; *District Director:* Jeffery Sligh
531-A Oxford Dr., Sumter, SC 29150; 803-774-0186; Fax: 803-774-0188; *Field Rep.:* Bobbie Williams
Committee Assignments: Financial Services; Oversight and Government Reform

Murphy, Patrick, D-Fla. (18)

Capitol Hill Office: 211 CHOB 20515; 225-3026; Fax: 225-8398; *Chief of Staff:* Eric Johnson
Web: patrickmurphy.house.gov
Facebook: www.facebook.com/CongressmanPatrickMurphy
Twitter: @RepMurphyFL
District Offices: 2000 PGA Blvd., #A3220, Palm Beach Gardens, FL 33408; 561-253-8433; Fax: 561-253-8436; *District Director:* Michael Kenny
121 S.W. Port St. Lucie Blvd., #187, Port St. Lucie, FL 34984; 772-336-2877; Fax: 772-336-2899; *Constituent Services Reps.:* Kalene Rowley and Jack Foster
171 S.W. Flagler Ave., Stuart, FL 34994 772-781-3266; Fax: 772-781-3267; *Constituent Services Reps.:* Kalene Rowley and Jack Foster
2300 Virginia Ave., #200A, Fort Pierce, FL 34982; 772-489-0736; Fax: 772-464-8392; *Constituent Services Reps.:* Kalene Rowley and Jack Foster
Committee Assignments: Financial Services; Permanent Select Intelligence

Murphy, Tim, R-Pa. (18)

Capitol Hill Office: 2332 RHOB 20515; 225-2301; Fax: 225-1844; *Chief of Staff:* Susan Mosychuk
Web: murphy.house.gov
Facebook: www.facebook.com/reptimmurphy
Twitter: @RepTimMurphy
District Offices: 2040 Frederickson Pl., Greensburg, PA 15601-9688; 724-850-7312; Fax: 724-850-7315; *Deputy Chief of Staff:* Lou Lazzaro
504 Washington Rd., Pittsburgh, PA 15228-2817; 412-344-5583; Fax: 412-429-5092; *Caseworker:* John Stinner
Committee Assignment: Energy and Commerce

Nadler, Jerrold, D-N.Y. (10)

Capitol Hill Office: 2110 RHOB 20515; 225-5635; Fax: 225-6923; *Washington Director; Administrative Asst.:* John Doty
Web: nadler.house.gov
Facebook: www.facebook.com/CongressmanNadler
Twitter: @RepJerryNadler
District Offices: 6605 Fort Hamilton Pkwy., Brooklyn, NY 11219; 718-373-3198; Fax: 718-996-0039; *Brooklyn Director:* Robert Gottheim
201 Varick St., #669, New York, NY 10014-7069; 212-367-7350; Fax: 212-367-7356; *Chief of Staff:* Amy Rutkin
Committee Assignments: Judiciary; Transportation and Infrastructure

Napolitano, Grace F., D-Calif. (32)

Capitol Hill Office: 1610 LHOB 20515-0538; 225-5256; Fax: 225-0027; *Chief of Staff:* Daniel S. Chao
Web: napolitano.house.gov
Facebook: www.facebook.com/RepGraceNapolitano
Twitter: @gracenapolitano
District Office: 4401 Santa Anita Ave., #201, El Monte, CA 91731; 626-350-0150; Fax: 626-350-0450; *District Director:* Perla Hernandez Trumkul
Committee Assignments: Natural Resources; Transportation and Infrastructure

Neal, Richard E., D-Mass. (1)

Capitol Hill Office: 341 CHOB 20515-2102; 225-5601; Fax: 225-8112; *Chief of Staff:* Ann M. Jablon
Web: neal.house.gov
Facebook: www.facebook.com/Congressman-Richard-Neal-325642654132598
Twitter: @RepRichardNeal
District Offices: 78 Center St., Pittsfield, MA 01201; 413-442-0946; Fax: 413-443-2792; *District Director:* William Powers
300 State St., #200, Springfield, MA 01105-1711; 413-785-0325; Fax: 413-747-0604; *Scheduler:* Elizabeth Quigley
Committee Assignment: Ways and Means

Neugebauer, Randy, R-Tex. (19)

Capitol Hill Office: 1424 LHOB 20515-4319; 225-4005; Fax: 225-9615; *Chief of Staff:* Jeanette Whitener
Web: randy.house.gov
Facebook: www.facebook.com/rep.randy.neugebauer
Twitter: @RandyNeugebauer
District Offices: 500 Chestnut St., #819, Abilene, TX 79602-1453; 325-675-9779; Fax: 325-675-5038; *District Rep.:* Bobbi Hanson
1510 Scurry St., Suite B, Big Spring, TX 79720-4441; 432-264-0722; Fax: 432-264-1838; *District Rep.:* Lisa Brooks
611 University Ave., #220, Lubbock, TX 79401-2206; 806-763-1611; Fax: 806-767-9168; *District Director:* Jay Ibarra
Committee Assignments: Agriculture; Financial Services; Science, Space, and Technology

Newhouse, Dan, R-Wash. (4)

Capitol Hill Office: 1641 LHOB 20515-4704; 225-5816; Fax: 225-3251; *Chief of Staff:* Carrie Meadows
Web: newhouse.house.gov
Facebook: www.facebook.com/RepNewhouse
Twitter: @repnewhouse
District Office: 402 E. Yakima Ave., #445, Yakima, WA 98901; 509-452-3243; Fax: 509-452-3438; *District Director:* Sharra Finley
3100 George Washington Way, #135, Richland, WA 99354; 509-713-7374; Fax: 509-713-7377; *District Rep.:* Josh Lozano
Committee Assignments: Agriculture; Natural Resources; Rules

Noem, Kristi, R-S.D. (At Large)

Capitol Hill Office: 1323 LHOB 20515; 225-2801; Fax: 225-5823; *Chief of Staff:* Jordan Stoick
Web: noem.house.gov
Facebook: www.facebook.com/kristiforcongress
Twitter: @RepKristiNoem
District Offices: 343 Quincy St., Rapid City, SD 57701-3797; 605-791-4673; Fax: 605-791-4679; *West River Director:* Brad Otten
300 N. Dakota Ave., #314, Sioux Falls, SD 57104; 605-275-2868; Fax: 605-275-2875; *Southeast Area Director:* Andrew Curley
818 S. Broadway, #113, Watertown, SD 57201; 605-878-2868; Fax: 605-878-2871; *Northeast Director, Watertown:* Mary Beth Hollatz
Committee Assignment: Ways and Means

Nolan, Rick, D-Minn. (8)

Capitol Hill Office: 2447 RHOB 20515; 225-6211; Fax: 225-0699; *Chief of Staff:* Jodie Torkelson
Web: nolan.house.gov
Facebook: www.facebook.com/UsRepRickNolan
Twitter: @USRepRickNolan
District Office: 11 E. Superior St., #125, Duluth, MN 55802; 218-464-5095; Fax: 218-464-5098; *District Director:* Jeff Anderson
Satellite Offices: 501 Laurel St., Brainerd, MN 56401-3595; 218-454-4078; Fax: 218-454-4096; *Constituent Services and Field Rep.:* Tom Whiteside
313 N. Main St., #103, Center City, MN 55012; 218-491-3131; *Field Rep.:* Rick Olseen
316 W. Lake St., #7, Chisholm, MN 55719; 218-491-3114; *Field Rep.:* Jordan Metsa
Committee Assignments: Agriculture; Transportation and Infrastructure

Norcross, Donald, R-N.J. (1)

Capitol Hill Office: 1531 LHOB 20515-3001; 225-6501; Fax: 225-6583; *Chief of Staff:* Michael Maitland
Web: norcross.house.gov
Facebook: www.facebook.com/DonaldNorcrossNJ
Twitter: @DonaldNorcross
District Office: 10 Melrose Ave., #210, Cherry Hill, NJ 08003; 856-427-7000; Fax: 856-427-4109; *District Director:* Karl Parker
Committee Assignments: Armed Services; Budget

Norton, Eleanor Holmes, D-D.C. (At Large)

Capitol Hill Office: 2136 RHOB 20515-5101; 225-8050; Fax: 225-3002; *Chief of Staff:* Raven Reeder
Web: norton.house.gov
Facebook: www.facebook.com/CongresswomanNorton
Twitter: @eleanornorton
District Offices: 2041 Martin Luther King Jr. Ave. S.E., #238, Washington, DC 20020-7005; 202-678-8900; Fax: 202-678-8844; *District Director:* Tristan Breaux
90 K St. N.E., #100, Washington, DC 20001; 202-408-9041; Fax: 202-408-9048; *District Director:* Tristan Breaux
Committee Assignments: Oversight and Government Reform; Transportation and Infrastructure

Nugent, Richard, R-Fla. (11)

Capitol Hill Office: 1727 LHOB 20515; 225-1002;
Fax: 226-6559; *Chief of Staff:* Justin Grabelle
Web: nugent.house.gov
Facebook: www.facebook.com/RepRichNugent
Twitter: @RepRichNugent
District Offices: 115 25th Ave. S.E., Ocala, FL 34471; 352-
351-1670; Fax: 352-351-1674; *Constituent Services
Rep.:* Shawna Williams
11035 Spring Hill Dr., Spring Hill, FL 34608; 352-684-
4446; Fax: 352-684-4484; *Constituent Services
Supervisor:* Janice Rickarts
8015 E. CR-466, The Villages, FL 32162; 352-689-4684;
Fax: 352-689-4621 *Constituent Services Rep.:*
Al Harrison
Satellite Office: 212 W. Main St., #204, Inverness, FL
34450; 352-341-2354; Fax: 352-341-2316
Committee Assignments: Armed Services; House
Administration

Nunes, Devin, R-Calif. (22)

Capitol Hill Office: 1013 LHOB 20515-0521; 225-2523;
Fax: 225-3404; *Chief of Staff:* Anthony Ratekin
Web: nunes.house.gov
Facebook: www.facebook.com/ Congressman-Devin-
Nunes-376470350795
Twitter: @DevinNunes
District Offices: 264 Clovis Ave., #206, Clovis, CA 93612-
1115; 559-323-5235; Fax: 559-323-5528; *Field Rep.:*
Anneka Sweeney
113 N. Church St., #208, Visalia, CA 93291-6300; 559-733-
3861; Fax: 559-733-3865; *Constituent Liaison:*
Melissa Semoes
Committee Assignments: Permanent Select Intelligence,
Chair; Ways and Means

Olson, Pete, R-Tex. (22)

Capitol Hill Office: 312 CHOB 20515-4322; 225-5951;
Fax: 225-5241; *Chief of Staff:* Tyler Nelson
Web: olson.house.gov
Facebook: www.facebook.com/PeteOlsonTX
Twitter: @PeteOlson
District Offices: 6302 W. Broadway St., #220, Pearland, TX
77581; 281-485-4855; Fax: 281-485-4850; *Field Rep.:*
Kial Vidic
1650 Hwy. 6, #150, Sugar Land, TX 77478-4921; 281-494-
2690; Fax: 281-494-2649; *District Director:*
Robert Quarles
Satellite Office: 22333 Grand Corner Dr., #151, Katy, TX
77494; 281-889-7134;
Committee Assignment: Energy and Commerce

O'Rourke, Beto, D-Tex. (16)

Capitol Hill Office: 1330 LHOB 20515; 225-4831;
Fax: 225-2016; *Chief of Staff:* David Wysong
Web: orourke.house.gov
Facebook: www.facebook.com/BetoORourkeTX16
Twitter: @RepBetoORourke

District Office: 303 N. Oregon St., #210, El Paso, TX
79901-1301; 915-541-1400; Fax: 915-541-1407; *District
Director:* Cynthia Cano
Committee Assignments: Armed Services; Veterans'
Affairs

Palazzo, Steven, R-Miss. (4)

Capitol Hill Office: 331 CHOB 20515-2404; 225-5772;
Fax: 225-7074; *Chief of Staff:* Casey Street
Web: palazzo.house.gov
Facebook: www.facebook.com/stevenpalazzo
Twitter: @congpalazzo
District Offices: 970 Tommy Munro Dr., Suite D, Biloxi,
MS 39532; 228-864-7670; Fax: 228-864-3099; Deputy
Chief of Staff; *District Director:* Hunter Lipscomb
641 Main St., #142, Hattiesburg, MS 39401-3478; 601-582-
3246; *Office Manager:* Anita Bourne
3118 Pascagoula St., #181, Pascagoula, MS 39567-4215;
228-202-8104; Fax: 228-202-8105; *Constituent
Liaison:* Debora Nelson
Committee Assignments: Approriations

Pallone, Frank, Jr., D-N.J. (6)

Capitol Hill Office: 237 CHOB 20515-3006; 225-4671;
Fax: 225-9665; *Deputy Chief of Staff:* Brian Laughlin
Web: pallone.house.gov
Facebook: www.facebook.com/RepFrankPallone
Twitter: @FrankPallone
District Offices: 504 Broadway, Long Branch, NJ 07740-
5951; 732-571-1140; Fax: 732-870-3890; *Chief of Staff:*
Janice Fuller
Kilmer Square, 67-69 Church St., New Brunswick, NJ
08901; 732-249-8892; Fax: 732-249-1335; *Constituent
Services Director:* Alexandra Maldonado
Committee Assignment: Energy and Commerce, Ranking
Minority Member

Palmer, Gary, R-Ala. (6)

Capitol Hill Office: 206 CHOB 20515-0106; 225-4921;
Fax: 225-2082; *Chief of Staff:* William Smith
Web: palmer.house.gov
Facebook: www.facebook.com/
USRepresentativeGaryPalmer
Twitter: @USRepGaryPalmer
District Office: 703 2nd Ave. North, P.O. Box 502,
Clanton, AL 35243; 205-280-6846; Fax: 205-968-1294;
District Director: Ray Melik
3535 Grandview Pkwy., #525, Birmingham, AL 35243;
205-968-1290; Fax: 205-968-1294; *District Director:*
Ray Melick
202 3rd Ave., Oneonta, AL 35121; 205-274-2136; *District
Director:* Ray Melik
Committee Assignments: Budget; Oversight and
Government Reform; Science, Space, and Technology

Pascrell, Bill, Jr., D-N.J. (9)

Capitol Hill Office: 2370 RHOB 20515-3008; 225-5751;
Fax: 225-5782; *Chief of Staff:* Benjamin Rich
Web: pascrell.house.gov

Facebook: www.facebook.com/pascrell
Twitter: @BillPascrell
District Offices: 330 Passaic St., 1st Floor, Passaic, NJ 07055-5815; 973-472-4510; Fax: 973-472-0852; *Field Rep.:* Celia Anderson
200 Federal Plaza, #500, Paterson, NJ 07505-1999; 973-523-5152; Fax: 973-523-0637; *Deputy Chief of Staff:* Assad Akhter
Satellite Offices: 367 Valley Brook Ave., Lyndhurst, NJ 07071; 201-935-2248; *Caseworker:* Shannon McGee
2-10 N. Van Brunt St., Englewood, NJ 07631; 201-935-2248; *Caseworker:* Shannon McGee
Committee Assignments: Budget; Ways and Means

Paulsen, Erik, R-Minn. (3)

Capitol Hill Office: 127 CHOB 20515-2303; 225-2871; Fax: 225-6351; *Chief of Staff:* Laurie Esau
Web: paulsen.house.gov
Facebook: www.facebook.com/CongressmanErikPaulsen
Twitter: @RepErikPaulsen
District Office: 250 Prairie Center Dr., #230, Eden Prairie, MN 55344-7909; 952-405-8510; Fax: 952-405-8514; *District Director:* John Paul Yates
Committee Assignment: Ways and Means, Joint Economic

Payne, Donald M., Jr., D-N.J. (10)

Capitol Hill Office: 103 CHOB 20515; 225-3436; Fax: 225-4160; *Chief of Staff:* LaVerne Alexander
Web: payne.house.gov
Facebook: www.facebook.com/DonaldPayneJr
Twitter: @RepDonaldPayne
District Offices: 253 Martin Luther King Jr. Dr., Jersey City, NJ 07305-3427; 201-369-0392; Fax: 201-369-0395; *Constituent Service Asst.:* Elizabeth Lorenzo
60 Nelson Pl., 14th Floor, Newark, NJ 07102; 973-645-3213; Fax: 973-645-5902; *District Director:* Michael Gray
Committee Assignments: Homeland Security; Small Business

Pearce, Stevan, R-N.M. (2)

Capitol Hill Office: 2432 RHOB 20515-3102; 225-2365; Fax: 225-9509; *Chief of Staff:* Todd D. Willens
Web: pearce.house.gov
Facebook: www.facebook.com/RepStevePearce
Twitter: @repstevepearce
District Offices: 1101 New York Ave., Room 115, Alamogordo, NM 88310-6923; 855-473-2723; *District Director:* Barbara Romero
200 E. Broadway St., #200, Hobbs, NM 88240-8425; 855-473-2723; *Field Rep.:* Bernadette Granger
570 N. Telshor Blvd., Las Cruces, NM 88011-8223; 575-522-0771; Fax: 575-522-0855; *District Director. Office Manager:* Mary Morris
3445 Lambros Loop, N.E., Los Lunas, NM 87031-6472; 855-473-2723; *Field Rep.:* Bridget Condon

1717 W. 2nd St., #110, Roswell, NM 88201-2029; 855-473-2723; *Field Rep.:* Gloria Salas
111 School of Mines Rd., Socorro, NM 87801-4533; 855-473-2723; Fax: 575-835-8985; *District Director:* Barbara Romero
Committee Assignment: Financial Services

Pelosi, Nancy, D-Calif. (12)

Capitol Hill Office: 233 CHOB 20515-0508; 225-4965; Fax: 225-8259; *Chief of Staff:* Nadeam Elshami
Web: pelosi.house.gov
Facebook: www.facebook.com/NancyPelosi
Twitter: @NancyPelosi
District Office: 90 7th St., #2-800, San Francisco, CA 94103-6723; 415-556-4862; Fax: 415-861-1670; *Chief of Staff:* Dan Bernal
Democratic Minority Leader

Perlmutter, Ed, D-Colo. (7)

Capitol Hill Office: 1410 LHOB 20515; 225-2645; Fax: 225-5278; *Chief of Operations:* Alison Inderfurth
Web: perlmutter.house.gov
Facebook: www.facebook.com/RepPerlmutter
Twitter: @repperlmutter
District Office: 12600 W. Colfax Ave., #B400, Lakewood, CO 80215-3779; 303-274-7944; Fax: 303-274-6455; *Chief of Staff:* Danielle Radovich-Piper
Committee Assignments: Financial Services; Science, Space, and Technology

Perry, Scott, R-Pa. (4)

Capitol Hill Office: 1207 LHOB 20515; 225-5836; Fax: 226-1000; *Chief of Staff:* Lauren Muglia
Web: perry.house.gov
Facebook: www.facebook.com/repscottperry
Twitter: @RepScottPerry
District Offices: 22 Chambersburg St., Gettysburg, PA 17325; 717-338-1919; Fax: 717-334-6314; *Constituent Services Rep.:* Holly Sutphin
730 N. Front St., Wormleysburg, PA 17043; 717-635-9504; Fax: 717-635-9861; *Director of Constituent Services:* Tyra Wallace
2209 E. Market St., York, PA 17402; 717-600-1919; Fax: 717-757-5001; *District Rep.:* Bob Reilly
Committee Assignments: Foreign Affairs; Homeland Security; Transportation and Infrastructure

Peters, Scott H., D-Calif. (52)

Capitol Hill Office: 1122 LHOB 20515-0550; 225-0508; Fax: 225-2558; *Chief of Staff:* Michelle Dorothy
Web: scottpeters.house.gov
Facebook: www.facebook.com/CongressmanScottPeters
Twitter: @RepScottPeters
District Office: 4350 Executive Dr., #105, San Diego, CA 92121; 858-455-5550; Fax: 858-455-5516; *District Director:* MaryAnne Pintar
Committee Assignments: Armed Services; Judiciary

Peterson, Collin C., D-Minn. (7)

Capitol Hill Office: 2109 RHOB 20515-2307; 225-2165; Fax: 225-1593; *Deputy Chief of Staff, Legislative Director:* Adam Durand
Web: collinpeterson.house.gov
Facebook: www.facebook.com/Collin-Peterson-6595227967
Twitter: @collinpeterson
District Offices: 714 Lake Ave., #107, Detroit Lakes, MN 56501-3057; 218-847-5056; Fax: 218-847-5109; *Chief of Staff, Communications Director:* Allison Myhre
1420 E. College Dr. S.W. / WC, Marshall, MN 56258-2065; 507-537-2299; Fax: 507-537-2298; *Staff Asst.:* Meg Louwagie
100 N. 1st St., Montevideo, MN 56265; 320-235-1061; *Staff Asst.:* Tom Meium
324 3rd St. S.W., #4, Willmar, MN 56201-3696; 320-235-1061; Fax: 320-235-2651; *Staff Asst.:* Mary Bertram
Committee Assignment: Agriculture, Ranking Minority Member

Pierluisi, Pedro, D-P.R. (At Large)

Capitol Hill Office: 2410 RHOB 20515-5401; 225-2615; Fax: 225-2154; *Chief of Staff:* Carmen M. Feliciano
Web: pierluisi.house.gov
Facebook: www.facebook.com/pedropierluisi
Twitter: @pedropierluisi
District Office: 157 Ave. de la Constitución, Ant. Edif. Medicina Tropical, San Juan, Puerto Rico 00901; 787-723-6333; Fax: 787-729-7738; *District Director:* Rosemarie Vizcarrondo
Committee Assignments: Judiciary; Natural Resources

Pingree, Chellie, D-Maine (1)

Capitol Hill Office: 2162 RHOB 20515-1901; 225-6116; Fax: 225-5590; *Chief of Staff:* Jesse Connolly
Web: pingree.house.gov
Facebook: www.facebook.com/ChelliePingree
Twitter: @chelliepingree
District Office: 2 Portland Fish Pier, #304, Portland, ME 04101; 207-774-5019; Fax: 207-871-0720; *Deputy Director of Communications:* Andrew Colvin
1 Silver St., Waterville, ME 04901; 207-873-5713; Fax: 207-873-5717; *Field Rep.:* Pamela Trinward
Committee Assignment: Appropriations

Pittenger, Robert, R-N.C. (9)

Capitol Hill Office: 224 CHOB 20515; 225-1976; Fax: 225-3389; *Chief of Staff:* Brad Jones
Web: pittenger.house.gov
Facebook: www.facebook.com/congressmanpittenger
Twitter: @RepPittenger
District Offices: 2701 Coltsgate Rd., #105, Charlotte, NC 28211; 704-362-1060; Fax: 704-365-6384; *District Director:* Robert Becker
116 Morlake Dr., #101A, Mooresville, NC 28117; 704-696-8188; Fax: 704-696-8190; *Regional Constituent Rep.:* Preston Curtis
Committee Assignment: Financial Services

Pitts, Joe, R-Pa. (16)

Capitol Hill Office: 420 CHOB 20515-3816; 225-2411; Fax: 225-2013; *Chief of Staff:* Gabe Neville
Web: pitts.house.gov
Facebook: www.facebook.com/CongressmanJoePitts
Twitter: @RepJoePitts
District Offices: 150 N. Queen St., #716, Lancaster, PA 17603-3562; 717-393-0667; Fax: 717-393-0924; *District Chief of Staff:* Thomas Tillett
Reading City Hall, 815 Washington St., Room 2-36, Reading, PA 19601; 610-374-3637; Fax: 610-444-5750; *Casework Asst.:* Jesse Stoepker
Committee Assignments: Commission on Security and Cooperation in Europe; Energy and Commerce

Plaskett, Stacey, D-Virgin Islands (At Large)

Capitol Hill Office: 509 CHOB 20515-5501; 225-1790; Fax: 225-5517; *Chief of Staff:* D. Jerry Garcia
Web: plaskett.house.gov
Facebook: www.facebook.com/repstaceyplaskett
Twitter: @staceyplaskett
District Office: 60 King St., Frederiksted, VI 00840; 340-778-5900; Fax: 340-778-5111; *District Director:* Elizabeth Centeno
9100 Port of Sale, #22, St. Thomas, VI 00802; 340-774-4408; Fax: 340-774-8033; *Field Rep.:* Vacant
Committee Assignments: Agriculture; Oversight and Government Reform

Pocan, Mark, D-Wisc. (2)

Capitol Hill Office: 313 CHOB 20515; 225-2906; Fax: 225-6942; *Chief of Staff:* Glenn Wavrunek
Web: pocan.house.gov
Facebook: www.facebook.com/repmarkpocan
Twitter: @repmarkpocan
District Office: 10 E. Doty St., #405, Madison, WI 53703-5103; 608-258-9800; Fax: 608-258-0377; *District Director:* Dane Varese
100 State St., 3rd Floor, Beloit, WI 53511; 608-365-8001; *District Director:* Dane Varese
Committee Assignments: Budget; Education and the Workforce

Poe, Ted, R-Tex. (2)

Capitol Hill Office: 2412 RHOB 20515; 225-6565; Fax: 225-5547; *Chief of Staff:* Gina Santucci
Web: poe.house.gov
Facebook: www.facebook.com/JudgeTedPoe
Twitter: @JudgeTedPoe
District Offices: 1801 Kingwood Dr., #240, Kingwood, TX 77339-3058; 281-446-0242; Fax: 281-446-0252; *Caseworker:* Amy Harrison
Committee Assignments: Foreign Affairs; Judiciary

Poliquin, Bruce, R-Maine. (2)

Capitol Hill Office: 426 CHOB 20515-1902; 225-6306; Fax: 225-2943; *Chief of Staff:* Matt Hutson
Web: poliquin.house.gov

Facebook: www.facebook.com/RepPoliquin
Twitter: @RepPoliquin
District Office: 631 Main St., #2, Presque Isle, ME 04769; 207-764-1968; Fax: 202-764-2822; *District Director:* Samantha Warren
179 Lisbon St., Lewiston, ME 04240; 207-784-0768; Fax: 207-784-5672; *District Director:* Samantha Warren
6 State St., #101, Bangor, ME 04401; 207-942-0583; Fax: 207-942-7101; *District Director:* Samantha Warren
Committee Assignment: Financial Services

Polis, Jared, D-Colo. (2)

Capitol Hill Office: 1433 LHOB 20515; 225-2161; Fax: 226-7840; *Chief of Staff:* Eve Lieberman
Web: polis.house.gov
Facebook: www.facebook.com/jaredpolis
Twitter: @RepJaredPolis
District Offices: 1644 Walnut St., Boulder, CO 80303-2668; 303-484-9596; Fax: 303-568-9007; *District Director:* Lisa Kaufmann
101 W. Main St., #101G, P.O. Box 1453, Frisco, CO 80443; 970-668-3240; Fax: 970-668-9679; *District Rep.:* Nissa Erickson
1220 S. College Ave., Fort Collins, CO 80525; 970-226-1239; Fax: 970-226-8597; *District Rep.:* Mara Brosy-Wiwecher
Committee Assignments: Education and the Workforce; Natural Resources; Rules

Pompeo, Mike, R-Kans. (4)

Capitol Hill Office: 436 CHOB 20515-1604; 225-6216; Fax: 225-3489; *Chief of Staff:* Jim Richardson
Web: pompeo.house.gov
Facebook: www.facebook.com/CongressmanPompeo
Twitter: @repmikepompeo
District Office: 7701 E. Kellogg Dr., #510, Wichita, KS 67207-1722; 316-262-8992; Fax: 316-262-5309; *Chief of Staff:* Jim Richardson
Committee Assignments: Energy and Commerce; Permanent Select Intelligence; Select on Benghazi

Posey, Bill, R-Fla. (8)

Capitol Hill Office: 120 CHOB 20515-0915; 225-3671; Fax: 225-3516; *Chief of Staff:* Marcus Brubaker
Web: posey.house.gov
Facebook: www.facebook.com/bill.posey15
Twitter: @CongBillPosey
District Office: 2725 Judge Fran Jamieson Way, Bldg. C, Melbourne, FL 32940-6605; 321-632-1776; Fax: 321-639-8595; *Scheduler; Community Relations Director:* Patrick Gavin
Committee Assignments: Financial Services; Science, Space, and Technology

Price, David E., D-N.C. (4)

Capitol Hill Office: 20515-3304; 225-1784; Fax: 225-2014; *Chief of Staff:* Asher Hildebrand

Web: price.house.gov
Facebook: www.facebook.com/David-Price-8338225975
Twitter: @RepDavidEPrice
District Offices: 1777 Fordham Blvd., #204, Chapel Hill, NC 27514; 919-967-7924; Fax: 919-967-8324; *District Director:* Asher Hildebrand
301 Green St., #315, Fayetteville, NC 28301; 910-323-0260; Fax: 910-339-0159; *Constituent Services Liaison:* William Munn
436 N. Harrington St., #100, Raleigh, NC 27603; 919-859-5999; Fax: 919-859-5998; *Constituent Services Liaison:* Robyn Winneberger
Committee Assignment: Appropriations

Price, Tom, R-Ga. (6)

Capitol Hill Office: 100 CHOB 20515; 225-4501; Fax: 225-4656; *Chief of Staff:* Kris Skrzycki
Web: tomprice.house.gov
Facebook: www.facebook.com/reptomprice
Twitter: @RepTomPrice
District Office: 85-C Mill St., #300, Roswell, GA 30075; 770-998-0049; Fax: 770-998-0500; *District Director:* Kyle McGowan
Committee Assignments: Budget, Chair; Ways and Means

Quigley, Mike, D-Ill. (5)

Capitol Hill Office: 1124 LHOB 20515-1305; 225-4061; Fax: 225-5603; *Chief of Staff:* Juan Hinojosa
Web: quigley.house.gov
Facebook: www.facebook.com/repmikequigley
Twitter: @RepMikeQuigley
District Office: 3223 N. Sheffield Ave., Chicago, IL 60657; 773-267-5926; *District Director:* Mary Ann Levar
4345 N. Milwaukee Ave., Chicago, IL 60641; 773-267-5926; Fax: 773-267-6583; *District Director:* Mary Ann Levar
Committee Assignments: Appropriations; Permanent Select Intelligence

Radewagen, Amata Coleman, R-Am. Samoa (At Large)

Capitol Hill Office: 1339 LHOB 20515-5201; 225-8577; Fax: 225-8757; *Chief of Staff:* Leafaina O. Yahn
Web: radewagen.house.gov
Facebook: www.facebook.com/congresswomanaumuaamata
Twitter: @RepAmata
District Office: 1 Fagatogo Sq., P.O. Box 5859, Pago Pago, AS 96799; 684-633-3601; Fax: 684-633-3607 *District Director:* Ae Ae
Committee Assignments: Natural Resources; Small Business; Veterans' Affairs

Rangel, Charles B., D-N.Y. (13)

Capitol Hill Office: 2354 RHOB 20515-3215; 225-4365; Fax: 225-0816; *Scheduler, Exec. Asst.:* Wendy Featherson
Web: rangel.house.gov
Facebook: www.facebook.com/CBRangel

Twitter: @cbrangel
District Office: 163 W. 125th St., #737, New York, NY 10027-4404; 212-663-3900; Fax: 212-663-4277; *District Director:* Geoffrey Eaton
Committee Assignments: Joint Taxation; Ways and Means

Ratcliffe, John, R-Tex. (4)

Capitol Hill Office: 325 CHOB 20515-4304; 225-6673; Fax: 225-3332; *Chief of Staff:* Daniel Kroese
Web: ratcliffe.house.gov
Facebook: www.facebook.com/RepRatcliffe
Twitter: @RepRatcliffe
District Office: 6531 Horizon Rd., Suite A, Rockwall, TX 75032; 972-771-0100; Fax: 972-771-1222; *District Director:* Jason Ross
100 W. Houston St., 2nd Floor, Sherman, TX 75090; 903-813-5270; Fax: 903-868-8613; *Regional Rep.:* Kristine McKinney
2600 N. Robison Rd., #190, Texarkana, TX 75599; 903-823-3173; Fax: 903-832-3232; *Regional Rep.:* Robbin Bass
Committee Assignments: Homeland Security; Judiciary

Reed, Tom, R-N.Y. (23)

Capitol Hill Office: 1504 LHOB 20515; 225-3161; Fax: 226-6599; *Chief of Staff:* Tim Kolpien
Web: reed.house.gov
Facebook: www.facebook.com/RepTomReed
Twitter: @RepTomReed
District Offices: 89 W. Market St., Corning, NY 14830-2526; 607-654-7566; Fax: 607-654-7568; *District Director:* Alison Hunt
433 Exchange St., Geneva, NY 14456; 315-759-5229; Fax: 315-325-4045; *Field Rep.:* Mary Green
2 E. 2nd St., #300, Jamestown, NY 14701; 716-708-6369; Fax: 716-708-6058; *Regional Director:* Jacqueline Chiarot
1 Bluebird Square, Olean, NY 14760-2500; 716-379-8434; Fax: 716-806-1069; *Constituent Services Specialist:* Lee James
401 E. State St., #304-I, Ithaca, NY 14850; 607-222-2027;
Committee Assignment: Ways and Means

Reichert, Dave, R-Wash. (8)

Capitol Hill Office: 1127 LHOB 20515; 225-7761; Fax: 225-4282; *Chief of Staff:* Jeff Harvey
Web: reichert.house.gov
Facebook: www.facebook.com/repdavereichert
Twitter: @davereichert
District Offices: 22605 S.E. 56th St., #130, Issaquah, WA 98029-5297; 425-677-7414; Fax: 425-455-3283; *District Director:* Sue Foy
5 S. Wenatchee Ave., #315, Wenatchee, WA 98801; 509-885-6615; *Constituent Services Liaison:* Tyler Mackay
Committee Assignment: Ways and Means

Renacci, Jim, R-Ohio (16)

Capitol Hill Office: 130 CHOB 20515-3516; 225-3876; Fax: 225-3059; *Chief of Staff:* Rick Limardo

Web: renacci.house.gov
Facebook: www.facebook.com/repjimrenacci
Twitter: @repjimrenacci
District Office: 1 Park Center Dr., #302, Wadsworth, OH 44281; 330-334-0040; Fax: 330-334-0061; *Community and Media Relations Rep.:* Thomas Queen
7335 Ridge Rd., #2, Parma, OH 44129; 440-882-6779; Fax: 440-882-6560;
Committee Assignments: Budget; Ways and Means

Ribble, Reid, R-Wisc. (8)

Capitol Hill Office: 1513 LHOB 20515-4908; 225-5665; Fax: 225-5729; *Chief of Staff:* McKay Daniels
Web: ribble.house.gov
Facebook: www.facebook.com/RepRibble
Twitter: @RepRibble
District Offices: 333 W. College Ave., Appleton, WI 54911-5898; 920-380-0061; Fax: 920-380-0051; *District Chief of Staff:* Rick Sense
550 N. Military Ave., #4B, Green Bay, WI 54303-4569; 920-471-1950; *Constituent Services Rep.:* Kerry Niemcek
Committee Assignments: Foreign Affairs; Transportation and Infrastructure

Rice, Kathleen, D-N.Y. (4)

Capitol Hill Office: 1508 LHOB 20515-3204; 225-5516; Fax: 225-5758; *Chief of Staff:* Nell Reilly
Web: kathleenrice.house.gov
Facebook: www.facebook.com/repkathleenrice
Twitter: @repkathleenrice
District Office: 300 Garden City Plaza, #200, Garden City, NY 11530; 516-739-3008; Fax: 516-739-2973; *Field Rep.:* Amanda Walsh
Committee Assignments: Homeland Security; Veterans' Affairs

Rice, Tom, R-S.C. (7)

Capitol Hill Office: 223 CHOB 20515; 225-9895; Fax: 225-9690; *Chief of Staff:* Jennifer Watson
Web: rice.house.gov
Facebook: www.facebook.com/reptomrice
Twitter: @RepTomRice
District Offices: 1831 W. Evans St., #300, Florence, SC 29501; 843-679-9781; Fax: 843-679-9783; *Field Rep.:* John Sweeney
2411 N. Oak St., #405, Myrtle Beach, SC 29577; 843-445-6459; Fax: 843-445-6418; *Field Rep.:* Andrew Mims
Committee Assignment: Ways and Means

Richmond, Cedric, D-La. (2)

Capitol Hill Office: 240 CHOB 20515; 225-6636; Fax: 225-1988; *Chief of Staff:* Virgil A. Miller
Web: richmond.house.gov
Facebook: www.facebook.com/RepRichmond
Twitter: @reprichmond
District Offices: 200 Derbigny St., #3200, Gretna, LA 70053-5876; 504-365-0390; *Deputy District Director:* DeShannon Cobb-Russell

2021 Lakeshore Dr., #309, New Orleans, LA 70122-3501; 504-288-3777; Fax: 504-288-4090; *District Director:* Enix Smith

1520 Thomas H. Delpit Dr., #126, Baton Rouge, LA 70802; 225-636-5600; Fax: 225-636-5680; *Deputy District Director:* Darlene Fields

Committee Assignments: Homeland Security; Judiciary

Rigell, Scott, R-Va. (2)

Capitol Hill Office: 418 CHOB 20515; 225-4215; Fax: 225-4218; *Chief of Staff:* John Thomas
Web: rigell.house.gov
Facebook: www.facebook.com/RepScottRigell
Twitter: @RepScottRigell
District Offices: 36312 Lankford Hwy., #5, Belle Haven, VA 23306; 757-442-4790; Fax: 757-442-4793; *District Director:* Shannon Kendrick

4772 Euclid Rd., Suite E, Virginia Beach, VA 23462-3800; 757-687-8290; Fax: 757-687-8298; *District Director:* Shannon Kendrick

1100 Exploration Way, #302R, Hampton, VA 23666; 757-687-8290; Fax: 757-687-8298; *District Director:* Shannon Kendrick

Committee Assignment: Appropriations

Roby, Martha, R-Ala. (2)

Capitol Hill Office: 442 CHOB 20515-0102; 225-2901; Fax: 225-8913; *Chief of Staff:* Stephen Boyd
Web: roby.house.gov
Facebook: www.facebook.com/Representative.Martha .Roby
Twitter: @RepMarthaRoby
District Offices: 505 E. Three Notch St., #322, Andalusia, AL 36420-3129; 334-428-1129; Fax: 334-222-3342; *Constituent Services Rep.:* Amelia McMahon

217 Graceland Dr., #5, Dothan, AL 36305-7376; 334-794-9680; Fax: 334-671-1480; *District Director:* Joe Williams

401 Adams Ave., #160, Montgomery, AL 36104-4340; 334-262-7718; Fax: 334-262-8758; *Constituent Services Rep.:* Charlotte Bent

Committee Assignments: Appropriations; Select on Benghazi

Roe, Phil, R-Tenn. (1)

Capitol Hill Office: 407 CHOB 20515-4201; 225-6356; Fax: 225-5714; *Chief of Staff:* Matthew Meyer
Web: roe.house.gov
Facebook: www.facebook.com/DrPhilRoe
Twitter: @drphilroe
District Offices: 205 Revere St., Kingsport, TN 37660; 423-247-8161; Fax: 423-247-0119; *District Director:* John A. Teague

1609 College Park Dr., #4, Morristown, TN 37813-1659; 423-254-1400; Fax: 423-254-1403; *Caseworker:* Cheryl Bennett; *Caseworker:* Angie Jarnagin

Committee Assignments: Education and the Workforce; Veterans' Affairs

Rogers, Hal, R-Ky. (5)

Capitol Hill Office: 2406 RHOB 20515-1705; 225-4601; Fax: 225-0940; *Chief of Staff:* Megan Bell
Web: halrogers.house.gov
Facebook: www.facebook.com/CongressmanHalRogers
Twitter: @RepHalRogers
District Offices: 48 S. KY Hwy. 15, Hazard, KY 41701; 606-439-0794; Fax: 606-439-4647; *Field Rep.:* Nick Camic

110 Resource Court, Suite A, Prestonsburg, KY 41653-7851; 606-886-0844; Fax: 606-889-0371; *Field Rep.:* Adam Rice

551 Clifty St., Somerset, KY 42503; 800-632-8588; Fax: 606-678-4856; *District Director:* Karen Kelly

Committee Assignment: Appropriations, Chair

Rogers, Mike, R-Ala. (3)

Capitol Hill Office: 324 CHOB 20515-0103; 225-3261; Fax: 226-8485; *Chief of Staff:* Chris Brinson
Web: mikerogers.house.gov
Facebook: www.facebook.com/Mike-Rogers-6406874733
Twitter: @RepMikeRogersAL
District Offices: Federal Bldg., 1129 Noble St., #104, Anniston, AL 36201-4674; 256-236-5655; Fax: 256-237-9203; *District Director:* Sheri Rollins

701 A Ave., #300, Opelika, AL 36801; 334-745-6221; Fax: 334-742-0109; *Field Rep.:* Cheryl Cunningham

Committee Assignments: Agriculture; Armed Services; Homeland Security

Rohrabacher, Dana, R-Calif. (48)

Capitol Hill Office: 2300 RHOB 20515-0546; 225-2415; Fax: 225-0145; *Chief of Staff:* Richard T. Dykema
Web: rohrabacher.house.gov
Facebook: www.facebook.com/danarohrabacher
Twitter: @DanaRohrabacher
District Office: 101 Main St., #380, Huntington Beach, CA 92648-8149; 714-960-6483; Fax: 714-960-7806; *District Director:* Kathleen Staunton

Committee Assignments: Foreign Affairs; Science, Space, and Technology

Rokita, Todd, R-Ind. (4)

Capitol Hill Office: 1717 LHOB 20515-1404; 225-5037; Fax: 226-0544; *Chief of Staff:* Renee Hudson
Web: rokita.house.gov
Facebook: www.facebook.com/RepToddRokita
Twitter: @toddrokita
District Office: 355 S. Washington St., 2nd Floor, Danville, IN 46122-1779; 317-718-0404; Fax: 317-718-0405; *District Director:* Joe McLain
Satellite Office: 230 N. 4th St., #4, Lafayette, IN 47901-1315; 765-838-3930; Fax: 765-838-3931; *District Director:* Joe McLain

Committee Assignments: Budget; Education and the Workforce; Transportation and Infrastructure

Rooney, Thomas J., R-Fla. (17)

Capitol Hill Office: 221 CHOB 20515; 225-5792; Fax: 225-3132; *Chief of Staff:* Pete Giambastiani

Web: rooney.house.gov
Facebook: www.facebook.com/reptomrooney
Twitter: @TomRooney
District Offices: 226 Taylor St., #230, Punta Gorda, FL 33950-4422; 941-575-9101; Fax: 941-575-9103 *District Director:* Leah Valenti
10008 Park Place Ave., Riverview, FL 33578; 813-677-8646; Fax: 941-575-9103; *Field Rep.:* David Garcia
4507 George Blvd., Sebring, FL 33875; 863-402-9082; Fax: 863-402-9084; *Field Rep.:* Sherry McCorkle
Committee Assignments: Appropriations; Permanent Select Intelligence

Ros-Lehtinen, Ileana, R-Fla. (27)

Capitol Hill Office: 2206 RHOB 20515-0918; 225-3931; Fax: 225-5620; *Chief of Staff:* Joshua Salpeter
Web: ros-lehtinen.house.gov
Facebook: www.facebook.com/voteileana
Twitter: @RosLehtinen
District Office: 4960 72nd Ave. S.W., #208, Miami, FL 33155; 305-668-2285; Fax: 305-668-5970; *District Director:* Maytee Sanz
Committee Assignments: Foreign Affairs; Permanent Select Intelligence

Roskam, Peter, R-Ill. (6)

Capitol Hill Office: 2246 RHOB 20515-1306; 225-1561, Fax: 225-1166; *Chief of Staff:* David Mork
Web: roskam.house.gov
Facebook: www.facebook.com/RepRoskam
Twitter: @PeterRoskam
District Office: 2700 International Dr., #304, West Chicago, IL 60185; 630-232-0006; Fax: 630-232 7393; *District Director:* Lee Campuzano
200 S. Hough St., 2nd Floor, Barrington, IL 60010; 847-656-6354; *Office Manager:* Tom Williamson
Committee Assignments: Select on Benghazi; Ways and Means

Ross, Dennis A., R-Fla. (15)

Capitol Hill Office: 229 CHOB 20515; 225-1252; Fax: 226-0585; *Chief of Staff:* Anthony Foti
Web: dennisross.house.gov
Facebook: www.facebook.com/dennis.ross.376
Twitter: @RepDennisRoss
District Office: 170 Fitzgerald Rd., #1, Lakeland, FL 33813-2607; 863-644-8215; Fax: 863-648-0749; *Director of Administration:* Shellee Meeker
110 W. Reynolds St., #101, Plant City, FL 33563; 813-752-4790; Fax: 863-648-0749; *Constituent Services Rep.:* Taunia Sebright
Committee Assignment: Financial Services

Rothfus, Keith, R-Pa. (12)

Capitol Hill Office: 1205 LHOB 20515; 225-2065; Fax: 225-5709; *Chief of Staff:* Alexander Shively
Web: rothfus.house.gov
Facebook: www.facebook.com/keithrothfus
Twitter: @KeithRothfus

District Offices: 650 Corporation St., #304, Beaver, PA 15009; 724-359-1626; Fax: 412-593-2022; *Field Rep.:* Jeremy Honhold
110 Franklin St., #150, Johnstown, PA 15901; 814-619-3659; Fax: 412-593-2022; *Field Rep.:* José Otero
6000 Babcock Blvd., #104, Pittsburgh, PA 15237; 412-837-1361; Fax: 412-593-2022; *District Director:* Alex Brunory
Committee Assignment: Financial Services

Rouzer, David, R-N.C. (7)

Capitol Hill Office: 424 CHOB 20515-3307; 225-2731; Fax: 225-5773; *Chief of Staff:* Melissa Murphy
Web: rouzer.house.gov
Facebook: www.facebook.com/RepRouzer
Twitter: @repdavidrouzer
District Office: 310 Government Center Dr., #1, Bolivia, NC 28422; 910-253-6111; Fax: 910-253-6114; *District Director:* Tyler Foote
2736 NC Hwy. 210, Johnston County Agriculture Center, Smithfield, NC 27577; 919-938-3040; Fax: 919-938-3540; *Office Coordinator:* Dwight Williams
230 Government Center Dr., #113, Wilmington, NC 28403; 910-395-0202; Fax: 910-395-0209; *Office Coordinator:* Chance Lambeth
Committee Assignments: Agriculture; Transportation and Infrastructure

Roybal-Allard, Lucille, D-Calif. (40)

Capitol Hill Office: 2330 RHOB 20515-0534; 225-1766; Fax: 226-0350; *Chief of Staff:* Victor Castillo
Web: roybal-allard.house.gov
Facebook: www.facebook.com/RepRoybalAllard
Twitter: @RepRoybalAllard
District Office: 500 Citadel Dr., #320, Commerce, CA 90040; 323-721-8790; Fax: 323-721-8789; *District Chief of Staff:* Ana Figueroa
Committee Assignment: Appropriations

Royce, Edward R., R-Calif. (39)

Capitol Hill Office: 2310 RHOB 20515-0540; 225-4111; Fax: 226-0335; *Chief of Staff:* Amy Porter
Web: royce.house.gov
Facebook: www.facebook.com/EdRoyce
Twitter: @RepEdRoyce
District Offices: 210 W. Birch St., #201, Brea, CA 92821; 714-255-0101; Fax: 714-255-0109; *District Director:* Sara Catalan
1380 S. Fullerton Rd., #205, Rowland Heights, CA 91748; 626-964-5123; Fax: 626-810-3891; *District Rep.:* Stephanie Hu
Committee Assignments: Financial Services; Foreign Affairs, Chair

Ruiz, Raul, D-Calif. (36)

Capitol Hill Office: 1319 LHOB 20515; 225-5330; Fax: 225-1238; *Chief of Staff:* Cookab Hashemi
Web: ruiz.house.gov
Facebook: www.facebook.com/CongressmanRaulRuizMD

Twitter: @CongressmanRuiz
District Office: 445 E. Florida Ave., 2nd Floor, Hemet, CA 92543; 951-765-2304; Fax: 951-765-3784; *Constituent Services Rep.:* Shelley Martin
43875 Washington St., Suite F, Palm Desert, CA 92211; 760-424-8888; Fax: 760-424-8993; *Staff Asst.:* Tony Aguilar
Committee Assignments: Natural Resources; Veterans' Affairs

Ruppersberger, C. A. (Dutch), D-Md. (2)

Capitol Hill Office: 2416 RHOB 20515-2002; 225-3061; Fax: 225-3094; *Chief of Staff:* Tara Oursler
Web: ruppersberger.house.gov
Facebook: www.facebook.com/DutchRupp
Twitter: @Call_Me_Dutch
District Office: 375 W. Padonia Rd., #200, Timonium, MD 21093-2130; 410-628-2701; Fax: 410-628-2708; *District Director:* Jennifer Driban
Committee Assignment: Appropriations

Rush, Bobby L., D-Ill. (1)

Capitol Hill Office: 2188 RHOB 20515-1301; 225-4372; Fax: 226-0333; *Chief of Staff:* Stanley Watkins
Web: rush.house.gov
Facebook: www.facebook.com/congressmanbobbyrush
Twitter: @RepBobbyRush
District Offices: 700 E. 79th St., Chicago, IL 60619-3102; 773-224-6500; Fax: 773-224-9624; *District Director:* Robyn Grange
3235 147th St., Midlothian, IL 60445-3656; 708-385-9550; Fax: 708-385-3860; *Deputy District Director:* Younus Suleman
Committee Assignment: Energy and Commerce

Russell, Steve, R-Okla. (5)

Capitol Hill Office: 128 CHOB 20515-3605; 225-2132; Fax: 226-1463; *Chief of Staff:* Steve Moffitt
Web: russell.house.gov
Facebook: www.facebook.com/RepRussell
Twitter: @RepRussell
District Office: 4600 29th St. S.E., #400, Del City, OK 73115; 405-602-3074; Fax: 405-602-3953; *District Director:* Craig Smith
Committee Assignments: Armed Services; Education and the Workforce; Oversight and Government Reform

Ryan, Paul, R-Wisc. (1)

Capitol Hill Office: 1233 LHOB 20515-4901; 225-3031; Fax: 225-3393; *Chief of Staff:* Danyell Tremmel
Speaker's Office: H-232 CAP 20515; 225-0600; *Chief of Staff:* Dave Hoppe
Web: paulryan.house.gov; www.speaker.gov
Facebook: www.facebook.com/SpeakerRyan
Twitter: @SpeakerRyan
Speaker's Office: H-232 CAP 20515-4901; 225-0600; *Chief of Staff:* Dave Hoppe

District Offices: 20 S. Main St., #10, Janesville, WI 53545-3959; 608-752-4050; Fax: 608-752-4711; *Chief of Staff:* Danyell Tremmel
5031 7th Ave., Kenosha, WI 53140-4129; 262-654-1901; Fax: 262-654-2156; *Field Rep.:* Vacant
216 6th St., Racine, WI 53403; 262-637-0510; Fax: 262-637-5689; *Office Admin.:* Teresa Mora
Committee Assignment: Speaker of the House

Ryan, Tim, D-Ohio (13)

Capitol Hill Office: 1421 LHOB 20515-3517; 225-5261; Fax: 225-3719; *Chief of Staff:* Ron Grimes
Web: timryan.house.gov
Facebook: www.facebook.com/timryan
Twitter: @RepTimRyan
District Offices: 1030 E. Tallmadge Ave., Akron, OH 44310-3563; 330-630-7311; Fax: 330-630-7314; *Economic Development Coord.:* Catey Breck
197 W. Market St., Warren, OH 44481-1024; 800-856-4152; Fax: 330-373-0098; *District Director:* Rick Leonard
241 W. Federal St., Youngstown, OH 44503-1207; 330-740-0193; Fax: 330-740-0182; *Communications Director:* Patrick Lowry
Committee Assignments: Appropriations; Budget

Sablan, Gregorio Kilili Camacho, D-M.P. (At Large)

Capitol Hill Office: 423 CHOB 20515-5601; 225-2646; Fax: 226-4249; *Chief of Staff:* Robert J. Schwalbach
Web: sablan.house.gov
Facebook: www.facebook.com/Gregorio-Kilili-Camacho-Sablan-153423912663
District Offices: P.O. Box 1361, Rota, MP 96951; 670-532-2647; Fax: 670-532-2649; *Staff Asst.:* Harry Masga
P.O. Box 504879, Saipan, MP 96950; 670-323-2647; Fax: 670-323-2649; *District Director:* Mike Tenorio
P.O. Box 520394, Tinian, MP 96952; 670-433-2647; Fax: 670-433-2648; *Staff Asst.:* Edward Hoffchneider
Committee Assignments: Education and the Workforce; Natural Resources

Salmon, Matt, R-Ariz. (5)

Capitol Hill Office: 2349 RHOB 20515; 225-2635; Fax: 226-4386; *Chief of Staff:* Lorissa Bounds
Web: salmon.house.gov
Facebook: www.facebook.com/RepMattSalmon
Twitter: @RepMattSalmon
District Office: 207 N. Gilbert Rd., #209, Gilbert, AZ 85234; 480-699-8239; Fax: 480-699-4730; *District Director:* Chuck Gray
Committee Assignments: Education and the Workforce; Foreign Affairs

Sánchez, Linda, D-Calif. (38)

Capitol Hill Office: 2329 RHOB 20515-0539; 225-6676; Fax: 226-1012; *Chief of Staff:* Lea Sulkala
Web: lindasanchez.house.gov

Facebook: www.facebook.com/
CongresswomanLindaSanchez
Twitter: @RepLindaSanchez
District Office: 12440 E. Imperial Hwy., #140, Norwalk,
CA 90650; 562-860-5050; Fax: 562-924-2914; *District
Director:* Yvette Sahinian
Committee Assignments: Ethics, Ranking Minority
Member; Select on Benghazi; Ways and Means

Sánchez, Loretta, D-Calif. (46)

Capitol Hill Office: 1211 LHOB 20515-0547; 225-2965;
Fax: 225-5859; *Chief of Staff:* Jennifer Warburton
Web: lorettasanchez.house.gov
Facebook: www.facebook.com/LorettaSanchez
Twitter: @LorettaSanchez
District Office: 12397 Lewis St., #101, Garden Grove, CA
92840-4695; 714-621-0102; Fax: 714-621-0401; *District
Director:* Carlos Urquiza
Committee Assignments: Armed Services; Homeland
Security

Sanford, Mark, R-S.C. (1)

Capitol Hill Office: 2201 RHOB 20515-4001; 225-3176;
Chief of Staff: Matthew Taylor
Web: sanford.house.gov
Facebook: www.facebook.com/RepSanfordSC
Twitter: @RepSanfordSC
District Office: 530 Johnnie Dodds Blvd., #201, Mt.
Pleasant, SC 29464; 843-352-7572; Fax: 843-352-7620;
Director of Constituent Services: April Derr
710 Boundary St., #1D, P.O. Box 1538, Beaufort, SC 29902;
843-521-2530; Fax: 843-521-2535; *Scheduler:*
Martha Morris
Committee Assignments: Budget; Transporation and
Infrastructure

Sarbanes, John, D-Md. (3)

Capitol Hill Office: 2444 RHOB 20515-2003; 225-4016;
Fax: 225-9219; *Chief of Staff:* Jason Gleason
Web: sarbanes.house.gov
Facebook: www.facebook.com/RepSarbanes
Twitter: @RepSarbanes
District Office: 600 Baltimore Ave., #303, Towson, MD
21204-4022; 410-832-8890; Fax: 410-832-8898;
Constituent Services Rep.: Fred Hassell
Satellite Office: Arundel Center, 44 Calvert St., #349,
Annapolis, MD 21401-1930; 410-295-1679; Fax: 410-
295-1682; *Community Relations Specialist:*
Robert Beans
Committee Assignment: Energy and Commerce

Scalise, Steve, R-La. (1)

Capitol Hill Office: 2338 RHOB 20515; 225-3015;
Fax: 226-0386; *Chief of Staff:* Charles Henry
Web: scalise.house.gov
Facebook: www.facebook.com/RepSteveScalise
Twitter: @SteveScalise

District Offices: 1514 Martens Dr., #10, Hammond, LA
70401; 985-340-2185; Fax: 985-340-3122; *Regional
Director:* Justin Crossie
8026 Main St., #700, Houma, LA 70360; 985-879-2300;
Fax: 985-879-2306; *Field Rep.:* Ramona Williamson
21454 Koop Dr., #2C, Mandeville, LA 70471; 985-893-
9064; Fax: 985-893-9707; *Field Rep.:* Danielle Evans
110 Veterans Memorial Blvd., #500, Metairie, LA 70005;
504-837-1259; Fax: 504-837-4239; *Field Rep.:*
Ramona Williamson
Committee Assignment: Energy and Commerce

Schakowsky, Jan, D-Ill. (9)

Capitol Hill Office: 2367 RHOB 20515-1309; 225-2111;
Fax: 226-6890; *Chief of Staff:* Cathy Hurwit
Web: schakowsky.house.gov
Facebook: www.facebook.com/janschakowsky
Twitter: @janschakowsky
District Offices: 5533 N. Broadway St., Chicago, IL 60640-
1405; 773-506-7100; Fax: 773-506-9202; *District
Director:* Leslie Combs
820 Davis St., #105, Evanston, IL 60201-4400; 847-328-
3409; Fax: 847-328-3425; *Grants Coord.; Constituent
Advocate:* Andrew Goczkowski
1852 Johns Dr., Glenview, IL 60025; 847-328-3409;
Fax: 847-328-3425; *Constituent Advocate:*
Abbey Eusebio
Committee Assignment: Energy and Commerce

Schiff, Adam, D-Calif. (28)

Capitol Hill Office: 2411 RHOB 20515-0529; 225-4176;
Fax: 225-5828; *Chief of Staff:* Jeff Lowenstein
Web: schiff.house.gov
Facebook: www.facebook.com/RepAdamSchiff
Twitter: @RepAdamSchiff
District Office: 245 E. Olive Ave., #200, Burbank, CA
91502; 818-450-2900; 323-315-5555; Fax: 818-450-
2928; *District Director:* Ann Peifer
Satellite Office: 5500 Hollywood Blvd., #416, Los Angeles,
CA 90028; 323-315-5555; *District Director:* Ann Peifer
Committee Assignments: Permanent Select Intelligence,
Ranking Minority Member; Select on Benghazi

Schrader, Kurt, D-Ore. (5)

Capitol Hill Office: 2431 RHOB 20515; 225-5711;
Fax: 225-5699; *Chief of Staff:* Paul Gage
Web: schrader.house.gov
Facebook: www.facebook.com/repschrader
Twitter: @repschrader
District Offices: 621 High St., Oregon City, OR 97045-
2240; 503-557-1324; Fax: 503-557-1981; *District
Director:* Suzanne Kunse
544 Ferry St. S.E., #2, Salem, OR 97301-3830; 503-588-9100;
Fax: 503-588-5517; *Caseworker:* Mary Ann Smith
Committee Assignment: Energy and Commerce

Schweikert, David, R-Ariz. (6)

Capitol Hill Office: 409 CHOB 20515-0305; 225-2190;
Fax: 225-0096; *Chief of Staff:* Oliver Schwab

Web: schweikert.house.gov
Facebook: www.facebook.com/repdavidschweikert
Twitter: @RepDavid
District Office: 10603 N. Hayden Rd., #108, Scottsdale, AZ 85260-5571; 480-946-2411; Fax: 480-946-2446; *District Director:* Kevin Knight
Committee Assignments: Financial Services; Joint Economic

Scott, Austin, R-Ga. (8)

Capitol Hill Office: 2417 RHOB 20515-1008; 225-6531; Fax: 225-3013; *Chief of Staff:* Joby Young
Web: austinscott.house.gov
Facebook: www.facebook.com/RepAustinScott
Twitter: @AustinScottGA08
District Offices: 127-B N. Central Ave., Tifton, GA 31794-4087; 229-396-5175; Fax: 229-396-5179; *District Director:* Alice Johnson
230 Margie Dr., #500, Warner Robins, GA 31088; 478-971-1776; Fax: 478-971-1778; *Field Rep.:* Donovan Head
Committee Assignments: Agriculture; Armed Services

Scott, David, D-Ga. (13)

Capitol Hill Office: 225 CHOB 20515-1013; 225-2939; Fax: 225-4628; Chief of Staff; *Press Secretary:* Michael Andel
Web: davidscott.house.gov
Facebook: www.facebook.com/RepDavidScott
Twitter: @RepDavidScott
District Offices: 173 N. Main St., Jonesboro, GA 30236-3567; 770-210-5073; Fax: 770-210-5673; *District Director:* Chandra Harris
888 Concord Rd., #100, Smyrna, GA 30080-4202; 770-432-5405; Fax: 770-432-5813; *Deputy District Director:* Isaac Dodoo
Committee Assignments: Agriculture; Financial Services

Scott, Robert C. (Bobby), D-Va. (3)

Capitol Hill Office: 1201 LHOB 20515-4603; 225-8351; Fax: 225-8354; *Chief of Staff:* Joni L. Ivey
Web: bobbyscott.house.gov
Facebook: www.facebook.com/CongressmanBobbyScott
Twitter: @repbobbyscott
District Offices: 2600 Washington Ave., #1010, Newport News, VA 23607-4333; 757-380-1000; Fax: 757-928-6694; *Legislative Asst.:* Demontre Boone
400 N. 8th St., #430, Richmond, VA 23219-4815; 804-644-4845; Fax: 804-648-6026; Legis. Asst.; *District Scheduler:* Nkechi Winkler
Committee Assignment: Education and the Workforce, Ranking Minority Member

Sensenbrenner, Jim, R-Wisc. (5)

Capitol Hill Office: 2449 RHOB 20515-4905; 225-5101; Fax: 225-3190; *Chief of Staff:* Bart Forsyth
Web: sensenbrenner.house.gov
Facebook: www.facebook.com/RepSensenbrenner
Twitter: @JimPressOffice

District Office: 120 Bishops Way, #154, Brookfield, WI 53005-6249; 262-784-1111; Fax: 262-784-9437; *District Director:* Loni Hagerup
Committee Assignments: Judiciary; Science, Space, and Technology

Serrano, José E., D-N.Y. (15)

Capitol Hill Office: 2227 RHOB 20515-3216; 225-4361; Fax: 225-6001; *Chief of Staff:* Matthew Alpert
Web: serrano.house.gov
Facebook: www.facebook.com/RepJoseSerrano
Twitter: @RepJoseSerrano
District Office: 1231 Lafayette Ave., 4th Floor, Bronx, NY 10474-5331; 718-620-0084; Fax: 718-620-0658; *District Director:* Amanda Septimo
Committee Assignment: Appropriations

Sessions, Pete, R-Tex. (32)

Capitol Hill Office: 2233 RHOB 20515-4332; 225-2231; Fax: 225-5878; *Chief of Staff:* Kyle Matous
Web: sessions.house.gov
Facebook: www.facebook.com/petesessions
Twitter: @petesessions
District Office: Park Central VII, 12750 Merit Dr., #1434, Dallas, TX 75251-1229; 972-392-0505; Fax: 972-392-0615; *District Director:* Matt Garcia
Committee Assignment: Rules, Chair

Sewell, Terri A., D-Ala. (7)

Capitol Hill Office: 1133 LHOB 20515-0107; 225-2665; Fax: 226-9567; *Chief of Staff:* Shashrina Thomas
Web: sewell.house.gov
Facebook: www.facebook.com/RepSewell
Twitter: @RepTerriSewell
District Offices: Two 20th St. North, #1130, Birmingham, AL 35203-4014; 205-254-1960; Fax: 205-254-1974; *District Director:* Chasseny Lewis
2501 7th St., #300, Tuscaloosa, AL 35401; 205-752-5380; 205-752-5899; *District Director:* Chasseny Lewis
101 S. Lawrence St., Montgomery, AL 36104; 334-262-1919; Fax: 334-262-1921; *Constituent Services Manager/Outreach Coordinator:* Melinda Williams
908 Alabama Ave., Federal Bldg., #112, Selma, AL 36701-4660; 334-877-4414; Fax: 334-877-4489; *Constituent Services Rep.:* Kennard Randolph
Committee Assignments: Financial Services; Permanent Select Intelligence

Sherman, Brad, D-Calif. (30)

Capitol Hill Office: 2242 RHOB 20515-0527; 225-5911; Fax: 225-5879; *Chief of Staff:* Don MacDonald
Web: sherman.house.gov
Facebook: www.facebook.com/CongressmanBradSherman
Twitter: @bradsherman
District Office: 5000 Van Nuys Blvd., #420, Sherman Oaks, CA 91403; 818-501-9200; Fax: 818-501-1554; *District Director:* Scott Abrams
Committee Assignments: Financial Services; Foreign Affairs

Shimkus, John, R-Ill. (15)

Capitol Hill Office: 2217 RHOB 20515; 225-5271;
  Fax: 225-5880; *Chief of Staff:* Craig A. Roberts
Web: shimkus.house.gov
Facebook: www.facebook.com/repshimkus
Twitter: @RepShimkus
District Offices: 201 N. Vermilion St., #218, Danville, IL
  61832; 217-446-0664; Fax: 217-446-0670; *Regional
  Director:* Charles Hantz
101 N. 4th St., #303, Effingham, IL 62401; 217-347-7947;
  Fax: 217-342-1219; *District Aide:* Michael Hall
110 E. Locust St., Room 12, Harrisburg, IL 62946-1557;
  618-252-8271; Fax: 618-252-8317; *District Director:*
  Jenny Pruett
15 Professional Park Dr., Maryville, IL 62062; 618-288-
  7190; Fax: 618-288-7219; *District Director:*
  Deb Detmers
Committee Assignment: Energy and Commerce

Shuster, Bill, R-Pa. (9)

Capitol Hill Office: 2268 RHOB 20515; 225-2431;
  Fax: 225-2486; *Chief of Staff:* Eric Burgeson
Web: shuster.house.gov
Facebook: www.facebook.com/Rep.Shuster
Twitter: @repbillshuster
District Offices: 100 Lincoln Way East, Suite D,
  Chambersburg, PA 17201-2274; 717-264-8308;
  Fax: 717-264-0269; *Constituent Services Rep.:*
  Nancy Bull
310 Penn St., #200, Hollidaysburg, PA 16648-2044; 814-
  696-6318; Fax: 814-696-6726; *District Director:*
  Jim Frank
827 Water St., #3, Indiana, PA 15701; 724-463-0516;
  Fax: 724-463-0518; *Constituent Services Rep.:*
  Ron Nocco
Committee Assignments: Armed Services; Transportation
  and Infrastructure, Chair

Simpson, Mike, R-Idaho (2)

Capitol Hill Office: 2312 RHOB 20515-1202; 225-5531;
  Fax: 225-8216; *Chief of Staff:* Lindsay J. Slater
Web: simpson.house.gov
Facebook: www.facebook.com/Mike-Simpson-
  96007744606
Twitter: @CongMikeSimpson
District Offices: 802 W. Bannock St., #600, Boise, ID
  83702-5843; 208-334-1953; Fax: 208-334-9533; *District
  Director, Communications Director:* Nikki Wallace
410 Memorial Dr., #203, Idaho Falls, ID 83402-3600; 208-
  523-6701; Fax: 208-523-2384; *Regional Director:*
  Ethan Huffman
275 S. 5th Ave., #275, Pocatello, ID 83201-6400; 208-233-
  2222; Fax: 208-233-2095; *Regional Director:*
  Ethan Huffman
1341 Filmore St., #202, Twin Falls, ID 83301-3392; 208-
  734-7219; Fax: 208-734-7244; *Community
  Development Coord.:* Linda Culver
Committee Assignment: Appropriations

Sinema, Kyrsten, D-Ariz. (9)

Capitol Hill Office: 1530 LHOB 20515; 225-9888;
  Fax: 225-9731; *Chief of Staff:* Meg Joseph
Web: sinema.house.gov
Facebook: www.facebook.com/CongresswomanSinema
Twitter: @RepSinema
District Offices: 2944 N. 44th St., #150, Phoenix, AZ
  85018; 602-956-2285; Fax: 602-956-2468; *District
  Director:* Michelle Davidson
Committee Assignment: Financial Services

Sires, Albio, D-N.J. (8)

Capitol Hill Office: 2342 RHOB 20515-3013; 225-7919;
  Fax: 226-0792; *Chief of Staff:* Gene Martorony
Web: sires.house.gov
Facebook: www.facebook.com/RepAlbioSires
Twitter: @RepSires
District Offices: 800 Anna St., Elizabeth, NJ 07201; 908-
  820-0692; Fax: 908-820-0694; *District Director:*
  Ada Morell
121 Newark Ave., #200, Jersey City, NJ 07302; 201-309-
  0301; Fax: 201-309-0384; *Communications Director:*
  Erica Daughtrey
5500 Palisade Ave., Suite A, West New York, NJ 07093-
  2124; 201-558-0800; Fax: 201-617-2809; *Congressional
  Aides:* Liz Victorin, Gabe Rodriguez
Committee Assignments: Foreign Affairs; Transportation
  and Infrastructure

Slaughter, Louise M., D-N.Y. (25)

Capitol Hill Office: 2469 RHOB 20515-3228; 225-3615;
  Fax: 225-7822; *Chief of Staff:* Liam Fitzsimmons
Web: louise.house.gov
Facebook: www.facebook.com/RepLouiseSlaughter
Twitter: @louiseslaughter
District Office: 3120 Federal Bldg., 100 State St., Rochester,
  NY 14614-1309; 585-232-4850; Fax: 585-232-1954;
  District Director: Patricia Larke
Committee Assignments: Commission on Security and
  Cooperation in Europe; Rules, Ranking Minority
  Member

Smith, Adam, D-Wash. (9)

Capitol Hill Office: 2264 RHOB 20515-4709; 225-8901;
  Fax: 225-5893; *Chief of Staff:* Shana M. Chandler
Web: adamsmith.house.gov
Facebook: www.facebook.com/RepAdamSmith
Twitter: @RepAdamSmith
District Office: 101 Evergreen Bldg., 15 S. Grady Way,
  Renton, WA 98057; 425-793-5180; Fax: 425-793-5181;
  District Director: Matt Perry
Committee Assignments: Armed Services, Ranking
  Minority Member; Select on Benghazi

Smith, Adrian, R-Neb. (3)

Capitol Hill Office: 2241 RHOB 20515; 225-6435;
  Fax: 225-0207; *Chief of Staff:* Monica Jirik
Web: adriansmith.house.gov

Facebook: www.facebook.com/AdrianSmithNE
Twitter: @RepAdrianSmith
District Offices: 1811 W. 2nd St., #275, Grand Island, NE 68803; 308-384-3900; Fax: 308-384-3902; *Director of Constituent Services:* Todd Crawford
416 Valley View Dr., #600, Scottsbluff, NE 69361-1486; 308-633-6333; Fax: 308-633-6335; *Office Coord.:* Lenora Brotzman
Committee Assignment: Ways and Means

Smith, Chris, R-N.J. (4)

Capitol Hill Office: 2373 RHOB 20515-3004; 225-3765; Fax: 225-7768; *Chief of Staff:* Mary Noonan
Web: chrissmith.house.gov
Twitter: @RepChrisSmith
District Offices: 4573 S. Broad St., Hamilton, NJ 08620; 609-585-7878; Fax: 609-585-9155; *District Director for Casework:* Jeff Sagnip
405 Pinehurst Rd., Plumsted, NJ 08514; 609-286-2571; Fax: 609-286-2630; *Public Policy Advisor:* Joan Schloeder
Raintree Shopping Center, 112 Village Center Dr., 2nd Floor, Freehold, NJ 07728; 732-780-3035; Fax: 732-780-3079; *District Director for Casework:* Jeff Sagnip
Committee Assignments: Commission on Security and Cooperation in Europe, Co-Chair; Congressional-Executive Commission on China, Co-Chair; Foreign Affairs

Smith, Jason, R-Mo. (8)

Capitol Hill Office: 1118 LHOB 20515-2508; 225-4404; Fax: 226-0326; *Chief of Staff:* Eric Bohl
Web: jasonsmith.house.gov
Facebook: www.facebook.com/repjasonsmith
Twitter: @repjasonsmith
District Office: 830 S. Bishop Ave., Suite A, Rolla, MO 65401-4340; 573-364-2455; Fax: 573-364-1053; *Communications Advisor:* Aaron Willard
2502 Tanner Dr., #205, Cape Girardeau, MO 63701; 573-335-0101; Fax: 573-335-1931; *Office Manager, Constituent Services Specialist:* Leslie Herbst
22 E. Columbia, P.O. Box 1165, Farmington, MO 63640; 573-756-9755; Fax: 573-756-9762; *District Office Director:* Donna Hickman
35 Court Square, #300, West Plains, MO 65775; 417-255-1515; Fax: 417-255-2009; *District Office Director:* Heather Peugh
Committee Assignment: Ways and Means

Smith, Lamar, R-Tex. (21)

Capitol Hill Office: 2409 RHOB 20515-4321; 225-4236; Fax: 225-8628; *Chief of Staff:* Ashlee Vineyard
Web: lamarsmith.house.gov
Facebook: www.facebook.com/LamarSmithTX21
Twitter: @LamarSmithTX21
District Offices: 2211 S. IH-35, #106, Austin, TX 78741; 512-912-7508; Fax: 512-912-7519; *Constituent Services Liaison:* Morgan McFall

301 Junction Hwy., #346C, Kerrville, TX 78028-4247; 830-896-0154; Fax: 830-896-0168; *Constituent Services Liaison; Service Academy Liaison:* Anne Overby
1100 N.E. Loop 410, #640, San Antonio, TX 78209; 210-821-5024; Fax: 210-821-5947; *District Director:* Mike Asmus
Committee Assignments: Homeland Security; Judiciary; Science, Space, and Technology, Chair

Speier, Jackie, D-Calif. (14)

Capitol Hill Office: 211 CHOB 20515-0512; 225-3531; Fax: 226-4183; *Chief of Staff:* Josh Connolly
Web: speier.house.gov
Facebook: www.facebook.com/JackieSpeier
Twitter: @RepSpeier
District Office: 155 Bovet Rd., #780, San Mateo, CA 94402; 415-566-5257; Fax: 650-375-8270; *District Director:* Brian Perkins
Committee Assignments: Armed Services; Permanent Select Intelligence

Stefanik, Elise, R-N.Y. (21)

Capitol Hill Office: 512 CHOB 20515-3221; 225-4611; Fax: 226-0621; *Chief of Staff:* Lindley Kratovil
Web: stefanik.house.gov
Facebook: www.facebook.com/RepEliseStefanik
Twitter: @RepStefanik
District Office: 23 Durkee St., Suite C, Plattsburgh, NY 12901; 518-561-2324; Fax: 518-561-2408; *Regional Director:* Reneé McFarlin
88 Public Square, Suite A, Watertown, NY 13601; 315-782-3150; Fax: 315-782-1291; *Regional Director:* Maddie Donovan
136 Glen St., Glens Falls, NY 12801; 518-743-0964; Fax: 518-743-1391; *Regional Director:* Matt Scollin
Committee Assignments: Armed Services; Education and the Workforce

Stewart, Chris, R-Utah (2)

Capitol Hill Office: 323 CHOB 20515; 225-9730; Fax: 225-9627; *Chief of Staff:* Brian Steed
Web: stewart.house.gov
Facebook: www.facebook.com/RepChrisStewart
Twitter: @repchrisstewart
District Offices: 420 E. South Temple St., #390, Salt Lake City, UT 84111; 801-364-5550; Fax: 801-364-5551; *District Director:* Gary Webster
253 W. St. George Blvd., #100, St. George, UT 84770; 435-627-1500; Fax: 435-627-1911; *Deputy Director:* Lisa Taylor
Committee Assignments: Appropriations; Permanent Select Intelligence

Stivers, Steve, R-Ohio (15)

Capitol Hill Office: 1022 LHOB 20515-3515; 225-2015; Fax: 225-3529; *Chief of Staff:* Courtney Whetstone
Web: stivers.house.gov
Facebook: www.facebook.com/RepSteveStivers
Twitter: @RepSteveStivers

District Office: 3790 Municipal Way, Hilliard, OH 43026; 614-771-4968; Fax: 614-771-3990; *District Director:* Grant Shaffer

123 S. Broad St., #235, Lancaster, OH 43130; 740-654-2654; Fax: 740-654-2482; *Military Rep.:* Ryan O'Connor

69 N. South St., Wilmington, OH 45177; 937-283-7049; Fax: 937-283-7052; *Caseworker:* Sherry Stuckert

Committee Assignments: Financial Services; Rules

Stutzman, Marlin, R-Ind. (3)

Capitol Hill Office: 2418 RHOB 20515-1403; 225-4436; Fax: 226-9870; *Chief of Staff:* John Hammond

Web: stutzman.house.gov

Facebook: www.facebook.com/CongressmanMarlinStutzman

Twitter: @RepStutzman

District Offices: 1300 S. Harrison St., #3105, Fort Wayne, IN 46802-3492; 260-424-3041; Fax: 260-424-4042; *District Director:* Bill Davis

700 Park Ave., Suite D, Winona Lake, IN 46590-1066; 574-269-1940; Fax: 574-269-3112; *Deputy District Director:* Allison McSherry

118 S. Johnson St., Bluffton, IN 46714; 260-824-1900; Fax: 260-824-1922;

Committee Assignments: Budget; Financial Services

Swalwell, Eric, D-Calif. (15)

Capitol Hill Office: 129 CHOB 20515; 225-5065; Fax: 226-3805; *Chief of Staff:* Ricky Le

Web: swalwell.house.gov

Facebook: www.facebook.com/CongressmanEricSwalwell

Twitter: @repswalwell

District Office: 5075 Hopyard Rd., #220, Pleasanton, CA 94588; 925-460-5100; Fax: 925-460-5320; *Sr. Field Rep.:* Josh Huber

1260 B St., #150, Hayward, CA 94541; 510-370-3322; *District Rep.:* Isabel Urbano

Committee Assignments: Permanent Select Intelligence; Science, Space, and Technology

Takai, Mark, D-Hawaii (1)

Capitol Hill Office: 422 CHOB 20515; 225-2726; Fax: 225-0688; *Chief of Staff:* Rod Tanonaka

Web: takai.house.gov

Facebook: www.facebook.com/RepMarkTakai

Twitter: @RepMarkTakai

District Office: 300 Ala Moana Blvd., #4-104, Honolulu, HI 96850; 808-541-2570; Fax: 808-533-0133; *Staff Asst.:* Carissa Nakamura

Committee Assignments: Armed Services; Small Business

Takano, Mark, D-Calif. (41)

Capitol Hill Office: 1507 LHOB 20515; 225-2305; Fax: 225-7018; *Chief of Staff:* Richard McPike

Web: takano.house.gov

Facebook: www.facebook.com/RepMarkTakano

Twitter: @RepMarkTakano

District Office: 3403 10th St., #610, Riverside, CA 92501; 951-222-0203; Fax: 951-222-0217; *District Director:* Rafael Elizalde

Committee Assignments: Education and the Workforce; Science and Space Technology; Veterans' Affairs

Thompson, Bennie, D-Miss. (2)

Capitol Hill Office: 2466 RHOB 20515-2402; 225-5876; Fax: 225-5898; *Chief of Staff:* I. Lanier Avant

Web: benniethompson.house.gov

Facebook: www.facebook.com/Congressman-Bennie-G-Thompson-7259193379

Twitter: @BennieGThompson

District Offices: 107 W. Madison St., Bolton, MS 39041; 601-866-9003; Fax: 601-866-9036; *Field Rep.:* Brenda Funches

910 Courthouse Lane, Greenville, MS 38701-3764; 662-335-9003; Fax: 662-334-1304; *Community Development Coord.:* Timla Washington

728 Main St., Suite A, Greenwood, MS 38930-5030; 662-455-9003; Fax: 662-453-0118; *Caseworker:* Ashley Beale

3607 Medgar Evers Blvd., Jackson, MS 39213-6364; 601-946-9003; Fax: 601-982-5337; *Caseworker:* Steven Gavin

263 E. Main St., P.O. Box 356, Marks, MS 38646; 662-326-9003; *Caseworker; Field Rep.:* Sandra Jamison

106 Green Ave., #106, Mound Bayou, MS 38762-9594; 662-741-9003; Fax: 662-453-0118; *Caseworker:* Geri Adams

Committee Assignment: Homeland Security, Ranking Minority Member

Thompson, Glenn (GT), R-Pa. (5)

Capitol Hill Office: 124 CHOB 20515-3805; 225-5121; Fax: 225-5796; *Chief of Staff:* Matthew Brennan

Web: thompson.house.gov

Facebook: www.facebook.com/CongressmanGT

Twitter: @CongressmanGT

District Offices: 3555 Benner Pike, #101, Bellefonte, PA 16823-8474; 814-353-0215; Fax: 814-353-0218; *Field Rep.:* Mike Glazer

127 W. Spring St., Suite C, Titusville, PA 16354-1727; 814-827-3985; Fax: 814-827-7307; *District Director:* Peter Winkler

Committee Assignments: Agriculture; Education and the Workforce; Natural Resources

Thompson, Mike, D-Calif. (5)

Capitol Hill Office: 231 CHOB 20515-0501; 225-3311; Fax: 225-4335; *Chief of Staff:* Melanie Rhinehart Van Tassell

Web: mikethompson.house.gov

Facebook: www.facebook.com/RepMikeThompson

Twitter: @RepThompson

District Offices: 2721 Napa Valley Corporate Dr., #2, Napa, CA 94558; 707-226-9898; Fax: 707-251-9800; *District Director:* Brad Onorato

2300 County Center Dr., #A100, Santa Rosa, CA 95403; 707-542-7182; Fax: 707-542-2745; *Sr. Field Rep.:* Sean Hamlin

985 Walnut Ave., Vallejo, CA 94592; 707-645-1888; Fax: 707-645-1870; *District Rep.:* Mel Orpilla

Committee Assignment: Ways and Means

Thornberry, Mac, R-Tex. (13)

Capitol Hill Office: 2208 RHOB 20515-4313; 225-3706; Fax: 225-3486; *Chief of Staff:* Josh Martin

Web: thornberry.house.gov

Facebook: www.facebook.com/repmacthornberry

Twitter: @MacTXPress

District Offices: 620 S. Taylor St., #200, Amarillo, TX 79101; 806-371-8844; Fax: 806-371-7044; *Deputy District Director:* Paul Simpson

2525 Kell Blvd., #406, Wichita Falls, TX 76308; 940-692-1700; Fax: 940-692-0539; *District Director:* Sandra Ross

Committee Assignment: Armed Services, Chair

Tiberi, Patrick J., R-Ohio (12)

Capitol Hill Office: 1203 LHOB 20515; 225-5355; Fax: 226-4523; *Chief of Staff:* Kelli Briggs

Web: tiberi.house.gov

Facebook: www.facebook.com/RepPatTiberi

Twitter: @pattiberi

District Office: 250 E. Wilson Bridge Rd., #100, Worthington, OH 43085; 614-523-2555; Fax: 614-818-0887; *District Director:* Mark Bell

Committee Assignment: Joint Economic, Vice-Chair; Ways and Means

Tipton, Scott, R-Colo. (3)

Capitol Hill Office: 218 CHOB 20515-0603; 225-4761; Fax: 226-9669; *Chief of Staff:* Joshua Green

Web: tipton.house.gov

Facebook: www.facebook.com/CongressmanScottTipton

Twitter: @reptipton

District Offices: 609 Main St., #105, Box 11, Alamosa, CO 81101-2557; 719-587-5105; Fax: 719-587-5137; *Field Rep.:* Brenda Felmlee

835 E. 2nd Ave., #230, Durango, CO 81301-5474; 970-259-1490; Fax: 970-259-1563; *Field Rep.:* Darlene Marcus

225 N. 5th St., #702, Grand Junction, CO 81501-2658; 970-241-2499; Fax: 970-241-3053; *Regional Director:* Brian Meinhart

503 N. Main St., #658, Pueblo, CO 81003-3132; 719-542-1073; Fax: 719-542-1127; *District Director:* Brian McCain

Committee Assignment: Financial Services

Titus, Dina, D-Nev. (1)

Capitol Hill Office: 401 CHOB 20515; 225-5965; Fax: 225-3119; *Chief of Staff:* Jay Gertsema

Web: titus.house.gov

Facebook: www.facebook.com/CongresswomanTitus

Twitter: @repdinatitus

District Office: 550 E. Charleston Blvd., Suite B, Las Vegas, NV 89104; 702-220-9823; Fax: 702-220-9841; *District Director:* Mike Naft

Committee Assignments: Transportation and Infrastructure; Veterans' Affairs

Tonko, Paul D., D-N.Y. (20)

Capitol Hill Office: 2463 RHOB 20515; 225-5076; Fax: 225-5077; *Chief of Staff:* Clinton Britt

Web: tonko.house.gov

Facebook: www.facebook.com/reppaultonko

Twitter: @RepPaulTonko

District Offices: 61 Columbia St., 4th Floor, Albany, NY 12210; 518-465-0700; Fax: 518-427-5107; *District Director:* Ryan Horstmyer

61 Church St., Room 309, Amsterdam, NY 12010-4424; 518-843-3400; Fax: 518-843-8874; *Caseworker:* Kelly Quist-Demars

105 Jay St., Room 15, Schenectady, NY 12305-1970; 518-374-4547; Fax: 518-374-7908; *Caseworker:* Cora Schroeter

Committee Assignments: Energy and Commerce; Science, Space, and Technology

Torres, Norma, D-Calif. (35)

Capitol Hill Office: 516 CHOB 20515-0535; 225-6161; Fax: 225-8671; *Chief of Staff:* Dara Postar

Web: torres.house.gov

Facebook: www.facebook.com/RepNormaTorres

Twitter: @NormaJTorres

District Office: 3200 Inland Empire Blvd., #200B, Ontario, CA 91764; 909-481-6474; Fax: 909-941-1362; *District Director:* Veronica Zendejas

Committee Assignments: Homeland Security; Natural Resources

Trott, Dave, R-Mich. (11)

Capitol Hill Office: 1722 LHOB 20515-2211; 225-8171; Fax: 225-2667; *Chief of Staff:* Jenny Gorski

Web: trott.house.gov

Facebook: www.facebook.com/CongressmanDaveTrott

Twitter: @Repdavetrott

District Office: 625 E. Big Beaver Rd., #204, Troy, MI 48083; 248-528-0711; Fax: 248-528-0714; *District Director:* Doug Tietz

Committee Assignments: Foreign Affairs; Judiciary

Tsongas, Niki, D-Mass. (3)

Capitol Hill Office: 1714 LHOB 20515-2105; 225-3411; Fax: 226-0771; *Chief of Staff:* Katie Enos

Web: tsongas.house.gov

Facebook: www.facebook.com/RepTsongas

Twitter: @nikiinthehouse

District Office: 126 John St., #12, Lowell, MA 01852; 978-459-0101; Fax: 978-459-1907; *District Director:* June Black

Satellite Offices: 10 Welcome St., #4, Haverhill, MA 01830; 978-459-0101; *Constituent Services Rep.:* Mabel Covarrubias-Doucette

15 Union St., #401, Lawrence, MA 01840; 978-459-0101; Fax: 978-682-6070; *Casework Manager:* Patrick Kenney

255 Main St., #106, Marlborough, MA 01752; 978-459-0101; *Constituent Services Rep.:* Mabel Covarrubias-Doucette

Fitchburg State University, Center for Professional Studies Office, 150 Main St., Fitchburg, MA 01420; 978-459-0101; *Constituent Services Rep.:* Mabel Covarrubias-Doucette

Committee Assignments: Armed Services; Natural Resources

Turner, Mike, R-Ohio (10)

Capitol Hill Office: 2239 RHOB 20515-3503; 225-6465; Fax: 225-6754; *Chief of Staff:* Adam Howard
Web: turner.house.gov
Facebook: www.facebook.com/RepMikeTurner
Twitter: @RepMikeTurner
District Office: 120 W. 3rd St., #305, Dayton, OH 45402-1819; 937-225-2843; Fax: 937-225-2752; *District Director:* Frank Debrosse
Committee Assignments: Armed Services; Oversight and Government Reform; Permanent Select Intelligence

Upton, Fred, R-Mich. (6)

Capitol Hill Office: 2183 RHOB 20515-2206; 225-3761; Fax: 225-4986; *Chief of Staff:* Joan Hillebrands
Web: upton.house.gov
Facebook: www.facebook.com/RepFredUpton
Twitter: @RepFredUpton
District Offices: 157 S. Kalamazoo Mall, #180, Kalamazoo, MI 49007-4861; 269-385-0039; Fax: 269-385-2888; *District Director:* Lynn Turner
720 Main St., St. Joseph, MI 49085-2182; 269-982-1986; Fax: 269-982-0237; *Sr. Constituent Services Rep.:* Janet Zielke
Committee Assignment: Energy and Commerce, Chair

Valadao, David G., R-Calif. (21)

Capitol Hill Office: 1004 LHOB 20515; 225-4695; Fax: 225-3196; *Chief of Staff:* Cole Rojewski
Web: valadao.house.gov
Facebook: www.facebook.com/CongressmanDavidValadao
Twitter: @RepDavidValadao
District Offices: 2700 M St., #250B, Bakersfield, CA 93301; 661-864-7736; Fax: 559-587-5527; *Field Rep.:* Alex Dominguez
101 N. Irwin St., #110B, Hanford, CA 93230; 559-582-5526; Fax: 559-582-5527; *District Director:* Justin Mendes
Committee Assignment: Appropriations

Van Hollen, Chris, D-Md. (8)

Capitol Hill Office: 1707 LHOB 20515-2008; 225-5341; Fax: 225-0375; *Chief of Staff:* Karen Robb
Web: vanhollen.house.gov
Facebook: www.facebook.com/chrisvanhollen

Twitter: @chrisvanhollen
District Office: 51 Monroe St., #507, Rockville, MD 20850-2406; 301-424-3501; Fax: 301-424-5992; *District Director:* Joan Kleinman
205 Center St., #206, Mount Airy, MD 21771; 301-829-2181; *Field Rep.:* Melissa Joseph
76 E. Moser Rd., Thurmont, MD 21788; 301-829-2181; Fax: 301-424-5992; *Field Rep.:* Vacant
Committee Assignment: Budget, Ranking Minority Member

Vargas, Juan, D-Calif. (51)

Capitol Hill Office: 1605 LHOB 20515; 225-8045; Fax: 225-2772; *Chief of Staff:* Tim Walsh
Web: vargas.house.gov
Facebook: www.facebook.com/RepJuanVargas
Twitter: @RepJuanVargas
District Office: 333 F St., Suite A, Chula Vista, CA 91910-2624; 619-422-5963; Fax: 619-422-7290; *Sr. Field Rep.:* Eddie Meyer
380 N. 8th St., #14, El Centro, CA 92243; 760-355-9900; Fax: 760-312-9664; *Sr. Field Rep.:* Tomas Oliva
Committee Assignments: House Administration; Financial Services; Joint Printing

Veasey, Marc, D-Tex. (33)

Capitol Hill Office: 414 CHOB 20515; 225-9897; Fax: 225-9702; *Chief of Staff:* Jane Hamilton
Web: veasey.house.gov
Facebook: www.facebook.com/CongressmanMarcVeasey
Twitter: @RepVeasey
District Offices: JP Morgan Chase Bldg., 1881 Sylvan Ave., #108, Dallas, TX 75208; 214-741-1387; Fax: 214-741-2026; *District Director:* Anne Hagan
La Gran Plaza Office Tower, 4200 S. Freeway, #412, Fort Worth, TX 76115; 817-920-9086; Fax: 817-920-9324; *Director of Constituent Services:* Jennifer Ward
Committee Assignments: Armed Services; Science, Space, and Technology

Vela, Filemon, D-Tex. (34)

Capitol Hill Office: 437 CHOB 20515; 225-9901; Fax: 225-9770; *Chief of Staff:* Perry Brody
Web: vela.house.gov
Facebook: www.facebook.com/UsCongressmanFilemonVela
Twitter: @RepFilemonVela
District Offices: 500 E. Main St., Alice, TX 78332; 361-230-9776; *District Director:* Jose Pereida
333 Ebony Ave., Brownsville, TX 78520; 956-544-8352; Cameron County District Director: Marisela Cortez
1390 W. Expressway 83, San Benito, TX 78586; 956-276-4497; Fax: 956-276-4603; *Hidalgo County District Director:* Sally Lara
500 S. Kansas Ave., Weslaco, TX 78596; 956-520-8273; Fax: 956-520-8277; *Caseworker:* Anissa Guajardo
Committee Assignments: Agriculture; Homeland Security

Velázquez, Nydia M., D-N.Y. (7)

Capitol Hill Office: 2302 RHOB 20515-3212; 225-2361; Fax: 226-0327; *Chief of Staff:* Michael Day
Web: velazquez.house.gov
Facebook: www.facebook.com/ Nydia-Velazquez-8037068318
Twitter: @NydiaVelazquez
District Offices: 266 Broadway, #201, Brooklyn, NY 11211-6215; 718-599-3658; Fax: 718-599-4537; *Exec. Asst.:* Lucy Morcelo
16 Court St., #1006, Brooklyn, NY 11241-1010; 718-222-5819; Fax: 718-222-5830; *Community Coord.:* Daniel Wiley
500 Pearl St., #973, New York, NY 10007; 212-619-2606; Fax: 212-619-4969; *Community Liaison:* Iris Quiñones
Committee Assignments: Financial Services; Small Business, Ranking Minority Member

Visclosky, Pete, D-Ind. (1)

Capitol Hill Office: 2328 RHOB 20515-1401; 225-2461; Fax: 225-2493; *Chief of Staff:* Mark Lopez
Web: visclosky.house.gov
Facebook: www.facebook.com/repvisclosky
Twitter: @repvisclosky
District Office: 7895 Broadway, Suite A, Merrillville, IN 46410-5529; 219-795-1844; Fax: 219-795-1850; *Chief of Casework:* Greg Gulvas
Committee Assignment: Appropriations

Wagner, Ann, R-Mo. (2)

Capitol Hill Office: 435 CHOB 20515; 225-1621; Fax: 225-2563; *Chief of Staff:* Christian Morgan
Web: wagner.house.gov
Facebook: www.facebook.com/RepAnnWagner
Twitter: @RepAnnWagner
District Offices: 301 Sovereign Court, #201, Ballwin, MO 63011-4442; 636-779-5449; Fax: 636-779-5457; *District Director:* Miriam Stonebreaker
Committee Assignment: Financial Services

Walberg, Tim, R-Mich. (7)

Capitol Hill Office: 2436 RHOB 20515; 225-6276; Fax: 225-6281; *Chief of Staff:* R.J. Laukitis
Web: walberg.house.gov
Facebook: www.facebook.com/RepWalberg
Twitter: @RepWalberg
District Office: 110 1st St., #2, Jackson, MI 49201; 517-780-9075; Fax: 517-780-9081; *District Director:* Dustin Krasny, Stephen Rajzer
Committee Assignments: Education and the Workforce; Oversight and Government Reform

Walden, Greg, R-Ore. (2)

Capitol Hill Office: 2185 RHOB 20515-3702; 225-6730; Fax: 225-5774; *Chief of Staff:* Brian C. MacDonald
Web: walden.house.gov
Facebook: www.facebook.com/repgregwalden
Twitter: @repgregwalden

District Offices: 1051 N.W. Bond St., #400, Bend, OR 97701-2061; 541-389-4408; Fax: 541-389-4452; *Director, Central Oregon Office:* Nick Strader
1211 Washington Ave., La Grande, OR 97850-2535; 541-624-2400; *Field Rep.:* Jorden Noyes
14 N. Central Ave., #112, Medford, OR 97501-5912; 541-776-4646; Fax: 541-779-0204; *Southern Oregon Office Director:* Riley Bushue
Committee Assignment: Energy and Commerce

Walker, Mark, R-N.C. (6)

Capitol Hill Office: 312 CHOB 20515-3306; 225-3065; Fax: 225-8611; *Chief of Staff:* Scott Luginbill
Web: walker.house.gov
Facebook: www.facebook.com/RepMarkWalker
Twitter: @RepMarkWalker
District Office: 809 Green Valley Rd., #104, Greensboro, NC 27408; 336-333-5005; *Office Manager:* Katie Sessoms
219 B W. Elm St., P.O. Box 812, Graham, NC 27253; 336-229-0159; Fax: 336-350-9514; *Constituent Services Liaison:* Jeanin Osbourne
Committee Assignments: Homeland Security; House Administration; Oversight and Government Reform

Walorski, Jackie, R-Ind. (2)

Capitol Hill Office: 419 CHOB 20515; 225-3915; Fax: 225-6798; *Chief of Staff:* Ben Falkowski
Web: walorski.house.gov
Facebook: www.facebook.com/RepJackieWalorski
Twitter: @RepWalorski
District Office: 202 Lincolnway East, #101, Mishawaka, IN 46544; 574-204-2645; Fax: 574-217-8735; *District Director:* Brian Spaulding
Satellite Office: 709 Main St., Rochester, IN 46975; 574-223-4373; Fax: 574-223-4374; *District Director:* Brian Spaulding
Committee Assignments: Agriculture; Armed Services; Veterans' Affairs

Walters, Mimi, R-Calif. (45)

Capitol Hill Office: 236 CHOB 20515-0545; 225-5611; Fax: 225-9177; *Chief of Staff:* David Bowser
Web: walters.house.gov
Facebook: www.facebook.com/RepMimiWalters
Twitter: @RepMimiWalters
District Office: 3333 Michelson Dr., #230, Irvine, CA 92612; 949-263-8703; Fax: 949-263-8704; *Deputy Chief of Staff:* Sam Oh; *Staff Asst.:* Hannah Hess
Committee Assignments: Judiciary; Transportation and Infrastructure

Walz, Tim, D-Minn. (1)

Capitol Hill Office: 1034 LHOB 20515; 225-2472; Fax: 225-3433; *Deputy Chief of Staff:* Sara Severs
Web: walz.house.gov
Facebook: www.facebook.com/TimWalz4Congress
Twitter: @RepTimWalz

District Offices: 527 1/2 S. Front St., Mankato, MN 56001-3573; 507-388-2149; Fax: 507-388-3174; *Chief of Staff:* Josh Syrjamaki

1202 1/2 7th St. N.W., #211, Rochester, MN 55901-1732; 507-388-2149; Fax: 507-206-0650; *Field Rep.:* John Pierce

Committee Assignments: Agriculture; Armed Services; Commission on China; Veterans' Affairs

Wasserman Schultz, Debbie, D-Fla. (23)

Capitol Hill Office: 1114 LHOB 20515; 225-7931; Fax: 226-2052; *Chief of Staff:* Tracie Pough
Web: wassermanschultz.house.gov
Facebook: www.facebook.com/RepDWS
Twitter: @RepDWStweets
District Offices: 19200 W. Country Club Dr., Aventura, FL 33180-2403; 305-936-5724; Fax: 305-932-9664; *Deputy District Director:* Laurie Flink

10100 Pines Blvd., Pembroke Pines, FL 33026-6040; 954-437-3936; Fax: 954-437-4776; *District Director:* Jodi Davidson

Committee Assignment: Appropriations

Waters, Maxine, D-Calif. (43)

Capitol Hill Office: 2221 RHOB 20515-0535; 225-2201; Fax: 225-7854; *Chief of Staff:* Twaun Samuel
Web: waters.house.gov
Facebook: www.facebook.com/MaxineWaters
Twitter: @MaxineWaters
District Office: 10124 S. Broadway, #1, Los Angeles, CA 90003-4535; 323-757-8900; Fax: 323-757-9506; *District Director:* Blanca Jimenez
Committee Assignment: Financial Services, Ranking Minority Member

Watson Coleman, Bonnie, D-N.J. (12)

Capitol Hill Office: 126 CHOB 20515-3012; 225-5801; Fax: 225-6025; *Chief of Staff:* James Gee
Web: watsoncoleman.house.gov
Facebook: www.facebook.com/RepBonnieWatsonColeman
Twitter: @bwatsoncoleman
District Office: 850 Bear Tavern Rd., #201, Ewing, NJ 08628; 609-883-0026; Fax: 609-883-2093; *Staff Asst.:* Yujin Lee
Committee Assignments: Homeland Security; Oversight and Government Reform

Weber, Randy, R-Tex. (14)

Capitol Hill Office: 510 CHOB 20515; 225-2831; Fax: 225-0271; *Chief of Staff:* Chara McMichael
Web: weber.house.gov
Facebook: www.facebook.com/TXRandy14
Twitter: @TXRandy14
District Offices: 505 Orleans St., #103, Beaumont, TX 77701; 409-835-0108; Fax: 409-835-0578; *Deputy District Director:* Blake Hopper

122 W. Way, #301, Lake Jackson, TX 77566-5245; 979-285-0231; Fax: 979-285-0271; *Community Liaison:* Dodie Armstrong

174 Calder Rd., League City, TX 77573; 281-316-0231; Fax: 281-316-0271; *District Director:* Jed Webb
Committee Assignments: Foreign Affairs; Science, Space, and Technology

Webster, Daniel, R-Fla. (10)

Capitol Hill Office: 1039 LHOB 20515-0908; 225-2176; Fax: 225-0999; *Chief of Staff, Acting:* Garrett Bess
Web: webster.house.gov
Facebook: www.facebook.com/RepWebster
Twitter: @RepWebster
District Offices: 685 W. Montrose St., Clermont, FL 34711; 352-383-3552; Fax: 407-654-5814; *Constituent Services Rep.:* Ann Drawdy

315 W. Main St., Tavares, FL 32778-3806; 352-383-3552; Fax: 407-654-5814; *Constituent Services Director:* Abigail Tyrrell

451 3rd St. N.W., Winter Haven, FL 33881; 863-453-0273; Fax: 407-654-5814; *Constituent Services Rep.:* Natali Knight

300 W. Plant St., Winter Garden, FL 34787-3009; 407-654-5705; Fax: 407-654-5814; *Constituent Services Director:* Abigail Tyrrell

Committee Assignment: Transportation and Infrastructure

Welch, Peter, D-Vt. (At Large)

Capitol Hill Office: 2303 RHOB 20515; 225-4115; Fax: 225-6790; *Chief of Staff:* Bob Rogan
Web: welch.house.gov
Facebook: www.facebook.com/PeterWelch
Twitter: @PeterWelch
District Office: 128 Lakeside Ave., #235, Burlington, VT 05401; 802-652-2450; Fax: 802-652-2497; *State Director:* George Twigg
Committee Assignments: Energy and Commerce; Oversight and Government Reform

Wenstrup, Brad, R-Ohio (2)

Capitol Hill Office: 1318 LHOB 20515; 225-3164; Fax: 225-1992; *Chief of Staff:* Derek Harley
Web: wenstrup.house.gov
Facebook: www.facebook.com/RepBradWenstrup
Twitter: @RepBradWenstrup
District Offices: 7954 Beechmont Ave., #200, Cincinnati, OH 45255; 513-474-7777; Fax: 513-605-1377; *District Director:* Jeff Groenke

170 N. Main St., Peebles, OH 45660; 513-605-1380; *Field Rep.:* Kaci Compton

4350 Alcholtz Rd., Cincinnati, OH 45255; *Field Rep.:* Jeff Uckotter

Committee Assignments: Armed Services; Permanent Select Intelligence; Veterans' Affairs

Westerman, Bruce, R-Ark. (4)

Capitol Hill Office: 130 CHOB 20515-0404; 225-3772; Fax: 225-1314; *Chief of Staff:* Vivian Moeglein
Web: westerman.house.gov
Facebook: www.facebook.com/RepWesterman

Twitter: @RepWesterman
District Office: 101 N. Washington St., #406, El Dorado, AR 71730; 870-864-8946; Fax: 870-864-8958; *Field Rep.:* Ben Gilmore
101 Reserve St., #200, Hot Springs, AR 71901; 501-609-9796; Fax: 501-609-9887; *District Director:* Jason D. McGehee
211 W. Commercial St., Ozark, AR 72949; 479-667-0075; Fax: 501-609-9887; *Field Rep.:* Robert Ballinger
100 E. 8th Ave., Room 2521, Pine Bluff, AR 71601; 870-536-8178; Fax: 870-536-8364; *Field Rep.:* Tracy Cross
Committee Assignments: Budget; Natural Resources; Science, Space and Technology

Westmoreland, Lynn, R-Ga. (3)

Capitol Hill Office: 2202 RHOB 20515-1003; 225-5901; Fax: 225-2515; *Chief of Staff:* Brad Bohannon
Web: westmoreland.house.gov
Facebook: www.facebook.com/CongressmanLynnWestmoreland
Twitter: @RepWestmoreland
District Office: 1601-B E. Hwy. 34, Newnan, GA 30265-1325; 770-683-2033; Fax: 770-683-2042; *District Director:* Andy Bush
Committee Assignments: Financial Services; Permanent Select Intelligence; Select on Benghazi

Whitfield, Ed, R-Ky. (1)

Capitol Hill Office: 2184 RHOB 20515; 225-3115; Fax: 225-3547; *Chief of Staff:* TayLor Booth
Web: whitfield.house.gov
Facebook: www.facebook.com/RepEdWhitfield
Twitter: @repedwhitfield
District Offices: 222 1st St., #224, Henderson, KY 42420-3181; 270-826-4180; Fax: 270-826-6783; *Field Rep.:* Ed West
1403 S. Main St., Hopkinsville, KY 42240-2017; 270-885-8079; Fax: 270-885-8598; *Field Rep./Caseworker:* Kate Prince
100 Fountain Ave., #104, Paducah, KY 42001-2771; 270-442-6901; Fax: 270-442-6805; *Field Rep.:* Janece Everett
200 N. Main St., Suite F, Tompkinsville, KY 42167; 270-487-9509; Fax: 270-487-0019; *Field Rep.:* Sandy Simpson
Committee Assignment: Energy and Commerce

Williams, Roger, R-Tex. (25)

Capitol Hill Office: 1323 LHOB 20515; 225-9896; Fax: 225-9692; *Chief of Staff:* Colby Hale
Web: williams.house.gov
Facebook: www.facebook.com/RepRogerWilliams
Twitter: @RepRWilliams
District Offices: 1005 Congress Ave., #925, Austin, TX 78701; 512-473-8910; Fax: 512-473-8946; *District Director:* John Etue
1 Walnut St., #145, Cleburne, TX 76033; 817-774-2575; Fax: 817-774-2576; *District Rep.:* Robert Camacho
Committee Assignment: Financial Services

Wilson, Frederica S., D-Fla. (24)

Capitol Hill Office: 208 CHOB 20515-0917; 225-4506; Fax: 226-0777; *Chief of Staff:* Kim Bowman
Web: wilson.house.gov
Facebook: www.facebook.com/RepWilson
Twitter: @RepWilson
District Offices: 18425 2nd Ave. N.W., #355, Miami Gardens, FL 33169-4534; 305-690-5905; Fax: 305-690-5951; *District Chief of Staff:* Alexis Snyder
10100 Pines Blvd., Bldg. B, 3rd Floor, Pembroke Pines, FL 33025; 954-450-6767; Fax: 954-450-6768; *Congressional Aide:* Walta Tolbert
West Park City Hall, 1965 S. State Rd. 7, West Park, FL 33023; 954-989-2688; *Congressional Aide:* Walta Tolbert
2300 Civic Center, Miramar, FL 33025; 954-602-4357; *Director of Field Operations:* Shirlee Moreau-La Fleur
Committee Assignment: Education and the Workforce

Wilson, Joe, R-S.C. (2)

Capitol Hill Office: 2229 RHOB 20515-4002; 225-2452; Fax: 225-2455; *Chief of Staff:* Jonathan Day
Web: joewilson.house.gov
Facebook: www.facebook.com/JoeWilson
Twitter: @RepJoeWilson
District Offices: 1930 University Pkwy., #1600, Aiken, SC 29801; 803-642-6416; Fax: 803-642-6418; *Special Asst.:* Sarah Beaulieu
1700 Sunset Blvd. (U.S. 378), #1, West Columbia, SC 29169; 803-939-0041; Fax: 803-939-0078; *District Director:* Butch Wallace
Committee Assignments: Armed Services; Education and the Workforce; Foreign Affairs

Wittman, Robert J., R-Va. (1)

Capitol Hill Office: 2454 RHOB 20515; 225-4261; Fax: 225-4382; *Chief of Staff:* Jamie Miller
Web: wittman.house.gov
Facebook: www.facebook.com/RepRobWittman
Twitter: @RobWittman
District Offices: 95 Dunn Dr., #201, Stafford, VA 22556; 540-659-2734; Fax: 540-659-2737; *District Rep.:* Kristin Baroody
508 Church Lane, P.O. Box 3106, Tappahannock, VA 22560; 804-443-0668; Fax: 804-443-0671; *District Rep.:* Chris Jones
401 Main St., P.O. Box 494, Yorktown, VA 23690; 757-874-6687; Fax: 757-874-7164; *District Director:* Joe Schumacher
Committee Assignments: Armed Services; Natural Resources

Womack, Steve, R-Ark. (3)

Capitol Hill Office: 1119 LHOB 20515; 225-4301; Fax: 225-5713; *Chief of Staff:* Beau T. Walker
Web: womack.house.gov
Facebook: www.facebook.com/RepSteveWomack
Twitter: @rep_stevewomack

District Offices: 423 N. 6th St., Ft. Smith, AR 72902; 479-424-1146; Fax: 479-424-2737; *Field Rep.:* Janice Scaggs
303 N. Main St., #102, Harrison, AR 72601-3508; 870-741-6900; Fax: 870-741-7741; *Field Rep.:* Teri Garrett
3333 Pinnacle Hills Pkwy., #120, Rogers, AR 72758-9100; 479-464-0446; Fax: 479-464-0063; *Field Rep.:* Jeff Thacker
Committee Assignments: Appropriations; Budget

Woodall, Rob, R-Ga. (7)

Capitol Hill Office: 1725 LHOB 20515-1007; 225-4272; Fax: 225-4696; *Chief of Staff:* Derick Corbett
Web: woodall.house.gov
Facebook: www.facebook.com/RepRobWoodall
Twitter: @RepRobWoodall
District Office: 75 Langley Dr., Lawrenceville, GA 30046; 770-232-3005; Fax: 770-232-2909; *District Director:* Debra Poirot
Committee Assignments: Budget; Rules; Transportation and Infrastructure

Yarmuth, John, D-Ky. (3)

Capitol Hill Office: 403 CHOB 20515-1703; 225-5401; Fax: 225-5776; *Chief of Staff:* Julie Carr
Web: yarmuth.house.gov
Facebook: www.facebook.com/Congressman-John-Yarmuth-KY-3-214258646163
Twitter: @RepJohnYarmuth
District Offices: Romano L. Mazzoli Federal Bldg., 600 Martin Luther King Jr. Pl., #216, Louisville, KY 40202; 502-582-5129; Fax: 502-582-5897; *District Director:* Carolyn Tandy
Southwest Government Center, 7219 Dixie Hwy., Louisville, KY 40258-3756; 502-933-5863; Fax: 502-935-6934; *Congressional Aide:* Shelley Spratt
Committee Assignments: Budget; Energy and Commerce

Yoder, Kevin, R-Kans. (3)

Capitol Hill Office: 215 CHOB 20515-1603; 225-2865; Fax: 225-2807; *Chief of Staff:* Dave Natonski
Web: yoder.house.gov
Facebook: www.facebook.com/CongressmanKevinYoder
Twitter: @RepKevinYoder
District Office: 7325 W. 79th St., Overland Park, KS 66204-2908; 913-621-0832; Fax: 913-621-1533; *District Director:* Molly Haase
Committee Assignment: Appropriations

Yoho, Ted, R-Fla. (3)

Capitol Hill Office: 511 CHOB 20515; 225-5744; Fax: 225-3973; *Chief of Staff:* Omar Raschid
Web: yoho.house.gov
Facebook: www.facebook.com/CongressmanTedYoho
Twitter: @RepTedYoho
District Offices: 5000 N.W. 27th Court, Suite E, Gainesville, FL 32606; 352-505-0838; Fax: 352-505-3511; *Deputy District Director:* Kat Cammack

35 Knight Boxx Rd., #1, Orange Park, FL 32065; 904-276-9626; Fax: 904-276-9336; *Constituent Advocate:* Dorothy Richardson
Committee Assignments: Agriculture; Foreign Affairs

Young, David, R-Iowa (3)

Capitol Hill Office: 515 CHOB 20515-1504; 225-5476; Fax: 226-1329; *Chief of Staff:* James Carstensen
Web: davidyoung.house.gov
Facebook: www.facebook.com/RepDavidYoung
Twitter: @RepDavidYoung
District Office: 208 W. Taylor St., Creston, IA 50801; 641-782-2495; *District Director:* Laura Hartman
601 E. Locust St., #204, Des Moines, IA 50309; 515-282-1909; *District Manager:* Sherill Whisenan
501 5th Ave., Council Bluffs, IA 51503; 712-325-1404; *Caseworker:* Charlie Johnson
Committee Assignment: Appropriations

Young, Don A., R-Alaska (At Large)

Capitol Hill Office: 2314 RHOB 20515-0201; 225-5765; Fax: 225-0425; *Chief of Staff:* Pamela A. Day
Web: donyoung.house.gov
Facebook: www.facebook.com/RepDonYoung
Twitter: @RepDonYoung
District Offices: 4241 B St., #203, Anchorage, AK 99503-5920; 907-271-5978; Fax: 907-271-5950; *State Director:* Chad Padgett
100 Cushman St., #307, Key Bank Bldg., Fairbanks, AK 99707; 907-456-0210; Fax: 907-456-0279; *Special Asst.:* Kim Stickler
Committee Assignments: Natural Resources; Transportation and Infrastructure

Young, Todd, R-Ind. (9)

Capitol Hill Office: 1007 LHOB 20515; 225-5315; Fax: 226-6866; *Chief of Staff:* John Connell
Web: toddyoung.house.gov
Facebook: www.facebook.com/RepToddYoung
Twitter: @RepToddYoung
District Offices: 320 W. 8th St., #114, Bloomington, IN 47404-3700; 812-336-3000; Fax: 812-336-3355; *Constituent Services Manager:* Harold Turner
300 S. Madison Ave., Greenwood, IN 46142; 812-350-8956; *District Director:* Deb Johannes
279 Quartermaster Court, Jeffersonville, IN 47130-3669; 812-288-3999; Fax: 812-288-3873; *Constituent Coordinator:* Becky Lambert
Committee Assignment: Ways and Means

Zeldin, Lee, R-N.Y. (1)

Capitol Hill Office: 1517 LHOB 20515-3201; 225-3826; Fax: 225-3143; *Chief of Staff:* Eric Amidon
Web: zeldin.house.gov
Facebook: www.facebook.com/RepLeeZeldin
Twitter: @RepLeeZeldin
District Office: 31 Oak St., #20, Patchogue, NY 11772; 631-289-1097; Fax: 631-289-1268; *Field Rep.:* Jennifer Disiena

Satellite Office: 30 W. Main St., #201, Riverhead, NY 11901; 631-209-4235;

Committee Assignments: Foreign Affairs; Transportation and Infrastructure; Veterans' Affairs

Zinke, Ryan, R-Mont. (At Large)

Capitol Hill Office: 113 CHOB 20515; 225-3211; Fax: 225-5687; *Chief of Staff:* Scott Hommel

Web: zinke.house.gov

Facebook: www.facebook.com/CongressmanRyanZinke

Twitter: @RepRyanZinke

District Office: 222 N. 32nd St., #900, Billings, MT 59101; 406-969-1736; Fax: 406-702-1182; *Scheduler:* Jocelyn Galt

910 N. Last Chance Gulch, Suite B, Helena, MT 59601; 406-502-1435; Fax: 406-502-1436; *Staff Asst.:* Caroline Boulton

710 Central Ave., Great Falls, MT 59401; 406-952-1210; Fax: 406-952-1211;

1008 South Ave., #2, Missoula, MT 59801; 406-540-4370; 406-540-4371;

Committee Assignments: Armed Services; Natural Resources

Vacant-Ohio (8)

Capitol Hill Office: 1011 LHOB 20515-3508; 225-6205; Fax: 225-0704; *Chief of Staff:* Ryan Day

Web: clerk.house.govmember_info/vacancies.aspx

District Offices: 12 S. Plum St., Troy, OH 45373-3282; 937-339-1524; Fax: 937-339-1878; *Field Rep.:* Frank DeBrosse

76 E. High St., 3rd Floor, Springfield, OH 45502; 937-322-1120; *Field Rep.:* Austin Bingham

7969 Cincinnati-Dayton Rd., Suite B, West Chester, OH 45069-6637; 513-779-5400; Fax: 513-779-5315; *Office Manager:* Sharon Hughes

Joint Committees of Congress

The joint committees of Congress follow. Each listing includes room number, office building, zip code, telephone number, Web address(es), key staffers, committee jurisdiction, and membership (in order of seniority) for each committee. Members are drawn from the Senate and House and from both parties. This information is current as of April 25, 2016.

Republicans, the current majority in both chambers, are shown in roman type; Democrats, in the minority, appear in italic. When a senator serves as chair, the vice chair usually is a representative, and vice versa. The location of the chair usually rotates from one chamber to the other at the beginning of each Congress. The area code for all phone and fax numbers is (202). A phone number and/or office number next to either the Majority or Minority Staff Director indicates a change from the full committee's office number and/or phone number. If no numbers are listed, the individual's office number and phone number are the same as for the full committee.

JOINT ECONOMIC COMMITTEE

Office: G-01 SDOB 20510-6075
Phone: 224-5171 **Fax:** 224-0240
Web: jec.senate.gov/republicans
Minority Web: www.jec.senate.gov/public
Majority Staff Director: Robert O'Quinn
Minority Staff Director: Corey Astill
   Jurisdiction: (1) make a continuing study of matters relating to the Economic Report of the President; (2) study means of coordinating programs in order to further the policy of this Act; and (3) as a guide to the several committees of the Congress dealing with legislation relating to the Economic Report, not later than March 1 of each year (beginning with the year 1947) to file a report with the Senate and the House of Representatives containing its findings and recommendations with respect to each of the main recommendations made by the president in the Economic Report, and from time to time to make other reports and recommendations to the Senate and the House of Representatives as it deems advisable.

Senate Members

Dan Coats, Ind., Chair
Mike Lee, Utah
Ted Cruz, Tex.
Bill Cassidy, La.
Tom Cotton, Ark.
Ben Sasse, Neb.

Amy Klobuchar, Minn.
Robert P. Casey Jr., Pa.
Martin Heinrich, N.M.
Gary Peters, Mich.

House Members

Pat Tiberi, Ohio, Vice Chair
Justin Amash, Mich.
Erik Paulsen, Minn.
Richard Hanna, N.Y.
David Schweikert
Glenn Grothman

Carolyn B. Maloney, N.Y.
John Delaney, Md.
Alma Adams, N.C.
Don Beyer, Va.

JOINT COMMITTEE ON THE LIBRARY

Office: 1309 LHOB 20515-6157
Phone: 225-8281 **Fax:** 225-9957
Web: cha.house.gov/jointcommittees/joint-committee-library

Majority Staff Director: Sean Moran
Minority Staff Director: Kyle Anderson, 225-2061, 1307 LHOB
   Jurisdiction: considers proposals concerning the management and expansion of the Library of Congress, the development and maintenance of the U.S. Botanic Garden, the receipt of gifts for the benefit of the Library, and certain matters relating to placing of statues and other works of art in the U.S. Capitol.

Senate Members

Roy Blunt, Mo., Chair
Pat Roberts, Kans.
Shelley Moore Capito, W.Va.

Charles E. Schumer, N.Y.,
Patrick Leahy, Vt.

House Members

Gregg Harper, Miss., Vice Chair
Candice S. Miller, Mich.
Tom Graves, Ga.

Robert Brady, Pa.
Zoe Lofgren, Calif.

JOINT COMMITTEE ON PRINTING

Office: 1307 LHOB 20515
Phone: 225-2061 **Fax:** 226-2061
Web: http://cha.house.gov/jointcommittees/joint-committee-on-printing
Minority Web: http://democrats.cha.house.gov/joint-committee-printing
Majority Professional Staff Member: Katie Ryan
Minority Professional Staff Member: Sean Moran, 225-8281, 1309 LHOB
   Jurisdiction: oversight of (1) the functions of the Government Printing Office and general printing procedures of the federal government; and (2) compliance by federal entities with Title 44 of the U.S. Code, and the Government Printing and Binding Regulations.

Senate Members

Roy Blunt, Mo., Vice Chair
Pat Roberts, Kans.
John Boozman, Ark.

Charles E. Schumer, N.Y.,
Tom Udall, N.M.

House Members

Gregg Harper, Miss., Chair   *Robert Brady, Pa.*
Candice S. Miller, Mich.   *Juan Vargas, Calif.*
Rodney Davis, Ill.

JOINT COMMITTEE ON TAXATION

Office: 502 FHOB 20515-6453
Phone: 225-3621   **Fax:** 225-0832
Web: www.jct.gov
Chief of Staff: Thomas A. Barthold
  Jurisdiction: involved with every aspect of the tax legislative process, including: (1) assisting congressional tax-writing committees and Members of Congress with development and analysis of legislative proposals; (2) preparing official revenue estimates of all tax legislation considered by the Congress; (3) drafting legislative histories for tax-related bills; (4) investigating various aspects of the federal tax system.

Senate Members

Orrin G. Hatch, Utah, Chair   *Ron Wyden, Ore.*
Chuck Grassley, Iowa   *Debbie Stabenow, Mich.*
Mike Crapo, Idaho

House Members

Kevin Brady, Tex., Vice Chair   *Sandy Levin, Mich.*
Sam Johnson, Tex.   *Charles B. Rangel, N.Y.*
David Nunes, Calif.

COMMISSION ON SECURITY AND COOPERATION IN EUROPE (HELSINKI COMMISSION)

Office: 234 FHOB 20515-6460
Phone: 225-1901   **Fax:** 226-4199
Web: www.csce.gov
Chief of Staff: Mark S. Milosch
Counsel for International Law: Erika B. Schlager
  Jurisdiction: Established in 1976 to monitor and encourage compliance with the Final Act of the Organization for Security and Cooperation in Europe (OSCE), concluded at Helsinki, Finland on August 1, 1975. The Commission responds to the changing nature of the Helsinki process by: convening public hearings with expert witnesses to discuss issues affecting the OSCE community; organizing official delegations to OSCE states to assess political, economic and human rights developments; providing accurate and relevant information on the OSCE to the Congress and the public; furnishing Congress and the public with reports on the current diplomatic initiatives in the OSCE; participating in training seminars and conferences on human rights and the rule of law for official and non-governmental representatives; bringing the OSCE-related concerns of private citizens and groups to the attention of U.S. government officials, the U.S. Congress, and other OSCE participating states; and providing an important base of technical and political analysis for policymakers at home and abroad.

Senate Members

Roger Wicker, Miss.,   *Benjamin L. Cardin, Md.*
  Co-Chair   *Sheldon Whitehouse, R.I.*
Richard Burr, N.C.   *Tom Udall, N.M.*
John Boozman, Ark.   *Jeanne Shaheen, N.H.*

House Members

Chris Smith, N.J., Chair   *Alcee L. Hastings, Fla.*
Joe Pitts, Pa.   *Louise M. Slaughter, N.Y.*
Robert B. Aderholt, Ala.   *Steve Cohen, Tenn.*
Michael C. Burgess, Tex.   *Alan Grayson, Fla.*
Randy Hultgren, Ill.

CONGRESSIONAL-EXECUTIVE COMMISSION ON CHINA

Office: 243 FHOB 20515-0001
Phone: 226-3766   **Fax:** 226-3804
Web: www.cecc.gov
CECC Political Prisoner Database: cecc.gov/resources/
  political-prisoner-database
International Human Rights Materials: cecc.gov/
  resources/international-human-rights-materials
Staff Director: Paul Protic, 226-3798
  Jurisdiction: Monitor China's compliance with international human rights standards, encourage the development of the rule of law in the People's Republic of China, and establish and maintain a list of victims of human rights abuses in China. The Commission's professional staff is made up of U.S. experts on China specializing in religious freedom, labor affairs, Tibet and ethnic minorities, the Internet and free-flow of broadcast and print information, and law and legal reform, including commercial law reform. The Commission submits an annual report to the congressional leadership and the president. To gather information for the report, the Commission holds formal hearings and informal issues roundtables that bring together academics, activists, government officials, business representatives, and other experts on issues related to the Commission's mandate. Staff members also make frequent trips to China to gather information, meet Chinese officials, scholars, and analysts, and consult about the human rights situation and the development of the rule of law in China with U.S. diplomats and others.

Senate Members

Marco Rubio, Fla., Co-Chair   *Sherrod Brown, Ohio*
James Lankford, Okla.   *Dianne Feinstein, Calif.*
Tom Cotton, Ark.   *Jeff Merkley, Ore.*
Steve Daines, Mon.   *Gary Peters, Mich.*
Ben Sasse, Neb.

House Members

Chris Smith, N.J., Chair   *Diane Black, Tenn.*
Robert Pittenger, N.C.   *Tim Walz, Minn.*
Trent Franks, Ariz.   *Marcy Katpur, Ohio*
Randy Hultgren, Ill.   *Mike Honda, Calif.*
   Ted Lieu, Calif.

Senate Committees

The standing and select committees of the U.S. Senate follow. This information is current as of April 25, 2016. Each listing includes room number, office building, zip code, telephone and fax numbers, Web address, minority Web address if available, key majority and minority staff members, jurisdiction for the full committee, and party ratio. Subcommittees are listed under the full committees. Members are listed in order of seniority on the committee or subcommittee. Many committees and subcommittees may be contacted via Web-based email forms found on their Web sites. A phone number and/or office number next to either the Majority or Minority Staff Director indicates a change from the full committee's office number and/or phone number. If no numbers are listed, the individual's office number and phone number are the same as for the full committee.

Republicans, the current majority, are shown in roman type; Democrats, in the minority, appear in italic. The top name in the italicized list is the Ranking Minority Member. Bernie Sanders, I-Vt., and Angus King, I-Maine, caucus with the Democrats and accrue committee seniority with Democrats; thus, they are counted with the Democrats in the party ratio, although (I) appears after their names. The partisan committees of the Senate are listed on page 876. The area code for all phone and fax numbers is (202).

AGRICULTURE, NUTRITION, AND FORESTRY

Office: 328A SROB 20510-6000
Phone: 224-2035 **Fax:** 228-2125
Web: ag.senate.gov
Minority Web: ag.senate.gov/newsroom/minority-news
Majority Staff Director: Joel Leftwich
Minority Staff Director: Joe Shultz

Jurisdiction: (1) agricultural economics and agricultural research; (2) agricultural extension services and agricultural experiment stations; (3) agricultural production, agricultural marketing, and stabilization of prices; (4) agriculture and agricultural commodities; (5) animal industry and animal diseases; (6) crop insurance and soil conservation; (7) farm credit and farm security; (8) food from fresh waters; (9) food stamp programs; (10) forestry and forest reserves and wilderness areas other than those created from the public domain; (11) home economics; (12) human nutrition; (13) inspection of livestock, meat, and agricultural products; (14) pests and pesticides; (15) plant industry, soils, and agricultural engineering; (16) rural development, rural electrification, and watersheds; (17) school nutrition programs. The committee shall also study and review, on a comprehensive basis, matters relating to food, nutrition, and hunger, both in the United States and in foreign countries, and rural affairs, and report thereon from time to time.
Party Ratio: R 11-D 9

Pat Roberts, Kans., Chair	*Debbie A. Stabenow, Mich.*
Thad A. Cochran, Miss.	*Patrick P. Leahy, Vt.*
Mitch McConnell, Ky.	*Sherrod Brown, Ohio*
John Boozman, Ark.	*Amy Klobuchar, Minn.*
John Hoeven, N.D.	*Michael F. Bennet, Colo.*
David Perdue, Ga.	*Kirstin Gillibrand, N.Y.*
Joni Ernst, Iowa	*Joe Donnelly, Ind.*
Thom Tillis, N.C.	*Heidi Heitkamp, N.D.*
Ben Sasse, Neb.	*Robert P. Casey Jr., Penn.*
Chuck Grassley, Iowa	
John Thune, S.D.	

Subcommittees

Commodities, Risk Management, and Trade
Office: 328A SROB 20510 **Phone:** 224-2035
John Boozman (Chair), Thad A. Cochran, John Hoeven, David Perdue, Chuck Grassley, John Thune
Joe Donnelly (Ranking Minority Member), Heidi Heitkamp, Sherrod Brown, Kirsten Gillibrand, Michael F. Bennet

Conservation, Forestry, and Natural Resources
Office: 328A SROB 20510 **Phone:** 224-2035
David Perdue (Chair), Thad Cochran, Mitch McConnell, John Boozman, Ben Sasse, Chuck Grassley
Michael F. Bennet (Ranking Minority Member), Amy Klobuchar, Patrick P. Leahy, Heidi Heitkamp, Robert P. Casey Jr.

Livestock, Marketing, and Agriculture Security
Office: 328A SROB 20510 **Phone:** 224-2035
Ben Sasse (Chair), Mitch McConnell, Joni Ernst, Thom Tillis, John Thune, Chuck Grassley
Kirsten Gillibrand (Ranking Minority Member), Patrick P. Leahy, Amy Klobuchar, Joe Donnelly, Robert P. Casey Jr.

Nutrition, Specialty Crops, and Agricultural Research
Office: 328A SROB 20510 **Phone:** 224-2035
John Hoeven (Chair), Mitch McConnell, John Boozman, Joni Ernst, Thom Tillis, Ben Sasse
Robert P. Casey Jr. (Ranking Minority Member), Patrick P. Leahy, Sherrod Brown, Kirsten Gillibrand, Michael F. Bennet

Rural Development and Energy
Office: 328A SROB 20510 **Phone:** 224-2035
Joni Ernst (Chair), Thad Cochran, John Hoeven, David Perdue, Thom Tillis, John Thune
Heidi Heitkamp (Ranking Minority Member), Sherrod Brown, Amy Klobuchar, Michael F. Bennet, Joe Donnelly

APPROPRIATIONS

Office: S-128 CAP 20510-6025
Phone: 224-7257   **Fax:** 224-2100
Web: appropriations.senate.gov
Minority Web: appropriations.senate.gov/minority
Majority Staff Director: Bruce Evans
Minority Staff Director: Charles Kieffer, 224-7363
   Jurisdiction: (1) appropriation of the revenue for the support of the government, except as provided in subparagraph (e); (2) rescission of appropriations contained in appropriation acts (referred to in section 105 of title 1, United States Code); (3) the amount of new spending authority described in section 401(c)(2) (A) and (B) of the Congressional Budget and Impoundment Control Act of 1974 which is to be effective for a fiscal year; (4) new spending authority described in section 401(c)(2) (C) of the Congressional Budget and Impoundment Control Act of 1974 provided in bills and resolutions referred to the committee under section 401(b)(2) of that Act.
Party Ratio: R 16-D 14

Thad A. Cochran, Miss., Chair	Barbara Mikulski, Md.
Mitch McConnell, Ky.	Patrick P. Leahy, Vt.
Richard Shelby, Ala.	Patty Murray, Wash.
Lamar Alexander, Tenn.	Dianne Feinstein, Calif.
Susan Collins, Maine	Richard J. Durbin, Ill.
Lisa Murkowski, Alaska	Jack D. Reed, R.I.
Lindsey Graham, S.C.	Jon Tester, Mont.
Mark Kirk, Ill.	Tom Udall, N.M.
Roy Blunt, Mo.	Jeanne Shaheen, N.H.
Jerry Moran, Kans.	Jeff Merkley, Ore.
John Hoeven, N.D.	Chris Coons, Del.
John Boozman, Ark.	Brian Schatz, Hawaii
Shelly Moore Capito, W.V.	Tammy Baldwin, Wisc.
Bill Cassidy, La.	Chris Murphy, Conn.
James Lankford, Okla.	
Steve Daines, Mont.	

Subcommittees

Agriculture, Rural Development, Food and Drug Administration, and Related Agencies
Office: 192 SDOB 20510   **Phone:** 224-5270
   Jerry Moran (Chair), Roy Blunt, Thad A. Cochran, Mitch McConnell, Susan Collins, John Hoeven, Steve Daines
   Jeff Merkley (Ranking Minority Member), Dianne Feinstein, John Tester, Tom Udall, Patrick P. Leahy, Tammy Baldwin

Commerce, Justice, Science, and Related Agencies
Office: 192 SDOB 20510   **Phone:** 224-7277
   Richard Shelby (Chair), Lamar Alexander, Susan Collins, Lisa Murkowski, Lindsey Graham, Mark Kirk, John Boozman, Shelley Moore Capito, James Lankford
   Barbara Mikulski (Ranking Minority Member), Patrick P. Leahy, Dianne Feinstein, Jack D. Reed, Jeanne Shaheen, Chris Coons, Tammy Baldwin, Chris Murphy

Defense
Office: 192 SDOB 20510   **Phone:** 224-6688
   Thad Cochran (Chair), Mitch McConnell, Richard Shelby, Lamar Alexander, Susan Collins, Lisa Murkowski, Lindsey Graham, Roy Blunt, Steve Daines, Jerry Moran
   Richard J. Durbin (Ranking Minority Member), Patrick P. Leahy, Dianne Feinstein, Barbara Mikulski, Patty Murray, Jack D. Reed, Jon Tester, Tom Udall, Brian Schatz

Energy and Water Development
Office: 138 SDOB 20510   **Phone:** 224-7260
   Lamar Alexander (Chair), Thad Cochran, Mitch McConnell, Richard Shelby, Susan Collins, Lisa Murkowski, Lindsey Graham, John Hoeven, James Lankford
   Dianne Feinstein (Ranking Minority Member), Patty Murray, Jon Tester, Richard J. Durbin, Tom Udall, Jeanne Shaheen, Jeff Merkley, Chris Coons

Financial Services and General Government
Office: 124 SDOB 20510   **Phone:** 224-2104
   John Boozman (Chair), Jerry Moran, James Lankford
   Chris Coons (Ranking Minority Member), Richard J. Durbin

Homeland Security
Office: 138 SDOB 20510   **Phone:** 224-4319
   John Hoeven (Chair), Thad Cochran, Richard Shelby, Lisa Murkowski, Lindsey Graham, Bill Cassidy
   Jeanne Shaheen (Ranking Minority Member), Patrick P. Leahy, Patty Murray, Jon Tester, Tammy Baldwin

Interior, Environment, and Related Agencies
Office: 124 SDOB 20510   **Phone:** 224-7233
   Lisa Murkowski (Chair), Lamar Alexander, Thad A. Cochran, Roy Blunt, John Hoeven, Mitch McConnell, Steve Daines, Bill Cassidy
   Tom Udall (Ranking Minority Member), Jack D. Reed, Dianne Feinstein, Patrick Leahy, Jon Tester, Jeff Merkley

Labor, Health and Human Services, Education, and Related Agencies
Office: 124 SDOB 20510   **Phone:** 224-7230
   Roy Blunt (Chair), Jerry Moran, Thad A. Cochran, Richard Shelby, Lamar Alexander, Lindsey Graham, Mark Kirk, Bill Cassidy, Shelley Moore Capito, James Lankford
   Patty Murray (Ranking Minority Member), Richard J. Durbin, Jack D. Reed, Barbara Mikulski, Jeanne Shaheen, Jeff Merkley, Brian Schatz, Tammy Baldwin

Legislative Branch
Office: 138 SDOB 20510   **Phone:** 224-9747
   Shelley Moore Capito (Chair), Mark Kirk, Jerry Moran
   Brian Schatz (Ranking Minority Member), Chris Murphy

Military Construction, Veterans Affairs, and Related Agencies
Office: 124 SDOB 20510   **Phone:** 224-5245
   Mark Kirk (Chair), Mitch McConnell, Susan Collins, John Hoeven, Lisa Murkowski, John Boozman, Shelley Moore Capito, Bill Cassidy
   Jon Tester (Ranking Minority Member), Patty Murray, Jack D. Reed, Tom Udall, Brian Schatz, Tammy Baldwin, Chris Murphy

State, Foreign Operations, and Related Programs
Office: 124 SDOB 20510 **Phone:** 224-2104

Lindsey Graham (Chair), Mitch McConnell, Mark Kirk, Roy Blunt, John Boozman, Jerry Moran, James Lankford, Steve Daines

Patrick P. Leahy (Ranking Minority Member), Barbara Mikulski, Richard J. Durbin, Jeanne Shaheen, Chris Coons, Jeff Merkley, Chris Murphy

Transportation, Housing and Urban Development, and Related Agencies
Office: 192 SDOB 20510 **Phone:** 224-5310

Susan Collins (Chair), Richard Shelby, Lamar Alexander, Mark Kirk, Roy Blunt, John Boozman, Shelley Moore Capito, Bill Cassidy, Steve Daines

Jack D. Reed (Ranking Minority Member), Barbara Mikulski, Patty Murray, Richard J. Durbin, Dianne Feinstein, Chris Coons, Brian Schatz, Chris Murphy

ARMED SERVICES

Office: 228 SROB 20510-6050
Phone: 224-3871 **Fax:** 228-0036
Web: armed-services.senate.gov
Majority Staff Director: Chris Brose
Minority Staff Director: Elizabeth L. King

Jurisdiction: (1) aeronautical and space activities peculiar to or primarily associated with the development of weapons systems or military operations; (2) common defense; (3) Department of Defense, the Department of the Army, the Department of the Navy, and the Department of the Air Force, generally; (4) maintenance and operation of the Panama Canal, including administration, sanitation, and government of the Canal Zone; (5) military research and development; (6) national security aspects of nuclear energy; (7) naval petroleum reserves, except those in Alaska; (8) pay, promotion, retirement, and other benefits and privileges of members of the armed forces, including overseas education of civilian and military dependents; (9) selective service system; (10) strategic and critical materials necessary for the common defense. The committee shall also study and review, on a comprehensive basis, matters relating to the common defense policy of the United States.
Party Ratio: R 14–D 12

John McCain, Ariz., Chair	*Jack D. Reed, R.I.*
James M. Inhofe, Okla.	*Bill J. Nelson, Fla.*
Jeff A. Sessions, Ala.	*Claire McCaskill, Mo.*
Roger Wicker, Miss.	*Joe Manchin, W.V.*
Kelly Ayotte, N.H.	*Jeanne Shaheen, N.H.*
Deb Fischer, Neb.	*Kirsten Gillibrand, N.Y.*
Tom Cotton, Ark.	*Richard Blumenthal, Conn.*
Mike Rounds, S.D.	*Joe Donnelly, Ind.*
Joni Ernst, Iowa	*Mazie K. Hirono, Hawaii*
Thom Tillis, N.C.	*Tim Kaine, Va.*
Dan Sullivan, Alaska	*Angus King, Maine (I)*
Mike Lee, Utah	*Martin Heinrich, N.M.*
Lindsey Graham, S.C.	
Ted Cruz, Tex.	

Subcommittees

Airland
Office: 228 SROB 20510 **Phone:** 224-3871

Tom Cotton (Chair), James M. Inhofe, Jeff A. Sessions, Roger Wicker, Mike Rounds, Joni Ernst, Dan Sullivan, Mike Lee, John McCain (ex officio)

Joe Manchin (Ranking Minority Member), Claire McCaskill, Kirsten Gillibrand, Richard Blumenthal, Joe Donnelly, Mazie K. Hirono, Martin Heinrich, Jack D. Reed (ex officio)

Emerging Threats and Capabilities
Office: 228 SROB 20510 **Phone:** 224-3871

Deb Fischer (Chair), Kelly Ayotte, Tom Cotton, Joni Ernst, Thom Tillis, Lindsey Graham, Ted Cruz, John McCain (ex officio)

Bill J. Nelson (Ranking Minority Member), Joe Manchin, Jeanne Shaheen, Kirsten Gillibrand, Joe Donnelly, Tim Kaine, Jack D. Reed (ex officio)

Personnel
Office: 228 SROB 20510 **Phone:** 224-3871

Lindsey Graham (Chair), Roger Wicker, Tom Cotton, Thom Tillis, Dan Sullivan, John McCain (ex officio)

Kirsten Gillibrand (Ranking Minority Member), Claire McCaskill, Richard Blumenthal, Angus King, Jack D. Reed (ex officio)

Readiness and Management Support
Office: 228 SROB 20510 **Phone:** 224-3871

Kelly Ayotte (Chair), James M. Inhofe, Deb Fischer, Mike Rounds, Joni Ernst, Mike Lee, John McCain (ex officio)

Tim Kaine (Ranking Minority Member), Claire McCaskill, Jeanne Shaheen, Mazie K. Hirono, Martin Heinrich, Jack D. Reed (ex officio)

SeaPower
Office: 228 SROB 20510 **Phone:** 224-3871

Roger Wicker (Chair), Jeff Sessions, Kelly Ayotte, Mike Rounds, Thom Tillis, Dan Sullivan, Ted Cruz, John McCain (ex officio)

Mazie K. Hirono (Ranking Minority Member), Bill J. Nelson, Jeanne Shaheen, Richard Blumenthal, Tim Kaine, Angus King, Jack D. Reed (ex officio)

Strategic Forces
Office: 228 SROB 20510 **Phone:** 224-3871

Jeff A. Sessions (Chair), James M. Inhofe, Deb Fischer, Mike Lee, Lindsey Graham, Ted Cruz, John McCain (ex officio)

Joe Donnelly (Ranking Minority Member), Bill J. Nelson, Joe Manchin, Angus King, Martin Heinrich, Jack D. Reed (ex officio)

BANKING, HOUSING, AND URBAN AFFAIRS

Office: 534 SDOB 20510-6075
Phone: 224-7391 **Fax:** 224-7391
Web: banking.senate.gov
Majority Staff Director: William Duhnke
Minority Staff Director: Mark Powden

BANKING, HOUSING, AND URBAN AFFAIRS
(continued)

Jurisdiction: (1) banks, banking, and financial institutions; (2) control of prices of commodities, rents, and services; (3) deposit insurance; (4) economic stabilization and defense production; (5) export and foreign trade promotion; (6) export controls; (7) federal monetary policy, including Federal Reserve System; (8) financial aid to commerce and industry; (9) issuance and redemption of notes; (10) money and credit, including currency and coinage; (11) nursing home construction; (12) public and private housing (including veterans' housing) (13) renegotiation of government contracts; (14) urban development and urban mass transit. The committee shall also study and review, on a comprehensive basis, matters relating to international economic policy as it affects U.S. monetary affairs, credit, and financial institutions; economic growth, urban affairs and credit, and report thereon from time to time.

Party Ratio: R 12-D 10

Richard Shelby, Ala., Chair	Sherrod Brown, Ohio
Mike Crapo, Idaho	Jack D. Reed, R.I.
Bob Corker, Tenn.	Charles E. Schumer, N.Y.
David Vitter, La.	Robert Menendez, N.J.
Pat Toomey, Pa.	Jon Tester, Mont.
Mark Kirk, Ill.	Mark R. Warner, Va.
Jerry Moran, Kans.	Jeff Merkley, Ore.
Tim Scott, S.C.	Elizabeth Warren, Mass.
Tom Cotton, Ark.	Heidi Heitkamp, N.D.
Mike Rounds, S.D.	Joe Donnelly, Ind.
Ben Sasse, Neb.	
Dean Heller, Nev.	

Subcommittees

Economic Policy
Office: 324 SHOB 20510   **Phone:** 224-6244
Dean Heller (Chair), Pat Toomey, Tom Cotton, Mike Rounds, Ben Sasse, Jerry Moran, Richard Shelby (ex officio)
Elizabeth Warren (Ranking Minority Member), Jeff Merkley, Jon Tester, Heidi Heitkamp, Sherrod Brown (ex officio)

Financial Institutions and Consumer Protection
Office: 248 SROB 20510 Phone: 224-4254
Pat Toomey (Chair), Mike Crapo, Dean Heller, Mike Rounds, Bob Corker, Tim Scott, David Vitter, Mark Kirk, Richard Shelby (ex officio)
Jeff Merkley (Ranking Minority Member), Jack D. Reed, Charles E. Schumer, Robert Menendez, Elizabeth Warren, Mark R. Warner, Joe Donnelly, Sherrod Brown (ex officio)

Housing, Transportation, and Community Development
Office: 167 SROB 20510   **Phone:** 224-6121
Tim Scott (Chair), Mike Crapo, Dean Heller, Jerry Moran, Bob Corker, Tom Cotton, Mike Rounds, David Vitter, Richard Shelby (ex officio)

Robert Menendez (Ranking Minority Member), Jack D. Reed, Charles E. Schumer, Jon Tester, Jeff Merkley, Heidi Heitkamp, Joe Donnelly, Sherrod Brown (ex officio)

National Security and International Trade and Finance
Office: 524 SHOB 20510   **Phone:** 224-2854
Mark Kirk (Chair), Tom Cotton, Ben Sasse, Richard Shelby (ex officio)
Heidi Heitkamp (Ranking Minority Member), Mark R. Warner, Sherrod Brown (ex officio)

Securities, Insurance, and Investment
Office: 239 SDOB 20510   **Phone:** 224-6142
Mike Crapo (Chair), Bob Corker, David Vitter, Pat Toomey, Mark Kirk, Tim Scott, Ben Sasse, Jerry Moran, Richard Shelby (ex officio)
Mark R. Warner (Ranking Minority Member), Jack D. Reed, Charles E. Schumer, Robert Menendez, Jon Tester, Elizabeth Warren, Joe Donnelly, Sherrod Brown (ex officio)

BUDGET

Office: 624 SDOB 20510-6100
Phone: 224-0642   **Fax:** 228-2007
Web: budget.senate.gov
Minority Web: budget.senate.gov/democratic
Majority Staff Director: Eric Ueland
Minority Staff Director: Warren Gunnels
Jurisdiction: (1) all concurrent resolutions on the budget (as defined in Section 3 (a) (4) of the Congressional Budget Act of 1974) and all other matters required to be referred to that committee under Titles III and IV of that Act, and messages, petitions, memorials, and other matters relating thereto. (2) The committee shall have the duty (A) to report the matters required to be reported by it under Titles III and IV of the Congressional Budget and Impoundment Control Act of 1974; (B) to make continuing studies of the effect on budget outlays of relevant existing and proposed legislation and to report the results of such studies to the Senate on a recurring basis; (C) to request and evaluate continuing studies of tax expenditures, policies, and programs with direct budget outlays, and to report the results of such studies to the Senate on a recurring basis; and (D) to review, on a continuing basis, the conduct by the Congressional Budget Office of its functions and duties.

Party Ratio: R 12-D 10

Mike Enzi, Wyo., Chair	Bernie Sanders, Vt. (I)
Jeff A. Sessions, Ala.	Patty Murray, Wash.
Chuck Grassley, Iowa	Ron Wyden, Ore.
Mike Crapo, Idaho	Debbie A. Stabenow, Mich.
Lindsey Graham, S.C.	Sheldon Whitehouse, R.I.
Rob Portman, Ohio	Mark R. Warner, Va.
Pat Toomey, Pa.	Jeff Merkley, Ore.
Ron Johnson, Wisc.	Tammy Baldwin, Wisc.
Kelly Ayotte, N.H.	Tim Kaine, Va.
Roger Wicker, Miss.	Angus King, Maine (I)
Bob Corker, Tenn.	
David Perdue, Ga.	

COMMERCE, SCIENCE, AND TRANSPORTATION

Office: 512 SDOB 20510-6125
Phone: 224-1251 **Fax:** 228-1259
Web: commerce.senate.gov
Minority Web: commerce.senate.gov/public/index.cfm/ minority-dems
Majority Staff Director: Nick Rossi
Minority Staff Director: Kim Lipsky, 224-0411, 425 SHOB
   Jurisdiction: (1) United States Coast Guard (Homeland Security); (2) coastal zone management; (3) communications; (4) highway safety; (5) inland waterways, except construction; (6) interstate commerce; (7) marine and ocean navigation, marine and ocean safety, and marine and ocean transportation, including navigational aspects of deepwater ports; (8) marine fisheries; (9) United States Merchant Marine and navigation; (10) non-military aeronautical and space sciences; (11) oceans, weather, and atmospheric activities; (12) Panama Canal and interoceanic canals generally, except as provided in subparagraph (c); (13) regulation of consumer products and services, including testing related to toxic substances, other than pesticides, and except for credit, financial services, and housing; (14) regulation of interstate common carriers, including railroads, buses, trucks, vessels, pipelines, and civil aviation; (15) science engineering, and technology research, development, and policy; (16) sports; (17) standards and measurement; (18) transportation; (19) transportation and commerce aspects of Outer Continental Shelf land. The committee shall also study and review, on a comprehensive basis, all matters relating to science and technology, oceans policy, transportation, communications, and consumer affairs.
Party Ratio: R 13-D 11

John Thune, S.D., Chair	*Bill J. Nelson, Fla.*
Roger Wicker, Miss.	*Maria Cantwell, Wash.*
Roy Blunt, Mo.	*Claire McCaskill, Mo.*
Marco Rubio, Fla.	*Amy Klobuchar, Minn.*
Kelly Ayotte, N.H.	*Richard Blumenthal, Conn.*
Dean Heller, Nev.	*Brian Schatz, Hawaii*
Ted Cruz, Tex.	*Edward J. Markey, Mass.*
Deb Fischer, Neb.	*Cory Booker, N.J.*
Dan Sullivan, Alaska	*Tom Udall, N.M.*
Jerry Moran, Kans.	*Joe Manchin, W.V.*
Ron Johnson, Wisc.	*Gary Peters, Mich.*
Cory Gardner, Colo.	
Steve Daines, Mont.	

Subcommittees

Aviation Operations, Safety and Security
Office: 253 SROB 20510   **Phone:** 224-1251
   Kelly Ayotte (Chair), Roger Wicker, Roy Blunt, Marco Rubio, Ted Cruz, Deb Fischer, Jerry Moran, Dan Sullivan, Ron Johnson, Dean Heller, Cory Gardner, John Thune (ex officio)
   Maria Cantwell (Ranking Minority Member)Amy Klobuchar, Richard Blumenthal, Brian Schatz, Edward J. Markey, Cory Booker, Tom Udall, Joe Manchin, Gary Peters, Bill J. Nelson (ex officio)

Communications, Technology, Innovation, and the Internet
Office: 253 SROB 20510   **Phone:** 224-1251
   Roger Wicker (Chair), Roy Blunt, Marco Rubio, Kelly Ayotte, Ted Cruz, Deb Fischer, Jerry Moran, Dan Sullivan, Dean Heller, Ron Johnson, Cory Gardner, Steve Daines, John Thune (ex officio)
   Brian Schatz (Ranking Minority Member)Maria Cantwell, Claire McCaskill, Amy Klobuchar, Richard Blumenthal, Edward J. Markey, Cory Booker, Tom Udall, Joe Manchin, Gary Peters, Bill J. Nelson (ex officio)

Consumer Protection, Product Safety, Insurance, and Data Security
Office: 253 SROB 20510   **Phone:** 224-1251
   Jerry Moran (Chair), Roy Blunt, Ted Cruz, Deb Fischer, Dean Heller, Cory Gardner, Steve Daines, John Thune (ex officio)
   Richard Blumenthal (Ranking Minority Member), Claire McCaskill, Amy Klobuchar, Edward J. Markey, Cory Booker, Tom Udall, Bill J. Nelson (ex officio)

Oceans, Atmosphere, Fisheries, and Coast Guard
Office: 253 SROB 20510   **Phone:** 224-1251
   Marco Rubio (Chair), Roger Wicker, Kelly Ayotte, Ted Cruz, Dan Sullivan, Ron Johnson, John Thune (ex officio)
   Cory Booker (Ranking Minority Member), Gary Peters, Maria Cantwell, Richard Blumenthal, Brian Schatz, Edward J. Markey, Bill J. Nelson (ex officio)

Space, Science, and Competitiveness
Office: 253 SROB 20510   **Phone:** 224-1251
   Ted Cruz (Chair), Marco Rubio, Jerry Moran, Dan Sullivan, Cory Gardner, Steve Daines, John Thune (ex officio)
   Gary Peters (Ranking Minority Member), Edward J. Markey, Cory Booker, Tom Udall, Brian Schatz, Bill J. Nelson (ex officio)

Surface Transportation and Merchant Marine Infrastructure, Safety, and Security
Office: 253 SROB 20510   **Phone:** 224-1251
   Deb Fischer (Chair), Roy Blunt, Roger Wicker, Kelly Ayotte, Jerry Moran, Dan Sullivan, Dean Heller, Steve Daines, Ron Johnson, John Thune (ex officio)
   Cory Booker (Ranking Minority Member), Richard Blumenthal, Maria Cantwell, Claire McCaskill, Amy Klobuchar, Brian Schatz, Edward J. Markey, Tom Udall, Bill J. Nelson (ex officio)

ENERGY AND NATURAL RESOURCES

Office: 304 SDOB 20510-6150
Phone: 224-4971   **Fax:** 224-6163
Web: energy.senate.gov
Majority Staff Director: Collin Hayes
Minority Staff Director: Angela Becker-Dippmann
   Jurisdiction: (1) coal production, distribution, and utilization; (2) energy policy; (3) energy regulation and energy conservation; (4) energy related aspects of deepwater ports; (5) energy research and development; (6) extraction of minerals from oceans and Outer Continental Shelf

ENERGY AND NATURAL RESOURCES
(continued)

lands; (7) hydroelectric power, irrigation, and reclamation; (8) mining education and research; (9) mining, mineral lands, mining claims, and mineral conservation; (10) national parks, recreation areas, wilderness areas, wild and scenic rivers, historic sites, military parks and battlefields, and on the public domain, preservation of prehistoric ruins and objects of interest; (11) naval petroleum reserves in Alaska; (12) non-military development of nuclear energy; (13) oil and gas production and distribution; (14) public lands and forests, including farming and grazing thereon, and mineral extraction therefrom; (15) solar energy systems; (16) territorial possessions of the United States, including trusteeships; international energy affairs and emergency preparedness; nuclear waste policy; privatization of federal assets; Trans-Alaska Pipeline System and other oil or gas pipeline transportation systems within Alaska; Alaska Native Claims Settlement Act of 1971; Alaska National Interest Lands Conservation Act of 1980; Antarctic research and energy development; Arctic research and energy development; Native Hawaiian matters. The Committee shall also study and review, on a comprehensive basis, matters relating to energy and resources development.

Party Ratio: R 12-D 10

Lisa Murkowski, Alaska, Chair	Maria Cantwell, Wash.
John Barrasso, Wyo.	Ron Wyden, Ore.
James E. Risch, Idaho	Bernie Sanders, Vt. (I)
Mike Lee, Utah	Debbie A. Stabenow, Mich.
Jeff Flake, Ariz.	Al Franken, Minn.
Bill Cassidy, La.	Joe Manchin, W. Va.
Cory Gardner, Colo.	Martin Heinrich, N.M.
Lamar Alexander, Tenn.	Mazie K. Hirono, Hawaii
Steve Daines, Mont.	Angus King, Maine (I)
Rob Portman, Ohio	Elizabeth Warren, Mass.
John Hoeven, N.D.	
Shelley Moore Capito, W.Va.	

Subcommittees

Energy
Office: 304 SDOB 20510   **Phone:** 224-4971

James E. Risch (Chair), Jeff Flake, Steve Daines, Bill Cassidy, Cory Gardner, John Hoeven, Lamar Alexander, Rob Portman, Shelley Moore Capito, Lisa Murkowski (ex officio)

Joe Manchin (Ranking Minority Member), Al Franken, Bernie Sanders, Debbie A. Stabenow, Mazie K. Hirono, Martin Heinrich, Angus King, Elizabeth Warren, Maria Cantwell (ex officio)

National Parks
Office: 304 SDOB 20510   **Phone:** 224-4971

Bill Cassidy (Chair), Rob Portman, John Barrasso, Mike Lee, Lamar Alexander, John Hoeven, Shelley Moore Capito, Lisa Murkowski (ex officio)

Martin Heinrich (Ranking Minority Member), Ron Wyden, Bernie Sanders, Debbie A. Stabenow, Angus King, Elizabeth Warren, Maria Cantwell (ex officio)

Public Lands, Forests, and Mining
Office: 304 SDOB 20510   **Phone:** 224-4971

John Barrasso (Chair), Shelley Moore Capito, James E. Risch, Mike Lee, Steve Daines, Bill Cassidy, Cory Gardner, Jeff Flake, Lamar Alexander, John Hoeven, Lisa Murkowski (ex officio)

Ron Wyden (Ranking Minority Member), Debbie A. Stabenow, Joe Manchin, Al Franken, Martin Heinrich, Mazie K. Hirono, Elizabeth Warren, Maria Cantwell (ex officio)

Water and Power
Office: 304 SDOB 20510   **Phone:** 224-4971

Mike Lee (Chair), Jeff Flake, John Barrasso, James E. Risch, Steve Daines, Cory Gardner, Rob Portman, Lisa Murkowski (ex officio)

Mazie K. Hirono (Ranking Minority Member), Ron Wyden, Bernie Sanders, Joe Manchin, Al Franken, Angus King, Maria Cantwell (ex officio)

ENVIRONMENT AND PUBLIC WORKS

Office: 410 SDOB 20510-6175
Phone: 224-6176   **Fax:** 224-1273
Web: epw.senate.gov
Minority Web: epw.senate.gov/public/index.cfm/latest-updates-democratic
Majority Staff Director: Ryan Jackson
Minority Staff Director: Bettina M. Poirier, 224-8832, 456 SDOB

Jurisdiction: (1) air pollution; (2) construction and maintenance of highways; (3) environmental aspects of Outer Continental Shelf lands; (4) environmental effects of toxic substances, other than pesticides; (5) environmental policy; (6) environmental research and development; (7) fisheries and wildlife; (8) flood control and improvements of rivers and harbors, including environmental aspects of deepwater ports; (9) noise pollution; (10) non-military environmental regulation and control of nuclear energy; (11) ocean dumping; (12) public buildings and improved grounds of the United States generally, including Federal buildings in the District of Columbia; (13) public works, bridges, and dams; (14) regional economic development; (15) solid waste disposal and recycling; (16) water pollution; (17) water resources. The committee shall also study and review, on a comprehensive basis, matters relating to environmental protection and resource utilization and conservation.

Party Ratio: R 11-D 9

James M. Inhofe, Okla., Chair	Barbara Boxer, Calif.
David Vitter, La.	Thomas Carper, Del.
John Barrasso, Wyo.	Benjamin L. Cardin, Md.
Shelley Moore Capito, W.Va.	Bernie Sanders, Vt. (I)
Mike Crapo, Idaho	Sheldon Whitehouse, R.I.
	Jeff Merkley, Ore.
	Kirsten Gillibrand, N.Y.

John Boozman, Ark.
Jeff A. Sessions, Ala.
Roger Wicker, Miss.
Deb Fischer, Neb.
Mike Rounds, S.D.
Dan Sullivan, Alaska

Cory Booker, N.J.
Edward J. Markey, Mass.

Subcommittees

Clean Air and Nuclear Safety
Office: 406 SDOB 20510   **Phone:** 224-6176
   Shelley Moore Capito (Chair), David Vitter, John Barrasso, Mike Crapo, Jeff A. Sessions, Roger Wicker, Deb Fischer, James M. Inhofe (ex officio)
   Thomas Carper (Ranking Minority Member), Benjamin L. Cardin, Bernie Sanders, Sheldon Whitehouse, Jeff Merkley, Edward J. Markey, Barbara Boxer (ex officio)

Fisheries, Water, and Wildlife
Office: 406 SDOB 20510   **Phone:** 224-6176
   Dan Sullivan (Chair), John Barasso, Shelley Moore Capito, John Boozman, Jeff A. Sessions, Roger Wicker, Deb Fischer, Mike Rounds, James M. Inhofe (ex officio)
   Sheldon Whitehouse (Ranking Minority Member), Thomas Carper, Benjamin L. Cardin, Bernie Sanders, Kirsten Gillibrand, Cory Booker, Edward J. Markey, Barbara Boxer (ex officio)

Superfund, Waste Management, and Regulatory Oversight
Office: 406 SDOB 20510   **Phone:** 224-6176
   Mike Rounds (Chair), David Vitter, Mike Crapo, John Boozman, Dan Sullivan, James M. Inhofe (ex officio)
   Edward J. Markey (Ranking Minority Member), Thomas Carper, Jeff Merkley, Cory Booker, Barbara Boxer (ex officio)

Transportation and Infrastructure
Office: 410 SDOB 20510   **Phone:** 224-6176
   David Vitter (Chair), John Barrasso, Shelley Moore Capito, Mike Crapo, John Boozman, Jeff A. Sessions, Roger Wicker, Deb Fischer, James M. Inhofe (ex officio)
   Barbara Boxer (Ranking Minority Member), Tom Carper, Benjamin L. Cardin, Bernie Sanders, Sheldon Whitehouse, Jeff Merkley, Kirsten Gillibrand

FINANCE

Office: 219 SDOB 20510-6200
Phone: 224-4515   **Fax:** 228-0554
Web: finance.senate.gov
Majority Staff Director: Christopher Campbell
Minority Staff Director: Joshua Sheinkman
   Jurisdiction: (1) bonded debt of the United States, except as provided in the Congressional Budget and Impoundment Control Act of 1974; (2) customs, collection districts, and ports of entry and delivery; (3) deposit of public moneys; (4) general revenue sharing; (5) health programs under the Social Security Act and health programs financed by a specific tax or trust fund; (6) national social security; (7) reciprocal trade agreements; (8) revenue measures generally, except as provided in the Congressional Budget and Impoundment Control Act of 1974;

(9) revenue measures relating to the insular possessions; (10) tariffs and import quotas, and matters related thereto; (11) transportation of dutiable goods.
Party Ratio: R 14-D 12

Orrin G. Hatch, Utah, Chair
Chuck Grassley, Iowa
Mike Crapo, Idaho
Pat Roberts, Kans.
Mike Enzi, Wyo.
John Cornyn, Tex.
John Thune, S.D.
Richard Burr, N.C.
Johnny Isakson, Ga.
Rob Portman, Ohio
Pat Toomey, Penn.
Dan Coats, Ind.
Dean Heller, Nev.
Tim Scott, S.C.

Ron Wyden, Ore.
Charles E. Schumer, N.Y.
Debbie A. Stabenow, Mich.
Maria Cantwell, Wash.
Bill J. Nelson, Fla.
Robert Menendez, N.J.
Thomas Carper, Del.
Benjamin L. Cardin, Md.
Sherrod Brown, Ohio
Michael F. Bennet, Colo.
Robert P. Casey Jr., Penn.
Mark R. Warner, Va.

Subcommittees

Energy, Natural Resources, and Infrastructure
Office: 219 SDOB 20510   **Phone:** 224-4515
   Dan Coats (Chair), Chuck Grassley, Mike Crapo, Mike Enzi, John Cornyn, John Thune, Richard Burr, Orrin G. Hatch (ex officio)
   Michael F. Bennet (Ranking Minority Member), Maria Cantwell, Bill J. Nelson, Thomas Carper, Robert P. Casey Jr., Ron Wyden (ex officio)

Fiscal Responsibility and Economic Growth
Office: 219 SDOB 20510   **Phone:** 224-4515
   Rob Portman (Chair), Mike Crapo, Richard Burr, Orrin G. Hatch (ex officio)
   Mark R. Warner (Ranking Minority Member), Ron Wyden (ex officio)

Health Care
Office: 219 SDOB 20510   **Phone:** 224-4515
   Pat Toomey (Chair), Chuck Grassley, Pat Roberts, Mike Enzi, Richard Burr, Dan Coats, Dean Heller, Tim Scott, Orrin G. Hatch (ex officio)
   Debbie A. Stabenow (Ranking Minority Member), Maria Cantwell, Robert Menendez, Benjamin L. Cardin, Sherrod Brown, Mark R. Warner, Ron Wyden (ex officio)

International Trade, Customs, and Global Competitiveness
Office: 219 SDOB 20510   **Phone:** 224-4515
   John Cornyn (Chair), Johnny Isakson, Chuck Grassley, Pat Roberts, John Thune, Rob Portman, Orrin G. Hatch (ex officio)
   Ron Wyden (Ranking Minority Member), Charles E. Schumer, Debbie A. Stabenow, Bill J. Nelson, Ron Wyden (ex officio)

Social Security, Pensions, and Family Policy
Office: 219 SDOB 20510   **Phone:** 224-4515
   Dean Heller (Chair), Pat Toomey, Johnny Isakson, Tim Scott, Orrin G. Hatch (ex officio)

FINANCE (continued)

Sherrod Brown (Ranking Minority Member), Charles E. Schumer, Ron Wyden (ex officio)

Taxation and IRS Oversight
Office: 219 SDOB 20510   **Phone:** 224-4515

Mike Crapo (Chair), Mike Enzi, Pat Roberts, John Cornyn, John Thune, Johnny Isakson, Rob Portman, Pat Toomey, Dan Coats, Dean Heller, Tim Scott, Orrin G. Hatch (ex officio)

Robert P. Casey Jr. (Ranking Minority Member), Charles E. Schumer, Bill J. Nelson, Michael F. Bennet (Chair), Robert Menendez, Thomas Carper, Benjamin L. Cardin, Mark R. Warner, Ron Wyden (ex officio)

FOREIGN RELATIONS

Office: 423 SDOB 20510-6225
Phone: 224-6797   **Fax:** 228-3612
Web: foreign.senate.gov
Minority Web: foreign.senate.gov/press/ranking
Majority Staff Director: Chris Tuttle
Minority Staff Director: Jodi Herman

Jurisdiction: (1) acquisition of land and buildings for embassies and legations in foreign countries; (2) boundaries of the United States; (3) diplomatic service; (4) foreign economic, military, technical, and humanitarian assistance; (5) foreign loans; (6) international activities of the American National Red Cross, and the International Committee of the Red Cross; (7) international aspects of nuclear energy, including nuclear transfer policy; (8) international conferences and congresses; (9) international law as it relates to foreign policy; (10) International Monetary Fund and other international organizations established primarily for international monetary purposes (except that, at the request of the Committee on Banking, Housing, and Urban Affairs, any proposed legislation relating to such subjects reported by the Committee on Foreign Relations shall be referred to the Committee on Banking, Housing, and Urban Affairs); (11) intervention abroad and declarations of war; (12) measures to foster commercial intercourse with foreign nations and to safeguard United States business interests abroad; (13) national security and international aspects of trusteeships of the United States; (14) oceans and international environmental and scientific affairs as they relate to foreign policy; (15) protection of United States citizens abroad and expatriation; (16) relations of the United States with foreign nations generally; (17) treaties, conventions, and international agreements, and executive agreements, except reciprocal trade agreements; (18) the United Nations and its affiliated organizations; (19) World Bank group, the regional development banks, and other international organizations established primarily for development assistance purposes. The committee shall also study and review, on a comprehensive basis, matters relating to national security policy, foreign policy, and international economic policy as they relate to the foreign policy of the United States, and matters relating to food, hunger and nutrition in foreign countries.
Party Ratio: R 10-D 9

Bob Corker, Tenn., Chair
James E. Risch, Idaho
Marco Rubio, Fla.
Ron Johnson, Wisc.
Jeff Flake, Ariz.
Cory Gardner, Colo.
David Perdue, Ga.
Johnny Isakson, Ga.
Rand Paul, Ky.
John Barrasso, Wyo.

Benjamin L. Cardin, Md.
Robert Menendez, N.J.
Barbara Boxer, Calif.
Jeanne Shaheen, N.H.
Christopher Coons, Del.
Tom Udall, N.M.
Chris Murphy, Conn.
Tim Kaine, Va.
Edward J. Markey, Mass.

Subcommittees

Africa and Global Health Policy
Office: 423 SDOB 20510   **Phone:** 224-6797

Jeff Flake (Chair), Johnny Isakson, Rand Paul, John Barrasso, Marco Rubio, Bob Corker (ex officio)

Edward J. Markey (Ranking Minority Member), Chris Coons, Tom Udall, Robert Menendez, Benjamin L. Cardin (ex officio)

East Asia, the Pacific, and International Cybersecurity Policy
Office: 423 SDOB 20510   **Phone:** 224-6797

Cory Gardner (Chair), Marco Rubio, Ron Johnson, Johnny Isakson, Jeff Flake, Bob Corker (ex officio)

Benjamin L. Cardin (Ranking Minority Member), Barbara Boxer, Chris Coons, Tom Udall

Europe and Regional Security Cooperation
Office: 423 SDOB 20510   **Phone:** 224-6797

Ron Johnson (Chair), Rand Paul, James E. Risch, Cory Gardner, John Barrasso, Bob Corker (ex officio)

Jeanne Shaheen (Ranking Minority Member), Christopher Murphy, Tim Kaine, Edward J. Markey, Benjamin L. Cardin (ex officio)

Multilateral International Development, Multilateral Institutions, and International Economic, Energy, and Environmental Policy
Office: 423 SDOB 20510   **Phone:** 224-6797

John Barrasso (Chair), David Perdue, James E. Risch, Jeff Flake, Cory Gardner, Bob Corker (ex officio)

Tom Udall (Ranking Minority Member), Barbara Boxer, Jeanne Shaheen, Edward J. Markey, Benjamin L. Cardin (ex officio)

Near East, South Asia, Central Asia, and Counterterrorism
Office: 423 SDOB 20510   **Phone:** 224-6797

James E. Risch (Chair), David Perdue, Rand Paul, Marco Rubio, Ron Johnson, Bob Corker (ex officio)

Christopher Murphy (Ranking Minority Member), Benjamin L. Cardin, Jeanne Shaheen, Tim Kaine

State Department and USAID Management, International Operations, and Bilateral International Development
Office: 423 SDOB 20510   **Phone:** 224-6797

David Perdue (Chair), James E. Risch, Johnny Isakson, Ron Johnson, Rand Paul, Bob Corker (ex officio)

Tim Kaine (Ranking Minority Member), Barbara Boxer, Chris Coons, Christopher Murphy, Benjamin L. Cardin (ex officio)

Western Hemisphere, Transnational Crime, Civilian Security, Democracy, Human Rights, and Global Women's Issues
Office: 423 SDOB 20510　**Phone:** 224-6797
　Marco Rubio (Chair), Jeff Flake, Cory Gardner, David Perdue, Johnny Isakson, Bob Corker (ex officio)
　Barbara Boxer (Ranking Minority Member), Tom Udall, Tim Kaine, Edward J. Markey, Benjamin L. Cardin (ex officio)

HEALTH, EDUCATION, LABOR, AND PENSIONS

Office: 428 SDOB 20510-6300
Phone: 224-5375　**Fax:** 228-5044
Web: help.senate.gov
Majority Staff Director: David Cleary
Minority Staff Director: Evan Schatz
　Jurisdiction: (1) measures relating to education, labor, health, and public welfare; (2) aging; (3) agricultural colleges; (4) arts and humanities; (5) biomedical research and development, including cloning and stem cell research; (6) child labor; (7) convict labor and the entry of goods made by convicts into interstate commerce; (8) domestic activities of the American National Red Cross; (9) equal employment opportunity; (10) Gallaudet University (Washington, D.C.), Howard University (Washington, D.C.), and St. Elizabeth's Hospital (Washington, D.C.); (11) individuals with disabilities; (12) labor standards and labor statistics; (13) mediation and arbitration of labor disputes; (14) occupational safety and health, including the welfare of miners; (15) private pension plans; (16) public health; (17) railway labor and railway retirement; (18) regulation of foreign laborers; (19) student loans; (20) wages and hours of labor. The committee shall also study and review, on a comprehensive basis, matters relating to health, education, and training, and public welfare.
Party Ratio: R 12-D 10

Lamar Alexander, Tenn., Chair	*Patty Murray, Wash.*
Mike Enzi, Wyo.	*Barbara Mikulski, Md.*
Richard Burr, N.C.	*Bernie Sanders, Vt. (I)*
Johnny Isakson, Ga.	*Robert P. Casey Jr., Pa*
Rand Paul, Ky.	*Al Franken, Minn.*
Susan Collins, Maine	*Michael F. Bennet, Colo.*
Lisa Murkowski, Alaska	*Sheldon Whitehouse, R.I.*
Mark Kirk, Ill.	*Tammy Baldwin, Wisc.*
Tim Scott, S.C.	*Chris Murphy, Conn.*
Orrin G. Hatch, Utah	*Elizabeth Warren, Mass.*
Pat Roberts, Kans.	
Bill Cassidy, La.	

Subcommittees

Children and Families
Office: 428 SDOB 20510　**Phone:** 224-5375
　Rand Paul (Chair), Lisa Murkowsi, Richard Burr, Mark Kirk, Orrin G. Hatch, Pat Roberts, Bill Cassidy, Lamar Alexander (ex officio)

　Robert P. Casey Jr. (Ranking Minority Member), Barbara Mikulski, Bernie Sanders, Al Franken, Michael F. Bennet, Patty Murray (ex officio)

Employment and Workplace Safety
Office: 428 SDOB 20510　**Phone:** 224-5375
　Johnny Isakson (Chair), Rand Paul, Tim Scott, Mark Kirk, Pat Roberts, Bill Cassidy, Lamar Alexander (ex officio)
　Al Franken (Ranking Minority Member), Robert P. Casey Jr., Sheldon Whitehouse, Tammy Baldwin, Patty Murray (ex officio)

Primary Health and Retirement Security Aging
Office: 428 SDOB 20510　**Phone:** 224-5375
　Mike Enzi (Chair), Richard Burr, Susan Collins, Mark Kirk, Tim Scott, Orrin G. Hatch, Pat Roberts, Bill Cassidy, Lisa Murkowski, Lamar Alexander (ex officio)
　Bernie Sanders (Ranking Minority Member), Barbara Mikulski, Michael F. Bennet, Sheldon Whitehouse, Tammy Baldwin, Chris Murphy, Elizabeth Warren, Patty Murray (ex officio)

HOMELAND SECURITY AND GOVERNMENTAL AFFAIRS

Office: 340 SDOB 20510-6250
Phone: 224-4751　**Fax:** 224-9603
Web: hsgac.senate.gov
Minority Web: hsgac.senate.gov/media/minority-media
Majority Staff Director: Keith Ashdown
Minority Staff Director: Gabrielle Batkin, 224-2627, 442 SHOB
　Jurisdiction: (1) Department of Homeland Security, except matters relating to: the Coast Guard, the Transportation Security Administration, the Federal Law Enforcement Training Center, or the Secret Service; and the United States Citizenship and Immigration Service; or the immigration functions of the United States Customs and Border Protection or the United States Immigration and Custom Enforcement or the Directorate of Border and Transportation Security; and the following functions performed by any employee of the Department of Homeland Security: any customs revenue function, including any function provided for in Section 415 of the Homeland Security Act of 2002; any commercial function or commercial operation of the Bureau of Customs and Border Protection or Bureau of Immigration and Customs Enforcement, including matters relating to trade facilitation and trade regulation; or any other function related to the above items that was exercised by the United States Customs Service on the day before the effective date of the Homeland Security Act of 2002; (2) archives of the United States; (3) budget and accounting measures, other than appropriations, except as provided in the Congressional Budget and Impoundment Control Act of 1974; (4) census and collection of statistics, including economic and social statistics; (5) congressional organization, except for any part of the matter that amends the rules or orders of the Senate; (6) federal civil service; (7) government information; (8) intergovernmental relations; (9) municipal affairs of

HOMELAND SECURITY AND GOVERNMENTAL AFFAIRS (continued)

the District of Columbia, except appropriations therefore; (10) organization and management of United States nuclear export policy; (11) organization and reorganization of the executive branch of the Government; (12) United States Postal Service; (13) status of officers and employees of the United States, including their classification, compensation, and benefits. The committee shall have the duty of (A) receiving and examining reports of the Comptroller General of the United States and of submitting such recommendations to the Senate as it deems necessary or desirable in connection with the subject matter of such reports; (B) studying the efficiency, economy, and effectiveness of all agencies and departments of the Government; (C) evaluating laws enacted to effect the reorganization of the legislative and executive branches of the Government; and (D) studying the intergovernmental relationships between the United States and the states and municipalities, and between the United States and international organizations of which the United States is a member.

Party Ratio: R 9-D 7

Ron Johnson, Wisc., Chair	*Thomas Carper, Del.*
John McCain, Ariz.	*Claire McCaskill, Mo.*
Rob Portman, Ohio	*Jon Tester, Mont.*
Rand Paul, Ky.	*Tammy Baldwin, Wisc.*
James Lankford, Okla.	*Heidi Heitkamp, N.D.*
Kelly Ayotte, N.H.	*Gary Peters, Mich.*
Mike Enzi, Wyo.	*Cory Booker, N.J.*
Joni Ernst, Iowa	
Ben Sasse, Neb.	

Subcommittees

Federal Spending Oversight and Emergency Management
Office: SD-342 SDOB 20510 **Phone:** 224-2254
Rand Paul (Chair), James Lankford, Mike Enzi, Kelly Ayotte, Joni Ernst, Ben Sasse, Ron Johnson (ex officio)
Tammy Baldwin (Ranking Minority Member), Claire McCaskill, Cory Booker, Gary Peters, Thomas Carper (ex officio)

Permanent Investigations
Office: SD-342 SDOB 20510 **Phone:** 224-3721
Rob Portman (Chair), John McCain, Paul Rand, James Lankford, Kelly Ayotte, Ben Sasse, Ron Johnson (ex officio)
Claire McCaskill (Ranking Minority Member), Jon Tester, Tammy Baldwin, Heidi Heitkamp, Thomas Carper (ex officio)

Regulatory Affairs and Federal Management
Office: SD-342 SDOB 20510 **Phone:** 224-4551
James Lankford (Chair), John McCain, Rob Portman, Mike Enzi, Joni Ernst, Ben Sasse, Ron Johnson (ex officio)
Heidi Heitkamp (Ranking Minority Member), Jon Tester, Cory Booker, Gary Peters, Thomas Carper (ex officio)

INDIAN AFFAIRS

Office: 838 SHOB 20510-6450
Phone: 224-2251 **Fax:** 228-5429
Web: indian.senate.gov
Majority Staff Director: Mike Andrews
Minority Staff Director: Anthony Walters
Jurisdiction: (1) all proposed legislation, messages, petitions, memorials, and other matters relating to Indian affairs shall be referred to the committee; (2) study any and all matters pertaining to problems and opportunities of Indians, including but not limited to, Indian land management and trust responsibilities, Indian education, Indian health, special services, and Indian loan programs, the National Indian Gaming Regulatory Act of 1988, the National Indian Gaming Commission, and Indian claims against the United States.

Party Ratio: R 8-D 6

John Barrasso, Wyo., Chair	*Jon Tester, Mont., Vice Chair*
John McCain, Ariz.	*Maria Cantwell, Wash.*
Lisa Murkowski, Alaska	*Tom Udall, N.M.*
John Hoeven, N.D.	*Al Franken, Minn.*
James Lankford, Okla.	*Brian Schatz, Hawaii*
Steve Daines, Mont.	*Heidi Heitkamp, N.D.*
Mike Crapo, Idaho	
Jerry Moran, Kans.	

JUDICIARY

Office: 224 SDOB 20510-6275
Phone: 224-5225 **Fax:** 224-9516
Web: judiciary.senate.gov
Majority Staff Director: Kolan L. Davis
Minority Staff Director: Kristine Lucius, 224-7703
Jurisdiction: (1) apportionment of Representatives; (2) bankruptcy, mutiny, espionage, and counterfeiting; (3) civil liberties; (4) constitutional amendments; (5) federal courts and federal judges; (6) government information; (7) holidays and celebrations; (8) immigration and naturalization; (9) interstate compacts generally; (10) judicial proceedings, civil and criminal, generally; (11) local courts in United States territories and possessions; (12) measures relating to claims against the United States; (13) national penitentiaries; (14) United States Patent and Trademark Office (Commerce); (15) patents, copyrights, and trademarks; (16) protection of trade and commerce against unlawful restraints and monopolies; (17) revision and codification of the statutes of the United States; (18) state and territorial boundary lines.

Party Ratio: R 11-D 9

Chuck Grassley, Iowa, Chair	*Patrick P. Leahy, Vt.*
Orrin G. Hatch, Utah	*Dianne Feinstein, Calif.*
Jeff A. Sessions, Ala.	*Charles E. Schumer, N.Y.*
Lindsey Graham, S.C.	*Richard J. Durbin, Ill.*
John Cornyn, Tex.	*Sheldon Whitehouse, R.I.*
Mike Lee, Utah	*Amy Klobuchar, Minn.*
	Al Franken, Minn.

Ted Cruz, Tex.
Jeff Flake, Ariz.
David Vitter, La.
David Perdue, Ga.
Thom Tillis, N.C.

Christopher Coons, Del.
Richard Blumenthal, Conn.

Subcommittees

Antitrust, Competition Policy and Consumer Rights
Office: 224 SDOB 20510   **Phone:** 224-5225
Mike Lee (Chair), David Perdue, Thom Tillis, Chuck Grassley, Orrin G. Hatch
Amy Klobuchar (Ranking Minority Member), Chris Coons, Al Franken, Richard Blumenthal

The Constitution
Office: 224 SDOB 20510   **Phone:** 224-5225
John Cornyn (Chair), Thom Tillis, Lindsey Graham, Ted Cruz, David Vitter
Richard J. Durbin (Ranking Minority Member), Sheldon Whitehouse, Chris Coons, Al Franken

Crime and Terrorism
Office: 224 SDOB 20510   **Phone:** 224-5225
Lindsey Graham (Chair), David Vitter, Jeff A. Sessions, John Cornyn, Jeff Flake
Sheldon Whitehouse (Ranking Minority Member), Charles E. Schumer, Amy Klobuchar, Al Franken

Immigration and the National Interest
Office: 224 SDOB 20510   **Phone:** 224-5225
Jeff A. Sessions (Chair), David Vitter, David Perdue, Chuck Grassley, John Cornyn, Mike Lee, Ted Cruz, Thom Tillis
Charles E. Schumer (Ranking Minority Member), Patrick P. Leahy, Dianne Feinstein, Richard J. Durbin, Amy Klobuchar, Al Franken, Richard Blumenthal

Oversight, Agency Action, Federal Rights, and Federal Courts
Office: 224 SDOB 20510   **Phone:** 224-5225
Ted Cruz (Chair), Chuck Grassley, Orrin G. Hatch, Jeff A. Sessions, Jeff Flake, Lindsey Graham, Mike Lee, David Vitter
Chris Coons (Ranking Minority Member), Dianne Feinstein, Richard J. Durbin, Charles E. Schumer, Sheldon Whitehouse, Amy Klobuchar, Richard Blumenthal

Privacy, Technology and the Law
Office: 224 SDOB 20510   **Phone:** 224-5225
Jeff Flake (Chair), Orrin G. Hatch, David Perdue, Mike Lee, Thom Tillis, Lindsey Graham
Al Franken (Ranking Minority Member), Dianne Feinstein, Charles E. Schumer, Sheldon Whitehouse, Chris Coons

RULES AND ADMINISTRATION

Office: 305 SROB 20510-6325
Phone: 224-6352   **Fax:** 224-1912
Web: rules.senate.gov
Majority Staff Director: Kelly Fado
Minority Staff Director: Stacy McHatton-McBride

Jurisdiction: (1) administration of the Senate office buildings and the Senate wing of the United States Capitol, including the assignment of office space for Senators and Senate Committees; (2) Senate organization relative to rules and procedures, and Senate rules and regulations, including Senate floor rules and Senate gallery rules; (3) corrupt practices; (4) credentials and qualifications of Members of the Senate, contested elections, and acceptance of incompatible offices; (5) federal elections generally, including the election of the President, Vice President, and Members of the Senate; (6) Government Printing Office, and the printing and correction of the Congressional Record, as well as those matters provided for under Rule XI; (7) meetings of the Congress and attendance of Members; (8) payment of money out of the contingent fund of the Senate or creating a charge upon the same (except that any resolution relating to substantive matter within the jurisdiction of any other standing committee of the Senate shall be first referred to such committee); (9) Presidential Succession Act of 1947; (10) purchase of books and manuscripts and erection of monuments to the memory of individuals; (11) Senate Library and statuary, art, and pictures in the United States Capitol and Senate office buildings; (12) services to the Senate, including the Senate restaurant; (13) United States Capitol and Senate office buildings, the Library of Congress, the Smithsonian Institution (and the incorporation of similar institutions), and the United States Botanic Garden. The committee shall also (A) make a continuing study of the organization and operation of the Congress of the United States and shall recommend improvements in such organization and operation with a view toward strengthening the Congress, simplifying its operations, improving its relationships with other branches of the United States Government, and enabling it better to meet its responsibilities under the Constitution of the United States; (B) identify any court proceeding or action which, in the opinion of the Committee, is of vital interest to the Congress as a constitutionally established institution of the Federal Government and call such proceeding or action to the attention of the Senate; (C) develop, implement, and update as necessary a strategic planning process and a strategic plan for the functional and technical infrastructure support of the Senate and provide oversight over plans developed by Senate officers and others in accordance with the strategic planning process.
Party Ratio: R 10-D 8

Roy Blunt, Mo., Chair
Lamar Alexander, Tenn.
Mitch McConnell, Ky.
Thad A. Cochran, Miss.
Pat Roberts, Kans.
Richard Shelby, Ala.
Ted Cruz, Tex.
Shelley Moore Capito, W.Va.
John Boozman, Ark.
Roger Wicker, Miss.

Charles E. Schumer, N.Y.
Dianne Feinstein, Calif.
Richard J. Durbin, Ill.
Tom Udall, N.M.
Mark R. Warner, Va.
Patrick P. Leahy, Vt.
Amy Klobuchar, Minn.
Angus King, Maine (I)

SMALL BUSINESS AND ENTREPRENEURSHIP

Office: 428A SROB 20510-6350
Phone: 224-5175   **Fax:** 224-5619
Web: sbc.senate.gov
Minority Web: sbc.senate.gov/public/index.cfm?
   p=RankingMember
Majority Staff Director: Zak Baig
Minority Staff Director: Robert Diznoff
   Jurisdiction: (1) all proposed legislation, messages, petitions, memorials and other matters relating to the Small Business Administration; (2) any proposed legislation reported by such committee which relates to matters other than the functions of the Small Business Administration shall, at the request of the chair of any standing committee having jurisdiction over the subject matter extraneous to the functions of the Small Business Administration, be considered and reported by such standing committee prior to its consideration by the Senate; and likewise measures reported by other committees directly relating to the Small Business Administration shall, at the request of the chair of the Committee on Small Business and Entrepreneurship, be referred to the Committee on Small Business and Entrepreneurship for its consideration of any portions of the measure dealing with the Small Business Administration, and be reported by this Committee prior to its consideration by the Senate; (3) study and survey by means of research and investigation all problems of small business enterprises.
Party Ratio: R 10-D 9

David Vitter, La., Chair	*Jeanne Shaheen, N.H.*
James E. Risch, Idaho	*Maria Cantwell, Wash.*
Marco Rubio, Fla.	*Benjamin L. Cardin, Md.*
Tim Scott, S.C.	*Heidi Heitkamp, N.D.*
Rand Paul	*Edward Markey, Mass.*
Deb Fischer, Neb.	*Cory Booker, N.J.*
Cory Gardner, Colo.	*Chris Coons, Del.*
Joni Ernst, Iowa	*Mazie K. Hirono, Hawaii*
Kelly Ayotte, N.H.	*Gary Peters, Mich.*
Mike Enzi, Wyo.	

VETERANS' AFFAIRS

Office: 412 SROB 20510-6375
Phone: 224-9126   **Fax:** 224-8908
Web: veterans.senate.gov
Minority Web: veterans.senate.gov/newsroom/minority-news
Majority Staff Director: Thomas Bowman
Minority Staff Director: Ethan Saxon, 224-2074, 825A SHOB
   Jurisdiction: (1) compensation of veterans; (2) life insurance issued by the government on account of service in the Armed Forces; (3) national cemeteries; (4) pensions of all the wars of the United States; (5) readjustment of service personnel to civil life; (6) soldiers' and sailors' civil relief, including oversight of and appropriate modifications to the Soldiers' and Sailors' Civil Relief Act of 1940; (7) veterans' hospitals, medical care and treatment

of veterans; (8) veterans' measures generally; (9) vocational rehabilitation and education of veterans.
Party Ratio: R 8-D 7

Johnny Isakson, Ga., Chair	*Richard Blumenthal, Conn.*
Jerry Moran, Kans.	*Patty Murray, Wash.*
John Boozman, Ark.	*Bernie Sanders, Vt. (I)*
Dean Heller, Nev.	*Sherrod Brown, Ohio*
Bill Cassidy, La.	*Jon Tester, Mont.*
Mike Rounds, S.D.	*Mazie K. Hirono, Hawaii*
Thom Tillis, N.C.	*Joe Manchin, W.Va.*
Dan Sullivan, Alaska	

SELECT ETHICS

Office: 220 SHOB 20510-6425
Phone: 224-2981   **Fax:** 224-7416
Web: ethics.senate.gov
Staff Director: Deborah Mayer
Deputy Staff Director: Annette Gillis
   Jurisdiction: (1) receive complaints and investigate allegations of improper conduct which may reflect upon the Senate, violations of law, violations of the Senate Code of Official Conduct, and violations of rules and regulations of the Senate, relating to the conduct of individuals in the performance of their duties as Members of the Senate, or as officers or employees of the Senate, and to make appropriate findings of fact and conclusions with respect thereto; (2) recommend, when appropriate, disciplinary action against Members and staff; (3) recommend rules or regulations necessary to insure appropriate Senate standards of conduct; (4) report violations of any law to the proper Federal and State authorities; (5) regulate the use of the franking privilege in the Senate; (6) investigate unauthorized disclosures of intelligence information; (7) implement the Senate public financial disclosure requirements of the Ethics in Government Act of 1978; (8) regulate the receipt and disposition of gifts from foreign governments received by Members, officers, and employees of the Senate; and (9) render advisory opinions on the application of Senate rules and laws to Members, officers, and employees.
Party Ratio: R 3-D 3

Johnny Isakson, Ga., Chair	*Barbara Boxer, Calif., Vice*
Pat Roberts, Kans.	*Chair*
James E. Risch, Idaho	*Chris Coons, Del.*
	Brian Schatz, Hawaii

SELECT INTELLIGENCE

Office: 211 SHOB 20510-6475
Phone: 224-1700   **Fax:** 224-1772
Web: intelligence.senate.gov
Majority Staff Director: Christopher Joiner
Minority Staff Director: Michael Casey
   Jurisdiction: (1) oversee and make continuing studies of the intelligence activities and programs of the United States Government, including, but not limited to, the Central Intelligence Agency Act of 1949, Classified Information Procedures Act of 1980, classified national security information, foreign intelligence electronic surveillance,

Foreign Intelligence Surveillance Act of 1978, National Security Act of 1947, National Security Agency Act of 1959, national security information, President's Foreign Intelligence Advisory Board (Executive Office of the President), Provide Appropriate Tools Required to Intercept and Obstruct Terrorism (PATRIOT) Act of 2001, security requirements for government employment; (2) submit to the Senate appropriate proposals for legislation; (3) report to the Senate concerning such intelligence activities and programs.
Party Ratio: R 10-D 9

Richard Burr, N.C., Chair
James E. Risch, Idaho
Dan Coats, Ind.
Marco Rubio, Va.
Susan Collins, Maine
Roy Blunt, Mo.
James Lankford, Okla.
Tom Cotton, Ark.
John McCain, Ariz.
  (ex officio)
Mitch McConnell, Ky.
  (ex officio)

Dianne Feinstein, Calif.,
  Vice Chair
Ron Wyden, Ore.
Barbara Mikulski, Md.
Mark R. Warner, Va.
Martin Heinrich, N.M.
Angus King, Maine (I)
Mazie K. Hirono, Hawaii
Jack D. Reed, R.I. (ex officio)
Harry Reid, Nev.,
  (ex officio)

SPECIAL AGING

Office: G-31 SDOB 20510-6050
Phone: 224-5364 **Fax:** 224-9926
Web: aging.senate.gov
Majority Staff Director: Priscilla Hanley
Minority Staff Director: Joel Eskovitz, 628 SHOB
  Jurisdiction: (1) conduct a continuing study of any and all matters pertaining to problems and opportunities of older people, including, but not limited to, assisted living, elder abuse, health care, identity theft, long-term care, Medicare, Older Americans Act, prescription drugs, retirement income security, retirement pensions, rural health care, Social Security, telemedicine, problems and opportunities of maintaining health, of assuring adequate income, of finding employment, of engaging in productive and rewarding activity, of securing proper housing, and when necessary, of obtaining care or assistance. No proposed legislation shall be referred to such committee, and such committee shall not have power to report by bill, or otherwise

have legislative jurisdiction. (2) The special committee shall, from time to time (but not less often than once each year), report to the Senate the results of the study conducted pursuant to paragraph (1), together with such recommendation as it considers appropriate.
Party Ratio: R 11-D9

Susan Collins, Maine, Chair
Orrin G. Hatch, Utah
Mark Kirk, Ill.
Jeff Flake, Ariz.
Tim Scott, S.C.
Bob Corker, Tenn.
Dean Heller, Nev.
Tom Cotton, Ark.
David Perdue, Ga.
Thom Tillis, N.C.
Ben Sasse, Neb.

Claire McCaskill, Mo.
Bill J. Nelson, Fla.
Robert P. Casey Jr., Pa.
Sheldon Whitehouse, R.I.
Kirsten Gillibrand, N.Y.
Richard Blumenthal, Conn.
Joe Donnelly, Ind.
Elizabeth Warren, Mass.
Tim Kaine, Va.

INTERNATIONAL NARCOTICS CONTROL CAUCUS

Office: 818-C SHOB 20510
Phone: 224-9032 **Fax:** 224-6020
Web: drugcaucus.senate.gov
  Purpose: The Senate Caucus on International Narcotics Control was created to "monitor and encourage United States Government and private programs seeking to expand international cooperation against drug abuse and narcotics trafficking" and to "monitor and promote international compliance with narcotics control treaties." As a formal organization of the U.S. Senate, the Caucus has the status of a standing committee. The Caucus exercises oversight on a wide range of issues, including international counternarcotics assistance and domestic drug prevention and treatment programs. The Caucus has held numerous hearings over the years and has issued a number of reports on U.S. narcotics control policy.
Party Ratio: D 4-R 3

Chuck Grassley, Iowa,
  Chair
John Cornyn, Texas
James E. Risch, Idaho
Jeff A. Sessions, Ala.

Dianne Feinstein, Calif.
Charles E. Schumer, N.Y.
Sheldon Whitehouse, R.I.

SENATE LEADERSHIP AND PARTISAN COMMITTEES

REPUBLICAN LEADERS

Majority Floor Leader: Mitch McConnell, Ky.
Majority Whip: John Cornyn, Texas

REPUBLICAN PARTISAN COMMITTEES

National Republican Senatorial Committee
Office: 425 2nd St. N.E. 20002-4914
Phone: 675-6000   **Fax:** 675-4730
Web: www.nrsc.org
Roger Wicker, Mo., Chair

Republican Conference
Office: 405 SHOB 20510-7060
Phone: 224-2764   **Fax:** 228-4276
Web: www.republican.senate.gov
John Thune, S.D., Chair
Roy Blunt, Mo., Vice Chair

Republican Policy Committee
Office: 347 SROB 20510-7064
Phone: 224-2946   **Fax:** 228-2628
Web: www.rpc.senate.gov
John Barrasso, Wyo., Chair

DEMOCRATIC LEADERS

Minority Floor Leader: *Harry Reid, Nev.*
Minority Whip: *Richard J. Durbin, Ill.*

DEMOCRATIC PARTISAN COMMITTEES

Democratic Policy and Communications Center
Office: S-318 CAP 20510
Phone: 224-2939   **Fax:** 228-5576
Web: www.dpcc.senate.gov
Charles E. Schumer, N.Y., Chair
Debbie A. Stabenow, Mich., Vice Chair

Democratic Senatorial Campaign Committee
Office: 120 Maryland Ave. N.E. 20002-5610
Phone: 224-2447   **Fax:** 969-0354
Web: www.dscc.org
Email: info@dscc.org
Jon Tester, Mo., Chair

Democratic Steering and Outreach Committee
Office: 712 SHOB 20510
Phone: 224-9048   **Fax:** 224-5476
Web: www.dsoc.senate.gov
Email: steering@dsoc.senate.gov
Amy Klobuchar, Minn., Chair
Jeanne Shaheen, N.H., Vice Chair

Senate Members' Offices

The following list gives Senate members and their party and state affiliation, followed by the address and telephone and fax numbers for their Washington office. The area code for all Washington, D.C., numbers is 202. A top administrative aide, a Web address, a Facebook page, and a Twitter account for each senator are also provided, when available. Most members may be contacted via the Web-based email forms found on their Web sites. These are followed by the address, telephone and fax numbers, and name of a key aide for the senator's district office(s). Each listing concludes with the senator's committee assignments. For partisan committee assignments, see page 876.

As of April 25, 2016, there were 54 Republicans, 44 Democrats, and 2 Independents who caucus with the Democrats in the Senate.

Alexander, Lamar, R-Tenn.

Capitol Hill Office: 455 SDOB 20510-4206; 224-4944; Fax: 228-3398; *Chief of Staff:* David Cleary

Web: www.alexander.senate.gov

Facebook: www.facebook.com/lamaralexander

Twitter: @senalexander

District Offices: Tri-Cities Regional Airport, 2525 Hwy. 75, #101, Blountville, TN 37617-6366; 423-325-6240; Fax: 423-325-6236; *Field Rep.:* Lana Moore

Joel E. Soloman Federal Bldg., 900 Georgia Ave., #260, Chattanooga, TN 37402-2240; 423-752-5337; Fax: 423-752-5342; *Field Rep.:* Evann Freeman

111 Murray Guard Dr., Suite D, Jackson, TN 38305-3628; 731-664-0289; Fax: 731-664-3129; *Field Rep.:* Matt Varino

Howard H. Baker Jr. U.S. Courthouse, 800 Market St., #112, Knoxville, TN 37902-2303; 865-545-4253; Fax: 865-545-4252; *State Director:* Patrick Jaynes

Clifford Davis and Odell Horton Federal Bldg., 167 N. Main St., #1068, Memphis, TN 38103-1858; 901-544-4224; Fax: 901-544-4227; *Field Rep.:* Chris Connolly

3322 West End Ave., #120, Nashville, TN 37203-6821; 615-736-5129; Fax: 615-269-4803; *State Scheduler and Office Manager:* Faye Head

Committee Assignments: Appropriations; Energy and Natural Resources; Health, Education, Labor, and Pensions; Rules and Administration

Ayotte, Kelly, R-N.H.

Capitol Hill Office: 144 SROB 20510-2907; 224-3324; Fax: 224-4952; *Chief of Staff:* Rick Murphy

Web: www.ayotte.senate.gov

Facebook: www.facebook.com/kellyayottenh

Twitter: @KellyAyotte

District Offices: 19 Pleasant St., #13B, Berlin, NH 03570-1917; 603-752-7702; Fax: 603-752-7704; *Special Asst. for Casework and Projects:* Mike Scala

1200 Elm St., #2, Manchester, NH 03101-2503; 603-622-7979; Fax: 603-622-0422; *State Director:* Bud Fitch

144 Main St., Nashua, NH 03060-2702; 603-880-3335; *Outreach Manager:* Matt Flanders

14 Manchester Square, #140, Portsmouth, NH 03801-7866; 603-436-7161; *Caseworker:* Kate Pyle

Committee Assignments: Armed Services; Budget; Commerce, Science, and Transportation; Homeland Security and Government Affairs; Small Business and Entrepreneurship

Baldwin, Tammy, D-Wisc.

Capitol Hill Office: 717 SHOB 20510; 224-5653; Fax: 224-9787; *Chief of Staff:* Bill Murat

Web: www.baldwin.senate.gov

Facebook: www.facebook.com/TammyBaldwin

Twitter: @tammybaldwin

District Offices: 402 Graham St., #206, Eau Claire, WI 54701-2633; 715-832-8424; *Field Rep.:* Kelly Westlund

205 5th Ave. South, Room 216, La Crosse, WI 54601; 608-796-0045; Fax: 608-796-0089; *Regional Coord.:* John Medinger

30 W. Mifflin St., #700, Madison, WI 53703-2568; 608-264-5338; Fax: 608-264-5473; *State Director:* Doug Hill

633 W. Wisconsin Ave., #1920, Milwaukee, WI 53203-2205; 414-297-4451; Fax: 414-297-4455; *Field Rep.:* Benjamin Juarez

2100 Stewart Ave., #250B, Wausau, WI 54401; 715-261-2611; *Outreach Rep:* Bryce Luchterhand

Committee Assignments: Appropriations; Budget; Health, Education, Labor, and Pensions; Homeland Security and Governmental Affairs

Barrasso, John, R-Wyo.

Capitol Hill Office: 307 SDOB 20510-5005; 224-6441; Fax: 224-1724; *Chief of Staff:* J. Dan Kunsman

Web: www.barrasso.senate.gov

Facebook: www.facebook.com/johnbarrasso

Twitter: @senjohnbarrasso

District Offices: 100 E. B St., #2201, Casper, WY 82601-7021; 307-261-6413; Fax: 307-265-6706; *Field Rep.:* Riata Little

2120 Capitol Ave., #2013, Cheyenne, WY 82001-3631; 307-772-2451; Fax: 307-638-3512; *State Director:* Kristi Wallin

324 E. Washington Ave., Riverton, WY 82501-4342; 307-856-6642; Fax: 307-856-5901; *Field Rep.:* Pam Buline

1575 Dewar Dr., #218, Rock Springs, WY 82901-5972; 307-362-5012; Fax: 307-362-5129; *Field Rep.:* Sandy DaRif

2 N. Main St., #206, Sheridan, WY 82801-6322; 307-672-6456; Fax: 307-672-6456; *Field Rep.:* Oaklee Anderson
Committee Assignments: Energy and Natural Resources; Environment and Public Works; Foreign Relations; Indian Affairs, Chair

Bennet, Michael F., D-Colo.

Capitol Hill Office: 458 SROB 20510-0608; 224-5852; Fax: 228-5097; *Chief of Staff:* Jonathan Davidson
Web: www.bennet.senate.gov
Facebook: www.facebook.com/senatorbennet
Twitter: @senbennetco
District Offices: 609 Main St., #110, Alamosa, CO 81101-2557; 719-587-0096; Fax: 719-587-0098; *Regional Rep.:* Charlotte Bobicki
409 N. Tejon St., #107, Colorado Springs, CO 80903-1163; 719-328-1100; Fax: 719-328-1129; *Regional Director:* Annie Oatman-Gardner
1127 Sherman St., #150, Denver, CO 80203-2398; 303-455-7600; Fax: 303-455-8851; *Deputy Chief of Staff:* Sarah Hughes
835 E. 2nd Ave., #203, Durango, CO 81301-5475; 970-259-1710; Fax: 970-259-9789; *Regional Director:* John Whitney
1200 S. College Ave., #211, Fort Collins, CO 80524-3746; 970-224-2200; Fax: 970-224-2205; *Regional Director:* James Thompson
225 N. 5th St., #511, Grand Junction, CO 81501-2656; 970-241-6631; Fax: 970-241-8313; *Constituent Advocate:* Aaron Torres
129 W. B St., Pueblo, CO 81003-3400; 719-542-7550; Fax: 719-542-7555; *Regional Director:* Dwight Gardner
Committee Assignments: Agriculture, Nutrition, and Forestry; Finance; Health, Education, Labor, and Pensions

Blumenthal, Richard, D-Conn.

Capitol Hill Office: 724 SHOB 20510-0704; 224-2823; Fax: 224-9673; *Chief of Staff:* Laurie Rubiner
Web: www.blumenthal.senate.gov
Facebook: www.facebook.com/SenBlumenthal
Twitter: @SenBlumenthal
District Offices: 90 State House Square, 10th Floor, Hartford, CT 06103; 860-258-6940; Fax: 860-258-6958; *State Director:* Rich Kehoe
915 Lafayette Blvd., Room 230, Bridgeport, CT 06604; 203-330-0598; Fax: 203-330-0608; *State Director:* Rich Kehoe
Committee Assignments: Armed Services; Commerce, Science, and Transportation; Judiciary; Special Aging; Veterans' Affairs, Ranking Minority Member

Blunt, Roy, R-Mo.

Capitol Hill Office: 260 SROB 20510-2508; 224-5721; Fax: 224-8149; *Chief of Staff:* Glen R. Chambers
Web: www.blunt.senate.gov
Facebook: www.facebook.com/SenatorBlunt
Twitter: @RoyBlunt

District Offices: 2502 Tanner Dr., #208, Cape Girardeau, MO 63703; 573-334-7044; Fax: 573-334-7352; *Office Director:* Tom Schulte
7700 Bonhomme Ave., #315, Clayton, MO 63105; 314-725-4484; Fax: 314-727-3548; *Office Director:* Mary Beth
1001 Cherry St., #104, Columbia, MO 65201-7931; 573-442-8151; Fax: 573-442-8162; *State Director:* Derek Coats
911 Main St., #2224, Kansas City, MO 64105-5321; 816-471-7141; Fax: 816-471-7338; *Office Director:* Matt Haase
2740B E. Sunshine St., Springfield, MO 65804-2016; 417-877-7814; Fax: 417-823-9662; *District Office Director:* Joelle Cannon
Committee Assignments: Appropriations; Commerce, Science, and Transportation; Joint Library, Chair; Joint Printing, Vice Chair; Rules and Administration, Chair; Select Intelligence

Booker, Cory, D-N.J.

Capitol Hill Office: 141 SHOB 20510; 224-3224; Fax: 224-8378; *Chief of Staff:* Matt Klapper
Web: booker.senate.gov
Facebook: www.facebook.com/corybooker
Twitter: @corybooker
District Offices: One Port Center, 2 Riverside Dr., #505, Camden, NJ 08101; 856-338-8922; *South Jersey Director:* Bill Moen
One Gateway Center, 23rd Floor, Newark, NJ 07102; 973-639-8700; Fax: 973-639-8723; *State Director:* George Helmy
Committee Assignments: Commerce, Science, and Transportation; Environment and Public Works; Homeland Security and Governmental Affairs; Small Business and Entrepreneurship

Boozman, John, R-Ark.

Capitol Hill Office: 320 SHOB 20510-0406; 224-4843; Fax: 228-1371; *Chief of Staff:* Helen Tolar
Web: www.boozman.senate.gov
Facebook: www.facebook.com/JohnBoozman
Twitter: @JohnBoozman
District Offices: 106 W. Main St., #104, El Dorado, AR 71730-5634; 870-863-4641; Fax: 870-863-4105; *Constituent Services Rep.:* Chase Emerson
1120 Garrison Ave., Suite B, Fort Smith, AR 72901-2617; 479-573-0189; Fax: 479-573-0553; *Casework Coord.:* Kathy Watson
300 S. Church St., #400, Jonesboro, AR 72401-2911; 870-268-6925; Fax: 870-268-6887; *Caseworker:* Diane Holm
1401 W. Capitol Ave., Plaza F, Little Rock, AR 72201-2942; 501-372-7153; Fax: 501-372-7163; *Grants Coord.:* Tim Riley
213 W. Monroe Ave., Suite N, Lowell, AR 72745-9451; 479-725-0400; Fax: 479-725-0408; *State Director:* Stacey McClure
1001 Hwy 62 East., #11, Mountain Home, AR 72653-3215; 870-424-0129; Fax: 870-424-0141; *Caseworker, Social Security Medicare:* Sarah Hartley

620 E. 22nd St., #204, Stuttgart, AR 72160-9007; 870-672-6941; Fax: 870-672-6962; *Field Rep.:* Ty Davis

Committee Assignments: Agriculture, Nutrition, and Forestry; Appropriations; Commission on Security and Cooperation in Europe; Environment and Public Works; Joint Printing; Rules and Administration; Veterans' Affairs

Boxer, Barbara, D-Calif.

Capitol Hill Office: 112 SHOB 20510-0505; 224-3553; Fax: 224-0454; *Chief of Staff:* Laura Schiller
Web: www.boxer.senate.gov
Facebook: www.facebook.com/senatorboxer
Twitter: @senatorboxer
District Offices: 2500 Tulare St., #5290, Fresno, CA 93721-1318; 559-497-5109; Fax: 202-228-3864; *State Director:* Tom Bohigian

312 N. Spring St., #1748, Los Angeles, CA 90012-4719; 213-894-5000; Fax: 202-224-0357; *Deputy State Director and Sr. Advisor:* Yvette Martinez

70 Washington St., #203, Oakland, CA 94607-3705; 510-286-8537; Fax: 202-224-0454; *Director of State Operations:* Nicole Kaneko

3403 10th St., #704, Riverside, CA 92501-3641; 951-684-4849; Fax: 202-228-3868; *Senior Advisor:* Alton Garrett

501 I St., #7-600, Sacramento, CA 95814-7308; 916-448-2787; Fax: 202-228-3865; *Deputy State Director; State Press Liaison:* Stacey Smith

600 B St., #2240, San Diego, CA 92101-4508; 619-239-3884; Fax: 202-228-3863; *San Diego County and Imperial County Director:* Caridad Sanchez

Committee Assignments: Environment and Public Works, Ranking Minority Member; Foreign Relations; Select Ethics, Vice Chair

Brown, Sherrod, D-Ohio

Capitol Hill Office: 713 SHOB 20510-3505; 224-2315; Fax: 228-6321; *Chief of Staff:* Sarah Benzing
Web: www.brown.senate.gov
Facebook: www.facebook.com/sherrod
Twitter: @sensherrodbrown
District Offices: 425 Walnut St., #2310, Cincinnati, OH 45202-3915; 513-684-1021; Fax: 513-684-1029; *Southwest Regional Director:* Brooke Hill

1301 E. 9th St., #1710, Cleveland, OH 44114-1869; 216-522-7272; Fax: 216-522-2239; *State Director:* John Ryan

200 N. High St., Room 614, Columbus, OH 43215-2408; 614-469-2083; Fax: 614-469-2171; *Central Ohio Regional Director:* Joe Gilligan

200 W. Erie Ave., #312, Lorain, OH 44052; 440-242-4100; Fax: 440-242-4108; *Constituent Service Liaison:* Margaret Molnar

Committee Assignments: Agriculture, Nutrition, and Forestry; Banking, Housing, and Urban Affairs, Ranking Minority Member; Congressional-Executive Commission on China; Finance; Veterans' Affairs

Burr, Richard, R-N.C.

Capitol Hill Office: 217 SROB 20510-3308; 224-3154; Fax: 228-2981; *Chief of Staff:* Dean Myers
Web: www.burr.senate.gov
Facebook: www.facebook.com/SenatorRichardBurr
Twitter: @senatorburr
District Offices: Federal Bldg., 151 Patton Ave., #204, Asheville, NC 28801-2689; 828-350-2437; Fax: 828-350-2439; *State Director:* Steven Green

City Hall, 181 South St., Room 222, Gastonia, NC 28052-4126; 704-833-0854; Fax: 704-833-1467; *Field Rep.:* Josh Ward

100 Coast Line St., Room 210, Rocky Mount, NC 27804-5849; 252-977-9522; Fax: 252-977-7902; *Constituent Advocate:* Esther Clark

201 N. Front St., #809, Wilmington, NC 28401-5089; 910-251-1058; Fax: 910-251-7975; *Constituent Advocate:* Brandon Hawkins

2000 W. 1st St., #508, Winston-Salem, NC 27104-4225; 336-631-5125; Fax: 336-725-4493; *State Director:* Vacant

Committee Assignments: Commission on Security and Cooperation in Europe; Finance; Health, Education, Labor, and Pensions; Select Intelligence, Chair

Cantwell, Maria, D-Wash.

Capitol Hill Office: 311 SHOB 20510-4705; 224-3441; Fax: 228-0514; *Chief of Staff:* Travis Lumpkin
Web: www.cantwell.senate.gov
Facebook: www.facebook.com/senatorcantwell
Twitter: @CantwellPress
District Offices: 2930 Wetmore Ave., #9B, Everett, WA 98201-4044; 425-303-0114; Fax: 425-303-8351; *Northwest Washington Director:* Joe Downs

825 Jadwin Ave., #206, Richland, WA 99352-3562; 509-946-8106; Fax: 509-946-6937; *Central Washington Director:* David Reeploeg

915 2nd Ave., #3206, Seattle, WA 98174-1011; 206-220-6400; Fax: 206-220-6404; *Staff Director:* Nate Caminos

920 W. Riverside Ave., #697, Spokane, WA 99201-1008; 509-353-2507; Fax: 509-353-2547; *Eastern Outreach Director:* Nate Strege

950 Pacific Ave., #615, Tacoma, WA 98402-4431; 253-572-2281; Fax: 253-572-5859; *Olympic Peninsula and Pierce County Director:* Rosa McLeod

1313 Officers Row, Vancouver, WA 98661-3856; 360-696-7838; Fax: 360-696-7844; *Southwest Outreach Director:* Dena Horton

Committee Assignments: Commission on Security and Cooperation in Europe; Energy and Natural Resources, Ranking Minority Member; Finance; Indian Affairs, Small Business and Entrepreneurship

Cardin, Benjamin L., D-Md.

Capitol Hill Office: 509 SHOB 20510-2004; 224-4524; Fax: 224-1651; *Chief of Staff:* Christopher W. Lynch
Web: www.cardin.senate.gov
Facebook: www.facebook.com/senatorbencardin
Twitter: @SenatorCardin

District Offices: 100 S. Charles St., Tower 1, #1710, Baltimore, MD 21201-2788; 410-962-4436; Fax: 410-962-4156; *State Director:* Carleton Atkinson

10201 Martin Luther King Jr. Hwy., #210, Bowie, MD 20720-4000; 301-860-0414; Fax: 301-860-0416; *Field Rep.:* Angel Colon-Rivera

13 Canal St., Room 305, Cumberland, MD 21502-3054; 301-777-2957; Fax: 301-777-2959; *Field Rep.:* Robin Summerfield

451 Hungerford Dr., #230, Rockville, MD 20850-4187; 301-762-2974; Fax: 301-762-2976; *Field Rep.:* Ken Reichard

212 W. Main St., #301C, Salisbury, MD 21801-4920; 410-546-4250; Fax: 410-546-4252; *Field Rep.:* Kim Kratovil

Committee Assignments: Commission on Security and Cooperation in Europe; Environment and Public Works; Finance; Small Business and Entrepreneurship; Foreign Relations, Ranking Minority Member

Carper, Tom, D-Del.

Capitol Hill Office: 513 SHOB 20510-0803; 224-2441; Fax: 228-2190; *Chief of Staff:* Bill Ghent

Web: www.carper.senate.gov

Facebook: www.facebook.com/tomcarper

Twitter: @senatorcarper

District Offices: 500 W. Loockerman St., #470, Dover, DE 19904-3298; 302-674-3308; Fax: 302-674-5464; *State Director:* Lori James

12 The Circle, Georgetown, DE 19947-1501; 302-856-7690; Fax: 302-856-3001; *Sussex County Regional Director:* Karen McGrath

301 N. Walnut St., #102L-1, Wilmington, DE 19801-3974; 302-573-6291; Fax: 302-573-6434; *New Castle County Regional Director:* Bonnie Wu

Committee Assignments: Environment and Public Works; Finance; Homeland Security and Governmental Affairs, Ranking Minority Member

Casey, Robert P. Jr., D-Pa.

Capitol Hill Office: 393 SROB 20510-3805; 224-6324; Fax: 228-0604; *Acting Chief of Staff:* Kristen Gentile

Web: www.casey.senate.gov

Facebook: www.facebook.com/SenatorBobCasey

Twitter: @SenBobCasey

District Offices: 840 Hamilton St., #301, Allentown, PA 18101-2456; 610-782-9470; Fax: 610-782-9474; *Regional Manager:* Carol Obando-Derstine

817 E. Bishop St., Suite C, Bellefonte, PA 16823-2321; 814-357-0314; Fax: 814-357-0318; *Regional Manager:* Kim Bierly

17 S. Park Row, #B-150, Erie, PA 16501-1162; 814-874-5080; Fax: 814-874-5084; *Regional Manager:* Kyle Hannon

22 S. 3rd St., #6A, Harrisburg, PA 17101-2105; 717-231-7540; Fax: 717-231-7542; *Director of Constituent Services:* Bonnie Seaman

2000 Market St., #610, Philadelphia, PA 19103; 215-405-9660; Fax: 215-405-9669; *State Director:* Gwen Kamp

Grant Bldg., 310 Grant St., #2415, Pittsburgh, PA 15219; 412-803-7370; Fax: 412-803-7379; *Southwestern PA Regional Director:* Elizabeth Fishback

417 Lackawanna Ave., #303, Scranton, PA 18503-2013; 570-941-0930; Fax: 570-941-0937; *State Scheduler:* Kathy Bell

Committee Assignments: Agriculture, Nutrition, and Forestry; Finance; Health, Education, Labor, and Pensions; Joint Economic; Special Aging

Cassidy, Bill, R-La.

Capitol Hill Office: B85 SROB 20510-1804; 224-5824; Fax: 228-5061; *Chief of Staff:* James Quinn

Web: www.cassidy.senate.gov

Facebook: www.facebook.com/billcassidy

Twitter: @billcassidy

District Offices: 3600 Jackson St., #115A, Alexandria, LA 70508; 318-448-7176; Fax: 318- 448-5175; *Central Louisiana State Director:* Tommie Seaton

5555 Hilton Ave., #100, Baton Rouge, LA 70808; 225-929-7711; Fax: 225-229-8720; *Field Rep.:* Shawn Hanscom

101 La Rue France, #505, Lafayette, LA 70508; 337-261-1400; Fax: 337-261-1490; *Regional Director:* Hunter Hall

1 Lakeshore Dr., #1155, Lake Charles, LA 70629; 337-493-5398; Fax: 225-247-5629; *State Director:* Brian McNabb

3421 N. Causeway Blvd., #204, Metairie, LA 70002; 504-838-0130; Fax: 504-838-0133; *Regional Director:* Mark Zelden

1651 Louisville Ave., #123, Monroe, LA 70201; 318-324-2111; Fax: 318-324-2197; *Regional Director:* Angela Robert

6425 Youree Dr., #415, Shreveport, LA 71105; 318-798-3215; Fax: 318-798-6959; *Regional Director:* Hunter Hall

Committee Assignments: Appropriations; Energy and Natural Resources; Health, Education, Labor, and Pensions; Joint Economic; Veterans' Affairs

Coats, Dan, R-Ind.

Capitol Hill Office: 493 SROB 20510-1405; 224-5623; Fax: 228-1820; *Chief of Staff:* Dean Hingson

Web: www.coats.senate.gov

Facebook: www.facebook.com/senatordancoats

Twitter: @SenDanCoats

District Offices: 11035 Broadway, Suite A, Crown Point, IN 46307; 219-663-2595; Fax: 219-663-4586; *Regional Director:* Dave Murtaugh

101 Martin Luther King Jr. Blvd., Evansville, IN, 47708; 812-465-6500; Fax: 812-465-6503; *Regional Director:* Brenda Goff

1300 S. Harrison St., #3161, Fort Wayne, IN 46802; 260-426-3151; Fax: 260-420-0060; *Regional Director:* Paul Lagenann

1650 Market Tower, 10 W. Market St., Indianapolis, IN 46204-2934; 317-554-0750; Fax: 317-554-0760; *State Director:* Ginny Cain

2 E. McClain Ave., #2-A, Scottsburg, IN, 47170; 812-754-0520; Fax: 812-754-0539; *Regional Director:* Justin Stevens

Committee Assignments: Finance; Joint Economic, Chair; Select Intelligence

Cochran, Thad A., R-Miss.

Capitol Hill Office: 113 SDOB 20510-2402; 224-5054; Fax: 224-9450; *Chief of Staff:* Keith Heard
Web: www.cochran.senate.gov
Facebook: www.facebook.com/pages/US-Senator-Thad-Cochran-R-MS/384626981575895
Twitter: @SenThadCochran
District Offices: 2012 15th St., #451, Gulfport, MS 39501-2036; 228-867-9710; Fax: 228-867-9789; *Southern District Director:* Myrtis Franke
190 E. Capitol St., #550, Jackson, MS 39201-2137; 601-965-4459; Fax: 601-965-4919; *Central District Director:* Brad White
Federal Bldg. and U.S. Courthouse, 911 E. Jackson Ave., #249, Oxford, MS 38655-3652; 662-236-1018; Fax: 662-236-7618; *Northern District Director:* Mindy Maxwell
Committee Assignments: Agriculture, Nutrition, and Forestry; Appropriations, Chair; Rules and Administration

Collins, Susan, R-Maine

Capitol Hill Office: 413 SDOB 20510-1904; 224-2523; Fax: 224-2693; *Chief of Staff:* Steve Abbott
Web: www.collins.senate.gov
Facebook: www.facebook.com/susancollins
Twitter: @senatorcollins
District Offices: 68 Sewall St., Room 507, Augusta, ME 04330-6554; 207-622-8414; Fax: 207-622-5884; *State Office Rep.:* Patricia Aho
202 Harlow St., Room 20100, Bangor, ME 04401; 207-945-0417; Fax: 207-990-4604; *State Office Rep.:* Carol Woodcock
160 Main St., Biddeford, ME 04005-2580; 207-283-1101; Fax: 207-283-4054; *State Office Rep.:* Cathy Goodwin
25 Sweden St., Suite A, Caribou, ME 04736-2149; 207-493-7873; Fax: 207-493-7810; *State Office Rep.:* Phil Bosse
55 Lisbon St., Lewiston, ME 04240-7117; 207-784-6969; Fax: 207-782-6475; *State Office Rep.:* Carlene Tremblay
One Canal Plaza, #802, Portland, ME 04101-4083; 207-780-3575; Fax: 207-828-0380; *State Office Rep.:* Sara Holmbom Lund
Committee Assignments: Appropriations; Health, Education, Labor, and Pensions; Select Intelligence; Special Aging, Chair

Coons, Christopher, D-Del.

Capitol Hill Office: 127A SROB 20510-0805; 224-5042; Fax: 228-3075; *Chief of Staff:* Adam Bramwell
Web: www.coons.senate.gov
Facebook: www.facebook.com/senatorchriscoons
Twitter: @ChrisCoons
District Offices: 500 W. Loockerman St., #450, Dover, DE 19904-3298; 302-736-5601; Fax: 302-736-5609; *Kent/Sussex Coord.:* Kate Rorher
1105 N. Market St., #100, Wilmington, DE 19801-1233; 302-573-6345; Fax: 302-573-6351; *State Director:* Jim Paoli
Committee Assignments: Appropriations; Foreign Relations; Judiciary; Select Ethics; Small Business and Entrepreneurship

Corker, Bob, R-Tenn.

Capitol Hill Office: SD-425 SDOB; 224-3344; Fax: 228-0566; *Chief of Staff:* Todd Womack
Web: www.corker.senate.gov
Facebook: www.facebook.com/bobcorker
Twitter: @senbobcorker
District Offices: 10 W. Martin Luther King Blvd., 6th Floor, Chattanooga, TN 37402-1813; 423-756-2757; Fax: 423-756-5313; *Field Rep.:* Claire McVay
800 Market St., #121, Knoxville, TN 37902-2349; 865-637-4180; Fax: 865-637-9886; *Field Director:* Jane Jolley
100 Peabody Pl., #1125, Memphis, TN 38103-3654; 901-683-1910; Fax: 901-575-3528; *Sr. Field Director:* Nick Kistenmacher
3322 W. End Ave., #610, Nashville, TN 37203-1096; 615-279-8125; Fax: 615-279-9488; *State Director:* Brent Wiles
91 Stonebridge Blvd., #103, Jackson, TN 38305; 731-664-2294; Fax: 731-664-4670; *Sr. Field Director:* Jennifer Weems
1105 E. Jackson Blvd., #4, Jonesborough, TN 37659; 423-753-2263; Fax: 423-753-3679; *Field Director:* Jill Salyers
Committee Assignments: Banking, Housing, and Urban Affairs; Budget; Foreign Relations, Chair; Special Aging

Cornyn, John, R-Tex.

Capitol Hill Office: 517 SHOB 20510-4305; 224-2934; Fax: 228-2856; *Chief of Staff:* Beth Jafari
Web: www.cornyn.senate.gov
Facebook: www.facebook.com/Sen.JohnCornyn
Twitter: @JohnCornyn
District Offices: Chase Tower, 221 W. 6th St., #1530, Austin, TX 78701-3403; 512-469-6034; Fax: 512-469-6020; *State Field Director:* David James
5001 Spring Valley Rd., #1125E, Dallas, TX 75244-3916; 972-239-1310; Fax: 972-239-2110; *Regional Director:* Collin McLochin
222 E. Van Buren, #404, Harlingen, TX 78550-6804; 956-423-0162; Fax: 956-423-0193; *Regional Director:* Ana Garcia
5300 Memorial Dr., #980, Houston, TX 77007; 713-572-3337; Fax: 713-572-3777; *Regional Director:* Jay Guerrero
Wells Fargo Center, 1500 Broadway, #1230, Lubbock, TX 79401-3114; 806-472-7533; Fax: 806-472-7536; *Regional Director:* Brent Oden
600 Navarro St., #210, San Antonio, TX 78205-2455; 210-224-7485; Fax: 210-224-8569; *Regional Director:* Jonathan Huhn
Regions Bank Bldg., 100 E. Ferguson St., #1004, Tyler, TX 75702-5706; 903-593-0902; Fax: 903-593-0920; *Regional Director:* Kathy Comer
Committee Assignments: Finance; Judiciary

Cotton, Tom, R-AK.

Capitol Hill Office: 124 SROB 20510-0405; 224-2353; Fax: 228-0908; *Chief of Staff:* Doug Coutts
Web: www.cotton.senate.gov

Facebook: www.facebook.com/TomCottonAR
Twitter: @TomCottonAR
District Offices: 11809 Hinson Rd., #100, Little Rock, AR 72212; 501-223-9081; Fax: 501-223-9105; *Deputy Chief of Staff:* Eliza Baker

1108 S. Old Missouri Rd., Suite B, Springdale, AR 72764; 479-751-0879; Fax: 479-927-1092; *Scheduler:* Catherine Wilkins

106 W. Main St., #410, El Dorado, AR 71730; 870-864-8582; Fax: 870-864-8571; *Communications:* Caroline M. Rabbitt

300 South Church, #338, Jonesboro, AR 72401; 870-933-6223; Fax: 870-933-6596; *Field Representative:* Vacant

Committee Assignments: Armed Services; Banking, Housing, and Urban Affairs; Joint Economic; Select Intelligence; Special Aging

Crapo, Mike, R-Idaho

Capitol Hill Office: 239 SDOB 20510-1205; 224-6142; Fax: 228-1375; *Chief of Staff:* Susan Wheeler
Web: www.crapo.senate.gov
Facebook: www.facebook.com/mikecrapo
Twitter: @mikecrapo
District Offices: 251 E. Front St., #205, Boise, ID 83702-7312; 208-334-1776; Fax: 208-334-9044; *Regional Chief of Staff:* John Hoehne

610 W. Hubbard St., #209, Coeur d'Alene, ID 83814-2287; 208-664-5490; Fax: 208-664-0889; *Regional Director:* Karen Roetter

410 Memorial Dr., #204, Idaho Falls, ID 83402-3600; 208-522-9779; Fax: 208-529-8367; *Regional Director:* Kathryn Hitch

313 D St., #105, Lewiston, ID 83501-1894; 208-743-1492; Fax: 208-743-6484; *State Director for Intergovernmental Affairs and Environment:* Mitch Silvers

275 S. 5th Ave., #225, Pocatello, ID 83201; 208-236-6775; Fax: 208-236-6935; *Regional Director:* Farhana Hibbert

202 Falls Ave., #2, Twin Falls, ID 83301-3372; 208-734-2515; Fax: 208-733-0414; *Regional Director:* Samantha Marshall

Committee Assignments: Banking, Housing, and Urban Affairs; Budget; Environment and Public Works; Finance; Indian Affairs; Joint Taxation

Cruz, Ted, R-Tex.

Capitol Hill Office: 185 SDOB 20510; 224-5922; Fax: 224-0776; *Chief of Staff:* Paul Teller
Web: www.cruz.senate.gov
Facebook: www.facebook.com/SenatorTedCruz
Twitter: @SenTedCruz
District Offices: 300 E. 8th St., #961, Austin, TX 78701-3226; 512-916-5834; Fax: 512-916-5839; *State Director:* Katharine McAden

Lee Park Tower II, 3626 N. Hall St., #410, Dallas, TX 75219; 214-599-8749; *Regional Director:* Jason Wright

808 Travis St., #1420, Houston, TX 77002; 713-718-3057; *Regional Director:* Jessica Hart

9901 IH-10W, #950, San Antonio, TX 78230; 210-340-2885; *Regional Director:* Javier Salinas

305 S. Broadway, #501, Tyler, TX 75702; 903-593-5130; *Regional Director:* Daniel Alders

200 S. 10th St., #1603, McAllen, TX 78501; 956-686-7339; *Regional Director:* Casandra Garcia

Committee Assignments: Armed Services; Commerce, Science, and Transportation; Joint Economic; Judiciary; Rules and Administration

Daines, Steve, R-Mont.

Capitol Hill Office: 1 SROB 20510-2605; 224-2651; Fax: 228-4619; *Chief of Staff:* Jason Thielman
Web: www.daines.senate.gov
Facebook: www.facebook.com/SteveDainesMT
Twitter: @SteveDaines
District Offices: 280 E. Front St., #100, Missoula, MT 59802; 406-549-8198; Fax: 406-926-2125; *Caseworker:* Bill Hilshey

220 W. Lamme St., #1D, Bozeman, MT 59715; 406-587-3446; *Deputy Director:* Liz Dellwo

222 N. 32nd St., #100, Billings, MT 59101; 406-245-6822; Fax: 406-702-1182; *Administrative Director:* Amber Heinz

104 4th St. North #302, Great Falls, MT 59401; 406-453-0148; *Liaison:* Robin Baker

30 W. 14th St., #206, Helena, MT 59601; 406-443-3189; *State Director:* Charles Robison

Committee Assignments: Appropriations; Commerce, Science, and Transportation; Energy and Natural Resources; Indian Affairs

Donnelly, Joe, D-Ind.

Capitol Hill Office: 720 SHOB 20510; 224-4814; Fax: 224-5011; *Chief of Staff:* Joel Elliott
Web: www.donnelly.senate.gov
Facebook: www.facebook.com/senatordonnelly
Twitter: @SenDonnelly
District Offices: 115 N. Pennsylvania St., #100, Indianapolis, IN 46204; 317-226-5555; Fax: 855-772-7518; *State Director:* Hodge Patel

205 West Colfax Ave., South Bend, IN 46601; 574-288-2780; Fax: 574-234-7476; *Regional Director:* Lauren Barga

702 North Shore Dr., #LL-101, Jeffersonville, IN 47130; 812-284-2027; Fax: 812-284-2044; *Regional Director:* Melanie Douglas

5400 Federal Plaza, #3200, Hammond, IN 46320; 219-852-0089; Fax: 219-852-0729; *Regional Director:* Justin Mount

203 East Berry St., #702-B, Fort Wayne, IN 46802; 260-420-4955; Fax: 260-420-4930; *Regional Director:* Jorge Ortiz

123 4th St., N.W. #417; Evansville, IN 47708; 812-425-5862; Fax: 812-425-5817; *Regional Director:* Jerry Parkinson

Committee Assignments: Agriculture, Nutrition, and Forestry; Armed Services; Banking, Housing, and Urban Development; Special Aging

Durbin, Richard J., D-Ill.

Capitol Hill Office: 711 SHOB 20510-1304; 224-2152; Fax: 228-0400; *Chief of Staff:* Patrick J. Souders
Web: www.durbin.senate.gov
Facebook: www.facebook.com/SenatorDurbin
Twitter: @SenatorDurbin
District Offices: 250 W. Cherry St., #115-D, Carbondale, IL 62901-2856; 618-351-1122; Fax: 618-351-1124; *Staff Asst.:* Melissa O'Dell-Olson

230 S. Dearborn St., #3892, Chicago, IL 60604-1505; 312-353-4952; Fax: 312-353-0150; *Office Manager:* Cynthia Bajjalieh

1504 3rd Ave., #227, Rock Island, IL 61201-8612; 618-351-1122; Fax: 618-351-1124 *Western Illinois Outreach Coord.:* Brad Middleton

525 S. 8th St., Springfield, IL 62703-1606; 217-492-4062; Fax: 217-492-4382; *State Director:* Bill Houlihan
Committee Assignments: Appropriations; Judiciary; Rules and Administration

Enzi, Mike, R-Wyo.

Capitol Hill Office: 379A SROB 20510-5004; 224-3424; Fax: 228-0359; *Chief of Staff:* Flip McConnaughey
Web: www.enzi.senate.gov
Facebook: www.facebook.com/mikeenzi
Twitter: @SenatorEnzi
District Offices: 100 E. B St., Room 3201, P.O. Box 33201, Casper, WY 82602; 307-261-6572; Fax: 307-261-6574; *Field Rep.:* Jenelle Garber

2120 Capitol Ave., #2007, Cheyenne, WY 82001-3631; 307-772-2477; Fax: 307-772-2480; *Field Rep.:* Debbie McCann

1285 Sheridan Ave., #210, Cody, WY 82414-3653; 307-527-9444; Fax: 307-527-9476; *State Director:* Karen McCreery

400 S. Kendrick Ave., #303, Gillette, WY 82716-3803; 307-682-6268; Fax: 307-682-6501; *Field Rep.:* DeAnna Kay

1110 Maple Way, Suite G, P.O. Box 12470, Jackson, WY 83002-2470; 307-739-9507; Fax: 307-739-9520; *Field Rep.:* Nikki Brunner
Committee Assignments: Budget, Chair; Finance; Health, Education, Labor, and Pensions; Small Business and Entrepreneurship

Ernst, Joni, R-Iowa

Capitol Hill Office: 111 SROB 20510-1502; 224-3254; Fax: 224-9369; *Chief of Staff:* Lisa Goeas
Web: www.ernst.senate.gov
Facebook: www.facebook.com/joniforiowa
Twitter: @joniforiowa
District Offices: 733 Federal Bldg., 210 Walnut St., Des Moines, IA 50309; 515-284-4574; Fax: 515-284-4937; *Administrative Director:* Emilie Sekine

111 7th Ave. S.E., #480, Cedar Rapids, IA 52401-2101; 319-365-4504; Fax: 319-365-4683; *Field Rep.:* Ryan S. Berger

1606 Brady St., #323, Davenport, IA 52803; 563-322-1338; Fax: 563-322-0417; *State Director:* Clarke Scanlon

Federal Bldg., 320 6th St., Room 110, Sioux City, IA 51101; 712-252-1550; Fax: 712-252-7104 *Field Rep.:* Josie Beecher
Committee Assignments: Agriculture, Nutrition and Forestry; Armed Services; Homeland Security and Governmental Affairs; Small Business and Entrepreneurship

Feinstein, Dianne, D-Calif.

Capitol Hill Office: 331 SHOB 20510-0504; 224-3841; Fax: 228-3954; *Chief of Staff:* Jennifer Duck
Web: www.feinstein.senate.gov
Facebook: www.facebook.com/SenatorFeinstein
Twitter: @senfeinstein
District Offices: 2500 Tulare St., #4290, Fresno, CA 93721-1331; 559-485-7430; Fax: 559-485-9689; *District Director:* Shelly Abajian

11111 Santa Monica Blvd., #915, Los Angeles, CA 90025-3343; 310-914-7300; Fax: 310-914-7318; *State Director:* Trevor Daley

880 Front St., #3296, San Diego, CA 92101-; 619-231-9712; Fax: 619-231-1108; *District Director:* Bill Kratz

One Post St., #2450, San Francisco, CA 94104-5240; 415-393-0707; Fax: 415-393-0710; *Deputy State Director:* Sean Elsbernd
Committee Assignments: Appropriations; Congressional-Executive Commission on China; International Narcotics Control Caucus, Ranking Minority Member; Judiciary; Rules and Administration; Select Intelligence, Vice Chair

Fischer, Deb, R-Neb.

Capitol Hill Office: 454 SROB 20510; 224-6551; Fax: 228-1325; *Chief of Staff:* Joe Hack
Web: www.fischer.senate.gov/public
Facebook: www.facebook.com/senatordebfischer
Twitter: @SenatorFischer
District Offices: 440 N. 8th St., #120, Lincoln, NE 68508; 402-441-4600; Fax: 402-476-8753; *State Director:* Dustin Vaughan

11819 Miracle Hills Dr., #205, Omaha, NE 68154; 402-391-3411; Fax: 402-391-4724; *Outreach Coord.:* Denise Barrett

20 West 23rd St., Kearney, NE 68847; 308-234-2361; Fax: 308-234-3684; *Constituent Services Director:* Julie Booker

1110 Circle Dr., #F2, Scottsbluff, NE 69361; 308-630-2329; Fax: 308-630-2321; *Constituent Services Director:* Brandy McCaslin
Committee Assignments: Armed Services; Commerce, Science, and Transportation; Environment and Public Works; Small Business and Entrepreneurship

Flake, Jeff, R-Ariz.

Capitol Hill Office: 413 SROB 20510; 224-4521; Fax: 228-0515; *Chief of Staff:* Chandler Morse
Web: www.flake.senate.gov
Facebook: www.facebook.com/senatorjeffflake
Twitter: @jeffflake

District Offices: 2200 E. Camelback Rd., #120, Phoenix, AZ 85016-9021; 602-840-1891; Fax: 602-840-4092; *State Director:* Matthew Specht

6840 N. Oracle Rd., #150, Tucson, AZ 85704-4252; 520-575-8633; Fax: 520-797-3232; *Southern Arizona Director:* Julie Katsel

Committee Assignments: Energy and Natural Resources; Foreign Relations; Judiciary; Special Aging

Franken, Al, D-Minn.

Capitol Hill Office: 309 SHOB 20510-2308; 224-5641; Fax: 224-0044; *Chief of Staff:* Jeff Lomonaco

Web: www.franken.senate.gov

Facebook: www.facebook.com/Sen.Franken

Twitter: @alfranken

District Offices: 515 W. 1st St., #104, Duluth, MN 55802-1302; 218-722-2390; Fax: 218-722-4131; *Constituent Services Rep.:* Janet Nelson

819 Center Ave., #2A, Moorhead, MN 56560; 218-284-8721; *Field Rep.:* Carson Ouellette

60 E. Plato Blvd., #220, St. Paul, MN 55107-1827; 651-221-1016; Fax: 651-221-1078; *State Director:* Alana Petersen

1202-1/27th St. North, #213, Rochester, MN 55901; 507-288-2003; *Communications Director:* Ed Shelleby

West Central Mobile Office; 651-788-5100; *Field Rep.:* Al Juhnke

Committee Assignments: Energy and Natural Resources; Health, Education, Labor, and Pensions; Indian Affairs; Judiciary

Gardner, Cory, R-Colo.

Capitol Hill Office: 354 SROB 20510-0608; 224-5941; Fax: 224-6471; *Chief of Staff:* Chris Hansen

Web: www.gardner.senate.gov

Facebook: www.facebook.com/SenCoryGardner

Twitter: @SenCoryGardner

District Offices: 102 S. Tejon St., #930, Colorado Springs, CO 80903; 719-632-6706; Fax: 202-228-7176; *Regional Director:* Brandon Gould

999 18th St., #1525, Denver, CO 80202; 303-391-5777; *Regional Director:* Rebecca Hartman-Rudder

144 S. Mason St., Fort Collins, CO 80524; 970-484-3502

801 8th St., Greeley, CO 80631; 970-352-5546; Fax: 970-352-5546; *Regional Director:* Dan Betts

400 Rood Ave., #220, Grand Junction, CO 81501; 970-245-9553; Fax: 970-245-9523; *Regional Director:* Betsy Bair

503 N. Main St., #426, Pueblo, CO 81003; 719-543-1324; Fax: 202-228-7174; *Regional Director:* Cathy Garcia

529 North Albany St., #1220, Yuma, CO 80759; 970-848-3095; Fax: 202-228-7175; *Regional Director:* Alan Foutz

Committee Assignments: Commerce, Science and Transportation; Energy and Natural Resources; Foreign Relations; Small Business and Entrepreneurship

Gillibrand, Kirsten, D-N.Y.

Capitol Hill Office: 478 SROB 20510-3205; 224-4451; Fax: 228-0282; *Chief of Staff:* Jess C. Fassler

Web: www.gillibrand.senate.gov

Facebook: www.facebook.com/KirstenGillibrand

Twitter: @SenGillibrand

District Offices: Leo W. O'Brien Federal Office Bldg., 11A Clinton Ave., Room 821, Albany, NY 12207-2202; 518-431-0120; Fax: 518-431-0128; *Regional Director:* David Connors

Larkin At Exchange, 726 Exchange St., #511, Buffalo, NY 14210-1485; 716-854-9725; Fax: 716-854-9731; *Regional Director:* James Kennedy

P.O. Box 273, Lowville, NY 13367; 315-376-6118; Fax: 315-376-6118; *Regional Director:* Susan Merrell

P.O. Box 893, Mahopac, NY 10541; 845-875-4585; Fax: 845-875-9099; *Regional Director:* Susan Spear

155 Pinelawn Rd., #250 N., Melville, NY 11747-3247; 631-249-2825; Fax: 631-249-2847; *Regional Director:* Kristen Walsh

780 3rd Ave., #2601, New York, NY 10017-2177; 212-688-6262; Fax: 866-824-6340; *State Director:* Emily Arsenault

Kenneth B. Keating Federal Office Bldg., 100 State St., Room 4195, Rochester, NY 14614-1318; 585-263-6250; Fax: 585-263-6247; *Deputy State Director:* Sarah Hart Clark

James M. Hanley Federal Bldg., 100 S. Clinton St., Room 1470, P.O. Box 7378, Syracuse, NY 13261; 315-448-0470; Fax: 315-448-0476; *Regional Director:* Colleen Deacon

Committee Assignments: Agriculture, Nutrition, and Forestry; Armed Services; Environment and Public Works; Special Aging

Graham, Lindsey, R-S.C.

Capitol Hill Office: 290 SROB 20510-4003; 224-5972; Fax: 224-3808; *Chief of Staff:* Richard S. Perry

Web: www.lgraham.senate.gov

Facebook: www.facebook.com/USSenatorLindseyGraham

Twitter: @GrahamBlog

District Offices: 508 Hampton St., #202, Columbia, SC 29201-2718; 803-933-0112; Fax: 803-933-0957; *Midlands Regional Director:* Yvette Rowland

McMillan Federal Bldg., 401 W. Evans St., #111, Florence, SC 29501-3460; 843-669-1505; Fax: 843-669-9015; *Pee Dee Regional Director:* Celia Urquhart

130 S. Main St., 7th Floor, Greenville, SC 29601-4870; 864-250-1417; Fax: 864-250-4322; *State Director:* Van Cato

530 Johnnie Dodds Blvd., #202, Mt. Pleasant, SC 29464-3029; 843-849-3887; Fax: 843-971-3669; *Low Country Regional Director:* Mason Sullivan

124 Exchange St., Suite A, Pendleton, SC 29670-1312; 864-646-4090; Fax: 864-646-8609; *Sr. Advisor:* Denise Bauld

235 E. Main St., #100, Rock Hill, SC 29730-4891; 803-366-2828; Fax: 803-366-5353; *Piedmont Regional Director:* Teresa Thomas

Committee Assignments: Appropriations; Armed Services; Budget; Judiciary

Grassley, Chuck, R-Iowa

Capitol Hill Office: 135 SHOB 20510-1501; 224-3744; Fax: 224-6020; *Chief of Staff:* Jill Kozeny

Web: www.grassley.senate.gov

Facebook: www.facebook.com/grassley
Twitter: @chuckgrassley
District Offices: 111 7th Ave. S.E., Box 13, #6800, Cedar Rapids, IA 52401; 319-363-6832; Fax: 319-363-7179; *Regional Director:* Fred Schuster
307 Federal Bldg., 8 S. 6th St., Council Bluffs, IA 51501; 712-322-7103; Fax: 712-322-7196; *Regional Director; Constituent Services Specialist:* Donna Barry
201 W. 2nd St., #720, Davenport, IA 52801-1419; 563-322-4331; Fax: 563-322-8552; *Regional Director:* Penny Vacek
721 Federal Bldg., 210 Walnut St., Des Moines, IA 50309-2140; 515-288-1145; Fax: 515-288-5097; *State Director:* Aaron McKay
120 Federal Bldg., 320 6th St., Sioux City, IA 51101-1244; 712-233-1860; Fax: 712-233-1634; *Regional Director:* Jacob Bossman
210 Waterloo Bldg., 531 Commercial St., Waterloo, IA 50701-5497; 319-232-6657; Fax: 319-232-9965; *Regional Director:* Valerie Nehl
Committee Assignments: Agriculture, Nutrition, and Forestry; Budget; Finance; International Narcotics Control Caucus, Chair; Joint Taxation; Judiciary, Chair

Hatch, Orrin G., R-Utah

Capitol Hill Office: 104 SHOB 20510-4402; 224-5251; Fax: 224-6331; *Chief of Staff:* Rob Porter
Web: www.hatch.senate.gov
Facebook: www.facebook.com/OrrinHatch
Twitter: @OrrinHatch
District Offices: 77 N. Main St., #112, Cedar City, UT 84720-2648; 435-586-8435; Fax: 435-586-2147; *Southern Utah Director:* William Swadley
1006 Federal Bldg., 324 25th St., Ogden, UT 84401-2341; 801-625-5672; Fax: 801-394-4503; *Northern Area Director:* Sandra Kester
51 S. University Ave., #320, Provo, UT 84601-4491; 801-375-7881; Fax: 801-374-5005; *Regional Director:* Ron Dean
8402 Federal Bldg., 125 S. State St., Salt Lake City, UT 84138-1191; 801-524-4380; Fax: 801-524-4379; *State Director:* Melanie Bowen
196 E. Tabernacle St., Room 14, St. George, UT 84770-3474; 435-634-1795; Fax: 435-634-1796; *Southern Utah Director:* William Swadley
Committee Assignments: Finance, Chair; Health, Education, Labor, and Pensions; Joint Taxation, Vice Chair; Judiciary; Special Aging

Heinrich, Martin, D-N.M.

Capitol Hill Office: 303 SHOB 20510; 224-5521; Fax: 228-2841; *Chief of Staff:* Joe Britton
Web: www.heinrich.senate.gov
Facebook: www.facebook.com/MartinHeinrich
Twitter: @martinheinrich
District Offices: 400 Gold Ave. S.W., #1080, Albuquerque, NM 87102; 505-346-6601; Fax: 505-346-6780; *Constituent Services Director:* Miguel Negrete
7450 E. Main St., Suite A, Farmington, NM 87402; 505-325-5030; Fax: 505-325-6035; *Field Rep.:* Jim Dumont

Loretto Towne Center, 505 S. Main St., #148, Las Cruces, NM 88001-1200; 575-523-6561; Fax: 575-523-6584; *Field Rep:* Dara Parker
200 E. 4th St., #300, Roswell, NM 88201; 575-622-7113; Fax: 575-622-3538; *Constituent Services Rep.:* Iris Chavez
123 E. Marcy St., #103, Santa Fe, NM 87501-2046; 505-988-6647; Fax: 505-992-8435; *Field Rep.:* Patricia Dominguez
Committee Assignments: Armed Services; Energy and Natural Resources; Joint Economic; Select Intelligence

Heitkamp, Heidi, D-N.D.

Capitol Hill Office: SH-110 SHOB 20510; 224-2043; Fax: 224-7776; *Chief of Staff:* Tessa Gould
Web: www.heitkamp.senate.gov
Facebook: www.facebook.com/SenatorHeidiHeitkamp
Twitter: @SenatorHeitkamp
District Offices: 228 Federal Bldg., 220 E. Rosser Ave., Bismarck, ND 58501-3869; 701-258-4648; Fax: 701-258-1254; *Regional Director:* Ross Keys
306 Federal Bldg., 657 2nd Ave. North, Fargo, ND 58102-4727; 701-232-8030; Fax: 701-232-6449; *State Director:* Ryan Nagle
33 S. 3rd St., Suite B, Grand Forks, ND 58201; 701-775-9601; Fax: 701-746-1990; *Regional Director:* Gail Hand
105 Federal Bldg., 100 1st St. S.W., Minot, ND 58701-3846; 701-852-0703; Fax: 701-838-8196; *State Rep.:* Norman McCloud
40 1st Ave. West, #202, Dickinson, ND 58601; 701-225-0974; Fax: 701-225-3287; *Southwest Area Director:* Shirley Meyer
Committee Assignments: Agriculture, Nutrition, and Forestry; Banking, Housing, and Urban Development; Homeland Security and Government Affairs; Indian Affairs; Small Business and Entrepreneurship

Heller, Dean, R-Nev.

Capitol Hill Office: 324 SHOB 20510-2806; 224-6244; Fax: 228-6753; *Chief of Staff:* Mac Abrams
Web: www.heller.senate.gov
Facebook: www.facebook.com/SenDeanHeller
Twitter: @SenDeanHeller
District Offices: 8930 W. Sunset Rd., #230, Las Vegas, NV 89148; 702-388-6605; Fax: 702-388-6501; *Southern Nevada Director:* Jack Finn
Bruce Thompson Federal Bldg., 400 S. Virginia St., #738, Reno, NV 89501-2125; 775-686-5770; Fax: 775-686-5729; *State Director:* Ashley Carrigan
3920 E. Idaho St., #2A, Elko, NV 89801; 775-738-2001; Fax: 775-738-2004; *Eastern Nevada Rep.:* Donna Bath
Committee Assignments: Banking, Housing, and Urban Affairs; Commerce, Science, and Transportation; Finance; Veterans' Affairs; Special Aging

Hirono, Mazie K., D-Hawaii

Capitol Hill Office: 330 SHOB 20510; 224-6361; Fax: 224-2126; *Chief of Staff:* Betsy Lin
Web: www.hirono.senate.gov

Facebook: www.facebook.com/mazie.hirono
Twitter: @maziehirono
District Office: 300 Ala Moana Blvd., Room 3-106, Honolulu, HI 96850; 808-522-8970; Fax: 808-545-4683; *State Director:* Alan Yamamoto
Committee Assignments: Armed Services; Energy and Natural Resources; Select Intelligence; Small Business and Entrepreneurship; Veterans' Affairs

Hoeven, John, R-N.D.

Capitol Hill Office: 338 SROB 20510-3406; 224-2551; Fax: 224-7999; *Chief of Staff:* Ryan Bernstein
Web: www.hoeven.senate.gov
Facebook: www.facebook.com/SenatorJohnHoeven
Twitter: @SenJohnHoeven
District Offices: U.S. Federal Bldg., 220 E. Rosser Ave., Room 312, Bismarck, ND 58501-3869; 701-250-4618; Fax: 701-250-4484; *State Director:* Don Larson
1802 32nd Ave. South, Room B, Fargo, ND 58103-6747; 701-239-5389; Fax: 701-293-5112; *Regional Director:* Jessica Lee
Federal Bldg., 102 N. 4th St., Room 108, Grand Forks, ND 58203-3738; 701-746-8972; Fax: 701-746-5613; *Field Rep.:* Tom Brusegaard
100 1st St. S.W., #107, Minot, ND 58701; 701-838-1361; Fax: 701-838-1381; *Regional Director:* Sally Johnson
Committee Assignments: Agriculture, Nutrition, and Forestry; Appropriations; Energy and Natural Resources; Indian Affairs

Inhofe, James M., R-Okla.

Capitol Hill Office: 205 SROB 20510-3603; 224-4721; Fax: 228-0380; *Chief of Staff:* Ryan Jackson
Web: www.inhofe.senate.gov
Facebook: www.facebook.com/jiminhofe
Twitter: @jiminhofe
District Offices: 302 N. Independence St., #104, Enid, OK 73701-4025; 580-234-5105; Fax: 580-234-5094; *Field Rep.:* Blake Wieland
215 E. Choctaw Ave., #106, McAlester, OK 74501-5069; 918-426-0933; Fax: 918-426-0935; *Field Rep.:* Ryan Martinez
1900 Expressway St. N.W., #1210, Oklahoma City, OK 73118; 405-608-4381; Fax: 405-608-4120; *State Director:* Brian Hackler
1924 S. Utica Ave., #530, Tulsa, OK 74104; 918-748-5111; Fax: 918-748-5119; *Field Rep.:* Michael Junk
Committee Assignments: Armed Services, Environment and Public Works, Chair

Isakson, Johnny, R-Ga.

Capitol Hill Office: 131 SROB 20510-1008; 224-3643; Fax: 228-0724; *Chief of Staff:* Joan Kirchner
Web: www.isakson.senate.gov
Facebook: www.facebook.com/isakson
Twitter: @SenatorIsakson
District Offices: One Overton Park, 3625 Cumberland Blvd., #970, Atlanta, GA 30339-6406; 770-661-0999; Fax: 770-661-0768; *State Director:* Edward Tate

Committee Assignments: Finance; Foreign Relations; Health, Education, Labor and Pensions; Select Ethics, Chair; Veterans' Affairs, Chair

Johnson, Ron, R-Wisc.

Capitol Hill Office: 328 SHOB 20510-4905; 224-5323; Fax: 228-6965; *Chief of Staff:* Tony Blando
Web: www.ronjohnson.senate.gov
Facebook: www.facebook.com/senronjohnson
Twitter: @SenRonJohnson
District Offices: 517 E. Wisconsin Ave., Room 408, Milwaukee, WI 53202-4510; 414-276-7282; Fax: 414-276-7284; *Regional Director:* Kris McHenry
219 Washington Ave., Oshkosh, WI 54901-5029; 920-230-7250; Fax: 920-230-7262; *State Director:* Julie Leschke
Committee Assignments: Budget; Commerce, Science and Transportation; Foreign Relations; Homeland Security and Governmental Affairs, Chair

Kaine, Tim, D-Va.

Capitol Hill Office: 231 SROB 20510; 224-4024; Fax: 228-6363; *Chief of Staff:* Mike Henry
Web: www.kaine.senate.gov
Facebook: www.facebook.com/timkaine
Twitter: @timkaine
District Offices: 121 Russell Road, #2, Abingdon, VA 24210; 276-525-4790; Fax: 276- 525-4792; *Regional Director:* Laura Blevins
919 E. Main St., #970, Richmond, VA 23219; 804-771-2221; Fax: 804-771-8313; *State Director:* John Knapp
222 Central Park Dr., #120, Virginia Beach, VA 23462-3023; 757-518-1674; Fax: 757-518-1679; *Regional Director:* Diane Kaufman
308 Craghead St., #102A, Danville, VA 24541; 434-792-0976; Fax: 434-792-0978; *Regional Director:* Chris Collins
611 S. Jefferson St., #5B, Roanoke, VA 24011; 540-682-5693; Fax: 540-682-5697; *Regional Director:* Gwen Mason
9408 Grant Ave., #202, Manassas, VA 20110; 703-361-3192; Fax: 703-361-3198; *Regional Director:* Joe Montano
Committee Assignments: Armed Services; Budget; Foreign Relations

King, Angus, I-Maine

Capitol Hill Office: 133 SHOB 20510; 224-5344; Fax: 224-1946; *Chief of Staff:* Kay Rand
Web: www.king.senate.gov
Facebook: www.facebook.com/SenatorAngusSKingJr
Twitter: @SenAngusKing
District Offices: 4 Gabriel Dr., #3, Augusta, ME 04330; 207-622-8292; *Regional Rep.:* Chris Rector
169 Academy St., Suite A, Presque Isle, ME 04769; 207-764-5124; *Regional Rep.:* Sharon Campbell
383 US Route 1, #1C, Scarborough, ME 04074; 207-883-1588; *Regional Rep.:* Travis Kennedy
Committee Assignments: Armed Services; Budget; Energy and Natural Resources; Rules and Administration; Select Intelligence

Kirk, Mark, R-Ill.

Capitol Hill Office: 524 SHOB 20510-1308; 224-2854; Fax: 228-4611; *Chief of Staff:* Kate Dickens
Web: www.kirk.senate.gov
Facebook: www.facebook.com/SenatorKirk
Twitter: @SenatorKirk
District Offices: 230 S. Dearborn St., #3900, Chicago, IL 60604-1480; 312-886-3506; Fax: 312-886-2117; *Deputy Chief of Staff:* Alissa McCurley
607 E. Adams St., #1520, Springfield, IL 62701-1635; 217-492-5089; Fax: 217-492-5099; *Outreach Coord.:* Randy Pollard
Committee Assignments: Appropriations; Banking, Housing, and Urban Affairs; Health, Education, Labor, and Pensions; Special Aging

Klobuchar, Amy, D-Minn.

Capitol Hill Office: 302 SHOB 20510-2307; 224-3244; Fax: 228-2186; *Chief of Staff:* Elizabeth Peluso
Web: www.klobuchar.senate.gov
Facebook: www.facebook.com/amyklobuchar
Twitter: @amyklobuchar
District Offices: 1200 Washington Ave. South, Room 250, Minneapolis, MN 55415-1588; 612-727-5220; Fax: 612-727-5223; *State Director:* Ben Hill
121 4th St. South, Moorhead, MN 56560-2613; 218-287-2219, Fax: 218-287-2930; *Regional Outreach Director:* Andy Martin
1130 1/2 7th St. N.W., #208, Rochester, MN 55901-2995; 507-288-5321; Fax: 507-288-2922; *Regional Outreach Director:* Chuck Ackman
Olcott Plaza, 820 9th St. North, Room 105, Virginia, MN 55792-2300; 218-741-9690; Fax: 218-741-3692; *Regional Outreach Director:* Ida Ruckavina
Committee Assignments: Agriculture, Nutrition, and Forestry; Commerce, Science, and Transportation; Joint Economic, Ranking Minority Member; Judiciary; Rules and Administration

Lankford, James, R-Okla.

Capitol Hill Office: 316 SHOB 20510-3604; 224-5754; Fax: 228-1015; *Chief of Staff:* Greg Slavonic
Web: www.lankford.senate.gov
Facebook: www.facebook.com/lankford.for.america
Twitter: @jameslankford
District Offices: 1050 N. Broadway, #310, Oklahoma City, OK 73102; 405-231-4941; *Scheduler:* Rachel King
The Remington Tower, 5810 E. Skelly Dr., #500, Tulsa, OK 74135; 918-581-7651; *Comm. Dir.:* D.J. Jordan
Committee Assignments: Appropriations; Homeland Security and Governmental Affairs; Indian Affairs; Select Intelligence

Leahy, Patrick P., D-Vt.

Capitol Hill Office: 437 SROB 20510-4502; 224-4242; Fax: 224-3479; *Chief of Staff:* John P. Dowd
Web: www.leahy.senate.gov
Facebook: www.facebook.com/SenatorPatrickLeahy
Twitter: @SenatorLeahy
District Offices: 199 Main St., 4th Floor, Burlington, VT 05401-8309; 802-863-2525; Fax: 802-658-1009; *Vermont Office Director:* John Tracy
87 State St., Room 338, Montpelier, VT 05602-9505; 802-229-0569; Fax: 802-229-1915; *Field Rep.:* Tom Berry
Committee Assignments: Agriculture, Nutrition, and Forestry; Appropriations; Joint Library; Judiciary, Ranking Minority Member; Rules and Administration

Lee, Mike, R-Utah

Capitol Hill Office: 316A SROB 20510-4404; 224-5444; Fax: 228-1168; *Chief of Staff:* Allyson Bell
Web: www.lee.senate.gov
Facebook: www.facebook.com/senatormikelee
Twitter: @SenMikeLee
District Offices: Wallace F. Bennett Federal Bldg., 125 S. State St., #4225, Salt Lake City, UT 84138-1188; 801-524-5933; Fax: 801-524-5730; *State Director:* Derek Brown
285 W. Tabernacle St., #200, St. George, UT 84770-3474; 435-628-5514; Fax: 435-628-4160; *Southern Utah Director:* Bette Arial
James V. Hansen Federal Bldg., 324 25th St., #1410, Ogden, UT 84401; 801-392-9623; *Northern Utah Director:* Ryan Wilcox
Committee Assignments: Armed Services; Energy and Natural Resources; Joint Economic; Judiciary

Manchin, Joe, D-W.Va.

Capitol Hill Office: 306 SHOB 20510-4803; 224-3954; Fax: 228-0002; *Chief of Staff:* Patrick Hayes
Web: www.manchin.senate.gov
Facebook: www.facebook.com/JoeManchinIII
Twitter: @Sen_JoeManchin
District Offices: 900 Pennsylvania Ave., #629, Charleston, WV 25302; 304-342-5855; Fax: 304-343-7144; *State Director:* Mara Boggs
261 Aikens Center, #305, Martinsburg, WV 25404-6203; 304-264-4626; Fax: 304-262-3039; *Office Manager:* Missy Phalen
48 Donley St., #504, Morgantown, WV 26501-5900; 304-284-8663; Fax: 304-284-8681; *Regional Coord.:* Missy Phalen
Committee Assignments: Armed Services; Commerce, Science, and Transportation; Energy and Natural Resources; Veteran Affairs

Markey, Edward J., D-Mass.

Capitol Hill Office: 255 SDOB 20510; 202-224-2742; *Chief of Staff:* Mark Bayer
Web: www.markey.senate.gov
Facebook: www.facebook.com/EdJMarkey
Twitter: @markeymemo
District Offices: 975 JFK Federal Bldg., 15 New Sudbury St., Boston, MA 02203; 617-565-8519; *State Director:* Mark Gallagher
222 Milliken Blvd., #312, Fall River, MA 02721; 508-677-0523; *Regional Rep.:* Christine Pacheco

1550 Main St., 4th Floor, Springfield, MA 01101; 413-785-4610; *Regional Rep.:* Vacant

Committee Assignments: Commerce, Science, and Transportation; Environment and Public Works; Foreign Relations; Small Business and Entrepreneurship

McCain, John, R-Ariz.

Capitol Hill Office: 218 SROB 20510-0303; 224-2235; Fax: 228-2862; *Chief of Staff:* Pablo Carrillo
Web: www.mccain.senate.gov
Facebook: www.facebook.com/johnmccain
Twitter: @senjohnmccain
District Offices: 2201 E. Camelback Rd., #115, Phoenix, AZ 85016-3446; 602-952-2410; Fax: 602-952-8702; *State Director:* Gina Gormley
122 N. Cortez St., #108, Prescott, AZ 86301-3022; 928-445-0833; Fax: 928-445-8594; *Staff Asst.:* Naomi King
407 W. Congress St., #103, Tucson, AZ 85701-1349; 520-670-6334; Fax: 520-670-6637; *Office Manager:* Cheryl Bennett
Committee Assignments: Armed Services, Chair; Homeland Security and Governmental Affairs; Indian Affairs

McCaskill, Claire, D-Mo.

Capitol Hill Office: 730 SHOB 20510-2507; 224-6154; Fax: 228-6326; *Chief of Staff:* Julie Dwyer
Web: www.mccaskill.senate.gov
Facebook: www.facebook.com/senatormccaskill
Twitter: @clairecmc
District Offices: 555 Independence St., Room 1600, Cape Girardeau, MO 63703-6235; 573-651-0964; Fax: 573-334-4278; *District Director:* Christy Mercer
28 N. 8th St., #500, Columbia, MO 65201; 573-442-7130; Fax: 573-442-7140; *Constituent Services Rep.:* Samantha Brewer
4141 Pennsylvania Ave., #101, Kansas City, MO 64111-3064; 816-421-1639; Fax: 816-421-2562; *Regional Director:* Corey Dillon
324 Park Central West, #101, Springfield, MO 65806-1218; 417-868-8745; Fax: 417-831-1349; *District Director:* David Stokley
5850 Delmar Blvd., Suite A, St. Louis, MO 63112-2346; 314-367-1364; Fax: 314-361-8649; *Deputy Chief of Staff:* Tod Martin
Committee Assignments: Armed Services; Commerce, Science, and Transportation; Homeland Security and Governmental Affairs; Special Aging, Ranking Minority Member

McConnell, Mitch, R-Ky.

Capitol Hill Office: 317 SROB 20510-1702; 224-2541; Fax: 224-2499; *Chief of Staff:* Brian McGuire
Web: www.mcconnell.senate.gov
Facebook: www.facebook.com/mitchmcconnell
Twitter: @McConnellPress
District Offices: Federal Bldg., 241 E. Main St., Room 102, Bowling Green, KY 42101-2175; 270-781-1673; Fax: 270-782-1884; *Field Rep.:* Tim Thomas

1885 Dixie Hwy., #345, Fort Wright, KY 41011-2679; 859-578-0188; Fax: 859-578-0488; *Field Rep.:* Shane Noem
771 Corporate Dr., #108, Lexington, KY 40503-5439; 859-224-8286; Fax: 859-224-9673; *Field Rep.:* Ethan Witt
300 S. Main St., #310, London, KY 40741-2415; 606-864-2026; Fax: 606-864-2035; *Field Rep.:* Donna McClure
601 W. Broadway, Room 630, Louisville, KY 40202-2228; 502-582-6304; Fax: 502-582-5326; *State Director:* Terry Carmack
100 Fountain Ave., #300, Paducah, KY 42001; 270-442-4554; Fax: 270-443-3102; *Field Rep.:* Martie Wiles
Committee Assignments: Agriculture, Nutrition, and Forestry; Appropriations; Rules and Administration; Select Intelligence

Menendez, Robert, D-N.J.

Capitol Hill Office: 528 SHOB 20510-3006; 224-4744; Fax: 224-2197; *Chief of Staff:* Fred Turner
Web: www.menendez.senate.gov
Facebook: www.facebook.com/senatormenendez
Twitter: @SenatorMenendez
District Offices: 208 White Horse Pike, #18, Barrington, NJ 08007-1322; 856-757-5353; Fax: 856-546-1526; *Deputy State Director:* Richard Lockliar
One Gateway Center, #1100, Newark, NJ 07102-5323; 973-645-3030; Fax: 973-645-0502; *Deputy Chief of Staff:* Vacant
Committee Assignments: Banking, Housing, and Urban Affairs; Finance; Foreign Relations

Merkley, Jeff, D-Ore.

Capitol Hill Office: 313 SHOB 20510-3705; 224-3753; Fax: 228-3997; *Chief of Staff:* Michael S. Zamore
Web: www.merkley.senate.gov
Facebook: www.facebook.com/jeffmerkley
Twitter: @SenJeffMerkley
District Offices: 131 Hawthorne Ave. N.W., #208, Bend, OR 97701-2958; 541-318-1298; *Field Rep.:* Phil Chang
405 E. 8th Ave., #2010, Eugene, OR 97401-2730; 541-465-6750; *Field Rep.:* Dan Whelan
10 S. Bartlett St., #201, Medford, OR 97501-7204; 541-608-9102; *Field Rep.:* Amy Amrhein
310 2nd St. S.E., #105, Pendleton, OR 97801-2263; 541-278-1129; *Field Rep.:* Karen Wagner
121 Salmon St. S.W., #1400, Portland, OR 97204-2948; 503-326-3386; Fax: 503-326-2900; *State Director:* Jessica Stevens
495 State St., #330, Salem, OR 97301-4384; 503-362-8102; *Field Rep.:* Katie Gauthier
Committee Assignments: Appropriations; Banking, Housing, and Urban Affairs; Budget; Congressional-Executive Commission on China; Environment and Public Works

Mikulski, Barbara, D-Md.

Capitol Hill Office: 503 SHOB 20510-2003; 224-4654; Fax: 224-8858; *Chief of Staff:* Shannon Kula
Web: www.mikulski.senate.gov
Facebook: www.facebook.com/SenatorMikulski

Twitter: @SenatorBarb

District Offices: 60 West St., #202, Annapolis, MD 21401-2448; 410-263-1805; Fax: 410-263-5949; *Asst. to Senator:* Rachel Jones

901 S. Bond St., #310, Baltimore, MD 21231-3358; 410-962-4510; Fax: 410-962-4760; *State Director:* Lori Albin

6404 Ivy Lane, #406, Greenbelt, MD 20770-1407; 301-345-5517; Fax: 301-345-7573; *Asst. to the Senator:* Nichelle Schoultz

32 W. Washington St., Room 203, Hagerstown, MD 21740-4804; 301-797-2826; Fax: 301-797-2241; *Asst. to the Senator:* Juliana Albowicz

The Gallery Plaza Bldg., 212 W. Main St., #200, Salisbury, MD 21801-5106; 410-546-7711; Fax: 410-546-9324; *Special Asst. to the Senator:* Linda Prochaska

Committee Assignments: Appropriations, Ranking Minority Member; Health, Education, Labor, and Pensions; Select Intelligence

Moore Capito, Shelley, R-W.Va.

Capitol Hill Office: 172 SROB 20510-4804; 224-6472; Fax: 224-7665; *Chief of Staff:* Joel Brubaker

Web: www.capito.senate.gov

Facebook: www.facebook.com/senshelley

Twitter: @SenCapito

District Offices: 217 W. King St., #307, Martinsburg, WV 25401-3211; 301-262-9285; Fax: 304-262-9288; *State Director:* Mary Elisabeth Eckerson

405 Capitol St., #508, Charleston, WV 25301-1749; 304-347-5372; Fax: 304-347-5371; *Communications Director:* Ashley Berrang

Committee Assignments: Appropriations; Energy and Natural Resources; Environment and Public Works; Joint Library; Rules and Administration

Moran, Jerry, R-Kans.

Capitol Hill Office: 521 SDOB 20510-1606; 224-6521; Fax: 228-6966; *Chief of Staff:* Todd Novascone

Web: www.moran.senate.gov/public

Facebook: www.facebook.com/jerrymoran

Twitter: @jerrymoran

District Offices: 1200 Main St., #402, Hays, KS 67601-3649; 785-628-6401; Fax: 785-628-3791; *Constituent Services Director:* Chelsey Ladd

923 Westport Pl., #210, Manhattan, KS 66502; 785-539-8973; Fax: 785-587-0789; *State Director:* Brennen Britton

23600 College Blvd., #201, Olathe, KS 66061-8709; 913-393-0711; Fax: 913-768-1366; *Kansas Scheduler:* Lisa Dethloff

306 N. Broadway St., #125, Pittsburg, KS 66762-4836; 620-232-2286; Fax: 620-232-2284; *District Rep.:* Pam Henderson

3450 N. Rock Rd., Bldg. 200, #209, Wichita, KS 67226-1352; 316-631-1410; Fax: 316-631-1297; *Deputy State Director:* Mike Zamrzla

Committee Assignments: Appropriations; Banking, Housing, and Urban Affairs; Commerce, Science and Transportation; Indian Affairs; Veterans' Affairs

Murkowski, Lisa, R-Alaska

Capitol Hill Office: 709 SHOB 20510-0203; 224-6665; Fax: 224-5301; *Chief of Staff:* Edward G. Hild

Web: www.murkowski.senate.gov

Facebook: www.facebook.com/SenLisaMurkowski

Twitter: @lisamurkowski

District Offices: 510 L St., #600, Anchorage, AK 99501-1956; 907-271-3735; Fax: 877-857-0322; *State Director:* Kevin Sweeney

101 12th Ave., #329, Fairbanks, AK 99701-6237; 907-456-0233; Fax: 907-451-7146; *Special Asst.:* James Parrish

800 Glacier Ave., #101, Juneau, AK 99801-1852; 907-586-7277; Fax: 907-586-7201; *Special Asst.:* Connie McKenzie

805 Frontage Rd., #105, Kenai, AK 99611-9104; 907-283-5808; Fax: 907-283-4363; *Special Asst.:* Michelle Blackwell

1900 First Ave., #225, Ketchikan, AK 99901; 907-225-6880; Fax: 907-225-0390; *Special Asst.:* Penny Pederson

851 E. Westpoint Dr., #307, Wasilla, AK 99654-7183; 907-376-7665; Fax: 907-376-8526; *Special Asst.:* Gerri Sumpter

Committee Assignments: Appropriations; Energy and Natural Resources, Chair; Health, Education, Labor, and Pensions; Indian Affairs

Murphy, Chris, D-Conn.

Capitol Hill Office: 136 SHOB 20510; 224-4041; Fax: 224-9750; *Chief of Staff:* Allison Herwitt

Web: www.murphy.senate.gov

Facebook: www.facebook.com/ChrisMurphyCT

Twitter: @ChrisMurphyCT

District Office: One Constitution Plaza, 7th Floor, Hartford, CT 06103; 860-549-8463; Fax: 860-524-5091; *State Director:* Kenny Curran

Committee Assignments: Appropriations; Foreign Relations; Health, Education, Labor, and Pensions

Murray, Patty, D-Wash.

Capitol Hill Office: 154 SROB 20510; 224-2621; Fax: 224-0238; *Chief of Staff:* Mike Spahn

Web: www.murray.senate.gov

Facebook: www.facebook.com/pattymurray

Twitter: @pattymurray

District Offices: 2930 Wetmore Ave., #903, Everett, WA 98201-4067; 425-259-6515; Fax: 425-259-7152; *Regional Director:* Ann Seabott

2988 Jackson Federal Bldg., 915 2nd Ave., Seattle, WA 98174-1003; 206-553-5545; Fax: 206-553-0891; *State Director:* Beth Osborne

10 N. Post St., #600, Spokane, WA 99201-0712; 509-624-9515; Fax: 509-624-9561; *Eastern Washington Director:* John Culton

950 Pacific Ave., #650, Tacoma, WA 98402-4450; 253-572-3636; Fax: 253-572-9488; *South Sound Director:* Kierra Phifer

Marshall House, 1323 Officers Row, Vancouver, WA 98661-3856; 360-696-7797; Fax: 360-696-7798; *Southwest Washington Regional Director:* David Hodges

402 E. Yakima Ave., #420, Yakima, WA 98901-2760; 509-453-7462; Fax: 509-453-7731; *Central Washington Director:* Raquel Crowley

Committee Assignments: Appropriations; Budget; Health, Education, Labor, and Pensions, Ranking Minority Member; Veterans' Affairs

Nelson, Bill J., D-Fla.

Capitol Hill Office: 716 SHOB 20510-0905; 224-5274; Fax: 228-2183; *Chief of Staff:* Peter J. Mitchell

Web: www.billnelson.senate.gov

Facebook: www.facebook.com/billnelson

Twitter: @senbillnelson

District Offices: 2555 Ponce De Leon Blvd., #610, Coral Gables, FL 33134; 305-536-5999; Fax: 305-536-5991; *Regional Director:* Loren Parra

3416 S. University Dr., Ft. Lauderdale, FL 33328-2022; 954-693-4851; Fax: 954-693-4862; *Regional Director:* Willowstine Lawson

2000 Main St., #801, Ft. Myers, FL 33901-5503; 239-334-7760; Fax: 239-334-7710; *Regional Director:* Vacant

1301 Riverplace Blvd., #2010, Jacksonville, FL 32207-9021; 904-346-4500; Fax: 904-346-4506; *Regional Director:* Katie Ross

225 E. Robinson St., #410, Orlando, FL 32801-4326; 407-872-7161; Fax: 407-872-7165; *Director of Constituent Services:* Sherry Davich

111 N. Adams St., Tallahassee, FL 32301-7736; 850-942-8415; Fax: 850-942-8450; *Director of Outreach:* Mary-Louise Hester

801 N. Florida Ave., 4th Floor, Tampa, FL 33602-3849; 813-225-7040; Fax: 813-225-7050; *Regional Director:* Digna Alvarez

413 Clematis St., #210, West Palm Beach, FL 33401-5319; 561-514-0189; Fax: 561-514-4078; *Regional Director:* Michelle McGovern

Committee Assignments: Armed Services; Commerce, Science, and Transportation, Ranking Minority Member; Finance; Special Aging

Paul, Rand, R-Ky.

Capitol Hill Office: 167 SROB 20510-1704; 224-4343; Fax: 228-6917; *Chief of Staff:* William Henderson

Web: www.paul.senate.gov

Facebook: www.facebook.com/SenatorRandPaul

Twitter: @SenRandPaul

District Offices: 1029 State St., Bowling Green, KY 42101-2652; 270-782-8303; Fax: 270-782-8315; *Constituent Services Director:* Bobette Franklin

541 Buttermilk Pike, #102, Crescent Springs, KY 41017-1689; 859-426-0165; *Field Rep.:* Billy Matthews

1100 S. Main St., #12, Hopkinsville, KY 42240-2079; 270-885-1212; *Deputy State Director:* Rachel McCubbin

771 Corporate Dr., #105, Lexington, KY 40503; 859-219-2239; *Field Rep.:* Mica Sims

600 Dr. Martin Luther King Jr. Pl., Room 1072B, Louisville, KY 40202-2230; 502-582-5341; *State Director:* Jim Milliman

423 Frederica St., #305, Owensboro, KY 42301-3013; 270-689-9085; *Field Rep.:* Jason Hastert

Committee Assignments: Foreign Relations; Health, Education, Labor, and Pensions; Homeland Security and Governmental Affairs; Small Business and Entrepreneurship

Perdue, David, D-Ga.

Capitol Hill Office: 383 SROB 20510-1007; 224-3521; Fax: 228-1031; *Chief of Staff:* Derrick Dickey

Web: www.perdue.senate.gov

Facebook: www.facebook.com/perduesenate

Twitter: @sendavidperdue

District Office: 1 Overton Park, #970, 3625 Cumberland Blvd., Atlanta, GA 30339; 770-661-0999; Fax: 770-661-0768; *Communications Director:* Megan Whittemore

Committee Assignments: Agriculture, Nutrition and Forestry; Budget; Foreign Relations; Judiciary; Special Aging

Peters, Gary, D-Mich.

Capitol Hill Office: 724 SROB 20510-2202; 224-6221; Fax: 202-224-1388; *Chief of Staff:* Eric Feldman

Web: www.peters.senate.gov

Facebook: www.facebook.com/PetersForMichigan

Twitter: @Peters4Michigan

District Offices: Patrick V. McNamara Federal Bldg., 477 Michigan Ave., #1860, Detroit, MI 48226; 313-226-6020; *Scheduler:* Angeli Chawla

124 West Allegan St., #1810, Lansing, MI 48933; 517-377-1508; *State Director:* Elise Lancaster

Gerald R. Ford Federal Bldg., 110 Michigan St. N.W., #720, Grand Rapids, MI 49503; 616-233-9150; *Regional Director:* Peter Dikow

407 6th St., Suite C, Rochester, MI 48307; 248-608-8040; *Regional Director:* Jeremy Mahrle

515 North Washington Ave., #401, Saginaw, MI 48607; 989-754-0112; *Regional Director:* Montel Menifee

818 Red Dr., #40, Traverse City, MI 49684; 231-947-7773; *Regional Director:* Leah McCallum

Committee Assignments: Commerce, Science, and Transportation; Congressional-Executive Commission on China; Homeland Security and Governmental Affairs; Joint Economic; Small Business and Entrepreneurship

Portman, Rob, R-Ohio

Capitol Hill Office: 448 SROB 20510-3506; 224-3353; Fax: 224-9075; *Chief of Staff:* Mark Isakowitz

Web: www.portman.senate.gov

Facebook: www.facebook.com/robportman

Twitter: @robportman

District Offices: 312 Walnut St., #3075, Cincinnati, OH 45202; 513-684-3265; *Southwest Ohio District Director:* Connie Laug

1240 E. 9th St., Room 3061, Cleveland, OH 44199-2001; 216-522-7095; *Northeast Ohio District Director:* Caryn Candisky

37 W. Broad St., Room 300, Columbus, OH 43215-4180; 614-469-6774; *State Director:* Teri Geiger

420 Madison Ave., Room 1210, Toledo, OH 43604-1221; 419-259-3895; *Communications Director:* Caitlin Conant

Committee Assignments: Budget; Energy and Natural Resources; Finance; Homeland Security and Governmental Affairs

Reed, Jack D., D-R.I.

Capitol Hill Office: 728 SHOB 20510-3903; 224-4642; Fax: 224-4680; *Chief of Staff:* Neil D. Campbell
Web: www.reed.senate.gov
Facebook: www.facebook.com/SenJackReed
Twitter: @SenJackReed
District Offices: 1000 Chapel View Blvd., #290, Cranston, RI 02920-5602; 401-943-3100; Fax: 401-464-6837; *State Director:* Raymond Simone

U.S. Courthouse, One Exchange Terrace, #408, Providence, RI 02903-1773; 401-528-5200; Fax: 202-224-4680; *Deputy Chief of Staff:* Cathy Nagle

Committee Assignments: Appropriations; Armed Services, Ranking Minority Member; Banking, Housing, and Urban Affairs; Select Intelligence

Reid, Harry, D-Nev.

Capitol Hill Office: 522 SHOB 20510-2803; 224-3542; Fax: 224-7327; *Chief of Staff:* Drew Willison
Web: www.reid.senate.gov
Facebook: facebook.com/HarryReid
Twitter: @SenatorReid
District Offices: 600 E. William St., #302, Carson City, NV 89701-4052; 775-882-7343; Fax: 775-883-1980; *Regional Rep.:* Yolanda Garcia

Lloyd D. George Bldg., 333 Las Vegas Blvd. South, #8016, Las Vegas, NV 89101-7075; 702-388-5020; Fax: 702-388-5030; *Southern Nevada Director:* Shannon Raborn

Courthouse and Federal Bldg., 400 S. Virginia St., #902, Reno, NV 89501-2109; 775-686-5750; Fax: 775-686-5757; *State Director:* Mary Conelly

Committee Assignment: Select Intelligence
Minority Floor Leader

Risch, James E., R-Idaho

Capitol Hill Office: 483 SROB 20510-1206; 224-2752; Fax: 224-2573; *Chief of Staff:* John A. Sandy
Web: www.risch.senate.gov
Twitter: @SenatorRisch
District Offices: 350 N. 9th St., #302, Boise, ID 83702-5409; 208-342-7985; Fax: 208-343-2458; *Regional Director:* Melinda Smyser

Harbor Plaza, 610 W. Hubbard St., #213, Coeur d'Alene, ID 83814-2288; 208-667-6130; Fax: 208-765-1743; *Regional Director:* Sid Smith

901 Pier View Dr., #202A, Idaho Falls, ID 83402-5070; 208-523-5541; Fax: 208-523-9373; *Regional Director:* Amy Taylor

313 D St., #106, Lewiston, ID 83501-1894; 208-743-0792; Fax: 208-746-7275; *Regional Director:* Mike Hanna

275 S. 5th Ave., #290, Pocatello, ID 83201-6410; 208-236-6817; Fax: 208-236-6820; *Regional Director:* Jeremy Field

1411 Falls Ave. East, #201, Twin Falls, ID 83301-3455; 208-734-6780; Fax: 208-734-3905; *State Director:* Mike Matthews

Committee Assignments: Energy and Natural Resources; Foreign Relations; Select Ethics; Select Intelligence; Small Business and Entrepreneurship

Roberts, Pat, R-Kans.

Capitol Hill Office: 109 SHOB 20510-1605; 224-4774; Fax: 224-3514; *Chief of Staff:* Jackie Cottrell
Web: www.roberts.senate.gov
Facebook: www.facebook.com/SenPatRoberts
Twitter: @senpatroberts
District Offices: 100 Military Plaza, P.O. Box 550 , Dodge City, KS 67801-4990; 620-227-2244; Fax: 620-227-2264; *District Rep.:* Martha Ruiz-Martinez

11900 College Blvd., #203, Overland Park, KS 66210-3939; 913-451-9343; Fax: 913-451-9446; *State Director:* Chad Tenpenny

Frank Carlson Federal Bldg., 444 Quincy St. S.E., #392, Topeka, KS 66683-3599; 785-295-2745; Fax: 785-235-3665; *District Director:* Gilda Lintz

155 N. Market St., #120, Wichita, KS 67202-1802; 316-263-0416; Fax: 316-263-0273; *District Director:* Tamara Woods

Committee Assignments: Agriculture, Nutrition, and Forestry, Chair; Finance; Health, Education, Labor, and Pensions; Joint Library; Joint Printing; Rules and Administration; Select Ethics

Rounds, Mike, R-S.D.

Capitol Hill Office: 502 SHOB 20510-4104; 224-5842; Fax: 224-7482; *Chief of Staff:* Rob Skjonsberg
Web: www.rounds.senate.gov
Facebook: www.facebook.com/mikerounds
Twitter: @senatorrounds
District Offices: 1313 W. Main St., Rapid City, SD 57701; 605-343-5035; Fax: 605-343-5348; *West River Director:* Jeff Marlette

320 N. Main Ave., Suite B, Sioux Falls, SD 57014; 605-336-0486; Fax: 605-336-6624; *East River Director:* Mark Johnston

514 S. Main St., #100, Aberdeen, SD 57401; 605-936-0092; *Senior Field Manager:* Josh Haeder

111 W. Capitol Ave., #210, Pierre, SD 57501; 605-224-1450; *Central South Dakota Director:* Josh Haeder

Committee Assignments: Armed Services; Banking, Housing, and Urban Affairs; Environment and Public Works; Veterans' Affairs

Rubio, Marco, R-Fla.

Capitol Hill Office: 284 SROB 20510; 224-3041; Fax: 228-0285; *Chief of Staff:* Alberto Martinez
Web: www.rubio.senate.gov
Facebook: www.facebook.com/SenatorMarcoRubio
Twitter: @SenRubioPress

District Offices: 1650 Prudential Dr., #220, Jacksonville, FL 32207-8149; 904-398-8586; *Regional Director:* Adele Griffin

8669 36th St. N.W., #110, Doral, FL 33166-6640; 305-418-8553; *Regional Director:* Alyn Fernandez

3229 E. Tamiami Trail, #106, Naples, FL 34112; 239-213-1521; *Constituent Services Rep.:* Zach Zampella

201 S. Orange Ave., #350, Orlando, FL 32801-3499; 407-254-2573; *State Director:* Vacant

1 N. Palafox St., #159, Pensacola, FL 32502-5658; 850-433-2603; *Regional Director:* Kris Tande

402 S. Monroe St., #2105E, Tallahassee, FL 32399-6526; 850-599-9100; *Regional Director:* Brian Mimbs

3802 Spectrum Blvd., #106, Tampa, FL 33612-9220; 813-977-6450; *Regional Director:* Ryan Patmintra

4580 PGA Blvd., #201, Palm Beach Gardens, FL 33418; 561-775-3360; *Regional Director:* Greg Langowski

Committee Assignments: Commerce, Science, and Transportation; Congressional-Executive Commission on China, Co-Chair; Foreign Relations; Select Intelligence; Small Business and Entrepreneurship

Sanders, Bernie, I-Vt.

Capitol Hill Office: 332 SDOB 20510-4504; 224-5141; Fax: 228-0776; *Chief of Staff:* Michaeleen Crowell
Web: www.sanders.senate.gov
Facebook: facebook.com/senatorsanders
Twitter: @SenatorSanders
District Offices: 1 Church St., #300, Burlington, VT 05401-4451; 802-862-0697; Fax: 802-860-6370; *Outreach Director:* Phil Fiermonte

357 Western Ave., #1B, St. Johnsbury, VT 05819; 802-748-0191; Fax: 802-748-0302; *Agriculture Policy Advisor:* Jenny Nelson

Committee Assignments: Budget, Ranking Minority Member; Energy and Natural Resources; Environment and Public Works; Health, Education, Labor, and Pensions; Veterans' Affairs

Sasse, Ben, R-Neb.

Capitol Hill Office: 386A SROB 20510-2707; 224-6551; Fax: 228-1325; *Chief of Staff:* Derrick Morgan
Web: www.sasse.senate.gov
Facebook: www.facebook.com/sassefornebraska
Twitter: @sensasse
District Offices: 115 Railway St., #C102, Scottsbluff, NE 69361; 308-632-6032; *Scheduler:* Raven Shirley

4111 Fourth Ave., #26, Kearney, NE 68845; 308-233-3677; *Field Rep.:* Tyler Grassmeyer

1128 Lincoln Mall, #305, Lincoln, NE 68508; 402-476-1400; *State Director:* James Wegmann

304 N. 168th Circle, #213, Omaha, NE 68118; 402-550-8040
Committee Assignments: Agriculture, Nutrition and Forestry; Banking, Housing and Urban Affairs; Homeland Security and Governmental Affairs; Joint Economic; Special Aging

Schatz, Brian, D-Hawaii

Capitol Hill Office: 722 SHOB 20510; 224-3934; Fax: 228-1153; *Chief of Staff:* Andrew Winer

Web: www.schatz.senate.gov
Facebook: www.facebook.com/BrianSchatz
Twitter: @brianschatz
District Office: 300 Ala Moana Blvd., Room 7-212, Honolulu, HI 96850; 808-523-2061; Fax: 808-523-2065; *Deputy Chief of Staff:* Malia Paul
Committee Assignments: Appropriations; Commerce, Science, and Transportation; Indian Affairs; Select Ethics

Schumer, Charles E., D-N.Y.

Capitol Hill Office: 322 SHOB 20510-3203; 224-6542; Fax: 228-3027; *Chief of Staff:* Mike Lynch
Web: www.schumer.senate.gov
Facebook: www.facebook.com/chuckschumer
Twitter: @chuckschumer
District Offices: Leo O'Brien Bldg., Room 420, Albany, NY 12207; 518-431-4070; Fax: 518-431-4076; *Regional Director:* Steve Mann

15 Henry St., Room 100 A-F , Binghamton, NY 13901; 607-772-6792; Fax: 607-772-8124; *Regional Rep.:* Amanda Spellicy

130 S. Elmwood Ave., #660, Buffalo, NY 14202-2371; 716-846-4111; Fax: 716-846-4113; *Regional Rep.:* Shannon Patch

145 Pine Lawn Rd., #300, Melville, NY 11747; 631-753-0978; Fax: 631-753-0997; *Regional Rep.:* Kyle Strober

780 3rd Ave., #2301, New York, NY 10017-2110; 212-486-4430; Fax: 202-228-2838; *State Director:* Martin Brennan

One Park Pl., #100, Peekskill, NY 10566; 914-734-1532; Fax: 914-734-1673; *Regional Rep.:* Cody Peluso

100 State St., Room 3040, Rochester, NY 14614-1317; 585-263-5866; Fax: 585-263-3173; *Regional Rep.:* Christopher Zeltmann

100 S. Clinton St., Room 841, Syracuse, NY 13261-7318; 315-423-5471; Fax: 315-423-5185; *Regional Rep.:* Joe Nehme

Committee Assignments: Banking, Housing, and Urban Affairs; Finance; International Narcotics Control Caucus; Joint Library, Vice Chair; Joint Printing, Chair; Judiciary; Rules and Administration, Ranking Minority Member

Scott, Tim, R-S.C.

Capitol Hill Office: 520 SHOB 20510-4004; 224-6121; Fax: 228-5143; *Chief of Staff:* Jennifer DeCasper
Web: www.scott.senate.gov
Facebook: www.facebook.com/SenatorTimScott
Twitter: @SenatorTimScott
District Offices: 1301 Gervais St., #825, Columbia, SC 29201-2435; 803-771-6112; Fax: 855-802-9355; *Regional Director:* Delores Dacosta

40 W. Broad St., #320, Greenville, SC 29601; 864-233-5366; Fax: 855-802-9355; *Constituent Services Director:* Deb Blickenstaff

2500 City Hall Lane, 3rd Floor, North Charleston, SC 29406; 843-727-4525; Fax: 855-802-9355; *State Director:* Joe McKeown

Committee Assignments: Banking, Housing, and Urban Affairs; Finance; Health, Education, Labor, and Pensions; Small Business and Entrepreneurship, Special Aging

Sessions, Jeff A., R-Ala.

Capitol Hill Office: 326 SROB 20510-0104; 224-4124; Fax: 224-3149; *Chief of Staff:* Rick A. Dearborn
Web: www.sessions.senate.gov
Facebook: www.facebook.com/jeffsessions
Twitter: @senatorsessions
District Offices: 341 Vance Federal Bldg., 1800 5th Ave. North, Birmingham, AL 35203-2171; 205-731-1500; Fax: 205-731-0221; *Field Rep.:* Virginia Amason
100 W. Troy St., #302, Dothan, AL 36303-4574; 334-792-4924; Fax: 334-792-4928; *Field Rep.:* Cecelia Meeks
200 Clinton Ave. N.W., #802, Huntsville, AL 35801-4932; 256-533-0979; Fax: 256-533-0745; *Field Rep.:* Lisa Montgomery
41 W. I-65 Service Rd. North, #2003-A, Mobile, AL 36608; 251-414-3083; Fax: 251-414-5845; *Field Rep.:* Valerie Day
7550 Halcyon Summit Dr., #150, Montgomery, AL 36117-7012; 334-244-7017; Fax: 334-244-7091; *Field Rep.:* Cecelia Meeks
Committee Assignments: Armed Services; Budget; Environment and Public Works; Judiciary

Shaheen, Jeanne, D-N.H.

Capitol Hill Office: 506 SHOB 20510-2906; 224-2841; Fax: 228-3194; *Chief of Staff:* Maura Keefe
Web: www.shaheen.senate.gov
Facebook: www.facebook.com/SenatorShaheen
Twitter: @SenatorShaheen
District Offices: 961 Main St., Berlin, NH 03570-3031; 603-752-6300; Fax: 603-752-6305; *Special Asst. for Constituent Services/Outreach:* Chuck Henderson
50 Opera House Square, Claremont, NH 03743-5407; 603-542-4872; Fax: 603-542-6582; *Special Asst. for Constituent Services/Outreach:* Vacant
340 Central Ave., #205, Dover, NH 03820-3770; 603-750-3004; *Special Asst. for Constituent Services/Outreach:* Cara Osborn
1589 Elm St., #3, Manchester, NH 03101-1261; 603-647-7500; *Acting State Director:* Sarah Holmes
60 Main St., Nashua, NH 03060-2720; 603-883-0196; *Special Asst. for Constituent Services/Outreach:* Letizia Ortiz
12 Gilbo Ave., Suite C, Keene, NH 03431; 603-358-6604; *Special Asst. for Constituent Services/Outreach:* Pam Slack
Committee Assignments: Armed Services; Commission on Security and Cooperation in Europe; Foreign Relations; Small Business and Entrepreneurship, Ranking Minority Member

Shelby, Richard, R-Ala.

Capitol Hill Office: 304 SROB 20510-0103; 224-5744; Fax: 224-3416; *Chief of Staff:* Alan R. Hanson
Web: www.shelby.senate.gov
Facebook: www.facebook.com/RichardShelby
Twitter: @SenShelby
District Offices: 321 Federal Bldg., 1800 5th Ave. North, #321, Birmingham, AL 35203-2113; 205-731-1384; Fax: 205-731-1386; *District Rep.:* Heather Adams
1000 Glenn Hearn Blvd., #20127, Huntsville, AL 35824-2107; 256-772-0460; Fax: 256-772-8387; *District Rep.:* Carrie Suggs
445 Federal Courthouse, 113 St. Joseph St., Mobile, AL 36602-3606; 251-694-4164; Fax: 251-694-4166; *District Rep.:* Tera Johnson
Frank M. Johnson Jr. Federal Courthouse, 15 Lee St., #208, Montgomery, AL 36104-4054; 334-223-7303; Fax: 334-223-7317; *District Rep.:* Vera Jordan
2005 University Blvd., #2100, Tuscaloosa, AL 35401; 205-759-5047; Fax: 205-759-5067; *District Rep.:* Kay Presley
Committee Assignments: Appropriations; Banking, Housing, and Urban Affairs, Chair; Rules and Administration

Stabenow, Debbie A., D-Mich.

Capitol Hill Office: 731 SHOB 20510-2204; 224-4822; Fax: 228-0325; *Chief of Staff:* Bill Sweeney
Web: www.stabenow.senate.gov
Facebook: www.facebook.com/stabenow
Twitter: @StabenowPress
District Offices: 719 Griswold St., #700, Detroit, MI 48226; 313-961-4330; Fax: 313-961-7566; *Regional Manager:* Barbara McCallahan
221 W. Lake Lansing Rd., #100, East Lansing, MI 48823-8661; 517-203 1760; Fax: 517-203-1778; *State Director:* Teresa Plachetka
432 Saginaw St., #301, Flint, MI 48502; 810-720-4172; Fax: 810-720-4178; *Regional Manager:* Adrian Walker
3280 Beltline Court, N.E., #400, Grand Rapids, MI 49525-9494; 616-975-0052; Fax: 616-975-5764; *Regional Manager:* Derrick Matthis
1901 W. Ridge St., #7, Marquette, MI 49855-3198; 906-228-8756; Fax: 906-228-9162; *Regional Manager:* Jeremy Hosking
3335 S. Airport Rd. West, #6B, Traverse City, MI 49684-7928; 231-929-1031; Fax: 231-929-1250; *Regional Manager:* Brandon Fewins
Committee Assignments: Agriculture, Nutrition, and Forestry, Ranking Minority Member; Budget; Energy and Natural Resources; Finance; Joint Taxation

Sullivan, Dan, R-Alaska

Capitol Hill Office: 702 SROB 20510-0204; 224-3004; Fax: 224-2354; *Chief of Staff:* Joe Balash
Web: www.sullivan.senate.gov
Facebook: www.facebook.com/DanSullivanforAlaska
Twitter: @dansullivan2014
District Offices: 851 E. Westpoint Dr., #309, Wasilla, AK 99654; 907-357-9956; Fax: 907-357-9964; *Regional Director:* Paul "Otto" Feather
Federal Bldg. 101, 12th Ave., #328, Fairbanks, AK 99701; 907-456-0261; Fax: 907-451-7290; *Special Assistant:* Leslie Hajdukovich

805 Frontage Rd., #101, Kenai, AK 99611; 907-283-4000; Fax: 907-283-4401; *Field Director:* Elaina Spraker

1900 First Ave., #225, Ketchikan, AK 99901; 907-225-6880; Fax: 907-225-0390; *Field Rep.:* Vacant

510 L St., #750, Anchorage, AK 99501; 907-271-5915; Fax: 907-258-9305; *State Director:* Kathlene Rowell

800 Glacier Ave., #101, Juneau, AK 99801; 907-586-7277; Fax: 907-586-7201; *Scheduler:* DeLynn Henry

Committee Assignments: Armed Services; Commerce, Science, and Transportation; Environment and Public Works; Veterans' Affairs

Tester, Jon, D-Mont.

Capitol Hill Office: 724 SHOB 20510-2604; 224-2644; Fax: 224-8594; *Chief of Staff:* James Wise

Web: www.tester.senate.gov

Facebook: www.facebook.com/senatortester

Twitter: @jontester

District Offices: 2900 4th Ave. North, #201, Billings, MT 59101; 406-252-0550; Fax: 406-252-7768; *Scheduler:* Jeanne Forrester

1 E. Main St., #202, Bozeman, MT 59715-6248; 406-586-4450; Fax: 406-586-7647; *Regional Director:* Jennifer Madgic

Silver Bow Center, 125 W. Granite St., #200, Butte, MT 59701-9215; 406-723-3277; Fax: 406-782-4717; *Field Rep.:* Erik Nylund

122 W. Towne St., Glendive, MT 59330-1735; 406-365-2391; Fax: 406-365-8836; *Regional Director:* Penny Zimmerman

119 1st Ave. North, #102, Great Falls, MT 59401-2568; 406-452-9585; Fax: 406-452-9586; *Regional Director:* Cheryl Ulmer

Capital One Center, 208 N. Montana Ave., #202, Helena, MT 59601-3837; 406-449-5401; Fax: 406-449-5462; *Veteran Liaison:* Bruce Knutson

14 3rd St. East, #230, Kalispell, MT 59901-4588; 406-257-3360; Fax: 406-257-3974; *Regional Director:* Virginia Sloan

130 W. Front St., Missoula, MT 59802-4304; 406-728-3003; Fax: 406-728-2193; *State Director:* Dayna Swanson

Committee Assignments: Appropriations; Banking, Housing, and Urban Affairs; Homeland Security and Governmental Affairs; Indian Affairs, Vice Chair; Veterans' Affairs

Thune, John, R-S.D.

Capitol Hill Office: 511 SDOB 20510-4105; 224-2321; Fax: 228-5429; *Chief of Staff:* Ryan P. Nelson

Web: www.thune.senate.gov

Facebook: www.facebook.com/johnthune

Twitter: @johnthune

District Offices: 320 S. 1st St., #101, Aberdeen, SD 57401-4168; 605-225-8823; Fax: 605-225-8468; *Northeast Regional Director:* Judy Vrchota

246 Founders Park Dr., #102, Rapid City, SD 57701; 605-348-7551; Fax: 605-348-7208; *West River Regional Director:* Qusi Al-Haj

5015 South Bur Oak, Sioux Falls, SD 57108; 605-334-9596; Fax: 605-334-2591; *Chief of Staff; State Director:* Ryan Nelson

Committee Assignments: Agriculture, Nutrition, and Forestry; Commerce, Science, and Transportation, Chair; Finance

Tillis, Thom, R-N.C.

Capitol Hill Office: 185 SDOB 20510-3309; 224-6342; Fax: 228-2563; *Chief of Staff:* Ray Starling

Web: www.tillis.senate.gov

Facebook: www.facebook.com/ThomTillis

Twitter: @ThomTillis

District Offices: 1520 S. Blvd., #205, Charlotte, NC 28203; 704-334-2448; Fax: 704-334-2405; *State Director:* Jordan Shaw

301 S. Evan St., #102, Greenville, NC 27858; 252-329-0371; Fax: 252-329-0290; *Regional Rep.:* Brian Brown

1 Historic Courthouse Square, #112, Hendersonville, NC 28792; 828-693-8750; Fax: 828-693-9724; *Regional Rep.:* Colton Overcash

1840 Eastchester Dr., #200, High Point, NC 27265; 336-885-0685; Fax: 336-885-0692; *Regional Rep.:* Vacant

310 New Bern Ave., #122, Raleigh, NC 27601; 919-856-4630; 919-856-4053; *Scheduler:* Austen Shearer

Committee Assignments: Agriculture, Nutrition, and Forestry; Armed Services; Judiciary; Special Aging; Veterans' Affairs

Toomey, Pat, R-Pa.

Capitol Hill Office: 248 SROB 20510-3806; 224-4254; Fax: 228-0284; *Chief of Staff:* Christopher T. Gahan

Web: www.toomey.senate.gov

Facebook: www.facebook.com/senatortoomey

Twitter: @sentoomey

District Offices: 1150 S. Cedar Crest Blvd., #101, Allentown, PA 18103-7937; 610-434-1444; Fax: 610-434-1844; *Deputy State Director:* Sue Zimskind

Federal Bldg., 17 S. Park Row, #B-120, Erie, PA 16501-1156; 814-453-3010; Fax: 814-455-9925; *Northwest Pennsylvania Regional Manager:* Sheila Sterrett

Federal Bldg., 228 Walnut St., #1104, Harrisburg, PA 17101-1722; 717-782-3951; Fax: 717-782-4920; *State Director:* Bob DeSousa

Richland Square III, 1397 Eisenhower Blvd., #302, Johnstown, PA 15904-3267; 814-266-5970; Fax: 814-266-5973; *Greater Johnstown Regional Manager:* John Frick

1628 JFK Blvd., 8 Penn Center, #1702, Philadelphia, PA 19103-2136; 215-241-1090; Fax: 215-241-1095; *Southeast Pennsylvania Director:* Mitch Vidovitch

100 W. Station Square Dr., #225, Pittsburgh, PA 15219-1180; 412-803-3501; Fax: 412-803-3504; *Western Pennsylvania Director:* Matthew Blackburn

538 Spruce St., #302, Scranton, PA 18503-1816; 570-941-3540; Fax: 570-941-3544; *Northeast Pennsylvania Regional Manager:* Brian Langan

Committee Assignments: Banking, Housing, and Urban Affairs; Budget; Finance

Udall, Tom, D-N.M.

Capitol Hill Office: 110 SHOB 20510-3103; 224-6621; Fax: 228-3261; *Chief of Staff:* Michael Collins
Web: www.tomudall.senate.gov
Facebook: www.facebook.com/senatortomudall
Twitter: @SenatorTomUdall
District Offices: 219 Central Ave. N.W., #210, Albuquerque, NM 87102; 505-346-6791; Fax: 505-346-6720; *State Director:* Bianca Wertheim
102 W. Hagerman St., Suite A, Carlsbad, NM 88220; 575-234-0366; Fax: 575-234-1507; *Field Rep.:* Beverly Allen-Ananins
201 N. Church St., #201B, Las Cruces, NM 88001; 575-526-5475; Fax: 575-523-6589; *Field Rep.:* Elizabeth Driggers
120 S. Federal Pl., #302, Santa Fe, NM 87501-1966; 505-988-6511; Fax: 505-988-6514; *Field Rep.:* Michele Jacquez-Ortiz
100 S. Ave. A, #113, Portales, NM 88130; 575-356-6811; *Field Rep.:* Jack Carpenter
Committee Assignments: Appropriations; Commerce, Science, and Transportation; Commission on Security and Cooperation in Europe; Foreign Relations; Indian Affairs; International Narcotics Control Caucus; Joint Printing; Rules and Administration

Vitter, David, R-La.

Capitol Hill Office: 516 SHOB 20510-1805; 224-4623; Fax: 228-5061; *Chief of Staff:* Kyle Ruckert
Web: www.vitter.senate.gov
Facebook: www.facebook.com/DavidVitter
Twitter: @DavidVitter
District Offices: Plaza 28, 6501 Coliseum Blvd., #700-A, Alexandria, LA 71303; 318-448-0169; Fax: 318-448-0189; *Regional Rep.:* Quint Carriere
858 Convention St., Baton Rouge, LA 70802-5626; 225-383-0331; Fax: 225-383-0952; *Regional Director:* Michael Wong
2201 Kaliste Saloom Rd., #201, Lafayette, LA 70508; 337-993-9502; Fax: 337-993-9567; *Deputy State Director:* Nicole Hebert
1424 Ryan St., Suite A, Lake Charles, LA 70601; 337-436-0453; Fax: 337-436-3163; *Regional Rep.:* Brooke David
2800 Veterans Blvd., #201, Metairie, LA 70002; 504-589-2753; Fax: 504-589-2607; *State Director:* David Doss
1651 Louisville Ave., #148, Monroe, LA 71201-5435; 318-325-8120; Fax: 318-325-9165; *Regional Rep.:* Hayden Haynes
920 Pierremont Rd., #113, Shreveport, LA 71106-2079; 318-861-0437; Fax: 318-861-4865; *Regional Director:* Chip Layton
Committee Assignments: Banking, Housing, and Urban Affairs; Environment and Public Works; Judiciary; Small Business and Entrepreneurship, Chair

Warner, Mark R., D-Va.

Capitol Hill Office: 475 SROB 20510-4606; 224-2023; Fax: 224-6295; *Chief of Staff:* David Hallock
Web: www.warner.senate.gov
Facebook: www.facebook.com/MarkRWarner
Twitter: @MarkWarner
District Offices: 180 W. Main St., Abingdon, VA 24210-2844; 276-628-8158; Fax: 276-628-1036; *Outreach Rep.:* Drew Lumpkin
101 W. Main St., #4900, Norfolk, VA 23510-1690; 757-441-3079; Fax: 757-441-6250; *Constituent Services Director:* Denise Goode
919 E. Main St., #630, Richmond, VA 23219-4600; 804-775-2314; Fax: 804-775-2319; *Director of Government & Community Affairs:* Keyanna Connor
129B Salem Ave. S.W., Roanoke, VA 24011-1203; 540-857-2676; Fax: 540-857-2800; *Deputy State Director:* Lou Kadiri
8000 Towers Crescent Dr., #200, Vienna, VA 22182-6203; 703-442-0670; Fax: 703-442-0408; *State Director:* Ann Rust
Committee Assignments: Banking, Housing, and Urban Affairs; Budget; Finance; Joint Printing; Rules and Administration; Select Intelligence

Warren, Elizabeth, D-Mass.

Capitol Hill Office: 317 SHOB 20510; 224-4543; Fax: 228-2072; *Chief of Staff:* Mindy Myers
Web: www.warren.senate.gov
Facebook: www.facebook.com/senatorelizabethwarren
Twitter: @senwarren
District Offices: 2400 John F. Kennedy Federal Bldg., 15 New Sudbury St., Boston, MA 02203; 617-565-3170; Fax: 617-723-7325; *State Director:* Roger Lau
1550 Main St., #406, Springfield, MA 01103-1429; 413-788-2690; *Regional Director:* Jeremiah Thompson
Committee Assignments: Banking, Housing, and Urban Affairs; Health, Education, Labor, and Pensions; Special Aging

Whitehouse, Sheldon, D-R.I.

Capitol Hill Office: 530 SHOB 20510-3905; 224-2921; Fax: 228-6362; *Chief of Staff:* Sam Goodstein
Web: www.whitehouse.senate.gov
Facebook: www.facebook.com/SenatorWhitehouse
Twitter: @SenWhitehouse
District Office: 170 Westminster St., #1100, Providence, RI 02903-2109; 401-453-5294; Fax: 401-453-5085; *State Director:* George Carvalho
Committee Assignments: Budget; Commission on Security and Cooperation in Europe; Environment and Public Works; Health, Education, Labor, and Pensions; Judiciary; Special Aging

Wicker, Roger, R-Miss.

Capitol Hill Office: 555 SDOB 20510-2404; 224-6253; Fax: 228-0378; *Chief of Staff:* Michelle Barlow Richardson
Web: www.wicker.senate.gov
Facebook: www.facebook.com/wicker
Twitter: @rogerwicker
District Offices: 2909 13th St., 3rd Floor, #303, Gulfport, MS 39501; 228-871-2017; Fax: 228-871-7196; *Southern Regional Director:* Brad Ferguson

321 Losher St., P.O. Box 385, Hernando, MS 38632-2124; 662-429-1002; Fax: 662-429-6002; *Constituent Liaison:* Kim Chamberlin

501 E. Court St., #3-500, Jackson, MS 39201-5037; 601-965-4644; Fax: 601-965-4007; *State Director:* Ryan Annison

330 W. Jefferson St., Suite B, Tupelo, MS 38803; 662-844-5010; Fax: 662-844-5030; *North Regional Director:* Drew Robertson

Committee Assignments: Armed Services; Budget; Commerce, Science, and Transportation; Commission on Security and Cooperation in Europe; Environment and Public Works; Rules and Administration

Wyden, Ron, D-Ore.

Capitol Hill Office: 221 SDOB 20510-3703; 224-5244; Fax: 228-2717; *Chief of Staff:* Jeff Michels
Web: www.wyden.senate.gov
Facebook: www.facebook.com/wyden
Twitter: @ronwyden
District Offices: The Jamison Bldg., 131 N.W. Hawthorne Ave., #107, Bend, OR 97701-2957; 541-330-9142; *Field Rep.:* Wayne Kinney

405 E. 8th Ave., #2020, Eugene, OR 97401-2733; 541-431-0229; *Field Rep.:* Juine Chada

SAC Annex Bldg., 105 Fir St., #201, La Grande, OR 97850-2661; 541-962-7691; *Field Rep.:* Kathleen Cathey

Federal Courthouse, 310 W. 6th St., #118, Medford, OR 97501-2700; 541-858-5122; *Field Rep.:* Molly McCarthy Skundrick

911 11th Ave. N.E., #630, Portland, OR 97232-4107; 503-326-7525; *State Director:* Lisa Rockower

707 13th St. S.E., #285, Salem, OR 97301-4087; 503-589-4555; *Field Rep.:* Fritz Graham

Committee Assignments: Budget; Energy and Natural Resources; Finance, Ranking Minority Member; Joint Taxation; Select Intelligence

House and Senate Caucuses

The following is a compilation of the most active caucuses in the House and Senate. A general staff contact is listed along with the phone number as well as a Web address when available. The area code for all phone numbers is (202). This information is current as of April 25, 2016.

HOUSE CAUCUSES

Ad Hoc Congressional Committee for Irish Affairs, Travis Osen-foss, 225-2464

Americans Abroad Caucus, Elizabeth Darnall, 225-7944; Web, https://americansabroad.org/issues/representation/americans-abroad-caucus

Bipartisan Congressional Pro-Life Caucus, Jason Day, 226-5701

Bipartisan Disabilities Caucus, Todd Adams, 225-2735; Web, http://disabilitiescaucus.langevin.house.gov

Bipartisan Working Group, Sheila Grant, 225-4165

Blue Dog Coalition, Richard Carbo, 225-5711; Web, http://bluedog.schrader.house.gov

Caucus for Congressional World-Bank Dialogue, Kelly Stone, 225-6631

Congressional Academic Medicine Caucus, John Martin, 225-6356; Web, www.aamc.org/camc

Congressional Addiction, Treatment, and Recovery Caucus, Anne Sokolov, 225-5261; Web, http://timryan.house.gov/addiction-treatment-and-recovery-caucus

Congressional Affordable Medicine Caucus, Caroline Ehret, 225-2065

Congressional Albanian Issues Caucus, Travis Osen-foss, 225-2464; Web, http://engel.house.gov/index.cfm?sectionid=143

Congressional Algae Caucus, Daniel Tanner, 225-0508; Web, http://scottpeters.house.gov/congressional-algaecaucus

Congressional Aluminum Caucus, Ben Barasky, 225-6311; Web, www.aluminum.org/advocacy/congressional-aluminum-caucus

Congressional Anti-Bullying Caucus, Helen Chung, 225-2631; Web, https://antibullyingcaucus-honda.house.gov

Congressional Army Caucus, Steve Gilleland, 225-3864; http://carter.house.gov/house-army-caucus1

Congressional Army Aviation Caucus, Stephen Davis, 225-4801; Web, http://armyaviationcaucus-brooks.house.gov

Congressional Asia-Pacific Economic Cooperation (APEC) Caucus, Jennifer Weinhart, 225-4901

Congressional Asthma and Allergy Caucus, Tonya Winters, (800) 878-4403; Web, http://www.allergyasthmanetwork.org/advocacy/congressional-allergy-asthma-caucus

Congressional Automotive Caucus, Jennifer Perrino, 225-4146

Congressional Balanced Budget Amendment Caucus, Mike Cosio, 225-7882; Web, http://coffman.house.gov/legislation/committees-and-caucuses/congressional-balanced-budget-amendment-caucus

Congressional Baseball Caucus, Sean Dillon, 225-9896

Congressional Bicameral High-Speed & Intercity Passenger Rail Caucus (HSIPR), Colleen Bell, 225-3615; Web, http://highspeedintercitypassengerrailcaucus-slaughter.house.gov

Congressional Biofuels Caucus, Miles Chiotti, 225-2371

Congressional Biomedical Research Caucus, Sophie Trainor, 225-2002; http://www.coalitionforlifesciences.org/cbrc

Congressional Border Caucus, Norma Salazar, 225-2435

Congressional Border Security Caucus, Alyssa Tenna, 225-4236

Congressional Brain Injury Task Force, Arthur Mandel, 225-5751; Web, http://pascrell.house.gov/issues/brain-injury-task-force

Congressional Career & Technical Education Caucus, Matthew Brennan, 225-570; http://www.acteonline.org/caucus

Congressional Caucus for Competitiveness in Entertainment Technology (E-TECH), Seth Extein, 225-7931

Congressional Caucus for Effective Foreign Assistance, Cate Sadler, 225-2501; Web, http://crenshaw.house.gov/index.cfm/congressional-caucus-for-effective-foreign-assistance

Congressional Caucus for Middle Market Growth, Jesse Walls, 225-2015

Congressional Caucus on Black Men and Boys, Lavell Brown, 225-5006

Congressional Caucus on Brazil, Sophia Lafargue, 225-3461; Web, www.brazilcouncil.org/congressionalbrazilcaucus

Congressional Caucus on Community Health, Amy Kelbick, 225-5111

Congressional Caucus on Ethnic and Religious Freedom in Sri Lanka, Ani Tourmajn, 225-4671

Congressional Caucus on Foster Youth, Jasmine Velazquez, 225-7084; Web, http://fosteryouthcaucus-karenbass.house.gov

Congressional Caucus on India and Indian-Americans, Jeremy Woodrum, 225-3965

Congressional Caucus on Innovation and Entrepreneurship, Eve Lieberman, 225-2161

Congressional Caucus on Intellectual Property Promotion and Piracy Prevention, Jonathan Pawlow, 225-8901

Congressional Caucus on Korea, Annie Yea, 225-2965

Congressional Caucus on Long Range Strike, Matthew Silver, 225-2777

Congressional Caucus on Macedonia and Macedonian-Americans, Jeff Orzechowski, 225-2106

Congressional Caucus on Malaria and Neglected Tropical Diseases, Cate Sadler, 225-2501

Congressional Caucus on Modern Agriculture, Matt Reynolds, 225-6435

Congressional Caucus on Orphans and Vulnerable Children (OVC), Lena Smith, 225-4576

Congressional Caucus on Parkinson's Disease, Christina Parisi, 225-7944; Web, http://parkinsonsaction.org/our-work/congressional-caucus

Congressional Caucus on Public-Private Partnerships (Congressional P3 Caucus), Forrest McConnell, 225-3261

Congressional Caucus on Shellfish, Meridith Sebring, 225-3311

Congressional Caucus on the Deadliest Cancers, Hannah Murphy, 225-8104; Web, www.pancan.org/advocate/the-congressional-caucus-on-the-deadliest-cancers

Congressional Caucus on the European Union, Philip Bednarcyck, 225-3461; http://transatlanticrelations.org/content/partnerships-congressional-caucus-european-union

Congressional Caucus on the Netherlands, Raaed Haddad, 225-4401

Congressional Caucus on Prescription Drug Abuse, Jim Gordan, 225-8273

Congressional Caucus on Unmanned Systems, Brandon Eden, 225-1956

Congressional Caucus on U.S.-Turkish Relations and Turkish Americans, Melissa Buchanan, 225-3115

Congressional Caucus on Vietnam, Annie Yea, 225-2965

Congressional Caucus on Women in the Military, Annie Yea, 225-2965

Congressional Caucus on Women's Issues, Margaret McCarthy, 225-7163; http://www.womenspolicy.org/our-work/the-womens-caucus

Congressional Caucus on Youth Sports, Susan Manchester, 225-2676

Congressional Central Africa Caucus, Laura Hughes, 225-3106

Congressional Childhood Cancer Caucus, Kelly Cotner, 225-2401; Web, https://childhoodcancer-mccaul.house.gov

Congressional Children's Caucus, Lindsay Manson, 225-7761; Web, https://reichert.house.gov/issue/childrens-health-care-caucus

Congressional Children's Health Care Caucus, Lindsay Manson, 225-7761; Web, http://reichert.house.gov/issue/childrens-health-care-caucus

Congressional China Caucus, Eric Lindsey, 225-6365; https://forbes.house.gov/chinacaucus

Congressional Clean Water Caucus, Don Walker, 225-5435

Congressional Coal Caucus, Greta Joynes, 225-5271

Congressional Coast Guard Caucus, Neil McKiernan, 225-2076

Congressional Coastal Communities Caucus, Seth Dawson, 225-9740; Web, http://www.asbpa.org/news/CCCCTalking%20PointsFinal.pdf

Congressional Contaminated Drywall Caucus, John Thomas, 225-4215; Web, http://contaminateddrywallcaucus-rigell.house.gov

Congressional Creative Rights Caucus, Linda Shim, 225-5464; Web, http://creativerightscaucus-chu.house.gov

Congressional Cybersecurity Caucus, Nick Leiferson, 225-2735; Web, http://cybercaucus.langevin.house.gov

Congressional Cystic Fibrosis Caucus, Matt Powell, 225-3731; Web, www.cff.org/GetInvolved/Advocate/CFCaucus

Congressional Deaf Caucus, Claire Viall, 225-2305; Web, www.ceasd.org/child-first/congressional-caucus

Congressional Diabetes Caucus, Polly Webster, 225-4431; Web, https://diabetescaucus-degette.house.gov

Congressional Disaster Relief Caucus, Jordan Blumenthal, 225-3026

Congressional Down Syndrome Caucus, Steffanie Bezruki, 225-5905; Web, http://mcmorris.house.gov/down_syndrome_caucus

Congressional Electromagnetic Pulse (EMP) Caucus, Andrew Braun, 225-4576

Congressional Emergency Medical Services (EMS) Caucus, Samantha Dercher, 225-2472; Web, www.naemt.org/advocacyems-caucus

Congressional Ethiopia Caucus, Alice Lim, 225-2631

Congressional Everglades Caucus, Chris Sweet, 225-4211; Web, http://mariodiazbalart.house.gov/issues/everglades-restoration

Congressional Financial Protection and Life Insurance Caucus, Jim Notter, 225-4131

Congressional Food Safety Caucus, Elise Ackley, 225-3661

Congressional Fragile X Caucus, Scot Malvaney, 225-5031; Web, http://harper.house.gov/about-gregg/fragile-x

Congressional Friends of Jordan Caucus, Kaitlin Sighinolfi, 225-2031

Congressional Friends of Liechtenstein Caucus, Susey Davis, 225-4636

Congressional Friends of Panama Caucus, Sean Brady, 225-5015

Congressional Friends of Spain Caucus, Chris Sweet, 225-4211

Congressional Friends of Switzerland Caucus, Caitlin Hodgkins, 225-6101

Congressional Friends of Thailand Caucus, Kelsey Aulakh, 225-4811

Congressional Friends of Transatlantic Trade and Investment, Brandon Casey, 225-5601

Congressional Friends of Wales Caucus, Adam Harbison, 225-3861

Congressional Future Caucus, Anthony Ching, 225-4906; Web, www.millennialaction.org/congressional-future-caucus

Congressional Gaming Caucus, Scott Hughes, 225-3252; Web, https://heck.house.gov/issues/congressional-gaming-caucus

Congressional Global Health Caucus, Jenn Holcomb, 225-6631

Congressional Health Caucus, Danielle Steele, 225-7772; Web, http://health.burgess.house.gov

Congressional Heart and Stroke Coalition, Cate Benedetti, 225-3765; Web, www.heart.org/HEARTORG/Advocate/Congressional-Heart-and-Stroke-Coalition_UCM_452967_Article.jsp

Congressional Hepatitis Caucus, Helen Chung, 225-2631; Web, http://honda.house.gov/priorities/congressional-hepatitis-caucus

Congressional Higher Education Caucus, Erica Powell, 225-4011

Congressional History Caucus, Scott Stephanou, 225-2265; Web, http://historycoalition.org/congressional-history-caucus

Congressional Homelessness Caucus, Carrie Swope, 225-8885

Congressional House Manufacturing Caucus, Anne Sokolov, 225-5261; Web, http://timryan.house.gov/manufacturing-caucus

Congressional House Ocean Caucus, Troy Phillips, 225-2861; Web, http://farr.house.gov/index.php/oceancaucus

Congressional Human Trafficking Caucus, Christina Parisi, 225-7944; Web, http://maloney.house.gov/issues/womens-issues/human-trafficking

Congressional Immigration Reform Caucus, Tim Tarpley, 225-6565

Congressional International Anti-Piracy Caucus, Lindsay Yates, 205-5431; Web, http://goodlatte.house.gov/pages/anti-piracy-caucus

Congressional International Conservation Caucus, Blair Rotert, 225-4111; Web, http://royce.house.gov/internationalconservation

Congressional International Religious Freedom Caucus, Lena Smith, 225-4576

Congressional Invasive Species Caucus, Meredith Sebring, 225-3311

Congressional Israel Allies Caucus, Ellie Stern, 225-4576; Web, www.israelallies.org/usa/member_directory

Congressional Job Creators' Caucus, Ben Kochman, 226-7386

Congressional Joint Strike Fighter Caucus, Donald Davidson, 225-5071

Congressional Kidney Caucus, Matt Powell, 225-373; Web, https://www.kidney.org/content/congressional-kidney-caucus

Congressional Kids Safety Caucus, Alexander McIntyre, 225-2611

Congressional Kurdish-American Caucus, Eve Lieberman, 225-2161

Congressional Labor and Working Families Caucus, Andrew Noh, 225-6676; Web, http://lindasanchez.house.gov/index.php/issues-27713/labor-and-working-families-caucus

Congressional LGBT Equality Caucus, Eve Lieberman, 225-2161; Web, https://lgbt-polis.house.gov

Congressional Library of Congress Caucus, Megan Meadley, 225-4867

Congressional Liquefied Natural Gas (LNG) Export Caucus, Jeffrey Wilson, 225-7742

Congressional Lupus Caucus, Cate Sadler, 225-5792; Web, http://rooney.house.gov/legislation/congressional-lupus-caucus

Congressional Maker Caucus, Anne Sokolov, 225-5261; Twitter, @MakerCaucus

Congressional Media Fairness Caucus, James Danford, 225-4236; Web, http://lamarsmith.house.gov/issues/media-fairness caucus

Congressional Men's Health Caucus, Kayla Priehs, 225-2701

Congressional Military Mental Health Caucus, Anne Sokolov, 225-5261; Web, http://militarymentalhealthcaucus-ryan.house.gov

Congressional Modeling and Simulation Caucus, Eric Lindsey, 225-6365; Web, http://forbes.house.gov/biography/mscaucus.htm

Congressional Multiple Sclerosis Caucus, Danielle Steele, 225-7772

Congressional Native American Caucus, Holmes Whalen, 225-6886; Web, https://cole.house.gov/issue/native-americans

Congressional Natural Gas Caucus, John Busovsky, 225-5121; Web, https://thompson.house.gov/issue/natural-gas-caucus

Congressional Navy and Marine Corps Caucus, Ian Staples, 225-2040

Congressional Nepal Caucus, Cate Sadler, 225-2501; Web, http://crenshaw.house.gov/index.cfm/ander-crenshaw12345

Congressional Neuroscience Caucus, Kristen Donheffner, 225-4811; Web, http://blumenauer.house.gov/index.php?option=com_content&view=article&id=2395:neurosciece&catid=80&Itemid=239

Congressional Oral Health Caucus, Nathan Greene, 225-5531; Web, www.fnidcr.org/patient/oralHealthCaucus.html

Congressional Out of Poverty Caucus, Emma Mehrabi, 225-2661; Web, http://outofpovertycaucus-lee.house.gov

Congressional Peace Corps Caucus, Ana Sorrentino, 225-2861; Web, www.peacecorpsconnect.org/advocacy/the-peace-corps-caucus

Congressional Pollinator Protection Caucus, Tracey Chow, 225-4540

Congressional Ports-to-Plains Caucus, Coleman Garrison, 225-4005; Web, http://randy.house.gov/issue/transportation

Congressional Pro-Choice Caucus, Polly Webster, 225-4431

Congressional Progressive Caucus, Michael Darner, 225-2435; Web, http://cpc.grijalva.house.gov

Congressional Public Health Caucus, Kristen O'Neill, 225-1688; Web, www.coausphs.org/advocacy/public-health-caucus

Congressional Public Transport Caucus, Michael Mansour, 226-5136

Congressional Puget Sound Recovery Caucus, Seth Dawson, 225-9740; Web, http://dennyheck.house.gov/legislative-work/puget-sound-recovery

Congressional Range and Testing Center Caucus, Robert Cogan, 225-4231; Web, http://rangeandtestingcaucus-black.house.gov

Congressional Refinery Caucus, Richard England, 225-7576; Web, http://olson.house.gov/congressional-refinery-caucus

Congressional Research and Development Caucus, Catherine Knowles, 225-2571; Web, http://research caucus.org

Congressional Rural Caucus, Matt Reynolds, 225-6435; Web, http://ruralcaucus-adriansmith.house.gov

Congressional Rural Healthcare Coalition, Andrew Malcolm, 225-6730; Web, http://walden.house.gov/rural-health-care

Congressional Rural Housing Caucus, Roberto Haddad, 225-253; Web, ruralcaucus-adriansmith.house.gov

Congressional Safe Climate Caucus, Rachel Gentile, 225-7924; Web, safeclimatecaucus-lowenthal.house.gov

Congressional Science, Technology, Engineering and Mathematics (STEM) Education Caucus, Shawn Kimmel, 226-5701; Web, http://stemedcaucus2.org

Congressional Sharing Economy Caucus, Ellen Schrantz, 225-3906

Congressional Shipbuilding Caucus, Jamie Glines, 225-4261; Web, http://shipbuilding-wittman.house.gov

Congressional Skin Cancer Caucus, Ann Waller Curtis, 225-4311

Congressional Small Business Caucus, Dustin Sherer, 225-4761

Congressional Social Work Caucus, Ma Keifer, 225-2661; Web, http://socialworkcaucus-lee.house.gov

Congressional Spectrum Caucus, Megan Jackson, 225-3501

Congressional Student Athlete Protection Caucus, Anna Hevia, 225-6131; Web, https://cardenas.house.gov/congressional-student-athlete-protection-caucus

Congressional Steel Caucus, Megan Adamcweski, 225-2461; Web, http://visclosky.house.gov/legislative-work/congressional-steel-caucus

Congressional Task Force on Alzheimer's Disease, Brenden Chainey, 225-4001; Web, http://act.alz.org/site/PageNavigator/congressionaltaskforce

Congressional Task Force on Childhood Obesity, Sarah Nasta, 225-7032

Congressional Task Force on Terrorism and Unconventional Warfare, Clark Fonda, 223-1976; Web, http://pittenger.house.gov/NationalSecurity

Congressional Technology Transfer Caucus, Jeremy Pederson, 225-5755

Congressional Tourette Syndrome Caucus, Randy Wadkins, 225-3265; Web, http://cohen.house.gov/congressional-tourette-syndrome-caucus

Congressional Transparency Caucus, Joseph Bushong, 225-4061; Web, https://transparencycaucus-quigley.house.gov

Congressional Travel & Tourism Caucus, Joe Millado, 225-5755; Web, http://farr.house.gov/index.php/travelcaucus

Congressional U.S.–Lebanon Friendship Caucus, Ellen Schrantz, 225-3906

Congressional U.S.–Mexico Friendship Caucus, Camilla Vogt, 225-2161

Congressional Urban Caucus, Christian Pierre-Caneo, 225-4001; Web, http://fattah.house.gov/urban-caucus

Congressional Victims' Rights Caucus, Blair Bjellos, 225-6565; Web, http://vrc.poe.house.gov

Congressional Vision Caucus, Sergio Espinosa, 225-1688; Web, www.preventblindness.org/congressional-vision-caucus

Congressional Watchdog Caucus, Justin Vogt, 225-3531; Web, http://speier.house.gov/index.php?option=com_content&view=article&id=950&Itemid=96

Congressional Western Caucus, Landon Stropko, 225-2311; Web, https://westerncaucus-lummis.house.gov

Congressional Wildlife Refuge Caucus, Alex Eveland, 225-5506; Web, http://nationalwildliferefugeassociation.com/new-issues/refugecaucus.html

Congressional Women's High Tech Caucus, Reagan Payne, 225-2276

Crime Prevention and Youth Development Caucus, Anna Hevia, 225-6131; Web, http://crimeprevention andyouthdevelopmentcaucus-cardenas.house.gov

Crohn's and Colitis Caucus, Cate Sadler, 225-2501; Web, http://crenshaw.house.gov/index.cfm/ander-crenshaw123

Defense Communities Caucus, Andrew Franke, 225-6601; Web, www.defensecommunities.org/federal-outreach/defense-communities-caucus

Financial and Economic Literacy Caucus, Jesse Walls, 225-2015; Web, http://financialandeconomic literacycaucus-hinojosa.house.gov

Friends of Norway Caucus, Mike Stober, 225-2871; Web, www.norway.org/Embassy/washington/Friends-of-Norway-Caucus/#.VP3PnnzF-Gc

Friends of Trans-Pacific Partnership Caucus, Kaitlin Sighinolfi, 225-2031

German-American Caucus, Kerry O'Brien, 225-3111; Web, www.gabcwashington.com/page/the-german-american-congressional-caucus

GOP Doctors Caucus, Matt Meyer, 225-6356; Web, http://doctorscaucus.roe.house.gov

Historic Preservation Caucus, Vince Erfc, 225-4811; Web, www.preservationaction.org/resources/congress/caucus

House Auto Caucus, Jenny Perrino, 225-4146

House Baltic Caucus, Christina Cheshier, 225-4176; Web, http://housebalticcaucus.webs.com

House Liberty Caucus, Poppy Nelson, 225-3831

House Organic Caucus, Megan DeBates, 225-6416; Web, www.nationalorganiccoalition.org/organic-caucus

House Recycling Caucus, Ani Toumain, 225-4671; Web, www.isri.org/policy-regulations/advocacy/congressional-recycling-caucus#.VP3sr3zF-Gc

House Retirement Caucus, Isaac Fong, 225-5406

House Small Brewers Caucus, Megan DeBates, 225-6416; Web, http://smallbrewers.defazio.house.gov

Law Enforcement Caucus, Dylan Sodaro, 225-5751; Web, https://reichert.house.gov/issue/law-enforcement-caucus

Lyme Disease Caucus, Cate Benedetti, 225-3765; Web, http://chrissmith.house.gov/lymedisease

National Guard and Reserve Components Caucus, Patrick Large, 225-5772; Web, http://ngrcc-hunter.house.gov

National Marine Sanctuary Caucus, Eliot Crafton, 225-3601; Web, http://www.nmsfocean.org/national-marine-sanctuary-caucus

Northeast-Midwest (NEMW) Congressional Coalition, Sam Breene, 225-5406; Web, www.nemw.org/index.php/congressional-coalitions-and-task-forces/northeast-midwest-congressional-coalition

Republican Study Committee, Scott Parkinson, 226-9717; Web, http://rsc.flores.house.gov

Republican Women's Policy Committee, Blair Ellis, 225-4531; Web, https://republicanwomenspolicy committee-ellmers.house.gov

Sustainable Energy and Environment Coalition, Chris Rackens, 226-5034; Web, http://seec-israel.house.gov

SENATE CAUCUSES

Senate Auto Caucus, Zachary Rudisill, 224-3353

Senate Cancer Coalition, Megan Thompson, 224-3841

Senate Caucus on International Narcotics Control, Kelly Lieupo, 224-3841; Web, http://drugcaucus.senate.gov

Senate Cultural Caucus, Renee Bender, 224-3424

Senate Republican High Tech Task Force, Matthew Sandgren, 224-5251

Senate Western Caucus, Brian Clifford, 224-6441; Web, www.barrasso.senate.gov/public/index.cfm/senate-western-caucus

HOUSE AND SENATE CAUCUSES

Coalition for Autism Research and Education (CARE), Hannah Malvin, 225-2135; Web, http://doyle.house.gov/issue/autism-caucus

California Democratic Congressional Delegation, Martin Radosevich, 225-3072; Web, www.cadem.org/about/congress

Commission on Security and Cooperation in Europe (Helsinki Commission), Stacy Hope, 225-1901; Web, www.csce.gov

Congressional Air Force Caucus, Jessica Calio, 225-6465; Web, http://secure.afa.org/grl/caucus.asp

Congressional Arts Caucus, Cheryl Hoffman, 225-3615; Web, http://artscaucus-slaughter.house.gov

Congressional Asian Pacific American Caucus (CAPAC), Krystal Kaai, 225-5464; Web, http://capac-chu.house.gov

Congressional Bi-Partisan Privacy Caucus, Amy Murphy, 225-2002; Web, http://joebarton.house.gov/congressional-bipartisan-privacy-caucus

Congressional Black Caucus, Edward Hill, 225-3101; Web, http://cbc-butterfield.house.gov

Congressional Farmer Cooperative Caucus, Dennis D'Aquila, 224-2321; Web, www.ncfc.org/letters-testimony-comments/congressional-farmer-cooperative-caucus-members

Congressional Fire Services Caucus, Dylan Sadaro, 225-5751; Web, www.cfsi.org/congress_legislation/caucus.cfm

Congressional Fire Services Institute, William Webb, Executive Director, 371-1277; Web, www.cfsi.org

Congressional Hispanic Caucus, Valeria Carranza, 225-2410; Web, www.chci.org

Congressional HIV/AIDS Caucus, Ma Keifer, 225-2661; Web, http://hivaidscaucus-lee.house.gov

Congressional Internet Caucus, Branden Ritchie, 205-5741; Web, www.netcaucus.org

Congressional Long Island Sound Caucus, Eric Anthony, 225-3661

Congressional Veterans Jobs Caucus, Christopher Bennett, 225-2472; Web, www.manchin.senate.gov/public/index.cfm/congressional-veterans-jobs-caucus-members

United States Association of Former Members of Congress, Peter M. Weichlein, Chief Executive Officer, 222-0972; Web, http://usafmc.org

Ready Reference

Government Hotlines

DEPARTMENTS

Agriculture,
Fraud, waste, and abuse hotline, (800) 424-9121
Meat and poultry safety inquiries, (800) 674-6854

Commerce,
Export enforcement hotline, (800) 424-2980
Fraud, waste, and abuse hotline, (800) 424-5197
Trade Information Center, (800) 872-8723

Defense,
Army Department's Casualty and Mortuary Affairs
Information Center, (800) 626-3317
Fraud, waste, and abuse hotline, (800) 424-9098
Military OneSource, (800) 342-9647

Education,
Fraud, waste, and abuse hotline, (800) 647-8733
Student financial aid information, (800) 433-3243

Energy,
Energy Efficiency and Renewable Energy Information
Center, (877) 337-3463
Fraud, waste, mismanagement, and abuse hotline,
(800) 541-1625

Health and Human Services,
Child Welfare Information Gateway, (800) 394-3366
Fraud hotline, (800) 447-8477
General health information, (800) 336-4797
HIV/AIDS, STDs, and immunization information,
including pandemic flu, (800) 232-4636
Medicare hotline (including prescription drug discounts),
(800) 633-4227
National Adoption Center, (800) 862-3678
National Cancer Institute cancer information,
(800) 422-6237
National Runaway Safeline, (800) 786-2929
Traveler's health information, (800) 232-4636

Homeland Security,
Disaster assistance, (800) 621-3362
Fraud, abuse, and mismanagement, (800) 323-8603
Investigations Tip Line, (866) 347-2423
National Emergency Training Center, (800) 238-3358
Security breaches, hazardous material, chemical, and oil
spills, (202) 267-2675
U.S. Immigration and Customs Enforcement suspicious
activity (866) 347-2423, detainees' rights, (855) 448-6903

Housing and Urban Development,
Fair Housing Complaints, (800) 669-9777

Justice,
Americans With Disabilities Act information,
(800) 514-0301; TTY, (800) 514-0383
Arson hotline, (888) 283-3473
Bomb information hotline (ATF), (888) 283-2662
Fraud, abuse, or misconduct hotline, (800) 869-4499
Illegal firearms activity hotline, (800) 283-4867
National Criminal Justice Reference Service, (800) 851-3420
National Institute for Corrections Information Center,
(800) 877-1461
Stolen firearms hotline, (888) 930-9275
Unfair employment practices hotline (immigration
related), (800) 255-7688

Transportation,
Auto safety hotline, (800) 424-9393
Aviation safety hotline, (800) 255-1111
Federal Aviation Administration consumer hotline,
(866) 835-5322

Treasury,
Comptroller of the Currency customer assistance hotline,
(800) 613-6743
Fraud, waste, mismanagement, and abuse hotline (IRS
programs), (800) 366-4484
Identity theft hotline, (800) 908-4490
Tax forms, tax refund information, and general
information, (800) 829-3676
Tax refund status, (800) 829-1954
Taxpayer Advocate Service, (877) 777-4778
Taxpayer assistance, (800) 829-1040

Veterans Affairs,
Benefits hotline, (800) 827-1000
Debt Management Center, (800) 827-0648
Fraud, waste, abuse, and mismanagement hotline,
(800) 488-8244
Insurance policy information, (800) 669-8477

AGENCIES

Consumer Product Safety Commission,
Product safety information, (800) 638-2772

Environmental Protection Agency,
Asbestos and small business hotline, (800) 368-5888
Endangered species hotline, (800) 447-3813
National Lead Information Center, (800) 424-5323
National Pesticides Information Center, (800) 858-7378
National radon hotline, (800) 767-7236
Ozone Protection hotline, (800) 296-1996
Safe drinking water hotline, (800) 426-4791
Superfund hotline, (800) 424-9346; (703) 412-9810
in Washington
Wetlands information hotline, (800) 832-7828

Export-Import Bank,
Export finance hotline, (800) 565-3946;
(202) 565-3946 in Washington

Federal Deposit Insurance Corporation,
Banking complaints and inquiries, (877) 275-3342

Federal Election Commission,
Campaign finance law information, (202) 694-1100

General Services Administration,
Federal Citizen Information Center, (800) 333-4636

Office of Special Counsel,
Prohibited personnel practices information,
(800) 872-9855

Small Business Administration,
Fraud, waste, abuse, and mismanagement hotline,
(800) 767-0385
Small business assistance, (800) 827-5722

Social Security Administration,
Fraud and abuse hotline, (800) 269-0271
Social Security benefits (including Medicare) information,
(800) 772-1213

Directory of Government Information on the Internet

Listed below are Web addresses that lead to executive, legislative, and judicial information on the Internet. These links were active as of April 25, 2016. Government information can also be explored online through the www.usa.gov, which is the U.S. government's official Internet portal to Web pages for federal and state governments, the District of Columbia, and U.S. territories.

EXECUTIVE BRANCH

The White House

Main: www.whitehouse.gov
Twitter: @whitehouse
Facebook: www.facebook.com/WhiteHouse
News: www.whitehouse.gov/briefing-room
President's Bio: www.whitehouse.gov/administration/president-obama
Vice President's Bio: www.whitehouse.gov/administration/vice-president-biden
First Lady's Bio: www.whitehouse.gov/administration/first-lady-michelle-obama
Contacting the White House: www.whitehouse.gov/contact
Blog: www.whitehouse.gov/blog

Agriculture Dept.

Main: www.usda.gov
Twitter: @usda
Facebook: www.facebook.com/USDA
About the Agriculture Dept.: www.usda.gov/about_usda
News: www.usda.gov/newsroom
Secretary's Bio: www.usda.gov/wps/portal/usda/usdahome?contentid=bios_vilsack.xml&contentidonly=true
Employee Directory: http://dc-directory.hqnet.usda.gov/DLSNew/phone.aspx
Link to Regional Offices: www.usda.gov/wps/portal/usda/usdahome?navtype=MA&navid=AGENCIES_OFFICES_C
Department Budget: www.usda.gov/wps/portal/usda/usdahome?navid=BUDGET
Blog: http://blogs.usda.gov

Commerce Dept.

Main: www.commerce.gov
Twitter: @CommerceGov
Facebook: www.facebook.com/Commercegov
About the Commerce Dept.: www.commerce.gov/about-department-commerce
News: www.commerce.gov/news; www.youtube.com/commercenews

Secretary's Bio: www.commerce.gov/directory/pennypritzker
Employee Directory: http://dir.commerce.gov
Links to State and Regional Offices:
 Census Bureau: www.census.gov/regions
 Commerce Dept.: www.commerce.gov/about-commerce/services
 Economic Development Administration: www.eda.gov/contacts.htm
Department Budget: www.osec.doc.gov/bmi/budget
Blog: www.commerce.gov/blog
Photos: www.flickr.com/photos/commercegov

Defense Dept.

Main: www.defense.gov
Twitter: @deptofdefense
Facebook: www.facebook.com/DeptofDefense
About the Defense Dept.: www.defense.gov/about
News: www.defense.gov/news/articles.aspx
Secretary's Bio: www.defense.gov/bios/biographydetail.aspx?biographyid=365
Directory of Senior Defense Officials: www.defense.gov/home/top-leaders
Department Budget: http://comptroller.defense.gov
Live Blog: www.dodlive.mil
Video: www.youtube.com/deptofdefense

Education Dept.

Main: www.ed.gov
Twitter: @usedgov
Facebook: www.facebook.com/ED.gov
About the Education Dept.: www2.ed.gov/about/landing.jhtml
News: www2.ed.gov/news
Secretary's Bio: www2.ed.gov/news/staff/bios/king.html
Employee Directory: http://wdcrobcolp01.ed.gov/CFAPPS/employee_locator
State Contacts and Information: www2.ed.gov/about/contacts/state/index.html
Department Budget: www2.ed.gov/about/overview/budget
Blog: www.ed.gov/blog
Video: www.youtube.com/usedgov

Energy Dept.

Main: www.energy.gov
Twitter: @energy
Facebook: www.facebook.com/energygov
About the Energy Dept.: www.energy.gov/about
News: www.energy.gov/news
Secretary's Bio: http://energy.gov/contributors/dr-ernest-moniz
Employee Directory: http://energy.gov/phonebook
Link to Regional Offices: www.energy.gov/contact-us/mailing-addresses-and-information-numbers-operations-field-and-site-offices
Department Budget: http://energy.gov/budget-performance

Health and Human Services Dept.

Main: www.hhs.gov
Twitter: @HHSGov
Facebook: www.facebook.com/HHS
About the Health and Human Services Dept.: www.hhs.gov/about
News: www.hhs.gov/news
Secretary's Bio: www.hhs.gov/about/leadership/secretary/sylvia-mathews-burwell
Employee Directory: http://directory.psc.gov/employee.htm
Link to Regional Offices: www.hhs.gov/about/agencies/regional-offices
Department Budget: www.hhs.gov/budget

Homeland Security Dept.

Main: www.dhs.gov
Twitter: @DHSgov
Facebook: www.facebook.com/homelandsecurity
About the Homeland Security Dept.: www.dhs.gov/about-dhs
News: www.dhs.gov/news
Secretary's Bio: www.dhs.gov/secretary-jeh-johnson
Leadership Directory: www.dhs.gov/leadership
Links to Regional Offices:
    Federal Emergency Management Agency: www.fema.gov
    U.S. Citizenship and Immigration Services: www.uscis.gov
    U.S. Secret Service: www.secretservice.gov/field_offices.shtml
Department Budget: www.dhs.gov/dhs-budget
Video: www.youtube.com/ushomelandsecurity

Housing and Urban Development Dept.

Main: www.hud.gov
Twitter: @HUDgov
Facebook: www.facebook.com/HUD
About the Housing and Urban Development Dept.: www.hud.gov/about
News: http://portal.hud.gov/hudportal/HUD?src=/press
Interactive Self-Assessment Tool: http://makinghomeaffordable.gov

Secretary's Bio: http://portal.hud.gov/hudportal/HUD?src=/about/principal_staff/secretary_castro
Employee Directory: www5.hud.gov:63001/po/i/netlocator
Link to Regional Offices: http://portal.hud.gov/hudportal/HUD?src=/states
Department Budget: http://portal.hud.gov/hudportal/HUD?src=/program_offices/cfo/budget
Video: www.youtube.com/hudchannel

Interior Dept.

Main: www.doi.gov
Twitter: @Interior
Facebook: www.facebook.com/USInterior
About the Interior Dept.: www.doi.gov/whoweare
News: www.doi.gov/news
Secretary's Bio: www.doi.gov/whoweare/secretaryjewell
Employee Directory: www.doi.gov/employees
Links to Regional Offices:
    Bureau of Indian Affairs: www.bia.gov
    Bureau of Land Management: www.blm.gov
    Bureau of Ocean Energy Management: www.boem.gov
    Bureau of Reclamation: www.usbr.gov
    National Park Service: www.nps.gov
    Office of Surface Mining: www.osmre.gov
    U.S. Fish and Wildlife Service: www.fws.gov
    U.S. Geological Survey: www.usgs.gov
Department Budget: www.doi.gov/budget
Video: www.youtube.com/USInterior

Justice Dept.

Main: www.justice.gov
Twitter: @TheJusticeDept
Facebook: www.facebook.com/DOJ
About the Justice Dept.: www.justice.gov/about/about.html
News: www.justice.gov/briefing-room.html
Attorney General's Bio: www.justice.gov/ag/meet-attorney-general
Links to Regional Offices:
    Drug Enforcement Administration: www.justice.gov/dea/contactinfo.htm
    Federal Bureau of Investigation: www.fbi.gov/contact-us/contact-us
    Federal Bureau of Prisons: www.bop.gov/about/contactus.jsp
Department Budget: www.justice.gov/about/bpp.htm
Video: www.youtube.com/thejusticedepartment

Labor Dept.

Main: www.dol.gov
Twitter: @USDOL
Facebook: www.facebook.com/departmentoflabor
About the Labor Dept.: www.dol.gov/dol/aboutdol/main.htm
News: www.dol.gov/dol/media
Secretary's Bio: www.dol.gov/_sec/welcome.htm

Employee Directory: www.dol.gov/dol/contact-phonekeypersonnel.htm
Links to Regional Offices:
    Bureau of Labor Statistics: www.bls.gov/bls/regnhome.htm
    Employment and Training Administration: http://wdr.doleta.gov/contacts
    Occupational Safety and Health Administration: www.osha.gov/dcsp/osp/index.html
Department Budget: www.dol.gov/dol/aboutdol/#budget
Video: www.youtube.com/usdepartmentoflabor

State Dept.

Main: www.state.gov
Twitter: @StateDept
Facebook: www.facebook.com/usdos
Mobile: http://m.state.gov
About the State Dept.: www.state.gov/aboutstate
News: www.state.gov/media
Secretary's Bio: www.state.gov/secretary
Employee Directory: www.state.gov/m/a/gps/directory
Link to Regional Offices: www.state.gov/ofm/ro
    Passport Services: http://iafdb.travel.state.gov
Department Budget: www.state.gov/s/d/rm/rls
Video: www.youtube.com/statevideo

Transportation Dept.

Main: www.dot.gov
Twitter: @usdot
Facebook: www.facebook.com/USDOT
About the Transportation Dept.: www.dot.gov/about.html
News: www.dot.gov/briefing-room.html
Secretary's Bio: www.dot.gov/secretary
Links to Regional Offices:
    Federal Aviation Administration: www.faa.gov/about/office_org
    Federal Highway Administration: www.fhwa.dot.gov/field.html
    Federal Railroad Administration: www.fra.dot.gov/Page/P0001
    Federal Transit Administration: www.fta.dot.gov/12926.html
    Maritime Administration: www.marad.dot.gov
    National Highway Traffic Safety Administration: www.nhtsa.gov/nhtsa/whatis/regions
Department Budget: www.dot.gov/budget
Video: www.youtube.com/user/usdotgov

Treasury Dept.

Main: www.treasury.gov/
Twitter: @USTreasury
Facebook: www.facebook.com/ustreasury
About the Treasury Dept.: www.treasury.gov/about
News: www.treasury.gov/press-center
Interactive Self-Assessment Tool: www.makinghomeaffordable.gov
Secretary's Bio: www.treasury.gov/about/Pages/Secretary.aspx

Directory of Treasury Officials: www.treasury.gov/about/organizational-structure/Pages/officials.aspx
Links to Regional Offices:
    Comptroller of the Currency: www.occ.treas.gov/about/organization/index-organization.html
    Financial Management Service: http://fms.treas.gov/aboutfms/locations.html
    Internal Revenue Service: www.irs.gov/uac/Contact-Your-Local-IRS-Office-1
    Veterans Benefits Administration: http://benefits.va.gov/benefits/offices.asp
Department Budget: www.treasury.gov/about/budget-performance
Video: www.youtube.com/USTreasGov

Veterans Affairs Dept.

Main: www.va.gov
Twitter: @DeptVetAffairs
Facebook: www.facebook.com/VeteransAffairs
About the Veterans Affairs Dept.: www.va.gov/about_va
News: www.va.gov/opa/pressrel
Secretary's Bio: www.va.gov/opa/bios/secretary.asp
Link to Regional Offices: www2.va.gov/directory/guide/home.asp?isFlash=1
Department Budget: www.va.gov/budget/products.asp
Blog: www.blogs.va.gov/VAntage
Video: www.youtube.com/deptvetaffairs

LEGISLATIVE BRANCH

Congress

Biographical Directory of the U.S. Congress: http://bioguide.congress.gov/biosearch/biosearch.asp
Election Statistics (1920–present): http://clerk.house.gov/member_info/electionInfo
How Laws Are Made: http://thomas.loc.gov/home/lawsmade.toc.html
Legislative Process: www.rules.house.gov; www.congress.gov
U.S. Constitution: www.archives.gov/exhibits/charters/constitution_transcript.html

House

Main: www.house.gov
Twitter: @HouseFloor
Schedule: www.house.gov/legislative/
Daily Business: http://clerk.house.gov/floorsummary/floor.aspx
Committees: http://clerk.house.gov/committee_info/commact.aspx
Committee Hearing Schedules: http://docs.house.gov/Committee/Calendar/ByWeek.aspx
Pending Business: http://clerk.house.gov/floorsummary/floor.aspx
Link to Roll Call Votes: http://clerk.house.gov/legislative/legvotes.aspx
Leadership: www.house.gov/leadership
Media Galleries: www.house.gov/content/media

Government of the United States

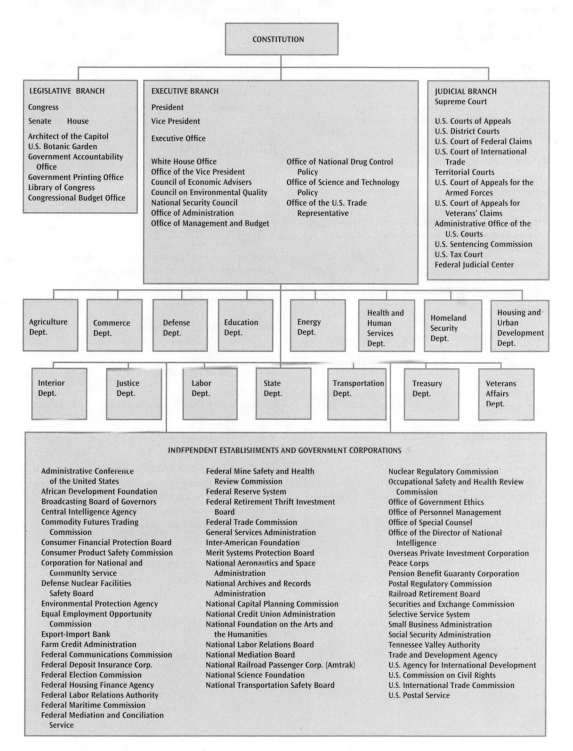

CONSTITUTION

LEGISLATIVE BRANCH

Congress

Senate   House

Architect of the Capitol
U.S. Botanic Garden
Government Accountability
    Office
Government Printing Office
Library of Congress
Congressional Budget Office

EXECUTIVE BRANCH

President

Vice President

Executive Office

White House Office
Office of the Vice President
Council of Economic Advisers
Council on Environmental Quality
National Security Council
Office of Administration
Office of Management and Budget

Office of National Drug Control
    Policy
Office of Science and Technology
    Policy
Office of the U.S. Trade
    Representative

JUDICIAL BRANCH
Supreme Court

U.S. Courts of Appeals
U.S. District Courts
U.S. Court of Federal Claims
U.S. Court of International
    Trade
Territorial Courts
U.S. Court of Appeals for the
    Armed Forces
U.S. Court of Appeals for
    Veterans' Claims
Administrative Office of the
    U.S. Courts
U.S. Sentencing Commission
U.S. Tax Court
Federal Judicial Center

Agriculture Dept.

Commerce Dept.

Defense Dept.

Education Dept.

Energy Dept.

Health and Human Services Dept.

Homeland Security Dept.

Housing and Urban Development Dept.

Interior Dept.

Justice Dept.

Labor Dept.

State Dept.

Transportation Dept.

Treasury Dept.

Veterans Affairs Dept.

INDEPENDENT ESTABLISHMENTS AND GOVERNMENT CORPORATIONS

Administrative Conference
    of the United States
African Development Foundation
Broadcasting Board of Governors
Central Intelligence Agency
Commodity Futures Trading
    Commission
Consumer Financial Protection Board
Consumer Product Safety Commission
Corporation for National and
    Community Service
Defense Nuclear Facilities
    Safety Board
Environmental Protection Agency
Equal Employment Opportunity
    Commission
Export-Import Bank
Farm Credit Administration
Federal Communications Commission
Federal Deposit Insurance Corp.
Federal Election Commission
Federal Housing Finance Agency
Federal Labor Relations Authority
Federal Maritime Commission
Federal Mediation and Conciliation
    Service

Federal Mine Safety and Health
    Review Commission
Federal Reserve System
Federal Retirement Thrift Investment
    Board
Federal Trade Commission
General Services Administration
Inter-American Foundation
Merit Systems Protection Board
National Aeronautics and Space
    Administration
National Archives and Records
    Administration
National Capital Planning Commission
National Credit Union Administration
National Foundation on the Arts and
    the Humanities
National Labor Relations Board
National Mediation Board
National Railroad Passenger Corp. (Amtrak)
National Science Foundation
National Transportation Safety Board

Nuclear Regulatory Commission
Occupational Safety and Health Review
    Commission
Office of Government Ethics
Office of Personnel Management
Office of Special Counsel
Office of the Director of National
    Intelligence
Overseas Private Investment Corporation
Peace Corps
Pension Benefit Guaranty Corporation
Postal Regulatory Commission
Railroad Retirement Board
Securities and Exchange Commission
Selective Service System
Small Business Administration
Social Security Administration
Tennessee Valley Authority
Trade and Development Agency
U.S. Agency for International Development
U.S. Commission on Civil Rights
U.S. International Trade Commission
U.S. Postal Service

Senate

Main: www.senate.gov
Twitter: @SenateFloor
Annual Calendar: www.republican.senate.gov/public/
index.cfm/senate-calendar
Daily Calendar: www.senate.gov/legislative/LIS/executive_
calendar/xcalv.pdf
Committees: www.senate.gov/pagelayout/committees/d_
three_sections_with_teasers/committees_home.htm
Committee Hearing Schedules: www.senate.gov/
pagelayout/committees/b_three_sections_with_
teasers/committee_hearings.htm
Link to Roll Call Votes: www.senate.gov/pagelayout/
legislative/a_three_sections_with_teasers/votes.htm
Leadership: www.senate.gov/pagelayout/senators/a_
three_sections_with_teasers/leadership.htm
Media Galleries: www.senate.gov/galleries
Executive Nominations: www.senate.gov/pagelayout/
legislative/a_three_sections_with_teasers/
nominations.htm

Government Accountability Office

Main: www.gao.gov
Twitter: @usgao
About the Government Accountability Office:
www.gao.gov/about/index.html
Comptroller General's Bio: www.gao.gov/cghome/
gdbiog.html
GAO Reports: www.gao.gov/docsearch/repandtest.html
Media: www.gao.gov/multimedia/video

Government Printing Office

Main: www.gpo.gov
Twitter: @usgpo
Facebook: www.facebook.com/USGPO
About the Government Printing Office: www.gpo.gov/
about
Video: www.youtube.com/gpoprinter

Library of Congress

Main: www.loc.gov/index.html
Twitter: @librarycongress
Facebook: www.facebook.com/libraryofcongress
Online Catalog: http://catalog.loc.gov
Thomas (Legislative Information on the Internet):
http://thomas.loc.gov
Copyright Office: www.copyright.gov
Video: www.youtube.com/libraryofcongress

JUDICIAL BRANCH

The Supreme Court

Main: www.supremecourt.gov
Twitter: @USSupremeCourt
About the Supreme Court: www.supremecourt.gov/
about/about.aspx
News: www.supremecourt.gov/opinions/slipopinions.aspx
Biographies of the Justices: www.supremecourt.gov/
about/biographies.aspx
Supreme Court Docket: www.supremecourt.gov/docket/
docket.aspx
Visiting the Supreme Court: www.supremecourt.gov/
visiting/visiting.aspx

Federal Judicial Center

Main: www.fjc.gov
History: www.fjc.gov/history/home.nsf

U.S. Federal Courts

Main: www.uscourts.gov
About the U.S. Federal Courts: www.uscourts.gov/
FederalCourts.aspx
News: http://news.uscourts.gov
Publications: www.uscourts.gov/FederalCourts/
PublicationsAndReports.aspx

Governors and Other State Officials

Political affiliations, when available, are indicated by (D) for Democrat, (R) for Republican, and (I) for Independent. For key officials of the District of Columbia and other Washington-area localities, see page 338.

Alabama   Web, www.alabama.gov

Gov. Robert Bentley (R), State Capitol, 600 Dexter Ave., #N-104, Montgomery 36130; (334) 242-7100; Fax, (334) 353-0004; Web, www.governor.alabama.gov; Facebook, www.facebook.com/GovernorRobertBentley; Twitter, @GovernorBentley

Lt. Gov. Kay Ivey (R), Alabama State House, 11 S. Union St., #725, Montgomery 36130; (334) 242-7900; Fax, (334) 242-4661; Web, www.ltgov.alabama.gov; Email, kay.ivey@ltgov.alabama.gov

Secy. of State John H. Merrill (R), State Capitol Bldg., 600 Dexter Ave., #S-105, Montgomery 36130; P.O. Box 5616, Montgomery 36103-5616; (334) 242-7200; Fax, (334) 242-4993; Web, www.sos.alabama.gov

Atty. Gen. Luther Strange (R), Alabama State House, 501 Washington Ave., Montgomery 36104; P.O. Box 300152, Montgomery 36130-0152; (334) 242-7300; Fax, (334) 242-4891; Web, www.ago.state.al.us

Treasurer Young Boozer (R), State Capitol, 600 Dexter Ave., #S-106, Montgomery 36104; (334) 242-7500; Fax, (334) 242-7592; Web, www.treasury.state.al.us; Email, alatreas@treasury.alabama.gov

In Washington, DC: Jill Boxler, Federal Relations Director, Washington Office of the Governor, State of Alabama, 444 N. Capitol St. N.W., #382A, 20001; (202) 220-1379

Alaska   Web, www.alaska.gov

Gov. Bill Walker (I), State Capitol, 3rd Floor, P.O. Box 110001, Juneau 99811-0001; (907) 465-3500; Fax, (907) 465-3532; Web, www.gov.alaska.gov; Facebook, www.facebook.com/Governor.BillWalker; Twitter, @AkGovBillWalker

Lt. Gov. Byron Mallott (D), State Capitol, 3rd Floor, Juneau 99811-0015; (907) 465-3520; Fax, (907) 465-5400; Web, www.ltgov.alaska.gov

(No office of Secretary of State)

Atty. Gen. Craig W. Richards (R), P.O. Box 110300, Juneau 99811-0300; (907) 465-3600; Fax, (907) 465-2075; Web, www.law.alaska.gov; Email, attorney.general@alaska.gov

In Washington, DC: Nathan Butzlaff, Director, Washington, Office of the Governor, State of Alaska, 444 N. Capitol St. N.W., #336, 20001-1512; (202) 624-5988; Fax, (202) 624-5857

Arizona   Web, www.az.gov

Gov. Doug Ducey (R), State Capitol, 1700 W. Washington St., 9th Floor, Phoenix 85007; (602) 542-4331; Fax, (602) 542-1381; Toll-free (in-state only), (800) 253-0883; Web, www.azgovernor.gov; Facebook, www.facebook.com/dougducey; Twitter, @DougDucey

(No office of Lieutenant Governor)

Secy. of State Michele Reagan (R), State Capitol, 1700 W. Washington St., 7th Floor, Phoenix 85007-2888; (602) 542-4285; Fax, (602) 542-1575; Web, www.azsos.gov

Atty. Gen. Mark Brnovich (R), 1275 W. Washington St., Phoenix 85007-2926; (602) 542-5025; Fax, (602) 542-4085; Toll-free (in-state only), (800) 352-8431; Web, www.azag.gov

Treasurer Jeff DeWit (R), 1700 W. Washington St., 1st Floor, Phoenix 85007; (602) 604-7800; Fax, (602) 542-7176; Toll-free, (877) 365-8310; Web, www.aztreasury.gov; Email, info@aztreasury.gov

Washington, DC Representative: Danny Seiden Deputy Chief of Staff, State Capitol, 1700 W. Washington, Phoenix 85007; (602) 542-3439

Arkansas   Web, www.arkansas.gov

Gov. Asa Hutchinson (R), State Capitol, 500 Woodlane Ave., #250, Little Rock 72201; (501) 682-2345; Fax, (501) 682-3597; Toll-free, (877) 727-3468; TTY, (501) 682-7515; www.governor.arkansas.gov; Facebook, www.facebook.com/asaforarkansas; Twitter, @AsaHutchinson

Lt. Gov. Tim Griffin (R), State Capitol, #270, Little Rock 72201-1061; (501) 682-2144; Fax, (501) 682-2894; Web, www.ltgovernor.arkansas.gov; Email, lg.staff@arkansas.gov

Secy. of State Mark Martin (R), State Capitol, #256, Little Rock 72201-1094; (501) 682-1010; Fax, (501) 682-3510; Web, www.sos.arkansas.gov; Email, generalinfo@sos.arkansas.gov

Atty. Gen. Leslie C. Rutledge (R), Tower Bldg., 323 Center St., #200, Little Rock 72201-2610; (501) 682-2007; Fax, (501) 682-8084; Toll-free, (800) 482-8982; Web, www.ag.arkansas.gov

Treasurer Dennis Milligan (R), State Capitol, #220, Little Rock 72201; (501) 682-5888; Fax, (501) 682-9692; Web, www.artreasury.gov; Email, info@artreasury.gov

Washington, DC Representative: Michael Lamoureux, Chief of Staff, Office of the Governor, State Capitol Bldg., Little Rock, AK 72201; (501) 682-2345

California   Web, www.ca.gov

Gov. Edmund G. (Jerry) Brown Jr. (D), State Capitol, #1173, Sacramento 95814; (916) 445-2841; Fax, (916) 558-3160; TTY (916) 464-1580; Web, www.gov.ca.gov;

Email, stateinformation@state.ca.gov; Facebook, www.facebook.com/jerrybrown; Twitter, @JerryBrownGov

Lt. Gov. Gavin Newsom (D), State Capitol, #1114, Sacramento 95814; (916) 445-8994; Fax, (916) 323-4998; Web, www.ltg.ca.gov

Secy. of State Alex Padilla (D), 1500 11th St., #600, Sacramento 95814; (916) 653-6814; Fax, (916) 653-4795; Web, www.sos.ca.gov; Email, secretary.padilla@sos.ca.gov

Atty. Gen. Kamala D. Harris (D), 1300 T St., Sacramento 95814-2929; P.O. Box 944255, Sacramento 94244-2550; (916) 322-3360; Fax, (916) 323-5341 Toll-free, (800) 952-5225; TTY, (800) 735-2929; TTY Spanish, (800) 855-3000; Web, www.oag.ca.gov

Treasurer John Chiang (D), 915 Capitol Mall, #110, C-15, Sacramento 95814; (916) 653-2995; Fax, (916) 653-3125; Web, www.treasurer.ca.gov

In Washington, DC: Katie Mathews, Deputy Director, Washington Office of the Governor, State of California, 444 N. Capitol St. N.W., #134, 20001; (202) 624-5270; Fax, (202) 624-5280

Colorado   Web, www.colorado.gov

Gov. John Hickenlooper (D), 136 State Capitol, Denver 80203; (303) 866-2471; Fax, (303) 866-2003; Web, www.colorado.gov/governor; Facebook, www.facebook.com/JohnHickenlooper; Twitter, @hickforco

Lt. Gov. Joseph Garcia (D), 130 State Capitol, Denver 80203; (303) 866-2087; Fax, (303) 866-5469; Web, www.colorado.gov/ltgovernor

Secy. of State Wayne W. Williams (R), 1700 Broadway, #200, Denver 80290; (303) 894-2200; Fax, (303) 869-4860; Web, www.sos.state.co.us

Atty. Gen. Cynthia H. Coffman (R), 1300 Broadway, 10th Floor, Denver 80203; (720) 508-6000; Fax, (720) 508-6030; Web, www.coloradoattorneygeneral.gov; Email, attorney.general@state.co.us

Treasurer Walker Stapleton (R), 140 State Capitol, Denver 80203; (303) 866-2441; Fax, (303) 866-2123; Web, www.colorado.gov/treasury

In Washington, DC: Jena Griswold, Washington Director, Office of the Governor State of Colorado, 444 N. Capitol St., #314, 20001; (202) 624-5278

Connecticut   Web, www.ct.gov

Gov. Dannel Malloy (D), State Capitol, 210 Capitol Ave., #202, Hartford 06106; (860) 566-4840; Fax, (860) 524-7395; Toll-free, (800) 406-1527; TTY, (860) 524-7397; Web, www.governor.ct.gov; Facebook, www.facebook.com/GovMalloyOffice; Twitter, @GovMalloyOffice

Lt. Gov. Nancy Wyman (D), State Capitol, 210 Capitol Ave., #304, Hartford 06106; (860) 524-7384; Fax, (860) 524-7304; Toll-free, (866) 712-6998; TTY, (860) 524-7397; Web, www.ct.gov/LtGovernor; Email, ltgovernor.wyman@ct.gov

Secy. of State Denise Merrill (D), 30 Trinity St., Hartford 06106; (860) 509-6200; Fax, (860) 509-6209; Web, www.sots.ct.gov

Atty. Gen. George C. Jepsen (D), 55 Elm St., Hartford 06106; (860) 808-5318; Fax, (860) 808-5387; Web, www.ct.gov/ag

Treasurer Denise L. Nappier (D), 55 Elm St., Hartford 06106-1773; (860) 702-3010; Fax, (860) 702-3043; Information, (860) 702-3000; Toll-free, (800) 618-3404; Web, www.ott.ct.gov

In Washington, DC: Dan DeSimone, Director, Washington Office of the Governor, State of Connecticut, 444 N. Capitol St. N.W., #317, 20001; (202) 403-8654

Delaware   Web, http://delaware.gov

Gov. Jack A. Markell (D), 150 Martin Luther King Jr. Blvd. South, 2nd Floor, Dover 19901; (302) 744-4101; Fax, (302) 739-2775; Web, www.governor.delaware.gov; Facebook,www.facebook.com/GovernorMarkell; Twitter, @GovernorMarkell

Lt. Gov. Vacant (D), Tatnall Bldg., 3rd Floor, Dover 19901; (302) 744-4333; Fax, (302) 739-6965

Secy. of State Jeffrey W. Bullock (D), 401 Federal St., #3, Dover 19901; (302) 739-4111; Fax, (302) 577-2694; Web, www.sos.delaware.gov

Atty. Gen. Matt Denn (D), Carvel State Office Bldg., 820 N. French St., Wilmington 19801; (302) 577-8400; Fax, (302) 577-6630; TTY (302) 577-5783; Web, www.attorneygeneral.delaware.gov; Email, Attorney.General@state.de.us

Treasurer Ken Simpler (D), 820 Silver Lake Blvd., #100, Dover 19904; (302) 672-6700; Fax, (302) 739-5635; Web, treasurer.delaware.gov; Email, statetreasurer@state.de.us

In Washington, DC: Garth Spencer, Director, Washington Office of the Governor, State of Delaware, 444 N. Capitol St. N.W., #230, 20001; (202) 624-7724; Fax, (202) 624-5495

Florida   Web, www.flgov.com

Gov. Rick Scott (R), The Capitol, 400 S. Monroe St., Tallahassee 32399-0001; (850) 488-7146; Fax, (850) 488-4042; TTY, (850) 922-7795; Web, www.flgov.com; Facebook, www.facebook.com/scottforflorida; Twitter, @flgovscott

Lt. Gov. Carlos Lopez-Cantera (R), The Capitol, 400 S. Monroe St., PL-05, Tallahassee 32399-0001; (850) 717-9331; Fax, (850) 487-0830; Web, www.flgov.com

Secy. of State Kenneth Detzner (R), R.A. Gray Bldg., 500 S. Bronough, #15, Tallahassee 32399-0250; (850) 245-6500; Fax, (850) 245-6125; Web, www.dos.myflorida.com; Email, SecretaryofState@DOS.MyFlorida.com

Atty. Gen. Pam Bondi (R), The Capitol, PL-01, 500 S. Bronough St., Tallahassee 32399-1050; (850) 414-3300; Fax, (850) 410-1630; Web, www.myfloridalegal.com

Chief Financial Officer Jeff Atwater (R), 200 E. Gaines St., Tallahassee 32399-0300; (850) 413-3089; Fax, (850) 413-4993; Web; www.myfloridacfo.com

In Washington, DC: Chris Hartline, DC Liaison, Washington Office, State of Florida, 444 N. Capitol St. N.W., #349, 20001; (202) 624-5885; Fax, (202) 624-5886

Georgia   Web, www.georgia.gov

Gov. Nathan Deal (R), 111 State Capitol, 206 Washington St., Atlanta 30334; Press, Brian Robinson, (404) 656-1776; Fax, (404) 657-7332; Web, www.gov.georgia.gov; Facebook, www.facebook.com/GovernorDeal; Twitter, @GovernorDeal

Lt. Gov. Casey Cagle (R), 240 State Capitol, Atlanta 30334; (404) 656-5030; Fax, (404) 656-6739; Web, www.ltgov.georgia.gov

Secy. of State Brian Kemp (R), 214 State Capitol Atlanta 30334; (404) 656-2881; Fax, (404) 656-0513; Web, www.sos.ga.gov

Atty. Gen. Sam Olens (R), 40 Capitol Square S.W., Atlanta 30334; (404) 656-3300; Fax, (404) 657-8733; Web, www.law.ga.gov; Email, AGOlens@law.ga.gov

Treasurer Steve McCoy (R), 200 Piedmont Ave., West Tower, #1204, Atlanta 30334; (404) 656-2168; Fax, (404) 656-9048; Web, www.ost.georgia.gov; Email, ostweb@treasury.ga.gov

In Washington, DC: Todd Smith, Washington Office of the Governor, State of Georgia, 1455 Pennsylvania Ave. N.W., #400, 20004; (202) 652-2299; Fax, (202) 347-1142

Hawaii   Web, www.hawaii.gov

Gov. David Ige (D), State Capitol, 415 S. Beretania St., Honolulu 96013, (808) 586-0034; Fax, (808) 586-0006; Web, www.governor.hawaii.gov; Facebook, www.facebook.com/GovernorIge; Twitter, @GovHawaii

Lt. Gov. Shan S. Tsutsui (D), State Capitol, 415 S. Beretania St., Honolulu 96813; (808) 586-0255; Fax, (808) 586-0231; Web, www.ltgov.hawaii.gov; Email, Shan.Tsutsui@hawaii.gov

(No office of Secretary of State)

Atty. Gen. Douglas Chin (D), 425 Queen St., Honolulu 96813; (808) 586-1500; Fax, (808) 586-1239; Web, www.ag.hawaii.gov; Email, hawaiiag@hawaii.gov

Budget and Finance Director Wesley Machida (D), 1 Capitol District Bldg., 250 S. Hotel St., Honolulu 96813; P.O. Box 150, Honolulu 96810; (808) 586-1518; Fax, (808) 586-1976; Web, www.budget.hawaii.gov; Email, hi.budgetandfinance@hawaii.gov

Washington, DC Representative: Elizabeth Kim, Special Advisor, State Capitol, Executive Chambers, Honolulu 96813; (808) 586-0034

Idaho   Web, www.state.id.us

Gov. C. L. (Butch) Otter (R), State Capitol, West Wing, 2nd Floor, Boise 83720-0034; (208) 334-2100; Fax, (208) 334-3454; Web, www.gov.idaho.gov; Facebook, www.facebook.com/Governor-C-L-Butch-Otter-292986829831; Twitter, @ButchOtter

Lt. Gov. Brad Little (R), State Capitol, #225, Boise 83720-0057; (208) 334-2200; Fax, (208) 334-3259; Web, www.lgo.idaho.gov; Email, info@lgo.idaho.gov

Secy. of State Lawerence Denney (R), 700 W. Jefferson, #E205, P.O. Box 83720, Boise 83720-0080; (208) 334-2300; Fax, (208) 334-2282; Web, www.sos.idaho.gov

Atty. Gen. Lawrence G. Wasden (R), 700 W. Jefferson St., #210, P.O. Box 83720, Boise 83720-0010, (208) 334-2400; Fax, (208) 854-8071; Web, www.ag.idaho.gov

Treasurer Ron G. Crane (R), 700 W. Jefferson St., #E126, P.O. Box 83720, Boise 83720; (208) 334-3200; Fax, (208) 332-2959; Web, www.sto.idaho.gov

Washington, DC Representative: David Hensley, Chief of Staff, 700 W. Jefferson St., 2nd Floor West Wing, Boise 83702; (208) 854-3005

Illinois   Web, www.illinois.gov

Gov. Bruce Rauner (R), 207 State House, Springfield 62706; (217) 782-0244; TTY, (888) 261-3336; Web, www.illinois.gov/gov; Facebook, www.facebook.com/GovRauner; Twitter, @GovRauner

Lt. Gov. Evelyn Sanguinetti (D), 214 State House, Springfield 62706; (217) 558-3085; Fax, (217) 558-3094; Web, www.illinois.gov/ltg

Secy. of State Jesse White (D), 213 State Capitol Springfield 62756; (217) 785-3000; Fax, (217) 785-0358; Web, www.ilsos.gov

Atty. Gen. Lisa Madigan (D), 500 S. 2nd St., Springfield 62706-1771; (217) 782-1090; TTY, (877) 844-5461; Web, www.illinoisattorneygeneral.gov

Treasurer Michael W. Frerichs (R), Capitol Bldg., 219 State House, Springfield 62706-1000; (217) 782-2211; Fax, (217) 785-2777; Web, www.treasurer.il.gov

In Washington, DC: Kathy Lydon, Director, Washington Office of the Governor, State of Illinois, 444 N. Capitol St. N.W., #400, 20001; (202) 624-7760; Fax, (202) 724-0689

Indiana   Web, www.in.gov

Gov. Mike Pence (R), 206 State House, 200 W. Washington St., Indianapolis 46204; (317) 232-4567; Web, www.in.gov/gov; Facebook, www.facebook.com/GovernorMikePence; Twitter, @GovPenceIN

Lt. Gov. Sue Ellspermann (R), 333 State House, 200 W. Washington St., Indianapolis 46204-2790; (317) 232-4545; Fax, (317) 232-4788; Web, www.in.gov/lg

Secy. of State Connie Lawson (R), 200 W. Washington St., #201, Indianapolis 46204-2790; (317) 232-6531; Fax, (317) 233-3283; Web, www.in.gov/sos

Atty. Gen. Greg Zoeller (R), Indiana Government Center South, 302 W. Washington St., 5th Floor, Indianapolis 46204-2770; (317) 232-6201; Fax, (317) 232-7979; Web, www.in.gov/attorneygeneral

Treasurer Kelly Mitchell (R), 242 State House, 200 W. Washington St., Indianapolis 46204; (317) 232-6386; Fax, (317) 233-1780; Web, www.in.gov/tos; Email, tosstaff@tos.state.in.us

In Washington, DC: Josh Pitcock, Federal Representative, Washington Office of the Governor, State of Indiana, 444 N. Capitol St. N.W., #411, 20001; (202) 624-1474; Fax, (202) 833-1587

Iowa   Web, www.iowa.gov

Gov. Terry Branstad (R), State Capitol, 1007 E. Grand Ave., Des Moines 50319; Press, Tim Albrecht, (515)

281-5211; Fax, (515) 725-3527; Web, www.governor.iowa.gov; Facebook, www.Facebook.com/TerryBranstad; Twitter, @TerryBranstad

Lt. Gov. Kim Reynolds (R), State Capitol, 1007 E. Grand Ave., Des Moines 50319; (515) 281-5211; Fax, (515) 725-3527; Web, www.ltgovernor.iowa.gov

Secy. of State Paul D. Pate (R), 1st Floor, Lucas Bldg., 321 E. 12th St., Des Moines 50319; (515) 281-5204; Fax, (515) 242-5952; Web, www.sos.iowa.gov; Email, sos@sos.iowa.gov

Atty. Gen. Tom Miller (D), Hoover Bldg., 2nd Floor, 1305 E. Walnut St., Des Moines 50319; (515) 281-5164; Fax, (515) 281-4209; Web, www.iowaattorneygeneral.gov; Email, webteam@ag.state.ia.us

Treasurer Michael L. Fitzgerald (D), Capitol Bldg., 1007 E. Grand Ave., Des Moines 50319; (515) 281-5368; Fax, (515) 281-7562; Web, www.iowatreasurer.gov; Email, treasurer@iowa.gov

In Washington, DC: Doug Hoelscher, Director, Washington Office of the Governor, State of Iowa, 400 N. Capitol St. N.W., #359, 20001; (202) 624-5479; Fax, (202) 624-8189

Kansas   Web, www.kansas.gov

Gov. Sam Brownback (R), Capitol, 300 S.W. 10th Ave., #241S, Topeka 66612-1590; (785) 296-3232; Fax, (785) 368-8500; Toll-free, (877) 579-6757; Web, www.governor.ks.gov; Facebook, www.Facebook.com/govsambrownback; Twitter, @govsambrownback

Lt. Gov. Jeff Colyer, MD (R), State Capitol, 2nd Floor, 300 S.W. 10th Ave., Topeka 66612-1590; (785) 296-2214; Fax, (785) 296-5669; TTY, (800) 766-3777; Web, www.governor.ks.gov

Secy. of State Kris Kobach (R), Memorial Hall, 1st Floor, 120 S.W. 10th Ave., Topeka 66612-1594; (785) 296-4564; Fax, (785) 296-4570; Web, www.sos.ks.gov

Atty. Gen. Derek Schmidt (R), Memorial Hall, 120 S.W. 10th Ave., 2nd Floor, Topeka 66612-1594; (785) 296-2215; Fax, (785) 296-6296; Toll-free, (888) 428-8436; Web, www.ag.ks.gov

Treasurer Ron Estes (R), Landon State Office Bldg., 900 S.W. Jackson St., #201, Topeka 66612-1235; (785) 296-3171; Fax, (785) 296-7950; Web, www.kansasstatetreasurer.com

In Washington, DC: Adam Nordstrom, Washington Representative, Washington Office of the Governor, State of Kansas, 500 New Jersey Ave. N.W., #400, 20001; (202) 715-2923; Fax, (202) 638-1045

Kentucky   Web, www.kentucky.gov

Gov. Matt Bevin (R), The Capitol Bldg., 700 Capitol Ave., #100, Frankfort 40601; (502) 564-2611; Fax, (502) 564-2517; TTY, (502) 564-9551; Web, www.governor.ky.gov; Facebook, www.facebook.com/GovMattBevin; Twitter, @GovMattBevin

Lt. Gov. Jenean Hampton (R), The Capitol Bldg., 700 Capitol Ave., #142, Frankfort 40601; (502) 564-2611; Fax, (502) 564-2849; Web, http://ltgovernor.ky.gov

Secy. of State Alison Lundergan Grimes (D), The Capitol Bldg., 700 Capitol Ave. #152, Frankfort 40601-3493; (502) 564-3490; Fax, (502) 564-5687; Web, www.sos.ky.gov

Atty. Gen. Andy Beshear (D), State Capitol, 700 Capitol Ave., #118, Frankfort 40601-3449; (502) 696-5300; Fax, (502) 564-2894; Web, www.ag.ky.gov

Treasurer Allison Ball (R), 1050 U.S. Hwy. 127 South, #100, Frankfort 40601; (502) 564-4722; Fax, (502) 564-6545; Web, www.kytreasury.com; Email, treasury.web@ky.gov

In Washington, DC: Leeann Veatch, Director, Washington Office of the Governor, State of Kentucky, 444 N. Capitol St. N.W., #380, 20001; (202) 220-1350; Fax, (202) 220-1359

Louisiana   Web, www.louisiana.gov

Gov. John Bel Edwards (R), State Capitol, 900 N. 3rd St., 4th Floor, Baton Rouge 70802-9004; P.O. Box 94004, Baton Rouge 70804-9004; (225) 342-7015; Fax, (225) 342-7099; Toll-free, (866) 366-1121; Web, www.gov.louisiana.gov; Facebook, www.facebook.com/LouisianaGov; Twitter, @LouisianaGov

Lt. Gov. Billy Nungesser (R), Capitol Annex Bldg., 1051 N. 3rd St., Baton Rouge 70802; P.O. Box 44243, Baton Rouge, 70804-4242; (225) 342-7009; Fax, (225) 342-1949; Web, www.crt.state.la.us/lt-governor; Email, ltgov@crt.la.gov

Secy. of State Tom Schedler (R), 8585 Archives Ave., Baton Rouge 70809; P.O. Box 94125, Baton Rouge 70804-9125; (225) 922-2880; Fax, (225) 922-2003; Web, www.sos.la.gov; Email, admin@sos.louisiana.gov

Atty. Gen. Jeff Landry (R), 1885 N. 3rd St., Baton Rouge 70802, P.O. Box 94005, Baton Rouge 70804; (225) 326-6079; Fax, (225) 326-6793; Web, www.ag.state.la.us; Email, Admininfo@ag.state.la.us

Treasurer John Neely Kennedy (R), 900 N. 3rd St., 3rd Floor, State Capitol, Baton Rouge 70802; P.O. Box 44154, Baton Rouge 70804; (225) 342-0010; Fax, (225) 342-0046; Web, www.treasury.state.la.us

Washington, DC Representative: Emily Monroe Wesley, Special Counsel, P.O. Box 94004, Baton Rouge 70804; (225) 342-7188

Maine   Web, www.maine.gov

Gov. Paul R. LePage (R), 1 State House Station, Augusta 04333-0001; (207) 287-3531; Fax, (207) 287-1034; TTY, (207) 287-6548; Web, www.maine.gov.governor; Email, governor@maine.gov; Facebook, www.facebook.com/mainesgov; Twitter, @Governor_LePage

Secy. of State Mathew Dunlap (D), Nash School Bldg., 103 Sewall St., 2nd Floor, Augusta 04333; Mailing address, 148 State House Station, Augusta 04333-0148; (207) 626-8400; Fax, (207) 287-8598; Web, www.maine.gov/sos; Email, sos.office@state.me.us

Atty. Gen. Janet T. Mills (D), Burton M. Cross Bldg., 6th Floor, 111 Sewall St., Augusta 04333; Mailing address, 6 State House Station, Augusta 04333-0006; (207) 626-8800; TTY, (207) 626-8865; Web, www.maine.gov/ag

Treasurer Terry Hayes (D), Burton M. Cross Bldg., 3rd
Floor, 111 Sewall St., Augusta 04333; Mailing address,
39 State House Station, Augusta 04333-0039; (207)
624-7477; Fax, (207) 287-2367; Web, www.maine.gov/
treasurer; Email, state.treasurer@maine.gov

Washington, DC Representative: Lance Libby, Legislative
Policy Coordinator, 1 State House Station, Augusta,
ME 04333; (207) 287-3533

Maryland   Web, www.maryland.gov

Gov. Larry Hogan (R), State House, 100 State Circle,
Annapolis 21401; (410) 974-3901; Toll-free, (800) 811-
8336; Web, www.governor.maryland.gov; Facebook,
www.facebook.com/larryhoganmd; Twitter,
@LarryHogan

Lt. Gov. Boyd K. Rutherford (R), State House, 100 State
Circle, Annapolis 21401-1925; (410) 974-2804;
Web, www.governor.maryland.gov/ltgovernor

Secy. of State John C. Wobensmith, Fred L. Wineland
Bldg., 16 Francis St., Annapolis 21401; (410) 974-5521;
Fax, (410) 974-5190; Web, www.sos.state.md.us

Atty. Gen. Brian E. Frosh (R), 200 St. Paul Pl., Baltimore
21202; (410) 576-6300; TTY, (410) 576-6372;
Web, www.oag.state.md.us

Treasurer Nancy K. Kopp (D), Goldstein Treasury Bldg.,
#109, 80 Calvert St., Annapolis 21401; (410) 260-7160;
Fax, (410) 974-3530; Toll-free, (800) 974-0468;
Web, www.treasurer.state.md.us

In Washington, DC: Tiffany Waddell Director,
Washington Office of the Governor, State of Maryland,
444 N. Capitol St. N.W., #311, 20001; (202) 624-1430;
Fax, (202) 783-3061

Massachusetts   Web, www.mass.gov

Gov. Charlie Baker (R), Executive Office, State House,
#280, Boston 02133; (617) 725-4005; Fax, (617) 727-
9725; Toll-free (in-state only), (888) 870-7770;
TTY, (617) 727-3666; Web, www.mass.gov/governor;
Facebook, www.facebook.com/CharlieBakerMA;
Twitter, @MassGovernor

Lt. Gov. Karyn Polito (R), State House, #360, Boston
02133; (617) 725-4005; Fax, (617) 727-9725;
Web, www.mass.gov/governor/administration/
lieutenant-governor-karyn-polito

Secy. of the Commonwealth William Francis Galvin (D),
One Ashburton Pl., #1611, Boston 02108-1512; (617)
727-7030; Fax, (617) 742-4528; Toll-free (in-state
only), (800) 392-6090; TTY, (617) 878-3889;
Web, www.sec.state.ma.us; Email, cis@sec.state.ma.us

Atty. Gen. Maura Healey (D), McCormack Bldg., One
Ashburton Pl., #2010, Boston 02108-1518; (617) 727-
2200; TTY, (617) 727-4765; Web, www.mass.gov/ago

Treasurer Deborah B. Goldberg (D), State House, #227,
Boston, 02133; (617) 367-6900; Fax, (617) 248-0372;
Web, www.mass.gov/treasury

In Washington, DC: Tiffany Watkins, Director of State and
Federal Relations, Washington Office of the Governor,
Commonwealth of Massachusetts, 444 N. Capitol St.
N.W., #208, 20001; (202) 624-7713; Fax, (202) 624-7714

Michigan   Web, www.michigan.gov

Gov. Rick Snyder (R), Romney Bldg., 111 S. Capitol Ave.,
P.O. Box 30013, Lansing 48909; (517) 373-3400;
Fax, (517) 335-6863; Web, www.michigan.gov/snyder;
Facebook, www.facebook.com/GovernorRickSnyder;
Twitter, @onetoughnerd

Lt. Gov. Brian Calley (R), Romney Bldg., 111 S. Capitol
Ave., 5th Floor, P.O. Box 30013, Lansing 48909; (517)
373-6800; Fax, (517) 241-3956; Web, www.michigan
.gov/calley

Secy. of State Ruth Johnson (R), Treasury Bldg., 430
W. Allegan St., 1st Floor, Lansing 48918-9900; (517)
322-1460; Fax, (517) 373-0727; Toll-free, (888) 767-
6424; Web, www.michigan.gov/sos

Atty. Gen. Bill Schuette (R), G. Mennen Williams Bldg.,
525 W. Ottawa St., 7th Floor, P.O. Box 30212, Lansing
48909; (517) 373-1110; Fax, (517) 373-3042; Web,
www.michigan.gov/ag; Email, miag@michigan.gov

Treasurer Nick Khouri (R), Treasury Bldg., 430 W. Allegan
St., Lansing 48922; (517) 373-3200; Fax, (517) 373-
4968; TTY, (517) 636-4999; Web, www.michigan.gov/
treasury

In Washington, DC: Bill McBride, Washington
Representative, Washington Office of the Governor,
State of Michigan, 444 N. Capitol St. N.W., #411,
20001; (202) 624-5840; Fax, (202) 624-5841

Minnesota   Web, www.state.mn.us

Gov. Mark Dayton (D), 116 Veterans Service Bldg., 20
W. 12th St., St. Paul 55155; (651) 201-3400; Fax, (651)
797-1850; Toll-free, (800) 657-3717; Web, www.mn
.gov/governor; Facebook, www.facebook.com/
GovMarkDayton; Twitter, @GovMarkDayton

Lt. Gov. Tina Smith (D), 116 Veterans Service Bldg. 20, W.
12th St., St. Paul 55155; (651) 201-3400; Fax, (651) 797-
1850; Web, www.mn.gov/governor

Secy. of State Steve Simon (D), Retirement Systems of
Minnesota Bldg., 60 Empire Dr., #100, St. Paul 55103;
(651) 296-2803; Fax, (651) 297-7067; Toll-free, (877)
551-6767; Web, www.sos.state.mn.us; Email, secretary
.state@state.mn.us

Atty. Gen. Lori Swanson (D), 1400 Bremer Tower, 445
Minnesota St., St. Paul 55101; (651) 296-3353;
Toll-free, (800) 657-3787; TTY, (800) 366-4812;
Web, www.ag.state.mn.us

Commissioner of Minnesota Myron Frans, 400
Centennial Bldg., 658 Cedar St., St. Paul, 55155;
(651) 201-8000; Fax, (651) 296-8685; TTY, (800) 627-
3529; Web, www.mn.gov/mmb; Email, info.mmb@
state.mn.us

Washington, DC Representative: Elizabeth Dressel, Policy
Coordinator and Federal Relations Director, 116
Veterans Bldg., 20 W. 12th St., St. Paul, MN 55155;
(651) 201-3420

Mississippi   Web, www.ms.gov

Gov. Phil Bryant (R), P.O. Box 139, Jackson 39215; (601)
359-3150; Fax, (601) 359-3741; Toll-free, (877) 405-
0733; Web, www.governorbryant.com; Email,

governor@governor.state.ms.us; Facebook,
www.facebook.com/im4phil; Twitter, @PhilBryantMS

Lt. Gov. Tate Reeves (R), New Capitol Bldg., #315, 400
High St., P.O. Box 1018, Jackson 39215-1018; (601)
359-3200; Fax, (601) 359-4054; Web, www.ltgovreeves
.ms.gov; Email, ltgov@senate.ms.gov

Secy. of State Delbert Hosemann (R), 401 Mississippi St.,
Jackson 39201; (601) 359-1350; Fax, (601) 359-1499;
Web, www.sos.ms.gov

Atty. Gen. Jim Hood (D), Walter Sillers Bldg., 550 High St.,
#1200, Jackson 39201, P.O. Box 220, Jackson 39205;
(601) 359-3680; Fax, (601) 359-3796; Web, www.ago
.state.ms.us

Treasurer Lynn Fitch (R), 1101-A Woolfolk Bldg., 501
N. West St., Jackson 39201, P.O. Box 138, Jackson
39205; (601) 359-3600; Fax, (601) 359-2001;
Web, www.treasurerlynnfitch.com

Washington, DC Representative: Lucien Smith, Chief of
Staff, P.O. Box 139, Jackson, MS 39205; (601) 359-3150

Missouri   Web, www.mo.gov

Gov. Jeremiah W. (Jay) Nixon (D), State Capitol, #216,
Jefferson City 65101; P.O. Box 720, Jefferson City
65102; (573) 751-3222; Web, www.governor.mo.gov;
Twitter, @GovJayNixon

Lt. Gov. Peter Kinder (R), State Capitol, #224, Jefferson
City 65101; (573) 751-4727; Fax, (573) 751-9422; Web,
www.ltgov.mo.gov; Email, ltgovinfo@ltgov.mo.gov

Secy. of State Jason Kander (D), 600 W. Main St.,
Jefferson City 65101; (573) 751-4936; Fax, (573) 751-
2490; Web, www.sos.mo.gov; Email, Info@sos.mo.gov

Atty. Gen. Chris Koster (D), Supreme Court Bldg., 207 W.
High St., P.O. Box 899, Jefferson City 65102; (573) 751-
3321; Fax, (573) 751-0774; Web, www.ago.mo.gov;
Email, attorney.general@ago.mo.gov

Treasurer Clint Zweifel (D), P.O. Box 210, Jefferson City
65102, (573) 751-8533; Fax, (573) 751-0343;
Web, www.treasurer.mo.gov

Washington, DC Representative: Dustin Allison, Deputy
Chief of Staff, State Capitol, 301 W. High St., #216,
Jefferson City, MO 39205; (573) 751-3222

Montana   Web, http://mt.gov

Gov. Steve Bullock (D), State Capitol, #204, P.O. Box
200801, Helena 59620-0801; (406) 444-3111; Fax, (406)
444-5529; Web, www.governor.mt.gov; Facebook,
www.facebook.com/GovernorBullock; Twitter,
@GovernorBullock

Lt. Gov. Mike Cooney (D), State Capitol, #207, P.O. Box
201901, Helena 59620-1901; (406) 444-5665; Fax, (406)
444-4648; Web, www.governor.mt.gov/Home/
LTGovernor

Secy. of State Linda McCulloch (D), State Capitol Bldg.,
1301 6th Ave., #260, Helena 59601; P.O. Box 202801,
Helena 59620; (406) 444-2034, Fax, (406) 444-3976;
Web, www.sos.mt.gov; Email, secretary@mt.gov

Atty. Gen. Tim Fox (R), Justice Bldg., 215 N. Sanders St.,
P.O. Box 201401, Helena 59620-1401; (406) 444-2026;

Fax, (406) 444-3549; Web, www.dojmt.gov; Email,
contactdoj@mt.gov

Director of Dept. of Administration Sheila Hogan, 125
N. Roberts St., P.O. Box 200101, Helena 59620-0101;
(406) 444-2511 or 444-2023; Fax (406) 444-6194;
Web, www.doa.mt.gov

Washington, DC Representative: Adam Schafer, Director
of Public Engagement and Senior Advisor, P.O. Box
200801, Helena, MT 59620; (406) 444-3111

Nebraska   Web, www.nebraska.gov

Gov. Pete Ricketts (R), State Capitol, 1445 K St., #2316,
P.O. Box 96848, Lincoln 68509; (402) 471-2244;
Fax, (402) 471-6031; Web, www.governor.nebraska
.gov; Facebook, www.facebook.com/
GovernorPeteRicketts; Twitter, @GovRicketts

Lt. Gov. Mike Foley (R), State Capitol, #2315, Lincoln,
P.O. Box 94848, 68509; (402) 471-2256; Fax, (402) 471-
6031; Web, www.ltgov.nebraska.gov

Secy. of State John A. Gale (R), State Capitol, 1445 K St.,
#2300, Lincoln; P.O. Box 94608, Lincoln 68509; (402)
471-2554; Fax, (402) 471-3237; Web, www.sos.ne.gov

Atty. Gen. Doug Peterson (R), 2115 State Capitol, Lincoln
68509; (402) 471-2683; Fax, (402) 471-3297;
Web, www.ago.nebraska.gov; Email, ago.info.help@
nebraska.gov

Treasurer Don Stenberg (R), State Capitol, #2005, P.O.
Box 94788, Lincoln 68509; (402) 471-2455; Fax, (402)
471-4390; Web, www.treasurer.nebraska.gov

Washington, DC Representative: Lauren Kintner, Policy
Director and General Counsel, State Capitol, #1319,
Lincoln, NE 68509; (402) 471-2244

Nevada   Web, www.nv.gov

Gov. Brian Sandoval (R), State Capitol Bldg., 101 N.
Carson St., Carson City 89701; (775) 684-5670;
Fax, (775) 684-5683; Web, www.gov.nv.gov; Facebook,
www.facebook.com/BrianSandoval; Twitter,
@GovSandoval

Lt. Gov. Mark Hutchinson (R), State Capitol Bldg., 101
N. Carson St., #2, Carson City 89701; (775) 684-7111;
Fax, (775) 684-7110; Web, www.ltgov.nv.gov; Email,
Ltgov@ltgov.nv.gov

Secy. of State Barbara Cegavske (R), State Capitol Bldg.,
101 N. Carson St., Carson City 89701-4786; (775) 684-
5708; Fax, (775) 684-5725; Web, www.nvsos.gov;
Email, sosmail@sos.nv.gov

Atty. Gen. Adam Paul Laxalt (R), Capitol Complex, 100
N. Carson St., Carson City 89701-4717; (775) 684-
1100; Fax, (775) 684-1108; Web, www.ag.nv.gov;
Email, aginfo@ag.nv.gov

Treasurer Dan Schwartz (R), Capitol Bldg., 101 N. Carson
St., #4, Carson City 89701-4786; (775) 684-5600;
Fax, (775) 684-5781; Web, www.nevadatreasurer.gov;
Email, statetreasurer@nevadatreasurer.gov

In Washington, DC: Ryan McGinness, Director,
Washington Office of the Governor, State of Nevada,
444 N. Capitol St. N.W., #209, 20001; (202) 624-5405

New Hampshire   Web, www.nh.gov

Gov. Maggie Hassan (D), State House, 107 N. Main St., Concord 03301; (603) 271-2121; Fax, (603) 271-7680; Web, www.governor.nh.gov

(No office of Lieutenant Governor)

Secy. of State William M. Gardner (D), State House, #204, 107 N. Main St., Concord 03301; (603) 271-3242; Fax, (603) 271-6316; Web, sos.nh.gov; Email, elections@sos.state.nh.us

Atty. Gen. Joseph Foster (D), 33 Capitol St., Concord 03301; (603) 271-3658; Fax, (603) 271-2110; TTY, (800) 735-2964; Web, www.doj.nh.gov; Email, attorneygeneral@doj.nh.gov

Treasurer William F. Dwyer (D), State House Annex, 25 Capitol St., #121, Concord 03301; (603) 271-2621; Fax, (603) 271-3922; Web, www.nh.gov/treasury; Email, treasury@treasury.state.nh.us

Washington, DC Representative: Pamela Walsh, Chief of Staff, State House, 107 N. Main St., Concord, #208, 03301; (603) 271-2121

New Jersey   Web, www.newjersey.gov

Gov. Chris Christie (R), State House, 125 W. State St., P.O. Box 001, Trenton 08625; (609) 292-6000; Web, www.state.nj.us/governor; Facebook, www.facebook.com/GovChrisChristie; Twitter, @GovChristie

Lt. Gov. & Secy. of State Kim Guadagno (R), 225 W. State St., P.O. Box 300, Trenton 08625; (609) 984-1900; Fax, (609) 777-1764; Web, www.nj.gov/governor/admin/lt/; Email, Feedback@sos.state.nj.us

Atty. Gen. John Jay Hoffman (acting) (R), 25 Market St., 8th Floor, West Wing, P.O. Box 080, Trenton 08625-0080; (609) 292-4925; Fax, (609) 292-3508; Web, www.nj.gov/oag

Treasurer Ford Scudder (acting) (R), State House, 125 W. State St., Trenton 08625; P.O. Box 002, Trenton 08625; (609) 292-6748; Web, www.state.nj.us/treasury

In Washington, DC: Dona De Leon, Director, Washington Office of the Governor, State of New Jersey, 444 N. Capitol St. N.W., #201, 20001; (202) 638-0631; Fax, (202) 638-2296

New Mexico   Web, www.newmexico.gov

Gov. Susana Martinez (R), State Capitol Bldg., 490 Old Santa Fe Trail, #400, Santa Fe 87501; (505) 476-2200; Fax, (505) 476-2226; Web, www.governor.state.nm.us; Facebook, www.facebook.com/SusanaMartinezFan; Twitter, @Gov_Martinez

Lt. Gov. John A. Sanchez (R), State Capitol Bldg., 490 Old Santa Fe Trail, #417, Santa Fe 87501; (505) 476-2250; Fax, (505) 476-2257; Web, www.ltgov.state.nm.us

Secy. of State Brad Winter (R), State Capitol North Annex, 325 Don Gaspar Ave., #300, Santa Fe 87501; (505) 827-3614; Fax, (505) 827-3611; Toll-free, (800) 477-3632; Web, www.sos.state.nm.us

Atty. Gen. Hector Balderas (D), Villagra Bldg., 408 Galisteo St., Santa Fe 87501; P.O. Drawer 1508, Santa Fe 87504-1508; (505) 827-6000; Fax, (505) 827-5826; Web, www.nmag.gov

Treasurer Tim Eichenberg (D), State Treasurer's Office, 2055 S. Pacheco St., #100 & 200, Santa Fe 87505-5135; (505) 955-1120; Fax, (505) 955-1195; Web, www.nmsto.gov

Washington, DC Representative: James Ross, Cabinet Director, State Capitol, 4th Floor, Santa Fe 87501; (505) 476-2200

New York   Web, www.ny.gov

Gov. Andrew Cuomo (D), NYS State Capitol Bldg., Albany 12224; (518) 474-8390; Web, www.governor.ny.gov; Facebook, www.facebook.com/GovernorAndrew Cuomo; Twitter, @NYGovCuomo

Lt. Gov. Kathy Hochul (D), Executive Chamber, State Capitol, Albany 12224-0341; (518) 474-8390; Fax, (518) 474-1513; Web, www.governor.ny.gov/meet-lieutenant-governor-kathy-hochul

Secy. of State Cesar A. Perales (D), One Commerce Plaza, 99 Washington Ave., Albany 12231-0001; (518) 473-3355; Fax, (518) 474-6572; Web, www.dos.ny.gov

Atty. Gen. Eric T. Schneiderman (D), State Capitol, Albany 12224-0341; (518) 474-7330; Toll-free, (800) 771-7755; Web, www.ag.ny.gov

Treasurer Eric Mostert (R), 110 State St., 2nd Floor, Albany 12207; P.O. Box 22119, Albany 12201-2119; (518) 474-4250; Fax, (518) 402-4118; Web, www.tax.ny.gov

In Washington, DC: Alexander Cochran, Director, Washington Office of the Governor, State of New York, 444 N. Capitol St. N.W., #301, 20001; (202) 434-7112; Fax, (202) 434-7110

North Carolina   Web, www.nc.gov

Gov. Pat McCrory (R), State Capitol, Raleigh 27699; Mailing address, 20301 Mail Service Center, Raleigh 27699; (919) 814-2000; Fax, (919) 733-2120; Web, www.governor.nc.gov; Facebook, www.facebook.com/OfficeofGovernorMcCrory; Twitter, @GovOfficeNC

Lt. Gov. Dan Forest (R), 310 N. Blount St., Raleigh 27601; 20401; Mailing address, Mail Service Center, Raleigh, 27699-0401; (919) 733-7350; Fax, (919) 733-6595; Web, ltgov.nc.gov

Secy. of State Elaine F. Marshall (D), 2 S. Salisbury St., Raleigh, 27601; Mailing address, P.O. Box 29622, Raleigh 27626; (919) 807-2000; Fax, (919) 807-2039; Web, www.sos.nc.gov

Atty. Gen. Roy Cooper (D), 114 W. Edenton St., Raleigh 27603; Mailing address, 9001 Mail Service Center, Raleigh 27699-9001; (919) 716-6400; Fax, (919) 716-6750; Web, www.ncdoj.gov

Treasurer Janet Cowell (D), 3200 Atlantic Ave., Raleigh 27603-1385; (919) 814-4000; Web, www.nctreasurer.com

In Washington, DC: Virginia Johnson, Policy Director, 444 N. Capitol St. N.W. #332, 20001; (202) 624-5833

North Dakota   Web, www.nd.gov

Gov. Jack Dalrymple (R), State Capitol, 600 E. Boulevard Ave., Bismarck 58505-0100; (701) 328-2200; Fax, (701) 328-2205; Web, www.governor.nd.gov; Facebook, www.facebook.com/NDGovDalrymple; Twitter, @NDGovDalrymple

Lt. Gov. Drew Wrigley (R), State Capitol, 600 E. Boulevard Ave., Dept. 101, Bismarck 58505-0100; (701) 328-2200; Fax, (701) 328-2205; Web, www.governor.nd.gov/lieutenant-governor-drew-wrigley

Secy. of State Al Jaeger (R), State Capitol, 600 E. Boulevard Ave., Dept. 108, Bismarck 58505-0500; (701) 328-2900; Fax, (701) 328-2992; Toll-free, (800) 352-0867; TTY, (800) 366-6888; Web, www.sos.nd.gov; Email, sos@nd.gov

Atty. Gen. Wayne Stenehjem (R), State Capitol, 600 E. Boulevard Ave., Dept. 125, Bismarck 58505; (701) 328-2210; Fax, (701) 328-2226; TTY, (800) 366-6888; Web, www.ag.nd.gov; Email, ndag@nd.gov

Treasurer Kelly L. Schmidt (R), State Capitol, 3rd Floor, 600 E. Boulevard Ave., Dept. 120, Bismarck 58505-0660; (701) 328-2643; Fax, (701) 328-3002; Web, www.nd.gov/treasurer; Email, treasurer@nd.gov

In Washington, DC: Krista Carman, Washington Representative, Washington Office of the Governor, State of North Dakota, 211 N. Union St., #100, Alexandria, VA 22314; (703) 519-1207; Fax, (202) 478-0811

Ohio   Web, www.ohio.gov

Gov. John R. Kasich (R), Vern Riffe Center, 30th Floor, 77 S. High St., Columbus 43215-6117; (614) 466-3555; Fax, (614) 466-9354; Web, www.governor.ohio.gov; Facebook, www.facebook.com/JohnKasich; Twitter, @JohnKasich

Lt. Gov. Mary Taylor (R), Vern Riffe Center, 30th Floor, 77 S. High St., Columbus 43215-6117; (614) 644-3379; Fax, (614) 644-9345; Web, www.governor.ohio.gov/About/LtGovernorTaylor

Secy. of State Jon Husted (R), 180 E. Broad St., 16th Floor, Columbus 43215; (614) 466-2655; Fax, (614) 466-3899; TTY, (614) 466-0562; Web, www.sos.state.oh.us

Atty. Gen. Mike DeWine (R), 30 E. Broad St., 14th Floor, Columbus 43215-3428; (614) 466-4320; Help line, (614) 466-4986; Web, www.ohioattorneygeneral.gov

Treasurer Josh Mandel (R), 30 E. Broad St., 9th Floor, Columbus 43215; (614) 466-2160; Fax, (614) 644-7313; TTY, (800) 228-1102; Web, www.tos.ohio.gov; Email, treasurer@tos.ohio.gov

Washington, DC Representative: R. David Frash III, Assistant Policy Director, Vern Riff Center, 77 S. High St, 30th Floor, Columbus 43215; (614) 466-3555

Oklahoma   Web, www.ok.gov

Gov. Mary Fallin (R), State Capitol, 2300 N. Lincoln Blvd., #212, Oklahoma City 73105; (405) 521-2342; Fax, (405) 521-3353; Web, www.ok.gov/governor; Facebook, www.facebook.com/GovernorMaryFallin; Twitter, @GovMaryFallin

Lt. Gov. Todd Lamb (R), State Capitol, 2300 N. Lincoln Blvd., #211, Oklahoma City 73105; (405) 521-2161; Fax, (405) 522-8694; Web, www.ok.gov/ltgovernor

Secy. of State Chris Benge (R), 2300 N. Lincoln Blvd., #101, Oklahoma City 73105; (405) 521-3912; Web, www.sos.ok.gov

Atty. Gen. E. Scott Pruitt (R), 313 N.E. 21st St., Oklahoma City 73105; (405) 521-3921; Fax, (405) 521-3921; Web, www.ok.gov/oag

Treasurer Ken Miller (R), State Capitol, 2300 N. Lincoln Blvd., #217, Oklahoma City 73105; (405) 521-3191; Web, www.ok.gov/treasurer

Washington, DC Representative: Katie Altshuler, Policy Director, Washington Office of the Governor, State of Oklahoma, 2300 N. Lincoln Blvd., #212, Oklahoma City, OK 73105; (405) 521-2342

Oregon   Web, www.oregon.gov

Gov. Kate Brown (D), 160 State Capitol, 900 Court St. N.E., Salem 97301-4047; (503) 378-4582; Fax, (503) 378-6827; Web, www.governor.oregon.gov; Facebook, www.facebook.com/OregonGovernor; Twitter, @OregonGovBrown

(No office of Lieutenant Governor)

Secy. of State Jeanne Atkins (D), 136 State Capitol, Salem 97301-0722; (503) 986-1523; Fax, (503) 986-1616; Web, www.sos.oregon.gov; Email, oregon.sos@state.or.us

Atty. Gen. Ellen F. Rosenblum (D), Justice Bldg., 1162 Court St. N.E., Salem 97301-4096; (503) 378-4400; Fax, (503) 378-4017; Web, www.doj.state.or.us

Treasurer Ted Wheeler (D), 900 Court St. N.E., #159, Salem 97301-4043; (503) 378-4329; Fax, (503) 373-7051; Web, www.Oregon.gov/treasury; Email, oregon.treasurer@state.or.us

Washington, DC Representative: Drew Johnston, Washington Office of the Governor State of Oregon, 444 North Capitol St., #134, 20001; (202) 508-3847

Pennsylvania   Web, www.state.pa.us

Gov. Tom Wolf (D), 508 Capitol Bldg., 501 N. 3rd St., Harrisburg 17120; (717) 787-2500; Fax, (717) 772-8284; Web, www.governor.pa.gov; Email, governor@pa.gov; Facebook, www.facebook.com/GovernorWolf; Twitter, @GovernorTomWolf

Lt. Gov. Michael Stack (D), 200 Capitol Bldg., 501 N. 3rd St., Harrisburg 17120-0002; (717) 787-3300; Fax, (717) 783-0150; Web, www.governor.pa.gov/lt-gov-mike-stack

Secy. of the Commonwealth Pedro A. Cortés (D), 302 North Office Bldg., Harrisburg 17120; (717) 787-6458; Fax, (717) 787-1734; Web, www.dos.pa.gov

Atty. Gen. Kathleen G. Kane (D), 11 N. 3rd St., Strawberry Square, 16th Floor, Harrisburg 17120; (717) 787-3391; Fax, (717) 783-8242; Web, www.attorneygeneral.gov

Treasurer Timothy A. Reese (D), 613 North St., 129 Finance Bldg., Harrisburg 17120; (717) 787-2465; Fax, (717) 783-9760; Web, www.patreasury.gov

Washington, DC Representative: John Hanger, Secretary of Policy and Planning, Main Capitol Bldg., #238, Harrisburg 20036; (717) 787-2500

Rhode Island   Web, www.ri.gov

Gov. Gina Raimondo (D), State House, 82 Smith St., Providence 02903-1196; (401) 222-2080; Fax (401) 228-8096; Web, www.governor.ri.gov; Email, governor@governor.ri.gov; Facebook, www.facebook.com/GinaMRaimondo; Twitter, @ginaraimondo

Lt. Gov. Daniel J. McKee (D), State House, #116, 82 Smith St., Providence 02903; (401) 222-2371; Fax, (401) 222-2012; Web, www.ltgov.ri.gov; Email, info@ltgov.state.ri.us

Secy. of State Nellie M. Gorbea (D), 82 Smith St., State House, #218, Providence 02903-1105; (401) 222-2357; Fax, (401) 222-1356; Web, www.sos.ri.gov; Email, secretarygorbea@sos.ri.gov

Atty. Gen. Peter Kilmartin (D), 150 S. Main St., Providence 02903-2856; (401) 274-4400; Fax, (401) 222-1302; Web, www.riag.ri.gov

Treasurer Seth Magaziner (D), State House, 82 Smith St., #102, Providence 02903; (401) 222-2397; Fax, (401) 222-6140; Web, www.treasury.ri.gov

Washington, DC Representative: Matt Bucci, Director, Washington Office of the Governor, State of Rhode Island, State House, Providence 02903; (410) 222-2080

South Carolina   Web, www.sc.gov

Gov. Nikki Haley (R), Office of the Governor, 1205 Pendleton St., Columbia 29201; Press, Rob Godfrey, (803) 734-2100; Fax, (803) 734-5167; Web, www.governor.sc.gov; Facebook, www.facebook.com/NikkiHaley; Twitter, @NikkiHaley

Lt. Gov. Henry McMaster (R), State House, 1st Floor, Columbia 29202; P.O. Box 142, Columbia 29202; (803) 734-2080; Fax, (803) 734-2082; Web, www.ltgov.sc.gov; Email, LtGovernor@scstatehouse.gov

Secy. of State Mark Hammond (R), 1205 Pendleton St., #525, Columbia 29201; P.O. Box 11350, Columbia 29211; (803) 734-2170; Fax, (803) 734-1661; Web, www.scsos.com

Atty. Gen. Alan Wilson (R), Rembert Dennis Bldg., 1000 Assembly St., #519, Columbia 29201; P.O. Box 11549, Columbia 29201; (803) 734-3970; Fax, (803) 253-6283; Web, www.scag.gov

Treasurer Curtis M. Loftis Jr. (R), Wade Hampton Office Bldg., 1200 Senate St., #118, Columbia 29201; P.O. Box 11778, Columbia 29211; (803) 734-2101; Fax, (803) 734-2690; Web, www.treasurer.sc.gov; Email, treasurer@sto.sc.gov

Washington, DC Representative: Josh Baker, Budget Director, Statehouse, 1205 Pendleton St., Columbia 29201; (803) 734-2100

South Dakota   Web, www.sd.gov

Gov. Dennis Daugaard (R), Capitol Bldg., 500 E. Capitol Ave., Pierre 57501; (605) 773-3212; Fax, (605) 773-4711; Web, www.sd.gov/governor; Twitter, @SDGovDaugaard

Lt. Gov. Matt Michels (R), Capitol Bldg., 500 E. Capitol Ave., Pierre 57501-5070; (605) 773-3212; Fax, (605) 773-4711

Secy. of State Shantel Krebs (R), Capitol Bldg., 500 E. Capitol Ave., #204, Pierre 57501-5070; (605) 773-3537; Fax, (605) 773-6580; Web, www.sdsos.gov; Email, sdsos@state.sd.us

Atty. Gen. Marty Jackley (R), 1302 E. Hwy. 14, #1, Pierre 57501-8501; (605) 773-3215; Fax, (605) 773-4106; TTY, (605) 773-6585; Web, www.atg.sd.gov

Treasurer Richard L. Sattgast (R), State Capitol, 500 E. Capitol Ave., #212, Pierre 57501-5070; (605) 773-3378; Fax, (605) 773-3115; Web, www.sdtreasurer.gov

Washington, DC Representative: Kelsey Webb, Deputy Policy Advisor, State Capitol, 500 E. Capitol Ave., Pierre 57501; (605) 773-3212

Tennessee   Web, www.tn.gov

Gov. Bill Haslam (R), State Capitol, 1st Floor, Nashville 37243-0001; (615) 741-2001; Fax, (615) 532-9711; Web, www.tn.gov/governor

Lt. Gov. Ron Ramsey (R), 1 Legislative Plaza, 301 6th Ave. North, Nashville 37243-0202; (615) 741-4524; Fax, (615) 253-0197; Web, www.ltgov.tn.gov; Email, lt.gov.ron.ramsey@capitol.tn.gov

Secy. of State Tre Hargett (R), State Capitol, 312 Rosa L. Parks Ave., Nashville 37243-1102; (615) 741-2819; Fax, (615) 741-5962; Web, www.tn.gov/sos

Atty. Gen. Herbert H. Slattery (R), Cordell Hull Bldg., 425 5th Ave. North, Nashville 37243-0485; P.O. Box 20207, Nashville 37202-0207; (615) 741-3491; Fax, (615) 741-2009; Web, www.tn.gov/attorneygeneral

Treasurer David H. Lillard Jr. (R), Tennessee State Capitol, 1st Floor, 600 Charlotte Ave., Nashville 37243-0225; (615) 741-2956; Web, www.treasury.state.tn.us

Washington, DC Representative: Beth Tipps, Deputy Director of Policy and Research, State Capitol, 1st Floor, Nashville, TN 37243; (615) 741-2001

Texas   Web, www.tx.gov

Gov. Greg Abbott (R), State Insurance Bldg., 1100 San Jacinto Blvd., #151B, Austin 78701; P.O. Box 12428, Austin 78711; (512) 463-2000; Fax, (512) 463-1849; Web, www.governor.state.tx.us; Facebook, www.facebook.com/TexasGovernor; Twitter, @GovAbbott

Lt. Gov. Dan Patrick (R), Capitol Station, P.O. Box 12068, Austin 78711-2068; (512) 463-0001; Fax, (512) 463-0677; Web, www.ltgov.state.tx.us

Secy. of State Carlos Cascos (R), 1100 Congress Capitol Bldg., #1E.8, Austin 78701; P.O. Box 12697, Austin 78701; (512) 463-5770; Fax, (512) 475-2761; Web, www.sos.state.tx.us

Atty. Gen. Ken Paxton (R), 300 W. 15th St., 8th Floor, Austin 78701; P.O. Box 12548, Austin 78711; (512) 463-2100; Fax, (512) 475-2994; Web, www.oag.state.tx.us; Email, public.information@oag.state.tx.us

Comptroller Glenn Hegar (R), Lyndon B. Johnson Bldg., 111 E. 17th St., Austin 78774-0100; P.O. Box 13528, Capitol Station, Austin 78711-3528; (512) 463-4000; Fax, (512) 475-0352; Web, www.window.state.tx.us; Email, texas.comptroller@cpa.state.tx.us

In Washington, DC: Jerry Strickland, Director, Office of State-Federal Relations, State of Texas, 10 G St. N.E., #650, 20001; (202) 638-3927; Fax, (202) 628-1943

Utah   Web, www.utah.gov

Gov. Gary Herbert (R), Utah State Capitol Complex, 350 N. State St., #200; P.O. Box 142220, Salt Lake City 84114-2220; (801) 538-1000; Fax, (801) 538-1528; Toll-free, (800) 705-2464; Web, www.utah.gov/

governor; Facebook, www.facebook.com/
GovGaryHerbert; Twitter, @GovHerbert

Lt. Gov. Spencer J. Cox (R), Utah State Capitol Complex,
#220; P.O. Box 142325, Salt Lake City 84114-2220;
(801) 538-1041; Fax, (801) 538-1133; Web, www.utah
.gov/ltgovernor

(No office of Secretary of State)

Atty. Gen. Sean D. Reyes (R), State Capitol Complex, 350
N. State St., #230; P.O. Box 142320, Salt Lake City
84114-2320; (801) 366-0260; Fax, (801) 538-1121;
Web, attorneygeneral.utah.gov; Email, uag@utah.gov

Treasurer Richard K. Ellis (R), State Capitol Complex, 350
N. State St., #180; P.O. Box 142315, Salt Lake City
84114-2315; (801) 538-1042; Fax, (801) 538-1465;
Web, www.treasurer.utah.gov

Washington, DC Representative: Wesley Smith, Director
State and Federal Regulations, 350 N. State St., #200,
Salt Lake City, UT 84114; (801) 538-1000

Vermont   Web, www.vermont.gov

Gov. Peter Shumlin (D), Pavilion Office Bldg., 109 State
St., Montpelier 05609-0101; (802) 828-3333; Fax, (802)
828-3339; TTY, (800) 649-6825; Web, www.governor
.vermont.gov; Facebook, www.facebook.com/
Governor.Peter.Shumlin; Twitter, @GovPeterShumlin

Lt. Gov. Phil Scott (D), 115 State St., Montpelier 05633-
5401; (802) 828-2226; Fax, (802) 828-3198;
Web, www.ltgov.vermont.gov

Secy. of State Jim Condos (D), 128 State St., Montpelier
05633-1101; Information, (802) 828-2363; Fax, (802)
828-2496; Web, www.sec.state.vt.us; Email,
jim.condos@sec.state.vt.us

Atty. Gen. William H. Sorrell (D), Pavilion Office Bldg.,
109 State St., Montpelier 05609-1001; (802) 828-3171;
TTY, (802) 828-3665; Web, www.ago.vermont.gov;
Email, ago.info@.state.vt.us

Treasurer Elizabeth (Beth) Pearce (D), Pavilion Office
Bldg., 109 State St., 4th Floor, Montpelier 05609-6200;
(802) 828-2301; Fax, (802) 828-2772; TTY, (800) 253-
0191; Web, www.vermonttreasurer.gov; Email,
Treasurers.Office@state.vt.us

Washington, DC Representative: Sue Allen, Secretary of
Civil and Military Affairs, Pavilion Office Bldg., 109
State St., 5th Floor, Montpelier, VT 05609-6200; (802)
828-3333

Virginia   Web, www.virginia.gov

Gov. Terence (Terry) R. McAuliffe (D), Patrick Henry
Bldg., 3rd Floor, 1111 E. Broad St., Richmond 23219;
P.O. Box 1475, Richmond, 23218; (804) 786-2211;
Fax, (804) 371-6351; TTY, (800) 828-1120; Web,
www.governor.virginia.gov; Facebook, www.facebook
.com/Governor-of-Virginia-61634046094; Twitter,
@GovernorVA

Lt. Gov. Ralph S. Northam (D), 102 Governor St.,
Richmond 23219; P.O. Box 1195, Richmond 23218;
(804) 786-2078; Fax, (804) 786-7514; Web, www.ltgov
.virginia.gov; Email, ltgov@ltgov.virginia.gov

Secy. of the Commonwealth Levar Stoney (D), 1111 E.
Broad St., 4th Floor, Richmond 23219; P.O. Box 2454,
Richmond 23218; (804) 786-2441; Fax, (804) 371-0017;
Web, www.commonwealth.virginia.gov

Atty. Gen. Mark R. Herring (D), 900 E. Main St.,
Richmond 23219; (804) 786-2071; Web, www.oag.state
.va.us

Treasurer Manju Ganeriwala (D), James Monroe Bldg.,
3rd Floor, 101 N. 14th St., Richmond 23219; P.O. Box
1879, 23219 (804) 225-2142; Fax, (804) 225-3187;
Web, www.trs.virginia.gov

In Washington, DC: Maribel Ramos, Director, Virginia
Office of Intergovernmental Affairs, Commonwealth of
Virginia, 444 N. Capitol St. N.W., #214, 20001; (202)
783-1769; Fax, (202) 783-7687

Washington   Web, www.access.wa.gov

Gov. Jay Inslee (D), Legislative Bldg., 2nd Floor, 1143
Capitol Way South; P.O. Box 40002, Olympia 98504-
0002; (360) 902-4111; Fax, (360) 753-4110; TTY (WA
only), (800) 833-6388; Web, www.governor.wa.gov;
Facebook, www.facebook.com/WaStateGov; Twitter,
@GovInslee

Lt. Gov. Brad Owen (D), Legislative Bldg., #220, 416 Sid
Snyder Ave. S.W.; P.O. Box 40400, Olympia 98504-
0400; (360) 786-7700; Fax, (360) 786-7749;
Web, www.ltgov.wa.gov; Email, ltgov@leg.wa.gov

Secy. of State Kim Wyman (R), Legislative Bldg., 2nd
Floor, 416 Sid Snyder Ave. S.W.; P.O. Box 40220,
Olympia 98504-0220; (360) 902-4151; Fax, (360) 586-
5629; TTY, (800) 422-8683; Web, www.sos.wa.gov;
Email, mail@sos.wa.gov

Atty. Gen. Bob Ferguson (D), 1125 Washington St. S.E.;
P.O. Box 40100, Olympia 98504-0100; (360) 753-6200;
Fax, (360) 664-0228; Web, www.atg.wa.gov

Treasurer James L. McIntire (D), Legislative Bldg., #230,
416 Sid Synder Ave. S.W.; P.O. Box 40200, Olympia
98504; (360) 902-9000; Fax, (360) 902-9037; TTY,
(360) 902-8963; Web, www.tre.wa.gov; Email,
watreas@tre.wa.gov

In Washington, DC: Sam Ricketts, Director, Washington
Office of the Governor, State of Washington, 444
N. Capitol St. N.W., #411, 20001; (202) 624-3691;
Fax, (202) 624-5841

West Virginia   Web, www.wv.gov

Gov. Earl Ray Tomblin (D), State Capitol, 1900 Kanawha
Blvd. East, Charleston 25305-0370; (304) 558-2000;
Toll-free, (888) 438-2731; Web, www.governor.wv.gov;
Twitter, @GovTomlin

Senate Pre. William Cole (R), Capitol Complex, Bldg.
1, #229M, Charleston 25305; (304) 357-7801;
Fax, (304) 357-7839; Web, www.legis.state.wv.us;
Email, bill.cole@wvsenate.gov

Secy. of State Natalie E. Tennant (D), Capitol Complex,
Bldg. 1, #157-K, 1900 Kanawha Blvd. East, Charleston
25305-0770; (304) 558-6000; Fax, (304) 558-0900;
Web, www.sos.wv.gov

Atty. Gen. Patrick Morrisey (R), Capitol Complex, Bldg. 1, #E-26, 1900 Kanawha Blvd. East, Charleston 25305; (304) 558-2021; Fax, (304) 558-0140; Web, www.ago.wv.gov

Treasurer John D. Perdue (D), Capitol Complex, Bldg. 1, #E-145, 1900 Kanawha Blvd. East, Charleston 25305; (304) 558-5000; Toll-free, (800) 422-7498; TTY, (304) 340-1598; Web, www.wvsto.gov

Washington, DC Representative: Larry Malone Director of Policy, Washington Officer of the Governor, 1900 Kanawha Blvd. East, Charleston, WV 25305; (304) 558-2000

Wisconsin   Web, www.wisconsin.gov

Gov. Scott Walker (R), 115 E. Capitol, Madison 53702-7863; (608) 266-1212; Fax, (608) 267-8983; TTY, (608) 267-6790; Web, www.walker.wisconsin.gov; Email, govgeneral@wisconsin.gov; Facebook, www.facebook.com/governorscottwalker; Twitter, @GovWalker

Lt. Gov. Rebecca Kleefisch (R), 19 E. Capitol; P.O. Box 2043, Madison 53702; (608) 266-3516; Fax, (608) 267-3571; Web, www.ltgov.wisconsin.gov; Email, ltgov@wisconsin.gov

Secy. of State Douglas La Follette (D), 30 W. Mifflin St., 10th Floor, Madison 53703; P.O. Box 7848, 53707; (608) 266-8888; X3 Fax, (608) 266-3159; Web, www.sos.state.wi.us; Email, statesec@sos.state.wi.us

Atty. Gen. Brad D. Schimel (R), 17 W. Main St., Madison 53702; P.O. Box 7857, Madison 53707-7857; (608) 266-1221; Fax, (608) 267-2779; Web, www.doj.state.wi.us

Treasurer Matt Adamczyk (R), B41 W. State Capitol, Madison 53703; P.O. Box 2114, Madison 53701; (608) 266-1714; Fax, (608) 261-6799; Web, www.statetreasury.wisconsin.gov; Email, Matt.Adamczyk@wisconsin.gov

In Washington, DC: Kyle Roskam, Director, Washington Office of the Governor, State of Wisconsin, 444 N. Capitol St. N.W., #613, 20001; (202) 624-5870; Fax, (202) 624-5871

Wyoming   Web, www.wy.gov

Gov. Matt Mead (R), Idelman Mansion, 2323 Carey Ave., Cheyenne 82002-0010; (307) 777 7434; Fax, (307) 632-3909; Web, www.governor.wyo.gov; Facebook, www.facebook.com/governormattmead; Twitter, @GovMattMead

(No office of Lieutenant Governor)

Secy. of State Ed Murray (R), 2020 Care Ave., #600, Cheyenne 82002-0020; (307) 777-7378; Fax, (307) 777-6217; Web, www.soswy.state.wy.us; Email, secofstate@wyo.gov

Atty. Gen Peter Michael (R), Kendrick Bldg., 2320 Capitol Ave., Cheyenne 82002; (307) 777-7841; Fax, (307) 777-6869; TTY, (307) 777-5351; Web, www.ag.wyo.gov; Email, attorneygeneral.state.wy.us

Treasurer Mark Gordon (R), 2020 Carey St., 4th Floor, Cheyenne 82002; (307) 777-7408; Fax, (307) 777-5411; Web, www.treasurer.state.wy.us

Washington, DC Representative: Tony Young, Washington Officer of the Governor, Deputy Chief of Staff, State Capitol, 200 W. 24th St., Cheyenne 82002; (307) 777-7434

U.S. TERRITORIES

American Samoa

Gov. HTC Lolo Matalasi Moliga (I), P. Lutali Executive Office Bldg., Pago Pago, American Samoa 96799; (011) 684-633-4116; Fax, (011) 684-633-2269

Lt. Gov. HC Lemanu Peleti Mauga (I)

Washington, DC Representative: Minnie Tuia, Deputy Chief of Staff, Executive Office Bldg., Pago Pago 96799; (011) 684-633-4116, ext. 233

Guam   Web, www.guam.gov

Gov. Eddie Baza Calvo (R), Ricardo J. Bordallo Governor's Complex, Adelup, Guam 96910; (671) 472-8931, (671) 472-8936; Fax, (671) 472-4826; Web, www.governor.guam.gov

Lt. Gov. Ray Tenorio (R), Ricardo J. Bordallo Governor's Complex, P.O. Box 2950, Hagåtña 96932; (671) 475-9380; Fax, (671) 477-2007; Web, www.lt.guam.gov

In Washington, DC: Margret Metcalfe, Director, Washington Office, Governor of Guam, 444 N. Capitol St. N.W., #619, 20001; (202) 434-4855; Fax (202) 434-4856

Northern Mariana Islands   Web, www.gov.mp

Gov. Eloy S. Inos (Covenant Party), Memorial Bldg., Capitol Hill, Caller Box 10007, Saipan, MP 96950; (670) 664-2280

Lt. Gov. Ralph Torres (R), Memorial Bldg., Capitol Hill, Caller Box 10007, Saipan, MP 96950; (670) 664-2280

Washington, DC Representative: Esther Fleming, Chief of Staff, Capitol Hill, Caller Box 10007, Saipan, MP 96950; (670) 664-2212

Puerto Rico   Web, www.pr.gov

Gov. Alejandro Garcia Padilla (Popular Democratic Party), Calle Fortaleza #63, Viejo San Juan; P.O. Box 9020082, San Juan 00902-0082; (787) 721-7000; Fax (787) 723-3287

Lt. Gov. and Secretary of State (Vacant)

In Washington, DC: Juan Eugenio Hernandez, Executive Director, Puerto Rico Federal Affairs Administration, 1100 17th St. N.W., #800, 20036; (202) 778-0710; Fax, (202) 822-0916

Virgin Islands   Web, www.vi.gov

Gov. Kenneth Mapp (I), St. Thomas and Water Island, 21-22 Kongens Gade, Charlotte Amalie, St. Thomas 00802; (340) 774-0001; Fax, (340) 774-1361

Lt. Gov. Osbert Potter (I), #18 Kongens Gade, St. Thomas, VI 00802; (340) 774-2991; Fax, (340) 774-6953

Washington, DC Representative: Rochelle Corneiro, Deputy Chief of Staff, Office of the Governor, 21-22 Kongens Gade, Charlotte Amalie, St. Thomas, VI 00802; (340) 774-0001

Foreign Embassies, U.S. Ambassadors, and Country Desk Offices

Following are key foreign diplomats in the United States, U.S. ambassadors or ranking diplomatic officials abroad, and country offices of the State Department that follow political, cultural, and economic developments. Also included is the African Union Commission. This information is current as of April 25, 2016.

For information on investing or doing business abroad, contact the Commerce Department's Trade Information Center at (800) USA-TRAD(E) (800-872-8723) or visit www.export.gov. The Office of the United States Trade Representative also offers trade information by region at www.ustr.gov/countries-regions.

Afghanistan   Web, www.embassyofafghanistan.org

Ambassador: Hamdullah Mohib
Chancery: 2341 Wyoming Ave. N.W. 20008; (202) 483-6410; Fax, (202) 483-6488; Email, info@embassyofafghanistan.org
U.S. Ambassador in Kabul: P. Michael McKinley
State Dept. Country Office: (202) 647-5175

African Union Commission

Web, www.au.int/en/commission

Chairperson: Dr. Nkosazana Dlamini Zuma
Ambassador: Amina Salum Ali
Chancery: 1640 Wisconsin Ave. N.W. 20007; (202) 293-8006; Fax, (202) 293-8007
U.S. Chargé d'Affaires in Addis Ababa, Ethiopia: Susan D. Page
State Dept. Country Office: (202) 647-0553

Albania

Web, www.embassyofalbania.org or www.ambasadat.gov.al/usa/en

Ambassador: Floreta Faber
Chancery: 2100 S St. N.W. 20008; (202) 223-4942; Fax, (202) 628-7342; Email, embassy.washington@mfa.gov.al
U.S. Ambassador in Tirana: Donald Lu
State Dept. Country Office: (202) 647-3747

Algeria   Web, www.algerianembassy.org

Ambassador: Madjid Bouguerra
Chancery: 2118 Kalorama Rd. N.W. 20008; (202) 265-2800; Fax, (202) 986-5906; Email, mail@algerianembassy.org
U.S. Ambassador in Algiers: Joan Polaschik
State Dept. Country Office: (202) 647-4371

Andorra

Web, www.exteriors.ad/en/embassies-of-andorra/andorra-usa-embassy

Ambassador: Elisenda Vives Balmaña

Chancery: 2 United Nations Plaza, 27th Floor, New York, NY 10017; (212) 750-8064; Fax, (212) 750-6630; Email, contact@andorraun.org or andorra@un.int
U.S. Ambassador: James Costos (resident in Madrid, Spain)
State Dept. Country Office: (202) 647-3151

Angola   Web, www.angola.org

Ambassador: Agostinho Tavares da Silva Neto
Chancery: 2100-2108 16th St. N.W. 20009; (202) 785-1156; Fax, (202) 822-9049
U.S. Ambassador in Luanda: Helen M. La Lime
State Dept. Country Office: (202) 647-9858

Antigua and Barbuda

Ambassador: Deborah-Mae Lovell
Chancery: 3216 New Mexico Ave. N.W. 20016; (202) 362-5122; Fax, (202) 362-5225; Email, embantbar@aol.com
U.S. Ambassador: Larry L. Palmer (resident in Bridgetown, Barbados)
State Dept. Country Office: (202) 647-4384

Argentina   Web, www.embassyofargentina.us

Ambassador: Martin Lousteau
Chancery: 1600 New Hampshire Ave. N.W. 20009; (202) 238-6400; Fax, (202) 332-3171; Email, eeeuu@mrecic.gov.ar
U.S. Ambassador in Buenos Aires: Noah B. Mamet
State Dept. Country Office: (202) 647-3402

Armenia   Web, www.usa.mfa.am

Ambassador: Grigor Hovhannissian
Chancery: 2225 R St. N.W. 20008; (202) 319-1976; Fax, (202) 319-2982; Email, contact@armembassy.org
U.S. Ambassador in Yerevan: Richard M. Mills Jr.
State Dept. Country Office: (202) 647-6576

Aruba   (See The Netherlands)

Australia   Web, www.usa.embassy.gov.au

Ambassador: Joe Hockey
Chancery: 1601 Massachusetts Ave. N.W. 20036; (202) 797-3000; Fax, (202) 797-3168

U.S. Ambassador in Canberra: John Berry
State Dept. Country Office: (202) 647-7828

Austria   Web, www.austria.org

Ambassador: Wolfgang Waldner
Chancery: 3524 International Court N.W. 20008; (202) 895-6700; Fax, (202) 895-6750; Email, inbox@austria.org
U.S. Ambassador in Vienna: Alexa L. Wesner
State Dept. Country Office: (202) 647-4782

Azerbaijan   Web, www.azembassy.us

Ambassador: Elin Suleymanov
Chancery: 2741 34th St. N.W. 20008; (202) 337-3500; Fax, (202) 337-5911; Email, azerbaijan@azembassy.us
U.S. Ambassador: Robert F. Cekuta
State Dept. Country Office: (202) 647-9677

Bahamas   Web, www.bahamasembdc.org

Ambassador: Eugene Glenwood Newry
Chancery: 2220 Massachusetts Ave. N.W. 20008; (202) 319-2660; Fax, (202) 319-2668; Email, embassy@bahamasembdc.org
U.S. Chargé d'Affaires in Nassau: Lisa Johnson
State Dept. Country Office: (202) 736-4322

Bahrain   Web, www.bahrainembassy.org

Ambassador: Shaikh Abdullah bin Mohammed bin Rashid Al Khalifa
Chancery: 3502 International Dr. N.W. 20008; (202) 342-1111; Fax, (202) 362-2192; Email, ambsecretary@bahrainembassy.org
U.S. Ambassador in Manama: William V. Roebuck
State Dept. Country Office: (202) 647-4709

Bangladesh   Web, www.bdembassyusa.org

Ambassador: Mohammad A. Ziauddin
Chancery: 3510 International Dr. N.W. 20008; Ambassador, (202) 244-2745; Main, (202) 244-0183; Fax, (202) 244-7830
U.S. Ambassador in Dhaka: Marcia Bernicat
State Dept. Country Office: (202) 647-2472

Barbados   Web, www.barbados.usembassy.gov

Ambassador: John Ernest Beale
Chancery: 2144 Wyoming Ave. N.W. 20008; (202) 939-9200; Fax, (202) 332-7467; Email, washington@foreign.gov.bb
U.S. Ambassador in Bridgetown: Linda Taglialatela
State Dept. Country Office: (202) 647-4384

Belarus   Web, www.usa.mfa.gov.by

Chargé d'Affaires: Pavel Shidlovsky
Chancery: 1619 New Hampshire Ave. N.W. 20009; (202) 986-1606; Fax, (202) 986-1805; Email, usa@mfa.gov.by
U.S. Chargé d'Affaires in Minsk: Scott M. Rauland
State Dept. Country Office: (202) 736-4443

Belgium   Web, www.diplobel.us

Ambassador: Johan Verbeke
Chancery: 3330 Garfield St. N.W. 20008; (202) 333-6900; Fax, (202) 333-4960; Email, washington@diplobel.fed.be
U.S. Ambassador in Brussels: Denise Bauer
State Dept. Country Office: (202) 647-6555

Belize   Web, www.embassyofbelize.org

Chargé d'Affaires: Ardelle Sabido
Chancery: 2535 Massachusetts Ave. N.W. 20008; (202) 332-9636; Fax, (202) 332-6888
Ambassador in Belmopan: Carlos R. Moreno
State Dept. Country Office: (202) 647-3519

Benin   Web, www.beninembassy.us

Ambassador: Omar Arouna
Chancery: 2124 Kalorama Rd. N.W. 20008; (202) 232-6656; Fax, (202) 265-1996; Email, info@beinembassy.us
U.S. Ambassador in Cotonou: Lucy Tamlyn
State Dept. Country Office: (202) 647-2637

Bhutan

The United States and Bhutan do not maintain formal diplomatic relations. Informal contact is made between the U.S. embassy and the Bhutanese embassy in New Delhi, India.
State Dept. Country Office: (202) 647-2941

Bolivia   Web, www.bolivia-usa.org

Chief of Mission: General Freddy Bersatti
Chancery: 3014 Massachusetts Ave. N.W., #2, 20008; Chief of Mission, (202) 232-8573; Main, (202) 482-4410; Fax, (202) 328-3712; Email, assistant@bolivia-usa.org
U.S. Chargé d'Affaires in La Paz: Peter Brennan
State Dept. Country Office: (202) 647-4193

Bosnia and Herzegovina
Web, www.bhembassy.org

Ambassador: Haris Hrle
Chancery: 2109 E St. N.W. 20037; (202) 337-1500; Fax, (202) 337-1502; Email, info@bhembassy.org
U.S. Ambassador in Sarajevo: Maureen Cormack
State Dept. Country Office: (202) 647-4277

Botswana   Web, www.botswanaembassy.org

Ambassador: David John Newman
Chancery: 1531-1533 New Hampshire Ave. N.W. 20036; (202) 244-4990; Fax, (202) 244-4164; Email, info@botswanaembassy.org
U.S. Ambassador in Gaborone: Earl R. Miller
State Dept. Country Office: (202) 647-9852

Brazil   Web, http://washington.itamaraty.gov.br/en-us

Ambassador: Luiz Alberto Figueiredo Machado

Chancery: 3006 Massachusetts Ave. N.W. 20008; (202) 238-2700; Fax, (202) 238-2827
U.S. Ambassador in Brasilia: Liliana Ayalde
State Dept. Country Office: (202) 647-4994

Brunei   Web, www.bruneiembassy.org

Ambassador: Dato Serbini Ali
Chancery: 3520 International Court N.W. 20008; (202) 237-1838; Fax, (202) 885-0560; Email, info@bruneiembassy.org
U.S. Ambassador in Bandar Seri Begawan: Craig Allen
State Dept. Country Office: (202) 647-1823

Bulgaria   Web, www.bulgaria-embassy.org

Ambassador: Elena Poptodorova
Chancery: 1621 22nd St. N.W. 20008; (202) 387-0174; Fax, (202) 234-7973; Email, office@bulgaria-embassy.org
U.S. Ambassador: Eric Seth Rubin
State Dept. Country Office: (202) 647-1457

Burkina Faso   Web, www.burkina-usa.org

Chargé d'Affaires: Seydou Sinka
Chancery: 2340 Massachusetts Ave. N.W. 20008; (202) 332-5577; Fax, (202) 667-1882; Email, contact@burkina-usa.org
U.S. Ambassador in Ouagadougou: Tulinabo S. Mushingi
State Dept. Country Office: (202) 647-2637

Burma   (See Myanmar)

Burundi   Web, www.burundiembassydc-usa.org

Ambassador: Ernest Ndabashinze
Chancery: 2233 Wisconsin Ave. N.W., #408, 20007; (202) 342-2574; Fax, (202) 342-2578; Email, burundiembusadc@gmail.com
U.S. Ambassador in Bujumbura: Dawn M. Liberi
State Dept. Country Office: (202) 647-4965

Cambodia   Web, www.embassyofcambodia.org

Ambassador: Bunrong Chum
Chancery: 4530 16th St. N.W. 20011; (202) 726-7742; Fax, (202) 726-8381; Email, camemb.usa@mfa.gov.kh
U.S. Ambassador in Phnom Penh: William A. Heidt
State Dept. Country Office: (202) 647-3095

Cameroon   Web, www.cameroonembassyusa.org

Ambassador: Joseph Bienvenu Charles Foe-Atangana
Chancery: 3400 International Dr. N.W. 20008; (202) 265-8790; Fax, (202) 387-3826; Email, mail@cameroonembassyusa.org
U.S. Ambassador in Yaounde: Michael S. Hoza
State Dept. Country Office: (202) 647-3139

Canada   Web, www.can-am.gc.ca/washington

Ambassador: David MacNaughton

Chancery: 501 Pennsylvania Ave. N.W. 20001; (202) 682-1740; Fax, (202) 682-7726
U.S. Ambassador in Ottawa: Bruce Heyman
State Dept. Country Office: (202) 647-2170

Cape Verde   Web, www.embcv-usa.gov.cv

Ambassador: Jose Luis Rocha
Chancery: 3415 Massachusetts Ave. N.W. 20007; (202) 965-6820; Fax, (202) 965-1207; Email, admin@caboverdeus.net
U.S. Ambassador in Praia: Donald L. Heflin
State Dept. Country Office: (202) 647-3468

Central African Republic
    Web, www.rcawashington.org

Ambassador: Stanislas Moussa-Kembe
Chancery: 2704 Ontario Rd. 20009; (202) 483-7800; Fax, (202) 332-9893
U.S. Ambassador in Bangui: Jeffrey Hawkins
State Dept. Country Office: (202) 647-4514

Chad   Web, www.chadembassy.us

Ambassador: Mahamat Nasser Hassane
Chancery: 2401 Massachusetts Ave. N.W. 20906; (202) 652-1312; Fax, (202) 758-0431; Email, info@chadembassy.us
U.S. Ambassador in N'Djamena: James Knight
State Dept. Country Office: (202) 647-2973

Chile   Web, www.chile-usa.org

Ambassador: Juan Gabriel Valdes
Chancery: 1732 Massachusetts Ave. N.W. 20036; (202) 785-1746; Fax, (202) 887-5579; Email, echile.eeuu@minrel.gov.cl
U.S. Ambassador in Santiago: Michael A. Hammer
State Dept. Country Office: (202) 647-2575

China   Web, www.china-embassy.org/eng

Ambassador: Cui Tiankai
Chancery: 3505 International Pl. N.W. 20008; (202) 495-2266; Fax, (202) 495-2138; Email, chinaembpress_us@mfa.gov.cn
U.S. Ambassador in Beijing: Max Baucus
State Dept. Country Office: (202) 647-9141

Colombia   Web, www.colombiaemb.org

Ambassador: Juan Carlos Pinzón
Chancery: 1724 Massachusetts Ave. N.W. 20036; (202) 387-8338; Fax, (202) 232-8643; Email, embassyofcolumbia@columbiaemb.org
U.S. Ambassador in Bogotá: Kevin Whitaker
State Dept. Country Office: (202) 647-3142

Comoros   Web, www.comorosembassy.org

Ambassador: Roubani Kaambi (in New York)

Chancery: 866 UN Plaza, #418, New York, NY 10017; (212) 750-1637; Fax, (212) 750-1657; Email, comoros@un.int
U.S. Ambassador: Robert T. Yamate (resident in Antananarivo, Madagascar)
State Dept. Country Office: (202) 736-9048

Congo, Democratic Republic of the (DRC)

Web, www.ambardcusa.org

Ambassador: François Nkuna Balumuene
Chancery: 1100 Connecticut Ave. N.W., #725, 20036; (202) 234-7690; Fax, (202) 234-2609; Email, ambassade@ambardcusa.org
U.S. Ambassador in Kinshasa: James C. Swan
State Dept. Country Office: (202) 647-2216

Congo, Republic of the

Web, www.ambacongo-us.org

Ambassador: Serge Mombouli
Chancery: 1720 16th St. N.W. 20009; (202) 726-5500; Fax, (202) 726-1860; Email, info@ambacongo-us.org
U.S. Ambassador in Brazzaville: Stephanie S. Sullivan
State Dept. Country Office: (202) 647-3138

Costa Rica   Web, www.costarica-embassy.org

Ambassador: Roman Macaya Hayes
Chancery: 2114 S St. N.W. 20008; (202) 499-2991; Fax, (202) 265-4795; Email, concr-us-wa@rree.go.cr
U.S. Ambassador in San Jose: S. Fitzgerald Haney
State Dept. Country Office: (202) 647-3519

Côte d'Ivoire   Web, www.ambaci-usa.org/en

Ambassador: Diabate Daouda
Chancery: 2424 Massachusetts Ave. N.W. 20008; (202) 797-0300; Fax, (202) 204-3967
U.S. Ambassador in Abidjan: Terence P. McCulley
State Dept. Country Office: (202) 647-2791

Croatia   Web, www.us.mvep.hr

Ambassador: Josip Josko Paro
Chancery: 2343 Massachusetts Ave. N.W. 20008; (202) 588-5899; Fax, (202) 588-8936; Email, Washington@mvep.hr
U.S. Ambassador in Zagreb: Julieta Valls Noyes
State Dept. Country Office: (202) 647-4987

Cuba   Web, www.cubadiplomatica.cu/eeuu/EN

Chargé d'Affaires: Jose Ramon Cabañas
Chancery: 2630 16th St. N.W. 20009; (202) 797-8518; Fax, (202) 797-8521; Email, recepcion@sicuw.org
U.S. Chargé d'Affaires in Havana: Jeffrey DeLaurentis
State Dept. Country Office: (202) 647-9272

Curacao   (See The Netherlands)

U.S. Chargé d'Affaires: Hormazd Kanga
State Dept. Country Office: (202) 647-4719

Cyprus   Web, www.cyprusembassy.net

Ambassador: George Chacalli
Chancery: 2211 R St. N.W. 20008; (202) 462-5772; Fax, (202) 483-6710; Email, info@cyprusembassy.net
U.S. Ambassador in Nicosia: Kathleen A. Doherty
State Dept. Country Office: (202) 647-6948

Czech Republic   Web, www.mzv.cz/washington

Ambassador: Petr Gandalovič
Chancery: 3900 Spring of Freedom St. N.W. 20008; (202) 274-9100; Fax, (202) 966-8540; Email, Washington@embassy.mzv.cz
U.S. Ambassador in Prague: Andrew H. Schapiro
State Dept. Country Office: (202) 647-3191

Denmark   Web, www.usa.um.dk

Ambassador: Lars Gert Lose
Chancery: 3200 Whitehaven St. N.W. 20008; (202) 234-4300; Fax, (202) 328-1470; Email, mwasamb@um.dk
U.S. Ambassador in Copenhagen: Rufus Gifford
State Dept. Country Office: (202) 647-8431

Djibouti   Web, www.embassy.org/embassies/dj.html

Ambassador: Mohamed Siad Doualeh
Chancery: 1156 15th St. N.W., #515, 20005; (202) 331-0270; Fax, (202) 331-0302
U.S. Ambassador in Djibouti: Thomas P. Kelly
State Dept. Country Office: (202) 647-6453

Dominica   Web, www.embassy.org/embassies/dm.html

Ambassador: Hubert John Charles
Chancery: 3216 New Mexico Ave. N.W. 20016; (202) 364-6781; Fax, (202) 364-6791; Email, embdomdc@aol.com
U.S. Ambassador: Larry L. Palmer (resident in Bridgetown, Barbados)
State Dept. Country Office: (202) 647-4384

Dominican Republic   Web, www.domrep.org

Ambassador: Jose Tomás Pérez
Chancery: 1715 22nd St. N.W. 20008; (202) 332-6280; Fax, (202) 265-8057; Email, embassy@us.serex.gov.do
U.S. Ambassador in Santo Domingo: James Brewster
State Dept. Country Office: (202) 647-5088

East Timor   (See Timor-Leste)

Ecuador   Web, www.ecuador.org

Ambassador: Francisco Borja Cevallos
Chancery: 2535 15th St. N.W. 20009; (202) 234-7200; Fax, (202) 333-2893; Email, embassy@ecudor.org
U.S. Ambassador in Quito: Todd Chapman
State Dept. Country Office: (202) 647-2807

Egypt   Web, www.egyptembassy.net

Ambassador: Yasser Reda

Chancery: 3521 International Court N.W. 20008; (202) 895-5400; Fax, (202) 244-5131; Email, embassy@egyptembassy.net
U.S. Ambassador in Cairo: R. Stephen Beecroft
State Dept. Country Office: (202) 647-4680

El Salvador   Web, www.elsalvador.org

Ambassador: Francisco Altschul Fuentes
Chancery: 1400 16th St. N.W., #100, 20036; (202) 595-7500; Fax, (202) 232-3763; Email, correo@elsalvador.org
U.S. Ambassador in San Salvador: Jean Elizabeth Manes
State Dept. Country Office: (202) 647-4161

Equatorial Guinea   Web, www.egembassydc.com

Ambassador: Miguel Ntutumu Evuna Andeme
Chancery: 2020 16th St. N.W. 20009; (202) 518-5700; Fax, (202) 518-5252; Email, eg_africa@yahoo.com
U.S. Ambassador in Malabo: Julie Furuta-Toy
State Dept. Country Office: (202) 647-4514

Eritrea   Web, www.embassyeritrea.org

Ambassador: Ghirmai Ghebremariam
Chancery: 1708 New Hampshire Ave. N.W. 20009; (202) 319-1991; Fax, (202) 319-1304; Email, embassyeritrea@embassyeritrea.org
U.S. Chargé d'Affaires in Asmara: Louis Mazel
State Dept. Country Office: (202) 647-6453

Estonia   Web, www.estemb.org

Ambassador: Eerik Marmei
Chancery: 2131 Massachusetts Ave. N.W. 20008; (202) 588-0101; Fax, (202) 588-0108; Email, Embassy.Washington@mfa.ee
U.S. Ambassador in Tallinn: James D. Melville Jr.
State Dept. Country Office: (202) 647-6582

Ethiopia   Web, www.ethiopianembassy.org

Ambassador: Girma Birru
Chancery: 3506 International Dr. N.W. 20008; (202) 364-1200; Fax, (202) 587-0195; Email, ethiopia@ethiopianembassy.org
U.S. Ambassador in Addis Ababa: Patricia M. Haslach
State Dept. Country Office: (202) 647-6473

European Union   Web: www.euintheus.org

Ambassador: David O'Sullivan
Chancery: 2175 K St., 20037; (202) 862-9500; Fax, (202) 429-1766
U.S. Ambassador to the EU: Anthony L. Gardner
State Dept. Country Office: (202) 647-1708

Fiji   Web, www.fijiembassydc.com

Ambassador: Winston Thompson
Chancery: 1707 L St. N.W., #200, 20036; (202) 466-8320; Fax, (202) 466-8325; Email, info@fijiembassydc.com
U.S. Ambassador in Suva: Judith Beth Cefkin
State Dept. Country Office: (202) 647-5156

Finland   Web, www.finland.org

Ambassador: Kirsti Kauppi
Chancery: 3301 Massachusetts Ave. N.W. 20008; (202) 298-5800; Fax, (202) 298-6030; Email, sanomat.was@formin.fi
U.S. Ambassador in Helsinki: Charles C. Adams Jr.
State Dept. Country Office: (202) 647-6582

France   Web, www.franceintheus.org

Ambassador: Gerard Araud
Chancery: 4101 Reservoir Rd. N.W. 20007; (202) 944-6000; Fax, (202) 944-6166; Email, info@ambafrance-us.org
U.S. Ambassador in Paris: Jane D. Hartley
State Dept. Country Office: (202) 647-4372

Gabon   Web, www.gabonembassyusa.org

Ambassador: Michael Moussa-Adamo
Chancery: 2034 20th St. N.W., #200, 20009; (202) 797-1000; Fax, (202) 332-0668; Email, info@gabonembassy.org
U.S. Ambassador in Libreville: Cynthia Akuetteh
State Dept. Country Office: (202) 647-3138

The Gambia   Web, www.gambiaembassy.us

Chargé d'Affaires: Sheikh Omar Faye
Chancery: Georgetown Plaza, 2233 Wisconsin Ave. N.W., Georgetown Plaza, #240, 20007; (202) 785-1399; Fax, (202) 342-0240; Email, info@gambiaembassy.us
U.S. Ambassador in Banjul: C. Patricia (Pat) Alsup
State Dept. Country Office: (202) 647-1596

Georgia   Web, www.usa.mfa.gov.ge

Ambassador: Archil Gegeshidze
Chancery: 1824 R St. N.W. 20009; (202) 387-2390; Fax, (202) 387-0864; Email, embgeo.usa@mfa.gov.ge
U.S. Ambassador in Tbilisi: Ian C. Kelly
State Dept. Country Office: (202) 647-6048

Germany   Web, www.germany.info

Ambassador: Peter Wittig
Chancery: 4645 Reservoir Rd. N.W. 20007; (202) 298-4000; Fax, (202) 298-4249
U.S. Ambassador in Berlin: John B. Emerson
State Dept. Country Office: (202) 647-4361

Ghana   Web, www.ghanaembassy.org

Ambassador: Lt. Gen. Joseph Henry Smith
Chancery: 3512 International Dr. N.W. 20008; (202) 686-4520; Fax, (202) 686-4527
U.S. Ambassador in Accra: Robert P. Jackson
State Dept. Country Office: (202) 647-0252

Greece   Web, www.mfa.gr/washington

Ambassador: Christos P. Panagopoulos
Chancery: 2217 Massachusetts Ave. N.W. 20008; (202) 939-1300; Fax, (202) 939-1324; Email, gremb.was@mfa.gr

U.S. Ambassador in Athens: David D. Pearce
State Dept. Country Office: (202) 647-6760

Greenland   (See Denmark)

Grenada   Web, www.grenadaembassyusa.org

Ambassador: E. Angus Friday
Chancery: 1701 New Hampshire Ave. N.W. 20009-2501; (202) 265-2561; Fax, (202) 265-2468; Email, embassy@ grenadaembassyusa.org
U.S. Ambassador: Larry L. Palmer (resident in Bridgetown, Barbados)
State Dept. Country Office: (202) 647-4384

Guatemala   Web, http://guatemalaembassyusa.org

Ambassador: Julio Ligorria Carballido
Chancery: 2220 R St. N.W. 20008; (202) 745-4953; Fax, (202) 745-1908; Email, info@guatemala-embassy.org
U.S. Ambassador in Guatemala City: Todd D. Robinson
State Dept. Country Office: (202) 647-3727

Republic of Guinea

Web, http://guineaembassyusa.com

Ambassador: Mamady Conde
Chancery: 2112 Leroy Pl. N.W. 20008, (202) 986-4300; Fax, (202) 986-3800; Email, acamara@guinea embassyusa.com
U.S. Ambassador in Conakry: Dennis B. Hankins
State Dept. Country Office: (202) 647-0252

Guinea-Bissau

There have been several attempts to establish diplomatic relations in recent years.
Contact: P.O. Box 33813, 20033; (301) 947-3958
The U.S. ambassador to Senegal, James P. Zumwalt, covers matters pertaining to Guinea-Bissau.
State Dept. Country Office: (202) 647-1597

Guyana

Web, www.guyana.org/govt/ foreign_missions.html

Ambassador: Bayney Ram Karran
Chancery: 2490 Tracy Pl. N.W. 20008; (202) 265-6900; Fax, (202) 232-1297; Email, guyanaembassydc@ verizon.net
U.S. Ambassador in Georgetown: Perry Holloway
State Dept. Country Office: (202) 647-4719

Haiti   Web, www.haiti.org

Ambassador: Paul Altidor
Chancery: 2311 Massachusetts Ave. N.W. 20008; (202) 332-4090; Fax, (202) 745-7215; Email, amb.washington@diplomatie.ht
U.S. Ambassador in Port-au-Prince: Peter F. Mulrean
State Dept. Country Office: (202) 647-9510
The Holy See
Ambassador: Christophe Pierre, Apostolic Nuncio

Office: 3339 Massachusetts Ave. N.W. 20008; (202) 333-7121; Fax, (202) 337-4036; Email, nuntiususa@ nuntiususa.org
U.S. Ambassador in Vatican City: Kenneth F. Hackett
State Dept. Country Office: (202) 647-3746

Honduras   Web, www.hondurasemb.org

Ambassador: Jorge Alberto Milla Reyes
Chancery: 3007 Tilden St. N.W. 20008; (202) 966-7702-2604; Fax, (202) 966-9751; Email, kescalante@hondurasemb.org
U.S. Ambassador in Tegucigalpa: James D. Nealon
State Dept. Country Office: (202) 647-3505

Hong Kong   (See China)

State Dept. Country Office: (202) 647-6300

Hungary   Web, www.washington.kormany.hu

Ambassador: Réka Szemerkényi
Chancery: 3910 Shoemaker St. N.W. 20008; (202) 362-6730; Fax, (202) 966-8135; Email, informacio.was@ mfa.gov.hu
U.S. Ambassador in Budapest: Colleen Bell
State Dept. Country Office: (202) 647-0425

Iceland   Web, www.iceland.is/iceland-abroad/us/wdc

Ambassador: Geir H. Haarde
Chancery: House of Sweden, 2900 K St. N.W., #509, 20007-1704, (202) 265-6653; Fax, (202) 265-6656; Email, icemb.wash@utn.stjr.is
U.S. Ambassador in Reykjavik: Robert C. Barber
State Dept. Country Office: (202) 647-8431

India   Web, www.indianembassy.org

Ambassador: Arun K. Singh
Chancery: 2107 Massachusetts Ave. N.W. 20008; (202) 939-7000; Fax, (202) 265-4351
U.S. Ambassador in New Delhi: Richard R. Verma
State Dept. Country Office: (202) 647-1112

Indonesia   Web, www.embassyofindonesia.org

Ambassador: Budi Bowoleksono
Chancery: 2020 Massachusetts Ave. N.W. 20036; (202) 775-5200; Fax, (202) 775-5365
U.S. Ambassador in Jakarta: Robert O. Blake Jr.
State Dept. Country Office: (202) 647-2301

Iran   Web, www.daftar.org

The United States severed diplomatic relations with Iran in April 1980. Iran's interests in the United States are represented by the Pakistani embassy.
Iranian Interests Section: 1250 23rd St. N.W., #200, 20037; (202) 965-4990; Fax, (202) 965-1073; Email, info@daftar.org
U.S. interests in Iran are represented by the Swiss embassy in Tehran.
State Dept. Country Office: (202) 647-2520

Iraq   Web, www.iraqiembassy.us

The United States and Iraq resumed diplomatic relations in June 2004.
Ambassador: Lukman Faily
Chancery: 3421 Massachusetts Ave. N.W. 20007; (202) 742-1600; Fax, (202) 333-1129
Consulate: 1801 P St. N.W. 20036; (202) 483-7500; Fax, (202) 462-5066
U.S. Ambassador to Baghdad: Stuart E. Jones
State Dept. Country Office: (202) 647-5692

Ireland   Web, www.embassyofireland.org

Ambassador: Anne Anderson
Chancery: 2234 Massachusetts Ave. N.W. 20008; (202) 462-3939; Fax, (202) 232-5993
U.S. Ambassador in Dublin: Kevin F. O'Malley
State Dept. Country Office: (202) 647-6591

Israel   Web, www.israelemb.org

Ambassador: Ron Dermer
Chancery: 3514 International Dr. N.W. 20008; (202) 364-5500; Fax, (202) 364-5423
U.S. Ambassador in Tel Aviv: Daniel B. Shapiro
State Dept. Country Office: (202) 647-3672

Italy   Web, www.ambwashingtondc.esteri.it

Ambassador: Armando Varricchio
Chancery: 3000 Whitehaven St. N.W. 20008; (202) 612-4400; Fax, (202) 518-2154; Email, stampa.washington@esteri.it
U.S. Ambassador in Rome: John R. Phillips
State Dept. Country Office: (202) 647-3746

Jamaica   Web, www.embassyofjamaica.org

Ambassador: Ralph Thomas
Chancery: 1520 New Hampshire Ave. N.W. 20036; (202) 452-0660; Fax, (202) 452-0036; Email, firstsec@jamaicaembassy.org
U.S. Ambassador in Kingston: Luis G. Moreno
State Dept. Country Office: (202) 736-4322

Japan   Web, www.us.emb-japan.go.jp/english/html

Ambassador: Kenichiro Sasae
Chancery: 2520 Massachusetts Ave. N.W. 20008; (202) 238-6700; Fax, (202) 328-2187
U.S. Ambassador in Tokyo: Caroline Kennedy
State Dept. Country Office: (202) 647-3152

Jordan   Web, www.jordanembassyus.org

Ambassador: Dr. Alia Hatoug-Bouran
Chancery: 3504 International Dr. N.W. 20008; (202) 966-2664; Fax, (202) 966-3110; Email, hkjembassydc@jordanembassyus.org
U.S. Ambassador in Amman: Alice G. Wells
State Dept. Country Office: (202) 647-1091

Kazakhstan   Web, www.kazakhembus.com

Ambassador: Kairat Umarov
Chancery: 1401 16th St. N.W. 20036; (202) 232-5488; Fax, (202) 232-5845; Email, washington@mfa.kz or Washington@kazakhembus.com
U.S. Ambassador: George A. Krol
State Dept. Country Office: (202) 647-6859

Kenya   Web, www.kenyaembassy.com

Ambassador: Robinson Njeru Githae
Chancery: 2249 R St. N.W. 20008; (202) 387-6101; Fax, (202) 462-3829; Email, information@kenyaembassy.com
U.S. Ambassador in Nairobi: Robert F. Godec
State Dept. Country Office: (202) 647-8913

Kiribati

Kiribati maintains a Permanent Mission to the United Nations.
Her Excellency: Makuritan Baaro
UN Chancery: 800 2nd Ave., #400A, New York, NY 10017; (212) 867-3310; Fax, (212) 867-3320.
U.S. Ambassador: Judith Beth Cefkin (resident in Suva, Fiji)
State Dept. Country Office: (202) 647-5156

Korea, Democratic People's Republic of (North)

North Korea maintains a Permanent Mission to the United Nations
UN Chancery: 515 E. 72nd St., #38F, New York, NY 10021; (212) 772-0712; Fax, (212) 772-0735
The United States does not maintain diplomatic relations with North Korea. The Swedish Embassy in Pyongyang represents the U.S. as a consular protecting power.
State Dept. Country Office: (202) 647-7717

Korea, Republic of (South)
   Web, http://usa.mofat.go.Kr/english

Ambassador: Ahn Ho-young
Chancery: 2450 Massachusetts Ave. N.W. 20008; (202) 939-5600; Fax, (202) 797-0595; Email, consular_usa@mofa.go.kr
U.S. Ambassador in Seoul: Mark Lippet
State Dept. Country Office: (202) 647-7717

Kosovo   Web, www.ambasada-ks.net/us

Ambassador: Vlora Çitaku
Chancery: 1101 30th St. N.W., #330, 20007; (202) 450-2130; Fax, (202) 735-0609; Email, embassy.usa@rks-gov.net
U.S. Ambassador in Pristina: Greg Delawie
State Dept. Country Office: (202) 647-0608

Kuwait   Web, www.kuwaitembassy.us

Ambassador: Salem Abdullah Al-Jaber Al-Sabah
Chancery: 2940 Tilden St. N.W. 20008; (202) 966-0702; Fax, (202) 364-2868

U.S. Ambassador in Kuwait City: Douglas A. Silliman
State Dept. Country Office: (202) 647-9005

Kyrgyzstan, Republic of Kyrgyz

Web, www.kgembassy.org

Ambassador: Kadyr Toktogulov
Chancery: 2360 Massachusetts Ave. N.W. 20008; (202) 449-9822; Fax, (202) 386-7550; Email, kgembassyusa@gmail.com
U.S. Ambassador in Bishkek: Sheila Gwaltney
State Dept. Country Office: (202) 647-9119

Laos   Web, www.laoembassy.com

Ambassador: Mai Sayavongs
Chancery: 2222 S St. N.W. 20008; (202) 332-6416; Fax, (202) 332-4923; Email, embasslao@gmail.com
U.S. Ambassador in Vientiane: Daniel A. Clune
State Dept. Country Office: (202) 647-2459

Latvia   Web, www.latvia-usa.org

Ambassador: Andris Razans
Chancery: 2306 Massachusetts Ave. N.W. 20008; (202) 328-2840; Fax, (202) 328-2860; Email, embassy.usa@mfa.gov.lv
U.S. Ambassador in Riga: Nancy Bikoff Pettit
State Dept. Country Office: (202) 647-9980

Lebanon   Web, www.lebanonembassyus.org

Chargé d'Affaires: Carla Jazzar
Chancery: 2560 28th St. N.W. 20008; (202) 939-6300; Fax, (202) 939-6324; Email, info@lebanonembassyus.org
U.S. Chargé d'Affaires in Beirut: Richard Henry Jones
State Dept. Country Office: (202) 647-1030

Lesotho, Kingdom of

Web, www.lesothoemb-usa.gov.ls

Ambassador: Eliachim Molapi Sebatane
Chancery: 2511 Massachusetts Ave. N.W. 20008; (202) 797-5533; Fax, (202) 234-6815; Email, lesothoembassy@verizon.net
U.S. Ambassador in Maseru: Matthew T. Harrington
State Dept. Country Office: (202) 647-9838

Liberia   Web, www.liberianembassyus.org

Ambassador: Jeremiah C. Sulunteh
Chancery: 5201 16th St. N.W. 20011; (202) 723-0437; Fax, (202) 723-0436
U.S. Chargé d'Affaires in Monrovia: Mark Bouleware
State Dept. Country Office: (202) 647-3469

Libya   Web, www.embassyoflibyadc.org

Chargé d'Affaires: Wafa Bughaighis
Chancery: 2600 Virginia Ave. N.W., #705, 20037; (202) 944-9601; Fax, (202) 944-9606; Email, info@embassyoflibyadc.org

The U.S. Embassy in Tripoli, Libya, closed on July 26, 2014. Diplomatic relations are handled from the U.S. Embassy in Tunis, Tunisia.
U.S. Ambassador to Tripoli: Peter W. Bodde
State Dept. Country Office: (202) 647-4674

Liechtenstein   Web, www.liechtensteinusa.org

Ambassador: Claudia Fritsche
Chancery: 2900 K St. N.W., #602B, 20007; (202) 331-0590; Fax, (202) 331-3221
U.S. Ambassador: Suzan G. LeVine (resident in Bern, Switzerland)
State Dept. Country Office: (202) 647-0425

Lithuania   Web, www.usa.mfa.lt

Ambassador: Rolandas Kriščiūnas
Chancery: 2622 16th St. N.W. 20009; (202) 234-5860; Fax, (202) 328-0466; Email, info@usa.mfa.lt
U.S. Ambassador in Vilnius: Deborah A. McCarthy
State Dept. Country Office: (202) 647-8378

Luxembourg   Web, www.washington.mae.lu/en

Ambassador: Jean-Louis Wolzfeld
Chancery: 2200 Massachusetts Ave. N.W. 20008; (202) 265-4171; Fax, (202) 328-8270; Email, luxembassy.was@mae.etat.lu
U.S. Ambassador in Luxembourg: David McKean
State Dept. Country Office: (202) 647-5674

Macau   (See China)

State Dept. Country Office: (202) 647-6300

Macedonia   Web, www.mfa.gov.mk/washington

Chargé d'Affaires: Oliver Krliu
Chancery: 2129 Wyoming Ave. N.W. 20008; (202) 667-0501; Fax, (202) 667-2131; Email, washington@mfa.gov.mk
U.S. Ambassador in Skopje: Jess L. Baily
State Dept. Country Office: (202) 647-3747

Madagascar   Web, www.madagascar-embassy.org

Chargé d'Affaires: Velotiana Rakotoanosy Raobelina
Chancery: 2374 Massachusetts Ave. N.W. 20008; (202) 265-5525; Fax, (202) 265-3034; Email, Malagasy.Embassy@verizon.net
U.S. Ambassador in Antananarivo: Robert T. Yamate
State Dept. Country Office: (202) 647-9048

Malawi   Web, www.malawiembassy-dc.org

Ambassador: Necton Mhura
Chancery: 2408 Massachusetts Ave. N.W. 20008; (202) 721-0270; Fax, (202) 721-0288
U.S. Ambassador in Lilongwe: Virginia E. Palmer
State Dept. Country Office: (202) 647-9857

Malaysia

Web, www.kln.gov.my/web/usa_washington/home

Ambassador: Awang Adek Bin Hussin
Chancery: 3516 International Court N.W. 20008; (202)
572-9700; Fax, (202) 572-9882; Email,
mwwashington@kln.gov.my
U.S. Ambassador in Kuala Lumpur: Joseph Y. Yun
State Dept. Country Office: (202) 647-4932

Maldives   Web, www.maldivesmission.com

Ambassador: Ahmed Sareer (in New York)
Chancery: 801 2nd Ave., #4202E, New York, NY 10017;
(212) 599-6194; Fax, (212) 661-6405
U.S. Ambassador: Atul Keshap (resident in Colombo,
Sri Lanka)
State Dept. Country Office: (202) 647-1078

Mali   Web, www.maliembassy.us

Ambassador: Tiena Coulibaly
Chancery: 2130 R St. N.W. 20008; (202) 332-2249;
Fax, (202) 332-6603; Email, tcoulibaly@maliembassy.us
U.S. Ambassador in Bamako: Paul A. Folmsbee
State Dept. Country Office: (202) 647-3469

Malta   Web, www.foreign.gov.mt

Ambassador: Pierre Clive Agius
Chancery: 2017 Connecticut Ave. N.W. 20008; (202) 462-
3611; Fax, (202) 387-5470; Email, maltaembassy
.washington@gov.mt
U.S. Ambassador in Valletta: G. Kathleen Hill
State Dept. Country Office: (202) 647-3151

Marshall Islands   Web, www.rmiembassyus.org

Ambassador: Charles R. Paul
Chancery: 2433 Massachusetts Ave. N.W. 20008; (202)
234-5414; Fax, (202) 232-3236; Email, info@
rmiembassyus.org
U.S. Ambassador in Majuro: Vacant
State Dept. Country Office: (202) 736-4683

Mauritania

Ambassador: Mohamed Lemine El Haycen
Chancery: 2129 Leroy Pl. N.W. 20008; (202) 232-5700;
Fax, (202) 319-2623
U.S. Ambassador in Nouakchott: Larry E. André Jr.
State Dept. Country Office: (202) 647-3468

Mauritius

Web, www.maurinet.com/tourist_information/
mauritius_embassies

Ambassador: Somduth Soborun
Chancery: 1709 N St. N.W. 20036; (202) 244-1491;
Fax, (202) 966-0983; Email, Mauritius.embassy@
verizon.net
U.S. Ambassador in Port Louis: Shari Villarosa
State Dept. Country Office: (202) 736-9048

Mexico   Web, www.embassyofmexico.org

Ambassador: Miguel Basáñez Ebergenyi
Chancery: 1911 Pennsylvania Ave. N.W. 20006; (202) 728-
1600; Fax, (202) 728-1698
U.S. Chargé d'Affaires in Mexico City: William H.
Duncan
State Dept. Country Office: (202) 647-8766

Micronesia   Web, www.fsmembassydc.org

Ambassador: Asterio Takesy
Chancery: 1725 N St. N.W. 20036; (202) 223-4383;
Fax, (202) 223-4391; Email, firstsecretary@
fsmembassydc.org
U.S. Ambassador in Kolonia: Vacant
State Dept. Country Office: (202) 736-4683

Moldova   Web, www.sua.mfa.md/about-embassy-en

Chargé d'Affaires: Veaceslav Pituşcan
Chancery: 2101 S St. N.W. 20008; (202) 667-1130;
Fax, (202) 667-2624; Email, washington@mfa.md
U.S. Ambassador in Chişinău: James D. Pettit
State Dept. Country Office: (202) 647-6733

Monaco   Web, www.monacodc.org

Ambassador: Maguy Maccario Doyle
Chancery: 4000 Connecticut Ave. N.W. 20008-3306;
Mailing address, 3400 International Dr. N.W.,
#2K–100, 20008; (202) 234-1530; Fax, (202) 244-7656;
Email, info@monacodc.org
U.S. Consulate General: Jane D. Hartley (resident in Paris,
France)
State Dept. Country Office: (202) 647-3072

Mongolia   Web, www.mongolianembassy.us

Ambassador: Bugaa Attangerel
Chancery: 2833 M St. N.W. 20007; (202) 333-7117;
Fax, (202) 298-9227; Email, washington@mfa.gov.mn
U.S. Ambassador in Ulaanbaatar: Jennifer Zimdahl Galt
State Dept. Country Office: (202) 647-7628

Montenegro

Web, www.mvpei.gov.me/en/sections/Missions/
Embassies-and-consulates-of-Montenegro/united-
states-of-america

Ambassador: Srđan Darmanović
Chancery: 1610 New Hampshire Ave. N.W. 20009; (202)
234-6108; Fax, (202) 234-6109
U.S. Ambassador in Podgorica: Margaret Ann Uyehara
State Dept. Country Office: (202) 647-7660

Morocco   Web, www.embassyofmorocco.us

Ambassador: Rachad Bouhlal
Chancery: 1601 21st St. N.W. 20009; (202) 462-7979;
Fax, (202) 462-7643; Email, ambmoroccoffice@gmail
.com
U.S. Ambassador in Rabat: Dwight L. Bush
State Dept. Country Office: (202) 647-1724

Mozambique   Web, www.embamoc-usa.org

Ambassador: Amelia Matos Sumbana
Chancery: 1525 New Hampshire Ave. N.W. 20036; (202) 293-7146; Fax, (202) 835-0245; Email, embamoc@aol.com
U.S. Ambassador in Maputo: H. Dean Pittman
State Dept. Country Office: (202) 647-9857

Myanmar (Burma)

Web, www.mewashingtondc.com

Ambassador: U Kyaw Myo Htut
Chancery: 2300 S St. N.W. 20008; (202) 332-3344; Fax, (202) 332-4351; Email, pyi.thayar@yahoo.com
U.S. Ambassador in Rangoon: Scot Marciel
State Dept. Country Office: (202) 647-0056

Namibia   Web, www.namibianembassyusa.org

Ambassador: Martin Andjaba
Chancery: 1605 New Hampshire Ave. N.W. 20009; (202) 986-0540; Fax, (202) 986-0443; Email, info@namibianembassyusa.org
U.S. Ambassador in Windhoek: Thomas F. Daughton
State Dept. Country Office: (202) 647-9858

Nauru   Web, www.un.int/nauru

Ambassador: Marlene I. Moses (in New York)
Chancery: 801 2nd Ave., 3rd Floor, New York, NY 10017; (212) 937-0074; Fax, (212) 937-0079; Email, nauru@onecommonwealth.org
U.S. Ambassador: Judith B. Cefkin (resident in Suva, Fiji)
State Dept. Country Office: (202) 647-5156

Nepal   Web, www.nepalembassyusa.org

Ambassador: Arjun Kumar Karki
Chancery: 2131 Leroy Pl. N.W. 20008; (202) 667-4550; Fax, (202) 667-5534; Email, info@nepalembassyusa.org
U.S. Ambassador in Kathmandu: Alaina B. Teplitz
State Dept. Country Office: (202) 647-2941

The Netherlands   Web, www.dc.the-netherlands.org

Ambassador: Henne Schuwer
Chancery: 4200 Linnean Ave. N.W. 20008; (202) 244-5300; Fax, (202) 362-3430; Email, info@dutchhelp.com
U.S. Ambassador at The Hague: Vacant
State Dept. Country Office: (202) 647-6555

New Zealand

Web, www.mfat.govt.nz/en/countries-and-regions/north-america/united-states-of-america/new-zealand-embassy-washington

Ambassador: Tim Groser
Chancery: 37 Observatory Circle N.W. 20008; (202) 328-4800; Fax, (202) 667-5227; Email, wshinfo@mfat.govt.nz
U.S. Ambassador in Wellington: Mark Gilbert
State Dept. Country Office: (202) 736-4745

Nicaragua   Web, www.consuladodenicaragua.com

Ambassador: Francisco Obadiah Campbell Hooker
Chancery: 1627 New Hampshire Ave. N.W. 20009; (202) 939-6570; Fax, (202) 939-6542
U.S. Ambassador in Managua: Laura F. Dogu
State Dept. Country Office: (202) 647-1510

Niger   Web, www.embassyofniger.org

Ambassador: Hassana Alidou
Chancery: 2204 R St. N.W. 20008; (202) 483-4224; Fax, (202) 483-3169; Email, communication@embassyofniger.org
U.S. Ambassador in Niamey: Eunice C. Reddick
State Dept. Country Office: (202) 647-2791

Nigeria   Web, www.nigeriaembassyusa.org

Chargé d'Affaires: Hakeem Balogun
Chancery: 3519 International Court N.W. 20008; (202) 986-8400; Fax, (202) 362-6541; Email, info@nigeriaembassyusa.org
U.S. Ambassador in Abuja: James F. Entwistle
State Dept. Country Office: (202) 647-1674

Norway   Web, www.norway.org

Ambassador: Kare R. Aas
Chancery: 2720 34th St. N.W. 20008; (202) 333-6000; Fax, (202) 469-3990; Email, emb.washington@mfa.no
U.S. Ambassador in Oslo: Samuel D. Heins
State Dept. Country Office: (202) 647-8178

Oman   Web, www.omani.info

Ambassador: Hunaina Sultan Ahmed Al-Mughairy
Chancery: 2535 Belmont Rd. N.W. 20008; (202) 387-1980; Fax, (202) 745-4933
U.S. Ambassador in Muscat: Marc Sievers
State Dept. Country Office: (202) 647-8821

Pakistan   Web, www.embassyofpakistanusa.org

Ambassador: Jalil Abbas Jilani
Chancery: 3517 International Court N.W. 20008; (202) 243-6500; Fax, (202) 686-1534; Email, info@embassyofpakistanusa.org
U.S. Ambassador in Islamabad: David Hale
State Dept. Country Office: (202) 647-9823

Palau   Web, www.palauembassy.com

Ambassador: Hersey Kyota
Chancery: 1701 Pennsylvania Ave. N.W., #300, 20006; (202) 452-6814; Fax, (202) 452-6281; Email, info@palauembassy.com
U.S. Ambassador in Koror: Amy Jane Hyatt
State Dept. Country Office: (202) 736-4683

Palestine Liberation Organization

Web, www.plodelegation.us

Ambassador: Maen Rashid Areikat

Chancery: 132 Wisconsin Ave. N.W. 20007; (202) 974-6360; Fax, (202) 974-6278; Email, info@plodelegation.us
U.S. Consul General in Jerusalem: Donald Blome
State Dept. Country Office: (202) 647-3746

Panama   Web, www.embassyofpanama.org

Ambassador: Emanuel Gonzalez Revilla
Chancery: 2862 McGill Terrace N.W. 20008; (202) 483-1407; Fax, (202) 483-8413; Email, info@embassyofpanama.org
U.S. Ambassador in Panama City: John D. Feeley
State Dept. Country Office: (202) 647-4992

Papua New Guinea   Web, www.pngembassy.org

Ambassador: Rupa Abraham Mulina
Chancery: 1779 Massachusetts Ave. N.W., #805, 20036; (202) 745-3680; Fax, (202) 745-3679; Email, info@pngembassy.org
U.S. Ambassador in Port Moresby: Catherine Ebert-Gray
State Dept. Country Office: (202) 647-5156

Paraguay
Web, www.mre.gov.py/embaparusa/en/index-eng.html

Ambassador: Igor Pangrazio
Chancery: 2400 Massachusetts Ave. N.W. 20008; (202) 483-6960; Fax, (202) 234-4508; Email, gabineteembaparusa@mre.gov.py
U.S. Ambassador in Asunción: Leslie A. Bassett
State Dept. Country Office: (202) 647-1551

Peru   Web, www.embassyofperu.org

Ambassador: Luis Miguel Castilla
Chancery: 1700 Massachusetts Ave. N.W. 20036; (202) 833-9860; Fax, (202) 659-8124; Email, sarboza@embassyofperu.us
U.S. Ambassador in Lima: Brian A. Nichols
State Dept. Country Office: (202) 647-4177

Philippines   Web, www.philippineembassy-usa.org

Ambassador: Jose L. Cuisia Jr.
Chancery: 1600 Massachusetts Ave. N.W. 20036; (202) 467-9300; Fax, (202) 467-9417; Email, info@philippinesusa.org
U.S. Ambassador in Manila: Phillip S. Goldberg
State Dept. Country Office: (202) 647-2927

Poland   Web, www.polandembassy.org

Ambassador: Ryszard Schnepf
Chancery: 2640 16th St. N.W. 20009; (202) 499-1700; Fax, (202) 328-6271; Email, washington.amb@msz.gov.pl
U.S. Ambassador in Warsaw: Paul W. Jones
State Dept. Country Office: (202) 647-4139

Portugal   Web, www.embassyportugal-us.org

Ambassador: Domingos Fezas Vital

Chancery: 2012 Massachusetts Ave. N.W. 20036; (202) 350-5400; Fax, (202) 462-3726; Email, info@embassyportugal-us.org
U.S. Ambassador in Lisbon: Robert A. Sherman
State Dept. Country Office: (202) 647-3746

Qatar

Ambassador: Mohammed Jaham Al Kuwari
Chancery: 2555 M St. N.W. 20037; (202) 274-1600; Fax, (202) 237-0061; Email, info@qatarembassy.net
U.S. Ambassador in Doha: Dana Shell Smith
State Dept. Country Office: (202) 647-2129

Romania   Web, www.washington.mae.ro/en

Ambassador: George Cristian Maior
Chancery: 1607 23rd St. N.W. 20008; (202) 332-4848; (202) 332-4846; Email, office@roembus.org
U.S. Ambassador in Bucharest: Hans G. Klemm
State Dept. Country Office: (202) 736-7152

Russia   Web, www.russianembassy.org

Ambassador: Sergei I. Kislyak
Chancery: 2650 Wisconsin Ave. N.W. 20007; (202) 298-5700; Fax, (202) 298-5735; Email, embassy@russianembassy.org
U.S. Ambassador in Moscow: John F. Tefft
State Dept. Country Office: (202) 647-9806

Rwanda   Web, www.rwandaembassy.org

Ambassador: Mathilde Mukantabana
Chancery: 1875 Connecticut Ave. N.W., #540, 20009; (202) 232-2882; Fax, (202) 232-4544
U.S. Ambassador in Kigali: Erica J. Barks-Ruggles
State Dept. Country Office: (202) 647-4965

Saint Kitts and Nevis   Web, www.embassy.gov.kn

Ambassador: Jacinth Lorna Henry-Martin
Chancery: 3216 New Mexico Ave. N.W. 20016; (202) 686-2636; Fax, (202) 686-5740; Email, stkittsnevis@embskn.com
U.S. Ambassador: Larry L. Palmer (resident in Bridgetown, Barbados)
State Dept. Country Office: (202) 647-4384

Saint Lucia   Web, www.govt.lc

Ambassador: Sonia M. Johnny
Chancery: 1001 19th St. North, #1234, Arlington, VA 22209; (202) 364-6792 or (571) 527-1375; Fax, (202) 364-6723 or (571) 384-7930; Email, embassydc@gosl.govt.lc or Sonia.johnny@govt.lc
U.S. Ambassador: Larry L. Palmer (resident in Bridgetown, Barbados)
State Dept. Country Office: (202) 647-4384

Saint Vincent and the Grenadines
Web, www.embsvg.com

Ambassador: La Celia Aritha Prince

Chancery: 1001 19th St. North, #1242, Arlington VA 22209; (202) 364-6730; Fax, (202) 364-6736; Email, mail@embsvg.com
U.S. Ambassador: Larry L. Palmer (resident in Bridgetown, Barbados)
State Dept. Country Office: (202) 647-4531

Samoa   Web, www.mfat.govt.ws

Ambassador: Aliʻioaiga Feturi Elisaia (in New York)
Chancery: 800 2nd Ave., #400j, New York, NY 10017; (212) 599-6196; Fax, (212) 599-0797; Email, samoa@un.int
U.S. Ambassador to Apia: Mark Gilbert (resident in Wellington, New Zealand)
State Dept. Country Office: (202) 736-4745

San Marino

Ambassador: Paolo Rondelli
Chancery: 1711 N St. N.W., 2nd Floor 20036; (202) 250-1535 San Marino is also represented by the Consul General Abigail (Abby) Rupp.
U.S. Ambassador: John R. Phillips (resident in Florence, Italy)
State Dept. Country Office: (202) 647-3072

São Tomé and Principe

Web, www.embstpusa.com

Ambassador: Ovidio Manuel Barbosa Pequeno
Chancery: 1211 Connecticut Ave. N.W., #300, 20036; (202) 775-2076, 2075; Fax, (202) 775-2077; Email, embstpusa@verizon.net
U.S. Ambassador in Libreville: Cynthia Akeuttah (resident in Libreville, Gabon)
State Dept. Country Office: (202) 647-3138

Saudi Arabia   Web, www.saudiembassy.net

Ambassador: Abdullah bin Faisal bin Turki bin Abdullah Al Saud
Chancery: 601 New Hampshire Ave. N.W. 20037; (202) 342-3800; Fax, (202) 944-5983; Email, info@saudiembassy.net
U.S. Ambassador in Riyadh: Joseph William Westphal
State Dept. Country Office: (202) 647-7550

Senegal   Web, www.ambasenegal-us.org

Ambassador: Babacar Diagne
Chancery: 2215 M St. N.W. 20037; (202) 234-0540; Fax, (202) 629-2961; Email, contact@ambasenegal-us.org
U.S. Ambassador in Dakar: James P. Zumwalt
State Dept. Country Office: (202) 647-1956

Serbia   Web, www.serbiaembusa.org

Ambassador: Djerdj Matkovic
Chancery: 2134 Kalorama Rd. N.W. 20008; (202) 332-0333; Fax, (202) 332-3933; Email, info@serbiaembusa.org
U.S. Ambassador in Belgrade: Kyle R. Scott
State Dept. Country Office: (202) 647-0310

Seychelles

Ambassador: Marie Louise Cecile Potter (in New York)
Chancery: 800 2nd Ave., #400G, New York, NY 10017; (212) 687-9766; Fax, (212) 972-1786; Email, Seychelles@un.int
U.S. Ambassador: Shari Villarosa (resident in Port Louis, Mauritius)
State Dept. Country Office: (202) 647-2791

Sierra Leone   Web, www.embassyofsierraleone.net

Chief of Mission: Bockari Kortu Stevens
Chancery: 1701 19th St. N.W. 20009-1605; (202) 939-9261; Fax, (202) 483-1798; Email, info@embassyofsierraleone.net
U.S. Ambassador in Freetown: John Hoover
State Dept. Country Office: (202) 647-1540

Singapore   Web, www.mfa.gov.sg/washington

Ambassador: Ashok Kumar Mirpuri
Chancery: 3501 International Pl. N.W. 20008; (202) 537-3100; Fax, (202) 537-0876; Email, singemb_was@sgmfa.gov.sg
U.S. Ambassador in Singapore: Kirk Wagar
State Dept. Country Office: (202) 647-1823

Slovakia   Web, www.mzv.sk/washington

Ambassador: Peter Kmec
Chancery: 3523 International Court N.W. 20008; (202) 237-1054; Fax, (202) 237-6438; Email, emb.washington@mzv.sk
U.S. Chargé d'Affaires in Bratislava: J. Liam Wasley
State Dept. Country Office: (202) 647-3191

Slovenia   Web, http://washington.embassy.si

Ambassador: Bozo Cerar
Chancery: 2410 California St. N.W., 20008; (202) 386-6601; Fax, (202) 386-6633; Email, vwa@gov.si
U.S. Ambassador in Ljubljana: Brent R. Hartley
State Dept. Country Office: (202) 647-4782

Solomon Islands

Web, www.un.int/wcm/content/site/solomonislands/pid/3603

Ambassador: Collin David Beck (in New York)
Chancery: 800 2nd Ave., #400L, New York, NY 10017; (212) 599-6192; Fax, (212) 661-8925; Email, simun@foreignaffairs-solomons.org
U.S. Ambassador: Catherine Erbert-Gray (resident in Port Moresby, Papua New Guinea)
State Dept. Country Office: (202) 647-5156

Somalia   Web, http://somalia.usvpp.gov

The Washington embassy ceased operations May 1991. The U.S. embassy in Mogadishu is unstaffed. Diplomatic relations are handled out of the U.S. embassy in Nairobi, Kenya.

U.S. Chargé d'Affaires: David H. Kaeuper
State Dept. Country Office: (202) 647-8284

South Africa   Web, www.saembassy.org

Ambassador: Mninwa Mahlangu
Chancery: 3051 Massachusetts Ave. N.W. 20008; (202) 232-4400; Fax, (202) 265-1607; Email, samees@dirco.gov.za
U.S. Ambassador in Pretoria: Patrick H. Gaspard
State Dept. Country Office: (202) 647-9862

South Sudan   Web, www.southsudanembassydc.org

Ambassador: Baak Valentino Akol Wol
Chancery: 1015 31st St. N.W., #300, 20007; (202) 293-7940; Fax, (202) 293-7941; Email, info@southsudanembassydc.com
U.S. Ambassador in Juba: Mary Catherine (Molly) Phee
State Dept. Country Office: (202) 647-4531

Spain

Web, www.spanish-embassy.com/washington.html

Ambassador: D. Ramón Gil Casares Satrustegui
Chancery: 2375 Pennsylvania Ave. N.W. 20037; (202) 452-0100; Fax, (202) 833-5670; Email, emb.washington@maec.es
U.S. Ambassador in Madrid: James Costos
State Dept. Country Office: (202) 647-3151

Sri Lanka   Web, www.slembassyusa.org

Ambassador: Prasad Karilyawasam
Chancery: 3025 Whitehaven St. N.W. 20008; (202) 483-4025; Fax, (202) 232-7181; Email, slembassy@slembassyusa.org
U.S. Ambassador in Colombo: Atul Keshap
State Dept. Country Office: (202) 647-1078

Sudan   Web, www.sudanembassy.org

Ambassador: Maowai Osman Khalid
Chancery: 2210 Massachusetts Ave. N.W. 20008; (202) 338-8565; Fax, (202) 667-2406
U.S. Chargé d'Affaires in Khartoum: Jerry P. Lanier
State Dept. Country Office: (202) 647-4531

Suriname   Web, www.surinameembassy.org

Ambassador: Subhas-Chandra Mungra
Chancery: 4301 Connecticut Ave. N.W., #460, 20008; (202) 244-7488; Fax, (202) 244-5878
U.S. Ambassador in Paramaribo: Edwin R. Nolan
State Dept. Country Office: (202) 647-4719

Swaziland

Ambassador: Rev. Abednego Mandla Ntshangase
Chancery: 1712 New Hampshire Ave. N.W. 20009; (202) 234-5002; Fax, (202) 234-8254; Email, info@swazilandembassyus.com or embassy@swaziland-usa.com
U.S. Ambassador in Mbabane: Lisa J. Peterson
State Dept. Country Office: (202) 647-9852

Sweden

Web, www.swedenabroad.com/en-GB/Embassies/Washington

Ambassador: Bjorn Lyrvall
Chancery: 2900 K St. N.W. 20007; (202) 467-2600; Fax, (202) 467-2699; Email, ambassaden.washington@gov.se
U.S. Ambassador in Stockholm: Azita Raji
State Dept. Country Office: (202) 647-8178

Switzerland   Web, www.swissemb.org

Ambassador: Martin Dahinden
Chancery: 2900 Cathedral Ave. N.W. 20008; (202) 745-7900; Fax, (202) 387-2564; Email, was.information@eda.admin.ch
U.S. Ambassador in Bern: Suzan G. LeVine
State Dept. Country Office: (202) 647-3238

Syria

On March 18, 2014, the Obama Administration ordered the Syrian government to suspend its diplomatic and consular missions in the United States.
Chancery (currently closed): 2215 Wyoming Ave. N.W. 20008; (202) 232-6313; Fax, (202) 234-9548; Email, info@syrembassy.net
U.S. Special Envoy in Damascus: Michael Ratney
State Dept. Country Office: (202) 647-2670

Taiwan   Web, www.taiwanembassy.org/US

Representation is maintained by the Taipei Economic and Cultural Representatives Office in the United States: 4201 Wisconsin Ave. N.W. 20016; (202) 895-1800; Email, tecroinfodc@tecro.us;
Representative of the Republic of China (in Taiwan): Lyushun Shun
The United States maintains unofficial relations with Taiwan through the American Institute in Taiwan.
American Institute: 1700 N. Moore St., #1700, Arlington, VA 22209-1385; (703) 525-8474; Kin W. Moy, Director
State Dept. Country Office: (202) 647-7711

Tajikistan   Web, www.tjus.org

Ambassador: Farhod Salim
Chancery: 1005 New Hampshire Ave. N.W. 20037; (202) 223-6090; Fax, (202) 223-6091; Email, tajikistan@verizon.net
U.S. Ambassador in Dushanbe: Elisabeth I. Millard
State Dept. Country Office: (202) 647-6757

Tanzania   Web, www.tanzaniaembassy-us.org

Ambassador: Wilson Mutagaywa
Chancery: 1232 22nd St. N.W. 20037; (202) 884-1080; Fax, (202) 797-7408; Email, ubalozi@tanzaniaembassy-us.org
U.S. Ambassador in Dar es Salaam: Mark Childress
State Dept. Country Office: (202) 647-8295

Thailand   Web, www.thaiembdc.org

Ambassador: Pisan Manawapat
Chancery: 1024 Wisconsin Ave. N.W. 20007; (202) 944-3600; Fax, (202) 944-3611; Email, information@ thaiembdc.org
U.S. Ambassador in Bangkok: Glyn T. Davies
State Dept. Country Office: (202) 647-2036

Timor-Leste   Web, www.timorlesteembassy.org

Ambassador: Domingos Sarmento Alves
Chancery: 4201 Connecticut Ave. N.W., #504, 20008; (202) 966-3202; Fax, (202) 966-3205; Email, info@ timorlesteembassy.org
U.S. Ambassador in Dili: Karen Clark Stanton
State Dept. Country Office: (202) 647-1823

Togo   Web, www.togoleseembassy.com

Ambassador: Edawe Limbiyè Kadangha Bariki
Chancery: 2208 Massachusetts Ave. N.W. 20008; (202) 234-4212; Fax, (202) 232-3190; Email, info@ togoembassy.us
U.S. Ambassador in Lomé: David R. Gilmour
State Dept. Country Office: (202) 647-2791

Tonga   Web, www.tongaconsul.com

Consul General (in California). Sela Tukia
Consulate-General: 1350 Old Bayshore Hwy., #610, Burlingame, CA 94010; (650) 685-1001
Tonga maintains a Permanent Mission to the United Nations.
Ambassador to the UN: Mahe'uli'uli Sandhurst Tupouniua
UN Chancery: 250 E. 51st St., New York, NY 10022; (917) 369-1025; Fax, (917) 369-1024; Email, tongaunmission@aol.com
U.S. Ambassador: Judith B. Cefkin (resident in Suva, Fiji)
State Dept. Country Office: (202) 647-5156

Trinidad and Tobago   Web, www.ttembassy.org

Ambassador: Neil Parsan
Chancery: 1708 Massachusetts Ave. N.W. 20036; (202) 467-6490; Fax, (202) 785-3130
U.S. Ambassador in Port-of-Spain: John Estrada
State Dept. Country Office: (202) 647-4384

Tunisia   Web, www.tunconsusa.org

Ambassador: Fayçal Gouia
Chancery: 1515 Massachusetts Ave. N.W. 20005; (202) 862-1850; Fax, (202) 862-1858; Email, info@ tunconsusa.org
U.S. Ambassador in Tunis: Daniel H. Rubinstein
State Dept. Country Office: (202) 647-4676

Turkey

Web, www.vasington.be.mfa.gov.tr/contactinfo.aspx or www.turkishembassy.org
Ambassador: Serdar Kilic

Chancery: 2525 Massachusetts Ave. N.W. 20008; (202) 612-6701; Fax, (202) 612-6744; Email, embassy .washingtondc@mfa.gov.tr
U.S. Ambassador in Ankara: John R. Bass
State Dept. Country Office: (202) 647-9749

Turkmenistan   Web, www.turkmenistanembassy.org

Ambassador: Meret B. Orazov
Chancery: 2207 Massachusetts Ave. N.W. 20008; (202) 588-1500; Fax, (202) 280-1003; Email, turkmenembassyus@verizon.net
U.S. Ambassador in Ashgabat: Allen P. Mustard
State Dept. Country Office: (202) 647-9024

Tuvalu

Ambassador: Aunese Makoi Simati
Chancery: 800 E. 2nd Ave., #400B, New York, NY 10017; (212) 490-0534; Fax, (212) 937-0692; Email, Tuvalu@ onecommonwealth.org
U.S. Ambassador: Judith B. Cefkin (resident in Suva, Fiji)
State Dept. Country Office: (202) 647-5156

Uganda

Web, www.washington.mofa.go.ug or www.ugandaembassy.com
Ambassador: Oliver Wonekha
Chancery: 5911 16th St. N.W. 20011; (202) 726-7100; Fax, (202) 726-1727; Email, washington@mofa.go.ug or info@ugandaembassy.org
U.S. Ambassador in Kampala: Deborah R. Malac
State Dept. Country Office: (202) 647-5924

Ukraine   Web, www.usa.mfa.gov.ua/en

Ambassador: Olexander Motsyk
Chancery: 3350 M St. N.W. 20007; (202) 349-2963; Fax, (202) 333-0817; Email, owonekha@ ugandaembassyus.org or emb_us@mfa.gov.ua
U.S. Ambassador in Kyiv: Geoffrey R. Pyatt
State Dept. Country Office: (202) 647-8671

United Arab Emirates   Web, www.uae-embassy.org

Ambassador: Yousef Al Otaiba
Chancery: 3522 International Court N.W., #400, 20008; (202) 243-2400; Fax, (202) 243-2432
U.S. Ambassador in Abu Dhabi: Barbara A. Leaf
State Dept. Country Office: (202) 647-6562

United Kingdom   Web, ukinusa.fco.gov.uk/en

Ambassador: Sir Nigel Kim Darroch
Chancery: 3100 Massachusetts Ave. N.W. 20008; (202) 588-6500; Fax, (202) 588-7870; Email, britishembassyenquiries@gmail.com
U.S. Ambassador to London: Mathew W. Barzun
State Dept. Country Office: (202) 647-6557

United Nations   Web, www.un.org/en

Secretary-General: Ban Ki-moon

Information Center: 1775 K St. N.W., #400, 20006; (202) 331-8670; Fax, (202) 331-9191; Email, unicdc@unic.org
U.S. Ambassador: Samantha Power
State Dept. Country Office: (202) 736-7555

Uruguay   Web, www.urueeuu.mrree.gub.uy

Ambassador: Carlos Pita Alvariza
Chancery: 1913 Eye St. N.W. 20006; (202) 331-1313; Fax, (202) 331-8142
U.S. Chargé d'Affaires in Montevideo: Brad Freden
State Dept. Country Office: (202) 647-1551

Uzbekistan   Web, www.uzbekistan.org

Ambassador: Bakhtiyar Gulyamov
Chancery: 1746 Massachusetts Ave. N.W. 20036; (202) 887-5300; Fax, (202) 293-6804; Email, info@uzbekistan.org
U.S. Ambassador in Tashkent: Pamela L. Spratlen
State Dept. Country Office: (202) 647-6765

Vanuatu   Web, www.un.int/vanuatu

Vanuatu maintains a Permanent Mission to the United Nations.
Ambassador to the UN: Odo Tevi
UN Chancery: 800 E. 2nd Ave., #400B, New York, NY 10017; (212) 661-4303; Fax, (212) 661-5544; Email, vanunmis@aol.com
U.S. Ambassador: Catherine Ebert-Gray (resident in Port Moresby, Papua New Guinea)
State Dept. Country Office: (202) 647-5156

Vatican City   (See The Holy See)

Venezuela   Web, www.eeuu.embajada.gob.ve

Chargé d'Affaires: Maximilien Sanchez Arvelaiz
Chancery: 1099 30th St. N.W. 20007; (202) 342-2214; Fax, (202) 342-6820; Email, despacho.embveus@mppre.gob.ve

U.S. Chargé d'Affaires in Caracas: Lee McClenny
State Dept. Country Office: (202) 647-4984

Vietnam   Web, www.vietnamembassy-usa.org

Ambassador: Pham Quang Vinh
Chancery: 1233 20th St. N.W., #400, 20036; (202) 861-0737; Fax, (202) 861-0917; Email, info@vietnamembassy.us
U.S. Ambassador in Hanoi: Ted Osius
State Dept. Country Office: (202) 647-4023

Western Samoa   (See Samoa)

Yemen   Web, www.yemenembassy.org

Chargé d'Affaires: Adel Alsunaini
Chancery: 2319 Wyoming Ave. N.W. 20008; (202) 965-4760; Fax, (202) 337-2017; Email, dcm@yemenembassy.org
U.S. Ambassador in Sana'a: Matthew H. Tueller
State Dept. Country Office: (202) 647-6558

Zambia   Web, www.zambiaembassy.org

Ambassador: Palan Mulonda
Chancery: 2200 R St. N.W. 20008; (202) 265-0757; Fax, (202) 332-0826; Email, info@zambiaembassy.org
U.S. Ambassador in Lusaka: Eric T. Schultz
State Dept. Country Office: (202) 647-9857

Zimbabwe

Ambassador: Ammon M. Mutembwa
Chancery: 1608 New Hampshire Ave. N.W. 20009; (202) 332-7100; Fax, (202) 483-9326; Email, info33@zimbabwe-embassy.us
U.S. Ambassador in Harare: Harry K. Thomas Jr.
State Dept. Country Office: (202) 647-9852

Freedom of Information Act

Access to government information remains a key issue in Washington. In 1966, Congress passed legislation to broaden access: the Freedom of Information Act, or FOIA (PL 89-487; codified in 1967 by PL 90-23). Amendments to expand access even further were passed into law over President Gerald Ford's veto in 1974 (PL 93-502).

Several organizations in Washington specialize in access to government information. See the "Freedom of Information" section in the Communications and the Media chapter for details (p. 103). The Justice Department electronically publishes a clearinghouse of FOIA information at www.justice.gov/oip/foia-resources.html.

1966 Act

The 1966 act requires executive branch agencies and independent commissions of the federal government to make records, reports, policy statements, and staff manuals available to citizens who request them, unless the materials fall into one of nine exempted categories:

- secret national security or foreign policy information
- internal personnel practices
- information exempted by law (e.g., income tax returns)
- trade secrets, other confidential commercial or financial information
- inter-agency or intra-agency memos
- personal information, personnel or medical files
- law enforcement investigatory information
- information related to reports on financial institutions
- geological and geophysical information

1974 Amendments

Further clarification of the rights of citizens to gain access to government information came in late 1974, when Congress enacted legislation to remove some of the obstacles that the bureaucracy had erected since 1966. Included in the amendments are provisions that:

- Require federal agencies to publish their indexes of final opinions on settlements of internal cases, policy statements, and administrative staff manuals. If, under special circumstances, the indexes are not published, they are to be furnished to any person requesting them for the cost of duplication. The 1966 law simply required agencies to make such indexes available for public inspection and copying.
- Require agencies to release unlisted documents to someone requesting them with a reasonable description (a change designed to ensure that an agency could not refuse to provide material simply because the applicant could not give its precise title).
- Direct each agency to publish a uniform set of fees for providing documents at the cost of finding and copying them. The amendment allows waiver or reduction of those fees when in the public interest.
- Set time limits for agency responses to requests: ten working days for an initial request; twenty working days for an appeal from an initial refusal to produce documents; a possible ten-working-day extension that can be granted only once in a single case.
- Set a thirty-day time limit for an agency response to a complaint filed in court under the act; provide that the courts give such cases priority attention at the appeal, as well as the trial, level.
- Empower federal district courts to order agencies to produce withheld documents and to examine the contested materials privately (in camera) to determine if they are properly exempted.
- Require annual agency reports to Congress, including a list of all agency decisions to withhold information requested under the act, the reasons; the appeals; the results; all relevant rules; the fee schedule; and the names of officials responsible for each denial of information.
- Allow courts to order the government to pay attorneys' fees and court costs for persons winning suits against them under the act.
- Authorize a court to find that an agency employee has acted capriciously or arbitrarily in withholding information; stipulate that disciplinary action is determined by Civil Service Commission proceedings.
- Amend and clarify the wording of the national defense and national security exemption to make clear that it applies only to properly classified information.
- Amend the wording of the law enforcement exemption to allow withholding of information that, if disclosed, would interfere with enforcement proceedings, deprive someone of a fair trial or hearing, invade personal privacy in an unwarranted way, disclose the identity of a confidential source, disclose investigative techniques, or endanger law enforcement personnel; protect from disclosure all information from a confidential source obtained by a criminal law enforcement agency or a lawful national security investigation.
- Provide that separable non-exempt portions of requested material be released after deletion of the exempt portions.
- Require an annual report from the attorney general to Congress.

1984 Amendments

In 1984 Congress enacted legislation that clarified the requirements of the Central Intelligence Agency (CIA) to respond to citizen requests for information. Included in the amendments are provisions that:

• Authorize the CIA to close from FOIA review certain operational files that contain information on the identities of sources and methods. The measure removed the requirement that officials search the files for material that might be subject to disclosure.

• Reverse a ruling by the Justice Department and the Office of Management and Budget that invoked the Privacy Act to deny individuals FOIA access to information about themselves in CIA records. HR 5164 required the CIA to search files in response to FOIA requests by individuals for information about themselves.

• Require the CIA to respond to FOIA requests for information regarding covert actions or suspected CIA improprieties.

All agencies of the executive branch have issued regulations to implement the Freedom of Information Act. To locate a specific agency's regulations, consult the general index of the *Code of Federal Regulations* under "Information availability" or search in http://www.USA.gov, "FOIA Regulations."

Electronic Freedom of Information Act of 1996

In 1996 Congress enacted legislation clarifying that electronic documents are subject to the same FOIA disclosure rules as are printed documents. The 1996 law also requires federal agencies to make records available to the public in various electronic formats, such as email, compact disc, and files accessible via the Internet. An additional measure seeks to improve the government's response time on FOIA requests by requiring agencies to report annually on the number of pending requests and how long it will take to respond.

Homeland Security Act of 2002

In 2002 Congress passed legislation that established the Homeland Security Department and exempted from FOIA disclosure rules certain information about national defense systems. Included in the act are provisions that:

• Grant broad exemption from FOIA requirements to information that private companies share with the government about vulnerabilities in the nation's critical infrastructure.

• Exempt from FOIA rules and other federal and state disclosure requirements any information about the critical infrastructure that is submitted voluntarily to a covered federal agency to ensure the security of this infrastructure and protected systems; require accompanying statement that such information is being submitted voluntarily in expectation of nondisclosure protection.

• Require the secretary of homeland security to establish procedures for federal agencies to follow in receiving, caring for, and storing critical infrastructure information

that has been submitted voluntarily; provide criminal penalties for the unauthorized disclosure of such information.

Executive Order 13392: Improving Agency Disclosure of Information

On December 14, 2005, President George W. Bush issued Executive Order 13392: Improving Agency Disclosure of Information. The order sought to streamline the effectiveness of government agencies in responding to FOIA requests and to reduce backlogs of FOIA requests. The order did not expand the information available under FOIA. The executive order provided:

• A chief FOIA officer (at the assistant secretary or equivalent level) of each government agency to monitor FOIA compliance throughout the agency. The chief FOIA officer must inform agency heads and the attorney general of the agency's FOIA compliance performance.

• A FOIA Requester Service Center that would serve as the first point of contact for a person seeking information concerning the status of a FOIA request and appropriate information about the agency's FOIA response.

• FOIA public liaisons, supervisory officials who would facilitate further action if a requester had concerns regarding how an initial request was handled by the center staff.

• Requirement that the chief FOIA officer review and evaluate the agency's implementation and administration of FOIA pursuant to the executive order. The agency head was mandated to report the findings to the attorney general and to the director of the Office of Management and Budget. The report also must be published on the agency's Web site or in the *Federal Register*. Initial reports were submitted in June 2006, with follow-up plans included in each agency's annual FOIA reports for fiscal years 2006 and 2007 and continuing thereafter.

• The attorney general shall review the agency-specific plans and submit to the president a report on government-wide FOIA implementation. The initial report was submitted in October 2006. The Justice Department publishes annual reports of federal agency compliance on its Web site.

Open Government Act of 2007

On December 31, 2007, President George W. Bush signed the "Openness Promotes Effectiveness in our National (OPEN) Government Act of 2007." The OPEN Government Act amends the Freedom of Information Act (FOIA) by:

• defining "a representative of the news media";
• directing that required attorney fees be paid from an agency's appropriation rather than from the U.S. Treasury's Claims and Judgment Fund;
• prohibiting an agency from assessing search and duplication fees if it fails to comply with FOIA deadlines; and establishing an Office of Government Information Services within the National Archives and Records Administration to review agency compliance with FOIA.

Executive Order 13526: Classified National Security Information

On December 29, 2009, an Executive Order on Classified National Security Information was issued. The Executive Order contains two parts:

- The government may classify certain types of information pertaining to the National Security interests of the United States, even after a FOIA request has been submitted. They may do so if they believe that keeping the information secret is necessary for National Security.
- Additionally, the order sets a timeline for automatic declassification of old information that has not been specifically tagged as needing to remain secret.

H.R. 4173: The Dodd – Frank Wall Street Reform and Consumer Protection Act

H.R. 4173 was passed in both the House and Senate and signed by President Barack Obama on July 21, 2010. The law has specific implications for the FOIA, and they are as follows:

- Section 9291 of the statute shields the Securities and Exchange Commission (SEC) from FOIA requests, because of the worry that FOIA requests could potentially hinder SEC investigations.

S. 3717, a Bill to Amend the Securities Exchange Act of 1934, the Investment Company Act of 1940, and the Investment Advisers Act of 1940 to Provide for Certain Disclosures Under Section 552 of Title 5, United States Code (Commonly Referred to as the Freedom of Information Act), and for Other Purposes

This legislation passed both the House and Senate in late September 2010, and it was signed by President Obama on October 5, 2010. The laws FOIA applications are as follows:

- The provision in S. 3717 essentially rolls back the shielding of the SEC from FOIA requests, as previously mandated by Section 9291 of H.R. 4173.

FOIA Oversight and Implementation Act of 2014 (the FOIA Act)

A bill introduced by the House on March 15, 2013 to amend the Freedom of Information Act to make it easier to request and receive information. This bill passed the House unanimously on February 25, 2014. Under the amendment, the Office of Management and Budget would be required to operate a free Web site where users could submit requests for records and receive information on the status of said request. The bill would also:

- Require agencies to determine whether the release of agency records would contribute significantly to public understanding of the operations or activities of government
- Require agencies to document additional search or duplication fees
- Require agencies to submit annual FOIA reports to the Director of the Office of Government Information Services, in addition to the Attorney General
- Expand the duties of the Chief FOIA Officer of each agency to require an annual compliance review of FOIA requirements
- Establish the Chief FOIA Officers Council to develop recommendations for increasing compliance with FOIA requirements
- Require each agency to update its FOIA regulations within 180 days of the enactment of this Act
- Requires the Inspector General of each federal agency to:

    ◆ Periodically review compliance with FOIA disclosure requirements, including the timely processing of requests, assessment of fees and fee waivers, and the use of disclosure exemptions; and
    ◆ Make recommendations to the head of an agency, including recommendations for disciplinary action. Makes the improper withholding of information under FOIA a basis for disciplinary action

FOIA Improvement Act of 2014

A bill introduced by the Senate on June 24, 2014 to improve the Freedom of Information Act. This bill passed the Senate unanimously on December 8, 2014. However, it was not brought to a vote by the House despite its resemblance to the FOIA Act. The legislation would:

- Require agencies to electronically make available disclosed agency records to the public
- Reduce the ability of an agency to charge fees for a request if the agency does not meet the FOIA deadline
- Limit the terms by which an agency can determine records exempt from FOIA

• Puts a time limit of twenty-five years on Exemption 5 (b5)

• Expand the duties of the Chief FOIA Officer of each agency to require an annual compliance review of FOIA requirements

• Expand the duties of the Chief FOIA Officer of each agency to require an annual compliance review of FOIA requirements

• Establish the Chief FOIA Officers Council to develop recommendations for increasing compliance with FOIA requirements

• Require each agency to update its FOIA regulations within 180 days of the enactment of this Act

• Requires the Inspector General of each federal agency to:

♦ Periodically review compliance with FOIA disclosure requirements, including the timely processing of requests, assessment of fees and fee waivers, and the use of disclosure exemptions; and

♦ Make recommendations to the head of an agency, including recommendations for disciplinary action. Makes the improper withholding of information under FOIA a basis for disciplinary action

Justice Dept. "Proactive Disclosure Pilot" of 2015

On July 4, 2015, the Justice Dept. announced a new pilot program at seven agencies designed to test the feasibility of posting online FOIA responses so that they are available to the individual requester as well as the general public. Agencies involved in the pilot program are the Millennium Challenge Corporation, the Office of the Director of National Intelligence, the Environmental Protection Agency, and sections of the Defense, Homeland Security and Justice Depts., the National Archives and Records Administration and the Office of Information Policy. The purpose of the pilot is to determine the policy implementation costs, the effect on staff, and the effect on government stakeholders, as well as the justifications for exceptions.

Privacy Legislation

Privacy Act

To protect citizens from invasions of privacy by the federal government, Congress passed the Privacy Act of 1974 (PL 93-579). The act permitted individuals for the first time to inspect information about themselves contained in federal agency files and to challenge, correct, or amend the material. The major provisions of the act:

● Permit an individual to have access to personal information in federal agency files and to correct or amend that information.

● Prevent an agency maintaining a file on an individual from making it available to another agency without the individual's consent.

● Require federal agencies to keep records that are necessary, lawful, accurate, and current, and to disclose the existence of all databanks and files containing information on individuals.

● Bar the transfer of personal information to other federal agencies for nonroutine use without the individual's prior consent or written request.

● Require agencies to keep accurate accountings of transfers of records and make them available to the individual.

● Prohibit agencies from keeping records on an individual's exercise of First Amendment rights unless the records are authorized by statute, approved by the individual, or within the scope of an official law enforcement activity.

● Permit an individual to seek injunctive relief to correct or amend a record maintained by an agency and permit the individual to recover actual damages when an agency acts in a negligent manner that is "willful or intentional."

● Exempt from disclosure records maintained by the Central Intelligence Agency; records maintained by law enforcement agencies; Secret Service records; statistical information; names of persons providing material used for determining the qualification of an individual for federal government service; federal testing material; and National Archives historical records.

● Provide that an officer or employee of an agency who violates provisions of the act be fined no more than $5,000.

● Prohibit an agency from selling or renting an individual's name or address for mailing list use.

● Require agencies to submit to Congress and to the Office of Management and Budget any plan to establish or alter records. Virtually all agencies of the executive branch have issued regulations to implement the Privacy Act.

To locate a specific agency's regulations, consult the general index of the Code of Federal Regulations under "Privacy Act" or search in www.USA.gov, "Privacy Act."

USA Patriot Act

Following the terrorist attacks of September 11, 2001, Congress passed the USA PATRIOT Act (Uniting and Strengthening America by Providing Appropriate Tools Required to Intercept and Obstruct Terrorism; PL 107-56). Included in the USA PATRIOT Act are provisions that:

● Amend the federal criminal code to authorize the interception of wire, oral, and electronic communications to produce evidence of chemical weapons, terrorism, and computer fraud and abuse.

● Amend the Foreign Intelligence Surveillance Act of 1978 (FISA) to require an application for an electronic surveillance order or search warrant certifying that a significant purpose (formerly, the sole or main purpose) of the surveillance is to obtain foreign intelligence information. The administration of President George W. Bush aggressively defended its use of wiretaps approved by the Foreign Intelligence Surveillance Court, which handles intelligence requests involving suspected spies, terrorists, and foreign agents. Established under FISA, this court operates secretly within the Justice Department.

USA Patriot Improvement and Reauthorization Act of 2005 and USA Patriot Act Additional Reauthorizing Amendments Act of 2006

Some provisions of the USA PATRIOT Act were set to expire at the end of 2005. After a lengthy battle Congress voted to reauthorize the act with some of the more controversial provisions intact, including the FISA amendments and the electronic wiretap provisions. Civil libertarians were concerned with issues regarding four provisions: sections 206 (roving wiretaps), 213 (delayed notice warrants), 215 (business records), and 505 (national security letters). The Senate addressed some of these concerns in a separate bill, S. 2271, USA PATRIOT Act Additional Reauthorizing Amendments Act of 2006.

On March 9, 2006, the president signed into law the USA PATRIOT Improvement and Reauthorization Act of 2005 as well as the USA PATRIOT Act Additional Reauthorizing Amendments Act of 2006.

The reauthorized USA PATRIOT Act allows for greater congressional oversight and judicial review of section 215 orders, section 206 roving wiretaps, and national security letters. In addition, the act included requirements for high-level approval for section 215 FISA orders for library, bookstore, firearm sale, medical, tax return, and educational records. The act also provided for greater judicial review for delayed notice ("sneak and peek") search warrants. Fourteen of sixteen USA PATRIOT Act provisions were made permanent, and a new sunset date of December 31, 2009, was enacted for sections 206 and 215.

On February 27, 2010, President Barack Obama signed a one-year extension of sections 206 and 215 of the USA PATRIOT Act.

On May 26, 2011, President Barack Obama signed three expiring provisions of the USA PATRIOT Act into law for four more years. These expiring provisions included sections 215, 206, and 6001.

Homeland Security Act of 2002

The Homeland Security Act of 2002 was also passed in the aftermath of the September 11, 2001, terrorist attacks. It contains provisions that:

• Establish the Homeland Security Department.

• Exempt from criminal penalties any disclosure made by an electronic communication service to a federal, state, or local government. In making the disclosure, the service must believe that an emergency involving risk of death or serious physical injury requires disclosure without delay. Any government agency receiving such disclosure must report it to the attorney general.

• Direct the secretary of homeland security to appoint a senior department official to take primary responsibility for information privacy policy.

Protect America Act and Subsequent Follow-Up Legislation

On August 5, 2007, President George W. Bush signed the Protect America Act, which amended the Foreign Intelligence Surveillance Act of 1978 (FISA), declaring that nothing under its definition of "electronic surveillance" shall be construed to encompass surveillance directed at a person reasonably believed to be located outside the United States. Prior to this act, no court permission was obtained for surveillance of parties located outside the United States, though a warrant was required for electronic surveillance of targets within the United States. The Protect America Act allowed the Attorney General or the Director of National Intelligence to direct a third party (i.e., telecommunications provider) to assist with intelligence gathering about individuals located outside the United States and shields such parties from liability without a warrant from the FISA Court. The act did provide FISA Court oversight via requiring the Attorney General to submit to the FISA Court the procedures by which the government determines that such acquisitions do not constitute electronic surveillance. The Attorney General was required to report to the congressional intelligence and judiciary committees semiannually concerning acquisitions made during the previous six-month period.

The Protect America Act was designed as a temporary act to allow intelligence policy officials six months to establish a permanent law. The act expired 180 days later in January; it was briefly reauthorized and expired in February 2008. The Senate passed the FISA Amendments Act of 2007 (S. 2248) in February, which would make many of the provisions of the Protect America Act permanent. However, House leadership objected to many of the provisions. Instead, the House supported its version, the Respected Electronic Surveillance That is Overseen, Reviewed and Effective (RESTORE) Act (H. 3773). This act authorizes the Attorney General and the Director of National Intelligence to conduct electronic surveillance of persons outside the United States in order to acquire foreign intelligence, but places limitations, including: the methods must be conducted in a manner consistent with the Fourth Amendment to the U.S. Constitution and it prohibits targeting of persons reasonably believed to be in the United States (with exceptions). As amended, the bill allowed for limited retroactive immunity for telecommunications service providers. It provides for greater court oversight for targeting procedures, minimization procedures, and guidelines for obtaining warrants. The act expired December 31, 2009, when certain provisions of the PATRIOT Act expired.

2013–2015 Supreme Court Cases Affecting Privacy

Fernandez v. California

Holding: The Court's decision in *Georgia v. Randolph*, holding that the consent of one occupant is insufficient to authorize police to search a premises if another occupant is present and objects to the search, does not apply when an occupant provides consent well after the objecting occupant has been removed from the premises.

Judgment: Affirmed, 6-3, in an opinion by Justice Alito on February 25, 2014. Justice Scalia and Justice Thomas filed concurring opinions. Justice Ginsburg filed a dissenting opinion in which Justice Sotomayor and Justice Kagan joined.

Navarette v. California

Issue: Whether the Fourth Amendment requires an officer who receives an anonymous tip regarding a drunken or reckless driver to corroborate dangerous driving before stopping the vehicle.

Judgment: Affirmed, 5-4, in an opinion by Justice Thomas on April 22, 2014. Justice Scalia filed a dissenting opinion, in which Justice Ginsburg, Justice Sotomayor, and Justice Kagan joined.

Riley v. California

Issue: Whether evidence admitted at petitioner's trial was obtained in a search of petitioner's cell phone that violated petitioner's Fourth Amendment rights. (Riley's petition had posed a general question about whether the Fourth Amendment allowed police without a warrant to search "the digital contents of an individual's cellphone seized from the person at the time of arrest." In granting review, the Court said it would only rule on this issue: "Whether evidence admitted at [his] trial was obtained in a search of [his] cellphone that violated [his] Fourth Amendment rights.") Judgment: Reversed and remanded, 9-0, in an opinion by Chief Justice Roberts on June 25, 2014. Justice Alito filed an opinion concurring in part and concurring in the judgment.

United States v. Wurie

Issue: Whether the Fourth Amendment permits the police, without obtaining a warrant, to review the call log of a cellphone found on a person who has been lawfully arrested.

Judgment: Affirmed, 9-0, in an opinion by Chief Justice Roberts on June 25, 2014. Justice Alito filed an opinion concurring in part and concurring in the judgment.

Name Index

Fathi, David, 554
Fattah, Chaka (D–Pa.), 783, 786, 787, 819
Faucher, Robert, 607
Fauci, Anthony S., 405, 629
Faust, Leona, 137, 745, 763
Favors, Ronnie, 66, 630
Fay, Kevin, 290, 665
Fay, Mary, 706
Fazio, Larry D., 53
Feagan, Sarah, 84
Fearns, Sean, 548
Feather, Paul "Otto", 893
Featherson, Wendy, 844
Fecso, Barbara, 13, 16
Federici, Michael P., 166
Fedrizzi, S. Richard, 431
Feffer, John, 43, 606
Feinberg, Sarah, 740
Feingold, Cathy, 226
Feingold, Ellen, 41
Feinstein, Deborah L., 524
Feinstein, Dianne (R–Calif), 780, 862, 864, 865, 872, 873, 875, 883
Feldman, Eric, 890
Feldman, Jay, 8
Feldman, Judy Scott, 144
Feliciano, Carmen M., 843
Fells, Robert M., 77
Felmlee, Brenda, 854
Fenneman, Rebecca A., 49
Fenton Ambrose, Laurie, 397, 407
Ferafini, Marilyn, 351
Ferber, Corrin, 476
Ferguson, Brad, 895
Ferguson, Charles D., 609, 645
Ferguson, Drew, 823
Ferguson, Fred, 811
Ferguson, Karen W., 233
Ferguson, Maria Voles, 187
Ferguson, Rodney, 11, 28, 249, 280, 300
Ferland, John, 807
Fernandez, Alyn, 892
Fernandez, Janelle, 217
Fernandez, Mai, 555
Ferniza, Sandra, 821
Fernkas, Robin, 214
Ferrante, Anthony, 725
Ferraro, John, 437
Ferraro, Nina M., 331
Ferrell, Robert, 96
Ferrell, Robert S., 625
Ferriero, David S., 96, 139, 141
Ferrini-Mundy, Joan E., 199
Ferro, Anne S., 733
Fertel, Marvin S., 259
Fessel, Ted, 226
Fetgatter, James A., 444, 488
Fettig, Jason K., 584
Fewins, Brandon, 893
Ficca, Nan, 134
Ficca, Raymond G. (Ray), 134
Field, Jeremy, 891
Fields, Darlene, 846
Fields, Evonne, 568
Fiermonte, Phil, 892
Figueroa, Ana, 847
Figueroa, Blanca, 810
Fildes, Annette Guarisco, 74, 233
Filip, Allan, 806
Filippone, Desiree, 153
Finberg, Max, 145, 198, 684
Fincher, Stephen (R–Tenn.), 783, 792, 819
Findlay, Joshua, 825
Fine, Camden, 61

Fine, Glenn, 326
Fink, Amber, 66
Finkle, Jeffrey, 429
Finlay, Brian, 602
Finley, Joan, 807
Finley, Patrick D., 437
Finley, Sharra, 840
Finn, Jack, 885
Finneran, Lisa, 487
Fiotes, Stella S., 430, 588
Firman, James P., 382, 442, 535, 697
Fischer, Deb (R–Neb.), 782, 865, 867, 869, 874, 883
Fischer, Kyle, 824
Fischer, Robert, 748
Fischer, Stanley, 32, 41, 59, 63
Fischetti, Michael, 332
Fise, Tom, 357, 700
Fiser, Randy, 432
Fish, Lisa H., 398
Fish, Terri, 807
Fishback, Elizabeth, 880
Fisher, Ann C., 50, 333, 761
Fisher, Barbara Loe, 350, 630
Fisher, Donald W., 365
Fisherow, W. Benjamin, 289, 292
Fiske, Susan T., 653, 675
Fitch, Brad, 765
Fitch, Bud, 877
Fitterer, Amy, 134
Fitz, Gregory K., 384, 414
Fitzgerald, Brian K., 38, 181, 468
Fitzgerald, Douglas C., 329
Fitzgerald, Jonna, 822
Fitzgerald, Pat, 818
Fitzmaurice, Brian, 707
Fitzpatrick, Kevin, 798
Fitzpatrick, Michael J., 503
Fitzpatrick, Mike (R–Pa.), 783, 791, 792, 819
Fitzpatrick, Paul, 837
Fitzsimmons, David, 818
Fitzsimmons, Liam, 851
Fix, Michael, 473
Flagg, Laura, 296
Flaggs, Christopher, 322
Flahaven, Richard S., 101
Flake, Jeff (R–Ariz.), 780, 868, 870, 871, 873, 875, 883
Flanagan, Jenny Rose, 751
Flanders, Matt, 877
Flannery, Mark J., 44, 60, 64, 82
Flannery, Todd, 762
Flaum, David M., 775
Fleet, Jamie, 794
Flegel, Rita, 441
Flein, Tom Van, 822
Fleischmann, Chuck (R–Tenn.), 783, 786, 787, 819
Fleming, John Mary, Sr., 189
Fleming, John (R–La.), 781, 787, 788, 796, 820
Fleming, Michael, 35
Fleming, Rick, 64, 761
Fletcher, A. Jerome, 82
Fletcher, Jerome, II, 81, 332
Fletcher, Nancy, 79
Fleur, Shirlee Moreau-La, 858
Flink, Laurie, 857
Flohe, Kevin, 806
Flood, Kathleen, 373
Flores, Antonio R., 193
Flores, Bill (R–Texas), 783, 790, 791, 820

Flores-Quilty, Alexandra, 183, 753
Florez, Alex, 814
Flowers, Carolyn, 742
Flynn, Mike P., 261, 294, 433
Flynn, Vickie, 818
Fogarty, Kevin C., 830
Fogel, Jeremy D., 515
Fogleman, Guy C., 658
Foley, Robert F., 570, 572
Fonda, Clark, 900
Fong, Isaac, 901
Fong, Phyllis, 326
Fong, Vincent, 836
Fontaine, Caitlin, 818
Foote, Tyler, 847
Foote, Virginia, 459
Forbes, J. Randy (R–Va.), 783, 787, 788, 795, 820
Forbes, Randy, 788
Ford, Betty, 839
Ford, Marty, 706
Ford, Molly, 809
Ford, Nelson M., 617
Forest, Don, 653
Forlenza, Vincent, 357
Forrester, Jeanne, 894
Forsyth, Bart, 850
Forte, Denise, 789
Fortenberry, Jeff (R–Neb.), 782, 786, 787, 820
Fortenberry, Norman L., 200, 661
Fortman, Laura A., 210
Fortune, Brandon, 128
Foscarinis, Maria, 562, 709
Foster, Bill (D–Ill.), 781, 792, 798, 820
Foster, Christian, 12
Foster, Jack, 839
Foster, Nancy, 29
Foster, Robert W., 96
Foster, Serrin M., 540
Foster, William Douglas, Jr., 322
Foti, Anthony, 847
Foutz, Alan, 884
Fowkes, Bob, 835
Fowler, John M., 136
Fowler, Kevin, 262
Fowler, Phil, 584
Fowler-Green, Melody, 481
Fox, Christopher H., 369
Fox, Madison, 804
Fox, Nancy, 820
Fox, Sarah, 207, 478
Foxx, Anthony, 317, 714
Foxx, Rhonda, 804
Foxx, Virginia (R–N.C.), 782, 789, 790, 797, 803, 820
Foy, Sue, 845
Fradkin, Judith E., 398
Fraker, Ford M., 509
Francerchi, Natasha S., 510
Francis, David J., 167, 196
Frank, Abe L., 152
Frank, Jim, 851
Frank, Martin, 391
Frank, Richard, 346
Frank, Robert L., 566
Franke, Andrew, 901
Franke, Myrtis, 881
Frankel, Lois (D–Fla.), 781, 793, 799, 800, 820
Frankel, Mark S., 645, 655
Frankel, Morgan J., 758, 760
Franken, Al (D–Minn.), 782, 868, 871, 872, 873, 884

Organization Index

Population Connection, 400
    ratings of members (box), 768
Population Institute, 400
Population Reference Bureau, 322, 400
Portland Cement Assn., 437
Postal Regulatory Commission, 334
    Financial Officer, 323
    General Counsel, 521
    Inspectors General, 327
    Library, 175
    Public Affairs and Government Relations, 50, 333, 761
Potomac Institute for Policy Studies, International Center for
    Terrorism Studies (ICTS), 636
Poverty and Race Research Action Council, 530, 688
Presbyterian Mission (U.S.A.), Office of Public Witness, 158
Preservation Action, 139
Preservation Directorate, 176
President Pro Tempore of the U.S. Senate, 757
President's Cancer Panel, c/o National Cancer Institute, 396
President's Commission on White House Fellowships, 168, 335
President's Committee on the Arts and the Humanities, 118
President's Committee on the International Labor
    Organization, 209
President's Export Council, 485
President's Intelligence Advisory Board and Intelligence
    Oversight Board, 453, 635
President's Park, White House Visitor Center, 143
President's Park (White House), national park service sites in the
    capital region, 141
Press Photographers Gallery, 110
Prevention of Blindness Society of Metropolitan
    Washington, 704
PricewaterhouseCoopers PAC, 770
Prince William Forest Park, national park service sites in the
    capital region, 141
Print Communications Professionals International Inc.
    (PCPI), 116
Printing Industries of America (PIA), 116
Prints and Photographs Division, 176
Prison Fellowship Ministries, 554
Private Equity Growth Capital Council (PEGCC), 40, 65
Professional Aviation Safety Specialists, 727
Professional Aviation Safety Specialists PAC, 769
Professional Services Council (PSC), 332
Program for Appropriate Technology in Health (PATH),
    358, 466
Progressive Majority, 770
Progressive National Baptist Convention Inc., 158
Progressives for Immigration Reform Blog, 613
Project on Government Oversight, 321
Project on Middle East Democracy (POMED), 509
Property Casualty Insurers Assn. of America, 74
Property Management Assn., 450
ProtectSeniors.Org, 233, 353
Provisions Library Resource Center for Arts and Social
    Change, 120
Psychiatric Rehabilitation Assn., 417, 707
Public Affairs Council, 775
Public Affairs Department, 226
Public and Indian Housing, 442
    Housing Voucher Management and Operations, 442
    Native American Programs, 441
    Public Housing and Voucher Programs, 443
    Public Housing Investments, 443
Public Broadcasting Service, 93, 109
Public Citizen, 765
    Congress Watch, 768, 775
    Energy Program, 260
    Health Research Group, 23, 235, 351
    Litigation Group, 544, 562
    ratings of members (box), 768
Public Company Accounting Oversight Board, 65
Public Employees for Environmental Responsibility (PEER), 275

Public Housing Authorities Directors Assn., 443
Public Justice Foundation, 52, 562
Public Knowledge, 108
Public Lands Council, 303
Public Religion Research Institute, 158
Public Risk Management Assn. (PRIMA), 340
Public Service Research Council, 229, 329
Public Technology Institute (PTI), 340, 653
Public Welfare Foundation, 688
Puerto Rican Resident Commissioner, 512
PYXERA Global, 493

Quota International, 150, 457

Rachel Carson Council Inc., 294
Radio Free Asia, 469
Radio Free Europe/Radio Liberty, 469
    internships, 217
Radio Television Digital News Assn., 102, 114, 605
Railroad Retirement Board, Legislative Affairs, 741
Rails-to-Trails Conservancy, 309
Railway Supply Institute (RSI), 742
Rainbow PUSH Coalition, Public Policy Institute, Government
    Relations and Telecommunications Project, 530, 775
Rainbow/PUSH Coalition, 528
RAND Corporation, 173, 244, 519, 604, 654
    Drug Policy Research Center, 549
    Health Unit, 351
RAND Homeland Security and Defense Center (DoD) (DHS),
    counterterrorism resources and contacts, 632
Rape, Abuse, and Incest National Network (RAINN), 547, 695
Rare Book and Special Collections Division, 176
Reading Is Fundamental, 188, 199
Real Estate Assessment Center, 449
The Real Estate Roundtable, 445
Rebuilding Together, Inc., 624
Recording Industry Assn. of America, 133
Recreation Vehicle Dealers Assn. of North America
    (RVDA), 737
Recreation Vehicle Industry Assn. (RVIA), 737
Reform Immigration for America Blog, 613
Refugees International, 466, 471
Regional Airline Assn., 723
Registry of Interpreters for the Deaf, 705
Regulatory Affairs Professionals Society, 351
Regulatory Information Service Center, 315
Rehabilitation Engineering and Assistive Technology Society of
    North America (RESNA), 378, 702
Reinsurance Assn. of America, 74
Religious Coalition for Reproductive Choice, 541
Renewable Fuels Assn., 266
Renewable Natural Resources Foundation, 300
Renwick Gallery, museum education programs, 126
Renwick Gallery of the Smithsonian American Art Museum, 128
Reporters Committee for Freedom of the Press, 114, 605
Reporters Without Borders (Reporters Sans Frontières), 114
Republican Governors Assn., 752, 778
Republican Jewish Coalition, 775
Republican Main Street Partnership, 778
Republican National Committee, internships, 217
Republican National Committee (RNC), 752, 778
    Communications, 778
    Counsel, 778
    Finance, 778
    Political, 753
Research!America, 392
Reserve Officers Assn. of the United States, 587
Resources for the Future, 246, 276, 278, 681
RESULTS, 28
Retail Industry Leaders Assn., 78
Reuters, 109
Ripon Society, 778
Risk Management Agency, 18
The Road Information Program (TRiP), 736

Subject Index

NOTE: Entries in **CAPITALS** are chapters.